GHAI Essential Pediatrics

Seventh Edition

Prof. OP Ghai

1928–2008

Visionary and Doyen of Pediatrics

GHAI

Essential Pediatrics

Seventh Edition

Editors

OP Ghai MD, FIAP, FAAP
Former Professor and Head, Department of Pediatrics, and
Dean, All India Institute of Medical Sciences, New Delhi

Vinod K Paul MD, PhD, FAMS, FAAP
Professor and Head, Department of Pediatrics
All India Institute of Medical Sciences, New Delhi

Arvind Bagga MD, FIAP, FAMS
Professor of Pediatrics
All India Institute of Medical Sciences, New Delhi

CBS Publishers & Distributors Pvt Ltd

New Delhi • Bangalore • Pune • Cochin • Chennai

Disclaimer

Medical knowledge is constantly changing. As new information becomes available, changes in treatment, procedures, equipment and the use of drugs become necessary. The contributors, editors and the publishers, as far as possible, have taken care to ensure that the information given in this text is accurate and up-to-date. However, the readers are strongly advised to confirm that the information, especially with regard to drug usage, complies with the latest legislation and standards of practice.

Notice

Research in treatment and drug therapy is continually in progress throughout the world. Recommendations and contraindications in dosage schedules require constant updating and change, both from year to year and country to country. Different drugs may have a similar name in other countries or the same drugs may be packed in different strengths. It is, therefore, advisable to consult the product information sheet provided with each drug, particularly in the case of new, foreign or rarely used drugs, to ensure that changes have not been made in the recommended dosages.

GHAI
Essential Pediatrics
Seventh Edition

ISBN: 978-81-239-1777-1

First Edition: 1982
Second Edition: 1990
Third Edition: 1993
Fourth Edition: 1996
Fifth Edition: 2000
Sixth Edition: 2004
Seventh Edition: 2009
Reprint: 2010

Published by Satish Kumar Jain and produced by Vinod K. Jain for
CBS Publishers & Distributors Pvt Ltd
Head off: CBS Plaza 4819/XI Prahlad Street, 24 Ansari Road, Daryaganj,
New Delhi 110 002, India.
Ph: 23289259, 23266861/67 Fax: +91-11-23243014
Website: www.cbspd.com
e-mail: delhi@cbspd.com; cbspubs@vsnl.com; cbspubs@airtelmail.in.

Branches

- Bangalore: Seema House 2975, 17th Cross, K.R. Road, Banasankari 2nd Stage, Bangalore 560 070, Karnataka
  Ph: +91-80-26771678/79 Fax: +91-80-26771680 e-mail: bangalore@cbspd.com
- Pune: Shaan Brahmha Complex, 631/632 Basement, Appa Balwant Chowk, Budhwar Peth, Next To Ratan Talkies, Pune 411 002, Maharashtra
  Ph: +91-20-24464057/58 Fax: +91-20-24464059 e-mail: pune@cbspd.com
- Cochin: 36/14 Kalluvilakam, Lissie Hospital Road, Cochin 682 018, Kerala
  Ph: +91-484-4059061-65 Fax: +91-484-4059065 e-mail: cochin@cbspd.com
- Chennai: 20, West Park Road, Shenoy Nagar, Chennai 600 030, TN
  Ph: +91-44-26260666, 26208620 Fax: +91-44-45530020 email: chennai@cbspd.com

Printed at: Thomson Press (India) Ltd.

to

our esteemed

teachers

Prof. Om Prakash Ghai

Prof. Om Prakash Ghai had a distinguished academic tenure at the All India Institute of Medical Sciences, New Delhi. He started the Department of Pediatrics in 1959 with six beds for children. Under his leadership, the department evolved into a multispecialty centre of international repute.

After his retirement as Dean of the Institute and Professor and Head of the Department of Pediatrics, he chaired the Department of Pediatrics at the University College of Medical Sciences, Delhi, where he served until 1991.

Prof. Ghai was President of the Indian Academy of Pediatrics in 1978 and President of the International College of Pediatrics from 1987 to 1990. The International Pediatric Association presented him the prestigious 'Insignia of Merit Medallion' (1977) for his outstanding contributions to child welfare. The Indian Council of Medical Research awarded him the Dr. Kamla Menon Prize (1983) and Amrut Mody Prize (1985). The Medical Council of India bestowed on him the Dr. BC Roy Memorial Award for 'Eminent Medical Teacher' (1987). He was also awarded the Dr. KC Choudhry Oration by Calcutta University (1984) and Prof. JB Chatterjee Oration (1990) by the Calcutta School of Tropical Medicine. He was awarded the honorary fellowships of the American Academy of Pediatrics, the National Academy of Medical Sciences and the Indian Academy of Pediatrics.

Prof. Ghai served as a short-term consultant to the World Health Organization and Asian Development Bank. He was a member of the Technical Advisory Group of the Control of Diarrheal Diseases Program of the World Health Organization, Geneva (1987-89). He has been a member of the Scientific Advisory Boards of the National Institutes of Nutrition, Cholera and Enteric Diseases, Public Cooperation and Child Development. He was member of the National Children's Board and several expert groups of the Government of India, UNICEF and Indian Council of Child Welfare. He was the editor of *Indian Pediatrics* and World Pediatrics and Child Care and member of the editorial advisory boards of the *Annals of National Academy of Medical Sciences* and *Indian Journal of Pediatrics*.

Professor Ghai was a teacher par excellence, an inspiring leader and a true visionary. His name shall always remain etched in the annals of pediatrics of our country.

Preface to the Seventh Edition

This edition of the *Essential Pediatrics* marks the completion of more than 25 years of its existence as a beacon of art and science of pediatrics in the country and beyond. *Essential Pediatrics* began in 1982 with Dr. OP Ghai as its lead author and founder editor. He directed and steered this book until his sudden passing away in May 2008. Dr. Ghai was actively involved in the preparation of this edition, which continues to bear an indelible imprint of his creative instinct and scholarship.

The present edition comes at a time of unprecedented focus and investments on child survival and health in the country. There is a heightened interest in child health education and training and a global endeavour for improving child health. It also comes at a juncture when subspecialties of pediatrics are taking root in the country. The coming years will mark a transition of pediatrics from the existing priorities such as nutrition and infectious diseases to emerging areas such as genetics, adolescence, intensive care and care of children with chronic systemic diseases.

This edition upholds and advances the traditional core values, focus and scope of the book even as it encompasses significant changes. There are major revisions in most chapters, aimed at meeting the contemporary needs of undergraduate and postgraduate medical and nursing students, and pediatricians. The chapters on growth and development have been rewritten with inclusion of fresh illustrations and WHO growth norms. Chapters on nutrition and neonatology have been completely revised with emphasis on practical and evidence-based management of common conditions. The chapter on infections has also been rewritten keeping in view their relevance for physicians practising in developing countries. The chapters on hematological, endocrine, nervous system and renal disorders have been thoroughly updated and reorganized. New sections on hypertension, interventional cardiology, newer vaccines, poisonings and accidents, national and WHO guidelines on management of common conditions and IMNCI are incorporated. The inclusion of multiple diagnostic and therapeutic algorithms shall serve as a useful educational resource. Fresh chapters on skin and ocular disorders, practical procedures and rights of children provide a comprehensive review on issues pertaining to the care of children.

Some of the best-known academics have contributed to *Essential Pediatrics* and we are indebted to them for their scholarly writings. They all have a remarkable understanding of the learning needs of the students, and their chapters reflect the essence of their knowledge and experience. We are grateful to Dr Aditi Sinha for meticulous work at every stage of the preparation of this edition. Through tireless effort, she ensured accuracy of contents and quality of presentation of this edition. Mrs Veena Arora accomplished the composing with great patience. We thank the technical team at our publishers, CBS Publishers & Distributors, for their tremendous effort in improving the presentation of this book.

Humbled by the faith reposed by the successive waves of our readers, we are ever conscious of our responsibility in ensuring this book's relevance in the changing health scenario, and in the backdrop of the advances in knowledge. We hope this edition would succeed in continuing to make a genuine and lasting contribution towards the health and well-being of children.

Vinod K Paul

Arvind Bagga

Preface to the First Edition

The health problems of the children in the third world are the most pressing. Physicians in these countries often have to work under constraints of poor resources and a lack of access to the modern diagnostic aids. They, therefore, of necessity require a more exhaustive training in clinical skills and a sharper clinical acumen than their counterparts more fortunately placed. The present textbook is primarily aimed to fulfil this need.

This book covers a broad spectrum of the subject, laying a special emphasis on the nutritional and infectious disorders. Rare diseases are referred to only briefly. This has helped to restrict the size of the book to a manageable level so that the undergraduate medical students may find it handy and useful.

The sections on the applied aspects of anatomy and physiology of the various body systems and pathophysiology of the disease processes affecting them will appeal to the postgraduate medical students. These may help them in understanding the biological basis of diagnosis and management. The sections on the use of drugs, clinical approach to the diagnosis and details of diagnostic and therapeutic procedures will be useful especially for the general practitioners and clinical residents.

Most references used in the preparation of the manuscript have been cited but if some have been left out through oversight, I offer my sincere apologies. I thank Prof. MMS Ahuja for the permission to include some excerpts from the chapter on "Nutrition" written by Dr. Tara Gopaldas and me from the book *Progress in Clinical Medicine*, Series IV, published by Arnold Heinemann, New Delhi.

I acknowledge my gratitude to all my colleagues in the department who gave me unstinted support and stood solidly beside me in our joint endeavour for upgrading the status of pediatric services in India. The erudition and scholarship of Professors KL Wig and V Ramalingaswami have been a great source of inspiration to me. I am grateful to Professors PN Taneja and Harish Chandra, who encouraged me to write this book.

I take this opportunity to thank Dr. PSN Menon, my erstwhile student, now a dear colleague, who helped me at every stage of preparation of this edition. The book bears an indelible imprint of his meticulous efforts. I am grateful to my colleague Dr. HS Wasir for his valuable suggestions on the section on hypertension. Drs RK Menon, Vedanarayanan and Anil Gupta read through several sections and made helpful suggestions.

Many medical students, especially Mr. Gurkirpal Singh, helped at several stages in preparation of the book. I am grateful to Messrs Ganguly, Mitra, Ghosh and Awasthi for their help in artwork. Shri Suraj Bhan did the typing work with great patience. Shri JN Mathur of Mehta Offset Works, toiled painstakingly to give the finishing touches to the book. Shri SN Mehta, our publisher, was very co-operative and took a special pride in publishing this volume.

OP Ghai

List of Contributors

Agarwala, Anuja
Dietitian
Department of Pediatrics
All India Institute of Medical Sciences
New Delhi
email: aanujaaiims@yahoo.com

Agarwal, Ramesh
Assistant Professor
Division of Neonatology, Department of Pediatrics
WHO-CC for Training and Research in Newborn Care
All India Institute of Medical Sciences
New Delhi
email: aranag@rediffmail.com

Aneja, S
Professor of Pediatrics
Lady Hardinge Medical College and
Kalawati Saran Children's Hospital
New Delhi
email: anejas@hotmail.com

Arora, Narendra Kumar
Executive Director
International Clinical Epidemiology Network
Ex-Professor
Department of Pediatrics
All India Institute of Medical Sciences
New Delhi
email: narendrakumararora@hotmail.com

Arya, LS
Senior Consultant, Pediatric Oncology and Hematology
Indraprastha Apollo Hospitals
Sarita Vihar, New Delhi
email: lsarya@rediffmail.com

Bajpai, Anurag
Consultant Pediatric and Adolescent Endocrinologist
Regency Hospital Limited
Sarvodaya Nagar
Kanpur
email: dr_anuragbajpai@yahoo.com,

Bagga, Arvind
Professor
Division of Nephrology
Department of Pediatrics
All India Institute of Medical Sciences
New Delhi
email: arvindbagga@hotmail.com

Bhat, S Rekha
Professor and Head
Division of Neonatology
Department of Pediatrics
St Johns Medical College, Bangalore

Bhatia, Vidyut
Senior Research Associate
Division of Gastroenterology
Department of Pediatrics
All India Institute of Medical Sciences
New Delhi
email: drvidyut@gmail.com

Bhatnagar, Shinjini
Sr. Scientist-III
Center for Diarrheal Diseases and Nutrition Research
Department of Pediatrics
All India Institute of Medical Sciences
New Delhi
email: shinjini.bhatnagar@gmail.com

Chawla, Deepak
Assistant Professor
Department of Pediatrics
Government Medical College and Hospital, Chandigarh
email: drdeepakchawla@hotmail.com

Das, Manoja Kumar
Program Consultant
International Clinical Epidemiology Network, New Delhi
email: dr_manojdas@rediffmail.com

Dawa, Natasha
National Consultant
World Health Organization, New Delhi
email: dawan@searo.who.int

Deorari, Ashok K
Professor
Division of Neonatology, Department of Pediatrics
WHO-CC for Training and Research in Newborn Care
All India Institute of Medical Sciences
New Delhi
email: ashokdeorari_56@hotmail.com

Dutta, Sourabh
Additional Professor
Department of Pediatrics
Postgraduate Institute of Medical Education and Research
Chandigarh
email: sourabhdutta@yahoo.co.in

Ghai, Kanika
Director, Division of Endocrinology
Lutheran General Children's Hospital
Assistant Professor, Pediatrics
Chicago Medical School
Chicago, Illinois, USA

Ghai, OP
Ex-Professor and Head
Department of Pediatrics, and
Dean, All India Institute of
Medical Sciences, New Delhi

Ghai, Vivek
Section Chief, Neonatology
Advocate Illinois Masonic Medical Center
Assistant Professor, Rush Medical College
Chicago, Illinois, USA
email: vicneo@gmail.com

Gulati, Ashima
Senior Research Associate
Division of Nephrology
Department of Pediatrics
All India Institute of Medical Sciences
New Delhi
email: ashnanya@gmail.com

Gulati, Sheffali
Associate Professor
Division of Neurology
Department of Pediatrics
All India Institute of Medical Sciences
New Delhi
email: sheffaligulati@gmail.com

Hari, Pankaj
Associate Professor
Division of Nephrology
Department of Pediatrics
All India Institute of Medical Sciences
New Delhi
email: pankajhari@hotmail.com

Jain, Ashish
Neonatologist
Department of Pediatrics
Hindu Rao Hospital, Delhi
email: drashishjain2000@yahoo.co.in

Jain, Richa
Senior Resident
Department of Pediatrics
All India Institute of Medical Sciences
New Delhi
email: richirich24@gmail.com

Jain, Vandana
Assistant Professor
Division of Endocrinology
Department of Pediatrics
All India Institute of Medical Sciences
New Delhi
email: drvandanajain@gmail.com

Kabra, Madhulika
Additional Professor
Division of Genetics
Department of Pediatrics
All India Institute of Medical Sciences
New Delhi
email: madhulikakabra@hotmail.com

Kabra SK
Professor
Division of Pulmonology and Intensive Care
Department of Pediatrics
All India Institute of Medical Sciences
New Delhi
email: skkabrahotmail.com

Kalra, Veena
Senior Consultant, Pediatric Neurology
Indraprastha Apollo Hospitals
Sarita Vihar
New Delhi
email: kalra.veena@gmail.com

Khanna, Neena
Professor
Department of Dermatology and Venereology
All India Institute of Medical Sciences
New Delhi
email: neena_aiims@yahoo.co.in

Kumar, Krishna
Professor and Head
Pediatric Cardiology
Amrita Institute of Medical Sciences and Research Center
Elamakkara
Cochin
email: rkrishnakumar@aims.amrita.edu

Kumar, Pawan
Senior Resident
Department of Pediatrics
All India Institute of Medical Sciences
New Delhi
email: drpawan_bhutani@rediffmail.com

Lodha, Rakesh
Assistant Professor
Division of Pulmonology and Intensive Care
Department of Pediatrics
All India Institute of Medical Sciences
New Delhi
email: rakesh_lodha@hotmail.com

Mathur, Prashant
Assistant Director General
Division of Non-communicable Diseases
Indian Council of Medical Research
New Delhi
email: drprashant.mathur@yahoo.com

Mehta, Rajesh
National Professional Officer – FCH
Office of WHO Representative to India
Nirman Bhawan, New Delhi
email: mehtaraj@searo.who.int

Menon, P Ramesh
Senior Lecturer
Department of Pediatrics
TD Medical College
Alappuzha, Kerala
email: rpmpgi@gmail.com

Menon, PSN
Consultant and Head
Department of Pediatrics
Jaber Al-Ahmed, Armed Forces Hospital
PO Box 5891, Salmiya 22069, Kuwait
email: psnmenon@hotmail.com

Mishra, Satish
Senior Research Associate
Division of Neonatology, Department of Pediatrics
All India Institute of Medical Sciences
New Delhi
email: drsatishmishra@rediffmail.com

Mondkar, Jayshree
Professor and Head of Neonatology
LTMG Medical College
Sion, Mumbai
email: jamond@vsnl.com

Mukhopadhyay, Sagori
Resident, Boston Combined Residency Program
Harvard University and Boston University
Boston, USA.

Nayar, Patanjali Dev
Chief Medical Officer, Hindu Rao Hospital
Delhi
email: nayarp@wpro.who.int

Patwari, Ashok K
Research Professor, International Health
Center for International Health and Development, School of Public Health
Boston University, USA

Paul, Vinod K
Professor and Head
Department of Pediatrics
WHO-CC for Training and Research in Newborn Care
All India Institute of Medical Sciences
New Delhi
email: vinodkpaul@hotmail.com

Raina, Neena
Regional Advisor
Adolescent Health
South East Regional Office
World Health Organization
New Delhi
email: rainan@searo.who.int

Rasool Seemab
Research Officer
Regional Research Institute of Unani Medicine
Okhla, New Delhi
email: mercurial72@rediffmail.com

Rohman, Grant T
Department of Otolaryngology-Head and Neck Surgery
University of Tennessee-Memphis
Memphis, TN 38163, USA

Samant, Sandeep
Associate Professor
Department of Otolaryngology-Head and Neck Surgery
University of Tennessee-Memphis
Memphis, TN 38163, USA

Sankar, Jhuma
Senior Research Associate
Department of Pediatrics
All India Institute of Medical Sciences
New Delhi
email: jhumaji@yahoo.com

Sankar, M Jeeva
Senior Research Associate
Division of Neonatology, Department of Pediatrics
All India Institute of Medical Sciences
New Delhi
email: jeevasankar@gmail.com

Sankhyan, Naveen
Senior Resident
Division of Neurology
Department of Pediatrics
All India Institute of Medical Sciences
New Delhi
email: nsankhyan@rediffmail.com

Sarthi, Manjunatha
Assistant Professor
Department of Pediatrics
SS Institute of Medical Sciences and Research Center
Jnanashankara
Davangere
email: msarthi@gmail.com

Seth, Pradeep
President
Seth Research Foundation
H 8/3 First Floor, DLF Phase I
Gurgaon
email: dr.pradeepseth@gmail.com

Seth, Rachna
Assistant Professor, Division of Oncology
Department of Pediatrics
All India Institute of Medical Sciences
New Delhi
email: drrachnaseth@yahoo.co.in

Seth, Rajeev
Senior Consultant Pediatrics
E 10, Green Park Main, New Delhi
email: sethrajeev @gmail.com

Seth, Tulika
Assistant Professor
Department of Hematology
BRA-IRCH Building
All India Institute of Medical Sciences
New Delhi
email: drtulikaseth@gmail.com

Sethi, Sidharth Kumar
Senior Resident
Department of Pediatrics
All India Institute of Medical Sciences
New Delhi
email: sidsdoc@gmail.com

Sharma, Pradeep Kumar
Senior Resident, Division of Neonatology
Department of Pediatrics
All India Institute of Medical Sciences
New Delhi
email: psaiims@yahoo.co.in

Singh, Surjit
Professor
Department of Pediatrics
Postgraduate Institute of Medical Education and Research, Chandigarh
email: surjitsinghpgi@rediffmail.com

Singhal, Tanu
Consultant Pediatrician
Kokilaben Dhirubhai Ambani Hospital and Medical Research Institute
Mumbai
email: tanusinghal@yahoo.com

Sinha, Aditi
Senior Research Associate
Division of Nephrology
Department of Pediatrics
All India Institute of Medical Sciences
New Delhi
email: aditisinha4@rediffmail.com

Srivastava, R N
Senior Consultant, Pediatric Nephrology
Indraprastha Apollo Hospitals
Sarita Vihar, New Delhi
email: rnsri@vsnl.net

Sivanandan, Sindhu
Senior Resident
Department of Pediatrics
All India Institute of Medical Sciences
New Delhi
email: drsindhu80@rediffmail.com

Tandon, R
Consultant Cardiologist
Sita Ram Bhartia Institute of Sciences and Research
Mehrauli
New Delhi

Tandon, Radhika
Professor of Ophthalmology
Dr. Rajendra Prasad Centre for Ophthalmic Sciences
All India Institute of Medical Sciences
New Delhi
email: radhika_tan@yahoo.com

Thompson, Jerome W
Department of Otolaryngology-Head and Neck Surgery
University of Tennessee-Memphis
Memphis
TN 38163
USA

Wadhwa, Nitya
Senior Research Officer
Division of Gastroenterology
Department of Pediatrics
All India Institute of Medical Sciences
New Delhi
email: nityawadhwa@gmail.com

Contents

Contents

Contents

Contents

Contents

1 Normal Growth and its Disorders

INTRODUCTION

Growth is an essential feature that distinguishes a child from an adult. The process of growth starts from the time of conception and continues until the child grows into a fully mature adult. During the early embryonic period of life, an exponential increase in the number of cells occurs. At the early embryonic stage, fetal cells divide and differentiate to form tissues and organs. In the later half of pregnancy and early childhood, there is additionally an increase in the cell size. This manifests as increase in the protein to DNA ratio. The cell size continues to enlarge until about ten years of age. After that, increase in cell size occurs rather slowly. The body cells remain in a state of dynamic equilibrium; hence ageing cells are continuously replaced by new cells. However, the rate of turnover of cells in different tissues is variable.

The terms "growth and development" are often used together. These are not interchangeable because they represent two different facets of the dynamics of change, i.e. those of quantity and quality. Growth and development usually proceed concurrently. While they are discussed separately, both growth and development are closely related, hence factors affecting one also tend to have an impact on the other.

The term **growth** denotes a net increase in the size or mass of tissues. It is largely attributed to multiplication of cells and increase in the intracellular substance. Hypertrophy or expansion of cell size contributes to a lesser extent to the process of growth. **Development** specifies maturation of functions. It is related to the maturation and myelination of the nervous system and indicates acquisition of a variety of skills for optimal functioning of the individual.

FACTORS AFFECTING GROWTH

Fetal Growth

Fetal growth is influenced primarily by fetal, placental and maternal factors. In humans, 40% of variation in the birth weight is due to genetic factors while the rest is due to environmental factors. The fetus has an inherent growth potential and under normal circumstances grows into a healthy appropriate sized newborn. The maternal-placental-fetal units act in harmony to provide the needs of the fetus.

Genetic potential: The parental traits are usually transmitted to the offspring. Thus, tall parents have tall children and so on. The size of the head is more closely related to that of parents than are the size and shape of hands and feet. Similarly, the structure of the chest and fatty tissue has better genetic association than other somatic characteristics.

Sex: Boys are generally longer and heavier than girls at the time of birth.

Fetal hormones: Human fetus secretes thyroxine from the 12th weeks of gestation onward. Thyroxine and insulin have an important role in regulation of tissue accretion and differentiation in the fetus. Both are required for normal growth and development particularly late in gestation. Glucocorticoids also play an important role, primarily towards the end of gestation. They influence the prepartum maturational events of organs such as liver, lungs and gastrointestinal tract, in preparation for extrauterine survival. Growth hormone though present in high levels in fetus is not known to influence fetal growth.

Fetal growth factors: A large number of growth factors have been identified in fetal tissues. Synthesized locally they act principally by autocrine and paracrine mechanisms. Their prime action is on cell division, though they also influence other aspects of tissue growth. These factors can be both growth promoting or inhibitory. The insulin like growth factor (IGF)-I and IGF-II are the most extensively studied fetal growth factors. Like IGF-I and IGF-II, growth promoting factors include epidermal growth factor (EGF), transforming growth factor (TGF-α), platelet derived growth factor (PDGF), fibroblast growth factor (FGF), nerve growth factor and other hemopoetic growth factors. Inhibitory factors include TGF-β, müllerian inhibitory substance, inhibin/activin family of proteins.

Placental factors: As in most species fetal weight directly correlates with placental weight at term. Fetal growth is highly dependent on the structural and functional integrity of the placenta. With advancing gestation, the

1

weight of the placenta increases to cater to the increased needs of the baby. There are important functional and structural changes in the placenta that makes this adaptation more efficient. The total villous surface area increases, the diffusion distance decreases, the fetal capillaries dilate and the resistance in fetoplacental vasculature falls. This positive remodeling facilitates the enhanced nutrient transport across the placenta.

Maternal factors: The mother's own fetal and childhood growth and her diet, nutrient intake and body composition at the time of conception as well as during pregnancy, plays an important role in determining the lifelong well-being of her children. Teenage or advanced age, recent pregnancy, high parity and anemia negatively influence fetal size and health. Maternal tobacco (smoked or chewed), drug or alcohol abuse also retards fetal growth. Obstetric complications such as pregnancy induced hypertension, pre-eclampsia and multiple pregnancies produce fetal growth restriction. Both pre-existing chronic systemic disorders (chronic renal failure, congestive heart failure) and acquired infections (rubella, syphilis, hepatitis B, HIV, CMV, toxoplasmosis) influence fetal growth.

Postnatal Period

The growth of the child during postnatal life is determined by genetic potential other than internal and external influences.

Sex: The pubertal growth spurt occurs earlier in girls. However, their mean height and weight are usually less than those in boys of corresponding ages at the time of full maturity.

Intrauterine growth retardation: About 20% of growth retarded newborns develop postnatal growth failure and short stature. Newborns that have asymmetrical growth retardation, with preserved length are more likely to have catch up growth in the first 2–3 years and subsequently normal stature.

Genetic factors: Both chromosomal disorders and other disorders related to gene mutation can affect growth. Chromosomal defects like Turner syndrome and Down syndrome manifest growth retardation. Mutation of a single or multiple genes may result in inherited retardation of growth, e.g. Prader Willi syndrome, Noonan syndrome. While most of these disorders lead to short stature, some of the genetic defects can also lead to tall stature, e.g. Klinefelter syndrome, Soto syndrome, etc.

Hormonal influence: Normal development cannot proceed without the right milieu of hormones in the body throughout childhood and adolescence. Absence of growth hormone, thyroxine or cortisol results is dwarfism, underscoring the importance of these factors in promoting growth. These factors influence both somatic and skeletal growth. During adolescence, androgens and estrogens have an important influence on the growth spurt and final adult height.

Nutrition: Growth of children suffering from protein-energy malnutrition, anemia and vitamin deficiency states is retarded. Among the nutrients, calcium, iron, zinc, iodine, vitamins A and D, have been closely related to disorders of growth and development and increase in adverse health events in children. On the other hand overeating and obesity accelerate somatic growth.

Infections: In India one of the commonest contributors to poor childhood growth are infections. Persistent or recurrent diarrhea and respiratory tract infections are common causes of growth impairment. Systemic infections and parasitic infestations may also retard the velocity of growth.

Chemical agents: Administration of androgenic hormones initially accelerates the skeletal growth. Ultimately, epiphyses of bones close prematurely and therefore, the bone growth ceases relatively early in these cases.

Trauma: Fracture of the end of bone may damage the growing epiphysis and thus hamper the skeletal growth.

Social Factors

Socioeconomic level: Children from families with high socioeconomic level usually have a superior nutritional state. They suffer from fewer infections because of more hygienic living conditions.

Poverty: Hunger, undernutrition and infections are closely associated with poverty.

Natural resources: Plentiful natural resources encourage industrial and agricultural enterprise in the country. Improved nutrition of children in the community is secured when there is a climb in gross national product and per capita income is high.

Climate: The velocity of growth may alter in different seasons and is usually higher in spring and low in summer months. Infections and infestations are common in hot and humid climate. Weather also has a pivotal effect on agricultural productivity, ready availability of food and capacity for strenuous labor by the population.

Emotional factors: Children from broken homes and orphanages do not grow and develop at an optimal rate. Anxiety, insecurity, lack of emotional support and love from the family prejudice the neurochemical regulation of the growth hormone. Parents who had happy childhood and carry a cheerful personality are more likely to have children with similar countenance.

Cultural factors: Methods of child rearing and infant feeding in the community are determined by cultural habits and conventions. There may be religious taboos against consumption of particular types of foodstuffs. These affect the nutritional state and growth performance of children.

Parental education: Mothers with more education are more likely to adopt appropriate health-promoting behaviors, having a direct and indirect influence on growth and development.

Consequences of Impaired Growth and Undernutrition

Maternal and child undernutrition is the underlying cause of 3–5 million deaths annually, and 35% of the disease burden in children younger than 5 years. It is estimated that India, has more than 61 million stunted children, 34% of the global total. Recent research suggests that several of the major disorders of later life including coronary heart disease, hypertension and type 2 diabetes, originate in impaired intrauterine growth and development. These diseases may be consequences of "programming," whereby a stimulus or insult at a critical, sensitive period of early life has permanent effects on structure, physiology and metabolism. The "fetal origins" hypothesis (Barker hypothesis) proposes that alterations in fetal nutrition and endocrine status result in developmental adaptations that permanently change structure, physiology and metabolism, thereby predisposing individuals to cardiovascular, metabolic and endocrine disease in adult life. As a result, infants born low birth weight have increased risk of diabetes, hypertension, coronary artery disease and hyperlipidemia in adult life.

LAWS OF GROWTH

a. Growth and development of children is a continuous and orderly process. There are specific periods in a child's life when the rate of growth is steady, accelerates and decelerates (Table 1.1). The fetus grows fast in the first half of gestation. Thereafter, the rate of growth is slowed down until the baby is born. In the early postnatal period the velocity of growth is high, especially in the first few months. Thereafter there is slower but steady rate of growth during mid-childhood. A second phase of accelerated growth occurs at puberty. Growth decelerates thereafter for some time after that and then ceases altogether.

   The Infancy-childhood-puberty (ICP) model proposed by Karlberg describes postnatal growth has 3 different biological/endocrinal periods of growth. It begins with infancy when growth is principally influenced by nutrition. This period is followed by the childhood period influenced by growth hormone and thyroid hormone. And finally the pubertal growth spurt influenced by sex steroids and growth hormone. Though simplistic, this model provides an instrument to detect and understand growth failure at various ages.

b. Growth pattern of every individual is unique. Order of growth in human beings is cephalocaudal and distal to proximal. During fetal life, growth of head occurs before that of neck and arms grow before legs. Distal parts of the body such as hands increase in size before upper arms. In the postnatal life, growth of head slows down but limbs continue to grow rapidly. Head control which involves the use of neck muscles develops early. It is followed by coordination of spinal muscles and effective use of hands. Creeping and crawling which entails the use of legs is learnt later.

c. Different tissues of the body grow at different rates (Fig. 1.1)

Table 1.1: Periods of growth

Prenatal period	
Ovum	0 to 14 days
Embryo	14 days to 9 weeks
Fetus	9 weeks to birth
Perinatal period	22 weeks of gestation to 7 days after birth
Postnatal period	
Newborn	First 4 weeks after birth
Infancy	First year
Toddler	1–3 years
Preschool child	3–6 years
School age child	6–12 years
Adolescence	
Early	10–13 years
Middle	14–16 years
Late	17–20 years

General body growth: The general body growth is rapid during the fetal life, first one or two years of postnatal life and also during puberty. In the intervening years of mid childhood, the somatic growth velocity is relatively slowed down.

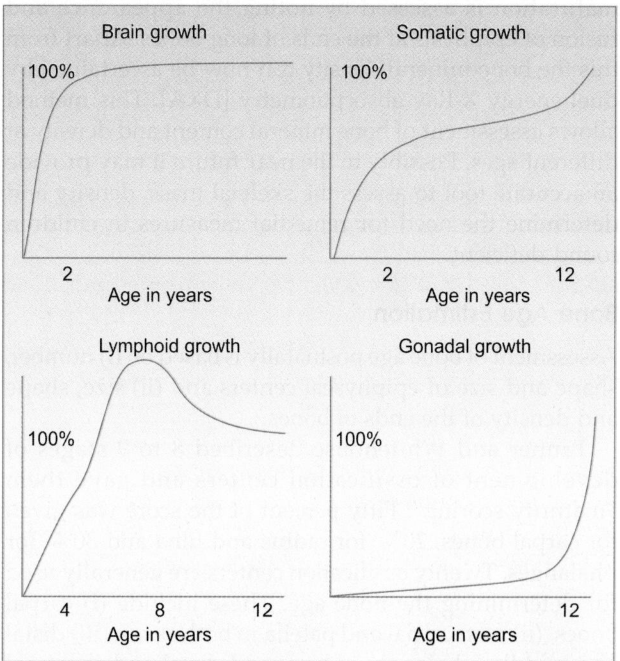

Fig. 1.1: Rates of growth of different tissues and organs

The brain growth: The brain enlarges rapidly during the latter months of fetal life and early months of postnatal life. At birth, the head size is about 65 to 70% of the expected head size in adults. It reaches 90% of the adult head size by the age of 2 years. Thus, the fetal phase and the first two years are crucial periods for brain development and thereafter for acquiring neuromotor functions and cognitive ability.

The growth of gonad: Gonadal growth is dormant during childhood and becomes conspicuous during pubescence.

Lymphoid growth: The growth of lymphoid tissue is most notable during mid-childhood. During this period, the lymphoid tissue is overgrown and its mass may appear to be larger than that of the fully mature adult. A sign of this accelerated lymphoid growth is the frequent finding of large tonsils and palpable lymph nodes in normal children between ages of 4 to 8 years.

SOMATIC GROWTH

Skeletal Growth

Skeletal growth is a continuous process occurring during the whole of childhood and adolescence. It is steady until the pubertal growth spurt when it accelerates and subsequently slows considerably. The skeleton is mature once the epiphysis or growth plates at the end of long bones fuse to the shaft or diaphysis. This occurs by 18 years or so in girls and by 20–22 years in boys. The degree of skeletal maturation closely correlates with the degree of sexual maturation. A child who has advanced sexual maturity will also have earlier skeletal maturation. Skeletal maturation is assessed by noting the appearance and fusion of epiphysis at the ends of long bones. Apart from this the bone mineral density can now be ascertained by duel energy X-Ray absorptiometry [DXA]. This method allows assessment of bone mineral content and density at different ages. Possibly in the near future it may provide an accurate tool to assess the skeletal mass, density and determine the need for remedial measures in children found deficient.

Bone Age Estimation

Assessment of bone age postnatally is based on (i) number, shape and size of epiphyseal centers and (ii) size, shape and density of the ends of bones.

Tanner and Whitehouse described 8 to 9 stages of development of ossification centers and gave them "maturity scoring". Fifty percent of the score was given for carpal bones, 20% for radius and ulna and 30% for phalanges. Twenty ossification centers are generally used for determining the bone age. These include (i) carpal bones, (ii) metacarpal and patella in both sexes, (iii) distal and middle 'phalanges in boys and distal and proximal phalanges in girls, and (iv) distal and proximal toes.

To determine the skeletal age, in infants between 3 and 9 months, radiograph of shoulder is most helpful. A single film of hands and wrists is adequate in children between the ages of 1 and 13 years. For children between 12 and 14 years, radiographs of elbow and hip give helpful clues.

Eruption of Teeth

Primary teeth: The teeth in the upper jaw erupt earlier than those in the lower jaw, except for lower central incisors.

Permanent teeth: These erupt in the following order; 1st molar 6–7 years; central and lateral incisors 6 to 8 years; canines and premolars 9 to 12 years; second molars 12 years; third molars 18 years or later.

Growth of body fat and muscle mass: Body tissues can be divided into fat and fat free components. The lean body mass includes muscle tissue, the internal organs and skeleton. It contains only a small amount of fat. The growth in lean body mass is primarily due to increase in muscle mass. Lean body mass further corelates closely with stature. Taller children have greater lean body mass than shorter children of the same age. After the pubertal growth spurt boys have greater lean body mass compared to girls.

Body fat is the storehouse of energy: It is primarily deposited in the subcutaneous adipose tissue. Girls have more subcutaneous adipose tissue than boys. Moreover the sites and quantity of adipose tissue differs in girls and boys. Girls tend to add adipose tissue to breasts, buttocks, thighs and back of arms during the adolescence.

ASSESSMENT OF PHYSICAL GROWTH

Weight: The weight of the child in the nude or minimal light clothing is recorded accurately on a lever or electronic type of weighing scale (Fig. 1.2). Spring balances are less accurate. The weighing scale should have a minimum unit of 100 gm. It is important that child be placed in middle of weighing pan. The weighing scale should be corrected for any zero error before measurement.

Length: Length is recorded for children under 2 years of age. The child is placed supine on a rigid measuring table

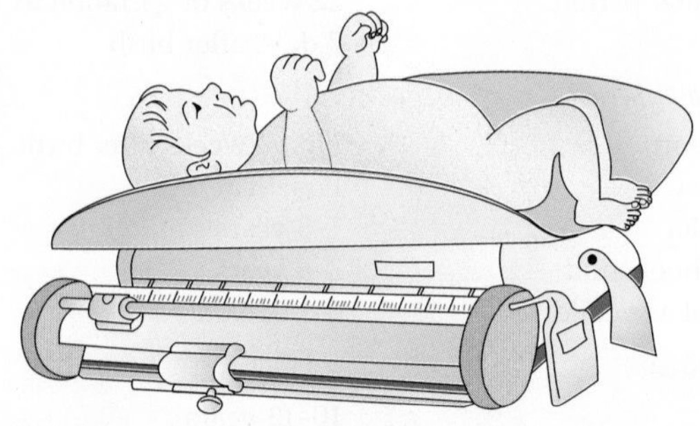

Fig. 1.2: Beam scale for accurate measurement of weight. The child should be nude or in minimal light clothing

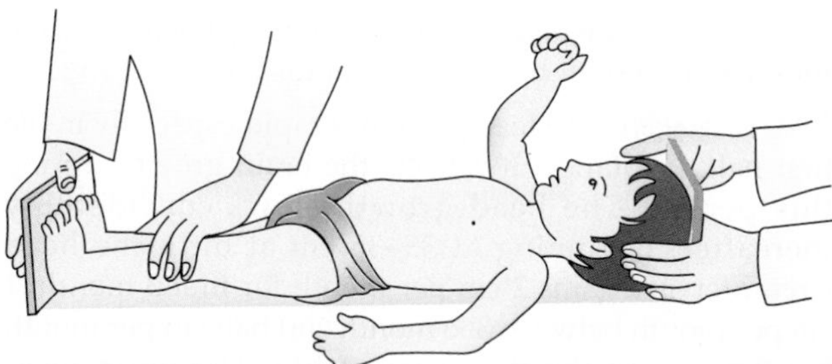

Fig.1.3: Measurement of length on an infantometer. Note how the knees are gently straightened while the head and feet are aligned

or an infantometer. The head is held firmly in position against a fixed upright head board. Legs are straightened, keeping feet at right angles to legs with toes pointing upward. The free foot board is brought into firm contact with the child's heels (Fig. 1.3). Length of the baby is measured from a scale, which is set in the measuring table. Measurement of length of a child lying on a mattress with cloth tapes is inaccurate and not recommended.

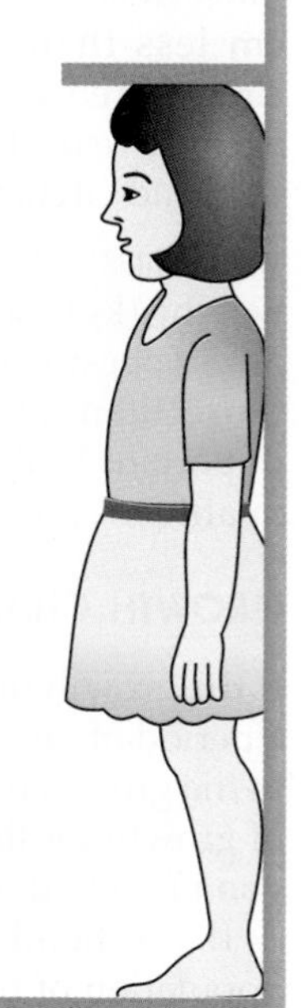

Fig. 1.4: Method of recording height. Note the erect posture and the bare feet flat on the ground. Back of heel, buttocks, shoulders and occiput touching the walls

Standing height: For the standing height, the child stands upright. Heels are slightly separated and the weight is borne evenly on both feet. Heels, buttocks and back are brought in contact with a vertical surface such as wall or height measuring rod or a stadiometer. The head is so positioned that the child looks directly forwards with the Frankfurt plane (the line joining floor of external auditory meatus to the lower margin of orbit) and the biauricular plane being horizontal. The head piece is kept firmly over the vertex to compress the hair. The measurement of height is then recorded (Fig. 1.4).

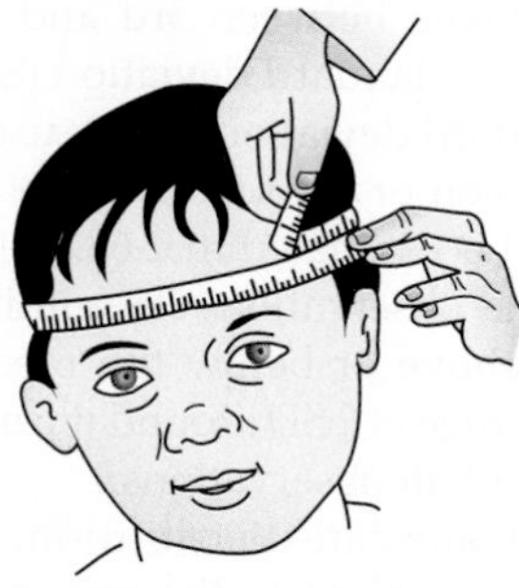

Fig. 1.5: Method of recording head circumference. Note the crossed tape method

Head circumference: Using a nonstretchable tape the maximum circumference of the head from the occipital protuberance to the supraorbital ridges on the forehead is recorded. The crossed tape method, using firm pressure to compress the hair is the preferred way to measure head circumference (Fig. 1.5)

Chest circumference: The chest circumference is measured at the level of the nipples, midway between inspiration and expiration. The crossed tape method as for head circumference measurement is used for measuring chest circumference (Fig. 1.6).

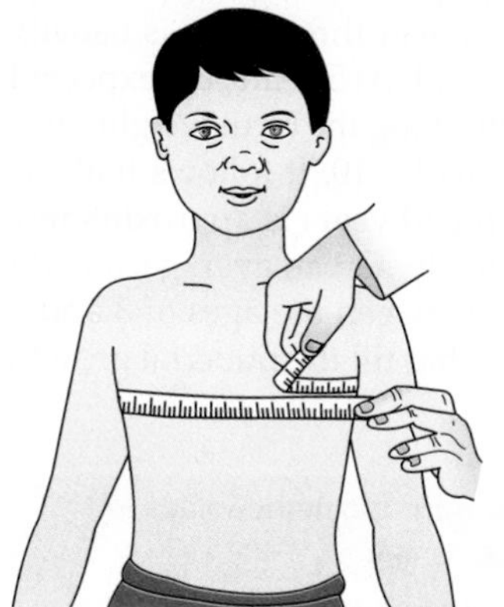

Fig. 1.6: Method of measurement of chest circumference at the level of nipples

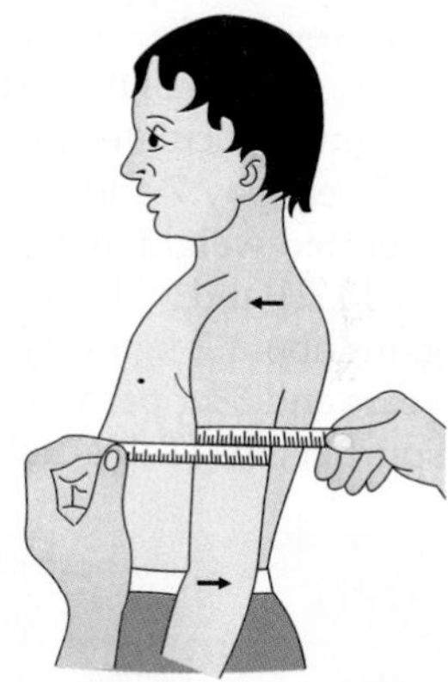

Fig. 1.7: Measurement of mid-arm circumference. Note how the anatomical landmarks are first located (arrows) to accurately measure the MAC

Mid-arm circumference: To measure the mid-arm circumference first mark a point midway between the tip of acromian process of scapula and the olecranon of ulna, while the child holds the left arm by his side (Fig. 1.7). Thereafter the crossed tape method as for head circumference measurement is used for measuring.

NORMAL GROWTH

It is difficult to precisely define the normal pattern of growth. Generally, it implies average of readings obtained in a group of healthy individuals along with a permissible range of variation, i.e. between the third and ninety-seventh percentiles. A child's percentile position on the growth chart is a function of the difference in his/her genetic background compared to that of children used to construct the charts.

Most healthy children maintain their growth percentile on the growth charts as the years pass by. Significant deviation in a child's plotted position on the growth chart can be due to a recent illness or over or under nutrition. It is also important to take into account the gestation age of infants born prematurely. The duration of prematurity is subtracted from the infant's chronological age. This correction, however, is not required after 2 years of age.

1

Weight: The average birth weight of neonates is about 3 kg. During the first few days after birth, the newborn loses extracellular fluid equivalent to about 10% of the body weight. Most infants regain their birth weight by the age of 10 days. Subsequently, they gain weight at a rate of approximately 25 to 30 g per day for the first 3 months of life. Thereafter they gain about 400 g weight every month, for the remaining part of the first year. An infant usually doubles his birth weight (taken as 3 kg) by the age of 5 months. The birth weight triples at 1 year and is four times at 2 years of age. Thus the weight at 5 months, one year and 2 years is approximately 6, 9 and 12 kg, respectively. The weight of a child at the age of three years is usually five times that of the birth weight. At 5 years, the expected weight is calculated by multiplying the birth weight by 6, at 7 years by 7 and at 10 years by 10. It follows that the expected weight at 3, 5, 7 and 10 years is approximately 15, 18, 21 and 30 kg, respectively. On an average, a child gains about 2 kg every year between the ages of 3 and 7 years and 3 kg per year after that till the pubertal growth spurt begins (Table 1.2).

Table 1.2: Approximate anthropometric values in relation to age

Age	*Weight (kg)*	*Length or height (cm)*	*Head circumference (cm)*
Birth	3	50	34
6 months	6 (doubles in 5 months)	65	42
1 year	9 (triples)	75	45
2 years	12 (quadruples)	85	47
3 years	14	95	49
4 years	16	100	50

Length or height: The infant measures 50 cm at birth, 60 cm at 3 months, 70 cm at 9 months, 75 cm at 1 year and 90 cm at 2 years. A normal Indian child is 100 cm tall at the age of 4 ½ years. Thereafter, the child gains about 6 cm in height every year, until the age of 12 years. After this, increments in height vary according to the age at the onset of puberty. There is a marked acceleration of the growth during puberty. The estimated target height is important to assess the child's growth potential. The correct acceptable range of height for a child is within two standard deviations of the target height percentile. Target height is calculated as follows:

Boys (cm)

$$= \frac{\text{Father's height (cm)} + \text{mother's height (cm)}}{2} + 6.5$$

Girls (cm)

$$= \frac{\text{Father's height (cm)} + \text{mother's height (cm)}}{2} - 6.5$$

A useful guide for normal range is target height $\pm$ 7 cm for girls and target height $\pm$ 8.5 cm for boys.

Head circumference: Head growth is rapid especially in the first half of infancy. It reflects the brain growth during this period. The head growth slows considerably thereafter. Beginning at 33–35 cm at birth the head circumference gains 2 cm per month for first 3 month, 1 cm per month between 3–6 month and half cm per month for the rest of the first year of life. The mean head circumference is 40 cm at 3 month, 43 cm at 6 month, 46–47 cm at 1 year, 48 cm at 2 years. By 12 years it is 52 cm.

Chest circumference: The circumference of chest is about 3 cm less than the head circumference at birth. The circumference of head and chest are almost equal by the age of 1 year. Thereafter the chest circumference exceeds the head circumference.

Body mass index (BMI): The formula to calculate BMI is weight (kg)/height (meter)^2. BMI is primarily used to assess obesity. BMI at or above the 95th centile for age or more than 30 is obesity. Obesity is emerging as an important health concern all over the world particularly in affluent populations.

GROWTH CHARTS

If the growth measurements are recorded in a child over a period of time and are plotted on a graph, the deviation in the growth profile of the child from the normal pattern of growth for that age can be easily interpreted. This is a good tool to diagnose deviation of growth from normal.

If the height or weight measurements in a large population of normal children are arranged in a regular order starting from the lowest, going to the highest, a bell shaped curve is formed. Most of the measurements fall around the middle of the curve, which tapers off on either side because only a few individuals have extreme measurements. If the selection and distribution of the sampled group is properly stratified and represents the group as a whole, the curve should be symmetrical with nearly half of the observations lying above and half below the median or the 50th percentile. This is called Gaussian distribution (bell-shaped curve).

Allowable normal range of variation in observations is conventionally taken between 3rd and 97th percentile curves or mean $\pm$ 2 standard deviation (SD).

The term standard deviation (SD) is used to denote the degree of dispersion or the scatter of observations away from the mean. It is estimated that 68.3% (approximately two-thirds) of the observations lie within one standard deviation (SD) above or below the mean value of the observations. A range of 2 SD around the mean is expected to include 95.4% of all observations.

In a typical Gaussian distribution, the median is expected to be equivalent to the arithmetic mean. The mean is obtained by dividing the sum of all observations by the number of observations. The median, on the other hand, indicates that 50% of observations are above and 50% are below this point.

Percentile curves represent frequency distribution curves. For example, 25th percentile for height in a population would mean that height of 75% of individuals is above and 24% are below this value. One standard deviation above the mean coincides with 84th percentile curve. Likewise 16th percentile curve represents one standard deviation below the mean.

Z scores: In a population with observations in a typical Gaussian distribution, any individual value can be expressed as how many standard deviations it lies above or below the mean. This is the Z score for that observation. Thus if a child's weight is at 2 SD below the mean, it is equivalent of -2Z. If the value lies above the mean, Z score is positive, otherwise it is negative. The formula for calculating the Z score is:

$$\text{Z score} = \frac{\text{Observed value} - \text{mean value}}{\text{Standard deviation}}$$

Z score allows comparison of different observations in an individual. For example, one can compare the height and weight of an individual by obtaining the respective Z score.

Growth Standards

Growth standards represent norms of growth and can be presented in tabular or graphical manner. These are obtained by either cross-sectional or longitudinal studies in large populations. Based on data obtained from US children, the National Center for Health Statistics (NCHS) developed growth charts in 1977, which were also adopted by the WHO for international use. In the year 2000 revised growth charts provided by CDC offered an improved tool to assess child health. But these charts were again based on data obtained from US children who were formula fed. Sensing the need for more internationally applicable growth standards, the WHO conducted the "Multicentre Growth Reference Study" (MGRS) and published the new growth charts in 2006. The MGRS was a community-based, multi-country project conducted in Brazil, Ghana, India, Norway, Oman, and the United States. The children included in the study were raised in environments that minimized constraints to growth such as poor diets and infection. In addition, their mothers followed healthy practices such as breastfeeding their children and not smoking during and after pregnancy.

The new WHO Child Growth Standards are unique on several accounts. They provide data on "how children should grow," and go beyond the traditional descriptive references. The new standards make breastfeeding the biological "norm" and establishes the breastfed infant as the normative growth model. The pooled sample from the six participating countries makes it a truly international standard (in contrast to the previous international reference based on children from a single country) and reiterates the fact that child populations grow similarly across the world's major regions when their needs for health and care are met. These standards also include new growth indicators beyond height and weight that are particularly useful for monitoring the increasing epidemic of childhood obesity, such as the skinfold thickness. The study's longitudinal nature will further allow the development of growth velocity standards, enabling the early identification of children in the process of becoming under or over-nourished.

Figures 1.8 to 1.17 provides percentile curves for weight, length/height, weight for height and head circumference for girls and boys upto 5 years of age based on WHO standards. Tables 1.3A and B and 1.4A and B summarize the data on length, weight and head circumference for these children. Tables 1.5A and B show data on height, weight and body mass index in girls and boys, respectively, between 5 to 10 years of age. Detailed growth charts are available at http://www.who.int/childgrowth/standards/en.

VELOCITY OF GROWTH

Plotting a child's height and weight on a growth chart helps to determine if he or she is within the expected normal range for his or her age. One time measurement, however, does not indicate if the rate of growth of the child has been normal in the recent past. Likewise, a clearly abnormal percentile position on the growth chart becomes evident only when the factors retarding growth are profound or if they have persisted for a considerable time. On the other hand serial measurements provide rate of growth per unit time. Plotting growth velocity is a useful supplement to monitor rate of growth in children. Growth velocity is a better tool for early identification of factors affecting growth and also for assessment of usefulness of social and remedial measures. Velocity of growth more accurately helps in predicting the ultimate adult height.

GROWTH MONITORING

The Indian Academy of Pediatrics has given guidelines to monitor growth during childhood (Table 1.6). During infancy the monitoring is conveniently done during visits for vaccination. Later it can be integrated into visits for vaccination, minor illnesses or into school health programme. During adolescence sexual maturity rating (SMR) staging is an additional measure to be monitored.

Suggested reading

1. World Health Organsiation. http://www.who.int/nutgrowthdb/en.
2. Guidelines on growth monitoring from birth to 18 years. IAP National Guidelines 2006.
3. Graham CB. Assessment of bone maturation—methods and pitfalls. Radiol Clin North Am 1972,10:185–202.
4. Agarwal DK, Agarwal KN et al. Physical and sexual growth pattern of affluent Indian children from 5–18 years of age. Indian Pediatrics 1992; 29: 1203–1282.
5. Agarwal DK, Agarwal KN et al. Physical growth assessment in adolescence. Indian Pediatrics 2001; 38: 1217–1235.

1

Table 1.3A: Summary table of length/height, weight and head circumference (HC) percentiles for girls aged 0–30 months

Month	*Length/height (cm)*			*Weight (kg)*			*HC (cm)*		
	3rd percentile	*50th centile*	*97th centile*	*3rd percentile*	*50th centile*	*97th centile*	*3rd percentile*	*50th centile*	*97th centile*
0	45.6	49.1	52.7	2.4	3.2	4.2	31.7	33.9	36.1
1	50.0	53.7	57.4	3.2	4.2	5.4	34.3	36.5	38.8
2	53.2	57.1	60.9	4.0	5.1	6.5	36.0	38.3	40.5
3	55.8	59.8	63.8	4.6	5.8	7.4	37.2	39.5	41.9
4	58.0	62.1	66.2	5.1	6.4	8.1	38.2	40.6	43.0
5	59.9	64.0	68.2	5.5	6.9	8.7	39.0	41.5	43.9
6	61.5	65.7	70.0	5.8	7.3	9.2	39.7	42.2	44.6
7	62.9	67.3	71.6	6.1	7.6	9.6	40.4	42.8	45.3
8	64.3	68.7	73.2	6.3	7.9	10.0	40.9	43.4	45.9
9	65.6	70.1	74.7	6.6	8.2	10.4	41.3	43.8	46.3
10	66.8	71.5	76.1	6.8	8.5	10.7	41.7	44.2	46.8
11	68.0	72.8	77.5	7.0	8.7	11.0	42.0	44.6	47.1
12	69.2	74.0	78.9	7.1	8.9	11.3	42.3	44.9	47.5
13	70.3	75.2	80.2	7.3	9.2	11.6	42.6	45.2	47.7
14	71.3	76.4	81.4	7.5	9.4	11.9	42.9	45.4	48.0
15	72.4	77.5	82.7	7.7	9.6	12.2	43.1	45.7	48.2
16	73.3	78.6	83.9	7.8	9.8	12.5	43.3	45.9	48.5
17	74.3	79.7	85.0	8.0	10.0	12.7	43.5	46.1	48.7
18	75.2	80.7	86.2	8.2	10.2	13.0	43.6	46.2	48.8
19	76.2	81.7	87.3	8.3	10.4	13.3	43.8	46.4	49.0
20	77.0	82.7	88.4	8.5	10.6	13.5	44.0	46.6	49.2
21	77.9	83.7	89.4	8.7	10.9	13.8	44.1	46.7	49.4
22	78.7	84.6	90.5	8.8	11.1	14.1	44.3	46.9	49.5
23	79.6	85.5	91.5	9.0	11.3	14.3	44.4	47.0	49.7
24	80.3	86.4	92.5	9.2	11.5	14.6	44.6	47.2	49.8
		Height							
25	80.4	86.6	92.8	9.3	11.7	14.9	44.7	47.3	49.9
26	81.2	87.4	93.7	9.5	11.9	15.2	44.8	47.5	50.1
27	81.9	88.3	94.6	9.6	12.1	15.4	44.9	47.6	50.2
28	82.6	89.1	95.6	9.8	12.3	15.7	45.1	47.7	50.3
29	83.4	89.9	96.4	10.0	12.5	16.0	45.2	47.8	50.5
30	84.0	90.7	97.3	10.1	12.7	16.2	45.3	47.9	50.6

Table: 1.3B: Summary table of height, weight and head circumference (HC) percentiles for girls aged 31–60 months

Month	*Height (cm)*			*Weight (kg)*			*HC (cm)*		
	3rd percentile	*50th centile*	*97th centile*	*3rd percentile*	*50th centile*	*97th centile*	*3rd percentile*	*50th centile*	*97th centile*
31	84.7	91.4	98.2	10.3	12.9	16.5	45.4	48.0	50.7
32	85.4	92.2	99.0	10.4	13.1	16.8	45.5	48.1	50.8
33	86.0	92.9	99.8	10.5	13.3	17.0	45.6	48.2	50.9
34	86.7	93.6	100.6	10.7	13.5	17.3	45.7	48.3	51.0
35	87.3	94.4	101.4	10.8	13.7	17.6	45.8	48.4	51.1
36	87.9	95.1	102.2	11.0	13.9	17.8	45.9	48.5	51.2
37	88.5	95.7	103.0	11.1	14.0	18.1	45.9	48.6	51.3
38	89.1	96.4	103.7	11.2	14.2	18.4	46.0	48.7	51.3
39	89.7	97.1	104.5	11.4	14.4	18.6	46.1	48.7	51.4
40	90.3	97.7	105.2	11.5	14.6	18.9	46.2	48.8	51.5
41	90.8	98.4	106.0	11.6	14.8	19.2	46.2	48.9	51.6
42	91.4	99.0	106.7	11.8	15.0	19.5	46.3	49.0.	51.6
43	92.0	99.7	107.4	11.9	15.2	19.7	46.4	49.0.	51.7
44	92.5	100.3	108.1	12.0	15.3	20.0	46.4	49.1	51.8
45	93.0	100.9	108.8	12.1	15.5	20.3	46.5	49.2	51.8
46	93.6	101.5	109.5	12.3	15.7	20.6	46.5	49.2	51.9
47	94.1	102.1	110.2	12.4	15.9	20.8	46.6	49.3	51.9
48	94.6	102.7	110.8	12.5	16.1	21.1	46.7	49.3	52.0
49	95.1	103.3	111.5	12.6	16.3	21.4	46.7	49.4	52.1
50	95.7	103.9	112.1	12.8	16.4	21.7	46.8	49.4	52.1
51	96.2	104.5	112.8	12.9	16.6	22.0	46.8	49.5	52.2
52	96.7	105.0	113.4	13.0	16.8	22.2	46.9	49.5	52.2
53	97.2	105.6	114.1	13.1	17.0	22.5	46.9	49.6	52.3
54	97.6	106.2	114.7	13.2	17.2	22.8	47.0	49.6	52.3
55	98.1	106.7	115.3	13.4	17.3	23.1	47.0	49.7	52.4
56	98.6	107.3	116.0	13.5	17.5	23.3	47.1	49.7	52.4
57	99.1	107.8	116.6	13.6	17.7	23.6	47.1	49.8	52.5
58	99.6	108.4	117.2	13.7	17.9	23.9	47.2	49.8	52.5
59	100.0	108.9	117.8	13.8	18.0	24.2	47.2	49.9	52.6
60	100.5	109.4	118.4	14.0	18.2	24.4	47.2	49.9	52.6

1

1

Table: 1.4A: Summary table of length/height, weight and head circumference (HC) percentiles for boys aged 0–30 months

Month	*Length/height (cm)*			*Weight (kg)*			*HC (cm)*		
	3rd percentile	*50th centile*	*97th centile*	*3rd percentile*	*50th centile*	*97th centile*	*3rd percentile*	*50th centile*	*97th centile*
0	46.3	49.9	53.4	2.5	3.3	4.3	32.1	34.5	36.9
1	51.1	54.7	58.4	3.4	4.5	5.7	35.1	37.3	39.5
2	54.7	58.4	62.2	4.4	5.6	7.0	36.9	39.1	41.3
3	57.6	61.4	65.3	5.1	6.4	7.9	38.3	40.5	42.7
4	60.0	63.9	67.8	5.6	7.0	8.6	39.4	41.6	43.9
5	61.9	65.9	69.9	6.1	7.5	9.2	40.3	42.6	44.8
6	63.6	67.6	71.6	6.4	7.9	9.7	41.0	43.3	45.6
7	65.1	69.2	73.2	6.7	8.3	10.2	41.7	44.0	46.3
8	66.5	70.6	74.7	7.0.	8.6	10.5	42.2	44.5	46.9
9	67.7	72.0	76.2	7.2	8.9	10.9	42.6	45.0	47.4
10	69.0	73.3	77.6	7.5	9.2	11.2	43.0	45.4	47.8
11	70.2	74.5	78.9	7.7	9.4	11.5	43.4	45.8	48.2
12	71.3	75.7	80.2	7.8	9.6	11.8	43.6	46.1	48.5
13	72.4	76.9	81.5	8.0	9.9	12.1	43.9	46.3	48.8
14	73.4	78.0.	82.7	8.2	10.1	12.4	44.1	46.6	49.0
15	74.4	79.1	83.9	8.4	10.3	12.7	44.3	46.8	49.3
16	75.4	80.2	85.1	8.5	10.5	12.9	44.5	47.0	49.5
17	76.3	81.2	86.2	8.7	10.7	13.2	44.7	47.2	49.7
18	77.2	82.3	87.3	8.9	10.9	13.5	44.9	47.4	49.9
19	78.1	83.2	88.4	9.0	11.1	13.7	45.0	47.5	50.0
20	78.9	84.2	89.5	9.2	11.3	14.0	45.2	47.7	50.2
21	79.7	85.1	90.5	9.3	11.5	14.3	45.3	47.8	50.4
22	80.5	86.0	91.6	9.5	11.8	14.5	45.4	48.0	50.5
23	81.3	86.9	92.6	9.7	12.0	14.8	45.6	48.1	50.7
24	82.1	87.8	93.6	9.8	12.2	15.1	45.7	48.3	50.8
		Height							
25	82.1	88.0	93.8	10	12.4	15.3	45.8	48.4	50.9
26	82.8	88.8	94.8	10.1	12.5	15.6	45.9	48.5	51.1
27	83.5	89.6	95.7	10.2	12.7	15.9	46.0	48.6	51.2
28	84.2	90.4	96.6	10.4	12.9	16.1	46.1	48.7	51.3
29	84.9	91.2	97.5	10.5	13.1	16.4	46.2	48.8	51.4
30	85.5	91.9	98.3	10.7	13.3	16.6	46.3	48.9	51.5

Table: 1.4B: Summary table of height, weight and head circumference (HC) percentiles for boys aged 31–60 months

Month	*Height (cm)*			*Weight (kg)*			*HC (cm)*		
	3rd percentile	*50th centile*	*97th centile*	*3rd percentile*	*50th centile*	*97th centile*	*3rd percentile*	*50th centile*	*97th centile*
31	86.2	92.7	99.2	10.8	13.5	16.9	46.4	49.0	51.6
32	86.8	93.4	100.0	10.9	13.7	17.1	46.5	49.1	51.7
33	87.4	94.1	100.8	11.1	13.8	17.3	46.6	49.2	51.8
34	88.0	94.8	101.5	11.2	14.0	17.6	46.6	49.3	51.9
35	88.5	95.4	102.3	11.3	14.2	17.8	46.7	49.4	52.0
36	89.1	96.1	103.1	11.4	14.3	18.0	46.8	49.5	52.1
37	89.7	96.7	103.8	11.6	14.5	18.3	46.9	49.5	52.2
38	90.2	97.4	104.5	11.7	14.7	18.5	46.9	49.6	52.3
39	90.8	98.0	105.2	11.8	14.8	18.7	47.0	49.7	52.4
40	91.3	98.6	105.9	11.9	15.0	19.0	47.0	49.7	52.4
41	91.9	99.2	106.6	12.1	15.2	19.2	47.1	49.8	52.5
42	92.4	99.9	107.3	12.2	15.3	19.4	47.2	49.9	52.6
43	92.9	100.4	108.0	12.3	15.5	19.7	47.2	49.9	52.7
44	93.4	101.0	108.6	12.4	15.7	19.9	47.3	50.0	52.7
45	93.9	101.6	109.3	12.5	15.8	20.1	47.3	50.1	52.8
46	94.4	102.2	109.9	12.7	16.0	20.4	47.4	50.1	52.8
47	94.9	102.8	110.6	12.8	16.2	20.6	47.4	50.2	52.9
48	95.4	103.3	111.2	12.9	16.3	20.9	47.5	50.2	53.0
49	95.9	103.9	111.8	13.0	16.5	21.1	47.5	50.3	53.0
50	96.4	104.4	112.5	13.1	16.7	21.3	47.5	50.3	53.1
51	96.9	105.0	113.1	13.3	16.8	21.6	47.6	50.4	53.1
52	97.4	105.6	113.7	13.4	17.0	21.8	47.6	50.4	53.2
53	97.9	106.1	114.3	13.5	17.2	22.1	47.7	50.4	53.2
54	98.4	106.7	115.0	13.6	17.3	22.3	47.7	50.5	53.3
55	98.8	107.2	115.6	13.7	17.5	22.5	47.7	50.5	53.3
56	99.3	107.8	116.2	13.8	17.7	22.8	47.8	50.6	53.4
57	99.8	108.3	116.8	13.9	17.8	23.0	47.8	50.6	53.4
58	100.3	108.9	117.4	14.1	18.0	23.3	47.9	50.7	53.5
59	100.8	109.4	118.1	14.2	18.2	23.5	47.9	50.7	53.5
60	101.2	110	118.7	14.3	18.3	23.8	47.9	50.7	53.5

Table 1.5A: Summary table of height, weight and body mass index (BMI) percentiles for girls aged 5–10 years

Year:Month	Height (cm)			Weight (kg)			BMI		
	3rd centile	50th centile	97th centile	3rd centile	50th centile	97th centile	3rd centile	50th centile	97th centile
5: 1	100.6	109.6	118.6	14.2	18.3	24.3	12.9	15.2	18.6
5: 2	101.1	110.1	119.2	14.3	18.4	24.6	12.9	15.2	18.6
5: 3	101.5	110.6	119.7	14.4	18.6	24.9	12.9	15.2	18.7
5: 4	102.0	111.2	120.3	14.5	18.8	25.1	12.9	15.2	18.7
5: 5	102.4	111.7	120.9	14.7	19.0	25.4	12.9	15.2	18.7
5: 6	102.9	112.2	121.5	14.8	19.1	25.7	12.8	15.2	18.7
5: 7	103.3	112.7	122.0	14.9	19.3	25.9	12.8	15.2	18.8
5: 8	103.8	113.2	122.6	15.0	19.5	26.2	12.8	15.3	18.8
5: 9	104.2	113.7	123.1	15.2	19.6	26.5	12.8	15.3	18.8
5: 10	104.6	114.2	123.7	15.3	19.8	26.7	12.8	15.3	18.9
5: 11	105.1	114.6	124.2	15.4	20.0	27.0	12.8	15.3	18.9
6: 0	105.5	115.1	124.8	15.5	20.2	27.3	12.8	15.3	18.9
6: 1	105.9	115.6	125.3	15.6	20.3	27.5	12.8	15.3	19.0
6: 2	106.3	116.1	125.8	15.8	20.5	27.8	12.8	15.3	19.0
6: 3	106.8	116.6	126.4	15.9	20.7	28.1	12.8	15.3	19.0
6: 4	107.2	117.0	126.9	16.0	20.9	28.4	12.8	15.3	19.1
6: 5	107.6	117.5	127.4	16.1	21.0	28.7	12.8	15.3	19.1
6: 6	108.0	118.0	127.9	16.3	21.2	28.9	12.8	15.3	19.2
6: 7	108.4	118.4	128.5	16.4	21.4	29.2	12.8	15.3	19.2
6: 8	108.9	118.9	129.0	16.5	21.6	29.5	12.8	15.3	19.3
6: 9	109.3	119.4	129.5	16.6	21.8	29.8	12.8	15.4	19.3
6: 10	109.7	119.9	130.0	16.8	22.0	30.1	12.9	15.4	19.3
6: 11	110.1	120.3	130.6	16.9	22.2	30.4	12.9	15.4	19.4
7: 0	110.5	120.8	131.1	17.0	22.4	30.8	12.9	15.4	19.4
7: 1	110.9	121.3	131.6	17.2	22.6	31.1	12.9	15.4	19.5
7: 2	111.4	121.8	132.1	17.3	22.8	31.4	12.9	15.4	19.6
7: 3	111.8	122.2	132.7	17.5	23.0	31.7	12.9	15.5	19.6
7: 4	112.2	122.7	133.2	17.6	23.2	32.1	12.9	15.5	19.7
7: 5	112.6	123.2	133.7	17.8	23.4	32.4	12.9	15.5	19.7
7: 6	113.1	123.7	134.3	17.9	23.6	32.8	12.9	15.5	19.8
7: 7	113.5	124.1	134.8	18.1	23.9	33.1	12.9	15.5	19.8
7: 8	113.9	124.6	135.3	18.2	24.1	33.5	13.0	15.6	19.9
7: 9	114.4	125.1	135.9	18.4	24.3	33.8	13.0	15.6	20.0
7: 10	114.8	125.6	136.4	18.6	24.5	34.2	13.0	15.6	20.0
7: 11	115.2	126.1	136.9	18.7	24.8	34.6	13.0	15.7	20.1
8: 0	115.7	126.6	137.5	18.9	25.0	34.9	13.0	15.7	20.2
8: 1	116.1	127.0	138.0	19.1	25.3	35.3	13.0	15.7	20.2
8: 2	116.5	127.5	138.5	19.2	25.5	35.7	13.1	15.7	20.3
8: 3	117.0	128.0	139.1	19.4	25.8	36.1	13.1	15.8	20.4
8: 4	117.4	128.5	139.6	19.6	26.0	36.5	13.1	15.8	20.4
8: 5	117.9	129.0	140.2	19.8	26.3	36.9	13.1	15.8	20.5
8: 6	118.3	129.5	140.7	20.0	26.6	37.4	13.1	15.9	20.6
8: 7	118.7	130.0	141.2	20.1	26.8	37.8	13.2	15.9	20.7
8: 8	119.2	130.5	141.8	20.3	27.1	38.2	13.2	15.9	20.7
8: 9	119.6	131.0	142.3	20.5	27.4	38.6	13.2	16.0	20.8
8: 10	120.1	131.5	142.9	20.7	27.6	39.1	13.2	16.0	20.9
8: 11	120.5	132.0	143.4	20.9	27.9	39.5	13.3	16.1	21.0
9: 0	121.0	132.5	144.0	21.1	28.2	40.0	13.3	16.1	21.1
9: 1	121.5	133.0	144.5	21.3	28.5	40.4	13.3	16.1	21.1
9: 2	121.9	133.5	145.1	21.5	28.8	40.9	13.3	16.2	21.2
9: 3	122.4	134.0	145.6	21.7	29.1	41.3	13.4	16.2	21.3
9: 4	122.8	134.5	146.2	21.9	29.4	41.8	13.4	16.3	21.4
9: 5	123.3	135.0	146.8	22.1	29.7	42.3	13.4	16.3	21.5
9: 6	123.8	135.5	147.3	22.3	30.0	42.7	13.4	16.3	21.6
9: 7	124.2	136.1	147.9	22.6	30.3	43.2	13.5	16.4	21.6
9: 8	124.7	136.6	148.4	22.8	30.6	43.7	13.5	16.4	21.7
9: 9	125.2	137.1	149.0	23.0	30.9	44.2	13.5	16.5	21.8
9: 10	125.7	137.6	149.5	23.2	31.2	44.7	13.6	16.5	21.9
9: 11	126.1	138.1	150.1	23.4	31.5	45.2	13.6	16.6	22.0
10: 0	126.6	138.6	150.7	23.7	31.9	45.7	13.6	16.6	22.1

Table 1.5B: Summary table of height, weight and body mass index (BMI) percentiles for boys aged 5–10 years

Year:Month	Height (cm)			Weight (kg)			BMI		
	3rd centile	50th centile	97th centile	3rd centile	50th centile	97th centile	3rd centile	50th centile	97th centile
5: 1	101.6	110.3	118.9	14.6	18.5	23.8	13.1	15.3	18.1
5: 2	102.1	110.8	119.5	14.7	18.7	24.0	13.1	15.3	18.1
5: 3	102.6	111.3	120.1	14.8	18.9	24.3	13.1	15.3	18.1
5: 4	103.1	111.9	120.7	15.0	19.0	24.5	13.1	15.3	18.1
5: 5	103.5	112.4	121.3	15.1	19.2	24.8	13.1	15.3	18.1
5: 6	104.0	112.9	121.8	15.3	19.4	25.1	13.1	15.3	18.1
5: 7	104.4	113.4	122.4	15.4	19.6	25.3	13.1	15.3	18.2
5: 8	104.9	113.9	123.0	15.5	19.8	25.6	13.1	15.3	18.2
5: 9	105.4	114.5	123.5	15.7	19.9	25.8	13.1	15.3	18.2
5: 10	105.8	115.0	124.1	15.8	20.1	26.1	13.1	15.3	18.2
5: 11	106.2	115.5	124.7	16.0	20.3	26.4	13.2	15.3	18.3
6: 0	106.7	116.0	125.2	16.1	20.5	26.7	13.2	15.3	18.3
6: 1	107.1	116.4	125.8	16.3	20.7	26.9	13.2	15.3	18.3
6: 2	107.6	116.9	126.3	16.4	20.9	27.2	13.2	15.3	18.4
6: 3	108.0	117.4	126.9	16.5	21.1	27.5	13.2	15.3	18.4
6: 4	108.4	117.9	127.4	16.7	21.3	27.8	13.2	15.4	18.4
6: 5	108.8	118.4	127.9	16.8	21.5	28.1	13.2	15.4	18.5
6: 6	109.3	118.9	128.5	17.0	21.7	28.3	13.2	15.4	18.5
6: 7	109.7	119.4	129.0	17.2	21.9	28.6	13.2	15.4	18.5
6: 8	110.1	119.8	129.5	17.3	22.1	28.9	13.2	15.4	18.6
6: 9	110.5	120.3	130.1	17.5	22.3	29.2	13.2	15.4	18.6
6: 10	111.0	120.8	130.6	17.6	22.5	29.5	13.2	15.4	18.7
6: 11	111.4	121.3	131.1	17.8	22.7	29.8	13.3	15.5	18.7
7: 0	111.8	121.7	131.7	17.9	22.9	30.1	13.3	15.5	18.8
7: 1	112.2	122.2	132.2	18.1	23.1	30.4	13.3	15.5	18.8
7: 2	112.6	122.7	132.7	18.2	23.3	30.7	13.3	15.5	18.8
7: 3	113.0	123.1	133.3	18.4	23.5	31.1	13.3	15.5	18.9
7: 4	113.4	123.6	133.8	18.5	23.7	31.4	13.3	15.6	18.9
7: 5	113.8	124.1	134.3	18.7	23.9	31.7	13.3	15.6	19.0
7: 6	114.3	124.5	134.8	18.8	24.1	32.0	13.3	15.6	19.0
7: 7	114.7	125.0	135.3	19.0	24.3	32.3	13.4	15.6	19.1
7: 8	115.1	125.5	135.9	19.1	24.6	32.7	13.4	15.6	19.2
7: 9	115.5	125.9	136.4	19.3	24.8	33.0	13.4	15.7	19.2
7: 10	115.9	126.4	136.9	19.5	25.0	33.3	13.4	15.7	19.3
7: 11	116.2	126.8	137.4	19.6	25.2	33.7	13.4	15.7	19.3
8: 0	116.6	127.3	137.9	19.8	25.4	34.0	13.4	15.7	19.4
8: 1	117.0	127.7	138.4	19.9	25.6	34.4	13.4	15.8	19.4
8: 2	117.4	128.2	138.9	20.1	25.9	34.7	13.5	15.8	19.5
8: 3	117.8	128.6	139.4	20.2	26.1	35.1	13.5	15.8	19.5
8: 4	118.2	129.0	139.9	20.4	26.3	35.5	13.5	15.8	19.6
8: 5	118.6	129.5	140.4	20.5	26.5	35.8	13.5	15.9	19.7
8: 6	119.0	129.9	140.9	20.7	26.7	36.2	13.5	15.9	19.7
8: 7	119.3	130.4	141.4	20.8	27.0	36.6	13.5	15.9	19.8
8: 8	119.7	130.8	141.9	21.0	27.2	37.0	13.5	15.9	19.9
8: 9	120.1	131.3	142.4	21.1	27.4	37.4	13.6	16.0	19.9
8: 10	120.5	131.7	142.9	21.3	27.6	37.8	13.6	16.0	20.0
8: 11	120.9	132.1	143.4	21.4	27.9	38.2	13.6	16.0	20.0
9: 0	121.3	132.6	143.9	21.6	28.1	38.6	13.6	16.0	20.1
9: 1	121.6	133.0	144.4	21.8	28.3	39.0	13.6	16.1	20.2
9: 2	122.0	133.4	144.9	21.9	28.6	39.4	13.7	16.1	20.2
9: 3	122.4	133.9	145.4	22.1	28.8	39.8	13.7	16.1	20.3
9: 4	122.8	134.3	145.8	22.2	29.1	40.3	13.7	16.2	20.4
9: 5	123.2	134.7	146.3	22.4	29.3	40.7	13.7	16.2	20.5
9: 6	123.5	135.2	146.8	22.6	29.6	41.1	13.7	16.2	20.5
9: 7	123.9	135.6	147.3	22.7	29.8	41.6	13.8	16.3	20.6
9: 8	124.3	136.1	147.8	22.9	30.1	42.0	13.8	16.3	20.7
9: 9	124.7	136.5	148.3	23.1	30.4	42.5	13.8	16.3	20.8
9: 10	125.0	136.9	148.8	23.2	30.6	43.0	13.8	16.4	20.8
9: 11	125.4	137.3	149.3	23.4	30.9	43.5	13.8	16.4	20.9
10: 0	125.8	137.8	149.8	23.6	31.2	43.9	13.9	16.4	21.0

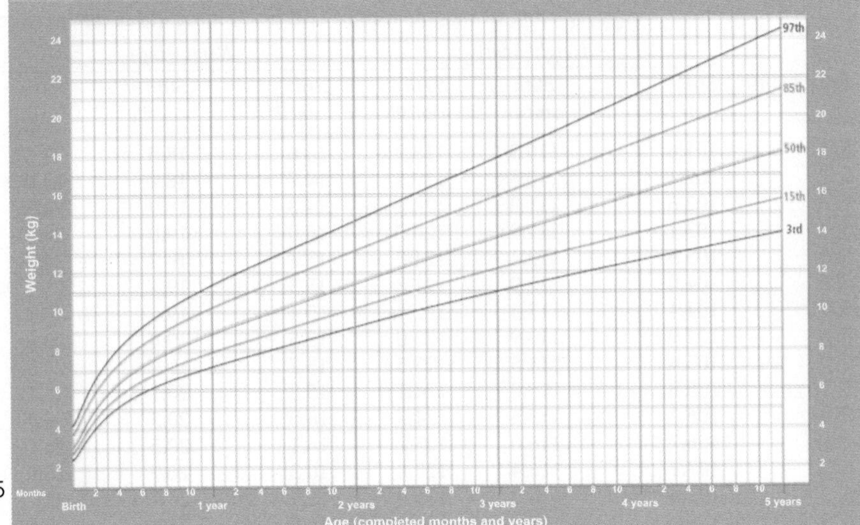

Fig. 1.8: Weight for age (girls) from birth to 5 years (percentiles)

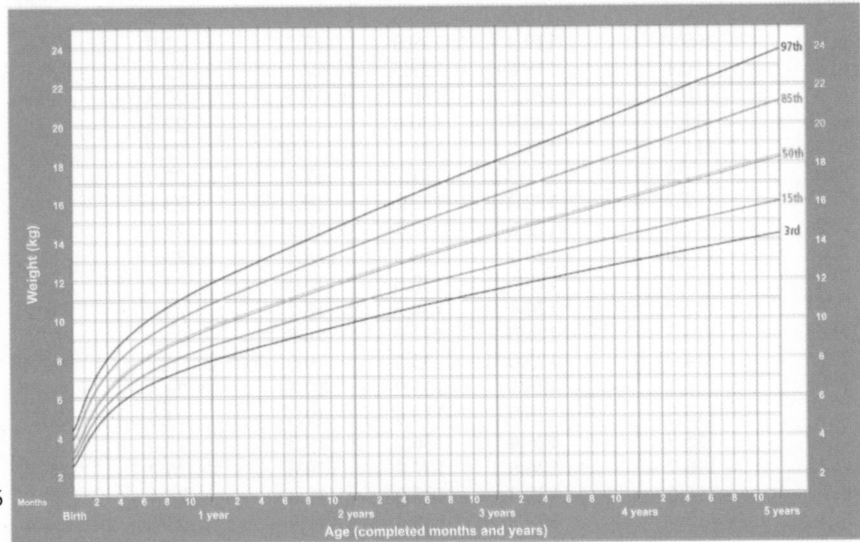

Fig. 1.9: Weight for age (boys) from birth to 5 years (percentiles)

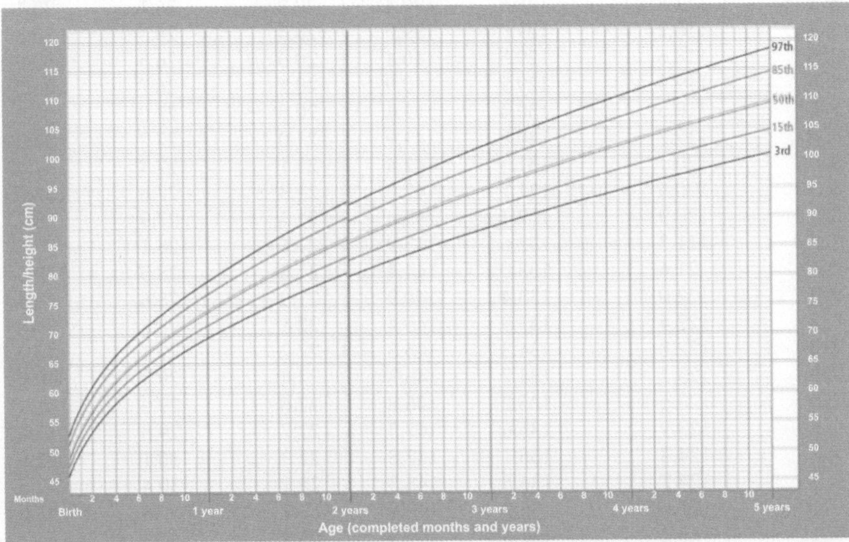

Fig. 1.10: Height for age (girls) from birth to 5 years (percentiles)

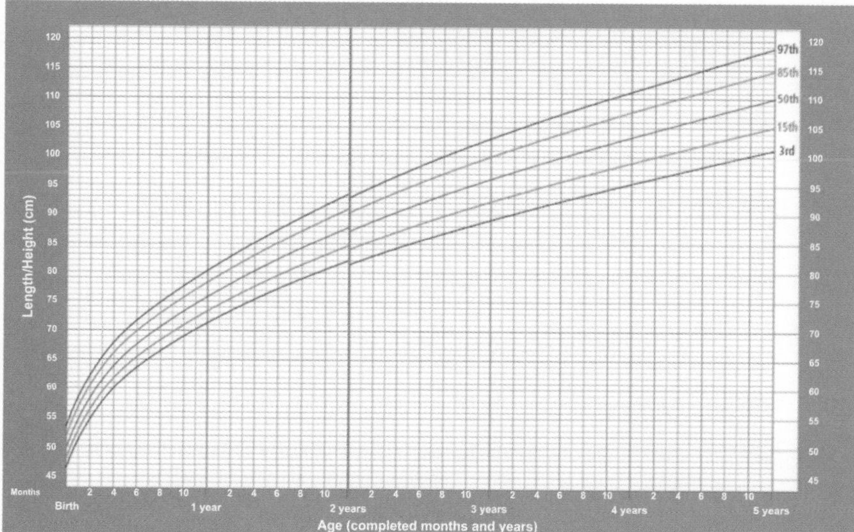

Fig. 1.11: Height for age (boys) from birth to 5 years (percentiles)

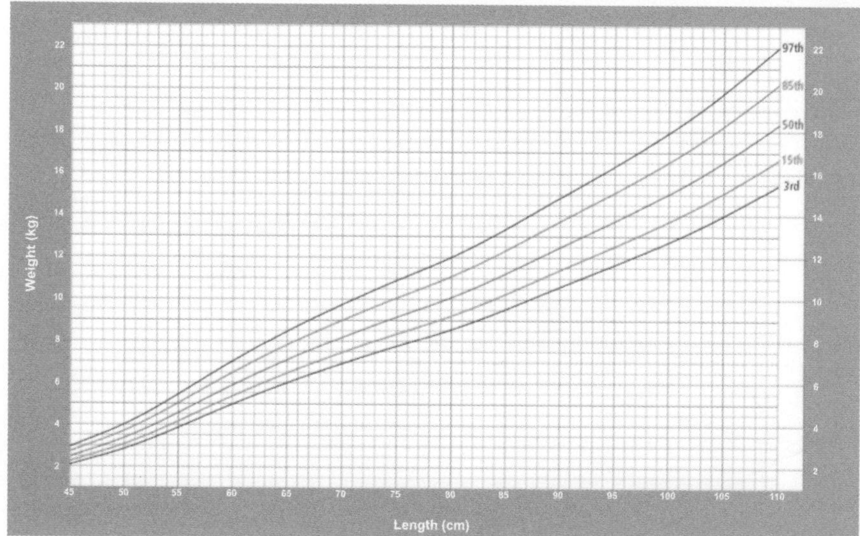

Fig. 1.12: Weight for height (girls) from birth to 2 years (percentiles)

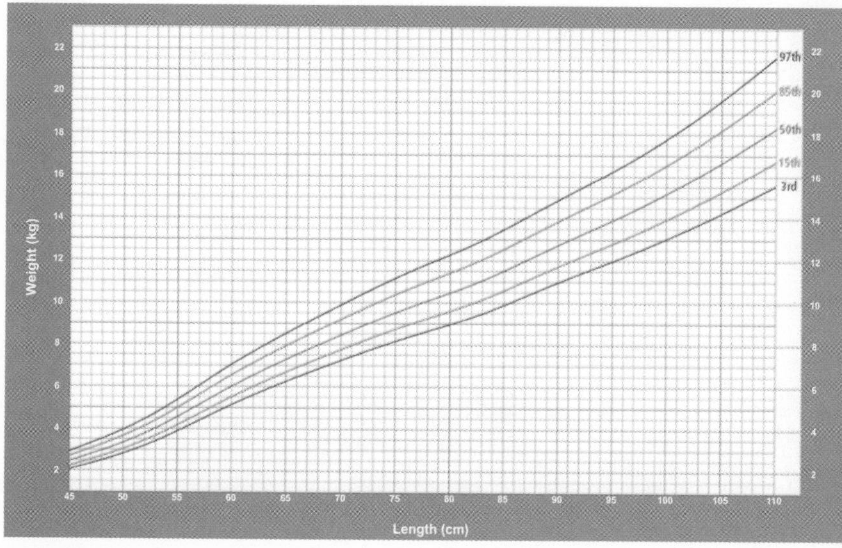

Fig. 1.13: Weight for height (boys) from birth to 2 years (percentiles)

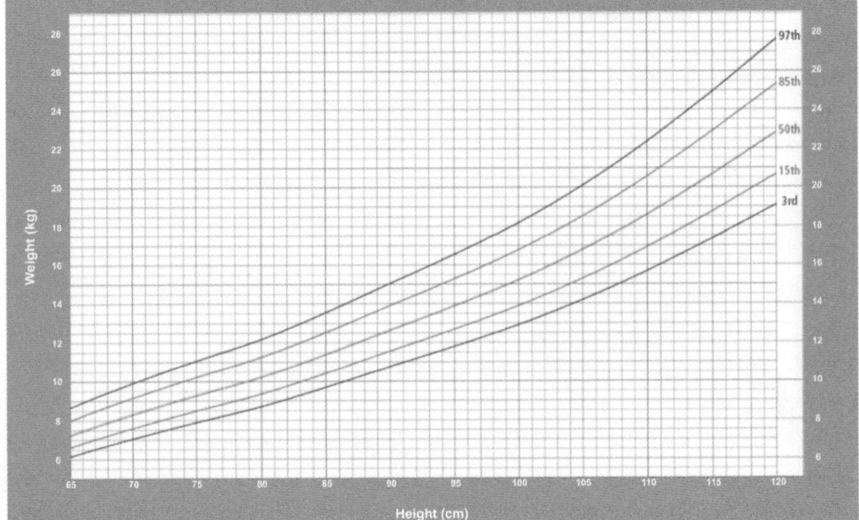

Fig. 1.14: Weight for height (girls) from 2 to 5 years (percentiles)

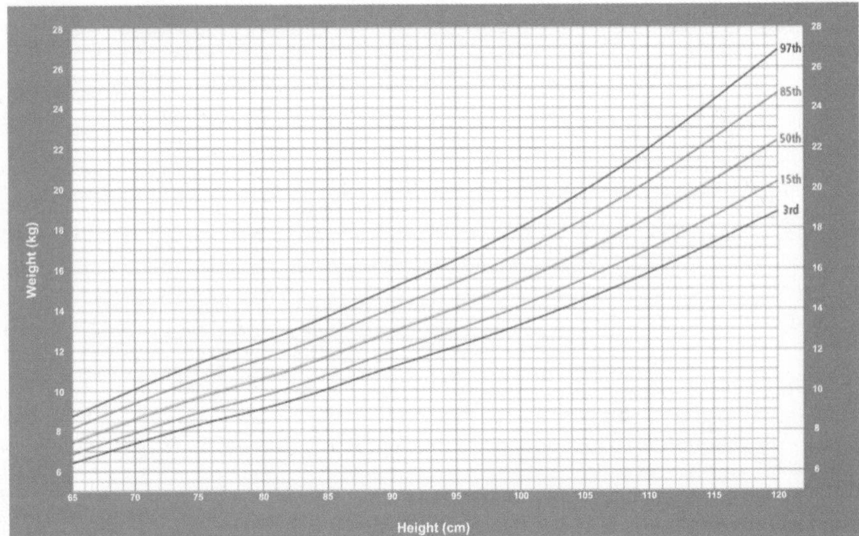

Fig. 1.15: Weight for height (boys) from 2 to 5 years (percentiles)

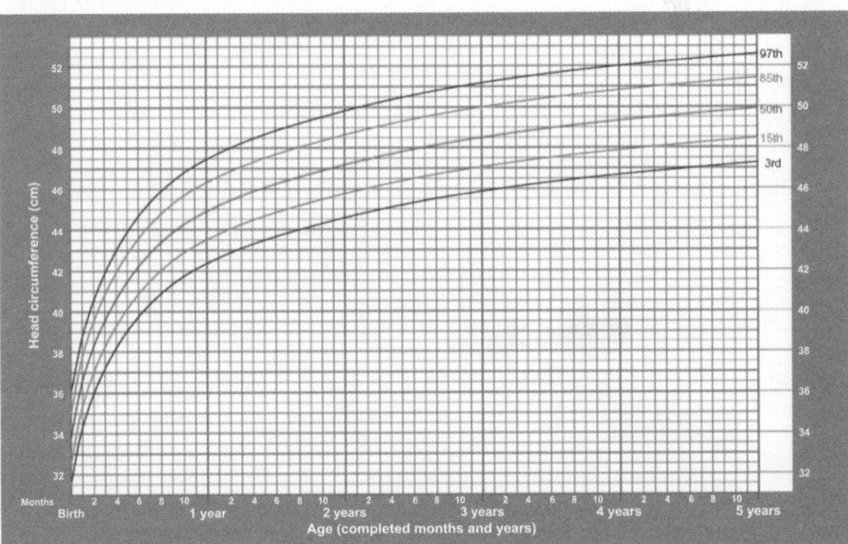

Fig. 1.16: Head circumference (girls) from birth to 5 years (percentiles)

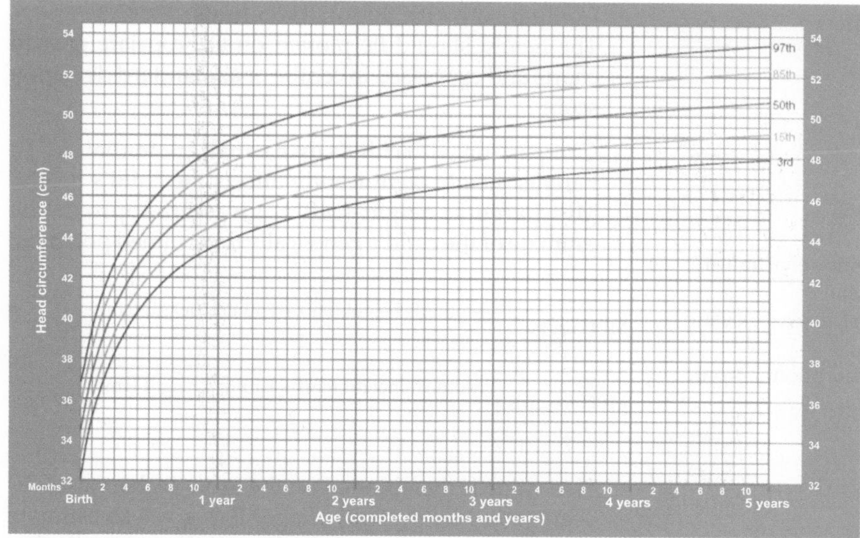

Fig. 1.17: Head circumference (boys) from birth to 5 years (percentiles)

Table 1.6: Suggested growth monitoring in children of different ages

Age	*Height/length*	*Weight*	*HC*	*Other*
Birth	✓	✓	✓	
1½, 3 ½, 6, 9, 15 mo	✓	✓	✓	
18 months–3 years	✓ (6 monthly)	✓ (6 monthly)	✓(6 monthly)	
3.5–5.5 years	✓ (6 monthly)	✓ (6 monthly)		
6–8 years (yearly)	✓ (6 monthly)	✓ (6 monthly)		BMI and SMR
9–18 yrs	✓ (yearly)	✓ (yearly)		BMI and SMR (yearly)

Adapted from guidelines given by Indian Academy of Pediatrics (2006)
BMI body mass index, SMR sexual maturity rating, HC head circumference

DISORDERS OF GROWTH

SHORT STATURE

Definition and Epidemiology

Short stature is defined as height below 3rd centile or more than 2 standard deviations below the median height for that age and sex according to the population standard.

As is evident from the definition, approximately 3% of children in any given populations will be short. Approximately half of these have physiological, i.e. familial or constitutional short stature and half have pathological short stature.

Etiology

Short stature can be due to a variety of causes (Table 1.7). Amongst the pathological causes, undernutrition and chronic systemic illness are the common etiological factors followed by growth hormone deficiency (GHD) and hypothyroidism.

Steps in Assessment of a Child who Presents with Short Stature

1. **Accurate height measurement**
   For children below 2 years, supine length should be measured using an infantometer with a rigid headboard on one side and a moveable footboard on the other side while holding the infant straight on the horizontal board.
   For older children, height should be measured with a stadiometer. Child should be asked to remove footwear and stand with both feet together. His heels, buttocks, scapulae and occiput should be touching the vertical support and head should be in Frankfurt plane, i.e. the line joining the inferior margin of orbit to external auditory meatus should be parallel to the ground. The horizontal headboard is then brought down to the vertex end reading is taken to the nearest millimeter.
2. **Assessment of body proportion**
   Short stature can be proportionate or disproportionate. The proportionality is assessed by upper segment (US):

1

Table 1.7: Causes of short stature

Physiological or normal variant short stature

a. Familial
b. Constitutional

Pathological short stature

a. Undernutrition
b. Chronic systemic illness
  - Renal: renal tubular acidosis, chronic renal failure, steroid dependent nephrotic syndrome
  - Cardiopulmonary: congenital heart disease, cystic fibrosis, asthma
  - Gastrointestinal and hepatic: malabsorption, chronic liver disease
  - Chronic severe infections
c. Endocrine causes
  - Growth hormone deficiency/insensitivity
  - Hypothyroidism
  - Cushing syndrome
  - Pseudohypoparathyroidism
  - Precocious or delayed puberty
d. Psychosocial dwarfism
e. Children born small for gestational age
f. Skeletal dysplasias, e.g. achondroplasia, rickets
g. Genetic syndromes, e.g. Turner syndrome, Down syndrome

lower segment (LS) ratio and comparison of arm span with height.

Technique of measurement: US can be measured by taking the sitting height of the child. Child is made to sit on a square stool placed against the vertical rod of the stadiometer. The headboard is brought down to the vertex similarly as for taking height. The height of the stool is subtracted from the reading obtained to get sitting height. LS can be obtained by subtracting US from height. Alternatively, LS can be measured by taking the length from pubic symphysis to the ground while the child is standing erect.

For measuring arm span, child is asked to stand straight with both arms extended outwards parallel to the ground. Length between the tips of the middle finger of the 2 outstretched hands is the arm span.

Interpretation: Normally, US : LS ratio is 1.7 at birth, 1.3 at 3 years, 1.1 by 6 years, 1 by 10 years and 0.9 in adults. Increase in US : LS ratio is seen in rickets, achondroplasia and untreated congenital hypothyroidism. Decrease in US : LS ratio is seen in spondyloepiphyseal dysplasia and vertebral anomalies. Arm span is shorter than length by 2.5 cm at birth, equals height at 11years and thereafter is greater than height.

3. **Assessment of height velocity**
   Height velocity is the rate of increase in height over a period of time expressed as cm/year. It varies with the age of the child. If height velocity is low, the child is more likely to be suffering from a pathological cause of short stature.

4. **Comparison with population norms**
   The height should be plotted on appropriate growth charts and expressed in centile or as standard deviation score.

5. **Comparison with child's own genetic potential**
   Parents' height significantly affects the child's height. Mid parental height (MPH) gives an approximate estimate of the child's genetically determined potential.

$$\text{MPH for boys} = \frac{\text{Mother's height (cm)} + \text{Father's height (cm)}}{2} + 6.5\text{ cm}$$

$$\text{MPH for girls} = \frac{\text{Mother's height (cm)} + \text{Father's height (cm)}}{2} - 6.5\text{ cm}$$

   This value is then plotted on the growth chart at 18–20 years (adult equivalent) of age. This gives an estimate of the target height for the child and the percentile that he/ she is likely to follow.

6. **Sexual maturity rating (SMR)**
   SMR stage should be assessed in older children. Height spurt is seen in early puberty in girls and mid-puberty in boys. Precious puberty can lead to early height spurt followed by premature epiphyseal fusion and ultimate short stature. On the other hand, delayed puberty can also present with short stature in adolescents as the height spurt is also delayed. This is especially common in children with constitutional delay in growth.

Diagnosis

Diagnosis is based on a detailed history, examination and laboratory evaluation.

History and examination: Careful history and examination can unravel many clues to the etiology of short stature (Tables 1.8 and 1.9).

Table 1.8: Clues to etiology of short stature from history

History	*Etiology*
Low birth weight	Small for gestational age
Polyuria	Chronic renal failure, renal tubular acidosis
Diarrhea, offensive greasy stools	Malabsorption
Neonatal hypoglycemia, jaundice, micropenis	Growth hormone deficiency
Headache, vomiting, visual problem	Pituitary/hypothalamic space occupying lesion
Lethargy, constipation, weight gain	Hypothyroidism
Dietary intake	Undernutrition
Social history	Psychosocial dwarfism
History for timing of puberty in parents	Constitutional delay of growth

Table 1.9: Clues to etiology of short stature from examination

Examination finding	*Etiology*
Disproportion	Skeletal dysplasia, rickets, hypothyroidism
Dysmorphism	Congenital syndromes
Pallor	Chronic anemia, chronic renal failure
Hypertension	Chronic renal failure
Frontal bossing, depressed nasal bridge, crowded teeth, small penis	Growth hormone deficiency
Goiter, coarse skin	Hypothyroidism
Central obesity, striae	Cushing syndrome

Investigations

The investigative work up to be done is guided by clues from history and physical examination.

Bone age (BA) assessment should be done in all children with short stature. The appearance of various epiphyseal centers and fusion of epiphyses with metaphyses tells about the skeletal maturity of the child. BA is conventionally read from radiograph of the hand and wrist using either Gruelich-Pyle atlas or Tanner-Whitehouse method. BA gives an idea as to what proportion of the adult height has been achieved by the child and what is the remaining potential for height gain.

BA is delayed compared to chronological age in almost all causes of short stature. Few exceptions to this are familial short stature, in which BA equals chronological age and precocious puberty, in which BA exceeds chronological age. In case of constitutional delay, undernutrition and systemic illness, BA is less than chronological age and equals height age. In cases of growth hormone deficiency (GHD) and hypothyroidism, BA may be even less than height age if the endocrine condition is diagnosed late.

In all children with disproportionate short stature, ***skeletal survey*** should be done to rule out skeletal dysplasia and rickets.

The essential screening investigations (also called level 1 investigations) that should be done in all children with short stature are listed in Table 1.10. If these investigations are normal and bone age is delayed, level 2 investigations should be done. If these investigations are also normal, then the diseases that still remain to be excluded are GHD and malabsorption. If the child's height is borderline short, i.e. between –2 and –3 SD, then it is prudent to wait for 6–12 months and observe for height velocity. On the other hand, if the child is significantly short (< –3SD) at presentation or if height velocity over 6–12 months is also low for age, one should proceed to level 3 investigations.

Table 1.10: Stepwise investigative work-up for short stature

Level 1 (essential) investigations for short stature

1. Complete hemogram with ESR
2. Bone age
3. Urinalysis including microscopy, osmolality and pH
4. Stool examination for parasites, steatorrhea and occult blood
5. Blood – urea, creatinine, venous gas, calcium, phosphate, alkaline phosphatase, fasting glucose, albumin and transaminases

Level 2 investigations for short stature

1. Serum thyroxin and thyroid stimulating hormone to rule out hypothyroidism
2. Karyotype to rule out Turner syndrome in girls

Level 3 investigations for short stature

1. Celiac serology (anti-endomysial or anti-tissue transglutaminase antibodies) and duodenal biopsy
2. Growth hormone stimulation test with clonidine or insulin and serum insulin-like growth factor-1 (IGF-1) levels.

Salient Clinical Features of Some Causes of Short Stature

Endocrine causes: These are discussed in the chapter on endocrinological disorders.

Familial Short Stature

Familial short stature is the condition in which child is short as per the definition of short stature (i.e. height is below the 3rd centile) but is normal according to his own genetic potential as determined by the parents' height. The child is short because the parents are short. These children have a normal height and weight at birth and then show a catch down growth, so that the height and weight come to lie on their target (mid-parental) centiles by the age of 2 years. Subsequently, the growth velocity remains normal throughout childhood and adolescence. The body proportion is appropriate and bone age equals the chronological age. Puberty is achieved at appropriate age and final height is within the target range.

Constitutional Growth Delay

These children are born with a normal length and weight and grow normally for the 1st 6–12 months of life. Their growth then shows a deceleration so that the height and weight fall below the 3rd centile for age. By 2–3 years of age, height velocity again accelerates and they continue to grow just below and parallel to the 3rd centile with a normal height velocity. The onset of puberty and adolescent growth spurt is also delayed in these children but final height is within normal limits. Bone age is lower than chronological age and corresponds to the height age. History of delayed puberty and delayed height spurt is usually present in one or both parents with eventual normal height.

1

Table 1.11: Comparison of constitutional delay and familial short stature

Feature	*Constitutional growth delay*	*Familial short stature*
Height	Short	Short
Height velocity	Normal	Normal
Family history	Of delayed puberty	Of short stature
Bone age	Less than chronological age	Normal
Puberty	Delayed	Normal
Final height	Normal	Low but normal for target height

Some of the differentiating features between constitutional delay and familial short stature are listed in Table 1.11

Undernutrition

This is one of the commonest cause for short stature in our country. Chronic undernutrition leads to stunting. A good dietary history and presence of other features of malnutrition such as low mid-arm circumference and low weight for height on examination suggest the diagnosis.

Skeletal Dysplasias

Inborn errors in the formation of various components of the skeletal system can cause disturbances of cartilage and bone, grouped under the general term chondrodysplasias or skeletal dysplasias. These conditions may be inherited or sporadic, and are usually associated with abnormal skeletal proportions and severe short stature (except hypochondroplasia, where growth retardation is mild). A careful elicitation of family history, measurement of body proportions, examination of the limbs and skull and skeletal survey are required for diagnosis.

Genetic Syndromes

Turner syndrome with an incidence of 1:2000 live births is a common cause of short stature in girls and should be ruled out in all short girls, even if the typical phenotypic features are absent. Some other syndromes associated with short stature are Down's, Prader-Willi, Russell-Silver and Seckel syndrome.

Psychosocial Dwarfism

This condition is also known as emotional deprivation dwarfism, maternal deprivation dwarfism or hyperphagic short stature. It is seen in children in unhappy homes where the emotional needs of the child are totally neglected.

It is characterized by functional hypopituitarism indicated by low IGF-1 levels and inadequate response of GH to stimulation. Therapy with GH is however, not beneficial. Good catch-up growth is usually seen when the child is placed in a less stressful environment and nurtured with love and affection.

Children Born Small for Gestational Age (SGA)

Birth weight below the 10th centile for gestational age can be caused by maternal, placental or fetal factors. Most of these babies show catch-up growth by 2 years of age. However, an estimated 20–30% of babies born SGA fail to show catch up growth and remain short. Subtle defects in the Growth hormone- Insulin-like growth factor (GH-IGF) axis are considered responsible for the short stature.

Management

The general principles of management for any child who presents with short stature include *counseling of parents and dietary advice*. Parents should be counseled to highlight the positive aspects in child personality and not put undue emphasis on stature. Intake of a balanced diet containing the recommended amounts of macro and micronutrients should also be recommended.

The specific management depends on the underlying cause. For physiological causes, reassurance and annual monitoring of height and weight is sufficient. Dietary rehabilitation for undernutrition and treatment of underlying condition such as renal tubular acidosis or celiac disease are generally associated with good catch up growth.

For skeletal dysplasias, limb lengthening procedures are offered at few orthopedic centers. For hypothyroidism, levothyroxine replacement is advised.

For GHD, treatment with daily subcutaneous injections of GH is recommended. GH therapy is also approved for several other conditions though the doses required are generally higher and improvement in final height smaller and more variable as compared to GHD. Some of these conditions are Turner syndrome; children born SGA who fail to show catch up growth by 2 years of age and children with chronic renal failure prior to transplant.

With any form of therapy, monitoring with regular and accurate recording of height is mandatory for a good outcome.

Suggested reading

1. Hintz RL. Management of disorders of size. In Brook CGD, Hindmarsh PC, eds. Clinical Pediatric Endocrinology. London: Blackwell Science, 2001:124-39.

2. Bhatia V. Normal and abnormal growth. In Desai MP, Bhatia V, Menon PSN eds Pediatric Endocrine Disorders. Hyderabad: Orient Longman,2001:41-83.

FAILURE TO THRIVE

Definition and Epidemiology

Failure to thrive (FTT) is a descriptive term rather than diagnosis and is used for infants and children up to 5 years of age whose physical growth is significantly less than their peers of same age and sex. FTT usually refers to weight below 3rd or 5th centile, failure to gain weight over a period of time or a change in rate of growth that has crossed two major centiles, e.g. 75th to 50th, over a period of time.

The prevalence of FTT varies according to the population sampled.

Etiology

Traditionally FTT is classified as organic, where the child has some known underlying medical condition and non-organic or psychosocial, where poor growth is the result of inadequate caloric provision and/ or emotional deprivation. Organic and non-organic etiological factors may co-exist, e.g. in children with cerebral palsy or multiple congenital anomalies. FTT is non-organic in up to 80% of cases. The common etiological factors are listed in Table 1.12.

Table 1.12: Causes of failure to thrive

Organic causes

- Gastrointestinal—gastroesophageal reflux, malabsorption, inflammatory bowel disease, pyloric stenosis
- Neurological—mental retardation, cerebral palsy
- Renal—renal tubular acidosis, chronic renal failure
- Cardiopulmonary—congenital heart disease, cystic fibrosis, asthma
- Endocrine—Hypothyroidism, diabetes mellitus, adrenal insufficiency
- Infections—chronic parasitic or bacterial infections of gastrointestinal tract, tuberculosis, infection with human immunodeficiency virus
- Genetic—Inborn errors of metabolism, chromosomal anomalies
- Miscellaneous—Lead poisoning, malignancy, collagen vascular disease

Non-organic causes

- Poverty
- Misperceptions or lack of knowledge about diet and feeding practices
- Lack of breastfeeding, feeding diluted formulae
- Dysfunctional parent-child relationship with child abuse and neglect

Clinical Features

These children present with poor growth, often associated with poor development and cognitive functioning. The degree of FTT is usually measured by calculating weight, height and weight for height as percentage of the median value for age based on appropriate growth charts.

Diagnosis

History, physical examination and observation of parent–child interaction are important. Detailed laboratory investigations are needed only if history and physical examination suggest that an organic cause is responsible for FTT and to localize the systems involved. For initial evaluation the following investigations are adequate:

Management

The goals of management are nutritional rehabilitation, treatment of organic causes if present and remedial measures for psychosocial factors involved.

Indications for hospitalization include: (i) severe malnutrition, (ii) diagnostic and laboratory evaluation needed for organic cause, (iii) lack of catch up growth during outpatient treatment (iv) Suspected child abuse or neglect

The management of these patients depends on the underlying cause. Nutritional rehabilitation is necessary. Weight gain in response to adequate calorie feeding establishes the diagnosis of psychosocial FTT.

Prognosis

If managed early and adequately, the prognosis for physical growth recovery is good. However, the outlook for cognitive, emotional and behavioral development is variable and less certain. The growth and development of these children should be monitored regularly.

Suggested reading

1. Frank D, Silva M, Needlman R. Failure to thrive: Mystery, myth and method. Contemporary Pediatrics 1993;10:114–9.
2. Hank DA, Jiesel SH. Failure to thrive. Pediatr Clin North Am 1998;35:1187–205.

2 Normal and Abnormal Development

Development, the maturation of function with age, is reflected by the sequential attainment of various milestones. Matching the formation of new synapses in the brain, increasingly complex skills are learnt starting from the more basic capabilities. Appropriate sensory input, e.g. through hearing and vision, and secure and responsive relationships help build a healthy brain architecture that provides a strong foundation for lifelong learning, behavior, and health.

RULES OF DEVELOPMENT

To understand this complex process, it would be pertinent to understand a few basic facts about human development. Development is a continuous process, starting in utero and progressing in an orderly manner until maturity. The sequence of attainment of milestones is essentially same in all children, e.g. all babies learn to babble before speaking words or sit before they stand. Variations exist only in the time and manner of attainment. As for growth, the process of development also progresses in a cephalocaudal direction. For example, head control precedes trunk control, which precedes lower limb control. The control of limbs proceeds in a proximodistal fashion, whereby hand use is learnt before finger control. Certain primitive reflexes have to be lost before relevant milestones are attained, e.g. palmar grasp is lost before voluntary grasp is attained.

The initial disorganized mass activity is gradually replaced by more specific and wilful activity, e.g. when shown a bright toy, a 3–4 month old will excitedly move all limbs, and squeal loudly whereas a 3–4 year old may just smile and ask for it.

FACTORS AFFECTING DEVELOPMENT

Development depends on a variety of mutually interactive factors such as hereditary endowment, biological integrity, physical and psychosocial milieu and emotional stimulation.

Prenatal Factors

Intelligence of parents has direct correlation on the final IQ of the child. Moreover, certain developmental patterns are observed to follow parental patterns like speech. Apart from these, parental attitudes, involvement, education and desire for the child also have an impact on the development of the child.

Genetic Factors

There are many genetic causes for developmental delay and subsequent mental retardation (MR). Prominent genetic factors include chromosomal abnormalities (e.g. Down syndrome), X-linked MR (fragile X and other mutations), subtelomeric deletions, single gene disorders causing disorders of brain formation (lissencephaly) and other metabolic disorders (phenylketonuria).

Maternal Factors

A host of factors which impair growth in utero also can potentially affect brain growth, particularly if they are severe and/or sustained. Prominent among these are maternal drug or alcohol abuse, pregnanacy induced hypertension, hypothyroidism, malnutrition and feto-placental insufficiency due to any cause. Acquired infections (e.g. STARCH— syphilis, toxoplasmosis, AIDS, rubella, CMV, herpes) can have a severe impact on fetal physical and brain growth. Exposure to free radicals and oxidants in utero (e.g. chorioamnionitis) has been incriminated in the causation of cerebral palsy and developmental impairment. It has been shown that the overall quality of maternal care can produce lasting changes in stress reactivity, anxiety, and memory in the child.

Neonatal Risk Factors

Low Birth Weight

Babies with low birth weight include premature babies and those growth retarded in utero. The latter are more likely to have developmental impairment. Premature babies are at risk due to other complications, including intracranial bleed, white matter injury, hypoxia, hyperbilirubinemia, hypoglycemia, etc.

Neonatal Seizures

The association of neonatal seizures with developmental impairment is related to the cause of seizures. Those with the adverse outcomes include malformations of brain, inborn errors of metabolism, severe hypoxia, hypoglycemia, intracranial bleeds and intracranial infections.

Post Neonatal Factors

Nutritional Factors

Severe calorie deficiency, as evident by stunting, is associated with apathy, less positive affect, lower levels of play and insecure attachment. Calorie deficiency is often associated with deficiency of vitamins (B1, B2, and niacin) that contribute to developmental impairment. Deficiency of iron is associated with anemia and also with impaired emotional and cognitive development.

Iodine deficiency is an important preventable cause of developmental delay and mental subnormality in our country.

Acquired Insults to Brain

Traumatic or infectious insults (meningitis, encephalitis, cerebral malaria) and other factors (near drowning, irradiation), particularly during early years of life, can have a permanent adverse effect on brain development.

Endocrine Factors

Hypothyroidism is an important preventable and treatable cause of developmental delay and should be considered in all cases with uncertain etiology for delay.

Associated Impairments

Impairments particularly those involving sensory inputs from the eyes or ears can have a significant impact on attainment of milestones. These impairments have to be actively sought in any child with delay as they offer opportunity for intervention.

Others

Environmental exposure to toxins (lead, mercury, pesticides) that can affect cognition may be important in certain regions of our country.

Social Factors

During the critical period of development and learning, several social factors have an important bearing on not only cognition but also attitudes, social-emotional competence and sensorimotor development.

Parenting

Cognitive stimulation, caregiver's sensitivity and affection (emotional warmth or rejection of child) and responsiveness to the child in the setting of other factors such as poverty, cultural values and practices have an important bearing on child development. Higher levels of maternal warmth and responsiveness are associated with higher cognitive ability and reduced levels of behavioral problems in young children.

Poverty

This is possibly the most common underlying factor for impaired child development worldwide. It acts throughout the lifetime of the individual and also affects the next generation.

Lack of Stimulation

Social and emotional deprivation and lack of adequate interaction and stimulation is an important cause of developmental impairment, particularly evident in the setting of poverty.

Violence and Abuse

Domestic and community violence are emerging threats to child development. Child abuse, physical and sexual, can have a profound psychological effect on the child. Problems of attention and cognition are more common in children exposed to violence or abuse. Apart from the direct effect, there are indirect consequences due to change in family dynamics and effect on the caregiver. Early life experiences have been shown to have a bearing on behavioral patterns later in life.

NORMAL DEVELOPMENT

Normal development is a complex process and has a multitude of facets. However, it is convenient to understand and assess development under the following domains:

i. gross motor development,
ii. fine motor skill development,
iii. personal and social development and general understanding,
iv. language, and
v. vision and hearing.

Gross Motor Development

Motor development progresses in an orderly sequence to ultimate attainment of locomotion and more complex motor tasks thereafter. In an infant it is assessed and observed as follows:

Supine and Pull to Sit

The infant is observed in supine and then gently pulled to sitting position. Control of head and curvature of the spine is observed. In the newborn period, the head completely lags behind and back is rounded (Fig. 2.1). Starting at 6 weeks, the head control develops and by 12 weeks there is only a slight head lag. The spine curvature also decreases accordingly (Fig. 2.2). The child has complete neck control by 20 weeks (Fig. 2.3). This can be ascertained by swaying him gently "side-to-side" when sitting. At this age, the baby loves to play with his feet, and may take his foot to mouth as well.

2

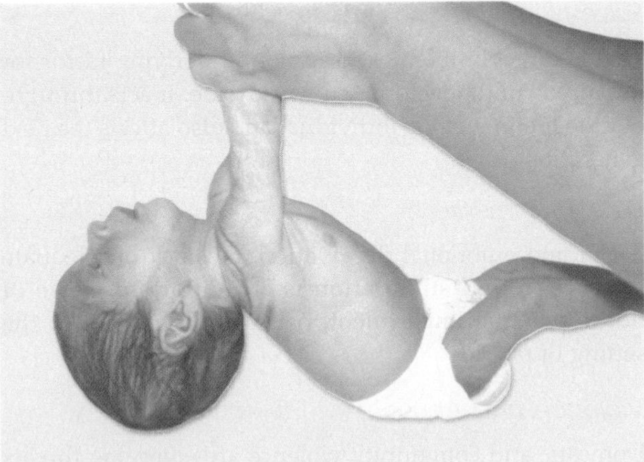

Fig. 2.1: Pull to sit; complete head lag in a newborn

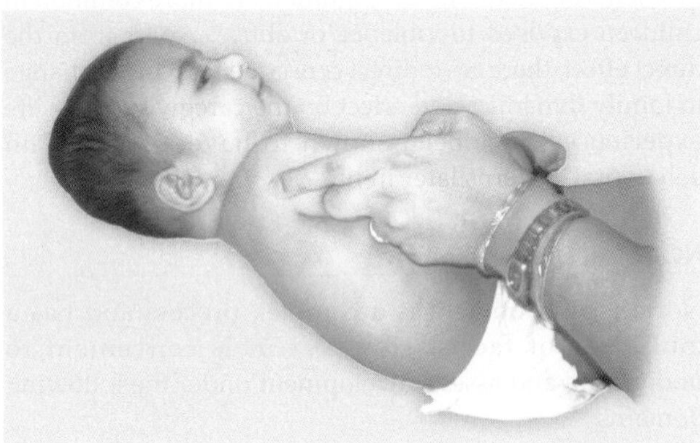

Fig. 2.2: Pull to sit; no head lag at 4 months

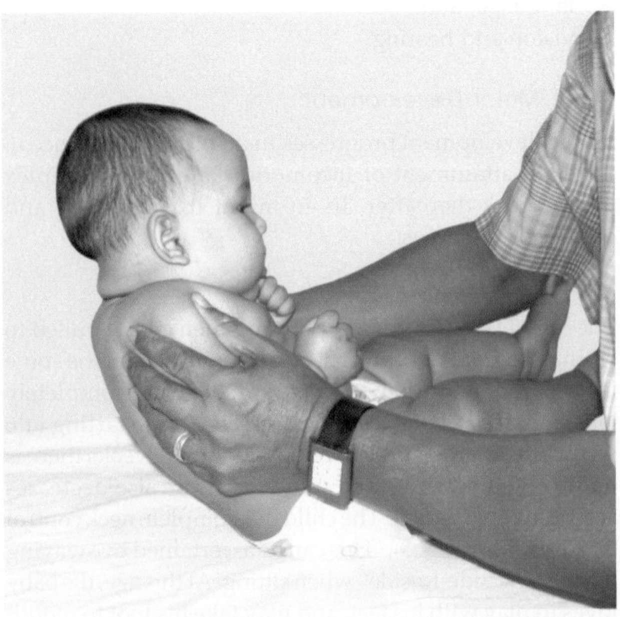

Fig. 2.3: Pull to sit; flexes the head on to chest at 5 months

Ventral Suspension

The child is held in prone position and then lifted from the couch, with the examiner supporting the chest and abdomen of the child with the palm of his hand. In the newborn the head flops down (Fig. 2.4). At 6 weeks the child momentarily holds head in the horizontal plane and by 8 weeks he can maintain this position well (Fig. 2.5). By 12 weeks he can lift his head above the horizontal plane (Fig. 2.6).

Prone Position

At birth or within a few days, the newborn turns the head to one side. At 4 weeks the child lifts the chin up momentarily in the midline. By 8 weeks, face is lifted up at 45° and by 12 weeks the child can bear weight on forearms with chin and shoulder off the couch and face up to 90° (Figs 2.7 and 2.8). At 6 months, he can lift his head and greater part of the chest while supporting weight on the extended arms (Fig. 2.9). Between 4 to 6 months, he learns to roll over, at first from back to side and then from back to stomach. By the age of 8 months, he crawls (with abdomen on the ground) and by 10 months, creeps (abdomen off the ground, with weight on knees and hands).

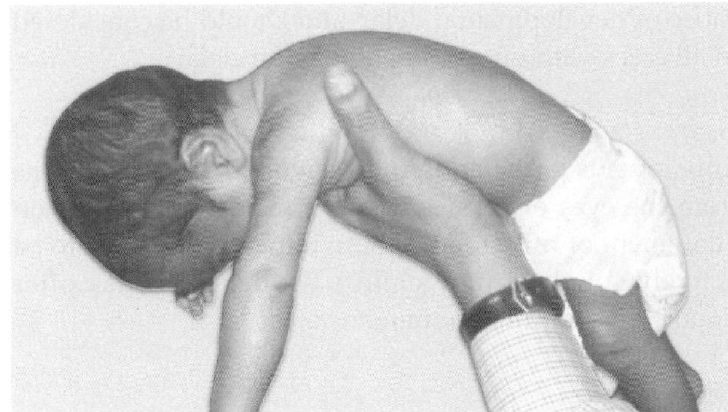

Fig. 2.4: Ventral suspension; unable to hold neck in the line with trunk at 4 weeks

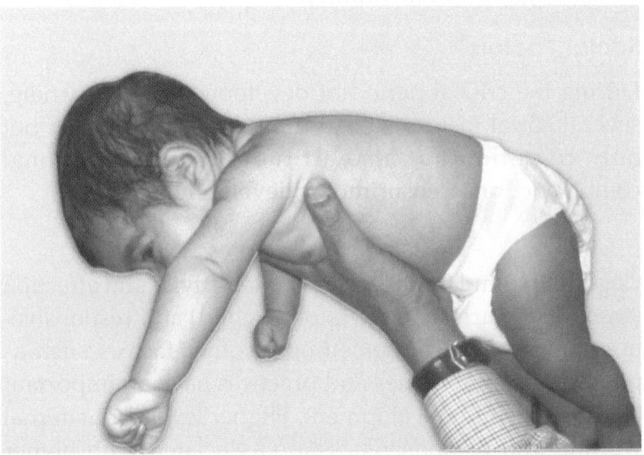

Fig. 2.5: Ventral suspension; head in line with the trunk at 8–10 weeks

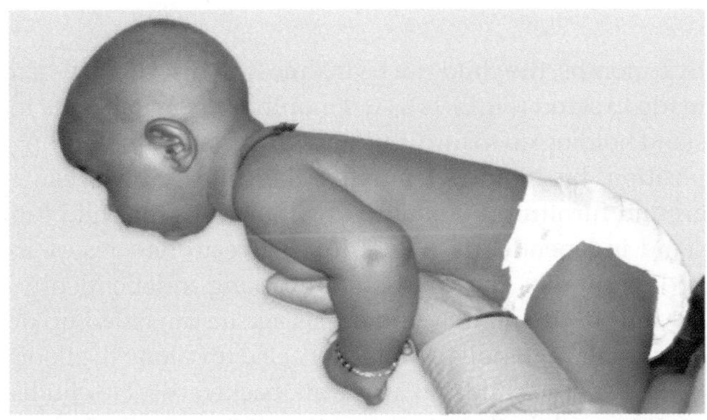

Fig. 2.6: Ventral suspension; head above the plane of trunk at 4 months

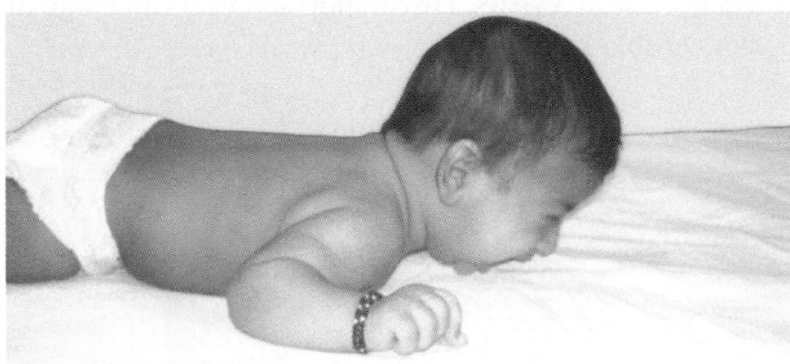

Fig. 2.7: In prone: face lifted to about 45° at 8 weeks

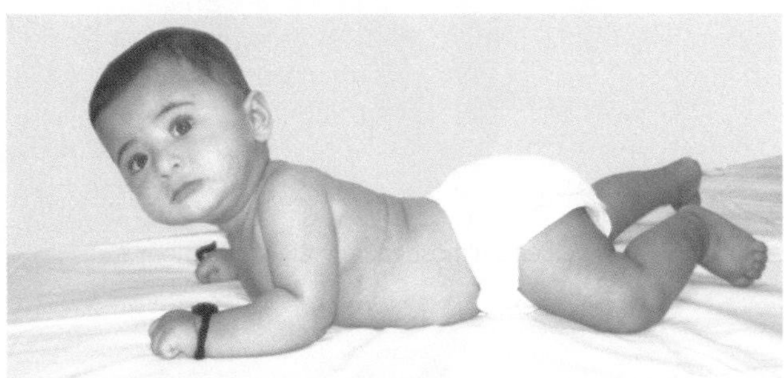

Fig. 2.8: In prone: face, head and chest off the couch at 4 months

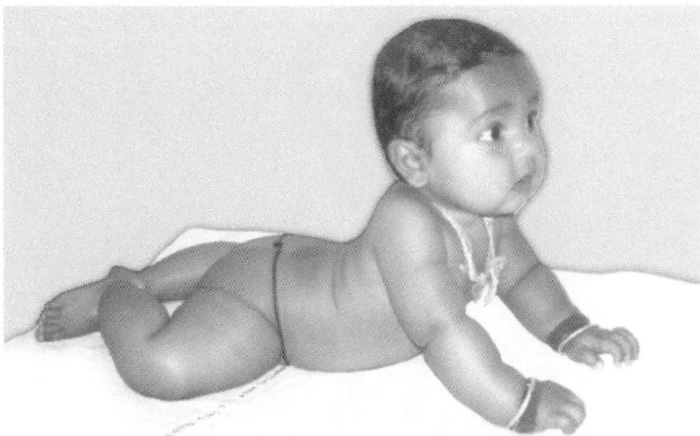

Fig. 2.9: In prone: weight on hands with extended arms at 6 months

Sitting

By the age of 5 months, the child can sit steadily with support of pillows or the examiner's hands (Figs 2.10 and 2.11). At first the back is rounded, but gradually it straightens (Figs 2.10 and 2.11). He independently sits with his arms forward for support (tripod or truly "sitting with support") by the age of 6–7 months (Fig. 2.12). Steady sitting without any support generally develops at around 8 months (Fig. 2.13). By 9–10 months he can pivot in sitting position to play around with toys (Fig. 2.14).

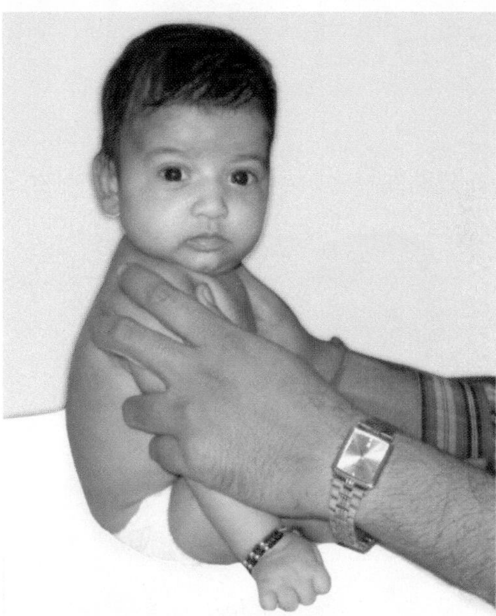

Fig. 2.10: Sitting; back rounded but able to hold head at 8 weeks

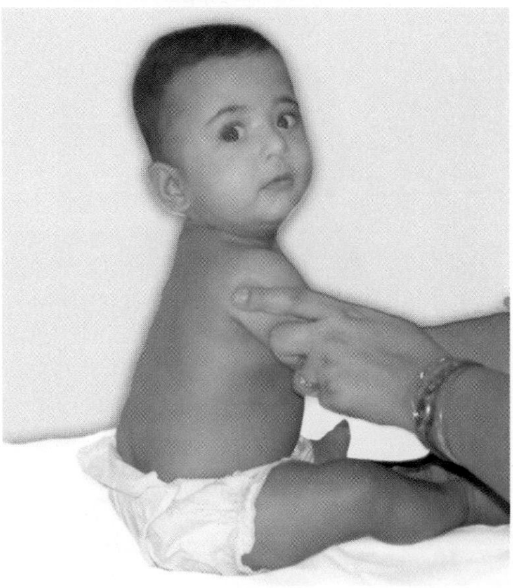

Fig. 2.11: Sitting; back much straighter at 4 months

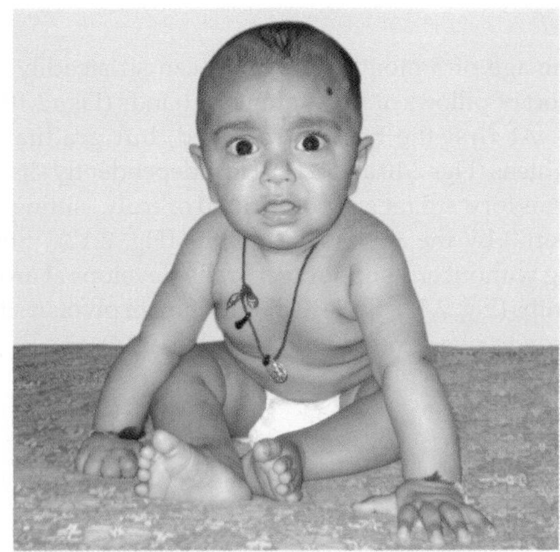

Fig. 2.12: Sitting with support of hands at 6 months

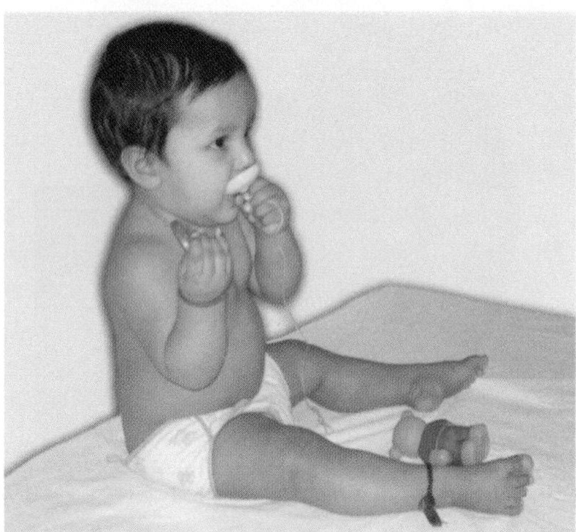

Fig. 2.13: Sitting without support at 8 months

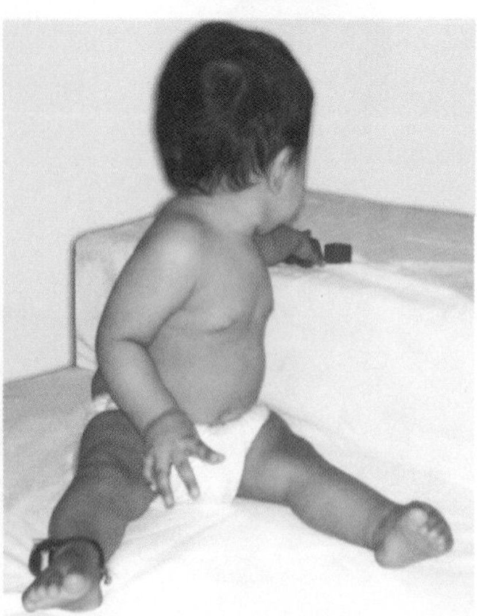

Fig. 2.14: Pivoting; turns around to pick up an object at 11 months

Standing and Walking

By 6 months, the child can bear almost all his weight when made to stand (Fig. 2.15). At 9 months, the child begins to stand holding on to furniture and pulls himself to standing position. By 10 and 11 months, the child starts cruising around furniture. At about 12 or 13 months the child can stand independently (Fig. 2.16). Between the ages of 13 and 15 months the child starts walking independently. He runs by 18 months, and at this age he can crawl up or down stairs and pulls a doll or wheeled toy along the floor. By 2 years the child can also walk backwards. He climbs upstairs with both feet on one step at 2 years. By 3 years he can climb upstairs with one foot per step and by 4 years he can move down the stairs in the same fashion. He can ride a tricycle at 3 years. He can hop at 4 years and skip at 5 years (Table 2.1).

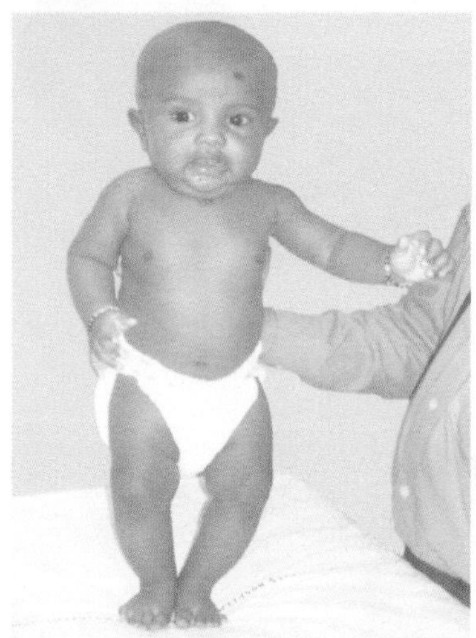

Fig. 2.15: Bears almost entire weight at 6 months

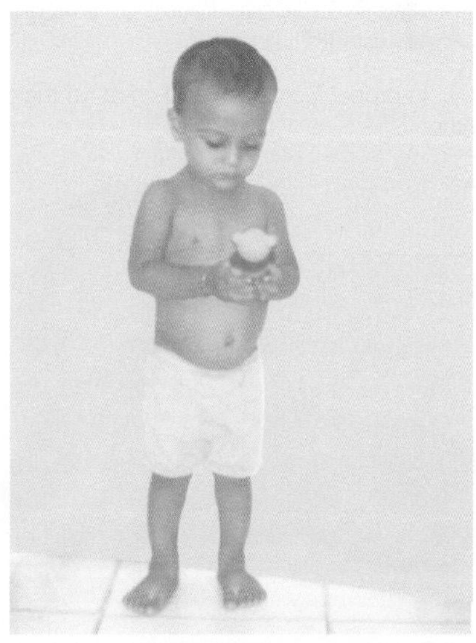

Fig. 2.16: Stands well at 15 months

Table 2.1: Key gross motor developmental milestones

Age	*Milestone*
3 months	Neck holding
5 months	Rolls over
6 months	Sits in tripod fashion (sitting with own support)
8 months	Sitting without support
9 months	Stands holding on (with support)
12 months	Creeps well; walks but falls; stands without support
15 months	Walks alone; creeps upstairs
18 months	Runs; explores drawers
2 years	Walks up and downstairs (2 feet/step); jumps
3 years	Rides tricycle; alternate feet going upstairs
4 years	Hops on one foot; alternate feet going downstairs

Fine Motor Development

This primarily involves the development of fine manipulation skills and coordination with age.

Hand Eye Coordination

Between 12 to 20 weeks the child observes his own hands very intently, this is called hand regard (Fig. 2.17). Its persistence after 20 weeks is considered abnormal. At 4 months, hands of the child come together in midline as he plays. If a red ring is dangled in front of him, he fixes his attention on it, and then tries to reach for it (Fig. 2.18). Initially he may overshoot but eventually he gets it and brings it to his mouth.

Grasp is best assessed by offering a red cube to the child. The 5–6 month old infant reaches and holds the cube (larger object) in a crude manner using the ulnar aspect of his hand (Fig. 2.19). He can transfer objects from one hand to other by 6–7 months. The child is able to grasp from the radial side of hand at 8–9 months (Fig. 2.20). By the age of 1 year mature grasp (index finger and thumb) is evident (Fig. 2.21).

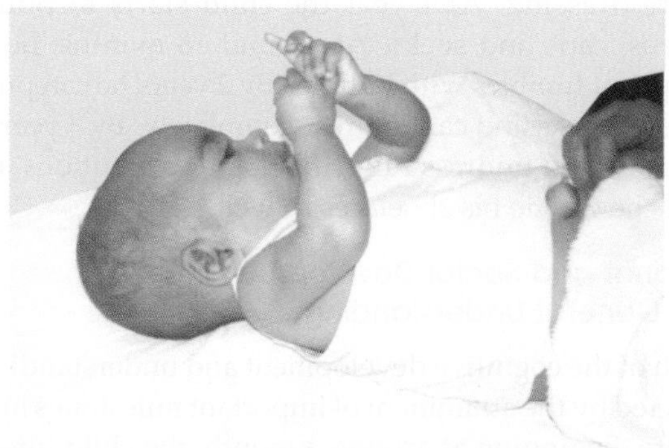

Fig. 2.17: Hand regard (between 12–20 weeks)

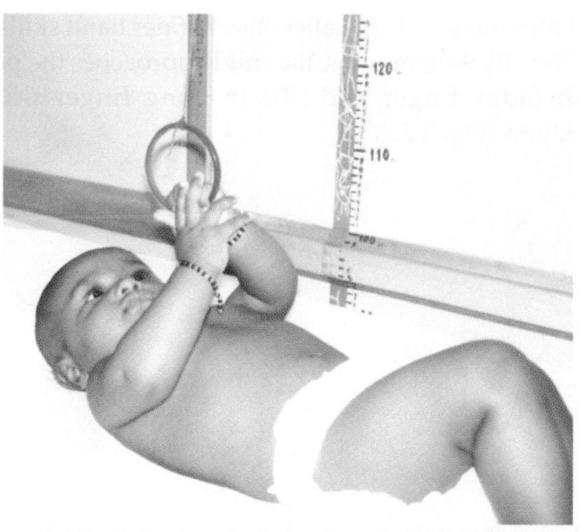

Fig. 2.18: Bidextrous grasp approach to a dangling ring at 4 months

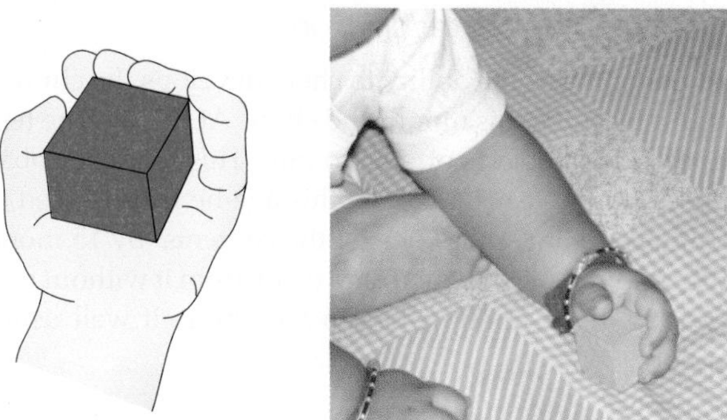

Fig. 2.19: Immature grasp at 6 months, palmar grasp

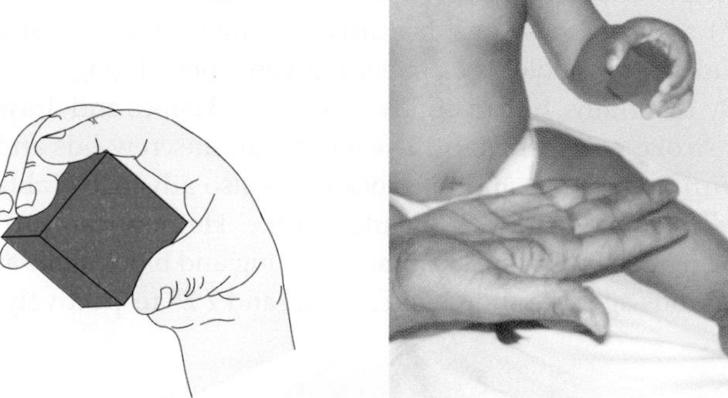

Fig. 2.20: Intermediate grasp at 8 months, beginning to use radial aspect of the hand

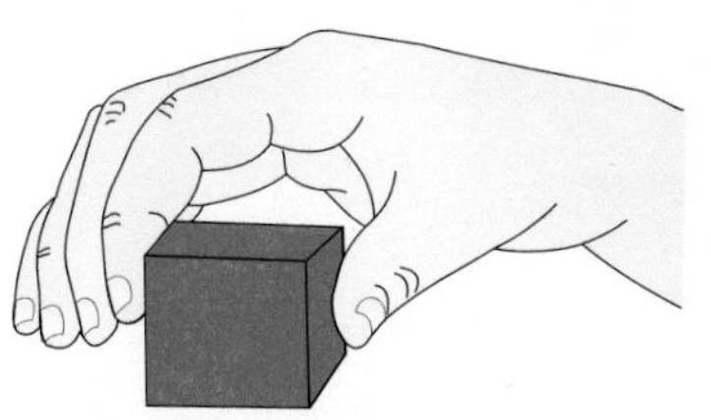

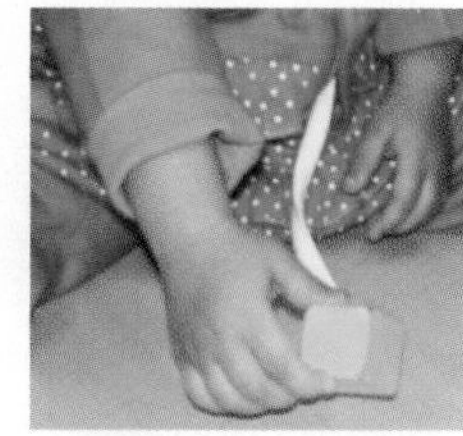

Fig. 2.21: Mature grasp at 1 year of age, note the use of thumb and index finger

By offering pellets (smaller object), finer hand skills are assessed. By 9–10 months, the child approaches the pellet by an index finger and lifts it using finger thumb apposition (Fig. 2.22).

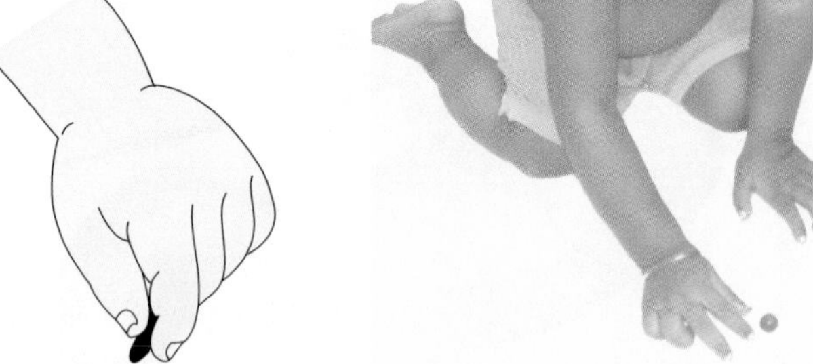

Fig. 2.22: Pincer grasp approach to small objects (index finger and thumb)

Hand to Mouth Coordination

At 6 months as the ability to chew develops the child can take a biscuit to his mouth and chew. At this age, he tends to mouth all objects offered to him. This tendency abates by around 1 year of age. By this age he tries to feed self from a cup but spills some of the contents. By 15 months the child can pick up a cup and drink from it without much spilling. By 18 months he can feed himself well using a spoon.

Advanced Hand Skills

With advancing age the child can use hands to perform finer activities. Much of the advanced skills depend partly on the opportunity given by the caretakers to the child. At around 15 months, he turns 2–3 pages of a book at a time and scribbles on a paper if given a pencil. (Fig. 2.23) By 18 months, he can build a tower of 2–3 cubes and draw a stroke with pencil. By 2 years, he can unscrew lids and turn door knobs and his block skills also advance (Table 2.2). He now draws a circular stroke. He now can turn pages of a book, one at a time. Drawing and block skills at various ages are shown in Figs 2.24 and 2.25 respectively.

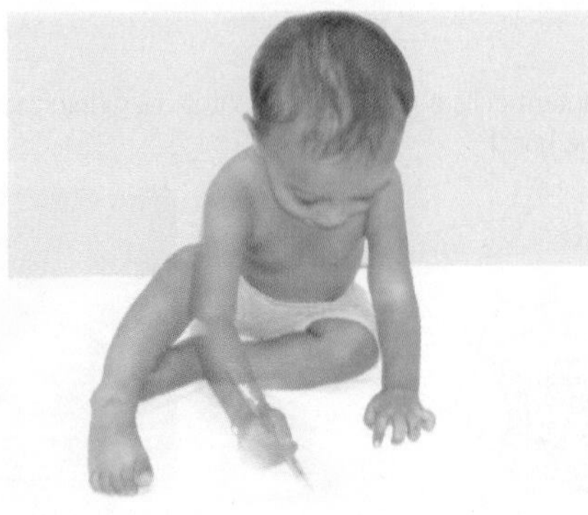

Fig. 2.23: Scribbles spontaneously at 15 months

Table 2.2: Key fine motor developmental milestones

Age	*Milestone*
4 months	Bidextrous reach (reaching out for objects with both hands)
6 months	Unidextrous reach (reaching out for objects with one hand); transfers objects
9 months	Immature pincer grasp; probes with forefinger
12 months	Pincer grasp mature
15 months	Imitates scribbling; tower of 2 blocks
18 months	Scribbles; tower of 3 blocks
2 years	Tower of 6 blocks; vertical and circular stroke
3 years	Tower of 9 blocks; copies circle
4 years	Copies cross; bridge with blocks
5 years	Copies triangle

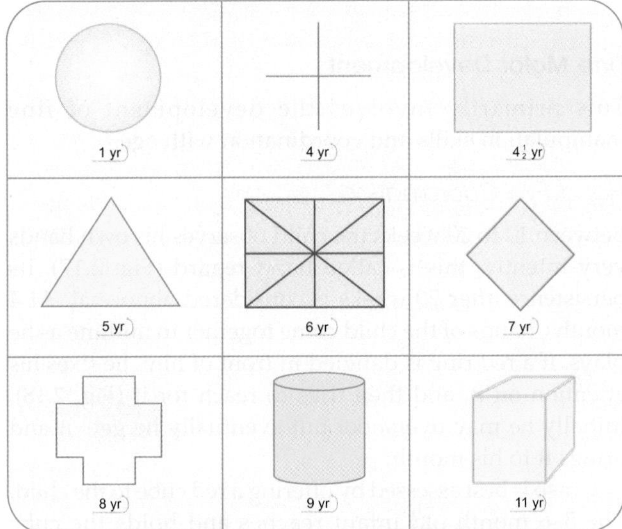

Fig. 2.24: Drawing skills at various ages

Dressing

Between 18–30 months of age, children are most eager to learn dressing skills. Undressing being easier, is learned before dressing. At 1 year the child starts to pull off mittens, caps and socks. At around 18 months, he can unzip, but fumbles with buttons. By 2 years he can put on shoes or socks and can undress completely. By 3 years he can dress and undress fully, if helped with buttons. By 5 years, he can tie his shoelaces as well.

Personal and Social Development and General Understanding

Much of the cognitive development and understanding is reflected by the attainment of important milestones in this sphere. Beginning at around 1 month, the child intently watches his mother when she talks to him (Fig. 2.26). He

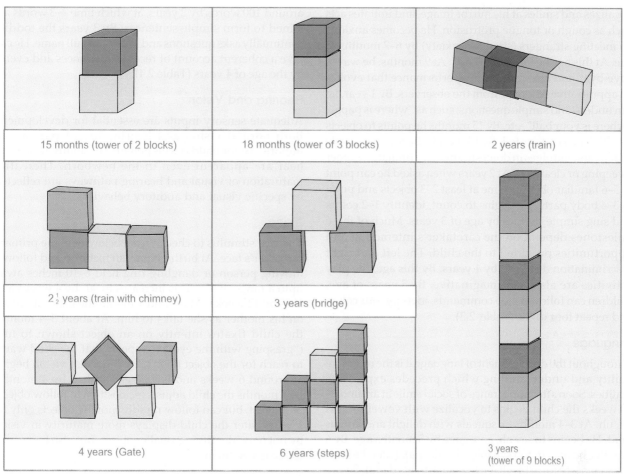

15 months (tower of 2 blocks)	18 months (tower of 3 blocks)	2 years (train)
$2\frac{1}{2}$ years (train with chimney)	3 years (bridge)	3 years (tower of 9 blocks)
4 years (Gate)	6 years (steps)	

Fig. 2.25: Block skills at various ages

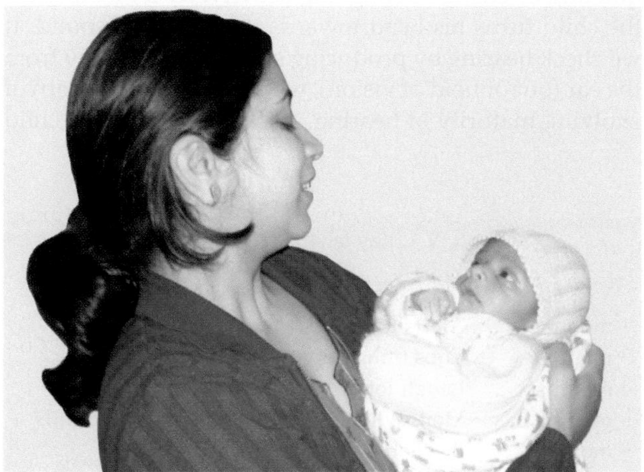

Fig. 2.26: At 1 month the baby showing intent regard of his mother's face as she talks to him

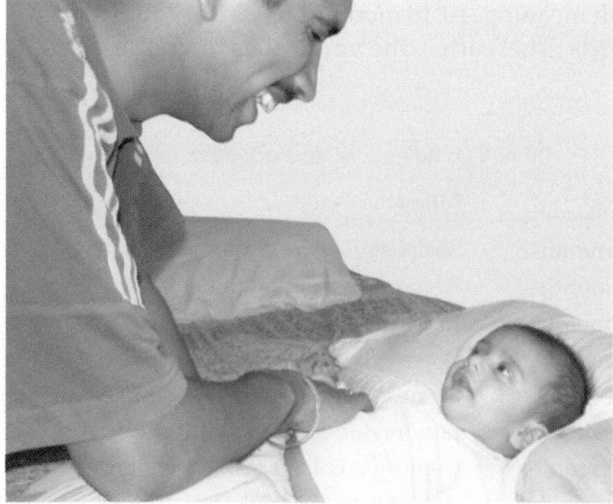

Fig. 2.27: Social smile

starts smiling back (social smile) when anyone talks to him or smiles at him by 6–8 weeks of age (Fig. 2.27). It is important to differentiate social smile from spontaneous smile (smile without any social interaction), which is present even in neonates. By 3 months he enjoys looking around and recognizes his mother. By 6 months, he vocalizes and smiles at his mirror image, and imitates acts such as cough or tongue protrusion. He becomes anxious on meeting strangers (stranger anxiety) by 6–7 months of age. At this age he inhibits to "no". At 9 months, he waves "bye-bye" and also repeats any performance that evokes an appreciative response from the observers. By 1 year, he can understand simple questions, such as "where is papa", "where is your ball", etc. By 15 months he points to objects in which he is interested. By 18 months he follows simple orders, and indulges in domestic mimicry (imitates mother sweeping or cleaning). At 2 years when asked he can point to 5–6 familiar objects, name at least 2–3 objects and point to 3–4 body parts. He begins to count, identify 1–2 colors and sing simple rhymes by age of 3 years. Much of these milestones depend on the caretaker's interaction and opportunities provided to the child. The left and right discrimination develops by 4 years. By this age, the play activities are also very imaginative. By 5 years of age, children can follow 3-step commands, identify four colors and repeat four digits (Table 2.3).

Language

Throughout the development of language it is the receptive ability and understanding which precedes expressive abilities. Soon after appearance of social smile at around 8–10 weeks the child begins to vocalize with vowel sounds ah, uh. At 3–4 months he squeals with delight and laughs loud. He begins to say ah, goo, gaga by 5 months age. By 6 months, he uses mono syllables (ba, da, pa). Later, he joins consonants to form bisyllables (mama, baba, dada). Before developing true meaningful speech, at around 9–10 months the child learns to imitate sounds derived from his native language. At his first birthday he can usually say 2–3 words with meaning. At 18 months he has a vocabulary of 10–15 words. Thereafter, the vocabulary increases rapidly to around 100 words by 2 years, at which time 2–3 words are joined to form simple sentences. By 3 years the toddler continually asks questions and knows his full name. He can give a coherent account of recent experiences and events by the age of 4 years (Table 2.4).

Hearing and Vision

Adequate sensory inputs are essential for development. Both normal vision and hearing are of paramount importance for child development. The ability to see and hear are apparent even in the newborn. Thereafter maturation of visual and hearing pathways are reflected by specific visual and auditory behaviors.

Vision

The best stimulus to check visual behavior is the primary caretaker's face. At birth a baby can fixate on and follow a moving person or dangling ring held 8–10 inches away upto a range of 45°. This increases to 90° by 4 weeks and 180° by 12 weeks. At around 1 month the baby can fixate on his mother as she talks to him. At about 3–4 months the child fixates intently on an object shown to him ("grasping with the eye") it appears that the child wants to reach for the object (Fig. 2.28). Binocular vision begins at around 6 weeks and is well established by 4 months. By 6 months the child adjusts his position to follow objects of interest, but can follow rapidly moving objects only by 1 year. Later the child displays more maturity in vision by not only identifying smaller objects but also being able to recognize them.

Hearing

Newborns respond to sounds by startle, blink, cry, quieting or change in ongoing activity. By 3 to 4 months the child turns his head towards the source of sound. If we check hearing by producing sound 1½ feet away from the ear (out of field of vision), we can observe a pattern of evolving maturity of hearing. At 5 to 6 months the child

Table 2.3: Key social and adaptive milestones

Age	*Milestone*
2 months	Social smile (smile after being talked to)
3 months	Recognizes mother; anticipates feeds
6 months	Recognizes strangers/stranger anxiety
9 months	Waves "bye bye"
12 months	Comes when called; plays simple ball game
15 months	Jargon
18 months	Copies parents in task (sweeping, etc.)
2 years	Asks for food, drink, toilet; pulls people to show toys
3 years	Shares toys; knows full name and gender
4 years	Plays cooperatively in a group; goes to toilet alone
5 years	Helps in household tasks, dresses and undresses

Table 2.4: Key language milestones

Age	*Milestone*
1 month	Alerts to sound
3 months	Coos (musical vowel sounds)
4 months	Laugh loud
6 months	Monosyllables (ba, da, pa), ah-goo sounds
9 months	Bisyllables (mama, baba, dada)
12 months	1–2 words with meaning
18 months	8–10 word vocabulary
2 years	2–3 word sentences, uses pronouns " I", "me", "you"
3 years	Asks questions; knows full name and gender
4 years	Says song or poem; tells stories
5 years	Asks meaning of words

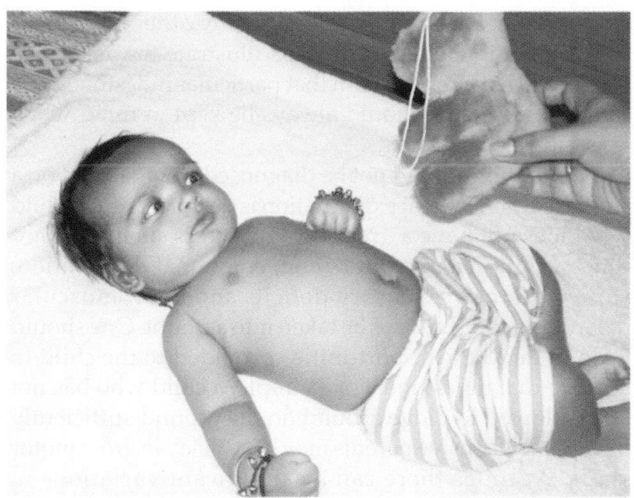

Fig. 2.28: Grasping with the eye at 3 months

turns the head to one side and then downwards if a sound is made below the level of ears. In a similar fashion, one month later he is able to localize sounds made above the level of ears. By the age of 10 months the child directly looks at the source of sound diagonally (Fig. 2.29).

EVALUATION OF DEVELOPMENT

Developmental delay is estimated to be present in about 10% of children. It is possible to recognize severe developmental disorders early in infancy. Speech impairment, hyperactivity and emotional disturbances are often not detected till the child is 3 to 4 years old. Learning disabilities are not picked up till the child starts schooling.

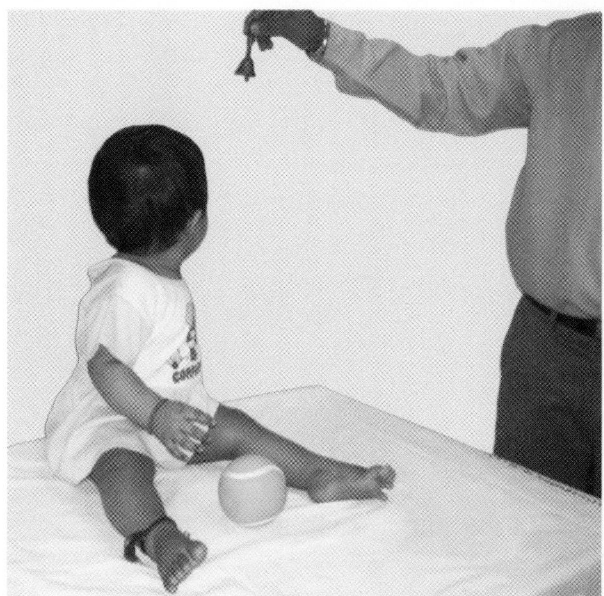

Fig. 2.29: Diagonal localization of the source of sound at 10 months

Prerequisites

The development assessment should be assessed in a place which is free from distractions. It is important that the child should not be hungry, tired, ill or irritated at time of development assessment. It would be most desirable to assess him when he is in a playful mood with his mother around. Adequate time should be spent in making the child and family comfortable. Observation for alertness, concentration and skills of the child is an integral part of assessment.

Equipment

A kit for development assessment typically contains commonly available articles, including (i) a red ring (diameter 6–7 cm) tied to a string, (ii) nine red cubes, (iii) paper pellets, (iv) spoon, (v) cup with handle, (vi) a book with thick pages, (vii) picture book, (viii) red pencil, paper and (ix) doll and mirror. It is a good idea to always carry a list of key milestones with normal age of their achievement (as provided in this chapter) for a ready reference, else one is likely to forget particularly the personal-social and linguistic domains.

Steps

History

A detailed history is the starting point for any development assessment. Observations by parents are fairly accurate. Hence a well taken history will help in (a) determining the details of probable risk factors affecting development, (b) evaluation of rate of acquisition of skills and differentiating between delay and regression, and (c) forming a gross impression about the development age of the child. This helps to choose the appropriate tools for further evaluation and confirmation.

Examination

This should be done to (a) assess physical growth and head circumference, (b) do a physical assessment, particularly for dysmorphism, stigmata of intrauterine infections and signs of hypothyroidism, (c) screen for vision and hearing and (d) neurological examination and primitive reflexes (if required).

Developmental Assessment

The maximum time should be spent observing when the baby is with the mother, especially social responsiveness, alertness, concentration, interest and distractibility. It would be most appropriate to assess vision and hearing at the outset so that further observations are not confounded by lack of sensory stimuli. The vocal responses, particularly the nature, frequency and quality of the vocalizations is noted. Subsequently, fine motor skills should be assessed, including the interest, alertness and rapidity of responses. The most annoying maneuvers, including assessment of reflexes, head circumference, ventral suspension and pull

2

to sit should be done at the end. It is preferable to perform the developmental assessment before the systemic examination so that the child's cooperation is solicited. By the end of the evaluation one should be able to arrive at a conclusion whether the neurological status and cognitive status are within normal range or not. Significant delays on screening are an indication for a detailed formal assessment of development status. By assessment one can assign developmental quotient (DQ) for any developmental sphere. It is calculated as

$$\frac{\text{Average age of attainment}}{\text{Observed age at attainment}} \times 100$$

A DQ below 70% is taken as delay and warrants detailed evaluation.

Interpretation

In babies born preterm corrected age, rather than postnatal age, is used for determining developmental status till two years of age. For example, a child born at 32 weeks gestation (gestational age) seen at 12 week of age (postnatal age) should be considered as a 4 week old child for development assessment (corrected age).

While drawing any conclusions about development, one should remember the wide variations in normality. For example, let us consider the milestone of "standing alone". The average age for attainment of this milestone in a WHO survey was 10.8 months. However, the 3rd and 97th centiles for normal children were 7.7 and 15.2 months respectively. The same is true for many other milestones as is shown in Fig. 2.30. The bars illustrate the age range for normal children to attain that particular milestone. This range of normalcy should always be kept in mind while assessing development.

Retardation should not be diagnosed or suggested on a single feature. Repeat examination is desirable in any child who does not have a gross delay. Factors such as recent illness, significant malnutrition, emotional deprivation, slow maturation, sensory deficits and neuromuscular disorders should always be taken into account. One should keep in mind the opportunities provided to the child to achieve that milestone. For example, a child who has not been allowed to move around on the ground sufficiently by the apprehensive parents may have delay in gross motor skills. At times there can be significant variations in attainment of milestones in individual fields, this is called "dissociation". For example, a 1 year old child who speaks 2–3 words with meaning, has finger thumb opposition (10–12 months), but cannot stand with support (less than 10 months). In such a situation, look for physical disorder affecting a particular domain of development. A child having normal development in all domains except language may have hearing deficit. Table 2.5 gives the upper limits by which a milestone must be attained. A child who does not attain the milestone by the recommended limit should be evaluated for cause of developmental delay.

The predictive value of different domains of development for subsequent intelligence is not the same.

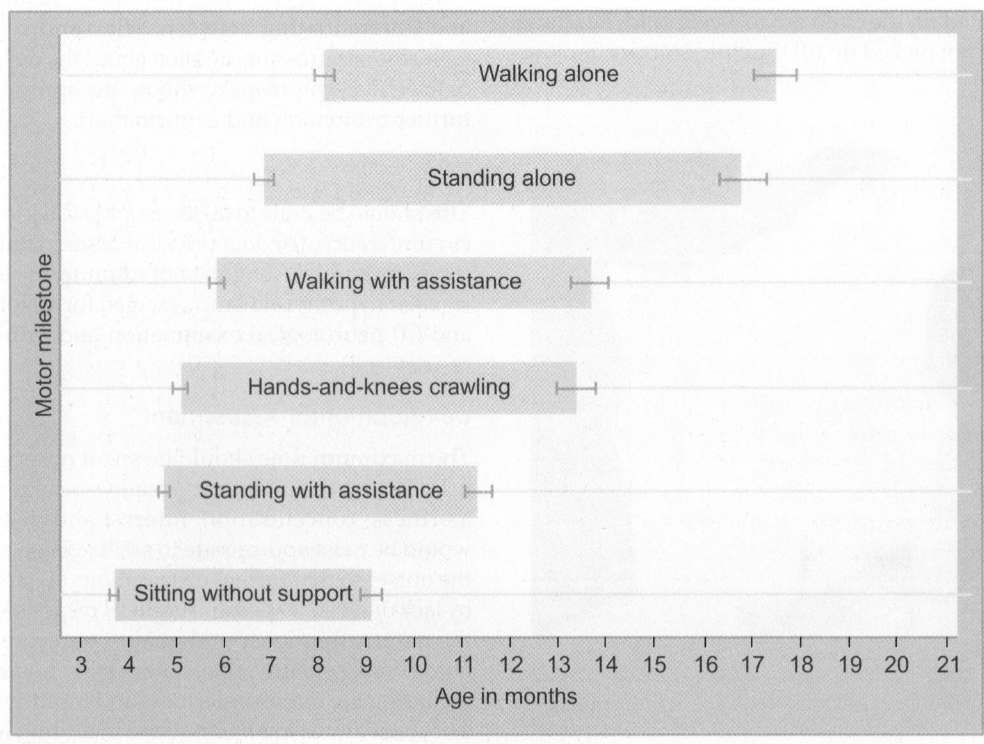

Fig. 2.30: Windows of achievement of six motor milestones (WHO; Multicenter Growth Reference Study Group)

The fine motor, personal-social and linguistic milestones predict intelligence far better than gross motor skills. In fact an advanced language predicts high intelligence in a child. Therefore, one should spend sufficient time in assessing these domains.

Table 2.5: Red flags signs in child development

Milestone	*Age*
No visual fixation or following by	2 months
No vocalization by	6 months
Not sitting without support by	9–10 months
Not standing alone by	16 months
Not walking alone by	18 months
No single words by	18 months
Lack of imaginative play at	3 years
Loss of comprehension, single words or phrases at any age	

Development Screening

Screening is a "brief assessment procedure designed to identify children who should receive more intensive diagnosis or assessment". Such an assessment aids early intervention services, making a positive impact on development, behavior and subsequent school performance. It also provides an opportunity for early identification of co-morbid developmental disabilities. Ideally, all children should be periodically screened but in in short of this at least those with perinatal risk factors should be screened.

Advantages of Screening

- They are standardized and the norms are explicitly stated
- They are more accurate to estimate developmental status than informal clinical impressions
- They reinforce the importance of development to caregiver
- They are an efficient way to record observations
- They help identify more children with delay

Limitations of Screening

Most limitations are due to inappropriate use of the tests
- The assessor may not be fully trained, may not follow the instructions or the scoring appropriately
- Relying on the screening test alone to make an assessment
- Using a screening test as a diagnostic tool (as distinct from a preliminary assessment)
- Not following the screening tests with further evaluations and interventions can be damaging

Developmental Surveillance

Child development is a dynamic process and difficult to quantitate by a one time assessment. During surveillance repeated observations on development are made by a skilled caregiver over time to see the rate and pattern of development. Periodic screening helps to detect emerging disabilities as a child grows. However, using clinical judgment alone has the potential for bias, and it has been suggested that it would be appropriate to use periodic screening tools during the course of ongoing developmental surveillance. The caregiver should choose a standardized developmental screening tool that is practical and easy to use in office setting. Once skilled with the tool, it can be used as screening method to identify at risk children. Some of the common screening tools include the following.

Phatak's Baroda Screening Test

This is India's best known development testing system that was developed by Dr. Promila Phatak. It is meant to be used by child psychologists rather than physicians. It is the Indian adaptation of Bayley's development scale. It requires several testing tools and objects. The test items are arranged according to age. The kit is available commercially.

Denver Development Screening Test

The revised Denver Development Screening Test (DDST) was restandardized and presented as the Denver II Test in 1992. The Denver II assesses child development in four domains, viz., gross motor, fine motor adaptive, language and persona1 social behavior, which are presented as age norms, just like physical growth curves.

Trivandrum Development Screening Chart

This is a simplified adaptation of the Border development screening system. It consists of 17 items selected from BSID Baroda norms. It is a simple test and can be administered in 5 minutes by a health worker. It is recommended to be used as a mass screening test.

CAT/CLAMS (Clinical adaptive test/Clinical linguistic and auditory milestone scale)

This is an easy to learn scale which can be used to assess the child's cognitive and language skills. It uses parental report and direct testing of the child's skills. It is used in ages of 0–36 months and takes 10–20 minutes to apply. It is useful in discriminating children with mental retardation (i.e. both language and visual motor delay) and those with communication disorders (low language scores).

Goodenough Harris Drawing Test

It is simple nonverbal intelligence test which only requires a pencil/pen and white unlined paper. It is useful as a group screening tool. Here the child is asked to draw a man in the best possible manner. Points are given for each detail that the child draws in the figure. One can then determine the mental age by comparing scores obtained and comparing with normative sample. This test allows a quick but rough estimate of a child's intelligence.

Definitive Tests

These tests are required once screening tests or clinical assessment is abnormal. They are primarily aimed to accurately define the impairments in both degree and sphere. For example, by giving scores for verbal, performance abilities, personal and social skills, these can be differentially quantified. The common scales used include

2

- Bayley Scale of Infant Development -II
- Stanford Binet Intelligence Scale
- Wechsler Intelligence Scale for Children-IV and Wechsler Preschool and Primary Scale of Intelligence
- Vineland Adaptive Behavior Scales
- DASII

Early Stimulation

Infants who show suspect or early signs development delay need to be provided opportunities that promote body control, acquisition of motor skills, language development and psychosocial maturity. These inputs, termed early stimulation, include measures such as making additional efforts to make the child sit or walk, giving toys to manipulate, playing with the child, showing objects, speaking to the child and encouraging him to speak and prompting the child to interact with others, etc.

Promoting Development by Effective Parenting

Provision of comprehensive care to children in coming decades would require a renewed focus on preventive efforts including child-rearing information to parents. Parenting has an immense impact on emotional, social and cognitive development, and also plays a role in the later occurrence of mental illness, educational failure and criminal behavior. Creating the right conditions for early childhood development is likely to be more effective and less costly than addressing problems at a later age.

Television Viewing and Development

Television viewing in younger children has been shown to retard language development. It is a passive mode of entertainment and impairs children's ability to learn and read, and also limits creativity. Children can pick up inappropriate language and habits by watching TV shows and commercials. Violence and sexuality on television can have a lasting impact on the child's mind. Parents need to regulate both the quantity and quality of TV viewing, limiting the time to 1–2 hours per day and ensuring that the content they see is necessary.

Child Development in the Developing World

Child development is a foundation for community development and economic development, as capable children become the foundation of a prosperous and sustainable society. In developing countries children younger than 5 years are exposed to multiple risks, including poverty, malnutrition, poor health, and unstimulating home environments, which impair their cognitive, motor, and social emotional development. These disadvantaged children are likely to do poorly in school and subsequently have low incomes, high fertility, and provide poor care for their children, thus contributing to the intergenerational transmission of poverty (Fig. 2.31).

Suggested reading

1. Developmental surveillance and screening of infants and young children. American Academy of Pediatrics, Committee on Children with Disabilities. Pediatrics 2001; 108: 192–196
2. Grantham-McGregor S, Cheung Y, Cueto S, Glewwe P, Richter L, Strupp B. Developmental potential in the first 5 years for children in developing countries. Lancet 2007; 369: 60–70
3. Walker S, Wachs T, Meeks Gardner J, et al. Child development: risk factors for adverse outcomes in developing countries. Lancet 2007; 369: 145–157.
4. Engle PL, Black MM, Jere R Behrman JR, et al. Strategies to avoid the loss of developmental potential in more than 200 million children in the developing world. Lancet 2007; 369: 229–242.

BEHAVIORAL DISORDERS

Pica

Pica is described in Diagnostic and Statistical Manual of mental disorders, fourth edition (DSM IV) as persistent eating of non-nutritive substances such as plaster, charcoal, paint and earth for at least 1 month in such a fashion that it is inappropriate to developmental level, is not part of a culturally sanctioned practice and is sufficiently severe to warrant independent clinical attention. It is a common problem in children less than 5 years of age.

The etiology of this disorder remains elusive. Several heterogeneous entities like mental retardation, psychosocial stress in the form of maternal deprivation, parental neglect and abuse and a variety of behavior disorders have been speculated to be predisposing factors for pica. Poor socioeconomic status, malnutrition and iron deficiency, so commonly associated with pica, have often been considered to have etiologic significance, however, the cause and effect relationship has never been established clearly.

Children with pica are at an increased risk for lead poisoning, iron-deficiency anemia and parasitic infestations and should be routinely screened for these. Management comprises alleviating the psychosocial stress if present and iron supplementation if deficiency is present.

Food Fussiness

Food fussiness is a common problem faced by parents of young children. However, many times it reflects an excessive need for control on the part of the parents about what the child eats. The best strategy to improve eating includes establishing regular meal timings, ensuring a pleasant atmosphere, offering a variety of foods and setting an example of enjoying the same food themselves.

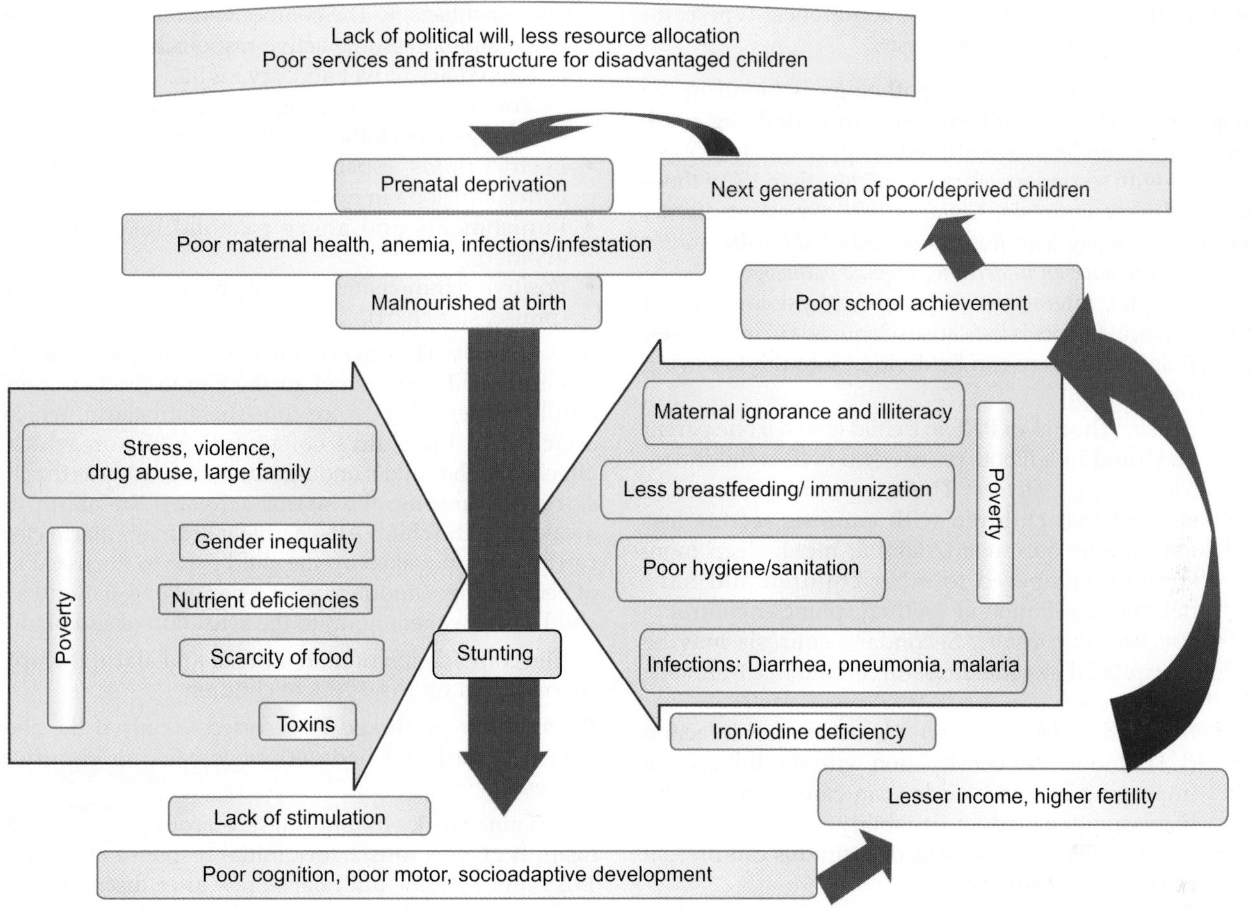

Fig. 2.31: Trans-generational cycle of poverty, illiteracy, malnutrition and hampered child growth and development in the developing countries

Offering small servings at a time, reducing between meal caloric intake and not pressurizing or force-feeding the child to finish a predecided quantity of food is also useful.

Parents should engage their children in conversation about benefits of healthy and balanced diet and discourage intake of junk foods.

Toilet Training, Enuresis

Difficulties with Toilet Training

If toilet training is begun arbitrarily by the parents before the child is developmentally ready to be trained, unnecessary power struggle between the child and parents sometimes ensues. Toilet training should be started after 2 years of age when the child has spontaneously started indicating bladder and bowel fullness and is able to follow simple instructions. The general ambience should be conducive to learning and free from pressure.

Refusal to defecate in the toilet with development of constipation is a common problem in children. This leads to parental frustration and increased pressure on the child. Parents should be advised for temporary cessation of toilet training and making a fresh beginning after some time. Consistency in the parents' approach and positive reinforcement by praising and encouraging the child go a long way in producing a positive outcome.

Enuresis

Definition and epidemiology: Enuresis is defined as urinary incontinence beyond the age of 4 years for daytime and 6 years for nighttime, or as the loss of continence after at least 3 months of dryness. The diagnosis of enuresis is made when wetting occurs twice a week for 3 consecutive months or child suffers significant distress because of it. Most children attain complete bladder control by the mental age of 5 years. The prevalence of enuresis is 7% in boys and 3% in girls at the age of 5 years and decreases to 3% for boys and 2% for girls by 10 years.

Classification: Enuresis is classified as **primary** in which the child has never been dry at night and **secondary** in which the child begins bedwetting after remaining continent for 6 months or more. Enuresis may be further classified into **nocturnal,** in which involuntary voiding occurs only during sleep at night and **diurnal** in which it occurs during daytime also while child is awake. Primary nocturnal enuresis (PNE) is the commonest type comprising 90% of all cases of enuresis.

Etiology: No specific organic pathology is found in the majority of children with enuresis. An underlying cause for enuresis can be demonstrated in approximately 5% of children with secondary enuresis and less than 1% of those with primary enuresis. *Children with persistent diurnal incontinence along with features of voiding difficulty are the most likely to have an underlying organic pathology.*

A complex interaction of genetic, physiological and psychological factors is the cause of enuresis in most cases. The etiological factors can be divided into the following subgroups:

- *Genetic*: The risk of PNE in a child is 40% if one parent had it and 70 % if both parents had PNE in childhood.
- *Physiological factors*: There is some evidence to suggest that children with enuresis secrete less antidiuretic hormone (ADH) at night, sleep more soundly compared to other children and have delayed maturation of urethral sphincter control.
- *Psychological factors:* Secondary enuresis may be precipitated by acute stressful condition or traumatic experience.
- *Increased bladder irritability*: Urinary tract infection (UTI) and severe constipation with the full rectum impinging on the bladder can cause enuresis by increasing the bladder irritability.
- *Polyuria*: Diabetes mellitus or insipidus can present as secondary enuresis.
- *Organic causes*: Spina bifida (neurological bladder dysfunction), ectopic ureter.
- *Giggle and stress incontinence* cause diurnal enuresis in young girls.
- *Micturition deferral* (waiting till the last minute to void) is a common cause of diurnal incontinence in younger children.

Assessment: A careful history should be taken to determine whether the enuresis is primary or secondary, whether any daytime symptoms are present and whether any voiding difficulty is present. In cases of secondary enuresis, history should be taken to rule out acute stressful conditions, polyuria and features of bladder irritability such as frequency and urgency. Physical examination should focus on spinal anomalies. Laboratory test should include complete urinalysis for all children and urine culture for all with secondary enuresis. Additional studies like radiograph of dorso-lumbar spine, ultrasonography or urodynamic study may be done if indicated by history or examination.

Treatment: No treatment is recommended in children below 6 years of age because of high spontaneous cure rate. The first line of treatment should be non-pharmacological.

Non-pharmacological therapy comprises motivational therapy and use of alarm devices.

Motivational therapy: The components of this therapy are:

- Child should assume active responsible role.
  - Keep diary of wet and dry nights.
  - Void urine before going to bed.
  - Change wet clothes and bedding.
- Restrict fluids, especially caffeinated drinks like tea, coffee and soda in evening.
- Punishments and angry parental responses to be avoided.
- Positive reinforcements to be given for each dry night (praise, star chart).

Alarm therapy: This involves using alarm systems to elicit a conditioned response of awakening to the sensation of a full bladder. This device consists of an alarm, which is attached to the child's collar, and a sensor, which is attached to the child's undergarments. As soon as the child starts micturating, the sensor activates the alarm thus awakening the child. Alternatively ordinary alarm clocks can be used to waken up the child prior to the usual time of bedwetting. Gradually after a period of 4–6 months the child starts wakening up to the sensation of full bladder.

The combination of motivational and alarm therapy is successful in up to 60-70% of children.

Pharmacotherapy should be resorted to only if the above measures fail and bedwetting is causing significant distress.

Imipramine works by altering the arousal-sleep mechanism. It gives a satisfactory initial response at a dose of 1–2.5 mg/kg/day, but relapse rate after discontinuation of therapy is high. Cardiac conduction disturbance is a serious adverse event effect. This medication is rarely used.

Oxybutinin is an anticholinergic drug that reduces uninhibited bladder contractions. It is useful in children who have significant daytime urge incontinence besides nocturnal enuresis. The dose is 10–20 mg/day.

Desmopressin (DDAVP) (10 μg orally or intranasally) works by reducing the volume of urine produced at night. The relapse rate is high after stopping of the drug. Its fast onset of action makes it a good choice for special occasions like staying out for the night. Water intoxication and hyponatremia are rare adverse effects.

Indiscipline and Temper Tantrums

A parent's ability to discipline and teach is central to raising emotionally healthy children who can learn societal rules, live, play and eventually work with others. Modelling desirable behavior by their own language and actions is the most effective tool for disciplining children. The reaction to unwanted behavior should be consistent, logical and reasonably immediate.

Punishment is best given in the form of loss of privileges such as not allowing to watch a favourite television show or playing with friends for a day. Physical punishment is commonly used by parents to make the child stop the unwanted behavior quickly. However, this gives the subconscious message to the child that aggression toward another person can get the desired results. Children may feel that the punishment has cancelled the crime, allowing the unwanted behavior to be repeated on some other occasion. Hence this form of punishment should be avoided.

Temper Tantrums

From the age of 18 months to 3 years, the child begins to develop autonomy and starts separating from primary caregivers. At this age they also develop *negativism*, that is, they do things opposite to what has been requested. When they cannot express their autonomy they become frustrated and angry. Some of these children show their frustration, opposition and defiance with physical aggression or resistance, such as biting, crying, kicking, pushing, throwing objects, hitting and head banging. This kind of behavior is known as temper tantrum. This behavior reaches its peak during second and third year of life and gradually subsides by the age of 3 to 6 years as the child learns to control his negativism.

Management: Parents should be asked to list situations where disruptive behavior are likely to occur and plan strategies to avoid these (for example, ensuring that child is rested and fed before taking him along for a shopping trip). . They should be calm, firm and consistent and not allow the child to take advantage for gains from such behavior.

During an attack the child should be protected from injuring himself or others. At an early stage, distracting his attention from the immediate cause and changing the environment can abort the tantrum. "Time out" procedure, i.e. asking the child to stay alone in a safe and quiet place for a few minutes (1 minute for each year of age with a maximum of 5 minutes) may be helpful. This helps the child to self-regulate his out-of-control emotional response. The reason for timeout should be clearly explained to the child. Timeout should be followed by time-in by welcoming him back into the social group with a hug and affectionate words.

Breath Holding Spells

Breath holding spells are reflexive events in which typically there is a provocative event that causes anger, frustration or pain and the child starts crying. The crying stops at full expiration when the child becomes apneic and cyanotic or pale. In some cases child may lose consciousness and muscle tone and fall. Some children may have a seizure because of cerebral anoxia. Breath holding spells are rare before 6 months of age, peak at 2 years and abate by 5 years of age. The affected children are often highly pampered by parents or grandparents. All their wishes, reasonable or unreasonable, are fulfilled, but once they are refused something or they are hurt physically or otherwise, they feel angry/ frustrated and exhibit breath holding.

Diagnosis is quite simple due to typical history and settings in most cases. The differential diagnoses include seizures, cardiac arrhythmias or brainstem tumor or malformation. History of provoking event, stereotyped pattern of events and presence of color change before loss of consciousness help in distinguishing breath holding spells from seizures. In case of pallid spells, electrocardiogram can be done to rule out conditions associated with cardiac arrhythmias such as long QT syndrome.

Management

Parents' worries are allayed by doing a thorough examination of the child and explaining the mechanism of breath holding spells. Both parents as also the grandparents if staying with the child should be counseled together. They should be asked to be consistent in their behavior with the child. During the episode, they should pinch the child at the onset of the spell and should not exhibit undue concern or excessively cuddle the child as this reinforces the 'gain' in attention. Iron supplementation (3 mg/kg/day) is definitely effective in children with iron deficiency. Its role in children without iron deficiency is not yet clear.

Suggested reading

1. Boris NW, Dalton R. Vegetative disorders. In Behrman RE, Kliegman RM, Jenson HR, eds. Nelson Textbook of Pediatrics. Philadelphia: Saunders, 2004: 73–80.
2. Rose EA, Porcerelli JH, Neale AV. Pica: common but commonly missed. J am Broad Fam Prac 2000; 13: 353–6.
3. Weaver A, Dobson P. Nocturnal enuresis in children. J Fam Health Care 2007;17:159–61.
4. Lottmann HB, Alova I. Primary monosymptomatic nocturnal enuresis in children and adolescents. Int J Clin Pract (suppl) 2007;155:8–16.

Habit Disorders and Tics

Habit disorders include repetitive pattern of movements such as head banging, rocking of body, thumb sucking, twisting of hair and grinding of teeth. Such movements are seen frequently in normally developing children between the age of 6 months and 2 years and are benign and generally self-limited. These movements seem to serve as a means for discharging tension in the children or providing extra self-nurturance.

As these children become older, they learn to inhibit some of their rhythmic habit patterns particularly in social situations. Undue attention from parents and forcing the child to give up these behaviors often leads to reinforcement of such behaviors and their persistence for a longer period.

Bruxism is clenching or grinding of teeth, which produces a high-pitched audible sound. This typically occurs at night, is quite common among young children and seems to be associated with daytime anxiety. Persistent bruxism may cause tenderness and pain in the muscles of mastication and temporomandibular joints and can lead to dental malocclusion.

Parents should be advised to talk to the child about his/ her fears or anxieties. Indulging in some enjoyable activity like reading a story to the child at bedtime helps him/her to relax.

Thumb sucking is normal behavior in infants and toddlers. It peaks between the ages of 18–21 months and most children spontaneously drop the habit by 4 years of age. Its persistence in older children is socially unacceptable and can lead to dental malalignment. Before 4 years of age, parents should be reassured and asked to ignore the habit. If it persists beyond the age of 4–5 years, the parents should gently motivate the child to stop thumb sucking and praise and encourage him when he tries to actively restrain himself from sucking the thumb. Application of noxious agents over the thumb is useful as an adjunctive second-line treatment in motivated children.

Tics are involuntary and purposeless movements or utterances that are sudden, spasmodic and repetitive. These mostly involve the muscles of eyes, mouth, face and neck. Tics can range from simple blinking of eyes or facial twitching to extreme ones like obscene gestures and vocalizations (coprolalia). The estimated prevalence of tic disorders is 1–2%, with a 2:1 male preponderance. It is most common in the school-aged children. According to DSM-IV, tic disorders are classified into transient, chronic, Tourette syndrome or 'tic disorder not otherwise specified'.

Transient tic disorders are characterized by mild tics which occur several times daily for a period ranging from 4 weeks to 12 months.

Chronic tic disorder is much more rarer. It is characterized by either motor or vocal tics which occur daily or intermittently for more than a year. The condition may persist in adulthood when tics appear during conditions of stress or fatigue.

Tourette syndrome is the severest of the tic disorders. It begins in early childhood with simple tics like blinking and facial tics. Over a period of time, the child also starts having complex motor tics like sudden squatting while walking. These are followed after 1–2 years by vocal tics like grunting, barking and coprolalia. Attention deficit hyperactivity disorder and obsessive compulsive disorders are common comorbid conditions. Dopaminergic antagonists like haloperidol and aypical antipsychotics like quiteapine are useful in relieving the symptoms.

Psychotherapy also has an adjunctive role.

Attention Deficit Hyperactivity Disorder

Definition and Epidemiology

It is the commonest neurobehavioral disorder of childhood affecting 3–5% of school-aged children. It is 3 times commoner in boys.

Etiology

For most children, no etiology is identified. Twin and family studies suggest that genetic factors may play a role. Molecular genetic studies have identified abnormalities in dopamine transporter gene and thyroid receptor beta gene in some patients.

Clinical Manifestations

These children display some or all of the following symptoms (Table 2.6).

- Inattention and early distractibility
- Impulsivity
- Motor restlessness and hyperactivity
- Difficulty with planning and organizing tasks
- Emotional lability

Examples of inattentive, hyperactive and impulsive behavior included within the criteria for diagnosis of ADHD are listed in Table 2.6. For making the diagnosis, the behavior must begin before 7 years of age, be present for at least 6 months, be pervasive (present in at least 2 different settings) and impair the child's ability to function normally. The symptoms should not be secondary to another disorder.

Diagnosis

Diagnosis is made primarily on clinical grounds after a thorough clinical interview of parents and use of behavior rating scales. Physical examination includes direct observation of the child and ruling out any chronic systemic illness that may affect child's attention span.

Neuropsychological evaluation using standard tests of general intelligence and educational achievement should also be done to exclude learning disorders or mental retardation, which may present as ADHD.

Management

The management of ADHD should begin with educating the parents about the effect of ADHD on child's learning, behavior and social skills and helping them in setting

Table 2.6: Examples of inattentive and hyperactive/ impulsive behavior included within the criteria for diagnosis of ADHD

Inattentive behavior
1. Early distraction by extraneous stimuli
2. Often makes careless mistakes in schoolwork or other activities
3. Often has difficulty sustaining attention in tasks or play activities
4. Often forgetful in daily activities
5. Does not seem to listen to what is being said to him
6. Often fails to finish schoolwork or other chores
Hyperactive/impulsive behavior
1. Runs about or climbs excessively in situations where it is inappropriate
2. Fidgets with hands and feet and squirms in seat
3. Has difficulty awaiting turn in games or group situations
4. Blurts out answers to questions

realistic goals of treatment. The treatment involves a combination of behavioral therapy and medications.

Behavioral therapy: Behavioral modification methods that have been used with variable success are

1. Clear and explicit instructions to the child about desirable and non-desirable behavior.
2. Positive reinforcement of desirable behavior by praise or small tangible rewards.
3. Punishment strategies like verbal reprimand, non-verbal gestures or 'time out' for undesirable behavior.
4. Extinction technique, i.e. systematic ignoring of undesirable behavior.

Providing a well-structured and organized routine for the child at home as well as school is helpful. At school, giving brief and consistent instructions to the child, clear and consistent response to the child's behavior, seating in an area with few distractions and allowing the child to change activities and move about periodically are helpful.

Medications

- *Stimulants:* The 2 main classes of stimulants are methylphenidate and its derivatives and amphetamine and its derivatives. These are the first line treatment for ADHD and are effective in amelioration of the chief complaints of inattention, hyperactivity and impulsivity in 70–80% of all children. However, no improvement is noted in academic achievement or social skills. Adverse effects are usually mild and include abdominal discomfort, loss of appetite and initial weight loss.
- *Antidepressants* like imipramine and bupropinone are considered second-line drugs that are effective in treatment of ADHD, especially in the presence of co-morbid depression.

Learning Disabilities

Learning disabilities are considered to arise from specific neurodevelopmental dysfunctions that prevent expectable learning in one or more academic areas. The important defining principle is that such disabilities are unexpected given the overall intellectual functioning of the child. These disorders are not the result of global developmental delay, major vision or hearing handicaps or consequences of major social or emotional stressors.

Dyslexia

Dyslexia or specific reading difficulty is the commonest learning disability. It is characterized by difficulty with accurate and/or fluent word recognition and by poor spelling and word decoding abilities. Word decoding is the ability to apply principles of phonetics to sound the words, i.e. understanding that each letter or letter combination in the word has a sound and by combining these, the word can be read and spelled. According to western estimates, 5–15% of school-aged children suffer from dyslexia.

Etiology: Genetic factors play a strong role. Up to 50% of children of a dyslexic parent and 50% of siblings of a dyslexic child have dyslexia. Functioning brain imaging in children with dyslexia shows that the temporoparieto-occipital regions of the left cerebral hemisphere do not function properly during reading compared to normal children.

Clinical manifestations: Dyslexic children have an inaccurate and labored approach to reading. They also have difficulty in spelling because of underlying problem with word decoding. Listening comprehension is typically normal. Dyslexia may co-occur with ADHD in 15–40% of children.

Diagnosis: Diagnosis of dyslexia is clinical based on presence of "unexpected" difficulties in reading at the level of phonologic processing of words.

Management: In younger children, the focus is on remediation. The affected children are best taught in small groups, by teachers trained in the principle of phonics. The children are taught how letters are linked to sounds. The stress is on improving phonemic awareness, i.e. the ability to focus on and manipulate phonemes (speech sounds) in spoken syllables and words. One or two phonemes are taught at a time with sufficient time spent on reading and writing words using those phonemes. Usually these programs improve the reading accuracy significantly and fluency to a lesser extent.

For older children, the management stresses more on accommodation rather than remediation, e.g. use of laptop computers with spell-check, recorded books and giving extra time for writing tests or multiple choice questions (MCQ) type of tests.

Language Delay and Disorders of Communication

Stuttering

Stuttering is a defect in speech characterized by hesitation or spasmodic repetition of some syllables with pauses. There is difficulty in pronouncing the initial consonants caused by spasm of lingual and palatal muscles. It is a common problem affecting up to 5% of children between 2–5 years of age, a period in which there is non-fluency of speech. Environmental and emotional stress or excitement may exacerbate stuttering.

Management: Parents of a young child with primary stuttering should be reassured that stuttering during the phase of non-fluent speech between the age of 2–5 years usually resolves on its own. Making the child conscious of his stutter or pressurizing him to repeat the word without stuttering will further increase the stress and the stutter.

In about 1% of children who continue to have significant stuttering, referral to a speech therapist should be advised. In older children with late onset of stuttering, the help of a child psychologist should also be sought.

Suggested reading

1. Reiff MI, Stein MT. ADHD: Evaluation and diagnosis. Pediatr Clin North Am 2003;50:801–16.
2. Boyce WT, Shonkoff JP. Developmental behavioral pediatrics. In: Rudolph AM, Hoffman JIE, Rudolpf CD eds, Rudolph's Pediatrics. Connecticut: Appleton and Lange, 1996: 87–196.
3. Shaywitz S. Current concepts: dyslexia. N Engl J Med 1998; 338: 307–12.

MAJOR PSYCHOPATHOLOGICAL DISORDERS

Autistic Disorder

Definition and Epidemiology

In the DSM-IV, autistic disorder is classified as one of the pervasive developmental disorders (PDDs). PDDs are a cluster of syndromes that share marked abnormalities in the development of social and communicative skills (Table 2.7).

Table 2.7: Pervasive developmental disorders
• Autistic disorder
• Rett syndrome
• Asperger syndrome
• Childhood disintegrative disorder
• Pervasive developmental disorder not otherwise specified.

Autistic disorder (AD) is the commonest of the PDDs. It is characterized by a qualitative impairment in verbal and nonverbal communication, in imaginative activity and in reciprocal social interactions that develops before the age of 3 years. According to western data, the prevalence ranges from 10 to 20 per 10000 children with a marked male preponderance (3–4:1). Other neurological disorders that can co-occur with AD are seizure disorder, tuberous sclerosis and fragile X syndrome.

Etiology

Etiology of autism is multifactorial. Genetic factors play a significant role as evidenced by a 60–90% concordance in monozygotic twins. Pre or perinatal brain injury is considered as an important risk-augmenting factor. Abnormalities in brain structure and function have also been suggested by neuroradiological and neurochemical studies. However, the findings of various studies are conflicting and there is no diagnostic imaging or other test for autism.

Clinical Features

Children with AD are diagnosable by 18 months of age by their poor eye contact, inability to engage socially or emotionally with caregivers, delayed speech, stereotypical body movements, marked need for sameness and preference for solitary play. Older children also show bizarre or unusual preoccupations and severe impairment in socialization. Seizures develop by adolescence in up to one-third of affected patients.

Intelligence is variable in children with AD though most children fall in the functionally retarded category by conventional psychological testing. Some children show an isolated remarkable talent.

Diagnosis

Diagnosis of AD is clinical. However, testing for associated neurological disorders such as tuberous sclerosis and fragile X is recommended. Conditions that should be differentiated from AD include mental retardation, deafness, selective mutism and ADND.

Treatment

The primary management is through "intensive behavioral therapy", starting before 3 years of age, applied at home as well as school focusing on speech and language development and good behavioral control.

Important principles of the educational approach to be applied at school are

- Teaching one-on-one using primary rewards such as food as motivation
- Teaching in small increments with repetitions
- Using 'total communication' i.e. teaching with a range of techniques such as spoken language, symbols and visual tools

The principles of behavioral modification programs to be applied at home by the parents are

- Identifying the manageable problems
- Finding a reward that works for the child
- Trying to modify the behavior consistently and repeatedly:

Older children and adolescents with relatively higher intelligence but poor social skills and psychiatric symptoms (e.g. depression, anxiety and obsessive-compulsive symptoms) may require psychotherapy and pharmacotherapy.

Prognosis

Factors associated with better prognosis include: (i) Early diagnosis and intensive behavioral therapy (ii) Higher intelligence level (iii) Presence of functional speech

Children with better prognostic factors may grow up to be self-sufficient and employed, though socially isolated. On the other hand, those with poor prognosis remain dependent on family or require placement in facilities outside home.

Munchausen by Proxy Syndrome

Munchausen by proxy syndrome is a disorder in which a caregiver, usually mother deliberately makes up a history of illness in her child and/or harms the child to create illness. The name is derived from the adult 'Munchausen syndrome' in which a person self-induces or acts out illness to gain medical attention. In Manchausen by proxy, the abusing caregiver gains attention from the relationships formed with health care providers or her own family as a result of the problems created.

Clinical manifestation: Most commonly, the victims are infants and young preverbal children. The child's symptoms, their pattern or response to treatment may not conform to any recognizable disease and always occurs when mother is with the child. Apnea, seizures (which may be induced by suffocating the child or injecting insulin), fever, diarrhea and skin conditions are the common symptoms. Confirmation of diagnosis needs careful history, reviewing of all past and current hospital records of the child. Monitoring by hidden television cameras in the ward may be useful. Once the diagnosis is made, the offending caregiver should be confronted, separated from the child and provided psychotherapy.

Suggested reading

1. Mitchell I, Brummet J, De Forest J. Apnea and factitious illness (Munchausen syndrome) by proxy. Pediatrics 1993;92:810–5.
2. American Academy of Neurology: Practice parameter: Screening and diagnosis of autism. Neurology 2000;55:468–79.

3 Adolescent Health and Development

Adolescence is described as the period in life when an individual is no longer a child, but not yet an adult. It spans the age group of 10 to 19 years.

The term adolescence is derived from the Latin word, *'adolescere'*; meaning *to grow, to mature.* Developmentally, this amounts to 'achieving an identity'. Adolescents constitute about 23% of population in India.

It is important to note that adolescents are *not a homogenous* group. Their needs vary with their sex, stage of development, life circumstances and the socio-economic conditions of their environment. These are highly formative years for development, behavioural patterns and activities that impact their present and future health.

WHO/UN definitions		
Adolescent	–	10–19 years
Youth	–	15–24 years
Young people	–	10–24 years

Adolescence is a critical period of biological and psychological changes for both boys and girls. It is a phase of life which has recently gained recognition as a distinct phase of life with its own special needs. It is a phase of development on many fronts: from the appearance of secondary sex characteristics (puberty) to sexual and reproductive maturity; the development of mental processes and adult identity; and the transition from total socio-economic and emotional dependence to relative independence.

Healthy development of adolescents is dependent on several complex factors: their socio-economic circumstances, the environment in which they live and grow, the quality of relationships with their families, communities and peer groups and the opportunities for education and employment, among others.

Salient attributes of adolescence

- Physical, psychological, emotional and social development
- Rapid but uneven physical growth and development
- Sexual maturity and the onset of sexual activity
- Desire for exploration and experimentation
- Development of adult mental processes and self identity
- Transition from dependence to relative independence.

Stages of Adolescence

Though there is an overlap, three main stages of adolescence can be discerned:

- **Early adolescence (10–13 years):** Characterized by a spurt of growth and the development of secondary sexual characteristics.
- **Mid adolescence (14–16 years):** This stage is distinguished by the development of a separate identity from parents, of new relationships with peer groups and the opposite sex, and of experimentation.
- **Late adolescence (17–19 years):** At this stage, adolescents have fully developed physical characteristics (similar to adults), and have formed a distinct identity and have well-formed opinions and ideas.

CHANGES DURING ADOLESCENCE

With the onset of puberty several changes start concurrently. Some of the prominent changes are summarized in Tables 3.1 and 3.2 below.

Table 3.1: Changes during adolescence

Boys	*Girls*
• Growth spurt	• Growth spurt
• Muscles develop	• Breasts develop
• Skin becomes oily	• Skin becomes oily
• Shoulders broaden	• Hips widen
• Voice cracks	• Underarm hair
• Underarm, chest hair	• Pubic hair appears
• Pubic hair appears	• Uterus, ovaries enlarge
• Facial hair appears	• External genitals enlarge
• Penis, testes enlarge	• Menarche, ovulation
• Erections in boys	• Sexual desire
• Sperm production, ejaculation	• Sexual attraction
• Sexual desire	• Initiation of sexual behaviors
• Sexual attraction	
• Initiation of sexual behaviors	

Table 3.2: Emotional and social changes

- Preoccupied with body image
- Want to establish own identity
- Fantasy/daydreaming
- Rapid mood changes, emotional instability
- Attention seeking behavior
- Curious, inquisitive
- Full of energy, restless
- Self exploration and evaluation
- Conflicts with family over control
- Peer group defines behavioral code
- Formation of new relationships

VULNERABILITIES DURING ADOLESCENCE

As seen earlier the very process of growth and development adds to their vulnerability and can have adverse impact on their health. Adjusting to the concurrently occurring physical, mental, emotional, social and behavioral changes may pose special challenges and opportunities. Some adolescents become anxious and stressed because of these changes. Owing to tendency to explore and experiment and express new identity some of them can pick up a variety of health risk behaviors.

Most young people lack access to age and sex appropriate health information, skills and services and have many misconceptions and myths that lead to high risk sexual behaviour, mental ill health and social problems. This ignorance and myths surrounding adolescence also make adolescents vulnerable to consequences of inappropriate sexual behaviors, sexual exploitation and abuse. Most adolescents lack experience and skills in self protection that can help them remain safe and healthy—such as access to health and counseling services and contraceptives like condoms. They may thus initiate sexual behavior and substance abuse during this age and are more likely to have sex with high risk partners or multiple partners but are least likely to use condoms.

Owing to rapid urbanization many adolescents accompany the immigrating rural population to cities. Adolescents that live on streets come in contact with various adults in largely unsupervised conditions and are exposed to new value systems, modern communications, and unfamiliar or hostile cultures. Adolescents between 10–14 years who are working are exposed to work related and work place hazards. Sexual violence and coercion are serious problems, often hidden and unspoken of. These can be severely detrimental to physical and mental health during their adult lives. A large number of adolescents, especially, girls are the victims of trafficking and organized prostitution. The need to recognize adolescents as a vulnerable target group and to develop strategies for promotion of adolescent health should be emphasized.

Adolescents' ability to avoid HIV, STIs, unintended pregnancy or substance abuse depends only partly on their own individual knowledge and skills. There are other social and economic factors that are beyond the individual's control and that can put young people at higher or lower risk of infection. Significant social changes that have affected the whole society have affected the situation of the adolescents. Some of these social changes relate to broadened opportunities for women who are going to school for longer period and entering the workforce in large numbers. Fostered by other changes like urbanization, liberalization and communication explosion, sexual activity during the premarital phase seems to be on the rise. This again has an impact on the health of the adolescents.

Often, diseases and injuries are a result of an unsafe environment beyond the control of the adolescents. Interpersonal environment (e.g. family and peers), physical environmental or community settings (e.g. schools), and societal (e.g. mass media, social and cultural norms) environment are important factors that contribute to the vulnerability of adolescents.

Some adolescents are especially vulnerable and hard to reach and therefore need extra support, they include those who are denied the opportunities to complete their education, live on street, commercial sex workers, with mental and physical disability, orphans, adolescents in conflict and war, and working adolescents.

ADOLESCENT 'BODY IMAGE' AND ITS IMPACT

Body image is an important factor that adds to the vulnerability of the adolescents. Many of the attitudes, actions and behaviours that adolescents develop have body image concerns as one of the major underlying factors. Body image is defined as "the way a person pictures his or her own body". It is an important ingredient of our self-concept, helping to determine whether we accept or reject ourselves, whether we feel confident in social relationships, and whether we have an idealized or realistic idea of our attractiveness, strength, skills, and sex appeal. Body image is comprised of *two dimensions:* the perceptual (evaluation of the *size* of one's body) and the affective/cognitive (evaluation of abilities).

Normal variations in physical growth, development and sexual maturation can be a cause of undue anxiety in some. Comparing themselves negatively to peers for one reason or the other may lead to loss of self-esteem and a feeling of inferiority. These may interfere with adolescents' day-to-day functioning and studies, and may lead to problems in relationships with peers and family, jealousy, arguments and other negative expressions. Some behaviors that may have adverse health outcomes, like early sexual initiation (including sex with commercial sex workers), are liable to be determined or influenced by body image concerns. Body image disturbances may also lead to anorexia nervosa, bulimia, and body dysmorphic disorders.

Body image is a powerful factor in coming to terms with how adolescents feel about themselves. Higher levels of body satisfaction are associated with higher levels of self-esteem. It is important to understand the troubling relationship between psychological health and body image while managing adolescents with body image concerns.

ADOLESCENT SEXUALITY AND SEXUAL BEHAVIOR

Adolescence brings about sexual changes and maturation which adds to the vulnerability of the adolescents. The sexual attitude, behaviour and practices of the adolescents make them vulnerable to many adverse health consequences. Sex drive begins to be expressed in clear terms during adolescence, which is a period of heightened feelings, arousal, urges and sexual feelings directed towards self and the others. During adolescence, sexual exploration and expression is common and normal. The awakened sexual drive and thoughts produce a certain restlessness of character in the youth and they are often considered by their elders as different or difficult. Spontaneous erections, nocturnal emissions and masturbation manifest in the mid or early adolescence in majority of boys. Increased vaginal discharge, tingling and pain in the breasts, masturbation and menstrual concerns may be troublesome for young girls. The mood may become variable and impulsive. Both boys and girls may be troubled, confused and feel guilty because of these changes and may find redressal through behaviors that may be high risk, like smoking, alcohol use and sexual engagement that is more likely to be unsafe increasing their vulnerability to STI, HIV, pregnancy and sexual exploitation. Similarly, they may find it difficult to concentrate and remain distracted. Often, their school performance or work suffers. This can lead to various kinds of social and family maladjustment.

IMPORTANT HEALTH PROBLEMS OF ADOLESCENTS

Challenges to adolescent health and development are numerous, and often underestimated. In general, adolescent mortality rates are lower than older age groups or childhood, because of which adolescents are generally believed to be healthy - they have survived the diseases of early childhood, and the health problems associated with ageing are still many years away. Table 3.3 lists major health problems faced by adolescents.

There are significant sex differences in adolescent morbidity and mortality rates. Boys worldwide have higher rates of morbidity and mortality from injuries due to interpersonal violence, accidents and suicide, while adolescent girls have higher rates of morbidity and mortality related to sexual and reproductive behaviors.

Adolescent Reproductive and Sexual Health

In India, 47% of women ages 20–24 years were married before the legal minimum marriage age of 18 years according to the National Family Health Survey III (NFHS 3; 2005–06). Overall, 12% of women age 15–19 years have already become mothers. Forty three percent of women and 11% of men aged 20–24 had sexual debut – including within marriage -by 18 years of age. Sexual activity among adolescents is much higher and begins at an earlier age than what is commonly believed. Adolescents thus are vulnerable and at risk of unwanted pregnancies due to ignorance and lack of access to contraceptives during early teens. Other reproductive health related problems are also on the rise amongst adolescents in the age group 15–19 years. About 10% women and 11% men aged 15–19 had self-reported prevalence of sexually transmitted infection (STI) or symptoms (NFHS-3). The HIV prevalence is 0.04% among 15–19 years and 0.18% among 20–24 year olds (NFHS-3).

Table 3.3: Important health problems

1. *Illness*
   - Problems related to growth and development like precocious or delayed puberty and short stature
   - Endemic infectious diseases like tuberculosis, malaria
2. *Consequences of risk taking behavior*
   - Unintended injuries: Automobile and sports related accidents
   - Intended injuries: Violence, homicide, suicide
   - STIs, HIV/AIDS
   - Substance abuse related: tobacco, alcohol, drugs
3. *Nutritional problems*
   - Undernutrition
   - Micronutrient deficiencies like iron deficiency anemia, iodine deficiency
   - Obesity
   - Eating disorders
4. *Reproductive health problems*
   - High maternal mortality
   - High perinatal mortality, high low birth weight rate
   - Abortion related problems
   - Menstrual problems
   - Reproductive tract infections
5. *Mental health and related problems*
   - Behaviour disorders
   - Stress, anxiety
   - Depression and suicide
   - Substance use
   - Violence
   - Other psychiatric disorders

Adolescent Nutrition

Adolescence is a significant period for physical growth and sexual maturation. The foundation of adequate growth and development is laid before birth and during childhood, and is followed in adolescence. Adolescent growth and development is closely linked to the diet received during childhood and adolescence. Adolescent growth spurt determines final adult size.

Proper food and good nutrition are essential for physical growth, mental development, performance, productivity, health and well-being of adolescents. The adolescent growth spurt places extra demand on nutritional requirements. Adolescent girls need additional iron to compensate for menstrual blood loss. Over 80% of adolescent growth (attained weight and height) is completed in the early part of adolescence (10–15 years).

Inadequate nutrition in adolescence can potentially retard growth and sexual maturation, over and above the adverse consequences of chronic malnutrition during infancy and childhood. Improper nutrition (e.g., junk foods) can also affect adolescents' current health as well as put them at high risk of chronic diseases later in life, particularly if combined with other adverse behaviors like sedentary lifestyle.

Undernutrition and Anemia

Anemia during adolescent age group is rampant; 56% girls and 30% boys have hemoglobin less than 13 g/dL (NFHS 3, 2005-06). Undernutrition prevalence is also quite significant; 47% girls and 58% boys of 15–19 years age have BMI less than 18 (NFHS 3, 2005-06). Anemia and undernutrition have adverse impact on reproductive health outcomes, scholastic performance, physical performance and general productivity. There is an inter-generational effect in terms of greater prevalence of low birth weight babies born to undernourished and anemic women.

Overweight and Obesity

Lifestyle changes related to high fat, high carbohydrate diet and low levels of physical activity have resulted in the rising prevalence of overweight and obese adolescents, particularly in urban areas. Overweight and obesity during childhood and adolescence continue into adulthood, increasing the likelihood of a range of health disorders such as cardiovascular diseases, diabetes, hypertension, stroke, gallbladder disease and some cancers. Obese teenagers are vulnerable to social discrimination. Poor self-esteem and body image are consistently associated with obesity in adolescents.

Eating Disorders

Most adolescents are conscious about the changes in their bodies. They want to conform to the "ideal" body image. As such, they try unhealthy diets and engage in unhealthy eating habits that can lead to eating disorders. Eating disorders such as *bulimia* are often caused by anxiety, tension or worry about one's weight. *Anorexia nervosa* is a psychological disorder where people suffer from the mistaken notion that they are fat even though they are actually thin and weak.

Anorexia and bulimia can have serious psychological and medical consequences such as metabolic disturbances, convulsions, renal failure, irregular heart beat and dental erosion. In adolescent girls, anorexia can delay the onset of menstruation, minimize stature and result in osteoporosis.

Mental Health and Adolescents

Emotional Problems

These include sadness (or grief), anxieties (or worries), anger and stress. Stress is very common among adolescents because of the rapid physical, psychological, social and sexual changes during adole-scence. They also face new challenges as they are expected to assume more responsibility, form or change relationships, and achieve greater independence.

Behavioral Problems

These include aggressive or disruptive behavior towards parents, teachers, siblings and friends. These types of behaviors are expressed either individually or in a group. Risky behavior (such as unsafe sex, hazardous/drunken driving, smoking), self-harm, physical inactivity, educational failure and school dropout are associated with mental health problems.

Scholastic Issues

Strong emphasis placed on educational achievement has put a lot of pressure on adolescents. This causes a lot of stress among adolescents, which could cause psychosomatic symptoms like headaches, eye strain, difficulties concentrating and sleep problems. Some adolescents are slow or retarded in their development and may not do well in school.

Identity Problems

Adolescence is also a time when adolescents establish their individual identities. In today's world where there is so much diversity, mobility and opportunities it is a challenge for adolescents to decide their identities.

Others

Early childbearing and parenthood, unwanted pregnancy, abortion, sexually transmitted infection, social stigma and isolation and loss of education opportunity may all impose considerable stress on adolescents and could lead to other mental health problems or disorders.

Tobacco, Alcohol and Other Substance Use Amongst Adolescents

It is estimated that the most drug users are in the age group of 16–35 years with a bulk in the 18–25 years age group. Of the nearly 1.15 billion smokers in the world today, low and middle-income countries account for 82% of all smokers. While smoking prevalence is declining steadily in most high income countries, the tobacco epidemic is expanding in developing counties. In most developing countries, a significant percentage of the population belongs to the adolescent and younger age groups. Tobacco use presently causes around 11,000 deaths every day and the number of deaths in the next three decades is projected at 10 million annually; 70% of these will occur in the developing countries.

It is established that almost all tobacco users commence use before the age of 18 years. Therefore the young in developing countries are now increasingly being targeted by the tobacco industry to increase sales in order to offset their losses in the developed countries.

In recent years, drug abuse and injectable drug use among young male adolescents has increased. The use of alcohol and other drugs is a major contributing factor to accidents, suicides, violence, unwanted pregnancies and STDs including HIV/AIDS among young people.

Violence, Injuries and Sexual abuse

Accidents, interpersonal violence and self-inflicted violence are a major cause of morbidity and mortality amongst adolescents. Maltreatment and abuse including sexual abuse is a significant, though usually "invisible" cause of injuries amongst adolescents. Apart from physical injuries such as bruises and welts, burns and scalds, lacerations and fractures, child and adolescent maltreatment is associated with a number of other consequences, including: (i) alcohol and drug abuse; (ii) delinquent, violent and other risk-taking behaviors; (iii) eating and sleep disorders; (iv) reproductive health problems; (v) post-traumatic stress disorder; (vi) depression and anxiety; and (vii) suicidal behavior and self-harm.

ADOLESCENT FRIENDLY HEALTH SERVICES

For healthy development, adolescents need safe and supportive environment whereby they are protected, respected and nurtured to live life to its full potential while minimizing predilection for acquiring behaviors that endanger health and safety. There exists an extensive degree of public health rationale to provide adolescents with specific services.

Access to health services for adolescents is an important issue. Adolescents are reluctant to go to health centers and seek help for a variety of reasons. Even if they go to a health center for help, they are unsatisfied with the way in which they are treated. Most health services do not cater to their needs, are not perceived to be friendly by adolescents and are poorly attended by them.

Urgent action is required to improve the ability of health workers to respond to needs of adolescent clients more effectively and with greater sensitivity and to make health services more accessible and acceptable to them. The phrase '*adolescent friendly health services*' (AFHS) has been coined to communicate this idea.

There are a growing number and variety of initiatives to develop adolescent-friendly services. These include (i) to set up adolescent or youth friendly health centers, (ii) to make existing ones more 'youth friendly' than they currently are, and (iii) to deliver services and supplies (in a 'friendly' manner) to young people outside the health setting, e.g., school linked clinics, market place clinics and workplace clinics, etc.

Suggested reading

1. WHO, Regional Office for South East Asia. Adolescent health at a glance in South East Asia Region 2007, Fact Sheets WHO/UNFPA/UNICEF. Programming for adolescent health and development: Report of a study group on programming for adolescent health. Geneva: World Health.
2. Organization 1999 (WHO Technical Report Series, No.886) WHO. Broadening the horizon: Balancing protection and risk for adolescents. World Health Organization, Geneva, 2001.

4 Fluid and Electrolyte Disturbances

BODY FLUIDS

Fluid Compartments

Total body water (TBW) constitutes approximately 75% of the body weight at birth and declines to about 60% from the age of 2 years onwards. TBW is compartmentalized into *intracellular* (ICF) and *extracellular* fluid (ECF). The extracellular fluid comprises (i) *plasma*, (ii) *interstitial* fluid and (iii) *transcellular* fluid. The proportion of extracellular water to body weight is about 40% at birth, 25% at 2 years of age and 20% after the age of 7 years. The proportion of plasma at all ages is about 6%, and that of transcellular water about 2 to 3%; whereas interstitial fluid (ISF) declines from a maximum at birth to about 18 to 20% of body weight by 2 years. Plasma along with blood cells constitutes the blood volume, and it transports substances to various parts of the body. ISF buffers changes in plasma volume, and is the medium of exchange of all substances between plasma and the cells. Transcellular fluid comprises cerebrospinal fluid, synovial fluid, digestive juices, intraocular, pleural, pericardial and peritoneal fluids; these have specialized functions.

Fluid Composition

The distribution of body fluid is determined by the composition of electrolytes and proteins in different compartments (Fig. 4.1). Electrolytes exist as ions, namely cations (positively charged) and anions (negatively charged). The concentrations of electrolytes are generally expressed as mEq per liter. The equivalent weight is calculated by dividing the atomic weight by the valence, which gives the weight of the substance (in g) that can combine with or displace 1 g of hydrogen. A thousandth part of this is a mEq, e.g. if calcium level in blood is 10 mg/dL (0.1 g/L), then for the atomic weight and valence of 40 and 2 respectively, the calcium level is expressed as 0.1/40/2 Eq/L or 5 mEq/L. The *osmolality* of solutions determines the movement of water across an intervening semipermeable membrane. Osmolality is expressed as mOsm/kg, but osmolarity (expressed as mMol/L) is close enough for clinical purposes.

The compositions of plasma and ISF are roughly similar (Fig. 4.1) except for the presence of protein in plasma. ECF has a high concentration of sodium, chloride and bicarbonate whereas potassium, magnesium and phosphate are predominant intracellular ions. It is important to note that despite the differences in composition, each compartment is electroneutral and all have similar osmolality (290 mOsm/kg). Water is freely permeable across capillaries and cell membranes. In a steady state, there is no movement of water across compartments, since water only moves down osmotic gradients. As the major osmotic agent in the ECF is sodium chloride, the regulation of body water is linked to the regulation of sodium. The ionic composition of some transcellular fluids is shown in Table 4.1.

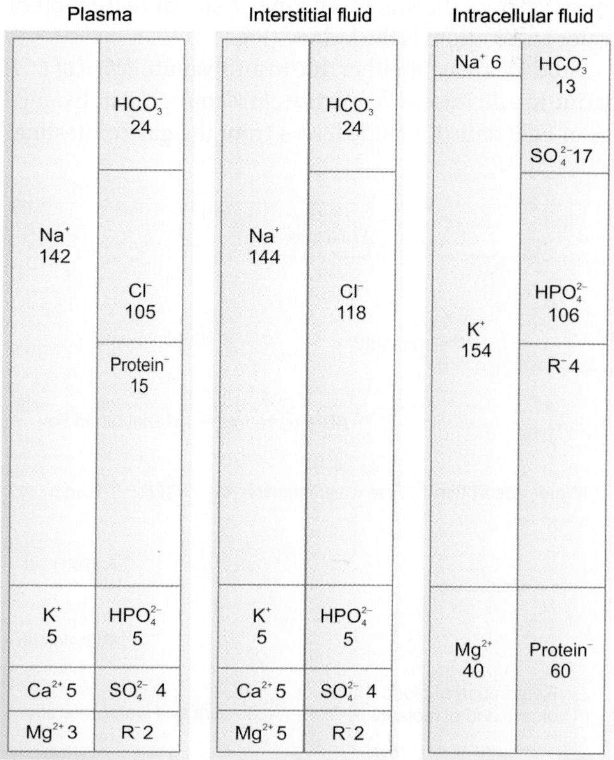

Plasma (cations)	Plasma (anions)	Interstitial fluid (cations)	Interstitial fluid (anions)	Intracellular fluid (cations)	Intracellular fluid (anions)
Na^+ 142	HCO_3^- 24	Na^+ 144	HCO_3^- 24	Na^+ 6	HCO_3^- 13
K^+ 5	Cl^- 105	K^+ 5	Cl^- 118	K^+ 154	SO_4^{2-} 17
Ca^{2+} 5	$Protein^-$ 15	Ca^{2+} 5	HPO_4^{2-} 5	Mg^{2+} 40	HPO_4^{2-} 106
Mg^{2+} 3	HPO_4^{2-} 5	Mg^{2+} 5	SO_4^{2-} 4		R^- 4
	SO_4^{2-} 4		R^- 2		$Protein^-$ 60
	R^- 2				

Fig. 4.1: Ionic compositions of major fluid compartments, figures represent concentration (mEq/L); sizes are not to scale

Table 4.1: Cations and anions in biological fluids (mEq/L)

Fluid	*Na⁺*	*K⁺*	*Cl⁻*
Gastric juice	60	10	85
Ileal fluid	130	10	115
Diarrheal stool*	10–90	10–80	10–110
Cerebrospinal fluid	140	3	120

* Upper end of the range for cholera stools, lower end for non-cholera

REGULATION OF BODY WATER AND ELECTROLYTES

The regulation of water and electrolytes is complex, involving close regulation of water, sodium, potassium and divalent ions.

4

Regulation of Water and Sodium Balance

For every 100 Calories metabolized, the body loses about 65 ml water in the urine, 40 ml by sweating, 15 ml from the lungs and about 5 ml in the feces; whereas it gains 15 ml from production in metabolic processes. Thus, the net need of water is 110 ml per 100 Calories metabolized. Loss of water through sweating depends on body surface area, temperature and environmental humidity, from the lungs varies with respiratory rate and humidity of inspired gases and that in the feces depends on the frequency and consistency of the stools. The major site of regulation of water and sodium is the kidney (Fig. 4.2).

Fluid loss may be either due to an absolute *deficit of ECF* or due to a *decrease in the effective circulating volume*. Examples of ECF deficit include losses from the gastrointestinal tract (diarrhea, vomiting), polyuria or decreased intake. Patients who have a decrease in the effective circulating volume may actually have a concomitant increase in total body water, e.g. nephrotic syndrome, cirrhosis with portal hypertension and congestive cardiac failure. Regulation of sodium and water balance is mediated through ADH, aldosterone and the thirst mechanism. *ADH* is synthesized in the anterior hypothalamus and secreted from the posterior pituitary. It acts upon the renal collecting ducts to retain free water. *Aldosterone* is secreted by the adrenal cortex in response to the production of renin and angiotensin by the kidney. It increases the reabsorption of sodium from the distal convoluted tubules in exchange for potassium; water passively follows the reabsorbed sodium. The intake of water is controlled by thirst. *Thirst* is regulated by the hypothalamus in response to ECF volume and osmolality. *Atrial natriuretic peptide,* released from right atrial myocytes, is important in disease states, e.g. congestive cardiac failure. The distension of the right atrium results in sodium and water loss, reducing cardiac preload.

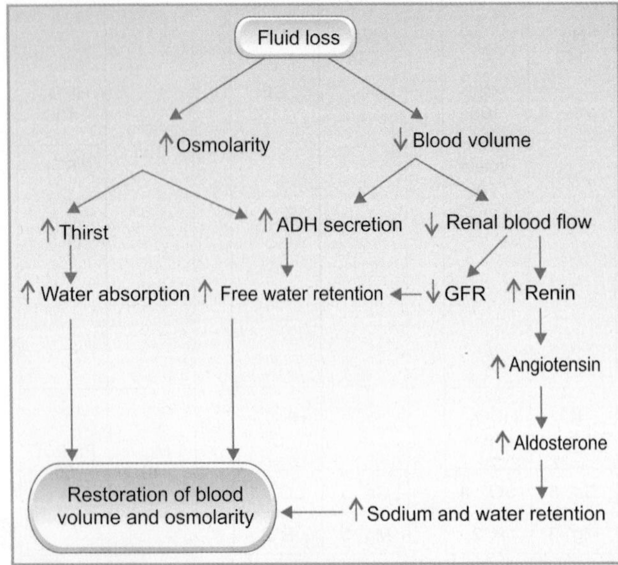

Fig. 4.2: Regulation of water and sodium balance in the body. ADH: antidiuretic hormone, GFR: glomerular filtration rate

Regulation of Potassium Balance

Potassium homeostasis is maintained by renal and extra-renal mechanisms (Fig. 4.3). Increased serum potassium stimulates the production of aldosterone. Aldosterone acts upon the distal convoluted tubules to reabsorb Na^+. To maintain electroneutrality, K^+ are excreted. Aldosterone also plays a role in extrarenal potassium homeostasis by causing potassium loss in the colon, in sweat and in saliva. Hyperkalemia also stimulates a non-mineralocorticoid dependent exchange of Na^+ and K^+ at the level of the distal convoluted tubule by a direct stimulation of the Na^+-K^+-ATPase pump. Conversely, an increased sodium load in the tubular lumen results in an attempt by the distal tubule to conserve Na^+; K^+ is lost in exchange. There are three important factors that enhance movement of K^+ into the cells. Alkalosis causes an efflux of H^+ from the cells, in

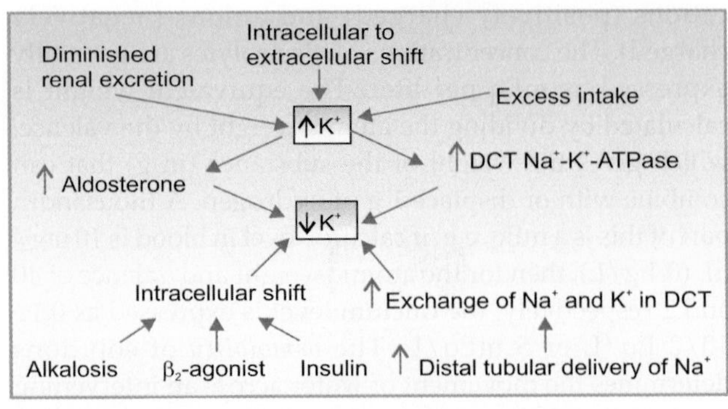

Fig. 4.3: Factors influencing potassium homeostasis. DCT distal convoluted tubule, ↑ K^+ increased serum potassium, ↓ K^+ decreased serum potassium

exchange K^+ moves intracellularly. Insulin increases potassium uptake by cells by directly stimulating Na^+-K^+-ATPase activity. β_2-agonists act by stimulating cyclic AMP via adenylate cyclase, which in turn activates the Na^+-K^+-ATPase pump.

Regulation of Calcium, Phosphate and Magnesium Balance

The key factors in the regulation of calcium, phosphate and magnesium balance are parathormone, 1,25-dihydroxyvitamin D3 (calcitriol) and calcitonin. The three key end-organs are bone, kidney and intestine (Fig. 4.4). Hypocalcemia is the most potent stimulator of parathormone production, whereas hypomagnesemia inhibits hypocalcemia-induced stimulation. Para- thormone, in the presence of calcitriol, acts on bone cells to release Ca^{2+}, and to a lesser extent phosphate into the serum. The increased ionized Ca^{2+} acts through calcitonin, a hormone produced by the parafollicular cells of the thyroid, to inhibit Ca^{2+} release from bones. Approximately half the Ca^{2+} in blood is bound to albumin. Hence, in hypoproteinemia, there is a decline in total serum Ca^{2+} levels, but there is no change in the unbound ionized Ca^{2+}. Since manifestations of Ca^{2+} disturbance are due to its ionized fraction, it is important to estimate the latter. This can either be directly assayed, or indirectly by either calculating the Q_oT_c interval on the ECG or by adjusting for the serum albumin level (for each 1 g/dL decline in albumin below 3.5 g/dl, there is a 0.8 mg/dL decline in Ca^{2+}). Q_oT_c is determined by estimating the Q_oT interval (beginning of Q wave to beginning of T wave) and corrected for heart rate by dividing by the square root of the RR interval; values greater than 0.22 suggest hypocalcemia.

ACID-BASE EQUILIBRIUM

A neutral solution has equal numbers of H^+ and OH^- ions. If the concentration of H^+, i.e. $[H^+]$, is higher than $[OH^-]$ in a given solution, that solution is acidic and if $[H^+]$ is less than $[OH^-]$ the solution is alkaline. Neutral solutions (e.g. plain water or sodium chloride dissolved in water) have 10^{-7} moles of H^+ per liter, and by definition an equal amount of OH^-. A convenient way to handle information regarding $[H^+]$ is to express it as *pH*, the negative logarithm of $[H^+]$. As the log of 10^{-7} is minus 7, the pH of a neutral solution is 7. Thus, a change in pH by one unit means a tenfold change in $[H^+]$.

Buffer systems are mixtures of a weak acid and its conjugate base. They resist marked changes in $[H^+]$, provided moderate amounts of acid or base are added to them. If a strong acid is added to a buffer system, the H^+ is taken up by the conjugate base to produce a weak acid. If a strong base is added, it combines with the weak acid to produce water and conjugate base. These systems are regulated by the *Henderson-Hasselbach equation*, which shows that the closer the pK of a buffer system is to the desired pH the more powerful is its buffering.

$$pH = pK + \log \frac{\text{base}}{\text{acid}}$$

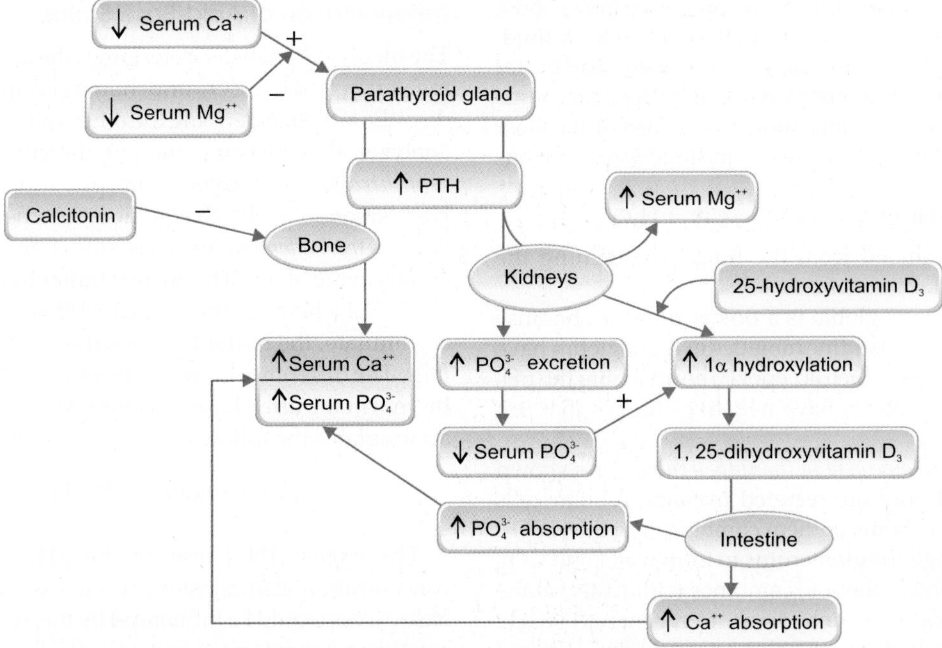

Fig. 4.4: Factors regulating calcium and phosphate balance

Table 4.2: Normal blood gas measurements

Parameter	*Arterial blood*	*Venous blood*
pH	7.38–7.45	7.35–7.45
pCO_2	35–45 torr	45–50 torr
HCO_3^-	23–27 mEq/L	24–25 mEq/L

Regulation of Acid-Base Equilibrium

The body maintains its arterial pH, pCO_2 and HCO_3^- within narrow range (Table 4.2).

Metabolic activity results in production of two types of acids, (i) *carbonic acid*, a volatile acid, which is derived from carbon dioxide, and (ii) *non-volatile acids*, including sulfuric acid (from metabolism of sulfur-containing amino acids), organic acids (incomplete combustion of carbohydrates and fats), uric acid (nucleoproteins), and inorganic phosphates (organic phosphates).

4

The principle mechanism for CO_2 handling is via the lungs. Hyperventilation results in CO_2 washout and drop in arterial pCO_2 (*respiratory alkalosis*); hypoventilation has the opposite effect (*respiratory acidosis*). The H^+ ions of non-volatile acids may either be buffered or excreted by several mechanisms. If these ions accumulate due to excess production or inadequate buffering, failure to excrete H^+, or loss of HCO_3^-, it results in *metabolic acidosis*. If the reverse occurs, it results in *metabolic alkalosis*.

The ECF has equal numbers of cations and anions, of which the easily measured are Na^+, K^+, Cl^- and HCO_3^-. The difference between the sums of (Na^+ + K^+) and (Cl^- + HCO_3^-) is comprised of unmeasured anions, called the *anion gap*. The value of the anion gap lies between 7 and 15. Metabolic acidosis is of two types: with or without increased anion gap.

The following buffer systems are operative in the body:

a. *Bicarbonate-carbonic acid buffer* in the extracellular fluid. The value of pK for the bicarbonate-carbonic acid buffer is 6.1. While this is a relatively weak buffer, it accounts for 55% of the buffering capacity because of its sheer abundance. When $[H^+]$ increases the following reactions occur:

$$H^+ + HCO_3^- \rightarrow H_2CO_3 \rightarrow CO_2 + H_2O$$

The CO_2 is exhaled from the lungs, dampening the change in pH.

b. *Hemoglobin:* Hemoglobin is a powerful buffer because its pK is 7.3. The histidine moieties in hemoglobin have negative charges, which accept H^+, normalizing the pH.

c. *Proteins:* The proteins have negative charges that can accept H^+.

d. *Bicarbonate-carbonic acid in the kidney tubules:* As shown in Fig. 4.5, H^+ ions are secreted from the tubular cells into the lumen. Some of them combine with the HCO_3^- filtered through the glomerulus to form water and CO_2. The CO_2 re-enters the cell, combines with water, in the presence of carbonic anhydrase, to regenerate HCO_3^- that is reabsorbed into the bloodstream. Thus, filtered HCO_3^- is conserved and H^+ is excreted.

e. *Monohydrogen phosphate-dihydrogen phosphate buffer:* This buffer system acts in the tubular lumen. It takes up H^+ ions secreted from the tubular cells, as follows:

$$H^+ + Na_2HPO_4 \rightarrow NaH_2PO_4 + Na^+$$

The weakly acidic NaH_2PO_4 is excreted in the urine.

f. *Sodium-hydrogen exchange in the distal tubule:* The distal tubular cells actively reabsorb Na^+; to maintain electroneutrality H^+ ions are exchanged. These ions combine with either monohydrogen phosphate or ammonia, and are excreted.

g. *Ammonia-ammonium buffer:* In the tubular cells, glutaminase breaks down glutamine in response to systemic acidosis to form glutamic acid and NH_3. The latter is secreted into the lumen combining with H^+ to form NH_4^+, which is excreted in urine.

The body is capable of compensating for various acid-base disturbances, with the singular aim of maintaining the pH in the normal range. Thus, in a patient who has respiratory acidosis, the kidneys retain bicarbonate to produce a *compensatory metabolic alkalosis*. On the contrary, in response to respiratory alkalosis the kidneys loose bicarbonate to effect a *compensatory metabolic acidosis*. In a patient who has metabolic acidosis, the respiratory rate and tidal volume increase to produce a *compensatory respiratory alkalosis*. The ventilation may decrease as a response to metabolic alkalosis, but this particular form of compensation is rarely ever seen. Respiratory compensation is rapid, whereas renal compensatory mechanisms may take several days to take effect. *Compensatory mechanisms do not overcorrect the primary disturbance.*

Determination of Acid-Base Status

The blood gas analyzer determines the acid-base status by measuring pH, pCO_2 and hemoglobin concentration directly; and then deriving the other values from these. The analyzer also measures the pO_2 directly. The *bicarbonate concentration* is derived from pH and pCO_2 using the Henderson-Hasselbach equation. Another useful derived value is the *buffer base*, which is a measure of the total buffer anions in the blood. The normal buffer base is 48 mMol/ L ($41.8 + 0.4 \times$ hemoglobin in g/dL). When non-volatile acids accumulate, the buffer base absorbs protons and its level falls. The difference between the observed buffer base and the normal buffer base is called *base excess*. When CO_2 accumulates the following reaction occurs:

$$CO_2 + H_2O \rightarrow H^+ + HCO_3^-$$

The excess $[H^+]$ lowers the pH, and the HCO_3^- concentration also registers an increase. Since the actual base excess would be influenced by this rise in the HCO_3, a correction factor is introduced to calculate the *standard base excess*. This gives us the base excess that would have been

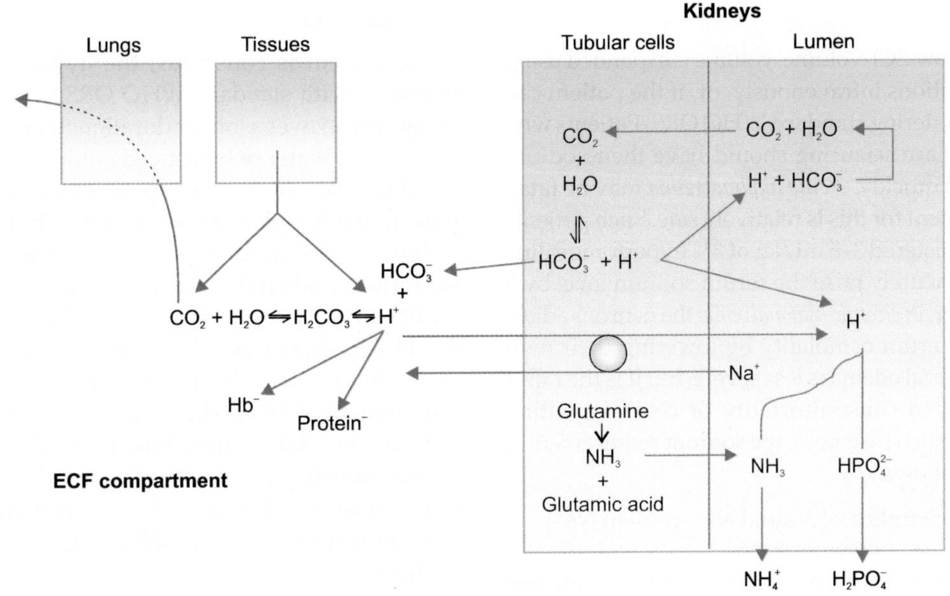

Fig. 4.5: Maintenance of acid-base equilibrium in the human body

there had the pH been 7.4 and had the pCO_2 been 40 torr. The standard base excess is used in calculating the dose of bicarbonate and estimate the renal contribution to bicarbonate retention.

Normal Maintenance Fluid and Electrolyte Requirements

The normal maintenance water requirement is equal to the insensible water losses and urinary losses. Insensible losses include losses through breathing and evaporative skin losses. As explained earlier, both insensible water losses and urinary losses depend on the metabolic activity of the individual. Assuming average calorie expenditure, the following guidelines for maintenance fluid requirements have been derived:

- For weight less than 10 kg: 100 ml/kg/day, e.g. an-8 kg child receives 800 ml/day
- For weight 10–20 kg: 100 ml/kg/d for the first 10 kg [1000 ml] + 50 ml/kg/d for every kg above 10 kg, e.g. a 14 kg child receives 1,200 ml/day
- For weight above 20 kg: 100 ml/kg for first 10 kg [1000 ml] + 50 ml/kg/d for next 10 kg [500 ml] + 20 ml/kg/d for every kg above 20 kg, e.g. a 25-kg child receives 1,600 ml/day

The normal daily sodium requirement is 3 mEq/kg, and for potassium and chloride 2 mEq/kg each. The daily glucose requirement is 5 g/kg.

Although, traditionally, hypotonic sodium containing fluids (usually N/5, see below) have been used for maintenance, evidence suggests that this may not be the best approach. A recent review showed that the odds of developing hyponatremia increased 17 times, when hypotonic maintenance fluids were used instead of isotonic saline.

DYSELECTROLYTEMIAS

Hyponatremia (Serum Sodium <130 mEq/L)

Causes

1. Reduced ECF volume and reduced total body Na^+: gastroenteritis, adrenal insufficiency, use of diuretics and cerebral salt wasting (CSW)
2. Increased ECF volume, normal total body Na^+ and low ADH: water intoxication
3. Increased ECF volume and high total body Na^+: cardiac failure, liver failure, portal hypertension, nephrotic syndrome, malnutrition
4. Increased ECF volume, normal total body Na^+ and high ADH: Syndrome of inappropriate antidiuretic hormone (SIADH). This is seen in the setting of neurological diseases, pulmonary diseases and rarely with certain drugs and malignancies. Patients with SIADH show weight gain, low serum osmolality and high urine osmolality.

Clinical Features

Hyponatremia may be symptomatic if the serum level is less than 120 mEq/L, more so if the onset of the hyponatremia is acute (< 24 hr). Fluid shifts from the ECF compartment, which is hypo-osmolar, into the neuronal cells. This results in cerebral edema, which causes headache, drowsiness, seizures and coma. Similar cerebral insults may cause either SIADH or CSW. The difference between the two is that SIADH has an expanded ECF while CSW has a depleted ECF compartment.

Management

In patients with low ECF volume, volume is expanded using isonatremic solutions intravenously, or, if the patient can drink, by administering standard WHO ORS. Patients who are comatose or are seizuring should have their sodium deficit corrected quickly. *Acute hyponatremia* may be fatal, whilst the treatment for this is relatively safe. Such patients should be administered 3–5 ml/kg of 3% hypertonic saline (500 mEq/L) to acutely raise the serum sodium level by 5 mEq/L. However, in *chronic hyponatremia* the neurons adjust to the lowered serum osmolality by lowering their own osmolality. Cerebral edema is less severe, but it is the rapid treatment that can cause mortality or central pontine myelinolysis. In such instances, the sodium requirement is determined as follows:

$$\text{Sodium deficit (mEq)} = [\text{desired Na}^+ - \text{present Na}^+] \times \text{weight} \times 0.6$$

The sodium deficit is repaired over 48 hr, at a rate less than 25 mEq/L over 48 hr.

SIADH is managed by restricting free water but not by giving more sodium, unless there are seizures. CSW is treated by administering both increased fluids and sodium. There are reports of the use of fludrocortisone in CSW.

Hypernatremia (Serum Sodium >150 mEq/L)

Causes

1. Decreased free water intake
2. High Na^+ intake: accidental salt administration in ORS or infant feeds
3. Increased free water loss
   i. Extra-renal: burns, sweating, tachypnea
   ii. Renal: central diabetes insipidus (craniopharyngioma, granulomatous diseases involving hypothalamus, postoperative); nephrogenic diabetes insipidus

Clinical Features

The signs of dehydration may be masked because fluid moves from the ICF compartment to the ECF down the osmotic gradient. ICF depletion results in a peculiar doughy feel of the skin, and a woody consistency of the tongue. Neuronal shrinkage causes alteration in sensorium, seizures and intracranial bleeds. In hypernatremia of more than a few hours duration, the neurons begin to generate *idiogenic osmoles* within the cells in an attempt to decrease the osmotic gradient.

Newborn babies may develop hypernatremic dehydration if they receive less breast milk. High breast milk sodium is indicative of lactation failure and this combined with poor intake may lead to excessive weight loss in the initial days and hypernatremia.

Management

If the patient is conscious, the hypernatremia is best managed with standard WHO ORS, with the correction being spread over a longer duration than the conventional 4–6 hr. Free water or breastfeeds should also be offered to the child. Neonates with hypernatremia need increase in milk intake. Supplementary feeds may be required.

Intravenous fluids are administered only if the patient's sensorium is altered. *Acute* hypernatremia, which has an onset within a few hours, may be treated with sodium free fluids. All other cases of hypernatremia must be corrected very slowly. The fluid deficit plus the maintenance requirement of 2 days should be given over a 48 hr period with an infusate which has a sodium concentration approximately equal to 40 mEq/L. Failure to correct the hypernatremia slowly may cause cerebral edema. Salt poisoning (serum Na^+ >180 mEq/L) requires urgent dialysis.

Hypokalemia (Serum Potassium <3.5 mEq/L)

Causes

1. Increased losses
   i. Diarrhea
   ii. Renal: Renal tubular acidosis, cystic kidneys
   iii. Endocrine: Cushing syndrome, hyper-aldosteronism
2. Decreased stores: malnutrition
3. Shift into intracellular compartment: alkalosis, high insulin state.

Clinical Features

Hypokalemia causes muscle weakness, hypotonia and paralytic ileus; EKG shows ST segment depression, T wave flattening or inversion, prominence of U waves and arrhythmias. Long standing hypokalemia causes a vacuolar nephropathy and polyuria. Malnourished children with diarrhea and dehydration may have severe hypokalemia.

Management

The deficit of K^+ should be corrected over a 24 hr period. Patients with depleted intracellular stores may require large amounts of K^+ as correction. Oral correction is always safer than intravenous correction. Intravenous correction is required when the patient is unable to take orally, the serum K^+ is less than or equal to 2.5 mEq/L or there are cardiac rhythm disturbances. The infused fluid should ideally not contain more than 40 mEq/L of potassium, or at most 60 mEq/L. The rate of infusion should not exceed 0.6 mEq/kg/hr. Relatively rapid correction may be required for profound hypokalemia, under continuous ECG monitoring.

Hyperkalemia (Serum Potassium >5.5 mEq/L)

Causes

1. Inadequate excretion
   i. Renal failure
   ii. Adrenal failure: Addison's disease, hypoaldosteronism
   iii. Potassium sparing diuretics
2. Shift of potassium from tissues
   i. Tissue damage: hemolysis, crush injuries
   ii. Acidosis
3. Drugs: digoxin, succinylcholine, β blockers.

Clinical Features

Hyperkalemia results in characteristic changes on the EKG, including peaked T waves, prolonged PR interval, widened QRS complex, heart blocks and ventricular fibrillation. Severe hyperkalemia may cause muscle weakness.

Management

Mild hyperkalemia (serum K^+ 5.5–6 mEq/L) is managed by stopping the intake of potassium and offending drugs such as potassium sparing diuretics. *Moderate hyperkalemia* (serum K^+ 6–8 mEq/L or peaked T waves) is managed by administering a glucose insulin infusion (0.5 g/kg glucose with 0.3 U regular insulin/g glucose, over 2 hr) and/or a sodium bicarbonate infusion (2 mEq/kg $NaHCO_3$ over 5–10 min), in addition to the measures already mentioned. Patients with *severe hyperkalemia* (serum K^+ >8 mEq/L or ECG changes) should be urgently administered IV calcium gluconate (10%) 0.5 ml/kg. This immediately reverses the cardiac effects of hyperkalemia. This should be followed up with the measures as for moderate hyperkalemia. Intravenous or nebulized salbutamol also rapidly lowers serum K^+. Dialysis is done if hyperkalemia is refractory to therapy. Sodium polystyrene sulphonate, a potassium binding ion exchange resin, can be used for the long-term management of hyperkalemia.

Hypocalcemia (Calcium <8 mg/dL or Ionized Calcium <4 mg/dL)

Causes

1. Vitamin D deficiency: (i) malnutrition; (ii) malabsorption; (iii) abnormal metabolism; (iv) prolonged phenytoin therapy
2. Increased losses: (i) idiopathic hypercalciuria; (ii) renal tubular acidosis; (iii) frusemide therapy; (iv) prolonged corticosteroid therapy
3. Metabolic: (i) hypoparathyroidism; (ii) pseudohypoparathyroidism; (iii) hypomagnesemia; (iv) hyperphosphatemia
4. Others: (i) metabolic alkalosis; (ii) hypoproteinemia; (iii) acute pancreatitis; (iv) prematurity; (v) infant of diabetic mother; (vi) neonates fed high phosphate milk

Clinical Features

Hypocalcemia may manifest with jitteriness, tetany, carpopedal spasms, laryngospasm and seizures. Latent tetany can be elicited by various maneuvers. Carpopedal spasm of the forearm and hand can be elicited by Trousseau sign, in which a blood pressure cuff on the arm is inflated to a pressure above the systolic pressure for 3 minutes to induce neuronal ischemia. Twitching of the orbicularis oculi and mouth can be elicited by tapping the facial nerve anterior to the external auditory meatus (Chvostek sign). Prolonged hypocalcemia can present with osteomalacia and rickets.

Management

Tetany, laryngospasm and seizures must be treated immediately with 2 ml/kg of 10% calcium gluconate, administered IV slowly under cardiac monitoring. Initially intravenous calcium boluses are given every 6 hr. Thereafter, oral calcium supplementation is provided at 40–80 mg/kg/day. Newborns with late onset hypocalcemia, due to high phosphate-containing milk intake, should be treated with supplemental calcium added to the milk to make the calcium: phosphorus ratio equal to 4:1. Vitamin D deficiency should be treated appropriately.

Hypercalcemia

Causes

1. Parathormone excess
   i. Parathyroid adenoma
   ii. Parathyroid hyperplasia: familial, sporadic, syndromic (MEN I and II)
   iii. Transient neonatal hyperparathyroidism
   iv. Paraneoplastic syndromes
2. Vitamin D excess; hypervitaminosis A
3. Sarcoidosis
4. William's syndrome
5. Subcutaneous fat necrosis
6. Thyrotoxicosis
7. Prolonged immobilization

Clinical Features

Hypercalcemia can have varied manifestations. Urinary stones are common and can present with colic and hematuria. Calcium can also deposit in the renal parenchyma to produce nephrocalcinosis. Non-specific manifestations include anorexia, fatigue, vomiting, constipation and weight loss. Polyuria and polydipsia may also be seen. Bony changes, especially in parathyroid disorders, may present as fractures, deformities and back pain. Severe hypercalcemia (>15 mg/dL) is extremely rare, and presents as stupor and coma.

Management

Forced saline diuresis with frusemide or peritoneal dialysis can rapidly lower serum calcium levels. Bisphosphonates have emerged as a modality of treatment of hypercalcemia in children. Pamidronate and etidronate have been used in the treatment of hypercalcemia due to malignancy, immobilization and hyperparathyroidism. The definitive surgical management of hyperparathyroidism is surgery.

Composition of commonly available fluids are given in Table 4.3.

FLUID THERAPY IN CLINICAL SITUATIONS

Diarrheal Dehydration

Fluid therapy can be subdivided under 3 headings, administered simultaneously.

4

Maintenance fluids: The required volumes and electrolyte requirements are described above. For every 1000 ml maintenance fluid in a 10-kg child, 30 mEq of sodium, 20 mEq of potassium and 20 mEq of chloride are required. This can be provided by 1000 ml of N/5 in 5% dextrose daily, with 1 ml potassium chloride per 100 ml fluid.

Deficit replenishment: This is best assessed by measuring acute weight loss. Weight loss occurring over a matter of hr or few days is assumed to be due to fluid deficit, because any significant weight change attributable to nutrition would occur over several days to weeks. The deficit volume should be replenished over 4–6 hr. If the baseline weight is not known, one has to take recourse to clinical assessment as mild, moderate or severe dehydration. The maintenance requirement may be added to the deficit, and this simplifies the fluid calculation. For a 10% fluid deficit in a 10-kg child, one requires a N/2 saline preparation with 2 ml KCl added per 100 ml fluid; 1,250 ml over 6 hr (1000 ml deficit and 250 ml maintenance for 6 hr) takes care of deficit and maintenance needs.

Ongoing losses: In a setting of diarrheal disease, stool losses need to be replaced on an ongoing basis. The standard WHO ORS solution given orally, with intermittent breastfeeds or free water, is the treatment of choice. However, if the losses have to be matched by IV fluids, the choice of fluid depends on the etiology of diarrhea. Cholera stools have 90 mEq/L sodium and non-cholera stool 40 mEq/L sodium; N/2 saline infusion providing sodium content between these figures (77 mEq/L) can be safely used.

Otherwise **Ringer's lactate** or **normal saline** is used to match the losses due to cholera. Keeping in mind the widespread availability of normal saline and the need to have simple guidelines for community-based treatment of dehydration, the WHO guidelines stress on the use of normal saline for simpler calculations. These are discussed elsewhere in this book.

Acute Renal Failure

To differentiate pre-renal from intrinsic renal failure, a fluid challenge should be administered to evaluate the response in urine output. The fluid chosen should be similar to ECF, hence *normal saline* is the fluid of choice. After a rapid infusion of 10 ml/kg of normal saline, an increase in urine output to greater than 1 ml/kg/hr is expected if it is pre-renal failure. If this fails, a second bolus may be given along with IV frusemide. If this too fails to elicit an increase in urine output, it is designated as intrinsic renal failure. For intrinsic renal failure, the maintenance fluid volume should be restricted to the insensible losses (30–40 ml/kg/day) plus the measured urine output of the previous day. Since patients with oliguric renal failure would generally have a urine output less than 0.5 ml/kg/hr, the upper limit of the daily urine volume is around 10 ml/kg. No electrolytes should added to this fluid. Hence, the fluid of choice is 5% *dextrose* at 45–55 ml/kg/day.

Table 4.3: Composition per 1000 ml of fluid

Fluid	*Na^+*	*K^+*	*Cl^-*	*Glucose*	*Others (mEq)*
5% Dextrose	–	–	–	50 g	–
10% Dextrose	–	–	–	100 g	–
Normal saline	154 mEq	–	154 mEq	–	–
N/2 saline	77 mEq	–	77 mEq	–	–
N/5 in 5% dextrose	30 mEq	–	30 mEq	40 g	–
3% saline	513 mEq	–	513 mEq	–	–
Ringer's lactate	130 mEq	4 mEq	109 mEq	–	Lactate 29
Isolyte-P	26 mEq	19 mEq	22 mEq	50 g	Acetate 24, PO_4^{3-} 3, Mg^{2+} 3
7.5% Sodium bicarbonate	1280 mEq	–	–	–	Bicarbonate 1280
Potassium chloride	–	2000 mEq	2000 mEq	–	–

Congestive Heart Failure

Patients with congestive heart failure are fluid overloaded. The daily maintenance fluids should be restricted to two-thirds of the routine guidelines. With the use of powerful diuretics, the restriction can be eased somewhat. These patients are often hyponatremic because of diuretic losses and dilution, and are hypokalemic because of diuretic usage. Increased sodium intake, on the other hand, can worsen the heart failure. Hence, the maintenance fluids should contain the normal amount of sodium and extra amounts of potassium. The fluid of choice for a 10-kg child thus is *N/5 in 5% dextrose* with 2 ml KCl per 100 ml fluid, at about 70 ml/kg/day.

Intestinal Obstruction

A child with intestinal obstruction should have an indwelling nasogastric tube to decompress the stomach. The gastric juices contain about 60 mEq/L of sodium (Table 4.1). Nasogastric aspirate should be replaced volume for volume with N/2 or N/3 saline, with added potassium. Post-ileostomy losses should be replaced volume for volume with normal saline or Ringer's lactate with added potassium.

DISTURBANCES IN ACID-BASE STATUS

Respiratory Acidosis

Causes

- Decreased respiratory drive-cerebral diseases, drugs, neuromuscular diseases
- Pulmonary diseases with alveolar hypoventilation
- Respiratory fatigue

Clinical Features

The manifestations of hypercapnia are not always obvious, unless it is severe. It causes obtundation, features of raised intracranial pressure, asterixis and plethora.

Management

The underlying disease must be treated and the patient must be mechanically ventilated. Bicarbonate must not be infused to treat the acidosis because it generates more CO_2.

Respiratory Alkalosis

Causes

- Hypoxia causing tachypnea: asthma, pneumonia, bronchiolitis
- Respiratory center stimulation: fever, anxiety, cerebral tumor

Clinical Features

Respiratory alkalosis is apparent only when it is severe and acute. It causes parasthesias, numbness and tetany.

Management

The underlying disorder should be treated.

Metabolic Acidosis

Causes

- *Increased anion gap*
  Lactic acidosis: hypoperfusion, hypoxia, septicemia
  Ketoacidosis: diabetic, starvation
  Poisoning: salicylate
  Metabolic disorders: aminoacidopathies, organic acidemias
  Renal failure
- *Normal anion gap*
  Renal tubular acidosis
  Loss of bicarbonate: diarrhea, acetazolamide use

Clinical Features

Patients with acute metabolic acidosis have deep and rapid breathing (Kussmaul breathing). Severe acidosis may cause confusion, drowsiness, myocardial depression and shock. Chronic metabolic acidosis causes fatigue and anorexia.

4

Management

It is important to identify the cause of metabolic acidosis and treat accordingly. Empirical therapy with bicarbonate without addressing the underlying cause is not recommended. Bicarbonate therapy has a role when the pH is less than 7.25 because pH in this range causes myocardial depression. The requirement of sodium bicarbonate (mEq) is as follows: *body weight (kg) × standard base excess × 0.3*

This amount is given over two days with the intention of correcting the acidosis over 48 hr. One ml of 7.5% $NaHCO_3$ contains 0.9 mEq of bicarbonate. Patients with congestive cardiac failure may not tolerate large amounts of Na^+. In these cases, the rate of infusion should be slow or THAM should be infused over 3–6 hr. Dose of THAM (ml) is: *weight (kg) × standard base excess.*

In cases of acidosis due to *volume depletion*, the volume deficit should be corrected. In *diabetic ketoacidosis*, insulin therapy generally corrects the acidosis. Acidosis due to *poisoning* or *metabolic disorders* may require dialysis. Correct treatment of the underlying metabolic disorder usually corrects the acidosis. Mild to moderate acidosis in *renal failure* improves on oral alkali therapy. There is no need to correct this acidosis completely. Overzealous correction in the setting of renal failure may precipitate tetany. *Renal tubular acidosis* should be fully corrected with $NaHCO_3$, Shohl's or other alkai solutions. The dose is 0.5 to 2 mEq/kg/d of bicarbonate in 3–4 divided doses. *Hypoadrenal states* require steroid replacement. Acidosis caused by *acetazolamide* or *potassium sparing diuretics* requires cessation of the drug, if the acidosis is significant.

Metabolic Alkalosis

Causes

- *Loss of volume and chloride*
  Recurrent vomiting, diuretic therapy, Bartter and Gitelman syndromes
  Hyperaldosteronism: primary, secondary
  Liddle syndrome, syndrome of mineralocorticoid excess, glucocorticoid remediable aldosteronism, congenital adrenal hyperplasia (non-sodium wasting forms)
  Cushing syndrome
- *Excess base intake:* overzealous bicarbonate therapy
- Severe hypokalemia

Clinical Features

Mild alkalosis has no signs and symptoms. Severe alkalosis causes apathy and stupor. Rapid development of alkalosis may precipitate hypocalcemic tetany. Symptoms of hypokalemia may also be present.

4

Management

Mild to moderate cases usually require no treatment. In patients with volume depletion due to recurrent vomiting, infusion of saline solutions is adequate. If there is concomitant potassium loss, as in diuretic therapy or vomiting, it should be replaced with potassium chloride. Adrenal dysfunction requires treatment of the underlying problem. Therapy of Bartter and Gitelman syndrome includes potassium supplements and indomethacin.

Suggested reading

1. Choong K, Kho ME, Menon K, Bohn D. Hypotonic versus isotonic saline in hospitalized children: a systematic review. Arch Dis Child 2006; 91: 828–835
2. Shaw NJ, Bishop NJ. Bisphosphonate treatment of bone disease. Arch Dis Child 2005; 90: 494–499
3. Albanese A, Hindmarsh P, Stanhope R. Management of hyponatremia in patients with acute cerebral insults. Arch Dis Child 2001; 85: 246–251
4. Clark BA, Brown RS. Potassium homeostasis and hyperkalemic syndromes. Endocrinol Metabol Clin N Amer 1995; 24:573–590

5 Nutrition

Nutrition, also called nourishment, is the provision, to cells and organisms, of the materials necessary in the form of food to support life. Our food is made up of essential, natural complex chemical substances called *nutrients*. There are seven major classes of nutrients: carbohydrates, fats, fiber, minerals, proteins, vitamins, and water. These nutrient classes can be grouped into the categories of macronutrients and micronutrients. The *macronutrients* are needed in large quantities (e.g. carbohydrates, fats and proteins), and are building blocks of the body. The *micronutrients* (e.g. minerals and vitamins), on the other hand, are needed in tiny quantities, and are crucial for their role in metabolic pathways and in enhancing immunity. Micronutrients are discussed in Chapter 6.

MACRONUTRIENTS

Carbohydrates

Carbohydrates are the main source of energy in the Indian diet contributing to 55–60% of total energy intake. Carbohydrates contribute taste, texture and bulk to the diet. Lack of carbohydrates (less than 30%) in the diet may produce ketosis, loss of weight, and breakdown of proteins. Carbohydrates are divided into *simple carbohydrates* (monosaccharide and disaccharides such as glucose and fructose in fruits, vegetables and honey, sucrose in sugar and lactose in milk) and *complex carbohydrates* (oligosaccharides and polysaccharides such as starch in cereals, millets, pulses and root vegetables). The main source of energy in the body is glucose derived from starch and sugars present in the diet. Glucose is used as a fuel by the cells and is converted to glycogen by liver and muscles. Excess carbohydrates are converted to fat. Carbohydrates provide 4 kcal of energy per gram.

Proteins

Proteins are the second most abundant substance in the body, after water. They are required for the growth and synthesis of tissues in the body; formation of digestive juices, hormones, plasma proteins, enzymes and hemoglobin; as buffers to maintain acid-base equilibrium in the body ; and as alternate source of energy for the body. Proteins are made of 20 different kinds of amino acids. Amino acids that can be adequately synthesized in the body are called non-essential amino acids, while others known as essential amino acids must be supplied in the diet because the body cannot synthesize them.

Essential amino acids include: leucine, isoleucine, lysine, methionine, phenylalanine, threonine, tryptophan and valine. Histidine and arginine are essential during infancy because the rate of their synthesis is inadequate for sustaining growth.

Protein Quality

Food proteins differ in their nutritional quality depending on their amino acid profile and digestibility. Cereal grains are deficient in the essential amino acids like lysine, threonine or tryptophan, whereas pulses are rich in lysine but are limiting in sulphur containing amino acids, mainly methionine. When cereals are taken in combination with the pulses, the deficiency in one is made good by an excess in other.

The following terms are used to describe protein quality:

$$\text{True digestibility (TD)} = \frac{\text{Nitrogen absorbed}}{\text{Nitrogen intake}} \times 100$$

$$\text{Biological value (BV)} = \frac{\text{Nitrogen retained}}{\text{Nitrogen absorbed}} \times 100$$

$$\text{Net protein utilization (NPU)} = \frac{\text{TD}}{100} \times \text{BV}$$

Egg protein has the highest values for BV and NPU and is therefore taken as the reference protein and the value of others is expressed as relative to egg (100). Generally, animal proteins have a higher BV than the plant proteins. The nutritive value of a mixture of two proteins may be higher than the arithmetic mean of the two because of the mutual supplementary effects.

Requirements: The protein allowances shown in Table 5.1 are given in terms of the mixed vegetable proteins contained in Indian diets, the NPU of which is assumed to be 65. Nearly 8–12 % of the total energy should be provided from protein sources. An intake of 8% proteins may be sufficient for those having a higher content of animal proteins or high value proteins in the diet. Proteins provide 4 kcal energy per gram.

Table 5.1: Recommended dietary allowances for Indian children

Group	*Particulars*	*Body weight (kg)*	*Energy (kcal/day)*	*Protein (g/day)*	*Fat (g/day)*	*Calcium (mg/day)*	*Iron (mg/day)*	*Vitamin A (µg/day)*		*Thiamine (mg/day)*	*Riboflavin (mg/day)*	*Nicotinic acid (mg/day)*	*Pyridoxine (mg/day)*	*Ascorbic acid (mg/day)*	*Folic acid (µg/day)*	*Vitamin B12 (µg/day)*
								Retinol	*β-carotene*							
Infants	0–6 months	5.4	108/kg	2.05/kg	*	500	79**	350	1200	55**	65**	710**	0.1	25	25	0.2
	6–12 months	8.6	98/kg	1.65 /kg	25	300	79**	350	1200	50**	60**	650**	0.4	25	25	0.2
Children	1–3 years	12.2	1240	22	25	400	12	400	1600	0.6	0.7	8	0.9	40	30	0.2–1.0
	4–6 years	19.0	1690	30	25	400	18	400	1600	0.9	1.0	11	0.9	40	40	0.2–1.0
	7–9 years	26.9	1950	41	25	400	26	600	2400	1.0	1.2	13	1.6	40	60	0.2–1.0
Boys	10–12 years	35.4	2190	54	22	600	34	600	2400	1.1	1.3	15	1.6	40	70	0.2–1.0
Girls	10–12 years	31.5	1970	57	22	600	19	600	2400	1.0	1.2	13	1.6	40	70	0.2–1.0
Boys	13–15 years	47.8	2450	70	22	600	41	600	2400	1.2	1.5	16	2.0	40	100	0.2–1.0
Girls	13–15 years	46.7	2060	65	22	600	28	600	2400	1.0	1.2	14	2.0	40	100	0.2–1.0
Boys	16–18 years	57.1	2640	78	22	500	50	600	2400	1.3	1.6	17	2.0	40	100	0.2–1.0
Girls	16–18 years	49.9	2060	63	22	500	30	600	2400	1.0	1.2	14	2.0	40	100	0.2–1.0

*adequately breastfed infants receive nearly 30 g fat per day

** µg/kg/day

Modified from Gopalan C, Rama Sastri BV, Balasubramanian SC, Narasinga Rao BS, Deosthale YG, Pant KC. Nutritive value of Indian foods. Hyderabad: National Institute of Nutrition; 1991.

Fats

Fats comprise a large and diverse group of compounds that are saponifiable esters of long-chain fatty acids (Fig. 5.1). The major functions of the fats are to act as major structural element of the cell membranes; major source of energy, carriers of fat soluble vitamins (A, D, E and K); precursors for biosynthesis of prostaglandins and hormones.

The fats present in the diet or in human body are in the form of fatty acids (triglycerides), phospholipids and cholesterol. The fatty acids are of different carbon chain length and may be either saturated or unsaturated. There is a great variety in the structure and characteristic of individual fats, giving different nutritional properties to them. Fats are grouped as saturated or polyunsaturated fats depending on the predominating fatty acids. Whether the fats are solids or liquids at room temperature is largely determined by the degree of their saturation. The more the level of saturation, more solid is the fat.

About 25–30% of energy intake should be from fat. However in malnourished children, up to 45% of calories can be provided from fat safely. In India, almost 10–15% of fat is derived from invisible fat. Therefore visible fat intake should be restricted to below 20%. Saturated fat should not exceed 7% of the total fat intake; polyunsaturated fat should be restricted to 10% and rest 13% should be derived from monounsaturated fats. A minimum of 3% energy should be derived from linoleic and 0.3% from linolenic acid. Fats provide 9 kcal of energy per gram.

Triglycerides

Triglycerides are divided on the basis of chain length into *medium chain triglycerides* (MCT; 6–12 carbon length) or *long chain triglycerides* (LCT; >12 carbon length). MCTs are an immediate source of energy as they are transported directly from the small intestine to liver by portal vein and are burned immediately. They comprise primarily of caprylic acid and capric acid. Sources of MCT are coconut oil, palm kernel oil and butter (15% of MCT). MCT improves endurance performance, promotes fat burning, spares muscle glycogen, increases metabolic rate and lowers blood cholesterol level. MCT is used in the dietary management of cystic fibrosis, pancreatic insufficiency, AIDS, epilepsy, gallstones, high blood cholesterol levels, fat malabsorption, intestinal lymphangiectasias and as energy booster in athletes. LCT provides essential fatty acids (EFAs) and requires carnitine to produce energy. It is best to provide a combination of both MCT along with LCT because MCT provides immediate energy to critically ill patients whereas LCT gives EFAs. Prolonged use of sole MCTs leads to EFA deficiency.

Essential Fatty Acids (EFA)

EFA cannot be synthesized in the body and have to be supplied through dietary fat. Linolenic acid, eicosapentanoic acid (EPA) and docosahexanoic acid (DHA) are omega-3 type of fatty acids. EPA and DHA have antithrombotic, anti-vasorestrictive, anti-hypertensive and anti-arrhythmic influences. Omega-3 fatty acids also have anti-inflammatory properties. They are important components of gray matter of the brain and improve intellectual performance. Infants fed omega-3 fatty acids have demonstrated better cognitive development than those who are not. It is recommended that omega-3 fatty acid content of the diet should be about 0.5 % of the total calories or 1.0–1.5 g/day. Most omega-6 fatty acids are consumed in the diet in the form of linoleic acid, which gets converted to γ-linolenic acid (GLA) in the body and then further broken down to arachidonic acid (AA). Excess amount of AA/ linoleic acid are unhealthy because they promote inflammation. In contrast, GLA reduces inflammation. Deficiency of EFAs leads to cessation of growth, alopecia, diarrhea, impaired wound healing, decreased calcium absorption, decreased calcium deposits in bones and decreased bone strength.

5

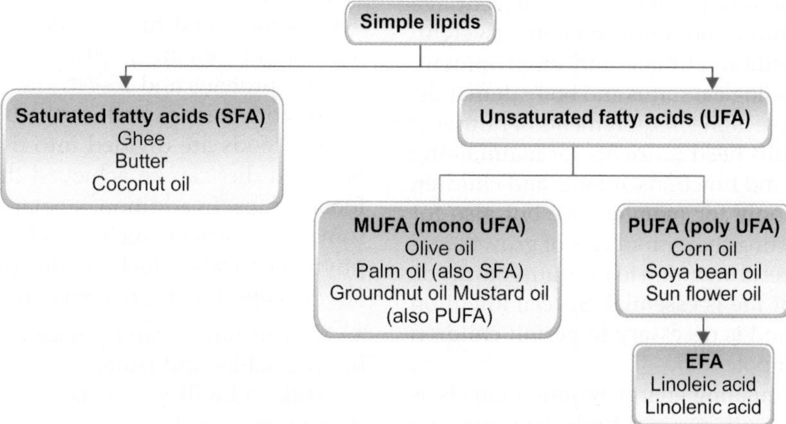

Fig. 5.1: Classification of fats. EFA—essential fatty acids

Cholesterol

Cholesterol is produced in the liver. It is a component of the cell membranes. Cholesterol also helps the body to produce steroid hormones and bile acids needed for digestion.

Fiber

Dietary fibers include polysaccharides such as cellulose, hemicelluloses, pectin, gums, mucilage and lignin. They have very little nutritional value as they are not digested by the enzymes in the gut. Fibers are essential for the normal functioning of the gut, elimination of waste, water holding, bile acid binding capacity and for maintaining the growth of normal intestinal microflora.

Energy

Energy needs of children are computed keeping in mind the constant and rapid increase in body size, increased BMR so as to regulate body temperature and to maintain high level of metabolic activities and marked developmental changes in organ function and composition. Energy requirements vary between infants and children because of variations in growth rate and physical activity. Although growth rate slows in toddlers, their activity levels are high, and appetite and food intake tends to be erratic. In older children, growth is more constant but energy needs vary within and between individuals. During adolescence, energy needs increase due to rapid growth and development. There are 3 critical periods in early life of a young child with regards to energy requirements; around 6 months when complementary feeding is initiated, between 1–2 years when physical activity is increased and between 10–12 years for girls and 15–18 years for boys) when puberty is attained.

Recommended Dietary Allowances (RDA)

A range of acceptable or safe intake levels have been established for almost all the important nutrients, which are recognized as "RDA" or "Recommended dietary allowances". RDAs are formulated based on the current knowledge of nutritional requirements of different age and sex groups depending on anthropometry (weight, height), body composition, climate and environment, physical activity, physiological status and body demands. Infants and children have higher requirements of nutrients than adults. While adults need nutrients for maintaining constant body weight and functions, infants and children require nutrients not only for maintenance but also for promoting and supporting their rapid rate of growth and development. Thus careful attention to the nutrients needs of children throughout life is essential. Special attention during the critical period is necessary to permit children to develop to their full potential.

A simple way of calculating energy requirements is as follows: For children with normal body weights, the energy requirements are 100 kcal/kg for the first 10 kg. Between 10–20 kg, the requirement is 1000 kcal plus 50 kcal/kg added for weight above 10 kg (e.g. for a 15 kg child, the requirement will be 1250 kcal). For weight more than 20 kg, 20 kcal/kg is added to 1500 kcal to estimate the requirements (e.g. for a 30 kg child the requirement is approximately 1700 kcal).

NORMAL DIET

Breastfeeding

An infant should be exclusively breastfed till six months of age. During this age, additional food or fluid is not required as breast milk is nutritionally complete for the child's growth and development and it protects from infections and strengthens immune system.

Complementary Feeding

After six months of age, breast milk alone is not enough to make an infant grow well. Complementary feeding refers to food which complements breast milk and ensures that the child continues to have enough energy, protein and other nutrients to grow normally. **Complementary feeding is started at six months of age, while continuing breastfeeding**, Breastfeeding is encouraged up to two years of age in addition to normal food. IMNCI recommendations for breastfeeding and complementary feeding are given in Table 5.2.

Balanced Diet

Balanced diet is defined as nutritionally adequate and appropriate; it provides all the nutrients in required amounts and proper proportions. Even at 9 months, infants need small portions of a mix of food groups to be included in their diet to ensure intakes of all macronutrients and micronutrients. A combination of carbohydrate rich food (any cereal, fruit and/or vegetable), a protein source (milk and milk products, pulse, egg, meat, fish, nuts) and a fat (visible oil/ghee) and/or sugar/salt should be used to make nutritionally adequate complementary food or feed. A balanced diet should be consumed by children and adolescents to ensure proper growth and development and to stay healthy and disease free. This diet should contain 55–60% calories from carbohydrates, 10–12% proteins and 25–30% fat.

For convenience and on the basis of similar nutritive values, foods are divided into five basic food groups. A balanced diet can be achieved through a blend of these food groups. In addition, a balanced diet should provide some non-nutrients such as dietary fiber, antioxidants and phytochemicals which render positive health benefits. *Food Groups:* Foods are conventionally grouped as:

a. Cereals, millets and pulses
b. Vegetables and fruits
c. Milk and milk products
d. Egg, meat, fish
e. Oils and fats

Table 5.2: IMNCI food box

Age (months)	Food
Upto 6 months	• Breastfeed as often as the child wants, day and night, at least 8 times in 24 hours • Do not give any other foods or fluids not even water *Remember:* Continue breastfeeding even if the child is sick
6–12 months	• Breastfeed as often as the child wants. • Give at least *one katori* serving at a time of: Mashed roti/bread/biscuit mixed in sweetened undiluted mild Or Mashed roti/rice/bread mixed in thick dal with added ghee/oil or Khichri with added oil/ ghee. Add cooked vegetables also in the servings Or Sevian/dalia/halwa/kheer prepared in milk or any cereal porridge cooked in milk OR Mashed boiled/fried potatoes • Offer banana/biscuit/cheeko/mango/papaya as snacks in between the serving *Frequency:* 3 times per day if breastfed; 5 times per day if not breastfed *Remember:* Keep the child in your lap and feed with your own hands Wash your own and child's hands with soap and water every time before feeding
12 months to 2 years	Breastfeed as often as the child wants Offer food from the family pot Give at least 1½ katori serving at a time of: Mashed roti/rice bread mixed in thick *dal* with added ghee/oil or *khichri* with added oil/ghee. Add cooked vegetables also in the servings OR Mashed roti/rice/bread/biscuit mixed in sweetened undiluted milk OR Sevian/dalia/halwa/kheer prepared in milk or any cereal porridge cooked in milk OR Mashed boiled/fried potatoes *Frequency:* 5 times a day • Offer banana/biscuit/cheeku/mango/papaya/as snacks in between the servings *Remember:* Sit by the side of child and help him to finish the serving Wash your child's hands with soap and water every time before feeding
2 years and older	Give family food as 3 meals each day. Also, twice daily, give nutritious food between meals, such as: banana/biscuit/cheeku/mango/papaya as snacks *Remember:* Ensure that the child finishes the serving Teach your child to wash his hands with soap and water every time before feeding

Cereals, millets and pulses are the major source of most nutrients in Indian diets. Milk provides good quality protein and calcium and hence, is an essential item of our diet. Eggs, flesh foods and fish enhance the quality of diet but Indians are predominantly a vegetarian society and most of our nutrients are derived from cereal/pulse and milk based diets. Oils and nuts are calorie rich foods and are useful in increasing the calorie density. Vegetables and fruits provide protective substances such as vitamins, minerals, fiber and antioxidants.

Factors to be Considered while Planning a Feed or Food for the Child

There are six cardinal factors to be considered while feeding the child:

1. *Energy density:* Most of our traditional foods are bulky and a child cannot eat large quantities at a time. Hence, it is important to give small energy dense feeds at frequent intervals to ensure adequate energy intakes by the child. Energy density of foods given to infants and young children can be increased without increasing the bulk by adding a *teaspoon of oil or ghee in every feed.* Fat is a concentrated source of energy and increases energy content of food without increasing the bulk. Sugar and jaggery can also be added in infant foods. *Amylase rich foods (ARF)* such as malted foods reduce the viscosity of the foods and therefore, the child can eat more quantities at a time (Malting is germinating whole grain cereal or pulse, drying and then grinding). Thin gruels do not provide enough energy; a young infant particularly during 6–9 months requires thick but smooth mixtures.
2. *Amount of feed:* At 6 months of age, feed should be started with small amount as much as 1–2 teaspoons and the quantity is increased gradually as the child gets older and starts to accept food better. Child should be

given time to adapt gradually to larger quantities from teaspoon to table spoon and then to a katori.

3. *Consistency of feed:* Infants can eat pureed, mashed and semi-solid foods beginning at six months. By 8 months, most infants can also eat "finger foods" (snacks that can be eaten by children alone). By 12 months, most children can eat the same types of foods as consumed by the rest of the family. Foods that can cause choking such as nuts, grapes, raw carrots should be avoided. For small children, the food should not contain particulate matter that may trigger gag reflex or vomiting.
4. *Frequency of feeding:* An average healthy breastfed infant needs complementary foods 2–3 times per day at 6–8 months of age and 3–4 times per day at 9–24 months. For children 12–24 months of age, additional nutritious snacks such as a piece of fruit should also be offered 1–2 times per day. Snacks are defined as foods eaten between meals, usually convenient and easy to prepare. If energy density or amount of food per meal is low, or the child is no longer breastfed, more frequent meals should be provided.
5. *Hygiene:* Good hygiene and proper food handling should be practiced to prevent children from infections and malnutrition. Simple hygiene practices like: (a) Washing hands before food preparation and eating, (b) Serving freshly cooked foods (cooked food should not be kept for more than 2–3 hours) (c) Using clean utensils and covered properly. (d) Using clean cups and bowls when feeding children, and (e) Avoiding use of feeding bottles. As the child grows older, he should be shifted to more appropriate foods suitable for his age.
6. *Helping the child:* Feeding the infants and children should be an active, engaging and interactive affair. Often the food is left in front of the child to eat. This approach is not appropriate. Mother/father should actively engage with the child in feeding. Make the child sit in the lap and feed him affectionately in small portions with spoon or with small morsels. Child is coaxed and encouraged to finish the desired amount of food.

Suggested reading

1. Ghafoorunissa, Krishnaswamy K. Diet and heart disease. Hyderabad, India: National Institute of Nutrition; 2004.
2. Dietary guidelines for Indians: a manual. Hyderabad, India: National Institute of Nutrition; 2005.
3. Gopalan C, Rama Sastri BV, Balasubramanian SC, Narasinga Rao BS, Deosthale YG, Pant KC. Nutritive value of Indian foods. Hyderabad: National Institute of Nutrition; 1991.
4. Venkatachalam PS, Rebello LM. Nutrition for mother and child. 4th ed. Hyderabad: National institute of Nutrition (ICMR); 1994.

UNDERNUTRITION

Undernutrition is a condition in which there is inadequate consumption, poor absorption or excessive loss of nutrients. Overnutrition is caused by overindulgence or excessive intake of specific nutrients. The term malnutrition refers to both undernutrition as well as overnutrition. However, sometimes the terms malnutrition and protein energy malnutrition (PEM) are used interchangeably with undernutrition. **In this chapter the term malnutrition is used while referring to undernutrition.**

Malnourished children may also suffer from numerous associated complications. They are more susceptible to infections, especially sepsis, pneumonia, and gastroenteritis. Vitamin deficiencies and deficiencies of minerals and trace elements can also be seen. Malnutrition in young children is conventionally determined through measurement of height, weight, skin-fold thickness (or subcutaneous fat) and age. The commonly used indices derived from these measurements are given in Table 5.3.

Table 5.3: Indicators of malnutrition

Indicator	*Interpretation*	
Stunting	Low height for age	Indicator of chronic malnutrition, the result of prolonged food deprivation and/or disease or illness.
Wasting	Low weight for height	Suggests acute malnutrition, the result of more recent food deficit or illness.
Under weight	Low weight for age	Combined indicator to reflect both acute and chronic malnutrition

Epidemiology

Childhood malnutrition is an underlying cause in an estimated 35% of all deaths among children under five and 11% of total global Disability Adjusted Life Years (DALYs) lost. According to the recently released National Family Health Survey, NFHS-3, carried out in 2005–06, 40% of India's children under the age of three are underweight, 45% are stunted and 23 % are wasted. Comparable figures for NFHS-2 (1998–99) are 43%, 51% and 20 %, respectively (Fig. 5.2).

The proportion of children who are stunted or underweight increases rapidly with the child's age (Fig. 5.3). During the first six months of life, when most babies are breastfed, 20–30% of children are already malnourished. By 18–23 months, when many children are being weaned from breast milk, 30% of children are severely stunted and one-fifth are severely underweight. This clearly shows that the onset of malnutrition in Indian children occurs early, possibly even in utero and is the consequence of maternal malnutrition and low birth weight.

Levels of malnutrition vary widely across Indian states. Punjab, Kerala, Jammu and Kashmir, and Tamil Nadu account for the lowest proportions of underweight children (27 to 33%); while Chhattisgarh, Bihar, Jharkhand,

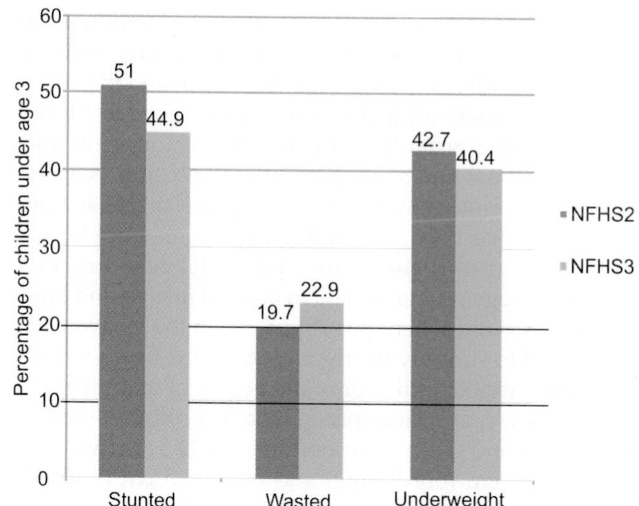

Fig. 5.2: Trends in nutritional status of children under 3 years in India

and Madhya Pradesh report the maximum levels of underweight children (52 to 60%).

Classification of Malnutrition in Children

Malnutrition ranges in severity from mild to severe depending upon the degree of loss of weight. Various classification schemes have been proposed over the last few decades in order to assess and classify children with malnutrition.

WHO Classification of Malnutrition

The assessment of nutritional status is done according to weight-for-height (or length), height (or length)-for-age and presence of edema (Table 5.4). The WHO recommends the use of Z-scores or standard deviation scores (SDS) for evaluating anthropometric data, so as to accurately classify individuals with indices below the extreme percentiles. The SD-score is defined as the deviation of the value for an individual from the median value of the reference population, divided by the standard deviation of the reference population. SD-score = [(observed value) –(median reference value)]/[standard deviation of reference population]. The calculation of the SDS gives a numerical score indicating how far away from the 50th centile for age the child's measurements falls. A score of –2 to –3 indicates moderate malnutrition and a score of +2 to +3 indicates overweight. A score of less than –3 indicates severe malnutrition and a score of more than +3 indicates obesity. Z-score percentile charts developed by the WHO are available at *http://www.who.int/childgrowth/standards/en*.

The earlier system of classification using percentiles has been given up because of unequal intervals from one percentile curve to another which means that in the visual monitoring of growth faltering; the crossing of percentile lines gives rise to different interpretations in different areas of the chart. The difficulty in plotting additional curves below the third percentile is a further disadvantage of the percentile-based chart.

Table 5.4: WHO classification of malnutrition

	Moderate malnutrition	*Severe malnutrition (type)*
Symmetrical edema	No	Yes (edematous malnutrition)
Weight-for-height	SD score between –2 to –3	SD score <–3 (severe wasting)
Height-for-age	SD score between –2 to –3	SD score <–3 (severe stunting)

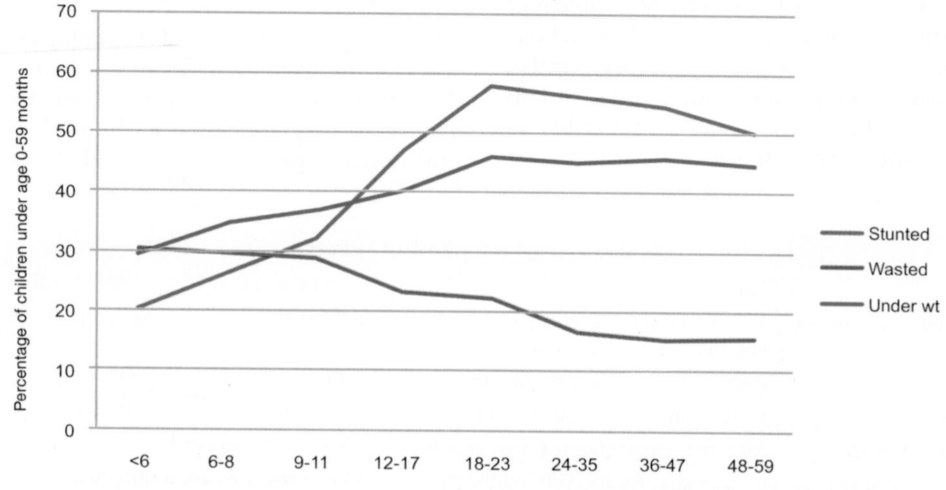

Fig. 5.3: Malnourished children according to age (NFHS-3)

The current classification includes kwashiorkor and marasmic kwashiorkor from older classifications. However, to avoid confusion with the clinical syndrome of kwashiorkor, which includes other features, the term "edematous malnutrition" is preferred.

IAP Classification

This is based on weight for age values (Table 5.5). The standard used in this classification for reference population was the 50th centile of Harvard standards. This classification scheme is used in the ICDS program.

Table 5.5: IAP classification of malnutrition

Grade of malnutrition	*Weight-for-age of the standard (median) (%)*
Normal	>80
Grade I	71–80 (mild malnutrition)
Grade II	61–70 (moderate malnutrition)
Grade III	51–60 (severe malnutrition)
Grade IV	<50 (very severe malnutrition)

Older Classifications

5

Older classification like the Waterlow and Gomez classifications do not take edema into account therefore cannot differentiate between marasmus and kwashiorkor. The Gomez classification also does not discriminate between wasting and stunting as height is not a part of it. These classifications are now rarely used.

Age Independent Indices

In many situations the child's age is not known, e.g. children from orphanages, street children, during natural disasters, etc., and this has prompted many attempts to devise methods of interpreting anthropometric data, which do not require knowledge of precise age. Some measures are relatively labile and susceptible to external influence while others are relatively insensitive. This fact has been applied in three ways to tackle the problem of interpreting anthropometric data in children whose chronological age is unknown. Various variables sensitive to external influences change only slowly over certain broad age ranges and thus they may be regarded as independent of age over these ranges.

Mid upper arm circumference (MUAC): It is a widely used measurement and requires minimum equipment. It increases rapidly in the first year (11–16 cm) and then been found to be relatively stable between the ages 1 to 5 years at a value of between 16 and 17 cm. Any value below 13.5 cm is abnormal and suggestive of malnutrition. A value below 11.5 cms is suggestive of severe malnutrition. Recently, it has been shown that MUAC may not be age independent and therefore, the WHO recommends MUAC-for-age reference data to be used in girls and boys 6–59 months old where possible. Certain tools have been developed to simplify the measurement for field workers and give a visible indicator of the degree of malnutrition. *Shakir tape method:* This special tape has coloured zones-red, yellow and green corresponding to <12.5 cm (wasted), 12.5 to 13.5 cm (borderline) and over 13.5 cm (normal) mid upper arm circumference respectively.

Bangle test: A bangle with internal diameter of 4 cm is passed above the elbow. In severe malnutrition it is passable above the elbow in normal children it is not.

Skinfold thickness: It is an indication of the subcutaneous fat. Triceps skin fold is the most representative of the total subcutaneous fat upto sixteen years of age. It is usually above 10 mm in normal children whereas in severely malnourished it may fall below 6 mm.

Ratios: In addition to the above indices, comparison of environmentally sensitive and environmentally insensitive measures may yield indicators of environmental influence which are independent of age. Examples of this approach are given in Table 5.6.

Etiology

The causes of malnutrition could be viewed as immediate, underlying and basic as depicted in Fig. 5.4.

Immediate Determinants

The immediate determinants of a child's nutritional status work at the individual level. They include inadequate dietary intake and illness. These two often work synergistically and have an immediate effect on the nutritional status of the individual.

Table 5.6: Age independent indices

Name of index	*Calculation*	*Normal value*	*Value in malnutrition*
Kanawati and McLaren's index	Mid arm circumference/ head circumference (cm)	0.32–0.33	Severely malnourished: < 0.25
Rao and Singh's index	(weight (in kg)/height^2 (in cm)) × 100	0.14	0.12–0.14
Dugdale's index	weight (in kg)/height$^{1.6}$ (in cm)	0.88–0.97	< 0.79
Quaker arm circumference measuring stick (quac stick)	Mid-arm circumference that would be expected for a given height	75–85%: malnourished <75%: severely malnourished	
Jeliffe's ratio	Head circumference/chest circumference	Ratio < 1 in a child > 1 year: malnourished	

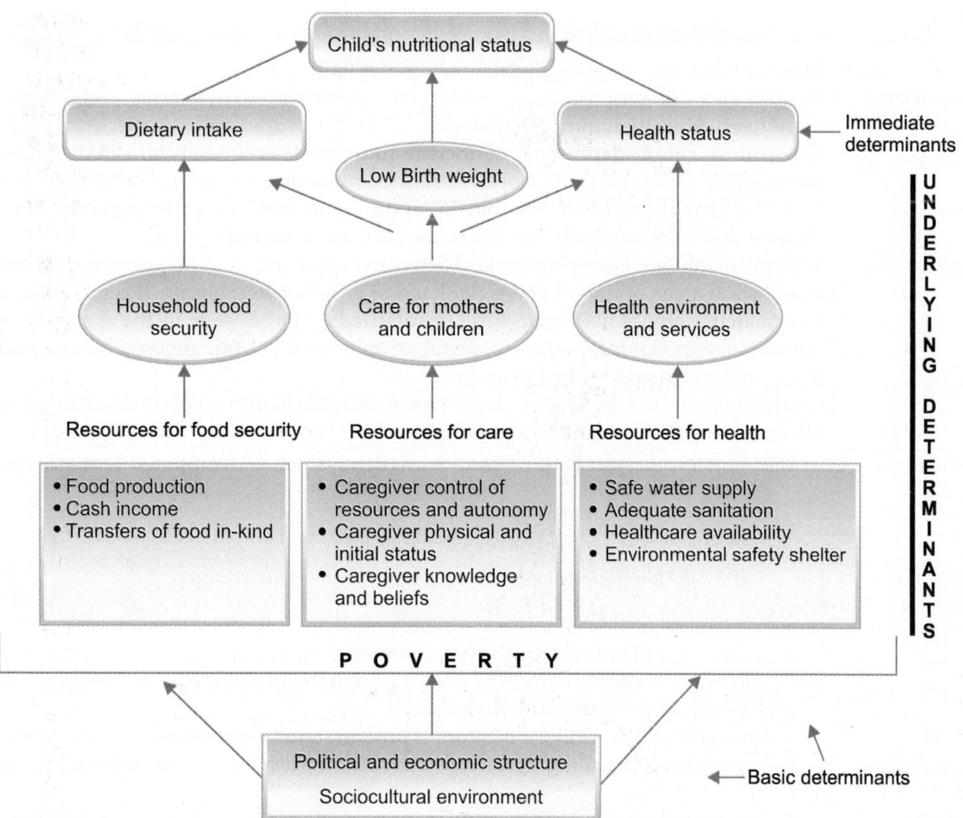

Fig. 5.4: Determinants of a child's nutrition status

Underlying Determinants

The immediate determinants are in turn influenced by three household-level underlying determinants namely food, health and care. *Food* refers to food security at the household level. It is the sustainable access to safe food of sufficient quality and quantity, paying attention to energy, protein and micronutrients. This in turn depends on having financial, physical and social access as distinct from mere availability. *Health* includes access to curative and preventive health services to all community members as well as a hygienic and sanitary environment and access to water. *Care* refers to a process taking place between a caregiver and the receiver of care. It translates food availability at the household level and presence of health services into good growth and development of the child. Analyses in several countries had demonstrated that there are households that had an abundance of children food but still manifested signs of malnutrition and this was attributed to other factors including care. Care includes care for women, breastfeeding and complementary feeding, home health practices, hygiene practices, psycho-social care, and food preparation. The factors that determine adequate household food security, care and health are related to resources, their control and a host of political, cultural, and social factors that affect their utilization. Resources include human, economic, and organizational resource. Embedded in human resources are skills, motivation and knowledge, which is also influenced by education.

Basic Determinants

Finally, the underlying determinants are influenced by the basic determinants.

Pathological and Biochemical Changes

Malnutrition affects almost all organ systems. The salient findings in various organs/tissues are elucidated in Table 5.7. A variety of biochemical indices have been devised to gauge the metabolic changes that may precede clinical evidences of malnutrition. A list of some of them is given in Table 5.8.

However, their use is not very popular because many of them are reduced by the acute phase protein response associated with trauma, injury and sepsis and their concentration is affected by a variety of other factors such as overhydration, dehydration, liver function and by specific pathological conditions (e.g. iron deficiency increases the circulating concentration of transferrin).

CLINICAL FEATURES OF MALNUTRITION

These vary with the degree and duration of undernourishment, the age of the child and associated vitamin, mineral and trace element deficiencies.

5

Table 5.7: Pathological changes in malnutrition in various organ systems

Upper GIT	Mucosa shiny and atrophic. Papillae of tongue flattened.
Small and large intestine	Mucosa and villi atrophic; brush border enzymes reduced; hypotonic, rectal prolapse
Liver	Fatty liver, deposition of triglycerides.
Pancreas	Exocrine secretion depressed; endocrine function less severely affected; glucagon production reduced; insulin levels low; atrophy and degranulation or hypertrophy of islets seen
Endocrine system	Elevated growth hormone; thyroid involution and fibrosis; adrenal glands atrophic and cortex thinned; increased cortisol; catecholamine activity unaltered
Lymphoreticular system	Thymus involuted; loss of distinction between cortex and medulla; depletion of lymphocytes; paracortical areas of lymph nodes depleted of lymphocytes; germinal centres smaller and fewer
CNS	Head circumference and brain growth retarded; changes seen in the dendritic arborization and morphology of dendritic spines; cerebral atrophy on CT/MRI; abnormalities in auditory brainstem potentials and visual evoked potentials.
CVS	Cardiac volume; muscle mass and electrical properties of the myocardium changes; systolic functions affected more than diastolic functions.

GIT gastrointestinal tract, CNS central nervous system, CVS cardiovascular system, CT computed tomography, MRI magnetic resonance imaging

Table 5.8: Biochemical indices in children with malnutrition

Index	*Status in malnutrition*
Transferrin	↓, < 0.45 mg/ml indicative of severe malnutrition.
Albumin	↓; Albumin concentration < 3 g/dl is associated with early illness; between 2.5 and 2.9 are low and below 2.5 g/dl are pathological.
Serum prealbumin, transthyretin and retinol binding protein	↓; Have short t½. Sensitive indicators of protein status; return to normal at beginning of nutritional therapy, therefore cannot be used as endpoint for terminating nutritional therapy.
Pattern of circulating amino acids in blood	Essential amino acids ↓; non essential amino acids are normal or ↑; therefore their ratio is↑. Mean value 1.5; subclinical illness 2–4; frank kwashiorkor > 3.5 $\text{Ratio} = \dfrac{\text{Glycine+serine+taurine+glutamine}}{\text{Valine+leucine+isoleucine+ methionine}}$
24 hr urinary 3-methylhistidine excretion	Present exclusively in skeletal muscle and white muscle fibres; released when actin and myosin catabolized; excreted in urine; reflects muscle mass. 24 hr excretion ↓ in malnutrition
Urinary creatinine height index (CHI)	Breakdown product of creatine; reflects muscle mass $\text{CHI} = \dfrac{\text{24 hour urine creatinine}}{\text{24 hour urine creatinine (normal child of same height)}}$ Ranges 0.25 – 0.75 in kwashiorkor and 0.33–0.85 in marasmus; recovered child ~ 1

Mild Malnutrition

It is most common between the ages of 9 months to 2 years. Main features are as follows.

a. *Growth failure:* This is manifested by slowing or cessation of linear growth; static or decline in weight; decrease in mid arm circumference; delayed bone maturation; normal or diminished weight for height z scores; and normal or diminished skin fold thickness.
b. *Infection:* A high rate of infection involving various organ systems may be seen, e.g. gastroenteritis, pneumonia, tuberculosis.
c. *Anemia:* May be mild to moderate and any morphological type may be seen.
d. *Activity:* This may be diminished.
e. *Skin and hair changes:* These may occur rarely.

Moderate to Severe Malnutrition

Moderate to severe malnutrition is associated with one of classical syndromes, namely, marasmus, kwashiorkor, or with manifestations of both (Table 5.9).

Table 5.9: Differences between kwashiorkor and marasmus

Clinical finding	*Marasmus*	*Kwashiorkor*
Occurrence	More common	Less common
Edema	–	+
Activity	Active	Apathetic
Appetite	Good	Poor
Liver enlargement	–	+
Mortality	Less than kwashiorkor	High in early stage
Recovery	Recover early	Long to recover
Infection	Less prone	More prone

Marasmus

It results from prolonged starvation. It may also result from chronic or recurring infections with marginal food intake.

a. The main sign is a **severe wasting.** The child appears very thin ("skin and bones") and has no fat. Most of the fat and muscle mass having been expended to provide energy.
b. There is severe wasting of the shoulders, arms, buttocks and thighs.
   i. The loss of buccal pad of fat creates the aged or wrinkled appearance that has been referred to as *"monkey facies"*
   ii. *"Baggy pants appearance"* refers to loose skin of the buttocks hanging down
   iii. Axillary pad of fat may also be diminished
c. Affected children may appear to be alert in spite of their condition
d. There is no edema

Kwashiorkor

It usually affects children aged 1–4 years. The main sign is pitting edema, usually starting in the legs and feet and spreading, in more advanced cases, to the hands and face. Because of edema, children with kwashiorkor may look "healthy" so that their parents view them as well fed.

i. *General appearance:* Child may have a fat *"sugar baby"* appearance.
ii. *Edema:* It ranges from mild to gross, and may represent up to 5–20% of the body weight.
iii. *Muscle wasting:* It is always present. The child is often weak, hypotonic and unable to stand or walk.
iv. *Skin changes:* The skin lesions consist of increased pigmentation, desquamation, and dyspigmentation. Pigmentation may be confluent resembling *'flaky paint'* or in individual spots *'enamel spots'*. The distribution is typically on buttocks, perineum and upper thigh. Petechiae may be seen over abdomen. Outer layers of skin may peel off and ulceration may occur. The lesions may sometimes resemble burns.
v. *Mucous membrane lesions:* Smooth tongue, cheilosis and angular stomatitis are common. Herpes simplex stomatitis may also be seen.
vi. *Hair:* Changes include dyspigmentation, loss of characteristic curls and sparseness over temple and occipital regions. Hairs also lose their lustre and are easily pluckable. A *'flag sign'* which is the alternate bands of hypopigmented and normally pigmented hair pattern is seen when the growth of child occurs in spurts.
vii. *Mental changes:* Includes unhappiness, apathy or irritability with sad, intermittent cry. They show no signs of hunger, and it is difficult to feed them.
viii. *Neurological changes:* These are seen during recovery (see section on the nutritional rehabilitation).
ix. *Gastrointestinal system:* Anorexia, sometimes with vomiting, is the rule. Abdominal distension is characteristic. Stools may be watery or semisolid, bulky with a low pH and may contain unabsorbed sugars.
x. *Anemia:* It may also be seen, as in mild PEM but with greater severity.
xi. *Cardiovascular system:* The findings include cold, pale extremities due to circulatory insufficiency and are associated with a prolonged circulation time, bradycardia, a diminished cardiac output and hypotension.
xii. *Renal function:* Glomerular filtration and renal plasma flow are diminished. There is an overflow aminoaciduria and inefficient excretion of acid load.

Marasmic Kwashiorkor

It is a mixed form of PEM, and manifests as edema occurring in children who may or may not have other signs of Kwashiorkor.

Suggested reading

1. World Health Organization. The management of nutrition in major emergencies. Geneva: World Health Organization; 2000.
2. Nutrition Subcommittee of the Indian Academy of Pediatrics. Report of Convener. Indian Pediatr. 1972;9:360.

5

MANAGEMENT OF MALNUTRITION

The management of malnutrition depends on its severity. While mild to moderate malnutrition can be managed on ambulatory basis, severe malnutrition is preferably managed in hospital. The management of low birth weight (LBW) infants is discussed in Chapter 7.

Mild and Moderate Malnutrition

Mild and moderate malnutrition make up the greatest portion of malnourished children and >80% of malnutrition associated deaths occur in such children. It is, therefore, vital to intervene in children with mild and moderate malnutrition at the community level before they develop complications.

The mainstay of treatment is provision of adequate amounts of protein and energy. Experience has shown that at least 150 kcal/kg/day should be given. In order to achieve these high energy intakes, frequent feeding (up to seven times a day) is often necessary. Because energy is so important , and because carbohydrate energy sources are bulky, oil is usually used to increase the energy in therapeutic diets.

It is being recognized increasingly that a relatively small increase over normal protein requirements is sufficient for rapid catch-up growth, provided energy intake is high. A protein intake of 3 g/kg/day is sufficient. Milk is the most frequent source of the protein used in therapeutic diets, though other sources, including vegetable protein mixtures, have been used successfully. Adequate minerals and vitamins should be provided for the appropriate duration. The best measure of the efficacy of treatment of mild and moderate malnutrition is weight gain.

Severe Malnutrition

The World Health Organization has developed guidelines for the management of severe malnutrition based on sound pathophysiological principles and extensive research and these have been adapted for Indian scenarios by the Indian Academy of Pediatrics. At the community level, the presence of severe wasting and/or edema or a Mid Upper Arm Circumference (MUAC) of <11.5 cm are suitable criteria to identify severely wasted children aged 6–59 months. For children < 6 months, in place of using anthropometric criteria visible severe wasting and/or bilateral edema should be used for determining severe malnutrition. **WHO recommends exclusive inpatient management of a severely malnourished child.**

Initial Assessment of the Severely Malnourished Child

History: The child with severe malnutrition has a complex backdrop - dietary, infective, social and economic. A history of events leading to the child's admission should be obtained. Particular attention should be given to

- The usual diet (before the current illness) including breastfeeding
- Presence of diarrhea (duration, watery/bloody),
- Information on vomiting, loss of appetite, chronic cough, and
- Contact with tuberculosis.

Malnutrition may the presentation of HIV infection. Socio-economic history and family circumstances should be explored to understand the underlying and basic causes.

Examination: Anthropometry provides the main assessment of the severity of malnutrition. Physical features of malnutrition as described above should be looked for. Detailed general and systematic examination should be undertaken to detect complications.

Clinical features shown to be of prognostic significance include

- Signs of dehydration
- Shock (cold hands, slow capillary refill, weak and rapid pulse)
- Severe palmar pallor
- Eye signs of vitamin A deficiency
- Localizing signs of infection including ear and throat infections
- Skin infection or pneumonia, signs of HIV infection, fever (temperature $\geq$ 37.5°C or $\geq$ 99.5°F)
- Hypothermia (rectal temperature <35.5°C or <95.9° F), mouth ulcers, skin changes of kwashiorkor.

Management of Severe Malnutrition

Children with severe malnutrition undergo physiologic and metabolic changes to preserve essential processes, which include reductions in the functional capacity of organs and slowing of cellular activities. Co-existing infections add to the difficulty of maintaining metabolic control. These profound changes put severely malnourished children at particular risk of death from hypoglycemia, hypothermia, electrolyte imbalance, heart failure and untreated infection.

The general treatment involves **ten steps** in **two phases**:

- The initial **stabilization phase** focuses on restoring homeostasis and treating medical complications and usually takes 2–7 days of inpatient treatment.
- The **rehabilitation phase** focuses on rebuilding wasted tissues and may take several weeks.

The ten essential steps and the time frame are shown in Fig. 5.5 and Table 5.10.

Steps	Stabilization		Rehabilitation
	Days 1–2	Days 3–7	Weeks 2–6
1. Hypoglycemia	→		
2. Hypothermia	→		
3. Dehydration	→		
4. Electrolytes	→	→	→
5. Infection	→	→	
6. Micronutrients	No iron	No iron	With iron
7. Initiate feeding	→	→	
8. Catch-up growth			→
9. Sensory stimulation	→	→	→
10. Prepare for follow-up			→

Fig. 5.5: The time frame for initiating/achieving 10 steps

Table 5.10: Summary of the management of severe malnutrition

1. Hypoglycemia	• Blood glucose level <54 mg/dl or 3 mmol/l • If blood glucose cannot be measured, assume hypoglycemia • Hypoglycemia, hypothermia and infection generally occur as a triad **Treatment** • In asymptomatic hypoglycemia → Give 50 ml of 10% glucose or sucrose solution orally or by nasogastric tube followed by the first feed → Feed with starter F-75 every 2 hourly day and night • In symptomatic hypoglycemia → Give 10% dextrose i.v. 5 ml/kg → Follow with 50 ml of 10% dextrose or sucrose solution by nasogastric tube → Feed with starter F-75 every 2 hourly day and night → Start appropriate antibiotics **Prevention** • Feed 2 hourly starting immediately • Prevent hypothermia
2. Hypothermia	• Rectal temperature less than <35.5°C or 95.5°F or axillary temperature less than 35°C or 95°F • Always measure blood glucose and screen for infections in the presence of hypothermia **Treatment** • Clothe the child with warm clothes • Ensure that the head is also covered well with a scarf or a cap • Provide heat using radiation (overhead warmer), conduction (skin contact) or convection (heat convector) • Avoid rapid rewarming as this may lead to disequilibrium • Feed the child immediately • Give appropriate antibiotics **Prevention** • Place the child's bed in a draught-free area • Always keep the child well covered. Ensure that head is also covered well • The child could also be put in the contact with the mother's bare chest or abdomen (skin to skin) as in kangaroo mother care to provide warmth • Feed the child 2 hourly starting immediately after admission
3. Dehydration	• Difficult to estimate dehydration status accurately in the severely malnourished child • Assume that all severely malnourished children with watery diarrhea have some dehydration • Low blood volume (hypovolemia) can co-exist with edema **Treatment** • Use reduced osmolarity ORS with potassium supplements for rehydration and maintenance • Amount depends upon how much the child wants, volume of stool loss, and whether the child is vomiting • Initiate feeding within two to three hours of starting rehydration with F-75 formula on alternate hours with reduced osmolarity ORS • Be alert for signs of overhydration **Prevention** • Give reduced osmolarity ORS at 5–10 ml/kg after each watery stool, between feeds to replace stool losses • If breastfed, continue breastfeeding • Initiate re-feeding with starter F-75 formula
4. Electrolytes	• Give supplemental potassium at 3–4 mEq/kg/day for at least 2 weeks • On day 1, give 50% magnesium sulphate (equivalent to 4 mEq/ml). IM once (0.3 ml/kg up to a maximum of 2 ml). Thereafter, give extra magnesium (0.8–1.2 mEq/kg daily) • Excess body sodium exists even though the plasma sodium may be low • Prepare food without adding salt
5. Infection	• Multiple infections common • Usual signs of infection such as fever often absent • Majority of the bloodstream infections due to gram negative bacteria • Assume serious infection and treat • Hypoglycemia and hypothermia are considered markers of severe infection

Contd.

	Treatment • Treat with parenteral ampicillin 50 mg/kg/dose 6 hourly for at least 2 days followed by oral amoxycilin 15 mg/kg 8 hourly for five days and gentamicin 7.5 mg/kg or amikacin 15–20 mg/kg I.M. or I.V. once daily for seven days • If no improvement within 48 hour change to IV cefotaxime (100–150 mg/kg/day 6–8 hourly) or ceftriaxone (50–75 mg/kg/day 12 hourly) • If other specific infections are identified, give appropriate antibiotics **Prevention** • Follow standard precautions like hand hygiene • Give measles vaccine if the child is >6 months and not immunized, or if the child is >9 months and had been vaccinated before the age of 9 months
6. Micronutrients	• Use up to twice the recommended daily allowance of various vitamins and minerals • On day 1 give Vitamin A orally (if age >1 year give 2 lakh IU; age 6–12 m give 1 lakh IU; age 0–5 m give 50,000 IU) • Folic acid 1 mg/d (give 5 mg on day 1) • Zinc 2 mg/kg/d • Copper 0.2–0.3 mg/kg/d • Iron 3 mg/kg/d, once child starts gaining weight; after the stabilization phase
7. Initiate feeding	• Start feeding as soon as possible as frequent small feeds • If unable to take orally, initiate nasogastric feeds • Total fluid recommended is 130 ml/kg/day; reduce to 100 ml/kg/day if there is severe, generalized edema • Continue breast feeding ad-libitum • Start with F-75 starter feeds every 2 hourly • F-75 contains 75 kcal/100ml with 1.0 g protein/100 ml • If persistent diarrhea, give a serial based low lactose F-75 diet as starter diet • If diarrhea continues on low lactose diets give F-75 lactose free diets (rarely needed)
8. Catch-up growth	• Once appetite returns in 2–3 days, encourage higher intakes • Increase volume offered at each feed and decrease the frequency of feeds to 6 feeds per day • Continue breast feeding ad-libitum • Make a gradual transition from F-75 to F-100 diet • F-100 contains 100 kcal/100ml with 2.5–3.0 g protein/100 ml • Increase calories to 150–200 kcal/kg/day, and the proteins to 4–6g/kg/day • Add complementary foods as soon as possible to prepare the child for home foods at discharge
9. Sensory stimulation	• A cheerful, stimulating environment • Age appropriate structured play therapy for at least 15–30 min/day • Age appropriate physical activity as soon as the child is well enough • Tender loving care
10. Prepare for follow-up	• **Primary failure to respond is indicated by:** → Failure to regain appetite by day 4 → Failure to start losing edema by day 4 → Presence of edema on day 10 → Failure to gain at least 5 g/kg/day by day 10 • **Secondary failure to respond is indicated by:** → Failure to gain at least 5 g/kg/day for consecutive days during the rehabilitation phase

Step 1: Treat/Prevent Hypoglycemia

All severely malnourished children are at risk of hypoglycemia (blood glucose level <54 mg/dl or 3 mmol/l), hence blood glucose should be measured immediately at admission. If blood glucose cannot be measured, one must assume hypoglycemia and treat.

Hypoglycemia may be asymptomatic or symptomatic. **Symptomatic hypoglycemia** manifesting as lethargy, unconsciousness, seizures, peripheral circulatory failure or hypothermia is more common in marasmus, where energy stores are depleted or when feeding is infrequent.

For correction of **asymptomatic** hypoglycemia, 50 ml of 10% glucose or sucrose solution (1 rounded teaspoon of sugar in 3½ tablespoons of water) should be given orally or by nasogastric tube followed by the first feed. For correction of **symptomatic** hypoglycemia, 5 ml/kg of 10% dextrose should be given intravenously. This should be followed with 50 ml of 10% dextrose or sucrose solution by nasogastric tube. Blood glucose levels must be estimated every 30 min till the glucose level becomes normal and stabilizes. Once stable, the 2 hourly feeding regimens should be started.

Feeding should be started with starter F-75 (Formula 75 which is a WHO recommended starter diet for severe acute malnutrition containing 75 kcal/100 ml of feed-described later) diet as quickly as possible and then continued 2–3 hourly day and night (initially 1/4th of the 2 hourly feed should be given every 30 minutes till the blood glucose stabilizes). Most episodes of symptomatic hypoglycemia can be prevented by frequent, regular feeds and one must ensure that the child is fed regularly throughout the night. Hypoglycemia, hypothermia and infection generally occur as a triad.

Step 2: Treat/Prevent Hypothermia

All severely malnourished children are at risk of hypothermia due to impairment of thermoregulatory control, lowered metabolic rate and decreased thermal insulation from body fat. Children with marasmus, concurrent infections, denuded skin and infants are at a greater risk. Hypothermia is diagnosed if the rectal temperature is less than 35.5°C or 95.9°F or axillary temperature is less than 35°C or 95°F. A low reading thermometer (range 29°C-42°C) should be used to measure the temperature of malnourished children. If the temperature does not register on a normal thermometer, hypothermia should be assumed and treated. It can occur in summers as well.

The child should be rewarmed providing heat using radiation (overhead warmer) or conduction (skin contact) or convection (heat convector). Rapid rewarming may lead to disequilibrium and should be avoided.

In case of severe hypothermia (rectal temperature <32°C) warm humidified oxygen should be given followed immediately by 5 ml/kg of 10% dextrose IV or 50 ml of 10% dextrose by nasogastric route (if IV access is difficult). If clinical condition allows the child to take orally, warm feeds should be given immediately or else the feeds should be administered through a nasogastric tube. If there is feed intolerance/contraindication for nasogastric feeding, maintenance IV fluids (pre warmed) should be started.

In a hypothermic child, hypoglycemia must be looked for and managed. The child's temperature should be monitored every 2 hours till it rises to more than 36.5°C. Temperature monitoring must be ensured especially at night when the ambient temperature falls.

In most cases, hypothermia may be prevented by frequent feeding. Therefore, the child should be fed immediately and subsequently, every 2 hourly. All children should be nursed in a warm environment, clothed with warm clothes and covered using a warm blanket. The head should also be covered well with a scarf or a cap. The child could also be put in contact with the mother's bare chest or abdomen (skin to skin) as in kangaroo mother care to provide warmth. Besides these measures, hypothermia can also be prevented by placing the child's bed in a draught free area away from doors and windows, minimizing exposure after bathing or during clinical examination, and keeping the child dry always.

Step 3: Treat/Prevent Dehydration

Dehydration tends to be overdiagnosed and its severity overestimated in severely malnourished children. Loss of elasticity of skin may either be due to loss of the subcutaneous fat in marasmus or loss of extracellular fluid in dehydration. In dehydration, the oral mucosa feels dry to the palpating finger gently rolled on the inner side of the cheek. Presence of thirst, hypothermia, weak pulses and oliguria are other signs of dehydration in severely malnourished children. It is important to recognize the fact that low blood volume (hypovolemia) can co-exist with edema. Since estimation of dehydration may be tricky in severely malnourished children, it is safe to assume that all such children with watery diarrhea have some dehydration.

The Indian Academy of Pediatrics has recommended the use of one single solution for all types of diarrhea in all clinical settings and there is evidence to suggest that new reduced osmolarity ORS (RO-ORS) with potassium supplements given additionally works in severe malnutrition.

Dehydration should be corrected slowly over a period of 12 hours. Some dehydration can be corrected with RO-ORS. Intravenous therapy should be given only for severe dehydration and shock or if the enteral route cannot be used. The RO-ORS should be given orally or by nasogastric tube at 5 ml/kg every 30 minutes for first 2 hours and then at 5–10 ml/kg every hour for the next 4–10 hours. The exact amount actually depends on how much the child wants, volume of stool loss, and whether child is vomiting. Ongoing stool losses should be replaced with approximately 5–10 ml/kg of the ORS after each watery stool. The frequent passage of small unformed stools should not be confused with profuse watery diarrhea as it does not require fluid replacement.

Breastfeeding should be continued during the rehydration phase. Refeeding must be initiated with starter F-75 formula within 2–3 hours of starting rehydration. The feeds must be given on alternate hours (e.g. hours 2, 4, 6) with reduced osmolarity ORS (hours 1, 3, 5). Once rehydration is complete, feeding must be continued and ongoing losses replaced with ORS.

The progress of rehydration should be monitored every half hourly for first 2 hours and then hourly for the next 4–10 hours. Pulse rate, respiratory rate, oral mucosa, urine frequency or volume and frequency of stools and vomiting should be monitored. One must be alert for signs of overhydration (increase in respiratory rate by 5/min and pulse rate by 15/min, increasing edema and periorbital puffiness), which can be dangerous and may lead to heart failure. In case of signs of overhydration, ORS should be stopped immediately and child reassessed after one hour. Diuretics must never be used in this setting. On the other hand a decrease in the heart rate and respiratory rate (if increased initially) and increase in the urine output indicate that rehydration is proceeding. The return of tears, a moist oral mucosa, less sunken eyes and fontanelle and improved skin turgor are also indicators of rehydration. Once any four signs of hydration (child less thirsty, passing urine, tears, moist oral mucosa, eyes less sunken, faster skin pinch) are present, ORS for rehydration must be stopped and continued only to replace the ongoing losses.

Severe Dehydration with Shock

It is important to recognize severe dehydration in severely malnourished children. All such children with severe dehydration with shock should be treated with intravenous fluids. Ideally, Ringer's lactate with 5% dextrose should be used as rehydrating fluid. If not available, half normal saline (N/2) with 5% dextrose or Ringer's lactate alone can be used. One should never use 5% dextrose alone. After providing supplemental oxygen, the rehydrating fluid should be given at a slow infusion rate of 15 ml/kg over the first hour with continuous monitoring of pulse rate, volume, respiratory rate, capillary refill time and urine output.

If there is improvement (pulse slows, faster capillary refill) at the end of the first hour of IV fluid infusion, a diagnosis of severe dehydration with shock should be considered and the rehydrating fluid repeated at the same rate of 15 ml/kg over the next hour. This should be followed by reduced osmolarity ORS at 5–10 ml/kg/hour, either orally or by nasogastric tube. One must also frequently monitor to look for features of overhydration and cardiac decompensation.

5

Septic Shock

If at the end of the first hour of IV rehydration, there is no improvement or worsening, septic shock must be considered and appropriate treatment started.

Step 4: Correct Electrolyte Imbalance

In severely malnourished children excess body sodium exists even though the plasma sodium may be low. Sodium intake should be restricted to prevent sodium overload and water retention during the initial phase of treatment. Excess sodium in the diet may precipitate congestive cardiac failure.

In addition, all severely malnourished children have deficiencies of potassium and magnesium which may take two weeks or more to correct. Severely malnourished children may develop severe hypokalemia and clinically manifest with weakness of abdominal, skeletal and even respiratory muscles. This may mimic flaccid paralysis. Electrocardiography may show ST depression, T waves inversion and presence of U waves. If serum potassium is <2 mEq/l or <3.5 mEq/l with ECG changes, correction should be started at 0.3–0.5 mEq/kg/hour infusion of potassium chloride in intravenous fluids, preferably with continuous monitoring of the ECG.

Once severe hypokalemia is corrected, all severely malnourished children need supplemental potassium orally at 3–4 mEq/kg/day for at least 2 weeks. Potassium can be given as syrup potassium chloride; the most common preparation available has 20 mEq of potassium / 15 ml.

In addition, magnesium also needs to be supplemented. On day 1, 50% magnesium sulphate (equivalent to 4 mEq/ml) should be given at 0.3 ml/kg up to a maximum of 2 ml intramuscularly. Thereafter, 0.8–1.2 mEq /kg magnesium should be given orally as a magnesium supplement mixed with feeds.

Step 5: Treat/Prevent Infection

Infection may not produce the classical signs of fever and tachycardia in severely malnourished children. Instead, severe infection may be associated with hypothermia. Localizing signs of infection are often absent. The most common sites for infection to occur are the skin, the alimentary tract, the respiratory tract (including the ears, nose and throat) and the urinary tract. Majority of the infections and septicemia are caused by gram negative organisms. Therefore, all severely malnourished children should be assumed to have a serious infection on their arrival in hospital. In addition, hypoglycemia and hypothermia are considered markers of severe infection in children.

Whenever and wherever feasible, the following investigations may be done for identifying the infections in severely malnourished children.

(i) Hb, TLC, DLC, peripheral smear, (ii) Urine analysis and urine culture, (iii) Blood culture, (iv) Chest X-ray, (v) Mantoux test, (vi) Gastric aspirate for AFB, (vii) Peripheral smear for malaria (in endemic areas), (viii) CSF examination (if meningitis suspected).

All children should be treated with broad spectrum parenteral antibiotics-ampicillin and gentamicin or amikacin (Table 5.11). Antimalarial and anti- tuberculosis treatment should only be given when the particular conditions are diagnosed.

Response to treatment will be indicated by resolution of initial symptoms and signs of infection, if any. The child's activity, interaction with parents and appetite should improve. If there is no improvement or deterioration of the symptoms/signs of infection, the child should be screened for infection with resistant bacterial pathogens, tuberculosis, HIV and unusual pathogens.

Prevention of Hospital Acquired Infection

The healthcare personnel should follow standard precautions. The effectiveness of hand hygiene should be emphasized to all health care providers, attendants and patients. It is essential that adequate safety measures are taken to prevent the spread of hospital acquired infections, since these children are at higher risk of acquiring infections due to their compromised immune status.

Step 6: Correct Micronutrient Deficiencies

All severely malnourished children have vitamin and mineral deficiencies. Micronutrients should be used as an

Table 5.11: Recommended antibiotics for infections in severely malnourished children	
Type of infection	*Recommended antibiotics*
No obvious infections or complications	Oral cotrimoxazole (5 mg/kg 12 hourly of trimethoprim) or oral amoxicillin 10 mg/kg 8 hourly for 5 days
Infected child or complications present	IV ampicillin 50 mg/kg/dose 6 hourly and IV gentamicin 2.5 mg/kg/dose 8 hourly Add IV cloxacillin 100 mg/kg/day 6 hourly if staphylococcal infection is suspected. Revise therapy based on the culture sensitivity report
For septic shock or no improvement or worsening in initial 48 hours	Add third generation cephalosporin i.e. IV cefotaxime 100 mg/kg/day 8 hourly
Meningitis	IV cefotaxime 200 mg/kg/day IV 6 hourly with IV amikacin 15 mg/kg/day 8 hourly
Dysentery	Ciprofloxacin 30 mg/kg/day in 2 divided doses. IV ceftriaxone 50 mg/kg/day in 24 or 12 hourly if child is sick or has already received nalidixic acid

adjunct to treatment in safe and effective doses. Up-to twice the recommended daily allowance of various vitamins and minerals should be used. Although anemia is common, iron should not be given initially due to danger of promoting free radical generation and bacterial proliferation. It should be added only after a week of therapy when the child has a good appetite and starts gaining weight.

Vitamin A deficiency is not an infrequent association and is an important cause of blindness caused by keratomalacia. Vitamin A should therefore be given to all severely malnourished children on day 1 at 50,000 IU, 100,000 IU and 200,000 IU for infants 0–5 month, 6–12 months and children > 1 year of age unless there is definite evidence that a dose has been given in the last month. In presence of xerophthalmia, the same dose should be repeated on the next day and 2 weeks later. Children > 1 year but weighing < 8 kg should receive half the age related dose. In presence of clinical evidence of xerophthalmia the administration of Vitamin A should be considered an emergency as the changes may progress to keratomalacia within hours.

Vitamin K should be administered in a single dose of 2.5 mg intramuscularly at the time of admission. Daily multivitamin supplements containing thiamin 0.5 mg/1000 kcal, riboflavin 0.6 mg/1000 kcal and nicotinic acid (niacin equivalents) 6.6 mg/1000 kcal should be given. It is better to give a formulation that is truly multi-vitamin (e.g. one that has vitamin A, C, D, E and B12). Folic acid 1 mg/day (5 mg on day 1), zinc 2 mg/kg/day and copper 0.2–0.3 mg/kg/day (a multivitamin/ mineral commercial preparation should be used) should be given daily. Iron 3 mg/kg/day should be added once child starts gaining weight, after the stabilization phase.

Emergency Treatment of Severe Anemia

If a severely malnourished child has severe anemia with a hemoglobin of less than 4 g/dl or hemoglobin (Hb) between 4 and 6 g/dl but with respiratory distress, a blood transfusion should be given with whole blood 10 ml/kg bodyweight slowly over 3 hours. Furosemide should be given at the start of the transfusion. If the severely anemic child has signs of cardiac failure, packed cells rather than whole blood should be transfused.

The hemoglobin concentration may fall during the first week of treatment. This is normal and no transfusion should be given. In mild to moderate anemia, iron should be given for two months to replete iron stores but this should not be started until after the initial stabilization phase has been completed.

Step 7: Initiate Re-feeding

Feeding should be started as soon as possible with a diet which has osmolarity less than 350 mOsm/l; lactose not more than 2–3 g/kg/day; appropriate renal solute load (urinary osmolarity <600 mOsm/l); initial percentage of calories from protein of 5%; adequate bioavailability of micronutrients; low viscosity, easy to prepare and socially acceptable; adequate storage, cooking and refrigeration.

5

Start Cautious Feeding

Feeding should be started as soon as possible as frequent small feeds. If child is unable to take orally with a cup and spoon or takes <80% of the target intake, nasogastric feeds should be initiated. Breastfeeding should be continued ad-libitum. The suggested starter formula and feeding schedules are designed to meet these targets. Milk-based formulas such as starter F-75 (with 75 kcal/100 ml and 0.9 gm of protein /100 ml) will suffice for most children. Older children could be started on cereal-based diets (Table 5.12).

One should begin with 80 kcal/kg/day and gradually increase to 100 kcal/kg/day. To fulfill this, start with 2 hourly feeds of 11 ml/kg/feed (Table 5.13). Night feeds are essential. The volume of feeds should be increased gradually while decreasing the frequency of administration. The calories should be increased only after the child is able to accept the increased volume of feeds.

Step 8: Achieve Catch up Growth

Once appetite returns, higher intakes should be encouraged. Starter F-75 feeds should be gradually replaced with feeds which have a higher calorie density (100 kcal/100 ml) and have at least 2.5–3.0 gm protein/100 ml. These feeds are called F-100 diets (Table 5.14). It is recommended that each successive feed is increased by 10 ml until some

Table 5.12: Starter diets

Diet contents (per 100 ml)	*F-75 Starter*	*F-75 Starter (Cereal based) Example: 1*	*F-75 Starter (Cereal based) Example: 2*
Cow's milk or equivalent (ml)	30	30	25
(Approximate measure of one katori)	(1/3)	(1/3)	(1/4)
Sugar (g)	9	6	3
(approximate measure of one level teaspoon)	(1 + ½)	(1)	(1/2)
Cereal: Powdered puffed rice* (g)	–	2.5	6
(approximate measure of one level teaspoon)		(3/4)	(2)
Vegetable oil (g)	2	2.5	3
(approximate measure of one level teaspoon)	(1/2)	(1/2+)	(3/4)
Water: make up to (ml)	100	100	100
Energy (kcal)	75	75	75
Protein (g)	0.9	1.1	1.2
Lactose (g)	1.2	1.2	1.0

* *Powdered puffed rice may be replaced by commercial pre-cooked rice preparations (in same amounts)*

Note:

1. *Wherever feasible, actual weighing of the constituents should be carried out. Household measure should be used only as an alternative, as they may not be standardized.*
2. *The above charts give the composition for 100 ml diet. Wherever there is a facility for refrigeration, 1 liter diet could be prepared by multiplying the requirement of each constituent by 10.*

5

Table 5.13: Feeding patterns in the initial days of rehabilitation

Days	*Frequency*	*Volume/kg/feed*	*Volume/kg/day*
1–2	2 hourly	11 ml	130 ml
3–5	3 hourly	16 ml	130 ml
6	4 hourly	22 ml	130 ml

Source: WHO guidelines

Table 5.14: Catch-up diets

Diet contents (per 100 ml)	*F-100 Catch-up*	*F-100 Catch-up (cereal based) Example*
Cows milk/toned dairy milk (ml)	95	75
(approximate measure of one katori)	(3/4+)	(1/2)
Sugar (g)	5	2.5
(approximate measure of one level teaspoon)	(1)	(1/2-)
Cereal: Puffed rice (g)	-	7
(approximate measure of one level teaspoon)		(2)
Vegetable oil (g)	2	2
(approximate measure of one level teaspoon)	(1/2)	(1/2)
Water to make (ml)	100	100
Energy (kcal)	101	100
Protein (g)	2.9	2.9
Lactose (g)	3.8	3

is left uneaten. The frequency of feeds should be gradually decreased to 6 feeds/day and the volume offered at each feed should be increased till the child is being offered 200 ml/kg/day and 4–6 g/kg/day of protein. Breastfeeding should be continued ad-libitum.

Complementary foods should be added as soon as possible to prepare the child for home foods at discharge. They should have comparable energy and protein concentrations once the catch-up diets are well tolerated. Khichri, dalia, banana, curd-rice and other culturally acceptable and locally available diets can also be offered liberally (see IMNCI Food Box, Table 5.2).

Special Diets for Diarrhea

For children with persistent diarrhea, who do not tolerate low lactose diets, lactose free diet can be started. In these diets, carbohydrates (rice, sugar and glucose) can be given in varying proportions according to the patients' individual level of carbohydrate to achieve optimal balance between osmolarity and digestibility.

Monitoring Progress during Treatment

If there is a good weight gain of >10 g/kg/day, the same treatment should be continued till recovery. If there is a moderate weight gain of 5–10 g/kg/day; food intake should be checked and the children should be screened for systemic infection. In case of poor weight gain of <5 gm/kg/day possible causes like inadequate feeding, untreated infection, psychological problems and coexisting infections like tuberculosis and HIV should be looked for and managed appropriately.

Ready to use Therapeutic Food (RUTF)

In the 1990s, the **RUTF (ready to use therapeutic food)** was developed which has allowed much of the management of severe malnutrition to move out of hospitals, by shortening the duration of in-patient treatment from an average of 6 weeks to only 5–10 days. This energy dense, mineral and vitamin enriched ready to use therapeutic food with a similar nutrient profile but greater energy and nutrient density than F-100 has greatly improved cost effectiveness of treating severe malnutrition. F-100 although extremely effective during rehabilitation phase in in-patient centers is very vulnerable to bacterial contamination and must be used within a couple of hours of being made.This restricts its use to in-patient facilities. RUTF is an oil based paste with extremely low water activity and, as such can be stored at home unrefrigerated with little risk of microbial contamination for several months.

Step 9: Provide Sensory Stimulation and Emotional Support

Delayed mental and behavioral development often occurs in severe malnutrition. In addition to the above management, one should encourage a cheerful, stimulating environment; structured play therapy for at least 15–30 min/day; physical activity as soon as the child is well enough and tender loving care.

Step 10: Prepare for Follow-up After Recovery

The child is said to have recovered when his weight for height is 90 % of the NCHS median and he has no edema. The child is still likely to have a low weight for age because of stunting.

Criteria for Discharge and Failure of Response

Criteria for Discharge

Ideally 6–8 weeks of hospitalization is required for complete recovery. The child is said to have recovered when his weight for height is 90 % of the NCHS median and he has no edema. The child may be discharged earlier if it is certain that the final stages of recovery will not be jeopardized by early discharge.

Severely malnourished children are ready for discharge when the child

- Is alert and active, eating at least 120–130 kcal/kg/day with a consistent weight gain (of at least 5 g/kg/day for 3 consecutive days) on exclusive oral feeding,
- Is receiving adequate micronutrients,
- Is free from infection,
- Has completed immunization appropriate for age and
- The caretaker has been sensitized to home care.

The caregiver should be advised to bring child back for regular follow-up checks, ensure booster immunizations, make sure that vitamin A is given every six months, feed frequently with energy-and nutrient-dense foods and give structured play therapy.

Criteria for Discharge before Recovery is Complete

For some children, earlier discharge may be considered if effective alternative supervision is available. Domiciliary care should only be considered if the child

- Is aged > 12 months,
- Has a good appetite with satisfactory weight gain,
- Has completed antibiotic treatment and
- Has taken 2-weeks of potassium /magnesium /mineral / vitamin supplement (or continuing supplementation at home is possible).

It is important to be sure that the mother/caretaker has the financial resource to feed the child, is specifically trained to give appropriate feeding (types, amount, frequency), lives within easy reach of the hospital, is trained to give structured play therapy and is motivated to follow advice given.

For children being rehabilitated at home, it is essential to give frequent meals with a high energy and protein content. One should aim at achieving at least 150 kcal/kg/day and adequate protein (at least 4 g/kg/day). This would require feeding the child at least 5 times per day with foods that contain approximately 100 kcal and 2–3 g protein per 100 g of food. A practical approach should be taken using simple modifications of usual staple home foods. Vitamin, iron and electrolyte/mineral supplements can be continued at home. High energy snacks should be given between meals (e.g. milk, banana, bread, biscuits). The child should be assisted and encouraged to complete each meal.

Primary failure to respond is indicated by (i) Failure to regain appetite by day 4, or (ii) Failure to start losing edema by day 4, or (iii) Presence of edema on day 10, or (iv) Failure to gain at least 5 g/kg/day by day 10. *Secondary failure to respond is indicated by:* Failure to gain at least 5 g/kg/day for 3 consecutive days during the rehabilitation phase.

Community-Based Therapeutic Care (CTC)

In the last five years, a growing number of countries and international relief agencies have adopted a new concept called the Community based Therapeutic Care (CTC) for the management of severe acute malnutrition. The CTC concept actually combines facility or in-patient management of severe acute malnutrition with complications and a community based management of severe acute malnutrition without complications or mild or moderate malnutrition. These facility-based and community-based components of management should be closely linked so that children who are too ill to be treated at the community level or who are not responding to treatment can be referred to the facility level, and those receiving facility based treatment who have regained their appetites can be transferred for continued care in the community. For this community based therapeutic care approach a suggested classification and treatment system for acute malnutrition is given in Table 5.15 .

Phenomena that may be encountered during Nutritional Rehabilitation

The following conditions are rarely seen now.

Pseudotumor Cerebri

Over-energetic nutritional correction in malnourished infants may be accompanied by transient rise of intracranial tension. The phenomenon is benign and self limiting.

Nutritional Recovery Syndrome

It refers to a sequence of events seen in children who are being treated with very high quantity of proteins during the course of rehabilitation. It presents as (1) abdominal distention, (2) increasing hepatomegaly, (3) ascites, (4) prominent thoraco-abdominal venous network, (5) hypertrichosis, (6) parotid swelling, (7) gynaecomastia, (8)eosinophilia, (9) splenomegaly.

Its development may be related to endocrinal disturbances, possibly by an increase in the estrogen level and by a variety of trophic hormones produced by the recovering pituitary gland.

5

Table 5.15: Suggested classification and treatment system for Malnutrition

Suggested classification	*Suggested treatment*
1. Severe acute malnutrition with complications like anorexia, lower respiratory tract infection, high fever, severe dehydration, severe anemia or lethargy.	Stabilization center (SC): in-patient care, also known as "phase 1 treatment", for acutely malnourished children with medical complications and no appetite using standard WHO guidelines.
2. Severe acute malnutrition without complications where the child is clinically well, alert and has a good appetite.	Outpatient therapeutic programme (OPT): home based treatment and rehabilitation with a specially formulated RUTF (ready to use therapeutic feed) provided on a weekly or two weekly basis, medical treatment using simplified medical protocols and regular follow up for children with severe acute malnutrition without complications
3. Moderate acute malnutrition without complications where weight-for-height is between 70–80% with no edema or MUAC is between 11–12.5 cm.	Supplementary feeding programme (SFP): take home ration for children with moderate acute malnutrition without complications.

Encephalitis Like Syndromes

Up to 1/5th of the children with kwashiorkor may become drowsy within 3–4 days after initiation of dietary therapy. Most often the condition is self limiting. Occasionally, it may be accompanied by progressive unconsciousness with fatal outcome. Even more rarely a transient phenomena marked by coarse tremors, parkinsonian rigidity, bradykinesia and myoclonus may appear several days after starting the dietary rehabilitation. These encephalitis states are considered to be the result of too much of proteins in the diet.

Suggested reading

Bhatnagar S, Lodha R, Choudhury P, Sachdev HP, Shah N, Narayan S, et al. IAP guidelines 2006 on hospital based management of severely malnourished children (adapted from the WHO Guidelines). Indian Pediatr. 2007; 44:443–61.

PREVENTION OF MALNUTRITION

Improvement of nutrition status of children is an essential component of health care.

Prevention at National Level

Nutrition supplementation: This can be done by improvement of food and feeding; by fortification of staple food; iodination of common salt and food supplementation.
Nutritional surveillance: Surveillance defines the character and magnitude of nutritional problems and selects appropriate strategies to counter these problems.
Nutritional planning: Nutritional planning involves a political commitment by the government, formulation of a nutrition policy and planning to improve production and supplies of food and ensure its distribution.

Prevention at Community Level

a. *Health and nutritional education:* Lack of awareness of the nutritional quality of common foods, irrational beliefs about certain foods, and cultural taboos about feeding contribute to the development of malnutrition. People should be informed of the nutritional quality of various locally available and culturally accepted low cost foods.
b. *Promotion of education and literacy in the community,* especially non formal education and functional literacy among village women.
c. *Growth monitoring:* The growth should be monitored periodically on growth cards. Velocity of growth is more meaningful than the actual weight of a child.
d. *Integrated health package:* Primary health care package should be made available to all sectors of population including preventive immunization, oral hydration, periodic deworming, and early diagnosis and treatment of common illnesses.
e. Vigorous promotion of *family planning programs* to limit family size.

Prevention at Family Level

a. Exclusive breastfeeding of infants for first 6 months of life should be vigorously promoted and encouraged.
b. Complementary foods should be introduced in the diet of infants at the age of 6 months.
c. Vaccination.
d. Iatrogenic restriction of feeding in fevers and diarrhea should be discouraged.
e. Adequate time should be allowed between two pregnancies so as to ensure proper infant feeding and attention to the child before the next conception.

National Nutrition Policy

The adoption of **National Nutrition Policy (NNP)** by the Government has been a significant achievement. Various programs have been launched or strengthened in pursuance of these policies. Few of them are mentioned here.

Integrated Child Development Services Programme (ICDS)

The ICDS programme is an inter-sectoral programme which seeks to directly reach out to children, below six years, especially from vulnerable groups and remote areas. The Scheme provides an integrated approach for converging basic services through community-based workers and helpers. The services are provided at a centre called the 'Anganwadi'. A package of six services is provided under the ICDS Scheme:

a. *Supplementary nutrition:* The norms are given in Table 5.16.
b. *Immunization:* Immunization of pregnant women and infants is done against the six vaccine preventable diseases
c. Non-formal pre-school education
d. *Health Check-up:* This includes health care of children less than six years of age, antenatal care of expectant mothers and postnatal care of nursing mothers. These services are provided by the ANM, Medical Officers under the RCH programme. The various health services include regular health check-ups, immunization, management of malnutrition, treatment of diarrhea, deworming and distribution of simple medicines, etc.
e. *Referral services:* During health check-ups and growth monitoring, sick or malnourished children, in need of prompt medical attention, are referred to the Primary Health Centre or its sub-centre.
f. Nutrition and health education.

However, the utilization of these services is still poor. According to the NFHS-3 survey, 72% areas surveyed were covered by an *anganwadi* centre; only 33% of children under 6 years of age received any kind of service from it.

Table 5.16: Norms for supplementary nutrition in ICDS

Beneficiaries	*Calories (kcal)*	*Protein (g)*
Children 3 yr	300	8–10
Children 3–6 yr	300	8–10
Severely malnourished children	Double of above	
Pregnant and lactating mothers	500	20–25

National Programme of Mid-day Meals in Schools

With a view to enhancing enrolment, retention and attendance and simultaneously improving nutritional levels among children, the National Programme of Nutritional Support to Primary Education (rechristened National Programme of Mid-Day Meals in Schools in 2007) was launched as a centrally sponsored scheme on 15th August 1995, initially in 2408 blocks in the country. The National Programme of Mid-Day Meals in Schools covers approximately 9.70 crore children studying at the primary stage of education in 9.50 lakh Government (including local bodies), Government aided schools and the centres run under Education Guarantee Scheme (EGS) and Alternative and Innovative Education (AIE) scheme.

The programme provides a mid-day meal of 450 kcal and 12 g of protein to children at the primary stage. For children at the upper primary stage, the nutritional value is fixed at 700 kcal and 20 g of protein. Adequate quantities of micronutrients like iron, folic acid and vitamin A are also recommended. The programme has helped in protecting children from classroom hunger, increasing school enrolment and attendance, improved socialization among children belonging to all castes, addressing malnutrition, and social empowerment through provision of employment to women.

National Nutrition Anemia Prophylaxis Programme

This programme was launched in 1970 to prevent nutritional anemia in mothers and children. Under this programme, the expected and nursing mothers as well as acceptors of family planning are given one tablet containing 100 mg elementary iron and 0.5 mg of folic acid. Children in the age group of 1–5 years are given one tablet containing 20 mg elementary iron (60 mg of ferrous sulphate) and 0.1 mg of folic acid daily for a period of 100 days.

Suggested reading

1. Kapil U, Pradhan R. Integrated child development services scheme (ICDS) in India: its activities, present status and future strategy to reduce malnutrition. J Indian Med Assoc. 2000;98:559–60.
2. Ghosh S. Integrated Child Development Services programme. Natl Med J India. 2003;16 Suppl 2:20–3.

5

6 Micronutrients in Health and Disease

INTRODUCTION

Originally, global nutrition concerns were dominated by vitamin deficiencies; however, the focus changed with time, and currently the concern is on both the macro- and micronutrient deficiencies. There is growing interest globally, on micronutrient deficiencies; mainly iodine, zinc, and vitamin A. Micronutrients play a central part in metabolism and in the maintenance of tissue function. An adequate intake, therefore' is necessary, but provision of excess supplements may be harmful. Single micronutrient deficiency states are comparatively easily recognized and treated. Subclinical deficiency, often of multiple micronutrients, is more difficult to recognize, and laboratory assessment is often complicated by the acute phase response. Clinical benefit is most likely in those children who are severely depleted and at risk of complications.

VITAMINS

A vitamin is an organic compound required as a nutrient in tiny amounts by an organism. A compound is called a vitamin when it cannot be synthesized in sufficient quantities by an organism, and must be obtained from the diet.

Vitamins have diverse biochemical functions, including function as hormones (e.g. vitamin D), antioxidants (e.g. vitamin E), and mediators of cell signaling and regulators of cell and tissue growth and differentiation (e.g. vitamin A). The largest number of vitamins (e.g. B complex vitamins) function as precursors for enzyme cofactor biomolecules (coenzymes), that help act as catalysts and substrates in metabolism. When acting as part of a catalyst, vitamins are bound to enzymes and are called prosthetic groups.

Vitamins are classified as either water-soluble, meaning that they dissolve easily in water, or fat-soluble vitamins, which are absorbed through the intestinal tract with the help of lipids (fats). In general, water-soluble vitamins are readily excreted from the body. Each vitamin is typically used in multiple reactions and, therefore, most have multiple functions.

In humans there are 13 vitamins: 4 fat-soluble (A, D, E and K) and 9 water-soluble (8 B vitamins and vitamin C).

MINERALS

Sixteen minerals are required to support human biochemical processes by playing roles in cell structure and function as well as electrolytes. These are calcium, chloride, cobalt, copper, iodine, iron, magnesium, manganese, molybdenum, nickel, phosphorus, potassium, selenium, sodium, sulfur and zinc.

Many elements, e.g. chromium have been suggested as essential, but such claims have not been confirmed. Definitive evidence for efficacy comes from the characterization of a biomolecule containing the element with an identifiable and testable function.

Essential trace elements are required by humans in amounts ranging from 50 micrograms to 18 milligrams per day. Acting as catalytic or structural components of larger molecules, they have specific functions and are indispensable for life. In addition to the long-known deficiencies of iron and iodine, signs of deficiency for chromium, copper, zinc and selenium have been identified. Marginal or severe trace element imbalances can be considered risk factors for several diseases of public health importance. Proof of cause and effect relationships will depend on a more complete understanding of the mechanisms of action and on better analytical procedures and functional tests.

FAT-SOLUBLE VITAMINS

The fat-soluble vitamins A, D, E and K control protein synthesis at either the transcriptional or post-transcriptional level. All of them are converted to active forms in the body, by oxidation, hydroxylation, reduction or simple ionization. Breast milk is deficient in both vitamins D and K and must be supplemented with these vitamins to protect breastfed infants.

VITAMIN A

Vitamin A refers generically to all compounds structurally related to retinol that have biological activity. Six isomers of retinol are known. In addition to the common all-trans retinol, there are 13-cis, 11-cis, 9-cis, 7-cis and 9, 13-cis retinols. The oxidation products of retinol, such as all-trans retinal, and all-trans retinoic acid are active forms of vitamin A. Carotenoids are provitamin A substances found in vegetables. Hundreds of carotenoids have been identified in nature, but only a handful can be converted to vitamin A. All-trans β-carotene is the most effective precursor of vitamin A and the most widely distributed.

Absorption and Metabolism

Vitamin A is absorbed in esterified form as part of chylomicrons. Absorption is affected by impaired chylomicron formation, or when fat absorption is altered. Retinol is absorbed as the free alcohol by an active transport system containing a cellular retinol binding protein CRBPII. The yellow β-carotene also requires bile salts for absorption and is converted to vitamin A in the intestinal tract. Once absorbed, vitamin A is stored in the liver as retinyl palmitate. The liver releases vitamin A to the circulation, bound to retinol-binding protein (RBP) and to a prealbumin (transthyretin).

Sources

The richest sources of preformed vitamin A include oils extracted from shark and cod liver. Carrots, dark-green leafy vegetables, squash, oranges, and tomatoes are also good sources. Many processed foods and infant formulas are fortified with preformed vitamin A.

Recommended Daily Allowance

The recommended daily allowance of vitamin A is as follow: Infants 300–400 µg; Children 400–600 µg; Adolescents 750 µg.

1 µg retinol= 1 retinol equivalent (RE)
1 µg β-carotene = 0.167 µg RE
1 µg other pro-vitamin A carotenoids = 0.084 µg RE

Physiological Functions

There are two main functions of vitamin A: (a) maintenance of vision, particularly night vision; and (b) maintenance of epithelial tissues and differentiation of many other tissues, particularly during reproduction and gestation.

The role of vitamin A in the vision cycle is specifically related to the retinal form. Within the eye, 11-*cis*-retinal is bound to rhodopsin (rods) and iodopsin (cones) at conserved lysine residues. As light enters the eye the 11-*cis*-retinal is isomerized to the all-"trans" form. The all-"trans" retinal dissociates from the opsin in a series of steps called bleaching. This isomerization induces a nervous signal along the optic nerve to the visual center of the brain. Upon completion of this cycle, the all-"trans"-retinal can be recycled and converted back to the 11-"cis"-retinal form via a series of enzymatic reactions. Additionally, some of the all-"trans" retinal may be converted to all-"trans" retinol form and then transported with an inter-photoreceptor retinol-binding protein (IRBP) to the pigment epithelial cells. Further esterification into all-"trans" retinyl esters allows this final form to be stored within the pigment epithelial cells to be reused when needed.

The final conversion of 11-*cis*-retinal will rebind to opsin to reform rhodopsin in the retina. Rhodopsin is needed to see black and white as well as see at night. It is for this reason that a deficiency in vitamin A will inhibit the reformation of rhodopsin and lead to night blindness.

The other functions of vitamin A are to maintain epithelial tissue, and to stimulate differentiation of a number of tissues by controlling gene expression.

Vitamin A Deficiency

In developing countries, it is estimated that 500,000 preschool children become blind every year owing to vitamin A deficiency, and that many of them, will die because of increased vulnerability to infections especially measles.

Defective dark adaptation is the most characteristic early clinical feature, resulting in night blindness. The syndrome of vitamin A deficiency in infants consists of Bitot spots, xerophthalmia, keratomalacia, corneal opacities, hyperkeratosis, growth failure and death. The deficiency disease in humans was called xerophthalmia (dry eyes) because of the prominence of the eye signs (Table 6.1).

Other findings include infertility, metaplastic bones and general keratinization of epithelial tissue particularly in the skin, genitourinary system and the lung. Urinary calculi are common and fetal abnormalities are seen in pregnancy. Diets consisting of polished rice with little or no vegetables or fruits increase the risk of xerophthalmia. Laboratory tests show a mild leukopenia occurring in vitamin A deficiency, with a serum retinol level of 15 µg/dl or less (normal 20 to 80 µg/dl). Clouding of the cornea in a child with vitamin A deficiency is a medical emergency and requires parenteral administration of 50,000 to 100,000 IU (15 to 30 mg retinol).

Table 6.1: WHO classification of xerophthalmia

Primary signs	*Secondary signs*
X1A Conjunctival xerosis	XN Night blindness
X1B Bitot's spots	XF Fundal changes
X2 Corneal xerosis	XS Corneal scarring
X3A Corneal ulceration(<1/3 of cornea)	
X3B Corneal ulceration(>1/3 of cornea)	

Hypervitaminosis A and Teratogenicity

Toxicity has been observed in children and adults ingesting more than 50,000 IU /day of vitamin A for several months. Pediatric toxicity is commonly related to excessive doses of fish liver oil or therapeutic vitamin preparations. In adolescents, its occurrence is related to excessive use of retinol or retinoic acid for various skin disorders, particularly globular acne. The presenting symptoms are fatigue, malaise, anorexia, vomiting, headache, and diplopia related to elevated cerebral spinal fluid pressure. Other findings are bone pain, dermatitis, hepatomegaly with liver abnormalities, hypercalcemia, hypo- prothrombinosis, and fetal abnormalities.

When taken by women at early stages of gestation at daily levels of more than 7500 μg, fetal anomalies and poor reproductive outcomes have been reported. The WHO expert group recommend that daily intakes in excess of 3000 μg or weekly intakes in excess of 7500 μg should not be taken at any period during gestation.

Carotenemia

Carotene is a pigment normally present in keratin and subcutaneous fat. When plasma carotene levels are above 250 μg, yellow pigmentation (carotenemia) shows in superficial areas of the skin, such as face, palms, and soles; however, yellow pigmentation is uncommon in mucosal areas such as the sclerae. This is the result of excessive dietary intake of carotene-containing foods, most commonly carrots and carrot-containing products.

β-Carotene is the most important precursor of vitamin A in vegetable-based diets. Six micrograms of β-carotene have the biological potency of 1 μg of retinol. Excessive intake of carotene does not produce symptoms other than yellow skin pigmentation, probably because it is not absorbed as well as vitamin A and is metabolized too slowly to cause hypervitaminosis. The peak time for the appearance of carotenemia is 6 months to 5 years of age. The skin color will return to normal within 2–6 weeks after discontinuing intake of carrots. The only known hazard of carotenemia is that it could be mistaken for jaundice and stimulates an unnecessary work-up for liver disease.

6

Treatment of Vitamin A Deficiency (VAD)

Specific treatment consists of oral vitamin A in a dose of 50,000, 1 lakh, and 2 lakh IU in children aged <6 months, 6–12 months, and > 1 year respectively. The same dose is repeated next day and 4 weeks later. Alternatively, parenteral water-soluble preparation can be administered in children with persistent vomiting or severe malabsorption (parenteral dose is half of the oral dose for children above 6–12 months and 3/4th in <6 months old). In addition, local treatment with antibiotic drops and ointment and padding of the eye enhances healing.

Prevention

The National Vitamin A Prophylaxis Program was started with the primary aim of reducing blindness in children. Under this program, sponsored by the Ministry of Health and Family Welfare, children between 1–5 years were given oral doses of 200,000 IU vitamin A every six months. Evaluation studies since then revealed inadequate coverage in most of the states. Currently, vitamin A is given only to children less than three years old who are at greatest risk, and the administration of the first two doses is linked with routine immunization to improve the coverage. A dose of 100,000 IU is given along with measles vaccine at nine months of age and 200,000 IU with DPT booster at fifteen months. Dietary improvement is, undoubtedly, the most logical and sustainable strategy to prevent VAD. Availability alone, however, does not ensure programmatic success. A change in dietary habits and increased access to vitamin A-rich foods are required.

VITAMIN D

Vitamin D is the generic term for a family of secosteroids with antirachitic activity. In the secosteroid rings, A, C and D are intact whereas the opened ring B is converted into a conjugated system of double bonds. All molecules with vitamin D activity have the same interrupted ring system but vary in their side chains.

Vitamin D comprises a family of fat-soluble vitamins and hormones that, when deficient in the diet, causes rickets from defective mineralization of growing bone, and osteomalacia in non-growing bones.

It is now known that vitamin D is a precursor of a hormone that is the active form of vitamin D (1,25-dihydroxycholecalciferol), synthesized in the kidney and secreted by the kidney under the control of parathyroid hormone and tissue phosphate concentration. Vitamin D is a facultative vitamin that is required in the diet when there is insufficient vitamin D3 made from 7-dehydrocholesterol in the skin by irradiation with ultraviolet light. In Northern and Western countries where sunlight is less available due to cloudiness of the poor angle of radiation, dietary vitamin D is essential. In the tropics, however, dietary vitamin D is not necessary when there is sufficient exposure to sunlight.

Absorption and Metabolism

Vitamin D is absorbed in the small intestine, mainly in the duodenum by an active transport system that delivers vitamin D to the enterocyte; there it is incorporated into chylomicrons for delivery to the liver. In the liver, vitamin D is hydroxylated to 25(OH)D3 and secreted in association with an α-2 globulin. This carrier transports all three forms of vitamin D of which 25(OH)D3 is in the highest concentration in plasma (20 to 40 ng/ml) whereas vitamin D itself is present in a concentration of 2 to 4 ng/ml and the hormone $1,25(OH)_2D3$ is present in very small amounts, normally 20 to 40 pg/ml.

Vitamin D is hydroxylated twice, once in the liver and then again in the kidney to produce the hormone 1,25-dihydroxycholecalciferol (Fig. 6.1). This hormone which is secreted by the kidney travels to the gut where it increases calcium absorption and to the bones where it increases calcium turnover.

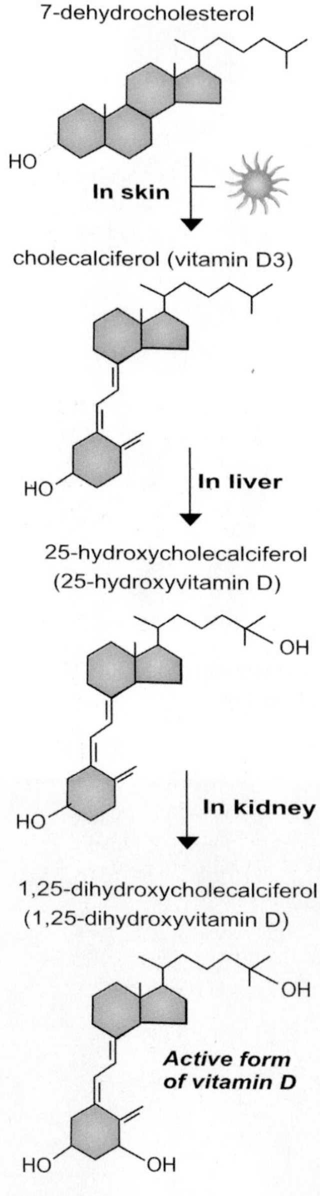

7-dehydrocholesterol

HO

In skin

cholecalciferol (vitamin D3)

HO

In liver

25-hydroxycholecalciferol
(25-hydroxyvitamin D)

OH

HO

In kidney

1,25-dihydroxycholecalciferol
(1,25-dihydroxyvitamin D)

OH

Active form of vitamin D

HO OH

Fig. 6.1: Vitamin D metabolism

Thus, vitamin D is a vitamin when sunlight is limiting, and its hydroxylated derivative, $1,25(OH)_2D3$, is a hormone.

The organs affected by vitamin D hormone in its control of calcium homeostasis are the intestine, kidney, and bones. In the intestine, the hormone induces a calcium transport system involving transport proteins and an intracellular calcium-binding protein (CBP) called calbindin, which aids in the transport of calcium across the enterocyte. In the kidney, vitamin D hormone enhances calcium reabsorption in the tubule by a mechanism similar to that in the gut. It also inhibits the synthesis of 1-α hydroxylase activity (to diminish hormone synthesis) and stimulates 25(OH)D3 24-hydroxylase activity which inactivates both the substrate and the product of 1-α hydroxylase; 1-α hydroxylase activity is also stimulated by parathormone (PTH) and low tissue phosphate concentrations.

Sources

Most foods contain only small amounts of preformed vitamin D. Fish, liver and oils are good sources. Human milk contains only 30–40 IU/L. Exposure to sunlight and vitamin D supplementation for the nursing mother can increase the vitamin D content in breast milk.

In addition to dietary sources, photoconversion by the action of sunlight in the ultraviolet band is an important source of vitamin D for infants and children. It is estimated that an infant needs to have about 20 cm^2 of skin exposed to sunlight for 15–20 minutes daily in order to synthesize enough vitamin D to prevent rickets. The cultural practice of keeping babies tightly covered may prevent adequate exposure. Persons with dark skin appear to have less capacity to photoconvert vitamin D than do fair-skinned individuals, but this limited capacity can be overcome by increasing exposure to sunlight.

Vitamin D Requirements

Since vitamin D3 is produced endogenously in the skin through the action of sunlight on 7-dehydrocholesterol, there is no nutritional requirement for vitamin D when sufficient sunlight is available. However, when shielded from sunlight, breast-fed infants will develop rickets unless supplemented with vitamin D.

The recommended daily allowance in infants is 5 μg (200 IU) per day and children 10 μg (400 IU) per day.

Human milk is deficient in vitamin D and contains only 30–40 IU per liter, mostly from 25(OH) D3. Breast-fed infants must receive an additional source of vitamin D.

Hypervitaminosis D

An epidemic of "idiopathic hypercalcemia" in infants, with anorexia, vomiting, hypertension, renal insufficiency, and failure to thrive in England in the 1950s was traced to an intake of vitamin D between 2,000 and 3,000 IU /day. In adults, dosages of 10,000 IU/day of vitamin D for several months have resulted in marked disturbances in calcium metabolism with hypercalcemia, hyperphosphatemia, hypertension, anorexia, nausea, vomiting, weakness, polyuria, polydipsia, azotemia, nephrolithiasis, ectopic calcification, renal failure and, in some cases, death.

Vitamin D Deficiency and Rickets

A lack of adequate mineralization of growing bones results in rickets, and that of trabecular bone in osteomalacia. Osteoporosis is due to proportionate loss of bone volume and mineral, which in children is often caused by excessive administration of corticosteroids.

In most developed countries nutritional rickets (vitamin D deficiency rickets) was virtually eradicated by fortification of milk or direct administration of vitamin D. In India and many other developing countries, however, nutritional rickets is still widely prevalent. Recent reports suggest that nutritional rickets is reappearing in the developed countries, particularly among dark-skinned infants who are exclusively breastfed for prolonged periods without additional vitamin supplements.

Rickets may result from the deficiency of either calcium or phosphorus, since both of these are needed for bone mineralization. The former results from insufficient amount of vitamin D, resulting in secondary hyperparathyroidism. Blood PTH levels are almost always raised. Besides a poor dietary intake and insufficient exposure to sunlight, vitamin D deficiency may result from its malabsorption. Prolonged total breastfeeding without vitamin D supplementation also contributes to the problem. Various malabsorption syndromes and chronic liver diseases (e.g. biliary atresia) impair intestinal absorption of vitamin D and calcium. Anticonvulsant drugs induce hepatic cytochrome P-450 oxidase that leads to conversion of 25(OH)D3 into its inactive metabolites. A state of vitamin D deficiency is thus induced and may lead to rickets.

Rickets may also occur secondary to severe dietary deficiency of calcium; such patients show normal serum concentrations of 25(OH)D3 but elevated levels of 1,25 (OH)D3. Calcium supplements alone lead to healing of rickets in such cases.

6

The clinical signs and symptoms of rickets include skeletal deformity; bowed legs (genu varum) in toddlers, knock-knees (genu valgum) in older children, craniotabes (soft skull), spinal and pelvic deformities, growth disturbances, costochondral swelling (rickety rosary or rachitic rosary), Harrison's groove, double malleoli due to metaphyseal hyperplasia, increased tendency for fractures, especially greenstick fractures, bone pain or tenderness, muscle weakness and dental problems (Fig. 6.2).

Radiologic changes are characteristically seen at the metaphysis. The first change to appear is 'loss of normal zone of provisional calcification' adjacent to metaphysis. This begins as an indistinctness of the metaphyseal margin, progressing to a 'frayed' appearance with widening of the growth plate, due to lack of calcification of metaphyseal bone (Fig. 6.3). Weight bearing and stress on uncalcified bone gives rise to 'splaying' and 'cupping' of metaphysis. Eventually a generalized reduction in bone density is seen.

Laboratory diagnosis of vitamin D deficiency is based on low circulating levels of 25(OH)D3. Values below 10 μg/ml are indicative of deficiency (Table 6.2). An increased plasma level of 1,25$(OH)_2$D3 indicates deficient intake of calcium or phosphorus. Blood levels of 25(OH)D3 are decreased in rickets, while serum alkaline phosphate is elevated. Calcium levels may be normal or low and phosphate level usually are unchanged or low.

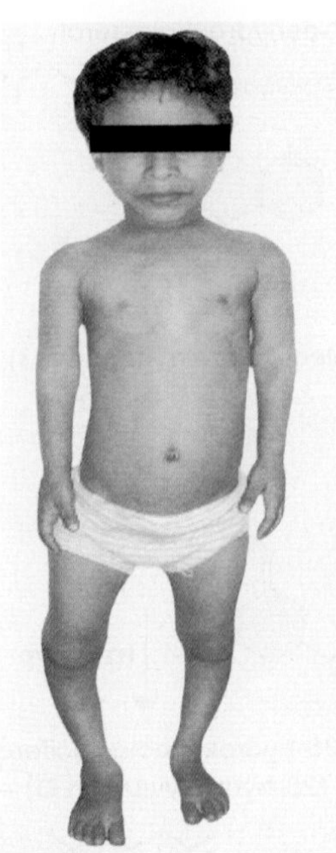

Fig. 6.2: A 4-year-old child with rickets with wide wrist and bow legs

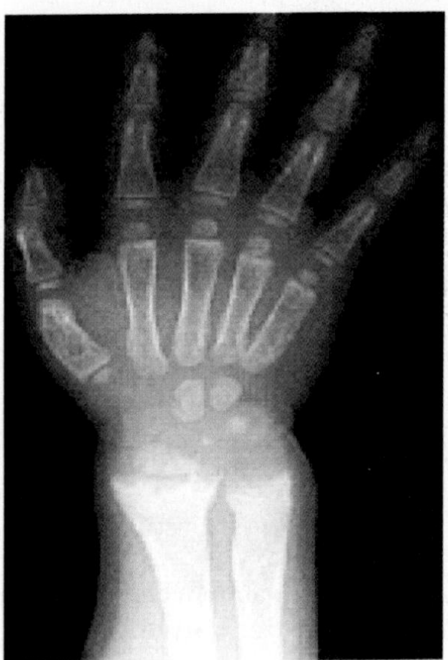

Fig. 6.3: Radiograph of wrist in 4-year-old boy with rickets. Note widening, cupping and fraying at the metaphyseal ends of forearm bones

Table 6.2: Vitamin D levels in serum

	25(OH)D level (ng/ml)
Deficient	Less than 10
Insufficient	10–20
Optimal	20–60
High	60–90
Toxic	Greater than 90

Vitamin D is administered orally either in a single dose of 600,000 IU or over 10 days (60,000 IU daily for 10 days) followed by a maintenance dose of 400 IU/day and oral calcium supplements (50–75 mg/kg/day).

Patients with vitamin D deficiency rickets show evidene of radiological healing (Fig. 6.4) within 4 weeks of therapy. Reduction in blood levels of alkaline phosphatase and resolution of clinical signs occur slowly.

If no healing can be demonstrated with 2 mega doses of vitamin D, patients should be evaluated for refractory rickets (Fig. 6.5).

Familial Hypophosphatemic Rickets

This is the most commonly inherited form of refractory rickets, being inherited as X-linked dominant with variable penetrance. The mother of affected children may have bowing of legs and short stature or fasting hypophosphatemia. Sporadic instances are frequent and an autosomal recessive inheritance has also been reported.

The gene for X-linked hypophosphatemic rickets has been cloned and termed the PHEX gene (phosphate regulating gene with homology to endopeptidases on the X-chromosome). The underlying defect involves impaired proximal tubular reabsorption of phosphate. Despite hypophosphatemia the blood levels of $1,25(OH)_2D3$ are

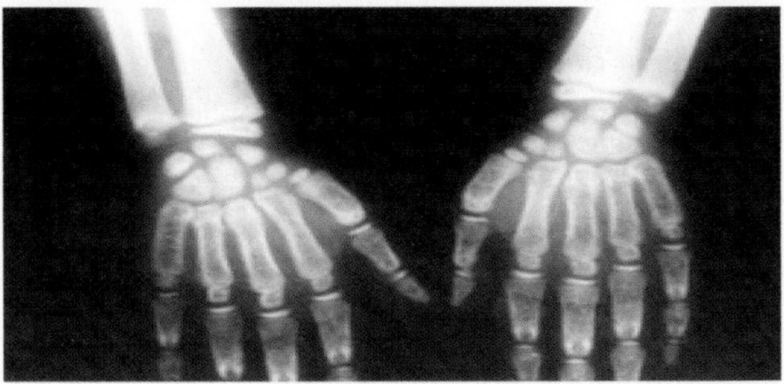

Fig. 6.4: Healing of the growth plate after vitamin D therapy

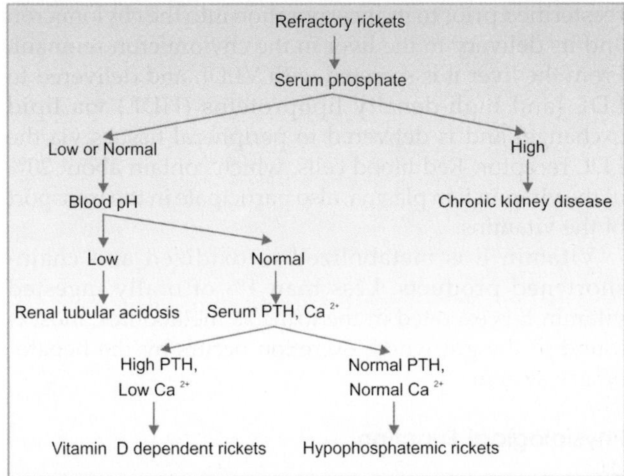

Fig. 6.5: Biochemical evaluation of a child with refractory rickets

low, which implies a deranged response of renal 1-α hydroxylase to a low phosphate signal. Limb deformities such as coxa vara, genu valgum, genu varum and short stature may occur. Abnormalities of maxillofacial region and premature fusion of cranial sutures may lead to deformities of skull. Dental abnormalities are commonly seen including pulp deformities with intraglobular dentine, and frequent dental abscesses. Symptoms of hypocalcemia (tetany and muscle weakness) are absent. Changes of active rickets in spine and pelvis are rarely seen even in advanced stages.

The level of serum calcium is normal or slightly low (9–9.5 mg/dl), that of phosphate decreased (1.5–3 mg/dl). Serum alkaline phosphatase level is raised. PTH levels are normal. Blood levels of $1,25(OH)_2D3$ are inappropriately low for the level of serum phosphate. Urinary phosphate excretion is increased with decreased tubular reabsorption of phosphate.

Oral phosphate and vitamin D supplements are administered. Phosphates are provided in a dosage of 30 to 50 mg/kg (total 1–3 g elemental phosphorus) divided into 5 to 6 equal parts and can be given in the form of Joulie's solution or as neutral phosphate effervescent tablets. Joulie's solution contains 30.4 mg of phosphate/ml. Diarrhea is a frequent problem with higher doses.

Vitamin D supplementation is necessary for healing of rickets. Treatment is started with alfacalcidiol at a dose of 25–50 ng/kg/day (maximum 2 μg/day) until there is biochemical and radiological evidence of healing of rickets. Periodic monitoring of serum and urine levels of calcium and phosphate is essential. A level of serum phosphate greater than 3.0 to 3.2 mg/dl is desirable.

6

Vitamin D Dependent Rickets (VDDR)

These rare autosomal recessively inherited rickets are seen in infants between 3 to 6 months of age, who have been receiving the usual amounts of vitamin D. Two forms are seen.

VDDR Type I

This condition is characterized by a deficiency of the enzyme, 25-hydroxyvitamin D-1-α-hydroxylase. Reduced blood levels of calcium, normal to low phosphate and elevated alkaline phosphatase are characteristic. Blood levels of 25(OH)D3 are normal but those of $1,25(OH)_2D3$ are markedly decreased despite hypocalcemia.

The clinical features are similar to vitamin D deficiency rickets and include hypotonia, growth failure, motor retardation (poor head control, delayed standing and walking), convulsions due to hypocalcemia, anemia and occasionally respiratory difficulty. Physical examination shows thickening of wrists and ankles, frontal bossing, widely open anterior fontanelle, rickety rosary, bony deformities, and positive Trousseau and Chvostek signs. Dentition is delayed and development of tooth enamel impaired.

The treatment of VDDR type I is with physiological doses of alfacalcidiol or calcitriol (1–2 μg daily). Most subjects require concomitant treatment with calcium with or without phosphate supplements. With appropriate therapy the serum calcium levels rise and radiological healing occurs within 6 to 8 weeks.

VDDR Type II

The features are similar to VDDR type I. There is end organ resistance to $1,25(OH)_2D3$. This leads to virtual abolition of actions of $1,25(OH)_2D3$, despite its markedly raised levels in circulation (secondary to hypocalcemia and low 24-hydroxylase activity).

Early onset of rickets, a high prevalence of alopecia and ectodermal defects (oligodontia, milia and epidermal cysts) are characteristic. Hypocalcemia, secondary hyperparathyroidism, elevated circulating levels of $1,25(OH)_2D3$ and an absence or decreased response to vitamin D analogs are seen.

The response to treatment in patients with VDDR type II is not satisfactory. An occasional patient may get clinical and biochemical improvement and radiological healing following long-term administration of large amounts of intravenous or oral calcium.

Other Causes of Rickets

Renal Tubular Acidosis

Proximal as well as distal renal tubular acidosis (RTA) are important causes of refractory rickets in children. The conditions are characterized by hyperchloremic metabolic acidosis with normal blood levels of urea and creatinine. Appropriate correction of acidosis with bicarbonate supplements and phosphate supplementation (in proximal RTA) results in healing of rickets.

6

Chronic Kidney Disease

Refractory rickets may occasionally be the presenting manifestation of chronic kidney disease (GFR below 30–35 ml/min/1.73 m^2), particularly in patients with tubulointerstitial disease. The clinical features of osteodystrophy depend on the patient's age and duration of disease. Elevated blood levels of creatinine and phosphate are characteristic. Therapy consists of restricting phosphate intake and providing supplements of calcium and active vitamin D analogs.

Oncogenous Rickets

Rarely benign mesenchymal tumors may secrete a circulating substance that results in phosphaturia, hypophosphatemia, rickets and muscle weakness. The tumor may be small and difficult to detect but its removal reverses the biochemical abnormalities and heals the rickets.

Metaphyseal Dysplasia

Several types of these disorders are described. Short stature with bowing of legs and waddling gait are prominent in some. There are no biochemical abnormalities except for the occasional presence of hypercalcemia in Jansen metaphyseal chondrodysplasia. Radiological changes resemble rickets. There is no treatment for these disorders.

Fluorosis

Endemic fluorosis occasionally presents with bony deformities and radiological features suggestive of rickets in school going children. Presence of pain in the limbs and spine, mottling of teeth and family history of a similar illness are important features. Osteosclerosis and calcification of ligaments may be found in older children and adults. Blood levels of alkaline phosphatase and parathormone are raised. Levels of fluoride are increased in the water consumed, urine and blood.

VITAMIN E

Vitamin E or tocopherol is a fat-soluble vitamin whose major function is as an antioxidant. In humans, the main manifestations of vitamin E deficiency are (a) a mild hemolytic anemia associated with increased erythrocyte hemolysis, and (b) spinocerebellar disease, mostly observed in children who have fat malabsorption due to abetalipoproteinemia, chronic biliary disease with cholestasis, or other types of malabsorption.

Absorption and Metabolism

Only 20% to 40% of orally ingested tocopherol and/or its esters are absorbed. Tocopherol esters are almost completely hydrolyzed by a duodenal mucosal esterase prior to absorption. The efficiency of absorption is enhanced by the simultaneous digestion and absorption of dietary lipids. Medium-chain triglycerides enhance absorption, whereas polyunsaturated fatty acids are some what inhibitory. Both bile and pancreatic juice are necessary for maximal absorption of vitamin E.

Unlike cholesterol or vitamin A, α-tocopherol is not reesterified prior to its incorporation into the chylomicron and its delivery to the liver in the chylomicron remnant. From the liver it is secreted with VLDL and delivered to LDL [and high-density lipoproteins (HDL) via lipid exchange] and is delivered to peripheral tissues via the LDL receptor. Red blood cells, which contain about 20% of the vitamin E in plasma, also participate in the transport of the vitamins.

Vitamin E is metabolized to oxidized and chain-shortened products. Less than 1% of orally ingested vitamin E is excreted in the urine as metabolites; most is found in the gut where excretion occurs by the hepatobiliary system.

Physiological Function

The principal function of vitamin E is to serve as a physiological membrane-bound antioxidant. Since radical-catalyzed lipid peroxidation seems to be a continual biologic process that damages cellular and intracellular structures, vitamin E appears to promote health by inhibiting this process and terminating radical chain reactions.

Nutritional Requirements

The vitamin E requirement of normal infants, estimated from the amount needed to prevent peroxidative hemolysis, is approximately 0.4 µg/kg body weight/day. For premature infants, 15 to 20 mg/day may be required to maintain normal plasma values. The RDA for infants increases from 3 to 6 mg of α-tocopherol from birth to 2 years of age. One mg of α-tocopherol provides 1.5 IU activity of vitamin E.

Sources

The most common sources of vitamin E are vegetable oils (corn, cottonseed, safflower) and their products (margarine). Other good sources include green leafy vegetables and nuts. Animal fat, fish and fruits are poor sources. Breast milk is rich in vitamin E, and colostrum contains even higher concentrations. Most infant formulas currently in use are fortified with tocopherol.

Vitamin E Deficiency

Infants are born in a state of relative tocopherol deficiency; smaller the infant, the greater the degree of deficiency. Term infants who are breast-fed quickly attain adult blood tocopherol values. The vitamin E-deficient state of premature infants during the first few weeks of life can be attributed to limited placental transfer of vitamin E, low tissue levels at birth, relative dietary deficiency in infancy, intestinal malabsorption and rapid growth. As the digestive system matures, tocopherol absorption improves and blood vitamin E levels rise.

Hemolytic anemia in premature infants may be a manifestation of vitamin E deficiency. The anemia presents with hemoglobin levels in the range of 7 to 9 g/dl and is accompanied by low plasma vitamin E levels, reticulocytosis and hyperbilirubinemia. In these children administration of iron may exacerbate red blood cell destruction unless vitamin E is also administered. This anemia has been associated with ingestion of formulas high in PUFA and low in α-tocopherol. Parenteral vitamin E improves the anemia and corrects the hemolysis.

In children and adults, fat malabsorption generally underlies vitamin E deficiency. Abetalipoproteinemia, caused by the genetic absence of apolipoprotein B, causes serious fat malabsorption and steatorrhea, with progressive neuropathy and retinopathy in the first two decades of life. Plasma vitamin E levels are sometimes undetectable. High-dose vitamin E has improved symptoms in young patients and arrested the neurological disorder in older patients.

Other manifestations include the neurologic syndrome of spinocerebellar ataxia with loss of deep tendon reflexes, truncal and limb ataxia, loss of vibration and position sense, ophthalmoplegia, muscle weakness, ptosis and dysarthria. A pigmented retinopathy may also occur.

A rare, isolated form of vitamin E deficiency without general fat malabsorption has been reported. Most of these malabsorption syndromes respond to massive doses of oral vitamin E (100 to 200 mg/kg/day) with amelioration of the deficiency and prevention of the neurological sequelae.

Hypervitaminosis E

Relatively large amounts of vitamin E, in the range of 400 to 800 mg of l-α-tocopherol, have been taken daily by adults for months to years without causing any apparent harm. Occasionally, muscle weakness, fatigue, nausea and diarrhea have been reported in persons taking 800 to 3,200 mg/day. The most significant toxic effect of vitamin E at dosages exceeding 1,000 mg/day is the antagonism to vitamin K action and the enhancement of the effect of oral coumarin anticoagulant drugs, with overt hemorrhage.

VITAMIN K

Vitamin K is a generic term for derivatives of 2-methyl-1, 4-naphthoquinone with procoagulation activity. The natural forms are substituted in position 3 with an alkyl side chain. Vitamin K1, called phylloquinone, has a phytol side chain in position 3 and is the only homologue of vitamin K in plants. Vitamin K2 is a family of homologues of 2-methyl-1, 4-naphthoquinone substituted in position 3 with isopropyl side chains. These are called menaquinones. The menaquinones synthesized by bacteria in the intestinal tract of humans can contribute to vitamin K requirements. Vitamin K is essential for humans because the 1, 4-naphthoquinone moiety cannot be synthesized in animal cells.

Absorption and Metabolism

The absorption of phylloquinone and the menaquinones requires bile and pancreatic juice for maximum effectiveness. Dietary vitamin K is absorbed in the small bowel, incorporated into chylomicrons, and delivered to the circulation via the lymph. The liver appears to be the primary target of administered vitamin K in animals and humans. The total body pool of vitamin K in animals and humans is surprisingly small, 80% of which is in the liver. The principal sites of uptake, after liver, are skin and muscle. The terminal oxidation of vitamin K and its epoxides involves chain shortening and excretion in urine and stool mainly as glucuronides of vitamin K lactones.

Physiological Function

The main role of vitamin K is as a cofactor in the posttranslational carboxylation of glutamic acid to form glutamate (Gla), which takes place in the liver. The physiological function of vitamin K is to carboxylate selected glutamic acids to the translation products of vitamin K-dependent proteins to produce γ-carboxyglutamates. Factors II (prothrombin), VII, IX, and X are procoagulant proenzymes whereas proteins C and S are anticoagulant proenzymes. The function of these proteins is to facilitate the chelation of calcium ions to Gla and platelet phosphatide, which is essential for the coagulation cascade to operate.

Nutritional Requirements

The vitamin K requirement is met by a combination of dietary intake and microbiological biosynthesis in the gut. The vitamin K-dependent coagulation factors are depressed to 30% of normal at birth in full-term infants and even lower in premature newborns. The vitamin K requirement for the normalization of prothrombin and other factor levels in newborns is 3 to 5 μg/day. Since breast milk contains only 2 μg phylloquinone per liter, breast-fed infants must be fortified with vitamin K in order to prevent the hemorrhagic disease of the newborn. The allowance for infants increases from 5 μg/day at birth to 10 μg/day at 2 years. The requirement for older children is in the range of 10 to 30 μg/day or 0.2 to 0.5 μg/kg/day.

Sources

6

Green leafy vegetables are rich in phylloquinone, while animal foods are intermediate, and cereals low, in this vitamin. The bacterial flora of the human intestine are capable of synthesizing substantial amounts of vitamin K, which presumably is sufficient to fulfill the daily requirements in adults with normal intestinal flora.

Vitamin K Deficiency

Most natural foods consumed by humans have a high vitamin K content relative to its low requirement. Thus, primary deficiency is very rare. Conversely, elimination of the bacterial flora of the intestine, or exclusive parenteral alimentation with no added vitamins K are reported mechanisms of secondary vitamin K deficiency. Among other conditions favoring deficiency are fat malabsorption, biliary obstruction, cystic fibrosis and short bowel syndrome.

The hemorrhagic disease of the newborn is a syndrome of gastrointestinal bleeding and ecchymoses appearing in the first week of life, predominating in breast-fed infants because of the low vitamin K content of human milk. Because of the routine administration of prophylactic vitamin K at birth, most cases of hemorrhagic disease of the newborn are of late onset (after 2 weeks of life) and are also associated with a variety of conditions such as antibiotic therapy, cholestasis, maternal use of antagonist drugs (primidone, warfarin, diphenylhydantoin), low dietary intake and fat malabsorption. Confirmation of the diagnosis depends on a rapid therapeutic response to administration of vitamin K intramuscularly.

The current guidelines recommend the prophylactic administration of vitamin K to all newborns, 0.5–1.0 mg i.m. and a weekly i.m. supplementation with 1 mg of vitamin K for parenterally fed infants and children.

Hypervitaminosis K

Menadione unsubstituted in the 3 position causes toxicity in children, expressed as jaundice, hemolysis and kernicterus. Phylloquinone is essentially nontoxic.

WATER-SOLUBLE VITAMINS

VITAMIN B GROUP

Thiamine (Vitamin B1)

Thiamine is water-soluble, composed of an imidazole and a pyrimidine ring, connected by a methylene link. Thiamine deficiency or beriberi has been known to affect people who consumed diets based on polished rice. Nowadays, refined cereals are fortified with thiamine.

Sources

Dietary sources include unrefined or fortified cereal grains, enriched bakery products, organ meats (liver, kidney), and legumes. The vitamin is sensitive to heat, sulfites, and pasteurization and sterilization. The thiamine content of human milk is relatively low (16 μg/ml) compared to cow's milk which contains 40–50 μg/ml. Freezing foods results in little loss.

Absorption and Metabolism

Thiamine is absorbed both actively and passively from the gastrointestinal tract, mainly the jejunum. It is dependent on the sodium ion for active absorption. Active absorption can be inhibited by ethanol, and unless higher doses are administered, the usually physiologic dose is insufficient to maintain normal levels in the chronic alcoholic.

Although thiamine deficiency during pregnancy has been described, the fetus appears to be protected by an active placental transport, and thiamine levels in cord blood are usually higher than in maternal blood.

Biologic Action

The active form of thiamine, thiamine pyrophosphate, is involved in several key enzymatic steps of carbohydrate metabolism. It acts as a cofactor for the oxidative decarboxylation of pyruvate to form acetyl-CoA, a step catalyzed by the pyruvate dehydrogenase complex. Thiamine pyrophosphate is also a cofactor for transketolase, an enzyme of the pentose pathway. This pathway is not directly involved in carbohydrate metabolism, but is the major source of five carbon compounds for nucleic acid synthesis and of the NADPH used in fatty acid synthesis. The transketolase reaction is affected rapidly in thiamine deficiency, and its rate in erythrocytes is used as an index of thiamine status.

Deficiency

Thiamine deficiency or beriberi occurs in adults when the level of intake drops below 1 mg/day. The classic signs of beriberi appear after prolonged periods of low thiamine intake. Three forma of beriberi have been described: dry, wet, and acute. The dry and wet (edematous) forms are different manifestations of a polyneuritis. The "dry" form has no edema, and typically includes severe muscle wasting and cardiomegaly.

Wet beriberi is characterized by peripheral edema, ocular paralysis, ataxia and mental impairment. The pathogenesis of edema in wet beriberi is unclear. Infantile beriberi may be more subtle than that found in adults. It occurs in breast-fed infants of thiamine-deficient mothers (who may not have signs of beriberi), or in other conditions of very low thiamine intake. The clinical picture is dominated by cardiac involvement, with cardiomegaly, cyanosis, dyspnea and aphonia. The disease when untreated may result in death after a few weeks, in the infantile form.

Diagnosis of Thiamine Deficiency

Thiamine deficiency may be suspected in all cases of malnutrition. The diagnosis may be confirmed by measurement of 24-hr urinary thiamine excretion which in children is normally about 40 to 100 µg /day. Values less than 15 µg /day are in the deficient range. Diagnosis of deficiency can also be based on the response of red cell transketolase to the addition of thiamine in vitro. Erythrocytes from deficient persons have a greater response to thiamine pyrophosphate addition than do those of normal controls. An increase in transketolase activity of less than 15% constitutes a normal status, 15–25% is considered mild deficiency, and responses of over 25% are defined as severely deficient.

Thiamine Requirements

Requirements are generally based on carbohydrate intake since thiamine functions primarily in the metabolism of carbohydrates. The recommended daily allowance is 0.4 mg/1000 kcal consumed.

Treatment of Beriberi

Treatment of beriberi with thiamine usually leads to resolution of neurologic and cardiac symptoms within 24 to 48 hr. Treatment of children with mild beriberi with an oral dose of 5 mg thiamine per day is usually satisfactory. Severely ill children should receive 10 mg intravenously twice daily. In the management of fulminant heart disease, higher doses with vigorous treatment of congestive heart failure are necessary.

Riboflavin (Vitamin B2)

Riboflavin is a flavoprotein which is widely distributed in plants.

Sources

Meat, poultry fish, and dairy products are good sources of riboflavin. Many cereals are also fortified or enriched with the vitamin. Among the vegetables, broccoli, spinach and asparagus are good sources. Riboflavin is quite resistant to oxidation and to heat, and is not destroyed by pasteurization or evaporation.

Human milk contains 40–70 µg/100 kcal of riboflavin, and cow's milk has around 250 µg/100 kcal. Maternal riboflavin supplementation may be used to increase concentration in breast milk in deficiency states.

Absorption and Metabolism

Riboflavin is absorbed efficiently from the small intestine by a site-specific, saturable, specialized transport process. Biliary obstruction, high dietary fiber, and antacids decrease the bioavailability of the vitamin.

Biologic Action

It is a constituent of two coenzymes involved in oxidation-reduction reactions: flavin adenine dinucleotide (FAD) and flavin mononucleotide (FMN). A number of important redox enzymes, including glutathione reductase and xanthine oxidase, require flavin coenzymes. The enzymes catalyzing the synthesis of niacin from tryptophan and the conversion of pyridoxal phosphate to an active coenzyme are also flavin-dependent, and thus, link riboflavin with these two vitamins. Riboflavin deficiency affects fatty acid synthesis, and causes a decrease in plasma levels of linoleic and linolenic acids. By impairing the conversion of phosphorylated vitamin B6 to its coenzyme, it affects reactions involved in amino acid metabolism requiring this vitamin.

Deficiency

Riboflavin deficiency may occur from inadequate intake or malabsorption. It takes 1–2 months to develop and is usually associated with other vitamin deficiencies. The classic presentation of ariboflavinosis includes photophobia, glossitis, angular stomatitis, seborrheic dermatitis, corneal vascularization and cataracts. Nonspecific symptoms of anorexia, weight loss, weakness, dizziness and confusion may precede. Late complications of ariboflavinosis are unusual with prompt therapy.

Diagnosis of Riboflavin Deficiency

Diagnosis should be considered with a history of dietary deficiency and clinical manifestations. A reliable, although not always practical indicator of riboflavin status is the 24-hour urinary excretion of the vitamin. Excretion of less than 10% of intake over 24 hours is indicative of deficiency.

Activity of glutathione reductase in the erythrocytes provides a functional index of flavin coenzyme activity. The enzyme activity in red cells is measured in vitro before and after the addition of FAD. A cofactor-induced increase of 20% above the basal level is indicative of deficiency.

Riboflavin Requirements

Requirements are often based on caloric intake. The recommended daily intake is 0.4 mg / 1000 kcal for infants and 0.8–1.2 mg / 1000 kcal for children.

Treatment of Riboflavin Deficiency

Children may be successfully treated with 1 mg riboflavin three times daily for several weeks, and infants respond to 0.5 mg twice daily. Often therapeutic doses of vitamin A will improve the corneal lesions more rapidly.

Niacin (Vitamin B3)

Nicotinic acid and nicotinamide, which are biologically equivalent vitamins, are both referred to as niacin.

Biosynthesis of this vitamin occurs in almost all organisms; and in humans the conversion ratio of tryptophan to nicotinic acid is only about 60 to 1, making it possible for large amounts of tryptophan to meet niacin requirements.

Sources

Niacin is distributed in plants and in animal food sources, only in its pyridine nucleotide form. Milk, cereals, leafy vegetable, fish, coffee, and tea are all good sources of niacin. The vitamin is quite resistant to heating. Human milk contains around 30 mg/100 kcal of niacin compared with only 0.12 mg/100 kcal in cow's milk.

Absorption and Metabolism

Niacin is absorbed in the proximal small bowel and incorporated into nicotinamide adenine dinucleotide (NAD) and its phosphate (NADP), two key coenzymes of cellular bioenergetics. Excess niacin is methylated in the liver, forming N^1-methylnicotinamide. This compound and its oxidation product, 2-pyridone, are the two major niacin metabolites found in urine.

Biological Role

NAD and NADP are coenzymes for oxidation-reduction reactions, for obtaining energy from protein, and in excision-repair mechanisms of DNA.

Niacin Deficiency

Niacin deficiency leads to pellagra, named after the pathognomonic skin changes that result: *pelle*, skin; *agro*, rough. It was originally thought to be caused by a factor deficient in maize, subsequently identified as nicotinic acid.

Clinical features of niacin deficiency are chronic, relapsing, and popularly characterized by three D's: dermatitis, diarrhea, and dementia. The cutaneous lesions consist of a pigmented rash aggravated by sunlight. More acute cases may progress to vesiculation, ulceration and secondary infection. Classically, the erythema progresses to roughening and keratosis with scaling. A characteristic red coloration of the tongue may also be seen. Although neurologic manifestations may appear without skin manifestations, they usually follow development of skin lesions. Neurologic symptoms include apathy, headaches and loss of memory. In most chronic forms, posterolateral cord degeneration and peripheral nerve lesions are seen. Only in the most severe and chronic cases do the neurologic lesions persist after adequate treatment with niacin.

Diagnosis of Niacin Deficiency

Diagnosis may be suspected by a history of inadequate diet, INH treatment, or chronic alcohol ingestion when the typical manifestations are present. Determination of urinary excretion of N^1-methylnicotinamide is the most helpful. Normal twenty-four hour excretion of N^1-methylnicotinamide is between 4 and 6 mg and values below 3 mg are indicative of deficiency state. In pellagra these values are usually 0.5 to 0.8 mg/day.

Niacin Requirements

Requirements are expressed in terms of "Niacin Equivalents" (NE). One NE equals 1 mg of niacin or 60 mg of tryptophan. RDA for niacin is related to dietary energy intake. The recommended intake is 6.4 to 8 NE / 1000 cal, human milk provides about 8 NE/1000 cal.

High doses of nicotinic acid (but not of nicotinamide) reduce serum cholesterol and triglyceride levels in humans. A number of side effects, including skin flares, hyperuricemia, hyperglycemia, and abnormal tests of liver function have been described.

Treatment of Pellagra

The usual daily dose for treatment is about 10 times the recommended dietary intake. Oral treatment with nicotinamide is preferred over nicotinic acid to avoid unpleasant side effects such as flushing, tachycardia. Parenteral therapy is considered when gastrointestinal absorption is deficient. Prevention of pellagra can be achieved by eating an adequate protein diet containing tryptophan and foods containing niacin.

Pyridoxine (Vitamin B6)

Pyridoxine aids in food assimilation and protein and fat metabolism, especially in the metabolism of essential fatty acids. It activates many enzyme systems and is involved in the production of antibodies against bacterial diseases. It is linked to cardiovascular health by decreasing the formation of homocysteine. It has been suggested that Pyridoxine might help children with learning difficulties, and may also prevent dandruff, eczema, and psoriasis. It is also required for absorption of vitamin B12 and for the production of hydrochloric acid and magnesium. Pyridoxine is required for the production of the monoamine neurotransmitters serotonin, dopamine, noradrenaline and adrenaline, as it is the precursor to pyridoxal phosphate: cofactor for the enzyme aromatic amino acid decarboxylase. This enzyme is responsible for converting the precursors 5-hydroxytryptophan (5-HTP) into serotonin and levodopa (L-DOPA) into dopamine, noradrenaline and adrenaline. As such it has been implicated in the treatment of depression and anxiety.

Lack of pyridoxine may cause anemia, nerve damage, seizures, skin problems, and sores in the mouth. Pyridoxine is given 10–50 mg/day to patients on INH (isoniazid) to prevent peripheral neuropathy and CNS effects that are associated with the use of isoniazid.

Vitamin B6 is absorbed mainly in the jejunum. Although the bacteria in the colon do synthesize vitamin B6, it is not absorbed to any significant extent. Small quantities of this vitamin are stored in the body. Rich sources of vitamin B6 include yeast, sunflower seeds, wheat germ, soya beans and walnuts.

Cobalamin (Vitamin B12)

The cobalamins share a common structure of four linked pyrrole rings, forming a core around a cobalt moiety. Cyanocobalamin is the most common commercially available form of vitamin B12, but the active forms in tissues are methylcobalamin arid 5' -deoxy-adenosyl cobalamin.

Methylcobalamin is a coenzyme in the reaction that transfers a methyl group to homocysteine to form methionine. The methyl group donor for this reaction is methyl folate, which is then regenerated to its active form, tetrahydrofolate. Vitamin B12 deficiency blocks this reaction, trapping folate into the inactive methyl form, and thus favoring the development of clinical folate deficiency.

The other coenzyme, 5′-deoxyadenosyl cobalamin, acts in the formation of succinyl-CoA, which is an essential step in the catabolism of valine, isoleucine, and other amino acids through the Kreb's cycle.

Sources

Vitamin B12 is only produced by microorganisms, and thus its presence in plant sources depends on contamination by microorganisms. Animals contain cobalamin either ingested with microorganisms or produced by bacteria in the upper segments of the intestine. Highest concentrations are in organs such as liver, kidney, and heart, followed by muscle meat. Clams and oysters are also excellent sources.

Concentrations of vitamin B12 in human milk parallel those of plasma, reaching about 0.6 µg/L.

Absorption and Metabolism

A very specific, receptor-mediated process operates at the ileum, involving a glycoprotein known as "intrinsic factor." This glycoprotein is produced in the stomach, and its absence causes pernicious anemia, an inability to absorb the ingested vitamin B12. Passive diffusion accounts for a very small fraction of total absorption, but has important therapeutic implications for the management of pernicious anemia with megadoses of vitamin. Cobalamin undergoes enterohepatic recirculation, and this process accounts for the very long half-life of the vitamin.

Vitamin B12 is transported in plasma bound to transcobalamin II, which delivers it to target tissues. The average total body pool in an adult is enough to sustain the daily vitamin B12 needs for several years.

Deficiency

Most of the deficiencies are caused by impaired absorption, due to the deficiency of the intrinsic factor, or intestinal or liver disease, and they are more common in adults and elderly persons. True dietary vitamin B12 deficiency occurs in persons who follow strict diets containing essentially no animal or fish products.

Vitamin B12 status is assessed by measurement of serum cobalamin levels, with values below 1.1 pmol/L indicative of negative vitamin B12 balance. The plasma levels of methylmalonic acid and homocysteine are increased, because of block in the vitamin B12-dependent steps of their metabolic pathway. Methylmalonic aciduria may also occur but is a less consistent finding.

Since the development of clinical vitamin B12 deficiency takes a long time, it is rare in young infants. Exclusively breast-fed infants of strict vegetarian mothers, however, may be at risk of deficiency, manifested by methylmalonic aciduria and/or megaloblastic changes. Other early signs of deficiency in infants and young children are low plasma cobalamin levels (less than 100 pg/ml) and neutrophil hypersegmentation, followed by megaloblastic anemia and pancytopenia.

A specific manifestation of vitamin B12 deficiency is a diffuse and progressive demyelination, which usually starts in peripheral nerves, and progresses to the posterior and lateral columns of the spinal cord and to the central nervous system. These lesions are possibly due to a generalized methyl group deficiency in the nervous system, and perhaps also to toxic accumulation of homocysteine.

Requirements

The recommended intake of vitamin B12 for infants is 0.3 µg/day. Older children should receive 0.5–1.5 µg/day, and adolescents 2.0 µg/day. These levels are easily met by virtually any mixed diet.

Folic Acid (Pteroylglutamic Acid)

Folic acid is the parent compound of a large group of naturally occurring, structurally related compounds collectively known as the folates. Folic acid participates in several important metabolic processes in the body. It is essential for the normal growth and maintenance of all cells because it acts as a coenzyme for normal DNA and RNA synthesis. Folate is vital for the reproduction of the cells within the fetus. A deficiency affects normal cell division and protein synthesis, especially impairing growth. Folic acid, with the collaboration of vitamin B12 converts homocysteine in methionine therefore reducing blood levels of homocysteine and lowering risks of heart disease. It also maintains nervous system's integrity and intestinal tract functions. It is involved in the production of neurotransmitters such as serotonin, which regulate mood, sleep and appetite. Leafy vegetables such as spinach, turnip greens, lettuces, dried beans and peas, fortified cereal products, sunflower seeds and certain other fruits and vegetables are rich sources of folate.

Deficiency of folic acid limits cell function (cell division and protein synthesis) and affects the normal growth and repair of all cells and tissues in the body. The tissues that have the fastest rate of cell replacement are affected first. Since folate deficiency limits cell division, erythropoiesis, is hindered and leads to megaloblastic anemia. Other symptoms are impaired brain and nerve functions especially memory problems. Deficiency of folate in pregnant women has been implicated in neural tube defects. Therefore peri-conceptional folic acid supplementation a month **before conception and at least 3 months afterward** is recommended to potentially reduce the risk of having a fetus with a neural tube defect.

Recommended Daily Allowance

The recommended daily allowance of folic acid is as follows

Age	*Micrograms of folic acid per day*
Infants	70
1–3 years	100
4–6 years	150
7–9 years	200
10–12 years	250
13–15 years	300
Pregnant and lactating women	400

Other Water-Soluble Vitamins

Biotin

Biotin is a coenzyme for carboxylation reactions. Four such reactions have been found to require biotin as an essential cofactor in mammals: (a) acetyl-CoA carboxylase synthesizes malonyl-CoA, the initial step in fatty acid synthesis; (b) pyruvate carboxylase forms oxaloacetate, a key intermediate of the Krebs cycle; (c) propionyl-CoA carboxylase forms methyl-malonyl-CoA, permitting the entry to the Krebs cycle of carbons derived from branched chain amino acids, fatty acids with odd-numbered carbon chains, and cholesterol; (d) methylcrotonyl-CoA carboxylase participates in the catabolism of leucine.

Dietary sources include liver, egg yolk, milk, yeast extracts and meat.

Biotin deficiency has been observed in individuals who consume large number of raw eggs (rich in avidin) for several months. The avidin is not hydrolyzed by gastrointestinal enzymes; it binds biotin, and prevents its absorption. Cooking of eggs destroys avidin.

Clinical features of biotin deficiency include anorexia, vomiting, dry scaly dermatitis, glossitis, and hypercholesterolemia. Long-term parenteral alimentation without biotin can also lead to deficiency in pediatric and adult patient. Multiple carboxylase deficiency is a genetic metabolite disorder affecting the activity of carboxylase synthetase, which catalyzes the transfer of biotin to the apocarboxylase moiety. This condition responds to large doses of biotin. Another genetic defect affects the activity of biotinidase, an enzyme involved in the recycling of biotin.

Requirements are difficult to determine since biotin is produced by bacteria in the gastrointestinal tract. Recommendations are 0.15 mg biotin in the multivitamin supplements for infants and children.

For **treatment** of biotin deficiency oral administration of 2 to 5 mg daily for 2 to 3 weeks is recommended for mild cases. A parenteral biotin dose of 200 μg daily for 2 to 5 days can be used in more severe cases.

Pantothenic Acid

Pantothenic acid (vitamin B5) is present in virtually all naturally occurring foods and is also synthesized by microorganisms from pantoic acid and β-alanine. Pantothenate is absorbed in the proximal small intestine; in the liver it becomes an integral part of coenzyme A, which is essential for acyl transfer reactions of fatty acid, steroids, and cholesterol synthesis, as well as for the metabolism of pyruvate and α-ketoglutarate.

As an isolated entity, pantothenate deficiency rarely occurs. In cases of extreme malnutrition, such a deficiency coexists with other vitamin deficiencies. Symptoms of isolated experimental deficiency include burning feet, insomnia, and gastrointestinal symptoms.

The suggested daily intake is 2–3 mg for infants and 3–5 mg for children.

VITAMIN C

Vitamin C or ascorbic acid is a six-carbon compound, structurally related to glucose. Although it appears to have multiple functions in humans, its specific biochemistry is not clearly defined. Its most striking property is its capacity for reversible oxidation-reduction. Humans and other primates do not synthesize vitamin C.

Sources

Dietary sources include vegetables (cauliflower, broccoli, cabbage) and fruits (strawberries, citrus). Much of the vitamin C in foods may be lost in cooking as a result of heat and oxidation. Ascorbate is relatively stable in canned and frozen foods.

Vitamin C in human milk ranges from 5–15 mg/ 100 kcal, compared with 0.2–2.0 mg/100 kcal in cow's milk.

Absorption and Metabolism

Ascorbic acid is absorbed by an active, sodium-dependent process in the upper small intestine. Ascorbic acid circulates in plasma in its free, anionic form and is widely distributed in the body, reaching the highest concentration in the adrenal and pituitary glands and in leukocytes. Vitamin C appears unchanged in the urine or as the sulfate when the renal threshold is exceeded.

Biologic Action

Vitamin C appears to function primarily as a strong reducing agent or in reactions involved in electron transport within biological systems. Ascorbic acid is also essential for the normal function of leukocytes, fibroblasts, osteoblasts, and microsomes, and it participates in the metabolism of carnitine, serotonin, and folate. In these systems, ascorbic acid affects the immune response, detoxification, collagen synthesis, and wound healing.

Deficiency

Prolonged vitamin C deficiency results in scurvy. It usually occurs in those who are deprived of citrus fruits, fresh vegetables, or vitamins for some cultural or geographic reasons.

In infancy, clinical features of scurvy (Barlow's disease) are anorexia, diarrhea, pallor, irritability and increased susceptibility to infections. Sub-periosteal hemorrhages and long bone tenderness (pseudoparalysis of the lower extremities) can occur. Radiologic abnormalities are the most frequent manifestations. In older children, hemorrhagic signs usually predominate, with bleeding of gums, conjunctiva, and the intestinal tract.

Diagnosis of Scurvy

Diagnosis can be made by the presence of characteristic physical findings and history of inadequate dietary intake of vitamin C. X-rays of long bones are diagnostic in infantile scurvy.

Vitamin C therapy often results in dramatic improvement within 24–48 hrs.

Requirements for Vitamin C

Daily requirements are 30 to 40 mg for infants and 40 to 70 mg for children.

CALCIUM AND MAGNESIUM

CALCIUM

Calcium is the most abundant mineral in the body, and is located primarily in bone tissue (98%). It is involved in coagulation cascade, nerve conduction and muscle stimulation. Intestinal absorption of calcium varies in inversely with intake and is regulated by 1,25(OH)D3, which controls the synthesis of calcium-binding protein at the brush border. In the presence of Vitamin D, calcium absorption can adapt to a wide range of dietary calcium intake, varying from less than 10–80% of available calcium. Calcium absorption also depends on the interaction of calcium with other dietary constituents, including fiber, phytate, oxalate, fat, and lactose.

The main sources of calcium for infants are milk and dairy products, with smaller amounts derived from grains and fruits once solid foods are introduced. Children consuming strict vegetarian diets may develop calcium deficiency, either alone or in combination with vitamin D deficiency. Strict vegetarian diets may provide as little as 250 mg of calcium per day, and include generous amounts of substances that inhibit calcium absorption, such as fiber and phytates. Secondary calcium deficiency may develop in association with steatorrhea, chronic malabsorption syndromes, or intestinal or renal abnormalities of calcium metabolism.

Children aged 1 to 10 years require an intake of 500 to 800 mg per day. During the pubertal growth spurt calcium requirements are as high as 1000 to 1200 mg per day. Pregnant and lactating women require 400 mg per day. Calcium deficiency may cause tetany characterized by muscle cramps, numbness and tingling in limbs. Rickets and osteoporosis may occur with chronic deficiency.

MAGNESIUM

Magnesium is essential for bioenergetic reactions controlling fuel oxidation, membrane transport, and signal transmission, contributing to the action of more than 300 enzymes. Over 80% of the total body magnesium is in bone and skeletal muscle. Rich sources of magnesium include legumes, nuts, bananas, and whole grains.

Magnesium is absorbed efficiently by the intestine primarily by diffusion. Regulation of magnesium balance depends mainly on renal tubular reabsorption. Deficiency is usually secondary to intestinal malabsorption, excessive gastrointestinal losses through fistulae or continuous suction or renal disease affecting tubular cation reabsorption. Clinical manifestations of magnesium deficiency include irritability, tetany and hypo or hyper-reflexia. Magnesium requirements in the first 6 months range between 40–50 mg/day; 60 mg/day for 6–12 months and approximately 200 mg/day for older children.

TRACE ELEMENT DEFICIENCIES

BIOLOGICAL FUNCTION OF THE TRACE ELEMENTS

Eleven "major" elements constitute 99% of human body weight. These essential-for-life elements are hydrogen carbon, nitrogen, oxygen, sodium, potassium, chlorine, calcium, phosphorus, sulfur, and magnesium. In addition, the body is composed of numerous "trace" elements. The term trace elements comprise an increasing number of compounds with proven or putative essentiality for human nutrition. Each of these contributes less than 0.01% of total body weight.

The major functions of the trace elements are related to enzyme systems where they may act either as cofactor for metal-ion-activated enzymes or as specific constituents of metalloenzymes.

This section provides an overview of all trace elements of established importance in human nutrition.

ZINC

Functions

Zinc is a component of over 100 zinc- metalloenzymes and participates exclusively in many biological processes. However, most attention has been directed to its catalytic role. There is growing evidence to support a structural role for zinc in biological membranes. Its role as an intracellular regulatory ion is analogous to the role of calcium.

It has been hypothesized that zinc functions as an intracellular hormone contributing to the regulation of cellular growth and also impacts on nucleic acid metabolism and protein synthesis. Thymidine kinase, DNA polymerase, and RNA polymerase have each been reported to be zinc dependent. Zinc has a crucial role in the conformation of the "ZiD fingers" that allows them to bind with DNA to initiate the transcription process.

Absorption and Metabolism

Zinc is absorbed throughout the small intestine probably by a process of facilitated diffusion. Most of the absorbed zinc is taken up temporarily by the liver, which plays a central role in zinc metabolism. Absorbed zinc is transported in the portal system attached to albumin or transferrin. In the systemic circulation, the major fraction of plasma zinc is loosely bound to albumin. Zinc is distributed in most tissues, but almost 90% of total body zinc is localized in bone and skeletal muscle.

Zinc status is regulated both at the absorptive step and by intestinal re-excretion. The major excretory route for endogenous zinc is via the feces. The quantity excreted in the feces depends on the quantity of dietary zinc absorbed and on zinc nutritional status.

Deficiency

More commonly, zinc deficiency develops as part of malnutrition or malabsorption syndromes, caused by low intake of zinc in the diet or by intestinal disease. Severe zinc deficiency syndromes have occurred in patients maintained on prolonged total intravenous feeding without adequate trace element supplements. Poor physical growth is a documented feature of zinc depletion in preschool and school-age children. Zinc supplementation has been reported to accelerate growth in adolescents suffering from intestinal malabsorption and sickle-cell disease. Delayed sexual maturation is also a prominent feature of zinc deficiency in adolescents. The typical syndrome of zinc deficiency in humans consists of growth retardation, hypogonadism, and anemia. Other major symptoms include diarrhea, hair loss, anorexia, dermatitis impaired immune function and skeletal abnormalities. Acrodermatitis enteropathica is an autosomal recessive syndrome of severe zinc deficiency, caused by defective intestinal absorption. Anorexia is a prominent feature of untreated acrodermatitis enteropathica. Pica may also be present in some cases. Impaired taste perception has been demonstrated in zinc-depleted children.

Catchup growth has followed the introduction of zinc therapy in patients with acrodermatitis enteropathica. Wound healing is delayed in zinc-deficient animals. Epithelialization of burns may also be improved with zinc therapy. Eye lesions that occur with zinc deficiency include photophobia, blepharitis, and corneal opacities.

A definitive diagnosis of zinc deficiency is difficult and is often derived from the combination of a dietary history of chronic low zinc intake and /or excessive intestinal losses, the presence of clinical signs compatible with zinc deficiency, such as growth delay or skin lesions, and low levels of zinc in plasma or hair.

Requirements

The requirements for infants range between 3.5 and 5.0 mg per day.

Treatment of Deficiency

Acquired zinc deficiency states can be treated with 0.5 to 1.0 mg elemental zinc/kg/day for several wks or months. Oral zinc can be administered as the sulfate or acetate. One mg of elemental zinc is equivalent to 4.5 mg zinc sulfate or 3 mg zinc acetate. Intravenous requirements for patients maintained on prolonged intravenous feeding approximate 50 µg of elemental zinc/kg body weight/day. These requirements can be considerably higher in the presence of excessive zinc losses. Zinc therapy should be monitored with plasma zinc and copper concentrations as excessive zinc therapy can lead to a copper deficiency syndrome.

Toxicity

Zinc is relatively nontoxic, but acute ingestion of large amounts may cause liver and kidney failure. Competitive interaction of zinc with other minerals in the intestinal lumen, may lead to copper deficiency in persons receiving chronic zinc supplementation at high doses.

COPPER

Copper is a component of several metalloenzymes that are required for oxidative metabolism, including cytochrome oxidase, ferroxidases, amine oxidases, superoxide dismutase, ascorbic acid oxidase and tyrosinase. Cytochrome oxidase, the terminal enzyme in the electron transport chain, is the key enzyme necessary for the production of most of the energy of metabolism in aerobic cells. Ceruloplasmin, a glycoprotein that contains eight copper atoms per molecule, accounts for more than 95% of the copper present in the blood plasma.

Absorption and Metabolism

Approximately 40% of ingested copper is absorbed in the stomach and small intestine. Absorbed copper is transported to the liver attached to albumin. In the liver it is utilized by the hepatocytes in the synthesis of ceruloplasmin, which is subsequently released into the systemic circulation. Biliary excretion plays an important role in copper homeostasis. Approximately one-third of fecal copper is contributed by copper in bile acids, the rest coming from unabsorbed copper and from epithelial desquamation. Urinary excretion of copper contributes minimally to copper balance.

Sources

The richest sources are meats, liver, seafood, nuts and seeds. Additional copper may enter the food chain through the use of copper-containing pesticides and by contamination of water by copper pipes and copper cooking utensils.

Deficiency

Primary dietary deficiency is infrequent. Secondary deficiency may develop in malabsorption syndromes, liver disease, peritoneal dialysis, and other conditions causing excessive copper losses. Classical manifestations of copper deficiency include a microcytic, hypochromic anemia unresponsive to iron therapy, neutropenia, and osteoporosis. Copper deficiency decreases the lifespan of the erythrocyte and impairs mobilization of stored iron from liver and bone marrow. Skeletal lesions include periosteal elevation, cupping and flaring of long-bone metaphyses with spur formation, and, in some cases, submetaphyseal fractures, flaring of the anterior ribs, and spontaneous fractures of the ribs. Deficient infants show pallor, depigmentation of skin and hair, prominent dilated superficial veins, skin lesions resembling seborrheic dermatitis, anorexia, diarrhea, and failure to thrive.

Copper transport is disrupted in two human diseases: Wilson disease and Menkes disease. Both have defects in copper transporting membrane proteins. Central nervous system manifestations include hypotonia, psychomotor retardation, and apneic episodes. In the Menkes's steely-hair syndrome there is severe neurological degeneration leading to a fatal outcome by early childhood. Laboratory findings include hypocupremia, low plasma ceruloplasmin, neutropenia and anemia.

Toxicity

Acute ingestion of large doses of copper cause diarrhea, abdominal pain, and may lead to liver and kidney failure. Chronic intoxication occurs from copper released from water piping, by extensive use of topical copper-containing medications, or by hemodialysis with solutions that have high copper content. Chronic copper intoxication has been proposed as the mechanism causing Indian childhood cirrhosis.

SELENIUM

Selenium is a constituent of glutathione peroxidase, an antioxidant system present in red blood cells and in other tissues. Glutathione peroxidase scavenges free hydroperoxides generated during fatty acid oxidation, thus protecting the cell from damage caused by free radical formation. Severe selenium deficiency is the major etiological factor in Keshan disease, which presents primarily as a cardiomyopathy in young children. Skeletal myopathies have also been reported. Mild selenium deficiency is associated with macrocytosis and loss of hair pigment.

CHROMIUM

Glucose intolerance, which complicates malnutrition in young children, has been attributed in part to chromium deficiency. Chromium acts in glucose homeostasis by potentiating insulin action, possibly by interacting with this hormone and its receptor, facilitating binding. Symptoms of chromium deficiency are usually seen in the setting of total parenteral alimentation with low chromium content for long periods of time and include glucose intolerance, peripheral neuropathy, and evidence of disturbed nitrogen and lipid metabolism.

IODINE

The term iodine deficiency disorders (IDD) refers to all the ill-effects of iodine deficiency in a population that can be prevented by ensuring an adequate intake of iodine. Iodine deficiency disorders (IDD) jeopardize children's mental health and often their very survival. Serious iodine deficiency during pregnancy can result in stillbirth, spontaneous abortion, and congenital abnormalities such as cretinism, a grave, irreversible form of mental retardation that affects people living in iodine-deficient areas. However, of far greater significance is IDD's less visible, yet pervasive, mental impairment that reduces intellectual capacity at home, in school and at work.

The effects of iodine deficiency on growth and development are summarized in Table 6.3.

Iodine Deficiency in the Fetus

Iodine deficiency in the fetus is the result of iodine deficiency in the mother. The consequence of iodine deficiency during pregnancy is impaired synthesis of thyroid hormones by the mother and the fetus. Since the physiologic role of thyroid hormones is to insure the timed coordination of different developmental events through specific effects on the rate of cell differentiation and gene expression, an insufficient supply of thyroid hormones to the developing brain may result in mental retardation.

Iodine Deficiency in the Neonate

The brain of the human infant at birth has only reached about one-third of its full size and continues to grow rapidly until the end of the second year. The thyroid hormone, dependent on an adequate supply of iodine, is essential for normal brain development. Apart from mortality, the importance of the state of thyroid function in the neonate relates to the fact that continuing presence of iodine deficiency is a threat to early brain development.

Neonatal chemical hypothyroidism is defined by serum levels of T4 lesser than 3 μg/dl and TSH greater than 100 μU/ml. In the most severely iodine-deficient environments in Northern India, where more than 50% of the population has urinary iodine levels below 25 μg per gram creatinine, the incidence of neonatal hypothyroidism is 75 to 115 per thousand births. In Delhi, where only mild iodine deficiency is present with low prevalence of goiter, the incidence drops to 6 per thousand. These observations have been made using blood taken from the umbilical vein just after birth.

Neonatal hypothyroidism persists into infancy and childhood if the deficiency is not corrected, and results in retardation of physical and mental development. These observations indicate a much greater risk of mental defect in severely iodine-deficient populations than is indicated by the presence of cretinism. They provide strong evidence for the need to correct the iodine deficiency.

Iodine Deficiency in Children

Investigations conducted in areas with moderate iodine deficiency have demonstrated the presence of definite abnormalities in the psychoneuromotor and intellectual development of children who are clinically euthyroid but who do not exhibit the other signs and symptoms of endemic cretinism that is the most severe form of brain damage caused by iodine deficiency. Some patients may show goiter (Fig. 6.6). Studies conducted in a moderately iodine-deficient area have also indicated that fine motor skills and visual problem solving improved in school-children after iodine repletion of the population.

Recommended Daily Intake of Iodine

The recommended daily allowance of iodine is as follows

- 90 μg for preschool children (0 to 59 months)
- 120 μg for school children (6 to 12 years)
- 150 μg for adults (above 12 years)
- 200– 250 μg for pregnant and lactating women.

Correction of Iodine Deficiency

Iodization of salt is the most practical option. Other options for correction of IDD are administration of iodized oil capsules every 6–10 months, direct administration of iodine solutions, such as Lugol's iodine at regular intervals, and iodization of water supplies by direct addition of iodine solution or via a special delivery mechanism.

Table 6.3: **Spectrum of iodine deficiency disorders, IDD**

Fetus	Abortions
	Stillbirths
	Congenital anomalies
	Increased perinatal mortality
	Endemic cretinism
Neonate	Neonatal goiter
	Neonatal hypothyroidism
	Endemic mental retardation
Child and adolescent	Goiter
	Subclinical hypothyroidism
	Impaired mental function
	Retarded physical development

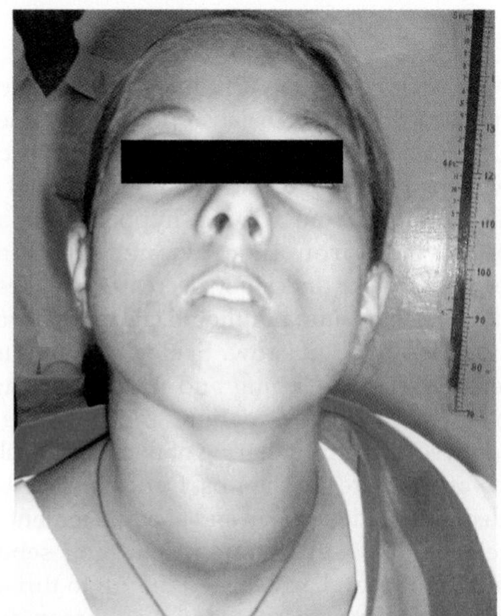

Fig. 6.6: A 14-year-old girl with goiter

The **National Goiter Control Program** (1962) was begun by the Ministry of Health in India for control of iodine deficiency disorders. It was started by establishment of salt iodination plants to ensure an adequate supply of iodized salt in the country. Based on an assumption of a mean intake of salt of 5 g/day, the recommended level of iodination is one part of iodine in 25,000 to 50,000 parts of salt.

IRON

Iron deficiency remains a major nutritional problem among infants and young children in India. The National Family Health Survey (NFHS) II, conducted in 1998–99, documented that about 74% children between the ages of 6–35 months were anemic. The NFHS III (2005–06) shows similar data.

Evidence indicates that iron deficiency anemia is associated with impaired performance on a range of mental and physical functions in children including physical coordination and capacity, mental development cognitive abilities, and social and emotional development. Other health consequences include reduced immunity, increased morbidity, increased susceptibility to heavy metal (including lead) poisoning. The precise effects vary with the age groups studied. The health consequences of iron deficiency during first two years of life are not only serious but also irreversible. It is evident that concerted efforts need to be undertaken to improve the scenario. There is an urgent need to initiate specific public health action to prevent iron deficiency in young children.

A detailed description of clinical features, diagnosis, treatment and prevention of iron deficiency anemia is given in chapter 11.

7 Newborn Infants

Newborn infants are unique in their physiology and the health problems that they experience. Neonatal period is characterized by transition to extrauterine life and exquisitely rapid growth and development. This is the phase in life with the greatest risk of mortality as well as the maximum potential for long-term physical and neurocognitive development. Almost half of under five child deaths occur in the neonatal period. Bacterial infections, manifesting as sepsis and pneumonia, are the foremost cause of death. Other causes of neonatal mortality are prematurity, birth asphyxia and congenital malformations. Almost three-fourths of all neonatal deaths occur among the low birth weight newborns. Of all the neonatal deaths, about 40% occur within 72 hours of birth. Health of the mother and her care during pregnancy and at childbirth has profound influence on neonatal outcome. Newborn health is indeed the key to child health and survival.

DEFINITIONS

Neonatal period: From birth to under four weeks (<28 days) of age. An infant is called a neonate during this phase. First week of life (<7 days or <168 hours) is known as early neonatal period. Late neonatal period extends from 7th to <28th day.

Post-neonatal period: Period of infancy from 28 days to <365 days of life.

Perinatal period: Perinatal period extends from 20th week of gestation (or weighing 500 g or more at birth) to less than 7 days of life.

Live birth: A product of conception, irrespective of weight or gestational age, that, after separation from the mother, shows any evidence of life such as breathing, heartbeat, pulsation of umbilical cord or definite movement of the voluntary muscle.

Fetal death: A fetal death is a product of conception that, after separation from the mother, does not show any evidence of life.

Still-birth: A fetal death at a gestational age of 20 weeks of more or weighing more than 500 g is designated as still-birth or still-born.

Term neonate: Any neonate born between 37 and <42 weeks (259–293 days) of gestation irrespective of the birth weight.

Pre-term neonate: Any neonate born before 37 weeks (<259 days) of gestation irrespective of the birth weight.

Postterm neonate: A neonate born at a gestation age of 42 weeks or more (294 days or more) gestation irrespective of the birth weight.

Low birth weight (LBW) neonate: Any neonate weighing less than 2500 g at birth irrespective of the gestational age.

Very low birth weight (VLBW) neonate: Any neonate weighing less than 1500 g at birth irrespective of the gestational age.

Extremely low birth weight (ELBW) neonate: Any neonate weighing less than 1000 g at birth irrespective of the gestational age.

Neonatal mortality rate (NMR): Deaths of infants under the first 28 days of life per 1000 live births.

RESUSCITATION OF A NEWBORN

Of the 25 million infants born every year in India, 3–5% experience asphyxia at birth. Asphyxia is characterized by progressive hypoxia, hypercapnia, hypoperfusion and acidosis. It may lead to multiorgan dysfunction including hypoxic ischemic encephalopathy (HIE) which might result in long-term neuromotor sequelae.

There is a broad consensus on the evidence-based resuscitation of newborn babies at birth. The American Heart Association (AHA) and the American Academy of Pediatrics (AAP) have recently updated the resuscitation guidelines that are being propagated worldwide through the Neonatal Resuscitation Program (NRP). A summary of the recommendations of AHA-AAP (2005) is provided here.

Physiology of Asphyxia

When an infant is deprived of oxygen, an initial brief period of rapid breathing occurs. If the asphyxia continues, the respiratory movements cease, the heart rate begins to fall, neuromuscular tone gradually diminishes, and the infant enters a period of apnea known as *primary apnea*. In most instances, tactile stimulation and exposure to oxygen during this period will induce respiration.

If the asphyxia continues, the infant develops deep gasping respiration, the heart rate continues to decrease, the *blood pressure begins to fall*, and the infant becomes nearly flaccid. The respirations become weaker and weaker until the infant takes a last gasp and enters a period of *secondary apnea*. The infant is now unresponsive to stimulation and will not spontaneously resume respiratory efforts unless resuscitation in the form of positive pressure ventilation is initiated.

It is important to note that as a result of fetal hypoxia, the infant may go through the phases of primary and secondary apnea *in-utero* itself. Thus an apneic infant at birth may be in either primary or secondary apnea. These two are virtually indistinguishable from one another. In both instances, the infant is not breathing and the heart rate may be below 100 beats per minute. The clinical significance of this is that when faced with an apneic infant at birth, one should assume that one is dealing with secondary apnea and be ready to undertake full resuscitation efficiently.

Lungs and Respiration

During intrauterine life the lungs do not play a role in gas exchange which is taken care of by the placenta. The lung alveoli in the fetus are filled with fluid. The process of fluid removal starts with onset of labor or even before. Contrary to what was previously thought, squeezing the infant's chest during a vaginal delivery plays only a minor role in clearing lung fluid. The majority of the fluid passes from the air spaces into perivascular space and is absorbed into the blood and lymphatic channels within the lungs. The process of labor may facilitate removal of lung fluid, whereas removal is slowed when labor is absent (as in elective cesarean section).

Removal of lung fluid from the air spaces is facilitated by respiration soon after birth. The first few breaths after birth are effective in expanding the alveoli and replacing the lung fluid with air. Problems in clearing lung fluid occur in infants whose lungs do not inflate well with the first few breaths such as those who are apneic at birth or have a weak initial respiratory effort as with prematurity and sedation.

Pulmonary Circulation

Oxygenation depends not only on air reaching the alveoli, but also on pulmonary blood flow. During intrauterine life, there is a very little blood flow in the pulmonary circulation since capillaries are in a state of vasoconstriction. After birth, pulmonary vasodilatation takes place resulting in fall in pulmonary vascular resistance and increased blood flow in the pulmonary circuit.

An asphyxiated infant has hypoxemia (low-oxygen content of the blood) and acidosis (a fall in pH). In the presence of hypoxemia and acidosis, the pulmonary arterioles remain constricted and ductus arteriosus remains open. This results in persistence of fetal circulation. As long as decreased pulmonary blood flow exists, proper oxygenation of the tissues of the body is impossible, even when the infant is being properly ventilated.

In mildly asphyxiated babies whose oxygen and pH are only slightly lowered, it may be possible to increase pulmonary blood flow by quickly restoring adequate ventilation. Pulmonary perfusion in severely asphyxiated infants may not improve with ventilation alone. The combination of oxygenation and correction of metabolic acidosis would result in opening the pulmonary arterioles and thereby an improvement in pulmonary blood flow.

Cardiac Function and Systemic Circulation

In asphyxia, there is redistribution of blood flow to preserve blood supply to vital organs. There is vasoconstriction in the bowel, kidney, muscles, and skin, thus preserving blood flow to the heart and brain.

As asphyxia is prolonged, myocardial function and cardiac output deteriorate, and blood flow to all organs is reduced. This sets in the stage for progressive organ damage. At this point it may be necessary to provide cardiac stimulants (epinephrine) and volume expanders (normal saline) to support the heart and circulation.

Being Prepared for Resuscitation

With careful consideration of antepartum and intrapartum risk factors, asphyxia can be anticipated in up to half of the newborns who will eventually require some form of resuscitation. In others, the need for resuscitation can come as a complete surprise. Therefore, each delivery should be viewed as an emergency, and basic readiness must be ensured to manage asphyxia. Preparation for delivery should include: (i) a radiant heat source ready for use; (ii) all resuscitation equipments immediately available and in working order (Table 7.1); and (iii) at least one person skilled in neonatal resuscitation.

Signs to Evaluate

Evaluation is based primarily on the following three signs: respiration, heart rate (HR) and color. Though all three signs are evaluated simultaneously, *low heart rate* is the most important sign for proceeding to the next step.

Role of Apgar Score in Resuscitation

The Apgar score is an objective method of evaluating the newborn's condition. It is generally performed at 1 minute and again at 5 minutes of age. However, resuscitation must be initiated before the 1-minute score is assigned. If the infant requires interventions based on assessment of respiration, heart rate, or color, they should not be delayed for want of Apgar score at 1 minute. Therefore, the Apgar score is not used to determine the need or the steps necessary for resuscitation.

Table 7.1: Neonatal resuscitation supplies and equipment

Suction equipment
Meconium aspirator
Mechanical suction
Suction catheters 10, 12 or 14 F
Bag and mask equipment
Neonatal resuscitation bags (Self-inflating)
Face-masks (for both term and preterm babies)
Oxygen with flow meter and tubing
Intubation equipment
Laryngoscope with straight blades no. 0 (preterm) and no. 1 (term)
Extra bulbs and batteries (for laryngoscope)
Endotracheal tubes 2.5, 3.0, 3.5 and 4.0 mm ID (internal diameter)
Stylet
Medications
Epinephrine
Normal saline or Ringer lactate solution
Naloxone hydrochloride
Sterile water
Miscellaneous
Stop-watch
Linen, shoulder roll, gauze
Radiant warmer
Stethoscope
Adhesive tape, scissors
Syringes 1, 2, 5, 10, 20, 50 mL
Feeding tube 6F
Umbilical catheters 3.5, 5F
Three way stopcocks
Gloves

7

While the Apgar score is not useful for decision making at the beginning of resuscitation, the change of score at sequential time points following birth can reflect how well the baby is responding to resuscitative efforts. Hence, additional scores should be obtained every 5 minutes for up to 20 minutes, if the 5-minute Apgar score is less than 7.

TABC of Resuscitation

The components of the neonatal resuscitation procedure related to the TABC of resuscitation are shown here:

T-Temperature: Provide warmth, dry the baby and remove the wet linen.

A-Airway: Position the infant, clear the airway (wipe baby's mouth and nose or suction mouth, nose and in some instances, the trachea). If necessary, insert an endotracheal (ET) tube to ensure an open airway.

B-Breathing: Tactile stimulation to initiate respirations, positive-pressure breaths using either bag and mask or bag and ET tube when necessary.

C-Circulation: Stimulate and maintain the circulation of blood with chest compressions and medications as indicated.

Resuscitation Algorithm

Figure 7.1 presents the algorithm of neonatal resuscitation. At the time of birth, one should ask him/herself 4 questions about the newborn.

1. Term gestation?
2. Clear amniotic fluid?
3. Breathing or crying?
4. Good muscle tone? *(flexed posture and active movement of baby denotes good tone)*

If answers to all the four questions are "Yes", then baby does not require any active resuscitation and **routine care** should be provided. Warmth is provided by putting the baby directly on the mother's chest after drying and covering with dry linen. Clearing of the upper airway can be done by wiping the baby's mouth and nose using a clean cloth. Providing skin-to-skin contact and allowing breastfeeding will help in easy transition to extrauterine environment.

If answer to any of the four questions is "No", then the baby requires resuscitation. After cutting the cord, the baby should be subjected to a set of interventions known as **"Initial steps".**

INITIAL STEPS

Provide Warmth

The baby should be placed under the heat source, preferably a radiant warmer. The radiant heat reduces heat loss. The baby should not be covered with blankets or towels to allow full visualization and to permit the radiant heat to reach the baby.

Positioning

The baby should be placed on her back or side with the neck slightly extended. This will bring the posterior pharynx, larynx, and trachea in line and facilitate air entry. Care should be taken to prevent hyperextension or flexion of the neck, since either may decrease air entry. To help maintain the correct position, one may place a rolled blanket or towel under the shoulders, elevating them ¾ or 1 inch off the mattress. This shoulder roll may be particularly helpful if the infant has a large occiput resulting from molding, edema, or prematurity (Fig. 7.2).

Clear Airway

The appropriate method for clearing the airway will depend on the presence or absence of meconium.

If no meconium is present, secretions may be removed from the airway by wiping the nose and mouth with a towel or by suctioning with a bulb syringe or suction catheter. The mouth is suctioned first to ensure that there is nothing for the infant to aspirate, if he/she should gasp when the nose is suctioned. If the infant has copious secretion from the mouth, the head should be turned to the side. This will allow secretions to collect in the mouth, from where they can be easily removed.

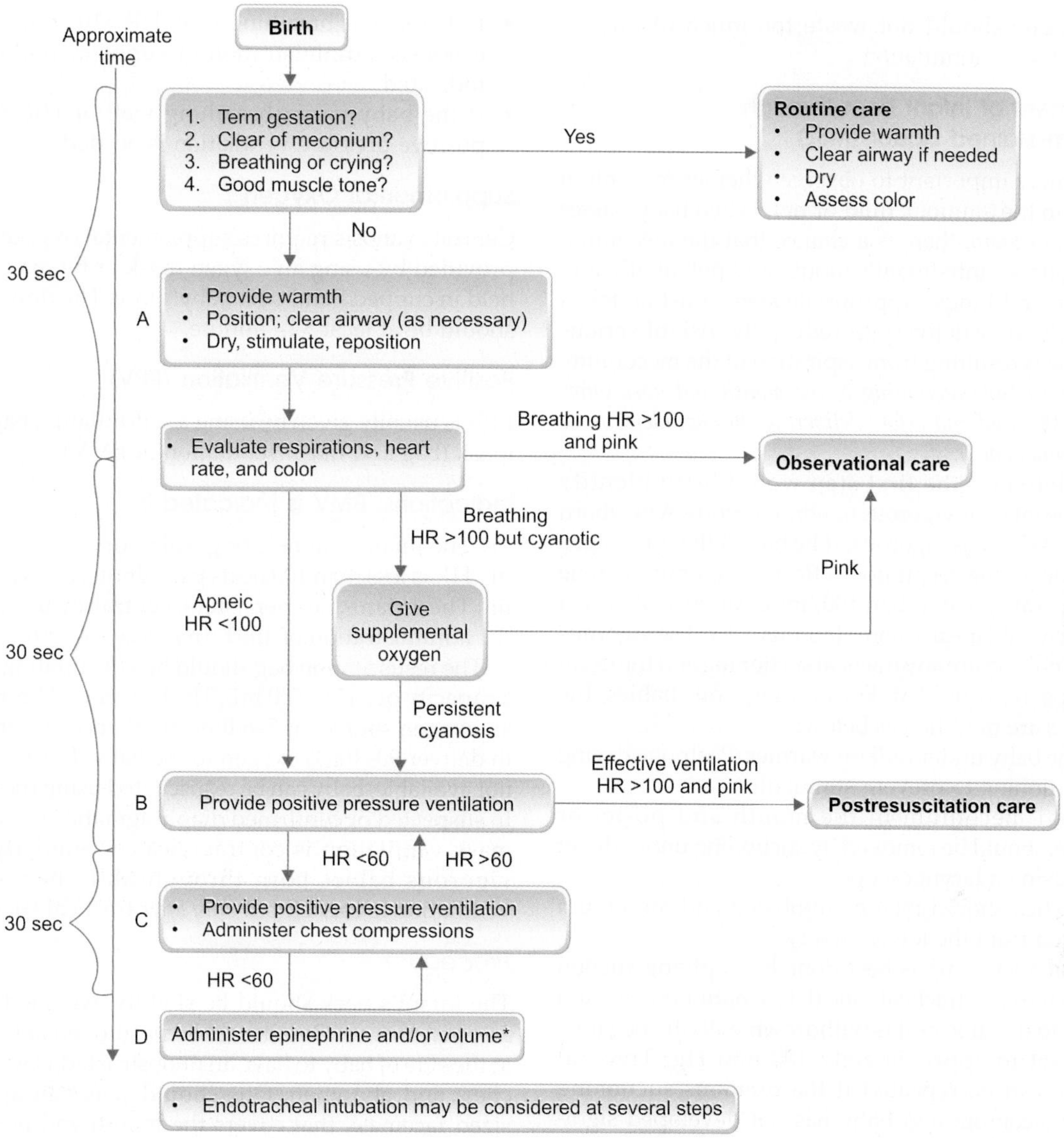

Approximate time

Birth

1. Term gestation?
2. Clear of meconium?
3. Breathing or crying?
4. Good muscle tone?

Yes → Routine care
- Provide warmth
- Clear airway if needed
- Dry
- Assess color

No

30 sec

A
- Provide warmth
- Position; clear airway (as necessary)
- Dry, stimulate, reposition

- Evaluate respirations, heart rate, and color

Breathing HR >100 and pink → Observational care

Breathing HR >100 but cyanotic → Give supplemental oxygen

Pink → Observational care

Apneic HR <100

30 sec

Persistent cyanosis

B Provide positive pressure ventilation

Effective ventilation HR >100 and pink → Postresuscitation care

HR <60 HR >60

30 sec

C
- Provide positive pressure ventilation
- Administer chest compressions

HR <60

D Administer epinephrine and/or volume*

- Endotracheal intubation may be considered at several steps

Fig. 7.1: Neonatal resuscitation. HR heart rate

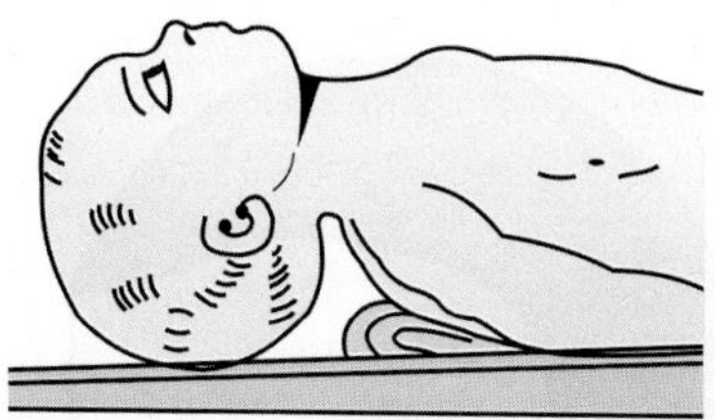

Fig. 7.2: Rolled towel under the shoulders

For suctioning, the size of suction catheter should be 12 or 14 Fr. The suction pressure should be kept around 80 mm Hg (100 cm water) and should not exceed 100 mm Hg (130 cm water). One should not insert the catheter too deep in mouth or nose for suction since stimulation of the posterior pharynx can produce a vagal response causing severe bradycardia or apnea. The catheter can be inserted up to a maximum of 3 and 5 cm in the nose and mouth respectively for suctioning. Also, the maximum time limit for suctioning is 15 seconds.

Clearing of the airways in babies born through meconium stained liquor is discussed separately later.

Dry, Stimulate and Reposition

After suctioning, the baby should be dried adequately using prewarmed linen to prevent heat loss. The wet linen should be removed away from the baby. The act of suctioning and drying themselves provides enough stimulation to initiate breathing. If the newborn continues to have poor respiratory efforts, additional tactile stimulation in form of flicking the soles or gently rubbing the back may be provided *briefly* to stimulate breathing.

However, one should not waste too much of time in providing tactile stimulation.

Management of Infant born through Meconium-stained Liquor (MSL)

It is extremely important to observe whether meconium is present in the amniotic fluid or not. When baby passes meconium *in utero*, there is a chance that the meconium will be aspirated into infant's mouth and potentially into the trachea and lungs. Appropriate steps must be taken immediately after delivery to reduce the risk of serious consequences resulting from aspiration of the meconium. *(Note: Intrapartum suctioning of the mouth and nose (after delivery of the head and before delivering the shoulders) is no longer recommended).*

After delivery, the first step would be to identify whether the infant is vigorous or non-vigorous. A newborn infant is classified as vigorous, if he has all the three signs that include strong respiratory efforts, good muscle tone and a heart rate greater than 100/min. Absence of even a single sign would mean a non-vigorous baby. The vigorous baby does not require any tracheal suctioning and the usual initial steps are provided. For non-vigorous babies, the initial steps are modified as below:

- Place the baby under radiant warmer. Postpone drying and suctioning to prevent stimulation.
- Residual meconium in the mouth and posterior pharynx should be removed by suctioning under direct vision using a laryngoscope.
- The trachea should then be intubated and meconium suctioned from the lower airway.

Tracheal suctioning is best done by applying suction directly to the endotracheal tube (ET). Continuous suction is applied to the tube as it is withdrawn with the negative pressure set to approximately 100 mm Hg. Tracheal suctioning can be repeated if the previous suctioning revealed meconium and baby has not developed significant bradycardia.

Evaluation

After providing initial steps, the baby should be evaluated for three vital signs—respiration, HR and color. Respiration is evaluated by observing the infant's chest movements. HR can be assessed by auscultating the heart or by palpating the umbilical cord pulsation for 6 seconds. The number of beats is multiplied by 10 to obtain the HR per minute (e.g. a count of 12 in 6 seconds is a HR of 120 per minute). Color is evaluated by looking at tongue, mucous membranes, and trunk. A blue hue to the lips, tongue, and central trunk indicates central cyanosis. Presence of cyanosis in extremities (acrocyanosis) does not have any value.

- If the baby has good breathing, HR >100 and pink color, then he does not require any additional intervention. He should be monitored frequently in a transitional area of the nursery (*observational care*).
- If the baby is breathing well, HR >100 but has central cyanosis, administration of supplemental oxygen is indicated.
- If the baby is not breathing well or HR <100, then positive pressure ventilation is needed.

Supplemental Oxygen

Central cyanosis requires supplemental oxygen, which is provided by using an oxygen mask or by oxygen tubing held in cupped hand over baby's face. The flow of oxygen should be at least 5 L/minute.

Positive Pressure Ventilation (PPV)

PPV is usually given by using a self-inflating bag and face mask (bag and mask ventilation or BMV).

Indications: BMV is Indicated if

i. The infant is apneic or gasping or
ii. HR is less than 100 beats per minute, even if breathing
iii. The infant has persistent central cyanosis despite administration of 100% free flow oxygen

The resuscitation bag should be self-inflating type with a capacity of 240 to 750 mL. The bag should be attached to an oxygen source (at 5–6 liter/min) and a reservoir so as to deliver 90–100% oxygen to the baby. In case oxygen is not available, baby can be resuscitated using room air also. In suspected or confirmed diaphragmatic hernia, bag and mask ventilation is contraindicated. Similarly, in non-vigorous babies born through MSL, bag and mask ventilation is carried out *only after* tracheal suctioning.

Procedure

The infant's neck should be slightly extended to ensure an open airway. One should be positioned at head end or at the side of baby to have an unobstructed view of infant's chest and abdomen. One should select an appropriate sized facemask that covers the mouth and nose but not eyes of the infant (Fig. 7.3). The facemask should be held firmly on face to obtain a good seal.

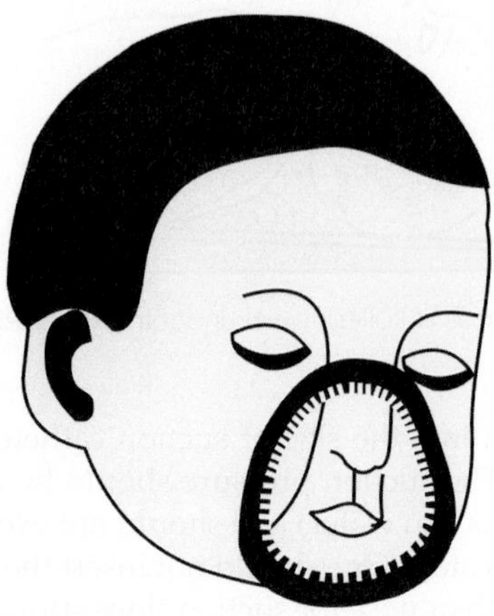

Fig. 7.3: Properly fitting mask

The bag should be compressed using fingers. One should observe for an appropriate rise of the chest. If chest does not rise, the steps outlined in Table 7.2 should be followed.

Table 7.2: Follow up action for absence of chest rise

Action	*Condition corrected*
1. Reapply mask	Inadequate seal
2. Reposition the infant's head	Blocked airway
3. Check for secretions; suction, if present.	Blocked airway
4. Ventilate with mouth slightly open	Blocked airway
5. Increase pressure slightly	Inadequate pressure

If chest still does not rise, one should get a new bag, check it, and try again. When normal rise of the chest is observed, one should begin ventilating. Ventilation should be carried out at a rate of 40 to 60 breaths per minute, following a "squeeze, … , two, ….., three, ….., squeeze" sequence. The best guide to adequate pressure during bag and mask ventilation is an easy rise and fall of the chest with each breath. Usual pressure required for the first breath is 30–40 cm of water. For subsequent breaths, pressures of 15–20 cm of water are adequate. After the infant has received 30 seconds of ventilation with 100% oxygen, one should evaluate the heart rate and take a follow up action as in Table 7.3.

Table 7.3: Follow up action for heart rate response

Heart rate	*Action*
Above 100	If spontaneous respiration is present, discontinue ventilation gradually. Provide tactile stimulation, and monitor heart rate, respiration and color.
60 to 100	Continue ventilation
Below 60	Continue to ventilate; start chest compressions

Improvement in the infant's condition is judged by increasing heart rate, spontaneous respiration and improving color. If the infant fails to improve, one should check adequacy of ventilation in form of adequate chest expansion and 100% oxygen delivery. If chest expansion is inadequate, one should take necessary action as described earlier.

Bag and mask ventilation causes abdominal distension as air or oxygen not only enters the lung, but also escapes into the stomach via esophagus. Distended stomach presses on the diaphragm and compromises ventilation. Therefore, if ventilation is continued for more than two minutes, an orogastric tube (feeding tube size 6–8Fr) should be inserted and left open to decompress the abdomen.

Chest Compressions

The heart circulates blood throughout the body delivering oxygen to vital organs. When an infant becomes hypoxic, the heart rate slows and myocardial contractility decreases. As a result there is diminished flow of blood and oxygen to the vital organs. Chest compressions help in mechanically pumping the blood to vital organs of the body. It must always be accompanied by BMV so that only oxygenated blood is being circulated during chest compressions.

Chest compressions consist of rhythmic compressions of the sternum that compress the heart against the spine, increase intrathoracic pressure and circulate blood to the vital organs of the body.

Chest compressions are indicated if heart rate is below 60 beats per minute even after 30 seconds of positive pressure ventilation with 100% oxygen.

Once the heart rate is 60 beats per minute or more, chest compressions should be discontinued.

Procedure

There are two techniques of chest compressions: (i) thumb technique (preferable), and (ii) two-finger technique. With the thumb technique (Fig. 7.4), the two thumbs are used to depress the sternum, with the hands encircling the torso and the fingers supporting the back. With the two-finger technique (Fig. 7.5), the tips of the middle finger and either the index finger or ring finger of one hand are used to compress the sternum. The other hand is used to support the infant's back, unless the infant is on a very firm surface.

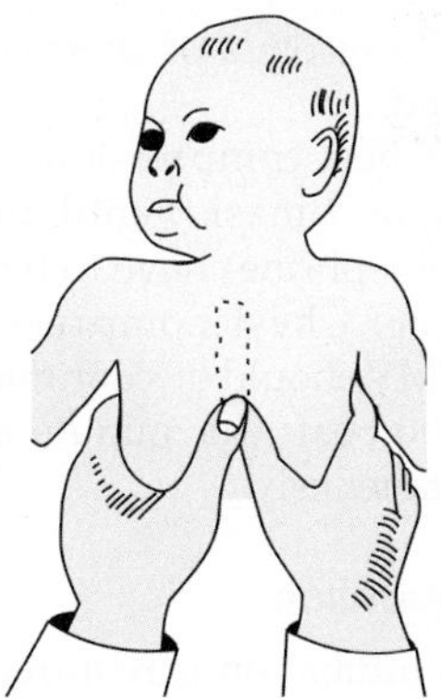

Fig. 7.4: Chest compression with thumb technique

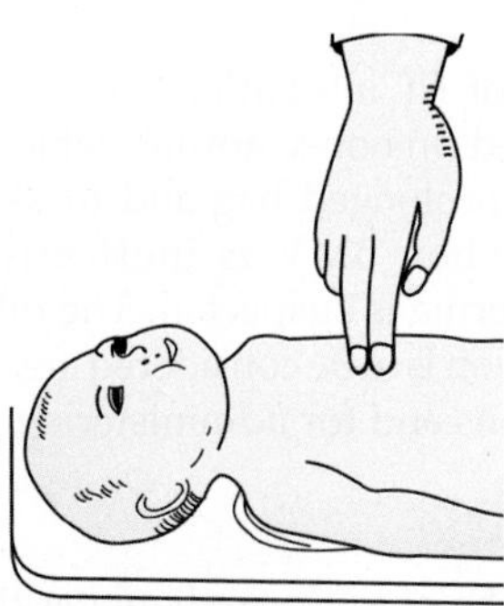

Fig. 7.5: Chest compression with two finger technique

7

When chest compressions are performed on a neonate, pressure is applied to the lower third of the sternum. Care must be used to avoid applying pressure to the xiphoid. To locate the area, slide your finger on the lower edge of thoracic cage and locate xiphisternum. The lower third of the sternum is just above it.

Rate

It is important to ventilate between chest compressions. A ventilation breath should follow every third chest compression. In one minute, 90 chest compressions and 30 breaths are administered, (a total of 120 events). To obtain the proper ratio of 90 compressions and 30 ventilations in 1 minute (3:1), you must compress the chest three times in 1½ seconds, leaving approximately ½ second for ventilation.

Your thumbs or the tips of your fingers (depending on the method you use) should remain in contact with the chest during compression and *release*. Do not lift your thumbs or fingers off the chest between compressions.

It is important to know whether the blood is being circulated effectively by chest compressions. To determine this, the carotid or femoral pulse should be checked periodically.

Chest compressions can cause trauma to the infant. The dangers of chest compressions are: broken ribs, laceration of liver and pneumothorax.

EVALUATION

After a period of 30 seconds of chest compressions, the heart rate is checked.

- **HR below 60:** Chest compressions should continue along with bag and mask ventilation. In addition, medications (epinephrine) have to be administered.
- **HR 60 or above:** Chest compressions should be discontinued. BMV should be continued until the heart rate is above 100 beats per minute and the infant is breathing spontaneously.

Endotracheal Intubation

Endotracheal (ET) intubation is required in only a small proportion of asphyxiated neonates. Intubation is a relatively difficult skill to master and it requires frequent practice to maintain mastery over this skill.

Indications

The indications of ET intubation are: (i) when tracheal suction is required (in non-vigorous babies born through MSL), (ii) when prolonged bag and mask ventilation is required, (iii) when BMV is ineffective, (iv) when diaphragmatic hernia is suspected. The other conditions where ET intubation is to be considered are: before starting chest compressions and for administering medications.

Endotracheal Tube

The tube should be of uniform diameter throughout the length of the tube (and not tapered near the tip) and have vocal cord guide and centimeter markings. ET tube size depends on the weight or gestation of the baby. Appropriate sizes of the tube for newborns of different gestation are shown in Table 7.4.

Table 7.4: Appropriate endotracheal tube size by gestational age

Tube size Inner diameter (mm)	*Weight (g)*	*Gestational age (weeks)*
2.5	<1000	<28
3.0	1000–2000	28–34
3.5	2000–3000	34–38
4.0	>3000	>38

Most endotracheal tubes currently manufactured for neonates have a black line near the tip of the tube which is called a vocal cord guide. Such tubes are meant to be inserted so that the vocal cord guide is placed at the level of the vocal cords. This usually positions the tip of the tube above the bifurcation of the trachea.

For intubation, a neonatal laryngoscope, with straight blades of sizes '0' (for preterm babies) and '1' (term babies) is required. Before intubating, the appropriate blade is attached to the handle of laryngoscope and the light is turned on.

Procedure

The infant's head should be in midline and the neck kept slightly extended. The laryngoscope is held in the left hand between the thumb and the first three fingers, with the blade pointing away from oneself. Standing at the head end of the infant, the blade is introduced in the mouth and advanced to just beyond the base of the tongue so that its tip rests in the vallecula. The blade is lifted (as shown in Fig. 7.6) and landmarks looked for; the epiglottis and glottis should come into view. The glottic opening is surrounded by vocal cords on the sides. Once the glottis and vocal cords are visualized, the ET tube is introduced into the right side of the mouth and its tip inserted into the glottis till the vocal cord guide is at the level of the glottis, thus positioning it halfway between the vocal cords and carina.

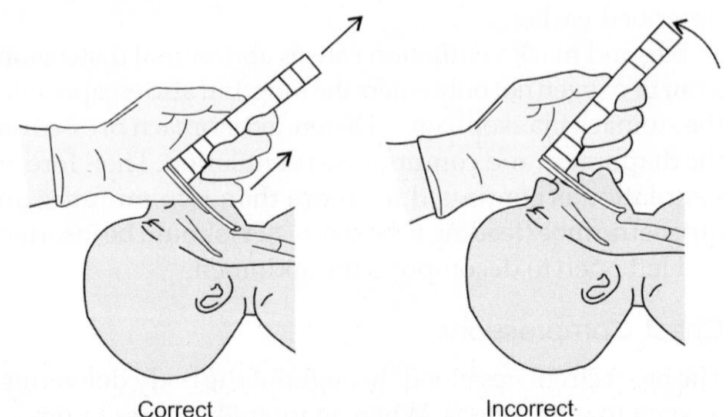

Fig. 7.6: Direction of pull on the laryngoscope

Medications

The majority of infants requiring resuscitation will have a response to prompt and effective ventilation with 100% oxygen. Only a few will require medications.

Medications used in resuscitation are epinephrine and volume expanders. Sodium bicarbonate and naloxone are indicated only for special circumstances (Table 7.5). There is no role of atropine, dexamethasone, calcium, mannitol and dextrose for resuscitation in the delivery room.

Route of medication: Since veins in scalp or extremities are difficult to access during resuscitation, umbilical vein is the preferred route via a catheter. No intracardiac injections are recommended in neonates.

For umbilical vein catheterization, 3.5 Fr or 5 Fr umbilical catheter (or a feeding tube in an emergency), is inserted into the umbilical vein such that its tip is just inside the skin surface and there is free flow of blood. There is no need to insert the catheter any further. Direct injection into the umbilical cord is undesirable and should not be attempted.

Epinephrine may be injected directly into the bronchial tree through endotracheal tube. Since absorption by this route is erratic, this method is to be used only if venous access cannot be obtained. The drug is injected by a needle or a feeding tube (5 Fr) into the endotracheal tube, flushed with 0.5 mL of normal saline and disseminated into the lung by positive pressure ventilation.

Indications

Use of adrenaline is indicated if heart rate remains below 60 despite adequate ventilation with 100% oxygen and chest compressions for 30 seconds.

Table 7.5 shows indications and effects of drugs used for neonatal resuscitation.

Suggested reading

Kattwinkel J. Textbook of Neonatal Resuscitation. *In:* Kattwinkel J (ed). 5th ed. American Academy of Pediatrics and American Heart Association, 2005.

CARE AT BIRTH AND DURING FIRST FEW WEEKS OF LIFE

Prevention of Infection

In every step of newborn care and for every person who comes in contact with neonates (especially health care staff, who come in contact with multiple neonates, and older children, who are ideal vehicles for infection transmission), the importance of maintaining cleanliness and asepsis cannot be overemphasized. A few simple and inexpensive ways to ensure this are:

- *Clean environment:* One should follow the "5 cleans" of birthing process, including clean hands, clean delivery surface, clean cord cut (using a sterile instrument or new blade to cut the umbilical cord), clean cord tie and clean cord stump.

Table 7.5: Medications: indications, dosages and effects

Medication (Concentration available in India)	*Indication*	*Effects*	*Concentration to be administered*	*Amount to dilute and prepare*	*Dose of the prepared solution*	*Route*
Epinephrine (1:1000)	HR <60/min after 30 secs of positive pressure ventilation and chest compressions	Inotropic; chronotropic; peripheral vasoconstrictor	1:10000 (i.e. diluted × 10)	0.5 mL in 5 mL 1.0 mL in 10 mL	0.1 mL/kg to 0.3 mL/kg	Intravenous: through umbilical vein (consider endotracheal route if IV access can not be obtained)
Volume expanders (Normal saline, Ringer lactate)	Evidence of acute bleeding with signs of hypovolemia	Increased intravascular volume, better tissue perfusion, less acidosis		40 mL in infusion set or multiple syringes	10 mL/kg	Umbilical vein
Naloxone (0.4 mg/mL)	Respiratory depression with history of narcotic administration 4 hrs before delivery. Administer only after positive pressure ventilation has restored oxygenation.	Narcotic antagonst	0.4 mg/mL	2 mL in a syringe	0.25 mL/kg (i.e. 0.1 mg/kg)	Intravenous: preferred; intramuscular: acceptable but delayed onset of action

Note: Use of sodium bicarbonate is required only if asphyxia is very prolonged and there is a documented metabolic acidosis even after the use of epinephrine and volume expanders. It should be remembered that the mainstay of therapy of metabolic acidosis is oxygenation and volume expansion, and not sodium bicarbonate. Sodium bicarbonate therapy, if used, must be preceded, accompanied and followed by ventilation.

- *Hand washing for care-givers:* It is the *single most effective* method to prevent nosocomial transmission of infection.
- *Strict asepsis* should be maintained during procedures.
- *No sharing:* Sharing of equipment, sheets, towels, medicines, syringes, etc. among neonates increases the chances of infection transmission significantly and should be avoided. Even in a facility with limited resources the cost of maintaining separate items for newborns is rarely ever higher than sepsis management and its consequences.
- *Parental education:* Parental counseling should be done to underline the importance of hygiene practice at home and illustrate methods in which it can be done.

Drying and Temperature Maintenance

Immediately following delivery, if the mother and baby's condition allow it, baby can be put on the mother's abdomen in direct skin to skin contact and then dried as the cord is being cut. Alternately, baby can be carried to a preheated area or under the radiant warmer. Wet skin can result in a large amount of heat loss with seriously detrimental hypothermia. Therefore, one of the first steps after birth is thorough drying of the body and especially the head, which constitutes a large part of the neonatal surface area. The vernix, the cheesy material stuck on newborn skin made of dead skin, hair and secretions, serves to conserve heat and protect the delicate newborn skin from environmental stress; no attempt is made to remove this. After examination, baby is wrapped in clothes including a cap, and given to mother to allow first breastfeed and gain heat from mother's proximity.

Cord Care

The umbilical cord is clamped soon after delivery without any undue haste or delay. After stabilization and drying of the baby, following method is used to cut cord:

Using two clean ligatures and a new blade, the first ligature is tied about 2 cm from the abdomen of the baby (to avoid inclusion of any gut wall present in the cord as part of undetected omphalocele, and to leave adequate length for umbilical catheter insertion, if required). Second ligature is tied 5 cm from the abdomen and the cord between the 2 ligatures is cut using a new blade (second ligature is applied to avoid spilling of blood). One should check the cut end of cord for normal anatomy, i.e. two arteries and one vein. The cord is left dry and open; one should not apply anything on the cord and avoid touching it (Fig. 7.7).

Eye Care

Eyes are cleaned with sterile normal saline-soaked cloth, using separate edges or pieces for the two eyes. The cloth is moved over the lower edge of eyelid from medial to lateral canthi. No application is recommended unless there was evidence of gonococcal infection in mother, in which case 1% silver nitrate is applied to both eyes.

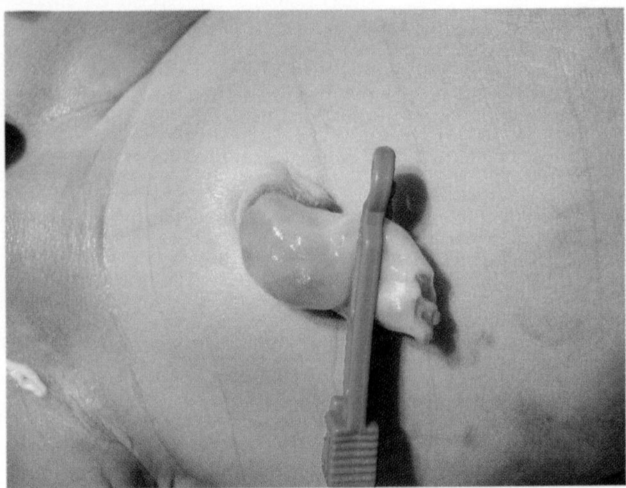

Fig. 7.7: Correct application of the umbilical clamp

Vitamin K Prophylaxis

Vitamin K is produced in the human body from bacteria colonizing the gut. In babies the relative absence of such microorganisms and the deficiency of vitamin K in breast milk predispose the baby to its deficiency. This deficiency can manifest as **vitamin K deficiency bleeding** with formation of subcutaneous hematomas, ecchymosis, mucosal bleeding and life-threatening intracranial bleed. Laboratory studies reveal prolonged prothrombin and activated partial thromboplastin time. In order to prevent this, vitamin K should be given intramuscularly at birth in a dose of 1 mg to all babies 1 kg or more and 0.5 mg to those <1 kg.

Nutrition

Breast milk is the best source of nutrition for infants until 6 months of age. Information regarding breastfeeding and its technique need to be discussed with the mother, both during antenatal and postnatal period, not just once but in every visit so that its importance is reinforced and all maternal concerns are addressed.

Common Concerns during Neonatal Care

- *Weight loss in first week:* Normally babies lose 8–10% of birth weight in the first week of life which is regained by 7–10 days age. Subsequently there should be a gain of 20 to 40 gram per day.
- *Crying during micturition:* The sensation of a full bladder is uncomfortable to many babies who cry *before* passing urine and stop as soon as micturition starts. Crying *during* passage of urine as opposed to *before* it should alert clinician to the possibility of urinary tract infection.
- *Bathing:* During the first week, till cord falls off, only sponging is recommended which can be given after the first 24 hrs of life. Later, bathing every 2–3 days is quite

sufficient. A draught-free warm room, warm water and quick completion of bath ensure that the baby doesn't get cold during bathing. The head constitutes a large surface area of the baby; therefore, it should be washed last and dried first. Bathing time can be used to inspect baby's cord, eyes and skin for any discharge, rash or redness.

- *Cosmetics:* Babies have a sensitive skin and use of cosmetics should be minimized. A low alkalinity, mild, non-perfumed/non-medicated soap should be used. Any oil except mustard oil can be used; massaging babies increases human touch and contact with baby and is beneficial. Sprinkling talc on babies can result in inhalation and so should be avoided; one should apply it sparingly if at all and avoid products containing boric acid (present in most prickly heat preparations). *Kajal* can be harmful to the baby's eyes and, therefore, should not be applied.
- *Redness around umbilicus:* Umbilical cord normally falls off in 7–10 days and the wound heals in about 15 days. It should be kept dry, without any application or bandaging. To avoid soiling, diaper should be folded such that its upper margin lies below stump. If soiled, the cord should be washed with clean water and soap and dried with a clean cloth.
  Any redness or induration around the umbilicus or pus drainage from it should alert the clinician to omphalitis. *Omphalitis* starts as a local infection of the umbilicus, usually from unclean handling or application of unclean substances to the cord. It can spread to cause life-threatening systemic sepsis. One should take a swab for gram staining and culture if any discharge is present. If the area of redness extends to <1 cm of surrounding area and no other sign of sepsis is present, local cleaning with antiseptic solution, followed by application of 0.5% gentian violet four times a day till redness subsides, usually suffices. If redness in surrounding area is >1 cm or there are signs of sepsis, then, in addition to local therapy, systemic antibiotic should be started as in management of septicemia.
- *Regurgitation:* Babies commonly regurgitate small amount of curdled milk soon after feeding. This behavior is normal and as long as the baby gains weight and passes urine 6–8 times a day it does not require any treatment other than reassurance.
- *Frequent stools:* During the first few days of life, the stool color in breastfed neonates changes from green meconium to yellow seedy stools by the end of the week. In between the stools appear loose ('transitional stools') and may cause unnecessary anxiety to the family. The stool frequency can increase to several times per day, and is attributed to the enhanced gastrocolic reflex in neonates which results in the passage of small stools just after feeding. If the baby remains well hydrated, has no signs of sepsis, feeds well, passes urine 6–8 times per day and gains weight, there is no cause for concern. The parents should be reassured accordingly to allay their anxiety.
- *Breast discharge:* Under the effect of transplacentally transmitted hormones, the breasts of both boys and girls may get hypertrophied and may even secrete a milk like fluid from the enlarged breast bud. Squeezing it causes pain and can harm the baby, hence it must be avoided. It resolves spontaneously in a few days and should cause no worry.
- *Rashes and skin peeling:* Papular lesions on an erythematous base can be seen in many babies; dispersed over the trunk and face, these are commonly seen on day two or three of life. These lesions called *erythema toxicum*, are eosinophil-filled sterile lesions that are normal, resolve spontaneously and require no treatment (Fig. 7.8). Pus filled lesions or pyoderma, on the other hand, are neutrophil-filled lesions occurring in response to local infection of glands in the skin, commonly in skin creases where dirt accumulates, like thigh fold, back of neck, etc. If these are <10 in number and there are no signs of sepsis, local cleaning with antiseptic solution and application of 0.5% gentian violet along with monitoring for resolution and new lesions suffices. Further investigation, and treatment as for sepsis, is indicated if there are >10 lesions, signs of sepsis or non-resolution after topical treatment. Skin peeling is another normal skin finding noted especially in post-term and IUGR babies. Oil massaging can decrease the flaking but no other intervention is required.
- *Physiological jaundice:* Almost 60% of normal newborn babies develop clinically detectable jaundice (>5 mg/dL). Onset is usually on day 2–3 of life, reaching a peak on day 3–4 and subsiding spontaneously within 7–10 days. However, in some babies this level can reach high enough to cause brain damage. Signs suggesting pathological jaundice are discussed later on page 147.

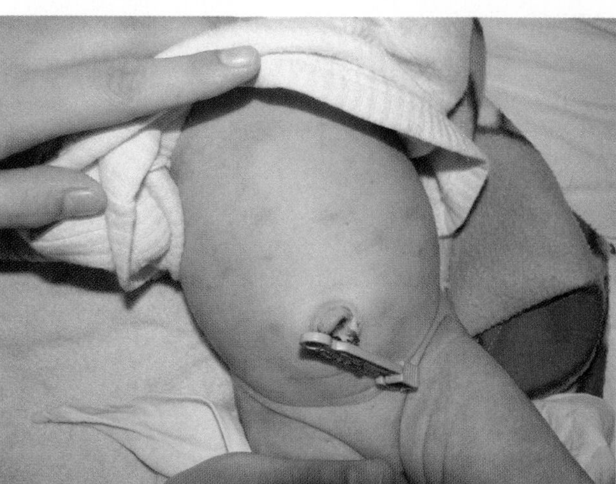

Fig. 7.8: Erythema toxicum

- *Oral thrush:* White patchy lesions on the oral mucosa and tongue that are difficult to wipe off and leave hemorrhagic points when removed suggest candidiasis. Neonatal period is the only time when candidiasis occurs in otherwise healthy babies. Nystatin application four times a day after feed, till 2 days after resolution, is recommended. Application of nystatin on mother's breast during this treatment ensures that mother is treated for any local infection and recurrent infection of baby is prevented.
- *Diaper rash:* Two types of diaper rash are seen, namely, ammoniacal and candidal. Their key features and treatment are shown in Table 7.6.

Table 7.6: Comparison of types of diaper rash

Feature	*Ammoniacal*	*Candidal*
Etiology	Dermatitis from prolonged skin contact with irritating chemicals in urine	Skin infection with candida; source being commensals from environment causing infection in predisposed normal newborns
Presentation	Skin creases are spared; red areas with or without blisters; painful	Skin creases are primarily affected; red lesions with edges showing satellite lesions
Treatment	Leave open; change diapers frequently; application of zinc oxide for soothing effect	Application of nystatin cream four times a day till lesions resolve.

- *Eye discharge:* Eye discharge is a common problem among neonates. It may represent minor problems such as sticky eyes or transient nasolacrimal duct obstruction, or may be due to serious infections (Table 7.7).

At Discharge

In cases of institutional delivery, the following should be ensured at discharge:

- Through counseling, parents have been enabled to be confident to look after the baby at home.
- BCG, OPV and hepatitis B vaccine have been administered, and information regarding when and where to come for future immunization given.
- The baby has been examined, at discharge, with special attention to the following:
  - Vital signs
  - Signs of illness (no 'danger signs')
  - Skin for jaundice
  - Cardiovascular system for new murmurs
- Parents have been explained the following 'danger signs', in presence of any of which they should bring the baby to the hospital:
  - Poor feeding
  - Fever or low body temperature
  - Lethargy or less movements
  - Yellowish discoloration of legs and hands
  - Fit(s)
  - Fast breathing
  - Excessive crying
- A date for follow up has been assigned: A normal newborn in whom breastfeeding is well established can be seen at 6 weeks of age when the next vaccinations are scheduled. In presence of any high risk factor (e.g. low birth weight, prematurity, jaundice, or feeding not established), the baby should be seen within 3 days of discharge.

EVALUATION OF NEWBORN

Most neonates are born healthy, normal and free from disease. Only a few (approx 3%) of them need observation in an intensive care in the nursery. The newborn examination yields different information at different times and hence, the newborn should be examined in detail at least at four points of time, namely, (1) soon after birth (2) at 24 hours of birth (3) before discharge from hospital and again (4) at follow up visit.

Immediately after birth, the Apgar scores are assigned at 1 and 5 minutes (Table 7.8). If the score is less than 7, it is assigned every 5 min until 20 minutes or till two successive score are 7 or greater. These scores rapidly assess the cardiopulmonary status; tell about need for resuscitation and its effectiveness. These scores may be falsely low in very preterms, maternal drug intake, congenital heart disease and central nervous system malformations. Hence, low Apgar scores should not be equated to asphyxia. The 1 min Apgar does not correlate with future outcome; a score of 0 to 3 at 5 minutes is associated with a risk of cerebral palsy (0.3% to 1%). Scores of less than 3 at 10, 15 and 20 minutes have a higher correlation but are nonspecific in the absence of other clinical correlates such as evidence of neuroencephalopathy.

If systemic examination reveals an abnormal finding, a more thorough physical examination and laboratory evaluation is warranted. Table 7.9 provides one of the sequences that can be used for the comprehensive history and examination of the newborn.

General Observation

The least disturbing examination should be done first; this gives an opportunity to assess the state, posture, spontaneous activity, color, any obvious respiratory distress or malformation. The five states of an infant are deep sleep, light sleep, awake and quiet, awake and active, and awake and crying. The states 2 and 3 (light sleep and quiet awake) are best for newborn examination.

A newborn with undue hypotonia may have an unflexed posture as seen in a baby with hypoxic encephalopathy. A clear note of the color of the baby,

Table 7.7: Conditions causing eye discharge in neonates

Condition	*History*	*Presentation*	*Gram staining and culture**	*Treatment*
Non-infectious causes				
Sticky eyes	Clear or white discharge in small amount resulting in sticking of eyelids	No redness, pus or swelling of eye and surrounding tissues	Sterile	An innocuous condition developing in some babies; requires only cleaning with a wet cloth.
Nasolacrimal duct obstruction	Clear watery discharge from eyes	No redness, pus or swelling of eye and surrounding tissues	Sterile	Due to narrow nasolacrimal duct formation. Massaging inner canthi of eye in a downward and lateral direction results in resolution of majority of cases.
Chemical conjunctivitis	History of some instillation in eye, most commonly silver nitrate	Redness and swelling present along with small amount of pus	Sterile	Resolves spontaneously.
Infectious causes				
Gonococcal conjunctivitis	Onset before 3rd day; h/o sexually transmitted disease in mother	Both eyes are grossly swollen, red with copius purulent discharge	Gram-positive diplococci	Clean eyes using sterile saline soaked cotton from inner canthi to out along the edge of eye. Injection ceftriaxone 25–50 mg/kg IM given once #
Chlamydial conjunctivitis	Onset after 3 days; h/o sexually transmitted disease in mother; starts as a watery discharge	Moderate amount of redness and swelling bilaterally	No organism/ no growth	Clean eyes as above. Oral erythromycin 50 mg/kg/day in 4 divided doses for 14 days. Topical treatment is ineffective and is not indicated. Untreated chlamydial conjunctivitis can progress to pneumonia in some infants.
Staphylococcal conjunctivitis	Onset after day 3	Unilateral with moderate redness and pus	Gram-positive cocci in clusters	Clean eyes as above. Antibiotic ointment containing various combinations of bacitracin, neomycin, ciprofloxacin or polymyxin several times a day for 7–10 days.

* In the absence of gram stain results in a case of suspected bacterial conjunctivitis, if baby <7 days treat for gonococcal, and if >7days or not responding to treatment for gonococcus, treat for Chlamydia.

Treat mother and sexual partner if not already treated.

Table 7.8: Apgar score

Sign	*0*	*1*	*2*
Heart rate	Absent	Slow (<100 beats/min)	Normal (>100 beats/min)
Respirations	Absent	Weak cry	Good strong cry
Muscle tone	Limp	Some flexion	Active movements
Reflex irritability	No response	Grimace	Cough or sneeze
Color	Blue or pale	Body pink, extremities blue	Completely pink

including cyanosis, pallor, jaundice, plethora and ashen color should be made. One should also look at the spontaneous movements shown by the baby.

Vital signs

In a sick baby vitals take a priority over all other examination. Temperature is measured in the apex of the baby's axilla by holding the thermometer for at least 3 minutes. Rectal temperature may be recorded to differentiate fever associated with infection and environmental hyperthermia. The finding of hypothermia (temperature

Table 7.9: Newborn history and examination: a format for case presentation

HISTORY	
General	Mother's name and age, parity, last menstrual period, expected date of delivery.
Past obstetric history	Past pregnancies: when, gestation, neonatal problems, present status.
Antenatal care	Registration, contacts (when, number), where/by whom, tests (Hb, urine albumin/sugar, cultures, ultrasound, blood group, VDRL, HIV, others), TT immunization, diet, supplements (iron, folic acid, calcium, iodine).
Obstetric/ medical complications	Obstetric complications (toxemia, UTI, twins/triplets, placenta previa, accidental hemorrhage); fetal problems (IUGR, hydrops, Rh isoimmunization); medical problems (diabetes, hypertension); investigations, medications, course.
Labor	Presentation, lie, onset of labor (spontaneous /induced), rupture of membranes (spontaneous/artificial), liquor (clear/ meconium stained); duration of first and second stage of labor; fetal heart rate (tachycardia, bradycardia, irregular).
Delivery	Place of delivery, conducted by whom, vaginal (spontaneous/forceps/vacuum), cesarean (indication, elective/emergency); local/general anesthesia; other drugs; duration of third stage; postpartum hemorrhage.
Immediate care at birth	Resuscitation, time of first breath /cry, Apgar scores if known; cord care; passage of urine/stool.
Feeding history	What feeds; breastfeeding (when initiated, frequency, adequacy); other feeds (what, how fed).
Postnatal problems	Any problems experienced (e.g. feeding problems, jaundice, eye discharge, fever, etc.), their course/investigations/treatment; any problems at present.
Family history	History of health problems in the family.
Past medical problems	History of past medical problems, if any.
Personal/ social history	Socioeconomic status, family support.
EXAMINATION	
Immediately after birth	Weight, gestation, congenital anomalies, sex assigning, Apgar scores, umbilical vessel examination, examination of placenta.
GENERAL	
Appearance	Overall appearance: well/sick look; alert/ unconscious.
Vital signs	Temperature, cold stress; respiratory rate, retractions, grunt/stridor; heart rate, palpable femorals; blood pressure, capillary refill time; cry; apneic spells.
Anthropometry	Weight, length, head circumference, chest circumference.
Gestation	Assessment by physical criteria; more detailed assessment by New Ballard. examination.
Classification by intrauterine growth	Appropriate/small/large for gestational age; symmetric or asymmetric small for gestational age; signs of IUGR (loose folds of skin, poor muscle mass, wrinkles over thighs/buttocks.
Congenital anomalies	Head to toe examination for malformations/ abnormalities.
Birth trauma	Search for trauma; cephalohematoma.
Common signs	Cyanosis, jaundice (extent), bleed, pustules, edema, pallor, bleeding, fontanel.
Special signs	Caput, eye discharge, umbilical examination (stump, discharge, redness), jitteriness, eye discharge, oral thrush development peculiarities (toxic erythema, Epstein pearls, breast engorgement, vaginal bleeding, capillary hemangiomas, Mongolian spot).
Feeding	Observe feeding on breast (check signs of positioning and attachment).
Reflexes	Moro, grasp, rooting.
SYSTEMIC EXAMINATION	
Chest	Shape, distress, retractions, air entry, adventitious sounds.
CVS	Precordium, apical impulse, heart sounds/ murmur.
Abdomen	Distension, wall edema, tenderness, palpable liver/spleen/kidneys, any other lump, ascites, hernial sites, gonads, genitalia.
Musculo-skeletal system	Deformities, tests for developmental dysplasia of hip, club foot.
Central nervous system	State; cranial nerve examination (vision, pupils, eye movement examination, facial sensation and motility, hearing, sucking and swallowing); motor examination (tone and posture, power, tendon reflexes)

UTI urinary tract infection, IUGR intrauterine growth retardation

of less than 36.5°C) in neonate has very important connotations. Cold stress is assessed by touching the abdomen and the palms/soles. In cold stress, palms and soles are colder to touch than the abdomen. Neonates have a normal respiratory rate of 40–60 breaths/minute. The heart rate is faster in preterms compared to term. The normal range is 110–160 beats per minute. Bradycardia (rate <80/min) may be associated with heart disease while tachycardia (rate >160/min) may be due to sepsis, anemia, fever or congestive cardiac failure. Blood pressure may be measured by the flush method, doppler monitoring or direct intravascular measurement. The measurement may be inaccurate due to activity of the baby or wrong cuff size (the cuff should ideally have a width 50–67% of arm length and bladder should cover the full limb). Capillary refill time is estimated by applying firm pressure on the sternum area for 5 seconds than releasing and observing the time taken to refill. The refill time is prolonged (more than 3 sec) in case of hypothermia and shock.

Assessment of Size and Growth

Depending on the weight the neonates are termed as low birth weight (less than 2500 g), very low birth weight (less than 1500 g) or extremely low birth weight (less than 1000 g). The aberrant growth pattern is assessed by plotting the weight against the gestational age on a standard intrauterine growth curve (which is different from postnatal growth curves used for normal babies), as shown in Fig. 7.9. A neonate whose weight falls between the 10th and 90th percentile is considered as appropriate for gestational age (AGA); if the weight falls below 10th percentile, the neonate is classified as small for gestational age (SGA); the neonate is classified as large for gestational age (LGA) if the weight falls above 90th percentile for gestational age.

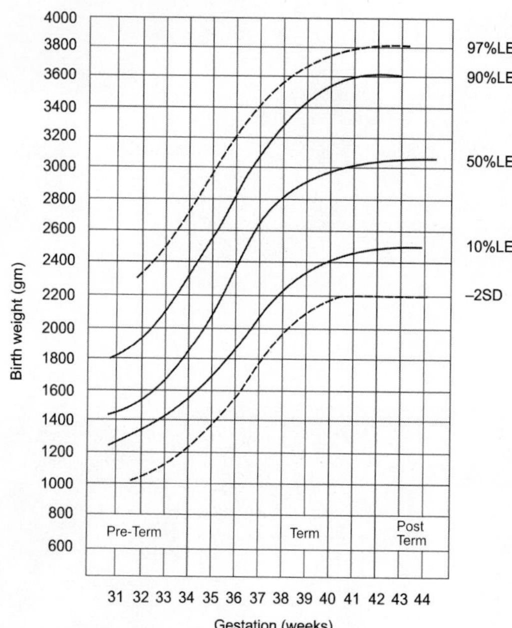

Fig. 7.9: Intrauterine growth curves

Anthropometry

The weight is measured in grams (g). Length is measured using an infantometer. The newborn baby at birth is about 50 cm long. Head circumference is measured by placing a soft non-stretchable tape around the head just above the eyebrows and finding the largest circumference over the occiput. This is 33–37 cm at birth in term babies (Fig. 7.10). Chest circumference at the level of nipples is about 3 cm less than HC. If this difference is more than 3 cm, it may be an indicator of intrauterine growth retardation. The Ponderal index (P.I.) is calculated by multiplying the

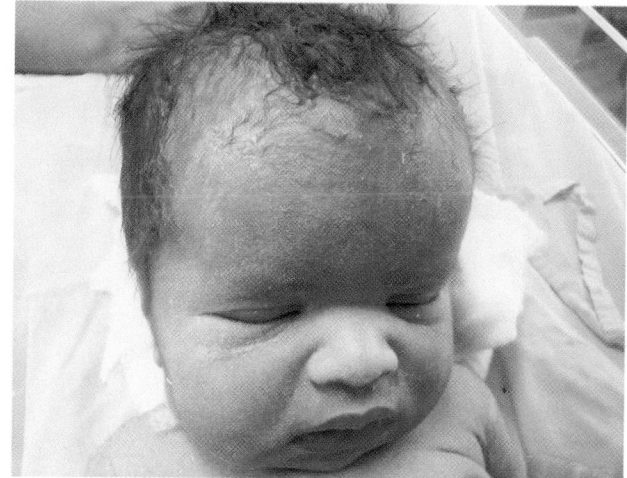

Fig. 7.10: A newborn infant with large head (macrocephaly); note bossings of both frontal eminences

weight in grams by hundred and then dividing by cube of length in cm $\frac{\text{Wt (gm)} \times 100}{\text{Length (cm)}^3}$. This parameter is usually less than 2 in asymmetrically growth retarded baby and 2 or more in a baby who has either normal growth or has symmetrical growth retardation.

Assessment of Gestational Age

The gestational age helps classify the neonates as preterm (<37 week), postterm (≥42 week) or term (37–41 completed weeks). In preterm infants (i) deep sole creases are absent or limited to anterior 1/3rd; (2) breast nodule is less than 5 mm; (iii) ear cartilage has poor elastic recoil; (iv) hair is fuzzy; (v) testes are at the external ring and scrotum has few rugosities; and labia majora in females are widely separated exposing labia minora and clitoris. Figs 7.11 (A) to (L) depict the differences in physical characteristics that help differentiate between preterm and term neonates at birth.

The detailed evaluation requires evaluation of physical features and neurological maturity. The scoring system commonly used is the Expanded New Ballard Scores (ENBS) which has a range of accuracy to within 1 week.

Regional General Examination

Skin and hair: The skin is examined with regard to scaliness, elasticity and thickness, and for edema, rashes and lesions like hemangioma. Jaundice is detected by compressing on the skin so that the color imparted by the hemoglobin in the blood vessels is eliminated and the yellow color due to billirubin is highlighted. The skin may exhibit minor clinical problems that are normal, innocuous and self-limiting. Ecchymoses or petechiae may relate to birth trauma, especially if present on head and necklace region. The hair should be observed carefully. Lanugo are the fine hair of fetal period that

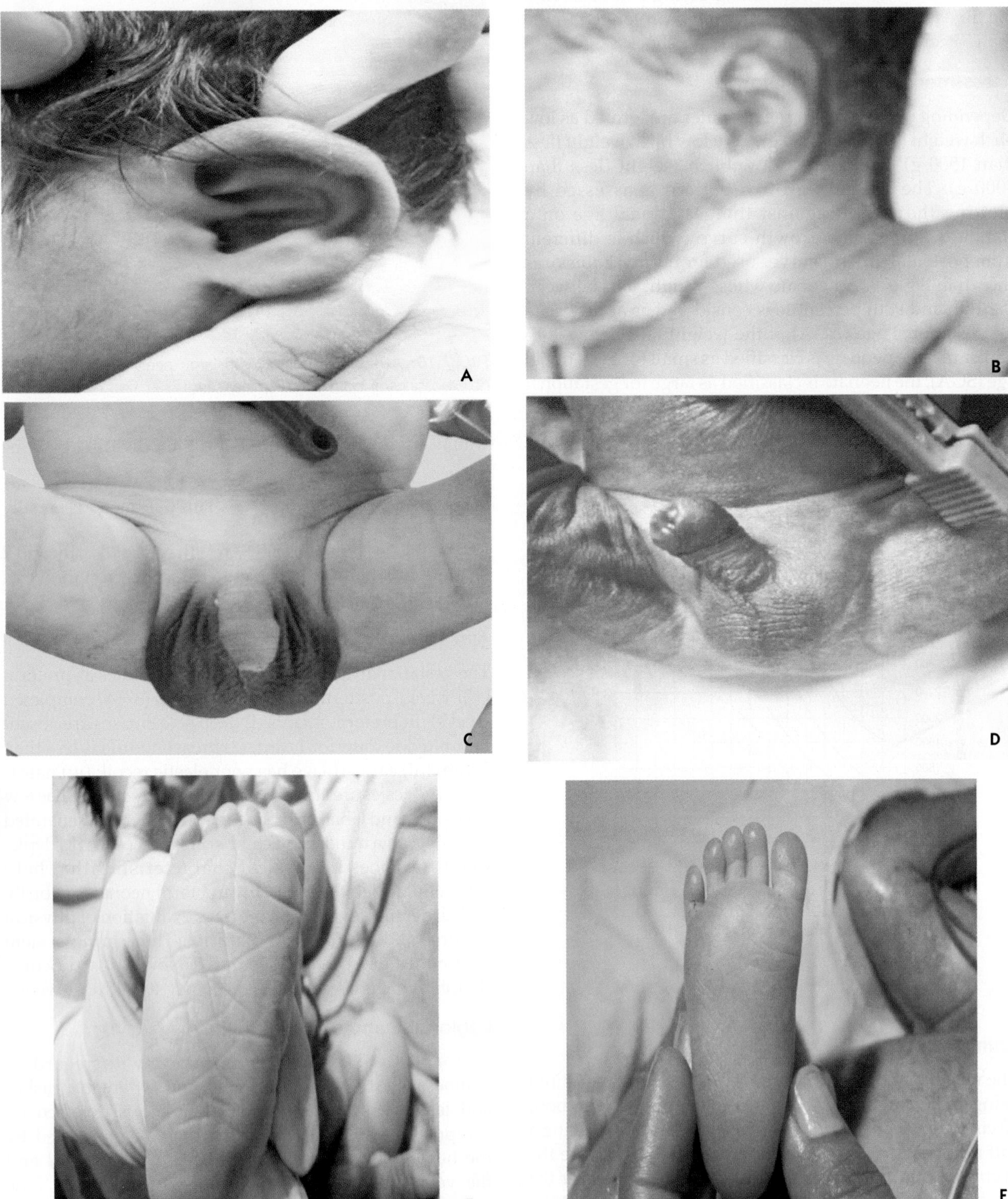

Figs 7.11A to F: Salient difference in physical characteristics of preterm and term neonates (A) Well-curved pinna, cartilage reaching up to periphery (B) Flat and soft pinna, cartilage not reaching up to periphery (C) Well pigmented and pendulous scrotal sacs, with fully descended testes (D) Light pigmentation and not yet descended testes (E) Deep transverse creases on the soles (F) Faint marks on the sole, no deep creases

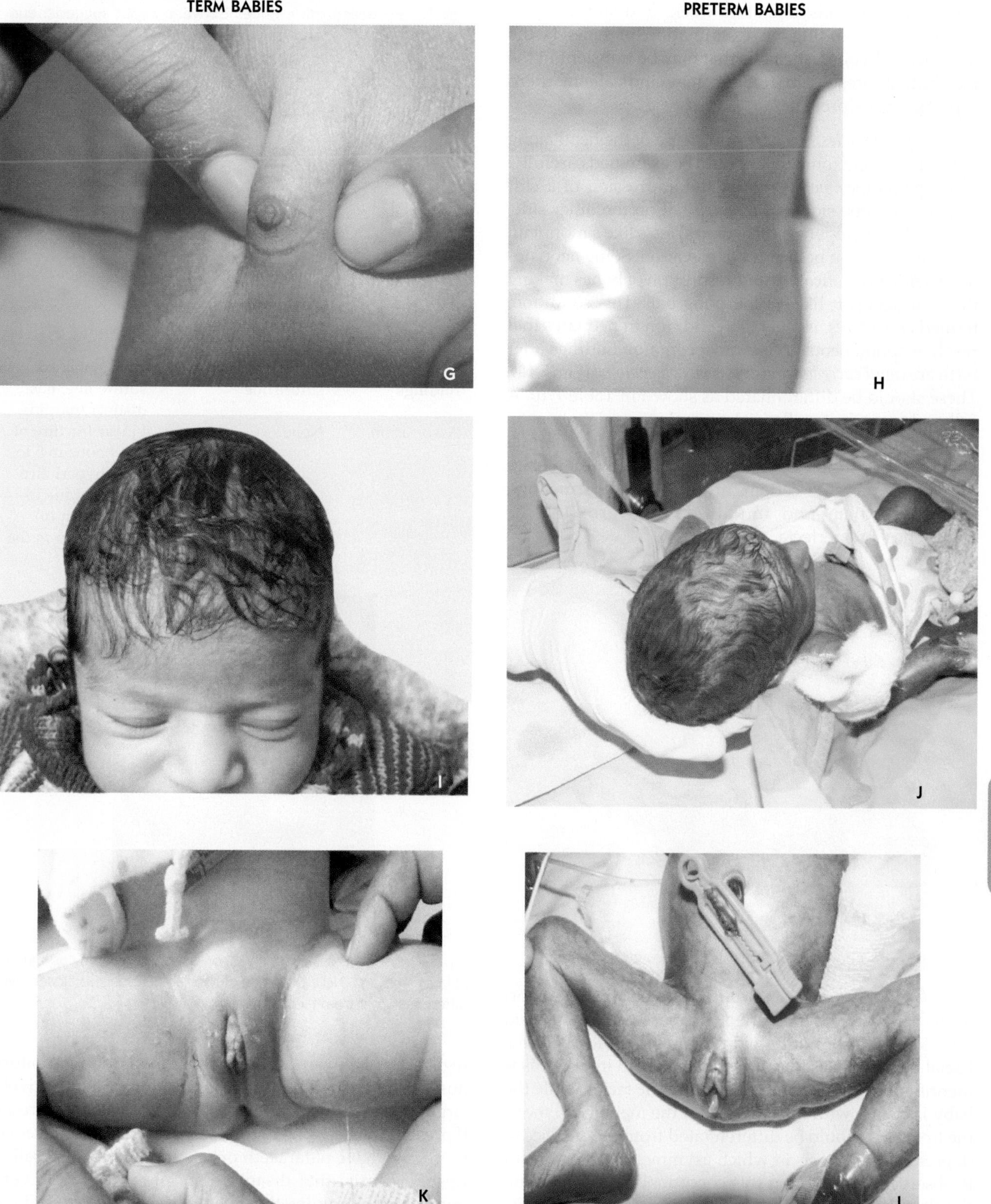

Figs 7.11G to L: Salient difference in physical characteristics of preterm and term neonates (G) Well formed breast bud (>5 mm) (H) Poorly developed breast bud (I) Silky hair-individual strands can be made out (J) Fuzzy hair (K) Labia majora covering clitoris and labia minora (L) Prominent labia minora and clitoris

shed in two periods; one at 28 weeks and later at term. The common finding on examination of nails is the presence of hypoplastic nails that may be transient in the toe, but, if present in fingers, may indicate in utero exposure to valproate.

Head and fontanelles: The size and shape of the head along with sutures and fontanelle should be examined carefully. Upon palpation, *molding* gives the impression of a cliff with rise on one side and a sharp fall on the other side, whereas a *synostosis* (fusion of bones) feels like a mountain range with rise on both sides of elevation. Some neonates have delayed ossification and resorption of bones making the skull feel soft like a ping pong ball. This condition, termed *craniotabes*, is a benign condition in neonates that resolves spontaneously. The most common findings after birth are *caput succedaneum* and *cephalohematoma* (Fig. 7.12). These should be differentiated as shown in Table 7.10. A full and tense fontanelle is abnormal in a quiet neonate. Large fontanelles and split sutures are most often normal variants but they can be associated with increased intracranial pressure, certain chromosomal abnormalities, hypothyroidism and impaired bone growth like osteogenesis imperfecta.

Table 7.10: Salient differences between caput succedaneum and cephalohematoma

Characteristic	*Caput succedaneum*	*Cephalohematoma*
Incidence	Common	Less common
Location	Subcutaneous plane	Located over parietal bones, between skull and periosteum.
Time of presentation	Maximum size and firmness at birth	Increasing size for 12– 24 hrs and than stable.
Clinical time course	Softens progressively from birth and resolves within 2 or 3 days	Takes 3 to 6 weeks to resolve
Characteristic findings	Diffuse, crosses suture line	Does not cross suture line, has distinct margins.
Association	None	Linear fracture of skull bone in 5 to 25%; hyperbilirubinemia (due to breakdown of hemoglobin in the bleed)

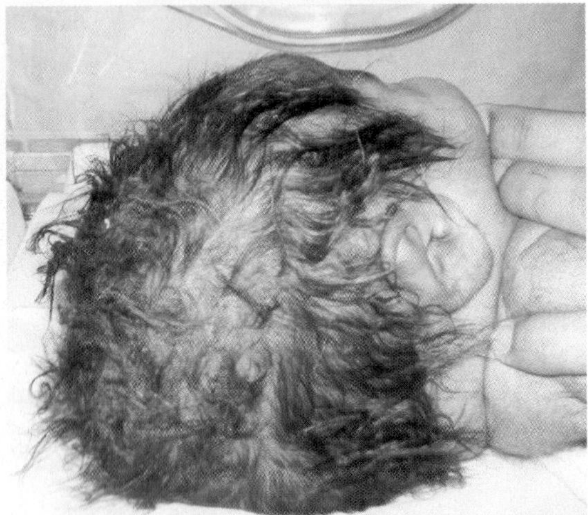

Fig. 7.12: Cephalohematoma: note the overlying bruising

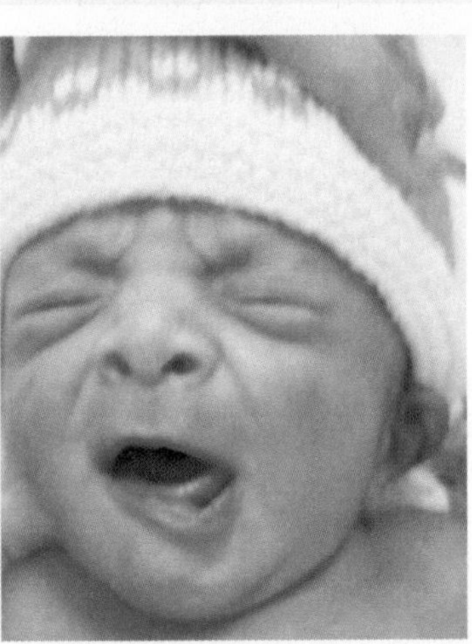

Fig. 7.13: Absent depressor anguli oris muscle depicting asymmetry of face on crying. Note presence of nasolabial folds and closed eyes differentiating it from facial palsy

Neck, face, eyes and ears: Newborns universally have short necks. The neck is examined for masses like enlarged thyroid gland, sternomastoid tumor and cystic hygroma. Facial nerve paresis may occur due to birth injury; this is identified by the presence of asymmetric facies while the baby is crying with open eyes, and the inability to move the lips. This should be differentiated from the absence of depressor anguli oris in which asymmetric crying facies is observed; however, in this condition, the eyes remain tightly shut while crying (Fig. 7.13). Nose is looked for its size, shape, secretions, patency and flaring. The patency of the nose can be checked by holding a wisp of cotton at the orifice while occluding the other nares. The flaring of the nostrils indicates an increase in respiratory efforts regardless of the cause. The newborn infants are obligatory nose breathers because of the apposition of the relatively large tongue to the palate. Hence, bilateral choanal atresia, if present, causes severe respiratory distress. The alveolar ridge may have natal teeth or retention cysts (also called Epstein pearls) that disappear in few weeks. It is very important to examine the palate for cleft. The eyes of the infant may be opened spontaneously with to and fro rocking during which the head is elevated; this permits eyes to be inspected and observed for visual tracking assessment of the examiner's face. The globe in a neonate is 70% the size in an adult and the cornea is 80% of the adult size. The two eyes and the space in between the eyes are in 1–1–1 relation. The nasolacrimal duct is not fully patent in most neonates, but epiphora is observed in only few newborns. Subconjunctival hemorrhages are common after vaginal delivery and resolve spontaneously. The cornea should be clear. Pupils should be equal in size, reactive to light, and symmetrical. The pupil should be inspected for the red reflex. The wide beam of the ophthalmoscope or a torch is used so that the circle of light covers both the eyes, and the focus is adjusted to give a distinct glow in the pupils. One should look for the brightness and position of the red reflex. A positive red reflex rules out lenticular and anterior or posterior chamber opacity.

Gross hearing is often inaccurately assessed by looking for blink on response to noise. More formal hearing screening for all newborns is now recommended. Accessory auricles and preauricular tags are a common finding that may be associated with renal anomalies.

Umbilicus, anus and spine: At birth it is important to inspect the number of vessels in the umbilical cord. A single umbilical artery may be found in 0.7% of live births; this may be associated with renal and gastrointestinal tract anomalies. In intrauterine growth retarded babies the cord is long and thin, with very little Wharton jelly. After cord separation the umbilicus is examined for evidence for complete healing and the presence of umbilical granuloma.

One should palpate the base of the umbilical cord for a hernia and estimate the diameter of the fascial opening (Fig. 7.14). The spine should be examined with fingers to exclude spina bifida, masses and any scoliosis. The anal opening should be examined for its patency and position.

Genitalia (male and female): The genital area is examined by the hips abducted in the supine position. The urethra and clitoris are examined for patency and cliteromegally respectively.

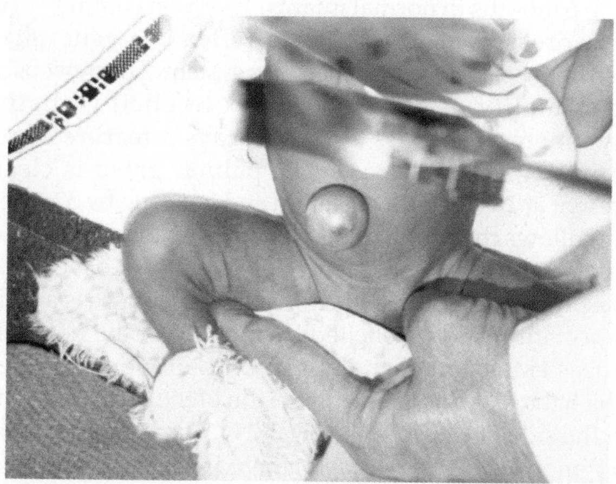

Fig. 7.14: Umbilical hernia

Extremities: One should make sure that the arms and limbs are fully movable with no evidence of dislocation or asymmetry of movements. The fingers are counted and any abnormality noted like nail hypoplasia, syndactyly, polydactyly, oligodactyly or unequal limbs. A calcaneo-valgus deformity is usually self-correcting within the next few months but equinovarus is much more sinister and should be brought to the notice of an orthopedic specialist (Fig. 7.15).

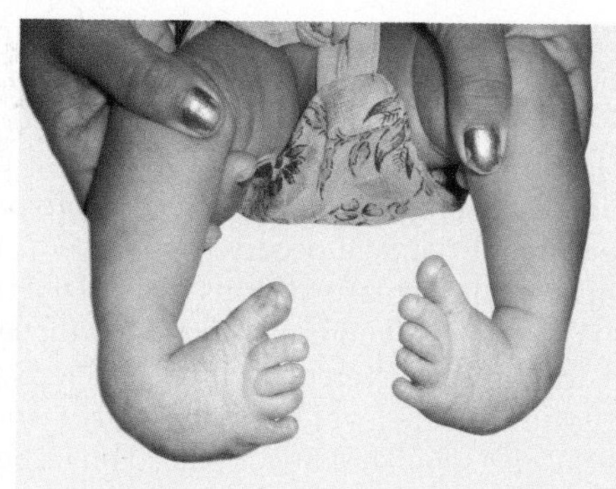

Fig. 7.15: Congenital talipes equinovarus deformity

Systemic Examination

Chest: The anteroposterior diameter of the neonate's chest is roughly same as the transverse diameter. Respiratory distress is indicated by nasal flaring, grunting, tachypnea and intercostal and subcostal retractions. Such distress may indicate pneumonia, respiratory distress syndrome (RDS), delayed reabsorption of lung fluid or any other cardiorespiratory cause. Stridor may be inspiratory, indicating large airway obstruction, or there may be expiratory prolongation, indicating a small airway obstruction. Percussion is rarely done in the newborn. Rarely, bowel sounds may be heard high in the chest in the absence of breath sounds. In this case emergency radiograph and surgical consultation are required to rule out diaphragmatic hernia.

Cardiovascular system: The findings in an infant with heart disease in the newborn period are tachypnea, cyanosis or both. The position of apical impulse is of prime importance in conditions like congenital diaphragmatic hernia and pneumothorax. Auscultation should be carried out in both cardiac and non-cardiac areas.

Abdomen: Inspection of abdomen may reveal unusual flatness or scaphoid shape of abdomen that may be associated with congenital diaphragmatic hernia. Visible gastric or bowel patterns may be seen indicating ileus or other obstruction. Abdominal palpation is carried out using one to two fingers and counter-pressure in the flank with other hand. Normally 1–2 cm of liver, tip of the spleen overlying the stomach and the lower pole of the left kidney are palpated. The size, shape, location, consistency and relation to mesenteric axis of any other abdominal mass palpated should be described in detail. Tenderness of abdomen is an important sign in necrotizing enterocolitis (NEC) and can be elicited during palpation. On percussion, rarely a fluid thrill may be obtained in cases of neonatal ascites. All the quadrants of the abdomen should be auscultated for sufficient time period (3 minutes) before making a comment on bowel sounds. The quantity, nature and location of bowel sounds should be described whenever they are present.

Musculoskeletal system: The common alterations are deformations caused by adverse mechanical factors in utero. Most positional deformities are mild and resolve in time. The hips are to be examined because physical examination is the only method of detecting hip problems before permanent damage occurs by one year of age.

Developmental dysplasia of hips girls, (DDH) occurs in 1 of 800 live births, more commonly in those with a family history and delivered by breech. There are two major tests to detect developmental dysplasia of hip (DDH). *Ortolani's sign:* The baby is placed on its back with the knees fully flexed and the hips flexed to a right angle. The thighs of the baby are grasped in both hands with the middle finger of each placed over the greater trochanter on the outside and with the thumb placed on the inner side. The thighs are then abducted and the middle fingers of the examining hands used to press forward on the greater trochanters. In DDH, the femoral head suddenly slips into the acetabulum with a distinctly palpable "clunk". If pressure is now applied with the thumbs outwards and backwards of the inner side of the thigh, the femoral head again slips over the posterior lip of the acetabulum. If the femoral head slips into the acetabulum again when the pressure is released, it is merely unstable, rather than dislocated. This test is important because the treatment in early neonatal life is simple and efficient, and consists simply in maintaining the hips in full abduction and at least 90° flexion with malleable metal splints. *Barlow maneuver:* This is done to dislocate the unstable hip joint. With the hip initially abducted, the right hand is positioned to apply a soft pressure in the directions necessary to dislocate the femoral head posteriorly. As the leg is adducted to at least 20° post midline, a lateral pressure is applied with the thumb and a posterior pressure with the hand to dislocate the hip. A positive test leads to knee height discrepancy.

Neurological examination: This consists of the assessment of the level of alertness (already discussed), cranial nerve examination, motor examination, sensory examination and the examination of the primitive neonatal reflexes. *Cranial nerves:* Neonates respond to cotton soaked in peppermint by 32 wks of gestation. By 26 weeks the infant consistently blinks in response to light, and by term, fixation and following are well established. The fluffy red yarn ball is seen to be a useful target in assessing this. Color vision is demonstrated as early as 2 months of age. Binocular vision and perception of depth also appear by 3 to 4 month postnatal age. Reaction to light begins to appear at 30 weeks but consistent response is seen to develop by 35 weeks. The tracking movements of the full term and post term infants at first are rather jerky and become smooth by third month of life. By 28 weeks the infant startles or blinks to loud noise. Sucking and swallowing are important aspects that should be examined as they give insight into the proper functioning of the V, VII, IX, X and XII cranial nerves. The act of sucking requires the concerted action of breathing, sucking and swallowing. Sucking and swallowing are coordinated sufficiently for oral feeding as early as 28 weeks. At an early stage, however, the synchrony of breathing with sucking and swallowing is not well developed, and thus oral feeding is difficult till 32 to 34 weeks of gestation. *Motor examination:* By 28 weeks there is minimal resistance to passive manipulation in all the limbs, and a distinct flexor tone is appreciated in lower extremities by 32 weeks. By 36 weeks flexor tone is palpable in both the lower and upper extremities. Differential hypotonia, in which there is selective hypotonia in the upper and proximal muscle group compared to the lower and distal group, is seen in the early phase of hypoxic ischemic encephalopathy. Ankle clonus of upto 5 to 10 beats is accepted as a normal finding in the newborn but clonus of more than a few beats beyond the 3 months of age is abnormal. The plantar response depends on the way it is elicited in the newborn. If elicited by thumbnail, a flexion response is obtained. If the same is elicited by pin drag, extension response is obtained 95% of the time. *Primary neonatal reflexes:* Moro reflex is best elicited by the sudden dropping of the baby's head in relation to trunk; the response consists of opening of the hands and extension and abduction of the upper extremities, followed by anterior flexion (embracing) of upper extremities with an audible cry (Figs 7.16A and B). The hand opening is present by 28 weeks, extension and abduction by 32 weeks and anterior flexion by 37 weeks. Audible cry appears at 32 weeks. Moro reflex disappears by 3–6 months in normal infants. The most common cause of depressed or absent Moro reflex is a generalized disturbance of the central nervous system. The most useful abnormality of the Moro reflex to elicit is distinct asymmetry, which is almost always a feature of root plexus or nerve disease. The palmar grasp is clearly present at 28 weeks of gestation and is strong by 32 weeks. This allows the lifting of the baby at 37 weeks of gestation. This becomes less consistent on development of voluntary grasping by 2 months. The tonic neck response is another important response elicited by rotation of the head, that causes extension of the upper extremity on the side to which the face is rotated and flexion of the upper extremity on the side of the occiput (Fig. 7.17). This disappears by 6 to 7 months. *Sensory examination:* Even a neonate of 28 weeks has the ability to discriminate touch and pain,

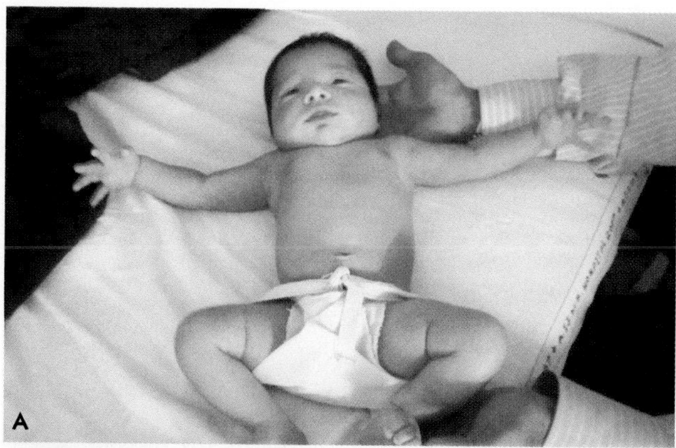

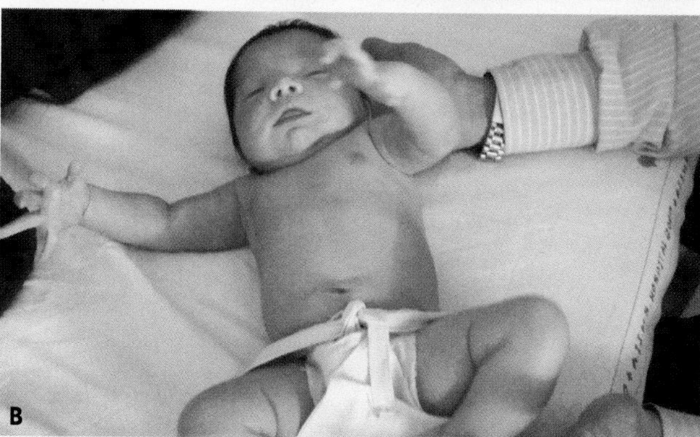

Figs 7.16A and B: Moro reflex (A) Abduction and extension of arms (B) Adduction and flexion component

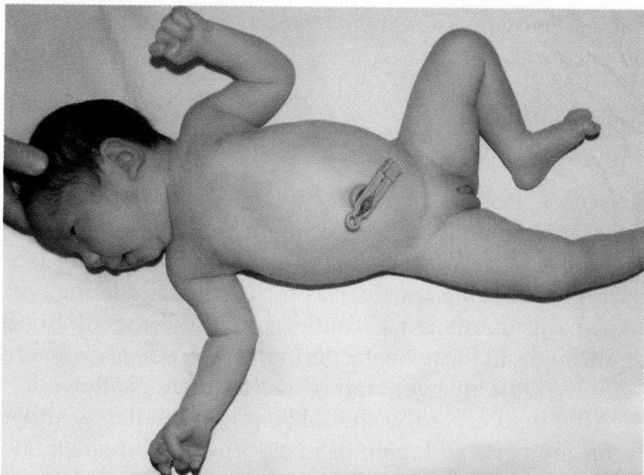

Fig. 7.17: Asymmetrical tonic neck reflex

wherein pain would result in alerting and slight motor activity and then later withdrawal and cry.

THERMAL PROTECTION

Newborn babies have poor heat regulating mechanisms making them prone to hypothermia and its ill effects. Hypothermia is responsible for much morbidity and mortality among neonates.

Sources of Heat Loss

During intrauterine life, the fetal temperature is 0.5° C higher than the maternal temperature due to metabolic reactions that generate heat. After birth the infant is exposed to air and environment which have lower temperature. Heat loss in a newborn occurs through 4 primary routes: radiation (to surrounding environment not in direct contact with baby), convection (to air flowing in surrounding), conduction (to substances in direct contact with baby), and evaporation (of amniotic fluid and moisture from baby's skin to atmosphere), a major contributor.

Reasons Why Newborns have Increased Susceptibility to Hypothermia

- Large surface area of babies compared to their weight: The head constitutes a significant portion of the newborn's surface area and can be a source of great heat loss.
- Limited heat generating mechanisms.
- Vulnerability to getting exposed, being dependant on others for early detection and rectification.

Additional Factors that Contribute to Heat Loss In LBW Babies

- Decreased subcutaneous fat and brown fat
- More permeable skin
- Even larger surface area than term babies
- Poorer homeostatic response to hypothermia and early exhaustion of metabolic stores like glucose.

Sources of Heat Production

On exposure to cold and wet environment, the neonate tries to generate heat by increased activity (crying with agitated movement) and a sympathetic surge that causes vasoconstriction and **non-shivering thermogenesis** in the brown fat. Brown fat is a well vascularized, sympathetically innervated lipid collection located in the axillae, groin, and nape of the neck, interscapular area and perirenal area. Cold stress causes the release of norepinephrine that uncouples beta-oxidation in fat, with resultant heat generation. Preterm and small for gestational age infants have immature thermogenic response because of scanty brown fat stores.

7

Response to hypothermia: Babies attempt to conserve heat by peripheral vasoconstriction. This leads to increased anaerobic metabolism at the ill-perfused areas with acidosis (Fig. 7.18). The latter predisposes to pulmonary vasoconstriction, raised pulmonary arterial pressure and further hypoxemia, with anaerobic metabolism and acidosis leading to a positively reinforcing vicious cycle. With continued hypothermia, usually when temperature drops to 32°C, oxygen cannot be released from hemoglobin, resulting in the blood having a bright red color, which should not be mistaken for good perfusion. With

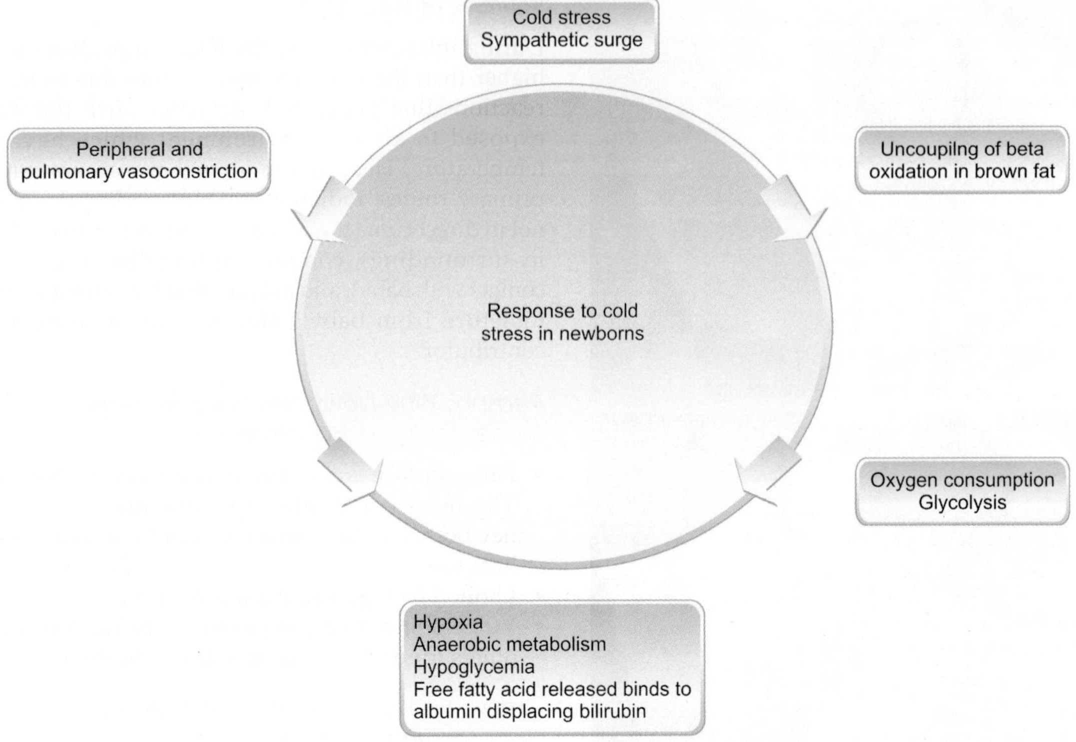

Fig. 7.18: Response to cold stress in sick neonate

severe hypothermia, hypoxemia, hypoglycemia and metabolic acidosis develop, leading to mortality.

Hyperthermia: An immature thermoregulating brain center and decreased ability to sweat also predispose newborns to hyperthermia. Overclothing, environmental exposure in summer, poor feeding, dehydration and sun exposure are common reasons that can lead to hyperthermia.

Definitions

Thermoneutral environment: This is a gestational and postnatal age specific temperature range in which the basal metabolic rate of the baby is at a minimum, oxygen utilization is least and baby thrives well.

Hypothermia: Axillary temperature of baby <36.5°C

- Cold stress 36.0–36.4°C
- Moderate hypothermia 32–35.9°C
- Severe hypothermia <32°C

Hyperthermia: Axillary temperature of baby >37.5°C

Measurement of Temperature

Recommended type of thermometer for measuring neonatal temperature should have low reading values till 30°C, so that degree of severe hypothermia can be accurately assessed. Methods of measurement are listed in Table 7.11.

Frequency of Measurement

Unless dictated by specific clinical needs, the frequency of temperature measurement can be once daily for healthy babies who are progressing well, two-three times daily for healthy small babies (2.4–1.5 kg), four times daily for very small babies (<1.5 kg) and every two hour for sick babies. Frequent assessment by mother using touch should be encouraged.

Hypothermia

Prevention

The most effective management strategy for hypothermia is its prevention, practised using the following:

- *Warm chain:* Warm chain is a sequence of ten steps (see Table 7.12) aimed at decreasing heat loss, initiating heat gain and ensuring that, from the time of birth throughout the neonatal period, no episode of exposure to hypothermia generating environment is allowed.
- After delivery, baby should be put immediately either on mother's abdomen or in a preheated bassinet; one should quickly dry body and head, discard the wet towel and use another dry warm sheet to wrap baby, using a head cap to cover head (Fig. 7.19).
- Skin-to-skin contact between baby and the mother, called as Kangaroo mother care (KMC).
- Breastfeeding; frequent feeding.
- Bathing and weighing postponed.
- During summer months term babies can be sponged after first 24 hours. During winters and for sick or LBW babies this can be postponed by several days usually until umbilical cord falls off, often by the end of first week. Dressing the baby in layers of warm light

Table 7.11: Methods of temperature measurement

Name	*Method*	*Timing*	*Comment*
Axillary	Bulb of the thermometer is placed against the roof of dry axilla, and baby's arm is held close to the body to keep thermometer in place. Read after 3 minutes.	Intermittent measurement	This is the standard method of temperature recording. Closely approximates core temperature.
Rectal	Bulb of a special rectal thermometer is lubricated and inserted in a backward and downward direction through the baby's anal opening upto a depth of 3 cm (2 cm in a preterm baby). Read after 2 minutes.	Intermittent measurement	Good measure of core temperature. Must **not** be employed in routine clinical practice.
Skin	The probe of the thermal sensor called thermister is attached to the skin over upper abdomen from where it reads the temperature and displays it on the panel.	Continuous monitoring	Purpose is for continuous monitoring of babies under servo control, radiant warmer, incubators, etc.
Human touch	Temperature is felt at the abdomen, feet and hands of the baby by back of hand of the examiner: • Abdomen, feet and hands are warm → normal • Abdomen is warm but feet and hands are cold → cold stress • Abdomen, feet and hands are cold → hypothermia	Intermittent measurement	Method cruder than others but helps mother and health worker get a quick idea about temperature without a formal measurement; accuracy improves with experience of the examiner

Table 7.12: Steps of warm chain

1. Warm delivery room
2. Warm resuscitation
3. Immediate drying
4. Skin to skin contact
5. Breastfeeding
6. Bathing postponed
7. Appropriate clothing
8. Mother and baby together
9. Professional alertness
10. Warm transportation

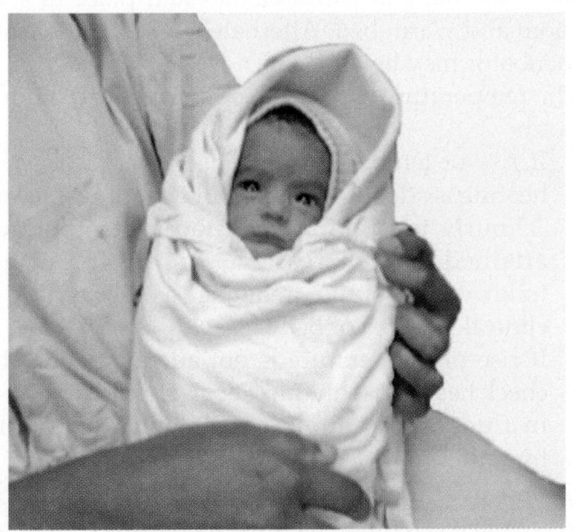

Fig. 7.19: A well clothed baby

garments gives better insulation and heat than single layer of heavy woolen clothing. Covering of the head is an important part of heat conservation.

- Mother and baby co-bedding: 'rooming in'.
- Warm transportation: This is the weakest link in the warm chain with greatest possibility of severe and undetected hypothermia.
- Training/awareness of healthcare providers: unless persons involved in the care of newborns realize the implications of hypothermia it cannot be detected or managed effectively.

Kangaroo mother care (KMC) or "Kangarooing" is an effective way to meet baby's needs for warmth, breastfeeding, clean environment, human contact and safety.

Incubators and radiant warmers: These equipments are used for maintenance of normal body temperature of sick or small neonates in a noenatal unit (Figs 7.20A and B). In an incubator the baby is warmed by circulating warmed and humidified air around the baby in a closed environment (a transparent plastic hood covers the baby). The mechanism of heat transfer is by convection. Temperature may be controlled thermostatically to regulate either the air or infant skin temperature. In a radiant warmer the neonate lies on a waist high bed and heated from above by a radiant heat source. The heater output can be regulated by a thermostatic skin servo control device. Compared to an incubator, infants under a radiant warmer have more insensibile water loss by evaporation; this can

7

Figs 7.20A and B: A very low birth weight (VLBW) baby being cared for in (A) an incubator and (B) radiant warmer. Note that baby is well clothed and the incubator is covered with a cloth to prevent excessive light or noise for adequate comfort of the baby

be reduced by using plastic sheets. This equipment is costly and requires proper maintenance for optimal functioning. It requires proper cleaning and disinfection for prevention of cross infection.

Radiant warmers and incubators should be used in the servo control mode with the abdominal skin temperature maintained at 36.2°C – 37°C depending on the birth weight of the neonate as shown in Table 7.13.

The cheaper alternatives of radiant warmers/incubators include oil-fin radiators, warm air blowers, heaters or simply electricity bulb that keep the environment warm. However, there is no servo controlled mechanism in these devices to control the heat output in response to baby's body temperature (servo mechanism), therefore, these devices carry a risk of hypo and hyperthermia in the baby.

Table 7.13: Set temperature for incubator

Birth weight (kg)	*Set temperature (°C)*
<1.0	37.0
1.0–1.5	36.8
1.5–2.0	36.6
2.0–2.5	36.4
>2.5	36.2

Signs and Symptoms

Peripheral vasoconstriction results in acrocyanosis, cool extremities and delayed peripheral capillary refill time (CRT). The baby becomes restless and then lethargic. Chronic or recurrent episodes of hypothermia results in poor weight gain. Cardiovascular manifestations may occur in the form of bradycardia, hypotension, raised pulmonary pressure with resultant hypoxemia, tachypnea and distress. Lethargy, poor reflexes, decreased oral acceptance and apnea denote CNS depression. Abdomen distension, vomiting and feeding intolerance makes maintaining enteral calorie intake difficult. Acidosis, hypoglycemia, oliguria, azotemia and even generalized bleeding can occur in severe cases, especially in predisposed babies who are sick or premature.

Management

Methods for temperature maintenance include skin to skin contact, warm room, radiant warmers, incubators and exposure to sources of heat such as hot air blowers, 200 watt bulb, etc.

Cold stress and moderate hypothermia

- One should remove the baby from the source causing hypothermia, such as cold environment including cold clothes, draught of air or wet nappy/sheet.
- If mother is available and baby's condition allows, skin to skin contact can be started. Otherwise, one should dress the baby in warm clothes and place in a warm room and warm bed. Alternately a radiant warmer or incubator may be used.
- The temperature should be measured every hour for 3 hours
  - If rise of temperature has been by 0.5° C/hr then heating is adequate; one should continue measuring 2 hourly temperature till normal temperature is attained, and thereafter 3 hourly for 12 hours, followed by routine frequency as dictated by other clinical features of baby.
  - If rise of temperature is not adequate, one should check heating technique. Sepsis should be suspected in fluctuating temperatures with unresponsive hypothermia.
- Supportive measures: One should maintain normoglycemia by frequent feeding; increase calorie intake if possible; monitor vitals.

Severe hypothermia

- One should remove all wet clothing and place baby in warm bed with warm clothes.
- Method of warming could be an incubator (air temp 35–36°C) or preheated radiant warmer or thermostatically controlled heated mattress set at 37–38°C. Alternately, one may use room heater or 200 watts bulb.
- Once baby's temperature reaches 34°C, the rewarming process should be slowed down.
- Temperature is measured every hour for 3 hours
  - If rise of temperature has been by 0.5°C/hr then heating is adequate and measuring is continued 2 hourly till normal temperature is attained and thereafter 3 hourly for 12 hours, followed by routine frequency as dictated by other clinical features of baby.
  - If rise of temperature is not adequate, one should check heating technique or change method.
- Supportive measure
  - Oxygen
  - Empirical antibiotics are started; investigations are sent for to rule out sepsis.
  - Saline bolus is given if hypotension present.
  - IV fluids are required for hypoglycemia correction and prevention.
  - Inj vit K 1 mg (0.5 mg for <1 kg weight baby) is given.
  - Temperature and vital signs should be monitored.

Suggested reading

1. Thermal protection of the newborn: A practical guide. WHO/FHW/MSM/97.2.
2. Guidelines for perinatal care. Second Edition, American Academy of Pediatrics and American College of Obstetricians and Gynecologists, 1998.

FLUID AND ELECTROLYTE MANAGEMENT IN NEONATES

Transition from fetal to extrauterine life is accompanied by remarkable changes in body fluid composition. Before assessing fluid and electrolyte balance and planning fluid therapy, it is important to understand normal postnatal changes in body fluid composition. In a neonate born at term gestation total body water (TBW) constitutes about 80% of body weight as compared to an adult in whom TBW constitutes 60% of body weight. Neonates are born with an excess of total body water, primarily in the extracellular fluid (ECF) compartment. This excess of TBW is normally lost by diuresis during first week of life. In neonates born at term gestation, this physiological diuresis results in a weight loss of 5–10% during first 3 to 5 days of life. Preterm neonates have proportionately higher TBW and, therefore, may lose up to 10–15% of birth weight during first week of life.

The heart, kidneys, the skin and the neuroendocrine system play the most important role in regulation of fluid and electrolyte balance in neonates. Neonates lose body water through kidneys or gastrointestinal tract. In neonates, kidneys have a limited capacity to concentrate or dilute urine, mainly due to lower glomerular filtration rate and reduced proximal and distal tubular sodium reabsorption. In addition to mandatory water loss by the kidneys and gastrointestinal system (termed as sensible loss), additional water losses occur due to evaporation from the skin and respiratory tract. This water loss is termed as insensible water loss (IWL). Insensible water losses tend to be higher in preterm infants. Evaporation loss through the skin usually contributes to 70% of IWL. The remaining 30% is contributed through losses from the respiratory tract. Fever, increased respiratory rate, radiant warmers and phototherapy increase IWL.

Guidelines for Fluid Therapy

Healthy neonates born at term gestation on oral feeds are able to self-regulate the fluid intake. Sick or very preterm neonates are started on intravenous (IV) fluid therapy.

Babies with birth weight ≥ 1500 grams: These infants on intravenous fluids would need to excrete a solute load of about 15 mosm/kg/day in the urine. To excrete this solute load at a urine osmolarity of 300 mosm/kg/day, the infant would have to pass a minimum of 50 mL/kg/day. Allowing for an additional IWL of 20 mL/kg, the initial fluids should be 60–70 mL/kg/day. The initial fluids should be 10% dextrose with no electrolytes in order to maintain a glucose infusion rate of 4–6 mg/kg/min. Hence total fluid therapy on day 1 would be 60 mL/kg/day. It is provided as 10% dextrose (Table 7.14). As the infant grows and receives enteral milk feeds, the solute load presented to the kidneys increases and the infant requires more fluid to excrete the solute load. Water is also required for fecal losses and for growth purposes. The fluid requirements increase by 15–20 mL/kg/day till a maximum of 150 mL/kg/day.

Babies with birth weight <1500 grams: The urine output in a preterm LBW baby is similar to a term baby. However, the fluid requirement is higher due to increased IWL and increased weight loss (extracellular fluid loss). Baby should be well dressed including use of caps and socks to reduce the IWL under the radiant warmer. Using this method, 80 mL/kg/day of 10% dextrose is adequate on day 1 of life (Table 7.14). As the skin matures in a preterm baby, the IWL progressively decreases and becomes similar to a term baby by the end of the first week. Hence,

Table 7.14: Daily fluid requirements during first week of life (mL/kg/day)

Birth weight	*Day 1*	*Day 2*	*Day 3*	*Day 4*	*Day 5*	*Day 6*	*Day 7 and onwards*
<1500 g	80	95	110	120	130	140	150
≥1500 g	60	75	90	105	120	135	150

7

the fluid requirement in a preterm baby, initially higher due to increased IWL, would become similar to a term baby by the end of the first week. Fluids need to be increased at 10–15 mL/kg/day till a maximum of 150 mL/kg/day.

Sodium and potassium should be added after 48 hours. Glucose infusion should be maintained at 4–6 mg/kg/min. 10% dextrose may be used in babies >1250 g and 5–7.5% dextrose in babies with birth weight <1250 g.

Intravenous fluid therapy: Indications for starting IV fluid therapy include birth weight less than 1200 g or gestation <30 wk, respiratory distress, feed intolerance, hemodynamic instability, gastrointestinal malformations (like tracheoesophgeal fistula, duodenal or ileal atresia, anorectal malformation, etc.) or any other severe illness precluding oral feeding. Peripheral intravenous line is the most common intravenous access method used to provide fluid therapy. In neonates 22–24 gauze cannula is inserted in peripheral veins on hands, antecubital fossa, feet or ankle. Fluid requirement is calculated based on birth weight, day of life and current fluid balance.

Risks of IV fluid therapy include local infection, systemic infection, phlebitis, accidental fluid overload and extravasation. Because IV fluid therapy is a major risk factor for nosocomial infection, all asepsis precautions must be followed during insertion of IV cannula or administering fluids. Administration of hypertonic and irritant medications like sodium bicarbonate and calcium gluconate should be minimized to prevent extravasation. Oral feeds should be started at the earliest possible opportunity when clinical condition of neonate improves and IV fluid should be stopped when oral feeds constitute about two-thirds of daily fluid requirement. IV sites should be inspected frequently to detect evidence of extravasation.

Monitoring of Fluid and Electrolyte Status

Fluid therapy should be monitored every 8–12 h in a baby on IV fluids. In a stable baby on oral fluids it can be monitored every 24 h (Table 7.15).

Body weight: Serial weight measurements can be used as a guide to estimate the fluid deficit in newborns. Term neonates lose 1–3% of their birth weight daily with a cumulative loss of 5–10% in the first week of life. Preterm neonates lose 2–3% of their birth weight daily with a cumulative loss of 10–15% in the first week of life. Failure to lose weight in the first week of life would be an indicator of excessive fluid administration. However, excessive weight loss (>3% in 24 hr) in the first 5–7 days or later would be non-physiological and would merit correction with fluid therapy.

Clinical examination: The usual physical signs of dehydration are unreliable in neonates. Infants with 10% (100 mL/kg) dehydration may have sunken eyes and fontanel, cold and clammy skin, poor skin turgor and oliguria. Infants with 15% (150 mL/kg) or more dehydration would have signs of shock (hypotension, tachycardia and weak pulses) in addition to the above features. Dehydration would merit correction of fluid and electrolyte status gradually over the next 24 hours.

Urine output, specific gravity: The capacity of the newborn kidney to either concentrate or dilute urine is limited and estimation of urine specific gravity would be useful to guide fluid therapy. The acceptable range for urine output would be 1–3 mL/kg/hr, for specific gravity between 1.005–1.012.

Biochemical tests: Serum sodium and plasma osmolality are helpful but not always essential in the assessment of the hydration status in an infant. Serum sodium values should be maintained between 135–145 mEq/L. Blood gases are not needed routinely for fluid management. However, they are useful in the acid base management of patients with poor tissue perfusion and shock. Hypoperfusion is associated with metabolic acidosis.

Suggested reading

Chawla D, Agarwal R, Deorari AK, Paul VK. Fluid and electrolyte management in term and preterm neonates. Indian J Pediatr. 2008;75:255–9.

Table 7.15: Monitoring of fluid therapy

Parameter	*Adequate fluid therapy*	*Inadequate fluid therapy*	*Excessive fluid therapy*
Weight	Physiological weight loss (1–3%/day) during first week after birth	Excessive weight loss (>3% day or >10% cumulative weight loss)	No weight loss or weight gain during first week after birth.
Urine output	Normal (1–3 mL/kg/h)	Decreased (<1 mL/kg/h)	Increased
Physical signs	None	Decreased skin turgor, sunken eyes and depressed anterior fontanel if >10% dehydration	Puffy eyelids, dependent edema
Serum sodium	Normal	Increased if excessive insensible water loss. Decreased if excessive loss through gastrointestinal tract or kidneys.	Decreased; increased if hypertonic saline administration.
Urine specific gravity	1.005–1.012	>1.012	<1.005

KANGAROO MOTHER CARE

Kangaroo mother care (KMC) is care of preterm or low birth weight infants carried skin-to-skin with the mother. KMC was initially conceived as an alternative to warmer care for stable low birth weight infants. KMC has now become standard of care either as an alternative to or an adjunct to technology-based care.

KMC was first suggested in 1978 by Dr Edgar Rey in Bogotá, Colombia . The term kangaroo care is derived from practical similarities to marsupial care-giving, i.e. the premature infant is kept warm in the maternal pouch and close to the breasts for unlimited feeding.

Components of KMC

Kangaroo Position

The kangaroo position consists of skin-to-skin contact between the mother and her infant in a vertical position, between the mother's breasts and under her clothes (Fig. 7.21).

It can be of two types depending upon the duration: continuous or intermittent. The continuous modality is usually employed as an alternative to minimal care in an incubator for infants who have already overcome major problems while adapting to extrauterine life, are able to suck and swallow properly and are thriving in neutral thermal environment. The kangaroo position should be maintained as long as possible, ideally 24 hr/day. The provider must be in a semi-reclining position to avoid reflux in the infants.

When continuous care is not possible, the kangaroo position can be used intermittently, providing the proven emotional and breastfeeding promotion benefits. The kangaroo position must be offered for as long as possible (1–2 hrs at least in a sitting). This 1–2 h span is important as it provides the stimulation that the mother needs to increase the milk volume and facilitate milk let-down. This is initiated in the hospital and continued at home.

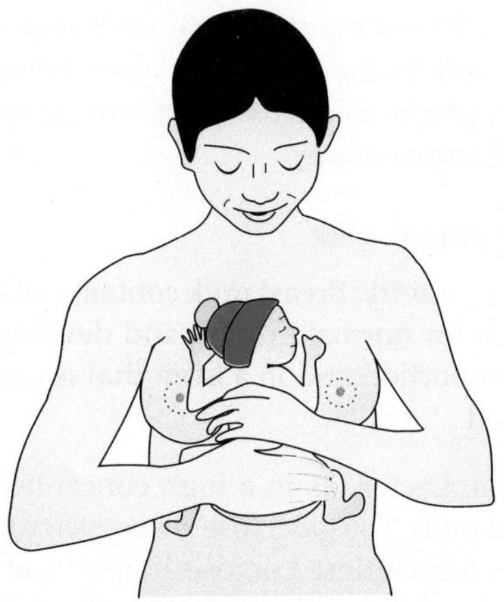

Fig. 7.21: Kangaroo positioning

Benefits of KMC

Physiological Benefits

Heart and respiratory rates, respiration, oxygenation, oxygen consumption, blood glucose, sleep patterns and behavior observed in preterm/LBW infants held skin-to-skin tend to be similar to or better than those observed in infants separated from their mothers.

Clinical Benefits

- KMC significantly increases milk production in mothers.
- KMC increases the exclusive breastfeeding rates.
- KMC reduces the incidence of respiratory tract and nosocomial infections.
- There is improved weight gain.
- It improves thermal protection in these infants and there is a reduced chance of hypothermia.
- It improves emotional bonding between the infant and mothers.
- KMC reduces duration of hospital stay.

Criteria for Eligibility of KMC

Baby

KMC is indicated in all stable LBW babies. However, very sick babies needing special care should be cared for under radiant warmer initially. KMC should be started after the baby is hemodynamically stable. Short KMC sessions can be initiated during recovery with ongoing medical treatment (IV fluids, oxygen therapy). KMC can be provided while the baby is being fed via orogastric tube or on oxygen therapy. Guidelines for practicing KMC include:

- *Birth weight >1800 g:* These babies are generally stable at birth. Therefore, in most of them KMC can be initiated soon after birth.
- *Birth weight 1200–1799 g:* Many babies of this group have significant problems in neonatal period. It might take a few days before KMC can be initiated.
- *Birth weight <1200 g:* Frequently, these babies develop serious prematurity-related morbidity, often starting soon after birth. It may take days to weeks before baby's condition allows initiation of KMC.

Mother

All mothers can provide KMC, irrespective of age, parity, education, culture and religion. The mother must be willing to provide KMC. The mother should be free from serious illness to be able to provide KMC. She should receive adequate diet and supplements recommended by her physician. She should maintain good hygiene. Mother would need family's cooperation to deal with her conventional responsibilities of household chores till the baby requires KMC.

7

Initiation of KMC

Counseling: When baby is ready for KMC, arrange a time that is convenient to the mother and her baby. The first few sessions are important and require extended interaction. Demonstrate to her the KMC procedure in a caring, gentle manner and with patience. Answer her queries and allay her anxieties. Encourage her to bring her mother/mother in law, husband or any other member of the family. It helps in building positive attitude of the family and ensuring family support to the mother which is particularly crucial for post-discharge home-based KMC. It is helpful that the mother starting KMC interacts with someone already practising KMC for her baby.

Mother's clothing: KMC can be provided using any front-open, light dress as per the local culture. KMC works well with blouse and sari, gown or shawl. Suitable apparel that can retain the baby for extended period of time can be adapted locally.

Baby's clothing: Baby is dressed with cap, socks, nappy, and front-open sleeveless shirt.

KMC Procedure

Kangaroo positioning: The baby should be placed between the mother's breasts in an upright position. The head should be turned to one side and in a slightly extended position. This slightly extended head position keeps the airway open and allows eye to eye contact between the mother and her baby. The hips should be flexed and abducted in a "frog" position; the arms should also be flexed. Baby's abdomen should be at the level of the mother's epigastrium. Mother's breathing stimulates the baby, thus reducing the occurrence of apnea. Support the baby's bottom with a sling/binder.

Monitoring: Babies receiving KMC should be monitored carefully, especially during the initial stages. Nursing staff should make sure that baby's neck position is neither too flexed nor too extended, airway is clear, breathing is regular, color is pink and baby is maintaining temperature. Mother should be involved in observing the baby during KMC so that she herself can continue monitoring at home.

Feeding: The mother should be explained how to breastfeed while the baby is in KMC position. Holding the baby near the breast stimulates milk production. She may express milk while the baby is still in KMC position. The baby could be fed with *paladai*, spoon or tube, depending on the condition of the baby.

Privacy: KMC unavoidably requires some exposure on the part of the mother. This can make her nervous and could be demotivating. The staff must respect mother's sensitivities in this regard and ensure culturally acceptable privacy standards in the nursery and the wards where KMC is practised.

Duration: Skin-to-skin contact should start gradually in the nursery, with a smooth transition from conventional care to continuous KMC (Figs 7.22A and B). Sessions that last less than one hour should be avoided because frequent handling may be stressful for the baby. The length of skin-to-skin contact should be gradually increased up to 24 hours a day, interrupted only for changing diapers. When the baby does not require intensive care, she should be transferred to the postnatal ward where KMC should be continued.

The mother can sleep with baby in kangroo position in reclined or semi-recumbent position about 15 degrees from horizontal. This can be done with an adjustable bed or with pillows on an ordinary bed. A comfortable chair with an adjustable back may be used for resting during the day.

When to Stop KMC

KMC is continued till the baby finds it comfortable and cosy. KMC is unnecessary once the baby attains a weight of 2500 g and a gestation of 37 weeks. A baby who, upon being put in the kangaroo position, tends to wriggle out, pulls limbs out, or cries/fusses, is not in need of KMC any more.

BREASTFEEDING

Breast milk is an ideal food for a normal neonate. It is the best gift that a mother can give to her baby. It contains all the nutrients for normal growth and development of a baby from the time of birth to the first six months of life. Ensuring exclusive breast feeding for six months has a potential to reduce under-5 mortality rate by 13%, by far the most effective intervention that are known to reduce newborn and child deaths.

To accrue the maximum benefits, the breastfeeding must be exclusive (only breast milk nothing other than breast milk except vitamin drops, if indicated), initiated within half an hour of birth, and continued through first six months after birth. Recently National Family Health Survey-3 documented that only a quarter of infants who were ever breastfed started breastfeeding within half an hour of birth. 57% of mothers gave additional drinks other than breast milk in the three days after delivery which is an improper practice. Exclusive breastfeeding rate is only 28% at 4–5 months of age.

Benefits of Breast Milk

Nutritional superiority: Breast milk contains all the nutrients a baby needs for normal growth and development, in an optimum proportion and in a form that is easily digested and absorbed.

Carbohydrates: Lactose is in a high concentration (6–7 g/dL) in breast milk. The galactose is necessary for formation of galactocerebrosides. Lactose helps in absorption of calcium and enhances the growth of lactobacilli in the intestine.

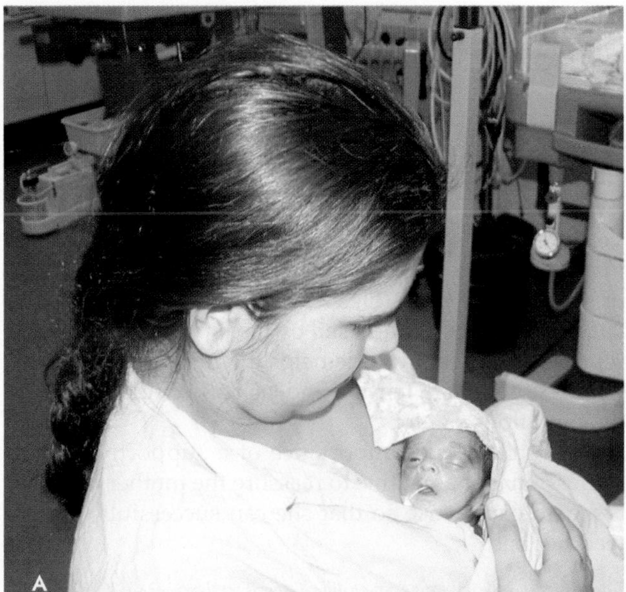

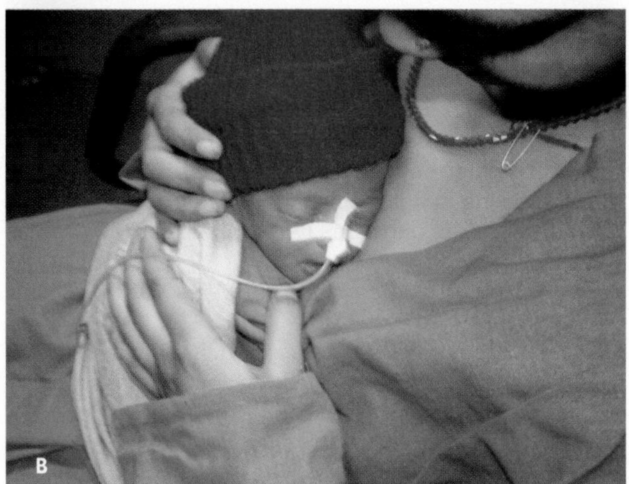

Figs 7.22A and B: Kangaroo mother care being provided in postnatal ward

Proteins: The protein content of breast milk is low (0.9–1.1 g/dL) as the baby cannot effectively metabolize a high protein load. Most of the protein is lactalbumin and lactoglobulin (60%), which is easily digested. Human milk contains amino acids like taurine and cysteine which are necessary for neurotransmission and neuromodulation. These are lacking in cow's milk and formula.

Fats: Breast milk is rich in polyunsaturated fatty acids, necessary for the myelination of the nervous system. It also contains omega 2 and omega 6 (very long chain fatty acids) which are important for the formation of prostaglandins and cholesterol, required as a base for steroid hormones.

Vitamins and minerals: The quantity and bioavailability of vitamins and minerals is sufficient for the needs of the baby in the first 6 months of life.

Water and electrolytes: Breast milk has a water content of 88% hence a breastfed baby does not require any additional water in the first few months of life even in summer months. The osmolality of breast milk is low, presenting a low solute load to the neonatal kidney.

Immunological superiority: Breast milk contains a number of protective factors which include immunoglobulin, mainly secretary IgA, macrophages, lymphocytes, lactoferrin, lysozyme, bifidus factor, interferon and other protective substances. Breastfed babies are less likely to develop infection. A breast-fed baby is 14.2 times less likely to die of diarrhea and 3.6 times less likely to die of respiratory infection.

Other benefits: Breast milk contains a number of growth factor, enzymes, hormones, etc. The epidermal growth factor in breast milk enhances the maturation of the intestinal cells and thus reduces the risk of allergy in later life. Enzymes like lipases increase the digestion of fats in the milk.

Protection against other illness: Breastfed babies have a lower risk of allergy, ear infections and orthodontic problems. They have a lower risk of diabetes, heart disease and lymphoma in later life.

Mental growth: Babies who are breastfed are better bonded to their mothers. Studies have shown that babies who were breastfed had a higher IQ than those babies who were given other forms of milk.

Benefits to mother: Breastfeeding soon after birth helps uterine involution, reducing chances of postpartum hemorrhage. It provides protection against pregnancy due to lactational amenorrhea. If the mother is exclusively breastfeeding her baby and not resumed menses then there is no need for any other contraception during initial 6 months after delivery.

Breastfeeding is most convenient and time saving. It reduces the risk of cancer of breast and ovary. Breastfeeding is the most effective way of shedding extra weight that mother has put on during pregnancy.

Breast Milk—Where and How it is Produced

Anatomy

The breast is made up of glandular tissue, supporting tissue and fat (Fig. 7.23). The glandular tissue consists of small clusters of sac-like spaces which produce milk. Around each sac is a basket-like array of muscle cells known as myoepithelial cells. Milk produced in the alveoli is carried along 20 small tubes or ducts towards the nipple. Before reaching the nipple, the ducts widen to form 10–15 lactiferous sinuses which store milk. The lactiferous sinuses lie beneath the circle of dark skin around the nipple called the areola.

The areola and nipples are extremely sensitive as they are supplied by a rich network of nerve endings. On the

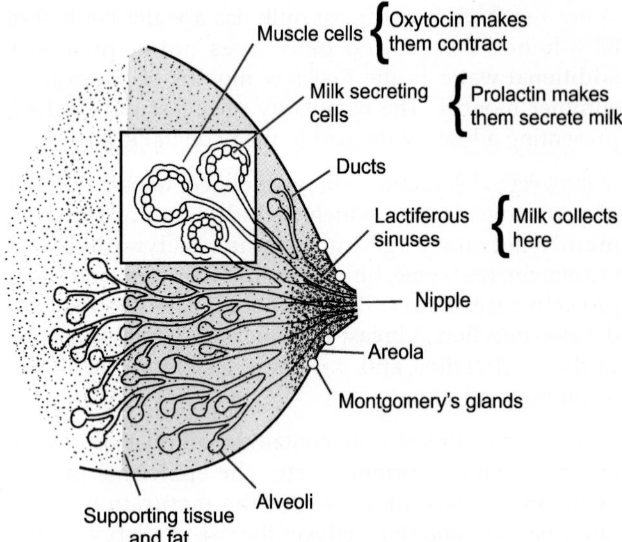

Fig. 7.23: Anatomy of breast

areola are small swellings of glands which produce an oily fluid to keep the nipple skin soft. Since the lactiferous sinuses lie beneath the areola, a baby must suck at the nipple and areola (gum line of the baby should rest at the junction of areola and rest of breast tissue in order to exert pressure on lactiferous sinuses) to draw out the milk.

The glandular tissue is responsible for production of milk. The fat and the supporting tissue are responsible for the size of the breast; hence a mother can produce enough milk despite small size of the breast.

Physiology

Milk is produced as a result of the interaction between hormones and reflexes. During pregnancy and lactation the glandular tissue is stimulated to produce milk due to various hormonal influences. Two hormones come into play during lactation.

Prolactin reflex (milk secretion reflex): Prolactin produced by the anterior pituitary gland is responsible for milk secretion by the alveolar epithelial cells (Fig. 7.24A). When the baby sucks, the nerve ending in the nipple carry message to the anterior pituitary which in turn release prolactin and that acts on the alveolar glands in the breast to stimulate milk secretion.

This cycle from stimulation to secretion is called the prolactin reflex or the milk secretion reflex. The more the baby sucks at the breast, the greater is the milk production. The earlier the baby is put to the breast, the sooner this reflex is initiated. The greater the demand, more is the milk produced. It is, therefore, important for mothers to feed early, frequently and completely empty the breasts at each feed and ensure that the baby is properly attached to the breast. Since prolactin is produced during night time, breastfeeding during night is very important for maintenance of this reflex. Even a single supplemental feeding would interfere with successful breast milk production.

Oxytocin reflex (milk ejection reflex): Oxytocin is a hormone produced by the posterior pituitary. It is responsible for contraction of the milk from the glands into the lactiferous sinuses and the lactiferous ducts. This hormone is produced in response to stimulation to the nerve endings in the nipple by suckling as well as by the thought, sight, or sound of the baby (Figs 7.24B and C).

Since this reflex is affected by the mother's emotions, a relaxed, confident attitude helps the milk ejection reflex. On the other hand, tension and lack of confidence hinder the milk flow.

This stresses the importance of a supportive health professional or a relative to reassure the mother and help her gain confidence so that she can successfully breastfeed her baby.

Factors which Lessen Milk Production

- Dummies, pacifiers, bottles. Studies have revealed that even one or two supplemental feed would hinder successful breastfeeding.
- Giving things like sugar water, gripe water, honey, breast milk substitutes or formula, either as prelacteal (before establishment of breastfeeding) feeds or supplemental (at any time later) feeds.
- Painful breast conditions like sore or cracked nipples and congested breast.
- Lack of night feeding, as it interferes with prolactin reflex
- Inadequate emptying of breast such as when sick or small baby is unable to suck on the mother's breast, and mother does not manually express breast milk.

Reflexes in the Baby

A baby is born with certain reflexes which help the baby to feed. These include rooting, sucking and swallowing reflexes.

The rooting reflex: When the mother holds her baby and her breast touches the baby's upper lip, cheek or the side of the mouth, the baby opens her or his mouth and searches for the nipple with an open mouth. This is called rooting reflex. This reflex helps the baby to find the nipple and helps in proper attachment to the breast.

The suckling reflex: This reflex which is very strong immediately after birth helps the baby draw out milk from the mother's breast. The sucking action consists of:

- Drawing in the nipple and areola to form an elongated teat inside the mouth.
- Pressing the stretched nipple and areola with the jaw and tongue against the palate (which is sensitive for the suckling action).
- Drawing milk from the lactiferous sinuses by wave-like peristaltic movement of the tongue on the

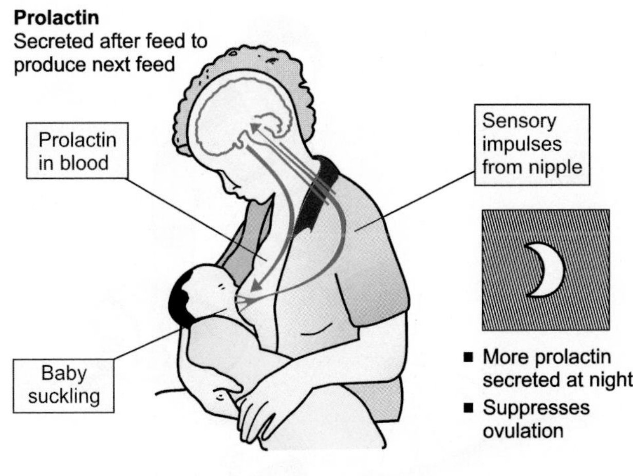

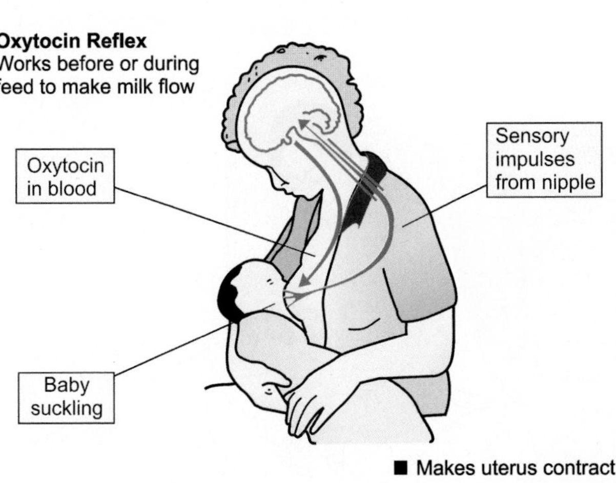

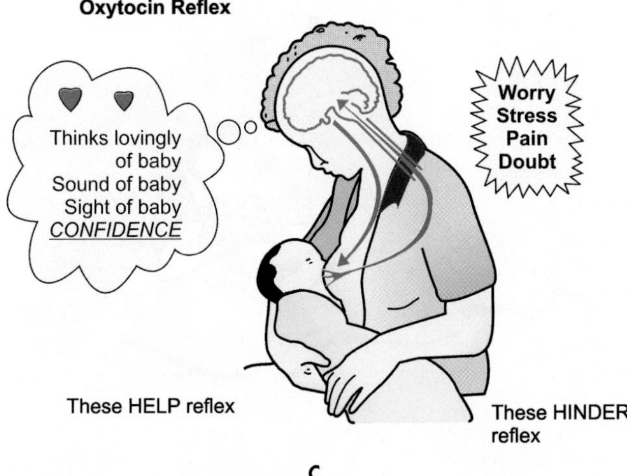

Figs 7.24A and B: Prolactin and oxytocin reflex (C) Factors which help and hinder oxytocin reflex

underneath of the areola and the nipple and compressing them against the palate above.

Ensuring a good attachment at breast is a skill which both the mother and the baby have to learn. To suckle effectively, the baby should be well attached (latched on) to the breast to be able to take both, the nipple and the areola, into the mouth for effective suckling.

The method of suckling at the breast and bottle is entirely different. Suckling on a bottle already filled with milk requires less effort to draw out milk. Here the baby uses the tongue only to control the flow of milk into the mouth. A baby who has been fed with a bottle finds it difficult and confusing to suckle at the breast, aptly termed as 'nipple confusion'.

The swallowing reflex: It may take one to three suckles to fill the baby's mouth with milk. When the mouth is filled with milk, the baby swallows the milk and then breathes. The suckle-swallow-breathe cycle lasts for about one second.

Composition of Breast Milk

The composition of breast milk varies at different stages after birth to suit the needs of the baby. Milk of a mother who has delivered a preterm baby is different from milk of a mother delivered a term baby.

1. Colostrum is the milk secreted during the initial 3–4 days after delivery. It is yellow and thick and contains more antibodies and cells and increased amounts of vitamins A, D, E and K.
2. Transitional milk is the milk secreted after 3–4 days and until two weeks. The immunoglobulin and protein content decreases while the fat and sugar content increases.
3. Mature milk follows transitional milk. It is thinner and watery but contains all the nutrients essential for optimal growth of the baby.
4. Preterm milk is the milk of a mother who delivers prematurely. It contains more proteins, sodium, iron, immunoglobulins and calories as they are needed by the preterm baby.
5. Fore-milk is the milk secreted at the start of a feed. It is watery and is rich in proteins, sugar, vitamins, minerals and water that satisfies the baby's thirst.
6. Hind-milk comes later towards the end of feed and is richer in fat content and provides more energy, and satisfies the baby's hunger. Thus, the composition of milk also varies during the phase of feeding. For optimum growth, the baby needs both fore and hind milk. The baby should, therefore, be allowed to empty a breast completely before switching over to the other breast.

Technique of Breastfeeding

Most mothers can successfully breastfeed. Some mothers are at a higher risk for problems in breastfeeding. These include primipara mothers, mothers who have had problems in breast-feeding in previous pregnancy, mothers with breast problems like retracted nipple and mothers who have not been motivated to breastfeed. These mothers require more support to have a successful breastfeeding.

Positioning

- *Position of the mother:* The mother can take any position that is comfortable to her and her baby. She could sit or lie down. Her back should be well supported and she should not be leaning on her baby (Figs 7.25A to C).
- *Position of baby:* Make sure that baby is wrapped properly in a cloth.
  - Baby's whole body must be well supported not just neck or shoulders.
  - Baby's head and body are in a line without any twist in the neck.
  - Baby's body turned towards the mother with the baby's abdomen touching the mother's abdomen.
  - Baby's nose is at the level of the nipple.

Attachment: After proper positioning, the baby's cheek is touched and that will make the baby open her mouth (rooting reflex). Allow the baby to have a wide open mouth and the baby should be quickly brought on to the breast ensuring that the nipple and most of the areola is within the baby's mouth (Fig. 7.26). It is important that baby is brought on the mother rather than mother leaning on to the baby.

Signs of good attachment

1. The baby's mouth is *wide open.*
2. Most of the nipple and areola in the mouth, only upper areola visible, not the lower one.
3. The baby's chin touches the breast.
4. The baby's lower lip is everted.

7

Effective suckling

- Baby suckles slowly and pauses in between to swallow. One may be able to see the movement of throat bones and muscles and hear the gulping sound indicating that baby is swallowing milk.
- Baby's cheeks are full and not hollow or retracting during sucking.

Problems in Breastfeeding

Inverted nipples: Flat or short nipples which protract well (become prominent or pull out easily) do not cause difficulty in breastfeeding. Inverted or retracted nipples sometimes make attachment to the breast difficult. These mothers need additional support to feed their babies. Treatment is started after birth of the baby. The nipple is manually stretched and rolled out several times a day. A pump or a plastic syringe is used to draw out the nipple and the baby is then put to the breast (Fig. 7.27).

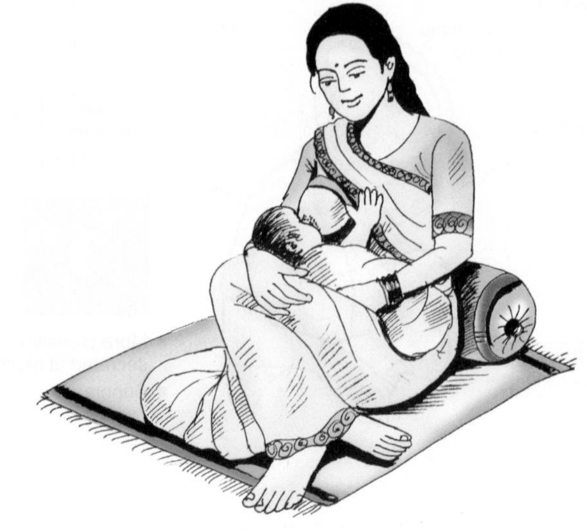

A

B

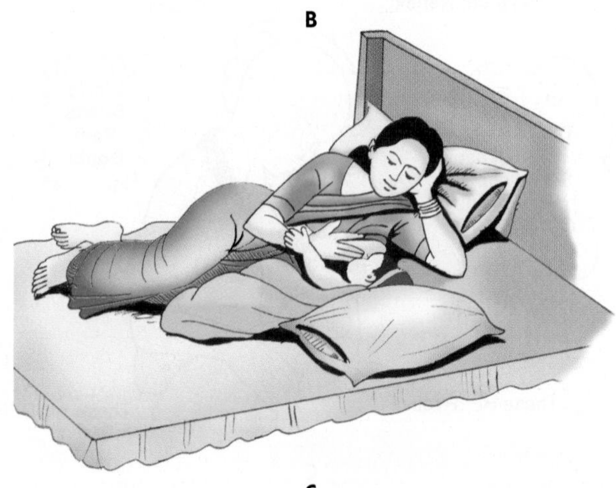

C

Figs 7.25A to C: Different postures of feeding

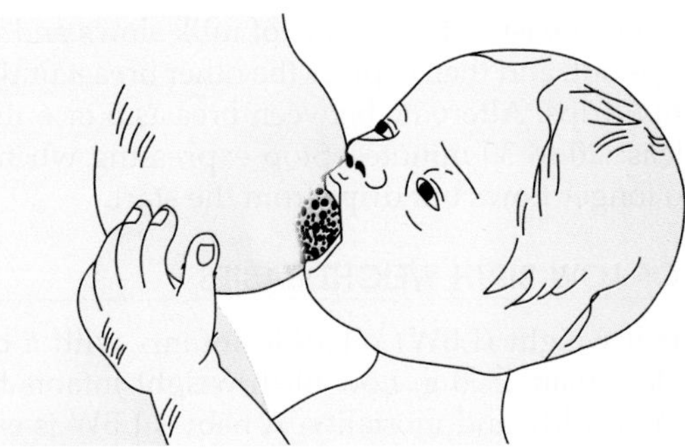

Fig. 7.26: Good attachment

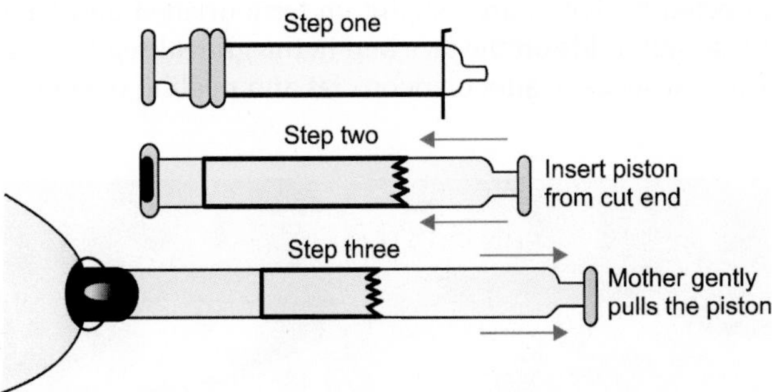

Fig. 7.27: Syringe treatment for inverted/flat nipple

Sore nipple: A sore nipple is caused by incorrect attachment of the baby to the breast. A baby who sucks only on the nipple rather than areola does not get enough milk. Therefore he sucks vigorously often in frustration and inflicts injury on the nipple causing soreness. Frequent washing with soap and water, pulling the baby off the breast while he is still sucking may also result in sore nipple. Candida infection of the nipple is also a cause of a sore nipple after the first few weeks.

Treatment consists of correct positioning and latching of the baby to the breast. A mother would be able to feed the baby despite sore nipple if the baby is attached properly. Hind milk should be applied to the nipple after a feed and the nipple should be aired and allowed to heal in between feeds. She should be advised not to wash nipple each time before/after feeding. She can clean breast and nipple once daily at time of bathing.

Breast engorgement: The milk production increases during the second and third day after delivery. If feeding is delayed or infrequent, or the baby is not well positioned at the breast, the milk accumulates in the alveoli. As milk production increases, the amount of milk in the breast exceeds the capacity of the alveoli to store it comfortably. Such a breast becomes swollen, hard, warm and painful and is termed as an 'engorged breast' (Fig. 7.28).

Breast engorgement can be prevented by early and frequent feeds and correct attachment of the baby to the breast. Treatment consists of local warm water packs,

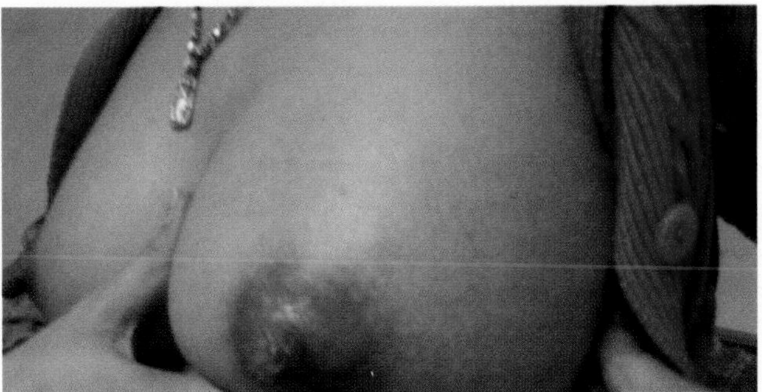

Fig. 7.28: Engorged breast. Note tense and shiny skin, nipple shows excoriation

breast massage and analgesics to the mother to relieve the pain. Milk should be gently expressed to soften the breast and then the mother must be helped to correctly latch the baby to the breast.

Breast abscess: If a congested, engorged breast, an infected cracked nipple, or a blocked duct and mastitis are not treated in the early stages, then an infected breast segment may form a breast abscess. The mother may also have high grade fever and a raised blood count.

Mother must be treated with analgesics and antibiotics. The abscess must be incised and drained. Breastfeeding must be continued.

Not enough milk: First make sure that the perception of "not enough milk" is correct. If baby is satisfied and sleeping for 2–3 hours after breastfeeding and passing urine at least 6–8 times in 24 hours and gaining weight, then the mother is producing enough milk.

There could be a number of reasons for insufficient milk such as incorrect method of breastfeeding, supplementary feeding, bottle feeding, no night breastfeeding, engorgement of breast, any illness, painful condition, stress or insufficient sleep in the mother.

Try to identify the possible reason and take an appropriate action. Advise mother to take sufficient rest and drink more fluids. Feed the baby on demand. Let the baby feed for as long as possible on each breast. Feed only at breast. Advise the mother to keep the baby with her.

Expressed Breast Milk

If a mother is not in a position to feed her baby (e.g. ill mother, preterm baby, working mother, etc.), she should express her milk in a clean wide-mouthed container and this milk should be fed to her baby. Expressed breast milk can be stored at room temperature for 6–8 hours, in a refrigerator for 24 hours and a freezer at –20°C for 3 months.

Method of Milk Expression

Ask the mother to wash her hands thoroughly with soap every time before she expresses. Make herself comfortable. Gently massage the breast (Fig. 7.29). Hold the container

Step 1: Massage the breasts gently toward the nipples
Step 2: Place the thumb and index finger opposite each other just outside the dark circle around the nipple
Step 3: Now press back toward the chest, then gently squeeze to release milk
Step 4: Repeat step 3 at different positions around the areola

Fig. 7.29: Four steps of breast milk expression

under her nipple and areola. Place her thumb on top of the breast at least 4 cm from the tip of the nipple, and the first finger on the under side of the breast opposite the thumb. Compress and release the breast tissue between her fingers and thumb a few times. If the milk does not appear she should reposition her thumb and finger closer to the nipple and compress and release the breast as before. Compress and release all the way around the breast, keeping her fingers the same distance from the nipple. Express one breast until the flow of milk slows and milk only drips out, and then express the other breast until the milk only drips. Alternate between breasts 5 or 6 times, for at least 20 to 30 minutes. Stop expressing when the milk no longer flows but drips from the start.

CARE OF LOW BIRTH WEIGHT BABIES

Low birth weight (LBW) refers to infants with a birth weight less than 2500 g. Low birth weight infants have higher morbidity and mortality. A baby's LBW is either the result of preterm birth (before 37 completed weeks of gestation) or due to intrauterine growth restriction (IUGR) or both. IUGR is similar to malnutrition and may be present in both term and preterm infants. Neonates affected by IUGR are usually undernourished and have loose skin folds on the face and in the gluteal region (Fig. 7.30), absence of subcutaneous fat and peeling of skin.

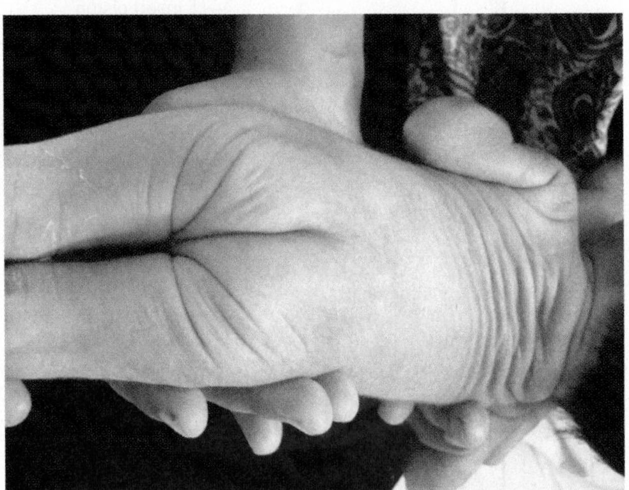

Fig. 7.30: IUGR baby showing many loose folds of skin

LBW babies can be classified according to their birth weight as,

- Low birth weight (LBW) <2.5 kg
- Very low birth weight (VLBW) 1–1.5 kg
- Extremely low birth weight (ELBW) <1 kg

Problems faced by a preterm and IUGR neonate are different; so a clear understanding of these groups is essential (Table 7.16).

Definitions

Prematurity: Gestational age <37 completed weeks

Low birth weight: Birth weight < 2500 g

IUGR (Intrauterine growth restriction): It is a deviation from an expected fetal growth pattern. IUGR can result from any adverse factor that affects the normal growth potential of the fetus. There are two patterns of IUGR:

- *Symmetric:* When insult on the fetal growth occurs early. The size of the head, body weight and length are equally

Table 7.16: Problems of preterm babies versus those in IUGR babies

Major problems encountered in preterm babies
- Hypothermia
- Birth asphyxia
- Respiratory (hyaline membrane disease, pulmonary hemorrhage, pneumothorax, bronchopulmonary dysplasia, pneumonia)
- Apnea of prematurity
- Metabolic (hypoglycemia, hypocalcemia)
- Hematologic (anemia, hyperbilirubinemia)
- Bacterial sepsis
- Feeding problems and poor weight gain

Major problems encountered in IUGR babies
- Perinatal asphyxia
- Meconium aspiration
- Hypothermia
- Hypoglycemia
- Feed intolerance
- Polycythemia
- Growth retardation

reduced. Causes include genetic and chromosomal, TORCH infections, etc.
- *Asymmetric:* The insult on the fetal growth occurs late during gestation producing a brain sparing effect. Head circumference is relatively preserved compared to length and weight. Causes include placental insufficiency, pregnancy-induced hypertension, maternal medical diseases. These infants are at greater risk for hypoglycemia and birth asphyxia.

Small for gestational age (SGA): It is a statistical definition and denotes an infant whose weight is less than 2 standard deviations or less than the tenth percentile of the population norms (plotted on a growth chart).

Special Requirements and Issues

Besides the pathologies that can affect all neonates irrespective of weight and gestation, additional complication occur in LBW which require special care and management.

Resuscitation

Problems
- Compromised intrauterine environment with higher chances of perinatal asphyxia
- Preterm babies have immature lungs that may be more difficult to ventilate and are also more vulnerable to injury by positive-pressure ventilation.
- Immature blood vessels in the brain are prone to hemorrhage
- Thin skin and a large surface area, which contribute to rapid heat loss
- Increased risk of hypovolemic shock caused by small blood volume

Management
- Prepare as high risk resuscitation
- Gentle resuscitation. Small bags for positive pressure ventilation, use of CPAP
- Use of food grade plastic sheets to cover them during resuscitation to avoid hypothermia.

Temperature Control

Problems
- Higher surface area to body weight ratio
- Low glycogen stores
- Low subcutaneous fat.

Management
- Frequent monitoring and educating parents for need to check temperature
- Warm chain maintenance
- Kangaroo mother care practice

Feeding and Nutrition

These have been discussed under the section on feeding.

Fluid and Electrolyte

These have been discussed under the section on fluid and electrolyte management.

Infection

Problems
- Immature defenses
- Greater probability of invasive interventions like mechanical ventilation, umbilical vessel catheterization.

Management
- Strict adherence to asepsis
- Hand washing
- Minimal handling of babies
- Low threshold for suspicion of sepsis, adequate and appropriate use of antibiotics
- Decreasing exposure to adults/other children with communicable diseases particularly respiratory.

7

Metabolic Derangements

Problems
- Low hepatic glycogen stores with rapid depletion in stress places these infants at increased risk of **hypoglycemia.**
- Immature glucose homeostatic mechanisms in premature babies can also lead to decreased inability to utilize glucose and resultant **hyperglycemia**, especially during stressful periods like infection.
- Early onset **hypocalcemia**: presenting within 3 days of life and is usually asymptomatic, detected on investigation. It is especially seen in premature babies, infants of diabetic mothers and those with birth asphyxia.
- Late onset hypocalcemia presents as classical neonatal tetany, jitteriness and seizures. Feeds with higher phosphate load such as cow's milk and some formulae,

result in hyperphosphatemia with subsequent hypocalcemia.

Management
This has been discussed in appropriate sections.

Jaundice

Problems
- Larger RBC volume for body weight
- Immaturity of hepatic enzymes and hepatic excretory capacity
- Immature blood brain barrier-increased risk for bilirubin encephalopathy

Management
This has been discussed in section on jaundice.

Hematological Abnormality

Problems
- *Polycythemia*: Placental insufficiency with intrauterine hypoxia leads to stimulation of erythropoiesis and resultant polycythemia, especially seen in IUGR babies. Polycythemia (>65% hematocrit) produces hyperviscosity with decreased organ perfusion. Manifestations include jitteriness, respiratory distress, cardiac failure, feeding intolerance, hypoglycemia, hypocalcemia and hyperbilirubinemia.
- *Anemia*: Accalarated destruction of fetal RBCs, low reticulocyte count and inadequate response of the bone marrow to erythropoietin cause anemia of premaurity. Low iron stores, higher incidence of sepsis and frequent blood sampling in LBW babies further predisposes to risk of severe anemia.

Management
- *Treatment of polycythemia:* Symptomatic infants or those with Hct > 75% require partial exchange transfusion. For others, management includes increasing the fluid intake.
- *Anemia:*
  - Iron supplementation: All LBW babies should be started of 2–3 mg/kg of iron from 2 months till 2 years of age.
  - Minimal sampling and quantification of amount removed
  - Transfusions as per institution protocol.

Immature Organ Systems in Preterms

Problem and management
- *Intraventricular hemorrhage*: Preterms have a fragile highly vascular collection of vessels near the lateral ventricle of brain. Respiratory distress, mechanical ventilation, vigorous resuscitation, etc. can cause rupture of these vessels leading to adverse neurological sequelae. Preventive measures include minimal and gentle handling, avoiding rapid changes in intravascular volume such as rapid boluses or infusion of hyperosmolar solutions, avoiding high pressures during ventilation and treating any bleeding diathesis. Treatment is essentially supportive and management of later complications such as hydrocephalus.
- *Retinopathy of prematurity:* Growth of retinal vessels occurs from the optic disc to the periphery from 18 weeks of gestation till term. Any injury to these vessels due to the still developing vessels of preterm retina when subjected to the premature transition of postnatal life especially high oxygen saturation as may be used during resuscitation, undergo pathological proliferation resulting in retinal damage with vision loss if left untreated. This complication can be decreased with rational use of oxygen, maintaining a SpO_2 between 85–95% and regular screening for early detection and treatment.
- *Hearing damage:* While not restricted to preterm infants in occurrence due to their immature systems, effect of hypoxia and renotoxic drugs is enhanced leading to a frequent occurrence of sensorineural hearing loss especially after long and eventful NICU stay. Adjustment of doses according to gestational age, checking drug levels and routine screening for early detection can minimize this complication.
- *Osteopenia of prematurity:* Low calcium, phosphorus and Vitamin D levels predispose premature babies to osteopenia and rickets early in neonatal period unless extra supplementation is given. All VLBW babies should be started on 200 mg/kg of calcium, 100 mg/kg of phosphorus and 400 IU of vitamin D as oral or parenteral supplementation.
- *Respiratory distress syndrome:* This has been described in detail later.

Associated Conditions

Problem
An IUGR birth itself might be an indication of a preexisting problem leading to such occurrence. Examples include intrauterine infections and chromosomal anomalies which result in IUGR babies. These usually constitute a subgroup of IUGR babies known as symmetrical IUGR; cause of growth restriction is due to conditions other than nutritional deficiency and onset occurs early in fetal life with proportionate restriction of head and body unlike the nutritionally restricted IUGR with onset in third trimester and sparing of head growth.

Management
- According to diagnosis.

Long Hospital Stay

Requirement for frequent monitoring and aggressive intervention in such high risk babies results in their separation from parents at birth, decreased contact and high expenditure. It is an emotionally and financially trying time for all families. Keeping parents involved in decision making with counseling sessions directed at their concerns helps greatly in management and the final outcome.

Discharge and Follow Up

- Screening tests before discharge or on follow up include those for ROP detection and auditory brainstem evoked response (ABER).
- Nutrition supplements including multivitamins, iron, calcium and vitamin D are started.
- Immunization with BCG, Hep B and OPV given. Many institutes prefer to delay immunization of Hep B and BCG till baby is 2 kg by weight.
- Weight gain should be consistently demonstrated for few days before discharge. Weight, length and head circumference should be noted at discharge and plotted on a growth chart which can be used in follow up to determine if growth is adequate.
- Baby should be feeding well; if on alternate feeding technique like paladai feeding the mother should be confident regarding its details.
- Absence of danger signs and completion of treatment like IV antibiotics; if baby is being discharged on oral medication then parents should be well educated regarding how to administer it and other details regarding it.
- Methods of temperature regulation, either KMC practice or other methods should be well known to parents and practised during hospital stay under supervision.
- All danger signs explained in detail to parents with information regarding whom and where to contact clearly highlighted.
  - History of difficulty in feeding
  - Movement only when stimulated
  - Temperature below 35·5°C or 37·5°C or more
  - Respiratory rate over 60 breaths per minute
  - Severe chest indrawing
  - History of convulsions
- Follow up within 3–7 days of discharge to ensure the baby has been adpted well to home environment. Detailed follow up discussed elsewhere.

FEEDING OF LBW BABIES

Nutritional management influences immediate survival as well as subsequent growth and development of low birth weight (LBW) infants. Early nutrition could also influence the long-term neurodevelopmental outcomes—Malnutrition at a vulnerable period of brain development has been shown to have deleterious effects in experimental animals.

Term infants with normal birth weight require minimal assistance for feeding in the immediate postnatal period. They are able to feed directly from mothers' breast. In contrast, feeding of LBW infants is relatively difficult because of the following limitations:

1. Though majority of these infants are born at term, a significant proportion are born premature with inadequate feeding skills. They might not be able to breastfeed and hence would require other methods of feeding such as spoon or gastric tube feeding.
2. They are prone to have significant illnesses in the first few weeks of life, the underlying condition often precludes enteral feeding.
3. Preterm infants have higher fluid requirements in the first few days of life due to excessive insensible water loss.
4. Since intrauterine accretion occurs mainly in the later part of the third trimester, preterm infants (particularly those born before 32 weeks of gestation) have low body stores of various nutrients at birth which necessitates supplementation in the postnatal period.
5. Because of the gut immaturity, they are more likely to experience feed intolerance necessitating adequate monitoring and treatment.

Methods

Direct and exclusive breastfeeding is the ideal method for feeding a LBW infant. However, because of the various limitations, not all LBW infants would be able to accept breastfeeding at least in the initial few days after birth. These infants have to be fed by either spoon/*paladai* or intragastric tube (gavage feeding); those babies who cannot accept oral feeds by even these methods would require intravenous fluids.

The appropriate method of feeding in a given LBW infant is decided based upon the following factors:

- Whether the infant is sick or not and
- Feeding ability of the infant (which depends upon the gestational maturity).

Level of Sickness

It is essential to categorize LBW infants into two major groups, *sick* and *healthy*, before deciding the initial method of feeding.

Sick infants: This group constitutes infants with respiratory distress requiring assisted ventilation, shock, seizures, symptomatic hypoglycemia, electrolyte abnormalities, renal/cardiac failure, surgical conditions of gastro-intestinal tract, necrotizing enterocolitis (NEC), hydrops, etc. These infants are usually started on intravenous (IV) fluids. Enteral feeds should be initiated as soon as they are hemodynamically stable with the choice of feeding method based on the infants' gestation and clinical condition (*see below*).

It is important to realize that enteral feeding is important even for sick neonates. Oral feeds should not be delayed in them without any valid reason. Even infants with respiratory distress and/or on assisted ventilation can be started on enteral feeds once the acute phase is over and the infants' color, saturation and perfusion have improved. Similarly, sepsis (unless associated with shock/ sclerema/NEC) is not a contraindication for enteral feeding.

Healthy LBW infants: Enteral feeding should be initiated immediately after birth in healthy LBW infants with the appropriate feeding method determined by their oral feeding skills and gestation.

Feeding Ability

Breastfeeding requires effective sucking, swallowing and a proper coordination between suck/swallow and breathing. These complex skills mature with increasing gestation. A mature sucking pattern that can adequately express milk from the breast is not present until 32–34 weeks gestation; the coordination between suck/swallow and breathing is not fully achieved until 37 weeks of gestation. The maturation of oral feeding skills and the choice of initial feeding method at different gestational ages are summarized in Table 7.17.

Table 7.17: Maturation of oral feeding skills and the choice of initial feeding method in LBW infants

Gestational age	*Maturation of feeding skills*	*Initial feeding method*
< 28 weeks	No proper sucking efforts No propulsive motility in the gut	Intravenous fluids
28–31 weeks	Sucking bursts develop No coordination between suck/ swallow and breathing	Oro-gastric (or naso-gastric) tube feeding with occasional spoon/*paladai* feeding
32–34 weeks	Slightly mature sucking pattern Coordination between breathing and swallowing begins	Feeding by spoon/*paladai*/ cup
>34 weeks	Mature sucking pattern More coordination between breathing and swallowing	Breastfeeding

However, it is important to remember that *not all* infants born at a particular gestation would have same feeding skills. Hence, the ideal way in a given infant would be to evaluate if the feeding skills expected for his/her gestation are present and then decide accordingly (Fig. 7.31).

All stable LBW infants, irrespective of their initial feeding method should be put on their mothers' breast. The immature sucking observed in preterm infants born before 34 weeks might not meet their daily fluid and nutritional requirements but helps in rapid maturation of their feeding skills and also improves the milk secretion in their mothers (*Non-nutritive sucking*).

Figures 7.32A and B show the method of *paladai* and intragastric tube feeding in babies.

Progression of Oral Feeds

All LBW infants, irrespective of their gestation and birth weight, should ultimately be able to feed directly from the mothers' breast. For preterm LBW infants started on IV fluids/OG tube/*paladai* feeding, the steps of progression to direct and exclusive breastfeeding are summarized in Fig. 7.33.

Term LBW infants started on IV fluids (because of their sickness) can be put on the breast once they are hemodynamically stable.

Choice of Milk

All LBW infants, irrespective of their initial feeding method should receive only breast milk. This can be ensured by giving expressed breast milk (mothers' own milk) for those infants fed by *paladai* or gastric tube.

Expressed breast milk (EBM): All mothers should be counseled and supported in expressing their own milk for feeding their preterm infants. Expression should ideally be initiated within hours of delivery so that the infant gets the benefits of feeding colostrum. Thereafter, it should be done 2–3 hourly so that the infant is exclusively breastfed and lactation is maintained in the mother. Expressed breast milk can be stored for about 6 hours at room temperature and for 24 hours in refrigerator. The steps of breast milk expression are given in Fig. 7.29.

Sick mothers/contraindication to breastfeeding: In these rare circumstances, the options available are

1. Formula feeds:
   a. Preterm formula – in VLBW infants and
   b. Term formula – in infants weighing >1500 g at birth
2. Animal milk, e.g. undiluted cow's milk

Once the mother's condition becomes stable (or the contraindication to breastfeeding no longer exists), these infants should be started on exclusive breastfeeding.

How Much to Feed?

Infants Who are Breastfed

Infants who are able to suckle effectively at the breast should be breastfed on demand. Small babies usually demand to feed every 2–3 hours, sometimes more frequently. A small infant, who does not demand to be fed for 3 hours or more, can be offered the breast and encouraged to feed.

Infants Who are Fed by Spoon/ Paladai or by Intragastric Tube

It is essential to know how much to feed, the amount of expressed breast milk to be given, for those infants who

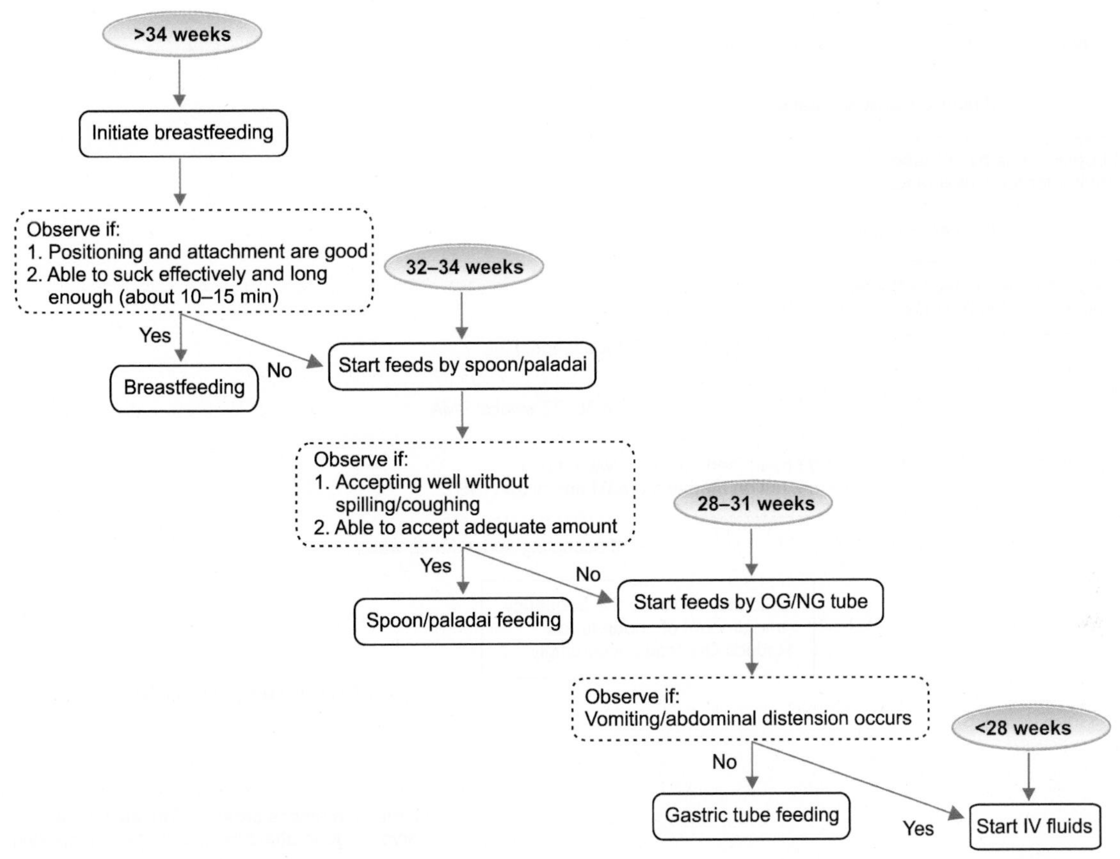

Fig. 7.31: Choosing initial methods of feeding

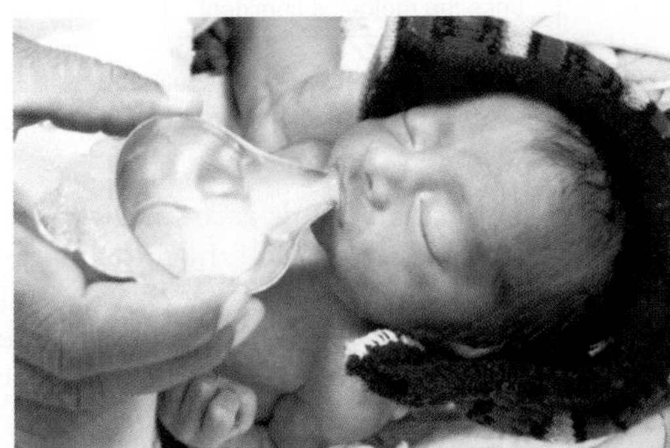

A

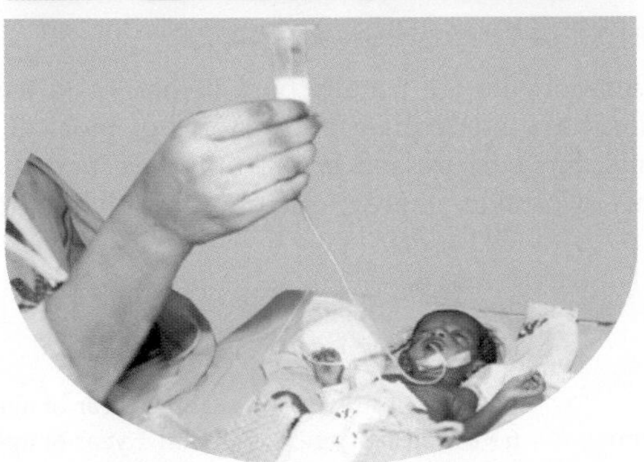

B

Figs 7.32A and B: (A) Paladai feeding; (B) Gavage feeding

are on alternative methods of feeding like gavage or spoon feeding.

The daily fluid requirement is determined based on the estimated insensible water loss, other losses, and urine output. Extreme preterm infants need more fluids in the initial weeks of life because of the high insensible water loss. It is usual clinical practice to provide VLBW infants (<1500 g) about 80 ml/kg fluids on the first day of life and increase by 10–15 ml/kg/day to a maximum of 160 ml/kg/day by the end of the first week of life. LBW infants ≥1500 g are usually given about 60 ml/kg fluids on the first day of life and fluid intake is increased by about 15–20 ml/kg/day to a maximum of 160 ml/kg/day by the end of the first week of life. After deciding the total daily fluid requirement, the individual feed volume to be given every 2 or 3 hours (by OG tube or *paladai)* can be determined.

Nutritional Supplementation

LBW infants, especially those who are born preterm, require supplementation of various nutrients to meet their high demands. Since the requirements of VLBW infants differ significantly from those with birth weights of 1500–2499 g, supplementation regimes for these two groups have been discussed separately.

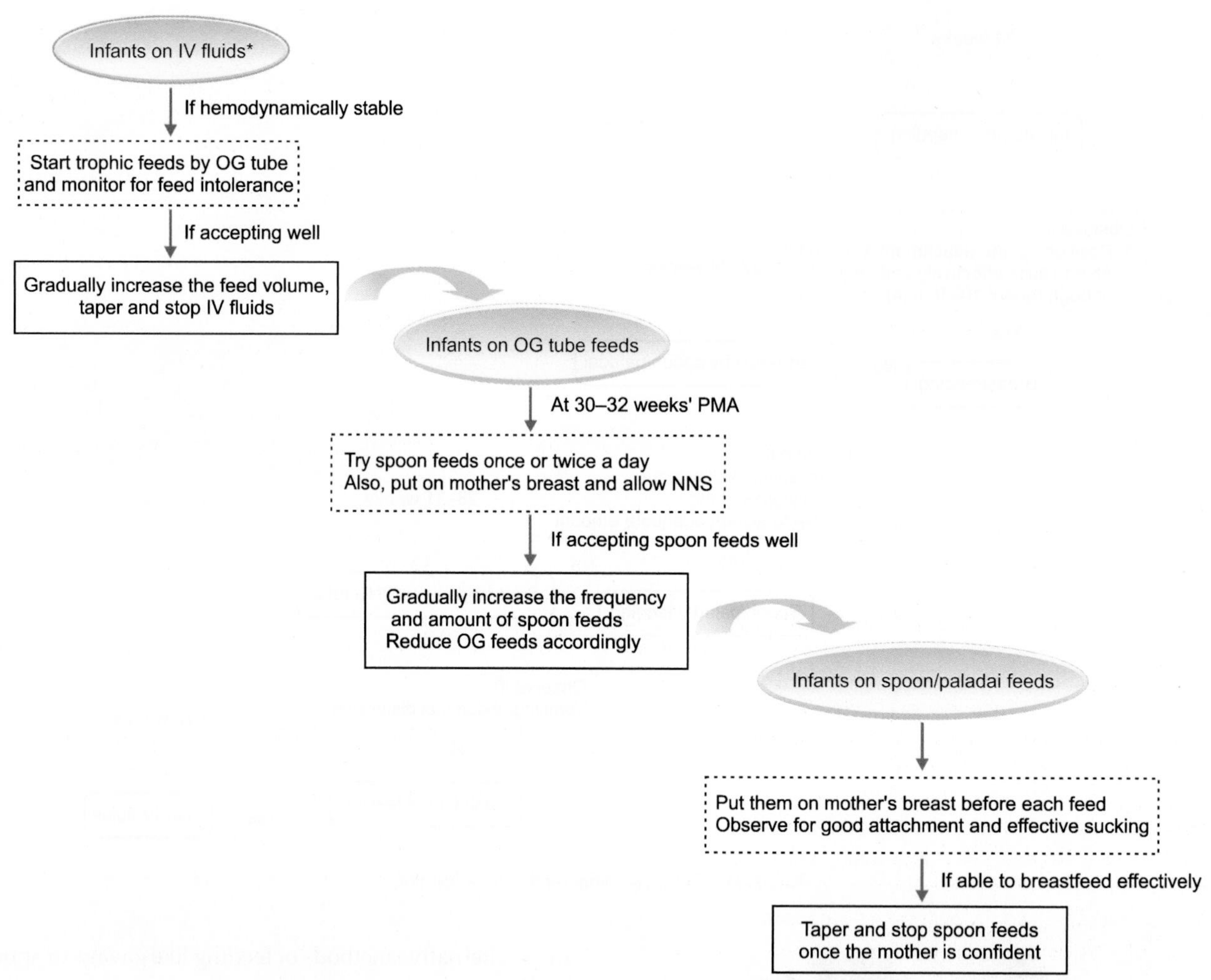

Fig. 7.33: Progression of oral feeding in preterm LBW infants. (IV, intravenous; OG, oro-gastric tube; PMA, postmenstrual age; NNS, non-nutritive sucking) * Term and near-term sick infants started on IV fluids can be initiated on breastfeeding once they are hemodynamically stable

7

Supplementation for Infants with Birth Weights of 1500–2499 g

These infants are more likely to be born at term or near term gestation (≥34 weeks) and are more likely to have adequate body stores of most nutrients. Therefore, they do not require multi-nutrient supplementation (unlike VLBW infants). However, vitamin D and iron might still have to be supplemented in them. While iron supplementation is mandatory for all infants, supplementation of vitamin D is contentious because of the paucity of the data regarding its levels and deficiency status in different populations. Some would argue that the daily requirement of vitamin D is met usually by *de novo* synthesis in the skin following exposure to sunlight and hence no supplementation is required. However, because LBW infants are more at risk of osteopenia than healthy term infants, most neonatal units tend to supplement vitamin D in the dose of 200–400 IU/day (Table 7.18).

Supplementation in VLBW Infants

These infants who are usually born before 32–34 weeks gestation have inadequate body stores of most of the nutrients. Since expressed breast milk has inadequate amounts of protein, energy, calcium, phosphorus, trace

Table 7.18: Nutritional supplements for infants with birth weights of 1500–2499 g

Nutrients	*Method of supplementation*	*Dose*	*When to start*	*Till when?*
Vitamin D*	Multivitamin drops/syrup	200–400 IU/day	2 weeks of life	Until 1 year of age
Iron	Iron drops/syrup	2 mg/kg/day (maximum 15 mg/day)	6 – 8 weeks of age	Until 1 year of age

elements (iron, zinc) and vitamins D, E and K, it is often not able to meet the daily recommended intakes of these infants. Hence, these infants need multi-nutrient supplementation till they reach term gestation (40 weeks, i.e. until the expected date of delivery). The following nutrients have to be added to the expressed breast milk in them:

1. Calcium and phosphorus (140–160 mg/kg/d and 70–80 mg/kg/d respectively for infants on EBM)
2. Vitamin D (400 IU/day), vitamin B complex and zinc (about 0.5 mg/day)–usually in the form of multivitamin drops
3. Folate (about 50 mcg/kg/day)
4. Iron (2 mg/kg/day)

Multi-nutrient supplementation can be ensured by one of the following methods:

1. Supplementing individual nutrients, e.g. calcium, phosphorus, vitamins, etc. These supplements should be added at different times in the day to avoid abnormal increase in the osmolality.
2. By fortification of expressed breast milk with human milk fortifiers (HMF): Fortification increases the nutrient content of the milk without compromising its other beneficial effects. Experimental studies have shown that the use of fortified human milk results in net nutrient retention that approaches or is greater than expected intrauterine rates of accretion in preterm infants. Preterm VLBW infants fed fortified human milk do not require any supplementation other than iron.

Fortification or supplementation of minerals and vitamins should be continued only till term gestation (40 weeks) in VLBW infants; after this period, only vitamin D and iron needs to be supplemented (similar to infants with birth weights of ≥1500 g).

Growth Monitoring of LBW Infants

Regular growth monitoring helps in assessing the nutritional status and adequacy of feeding in LBW infants; it also identifies those infants with inadequate weight gain.

All LBW infants should be weighed daily till the time of discharge from the hospital. Other anthropometric parameters such as length and head circumference should be recorded weekly.

Both term and preterm LBW infants tend to lose weight (about 10% and 15% respectively) in the first 7 days of life; they regain their birth weight by 10–14 days. Thereafter, the weight gain should be at least 15–20 g/kg/day till a weight of 2–2.5 kg is reached. After this, a gain of 20 to 30 g/day is considered appropriate.

Growth charts: Using a growth chart is a simple but effective way to monitor the growth. Serial plotting of weight and other anthropometric indicators in the growth chart allows the individual infant's growth to be compared with a reference standard. It helps in early identification of growth faltering in these infants.

Two types of growth charts are commonly used for growth monitoring in preterm infants: intrauterine and postnatal growth charts. Of these, the postnatal growth chart is preferred because it is a more realistic representation of the true postnatal growth (than an intrauterine growth chart) and also shows the initial weight loss that occurs in the first two weeks of life. The two postnatal charts that are most commonly used for growth monitoring of preterm VLBW infants are: Wright's and Ehrenkranz' charts. Once the preterm LBW infants reach term gestation (40 weeks), WHO growth charts should be used for growth monitoring.

Management of Inadequate Weight Gain

Inadequate weight gain is a common and pertinent problem in LBW infants. It starts at the time of initial admission and continues after discharge resulting in failure to thrive and wasting in the first year of life. The common causes are summarized in Table 7.19.

Table 7.19: Causes of inadequate weight gain

1. Inadequate intake
Breastfed infants:
Incorrect feeding method (improper positioning/attachment)*
Less frequent breastfeeding, not feeding in the night hours*
Infants on spoon/paladai feeds:
Incorrect method of feeding* (e.g. excess spilling)
Incorrect measurement/calculation
Infrequent feeding*
Not fortifying the milk in VLBW infants
2. Increased demands
Illnesses such as hypothermia/cold stress*, bronchopulmonary dysplasia
Medications such as corticosteroids

*Common causes

Management of inadequate weight gain consists of the following steps:

1. Proper counseling of mothers and ensuring adequate support for breastfeeding their infants; includes assessment of positioning/attachment, managing sore/flat nipple, etc.
2. Explaining the frequency and timing of both breast-feeding and spoon/*paladai* feeds: Infrequent feeding is one of the commonest causes of inadequate weight gain. Mothers should be properly counseled regarding the frequency and the importance of night feeds. A time-table where mother can fill the timing and amount of feeding is very helpful in ensuring frequent feeding.
3. Giving EBM by spoon/*paladai* feeds after breastfeeding also helps in preterm infants who tire out easily while sucking from the breast.

4. Proper demonstration of the correct method of expression of milk and *paladai* feeding: It is important to observe how the mother gives *paladai* feeds; the technique and amount of spillage should be noted. This should be followed by a practical demonstration of the proper procedure.
5. Initiating fortification of breast milk when indicated
6. If these measures are not successful, increase either the
   a. Energy (calorie) content of milk by adding MCT oil, corn starch, etc. Infants on formula feeds can be given concentrated feeds (by reconstituting 1 scoop in 25 mL of water), OR
   b. Feed volume – to 200 mL/kg/day.

Suggested reading

1. Nutrition. In: Edmond K, Bahl R (Eds). Optimal feeding of low-birth-weight infants—Technical Review. World Health Organization 2006; p42.
2. Sankar MJ, Agarwal R et al. Feeding of low birth weight infants. Indian J Pediatr 2008;75:459–69.

NEONATAL SEPSIS

When pathogenic organisms gain access into the blood stream, they may cause an overwhelming infection without much localization (septicemia), or may get predominantly localized to the lung (causing pneumonia) or the meninges (causing meningitis). Systemic bacterial infections are known by the generic term neonatal sepsis (NNS), which incorporates septicemia, pneumonia and meningitis of the newborn.

NNS is one of the most important morbidities seen at the community and facility levels. It is also the most important cause of neonatal deaths in the community. If diagnosed early and treated aggressively with antibiotics and, equally importantly, with good supportive care, it is possible to save most cases of neonatal sepsis.

7

Etiology

Escherichia coli, *Staphylococcus aureus* and *Klebsiella sp*. are responsible for most cases of neonatal sepsis.

Early vs Late Sepsis

Early-onset sepsis (EOS) (less than 72 hr) infections are caused by organisms prevalent in the maternal genital tract or in the delivery area. The predisposing factors include low birth weight (LBW), prolonged rupture of membranes, foul smelling liquor, multiple per vaginum examinations, maternal fever, difficult or prolonged labor and aspiration of meconium. EOS manifests frequently as pneumonia and less commonly as septicemia or meningitis.

Late-onset sepsis (LOS) (greater than 72 hr) infections are caused by the organisms thriving in the external environments of the home or the hospital. The infection is often transmitted through the hands of the care-providers. The presentation is that of septicemia, pneumonia or meningitis. The predisposing factors include LBW, lack of breastfeeding, poor cord care, superficial infections (pyoderma, umbilical sepsis), aspiration of feeds, and disruption of skin integrity with needle pricks and use of intravenous fluids.

When to Suspect NNS?

The manifestations of NNS are often vague and ill-defined, and, therefore, demand a high index of suspicion for early diagnosis. A common and early but non-specific manifestation is an alteration in the established feeding behavior. The baby, who had been active and sucking normally, gradually or suddenly refuses to suck and becomes lethargic, inactive or unresponsive. Poor cry, hypothermia, abdominal distension, vomiting and apneic spells are other common manifestations. Diarrhea is uncommon. Fast breathing, chest retractions and grunt indicate pneumonia. Most cases of meningitis do not have any distinct clinical picture per se, making it mandatory to suspect meningitis in practically all cases suspected of sepsis. Presence of excessive or high-pitched crying, fever, seizures, blank look, neck retraction or bulging anterior fontanel are highly suggestive of meningitis. Shock, bleeding, sclerema and renal failure are indicators of overwhelming sepsis.

A host of conditions like hypothermia, hyperthermia, hypoglycemia, hypoxia, late metabolic acidosis, congestive heart failure, and even a simple condition like nasal block may mimic sepsis. A careful clinical examination and relevant investigations are necessary to differentiate these conditions from NNS.

Investigations

No investigation is required as a prerequisite to start treatment in a clinically obvious case. Blood culture is of help in guiding therapy. A panel of tests consisting of total leukocyte count (TLC), absolute neutrophil count (ANC), immature to total neutrophil ratio (I/T ratio), CRP and micro ESR constitutes a useful sepsis screen for clinically doubtful cases. Sepsis screen is considered positive if two of these parameters are positive. Value of sepsis screen is more for exclusion of diagnosis of NNS. The diagnosis of sepsis can be reasonably excluded if two screens 12–24 hr apart are negative.

Blood Culture

Blood culture should be taken before starting antimicrobial therapy. After cleaning with alcohol, povidone-iodine and again alcohol, a specimen of 0.5 to 1.0 ml of blood can be taken in a small culture media bottle containing 5 to 10 ml of the liquid broth.

Lumbar Puncture (LP)

1. LP should be performed in all cases suspected of NNS except in asymptomatic babies being investigated for maternal risk factors.
2. Table 7.20 depicts the normal CSF parameters in neonates.

Table 7.20: Normal CSF examination in neonates [(mean (range)]

Test	Term	Preterm
Cells		
WBCs	7 (0–32)	9 (0–29)
Polymorphonuclear cells	61%	57%
Protein (mg/dl)	90 (20–170)	115 (65–150)
Glucose (mg/dl)	52 (34–119)	50 (24–63)

Indirect Markers of Neonatal Infection

1. *TLC:* There is a wide range of normal TLC, from 8000 to 20,000 per cu mm and high counts are often of no value. Neonatal sepsis is associated with leukopenia (TLC < 5000/cu mm).
2. *ANC:* ANC includes both immature and mature neutrophils. ANC is obtained by doing a differential leukocyte count on a stained smear or preferably by the automatic Coulter counter (after correction for nucleated red cells). ANC below 1800 per cubic mm is believed to be the best predictor of sepsis, while neutrophilia does not correlate well.
3. *I/T ratio:* An I/T ratio of over 0.2 is a highly sensitive marker of NNS. It is obtained by examining the peripheral blood smear, counting the immature and mature neutrophils separately. A mature neutrophil has segmented nucleus and the segments are connected by characteristic thin filamentous strands. In contrast, the nucleus of a band cell is indented by more than one half of its breadth giving a uniform diameter (band-like configuration or a lobulated appearance) in which the isthmus between the lobules is broad enough to reveal two distinct margins with nuclear material between them. Occasionally, metamyelocytes, which are less mature neutrophils than bands, may also spill into peripheral blood. The nucleus of a metamyelocyte shows only marginal identation. All bands and other cell forms which are less mature than bands are classified as immature neutrophils.
4. *C-reactive protein (CRP):* A concentration above 1 mg/dL would indicate NNS.
5. *Micro ESR:* mESR is obtained by collecting capillary blood in a standard preheparinized microhematocrit glass tube (75 mm length, internal diameter 1.1 mm, outer diameter 1.5 mm), placing it vertically and reading the fall in the red cell column after one hour. The normal value (mm 1st hour) is equal to the postnatal day of life plus 3 mm (thus it is 5 on day 2 and 10 on day 7). Peak value is 15 mm at the end of 1st hour during neonatal period. High mESR is a specific test but it has only moderate sensitivity. The value is spuriously high in neonates with hemolysis and low in babies with disseminated consumptive coagulopathy.

Treatment

Institution of prompt treatment is essential for ensuring optimum outcome of neonates with sepsis who often reach the health care facilities late and in a critical condition. Supportive care and antibiotics are the two *equally important* components of treatment. It should be realized that antibiotics take at least 12 to 24 hours to show any effect and it is the supportive care that makes the difference between life and death early in the hospital course.

Supportive Care

Good supportive care plays a vital role in management of sick babies. Meticulous attention is required to various aspects of it.

- Provide warmth; ensure consistently normal temperature (36.5°C–37.5°C). Kangaroo mother care (KMC) is a useful modality to maintain temperature of small and sick babies.
- Start oxygen by hood or mask, if cyanosed or grunting. Provide bag and mask ventilation with oxygen if breathing is inadequate. Instilling normal saline drops in nostrils may help clear the nasal block.
- Assess peripheral perfusion by palpating peripheral pulses, assessing capillary refill time (CRT) (normal less than 2–3 seconds), and skin color. Serial measurement of urine output is helpful for this purpose. Infuse normal saline or Ringer lactate 10 ml/kg over 5–10 minutes, if perfusion is poor as evidenced by CRT of more than 3 seconds. Repeat the same dose 1–2 times over the next 30–45 minutes, if perfusion continues to be poor. Dopamine and dobutamine may be required to maintain normal perfusion in sick babies.
- Start intravenous line. If hypoglycemia is suspected, infuse glucose (10%) 2 ml/kg stat. Do not use glucose boluses routinely. Provide maintenance fluid, electrolytes and glucose (4–6 mg/kg/min). Add potassium to IV fluids once normal flow of urine is documented.
- Ensuring optimal nutrition is extremely helpful in sick babies. Enteral feeds should be initiated early if there is no abdominal distension and baby is hemodynamically stable. Feed mother's milk. Consider parenteral nutrition, if available.
- Administer vitamin K 1 mg intramuscularly.
- Transfuse packed cells, if baby has a low hematocrit (less than 35–40%). Do not use blood/plasma transfusion on routine basis for 'boosting' immunity.

Approach to Antimicrobial Therapy

Antimicrobial therapy constitutes the mainstay of treatment of sepsis. In a seriously sick neonate suspected of sepsis, appropriate antibiotics therapy should be initiated without any delay after obtaining blood samples for culture and sepsis screen. One need not await the results of sepsis screen for antibiotics treatment. However, in a baby who is stable otherwise or suspected of sepsis because of maternal risk factors, it is desirable to await results of sepsis screen before initiation of antibiotics. Since symptoms suggestive of sepsis may be caused by a variety of other illnesses, confirmation of sepsis by sepsis screen may help avoiding unnecessary antibiotics therapy.

Empiric therapy when etiologic agent is not known: The empiric therapy of NNS should cover the major causative pathogens while awaiting reports of culture studies. Since the antimicrobial spectrum and susceptibility profile is different in different newborn services, there cannot be a universal recommendation of a single empiric regimen. Antibiotics are often used in neonates on the slightest suspicion of sepsis because of the grave and fulminant nature of neonatal sepsis. But unbridled overuse of antibiotics is associated with the serious risk of emergence of resistant strains of pathogens. Most newborn units in the country are facing the problem of overwhelming resistance to commonly used antibiotics including third generation cephalosporins. Rational use of antibiotics is, therefore, the responsibility of every physician.

Each treating unit should adopt a suitable policy. Based on changes in the spectrum of etiologic agents and the antibiotics sensitivity pattern, the choice of antibiotics must be periodically reviewed and modified. Table 7.21 provides possible regimen of empiric antibiotics.

Therapy after an etiologic agent is known: Antimicrobial therapy can be made specific once a positive culture and sensitivity report is available. However, this would be known only after 2–3 days. Even in best institutions well over 50% blood cultures are negative.

7

Table 7.21: Initial antibiotic therapy (individualized and later modified as per the clinical course and culture reports)

Clinical situation	*Septicemia and pneumonia*	*Meningitis*
First line		
Community-acquired; resistant strains unlikely	Ampicillin or penicillin and gentamicin	Cefotaxime and gentamicin
Second line		
Hospital-acquired or when there is a low to moderate probability of resistant strains	Ampicillin or cloxacillin and amikacin	Cefotaxime and amikacin
Third line		
Hospital-acquired sepsis or when there is a high probability of resistant strains	Cefotaxime and amikacin	Cefotaxime and amikacin

Mode of Administration and Dosage

Antibiotics should preferably be administered parenterally. In a baby with septicemia or pneumonia (but not meningitis), who has received intravenous ampicillin and gentamicin initially and is clinically well after 3 days, the physician may consider on individual basis switching over to oral amoxycillin along with single-dose intramuscular gentamicin therapy for the rest of the course. Studies are needed to confirm the efficacy of this approach.

Adjunct Therapy

Exchange blood transfusion (EBT): EBT using fresh whole blood in sick infected babies in the presence of sclerema, disseminated coagulation, hyperbilirubinemia or rapid clinical deterioration has been shown to be effective. Since the candidate babies are likely to be unstable, it is important to monitor them carefully during the procedure.

Intravenous immunoglobulin (IVIG): The use of IVIG as a prophylaxis or in treatment of NNS is not recommended. It has doubtful beneficial immune-enhancement effect and may be associated with harmful side effects.

Monitoring

Intensive care and monitoring is the key determinant of improved survival of neonates. The elements of monitoring in sepsis are not different from those in other lifethreatening conditions, and enable detection of complications at the earliest in order to ensure timely intervention. The periodicity of documenting the various parameters should be individualized.

Prognosis

The outcome depends upon weight and maturity of the infant, type of etiologic agent, its antibiotic senstivity pattern; and adequacy of specific and supportive therapy. The early-onset septicemia carries adverse outcome. The reported mortality rates in neonatal sepsis in various studies from India ranges between 45–58%. The institution of sepsis screen for early detection of infection, judicious and early antimicrobial therapy, close monitoring of vital signs and intensive supportive care are the most crucial factors responsible for a better outcome.

Suggested readings

Sankar MJ, Agarwal R, Deorari AK, Paul VK. Sepsis in the newborn. Indian J Pediatr. 2008 Mar;75(3):261–6.

NECROTIZING ENTEROCOLITIS

Necrotizing enterocolitis occurs among premature infants under stress in the first week of life. The clinical picture closely resembles neonatal septicemia because of the association of abdominal distension, apnea, bradycardia, instability of temperature, cyanosis and lethargy.

Pathogenesis: Several factors are implicated.

1. *Mucosal injury:* This is attributed to (i) ischemic damage to the intestinal mucosal barrier, as a result of fetal distress, perinatal asphyxia, respiratory distress syndrome -hypothermia, vascular spasm or following exchange transfusion for hyperbilirubinemia, (ii) diarrhea and (iii) bacterial infections of the injured gut with *E. coli, Klebsiella, Pseudomonas* or *Salmonella*. More recently, infection with clostridia, *C. perfringens* and *C. butyricum* have been incriminated. Stasis of intestinal contents favors bacterial overgrowth.
2. *Formula feeding:* Almost all patients of neonatal necrotizing enterocolitis are artificially fed prior to the onset of illness. Breast milk appears to be protective for NEC. It appears that there must be a substrate in the formula feed which facilitates gas production in the intestinal flora. Poor systemic and gastrointestinal immunological protection against bacterial infections in the preterm babies predisposes them to infection of the gut.

Clinical features: The illness usually develops after the first week of life. The course may be very fulminant with death occurring in a few hours, mortality rate being around 40–50%. Clinical manifestations may be described in three stages:

Stage 1: Suspected NEC: Unstable temperature, apnea, bradycardia, lethargy, mild abdominal distension, vomiting. In stage 1B, blood is present in stools. X-ray shows mild intestinal distension in stage lA and 1B.

Stage 2: Clinical signs as above. Bowel sounds are diminished with or without abdominal tenderness. In more severe cases of this stage **(2B)**, there may be metabolic acidosis and mild thrombocytopenia. Pneumatosis intestinalis (gas in intestinal wall) and dilatation of intestines are seen on abdominal X-ray (Fig. 7.34).

Stage 3: In addition to the above, the infant has low blood pressure, bradycardia, apnea, acidosis, disseminated intravascular coagulation and even anuria. There are frank signs of peritonitis with abdominal wall redness. Pneumoperitoneum is present in abdominal X-ray.

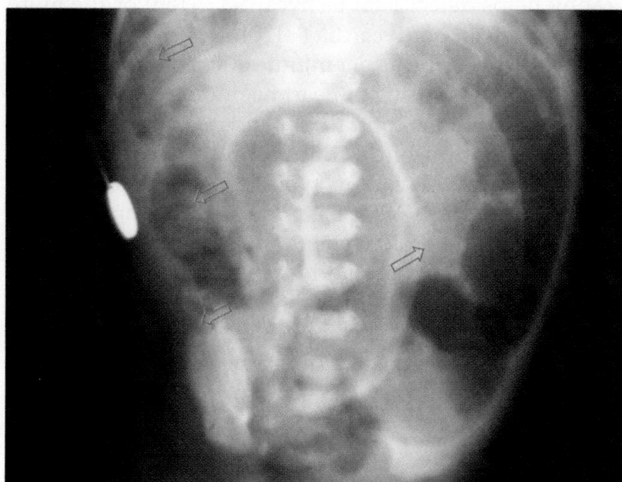

Fig. 7.34: Necrotizing enterocolitis showing dilated bowel loops and pneumatosis intestinalis (arrows)

Management: All oral feeding should be withheld. A nasogastric tube is inserted to relieve distension and aspirate stomach contents. Fluids and electrolytes in adequate quantities should be administered. Parenteral alimentation may be administered to provide nutrition.

The blood, cerebrospinal fluid, urine and stools are cultured. Shock is managed by replacement of fluids and use of vasopressor agents. Plasma and platelet transfusion are used to prevent bleeding tendency.

Perforation is suggested if there is free intra-abdominal gas and liver dullness is obliterated. Surgical intervention is necessary in these cases.

Sequelae: Intestinal strictures may be left in survivors. These manifest with bloody stools, vomiting and abdominal distention. Shortened bowel leads to malabsorption.

POST-RESUSCITATION MANAGEMENT OF ASPHYXIATED NEONATES

Perinatal Asphyxia

Perinatal asphyxia is an insult to the fetus or newborn due to a lack of oxygen (hypoxia) and/or a lack of perfusion (ischemia) to various organs. It is often associated with tissue lactic acidosis and hypercarbia.

There is no universally accepted definition of perinatal asphyxia. The American Academy of Pediatrics Committee on Fetus and Newborn has suggested essential criteria (Tables 7.22 and 7.23) of defining a case of perinatal asphyxia.

Table 7.22: Essential criteria for perinatal asphyxia

- Prolonged metabolic or mixed academia (pH <7.0) on an umbilical arterial blood sample
- Persistence of apgar score of 0–3 for >5 min
- Neurological manifestations, e.g. seizures, coma, hypotonia or hypoxic ischemic encephalopathy (HIE) in the immediate neonatal period
- Evidence of multiorgan dysfunction in the immediate neonatal period

Table 7.23: Multiorgan dysfunction in perinatal asphyxia

CNS	HIE, cerebral edema, seizures, long-term neurological sequelae
Pulmonary	Pulmonary hypertension, meconium aspiration, surfactant disruption
Renal	Oliguria, acute renal failure
Metabolic	Metabolic acidosis, hypoglycemia, hypocalcemia, hyponatremia
Gastrointestinal	Necrotizing enterocolitis, hepatic dysfunction
Hematological	Thrombocytopenia, disseminated intravascular coagulation

HIE: Hypoxic ischemic encephalopathy

In the absence of such quantification it is better to use the term 'neonatal depression', which refers to a condition of the infant in the immediate postnatal period (approximately 1st hour) without making any association with objective evidence.

National Neonatology Forum of India (NNF) and WHO use an Apgar of 0–3 and 4–7, at 1 minute, to define severe and moderate birth asphyxia respectively (1985). For the community settings NNF defines asphyxia as absence of cry at 1 minute and severe asphyxia as absent or inadequate breathing at five minutes.

Neuropathology

These differ according to gestation (Table 7.24) and are of the following main types:

Table 7.24: Neurological patterns of hypoxic ischemic encephalopathy (HIE)

Premature newborns
Selective subcortical neuronal necrosis
Periventricular leukomalacia
Focal and multifocal ischemic necrosis
Periventricular hemorrhage infarction
Term newborn
Selective cortical neuronal necrosis
Status marmoratus of basal ganglia and thalamus
Parasagittal cerebral injury
Focal and multifocal ischemic cerebral necrosis

Term

Selective neuronal necrosis involves cerebral cortex, hippocampus, basal ganglia, cerebellum and anterior horn cells of spinal cord. Seen predominantly in term infants and depending on site, this manifests clinically as diminished consciousness, seizures, and abnormalities of feeding, breathing, etc. Status marmoratus is a variant of selective neuronal necrosis involving only basal ganglia and thalamus, having long term sequelae such as choreoathetosis, spastic quadriparesis and retardation. Focal necroses are commonly thromboembolic and involve the left middle cerebral artery. Parasagittal area serves as the watershed area for many arteries and hence is vulnerable to ischemia resulting in proximal limb weakness (upper > lower) that later may develop into spastic quadriparesis.

Preterm

Selective neuronal necrosis is rare in preterms; diencephalic neuronal necrosis restricted to thalamus and brainstem with or without hypothalamus and lateral geniculate body is seen. Hypoxia and acidosis followed by hyperoxia demonstrates a unique pattern of injury involving pontine nucleus and subiculum of the hippocampus.

Periventricular leukomalacia (PVL) results from HIE insult leading to coagulative necrosis and infarction of periventricular white matter that is the watershed area between various arteries. Two areas frequently involved are the posterior white matter, involving the occipital radiation at trigone and anteriorly around the foramen of Munro. Relative sparing of the cerebral cortex is seen due to its rich supply of arteries. Long-term sequels include spastic diplegia and quadriplegia (lower limbs > upper limbs) and visual impairment. Posthemorrhagic infarcts are usually associated with severe intraventricular bleeds and result from venous infarction due to occlusion of medullary and terminal veins by the large bleed. Other lesions include small infarcts secondary to blocking of end arteries resulting in porencephaly, hydrancephaly or multicystic encephalomalacia.

Diagnosis and Approach

Hypoxia is an evolving process that starts at the onset of the insult and continues after resuscitation and thereafter manifests in form of sequelae. Management thus depends on which point in this evolution it is detected; with the preventive approach beginning in the prenatal period and then continuing in the form of a long follow up much after the stabilization of the initial condition.

Antenatal Assessment

Meticulous antenatal check up with early detection and management of high risk mothers such as those with diabetes, hypertension, or bad obstetric history help both reduce complications and allow the mother and the treating doctor to prepare adequately.

Perinatal Assessment

Anticipating problems and being prepared for intervention require rigorous monitoring during labor which may include, depending on availability of resources, the following—fetal movement, non-stress test, fetal biophysical profile, fetal heart rate alternation, and fetal acid-base status.

Fetal heart rate monitoring clinically or by tococardiography helps detect fetal tachycardia (>160) or the more worrisome fetal bradycardia (<120). Normal beat-to-beat variability is 6–25 beats per minute. Most ominous are late deceleration (a slowing of heart beginning 15–30 seconds after onset of uterine contractions and returning to baseline after contraction ends) and combination of loss of variability with the various types of deceleration.

Fetal scalp pH < 7.0 or base deficit > 12 is an evidence of significant and prolonged intrauterine asphyxia and are indications of urgent delivery. Meconium passage suggests fetal hypoxia though 10–20% of normal pregnancy and 25–50% of uncomplicated postdated pregnancies may also have meconium-stained liquor. Fetal nails and cord staining indicate > 4 to 6 hrs of exposure.

Delivery Room

Prevention of heat loss and rapid establishment of effective ventilation and circulation are the cornerstones to neonatal resuscitation. The details of resuscitation have been

7

discussed previously. Hyperthermia should also be avoided as it may lead to further neurological damage.

Other conditions that may be considered in the delivery room and thereafter include: the effect of maternal drugs or anesthesia; acute blood loss; acute intracranial bleeding; CNS malformation; neuromuscular disease; cardiopulmonary disease; mechanical impediments to ventilation; and infection (including septic shock and hypotension).

Postnatal Assessment

Risk factors noted in ante and intrapartum period along with post delivery resuscitation, Apgar and neurological examination help in diagnosis of most cases. Laboratory methods help quantify the damage and can predict outcome to some extent.

A wide spectrum of clinical manifestations is seen depending on the severity of injury. These manifestations change over time and are clinically noted in babies of gestational age >36 weeks by classification on the basis of Sarnat stages of HIE (1976). This helps both note the evolution of the state and predict outcome. No baby in stage 1 has a poor outcome, in stage 2, 20–40% may have adverse outcome while stage 3 has a universally poor outcome (Table 7.25).

In acute severe HIE the sequence seen is:

- During 1st 12 hrs—Evidence of bilateral hemispheric dysfunction with decreased consciousness.
- Between 12–24 hrs—apparent improvement in level of consciousness but with associated worsening of other aspects such as seizures or apnea.
- During the first 3 days of life—signs of brainstem dysfunction worsening like ophthalmoplegia, bulbar involvement and arrest may occur.
- After 3–4 days—if patient survives, gradual improvement in the neurological status occurs. Persistent sequelae that commonly remain include dullness, feeding problems, obstructive apnea and abnormal muscle tone.

  Milder presentations include hyper alert states with jitteriness, excessive crying, exaggerated Moro and hyperreflexia.

Involvement of other systems, most commonly renal and cardiac, significantly add to the clinical picture and point to substantial perinatal insult.

Management of Hypoxic-ischemic Injury

Initial management includes effective resuscitation at the delivery room followed by supportive care under frequent monitoring. The aim is to keep all parameters within *normal* range except for fluids, which may be restricted in case of syndrome of inappropriate antidiuretic hormone (SIADH).

1. *Temperature:* Even though hypothermia has been recently investigated for its neuroprotective actions presently recommended temperature remains the thermoneutral zone for the baby.
2. *Oxygen (PaO_2):* Both hypoxia and hyperoxia can damage neurons; hence percent O_2 saturation (SpO_2) or preferably arterial oxygen levels should be monitored and kept in normal range.
3. *Carbon-dioxide ($PaCO_2$):* Hypercarbia causes cerebral acidosis and vasodilatation, which leads to shunting of blood away from compromised areas (steal phenomenon) increasing infarct size. Hypocapnia of <25 mm Hg decreases cerebral perfusion and can cause infarction. Both should be avoided and this requires blood gas monitoring.
4. *Perfusion:* Cerebral perfusion pressure (CPP) reflects systemic blood pressure in a pressure passive manner. Hence to maintain the desired range of CPP a systemic mean arterial pressure of 45–50 mm Hg (term), 35–40 (1–2 kg weight) and 30–35 mmHg (< 1 kg weight) is required. Blood pressure measurement should be taken in all babies. A central venous pressure of 5–8 mm Hg in term and 3–5 mm Hg in preterm babies is ideal. Free water administration should be restricted. In case of poor perfusion, bolus administration should be done slowly and along with monitoring to avoid overhydration. Judicious use of pressors can help maintain adequate BP. Hyperviscosity due to a hematocrit of 65 or more should be corrected by partial exchange with normal saline.

Table 7.25: Sarnat and Sarnat stages of HIE

Stage	*Stage 1 (Mild)*	*Stage 2 (Moderate)*	*Stage 3 (Severe)*
Level of consciousness	Hyperalert; irritable	Lethargic or obtunded	Stuporous, comatose
Muscle tone	Normal	Mild hypotonia	Flaccid
Autonomic function	Generalized sympathetic	Generalized parasympathetic	Both system depressed
Pupils	Mydriasis	Miosis	Midposition, often unequal; poor light reflex
Seizures	None	Common focal or multifocal (6 to 24 hours of age)	Uncommon (excluding decerebration)
Duration of symptoms	<24 hours	2 to 14 days	Hours to weeks
Outcome	About 100% normal	80% normal; abnormal if symptoms more than 5 to 7 days	About 50% die; remainder with severe sequalae

5. *Glucose:* Levels between 75–100 mg/dl are recommended. Higher levels enhance cerebral edema and compromise perfusion, while hypoglycemia potentiates excitotoxic damage. Hypoglycemia is commonly seen in asphyxiated infants and must be regularly monitored and rigorously corrected. Seizures caused by hypoglycemia should not be used for Sarnat classification.
6. *Metabolic profile:* Hypocalcemia and electrolyte disturbances should be regularly looked for till stabilization of baby and corrected as indicated.
7. *Cerebral edema:* Intracranial pressure (ICP) can be estimated by measuring the vertical distance between the anterior fontanel and the heart at the point that the midportion of the fontanel flattens when the baby is tilted up. (Normal = 50 mm H_2O or lower). The main cause of edema is cytotoxic injury and treatment directed at reducing the edema per se has not shown to be useful. However factors enhancing it should be prevented.
8. *Seizures:* 20–50% of infants with HIE develop seizures during day 1 or 2. Seizures are commonly focal or multifocal. Metabolic disturbances such as hypoglycemia, hypocalcemia and hyponatremia must be ruled out. Seizures may be intractable initially but usually burn themselves out by 48 hours. Major differential diagnosis includes pyridoxine deficiency and drug toxicity. Subtle seizures lasting short durations need not be treated.
   Once the baby is seizure free for 3–4 days anticonvulsants are stopped in the same order as they were started, except phenobarbitone. Phenobarbitone is stopped at discharge if neurological examination is normal and baby is feeding well on breast. If neurological examination is not normal, then phenobarbitone is continued until one month. At one month if baby is normal neurologically, phenobarbitone is tapered off over a couple of days. If neurological function is abnormal but EEG shows no seizure activity, tapering of phenobarbitone may still be tried. If EEG shows seizure activity, reevaluation is done at 3 months.

Prognosis

The following predict a poor outcome:

- Lack of spontaneous respiratory effort within 20–30 minutes of birth is associated with almost uniform mortality
- Sarnat stage 3
- Abnormal neurological findings persisting beyond the first 7–10 days of life
- Oliguria (<1ml/kg/day) during the first 36 hours
- Interictal burst suppression or isoelectrical pattern on EEG.
- Persistent hypodensities on CT after 1 month of injury.

Thus all these babies should have regular follow up with monitoring of neuro developmental milestones to detect any deficits early and to intervene effectively.

Suggested reading

Agarwal R, Jain A, Deorari AK, Paul VK. Post-resuscitation management of asphyxiated neonates. Indian J Pediatr 2008; 75:175–80.

RESPIRATORY DISTRESS

Respiratory distress in the neonate is common problem and when severe, it can be a serious neonatal emergency. It can be due to respiratory (Table 7.26) and non-respiratory causes (Table 7.27). Early recognition and prompt treatment is essential to improve outcome.

Approach

Respiratory distress in a neonate can be recognized by the presence of varying combinations of tachypnea (RR>60/min), chest retractions, grunting, flaring of alae nasi and cyanosis. Severity of distress can be assessed by

7

Table 7.26: Pulmonary causes of respiratory distress

Cause	*Time of onset*	*Remarks*
Respiratory distress syndrome	First 6 hours of life	Common in preterm neonates
Meconium aspiration syndrome	First few hours of life	Common in term, post-term and SFD babies; history of meconium stained liquor present
Pneumonia	Can occur at any age	Often bacterial, neonates may be septic
Transient tachypnea of newborn	First 6 hr after birth	High rates, mainly tachypnea, minimal distress; lasts for less than 48–72 hr
Persistent pulmonary hypertension	Any age	Severe cyanosis and severe distress
Pneumothorax	Any age	Seen often in ventilated babies, and in those received assisted ventilation during resuscitation at birth; sudden deterioration.
Congenital malformations: trachea-esophageal fistula (TEF), diaphragmatic hernia, lobar emphysema, etc.	Any age	Dysmorphic features, other malformations, polyhydramnios in TEF
Upper airway obstruction: bilateral choanal atresia, vascular rings, etc.	Usually first 24 hours of life	Associated with stridor

Table 7.27: Non-pulmonary causes of rapid breathing	
Cardiac	CHF, congenital heart disease.
Metabolic	Hypothermia, hypoglycemia, metabolic acidosis.
CNS	Asphyxia, cerebral edema, hemorrhage.
Chest wall problem	Asphyxiating thoracic dystrophy, Werdnig Hoffman disease.

CHF: congestive heart failure, CNS: central nervous system

using the respiratory distress score (Table 7.28). The gestation, age at onset, severity of distress and presence of associated clinical features help in arriving at a diagnosis. It should be noted that chest retractions are mild or absent in respiratory distress due to non-respiratory causes.

Cardiac diseases: Cardiac etiology for respiratory distress should be suspected if a neonate with distress has cyanosis or hepatomegaly. Congenital heart disease and cardiac arrhythmias can present as congestive cardiac failure in the neonatal period. Transposition of great vessels (TGV) and hypoplastic left heart syndrome usually present on day one with progressive distress. Most other cardiac conditions present after the first week of life. A preterm neonate having a systolic murmur with tachypnea and hepatomegaly is likely to have patent ductus arteriosus (PDA).

Metabolic causes: Metabolic acidosis is one of the common causes of tachypnea in a neonate. Sepsis, asphyxia, diarrhea and dehydration can predispose a neonate to develop metabolic acidosis. These neonates usually have tachypnea and minimal distress.

CNS causes: Neonates with birth asphyxia, cerebral hemorrhage, or meningitis can present with tachypnea and respiratory distress. These neonates are usually lethargic with poor neonatal reflexes.

Respiratory causes: All respiratory diseases listed in Table 7.26 can occur both in preterm and term babies. However, if a preterm baby has respiratory distress within the first few hours of life the most likely cause is respiratory distress syndrome (RDS). Similarly if a term baby born to a mother with meconium stained liquor develops respiratory distress within the first 24 hours, the most likely cause is meconium aspiration syndrome (MAS). A term baby with uncomplicated birth developing tachypnea in the first few hours of birth is likely to have transient tachypnea of newborn. Presence of suprasternal recessions with or without stridor indicates upper airway obstruction.

Respiratory Distress Syndrome (RDS) or Hyaline Membrane Disease (HMD)

RDS is common in preterm babies less than 34 weeks of gestation. The overall incidence is 10–15% but can be as high as 80% in neonates <28 weeks. In addition to prematurity, asphyxia, acidosis, maternal diabetes and cesarean section can increase the risk of RDS.

Etiopathogenesis

In RDS, the basic abnormality is surfactant deficiency. Surfactant is a lipoprotein containing phospholipids like phosphatydylcholine and phosphatydylglycerol and proteins. Surfactant is produced by type II alveolar cells of lungs and helps reduce surface tension in the alveoli. In the absence of surfactant, surface tension increases and alveoli tend to collapse during expiration. During inspiration more negative pressure is needed to keep alveoli patent. There is inadequate oxygenation and increased work of breathing. Hypoxemia and acidosis result in pulmonary vasoconstriction and right to left shunting across the foramen ovale. This worsens the hypoxemia and the neonate eventually goes into respiratory failure. Ischemic damage to the alveoli causes transudation of proteins into the alveoli. Surfactant production starts around 20 weeks of life and peak at 35 weeks gestation. Therefore any neonate less than 35 weeks is prone to develop RDS.

Clinical Features

Respiratory distress usually occurs within the first 6 hours of life. Clinical features include tachypnea, retractions, grunting, cyanosis, and decreased air entry. Diagnosis can be confirmed by chest X-ray. Radiological features include reticulogranular pattern, ground glass opacity, low lung volume, air bronchogram (Fig. 7.35), and white out lungs in severe disease.

Table 7.28: Scoring system to evaluate severity of respiratory distress

Clinical sign	*Score*		
	0	*1*	*2*
Respiratory rate (per minute)	<60	60–80	>80
Cyanosis	Absent	Absent with upto 40% oxygen	Requires >40% oxygen
Retractions	Absent	Mild	Moderate to severe
Grunting	Absent	Audible with stethoscope	Audible without stethoscope
Breath sounds	Good	Decreased	Barely audible

(Mild 0–3, Moderate 4–6, Severe 7–10).

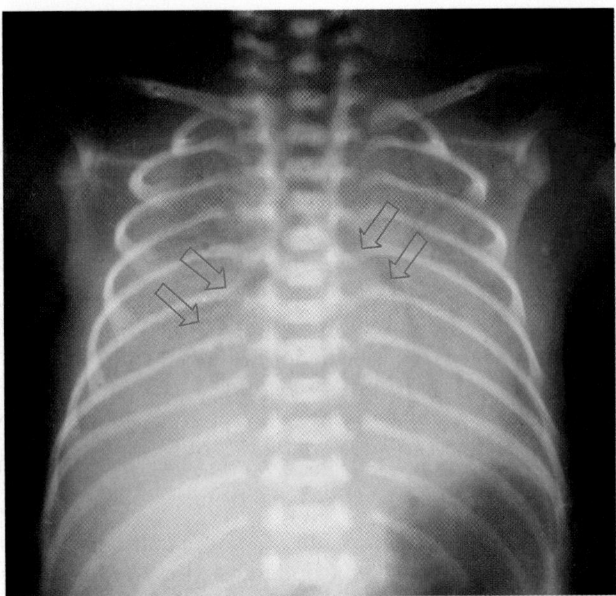

Fig. 7.35: Moderate to severe hyaline membrane disease: note homogenous opacification of lungs obscuring heart borders and presence of air bronchogram (arrows)

Prenatal diagnosis can be made by determining the lecithia lecithin/sphingomyelin (L/S) ratio in the amniotic fluid. L/S ratio > 2.0 indicates adequate lung maturity. A simple bedside test, the shake test, can be done on the amniotic fluid or gastric aspirate to determine lung maturity. The gastric or amniotic fluid is mixed with absolute alcohol, shaken for 15 secs and allowed to settle. Bubbles are formed in the presence of adequate surfactant indicating extent of lung maturity.

Management

Neonates suspected to have RDS need to be cared for in neonatal intensive care unit with IV fluids, and oxygen. Mild to moderate RDS can be managed with continuous positive airway pressure (CPAP). CPAP is a non invasive modality of support where a continuous distending pressure (5–7 cm of water) is applied at nostril level to keep the alveoli open in a spontaneously breathing baby. This is an excellent modality of respiratory support which minimizes lung injury and other complications such as air leak and sepsis. Preterm babies developing severe RDS often require mechanical ventilation in form of synchronized intermittent mandatory ventilation (SIMV). Preterm babies are at risk of lung injury by excessive pressure and high oxygen. High saturations of oxygen (above 95%) can produce retinopathy of prematurity (ROP) which can blind the infant.

RDS has generally a good prognosis if managed appropriately. Survival is as high as 90% in very low birth weight babies (<1500 g). In the absence of ventilatory support, most neonates with severe disease will die.

Since surfactant deficiency is the basis of RDS, exogenous surfactant is now recommended as the treatment of choice in neonates with RDS. Surfactant is indicated in all neonates with moderate to severe RDS. The route of administration is intratracheal. It can be given as a rescue treatment (when RDS actually develops) or prophylactically (all neonates less than 29 weeks irrespective of presence or absence of RDS). Even those babies who have been given surfactant will need ventilator support. Surfactant decreases duration and level of support of ventilation in neonates and therefore improves outcome. The practice of giving surfactant and then putting the infant on CPAP immediately (InSurE approach) is showing a promise in developing countries.

Prevention of RDS

Administration of antenatal steroids to mothers in preterm labor (<35 wk) has been a major breakthrough in management of preterm infants. Antenatal steroids are effective in decreasing RDS, intraventricular hemorrhage and mortality in these neonates (Table 7.29).

Table 7.29: Antenatal corticosteroids in preterm labor

Benefits
• 50% reduction in the incidence of respiratory distress syndrome • 50% reduction in the incidence of intraventricular hemorrhage (IVH) • 40% reduction in mortality
Indications
• All women with preterm labor between 24 and 34 weeks of gestation
Contraindication
• Clinical chorioamnionitis • Eclampsia [Maternal hypertension and diabetes mellitus are not contraindications. Careful monitoring and management of hypertension and hyperglycemia should be ensured]
Drug regimens
• Inj. Betamethasone 12 mg IM every 24 hours, 2 doses (preferred) • Inj. Dexamethasone 6 mg IM every 12 hours, 4 doses (only if betamethasone cannot be arranged) • Maximum effect is seen between 24 h and 7 days of administration of antenatal steroids. However, benefits still accrue beyond these time limits.
One should avoid multiple courses of antenatal steroids, if the women remain undelivered after the first course.

Meconium Aspiration Syndrome (MAS)

Meconium staining of liquor occur in 10–14% of pregnancies. Neonates born through meconium stained liquor can aspirate the meconium into the lungs and develop respiratory distress. This is known as meconium aspiration syndrome (MAS). Aspiration of meconium can occur in utero, during birth or immediately after birth. Thin meconium can cause chemical pneumonitis. Thick meconium aspiration can block the large and small airway causing areas of atelectasis and emphysema which can progress to develop air leak syndromes like pneumothorax. Presence of atelectasis and emphysema can cause ventilation perfusion mismatch in these babies that can progress to respiratory failure.

Clinical Features and Course

MAS usually occurs in term or post term babies and small for dates babies. These babies usually develop respiratory distress in the first few hours of life, that often deteriorates in next 24–48 hours. If untreated, distress can progress to respiratory failure. Complications include pneumothorax, other air leak syndromes (pneumopericardium, pneumomediastinum) and persistent pulmonary hypertension. Chest X-ray shows bilateral heterogeneous opacities, areas of hyperexpansion and atelectesis and air leak (Fig. 7.36).

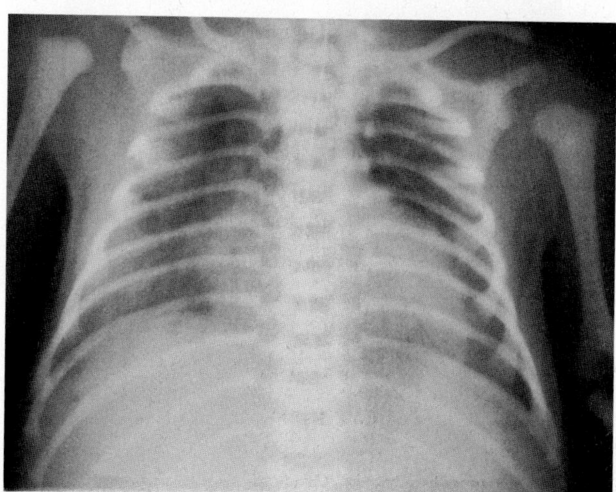

Fig. 7.36: Meconium aspiration syndrome-note hyperexpansion of lungs and heterogeneous opacities in right lung

Management

Clinical course in these babies can be complicated by severe pulmonary hypertension, which is a difficult condition to treat. IV fluids and oxygen are needed for mild distress and ventilatory support for severe disease. A good supportive care in terms of maintenance of normal body temperature, blood glucose and calcium level, ensuring analgesia and avoiding unnecessary fiddling pays good dividends. With ventilatory support, 60–70% neonates survive, but in the absence of ventilatory support, mortality is high in severe disease.

Persistent Pulmonary Hypertension (PPHN)

Also known as persistent fetal circulation, it is caused by a persistent elevation in pulmonary vascular resistance resulting in right to left shunt across the foramen ovale and/or ductus. The disease is more common in term and post-term babies and occurs as a result of persistent hypoxia and acidosis. Hypoxia and hypercarbia cause pulmonary vasoconstriction. This increases pulmonary vascular pressure and results in right to left shunting.

Common causes include asphyxia, respiratory distress due to MAS, RDS, diaphragmatic hernia, etc. Primary pulmonary hypertension can also occur because of an abnormal pulmonary vasculature secondary to chronic intrauterine hypoxia.

The neonate usually presents with severe respiratory distress and cyanosis. It is often difficult to differentiate PPHN from cyanotic congenital heart disease. Echocardiography helps in ruling out congenital heart disease and may demonstrate right to left shunt across the foramen ovale.

Ventilatory support is mandatory. Nitric oxide, a pulmonary vasodilator, may help. Prognosis is poor even with ventilatory support.

Pneumonia

Pneumonia is a common cause of respiratory distress in both term and preterm babies and is caused by bacteria such a *E. coli*, *S. aureus* and *K. pneumoniae*. Neonatal pneumonia may be due to aspiration or occasionally due to viral or fungal infection. Though group B streptococcal pneumonia is common in the West, it is uncommon in India.

The neonate has features suggestive of sepsis in addition to respiratory distress. Chest X-ray shows pneumonia (Fig. 7.37), blood counts are raised and blood culture may be positive. Treatment includes supportive care and specific antibiotic therapy. Ampicillin or cloxacillin with gentamicin is usually used. If the pneumonia is due to hospital acquired infection, antibiotics like cephalosporins with

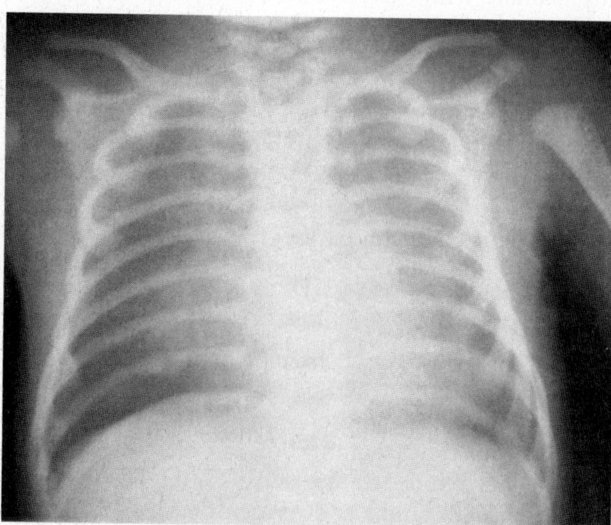

Fig. 7.37: Pneumonia-note heterogeneous opacities in both the lung fields

amikacin may have to be used. Survival is 60–70%, if treated early with appropriate antibiotics.

Transient Tachypnea of Newborn (TTN)

Transient tachypnea of the newborn is a benign self-limiting disease occurring usually in term neonates and is due to delayed clearance of lung fluid. These babies have tachypnea with minimal or no respiratory distress. Chest X-ray may show hyperexpanded lung fields, prominent vascular marking and prominent interlobar fissure (Fig. 7.38). Oxygen treatment is often adequate. Prognosis is excellent.

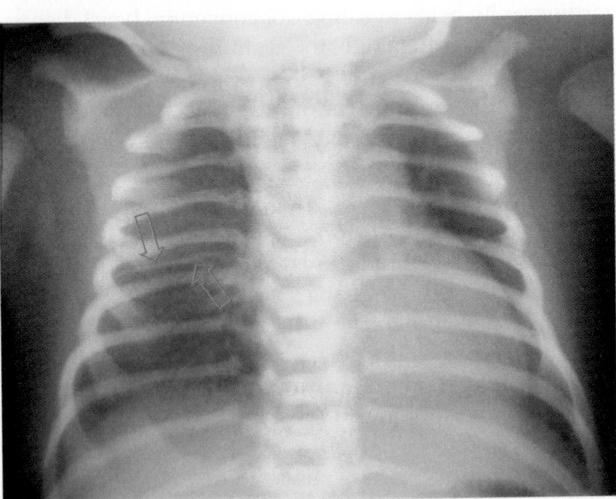

Fig. 7.38: Transient tachypnea of newborn. Note hyperinflated lungs, prominent bronchovascular markings and horizontal fissure (arrow)

7

Surgical Problems

Tracheo-esophageal fistula (TEF) should be suspected in any neonate with excessive frothing. Diagnosis can be confirmed by a plain X-ray with a red rubber catheter (not infant feeding tube); the catheter generally stops at 10th thoracic vertebrae in presence of TEF.

Diaphragmatic hernia should be suspected in any neonates who has severe respiratory distress and has a scaphoid abdomen. This condition can be detected during antenatal ultrasonography. Chest X-ray shows presence of bowel loops in the thoracic cavity.

Chronic Lung Disease (CLD) or Bronchopulmonary Dysplasia (BPD)

Diagnosis is suspected when a preterm neonate continues to have respiratory distress and remains oxygen or ventilator dependent for a long time. Criteria for diagnosis are oxygen requirement beyond 36 weeks post conceptional age or beyond 28 days of life. CLD occurs because of barotrauma and oxygen toxicity that causes damage to the alveolar cells, interstitium and blood vessels. Inflammatory mediators are released and there is increased permeability causing leakage of water and protein. In later stages there is fibrosis and cellular hyperplasia. Severe lung damage leads to respiratory failure. These babies continue to require prolonged oxygen therapy.

Pneumothorax

Presence of air in the pleural cavity (pneumothorax) is most common in babies with meconium aspiration syndrome and those being ventilated (Fig. 7.39). Transillumination of the chest can help in diagnosis. Needle aspiration or chest tube drainage is a life saving procedure in this situation.

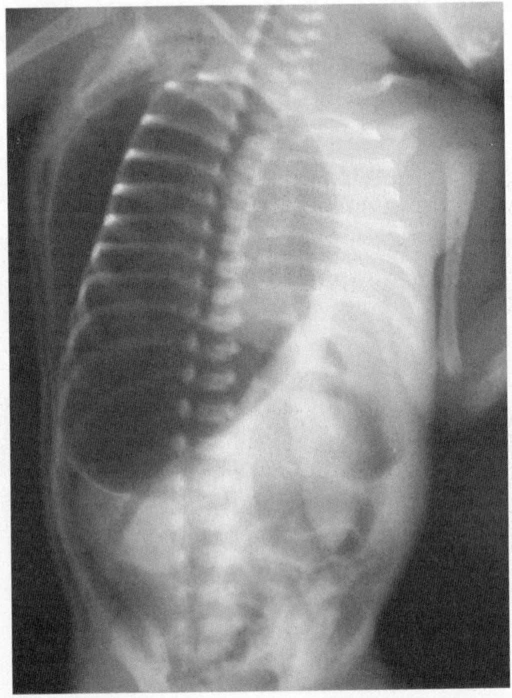

Fig. 7.39: Tension pneumothorax on right side displacing mediastinum and pushing the diaphragm down

Apnea

Apnea may be defined as cessation of respiration for 20 seconds with or without bradycardia and cyanosis or for shorter periods if it is associated with cyanosis or bradycardia. Apnea is a common problem in preterm neonates. It could be central, obstructive or mixed.

Apnea of prematurity occurs in preterm neonates between the 2nd to 5th days of life and is because of the immaturity of the developing brain. Central apnea can also occur because of pathological causes like sepsis, metabolic problems (hypoglycemia, hypocalcemia), temperature instability, respiratory distress, anemia and polycythemia. Obstructive apnea can occur because of block to the airway by secretion, improper positioning, etc.

Treatment is supportive and involves correction of underlying cause. Drugs used include aminophylline and caffeine. Prognosis is good in apnea of prematurity. In other cases it depends on the underlying cause.

Suggested readings

1. Bhutani VK. Differential diagnosis of neonatal respiratory disorders. In: Intensive of the Fetus and Neonate. Ed Spitzer AR. Mosby Year Book 1996; 494–505.
2. Greenough A, Roberton MRC. Respiratory distress syndrome. In: Neonatal Respiratory Disorders. Eds Greenough A, Roberton NRC, Milner AD. Arnold 1996; 238–279.
3. Singh M, Deorari AK. Pneumonia in newborn babies. Indian J Pediatr 1995; 62: 293–306.

JAUNDICE

Jaundice is an important problem in the first week of life. It is a cause of concern for the physician and a source of anxiety for the parents. High bilirubin levels may be toxic to the developing central nervous system and may cause neurological impairment even in term newborns. Nearly 60% of term newborn becomes visibly jaundiced in the first week of life. In most cases, it is benign and no intervention is required. Approximately 5–10 % of them have clinically significant jaundice mandating the use of phototherapy or other therapeutic options.

Physiological Versus Pathological Jaundice

Physiological jaundice represents physiological immaturity of the neonates to handle increased bilirubin production. Visible jaundice usually appears between 24–72 hours of age. Serum total bilirubin (STB) level usually peaks by 3 days of age and then falls in term neonates. STB levels are below the designated cut-offs for phototherapy. It does not require any treatment.

Pathological jaundice is referred to as an elevation of STB levels to the extent where treatment of jaundice is more likely to result into benefit than harm. There is no clear cut demarcation between pathological and physiological jaundice. STB levels have been arbitrarily defined as pathological if it exceeds 5 mg/dL on first day, 10 mg/dL on second day, or 12–13 mg/dl thereafter in term babies. Such jaundice warrants investigation for a cause and therapeutic interventions such as phototherapy. Appearance of jaundice within 24 hours, STB levels above the expected normal range, presence of clinical jaundice beyond 3 weeks and conjugated bilirubin (dark urine staining the nappy) would be categorized under this category.

Breastfeeding Jaundice

Exclusively breastfed infants have a different pattern of physiological jaundice as compared to artificially-fed babies. Jaundice in breast-fed babies usually appears between 24–72 hours of age, peaks by 5–15 days of life and disappears by the third week of life. One-third of all breastfed babies are detected to have mild clinical jaundice in the third week of life, which may persist into the 2nd to 3rd month of life in a few babies. This increased frequency of jaundice in breastfed babies is not related to characteristics of breast milk but rather to inadequate breastfeeding (breastfeeding jaundice). Ensuring optimum breastfeeding would help decrease this kind of jaundice.

Breast Milk Jaundice

Approximately 2–4% of exclusively breastfed term babies have jaundice in excess of 10 mg/dL beyond third-fourth weeks of life. These babies should be investigated for prolonged jaundice. A diagnosis of breast milk jaundice should be considered if this is unconjugated (not staining nappies); and other causes for prolongation such as continuing hemolysis, extravasated blood, G6PD deficiency and hypothyroidism have been ruled out. Mothers should be advised to continue breastfeeding at frequent intervals and STB levels usually decline over a period of time. Some babies may require phototherapy. Breastfeeding should not be stopped either for cessation or treatment of breast milk jaundice.

Clinical Quantification

Originally described by Kramer, dermal staining of bilirubin may be used as a clinical guide to the level of jaundice. Dermal staining in newborn progresses in a cephalocaudal direction. The newborn should be examined in a good daylight. The skin of forehead, chest, abdomen, thighs, legs, palms and soles should be blanched with digital pressure and the underlying color of skin and subcutaneous tissue should be noted (Fig. 7.40). STB levels are approximately 4–6 mg/dL (zone 1), 6–8 mg/dL (zone 2), 8–12 mg/dL (zone 3), 12–14 mg/dL (zone 4) and >15 mg/dL (zone 5). In general, the estimation of STB levels

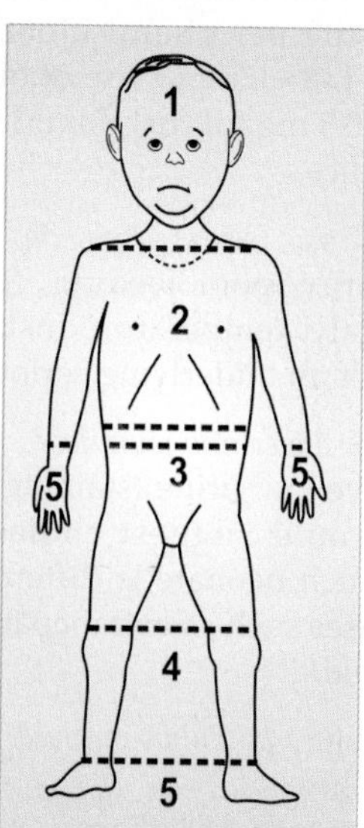

Fig. 7.40: Dermal zones for estimation of serum total bilirubin levels

7

by dermal zones is unreliable particularly at higher STB levels, after phototherapy and when it is carried out by an inexperienced observer. STB can be assessed noninvasively by a transcutaneous handheld device. Transcutaneous bilirubinometry is useful to identify significantly jaundiced neonates and helps decrease the need for frequent lab estimation of STB.

Measurement of Bilirubin Levels

Newborns detected to have yellow discoloration of the skin beyond the legs, or when their clinically assessed STB levels approach phototherapy range, should have lab confirmation of STB. STB assessment has a marked interlaboratory variability.

Causes

Important causes of jaundice in neonates include:

1. Hemolytic: Rh incompatibility, ABO incompatability, G6PD deficiency, thalassemias, hereditary spherocytosis.
2. Non-hemolytic: prematurity, extravasated blood, inadequate feeding, polycythemia, idiopathic, breast milk jaundice.

Clinical Approach

Is the newborn term or preterm?

Basic pathophysiology of jaundice is same in term and preterm neonates but babies at lower gestation are at a higher risk of developing brain damage at lower levels.

Is there any hemolysis?

Setting of Rh (mother Rh negative and baby with Rh positive) or ABO incompatibility (mother O group with baby either A or B group), onset of jaundice within 24 hours, presence of pallor, hepatosplenomegaly, presence of hemolysis on the peripheral blood smear, raised reticulocyte count (>8%), rapid rise of bilirubin (>5 mg/dl in 24 hours or >0.5 mg/dl/hr) should raise a suspicion of hemolytic jaundice.

Is the baby otherwise sick (sepsis, asphyxia) or healthy?

Presence of lethargy, poor feeding, failure to thrive, hepatosplenomegaly, temperature instability or apnea may be a marker of an underlying serious disease.

Does the infant have cholestatic jaundice?

Presence of dark yellow urine (staining clothes) or pale colored stools would suggest cholestatic jaundice. Management of such neonate is different and requires evaluation for causes such as extrahepatic biliray atresia, sepsis, galactosemia.

Does the baby have any bilirubin-induced brain dysfunction (kernicterus)?

These include presence of lethargy, poor feeding and hypotonia. Advanced signs include seizures, retrocollis, paralysis of upward gaze, and shrill cry.

Risk Factors for development of severe hyperbilirubinemia

1. Pre-discharge STB in the high-risk zone.
2. Jaundice observed in the first 24 h.
3. Blood group incompatibility with positive direct antiglobulin test (DCT), other known hemolytic disease (e.g. G6PD deficiency).
4. Gestational age 35–36 weeks.
5. Previous sibling received phototherapy.
6. Cephalohematoma or significant bruising.
7. If breastfeeding is inadequate with excessive weight loss.

Management

Investigation

The aim of performing investigations is to confirm the level of jaundice, identify the cause and follow response to treatment.

- Serum total bilirubin (STB) (and its fractions, if jaundice is prolonged or there is yellow staining of nappies): All cases with suspected pathological levels either clinically or by trancutaneous measurements need confirmation by blood examination for serum bilirubin levels.
- Blood group of mother and baby: detects any incompatibility.
- Direct Coombs test: detects presence of antibody coating on fetal RBC.
- Indirect Coombs test: detects presence of antibodies against fetal RBC in maternal serum.
- Hematocrit: decreased in hemolysis.
- Reticulocyte count: increased in hemolysis.
- Peripheral smear: evidence of hemolysis.
- G6PD levels in RBC.
- Others: sepsis screen; thyroid function test; urine for reducing substances to rule out galactosemia; specific enzyme/genetic studies for Crigglar Najjar, Gilbert and other genetic enzyme deficiencies, as per indications.

Prevention

- Antenatal investigation should include maternal blood grouping. Rh positive baby born to a Rh negative mother is at higher risk for hyperbilirubinemia and requires greater monitoring. Anti D (RhoGam) injection after first obstetrical event ensures decreased risk of sensitization in future pregnancies.
- Ensuring adequate breastfeeding.
- Parent education regarding danger signs should include yellowish discoloration below knees and elbows or persistent jaundice beyond 15 days as reason for immediate checkup by health personnel.
- High risk babies such as with large cephalohematoma or family history of jaundice should be asked to come for follow up after 3 days of discharge and reassessed.

Physiological Jaundice

The parents should be explained about the benign nature of jaundice. The mother should be encouraged to breastfeed frequently. The newborn should be exclusively breastfed with no top feeds, water or dextrose water. Mother should be told to bring the baby to the hospital if the baby looks deep yellow or palms and soles also have yellow staining.

Any newborn discharged prior to 72 hours of life should be evaluated again in the next 48 hours for assessment of adequacy of breastfeeding and progression of jaundice.

Pathological Jaundice

Term and Near Term Neonates

The American Academy of Pediatrics (AAP) has laid down criteria for managing babies with elevated serum bilirubin. Guidelines for phototherapy and exchange transfusion are provided in Figs 7.41 and 7.42 respectively. Both the figures have age in hours on the X-axis and STB levels on Y-axis. There are three curves on each figure representing three risk categories of babies defined by gestation and other risk factors.

Preterm Neonates

Table 7.30 provides cut-offs for exchange transfusion and phototherapy in preterm neonates below 35 weeks of gestation.

Prolonged Jaundice beyond 3 Weeks

This is defined as persistence of significant jaundice (10 mg/dL) beyond three weeks in a term baby. The common causes include breast milk jaundice, extravasated blood (cephalohematoma), ongoing hemolytic disease, G6PD deficiency and hypothyroidism. One should rule out cholestasis by noting the urine and stool color and checking the level of direct bilirubin. The diagnostic work up in such a newborn includes:

- Investigations to rule out cholestasis (stool color, urine color, direct and indirect bilirubin levels).
- Investigations to rule out ongoing hemolysis, G6PD screen.

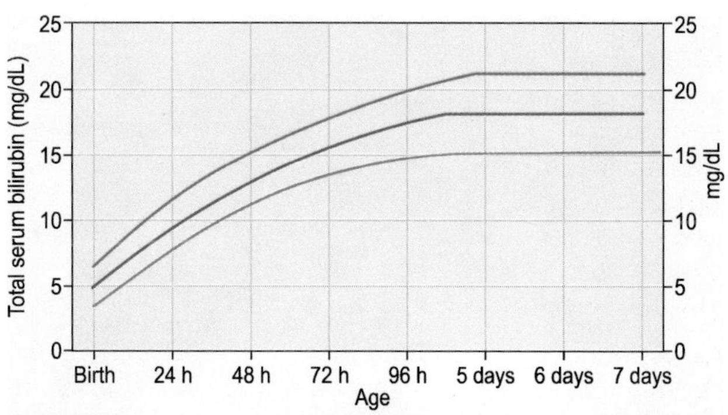

Fig. 7.41: Guidelines for phototherapy in hospitalized infants of 35 or more weeks' gestation. — Infants at lower risk (> 38 wk and well) — Infants at medium risk (> 38 wk + risk factors or 35-37 6/7wk and well) — Infants at higher risk (35-37 6/7 wk + risk factors)

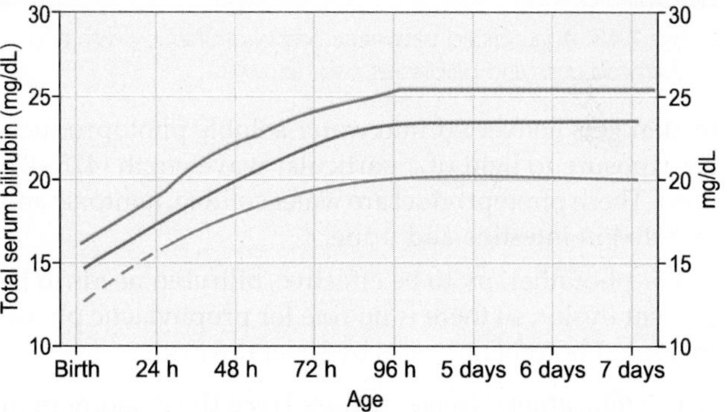

Fig. 7.42: Guidelines for exchange transfusion in infants 35 or more weeks' gestation. — Infants at lower risk (> 38 wk and well) — Infants at medium risk (> 38 wk + risk factors or 35–37 6/7 wk and well) — Infants at higher risk (35–37 6/7 wk + risk factors)

- Investigations to rule out hypothyroidism.
- Investigations to rule out urinary tract infection.

Treatment Options

Phototherapy

Phototherapy has been found to be effective in treating jaundice in neonates (Fig. 7.43). Unconjugated bilirubin

Table 7.30: Guideline for management of jaundiced preterm neonates

Birth weight	*Total serum bilirubin (mg/dL)*			
	Healthy baby		*Sick baby*	
	Phototherapy	*Exchange transfusion*	*Phototherapy*	*Exchange transfusion*
<1000 gm	5–7	11–13	4–6	10–12
1001–1500 gm	7–10	13–15	6–8	11–13
1501–2000 gm	10–12	15–18	8–10	13–15
2001–2500 gm	12–15	18–20	10–12	15–18

Adapted from Halamek LP, Stevenson DK. Neonatal Jaundice. In Fanroff AA, Martin RJ (Eds): Neonatal Perinatal Medicine. Diseases of the fetus and Infant. 7ed. St Louis, Mosby Year Book 2002. pp 1335.

1. Treatment decisions are based on serum total bilirubin (STB).
2. Gestation is more important than birth weight of the baby in deciding need for phototherapy or exchange transfusion. A higher cutoff can be used for a small for date baby.
3. Postnatal age should also be considered when deciding for treatment. Jaundice appearing on first day of life is more likely to need treatment than that appearing later.
4. Sick baby refers to presence of asphyxia, hypothermia, sepsis, acidosis, hypoxia, hypercapnia and evidence of hemolysis.

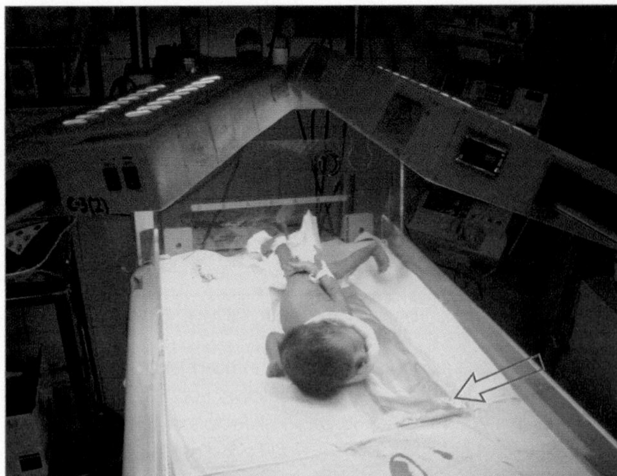

Fig. 7.43: A jaundiced baby receiving phototherapy with two overhead units and biliblanket pad (arrow)

in skin gets converted into water-soluble photoproducts on exposure to light of a particular wavelength (425–475 mm). These photoproduct are water soluble, nontoxic and excreted in intestine and urine.

For phototherapy to be effective, bilirubin needs to be present in skin so there is no role for prophylactic phototherapy. Phototherapy acts by several ways:

- *Configurational isomerization:* Here the Z-isomers of bilirubin are converted into E-isomers. The reaction is instantaneous upon exposure to light but reversible as bilirubin reaches into the bile duct. After exposure of 8–12 hrs of phototherapy, this constitutes about 25% of STB, which is nontoxic. Since this is excreted slowly from body this is not a major mechanism for decrease in STB.
- *Structural isomerization:* This is an irreversible reaction where the bilirubin is converted into lumirubin. The reaction is directly proportional to dose of phototherapy. This product forms 2–6% of STB which is rapidly excreted from body thus is mainly responsible for phototherapy induced decline in STB.
- *Photo oxidation:* This is a minor reaction, where photoproducts are excreted in urine.

Types of light: The most effective lights are those with high-energy output near the maximum adsorption peak of bilirubin (450–460 nm). Special blue lamps with a peak output at 425–475 nm are the most efficient. Cool daylight lamps with a principal peak at 550 to 600 nm are most commonly used but not very effective phototherapy units in our country. The lamps should be changed every 3 months or earlier if irradiance is being monitored. Double surface phototherapy is more effective than the single surface. Double surface phototherapy can be provided either by double surface special blue lights or by conventional blue light and undersurface fiberoptic phototherapy.

Efficacy of phototherapy depends upon irradiance, surface area exposed, distance from phototherapy unit, initial STB level and adequacy of breastfeeding. One must periodically check irradiance of phototherapy units. Sunlight is relatively ineffective because of low blue content of light. Besides, hyperpyrexia and skin burns can occur in prolonged sunlight exposure.

Procedure of providing phototherapy: Undress the baby completely. Cover the eyes and genitalia (in males only) to prevent damage by bright lights. Keep baby at a distance of 30–45 cm from the light source. Turn the baby after each feed to expose maximum surface area of baby to light. Monitor temperature every two to four hours or more frequently if fluctuation in temperature is noted. Ensure adequate breastfeeding. Record body weight daily and ensure that baby passes adequate amount of urine (6–8 times per day). Phototherapy should be provided continuously except during breastfeeding sessions when it can be switch off. Monitor STB levels at least once a day. Discontinue phototherapy when STB falls below age-specific phototherapy cut-offs. Monitor clinically for rebound STB rise after 24 hours of stopping phototherapy for babies with hemolytic disorders.

Side effects: Phototherapy is in use since the last 40 years and has an excellent safety record. The predominant adverse effects of phototherapy include rash, overheating, dehydration and diarrhea.

Exchange Transfusion

Rh isoimmunization: Blood used for exchange transfusion in neonates with Rh isoimmunization should be Rh negative and baby's blood group or 'O' group.

ABO incompatibility: Only O group blood should be used for exchange transfusion in neonates with ABO incompatibility. The best choice would be O group (Rh compatible) packed cells suspended in AB plasma or O group whole blood (Rh compatible with baby).

Other situations: Cross-matched with baby's blood group. Blood volume used:

- Double volume exchange: 2 × (80–100 ml/kg) × birth weight in kg (arrange 70% packed red blood cells and 30% fresh frozen plasma, so that PCV of whole arranged blood ~ 50–55)

Pharmacological Treatment

1. *Phenobarbitone:* Phenobarbitone induces glucuronyl transferase enzyme thus improves conjugation as well as uptake and excretion of bilirubin by liver cells. There is no role for routine use of phenobarbitone in management of jaundice.
2. *High dose intravenous immunoglobulin:* High dose intravenous immunoglobulin therapy is effective in reducing need for exchange transfusion in hemolytic jaundice such as in Rh or ABO incompatibility. It blocks the Fc receptors thereby inhibiting hemolysis. Intravenous immunoglobulin is given in dose of 500–1000 mg/kg as slow infusion over 2 hours.

Follow-Up

Babies with serum bilirubin ≥20 mg/dl and those who require exchange transfusion should be kept under follow-up in the high-risk clinic for neurodevelopmental outcome. Hearing assessment (BERA) should be done at 3 months of age. With prompt treatment, even very elevated serum bilirubin levels within the range of 25 to 29 mg/dl are not likely to result in long-term adverse effects on neurodevelopment.

CONGENITAL MALFORMATIONS

Tracheoesophageal Fistula, Esophageal Atresia

Upper part of esophagus is developed from retro-pharyngeal segment and the lower part from pregastric segment of the first part of the primitive gut. At four weeks of gestation, the laryngotracheal groove is formed. Later, two longitudinal furrows develop to separate the respiratory primordium from the esophagus. Deviation or altered cellular growth in this septum results in formation of tracheoesophageal fistulae.

Five types of tracheoesophageal fistulae are recognized. (i) In the most common variety (over 80% of cases), the upper part of the esophagus ends blindly and the lower part is connected to the trachea by a fistula. Incidence is 1 in 4000 live births. (ii) In the second type, there is no fistulous connection between either the upper or the lower part of the esophagus and trachea. (iii) In the third variety, there is no esophageal atresia, but there is a fistulous tract between the trachea and esophagus (H type). (iv) The variety in which the upper segment of esophagus opens into trachea is uncommon. (v) In the least common variety, both segments open into the trachea.

Clinical Features

The presence of maternal polyhydramnois and single umbilical artery should alert the pediatrician to look for atresia of the upper digestive tract. Association of congenital anomalies of vertebrae, anorectal region, heart, kidneys or limbs should also arouse suspicion. The newborn baby has excessive drooling, saliva is frothy and there is choking and cyanosis with the first feed. Overflow of milk and saliva from esophagus, and regurgitation of secretions through the fistulous tract (when present) into the lungs results in pneumonia.

Diagnosis

A large size 8 or 10 Fr plastic orogastric tube cannot be passed into stomach as it gets arrested at a distance of 7–10 cm from the mouth (Fig. 7.44). A polythene catheter may get coiled up in the upper pouch of the esophagus. Accumulated secretions aspirated on suction may be mistaken as stomach contents. The latter should have acidic pH. A skiagram may be obtained after instilling 1–2 ml of air through the tube or by using a catheter with radiopaque end. It is not advisable to use barium as a contrast material since it may be aspirated in lungs. On X-ray, an air bubble is seen in the stomach if there is communication between the lower part of the esopagus and trachea which occurs in the commonest variety of tracheo-esophageal fistula. Lungs show atelectasis or pneumonia in the right upper zone.

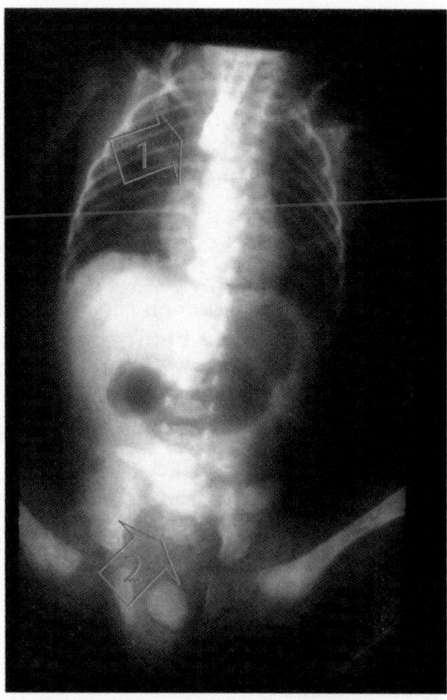

Fig. 7.44: Esophageal atresia with tracheo-esophageal fistula. Note the red rubber catheter stopping at T4 level (arrow 1). There is a double gas bubble sign indicating presence of concomitant duodenal atresia (arrow 2)

Prognosis

The prognosis is unsatisfactory and depends upon (a) how soon the diagnosis is made, (b) whether pneumonitis has occurred or not, (c) the size and maturity of the baby, (d) existence of serious anomalies such as congenital heart disease and urogenital defects, (e) experience of the surgeon and (f) standard medical and nursing care.

Management

The baby should be nursed supine or in an upright position and esophageal pouch should be gently sucked every five minutes, or continuously using a slow suction device. Intravenous fluids should be administered and infection, if any should be treated. Surgical repair should be undertaken as early as possible.

Anorectal Anomalies

A variety of anorectal anomalies have been described. These may be anatomically classified as high, intermediate or low. The position is determined by the relation of terminal part of bowel to the puborectalis sling. High or intermediate lesions are more common in males. Anal stenosis or covered anus, anocutaneous fistulae are common in both sexes. Anovestibular fistula (low lesion) in females and anorectal agenesis with rectoprostatic urethral fistula (high lesion) are common in male infants.

Among the males with high or intermediate lesions, 80% are rectovesical fistulae, but among the females with high defect, 80% have a rectovaginal fistula. There are significant chances of associated anomalies in case of higher anorectal anomalies.

An X-ray film of the abdomen is obtained 12–24 hours after birth, with the baby being kept in an inverted position. A lateral picture of the pelvis should be obtained to define whether the rectal pouch is above or below a line drawn from the pubis to the coccyx. Abdominal ultrasound should be done to detect associated urinary tract anomalies. Intravenous pyelogram and micturating cystourethrogram should also be done to exclude vesiocoureteral reflux. Meconium may be passed from vagina and unless a careful examination of the perineum is done, the diagnosis of anorectal anomaly may be missed in female infants. Urinary infection often supervenes in rectovesical fistulae.

Treatment is surgical. Prognosis is better with low defects. About 80 to 90% of patients become continents after surgery for low defects. More than two-thirds of patients are incontinent after surgery of high defects.

Neural Tube Defects

Anencephaly: Anencephaly is due to a defect in the development of neural axis and is not compatible with life.

Encephalocele: In encephalocele, the brain and/or its coverings herniate through a defect in the skull.

7

Congenital hydrocephalus: Congenital hydropcephalus is due to occlusion of aqueduct of sylvius or basal cisterns. This usually follows intrauterine infections such as toxoplasmosis, rubella, cytomegalovirus and syphilis, but may also be the result of a congenital malformation of the aqueduct, Dandy-Walker syndrome (posterior fossa cyst and a defect of cerebellar vermis), Arnold-Chiari malformation (displacement of brainstem and cerebellum in the spinal canal) or multiple congenital malformations of the nervous system.

Diagnosis should be suspected if the head circumference increases rapidly (more than 1 cm in a fortnight during the first three months). CT or MRI scan should be done to confirm the diagnosis. The type of dilatation of ventricles indicates the site of obstruction. Isolated aqueductal stenosis has better prognosis.

Treatment should be directed at the specific cause if amenable to therapy and surgical intervention such as ventriculocaval or ventriculoperioneal shunt. Infection of shunt is common.

Myelomeningocele: It presents as membranous protrustion near the lumbosacral region and contains meninges, cerebrospinal fluid, nerve roots and a dysplastic spinal cord. There is a distinct line of demarcation between the skin and the protruding membranous sac. In contrast, meningocele is covered with only skin. The covering cannot be demarcated into two different areas of skin and meninges. There may be no associated neurological deficit, but Arnold-Chiari malformation and congenital hydrocephalus are often associated. Severe motor and sensory deficit are common and urinary and fecal incontinence are usually present. Meningomyclocele is operated only if there is no paralysis of lower limbs and if there is no bladder/bowel involvement.

Cleft Lip and Cleft Palate

Cleft lip is recognized readily (Fig. 7.45), but a careful inspection of the oral cavity is necessary to identify cleft palate. A cleft of the soft palate can be easily missed unless the baby is examined carefully. Ventricular septal defect is a common associated anomaly with cleft palate.

In Pierré-Robin syndrome, cleft palate is associated with retracted jaw (micrognathia) and large tongue, with a tendency for glossoptosis. In these cases, tongue should be stabilized early in life by surgery to maintain an adequate airway. Feeding is difficult in cases of cleft palate. For the first few days, gavage feeding or spoon-feeding may be done. Bottle feeding may be tried with a soft nipple with rubber flange, which close the cleft and help the baby in sucking. If this is not successful, palatal prosthesis may be used. The baby should be kept under constant surveillance for maintaining nutrition and adequate growth and development. These babies are prone to develop otitis media and should be carefully watched and treated as and when required. Despite successful repair of cleft palate, residual speech defects may be present, necessitating help of a speech therapist.

Management: Management of cleft palate requires a team effort involving a pediatrician, a plastic surgeon,

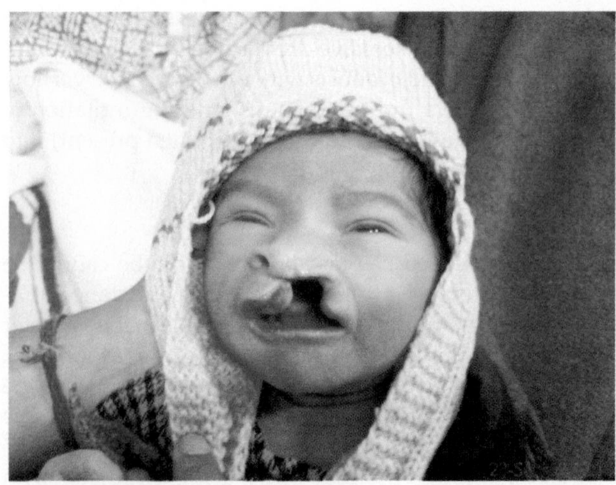

Fig. 7.45: Unilateral cleft lip and cleft palate

orthodontist, ENT specialist and speech therapist. Cleft lip is repaired in the neonatal period. Operation for cleft palate is generally deferred until the second year.

Diaphragmatic Hernia

Diaphragmatic hernia occurs because of failure of closure of the pleuroperitoneal membrane. This allows intestinal loops to ascend to the thorax that compress the developing lung and can result in pulmonary hypoplasia (Fig. 7.46). These babies can present at any time after birth. At birth a baby may be suspected to have diaphragmatic hernia if there is respiratory distress and a scaphoid abdomen. Bag and mask ventilation should be avoided in these babies. Surgical repair after stabilization is the treatment of choice.

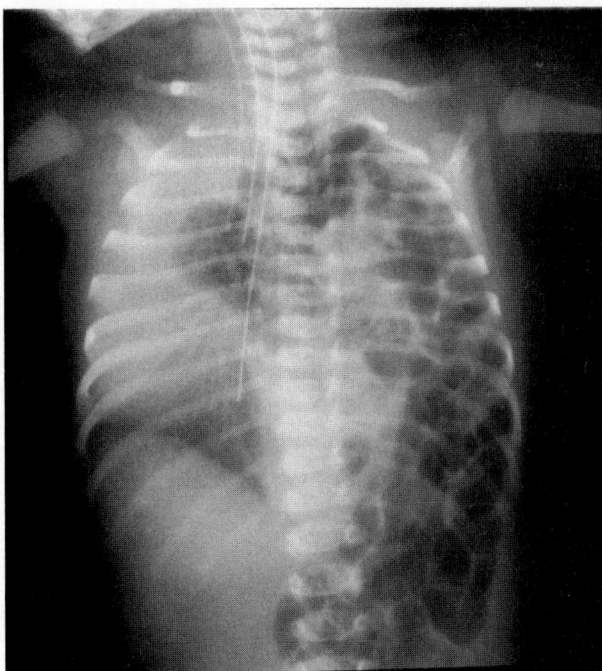

Fig. 7.46: Diaphragmatic hernia: Note multiple air filled cysts in left hemithorax, shift of mediastinum to the right and the absence of outline of the left diaphragm

TRANSPORT OF NEONATES

Transport is an important component of sick newborn care and improves their chances of survival. It requires careful attention to vital parameters, temperature and blood glucose levels as well as coordination with the receiving hospital.

If the birth of an at-risk neonate is anticipated, the mother should be transported (in-utero transport) to a facility with optimum maternal and neonatal care before delivery (in-utero transfer). However, if referral of a neonate is unavoidable, efforts should be made to do the best possible job.

The principles of efficient transport are:

1. To make a correct assessment of the baby.
2. To make sure that there is a genuine indication for referral. One should explain the condition and reasons for transport to the family.
3. One should correct hypothermia before transporting, since it may even worsen on the way.
4. One should stabilize the baby as much as possible.
5. A precise note should be written providing details of the baby's condition, need for referral and treatment given to the baby.
6. The mother should be encouraged to accompany the baby. In case she cannot accompany immediately, she should be encouraged to reach the facility at the earliest.
7. A doctor/nurse/dai/health worker should accompany the baby, if feasible, to provide care en route.
8. One should ensure warmth on the way:
   - The baby should be covered fully with clothes (or cotton) including the head and the limbs.
   - If the baby passes urine or stool he should be dried up quickly.
   - Different workers have suggested the use of thermocol box, basket, padded pouch, polythene covering, etc. for ensuring temperature stability during transport.
   - The ideal modality of transport incubator is a rarity in most situations.
   - The use of hot water bottle is fraught with considerable danger due to accidental burns to the baby if the bottle is not wrapped properly and remains in touch with baby's body. It is best avoided, but if no other means are available, this method may be employed. But the accompanying members of the team should be explained to take care of the bottle on the way.
   - One of the best methods to provide warmth to the neonates is to use skin-to-skin contact. The naked baby is kept on the mother's (or another adult's) chest.
9. The accompanying family members should be explained how to care for the baby on the way. The accompanying person should be explained to ensure the following:
   a. The baby's trunk as well as soles and palms are warm to touch.
   b. The neck of the baby is in slight extension.
   c. Baby's mouth and nose are not covered and the secretions therein are gently wiped with a cotton covered finger.
   d. Baby's breathing is regular; if required, physical stimulation at the soles should be given to break apnea.
   e. If baby is in a position to suck on breast, baby should be breastfed. If he can take *katori*-spoon feeding, expressed breast milk should be provided. If the distance is long, a stomach tube may be inserted and gavage feeding given. However, it is not easy to train

f. If intravenous fluids are being provided, one should make sure that the attendants know how many drops of infusion are to be given every minute; they should also be explained how to close the regulator to stop the infusion once the bottle empties.

the accompanying members in this modality of care within minutes.

10. One should take the baby to the nearest referral facility (inform them in advance on phone or otherwise), by the shortest route, using the fastest possible and affordable mode of transport.

FOLLOW-UP OF HIGH RISK NEONATES

Improved perinatal and neonatal care has resulted in improved survival of many sick and small neonates who are at-risk for long-term morbidities such as growth failure, developmental delay and visual/hearing problems. A proper and appropriate follow-up program would help in prevention, early detection and appropriate management of these problems, thereby ensuring disability and morbidity free survival.

Who Needs Follow-Up Care?

Table 7.31 lists the cohort of high risk infants who require follow up services.

Table 7.31: High risk neonates who need follow-up care

1. Babies with <1800 g birth weight and/or gestation <35 weeks
2. Small for date (<3rd centile) and large for date (>97th centile)
3. Perinatal asphyxia–Apgar score 3 or less at 5 min and/ or hypoxic ischemic encephalopathy
4. Mechanical ventilation for more than 24 hours
5. Metabolic problems—symptomatic hypoglycemia and hypocalcemia
6. Seizures
7. Infections–meningitis and/or culture positive sepsis
8. Shock requiring inotropic/vasopressor support
9. Infants born to HIV-positive mothers
10. Hyperbilirubinemia > 20 mg/dl or requirement of exchange transfusion
11. Major malformations

When to Follow Up

The following should be the follow-up schedule:

- 2 weeks after discharge
- At 6, 10, 14 weeks of postnatal age
- At 3, 6, 9, 12 and 18 months of corrected age and then 6 monthly.

The influence of environmental factors on performance is less at 12 months corrected age and biomedical issues such as oxygen supplementation for chronic lung disease have resolved. By 12 months corrected age the cognitive and language assessment can also be done. However, cognitive and motor functions are still evolving at 12 months corrected age and the period of acquisition of developmental milestone is variable. Also, some neurologic abnormalities that are identified in the first year of life are transient or improve whereas findings in other children may worsen over time. By 18–24 months corrected age the environmental factors begin to exert a stronger influence on test results, cognitive and motor abilities diverge, language and reasoning skills are developing and there is improved prediction to early school age performance. Standard follow-up for many multicenter networks is currently at 18–24 months corrected age. The correction for gestational immaturity at birth should be done till 24 months age.

What should be Done at Follow-Up?

1. *Assessment of feeding and dietary counseling:* Parents should be asked about the infants' diet and offered dietary counseling at each visit. Breastfeeding frequency and adequacy should be assessed. The amount, dilution and mode of feeding should be noted if supplemental feeding is given. It is also important to record the duration of exclusive breastfeeding. If a baby is not gaining adequate weight on exclusive breastfeeding, take care of any illness or maternal problems which may interfere with feeding and milk output. If poor weight gain persists despite all measures to improve breast milk output supplementation can be considered. Complementary feeding should be started at 6 months corrected age. Initially, semisolids should be advised in accordance with the local cultural practices.
2. *Growth monitoring:* Growth (including weight, head circumference, mid-arm circumference and length) should be monitored and plotted on an appropriate growth chart at each visit.
3. *Developmental assessment:* Assessment of developmental milestones should be done according to the corrected age. The milestones should be assessed in four domains —gross motor, fine motor, language, and personal-social. Infants who lag behind in any domain should undergo a formal developmental evaluation by a clinical psychologist using tests such as Developmental assessment of Indian Infant II (DASII II). Age appropriate stimulation should be provided to these babies.
4. *Immunization:* Immunization should be ensured according to chronological age. Parents should be offered the option of using additional vaccines such as *Hemophilus influenzae* B, typhoid, MMR.
5. *Ongoing problems:* Ongoing morbidities such as diarrhea, pneumonia occur more frequently in these babies and should require appropriate treatment.
6. *Neurological assessment:* Muscle tone should be assessed, any asymmetry between the extremities should also be

recorded. Any history of seizures or involuntary movements should also be recorded.

7. *Eye evaluation*: An ophthalmologist should evaluate the baby for vision, squint, cataract and optic atrophy. Subjective visual assessment can be made from clinical clues as inability to fixate eyes, roving eye movements and nystagmus. Objective visual assessment should be done with the Teller Acuity Card.
8. *Hearing evaluation*: High risk infants have higher incidence of moderate to profound hearing loss (2.5–5% *versus* 1%). Since clinical screening is often unreliable, brainstem auditory evoked responses (BAER/BERA) should be performed between 40 weeks PMA and 3 months postnatal age.

METABOLIC DISORDERS

Hypoglycemia

Hypoglycemia is a common preventable disorder seen in 1–3 per 1000 neonates. A blood glucose value of less than 40 mg/dL (plasma glucose less than 45 mg/dL) is considered as hypoglycemia in most of the situations.

Blood glucose levels are maintained by gluconeogenesis. Neonatal hypoglycemia occurs in infants with impaired gluconeogenesis, brought about by increased insulin production, altered counter-regulatory hormone or an inadequate substrate supply.

Screening for hypoglycemia is recommended in high risk situations (Table 7.32). These babies should be screened for hypoglycemia at 2, 6, 12, 24, 48 and 72 hours after birth with reagent strips (dextrostix). Babies showing blood sugar value of less than 40 mg/dL on reagent strip should be treated for hypoglycemia but should have confirmation of hypoglycemia by a lab test as reagent strips have high false positive rates. Appropriate for gestational age babies who are breastfeeding adequately do not require any screening for hypoglycemia.

Clinical Features

Clinically the hypoglycemia may be asymptomatic or may manifest with a range of clinical features like stupor, tremors, apathy, cyanosis, convulsions, apneic spells, tachypnea, weak and high pitched cry, lethargy, difficulty in feeding, eye rolling, episodes of sweating, sudden pallor, hypothermia, and rarely, cardiac arrest.

Table 7.32: Common causes of hypoglycemia

- Inadequate substrate: Small for gestational age (weight for gestation <3rd percentile), preterm babies (<35 wk), low birth weight babies (<2000 g).
- Relative hyperinsulinemia: infants of diabetic mother, large for date babies (weight for gestation >97th percentile), Rh isoimmunization.
- Sickness: hypothermia, sepsis, asphyxia, etc.

Management of Hypoglycemia

Prevention of hypoglycemia: All high risk babies should receive proper breastfeeding counseling and support. Adequacy of breastfeeding should be assessed and small babies not able to suck effectively on the breast, should receive expressed breast milk by alternate methods.

Asymptomatic babies: If the blood sugar is more than 20 mg/dL in an asymptomatic baby, a trial of oral feeds/ fortified feeds (prepared by adding 5 g sugar in 100 ml of milk) is given and blood sugar be tested after 30–45 minutes. If repeat blood sugars are above 40 mg/dL, frequent feeding is ensured with 6 hourly monitoring of blood sugar for 48 hrs. However if blood sugar values persists below 40 mg/dL, baby should receive IV glucose infusion.

If the initial blood sugar value is less than 20 mg/dL, then intravenous glucose infusion is started.

Symptomatic babies: A bolus of 2 mL/kg of 10% dextrose should be given, followed immediately by glucose infusion at an initial rate of 6 mg/kg/min. Blood sugar is checked after 30–45 minutes and then 6 hourly. Repeat hypoglycemic episodes may be treated by increasing the glucose infusion rate by 2 mg/kg/min until a maximum of 12 mg/kg/min. If two or more consecutive values are >50 mg/dl after 24 hours of parenteral therapy, the infusion can be tapered off at the rate of 2 mg/kg/min every 6 hours, with glucose monitoring. Tapering has to be accompanied by concomitant increase in oral feeds. Once a rate of 4 mg/kg/min of glucose infusion are reached and sugar values are consistently >50 mg/dL the infusion can be stopped.

Follow Up and Outcomes

Hypoglycemia is been linked to long term adverse outcomes. These babies are followed up and assessed at one month corrected age for vision/eye evaluation and at 3, 6, 9, 12 and 18 months corrected age for growth, neurodevelopment, and vision and hearing loss.

Hypocalcemia

Calcium is transferred from mother to the fetus by active transport. Parathyroid hormone (PTH) and calcitonin (CT) do not cross the placental barrier. The PTH related peptide (PTHrP) is the main regulator of the calcium balance in fetus. After delivery, calcium levels start decreasing (more significantly in preterms) and reach a nadir of 7.5–8.5 mg/dl in term babies, by 2nd day of life. The drop in postnatal serum calcium may be related to hypoparathyroidism, end organ unresponsiveness to parathyroid, abnormalities of vit D metabolism, hyperphosphatemia, hypomagnesemia and hypercalcitocalcitonemia which occurs by 12–24 hours of age. PTH levels increase gradually in the first 48 hours of life and normal levels of serum calcium are regained by day 3 of life.

Definition

Hypocalcemia is defined as total serum calcium < 7 mg/dL or ionized calcium < 4 mg/dL. Hypocalcemia may be of early onset (< 72 hr) or rarely late onset (>72 hr).

Early onset neonatal hypocalcemia (ENH): Commonly seen in preterms less than 32 weeks, infants of diabetic mothers, perinatal asphyxia and maternal hyperparathyroidism. Such babies are at increased risk of hypocalcemia.

Late onset hypocalcemia (LNH): Neonates born to mothers with vitamin D deficiency, babies on anticonvulsant therapy or with malabsorption, those on cow milk feeding, or with hypoparathyroidism are at risk of LNH.

Clinical Presentation

ENH is usually asymptomatic unlike the LNH variety and is diagnosed on routine screening. The symptoms when present may be of neuromuscular irritability: myoclonic jerks, jitteriness, exaggerated startle, seizures. They may represent the cardiac involvement like tachycardia, heart failure, prolonged QT interval, decreased contractibility. Apnea, cyanosis, tachypnea, vomiting and laryngospasm are other rare symptoms.

Treatment

Patients at increased risk of hypocalcemia: They should receive 40 mg/kg/day of elemental calcium (4 ml/kg/day of 10% calcium gluconate). Infants tolerating oral feeds may receive this calcium orally q 6 hourly. Therapy should be continued for 3 days.

Patients diagnosed to have asymptomatic hypocalcemia: They should receive 80 mg/kg/day elemental calcium for 48 hours. This may be tapered to 50% dose for another 24 hours and then discontinued.

Patients diagnosed to have symptomatic hypocalcemia: They should receive a bolus dose of 2 ml/kg/dose. This should be followed by a continuous IV infusion of 80 mg/kg/day elemental calcium for 48 hours. Calcium infusion should be dropped to 50% of the original dose for the next 24 hours and then discontinued. The infusion may be replaced with oral calcium therapy on the last day. Normal calcium values should be documented at 48 hours before weaning the infusion.

Bradycardia and arrhythmia are known side effects of bolus IV calcium administration and bolus doses of calcium should be diluted 1:1 with 5% dextrose and given under cardiac monitoring. Skin and subcutaneous tissue necrosis may occur due to extravasations. Hence IV sites where calcium is being infused should be checked at least q2 hourly to monitor for extravasation and avoid subcutaneous tissue necrosis.

EFFECT OF MATERNAL CONDITIONS ON FETUS AND NEONATES

Infant of Diabetic Mother (IDM)

Diabetes is one of the most common endocrine disorders affecting women during pregnancy. The following complications are likely to occur during pregnancy of a diabetic mother.

1. Fetus may suddenly die during the last trimester of pregnancy
2. Preterm delivery may have to be induced to avoid third trimester fetal death
3. Macrosomia or large size of the body (Fig. 7.47) and its attending risks during delivery such as birth trauma, asphyxia and increased possibilities of cesarean section
4. Neonatal respiratory distress
5. Hypoglycemia
6. Hypocalcemia
7. Hyperbilirubinemia
8. Polycythemia and increased viscosity of blood
9. Higher risk of congenital anomalies. (Infants of mothers with diabetes are 20 times more at risk to develop cardiovascular defects)
10. Cardiomyopathy and persistent pulmonary hypertension
11. Lazy left colon syndrome.

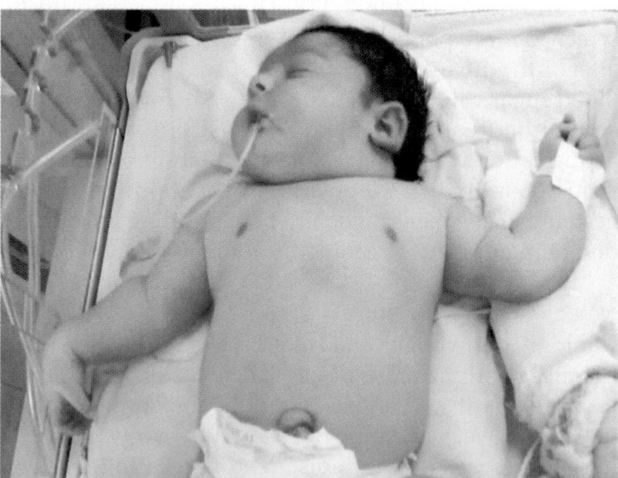

Fig. 7.47: Infant of diabetic mother: Note the large size of the baby with broad shoulders and torso and a relatively smaller head

Pathogenesis

Maternal hyperglycemia leads to fetal hyperglycemia. This stimulates fetal pancreatic beta cells and increased production of insulin by the fetus. Insulin C peptide plasma concentration of the fetus is elevated. Insulin is an anabolic hormone and promotes growth. Mother's insulin turnover rate is increased during pregnancy due to the proteolytic degradation of insulin by the placenta and opposing effects of human placental proactin, progesterone and cortisol. This is how latent diabetes in the mother may become apparent diabetes during pregnancy. Excess maternal glucose and amino acids provide the substrate for increased synthesis of protein, lipids and glycogen in the fetus. Most part of the large fetal size is due to the accumulation of fat. (Intrauterine growth retardation observed in some infants of diabetic mothers may be due to maternal placental vascular insufficiency).

The basic mechanism of hypoglycemia in these cases is diminished production of glucose and increased removal by insulin. The cause of hypocalcemia is not clear but is probably due to diminished production of parathormone. Hypomagnesemia as seen in infants of the diabetic mother may be due to increased losses of magnesium in the urine of diabetic mothers. Hyperbilirubinemia may be due to the breakdown of hemoglobin from collection of blood in cephalohematoma which is usual in the delivery of large babies. Since insulin blocks induction of enzyme system, this may explain lower production of surfactant. This along with higher risk of preterm deliveries explains higher risk of respiratory distress syndrome. Increased smooth muscles in pulmonary arteries may explain persistent pulmonary hypertension. Infants of diabetic mothers have one to nine percent incidence of diabetes in later life.

Hypertensive Disorder of Pregnancy

Hypertension during the pregnancy causes uterine vasculature remodeling and activation of rennin-angiotensin system. Preeclampsia-eclampsia is severe form of pregnancy induced hypertension. The fundamental abnormality recognized in preeclampsia-eclampsia is uteroplacental ischemia. The following complications are likely to occur during pregnancy of a hypertensive mother.

1. Intrauterine growth retardation.
2. Increased perinatal mortality.
3. Increased incidence of spontaneous and/or iatrogenic prematurity.
4. Respiratory depression of the fetus due to the use of sedatives.

Disorder of Thyroid Functions during Pregnancy

Hyperthyroidism occurs in approximately 0.2% of pregnancies and results in significant increase in the prevalence of low-birth-weight delivery and a trend toward higher neonatal mortality. Most common cause of thyrotoxicosis (85% of cases) in women of child bearing age is Graves disease. Pathogenesis of Graves disease is not fully understood but it probably represent an overlapping spectrum of disorders that are characterized by production of polyclonal antibodies. Measurement of thyroid-stimulating antibodies (TSAbs) is useful in predicting whether the fetus will be affected.

Hypothyroidism during pregnancy is not a significant problem and treatment with replacement doses of thyroid hormone is usually well tolerated and easily titrated. Hypothyroidism has occurred in fetus whose mothers have inadvertently received radioactive iodine during pregnancy. There is currently no reliable method for diagnosing hypothyroidism *in utero*.

Maternal Immunologic Diseases

Autoimmune diseases are characterized by an immune attack on tissues of the body in the apparent absence of active infection. Symptoms arise from the resulting impairment of cell or organ function. The autoantibody mediated diseases can have direct consequences on the fetus and neonate because the antibodies are usually of the immunoglobulin G (IgG) type, which are transported across the placenta to the fetal circulation. Diseases in this class include myasthenia gravis, Goodpasture syndrome, Graves' disease, antiphospholipid antibody syndrome (APS), immune thrombocytopenic purpura (ITP), and systemic lupus erythematosus (SLE).

APS is an autoimmune disease associated with thrombophilia and recurrent pregnancy loss. Antiphospholipid antibodies and APS are usually seen in association with SLE and other rheumatic diseases. Vasculopathy, infarction, and thrombosis have been identified in placentas from women who had failed pregnancies and APS. Treatment trials have focused on immunomodulation (e.g. corticosteroids and intravenous immune globulin [IVIG]) and anticoagulation (e.g. low-dose aspirin, heparin, low-molecular weight heparin).

ITP in pregnant women usually induces moderate thrombocytopenia in the fetus or the newborn. The frequency of intracranial hemorrhage has been estimated to be about 1% and is less frequent in autoimmune thrombocytopenia than in neonatal allo-immune thrombocytopenia (10%). No significant correlation has been observed between neonatal thrombocytopenia and maternal platelet autoantibodies. The history of a previous infant who had thrombocytopenia is the only important factor in estimating the risk of fetal thrombocytopenia. After birth, thrombocytopenia in the neonate usually worsens during the first days of life. Postnatal management typically involves observation when the platelet count is greater than $20 \times 10^3/\mu L$ ($20 \times 10^9/L$) in a child who exhibits no clinical bleeding. For infants who have evidence of hemorrhage, single-donor irradiated platelets may be administered to control bleeding, even though the platelet count may not show a sustained increase. In addition, the infant may benefit from an infusion of IVIG.

Neonatal lupus erythematosus is a model of passively acquired autoimmunity in which immune abnormalities in the mother lead to the production of anti-SSA/Ro-SSB/La antibodies that cross the placenta and presumably injure fetal tissue. The most serious manifestation is damage to the cardiac conducting system that results in congenital heart block (CHB), which is usually third degree. No serologic profile is unique to mothers of affected children, but compared with mothers of healthy children, anti-SSA/Ro antibodies are usually of high titer. For the fetus in whom a block is identified, there are several guidelines for treatment, but no definitive approach. If the fetus has been in complete block for more than 3 weeks and there is no sign of myocardial dysfunction or hydrops, it might be prudent to monitor with frequent echocardiograms and not institute any medication. For incomplete blocks, very recently identified blocks, or complete blocks associated with dysfunction or hydrops, 4 mg daily of maternal dexamethasone is a reasonable consideration. Children (affected or unaffected) whose mothers have anti-SSA/Ro or SSB/La antibodies do not appear to have an increased risk of developing systemic rheumatic diseases during adolescence and early adulthood.

Other Maternal Disorders and Possible Adverse Effects on the Fetus

Complications related to pregnancy, maternal malnutrition and certain systemic infections in the mother adversely influence the growth of the fetus and the newborn (Table 7.33). Awareness of this interrelationship helps the physician to anticipate any morbidity in the fetus or the newborn and to facilitate prompt remedial measures.

Drug Therapy and Breastfeeding

Although all medications transfer into human milk, most do so in amounts that are subclinical. The clinician should evaluate each medication carefully, examine published data on the drug, and advise the mother carefully about the use of medications while breastfeeding. In each case, the clinician also must evaluate the relative risk to the infant by considering the absolute dose transferred via milk, the age and maturity of the infant, and the ability of the infant to clear the normally minimal concentrations of medications found in milk. In most cases, the amount of drug in milk is far less than 4% of the maternal dose and often is extremely subclinical. In almost all situations, numerous medications can be used safely for specific syndromes, and drugs should be chosen carefully with the breastfeeding mother in mind. Most importantly, discontinuing breastfeeding and changing to formula may predispose the infant to a number of significant risks. Formula feeding may predispose infants to increased risk of GI tract syndromes, allergies, deficits in neurobehavioral outcomes, and major increases in infectious disease. Table 7.34 enlist the maternal medications which possesses high risk to the breastfeeding infants.

Table 7.33: Maternal disorders and possible adverse effects on the fetus

Maternal disorders	*Possible adverse effects*	*Remarks*
Antepartum hemorrhage	Fetal and birth asphyxia, premature labor, anemia.	Anticipate birth asphyxia Monitor baby's Hb levels.
Poly-hydramnios	Anencephaly, high intestinal obstruction, ectopia vesicae	Exclude esophageal atresia at birth.
Oligo-hydramnios	Bilateral renal agenesis, obstructive uropathy, deformed limbs or face	Need for ventilation due to risk of pulmonary hypoplasia.
Prolonged rupture of membranes	Risk of pneumonia or septicemia.	Obtain gastric aspirate for leukocyte count.
Malnutrition	Intrauterine growth retardation, risk of anemia, due to inadequate stores of iron	Pregnant mothers should receive supplement of 350 kcal/day, iron, folic acid and vitamins.
Maternal infections (viruses, protozoal, spirochetal)	Abortion, intrauterine death, fetal growth retardation, multisystem involvement, e.g. hepatitis, meningoencephalitis, anemia, thrombocytopenia, microcephaly or hydrocephaly.	

Maternal Medications and Fetal Hazards

The available scientific information on the placental transfer of drugs and their metabolism in the fetus is incomplete. It appears that most of the soluble constituents of drugs in the maternal serum cross the placental barriers by simple or facilitated diffusion. However, poorly diffused constituents may be actively transported to the fetus through pinocytosis. The immaturity of fetal enzymes and of transport system, may handicap the metabolism of drugs by the fetus.

The risk by exogenous agents to the fetus is most pronounced during the period of embryogenesis and may result in abortion or congenital malformation. In the late part of pregnancy, these agents only cause organ dysfunction or disturbances of enzyme systems. However, some drugs used by the mother, e.g. barbiturates have the potential of inducing fetal enzyme systems. As a general principle, the use of drugs during pregnancy

Table 7.34: Maternal medications of high risk to breastfeeding infants*

Amiodarone	Significant risk of accumulation; thyroid suppression and cardiovascular toxicity.
Anticancer agents	Some anticancer agents that have short half-lives may permit breastfeeding with a brief interruption.
Doxepin	Sedation and respiratory arrest.
Drugs of abuse	Cocaine, amphetamines, phencyclidine, heroin, and others should be avoided.
Ergotamine, cabergoline, bromocriptine	Ergotism has been reported in breastfed infants. Likely suppression of prolactin and milk cessation.
Sodium or potassium iodide; povidone iodide solutions	Massive concentration of iodine in milk; thyroid suppression in infant.
Methotrexate	Immune suppression; concentration in gastrointestinal tract of infant.
Lithium	Lithium concentrations in milk are high. Infant plasma likely has 33% to 40% of maternal plasma levels; monitor infant and mother closely if used.
Radioisotopes	Brief interruptions are advised; consult nuclear regulatory commission recommendations.
Tetracycline	Short-term use (<3 to 4 wk) not harmful

*Many of these medications can be used in breastfeeding mothers if followed by brief periods of interruption.

Table 7.35: Common teratogenic drugs

Drugs or chemical	*Teratogenic effect*
Alcohol	Growth retardation; cardiac, limb and facial anomalies
Amphetamines	Learning disability, motor incoordination, hepatic calcification
Androgens	Cleft lip-palate, tracheoesophageal fistula, CHD, masculinization
Barbiturates	Cleft lip-palate, CHD, induction of hepatic microsomal enzymes, respiratory depression, withdrawal symptoms
Chloroquine	Deafness after prolonged use, hemolysis in susceptible individuals
Diazepam	Cleft lip-palate, apnea, hypothermia
Dicumarol	Bleeding, fetal death, depressed nasal bridge, stippling of phalanges, choanal atresia; cardiac, renal and ophthalmic defects
Diphenylhydantoin	Facial, cardiac and limb anomalies
Excessive smoking	Growth retardation
Gentamicin	Eighth nerve damage
Heroin	Intrauterine death, low birth weight, sudden infant death
Indomethacin	Low birth weight, platelet dysfunction
Iodides	Hypothyroidism, goiter
Lithium carbonate	CHD, goiter
Propylthiouracil	Hypothyroidism
Methotrexate	Congenital malformation, abortion.
Oral contraceptives	Cardiac, limb and visceral anomalies
Progestins	Masculinization, advanced bone age
Quinine	Deafness, neurologic anomalies, thrombocytopenia
Radiation	Microcephaly, mental retardation
Tetracycline	Staining of teeth, enamel hypoplasia, inhibition of bone growth, congenital cataracts
Tolbutamide	Fetal death, thrombocytopenia
Vitamin D (heavy dose)	Mental retardation, supravalvular aortic stenosis, ventricular opacities, elfin facies

CHD: Congenital heart disease

should be minimized. The benefits of medication to the mother must always be carefully weighed against the risk to the fetus.

Drugs listed in Table 7.35 are known to be or suspected to be teratogenic when given during the first trimester of pregnancy.

8 Immunity and Immunization

The word 'immunity' (Latin immunis) means the state of protection from infectious disease. The immune system has evolved as defence system to protect animals from invading microorganisms and malignant disorders. It first recognizes a microorganism or any other foreign material, discriminates it from self, and then mounts an appropriate response to eliminate it. Two broad categories of immune system act in concert to eliminate microorganisms: innate immune system and adaptive immune system. The former is primitive, non-specific, has no memory and provides the first line of defense against infections. The adaptive immune system is highly evolved, specific and has memory characterized by a rapid rise in immune response that serves to eliminate the microorganism.

INNATE IMMUNE SYSTEM

The skin and mucous membranes provide an important mechanical barrier. Gastric acidity is an effective physiologic barrier as very few microorganisms can survive the low acidic pH in stomach. The complement system is a complex system of multiple proteins circulating in the blood. Most of these are in inactive form; once activated, they interact in a cascade activating each other sequentially. There are two pathways by which complement activation is initiated. The classical pathway is activated by antibody-antigen complexes, polyanions (heparin, protamine, nucleic acids from apoptotic cells), gram negative bacteria and C-reactive protein. The alternative pathway is initiated when a previously activated complement component binds to the surface of a pathogen (e.g. yeast walls, bacterial cell wall lipopolysaccharides/endotoxin).

Activation of complement generates molecules that have a number of important effects. For example, activation of C3 results in formation of the membrane attack complex, which binds to the surface of cells including bacteria, fungi and viruses leading to their lysis. C3b component can bind to the immune complexes or the foreign cell surface resulting in their opsonization. Binding of anaphylotoxins (C3a, C4a, C5a) to receptors on mast cells and basophils result in their degranulation and release of histamine, other mediators and intracellular enzymes, inducing anaphylaxis. C3a and C5a regulate monocyte-macrophage and neutrophil activities by inducing their adherence to vascular endothelial cells, extravasation and chemotaxis at the site of inflammation. Activation of the classical pathway results in low levels of C4, C2 and C3; activation of alternative pathway is characterized by reduced levels of C3 and normal levels of C4 and C2.

Cellular components of the innate immune system comprise of mononuclear phagocytic cells (polymorphonuclear leukocytes, macrophages and NK cells). They ingest extracellular material by phagocytosis, which fuses with the lysosomes, forming phagolysosomes. Activation of myeloperoxidase in phagolysosomes results in production of superoxide that oxidizes and inactivates microbial proteins. In the presence of chlorine, superoxide forms another toxic compound, hypochlorous acid.

ADAPTIVE IMMUNE SYSTEM

Adaptive immune system requires cooperation between lymphocytes and antigen presenting cells. Adaptive immune response develops to specific antigenic challenge, shows tremendous diversity and exhibits immunological memory. Cellular components of the immune system comprise of lymphocytes, macrophages and antigen presenting cells, organized into organs and tissues that are distributed throughout the body. All cells of the immune system develop and mature in the primary lymphoid organs (bone marrow, thymus) and interact with foreign antigens in the secondary lymphoid organs (spleen, lymph nodes, mucosa associated lymphoid tissues including tonsils and Peyer patches).

Lymphocytes constitute 20–40% of white cells in the peripheral blood. Based on function and specific cell surface receptors, these are divided into B cells, T cells and NK cells. T cells are identified by the presence of T cell antigen receptor (TCR) which is associated with CD3 complex to form the TCR-CD3 complex. Each T cell has a unique receptor that remains unchanged during cell division. T cells recognize antigen only when it is bound to MHC molecules on the surface of antigen presenting cells.

Mature T lymphocytes are distinguished into CD4+ cells and CD8+ cells by the presence of one of the two

adjuvants in the diphtheria pertussis tetanus (DPT) vaccine.

If a large number of susceptible individuals are simultaneously protected from a particular infectious disease by immunization at the same point of time, the transmission chain of the infectious agent can be broken, thus decreasing the risk of disease in the unimmunized children as well. This is called the *herd effect* of immunization. Vaccines that protect only against disease (e.g. diphtheria) have a lower herd effect than vaccines that protect against both disease and infection (e.g. measles and OPV). Vaccines that have low protective efficacy (e.g. pertussis and typhoid) will similarly have no significant herd effect. The herd effect is utilized as one of the strategies for eradication of poliovirus, and may be used to interrupt transmission in measles epidemics.

TYPES OF VACCINES

Vaccines may consist of live attenuated organism, killed or inactivated organism, modified toxins or toxoids, or subunits of antigens. Some examples of each of these are listed in Table 8.3.

Live Vaccines

These vaccines actually infect the recipient but do not cause disease because the potency of the organism has been attenuated. If residual maternal antibody is present in the infant's serum, it may neutralize the organism before infection occurs, thus interrupting the "take" of a vaccine; hence, vaccines like measles and measles, mumps, rubella (MMR) are administered beyond 9 months of age. BCG and oral poliovirus vaccine (OPV) are exceptions as the maternally derived immunity does not interfere with the vaccine "take". There is no interference with response to BCG because it induces cell mediated immunity which is not transferred from mother to fetus; hence, it may be given shortly after birth. OPV infects the gut mucosa and residual maternal antibody does not interrupt this infection.

With live vaccines, usually a single dose is sufficient to induce immunity; OPV is an exception where multiple doses are required because infection of intestinal mucosa is required. Storage and transportation conditions are critical to the potency of live vaccines.

Killed Vaccines

The chief advantage with killed vaccines is the stability of these vaccines. However, the immunity induced is usually not permanent and multiple doses, including booster doses, are required to ensure prolonged protection. Most killed bacterial and some killed viral vaccines (like influenza) are associated with significant local and systemic reactions.

Toxoids

Toxoids are modified toxins that, if well purified, are non toxic to the recipient. Primary immunization is in form of multiple divided doses in order to decrease the adverse effects at each administration, and to provide high antibody titres that occur with repeated exposure to the same antigen. Booster doses are required to sustain the protection.

Subunit Vaccines

Other non replicating antigens include capsular polysaccharide and viral or bacterial subunits. Capsular polysaccharides are carbohydrate antigens that elicit humoral response by stimulating B cells directly, without modulation by helper T cells. Hence, there is no immunological memory, and the antibodies produced are of the IgM class alone, rather than an IgG response.

PRINCIPLES OF IMMUNIZATION

A good vaccine is one that is easy to administer, induces permanent immunity, is free of toxic substances, has minimal side effects, is easy to produce and is stable at different environmental conditions. The choice of a vaccine for any immunization program depends on the utility or

8

Table 8.3: Type of vaccines

Description		*Example*
Live attenuated organism	Bacterial	BCG, oral typhoid (*S. typhi* Ty21a)
	Viral	OPV, measles, MMR, varicella
Killed or inactivated organism	Bacterial	DTPw, whole cell killed typhoid
	Viral	Inactivated polio vaccine, rabies, hepatitis A vaccine
Modified bacterial toxins or toxoids		Diphtheria toxoid, tetanus toxoid
Subunit	Bacterial capsular polysaccharide	*S. typhi* (Vi), Hemophilus influenza type b, meningococcal, pneumococcal
	Viral	Hepatitis B (surface antigen)

BCG Bacillus Calmette Guerin vaccine, OPV oral poliovirus vaccine, MMR measles mumps and rubella vaccine, DTPw diphtheria toxoid tetanus toxoid whole cell killed pertussis vaccine

Table 8.4: Basic principles of immunization

- A minimum interval of 4 weeks is recommended between the administrations of 2 live antigens, if not administered simultaneously. Exceptions are OPV and MMR, and OPV and oral typhoid (Ty21a), where administration of one before or after another is permissible if indicated.
- Two or more killed antigens may be administered simultaneously or at any interval between the doses. However, a minimum gap of 3–4 weeks is recommended between two doses of cholera or yellow fever vaccine.
- There is no minimum recommended time interval between two types of vaccines. A live and an inactivated viral vaccine can be administered simultaneously at two different sites.
- A delay or lapse in the administration of a vaccine does not require the whole schedule to be repeated; the missed dose can be administered to resume the course at the point it was interrupted.
- If the immunization status of a child is not known, he may be administered age appropriate vaccines.
- The recommended dose of each vaccine should be adhered to; excessive dose may result in adverse events while an inappropriately low dose may not evoke the required immune response.
- Mixing of vaccines in the same syringe is not recommended.
- There is no evidence to suggest that combination vaccines are more efficacious than individual vaccines.
- The following are not contraindications to immunization: minor illnesses such as upper respiratory tract infection and diarrhea, mild fever, prematurity, allergy to penicillin, history of allergies, malnutrition, recent exposure to infection and current therapy with antibiotics.
- Immunoglobulins interfere with the immune response to measles and MMR; hence, the vaccine should not be given to children who have received such agents in the last 3 months. Immunoglobulins do not interfere with the immune response to OPV and yellow fever vaccine. Hepatitis B, tetanus and rabies vaccine or toxoid may be administered concurrently with their corresponding immunoglobulin.
- Congenital immunodeficiency, therapy with high dose steroids and illnesses associated with considerable immunosuppression are contraindications to the administration of BCG and live viral vaccines. Live viral vaccines should be avoided in children with symptomatic HIV (AIDS); they may be given after short courses (less than 2 weeks) of low dose steroids. OPV should be avoided in healthy siblings of immunocompromised children due to the risk of feco-oral transmission to the immunocompromised child.
- Risk of adverse events following whole cell pertussis vaccine is increased in infants with progressive neurological disease, and in those with convulsions following a previous dose of the vaccine. Active immunization should be carried out following exposure to rabies, measles, varicella, tetanus and hepatitis B.

necessity in terms of prevalence and severity of disease it helps prevent, efficacy, and safety profile. The timing of administration depends on the age at which the disease is anticipated and feasibility. Basic principles of immunization are listed in Table 8.4.

VACCINE STORAGE AND COLD CHAIN

The potency of a vaccine is maintained by cold chain, which refers to the proper system of transporting, storing, and distributing vaccines at the recommended temperatures from the point of manufacture to the point at which they are administered. Maintenance of appropriate temperature is critical to the viability and potency of a vaccine. While BCG, OPV and measles are very sensitive to heat and can be frozen without harm, vaccines like tetanus toxoid are less sensitive to heat and may in fact be damaged by freezing. Other vaccines that must not be frozen include DT, DPT, Td, hepatitis B, hepatitis A, Hemophilus influenza b, and whole cell killed typhoid vaccine. In the refrigerator, OPV vials are stored in the freezer compartment (0 to –4°C). In the main compartment (4–10°C) BCG, measles and MMR are kept in the top rack (below the freezer); other vaccines like DPT, DT, TT, hepatitis A and typhoid are stored in the middle racks; while hepatitis B, varicella and diluents are stored in the lower racks.

BCG VACCINE

The Bacillus Calmette Guérin (BCG) vaccine continues to be the only effective vaccine against tuberculosis. Currently several strains are in use; the common ones include Copenhagen (Danish 1331) and Pasteur. The Danish 1331 strain was being produced in India at Guindy, Tamil Nadu till recently.

The protective efficacy of the BCG vaccine is variable. Its efficacy against severe forms of tuberculosis like miliary tuberculosis and tubercular meningitis is about 50–80%, but protection against development of pulmonary tuberculosis is less than 50%. BCG does not protect against other mycobacterial diseases like leprosy. BCG induces primarily cell mediated immunity, and there is no interference by maternal antibody. It is usually administered at or soon after birth to provide early protection and to utilize the opportunity of the infant being available; some believe that the adverse events are also less frequent in neonatal period.

The vaccine is supplied in the form of a lyophilized or freeze dried powder, in a vacuum-sealed dark-colored multidose vial. The vaccine is reconstituted with sterile normal saline. Any unused vaccine must be discarded after 4 hours, otherwise bacterial contamination may occur. The vaccine is extremely sensitive to light and heat. The cold chain should be maintained at all points in transit. In the lyophilized form the vaccine remains potent for up to a year at 2–8°C, but the potency drops rapidly after reconstitution.

Each dose of the vaccine contains 0.1 to 0.4 million live viable bacilli. The recommended volume is 0.1 ml at all ages. Conventionally, the vaccine is administered on the convex aspect of the left shoulder at the insertion of the deltoid, to allow for easy identification of the BCG scar. The intradermal route should be used to raise a wheal about 5 mm. Subcutaneous administrations may cause lymphadenopathy. At the injection site, BCG bacilli multiply and form a papule at about 2–3 weeks, which enlarges to 4–8 mm size at 5–6 weeks; this papule ulcerates and then heals by scarring at around 6–12 weeks. Adverse effects include persistent ulcer with delayed healing, ipsilateral axillary or cervical lymphadenopathy, and rarely, abscess and sinus formation. Children with severe deficiencies in cellular immunity may develop disseminated BCG disease. Majority of children will show a positive reaction to tuberculin test 4 to 12 weeks after immunization.

Children who are tuberculin positive have an accelerated and enhanced response to BCG administration, and this 'BCG" test has been used by some as a diagnostic test for tuberculosis. Although it is considered more sensitive than tuberculin test, it is associated with the risk of severe reactions like ulceration, and is used rarely.

POLIOMYELITIS VACCINES

Two types of vaccines are available worldwide for prevention of poliomyelitis, the live attenuated oral poliovirus vaccine (OPV) developed by Salk and the inactivated or killed poliovirus vaccine (IPV) developed by Sabin. Both vaccines are available as trivalent preparations containing the three types of poliovirus, and both, when used as recommended, provide good protection from paralytic poliomyelitis as well as control of the disease in the community.

Oral Polio Vaccine (OPV)

The OPV is a suspension of over 10^5–10^6 median cell culture infectious doses of the attenuated poliovirus types 1, 2 and 3 in each liquid dose, which is two drops in India, and 0.5 ml in some countries like the USA. OPV has also been formulated as a monovalent vaccine (mOPV). The mOPV type 1 vaccine has been used in India for the first time in specific areas where surveillance showed P1 wild virus transmission in 2005.

Once administered, the vaccine viruses reach the intestines where they must establish an infection of the mucosal cells to elicit an immune response; this is termed the "take" of the vaccine virus. Theoretically, one dose should suffice, but due to various reasons like interruptions in the cold chain, interference due to intestinal infection with other enteroviruses, or the presence of diarrhea that causes excretion of the virus before it can attach to the mucosal cells, 'take' rates may be variable and several doses may be required. Seroconversion rates after 3 doses of OPV are 73%, 90% and 70% for serotypes 1, 2 and 3. Hence the number of doses should be increased to decrease the frequency of vaccine failure. For this reason the IAP recommends five doses in infancy and two booster doses at 15–18 months and again at 5 years. The first dose of OPV may be administered to the neonate, three doses are given 4 weeks apart along with DPT at 6, 10 and 14 weeks, and the opportunity for measles immunization at 9 months can be utilized for OPV administration, too. In addition to the routine OPV doses, "pulse polio" doses on every National Immunization Day (NID) and sub-National Immunisation Day (sNID) until the age of 5 years are also mandatory.

Where poliovirus circulation is intensive, paralytic poliomyelitis is a disease almost exclusively seen in infants and children, and adults are immune. Simultaneous administration of OPV to all susceptible infants and children interferes with the circulation of the wild poliovirus in the community. In order that no wild poliovirus remains in circulation, NIDs are organized each year for this purpose. Organization of such mass campaigns is one of the 4 key strategies for eradication of polio; the others are maintaining high routine infant immunization coverage with OPV, organization of mop-up campaigns in event of an outbreak, and maintaining a sensitive system of surveillance for acute flaccid paralysis (AFP).

The vaccine contains magnesium chloride as a stabilizing agent, and is therefore stable for 3–4 months at 4–8°C and for 1–2 years at –20°C; the potency is decreased with temperature fluctuations, especially to above 8°C. Vaccine potency can be effectively monitored with the vaccine vial monitor (VVM), displayed on the label of the vial.

Breastfeeding and mild diarrhea are not contraindications for the administration of OPV. OPV is an excellent vaccine and is the vaccine of choice for the eradication of poliovirus in developing countries like India, where it should continue to be used till wild poliovirus circulation ceases. However, OPV (especially the type 2 strain) is associated with the risk of vaccine associated paralytic poliomyelitis (VAPP), which occurs in 1 in a few million vaccines, resulting in 250–800 cases every year globally. The emergence of outbreaks caused by vaccine-derived virus is a relatively recent phenomenon, and has been seen in the Dominican Republic, Egypt, Haiti, Madagascar and the Philippines. It is a virus that has mutated from the original Sabin strain by more than 1% and reverted to neurovirulence. Two types of vaccine-derived poliovirus (VDPV) have been recognized: iVDPV (i for immunodeficient), which is isolated from immunodeficient individuals and cVDPV (c for circulating), which is isolated from outbreaks and has similar epidemiological and biological characteristics as the wild viruses.

Inactivated Polio Vaccine (IPV)

IPV is a suspension of formaldehyde killed and purified poliovirus grown in monkey kidney or human diploid cell culture. The potency is measured by 'D' antigen content. Currently used IPV vaccines have enhanced potency compared to previously used IPVs, and contain 40D, 8D and 32D units of the types 1, 2 and 3 polioviruses respectively. The vaccine is highly immunogenic; it produces excellent humoral immunity, and also induces local pharyngeal and, possibly, intestinal immunity as well. Seroconversion is seen in 90–95% cases when 2 doses of the vaccine are given 2 months apart beyond 2 months age, while 3 doses, given beyond 6 weeks age and only 4 weeks apart, are associated with seroconversion in 99% cases. Hence the vaccine can be given in 3 doses along with DTP beginning at 6 weeks age, without decrease in seroconversion or increase in side effects. Since IPV induces only low levels of immunity (via secretary IgA) in the gut, IPV is less reliable in control of spread of wild virus. However, observations from use of the vaccine in the USA and other developed countries indicate that IPV has excellent herd effect. IPV is also very safe. The vaccine is administered intramuscularly in 0.5 ml volume, singly or as a combination (available with DTaP/ Hib in India).

The recommendations of the polio eradication committee of the Indian Academy of pediatrics (IAP) highlight the potential utility of IPV in two key areas; firstly, to curb wild virus transmission in UP and Bihar, and secondly, to switch to IPV DPT combination in polio free states in preparation for the post polio eradication era.

IAPCOI had previously recommended use of IPV in conjunction with OPV in children after one to one discussion with parents; IAPCOI now recommends offering additional use of IPV with OPV in all children who can afford the vaccine. Recommending wider use of IPV is in view of the excellent immunogenicity, efficacy and safety of IPV and the inevitability of switch to IPV in the post polio eradication era. The IAPCOI recommends continued use of OPV in concordance with the government policy of using OPV for polio eradication, evidence to suggest that mucosal immunity (as measured by stool excretion of virus after monovalent OPV1 challenge) is superior with combination of OPV and IPV as compared to IPV alone, and to avoid confusion in the minds of parents whose children receive only IPV about the efficacy and safety of OPV. The latter may adversely influence the turn-up for OPV on NID's; there might be individuals who do not give immunization with OPV due to fear of side effects and neither give IPV due to non-affordability. The advantage of combining use of IPV and OPV is that the risk of VAPP is extremely low as the child receives OPV at the time when he/she is protected against VAPP by maternal antibodies, and subsequently, he/she is protected from VAPP by IPV. An all IPV schedule would keep the child at a small risk for VAPP through exposure to the OPV virus through contacts/ environment before he/ she receives his/her first dose of IPV. Hence, the combined OPV and IPV schedule strives to provide the best protection to an individual child while not deviating from the national immunization policies.

IAP recommends that the birth dose of OPV and all doses on the NIDs be given to the child. Hence, a child should receive OPV at birth, OPV and IPV at 6, 10 and 14 weeks, OPV and IPV at 15–18 months, OPV at 5 years, and OPV on all NID's and SNID's. A child less than 5 years of age who has completed primary immunization with OPV may be offered IPV as catch up vaccination as three doses; 2 doses at 2 month interval followed by a third dose 6 months after the first dose. OPV need not be given with these IPV doses, but should be given with the first and 2nd boosters of DTP and on all NID's and SNID's. IPV is the vaccine of choice in patients with immunodeficiency including symptomatic HIV, and in siblings and close contacts of such patients; OPV should be avoided especially in patients with B cell immunodeficiency. The primary immunization and first IPV booster are as discussed above; a second booster dose of IPV at 5 years is also recommended. Once poliovirus eradication is achieved, the country should switch to IPV usage and OPV use should be discontinued.

DIPHTHERIA VACCINE

Natural immunity to diphtheria is often acquired through apparent or inapparent infections. However, even apparent infections may not confer protection against subsequent infections. Maternal antibodies protect the infant against disease and also interfere with immune response to vaccination for several weeks after birth. Hence vaccination beginning some weeks after birth is required, in multiple doses to ensure protection. Diphtheria antitoxin titre of >0.1 IU/ml is said to be associated with protection from disease.

Diphtheria vaccine is a toxoid vaccine, containing the diphtheria toxin (DT) that has been modified and adsorbed onto aluminium hydroxide, which acts as an adjuvant. It has been in use for about six decades as a combination vaccine with tetanus toxoid (TT) and whole cell killed pertussis vaccine as DTPw. The quantity of toxoid contained in a vaccine is expressed as its limit of flocculation (Lf) content. Each dose of the vaccine contains 20–30 Lf of DT, 5–25 Lf of TT and >4 IU of whole cell pertussis in 0.5 mL volume. The vaccine should be stored at 2–8°C. It is administered intramuscularly in the anterolateral thigh.

Common adverse effects include fever, local pain and induration; rarely, incessant crying and encephalopathy are seen. All adverse effects are related chiefly to the pertussis component.

Primary immunization requires 3 doses to be given 4–8 weeks apart; in our country this is carried out at 6, 10 and 14 weeks. After 3 doses, antitoxin response to DT and TT is seen in over 95%, but protective efficacy against pertussis is lower at about 70–90%. Immunization does not eliminate *Corynebacterium diphtheriae* from the skin or nasopharynx.

Booster doses of DTP are required to achieve a protective antibody titer of 0.1 IU/ml which confers protection against diphtheria in the first decade of life. Immunity following primary immunization with DTP or one booster wanes over the next 6–12 years. IAPCOI recommends a total of 5 doses of DTP vaccine; three in infancy as part of primary immunization and two booster doses at 18 months and 5 years. If given beyond 7 years of age, primary immunization or booster doses should be in the form of Td or Tdap, which contains smaller amounts of diphtheria toxoid (2 Lf) and acellular pertussis vaccine.

PERTUSSIS VACCINE

Pertussis is an important cause of childhood morbidity and mortality in children and remains endemic all over the world despite routine childhood immunization, affecting principally infants and, to a lesser extent, adolescents. Natural infections as well as immunization induce immunity that lasts up to 10 years, necessitating revaccination for continued protection.

The vaccine has been traditionally available as DTPw or "triple antigen", as described above. For primary immunization, three doses of the vaccine are administered at 6, 10 and 14 weeks. However, the protective efficacy of pertussis vaccine is only 70–90%, even after three doses. Immunity following primary immunization or booster dose of pertussis vaccine wanes over next 6–12 years, making re-immunization essential for continued production.

The local (pain and redness) and systemic (fever) reactions commonly seen with DTPw is chiefly because of the pertussis component. The incidence of these adverse effects increases with the number of doses administered, hence the vaccine is not used beyond 5 doses, and beyond 7 years of age. DTPw has also been rarely incriminated in the induction of serious neurological complications, though no conclusive evidence is available. No causal relationship has been demonstrated between the administration of the vaccine and development of chronic neurological disease. The vaccine is relatively contraindicated in children with progressive neurological disease, but children with stable neurological diseases like developmental delay, cerebral palsy and idiopathic epilepsy may be vaccinated. Absolute contraindications to the administration of further doses of the vaccine include immediate anaphylaxis, or the development of encephalopathy lasting >24 hours within 7 days of vaccination. If a child develops persistent inconsolable crying lasting more than 3 hours, hypotensive-hyporesposive episode, or hyperpyrexia (temperature > 40.5°C) within 48 hours of DTPw administration, or febrile or afebrile seizures within 72 hours of DTPw administration, parents should be counseled about risk of recurrence of these adverse events with further doses of the vaccine. If such an event recurs after a subsequent dose, the vaccine is contraindicated in the future.

DT contains the same doses of diphtheria and tetanus toxoids as DTP, but is devoid of the pertussis component. It is indicated for immunization of individuals with a known contraindication to DTP, such as progressive neurological disease or encephalopathy lasting more than 24 hours within 7 days of administration of DTP previously. It is recommended for use up to the age of 7 years, beyond which Td must be used, as described below.

Acellular Pertussis Vaccine (DTPa)

The suspicion that the active pertussis toxin and endotoxin are responsible for the high incidence of adverse events associated with DTPw administration led to the development of various types of purified acellular pertusssis vaccine DTPa. The available DTPa vaccines contain inactivated pertussis toxin (PT) and one or more additional pertussis antigens, like filamentous hemagglutinin (FHA), pertactin, fimbrial protein and a non-fimbrial protein. Trials have demonstrated that these vaccines have similar efficacy compared to DTPw vaccine, but are associated with significantly fewer systemic and local side effects. The PT component of these vaccines is > 4 IU (10–25 mg), while the DT content is between 6.7–25 Lf in each 0.5 ml dose.

The vaccine is not recommended for routine use in our country because of the high cost; the IAPCOI endorses the continued use of the DTPw in the National Program in India in view of its proven efficacy. The DTPa may be administered to children when parents opt for it in view of the advantage of fewer side effects, or are reluctant to the administration of further doses of DTPw after an adverse effect with a previous dose. DTPa is absolutely contraindicated if a previous dose of DTPw or DTPa was associated with immediate anaphylaxis, or the development of encephalopathy lasting >24 hours within 7 days of vaccination. In case of anaphylaxis, all vaccines containing any of the three components of the vaccine are to be avoided in the future. Children who develop encephalopathy should receive DT instead of DTPw or DTPa.

Reduced Antigen Acellular Pertussis Vaccine (Tdap) and Reduced Antigen Diphtheria Toxoid Vaccine (Td)

Both natural infection with pertussis and routine immunization in infancy induce an immunity that wanes by adolescence. This results in a second peak of the disease associated morbidity in adolescence. Pertussis control is unlikely to be achieved if adolescents and adults are not protected against the disease, because they are the source of infection to susceptible individuals. The availability of Tdap offers the prospect of reducing disease burden in the community. The rationale for its use is that the reduced antigen content causes less severe adverse effects while being sufficient to induce protective response in a previously immunized individual (booster effect).

Immunity against diphtheria wanes with time, too, and the only effective way to control the disease is through immunization throughout life to provide constant protective antitoxin levels. While standard dose DT is recommended for primary immunization against diphtheria because of its superior immunogenicity and minimal reactogenicity, the adult preparation Td (or dT) containing a lower content of the toxoid is recommended in individuals 7 years of age or older, because it is adequately immunogenic and reactogenicity is known to increase with age.

The available Tdap vaccine in India contains tetanus toxoid 5 Lf, diphtheria toxoid 2 Lf and three acellular pertussis components namely, pertussis toxoid 8 μg, filamentous hemagglutinin 8 μg and pertactin 2.5 μg. Td contains 5 Lf of tetanus toxoid and 2 Lf of diphtheria toxoid. The reduced antigen diphtheria toxoid vaccine (Td) contains diphtheria toxoid 2 Lf and tetanus toxoid 5 Lf. The contraindications to Tdap are serious allergic reaction to any component of the vaccine or history of encephalopathy not attributable to an underlying cause within 7 days of administration of a vaccine with pertussis component. Td is not associated with significant adverse effects.

Tdap should be administered as a single dose at the age of 10–12 years. The single booster dose of Tdap may be followed by Td boosters every 10 years. There is no data at present to support repeat doses of Tdap. Tdap may also be used as replacement for Td/TT booster in children above 10 years and adults of any age if they have not received Tdap in the past and 5 years have elapsed since the receipt of previous TT/Td vaccine. If less than 5 years have elapsed since Tdap administration, TT is not required for wound prophylaxis. Tdap is also used for primary immunization of children above 7 years, using one dose of Tdap followed by two doses of Td at 0, 1 and 6 months. The IAPCOI recommends the use of DTPw or DTPa, and not Tdap, as second booster in children below 7 years of age. Td may be used whenever TT is indicated in children above 7 years of age.

TETANUS VACCINE

In many developing countries including ours, neonatal tetanus remains an important cause of neonatal mortality. Using two dose tetanus toxoid (TT) to immunize pregnant women or women of child bearing age is an important strategy to reduce the incidence of this disease, because IgG antibodies are passively transferred across the placenta to the fetus and protect the newborn. The last dose of TT should have been received at least 2 weeks prior to delivery. This constitutes passive immunization for the child. Since tetanus can occur at any age, primary immunization is essential, for which three doses of the vaccine (as DPT) are given one month apart. Boosters are given at 18 months and at 5, 10 and 16 years of age. The efficacy of TT vaccine varies between 80–100%. Tetanus antitoxin level of 0.01 IU/mL is considered the minimum protective level in animals; in humans, the level of antitoxin required depends on the toxin load. For previously unimmunized school children, 2 doses of TT given 1 month are sufficient. TT should not be administered after every injury if immunization is complete and last dose is received within last 10 years. For previously immunized pregnant women, 1 dose of TT is sufficient if the second pregnancy within the next 5 years, but would need to be administered 2 doses if the interval exceeds 5 years.

Tetanus toxin, which is highly toxic, is inactivated by formalin to make tetanus toxoid (TT), and adsorbed onto aluminium salts to enhance its immunogenicity. TT vaccine contains 5 Lf of the toxoid. It is a heat stable vaccine that remains potent for a few weeks even at 37°C. Tetanus toxoid is administered with diphtheria toxoid and pertussis killed vaccine as a combination called DPT; DT, Td and TT are also available.

Recommendations for routine tetanus prophylaxis in wound management and indications of tetanus immunoglobulin (TIG) are listed in Table 8.5.

Table 8.5: Guide to tetanus prophylaxis in routine wound management

Past doses of TT	*Clean minor wound*		*All other wounds*	
	TT	TIG*	TT	TIG*
Unknown or < 3 doses	Yes	No	Yes	Yes
>/= 3 doses	No**	No	No***	No

For children < 7 years DTPw or DTPa may be given while TT or Td may be used in older children.
*TIG: Tetanus immunoglobulin (250 IU i/m)

**Yes if > 10 years since last dose
***Yes if > 5 years since last dose

8

MEASLES VACCINE

Measles vaccine is a live attenuated vaccine. The strain used in our country is derived from the Edmonston Zagreb strain of vaccine virus grown in human diploid cell culture. A heat sensitive vaccine, it is stored frozen, and has a shelf life of 1 year at 4–8°C. The vaccine should be used within 4 hours of reconstitution as the potency drops rapidly after reconstitution. Proper aseptic precautions should be taken in reconstituting the vaccine because cases of staphylococcal sepsis and toxic shock syndrome have been seen due to bacterial contamination; any unused vaccine must therefore be discarded.

The vaccine is administered subcutaneously or intramuscularly over the anterolateral thigh or the upper arm. An attenuated infection ensues, and 10–20% children may have a mild illness with fever and a macular rash 7–10 days after vaccination; the illness lasts 1–3 days. Since maternal immunity may interfere with the immune response to the vaccine, the vaccine is administered in our country at 9 months so as to keep a balance between the needs of early protection and high seroconversion. Adequate titers of antibody are generated in 85–90% at 9 months age. In case of an outbreak, vaccine administration as early as 6 months of age may be carried out, with a repeat dose at 12 to 15 months as part of measles or MMR vaccine.

Patients with HIV infection may be vaccinated. Contraindications to measles vaccine include malignancies, therapy with alkylating agents or high dose corticosteroids, untreated tuberculosis and severe immunodeficiencies like severe forms of HIV infection.

Post exposure prophylaxis (PEP) with immunoglobulin (0.25–0.5 ml/kg) within 5 days of exposure is indicated for all immunocompromised contacts irrespective of immunization status and susceptible contacts aged 6–12 months. For susceptible immunocompetent contacts aged more than 12 months, administration of vaccine within 72 hours of exposure is recommended.

MEASLES MUMPS RUBELLA VACCINE

Most countries use a combination of these three vaccines rather than measles vaccine alone. Each 0.5 ml dose of the vaccine contains 1000, 5000 and 1000 TCID50 of measles, mumps and rubella respectively, and is dispensed as single and multiple dose preparations. The vaccine is a lyophilized preparation, best stored between 2 to 8°C. It should be used within 4 hours of reconstitution in view of risk of loss of potency. The vaccine is also sensitive to light.

The need for mumps immunization stems from the risk of oophoritis and orchitis that may be seen when mumps occurs in adulthood. Some recommend that the vaccine be given to all young adults who have not had the disease earlier. The mumps component contains live attenuated mumps virus derived from the Jeryl Lynn strain grown in chick embryo or human diploid cell cultures. Clinical efficacy is 75 to 90%. The vaccine is safe; there is no association of the vaccine with autism or Crohn's disease as postulated previously. Aseptic meningitis may occur with 1 in 10^4 to 10^5 doses, but is mild and often subclinical. Monovalent mumps vaccine is not available in India, and is low in priority as a vaccine for the country because we need vaccines against other more severe diseases.

Rubella vaccination is mainly directed at prevention of the congenital rubella syndrome (CRS) and not prevention of primary rubella infection, which is a benign illness. Rubella vaccines currently available are derived from the RA 27/3 strain of the virus, grown in human diploid or chick embryo cell culture. The vaccine is highly immunogenic with a seroconversion rate of over 95%; the resulting immunity is long-term and, possibly, lifelong. Adverse effects that may be seen following immunization are mild and may include lymphadenopathy, arthralgias and a transient skin rash. The vaccine is contraindicated in pregnant women and in immunocompromised persons. However, MMR vaccine is recommended to asymptomatic and symptomatic individuals infected with HIV who are not severely immunocompromised.

Haphazard use of rubella or MMR vaccine in children without ensuring optimal immunization coverage may result in an epidemiological shift of disease with more clinical cases in adulthood and a paradoxical increase in CRS. Hence the vaccine should be introduced in the National Program only after ensuring that the routine immunization coverage is at least 80%.

The vaccine is recommended for use beyond 12–15 months of age because maternal antibodies interfere with response to the vaccine if given earlier. IAPCOI recommends two doses of MMR vaccine, the first at 15 months and the second MMR after 8 weeks; this should decrease the risk of primary vaccine failure to the mumps and rubella component of the vaccine.

HEPATITIS B VACCINE

India has intermediate endemicity for hepatitis B virus (HBV), with about 4% individuals being chronic carriers of the virus. Studies in adults in India demonstrate that HBV is the single most common etiological agent responsible for chronic hepatitis, cirrhosis, and hepatocellular carcinoma. Infection with HBV may occur by the perinatal route from infected mothers (vertical transmission), during childhood by unclear routes through close contact with infected family members (horizontal transmission), through transfusions or use of infected needles (nosocomial) and by sexual contact. Infection at a younger age is associated with higher risk of chronic carriage and chronic liver disease. In regions of high and intermediate endemicity, vertical and horizontal transmissions are major modes of infection. Both are prevented if the available vaccine is used judiciously. Hence the WHO recommends universal Hepatitis B (HB) vaccination. The Government of India has initiated the incorporation of HB vaccine in the National Immunization Schedule in a phased manner.

The current HBV vaccine is a highly purified vaccine produced by recombinant DNA techniques in yeast species. It contains aluminium salts as adjuvant. The vaccine should be stored at 2–8°C and should not be frozen. The vaccine is administered intramuscularly in anterolateral thigh in children and in deltoid in adults. The dose is 0.5 mL, containing 10 μg of antigenic component, in children upto 19 years of age and 1 mL (20 μg) in older persons. It is recommended that the dose be doubled in patients on hemodialysis, immunocompromised individuals and those with malignancies. Seroconversion rates are > 95% after three doses. An antibody titre of >10 mIU/mL is considered protective.

HB vaccine is given in three doses. It is known that immunization at birth prevents horizontal transmission. Immunization at birth, 1 and 6 months is considered ideal in terms of its proven immunological efficacy. Attempts at integrating HB vaccination into the National Schedule without increasing number of contacts have led to trials of other schedules which have been found to provide good efficacy. Hence the vaccine may be given at birth, 1 month and 6 months of age, at birth, 6 weeks and 14 weeks of age, or at birth, 6 weeks and 6 months of age. Where birth dose has been missed, it may be given at 6, 10 and 14 weeks of age. Currently, there is no evidence to suggest that booster doses are required.

Hepatitis B surface antigen (HBsAg) screening should be offered to all pregnant women. If the mother is known to be HBsAg negative, it is not essential that HB vaccine be given to the newborn at birth, vaccination of the child may safely begin at 6 weeks. Where the mother's status is not known, it is safer to vaccinate the newborn within a few hours of birth. If the mother is known to be HBsAg positive, the child must receive the vaccine within a few hours of birth, along with Hepatitis B immunoglobulin (HBIG) within 24 hours of birth. Administration of HBIG up to 5 days after birth may be effective. If HBIG has been administered, any of the schedules incorporating a birth dose of the vaccine can be used. If HBIG is not administered, the baby should be immunized in an accelerated schedule at 0, 1 and 2 months, along with an additional dose at 9–12 months. HBIG and HB vaccine should be administered at separate sites.

Vaccination of older children and adults requires three doses at 0, 1 and 6 months, where 0 refers to the date of administration of the first dose.

HBIG provides immediate passive immunity and is used in circumstances where an acute exposure to HBsAg positive material has occurred. Concurrent use of HBIG and HB vaccination, i.e. combined passive and active immunization, results in 90% decrease in the risk of transmission of HBV. Such circumstances include needle stick injuries, sexual exposure, use of blood product not screened for HBV, etc. HBIG is administered intramuscularly at a site away from the site of HB vaccination, in a dose of 0.5 mL in newborns, and 0.06 mL (32–48 IU) per kilogram body weight for all other ages. Following exposure, HBIG should be administered as soon as possible, preferably within 48 hours.

RABIES VACCINE

Rabies is endemic in India and 50% of the deaths attributable to this disease occur in our country. Currently three types of vaccines are available against the virus. Nerve tissue vaccines are no longer recommended because of poor efficacy and high incidence of serious adverse effects, like neuroparalytic reactions. The purified duck embryo vaccine (PDEV) has been available for several decades and continues to be used. It is free from myelin basic protein and considered safe for use. Its immunogenicity is comparable to modern tissue culture vaccines. Modern tissue culture vaccines (MTCV) include purified chick embryo cell (PCEC) vaccine (Rabipur), human diploid cell vaccine (HDCV) (Rabivax) and purified vero cell vaccine (PVRV) (Verorab, Abhayrab). All tissue cell culture vaccines are equally efficacious and safe, and any one of these may be used. The vaccine is stored at 2–8°C. Common adverse effects include local pain, swelling and induration. Systemic manifestations like fever, malaise, abdominal pain and headache are less common and transient.

In case of an animal bite, one should immediately clean the wound thoroughly with soap, irrigate the wound with running water for 10 minutes, and then apply povidone iodine, 70% alcohol or tincture iodine. All individuals should receive post exposure prophylaxis as detailed below. All patients with wound category III (WHO recommendations) should also receive rabies immunoglobulin (RIG); these include all transdermal bites or scratches and contamination of mucous membranes with saliva (e.g. licks). RIG is not required in case of licks on intact or broken skin, nibbling of uncovered skin and minor scratches or abrasions without bleeding. Wound suturing should be avoided. If suturing is essential for hemostasis, it should be done after administration of RIG.

RIG provides passive immunity by immediately neutralizing the rabies viruses on contact so that neural infection is prevented. The dose of RIG is 20 U/kg for human (HRIG) and 40 U/kg for equine (ERIG) immunoglobulin. RIG should be infiltrated in and around the wound; in case of large or multiple wounds, RIG may be diluted with normal saline so as to infiltrate all wounded areas. Any remaining immunoglobulin should be administered intramuscularly at a site away from vaccine site; usual sites include the deltoid and anterolateral thigh. HRIG is very expensive and not available easily. ERIG is associated with a high risk of adverse effects including anaphylaxis; therefore skin testing is recommended before its use.

There are various schedules for administration of rabies vaccine for post-exposure prophylaxis, using the intramuscular and intradermal routes (Table 8.6). The anterolateral thigh and deltoid region are preferred sites for intramuscular administration; the gluteal region should not be used. The dose is 1 mL for all modern tissue culture vaccines except PVRV in which case the dose is 0.5 mL. The intradermal dose is one-fifth of the intramuscular dose.

In India, the *Essen schedule* or *WHO standard schedule* is most commonly practised. The Zagreb schedule induces an early immune response, but the long term efficacy is poor if administered along with RIG. TRC-ID schedule is a cost effective and efficacious schedule that is now approved for use in India, using either PCEC or PVRV, in centers with adequate training and frequent use of the vaccine.

Pre-exposure prophylaxis is offered to individuals at high risk of rabies due to contact with animals, e.g. veterinary doctors, wildlife workers, dog handlers, taxidermists, postmen, animal laboratory workers, municipal workers etc. Three doses are recommended to be given intramuscularly on days 0, 7 and 21 or 28. A booster dose is required after 1 year and every 5 years thereafter. In case of re-exposure after completed pre or post-exposure prophylaxis, two doses are recommended on days 0 and 3. The intradermal schedule using MTCV is also acceptable; here the boosters are required yearly.

Since human rabies immunoglobulin (HRIG) is required in addition to the vaccine for most animal bites, and the availability, cost and knowledge regarding use of HRIG is limited, IAPCOI recommends that pre-exposure prophylaxis against rabies be offered to all children at high risk for rabies. Pre-exposure prophylaxis will obviate the need for use of HRIG and will restrict the number of post-exposure doses to 2 on day 0 and day 3.

VARICELLA VACCINE

Chicken pox (varicella) chiefly affects children and young adults in whom it is usually a benign and self limiting infection. The disease may be associated with complications when it occurs in adults, pregnant women and immunocompromised individuals. The available vaccines are live attenuated vaccines derived from the Oka strain, originally developed in Japan. The vaccine induces good cellular and humoral immune response and high (95–99%) protective efficacy which is long lasting.

The varicella vaccine is not recommended for universal immunization in our country because of the benign nature of the disease in children; it may be offered to children from affording families on an individual basis after discussion with parents. It is recommended for all children with chronic cardiac or pulmonary disease, immunodeficiency, HIV infection (with CD4 counts more than 15% for age), leukemia (while disease is in remission and chemotherapy has been discontinued at least 3–6 months back), and those on long-term salicylates or high dose steroids. Household contacts of immunocompromised children should also be immunized. It may be considered in children attending crèches and day care facilties, and in adolescents who have not had varicella in the past or are known to be seronegative for varicella IgG. It may be administered to household contacts of patients with varicella but the vaccine must be given within 72 hours and the efficacy is not guaranteed. Susceptible adolescents and adults should also be vaccinated if they stay or work in an institutional setting, e.g. school, hospital or military establishment.

The vaccine is administered subcutaneously or intramuscularly in a dose of 0.5 ml (containing at least 1000 plaque forming units). Two doses of the vaccine are given 4–8 weeks apart in children older than 13 years. Previously a single dose was considered sufficient in children between 1 and 13 years of age, but the American Academy of Pediatrics now recommends two doses, as for older children, in view of increasing reports of breakthrough varicella following vaccination. However, in the absence of sufficient data on changing epidemiology of chicken pox, the IAPCOI continues to recommend single dose of varicella vaccine in children aged below 13 years. The vaccine should not be administered to children below one year of age. The vaccine should be stored at 2–8°C. It should be protected from light and used within 30 minutes of reconstitution. Adverse reactions include fever, rash and local pain, redness and swelling.

Table 8.6: Various schedules for administration of rabies vaccine for post-exposure prophylaxis*

Schedule (route) / Day of vaccination	*D0*	*D3*	*D7*	*D14*	*D21*	*D28*	*D90*
Essen (intramuscular)	1	1	1	1	-	1	+/-**
Zagreb (intramuscular)	2	-	1	-	1	-	-
Oxford (intradermal)	8	-	4	-	-	1	1
Thai Red Cross (intradermal) (TRC-ID)	2	2	2	-	-	1	1
Updated Thai Red Cross (intradermal)	2	2	2	-	-	2	-
Bangalore/ KIMS modification of TRC-ID (intradermal)	2	2	2	2	-	2	

* Day 0 refers to the day of administration of the first dose. Numbers indicate number of doses required on a particular day. Where multiple doses are to be administered on the same day, different sites should be used.

** This additional dose is recommended for immunocompromised or severely malnourished patients.

8

Varicella zoster immunoglobulin (VZIG) provides passive immunity to non-immune individuals who are exposed to varicella and are at significant risk of complications. Post-exposure prophylaxis is recommended for susceptible contacts with significant exposure to varicella or herpes zoster who are at risk for severe disease. This group includes pregnant women, neonates whose mother has developed varicella 5 days before or 2 days after delivery and immunocompromised children and adults. Post-exposure prophylaxis is best achieved by administering varicella zoster immunoglobulin (VZIG) now available as an IV preparation at a dose of 0.2–1 ml/ kg (5–25 units/kg) of body weight, or 125 units/ 10 kg body weight, within 96 hr of exposure.

TYPHOID VACCINE

Enteric fever is an important public health problem in our country. Three types of typhoid vaccines have been developed, as described below. The efficacy of all vaccines ranges between 50–70%.

The whole cell inactivated typhoid vaccines (TA/TAB) are inexpensive vaccines that have been available for several decades as either a heat-killed phenol-preserved vaccine or as an acetone-inactivated vaccine. The acetone-inactivated vaccine is more immunogenic but is also associated with more adverse effects. Both vaccines contain 1000 million particles of inactivated whole cell *Salmonella typhi* in each mL. The vaccine induces antibodies against the cell wall somatic (O) antigen and the flagellar (H) antigen. The antibody response can be used as indicative of response to the vaccine, but the same may interfere with the interpretation of Widal test in vaccinated individuals. The vaccine is safe and immunogenic in children older than 6 months. Primary immunization comprises of two doses given at least 4 weeks apart, by the subcutaneous route. Dose is 0.25 mL in children between 6 months–10 years, and 0.5 mL in an older individual. Protective efficacy is 50–70%, and ensues 4 weeks after administration. Re-vaccination is required every 2–3 years, and should be done preferably before the peak season. Adverse effects include fever, local pain and malaise; these are more common with the vaccine containing TA/TAB than with the pure *S. typhi* vaccine. The vaccine should be stored at 2–8°C and should not be frozen. Currently this vaccine is not available in our country.

The Vi capsular polysaccharide of *S. typhi* has an important role in the virulence of the organism as it prevents phagocytosis and inhibits serum bactericidal action. The purified antigen is incorporated in the Vi capsular polysaccharide vaccine, an unconjugated polysaccharide vaccine that can be used in children older than 2 years of age. The vaccine has an efficacy of 50–60%, seen after 2 weeks of administration. Vaccination elicits immune response in form of anti-Vi antibodies. A single dose is recommended to be administered either intramuscularly or subcutaneously, in a dose of 0.5 mL, which contains 25 μg of the antigen. The vaccine should be stored at 2–8°C and should not be frozen. The vaccine is associated with mild adverse effects like local pain and swelling. The IAPCOI recommends the administration of the currently available Vi polysaccharide vaccine to all children every three years beginning by the age of 2 years till age of 18 years.

An oral vaccine has been developed recently, using the live attenuated Ty21a strain of *S. typhi*. This strain has a genetically stable mutation in the gal E gene; its reversion to virulence is unlikely. The vaccine acts by inducing local gut immunity; hence there is no immunological marker of its efficacy. Vaccine efficacy is 50–60% with the available formulation, and is present within 7 days of primary immunization. Primary immunization consists of three doses given on alternate days on an empty stomach. Since the bacteria are inactivated by gastric acidity, the vaccine is available as enteric coated capsules which must be swallowed intact and not chewed or opened. For this reason the vaccine is suitable for use only in children above 6 years of age. Antibiotics are contraindicated between 3 days before to 7 days after the vaccine administration as their use may compromise the vaccine "take". The vaccine should be stored at 2–8°C. Vaccination has to be repeated every 3–5 years. Currently the vaccine is not available in India.

HEPATITIS A VACCINE

Infection with hepatitis A (HA) virus is endemic in India, and is usually benign in children; among children who acquire the infection below 5 years of age, 50–85% have non-specific manifestations like any viral illness. Disease severity, rate of complications and mortality are higher in those with underlying chronic liver disease, and in adults.

Available HA vaccines are formalin inactivated vaccines derived from strains grown on human diploid cell lines. Aluminium hydroxide is used as an adjuvant. The vaccine is administered intramuscularly in two doses 6 months apart; no boosters are required as immunity appears to be long lasting. The vaccine has protective efficacy of 94–100%. Since maternal antibody may interfere with immune response to the vaccine, hence the vaccine should be administered beyond 18 months of age. Local pain and induration are the adverse reactions commonly noted. All available brands of hepatitis A vaccines have similar efficacy and safety.

The HA vaccine is not recommended for universal immunization in our country because of the benign nature of the disease in children; it may be offered to children from high socio-economic strata on an individual basis after discussion with parents. It is recommended for all children with chronic liver disease who are seronegative for HA virus. It may be considered in children attending crèches and day care facilities, in travelers from abroad attending endemic areas, and in adolescents who have not had viral hepatitis in the past or are known to be seronegative for HA virus. It may be administered to household contacts of patients with HA virus infection but the vaccine must be given within 10 days of the index case being infected.

ROTAVIRUS VACCINE

Rotavirus is a major cause of diarrhea related morbidity and mortality in children worldwide. Rotavirus is an RNA virus with 7 serogroups (A-G), of which group A rotaviruses cause most human disease. Epidemiologic studies from India indicate that rotavirus is responsible for 6–45% of all childhood diarrheas that need hospitalization. The first clinically licensed rotavirus vaccine was Rotashield, a live oral tetravalent vaccine which was withdrawn soon after its introduction in 1998 due to occurrence of vaccine associated intussusception. Currently, two live oral vaccines, namely Rotarix and RotaTeq, are licensed and marketed worldwide, while a vaccine based on Indian neonatal strains is undergoing clinical trials.

Rotarix is a monovalent attenuated human rotavirus vaccine derived from human rotavirus strains, and contains the G1P1A(8) strain. It is administered orally in a 2-dose schedule to infants at 2 and 4 months of age. RotaTex is a human bovine reassortant vaccine and consists of five reassortants between the bovine WC23 strain and human G1, G2, G3, G4 and P1A(8) rotavirus strains. It is administered orally in a three dose schedule at 2, 4 and 6 months. In trials conducted elsewhere, both vaccines have shown 85–98% efficacy against severe rotavirus gastroenteritis and have been demonstrated to be safe with no increased risk of intussusception as compared to placebo. Efficacy trials in developing countries of Africa and Asia are ongoing. Shedding of the vaccine virus is observed in 10% of vaccinees with Rotateq and more than 50% of vaccinees with Rotarix. Simultaneous administration of rotavirus vaccines with OPV does not appear to affect adversely the efficacy of either vaccine.

The morbidity and mortality burden of rotavirus in India is huge and an efficacious rotavirus vaccine is required. However, given the tremendous diversity in circulating strains of the virus and the lack of efficacy studies from India, the results of efficacy trials of the currently licensed for use vaccines cannot be extrapolated to India. The IAPCOI recommends that any decision to administer the vaccine be based on a one to one discussion with parents.

Vaccination should be strictly as per schedule; there is a potential risk of intussusception if vaccines are given to older infants. The first dose of Rotarix can be given at 6 weeks and no later than at 12 weeks; the interval between the 2 doses should be at least 4 weeks, and two doses should be completed by age 16 weeks, and no later than by 24 weeks of age. The first dose of Rotateq should be administered between ages 6–12 weeks and subsequent 2 doses at intervals of 4–8 weeks; vaccination should not be initiated for infants aged >12 weeks, and all 3 doses should be administered before the age of 32 weeks.

Vaccination should be postponed in infants with acute gastroenteritis as it might compromise efficacy of the vaccine. Risks versus benefits of vaccination should be considered while considering vaccination for infants with chronic gastrointestinal disease, gut malformations, previous intussusception and immunocompromised infants.

HEMOPHILUS INFLUENZA B VACCINE

Worldwide, hemophilus influenza type b (Hib) is an important cause of invasive infections like pneumonia, meningitis and bacteremia, especially in children below 2 years of age. A study of pathogens from six centers in India (the Invasive Bacterial Infections Study) showed that Hib is an important cause of meningitis. Effective vaccines are available, and their incorporation into the immunization schedule of developed countries has resulted in a significant decline in morbidity and mortality attributable to invasive disease due to Hib.

The capsular polysaccharide is the moiety used as the antigen in the available vaccines. Since polysaccharide antigens are poorly immunogenic in children below 2 years of age, it is conjugated to a protein antigen in order to enhance the immunogenicity. The PRP-T vaccine has the tetanus toxoid as the conjugate, the Hb-OC has the mutant CRM 197 diphtheria toxin, while PRP-OMP incorporates the outer membrane protein of meningococcus as conjugate. PRP-OMP is a more immunogenic vaccine than the other two, but is not available in India. Conjugate vaccines for hemophilus influenza containing diphtheria toxoid do not contain enough toxoid to be a substitute for DTP or DT.

The IAP-COI recommends that Hib vaccine be administered to all children; however, given the epidemiological profile of infections with Hib, unimmunized children above 5 years of age should not receive the vaccine. Vaccination is particularly recommended prior to splenectomy and in patients with sickle cell disease.

Vaccination schedule depends on the age of the child at the time immunization is initiated. Three doses are recommended in a child below 6 months, 2 doses in a child between 6–12 months, and one dose in a child aged between 12–15 months; a booster should be administered in these children at 18 months of age. When immunization is delayed beyond 15 months, one dose is considered sufficient. Two doses of the vaccines should be at least 4 weeks apart. The vaccine is safe and immunogenic, and has a protective efficacy of over 95%.

PNEUMOCOCCAL VACCINE

Worldwide, *S. pneumoniae* is responsible for 15–50% of all episodes of community acquired pneumonia, 30–50% of all cases of acute otitis media, and 50% of deaths due to pneumonia every year. Among 90 known serotypes of *S. pneumoniae*, 7 serotypes (14, 6, 19, 18, 9, 23 and 7) are responsible for 85% of invasive pneumococcal disease in the developed world. In India, it has been demonstrated that serotypes 6, 1, 19, 14, 4, 5, 45, 12, 7, 23 are the most prevalent, and serotypes 1 and 5 account for 30% of invasive pneumococcal disease.

Children under the age of 2 years are at greatest risk for invasive pneumococcal disease (IPD). Children at high risk for pneumococcal disease include those with congenital immunodeficiency, HIV, children on immunosuppressive therapy, organ transplant recipients, sickle cell disease, asplenia or hyposplenia, chronic cardiac, liver, or pulmonary disease (excluding asthma unless on high dose oral steroids), chronic renal failure, nephrotic syndrome, diabetes mellitus, and children with cerebrospinal fistula or cochlear implants. Currently, two vaccines are available, the unconjugated pneumococcal polysaccharide vaccine and the conjugate vaccines.

The unconjugated polysaccharide vaccine is a 23 valent vaccine (PPV23). Since capsular polysaccharides stimulate B cells directly independent of T cell stimulation, the vaccine is poorly immunogenic below the age of 2 yrs, and immunological memory is low. The vaccine does not reduce nasopharyngeal carriage of *S. pneumoniae*; therefore, it does not provide herd immunity. Its efficacy against prevention of IPD in the high-risk population is less than 70%. The vaccine is administered intramuscularly in a dose of 0.5 mL; more than two life time doses should not be given.

Pneumococcal conjugate vaccine (PCV) is available as a 7 valent pneumococcal conjugate vaccine (PCV7) containing 7 polysaccharide antigens linked to a protein carrier. These antigens are from serotypes (4, 6B, 9V, 14, 18C, 19F and 23) that account for 85% of invasive disease in USA, where efficacy trials demonstrated >95% reduction in IPD and 30% reduction in pneumonia. A herd effect results from reduction in nasopharyngeal carriage of *S. pneumoniae*; a significant decline in pneumococcal disease has been seen in unvaccinated contacts of the vaccinees after introduction of the vaccine in the immunization program of developed nations. The current PCV7 covers only 55% of pneumococcal serotypes prevalent in India. Conjugated vaccines with broader serotype vaccines should be available in future.

Since pneumococcus is a cause of significant morbidity and mortality in children (especially those <2 years), the IAPCOI recommends the use of the currently available conjugate pneumococcal vaccine (PCV7) after one to one discussion with parents in healthy children aged <2 years; vaccination of healthy children >2 years is likely to be associated with less benefits due to the low risk of invasive pneumococcal disease in these children. There is no data to support the use of pneumococcal vaccine in healthy children aged >5 years, and it should not be given. PCV is given in a dose of 0.5 ml intramuscularly, as three doses at 6, 10 and14 weeks, with a booster at 15–18 months. Children between 6–12 months should be administered 2 doses 4–8 weeks apart and 1 booster at 15 –18 months, those between 12–23 months get 2 doses 8 weeks apart; while those between 2–5 years should receive a single dose.

The IAPCOI recommends administration of both PCV and PPV23 in all high-risk children who can afford the vaccine, because while PCV provides robust immune response and immune memory, the PPV23 provides expanded serotype coverage. Where the cost of PCV is a limiting factor at least PPV23 should be given to high-risk children >2 years of age. If affordable, PCV should be given first, in the schedule described above; for children over 5 years a single dose of PCV is recommended. In children aged >2 years, PPV 23 should also be given as a single dose. A gap of 2 months must be maintained between PCV and subsequent PPV 23. Only one repeat dose of PPV23 is recommended in high risk children; this may be given after 3–5 years if the child is less than 10 years of age and after 5 years if child is aged more than 10 years.

MENINGOCOCCAL VACCINE

Neisseria meningitides is a major cause of bacterial meningitis accounting for 30–40% of cases in children below 15 years. Endemic cases and severe meningococcal disease are primarily seen in children and adolescents; attack rates are highest in infants between 3–12 months of age. Even with treatment, case fatality rates are high (5–15%). The infection is usually due to serogroups A, B, C, Y and W135; serogroup A (and sometimes C) may cause epidemics. In India endemic cases are chiefly due to serogroup B. Infection results in serogroup specific immunity.

Two types of vaccines have been developed: the unconjugated polysaccharide vaccines and a conjugate group C vaccine. Unconjugated vaccines contain group specific capsular polysaccharides, which, like other polysaccharide vaccines, are T cell independent and do not induce immunological memory, and are not very immunogenic below 2 year of age. Bivalent (containing group A and C) and tetravalent (containing groups A, C, Y and W135) vaccines are available.

The meningococcal vaccine is indicated in close contacts of patients with meningococcal disease (as an adjunct to chemoprophylaxis), certain high risk groups (complement deficiency, sickle cell anemia, asplenia, before splenectomy), during disease outbreaks (when caused by a serogroup included in the vaccine), and before travel to the high endemicity belt in Africa.

The vaccine is administered in a dose of 0.5 ml intramuscularly or subcutaneously in a single dose. If required, revaccination may be considered after 3–5 years. Fever and pain at injection site are the commonly reported adverse events. The vaccine is not recommended for universal immunization in India. During epidemics, children above 2 years of age may be administered the vaccine. If the vaccine is given to younger children (e.g. close household contact), protective efficacy is likely to be low.

The conjugated group C vaccine has been marketed in some countries where group C is the most common isolate in meningococcal disease. Three doses of the vaccine are administered 4–8 weeks apart in children below 6 months, while 2 doses suffice for 6–12 months age and 1 dose is enough in older children.

JAPANESE B ENCEPHALITIS VACCINE

Japanese encephalitis is an important cause of viral encephalitis in our country; being responsible for 2000–3000 cases and 500–600 deaths annually. In absence of specific therapy, vaccination remains the most important control measure, and is indicated in all children between 1–15 years of age residing in highly endemic areas like Andhra Pradesh, Uttar Pradesh and Karnataka. It should also be given to visitors to endemic areas if duration of stay is expected to be more than 4 weeks. Three types of vaccine are available, the mouse brain-derived inactivated vaccine, the cell culture-derived inactivated vaccine and the cell culture-derived live attenuated vaccine.

The mouse brain-derived vaccine is an inactivated vaccine administered subcutaneously in a dose of 0.5 ml for children between 1–3 years and 1 ml in an older child. Primary immunization consists of 3 doses; the second and third doses are given 7 and 30 days after the first dose. Booster doses are to be administered at 1 year after primary immunization and every 3 years subsequently. Common adverse events include fever, malaise and local tenderness and redness. Reports of a temporal relationship of vaccination to acute encephalitis and anaphylactic reactions in recipients have resulted in decline in usage of this vaccine.

An inactivated vaccine derived from primary hamster kidney cell line was popular in China, but its use was discontinued following availability of the live cell culture derived vaccine. The cell culture derived live vaccine is based on a stable neuro-attenuated strain of JE virus, the SA–14–14–2, which was first used in China and is currently in use in Nepal and South Korea. The vaccine has high efficacy; initial studies demonstrated 80% efficacy with one dose and 98% with two doses, but recent studies suggest efficacy of upto 99% even with a single dose. The vaccine is administered in a dose of 0.5 ml subcutaneously. Other than anaphylaxis, there are no reported serious adverse events. The vaccine has been used in pilot projects initiated by the Government of India in hyperendemic districts of Uttar Pradesh, West Bengal, Assam and Karnataka, and found to be safe.

INFLUENZA VACCINE

The influenza virus has three antigenic types (A, B and C) and several subtypes (based on the surface antigens hemagglutinin and neuraminidase), with frequent mutations due to antigenic drifts and antigenic shifts, resulting in frequent changes in the strains in circulation. Since the available vaccines elicit a strain specific humoral immune response, this is the only vaccine whose composition has to be altered yearly according to the expectation of the prevalent strain in the next peak season.

Influenza vaccines are inactivated vaccines derived from viruses grown in embryonated hen's eggs, and are of three types. Whole virus vaccines that were available previously were associated with significant adverse effects, especially in children; hence they are no longer used. Split product vaccines are produced from detergent treated highly purified influenza viruses. Surface antigen vaccines are subunit vaccines containing the purified antigens hemagglutinin and neuraminidase. Current vaccines are highly immunogenic and associated with minimal adverse events. The vaccines are usually trivalent, containing two influenza A subtypes and one influenza B strain. The composition of the vaccine is reviewed by the WHO six-monthly to update antigens contained in the vaccine based on the prevalent circulating strains.

The vaccine is recommended for use in high risk children, including those with chronic cardiac or pulmonary disease, immunodeficiency, HIV infection, sickle cell disease, diabetes mellitus, systemic lupus erythematosus, long-term aspirin therapy, and children with severe asthma who frequently require oral corticosteroids. Primary immunization requires two doses to be given in children between 6 months and 8 years of age, while a single dose suffices in older children. Revaccination is required annually; the dose should be given prior to the peak influenza season. The vaccine is administered intramuscularly, in a dose of 0.25 ml in children < 3 years and 0.5 ml in an older child.

HUMAN PAPILLOMA VIRUS (HPV) VACCINE

Cervical cancer is the second most common cancer and the leading cause of cancer related deaths in women. Cervical cancer is almost always caused by persistent infection with oncogenic human papillomavirus (HPV). Among 100 known serotypes of HPV, about 20 are oncogenic, with serotypes 16 and 18 being associated with 70% cases of invasive cervical cancer. Additionally, oncogenic serotypes of HPV may have a causal role in the pathogenesis of anal, vulvar, vaginal, penile and oropharyngeal cancers. Nononcogenic HPV serotypes 6 and 11 cause 90% of anogenital warts.

The available vaccines against HPV are self-assembling virus like particles (VLP) constituted of recombinant L1, the major capsid protein of HPV. Since these do not contain any nucleic acid, these empty capsids are non-infectious but capable of eliciting a host immune response. VLP based vaccines prevent more than 90% new infections with the serotypes included in the vaccines. The vaccines do not protect against serotypes with which infection has already occurred before vaccination.

Two vaccines are currently licensed; these include Gardasil, a quadrivalent vaccine active against HPV strains 6, 11, 16 and 18, and Cervarix, a bivalent vaccine targeting only HPV 16 and 18. Clinical trials with both vaccines have shown good efficacy against types 16, 18 related CIN grades 2 and 3 and adenocarcinoma in situ (AIS), and Gardasil is also effective in preventing vaccine type related genital warts, vaginal intraepithelial neoplasia and vulvar intraepithelial neoplasia. Persistent protection for up to 5 years has been demonstrated, as also a good response to booster immunization. Local adverse effects with both vaccines include mild to moderate pain at the injection site, and swelling and erythema; systemic adverse effects such as fever are rare. No serious adverse events following immunization have been attributable to the vaccines.

The vaccine is of public health importance in a country like India where compliance with routine screening for cervical cancer is low and several women are diagnosed with the cancer every year. However, several issues pertaining to the vaccine remain unresolved. The duration of protection provided, and hence, the ideal age at vaccination and need of booster doses, if any, are not known. The vaccine is not expected to be effective in women already persistently infected with the virus. Any cross protection against other strains is likely to be modest. Socio-cultural issues related to the vaccine being protective against a sexually transmitted disease may limit its acceptability. Importantly, immunization status should not create a false complacency resulting in a decline in routine screening for cervical cancer, especially when routine immunization has not been ensured, because this may result in a paradoxical rise in cervical cancer related mortality. Screening programs should therefore continue as per recommendations.

The IAPCOI recommends that the HPV vaccines should be offered to all females who can afford the vaccine, given prior to sexual debut, as a cervical cancer preventing vaccine and not as a vaccine against a sexually transmitted infection (STI). The dose is 0.5 mL intramuscular in the deltoid. The recommended age for initiation of vaccination is 10–12 years, while catch up vaccination may be permitted up to 26 years of age. Gardasil is given in three doses at 0, 2 and 6 months (with a minimum interval of 4 weeks between 1st and 2nd dose, and 12 weeks between the second and third dose), while Cervarix is given at 0, 1 and 6 months. Both vaccines are contraindicated in patients with history of hypersensitivity to any vaccine and should be avoided in pregnancy. The vaccines may have a lower immunogenicity and efficacy in immunocompromised hosts. At present boosters are not recommended.

RECOMMENDATIONS OF THE INDIAN ACADEMY OF PEDIATRICS COMMITTEE ON IMMUNIZATION (IAPCOI)

The IAPCOI endorses and fully supports the National immunization program, but recommends additional vaccines for children to meet the immunization needs of our population. The Academy also suggests certain optional vaccines that may be administered after discussion with parents regarding their utility and costs. The IAPCOI categorizes the childhood vaccines as listed in Table 8.7 . The differences in the national immunization program and the recommendations of the IAP are highlighted in Table 8.8.

COMBINATION VACCINES

With the advent of several new vaccines, a child needs to be administered more than twenty antigens to avail protection against vaccine preventable diseases. The ideal vaccine, as proposed by the CVI, would be one that shall provide all indicated antigens in a single dose, shall be administered preferably orally, shall be heat stable, shall be effective if administered soon after birth, and shall be

Table 8.7: Categorization of vaccines by the Indian Academy of Pediatrics

Category 1: Vaccines in EPI
- BCG, OPV, DTPw, Measles, TT
- New additions: Hepatitis B, MMR in certain districts

Category 2: IAP recommended vaccines (in addition to EPI vaccines)
- Hepatitis B, Hib, MMR, typhoid, Td
- New additions: Tdap, IPV, HPV

Category 3: Vaccines to be given after one to one discussion with parents
- Hepatitis A, varicella, PCV7, DTPa
- New addition: Rotavirus

Category 4: Vaccines under special circumstances
- Influenza, PPV23, meningococcal vaccine, JE vaccine

BCG Bacillus Calmette Guérin vaccine; OPV oral poliovirus vaccine; DTPw diphtheria toxoid, tetanus toxoid, whole cell killed pertussis vaccine; TT tetanus toxoid; Hib hemophilus B vaccine; MMR measles mumps and rubella vaccine; Td tetanus toxoid with reduced dose diphtheria; Tdap tetanus toxoid with reduced dose diphtheria and acellular pertussis vaccines; IPV inactivated polio vaccine; HPV human papilloma virus vaccine; PCV7 pneumococcal heptavalent conjugate vaccine; DTPa diphtheria toxoid, tetanus toxoid, acellular pertussis vaccine; PPV23 23 valent pneumococcal polysaccharide vaccine; JE Japanese encephalitis.

Table 8.8: Comparison of the National Immunization Program with the recommendations of the Indian Academy of Pediatrics (IAP) Committee on Immunization

Age	*National Immunization Program*	*IAP recommendation*	
0 (at birth)	BCG, OPV_0	BCG, OPV_0, Hep B_1	
6 weeks	$DTPw_1$, OPV_1 (and BCG, if not given at birth)	$DTPw_1/DPTa_1$, $OPV_1^{\$}$, Hep B_2, Hib_1	
10 weeks	$DTPw_2$, OPV_2	$DTPw_2/DPTa_2$, $OPV_2^{\$}$, Hib_2	
14 weeks	$DTPw_3$, OPV_3	$DTPw_3/DPTa_3$, $OPV_3^{\$}$, Hep B_3^{*}, Hib_3	
9 months	Measles	Measles	
15–18 months		DTPw B_1/DPTa B_1, $OPV_4^{\$}$, Hib B_1, MMR_1	
18–24 months	DTPw B_1, OPV B_1	-	
2 years	–	Typhoid**	
5 years	DT B_2^{***}	DTPw B_2/DPTa B_2, OPV_5, $MMR_2^{\#}$	
10 years	TT##	Td$$/Tdap/TT	
16 years	TT##	Td$$/TT	
Pregnant women	2 doses of TT 1 month apart	2 doses of Td$$/TT	
Optional vaccines	None	Varicella	> 15 months
		Hepatitis A	> 18 months
		PCV 7	> 6 weeks
		Rotavirus	> 6 weeks

BCG Bacillus Calmette Guérin vaccine; OPV oral poliovirus vaccine; Hep B hepatitis B vaccine; DTPw diphtheria toxoid, tetanus toxoid, whole cell killed pertussis vaccine; DTPa diphtheria toxoid, tetanus toxoid, acellular pertussis vaccine; Hib hemophilus b vaccine; B1 1st booster dose; MMR measles, mumps and rubella vaccine; B2 2nd booster dose; DT diphtheria toxoid with tetanus toxoid; TT tetanus toxoid; Td tetanus toxoid with reduced dose diphtheria; Tdap tetanus toxoid with reduced dose diphtheria and pertussis vaccine; PCV7 pneumococcal heptavalent conjugate vaccine

$ OPV + Inactivated polio vaccine (IPV) where affordable

* May be given at 6 months of age

** Revaccination required every 3 years

*** Give a second dose after 1 month if there is no clear history of prior immunization with DTP

\# The second dose of MMR may be given any time 8 weeks after the first dose

\## Give a second dose after 1 month if there is no clear history of prior immunization with DTP/DT/TT

$$ Td preferred over TT

affordable to families of all economic strata. While such a vaccine remains a dream, ongoing research is addressing these needs of simplification and expansion of the immunization program through a variety of combination vaccines.

A combination vaccine consists of 2 or more separate immunogens that have been physically combined in a single preparation. These immunogens may be antigens or serotypes of the same pathogen (e.g. trivalent polio vaccine) or different pathogens (e.g. DTP vaccine). This concept is distinct from simultaneous vaccination, which implies the administration of multiple physically separate vaccines, at the same time, at separate sites or by different routes.

Studies on the diversity of antigen receptors indicate that the immune system of an infant can respond to a large number of antigens simultaneously. There is no evidence that the efficacy of any currently recommended vaccine is altered by its concurrent administration with another vaccine recommended for administration at the same age. There are several benefits of combining vaccines. Use of combination vaccines shall mean a decrease in the number of injections for a child resulting in decreased pain and local adverse effects, fewer visits required for immunization, higher compliance to the immunization schedule and enhanced immunization coverage, less need for storage space and an overall decrease in expense on packaging, handing and transportation of vaccines.

The concept of combination vaccines is not novel; those in common use include DTP, DT or Td, OPV, IPV and MMR. Combination vaccines that have been recently licensed as well as those in final stages of development are listed in Table 8.9.

There are several challenges in the development of combination vaccines. The antigens combined together in a vaccine should be compatible with each other, should not interfere with each other's immunological 'take' (relevant especially for live viral vaccines) and should be indicated at the same time in the immunization schedule. Some antigens may require an adjuvant to be present in the combination. The total volume of the vaccine thus produced should not be excessive, and the final product should be stable for at least 18–24 months. Before recommending a particular combination vaccine, its efficacy should be evaluated in clinical trials, and its inclusion into the immunization program of a country should follow a cost benefit analysis.

Table 8.9: Combination vaccines for use in children and infants, recently introduced or in final stages of development

Newer combination vaccines	*Available in India*	*Available outside India*
	DTPw + Hib	DTPw + Hib + IPV
	DTPw + HepB	DTPw + IPV
	DTPw + Hib + HepB	DTPa + Hib + HepB + IPV
	DTPa + Hib	DTPa + IPV
	HepA + HepB	MMR + Varicella
Combination vaccines being developed	DTPa + Hib + HepB + IPV + HepA	
	PnC + MnC	
	PnC + MnC + Hib	

DTPw diphtheria toxoid, tetanus toxoid, whole cell killed pertussis vaccine; HiB hemophilus b vaccine; IPV inactivated polio vaccine; HepB hepatitis B vaccine; DTPa diphtheria toxoid, tetanus toxoid, acellular pertussis vaccine; HepA hepatitis A vaccine; MMR measles, mumps and rubella vaccine; PnC pneumococcal conjugate vaccine; MnC meningococcal conjugate vaccine

Combination Vaccines of the Future

With advances in molecular technology, it is likely that combination vaccines in the future shall be based on genomic technology, in form of either pox virus based or virosome based vaccines. The pox virus genome can be manipulated to incorporate genes for multiple foreign antigens, suggesting the possibility of its modification into a multivalent vaccine candidate. Immunopotentiating reconstituted influenza virosomes (IRIV) are liposomes that contain glycoproteins hemagglutinin and neuraminidase and can be used as carriers for multiple antigens, which can be covalently attached to the liposomes. The glycoproteins can be used to bring the antigens into antigen presenting cells the same way as they mediate infection with influenza virus. Thus IRIV may be used as an alternative adjuvant for multivalent vaccines, e.g. influenza A and B, hepatitis A, tetanus and diphtheria vaccines, which are alum precipitated products.

Suggested reading

1. IAP Committee on Immunization (IAPCOI). Consensus Recommendations on Immunization, 2008. Indian Pediatrics 2008; 45: 635–648.
2. Vaccination- Present status and future challenges, Guest Ed Dutta AK. Indian J Pediatr 2007; 74: SS No. 2.

8

9 Infections and Infestations

FEVER

Fever is a controlled increase in body temperature over the normal values for an individual. The normal body temperature in children is higher as compared to adults, exhibits a normal circadian diurnal variation and varies between 36.1°C to 37.8°C (97°F–100°F) on rectal measurement. There is a normal diurnal variation in the body temperature; it is lowest between 0 and 0600 hours and maximum between 1700 and 1900 hours.

Measurement and Definition

The core body temperature can be measured at several sites including the oral cavity, axilla, rectum, ear canal and over the temporal artery. The rectal method is the most accurate method for measurement of temperature and fever is defined as rectal temperature of more than 38°C or 100.4°F. However, measurement of rectal temperature is not always possible in clinical practice. In children below the age of 4-5 years, axillary temperature may be used if taken correctly. The axillary temperature is on an average 0.5–1°C or 1–2°F lower than the rectal temperature. Fever, if measured in the axilla, is defined as temperature more than 37.2°C or 99°F. In infants below the age of 3 months, if the axillary method shows fever, rectal temperatures should be measured as this is of serious concern and mandates investigations as discussed later.

In children above the age of 4–5 years, the oral method is suitable. The oral temperature is on an average 0.5–1°F or 0.25–0.5°C lower than rectal temperature. Fever as measured in the oral cavity is defined as temperature more than 37.5°C or 99.5°F.

Both mercury and electronic thermometers are available. The electronic thermometers take only 30 seconds for recording temperature, are convenient to use but are subject to calibration errors. The mercury thermometers take 2–4 minutes to record temperature, are cheaper and especially suitable for home use where regular calibration of electronic thermometers is not possible. The infrared thermometers used for measurement of ear/temporal artery temperatures are very quick and closely approximate rectal temperatures but are expensive.

Etiopathogenesis

Fever may be caused by multiple causes including infection, vaccines, biologic agents, tissue injury, malignancy, drugs, autoimmune diseases, granulomatous diseases, metabolic disorders (gout) and genetic disorders such as familial Mediterranean fever. All these insults result in the production of endogenous pyrogens, such as interleukin (IL)-1, IL-6, tumor necrosis factor (TNF)–α, interferon-β and interferon-γ and lipid mediators such as prostaglandin E_2, which alter the temperature set point in the anterior hypothalamus leading to elevation in body temperature. In contrast to fever, the high body temperature in *heat illness* is due to increased heat production or reduced heat loss, with the hypothalamic set point being normal. Here, the core temperatures can rise to beyond 106°F. Common causes of heat illness are hyperthy roidism, anhidrotic ectodermal dysplasia, drugs such as anticholinergics and phenothiazines, heat stroke and malignant hyperthermia.

Evaluation of a Febrile Patient

Fever is a symptom and not a disease; hence, evaluation for cause is important. If temperatures are very high, heat illness should be suspected. It is useful to classify fevers as short duration fevers and prolonged fevers as etiology and management strategies differ. The pattern of fever is only sometimes useful in arriving at a diagnosis. Intermittent fevers are characteristic of malaria; biphasic fevers are seen in illnesses such as dengue and leptospirosis; and periodic fevers (fever syndromes with regular periodicity) are seen in cyclic neutropenia, PFAPA syndrome (periodic fever, adenopathy, pharyngitis, aphthous ulcers) and hyperimmunoglobulin (Ig) D syndromes.

Management

Fever is a symptom and, therefore, treatment of the underlying cause is important. Treatment of fever *per se* may not always be needed. Fever has been shown to improve the immunologic response to certain infections in experimental models; whether this is clinically significant is unknown. However, fever may be associated with adverse effects such as paradoxical suppression of immune response, increased insensible water losses, cardiopulmonary stress and triggering febrile seizures in predisposed patients.

Reduction of fever should be a priority in patients with past/family history of febrile seizures, those critically ill, those with cardiorespiratory failure, those with disturbed fluid and electrolyte balance, or with temperature exceeding 40°C (104°F). For the rest, treatment should be individualized; parental counseling is important.

The two commonly used drugs for antipyresis in children are paracetamol and ibuprofen. Other agents such as aspirin, nimesulide and mefenamic acid are associated with high incidence of adverse effects and are better avoided. Ibuprofen decreases fever at the same rate as paracetamol, the nadir with ibuprofen is slightly lower and duration of action is longer (6 hr) as compared to paracetamol (4 hr). However, the risk of side effects such as acute renal failure and gastrointestinal bleeding is theoretically higher with ibuprofen (not substantiated by observational studies). Conversely, the consequences of paracetamol overdose (hepatic failure) are more sinister than those with ibuprofen (renal failure, neurological depression). Considering all factors, it is reasonable to use paracetamol at a dose of 15 mg/kg every 4 hours (max. 5–6 doses/day) as the first-line drug for fever management. It is reasonable to shift to ibuprofen in those patients who have not adequately responded to paracetamol, at a dose of 10 mg/kg every 6 hr. There is no evidence at present to support alternating or combined use of paracetamol and ibuprofen.

Tepid water sponging may be used as a complementary method to drug therapy in bringing down fever quickly in some children.

Heat illness is a medical emergency. The high temperatures can cause irreversible organ damage and should be brought down quickly. Since the hypothalamic set point is not altered, non-steroidal anti-inflammatory drugs, which act by reducing prostaglandin production, are ineffective. External cooling is needed with ice water sponging, cooling blankets, cold water enemas and gastric washes. At the same time, measures should be taken to correct the underlying condition.

Suggested reading

1. Lorin MI. Fever: pathogenesis and treatment. In: Feigin RD, Cherry JD, eds. Textbook of Pediatric Infectious Diseases, 4th edn. Philadelphia, WB Saunders, 89–94
2. Crocetti M, Moghbeli N, Serwint J. Fever phobia revisited: Have parental misconceptions about fever changed in 20 years? Pediatrics 2001; 107: 1241-6

SHORT DURATION FEVERS

Short duration fevers lasting for less than 5–7 days are one of the most common reasons for pediatric outpatient visits. The overwhelming majority are due to viral infections. Of greater concern are fevers without localizing signs/without focus in children below the age of 3 years (especially below 3 months) as they may indicate an underlying serious bacterial infection (SBI). Since *H. influenzae* and *S. pneumoniae* are important causes of SBI the algorithms suggested here may change with increasing immunization with *H. influenzae* and *S. pneumoniae* vaccines.

Fever without Focus in Less than 1 Month

Fever in a neonate (< 1 month of age) is generally a medical emergency. This is because of (i) 5–15% risk of serious bacterial infection such as sepsis, bacteremia, urinary tract infections, pneumonia, enteritis and bacterial meningitis, (ii) neonates may look well and still have serious bacterial infection and (iii) the implications of missing or delaying diagnosis of sepsis are serious.

A detailed clinical assessment should be performed (Fig. 9.1). A toxic neonate is at high risk of serious bacterial infections and should be treated aggressively. The patient

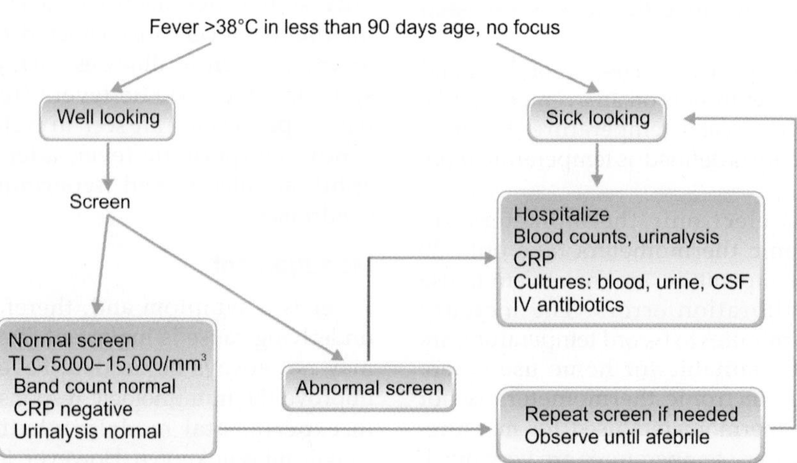

Fig. 9.1: Evaluation of fever in a patient less than 3-months-old; CSF cerebrospinal fluid; TLC total leukocyte count; CRP C reactive protein

9

should be hospitalized to undergo a complete septic work up and administered antibiotics without waiting for the results of investigations. Other supportive therapy should be instituted, if required.

Sometimes neonates get fever due to overclothing and warm weather ('dehydration fever') in which the baby looks well and active. This only warrants frequent feeding and nursing in less warm environment. The infant is kept under observation for other signs of sepsis and investigated if in doubt.

Fever without Focus in an Infant 1–3 Months of Age

Infants in this age group like those aged less than 1 month are at high risk of serious bacterial disease (10%, with 2–3% risk of bacteremia). Also, they may look well and still have bacterial disease. The algorithm for management of these babies is fairly similar to those less than 1 month (Fig. 9.1). A detailed clinical assessment should be performed. A history of recent immunizations is obtained as fever may be related to the immunization.

All toxic/ill-appearing babies should be managed as an infant less than 1 month (discussed earlier). A well-looking infant 1–3 months of age should undergo a complete sepsis evaluation while in the outpatient department including leukocyte and platelet counts, band cell count, C-reactive protein, urinalysis, urine and blood cultures and if indicated smear for malarial parasite, and chest X-ray. CSF examination may be undertaken if no other clue to focus of infection is found. If the screen is positive, the patient is hospitalized and treated with antibiotics. A well-looking infant with no clinical focus of infection and a negative screen (leukocyte count <15,000 cu mm, band count <20%, C-reactive protein negative, urine white cells <10/HPF) can be observed at home without antibiotics, provided the care takers are reliable and agree to bring the infant for reassessment 24 hours and 48 hours later.

Fever without Focus in Children Aged 3–36 Months

The risk of serious bacterial infections decreases with advancing age and in this age group it is 5%. A child presenting with fever without focus should be assessed completely. Detailed history is taken about vaccination, history of sick contacts in family and the condition of the child when fever is down. If the patient looks toxic, he should be hospitalized and undergo appropriate evaluation and treatment. In a non-toxic child with fever less than 39°C, one can merely observe. In children with fever more than 39°C, the risk of bacteremia is higher and it is recommended to do a leukocyte count and examine smear for malarial parasite. If the leukocyte count is >15,000/cu mm, blood culture should be sent and the patient administered IV ceftriaxone on either an inpatient or outpatient basis. If the count is less than 15,000/cu mm, observation is continued. Most patients with a febrile illness shall develop a focus in the next 1–2 days.

Suggested reading

1. Baraff LJ, Schriger DL, Bass JW, Fleisher GR, Klein JO, McCracken, Jr GH, Powell KR. Practice guideline for the management of infants and children 0 to 36 months of age with fever without source. Pediatrics 1993; 92; 1-12.
2. Baker MD. Evaluation and management of infants with fever. Pediatr Clin North Am 1999; 46:1061–72.

FEVER OF UNKNOWN ORIGIN

Definition

The definition of fever of unknown origin (FUO) is fever >101°C lasting for 3 weeks or more for which no cause is apparent after 1 week of outpatient investigation. A practical definition of FUO is simply fever >101°F measured on several occasions over a 7-day period.

Causes

The principal causes of FUO are listed in Table 9.1. Infections account for most of the cases of FUO in children (60–70%). Most common among infectious causes are enteric fever, malaria, pulmonary or extrapulmonary tuberculosis and urinary tract infections. Malignancies chiefly leukemia and autoimmune diseases chiefly juvenile rheumatoid arthritis account for the remaining cases. Relatively rare causes include drug fever, temperature dysregulation, diabetes insipidus, sarcoidosis, ectodermal dysplasia, sensory autonomic neuropathies, etc. Even with extensive investigations the cause of FUO remains undiagnosed in 10–20% of the cases.

Table 9.1: **Causes of fever of unknown origin**
Infections
Enteric fever, malaria, urinary tract infections, tuberculosis, chronic hepatitis, HIV inection, hidden abscesses (liver, pelvic), mastoiditis, sinusitis, osteomyelitis, meningitis, infectious mononucleosis, infective endocarditis, brucellosis, cytomegalovirus, toxoplasmosis, kala azar
Autoimmune
Systemic onset juvenile rheumatoid arthritis, Kawasaki disease, systemic lupus erythematosus, inflammatory bowel disease, polyarteritis nodosa
Malignancies
Leukemia, lymphoma, Langerhan cell histiocytosis

Approach to FUO

The first step is to identify sick patients who need stabilization and urgent referral to a tertiary care centre. Subsequently all attempts should be made to reach an etiologic diagnosis. A detailed history is of paramount importance. History should include

- Whether and how fever was documented (it is not uncommon to find children with history of prolonged fever not to have fever documented by a thermometer)

- Duration and pattern of fever (distinguish from recurrent fever)
- Symptoms referable to all organ systems, weight loss
- History of recurrent infections, oral thrush (HIV infection)
- History of joint pain, rash, photosensitivity (autoimmune disease)
- History of contact with tuberculosis and animals (brucellosis)
- Travel to endemic zones (kala azar)
- Drug history particularly anticholinergics (drug fever)

History is followed by a complete physical examination. Documentation of fever is necessary, followed by assessment of general activity, nutritional status and vitals. A head to toe examination, after removing all clothes, is vital. The physical examination should be repeated on daily basis as new findings may emerge that provide a clue to the etiology.

Preliminary investigations, which should be done in all patients with FUO include complete blood counts, peripheral smear, malarial parasite, ESR, blood cultures, Widal test, chest X-ray, tuberculin test, urinalysis and culture, hepatic transaminases and abdominal ultrasound. Specialized investigations are done, depending on clinical clues.

If a diagnosis is established on the basis of the above approach, appropriate treatment should be instituted. If no diagnosis is made, clinical reassessment and further investigations are merited. While second line investigations are being planned and executed, treatment with IV ceftriaxone may be considered as enteric fever is an important cause of FUO in our country, especially in those cases with negative clinical/preliminary investigations.

Second-line investigations include HIV ELISA, contrast enhanced CT of chest and abdomen, bone marrow histology and cultures, 2D echocardiogram, complement level, antinuclear and rheumatoid factors, tissue biopsies if indicated. Other serologic tests that may be done include brucella serology, HBsAg, Paul Bunnel/Monospot test/IgM VCA for infectious mononucleosis. Tests which are of no clinical value include serology, and PCR in blood for *M. tuberculosis* or other organisms.

It should be possible to make a diagnosis of the etiology of FUO in most cases. In a small number of cases, it may not be possible to arrive at the etiologic diagnosis. In such cases periodic reassessments should be done as the disease may finally surface (e.g. lymphoma, systemic onset juvenile rheumatoid arthritis). Some cases of FUO may self resolve over time. Empirical antitubercular therapy with four drugs for four weeks may be tried if it is not possible to arrive at an etiologic diagnosis after exhaustive work up. Empirical use of steroids should be avoided.

Suggested reading

Miller ML, Szer I, Yogev R, Bernstein B. Fever of unknown origin. Pediatr Clin North Am 1995; 42: 999–1015.

FEVER WITH RASH

Fever with rash is a common and vexing problem. It may signify a serious disorder such as meningococcemia or dengue hemorrhagic fever or may be associated with a minor drug allergy. There are multitudinous infectious and non-infectious causes of fever with rash; the common causes are listed in Table 9.2.

Evaluation

The most important factor that helps to determine the etiology of an exanthematous febrile illness is the nature of rash. Rashes may be macular, maculopapular, vesicular, nodular, urticarial or purpuric (Table 9.2). These are not watertight compartments and considerable overlap may occur with one etiology having varying presentations. Other factors that help in arriving at a diagnosis are local epidemiology, season, history of exposure, incubation period, age, vaccination status, previous exanthems, nature of prodromal symptoms and relation of rash with fever, distribution and progression of the rash, involvement of mucous membranes, history of drug intake, associated symptoms and laboratory findings. Details of each of these conditions are discussed later.

Table 9.2: Common causes of exanthematous illnesses in India

Macular or maculopapular rash
Measles, rubella, dengue, roseola infantum, erythema infectiosum, drug rash, infectious mononucleosis, chikungunya, *adenoviral infections, enteroviral infections,* mycoplasma infections, secondary syphilis, brucellosis, scrub typhus, chronic hepatitis B, cytomegalovirus infection, HIV infection, systemic lupus, juvenile rheumatoid arthritis
Diffuse erythema with peeling or desquamation
Scarlet fever, *Steven Johnson syndrome, drug-induced toxic epidermolysis,* staphylococcal and streptococcal toxic shock syndrome, *Kawasaki disease*
Vesicular rash
Varicella, herpes simplex, herpes zoster, *enteroviral infections,* papulonecrotic tuberculids
Petechial or purpuric rash
Meningococcemia, dengue hemorrhagic fever, gonococcemia, hemorrhagic measles or varicella, cutaneous vasculitis, *Henoch Schonlein purpura*
Urticarial rash
Scabies, cutaneous larva migrans, *insect bites,* pediculosis
Nodular rash
Molluscum contagiosum, disseminated histoplasmosis, cryptococcosis, *erythema nodosum* (secondary to tuberculosis, drugs, sarcoidosis, inflammatory bowel disease, leprosy)

Common and serious conditions are italicized

Management

All efforts should be made to arrive at a specific diagnosis followed by institution of specific therapy. However, on several occasions a specific diagnosis is not possible. In this situation symptomatic therapy, close observation, explanation of danger signs to parents and staying away from school until the rash resolves is recommended.

Suggested reading

Cherry JD. Cutaneous manifestations of systemic Infections. In: Feigen RD, Cherry JD, eds. Text book of Pediatric Infectious Diseases, 4th edn. Philadelphia, WB Saunders; 713–37.

COMMON VIRAL INFECTIONS

MEASLES

Measles is a common and serious childhood exanthematous illness, which still causes approximately 350,000 childhood deaths in developing countries of which 80,000 occur in India alone.

Etiopathogenesis

Measles is caused by an RNA virus belonging to the paramyxovirus family. The virus is transmitted by droplet spread from the secretions of the nose and throat usually 4 days before and 5 days after the rash. The disease is highly contagious with secondary attack rates in susceptible household contacts exceeding 90%. The portal of entry is the respiratory tract where the virus multiplies in the respiratory epithelium. Primary viremia occurs resulting in infection of the reticuloendothelial system followed by secondary viremia, which results in systemic symptoms. The incubation period is around 10 days.

Features

The disease is most common in preschool children; infants are protected by transplacental antibodies, which generally decay by 9 months (hence the rationale for vaccination at this age). The prodromal phase is characterized by fever, rhinorrhea, conjunctival congestion and a dry hacking cough. Koplik spots considered as pathognomonic of measles appear on the 2nd or 3rd day of the illness as gray/white grains of sand-like lesions with surrounding erythema opposite the lower second molars on the buccal mucosa. The rash usually appears on the fourth day with rise in fever as faint reddish macules behind the ears, along the hairline and on the posterior aspects of the cheeks. The rash rapidly becomes maculopapular and spreads to the face, the neck, chest, arms, trunk, thighs and legs in that order over the next 2–3 days. It then starts fading in the same order that it appeared and leaves behind branny desquamation and brownish discoloration, which fades over the next 10 days. Modified measles seen in partially immune individuals is a much milder and shorter illness. Hemorrhagic measles is characterized by a purpuric rash and bleeding from the nose, mouth or bowel.

Complications

Widespread mucosal damage and significant immunosuppression induced by measles account for the frequent complications seen with this viral infection. Complications are more frequent in the very young, the malnourished and the immunocompromised. The most common complications are otitis media and bacterial bronchopneumonia. Other respiratory complications include laryngitis, tracheitis, bronchitis, giant cell pneumonia, bronchiectasis and flaring up of latent *M. tuberculosis* infection. Transient loss of tuberculin hypersensitivity reaction is common following measles. Gastrointestinal complications include persistent diarrhea, appendicitis, hepatitis and ileocolitis. Measles can precipitate malnutrition and can cause noma or gangrene of the cheeks.

Acute encephalitis occurs in measles at a frequency of 1–2/1000 cases most commonly during the period of the rash, consequent to direct invasion of the brain. Post measles encephalitis occurs after recovery and is believed to be due to an immune mechanism, similar to other para-infectious/demyelinating encephalomyelitis. Measles is also responsible for the almost uniformly fatal subacute sclerosing panencephalitis (SSPE) seen several years after infection at a frequency of 1/100,000 cases.

Diagnosis

The diagnosis is clinical; it may be confirmed by estimating the levels of IgM antimeasles antibody that is present 3 days after the rash and persists for 1 month. Measles needs to be differentiated from other childhood exanthematous illnesses. The rash is milder and feverless prominent in rubella, enteroviral and adenoviral infections. In roseola infantum, the rash appears once fever disappears while in measles the fever increases with rash. In rickettsial infections, the face is spared which is always involved in measles. In meningococcemia, the upper respiratory symptoms are absent and the rash rapidly becomes petechial. Drug rashes have history of antecedent drug intake. In Kawasaki disease, glossitis, cervical adenopathy, fissuring of lips, extreme irritability, edema of hands and scaling are distinguishing clinical features.

Treatment

Treatment is mainly supportive and comprises antipyretics, maintenance of hygiene, ensuring adequate fluid and caloric intake, humidification, etc. Vitamin A reduces morbidity and mortality of measles and a single oral dose of 100, 000 units below 1 year and 200,000 units over the age of 1 year is recommended. Complications should be managed appropriately.

Prevention

Measles is a preventable and potentially eradicable disease through universal immunization, as discussed in chapter 8.

VARICELLA (CHICKEN POX)

Chicken pox is a mild exanthematous illness in most healthy children but can be a serious disease in neonates, immunocompromised, pregnant women and even healthy adults.

Etiopathogenesis

Chicken pox is caused by the varicella zoster virus (VZV), a DNA virus of the herpes virus family. The virus is present in respiratory secretions and the skin lesions of an affected child and is transmitted either by air-borne spread or through direct contact. The portal of entry is the respiratory tract. During the incubation period of 10–21 days, the virus replicates in the respiratory mucosa followed by viremic dissemination to the skin and various organs. The host immune response limits infection and promotes recovery. In immunocompromised children, unchecked replication and dissemination of virus leads to complications. During the latter part of the incubation period, the virus is transported to the respiratory mucosa and leads to infectivity even prior to appearance of the rash. The period of infectivity lasts from 24–48 hours before the rash until all the vesicles are crusted (the scabs are not infective unlike small-pox). The disease is highly contagious with secondary attack rates of 80% among household contacts. VZV establishes lifelong latent infection in the sensory ganglia. Reactivation, especially during periods of depressed immunity, leads to the dermatomal rash of herpes zoster.

Features

Chicken pox is rarely subclinical; however, in some children only a few lesions may be present. The peak age of disease is 5–10 years. The prodromal period is short with mild to moderate fever, malaise, headache and anorexia. The rash appears 24–48 hours after the prodromal symptoms as intensely pruritic erythematous macules first on the trunk. The rash rapidly spreads to the face and extremities while it evolves into papules, clear fluid-filled vesicles, clouded vesicles and then crusted vesicles. Several crops of lesions appear and simultaneous presence of skin lesions in varying stages of evolution is a characteristic of varicella. The median number of lesions is around 300 but may vary from 10–1500. Systemic symptoms persist for 2–4 days after appearance of the rash. The rash lasts 3–7 days and leaves behind hypopigmented or hyperpigmented macules that persist for days to weeks. Scarring is unusual unless lesions are secondarily infected.

Complications

Secondary bacterial infections of the skin lesions may occur, occasionally resulting in necrotizing fascitis. Neurologic complications include meningoencephalitis, acute cerebellar ataxia, transverse myelitis, LGB syndrome and optic neuritis. Other complications include purpura fulminans due to antibodies against protein C, CNS vasculitis leading to stroke, autoimmune thrombocytopenic purpura and Reye syndrome.

The progressive varicella syndrome is a dreaded complication of chicken pox in the immunocompromised, neonates, pregnant women and even healthy adults and adolescents. This syndrome is characterized by continued development of lesions, hemorrhagic lesions, coagulopathy and visceral organ involvement including hepatitis, pneumonia and encephalitis; mortality rate are high despite therapy.

Chicken pox in pregnancy is associated with an increased risk of severe disease in the mother. Congenital varicella syndrome may occur following infection in the 1st and 2nd trimester at a frequency of 0.4–2% characterized by skin scarring, malformed extremities, cataracts and brain abnormalities (e.g. aplasia, calcifications). Finally, if the disease occurs in the mother 5 days before and 2 days after delivery, severe and often fatal neonatal disease may result.

Herpes zoster in children is characterized by a mild vesicular rash with dermatomal distribution; unlike adults pain is less and post-herpetic neuralgia unusual. The risk of herpes zoster is more in children who acquire chicken pox in infancy, those whose mothers developed varicella in the third trimester and in the immunocompromised.

Diagnosis

The diagnosis is clinical and usually not difficult. Chicken pox should be differentiated from other vesicular exanthemata such as herpes simplex, enteroviral infections, insect bites and drug reactions. In atypical cases, the diagnosis is made on Tzanck smear of the lesions (showing multinucleated cells) and presence of anti IgM antibodies to varicella.

Treatment

Management is symptomatic and includes antipyretics (aspirin is contraindicated due to risk of Reye syndrome), antipruritic agents and good hygiene. The child should not attend school until no new lesions appear and all lesions have crusted. Administration of oral acyclovir (20 mg/kg/dose four times a day for 5 days) within 24 hours of onset of rash in healthy children reduces the duration of rash by one day and lesions by 25%. IV acyclovir (10 mg/kg every 8 hours for 14–21 days) is given to patients with complicated varicella and illness in high risk patients (neonates, immunocompromised children, pregnant women).

Prevention

Prevention against varicella with the live attenuated varicella vaccine and use of varicella zoster immune globulin (VZIG) for post exposure prophylaxis are detailed in chapter 8. VZIG is fairly expensive and not always available. Other options, which have not been evaluated, include the use of intravenous immunoglobulin and oral acyclovir.

Suggested reading

Arvin AM. Varicella zoster virus. Clin Microbiol Rev 1996; 9:361-8.

INFECTIOUS MONONUCLEOSIS

Infectious mononucleosis (IM), a syndrome characterized by fever, fatigue, sore throat and lymphadenopathy, is most often caused by a herpes virus, Epstein Barr virus (EBV). Infectious mononucleosis-like illness can also be caused by toxoplasma, CMV, adenoviruses and primary HIV infection.

Epidemiology

The epidemiology of IM is related to the age of primary acquisition of EBV infection. In developing countries, most of EBV infection occurs in infancy and early childhood when it is either asymptomatic or similar to other childhood infections. For this reason, IM is uncommonly seen or reported in India. In developed countries, the age of acquisition of EBV infection shifts upwards and thus IM is seen more commonly.

The EBV virus, a DNA virus of the herpes virus family, is transmitted in oral secretions by close intimate contact like kissing or exchange of saliva from close child contact. The virus replicates in the oral epithelial cells then spreads to salivary glands with eventual viremia to the B lymphocytes in the blood and lymphoreticular system including liver and spleen. The CD8 lymphocytes proliferate to check this replication of virus in the B lymphocytes and represent the atypical lymphocytes seen in EBV infection. Like other herpes viruses, EBV establishes lifelong latent infection after the primary infection with frequent asymptomatic reactivations.

Features

Symptomatic EBV infections in older children and adults are characterized by insidious onset with symptoms such as malaise, fatigue, fever, headache, nausea, sore throat, abdominal pain and myalgia. Examination shows pharyngeal inflammation with exudates and petechiae at the junction of soft and hard palate, generalized lymphadenopathy (cervical, less often axillary and inguinal), mild splenomegaly (50%) and hepatomegaly (10%). Maculopapular rashes are seen in 3–15% and in 80% of those who have received ampicillin or amoxicillin.

Complications are rare and include splenic rupture following minor trauma, airway obstruction due to enlargement of oropharyngeal lymphoid tissue, meningitis, seizures, ataxia, myocarditis, hemolytic anemia, thrombocytopenia, neutropenia, aplastic anemia, interstitial pneumonitis and pancreatitis.

Diagnosis

Most patients show leukocytosis and absolute lymphocytosis, with presence of atypical lymphocytes. The platelet counts are mildly low and hepatic transaminases mildly elevated in 50% patients. The Paul Bunnel (heterophile antibody test) is used for screening. This test is based on agglutination of sheep/horse red cells by heterophile antibodies present in the serum of patients with EBV infection. This test may have false negative rates of 10% and remains positive for few months to 2 years after infection. IgM antibody to viral capsid antigen is a confirmatory test to diagnose acute EBV infection.

IM should be differentiated form other causes of similar illness enumerated earlier, from streptococcal pharyngitis and acute leukemia.

Treatment

Rest and symptomatic therapy are mainstays of management. Participation in strenuous activities and contact sports should be prohibited in the first 2–3 weeks of illness due to risk of splenic rupture. Treatment with prednisolone (1 mg/kg/day for 7 days) is advised for complications such as hemolytic anemia, airway obstruction, meningitis and thrombocytopenia with bleeding.

Other Manifestations of EBV Infections

EBV has oncogenic potential and has been causally associated with aggressive proliferative disorders such as virus associated hemophagocytic syndrome, oral hairy leukoplakia and lymphoid interstitial pneumonitis in patients with AIDS, nasopharyngeal carcinoma, Burkitt lymphoma, Hodgkin disease and tumors in immunocompromised patients (e.g. X-linked lymphoproliferative disease, leiomyosarcoma, CNS lymphoma).

MUMPS

Mumps is an acute viral infection characterized by painful enlargement of the salivary glands (most characteristically the parotid glands). Mumps is caused by an RNA virus of genus Paramyxovirus in the family Paramyxoviridae; only one serotype is known.

Epidemiology

Most cases occur between the ages of 5 and 15 years; infants are rarely affected due to presence of transplacentally acquired maternal antibodies. The incidence is higher in winter and spring. Man is the only reservoir of infection; carrier state does not exist.

The virus has a predilection for salivary glands and nervous tissue, but can also infect the breast, liver, joints and the heart. The disease is mild in the majority; in 10% the infection is associated with aseptic meningitis or encephalitis.

The virus is spread from human reservoir by direct contact, air-borne droplets and fomites contaminated by saliva and urine. The virus proliferates in the respiratory epithelium and enters the circulation; it then gets localized to the glandular and neural tissue. The virus has been isolated from saliva as long as 6 days before and 9 days after appearance of salivary gland swelling. The secondary infection rate is as high as 80%. Mumps infection or immunization is believed to confer lifelong immunity.

Features

Following an incubation period of 2–4 weeks, the symptoms begin acutely with fever, malaise and headache. Mumps infection is characterized by unilateral or bilateral parotitis. This presents as earache, jaw tenderness while chewing, dryness of mouth and swelling at the angle of jaw. The ear lobe may appear to be pushed upwards and outwards. The defervescence and resolution takes about a week. Occasionally other salivary glands including the submaxillary and sublingual glands are affected.

The occurrence of epididymo-orchitis is more common in adolescent boys or postpubertal men (unilateral in 85% cases) and occurs 1–2 weeks after parotitis. The testes are enlarged and tender. Some degree of atrophy develops in the testes affected by this viral infection but sterility is rare.

CNS involvement in the form of aseptic meningitis is seen in about 1–10% patients with parotitis. Recovery is generally uneventful. Mumps is perhaps the commonest cause of aseptic meningitis in children. The risk of encephalitis is between 0.02–0.3% cases. Mumps encephalitis has a satisfactory prognosis with a mortality rate of less than 2%. Other CNS manifestations include auditory nerve damage leading to deafness, cerebellar ataxia, facial neuritis, transverse myelitis and Guillain Barre syndrome.

Uncommon presentations include pancreatitis (5% may trigger insulin dependent diabetes mellitus), mastitis, oophoritis, nephritis and myocarditis.

Diagnosis

The diagnosis is based on clinical features. Serum amylase is elevated in almost 90% patients. The diagnosis may be confirmed on isolation of the virus on tissue culture inoculated with throat washings, spinal fluid and urine. ELISA or the hemagglutination inhibition test is used to demonstrate antibodies to S and V antigens of mumps virus. Mumps parotitis needs to be differentiated from suppurative parotitis, recurrent parotitis, calculus in Stensen duct and other viral infections causing parotitis, e.g. coxsackie A and cytomegalovirus.

Treatment

Symptomatic treatment is given in the form of antipyretics and warm saline mouthwashes. Orchitis is treated by bed rest and local support. Steroids may be used for symptomatic relief of orchitis and arthritis but does not alter the course of disease.

Prevention

The affected patient should be isolated until the parotid swelling has subsided. Mumps can be prevented by timely immunization (Chapter 8).

POLIOMYELITIS

The polioviruses belong to the genus Enterovirus in the family Picornaviridae and comprise three related serotypes: types 1, 2 and 3, all of which can cause paralysis. Type 1 is most frequently responsible, type 3 plays a lesser role and type 2 is only rarely involved.

Epidemiology

The disease is seasonal, occurring more commonly in summer and early autumn in temperate climates. In tropical countries, seasonality is less clearly defined; some areas experience increase during the rainy season. Three regions of the world were certified as free from the indigenous circulation of the wild poliovirus: the Americas in 1994, the Eastern Pacific in 2000 and Europe in 2002. A dramatic increase in cases was seen in 2004 because Nigeria interrupted its national vaccination campaigns, which caused not only an increase in the number of cases in that country, but also led to the emergence of cases in countries that previously had eliminated polio.

Feco-oral transmission of the poliovirus is the predominant mode in the developing countries where sanitation is poor, whereas oral-pharyngeal transmission is more likely to predominate in industrialized countries and during outbreaks. The virus is shed in stools for six to eight weeks. On average, the incubation period of the disease is 7–10 days (range, 4–35 days). The virus spreads rapidly to non-immune persons; transmission is usually widespread in the community by the time of onset of paralysis in a child. Humans are the only reservoir of poliovirus, and infection is spread from person to person.

Infants born to mothers with antibodies are protected naturally against paralytic disease for a few weeks. Immunity is acquired through infection with the wild virus and through immunization. Immunity following natural infection or administration of a complete series of live oral polio vaccine (OPV) results in both humoral and local intestinal cellular responses. This immunity is lifelong and can serve to interrupt the chain of transmission. The inactivated poliovirus vaccine (IPV) confers humoral immunity but relatively less intestinal immunity. There is little or no cross-immunity between the poliovirus types.

The Global Polio Eradication Initiative has significantly reduced the number of cases in the world, from an estimated 350,000 in 1988 to 1308 in 2007 out of which 866 were reported from India (Fig. 9.2).

Pathogenesis

The mouth is the usual portal of entry. It is usually present in the pharynx and in the stool before the onset of paralytic

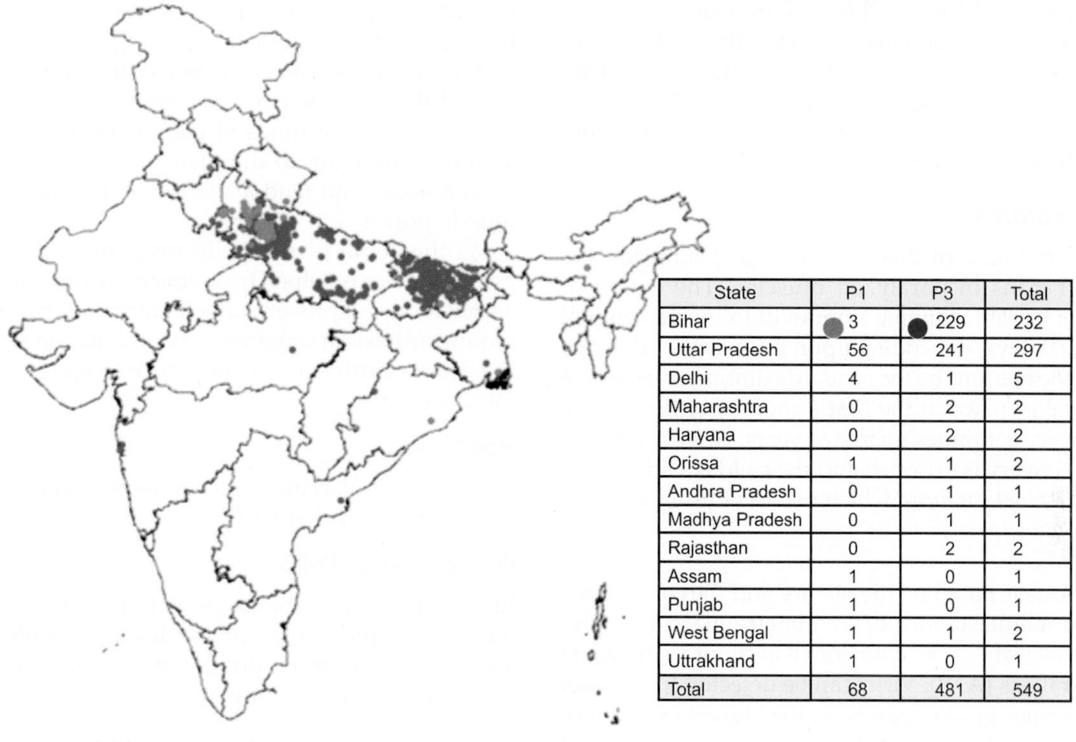

State	P1	P3	Total
Bihar	3	229	232
Uttar Pradesh	56	241	297
Delhi	4	1	5
Maharashtra	0	2	2
Haryana	0	2	2
Orissa	1	1	2
Andhra Pradesh	0	1	1
Madhya Pradesh	0	1	1
Rajasthan	0	2	2
Assam	1	0	1
Punjab	1	0	1
West Bengal	1	1	2
Uttrakhand	1	0	1
Total	68	481	549

Fig. 9.2: Cases of poliomyelitis reported from India in 2008. P1 poliovirus type 1, P3 poliovirus type 3

illness. It invades local lymphoid tissue, enters the bloodstream and invades certain nerve cells. It may damage or destroy the nerve cells.

Clinical Features

In 90–95% of infected individuals, poliovirus infection is inapparent. In the remaining 5–10% of individuals infected by poliovirus, one of the following syndromes may occur.

Abortive polio occurs in 4–8% of infections and is characterized by a minor illness with low grade fever, sore throat, vomiting, abdominal pain, loss of appetite and malaise. Recovery is rapid and complete; there is no paralysis. It cannot be distinguished from other viral infections.

Non-paralytic aseptic meningitis occurs in 1–2% of infections, with headache, neck, back, and leg stiffness several days after a prodrome similar to abortive polio. Recovery occurs within 2–10 days.

Paralytic poliomyelitis occurs in 0.5–1% of infections. Symptoms occur in two phases, minor and major, separated by several days without symptoms. The minor phase consists of symptoms similar to those of abortive poliomyelitis. The major phase of illness begins with muscle pain, spasms and the return of fever. This is followed by rapid onset of flaccid paralysis that is usually complete within 72 hours.

Polio encephalitis is characterized by irritability, delirium and loss of consciousness; seizures may occur. The paralysis may be of the upper motor neuron type.

There are 3 types of paralytic poliomyelitis.

Spinal paralytic poliomyelitis is the most common form of paralytic poliomyelitis, accounting for approximately 80% cases. It results from a lower motor neuron lesion of the anterior horn cells of the spinal cord and affects the muscles of the legs, arms and/or trunk. Severe cases may develop quadriplegia and paralysis of the trunk, abdominal and thoracic muscles. The affected muscles are floppy and reflexes are diminished. The sense of pain and touch are normal. Paralysis is often asymmetrical, affecting legs more often than arms. Paralytic manifestation in extremities begins proximally and progresses to involve distal muscle groups (i.e. descending paralysis). Residual flaccid paralysis is usually present after 60 days.

Bulbar polio accounts for 2% cases and results from a cranial nerve lesion, resulting in respiratory insufficiency and difficulty in swallowing, eating or speaking.

Bulbospinal polio accounts for 20% cases and is a combination of spinal paralytic and bulbar polio.

Depending on the strain of poliovirus, the ratio between subclinical and clinical infections is estimated to range between 100:1 and 1000:1. Older children and adults run a greater risk of developing paralytic illness. The case-fatality rate ranges between 2–20% among persons who do develop the paralytic form of the disease. However, if there is bulbar or respiratory involvement, the case-fatality rate may be as high as 40%.

Residual Paralysis

As the acute phase of illness (0–4 weeks) subsides, the recovery begins in paralyzed muscles. The extent of recovery is variable ranging from mild to severe residual paresis at 60 days, depending upon the extent of damage caused to the neurons by the virus. Maximum neurological recovery takes place in the first 6 months of the illness; slow recovery continues up to two years. After two years, no more recovery is expected and the child is said to have *post polio residual paralysis*, which persists throughout life.

Diagnosis

The diagnosis is based on the history and the characteristic clinical manifestations of asymmetric flaccid paralysis. *Stool examination* is recommended in every case of acute flaccid paralysis (AFP). Virus can be detected from onset to 8 or more weeks after paralysis; the highest probability of detection is during the first 2 weeks after onset of paralysis. Examination of the *cerebrospinal fluid* (cell count, gram stain, protein and glucose) is useful in eliminating other conditions that cause AFP. Current *serologic tests* cannot differentiate between wild and vaccine virus strains. Collection of blood specimens for culture or serology is not recommended.

Differential Diagnosis

The two diseases most commonly confused with polio are Guillain-Barré syndrome and transverse myelitis. Other conditions with a presentation similar to those of paralytic poliomyelitis include traumatic neuritis, less frequently, meningitis /encephalitis, as well as illnesses produced by a variety of toxins (diphtheria, botulism).

Treatment

Treatment should be early and appropriate to the stage and degree of paralysis. Children with bulbospinal polio and respiratory paralysis require hospitalization. In acute stage children with isolated limb/limbs paralysis can be managed at home. They should be advised complete rest, proper positioning of the affected limb and passive range of movement at the joints. Massage and intramuscular injection should be avoided during acute phase of illness. Frequent change of the posture of the patient is must. The child should be made to lie on firm bed and maintain limbs in neutral position. The child should lie with trunk and hip straight with slight flexion (5–10°) at knees and feet at right angle at the ankle joint. This position can be maintained with pillows, rolled towels or sand bags. Warm moist fomentations can be given with soft towels, dipped in warm water to relieve pain and spasms (Sister Kenny's treatment). Analgesics can also be given to relieve pain and fever. All the joints of affected limb/limbs should be moved through their passive range of movements, 2–3 times/day for 10 times at each joint, to prevent joint stiffness. This helps to stimulate proprioceptive impulses from muscles and tendons thus helping improvement in muscle power.

As the acute phase of illness subsides, recovery in muscle power is helped by giving physiotherapy, helping ambulation and prevention of deformities. Some children require orthosis at some stage for ambulation. Others with fixed deformities and contractures require orthopedic intervention.

9

Vaccines

The available vaccines and the recommended schedule are discussed in chapter 8.

Eradication of Polio

Eradication is possible because polio affects only man, immunity is lifelong, a safe vaccine is available and there are no carriers or reservoirs of the infection. The strategies for achieving this goal are:

Attaining High Routine Immunization

Immunize every child aged <1 year with at least three doses of oral poliovirus vaccine (OPV).

National Immunization Days (NIDs)

On these days, under the Pulse Polio Immunization (PPI) program, additional OPV doses are administered to every child <5-year-old. The aim of NIDs/PPI is to "flood" the community with OPV within a very short period, thereby interrupting transmission of virus throughout the community. Intensification of the PPI program is accomplished by the addition of extra immunization rounds, adding a house-to-house "search and vaccinate" component in addition to providing vaccine at a fixed post. The number of PPI rounds conducted during any particular year is determined by the extent of poliovirus transmission in the state/district.

Mopping-up immunization

When poliovirus transmission is reduced to well-defined and focal geographic areas, intensive house-to-house, child-to-child immunization campaigns are conducted over a period of days to break the final chains of virus transmission.

Acute Flaccid Paralysis Surveillance

Under the Global Polio Eradication Initiative, surveillance for polio is conducted through investigation of patients with AFP. AFP surveillance helps to detect reliable areas where poliovirus transmission is occurring.

Acute flaccid paralysis (AFP) is defined as sudden onset of weakness and floppiness in any part of the body in a child <15-year old or paralysis in a person of any age in whom polio is suspected. In other parts of the world, at least one case of AFP (excluding polio) occurs annually for every 100,000 children less than 15-years of age (background AFP rate). The non-polio causes of AFP account for this background rate. Sensitive surveillance will detect a background AFP rate of 1/100,000 children. In our country, where the incidence of conditions such as traumatic neuritis and AFP caused by other non-polio enteroviruses is very high, the background non-polio AFP rate is higher.

The Ministry of Health & Family Welfare, Government of India issued an official instruction that all health facilities, clinicians and other practitioners are required to notify AFP cases immediately to the District Immunization Officer (DIO), by the fastest available means. All cases with AFP should be reported and their stools must be collected within 14 days of onset. If it is not possible to collect stool specimens within 14 days, the specimens should still be collected up to 60 days after onset of paralysis. Upon verification that the case meets the AFP case definition, the DIO initiates the case investigation. As part of the investigations two stool samples are collected from the child at a minimum interval of 24-hr. A sixty day follow-up is done between the 60th and 90th day in certain categories of AFP cases to determine the presence/absence of residual paralysis. The presence of residual paralysis at this time is further evidence that the cause of paralysis is likely to be due to poliovirus.

An AFP case is "confirmed" as polio only by the isolation of wild poliovirus from any stool specimen. An AFP case is classified as "non-polio AFP" if wild poliovirus is not isolated from adequate stool specimens. If stool specimens are inadequate, final classification of the AFP case as either non-polio AFP or compatible with polio will depend on the results of the 60-day examination. If the 60-day follow-up examination shows no residual weakness, the case is classified as non-polio AFP.

Suggested reading

1. National Polio Surveillance Project. Available at: http://www.npspindia.org/index.asp
2. Poliomyelitis Eradication Field Guide, 3rd edn. Available at http://www.paho.org/english/ad/fch/im FieldGuide_Polio.pdf
3. Singhal T, Amdekar YK, Thacker N and Indian Academy of Pediatrics. IAP Committee on immunization. Ind Pediatr 2007; 44: 390–2.

VIRAL HEPATITIS

Hepatitis is a general term meaning inflammation of the liver and can be caused by a variety of different viruses such as hepatitis A, B, C, D and E. Hepatitis A and E are responsible for most of the water-borne (community acquired) hepatitis while B, C and D are responsible for post-transfusion hepatitis. Since a considerable number of cases of both post-transfusion and community-acquired hepatitis are not identified as being caused by hepatitis A–E, investigators have sought to identify other potentially hepatotropic viral agents, including hepatitis G virus, TT virus and SEN virus.

HEPATITIS A

Hepatitis A is caused by infection with the hepatitis A virus (HAV), a nonenveloped RNA virus, first identified by electron microscopy in 1973. It is classified within the genus hepatovirus of the picornavirus family. In humans, a single serotype of HAV exists. HAV infection induces lifelong protection against reinfection. HAV is extremely resistant to degradation by environmental conditions, a property that allows its maintenance and spread within populations. In developing countries with poor environmental hygienic conditions, nearly all children are infected with HAV before 9-years of age. It is spread via the fecal oral route through contaminated food and water, and person-to-person spread under poor sanitary conditions. Infections occur early in life in areas where HAV is highly endemic.

Clinical Features

The course of hepatitis A is extremely variable. The severity of the disease increases with age at time of infection. The course of acute hepatitis A can be divided into four clinical phases:

- *Incubation or preclinical period* ranging from 10 to 50 days (median 30 days), during which the patient remains asymptomatic despite active replication of the virus.
- *Prodromal or pre-icteric phase* ranging from several days to more than a week, characterized by symptoms like loss of appetite, fatigue, abdominal pain, nausea and vomiting, fever, diarrhea, dark urine and pale stools. Children generally belong to this group.
- *Icteric phase*, during which jaundice develops at total bilirubin levels exceeding 2–4 mg/dl. The icteric phase generally begins within 10 days of the initial symptoms. Fever improves after the first few days of jaundice. The mortality rate is low (0.2% patients with jaundice) and the disease resolves.
- *Convalescent period*, where resolution of the disease is slow, but patient recovery uneventful and complete.

Occasionally, extensive necrosis of the liver occurs during the first 6–8 weeks of illness. In this case, high fever, marked abdominal pain, vomiting, jaundice and the development of hepatic encephalopathy associated with coma and seizures occur. These are the signs of fulminant hepatitis, leading to death in 70–90% of the patients. In patients who survive, neither functional nor pathologic sequelae are common despite the widespread necrosis. Infection with HAV does not lead to chronic or persistent hepatitis. Relapsing hepatitis occurs in 3–20% of patients 4 to 15 weeks after the initial symptoms have resolved.

In acute hepatitis A, the presence of anti-HAV IgM is detectable about 3 weeks after exposure, its titer increases over 4 to 6 weeks, then declines to non-detectable levels within 6 months of infection.

Diagnosis

The specific diagnosis of acute hepatitis A is made by finding anti-HAV IgM in the serum of patients. As IgG anti-HAV persists lifelong after acute infection, detection of IgG anti-HAV alone indicates past infection. Laboratory evaluation of liver function includes estimation of total and direct bilirubin, transaminases, alkaline phosphatase, prothrombin time, total protein and albumin.

Immune Prophylaxis

The administration of immunoglobulin can reduce the incidence of hepatitis A up to 90%, and it is most effective if given before exposure. Its use is declining, since there is increasing use of HAV vaccines. Immunoglobulin G may be used for postexposure prophylaxis. If administered within two weeks of exposure it either prevents development of disease or reduces its severity.

Active Immunization

Inactivated HAV vaccines are available that are safe, highly immunogenic and provide long-term protection from infection. The vaccine is highly effective and provides seroconversion rates of more than 99% when given as a single primary immunization, followed by a booster dose 6 months later.

Treatment

As no specific treatment exists, prevention is the most effective approach against the disease. Therapy is supportive and is aimed at maintaining adequate nutrition. There is no evidence to suggest that restriction of fats has any beneficial effect on the course of the disease. Eggs, milk and butter may actually help provide a correct caloric intake. Antiviral agents have no role because the hepatic injury appears to be immunopathologically mediated. Referral to a liver transplant centre is appropriate for patients with fulminant hepatitis A. Temporary auxiliary liver transplantation for subacute liver failure may be a way to promote native liver regeneration.

HEPATITIS B

Hepatitis B virus is a 3.2 kb, circular, partially double stranded DNA virus. HBV contains four open reading frames, which encode major structural and nonstructural proteins for HBV.

Epidemiology of HBV Infection

HBV infection is prevalent in Asia, Africa, Southern Europe and Latin America, where the HBsAg seropositive rate ranges from 2 to 20%. In hyperendemic areas, HBV infections occur mainly during infancy and early childhood. In Asia, perinatal transmission from HBsAg carrier mothers to their infants is a very important route of transmission, leading to chronicity. Approximately 90% of the infants of HBeAg seropositive carrier mothers become HBsAg carriers, irrespective of a high or low HBsAg carrier rate in the population. In areas of low endemicity, horizontal infection is the main route of transmission.

Pathogenesis and Natural Course

HBV has an incubation period of 2 to 6 months. Following a primary HBV infection, the host may run an acute, fulminant or chronic course.

Acute and Fulminant Hepatitis

Acute hepatitis is marked by symptoms similar to other acute hepatitis illnesses, i.e. fever, vomiting, jaundice and anorexia. Recovery is marked by hepatitis B surface antibody (anti-HBs) seroconversion. Fulminant hepatitis is heralded by pathologic mental status changes within 2 to 8 weeks after the initial symptoms in an otherwise healthy child. About two-thirds of children with fulminant hepatitis B present in infancy.

Chronic Infection

Children with chronic HBV infection are mostly asymptomatic. They are generally active and grow well. Although liver damage is usually mild during childhood, serious sequelae, including cirrhosis and hepatocellular carcinoma, may develop insidiously at any age. An immune-mediated process is the main mechanism for cell damage. During acute exacerbations of chronic HBV infections, CD8+ T lymphocytes are the predominant cells in the liver in the areas of piecemeal necrosis. Since HBeAg is an important marker reflecting active viral replication and infectivity, its clearance is used as a marker for the success of antiviral therapy. Children with chronic HBV infection are HBeAg seropositive at the initial stage of infection; this antigenemia can persist for years after primary infection (Fig. 9.3). Spontaneous clearance of HBeAg occurs gradually with increasing age. Viral replication is reduced during this process. This process of HBeAg seroconversion takes place subclinically in most individuals for a period of 2 to 7 years (Table 9.3). This process is usually preceded by an elevation of aminotransferases. After HBeAg clearance, aminotransferase levels return to normal levels and anti-HBe develops. Long-term follow-up of HBsAg carrier children shows that the rate of HBsAg clearance is low (0.6% annually), and occurs only after clearance of HBeAg.

During the early phase of infection, the amount of virus in the liver and blood is usually large, whereas the liver damage is mostly mild. The host immune system gradually recognizes the virus and starts to clear the virus.

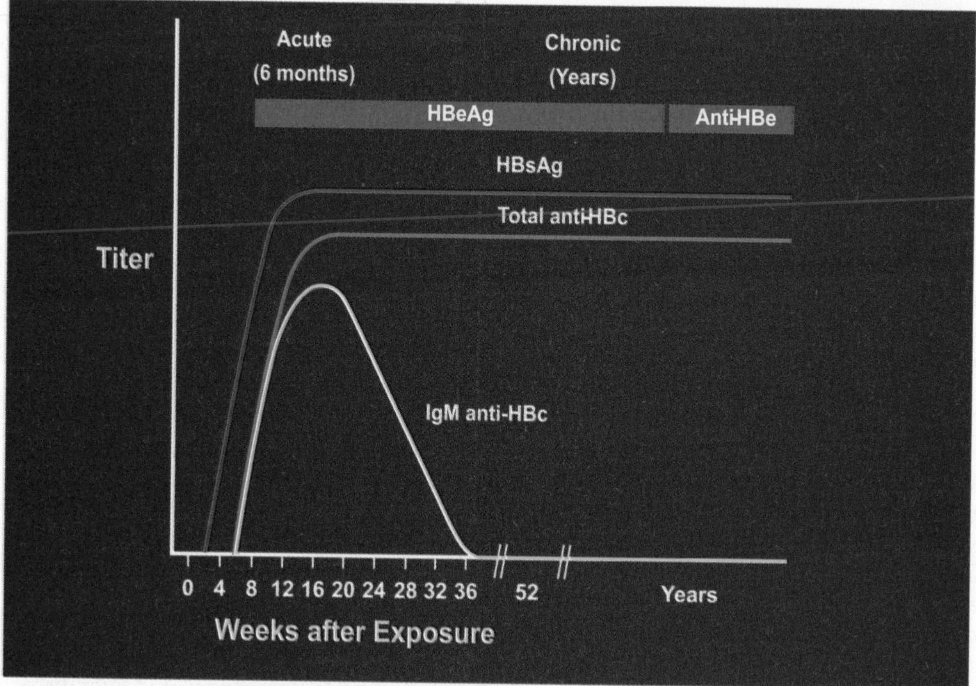

Fig. 9.3: Progression to chronic hepatitis B virus infection

Table 9.3: Common seropatterns of hepatitis B infection

HBsAg	*Anti HBs*	*Anti HBc*	*HBeAg*	*Anti HBe*	*Interpretation*
+	–	IgM	+	–	Acute infection
–	–	IgM	+/–	+/–	Acute infection; antiHBc window
+	–	IgG	+	–	Chronic infection; high infectivity
+	–	IgG	–	+	Chronic infection; low infectivity
+	–	+/–	–	–	Precore/core mutant infection
+	–	IgG	–	+/–	Hepatitis B carrier
–	+	IgG	–	+/–	Recovery from infection
–	+	–	–	–	Immunization; false positive; infection in remote past

It results in active inflammation of the liver and elevation of serum aminotransferases. Repeated episodes of elevation of aminotransferases is followed by HBeAg seroconversion. After HBeAg seroconversion, viral replication declines and the liver inflammation gradually becomes inactive.

Hepatitis D

Hepatitis delta virus (HDV) was first detected as a new nuclear antigen in the hepatocytes of patients infected with hepatitis B virus (HBV) and was frequently associated with severe acute or chronic hepatitis. Transmission of HDV requires either co-infection with HBV or superinfection in individuals who are HBV carriers. Although HDV infection is closely associated with HBV, HDV clearly belongs to a distinct virus group. Currently, HDV is assigned a floating genus, Deltavirus.

Immunoprophylaxis

Hepatitis B immunoglobulin (HBIG) is used in the post-exposure prophylaxis of newborns of HBV infected women. It is administered intramuscularly and may be given concurrently with HBV vaccine, at a different site. The dose for infants is 0.5 mL. Combination of HBIG and HBV vaccination in infants born to HBsAg positive mothers prevents transmission in approximately 95% of those at risk.

Treatment

There are two approved therapies for *chronic hepatitis B* in children: interferon (IFN) and lamivudine. Interferons are a group of naturally occurring agents with antiviral, antineoplastic and immunomodulatory properties. IFNα2a achieves seroconversion in approximately one-

9

third of cases; those most likely to respond have high ALT activity and a greater histological activity index score in the liver biopsy before treatment. Children younger than 6 years have an enhanced response to IFNα2b treatment. Side effects of IFN in children are flu-like symptoms, headache, depression, loss of appetite, anemia, leukopenia and thrombocytopenia. Promising results are emerging using pegylated IFN in adults with chronic hepatitis B, but data in children are lacking.

Lamivudine monotherapy for 1 year provides satisfactory results in children with chronic hepatitis B. Children with higher pretreatment ALT levels and histologic activity index scores are most likely to respond to lamivudine. The medication is well tolerated, has minimal side effects and is easy to administer. However, the development of resistant viral mutants (YMDD) limits the benefit of long-term monotherapy. Combinations of either INFα2a or INFα2b with lamivudine have comparable effects and slightly better results than monotherapy in children affected by chronic hepatitis. Other drugs including adefovir, entecavir and dipivoxil have documented clinical activity against wild and lamivudine resistant HBV, but needs to be further evaluated in children.

HEPATITIS C

Hepatitis C virus (HCV) was recognized in 1989 as a major cause of non-A, non-B hepatitis. HCV is an enveloped, single-stranded, positive-sense ribonucleic acid (RNA) virus, classified as an independent genus (*Hepacivirus*) within the Flavivirus family. The HCV genome encodes for a polyprotein, which undergoes proteolysis by viral and host-encoded proteases, resulting in the formation of the various HCV proteins. The HCV genome is organized so that its 52 end encodes for the structural proteins including the core (or capsid) and envelope proteins (E1 and E2), whereas the nonstructural (NS) or functional viral proteins (NS2-NS5) are encoded by the larger subsequent 32 segment.

Viral Variants

9

The HCV RNA-dependent RNA polymerase lacks proofreading ability, which results in HCV being genetically heterogeneous. Based on analysis of HCV sequences, six major HCV genotypes are recognized. HCV genotypes 1 and 2 are the most prevalent worldwide. HCV genotype 3 is most common in Australia and the Indian subcontinent. The viral genotypic distribution in children generally parallels that reported regionally in adults. HCV genotype 1 correlates with higher serum viral levels and a less favorable response to antiviral treatment.

Epidemiology

The worldwide prevalence of HCV infection is approximately 3%, which represents an estimated 170 million infected persons. Children who received transfusions of potentially contaminated blood products prior to the institution of routine screening have seroprevalence rates upto 95%.

Presentation

The mean incubation period of post-transfusion acute HCV infection is 7 to 8 weeks, with a range of 2 to 26 weeks. Acute HCV is usually anicteric or subclinical and only one-third of patients develop jaundice or symptoms. Fulminant hepatic failure due to HCV is rare. In adults, 85% of patients exposed to HCV will develop chronic infection, of which approximately 10 to 20% develop cirrhosis. In children, the course of HCV infection is generally benign. Most children with acute hepatitis C are asymptomatic.

When symptoms are present, they are often nonspecific (malaise, anorexia) or mild; jaundice is present in 25%. Most children exposed to HCV are at risk to become chronically infected based on persistently detectable serum anti-HCV antibodies and HCV RNA. Children with chronic HCV infection may also remain asymptomatic. Progression to decompensated liver disease in children is rare. Biochemical markers such as serum alanine aminotransferase (ALT) typically fluctuate in HCV patients. Normal or only minimally increased ALT levels are reported with chronic HCV infection, and serum ALT levels can remain elevated despite anti-HCV seronegativity. Liver histology shows portal lymphoid aggregates, bile duct injury and steatosis; necroinflammatory activity is mild.

Perinatal Transmission

The rate of vertical transmission is approximately 5–6%, which is low compared to that for hepatitis B virus and human immunodeficiency virus (HIV). High-titer maternal viremia correlates with higher transmission rates.

Diagnosis

The diagnosis of HCV infection is based on detection of antibodies against recombinant HCV antigens by enzyme immunoassay or recombinant immunoblot assay or by detection of HCV RNA using nucleic acid tests. Enzyme immunoassay is limited by frequent false-positive results, particularly in patients with elevated globulin levels such as those with autoimmune hepatitis. Recombinant immunoblot assay detects HCV immunoglobulin IgG antibodies against synthetic HCV recombinant antigens and synthetic peptides immobilized on a solid matrix. Recombinant immunoblot assays are less sensitive but more specific than enzyme immunoassay in detecting anti-HCV antibodies. Recombinant immunoblot assay is, therefore, not recommended for initial HCV screening and are useful to confirm viral infection. Nucleic acid tests directly detect circulating virus; two tests are currently used for the detection of HCV that rely on different amplification schemes, namely target and signal amplification. Nucleic acid tests identify the presence of HCV very early in the course of infection, and, therefore, are used to diagnose infection even before the anti-HCV antibodies have appeared. These tests are also necessary to detect HCV in infants born to infected mothers, in whom HCV antibodies may be of maternal origin and in immunocompromised patients whose ability to produce HCV antibodies may be impaired.

Therapy

Sustained virologic responses are achieved in only 8–35% of patients given recombinant interferon monotherapy. However, significantly higher sustained virologic responses are attained (30–40%) by combining interferon with ribavirin at 15 mg/kg/d. Longer-acting pegylated interferons have been subsequently developed based on the premise that more sustained drug levels would result in greater antiviral activity. Several randomized clinical trials in adults verify considerably better virologic responses (50–60%) with the use of pegylated interferons, particularly when given in conjunction with ribavirin. However, in general, sustained virologic response rates in children treated with interferon alone (30–60%) appear to be two- to threefold higher than in similarly treated adults. Importantly, biochemical and virologic responses have been accompanied by significant histologic improvement in all treated patients included in these trials, and interferon has been well tolerated in children.

HEPATITIS E

Hepatitis E virus was first described in 1978 after an epidemic affecting 52,000 individuals in Kashmir. Hepatitis E is caused by infection with the hepatitis E virus (HEV), a single-stranded RNA virus. The virion is nonenveloped and with a diameter of 27–34 nm, is composed entirely of viral protein and RNA. Just like HAV, HEV is transmitted from person-to-person via the fecal oral route. It is usually transmitted through contaminated drinking water. Hepatitis E virus causes acute sporadic and epidemic viral hepatitis. Symptomatic HEV infection is most common in young adults aged 15–40 years and is uncommon in children since it is mostly asymptomatic and anicteric.

Presentation

The incubation period following exposure to HEV ranges from 3 to 8 weeks, with a mean of 40 days. The clinical presentation of hepatitis E is similar to hepatitis A. The severity of an HEV infection is generally greater than the severity of an HAV infection. In pregnant women, the disease is particularly severe where mortality approaches 20% with infections in the third trimester. Premature deliveries with high infant mortality up to 33% are observed. No evidence of chronic inflammation or of a healthy chronic carrier state has been detected, and no recurrence of hepatitis E has been reported.

Diagnosis

Laboratory evaluation of HEV is similar to that of HAV. The antibody elevated in acute hepatitis E is IgM anti-HEV. The viral proteins pORF2 and pORF3 detected by enzyme immunoassay or ELISA form the basis for diagnosis. To confirm the results of these tests, Western blot assays to detect IgM and IgG anti-HEV in serum can be used, along with polymerase chain reaction tests for the detection of HEV RNA in serum and stool and liver, and immune electron microscopy to visualize viral particles in feces. Antibodies to HEV (IgM and IgG) develop at the time symptoms occur, usually before the development of jaundice. IgM anti-HEV titer declines rapidly during early convalescence, while IgG anti-HEV persists for long duration and provides protection against subsequent infections.

Vaccines

At present, there are no commercially available vaccines for the prevention of hepatitis E.

Prevention

As with HAV good personal hygiene, high quality standards for public water supplies and proper disposal of waste have resulted in a low prevalence of HEV infections in developed countries.

Treatment

As no specific therapy is capable of altering the course of acute hepatitis E infection, prevention is the most effective approach against the disease.

HEPATITIS DUE TO OTHER VIRUSES

Certain cases of post transfusion (10%) and community acquired hepatitis (20%) are of unknown origin. There are three viruses that have been potentially associated with liver disease but no conclusive evidence exists to support them as a cause for these cases. These viruses are HGV/GB virus C, TT virus and SEN virus. GB virus C (GBV-C), or HGV, is a recently discovered enveloped RNA virus that belongs to the Flavivirus family. GBV-C and HGV were independently isolated and reported by two different groups of researchers; they are 96% similar, indicating that they are two genotypes of the same virus. This virus has a predominant parenteral mode of transmission. It is found throughout the world, with a high prevalence in both healthy populations and in different patient groups. This has called into question its actual role in acute or chronic hepatitis. The tissue tropism of HGV is also not clearly established, however, it may replicate in human mononuclear cells rather than in hepatocytes. Overall, most infections are asymptomatic, and whether HGV is truly a cause of *'non A to E' hepatitis* is unlikely. TTV is a non-enveloped single-stranded DNA virus. Although TTV is found in patients with *non A to E hepatitis*, its overall prevalence has not been different between healthy individuals and patients with liver disease. It has both parenteral and non-parenteral routes of transmission. The data available for TTV does not support a significant role for this virus in children. SENV is a single-stranded DNA virus from the Circovirus family that bears some similarity to TTV. The prevalence of SENV infection is shown to increase with the volume of transfused blood, supporting the parenteral mode of transmission. About 15% of SENV-infected patients develop acute *non A to E hepatitis* temporally related to the appearance of viremia, whereas the rest do not. Several studies have documented a high prevalence of SENV infection in healthy individuals and those with acute or chronic liver disease, and have also suggested non-parenteral transmission.

Suggested reading

1. Hsu EK, Murray KF. Hepatitis B and C in children. Nat Clin Pract Gastroenterol Hepatol 2008; 5: 311-20.
2. Price N, Boxall EH. Treatment of children persistently infected with hepatitis B virus: seroconversion or suppression. J Antimicrob Chemother 2007; 60: 1189–92.
3. Koff RS. Review article: vaccination and viral hepatitis - current status and future prospects. Aliment Pharmacol Ther 2007; 26: 1285–92.
4. Heller S, Valencia-Mayoral P. Treatment of viral hepatitis in children. Arch Med Res. 2007; 38: 702–10.

DENGUE FEVER, DENGUE HEMORRHAGIC FEVER, DENGUE SHOCK SYNDROME

Dengue fever is an acute febrile illness caused by viruses belonging to the Flaviviridae family and is characterized by biphasic fever, myalgia, arthralgia and rash. Dengue hemorrhagic fever (DHF) is characterized by abnormalities in hemostasis and by marked leakage of plasma from the capillaries; the latter may lead to shock (dengue shock syndrome).

Epidemiology

The global prevalence of dengue has grown dramatically in recent decades. The disease is now endemic in more than 100 countries in Africa, the Americas, the Eastern Mediterranean, South-east Asia and the Western Pacific. South-east Asia and the Western Pacific are most seriously affected. Nearly 2.5 billion people are at risk from dengue. WHO currently estimates there may be 50 million cases of dengue infection worldwide every year.

9

During epidemics of dengue, attack rates among susceptibles are often 40–50%, but may reach 80–90%. An estimated 500,000 cases of DHF require hospitalization each year, of whom a very large proportion are children. At least 2.5% of cases die, although case fatality could be twice as high. Without proper treatment, DHF case fatality rates can exceed 20%. With modern intensive supportive therapy, such rates are reduced to less than 1%.

The spread of dengue is attributed to expanding geographic distribution of the four dengue viruses and of their mosquito vectors, the most important of which is the predominantly urban species *Aedes aegypti*. A rapid rise in urban populations is bringing ever greater numbers of people into contact with this vector, especially in areas that are favorable for mosquito breeding, e.g. where household water storage is common and where solid waste disposal services are inadequate.

Virus

Dengue fever and dengue hemorrhagic fever (DHF) are caused by infection due to any of the four serotypes of dengue viruses. Dengue viruses are arboviruses that belong to the family Flaviviridae. These viruses are spherical particles approximately 50 nm in diameter. Dengue RNA has approximately 11,000 nucleotides. The envelop protein bears epitopes that are unique to the serotypes; the antibodies to these unique epitopes neutralize by interfering with the entry of the virus into the cells. There are other epitopes that are shared between dengue viruses (dengue subgroup antigens) and other flaviviruses (group antigens).

Four well-defined types of dengue virus have been identified, called DENV-1, DENV-2, DENV-3 and DENV-4, respectively; these have distinctive genetic structures. Genotyping has been used to trace the movement of dengue viruses between different geographic regions.

Transmission

Dengue viruses are transmitted to humans through the bites of infective female *Aedes* mosquitoes. Mosquitoes generally acquire the virus while feeding on the blood of an infected person. After virus incubation for 8–10 days, an infected mosquito is capable, during probing and blood feeding, of transmitting the virus, to susceptible individuals for the rest of its life. Infected female mosquitoes may also transmit the virus to their offspring by transovarial (via the eggs) transmission, but the role of this in sustaining transmission of virus to humans has not yet been delineated.

Humans are the main amplifying host of the virus, although studies have shown that in some parts of the world monkeys may become infected and perhaps serve as a source of virus for uninfected mosquitoes. The virus circulates in the blood of infected humans for two to seven days, at approximately the same time as they have fever; *Aedes* mosquitoes may acquire the virus when they feed on an individual during this period.

Pathophysiology of the Infection and Its Consequences

The major pathophysiologic changes that determine the severity of disease in DHF and differentiate it from dengue fever are plasma leakage and abnormal hemostasis leading to rising hematocrit values, moderate to marked thrombocytopenia and varying degrees of bleeding manifestations. The cause of abnormal leakage of plasma is not entirely understood. However, rapid recovery without residual abnormality in vessels suggests it to be the result of release and interaction of biological mediators, which are capable of producing severe illness with minimal structural injury.

The pathogenesis of DHF/DSS is not clear. It has been observed that sequential infection with any two of the four serotypes of dengue virus results in DHF/DSS in an endemic area. How a second dengue infection causes severe disease and why only some patients get severe disease remains unclear. It is suggested that the residual antibodies produced during the first infection are able to neutralize a second viral infection with the same serotype. However, when no neutralizing antibodies are present (i.e. infection due to another serotype of dengue virus), the second infection is under the influence of enhancing antibodies and the resulting infection and disease are severe. An alternative explanation is that certain strains (south-east Asian) of the dengue virus may be inherently capable of supporting severe antibody-enhanced infection than viruses in other geographic area.

Serotype cross-reactive antibodies generated from previous primary infection with a particular dengue viral serotype are not highly specific for the other serotypes involved in secondary infections. Hence, they bind to the virions but do not neutralize them, and instead increase their uptake by cells, which express Fcγ receptors on their surfaces, like tissue dendritic cells, monocytes and macrophages. Such antibody-coated virions are taken up more rapidly than uncoated virus particles and this leads to enhanced antigen presentation by the infected dendritic cells to the T cells, leading to the more rapid activation and proliferation of memory T cells. The cytokines produced by the activated T cells have several important effects that lead to the pathogenesis of the DHF/DSS.

Cytokines are also implicated in the pathogenesis of vascular compromise and hemorrhage in dengue virus infection. Endothelial cell dysfunction in dengue virus infection manifests as diffuse increase in capillary permeability, which is responsible for the microvascular leakage, hemoconcentration and circulatory insufficiency. The transient nature of plasma leakage suggests that it could be mediated by a soluble mediator.

Dengue viral infection is commonly associated with thrombocytopenia, the cause of which is molecular mimicry between dengue virus proteins and endogenous self-proteins. There is generation of antibodies against dengue virus proteins (especially NS1), which cross-react with platelet surface proteins and thus cause thrombocytopenia. There is activation of blood clotting and fibrinolytic pathways. Mild disseminated intravascular coagulation, liver injury and thrombocytopenia together contribute to hemorrhagic tendency. Central nervous system involvement also has been identified and has been attributed to direct neurotropic effect of dengue virus.

Pathology

There are usually no gross or microscopic lesions that may account for death, except when massive gastrointestinal or intracranial bleeding causes death. Presence of viruses in tissues mainly leads to hemodynamic alterations with generalized vascular congestion and increased permeability, and mast cell recruitment in lungs. These findings have also been seen in animal models.

Variable hepatic involvement has been reported—diffuse hepatitis with midzonal necrosis and steatosis, focal areas of necrosis, and normal histology in some children. Dengue virus antigen can be detected using immunohistochemistry in hepatocytes from necrotic areas. Absence of recruitment of polymorphonuclear cells and lymphocytes has been observed in the liver lesions of patients who died from DHF.

Clinical Features

DHF and dengue shock syndrome (DSS) are serious clinical manifestations of the dengue infection. It is estimated that during outbreaks, about 150–200 mild to silent infections occur in the community for each case of DSS seen in the hospital.

The clinical manifestations of dengue virus infection vary from asymptomatic to severe life-threatening illness in the form of DHF/DSS (Fig. 9.4). Most dengue infections in young children are mild and indistinguishable from other common causes of febrile illnesses. Fever, headache, myalgia, arthralgia, skin rashes and malaise characterize the illness.

Some patients with dengue infection have varying degrees of mucosal and cutaneous bleeds with thrombocytopenia. These patients may not show other criteria for diagnosis of DHF/DSS, i.e. hemoconcentration or objective evidence of fluid leak (e.g. ascites, pleural effusion). These patients are classified as *dengue fever with unusual bleeding*. Patients falling in this category may be seen in significant numbers in epidemics. Since hypovolemia and hypotension do not occur in this group of children, fluid requirement is lesser than in DHF. It is therefore, important to distinguish these children from classical DHF.

DHF can occur in all age groups including infants. Risk factors for DHF/DSS are (i) virus strain: risk is greatest for DENV-2 followed by DENV-3, DENV-4 and DENV-1; (ii) pre-existing anti-dengue antibody; (iii) age of host: younger children are at increased risk; (iv) secondary infection; (v) genetics: there may be existence of human dengue resistance gene, which offer protection; and (vi) hyperendemicity—two or more serotypes may be circulating simultaneously at high level.

Typically, after an incubation period of 4–6 days the patients may develop abrupt onset of high-grade fever, facial flushing and headache. Anorexia, vomiting, pain in abdomen and tenderness over the right costal margin are common. There may be varying degrees of tender hepatomegaly. Spleen is less commonly enlarged. All

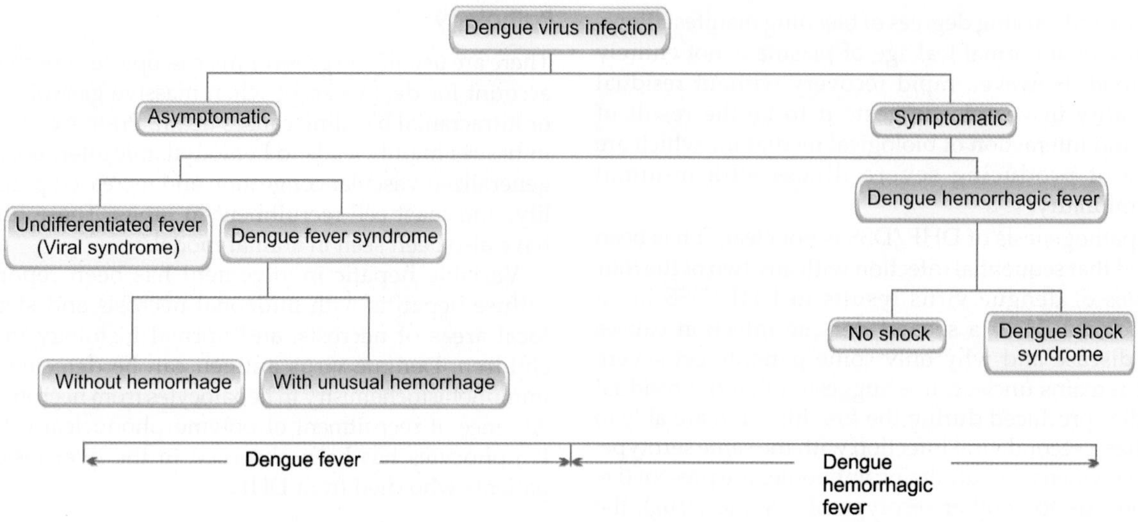

Dengue virus infection
Asymptomatic
Symptomatic
Undifferentiated fever (Viral syndrome)
Dengue fever syndrome
Dengue hemorrhagic fever
Without hemorrhage
With unusual hemorrhage
No shock
Dengue shock syndrome
Dengue fever
Dengue hemorrhagic fever

Fig. 9.4: Manifestations of dengue virus infection

patients have some hemorrhagic phenomena in form of positive tourniquet test, petechial spots, bruising at venepuncture sites, bleeding from gums, epistaxis, hemetemesis or melena. Occasionally, adolescent girls may have bleeding per vaginum that mimics menstrual bleeding. Rarely bleeding from ears, muscle hematoma, hematuria or intracranial hemorrhage may occur.

Fever may subside after 2–7 days. At this stage, the child may show varying degrees of peripheral circulatory failure, characterized by excessive sweating, restlessness and cold extremities. Initially the pulse pressure is narrow; the blood pressure later starts falling, leading to unrecordable blood pressure and irreversible shock. Prior to the child becoming afebrile, thrombocytopenia and a rise in hematocrit occur; these features are characteristic of the disease. Patients with shock and bleeding manifestations, usually show increase in hematocrit and thrombocytopenia. Unusual manifestations of DHF/DSS include hepatitis, encephalitis and glomerulonephritis. Myocardial dysfunction has also been reported.

Grading of DHF

The presence of thrombocytopenia with concurrent hemoconcentration differentiates DHF from dengue fever. Based on clinical features, DHF is classified into four grades of severity. Grades III and IV define DSS (Table 9.4).

Diagnosis

Diseases which may mimic DHF/DSS include infections due to gram-negative organisms such as meningococcemia, typhoid and rarely plague. Occasionally, falciparum malaria may manifest with fever and bleeding, but is distinguished by the presence of splenomegaly and pallor. The following features are useful for making a provisional diagnosis of DHF/DSS:

Clinical

Acute onset high fever, hemorrhagic manifestations (at least a positive tourniquet test), hepatomegaly and shock

Table 9.4: Grading of dengue hemorrhagic fever (DHF)

	Clinical features	*Bleeding manifestations*	*Hemodynamic status*
Grade I	Fever with non-specific constitutional symptoms	Positive tourniquet test* and/or easy bruising	Tachycardia; normal blood and pulse pressures
Grade II	Fever with non-specific constitutional symptoms	Spontaneous bleeding, usually in form of skin/other bleeds	Tachycardia; normal blood and pulse pressures
Grade III DSS	Same as Grade I/II; may present with cold peripheries	Spontaneous bleeding may be present	Circulatory failure: rapid weak pulse, narrow pulse pressure, hypotension, cold clammy skin, restlessness
Grade IV DSS	Same as Grade I/II; may present with cold peripheries and features of organ hypoperfusion	Spontaneous bleeding may be present	Profound shock; undetectable blood pressure or peripheral pulse

DSS dengue shock syndrome

*An appropriate sized cuff is applied to the arm, and inflated to between the systolic and diastolic blood pressures for five minutes. The test is positive if there are more than 20 petechiae/ square inch.

Laboratory

Thrombocytopenia (less than 100,000 cells/mm^3), hemoconcentration (hematocrit elevated at least 20% above the standard for age, sex and population baseline or baseline hematocrit)

Two clinical features and one laboratory finding (or rising hematocrit) are sufficient to make a provisional diagnosis of DHF. A rise in hematocrit of 20% over the baseline can be documented if the hematocrit is monitored regularly from the early stages of illness. Since patients are likely to present with symptoms suggestive of DHF, a drop in hemoglobin or hematocrit of more than 20% following volume replacement therapy can be taken as an indication of previous hemoconcentration. Hematocrit can, however, be affected by various factors including baseline anemia, time of hematocrit estimation during illness and blood loss. In monitoring hematocrit, one should bear in mind the possible effects of pre-existing anemia, severe hemorrhage or early volume replacement therapy.

Presence of pleural effusion on X-ray film of chest or hypoalbuminemia provide supportive evidence of plasma leakage, the distinguishing feature of DHF. In a patient with suspected DHF, the presence of shock suggests the diagnosis of DSS.

Investigations

Demonstration of dengue virus on culture or demonstration of antibodies against dengue virus are required for confirming dengue infection (Table 9.5). Viral isolation is recommended if the blood sample is taken within 5 days of the onset of fever while serologic methods are used if blood samples are taken after defervescence or during convalescence.

Commonly used serologic tests to detect antibodies include MAC-ELISA test and hemagglutination inhibition test. MAC-ELISA test measures dengue specific IgM antibodies and suggests recent infection with dengue virus. The hemagglutination inhibition test measures IgG antibodies; it is a simple, sensitive and reproducible test but requires paired sera collected at interval of 1–2 weeks. Positive test result indicates a recent infection due to flavivirus. A strip test is commercially available, which requires a drop of serum and gives results within few minutes. Quantitation of the IgG and IgM antibodies may help in differentiating between primary and secondary dengue virus infections. IgG antibodies will be abundant in secondary infection unlike primary infection.

Table 9.5: Diagnostic tests for dengue fever

Period	*Tests*
Within first 5 days of onset of fever	Viral isolation from blood (inoculated either in suckling mice, tissue cultures of mammalian or mosquito origin)
After defervescence or in convalescent phase	*Serologic tests* IgM: MAC-ELISA; strip test IgG: Hemagglutination inhibition test; strip test

Meticulous attention has to be paid towards sample collection and transport of clinical samples for virus isolation. Samples may be inoculated either in suckling mice or in various tissue cultures of mammalian or mosquito origin.

Children with DHF/DSS show increasing hemotocrit, thrombocytopenia, increased white cell counts with relative lymphocytosis. The peripheral smear may show transformed lymphocytes. In severe illness with prolonged shock, there may be evidence of disseminated intravascular coagulation. Blood levels of total protein and albumin are low, especially in patients with shock. Levels of transaminases are raised; a higher increase in levels of SGOT than SGPT suggests the possibility of DHF rather than hepatitis due to other virus. In severe cases, there may be hyponatremia, acidosis and increased blood levels of urea and creatinine.

X-ray film of the chest may show varying degrees of pleural effusion, commonly on the right side, occasionally bilateral. Ultrasonography of abdomen may show enlarged gall bladder due to wall edema. Abnormal electrocardiogram and myocardial dysfunction on echocardiogram have been reported.

Treatment

The treatment of dengue fever is symptomatic. Fever is treated with paracetamol. Salicylates and other nonsteroidal anti-inflammatory drugs should be avoided as these may predispose a child to mucosal bleeds. In an epidemic setting, all patients with dengue fever need regular monitoring by a primary care physician for early detection of DHF. The primary care physician/health care worker should monitor the patient for clinical features of DHF/DSS along with hematocrit and platelet counts, if possible. Any patient developing cold extremities, restlessness, acute abdominal pain, decreased urine output, bleeding and hemoconcentration should be admitted in a hospital. Children with rising hematocrit and thrombocytopenia without clinical symptoms should also be admitted. Children should be encouraged to improve the oral fluid intake. Electrolyte solutions such as WHO oral rehydration salt solutions may be preferred over plain water.

DHF/DSS

The management discussed here is based on guidelines issued by the WHO. The WHO guidelines are useful in that they offer an algorithmic approach to fluid resuscitation of DHF and DSS. As there are no specific antiviral medications for dengue infections, supportive and aggressive fluid therapy are the cornerstone of management. Early recognition of these conditions is crucial for decreasing the case fatality rates.

In the hospital, all children without hypotension (DHF grades I and II) should be given Ringer's lactate infusion at the rate of 7 ml/kg over one hour. After one hour if hematocrit decreases and vital parameters improve, fluid infusion rate should be decreased to 5 ml/kg over next hour and to 3 ml/kg/hour for 24–48 hours. When the patient is stable as indicated by normal blood pressure, satisfactory oral intake and urine output, the child can be discharged (Fig. 9.5).

If at one hour the hematocrit is rising and vital parameters do not show improvement, fluid infusion rate is increased to 10 ml/kg over next hour. In case of no improvement fluid infusion rate is further increased to 15 ml/kg over the third hour. Patients showing no improvement in vital parameters and hematocrit at end of 3 hours, should be treated with colloids or plasma infusion (10 ml/kg) (Fig. 9.5). Once the hematocrit and vital parameters are stable, the infusion rate is gradually reduced and discontinued over 24–48 hours.

In children with hypotension (DSS grade III) Ringer's lactate solution, 10–20 ml/kg is infused over one hour or as bolus if blood pressure is unrecordable (DSS grade IV). The bolus may be repeated twice if there is no improvement. If there is no improvement in vital parameters and hematocrit is rising, colloids 10 ml/kg are rapidly infused. If the hematocrit is falling without improvement in vital parameters, blood is transfused presuming that lack of improvement is due to occult blood loss (Fig. 9.6). Once improvement starts then fluid infusion rate is gradually decreased. In addition to fluids, oxygen should be administered to all patients in shock.

For uncontrolled bleeding in DHF or DSS, the role of plasma or platelet infusion remains unclear. Infusion of fresh frozen plasma and platelet concentrates may be beneficial in patients with disseminated intravascular coagulation.

Monitoring

In view of the rapid course in DHF and DSS, close monitoring of the patient is crucial in the first few hours of illness. Heart rate, respiratory rate, blood pressure and pulse pressure should be measured every 30 minutes until the patient is stable and thereafter every 2–4 hours. Central venous pressure monitoring is desirable in children who develop hypotension. Difficulties are often encountered in insertion of central lines in critically ill small children.

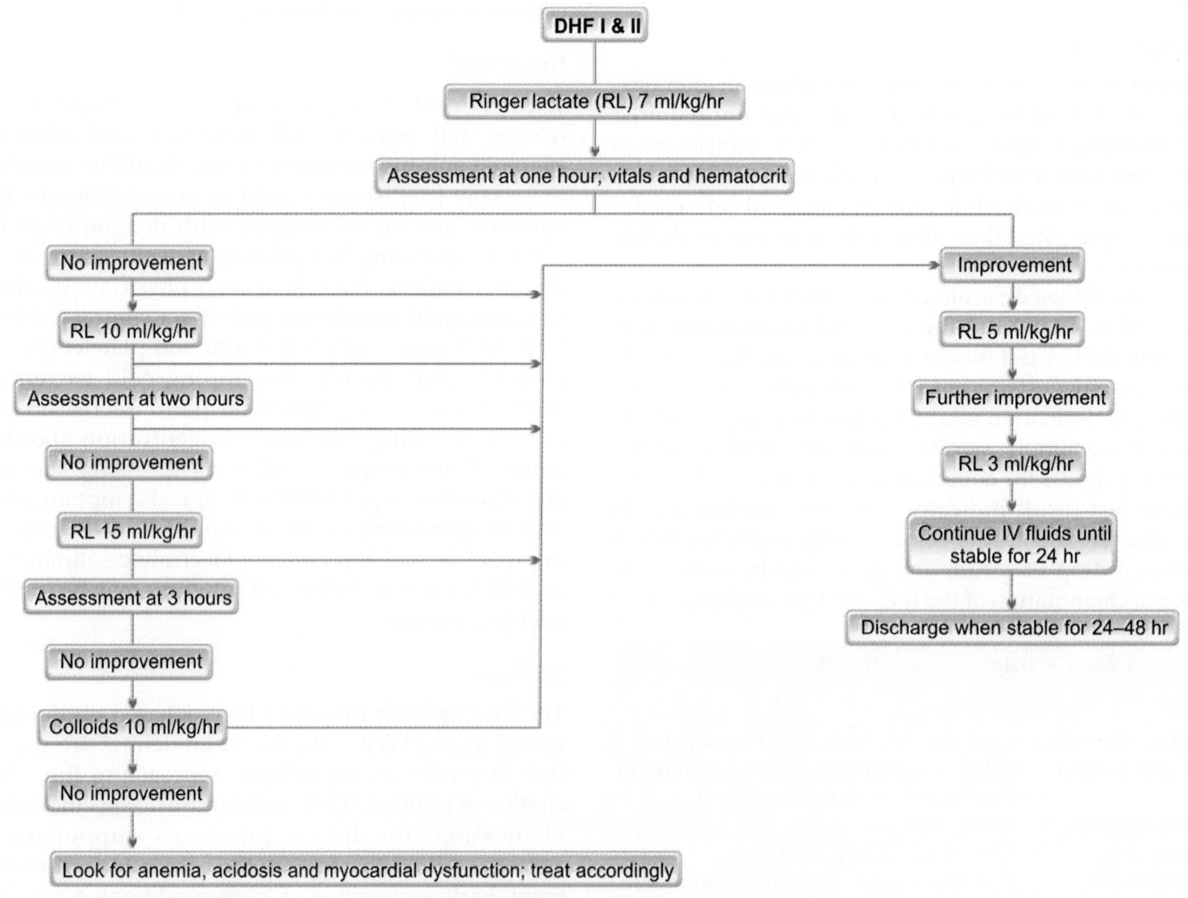

Fig. 9.5: Intravenous fluid therapy in patients with DHF

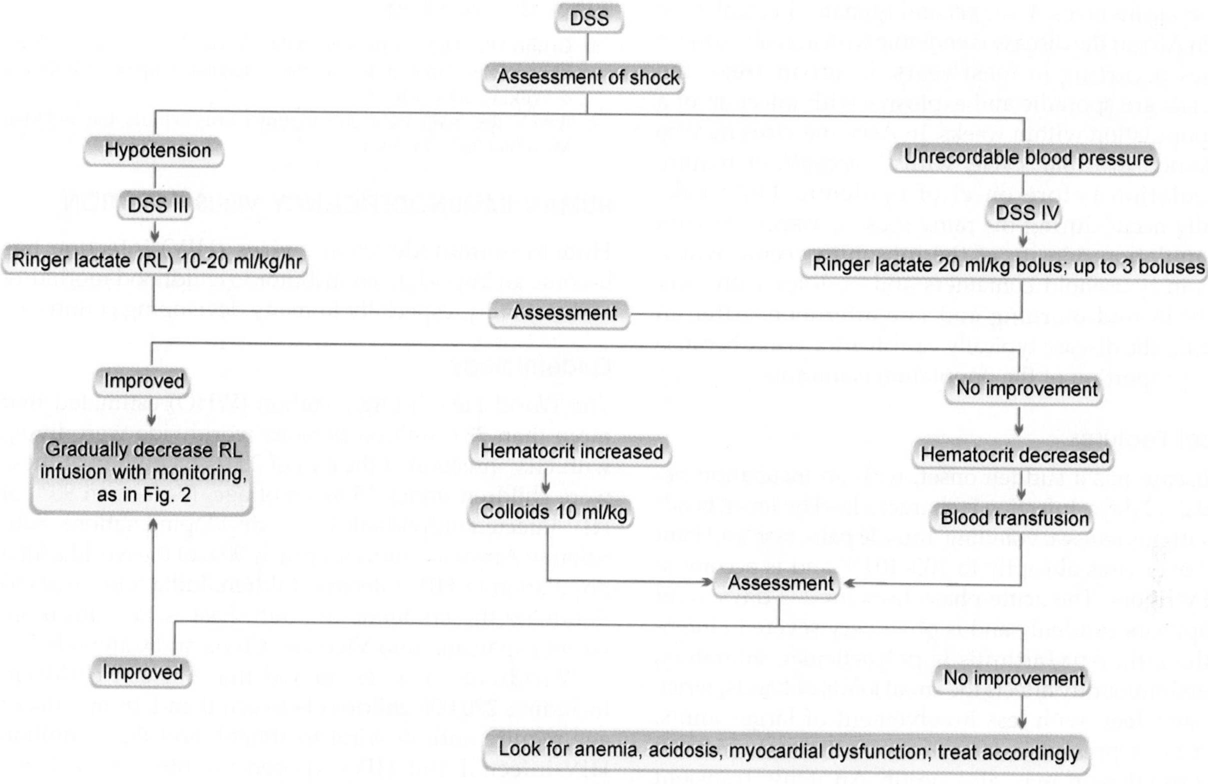

Fig. 9.6: Treatment of patients with dengue shock syndrome (DSS)

Laboratory monitoring includes hematocrit measurement every 2-hours for the first 6 hours or until stable. Platelet counts are estimated daily until they show a rising trend. These may be repeated and coagulation studies performed if there is uncontrolled bleeding. If insertion of a central line is not feasible, clinical and hematocrit monitoring every 30 minutes, guides the rate of fluid infusion. It is emphasized that infusion rates decrease rapidly in the first 6-hours following intervention in most patients with DSS and DHF.

Prognosis

If left untreated, the mortality in patients with DHF or DSS may be as high as 40–50%. Early recognition of illness, careful monitoring and appropriate fluid therapy alone has resulted in reduction in mortality to 1–5%. Early recognition of shock is of paramount importance as the outcome in DSS depends on the duration of shock. If shock is identified and treated early (e.g. when pulse pressure starts getting narrow), the outcome is excellent. Recovery is fast and majority of the patients recover in 24–48 hours without sequelae. The outcome may not be as good once patient develops cold extremities. The prognosis is unsatisfactory in patients with prolonged shock and if blood pressure is not recordable.

Suggested Reading

1. Nimmannitya S. Clinical manifestations of dengue/dengue hemorrhagic fever. In: Monograph on dengue/dengue hemorrhagic fever. New Delhi, World Health Organization, 1993; 48–54.
2. Dengue haemorrhagic fever, diagnosis, treatment, prevention and control; 2nd edn, Geneva, World Health Organization, 1997; pp 12–23.
3. Kabra SK, Jain Y, Pandey RM, *et al.* Dengue hemorrhagic fever in children in the 1996 Delhi epidemic. Trans Royal Society Trop Med Hygiene 1999: 93: 294–8.

CHIKUNGUNYA

Chikungunya is an acute disease, which results in fever, arthritis and skin rash, caused by an enveloped virus capable of replicating in mosquitoes. Because of severe arthritic symptoms, the disease is given the Swahili name of chikungunya (that which bends up). Since an outbreak of chikungunya in Tanzania in 1952, large epidemics were reported in South Africa, India (1971), South East Asia and Philippines. Re-emergence of chikungunya disease occurred in India during 2005–06, causing 1.3 million cases in 13 states, chiefly Andhra Pradesh and Karnataka.

9

Epidemiology

The rural cycle of chikungunya transmission involves *Aedes africans*, *A. fancifer*, and wild primates, while the urban cycle involves *A. aegypti* and humans. In rural cycle (seen in Africa) the disease is endemic with a small number of cases occurring in most years. In urban areas, the outbreaks are sporadic and explosive with infection of a large population within weeks. In Asia, the virus may be maintained in urban cycle, with *A. aegypti*, or require reinoculation before onset of epidemic. Outbreaks typically occur during the rainy season, associated with the population density of the mosquito vector, which breeds in household containers and puddles with peak activity in mid-morning and late afternoon. After an epidemic, the disease typically vanishes for years, because a large proportion of the population is immune.

Clinical Features

The disease has a sudden onset, with an incubation period of 2–12 days. Infection is characterized by fever, headache, fatigue, nausea, vomiting, muscle pain, rash and joint pain. Fever rises abruptly to 103–104°F and is accompanied by rigors. The acute phase lasts for 2–3 days. Joint pain appears suddenly and is often very severe in intensity; the arthralgia/arthritis is polyarticular, migratory, and predominantly affects the small joints of hands, wrist, ankle and feet, with less involvement of larger joints. Headache is present in 80% of cases. Photophobia and retro-orbital pain may also occur. An itchy, transient maculopapular rash appears 4–8 days later affecting the trunk and limbs. Inguinal lymph nodes may be enlarged. The joint pains may continue for many months after the illness. Fatalities are rare and associated with young age, thrombocytopenia and shock.

Diagnosis

Chikungunya should be suspected in patients who presents with the characteristic triad of fever, rash and arthritis. Viremia is present in most patients during the initial 2–4 days of disease and may be isolated in cell cultures. Polymerase chain reaction can be used to confirm the infection. Virus specific IgM antibodies may be detected by capture ELISA and haemagglutination inhibition assays by 5–7 days of illness.

Treatment

No specific treatment is available. Symptomatic treatment in the form of rest, fluids, and ibuprofen, naproxen, acetaminophen, or paracetamol may relieve symptoms. Aspirin should be avoided during acute phase of illness.

Prevention and Control

Strategies for prevention and control include breaking the transmission cycle of *A. aegypti* and by holding the mosquito population at extremely low levels. A live attenuated vaccine, developed recently, which induces long-term production of neutralizing antibodies, is being examined.

Suggested reading

1. Griffin DE. Alphaviruses. In: MD, Howley PM. Fields Virology, Philadelphia 5th edn; Knipe. Phialadelphia: Lippincott Williams & Wilkins; 2007: 1047–8.
2. Ravi V. Reemergence of chikungunya virus in India. Indian J Med Microbiol 2006; 24: 83–4.

HUMAN IMMUNODEFICIENCY VIRUS INFECTION

Human immunodeficiency virus (HIV) infection has become an important contributor to childhood morbidity and mortality, especially in many developing countries.

Epidemiology

The World Health Organization (WHO) estimated that more than 38.6 million persons worldwide were living with HIV infection at the end of 2007; 2.3 million of these were children under 15 years of age. More than 90% of HIV-infected individuals live in developing nations. Sub-Saharan Africa accounts for nearly 90% of the world's total population of HIV-infected children. India and Thailand dominate the epidemic in South-East Asia, with more recent expansion into Vietnam, China and Cambodia.

Worldwide, it is estimated that 660,000 children, including 270,000 children between 0 and 18 months of age require antiretroviral treatment, and that 4 million HIV-infected and HIV-exposed infants and children require cotrimoxazole prophylaxis from 6 weeks of age to prevent *Pneumocystis jiroveci* pneumonia. Without access to antiretroviral therapy, 20% of vertically infected children will progress to acquired immunodeficiency syndrome (AIDS) or death in their first year of life and more than half of HIV-infected children will die before their fifth birthday.

HIV-1 and HIV-2

HIV-1 and HIV-2 are members of the Retroviridae family and belong to the *Lentivirus* genus. The HIV-1 genome is single-stranded RNA that is 9.2 kb in size. The genome has three major sections: the gag region, which encodes the viral core proteins (p24, p17, p9, p6; these are derived from the precursor p55), the pol region, which encodes the viral enzymes (reverse transcriptase [p51], protease [p10], and integrase [p32]); and the env region, which encodes the viral envelope proteins (gp120 and gp41).

The major external viral protein of HIV-1 is a heavily glycosylated gp120 protein which contains the binding site for the CD4 molecule, the most common T lymphocyte surface receptor for HIV. Most HIV strains have a specific tropism for one of the chemokines: the fusion-inducing molecule, CXCR-4, which has been shown to act as a co-receptor for HIV attachment to lymphocytes, and CCR-5, a β chemokine receptor that facilitates HIV entry into macrophages.

Following viral attachment, gp120 and the CD4 molecule undergo conformational changes, allowing gp41 to interact with the fusion receptor on the cell surface. Viral fusion with the cell membrane allows entry of viral RNA into the cell cytoplasm. Viral DNA copies are then transcribed from the virion RNA through viral reverse transcriptase enzyme activity, and duplication of the DNA copies produces double-stranded circular DNA. Because the HIV-1 reverse transcriptase is error-prone, many mutations arise, creating wide genetic variation in HIV-1 isolates even within an individual patient. The circular DNA is transported into the cell nucleus where it is integrated into chromosomal DNA; this is called as the provirus. The provirus can remain dormant for extended periods.

HIV-1 transcription is followed by translation. A capsid polyprotein is cleaved to produce, among other products, the virus-specific protease (p10). This enzyme is critical for HIV-1 assembly. The RNA genome is then incorporated into the newly formed viral capsid. As the new virus is formed, it buds through the cell membrane and is released.

HIV-2 is a rare cause of infection in children. It is most prevalent in Western and Southern Africa. If HIV-2 is suspected, a specific test that detects antibody to HIV-2 peptides should be used.

Transmission

Transmission of HIV-1 occurs via sexual contact, parenteral exposure to blood, or vertical transmission from mother to child. The primary route of infection in the pediatric population is vertical transmission. Most large studies in the United States and Europe have documented mother-to-child transmission rates in untreated women between 12–30%. In contrast, transmission rates in Africa and Asia are higher, up to 50%.

Vertical transmission of HIV can occur during the intrauterine or intrapartum periods, or through breastfeeding. Up to 30% of infected newborns are infected in utero. The highest percentages of HIV-infected children acquire the virus intrapartum. Breastfeeding is an important route of transmission, especially in the developing countries. The risk factors for vertical transmission include preterm delivery (<34 wk gestation), a low maternal antenatal CD4 count, use of illicit drugs during pregnancy, >4 hours duration of ruptured membranes and birth weight <2500 g.

Transfusions of infected blood or blood products have accounted for a variable proportion of all pediatric AIDS cases. Heat treatment of factor VIII concentrate and HIV antibody screening of donors has virtually eliminated HIV transmission to children with hemophilia. Blood donor screening has dramatically reduced, but not eliminated, the risk of transfusion-associated HIV infection. Sexual contact is a major route of transmission in the adolescent population.

Natural History

Before highly active antiretroviral therapy (HAART) was available, three distinct patterns of disease were described in children. Approximately 10–20% of HIV-infected newborns in developed countries presented with a rapid disease course, with onset of symptoms of AIDS during the first few months of life and, if untreated, death from AIDS-related complications by 4 years of age. In resource-poor countries, >85% of the HIV-infected newborns may have such a rapidly progressing disease.

It has been suggested that if intrauterine infection coincides with the period of rapid expansion of CD4 cells in the fetus, it could effectively infect the majority of the body's immunocompetent cells. Most children in this group have a positive HIV-1 culture and/or detectable virus in the plasma in the first 48 hours of life. This early evidence of viral presence suggests that the newborn was infected in utero. In contrast to the viral load in adults, the viral load in infants stays high for at least the first 2 years of life.

The majority of perinatally infected newborns (60–80%) present with a second pattern that of a much slower progression of disease with a median survival time of 6 years. Many patients in this group have a negative viral culture or PCR in the 1st week of life and are, therefore, considered to be infected intrapartum. In a typical patient, the viral load rapidly increases by 2–3 months of age (median 100,000 copies/mL) and then slowly declines over a period of 24 months. This observation can be explained partially by the immaturity of the immune system in newborns and infants. The third pattern of disease (i.e. long-term survivors) occurs in a small percentage (<5%) of perinatally infected children who have minimal or no progression of disease with relatively normal CD4 counts and very low viral loads for longer than 8 years.

HIV-infected children have changes in the immune system that are similar to those in HIV-infected adults. CD4 cell depletion may be less dramatic because infants normally have a relative lymphocytosis. Therefore, for example, a value of 1,500 CD4 cells/mm^3 in children <1 year of age is indicative of severe CD4 depletion and is comparable to <200 CD4 cells/mm^3 in adults. Lymphopenia is relatively rare in perinatally infected children and is usually only seen in older children or those with end-stage disease.

B-cell activation occurs in most children early in the infection as evidenced by hypergammaglobulinemia associated with high levels of anti-HIV-1 antibody. This response may reflect both dysregulation of T-cell suppression of B-cell antibody synthesis and active CD4 enhancement of B-lymphocyte humoral responses.

CD4 depletion and inadequate antibody responses lead to increased susceptibility to various infections and the clinical manifestations vary with the severity of immunodeficiency.

Clinical Manifestations

The clinical manifestations of HIV infection vary widely among infants, children, and adolescents. In most infants, physical examination at birth is normal. Initial signs and symptoms may be subtle and non-specific, such as lymphadenopathy, hepatosplenomegaly, failure to thrive, chronic or recurrent diarrhea, interstitial pneumonia, or oral thrush, and may be distinguishable from other causes only by their persistence. Whereas systemic and pulmonary findings are common in the United States and Europe, chronic diarrhea, wasting, and severe malnutrition predominate in Africa. Symptoms found more commonly in children than adults with HIV infection include recurrent bacterial infections, chronic parotid swelling, lymphocytic interstitial pneumonitis (LIP) and early onset of progressive neurologic deterioration.

The HIV classification system is used to categorize the stage of pediatric disease by using two parameters: clinical status (Table 9.6) and degree of immunologic impairment (Table 9.7).

Opportunistic Infections

Children with HIV infection and advanced or severe immunosuppression are susceptible to develop various opportunistic infections. The important pathogens are

Table 9.6: WHO clinical staging of HIV/ AIDS for children with confirmed HIV infection

Clinical Stage 1	
Asymptomatic	Persistent generalized lymphadenopathy
Clinical Stage 2	
Unexplained persistent hepatosplenomegaly	Papular pruritic eruptions
Fungal nail infection	Angular cheilitis
Lineal gingival erythema	Extensive wart virus infection
Extensive molluscum contagiosum	Recurrent oral ulceration
Unexplained persistent parotid enlargement	Herpes zoster
Recurrent or chronic upper respiratory tract infections (otitis media, otorrhoea, sinusitis, tonsillitis)	
Clinical Stage 3	
Unexplained moderate malnutrition or wasting not adequately responding to standard therapy	
Unexplained persistent diarrhoea (14 days or more)	
Unexplained persistent fever (above 37.5° C intermittent or constant, for longer than one month)	
Persistent oral candidiasis (after the first 6–8 weeks of life)	
Oral hairy leukoplakia	
Acute necrotizing ulcerative gingivitis or periodontitis	
Lymph node or pulmonary tuberculosis	
Severe, recurrent bacterial pneumonia	
Symptomatic lymphoid interstitial pneumonitis	
Chronic lung disease including bronchiectasis	
Unexplained anemia (<8 g/dl), neutropenia (<0.5 × 10^9/L) or chronic thrombocytopenia (<50 × 10^9/L)	
Clinical Stage 4	
Unexplained severe wasting, stunting or severe malnutrition not responding to standard therapy	
Pneumocystis pneumonia	
Recurrent severe bacterial infections (e.g. empyema, pyomyositis, bone or joint infection, meningitis)	
Chronic herpes simplex infection (orolabial, cutaneous >1 month duration or visceral at any site)	
Esophageal candidiasis (or candidiasis of trachea, bronchi, lungs)	
Extrapulmonary or disseminated TB	
Kaposi sarcoma	
Cytomegalovirus infection: retinitis or CMV infection affecting another organ, with onset at age >1 month	
Central nervous system toxoplasmosis (after one month of life)	
Extrapulmonary cryptococcosis (including meningitis)	
HIV encephalopathy	
Disseminated endemic mycosis (extrapulmonary histoplasmosis, coccidioidomycosis)	
Disseminated non-tuberculous mycobacterial infection	
Chronic cryptosporidiosis (with diarrhea)	
Chronic isosporiasis	
Cerebral or B cell non-Hodgkin lymphoma	
Progressive multifocal leukoencephalopathy	
Symptomatic HIV-associated nephropathy or HIV-associated cardiomyopathy	

Unexplained refers to where the condition is not explained by other causes
[a] Some additional conditions can also be included in regional classifications (e.g. reactivation of American trypanosomiasis in Americas region, penicilliosis in Asia and HIV-associated rectovaginal fistula in Africa)

Table 9.7: Classification of severity of immune suppression in relation to CD4 levels

	Age-related CD4 cell values			
	<11 months (CD4%)	*12–35 months (CD4%)*	*36–59 months (CD4%)*	*≥ 5 years (cells/mm^3)*
Not significant	>35	>30	>25	>500
Mild	30–35	25–30	20–25	350–499
Advanced	25–30	20–25	15–20	200–349
Severe	<25% or <1500/mm^3	<20% or <750/mm^3	<15% or <350/mm^3	<15% or <200/mm^3

Pneumocystis jiroveci, cryptosporidium, cryptococcus, isospora and CMV.

P. jiroveci (previously *P. carinii*) *pneumonia* (PCP) is the opportunistic infection that led to the initial description of AIDS. PCP is one of the commonest AIDS-defining illnesses in children in the US and Europe. However, data regarding the incidence of PCP in children in other parts of the world are scarce. The majority of the cases occur between 3rd and 6th months of life. Even if a child develops PCP while on prophylaxis, therapy may be started with TMP/SMX. This is because the prophylaxis may have failed because of poor compliance, or unusual pharmacokinetics. Untreated, PCP is universally fatal. With the use of appropriate therapy, the mortality decreases to less than 10%. The risk factors for mortality are the severity of the episode, and the severity of the immunosuppression.

Recurrent bacterial infections: In various studies from developing countries, up to 90% of HIV-infected children had history of recurrent pneumonias. Initial episodes of pneumonia often occur before the development of significant immunosuppression. As the immunosuppression increases the frequency increases. The common pathogens for community-acquired pneumonia in these children are *S. pneumoniae, H. influenzae* and *S. aureus*. However, in children with severe immunosuppression and in hospital-acquired infections, gram negative organisms, such as, *P. aeruginosa* gain importance. The clinical features of pneumonia in HIV-infected children are similar to those in uninfected children. However, in severely immunocompromised children, the signs may be subtle. The response to therapy is usually slow, bacteremia is common and relapse rates are high.

The choice of appropriate therapy is based on the local patterns of etiologies. In many settings, an appropriate choice would be a combination of a broad-spectrum cephalosporin and an aminoglycoside. In areas where a large proportion of *S. aureus* isolates are resistant to antistaphylococcal antibiotics (MRSA), then the empiric inclusion of vancomycin, clindamycin, linezolid, or other drugs to which community-acquired MRSA is usually susceptible should be considered. Children with non-severe pneumonia can be managed as outpatients using a second- or a third-generation cephalosporin or a combination like- amoxicillin-clauvulanic acid. Since *P. jiroveci* pneumonia cannot be excluded at the outset in most HIV-infected children with severe respiratory infections, cotrimoxazole should be added unless another diagnosis has been definitively made.

The principles of supportive care of HIV-infected children admitted with severe pneumonia are similar to those in non-HIV-infected children.

Tuberculosis is an important infection associated with HIV. Co-existent TB and HIV infections accelerate the progression of both the diseases. HIV-infected children are more likely to have extrapulmonary and disseminated tuberculosis; the course is also likely to be more rapid. The overall risk of active TB in children infected with HIV is at least 5- to 10-fold higher than that in children not infected with HIV. All HIV-infected children with active TB should receive antitubercular therapy for 9–12 months. A close follow-up is essential to diagnose non-response/drug resistance early.

Viral infections due to respiratory syncytial virus (RSV), influenza and parainfluenza viruses result in symptomatic disease more often in HIV-infected children in comparison to non-infected children. Infections with other viruses such as adenovirus and measles virus are more likely to lead to serious sequelae than with the previously mentioned viruses. As RSV infections most often occur in children in the first 2 years of life, during which many of these may not be severely immunocompromised, the severity of illness may not be different from the non-HIV-infected children. In children with AIDS, disseminated CMV is a known opportunistic infection, but pneumonia caused by this virus is rare. The principles of diagnosis and treatment of these infections in HIV-infected children are similar to those in non-HIV-infected children.

Fungal infections usually present as a part of disseminated disease in immunocompromised children. Pulmonary candidiasis should be suspected in any sick HIV-infected child with lower respiratory tract infection that does not respond to common therapies.

Lymphoid Interstitial Pneumonitis (LIP)

LIP is recognized as a distinctive marker for pediatric HIV infection and is included as a Class B condition in the revised criteria for AIDS in children. In absence of antiretroviral therapy, nearly 20% of HIV-infected children developed LIP. The pathogenesis of LIP are not well understood, but might include an exaggerated immunologic response to inhaled or circulating antigens, and/or primary infection of the lung with HIV or Epstein-Barr virus (EBV).

LIP is characterized by nodule formation and diffuse infiltration of the alveolar septae by lymphocytes, plasmacytoid lymphocytes, plasma cells and immunoblasts. There is no involvement of the blood vessels or destruction of the lung tissue. Children with LIP have a relatively good prognosis compared to other children who meet the surveillance definition of AIDS. LIP is usually diagnosed in children with perinatally acquired HIV infection when they are older than 1-year of age, unlike PCP. Most children with LIP are asymptomatic. Tachypnea, cough, wheezing and hypoxemia may be seen when children present with more severe manifestations; crepitations are uncommon. Clubbing is often present in advanced disease. These patients can progress to chronic respiratory failure. Long standing LIP may be associated with chronic bronchiectasis. The presence of a reticulonodular pattern, with or without hilar lymphadenopathy that persists on chest radiograph for 2 months or more, or is unresponsive to antimicrobial therapy is considered presumptive evidence of LIP. Care should be taken to exclude other possible etiologies. A definitive diagnosis is made on histopathology.

Early disease is managed conservatively. The effect of antiretrovirals on LIP is probably limited. Steroids are indicated if children with LIP have symptoms and signs of chronic pulmonary disease, clubbing and/or hypoxemia. Treatment usually includes an initial 4- to 12-week course of prednisolone (2 mg/kg/d) followed by a tapering dose, using oxygen saturation and clinical status as a guide to improvement. This is then followed by chronic low dose prednisolone.

Gastrointestinal Disease

The pathologic changes in the gastrointestinal tract of children with AIDS are variable and can be clinically significant. A variety of microbes can cause gastrointestinal disease, including bacteria (salmonella, campylobacter, *Mycobacterium avium intracellulare* complex), protozoa (giardia, cryptosporidium, isospora, microsporidia), viruses (CMV, HSV, rotavirus), and *Candida*. The protozoal infections are most severe and can be protracted in children with severe immunosuppression. Children with cryptosporidium infestation can have severe diarrhea leading to hypovolemic shock; this may merit admission to PICU. AIDS enteropathy, a syndrome of malabsorption with partial villous atrophy not associated with a specific pathogen, is probably the result of direct HIV infection of the gut.

Chronic liver inflammation is relatively common in HIV infected children. In some children, hepatitis caused by CMV, hepatitis B or C viruses, or mycobacteria (MAC) may lead to liver failure and portal hypertension. It is important to recognize that several of the antiretroviral drugs such as didanosine, and protease inhibitors may also cause reversible elevation of transaminases.

Pancreatitis is uncommon in HIV infected children. This may be the result of drug therapy, e.g. didanosine, lamivudine, nevirapine or pentamidine. Rarely, opportunistic infections such as MAC or CMV may be responsible for acute pancreatitis.

Neurologic Invovement

The incidence of central nervous system (CNS) involvement in perinatally infected children may be more than 50% in developing countries but lower in developed countries, with a median onset at about one and a half years of age. The most common presentation is progressive encephalopathy with loss or plateau of developmental milestones, cognitive deterioration, impaired brain growth resulting in acquired microcephaly, and symmetric motor dysfunction. CNS infections- meningitis due to bacterial pathogens, fungi such as *Cryptococcus* and a number of viruses may be responsible for clinical presentations that are indications for ICU admissions. CNS toxoplasmosis is exceedingly rare in young infants, but may occur in HIV-infected adolescents; the overwhelming majority of these cases have serum IgG antitoxoplasma antibodies as a marker of infection. The management of these conditions is similar to that in non HIV-infected children; the response rates and outcomes may be poorer.

Cardiovascular Involvement

Cardiac abnormalities in HIV-infected children are common, persistent, and often progressive; however, the majority of these are sub-clinical. Left ventricular (LV) structure and function progressively may deteriorate in the first 3 years of life, resulting in subsequent persistent mild LV dysfunction and increased LV mass in HIV-infected children. Children with encephalopathy or other AIDS-defining conditions have the highest rate of adverse cardiac outcomes. Resting sinus tachycardia is reported in up to nearly two-thirds and marked sinus arrhythmia in one-fifth of HIV-infected children. Gallop rhythm with tachypnea and hepatosplenomegaly appear to be the best clinical indicators of congestive heart failure (CHF) in HIV-infected children; anticongestive therapy is generally very effective, especially when initiated early. Electrocardiography and echocardiography are helpful in assessing cardiac function before the onset of clinical symptoms.

Renal Involvement

Nephropathy is an unusual presenting symptom of HIV infection, more commonly occurring in older symptomatic children. Nephrotic syndrome is the most common manifestation, with edema, hypoalbuminemia, proteinuria and azotemia with normal blood pressure. Polyuria, oliguria and hematuria have been observed in some patients.

Diagnosis

All infants born to HIV-infected mothers test antibody-positive at birth because of passive transfer of maternal HIV antibody across the placenta. Most uninfected infants lose maternal antibody between 6 and 12 months of age. As a small proportion of uninfected infants continue to have maternal HIV antibody in the blood up to 18 months of age, positive IgG antibody tests cannot be used to make a definitive diagnosis of HIV infection in infants younger than this age. In a child older than 18 months of age, demonstration of IgG antibody to HIV by a repeatedly reactive enzyme immunoassay (EIA) and confirmatory test (e.g., Western blot or immunofluorescence assay) can establish the diagnosis of HIV infection. Although serologic diagnostic tests were the most commonly used in the past, tests that allow for earlier definitive diagnosis in children have replaced antibody assays as the tests of choice for the diagnosis of HIV infection in infants.

Specific viral diagnostic assays, such as HIV DNA or RNA PCR, HIV culture, or HIV p24 antigen immune dissociated p24 (ICD-p24), are essential for diagnosis of young infants born to HIV infected mothers. By 6 months of age, the HIV culture and/or PCR identifies all infected infants, who are not having any continued exposure due to breastfeeding. HIV DNA PCR is the preferred virologic assay in developed countries. Plasma HIV RNA assays may be more sensitive than DNA PCR for early diagnosis, but data are limited. HIV culture has similar sensitivity to HIV DNA PCR; however, it is more technically complex and expensive, and results are often not available for 2–4 week compared to 2–3 days with PCR. The p24 antigen assay is less sensitive than the other virologic tests. Figure 9.7 shows the suggested algorithm for diagnosis of HIV infection in infants.

Management

The management of HIV infected child includes antiretroviral therapy, prophylaxis and treatment of opportunistic infections and common infections, adequate nutrition and immunization.

Antiretroviral Therapy

Decisions about antiretroviral therapy for pediatric HIV-infected patients are based on the magnitude of viral replication (i.e. viral load), CD4 lymphocyte count or percentage, and clinical condition. A child who has WHO stage 3 or 4 clinical disease should receive ART irrespective of the immunologic stage. Children who are asymptomatic or have stage 1 or 2 disease may receive ART if they have evidence of advanced or severe immunosupression.

The availability of antiretroviral therapy has transformed HIV infection from a uniformly fatal condition to a chronic infection, where children can lead a near normal life. The currently available therapy does not eradicate the virus and cure the child; it rather suppresses the virus replication for extended periods. The 3 main groups of drugs are nucleoside reverse transcriptase inhibitors (NRTI), non-nucleoside reverse transcriptase inhibitors (NNRTI) and protease inhibitors (PI). Highly active antiretroviral therapy (HAART) is a combination of 2 NRTIs with a PI or a NNRTI. The details of the antiretroviral drugs are shown in Table 9.8.

Cotrimoxazole Prophylaxis

In resource-limited settings, cotrimoxazole prophylaxis is recommended for all HIV exposed infants starting at 4–6 weeks of age (or at first encounter with the health care system) and continued until HIV infection can be excluded. Cotrimoxazole is also recommended for HIV-exposed breastfeeding children of any age, and cotrimoxazole prophylaxis should be continued until HIV infection can be excluded by HIV antibody testing (beyond 18 months of age) or virological testing (before 18 months of age) at least six weeks after complete ceszation of breastfeeding.

All children younger than one year of age documented to be living with HIV should receive cotrimoxazole prophylaxis regardless of symptoms or CD4 percentage. After one year of age, initiation of cotrimoxazole prophylaxis is recommended for symptomatic children (WHO clinical stages 2, 3 or 4 for HIV disease) or children with CD4 <25%. All children who begin cotrimoxazole prophylaxis (irrespective of whether cotrimoxazole was initiated in the first year of life or after that) should continue until the age of five years, when they can be reassessed.

Nutrition

It is important to provide adequate nutrition to HIV-infected children. Many of these children have failure to thrive. These children will need nutritional rehabilitation. In addition, micronutrients like zinc may be useful.

Immunization

The vaccines that are recommended in the national schedule can be administered to HIV infected children except that symptomatic HIV infected children should not be given OPV and BCG.

Prevention of Mother to Child Transmission (MTCT)

The risk of MTCT can be reduced to under 2% by interventions that include antiretroviral (ARV) prophylaxis given to women during pregnancy and labor and to the infant in the first weeks of life, obstetrical interventions including elective cesarean delivery (prior to the onset of labor and rupture of membranes), and complete avoidance of breastfeeding.

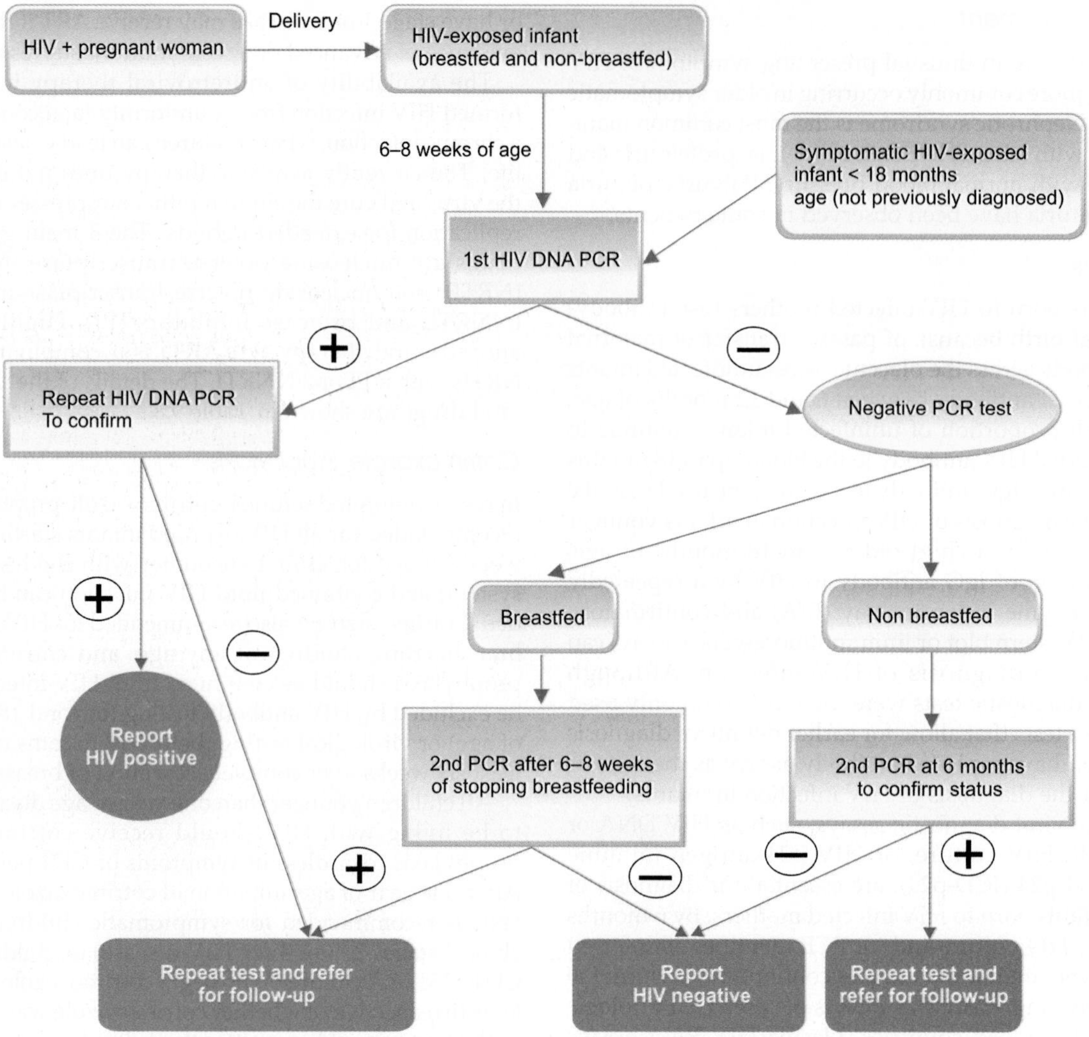

Fig. 9.7: HIV diagnosis in children below the age of 18 months with DNA-PCR

Antiretroviral Drug Regimens for Treating Pregnant Women

Recommended regimen for pregnant women with indication for antiretroviral therapy (ART) is combination of zidovudine (AZT), lamivudine (3TC) and nevirapine (NVP) in antepartum, intrapartum and postpartum period. The recommended regimen for pregnant women who are not eligible for ART, but for preventing MTCT is:

- *Antepartum:* AZT starting at 28 weeks of pregnancy
- *Intrapartum:* A combination of single dose (Sd) NVP, AZT and 3TC
- *Postpartum:* A combination of AZT and 3TC for 7 days.

The recommended treatment for pregnant women in labor and who have not received ART is:

- *Intrapartum:* A combination of Sd-NVP, AZT and 3TC
- *Postpartum:* A combination of AZT and 3TC × 7 weeks

Omission of the Sd-NVP for the mother may be considered for women who receive at least four weeks of AZT before delivery. When Sd-NVP is used to prevent MTCT, either alone or in combination with AZT, the rationale of giving AZT and 3TC intrapartum and for seven days postpartum is to prevent resistance to NVP.

ARV Regimens for Infants Born to HIV Positive Mothers

The recommended regimen for infants is Sd-NVP + AZT for one week. When delivery occurs within two hours of a woman taking Sd-NVP, the infant should receive Sd-NVP immediately after delivery and AZT for four weeks. If the mother receives less than four weeks of antenatal ART, then four weeks rather than one week of AZT is recommended for the infant.

Table 9.8: Commonly used antiretroviral drugs

Drug	*Dose*	*Side effects*
Nucleoside reverse transcriptase inhibitors		
Abacavir	3 mo–13 yr: 8 mg/kg/dose q12 hr; >13 yr: 300 mg/dose q12 hr (max 300 mg/dose)	Hypersensitivity
Didanosine	0–3 mo: 50 mg/m^2/ dose q12 hr 3 mo–13 yr: 90–150 mg/m^2 q 12 hr (max dose 200 mg/dose) >13 yr; <60 kg: 125 mg tablets q12 hr >13 yr; >60 kg: 200 mg tablet q12 hr	Peripheral neuropathy, pancreatitis, abdominal pain, diarrhea
Lamivudine (3TC)	1 mo-13 yr: 4 mg/kg q12 hr >13 yr; <50 kg: 4 mg/kg/dose q12 hr >13 yr; >50 kg: 150 mg/kg/dose q12 hr	Pancreatitis, neuropathy, neutropenia
Stavudine (d4T)	1 mo-13 yr: 1 mg/kg q12 hr >13 yr; 30–60 kg: 30 mg/dose q12 hr >13 yr; >60 kg: 40 mg/dose q12 hr	Headache, GI upset, neuropathy
Zalcitabine	<13 yr: 0.01 mg/kg/dose q8 hr >13 yr: 0.75 mg q8 hr	Rash, peripheral neuropathy, pancreatitis
Zidovudine	Neonates: 2 mg/kg q6 hr 3 mo–13 yr: 90–180 mg/m^2 q6-8 hr >13 yr: 200 mg q8 hr or 300 mg q12 hr	Anemia, myopathy
Non-nucleoside reverse transcriptase inhibitors		
Nevirapine (NVP)	2 mo–13 yr: 120 mg/m^2 (max 200 mg) q24 hr for 14 days, followed by 120–200 mg/m^2 q12 hr >13 yr: 200 mg q24 hr for 14 days, then increase to 200 mg q12 hr if no rash or other side effects	Skin rash, Steven Johnson syndrome
Efavirenz*	10- <15 kg: 200 mg q24 hr 15- <20 kg: 250 mg q24 hr 20- <25 kg: 300 mg q24 hr 25–<32.5 kg: 350 mg q24 hr 32.5- <40 kg: 400 mg q24 hr >40 kg: 600 mg q24 hr	Skin rash, CNS symptoms, increased transaminases
Protease inhibitors		
Amprenavir	4–16 yr and <50 kg: 22.5 mg/kg q12 hr (oral solution) or 20 mg/kg q12 hr (capsules) >13 yr and >50 kg: 1200 mg q12 hr (capsules)	
Indinavir	500 mg/m^2 q8 hr >13 yr: 800 mg q8 hr	Hyperbilirubinemia, nephrolithiasis
Lopinavir/ ritonavir	*6 mo–12 yr* 7- < 15 kg: 12 mg/kg lopinavir; 3 mg/kg ritonavir q12 hr with food; 15–40 kg: 10 mg/kg lopinavir; 2.5 mg/kg ritonavir q12 hr; *>12 yr*: 400 mg lopinavir; 100 mg ritonavir q12 hr	Diarrhea, fatigue, headache, nausea, increased cholesterol and triglycerides
Nelfinavir	<13 yr: 50–55 mg/kg q12 hr >13 yr: 1250 mg q12 hr (max 2000 mg)	Diarrhea, abdominal pain
Ritonavir	<13 yr: 350–400 mg/m^2 q12 hr (starting dose 250 mg/m^2) >13 yr: 600 mg q12 hr (starting dose 300 mg)	Bad taste, vomiting, nausea, diarrhea; rarely hepatitis
Saquinavir	50 mg/kg q8 hr; >13 yr: soft gel capsules 1200 mg q8 hr	Diarrhea, headache, rash

*Efavirenz should not be used below 3 yr of age

Intrapartum Interventions

Avoid ARM unless medically indicated. Delivery by elective cesarean section at 38 weeks before onset of labor and rupture of membranes should be considered. Avoid procedures increasing risk of exposure of child to maternal blood and secretions like use of scalp electrodes.

Breastfeeding

Breastfeeding is an important modality of transmission of HIV infection in developing countries. The risk of HIV infection via breastfeeding is highest in the early months of breastfeeding. Factors that increase the likelihood of transmission include detectable levels of HIV in breast

9

milk, the presence of mastitis and low maternal CD4+ T cell count. Exclusive breastfeeding has been reported to carry a lower risk of HIV transmission than mixed feeding. According to current UN recommendations (WHO, 2001) when replacement feeding is *acceptable, feasible, affordable, sustainable and safe*, avoidance of all breastfeeding by HIV-infected mothers is recommended. Otherwise, exclusive breastfeeding is recommended during the first months of life. WHO recommends that the transition between exclusive breastfeeding and early cessation of breastfeeding should be kept as short as possible, "early and abrupt cessation" bearing in mind that mixed feeding during this period carries a 70% greater risk of MTCT. Replacement feeding should be given by *katori* spoon.

Suggested reading

1. WHO/UNAIDS. AIDS epidemic update Dec 2007.
2. WHO. Antiretroviral therapy of HIV infection in infants and children in resource-limited settings: towards universal access. WHO 2006.

COMMON BACTERIAL INFECTIONS

TUBERCULOSIS

Tuberculosis is a chronic infectious disease caused by *Mycobacterium tuberculosis*. Tuberculosis still is one of the deadliest diseases in the world killing nearly 2 million people every year. More than ninety percent of all tuberculosis cases occur in the developing countries, where limited resources are available for optimal treatment. Tuberculosis continues to be an important cause of morbidity and mortality for children worldwide.

Magnitude of the Problem

Since most children acquire the organism from adults in their surroundings, the epidemiology of childhood tuberculosis follows that in adults. Because of the difficulty of confirming the diagnosis the global burden of childhood tuberculosis in the world is unclear. Another important reason is that children do not make a significant contribution to the spread of tuberculosis. Several estimates make use of an arbitrary calculation assigning 10% of the tuberculosis burden to children. Tuberculosis infection and disease among children are much more prevalent in developing countries, where resources for control are scarce. It is estimated that in developing countries the annual risk of tuberculosis infection in children is 2–5%. The estimated lifetime risk of developing tuberculosis disease for a young child infected with *M. tuberculosis* as indicated by positive tuberculin test is about 10%. About 5% of those infected are likely to develop disease in the first year after infection and the remaining 5% during their lifetime. These rates increase about six fold in HIV infected individuals. Nearly 8–20% of the deaths caused by tuberculosis occur in children. The age of the child at acquisition of infection has a great effect on the occurrence of tuberculosis disease. Approximately 40% of infected children less than 1 year of age if left untreated develop radiologically significant lymphadenopathy or segmental lesions compared with 24% of children between 1–10 years and 16% of children 11–15 years of age. In India, over 100,000 children die from tuberculosis every year.

The important reasons for a recent worldwide increase in childhood tuberculosis include inadequate treatment facilities for tuberculosis, inadequate facilities to prevent tuberculosis infection in children, HIV pandemic, and emergence of drug resistance with nearly 170,000 children dying of it every year. Due to improved standard of living and better sanitation, the incidence of tuberculosis has steadily declined in the affluent and highly developed countries. However, it is still a major public health problem in the economically underprivileged countries of Asia, Africa and South America.

Epidemiology

Agent

All patients of pulmonary tuberculosis and most cases of extrapulmonary disease are caused by human type strain of *Mycobacterium tuberculosis*. A few cases of extrapulmonary illness particularly the tubercular lymphadenitis may be due to the bovine strain.

Reservoir of Infection

The infection is spread by the tuberculous patient, who discharges tubercle bacilli in his sputum or nasopharyngeal secretions during bouts of coughing or sneezing, etc. Such patients are open or infective cases. In the pediatric age groups, few infections may also occur by the transplacental route (congenital tuberculosis).

Mode of Infection

The usual mode of infection is through inhalation of droplets of infected secretions. The infected sputum spitted carelessly by open cases of tuberculosis dries up and the tubercle bacilli are resuspended in the dust and air. This may be a source of infection through breathing. Infection through ingestion of infected material is rare. Rarely infection may be transmitted through skin, mucous membrane or transplacentally.

Host Factors

Age: No age is exempt from tuberculosis. Tubercle bacilli are not transferred across the healthy placenta but the fetus may be infected from the infected placenta. Frequency of infection with tubercle bacilli increases progressively as the child grows in age. As discussed above, an infant is more likely to develop disease after an infection compared with an older child.

Sex: The adolescent children especially the girls are more prone to develop active tuberculosis disease during puberty.

Malnutrition

Undernourished children are more susceptible to develop tuberculosis, probably due to depressed immunological defenses. Tuberculosis may precipitate kwashiorkor/ marasmus in an infant with borderline undernutrition. A malnourished patient, who does not respond to the dietary therapy should be promptly investigated for tuberculosis.

Immune deficiency: Children with primary or secondary immune deficiencies (including HIV) are more likely to develop disseminated disease. The diseases that affect the cell mediated immunity are more likely to increase the susceptibility.

Intercurrent infections: A quiescent tuberculous infection may flare up after an attack of measles or pertussis. Measles may depress delayed hypersensitivity to tubercular proteins.

Environment: The risk of acquiring infection has been associated consistently with the extent of contact with the index case, the burden of organisms in the sputum, and the frequency of cough in the index case. Patients with smear positive pulmonary tuberculosis are more likely to transmit infection. An increased risk of developing infection has been seen in institutional settings, including nursing homes, correctional institutions and homeless shelters.

Pathology

The inhaled tubercle bacilli may lodge in the pulmonary alveoli and cause inflammation with hyperemia and congestion. Initially, the polymorphonuclear leukocytes infiltrate at the site of lesion. The phagocytic ability of these cells is poor and they are soon eliminated.

Further course of the infection depends on the immune response of the host. If the host resistance is good, the inflammatory exudate around the primary focus is absorbed and the caseous area inspissated. Healing occurs by fibrosis and calcification. When the cell mediated immune response is weak, the bacilli continue to multiply and the inflammatory process extends to the contiguous areas. Progressive primary disease is a serious complication of the pulmonary primary complex (PPC) in which the PPC, instead of resolving/calcifying, enlarges steadily and develops large caseous center. The center then liquefies; this may empty into an adjacent bronchus leading to formation of a cavity. This is associated with large numbers of tubercle bacilli. From this stage, the bacilli may spread to other parts of the lobe or the entire lung. This may lead to consolidation of area of lung or bronchopneumonia. Cavitary disease is uncommon in children. It may be difficult to differentiate PPD from a simple tuberculous focus with superimposed acute bacterial pneumonia. Appearance of a segmental lesion is fan shaped on a roentgenogram, representing mainly atelectasis and involves the segment occupied by the primary pulmonary focus.

Some of the events may occur because of involvement of lymph nodes. The enlarged lymph nodes may compress the neighbouring airway. Ball-valve effect due to incomplete obstruction may lead to trapping of air distal to obstruction (emphysema). Enlarged paratracheal nodes may cause stridor and respiratory distress. Subcarinal nodes may impinge on the esophagus and may cause dysphagia. If the obstruction of bronchus is complete, atelectasis occurs.

Outcome of Bronchial Obstruction

i. Complete expansion and resolution of chest X-ray findings.
ii. Disappearance of the segmental lesions.
iii. Scarring and progressive compression of the lobe or segment leading to bronchiectasis.

A caseated lymph node may erode through the wall of the bronchus, leading to tuberculous bronchitis/ endobronchial tuberculosis. Fibrosis and bronchiectatic changes may supervene. Discharge of the bacteria into the lumen may lead to its bronchial dissemination.

Hematogenous dissemination of *M. tuberculosis* occurs early in the course of the disease; this results when the bacilli find their way into bloodstream through lymph nodes. This may result in foci of infection in various organs. If the host immune system is good, then these foci are contained and disease does not occur. Seeding of apex of lungs leads to development of *Simon's focus*. Lowering of host immunity may lead to activation of these metastatic foci and development of disease. This is especially seen in young infants, severely malnourished children and children with immunodeficiency. Massive seeding of blood stream with *M. tuberculosis* leads to miliary tuberculosis, where all lesions are of similar size. This usually occurs within 3–6 months after initial infection.

Pulmonary tuberculosis resulting from endogenous reactivation of foci of infection is uncommon in children; but may be seen in adolescents. The commonest site for this type of disease is the apex of the lung (Puhl's lesion), because the blood flow is sluggish at apex. Regional lymph nodes are usually not involved. Miliary and meningeal tuberculosis usually occur within a year of the primary lesion.

Clinical Features

The incubation period varies between 4 and 8 weeks. The clinical features usually start with the development of hypersensitivity to tubercular proteins. Childhood tuberculosis can be divided into those involving the intra- and extrathoracic sites.

Intrathoracic Tuberculosis

The diagnosis of tuberculosis in a child is often difficult because of absence of typical symptoms signs and of microbiologic evidence in the majority of children with pulmonary tuberculosis. The onset of symptoms is generally insidious, but may be relatively acute in miliary tuberculosis.

Primary infection usually passes off unrecognized. Asymptomatic infection is defined as infection associated with tuberculin hypersensitivity and a positive tuberculin test but with no striking clinical or roentgenographic manifestations.

Most symptoms in children with **primary complex** (PPC) are constitutional in the form of mild fever, anorexia, weight loss, decreased activity. Cough is an inconsistent symptom and may be absent even in advanced disease. Irritating dry cough can be a symptom of bronchial and tracheal compression due to enlarged lymph nodes. In some children, the lymph nodes continue to enlarge even after resolutions of parenchymal infiltrate. This may lead to compression of neighboring regional bronchus. The PPC may be picked up accidentally during evaluation of intercurrent infections.

Progressive primary disease (PPD) is the result of the progression of primary disease. Children with PPD may present with high-grade fever and cough. Expectoration of sputum and hemoptysis are usually associated with advanced disease and development of cavity or ulceration of the bronchus. Abnormal chest signs consist mainly of dullness, decreased air entry and crepitations. Cavitating pulmonary tuberculosis is uncommon.

Children with ***endobronchial tuberculosis*** may present with fever, troublesome cough (with or without expectoration). Dyspnea, wheezing and cyanosis may be present. Occasionally, the child may be misdiagnosed as asthma. In a wheezing child less than 2- yr-old, the possibility of endobronchial tuberculosis should always be considered. Partial compression of the airway can lead to emphysema. Features of collapse may be present if a large airway is completely compressed.

Miliary tuberculosis is an illness characterized by heavy hematogenous spread and progressive development of innumerable small foci throughout the body. The disease is most common in infants and young children. The onset of illness is often sudden. The clinical manifestations depend on the numbers of disseminated organisms and the involved organs. The child may have high-grade fever, which is quite unlike other forms of tuberculosis. The child may also have dyspnea and cyanosis. There are hardly any pulmonary findings but fine crepitations and rhonchi may be present. These findings may occasionally be confused with other acute respiratory infections of childhood. The illness may be severe, with the child having high fever, rigors and alteration of sensorium. In addition, these children may have lymphadenopathy and hepatosplenomegaly. The other presentation of miliary tuberculosis may be insidious with the child appearing unwell, febrile and losing weight. Choroid tubercles may be seen in about 50% children. Meningitis may occur in 20–30% of cases.

Pleural effusion follows the rupture of a subpleural focus into the pleural cavity. The pleura may also be infected by hematogenous spread from the primary focus. The effusion usually occurs because of hypersensitivity to tuberculoproteins. If the sensitivity is high, there is significant pleural effusion along with fever and chest pain on affected side. Minor effusions associated with the rupture of primary foci are usually not detected. Tuberculous effusion is uncommon in children younger than 5-years of age, is more common in boys, and is rarely associated with segmental lesion and miliary tuberculosis. The onset may be insidious or acute with rise in temperature, cough, dyspnea and pleuritic pain on the affected side. There is usually no expectoration. Pain in chest may disappear once the fluid separates the inflamed pleural surfaces; this may be replaced by some discomfort. Increase in effusion may make breathing shallow and difficult. The clinical findings depend on the amount of fluid in the pleural cavity. In early stages, a pleural rub may be present. Early signs include decreased chest wall movement, impairment of percussion note and diminished air entry on the affected side. As the fluid collection increases, the signs of pleural effusion become more definite.

Extrathoracic Tuberculosis

The most common forms of extrathoracic disease in children include tuberculosis of the superficial lymph nodes (scrofula) and the central nervous system. Other rare forms of extrathoracic disease in children include osteoarticular, abdominal, gastrointestinal, genitourinary, cutaneous and congenital disease.

TB of the superficial lymph nodes can be associated with drinking unpasteurized cow's milk or can be caused by extension of primary lesions of the upper lung fields or abdomen leading to involvement of the supraclavicular, anterior cervical, tonsillar and submandibular nodes. Although lymph nodes may become fixed to surrounding tissues, low grade fever may be the only systemic symptom. A primary focus is visible radiologically only 30 to 70% of the time. Tuberculin skin test results usually are reactive. Although spontaneous resolution may occur, untreated lymphadenitis frequently progresses to caseating necrosis, capsular rupture, and spread to adjacent nodes and overlying skin, resulting in a draining sinus tract that may require surgical removal.

Central nervous system disease is the most serious complication of tuberculosis in children and arises from the formation of a caseous lesion in the cerebral cortex or meninges that results from occult lymphohematogenous spread. Infants and young children are likely to experience a rapid progression to hydrocephalus, seizures and cerebral edema. In older children, signs and symptoms progress over the course of several weeks, beginning with fever, headache, irritability and drowsiness. The disease advances with symptoms of lethargy, vomiting, nuchal rigidity, seizures, hypertonia and focal signs. The final stage of disease is marked by coma, hypertension, decerebrate and decorticate posturing, and death. Rapid confirmation of tuberculous meningitis can be difficult because of the wide variability in cerebrospinal characteristics, nonreactive tuberculin skin tests in 40% and normal chest radiographs in 50%. Because improved outcomes are associated with early treatment, empiric antituberculous therapy should be considered for any child with basilar meningitis, hydrocephalus or cranial nerve involvement that has no other apparent cause.

Tuberculosis of abdomen is often due to hematogenous spread from the primary focus in the lungs. It may, however, be secondary to swallowing of the infected sputum by a patient with pulmonary lesions. Primary tuberculosis of the intestines due to ingestion of the food contaminated by tubercle bacilli is relatively less common in India as the milk is generally boiled before use.

Patients with abdominal tuberculosis may remain asymptomatic initially. Symptomatic patients show evidence of tuberculous toxemia and may present with colicky abdominal pain, vomiting and constipation. The abdomen feels characteristically doughy. The abdominal wall is not rigid but appears tense, so that the abdominal viscera cannot be palpated satisfactorily. The rolled up omentum and enlarged lymph nodes may appear as irregular nodular masses with ascites. The liver and spleen are often enlarged. Histological examination of the liver may show granulomatous hepatitis and fatty change.

Diagnosis

The diagnosis of tuberculosis in children is usually based on clinical signs and symptoms, chest roentgenogram, tuberculin testing and history of contact with adult patients. Clinical features may be nonspecific and chest radiograph and Mantoux test are difficult to interpret. In addition, these do not give conclusive evidence for the disease. Although demonstration of mycobacterium in various clinical specimens remains gold standard, this is often not possible in children due to the pauci-bacillary nature of the illness.

A *history of contact with an infective case contact* is defined as any child who lives in a household with an adult taking antitubercular therapy or has taken such therapy in past 2-years. A history of contact is available in less than one-third of the patients. Contacts can often be traced to maidservant, cook, domestic aid or gardener in case of tuberculous children from well-to-do families with healthy parents. Tracing of contact is important not only for confirming the diagnosis but also for protection of other vulnerable children from the disease.

Various scoring systems have been developed for diagnosis of tuberculosis. In these scoring system more weightage is given to laboratory tests, i.e. demonstration of acid fast bacilli, tubercles on histology, suggestive radiology and tuberculin test >10 mm induration. These scoring systems are not used routinely.

Laboratory Tests

The diagnostic tests for pulmonary tuberculosis can be divided into 2 categories: (a) demonstration or isolation of *M. tuberculosis* or one of its components; (b) demonstration of host's response to exposure to *M. tuberculosis.*

Demonstration of M. tuberculosis or its components

M. tuberculosis can be demonstrated by (i) Ziehl Neelson (ZN) staining, (ii) special stains, (iii) cultures, (iv) polymerase chain reaction and (v) other methods. The above methods can be used on sputum, gastric lavage, bronchoscopic lavage fluid, or pleural fluid. The best specimen for demonstration of *M. tuberculosis* in children is the early morning gastric aspirate obtained by using a nasogastric tube before the child arises. The yield of *M. tuberculosis* on ZN stain is less than 20% and depends on extent of pulmonary disease and number of specimen tested. For better results 3 consecutive specimen of gastric aspiration are recommended. If a delay in the processing of specimen is expected the GA should be neutralized with sodium bicarbonate for higher yield.

Culture

Lowenstein- Jensen (LJ) medium is the most widely used medium for determination of characteristic features of colonial morphology, growth rate and pigment production. Though the culture technique is simple, 7–10 week of incubation may be necessary for detection of organisms. Microscopic examination of thin layer culture plate may lead to detection of microcolonies of *M. tuberculosis* as early as after 7 days. The yield of culture of gastric aspirate varies from 30–50% in children with tuberculosis. Excessively long period required for isolation of *M. tuberculosis* by conventional culture techniques has led to the development of other techniques for culture such as BACTEC radiometric assay, Septichek AFB system and mycobacterial growth indicator tube system.

Polymerase Chain Reaction (PCR)

PCR is the most commonly used technique of nucleic acid amplification, for diagnosis of tuberculosis. The PCR may be used to (i) diagnose tuberculosis rapidly by identifying DNA from *M. tuberculosis* in clinical samples that are negative by microscopic examination; (ii) determine rapidly whether acid-fast organisms identified by microscopic examination in clinical specimens are *M. tuberculosis* or atypical mycobacteria; and (iii) identify the presence of genetic modifications known to be associated with resistance of some antimycobacterial agents. The most commonly used target for detection of *M. tuberculosis* is the insertion sequence IS6110. The sensitivity ranges from 4–80% and the specificity 80–100%.

PCR gives rapid results and has a greater sensitivity compared with traditional microbiological methods. This makes PCR a suitable technique in childhood tuberculosis, especially when diagnosis is difficult or needed urgently. However, the possibility of false positive results must be considered, especially when the clinical symptoms and history of exposure of the child make the diagnosis improbable.

Serodiagnosis

In absence of good diagnostic method for childhood tuberculosis, a lot of interest has been generated in serodiagnosis. ELISA has been used in children to detect antibodies to various purified or complex antigens of *M. tuberculosis*. Despite a large number of studies published, serology has found little place in the routine diagnosis of tuberculosis in children, even though it is rapid and does not require specimen from the site of disease. Sensitivity and specificity depend on the antigen used, gold standard for the diagnosis, and the type of tubercular infection. At present, serodiagnosis does not have any role in diagnosis of childhood pulmonary tuberculosis.

Methods to Diagnose Latent Tuberculosis Infection

Till date, tuberculin skin test was the only method to diagnose latent tuberculosis infection. Recently, a new test QuantiFERON®-TB test (QFT) was approved by the Food and Drug Administration as an aid for detecting latent *M. tuberculosis* infection. This is an *in vitro* diagnostic aid that measures a component of cell-mediated immune reactivity to *M. tuberculosis*, and is based on the quantification of interferon-gamma (IFN-gamma) released from sensitized lymphocytes in whole blood incubated overnight with purified protein derivative (PPD) from *M. tuberculosis* and control antigens. Similarly, another in vitro test- ELISPOT is also available for diagnosis of latent infection.

Radiology

Chest radiograph has an important role in diagnosis of childhood tuberculosis, especially pulmonary tuberculosis. In extra-pulmonary tuberculosis, presence of lesions on chest radiograph supports diagnosis.

9

The typical chest X-ray appearance of a pulmonary primary complex is that of an airspace consolidation of variable size, usually unifocal and homogenous (Fig. 9.8). Enlarged lymph nodes are usually seen in the hila, right paratracheal region. Adenopathy alone may be the sole manifestation of primary tuberculosis. There is no consensus regarding the most common site of involvement.

Consolidation in progressive primary disease (PPD) is usually heterogenous, poorly marginated with predilection of involvement of apical or posterior segments of upper lobe or superior segment of lower lobe (Fig. 9.9). There may be features of collapse as well (Fig. 9.10). Bronchiectasis may occur in PPD because of (i) destruction and fibrosis of lung parenchymal resulting in retraction and irreversible bronchial dilatation, and (ii) cicatricial bronchostenosis secondary to localized endobronchial infection resulting in obstructive pneumonitis and distal bronchiectasis. In children, cavitary disease is uncommon and occurs rarely in children.

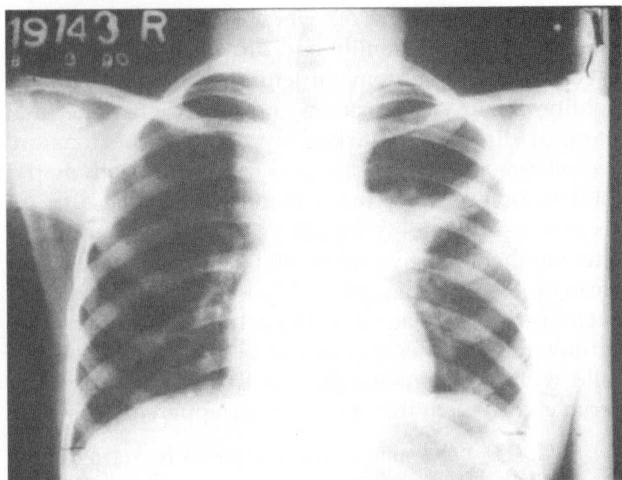

Fig. 9.8: X ray film of PPC showing left hilar adenopathy with ill defined parenchymal lesion

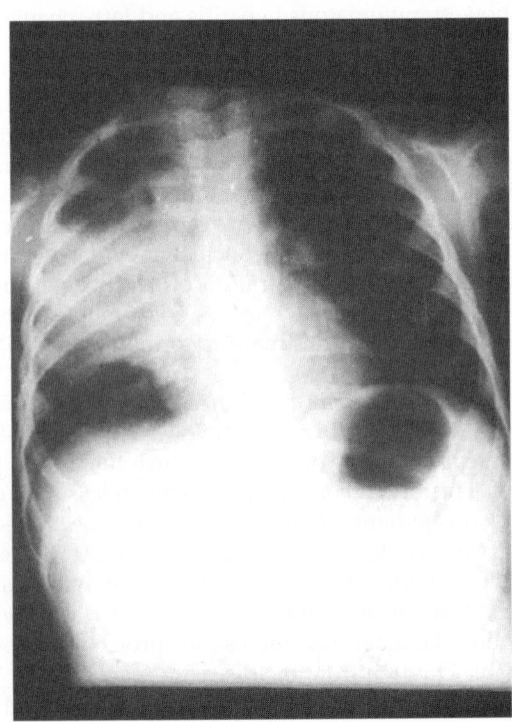

Fig. 9.9: PPD showing consolidation

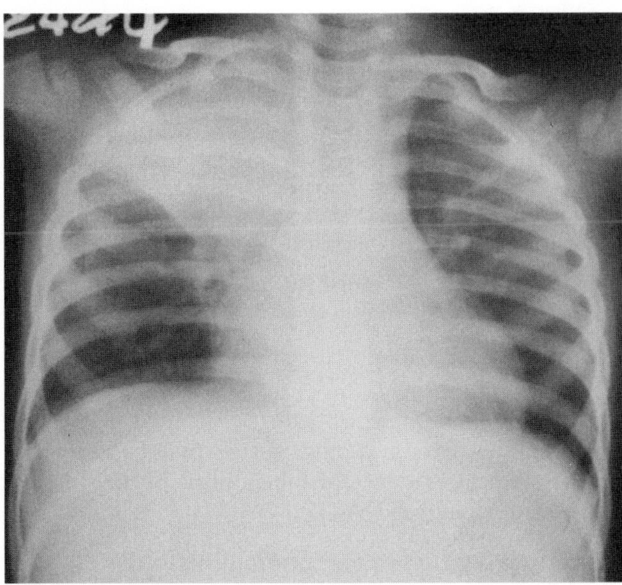

Fig. 9.10: Showing collapse consolidation of right upper lobe

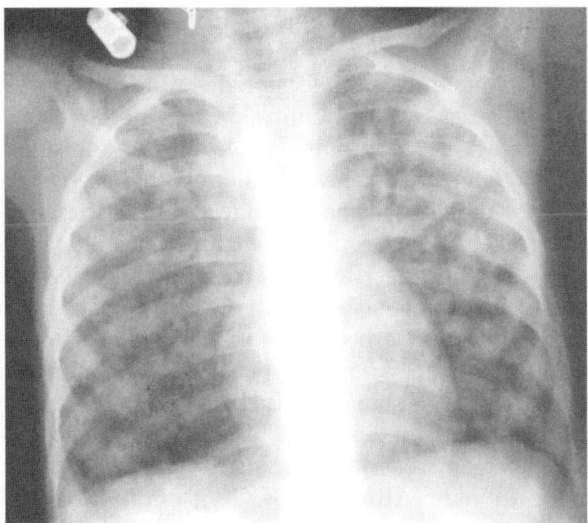

Fig. 9.12: Showing miliary shadows with right paratracheal adenopathy

Pleural effusion may occur with or without lung lesion (Fig. 9.11). In miliary tuberculosis, there are multiple lesions of size 2–5 mm (Fig. 9.12). Occasionally, the chest radiograph may be normal and lymphadenopathy may be detected on computed tomography (CT), which is not evident radiographically. In addition, CT features such as low attenuation lymph nodes with peripheral enhancement, lymph node calcification, branching centrilobular nodules and miliary nodules are helpful in suggesting the diagnosis in cases where the radiograph is normal or equivocal. Other features such as segmental or lobar consolidation and atelectasis are non-specific. Contrast enhanced MRI is emerging as a very useful technique for diagnosing CNS tuberculosis, as it demonstrates the localized lesions, meningeal enhancement and the brain stem lesions.

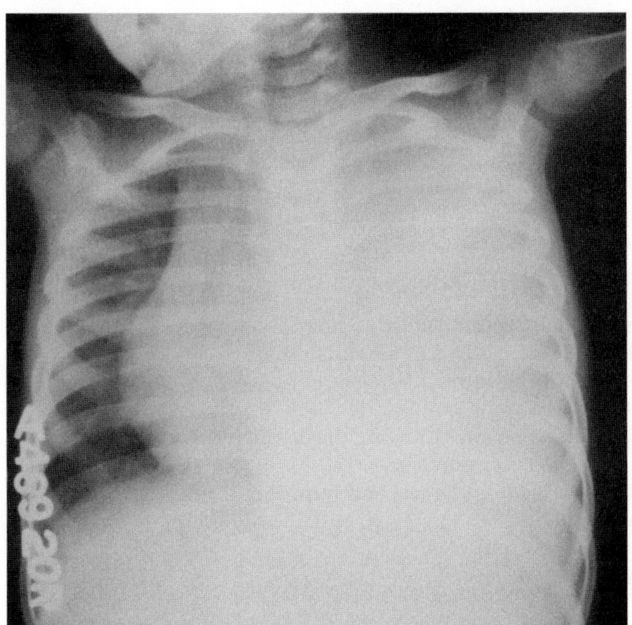

Fig. 9.11: Showing massive pleural effusion on left side

Tuberculosis Skin Test

The tuberculin skin test (Mantoux text) is the test most commonly used for establishing the diagnosis of tuberculosis in children. Although currently available tuberculin skin test antigens are not 100 percent sensitive or specific, no better diagnostic test is widely available. The positive and negative predictive values of the tuberculin skin test are affected significantly by a number of factors. Infection with *M. tuberculosis* produces a delayed-type hypersensitivity reaction to specific antigenic components of the bacilli. All PPD lots are bio-assayed to demonstrate equal potency. Thus, the standard test dose of a commercially available preparation is defined as the dose of that product that is biologically equivalent to 5 TU of PPD-S or 2 TU of tuberculin PPD RT23. The reaction to tuberculin typically begins 5 to 6 hours after the patient receives the injection and reaches maximal induration at 48 to 72 hours. In some individuals, the reaction may peak after 72 hours. In these instances, the tuberculin skin test should be measured again and interpretation of the test should be based on the larger, later reading. Rarely, vesiculation and necrosis may occur. In these cases, repeat tuberculin testing should be avoided. Variability of the tuberculin skin test may be reduced by giving careful attention to details of administration and reading. A one-quarter to one-half inch, 26-gauge needle and tuberculin syringe are used to inject 0.1 mL of PPD intradermally into the volar aspect of the forearm. Forty-eight to seventy-two hours after the injection is given, the diameter of induration should be measured transversely to the long axis of the forearm and recorded in millimeters. A trained health care professional should read all skin tests. A non-reactive tuberculin skin test does not exclude latent or active tuberculosis. Numerous factors can diminish tuberculin reactivity, resulting in a false-negative reaction. Numerous factors also have been associated with false positive tuberculin reactions and decreased tuberculin test specificity (Table 9.9). Because some antigens in PPD are shared with other mycobacteria and Bacille Calmette-Guerin (BCG), false-positive reactions can occur in children who have been infected with other mycobacterium or have received BCG vaccination. No reliable method for distinguishing BCG-induced cross-reactivity from reactivity secondary to mycobacterial infection exists. Although BCG vaccination of older children or adults results in greater initial and more persistent cross-reactivity, most of these individuals lose cross-reactivity within 10 years of receiving the vaccination. Interpretation of tuberculin skin test reactions is based on risk of infection and progression to disease (Table 9.10).

BCG test

An accelerated response after injection of the vaccine is observed in individuals suffering from tuberculosis. An induration of more than 5–6 mm after 3 days of BCG vaccine is considered a positive reaction. The Indian Academy of Pediatrics does not recommend BCG test for diagnosis of tuberculosis.

Table 9.10: Interpretation of Mantoux test

Size of induration	*Interpretation*
<10 mm	Negative; no active disease
5–10 mm	Borderline; consider positive in immunocompromised host; contact with adult patient with sputum AFB positive tuberculosis
>10 mm	Positive; suggests disease in presence of clinical features

Histopathology

Lymph nodes, liver and other tissues may be examined for histological evidence of tuberculosis by fine needle aspiration cytology (FNAC).

Diagnostic Algorithm for Tuberculosis

The diagnosis of tuberculosis disease in children continues to be challenging. Even in the advanced nations, the diagnosis is most often made by combination of a positive tuberculin skin test, chest radiograph, physical examination and history of contact with adult patient with tuberculosis. Newer diagnostic methods such as PCR, chromatography and serodiagnosis have not given encouraging results. Newer staining and culture methods have found their place in the management of tuberculosis. There is a need to develop better techniques for diagnosis of tuberculosis in children. The suggested algorithm for

Table 9.9: Causes of false positive and false negative Mantoux test

False Positive Results

Infections due to atypical mycobacteria
BCG vaccination
Infection at the site of test

False Negative Results

Infections
Viral (measles, mumps, chicken pox, HIV)
Bacterial (typhoid fever, brucellosis, typhus, leprosy, pertussis, overwhelming tuberculosis)
Live virus vaccinations (measles, mumps, polio, varicella)
Metabolic derangements
Chronic renal failure, liver failure, severe malnutrition
Diseases affecting lymphoid organs
Hodgkin disease, lymphoma, chronic leukemia, sarcoidosis
Drugs: Corticosteroids, other immunosuppressive agents
Age: Newborns, elderly patients
Stress: Surgery, burns, mental illness, graft-versus-host reactions

Factors related to the tuberculin used
Improper storage (exposure to light and heat)
Improper dilutions
Chemical denaturation
Contamination
Adsorption (partially controlled by adding Tween 80)
Factors related to the method of administration
Injection of too little antigen
Subcutaneous injection
Delayed administration after drawing into syringe
Injection to close to other skin tests
Factors related to reading the test and recording results
Inexperienced reader
Conscious or unconscious bias
Error in recording

diagnosis of pulmonary tuberculosis is given in Fig. 9.13.

Treatment

The principles of therapy in children with tuberculosis are similar to that of adults.

Commonly Used Drugs in Childhood Tuberculosis

The drugs used for treatment of tuberculosis in children are given in Table 9.11.

Drug Regimens

During the last few years, changes have occurred in the therapeutic approach to childhood tuberculosis as a result of large number of treatment trials for children and concern about the development of resistance to antituberculosis drugs. Short-course chemotherapy, with the treatment duration as short as 6 months, has become the standard practice. Intermittent regimens have been documented to be as effective as daily regimen in the paediatric population.

The major problem in inclusion of children in Directly Observed Treatment Short course (DOTS) program has been a difficulty in demonstration of AFB and classification of different clinical manifestations according to categories described for adults. There have been efforts to develop classification of different types of childhood tuberculosis into 3 categories similar to those for adults.

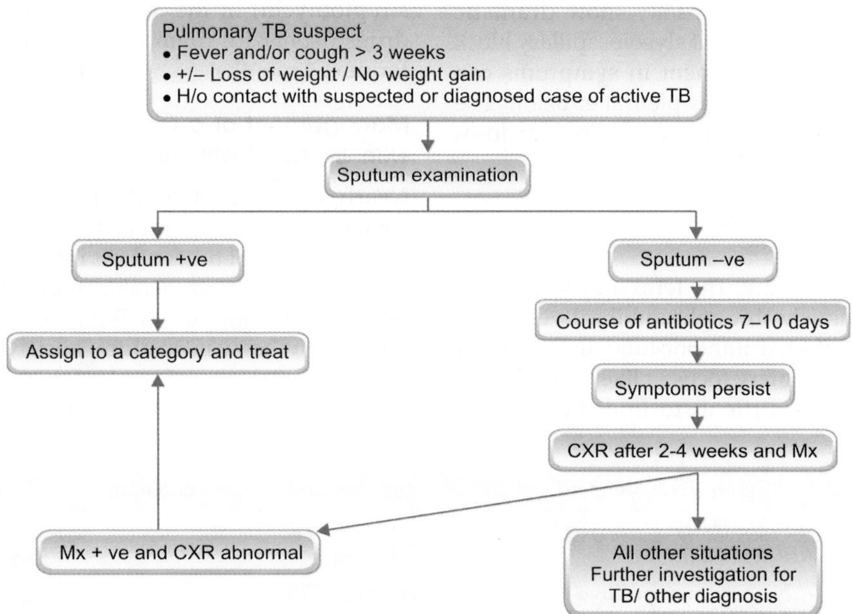

Fig. 9.13: Diagnostic algorithm for pediatric tuberculosis (TB). CXR Chest X-ray, Mx Mantoux/tuberculin test

Table 9.11: Doses and important side effects of antitubercular drugs

Drugs	*Dose (mg/kg/day; frequency)*	*Side effects*
Isoniazid	5; q 24 h	Hepatotoxicity, hypersensitivity rash, fever, peripheral or optic neuritis, psychosis, seizures
Rifampicin	10; q 24 h	Nausea, vomiting, hepatotoxicity, flu-like syndrome, blood dyscrasia, arthralgia, wheezing
Streptomycin	10–30; q 24 h	Ototoxicity: vestibular or hearing loss, rash, fever, arthralgia, neuromuscular blockade, peripheral neuritis, anaphylaxis
Ethambutol	15–25; q 12 h	Hypersensitivity reaction: rash, fever, joint pain, optic neuritis, GI upset, confusion, dizziness.
Pyrazinamide	25–35; q 24 h	GI upset, hepatotoxicity, hyperuricemia, photosensitivity, dysuria, malaise, arthralgia, fever, thrombocytopenia
Ethionamide	15–20; q 12 h	GI upset, hepatotoxicity, peripheral neuropathy, gynaecomastia, rash, alopecia, headache, depression, diplopia, blurred vision, tremors
Cycloserine	15–20; q 12 h	Seizures, psychosis, peripheral neuritis

9

Recently a consensus statement jointly prepared by Indian Academy of Pediatrics and Revised National Tuberculosis Control Program (RNTCP) has also proposed a classification of different types of tuberculosis in children into three categories.

Table 9.12 gives standardized categories given by WHO along with suggested clinical condition in children.

Corticosteroids

Corticosteroids, in addition to antitubercular drugs, are useful in treatment of patients with CNS tuberculosis and occasionally pulmonary tuberculosis. These are useful in settings where the host inflammatory reaction contributes significantly to tissue damage. Short courses of corticosteroids are indicated in children with endobronchial tuberculosis that causes localized emphysema, segmental pulmonary lesions or respiratory distress. Some children with severe miliary tuberculosis may show dramatic improvement with corticosteroids if alveolocapillary block is present. Significant improvement in symptoms can occur in children with tuberculous pleural effusion. The most commonly used medication is prednisolone, at doses of 1–2 mg/kg/day for 4–6 weeks.

Management of an Infant born to Mother with Tuberculosis

Congenital tuberculosis is rare. The fetus may be infected either by hematogenously through umbilical vessels or through ingestion of infected amniotic fluid. In the former situation, there will be primary focus in liver and in latter it will be in lungs. It is difficult to find the route of transmission in a newborn with multiple focus of infection. It is difficult to differentiate between congenital and postnatally acquired tuberculosis.

Infants born to mothers with active tuberculosis should be screened for evidence of disease by a thorough physical examination, tuberculin test and X-ray film of chest. If physical examination and investigations are negative for disease, the infant should be started on isoniazid prophylaxis at doses of 5 mg/kg/day for 6 months. After three months, the patients should be examined for evidence of infection and a repeat tuberculin test is done. If tuberculin test is negative, the infant can be immunized with BCG and INH can be stopped. If tuberculin test is positive but the infant is asymptomatic, INH prophylaxis is continued for another 3 months.

Infants with congenital tuberculosis should be treated with four drugs (isoniazid, rifampicin, pyrazinamide, streptomycin) in the intensive phase followed by two drugs (isoniazid, rifampicin) during maintenance phase for next 4 months.

Management of a Child in Contact with an Adult with Tuberculosis

Nearly one-third of children (aged less than 5 years) in contact with adults with active tuberculosis disease may have evidence of tuberculosis infection. The infection was more commonly associated with younger age, severe malnutrition, absence of BCG vaccination, contact with an adult who was sputum positive and exposure to environmental tobacco smoke. It is suggested that children below 5 years of age in contact with adult patients with

Table 9.12: Standardized clinical categories and clinical conditions

Categories	*As suggested by WHO for adults*	*Suggested conditions in children*	*Suggested regimens#*
Category I	– New sputum positive Pulmonary TB Serious extrapulmonary	PPC, PPD, TBL Pleural effusion Abdominal TB Osteoarticular TB Genitourinary TB CNS TB Pericardial TB	2HRZE + 4 HR or 2SHRZ + 4HR
Category II	– Relapse – Treatment failure – Return after adult default (Interrupted treatment)	Relapse Treatment failure Interrupted treatment	2SHRZE + 1HRZE + 5HRE
Category III	– Sputum negative pulmonary with limited parenchymal involvement – Extrapulmonary TB (less severe forms)	Single lymph node Small effusion Skin TB	2HRZ + 4 HR

PPC-pulmonary primary complex, PPD-Progressive primary disease,
TBL-Tubercular lymphadenitis, CNS TB-Central nervous system tuberculosis
H-Isonizid, R-Rifampin, Z-Pyrizinamide, E-Ethambutol, S-Streptomycin
#the numerical denotes number of months for which the drug is to be given; e.g. 4 HR means giving 4 months of INH and rifampin

sputum positive tuberculosis should receive 6 months of isoniazid prophylaxis. It is mandatory to screen all children in the household of an adult patient with sputum positive tuberculosis for evidence of tuberculosis.

Monitoring of Therapy

Response to treatment can be judged by using the following criteria: clinical, radiological, bacteriological, and laboratory test.

Clinical Criteria

Clinical improvement in a child on ATT is the mainstay of judging response of therapy. The child should be seen every 2–4 weeks initially, then every 4–8 weeks. On each visit, improvement in fever, cough, appetite and subjective well-being is assessed. The child is examined for weight gain and improvement in chest findings. Compliance is assessed by talking to parents, checking medications on each visit. Majority of children show improvement in symptoms within a few weeks.

In the presence of poor response or worsening of symptoms or signs, the initial basis of diagnosis is reviewed, especially, if there are no problems with compliance. Assessment for possibility of drug resistant tuberculosis should be made. After the treatment is over, follow-up every 3–6 months for next 2 years is desirable.

Radiological Criteria

Clinical improvement precedes radiological clearance of lesion on chest X-ray films. The first chest X-ray during therapy should be done after 8 weeks, i.e. at the end of intensive phase. In patients who show increase or little change in radiological features coupled with delayed clinical response, prolongation of intensive phase by a month is suggested. Further films are taken after 4 weeks and child, if better, should be shifted to continuation phase; else the child is investigated for failure of treatment and drug resistance. The degree of radiological clearance can be graded as (1) complete clearance, (2) moderate to significant clearance (1/2–2/3 clearance), (3) mild clearance (1/3 decrease in size) or (4) no clearance or appearance of new lesion. One should not attempt to treat till complete radiological clearance, improvement in the X-ray may continue to occur even after stoppage of therapy.

Microbiological Criteria

Most of the childhood pulmonary tuberculosis is paucibacillary. In children, where isolation of *M. tuberculosis* was possible at the time of diagnosis, every effort should be made to document disappearance of bacilli during therapy.

When to Suspect Drug Resistant Tuberculosis?

It is important to keep a high index of suspicion of drug resistant tuberculosis. Children in following category are at risk of developing drug resistant tuberculosis: children in contact with adult patients who have proven drug resistant tuberculosis, children with tuberculosis getting antituberculosis drugs but not responding and children who respond to antituberculosis drugs in the beginning and then show deterioration. Appearance of new lymph nodes on treatment, persistence of shadow or isolated non clearance of X-ray film of the chest should not be considered indicator of drug resistant tuberculosis.

Diagnosis of Drug resistant Tuberculosis

It is important that a clinician should not miss or should not make over diagnosis of particular disease. Problems with over diagnosis of drug resistant tuberculosis and its treatment are manyfold as the second line drugs are less effective and have more side effects as well as they are more costly.

A physician can suspect drug resistant tuberculosis on basis of criteria given above, but before making a diagnosis all attempts should be made to demonstrate AFB from appropriate samples and get its culture and sensitivity. If the diagnosis is confirmed or could not be established due to any reason, these patients should be referred to a center that is treating children with drug resistance. These children should not be treated by a person who does not have experience of management of drug resistant tuberculosis.

Suggested reading

1. Seth V, Kabra SK (Eds). Essentials of tuberculosis in children, 3rd ed. New Delhi; Jaypee Publishers, 2006.
2. Chauhan LS, Arora VK. Management of Pediatric Tuberculosis under the Revised National Tuberculosis Control Program (RNTCP). Indian Pediatrics 2004; 41:901–5.

DIPHTHERIA

Diphtheria is an acute bacterial infection caused by gram-positive bacillus, *Corynebacterium diphtheriae.* The infection is characterized by local inflammation of the epithelial surface, formation of membrane and toxemia.

The secretions and discharges from infected person or carrier are the main source of infection. Asymptomatic individuals harboring the infection in their respiratory tract are the chief reservoir of infection. The infection is transmitted by contact or via droplets of secretion. The portal of entry is commonly the respiratory tract. Uncommonly, the conjunctiva or skin wound may serve as portals of entry. The period of infectivity persists till the virulent bacilli are present in the lesions, which is around 2–4 weeks. The incubation period of the disease is 2–5 days.

Pathology

Corynebacterium diphtheriae proliferate and liberate powerful exotoxin which is the principal cause of systemic and local lesions. The exotoxin causes necrosis of the epithelial cells and liberates serous and fibrinous material which forms a grayish white pseudomembrane which bleeds on being dislodged. The surrounding tissue is inflamed and edematous.

The organs principally affected by the exotoxin include the heart, kidney and myocardium.

Clinical Features

The onset is generally acute with fever, malaise and headache. The child has a toxic look. Shock may occur due to myocarditis or adrenal insufficiency.

The local manifestations depend on the site of involvement.

Nasal Diphtheria

This is characterized by unilateral/bilateral sero-sanguinous discharge from the nose and excoriation of upper lip. The child does not look too sick.

Faucial Diphtheria

There is redness and swelling over the fauces. The exudates coalesce to form a grayish white pseudo-membrane, which extends to surrounding areas. Sore throat, dysphagia and muffled voice are frequently present.

Laryngotracheal Diphtheria

Membrane over the larynx results in brassy cough and hoarse voice. The respiration becomes laboured and noisy. There is increased respiratory effort. The use of accessory muscles of respiration herald the onset of respiratory obstruction and respiratory failure may ensue.

Diphtheritic lesions may also be found in skin and conjunctiva.

Complications

Myocarditis generally occurs by second week of illness and is manifested by abdominal pain, vomiting, dyspnea, systemic venous congestion, tachycardia/bradycardia, extrasystoles, thready pulse, and muffled heart sounds.

Neurological complications include: (a) palatal palsy, which occurs in second week and is clinically manifested by nasal twang and nasal regurgitation; (b) ocular palsy in third week; (c) loss of accommodation, manifested by visual blurring and inability to read; (d) generalized polyneuritis occurs by 3rd to 6th weeks of illness.

Renal complications include oliguria and proteinuria.

Diagnosis

There should be a high index of suspicion. The diagnosis is suspected on the basis of clinical examination and identification of diphtheria bacilli from the site of lesion. The diagnosis is confirmed by culture of bacilli from the swab from larynx or pharynx. Culture, however, takes eight hours to become available. Rapid techniques like the fluorescent antibody technique may be used to identify diphtheria bacilli.

Nasal diphtheria should be differentiated from foreign body nose or congenital syphilis. Faucial diphtheria should be differentiated from acute streptococcal membranous tonsillitis (patients have high fever but are less toxic and the membrane is confined to the tonsils), viral (adenovirus) membranous tonsillitis (high fever, sore throat, membranous tonsillitis with normal leukocyte count, self limited course of 4–8 days), herpetic tonsillitis/aphthous stomatitis (extremely painful condition that responds to levimasole), thrush (moniliasis), infectious mononucleosis (generalized rash, lymphadenopathy, abnormal lymphocytosis, positive Paul Bunnel test), agranulocytosis and leukemia. Laryngeal diphtheria should be differentiated from croup, acute epiglottitis, laryngotracheobronchitis, retropharyngeal abscess, peritonsillar abscess and bronchopneumonia.

Management

The broad principles of management include

i. Neutralization of free circulating toxins by administration of antitoxin
ii. Antibiotics to eradicate bacteria
iii. Supportive and symptomatic treatment
iv. Management of complications

Diphtheria antitoxin (IV/IM) should be administered as soon as infection with diphtheria bacilli is suspected. Antitoxin should be administered even earlier than bacteriological confirmation before the bacteria have fixed to the tissues. The degree of protection offered by the diphtheria antitoxin is inversely proportional to the duration of clinical illness. The recommendations for antitoxin dosage by the Committee on Infectious Diseases of American Academy of Pediatrics are as follows: Pharyngeal or laryngeal diphtheria of 48 hours duration 20,000–40,000 units, nasopharyngeal lesions 40,000–60,000 units, extensive disease of 3 or more days duration or patients with swelling of the neck 80,000–120,000 units. Repeat doses of antitoxin may be given if clinical improvement is suboptimal.

Antibiotics such as penicillin or erythromycin may be used to terminate toxin production, limit proliferation of bacteria, to prevent spread of organism to contacts and to prevent the development of carriers. Procaine penicillin 3–600,000 units IM at 12 hourly intervals until the patient can swallow, followed by oral penicillin (125–250 mg qid) or erythromycin (25–30 mg/kg/day) to complete a total duration of antibiotic course to 14 days. Three consecutive cultures, 24 hours apart should be negative for diphtheria bacilli before the patient is declared free of disease. This should be followed by active immunization as clinical disease does not confer active immunity.

Bedrest is advocated for two to three weeks. Sudden exertion should be avoided and changes in rate and rhythm of heart should be looked for.

Treatment of Complications

Respiratory obstruction: Humidified oxygen is used. Airway obstruction should be suspected if the child has inspiratory stridor and there is a change in the quality of voice. Severe respiratory distress ensues. Obstruction should be relieved by tracheostomy.

Myocarditis: Intake of fluids and salt should be restricted. The patient should be asked to take bedrest and enforced restricted exertion. Diuretics and digoxin may be used.

Neurological complications: Children with palatal palsy should be fed by nasogastric feeding. Generalized weakness due to polyneuritis is treated as for poliomyelitis or Guillain Barre syndrome.

Prevention and Control

The patient should be isolated until two successive cultures of throat and nose are negative for diphtheria bacillus. All contaminated articles from discharges should be disinfected. All household/other contacts should be observed carefully for development of active lesions, cultured for *C. diphtheria* and given chemoprophylaxis with oral erythromycin (40–50 mg/kg/day for 7 days) or benzathine penicillin (60,000–120,000 units IM). Previously immunized asymptomatic patients should receive a booster dose of diphtheria toxoid. Those not fully immunized but asymptomatic contacts should receive immunization for their age. Immunization is discussed in chapter 8.

Suggested reading

Panchereon C. Clinical features of diphtheria in Thai children: a historic perspective. Southeast Asian J Trop Med Public Health 2002; 33: 352–4.

PERTUSSIS (WHOOPING COUGH)

Pertussis is an acute highly contagious respiratory tract infection, caused by *Bordetella pertussis*. It may affect any susceptible host but is more common and serious in infancy and early childhood. The disease is characterized by intense spasmodic cough. Similar illness is also caused by *B. parapertussis, B. brochiseptica* and adenoviral infections 1, 2, 3 and 5. The worldwide prevalence of the illness has declined following widespread vaccination.

Epidemiology

Pertussis is extremely contagious with attack rates as high as 100% in susceptible individuals exposed to aerosol droplets. *B. pertussis* does not survive for prolonged periods in the environment. Chronic carriage in humans is not known. After intense exposure as in households, the rate of subclinical infection is as high as 80% in fully immunized and naturally immune individuals. Protection against typical disease wanes 3–5 years after vaccination and is unmeasurable after 12 years. Coughing adolescents and adults are the major reservoir of *B. pertussis* and are the usual sources for index cases in infants and children.

Features

The incubation period of the disease is 7–14 days. The clinical presentation can be divided into three stages.

Catarrhal

This lasts for 1–2 weeks and is the most infectious period. The initial manifestations are indistinguishable from upper respiratory tract infections. The child has cough, coryza with little nasopharyngeal secretions. Unlike the upper respiratory infections, the cough does not improve in a few days but becomes more severe and frequent with the passage of time. Though the cough may not be typically paroxysmal in early stages, it tends to be annoying and frequent at night. The paroxysmal nature of the cough is suspected towards the latter part of this phase.

Paroxysmal

This stage lasts for 2–6 weeks in which cough progresses to episodic paroxysms of increasing intensity ending with high-pitched inspiratory whoop. The whoop is produced by the air rushing in during inspiration through the half-open glottis. The whoop may not always be present in infants who present with apneic or cyanotic spells. The child coughs up thick tenacious mucus. The paroxysms of cough may occur frequently and terminate by vomiting. Repeated thrusting of tongue over the teeth causes ulceration of the frenulum of the tongue. Paroxysms of cough are precipitated by food, cold air and cold liquids. In infants <3 months, this stage may be considerably prolonged.

Convalescent

The intensity and paroxysms of cough decrease gradually over 1–4 weeks. The vomiting becomes less frequent. Appetite, general condition and health gradually improve.

Complications

- Respiratory complications include otitis media, pneumonia, atelectasis, emphysema, bronchiectasis, pneumothorax and pneumomediastinum
- Neurological complications include seizures and encephalopathy (2–7%)
- Bleeding episodes, e.g. epistaxis, retinal or subconjunctival bleeds, intracranial hemorrhage
- Inguinal hernia, rectal prolapse
- Malnutrition due to persistent vomiting and disinclination to eat because of fear of paroxysms of cough with attempts at feeding
- Flare up of tuberculosis

Diagnosis

The diagnosis of whooping cough is based on clinical features. There may be a lymphocytic leukocytosis and low ESR. Specific diagnosis depends on isolation of the organism from nasopharyngeal swab or cough plate cultured on Bordet-Gengou medium, which is often positive in the catarrhal and paroxysmal stage. Rapid tests like direct fluorescent antibody and counter immuno-electrophoresis exist but are not available routinely. Other conditions that present with prolonged episodes of spasmodic cough include adenoviral infection, endobronchial tuberculosis, inhaled foreign body and reactive airway disease.

Management

General measures include providing adequate nutrition and hydration and avoiding factors aggravating cough. The antibiotic of choice is erythromycin (40–50 mg/kg/day in 3 divided doses) given for 14 days. It terminates the respiratory tract carriage of *B. pertussis* thus reducing the period of communicability but does not shorten the course of illness. Nebulization with salbutamol is effective in reducing bronchospasm and controlling bouts of cough. If nebulization is not possible, salbutamol may be given orally. Cough suppressants and antihistaminic agents should be avoided.

Prevention

Chemoprophylaxis with erythromycin is recommended for close family contacts especially children <2-year-old. Children under 7 years of age should be vaccinated, as discussed in chapter 8.

ENTERIC FEVER

The term enteric fever includes typhoid fever caused by *Salmonella enterica* var *typhi* and paratyphoid fever caused by *S. enterica* var *paratyphi* A, B or C. Paratyphoid infections constitute about 20% of all cases of enteric fever worldwide. As enteric fever is a disease transmitted by the feco-oral route, its greatest burden is in resource-limited countries where water supply and sanitary conditions are poor. In a community-based study in urban slums of Delhi the incidence was estimated to be 980/100 000 population.

Etiopathogenesis

S. enterica serotype *typhi/paratyphi* is a gram-negative, non-lactose fermenting, flagellate bacterium. The somatic or O antigen is shared among various salmonellae; the flagellar or H antigen is specific to the serovar. *S. enterica* var *typhi* also possesses a Vi polysaccharide capsule.

The infective dose of typhoid/paratyphoid bacillus varies from 10^3 to 10^6 organisms. The organism must survive the gastric barrier to reach the small intestine; hence, conditions which reduce gastric acidity, such as use of antacids, H2 receptor blockers and proton pump inhibitors, reduce the infective dose. On reaching the small intestine, the organism penetrates the mucosa and infects the lymphoid follicles and subsequently the draining mesenteric lymph nodes and the liver and spleen. It multiplies in the reticuloendothelial system and after incubation period varying from 7–14 days spills into the bloodstream and is widely disseminated, especially to liver, spleen, bone marrow, gallbladder and the Peyers patches of the terminal ileum. This spill marks the onset of clinical manifestations of enteric fever. Infection leads to both local and systemic immune responses, which are, however, inadequate to prevent relapse or reinfection.

Clinical Features

There is no appreciable difference between the manifestations of typhoid and paratyphoid fever. The hallmark of enteric fever is fever which starts as a low grade fever and then shows stepwise increase peaking to as high as 103–104°C by the end of the first week. This pattern differentiates it from viral fever where the peak is usually at the onset of fever. With fever, there is associated malaise, dull headache, anorexia, nausea, poorly localized abdominal discomfort, mild cough and malaise. There may be diarrhea; constipation in children is rare. Physical findings are unremarkable with the exception of a coated tongue, tumid abdomen and sometimes hepatosplenomegaly. The rash described in Western textbooks is seldom or never seen in Indian subjects. Infants and young children with enteric fever may have diarrhea as a predominant manifestation or a short-lasting undifferentiated febrile illness. In the absence of treatment fever may continue for 3–4 weeks followed by natural remission or by development of complications.

Complications

The commonest intestinal complications are bleeding or perforation seen in the 2nd or 3rd week of illness in 10–15% adult patients, but less frequently in children. Bleeding is due to erosion of a necrotic Peyers patch through the wall of a vessel and is usually mild but can, sometimes, be life-threatening. Perforation is a dreaded complication manifesting as acute abdomen, with high mortality unless appropriately treated.

The term severe or complicated enteric fever is used for patients presenting with neurological complications such as delirium/coma/obtundation/stupor and/or shock and is associated with mortality rates as high as 50%. Other complications of enteric fever include splenic abscesses, hepatitis, cholecystitis, pneumonia, disseminated intravascular coagulation and other manifestations such as psychosis/ ataxia or meningitis. The case fatality rate is less than 1% in appropriately treated cases but may be 10–20% in inadequately treated or complicated cases.

Relapse

Relapse may occur in 5–15% of treated cases, usually due to the organism with the same susceptibility as the original attack and is relatively a milder illness. Rate of relapse is dependent on choice of drug therapy. It is higher with beta lactams such as cefixime or ceftriaxone as compared to quinolones and azithromycin.

Carrier State

Although 5–10% adult patients may shed salmonella in stool following an acute attack for up to 3 months, only 1–4% excrete bacilli for more than 1 year. These individuals are potential sources of infection for family members and contacts and for the community if they are in occupations that involve food-processing. There is no data on carrier prevalence in children and routine examination of stool following recovery from enteric fever is not recommended.

Diagnosis

Leukocyte counts may be normal to low with absolute eosinopenia and neutrophilic predominance. Anemia and thrombocytopenia may occur in advanced illness. There may be mild elevation of transaminases to 2–3 times normal. The gold standard for diagnosis is blood culture. The sensitivity is greatest in the first week at around 90% but drops to 40% in the 4th week. Its overall sensitivity is 60%, which reduces to 20–40% after antibiotics. *Salmonella* is an easy organism to culture and use of bile broth media and automated culture systems such as BACTEC improve recovery. Sufficient blood should be collected (10 ml in adults and 5 ml in children) and a blood: media ratio of 1:5 should be maintained. The use of clot culture methods does not significantly improve recovery rates. Bone marrow cultures have higher yield as compared to peripheral blood cultures as salmonella is a pathogen of the reticuloendothelial system and should be done when patients present in later stages of the illness. Owing to very low recovery rates, stool cultures and urine cultures are not recommended. Antimicrobial susceptibility testing of the isolate is important in the era of multidrug resistance.

The Widal test has been in use for around 100 years for the serological diagnosis of typhoid. It detects presence of IgG and IgM antibodies to H (flagellar antigen) of *S. enterica* var *typhi* and *paratyphi* A and B, and O (somatic antigen) common to typhi and paratyphi A and B. Anti O titers are both IgG and IgM that rise and decline early, while anti H are primarily IgG that rise and decline late in course of the disease. The conventional method of interpretation of the Widal test has been to demonstrate fourfold rise in antibody titers in two samples. Since this is often not practical, a single titer of at least 1: 160 for both O and H is considered positive. Even with this compromise, the Widal test has several limitations. Sensitivity is low in the first week of illness and in patients treated with prior antibiotics. Specificity is low owing to anamnestic reactions, prior vaccination, cross reactivity with other *Enterobacteriaceae* and subclinical infections in endemic areas. Other tests such as Tubex and Typhidot that detect IgM antibodies against typhoid have not proven to be superior to the Widal test.

In summary, blood culture is the most important investigation in diagnosis of enteric fever. The blood culture is 100% specific, gives information on antimicrobial susceptibility of the isolate, is cost effective in the long run and is particularly important as other diagnostic methods are suboptimal.

Treatment

Indications for Inpatient Treatment

Most cases of enteric fever can be managed at home with oral antibiotics and advice to seek medical follow up in case of failure to respond to therapy or development of complications. Children with persistent vomiting, inability to take orally, severe diarrhea or abdominal distension usually require intravenous antibiotics therapy and intravenous fluids, necessitating admission to hospital.

Antimicrobial Susceptibility

The antimicrobial sensitivity of *S. typhi/paratyphi* has shown changes over the decades. Though resistance to chloramphenicol was first noted soon after its first use in the 1940's, it was not until 1972 that chloramphenicol-resistant typhoid fever became a major problem. Multi Drug Resistant typhoid fever (MDRTF) became a common occurrence by the end of 1990s, with emergence of *S. typhi* simultaneously resistant to all the drugs that were used as first-line treatment (chloramphenicol, trimethoprim, sulfamethoxazole and ampicillin). Fluoroquinolones were introduced in the late 1980's and early 1990's and produced very good results initially, but the past decade has seen a progressive increase in the minimum inhibitory concentrations (MIC) of ciprofloxacin in *S. typhi* and *paratyphi*. Since the current MICs are still below the standard susceptibility breakpoint, laboratories continue to report bacteria as sensitive to fluoroquinolones, but the use of fluoroquinolones in this scenario is associated with a high incidence of clinical failure because drug levels needed to kill organisms with such high MICs are not achieved with standard doses, and often, even with highest tolerated doses. Resistance to nalidixic acid has been suggested as a surrogate marker for high ciprofloxacin MICs that predict fluoroquinolone failure. Hence resistance to nalidixic acid may be used to guide antibiotic therapy, especially where MIC testing is not available (i.e. if resistance to nalidixic acid is present, quinolones should not be used or, if used, high doses should be given, irrespective of the results of ciprofloxacin/ofloxacin sensitivity). Alongside the recent rise in resistance to quinolones, there has been some return in sensitivity to first-line antibiotics such as chloramphenicol, cotrimoxazole and ampicillin. However, concerns of toxicity and inconsistent reports of sensitivity preclude their widespread use.

Currently, third-generation cephalosporins such as ceftriaxone and cefixime are the first-line agents for therapy of enteric fever. Azithromycin is a new drug that is being used as an alternative agent. Often there is discordance between *in vitro* and *in vivo* susceptibility in *S. enterica*; salmonella may show *in vitro* susceptibility to aminoglycosides and second-generation cephalosporins, but good *in vivo* responses may not be seen; therefore, these drugs should not be used to treat enteric fever.

Choice for Empirical Therapy

Where enteric fever is clinically suspected but cultures have not been sent for, reports are awaited or are sterile, empirical therapy may be started. Choice for empirical therapy is guided by various factors including the severity of the illness, inpatient/outpatient therapy, presence of complications and local sensitivity patterns.

For uncomplicated enteric fever, oral cefixime in a dose of 20 mg/kg/day is the drug of choice, both for sensitive and multidrug resistant *S. typhi*. In areas where nalidixic acid resistance is infrequent (rare at the moment in India), fluoroquinolones may still be considered the drugs of choice; however, if both nalidixic acid resistance and resistance to other drugs (like amoxicillin, chloramphenicol, cotrimoxazole) are widespread, the only options are oral cefixime or azithromycin. If the local resistance pattern is unknown, chances of failure are likely to be least if either cefixime or azithromycin is used.

Azithromycin (10–20 mg/kg/day) is a good second choice agent; chloramphenicol (50 mg/kg/day), amoxicillin and cotrimoxazole are other second-line agents. Clinical efficacy is more or less the same with all these drugs with each drug having its own advantages and limitations. The choice of medication depends on individual preference, experience, and level of comfort and cost considerations. Once culture results are available, therapy can be modified. There is no data at present to support use of combination therapy in enteric fever.

For severe illness and where complications are present, intravenous ceftriaxone and cefotaxime are used in a dose of 100 mg/kg/day. In patients with history of penicillin or cephalosporin allergy, aztreonam, chloramphenicol (in higher than usual doses) or cotrimoxazole (in higher than usual doses) are used as second-line agents. Parenteral treatment is continued until defervescence has occurred, oral intake has improved and complications resolved. Thereafter, therapy can be switched to oral cefixime to complete a total duration of 14 days. Other oral drugs that may be used for switch over therapy include cefpodoxime, azithromycin, cotrimoxazole and amoxicillin. However, the experience with cefpodoxime is limited, and the other agents require switch to a different class of antimicrobials than cephalosporins.

If cultures are positive and show nalidixic acid sensitivity, therapy should be changed to ciprofloxacin at a dose of 20 mg/kg/day as quinolones are associated with faster defervescence and lower relapse rates as compared to ceftriaxone. If cultures are positive and show nalidixic acid resistance as well as sensitivity to other drugs (ampicillin, chloramphenicol and cotrimoxazole), it is prudent to continue with ceftriaxone alone rather than change because the older drugs do not offer any advantage over ceftriaxone. If cultures are negative and defervescence has not occurred by day 7, a thorough search for alternative etiology for fever should be made and ceftriaxone continued. There is no role for changing the antimicrobial agent or adding another drug, since ceftriaxone resistance is currently anecdotal.

Therapy of Relapses

Relapse rates vary with the type of drug and are most common with beta lactams (ceftriaxone, cefixime) especially if shorter duration of therapy is used. Usually relapses may be satisfactorily treated with the same drug as used for primary therapy but for at appropriate dose and duration. However, if the isolate is nalidixic acid sensitive and fluoroquinolones were not used for primary therapy, they should be used for treatment of the relapse. Azithromycin is likely to be a promising agent for this purpose.

Therapy of Carriers

The carrier state is uncommon in children and testing for chronic carriage 3 months after an episode of enteric fever is not routinely recommended in children. However, if chronic carriage is demonstrated, treatment with amoxicillin (100 mg/kg/d) with probenecid (30 mg/kg/d) or cotrimoxazole (10 mg/kg/d) for 6–12 weeks is recommended. If the strain is nalidixic acid sensitive, quinolones for 28 days is a better option.

Prevention

The most effective and desirable method for preventing enteric fever is by improving hygiene and sanitation. This will yield additional dividends of reduction in the burden of other water-borne illnesses as well. Since this is unlikely in the near future in developing countries, vaccination is a major preventive strategy, as detailed in chapter 8.

Suggested reading

1. Parry CM, Hien TT, Dougan G, White NJ, Farrar JJ. Typhoid fever. N Eng J Med 2002; 347: 1770–82.
2. Kundu R, Ganguly N, Ghosh TK, Yewale VN, Shah RC, Shah NK; IAP Task Force. Report: management of enteric fever in children. Indian Pediatr 2006; 43: 884–7.
3. Kundu R, Ganguly N, Ghosh TK, Yewale VN, Shah RC, Shah NK; IAP Task Force. Report: diagnosis of enteric fever in children. Indian Pediatr 2006; 43: 875–83.

LEPTOSPIROSIS

Leptospirosis is an emerging zoonotic disease of worldwide distribution, caused by spirochetes of the genus *Leptospira*. The infection has a broad spectrum of clinical manifestations, varying from an influenza-like mild acute febrile illness with headache and severe muscular pain, to severe leptospirosis causing jaundice, renal failure, and severe hemorrhagic manifestations like pulmonary hemorrhage with respiratory distress, myocarditis with arrhythmias, meningitis and meningoencephalitis.

Most cases of leptospirosis occur in tropical and subtropical countries. While rats are the principal source of human infection, dogs, cats, livestock and wild animals are other important animal reservoirs. Infected animals may excrete spirochete in urine for several weeks. The survival of excreted organisms depends on the moisture content and temperature of the soil. Humans acquire infection after getting exposure to water or soil contaminated with rat urine. Agricultural workers, veterinarians, meat handlers, rodent control workers and laboratory personnel are at higher risk of getting infected because of occupational exposure.

Pathogenesis

Leptospira enter the body through abrasions and cuts in skin or through mucus membranes, and spread to all organs hematogenously. The organisms damage the endothelial lining of small blood vessels, with leakage and extravasation of blood cells, hemorrhage, and ischemic damage to various organs including liver, kidneys, meninges and muscles.

Clinical Features

Human infection with *Leptospira* may range from asymptomatic infection to a severe multiorgan involvement which is often fatal. Symptomatic infection is a relatively mild and anicteric febrile illness in over 70% of patients; about 20% present as aseptic meningitis, while severe leptospirosis with hepatorenal dysfunction (Weil's disease) develops in 5–10% of individuals. The incubation period is usually 1–2 weeks.

The illness is often biphasic. In the initial or septicemic phase lasting 2–7 days, fever and non-specific symptoms predominate, and organisms may be isolated from blood, cerebrospinal fluid and other involved tissues. After a brief asymptomatic phase, the second phase, called the immune or leptospiruric phase, becomes manifest wherein *Leptospira* localize to various tissues to cause tissue specific signs and symptoms. In this phase, circulating autoantibodies to *Leptospira* are present; organisms can no more be isolated from blood or CSF but persist in tissues like kidneys and aqueous humor.

Anicteric leptospirosis: Onset is abrupt with high grade fever with rigors and chills, lethargy, severe myalgia, headache, nausea, vomiting. Patient may have conjunctival suffusion with photophobia and orbital pain, generalized lymphadenopathy and hepatosplenomegaly. Transient maculopapular erythematous rash may be seen in <10% cases. Hypotension with bradycardia and circulatory collapse is rarely seen. Most patients become asymptomatic within one week. During the immune phase, some children may develop aseptic meningitis or uveitis with recurrence of fever. Encephalitis, cranial nerve palsies, paralysis and papilledema are rare manifestations. Central nervous system abnormalities usually normalize within 1 week; mortality is rare.

Icteric leptospirosis (Weil's syndrome): This is the most severe form of leptospirosis, characterized by jaundice, renal dysfunction, hemorrhagic diathesis and high mortality. Initial symptoms same as anicteric leptospirosis but after 1–2 weeks, hepatic, renal and vascular dysfunction develops. Hepatomegaly and tenderness in right upper quadrant are usually detected. Splenomegaly found in 20% of cases. Renal failure may develop, often during the second week of illness. All patients have abnormal urinary finding on urinalysis in the form of hematuria, proteinuria and casts. Azotemia is common, often associated with oliguria or anuria. Hemorrhagic manifestations are rare but when present, may include epistaxis, hemoptysis and gastrointestinal and adrenal hemorrhage. Transient thrombocytopenia may occur. Mortality is 5–15%.

Diagnosis

The diagnosis is established by serologic testing and by isolation of infecting organism. Serologic tests for leptospira are microscopic agglutination test (MAT), read by dark-field microscopy for agglutination, and titers are determined. Enzyme-linked immunosorbant assay methods, including an IgM-specific dot ELISA test, have also been developed. Leptospira can be isolated from blood and/or CSF during the first 10 days of illness and from urine for several weeks beginning at around 1 week. Warthin-Starry silver staining and immunoflouroscent and immunohistochemical methods permit identification of leptospira in infected tissue or body fluids. Spirochete may also be demonstrated by phase contrast or dark-field microscopy, but these are insensitive.

Treatment

Treatment should be initiated as early as possible. For a severe case of leptospirosis, parentral penicillin G (6–8 million U/m^2/24 hr q 4 hr IV for 7 days) is the drug of choice. Tetracycline oral or IV (10–20 mg/kg/24 hr q 6hr) can be used as an alternative for patients allergic to penicillin.

TETANUS

Tetanus is caused by the bacterium *Clostridium tetani*, a spore forming, anerobic, gram-positive motile bacillus, found in human and animal feces. Its spores are widespread in the environment. The organism produces a potent neurotoxin tetanospasmin, under certain conditions, which leads to the clinical manifestations of the disease. Tetanus commonly occurs in areas where soil is cultivated, in rural areas, in warm climates, and during summer months. According to WHO estimates, it contributes to almost 8% of vaccine preventable deaths.

Pathogenesis

C. tetani is a noninvasive organism. The spores of the organism remain nonpathogenic in soil or contaminated tissues until conditions are favorable for transformation into vegetative form. Transformation occurs in the presence of locally decreased oxygen reduction potential, typically in devitalized tissue, in the presence of a foreign body, trauma and crush injury and suppurative infections. Two types of toxins are produced by the organism, *tetanolysin* and *tetanospasmin*.

Tetanolysin is a hemolytic toxin, which potentiates infection, but does not contribute to the disease process *per se*. *Tetanospasmin*, a 150 kDa protein coded by a plasmid, is the main toxin responsible for the manifestations of the disease. It binds to the neuromuscular junction at the site of injury, and undergoes retrograde axonal transport to reach the presynaptic nerve terminal where it prevents the release of inhibitory neurotransmitters glycine and GABA. In a normal state, these transmitters prevent release of acetylcholine from excitatory neurons thus inhibiting muscle contraction. In the presence of the toxin, these inhibitory impulses are prevented, leading to uncontrolled contraction of muscles.

Clinical Features

Tetanus mainly affects the unimmunized and partly immunized individuals. The disease may occur in various forms: neonatal, generalized, localized, and cephalic. The most common forms are generalized and neonatal tetanus.

Generalized tetanus has an incubation period of approximately 8 days (range 2–14 days). However, the disease may occur months after the initial injury. The incubation period depends on the distance of the site of injury from the central nervous system. The faster is the onset of symptoms, the poorer is the prognosis. Characteristically, there is descending paralysis, with initial involvement of the jaw muscles. There is spasm of the masseters leading to trismus or lockjaw. Subsequent involvement of the neck, back and abdominal muscles occurs, soon involving the whole body. As the disease progresses, minimal stimuli may lead to generalized spasms, which are the hallmark of the disease, and contribute to serious complications and eventually death. Typically, the sensorium of the patient is preserved. There is difficulty in swallowing. Autonomic instability may occur, with blood pressure fluctuations in the form of hypertension or hypotension, diaphoresis and arrhythmias. Recovery usually begins after 3 weeks and approximately takes four weeks. Recovery from tetanus occurs by sprouting new nerve terminals in the spinal cord leading to relaxation of the contracted muscles.

Neonatal tetanus is a major cause of mortality in developing countries. It occurs as a result of unhygienic birth practices, most commonly when the umbilical cord is contaminated at the time of cutting after delivery. Symptoms usually appear by the third day after birth, never in the first two days of life and rarely after the age of two weeks. Excessive unexplained crying followed by refusal of feeds and apathy are the common initial symptoms. The baby develops progressive feeding difficulty, becomes rigid, develops paralysis, and may develop opisthotonic posturing and experience painful spasms. The mouth is kept slightly open due to pull and spasm of the neck (Fig. 9.14). Reflex spasm of the masseter makes feeding painful. Pharyngeal muscles go into spasm and cause dysphagia and choking, lockjaw or reflex trismus followed by spasms of limbs. There is generalized rigidity and opisthotonus in extension. Spasm of larynx and respiratory muscles are characteristically induced by stimuli such as touch, noise and bright light, resulting in episodes of apnea and cyanosis. Constipation persists until the spasms are relieved. Intercurrent infections, dehydration and acidosis may complicate the clinical picture. It has a very high case fatality rate of 70 to 100%.

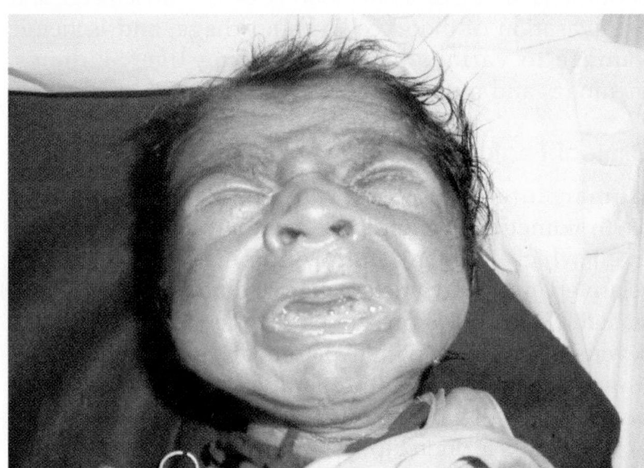

Fig. 9.14: Neonatal tetanus (Courtesy Dr. Amarjeet Mehta, Jaipur)

Localized tetanus is less severe in comparison, and is characterized by rigidity and pain confined to the muscles adjacent to the wound. It may lead to generalized tetanus later. In patients with isolated localized tetanus, the mortality is less than 1%. *Cephalic tetanus* is a form of local tetanus, which occurs due to injury of the bulbar muscles. It has a poor prognosis.

Treatment

Most patients require intensive care management and good supportive care. The aims of treatment are airway maintenance, prevention of further toxin absorption, relieving clinical features, e.g. spasms, controlling autonomic instability and antibiotics. Airway management may require intubation and mechanical ventilation, especially in severe cases and if the infant gets frequent episodes of largyngeal spasms, apneic attacks with cyanosis or central respiratory failure. Spasms are precipitated by minimal stimuli, therefore, efforts should be made to avoid noxious stimuli including bright lights, pain, and loud noises. Patient should be kept in a dark, quiet and isolated room, which should be lighted well to permit observation of the child; handling should be minimum. Intramuscular injections must be avoided. Temperature should be maintained within normal limits. Relief of spasms is done by using benzodiazepines. The most commonly used agent is diazepam, either as an intermittent IV bolus or as continuous infusion. Diazepam leads to prevention of further spasms by causing GABA-mediated central inhibition. It also helps by reducing anxiety and promoting muscle relaxation. Other agents used for severe spasms include pancuronium bromide.

Neutralization of free toxin is done by administering human tetanus immunoglobulin (TIG); however, antitoxin cannot dislodge the toxin already fixed to the nerve roots. The route of administration is intramuscular or intrathecal. The usual dose is 500 to 1000 IU. Supportive care includes maintaining adequate hydration, early detection of myoglobinuria, and prevention of renal shutdown. Oropharyngeal secretions should be sucked periodically. Maintenance of oxygen is important. Oral feeding should be stopped and an IV line should be established for providing adequate fluids, calories and electrolytes and for administration of various drugs. After three to four days of treatment, milk feeding through nasogastric tube may be started.

Antibiotic therapy is needed to abolish the bacteria from the wound site. The commonly used antibiotics are crystalline penicillin or metronidazole. Autonomic instability is controlled with the use of alpha and beta adrenergic blockers, like propranolol and labetalol. Intravenous magnesium has also been used, and found to be effective in decreasing autonomic instability, and treat muscle spasms.

Prognosis

The disease has high mortality rate in spite of adequate supportive care, which may reach up to 50% in severe generalized tetanus and 90% in neonatal form. The outcome depends on the incubation period, the site of injury, the rate of progression of illness, and presence of autonomic instability. Survivors do not manifest any neurological sequelae, except when apneic episodes are unduly prolonged and unattended. The prognosis in neonatal tetanus is worse if the (i) onset of symptoms occurs within the first weeks of life, (ii) interval between lockjaw on onset of spasms is less than 48 hours, (iii) high fever and tachycardia are present, (iv) spasms, especially of larynx resulting in apnea are severe and frequent.

All patients should receive a complete course of immunization with tetanus toxoid once recovered, as the disease does not induce protective antibodies.

Prevention

Immunization with tetanus toxoid leads to induction of protective antibodies, and is discussed in chapter 8. Maternal and neonatal tetanus can be effectively prevented by immunizing the mother during pregnancy, and ensuring clean delivery and cord care.

Suggested reading

1. Bunch TJ, Thalji MK, Pellikka PA et al. Respiratory failure in tetanus: Case report and review of a 25-year experience. Chest 2002; 122: 1488–92.
2. Singhi S, Jain V, Subramanian C. Post-neonatal tetanus: issues in intensive care management. Indian J Pediatr. 2001; 68: 267–72.
3. Okoromah CN, Lesi FE. Diazepam for treating tetanus. Cochrane Database Syst Rev 2004; CD003954.

PROTOZOAL INFECTIONS

MALARIA

Malaria is an important tropical disease, afflicting 350–500 million patients annually with over one million deaths. Of regions endemic for malaria, >70% cases are in Sub-Saharan Africa. Malaria is an important cause of morbidity and mortality in South Asia. Presently, about 2 million cases and 1000 deaths due to malaria are reported annually in India; 50% of these cases are due to infection with *Plasmodium falciparum*. Large numbers of cases are reported from Orissa, Chhattisgarh, West Bengal, Karnataka, Jharkhand, Madhya Pradesh, Uttar Pradesh, Assam, Gujarat and Rajasthan. About 10% cases are reported from the urban areas, due to construction activities, population migration, and inappropriate water storage and disposal. The National Health Policy (2002) and Millennium Development Goals aim for reduction in malaria mortality by 50% by year 2010.

Etiology

There are four species of *Plasmodium* that cause human malaria: *P. falciparum, P. vivax, P. malariae* and *P.ovale. P. falciparum* and *P. vivax* are the most common. Infection due to *P. falciparum* is the most serious, being responsible for deaths among children in Africa and in India. Infections due to *P. malariae* and *P. ovale* are clinically similar to *P. vivax*. The infectious stage of the parasite, the sporozoite, is transmitted to the host by the bite of the female anopheline mosquito. Transmission may also occur transplacentally and rarely through blood transfusions. Six species of anopheline mosquitoes are important in the transmission of the disease, namely *Anopheles culicifacies* (rural), *A. fluvitalis, A. stephensi* (urban), *A. minimus, A. philippinesis* and *A. sundaicus*. To enable development of parasites in the vector's body and make it capable of transmitting the disease, the vector must be susceptible, feed on human blood and live at least for 10–12 days after an infective blood meal. The vector should be present in large number or sufficient density to be of importance. Resting habits of the mosquito are important for planning control measures. Mosquitoes usually breed in edges of streams, water tanks, pits, cisterns and overhead tanks. *A. stephensi* breed in wells, cisterns, fountains and overhead tanks, *A. fluviatilis* in moving water and *A. sundaicus* in brackish water. Breeding sites such as burrowed pits, pools, ponds, marshy areas and unregulated irrigation channels are conducive to mosquito breeding and spread of malaria. Mosquitoes thrive best in temperature between 20–30 °C, relative humidity 60% and in areas with good rainfall. The peak transmission season of malaria is between July and November. Malaria is uncommon at altitudes over 2000 m above sea level.

Prevalence of Malaria in the Community

A number of indices are used to estimate the prevalence of malaria in the community. *Splenic index* is the prevalence of malaria in the community as measured by the rate of palpable spleen in children between the ages of 2–10 year. If less than 10% of children have palpable spleen, the incidence of malaria is considered low; hyperendemic areas show palpable spleens in >50% and holoendemic in >75%. *Parasite rate* is percentage of children between 2–10 years of age who show malarial parasites in blood films. *Proportionate case rate* is an index that measures the number of cases diagnosed with clinical malaria for every 100 patients reporting to the health facility.

Life Cycle of the Parasite

The life cycle of the malarial parasite involves two hosts.

Hepatic or Tissue Phase

When an infectious mosquito bites a human, it injects sporozoites, which circulate and invade hepatocytes and reticuloendothelial tissues within 30 minutes of the bite. During hepatic infection, *P. vivax* produces 2000–15000 merozoites and *P. falciparum* produces 40000 merozoites by repeated divisions. These merozoites are released and invade erythrocytes at end of the hepatic phase. In infection due to *P. vivax* and *P. ovale*, a dormant stage (hypnozoite) can persist in the liver and cause relapses by invading the bloodstream weeks or even years later. This intermittent release of schizonts in case of *P. vivax* and *P. ovale* may last for 2–3 years and for *P. malariae* for 10–20 years. The first exoerythrocytic cycle or the hepatic phase is asymptomatic and constitutes the incubation period. This cycle lasts at least 10 days (1–2 weeks for falciparum infection).

Erythrocytic Phase

After replication in the liver (exoerythrocytic schizogony), the parasites undergo asexual multiplication in the erythrocytes (erythrocytic schizogony). In erythrocytes, parasites develop into ring forms, mature trophozoites and then multinucleated schizonts, which rupture and release more merozoites. Repeated cycles of erythrocyte invasion and rupture lead to chills, fever, headache, fatigue, nonspecific symptoms and, with severe malaria, signs of organ dysfunction (Table 9.13).

A key feature of the life cycle of *P. falciparum* is cytoadherence, whereby erythrocytes infected with mature parasites adhere to endothelial cells in the microvasculature. This process is presumably advantageous to the parasite, since it prevents the passage of abnormal erythrocytes through the spleen. High concentrations of *P. falciparum* infected erythrocytes in the microvasculature and a complex interplay of host and parasite factors lead to the manifestations of severe malaria, including cerebral malaria, noncardiogenic pulmonary edema and renal failure. Because of the ability of mature *P. falciparum* organisms in the erythrocytic stage to adhere to endothelial cells, only ring forms circulate (except in very severe infections), and levels of peripheral parasitemia may be low despite substantial infection. Termination of the erythrocytic schizogony does not necessarily terminate the infection with malaria because merozoites of *P. vivax*, but not those of *P. falciparum*, may go into exoerythrocytic schizogony after the erythrocytic cycle. This explains why relapses are frequent after vivax but not falciparum malaria.

Sexual Reproduction

After several stages of schizogony, some parasites develop into gametocytes, which may be taken up by mosquitoes,

Table 9.13: Characteristics of severe malaria; features associated with a poor prognosis

Physical findings	*Laboratory abnormalities*
Prostration	Severe anemia: hematocrit <15, hemoglobin <5 g/dL
Impaired consciousness, coma	Hypoglycemia: glucose <40 mg/dL
Respiratory distress, tachypnea, dyspnea	Metabolic acidosis (bicarbonate <15 mEq/L, pH <7.25)
Pulmonary edema	Hyperlactatemia: venous lactate >36 mg/dL
Repeated seizures ≥3 seizures in 24-hr	Hyperparasitemia: >500 000 parasites/mm^3, or >5–10% red cells parasitized
Abnormal bleeding, retinal hemorrhages	Disseminated intravascular coagulation
Systolic pressure <80 mm Hg after volume repletion	Elevated aminotransferase levels >3 times normal
Jaundice	Bilirubin level >3 mg/dL
Acute renal failure	Renal insufficiency: creatinine >2.5–3 mg/dL

9

in which sexual reproduction and further development of the parasites lead to the generation of a new set of infectious sporozoites. The gametocytes are ingested by an Anopheles mosquito during a blood meal. Only the gametocyte forms survive in the stomach of the mosquito; all other stages are destroyed. The parasites' multiplication in the mosquito is known as the sporogonic cycle. While in the mosquito's stomach, fertilization of female gametes generates motile and elongated zygotes (ookinetes) that invade the midgut wall and develop into oocysts (resting stage). These oocysts grow, rupture and release sporozoites, which make their way to the mosquito's salivary glands. Inoculation of the sporozoites into a new human host perpetuates the malaria life cycle.

Pathophysiology

Innate Resistance

In countries where malaria is endemic, a large number of people suffer from the infection but a proportion of them are relatively immune, even though they are exposed to the similar environment. Some individuals are vulnerable to infection with one species of plasmodium but not to the other, due to the differences in genetic constitution of the species. The natural capacity of the host to resist infection with malaria is called the innate resistance, and this may be due to differences in the surface receptor, intraerythrocytic factors or yet unknown causes.

Differences in the cell membrane determine whether a merozoite can attach to the surface receptors or the cell membrane and invade the cells. Epidemiologic observations suggest that patients with sickle cell trait, thalassemia and glucose-6-phosphate dehydrogenase deficiency are relatively immune to malaria. It has been postulated that intraerythrocytic factors may (i) resist penetration of red cells by merozoites, (ii) impede development of merozoites and (iii) assist in their removal by the reticuloendothelial system. Homozygotes of sickle cell disease are not protected from malaria but heterozygotes are immune. Variations in HLA frequency may also determine the prevalence of malaria.

Acquired Resistance to Malaria

Sporozoites injected into the host localize to the liver cells within a few minutes. Apparently, there is no immunological defense against the naturally transmitted sporozoites in the blood or in the liver cells. Immunological defences start operating when merozoites invade erythrocytes. The first response to malarial infection is *phagocytosis* in the spleen or the hyperplastic reticuloendothelial cells. *Cell-mediated immunity* has an important role in protection, through activated macrophages that attack the parasitized erythrocytes. As host defences develop sufficiently, the parasite level falls abruptly and a crisis occurs with defervescence of temperature.

Following infection, serum immunoglobulins are elevated, with most *protective antibodies* against merozoites being of IgM type. The complement system, however, is not involved. Schizont-infested erythrocytes are phagocytosed rapidly if they have been sensitized with specific anti-malarial (opsonin) antibody. Antibodies against the toxins of malarial parasite protect the host from the toxic products of *P. falciparum*. Antimalarial antibodies and malarial antigens in maternal blood may be transmitted transplacentally to the fetus. While the former protect the newborn of the immune mother from malaria, antigens or antigen-antibody complexes help the infant to acquire immunity against malaria.

Immune Evasion by the Parasite

Though the parasite stimulates antimalarial antibodies in the host, yet the infection may continue for long periods due to the ability of the malarial parasites to survive in the host. The reasons for the survival of the parasites include: (i) antibodies against the parasite may promote their survival instead of destruction; (ii) the infection may impair antibody synthesis; (iii) handling and processing of the antigens by macrophages is impaired, and (iv) sporozoites, schizonts and gametocytes are not destroyed by immune defences of the host.

Immunopathology

Some pathological lesions in malaria are explained as being due to immunological mechanisms. Anemia is disproportionate to the damage to red blood cells by the parasites. It is due to the formation of autoantibodies to the erythrocytes and immune binding or adherence of the circulating malaria antigen-antibody complexes to uninfected erythrocytes. Hemolysis associated with blackwater fever is attributed to drug hypersensitivity. Damage to the kidneys is of two types: (i) acute transient lesions in which proteinuria develops a week or two after the infection and responds to antimalarial treatment. Renal biopsy shows immune complex deposits in the glomeruli. Proteinuria and immunological abnormalities disappear in 4–6 weeks, (ii) chronic progressive nephritic syndrome observed secondary to *P. malariae* infections (quartan malaria). Glomerular lesions are due to deposits of the soluble immune complexes in the basement membrane of the glomerular capillaries.

The spleen plays an important part in defence against malaria. The spleen is enlarged in malaria and returns to normal as infection is controlled. Splenomegaly due to malaria is associated with elevated levels of IgM and lymphocytosis in peripheral blood, bone marrow and liver sinusoids. Splenectomy results in relapse of the latent infection.

Cerebral malaria occurs frequently in the preschool children, but is relatively rare in those with protein-energy malnutrition. Histopathological studies show plugging of the cerebral capillaries with infected erythrocytes, hemorrhages and deposition of fibrin in the vessels. Changes may be due to mechanical factors, altered capillary permeability and intravascular coagulation.

Autoimmunity in malaria: Autoantibodies are increasingly observed in patients living in the endemic zones. The circulating antiglobulins may be produced in response to the circulating malarial immune complexes. Antinuclear antibodies are probably cross-reacting antibodies induced by the malarial DNA. Presence of these antibodies may be due to the release of the cross-reacting antigens, or alteration of the host tissue. As the parasite may have similar antigens as in the host, presence of these serological abnormalities should be interpreted with caution in areas endemic for malaria.

Immunosuppressive Effects

Individuals infected with malaria respond poorly to the other antigens, e.g. tetanus toxoid. Collagen vascular disorders such as rheumatoid arthritis and lupus are uncommon in malarial endemic zones. Measles and toxoplasmosis are generally more virulent. It is proposed that the immunological effects of malaria might allow Epstein-Barr virus to give rise to lymphoproliferative disorders.

Clinical Features

The incubation period of malaria varies between 9 and 30 days, being the least for *P. falciparum* and longest for *P. malariae* infections. The onset of the disease is not as characteristic as is believed, especially in infections with *P. falciparum.* The onset of the disease is sudden with fever, headache, loss of appetite, lassitude and pain in the limbs. The fever may be continuous or remittent for several days before it becomes classically intermittent. The illness, then, is characterized by a *cold stage* (chills and rigors with headache, nausea, malaise and anorexia); *hot stage* (dry flushed skin, rapid respiration and marked thirst); and *sweating stage* (temperature falls by crisis). There is no fever for 24–48 hr, and subsequently the fever depends on the type of malarial parasite causing the infection. The fever occurs on alternate days in falciparum and vivax malaria, and on the fourth day with *P. malariae* infection. Several paroxysm of fever may occur more or less regularly in a primary attack of malaria.

Non Immune Children

In children, the clinical presentation of malaria may not be typical. Even in the non immune children, many clinical features of classical malaria are masked. Initially, the child appears restless, drowsy or listless, refuses food and complains of nausea and headache. During the hot stage of illness, sweating is marked. Temperature may be variable moderate to high, continuous or irregular. The stools are often loose and vomiting is pronounced. Many children are acutely distressed due to abdominal pain. The liver is usually enlarged and after some days, the spleen also becomes palpable. This occurs relatively earlier in the vivax infection but may be late in falciparum malaria. Renal manifestations with proteinuria and casts in the urine may occur. Convulsions usually occur even though the fever is only moderately high. The diagnosis of cerebral malaria should be considered seriously in the endemic zones if the consciousness does not return soon in a febrile patient who develops convulsions. The children look pale. During fever they appear flushed and sweat freely.

Clinical Pattern in Endemic Zones

The clinical profile of malaria from the highly endemic zones is atypical. Since these patients have already some degree of tolerance to malaria, the parasitemia is minimal and symptoms are generally mild. The patient may appear restless and pale. Appetite is poor and temperature rises only occasionally. After some time, the inherited immunity may diminish and as these patients are continuously exposed to heavy doses of infection with plasmodia and have poor immunological defence, a severe clinical disease may then occur. At this stage, the patient may even die of cerebral malaria. After several episodes of malaria, some degree of tolerance again develops and then the clinical picture becomes mild, with low grade fever, easy fatigability and irritability. The liver and spleen are enlarged. During this phase the patient may succumb to associated malnutrition, anemia and intercurrent bacterial infections. Patients in highly endemic zones may develop *chronic malaria* in which the liver and spleen are markedly enlarged. They look wasted and pale with either no fever or only a moderate elevation of temperature.

Relapse

Relapse is defined as the recrudescence of fever after a period which is greater than the normal periodicity of malarial fever. Relapses are rare in falciparum malaria as the plasmodia do not go into the exoerythrocytic phase after the erythrocytic schizogony. These are however, frequent in vivax malaria because they can start erythrocytic schizogony, resulting in relapse of the clinical illness.

Complications

Cerebral Malaria

The onset may be sudden or gradual. The child develops convulsions and becomes unconscious. Cerebrospinal fluid is normal. Cerebral malaria is due to blockage (sequestration) of capillaries with parasitized erythrocytes and terminally, thrombosis may occur. Three separate receptors of parasitized erythrocytes have been identified (ICAM-11, CD 36 and thrombospondin). These cause foci of cerebral damage. The illness may be confused with meningitis, encephalitis, head injury or tetanus. Mortality of cerebral malaria is high (about 15–16%) and the surviving children may be left with major neurological residua in about 9% of cases. Hypoglycemia associated with cerebral malaria carries bad prognosis.

Anemia

The anemia is severe and out of proportion to the degree of parasitemia.

Gastrointestinal illness

Marked vomiting (characteristic of malaria in infants), diarrhea, dehydration, dyselectrolytemia are present. The stools are dark green and brownish and are sometimes tinged with blood. The symptoms subside quickly with the antimalarial drugs.

Algid Malaria

This is characterized by peripheral circulatory failure and shock and usually occurs with falciparum infections in the non-immune children.

Blackwater Fever

The blackwater fever is characterized by sudden severe hemolysis, hemoglobinuria and renal failure. Hypersensitivity to drugs is the most likely cause of this syndrome.

Renal Lesions

Acute transient nephritis or chronic nephritic syndrome (*P. malariae* infection) may be associated.

Diagnosis

The clinical picture of malaria in children in endemic zones may often be atypical, and a high index of suspicion for malaria is required. The diagnosis should be established by demonstrating the parasites in blood. The microscopic tests involve staining and direct visualization of the parasite under the microscope.

Peripheral Smear: A careful examination of a well-prepared and well-stained blood film currently remains the "gold standard" for malaria diagnosis. Sometimes no parasites can be found in peripheral blood smears from patients with malaria, due to partial antimalarial treatment or sequestration of parasitized cells in deep vascular beds. In these cases, parasites, or malarial pigment may be found in the bone marrow aspirates, in circulating neutrophils or monocytes.Thick and thin smears are usually prepared. Thick smears are used for screening of parasites with a sensitivity of 5–10 parasites/µL.; thin smears for identifying the species and for the stippling of infected red cells and have a sensitivity of 200 parasites/µL. In thick blood film, infected erythrocytes are counted in relation to a predetermined number of WBCs (200 leucocytes are counted in 100 fields). All parasite species and forms including both sexual and asexual forms are counted together. In thin blood film the percentage of parasitaemia is calculated for *P. falciparum*. The number of infected red cells (and not number of parasites) in 1000 RBCs is converted to percentage. This method estimates the percentage of red blood cells infected with malarial parasites. The smear is scanned carefully, one 'row' at a time, and the total number of red cells and the number of parasitized red cells are tabulated separately. If 1000 red cells are counted, then divide the number of parasitized red cells by 10 to get the percentage (i.e. if 30 out of 1000 cells are parasitized, then the parasitized red cell count is 3%).

Quantitative Buffy Coat (QBC) test is a new method for identifying the malarial parasite in the peripheral blood. It involves staining of the centrifuged and compressed red cell layer with acridine orange and its examination under UV light source. It is fast, easy and claimed to be more sensitive than the traditional thick smear examination. About 60 microliters of blood from a finger, ear or heel puncture is sufficient. The key feature of the method is centrifugation and thereby concentration of the red blood cells in a predictable area of the QBC tube, making detection easy and fast. Red cells containing *Plasmodia* are less dense than normal ones and concentrate just below the leukocytes, at the top of the erythrocyte column. A precisely made cylindrical float, occupies 90% of the internal lumen of the tube, causes the leukocyte and thrombocyte cell band widths and the top-most area of red cells to be enlarged to 10 times normal. The parasites contain DNA which takes up the acridine orange stain, Fluorescing parasites can be observed at the red blood cell/white blood cell interface using the standard white light microscope. Virtually all of the parasites found in the 60 microliter of blood can be visualized by rotating the tube under the microscope. A negative test can be reported within one minute and positive result within minutes.

Rapid diagnostic tests detect malaria antigens (PfHRP2/PMA/pLDH) from asexual and/or sexual forms of the parasite. The presence of parasite antigen in blood is detected by color changes on antibody coated lines on the strip test such as the OptiMAL (DiaMed; under license from Flow, Inc., Portland, Oreg.) assay and Para Sight F test are being increasingly employed. In general, these are quick and simple to use, distinguish between the major forms of human malaria, and may have some advantages over microscopy, particularly in children with low density parasitaemia. Table 9.14 highlights the differences between microscopy and rapid diagnostic tests.

OptiMAL is a patient point-of-care immunochromatographic test that can be performed with a drop of finger stick blood. The test detects parasite lactate dehydrogenase, a parasite glycolytic enzyme produced by all species of metabolizing *Plasmodium* parasites. The test can distinguish between *P. falciparum* and non-falciparum species, but differentiation between the 3 non-falciparum species is not possible. The detection limit of the test is >100–200 parasites/µL for *P. falciparum* and *P. vivax*; it may be higher for *P. malariae* and *P. ovale*. A positive test indicates presence of viable parasitemia. The entire process

Table 9.14: Comparison of peripheral blood smear examination and rapid diagnostic tests for malaria

	Peripheral smear	*Rapid diagnostic tests*
Format	Slides with blood smear	Test strip
Equipment	Microscope	Kit only
Training	Trained microscopist	'Anyone with a little training'
Test duration	20–60 minutes or more	5–30 minutes
Test result	Direct visualization of the parasites	Color changes on antibody coated lines
Capability	Detects and differentiates all plasmodia at different stages	Detects malaria antigens (PfHRP2/ PMA/pLDH) from asexual and/or sexual forms of the parasite
Detection threshold	5–10 parasites/µL of blood	100–500/µL for *P. falciparum*, higher for non-falciparum
Species differentiation	Possible	Cannot differentiate among non-falciparum species; mixed infections of *P. falciparum* and non-falciparum appear as *P. falciparum*
Quantification	Possible	Not possible
Differentiation between sexual and asexual stages	Possible	Not possible
Disadvantages	Availability of equipment and skilled microscopists, particularly at remote areas and odd hours	Unpredictable efficiency at low and very high parasitemia; cross reactions among plasmodial species and with auto-antibodies; persistence of antigens
Status	Gold standard	Not yet approved by the FDA

takes approximately 15 min, and results are visually interpreted. The presence of a positive control line verifies that the test strip is functional (Fig. 9.15). The test remains positive for 1–3 weeks after treatment.

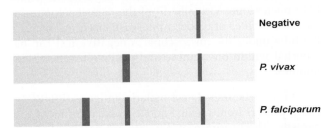

Fig. 9.15: OptiMAL test for rapid diagnosis of malaria. Expected reaction patterns on the OptiMAL test strip for a negative patient, a patient with *P. vivax* malaria, and a patient with *P. falciparum* malaria.

Two other rapid diagnosis tests are available; these are based on the histidine rich protein 2 of *P. falciparum* (PfHRP2), a water soluble protein expressed on RBC membrane of *P. falciparum*, and pan-specific Plasmodium aldolase (PMA), a parasite glycolytic enzyme produced by all species. One test utilises PfHRP2 alone, while another test uses both PfHRP2 and PMA. Hence the former can only detect *P. falciparum*, with a detection limit of >40–100 parasites/µL. The latter test is positive in presence of any of the four species, with differentiation possible between *P. falciparum* and non-falciparum species (but differentiation between the 3 non-falciparum species is not possible). The detection limit of this test is higher for non-falciparum species than for *P. falciparum*. These tests do not provide any indication of parasite viability, unlike the LDH based test.

Polymerase chain reaction (PCR) has been found to be highly sensitive and specific for detecting all species of malaria, particularly in cases of low level parasitemia and mixed infections. The PCR test is reportedly 10–fold more sensitive than microscopy. The PCR test has also been found useful in unraveling the diagnosis of malaria in cases of undiagnosed fever. *Antibodies to the asexual blood stages* appear a few days after malarial infection, increase in titer over the next few weeks, and persist for months or years in semi-immune patients in endemic areas, where re-infection is frequent. In non-immune patients, antibodies fall more rapidly after treatment for a single infection and are undetectable in 3–6 months. These antibodies can be detected by immunofluorescence or enzyme immunoassay. Fluorescent antibody technique, which detects species-specific IgG antibodies, may remain positive for several months after cure of the illness. It is useful in epidemiological surveys, for screening potential blood donors and occasionally for providing evidence of recent infection in non-immunes. *Intraleukocytic malaria pigment* has been suggested as a measure of disease severity. *Flowcytometry* and automated hematology analyzers have been found to be useful in indicating a diagnosis of malaria during routine blood counts. In cases of malaria, abnormal cell clusters and small particles with DNA fluorescence, probably free malarial parasites, have been seen on automated hematology analyzers and it is suggested that malaria can be suspected based on the scatter plots produced on the analyzer.

Other investigations including complete blood counts, and blood levels of glucose, bilirubin, urea, creatinine, transaminases, prothrombin time, urinalysis may be done as required.

If laboratory confirmation is not available, it is appropriate to give a therapeutic trial with antimalarial drugs. Proven resistance to antimalarial drugs however, is not uncommon. There is leukopenia with an increase in proportion of large mononuclear cells. Administration of subtherapeutic doses of antimalarial drugs makes it difficult to interpret the clinical or laboratory findings.

Differential Diagnosis

The early invasive phase of malaria can be confused with typhoid fever, non-icteric hepatitis and septicemia. The paroxysmal phase of malaria should be distinguished from urinary tract infections, gram negative septicemia and liver abscess. Simultaneous infection with two strains of plasmodia may cause difficulty in diagnosis in some cases. Cerebral malaria may be mistaken for meningitis, encephalitis, lead encephalopathy or heat stroke. Gastrointestinal forms may be misdiagnosed as non-specific gastroenteritis, cholera, *E. coli* diarrhea or abdominal emergencies. Algid form resembles shock due to septicemia. Chronic malarial fever with splenomegaly may be confused with tuberculosis, kala azar and leukemia.

Treatment

Management of a child with malaria at the primary health facility involves making a clinical diagnosis of malaria on the basis of signs and symptoms, confirmation of malaria by lab tests/rapid diagnostic kits, referral to a secondary/ tertiary level of care in case of complications, and education of patient or family. Health education of the family should include instructions about administration of drugs (Table 9.15), danger symptoms (Table 9.13), when to report to health facility, and prevention of malaria.

Table 9.15: Pharmacotherapy of malaria in National Anti-Malaria Drug Policy

Drug categories

Schizonticidal drugs (used for clinical and parasitological cure)	Chloroquine, amodiaquine, quinine, pyrimethamine, trimethoprim, proguanil, sulfa-pyrimethamine, mefloquine, halofantrine, artemisinine and its derivatives
Gametocytocidal and antirelapse drugs	Primaquine, 8-aminoquinoline group

Practice followed

	Microscopy or Rapid diagnostic kit test (RDK)		**Clinical malaria (No microscopy or RDK)**	
	P. vivax positive	*P. falciparum positive*	*Low risk area*	*High risk area*
Chloroquine	25 mg/kg over 3 days	25 mg/kg over 3 days	25 mg/kg over 3 days	25 mg/kg over 3 days
Primaquine (contra-indicated in pregnant woman and infants)	0.25 mg/kg/day × 14 days under medical supervision (to prevent relapse)	0.75 mg/kg on day 1	–	0.75 mg/kg on day 1
Artesunate sulfa-pyrimethamine (Artesunate-based combination therapy, ACT)*		4 mg/kg/day of artesunate daily × 3 days + 25 mg/ kg of sulphadoxine or sulphalene + 1.25 mg/ kg of pyrimethamine on day 1		

Treatment categories

- Drugs for first-line treatment: Given to clinical or confirmed malaria, e.g. chloroquine
- Drugs for second-line treatment: Given to treatment failure, severe and complicated malaria, pregnant women, and travelers. e.g. Artesunate + sulpha pyrimethamine (artesunate-based combination therapy, ACT) combination, quinine
- Mass treatment: Recommended in epidemics

* **Indications for alternative /second-line antimalarial drug** (artesunate-sulfa-pyrimethamine (ACT) combination)

- The area/PHC showing a treatment failure more than 10% (both early and late treatment failure) to chloroquine in the minimum sample of 30 cases
- Suspected resistance: If despite full treatment, with no history of vomiting or diarrhea, patient does not respond within 72 hours parasitologically
- In areas with high disease burden, high proportion of *P. falciparum*, inadequate facilities for laboratory diagnosis, inaccessibility and relatively poor communication facilities and the presence of *P. falciparum* chloroquine resistant pockets, based on clinical diagnosis of malaria by a trained medical officers or trained paramedical personnel after excluding other common causes of fever.

Artesunate tablets should not be administered as monotherapy; primaquine may not be given with ACT combination as artesunate reduces gametocyte carriage.

Dispensing the correct drugs of assured quality (first dose may be given preferably by dispenser), and ensuring patient compliance are important. The classical manifestations of malaria may not occur, especially in children; hence, any case of fever in the endemic areas during transmission season may be considered as malaria.

Management of Severe Malaria

Although most cases of *P. falciparum* malaria in patients presenting to health services are uncomplicated, up to 10% become severe and life threatening malaria, principally because of delays in diagnosis and inadequate treatment. In severe disease, the clinical spectrum, complications and management in children considerably differ from those in adults. Complications such as multiple convulsions, Kussmaul's breathing (indicating metabolic acidosis) and severe anemia are more common in children than in adults; while jaundice, a common complication in adults with severe malaria, is rarely seen in children, and renal failure and pulmonary edema occur even more infrequently than in adults.

Immediate Management

The initial stabilization of the patient involves the use of advanced life support techniques. The key steps include the following:

- Assessment of airway, breathing and circulation and intervention as required.
- Diagnosis and treatment of hypoglycemia and other dyselectrolytemias (Table 9.16)
- Assessment of vital and consciousness (Glassgow Coma Scale)
- Assessment of hydration.
- Management of unconsciousness patients should include placement of nasogastric tube and emptying of gastric contents (to prevent aspiration), urinary catheterization (to measure urine output), and placement of central vascualr access (to measure central venous pressure) and lumbar puncture (LP), should be performed to rule out acute bacterial meningitis (Table 9.16); LP should be deferred if signs of raised intracranial pressure are present.

Criteria for admission to the intensive care unit are outlined in Table 9.17.

Anti-malarial Therapy

Treatment with effective anti-malarial agents is the only therapeutic intervention that has been shown to reduce mortality in severe malaria. Anti-malarial agents should be administered parenterally to patients with severe malaria, since gastrointestinal absorption may be erratic. In a life-threatening situation such as severe malaria, all efforts should be directed to ensure that effective levels of these drugs are attained in patients. The cinchona alkaloids (e.g. quinine) or artemisinin derivatives are the usual drugs of choice in such a situation.

Table 9.16: Investigations to detect complications of severe malaria

Blood
Parasite count
Blood glucose level
Complete hemogram (hemoglobin estimation, white cell count and platelet count)
Blood group determination and cross match
Blood gas analysis
Serum electrolyte estimation
Blood urea and creatinine level
Blood culture
Coagulation indices
Estimation of serum/plasma levels of liver enzymes
CSF
Microscopic examination including cell count
Estimation of CSF levels of glucose and protein (to exclude other infections of the central nervous system)
Urine
Determination of specific gravity
Microscopic examination including cell count
Chest X-ray
Evidence of pulmonary edema or pneumonia

Table 9.17: Criteria for admission of patients with severe malaria to ICU

Acidosis	Base excess <-8
Parasitaemia	Endemic areas: >20% Non-endemic areas: >10%
Coma	Glasgow Coma scale $\leq$ 8
Hypoglycemia	Blood glucose level < 2.2 mmol/l
Renal dysfunction	Urine output < 0.5 ml/kg/hr
Pulmonary edema	

Quinine: Quinine can be administered intravenously, intramuscularly or orally, but only the parenteral routes are recommended in the presence of severe malaria. Quinine dihydrochloride salts are used parentally as the first line of treatment in most parts of the world. It acts on the mature trophozoite stages only. Quinine has 85% bioavailability when given intramuscularly, even in young children but the intramuscular route is avoided in view of the associated pain. A loading dose of intravenous quinine allows for parasiticidal concentrations to be achieved quickly. It reduces fever clearance time and parasite clearance time (Table 9.18). Once the child is able to take orally, parenteral quinine is substituted with oral quinine in a dose of 10 mg/kg/dose given 8 hourly to complete 7 days of therapy with quinine.

Table 9.18: Parenteral anti-malarial therapy for severe falciparum malaria

Antimalarial	Loading dose	Maintenance dose
Cinchona alkaloids		
Quinine dihydrochloride	20 mg salt /kg over 4 hr IV	10 mg salt /kg over 4 hr repeated every 8 hr
Quinidine gluconate† IV	20 mg salt/kg IV infused over 4 hr	10 mg salt/kg infused over 4 hours every 8–12 hr
Artemisin derivatives		
Artesunate IV route	2.4 mg/kg	1.2 mg/kg repeated at 12 and 24 hr, then 1.2 mg/kg/d
Artemether IM route	3.2 mg/kg	1.6 mg/kg repeated 12–24 hr

*The loading dose is to be avoided in a patient who has received quinine, mefloquine or quinidine within the last 24 hours.
†Monitor the QRS and QTc during treatment
Oral quinine (tablets or syrup) is unpalatable; hence it should never be prescribed for young children.

Quinine has a strong stimulant effect on pancreatic insulin secretion and leads to iatrogenic hypoglycemia. In the doses used for the treatment of malaria it does not appear to cause significant cardiotoxicity, but it is advisable to monitor the electrocardiogram while the loading dose is administered. ***Cinchonism*** (tinnitus, high-tone hearing impairment, nausea, dysphoria and vomiting) often leads to poor compliance with the seven-day regime. Although quinine may cause contractions of the pregnant uterus and has been associated with effects on the fetus, it remains the most widely used drug for the treatment of severe malaria during pregnancy.

Quinidine: Quinidine, a d-isomer of quinine, is more effective than quinine as an antimalarial but is also more cardiotoxic. Systemic hypotension and significant QTc prolongation are more commonly seen with quinidine. It is used mainly in the USA. It is rarely used in other parts of the world and except when quinine and artemisinin derivatives are not available.

Artemisinin derivatives: Artemether and artesunate are increasingly being used in the treatment of severe malaria. Treatment is initiated with a loading dose that is followed by a once-daily dose regimen. Such a schedule is more convenient than that used for the administration of cinchona alkaloids. Artemisinin derivatives have the advantage of clearing the parasitemia at a faster rate than that seen with quinine, because artemisinin and its derivatives are fatal for all stages of the parasite. However, there is to date no difference in the efficacy and safety of quinine and artemether, as shown by mortality or frequency or severity of residual neurological sequelae. The artemisinin derivatives have relatively few side-effects, although severe allergic reactions have been reported. The reticulocyte count may drop transiently in the first week of treatment, although this does not appear to aggravate the anemia associated with malaria. Artemisinin-induced neurotoxicity was detected in animal models, although there have been no reports of neuro-toxicity in human subjects. These compounds should be used in combination with other anti-malarials to prevent the development of resistance.

Other anti-malarials: Other anti-malarial drugs such as halofantrine, mefloquine, atavaquone, SP, doxycycline, and tetracycline are not recommended in severe and complicated malaria as primary treatment. Parasite resistance has developed to these drugs, when they are used alone. Mefloquine administered by the nasogastric route in patients with CM showed rapid but incomplete absorption suggesting that this route is unreliable in patients with severe malaria. These anti-malarials may be used in the latter stages of the management of severe malaria to reduce the period of parenteral treatment, improve compliance and cure, and prevent the development of resistance to the parenteral anti-malarials.

Supportive Therapies

Adjunct therapy may reduce mortality since over a third of the patients die within 12 hours of admission, before the antimalarials have had time to work. Supportive therapy is aimed at reversal or termination of patho-physiological mechanisms that lead to potentially fatal complications.

Antibiotics: Blood cultures have detected bacteremia in 7–14% of patients admitted with severe malaria. Non-typhoid Salmonella septicaemia is the most common co-infection in children with severe malaria. In patients with a reduced level of consciousness, the differential diagnosis of meningitis must be entertained and broad-spectrum anti-microbial agents should be administered until the diagnosis can be excluded.

Anticonvulsants: Seizures are common in children with severe falciparum malaria, but occur less frequently in adults. The pathogenesis of seizures in severe malaria is not clear, but they may be caused by the sequestration of parasites in the brain, hypoglycemia, hyperpyrexia (in children prone to febrile seizures), and sepsis or meningitis. Seizures may not be detected clinically; particularly in cerebral malaria. Prophylactic phenobarbitone is associated with an increased risk of mortality in children. The management of seizures should include correction of the underlying cause, such as hypoglycemia. Anticonvulsants should be administered for seizures lasting more than five minutes. Benzodiazepines are the most widely used and available anticonvulsants, but may cause respiratory depression. Other anticonvulsants, e.g. paraldehyde have less deleterious effects on respiration. With repeated or prolonged seizures, phenytoin, phenobarbitone, fosphenytoin, chlormethiazole and thiopentone have been used. These longer acting anticonvulsants require continued monitoring of vital signs for at least 4 hours after administration.

Blood transfusion and exchange transfusion: Blood transfusion is life-saving in severe malarial anemia. In malaria endemic areas, children with hemoglobin concentration less than 4 g/dl or presence of respiratory distress or parasitemia greater than 10%, with hemoglobin concentration between 4 and 5 g/dl should receive blood transfusion. The role of loop diuretics in children during transfusion is not established. The clinical condition of these individuals should be closely monitored to detect the development of fluid overload. Small doses of loop diuretics may avoid circulatory overload. Exchange transfusion has been thought to benefit patients with high parasite counts. The rationale is to remove infected red cells and thereby reduce the parasite burden, to reduce antigen load, to remove parasite-derived toxins and metabolites, and to correct anemia. In non-immune patients with severe falciparum malaria, indications for undertaking exchange transfusions include parasitemia exceeding 30%, irrespective of clinical features, response to therapy or absence of poor prognostic features. It is recommended that the procedure should be undertaken even if parasitemia is above 10%, if the patient has features suggestive of severe disease or if the individual has demonstrated failure to respond to treatment after 12–24 hours or if poor prognostic factors such as advanced age, or presence of late-stage parasites (schizonts) in the peripheral blood are present. Patients with anemia with circulatory overload may benefit from an exchange transfusion. This procedure, justified by convention, should be attempted only in units that can supply pathogen-free compatible fresh blood and when facilities for hemodynamic monitoring during and after the procedure are available.

Dialysis: The indications for dialysis in acute renal failure due to severe falciparum malaria are similar to other causes of renal failure. The mortality in acute renal failure without dialysis is 50–75%. Early diagnosis and treatment is important in preventing mortality. A rapidly rising creatinine level is the most sensitive indicator of the need for dialysis. Peritoneal dialysis reduces mortality, but hemofiltration is even more effective and is associated with an improved outcome.

Fluids: The role of fluids in severe falciparum malaria is controversial and appears to be different in children as compared to adults. The fluid requirements must be assessed in each patient. Hypovolemia is corrected by boluses of fluids that improve circulation. Children rarely develop pulmonary edema. Fluid administration should be stopped and diuretics given if pulmonary edema is suspected. Monitoring the CVP is very helpful during the administration of fluids. There is no evidence to show that fluid restriction improves the outcome in cerebral malaria.

Electrolyte derangements, particularly hyponatremia are an important consideration in the choice of fluids to be administered. Isotonic (0.9%) saline is used to correct hypovolemia. Maintenance fluids must contain sufficient glucose to prevent hypoglycemia. When anemia is present, blood transfusion should be considered as a therapeutic intervention. Fresh blood improves acidosis and red cell deformability found in falciparum malaria. Hypocalcemia (<2 mmol/l) should be managed with 0.3 ml/kg 10% calcium gluconate administered intravenously over 30 minutes, while hypomagnesemia (<0.75 mmol/l) is treated with 0.2 ml/kg 50% $MgSO_4$ administered intravenously over 30 minutes. Hypokalemia should be looked for and treated if present.

Inotropic support: Although shock (algid malaria) is rare, it is fatal. Dopamine appears to provide better inotropic support than adrenaline.

Hypoglycemia: Hypoglycemia is a common complication, particularly in children and pregnant women. Often, it cannot be detected clinically; hence frequent checking of blood glucose levels is mandatory, particularly in patients with impaired consciousness. Correction with 50% dextrose appears to be safe in adults, but this has not been established in children. Any blood sugar < 3 mmol/liter should be treated with 5 ml/kg of 10% dextrose intravenously.

Raised intracranial pressure: Raised intracranial pressure (ICP) is frequent in children with cerebral malaria, especially in Africa. Recent studies from India suggest that brain swelling, is common in adults. The treatment of raised ICP in malaria remains controversial. Mannitol may reduce the ICP but with no effect in reducing sequelae or mortality.

Ventilation: Prompt endotracheal intubation by experienced personnel and mechanical ventilation may be a life-saving procedure. Acute respiratory distress syndrome, poor respiratory effort, aspiration pneumonia, acute pulmonary edema and deep coma may benefit from ventilatory support.

Therapies not Recommended for the Treatment of Malaria

There are many therapies that have been tried in severe malaria, but there is insufficient evidence to recommend their use.

Antipyretics use remains controversial, since studies in patients with non-severe malaria showed that use of antipyretics, e.g. paracetamol, (only) prolonged parasite clearance in two studies of uncomplicated malaria, but has not been studied in severe disease. Ibuprofen appears to be more effective than paracetamol in uncomplicated malaria but should be avoided in patients with abnormal bleeding.

Corticosteroids have not shown any benefit when used in cerebral malaria, and their use was associated with significant side-effects. There is no evidence to support the use of low molecular weight dextran, adrenaline, cyclosporin A, and hyperimmune serum in patients with cerebral malaria. Use of dichloroacetate and anti-TNF antibodies has not shown any beneficial effects on survival in malaria.

National Anti-malaria Drug Policy (2007)

- All cases of fever should be investigated for malaria by microscopy or a rapid diagnostic kit (RDK).
- Patients should be treated according to the diagnosed species. However, if RDK for only *P. falciparum* is used, negative cases showing sign and symptom of malaria without any other obvious causes should be considered as clinical malaria.
- In patients resistant to chloroquine and artesunate sulpha pyrimethamine combination, oral quinine with tetracycline or doxycline can be prescribed.
- Mefloquine should be administered to patients with chloroquine or multiresistant uncomplicated *P. falciparum* malaria, only in standard doses as prescribed by the WHO. This drug should be made available through the depot system and only provided to patients against the prescription of medical practitioners supported by laboratory report showing asexual stage of *P. falciparum* parasite and not gametocyte alone and other species.
- Chemoprophylaxis with chloroquine is recommended in selected cases, including (i) pregnant women in high-risk areas and (ii) travelers including service personnel who temporarily go on duty to high malarious areas. In chloroquine resistant areas, it should be supplemented by daily dose of proguanil. However, chemoprophylaxis should not exceed 3 years due to the cumulative toxic effect of chloroquine.
- Patients with severe and complicated *P. falciparum* malaria should be treated with IV quinine or parenteral artemisinine derivatives, irrespective of chloroquine resistance status. In case of non-availability of the above drugs, chloroquine 10 mg/kg body weight in isotonic saline should be infused over 8-hours followed by 15 mg/kg body weight in the next 24-hr. This treatment may continue until such time quinine or artemesinine derivatives become available.
- Artesunate should be combined with sulpha-pyrimethamine tablets in prescribed dosages.

Suggested reading

Management of severe malaria in children: proposed guidelines for the United Kingdom. Maitland K, Nadel S, Pollard AJ, Williams TN, Newton CRJC, Levin M. Br Med J 2005; 331: 337–43.

LEISHMANIASIS

Leishmaniasis is a disease caused by parasites of the genus *Leishmania,* which are transmitted by the bites of female sandflies. There are three major clinical forms of leishmaniasis: visceral leishmaniasis (VL), cutaneous leishmaniasis, and mucocutaneous leishmaniasis (espundia). Visceral and cutaneous forms of the disease are seen in India. Kala-azar, the Indian term for the visceral form of leishmaniasis, denotes hyperpigmentation seen in these patients (*Kala*–black; *Azar*–sickness).

Etiology and Transmission

Leishmania is a protozoan parasite that infects animals, humans and sandflies; about 30 species of *Leishmania* are known to infect humans, of which each may cause a disease specific to the species and the host response. Organism prevalence differs by geographical distribution. VL is most often caused by *L. donovani* (in Indian subcontinent and Kenya), *L. infantum* (in Southern Europe, Middle East, North Africa and China), and *L. chagasi* (in South America).

The parasite exists in the human or animal reservoir as amastigotes, which are nonflagellated, round or oval in shape (Leishman-Donovan bodies), and in the sandfly and in the culture medium as flagellated promastigotes. The female sandfly, the vector of the disease, ingests amastigotes into its digestive tract when feeding on an infected animal. The amastigote develops into a promastigote in the digestive tract, migrates to the proboscis (salivary glands) and is injected into the susceptible host when the sandfly takes its next feed. Within the host, promastigotes infect macrophages where they develop into amastigotes. These amastigotes multiply in the cells of the mononuclear phagocyte system including blood monocytes, macrophages, histiocytes, Kupffer cells and reticuloendothelial cells in spleen and lymphoid tissue.

About 70 different species of sandfly can transmit leishmaniasis; these sandflies most commonly belong to the genus *Phlebotomus* and *Lutzomyia*. Male sandflies feed on fruit juices and do not suck blood. The female sandfly characteristically feeds at dusk, and tends to remain close to its breeding area. The feeding and resting patterns of sandflies are important in formulating control strategies. Rarely, VL can be transmitted by blood transfusion, sexual intercourse, accidental needle prick or congenitally.

The reservoirs of the disease are animals like canines, cats and rodents (zoonotic cycle). In countries such as India and Sudan humans are the chief reservoir (anthroponotic cycle). Although disease occurs irrespective of age, children aged 1–4 years appear to be more susceptible.

Prevalence

Leishmaniasis is endemic in more than 60 countries worldwide, and is seen in all continents except Australia and Antartica. Over 90% cases of visceral leishmaniasis (VL) are seen in India, Bangladesh, Nepal, Sudan and Brazil, while cutaneous leishmaniasis is seen in Afghanistan, Pakistan, Syria, Saudi Arabia, Algeria, Iran, Brazil, and Peru. In India, annually about 1–3 lakh cases of Kala-azar are reported, most often from Bihar and eastern UP.

Disease Patterns

The disease is seen in three main patterns: visceral, cutaneous and mucocutaneous leishmaniasis. Other less common disease patterns include post-kala azar dermal leishmaniasis, leishmaniasis recidivans and diffuse cutaneous leishmaniasis. The type of disease expressed depends both on the type of Leishmania species and on the zymodeme (electrophoretic isoenzyme pattern) expressed on that species. Thus, one zymodeme may cause visceral leishmaniasis while another zymodeme of the same species may cause cutaneous leishmaniasis.

Clinical Features

Visceral Leishmaniasis

The incubation period is generally 3 to 8 months (range 10 days-34 months). Features include high grade fever, weight loss, hepatosplenomegaly, abdominal discomfort, lymphadenopathy, and pallor. Fever may be high or low grade, remittent, intermittent or continuous; the *'double-rise'* of temperature in a day (*double quotidian*), although characteristic, is uncommon. There are no rigors and the patient does not appear 'toxic'. Splenohepatomegaly, with the spleen much larger than the liver, is usual. Spleen is usually huge, firm, smooth and nontender and is palpable by the end of first month of illness. Moderate hepatomegaly is seen in over 80% of cases. Unlike African VL, lymphadenopathy is infrequent in Indian VL (<5%). Hyperpigmentation of skin is characteristically a feature of Indian VL and occurs in about two-thirds of patients in late stages of disease, affecting the face, hands and upper trunk. Progressive emaciation occurs in all cases of VL, though appetite is well preserved. Cough and diarrhea are common. Bleeding manifestations in the form of petechial hemorrhages, epistaxis and gum bleeding may be seen. Pedal edema may occur due to hypoalbuminemia. Jaundice is uncommon. Diminished cell mediated immunity in VL may account for the high incidence of secondary infections, mainly pneumonia, septicemia, measles, tuberculosis, dysentry, otitis media and cancrum oris. Some cases of visceral leishmaniasis present atypically and cases have been reported which involve the lungs, pleura, oral mucosa, larynx, esophagus, stomach, small intestine, skin and bone marrow.

Pancytopenia and hypergammaglobulinemia are characteristic. Anemia is attributed to autoimmune hemolysis, hypersplenism, ineffective erythropoiesis, co-existing nutritional deficiencies and gastrointestinal blood loss.

The disease may begin insidiously and be asymptomatic initially, but usually runs a chronic course that may be fatal without or despite treatment. Death usually occurs within 2 years in 75–95% cases, because of severe secondary bacterial infections or gastrointestinal bleeding in advanced disease.

Post Kala-azar Dermal Leishmaniasis (PKDL)

Post-kala azar dermal leishmaniasis (PKDL) develops after resolution of visceral leishmaniasis and is seen in a small percentage of patients in Africa and India. This is usually due to infection by the *L. donovani* cluster. The time interval to development of PKDL is variable; it usually occurs 1–10 years after successful treatment of VL. Hypopigmented macular, maculo-papular or nodular skin lesions are seen first in the perioral area, chin and lips, and later appear over the neck, extensor surfaces of the arms, trunk, and legs. Lesions spare the scalp, palms, soles, axillae and perineum. Lepromatous leprosyis a close differential, but peripheral nerves are spared. Skin lesions may persist for upto 20 years. These patients may act as chronic reservoir of infection.

Cutaneous Leishmaniasis

This initially starts as a papule at the site of a sandfly bite, which increases in size, crusts, and eventually ulcerates. The lesion may take 3–18 months to heal in over 90% of cases. The incubation period is between 2 weeks to several months, with longer incubation period up to 3 years in Old World cases.

Variations of Cutaneous Leishmaniasis

Leishmaniasis recidivans is characterized by tuberculoid lesions developing around scars of healed cutaneous ulcers, revealing a low parasite count on biopsy. Infections tend to be resistant to treatment.

Diffuse cutaneous leishmaniasis is a rare manifestation, wherein dissemination of skin lesions occurs over the face, hands and feet, and lesions reveal high parasite numbers due to poor cell-mediated immune response. This is more common in the New World Leishmania but also occurs with L aethiopica in East Africa.

Mucocutaneous leishmaniasis is characterized by mucosal involvement of the nose, oral cavity and pharynx are seen, causing difficulty with eating and an increased risk of secondary infection which carries a significant mortality. This form of leishmaniasis has an incubation period of 1–3 months, but may occur many years after the initial cutaneous ulcer has healed.

Pathogenesis

The protective immune response in VL is primarily cell mediated immunity (CMI) which results in subclinical infection and spontaneous cure in majority of cases. Failure of CMI to develop leads to the clinical syndrome of VL. For every case of VL, there are about 30 subclinical infections. Malnutrition and HIV predispose to clinical disease.

Anti-leishmanial antibodies are not protective in nature. The *leishmanin skin test* (*Montenegro test*) detects delayed-type hypersensitivity to leishmanial antigens. The test is negative during active VL and becomes positive 3–6 months after recovery.

After infection, the organism lies exclusively intracellularly, mainly inside macrophages as replicating amastigotes. The outcome of infection depends on whether the host mounts primarily a T-helper (Th)-1 or Th2 response. Studies suggest that the Th1 response produces interferon c (IFNc), which mediates resistance, whilst Th2 cells producing interleukin-4 confer susceptibility to infection. In the Th1 response, promastigotes attach to reticuloendothelial cells and Th1 response activates macrophages leading to phagocytosis of promastigotes. Defective CMI correlates with increased suppressor cell activity and decreased production of IFN-γ, interleukin-1 and interleukin-2 by mononuclear cells. Host genetics influence the type of immune response. Genes coding for natural resistance associated macrophage protein 1 (NRAMP1), TNF or the major histocompatibility complex are thought to play a major role in the outcome of infection. Thus the interplay between the host-determined delayed-type hypersensitivity, antigen-specific T-cell reactivity and cytokine secretion, and the type and virulence of the particular infecting Leishmania species determine what type of disease expression develops in the host.

Diagnosis

Visceral Leishmaniasis

Demonstration of parasites: Diagnosis in visceral leishmaniasis is usually based on microscopic detection of amastigotes in smears of tissue aspirates or biopsy samples. Bone marrow aspirate or biopsy is frequently the tissue of choice with sensitivity between 55–97%. Lymph node aspirate smears (sensitivity 60%) or biopsy, liver biopsy (sensitivity 85%) and splenic aspirates (sensitivity 97%) may also be used for diagnosis. Though splenic aspirate has the highest sensitivity, the procedure may result in life-threatening hemorrhage; the procedure is contraindicated if the prothrombin time exceeds control value by 5 seconds or more or platelet count is below 40,000/mm^3.

Sometimes the parasite can be cultured from microscopy negative tissue samples on special media like Novy, McNeal and Nicolle (NNN) medium or inoculated into animals such as hamsters. Leishmania DNA can also be detected in tissue aspirates and peripheral blood by polymerase chain reaction (PCR), with sensitivity of 70–93% in peripheral blood. High sensitivities of even upto the level of one parasite have been reported.

Serological tests: Leishmania antibody may be detected by the direct agglutination test with a sensitivity of 72–94% and a specificity of 86–94%. Some cross-reactivity is seen with leprosy, Chagas disease, malaria, and schistosomiasis, while a false negative test result may be seen in HIV. Immunochromatographic strip (dipstick ELISA) testing of blood from a finger prick for leishmanial anti-K39 antibody has been used successfully in field serodiagnosis with a sensitivity of 90–100 % (~93%) in symptomatic patients, and a high specificity (90.6%). The test uses a recombinant K-39 (rK39) antigen incorporated into the strip. However, low sensitivity of the test has been reported in studies from Sudan. Titers to rK39 decrease following successful therapy and tend to rise in cases of relapse, thus making it useful to recognize treatment failures. This test is useful in clinical management in resource-poor areas. Newer methods with high sensitivity and specificity include the detection of Leishmania antigen and antibody in the urine.

Napier's aldehyde test has been traditionally used as a non-specific test for diagnosing kala-azar. It depends on the presence of increased levels of IgG and IgM in the blood. One or two drops of commercial formalin (40% formaldehyde) are added to 1 mL of the serum in a test tube. The serum becomes solid and opaque within 20 minutes in a strongly positive reaction and within 24 hours in a weakly positive test. Solidification without opacification is not diagnostic. The major limitation of the aldehyde test is its poor sensitivity and specificity.

Cutaneous Leishmaniasis

Diagnosis is usually based on microscopic examination of skin scrapings or biopsy specimens taken from the edge of lesions. The method is rapid and low-cost, but has limited sensitivity, especially in chronic lesions. Cultures of the lesions are more sensitive, but may become contaminated by bacterial and fungal elements in the biopsy specimen itself. Direct analysis of clinical specimens is better achieved by using PCR, which is rapid, with high specificity and sensitivity. Serology has limited role because of the poor antibody response in cutaneous leishmaniasis. The Montenegro (leishmanin) skin test has also been used which detects specific cutaneous delayed-type hypersensitivity to leishmania antigen. However, the test cannot be used to distinguish between current and past infection, and false positive results have been reported in other skin infections.

Treatment

Visceral Leishmaniasis

Treatment of VL is largely based on pentavalent antimonials; however, increasing resistance to antimonials is a major problem, most evident in North Bihar, where the failure rate for this treatment is more than 50%. Pentavalent antimony [Sb (V)] can be given in the form of sodium stibogluconate [Sb (V) 100 mg/ml] or meglumine antimonate [Sb (V) 85 mg/ml]; both may be given intravenously or intramuscularly with equal efficacy (Table 9.19). The dose of Sb (V) is 20 mg/kg for 28 days; however, a recent randomized trial showed a shorter, 10–day course to be equally effective. IM injections are painful and better avoided. IV injections should be diluted 1:10 with 5% dextrose and infused slowly over 20 minutes. Adverse effects include vomiting, fatigue, arthralgia, myalgia, abdominal pain, elevated serum transaminases, lipase and amylase levels, bone marrow depression, and ECG abnormalilties, including non-specific ST and T-wave changes and T-wave flattening or inversion. Rarely, there may be prolongation of QTc. Weekly ECG monitoring is recommended during therapy. Some recommend a maximum dose of 850 mg daily in order to minimize side effects such as arrhythmias; others, however, believe that this might predispose to resistance. In some resistant cases, addition of IFNγ to Sb (V) has been successful in inducing remission.

Amphotericin B is an effective treatment used in Sb (V)-resistant cases. It is toxic and requires admission to the hospital for a prolonged period. The main side effects include fever, chills, thrombophlebitis, hypokalemia, and renal failure. The alternative is to use the liposomal form, which is highly effective and less toxic, but continues to be very expensive. Liposomal amphotericin B is currently the drug of choice for antimony resistant VL. Compared to conventional amphotericin, its concentration in reticuloendothelial cells is tenfold more, and it is ten times less toxic. Recent studies using lower doses of this agent show that it may be cost-effective even in resource poor areas with high antimonial resistance.

Miltefosine is the first effective orally active drug against leishmaniasis. Studies of treatment with this drug for 3 or 4 weeks have shown a cure rate of 95–100%; cure rates at 6 months' follow-up are also comparable to amphotericin B. It has the added benefit of a very good safety profile; the chief adverse effects being gastrointestinal side effects, which are frequent but mild. This agent has the potential to be used in the treatment of patients as outpatients in resource-poor areas, though there are concerns about compliance and eventual resistance.

Other effective drugs used in treating leishmaniasis include pentamidine and paromomycin. Pentamidine is used in treatment-resistant cases of visceral leishmaniasis. Its use is limited by its substantial toxicity, including hypotension, hypoglycemia, renal damage, injection abscess, and diabetes, necessitating close inpatient monitoring. Paromomycin (aminosidine) has been used effectively in resistant cases in north Bihar. Though the drug is inexpensive, nephrotoxicity and ototoxicity are concerns with its use. Sitamaquine, another oral agent, is currently being evaluated in phase II studies in our country and has been associated with a 50–67% cure rate. Imidazole and triazole drugs are not recommended for use in visceral leishmaniasis. Recommended treatment regimens are summarized in Table 9.19.

Supportive care: Severe anemia and thrombocytopenia may necessitate packed cell and platelet transfusion. The child should receive a nutritious diet, and co-existing nutritional deficiencies should be corrected. Concurrent infections should be treated using appropriate antimicrobial agents.

Response to treatment: Fever, spleen size, hemoglobin, blood cell counts, serum albumin, and body weight are monitored for response to therapy. In most patients, the fever subsides within 7 days, blood counts and hemoglobin levels rise, the patient feels better, and spleen becomes smaller within 2 weeks. Parasitological cure should be documented at the end of therapy by splenic or bone marrow aspiration. As relapses are common in this disease, patient should be followed for at least 6 months before a long term definite cure is pronounced. The spleen may take 6 months to 1 year to regress completely. Relapse is suggested by an increase of spleen size, a fall in hemoglobin levels and should be confirmed by the demonstration of parasites.

Treatment of other Forms of Leishmaniasis

In PKDL, treatment is indicated only for those who have severe and prolonged disease. Pentavalent antimonials (2 month course) and liposomal amphotericin B are both effective.

Cutaneous leishmaniasis in the Old World cutaneous leishmaniasis is not a life threatening disease and 90% of patients heal spontaneously within 3–18 months. Treatment of cutaneous leishmaniasis accelerates cure and reduce scarring, which may improve cosmetic outcome.

Table 9.19: Treatment of visceral leishmaniasis

Drug	*Dose*	*Duration*
Pentavalent antimony (as sodium stibogluconate or meglumine antimonate)	20 mg/kg/day IM or IV	28 days
Amphotericin B	1 mg/kg IV on aleternate days	28 days
Liposomal amphotericin B	2 mg/kg/day IV	5 days
Miltefosine	2.5 mg/kg/day PO (od or bd)	28 days
Pentamidine	4 mg/kg IV or IM three times a week	8 weeks
Aminosidine (paromomycin)	16–20 mg/kg/day IV or IM	21 days

Options include local or systemic treatment. Local treatment is preferred for Old World cutaneous leishmaniasis, small single lesions, lack of lymph node metastases and *L mexicana* lesions. New World lesions except *L mexicana*, mucosal or lymph node involvement and lesions refractory to local treatment are indications for systemic treatment. Options of local treatment include cryotherapy, local infrared heat lamps, paromomycin (aminosidine) ointment with methylbenzethonium chloride, intralesional infiltration of the dermis and base of the lesion with pentavalent antimony and imiquimod in combination with meglumine antimonite. Systemic treatment with antimonials in general requires a 20– day course. Pentamidine, meglumine antimonat, oral fluconazole, ketoconazole, and oral miltefosine are other agents that have been studied.

Treatment of mucocutaneous leishmaniasis with antimonials is unsatisfactory; especially in severe disease. Amphotericin B and liposomal amphotericin B have been used in difficult cases with success. Steroids may be used in cases where respiratory compromise is likely.

Leishmania-HIV Coinfection

VL may occur in HIV infected persons, either as an opportunistic infection or as a result of reactivation of subclinical infection. A high index of suspicion is required in patients with HIV with the typical presentations of visceral leishmaniasis such as pyrexia, pancytopenia and hepatosplenomegaly. However, the presentation may be atypical with prominent gastrointestinal or upper respiratory tract involvement, and absence of hepatosplenomegaly. Diagnosis is reached as for non-HIV patients except that the Leishmania antibody test (direct agglutination test) is frequently negative. The main risk group is intravenous drug users where an anthroponotic cycle is involved, with Leishmania organisms present in used syringes being inoculated intravenously.

In leishmania–HIV coinfection, the Leishmania infection is often intractable, and is associated with a high relapse rate. Visceral leishmaniasis in HIV infection is being proposed for inclusion in the Centers for Disease Control and Prevention CDC clinical category C for the definition of AIDS as an indicator disease. Although treatment of coinfection has not been adequately studied, pentavalent antimonials are still used commonly. Meglumine antimonite, liposomal amphotericin and oral miltefosine have only been used in small studies. Secondary prophylaxis, using pentavalent antimonials administered once every 28 days or liposomal amphotericin B every 21 days, prevents relapse and improves survival. Secondary prophylaxis should be continued at CD4 counts below 200/ml. Antiretroviral treatment has been effective in decreasing relapses of visceral leishmaniasis.

Prevention and Control

Control of leishmaniasis involves controlling the source of infection and eradicating the vector, and depends on local epidemiology. Where sandflies are mostly endophilic (rest mostly indoors after feeding), spraying houses with insecticide is effective, while use of treated and untreated bed nets is effective where sandflies are endophagic (feed mainly indoors). Insecticide treatment of dogs and dog collars is useful where canines are important reservoirs. In India, where anthroponotic transmission is important, effective treatment of patients, especially those with PKDL (who may act as long-term reservoirs), has been found to be effective in controlling transmission when combined with vector control.

There is no effective vaccine for prevention of leishmaniasis. The safety and efficacy of live-attenuated and killed vaccines has been debated. Killed vaccines were favoured in the 1990s because of safety problems with live attenuated vaccines; however, recent advances in manipulation of the Leishmania genome may make development of a live attenuated vaccine more feasible. Recent approaches include working on recombinant DNA derived antigen vaccines and protein or peptide-based vaccines, made possible by the Leishmania Genome Project. However, most vaccine research is targeted against cutaneous leishmaniasis; any effectiveness against visceral leishmaniasis is uncertain.

Suggested reading

1. Piscopo TV, Azzopardi CM. Leishmaniasis.Postgrad Med J 2006; 82: 649–57.
2. Murray HW, Berman JD, Davies CR, et al. Advances in leishmaniasis. Lancet 2005; 366:1561–77.
3. Davies CR, Kaye P, Croft SL, et al. Leishmaniasis: new approaches to disease control. BMJ 2003;326:377–82.
4. Guerin PJ, Olliaro P, Sundar S, et al. Visceral leishmaniasis: current status of control, diagnosis, and treatment, and a proposed research and development agenda. Lancet Infect Dis 2002;2:494–501.
5. Herwaldt BL. Leishmaniasis. Lancet 1999; 354: 1191–9.
6. Paredes R, Munoz J, Diaz I, et al. Symposium: Leishmaniasis in HIV infection. J Postgrad Med 2003; 49:39–49.

AMEBIASIS

Amebiasis is defined as infection with *Entamoeba histolytica*. Clinical features of amebiasis due to *E. histolytica* range from asymptomatic colonization to amebic dysentery and invasive extraintestinal amebiasis, which occurs most commonly in the form of liver abscess.

Epidemiology

Amebiasis is associated with a high morbidity and mortality and is a major public health problem globally, especially in Central and South America, Africa, and the Indian subcontinent. Poverty, ignorance, overcrowding, poor sanitation and malnutrition favor transmission. In developed countries, high-risk groups include travelers, immigrants from areas of endemicity, and men who have sex with men. Asymptomatic individuals account for almost 90% of the infections. Invasive disease with *Entamoeba histolytica* is a leading parasitic cause of human mortality, causing 100,000 deaths every year globally.

E. histolytica is thought to infect 10% of the world's population, and 2–55% Indians. However, these may be overestimates, because two morphologically identical, genetically distinct but apparently nonpathogenic Entameba species, namely *E. dispar* and *E. moshkovskii*, are now being recognized as causing most of the asymptomatic cases.

The organism exists in nature as a cyst or a trophozoite. Cysts are oval or round, asymmetric with four nuclei, resistant to chlorination and low environmental temperatures, but susceptible to destruction with most disinfectants and to heating to 55°C. Asymptomatic human cyst carriers are the principal reservoir of infection. The infection is transmitted by feco-oral route by cysts of *Entameba*. The disease may occur months to years after exposure. Humans are the only host. Young, immunocompromized and malnourished children are at a higher risk of severe *E. histolytica* infection.

Pathogenesis

Each ingested cyst excysts in the small intestine to produce eight trophozoites, that colonize the mucosa of the large intestine. Trophozoites may cause tissue invasion and destruction through several virulence factors, with little or no local inflammation, resulting in characteristic flask-shaped ulcers, seen commonly in cecum, transverse colon and sigmoid colon.

Extra-intestinal complications occur when trophozoites invade the bloodstream and migrate through the portal circulation, to lodge usually in the liver. *Amebic liver abscess* is usually single (95%) and more frequently involves the right lobe of the liver (posterosuperior part) which receives most of the blood draining the cecum and ascending colon. Amebae are located at the periphery of abscess, while the inside contains viscid necrotic tissue, which is sterile and devoid of any neutrophils. The abscess may regress, rupture or disseminate; transdiaphragmatic rupture may cause amebic empyema and pulmonary amebiasis. Rare extra-intestinal complications include amebic involvement of peritoneum, pericardium, pleura, lungs, brain, genitourinary system and skin.

Clinical Features

Asymptomatic Colonization

Asymptomatic cyst passage is the most common manifestation of *E. histolytica, accounting for 90% of human infection*. In most cases, the infection resolves spontaneously, but uncommonly, these individuals may later present with amebic dysentery and other invasive manifestations.

9

Dysentery/Amebic Colitis

After a variable incubaton period of weeks to months, about 10% individuals colonized with *E. histolytica* develop symptomatic disease, in form of colitis or extraintestinal disease. Amebic colitis presents as abdominal pain or tenderness (seen in 80%), with watery, bloody or mucous diarrhea. Some may have only intermittent diarrhea alternating with constipation. Fever is unusual. Occasionally fulminant amebic colitis may occur, with profuse bloody diarrhea, fever, widespread abdominal pain, diffuse tenderness and pronounced leukocytosis. Toxic megacolon, ameboma, cutaneous amebiasis and rectovaginal fistulae can occur as complications of intestinal amebiasis.

Extraintestinal Amebiasis

Amebic liver abscess (ALA), seen in about 1% of infected individuals, is the most common extraintestinal manifestation, and may occur months to years after infection. While some individuals may have concurrent amebic colitis, more commonly there are no bowel symptoms. The child usually presents with fever with chills and rigors and right upper quadrant pain of acute onset (<10 days). Examination reveals toxic appearance, right upper quadrant tenderness and hepatomegaly; jaundice is unusual (10–15%). Cough, along with dullness or crepitations in the right lung base may be present. With early diagnosis and therapy, the mortality from uncomplicated ALA is less than 1%. Complications include rupture into the pleura, which has a relatively good prognosis, and rupture into the pericardium and superinfection with bacteria, which are more serious.

Investigations

In all cases, the combination of serological tests with detection of the parasite offers the best approach to diagnosis.

Parasite Detection

The most common microscopic techniques employed for the identification of *E. histolytica* is direct saline (wet) mount of feces. The sample is examined within 1 hour of collection to look for motile trophozoites. At least 3 stool specimens taken on consecutive days should be examined because the test has poor sensitivity (<60%; ~90% with 3 fresh samples). Stool contains plenty of erythrocytes but few leukocytes. Presence of ingested erythrocytes within trophozoites is pathognomic for *E. histolytica*, which is otherwise indistinguishable from *E. dispar*. Patients with asymptomatic carriage generally have only cysts in the fecal sample. Microscopy is a less sensitive method of identifying *Entameba* species than antigen detection tests; specificity is also low due to misidentification of macrophages as trophozoites, polymorphonuclear cells as cysts and other *Entameba* species such as *E. dispar*.

Various culture techniques for *E. histolytica* have been available using fecal specimens, rectal biopsy specimens or liver abscess aspirates. However, it is not undertaken routinely in view of low sensitivity (50–70%) and technical difficulties.

Antibody Detection Tests

Serological tests are routinely employed for diagnosis of extra-intestinal disease with *E. histolytica*. They are positive in 70–80% patients with invasive disease at presentation, and in >90% cases beyond first week of symptoms. IgG antibodies persist for years after *E. histolytica* infection, whereas the IgM antibodies indicate present or current infection. Serological tests that detect total antibodies are therefore useful in non-endemic areas, but have limited role in areas where infection is endemic because of their inability to distinguish past from current infection.

Among the many different assays that are commercially available, complement fixation test is less sensitive than others, is costly and not available routinely; latex agglutination test is commercially available as a rapid kit test, but has low specificity due to nonspecific reactions; and immunoelectrophoresis and immunodiffusion are highly sensitive but time-consuming. In extra-intestinal amebiasis, antibody detection by ELISA is the most sensitive test. Serological response as detected by ELISA becomes negative 6–12 months after infection. The IHA test is simple to perform and has been shown to be highly specific (~99%), and is among the most sensitive serological test available. However, IHA may stay positive for as long as 10 years following complete recovery, limiting its utility in endemic areas. The IFA test is rapid, reliable, reproducible and helps to differentiate ALA from other nonamebic etiologies; it has also been shown to differentiate between past (treated) and present disease.

Antigen Detection Tests

ELISA kits have been devised to detect *E. histolytica* antigen in stools with better sensitivity (>90%) and specificity than traditional stool microscopy. These kits are commercially available in several countries, are used in epidemiological studies, and may be useful in endemic areas where diarrheal diseases are common and molecular techniques are not available. However, its specificity for *E. histolytica* has been questioned because of cross-reaction with other *Entameba* species. Antigen detection by ELISA in the serum is the ideal test because of its high sensitivity and specificity, ability to distinguish current from past infection, and ability to distinguish *E. histolytica* from *E. dispar*. However, the test is not available routinely.

PCR Techniques

Molecular tools, including PCR and real-time PCR, to detect *E. histolytica* DNA in stool or liver abscess samples has made accurate diagnosis possible, but these assays are available only in research laboratories and clinical laboratories in developed countries.

Other Tests

In case of a liver abscess chest radiograph shows elevated diaphragm and pleural reaction on the right side. Ultrasound, CT, MRI, or isotope scan can localize the abscess in most cases. Sigmoidoscopy followed by aspiration of mucosal lesions or biopsy is valuable in symptomatic sick patients, where other tests fail to provide conclusive evidence. Leukocytosis without eosinophilia, mild anemia, raised alkaline phosphatase, and a high erythrocyte sedimentation rate (ESR) are common laboratory findings in a patient with ALA. Diagnosis of brain abscess is usually by brain biopsy or at autopsy by the microscopic detection of parasites.

Treatment

Antiamebic drugs are classified into luminal and tissue amebicides. Tissue amebicides including 5-nitroimidazoles, chloroquine and dehydroemetine, are effective in the treatment of invasive amebiasis but are less effective for luminal clearance. Nitroimidazoles are the drug of choice for treating invasive amebiasis; all agents including metronidazole, tinidazole, secnidazole and ornidazole are equally effective. Nitroimidazoles are ineffective against cysts. Chloroquine is used along with metronidazole/emetine in cases of hepatic amebiasis, but emetine is rarely used on account of its toxicity. Luminal amebicides include diloxanide furoate, diiodoquinol and paromomycin. Diloxanide furoate is the mainstay for treating asymptomatic cyst carriers. A combination of a luminal and a tissue amebicide is advocated for complete parasite clearance in invasive disease. Metronidazole is the most popular drug for management of both intestinal and extra-intestinal forms of amebiasis. Till date, there is no evidence of resistance against this agent.

Amebic colitis is treated by metronidazole, followed by a luminal agent (paromomycin, iodoquinol, or diloxanide furoate) to eradicate colonization (Table 9.20). When possible, fulminant amebic colitis, even with perforation, is managed conservatively, with the addition of antibiotics to deal with bowel flora. Radiographic monitoring of the abdomen by CT scan, coupled with the judicious use of percutaneous catheter drainage to obtain suspect fluid, might aid in management.

Asymptomatic intestinal carriage is treated with a luminal agent, but reinfection is quite common even after complete cure. It is recommended that persons harboring *E. histolytica* should be specifically identified and treated; treatment of individuals with only *E. dispar* is unnecessary. Asymptomatic individuals with documented *E histolytica* cyst passage require to be treated; because they are at risk for development of invasive disease, and are a risk to public health. *E. dispar* infection does not require treatment, but indicates exposure to fecally contaminated food or water.

Most amebic liver-abscesses, even large ones, can be cured without drainage. Most patients show a response to treatment (reduced fever and abdominal pain) within 72–96 hours. Individuals with amebic liver abscess should also receive a luminal agent to eliminate intestinal colonization. The role of ultrasound or percutaneous

Table 9.21: Treatment of amebiasis

Medication		*Pediatric dose*		*Adult dose*
Invasive disease		Colitis	Liver abscess	
Tissue amebicide	Metronidazole	35–50 mg/kg/day for 7–10 days (in 3 divided doses)	35–50 mg/kg/day for 7–10 days (in 3 divided doses)	750 mg 8 hourly
	OR			
	Tinidazole	50 mg/kg/day for 3 days (once daily)	50 mg/kg/day for 3–5 days (once daily)	2 g once a day
Followed by				
Luminal amebicide	Paromomycin	25–35 mg/kg/day for 7 days (in 3 divided doses)	25–35 mg/kg/day for 7 days (in 3 divided doses)	25–35 mg/kg/day (in 3 divided doses)
	OR			
	Diloxanide furoate *OR*	20 mg/kg/day for 7 days (in 3 divided doses)	20 mg/kg/day for 7 days (in 3 divided doses)	500 mg 8 hourly
	Iodoquinone	30–40 mg/kg/day for 20 days (in 3 divided doses)	30–40 mg/kg/day for 20 days (in 3 divided doses)	650 mg 8 hourly
Asymptomatic intestinal colonization				
	Paromomycin *OR*	As above		
	Diloxanide furoate *OR*	As above		
	Iodoquinone	As above		

therapeutic aspiration guided by CT in the treatment of uncomplicated amebic liver abscess is controversial. Large amebic liver abscesses (>300 mL) may benefit from aspiration with decrease in duration of hospital stay and faster clinical improvement recovery when compared to those managed medically alone. Abscess cavity resolves slowly over a period of several months.

Aspiration is usually reserved for individuals in whom diagnosis is uncertain (where pyogenic abscess or bacterial superinfection is a concern), those who have not responded to metronidazole therapy (persistent fever or abdominal pain after 4 days of treatment), individuals with large left lobe abscesses (because of the risk of rupture into the pericardium), size more than 8–10 cm (suggesting impending rupture) and severely ill patients with an accelerated clinical course and large abscesses suggesting imminent rupture. Aspiration, percutaneous catheter drainage, or both, improve outcomes in the treatment of amebic empyema after liver abscess rupture, and percutaneous catheter (or, if necessary, surgical) drainage could be lifesaving in the treatment of amebic pericarditis. ALA rupture into the peritoneum is managed conservatively, along with percutaneous catheter drainage for localized collections of fluid.

9

Suggested reading

1. Stanley SL. Amoebiasis.The Lancet 2003; 361:1025–1034.
2. Fotedar R, Stark D, Beebe N, Marriott D, Ellis J, Harkness J. Laboratory diagnostic techniques for *Entamoeba* species. Clin Microbiol Rev. 2007; 20: 511–32.

GIARDIASIS

Giardiasis, caused by *Giardia lamblia* (also known as *G. intestinalis* or *G. duodenalis*), is a major cause of diarrhea in children and in travelers. *G. lamblia* is a flagellated protozoan that infects the duodenum and small intestine of humans and causes varied clinical manifestations. Human infection may range from asymptomatic shedding of giardial cysts to symptomatic giardiasis, being responsible for abdominal cramps, nausea, acute or chronic diarrhea, with malabsorption and failure of children to thrive.

Epidemiology

The infection is endemic in developing countries with poor sanitation. In developed countries, the infection is common in institutional settings like daycare facilities and sanitaria etc, or as localized outbreaks associated with contamination of drinking water with cysts. Breast milk protects against giardiasis by virtue of the glycoconjugates and secretary IgA that it contains. Individuals with malnutrition, humoral immunodeficiencies and cystic fibrosis are particularly susceptible. Children appear to be more severely affected than adults.

Pathogenesis

Giardia exists in two stages, cysts and trophozoites. Outside the human body it exists in the form of cysts. Cysts are hardy, capable of surviving in cool, moist environments for up to 2 months and in water that has been routinely chlorinated, but are destroyed by boiling for 10 minutes. Transmission of infection is through cysts, which may be ingested in contaminated water or food or spread by direct person to person contact. Ingestion of 10–100 cysts is sufficient for causing infection. Low pH of the duodenum facilitates excystation and release of trophozoites. Trophozoites colonize the duodenum and proximal jejunum of the host, where they attach to the intestinal brush border. A ventral disk on the concave surface mediates the attachment of the protozoa to the intestinal wall, and also causes mechanical irritation and damage to the microvilli of the small bowel mucosa.

The host-microbial interactions that govern the outcome of infection remain incompletely understood. Unlike amebiasis, there are no invasive or locally destructive lesions. It is believed that the infection causes diarrhea via a combination of intestinal malabsorption and hypersecretion. *Giardia* induce disruption of epithelial tight junctions and enterocyte apoptosis, which activate T lymphocytes causing further enterocyte injury, resulting in intestinal permeability and diffuse shortening of epithelial microvilli. These effects cause malabsorption and maldigestion and, in addition, may facilitate the development of chronic enteric disorders, including inflammatory bowel disease, irritable bowel syndrome, and allergies, via mechanisms that remain poorly understood. It has been incriminated for the reported steatorrhea and decreased tryptic activity. Steatorrhea that is often seen may occur due to pancreatic involvement, or due to bacterial overgrowth in the duodenum and upper jejunum, and bile salt deconjugation liberating free bile acids.

Clinical Features

The incubation period after ingestion of cysts is 1–2 weeks. Most infections in both children and adults are *asymptomatic*. *Symptomatic* infections are more common in children than in adults, and usually take the form of acute diarrhea with sudden onset of explosive, watery, foulsmelling stools, along with nausea and anorexia; others may also have abdominal distension, flatulence, epigastric cramps and mild fever. There is no blood or mucus in stools. The illness may last 3–4 days and is usually self-limiting in normal immunocompetent children. Variable degree of malabsorption may occur. Some patients may have a protracted course, with persistent or recurrent mild to moderate symptoms such as brief episodes of loose foul smelling stools alternating with constipation. Persistent diarrhea may be seen in 30–50% cases. A few children may develop chronic diarrhea, lactose and fat malabsorption and failure to thrive.

Diagnosis

Diagnosis of giardiasis is traditionally established by microscopic examination of stools. At least three fresh specimens of stools collected on alternate days should be examined to achieve sensitivity of 90%, because the multiplication and passage of the giardial cysts is often intermittent. There is no blood or leucocytes in stools. Enzyme immunoassay (EIA) and direct fluorescent antibody test for *Giardia* antigens in stools have been reported to have better sensitivity and require less expertise than traditional microscopy. Where diagnosis is strongly suspected but stool testing is negative, duodenal aspirate or biopsy may yield high concentration of *Giardia* when fresh wet mount is examined for trophozoites. Where duodenal aspirate is negative, intestinal biopsy may be considered in presence of any suggestive feature like lactose malabsorption or abnormal radiographic findings (edema or segmentation in small intestine), or a suggestive setting like absent secretory IgA or hypogammaglobulinemia.

Treatment

All symptomatic cases—acute and persistent diarrhea, failure to thrive and malabsorption syndrome—require drug treatment. Asymptomatic cyst carriers are not treated except in specific situations like for outbreak control or for prevention of spread from toddlers to immunocompromised family members. At present, treatment options include the nitroimidazoles derivatives, especially metronidazole and tinidazole, and nitazoxanide. Metronidazole is given in a dose of 15 mg/kg/day for 5–7 days; it has 80–90% efficacy and is inexpensive, but has frequent adverse effects and has to be given threee times a day. Tinidazole has the advantage of high efficacy (>90%) and single dose treatment (50 mg/kg once), while nitazoxanide has high efficacy (80–90%), low incidence of adverse effects and is available in suspension form. Nitazoxanide is given for 3 days, in two doses, with the dose depending on age (100 mg bid for 1–4 years, 200 mg bid for 4–12 years, 500 mg bid for >12 years). Second-line alternatives include albendazole, furazolidone, paromomycin and quinacrine.

Suggested reading

1. Kiser JD, Paulson CP, Brown C. Clinical inquiries. What's the most effective treatment for giardiasis? J Fam Pract 2008; 57: 270–2.
2. Buret AG. Pathophysiology of enteric infections with Giardia duodenalis. Parasite. 2008; 15: 261–5.
3. Escobedo AA, Cimerman S. Giardiasis: a pharmacotherapy review. Expert Opin Pharmacother. 2007; 8: 1885–902.

AMEBIC MENINGOENCEPHALITIS

The term amebic meningoencephalitis refers to the infection of the central nervous system by free-living amebae. The disease occurs in two clinical forms: primary amebic meningoencephalitis (PAM) caused by *Naegleria fowleri* and granulomatous amebic encephalitis (GAE) induced by amebae of spp. of *Acanthamoeba* and *Balamuthia*. These organisms are ubiquitous, found in fresh and brackish water including ponds, lakes, wells, springs and swimming pools. Infections have been reported throughout the world and are usually fatal.

9

Primary Amebic Meningoencephalitis (PAM)

Naegleria fowleri causes a fulminating meningoencephalitis, mostly in children and healthy young adults who have a recent history of swimming in fresh water lakes, pools and ponds, usually during hot summer months. Rarely, infection may occur either by inhalation of air-borne cysts or by washing face in contaminated water. The amebae enter the nose through contaminated water (or air), penetrate the nasal mucosa and the cribriform plate and travel along the olfactory nerves to the brain. Within the brain they provoke inflammation and cause extensive destruction of tissue leading to a diffuse hemorrhagic necrotizing meningoencephalitis. The incubation period ranges from 3 days to 2 weeks.

Signs and symptoms are suggestive of acute pyogenic meningitis, including high grade fever, headache, vomiting, seizures, altered sensorium, cranial nerve palsies and signs of meningeal irriation. Disease progression is usually rapid; this along with the limited awareness about the disease and consequent non-institution of specific therapy, leads to death within 5–10 days; however, survivors have been reported occasionally.

Microscopic demonstration of motile amebae in fresh cerebrospinal fluid is required for diagnosis. The organism is seen in the CSF in the form of a 10–15 μm trophozoite with nonprominent karyosome and a broad pseudopod. CSF evaluation is otherwise similar to that seen with acute pyogenic meningitis with a high WBC count (usually in thousands) with a polymorphonuclear predominance, and elevated proteins.

Though PAM is rare, the disease has a grave prognosis if treatment is delayed. Hence, infection with *Naegleria* must be considered in differential diagnosis of a patient with pyogenic meningitis presenting with history of swimming in fresh water, non-specific cerebral edema on CT, and no evidence of bacteria on Gram's stain, antigen detection assays and culture. A careful examination of CSF wet prepration is the key to the rapid diagnosis of *Naegleria* infection. A combination of high dose amphotericin B, rifampicin, and chloramphenicol has been employed for therapy successfully in occasional patients. Good results have also been obtained with combinations of ampotericin B, fluconazole and rifampicin, and amphotericin B and azithromycin.

Granulomatous Amebic Encephalitis (GAE)

This is an infection with *Acanthamoeba* species (and, rarely, *Balamuthia* species) that is acquired through lung or skin and spreads hematogenously. The infection is usually seen in immunocompromised children like those with AIDS, SLE or post-renal transplant. Clinically, GAE runs a subacute or chronic course similar to tubercular meningitis, and if untreated, is fatal. CSF examination reveals motile trophozoites or cysts of *Acanthamoeba*, in addition to elevated proteins and lymphocytic leukocytosis. The trophozoite of *Acanthamoeba* is 25–30 μm in size, with a prominent karyosome and vacuolated cytoplasm.

A triplex real time TaqMan PCR assay for simultaneous identification of *Acanthamoeba* spp., *Balamuthia mandriallaris*, and *N. fowleri* has been developed and it could be useful for fast laboratory diagnosis. CT scan of brain may reveal granulomatous lesions and ventricular dilatation. Treatment has been attempted with fluconazole, ketoconazole, sulfonamides and cotrimoxazole, but prognosis is poor.

9

Suggested reading

1. Kaushal V, Chhina DK, Ram S, Singh G, Kaushal RK, Kumar R. Primary amebic meningoencephalitis due to Naegleria fowleri. J Assoc Phys India 2008: 56: 459–62.
2. Ma P. Naegleria and acanthamoeba infection: Review. Rev Infect Dis 1990; 12: 490–504.

HELMINTHIC INFESTATIONS

Helminthic infestations contribute to significant disease burden in children particularly in the underprivileged and in developing countries. Helminthiasis is caused by three groups of worms, nematodes (roundworms), cestodes (tapeworms) and trematodes (flukes). All these groups differ significantly in life cycle, mode of infection, pathogenesis and clinical manifestations and are considered separately. Trematode infections are uncommon in India and will not be considered further.

NEMATODES

Nematodes may be further classified as intestinal nematodes and tissue nematodes.

Intestinal Nematodes

Intestinal nematodes are the commonest type of helminthic infestations. This group includes *Ascaris lumbricoides* (roundworm), *Enterobius vermicularis* (pinworm, thread worm), *Ankylostoma duodenale* (Old world hookworm) *Nectar americanus* (New world hookworm), *Trichuris trichura* (whipworm) and *Strongyloides stercoralis.* These infections are common where hygiene and sanitation are poor and where there is improper disposal of sewage.

Life Cycle

Ascaris, Strongyloides, Necator and *Ankylostoma* inhabit the small intestine, *Enterobius* is lodged in the cecum and *Trichuris* inhabits the large intestine. Eggs are released in the feces with the exception of *Enterobius* where they are released on the perianal skin. The eggs embryonate in the environment and become infective. In *Ascaris, Enterobius* and *Trichura,* infection occurs by ingestion of embryonated eggs. The larvae are released in the intestines and mature into adult worms locally in case of trichuriasis and enterobiasis, while in case of ascariasis they migrate through the intestinal wall, into the portal circulation, the liver, heart, lungs, trachea, swallowed into the pharynx and finally mature into adult worms in the small intestine. In case of *Necator, Ankylostoma* and *Strongyloides* infection occurs by penetration of the skin by filariform larvae which through the systemic circulation reach the heart, the lungs, trachea, pharynx and finally mature into adult worms in the intestines. *Strongyloides* is unique among the intestinal nematodes in several respects; larvae divide parthenogenetically in the small intestine, development of the eggs into infective larvae occurs within the intestine leading to autoinfections and retroinfections.

Clinical Manifestations

Clinical manifestations depend on the worm burden and vary from asymptomatic infection to severe morbidity. Penetration of the skin by the larvae of *Ancylostoma, Necator* and *Strongyloides* may cause a maculopapular itchy rash. Migration of the larvae through the lungs in case of ascariasis and hookworm may cause Loeffler's syndrome characterized by fever, cough, dyspnea, wheeze, urticaria, eosinophilia and lung infiltrates. Other causes of Loeffler's syndrome include tropical pulmonary eosinophilia, visceral larva migrans, schistosomiasis and allergic bronchopulmonary aspergillosis.

Ascaris being the largest worm has the most prominent intestinal manifestations. Heavy infestation can lead to vague abdominal discomfort, abdominal distension, vomiting, irritability, poor growth and nutritional deficiencies. A large mass of worms may cause bowel obstruction and migration of the worms can result in cholecystitis, cholangitis, pancreatitis and rarely intrahepatic abscess.

Hookworms (*Ankylostoma, Necator*) suck blood from the intestine and lead to iron deficiency anemia, hypoalbuminemia and edema. The severity of anemia varies and with heavy infestations, transfusion may be needed.

Heavy infestation with *Trichuris* may cause dysentery, anemia, rectal prolapse, abdominal pain, distension, hypoproteinemia and growth retardation. Manifestations of enterobiasis include perianal or vulval itching caused by migration of the gravid females to the perianal skin to lay eggs. Strongyloides is associated with abdominal pain, vomiting, diarrhea, bleeding, steatorrhea and weight loss. Ulceration and strictures of the duodenum may occur. Hyperinfection syndrome occurs in the immunocompromised and is characterized by dissemination of massive numbers of larvae into various body organs, sepsis and high mortality.

Diagnosis

The diagnosis of most intestinal nematodes is by examination of feces for the characteristic eggs. In enterobiasis, the eggs are present on the perianal skin from which they can be lifted using the scotch tape method. In strongyloidiasis fresh stool should be examined for larvae as eggs are rarely present. Peripheral blood examination may reveal eosinophilia (striking in *Strongyloides*). In ascariasis, the worms may be incidentally observed in the biliary/ pancreatic ducts by ultrasound or in the intestines during contrast studies of the gastrointestinal tract.

Treatment

Several antiparasitic drugs are available, of which the most convenient is treatment with albendazole at a single bed time dose of 400 mg. Other drugs include mebendazole 100 mg twice a day for 3 days or 500 mg single dose (for enterobiasis, single dose of 100 mg and repeated two weeks later), or pyrantel pamoate at 11 mg/kg for 1 day (for ascariasis, enterobiasis) to 3 days (for hookworm). Pyrantel pamoate is not very effective against trichuriasis. Strongyloides is preferably managed with ivermectin at a dose of 200 μg/kg for 2 days (7–10 days in hyperinfection syndromes). Nitazoxanide is a newly available broad spectrum antiparasitic drug.

Prevention

Eradication of intestinal nematodes is possible only with improvement of hygiene and sanitation and appropriate disposal of sewage. There is limited rationale for periodic deworming in healthy children.

Suggested reading

1. Eziefula AC, Brown M. Intestinal nematodes: disease burden, deworming and the potential importance of co-infection. Curr Opin Infect Dis 2008; 21: 516–22.
2. Feigin R, Cherry J, Demmler-Harrison G, Kaplan S. Nematodes. In: Textbook of Pediatric Infectious Diseases Eds. Feigin R, Cherry J, Demmler-Harrison G, Kaplan S. Saunders 2003; 5th ed.

CESTODES

The cestodes that infect humans include giant tapeworms like *Taenia saginata, T. solium* and *Diphyllobothriurn latum,* dwarf tapeworms like *Hymenolepis nana* and zoonotic cestodes like *Echinococcus granulosus* and *E. multilocularis*. Infection with *T. saginata* and *T. solium* is acquired through ingestion of cysticerca in contaminated food, while *Echinococcus* infection is through ingestion of eggs, and *D. latum* infection is carried to man by ingestion of cysts in freshwater fish.

Taeniasis and Cysticercosis

Two species of tapeworms infest humans, *Taenia solium* or the pork tapeworm and *T. saginata* or beef tapeworm, the names reflecting the principal intermediate hosts for each of them. Man is the only definitive host for both the parasites. While the pork tapeworm has a scolex with suckers and hooks that aid its attachment to the intestinal wall, hooks are absent in *T. saginata*. Taeniasis refers to intestinal infection by the adult tapeworm, and cysticercosis results from larval lodging in various sites.

Epidemiology

Cysticercosis is the most common parasitic disease worldwide, with an estimated prevalence of more than 50 million persons. It is endemic in Mexico, Central and South America, and parts of Africa, Asia, and India. Neurocysticercosis, the neurologic manifestation of cysticercosis, is the most prevalent infection of the brain worldwide and may be resposible for upto 20–50% of all seizures.

Pathogenesis

The life cycle of *Taenia solium* begins as a larva in pigs, and human infection is acquired by ingestion of *T. solium* cysts in undercooked pork. The larvae attach to the human gut and grow into adult tapeworms. The adult tapeworm sheds proglottids containing hundreds of tapeworm eggs into human feces. When ingested by pigs, these eggs develop into larvae that invade the intestinal wall, enter the bloodstream and lodge in various tissues to develop into cysts.

The eggs of beef tapeworm are not infectious to humans. Humans may ingest *T. solium* eggs, usually by feco-oral transmission (via contamination of food by food handlers with poor hand hygiene, or by ingestion of raw fruits or vegetables fertilized with contaminated human waste), or sometimes through autoinfection (by reflux of eggs from intestine into the stomach by reverse peristalsis). Thus humans become dead-end hosts of the larval stage of the parasite, and develop cysticercosis in various body tissues. Ingestion of encysted pork does not directly cause cysticercosis; rather, it causes an intestinal infection with the adult tapeworm and a human reservoir for *T. solium* eggs. Cysticercosis can occur in persons who do not eat pork by feco-oral route described above. Infection with adult tapeworm (taeniasis), on the other hand, is acquired by ingestion of undercooked pork or beef containing infectious cysticerci.

Initially the larvae become encysted, which helps viable cysts avoid initial host reaction and destruction by the host. This phase, which may last for 5–10 years, is often clinically silent except when cyst location or size causes signs or symptoms. Degenerating cysts release larval antigens that produce a vigorous host response with release of inflammatory mediators and surrounding edema. After this phase, the encysted larvae degenearte entirely, die and often calcify. Calcified cysts can produce symptoms by unclear mechanisms.

Clinical Features

Infection with adult worm is mostly symptomatic, but some children may have non-specific symptoms like nausea, abdominal pain and diarrhea. These patients may also develop cysticercosis through auto-infection.

The clinical features of cysticercosis depend on the location of the cysts and overall cyst burden. In about 2 months, the larvae mature into cysticerci of about 2 mm to 2 cm size. Cysts can lodge in the brain, skeletal muscle, subcutaneous tissues, spinal column and eyes. The two sites associated with high morbidity are the brain, the most common (60–90 %) location for cysts, and the eye, the least common site (1–3 %).

Cysts in the brain parenchyma (parenchymal neurocysticercosis) cause focal or generalized seizures and, less commonly, headache, focal neurologic deficits, or behavioral abnormality. Heavy cyst burden can cause encephalopathy with fever, headache, nausea, vomiting, altered mental status and seizures. Cysts in the subarachnoid or ventricular spaces may cause meningeal signs and symptoms, obstructive hydrocephalus or cranial nerve palsies (by nerve entrapment); those located in the spinal column can cause radicular pain or paresthesias. Ocular cysts in the subretinal space or vitreous humor can impair vision by inflammation or through retinal detachment, while those in the extraocular muscles may limit the range of eye movements. Skeletal muscle or subcutaneous cysticercosis may be either asymptomatic or cause localized pain and nodules.

Diagnosis

The diagnosis of taeniasis is established by the demonstration of eggs or proglottids in the stools. Patients may pass motile segments of worms through anus.

Diagnosis of neurocysticercosis is based on CT, with or without contrast, or MRI of brain. Demonstration (by CT/MRI) of a solitary contrast-enhancing lesion less than 20 mm in diameter and producing no midline shift is highly sensitive for neurocysticercosis; if the scolex is visible, it is pathognomonic for neurocysticercosis. Cystic, nonenhancing lesions suggest viable, nondegenerating cysts; cystic, enhancing lesions indicate degenerating cysts with some surrounding inflammation; and calcified cysts suggest old cysts that have already died. MRI is superior to CT in demonstrating spinal, brainstem, or intraventricular lesions. Ocular or extraocular muscle cysticercosis can be picked up on CT or ultrasound, or by dilated ophthalmologic examination.

Detection of antibodies by enzyme-linked immunoblot assay or enzyme-linked immunosorbent assay of the serum or cerebrospinal fluid has a sensitivity of 65–98% and a specificity of 67–100%, varying with the cyst burden, location, and phase of the infection; the immunoblot assay is the preferred test.

Biopsy of the skin or muscle provides a definitive diagnosis in ambiguous situations, and may be the diagnostic method of choice for ocular, extraocular muscle, or painful muscular/subcutaneous cysts.

Treatment

Infestation with the adult tapeworm (taeniasis) is treated with praziquantel (5–10 mg/kg once) or niclosamide (50 mg /kg once).

Therapeutic options in neurocysticercosis include medications, surgery, or watchful waiting. The decision depends upon multiple factors, including symptoms and the location, number, stage, and size of cysts. Although active parenchymal lesions usually resolve spontaneously and thus may not require anticysticercal drugs, a meta-analysis demontrates that cysticidal drug therapy is associated with reduced seizures and increased resolution of lesions in the brain parenchyma. Two effective anticysticercal drugs are available: albendazole (15 mg/kg/day bid for 30 days) and praziquantel (50 mg/kg/day tid for 30 days). Albendazole is more effective than praziquantel. A 7-day course of albendazole is perhaps as effective as a 14- or 28-day course, though longer courses are preferred when more than a few lesions are present. Massive infections generally are not treated with antihelminthic medications because of the risk of an overwhelming inflammatory response from degenerating cysts. This can be prevented by giving steroids for 2–3 days before and during treatment. Watchful waiting is indicated for calcified cysts because they are already dead, hence children with seizures and calcified inactive lesions on CT do not require specific therapy apart from anticonvulsants. The commonly used antiepileptics are phenytoin and carbamazepine, which should be continued for at least one year and then tapered or continued based on symptoms.

Treatment of subarachnoid and intraventricular neurocysticercosis is complicated and risky. Cysts in these locations are usually managed surgically because medical treatment is associated with the risk of inflammation; however, recent reports suggest that high-dose albendazole (30 mg/kg/day) is associated with clearance of these cysts. A ventriculoperitoneal shunt should be placed in all patients with evidence of significant obstructive hydrocephalus.

Surgical removal of the cyst is considered the treatment of choice for intraocular cysts; antihelminthic medication should be avoided because therapy may induce inflammation that may threaten vision. Cysts in the extraocular muscle may be treated with albendazole and steroids, or surgically excised. Isolated skeletal muscle or subcutaneous cysticercosis requires no specific treatment unless it is painful, and then simple excision may suffice.

Suggested reading

1. Kraft R. Cysticercosis: an emerging parasitic disease Am Fam Physician 2007; 76: 91–6.
2. Castillo M. Imaging of neurocysticercosis. Semin Roengenol 2004; 39: 465–73.
3. Hawk MW, Shahlaie K, Kim KD, Theis JH. Neurocysticercosis: a review. Surg Neurol 2005; 63: 123–32.
4. Singhi P, Ray M, Singhi S. Clinical spectrum of 500 children with neurocysticercosis and response to albendazole therapy. J Child Neurol 2000; 15: 207–13.

Hymenolepiasis

Infection with *Hymenolepis nana*, also known as the dwarf tapeworm, is very common in developing countries. Man acts as both definitive and intermediate host because the entire life cycle may be completed in human host; however, rodents, ticks and fleas may serve as the intermediate host. The infestation usually results form poor hygiene. The adult worm lives in the jejunum. Transmission is mainly feco-oral, but auto-infection may also occur, such that one host may harbor upto thousands of adult worms. Symptoms are usually non-specific, including mild abdominal discomfort and poor appetite; some have linked growth retardation to *H. nana* infection. The infection is a major cause of eosinophilia. The diagnosis is based on the demonstration of characteristic eggs in stools. Treatment is with praziquantel (25 mg/kg once) or niclosamide (50 mg/kg once, maximum 2 g).

Echinococcosis (Hydatid Disease)

Human echinococcosis is a common infestation caused by larval stages of members of the genus *Echinococcus*, and is characterized by production of unilocular or multilocular cysts in the lung and liver. Echinococcosis is endemic in most contintents of the world, with hyperendemic areas in Western China, North Africa, West Asia and areas of South America.

Pathogenesis

Hydatidosis is a zoonosis caused by two *Echinococcus* species, *E. granulosus* and *E. mulilocularis*. The parasite eggs are transmitted from members of the canine family like dogs and wolves, to various wild and domestic animals like sheep, cattle and goats, which act as intermediate hosts. Humans are accidental hosts. Adult worm is a small tapeworm with 2–6 proglottids, which resides in the intestine of dog. Eggs from the adult worm are passed in the stools that may contaminate the water and soil, and also the fur coats of dogs. Ingestion of food or water contaminated with eggs or direct contact with infected dogs may result in humans being infected accidentally. Eggs hatch in the intestines to release larvae that penetrate the intestinal mucosa, and traverse the venous or lymphatic system to reach the liver, lungs and, less commonly, other target organs.

In the target organs, larvae develop into characteristic multiloculated fluid-filled cysts, called *hydatid cysts*. In children lung cysts are common, whereas in adults cysts are more commonly seen in the right lobe of the liver. Other tissues that may be involved include bone, brain, genitourinary tract, intestines and subcutaneous tissue. A cyst has two walls; a thick lamellated layer supports an inner germinal layer. From the inner aspect of the germinal layer multiple juvenile stage parasites or protoscolices may be produced, which, in turn, may give rise to daughter cysts within the primary cyst capsule. An outer tough fibrous capsule is produced by host reaction to the organism. The fluid in a hepatic cyst is clear, colorless and watery, but it may become thick and bile stained with treatment or with secondary bacterial infection. The cyst may keep on expanding over several years.

Life cycle of *E. multilocularis* is the same except that rodents and mice serve as intermediate hosts. The organism produces multilocular alveolar cysts with exogeneous proliferation, progressively invading the liver parenchyma and other tissues of the body. The cyst is not confined to a single defined structure because the daughter cysts bud externally, the cyst structures are poorly demarcated from the target organ tissues, making surgical removal difficult, and daughter cysts metastasize to distant organs. The infection often mimics a malignancy.

Clinical Features

Symptoms depend on the target organ involved. Very often, liver cysts may regress spontaneously without becoming symptomatic. Otherwise, cysts may become symptomatic after several years when significant mass effect results in abdominal pain vomiting, increase in abdominal girth and a palpable mass; jaundice is rare. Alveolar cysts have a more malignant course. Direct spread of infected tissue may result in cysts in the peritoneal cavity, kidneys, adrenal gland or bones. Lung cyst may present with chest pain, cough, hemoptysis and breathlessness. Involvement of the genitourinary tract may manifest as passage of cysts in the urine (hydatiduria) and hematuria. Rupture or leakage from a hydatid cyst may cause anaphylaxis, manifest as fever, itching and rash, and results in dissemination of infectious scolices. Rare but potentially serious complications include compression of important structures in the central nervous system, bone, heart, eyes or genitourinary tract.

Diagnosis

Physical examination may reveal a palpable mass, hepatomegaly or subcutaneous nodules. Ultrasonography is the most valuable tool in diagnosing echinococcal cysts. Imaging findings of echinococcosis caused by *E. granulosus* are single, unilocular cyst or multiseptated cysts, showing "wheel-like", "rosette-like" or "honeycomb-like" appearances. There may be "snow-flakes" sign, reflecting free floating protoscoleces (hydatid-sand) within the cyst cavity. Degenerating cysts show wavy serpentine bands or floating membranes representing detached or ruptured membranes, or heterogeneous, solid-looking pseudotumor with a "ball of wool sign". Dead cysts may show calcified cyst wall. Imaging findings of Echinococcosis caused by *E. multilocularis* are ill-defined infiltrating lesions of the liver parenchyma, consisting of multiple small clustered cystic and solid components. On sonography, lesions are heterogeneous with indistinct margins, showing "hailstorm appearance" or "vesicular or alveolar appearance". CT and MR imaging displays multiple, irregular, ill-defined lesions. Multiple small round cysts with solid components or large lesions with "geographical map"appearance may be seen, with frequent calcifications, appearing as peripheral calcification or punctuate scattered calcific foci. Invasion into the bile ducts, portal vein or hepatic vein may occur. Lung hydatid cyst is often apparent on a chest X-ray film. Diagnostic aspiration is generally contraindicated because of risk of infection and anaphylaxis. Antibody detection by ELISA is more sensitive but less specific. The test uses partially purified antigens that cross-reacts with other parasites such as cysticercosis and schistosomiasis.

Management

Surgical excision has for long been considered the treatment of chice. For simple and easily accessible cysts, USG-or CT-guided *p*ercutaneous *a*spiration, *i*nstillation of hypertonic saline or another scolicidal agent; and *r*easpiration after 15 minutes (PAIR) is now the preferred therapy. The risk of spillage with PAIR is minimal, and the risk of anaphylaxis is further decreased by prophylactic medical therapy beginning before PAIR and continuing for a month thereafter. PAIR, when combined with medical therapy, results in shorter hospital stay and faster resolution of cyst compared to surgical excision. PAIR is contraindicated in pregnancy (where scolicidal therapy is contraindicated) and in bile-stained cysts (wherein risk of biliary complications is high). The standard surgical approach is partial capsulectomy, drainage, and epiploplasty, and remains the most frequent operative method. Problems with this approach such as disease recurrence and a residual cavity have led to more radical operations such as total pericystectomy. Laparoscopic and endoscopic approaches (endoscopic retrograde cholangiopancreatography and sphincterotomy) have a role when the location of the cyst or the patient's status does not permit more radical approaches. In all approaches, care is taken to avoid spillage of cyst contents, which is associated with dissemination of infection and with risk of anaphylaxis. Alveolar hydatidosis is difficult to remove, and require more radical surgeries like partial hepatectomy.

Medical therapy alone may be attempted in patients where surgery and PAIR are contraindicated. Albendazole is also given both before and after percutaneous drainage of hydatid cysts. Albendazole is administered in a dose of 15 mg/kg/day in two divided doses (maximum 800 mg) for 2 weeks, repeated for 3–12 courses with 15 days drug-free interval in-between two courses. The efficacy rate is 40–60%. Albendazole therapy is safe. Common side effects include elevated transaminases and abdominal pain, and rarely, headache, abdominal distension or alopecia. The response to medical therapy is monitored by serial ultrasonography, which demonstrates a change in shape from spherical to elliptical or flat, progressive increase in echogenicity, and separation of membranes from the capsule (*water lily sign*).

Suggested reading

1. Czemak BV, Akhan O, Hiemetzberger R, Zelger B, Vogel W, Jaschke W et al. Echinococcosis of the liver Abdom Imaging. 2008; 33:133–43.
2. Akhan O, Ozmen MN. Percutaneous treatment of liver hydatid cysts. Eur J Radiol 1999; 32: 76–85.

9

10 Diseases of Gastrointestinal System and Liver

GASTROINTESTINAL TRACT

COMMON SYMPTOMS AND SIGNS OF GASTROINTESTINAL TRACT DISORDERS

Vomiting

Vomiting encompasses all retrograde ejection of gastrointestinal contents from the mouth. Vomiting may be caused by a wide variety of conditions, some of which may be catastrophic and life-threatening (Table 10.1).

Table 10.1: Causes of vomiting in children

Neonatal period	
Atresia/stenosis	Bacterial meningitis
Malrotation	Birth asphyxia
Volvulus	Hydrocephalus
Nectrotizing enterocolitis	Gastric irritation due to swallowed blood*
Meconium plug	
Gastroesophageal reflux	Faulty feeding technique*
Inborn errors of metabolism	Posseting*
Infancy	
Congenital hypertrophic pyloric stenosis	CNS space occupying lesions
Malrotation	Hydrocephalus
Volvulus	Subdural hematoma
Intussusception	Inborn errors of metabolism
Gastroesophageal reflux	
Gastroenteritis	Uremia
CNS infections	Cow milk protein allergy
Peritonitis	Over feeding*
Urinary tract infections	Faulty feeding technique*
Childhood	
Gastroenteritis	CNS space occupying lesions
Intestinal obstruction	
Gastroesophageal reflux	Hydrocephalus
Intussusception	Diabetic ketoacidosis
Urinary tract infections	Uremia
Hepatitis	Toxins
Pneumonia	Post nasal dripping
Peritonitis	Psychogenic*

* Non-organic causes

Determining the cause of vomiting in a child is, therefore, of major importance.

Approach to a Child with Vomiting

Given the wide spectrum of disorders that cause vomiting in a child, it is important to arrive at correct diagnosis. Figure 10.1 gives an approach for evaluation of a child with vomiting. The following information should be derived from a good history and examination:

1. Vomiting due to benign non-organic causes does not lead to dehydration or loss of weight, but may cause considerable anxiety to the parents. Posseting may at times be persistent and even forceful. However, these infants do not regurgitate whole of feed and do not lose weight.
2. Recurrent and severe vomiting results in disturbances of fluids and electrolytes. Excessive loss of gastric contents may cause alkalosis. This may be compensated partially by metabolic acidosis because of starvation. Hypokalemia is characteristic.
3. An occasional vomit at the onset of most acute fevers should be disregarded and does not require any specific therapy.
4. The following features suggest an organic basis for vomiting and every effort should be made to find the cause: (a) persistent vomiting with or without fever; (b) excessive drowsiness; (c) failure to suck, swallow or demand feeds; (d) marked abdominal distension; (e) visible peristalsis; (f) palpable mass in the abdomen; and (g) bulging fontannel, headache or convulsions.
5. *Age*: Vomiting in the newborn period may be serious. The possibility of a surgically correctable lesion should be considered and excluded. During infancy and early childhood, most of the causes of vomiting are due to general rather than local factors. Gastroenteritis is the commonest cause of vomiting in this age period. Generalized and distant infections such as tonsillitis, otitis media, appendicitis, urinary infections and meningitis may be responsible for vomiting in a significant proportion.
   In older children usually above the age of 7 years, acute appendicitis, migraine and gastrointestinal disturbances should be considered.

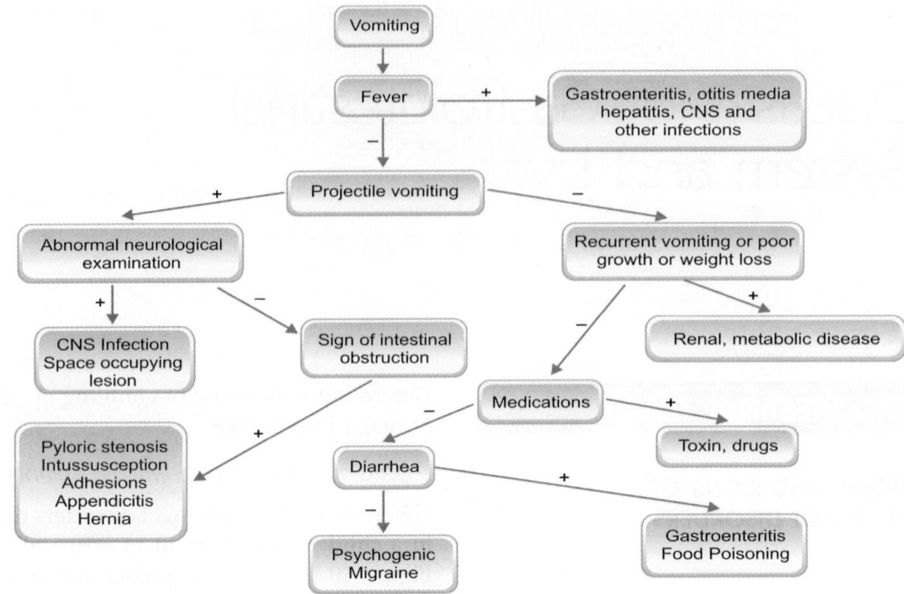

Fig. 10.1: Approach to a child with vomiting

6. *Site of lesion*: In esophageal atresia (tracheo-esophageal fistula) and stenotic lesions of the esophagus, the infant has excessive frothing soon after birth. He may choke on attempted feeding. It may not be possible to pass a soft rubber catheter beyond the obstruction. The swallowed milk is returned promptly, often relatively undigested and unchanged. In achalasia cardia, the vomiting is relieved on feeding in propped up position.
   Stomach: The child may vomit immediately or after some hours. The infant may regurgitate soon after the feed. Vomiting is not forceful. The milk is curdled but is not bile stained.
   Intestine: Vomitus is bile stained, greenish, if the obstruction is beyond the ampulla of Vater. Feculent vomiting suggests intestinal obstruction or paralytic ileus.
   Vomiting due to central causes: There is generally no preceding cause. Vomiting is often sudden, unexpected and forceful. Persistent headache and signs of increased intracranial pressure may be evident.

Management

Most children vomit occasionally for trivial reasons. This need not cause undue alarm. Sips of cold, clear fluids are better tolerated than the hot beverages like coffee and tea. Carbonated beverages may increase vomiting. Children with recurrent and persistent vomiting and associated features suggestive of an organic cause of vomiting should be evaluated properly and appropriate medical and surgical remedial measures should be instituted.

Recurrent vomiting may cause failure to thrive. Therefore, diet should be nutritious. Intravenous alimentation may be resorted to in case of persistent vomiting. Metoclopramide and domperidone are useful in vomiting because these increase gastric emptying. Ondansetron is increasingly used for intractable or refractory vomiting. However, drug therapy is only symptomatic and effort should be to identify the underlying cause. Symptomatic therapy of vomiting with phenothiazine without definitive assessment of the cause of vomiting is never advisable.

Cyclical Vomiting Syndrome (CVS)

Children experience bouts or cycles of severe nausea and vomiting that last for hours or even days and alternate with longer periods of no symptoms. CVS has no known cause and each episode is similar to the previous ones. The episodes tend to start at about the same time of day, last the same length of time, and present the same symptoms at the same level of intensity. Episodes can be severe enough to restraint the child to bed for days. The most common trigger is an infection, but emotional stress or excitement, and other physical agents can also set off episodes. Some patients may have a family history of migraine. CVS is difficult to diagnose because there are no diagnostic tests. The condition is suspected by consistency and relapsing nature of symptoms and excluding other organic causes. Patients are advised to get enough rest and sleep. In cases of frequent and long-lasting episodes, medications like propranolol, cyproheptadine and amitriptyline have been tried with limited success.

Congenital Hypertrophic Pyloric Stenosis

Hypertrophic pyloric stenosis is the commonest surgical disorder of the stomach during infancy. This condition is five times more common in boys than in girls. The pylorus is thickened and elongated and its lumen is narrowed due to hypertrophy of the circular muscle fibers of pylorus (Fig. 10.2).

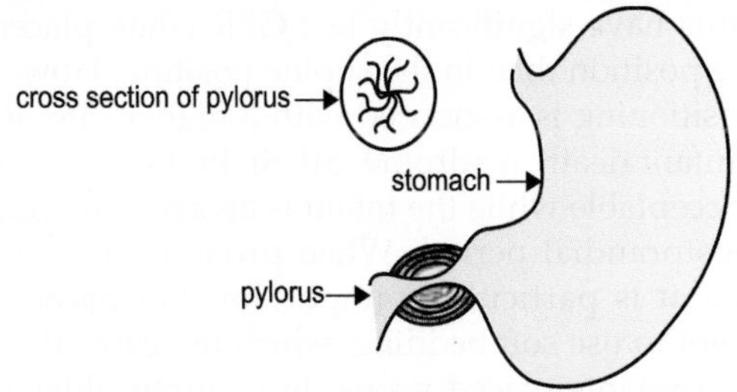

Fig. 10.2: Hypertrophic pyloric stenosis

Clinical features: Though etiology is not yet understood, it is now known that hypertrophic pyloric stenosis is not a congenital disorder. Recent evidence suggests that the local enteric innervation is involved and that primarily argyrophilic nitrergic neurons are affected. The classical presentation is of non-bilious vomiting beginning usually at 3–6 weeks of age. Vomiting gradually increases in frequency and severity to become projectile. Persistent vomiting leads to malnutrition, dehydration and hypochloremic alkalosis. Constipation is usual. The stomach muscles contract forcibly to overcome the obstruction. Vigorous peristaltic waves moving from the left hypochondrium to umbilicus are visible. A small mass due to pyloric thickening might be palpable in the transpyloric plane on the right side. The examiner should palpate the tumor with the index and middle fingers of the left hand, approaching the baby from the left side while the baby is sucking the left breast of the mother.

Diagnosis: The diagnosis is based on clinical history and palpability of the mass. A radiograph of upper abdomen after barium meal should be obtained. The classical findings are dilatation and hypertrophy of stomach, delayed passage of barium through narrow pylorus, *string sign* or *double track*. Ultrasound examination of abdomen reveals dome-shaped, thickened pyloric sphincter.

Treatment: Dehydration and dyselectrolytemia should be corrected rapidly. Hypokalemia is frequently observed, which might require correction. The stomach is washed with isotonic saline till clear fluid is returned. The stomach tube is left *in situ*. Treatment of choice is Ramstedt's operation (pyloromyotomy). The hypertrophied circular muscle fibers are cut longitudinally completely without damaging the mucosa. After the child comes out of system anesthesia, oral feeding is started in a stepwise manner, starting initially with one or two teaspoon of a clear solution, like 5% glucose solution, given every 2 hours for about 8 hours, provided the baby does not start vomiting. Laparoscopic surgery has improved the outcome and reduced the hospital stay. Medical treatment is not a substitute for surgery. However, if the diagnosis of stenosis is in doubt and pylorospasm is a possibility, medical therapy with atropine, methyl nitrate, metoclopramide and cisapride may be used.

Gastroesophageal Reflux (GER)

Gastroesophageal reflux (GER), defined as retrograde passage of gastric contents into the esophagus, is a normal physiologic process that occurs throughout the day in healthy infants, children, and adults. It refers to immaturity of lower esophageal sphincter function manifested by frequent transient relaxations. Most episodes of reflux are brief and asymptomatic, not extending above the distal esophagus. As many as 60–70% of infants experience emesis during at least one feeding per 24 hours period by 3–4 months. The distinction between physiologic GER and pathologic GER in infancy and childhood is determined by presence of reflux-related complication, including failure to thrive, erosive esophagitis, esophageal stricture formation and chronic respiratory disease.

Gastroesophageal reflux disease (GERD) occurs when gastric contents reflux into the esophagus or oropharynx and produce symptoms. During infancy GER is common and most often manifest as vomiting and by 1st year of age, it resolves spontaneously in nearly 90% infants. Symptoms that persist after 18 months of age suggest a higher likelihood of GERD.

Typical symptoms (e.g., heartburn, vomiting, and regurgitation) in the adults cannot be readily assessed in infants and children. Children with GER typically cry and report sleep disturbance and decreased appetite. They have recurrent vomiting, regurgitation, weight loss or poor weight gain and irritability. Infants with GERD present with anorexia, dysphagia (difficulty swallowing), odynophagia (painful swallowing), arching of the back during feedings, irritability, hematemesis, anemia or failure to thrive. GER in preschool age children may manifest as intermittent vomiting. Older children are more likely to have the adult-type pattern of chronic heartburn or regurgitation with reswallowing and esophagitis. Older children may present occasionally as dysphagia or food impaction due to secondary strictures in the middle or lower esophagus. Other symptoms of GER are chest pain, hematemesis, recurrent pneumonia, apnea, wheezing, stridor, hoarseness, cough, abnormal neck posturing (Sandifer syndrome). GER has been associated with significant respiratory symptoms in infants and children. Hence, diagnostic and therapeutic approaches vary with the age of the patient and the presenting signs or symptoms.

History and Physical Examination

In most infants with vomiting, and in older children with regurgitation and heartburn, a history and physical examination are sufficient to reliably suspect GER, associated complications, and initiate management. In many of the cases, anemia may be present. Vomiting is a symptom associated with many disorders. If vomitus is bilious or associated with diarrhea, hepatosplenomegaly or neurological features, other diagnosis should be considered. Other differentials include duodenal atresia, intestinal malrotation and other gastrointestinal surgical conditions, occasionally food allergies and intestinal motility disorders.

Investigations

Radiography: The upper gastrointestinal barium series is neither sensitive nor specific for the diagnosis of GER, but is useful for the evaluation of the presence of anatomic abnormalities, such as pyloric stenosis, malrotation and annular pancreas in the vomiting infant, as well as hiatal hernia and esophageal stricture in the older child.

Scintigraphy: A nuclear scintiscan is performed by the oral ingestion or instillation of technetium-labeled formula or food into the stomach. Scintigraphy also provides information about gastric emptying.

Esophageal pH monitoring: Esophageal pH monitoring is widely used as an index of esophageal acid exposure (pH <4), measures the frequency and duration of episodes of acid reflux. This test has been considered gold standard for diagnosis of GER. It helps establishing temporal association between acid reflux and frequently occurring symptoms, and to assess the adequacy of therapy. Intramural esophageal electrical impedance is a recently developed test useful for detecting both acid and non-acid reflux by measuring the retrograde flows in the esophagus.

Endoscopy and biopsy: Endoscopy enables both visualization and biopsy of the esophageal epithelium. Endoscopy and biopsy can determine the presence and severity of esophagitis, strictures and Barrett's esophagus, as well as exclude other disorders. A normal appearance of the esophagus during endoscopy does not exclude histopathological esophagitis; subtle mucosal changes such as erythema and pallor may be observed in the absence of macroscopic esophagitis. Esophageal biopsy is recommended when endoscopy is performed to detect microscopic esophagitis and to exclude causes of esophagitis other than GER.

Management

Since most causes of GER are functional, reassurance is a major part of treatment. Conservative measures may include upright positioning at least in the first postprandial hour, elevating the head end of the bed, prone positioning (>6 months) and providing small frequent feeds thickened with cereal.

Diet changes in the infant: Milk-thickening agents (rice cereals) do not improve reflux index scores but do decrease the number of episodes of vomiting. Thickening of food thus provides therapeutic advantage and prompts weight gain. Use of hypoallergenic formula in formula fed infants with vomiting help in cases of cow milk allergy.

Positioning: Esophageal pH monitoring has demonstrated that infants have significantly less GER when placed in the prone position than in the supine position. However, prone positioning is associated with a higher rate of the sudden infant death syndrome (SIDS). Prone positioning may be acceptable while the infant is awake, particularly in the postprandial period. When prone positioning is necessary, it is particularly important that parents be advised not to use soft bedding, which increases the risk of SIDS in infants placed prone. In children older than one year, left lateral positioning during sleep and elevation of the head end (25–45°) help in reducing GER.

Lifestyle changes in the child and adolescent: Children and adolescents with GERD should avoid caffeine, chocolate and spicy foods that provoke symptoms. Obesity, exposure to tobacco smoke and alcohol are also associated with GER. The magnitude of additive benefit due to lifestyle changes in patients receiving pharmacological therapy is exactly not known.

Pharmacotherapy

Acid-suppressant therapy: Histamine-2 receptor antagonists and proton pump inhibitors produce relief of symptoms and healing of esophagitis. Chronic antacid therapy is generally not recommended, but commonly used for the short-term relief of intermittent symptoms of GER.

Prokinetic therapy: Cisapride reduces esophageal acid exposure and enhanced esophageal acid clearance resulting in improvement in frequency of symptoms and esophageal histopathology. However, the use of cisapride is discouraged due to potential for serious cardiac arrhythmias in patients receiving cisapride. Appropriate patient selection and monitoring as well as proper use, including correct dosage (0.2 mg/kg/dose QID) and avoidance of co-administration of contraindicated medications are important. Presently, mosapride is gaining popularity in place of cisapride. Other prokinetic agents like metoclopramide, domperidone and bethanechol have not been shown to be effective in the treatment of GERD in children.

Surgical therapy: Surgery is considered for a small proportion of patients with GERD with persistence of symptoms on medical management or those unable to be weaned from medical therapy. The Nissen fundoplication (a gastric wrap procedure) is the most popular of the many surgical procedures that have been used. The stomach is wrapped and sutured 360° around the distal esophagus. As the stomach distends, the pressure at the junction compresses the distal esophagus.

Prognosis

Most cases of GER in infants and very young children are benign and 80% resolve by 18 months. In patients in whom

GER persists into later childhood, long-term therapy with proton pumps inhibitors is required. Children with neurodevelopmental disabilities including cerebral palsy have an increased prevalence of GER and high likelihood of developing long-term feeding disorders.

Suggested reading

1. North American Society for Pediatric Gastroenterology and Nutrition. Pediatric GE Reflux Clinical Practice Guidelines. J Pediatr Gastroenterol Nutr 2001; 32: Suppl. 2, S1–31.
2. Orenstein SR. Esophageal disorders in infants and children. Curr Opin Pediatr 1993; 5: 580-89.

Constipation

Constipation is defined as a delay or difficulty in defecation, present for 2 or more weeks and sufficient to cause significant distress to the patient. Constipation is characterized by infrequent bowel evacuations; hard, small feces, or difficult or painful defecation. Chronic constipation is a source of anxiety for parents who worry that a serious disease may be causing the symptom. Only a minority of children have an organic cause for constipation. In about 95% of children with constipation, no obvious anatomic, biochemical or physiologic abnormalities are identified. Many of these children have functional constipation resulting from intentional withholding of stool. In such children, an unpleasant event may precipitate desire to withhold stool. A change of milk formula, coercive toilet training or unpleasant toilet practices may lead to deliberate withholding.

Causes

Constipation may be *functional* (non-organic) or *organic*. Organic causes of constipation are listed below in Table 10.2.

The normal stool frequency decreases from 4 or more per day during infancy to once per day at 4 years of age. Stool frequency of less that 3 times per week at any age is abnormal. Many children with constipation pass large, hard stool and display stool withholding behavior, characterized by stiffening of whole body and screaming in infants, to walking on tiptoes, or tightening of buttocks in older children. Abdominal pain and overflow incontinence (encopresis) may also be presenting symptoms in older children.

Table 10.2: Organic causes of constipation

Intestinal	Hypothyroidism
Hirschsprung disease	Panhypopituitarism
Anal/rectal stenosis	*Neuromuscular*
Anal fissure	Cerebral palsy
Anteriorly displaced anal opening	Psychomotor retardation
Stricture	Spinal cord lesions
	Myotonic dystrophy
Drugs	Neuropathy or myopathy of GI tract
Narcotics	
Vincristine	*Other causes*
Psychotropics	Low fibre diet
Metabolic/Endocrine	Milk protein allergy
Cystic fibrosis	

Evaluation

A thorough history including family, psychological, school performance and medications is recommended as part of a complete evaluation of a child with constipation. History should include age of onset of symptoms; infants who fail to pass meconium within first 48 hours of life are likely to have Hirschsprungs disease than infants whose constipation began after being weaned from breast milk. Physical examination for systemic abnormalities and perineal and anal abnormalities are must. At least one digital examination of the anorectum is necessary to assess perianal sensation, anal tone, the size of the rectum, the presence of an anal wink, amount and consistency of stool and its location within the rectum. Children with rectal stenosis or Hirschsprung disease have tight anus, distended abdomen and empty rectum.

An abdominal radiograph is not indicated to establish the presence of fecal impaction if the rectal examination reveals the presence of large amounts of stool. Barium enema is mandatory when constipation is since birth. Barium enema, ano-rectal manometry and full thickness rectal biopsy (absence of ganglionic cells in Hirschsprung disease) may be required. In endemic areas, tests to rule out hypothyroidism must be undertaken for all children with constipation.

Management

The parents should be reassured of the benign nature of simple constipation and the patient helped to develop normal bowel habits. Parents are encouraged to maintain a consistent positive and supportive attitude in all aspects of treatment.

Rectal disimpaction of the hard fecoliths if present may be performed by the oral route (mineral oil, polyethylene glycol electrolyte solutions), the rectal route (phosphate soda enemas, saline enemas, or mineral oil enemas, suppositories—glycerin in infants and bisacodyl in older children). These interventions help in providing immediate relief, but need to be followed by maintenance therapy.

Once the fecal impaction is been removed, the treatment focuses on prevention of and recurrence of impaction. The goal is to achieve one soft stool per day and the minimum acceptable is 3 or more stools per week with no pain or soiling.

Maintenance therapy has four components: fluid and dietary interventions, toileting programmes, medication and follow up. Maintenance therapy consists of dietary interventions, behavioral modification, and laxatives to assure that bowel movements occur at normal intervals with good evacuation. Increasing fluid intake (at least 6–8 cups of per day), using high residue diets (whole wheat flour, fruit and vegetables) help in relieving the constipation. Excessive milk drinking may worsen constipation.

Behavior modification and regular toilet habits are an important component of treatment. It may be supplemented with maintaining stool diary and reward system. Child should be encouraged to use toilet regularly, without hurry or distractions.

When necessary, daily medication with mineral oil (a lubricant) or magnesium hydroxide, lactulose, sorbitol, polyethylene glycol (PEG) (osmotic laxatives), or a combination of lubricant and laxative is recommended. All these agents are extensively studied and are effective and safe for long-term use. PEG 3350 appears to be superior to other osmotic agents in palatability and acceptance by children. Phenolphthalein compounds are better avoided. Lactulose solution 15 to 30 mL at breakfast relieves constipation. The medications can be weaned off when the child has been regularly passing soft formed stools for at least 6 months. Patience and persistence of the physician and care provider are the keys to success of medical therapy. Consultation with a pediatric gastrointestinal specialist becomes necessary when the therapy fails, when there is concern that an organic disease exists, or when management is complex.

Suggested reading

Evaluation and Treatment of Constipation in Infants and Children: Recommendations of the North American Society for Pediatric Gastroenterology, Hepatology and Nutrition. J Pediatric Gastroenterol and Nutr 2006; 43:e1–e13.

Hirschsprung Disease

Hirschsprung disease is the congenital absence of ganglion cells in the submucosal and myenteric plexuses of the distal intestine. The distal rectum is aganglionic and the aganglionosis extends proximally usually ending in transition zone in the rectosigmoid colon. The length of aganglionosis may vary from short segment to total colon. The aganglionic segment is not capable of coordinated peristalsis and fails to relax, this leads to mechanical obstruction. The most important association is with Down syndrome.

Failure to pass meconium within first 48 hours of life, abdominal distension, vomiting, constipation starting in neonatal age and poor feeding are the usual symptoms. Diarrhea may be there in 1/3rd of infants and commonest cause of death. Abdominal distension, an empty rectum on digital examination or rectal impaction is the common physical findings. Rapid expulsion of feces often follows digital examination.

The differential diagnosis in the neonatal period include meconium plug syndrome, microcolon, hypothyroidism, sepsis and cystic fibrosis. In neonatal period, plain abdominal radiograph film reveals bowel distension with multiple air-fluid levels, and paucity of air in pelvis. A barium enema usually shows the narrow aganglionic bowel with dilated proximal bowel. However, a normal study does not exclude Hirschsprung disease. Rectal manometry helps in diagnosis in older infants. Rectal biopsy is the gold standard in diagnosing Hirschsprung disease. Full thickness biopsy is ideal, but submucosal biopsy also suffices in most cases. Recognition of the absence of ganglionic cells in the myenteric and submucosal plexi is essential for the diagnosis. Hypertrophied nerves are observed in the aganglionic segment.

The management is essentially surgical; the role of medical management is restricted to stabilize the general condition of the child. Initially, a colostomy in the ganglionic bowel is performed to relieve the obstruction and allow the dilated hypertrophied proximal bowel to return to normal. Subsequently, definitive surgery is performed. This consists of excision of the aganglionic segment with a "pull through" procedure enabling an anastomosis to be performed between the ganglionic colon and the anus.

The most frequently performed surgeries are those described by Swenson, Duhamel, Soave and Boley. Though the long-term bowel control is excellent, soiling and constipation may occur in initial period. Use of laparoscopes in neonatal colectomy has helped in rapid recovery and less adhesions.

Suggested reading

Rescoria FJ, Morrison AM, Engles D, et al. Hirschsprung disease: Evaluation of mortality and long-term function in 260 cases. Arch Surg 1992; 127: 934–42.

Protuberant Abdomen

Protuberance of abdomen is not an uncommon sign in infants and young children who often present with a pot belly. The mothers are often very concerned about it and this may be the main reason for seeking medical consultation. These children require a systematic evaluation as per the list of causes outlined in Table 10.3.

Abdominal Pain

Abdominal pain in children is a common and challenging complaint. At least 20% of the children will consult a physician for abdominal pain by the age of 15 years.

Acute Abdominal Pain

The pediatrician evaluating the child with acute abdomen must decide early whether the child has a "surgical abdomen", a serious medical disorder requiring admission, or a process that can be managed on an outpatient basis (Table 10.4 and Fig. 10.3).

Table 10.3: Causes of protuberant abdomen*

Abdominal wall
Hypotonia of the abdominal muscles due to malnutrition, rickets, hypokalemia Obesity
Gastrointestinal system
Aerophagy Constipation, Hirschsprung disease Malabsorption: celiac disease, lactose intolerance, cystic fibrosis Intestinal obstruction: meconium ileus and peritonitis, imperforate anus, volvulus with malrotation Dilatation of the stomach, e.g. following abdomen surgery Intestinal ileus: septicemia, necrotizing enterocolitis, hypokalemia
Peritoneum, omentum and mesentery
Peritonitis Mesenteric cysts Ascites due to portal hypertension, renal disorders, pericarditis, tuberculosis
Other viscera in the abdomen
Kidney: ectopic kidney, hydronephrosis, Wilm's tumor, polycystic kidney Neuroblastoma Ovarian cyst Pancreatic cyst All causes of hepatosplenomegaly

*Patients with lumbar lordosis appear to have protuberant abdomen

Table 10.4: Causes of acute abdominal pain

Surgical causes	*Medical causes*
Children <2-yr-old	
Malrotation Volvulus Intussusception Incarcerated inguinal hernia Appendicitis Necrotizing enterocolitis	Gastroenteritis Pneumonia (lower lobe) Urinary tract infection Hepatitis Spontaneous bacterial peritonitis
Children >2-yr-old	
Appendicitis Intestinal obstruction Meckel's diverticulum Peritonitis Cholecystitis Incarcerated inguinal hernia Trauma Henoch Schölein purpura Primary peritonitis	Non-specific abdominal pain Gastroenteritis Inflammatory bowel disease Hepatitis Pancreatitis Urinary tract infection Lead poisoning Mesenteric lymphadenitis

Management: It is done as per suspected etiology and the severity of pain. Administrtion of narcotics should be avoided. Analgesics and antispasmodics are mostly used to alleviate pain. Care must be taken to rule out surgical conditions.

Chronic and Recurrent Abdominal Pain

The term chronic and recurrent abdominal pain used interchangeably represents a description and not a diagnosis. Many diseases can cause chronic abdominal pain (Table 10.5).

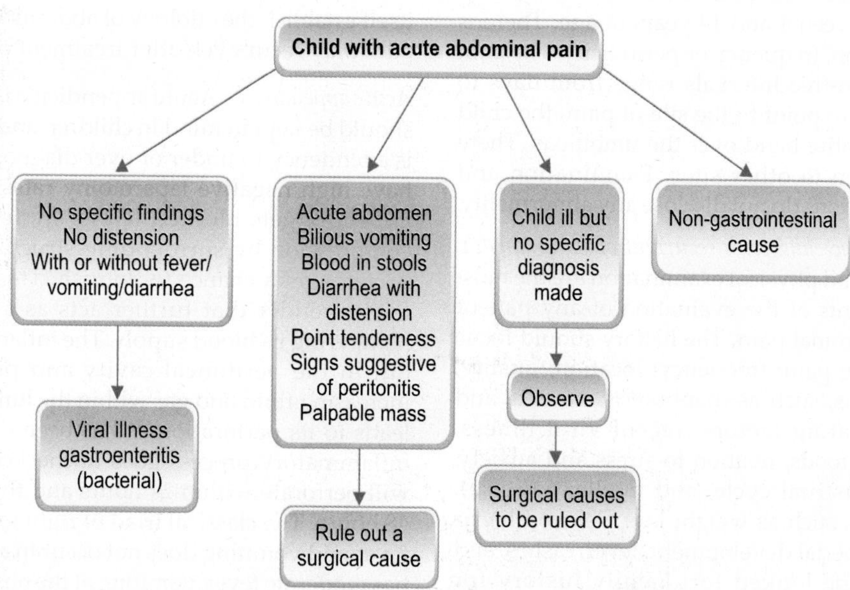

Fig. 10.3: Evaluation of acute abdominal pain in a child

10

Table 10.5: Causes of chronic and recurrent abdominal pain

Children <2-yr-old	*Children >2-yr-old*
Colic	Functional pain
Malabsorption	Constipation
Milk allergy	Giardiasis
Rotational defects	Intra-abdominal abscess
Hirschsprung disease	Lead poisoning
Esophagitis	Pancreatitis
	Abdominal migraine/ epilepsy
	Urolithiasis

Chronic abdominal pain is defined as presence of at least three bouts of pain severe enough to affect activities over a period of at least 3 months. The cause of pain may be functional or organic (disease-based). Nearly 10% to 15% of school-aged children experience recurring abdominal pain at some time.

The commonest cause of chronic abdominal pain in older children is functional. The following features are clues to an organic cause: (i) localized pain in non-periumbilical region; (ii) referred pain; (iii) pain awakens the child from sleep; (iv) sudden onset of severe pain; (v) high grade fever; (vi) dysuria; (vii) jaundice; (viii) anorexia/weight loss; (ix) specific physical findings; and (x) reduced activity level.

Functional abdominal pain is defined as abdominal pain without demonstrable evidence of a pathologic condition, such as an anatomic, metabolic, infectious, inflammatory or neoplastic disorder. The perception of recurrent abdominal pain is the summation of sensory, emotional and cognitive input. Psychosocial stress, child's personality type and reinforcement of illness behavior within the family affect the pain intensity and quality. Onset is usually between 4 and 14 years of age. There is no consistent duration, frequency or periodicity. The pain is usually brief; pain-free intervals range from days to weeks. When asked to point to the site of pain, the child usually places the entire hand over the umbilicus. There is often no radiation to other sites. Examination and laboratory investigations do not disclose any abnormality.

General approach to the child with recurrent abdominal pain: A complete history and physical examination are the most important components of the evaluation of any patient with recurrent abdominal pain. The history should focus on the timing of the pain; frequency; location; quality; associated symptoms, such as diaphoresis, nausea, and dizziness; precipitating factors (recent viral illness, ingestion of certain foods, relation to stress and anxiety, relation to the menstrual cycle, and medication use). Systemic symptoms, such as weight loss, delayed linear growth, delayed pubertal development, fever, rashes, and joint pain should be looked for. Family history for inflammatory bowel disease, peptic ulcer disease should be asked for. Clubbing, rashes, arthritis, and perirectal inflammation are important signs. The abdominal examination should look for distension, tenderness, organomegaly, any other mass, bowel sounds and bruit. A structured investigatory approach is needed in all cases. It has a reassuring impact on the family and the child that the symptoms are being seriously considered. Children with red flag symptoms and signs require more extensive investigations including endoscopy and contrast studies.

Management: Organic causes should be excluded. The parents and child should be assured about absence of major illness, once features of organic causes are absent. Help of a child psychologist should be sought for management is suspected psychiatric problem, maladaptive family and poor response to conservative therapy. Patients with functional abdominal pain do not need any medications. Hospitalization and drug therapy in such patients might reinforce the pain behavior. Unless documented, therapy for helminthiasis, protozoal infections, *H. pylori* and acid-peptic disease is not useful. Severe acute pain may be relieved by anticholinergic agents, but it should be used judiciously to avoid prolonged side effects.

Suggested reading

1. McCollough M, Sharieff GQ. Abdominal pain in children. Pediatr Clin N Am 2006;53:107–37.
2. Mittal SK, Verma IC. Abdominal pain in children. Indian J Pediatr 1994; 7: 1–15.

Gastrointestinal Causes of Pain

Parasitic infestations: The usual helminthic infestations are rarely responsible for abdominal pain; *Giardia lamblia* and *Entameba histolytica* infestations are often incriminated. A bunch of roundworms may cause acute intestinal obstruction. Demonstration of the infestation does not by itself establish the etiology of abdominal pain. Abdominal pain may recur even after treatment of the infestations.

Acute appendicitis: Acute appendicitis is rare in infancy but should be kept in mind in children and adolescents. There is a tendency to under or over diagnose appendicitis and have high negative laparotomy rates. The lumen of the appendix gets blocked (either by fecoliths or external compression by surrounding structures) and intestinal bacteria get a chance to flourish. This leads to edema of the appendix that further acts as a constriction, thus hampering its blood supply. The inflammatory fluid leaks out in the peritoneal cavity and produces pain. The increasing fluid and gas within the lumen of the appendix leads to its perforation. It has been estimated that if the inflammatory process goes unchecked, about 20% cases will perforate within 24 hours and the remaining 80% in 48 hours. The classical triad of right lower quadrant pain, fever and vomiting does not occur in all cases. The patient has moderate fever, vomiting at the onset, abdominal pain, distension and local tenderness over the McBurney's point in the right iliac fossa. Retrocecal appendicitis is difficult to diagnose clinically. Diarrhea and colicky abdominal pain may be the only symptoms in these patients.

Acute appendicitis is a clinical diagnosis, and no single investigation is confirmatory. Other possible causes and associations (urinary tract infection) should be ruled out. An erect X-ray abdomen may reveal calcification in the appendix, deviation of spinal curvature to the right and a dilated caecum and gas under diaphragm. In children below 2 years of age an X-ray examination is helpful in the absence of reliable clinical signs. An ultrasound examination may show a non-compressible appendix, peri-appendiceal fluid collection and a thickened appendix. CT scan examination is also useful. Appendicectomy at diagnosis is recommended.

Acute mesenteric lymphadenitis: The clinical features resemble acute appendicitis. There is history of preceding respiratory or enteric disease possibly due to infection with *Yersinia pseudotuberculosis* or *Yersinia enterocolitica.* Pain is poorly localized and there is fever. In mesenteric adenitis, area of tenderness shifts when the patient is rolled from side to side but in appendicitis it is fixed. Treatment is symptomatic.

Obstructive lesions of the gut: Incomplete intestinal obstruction as in tuberculosis of abdomen, intestinal malrotation, Meckel's diverticulum, volvulus, diverticulum and duplication of gut are occasionally responsible also for recurrent abdominal pain, which is typically colicky. Abdominal distension and vomiting (bilious or at times fecal, depending on the site of obstruction) are associated. Bowel sounds are loud and exaggerated. Plain X-ray films of the abdomen reveal gas filled loops of the bowels and multiple air fluid levels. Ultrasonography of abdomen should be done.

Intussusception in infants: Intussusception presents as acute intestinal obstruction in infancy, mostly between 6–11 months. Intermittent colicky abdominal pain, vomiting and bloody mucous stools (*currant jelly*), the classic triad is encountered in only 20% to 40% of cases. History of recent change of milk formula, upper respiratory tract infection, or vaccination may be present in a small proportion of patients. Severe colicky abdominal pain manifests as crying episodes and it may be associated with vomiting depending on the level of obstruction. A sausage-shaped mass may be palpable usually in the right quadrant of the abdomen; right iliac fossa may appear empty. Rectal examination may show the tip of the intussusceptum. Barium enema X-ray film shows cupping, as it is obstructed by the intussusceptum; the obstruction may be relieved following the procedure. Ultrasonography may be useful.

Intussusception is a surgical emergency and the aim is reduction of the obstructed bowel. Shock is treated and the patient is rehydrated. In intussusception of short duration, hydrostatic pressure of the barium enema (both diagnostic and therapeutic) or saline enema usually relieve intussusception. Air enema is used in some centers due to ease of administration and low radiation exposure when done under fluoroscopy. Reduction by enema is not possible in ileoileal intussusception. Clinical signs of peritonitis, perforation, or hypovolemic shock are clear contraindications to enema and mandate surgical exploration. Prolonged symptoms (>24 hr), evidence of obstruction such as air fluid levels on plain abdominal films, and ultrasonography findings of intestinal ischemia or trapped fluid are relative contraindications to performing enema. Surgical management of intussusception carries very good outcome.

Peptic ulcer: Peptic ulcer was believed to be infrequent in children. Several well-documented series on peptic ulcer in childhood have been published. Most Indian studies on recurrent abdominal pain do not find peptic ulcers as an important cause. Acute gastric ulceration may follow intake of drugs such as aspirin, steroids, potassium chloride, toxins, stress (burns, intracranial lesions), sepsis and shock. *Helicobacter pylori* has been implicated in the etiology of acute and chronic gastritis and duodenitis with ulcer formation. Zollinger Ellison syndrome associated with increased production of gastric acid result in gastric and duodenal ulcer. Peptic ulcers may be primary or secondary to a severe underlying disease. The latter often require emergency surgery for perforation or hemorrhage. In children with primary peptic ulcer, early symptoms are mild but there is a high incidence of recurrent symptoms. In early childhood, ulcer is more often gastric and hematemesis is the major presentation. Duodenal ulcer is usually found in older children (>9 years). They complain of epigastric pain which may or may not have consistent relationship to meal. Pain is usually periumbilical and vomiting may be present. Diagnosis is confirmed by endoscopy. Most duodenal ulcers are localized on the posterior wall of the duodenum.

Treatment: The child is kept on a bland diet for a few days. Thereafter, a more liberal diet is permitted. Frequent small feeds are desirable. Use of antacids between meals and anticholinergic drugs is recommended. Most ulcers heal in 3 to 4 weeks. H_2 receptor antagonists or proton pump inhibitors (PPI) are used to reduce gastric acid secretion. Although current evidence does not establish a cause-effect relationship between infection and recurrent abdominal pain, symptomatic children with positive evidence of *H. Pylori* infection should be treated with amoxicillin, clarithromycin and omeprazole for 1–2 weeks. Peptic ulcer may perforate in a few children. These require surgical closure. Blood transfusion may be required to maintain the hematocrit in case of bleeding peptic ulcers.

Gastrointestinal allergy: Allergic response to specific foods may cause diarrhea, nausea, vomiting and colicky abdominal pain. Allergy to cow's milk protein is not unusual in the first few months of life. Babies could even be sensitized in utero. Three main factors contribute to the development of allergy, viz. genetic predisposition, allergen exposure and contributory factors such as immunologic defects, gastrointestinal disease, infection and non-specific irritants.

Amebic liver abscess: Clinical manifestations include fever with loss of appetite and right upper abdominal pain. Liver is enlarged and tender; jaundice is absent or minimal. Metronidazole, 20 to 50 mg/kg/day in divided doses for 7 days is effective in treatment.

Passive congestion of the liver: In congestive cardiac failure and constrictive pericarditis, there is pain and tenderness in the right hypochondrium.

Choledochal cyst: There is a partial and intermittent obstruction to the flow of bile through the ampulla of Vater. The common bile duct is dilated into a cystic enlargement. Patients have history of abdominal pain and jaundice intermittently. A cystic swelling may be felt in the right upper quadrant of abdomen. The diagnosis is confirmed by ultrasonography and endoscopic retrograde cholangio-pancreatography (ERCP) or magnetic resonance cholangio-pancreatography (MRCP). Treatment is surgical.

Acute pancreatitis: Acute pancreatitis may follow mumps, biliary tract disease, trauma, drugs, congenital anomalies and generalized infections. Blunt abdominal trauma is an important cause of acute pancreatitis in childhood. It should be suspected in patients with sudden severe abdominal pain, tenderness in epigastrium or left upper quadrant, vomiting, fever and extreme prostration. Serum and urinary amylase levels are elevated. Vigorous symptomatic and supportive. treatment is necessary. Mortality is 10 to 15% and complications including pseudocyst occur in up-to 15%. Disease is generally self-limiting and supportive treatment is necessary. Surgical treatment is reserved for pancreatic abscess and necrotic pancreatitis.

Disorders of genitourinary system: Acute glomerulonephritis, acute pyelonephritis, acute cystourethritis, urinary calculi, hydronephrosis, and ectopic kidney may present with acute abdominal pain *(Dietel's crisis)*. Abdominal pain in kidney disease is usually present in the back, flanks and lower abdomen. Pain due to ureteric calculi radiates along the course of ureters. Passage of blood clots across the ureter may also cause clot colic. Acute salpingitis, torsion of ovaries and hematocolpos should be considered in differential diagnosis of abdominal pain in girls. Girls often suffer from severe abdominal pain with each menstrual period, especially around menarche. Torsion of testis is an acute surgical emergency. It requires immediate intervention otherwise permanent damage occurs.

Causes of pain outside the abdomen: Basal pneumonia, diaphragmatic pleurisy, rheumatic fever, pericarditis, subacute bacterial endocarditis, abdominal epilepsy, hemolytic crisis in sickle cell disease and hereditary spherocytosis may be responsible for abdominal pain.

Metabolic causes: Lead poisoning, diabetic keto-acidosis, anaphylactoid purpura can also manifest with pain abdomen. The treatment is directed at the specific cause.

DIARRHEA

Acute diarrhea is a leading cause of under-five mortality in India. Diarrhea is the passage of watery stools at least three times in a 24 hour period. However, recent change in the consistency of the stools is more important than the frequency. Mothers usually know when their children have diarrhea and provide useful working definitions in local situations.

Clinical Types of Diarrheal Diseases

Four clinical types of diarrhea can be recognized, each reflecting the basic underlying pathology and altered physiology:

- *Acute watery diarrhea* (including cholera) starts suddenly and lasts several hours or days. The main danger is dehydration; weight loss may occur if feeding is not continued.
- *Acute bloody diarrhea* (dysentery) is similar to acute watery diarrhea, but associated with gross blood in stool. The main dangers are intestinal damage, sepsis and malnutrition; other complications, including dehydration, may also occur.
- *Persistent diarrhea* starts as acute watery diarrhea and lasts 14 days or longer. The main danger is malnutrition and serious non-intestinal infection; dehydration may also occur.
- *Diarrhea with severe malnutrition* (marasmus or kwashiorkor) carries risk of severe systemic infection, dehydration, heart failure and vitamin and mineral deficiency.

The two main risks of diarrhea are malnutrition and death. While dehydration is the most common cause of death, several deaths occur as a result of malnutrition consequent to a series of diarrheal episodes. A child may lose almost as much water and electrolytes from the body during an episode of diarrhea as an adult, since the length and surface area of intestinal mucosa of a child from where the diarrheal fluids are lost, are as large as in adults. However, loss of one liter of fluids from the body of a child weighing 7 kg (approximately 15% of body weight loss) is much more hazardous than similar depletion from an adult of 70 kg weight (approximately 1.47% body weight loss). Significant dehydration disturbing the balance of electrolytes and acid–base status of the body occurs in about 2 to 5% of all cases of diarrhea, and may be fatal, if fluids and electrolytes are not replaced.

While any infection is associated with higher morbidity and mortality in a malnourished child, diarrheal illnesses are important contributors to malnoutration. Diarrhea can cause undernutrition and worsen milder forms of malnutrition because:

- Impaired intestinal absorption causes loss of macro and micronutrients (zinc);
- Urinary loss of specific nutrients occurs (vitamin A);
- There is increased catabolism due to infection;
- A child with diarrhea is often not hungry;
- Mothers often make the mistake of not feeding the child enough food during diarrhea or even for some days after recovery; and
- Doctors often do not emphasize on the need for continued feeding during the diarrhea episodes.

What Causes Acute Diarrhea?

Causative agents of acute diarrhea can now be identified in nearly 70–80% episodes of acute diarrhea in sophisticated laboratories. In India, rotavirus and enterotoxigenic *E. coli* account for nearly half the total diarrheal episodes among children. Rotavirus is more frequently isolated in children with severe disease than in mild cases. Cholera accounts for 5–10% cases; it is endemic in some parts and may occur in outbreaks. The importance of cholera lies in the rapidity with which severe dehydration may set in within hours. Apart from enterotoxin producing *E. coli* (ETEC), which account for nearly 20% of childhood diarrhea, other forms of diarrheagenic *E. coli* are enteroinvasive (EIEC), enterohemorrhagic (EHEC), attaching effacing *E. coli* or localized adherent (LA-EC), diffusely adherent *E. coli* (DA-EC) and aggregative adherent *E. coli* (Agg-EC). EIEC and EHEC can cause dysentery. EHEC is a cause of hemolytic uremic syndrome. *Shigella* and *Salmonella* species are isolated in 3–7% of childhood diarrheas. Shigella accounts for majority of cases of dysentry. The other bacterial agents causing diarrhea include *C. jejuni, Y. enterocolitica* and *A. hydrophilia. E. histolytica* accounts for nearly 5% of dysentery. *Giardia lamblia* rarely causes acute diarrhea. Intestinal helminthes do not usually cause of acute diarrhea; their frequent presence in stools simply reflects their high prevalence in the population.

How does Diarrhea Cause Significant Physiological Disturbances in the Body?

Approximately 60% of child's body weight is present in two fluid compartments: the extracellular fluid (ECF) and intracellular fluid (ICF). The extracellular compartment includes circulating blood, intestinal fluid and secretions. Diarrheal losses come from ECF and replacement fluids should be of similar composition: relatively rich in sodium with lower potassium. Kidneys regulate the electrolyte content of the extracellular compartment by filtering, -concentrating, diluting and reabsorbing fluids and metabolites from the circulation. Functional ability of the kidney of very young infants is not fully developed as compared to older children.

Large amount of water and water soluble nutritive substances such as electrolytes, metabolites and vitamins are lost from the body during diarrhea episodes. Loss of water from the body causes a reduction or shrinkage in the volume of extracellular compartment. In about half of these cases, the concentration of sodium in the plasma or extracellular compartment remains nearly normal (about 140 mEq/L). Since excessive sodium may be lost in the stools in another 40 to 45% of cases, there is a relative decline in the serum and ECF sodium level (hyponatremia). Sodium is a major osmotic determinant of ECF. Therefore, the osmolality of ECF falls, causing movement of water from the extracellular to intracellular compartment. This causes further shrinkage of the already reduced extracellular compartment volumes (Fig. 10.4).

Skin turgor or elasticity is normally maintained by the presence of water and fat in the tissues. Shrinkage of extracellular water in both hypo- and isonatremic types of dehydration impairs the skin elasticity. The skin appears to be wrinkled like that of an old man. On pinching, it takes a few seconds for the skin fold to return to normal. In about 5% of diarrhea cases (especially if the child has been given fluids with more salts), serum sodium levels may be elevated to more than 150 mEq/L. In these patients, the osmotic pressure of ECF is relatively higher. Therefore, water comes from inside the cells to the extracellular fluid and, therefore, partially masks loss of

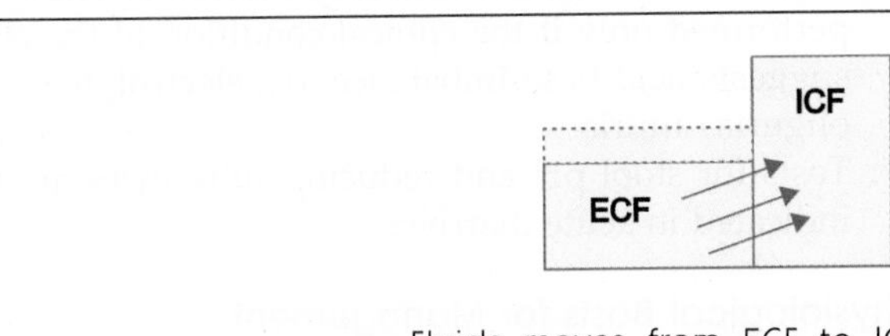

Fluids moves from ECF to ICF compartment in hyponatremic dehydration accentuating fluid depletion in ECF

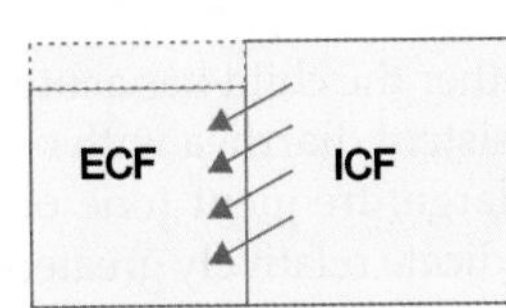

Fluid moves from ICF to ECF compartment in hypernatremic (hypertonic) dehydration, thus partially compensating from fluid depletion of ECF compartment

Fig. 10.4: Fluid shifts in hypo- and hypernatremic dehydration.

skin turgor. The skin may appear soggy, doughy or leathery. The physician is likely to erroneously underestimate a severe case of hypernatremic dehydration as mild dehydration unless he/she takes into account the other more important sequelae of dehydration such as circulatory or renal impairment. As the extracellular compartment is depleted, the blood volume is reduced. This results in a weak, thready pulse and a fall in blood pressure. Extremities appear cold. Because of low hydrostatic pressure in the renal glomeruli, the filtration of urine is reduced. This is ominous because poorly functioning kidneys cannot regulate the metabolic derangements. Urine flow is a good indicator of the severity of illness. In severe cases, renal failure may eventually set in.

Diarrhea stools contain large amounts of potassium. Therefore, the serum potassium level invariably falls if diarrhea persists for more than a few days. This is more pronounced in children with severe malnutrition. The affected children present with abdominal distension, paralytic ileus and hypotonia of muscles. Electrocardiogram may show ST depression and flat T waves. Since intestinal secretions are alkaline and considerable bicarbonate is lost in diarrheal stools, acidemia usually accompanies the diarrheal dehydration. Patient in such cases remains asymptomatic till the base excess falls to 12 mMol/L. As the base excess falls below this level, the breathing becomes deep and rapid (Kussmaul breathing).

To sum up, in early and mild cases of diarrhea, the child may be thirsty and slightly irritable. As the diarrhea continues and dehydration worsens, the child becomes more irritable and develops a pinched look. The fontanele, if open, is depressed, the eyes appear sunken, and the tongue and the inner side of cheeks appear dry. Abdomen may become distended in hypokalemia. The child passes urine at longer intervals. As acidosis worsens, the breathing becomes deep and rapid. In extreme cases, the child appears moribund, pulse appears to be weak and thready, blood pressure falls and the quantity of urine passed is markedly reduced. Children with severe dehydration may succumb rapidly, if they are not promptly treated.

Assessment of Child with Diarrhea

History

A careful history should elicit whether the child has acute watery diarrhea, dysentery or persistent diarrhea with or without growth failure. Watery, large, frequent (one or more stools every 3 hours) stools indicate relatively greater severity of illness. The following questions are important to plan therapy: Did the child vomit during the preceding 6–8 hours? Did he pass urine during the same period? What is the nature of fluids that the child has been taking? Was the child receiving optimum feeding before the illness? Has feeding been reduced or modified during diarrhea in a way that reduced the quantity of total energy intake or the quality of food consumed?

10

Assess in the examination: (i) physical signs of dehydration; (ii) nutritional status of the child; weight is the best parameter; and (iii) presence of pneumonia, otitis media or other associated infections.

Clinical Approach to Etiologic Diagnosis

In rotavirus diarrhea, vomiting is an early feature and diarrhea is more severe. Most patients have mild to moderate fever. Norwalk virus infection occurs in slightly older infants and preschool children. Stools are large and watery in secretory diarrhea due to infection with toxigenic strains of *E. coli* or *Vibrio cholerae.* The fecal matter appears as curdy deposits. Vomiting is common in cases of cholera. Fever, abdominal cramps and tenesmus with passing of blood and mucus in stools indicate dysentery (colitis), often due to infection with *Shigella.* Small amounts of blood in stools may be seen in infection with *Shigella, Salmonella, Campylobacter* or invasive stains of *E. coli.* Infection of the gut with Staphylococci, *Candida albicans* or *Clostridium difficile* should be suspected in severe cases of diarrhea in very sick infants, who have received prolonged treatment with broad spectrum antibiotics.

Laboratory Investigations

The large majority of acute diarrhea episodes can be managed effectively even in absence of laboratory investigations:

i. *Stool microscopy*: Fecal leukocyte counts of >10/hpf are suggested as an indicator of invasive diarrheas requiring antibiotic therapy. However, the major problem is low specificity, being often positive in viral diarrheas, where antibiotics are of no value.
ii. *Stool culture*: This is of little value in routine management of acute diarrhea. To identify cases for antibiotic especially infections with *Shigella* and *V. cholerae,* the presence of gross blood in stools and a cholera like clinical picture are more useful than culture. *E. coli* is often reported on stool cultures but most laboratories lack the ability to identify whether these are diarrheagenic or commensals.
iii. Blood gas estimations, serum electrolytes, renal function tests are not routinely indicated. These are performed only if the clinical condition of the child suggests acid-base imbalance, dyselectrolytemia or oliguria/anuria.
iv. Tests for stool pH and reducing substances are not indicated in acute diarrhea.

Physiological Basis for Management

In most cases of acute diarrhea, electrolytes such as chloride and sodium besides water are actively secreted from the gut mucosa and are, thus, lost in stools. Physiologists observed that while water and sodium were being lost, nutrients such as glucose, amino acids and dipeptides continued to be absorbed without difficulty in the majority of cases. The uptake of glucose and other nutrients in the intestinal cells is an enzyme-mediated active physiological process. The carrier mechanisms for the transport of glucose and sodium across the cell membrane are interlinked. As glucose is absorbed, sodium is also absorbed in the small gut, even though sodium is being actively lost at the same time in stools of secretory diarrheas due to the effects of the toxin elaborated by enterotoxigenic strains of *Escherichia coli* and *Vibrio cholerae*. Sodium absorption also promotes absorption of water. This is the physiological basis of oral rehydration therapy, which is a fascinating advance of modem medicine and has probably saved more lives than any other treatment modality.

What is Oral Rehydration Therapy (ORT)?

Oral rehydration therapy (ORT) today is at the core of management of diarrhea. The term ORT includes (Table 10.6):

a. Complete oral rehydration salt (ORS) solution with composition within the WHO recommended range;
b. Solutions made from sugar and salt;
c. Food-based solutions; and
d. In presence of continued feeding, a variety or commonly available, culturally acceptable fluids irrespective of presence of glucose or without salt when the former are present. The term ORS for facilitating understanding, refers to the complete oral rehydration salt mixture recommended by the WHO.

Since 2004, based on the WHO/UNICEF and IAP recommendations, the Government of India has adopted the low osmolarity ORS as the single universal ORS to be used for all ages and all types of diarrhea. The low osmolarity ORS is different from the previous ORS in sodium content and osmolarity. The comparison between the two ORS is given in Table 10.7. There were concerns of hypernatremia when old WHO-ORS was used in

Table 10.7: Comparison between low osmolarity ORS and WHO-ORS

Ingredients of ORS solution	*Concentration of various ingredients in ORS solution (mmol/L)*	
	Low osmolarity ORS (new)	*WHO-ORS (old)*
Sodium	75	90
Potassium	20	20
Chloride	65	80
Citrate*	10	10
Glucose	75	111

* One mmol of citrate provides 3 mEq of base.

Oral rehydration solution (ORS) should preferably be given with a teaspoon or consumed in small sips from a cup or tumbler. A child with profuse vomiting is more likely to retain the fluid if it is consumed in small sips. Large gulps of fluids stimulate gastrocolic reflex resulting in a quick passage of stools and often vomiting.

Table 10.6: Oral rehydration therapy

Type of ORT	*Composition per liter*	*Appropriate use*
• What is ORT? **Home made fluids with substrate and salt** Sugar and salt solution*	Sugar (sucrose) 40 g, salt (NaCl) 4 g	Prevention of dehydration
Food based solutions Rice water* with salt	Rice approximately 50 g (precise measurement not required), salt 40 g	Prevention of dehydration
Lassi (butter-milk) with salt		
Home fluids without insisting on both a glucose precursor and salt or their presence in specified amounts i. Plain water, lemon water, coconut water, soups. ii. Thin rice kanji, dal water without salt.		Prevention of dehydration; most useful in presence of continued feeding which provides both absorbable substrate and some salt.
• What is not ORT? Glucose water without salt. Fluids without starch or sugar and salt in children who are starved. Fluids consumed in very small quantities, e.g. tea.		

* May be used for treatment of dehydration when ORS is not available and while the child is being taken to a facility where ORS is available.

children with non-cholera diarrhea or with edema. The reduced osmolarity solution promotes water and sodium absorption more efficiently than the old WHO-ORS. Meta-analysis of trials of reduced osmolarity ORS revealed reduced need of IV fluids, reduction in stool output, lower vomiting, and no significant hyponatremia. In addition, no significant problems were observed in children with acute cholera diarrhea. Similarly, no significant hyponatremia was noticed in adults with cholera.

Assessment of Severity of Dehydration

A child's dehydration status should be classified as no dehydration, some dehydration or severe dehydration according to the WHO criteria (Table 10.8).

Treatment Plan A: Patients without Physical Signs of Dehydration

The mother should be educated to use increased amount of culturally appropriate home available fluids (Table 10.6). In addition, they should be given ORS packets for use at home (Table 10.9). ORS is appropriate for both prevention and treatment of dehydration. When ORS packets are given to the mother at treatment center or by other health care providers, she is less likely to demand or desire antidiarrheals. The mother should be asked to take the child to the health worker if the child does not get better in 3 days or develops any of the following *danger signs:* many watery stools; repeated vomiting, marked thirst, eating or drinking poorly, fever, and blood in stool.

Table 10.8: Assessment of dehydration in patients with diarrhea

LOOK AT	Condition[1]	Well alert	"Restless, irritable"	"Lethargic or unconscious"; floppy
	Eyes[2]	Normal	Sunken	Very sunken and dry
	Tears	Present	Absent	Absent
	Mouth and Tongue[3]	Moist	Dry	Very dry
	Thirst	Drinks Normally, not thirsty	"Thirsty, drinks eagerly"	"Drinks poorly, or not able to drink"
FEEL	Skin pinch[4]	Goes back quickly	"Goes back slowly"	"Goes back very slowly"
DECIDE		The patient has No signs of dehydration	If the patient has two or more signs, including at least one "sign", there is some dehydration	If the patient has two or more signs, including at least one "sign", there is severe dehydration
TREAT		Use treatment **Plan A**	Weigh the patient, if possible, and use treatment **Plan B**	Weigh the patient and use treatment **Plan C** urgently

1. *Being lethargic and sleepy are not the same. A lethargic child is not simply asleep: the child's mental state is dull and the child cannot be fully awakened; the child may appear to be drifting into unconsciousness.*
2. *In some infants and children the eyes normally appear somewhat sunken. It is helpful to ask the mother if the child's eyes are normal or more sunken than ususal.*
3. *Dryness of the mouth and tongue can also be palpated with a clean finger. The mouth may be dry in a child who habitually breathes through the mouth. The mouth may be wet in a dehydrated child owing to recent vomiting or drinking.*
4. *The skin pinch is less useful in infants or children with marasmus (severe wasting) or kwashiorkor (severe malnutrition with edema), or obese children.*

Table 10.9: Oral rehydration therapy to prevent dehydration (Plan A)

Age	*Amount of ORS or other culturally appropriate ORT fluids to give after each loose stool*	*Amount of ORS to provide for use at home*
Less than 24 months	50–100 mL	500 mL /day
2 up to 10 years	100–200 mL	1000 mL /day
10 year or more	As much as wants	2000 mL/day

- *Describe and show the amount to be given after each stool using a local measure. Show the mother how to mix ORS. Show her how to give ORS.*
- *Give a teaspoonful every 1–2 minutes for a child under 2 years.*
- *Give frequent sips from a cup for an older child.*
- *If the child vomits, wait for 10 minutes. Then give the solution more slowly (for example, a spoonful every 2–3 minutes).*
- *If diarrhea continues after the ORS packets are used up, tell the mother to give other fluids as described above or return for more ORS.*

Treatment Plan B: Patients with Physical Signs of Dehydration

All cases with obvious signs of dehydration need to be treated in a health center or hospital. However, oral fluid therapy must be commenced promptly and continued during transport. The fluid therapy for dehydration has three components:

a. Correction of the existing water and electrolyte deficit as indicated by the presence of signs of dehydration *(rehydration therapy).*
b. Replacement of ongoing losses due to continuing diarrhea to prevent recurrence of dehydration *(maintenance therapy).*
c. Provision of normal daily fluid requirements.

Deficit Replacement/Rehydration Therapy

Give 75 mL/kg of ORS in the first 4 hours. Use child's age only when you do not know the weight. Approximate fluid estimates for deficit replacement are given in the Table 10.10.

Maintenance Fluid Therapy

This begins when signs of dehydration disappear, usually within 4 hours. ORS should be administered in volume equal to diarrhea losses; approximately 10–20 mL per kilogram body weight for each liquid stool. ORS is administered in this manner till diarrhea stops. Offer plain water in between.

Breastfeed even during rehydration and offer semisolid foods soon after deficit replacement. Similarly, in non-breastfed babies, milk preferably mixed with cereals can be used together with other semisolid foods after they have been rehydrated. If the child continues to have some dehydration after 4 hours, repeat another 4 hours treatment with ORS solution (as in rehydration therapy) and start to offer feeds, milk and breastfeed frequently.

How Effective is ORT?

In infants and children with clinical evidence of some dehydration, oral rehydration therapy is effective in 95–97% cases.

When is Oral Rehydration Therapy Ineffective?

- *High stool purge,* more than 5 ml/kg body weight/ hour.
- *Persistent vomiting,* greater than 3 vomitings per hour. Children with less frequent vomiting tolerate ORS well.
- *Incorrect preparation* or administration of ORS solution; a very concentrated solution is unsafe due to high osmolality and a very dilute solution may be ineffective.
- *Abdominal distension* and ileus.
- *Glucose malabsorption:* Rarely, and especially in undernourished patients, significant glucose malabsorption may occur during acute diarrhea. The use of ORS solution in such patients results in a marked increase in watery diarrhea with large amounts of glucose in the stools. The patient is very thirsty and signs of dehydration do not improve, become worse or reappear. When ORS solution is discontinued, the stool volume decreases. If this occurs, IV fluid should be used for 24–28 hours, after which ORS solution can be tried again.

Treatment Plan C: Children with Severe Dehydration

- Start IV fluids immediately. While the drip is being set up, give ORS solution if the child can drink.
- The best IV fluid solution is Ringer's lactate solution. An ideal preparation would be Ringer's lactate with 5% added dextrose, however, it is not available. If plain Ringer's lactate is also not available, normal saline solution (0.9% NaCl) can be used. Dextrose on its own is not effective.
- Give 100 ml/kg of the chosen solution (Table 10.11).

All children should be started on some ORS solution (about 5 ml/kg/h) when they can drink without difficulty during the time they are getting IV fluids (usually within 3–4 hours for infants or 1–2 hours for older children). If one is unable to give IV fluids (for reasons of access, logistic availability or during transport), immediately start rehydration with ORS using nasogastric tube at 20 ml/kg/h (total of 120 mL/kg). Reassess the child every 1–2 hours: if

Table 10.10: Guidelines for treating patients with some (but not severe) dehydration

When body weight is not known (Plan B)
Approximate amount of ORS solution to give in the first 4 hours

Age	*Less than 4 months*	*4–11 months*	*12–23 months*	*2–4 years*	*5–14 years*	*15 years or older*
Approx. (weight in kg)	Less than 5 kg	5–8	8–11	11–16	16–20	>30
ORS in ml	200–400	400–600	600–800	800–1200	1200–2200	>2200
Local measure (glass)	1–2	2–3	3–4	4–6	6–11	12–20

- *The approximate amount of ORS required (in ml) can also be calculated by multiplying the patient's weight (in kg) times 75.*
- *For infants under-6 months who are not breastfed, also give 100–200 ml clean water during this period.*
- *Encourage breastfeeding.*

10

Table 10.11: Intravenous fluid therapy in severe dehydration

Age	*First give*	*Then give*
<12 months	30 ml/kg in 1 hour*	70 ml/kg in 5 hours
12 months up to 5 years	30 ml/kg in 30 minutes*	70 ml/kg in 2½ hours

* *Repeat again if the radial pulse is still very weak or not detectable.*

there is repeated vomiting or abdominal distension, give the fluids more slowly. If there is no improvement in hydration after 3 hours, try to start IV fluids as early as possible.

Monitoring

Reassess the child every 15–30 minutes until a strong radial pulse is present. If hydration is not improving, give the IV solution more rapidly. When the full amount of IV fluid has been given, reassess the child's hydration status, and

- If signs of severe dehydration are still present, repeat the IV fluid infusion as outlined earlier.
- If the child is improving but still shows signs of some dehydration, discontinue IV treatment and give ORS solution for 4 hours (as for Plan B). If the child is normally breastfed, encourage the mother to continue breastfeeding frequently.
- Observe the child for at least 6 hours before discharge, to confirm that the mother is able to maintain the child's hydration by giving ORS solution.

Unique Problems in Infants Under 2 Months of Age

Breastfeeding must continue during the rehydration process, whenever the infant is able to suck. Complications like septicemia, paralytic ileus, and severe electrolyte disturbance are more likely in young infants with diarrhea than at later ages. Diarrhea in these infants should be ideally treated as inpatients by experienced physicians at treatment centers with appropriate facilities. This allows for careful assessment for need for systemic antibiotics and careful monitoring.

Nutritional Management of Diarrhea

A considerable quantity of nutrients is lost in the diarrheal stools. Appetite is impaired and food is often withheld from the child by the mother because of an erroneous belief that rest to the bowel promotes early recovery. Some hydrolytic (disaccharidases) enzymes and absorptive mechanisms for glucose and amino acids may be partially compromised during viral diarrhea. Transient carbohydrate malabsorption may occur. Carbohydrates may pass unchanged in the lower gut, these raise intraluminal osmotic pressure and draw water from the gut by osmosis and increase the severity of diarrhea. Unabsorbed carbohydrates are also metabolized to short-chain fatty acids by colonic bacteria and are then absorbed from the colon. These pathological changes are transient and do not last for more than a few days in most cases. Therefore, it is safe and desirable to continue feeding in acute diarrhea. Since children with diarrhea may develop protein-energy-malnutrition, the diet should be easily digestible and nutritionally balanced. Presence of nutrients in the gut promotes absorption of sodium and water and hastens recovery of the intestinal epithelium because food in the intestine stimulates rapid cell turn over and renewal of intestinal lining. More lives are lost because of unnecessary starvation in diarrhea. Following are the *recommendations on dietary management of acute diarrhea:*

1. Children should continue to be fed during acute diarrhea because feeding is physiologically sound and prevents or minimizes the deterioration of nutritional status that normally accompanies such illness.
2. In acute diarrhea, breastfeeding should be continued uninterrupted even during rehydration with ORS.
3. Optimally energy dense foods with the least bulk that are recommended for routine feeding and available in the household should be offered during diarrhea, in small quantities but frequently, at least once every 2–3 hours.
4. Staple foods do not provide optimal calories per unit weight and these should be enriched with fats and oils or sugar, e.g. *khichri* with oil, rice with milk or curd and sugar, mashed banana with milk or curd, mashed potatoes with oil and lentil.
5. Foods with high fiber content, e.g. coarse fruits and vegetables should be avoided.
6. In non-breastfed infants, cow or buffalo milk can be given undiluted after correction of dehydration together with semisolid foods. Milk should not be diluted with water during any phase of acute diarrhea. Alternatively, milk cereal mixtures, e.g. dalia, sago, milk-rice mixture, can be used.
7. Routine lactose-free feeding, e.g. soy formula is not required during acute diarrhea even when reducing substances are detected in the stools. Lactose malabsorption meriting dietary modification is very uncommon in acute diarrhea. It may be required in very few infants in whom diarrhea persists beyond 8–10 days with progressive weight loss and ≥1% reducing substances in stools.
8. During recovery, an intake of at least 125% of normal RDA should be attempted with nutrient dense foods; it should continue until the child reaches pre-illness weight and ideally until the child achieves normal nutritional status, as measured by expected weight for height or weight for age. This might take several weeks or longer, depending on the degree of deficit.

Drug Therapy in Acute Diarrhea

Most episodes of diarrhea are self-limiting and no medication is necessary except in a few situations. Drugs have very limited use.

Antibiotics and Chemotherapeutic Agents

Since a large majority of cases of diarrhea are caused by viruses or toxigenic bacteria and there is little evidence of inflammation of gut mucosa, it is neither necessary nor desirable to use antibacterial drugs. Antibiotics do not shorten the duration of illness except in cases of cholera. Their indiscriminate use leads to emergence of resistant strains of harmful bacteria and eliminates resident flora which protects the gut. Furthermore all drugs are potentially toxic and hazardous. Antimicrobial should be used only for infectious agents such as *Shigella, Vibrio cholerae* (Table 10.12), *Entameba histolytica* and *Giardia.* In dysentery, empiric treatment can be initiated with cotrimoxazole (TMP-SMX) or ampicillin for 5 days. If there is no improvement after 48 hours, resistance to initial antimicrobial is assumed and the child should be given the second-line antimicrobial, e.g. nalidixic acid [15 mg/kg/dose 4 times a day] for a period of 5 days (Fig. 10.5). *Escherichia coli* are normal resident flora of intestines. Their growth on culture of stools is not an indication for antibiotics.

Table 10.12: Antimicrobials used in the treatment of cholera

Antimicrobial	*Dose*
Tetracycline*	12.5 mg/kg/dose 4 times/day for 3 days
Cotrimoxazole (TMP-SMX)	TMP 5 mg/kg/dose + SMX 25 mg/kg/dose 2 times/day for 3 days
Erythromycin	12.5 mg/kg/dose 4 times/day for 3 days
Furazolidone	1.25 mg/kg/dose 4 times/day for 3 days

* Not recommended in case of infants.

Indications for antibiotics for suspected extra-intestinal infections (Diarrhea): Malnourished or prematurely born young infants with diarrhea must be presumed to have sepsis and should receive adequate days of inpatient care and systemic antibiotics appropriate for generalized sepsis at this age without any delay. In well-nourished infants with diarrhea, if after correction of dehydration, any of the following are present systemic antibiotics should be considered: (i) sucking is poor or absent or attachment to breast is poor; (ii) abdominal distension; (iii) fever or hypothermia; (iv) fast breathing; (v) significant lethargy or inactivity.

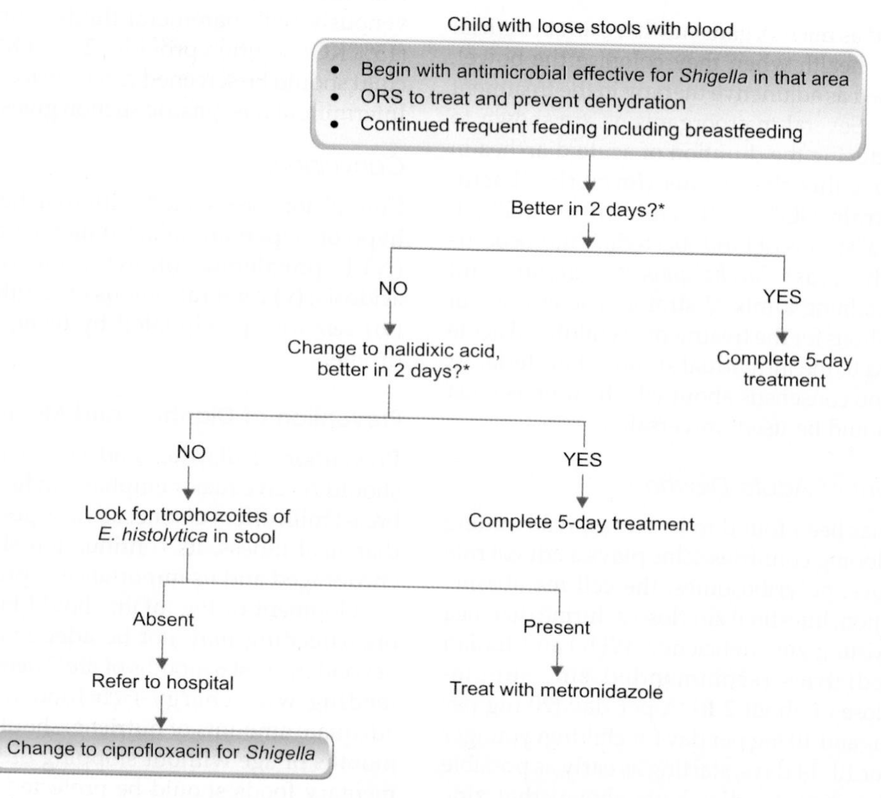

Fig 10.5: Algorithm for management of dysentery—*Disappearance of fever, less blood in stools, fewer stools, returns to normal activity

10

Binding Agents

So far there is little scientific evidence that formulations based on pectin, kaolin or bismuth salts are useful. These agents do not reduce excessive losses of fluids and electrolytes, even though the stools appear more solid and the parents are psychologically reassured.

Anti-motility Agents

Synthetic analogues of opiates such as diphenoxylate hydrochloride (lomotil) and loperamide (imodium) reduce peristalsis or gut motility. Reduction of gut motility does not abort an attack. On the other hand, it may give more time for the harmful bacteria to multiply in the gut. Therefore, the course of illness is often prolonged following their use. These drugs may also cause distension of abdomen and other undesirable side -effects of opiates. They can be dangerous (even fatal) if improperly used in infants, causing paralytic ileus, abdominal distension, bacterial overgrowth and sepsis.

Anti-secretory Agents

Racecadotril (acetorphan) is an antisecretory drug that exerts its antidiarrheal effects by inhibiting intestinal enkephalinase. Recent studies reported some advantage of this agent, but its use should be restricted until large enough evidence on efficacy and safety is available.

Probiotics

Probiotics, defined as microorganisms that exert beneficial effects on human health when they colonise the bowel, have been proposed as adjunctive therapy in the treatment of acute diarrhea. Several microorganisms are shown to be effective in reducing the duration of acute diarrhea in children: Lactobacillus rhamnosus (formerly "Lactobacillus casei strain GG" or "Lactobacillus GG"), L plantarum, several strains of bifidobacteria, Enterococcus faecium SF68, the yeast *Saccharomyces boulardii*, and preparations containing a mix of strains. The efficacy of probiotic preparations for the treatment of childhood acute diarrhea is related to the individual strains of bacteria. At present, there is no consensus about which strain is most beneficial and should be used universally.

Zinc in Treatment of Acute Diarrhea

Zinc deficiency has been found to be widespread among children in developing countries. Zinc plays a critical role in metalloenzymes, polyribosomes, the cell membrane, and cellular function. Intestinal zinc losses during diarrhea aggravate pre-existing zinc deficiency. WHO and Indian Academy of Pediatrics recommended zinc supplementation at a dose of about 2 RDA per day (20 mg per day for >6 months and 10 mg per day for children younger than 6 months) for 10–14 days, starting as early as possible after onset of diarrhea. Studies have shown that zinc supplementation during acute diarrhea leads to 16% faster recovery and 31% reduction in stool output. There is 1/3rd reduction in the episode lasting for more than 7 days. Zinc supplementation is now part of the standard care along with ORS in children with acute diarrhea.

Symptomatic Treatment

Vomiting

An occasional vomit in a child need not be treated. In such cases the children can easily tolerate sips of cold water or oral rehydration solution. If a child vomits during oral rehydration therapy, it is best to stop ORT for ten minutes and then restart ORT by spoon. If vomiting is persistent, it may be better to delay feeding for a few hours, while at the same time giving clear fluids with a teaspoon or in small sips. One or more doses of metoclopramide (0.1 to 0.2 mg/kg) or phenothiazine (0.5 mg/kg) may be given in cases of severe vomiting, but should be avoided since these can cause oculogyric spasms.

Abdominal Distension

If bowel sounds are present and the abdominal distension is mild, no specific treatment is necessary. Paralytic ileus due to hypokalemia, necrotizing enterocolitis or septicemia should be suspected if intestinal sounds are absent and distension is gross. In these cases oral intake should be withheld for some time. Hypokalemia along with paralytic ileus necessitates intravenous fluids. Potassium chloride (30–40 mEq/L) should be administered intravenously with parenteral fluids if urine is being passed (15% KC1 solution provides 2 mEq K^+/mL). The affected child should be screened carefully for any occult infection. Intermittent nasogastric suction gives symptomatic relief.

Convulsions

Convulsions associated with diarrhea may be due to (i) hypo or hypernatremia; (ii) meningitis; (iii) encephalitis; (iv) hypokalemia following bicarbonate therapy for acidosis; (v) cerebral venous or sagittal sinus thrombosis; (vi) seizures, precipitated by fever; or (vii) Reye's syndrome.

Prevention of Diarrhea and Malnutrition

Prevention of diarrhea and its nutritional consequences should receive major emphasis in health education. Since breast milk offers distinct advantages and protection from diarrheal illness, its continuation should be vigorously encouraged and its importance in promoting growth and development of the infant should be stressed. Exclusive breastfeeding may not be adequate to sustain growth beyond the first 6 months of life. Therefore, supplementary feeding with energy-rich food mixtures containing adequate amounts of nutrients should be introduced by 6 months of age without stopping breastfeeding. Complementary foods should be protected from contamination during preparation, storage, or at the time of administration. Emphasis should be given for maintaining sanitation and hygiene. Three 'C's; clean hands, clean container and clean environment are the key messages. Mother should be properly guided to avoid this risk by concrete recommendations such as the use of clean containers, avoiding exposure of food to dust, flies or cockroaches. Hands should be washed and dried with paper towel or clean towel and not by repeatedly used towels, before administration of food to the baby. Water given to the child or used for preparing feds should be clean, potable, preferably boiled. Vegetables and fruits should be washed and peeled before these are fed to the child. Improvement of environment sanitation, good water supply, adequate sewage disposal system and protection of food from exposure to bacterial contamination are effective long-term strategies for control of all infectious illnesses including diarrhea. These measures should be sustained to achieve the desired goals.

Suggested reading

1. The Treatment of Diarrhea: A Manual for Physicians and Other Senior Health Workers. WHO (2005). WHO/CDD/SER/80.2.
2. Consensus Statement of IAP National Task Force: Status Report on Management of Acute Diarrhea. Indian Pediatrics 2004; 41: 335–348.

PERSISTENT DIARRHEA

Diarrhea that starts as an acute episode, and lasts at least 14 days is said to be persistent (PD). This definition excludes specific conditions like celiac disease, tropical sprue, or other congenital, biochemical or metabolic disorders. The predominant causes of persistent diarrhea are listed below:

i. Persistent infection with one or more enteric pathogens.
ii. Malabsorption particularly of carbohydrates and fat, due to a combination of malnutrition and enteric infection.
iii. Infrequently, dietary protein intolerance.

Majority of patients with persistent diarrhea pass several loose stools daily but remain well hydrated. Dehydration develops only in some patients because of the high stool output or when oral intake is reduced due to associated systemic infection. The major consequences of PD are *growth faltering, worsening of malnutrition and death during subsequent diarrheal or non-diarrheal illness.*

Persistent diarrhea is more common in malnourished infants and young children. The growth failure associated with PD is not exclusively the result of malabsorption, it also occurs due to inadequate energy intake during the diarrheal episode. This results from anorexia associated with the illness, faulty feeding practices and incorrect advice by physicians. Nearly two-thirds of PD patients can be treated at home but it is better to hospitalize when following are present:

i. Age less than 4 months and not breastfed.
ii. Presence of dehydration.
iii. Severe malnutrition (weight-for-length <70%, or weight-for-age <60% of the WHO-growth medians or the presence of pedal edema involving at least the feet).
iv. Presence or suspicion of systemic infection.

Management

Assess the child for signs of dehydration and give fluids according to Treatment Plan A, B or C (for acute diarrhea), as appropriate. *The mainstay of therapy of persistent diarrhea is dietary management.*

Dietary Algorithm for the Treatment of PD

The Initial Diet A

[Reduced lactose diet; milk rice gruel, milk sooji gruel, rice with curds, dalia]. Clinical trials at AIIMS have clearly shown that reduced lactose diet is as well tolerated as totally lactose-free diet, without significantly increasing stool output or increasing risk of dehydration (Table 10.13). Milk

Recommendations for Dietary Management

Infants aged less than 6 months: Persistent diarrhea occurs rarely in infants below 6 months who are exclusively breastfed. A breastfed infant could normally be passing several soft or mushy stools each day. In such cases the change in character of stools will be important. The principles of treatment are summarized below:

i. Encourage exclusive breastfeeding.
ii. Help mothers who are not breastfeeding to reestablish lactation.
iii. If only animal milk must be given, replace it with curds or a lactose-free milk formula (gives with a cup and spoon).
iv. If required, cooked rice can be mixed with milk/curd/lactose-free formula.

Older infants and young children: Breastfeeding should be continued during PD. Breastfed infants continue to gain some weight even while passing abnormal stools for a few extra days after an acute episode of gastroenteritis. In the second and later years, the breast milk output is less and optimal feeding of a mixed diet is more important.

Table 10.13: The initial diet A for persistent diarrhea (Reduced Lactose)

Ingredients	*Measures*	*Weight/ volume*
Milk	1/3 katori	50 mL
Sugar	1½ tsp	7 g
Oil	1 tsp	4.5 g
Puffed rice powder*	2 tsp	6.0 g
Water	2/3 katori	100 mL
Calories/100 g	85 kcal	
Proteins/100 g	2.0 g	

*It can be substituted by cooked rice or sooji.
Preparation: Mix milk, sugar, rice together. Add boiled water and mix well. Add oil. The feed can now be given to the child.

10

cereal mixtures can be highly palatable, are consumed in large amounts, provide good quality proteins and some micronutrients, and result in faster weight gain than milk-free diets.

- If the patient is fed entirely on animal milk, the quantity should be reduced. Total elimination of animal milk is not required routinely. Limit daily intake of milk to 50–60 mL/kg providing not more than 2 g of lactose/kg/day. To reduce lactose concentration in animal milk, do not dilute it with water as it reduces energy density critically. Milk can be mixed with cereals, e.g. milk or curd, rice gruel, milk soojii gruel, or *dalia*.
- Start feeding as soon as the child can eat.
- Offer 6–7 feeds per day and a total daily energy intake of 110 kcal/kg to begin with, increase energy intake steadily, up to 150 kcal/kg over next two weeks if required to achieve weight gain.
- Many children will eat poorly, until any serious infection is treated for 24–48 hr. Use nasogastric feeding initially in such situations.

The Second Diet B

[Lactose-free diet with reduced starch]. About 65-70% of children improve on the initial Diet A. Remaining children, if free of systemic infection are changed to Diet B which is milk (lactose) free and provides carbohydrates as a mixture of cereals and glucose (Table 10.14). Milk protein is replaced by chicken, egg or protein hydrolysate.

Table 10.14: The second diet B for persistent diarrhea (Lactose-free)

Ingredients	*Measures*	*Approx weight/ volume*
Egg white	3 tsp	(½ egg white)
Puffed rice powder*	3 tsp	(9 g)
Glucose	1½ tsp	(7 g)
Oil	1½ tsp	(7 g)
Water	¾ katori	(120 mL)
Calories/100 g	90 kcal	
Proteins/100 g	2.4 g	

* It can be substituted with cooked rice.
Preparation: Whip the egg white well. Add puffed rice powder, glucose; oil and mix well. Add boiled water and mix rapidly to avoid clumping.

Basis for diet B: Some children do not respond well to the initial low lactose diet. They may have impaired digestion of starch and disaccharides other than lactose. Therefore, not only is milk eliminated but the starch is reduced and partially substituted by glucose. Substituting only part of the cereal with glucose increases the digestibility but at the same time does not cause a very high osmolarity, which would be the case if all the cereals were to be replaced by glucose.

The Third Diet C (Monosaccharide-based Diet)

Overall, 80–85% of patients with severe persistent diarrhea will recover with sustained weight gain on the initial diet A or the second diet B. A small percentage may not tolerate a moderate intake of the cereal in diet B. These children are given the third diet (diet C) which contains only glucose and a protein source as egg white or chicken or commercially available protein hydrolysates (Table 10.15). Energy density is increased by adding oil to the diet.

Table 10.15: Diet C for persistent diarrhea (Monosaccharide Based)

Ingredients	*Measures*	*Approx. Weight / volume*
Chicken puree Or	5 tsp	(15 g)
Egg white	3 tsp	(½ egg white)
Glucose	1½ tsp	(7 g)
Oil	1½ tsp	(7 g)
Water	1 katori	(150 mL)
Calories/100 g	67 kcal	
Proteins/100 g	3 g	

Preparation: Boil chicken, remove the bones and make chicken puree. Mix chicken puree with glucose and oil. Add boiled water to make a smooth flowing feed.

Supplemental Vitamins and Minerals

Supplemental multivitamins and minerals, about twice the RDA should be given daily to all children for at least two to four weeks. Iron supplements should be introduced only after the diarrhea has ceased. At the least, provide vitamin A (as a single large dose) and zinc, as these have been shown to effect recovery from persistent diarrhea.

Vitamin A: A single dose of 2,00,000 IV of vitamin A for children >12 months or 100,000 IV for children 6–12 months orally should be given routinely. Children weighing less than 8 kg, irrespective of their age, should be given 1,00,000 IV of vitamin A.

Zinc: Give 10–20 mg per day of elemental zinc for at least 2 weeks to children between 6 months and 3 years of age.

Additional Recommendations for the Severely Malnourished Infants and Children with PD

Intramuscular administration of a 50% solution of magnesium sulphate 0.2 mL/kg/dose twice a day is advised for a period of 2–3 days. Potassium is administered 5-6 mEq/kg/day orally or as part of intravenous infusion during the initial stabilization period. This is higher than the usual requirement of 2–3 mEq/kg/day.

Monitoring the Response to Treatment in the Hospital

Successful treatment is characterized by (i) diminished number of diarrheal stools (≤2 liquid stools/day for 2 consecutive days); (ii) adequate food intake; and (iii) weight gain. Most children will lose weight in the initial 1–2 days, and then show steady weight gain, as associated infections are treated and diarrhea subsides. They may return home, but should be followed regularly to ensure continued weight gain and compliance with feeding advice.

Indications for Change from the Initial Diet (Diet A) to the Second Diet (Diet B) or Diet B to Diet C?

In the absence of initial or hospital acquired systemic infection, the diet should be changed when there is treatment failure, defined as: (i) a marked increase in stool frequency (usually more than 10 watery stools/day) any time after at least 48 h of initiating the diet; or (ii) return of signs of dehydration any time after initiating treatment; or (iii) a failure to establish weight gain by day 7. Unless signs of treatment failure occur earlier, each diet should be given for a minimum period of 7 days.

Resumption of Regular Diet after Discharge

Children discharged on diet B should be given small quantities of milk as part of a mixed diet after 10 days. If they have no signs suggestive of lactose intolerance (diarrhea, vomiting, abdominal pain, abdominal distension, excessive flatulence) milk can be gradually increased over the next few days. A normal diet appropriate for age can be resumed over the next week.

Recommendations for Antimicrobial Therapy in PD

Antimicrobial therapy in persistent diarrhea is indicated in following situations:

- In the presence of gross blood in stools or for specific enteric pathogens against which such therapy is known to be beneficial, e.g. Shigella. Effective anti-shigella agents such as nalidixic acid or other quinolones should be given (see algorithm for dysentery).
- Associated systemic infection—combination of parenteral penicillin or cephalosporin and aminoglycosides is usually appropriate.
- Severe malnutrition—use combination of penicillin or cephalosporin and an aminoglycoside as for associated systemic infection, even if uncertain about presence of systemic infection
- If possible, screen for urinary tract infection (UTI). 10–15% of children with PD and malnutrition require antibiotics for associated lower UTI.
- When group B salmonella are isolated in stool, treat with systemic antibiotics only when there is a suspicion of systemic infection.

Additional drugs: Antimotility and antisecretory agents and bile salt binding resins have not been shown to give any significant clinical benefit when used to treat PD. Probiotics have not been systematically evaluated for the treatment of persistent diarrhea.

Value of Laboratory Investigations

Patients with PD can be managed without elaborate laboratory tests using the algorithm outlined above with very high levels of success. Stool microscopy helps in identifying trophozoites of *E. histolytica* and G. *lamblia*. Majority of patients who have cysts of *E. histolytica* are now known to have non-pathogenic *E. dispar*. Acid-fast staining with modified Ziehl-Neelsen technique will identify *Cyclospora*, *Isospora* and *Cryptosporidium*. Large number of pus cells (>20/hpf) in stool suggests invasive diarrhea but a majority of patients with persistent diarrhea do not have these. Stools cultures for *Salmonella* and *Shigella* should be done if feasible. Isolation of *E. coli* is not helpful as most laboratories cannot characterize for virulence properties. Stool pH and reducing substances help in determining carbohydrate intolerance. In a non-hospital setting, detecting reducing substances is often difficult as tests cannot be done promptly and several stools need to be examined for sufficient sensitivity. It is, therefore, more practical to use clinical criteria to decide a change in diet as discussed above. The fact that diet A has reduced lactose already assumes that some secondary lactose intolerance exists in children with PD and malnutrition.

Prognosis

Most patients with persistent diarrhea recover with the algorithmic approach outlined above. However 2–5% patients may require parenteral nutrition and extensive work up. These patients generally have high purge rates, continue to loose weight, do not tolerate oral feeds and should be sent to specialized pediatric gastroenterology centers.

CHRONIC DIARRHEA AND MALABSORPTION SYNDROMES

Malabsorption syndromes are characterized by the association of chronic diarrhea, abdominal distension and failure to thrive. Chronic diarrhea is the direct consequence of malabsorption, which in turn results in malnutrition and failure to thrive. Chronic diarrhea has to be differentiated from persistent diarrhea which is very common. (Refer previous section). Chronic diarrhea here refers to primarily conditions associated with "abnormal stools" which continues or recurrently occurs over several months. Dehydration is rare.

Stools may be loose and bulky in celiac disease, greasy and yellowish in exocrine pancreatic insufficiency, as liquid as water and mistaken for urine in infants with congenital chloride diarrhea or passed noisily with flatus in cases of sugar intolerance.

Non-specific chronic diarrhea or *toddler's diarrhea* is characterized by periods of frequent, heterogenous, often mucus containing, foul smelling stools, often alternating with periods of normal stools and most importantly a normal state of nutrition.

Chronic diarrhea is differentiated into *three major pathophysiologic categories:* impaired intraluminal digestion, intestinal malabsorption and fermentation (Tables 10.16 to 10.18).

Table 10.16: Chronic diarrhea due to impaired intraluminal digestion

Impaired digestion	*Conditions*
All nutrients	Cystic fibrosis, other pancreatic exocrine deficiencies.
Fat	Isolated lipase or co-lipase deficiency, bile duct atresia, interrupted enterohepatic circulation (e.g. ileal resection; Crohn's disease).
Proteins	Congenital trypsinogen deficiency, congenital enterokinase deficiency.

Table 10.17: Chronic diarrhea due to intestinal malabsorption

Mucosal changes	*Condition*
Total villous atrophy	Celiac disease
Partial villous atrophy	Food protein sensitivity, Giardia lamblia infestation, immunodeficiency, bacterial overgrowth, tropical enteropathy, malnutrition
Specific changes	
– Fat filled enterocytes	Abetalipoproteinemia
– Villi distorted by ectatic lymphatics	Lymphangiectasia

Table 10.18: Chronic diarrhea due to fermentation

Intestinal mucosal status	*Condition*
Normal biopsy	Congenital deficiency of mucosal enzymes digesting mono-disaccharides.
Non-specific inflammatory changes	All conditions associated with total and partial villous atrophy have carbohydrate malabsorption and fermentation.

Diarrhea due to exocrine pancreatic insufficiency is remarkable by the macroscopic appearance of the stools; these are more frequently loose and pasty than liquid, often obviously greasy with undigested fat oozing like oil from the stool when it is passed in a pot or floating on the surface of the water in the toilet, pale, with an offensive cheese smell. Massive steatorrhea occurs most frequently in exocrine pancreatic insufficiency and from acquired surgical conditions like short bowel syndrome.

Diarrhea due to intestinal malabsorption is loose or liquid, often with an acidic smell, rarely greasy. These patients have modest steatorrhea, abnormal d-xylose test and abnormal intestinal histology. Intestinal biopsy is necessary to differentiate chronic diarrhea due to different pathophysiologic reasons. Histologic changes in intestinal malabsorption vary according to clinical conditions, these changes may be specific or non-specific.

Diarrhea due to fermentation is liquid, acidic (pH less than 5.5) and often passed with flatus, and its volume is variable, roughly proportionate to the amount of malabsorbed carbohydrate that has been ingested.

Evaluation of a child with chronic diarrhea: Work up of a child suspected to have chronic diarrhea and malabsorption includes the following investigations:

- Repeated stool examination especially for giardia;
- Fecal fat excretion studies;
- D-xylose test (blood levels and urinary excretion);
- Intestinal biopsy; and
- Specific tests, e.g. sweet chloride for cystic fibrosis; exocrine pancreatic function tests; serology for celiac disease; breath analysis for carbohydrate malabsorption.

Celiac Disease

Celiac disease (CD) is a permanent sensitivity to gluten in genetically susceptible individuals. The disease is an immunologically mediated small intestinal enteropathy. The mucosal lesions suggest both cell-mediated and humoral immunological over stimulation. Cell-mediated mechanisms have a key role in the induction of mucosal damage. There is strong evidence of association with dermatitis herpetiformis, dental enamel defects, type 1 diabetes, IgA deficiency, autoimmune thyroiditis, Down syndrome, Turner syndrome, and Williams syndrome. The strong genetic influence on the susceptibility to celiac disease is further suggested by the occurrence of multiple cases in families. The major genetic association of celiac disease is with genes and gene products of the major histocompatibility complex locus on chromosome 6. The common associations are with B8, DR3, DR7, DQ2, DQ8.

Clinical Presentation

The clinical presentations vary with the age of the patient, the duration and extent of disease, and the presence of extraintestinal complications. The classic form of CD in children consists of gastrointestinal symptoms starting between 6 and 24 months of age, after the introduction of wheat (gluten) in the diet. Infants and young children typically present with chronic diarrhea, anorexia, abdominal distension, abdominal pain, poor weight gain or weight loss and vomiting. Older children usually present with diarrhea, nausea and vomiting, abdominal pain, bloating, weight loss and constipation. But there is little information currently available about the prevalence of CD in children with these specific types of GI symptoms.

Nongastrointestinal manifestations: Extraintestinal symptoms are more common in children who present late. In these children, short stature and iron deficiency anemia, resistant to oral iron supplementation are the commonest presentation. There may be associated dermatitis herpetiformis, dental enamel hypoplasia, osteopenia, delayed puberty, hepatitis (elevated liver enzymes), arthritis, and epilepsy.

Diagnosis

The initial work-up of these children involves complete hemogram, serum chemistry and tests measuring intestinal absorption, such as d-xylose absorption, fecal fat excretion. Diagnostic evaluation specific to the CD include serological tests and histopathological changes in intestinal mucosa.

Serological tests: Commercially available tests include anti-gliadin IgA and IgG (AGA IgA and AGA IgG), anti-reticulin IgA (ARA), anti-endomysium IgA (EMA) and anti-tissue transglutaminase IgA (TTG) antibodies. Table 10.19 shows the efficacy of different antibodies used for diagnosing CD.

Table 10.19: Sensitivity and specificity of the serological tests for CD

Antibodies	*Sensitivity (%)*	*Specificity (%)*
AGA IgA	52–100	92–97
AGA IgG	52–100	50
EMA	88–100	91–100
TTG	92–100	91–100

Intestinal biopsy and histopathology: For confirmation of the diagnosis of CD, intestinal biopsy is required in all cases. As the histologic changes in CD may be patchy, it is recommended that multiple biopsy specimens be obtained from the second or more distal part of the duodenum. There is good evidence that villous atrophy is a characteristic histopathologic feature of CD, but there can be infiltrative changes in the submucosa. The two requirements mandatory for the diagnosis of celiac disease are (i) villous atrophy with hyperplasia of the crypts and abnormal surface epithelium while the patient is eating adequate amounts of gluten; and (ii) a full clinical and histological remission after withdrawal of gluten from the diet. A positive serological test that reverts to negative after treatment with a strict gluten-free diet (GFD) in such cases is further supportive evidence for the diagnosis of CD. In patients with selective IgA deficiency, serologic diagnosis may become difficult as IgA antibodies will be negative. So in patients who are strongly suspected to be CD, but regular IgA based marker is negative; IgA level should be done. IgG antibody tests along with intestinal biopsy are needed for the diagnosis of CD in these cases.

Management

Treatment with a strict gluten-free diet (GFD) is recommended for all symptomatic children with characteristic intestinal histopathologic abnormalities and also for asymptomatic children with a condition associated with CD and characteristic histologic findings on small intestinal biopsy. A GFD for life remains the only scientifically proven treatment available for symptomatic individuals with CD. It is recommended that treatment be started only after the diagnosis has been confirmed by intestinal biopsy. Even small amounts of gluten containing grains (wheat, rye and barley) ingested on a regular basis lead to mucosal changes on intestinal biopsy and persistence of clinical symptoms. Rice and maize are nontoxic and act as wheat substitutes. The clinical response to gluten withdrawal is dramatic. The growth velocity improves rapidly. The major problem is of noncompliance especially in teenagers. Most newly diagnosed children will tolerate ingestion of lactose, particularly in moderate amounts; therefore, dietary lactose restriction is not usually necessary. Young children with more severe disease may benefit from an initial lactose-free diet.

Children with CD are to be monitored periodically for assessment of symptoms, growth, physical examination and adherence to a GFD. It is also recommended to measure TTG or EMG after 6 months of treatment with a GFD to demonstrate a decrease in antibody titer as an indirect indicator of dietary adherence and recovery.

Suggested reading

Guideline for the Diagnosis and Treatment of Celiac Disease in Children: Recommendations of the North American Society for Pediatric Gastroenterology, Hepatology and Nutrition. J Pediatr Gastroentero Nutri 2005; 40: 1–19.

Disaccharide Malabsorption

Pathophysiology

Intestinal disaccharidases are located in the brush border of epithelial cells of small intestinal mucosa. The superficially located enzyme is very vulnerable to damage by a wide variety of agents. In the absence of these digestive enzymes, disaccharides are not hydrolyzed into simpler sugars and these pass unchanged into the lower gut, where these draw water from the gut wall through osmosis and cause catharsis. The unabsorbed sugar is fermented by colonic bacteria leading to production of H_2, methane, CO_2 and low molecular weight organic acids. H_2 and CO_2 diffuse into the blood and are exhaled in breath. The gases cause abdominal distension and frothy character of loose stools. Older children with lactose deficiency may suffer from cramps on taking milk but may not have diarrhea.

Causes of Disaccharidases Deficiency

Congenital deficiency of disaccharidases is very rare. Primary late onset deficiency of lactase is not uncommon in India and many Asian countries. A variety of conditions such as acute viral or bacterial gastroenteritis, protein energy malnutrition, and prolonged use of drugs like neomycin, celiac disease, cow's milk protein intolerance and cystic fibrosis may cause secondary transient deficiency of disaccharidases.

Diagnosis

The diagnosis is based on (i) presence of more than 1/2 percent of reducing substance in the fresh stools (prior hydrolysis with HCl is necessary before stools are tested for the reducing substance); (ii) acidic stools (pH below 5.5) while the child is on a milk or diet containing offending carbohydrate; (iii) abnormal oral sugar tolerance test (blood glucose rise of less than 20 mg/dl above fasting level with a disaccharide load of 2 g/kg); (iv) breath H_2 excretion of more than 11 parts per million following a loading dose of lactose or the offending carbohydrate; and (v) enzyme assay on mucosal biopsies showing low levels of disaccharidases.

Treatment

As majority of cases in clinical practice have secondary transient lactose intolerance, symptoms usually subside while the child is kept on a low lactose formula. Lactose content of the diet can be gradually increased within days (as in post-enteritis syndromes) or weeks in more severe cases. Lactose in the diet may be reduced by (i) preparation of milk cereal mixtures, e.g. sooji-porridge, and (ii) for severe cases, use of a formula based on either soy protein, comminuted chicken meat or calcium caseinate. Carbohydrates are provided as glucose or sucrose or simple carbohydrate like rice.

Defects of Monosaccharide Transport

These include inborn and acquired forms of glucose and galactose intolerance. The former are rare. The basic disturbance is a defect in the transport mechanisms. The treatment of these inborn errors consists of exclusion of glucose and galactose from the diet. The diet is difficult and monotonous and consists of calcium caseinate, vegetable oils, fructose, salts and vitamins. Secondary forms of monosaccharide transport defects occasionally follow enteritis and celiac disease. Risk for these defects is particularly high in severely malnourished children. In chronic enteritis, the bacterial flora deconjugates the bile acids which interfere with the absorption of glucose and galactose.

Cystic Fibrosis

Cystic fibrosis (CF) is an inherited disorder with autosomal recessive transmission. CF was thought to be extremely rare in India. However, recent reports suggest that CF is probably more common than previously believed, but precise prevalence is not known. In majority of cases it is not diagnosed because of low index of suspicion and lack of wide availability of confirmatory tests. The pathogenesis, diagnosis and therapy of CF are discussed in Chapter 13.

The cystic fibrosis gene is on the chromosome 7 (at 7q13); there are more than 400 mutations at CF locus, of which Delta F508 (which denotes a single deletion at 508 position of the protein) is the commonest. The mutation affects the gene's protein product, cystic fibrosis transmembrane regulator (CFTR), which acts as a chloride channel regulator and affects other aspects of transmembrane movement of water and ions.

CF is a syndrome of apparent exocrine gland dysfunction characterized by abnormality in mucus and electrolyte secretion leading to obstructive lesions in multiple organs. Abnormal transmembrane transport of sodium and chloride leads to thick inspissated secretion in the epithelial linings of lungs, sweat glands, pancreas and intestinal mucosa. These trigger inflammatory process leading to fibrosis. In the lungs, thick mucus plugs obstruct bronchioles leading to collapse, stasis and infection. Parenchymal and bronchial damages together lead to chronic pulmonary disease. In the newborn period, thick meconium plugs which have not been liquefied by the pancreatic juice in the intestinal tract of fetus, may cause intestinal obstruction or meconium ileus. The patients with malabsorption usually have insufficient or low bicarbonate with low pH in the intestines. Increased secretion of chlorides in the sweat may be an independent associated defect.

Clinical Features

Intestinal obstruction may be an initial manifestation in the neonatal period (meconium ileus). This may be due to the presence of abnormal protein and mucoprotein secreted by the pancreatic enzymes. Later these children tend to retain the food residue in the ileum, caecum and colon and these may form firm masses. Respiratory system is most commonly affected and they manifest with recurrent and persistent pneumonia. In addition, other systems like gastrointestinal, reproductive, endocrinal are also affected significantly.

The gastrointestinal manifestations of cystic fibrosis are as follows:

Gastrointestinal: Meconium ileus, chronic diarrhea, malabsorption, steatorrhoea, pain abdomen, constipation, distal intestinal obstructive syndrome, Ileo-cecal intussusception, fibrosing colonopathy and rectal prolapse;

Hepatobiliary: Fatty liver, jaundice, portal hypertension, multilobular biliary cirrhosis, hepatic failure, and gall stones;

Pancreatic: Recurrent/chronic pancreatitis, exocrine and endocrine pancreatic dysfunction.

Nutritional: Vitamin deficiency (primarily fat-soluble), micronutrient deficiency (zinc, iron and copper), and failure to thrive.

Diagnosis

The diagnosis is suspected from the onset of diarrhea early in infancy, usually associated with recurrent respiratory infections. D-xylose absorption test is normal as this monosaccharide does not need hydrolysis before absorption. Trypsin in the duodenal juice and stools is reduced. X-ray film of the chest shows pulmonary involvement. Analysis of the sweat for chlorides is a reliable diagnostic test. Level of chlorides above 60 mEq/L in sweat obtained by *pilocarpine iontophoresis* is suggestive of the diagnosis. Specific mutations can now be identified. Genetic detection of mutations (like delta F508) help in confirming the diagnosis.

Treatment

There is no definite treatment. Supportive treatment depends on the severity of disease and associated complications and usually involves a combination of medicines and home treatment. Home treatments include getting rid of mucus, eating healthy foods, and exercising to help prevent infections and complications.

Nutrition: A child with CF should be offered a calorie dense diet (130–150% of RDA) with adequate carbohydrate and protein content. Fat should be more from vegetable origin and rich in polyunsaturated fatty acids. Medium chain triglycerides use is quite beneficial in CF children showing failure to thrive due to malabsorption. Fat-soluble vitamins to be supplemented at two times RDA.

Medical treatment: Pancreatic supplement (enteric coated, acid resistant, microsphere preparation) is given along with feed/meal depending on the patient's clinical response. The usual dosage of enzyme supplement is;

Infants: 2000–4000 Units lipase/120 ml formula or with each nursing or 450–900 units lipase/gram of dietary fat;

Children 1–4 years: 1,000–2,000 Units lipase/kg/meal or 500–4,000 Units lipase/gm of dietary fat; and

Children >4 years: 500–2000 Units lipase/kg/meal or 500–4,000 Units lipase/gm of dietary fat.

Use of antacids, sodium bicarbonate and antihistamine along with the enzyme is desirable. If the diarrhea persists in spite of adequate therapy, other causes like secondary disaccharide intolerance can be considered and managed accordingly. Taurine and lecithine supplements should be given to provide substrate for increased hepatic synthesis of bile acids. In resistant cases, misoprostol, a prostaglandin analogue had been used to inhibit gastric acid secretion and stimulate bicarbonate secretion in upper gut.

Long-term antibiotics are essential for preventing pulmonary complications as discussed in Chapter 13. Humidification of the inspired air helps. Aerosol therapy with mucolytic agents such as DNase (inhalation), acetylcystein (oral) may promote clearing the viscid secretions. Ursodeoxycholic acid (UDCA) is a hydrophilic bile acid which improves bile flow by reducing bile viscosity and has been used for CF patients with liver involvement. Breathing exercises with chest physiotherapy are encouraged.

In tropical countries, additional salt (1–2 gm/day) should be provided to compensate for excessive loss of chlorides.

Bleeding Per Rectum

Rectal bleeding (hematochezia) refers to passage of bright red blood from the anus, often mixed with stool and/or blood clots. Rectal bleeding in infants and children is an alarming symptom for the parents and requires additional investigation. Practically, localization of hemorrhage relative to the Treitz ligamentum directs the initial evaluation and resuscitation. The presentation depends on severity of bleeding. Moderate or severe rectal bleeding, associated with passage of clots, can quickly deplete a patient's body of blood, leading to symptoms of weakness, and hypotension and may shock.

Most rectal bleeding comes from the colon, rectum, or anus. The color of the blood during rectal bleeding often depends on the location of the bleeding in the gastrointestinal tract. Thus, bleeding from the anus, rectum, and the sigmoid colon tend to be bright red, whereas bleeding from the transverse colon and the right colon tend to be dark red or maroon. In some patients bleeding from the right colon can be black, "tarry" (sticky) and foul smelling. The black, smelly and tarry stool is called melena. Melena occurs when blood stays for longer time in the colon for bacterial degradation and usually indicates bleeding site to be the upper gastrointestinal tract (above Treitz ligament). But, melena also may occur with bleeding from the right colon. Rarely, massive bleeding from the upper gastrointestinal tract can cause rapid transit of the blood resulting in bright red rectal bleeding. Sometimes the bleeding may be too slow to cause either rectal bleeding or melena and detectable by testing for occult blood in stool.

Causes

Common causes of rectal bleeding in children include anal fissures, hemorrhoids (associated with portal hypertension), polyps of the rectum and colon, ulcerative colitis, ulcerative proctitis, Crohn's colitis, infectious colitis, ischemic colitis, diverticulosis, abnormal blood vessels (angiodysplasia), Meckel's diverticula and rarely cancers. In India and other similar communities, infectious colitis is the commonest cause of rectal bleeding.

Evaluation

Accurately diagnosing the location and the cause of rectal bleeding is important for directing treatment. Diagnosis with rectal bleeding relies on the history and physical examination, blood tests, proctoscopy/anoscopy, flexible sigmoidoscopy, colonoscopy, radionuclide scans and angiograms.

History

Age of onset, relation to stool, progression, associated fever, pain abdomen, diarrhea, tenesmus (pain while defecation), dietary (milk intake) and family history are important pointers towards the etiology.

Investigations

Blood tests such as a complete blood count (CBC) are necessary to assess the severity of anemia/ blood loss and whether bleeding is acute or chronic. Microscopic stool examination helps to rule out protozoal and helminthic infestations. Stool culture may be asked for if infectious colitis is suspected. Biochemical liver function tests may point towards the associated systemic abnormality.

Anoscopy/ proctoscopy helps in identifying internal hemorrhoids and anal fissures.

Flexible colonoscopy enable evaluation of the entire colon and is the most widely used procedure for evaluating rectal bleeding as well as occult bleeding. It helps in detecting polyps, cancers, diverticulosis, ulcerative colitis, ulcerative proctitis, Crohn's colitis, ischemic colitis, and angiodysplasias throughout the entire colon and rectum. It is diagnostic (direct visualization of the bleeding site, taking biopsy from the mucosa) and can be therapeutic (polypectomy, coagulation of bleeding sites) at the same time.

Radionuclide scan helps in identifying the bleeding site where colonoscopy fail to identify the exact location of bleeding. It includes two types of scan; Meckel's scan, and 99mTc–labeled red blood cell (RBC) scan. The Meckel's scan detects Meckel's diverticulum, where the radioactive chemical is picked up and concentrated by the acid-secreting tissue and appears as a "hot" area in the right lower abdomen on the scan. 99mTc–labeled RBC scans are used to determine the location of the gastrointestinal bleeding. If there is active gastrointestinal bleeding, the radioactive red blood cells leak into the intestine where the bleeding is occurring and will appear as a hot area on the scan. The problems with this scan are; (i) it will not show a hot area if there is no active bleeding at the time of the scan and thus, it may fail to diagnose the site of bleeding if bleeding is intermittent, and (ii) it may fail to detect bleeding if bleeding is too slow.

Double-contrast barium enema can help in finding the anatomical mucosal abnormalities and is indicated only for elective evaluation of unexplained lower GI bleeding. This should not be conducted in the acute hemorrhage phase because it makes subsequent diagnostic evaluations, including angiography and colonoscopy, very difficult.

Elective contrast radiography of the small bowel and/or enteroclysis is often valuable in investigation of long-term, unexplained lower GI bleeding.

Mesenteric angiogram is more sensitive to locate the vascular cause of gastrointestinal bleeding as compared to colonoscopy or radionucleide scan. It can have therapeutic utility also; embolization of the vessel can be done if the bleeding is not controlled by laser coagulation via colonoscopy. Angiogram is asked for when other investigations fail to localize the bleeding or for therapeutic indications.

Additional special tests are guided by the clinical possibilities and results of other investigations.

Management

Treatment for rectal bleeding includes (i) correcting the low blood volume and anemia, (ii) diagnosing the cause and the location of the bleeding, and (iii) stopping active bleeding and preventing re-bleeding. First aim is hemodynamic stabilization of the patient with fluids and/ or blood transfusions so that diagnostic tests and procedures such as colonoscopies and angiograms can be performed safely. Identification of the cause of bleeding guides the specific treatment modality.

Rectal and colonic polyps can be removed endoscopically. Polyposis coli require surgical resection of the involved segment of large bowel. Surgical treatment is also indicated if the patient continues to bleed profusely and if nonoperative management is unsuccessful or unavailable.

Inflammatory Bowel Disease

Inflammatory bowel disease (IBD) encompasses two major forms of chronic intestinal inflammation: Crohn's disease (CD) and ulcerative colitis (UC). In UK about 4% of children presenting with IBD were under 5 years and 17% were between 5 and 10 years of age, stressing on the importance of considering the diagnosis of IBD in very young children. The incidence and prevalence of IBD in children is not known in India. More children in India are being diagnosed to have IBD, but it is not clear whether this increase is a genuine phenomenon or merely reflective of changing referral patterns or improved diagnosis.

Etiology

The pathogenesis of IBD is presently unknown. Current theories speculate a multifactorial aetiology encompassing genetic pre-disposition, environmental influences and immune system disorders. The role of each of these components is believed to be different in UC and CD. There is a genetic association with high frequency of IBD in first-degree relatives, but not a clearly defined inheritance pattern. Approximately 25% cases of CD can be explained by mutations in the NDDZ gene. This gene regulates the innate immune response to bacteria and other pathogens. Other HLA correlations are HLA DR3 and DQ2 in determining the extent of the disease and HLA DR103 in predicting severity. Apparently pathogenesis is due to immunological abnormalities, which may be primary defects or just secondary phenomena. Defect is probably in cell-mediated immunity. It seems that environmental factor or factors are also necessary to trigger and maintain the diseases. Environmental factors may include bacterial pathogens or their products, dietary components, childhood infections, as well as a host of other possibilities. Cell wall-deficient *Mycobacteria* have been isolated from surgical specimens resected from Crohn's disease, but role of *Mycobacteria* in etiopathogenesis is not proven.

Pathology

Ulcerative colitis is a diffuse mucosal inflammation of the colon; it invariably affects the rectum and extends proximally for a variable distance in symmetric, uninterrupted pattern to involve part or the entire large bowel. Compared with adult-onset UC, childhood-onset disease is far more likely to be extensive, with 60–80% of children having a pan-colitis. The microscopic features of UC include diffuse inflammation confined to the mucosa or submucosa. Typically, there are acute and chronic inflammation of the mucosa by polymorphonuclear leukocytes and mononuclear cells, crypt abscesses, distortion of the mucosal glands, and goblet cell depletion.

In contrast to UC, *Crohn's disease* is characterized by patchy, transmural chronic inflammation which may affect any part of the gastrointestinal tract from the oral cavity to the anus. Lesions are focal and asymmetrical. Similar to UC, CD in children is more likely to be extensive than CD in adults, most commonly involving both the ileum and colon. Microscopically, the changes in CD extend into the submucosa/transmurally. The inflammation is focal and patchy, both in location and severity. Findings that clearly distinguish CD from UC include the presence of transmural inflammation with fissuring ulcers, fistulas, non-caseating granulomas, and vasculitis.

Clinical Features

The clinical presentation of IBD depends on the site and extent of mucosal inflammation.

Ulcerative colitis: The most common presenting symptoms in UC include passage of blood and mucus mixed with stools, diarrhea, pain abdomen, tenesmus (pain while defecation), fever, anorexia, and weight loss. The onset may either be insidious or explosive with high, prostration and continuous bloody diarrhea. Abdominal distension, guarding, and rebound tenderness to palpation with decrease in bowel sounds requires close supervision due to the impending risk of developing toxic megacolon. Non-specific symptoms of anorexia, fatigue, delayed sexual maturation, and decreased linear growth may be present but not immediately noticed and if noticed may not prompt a workup for IBD because of their nonspecific nature. Extraintestinal manifestations are common in both adults and children with IBD, affecting 25%–35% of patients

Crohn's disease: In contrast to UC, the presentation in CD often is subtle, leading to a delay in diagnosis. Gastrointestinal symptoms depend on the location, extent, and severity of involvement. The disease is most often seen in teenagers but it has been also reported during infancy. Crampy abdominal pain (usually postprandial) either in the periumbilical area or right lower quadrant is the usual early symptom. Patients commonly have fever, anorexia, pallor and weight loss. Colonic CD may mimic UC. Chronic diarrhea is the presenting symptom in nearly one-third of cases. Delayed growth is more common in CD (60 to 88%) than in UC (6 to 12%), with the greatest frequency found in prepubertal children. Perianal disease is common, as are anal tags, deep anal fissures, and fistulae. Examination may localize tenderness to the right lower quadrant, and an inflammatory mass is occasionally felt. Clubbing is seen most frequently in children with extensive small bowel disease. Extraintestinal symptoms of arthritis, uveitis, stomatitis and erythema nodosum may be seen in some cases.

Extraintestinal manifestation:

Generalized:	Fever, weight loss, malaise, anorexia, fatigue
Ocular:	Uveitis, episcleritis, iritis, conjunctivitis
Oral:	Cheilitis, stomatitis, aphthae
Pulmonary:	Pulmonary vasculitis, fibrosing alveolitis
Vascular:	Vasculitis, thrombosis
Hepatobiliary:	Primary sclerosing cholangitis, hepatitis, cholelithiasis
Pancreatic:	Pancreatitis
Renal/Urinary:	Nephrolithiasis, obstructive hydronephrosis, enterovesical fistula, UTI, amyloidosis
Hematologic:	Iron deficiency anemia, thrombocytosis, Vit B12 deficiency, autoimmune hemolytic anemia
Endocrine:	Decreased growth velocity, delayed sexual maturation
Skin:	Erythema nodosum, pyoderma gangrenosum, perianal disease
Musculoskeletal:	Osteopenia and osteoporosis, arthritis/arthralgias, ankylosing spondylitis

Diagnosis

Complete blood count may give important clues to the diagnosis, particularly if a high platelet count, anemia and neutrophil leucocytosis, are noted. Raised inflammatory markers such as C reactive protein and erythrocyte sedimentation rate also support the diagnosis. Liver function tests and serum proteins (albumin and globulin) should be done to look for hepatic involvement and hypoproteinemia.

Perinuclear anti-neutrophil cytoplasmic auto-antibodies (pANCA) and anti-*Saccharomyces cerevisiae* antibodies (ASCA) are shown to be useful in differentiating CD and UC. ASCA are directed against *Saccharomyces cerevisiae* wall oligomannosidic epitopes while pANCA recognize a nuclear membrane antigen of 50 kDa. These tests may have two different serologic profiles: (i) "ASCA+/ pANCA–" correlates with CD and (ii) "ASCA/ pANCA +" is associated to UC.

Radiological studies for evaluation of suspected IBD include barium enema and upper gastrointestinal series. In ulcerative colitis, there is granularity of mucosa with punctate collection of contrast material lodged in small ulcers. As the severity increases, the colonic mucosa develops irregularity with spiculations and deeper ulcers. The typical radiological features of Crohn's disease are nodularity, ulceration, narrowing and irregularity of the lumen *(String sign)*.

A computed tomography (CT) scan is helpful in the diagnosis and management of patients presenting with acute onset of symptoms or an exacerbation of their disease. CT can assess both intestinal abnormality and extraluminal abnormalities such as abscess formation. Ulcerative colitis is associated with mural thickening <1.5 cm, no thickening of the small bowel, increased perirectal and presacral fat, target appearance of the rectum, and lymphadenopathy. Findings consistent with CD include mural thickening >2 cm, involvement of the small bowel, mesenteric fat-stranding, perianal disease, abscesses, fistulas, and adenopathy.

Endoscopic evaluation is an essential tool in the workup of IBD. Colonoscopic examination with multiple mucosal biopsies is most important to establish the diagnosis. In ulcerative colitis, the mucosa is hyperemic, edematous and friable; ulcerations and granular pattern may be seen. The mucosal changes start from rectum and extend into colon with no normal mucosa in between. In Crohn's disease, the mucosal changes are patchy and cobblestones like with normal tissue in between and can have fissures, strictures and fistula openings. Current opinion suggests that an upper intestinal endoscopy should be performed at the same time as a colonoscopy, as a majority of patients with IBD may show endoscopic and histological abnormalities in the upper gastrointestinal tract.

Histopathologic features help to distinguish between the two types of IBD as described in pathology section. In approximately 5% of inflammatory bowel disease cases, a definite diagnosis of ulcerative colitis or Crohn's disease cannot be established, in which case the term "indeterminate" colitis is used.

Treatment

The goals of treatment of IBD in children are; (i) induce remission of the active disease, (ii) to prevent relapse, (iii) promoting growth and development including pubertal development, and (iv) prevent long-term side-effects of pharmacological treatments. An individualised treatment plan, based on type, severity and location of inflammation, age and psychological factors, is devised for each child.

Nutritional support: In addition to growth supportive function, nutritional therapy is the first-line treatment used by the majority of paediatric gastroenterologists to induce remission in active CD. It is effective in both small and large bowel CD disease. It does not induce remission in UC but is essential along with pharmacotherapy. The mechanism of action for induction of remission is still not clear. To ensure adequate growth, provide nutrients 125-150% of RDA with liberal amounts of micronutrients. During acute exacerbations of IBD, parenteral nutrition may be necessary but has the associated disadvantages of being more invasive, risk of infection and more expensive. There patients can also be given enteral feeding: elemental or polymeric. The usual course of specific nutritional therapy during exacerbations lasts for 6 weeks, followed by a gradual reintroduction of normal oral diet.

Anti-inflammatory drugs

Steroids: Systemic corticosteroid (prednisone or methylprednisolone) therapy is the mainstay of inducing remission in moderate to severe UC. It is also effective in inducing clinical remission in CD with up to a 90% rate of improvement. The dose is 1–2 mg/kg per day prednisone equivalent (max 40–60 mg/ day) for four to six weeks and then taper. Although corticosteroids act rapidly to alleviate symptoms, they do not heal mucosal lesions and are of no benefit for maintenance therapy. In addition to oral and parenteral forms of steroids, steroid enemas have been used with success in children with distal bowel involvement. The steroid enema preparation should have low systemic absorption and bioavailability, so as to reduce the risk of systemic complications.

Aminosalicylates (sulfasalazine): The 5-aminosalicylic acid agents sulfasalazine (50–100 mg/kg/day) and mesalamine (40–60 mg/kg/day) are the most widely used amino salicylate preparations used to treat ulcerative colitis and Crohn's disease. They are effective as monotherapy to induce remission in mild to moderate colitis. In patients with moderate to severe disease who are refractory to the aminosalicylates, corticosteroids may induce remission. These agents are continued in the maintainance phase.

Immunosuppressive drugs: In patients who have achieved remission with corticosteroids, immunomodulators, including azathioprine (1.5-2.5 mg/kg/day) 6-mercaptopurine (1–1.5 mg/kg/day), and methotrexate are helpful in maintaining remission. Immunosuppressive drugs are used because of their steroid sparing effect.

Biologic therapy: Tumor necrosis factor (TNF) plays an important role in the initiation and perpetuation of the inflammatory process in patients with IBD, more so with patients with CD. Infliximab (monoclonal anti-TNF antibody) has been approved for use in children with moderate to severe inflammatory CD refractory to conventional therapy and with actively draining external fistulas. It can be used as an alternative to prednisone to induce remission or as a first-line therapy in CD with severe perianal fistulizing disease or in patients with intolerance to corticosteroids. It has also been used in children with severe and steroid refractory ulcerative colitis with positive response.

Surgery: Surgical resection is curative in ulcerative colitis but is reserved for those with severe, acute complications; colonic dyplasia, persistent disease unresponsive to medical management and severe growth retardation. Surgery is usually avoided in CD as it is not curative. However, it is indicated for complications of the disease; such as perforation/abscess, obstruction, stricture, fistula, toxic megacolon, or malignancy. Stricture resection or stricturoplasty is used to treat.

Psychological support: Emotional and behavioral issues are common and stem from the chronic nature of the disease. Anxiety, depression, and antisocial and dependent behavior are all common. Due to illness and disease exacerbation, lifestyle changes including school attendance may suffer. These issues need to be addressed carefully and parents and older children need to be aware about the nature and course of disease.

Prognosis

In cases with IBD, the course is associated with intermittent exacerbations. There is an increased risk of cancer in both CD and UC patients. The risk is especially high in those patients diagnosed at younger age, extensive bowel involvement, and length of time since diagnosis (>10 years). So in the cases if IBD, after remission colonoscopy should be done at regular interval to detect malignancy early. Occasionally patients may develop severe extraintestinal diseases, e.g. chronic liver disease. Hence all IBD patients should remain on regular follow up and screening program.

Suggested readings

1. Diefenbach KA, Breuer CK. Pediatric inflammatory bowel disease. World J Gastroenterol 2006; 12: 3204–3212.
2. Abdel-Hady M, Bunn SK. Inflammatory bowel disease. Current Paediatr 2004; 14: 598–604.

LIVER

HEPATOMEGALY AND SPLENOMEGALY

A palpable liver does not always indicate enlargement. It only reflects the relation of the liver to adjacent structures. In normal children, the liver is palpable 1 cm below the costal margin and in infants it may be felt up to 2 cm below the rib margin. When the costal angle is wide, liver may not be palpable, and may be more than 2 cm below the rib margin if the costal angle is narrow. Liver is pushed down in pneumothorax, bronchiolitis and emphysema. Visceroptosis associated with rickets and Riedel's lobe cause pitfalls in the interpretation of the liver size. It is, therefore, important to measure the liver span to determine presence of hepatomegaly.The liver span in different age groups is: infants—5–6.5 cm; 1–5 years—6–7 cm; 5–10 years—7–9 cm; and 10–15 years—8–10 cm. Besides the size and shape of the liver, consistency and character of the surface and palpable margin should be evaluated for the assessment of hepatomegaly. Liver should be examined for tenderness and also auscultated for any murmurs or bruit. Abdomen should be palpated for other masses or enlargement of the spleen.

Pathogenesis of Liver Enlargement

The liver may be enlarged due to: (a) inflammation, (b) fatty infiltration, (c) Kupffer cell hyperplasia, (d) congestion, (e) cellular infiltration, and (f) storage of metabolite (Table 10.20).

Splenomegaly

Spleen is enlarged in a large proportion of patients with chronic liver diseases particularly when portal hypertension is present. In extrahepatic portal venous

Table 10.20: Causes of hepatomegaly in children
Infancy
Infections Intrauterine (TORCH) infection, septicemia, neonatal hepatitis
Storage disorders/metabolic Glycogen storage disease, galactosemia, peroxisomal disorders, α_1 antitrypsin deficiency, mucopolysaccharidosis, hemochromatosis
Biliary obstruction EHBA, infiltration, erythroblastosis fetalis, histiocytosis, tumors
Others Congestive cardiac failure
Older children
Infections: Acute hepatitis, chronic viral hepatitis, pyogenic/amebic liver abscess, infectious mononucleosis, hydatid cyst
Fatty infiltration: Kwashiorkor, tetracycline toxicity, tuberculosis, cystic fibrosis
Cellular infiltration: Lymphoreticular malignancies, hepatic neoplasms, metastasis, histiocytosis
Storage/metabolic disorders: Glycogen storage disorders, mucopolysaccharidoses, lipidoses, α-1 antirypsin deficiency, Wilson's disease
Congestion: Congestive cardiac failure, pericardial diseases, Budd Chiari syndrome, veno-occlusive disease of the liver

EHBA: Extrahepatic biliary atresia

obstruction, while liver size remains within normal range, massive enlargement of spleen may occur due to associated portal hypertension. Significant splenomegaly with lesser enlargement of liver is present in the following conditions.

Infections

Malaria and kala azar, infectious mononucleosis, toxoplasmosis, cytomegalovirus disease, tuberculosis and brucellosis.

Cellular infiltrations

Leukemia, lymphoma, thalassemia, sickle cell disease (spleen may not be palpable; absent due to repeated infarcts with fibrosis) and histiocytosis.

METABOLIC LIVER DISEASE

Liver has a central role in synthetic, degradative and regulatory pathways involving carbohydrates, proteins and lipids. Defects in the degradation of fructose, galactose, glycogen, amino acid, fatty acids and ketone can lead to significant liver dysfunction by causing pathologic alteration of blood glucose, ammonia, lactate and ketone levels and pH. Metabolic diseases account for up to 15–20% patients of chronic liver disease.

Etiology

Table 10.21 provides the profile of metabolic liver diseases documented in North India. In India, Wilson's disease is reported to be the most frequent cause of metabolic liver disease in childhood followed by glycogen storage disorders.

Alpha-1-antitrypsin deficiency appears to be rare in the Indian population. In a large scale study conducted at AIIMS, none of the patient had abnormal alpha-1-antitrypsin deficiency genotype or phenotype.

Table 10.21: Etiology of metabolic liver diseases in children (AIIMS 1991–2004; n–159)

Etiology	%
Wilson's disease	47.7
Glycogen storage disease	14.4
Hereditary fructose intolerance	8.8
Lipid storage disorder	8.1
Gaucher's disease	3.7
Bile acid metabolic defect	3.7
Tyrosinemia	1.2
Hemochromatosis	2.5
Organic acidemia	2.5
Galactosemia	1.2
Indian childhood cirrhosis	1.2
Byler's disease	1.2
Niemann Pick disease	1.2
Unknown	1.8

Clinical Features

Specific symptoms are often obscured by the consequences of nonspecific responses of the liver to injuries that lead to hepatocellular damage, decreased liver function, cholestasis and hepatomegaly. Metabolic liver diseases can broadly be classified under 4 main headings on the basis of their dominant clinical presentation: cholestasis, hepatocellular necrosis (acute/subacute), cirrhosis and hepatomegaly. Clinical signs and symptoms of most metabolic liver diseases are similar and indistinguishable from those seen in acquired hepatic disorders such as infection, intoxication, and immunologic disease. Most of the metabolic diseases affecting liver present with hepatomegaly documented incidentally with or without splenomegaly. Most of them are asymptomatic and anicteric. It may be associated with failure to thrive, diarrhea, fever, etc.

Diagnosis

Confirmation of the diagnosis of specific metabolic liver disease has important implications, not only clinically and therapeutically, but also for family screening. The significance of early detection stems from the availability of specific therapy for some conditions and the option of providing genetic counseling for future pregnancies. A very high index of suspicion is required for timely diagnosis of metabolic liver diseases. History of consanguinity, ethnicity and neonatal deaths in the family should alert the treating physician to strongly consider metabolic cause. Diagnostic laboratory evaluation of liver diseases must be broad and should include work up of most common metabolic causes, especially so in neonates. Diagnosis of metabolic liver disease requires availability of specific tests.

Features of Metabolic Liver Disease

- Hypoglycemia, lactic acidemia, hyperammonemia
- Recurrent vomiting, failure to thrive, dysmorphic facies
- Rickets, unusual odors, cataracts, cardiac dysfunction
- Developmental delay, hypotonia, neuromuscular deterioration, seizures

The pointers towards metabolic liver disease are younger age (<2 years), hepatomegaly with no jaundice, associated hypoglycemia, metabolic acidosis, vacuolated hepatocyte cytoplasm or intracellular deposits on liver biopsy. Many a times the liver biopsy suggests the possibility and further evaluation is needed to establish the cause. It is important to establish the exact etiology as management is etiology specific.

Specific Investigations

These include serum/plasma galactose-1-phosphate uridyl transferase (GALT) assay—qualitative and quantitative, aminoacidogram, ammonia, pH and bicarbonate, lactate, pyruvate, 3–hydroxybutyrate, acetoacetate, transferrin saturation, ferritin, alpha fetoprotein, and very long chain fatty acids, urine succinylacetone, ketones, organic acids— esporotic acid and bile acids, and sweat chloride.

Management

Management is two pronged; specific treatment of the underlying disease and supportive therapy for arrest and reversal of liver damage. Whenever specific therapy is available and affordable, it must be offered, e.g. chelation therapy for Wilson's disease and 2–nitro 4-trifluoromethylbenzoyl-1,3–cyclohexanedione (NTBC) for tyrosinemia. Supportive therapy with hepatoprotective agents, antioxidants, nutritional support and vaccines should be offered even if the specific therapy is not available. Liver transplantation has emerged as the definite treatment modality of most of the metabolic diseases and outcomes are encouraging.

NON-ALCOHOLIC FATTY LIVER DISEASE

Non-alcoholic fatty liver disease (NAFLD) describes a spectrum of liver disease in persons who have not consumed alcohol in significant amounts so as to cause liver damage, and in whom no other known etiology for fatty liver is present. The pathological spectrum ranges from simple hepatic steatosis, to infiltration by inflammatory cells and mild to moderate fibrosis (non-alcoholic steatohepatitis—NASH) leading to cirrhosis.

Although the exact prevalence of NASH/NAFLD is not known, the prevalence of NAFLD in obese children is reported to range from 20 to 77%.

Etiology

The causes of fatty liver in children include:

Hepatic Causes

a. Overweight and obesity related
b. Metabolic liver diseases (Wilson disease, galactosemia, hereditary fructose intolerance, glycogen storage disorders, etc.)
c. Syndromes (Schwachman-Diamond syndrome, Bardet-Biedel syndrome, lipodystrophy syndromes, Turner syndrome, Prader-Willi syndrome)
d. Chronic viral hepatitis C
e. Autoimmune hepatitis, sclerosing cholangitis.

Non-Hepatic Causes

a. Nutritional: prolonged protein calorie malnutrition, total parenteral nutrition, starvation
b. Infections: HIV
c. Drugs (glucocorticoids, hypervitaminosis A, methotrexate, L-asparginase, zidovidune) and toxins (*Amanita phalloides*)
d. Diabetes mellitus
e. Inflammatory bowel disease, cystic fibrosis, celiac disease, nephrotic syndrome.

Diagnosis

These children are mostly asymptomatic and detected to have incidental hepatomegaly or raised transaminases while evaluating for abdominal pain or some other cause. ALT and AST levels may be elevated to up to 5 times the upper limit of normal. Ultrasonography, CT and MRI scanning are reliable for detecting moderate to severe fatty changes in the liver but no imaging method is able to distinguish between simple steatosis and NASH and/or indicate the stage of fibrosis. Liver biopsy changes include microvesicular steatosis, perisinusoidal, or pericellular fibrosis, foci of lobular inflammation, lipid granulomas, Mallory hyaline and megamitochandria. Diagnosis is made after clinicopathologic correlation and exclusion of other causes.

Management

The key principles of NASH management are weight reduction and hepatocyte protection. Normalization of serum aminotransferases and steatosis occurs with weight reduction. Dietary modification, changes in lifestyle with increasing physical activity is the key for this effort. Ursodeoxycholic acid and vitamin E have been used in NASH with promising effects.

ACUTE HEPATITIS

Viral hepatitis is caused by the known hepatotropic viruses, hepatitis viruses A, B, C, D, and E being the most common. Infrequent causes of viral hepatitis include adenovirus, cytomegalovirus, Epstein-Barr virus, rarely, herpes simplex virus infection. Hepatitis A and E are self-limiting, but infection with hepatitis B and C lead to chronic hepatitis. Although most acute infections are asymptomatic, when symptoms are present they appear to be similar irrespective of the etiology. It is important to establish the virus involved as risks of progression differ. Acute symptomatic infection with a hepatitis virus may result in conditions ranging from sub-clinical disease to selflimited symptomatic disease to fulminant hepatic failure.

About 60–75% of children with presentation like acute hepatitis are water borne infections. Among the rest 5–15% is parenteral infection related, 2–5% is drug and toxin related and in 1–2% chronic liver disease presents like acute hepatitis. For details on specific viral infections, refer to Chapter 9.

CHRONIC LIVER DISEASE (CLD)

CLD is not a single entity, but a clinical and pathological syndrome, which has several causes and is characterized by varying degrees of hepatocellular necrosis, inflammation and fibrosis. It may be defined as a continuing inflammatory lesion of the liver with the potential to either progress to more severe disease, to continue unchanged, or to subside, spontaneously or with treatment. This definition covers any inflammatory disease of the liver not due to acute self-limiting infection or to past drug exposure. The possibility of CLD should be considered if clinical and biochemical abnormalities persist beyond the expected period of recovery from the acute liver disease.

The commonly used basis of using apparent duration of the disease (of greater than 6 months) is often misleading in children. Irreversible liver damage may have already taken place before any symptoms of the liver disease are noticed and in the absence of clinical or laboratory feature of chronic liver disease. Many disorders like autoimmune hepatitis and metabolic disorders should be considered CLD at first contact, since left untreated, they have the potential to progress to severe and incurable liver disease. However, the 6 month cutoff seems appropriate for chronic viral hepatitis due to B and C infection.

Grading and Staging of Chronic Hepatitis Activity

Grading may be used to describe the severity of necroinflammatory activity in chronic hepatitis. Staging, on the other hand, is a measure of fibrosis and architectural alteration, i.e. structural progression of the disease. The rationale of staging and grading is to record those features which indicate the severity and the progression of chronic hepatitis, and which might also be of prognostic significance.

Etiology

The causes of CLD in childhood include chronic hepatitis with viral agents (HBV, HCV), autoimmune liver disease, drug induced liver disease, metabolic etiologies and biliary malformations (Table 10.22).

Until the early 1980's, Indian childhood cirrhosis (ICC) accounted for almost 50% of all cases of CLD. The incidence of ICC has declined in recent years and is no more a major cause of CLD in Indian children.

Viral causes of hepatitis, mainly HBV contribute about 8-15% of patients with CLD. Up to one-fourth of CLD patients may have metabolic etiologies of which Wilson's disease is the commonest. Autoimmune liver disease has been reported in about 2–4% of children with CLD. In up to 30–65% of children with suspected liver disease, no cause can be identified.

Table 10.22: Etiology of chronic liver disease

Chronic viral hepatitis
- Chronic hepatitis B
- Chronic hepatitis C

Autoimmune liver disease
- Autoimmune hepatitis·
- Sclerosing cholangitis·
- Primary biliary cirrhosis·
- Overlap syndromes

Metabolic liver disease
- Wilson disease
- Hemochromatosis
- Indian childhood cirrhosis
- Cystic fibrosis
- Hereditary fructose intolerance
- Galactosemia
- Gaucher disease
- Niemann Pick disease
- Wolman disease
- Glycogen storage disease

Hepatic venous outflow tract obstruction
- Budd Chiari syndrome
- Veno-occlusive disease

Drug-induced biliary malformations
- Choledochal cyst
- Congenital hepatic fibrosis
- Caroli's disease

Cryptogenic

Clinical Features

Insidious Onset

The patient may have clinical features of prolonged/ repeated episodes of jaundice, features of portal hypertension, upper gastrointestinal bleed, abdominal distension, failure to thrive, shrunken or enlarged liver, presence of splenomegaly, ascites and cutaneous porto-systemic shunts. Laboratory investigations may show elevated transaminases, and elevated serum bilirubin, with or without the reversal of A: G ratio.

Acute Hepatitis

Occasionally, CLD is diagnosed when a child presents with acute viral hepatitis like features. Some features in history and examination may lead to suspicion of presence of an underlying chronic liver disease. Metabolic and genetic disorders like Wilson disease, α_1 antitrypsin deficiency and autoimmune hepatitis may present as acute viral hepatitis for the first time.

Asymptomatic Presentation

Occasionally, the condition is discovered in patients with no current or past history of jaundice. The only presenting feature might be hepatosplenomegaly with or without failure to thrive. Elevation of transaminases is detected incidentally. Almost 40–50% of children with CLD may have such presentations, particularly those with MLD.

Patients with any of the following features in the history should be suspected of having a CLD: history of conjugated hyperbilirubinemia in infancy; family history of chronic liver disease; inherited or autoimmune disorders and relapse of apparent acute hepatitis or persistence of clinical features of acute hepatitis for more than 3 months. Children who present with hepatosplenomegaly or isolated hepatomegaly with previous history of hepatitis B, C, or non-A, non-B hepatitis should be evaluated in detail. Clinical examination suggestive of CLD include shrunken liver with enlarged left lobe; hard or nodular liver; ascites; edema; cutaneous portosystemic shunts; gastrointestinal bleeding; growth failure; muscle wasting; cutaneous features (facial telangiectasia, palmar erythema, clubbing, papular acrodermatitis); extrahepatic manifestations of autoimmune chronic hepatitis and presence of Kayser-Fleischer rings (Wilson's disease).

Diagnosis

The diagnostic work up of a child with CLD includes determination of the etiology and evaluation of liver function. The clinical features do not help differentiate between various etiologies. Investigations for diagnosis and monitoring of liver function include estimation of blood levels of bilirubin, transaminases, alkaline phosphatase, serum proteins, prothrombin time and sugar. Abdominal ultrasonography and upper gastrointestinal endoscopy are necessary. Liver biopsy is required in almost 1/5th of patients of suspected CLD to establish or rule out the disease. It is particularly useful in marker negative acute hepatitis and children with suspected metabolic liver diseases.

Specific investigations for etiological diagnosis are: viral markers (HBsAg, HBeAg, anti HCV); autoantibodies (anti SMA, ANA, Anti LKM-1, p-ANCA); serum ceruloplasmin, 24 hr urinary copper following penicillamine challenge, and slit lamp examination for KF ring; liver biopsy; urinary reducing sugars and urinary aminoacidogram; GALT assay (for galactosemia) and fructose tolerance test (for hereditary fructose intolerance).

Additional investigations in some cases may be required depending upon the results of the initial investigations. These are HBV DNA, HCV RNA, magnetic resonance cholangiopancreatography (MRCP) or endoscopic retrograde cholangiography (ERCP), sigmoidoscopy or colonoscopy, bone marrow aspiration for abnormal storage materials and enzyme activity in leucocytes or fibroblasts for specific metabolic liver disease.

Suggested reading

Arora NK, and Bhatia V. Chronic liver disease in India. Indian J Pediatrics. 2008; 75: S69-S73.

CHRONIC HEPATITIS

Chronic hepatitis describes ongoing active hepatic injury for more than 6 months. Hepatitis B virus and hepatitis C virus are the infective causes of chronic hepatitis in children. These are also discussed in Chapter 9.

Chronic Hepatitis B

Persistence of HBAg HBeAg and HBV DNA in high titer for more than 6 months implies progression to chronic HBV infection. It is estimated that about 350 million individuals have chronic hepatitis B infection globally. Important routes of transmission of HBV are perinatal (vertical) and horizontal. In India, perinatal transmission of HBV is responsible for about 20% of HBV infection in children while bulk of the infection might be through horizontal routes. The risk of vertical transmission is best correlated with the HBeAg positivity and viral load among pregnant women. Most of the transmission occurs during labor and delivery, while in-utero and breast milk related infection is rare. Chronicity due to HBV is an age dependent process, and in those who acquire the infection before the age of 1 year almost 90–95% become chronic cases, and between 1 and 5 years of age it is 30–50%.

The patient may experience the chronic active hepatitis phase or chronic inactive carrier phase. Chronic active hepatitis patients can be categorized as either HBeAg positive (HBsAg +, HBeAg +, antiHBe antibody+ or –, and DNA+) and HBeAg-negative (HBsAg +, HBeAg–, antiHBe antibody + or – , and DNA+) and both showing features of hepatic injury (elevated transaminases and histologic features of ongoing inflammation, hepatocyte necrosis and fibrosis on liver biopsy). The inactive HBsAg *carrier state* is diagnosed by HBsAg+, HBeAg negative, anti–HBe + or –, no or low levels of HBV DNA, repeatedly normal ALT levels for more than 6 months and minimal or no histologic changes on liver biopsy. However, 15–40% of carriers are at increased risk of developing cirrhosis, liver decompensation hepatocellular carcinoma over the course of ensuing 15–20 years.

A child can be discovered to be HBsAg positive accidentally while being investigated for some other reasons with no history, symptoms or signs of liver disease, and could have acquired the infection from the mother, by close contact with an unknown HBV-infected person or through contaminated parenteral exposure. The following are recommended for evaluation of a child suspected with chronic HBV infection:

History

- Assessment of route of acquiring HBV infection: via perinatal, horizontal or sexual route
- Family history of hepatitis B infection particularly in the mother or any other liver disease.
- The index child's hepatitis B vaccination status
- Past history of liver disease in the child or intake of drugs or injections or IV fluids or blood products.

Investigations

- Hepatitis B replication markers: HBsAg, HBeAg, Anti-HBeAg and HBV DNA
- Other infections: hepatitis C antibody, HIV antibody HBeAg seroconversion (disappearance of HBeAg and

appearance of Anti-HBeAg antibody) is a key event in the evolution of chronic hepatitis B followed by resolution of biochemical and histologic signs of inflammatory activity. But recovery from infection is not same as seroconversion and normally evidenced by the appearance of anti-HBeAg and anti-HBsAg antibodies and disappearance of HBV DNA and HBsAg in the blood. It is estimated that about 2–3% of chronic hepatitis patients spontaneously clear the infection naturally every year, but it is difficult to predict for an individual patient. Emerging reports suggest that mutants share significant proportion of chronic HBV infection in children and pose problems of diagnosis, treatment failure and drug resistance.

Management

The aims of treatment are sustained cessation of viral replication and remission of liver disease. Currently, only two drugs are approved for use in children beyond 2 years of age: interferon and lamivudine. The overall response rate of a combination therapy of interferon and lamivudine varies between 40–60%. Favorable predictors of response at the time of initiating therapy are: higher age, elevated ALT levels and high HBV DNA levels.

Prognosis

The factors which influence outcome of chronic hepatitis B are viral (HBV replication status, virus genotype and mutants, co-infection like HCV or HIV) and clinical (mode of transmission, age at diagnosis, gender, stage of liver disease at presentation, recurrent flares of hepatitis and associated hepatic and non-hepatic co-morbidity).

Suggested reading

1. Lok ASF, MacMohan BJ. Chronic hepatitis B AASLD Practice Guidelines. Hepatology 2001; 1225
2. Broderick AL, Jonas MM. Hepatitis B in children. Semin Liver Dis. 2003; 23:59-68.
3. Elisofon SA. Jonas MM, Hepatitis B and C in children: Current treatment and future strategies. Clin Liver Dis 2006; 10:133–48.

Chronic Hepatitis C

Hepatitis C is caused by an RNA virus, transmitted mainly through parenteral route, though in childhood perinatal transmission is also important. Vertical transmission of HCV occurs in 4 to 5% of infants born to viremic mothers but is significantly higher (20%) when mothers are co-infected with untreated HIV. Chronic hepatitis C is reported to be in about 175 million people worldwide with wide geographic variability in its prevalence; low in developed countries (1–2%) and higher in Asian countries (up to 6% in Thailand). Hepatocellular carcinoma is likely to develop in about 20–30% of these patients over a period of 10-20 years, but data on children is not available.

10

Children with chronic hepatitis C are mostly asymptomatic and have normal or mildly elevated or mildly fluctuating serum transaminases. Severe liver disease and decompensated cirrhosis are rare during childhood. The diagnosis is based on the presence of anti-HCV antibodies in the blood and detection of HCV RNA. In addition, liver biopsy is required to look for histological changes of chronic hepatitis and progressive fibrosis. Adequate investigations should be done to rule out other associated comorbidities. There are 6 genotypes of HCV identified worldwide, of which genotypes 1, 2 and 3 are mostly studied. In India, genotype 3 is the commonest genotype amongst adult patients with chronic HCV.

Given the significant morbidity and mortality with long-standing hepatitis C infection, treatment should be considered for childhood infection. Combination therapy with IFN-α and ribavirin is approved for treatment of children aged 3 to 17 years who have chronic HCV infection. Overall sustained viral response rate is 50–64%, but higher response rates (>80%) have been reported for genotypes 2 and 3.

Suggested reading

1. Arora NK, Das MK, Mathur P. Mishra R. Hepatitis C virus in children. Intern Semin Pediatr Gastroenterol 2005; 12: 3–8.
2. Jonas MM. Children with hepatitis C. Hepatology 2002; 36: S173–8.

AUTOIMMUNE HEPATITIS

Autoimmune hepatitis (AIH) is a progressive inflammatory liver disease with clinical, serological, biochemical and histological findings suggestive of immunologic reaction against antigens of the host liver leading to irreversible changes. It is characterized by the presence of interface hepatitis and portal plasma cell infiltration on histologic examination, hypergammaglobulinemia, and circulating organ nonspecific autoantibodies. Females are affected more than men, and all ages and ethnic groups are susceptible. It occurs infrequently in childhood and constitutes up to 4–6% of children with chronic liver disease. It is uncommonly diagnosed below 2 years of age and peaks at 10 to 30 years of age. Autoimmune hepatitis can occur along with sclerosing cholangitis (overlap syndrome). It can also develop *de novo* in patients who have undergone liver transplantation.

Manifestations

Clinical presentation of AIH is varied. An acute viral hepatitis like onset is seen in almost 40-60%, chronic insidious onset in 30–40% and rapid acute liver failure in 10–15% of children. Features suggesting the presence of AIH include associated autoimmune thyroiditis, arthritis, hemolytic anemia, vitiligo, nephrotic syndrome, ulcerative colitis and insulin dependent diabetes mellitus. The condition progresses rapidly into cirrhosis and portal hypertension. Hepatocellular carcinoma occurs rarely.

Diagnosis

AIH has been classified on the basis of presence of autoantibodies and immunogenetic markers into 3 types.

Type 1: These patients are positive for ANA/SMA autoantibodies and this is the commonest type seen in childhood.

Type 2: LKM1 autoantibodies are present in this group of patients.

Type 3: This is characterized by the presence of anti-SLA (soluble liver antigen).

Management

The disease process appears to be more severe in children as compared to adults, and about 50% pediatric patients have cirrhosis at the time of diagnosis. The goal of therapy is control of the disease. Currently, immunosuppression is achieved by corticosteroids and azathioprine, either singly or in combination. Prednisolone at 1–2 mg/kg/day (maximum 60 mg per day) and azathioprine at 1.5–2 mg/kg/day are administered orally. Remission is achieved with prednisolone given every day for 8–12 weeks followed by gradual tapering over 6–8 weeks till a maintenance dose of 0.1–0.2 mg/kg/day or 5 mg per day. Azathioprine has steroid sparing effect and is added either at the beginning or while tapering steroids. The drug doses are adjusted so as to minimize drug associated adverse effects and maintain remission. Flares in disease activity, as assessed by an increase in serum aminotransferase level, are treated with a temporary increase in corticosteroid dose.

Most children demonstrate improvement in liver tests within the first 2 to 4 weeks of treatment and 80% to 90% achieve laboratory remission in 6 to 12 months. Histologic improvement lags behind clinical and laboratory improvement by 3 to 6 months, and treatment should be continued for at least this period. Medications can be stopped if liver tests are normal for 1–2 years, no flare during medication and no inflammation on liver biopsy.

Prognosis

Despite the severe disease at presentation, the response to treatment is generally excellent and normalization of liver function tests is noted after 6 to 9 months of therapy in 75% to 90%. The 10 years survival rate in treated pediatric patients is over 90%, and the remission rate on therapy is approximately 80%.

Suggested reading

1. Mieli-Vergani G, Vergani D. Autoimmune hepatitis in children. Clin Liver Dis 2002; 6: 335–46.
2. Czaja AJ, Freese DK. Diagnosis and treatment of autoimmune hepatitis-AASLD guidelines. Hepatology 2002; 36: 479–97.

LIVER FAILURE

Liver failure is a clinical syndrome rather than a specific disease entity. It represents the consequences of severe hepatocyte dysfunction and hepatocellular necrosis. Impairment in liver function is indicated by deranged synthesis (coagulation), detoxification and consequent encephalopathy. There are a multitude of causative factors, which differ between children and adults. Regardless of the antecedent cause, the clinical presentation is similar. The mortality is between 60–80% despite adequate care.

Definitions: Based on the natural course and clinical presentation, several nomenclatures are used in clinical practice. They are listed below:

- *Acute liver failure*: This term is used for multisystem disorder in which severe impairment of liver function (INR $\geq$ 1.5 with encephalopathy or INR $\geq$ 2 with or without encephalopathy) occurs in association with hepatocellular necrosis in a patient with no recognized underlying chronic liver disease, within 8 weeks of the initial symptoms.
- *Fulminant liver failure (FHF)*: This term is used to describe patients without previous liver disease who develop a rapidly progressive liver failure within four weeks of onset of symptoms.
- *Hyperacute liver failure*: If the features of acute liver failure are evident within one week of onset of symptoms, it is termed as hyperacute liver failure.
- *Sub-acute liver failure (SAHF)*: When the features of liver failure are gradual occurring over four weeks to six months after onset of symptoms and associated with persistent icterus, ascites and/or encephalopathy.
- *Chronic liver failure (CLF)*: Appearance of signs of liver failure such as hepatic encephalopathy and/or clinically detectable ascites at least six months after onset of hepatic illness.

The survival appears to be inversely related to the duration of illness: survival with hyperacute liver failure is 36%, and sub-acute liver failure is 14%.

ACUTE LIVER FAILURE

Epidemiology

The true incidence of ALF in children is not known. Approximately 0.2% to 1.0% of all acute hepatitis can progress to liver failure. Liver failure in children is different from that in adults; in children, especially in infancy, not only it is very difficult to identify signs of early encephalopathy but also encephalopathy can be a late presentation.

Etiology

Etiology of ALF not only provides indication of prognosis but also guides specific management options. In neonates, infections or inborn errors of metabolism are common, while viral hepatitis and metabolic causes are more likely in older children. Table 10.23 summarizes causes of acute liver failure in infancy and childhood.

Hepatitis A is the most common form of hepatitis worldwide but it progresses to acute liver failure only in 0.35% of cases. Patients with fulminant hepatitis A have a better prognosis with appropriate management than do those with acute liver failure due to any other cause; up

Table 10.23: Etiology of acute liver failure
Viral hepatitis (Isolated/mixed)
• Hepatitis A, B, C, D, E, and others
• Herpes simplex
• Epstein Barr virus
• Parvovirus B19
• Varicella zoster
• Cytomegalovirus
• Adenovirus
• Echovirus
• Coxsackie virus
Drug induced
• Acetaminophen (paracetamol)
• Isoniazid
• Halothane
• Sodium valproate
• Phenytoin
Metabolic causes
• Wilson disease
• Neonatal hemochromatosis
• Tyrosinemia type 1
• Mitochondrial disorders
• Hereditary fructose intolerance
• Alpha-1 antitrypsin deficiency
• Niemann-Pick disease
• Indian childhood cirrhosis
• Glycogen storage disease type IV
• Urea cycle defect
• Galactosemia
Hypoperfusion
• Budd Chiari syndrome
• Venoocclusive disease
• Right sided congestive heart failure
• Cardiogenic shock
Autoimmune hepatitis
Mixed: Viral infection on underlying chronic liver disease
Unknown causes

to 70% of them may survive without resorting to transplantation. Hepatitis E is increasingly being labeled as the causative agent responsible for acute liver failure. Hepatitis B is the most common identifiable viral agent responsible for acute liver failure worldwide with fulminant hepatitis occurring in approximately 1% of cases. Absence of HBeAg and presence of anti-HBeAg seems to increase the risk of acute liver failure in newborns and infants who have acquired the infection vertically from their mothers. Reactivation of latent HBV infection may lead to fulminant disease, and this usually occurs in immunocompromised patients. Risk of acute liver failure increases by 7–8 times with co-infection or super-infection of HDV and HBV. Super-infection with HDV also carries greater risk of fulminant hepatitis than simultaneous infection. HCV is a rare cause of acute liver failure.

Autoimmunne liver disease may also present as acute liver failure. Intake of hepatotoxic drugs in a child with preexisting liver disease of any etiology might enhance the probability of precipitating acute liver failure. Infection with HAV or HEV in a child with underlying occult liver disease, e.g. Wilson's disease increases the risk of liver failure.

Precipitating Factors

The precipitating factors of acute liver failure in patients with acute hepatitis include infections, persistent fever, persistent vomiting, hypovolemia, use of hepatotoxic drugs (anti-tubercular, antipyretics and anticonvulsants, etc.) and zinc deficiency.

Clinical Presentation

Most patients with acute liver failure may have no elicitable history of any major medical problems or blood transfusion. Initially the child has non-specific prodromal symptoms such as malaise, nausea, fatigue, loss of appetite, followed by dark urine and jaundice.

Hepatic encephalopathy is one of the most important presentations of acute liver failure. However, the clinical appearance of hepatic encephalopathy is variable, depending on the extent and rapidity of hepatic damage, the degree of portosystemic shunting, and the contribution of precipitating factors. Initial symptoms of encephalopathy may be subtle and are likely to be passed off for the behavioral aberration of the child. Change in personality is one of the earliest signs of hepatic encephalopathy. A child with acute onset of combative behavior, irrelevant talking, euphoria or being irritable without reason should always be screened for hepatic failure. Changes in sleep pattern and motor coordination are other early markers of hepatic encephalopathy. In younger patients, the presence of coagulopathy is accepted as fulfilling the definition of acute liver failure. Hepatic encephalopathy is staged into 4 grades, grade I through IV, as given in Table 10.24.

The patients with acute liver failure are at high risk for metabolic (hypoglycemia) and electrolyte imbalance and infections. Presence of fever, leukocytosis, unexplained hypotension, azotemia, oliguria, worsening encephalopathy, severe acidosis and DIC indicates sepsis and warrants aggressive investigations for infections and appropriate management. Most often the infecting organism is a bacterial agent (staphyloccoci or gram-negative organisms) but fungal infections are not uncommon.

Cerebral edema is a major cause of mortality in patients with acute liver failure. A sustained rise of ICP to 30 mmHg or more is taken as an indication of raised ICP. Paroxysmal or sustained systemic hypertension and increase in the tone of the muscles of the arms and/or legs are probably the earliest signs of raised ICP.

Management

Acute liver failure is a medical emergency associated with an unpredictable and an often fatal course; survival

Table 10.24: Staging of hepatic encephalopathy

Stage	*Clinical manifestation*	*Asterixis*	*EEG*
Stage I	Slowness in mentation, disturbed sleep-wake cycle, incoordination.	No	Minimal change
Stage II	Drowsiness, confusion, inappropriate behavior, disorientation, mood swings	Easily elicited	Usually generalized slowing of rhythm
Stage III	Very sleepy but arousable, unresponsive to verbal commands, markedly confused, delirious, hyrerreflexia, positive Babinski sign	Present	Grossly abnormal slowing
Stage IV	Unconscious, decerebrate or decorticate response to pain or no response to pain in severe cases	Usually absent	Appearance of delta waves, decreased amplitudes.

depends not only on the etiology, degree of hepatocyte damage, capacity of the liver to regenerate, but also on the intensive supportive medical care. The goals in the evaluation of any child with ALF are:

- To determine the etiology, since it might impact on treatment and prognosis.
- To assess the severity of liver failure and the need for liver transplant.
- To provide hepatic support till child recovers spontaneously or has liver transplantation.
- To anticipate and prevent complications.

The child must be cared for preferably in an ICU setting. This provides a calm and quite environment, intensive monitoring facilities and quick access to life supporting systems.

Initial workup of the child should include identification of the stage of hepatic encephalopathy, assessment of metabolic derangements and also the presence of the precipitating factors. Work up for etiology can be deferred till the patient is stabilized because the immediate outcome is determined by the degree of derangements in the hemodynamic parameters (circulating fluid volume, urine output) and biochemical abnormalities (blood sugar, urea, creatinine, and electrolytes). Investigations that are necessary for the immediate management of the patient include those to assess hepatocyte function (liver function tests—SGOT, SGPT, alkaline phosphatase, bilirubin, prothrombin time), blood chemistry (electrolytes, urea, creatinine, sugar, calcium, phosphate) and evidence of infection (cultures, blood counts and X-rays).

After initial stabilization, further investigations are better if done simultaneously because stepwise investigation protocol causes unnecessary delays in arriving at a working diagnosis. Specific therapy is available for Wilson's disease and autoimmune hepatitis and helps in retarding the liver cell failure.

Monitoring

A monitoring protocol for patients with acute liver failure is necessary (Table 10.25).

Table 10.25: Monitoring of patients with acute liver failure

Clinical examination (4 hourly)
Pulse rate, respiratory rate, BP and temperature.
Fluid intake/output charting (6 hourly)
Neurological/coma grading (12 hourly)
Biochemical testing (12 hourly)
Electrolytes, sugar, urea, pH, bicarbonate
Parameters to be monitored (once daily)
Weight, liver span, ascites, evidence of bleeding or infection; prothrombin time
Parameters to be monitored (twice weekly)
LFT, creatinine, calcium, phosphate
Parameters to be monitored (as required)
Evidence of infection: Chest X-ray, blood counts, blood and urine cultures, ESR and CRP
Urinary electrolytes, creatinine and osmolality

Fluid and Metabolic Disturbances

Hemodynamic status is characterized by hyperdynamic circulation with systemic peripheral vascular resistance similar to systemic inflammatory response syndrome (SIRS). Hypoglycemia (symptomatic or asymptomatic) along with electrolyte and acid-base imbalance is present in majority of patients. Appropriate management of fluid and metabolic abnormalities is important for improving outcomes (Table 10.26).

Infections

Patients with acute liver failure are at increased risk for infections, attributed to impaired immune system, but may not show fever and leukocytosis. Infections are the cause of death in about one-fifth of these patients. The choice of antibiotics depends on the offending agent if identified but in general, it should cover both gram-negative bacteria and staphylococci. The empiric practice is to use a combination of third generation cephalosporins and cloxacillin. Aminoglycosides are administered if renal functions are normal. If there is no improvement within 72 hr, it is prudent to step up antibiotics to cover *Pseudomonas aeruginosa*, anaerobic organisms and/or fungi depending upon individual patient requirements.

Cerebral Edema

Cerebral edema is a serious complication, found in up to 80% of patients dying from acute liver function.

Table 10.26: Management of fluid and metabolic complications in acute liver failure

Fluid intake: Normal maintenance requirement (10% dextrose in N/5 saline)

Hypotension
- Resuscitate with normal saline, Ringer lactate, plasma or blood
- If mean arterial pressure (diastolic pressure + 1/3 pulse pressure) is <60 mmHg start dobutamine

Metabolic acidosis
- Suspect fluid deficit ; evaluate for sepsis

Hypokalemia
- Give KCl infusion/100 ml IV fluid according to serum K^+ level
  3 mEq (1.5 ml) if serum K^+ 3–3.50 mEq/L
  4 mEq (2.0 ml) if serum K^+ 2.5–3 mEq/L
  5 mEq (2.5 ml) if serum K^+ 2–2.5 mEq/L
  6 mEq (3.0 ml) if serum K^+ < 2 mEq/L

Hyponatremia (Na^+ <120 mEq/L)
- Restrict fluids to 66–75% maintenance
- Restrict Na^+ infusion to less than 2 mEq/Kg/day

Hypernatremia (Na^+ >150 mEq/L)
- May be precipitated with lactulose administration: reduce/stop lactulose
- Replace deficit and maintenance fluids with N/3–N/4 saline

Hypoglycemia (Blood glucose <40 mg/dl)
- Infuse 50% dextrose @ 1 ml/kg
- Increase dextrose concentration to maintain sugar between 100–200 mg/dl

Monitoring intracranial pressure (ICP) in these patients is important because clinical signs and computed tomography scans are insensitive diagnostic methods for determining increase in the ICP. The aim of management is to maintain ICP below 20–25 mmHg and cerebral perfusion pressure (mean arterial blood pressure—ICP) at >50 mm Hg. Mannitol is the drug of choice and should be used as a rapid bolus of 0.5 g/kg as a 20% solution over a 15-minute period. The dose can be repeated if the serum osmolality is less than 320 mOsm/kg. In cases of mannitol-resistant cerebral edema, sodium thiopental can be used at a bolus dose of 2–4 mg/kg over 15 minutes followed by a slow intravenous infusion of between 1–2 mg/kg/hr. Patients are nursed with raised head end (30–45%) and head placed in a neutral position. There should be minimal handling of patients. Hyperventilation and maintaining arterial pCO_2 level of 22–26 mmHg has been shown to be effective in reducing the cerebral edema.

10

Hepatic Encephalopathy

The reduced ability to metabolize ammonia, resulting in hyperammonemia, has been ascribed as a major pathway for development of encephalopathy and cerebral edema. Colonic bacteria produce a significant amount of ammonia in the body and reducing ammonia production has been a treatment modality for controlling hepatic encephalopathy. Bowel cleansing helps in decreasing the amount of ammonia in the gut by decreasing the colonic bacterial counts and changing the colonic milleu to acidic. To achieve adequate cleansing of the bowel, bowel washes need to be given 6–8 hourly with acidic fluid (1 teaspoon vinegar in 0.5 liter of plain water). In addition, lactulose may be administered either orally or with NG tube at a dose of 0.5–2 ml/kg/dose (maximum 30 ml/dose) 6 hourly adjusted to produce 2–4 loose acidic stools per day. Lactulose reaches the colon undigested, and is broken down by the bacteria into monosaccharide sugars. This increases the local osmolality and acidity, thus causing stools to become loose and acidic. Antibiotics (neomycin) solution has also been used in patients with acute liver failure. In patients with more than grade II encephalopathy, protein intake should be restricted. Hypothermia (core body temperature of 32°C), selective head cooling and hypernatremia (145–155 mEq/L) are other suggested modalities of management of severe intracranial hypertension. No sedatives should be given as they interfere with the assessment of the status of consciousness of the child. Anticonvulsants like phenytoin or phenobarbitone may be required if seizures are present. Patient should be ventilated electively if encephalopathy progresses to grade III or more.

Coagulopathy

Coagulation defects require administration of fresh frozen plasma or blood, preferably fresh. Platelets should be given in cases with thrombocytopenia. Vitamin K at doses of 5–10 mg is administered intravenously or subcutaneously daily to increase the concentration of vitamin K dependent coagulation factors. Gastrointestinal bleeds may respond to cold saline washes, parenteral H_2-blockers and antacids. Plasmapheresis causes a rapid improvement of coagulation abnormalities and may remove anticoagulant or fibrinolytic products released during hepatocellular necrosis.

Renal Failure and Hepatorenal Syndrome

Acute renal failure is noticed in 10–15% children with acute liver failure and can be of prerenal or renal etiology. The hepatorenal syndrome is indicated by decreasing urine output and rising blood urea and creatinine. The urinary Na^+ is <10 mEq/L with urinary creatinine: plasma creatinine ratio more than 30 and urinary osmolality higher than plasma. There is no effective therapy, but salt and fluid restriction along with hemodialysis/peritoneal dialysis may be required.

Specific Treatment of Acute Liver Failure

Encouraging results have been reported with use of N-acetylcysteine (NAC) in children with non-acetaminophen induced liver failure. Bioartificial liver support systems have been developed which temporarily take over the functions of the liver without resorting to liver transplantation, thus giving the injured liver time to regenerate. These are of two types, bioartificial and artificial. Bioartificial devices include the extracorporeal liver assist device (ELAD) and the bioartificial liver (BAL) which uses dialysis like cartridge, which house human hepatoblastoma cell line (ELAD) or porcine hepatocytes (BAL). The artificial device mostly used is the molecular adsorbent recycling system (MARS). Availability of these devices is limited in the country at present. The treatment of choice for these patients is liver transplantation. Overall survival rate for liver transplantation in children with acute liver failure is 60–70% as compared to 90% in children with chronic liver disease.

Prognosis

Despite supportive care and nursing in intensive care units, 40–70% children with acute liver failure die. Poor prognostic markers are grade III or more hepatic encephalopathy, prothrombin time more than 40 seconds, presence of sepsis or chest infection. Hyperacute and acute liver failure has significantly less mortality (40–60%) compared to subacute hepatic failure (60–80%).

Suggested reading

1. Kelly DA. Managing liver failure. Postgrad Med J 2002; 78: 660–667.
2. Arora NK, Mathur P, Ahuja A, Oberoi A. Acute liver failure in children. Indian J Pediat 2003; 70: 73–79.
3. Bansal S, Dhawan A. Acute Liver Failure. Indian J Pediatr 2006; 73 : 931–934.
4. Cochran JB and Losek JD Acute liver failure in children. Pediatric Em Care 2007; 23:129–135.

PORTAL HYPERTENSION

Portal hypertension (PH) is the commonest cause of gastrointestinal bleeding in children of India. PH is defined a clinical syndrome in which the pressure in the portal vein rises above 10–12 mmHg (normal value being 7 mmHg).

Causes

PH can be caused by obstruction to the portal blood flow anywhere along its course. According to the anatomical site of obstruction, causes of PH can be classified into (i) pre-hepatic, (ii) hepatic and (iii) post-hepatic causes though there are many overlaps (Table 10.27).

Due to availability of different sensitive and sophisticated diagnostic facilities, the etiology can be found in 90% of cases. There is a remarkable difference in the etiology of portal hypertension between developing and developed nations. Studies reveal that extrahepatic portal venous obstruction (EHPVO) is the predominant cause of PH in children in India compared to hepatic causes in developed countries.

Table 10.27: Causes of portal hypertension

Presinusoidal or prehepatic	
Extrahepatic	Portal vein or splenic vein thrombosis, splenic AV fistula, massive splenomegaly
Intrahepatic	Sarcoidosis, schistosomiasis, congenital hepatic fibrosis, myeloproliferative disorders, nodular regenerative hyperplasia, idiopathic portal fibrosis
Sinusoidal or intrahepatic	
Cirrhosis due to any cause	
Postsinusoidal or posthepatic	
Budd Chiari syndrome, right heart failure, constrictive pericarditis, web in interior vena cava	

EHPVO indicates obstruction in the portal vein outside liver and may be at any part in the course of the portal vein. Portal venous thrombosis can occur in cases with infections and inflammation (umbilical infection with or without catheterization, acute appendicitis, primary peritonitis, pancreatitis, portal pyemia), hypercoagulable states (acute dehydration, polycythemia and inherited and acquired deficiencies of anticoagulant proteins like protein C, protein S and antithrombin III), trauma to portal vein and invasion or compression by tumor or pancreatic mass.

Hepatic venous outflow (Budd Chiari syndrome) may be congenital or acquired and the obstruction can be anywhere between the hepatic veins and right atrium.

Clinical Presentation

PH leads to many clinical complications like portosystemic vascular shunting and related problems and ascites. Portosystemic vascular shunting is an attempt of the body to decompress the portal hypertension by forming shunts between collaterals from portal vascular channel and systemic caval venous channels. These shunts are formed at various sites of the body. The most serious consequence of PH is gastrointestinal bleeding usually from the varices around the proximal stomach and distal esophagus (gastroesophageal varices). The mortality after hematemesis in variceal bleeding is 30% and after recurrent variceal bleeding is as high as 70% and depends on the degree of hepatic function. The clinical presentation of PH is similar, but the underlying cause may also have the specific features. Patients with EHPVO usually present about 5–6 years of age with hematemesis with or without melena. A febrile or upper respiratory illness or drug intake may predispose to upper GI bleeding. Splenomegaly is almost universal in patients with EHPVO and size of spleen is usually dependent on the duration of the blockage. Liver is usually normal in size. Ascites is usually rare in these patients. Children with EHPVO also have variable extent of growth retardation.

The cases of sinusoidal and postsinusoidal portal hypertension often present with hepatomegaly, ascites and splenomegaly, along with the stigmata of chronic liver disease. Ascites is directly related to the development of sinusoidal or postsinusoidal hypertension. Dilated collaterals on abdominal wall radiating outward from the umbilicus, "caput medusae" may be seen. Some may even have presence of anorectal varices, masquerading as hemorrhoids. Some children, especially those less than 5 years of age, may be suspected to have PH even in absence of history of upper GI bleeding if splenomegaly is present. These children should be investigated for presence of portosystemic collaterals and for possible etiology.

Diagnosis

The clinical features of portal hypertension are easy to detect but confirmation and identification of the underlying etiology may require more detailed investigations. Additionally, the investigations are to be directed towards assessment of the hematological status, liver function and etiology of the liver disease, status of the portal vein and hepatic vein, demonstration and identification of the varices and site of bleeding collaterals.

Investigations

1. Complete hemogram for degree of anemia and evidence of hypersplenism.
2. Liver function tests; prothrombin time; specific tests and liver biopsy to identify the exact etiology.
3. Radiology: For demonstration of hepatic vasculature, collaterals and shunts various noninvasive and invasive imaging techniques are used. *Noninvasive techniques* are ultrasound with duplex Doppler, CT scan and MRI to identify the liver and splenic morphology, status of the splenic and hepatic vein and flow. *Invasive techniques* include splenoportovenography, arterioportography, percutaneous transhepatic portography and inferior venocavography for detailed delineation of the vasculature. Barium swallow is helpful in demonstrating varices, but not frequently done.
4. Esophagogastroduodenal endoscopy to demonstrate the varices and identify the exact site of bleeding. This also gives opportunity to do therapeutic procedures (ligation or sclerotherapy) to stop bleeding.

Management

Management of PH includes treatment of acute upper GI bleeding and definite treatment to relieve the portal hypertension.

Treatment of the Acute Upper GI Bleeding

Upper GI bleeding is an emergency and treatment consists of the general resuscitative measures such as volume and blood replacement, and specific measures to stop the bleeding. Vitals (heart rate, respiratory rate, blood pressure, sensorium) and urine output should be monitored.

Resuscitation and monitoring: For resuscitation, adequate venous access should be established and intravenous fluids and/or packed cells infused. Vitamin K, infusion of fresh frozen plasma, and/or platelets may be required to correct the coagulopathy. Nasogastic tube should be placed and continuous aspiration is done to clear the stomach and assess ongoing bleeding. A H2-receptor antagonist is administered IV to reduce the risk of bleeding from gastric erosions.

Managing Variceal Bleeding

Various pharmacological, mechanical and surgical modes of arresting variceal hemorrhage are used.

Pharmacological therapy: Vasoconstrictive drugs commonly used to stop bleeding include vasopressin, or their longer-acting analogues such as glypressin and terlipressin. These drugs induce generalized arteriolar and venous constriction, with resultant decreased portal venous flow and thus pressure, and at least temporary cessation of bleeding in 50–80% of cases. However, the generalized vasoconstriction also may result in peripheral vascular ischemia, myocardial ischemia or infarction and renal tubular damage. Concurrent administration of arteriolar vasodilators (e.g. nitroglycerine) is used to attenuate some of these side effects. The other drugs used for this purpose are somatostatin or their longer-acting analogues such as octreotide. These drugs are considered to be safer with minimal systemic vasoconstriction effect compared to vasopressin. Whatever drug is used, it is generally advised to continue drug therapy till a bleeding free interval of 24–48 hours is achieved.

Mechanical therapy: Mechanical modes of therapy include inflatable balloons for direct compression of the varices. The commonly used Sengstaken-Blakemore tube has both an esophageal and a small gastric balloon which are inflated to compress the varices. The complications of esophageal balloon therapy for varices include aspiration, esophageal perforation and ischemic (pressure) necrosis of the mucosa.

Endoscopic therapy: The most common and probably the most effective nonsurgical therapies are endoscopic variceal sclerotherapy and ligation. Highly irritant solutions such as ethanolamine, polidocanol or even absolute ethanol are injected through endoscopic direct vision into and around the bleeding varix. The subsequent inflammation leads to eventual thrombosis and fibrosis of the varix lumen. Endoscopic ligation or banding of the varices using rubber bands is a relatively safer method to occlude the varices followed by fibrosis. The combination of endoscopic therapy and either balloon tamponade or drug therapy to control actively bleeding varices is successful in 80–95% of cases.

Surgical methods: When all the above measures fail, emergency surgery is indicated. The surgical procedures include devascularization or transaction of the esophagus which blocks the blood flow to the varices. Another type of "surgery" is the transjugular intrahepatic portal-systemic shunt (TIPS). In this procedure, a temporary shunt is created between branches of the hepatic and portal veins via a catheter under fluoroscopy to decompress the portal pressure.

Prophylaxis of Variceal Bleeding

Administration of a β-blocker (propranolol, 1–2 mg/kg/day) reduces the risk of initial bleeding as well as recurrent variceal hemorrage. Heart rate should be monitored.

Associated Problems

Hypersplenism

Massive splenomegaly may cause excessive destruction of the pooled blood cell components leading to thrombocytopenia, leukopenia and anemia. It may need splenectomy.

Liver Transplantation

If the cause of portal hypertension is cirrhosis and hepatic failure, liver transplantation is the definite management.

Suggested reading

Arora NK, Lodha S, Gulati S, et al. Portal hypertension in North Indian children. Indian J Pediatr 1998; 65: 585–91.

WILSON DISEASE

Wilson's disease (WD) is an inborn error of metabolism characterized by toxic accumulation of copper in liver, brain, cornea and other tissues. The hallmarks of the disease are the presence of liver disease, neurological symptoms and Kayser-Fleischer corneal rings. It occurs worldwide with an estimated prevalence of 1 in 3,0000–50,000. The abnormal gene in WD, *ATP7B*, located on chromosome 13 encodes a metal-transporting P-type adenosine triphosphatase (ATPase). This enzyme is expressed mainly in hepatocytes and functions in the transmembrane transport of copper within hepatocytes. Absent or reduced function of ATP7B protein leads to decreased hepatocellular excretion of copper into bile.

With the declining incidence of Indian childhood cirrhosis (ICC), WD has become one of the important causes of chronic liver disease in India. This disease is interesting and important for pediatricians as it is treatable, presents with variable clinical features and importance of diagnosis in asymptomatic siblings.

Clinical Features (Table 10.28)

The condition presents with liver disease more often in children and younger adult patients than in older adults, but symptoms at any age are frequently nonspecific. The majority of patients with WD present with either predominantly hepatic or neuropsychiatric symptoms. Most of the patients with neuropsychiatric manifestation have either clinically asymptomatic or symptomatic liver involvement.

Hepatic Disease

Children and adolescents usually present with primary hepatic involvement. In general, the younger the age of the patient at symptom onset, the greater the degree of liver involvement. Liver disease may mimic all forms of common liver conditions, including asymptomatic transaminasemia, acute or chronic hepatitis, fulminant hepatic failure and cirrhosis. The degree of liver involvement is variable, ranging from asymptomatic hepatosplenomegaly with mild elevations of certain liver enzymes, to complete liver failure. Associated symptoms include nonspecific general symptoms, ascites and jaundice, and symptoms such as hematemesis and melena that are caused by portal hypertension. The patients may have jaundice, hepatomegaly with or without splenomegaly and features of portal hypertension.

Table 10.28: Clinical features in patients with Wilson disease

Hepatic	Asymptomatic hepatomegaly Isolated splenomegaly Persistently elevated liver enzymes (AST, ALT) Acute liver failure	Fatty liver Acute hepatitis Resembling autoimmune hepatitis Cirrhosis
Neurological	Movement disorders (tremor, involuntary movements) Drooling, dysarthria Rigid dystonia Pseudobulbar palsy	Dysautonomia Migraine headaches Insomnia Seizures
Psychiatric	Depression Neurotic behaviors	Personality changes Psychosis
Other systems	Ocular: Kayser-Fleischer rings, sunflower cataracts Cutaneous: lunulae ceruleae Renal tubular acidosis, nephrolithiasis Hematological: hemolytic anemia	Cardiomyopathy, dysrhythmias Pancreatitis Hypoparathyroidism Rickets, osteomalacia and arthritis Cholelithiasis

Neuropsychiatric Disease

Neurological symptoms usually develop after 2nd decade, but may present in early childhood. The initial symptoms are subtle, such as mild tremor and speech and writing problems, and are frequently misdiagnosed as behavioral problems. The usual presentations are characterized by difficulties in speech and swallowing, and drooling. Abnormal posturing caused by limb dystonia interferes with writing and walking, and may simulate Parkinsonism. About one-third of patients may experience psychiatric disturbances, e.g. changes in school-related or work-related performance, attention deficit hyperactivity disorder, impulsivity, paranoid psychosis, obsessive behavior, depression and bizarre behavior. Rarely, patients exhibit chorea, and myoclonic or tonic-clonic seizures.

Ocular Features

KF rings represent deposition of copper in Descemet's layer of the cornea. A slit-lamp examination is required to identify KF rings. Rarely may it be visible by direct inspection as a band of golden-brownish pigment near the limbus. They are not entirely specific for WD, and may be found in patients with neonatal cholestasis. KF rings are invariably present in patients with a neurological presentation. In older patients a sunflower cataract may be seen.

Other Features

Less common features include resistant rickets, osteomalacia, spontaneous fractures, arthropathy and muscular weakness. Proximal renal tubular acidosis is often associated. WD can present with acute or recurrent Coombs negative hemolytic anemia with or without associated liver dysfunction. Gall stones are common.

Investigations

Serum ceruloplasmin may be in the low to normal range in up to 45% of patients with hepatic WD. A low ceruloplasmin level alone is not diagnostic in the absence of Kayser-Fleischer rings. The level of serum ceruloplasmin in normal individuals is 20–40 mg/dl, and levels below 20 mg/dl may suggest WD. Serum ceruloplasmin may be low in cases of severe malnutrition, protein losing states and acute liver failure of any etiology.

Urinary copper excretion beyond 100 µg/day is suggestive of WD. Estimation of urinary copper after a d-penicillamine challenge (500 mg given orally before and repeated 12 hr into the urine collection) help differentiate WD from other causes of raised urinary copper; excretion >1000 µg/day is characteristic of WD.

10

Serum-free copper (nonceruloplasmin toxic copper in the blood) increases in WD to >25µg/dl in parallel with the increased urinary copper excretion. It is valuable in cases with falsely high levels of serum ceruloplasmin, and if estimation of urinary copper is difficult to obtain. Radioactive copper (Cu63, Cu65) has been used to document hepatic copper clearance which is defective in WD.

Liver histopathology findings are generally nonspecific and are not much helpful for the diagnosis of WD. Detection of focal copper deposition is a pathognomonic feature of WD, but is present in a minority of patients. The hepatic copper content is increased and usually exceeds 250 µg/g dry weight (normal, up to 50 µg/g dry weight). In asymptomatic siblings with WD, the liver copper content may be borderline elevated. Hepatic copper is the most important test in the diagnosis of WD, but it is not widely available.

Mutation analysis by whole-gene sequencing is possible and should be performed on individuals in whom the diagnosis is difficult to establish by clinical and biochemical testing. Haplotype analysis or specific testing for known mutations can be used for family screening of first-degree relatives of patients with WD. This helps in labeling the sibling as normal, carrier or affected even at birth.

With a diagnosis of WD, it is mandatory to counsel family members on the importance of biochemical or genetic screening of siblings and other family members. Assessment should include: clinical history relating to jaundice, liver disease, and subtle features of neurological involvement; physical examination; serum copper, ceruloplasmin, liver function tests; slit-lamp examination of the eyes for KF rings; and basal 24-hour urinary copper. Individuals without KF rings who have subnormal ceruloplasmin and abnormal liver tests undergo liver biopsy to confirm the diagnosis. If available, molecular testing for *ATP7B* mutations or haplotype studies should be obtained.

Management

The aim of treatment for WD is to remove the toxic deposit of copper from the body to produce a negative copper balance (initial therapy) and to prevent its reaccumulation (maintenance therapy). Initial therapy usually takes 4 to 6 months. Copper chelating agents are the first-line therapy for WD.

Penicillamine is the drug of choice. Penicillamine reduces copper chelates and increases its excretion in the urine. Most symptomatic patients respond within months of starting treatment. The usual dose of penicillamine is 10 mg/kg/day (maximum 1 g/day) given in 3–4 divided doses one hour before meals; the dose is reduced after a few months. Penicillamine may be associated with immune mediated side effects like leukopenia and thrombocytopenia, systemic lupus erythematosus, nephritis, pemphigus, buccal ulcerations, myasthenia gravis, optic neuritis or direct, dose-dependent side-effects like pyridoxine deficiency and interference with collagen and elastin formation. Pyridoxine should be supplemented at a dose of 50 mg/week.

Trientine is also a copper chelator, acting primarily by enhancing urinary copper excretion. Trientine is as effective as penicillamine with far fewer side-effects and is used in cases refractory or allergic to penicillamine. The usual dose is 25 mg/kg/day in 2–3 divided doses one hour before meals. Ammonium tetrathiomolybdate acts by preventing the absorption of copper from GI tract and preventing its availability for cellular uptake. The experience with this drug in children is limited. Zinc prevents intestinal absorption of copper and excretion in the feces. The usual dose is 25–50 mg of elemental zinc daily, taken 1 hr before meals.

Patients should avoid copper-rich food such as chocolate, nuts, shellfish and liver, and abstain from cooking or taking food from copper bowls and plates.

Liver transplantation is the treatment of choice in patients with fulminant WD and in those with decompensated cirrhosis. In addition to improving survival, liver transplantation also corrects the biochemical defect. Liver transplantation is also indicated in the absence of liver failure in patients with neurological WD in whom chelation therapy has proved ineffective.

Prognosis

WD has a fatal outcome if not treated timely and appropriately. Symptomatic patients require lifelong treatment. Early initiation of therapy leads to symptomatic recovery and normal life expectancy. Residual hepatic and neurological sequelae depends on the degree of damage at the time of initiation of treatment.

Suggested reading

1. P. Ferenci. Diagnosis and current therapy of Wilson's disease. Aliment Pharmacol Ther 2004; 19: 157–165.
2. Roberts EA, Schilsky ML. Diagnosis and Treatment of Wilson's Disease: An Update. Hepatology 2008; 47: 2089–2111.

NEONATAL CHOLESTASIS

Cholestatic jaundice in infancy is potentially life-threatening problem that indicates severe hepatobiliary dysfunction. Any infant who is jaundiced beyond 2 weeks of age needs to be evaluated extensively and urgently to rule out neonatal cholestasis. Cholestasis is defined if absolute direct bilirubin value is greater than 2.0 mg/dl with total bilirubin more than 10 mg/dl, or a value of direct bilirubin that represents more than 20% of the total bilirubin if the total bilirubin is less than 10 mg/dl. It is often associated with dark urine and pale stool. Cholestatic jaundice is always pathological.

Broadly there are four pathophysiological patterns of neonatal cholestasis in neonates and young infants; (a) obstructive—extrahepatic biliary atresia (EHBA), (b) neonatal/giant cell hepatitis, (c) paucity of bile ducts, and (d) special categories of cholestasis (metabolic, cholestasis in premature infants, total parenteral nurtition associated cholestasis, Alagille syndrome, and progressive familial intrahepatic cholestasis—Byler's disease). Table 10.29 lists the causes of cholestasis in infancy.

Clinical Features

The infant shows jaundice (conjugated hyperbilirubinemia), the yellow urine and/or hypopigmented (acholic/pale/clay colored) stools noticed by the parents or primary care physician. Infants with EHBA are often full term appropriate for date, and look apparently healthy except for jaundice. Those with neonatal hepatitis are small for date or growth retarded, and show have increased association with infections and genetic abnormalities. Cholestatic jaundice is often misdiagnosed as associated with breastfeeding.

Table 10.29: Etiologies of neonatal cholestasis
Infections
Viral: HBV, HCV, CMV, rubella virus, reovirus-3, adenovirus, coxsackievirus, human herpes virus-6, varicella zoster virus, herpes simplex virus, parvovirus, HIV
Bacterial: Sepsis, urinary tract infection, syphilis, listeriosis, tuberculosis
Parasitic: Toxoplasmosis, malaria
Bile duct anomalies
Extrahepatic biliary atresia (EHBA) Choledechal cyst
Alagille syndrome
Non-syndromic bile duct paucity
Inspissated bile syndrome
Caroli's disease
Choledocholithiasis
Neonatal sclerosing cholangitis
Metabolic disorders
Galactosemia, Glycogen storage disease, hereditary tyrosinemia, neonatal hemochromatosis, hereditary fructosemia, bile acid synthesis disorders, progressive familial intrahepatic cholestasis, cystic fibrosis, Dubin-Johnson syndrome, Rotor syndrome, Niemann Pick disease, Gaucher disease, Zellweger's syndrome, α_1-antitrypsin deficiency
Endocrinopathies
Hypothyroidism, hypopituitarism
Chromosomal disorders
Turner syndrome, trisomy 18, trisomy 21, trisomy 13, Donahue syndrome
Neoplasia
Neonatal leukemia, histiocytosis-X, neuroblastoma, hepatoblastoma, erythrophagocytic lymphohistiocytosis
Miscellaneous
Neonatal lupus erythematosus, Indian childhood cirrhosis, perinatal asphyxia, congestive heart failure, Budd Chiari syndrome
Idiopathic neonatal hepatitis

Evaluation of Infant with Cholestasis

Several questions arise in a neonate with hyperbilirubinemia, including (1) Is the jaundice physiological or pathological, (2) What is the etiology, (3) Which babies require further investigation, (4) What are the investigations required, (5) Is the jaundice a threat to the infant, (6) What is the treatment, and (7) What is the prognosis?

The evaluation of the infant with cholestasis is a multistep process that should follow a logical sequence, which helps us differentiate the broad categories of neonatal cholestasis without wasting time and at minimal cost. It is important to recognize disorders for which specific treatment is available. Initial evaluation should focus on establishing the patency of the biliary tree. It is important to diagnose biliary atresia earlier than 2 months of age because the success of surgery and outcome is dependent on the age of surgery. Beyond 2 months, adequate biliary drainage is achieved in less than one-third of infants with EHBA.

Physical examination shows hepatomegaly or hepatosplenomegaly. Liver span is more important than the liver palpable below costal margin. Hepatomegaly is present in all these patients and those with severe liver disease show signs of portal hypertension and end stage liver disease. Eye examination for chorioretinitis, posterior embryotoxon, cataract, and cherry red spot is done to evaluate for metabolic disorders and intrauterine infections. Laboratory work up is carried out with the aim of: (1) establishing cholestasis and hepatocellular dysfunction; (2) arriving at a specific diagnosis; and (3) differentiate obstructive lesions from neonatal hepatitis as detailed in Table 10.30.

Table 10.30: Investigations for neonatal cholestasis

Liver Function
Serum bilirubin (total/conjugated/unconjugated)
Serum transaminases, alkaline phosphatase
Gamma glutamyl transpeptidase
Serum proteins, albumin
Prothrombin time
Infections
TORCH screen-IgM antibodies
Hepatitis B surface antigen, anti-hepatitis C antibodies
Evidence of sepsis
Others
Ultrasound of hepatobiliary tree
Hepatobiliary scintigraphy (HIDA) scan
Liver biopsy
Per-operative cholangiogram
Cholangiopancreatography: MR, endoscopic
Hematological
Hemoglobin, leukocyte and platelet count
Reticulocyte count
Metabolic disorders
Urine for amino acids, reducing substances
Blood, urine pH; bicarbonate
Investigations for: tyrosinemia, galactosemia, hereditary fructose intolerance, alpha-1 anti-trypsin
Urine aminoacidogram
Endocrine disorders
TSH level

Differentiation between Obstructive Lesion and Neonatal Hepatitis

Patients with obstructive lesion should be identified before 2 months to prevent irreversible damage and for possible surgical intervention. The key challenges to differentiate obstructive lesion (EHBA) from neonatal hepatitis are: (1) similarity in clinical presentation and overlapping values of routine biochemical investigations; (2) one-third of each are due to mild neonatal hepatitis, severe neonatal hepatitis and obstructive causes; (3) investigations like HIDA scan, ERCP/MRCP indicate obstructive lesions but do not help to differentiate with certainty between severe neonatal hepatitis and obstructive causes; and (4) a proportion of patients with EHBA show TORCH antibodies.

10

Radionuclide hepatobiliary scintigraphy [HIDA] is used to assess the continuity of the biliary tract with the small intestine. Non-visualization of radioactivity within 24 hours after injection is considered to be abnormal, indicating biliary obstruction or severe hepatocellular dysfunction. Priming of liver with phenobarbitone (5 mg/kg/day) and betamethasone (0.5 mg/kg/day) for a period of 5–7 days before imaging increases its specificity for the diagnosis of EHBA.

The combination of a non-excreting HIDA scan along with GGTP levels $\geq$ 50 IU/L are highly suggestive of EHBA. Liver biopsy is considered as the most accurate (90–95%) diagnostic test for differentiating biliary atresia from other causes of neonatal cholestasis. In biliary atresia, ductular proliferation and fibrosis are seen, whereas in neonatal hepatitis, there is alteration in lobular architecture, focal hepatocellular necrosis, and giant cells with ballooning of their cytoplasm. These changes are prominent after 6 weeks of age.

Currently, peroperative cholangiography (exploratory or laparoscopically) remains the gold standard to differentiate between EHBA and neonatal hepatitis.

Management

Medical management is usually directed at the specific cause identified, in addition to the supportive therapy for the cholestasis and treatment of sequelae of cholestasis. Most case of neonatal hepatitis cannot be offered definitive therapy; therefore, supportive care is the mainstay of therapy.

Nutritional support is important. The goal should be caloric intake of 150% of RDA based on ideal body weight with 25–35% calories derived from fat. Medium chain triglycerides are more water soluble and do not require bile salts for absorption. Supplementation of fat soluble vitamins is essential as their absorption is impaired in cholestasis. Adequate protein intake (2–3 g/kg/day) is advised.

Drugs: Ursodeoxycholic acid (UDCA) is a hydophilic bile acid, and at a dosage of 20–30 mg/kg/day in two divided doses has been shown to be beneficial. It is recommended that high dose (five times of RDA) of fat soluble vitamins along with vitamin E and two times RDA of water soluble vitamins should be supplemented for these infants. A weekly dose of parenteral vitamin K and D is helpful in infants with severe cholestasis.

Surgery: EHBA and choledochal cyst can be surgically corrected if the liver disease has not progressed to cirrhosis. Kasai's portoenterostomy is done for EHBA to reestablish the biliary flow into gut. Outcomes are good if surgery is done before 2 months of age.

Patients developing portal hypertension, ascites, infection and hepatic encephalopathy should be managed accordingly. Cholestatic infants should be treated aggressively for infections whenever suspected.

Suggested reading

1. Arora NK, Kohli R, Bal CS, Gupta AK, Gupta SD. Hepatic technetium-99m-meberferrin imidioacetate scans and serum γ-glutamyl transpeptidase levels interpreted in series to differentiate between extrahepatic biliary atresia and neonatal hepatitis. Acta Pediatr 2001; 90: 975–981.
2. Venigalla S, Gourley GR. Neonatal cholestasis. Semin Perinatol 2004; 28: 348–355.
3. Guideline for the evaluation of cholestatic jaundice in infants: Recommendations of the North American Society for Pediatric Gastroenterology, Hepatology and Nutrition. J Pediatr Gastroenterol Nutr 2004; 39:115–128.

PEDIATRIC LIVER TRANSPLANTATION

Liver transplantation has become the definitive treatment modality for patients with end-stage liver diseases. This can be achieved by a cadaveric transplant (transplanting liver from a dead donor), living related donor (taking out a part of the liver from a living donor) or hepatocyte transplant (injecting hepatocytes-experimental stage).

The clinical situations where transplantation is often required include progressive primary liver disease, stable liver disease with significant morbidity, metabolic liver disease and fulminant hepatic failure due to known or unknown cause. Biliary atresia is the commonest indication (80%) for transplantation in patients below 2 years of age and overall 50% among all pediatric liver transplants. Contraindications to liver transplantation are coma with irreversible brain injury, uncontrolled systemic infection, extrahepatic metastasis in liver tumors, and terminal progressive systemic disease, inadequate cardiac or pulmonary function, and HIV infection.

The process of liver transplant requires a multi-disciplinary approach, integrating all resources available with the medical fraternity and society. Children usually are seen at an initial consultation by a pediatric hepatologist, transplant surgeon, and a transplant coordinator. A social worker meets the family and relevant psychosocial issues are addressed. An extensive baseline assessment is necessary before taking up a child for transplant and dependent on the underlying cause of liver disease.

Drugs, such as corticosteroids, azathioprine, cyclosporine, tacrolimus, sirolimus, and mycophenolate mofetil are used for maintenance immunosuppression. Pediatric protocols that are steroid sparing or devoid of steroids are gaining favor and are being used. Apart from the drugs, a careful clinical observation is required for detecting the complication and early signs of graft rejection. Aggressive nutritional rehabilitation is mandatory in the pretransplant and posttransplant phase.

Long-Term Outcome

The long term survival of transplant patients varies from center to center and its experience. Outcome has improved over the decades and now reaches up to 90% in the first years of transplant. Thereafter, the survival rates vary between 60–80% till 5 years. The main factors which affect the survival rates are age (those younger than 1 year have better survival), nutritional status and severity of the disease in the postoperative period.

Suggested reading

1. Ferreira CT, Vieira SMG, da Silveria T. Liver transplantation. J Pediatr (Rio J) 2000; 76 (Suppl 2): S198–S208.
2. McDiarmid SV. Current status of liver transplantation in children. Pediatr Clin N Am 2003; 50: 1335–74
3. Kerkar N. Emre S. Issues unique to pediatric liver transplantation. Clin Liver Dis 2007; 11: 323–35.

11 Hematological Disorders

APPROACH TO ANEMIA

Anemia is a sign, which can present at any age. It is important to investigate the cause of anemia to exclude a serious underlying ailment and to define the correct management approach.

Definition

Anemia is present when the hemoglobin level in the blood is two standard deviations below the mean for the particular age and sex being evaluated (Table 11.1). The physiologic definition of anemia is a condition in which tissue hypoxia occurs due to inadequate oxygen carrying capacity of blood. According to the National Family Health Survey (NHFS-3) data the incidence of anemia in urban children is 71%, rural is 84% and overall is 79%.

Physiological Adaptations

Anemia leads to decreased oxygen-carrying capacity of the blood and compensatory physiological adjustments. Tissue hypoxia develops when the enhanced release of oxygen from hemoglobin and increase of blood flow to the tissues is insufficient to meet requirements. The maintenance of blood volume occurs by an increase in the volume of plasma and redistribution of blood flow. Cardiac output increases in anemia as a consequence of increased stroke volume; this high output state increases oxygen delivery to tissues by increasing the flow of blood. Diversion of blood flow occurs from tissues with lesser oxygen requirements to those with greater needs. Thus skin blood flow is reduced, while cerebral and muscle blood flow are increased.

Clinical Approach

The history can give many important clues for the etiology of anemia, causes vary with age, and in some cases the etiology may be multifactorial (Table 11.2). A family history of anemia, requirement for blood transfusions and demise of children, may lead the diagnosis towards thalassemia major; history of gallstones and recurrent episodes of jaundice are found in many types of hemolytic anemia in particular hereditary spherocytosis; only affected males can be a clue to an X-linked disorder like glucose 6 phosphate dehydrogenase (G6PD) deficiency.

Table 11.1: Hemoglobin and hematocrit in infancy and childhood

	Mean and lower limit of normal (–2 SD)			
	Hemoglobin (g/dL)		*Hematocrit (%)*	
Age	Mean	–2 SD	Mean	–2 SD
Birth (cord blood)	16.5	13.5	51	42
1–3 day (capillary)	18.5	14.5	56	45
1 week	17.5	13.5	54	42
2 week	16.5	12.5	51	39
1 month	14.0	10.0	43	31
2 month	11.5	9.0	35	28
3–6 month	11.5	9.5	35	29
0.5–2 year	12.0	10.5	36	33
2–6 year	12.5	11.5	37	34
6–12 year	13.5	11.5	40	35
12–18 yr, female	14.0	12.0	41	36
12–18 yr, male	14.5	13.0	43	37

Table 11.2: Information for evaluation of anemia

Infants	History of maternal infections, anemia or collagen vascular diseases. Prematurity, blood loss, jaundice (ABO or Rh incompatibility, glucose 6 phosphate dehydrogenase deficiency, sepsis. Hemangiomas, cephalhematoma. Intake of breast milk, formula, cow or goat milk; intake of vitamins and hematinics.
Young children	Diet, timing and nutritional quality of weaning foods. Blood loss, worms, epistaxis, hematuria, etc. Family history of thalassemia/sickle cell anemia. History of jaundice-hereditary hemolytic anemias (e.g. hereditary spherocytosis). Infections, e.g. malaria, tuberculosis. Other chronic illness, e.g. juvenile rheumatoid arthritis, etc. Medications, e.g. anticonvulsants, etc.

A dietary history is useful; early initiation of cow's milk and predominantly milk based diet results in poor iron intake or cow's milk allergy leading to anemia. Nutritional iron deficiency anemia often occurs between 6 months to 2 years due to inadequate weaning, chronic diarrhea or cow's milk allergy. Adolescents with growth spurt, menstruating and pregnant teens are also at risk for iron deficiency anemia. A pure vegetarian diet and use of goat's milk may result in megaloblastic anemia. History of pica, drug intake, chronic diarrhea, prior surgery, acute and prolonged infections, liver and renal disease, transfusions and age of onset of symptoms should be taken. History of iron supplements and a lack of response may suggest thalassemia. Thalassemia major usually presents at 2–3 months of age, and 70% of these children will present with symptoms by 6 months. Diamond-Blackfan (pure red cell) anemia usually presents at 3 months and shows a consistently low reticulocyte count and absence of erythroid precursors in the bone marrow. Fanconi anemia has a more variable and later onset, with children presenting at 3–4 years of age or even in adulthood. Lead toxicity by exposure to lead based paints and chemicals can occur in children.

Clinical Features

The hemoglobin level at which symptoms of anemia develop depends on two main factors, i.e. the rate of development of the anemia and state of the cardiovascular system of the patient. In general, symptoms occur at a higher hemoglobin level with rapidly developing anemia, e.g. due to acute hemorrhage.

Tiredness, lassitude, easy fatigability and generalized muscular weakness are the most common, and frequently the earliest symptoms of anemia. In children, this can present as poor feeding, irritability and inadequate school performance. Pallor is the most prominent and characteristic sign. Pallor of the nail beds, oral mucous membranes and conjunctivae are a more reliable indication of anemia. Conjunctival pallor is sought by pulling down the lower eyelid. Observing palmer creases and skin pallor, is insufficient in children as the skin creases do not show pigmentation. Facial pallor varies with skin pigmentation and presence of facial edema. Dyspnea on exertion, tachycardia and palpitation are common symptoms. Murmurs become more prominent as the degree of anemia increases. They may be caused entirely by the hemodynamic changes secondary to the anemia itself (hemic murmurs), by underlying heart disease or a combination of both factors. Hemic murmurs are mid-systolic 'flow' murmurs, reflecting the increased velocity of blood passing through the valves. They are common in the pulmonary area, but can be heard in areas corresponding to any of the heart valves. Very severe anemia can precipitate cardiac failure even in individuals with a normal cardiovascular system. Systolic bruits and postural hypotension can be demonstrated in patients with moderate to severe anemia.

Severe anemia is characterized by a high output state with an elevated pulse pressure and a 'collapsing' character to the pulse. Electrocardiographic changes may be found in approximately 30% patients with hemoglobin less than 6 g/dl, including depression of the S-T segments, and flattening or inversion of T waves.

Central nervous system symptoms such as dizziness, headache, humming in the ears, fainting, tinnitus, lack of concentration and drowsiness, and with severe anemia, clouding of consciousness may occur. Examination should be done to find etiological clues to the cause of anemia such as radial limb abnormalities seen in bone marrow failure syndromes, presence of splenomegaly may be found in infants or may indicate hemolytic anemia, infection and storage diseases, lymphadenopathy and hepatosplenomegaly may be seen in malignancies or infections, e.g. malaria and tuberculosis. Petechiae, purpura, icterus or bossing may help to diagnose the cause of anemia.

Laboratory Investigation

It is important to know the age and detailed history of the child, this information will provide direction to the laboratory investigation. The complete hemogram will reveal if there is isolated anemia, or if other cell lines are affected. The red cell indices will demonstrate the type of anemia, mean corpuscular volume (MCV) denotes the size of the red cells, the mean corpuscular hemoglobin (MCH) and mean corpuscular hemoglobin content (MCHC) provide information on red cell hemoglobinization (Table 11.3). Using the MCV, anemias can be classified into microcytic, normocytic or macrocytic anemia (Figs 11.1, 11.2, 11.3). Abnormal red cell indices can exist in subjects even when the underlying disorder is not sufficiently severe to cause anemia. In thalassemia minor or iron deficiency, the MCV, MCH and MCHC are low and in megaloblastic anemia, the MCV is elevated. The red cell distribution width (RDW) denotes the variation in size of red blood cells, low RDW means all the red blood cells are uniform in size, while a large RDW shows that the cells vary in size greatly. Examination of the peripheral smear will reveal the red cell morphology, presence of schistocytes, polychromasia, specific red cell morphology or presence of parasites may help in making the diagnosis. The reticulocyte count helps to determine if anemia is caused by red cell destruction or decreased production, the corrected or absolute reticulocyte count is more useful (Table 11.4). When nutritional anemias are suspected, iron status, vitamin B12 and folic acid levels are determined. The reticulocyte count is decreased in bone marrow failure syndromes, transient erythroblastopenia of infancy and infections, e.g. parvovirus. In cases of anemia with increased reticulocyte count, a Coombs test will help to identify if this is due to immune or hereditary hemolytic anemia.

11

Table 11.3: Normal red cell indices in infancy and childhood

Age	*Red cell count (10^{12}/L)* Mean	–2 SD	*MCV (fl)* Mean	–2 SD	*MCH (pg)* Mean	–2 SD	*MCHC (g/dL)* Mean	–2 SD
Birth (cord blood)	4.7	3.9	108	98	34	31	33	30
1–3 d (capillary)	5.3	4.0	108	95	34	31	33	29
1 week	5.1	3.9	107	88	34	28	33	28
2 week	4.9	3.6	105	86	34	28	33	28
1 month	4.2	3.0	104	85	34	28	33	29
2 month	3.8	2.7	96	77	30	26	33	29
3–6 month	3.8	3.1	91	74	30	25	33	30
0.5–2 year	4.5	3.7	78	70	27	23	33	30
2–6 year	4.6	3.9	81	75	27	24	34	31
6–12 year	4.6	4.0	86	77	29	25	34	31
12–18 year, female	4.6	4.1	90	78	30	25	34	31
12–18 year, male	4.9	4.5	88	78	30	25	34	31

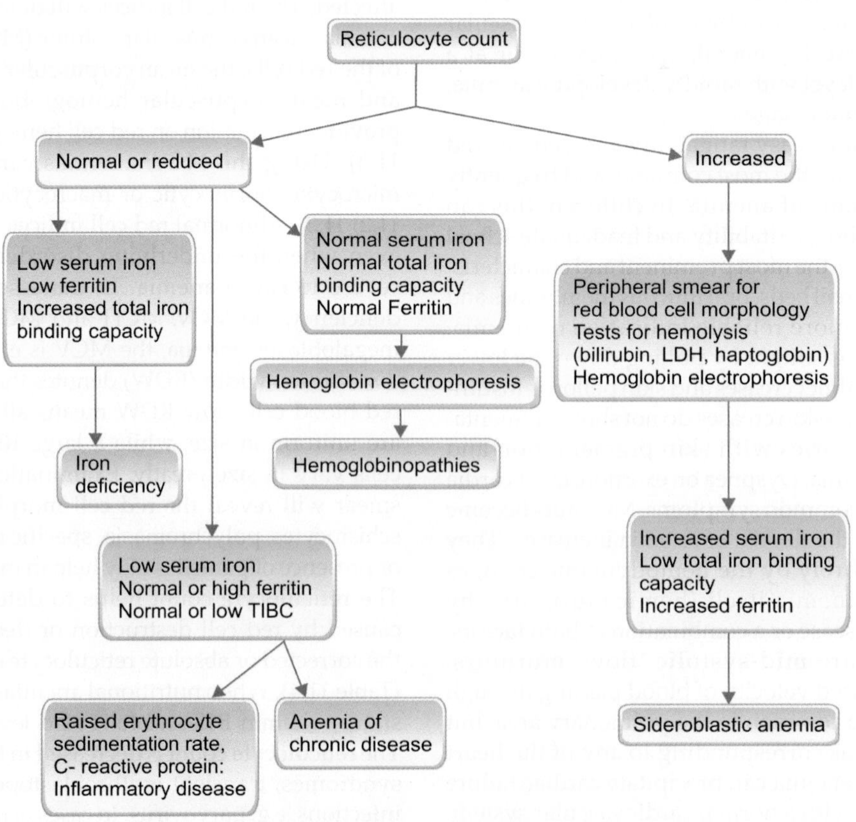

Fig. 11.1: Approach to microcytic anemia

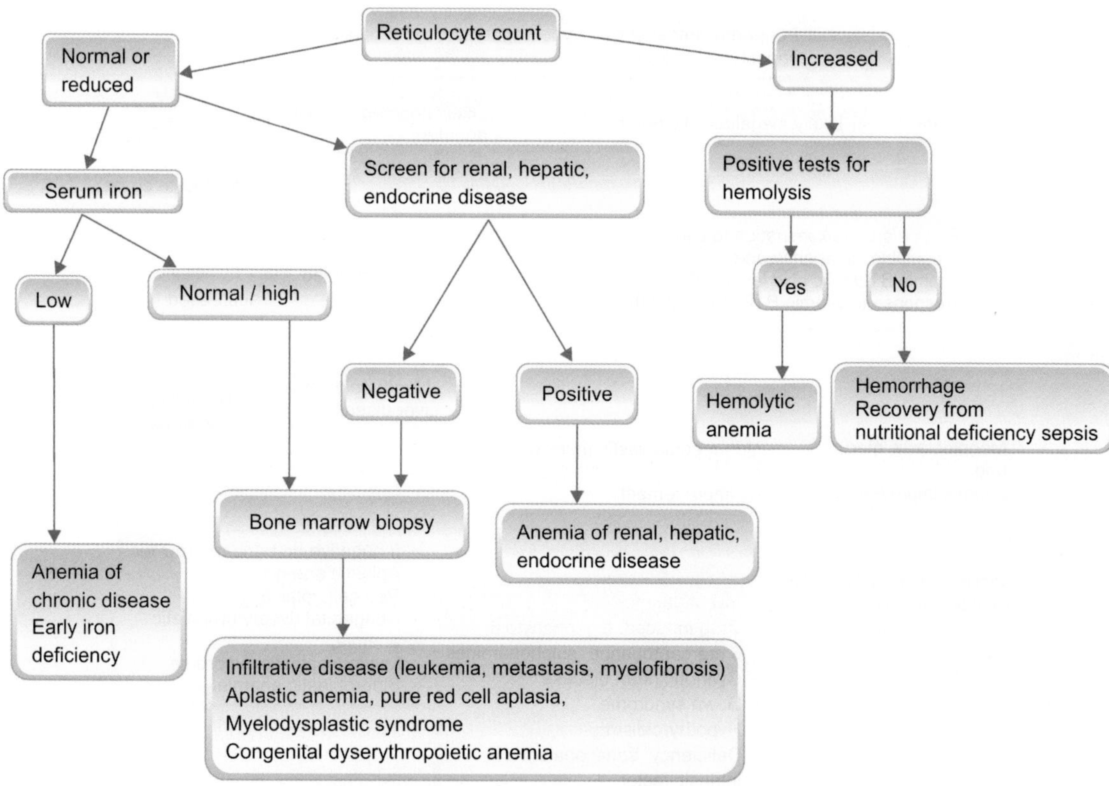

Fig. 11.2: Approach to normocytic anemia

Table 11.4: The utility of reticulocyte count for the evaluation of anemia

Normal reticulocyte count
Newborn 2–6%
Children 0.5–2%
Reticulocyte count should be corrected for the degree of anemia

$$\text{Corrected reticulocyte count} = \text{Patient reticulocyte count} \times \frac{\text{Patient hematocrit}}{\text{Normal hematocrit}}$$

Low reticulocyte count
Congenital or acquired, aplastic/hypoplastic anemia
Transient eythroblastopenia of childhood
Pure red cell aplasia
Bone marrow infiltration, e.g. malignancy, storage disorder

High reticulocyte count
Hemolysis
Hemorrhage
Splenic sequestration
Recovery from vitamin or iron deficiency
Sepsis

Suggested reading

1. NHFS-3 (2007) Government of India, WEBSITE http://www.nfhsindia.org/abt.html
2. Lokeshwar MR, Shah NK. IAP Speciality Series on Pediatric Hematology and Oncology (under IAP President Action Plan) (2006), *Approach to Anemia*, 3–17.

IRON DEFICIENCY ANEMIA

Iron deficiency anemia occurs when there is a decrease in total body iron content, severe enough to diminish erythropoiesis and cause anemia.

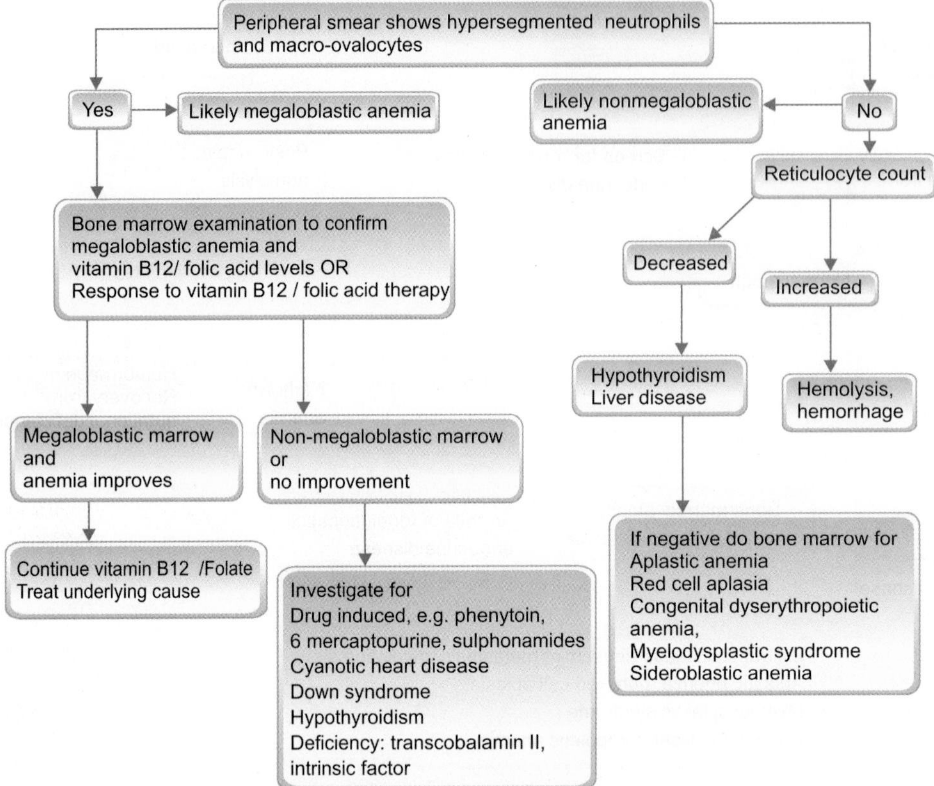

Fig. 11.3: Approach to macrocytic anemia

Pathophysiology

Diminished dietary iron absorption in the proximal small intestine or excessive loss of body iron can result in iron deficiency. Iron is essential for multiple metabolic processes, including oxygen transport, DNA synthesis, and electron transport. In severe iron deficiency, the iron containing enzymes are low and this can affect immune and tissue function. Iron deficiency anemia can result in diminished growth and learning and have serious consequences in children. Numerous dietary constituents make non-heme iron unabsorbable, e.g. phytates, phosphates and tannates.

Healthy newborn infants have a total body iron of 250 mg (approximately 80 parts per million, ppm); this decreases to approximately 60 ppm in the first 6 months of life. Body iron is regulated carefully by absorptive cells in the proximal small intestine, which alter iron absorption to match body losses of iron. Breast milk iron content is more bioavailable than cow's milk. Besides this fact, infants who consume cow's milk have more iron deficiency because bovine milk has a higher concentration of calcium, which competes with iron for absorption and they may have gastrointestinal blood loss due to cow's milk allergy. Multiple intercurrent infections such as hookworm infestation and malaria compound the problem.

Clinical Evaluation

A careful dietary history is important; enquire about type of milk, weaning foods and supplements. Pica increases the risk of helminthic parasites and lead poisoning. The common features of anemia are present in proportion to the severity and rate of development. Behavioral symptoms such as irritability, anorexia usually precede weakness, fatigue, leg cramps breathlessness and tachycardia. Congestive cardiac failure and splenomegaly may occur with severe, persistent, untreated iron deficiency anemia. Angular stomatitis, glossitis, koilonychia and platynychia are also seen in severe iron deficiency.

Laboratory Diagnosis

The evaluation of the peripheral blood smear (Figs 11.4 and 11.5) shows that red cells are microcytic, hypochromic, and show anisocytosis, poikilocytosis and increased RDW. The MCV and MCHC are reduced. Red cell number is reduced, unlike in thalassemia trait/minor where it is increased.

The serum iron is reduced while the total iron binding capacity (TIBC) is increased, transferrin saturation is reduced to less than 16% (normal range 25–50%). The reduction in serum ferritin occurs early, and correlates well with the total body iron stores. However, ferritin is an acute phase reactant and elevated in inflammatory

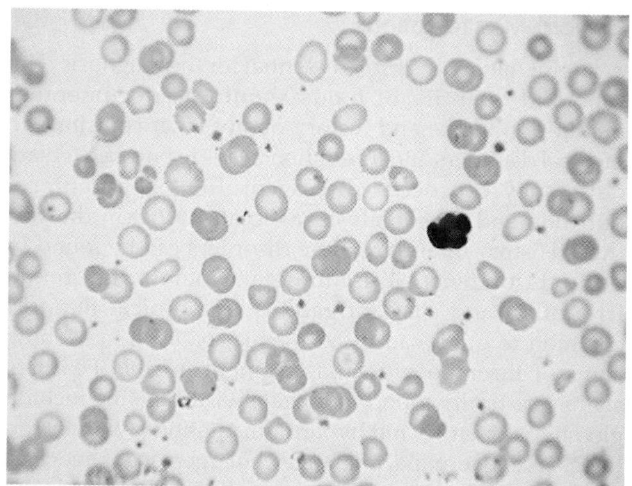

Fig. 11.4: Peripheral smear from a child with iron deficiency anemia, shows microcytosis (the red blood cells are smaller than the small lymphocyte in the field), hypochromia (central pallor >1/3rd of cell diameter), thrombocytosis, and a few ovalocytes and tear drop cells (moderate anisopoikilocytosis). Jenner-Giemsa x 1000

conditions hence may be falsely elevated in a sick child. High free erythroprotoporphyrin (FEP) is seen before anemia develops.

Treatment

The cause of anemia should be identified and corrected. Hookworm infestation is the most common cause of occult gastrointestinal blood loss in the rural population of India at all ages. Dietary counselling and treatment of any other causative factors are required to prevent recurrence or failure of therapy. Close follow-up is required to assess for adequate response and correction of anemia, this will help to identify iron therapy failure (Table 11.5).

Oral Medication

Oral iron preparations should be taken on an empty stomach or in between meals for best absorption. About 10–20% patients will develop gastrointestinal side effects such as nausea, epigastric discomfort, vomiting, constipation and diarrhea. Enteric-coated preparations have fewer side effects, but are also less efficacious and more expensive. The most effective and economical oral preparation is ferrous sulfate (20% elemental iron). In children, the dose for treatment of anemia is 3–6 mg/kg/day iron. The reticulocyte count increases within 72–96 hr after initiating therapy. After correction of anemia, oral iron should be continued for 4–6 months to replenish iron stores.

Table 11.5: Causes of refractory iron deficiency anemia

Poor compliance with therapy
Poorly absorbed iron preparations, e.g. enteric coated
Use of antacids or H_2 blockers causing achlorhydria
Interaction with food and medications
Associated vitamin B12 or folic acid deficiency
Underlying hemolytic anemia, inflammation or infections
Malabsorption states, e.g. celiac disease, giardiasis, *H. pylori* infection, autoimmune gastritis
High rate of ongoing blood loss
Sideroblastic anemia.

Parenteral Iron

The indications of parenteral iron therapy are limited to conditions such as (1) intolerance to oral iron, (2) malabsorption states and (3) ongoing blood loss at a rate where the oral replacement cannot match iron loss. If parenteral iron is indicated, then IV preparations are preferred over IM; iron sucrose IV preparations are safe and effective. They have been used in children with end stage renal disease on dialysis and inflammatory bowel disease. Iron sucrose is administered at a dose of 1–3 mg/kg diluted in 150 ml normal saline as a slow IV infusion over 30–90 minutes.

Dose for parenteral iron: The total dose of parenteral iron in milligrams is calculated as follows:
Iron required = Wt (kg) × 2.3 × (15 – patient hemoglobin in g/dl) + (500 to 1000) mg

The total calculated dose is given as divided doses.

Blood Transfusions

As iron deficiency anemia is readily corrected with medication, blood transfusions should be avoided in young, stable patients. Red cell transfusions are needed in emergency situations such as in patients where the rate of blood loss exceeds the expected rise of hemoglobin, for urgent surgery, hemorrhage or severe anemia with congestive cardiac failure. In very severe anemia with congestive cardiac failure, transfusions must be given slowly (2–3 ml/kg) with monitoring and diuretic therapy if necessary.

Suggested reading

1. Sachdeva HPS, Gera T, Nestel P. Effect of iron supplementation on mental and motor development in children: systemic review of randomized controlled trials. *Public Health Nutr* 2005; 8: 117–132.
2. Kapil US. Technical consultation on "Strategies for prevention and control of iron deficiency anemia amongst under three children in India". *Indian Pediatr* 2002;39:640–647.
3. Leijn E, Monnens LA, Cornelissen EA. Intravenous iron supplementation in children on hemodialysis. *J Nephrol* 2004; 17: 423–426.

MEGALOBLASTIC ANEMIA

Megaloblastic anemia is characterized by macrocytic red cells and erythroid precursors, which show nuclear dysmaturity. The common causes are deficiency of vitamin B12, (derived from cobalamin) and folic acid. The incidence varies with the dietary practices and socio-economic patterns. A study has put the incidence of folate deficiency as 6.8%, vitamin B12 as 32% and combined deficiency as 20% in north Indian children.

Pathophysiology

Megaloblastic changes affect all hematopoietic cell lines resulting in anemia, thrombocytopenia and leukopenia. DNA synthesis is impaired because of lack of methyltetrahydrofolate (a folate derivative), vitamin B12 plays an important role as cofactor, which is necessary for DNA base synthesis. The role of vitamin B12 as an enzyme cofactor and its effect on hematopoiesis is overcome by large doses of folic acid which may mask anemia but aggravate the neurological complications due to vitamin B12 deficiency.

Etiology

The two most common causes of megaloblastic anemia are vitamin B12 deficiency (cobalamin) and folic acid deficiency. Folate deficiency can be caused by decreased ingestion, impaired absorption (e.g. celiac disease, malabsorption states), impaired utilization (e.g. methotrexate, 6-mercaptopurine, trimethoprim, azathioprine, phenytoin and other anticonvulsants) (Table 11.6) and increased requirement (e.g. infancy, hyperthyroidism and chronic hemolytic disease). Vitamin B12 deficiency can be caused by decreased ingestion, impaired absorption (e.g. intestinal parasites, intrinsic intestinal disease, failure to release B12 from protein, intrinsic factor deficiency), or impaired utilization (congenital enzyme deficiencies, e.g. orotic aciduria). In recent years, vitamin B12 deficiency has been described in patients with HIV infection, with or without acquired immunodeficiency syndrome (AIDS).

Nutritional deficiency is far more common in vegan families (vegetarian with little or no dairy products) and those who consume only goat's milk (folate deficient). In infants, it is related to maternal deficiency with resultant inadequate body stores and prolonged exclusive breastfeeding (breast milk is a poor source of B12 and is associated with reduced access to other foods). Giardia infection has been demonstrated to cause folate malabsorption. *Helicobacter pylori* infections have been implicated in B12 malabsorption amongst adults.

Table 11.6: Drugs that cause megaloblastic anemia
Anticonvulsants: Phenytoin, phenobarbital, primidone.
Purine analogs: 6-Mercaptopurine, 6-thioguanine, azathioprine.
Antifolates: Methotrexate.
Ribonucleotide reductase inhibitors: Hydroxyurea, cytarabine arabinoside.
Pyrimidine analogs: Zidovudine, 5-fluorouracil.
Drugs that depress folate metabolism: trimethoprim, pyrimethamine.
Drugs that affect cobalamin metabolism: p-Aminosalicylic acid, metformin, neomycin.

Clinical Manifestations

A careful dietary history is essential for the diagnosis. The type and quantity of foods should be documented. Medication intake and history of any other contributing medical disorders and infestation needs to be taken. Folate deficiency can occur during prolonged parenteral nutrition and hemodialysis, as folate is lost in dialysis fluid. History of autoimmune disorders can be found in patients of pernicious anemia. Anemia, anorexia, irritability and easy fatigability are clinical features common to other causes of anemia; patients may show signs of thrombocytopenia and neutropenia. Features characteristically found in megaloblastic anemia include glossitis, stomatitis and hyperpigmentation of the skin on knuckles and terminal phalanges, enlargement of liver and spleen (30–40% cases). Neurologic signs may precede the onset of anemia. Petechiae and hemorrhagic manifestations are reported in 25%. Pancytopenia and hepatosplenomegaly can make it difficult to differentiate from leukemia. The child should be evaluated for signs of malabsorption such as weight loss, abdominal distention, diarrhea and steatorrhea. Abdominal scars from ileal resections may be present. Rarely inherited metabolic disorders may cause megaloblastic anemia (Table 11.7).

Neurologic examination may reveal loss of position and vibratory sensation, which are the earliest neurologic signs. Later other posterior and lateral column deficits may be found. Memory loss, confusion and neuropsychiatric symptoms can occur. Persistence of neurological sequelae can be found even after treatment of the deficiency.

Laboratory Evaluation

A complete hemogram with red cell indices reveal macrocytic red cells (>110 fl highly suggestive of

Table 11.7: Metabolic causes of megaloblastic anemia
Inborn errors of cobalamin metabolism
Selective malabsorption of cobalamin with normal secretion of intrinsic factor (Imerslünd-Grasbeck syndrome).
Other causes: Congenital intrinsic factor deficiency, TCII deficiency.
Methylmalonic aciduria.
Homocystinuria.
Inborn errors of folate metabolism
Congenital folate malabsorption
Dihydrofolate reductase deficiency.
N5-methyl tetrahydrofolate—Homocysteine methyltransferase deficiency.
Other inborn errors
Hereditary orotic aciduria.
Lesch-Nyhan syndrome.
Thiamine-responsive megaloblastic anemia.

megaloblastic anemia) and cytopenias. Hypersegmented neutrophils (nuclei with ≥ 6 lobes) may be seen. The reticulocyte count is important and should be performed. If available, serum B12 and folate levels are assayed. Investigation for contributing cause if indicated should be performed. The Schilling test requires radioactive labelled B12 for identification of pernicious anemia and evaluation of deficiency states, rarely needed in children.

Bone marrow evaluation should be performed in patients with more than one abnormal hematological cell line. It can help to rule out other disorders such as leukemia, myelodysplasia and aplastic anemia. In megaloblastic anemia the bone marrow is cellular (Fig. 11.5) and show red cell precursors with nuclear-cytoplasmic asynchrony; granulocyte precursors may also be abnormal. Serum chemistry shows elevated lactate dehydrogenase and bilirubin.

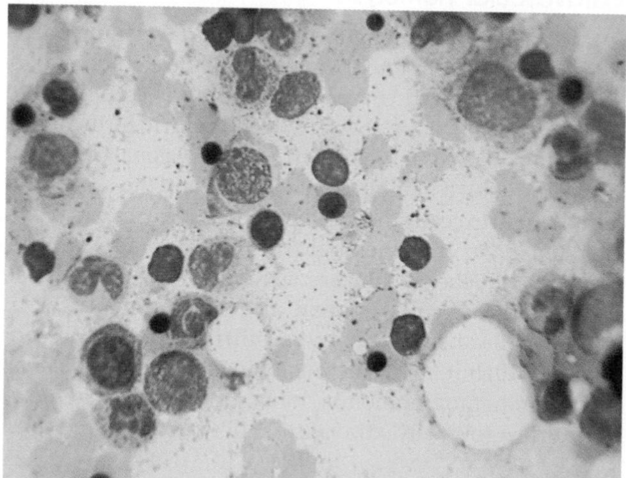

Fig. 11.5: Bone marrow aspirate from a patient with vitamin B12 deficiency shows erythroid hyperplasia, megaloblastosis and a giant myeloid form (top left). Jenner-Giemsa x 1000

Differential Diagnosis

Other causes of macrocytosis should be considered in the differential diagnosis. These include aplastic anemia and other marrow failure syndromes (pure red cell aplasia, Fanconi anemia, transient erythroblastopenia of childhood), congenital dyserythropoietic anemia, chronic liver disease, hypothyroidism, cold agglutinin disease, myelodysplastic syndrome and HIV infection.

Treatment

The treatment depends on the underlying cause. If the cause cannot be elucidated, therapeutic doses of folate (1–5 mg/day) should be administered with addition of vitamin B12 (1000 μg). Only folate therapy may correct the anemia, but will not correct cobalamin-induced neurological disorder and result in the progression of neuropsychiatric complications. Folate deficiency due to dietary insufficiency or increased demands is best treated with folate supplements. Folate deficiency caused by the use of anti-folate medications is best remedied by reducing or eliminating the implicating drug and addition of supplementation. In celiac disease, treatment requires exclusion of dietary gliadin and adequate supplementation. Folate is available as a 5 mg tablet and overdose is not associated with adverse effects; a dose of 1–5 mg/day is recommended for 3–4 weeks.

Vitamin B12 is administered parenterally at a dose of 1 mg (1000 μg) IM. Follow up will show decrease in MCV, reticulocytosis and improvement in platelet and neutrophil counts within a few days of therapy. In one study, tremors and extrapyramidal toxicity have been reported in young children, lower doses (250 μg) can be used in infants. In patients with pernicious anemia and malabsorption, vitamin B12 (1000 μg) is given parenterally daily for 2 weeks, weekly until the hematocrit value is normal and then monthly for life. Patients with neurological complications should receive 1000 μg every day for 2 weeks, then every 2 weeks for 6 months and monthly for life. Oral supplements can be administered; however absorption is variable and may be insufficient in some patients. In dietary insufficiency, no standard duration of therapy has been defined. Dietary counselling may be attempted; however diet may not be altered due to social and cultural reasons. Following correction of anemia, vitamin B12 supplements are recommended lifelong (oral supplements daily or parenteral dose every 3–12 months).

Suggested reading

1. Chandra J, Jain V, Narayan S, Sharma S. Folate and cobalamin deficiency in megaloblastic anemia in children. Indian Pediatrics 2002; 39: 453–457.
2. Stabler SP, Allen RH. Vitamin B_{12} deficiency as a world wide problem. Annu Rev Nutr 2004;24:299–326.

APPROACH TO HEMOLYTIC ANEMIAS

The term hemolytic anemia is limited to conditions in which the rate of red cell destruction is accelerated and the ability of the bone marrow to respond to the anemia is unimpaired. Under maximal stimulation, the normal marrow is capable of increasing its production rate about six to eight times its basal level. The reticulocyte count is useful in determining the rate of erythroid regeneration in response to red cell destruction. The normal reticulocyte count value in the newborn is 3.2 ± 1.4% and in children 1.2 ± 0.7%.

Clinical Signs

In acute hemolysis, symptoms are related to the rate of fall of hemoglobin. In rapidly occurring hemolysis the symptoms are more numerous and pronounced. Evidence of anemia as seen by weakness, pallor, fatigue may be seen. In some hemolytic anemias, jaundice is a prominent finding and red urine occurs in intravascular hemolysis. Splenomegaly is seen in autoimmune and many congenital types of hemolytic anemias. The presence of gall stones (spherocytosis), hemolytic or thalassemic facies (Fig. 11.6)

11

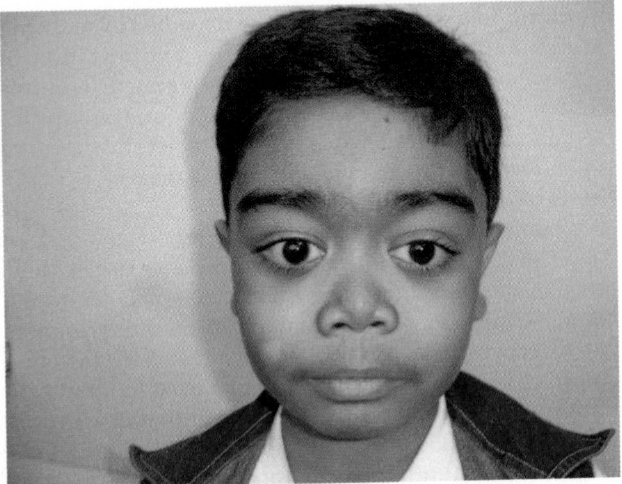

Fig. 11.6: Hemolytic anemia. Child with hemolytic anemia, showing hemolytic facies and icterus

and leg ulcers (sickle cell), if present can help to lead the laboratory investigations, however confirmatory tests are still required.

Laboratory Manifestations

Laboratory findings in hemolytic anemia can be divided into: (i) increase in erythrocyte destruction, (ii) compensatory increase in the rate of erythropoiesis, and (iii) specific features for particular types of hemolytic anemia (Tables 11.8 and 11.9).

An elevated corrected reticulocyte count may be the only manifestation of mild hemolytic anemia. A direct antiglobin (direct Coombs) test is positive in most patients with immune hemolytic anemias. A positive test means that the erythrocyte is coated with IgG or C3 component of complement. The test may be negative in 2–5% patients with immune hemolytic anemia. Haptoglobin and hemopexin are proteins, which bind to hemoglobin and heme released from red cells following their destruction. The protein complexes formed after intravascular hemolysis are removed by circulation. As a consequence, haptoglobin and hemopexin levels are low in patients who have hemolytic anemia. When haptoglobin is saturated, free plasma hemoglobin can be detected. While elevated indirect bilirubin levels are suggestive of hemolysis, the levels are elevated only when liver function is impaired or if hemolysis is extensive.

Table 11.8: Laboratory signs of accelerated erythrocyte destruction
Fall in blood hemoglobin level at a rate > 1.0 g/dl/week
Increased catabolism of heme
Increased serum unconjugated bilirubin level
Increased rate of urobilinogen excretion
Increased serum lactate dehydrogenase
Reduced haptoglobin and hemopexin
Reduced glycosylated hemoglobin
Decreased erythrocyte life span (radio-isotope labeling Cr^{51})

Table 11.9: Laboratory signs of accelerated erythropoiesis
In peripheral blood
Polychromasia /reticulocytosis
Macrocytosis
Increased nucleated red cells
Bone marrow
Erythroid hyperplasia
Ferrokinetic
Increased plasma iron turnover
Increased erythrocyte iron turnover

Features of Intravascular and Extravascular Hemolysis

Intravascular hemolysis occurs when the lysing RBCs release hemoglobin into the plasma (hemoglobinemia). A part of the circulating free hemoglobin is converted to methemoglobin, which binds with albumin to form methemalbumin, this confers a brown color to plasma for several days following a hemolytic episode. When the amount of hemoglobin exceeds the haptoglobin binding capacity it is excreted in the urine (hemoglobinuria), to some extent it is reabsorbed in the proximal renal tubules. The loss of heme laden tubular cells is seen as hemosiderinuria. In extravascular hemolysis, hyperbilirubinemia is present (Table 11.10) but no free hemoglobin is seen in the plasma. Hence no hemoglobinemia, hemoglobinuria or hemosiderinuria is found in extravascular destruction of red cells.

Table 11.10: Features of intravascular hemolysis
Increased unconjugated bilirubin
Hemoglobinemia
Hemoglobinuria
Hemosiderinuria
Reduced serum haptoglobin, hemopexin
Methemalbumin

The peripheral smear is useful in evaluation; it may show malarial parasites, spherocytes are seen in hereditary spherocytosis, autoimmune hemolytic anemia and following transfusion, presence of bite cells suggest glucose-6-phosphate dehydrogenase enzyme (G6PD) deficiency, microcytosis with fragmented red cells suggest thalassemia and thrombocytopenia with schistocytes (fragmented red cells) in disseminated intravascular coagulation. Specific tests such as hemoglobin electrophoresis, osmotic fragility, enzyme assays for G6PD and pyruvate kinase deficiency, assay for CD55/59 for paroxysmal nocturnal hemoglobinuria are required for the workup (Table 11.11).

Table 11.11: Causes of hemolytic anemias

Acquired
Mechanical Macroangiopathic: Artificial heart valves, march hemoglobinuria. Microangiopathic: Disseminated intravascular coagulation, hemolytic uremic syndrome, thrombotic thrombocytopenic purpura. *Infections*: malaria, kala azar, *Clostridium welchii*, etc. *Antibody mediated* Warm/cold type autoimmune hemolytic anemia. Transfusion reactions, hemolytic disease of newborn. Drugs, e.g. cefotetan, ceftriaxone. *Hypersplenism* *Cryopathic states*: cold agglutinin disease, paroxysmal cold hemoglobinuria. *Physical and chemical injury:* burns, snake bite; lead, arsenic toxicity. *Red cell:* Paroxysmal nocturnal hemoglobinuria
Hereditary
Hemoglobinopathies: thalassemia, sickle cell disease *Red cell enzyme defects*: glucose-6-phosphate dehydrogenase deficiency *Cytoskeletal membrane disorders*: hereditary spherocytosis. *Unstable hemoglobinopathies.* *Lipid membrane defects*: abetalipoproteinemia *Porphyrias.*

Hemolytic disorders may be divided into inherited and acquired varieties. This classification has a pathogenetic significance because the nature of hereditary lesions differs from that of acquired. Most intrinsic defects are inherited; extrinsic defects are acquired. Exceptions to this generalization include paroxysmal nocturnal hemoglobinuria, an acquired disorder characterized by an intrinsic red cell defect.

Management

During an acute attack of hemolysis, it is important to maintain fluid balance and renal output. Management of shock is by the usual appropriate measures, but blood transfusions, so useful in acute anemia of other types, must be used with caution in the treatment of patients with acquired hemolytic anemias. Even with careful blood matching, destruction of the transfused blood with an increase in the burden on the kidneys and sometimes thromboses may occur. Acute autoimmune hemolytic anemia is treated with steroids (prednisone 1–2 mg/kg/day), which should be tapered over several months, once the patient has demonstrated resolution of ongoing hemolysis. In chronic hemolysis the etiology should be investigated and treated appropriately.

HEREDITARY SPHEROCYTOSIS

Several membrane protein defects have been identified in hereditary spherocytosis. Many of these result in instability of spectrin and ankyrin, the major skeletal membrane proteins. The degree of skeletal membrane protein deficiency correlates with the degree of hemolysis. Structural changes due to membrane protein deficiency, lead to membrane instability, loss of surface area, abnormal membrane permeability and reduced red cell deformability. These defects are accentuated by metabolic depletion; this is demonstrated by the increase in osmotic fragility after a 24–hr incubation of blood at 37°C. The spleen is the site of destruction of these non-deformable erythrocytes.

Patients with hereditary spherocytosis have a mild to moderate chronic hemolytic anemia. The MCV is decreased and MCHC is increased due to cellular dehydration. The red cell distribution width is increased due to the presence of spherocytes and increased reticulocytes. These patients present with jaundice, the degree and age of onset varies. Splenomegaly is found in over 75% patients. Gallstones are frequently found, the risk of pigment calculi increases with age.

Patients require life long folic acid supplementation at a dose of 1–5 mg/day to ensure that they do not become folate deficient due to the high turnover rate of erythropoiesis. Splenectomy does not cure the hemolytic disorder but may reduce the degree of hemolysis. It is the treatment of choice in patients who have severe hemolysis and high transfusion requirement. In patients with mild hemolysis, splenectomy should be delayed or avoided. In certain patients who have an excessively large spleen, splenectomy may diminish the risk of traumatic splenic rupture. In general splenectomy is performed after 6 yr of age with pre-surgical immunization for *Hemophilus influenzae* type B, *Streptococcus pneumoniae* and *Neisseria meningitidis*. Following splenectomy, prophylactic penicillin is administered to prevent sepsis till early adulthood.

As with other hemolytic anemias, patients with hereditary spherocytosis are susceptible to aplastic crisis secondary to infection with human parvovirus B19. This organism selectively invades erythroid progenitor cells and causes a transient arrest in red cell production. Patients usually recover in 4–6 weeks.

ABNORMALITIES IN RED CELL GLYCOLYSIS

Glucose is the primary metabolic substrate for erythrocytes. Since the mature red cells do not contain mitochondria, glucose is metabolized by two chief anerobic pathways: the Embden Meyerhof pump and the hexose monophosphate shunt. The former accounts for 90% of glucose utilization. The inability to maintain enough ATP required for cellular functions such as deformability, membrane lipid turnover and permeability results in shortened red cell life. The hexose shunt is responsible for the remaining 10% of glucose metabolism, this generates substrates which protect the red cells against oxidant injury. A defective pathway causes accumulation of oxidized hemoglobin (Heinz bodies), lipids and membrane proteins in red cells, resulting in hemolysis. The

11

reticulocyte count is raised and bone marrow shows erythroid hyperplasia. A useful screening test is autohemolysis and diagnosis is by specific enzyme assays.

Pyruvate Kinase Deficiency

Pyruvate kinase deficiency is the most common Embden Meyerhof pump enzyme defect, inherited in an autosomal recessive manner. Homozygotes present with splenomegaly, icterus and hemolytic anemia and heterozygotes are asymptomatic. The clinical spectrum is variable. Splenectomy is a therapeutic option in pyruvate kinase deficient patients. The reticulocyte count increases dramatically after splenectomy. Folic acid supplementation is required to prevent megaloblastic complications due to relative folate deficiency. Splenectomy does not stop the hemolytic process.

Glucose-6-phosphate Dehydrogenase Deficiency

Glucose-6-phosphate dehydrogenase (G6PD) deficiency is the most common red cell enzyme deficiency. It is a sex linked disorder with full expression in affected males. Many variants of G6PD deficiency have been identified by their biochemical and molecular differences. They vary in antioxidant reserve and enzyme levels. After an oxidant exposure, hemoglobin is oxidized to methemoglobin and denatured to form intracellular inclusions also known as Heinz bodies. These Heinz bodies get attached to the red cell membrane and aggregate intrinsic membrane proteins such as band 3. The reticuloendothelial cells identify these changes as a new antigenic site on the red cell membrane. They ingest a part of the red cell, resulting in a partially phagocytozed 'bite cell'; this process shortens the life of the erythrocyte. The hallmarks of a hemolytic crisis are pallor, icterus, hemoglobinemia, hemoglobinuria and splenomegaly. Plasma haptoglobin and hemopexin are low. The child may present with jaundice in the neonatal period. The peripheral blood smear shows fragmented bite cells and polychromasia. Special stains demonstrate Heinz bodies during the initial few days of hemolysis. The diagnosis of G6PD deficiency is based on family history, clinical findings, laboratory features and exposure to oxidants prior to the hemolytic event. Confirmation of the diagnosis is by quantitative enzyme assay or molecular gene analysis. Management consists of supportive care for the acute crisis (hydration, transfusions if needed and monitoring) along with folic acid supplementation. Counselling to avoid oxidant drugs in the future is imperative (Table 11.12).

AUTOIMMUNE HEMOLYTIC ANEMIA

This arises as an autoimmune phenomenon targeting the red cells. It may arise as an isolated problem or as a complication of an infection (viral hepatitis B, upper respiratory tract viral infections, mononucleosis and cytomegalovirus infection); systemic lupus erythematosus (SLE) or other autoimmune syndromes; immunodeficiency states; or malignancies.

Table 11.12: Drugs which can cause oxidant stress and hemolysis in glucose-6-phosphate dehydrogenase deficient patients

Sulfonamides: Sulfamethoxazole
Antimalarials: Primaquin, pamaquin
Others: Nitofurantoin, dapsone, nalidixic acid, furazolidine.

Features

The disease usually has an acute onset, manifested by weakness, pallor, fatigue and dark urine. Jaundice is a prominent finding and splenomegaly is often present (Table 11.13). Some cases are chronic. Clinical evidence of an underlying causative disease (e.g. SLE, HIV) may be present.

Table 11.13: Clinical and laboratory features for diagnosis of autoimmune hemolytic anemia

Pallor, fatigue, jaundice and dark urine
Splenomegaly
Positive direct Coombs test
Reticulocytosis
Spherocytosis

Laboratory Findings

The anemia is normochromic and normocytic. It may vary from mild to severe (hemoglobin <5 g/dL); the reticulocyte count is increased. Spherocytes and nucleated red cells may be seen on the peripheral blood smear. Other laboratory data consistent with hemolysis may be present such as increased lactic dehydrogenase, indirect and total bilirubin, aspartate aminotransferase and urinary urobilinogen. Intravascular hemolysis is indicated by hemoglobinemia or hemoglobinuria. Examination of the bone marrow shows marked erythroid hyperplasia, but is seldom required.

Serologic studies are helpful in defining pathophysiology, planning therapeutic strategies, and assessing prognosis. In almost all cases, the direct Coombs test is positive. Further evaluation allows distinction into one of three syndromes. The presence of IgG on the patient's red blood cells, maximal *in vitro* antibody activity at 37°C, specificity for Rh-like antigen constitute warm autoimmune hemolytic anemia with extravascular destruction by the reticuloendothelial system. In contrast, the detection of complement alone on red blood cells, optimal reactivity *in vitro* at 4°C, i or I antigen specificity are diagnostic of cold autoimmune hemolytic anemia with intravascular hemolysis. Paroxysmal cold hemoglobinuria usually is identical to cold autoimmune hemolytic anemia except for antigen specificity -P and the exhibition of *in vitro* hemolysis. Paroxysmal cold hemoglobinuria is associated with significant infections, such as mycoplasma, Epstein-Barr virus and cytomegalovirus.

Complications

The anemia may be very severe and result in cardiovascular collapse, requiring emergency management. The complications of the underlying disease such as SLE or immunodeficiency states may be present.

Treatment

Medical management of the underlying disease is important. Most patients with warm autoimmune hemolytic anemia (in which hemolysis is extravascular) respond to prednisone 1 mg/kg for 4 weeks or till hemoglobin is stable. After the initial treatment, the dose of corticosteroids is tapered slowly over 4–6 months. Patients may respond to 1 g of intravenous immune globulin (IVIG) per kilogram per day for 2 days, however the response to IVIG is not sustained. Although the rate of remission with splenectomy may be as high as 50% particularly in warm autoimmune hemolytic anemia, this should be carefully considered in younger patients and avoided until other treatments have been tried. In severe cases unresponsive to more conventional therapy, immunosuppressive agents such as cyclophosphamide, azathioprine and cyclosporine may be tried alone or in combination with corticosteroids. Danazol is effective in 50–60% of cases of chronic hemolytic anemia. Refractory cases may respond to rituximab (monoclonal antibody to CD20) or hematopoietic stem cell transplantation.

Patients with cold autoimmune hemolytic anemia and paroxysmal cold hemoglobinuria are less likely to respond to corticosteroids or IVIG. These syndromes are associated with infections and have an acute, self-limited course; supportive care may be all that is necessary. Plasma exchange is effective in severe cold autoimmune (IgM) hemolytic anemia and may be helpful in severe cases because the offending antibody has an intravascular distribution.

Transfusion may be necessary because of the complication of severe anemia but should be monitored closely. In most patients, cross match compatible blood will not be found, and the least incompatible unit should be identified by the blood bank. Transfusions must be conducted carefully, beginning with a test dose.

Prognosis

In general, children with warm autoimmune hemolytic anemia are at greater risk for more severe and chronic disease with higher morbidity and mortality rates. Hemolysis and positive Coombs test may continue for months or years. Patients with cold autoimmune hemolytic anemia or paroxysmal cold hemoglobinuria are more likely to have acute self-limited disease (<3 months). Paroxysmal cold hemoglobinuria is almost always associated with infection (e.g. with mycoplasma, cytomegalovirus or Ebstein Barr virus).

Suggested reading

Ware RE, Gallager PG, Lux SE, Mentzer WC, Luzzatto L. Hemolytic anemias. In: *Nathan and Oski's Hematology of Infancy and Childhood*, 6th edn. Eds Nathan DG, Orkin SH, et al. WB Saunders, Philadelphia, 2003;519–712.

THALASSEMIAS

The word thalassemia is a Greek term derived from *thalassa,* which means 'the sea' (referring to the Mediterranean sea), and *emia,* which means 'related to blood'. Thalassemias are the commonest monogenic diseases, due to globin gene defects. The molecular biology and genetics of the thalassemia syndromes have revealed more than 200 mutations. These diseases are also commonly found in population from Southeast Asia to Africa. The carrier rates for β thalassemia reported in North Indians, varies in different ethnic groups from 3–17%. This section will discuss β thalassemia.

The major hemoglobin (Hb) found in children after one year of age, Hb A, constitutes approximately 95%, and a minor component, Hb A_2, accounts for 2–3%. The main hemoglobin in fetal life is HbF of which only traces remain after one-year of life.

Pathophysiology

The thalassemias are inherited disorders of hemoglobin synthesis that result from an alteration in the rate of globin chain production. A decrease in the rate of production of a globin (α, β, γ, δ) impedes hemoglobin synthesis and creates an imbalance with normally produced globin chains. Because two types of chains (α and non-α) pair with each other at a ratio close to 1:1 to form normal hemoglobin, an excess of the normally produced type is present and accumulates in the cell as an unstable product, leading to the early destruction of the red cell.

The type of thalassemia usually carries the name of the under produced chain or chains. The reduction may vary from a slight decrease to a complete absence. When β chains are produced at a lower rate, the thalassemia is termed β+, whereas β–0 thalassemia indicates a complete absence of production of β chains from the involved allele. The disease is inherited in a Mendelian recessive fashion. Advances in knowledge of molecular genetics have led to considerable progress in control of thalassemias. Carriers are relatively easy to identify and screen. Prenatal diagnosis and genetic counselling programs in many countries have lead to a dramatic reduction in the frequency of births of children with thalassemias major. More awareness is required amongst health professionals and the public to control this disease in India.

Presentation

Thalassemia should be considered in any child with hypochromic, microcytic anemia that does not respond to iron supplementation. Children with β thalassemia major usually demonstrate no symptoms until about three to six months of age (when β chains are needed to pair with α chains to form Hb A, after γ chains production is turned off). However the condition may not be recognized because of the delay in cessation of Hb F production till 3–5 years of age in some cases. Severe pallor and hepatosplenomegaly are almost always present. Icterus is usually not present but mild to moderate jaundice may be found due to liver dysfunction from iron overload and chronic hepatitis.

Symptoms of severe anemia such as intolerance to exercise, irritability, heart murmur or even signs of frank heart failure may be present. Bony abnormalities, such as frontal bossing, prominent facial bones and dental malocclusion are usually present (Fig. 11.6). The ineffective erythropoiesis creates a hypermetabolic state associated with fever and failure to thrive. Hyperuricemia may be encountered.

Spectrum of Thalassemia

Thalassemia Trait

Patients have mild anemia, abnormal red blood cell indices, and abnormal hemoglobin HPLC results with elevated levels of Hb A_2 or Hb F, or increase of both. The peripheral blood film examination usually reveals marked hypochromia, microcytosis (without anisocytosis which is usually found with iron deficiency anemia) and presence of target cells.

Thalassemia Intermedia

This condition is usually due to a compound heterozygous state, resulting in anemia of intermediate severity, which usually does not require regular blood transfusions. This is primarily a clinical diagnosis and requires monitoring of the child over time to see the clinical evolution of disease.

Thalassemia Major

This condition is characterized by transfusion-dependent anemia, splenomegaly, bone deformities, growth retardation and hemolytic facies in untreated or inadequately treated individuals. Examination of the peripheral blood smear shows severe hypochromia, microcytosis, marked anisocytosis, fragmented red blood cells, polychromasia, nucleated RBCs and occasionally immature leukocytes. Organomegaly is reduced in well transfused patients, but is marked in patients receiving irregular or inadequate transfusion support.

Thalassemia associated with β chain Structural Variants

The most significant condition in this group of thalassemic syndromes is the Hb E/b thalassemias. Patients with Hb E/b thalassemia may present with severe symptoms identical to that of patients with b thalassemia major or a milder course similar to that of patients with thalassemia intermedia or minor. The variation in severity can be explained because of the different genotypes, (i.e. b+ or b0), the co-inheritance of an a thalassemia gene, level of Hb F and the presence of other modifying genes.

Laboratory Studies

Complete blood count and peripheral blood film examination is usually sufficient to suspect the diagnosis. In thalassemias major/intermedia, the Hb level ranges from 2–8 g/dL. MCV and MCH are significantly low. Reticulocyte count is elevated to 5–8% and leukocytosis is usually present. A shift to the left is also encountered, reflecting the hemolytic process. The platelet count is usually normal, unless the spleen is markedly enlarged and causing hypersplenism.

Peripheral blood film examination reveals hypochromasia and microcytosis, polychromatophilic cells, nucleated red blood cells, basophilic stippling, and occasional immature leukocytes (Figs 11.7 to 11.9). A hemoglobin high performance liquid chromatography

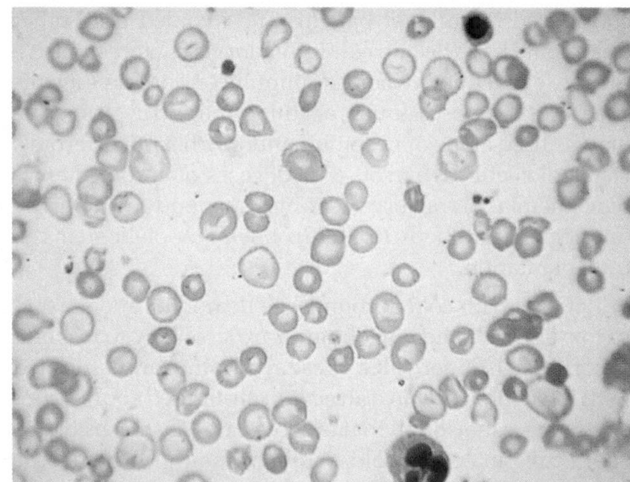

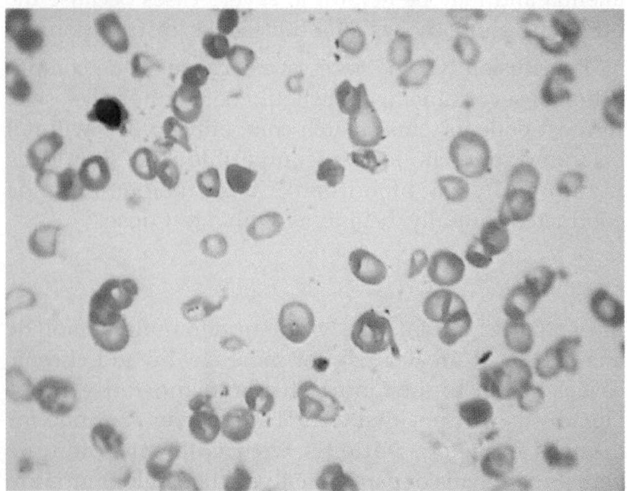

Figs 11.7 and 11.8: Perpheral smears from a transfusion dependent patient with beta thalassemia major showing marked anisopoikilocytosis, microcytosis, hypochromia, polychromatophilia, nucleated red blood cells and few fragmented erythrocytes. Jenner-Giemsa x 1000

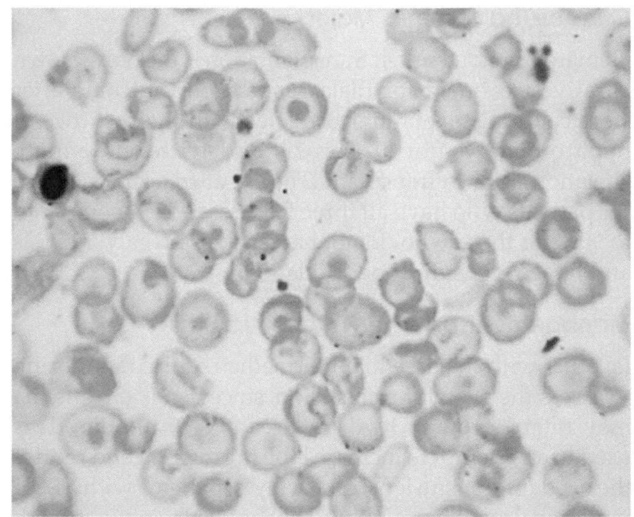

Fig. 11.9: Peripheral smear from an asymptomatic patient with hemoglobin E disease, showing microcytosis, hypochromia, target cells and a nucleated red blood cells. Jenner-Giemsa x 1000

(HPLC) must be sent prior to the first blood transfusion. The HPLC evaluation confirms the diagnosis in β thalassemia. There is absence of HbA and elevation of HbF; the level of Hb A2 is not important for the diagnosis of thalassemia major. Elevated Hb A2 fraction (> 3.5–3.9%)is an important finding for the diagnosis of thalassemia trait.

Management and Common Complications

The introduction of hematopoietic stem cell transplantation offers the possibility of cure in severe forms of thalassemia, however this is available only to a relatively small number of patients. Regular treatment with blood transfusion and iron-chelating agents, if pursued vigorously, will allow these children to survive into adulthood. The major problems to be resolved are the safety of blood supply and huge cost of life long iron chelating medications.

Patients with severe thalassemia require transfusion therapy. Blood transfusion should be initiated at an early age when the child is asymptomatic and attempts should be made to keep pre-transfusion hemoglobin above 9–10 g/dl (to promote growth and prevent deformity). Chelation therapy to deal with the accumulated iron overload is vital to prevent iron overload and organ dysfunction. A normal diet is recommended, with supplements of folic acid, ascorbic acid and alpha-tocopherol (vitamin E). Iron preparations should not be given. Drinking tea with meals has been shown to decrease absorption of iron in the gut.

Blood Transfusions and Infections

After multiple transfusions many patients develop reactions, these may be minimized by using leukocyte filters during transfusion or better still by having the blood bank preparing leukocyte poor packed red cells. Administration of acetaminophen and diphenhydramine hydrochloride before each transfusion will minimize febrile or allergic reactions. The major complications of blood transfusions are those related to transmission of infections-hepatitis B, C and HIV. Hepatitis B vaccination and regular assessment of the hepatitis and HIV status are part of routine care. Folate supplementation is required as with other hemolytic anemias for all of these patients and regular ferritin levels to monitor iron overload status.

Lactoferrin is a prominent component of the granules of polymorphonuclear leukocytes, it is bacteriostatic for many pathogens. The very high transferrin saturations attained in patients with iron overload compromise the bacteriostatic properties of the protein. *Yersenia enterocolitica* infection can occur in iron overloaded patients. This infection presents with fever, diarrhea and should be treated with gentamicin and cotrimoxazole. Other important infections which may occur are mucormycosis (*Rhizopus oryazae*) and *Listeria monocytogenes.*

Iron Overload

Iron overload is the major cause of morbidity and organ toxicity. The excessive load of iron is due to increased gastrointestinal iron absorption as well as repeated transfusions. Hence, avoidance of transfusions, as is done by many families, will not eliminate the iron overload. Patients with iron overload demonstrate signs of endocrinopathy caused by iron deposits. Diabetes, and dysfunction of thyroid and parathyroid glands, decreased growth and lack of sexual maturation are common.

The simplest method for monitoring of iron status is by serum ferritin measurements, however liver and cardiac iron may be underestimated by this test. For correct iron status evaluation a liver biopsy, liver MRI and echocardiography can be done. A highly accurate and noninvasive tool to assess the heart iron status is the cardiac T2 magnetic resonance (CMR). Results on CMR do not correlate well with other methods, suggesting that cardiac iron overload is poorly estimated by the surrogate measurements.

Chelation Therapy

The introduction of chelating agents capable of removing excess iron from the body has dramatically increased life expectancy. The cost however has resulted in poor compliance and inadequate dosing of iron chelators in many Indian patients. The standard medication, deferoxamine, must be administered parenterally because of its short half-life; prolonged subcutaneous infusion is the most effective route. A total dose of 40–60 mg/kg/day is infused over 8–12 hr during the night for 5–6 days/week by a mechanical pump. Patients should be warned that their urine will become orange, due to the iron-deferoxamine complex (ferrioxamine). Higher doses of deferoxamine 6–10 g may be administered IV when serious iron overload such as cardiac failure occurs. The optimal time to initiate chelation therapy is dictated by the amount of accumulated iron. This usually occurs after 1–2 yr of transfusions when ferritin level is 1000 to 1500 μg/L. Severe toxicity may develop if chelation is started prematurely. Eye examination, hearing tests and renal function tests are required to monitor the effects of therapy.

Deferiprone is an oral chelating agent, although less effective than deferoxamine in preventing organ damage. It may cause arthritis and agranulocytosis. It is administered at a dose of 75 mg/day. Deferasirox is a new oral chelating agent, which has now become available in India. The molecule is a tridentate ligand that binds iron with a high affinity, forming a 2:1 complex that is excreted in bile and eliminated primarily *via* the feces. It has shown efficacy similar to parenteral agent deferoxamine in maintaining or reducing liver iron. This orally active chelator is highly selective for iron; it chelates intracellular and extracellular excess iron throughout the body, including liver, heart reticuloendothelial system and circulation. It can lead to rash, gastrointestinal, renal and hepatic toxicity, hence creatinine, liver function tests and proteinuria should be monitored. The recommended starting dose is 20 mg/kg/day.

The spleen acts as a store for nontoxic iron, protecting the body from extra iron, thus early removal of the spleen may be harmful. Splenectomy is justified only in patients with hypersplenism, leading to excessive destruction of erythrocytes and increasing the need for frequent blood transfusions, resulting in further iron accumulation. Patients who require more than 200–250 mL/kg of packed red blood cells annually benefit from this procedure. This is rarely required in children receiving adequate transfusion therapy.

Other Complications

Bone Problems

The classic 'hair on end' radiologic appearance of the skull, results from widening of the diploic spaces and maxillary overgrowth, resulting in maxillary overbite and prominence of the upper incisors. These changes contribute to the classic hemolytic/chipmunk facies observed in patients with thalassemia major. Osteoporosis and osteopenia may result in fractures; the child may need treatment with calcium, vitamin D and bisphosphonates to improve bone density.

Extramedullary Hematopoiesis

These occur in patients with severe anemia not receiving transfusion therapy. They may cause neuropathy or paralysis from compression of the spine or peripheral nerves. Compression fractures and paravertebral expansion of extramedullary masses, which behave clinically like tumors, are found during the second decade of life.

Psychosocial

As these children survive into adulthood, problems related to employment, marriage, having families, and the stress of chronic illness need to be addressed.

Cure of Thalassemia Major

Hematopoietic stem cell transplantation is the only known curative treatment for thalassemia. Poor outcome after stem cell transplantation correlates with the presence of hepatomegaly, portal fibrosis and with inadequate chelation prior to transplant. The event-free survival rate for patients who have all three features is 59%, compared to 90% for those who do not have hepatomegaly, fibrosis and have received proper chelation.

Management of Other Thassemia States

Patients with thalassemia intermedia require monitoring to assess the need for transfusion, since persistent anemia may retard growth. Hydroxyurea (15–20 mg/kg/d) is used in an attempt to increase HbF production and reduce the need for transfusions, especially in patients with XLM1 mutation. Iron therapy should not be used in patients with thalassemia trait unless its deficiency is confirmed. Genetic counselling is necessary to create awareness and prevent thalassemia major in offspring.

Suggested reading

1. Nadkarni A, Gorakshakar AC, Krishnamoorthy R, Ghosh K, Colah R, Mohanty D. Molecular pathogenesis and clinical variability of beta thalassemia syndromes among Indians. Am J Hematol 2001;68:75–80.
2. Sarnaik SA. Thalassemia and related hemoglobinopathies. Indian J Pediatr 2005;72:319–324.

SICKLE CELL ANEMIA

Sickle cell anemia though rare in India with a gene frequency of 4.3%, occurs in a wide geographical distribution from Orissa, Maharashtra, Madhya Pradesh and Jharkand. These patients can present with serious and varied hematological manifestations.

Pathophysiology

Sickle cell anemia is an autosomal recessive disease that results from the substitution of valine for glutamic acid at position 6 of the β-globin gene. The sickle red blood cells are less deformable and obstruct the microcirculation, resulting in tissue hypoxia that further promotes sickling. Deoxygenation of the heme moiety of sickle hemoglobin leads to hydrophobic interactions between adjacent sickle hemoglobin (HbS) molecules that aggregate into larger polymers. Sickle-shaped red blood cells are rapidly hemolyzed and have a lifespan of only 10–20 days (compared to normal 120 days). Patients who are homozygous for the HbS gene have sickle cell disease. Patients who are heterozygous for the HbS gene have sickle trait.

Clinical Evaluation

A complete history should be taken for the site, frequency, duration, character and severity of pain, e.g. pleuritic in acute chest syndrome, joint/bone pain in arthritis or osteomyelitis. History of previous similar episodes should be inquired, as pain crises tend to recur. History of trigger should be searched for, whether dehydration, fever, etc. Pain is the most common presentation of vaso-occlusive crisis. Presence of fever, cough and urinary symptoms may help in the identification of infection. Shortness of breath or dyspnea is suggestive of an acute chest syndrome. Neurological symptoms such as unilateral weakness, aphasia, paresthesias, visual symptoms (retinal hemorrhage) may suggest stroke or infarct. Sudden increase in pallor, syncope or sudden pain or increase in left sided abdomen mass indicate a splenic sequestration crisis.

Icterus due to elevated unconjugated hyperbilirubinemia; pallor and mild splenomegaly in a young child are the usual presentations. The disease may manifest as a febrile episode as patients are prone to pneumococcal, salmonella and other bacterial infections. Every episode of fever needs to be investigated for focus of infection and treated. Tachypnea suggests pneumonia, congestive heart failure or acute chest syndrome. Hypoxia is commonly seen in patients with acute chest syndrome. Severe anemia may occur with aplastic crisis, patients show signs of congestive heart failure. Hypotension and tachycardia may be signs of septic shock or sequestration crisis. Growth retardation and gallstones are common in these children and need medical attention. The spleen undergoes auto-infarction and is usually not palpable beyond 6 years of age.

Types of Crisis

Vaso-occlusive Crisis

A vaso-occlusive crisis occurs when the microcirculation is obstructed by sickled red blood cells, resulting in ischemic injury. Pain is the major complaint; bones (e.g. femur, tibia and lower vertebrae) are frequently involved. Vaso-occlusion may present as dactylitis, hand and foot syndrome (painful and swollen hands and/or feet in children) or mimic an acute abdomen. The spleen develops auto-infarcts and becomes fibrotic and functionless. In the kidney, it results in papillary necrosis, which results in isosthenuria (inability to concentrate urine). Vaso-occlusive crises can involve the lungs and cause acute chest syndrome; retinal hemorrhages in the eye and involvement of corpus cavernosum, leading to priapism. Involvement of the femoral head results in avascular necrosis. Recurrent cerebrovascular accidents may occur.

Acute Chest Syndrome

In this condition a new pulmonary infiltrate is found, the child may have chest pain, cough, tachypnea, dyspnea, hypoxemia and fever. It is a type of vaso-occlusive crisis, which may be associated with pneumonia. This requires urgent admission and supportive care.

Sequestration Crisis

Sickled cells block splenic outflow, leading to the pooling of peripheral blood in the engorged spleen resulting in splenic sequestration.

Infections

Patients have increased risk of infection with encapsulated organisms (e.g. *H. influenzae, S. pneumoniae*). They are also at risk of other common infectious organisms such as *Salmonella, M. pneumoniae, S. aureus* and *E. coli*.

Aplastic Crisis

Aplastic crises occur when the bone marrow stops producing red blood cells. This is most commonly seen in patients with infection or folate deficiency. This is usually self-limited and may follow viral infections of which parvovirus B19 is the most commonly implicated. Supportive care and occasionally packed red cell transfusions are required.

Laboratory Studies

Anemia and thrombocytosis are commonly found. Leukocytosis occurs in patients with sickle cell anemia. However a rise in the white blood cell count (>20,000 per mm^3) with a left shift is indicative of infection. In the peripheral smear, sickle-shaped red blood cells are found along with target cells. Presence of Howell-Jolly bodies indicates that the patient is functionally asplenic. The baseline indirect bilirubin level may be elevated.

If the diagnosis of sickle cell anemia has not been made, a sickling test will establish the presence of sickle hemoglobin. Hemoglobin electrophoresis is the test that can differentiate between individuals who are homozygous or heterozygous. A homozygous patient will have hemoglobin SS (HbSS, 80–90%), carriers will have HbSS (35–40%). This needs to be done prior to giving blood transfusion.

Assessment during Acute illness

In a sick child, a type and cross-match is required for probable transfusion. A chest X-ray, blood culture and X-rays of bones if pain crisis is present are indicated. Oxygen saturation monitoring and arterial blood gases should be ordered in patients who are in respiratory distress. Assess hemoglobin levels; a major drop in hemoglobin (more than 2 g/dL) from baseline indicates a splenic sequestration or aplastic crisis. A reticulocyte count and examination of spleen size will help to differentiate between these two conditions. An ECG must be performed if patient has chest pain or pulse irregularities.

Hospital Management

Hydration and analgesia are the mainstays of treatment in a pain crisis. Administer oral hydration if the patient is not vomiting and can tolerate oral fluids. Narcotic analgesia is most frequently used. In severe dehydration, administer intravenous fluids. Take care not to overload the patient and ensure accurate intake-output monitoring. A simple blood transfusion is indicated in patients in aplastic crisis and acute sequestration crisis. Oxygen supplementation is of benefit if the patient has hypoxia. Intubation and mechanical ventilation may be required in children in whom cerebrovascular accidents have occurred, or with acute chest syndrome. Exchange transfusion consists of replacing the patient's red blood cells by normal donor red blood cells, decreasing sickle hemoglobin (HbS) to less than 30%. Exchange blood transfusions are indicated in cases of cerebrovascular accidents and acute chest syndrome. They may be performed in patients with acute sequestration crisis or in priapism that does not resolve after adequate hydration and analgesia.

Preventive Care

All children require prophylaxis with penicillin/amoxicillin, atleast until 5 years of age. They should receive immunizations of pneumococcal, meningococcal and *H. influenzae* vaccines. They should receive life long folate supplementation. Hydroxyurea is a cytotoxic agent, which can increase HbF and reduce episodes of pain crises and acute chest syndrome; this may be tried after 5 years of age. Parents need to learn how to identify complications, be informed for necessity and indications for admission and screened for gallstones and stroke. Genetic counselling and testing should be offered.

Suggested reading

1. Sachdeva A, Sharma SC, Yadav SP. Sickle cell disease. In: IAP Speciality series on Pediatric Hematology and Oncology 2006; 77–96.
2. Steinberg MH. Management of sickle cell disease. N Engl J Med 1999;340: 1021–1030.

APLASTIC ANEMIA

Aplastic anemia is a group of disorders of the hematopoietic stem cells that involve one or more cell line (erythroid, myeloid, megakaryocytic). Aplastic anemia can be inherited or acquired. It can involve just one or all hematopoietic cell lines. The prevalence of bone marrow failure (hypoplastic, aplastic anemia) is 2–6 cases/million population in western literature. In India, the prevalence is higher, although exact data is not available.

Etiopathogenesis

Hematopoietic stem cells are damaged by various mechanisms (1) an acquired stem cell injury from viruses, toxins or chemicals; (2) abnormal cellular control of hematopoiesis; (3) an abnormal marrow microenvironment; (4) immunologic suppression of hematopoiesis (i.e. mediated by antibodies, cytotoxic T cells), and (5) mutations in genes, resulting in inherited bone marrow failure syndromes.

Differential Diagnosis

Family and past medical histories help distinguish inherited from acquired causes. Inherited bone marrow failure syndromes are usually diagnosed in childhood or young adults. They may have characteristic physical anomalies, familial incidence or thrombocytopenia at birth. Acquired aplasia can occur due to exposure to toxins, drugs like chloramphenicol, environmental hazards and viral infections (e.g. hepatitis B, C). Single lineage cytopenias need to be differentiated from transient erythroblastopenia of childhood.

Clinical Manifestations

Physical examination reveals pallor and/or signs of congestive heart failure. Ecchymoses, petechiae, gum bleeding and nose bleeds are associated with thrombocytopenia. Fever, pneumonia or sepsis, are due to neutropenia. The child should be evaluated for the stigmata of congenital bone marrow failure syndromes (Table 11.14, Figs 11.10 and 11.11). However, Fanconi anemia may be present even without abnormal phenotypic features.

Laboratory Studies

Hematological features of bone marrow failure include single cytopenia, as seen in pure red cell aplasia and amegakaryocytic thrombocytopenic purpura, while in aplastic anemia, pancytopenia or bilineage involvement is present. Peripheral blood smear findings are anemia, occasionally with macrocytosis (<110 fl) thrombocytopenia and agranulocytosis. The corrected reticulocyte count is less than 1%, indicating reduced red cell production. Bone marrow aspirate and biopsy are essential for proper diagnosis and evaluation of bone marrow cellularity (Fig. 11.12). In general, the marrow is replaced with fat cells and lymphocytes, with very few hematopoietic cells.

Special Tests

The Ham's test, or sucrose hemolysis test, may be positive in a patient with underlying paroxysmal nocturnal hemoglobinuria (red cells lysed by patient's acidified sera); and type II congenital dyserythropoietic anemia (CDA) (red cells lysed by other acidified sera but not patient sera), but a recent transfusion with packed red blood cells may induce a false-negative test result. A more specific test for paroxysmal nocturnal hemoglobinuria is the assay for two complement regulatory proteins usually present on red blood cells, CD55 (decay accelerating factor) and CD59 (membrane inhibitor of reactive lysis) are required for the diagnosis of paroxysmal nocturnal hemoglobinuria. The deficiency of CD55/59 markers on red blood cells is the specific hallmark of paroxysmal nocturnal hemoglobinuria. The peripheral blood cells in Fanconi anemia show characteristic hypersensitivity and chromosomal breakage with crosslinking agents (e.g. mitomycin C and diepoxybutane). This test for chromosomal fragility may be positive even in Fanconi anemia patients who lack the physical stigmata of the disease.

Treatment

Supportive care such as packed red cells for anemia, platelets for thrombocytopenia and antibiotics for infection are needed. Hematopoietic stem cell transplant is the only

11

Table 11.14: Congenital syndromes associated with bone marrow failure

Condition	Inheritance	Associated features	Risk of malignancy
Syndromes associated with pancytopenias			
Fanconi anemia	AR	Absent thumbs, absent radius, microcephaly, renal anomalies, short stature, café au lait spots, skin pigmentation	High risk of acute myeloid leukemia, myelodysplasia, oral and liver cancers
Dyskeratosis congenita	X-linked recessive, AD, AR	Nail dystrophies, leukoplakia	Cancer (usually squamous cell) and myelodysplasia.
Single lineage cytopenias			
Amegakaryocytic thrombocytopenia	AR	Usually none	None
Diamond-Blackfan (PRCA)	AD, AR	Short stature, congenital anomalies in 1/3 children, macrocytosis, elevated Hb F, raised adenosine deaminase	Leukemia, myelodysplasia and other cancers
Thrombocytopenia absent radii (TAR)	AR	Absent radius	None

AR autosomal recessive, AD autosomal dominant, Hb F fetal hemoglobin.

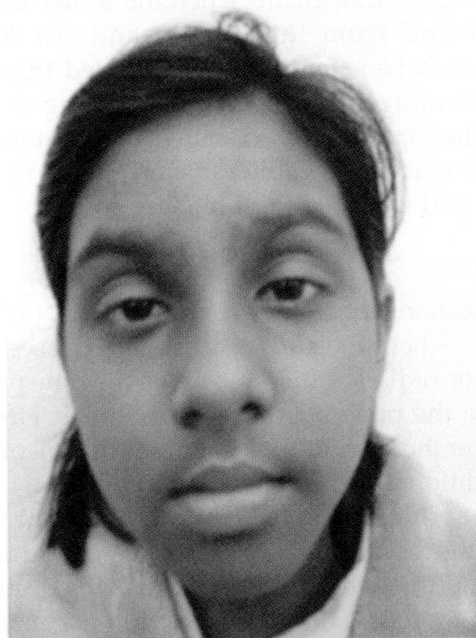

Fig. 11.10: Child with Fanconi anemia. The child had hyperpigmentation, microcephaly and microphthalmia. She also demonstrated radial ray defects and growth retardation

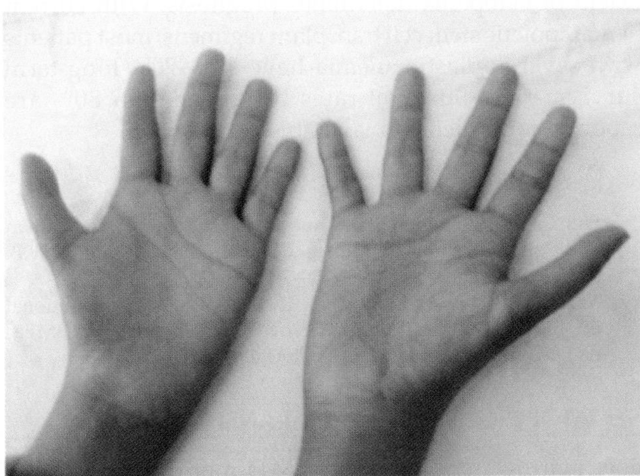

Fig. 11.11: Radial ray defects present in a wide spectrum they include absent or hypoplastic thumbs. The thenar hypoplasia may be missed unless carefully examined

curative therapy. Criteria for referral for hematopoietic stem cell transplant are (i) patients who are young, (ii) severe aplastic anemia and (iii) a matched related sibling donor. Patients with severe acquired aplastic anemia who cannot undergo a hematopoietic stem cell transplant, may benefit from antithymocyte globulin (ATG) or antilymphocyte globulin (ALG) with the addition of cyclosporine. Granulocyte colony-stimulating factor (G-CSF) is indicated in patients with neutropenia with infection. However if the neutrophil count does not increase with granulocyte colony-stimulating factor, this should be discontinued after a seven day trial, prolonged use has been associated with risk of malignant transformation.

In children with Fanconi anemia, therapy with ATG or cyclosporine is contraindicated. The only curative treatment is stem cell transplantation. However, this does not cure the physical and renal manifestations of the disease, nor prevent the risk of cancer in the future. Oral androgens have been used, as palliative therapy, for patients of Fanconi anemia who cannot undergo stem cell transplantation.

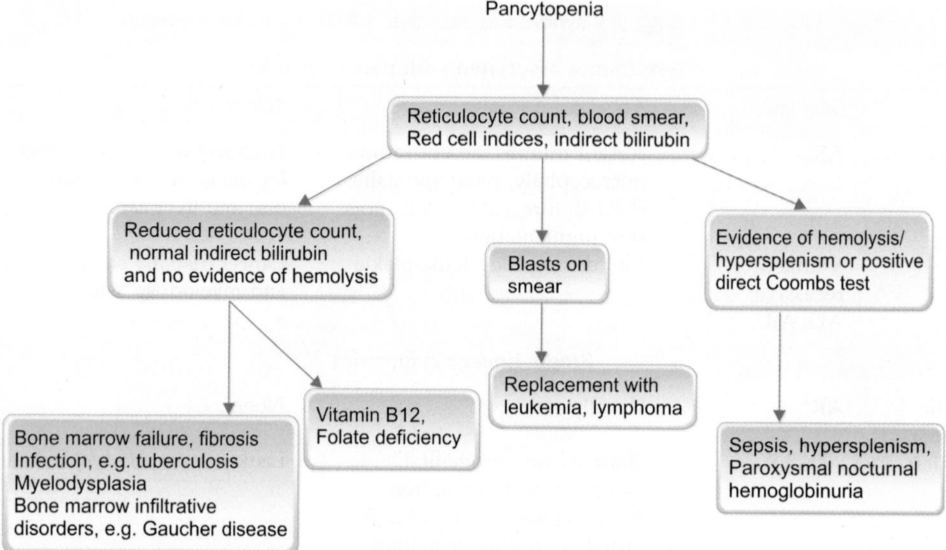

Fig. 11.12: Algorithm for evaluation of pancytopenia

Prognosis

Severe anemia can result in cardiac failure, neutropenia can lead to bacterial and fungal infections; severe bleeding can occur due to thrombocytopenia. The severity and extent of cytopenia determines prognosis. With current hematopoietic stem cell transplant regimens, most patients with severe aplastic anemia have a 60–70% long-term survival rate. Survival rates of higher than 80% are reported for patients in favorable subgroups.

Suggested reading

1. Shimamura A, Guinan EC. Acquired aplastic anemia. In: Nathan and Oski's Hematology of Infancy and childhood, 6th edn. W.B. Saunders, Philadelphia; 2003;256–79.
2. Varma N, Varma S, Marwaha RK, et al. Multiple constitutional etiological factors in bone marrow failure syndrome (BMFS) patients from north India. *Indian J Med Res* 2006;124:51–56.

HEMATOPOIETIC STEM CELL TRANSPLANTATION

Bone marrow transplantation (BMT), more correctly called hematopoietic stem cell transplantation (HSCT), is an established life saving procedure for many malignant and non-malignant diseases. HSCT are of the following types: (i) Autologous transplant- when the source of stem cells is harvested from the patient and (ii) Allogeneic transplant- when stem cells are collected from a human leukocyte antigen (HLA) matched sibling or unrelated donor. The commonly used sources of hematopoietic stem cells are cytokine mobilized peripheral blood, bone marrow and umbilical cord blood.

Indications

The indications for HSCT are (Table 11.15): (a) Malignant disorders – here the cure is by the high doses of chemotherapy or radiation therapy, while the transplant serves to rescue the patient from the myelotoxic effects of the anti cancer therapy. In allogeneic type of transplants, there is an additional benefit of the immunological response of 'graft versus cancer effect', which contributes to controlling the disease; (b) Non-malignant diseases – In these conditions the abnormal marrow is destroyed and replaced by the healthy unaffected donor marrow. This corrects genetic or acquired disease of blood and bone marrow.

Table 11.15: Indications for stem cell transplantation

Malignant Disorders	*Non Malignant Disorders*
Acute myeloid leukemia	Thalassemia
Chronic myeloid leukemia	Aplastic anemia
Acute lymphoblastic leukemia	Fanconi anemia
Hodgkin lymphoma (relapsed, refractory)	Immune deficiency syndromes
Non-Hodgkin (relapsed or refractory) lymphoma	Inborn errors of metabolism
Neuroblastoma	
Ewing sarcoma	
Myelodysplastic syndromes	
Gliomas, other solid tumors	

Allogeneic Hematopoietic Bone Marrow Transplant

Donor Requirement

For an allogeneic transplant, a HLA identical sibling is the ideal donor. In spite of HLA identity, there is always variation in the minor histocompatibility loci. These antigenic differences may lead to graft rejection or graft versus host disease. It is also possible to have a successful transplant using a partially matched sibling as a donor, or an unrelated HLA identical donor, but the complications of graft versus host disease and graft rejection are very severe. Most centers in India are not conducting unrelated transplants. Unlike most other organ transplants, in hematopoietic transplantation, ABO blood group compatibility is not essential. After successful hematopoietic transplantation, the blood group of the recipient will change to that of the donor group.

Conditioning Procedure

Myeloablative conditioning: The standard preparatory regimens given prior to hematopoietic transplantation are myeloablative (suppression of bone marrow). Patients receive extremely high doses of chemotherapy. The aim is threefold: (a) eradication of malignant cells or abnormal clone of cells, (b) suppression of the immune system of the host so that the allograft is not rejected, and (c) clearing a "physical space" to allow adequate growth of the donor stem cells.

Non-myeloablative conditioning: The curative potential of allogeneic hematopoietic transplantation is mediated in part by an immune mediated graft-versus-tumor effect. This has prompted some workers to focus on the use of donor T cells to eradicate both nonmalignant and malignant cells of host origin, without the use of myeloablative conditioning regimens. This non-myeloablative conditioning, aims to suppress the immunity of the recipient sufficiently to allow allogeneic engraftment, without destroying the recipient's marrow, with lower regimen related toxicity.

Technical Aspects

The donor's marrow is harvested by repeated aspiration from the posterior and anterior iliac crests, under general or spinal anesthesia. The marrow is collected in a bag with anticoagulant. The number of marrow cells or total nucleated cells required for successful engraftment is estimated to be at least 1 to 3 × 10^8 per kg of recipient's body weight. Bone marrow is transfused through the veins and the donor cells home into the recipient's marrow space and start engrafting. Engraftment is considered established when the peripheral neutrophil count reaches 500/cu mm on three successive days.

Supportive Care

Protective isolation: After transplantation of the marrow, it takes 2–3 weeks before engraftment occurs, the time when the stem cells start producing adequate number of neutrophils, platelets and erythrocytes. During this period, intensive support is required.

Venous access: The transplant process typically involves the use of a long term, silastic, multi-lumen, flexible catheter for chemotherapy administration, infusion of stem cells and supportive care management including frequent blood sampling, IV antibiotics, blood components and parenteral nutrition.

Early infections: Infection remains an important cause of morbidity and mortality, with bacterial and fungal infections being the predominant cause. Early institution of empirical antibiotics to cover gram-negative and gram-positive bacteria, with addition of antifungal drugs like amphotericin if fever persists, is practiced in most centers.

Blood component support: After conditioning therapy, patients require multiple red cell and platelet transfusions during the 2–4 week period of pancytopenia, until engraftment occurs. Patients are immunosuppressed and at risk of developing transfusion associated—graft versus host disease (TA-GVHD) after receiving cellular blood products. To prevent this, all cellular blood products should be irradiated prior to transfusion, to inactivate donor lymphocytes. As BMT can be performed even with ABO incompatibility, hemolysis may occur during infusion of ABO-incompatible stem cells, or later as a result of the production by donor lymphocytes of isoagglutinins directed against recipient ABO-antigens.

Hematopoietic growth factors: Hematopoietic colony stimulating factors, such as granulocyte colony stimulating factor are often administered to patients after infusion of stem cells in order to reduce the duration of neutropenia.

Toxicity Related to Conditioning

The conventional myeloablative therapy, given before infusion of the bone marrow causes complications: (a) veno-occlusive disease of the liver characterized by (i) jaundice, (ii) hepatomegaly and right upper quadrant pain, (iii) ascites or unexplained weight pain; (b) hemorrhagic cystitis characterized by the presence of hematuria, dysuria, and urinary frequency in a patient with sterile urine; (c) seizures-usually drug induced (cyclosporine, busulphan) or due to infections; (d) pulmonary complications; (e) skin and mucosal changes like alopecia, nail changes and oral mucositis.

Failure of Engraftment

Failure to engraft after hematopoietic stem cell transplantation (graft dysfunction) or inability to sustain graft (graft rejection) is a formidable complication. The causes of this include inadequate stem cell dose, infections, graft-versus-host disease and immunological mediated processes. Fortunately, this complication is uncommon. The incidence is higher in unrelated donor and HLA mismatched transplant.

Graft Versus Host Disease

In allogeneic bone marrow transplant patients, a unique complication occurs, graft versus host disease (GVHD), which may be acute or chronic. Acute GVHD occurs within the first 3 months after transplant. It classically affects three tissues, namely the skin, gut and liver and may be accompanied by fever. The severity can be graded according to the extent of skin involvement, degree of hyperbilirubinemia and severity of diarrhea. Chronic GVHD develops later than 100 days after transplant and often follows acute GVHD but may also develop *de novo*; it is classified as limited or extensive. Clinically it resembles autoimmune disorders like scleroderma with skin rash, sicca complex, sclerosing bronchioloitis and hepatic dysfunction. The mortality varies from 20–40%. Management is with immunosuppressive agents like cyclosporine, prednisolone, azathioprine, methotrexate and cyclophosphamide in various combinations. Most patients develop self tolerance and after a year or more these drugs can be tapered off. GVHD is more common in older patients and those with one or more HLA mismatches or unrelated HLA identical transplants.

Tumor Relapse

A successful hematopoietic stem cell transplant does not always mean that the primary disease is cured. A certain number of patients will relapse from the original malignancy, as the tumor cells survive the chemo/radiotherapy and graft versus tumor effect.

Late Infections

Infections remain a major complication in the post transplant period. Viral infections are important causes of morbidity and mortality after allogeneic stem cell transplant, the most important infections being cytomegalovirus, herpes simplex virus and varicella zoster infection. Bacterial infections with encapsulated organisms occur after 3–6 months.

Autologous Stem Cell Transplantation

Autologous bone marrow or peripheral blood stem cell transplantation is a procedure similar to allogeneic bone marrow transplant, the major difference being that the patient's own stem cells are used for engraftment. The concept of performing autologous stem cell transplant is to permit administration of very high doses of chemo or radiotherapy, which would otherwise be fatal, due to severe myelosuppression. First the patient's marrow or stem cells are collected prior to chemotherapy, they are then used to 'rescue' the patient from the myelotoxicity after the chemotherapy. The procedure is only indicated for malignancies which are chemo/radiosensitive, e.g. leukemia, lymphoma, neuroblastoma and other solid tumors. Peripheral blood stem cell transplantation (see below) have virtually replaced bone marrow for autologous stem cell transplantation. Engraftment takes place more rapidly when peripheral stem cells are used instead of bone marrow cells. The advantage of autologous transplant over allogeneic transplant is that there is no GVHD and once engraftment occurs, graft rejection is unlikely. Thus, there is a significant decrease in the complication rates. However, there is a higher risk of tumor relapse as compared to allogeneic transplants.

Peripheral Blood Stem Cell Transplantation

In the past few years an increasing number of peripheral blood stem cell transplantations (PBSCT) are being performed. The procedure is similar to bone marrow transplant except for differences in the method of collection of the stem cells and slight changes in the engraftment potential. It is known that the peripheral blood contains a small proportion of stem cells, approximately 0.1%. This number can be increased by administration of colony stimulating factors, e.g. G-CSF.

PBSCT can be autologous or allogeneic. For allogeneic donors, G-CSF is administered for 4 to 5 days, this results in high circulating stem cells which can be collected by a cell separator (apheresis) machine. The procedure requires venous access and takes two to four hours. The donor need not be admitted, does not require anesthesia and is spared the pain of marrow aspiration. For autologous PBSCT, the stem cells are collected in a similar fashion, but chemotherapy is also usually given prior to the harvest to reduce the tumor contamination and to yield a higher proportion of stem cells.

Cord Blood Stem Cell Transplantation

Placental blood, which is routinely discarded in clinical practice, is potentially a rich source for allogeneic hematopoietic stem cells. Cord blood stem cells have distinctive proliferative advantages which include: (a) enriched proportion of immature stem cells, (b) higher clonogenic growth advantage, (c) increased cell cycle rate, (d) autocrine growth factors production and (e) increased telomere length. The small number and relative immaturity of naive T cells of cord blood lymphocytes is expected to reduce the risk and severity of GVHD. The activation pattern of cord blood T cells is less in magnitude than that in adult counterparts. The main limitation of cord blood transplants is the limited number of nucleated cells available in a unit. Compared to bone marrow transplantation, the time for engraftment in cord blood transplantation is much longer, taking a month for neutrophilic engraftment and more than fifty days for platelet engraftment. There is also a higher incidence of non-engraftment. This leads to high transplant related mortality. The nucleated cell dose available in a cord blood unit is critical, being one log less than in a bone marrow transplant. The main advantage of cord blood transplant is a lower incidence and severity of GVHD. This allows a 1–2 HLA antigen mismatch even in unrelated cord blood transplant.

In India, the first bone marrow transplant was performed in Tata Memorial Hospital (Mumbai) in March 1983. Christian Medical College (Vellore) is the largest center in the country performing allogeneic bone marrow transplants. Other centers in the country involved in these procedures include All India Institute of Medical Sciences (New Delhi) and Apollo Hospital (Chennai).

Suggested reading

1. Copelan EA. Hematopoietic stem-cell transplantation. *N Engl J Med* 2006; 354:1813–1826.
2. Chandy M, Srivastava A, George B, *et al.* Allogeneic bone marrow transplantation in the developing world: experience from a center in India. *Bone Marrow Transplant* 2001;27:785–790.

APPROACH TO A BLEEDING CHILD

When a child with acute bleeding presents the most important initial step is to stabilize the child. Assessment of the vitals will give an important clue to the severity of the disorder and magnitude of blood loss. Adequate administration of replacement fluids and monitoring should be done. Following this, the child should be evaluated for the cause of bleeding, which may be due to platelet factors (Table 11.16), coagulation defects (Table 11.17) or fibrinolytic dysfunction. Clinical assessment and initial screening tests can help identify the cause, so that specific management can be initiated.

Table 11.16: Classification of platelet dysfunction

Quantitative disorders
Decreased production
Increased destruction
Qualitative disorders
Inherited disorders
Glanzmann thrombasthenia
Bernard Soulier syndrome
Gray platelet syndrome
Wiskott Aldrich syndrome
Acquired disorders
Medications
Chronic renal failure
Cardiopulmonary bypass

Table 11.17: Common coagulation disorders

Inherited disorders
Hemophilia A and B
von Willebrand disease
Factor VII, X, XIII deficiency, Afibrinogenemia
Acquired disorders
Liver disease
Vitamin K deficiency
Warfarin overdose
Disseminated intravascular coagulation

Pathogenesis

The process of hemostasis is divided into cellular and fluid phases. The former involves platelets and the vascular wall, while the latter involves plasma proteins. The physiology of hemostasis is complex and involves a fine balance between flow of blood (i.e. fluid) and local responses to vascular injury (i.e. clotting). The fluid phase is divided into three processes: (i) the multiple-step zymogen pathway that leads to thrombin generation, (ii) thrombin-induced formation of fibrin clot, and (iii) complex fibrinolytic mechanisms, which limit clot propagation. The physiology of hemostasis includes the generation of insoluble fibrin and activation of platelets to form a hemostatic plug. Pro- and anticoagulant pathways, platelet number and function, vascular factors and other metabolic processes control this process. The coagulation cascade is depicted as involving two pathways, intrinsic and extrinsic. The extrinsic pathway is the primary initiating pathway for coagulation and is measured by the prothrombin time (PT). The intrinsic system works as a regulatory amplification loop, measured by the activated partial thromboplastin time (aPTT) (Fig. 11.13).

Clinical Evaluation

It is important to know the age of onset of bleeding, type of bleeding (mucosal: epistaxis, oral and skin bleeds; or deep: joints or muscle), spontaneous, or after an intervention (e.g. dental extraction, surgery or circumcision), site of bleeding, local causes, duration and frequency (Table 11.18). In the case of new onset bleeding, history of antecedent infections, rash (Henöch Schönlein purpura, varicella), icterus (liver failure, hepatitis B and C), diarrhea, (hemolytic uremic syndrome) and medicine intake should be taken. Some important medications that may commonly cause bleeding problems are anticonvulsants, penicillins, warfarin, aspirin, non steroidal anti inflammatory drugs and heparin. The possibility of dengue or disseminated intravascular coagulopathy should be considered in patients who have history of prior fever and are sick. The family history is important, documentation of the gender of affected members and details of their bleeding manifestations should be noted (Fig. 11.14). The pedigree should include the sex of any stillborn or dead children as well. Only male affected children will suggest an X-linked disorder such as hemophilia, females with bleeding conditions may be seen in autosomal dominant conditions (von Willebrand disease). Specific types of bleeding may give a clue to assist in the diagnosis, e.g. poor wound healing and prolonged bleeding from the umbilical stump suggests factor XIII deficiency.

Examination is done for degree of anemia, and presence of ecchymoses (Fig.11.15), petechiae, vascular malformations and rashes. Presence of splenomegaly suggests infections, malignancy, collagen vascular disorders or hypersplenism rather than a primary bleeding defect. Rashes may be seen secondary to drug exposure,

11

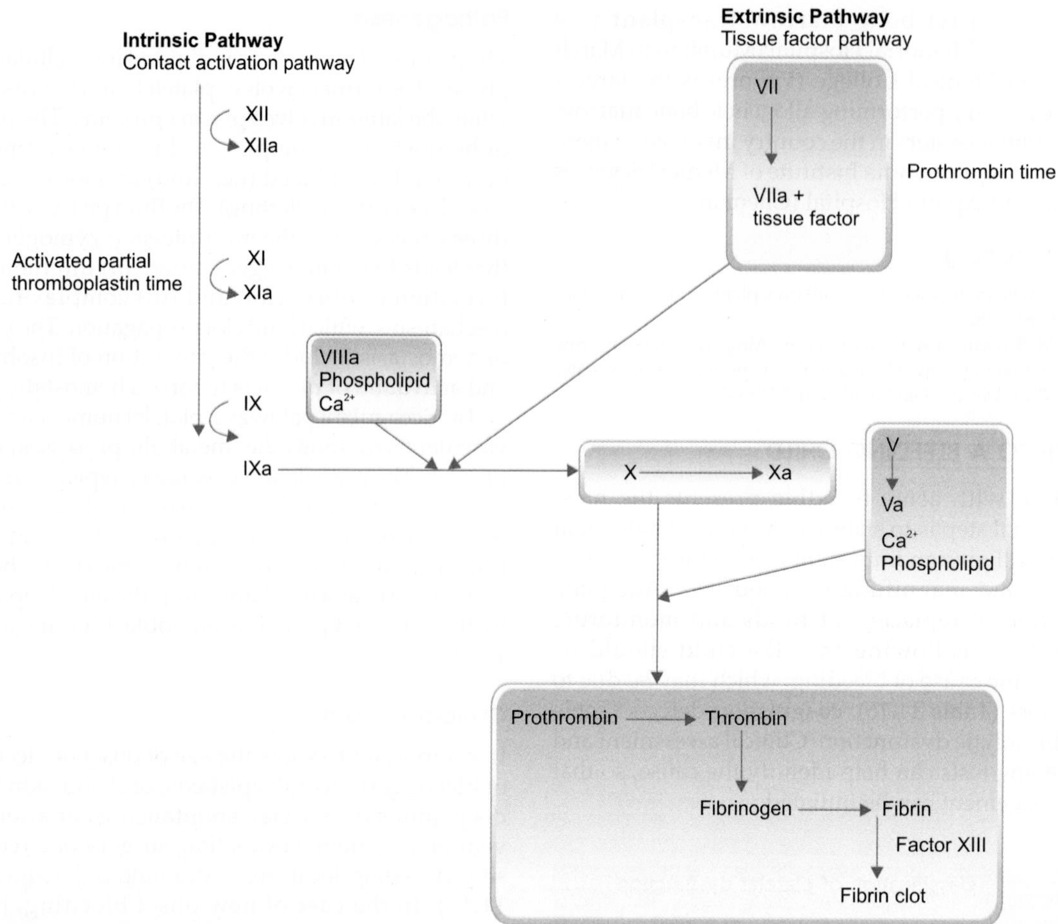

Fig. 11.13: In vivo coagulation cascade

Table 11.18: Differences in bleeding patterns in platelet disorders versus coagulation disorders

	Platelet disorder	*Coagulation disorder*
Site of bleeding	Skin, mucous membranes (epistaxis, oral, GI tract)	Deep in soft tissues, joints, muscles
Petechiae	Yes	No
Ecchymoses	Small, superficial	Large, deep
Hemarthrosis/muscle bleeding	Extremely rare	Common
Bleeding after minor trauma	Yes	No
Bleeding after surgery	Immediate, usually mild	Delayed (1–2 days), often severe
Examples	von Willebrand disease Idiopathic thrombocytopenic purpura	Hemophilia A Hemophilia B

infections, collagen vascular disorders, Langerhans cell histiocytosis and Wiskott Aldrich syndrome. The mouth and nose should be carefully examined to rule out local causes of bleeding. Hemangiomas and telangiectasias, may lead to mucocutaneous bleeding in Kasabach Merritt syndrome and hereditary telangiectasia.

Laboratory investigation

A complete hemogram is done for platelet count; peripheral smear examination shows platelet and red cell morphology. The optimal peripheral smear is made from a fresh finger stick, this avoids any artefactual errors due to EDTA anticoagulated blood. Initial coagulation screening tests include the PT and aPTT. Specific factor assays can be done to identify factor deficiencies, the degree of factor VIII and IX deficiency will dictate the management. The aPTT is used for monitoring heparin therapy; PT and its international normalized standard (INR) are used to assess therapeutic warfarin effect. Bleeding time is now rarely used due to the problems of reproducibility and reliability. This test is abnormal if the platelet count is below 100,000/cu mm (Table 11.19). In systemic vasculitides (e.g.

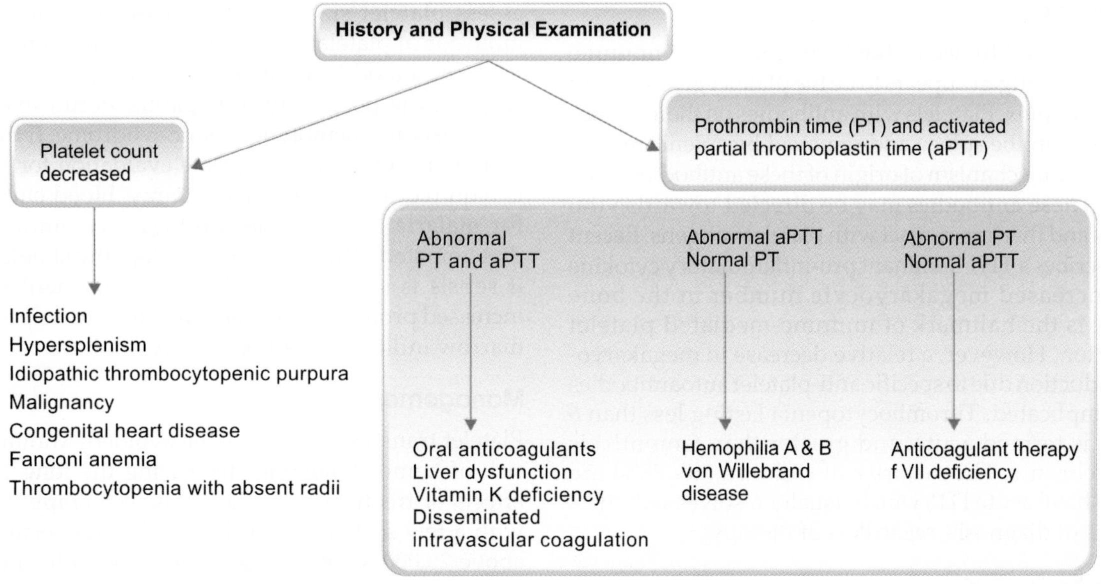

Fig. 11.14: Workup of a child with bleeding

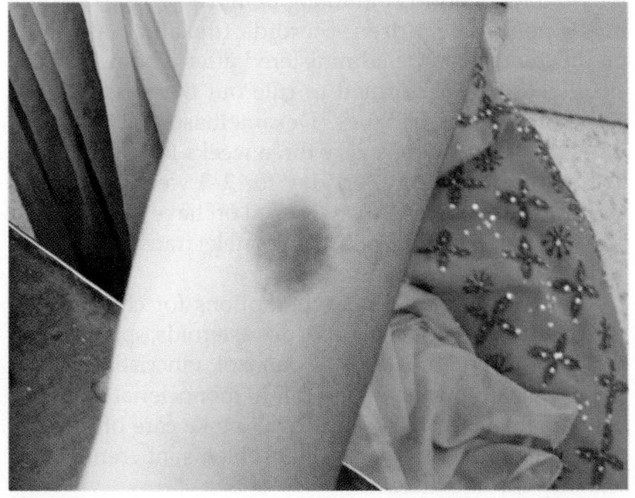

Fig. 11.15: Large ecchymotic patch on young girl with a von Willebrand disease

Table 11.19: Causes of thrombocytopenia
Idiopathic thrombocytopenic purpura
Congenital infections—TORCH
Infections: Disseminated intravascular coagulation, malaria, kala azar, dengue hemorrhagic fever, hepatitis B and C, HIV
Medications: Valproic acid, penicillins, heparin, quinine, digoxin
Malignancies: Leukemia, lymphoma, neuroblastoma
Collagen vascular disorders: systemic lupus erythematosus, Henoch Schonlein purpura
Immunodeficiency syndrome: Wiskott Aldrich syndrome
Bone marrow failure syndromes: thrombocytopenia with absent radii, Fanconi anemia, Shwachman—Diamond syndrome
Marrow replacement: osteopetrosis, Gaucher syndrome
Others: hypersplenism, hemolytic uremic syndrome, Kasabach Merritt syndrome

Henöch Schönlein purpura) and connective tissue defects (Ehlers Danlos syndrome), the bleeding time is also prolonged (Table 11.20). Bleeding time is largely being replaced by platelet aggregation studies for inherited and acquired platelet dysfunction. For evaluation of von Willebrand disease, the tests required include: von Willebrand cofactor assay, quantitation of von Willebrand antigen, factor VIII assay, ABO blood group (since vW antigen level varies with blood group) and electrophoretic analysis of von Willebrand multimeric subtypes. In a sick child, evaluation for disseminated intravascular coagulopathy might need to be performed.

Table 11.20: Vascular causes of bleeding
Henöch Schönlein purpura
Connective tissue disease
Scurvy
Prolonged steroid use/Cushing's disease
Hereditary hemorrhagic telangiectasia

Suggested reading

Lusher JM. Clinical and laboratory approach to the patient with bleeding. In: *Nathan and Oski's Hematology of Infancy and Childhood*, 6th edn. Eds. Nathan DG, Orkin SH, et al. WB Saunders, Philadelphia, 2003;1515–1526.

IDIOPATHIC THROMBOCYTOPENIC PURPURA

Idiopathic thrombocytopenic purpura (ITP) is the commonest bleeding disorder presenting in children between 1–7 years of age. It is important to correctly diagnose this entity and differentiate it from more ominous conditions. Normal platelet counts are 150–400000/cu mm in all children above one week of age.

11

Pathogenesis

ITP is proposed to occur due to an overactive immune system. The antigen appears to be the platelet glycoprotein IIb/IIIa complex. Platelets with antibodies on their surface are trapped in the spleen and removed by splenic macrophages. The mechanism of origin of these antibodies is not known. These antibodies may be directed towards viral antigens and then cross-react with platelet antigens. Recent data describes a TH1 dominant pro-inflammatory cytokine state. Increased megakaryocyte number in the bone marrow is the hallmark of immune-mediated platelet destruction. However, a relative decrease in megakaryocyte production due to specific anti-platelet autoantibodies is also implicated. Thrombocytopenia lasting less than 6 months is termed acute, and greater than 6 months is termed chronic. The majority of children (60–75%) are likely to have acute ITP, which usually resolves within 2–4 months of diagnosis, regardless of therapy.

Clinical Evaluation

There is often an antecedent history of febrile illness, but the child on presentation is usually a febrile and well. There is often a seasonal clustering of cases, more frequent during the change in seasons. Children present with a sudden appearance of bruises and mucosal bleeding (epistaxis, oral oozing) and prolonged bleeds with superficial trauma. It is important to estimate the total duration of symptoms and confirm if this is the initial episode or if there have been prior events, as seen in the relapsing course of chronic ITP.

The patient should be examined for features of bone marrow failure, e.g. Fanconi anemia (hypoplastic/absent thumb, short stature, hyperpigmentation), thrombocytopenia with absent radii presents with radial bone abnormality, but the thumb is present. Infants should be examined for presence of hemangiomas and ultrasound of abdomen may be useful. The presence of splenomegaly or lymphadenopathy may make the diagnosis of infection, malignancy or collagen vascular disorder more likely. Hypersplenism and hepatitis C may also cause thrombocytopenia.

Symptoms and signs depend on the platelet count. Bleeding is usually mild unless the platelet count drops below 20,000/cu mm. With platelet counts from 20,000–50,000/cu mm, petechiae and ecchymoses are observed following mild trauma. Physical examination shows petechiae and ecchymoses. The presence of lymphadenopathy or splenomegaly suggests other causes of thrombocytopenia, rather than ITP.

Laboratory Evaluation

The complete blood count shows that only the platelet count is diminished and other hematological parameters are normal. A peripheral smear will help to check for abnormal cells such as blasts, malarial parasites and importantly to know the precise platelet count, and exclude spurious thrombocytopenia. It will also help to assess platelet size: larger platelets are young and an indicator of platelet production. Liver and renal function tests and blood level of lactic dehydrogenase is done to rule out the possibility of hepatitis, occult malignancy, hemolysis and hemolytic uremic syndrome. If the child is febrile and ill then appropriate evaluation for infections is required; this include chest X-ray, blood culture, tests for malaria and dengue serology. Screening tests for disseminated intravascular coagulopathy should be done if sepsis is suspected. A bone marrow will show the increased production megakaryocytes and help to exclude marrow infiltration or bone marrow failure.

Management

Platelet transfusions need to be avoided. Minimizing the risk of hemorrhage and decreasing the long term side effects of treatment are the goals of therapy. In a child with a few scattered petechiae or bruises, platelet count above 20,000/cu mm and no bleeding only close observation is required. For children with bleeding, treatment includes intravenous immunoglobulin (IVIG) 1g/kg/day for 1–2 days or anti-D immunoglobulin 50–75 mg/kg only in Rh positive children. Steroids (dexamethasone or prednisolone) can be administered after a bone marrow examination is performed to rule out the possibility of hematological malignancy. Dexamethasone 20 mg /m^2 (total dose) for 4 days every three weeks for 4–6 courses, or prednisone 1–2 mg/kg/day for 2–3 weeks or 4 mg/kg/day for 7 days and then tapered off have been used. If serious hemorrhage occurs, then platelet transfusions may be used under cover of steroids.

There are many therapeutic options for chronic ITP; these include alternate day low dose steroids, splenectomy and various combinations of danazol, vincristine, cyclosporine, azathioprine or anti-CD20 monoclonal antibody (rituximab). The physician needs to take care of growth, bone density and psychosocial problems inherent in this and any chronic disease.

Suggested reading

Nugent, Diane ASH education book 2006. www.asheducation book.org/cgi/reprint/2006/1/97/pdf.

HEMOPHILIA

Hemophilias are the commonest hereditary clotting deficiency. They are X-linked recessive disorders. Hemophilia A is due to factor VIII deficiency and Hemophilia B due to insufficient factor IX; their clinical manifestations are similar. The presentation depends on the level of factor present. In mild cases, the factor level is enough to prevent minor spontaneous bleeds and patients manifest symptoms if they have surgery or severe trauma. In severe cases where factor levels are less than 1%, repeated, spontaneous, debilitating joint bleeds (hemarthroses, Fig. 11.16) lead to severe handicap and intracranial bleeds can be life threatening. Treatment requires appropriate factor

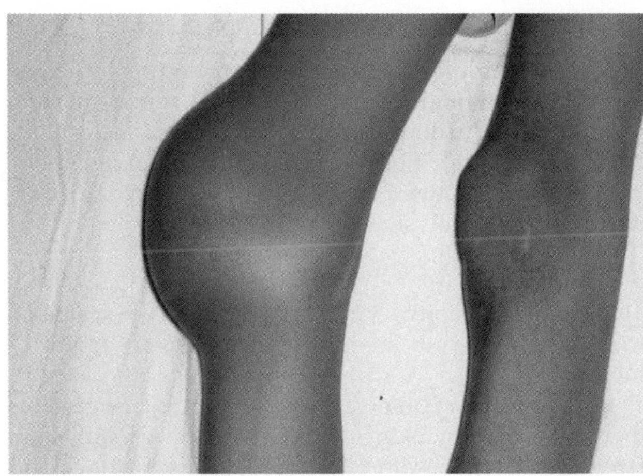

Fig. 11.16: Child with hemophilia with knee hemarthrosis. This shows signs of inflammation, severe pain and may lead to permanent disability

replacement, judicious physiotherapy to prevent chronic joint disease, counselling for injury prevention and monitoring for inhibitor development. Children with hemophilia should be managed in centers equipped for their special needs.

Replacement therapy for children with hemophilia with concentrates of factor VIII or IX is expensive and difficult to obtain in remote areas. Cryoprecipitate and fresh frozen plasma (FFP) can be used to control bleeding but carry the risk of transmitting HIV, hepatitis B and C. Cryoprecipitate contains factor VIII, fibrinogen and von Willebrand factor, but no factor IX. As fresh frozen plasma is frozen, it retains all factors at their hemostatic levels including the labile factors V and VII. Each unit of factor VIII/kg increases the level by 2%. To achieve a target of 30% factor VIII, which is required for management of most hemarthroses, a dose of 15 U/kg every 12–24 hr for 1–2 days is required. In major bleeds, e.g. intracranial hemorrhage, the target for factor level is 80–100% correction; the dose needed to achieve this is 50 U/kg every 8–12 hr for approximately 7–14 days. However, practically lower doses can be used in case of financial constraints, as some factor support is better than no replacement. Epsilon aminocaproic acid (Amicar) or tranexemic acid may be effective as adjunct therapy in mild cases of hemophilia. The principles of therapy of hemophilia B are similar; except factor IX is used for replacement, one unit of factor IX per kg raises factor level by 1%. In emergencies when factor IX is unavailable, only fresh frozen plasma can be used, as cryoprecipitate does not contain factor IX.

Primary prophylaxis is a better mode of management; patients with severe hemophilia (less than 1% measurable factor level) are given factor replacement 2–3 times a week to reduce the risk of bleeds. This results in less deformity and allows the child to play normally. This is an expensive mode of treatment, but provides good quality of life. All children should receive hepatitis B immunizations, vaccines are given subcutaneously and the parents are counselled regarding injury prevention. Genetic counselling is required and families should be informed of the availability of prenatal diagnosis.

Suggested reading

Roberts HA, Escobar M, White II GC. Hemophilia A and hemophilia B. Williams Hematology, 7th edn. Eds. Lichtman, Beutler, et al. McGraw-Hill Medical, 2006;1867–1886.

VITAMIN K DEFICIENCY

Phytonadione or vitamin K_1 is lipid-soluble vitamin that plays a vital role in production of vitamin K dependent coagulation factors. These are factor II (prothrombin), VII, IX, X, protein C and S. Vitamin K is found in green leafy vegetables, oils such as soyabean and canola and is synthesized by the colonic bacteria. Deficiency frequently occurs in newborn due to the low transmission of vitamin K across the placenta, paucity in the breast milk, sterile intestines and a premature liver. Later in life, vitamin K deficiency occurs due to antibiotic use, parenchymal liver disease, prolonged total parenteral nutrition and malabsorption. The classic vitamin K deficiency bleeding occurs in 0.25–1.7% of infants. The prevalence of late vitamin K deficiency bleeding in breastfed infants without prophylaxis is 20 cases per 100,000 live births.

Deficiency of vitamin K dependent factors leads to a prolonged prothrombin (PT) and activated partial thromboplastin time (PTT). Precise diagnosis may be made by measurement of protein in vitamin K absence assay (PIVKA assay), but this is usually not required. For prophylaxis against hemorrhagic disease of the newborn, administration of vitamin K as a single subcutaneous dose of 1 mg is required. In treatment of babies who did not receive prophylaxis or suffer from anticoagulant overdose larger doses of vitamin K (2–10 mg) can be given and repeated till coagulation studies are normal. Fresh frozen plasma can be used if there is overt bleeding, or liver dysfunction is suspected. Prophylaxis with vitamin K is safe and fears of leukemia are unsubstantiated.

Suggested reading

American Academy of Pediatrics. Controversies concerning vitamin K and the newborn. *Pediatrics* 2003;112:191–192.

NEONATAL ALLOIMMUNE THROMBOCYTOPENIA

Thrombocytopenia in the neonate has varied causes; a sick newborn may have sepsis, meconium aspiration, TORCH infection, etc. In a well looking infant, the causes may be due to medications taken by the mother or immunologic causes like maternal lupus erythematosus or neonatal alloimmune thrombocytopenia. In neonatal alloimmune thrombocytopenia the fetal platelets are destroyed by passage of maternal antibodies against paternally inherited antigens present on fetal platelets. Many platelet antigens like HPA-1a and HPA-5b have been identified. No prior pregnancy is required to sensitize the mother, hence 50% cases may occur with the first pregnancy. A high index of suspicion is required to correctly identify this condition, since this is a serious entity, which can result in intracranial hemorrhage. As there are few specific tests for its diagnosis it is primarily a diagnosis of exclusion. Postnatal management requires transfusion of washed, maternal platelets (preferably irradiated if facilities are available) and close monitoring till the platelet counts normalize). In subsequent pregnancies, the risk for neonatal thrombocytopenia increases. The fetus will need serial ultrasound examinations to see for intracranial hemorrhage; the mother may be given IV immunoglobulin (1 g/kg repeated every four weeks) with addition of oral dexamethasone if there is no response.

DISSEMINATED INTRAVASCULAR COAGULOPATHY

Disseminated intravascular coagulopathy or coagulation (DIC) is an acquired disorder of dysregulation of hemostasis. The presentation ranges from only an isolated derangement of laboratory parameters to a condition of severe bleeding from multiple sites, associated with high mortality. DIC is triggered by a variety of conditions all of which result in activation of the clotting cascade, this leads to deposition of fibrin in the microcirculation resulting in consumption of platelets and clotting factors. The diagnosis of DIC is clinical (Fig. 11.17). Laboratory tests merely provide confirmatory evidence.

Pathophysiology

There are three main pathologic processes involved.

Initiation of Fibrin Deposition

Thrombin generation in DIC is mediated by the extrinsic (tissue factor) pathway. The tissue factor accumulates on activated platelets by binding to platelet P-selectin which results in thrombin generation.

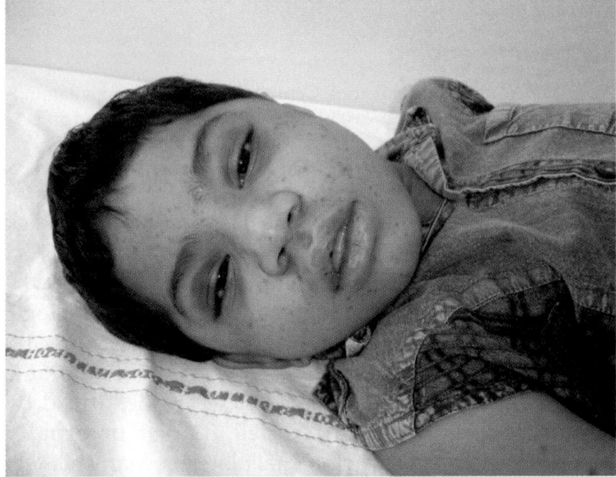

Fig. 11.17: Ill child with disseminated intravascular coagulation. Shows ecchymoses, purpura and subconjunctival hemorrhages

Amplification Role of Thrombin

Thrombin amplifies inflammation and clotting by activation of platelets, and factors V, VIII and IX leading to more thrombin production. Activated factor XIII leads to its cross-linking with fibrin clots making them insoluble, while thrombin activable fibrinolysis inhibitor makes clots resistant to fibrinolysis.

Propagation of Fibrin Deposition

There is suppression of fibrinolysis secondary to sustained increase in plasma levels of plasminogen-activator inhibitor (PAI-1).

Following injury, infection or other precipitating factors there is release of cytokines, which change the endothelium from an anticoagulant to a procoagulant surface and interfere with fibrinolysis. Many of the effects of DIC like hypotension or acute lung injury are due to the effects of these cytokines. As DIC continues, fibrinogen, prothrombin, platelets and other clotting factors are consumed beyond the capacity of the body to compensate and bleeding ensues. Activated protein C has an anti-inflammatory effect and down regulates the tissue factor and decreases calcium ion flux. It is consumed in DIC and its supplementation may have an important role in DIC due to sepsis.

Causes

The main groups of illnesses causing DIC are infections, malignancy, tissue necrosis, ABO incompatible blood transfusion and snakebites (Table 11.21).

In acute DIC, the patient is critically sick and bleeding predominates. Chronic DIC occurs due to a weak or intermittent stimulus. The process of destruction and production of clotting factors and platelets is balanced, and coagulopathy is compensated. Chronic DIC occurs in patients with giant hemangiomas, vasculitides and some solid tumors.

Laboratory Features

Screening tests include (i) peripheral blood film examination and hemogram, which reveal schistocytes and thrombocytopenia; (ii) prothrombin time (PT), activated partial thromboplastin time (aPTT) and thrombin time (TT) are prolonged, and fibrinogen level is low. There is increase in fibrin degradation products or D-dimers. No single test is diagnostic of DIC. The presence of thrombocytopenia and hypofibrinogenemia (50% reduction) are the most sensitive in making a laboratory diagnosis. A DIC scoring system has been proposed (Table 11.22). An underlying disorder known to be associated with DIC is a prerequisite for the use of this algorithm.

Treatment

The underlying disease must be managed appropriately. In cases of sepsis, antibiotics are required; anti-snake venom is administered in patients with snake bite. Tissue perfusion and respiratory function must be maintained by replacement with IV fluid and provision of oxygen support

11

Table 11.21: Disorders which cause acute or chronic disseminated intravascular coagulopathy

	Acute DIC	*Chronic DIC*
Medical	Septicemia/infections* Fulminant hepatic failure Heat stroke, hyperpyrexia Severe burns Malignancy-acute promyelocytic leukemia, acute myeloid leukemia, neuroblastoma Reye syndrome Hereditary protein C deficiency Snake bite Hemolytic uremic syndrome Kawasaki disease Collagen vascular disorders	Solid tumors Kasabach-Merritt syndrome Liver cirrhosis
Surgical	Severe renal graft rejection Severe trauma-crush injury, multiple fractures with fat emboli Major operations Brain injury	↑Vascular tumors ↑Aortic aneurysm
Transfusion medicine	Acute transfusion reaction Massive transfusion Heparin induced thrombosis	Artificial surfaces

* Septicemia/infections due to:
Bacterial: Meningococcus, gram-negative bacteria, gram-positive bacteria (group B streptococci).
Viral: Arboviruses, varicella, variola, rubella, paramyxoviruses, HIV, Ebola virus
Parasitic: Malaria
Mycotic: Candida, aspergillus.
Rickettsial: Rocky Mountain spotted fever

Table 11.22: The disseminated Intravascular coagulation score

Risk assessment

Does the patient have an underlying disorder known to be associated with disseminated intravascular coagulopathy. (If yes, proceed. If no, do not use this algorithm).

Coagulation tests (platelet count, prothrombin time, fibrinogen, soluble fibrin monomers /fibrin degradation products)

Score global coagulation test results

a. Platelet count: >100,000/cu mm = 0
50,000–100,000/cu mm =1
<50,000/cu mm = 2

b. Elevated fibrin-related marker (soluble fibrin monomers/fibrin degradation products) *
(no increase = 0, moderate increase = 2, strong increase = 3)

c. Prolonged prothrombin time: (<3 sec = 0, >3 but <6 sec = 1, >6 sec = 2)

d. Fibrinogen level: (>1g/L = 0, <1g/L = 1)

Calculate score
(a) If score ≥ 5: compatible with overt DIC; repeat scoring daily.
(b) If <5 suggestive (not affirmative) of non-overt DIC; repeat in 1–2 days

* In the prospective validation studies, D-dimer assays were used and a value above the upper limit of normal was considered moderately elevated, whereas a value above 5 times the upper limit of normal was considered as a strong increase.

to correct hypoxia. Coagulopathy may be compounded by vitamin K deficiency, hence vitamin K should be given.

In patients who have low levels of platelets, fibrinogen and other clotting factors as revealed by prolonged PT, aPTT and TT, replacement of deficient component is useful. Replacement therapy is not indicated if there is no clinical bleeding and if no invasive procedures are planned.

11

Monitoring is essential for guiding management and checking adequacy of replacement component support. The blood components commonly used in DIC are fresh frozen plasma, cryoprecipitate, platelet concentrates and packed red cells (Table 11.23). The required doses depend on rate and degree of consumption. Replacement therapy can be halted when stabilization in platelet counts, fibrinogen levels and fall in fibrin degradation products are observed.

For a patient who is actively bleeding, *heparin* aggravates the bleeding. In typical cases of acute DIC (95% or more) therapy with heparin has not proved useful and may be harmful. Indications of heparin therapy include presence of arterial or large vessel venous thrombosis. Supplementation with activated protein C has shown promise in critically ill patients and has anti inflammatory properties. Patients with DIC have an acquired deficiency of antithrombin and administration of this agent in supraphysiologic doses showed benefit in neonates. Despite early results, administration of the tissue factor pathway inhibitor has not shown benefit in DIC in clinical trials. Novel antithrombin–independent inhibitors of thrombin (e.g. desirudin are being examined. Gabexate mesylate, a synthetic inhibitor of serine protease, is also being tested.

Suggested reading

1. Levi M. Disseminated intravascular coagulation: What's new? *Crit Care Clin* 2005;21:449–467.
2. Taylor FB, Toh CH, Hoots WK, et al. Towards definition, clinical and laboratory criteria and a scoring system for disseminated intravascular coagulation. *Thromb Haemost* 2001;86:1327–1330.

APPROACH TO THROMBOSIS IN CHILDREN

The incidence of thrombosis is lower in children than adults, however morbidity and mortality are significant. Children until 6 months of age have lower levels of the vitamin K dependent coagulation factors II, IX, and X compared to adults. Levels of thrombin inhibitors, such as antithrombin and heparin cofactor II, plasminogen, protein C and S are low at birth. Protein S levels approach adult values by the age of 3–6 months, but protein C levels remain low in childhood. Thrombin generation is decreased (because of low prothrombin levels) and delayed in newborns compared with adults. The incidence of thrombosis is maximum in infants and during adolescence.

Clinical Evaluation

Enquire for a history or symptoms suggestive of congenital heart disease and/or recent cardiac catheterization, which

Table 11.23: Types of blood component therapy, their constituents and guidelines for use

Component	*Constituents*	*Indication*	*Dose*	*Precautions*
Fresh frozen plasma (FFP)	All coagulation factors as in normal plasma. 0.7 –1.0 U/ml of factors II, V, VII, VIII, IX, X, XI, XII, XIII and 2.5 mg/ml fibrinogen	Treatment of many coagulation factor deficiency states (prolonged prothrombin time) and thrombotic thrombocytopenic purpura.	15 ml/kg or 1 bag per 10 kg as initial treatment (constitutes 25–30% replacement therapy for coagulation factors)	Infuse soon after thawing, may lead to fluid overload. Need ABO compatible units.
Cryoprecipitate	Fibrinogen (150 mg/bag), Factor VIII (80–120 units/ bag), Factor XIII, vWD (contains no factor IX)	Fibrinogen deficiency or consumption, factor VIII deficiency (hemophilia A), vWD, Factor XIII deficiency.	1 bag per 5 kg will raise fibrinogen levels by 70 mg/dl	
Random donor platelets (RDP)	Platelets, contains at least 5.5×10^{10} platelets	Thrombocytopenia	One unit raises platelet counts by 5–10,000/cu mm. Dose 1 unit/10 kg to raise counts by 30,000 to 50,000/cu mm	Infuse rapidly, do NOT refrigerate prior to transfusion.
Single donor platelets (SDP)	Platelets, contains at least 3×10^{11} platelets.	Thrombocytopenia	One collection is equivalent to approximately 6 units of random platelets.	Precautions as for random donor platelets.
Fresh blood	All components of blood	To replace acute, massive blood loss	Only to be used in severe trauma	Not a good source for platelets or coagulation factors.

are the most common causes of arterial thrombosis in children. History of fever, recent surgery, trauma, central venous catheter use, nephrotic syndrome, dehydration, varicella and other infections, and family history is taken. The age at which thrombosis occurred and the type of thrombosis (deep vein thrombosis, arterial thrombosis or stroke) should be documented.

Symptoms due to deep vein thrombosis include pain and swelling of the limb. Pulmonary embolism may present with anxiety, breathlessness, pleuritic chest pain, fever and cough. Symptoms of central nervous system thrombosis include vomiting, lethargy, seizures or weakness in an extremity. Strokes may occur *in utero*; newborns will present with seizures and lethargy. Older children present with headaches and acute onset of weakness in an extremity or hemiplegia. Precipitating factors like infection, dehydration and trauma are common. Patients with renal vein thrombosis may present with flank pain and hematuria. Limb edema, erythema and tenderness on dorsiflexion of the foot (positive Homan's sign) are present in deep vein thrombosis. Signs of pulmonary embolism are nonspecific and include diaphoresis, tachycardia and tachypnea. Signs of arterial thrombosis include diminished or absent peripheral pulses and cool extremities.

Laboratory Evaluation

Many clotting factors are consumed in an acute thrombosis, and a low factor level may be the result of the preexisting thrombosis. The child should be evaluated to rule out DIC with complete blood count, peripheral blood smear, prothrombin time, activated partial thromboplastin time and fibrinogen level (Table 11.24).

Imaging studies include: (i) color Doppler imaging signals are absent in thrombosed vessels and the lumen cannot be compressed with direct pressure. However, this may not be sufficiently sensitive to detect thrombosis in vessels such as subclavian veins, superior vena cava or brachiocephalic veins; (ii) echocardiography is useful for vena caval and proximal subclavian vein thrombosis; (iii) computerized tomography of the head with IV contrast is useful for detecting venous sinus thrombosis. Both MRI and MRA are better at detecting early arterial ischemic strokes; (iv) chest radiograph may reveal findings of pulmonary embolism, which include small pleural effusions with wedge shaped, pleural opacity of pulmonary infarction; (v) ventilation perfusion (V/Q) scintigraphy is the procedure of choice in children with suspected pulmonary embolism.

Management

Urgent stabilization is required, if possible screening tests for hypercoagulable state (Table 11.25) should be sent prior to initiating anticoagulation therapy. If respiratory distress or neurological problems exist then management in an intensive care unit is required. Children with lower-extremity deep vein thrombosis can be provided compression stockings. Initial therapy requires heparin (unfractionated or low molecular weight) followed by oral warfarin therapy. Close monitoring is required to prevent overdosage and risk of bleeding, underdosing will hamper resolution of the thrombus. The international normalized ratio, which is patient's PT compared to a standard, is the most useful test for monitoring anticoagulation. The INR therapeutic range is 2–3. The duration of therapy depends on the risk of recurrence, assessed by testing for thrombo-

Table 11.24: Initial workup for thrombosis to evaluate for hypercoagulable state*
Complete blood count
Prothrombin time, activated partial thromboplastin time
Radiology as indicated by symptoms
Activated protein C resistance, factor V Leiden mutation
Antithrombin
Lupus anticoagulant (which may be screened by using the dilute Russell viper venom test)
Anticardiolipin antibodies
Prothrombin gene 20210A mutation
Lipoprotein (a) level
Plasma homocysteine values
Protein C (Usually decreased in acute thrombosis)
Free and total protein S (Usually decreased in acute thrombosis)

*Heparin therapy affects antithrombin, protein C, protein S and activated protein C resistance tests.
Warfarin affects protein C, protein S and antithrombin.
Neither drug affects results of anticardiolipin antibodies, factor V Leiden, the prothrombin mutation or lipoprotein(a) or homocysteine levels.

Table 11.25: Common pre-existing factors which increase risk of thrombosis in children
Acquired conditions
Sepsis-viral, bacterial
Disseminated intravascular coagulation
Dehydration
Central venous catheter
Surgery, trauma
Congenital heart disease
Antiphospholipid antibody syndrome
Malignancy- acute lymphoblastic therapy (L-asparaginase and steroids)
Nephrotic syndrome
Inherited prothrombotic disorders
Resistance to activated protein C
Factor V Leiden
Protein C deficiency
Protein S deficiency
Antithrombin deficiency
Prothrombin gene 20210A mutation
Elevated lipoprotein (a) level
Hyper homocysteinemia

philia status 3 months after stopping anticoagulants. Unfractionated heparin exhibits antithrombin and anti-Xa activity, whereas low molecular weight heparin has primarily anti-Xa function.

Suggested reading

1. Tormene D, Gavasso S, Rossetto V, Simioni P. Thrombosis and thrombophilia in children: a systematic review. *Semin Thromb Hemost* 2006; 32: 724–728.
2. Saxena R, Kannan M, Choudhry VP. Laboratory studies in coagulation disorders. *Indian J Pediatr* 2007;74:649–655.

WHITE BLOOD CELLS

Evaluation of quantitative and qualitative changes in the lymphocytes and myeloid series will help to diagnose many infectious, immunologic, malignant and even endocrine disorders. A detailed history of onset, duration, fever, rashes, lymphadenopathy, organomegaly must be taken. The complete history, including family history and examination will contribute to the diagnosis.

Quantitative changes are a frequent anomaly on the hemogram report. The differential count will help pinpoint the expanded population of cells. The percentage increase over normal range is important, very high counts are indicative of leukemoid reaction or leukemias. The absolute count is required in certain cases, e.g. absolute eosinophil count for diagnosis of hypereosinophilic syndromes and neutrophil count for degree of immunodeficiency. The morphology of cells may reveal abnormal size, immaturity, change in nuclear cytoplasmic ratio, inclusions and abnormal granules. For example, Howell Jolly bodies are found in cases of absent splenic function due to asplenia or post splenectomy, toxic granulations and left shift suggests sepsis, Epstein Barr virus infection results in large monocytoid cells, which can be confused for blasts in the peripheral smear. It is also important to know if other hematopoietic cell lineages are affected.

Leukocytosis

The onset and duration of illness may provide a clue to the diagnosis; a history of medications and prior hospitalization may be contributory. Evaluate the child for infections, inflammatory, malignant and metabolic disorders.

Neutrophils increase in acute bacterial infections, acute blood loss, hemolysis and diabetic ketoacidosis (Table 11.26). Leukocyte alkaline phosphatase (LAP) is an enzyme present in mature neutrophils, on staining blue granules become visible. This is increased in infections and leukemoid reaction (very high white blood cell response to infection). In chronic myeloid leukemia, the neutrophils are LAP deficient so the score is low.

The circulating tissue macrophage precursors are the monocytes. These cells migrate to different tissues and transform into macrophages, e.g. Kupffer cells. These cells are important for ingestion and killing of many pathogenic bacteria and parasites like *M. tuberculosis* and *Leishmania* (Table 11.27). Monocytes are the first granulocytic cells to recover in post chemotherapy states when white cell counts recover. Abnormality of macrophage activation leads to disorders like familial hemophagocytic syndrome. *Basophilia* is seen in hypersensitivity reactions, chronic myeloid leukemia, Hodgkin lymphoma, varicella infection, nephrotic syndrome, hypothyroidism and following antithyroid medications. *Eosinophilia* occurs in many conditions, including allergic disorders (e.g. atopic dermatitis, asthma), systemic inflammatory conditions (e.g. inflammatory bowel disease, rheumatoid arthritis), malignancies (e.g. Hodgkin lymphoma). Parasites which invade tissue are more likely to cause eosinophilia, e.g. toxocara which causes visceral larva migrans (Table 11.28). Elevated sustained eosinophil counts are associated with cardiac toxicity. Moderate elevated absolute eosinophil

Table 11.26: List of common causes of neutrophilia

Acute
Infection—many acute bacterial infections
Drugs—epinephrine, corticosteroids, granulocyte colony stimulating factor
Hemorrhage
Hypoxia
Hemolysis
Stress—Trauma, burns, exercise, heat stroke
Kidney failure, diabetic ketoacidosis, hepatic failure
Leukemoid reaction
Hodgkin's lymphoma, chronic myeloid leukemia
Chronic
Chronic myeloid leukemia
Rheumatological/inflammatory diseases
Hemolytic anemia—sickle cell anemia
Post splenectomy state
Chronic blood loss
Endocrine-thyrotoxicosis
Genetic causes/syndromes
Down syndrome
Asplenia
Chronic idiopathic neutrophilia
Leukocyte adhesion defect

Table 11.27: List of common causes of monocytosis

Infections: tuberculosis, typhoid, malaria, bacterial endocarditis, brucella, kala azar
Rheumatological/inflammatory diseases: Systemic lupus erythematosus, rheumatoid arthritis, ulcerative colitis
Post splenectomy state, hemolytic anemia
Malignancy: Lymphomas, chronic myeloid leukemia, juvenile myelomonocytic leukemia, myelodysplasia
Myxedema

Table 11.28: List of common causes of eosinophilia

Acute
Atopic and allergic disorders: e.g. asthma, urticaria, drug hypersensitivity reactions. Parasitic infestations: toxocara, ascaris, amoebic, strongyloidiasis, filarial, toxoplasmosis, trichinosis, malaria scabies. Fungal infections: Bronchopulmonary aspergillosis, coccidiomycosis Malignancy: Hodgkin lymphoma, acute myeloid leukemia, myeloproliferative syndrome, brain tumors, hypereosinophilic syndrome
Chronic
Atopic and allergic disorders: pemphigus, dermatitis herpetiformis Rheumatologic/inflammatory disorders: Inflammatory bowel disease, rheumatoid arthritis Malignancy, myeloproliferative syndrome, hypereosinophilic syndrome Addison disease Kidney rejection, peritoneal dialysis Hyper IgE syndrome, Loeffler syndrome, Wiskott Aldrich syndrome, Omenn syndrome Thrombocytopenia with absent radii syndrome

count are above 1500–5000/cu mm, and severe eosinophilia is >5000 cells/cu mm. *Lymphocytosis* is a feature of many infections in children (Table 11.29).

Table 11.29: List of common causes of lymphocytosis

Infections: Infectious mononucleosis, infectious hepatitis, cytomegalovirus, tuberculosis, pertussis
Endocrine: Thyrotoxicosis, Addison disease
Malignancy (lymphoblasts): Acute lymphoblastic leukemia, lymphoma

Leukopenia

Usually found in conjunction with pancytopenia, e.g. aplastic anemia, megaloblastic anemia, bone marrow replacement or infiltration (malignancy, Gaucher disease, osteopetrosis) or hypersplenism, which must be evaluated in the work up.

When the neutrophil count is two standard deviations below the normal for that age, the child has neutropenia.

Absolute neutrophil count = WBC count/cu mm × percentage of (neutrophils + band forms).

Severe neutropenia occurs when the absolute neutrophil count is below 500. Neutropenia can be due to infections, inflammatory conditions, bone marrow failure, malignancy or as a consequence of treatment for a malignancy. It can also be due to metabolic disorders like glycogen storage disease type 1b, Shwachman-Diamond syndrome and Kostmann syndrome (Table 11.30).

Table 11.30: List of common causes of neutropenia

Acute
Infections: Many viral, bacterial, protozoan, fungal and rickettsial organisms. *Drugs:* Sulfonamides, phenytoin, phenobarbital, penicillin, phenothiazines Hypersplenism *Bone marrow replacement:* Leukemia, lymphoma, neuroblastoma Cancer chemotherapy agents, e.g. busulphan, cyclophosphamide
Chronic
Inherited disorders Cyclic neutropenia Familial benign neutropenia Kostmann syndrome Shwachman- Diamond syndrome Chediak Higashi syndrome Glycogen storage disease type 1b
Autoimmune and isoimmune neutropenia
Vitamin B_{12} and folate deficiency
Immune deficiencies: HIV
Metabolic disease: Tyrosinemia, methylmalonic aciduria
Bone marrow failure: Fanconi anemia
Myelodysplasia

Lymphopenia is found frequently in inherited immunodeficiency syndromes due to decreased production of B or T lymphocytes and Wiskott Aldrich syndrome, due to increased T cell destruction. It is also found in acquired immunodeficiency syndrome, post anti-thymocyte globulin treatment for aplastic anemia, after use of corticosteroids for systemic lupus erythematosus and protein losing enteropathy.

Qualitative Defects

These give rise to immune deficiencies; some like ***Chediak Higashi syndrome*** can be identified by the characteristic morphology of giant lysosomes in the granulocytes (Fig. 11.18) and oculocutaneous albinism. It is due to a defect in *CHS1* gene that encodes for lysosomal trafficking, results in ineffective granulopoiesis, delayed degranulation and defects in chemotaxis resulting in increased bacterial infections. In the accelerated phase, there is lymphohistiocytic infiltration of organs.

Leucocyte adhesion defect has deficiency of CD11 and CD18 on the neutrophils, resulting in defects in adhesion, chemotaxis and C3bi mediated phagocytosis. This causes delayed umbilical cord separation in the newborn and leads to repeated, severe infections and periodontitis later in life. ***Chronic granulomatous disease*** is an X-linked or rarely autosomal recessive, inherited defect of the respiratory burst oxidase in the granulocytic cells. It results in deep-seated granulomatous infections in the lungs, skin

11

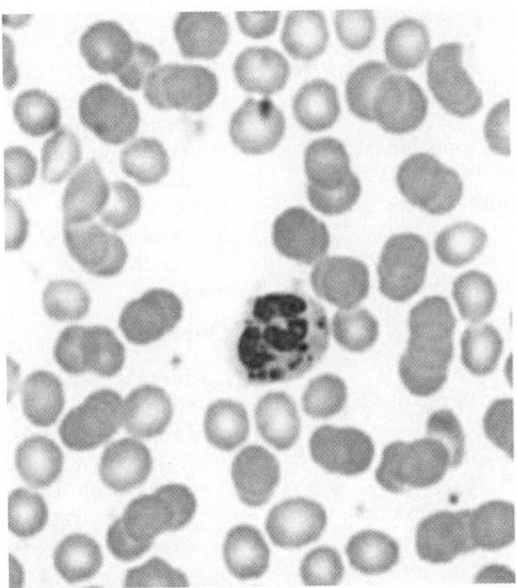

Fig. 11.18: Chediak Higashi syndrome. Neutrophils showing intracytoplasmic granules in a child with history of repeated infections

and gastrointestinal tract due to *S. aureus*, aspergillus spp. and *S. marcescens*. Many other primary immunodeficiencies have quantitative defects in T, B or both lymphocyte subsets with maturation or functional defects, which lead to life threatening infections.

Suggested reading

Dinauer MC. The phagocytic system and disorders of granulopoiesis and granulocytes function. In: Nathan and Oski's, Hematology of Infancy and Childhood, 6th edn. Eds. Nathan DG, Orkin SH, *et al.* WB Saunders: Philadelphia, 2003; 923–1010.

12 Diseases of Ear, Nose and Throat

DISEASES OF THE EAR

OTITIS MEDIA

Otitis media is one of the most common infections of early childhood. Anatomic features which make this age group particularly susceptible to ear infections include shorter, more horizontally placed and compliant eustachian tubes, which permit reflux of nasopharyngeal secretions into the middle ear. A high incidence of bacterial carriage in the adenoids may also contribute to the frequency of otitis media in children. Other risk factors include exposure to cigarette smoke, overcrowding, bottle-feeding, cleft palate, allergic rhinitis, Down syndrome and disorders of mucociliary transport. The same risk factors are operative in the pathophysiology of the two common varieties of otitis media seen in children: acute otitis media (AOM) and otitis media with effusion (OME).

Acute Otitis Media

Childhood acute otitis media (AOM) tends to occur in a bimodal age distribution, with children between ages 12 and 24 months and between ages 5 and 6 years at greatest risk.

Etiology

Streptococcus pneumoniae and *Hemophilus influenzae* are the two most common causative organisms of acute otitis media (AOM), accounting for approximately 65% of all cases. About 15% of the cases are due to *Moraxella catarrhalis*, *Streptococcus pyogenes* and *Staphylococcus aureus* infection. Respiratory viruses may play an important role in initiating otitis media and may be the only pathogens involved in some cases, as up to 20% of middle ear aspirates are sterile.

Diagnosis

AOM is characterized by the rapid onset of local and/or systemic signs and symptoms in the presence of a middle ear effusion. There is often a history of recent upper respiratory tract infection. Other symptoms include ear pain, ear tugging or rubbing, fever, excessive crying or poor appetite. Older children may report impaired hearing in the affected ear. The presence of ear pain has been found to be the most consistent symptom, while the presence or absence of fever is of variable utility.

Otoscopic examination generally reveals a red and bulging tympanic membrane with reduced tympanic membrane mobility as measured by either insufflation through the otoscope (pneumatic otoscopy) or tympanometry. A bulging tympanic membrane is the most reliable physical exam sign of AOM. Bulging and reduced mobility may help to differentiate AOM from redness of the tympanic membrane due to other causes, e.g. crying, viral myringitis, or trauma from aggressive ear cleaning. Suppuration (rupture of the drum with ear discharge) may have already occurred, in which case reddish brown fluid may be seen filling the ear canal. Cleaning of this fluid usually reveals an intact drum, as the rupture is small and closes promptly after spontaneous perforation.

Treatment

Antimicrobial therapy is the mainstay of treatment. Adjuvant treatment with oral decongestant drugs has not been shown to be efficacious, and the use of this class of drugs is not recommended. Topical decongestants, though frequently prescribed, are detrimental due to rebound congestion and nasal and nasopharyngeal mucosal irritation. Another frequently misused class of drugs is antihistamines, which contribute little to the resolution of otitis media and may precipitate sinus infections due to their drying effect on mucosal secretions.

Amoxicillin or co-trimoxazole form the first-line therapy for AOM. More expensive agents with β-lactamase resistance, e.g. amoxicillin-clavulanic acid, cefaclor, cefuroxime or other newer cephalosporins are useful second-line agents for unresponsive infections, and their routine first-line use should be limited to communities or patient populations with a demonstrated prevalence of β-lactamase producing *H. influenzae* or *B. catarrhalis*.

In the presence of complicated AOM such as intracranial spread of infection, acute mastoiditis, or neonatal otitis media, aspiration of the middle ear fluid (tympanocentesis) may be performed with an 18-gauge spinal needle and submitted for microbiology.

Initial antibiotic therapy should last at least 7 days, with reexamination indicated after 3–4 days and at 3 weeks. Many children present with *recurrent episodes of acute otitis media*. If particularly troublesome, this condition may be treated either with prolonged antibiotic prophylaxis (e.g. amoxicillin for 3–6 months) or insertion of tympanostomy tubes. Randomized trials have proved that both of these options are superior to placebo therapy, and that they appear to have equivalent efficacy in comparison to each other. If a child requires a second set of tympanostomy tubes, adenoidectomy is often simultaneously performed. This not only removes the bacterial reservoir that may contribute to recurrent otitis media, but also relieves possible obstruction of the eustachian tubes in the nasopharynx.

Otitis Media with Effusion (OME)

Following an episode of AOM, serous or mucoid middle ear effusions may be seen in a number of children. Effusion has been found to persist in up to 40% of children 1 month after their first episode of otitis media and in 10% after 3 months. However, many children with fluid effusion in the middle ear do not have any history of acute middle ear infections in the past. Pathogenesis of this condition has not been clearly established, but infectious, allergic or immunologic mechanisms may be at play.

Mild to moderate hearing loss and sensation of ear blockage or pressure are the chief complaints, although the condition may also be asymptomatic. As opposed to AOM, ear pain is generally not present in children with OME. Otoscopy reveals a dull tympanic membrane with or without a fluid level (Fig.12.1). Diagnosis is established by demonstrating reduced mobility of the tympanic membrane with either pneumatic otoscopy or a type B pattern on tympanometry. Since 50% of serous middle ear effusions resolve spontaneously within 3 months, newly diagnosed effusions should be observed for this period in nearly all cases. Most practitioners prescribe antibiotics during this period, though evidence supporting this practice is not incontrovertible. Use of antihistamines and decongestants is not recommended. The benefit of brief steroid administration has also not been proven.

If effusion persists beyond 3 months, tympanostomy tube insertion may be considered for significant hearing loss (>25 dB) (Fig. 12.2). Other indications of tube placement are ear discomfort or pain, altered behavior, speech delay, recurrent acute otitis media or impending cholesteatoma formation from tympanic membrane retraction. Improvement in hearing as well as ear discomfort is immediate and quite gratifying, but lasts only as long as the tubes are in place. Mean time before extrusion is usually between 6 and 9 months. The majority of the ears recover by the time the tubes extrude, but some children require repeated tube placements. Insertion of long-term tubes (of T-tube design) or adenoidectomy may be considered in cases of persistent symptomatic effusion. Although many otolaryngologists permit surface swimming (but not diving), it is probably safer for children to avoid swimming altogether to prevent contamination of the middle ear space.

Chronic Suppurative Otitis Media: The Draining Ear

Persistent or recurrent ear discharge is generally due to chronic inflammation of the middle ear space or mastoid air cells. Such infection invariably presents with perforation of the tympanic membrane, which allows egress of the suppurative material. Chronic suppurative otitis media (CSOM) most often results from neglected acute middle ear infections, and is, therefore, much more common in children with inadequate access to primary health care. It most often occurs in the first five years of life, as eustachian tube dysfunction plays a central role in the pathophysiology.

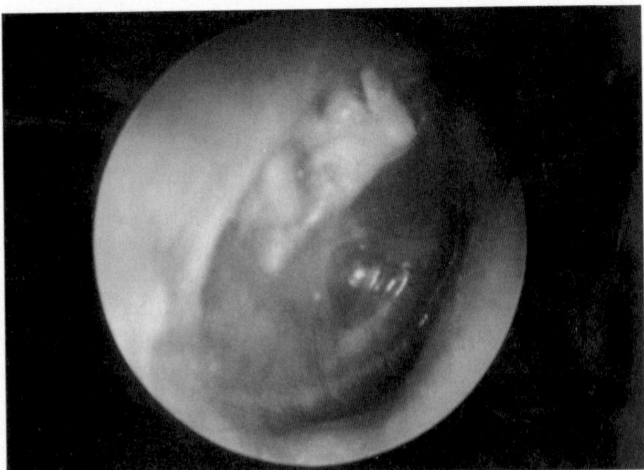

Fig. 12.1: Otitis media with effusion. Note the retraction and thinning of the tympanic membrane, the draping of the tympanic membrane over the long process of incus, distortion of the light reflex, and an impression of fluid being present behind the drum

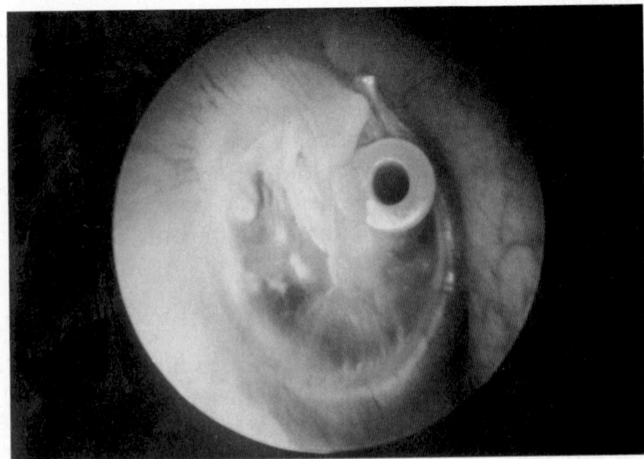

Fig. 12.2: A tympanostomy tube in place. The tube is beginning to get extruded, thus appearing higher than the site of its insertion (anteroinferior quadrant)

The most common complication of CSOM is hearing loss, which may affect a young child's language development and school performance. The hearing loss is usually a conductive loss, resulting from edema/fluid in the middle ear and tympanic membrane perforation. However, some recent studies have also suggested sensorineural hearing loss as a possible sequela of CSOM, presumably through direct extension of inflammatory mediators into the inner ear.

Etiology

Pseudomonas aeruginosa is the most commonly isolated organism in CSOM. Other organisms commonly identified include *Staphylococcus aureus*, gram-negative organisms such as *Proteus* species and *E. coli*, and anaerobes. Fungi are also thought to play a role in CSOM, especially *Aspergillus* and *Candida* species.

Diagnosis

Chronic ear discharge is the hallmark of CSOM. Otoscopy reveals perforation of the tympanic membrane (Fig. 12.3). A chronically draining ear may also be seen with cholesteatoma, which is a sac of squamous epithelium extending from the tympanic membrane into the middle ear (Fig. 12.4). Most cholesteatoma is acquired, although whether it arises from extension of a tympanic membrane retraction pocket, or from aberrant inward migration of the normal eardrum epithelium, remains unclear. Rarely, the cholesteatoma may be congenital, arising *de novo* in the middle ear space. Though not malignant, cholesteatoma may cause serious complications by slow expansion and local destruction. These complications are discussed further in the next section.

Treatment

Medical therapy consists primarily of: (i) topical antibiotics, and (ii) aural toilet. Topical quinolones are the preferred local antibiotic. Ciprofloxacin or ofloxacin ear drops three time a day for about 2 weeks are often effective. Aural toilet is provided by keeping the ear as dry as possible by wicking at least three times a day. Roll a clean absorbent cloth or strong tissue paper into a wick, place it in the child's ear, remove when wet, replace the wick with a clean one, and repeat these steps until the ear is dry.

The use of systemic antibiotic therapy should be reserved for infections showing signs of complications or for the presence of systemic involvement. Instructions to parents to avoid water entering the affected ear should also be given. Of note, secondary fungal otitis externa has been reported as a complication of topical antibiotic treatment. Otolaryngology referral is mandatory for ruling out cholesteatoma.

Surgery is usually indicated for most cases of CSOM that do not respond to conservative treatment. Surgical therapy involves repair of the tympanic membrane perforation (tympanoplasty) with or without a mastoidectomy. If cholesteatoma is suspected, ear exploration via mastoidectomy and cholesteatoma removal is mandatory. The primary goal of surgical therapy for cholesteatoma is to create a "safe ear" by removal of all cholesteatoma. Hearing preservation is a secondary goal of the procedure. In simple tympanic membrane perforations without cholesteatoma, surgical repair is now considered appropriate treatment in children older than 8 years of age. Tympanic membrane repair protects the ear from further contamination and infection, often improves hearing, and may have a positive effect on the quality of the child's life. The previously held dictum that tympanoplasty should be delayed until adulthood has been challenged by the results of several studies demonstrates equivalent success rates of surgical repair in children older than 6 to 8 years.

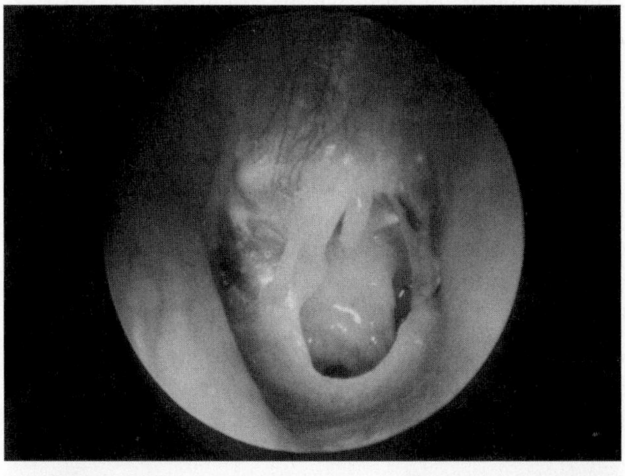

Fig. 12.3: Chronic suppurative otitis media with a dry, central perforation. The long process of incus and the stapedius tendon attaching to the neck of stapes are seen through the perforation. Also seen is the round window posteriorly

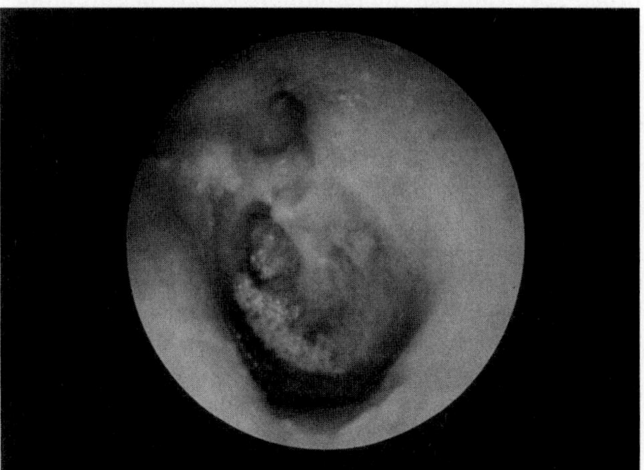

Fig. 12.4: Attic cholesteatoma. The entrance of an attic cholesteatoma sac (attic perforation) showing wet debris inside. The pars tensa shows retraction and tympanosclerosis (whitish plaque antero-inferiorly)

12

Complications of Otitis Media

Untreated otitis media may occasionally cause complications that, while occurring rarely, have potentially dire consequences. These complications can be further classified as either intracranial or extracranial (Table 12.1). AOM and its complications are more common in young children, while complications due to CSOM with or without cholesteatoma are more common in older children.

Table 12.1: Complications of otitis media

Intracranial complications
Meningitis
Brain abscess
Epidural abscess
Dural venous (sigmoid sinus) thrombosis
Otitic hydrocephalus
Extracranial complications
Subperiosteal abscess
Labyrinthine fistula
Facial nerve paralysis
Acute coalescent mastoiditis

Meningitis is the most common intracranial complication of both acute and chronic otitis media. Furthermore, AOM is the most common cause of secondary meningitis. While this is a serious complication, the mortality rate from otitic meningitis has decreased significantly. Of pertinent interest is the fact that meningitis is the most common cause of acquired sensorineural hearing loss in children.

Brain abscess is a potentially lethal complication of otitis media. Unlike meningitis, which is caused more frequently by AOM, brain abscesses result almost exclusively from chronic otitis media. Imaging plays an important role. Broad-spectrum parenteral antibiotics are begun immediately, and surgical drainage is paramount. Thrombosis of the sigmoid or transverse sinus is another important intracranial complication of otitis media. Patients typically present with headache, malaise, and high spiking fevers in a "picket fence" pattern. Treatment involves parenteral antibiotics and surgical drainage of the mastoid.

Acute coalescent mastoiditis occurs due to the spread of infection into the mastoid bone. This entity should be differentiated from fluid effusion within mastoid air cells, which is sometimes mistakenly noted radiologically as "mastoiditis". Such opacification is commonly seen with both acute and chronic OM, is readily apparent on CT scans, and is of little clinical significance. Coalescent mastoiditis, on the other hand, presents with postauricular erythema, tenderness, and edema, and an auricle that is generally displaced inferiorly and laterally. If acute coalescent mastoiditis is suspected, a CT scan should be performed, which would show clouding or coalescence of the mastoid air cells. Differential diagnosis must include a severe case of otitis externa, as both processes may present with swelling and tenderness of the ear canal, postauricular region and mastoid process. Untreated, this may progress to an abscess within the confines of the mastoid cells, or spread externally, leading to the formation of subperiosteal or deep neck abscesses.

Acute coalescent mastoiditis should initially be treated with parenteral antibiotics directed against the aforementioned pathogens related to AOM, adding coverage for gram-negative and anaerobic organisms only if mastoiditis is superimposed upon a history of a chronically discharging ear, where colonization with such bacteria is common. The presence of an abscess mandates surgical intervention. Surgery in the form of a cortical mastoidectomy is also indicated for cases with poor response to parenteral antibiotic therapy, an intracranial complication or acute mastoiditis in a chronic ear.

Other extracranial complications of otitis media include *labyrinthine fistula* and *facial nerve paralysis.* Labyrinthine fistula, in which a cholesteatoma has eroded into the inner ear, presents with vertigo and possibly a sensorineural hearing loss. Facial nerve paralysis secondary to otitis media is usually treated with appropriate antibiotics and myringotomy. If the paralysis is secondary to cholesteatoma, mastoidectomy is indicated.

OTITIS EXTERNA

Acute diffuse otitis externa (swimmer's ear) presents with itching, pain and fullness in the affected ear. Erythema and edema of the canal skin and tenderness on moving the pinnae or tragus are diagnostic features. Otorrhea is common, especially in bacterial infections. Swimming is a risk factor, but the infection can also result from impacted cerumen, hearing aid use, or self-induced trauma from foreign objects such as hairpins or cotton swabs. The etiologic agents of otitis externa are listed in Table 12.2. Treatment consists of ear canal cleaning by experienced personnel and topical antibiotic drops. Topical antibiotics are highly effective for acute otitis externa with clinical cure rates up to 80%. If edema is significant, ribbon gauze or a premanufactured "wick" may be placed in the external auditory canal to allow wick-like delivery of the antibiotic agent. Oral and parenteral antibiotics are reserved for cases with complications. A chronic form of diffuse otitis externa may also be seen.

Localized otitis externa or *furunculosis* presents as an exquisitely painful, superficial abscess in the outer portion

Table 12.2: Etiology of otitis externa

Pseudomonas aeruginosa	40%
Staphylococcus species	25%
Gram-negative rods (e.g. *Proteus, E. coli*)	9%
Other bacteria	13%
Aspergillus/Candida	2%

of the ear canal. Such infection is commonly staphylococcal in origin. Oral antistaphylococcal antibiotics and analgesics bring about prompt relief. Occasionally, incision and drainage of a pointing abscess may be necessary.

Eczematous or *psoriatic otitis externa* describes a group of inflammatory conditions in which there is drainage, pruritis and/or scaling of the ear canal skin. Underlying causes include contact dermatitis, atopic dermatitis and seborrheic dermatitis. To treat this condition effectively, the primary dermatologic disorder must be addressed.

Otomycosis or *fungal otitis externa* is most common in humid weather and presents with pain and pruritus of the affected ear. These infections are often considered to be opportunistic, as they are frequently seen subsequent to treatment of a bacterial infection. Examination reveals fungal spores and filaments along with cloudy discharge (Fig. 12.5). *Aspergillus* and *Candida* are the most common pathogens, though other fungi may be implicated. Aural toilet and application of a topical antifungal (e.g. clotrimazole) are curative.

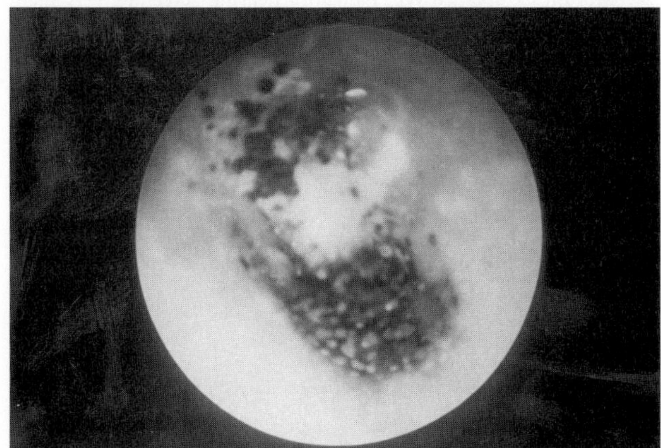

Fig. 12.5: Otomycosis. Fungal debris (hyphae and dark-colored spores) filling the deeper end of the external auditory meatus

HEARING LOSS

The importance of early detection of pediatric hearing loss should not be underestimated. Unrecognized early hearing loss can impede development of speech, language, and cognitive skills. Separate differential diagnoses exist for deficits of both the conductive and sensorineural components of the hearing mechanism. Pediatric hearing loss can be further classified as either *congenital* or *acquired*. A comprehensive discussion of the various causes of pediatric hearing loss exceeds the scope of this discussion. However, several important clinical points are presented below.

Conductive Hearing Loss

Any process that interferes with the conductive mechanism of the ear canal, tympanic membrane, or ossicles may cause a conductive hearing loss. The most common cause of conductive deafness in children is otitis media with effusion, and is typically of mild to moderate severity. Several congenital syndromes may also be associated with middle ear abnormalities, such as Apert, Crouzon and Treacher-Collins syndromes.

Sensorineural Hearing Loss

Sensorineural hearing loss (SNHL) is caused by a lesion of the cochlea, auditory nerve, or central auditory pathway. SNHL can be *acquired* or *congenital*. The majority of pediatric SNHL falls into the acquired (noncongenital) category.

The most common postnatal cause of acquired sensorineural hearing loss is meningitis, while the most common prenatal cause is intrauterine infection (e.g. TORCH infections, syphilis, mumps, measles). Other causes of acquired hearing loss include prematurity, hyperbilirubinemia, perinatal asphyxia/hypoxia, head trauma, acquired immunodeficiency syndrome and ototoxic medications (aminoglycosides, loop diuretics).

Congenital causes of sensorineural hearing loss can be further divided into *syndromic* and *nonsyndromic* types. Although the majority of congenital hearing loss is nonsyndromic, there are over 300 genetic syndromes identified to date that are associated with SNHL. Some of the most common genetic syndromes associated with deafness include Pendred syndrome, in which patients have thyroid enlargement, and Usher syndrome, which is associated with retinitis pigmentosa and blindness. Alport syndrome and Waardenburg syndrome are also implicated.

Most cases of congenital hearing loss are nonsyndromic, and the recent sequencing of the human genome has rapidly advanced our understanding of these disorders. To date more than 110 chromosome loci and at least 65 genes have been identified that are associated with genetic hearing loss. Mutations in a single gene, *GJB2*, may be responsible for up to 50% of nonsyndromic congenital hearing loss. *GJB2* encodes the protein connexin 26, which is widely expressed in cells of the inner ear. Screening tests for the connexin 26 mutation have recently become available as a means for detecting congenital hearing loss.

Neonatal Screening

All neonates with risk factors for hearing loss must be screened with an auditory brainstem response (ABR) or otoacoustic emissions (OAE) test to exclude hearing impairment. It must be recognized, however, that use of clinical indicators to focus hearing screens will miss as many as 50% of all cases of impairment. As a result, universal newborn hearing screen programs are becoming commonplace over the last 10 years in the United States and Europe, though not yet in India. The importance of neonatal screening cannot be overemphasized. Infants in whom treatment for hearing loss is initiated by 6 months of age are able to maintain language and social development in line with their physical development. This is in stark contrast to those whose hearing loss is identified after 6 months of age.

One limitation of newborn screening is that some forms of early-onset hearing loss are not apparent at birth. To address this issue, the Joint Committee on Infant Hearing in the United States has identified 10 risk indicators (Table 12.3) that should prompt continued monitoring of hearing status even in the face of normal neonatal screens.

Table 12.3: Indications for continued hearing monitoring with normal hearing on newborn hearing screen

Parental or caregiver concern regarding the child's speech or development
Family history of childhood hearing loss
Findings of a syndrome known to be associated with hearing loss
Postnatal infections known to be associated with hearing loss (e.g. meningitis)
In-utero infections such as CMV, rubella, syphilis, herpes, and toxoplasmosis
Hyperbilirubinemia requiring exchange transfusion, persistent pulmonary hypertension of the newborn, or conditions requiring ECMO
Syndromes associated with progressive hearing loss (e.g. neurofibromatosis)
Neurodegenerative disorders (e.g. Hunter syndrome or Friedrich ataxia)
Head trauma
Recurrent or persistent OME for at least 3 months

Screening in Older Children

Clinical evaluation of hearing at routine well child assessments is critical in early detection of hearing impairment. Examination should include otoscopy with attention to middle ear pathology such as OME and CSOM. Any doubtful cases must be referred for detailed audiologic evaluation at the earliest opportunity in order that timely intervention for hearing rehabilitation may begin.

Multiple techniques exist to assess hearing sensitivity and are selected based on the age and the abilities of the child. For younger children unable to understand instructions, visual-reinforcement audiometry is usually performed. Pure-tone audiometry is usually possible in children >5 years. Tympanometry may be performed in nearly all children to assess ear drum mobility.

Treatment of Hearing Loss

Once the diagnosis has been established, treatment of hearing loss is based on the extent of deficit and on the underlying pathology. For very mild or unilateral hearing loss, treatment may consist simply of preferential seating in school. For significant conductive hearing loss, treatment may consist simply of tympanostomy tubes or tympanoplasty if a perforation is present.

SNHL, in contrast, is generally more difficult to correct than conductive hearing loss. Treatment of significant SNHL may require the use of assistive hearing devices such as hearing aids from as early as 3 months of age. The development of cochlear implants has rapidly reshaped the management of childhood hearing loss. Cochlear implantation may be considered for infants as young as 12 months of age who have a profound bilateral hearing loss, and may be considered even earlier if the child's hearing loss is due to meningitis. Lip reading, sign language, and deaf education programs should be considered for children who are not candidates for or cannot afford cochlear implantation.

Suggested reading

1. Flynn CA, Griffin GH, Schultz JK. Decongestants and antihistamines for acute otitis media in children. Cochrane Database Syst Rev 2007;18: 1727.
2. Kenna MA. Otitis media and the new guidelines. J Otolaryngol 2005; 34 Suppl 1: S24–32.
3. Leach AJ, Morris PS. Antibiotics for the prevention of acute and chronic suppurative otitis media in children. Cochrane Database Syst Rev 2006;18: 4401.
4. Morton CC, Nance WE. Newborn hearing screening – A silent revolution. N Engl J Med 2006; 354: 2151–64.
5. Powers JH. Diagnosis and treatment of acute otitis media: Evaluating the evidence. Infect Dis Clin N Am 2007; 21: 409–26.
6. Rosenfeld RM, et al. Systematic review of topical antimicrobial therapy for acute otitis externa. Otolaryngol Head Neck Surg 2006; 134 Suppl 4: S24–S48.
7. Smith JA, Danner CJ. Complications of chronic otitis media and cholesteatoma. Otolaryngol Clin N Am 2006; 39: 1237–55.
8. Verhoeff M, et al. Chronic suppurative otitis media: a review. Int J Pediatr Otorhinolaryngol 2006; 70: 1–12.
9. Government of India. Integrated Management of Neonatal and Childhood Illness. Chart book. 2003

DISEASES OF THE NOSE AND SINUSES

RHINITIS

Allergic Rhinitis

Allergic rhinitis is an inflammatory disorder characterized by sneezing, itching, nasal blockage, and clear rhinorrhea. The pathophysiology involves an IgE-mediated reaction in response to a specific allergen. Symptoms may be seasonal (hay fever) or perennial. Examination reveals a pale and edematous nasal mucosa, congested nasal turbinates, and mucoid rhinorrhea. Conjunctival itching and redness are sometimes present. Inhaled allergens (e.g. pollen, spores, and dust mites) are the most common causes. Though the above symptomatology is characteristic, accurate diagnosis may require demonstration of eosinophilia in a nasal smear, or the use of skin/serologic tests to show specific IgE response to a variety of allergens (allergy tests). These tests establish the atopic etiology and help differentiate from other conditions causing similar symptoms, e.g. vasomotor rhinitis, viral rhinitis and adenoid hypertrophy.

Treatment includes avoidance of known allergens, use of topical cromolyn sodium and steroid sprays for prevention, and antihistamines for relief of symptoms. The use of oral decongestants is controversial. Topical decongestants should also generally be discouraged as they cause rebound congestion (short-term) and chemical rhinitis or rhinitis medicamentosa (long-term). Immunotherapy may be beneficial for refractory cases, but its application is now less frequent owing to the success of steroid sprays.

Viral Rhinitis

Viral rhinitis or "the common cold," is the most common cause of both nasal obstruction and rhinorrhea in children. Children average between six and eight of these upper respiratory infections per year. Parents often need reassurance that such frequent colds are not abnormal, provided their child has an otherwise normal growth pattern. Malaise, low to moderate grade fever, nasal congestion, and rhinorrhea are the presenting symptoms. A number of different viruses may be responsible, including rhinovirus and adenovirus. Treatment is symptomatic and requires paracetamol and a judicious use of oral decongestants. Antihistamines are contraindicated. Otitis media and sinusitis are frequent complications.

SINUSITIS

Sinusitis can be classified as either acute or chronic sinusitis. The ethmoid and maxillary sinuses are the earliest to develop and are the ones most commonly involved by sinusitis in infancy and early childhood. The frontal sinuses may become involved only after 5–6 years of life. Isolated sphenoid disease is rare, but can behave as a distinct clinical entity from other types of sinusitis. The ethmoids are now recognized to be the primary site of origin of inflammation in most cases of sinusitis.

Risk factors associated with sinusitis include recurrent upper respiratory infections (URI), allergic rhinitis, cystic fibrosis, immunodeficiency, ciliary dyskinesia, daycare attendance, and exposure to tobacco smoke. The most significant factor is the presence of a URI, as 5–10% of these are complicated by sinusitis. A sinus infection should be considered in any child whose cold symptoms have not resolved by 7–10 days.

Etiology

The most common isolates in acute sinus infections are *S. pneumoniae*, *H. influenzae* and *M. catarrhalis*. These same bacteria are implicated in chronic sinusitis, as are *S. aureus*, anaerobes and occasionally fungi. The adenoid pad plays an important role in the pathophysiology of sinusitis, as several studies have demonstrated its role as a bacterial reservoir for the paranasal sinuses.

Diagnosis

Acute rhinosinusitis typically presents as a URI with worsening of nasal discharge and cough 7 to 10 days after onset of symptoms. A severe URI with fever and purulent rhinorrhea also meets the diagnostic criteria for acute sinusitis. Chronic sinusitis is defined as either symptoms of sinusitis lasting longer than 3 months, or a patient with recurrent episodes of acute sinusitis. Nasal obstruction, halitosis, and headache may all be additional features of chronic rhinosinusitis. Imaging should not be used for the routine diagnosis of sinusitis and should be reserved for cases with complications and those being considered for surgery. CT scan has been proven to be far superior to plain X-rays in the imaging of the paranasal sinuses.

Allergic fungal sinusitis is an increasingly recognized condition in atopic, immunocompetent patients. Older children and adolescents are typically affected. The cause is hypersensitivity to fungal antigens. This results in a form of chronic rhinosinusitis that is difficult to manage medically and usually requires surgical intervention.

Complications of rhinosinusitis include orbital or intracranial spread of infection. Orbital complications typically result from direct extension from an ethmoid sinusitis. Early orbital complications manifest as periorbital (preseptal) cellulitis, while more severe complications include orbital abscess or cavernous sinus thrombosis. Ophthalmoplegia, loss of vision and severe toxemia indicate a potentially life-threatening spread of infection to the cavernous sinus. Intracranial complications such as meningitis and abscesses may also occur and are more commonly associated with infections of the frontal and sphenoid sinuses.

Treatment

Although a significant number of acute sinusitis episodes will resolve spontaneously, most authors recommend antibiotics as the cornerstone of treatment. As in acute otitis media, amoxicillin should be the first-line of medical therapy for acute sinusitis. The exact duration of therapy is not clear, but most clinicians feel that if symptoms have already persisted for 7–10 days, the infection should be treated for at least 14 days. Longer courses and second-line antibiotic agents are indicated for refractory infections, and parental antibiotics are the agents of choice for sinusitis with orbital or intracranial complications. Other adjuvant measures that may have a possible benefit include oral decongestants, mucolytic agents, and topical nasal saline. Topical decongestants may be used in sinusitis with complications. Antihistamines are detrimental due to their drying effect on mucosal secretions and are best avoided.

Antibiotics are also the mainstay of treatment for chronic sinusitis. As most of these patients have already failed a course of standard-dose amoxicillin, initial therapy may consist of amoxicillin/clavulanate, high-dose amoxicillin, or cefuroxime. The duration of treatment is longer than for acute sinusitis, typically 3 to 6 weeks. Patients who have a true penicillin allergy may be treated with a macrolide antibiotic, although there is increasing resistance of sinus pathogens to these drugs. Topical nasal steroids may also play a role in the treatment of chronic sinusitis.

Surgical intervention for acute sinusitis is limited to those with orbital or intracranial complications. Surgery may also be considered for patients with chronic sinusitis who have not responded to aggressive medical management. First-line surgical therapy usually consists of adenoidectomy to remove the adenoid pad as a bacterial reservoir for the sinuses. Significant controversy exists regarding the indications for endoscopic sinus surgery (ESS) in pediatric patients. Selected circumstances in which ESS may be of benefit include patients with sinonasal polyposis, cystic fibrosis, or those whose symptoms have not responded to adenoidectomy.

NASAL OBSTRUCTION

Causes

Chronic mouth breathing in children, is generally caused by blockage of nasal airflow. The site of nasal blockage is more often in the nasopharyngeal area due to adenoid hypertrophy, than in the nose itself. Intranasal causes of obstruction include allergic rhinitis, recurrent sinusitis, nasal septum deviation, turbinate hypertrophy, nasal polyps, and less commonly, neoplasms. As a rule, bilateral nasal polyps do not occur in normal children and their presence should prompt testing for cystic fibrosis. Congenital causes of nasal airway obstruction include choanal atresia, dermoid cysts, teratomas, encephaloceles, and pyriform aperture (bony opening to the nasal cavity in the skull) stenosis.

Diagnosis

Adenoid enlargement should be suspected in children, usually older than 2 years, who present with nasal blockage, mouth breathing, sleep disturbance and chronic nasal discharge. Examination must rule out nasal pathology such as septal deviation or polyposis. Neonates with pyriform aperture stenosis may present with a single midline maxillary incisor. CT scan confirms the diagnosis.

Treatment

Adenoidectomy is recommended for symptomatic younger children. In older children, it is useful to remember that pubertal growth of the midface and regression of adenoid size tends to result in relief of adenoid-related nasal obstruction from around the age of 9 years. Pyriform aperture stenosis is treated with surgical drilling of the bony pyriform aperture. Treatment for sinonasal polyposis includes topical and systemic steroids for limited disease. Larger, obstructing polyps usually require surgical intervention.

Generally speaking, surgery on the nasal septum should be avoided in prepubertal children, as it may lead to retardation in midface growth and saddling of the nasal dorsum. However, on rare occasions, a very conservative operation to correct a limited portion of the septum may be justified in a particularly symptomatic child. Turbinate hypertrophy usually responds to treatment of allergy, though in refractory cases electrocautery may be used for reduction of turbinate size.

EPISTAXIS

Bleeding from the nose occurs frequently in children, most ofen from the anterior portion of the nasal septum at a confluence of arterial vessels known as *Little's area* (or Kiesselbach's plexus). Local trauma, especially nose-picking, is the most common cause of epistaxis in children. Reduced ambient humidity, as seen during the winter months in some climates, also places the patient at risk. Examination reveals prominent vessels in Little's area that bleed promptly when touched with a cotton-tipped probe. Digital pressure by pinching the nose invariably stops the bleeding. Avoidance of nose picking, application of an antibiotic ointment for lubrication, and, for refractory cases, cauterization with topical silver nitrate or electrocautery are curative. Bleeding disorders must be suspected in children with a suggestive family history, a history of frequent bleeding from other sites, or any nasal bleeding which does not respond in the usual fashion.

Less frequent causes of recurrent epistaxis include nasopharyngeal angiofibroma and hereditary hemorrhagic telangiectasia (HHT). Nasopharyngeal angiofibroma is a tumor occurring exclusively in adolescent males that can cause profuse, brisk bleeding. HHT, also known as Osler-Weber-Rendu syndrome, is a genetic defect in blood vessel structure resulting in arteriovenous malformations. Patients may suffer from severe, recurrent epistaxis, as well as gastrointestinal bleeds and pulmonary hemorrhage.

CHOANAL ATRESIA

Congenital failure of the nasal cavities to open posteriorly into the nasopharynx (choanae) is called choanal atresia. It is caused by failure of resorption of the buccopharyngeal membrane during embryonic development. This process may be unilateral or bilateral. Bilateral choanal atresia usually presents immediately after birth with respiratory distress, which is due to the fact that neonates are obligate nose-breathers. The affected baby cycles between spells of cyanosis and crying. Attempts at suckling immediately precipitate cyanosis.

Bilateral choanal atresia requires urgent management. The airway may be established immediately by inserting a finger in the baby's mouth; this can be replaced with a plastic oropharyngeal airway or a McGovern nipple. Failure of these measures to secure a satisfactory airway may necessitate endotracheal intubation or tracheostomy.

Flexible nasal endoscopy confirms the diagnosis. When endoscopy is not available, attempts to pass an 8 French catheter can aid in diagnosis. Dye or contrast studies are not routinely used since the advent of endoscopy. A CT scan will demonstrate the thickness of the atretic plate and whether it is a bony or membranous atresia.

Bilateral atresia can present as part of the CHARGE association, consisting of *c*oloboma, *h*eart abnormalities, choanal *a*tresia, *r*etardation of growth and development, *g*enitourinary defects, and *e*ar anomalies.

Unilateral choanal atresia is a more indolent process and may present later in infancy or early childhood with unilateral nasal discharge or blockage. Atresia typically becomes apparent when the opposite nasal passage becomes blocked due to rhinitis or adenoid hypertrophy.

Treatment of choanal atresia is surgical. The two primary approaches are transpalatal and transnasal. Transnasal endoscopic repair is often attempted first as it is less invasive. Transpalatal repair, which involves removal of the posterior hard palate, is often reserved for failed endoscopic repair. Stents are placed in the nasal passages to prevent restenosis, and are typically left in place for 3 to 6 weeks postoperatively.

Suggested reading

1. Belenky WM, Madgy DN, Haupert MS. Nasal obstruction and rhinorrhea. In: Bluestone CD and Stool SE. Pediatric Otolaryngology, 4th ed. Philadelphia: Saunders, 2003: 908–21.
2. Daniel SJ. The upper airway: Congenital malformations. Paed Resp Reviews 2006; 7S: S260–S263.
3. Lieser JD, Derkay CS. Pediatric sinusitis: when do we operate? Curr Opin Otolaryngol Head Neck Surg 2005; 13: 60–6.
4. Lusk R. Pediatric chronic rhinosinusitis. Curr Opin Otolaryngol Head Neck Surg 2005; 14: 393–6.

DISEASES OF THE ORAL CAVITY AND PHARYNX

ORAL CAVITY

Inflammatory Disorders

Recurrent aphthous stomatitis is a disorder common in children that presents as painful white ulcers of variable size on the oral mucosa. The ulcers resolve spontaneously over several days; topical steroids, tetracycline, and analgesics are of doubtful benefit. The exact etiology is unknown, although multiple causes have been speculated.

Herpetic stomatitis presents in children with small, painful vesicles that evolve into gray pseudomembranous mucosal ulcers. Antiviral medications may be used to hasten recovery, though the lesions usually heal spontaneously within 10–14 days.

Oral candidiasis (*thrush*) appears as small, white, curd-like lesions on the tongue and oral mucosa. *Candida* is the typical etiological agent. It can be a benign finding in children who are under age 6 months or who have just completed antibiotic treatment. However, it can also be related to systemic disease such as diabetes or immunodeficiency. Topical nystatin suspension as well as oral antifungal agents are effective.

Congenital Disorders

Cleft palate may appear with or without *cleft lip* and can cause serious feeding difficulties in children. These malformations are believed to be multifactorial. Treatment should include staged reconstruction of the lip and palate defects and multidisciplinary management.

Micrognathia refers to a small mandible. If severe, the tongue may become displaced posteriorly and cause respiratory distress in the neonate. Congenital micrognathia is most commonly seen with the Pierre Robin sequence, in which patients also have cleft palate and glossoptosis. If the condition is severe, the neonate may require tracheostomy. Mandibular distraction, in which the jaw is surgically advanced forward, has been recently proposed as an alternative to tracheostomy in selected patients.

Ankyloglossia (tongue tie) is a limitation of anterior tongue mobility caused by a congenitally short tissue band (frenulum) under the tongue. Indications for surgical correction include speech impairment and feeding difficulties.

Macroglossia may be idiopathic or associated with syndromes such as neurofibromatosis and Down syndrome. If significant, the enlarged tongue may cause drooling, speech impairment, stridor, and airway obstruction. Surgical reduction may be undertaken if symptomatic.

Lingual thyroid may present as a posterior midline tongue mass and is caused by an abnormality in the descent of the thyroid from the primitive tongue base *in utero*. It may present with respiratory distress in the newborn. If removed, patients may require thyroid hormone supplementation, as lingual thyroid often represents the patient's only functioning thyroid tissue.

A multitude of congenital cysts may be found on the oral mucosal. Nearly all are benign and are treated with either simple excision or observation.

Systemic Processes

Although oral and oropharyngeal lesions are frequently caused by primary local disease, they may also indicate the presence of a systemic illness. Mucosal ulcerations, bleeding, and xerostomia should raise the consideration of systemic disease in one's differential diagnosis. Inflammatory processes with oral manifestations include Crohn's disease, systemic lupus erythematosus, and Kawasaki disease. Systemic infections with oral cavity symptoms include varicella, Epstein-Barr virus, and measles. Thrombocytopenia, clotting factor deficiencies and von Willebrand's disease may cause recurrent or persistent oral bleeding, especially along the gum line. Mucosal pigmentation may suggest Peutz-Jaeger disease, neurofibromatosis, or intoxication with lead or other heavy metals.

12

PHARYNX

The Sore Throat

All children will complain of sore throat at some time. Viral pharyngitis is by far the most common culprit. Important considerations in evaluating the child with sore throat should include hydration and nutritional status as well as the presence of any airway compromise.

Viral pharyngitis is very common and is caused by a number of different pathogens including adenovirus, enterovirus, coxsackievirus, and parainfluenza virus. It typically presents with nonexudative pharyngeal erythema and tender cervical adenopathy. It is frequently associated with other upper respiratory complaints such as rhinorrhea, nasal obstruction, cough and fever. Treatment is supportive, as this is nearly always a self-limited process.

Infectious mononucleosis (IM) is a condition caused by the Epstein-Barr virus (EBV) that presents with sore throat, gray pharyngeal exudate and edematous soft palate. IM is usually associated with significant systemic adenopathy and hepatosplenomegaly. Cervical adenopathy can be massive and give a "bull neck" appearance. Demonstration of heterophile antibody against sheep erythrocytes (Monospot or Paul-Bunnell test) is a useful screening test. Diagnosis is confirmed by EBV titer. Medical treatment is supportive and may include steroids for respiratory difficulty or severe dysphagia. Up to 50% of patients with IM may develop a maculopapular rash if amoxicillin is taken.

Acute bacterial pharyngotonsillitis is usually caused by group A β-hemolytic streptococci (strep throat). Less common pathogens include non-group A streptococcus, *S. aureus, H. influenzae, M. catarrhalis,* diphtheriae, gonococci, chlamydia, and mycoplasma. Streptococcal pharyngitis typically presents as bilateral tonsil hypertrophy and erythema with a characteristic whitish exudate. It is difficult to distinguish between viral and bacterial pharyngotonsillitis on clinical grounds alone. Thus, a rapid strep test should be obtained, though a negative result should be confirmed by throat culture. Treatment is with a ten-day course of oral penicillin V, macrolide or first-generation cephalosporin, though it should be noted that penicillin resistance is rapidly emerging. Both suppurative and nonsuppurative complications can result from untreated or incompletely treated streptococcal pharyngitis. Nonsuppurative complications include scarlet fever, acute rheumatic fever and post-streptococcal glomerulonephritis. Suppurative complications include peritonsillar, parapharyngeal, or retropharyngeal cellulitis or abscess.

Peritonsillar Abscess

Peritonsillar abscess may develop as a sequela of bacterial tonsillitis. Patients typically present with a muffled voice, trismus, and decreased oral intake. Physical examination reveals a unilateral bulge in the soft palate and peritonsillar region and uvular deviation to the opposite side. CT scan may aid in diagnosis in young, uncooperative patients. Treatment consists of aspiration or incision and drainage by experienced personnel. This should be followed by a 7–10 day course of oral or parenteral penicillin or clindamycin. Recent literature has supported a role for steroids as an adjunctive therapy, as they may significantly reduce pain and fever. Immediate tonsillectomy may be performed, especially in young patients who will already be under general anesthesia for drainage of the abscess. A single peritonsillar abscess is a relative indication for tonsillectomy, and patients with recurrent abscesses should always be considered for removal of the tonsils.

Pharyngeal Injury

Pharyngeal injury may occur in children after falling with a pen, stick or other sharp object in the mouth. Examination reveals a puncture or laceration of the soft palate, tonsil, or pharyngeal wall. The most significant risk is from carotid injury. The presence of significant bleeding, neurologic findings, or a puncture lateral to the exposed tonsil should prompt immediate consultation.

Adenotonsillectomy

Removal of the tonsils and adenoids is one of the most commonly performed operations in children. It is often recommended for patients who suffer from recurrent episodes of tonsillitis. More than 5 episodes of tonsillitis in a year or significant missed time from school or work should prompt consideration for tonsillectomy. Other indications include obstructive sleep apnea (OSA) and suspicion of malignancy. Previous peritonsillar abscess may be a relative indication. Surgery may be performed on an outpatient basis in older children. Adenoidectomy is indicated for OSA, chronic otitis media, and chronic sinusitis. The most significant risk of tonsillectomy is postoperative hemorrhage.

Obstructive Sleep Apnea

Obstructive sleep apnea (OSA) is characterized by episodic obstruction of airflow through the upper airway during sleep. The most common cause for OSA in children is adenotonsillar hypertrophy. Congenital nasal masses may be responsible for OSA in the neonate. Physiologic sequelae may include hypoxemia, hypercapnia and acidosis. The most severely affected patients may develop cor pulmonale, right ventricular hypertrophy, congestive heart failure, pulmonary hypertension and failure to thrive.

Diagnosis

Patients with OSA often present with noisy breathing, specifically *stertor*, a term used to describe sonorous breathing in the upper airway. Other symptoms include pauses, breathholding, or gasping during sleep, as well as enuresis. Daytime manifestations include morning headache, halitosis and, most importantly, behavioral and neurocognitive disorders. Physical examination often reveals audible breathing with open mouth posture, hyponasal speech, drooling, and tonsillar hyperplasia. A strong clinical picture may be enough to establish the diagnosis, but *polysomnography* (sleep study) remains the gold standard for objective correlation of ventilatory abnormalities with obstructive symptoms.

Treatment

Adenotonsillectomy is generally considered first-line therapy in most children with OSA. Improvement following adenotonsillectomy has been demonstrated in children with preoperative enuresis and behavioral issues. Postoperative improvement can also be seen on polysomnography. In neonates in whom congenital nasal masses may be responsible for their OSA, removal of the mass is curative. Rarely, in the most severe and refractory cases of OSA, tracheostomy may be considered.

Suggested reading

1. Darrow DH. Surgery for pediatric sleep apnea. Otolaryngol Clin N Am 2007; 40: 855–875.
2. Johnson RF, Stewart MG. The contemporary approach to diagnosis and management of peritonsillar abscess. Curr Opin Otolaryngol Head Neck Surg 2005; 13: 157–160.
3. Mueller DT, Callanan VP. Congenital malformations of the oral cavity. Otolaryngol Clin N Am 2007; 40: 141–160.
4. Tewfik TL, Al Garni M. Tonsillopharyngitis: clinical highlights. J Otolaryngol 2005; 34 Suppl 1: S45–9.

DISEASES OF THE LARYNX AND TRACHEA

THE STRIDOROUS CHILD

The term *stridor* refers to the physical finding of excessively noisy breathing and is generally due to upper airway obstruction. The relationship of stridor to the respiratory cycle often provides a clue to its etiology: *inspiratory stridor* suggests obstruction above the vocal cords (supraglottis), while *expiratory stridor* usually originates from the distal trachea. *Biphasic* (inspiratory and expiratory) stridor usually originates from a subglottic or proximal tracheal lesion. Most stridor in children originates from supraglottic lesions. Table 12.4 lists the differences between stridor due to supraglottic and tracheal obstruction.

Evaluation of the stridorous child should include a thorough history that is frequently diagnostic. Physical findings associated with stridor include nasal flaring and suprasternal or intercostal retractions. Radiographs such as chest X-rays or lateral neck films may confirm a diagnosis such as retropharyngeal abscess, epiglottitis, or croup. Barium esophagram may rule out extrinsic compression by a vascular anomaly. Flexible and rigid

Table 12.4: Supraglottic vs. tracheal obstruction

Supraglottic obstruction
Inspiratory stridor Weak cry/voice Dyspnea is generally mild Less pronounced cough
Tracheal obstruction
Biphasic or expiratory stridor Normal cry/voice May have severe dyspnea Deep barking, brassy cough

endoscopy is generally needed to confirm the clinician's diagnostic impressions.

There are a variety of different processes that can cause airway obstruction in children. These can be roughly divided into infectious, congenital, neoplastic, and miscellaneous causes.

Infections

Croup (laryngotracheobronchitis) is a viral infection of the upper respiratory tract and often presents in children 1–5 years of age with biphasic stridor, brassy or "barking" cough, and low-grade fever. Onset of symptoms is usually over several days. Chest X-ray reveals a characteristic narrowing of the subglottic region known as the "steeple sign" (Fig. 12.6).

Most cases of croup are mild and resolve within 1 to 2 days. Conservative management should include reassurance and oral hydration. Children with stridor at rest should be hospitalized for close observation and supplemental oxygen. Steroids are helpful in moderate to severe cases. Antibiotics may be indicated if the child fails to improve or if purulent secretions are present. Coverage should be directed towards *Staphylococcus* and *H. influenzae*.

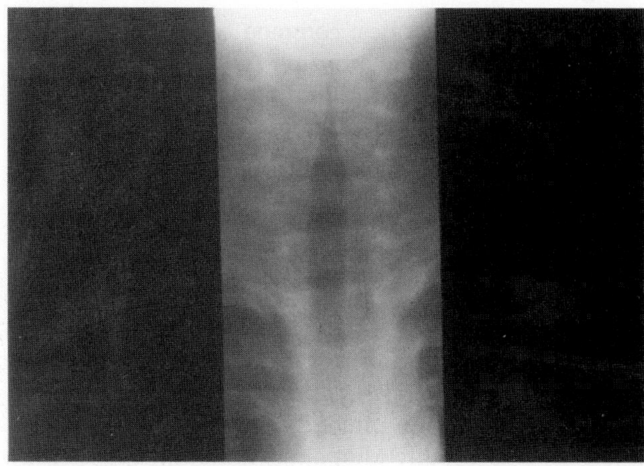

Fig. 12.6: Laryngotracheobronchitis (croup). 'Steeple sign'

Acute epiglottitis (often called *supraglottitis*), although less common than croup, typically presents with a greater degree of airway compromise. Patients typically present with acute onset (over several hours) of sore throat, marked dysphagia, and high fever. Patients are often encountered leaning forward in a "tripod" position, frequently toxic-appearing and drooling. Unlike croup, cough is frequently absent. Lateral X-ray of the neck reveals a characteristic thumb-like thickening of the epiglottis or other supraglottic structures. *H. influenzae* type b is the major etiologic organism.

Rapid airway management is essential and includes intubation by skilled personnel. Instrumentation of the throat with tongue depressors is not advised as this can precipitate a fatal laryngospasm. Management includes securing the airway and broad-spectrum IV antibiotics such as cefuroxime directed against *H. influenzae* and gram-positive organisms. The incidence of epiglottitis has decreased with the use of *H. influenzae* vaccine.

Bacterial tracheitis is typically seen in young children following a viral upper respiratory tract infection. The child appears toxic with a brassy cough and stridor. Bronchoscopy is both diagnostic and therapeutic, as it shows purulent tracheal secretions that can be mechanically debrided. Bacterial tracheitis is a relative medical emergency, as life-threatening obstruction may develop from tracheal secretions. The responsible pathogen is usually *S. aureus*.

Retropharyngeal abscess is a potential suppurative complication of bacterial pharyngitis that may also present with stridor. Patients may have high fever, reduced mobility of the neck, and are often toxic-appearing. Complications of retropharyngeal abscess include spread of infection into the mediastinum and a potentially fatal mediastinitis. Lateral neck radiograph reveals a soft tissue bulge in the posterior pharyngeal wall. Treatment is by surgical drainage and broad-spectrum parenteral antibiotics.

Congenital Causes of Stridor

Laryngomalacia is the most common congenital anomaly of the larynx, accounting for up to 60% of all anomalies. Inspiratory stridor is the hallmark of the condition. Symptoms are typically aggravated when the child is supine or crying. Examination reveals partial collapse of a flaccid supraglottic airway with inspiration (Fig. 12.7). The condition is generally benign and self-limited, as most cases resolve by 18 months of age. Severe cases may require surgical intervention if the distress prevents adequate feeding.

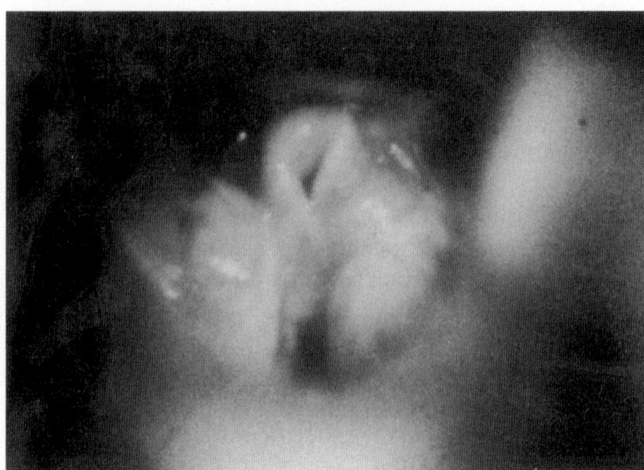

Fig. 12.7: Laryngomalacia, showing a collapse of the supraglottic airway

Vocal cord paralysis is the second most common congenital laryngeal anomaly. *Bilateral vocal cord paralysis* usually presents with a high-pitched inspiratory stridor and cyanosis. It is usually idiopathic, although causes may include Arnold-Chiari malformation, hydrocephalus, or hypoxia. *Unilateral vocal cord paralysis,* in contrast, may present with a mild stridor or with signs of aspiration. Accidental injury during ligation of patent ductus arteriosus is a frequent cause of unilateral paralysis in infants. Tracheostomy is required to secure the airway in bilateral paralysis, though generally not in unilateral paralysis unless there is excessive aspiration.

Congenital subglottic stenosis is the third most common congenital laryngeal anomaly. It results from incomplete recanalization of the laryngotracheal tube during embryonic development. Congenital subglottic stenosis may present as recurrent episodes of stridor within the first 6 months of life and may be mislabeled as "croup." Many cases resolve spontaneously as the child grows, while severe cases usually require tracheostomy. Surgical excision of the stenosis may be necessary to relieve the obstruction.

Vascular ring is an anomaly of the great vessels that causes extrinsic compression of both the trachea and the esophagus. The child with vascular ring anomaly usually presents with dysphagia as well as stridor. Contrasted swallowing studies (e.g. esophagram) may reveal the diagnosis. Treatment for vascular anomalies is surgical.

Subglottic hemangioma is a benign vascular tumor that may be found on the skin as well as in the trachea. Infants usually become symptomatic between 3–6 months of life as the hemangioma is in its proliferative phase. Symptoms include biphasic stridor and a barking cough. Up to half of patients may have concurrent cutaneous hemangiomas of the head and neck. Imaging may reveal asymmetric subglottic narrowing, and the diagnosis in confirmed with endoscopy. Treatment options include tracheostomy, systemic or intralesional steroids, CO_2 laser excision and open surgical excision.

Congenital saccular cyst, laryngeal web and *laryngeal atresia* are rare anomalies of the larynx that can present with varying degrees of airway obstruction.

Iatrogenic Causes of Stridor

Acquired subglottic stenosis is the most common cause of acquired stridor in children. It most often results from long-term endotracheal intubation and resulting scar formation. Treatment varies by the severity of the lesion. Minor stenoses may be observed, while more severe stenoses may be treated by a variety of surgical methods including tracheostomy, widening of the stenosis with cartilage grafts, and excision of the stenotic segment.

Laryngeal granuloma may also result from prolonged intubation. Endoscopy reveals a granuloma that is typically found on the vocal cord. These are often amenable to endoscopic removal.

Neoplasms

Recurrent respiratory papilloma (RRP) is the most common benign tumor of the larynx and presents with symptoms related to gradual airway obstruction. Endoscopy reveals single or multiple irregular, wart-like masses in the larynx or pharynx. RRP is caused by human papillomavirus (HPV) types 6 and 11, which also cause genital condyloma in adults. Transmission is believed to be from the passage of the fetus through an infected birth canal. Treatment is with CO_2 laser ablation or microdebrider excision of the papillomas. Adjunctive therapies include alpha-interferon and intralesional cidofovir, a potent antiviral agent. Multiple surgical procedures are usually necessary as the disease has a propensity to recur. Tracheostomy is to be avoided if possible, as it may potentiate spread of the virus into the distal airway. The clinical course is highly unpredictable, and death may occur in some children due to distal tracheobronchial spread and pulmonary involvement. The recent development of vaccines against HPV holds promise for prevention of this disease.

Foreign Body

Foreign body aspiration should always be considered as a potential cause of stridor and airway obstruction in children. Foreign bodies aspirated most commonly in children are food and coins. Young age is the greatest risk factor for injury or death from a foreign body in the aerodigestive tract. Conforming objects such as balloons pose the greatest risk of choking death, followed by round nonfood objects such as balls or marbles. After establishing airway security, treatment consists of endoscopic visualization and removal by an experienced surgeon.

Pediatric Tracheostomy

The most common indications for tracheostomy in children are ventilator dependence and airway obstruction. Although it may clearly be life-saving in the appropriate circumstances, tracheostomy carries a higher complication rate in children, particularly preterm infants, than it does in adults. The most common complications are tube obstruction or accidental decannulation that can occur months after the initial surgery. Preventive management is imperative in the child with tracheostomy and includes adequate tube cleaning, humidification, and thorough instructions to home care providers. Long-term tracheostomy in children may also affect speech and language development.

HOARSENESS

The differential diagnosis for hoarseness is quite long and can be divided into congenital, neurogenic, neoplastic, inflammatory, and traumatic causes. The more common entities among these categories have been previously discussed in the context of stridor; however, several additional disorders bear mention.

Vocal nodules are the most common cause of hoarseness in children, and are generally caused by vocal abuse. The severity of hoarseness fluctuates, worsening with vocal abuse and improving with rest. They are seen more frequently in habitually shouting or screaming children. Endoscopy reveals small, bilateral, opposing nodules, usually at the junction of the anterior and middle thirds of the vocal cord. Speech therapy is usually effective in older children. Surgery is rarely indicated.

Reflux laryngitis may result from gastric secretions spilling onto the larynx. Reflux has been implicated in numerous conditions, including laryngitis, subglottic stenosis, chronic sinusitis and otitis media with effusion. Diagnosis is established with 24 hour pH monitoring. Medical management is usually effective, though surgical fundoplication may be needed in severe cases.

Hypothyroid myxedema may occasionally cause an increase in vocal fold edema and present as hoarseness or stridor. Thyroid function tests should be measured in the hoarse child with a clinical history suggestive of hypothyroidism.

Laryngotracheal cleft (LTC) is a rare congenital defect in the posterior cricoid cartilage of the larynx. In its mildest form, children experience feeding difficulty, recurrent respiratory tract infection, or hoarseness. In its more severe forms, the cleft may extend inferiorly between the entire trachea and esophagus. Severe clefts usually cause significant aspiration pneumonias, and are often not compatible with life. LTC may be associated with hereditary conditions such as Opitz-Frias or Pallister-Hall syndromes. Management of symptomatic clefts is surgical.

Suggested reading

1. Ahmad SM, Soliman A. Congenital anomalies of the larynx. Otolaryngol Clin N Am 2007; 40: 177–91.
2. Brodsky L, Carr MM. Extraesophageal reflux in children. Curr Opin Otolaryngol Head Neck Surg 2006; 14: 387–92.
3. Carr MM, et al. Complications in pediatric tracheostomies. Laryngoscope 2001; 111: 1925–8.
4. Daniel SJ. The upper airway: Congenital malformations. Paed Resp Rev 2006; 7S: S260–S263.

5. McMurray JS. Disorders of phonation in children. Pediatr Clin North Am 2003; 50(2): 363–80.
6. Rafei K, Lichenstein R. Airway infectious disease emergencies. Pediatr Clin North Am 2006; 53(2): 215–42.
7. Stamataki S, et al. Juvenile recurrent respiratory papillomatosis: Still a mystery disease with difficult management. Head Neck 2007; 29: 155–62.

NECK MASSES

Neck masses in pediatric patients are quite common. The etiology can usually be assigned to one of three categories: congenital, inflammatory or neoplastic. Although malignancy is not as common as in adults presenting with neck masses, the possibility of a malignancy should always remain in the differential diagnosis.

CONGENITAL NECK MASSES

Branchial cleft cysts are relatively common and may comprise up to one-third of all congenital neck masses. Branchial cleft cysts are named according to the associated branchial cleft or pouch (e.g. first, second or third branchial cleft cysts). Second branchial cleft cysts are the most common, and typically present as a lateral neck mass just anterior to the sternocleidomastoid muscle. Imaging with ultrasound or CT scan reveals the cystic nature of the mass. Treatment is surgical excision. If possible, infected cysts should be managed with antibiotics prior to excision.

Thyroglossal duct cysts present as a midline neck mass in the region of the hyoid bone. Together with branchial cleft cysts, they comprise over half of congenital neck masses. They form as a remnant of the thyroid descent tract from the tongue base into the lower neck, where some tissue may also persist as a pyramidal lobe of the thyroid. Most thyroglossal duct cysts are in the midline, but they can occasionally present laterally. The cyst will often move upon tongue protrusion by the patient, due to its origin from the tongue base. Occasionally this may represent the patient's only functioning thyroid tissue, and preoperative imaging of the thyroid is recommended. Treatment is with the Sistrunk operation, where the cyst is removed along with the central portion of the hyoid bone. Removing the cyst alone without the hyoid bone leads to high rates of cyst recurrence.

Lymphangiomas, formerly termed cystic hygromas, are congenital malformations of lymph tissue. They present as a slow growing, painless, compressible mass that can be transilluminated on physical exam. They may become quite large causing significant functional deficits, airway compromise, and cosmetic deformity. CT or MRI should be obtained to assess the extent of the lesion. Treatment is with surgical excision, although injection of sclerosing agents has been reported with some success.

Hemangiomas are benign vascular lesions that represent the most common benign tumor of infancy. They typically present at birth, rapidly proliferate during the first year of life, and then slowly involute over the first decade of the child's life. Since up to 70% of these lesions completely resolve by age 7, the usual treatment is observation. Indications for surgery include functional impairment and bleeding. Surgery may also be useful when cosmetic deformities remain after involution. Stridor in a patient with a head and neck hemangioma should prompt consideration of a subglottic hemangioma.

Less common congenital neck masses include *teratomas, dermoid cysts* and *thymic cysts*.

INFLAMMATORY NECK MASSES

Cervical lymphadenopathy from an infective process is by far the most common neck mass in children. The etiology may be either viral or bacterial, and an upper respiratory infection is often the cause. Infected lymph nodes are characteristically tender on physical exam. Lymph nodes infected with *S. aureus* or *S. pyogenes* may suppurate and form an abscess. Incision and drainage and antibiotics are indicated in these cases. If an abscess is not present, management is observation to ensure resolution of the adenopathy.

Cat-Scratch disease is caused by the bacteria *Bartonella henslae*. Lymphadenopathy is a prerequisite for diagnosis, and the head and neck are involved in about one-fourth of cases. Patients may have mild fever or malaise, and there is usually a history of feline contact with or without scratches. Diagnosis is confirmed by serologic testing for antibodies against *Bartonella*. Treatment is with a macrolide or aminoglycoside antibiotic. Surgical treatment is rarely necessary.

Mycobacterial cervical adenitis is not infrequently seen in children. It should be suspected when patients fail standard antibiotic therapy. The etiologic agent is usually an atypical (non-tuberculous) mycobacterium. On physical exam, the skin overlying the adenopathy may show discoloration. Skin testing can aid in diagnosis. Treatment includes either complete surgical excision of the involved nodes, or incision and curettage. Anti-mycobacterial therapy is necessary in some cases .

Less frequent etiologies of inflammatory neck masses include tularemia, brucellosis, Kawasaki disease and sarcoidosis.

NEOPLASMS

Lymphomas are the most common pediatric head and neck malignancy. They may be divided into two histologic categories, Hodgkin's and non-Hodgkin's.

The most common clinical presentation is asymptomatic, unilateral lymphadenopathy. Fever, weight loss, and night sweats are usually not seen until late in the course of disease. After diagnosis is established by biopsy, treatment is with chemotherapy or radiation therapy.

Rhabdomyosarcoma is the most common soft-tissue sarcoma, and the second most common head and neck malignancy in children. Commonly involved sites include the orbit, nasopharynx, and temporal bone. Treatment involves a combination of surgery, chemotherapy and radiation.

Thyroid carcinoma is the third most common neck malignancy in children. Previous exposure to ionizing radiation is a critically important risk factor. The most common histologic type is papillary thyroid carcinoma. Children with thyroid cancer typically present with more advanced disease than do adults. Nonetheless, with appropriate management, the prognosis is excellent.

More rare malignancies that should remain in the differential diagnosis of a pediatric neck mass include salivary gland malignancies, nasopharyngeal carcinoma, and neuroblastoma.

Suggested reading

1. Bauer PW, Lusk RP. Neck masses. In: Bluestone CD and Stool SE. Pediat Otolaryngology, 4th ed. Philadelphia: Saunders, 2003: 1629–1647.
2. MacArthur CJ. Head and neck hemangiomas of infancy. Curr Opin Otolaryngol Head Neck Surg 2006; 14: 397–405.
3. Tracy TF Jr, Muratore CS. Management of common head and neck masses. Semin Pediatr Surg 2007; 16: 3–13.

DISEASES OF THE SALIVARY GLANDS

Clinical Anatomy

The major salivary glands consist of three paired structures: the parotid glands, the submandibular glands and the sublingual glands. In addition, there are numerous minor salivary glands located submucosally throughout the oral cavity and pharynx. With the exception of viral parotitis, most salivary gland disease is more common in adults than children. However, there are certain neoplastic, non-neoplastic, and systemic disorders of the salivary glands that are relevant to pediatric practice.

Infections

Bacterial parotid sialoadenitis is frequent in small children and presents with painful unilateral parotid swelling. Purulent material may be expressed from the parotid duct intraorally with parotid massage. The condition is usually caused by dehydration, which leads to staphylococcal overgrowth in the duct system. Treatment includes oral antibiotics as well as hydration, sialogogues, massage and warm compresses.

Viral parotitis is caused most often by the mumps virus, although other viruses may mimic its presentation. Patients generally present with painful parotid enlargement and fever. They may also present with an acute unilateral hearing loss or vestibular weakness. Systemic manifestations such as meningoencephalitis, pancreatitis, and orchitis may also be present. The incidence of mumps has decreased following use of the vaccine.

Tuberculosis is the most common granulomatous inflammation of the parotid. It may be limited to the salivary glands without lung involvement. Treatment is with antituberculous drugs. *Sarcoidosis* may also present with unilateral or bilateral parotid swelling. It is usually seen in association with systemic symptoms and peripheral adenopathy. A variety of laboratory tests and radiological studies including chest radiograph support the diagnosis. Steroids are of value in treating sarcoid-associated xerostomia.

Human Immunodeficiency Virus (HIV) involvement of the parotid glands is common. HIV-associated salivary gland disease usually appears as bilateral intraglandular cysts, although it may be unilateral clinically. Management usually consists of observation, as the cysts invariably recur after aspiration. Occasionally, surgery may be indicated for cosmesis alone, as parotid enlargement may be severe enough to cause facial disfigurement.

Primary Non-neoplastic Diseases

Sialectasis presents as recurrent episodes of painful unilateral or bilateral parotid swelling associated with systemic signs and symptoms of infection. Episodes typically resolve promptly with antibiotic therapy. Onset may be within the first few years of life, and episodes of recurrent infection tend to remit spontaneously around puberty. The exact etiology is unknown.

Acute unilateral pain and swelling of the parotid or submandibular gland with eating may be due to ductal *stricture* or to *sialolithiasis* (stones in the salivary ducts). While stricture affects both parotid and submandibular glands, salivary gland calculi are found far more often in the submandibular glands. Both stricture and sialolithiasis are treated most commonly by surgery. However, salivary gland lithotripsy has also described recently and may prove to be of value in the future.

Most *cysts* of the salivary glands are in the parotid and may be congenital, post-traumatic, neoplastic or infectious. A congenital parotid cyst is most likely to be a first branchial arch derivative; this may present as a recurrent, acutely infected, fluctuant mass that may spontaneously rupture and drain. The etiology of a post-traumatic cyst is suggested by history. A slow, progressive, unilateral cyst should be aspirated for cytology to rule out malignancy. HIV positive status should be suspected for polycystic changes in the parotids (see above).

Mucous retention cysts are derived from minor salivary glands and are found on the lips or mucous membranes.

12

They usually appear as bluish masses up to 2 centimeters in size and are treated surgically.

Ranulas are cystic lesions of the floor of the mouth. They are generally thought to be caused by salivary leakage from the sublingual with a resulting mucocele. They appear as a blue, fluctuant swelling in the floor of the mouth lateral to the midline. They may be limited to the floor of the mouth or extend into the upper aspect of the neck (known as a *plunging ranula*). Treatment is by either surgical excision or marsupialization.

Salivary Gland Neoplasms

The most common tumors of the salivary glands in children are vascular: parotid hemangioma and lymphangioma. Though most major salivary neoplasms in adults are benign, up to 57% of pediatric salivary gland tumors (excluding vascular lesions) are malignant. Mucoepidermoid carcinoma accounts for over half of pediatric salivary gland malignancies, followed in order of frequency by acinar cell carcinoma (12%). After hemangioma, pleomorphic adenoma is the most common benign salivary gland tumor in pediatric patients. Intraparotid lymph nodes may also harbor metastatic disease from the scalp or face.

Clinical features of salivary gland masses such as associated nerve weakness are suggestive of malignant disease. Definitive diagnosis of a mass is accomplished by fine needle aspiration. Incisional biopsy of salivary gland masses is rarely, if ever, indicated.

Aggressive surgical excision is generally performed if malignant disease is suspected. Hemangiomas are typically observed, as they most often involute within the first decade of life. Lymphangiomas, on the other hand, are progressive in their growth; surgical excision is the recommended treatment, though complete excision may not always be possible.

THE DROOLING CHILD

Drooling (sialorrhea) is a frequent and generally self-limited finding in young children. If problematic, drooling may be controlled in selected cases with speech and swallowing therapy. However, in children with neuromuscular disorders such as cerebral palsy, dyscoordinated swallowing and poor lip closure may result in chronic drooling, even in the presence of normal saliva production. Drooling may increase the difficulty of patient care and compromise social interactions. Moreover, if the swallowing mechanism is abnormal, pooling of secretions may allow chronic aspiration, which, in turn, can lead to pneumonia or other complications.

Medical therapy for drooling not controlled with speech therapy consists of drying agents such as glycopyrrolate and antihistamines. These medications may be associated with significant side effects. Refractory cases of drooling may be treated surgically with salivary gland excision, ductal ligation or rerouting, destruction of parasympathetic fibers, or some combination of the above. At present, the preferred surgical treatment is bilateral submandibular gland excision with parotid duct ligation. Tracheostomy or complete permanent separation of the trachea from the upper airway is reserved for profound and life-threatening chronic aspiration.

Suggested reading

1. Lal D, Hotaling AJ. Drooling. Curr Opin Otolaryngol Head Neck Surg 2006; 14: 3816.
2. Mehta D, Willging JP. Pediatric salivary gland lesions. Semin Pediatr Surg 2006; 15(2): 76–84.

13 Disorders of Respiratory System

DEVELOPMENTAL PHYSIOLOGY OF THE RESPIRATORY SYSTEM

The newborn has to contend with sudden transition from fetal life to extrauterine existence at the time of birth. In childhood, the lungs have to keep pace with the ordered growth of the body. During fetal life, the placenta helps in the gas exchanges. Therefore the fetal oxygen tension remains constant, independent of the maternal levels of oxygen. As the lungs are fluid filled, there is no air fluid interface.

By 24 weeks of gestation, the surfactant precursors appear as inclusion bodies in the alveolar lining cells. Prior to 28–32 weeks of gestation, the lungs have an inherent tendency to collapse. They are unable to retain any air. The surfactant, a protein in the alveolar lining layer decreases the alveolar surface tension and imparts finite elasticity to the interface. As a result less pressure is needed to distend the lungs. When the lung is inflated from a small or negligible volume such as in atelectasis or from a situation when the alveoli are filled with liquid as happens during the first breath at birth, lesser force is required to open up the alveoli if there is low surface tension at the air liquid interface and if the radius of the terminal units of the lung is adequate.

Although surfactant can be detected in lung exudates from human fetuses as early as 24 weeks, the quantity increases greatly towards the end of the term. Deficiency of surfactant leads to the respiratory distress syndrome.

Gas Transport in Fetal Life

Carbon dioxide tension falls from 35.5 mm Hg at the 10th week of gestation to 28 mm Hg at full term. The difference in oxygen dissociation curves and increase in the hemoglobin concentration enable the fetus to carry out effective oxygenation of the tissues. Recently it has been found that 2,3 diphosphoglycerate (2,3 DPG) in the surrounding medium seems to increase affinity of fetal hemoglobin for oxygen. The uptake of CO_2 also shifts the oxygen dissociation curve to the right and therefore adequate O_2 delivery is ensured by the high tissue levels of CO_2.

Onset of Respiration

The mechanisms of the onset of respiration at birth are multifactorial. Hypoxia, hypercapnia (more CO_2 in blood) and sudden increase in the sensitivity of chemoreceptor due to increased sympathetic activity after the cord is clamped, appears to be the main factors responsible for initiation of respiration at birth.

Respiratory Function in the Newborn

Before birth, the lungs are filled with fluid. This has to be replaced by air. Some of the fluid is extruded from the mouth and some is absorbed by the lymphatics.

Intrapleural negative pressure required for the first breath is 40 to 100 cm of water. This pressure is higher initially, because of the low compliance of the newborn lung (1.5 ml/cm H_2O at birth). The compliance of the lungs increases in the first few hours to 6 ml/cm H_2O and resistance to the air flow decreases. The tidal volume of a 3 kg infant is approximately 16 ml at about 28 breaths per minute. Resting lung volume also gradually increases in the first few hours and reaches a maximum of 80 ml within 24 hours.

Gas Exchange in Newborn

The normal newborn requires about 7 ml of oxygen/minute/kg. This is almost double the O_2 requirements of an adult on a relative weight basis.

The uptake of oxygen is a complex process involving transport across the alveolar capillary membrane. This process known as diffusion is virtually the same as in the adult in relation to the surface area. The dead space of the newborn in about 2 ml/kg with the resting tidal volume being 20 ml; 35% of the breath is wasted as compared to 30% in the adults. Persisting fetal channels and the ventilation perfusion problems in a newborn lead to increase in the right to left shunt.

Gas Transport

Relative hypoxia in a newborn is corrected in 5 minutes, hypercapnia by 20 minutes and acidosis in 24 hours. The initial acidosis is partly metabolic in origin, due to the elevated blood lactate levels. The higher hemoglobin concentration in the newborn, and the shift to the left of the O_2 dissociation curve allow the newborn baby to carry higher concentration of oxygen than in the adult.

Mechanical Function Throughout Childhood

The total lung capacity in a newborn is 150 ml as compared to that in an adult which is around 5000 ml. With the growth of the lungs, there is multiplication of the alveoli and increase in the size of alveoli and airways. Pores of Cohn or interalveolar communications also develop, with increasing age. There is a large increase in compliance and a fall in resistance. The reciprocal of resistance, i.e., conductance rises in proportion to the increase in the lung volumes. Increase in minute ventilation reflects the increase in the metabolic rate. The dead space, the tidal volume and the frequency changes reflect changes in the mechanics of the lungs.

Gas Transport in Childhood

The rise of pH and pCO_2 together means that the buffer base of the blood also increases. Bicarbonate rises from 19 mEq/L at the age of 2 years to 24 mEq/L at 16 years of age. Arterial pO_2 is about 75 mm Hg in the newborn period and around the age of 5 years it reaches the adult level of 95 mm Hg.

Suggested reading

Tooley WH and Kilterman J: Lung growth and functional development of the fetal respiratory system and the onset of air breathing. In: Rudolph AM. Pediatrics Connecticut, Prentice Hall International Inc, 1987;1359–1369.

COMMON RESPIRATORY SYMPTOMS

Cough

After maximal inspiration, the air is suddenly released through the partially closed glottis, because of forceful contraction of the expirtory muscles. This produces a bout of cough. The cough reflex is controlled by a center in the medulla. Irritation of the pharynx, larynx, trachea, bronchi and pleura transmit the afferent impulses through the vagus or glossopharyngeal nerves. Efferent pathways are in the nerve supply to the larynx and respiratory muscles.

Cough is an important defense mechanism of the respiratory system and helps to bring out the infected secretions from the trachea and bronchi. Cough should not be suppressed in younger children as retention of secretions in their lungs may result in atelectasis and pulmonary complications. On the other hand, persistent cough interferes with the sleep and feeding. It fatigues the child and may result in vomiting. A balanced approach is necessary in the management of cough.

Causes of Acute Cough

- Upper respiratory tract infection. Common cold, postnasal discharge due to sinusitis (in older children), rhinitis, pharyngitis, laryngitis and tracheobronchitis
- Nasobronchial allergy and asthma
- Bronchiolitis, pneumonia and pulmonary suppuration
- Measles.
- Whooping cough.
- Foreign body in the air passages.
- Empyema.

Causes of Chronic or Recurrent Cough

- Inflammatory disorders of airway
  1. Asthma and Loeffler's syndrome
  2. Infection-viral, bacterial, chlamydia, mycoplasma, tuberculosis, parasitic
  3. Inhalation of environmental irritants such as tobacco smoke, dust
- Suppurative lung disease
  1. Bronchiectisis, cystic fibrosis
  2. Foreign body retained in bronchi
  3. Congenital malformations, sequestrated lobe, bronchomalacia
  4. Immune deficiency, primary ciliary dyskinesia.
- Anatomic lesions, tumors, tracheal stenosis, H-type tracheo-esophageal fistula
- Psychogenic, habit cough
- Post-nasal discharge, sinusitis
- Gastroesophageal reflux disease
- Interstitial lung disease.

Expectoration

Children, as such, are not able to expectorate. They swallow the respiratory secretions. Older children with chronic respiratory problems may be able to bring out expectoration. Common causes of significant expectoration include bronchiectasis due to various causes, bronchitis, asthma and tuberculosis. The amount and nature of expectoration may gave clue about the cause of respiratory disease. Further investigation such as cell count, gram stain and culture or stain for AFB and culture may help in diagnosis and guide for treatment.

Hemoptysis

Hemoptysis is defined as blood stained expectoration. Children are not able to bring out expectoration, therefore hemoptysis as a clinical symptom in children is uncommon. Causes of hemoptysis may be necrotizing pneumonia, foreign body aspiration, bleeding diathesis, cavitatory tuberculosis, idiopathic pulmonary hemosiderosis, mitral stenosis, dilated cardiac myopathy and vascular malformation.

RESPIRATORY NOISES

Various types of sounds originating from respiratory system may be heard without the help of stethoscope. The intensity and pitch of these sounds alter depending on their site of origin within the respiratory tract. The general dictum is that the pitch of the sound keeps on increasing and the intensity keeps on decreasing as one goes down lower into the respiratory tract. For example, snoring is a highly intensive but low pitched sound because it results from the region of oropharynx. On the other hand wheeze is a high pitched, less intense sound originating from lower airway obstruction. Various sounds are described in Table 13.1.

Table 13.1: Respiratory sounds

Sound	*Causes*	*Character*
Snoring	Oropharyngeal obstruction	Inspiratory, low pitched irregular
Grunting	By partial closure of glottis	Expiratory, occurs in hyaline membrane disease
Rattling	Secretions in trachea/bronchi	Inspiratory, coarse. This sound can also be felt by placing hands over the chest
Stridor	Obstruction larynx/trachea	Inspiratory sound, may be associated with an expiratory component
Wheeze	Lower airway obstruction	Continuous musical sound predominantly expiratory in nature

Rattling

Rattling is due to excessive secretions in the pharynx or tracheobronchial tree during breathing. It is present in asthma, bronchitis and tracheobronchial stenosis. Inhalation of gastrointestinal content into the tracheobronchial tree can also result in rattling. Some normal infants may have transient rattling but prolonged rattling is always pathological.

Wheezing

Wheezing refers to high pitched whistling sounds audible without auscultation by the stethoscope. Wheezing causes considerable anxiety to the parents. Partial obstruction of the bronchi and bronchioles leading to narrowing produces wheezing. Sufficient air must flow through the narrowed airway to produce the wheezing sound. This may be due to causes within the lumen or in the walls of the bronchi. Pressure from outside the bronchi may also be responsible in some cases.

Common Causes

- **Wheeze associated lower respiratory tract infection (WALRI)** All that wheezes is not asthma. Wheezing is most often due to heightened sensitivity of the respiratory tract. Infections of the lower respiratory passages may cause bronchospasm in these patients. Attacks of wheezing are always preceded by a cold or acute respiratory disease. These are most frequent between 3 to 8 years of age and become less frequent thereafter. These attacks are relieved by simple antispasmodic drugs.
- **Bronchiolitis**
- **Bronchial asthma**
- **Tropical eosinophilia:** This is more frequent in adults than in children. It is an unusual form of infection with filariasis, e.g. *Dirofilaria imitis, W. bancrofti, B. malayi.* Clinical features simulate chronic recurrent asthma. X-ray films of the lungs show fine infiltration with snowflake like appearance. This should be distinguished from miliary tuberculosis. The leucocyte count shows eosinophilia. Absolute eosinophil count may be more than 1500/mm^3. The patients are treated with diethylcarbamazine (10 mg/kg) in 3 divided doses orally for 2 to 3 weeks. Two or three spaced courses may be required.
- **Loeffler's syndrome:** The pulmonary phase of migration of ascaris larvae may cause wheezing, pulmonary problems and eosinophilia in the blood. These features are characteristically transient. Visceral larva migrans due to larval form of toxocara infection do not usually involve the lungs.
- **Hypersensitivity pneumonitis.**

13

Rare Causes

- Inhaled foreign bodies cause unilateral localized wheeze which begin suddenly. Wheezing tends to be continuous and becomes worse with crying, during excitement and with cold.
- Pressure from enlarged mediastinal nodes.
- Pressure from anomalous left pulmonary artery compressing the right main bronchus.
- Cystic fibrosis. Recurrent wheezing, productive cough and malabsorption are the usual features.
- Pulmonary hemosiderosis.
- Tuberculous lymph glands producing compression of airways.
- Mediastinal cysts and tumors causing narrowing of airways due to external compression.

Stridor

Stridor indicates upper respiratory obstruction and is usually accompanied by hoarseness, brassy cough, dyspnea, retraction of the chest during inspiration and restlessness. Accessory muscles of respiration are usually working.

Stridor is frequently seen in infants and is often attributed to (i) small size of the larynx, (ii) loose submucous connective tissue around the glottic region, and (iii) rigid cricoid cartilage encircling the subglottic zone.

Acute Stridor

Acute upper airway obstruction occurring in the region of glottis, which is produced by inflammation and edema, may be life threatening. The obstruction may either be supraglottic as in case of epiglottitis or may be subglottic, e.g. in infectious croup, which can be differentiated (Table 13.2).

A detailed discussion on acute and chronic stridor is given in Chapter 12.

Table 13.2: Distinguishing between stridor due to supraglottic and tracheal obstruction

Clinical features	*Supraglottic obstruction*	*Tracheal obstruction*
Stridor	Inspiratory and often less serious	Usually expiratory and more serious
Cry	Muffled	Normal
Dyspnea	Less severe	More marked
Cough	Less marked	Deep barking or brassy

13

Dyspnea

Tachypnea means abnormally rapid respiration. Dyspnea means labored or difficult breathing, usually accompanied by pain and air hunger.

Causes of Dyspnea

Respiratory system

- **Newborn:** Respiratory distress syndrome, hypoplastic lung, diaphragmatic hernia and eventration, meconium aspiration.
- **Infants and childhood:** Pneumonia, bronchiolitis, bronchial asthma, aspiration, pneumothorax, pleural effusion, collapse, obstructive emphysema, smoke inhalation.

Cardiovascular system

Congenital heart disease, myocarditis, pulmonary edema, pericarditis.

Miscellaneous

Guillian Barré syndrome, myasthenia gravis, neuromuscular disease, obesity, painful breathing (fractured ribs, pleuritis), acidosis (diabetes, uremia, salicylate toxicity), anemia.

Suggested reading

1. Kabra SK. History taking and physical examination In; Essential Pediatric Pulmonology, Kabra SK, Lodha R (Eds). Nobel Vision, New Delhi 2006;1–10.
2. Phelan PD, Olinksy A, Robertson CF: Rattling and its clinical significance. In. Respiratory Illness in Children. London. Blackwell Scientific publications, 1994;109–110.

INVESTIGATIONS FOR DIAGNOSIS OF RESPIRATORY ILLNESSES

Various investigations required for diagnosis of respiratory illness in children include: imaging, microbiological tests, bronchoscopy, pulmonary function test, arterial blood gas analysis and sweat chloride estimation, etc.

Bronchoscopy

Bronchoscopy can be of two types, fiberoptic and rigid. Fiberoptic bronchoscopy is done under local anesthesia and sedation. This is used for diagnosis of structural abnormality of airways, foreign body in respiratory tract and obtaining bronchoalveolar lavage samples to identify cell type and infective etiology of lower respiratory tract. Rigid bronchoscopy can be used in place of fiberoptic bronchoscopy; the procedure requires general anesthesia. This is commonly used for removal of foreign bodies from airways.

Pulmonary Function Tests

Pulmonary function tests are important tools for monitoring of a patient with chronic respiratory illness. Flow rates and lung volumes are measured. The procedure requires cooperation of the patient. They can be measured in children above the age of 5–7 years. Commonly used parameters include: forced expiratory volume in first second (FEV1), forced vital capacity (FVC), mid expiratory flow rate (FEF25–75) and ratio of FEV1/FVC. Normal FEV1/FVC ratio is between 0.8–1.0. In obstructive diseases (asthma) the ratio is reduced. In restrictive lung diseases (interstitial lung disease) the ratio of FEV1/FVC is normal but FVC is reduced below 80% of predicted.

Blood Gas Analysis

Estimation of partial pressures of oxygen and carbon dioxide in blood along with blood pH gives fair idea about the pulmonary functions. Arterial blood gas analysis is used for making a diagnosis of respiratory failure as well as monitoring of a child with acute and chronic respiratory failure. Partial pressures of oxygen less than 60 and of carbon dioxide more than 50 mm of Hg suggest acute respiratory failure.

Imaging

X-ray film and newer imaging like computerized tomography are non invasive diagnostic methods. X-ray films help in diagnosis of soft tissue and bony abnormalities. This is most commonly used modality for making a diagnosis of pulmonary infection. A particular pattern of pneumonia may suggest the etiological agent of pneumonia. Lobar consolidation suggest infection due to *Streptococcus pneumoniae* while evidence of hilar or mediastinal adenopathy suggest a possibility of tubercular infection. Computerized tomographic scans are used for visualization of lymph nodes, tumors, bronchiectasis and pleural pathologies.

Sweat Chloride Test

Sweat chloride is estimated by quantitative pilocarpine iontophoresis. Chloride in sweat is increased in children suffering from cystic fibrosis. In normal children sweat chloride values are less than 40 mEq/l. In children with cystic fibrosis it is more than 60 mEq/l. A value of 40–60 mEq/l is borderline and should be repeated.

Suggested reading

1. Beydon N, Davis SD, Lombardi E, et al. An official American Thoracic Society/European Respiratory Society statement: pulmonary function testing in preschool children. Am J Respir Crit Care Med 2007;175: 1304-45.

2. Copley SJ. Application of computed tomography in childhood respiratory infections. British Medical Bulletin 2002; 61:263–279.
3. Kabra SK, Kabra M, Gera S, Lodha R, Sridevi KN, Chacko S, Mathew J, Shastri S, Ghosh. M. An indigenously developed method for sweat collection and estimation of chloride for diagnosis of cystic fibrosis. Indian Pediatrics 2002; 39:1039–1043.
4. Kabra SK, Lodha R. Investigations in Pulmonology. In Essential Pediatric Pulmonology, New Delhi Nobel Vision, 2006;11–30.
5. LeGrys VA, Yankaskas JR, Quittell LM, Marshall BC, Mogayzel PJ Jr;. Cystic Fibrosis Foundation. Diagnostic sweat testing: the Cystic Fibrosis Foundation guidelines. J Pediatr 2007;151:85–9.
6. Midulla F, de Blic J, Barbato A, Bush A, Eber E, Kotecha S, Haxby E, Moretti C, Pohunek P, Ratjen F: ERS Task Force. Flexible endoscopy of paediatric airways. Eur Respir J 2003; 22: 698–708.

COMMON COLD OR NASOPHARYNGITIS

Common cold is the most frequent medical problem in childhood and is usually due to infection of the upper respiratory tract with adenoviruses, influenza, rhinovirus, parainfluenza or respiratory syncytial viruses. These are spread by droplet infection. Predisposing factors include chilling, sudden exposure to cold air, and overcrowding. Rhinitis could also be due to allergy.

Clinical Features

These include fever, thin nasal discharge and irritability. Cervical lymph nodes may enlarge. Nasopharyngeal congestion causes nasal obstruction and respiratory distress. The latter is more common in young infants. Eustachian tube opening may be blocked leading to serous otitis media and congestion of tympanic membrane. In allergic rhinitis there is a clear mucoid discharge with sneezing. There is no contact with an infected patient and history of allergy is usually present. There is increasing recognition of the role of upper respiratory infections in the etiopathogenesis of bronchial asthma.

Narrowing of the airway and pharyngeal irritation causes dry hacking cough. Excessive lacrimation is due to the blocked lacrimal ducts in the nose. Purulent discharge does not necessarily mean secondary infection all the time as it can result from shedding of epithelial and inflammatory cells resulting from viral infection itself. The illness usually lasts for three days but cold may persist up to two weeks. Rhinitis and stuffy nose could become chronic and last for several weeks.

Complications

Otitis media, laryngitis, sinusitis, bronchiolitis, exacerbation of asthma and bronchopneumonia.

Differential Diagnosis

Foreign body: Unilateral serosanguineous or purulent discharge from the nose indicates presence of foreign body.

Drugs: Intermittent use of rifampicin may cause flu-like syndrome in some children. Drugs like reserpine and prochlorperazine cause nasal stuffiness.

Snuffles: Clear mucoid discharge from the nose in the first few weeks of life is called snuffles. The cause is unknown. There is no evidence for allergy or infections. "Snuffles" of congenital syphilis is severe rhinitis with bilateral serosanguineous discharge commonly excoriating the upper lip and leaving fine scars. Nasal septum may ulcerate leaving a flat nasal bridge.

Treatment

To relieve nasal congestion: Babies sneeze and blow out the nasal discharge, if their anterior nares are tickled by the tip of a handkerchief. Nose drops of saline may give symptomatic relief. Nasal decongestants (ephedrine, xylomatozoline) may cause rebound congestion. If congestion is severe then these should not be used for more than a few days. Oral nasal decongestants such as pseudoephedrine hydrochloride may be tried in resistant cases however routine use should be discouraged. Antihistaminics are increasingly being used for allergic colds. Antihistaminics dry up the thin secretions and relieve sneezing. Newer non sedating antiallergic drugs including loratidine and cetirizine may be useful in allergic rhinitis. Terfenadine should not be prescribed in children because of potential cardiac toxicity.

Fever is controlled by antipyretics such as paracetamol (acetaminophen).

Do not give cough syrups: If the cough is suppressed in infants and young children, mucoid secretions may be retained in the bronchi and this may predispose to spasmodic cough wheezing, atelectasis and suppuration.

Antibiotics are of little value in viral infections. These are used if the secretions become purulent, the fever continues to rise and if the child develops bronchopneumonia. There is no conclusive evidence that large doses of vitamin C are helpful.

Nursing: These children are best nursed prone (on their belly) so that there is no postnasal drip causing irritation of the throat. The children should be protected from sudden exposure to chills and kept warm during the winter months.

ACUTE TONSILLOPHARYNGITIS

Sore throat is due to acute inflammation of the pharynx and tonsils. Most often, it is associated with the viral infections of the upper respiratory tract such as adenovirus, influenza, para influenza virus, enterovirus and Ebstain Barr virus. It may, however, be a prodrome of measles and rubella or may be caused by *Streptococcus pyogenes* especially group A beta-hemolytic streptococci. *Mycoplasma pneumoniae* and *Candida albicans* have also been incriminated. Irritant fumes and smoke also cause irritation of the throat.

Clinical Features

Clinical features include fever, malaise, headache, nausea, and sore throat. It is difficult to distinguish the clinical syndromes due to viral or streptococcal infections. Hoarseness, cough and rhinitis are more common in viral infection. In these, the onset is gradual and there is less toxemia. In streptococcal infections, cervical lymph nodes are enlarged and illness is more acute with high fever, which typically lasts for 4–5 days.

Tonsils become swollen and covered with exudates in both types of infections. Younger children may not complain of sore throat but often refuse to feed normally.

Complication

Acute glomerulonephritis, rheumatic fever, otitis media, sinusitis, peritonsillar and retropharyngeal abscesses. The infection may spread down the tracheobronchial tree and cause tracheobronchitis and pneumonia.

Diagnosis

A possibility of acute pharyngitis due to group A beta hemolytic streptococci may be considered in a child who has exudates in throat, tender enlarged cervical nodes along with absence of nasal or conjunctival congestion. Throat swab culture for group A beta hemolytic streptococci help in the definitive diagnosis. Neutrophil count in the peripheral blood is elevated in streptococcal infections. Rapid diagnostic test for identification of group A beta hemolytic streptococcus may give the result within 10 minutes.

Differential Diagnosis

Narrowing and spasm of trachea and bronchi may also cause sensation of sore throat with a constant desire to clear the throat.

Herpangina: Herpangina is an acute febrile illness due to the group 'A' Coxsackie virus. Patients have dysphagia, sore throat and papulovesicular lesions surrounded by erythema over the tongue, pharynx, anterior tonsillar pillars and soft palate. Pharynx appears congested.

Diphtheria: There is moderate fever, severe toxemia, sore throat and membrane formation over the fauces or palate.

Agranulocytosis: Blood count shows neutropenia.

Pharyngoconjunctival fever: Patients have fever, conjunctivitis, pharyngitis and cervical lymphadenitis due to infection with adenovirus type III.

Infectious mononucleosis: Infectious mononucleosis is characterized by lymphadenopathy, morbilliform rash, hepatosplenomegaly and sometimes aseptic meningitis.

Treatment

Symptomatic: Warm saline gargles are prescribed for older children. Younger children are encouraged to sip warm tea. Paracetamol is administered for fever. Soft food such as custard or rice and lentil gruel is given because swallowing is painful. Rest in bed accelerates recovery.

Specific: Antibiotics are not used for viral infections. Infections with beta hemolytic streptococci are treated with penicillin V orally, injections of procaine penicillin, oral erythromycin or oral amoxicillin in adequate doses for at least 10 days. Parents are likely to stop medication after two to three days as the child begins to improve clinically. If compliance is a problem, single dose of benzathine penicillin by intramuscular route is preferred treatment. Cotrimoxazole which is being commonly used for sinusitis and otitis media is not an appropriate choice and should not be used for sore throat.

Recurrent Attacks of Sore Throat

Parents often seek the advice of a physician for the treatment of recurrent sore throat in their children. In such cases, a detailed history should be obtained and physical examination conducted for proper evaluation. Para-nasal sinuses and ears should be examined for the foci of infection and if present, these should be adequately treated. Smoky and dusty atmosphere should be avoided. Dampness in the environment and overcrowding predispose the child to recurrent upper respiratory tract infections. The child's general health should be improved by good nutritious diet.

Every episode of bacterial pharyngitis should be treated with adequate doses of antibiotics for at least 10 days, so that no residua of infection are left. Usually single dose of Benzathin penicillin by IM route or penicillin V orally are the drugs of choice. Presence of beta lactamase producing bacteria in the pharynx may inactivate penicillin and lead to recurrent sore throat. This should be treated with amoxycillin plus clavulinic acid. Clindamycin is an effective agent to eradicate the carrier state. In resistant cases, long term penicillin prophylaxis should be carried out especially if group A beta hemolytic streptococcal infection is present. Although the principle of its use is the same as in rheumatic fever, a shorter course of therapy for 3 to 6 months suffices to break the vicious circle.

Tonsillectomy does not prevent recurrence of pharyngeal infections. A detailed discussion on indications of tonsillectomy is given in Chapter 12.

Suggested reading

1. Casey JR, Pichichero ME. Metaanalysis of short course antibiotic treatment for group a streptococcal tonsillopharyngitis. Pediatr Infect Dis J 2005; 24: 909–17.
2. Aroll B. Antibiotics for upper respiratory tract infections: An overview of Cochrane reviews. Respir Med 2005;99:255–61.
3. Bisno AL, Gerber MA, Gwaltney JM, Kaplan EL, Schwartz RL. Practice Guidelines for the Diagnosis and Management of Group A Streptococcal Pharyngitis. Clinical Infectious Diseases 2002;35:113–125
4. Tiewsoh K, Kaur J, Lodha R, Kabra SK, Management of upper respiratory tract infection. Indian J Pediatrics 2007; 73: supplement.

ACUTE LOWER RESPIRATORY TRACT INFECTIONS

Acute lower respiratory tract infections are the leading cause of death in children below 5 years of age. The diseases included under this heading include: croup syndromes, bronchitis, bronchiolitis and pneumonia.

CROUP

The term croup is used for a variety of conditions in which a peculiar brassy cough is the main presenting feature. Inspiratory stridor, hoarseness or respiratory distress may not always be associated with croup. The diseases included are acute epiglottitis, laryngitis, laryngotracheobronchitis and spasmodic laryngitis.

Epiglottitis: Supraglottitis includes both epiglottitis and inflammatory edema of the hypopharynx. Hemophilus influenzae type B is the most frequent causative agent. Other microbes like pneumococcus, beta-hemolytic streptococcus and staphylococcus are not important in etiology. The illness usually starts with a minor upper respiratory tract illness, which progresses rapidly within the course of a few hours. The child suffers from high fever and has difficulty in swallowing. The breathing becomes noisy but is generally softer than in case of laryngotraceobronchitis. The child is not able to phonate and often sits up leaning forwards with his neck extended and saliva dribbling from his chin which appears to be thrust forwards. The accessory muscles of respiration are active and there is marked suprasternal and subcostal retraction of the chest. As the child becomes fatigued, the stridor diminishes. The diagnosis of epiglottitis is made by a cautious direct laryngoscopy, wherein the epiglottis appears angry red, and swollen. Injudicious attempt to examine the throat may, at times cause death by sudden reflex spasm of the larynx. It is therefore prudent not to force a child, panting for breath, to lie down for throat examination or to send him to the radiology department for an urgent X-ray film if the clinical diagnosis is otherwise obvious. In case these procedures are considered essential, the equipment and personnel for respiratory resuscitation should always be readily available.

Laryngitis and laryngotracheobronchitis (infectious croup): These conditions are nearly always caused by viral infections, usually with parainfluenza type 1. Other viruses incriminated include respiratory syncytial and parainfluenza types 2 and 3, influenza virus, adenovirus and rhinovirus. Bacterial etiology or bacterial superinfection are unusual. In infectious croup, the onset of the illness is more gradual. Usually, there is a mild cold for a few days before the child develops a brassy cough and mild inspiratory stridor. As the obstruction increases, the stridor becomes more marked and the suprasternal and sternal recession become evident. The child becomes restless and anxious with fast breathing due to increasing hypoxemia. Eventually cyanosis appears. As the obstruction worsens, breath sounds may become inaudible and stridor may apparently decrease. This may unfortunately be misinterpreted as clinical improvement by the unwary physician.

Spasmodic croup: It occurs in children between the age of 1 and 3 years. There may not be preceding coryza. The child wakes up suddenly in the early hours of the morning with brassy cough and noisy breathing. The symptoms improve within a few hours. The illness may recur on subsequent days. The course is generally benign and patients recover completely. The cause is unknown. Humidification of the room in which the child is nursed is all that is necessary.

Differential diagnosis of croup: The syndromes of croup should be distinguished from each other and also from the croup associated with diphtheria in which a membrane is seen on laryngoscopy or occasionally with measles. Rarely the croup may result from angioneurotic edema. A retropharyngeal abscess may cause respiratory obstruction. Aspiration of a foreign body is an important cause of obstruction. It may be rarely confused with wheezing in asthma.

Management of croup: A child with epiglottitis needs hospitalization. Humidified oxygen should be administered by hood. Face masks are not well tolerated by these children. As oxygen therapy masks cyanosis, a careful watch should be kept on patient for other evidences of impending respiratory failure. Sedatives should not be given. Unnecessary manipulation of the patient may induce laryngeal spasm. Fluids should be administered for adequate hydration of the patient by intravenous route. Antibiotics such as ampicillin 100 mg/kg/day or chloramphenicol 50 mg/kg/day may be useful in cases of epiglottitis but not in laryngotracheobronchitis or laryngitis. A single daily dose of intravenous ceftriaxone is a satisfactory alternative. Endotracheal intubation or tracheostomy may be indicated, if the response to antibiotics is not adequate and obstruction is worsening.

Child with acute laryngotracheobronchitis should be assessed for severity of illness on basis of general appearance, stridor (audible with/without stethoscope), oxygen saturation and respiratory distress (Table 13.3).

Mild cases can be managed on ambulatory basis with symptomatic treatment for fever and encouraging the child to take liquids orally. Parents may be explained about the progression of diseases and to bring the child back to hospital in case of worsening of symptoms. Antibiotics do not have any role.

Moderately severe patient may need hospitalization and treatment with racemic epinephrine (2.25%) diluted with water (1:8) administered through nebulizer for immediate relief of symptoms. Recent studies have shown that a single intramuscular dose of dexamethasone (0.3–0.6 mg/kg) reduces overall severity during first 24 hours.

13

Table 13.3: Severity of acute laryngotracheobronchitis

	Mild	*Moderate*	*Severe*
General appearance	Happy, feeds well, interested in surrounding	Irritable but can be comforted by parents	Restless or agitated or altered sensorium
Stridor	Stridor on coughing, No stridor at rest,	Stridor at rest and get worse when agitated	Stridor at rest and worsens on agitation
Respiratory distress	No distress	Tachypnea and chest retractions	Marked tachypnea with chest retractions
Oxygen saturation	>92% in room air	>92% in room air	<92% in room air, may be cyanosed

More recently inhalation of budesonide in doses of 1 mg twice a day for two days has shown good results. Antibiotics do not have any role.

Severe croup may need hospitalization, preferably in Pediatric Intensive care, with oxygen inhalation, steroids (similar to moderate severity). Worsening distress may need short term ventilation. Antibiotics do not have any role unless some bacterial infection is suspected.

Suggested reading

1. Russell K, Wiebe N, Saenz A, Ausejo SM, Johnson D, Hartling L, Klassen TP. Glucocorticoids for croup. Cochrane Database Syst Rev. 2004;(1):CD001955.
2. Knutson D, Aring A. Viral croup. Am Fam Physician 2004;69: 535–40.

PNEUMONIA

Pneumonia may be classified anatomically as lobar or lobular pneumonia, bronchopneumonia and interstitial pneumonia.

Pathologically, there is a consolidation of alveoli or infiltration of the interstitial tissue with inflammatory cells or both.

Etiology

Viral: Viral pneumonia caused by RSV, influenza, parainfluenza or adenovirus may be responsible for about 40% of the cases.

Bacterial: In over two-third of the cases, common bacteria cause pneumonia. In first 2 months the common agents include klebsiella, *E coli* and staphylococci. Between 3 months to 3 years common bacteria include *S. pneumoniae*, *H. influenzae* and staphylococci. After 3 years of age common bacterial pathogens include *S. pneumoniae* and staphylococci. Gram negative organisms cause pneumonia in early infancy, severe malnutrition and immunocompromised children.

Atypical organisms: More and more evidence are available to suggest important role of chlamydia spp and mycoplasma in community acquired pneumonia in adults and children. *Pneumocystis carinii:* causes pneumonia in immunocompromised children.

Clinical Features

The risk factors for pneumonia include low birth weight, malnutrition, vitamin A deficiency, lack of breast-feeding, passive smoking, large family size, family history of bronchitis, advanced birth order, crowding, young age and air pollution. Recent reviews suggest that indoor air pollution is one of the major risk factor for acute lower respiratory tract infection in children in developing countries. Onset of pneumonia may be insidious starting with upper respiratory tract infection or may be acute with high fever, dyspnea and grunting respiration. Respiratory rate is always increased.

Rarely, pneumonia may present with symptoms of acute abdominal emergency. This is attributed to referred pain from the pleura. Apical pneumonia may sometimes be associated with meningismus and convulsions. In these patients the cerebrospinal fluid is always clear.

On examination, there is flaring of alae nasi, retraction of the lower chest and intercostal spaces. Signs of consolidation are observed in lobar pneumonia.

Pneumococcal Pneumonia

Respiratory infection due to *S. pneumoniae* are transmitted by droplets and are more common in the winter months. Overcrowding and diminished host resistance predisposes children to infection with pneumococci.

Pathology: Bacteria multiply in the alveoli and an inflammatory exudate is formed. Scattered areas of consolidation occur, which coalesce around the bronchi and later become lobular or lobar in distribution. There is no tissue necrosis. Pathological process passes from the stage of congestion to red and gray hepatization before the final stage of resolution.

Clinical features: Incubation period is 1 to 3 days. The onset is abrupt with headache, chills, cough and high fever. Cough is initially dry but may be associated with thick rusty sputum. The latter is uncommon in children. Pleural pain is complained of and this may be referred to the shoulder or abdomen. Respiration is rapid. In severe cases there may be grunting chest indrawing, difficulty in feeding and cyanosis. Percussion note is impaired, air entry is diminished, crepitations and bronchial breathing may be heard over areas of consolidation. Bronchophony and whispering pectoriloquy may be observed. Meningismus may be present in apical pneumonia.

Diagnosis: The diagnosis is based on history, physical examination, X-ray findings of lobar consolidation (Fig. 13.1) and leukocytosis. Bacteriological confirmation is

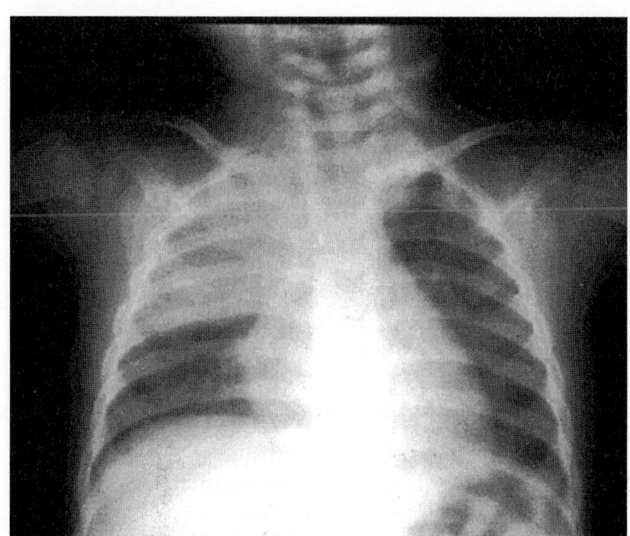

Fig. 13.1: Consolidation of right upper lobe due to infection with *Streptococcus pneumoniae*

difficult but sputum may be examined by Gram staining and culture. Blood culture may be positive in 5–15% of cases. Demonstration of polysaccharide antigen in urine and blood are attractive investigations but do not have sufficient sensitivity and specificity for confirming pneumococcal pneumonia.

Treatment: Penicillin G 50,000 units/kg/day is given intravenously or intramuscular in divided doses for 5–7 days. Procaine penicillin 600,000 units intramuscular per day or Penicillin V may be used orally instead. Oxygen should be given if cyanosis and respiratory distress are present. Alternative may be amoxycillin or ampicillin In patients allergic to penicillin, the alternatives are chloramphenicol or cephalosporins (Ceftrioxone/cefotaxime). The latter should be given with caution as cross sensitivity to penicillin may occur.

Staphylococcal Pneumonia

Staphylococcal pneumonia occurs in infancy and childhood. The pulmonary lesion may be primary infection of the parenchyma; or may be secondary to generalized staphylococcal septicemia. It may be a complication of measles, influenza and cystic fibrosis of the lungs or may follow minor staphylococcal pyoderma. Debilitating conditions including malnutrition, diabetes mellitus, macrophage dysfunction predispose the children to infection with staphylococci.

Pathology: In infants, the pneumonic process is diffuse initially, but soon the lesions suppurate, resulting in bronchoalveolar destruction. Multiple microabscesses are formed, which erode the bronchial wall and discharge their contents in the bronchi. Several pneumatoceles may form and they may fluctuate in size over the time, ultimately resolving and disappearing within a period of few weeks to months. Epithelialization of the walls of the air cysts may occur. Staphylococcal abscesses in the lungs may erode into the pericardium causing purulent pericarditis. Empyema in a child below two years of age is nearly always staphylococcal in etiology.

Clinical manifestations: The illness usually follows upper respiratory tract infection, pyoderma or other associated purulent disease. Besides the usual features of pneumonia, i.e. grunting respiration, the child has fever and anorexia, is listless and irritable. Abdomen is usually distended due to septicemia and ileus. This may distract the attention of the observer from the respiratory illness. Cyanosis may be present. Progression of the symptoms and signs is rapid. Rarely, the onset may be less abrupt, the course may be protracted and temperature may be only moderately elevated. Sometimes pulmonary infection may be complicated by disseminated disease, i.e. involvement of more than 2 anatomically different sites. This may manifest as metastatic abscesses into joints, bone, muscles, pericardium, liver, mastoid or brain.

Diagnosis: The diagnosis of staphylococcal pneumonia is suspected in a newborn or an infant with respiratory infection who has evidence of staphylococcal infection elsewhere in the body. The characteristic complications of pyo-pneumothorax and pericarditis in an infant are highly suggestive of the diagnosis. Pneumatoceles are present in X-ray films of the lung, characteristically in pneumonia due to staphylococci and klebsiella. These pneumatoceles are present in X-ray films of the lung (Fig. 13.2) characteristically in pneumonia due to staphylococci and klebsiella. These pneumatoceles persist as thin walled asymptomatic cysts for several weeks. Often staphylococci can be grown from the blood.

Treatment: The child should be immediately hospitalized and isolated to prevent the spread of resistant

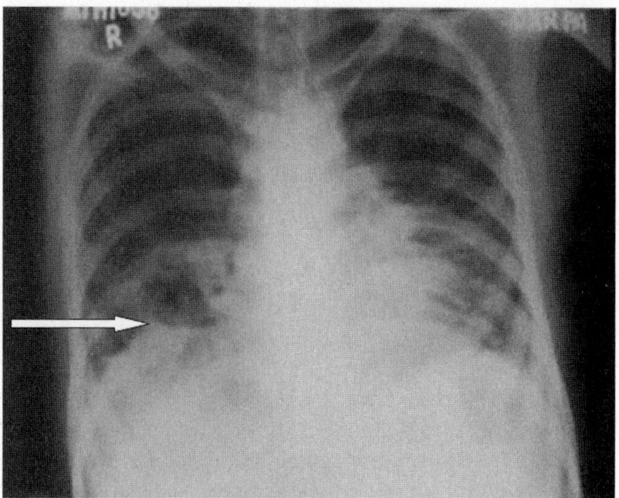

Fig. 13.2: *Staphylococcal pneumonia.* Note multiple pneumatoceles (arrow)

staphylococci to the other patients. Fever is controlled with antipyretics and hydration is maintained by intravenous infusion of electrolyte solutions in 5% dextrose. Oxygen is administered to relieve the dyspnea and cyanosis.

Specific: Empyema is aspirated and the pus is sent for culture and tests for sensitivity to antibiotics. Vigorous antibiotic therapy is carried out with penicillin G, erythromycin, cloxacillin or cephalosporin. The latter are preferred for infections with beta lactamase producing staphylococci. If the patient does not respond soon, vancomycin or ticoplanin may be introduced. Therapy should continue till all the evidence of the disease disappears both clinically and radiologically, which usually takes two to six weeks or even longer. After initial intravenous antibiotics remaining course may be completed with oral antibiotics. Prolonged therapy is desirable as the bacteria persist in the necrotic area.

Complications: Pneumatoceles do not require specific measures. Intercostal decompression may be done for the large pneumatoceles causing respiratory distress. Empyema and pyopneumothorax are treated by intercostal drainage under water seal or low pressure aspiration may be done. Metastatic abscesses require surgical drainage. Significant pleural thickening that is preventing complete expansion of underlying lung may require decortication. It can be done by open thoracotomy or by thoracoscopic surgery. An early thoracoscopic drainage of empyema may help in prevention of pleural thickening. Instillation of streptokinase or urokinase in pleural cavity when pleural fluid is thin may also help in prevention of pleural thickening.

Hemophilus Pneumonia

Infections occur usually between the age of three months and three years and are nearly always associated with bacteremia.

Infection with *H. influenzae* usually begins in the nasopharynx and spreads locally or through the blood stream. Most nasopharyngeal infections are mild and confer immunity from subsequent serious illness after the early months of life. As the infants have transplacentally transferred antibodies during the first 3 to 4 months of life, infection with *H. influenzae* is relatively less frequent during this period.

Pathology: Pathology is similar to that of infections with pneumococci. There is extensive destruction of bronchial epithelium and hemorrhagic edema extending into interstitial area.

Clinical features: The onset of the illness is gradual with nasopharyngeal infection. Certain viral infections as those due to influenza virus probably act synergistically with *H. influenzae*. These alter the respiratory epithelial resistance and therefore promote proliferation of the bacteria in the damaged respiratory epithelium.

The child has moderate fever, dyspnea, grunting respiration and retraction of the lower inter-costal spaces. Presentation may mimic acute bronchiolitis. The course is subacute and prolonged. Complications of *Hemophilus influenzae* pneumonia include bacteremia, pericarditis, empyema, meningitis and polyarthritis.

Treatment: *H. influenzae* pneumonia is best treated with ampicillin in a dose of 100 to 150 mg/kg/day and chloramphenicol 50 mg/kg/day in four divided doses. Cefotaxime (100 mg/kg/day) or ceftrioxone (50–75 mg/kg/day) are other alternative in seriously ill patients.

Streptococcal Pneumonia

Streptococcal infection of the lungs by group A beta hemolytic streptococci is usually secondary to measles, chicken pox, influenza or whooping cough.

Clinical features: The onset is abrupt fever, chills, dyspnea, rapid respiration, blood streaked sputum, cough and extreme prostration characterize the illness. Signs of bronchopneumonia are generally less pronounced, as the pathology is usually interstitial.

Complications: Thin serosanguineous or purulent empyema is a usual complication. Pulmonary suppuration is less frequent. Ten percent of the patients have bacteremia. When pneumatoceles are present, the condition mimics staphylococcal pneumonia.

Diagnosis: X-ray film shows interstitial pneumonia, segmental involvement, diffuse peribronchial densities or an effusion. (This should be distinguished from primary atypical pneumonia due to mycoplasma). Blood counts show increased neutrophils, and the patient looks more ill in streptococcal pneumonia.

Treatment: Penicillin G should be given in doses of 50,000 to 100,000 units/kg of body weight, daily in divided doses for 7–10 days. The response is gradual but recovery is generally complete.

Empyema is treated by closed drainage with indwelling intercostal tube.

Primary Atypical Pneumonia

The etiological agent of primary atypical pneumonia is *Mycoplasma pneumoniae*. The disease is transmitted by droplet infection. It occurs in epidemics chiefly in the winter months. The children living in overcrowded environments are more prone to develop pneumonia. The disease is uncommon in children below the age of four years, although subclinical and mild infections have been reported in infants.

Clinical features: Incubation period is 12 to 14 days. Onset may be insidious or abrupt. Initial symptoms are malaise, headache, fever, sore throat, myalgia and cough. Cough is dry at first but later it is associated with mucoid expectoration which may be blood streaked. Dyspnea is unusual. There are very few physical signs, except mild pharyngeal congestion, cervical lymphadenopathy and a few crepitations. Extrapulmonary manifestations include: hemolytic anemia.

X-ray: X-ray findings are more extensive than suggested by the physical findings. Poorly defined hazy or fluffy exudates radiate from the hilar regions. Enlargement of the hilar lymph nodes and pleural effusion have been reported. Infiltrates involve one lobe, usually the lower.

Diagnosis: It is difficult to distinguish *M. pneumonia* from viral or rickettsial pneumonia. The leukocyte count is usually normal. Cold agglutinins are elevated. *M. pneumoniae* may be recovered from the pharynx and sputum. The diagnosis is made rapidly by demonstration of IgM antibody by ELISA during the acute stage. IgG antibodies are demonstrable by complement fixation after one week of illness and shows increase in titers over 2–4 weeks.

Treatment: Patients are treated with macrolide antibiotics (erythromycin/roxithromycin/azithromycin/ clarithromycin) or tetracycline for older children for 7 to 10 days.

Pneumonia due to Gram-Negative Organisms

The etiological agents are *E. coli*, klebsiella and pseudomonas. These organisms affect small children (< 2 months of age) or children with malnutrition and poor immunity. Pseudomonas may colonize airways of patients with cystic fibrosis and causes recurrent pulmonary exacerbations.

Pathology: Well demarcated areas of consolidation and necrosis occur due to vasculitis. There is little inflammatory response.

Clinical features: Onset is gradual and assumes life threatening proportions during its course. Signs of consolidation are minimal, particularly in infants. Constitutional symptoms are more prominent than respiratory distress.

Diagnosis: Radiological signs are extensive in a form of massive consolidation. *E. coli* or klebsiella pneumonia may have pneumatoceles.

Treatment: Intravenous use of a third generation cephalosporin (cefotaxime or ceftriaxone, 75–100 mg/kg/day) with or without an aminoglycoside is recommended for 10 to 14 days. In case of suspected pseudomonas infection, ceftazadime may be drug of choice.

Viral Pneumonia

Respiratory syncytial virus is the most important cause in infants under 2 years of age. At other ages, influenza, parainfluenza and adenoviruses are common. The bronchial tree or alveoli are involved resulting in interstitial pneumonia. There is no clinical evidence of consolidation. Radiological signs consist of perihilar and peribronchial infiltrates.

Hydrocarbon Pneumonia

Kerosene exerts its toxic effects on the lungs and the central nervous system. It is poorly absorbed from the gastrointestinal tract. Milk and alcohol promote its absorption. It has low viscosity and less surface tension and therefore it diffuses quickly from the pharynx into the lungs. Administration of oil apparently decreases the absorption from the gastrointestinal tract but it is not used as a therapeutic measure. Clinical features of hydrocarbon pneumonia include cough, dyspnea, high fever, vomiting, drowsiness and coma. Physical signs in lungs are minimal. X-ray film of the chest shows ill defined homogeneous or patchy opacities, resembling miliary mottling of the lungs.

Treatment: Vomiting is not induced. Gastric lavage is usually avoided to prevent inadvertent aspiration. The patient is kept on oxygen. Routine antibiotics are not indicated. Corticosteroids have little beneficial effect.

Loeffler's Syndrome

Larvae of many nematodes (intestinal parasites) during their life cycle enter the portal circulation, liver and pass through the hepatic vein and inferior vena cava into the heart and lungs. In the lungs, the larvae penetrate the capillaries, enter the alveoli, plug the bronchi with mucus and eosinophilic material due to allergic reaction. There are fleeting patchy pulmonary infiltrations. Some cases may be due to drug reaction to aspirin, penicillin, sulfonamide or imipramine.

The clinical features include cough, low fever and scattered crepitations. There is eosinophilia in the blood and X-ray of the lungs shows pulmonary infiltrates of varying size but these may superficially resemble miliary tuberculosis. Treatment is symptomatic.

Suggested reading

1. Broor S, Pandey RM, Ghosh M, Maitreyi RS, Lodha R, Singhal T, Kabra SK. Risk factors for severe acute lower respiratory tract infection in under-five children. Indian Pediatr. 2001;38: 1361-9.
2. Chaudhary R, Nazima N, Dhawan B, Kabra SK. Prevalence of mycoplasma pneumonia and chlamydia pneumoniae in children with community acquired pneumonia. Indian J Pediatr 1998; 65: 717–721.
3. Kabra SK, Lodha R, Broor S, Chaudhary R, Ghosh M, Maitreyi RS Etiology of acute lower respiratory tract infection. Indian J Pediatr. 2003;70:33–6.
4. Kabra SK, Lodha R, Pandey RM.Antibiotics for community acquired pneumonia in children. Cochrane Database Syst Rev. 2006 Jul 19;3:CD004874
5. Kabra SK, Singhal T, Lodha R. Pneumionia. Indian J Pediatr 2001; 68 (supplement 3): S19– S23.
6. Maitreyi RS, Broor S, Kabra SK, Ghosh M, Seth P, Dar L, Prasad AK. Rapid detection of respiratory viruses by centrifugation enhanced cultures from children with acute lower respiratory tract infections. J Clin Virology 2000; 16: 41–47.

13

13

ACUTE RESPIRATORY TRACT INFECTION (ARI) CONTROL PROGRAMME

Acute lower respiratory tract infections (LRTI) are a leading cause of mortality in children below 5 years of age. It has been shown in various studies from developing countries that the etiological agents in LRTI is bacterial in 50–60% of children. The common bacteria causing LRTI in preschool children include *H. influenzae, S. pneumoniae* and staphylococci. All these are sensitive to antibacterials like cotrimoxazole. Hence judicious use of cotrimoxazole in children suffering from LRTI may prevent deaths due to pneumonia. The World Health Organization (WHO) has recommended certain clinical criteria for diagnosis of pneumonia in children at primary health care level for control of LRTI deaths in countries where the infant mortality is more than 40/1000 live births. The clinical criteria for diagnosis of pneumonia include rapid respiration with or without difficulty in respiration. Rapid respiration is defined as respiratory rate of more than 60, 50 or 40/minutes in children below 2 months of age, 2 months to 1 year and 1 to 5 years of age respectively.

Difficulty in respiration is defined as lower chest in drawing. The WHO recommends that in a primary care setting if a child between 2 months to 5 years of age presents with cough he should be examined for rapid respiration and difficulty in breathing along with presence of cyanosis or difficulty in feeding (Table 13.4). If the respiration is normal, no chest indrawing and he/she is feeding well, child is assessed to be suffering from upper respiratory tract infection and can be managed at home. If the child has rapid respiration but there is no chest indrawing, he/she is suffering from pneumonia and can be managed on ambulatory basis with oral cotrimoxazole for 5 days.

If child has chest indrawing, he/she is assessed to be suffering from severe pneumonia and needs hospitalization. In hospital, the child is managed with IV/IM penicillin.

Presence of severe chest indrawing or cyanosis indicates very severe pneumonia. Such children are admitted in hospital and treated with IV chloramphenicol along with supportive care (Table 13.4). Recent reports suggest that common causative agents of pneumonia are getting resistant to cotrimoxazole and chloramphenizol. In future these drugs may be replaced with amoxicillin and penicillins.

In children below 2 months of age, the presence of any of the following indicates severe disease: fever (38°C or more), convulsions, abnormally sleepy or difficult to wake, stridor in calm child, wheezing, not feeding, tachypnea, chest indrawing, altered sensorium, central cyanosis grunting, apneic spells or distended abdomen. Such children should be referred to hospital for admission and treated with injection ampicillin and gentamicin and supportive care.

Suggested reading

Technical bases for WHO recommendations on the management of pneumonia in children at first level health facilities. WHO/ARI/91.20 Geneva: World Health Organization, 1991.

BRONCHIOLITIS

It is one of the common serious acute lower respiratory infection in infants. Affected infants are between the ages of 1 and 6 months, but the disease can affect children up to their second birthday. Disease usually occurs in winter and spring. Respiratory syncytial virus (RSV) is implicated in most cases. Other causative organisms include parainfluenza virus, adenovirus, influenza viruses and *M. pneumoniae.*

Protection against RSV is mediated by antibodies of IgG3 subclass. These antibodies have shorter half life and do not cross the placenta in substantial amount so as to offer protection to the infant. High quantities of secretary IgA antibodies to RSV are present in the colostrum and breast feeding reduces the likelihood of an infant being hospitalized with acute bronchiolitis.

Table 13.4: Children aged 2 months to 5 years with cough or difficult breathing: Clinical classification to facilitate treatment decisions

Signs and symptoms	*Classification*	*Therapy*	*Where to treat*
Cough or cold No fast breathing No chest indrawing or indicators of severe illness	No pneumonia	Home remedies	Home
Respiratory rate RR/minute; Age 60 or more; <2 months 50 or more; 2–12 months 40 or more; 12–60 months	Pneumonia	Cotrimoxazole	Home
Chest indrawing	Severe pneumonia	IV/IM Penicillin	Hospital
Cyanosis, severe chest indrawing inability to feed	Very severe pneumonia	IV Chloramphenicol	Hospital

Pathogenesis and Clinical Features

The inflammation of the bronchiolar mucosa leads to edema, thickening, formation of mucus plugs and cellular debris. Bronchiolar spasm occurs in some cases. The bronchial lumen, which is already narrow in the infants, is further reduced. As the airway resistance is inversely related to the fourth power of the radius of the bronchiolar lumen, even slight further narrowing causes marked increase in the airway resistance and reduction of airflow. Resistance to the airflow is increased both during inspiration and expiration. During expiration, the bronchioles are partially collapsed and therefore the egress of the air from the lungs is severely restricted during this phase. This leads to trapping of the air inside the alveoli causing emphysematous changes. When obstruction becomes complete, the trapped air in the lungs may be absorbed causing atelectasis.

Due to diminished ventilation and diffusion, hypoxemia is produced in almost all of these infants. In severely hypoxemic infants, retention of carbon dioxide leads to respiratory acidosis. In the milder cases, compensation occurs due to hyperventilation of the normal alveoli. The presence of eosinophils in the blood and respiratory secretions suggest that the virus infection initiates the wheezing attack in a child who is already sensitized.

The disease ushers in with an upper respiratory tract infection. After a few days, the breathing becomes fast and respiratory distress develops. Majority of infants has mild symptoms and recover in 3–7 days. Those with severe disease may develop retraction of lower intercostal spaces and suprasternal notch on 3–5 days.

In severe infection the infant pants for breath and may appear cyanosed. The fever is moderately high. Accessory muscles of respiration are working. Expiration is prolonged, fine crepitations and rhonchi are auscultated. Breath sounds may be faint, or inaudible in severe cases. Respiratory distress is out of proportion to the extent of the physical signs in the lungs.

As the air is trapped in the lungs leading to emphysema, the liver and spleen are pushed down. When the chest becomes over inflated, the anteroposterior diameter of the chest is increased and hyper resonance is noted on percussion.

Investigations

X-ray chest shows hyperinflation and infiltrates (Fig. 13.3); diaphragm is pushed down. The lung fields appear abnormally translucent. The leukocyte count is normal or slightly elevated. A rapid test using monoclonal antibodies against respiratory syncytial virus on nasopharyngeal aspirate can identify RSV at bed site.

Bronchiolitis is generally a self-limiting illness. The symptoms subside in three to seven days. Death may occur in one percent of the severely ill patients due to respiratory failure. The relationship of acute bronchiolitis to bronchial asthma in later life has been observed in about one-fourth of the cases of acute bronchiolitis. Bronchial asthma is more likely in children with personal or family history of an allergic illness.

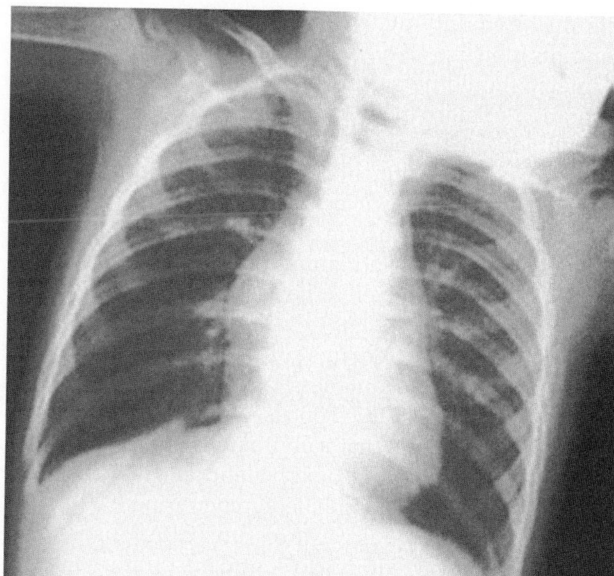

Fig. 13.3: Chest X-ray. Bronchiolitis showing hyperinflation

Differential Diagnosis

Bronchiolitis is often confused with bronchial asthma. The latter is unusual below the age of one year. There is often a family history of asthma. Several attacks occur in the same patient. Bronchial asthma may occur without a preceding respiratory infection. Response to bronchodilators is more consistent in children with asthma as compared to children with bronchiolitis.

Congestive heart failure is suggested, if there is cardiomegaly on X-ray film of chest, tachycardia, large tender liver, raised JVP, edema and rales in the bases of the lungs. Foreign bodies in trachea are diagnosed by the history of aspiration of foreign body, localized wheeze, and signs of collapse or localized obstructive emphysema. In bacterial pneumonia, the signs of obstruction are less pronounced, fever is high and adventitious sounds in the lungs are prominent.

Treatment

Treatment of bronchiolitis is essentially symptomatic. The child should be nursed in a humid atmosphere preferably in sitting position at angle of 30° to 40° with head and neck elevated.

Infants with mild disease can be cared for at home in a humidified atmosphere. If respiratory distress increases or feeding problems appear, child should be hospitalized.

In hospital moist oxygen inhalation remains the mainstay of treatment. It is administered continuously even in the absence of cyanosis. Fluids and electrolyte balance should be maintained. Very sick infants may need a concentration of 60% oxygen given through a hood. Pulse oximetry should be performed regularly to keep oxygen saturation of more than 95%.

Antibiotics have no role. Ribavirin, an antiviral agent has no role in the treatment of infants who were previously healthy. Ribavirin, however, shortens the course of illness in infants with underlying congenital heart disease, chronic lung disease and immunodeficiency. Ribavirin is delivered by a nebulizer 16 hours a day for 3–5 days in such cases.

Beta 2 adrenergic drugs and ipratropium are not recommended for infants less than 6 months. A recent analysis of all the studies on use of bronchodilators in bronchiolitis suggest that salbutamol with ipratropium inhalation may provide some benefit and there may be some beneficial effect of inhaled epinephrine.

Continous positive airway pressure (CPAP) or assisted ventilation may be required to control respiratory failure. Extracorporeal membrane oxygenation is effective, when respiratory failure is not controlled by mechanical ventilation.

Suggested reading

1. Blom D, Ermers M, Bont L, van Aalderen WM, van Woensel JB.Inhaled corticosteroids during acute bronchiolitis in the prevention of post-bronchiolitic wheezing. Cochrane Database Syst Rev. 2007;:CD004881
2. Calogero C, Sly PD. Acute viral bronchiolitis: to treat or not to treat-that is the question. J Pediatr. 2007;151:235–7.
3. Chávez-Bueno S, Mejías A, Welliver RC.Respiratory syncytial virus bronchiolitis : current and future strategies for treatment and prophylaxis. Treat Respir Med. 2006;5:483–94.
4. Spurling GK, Fonseka K, Doust J, Del Mar C.Antibiotics for bronchiolitis in children. Cochrane Database Syst Rev. 2007 Jan 24;(1):CD005189.

BRONCHIAL ASTHMA

Bronchial asthma is a disease characterized by an increased responsiveness of the airways to various stimuli. It manifests by widespread narrowing of the airways causing paroxysmal dyspnea, wheezing or cough. The diffuse obstruction to the airflow is reversible in a large majority of cases, either spontaneously or in response to treatment. Bronchial reactivity is a necessary component of asthma. Asthma is a result of multifactorial inheritance.

PATHOPHYSIOLOGY

Airway obstruction in asthma is caused by (i) edema and inflammation of mucous membrane lining the airways, (ii) excessive secretion of mucus, inflammatory cells and cellular debris and (iii) spasm of the smooth muscle of bronchi. Obstruction is diffuse but not uniform.

Asthma has been classified as extrinsic (IgE mediated, triggered by allergens) and intrinsic (non IgE mediated, triggered by infection).

Inhalation of an allergen leads to a biphasic response with early and late reactions ultimately causing broncho-constriction.

Early reaction starts within 10 minutes of the exposure to allergen. It is characterized by release of histamine, leukotrienes C,D,E, prostaglandins, platelet activating factor and bradykinin from the mast cells following the interaction of allergen with specific mast cell bound IgE. All these substances cause bronchoconstriction, mucosal edema and mucus secretion which manifests as airway obstruction. This phase is inhibited by Beta 2 agonist drugs.

Late phase occurs in about two-third of patients. It develops 3–4 hours later with peak at 8–12 hours. Again there is a release of mast cell mediators. This phase is not prevented by premedication with Beta 2 agonist drugs. However, it is inhibited by premedication with steroids suggesting that airway narrowing is mainly due to an inflammatory reaction and mucosal edema. This phase presents as clinical asthma.

Airway resistance is increased more so during exhalation because airways close prematurely during expiration. As a result lungs are hyperinflated; elasticity and frequency-dependent compliance of the lungs are reduced. Breathing involves more work resulting in dyspnea. Perfusion of inadequately ventilated lungs causes low PaO_2.

In early stages of illness $PaCO_2$ also falls because of hyperventilation caused by dyspnea. When obstruction becomes more severe, alveolar hypoventilation supervenes. This leads to retention of CO_2 with a rise of $PaCO_2$. With the exhaustion of buffer mechanisms, pH of blood falls (respiratory acidemia).

Bronchial hyperresponsiveness and asthma: Bronchial hyperresponsiveness is one of the most characteristic features of asthma. This is attributed to one or more of the following abnormalities:

i. defect in the airway,
ii. abnormal neural control of the airways, and
iii. bronchial inflammation

It is suggested that an imbalance between excitatory (cholinergic, alpha-adrenergic and non-cholinergic) and inhibitory mechanisms (adrenergic and non-adrenergic) increases bronchial reactivity. Bronchoconstriction results from increased cholinergic activity causing bronchial smooth muscle to contract and bronchodilatation results from non-adrenergic system and endogenous catecholamines acting on the beta adrenergic receptors and prostaglandin E2. There are both inhibitory and excitatory non-adrenergic non-cholinergic nerves which secrete certain neuropeptides. Two of these have been well studied. Vasoactive intestinal peptides (VIP) relax smooth muscles of bronchi while substance-P increases smooth muscle tone, mucus hypersecretion and microvascular leakage.

PATHOLOGY

Airway inflammation is now considered to be the basic pathology in asthma: This is initiated by degranulation of mast cells. Degranulated mast cells release various mediators of inflammation as discussed earlier. These mediators damage the wall of the airways leading to epithelial shedding and mucus secretion. Inflammatory mediators also influence reactivity via neural mechanisms.

Triggers of an attack of asthma: Only a few cases of asthma in children are directly related to the specific allergen exposure.

Exposure to allergens in the environment that are inhaled, plays a significant role in the pathogenesis of chronic asthma. A marked increase in the incidence of asthma occurred in areas in which high levels of aeroallergens such as house dust mites (dermatophagoids), molds such as alternaria or other industrial allergens were present. Smoke, hydrocarbons, drugs such as aspirin, non-steroidal-anti-inflammatory drugs, tartarazine trigger an attack. Prolonged allergen avoidance reduces allergen specific and mediator induced bronchial reactivity.

Viral infections: Viral infections in the young children and exercise in older child or adult appear to be more frequent triggers of airway narrowing. Exact mechanism by which viral infections (mainly RSV) induce temporary bronchoconstriction is not clear. Probably viral infections interefere with the integrity of mucosal surface by opening up the tight intraepithelial cell junctions and thus inducing the shedding of epithelium. It results in mucosal edema and mucus secretion.

Role of exercise: Exercise induced asthma occurs in genetically susceptible individuals with hyper-reactive airways because of the loss of water and heat from the respiratory tract following exercise. Water loss induces mucosal hyperosmolarity which stimulates mediator release from mast cells.

Role of weather change: Sudden weather change may result in (i) loss of heat and water from lower airways and (ii) sudden release of airborne allergens in atmosphere thus resulting in exacerbation of asthma.

Emotional factors: Emotional stress operated through vagus, initiating bronchial smooth muscles to contract.

Role of food: Allergy to food proteins or additives in food plays an insignificant role in the pathogenesis of asthma. These should be incriminated only on a very strong association with the illness.

Endocrine factors: Some endocrinal changes may increase symptoms of asthma. Children may get increase in symptoms during puberty.

CLINICAL FEATURES

The clinical features of asthma are variable. Symptoms vary from simple recurrent cough to severe wheezing. Children may present with recurrent cough with or without wheezing. The symptoms occur with change in season, aggravated by exercise and more in nights. Acute asthma may usually begin with a cold, or bouts of spasmodic coughing more so at night. In early phase of the attack cough is non-productive. The patient becomes dyspneic, with prolonged expiration and wheezing. Accessory muscles of respiration are excessively used. The child sweats profusely, may develop cyanosis and becomes apprehensive and restless and may appear fatigued.

In severe episodes the child may show air hunger. The chest is hyper-resonant because of excessive air trapping. As the obstruction becomes severe, the airflow decreases markedly. As a result the breath sounds become feeble. Wheezing which was earlier audible may disappear. This is an ominous sign. Absence of wheezing in the presence of cyanosis and respiratory distress should not be considered as an evidence of clinical improvement. As the child starts improving clinically, the airflow increases and wheezing may reappear. With the remission of the attack wheeze again disappears.

Severe hypoxemia in asthma results in cyanosis and cardiac arrhythmias. Pulsus paradoxus indicates severe illness. Mucus plugs occluding the bronchial tubes cause collapse of small segments of the lung.

Persistence of hyperinflation of the chest even after subsidence of asthmatic attack signifies that the apparent relief from bronchospasm will be short lived. In severe persistent cases the chest becomes barrel shaped. Clubbing of fingers, however, is unusual in uncomplicated cases.

DIAGNOSIS

A prolonged whistling sound heard at the mouth during expiration is called a wheeze. Recurrent attacks of wheezing indicate bronchial asthma. Although intermittent attacks of coughing may be due to recurrent viral infections, diagnosis of bronchial asthma must be considered. Cough, which is associated with asthma generally, worsens after exercise. Sputum is generally clear and mucoid but expectoration of yellowish sputum does not exclude the diagnosis of asthma. This may be attributed to large number of eosinophils in the sputum. Chronic spasmodic cough may suggest occult asthma.

Investigations

Pulmonary function test (PFT): The diagnosis of asthma is clinical in most cases, hence PFTs may not play significant role. However PFTs play an important role in diagnosis of doubtful cases and in monitoring of response to treatment. The important parameters in spirometry include PEFR, FEV1, FVC and FEV25–75. In asthma FEV_1/FVC is less than 0.8 (normal 0.8-1) FEV1 is commonly used parameter for documentation of severity of asthma. FEV25–75 is effort independent and is probably more sensitive indicator of airway obstruction. PEFR can be measured easily with peak expiratory flow meter, while for other parameters spirometer is required. PEER may be used as diagnostic tool in doubtful cases as well as monitoring of treatment. Abnormality in PEFR suggestive of asthma include: a diurnal variation of more than 20%,

≤ 80% of predicted and improvement of ≥ 20% after bronchodilator therapy.

Absolute eosinophil counts: Significance of eosinophilia for distinguishing between allergic, vasomotor or infectious nature of the chronic respiratory obstructive disease is limited. When eosinophilia is present, bronchial obstruction generally responds well to antispasmodic therapy and the condition is often reversible. The eosinophil count may be low in cases associated with infection. Steroid medication in asthma causes eosinopenia.

Chest X-ray film: The X-ray film of the chest shows bilateral and symmetric air trapping in case of asthma. Patches of atelectasis of varying sizes due to mucus plugs are not unusual. Main pulmonary artery is prominent due to pulmonary hypertension. Bronchial cuffing may occur due to the presence of edema fluid in perivascular and peribronchial interstitial space. Extensive areas of collapse or consolidation should suggest an alternative diagnosis. Chest X-ray film may be normal.

Allergy test: Skin test and RAST (radio-allergo-sorbent allergen specific IgE) have limited usefulness. Few children need skin tests to identify sensitivity to different antigens since the role of desensitization in therapy is not fully established.

Differential Diagnosis

Bronchiolitis: Bronchiolitis always occurs within the first 2 years, usually within the first 6 months of life. It is commoner in winter or spring months. Generally there is a single attack. Repeated attacks indicate asthma. Hyperinflation of chest with scattered areas of infiltration may be seen in chest X-ray. On the other hand, asthma may start at any age; more than 3 episodes are usual and wheezing is prominent. Infants diagnosed as bronchiolitis who present with family history of allergy have eczema or whose IgE levels are elevated, are most likely candidates for developing asthma.

Congenital malformations causing obstruction viz., vascular rings such as aberrant right subclavian artery or double aortic arch, bronchogenic cysts and tacheomalacia should be excluded in differential diagnosis.

Aspiration of foreign body: Wheeze, if present is generally localized. The history of foreign body aspiration may be forgotten. An area with diminished air entry, with or without hyperresonance on percussion especially in children, may be due to obstructive emphysema because of a check-valve type of obstruction due to the foreign body. Most children develop frequent infections in the lung around the foreign body.

Hypersensitivity pneumonitis: A puzzling acute or chronic lung disease may be observed following inhalation of organic dust such as molds, wood or cotton dust, bird droppings, fur dust, grain, or following exposure to certain chemicals or drugs such as epoxy resins, PAS, sulfonamide and nitrofuran, etc. In the acute form of illness, these children suffer from fever, chills, dyspnea, malaise, aches and pain, loud inspiratory rales (crackles) at bases of lung and weight loss. X-ray of the chest shows interstitial pneumonia. Bronchial markings are prominent. The levels of IgE antibodies to the specific antigen are increased. The skin test shows arthus phenomenon with local hemorrhage, edema and local pain within 8 hours of the test. Diagnosis is established by lung biopsy.

Cystic fibrosis: Children with cystic fibrosis may present with recurrent wheezing but over a period of time they develop clubbing, there may be history of passing large foul smelling stools suggesting malabsorption. X-ray film may show evidence of hyperinflation, peribronchial cuffing and pneumonia. Diagnosis can be established by doing sweat chloride estimation.

MANAGEMENT

Goals of therapy are (i) Maintenance of near normal pulmonary function (ii) Maintenance of near normal physical activity (iii) Prevention of night-time cough or wheezing with minimal chronic symptoms (iv) Prevention of exacerbation of asthma and (v) Avoiding adverse effects of medication.

Effective long-term management of asthma involves three major areas:

1. Identification and elimination of exacerbating factors.
2. Pharmacological therapy.
3. Education of patient and parents about the nature of disease and the steps required to avoid acute exacerbation.

Identification and Elimination of Exacerbating Factors

Common factors associated with development and precipitation of asthma include passive smoking, associated allergic disorders, inadequate ventilation at home leading to dampness, cold air, cold food, smoke, dust and pets in the family. Acute respiratory infection due to viruses is the most common cause of exacerbation of asthma.

Following measures may help in decreasing the triggers:

1. The bedroom of the child should be kept clean and as free from dust as possible. Wet mopping of the floor should be done because dry dusting increases exposure of the child to house dust.
2. Heavy tapestry attracts dust and therefore light plain cloth sheets should be used as curtains in the child's room.
3. Carpets, stuffed furniture, loose clothing, wall hangings, calendars and books attract lot of dust and should be regularly cleaned at periodic intervals.
4. The bed of the child should be made of light material and should be aired regularly.

5. Keeping of animal pets should be discouraged, as the child may be sensitive to their fur.
6. Generally, it is not necessary to restrict the diet of the child because bronchial asthma due to food allergy is unusual.
7. Adolescent patients should be advised to refrain from smoking.
8. Exposure to strong or pungent odors such as wet paint, dissinfectants and smoke should be minimized.
9. The child should not go to attics or basements, especially if these were unoccupied and kept closed for some days. These should be properly cleaned and aired for some time, before the asthmatic patient goes there.

Pharmacotherapy

The pharmacological therapy of bronchial asthma involves use of drugs that relax smooth muscle and dilate the airways and drugs that decrease inflammation and thereby prevent exacerbations. The medications used for long-term treatment of asthma include bronchodilators, steroids, mast cell stabilizers, leukotriene modifiers and theophylline. They have been described in a tabular form in Table 13.5.

Bronchodilators

This group of drugs provides symptomatic relief. They may be short acting and long acting. The commonly used short acting bronchodilators are adrenaline, terbutaline and salbutamol. All of these have quick onset of action. Adrenaline stimulates α and both β receptors; thus causes cardiac side effects. Terbutaline and salbutamol are specific β-2 agonist and hence, have least cardiac side effects. Adrenaline is given subcutaneously. The other two agents can be administered by oral/inhalation or parenteral route. Inhalation route is preferred because of quick onset of action and least side effects.

Long acting beta agonists include salmeterol and formoterol. Both these drugs are specific beta 2 agonist and have a longer duration of action of 12–24 hours. Its efficacy has been demonstrated in children above four years of age.

Corticosteroids

Asthma is a chronic inflammatory disease of airways. Corticosteroids being potent anti-inflammatory agents, are the corner stone of long-term treatment of asthma. Systemic glucocorticoids used early in the treatment of acute exacerbation can lessen the need for visits to emergency department and hospitalization. The advantage of inhaled administration of corticosteroids is application of the potent medication to the sites where it is specifically needed. This potentially reduces the risk for systemic adverse effect of these medications.

The commonly used inhaled steroids include beclomethasone, budesonide and fluticasone. Beclomethasone (BDP) or budesonide (BDS) has almost the same effect. The newer inhalation steroid, fluticasone is considered to be superior to BDP/BDS.

The main concern with the use of inhalation steroids is the effect on growth. An approximately 20 percent reduction in the growth velocity during the first year of treatment with inhaled steroids is reported. Subsequently the growth velocity recovers and children ultimately attain predicted adult height.

Mast Cell Stabilizers

In this group the drugs included are cromolyn sodium, nedocromil sodium and ketotifen.

Cromolyn sodium belongs to chromone group of chemicals. It reduces bronchial reactivity and symptoms induced by irritants, antigens and exercise. Indications for use of cromolyn includes mild to moderate persistent asthma and exercise induced asthma. It should be given at least for 6–8 weeks before declaring it ineffective. Now it is not available in the market.

Nedocromil is another nonsteroidal drug used for control of mild to moderate asthma. Ketotifen is another mast cell stabilizer. It is administered orally. Significant clinical improvement may be evident after 14 weeks of therapy.

Leukotriene Modifiers

Leukotriene inhibitors are new pharmacological agents for the treatment of mild to moderate persistent asthma and exercise-induced asthma. Leukotriene inhibitors act either by decreasing the synthesis of leukotrienes (Zileuton) or by antagonizing the receptors (Montelukast and Zafirlukast).

Montelukast and zafirlukast have received approval for use in pediatric asthma patients. Montelukast can be used in children above one year of age while zafirlukast above 6 years of age.

Theophylline

Theophylline has concentration-dependent bronchodilator effects. The bronchodilator effect is exerted by inhibition of phosphodiesterase. In addition, theophylline has anti-inflammatory and immunomodulatory effects at therapeutic serum concentration that appears to be distinct from its bronchodilator properties. Most recent guidelines recommend theophylline as an alternative second inferior drug for mild persistent asthma. It can also be used as adjunctive therapy (largely for control of nocturnal symptoms) in moderate or severe persistent asthma.

Immunotherapy

This consists of giving gradually increasing quantities of an allergen extract to a clinically sensitive subject, so as to ameliorate the symptoms associated with subsequent exposure to causative allergen. This is considered only occasionally in highly selected children who are sensitive to a specific allergen such as grass pollen, mites, etc. It is done only under specialist supervision and must, usually be given for 3 years.

13

Table 13.5: Medications for long-term treatment of asthma

Medication, route of administration	*Side effects*	*Dose*	*Comments*
Bronchodilators			
Salbutamol 100 μg/puff MDI Respirator solution 5 mg/ml Respules 2.5 mg/3 ml Dry powder capsules 200 μg/cap (*Rotacap*) ***Terbutaline*** 250 μg /puff *MDI*	Tachycardia, tremors, headache, hypokalemia hyperglycemia (minimal when used by inhalation)	1–2 puff 4–6 hourly 0.15–0.2 mg/kg/dose nebulization 1–2 puff 4–6 hourly	Drug of choice for acute attack. Prior to exercise to prevent exercise induced bronchospasm
Salmeterol 25 μg/puff *MDI* Dry powder capsules 50 μg/cap (Rotacap)	Tachycardia, tremors, headache, hypokalemia, hyperglycemia (minimal with inhalation route)	1–2 puffs 12–24 hourly 1 dry powder cap inhalation 12–24 hourly	Long-term prevention of symptoms. Particularly useful for nocturnal symptoms exercise induced bronchospasm
Formoterol 12μg/puff *MDI* Dry powder capsules 12 μg/cap (Rotacap)		1–2 puffs 12–24 hourly 1–2 dry powder cap inhalation 12–24 hourly	Not for treatment of acute symptoms. Used with anti-inflammatory therapy not as substitute.
Theophylline 100, 150, 200, 300 mg tablets Oral	Toxicity at >20 μg/ml, nausea, headache, tachycardia, drowsiness, seizures	5–15 mg/kg/day 2 divided dose	Drug interactions (anti-tubercular, anticonvulsants, ciprofloxacin). May be used in step II when inhalation route not possible
Mast cell stabilizers			
Sodium cromoglycate 5 mg/puff MDI	Medicinal taste Reflex coughing	5 mg/puff	Continuous prophylaxis for control of symptoms. May take 4–6 weeks for clinically evident effect.
Nedocromil sodium inhalation	Bitter taste, cough	1–2 puffs 3–4 times a day	
Ketotifen 1 mg tab and 1 mg/5 ml	May cause sedation and weight gain	1 mg twice a day	
Corticosteroids			
Inhaled corticosteroids ***Beclomethasone*** 50,100,200,250 μg/puff	Cough, dysphonia, oral thrush (gargling, spacer use minimizes effects)	50–800 μg/day in 2–3 divided doses 50–800 μg/day in 2 doses	Not recommended as relievers. Budesonide and fluticasone almost completely inactivated during first pass metabolism and thus have minimal systemic side effects
Budesonide 50, 100, 200, μg/puff MDI Respules–0.5 and 1 mg/ml Rotacaps 100/200/400 μg/cap	At dose of 400–800 μg/day negligible side effects	25–400 μg/ day in 2 divided doses	
Fluticasone 25,50,125 μg/puff MDI Dry powder capsules: 50, 100, 250 μg/cap Respules: 0.5 and 1 mg per ml	May cause systemic side effects		High dose for long duration Use minimum required dose preferably alternate day
Montelukast 4, 5, 10 mg tabs	Generally well tolerated Churg-Strauss syndrome reported	2–5 years: 4 mg per day 5–12 years 5 mg per day >12 years 10 mg per day	Exercise induced asthma Alternative to long acting β-agonist

PHARMACOLOGICAL MANAGEMENT

Assessment of Severity

Successful management of asthma requires grading the severity of the disease according to the frequency and severity of symptoms and functional impairment. This is assessed by asking the frequency of symptoms including disturbance of sleep, effect on day-to-day activity of child and need for medication, hospital visit and hospitalization. Result of pulmonary function tests (PFTs) by spirometer provides objective evidence of severity. PEFR measurement is an easy alternative to spirometry in day-to-day practice. PEFR is easier to perform and can be performed in children older than 5–6 years of age.

Children with asthma can be classified into 4 groups on the basis of information obtained from parents and

PEFR measurement, i.e. intermittent, mild persistent, moderate persistent and severe persistent asthma. This is presented in a tabular form in Table 13.6.

Table 13.6: Classification of asthma according to severity

	Symptoms	*Night time symptoms*	*PEFR*
Step 4 Severe persistent	Continuous Limited physical activity	Frequent	≤60% predicted variability >30%
Step 3 Moderate persistent	Daily use β_2 agonist attack affect activity	> 1 times a week	>60% <80% predicted; variability >30%
Step 2 Mild persistent	> 1 time a week but < 1 time a day	>2 times a month	≥80% predicted; variability 20–30%
Step 1 Intermittent	<1 time a week Asymptomatic and normal PEFR between attack	≤2 times a month	≥ 80% predicted; variability <20%

Selection of Medication

After the assessment of severity, appropriate anti asthma drugs are selected. The stepwise treatment of asthma according to the severity is given in tabular form in table 13.7.

Table 13.7: Step wise treatment of asthma

	Long term prevention
Step 4 Severe Persistent	Inhaled short acting β-agonist as required + Inhaled corticosteroids Budesonide/ Beclomethasone, 400 µg twice daily may increase up to 1000 µg/day + Long acting bronchodilator: long acting inhaled β_2 agonist and/ or sustained release theophylline +corticosteroids low dose alternate day (if no relief with above treatment)
Step 3 Moderate persistent	**Inhaled short acting β-agonist as required +** Inhaled corticosteroids Budesonide/ beclomethasone, 200–400 µg divided twice daily. If needed long acting bronchodilator: long acting inhaled β_2 agonist salmeterol 50 µg once/twice daily and/or sustained release theophylline
Step 2 Mild persistent	**Inhaled short acting β-agonist as required +** Inhaled corticosteroids Budesonide/beclomethasone, 100–200 µg or cromolyn or sustained release theophylline or leukotriene modifiers
Step 1 Intermittent	Inhaled short acting β-agonist as required for symptoms relief. If they are needed more than 3 times a week move to step 2.

Mild episodic asthma should be treated with salbutamol or terbutaline as and when required. If inhalation cannot be used due to any reason oral route can be used.

Mild persistent asthma needs daily treatment with maintenance medication. They can be cromolyn sodium 5–10 mg by inhalation route, 6–8 hourly or inhalation steroids (BPD, BDS) in the dose of 200 µg/day in two divided doses or slow release theophylline 5–15 mg/kg/day in two divided doses. The selection of either preparation is based on feasibility for inhalation, problems of compliance and cost of medications. The drug of choice in mild persistent asthma is a low dose inhaled steroid. If inhalation is not feasible due to any reason (cost of medication/ not able to take inhalation) a trial of leucotriene modifiers or oral theophylline can be given.

Moderate persistent asthma needs to be treated with inhalation steroid 200–400 µg/day in 2 divided doses and long acting β-agonist (formoterol/salmeterol). Montelukast can be used at this step as add on treatment for better control of asthma symptoms.

Severe persistent asthma needs inhalation steroids in the dose of 400–800 µg/day in 2–3 divided doses. For relief of symptoms long acting β-agonist and slow release theophylline needs to be given regularly. Montelukast can be used at this step as add on treatment for better control of asthma symptoms. If there is persistence of symptoms low dose prednisolone may have to be used, preferably alternate day.

Selection of Appropriate Inhalation Device

Drugs used as maintenance treatment of asthma can be administered by inhalation or oral route. Drugs used by the inhalation route are more effective, i.e. have a rapid onset of action, and have fewer side effects. Most important in the delivery of effective therapy to asthmatic children is the optimal use of appropriate inhalation devices. Commonly available inhalation devices are as follows:

Metered Dose Inhaler

An MDI is a device, which delivers a fixed amount of medication in aerosol form each time it is activated (Fig. 13.4). It can be used for exacerbation and maintenance therapy. They are effective but require considerable co-ordination, i.e. press and-breath co-ordination. This may not be possible in young children. After actuation the drug comes out at a pressure and a significant amount of the drug gets deposited in the oropharynx. To overcome this problem of co-ordination it is used with spacer. MDIs continue to work past the labeled number of doses because of excess propellant. Therefore, a track of number of actuations should be kept to ensure that children receive adequate therapy when needed.

Metered Dose Inhaler With Spacer

Use of spacer inhalation device with a MDI should be encouraged as it results in a larger proportion of the

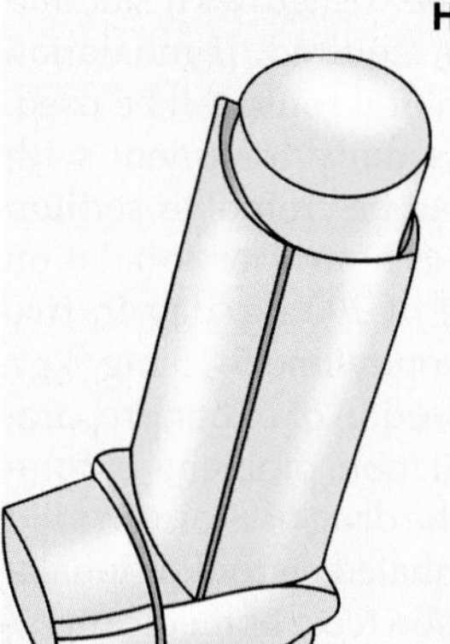

How to use metered dose inhaler

1. Remove cap and shake inhaler in vertical direction
2. Breathe out gently
3. Put mouthpiece in mouth and at start of inspiration which should be slow and deep, press canister down and continue to inhale deeply
4. Hold breath for 10 seconds or as long as possible then breathe out slowly
5. Wait for few seconds before repeating steps 2–4.

Fig. 13.4: Metered dose inhaler

medication being deposited in the lung, with less impaction in the oropharynx (Fig. 13.5). They also overcome the problems of poor technique and coordination of actuation and inspiration, which occur, with the use of MDIs alone. Furthermore, use of spacer allows MDI to be used for the young patient. MDI used with spacer has been found to be comparable to nebulizer in delivering salbutamol in acute exacerbation of asthma in children. Spacers have the limitation of being bulky, relatively costly and cannot be used in young infants and toddlers. A home-made spacer prepared from mineral water bottle has been shown to be equally effective in delivering salbutamol in acute exacerbation.

Metered Dose Inhaler with Spacer with Facemask

Attaching a facemask to the spacer facilitates their use in very young infants (Fig. 13.6).

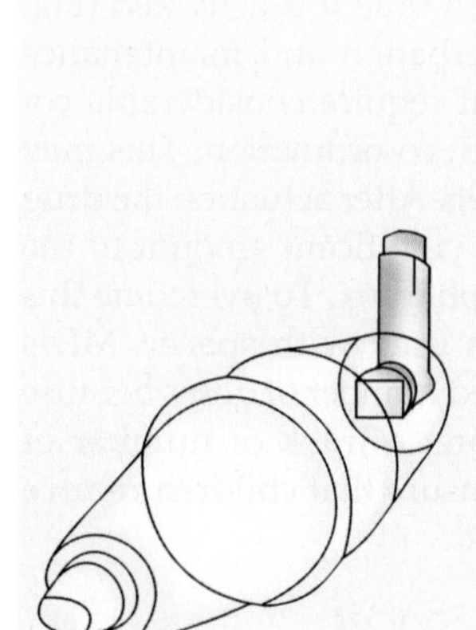

How to use metered dose inhaler with spacer device

1. Remove cap of MDI shake it and insert into spacer device
2. Place mouth piece of spacer in mouth
3. Start breathing in and out gently and observe movements of valve
4. Once breathing pattern is established press canister and continue to breathe 5–10 times (tidal breathing)
5. Remove the device from mouth and wait for 30 seconds before repeating steps 1–4

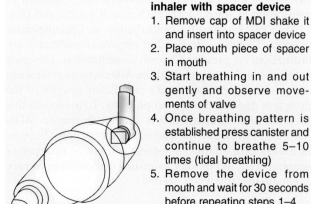

Fig. 13.5: Metered dose inhaler with spacer

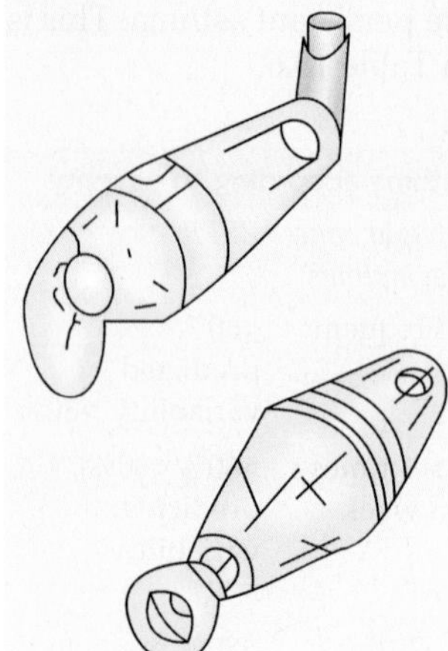

How to use MDI + spacer + baby mask?

1. Attach baby mask to the mouth end of spacer
2. Shake MDI and insert it in the MDI end of spacer device
3. Cover baby's mouth and nose with baby mask
4. Press canister and encourage the child to take tidal breathing with mouth open (if possible) 5-10 times
5. Remove baby mask and wait for 30–60 seconds before repeating steps 1–4

Fig. 13.6: Metered dose inhaler with spacer and baby mask

Dry Powder Inhaler (DPI)

These are breath-activated devices like Rotahaler (Fig. 13.7), Diskhaler, Spinhaler, Turbohaler and Acuhaler. They can be used in children above 4–5 years of age. They have the advantage of being portable and eliminate the need to co-ordinate actuation with breathing. In addition they are environmental friendly, as they do not contain CFC. Moreover, the effect of powder inhalers is dependent upon a certain inspiratory flow rate and therefore there is a risk of reduced effect during episodes of acute wheeze or in children with low pulmonary function.

Nebulizers

Nebulizers with air compressors are bulky and inefficient aerosol delivery systems (Fig. 13.8). With the advent of efficient spacer systems, the need for nebulizers has greatly diminished. There is a place for the use of nebulized

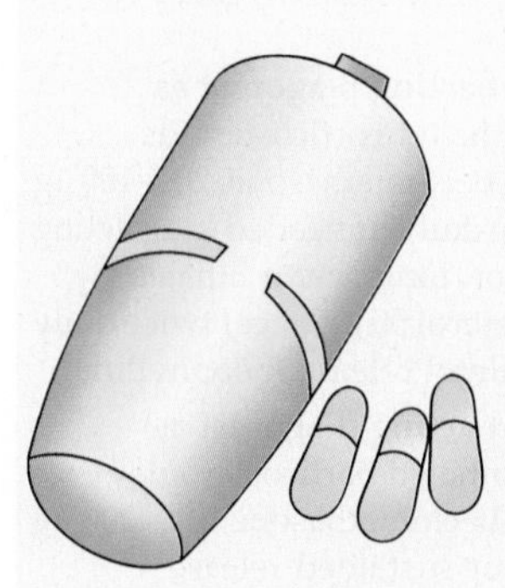

How to use rotahaler?

1. Hold rotahaler vertically and insert capsule (clear end first) into square hole, make sure that top of the capsule is level with top of hole
2. Hold rotahaler horizontally, twist barrel in clockwise and anticlockwise direction, this will split the capsule in to two
3. Breathe out gently and put mouth end of rotahaler in mouth and take deep inpiration
4. Remove rotahaler from mouth and hold breath for 10 seconds

Fig. 13.7: Rotahaler

How to use nebulizer?

1. Connect nebulizer to mains
2. Connect output of compressor to nebulizer chamber by the tubings provided with nebulizer
3. Put measured amount of drug in the nebulizer chamber and add normal saline to make it 2.5–3 ml

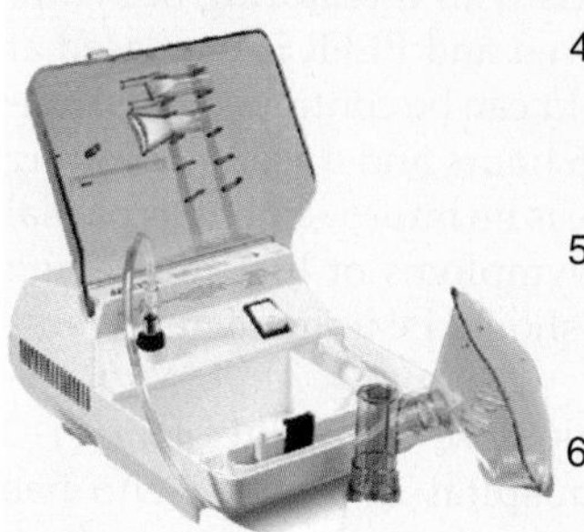

4. Switch on the compressor and look for aerosol coming out from other end of nebulizer
5. Attach face mask to this end of nebulizer chamber and fit it to cover nose and mouth of the child
6. Encourage child to take tidal breathing with open mouth

Fig. 13.8: Nebulizer

β-agonist in acute severe asthma in young irritable and hypoxic children who do not tolerate MDI used with spacer and facemask, because this allows the delivery of a large dose. The following measures can improve the amount of drug delivered to the lung by nebulizer: the total fill volume should be about 3–5 ml. Tapping the side of nebulizer chamber during operation induces the droplets on the sides to fall back into the reservoirs, minimizing the loss. The optimal flow rate is 6–12 l/min; at this flow, 30–50% of aerosol is in the respirable range of 1–5 mm. Creating a hole in the gas supply tube so that nebulization will occur only during inhalation, when the hole is closed, also decreases the aerosol loss. Slow, deep inhalations and breath holding can improve delivery.

It is very important to select an appropriate device by which the maintenance medication has to be administered. Inhalation method should be chosen on individual basis but the rough guideline is as follows:

- *Children below 4 years of age:* MDI with spacer with facemask can be used successfully
- *For children above 4 years of age:* MDI with spacer is preferred.
- *For children above 12 years of age:* MDI may be used directly. However use of spacer improves drug deposition in airways.

Monitoring and Modification of Treatment (Step-up, Step-down)

After starting appropriate treatment patients should be seen every 4–12 weeks. On each visit a detailed history regarding frequency of symptoms, sleep disturbance, physical activity, school absenteeism, visit to a doctor, need for bronchodilators (rescue drug), and PEFR is recorded. The patient or parents should be encouraged to maintain a symptom diary. Inhalation technique and compliance should be checked each time.

On each visit physician should examine the child, look for adverse effects of drugs and record height and weight. PEFR/PFTs should be measured in older children. The status of disease is assessed and recorded.

Control of asthma may be classified as controlled, partially controlled or uncontrolled. (Table 13.8). The causes of uncontrolled asthma could be: poor compliance, wrong technique of inhalation, continued use of empty canister, inappropriate doses, infection (otitis media, sinusitis, pneumonitis) continued exposure to allergens or under assessment of illness. Many asthmatic children have allergic rhinitis and its treatment has a beneficial effect on asthma. Asthmatic children also have a higher incidence of sinusitis, which may trigger asthma. Bronchial hyper responsiveness and asthma symptoms improve with therapy for these upper respiratory diseases.

If no cause is found a step up, i.e. increase in dose and frequency of medication is required. Step down if control is sustained for at least 3 months and follow a gradual stepwise reduction in treatment.

Exercise-induced Bronchoconstriction

Some children in addition to varying severity of asthma may develop bronchoconstriction after exercise. To avoid unpleasant experience they avoid participation in outdoor games. These children may be treated with appropriate stepwise management, may require additional medications like short and long acting beta agonists or

Table 13.8: Assessment of control of asthma

Feature	*Controlled (All of the following)*	*Partly controlled (Any feature present in any week)*	*Uncontrolled*
Daytime symptoms	None (twice or less/week)	More than twice/week	Three or more features of partly controlled asthma present in any week
Limitations of activities	None	Any	
Nocturnal symptoms/ awakening	None	Any	
Need for reliever/ rescue treatment	None (twice or less/week)	More than twice/week	
Lung function (PEF or FEV1)	Normal	<80% predicted or personal best (if known)	
Exacerbations	None	One or more/year	One in any week

13

leucotriene modifiers. Short acting beta agonists should be taken before going for exercise, as their duration of action is short. Long acting beta agonists can be taken in the morning and they continue to prevent exercise-induced bronchoconstriction throughout day time, hence preferable in children who find it difficult to take short acting beta agonists before exercise in school. Leucotriene modifiers are alternative to long acting beta agonists.

Seasonal Asthma

13

A small proportion of children get symptoms of asthma for a shorter period in a particular season. They remain asymptomatic for the rest of the year. These children can be started on maintenance treatment 2 weeks in advance. Medications are selected according to severity of asthma. These children should be examined again after discontinuing the medications after the season is over.

EDUCATION OF PARENTS

Education of parents is an important aspect of asthma treatment. A description of the pathogenesis of asthma in plain language should be made. Also, it needs to be emphasized that there is a wide spectrum of severity of asthma and that most children can lead active and normal lives. Parents also need to be involved in the steps required to minimize exposure to potential environmental triggers. Avoidance of all kinds of smoke at home including tobacco smoke, wood burning and kerosene stove. Parents should be advised regarding minimal use of carpets, curtains and other dust attracting articles.

Parents should also be asked to maintain a record of daily symptoms such as cough, coryza, wheeze and breathlessness. A record of sleep disturbances, absence from school due to illness and medication required to keep the child symptom free is advised. These records help in stepping up or down the pharmacotherapy of the asthmatic child.

Regarding pharmacological therapy it is important that the parents understand how the medicines work and how to take the medicines including the use of spacer and also the potential harmful effects of drugs. Parents concerned about the use of steroids needs to be reassured that in the conventional inhalation dosage, the risk of serious asthma outweighs the side effects of medication. Peak flow monitoring done properly by informed parents can help by:

1. Detecting early deterioration in lung function.
2. Managing asthma in patients who have difficulty in sensing the changes in severity of airway obstruction.
3. Managing patients whose asthma severity changes very rapidly.

Home Treatment of Acute Exacerbation

An important part of health education is instructing the parent/patient on how to recognize and manage acute exacerbation of asthma at home. A written action plan should be given to them. Acute exacerbation can be identified by increase in cough, wheeze and breathlessness. PEFR, if measured, may be decreased by 15% from the baseline. For acute exacerbation parents should administer short acting β_2 agonists by MDI ± spacer ± facemask, one puff at a time, repeated every 30–60 seconds up to a maximum of 10 puffs with monitoring of symptoms. If symptoms are relieved and PEFR is increased at the end of inhalation the child can be continued on salbutamol/terbutaline every 4–6 hours and a visit to treating physician is planned. If there is no improvement or partial improvement or there are symptoms of life threatening attack at any time, the child should be immediately transferred to a hospital.

Administration of a single dose of prednisolone (1–2 mg/kg) before going to hospital in a child who has symptoms of life threatening asthma or does not show satisfactory improvement after inhalation therapy at home may be useful.

MANAGEMENT OF ACUTE EXACERBATION OF ASTHMA

Increase in the symptoms in form of cough, wheeze and/or breathlessness is termed as exacerbation of asthma. The severity of exacerbation is variable and can be classified as mild, moderate, severe or life threatening on the basis of physical examination, measurement of PEFR/FEV_1 and oxygen saturation (Table 13.9).

Treatment of Life-Threatening Asthma

Presence of any of the following indicates a life-threatening asthma.

Cyanosis, silent chest, poor respiratory efforts, exhaustion/fatigue, altered sensorium, PEFR<30% of predicted and oxygen saturation of <90%.

Table 13.9: Grading of severity of acute asthma

Feature	*Mild*	*Moderate*	*Severe*
Color	Normal	Normal	Pale
Sensorium	Normal	Anxious	Agitated
Respiratory rate	Increased	Increased	Increased
Dyspnea	Absent can speak sentences	Moderate can speak in phrases	Severe difficulty in speech
Accessory muscles	Nil or minimal	Chest indrawing; alae nasii flare	Chest indrawing
Pulsus paradoxus	<10 mm	10–20 mm	>20 mm
Rhonchi	Expiratory	Expiratory inspiratory	Expiratory, inspiratory or absent
PEFR	>80%	60–80%	<60%
SaO_2	>95%	90–95%	<90%

Such patients should be immediately be started on oxygen inhalation injection of terbutalin or adrenaline is given subcutaneously, inhalation of salbutamol or terbutalin and ipratropium is started, an injection of hydrocortisone 10 mg/kg is given and an arrangement is made to transfer the patient to ICU preferably with an accompanying physician. In ICU if patient shows improvement the salbutamol/ terbutalin inhalation is continued every 20–30 minutes, 5 mg/kg of hydrocotisone is continued every 6–8 hourly till patient start accepting orally. If patient does not improve or deteriorates a loading dose of theophylline is infused. Another drug that can be used in such a situation is magnesium sulphate in doses of 50 mg/kg as intravenous infusion over 30 minutes. If there is no improvement with this management, patient is prepared for mechanical ventilation. Patient is also screened for causes of poor response such as acidosis, pneumothorax, electrolyte imbalance and infection and treated accordingly.

Treatment of Mild Acute Asthma

Patients with mild exacerbation have cough, rapid respiration and some wheezing but no chest indrawing and is able to speak and drink well. PEFR if can be measured is > 80% of predicted and oxygen saturation is more than 95% in room air.

Such patients should be given beta 2 agonists by nebuliser or MDI + Spacer with or without face mask. If later is used than one puff of medicine is repeated every minute up to 10 puffs. In case of significant improvement the patient can be sent home on inhalation or oral beta agonists every 6–8 hours along with general instructions and called back after 1–2 weeks for reassessment and long-term treatment. In case of no response or poor response the patient should be treated as moderate exacerbation.

Treatment of Acute, Moderate and Severe Asthma

These patients have rapid respiration, chest indrawing, wheezing, pulsus paradoxus, difficulty in speech and feeding, PEFR and oxygen saturation is decreased. The sensorium is normal.

Such patients should be treated with inhalation beta agonist as described in treatment of mild asthma. It is repeated every 20 minutes, oxygen inhalation is started and oral dose of prednisolone 1–2 mg/kg is given. At end of one hour the patient is assessed for improvement. In case of improvement the child is continued on inhalation of beta 2 agonists every 30 minutes and the interval is gradually increased to every 4–6 hourly. Oxygen inhalation is stopped if the patient is able to maintain oxygen saturation of >95%. Prednisolone is continued once daily for 5–7 days and then stopped without tapering. The patient can be discharged from hospital when the need for bronchodilators is every 4–6 hourly, able to feed and speak well and maintains oxygen saturation of >95% in room air. These patients should be educated about the disease, need for regular follow-up and avoidance of triggers. They should be assessed for long term treatment. In case of no improvement at end of one hour the inhalation of salbutamol is continued and ipratropium 250 microgram is also added every 20 minutes. An injection of hydrocortisone 10 mg/ kg is given and reassessed at end of two hours. If there is good response the patient is treated like the early responders. In case of no response; injectable theophylline bolus followed by continuous infusion is started. Such patients may respond well to magnesium infusion in doses of 50 mg/kg dissolved in dextrose over 30 minutes. If no improvement these patients should be prepared for possible mechanical ventilation.

Monitoring Treatment

Repeat PEF/PFTs measurement 15–30 minutes after starting treatment. Chart PEFR before and after the child is given nebulized beta-agonist and at least 4 times daily throughout the hospital stay. Pulse oximetry to maintain SaO_2 above 92%.

Transfer to Intensive Care Unit

The patient should be accompanied by a doctor prepared to intubate if FEV_1 is deteriorating, hypoxia or hypercapnia are worsening or persistent and in cases with exhaustion, feeble respiration, confusion, drowsiness, coma or respiratory arrest.

When to Discharge from the Hospital

Patient should have been on discharge medication for 24 hours and had inhaler technique checked and recorded. Treatment should include soluble steroids tablets and inhaled steroids in addition to the broncholdilator. The patient should be given a self management plan or instructions should be given to the parents.

Suggested reading

1. Kabra SK, Lodha R, P Ramesh: Long term management of asthma. Indian J Pediatr 2006;71: S43–S50.
2. Singhal T, Singh H, Gupta P, Lodha R, Pandey RM, Kabra SK: Home made v/s commercial spacer in children with asthma. Indian J Pediatr 2001;68: 37–40.
3. Lodha R, Puranik M, Kattal N, Kabra SK. Social and economic impact of childhood asthma. Indian Pediatr 2003;40:874–9
4. IAP Respiratory chapter. Consensus statement on diagnosis and management of asthma in children. An IAP chapter publication, 2003.
4. British Thoracic Society; Scottish Intercollegiate Guidelines Network. British guideline on the management of asthma. Thorax. 2003; 58 Suppl 1: i1–94.
5. Global Strategy for Asthma Management and Prevention 2007: Available on www.ginasthma.org.

FOREIGN BODY ASPIRATION

Young children between 1 and 4 years of age are especially prone to aspirate small objects in their air passages. Unless recognized and treated, these children have significant respiratory morbidity, such as recurrent wheezing, cough and pneumonia. Immediate response to foreign body

13

aspiration is a choke, gag, cough or localized wheeze. After the initial episode, symptoms may improve for some time and the whole episode may be forgotten. Subsequently, the course of illness depends on the nature of foreign body, its size, extent and the site of obstruction. Foreign bodies of organic or vegetable source swell up and cause more symptoms. A partial obstruction may cause ball valve type effect leading to localized hyperinflation. The overlying chest wall may show hyperresonance, diminished vocal resonance and poor air entry. In small children, it may be difficult to elicit hyperresonance. Thus a localized area of poor air entry in a child with chronic respiratory illness should arouse suspicion of a foreign body. Complete obstruction and surrounding inflammation cause distal atelectasis and suppuration of the surrounding parenchyma of the lungs. The elastic recoil of the bronchi is lost and the bronchi show segmental dilatation with eventual development of bronchiectasis. In children incidence of right and left bronchial location of foreign body is nearly equal. These children are treated by removal of foreign body through a rigid bronchoscope. Appropriate antibiotics are given for secondary infection. Bronchoscopy should be undertaken if the clinical and radiological picture suggests the diagnosis even when the history of foreign body aspiration is not forthcoming.

Suggested reading

1. Yadav SP, Singh J, Aggarwal N, Goel A. Airway foreign bodies in children: experience of 132 cases. Singapore Med J 2007 48: 850-3.
2. Pinzoni F, Boniotti C, Molinaro SM, Baraldi A, Berlucchi M. Inhaled foreign bodies in pediatric patients: Review of personal experience. Int J Pediatr Otorhinolaryngol. 2007;71:1897–1903.

LUNG ABSCESS

Lung abscess in children is most frequently a complication of bacterial pneumonia especially those due to S. aureus and pneumoniae. It may also develop in sequestration of lung tissue or in association with foreign bodies, bronchial cysts or stenosis. Staphylococcal lungs abscess are often multiple, while those complicating aspiration are solitary. The abscess may rupture into the pleural space leading to pyopneumothorax. The main pathological changes are of necrosis and liquefaction with inflammation in the surrounding lung tissue.

Clinical Features

The patient has fever, anorexia, lethargy, pallor, cough with foul smelling expectoration. Physical signs may be minimal. Amphoric breath sounds, coarse crepitations and whispering pectoriloquy are characteristic but often not elicitable. The diagnosis is confirmed by plain X-ray film and CT scan of chest.

Treatment

Appropriate antibiotics to which the organisms isolated from the sputum or bronchoscopic aspirate are sensitive, are administered for 4 to 6 weeks. Physiotherapy is carried out for effective drainage of the pus. Surgical resection of the involved area of lung is indicated if medical therapy is not effective.

BRONCHIECTASIS

Bronchiectasis is a chronic suppurative disease characterized by destruction of the bronchial and peribronchial tissues, dilatation of the bronchi and accumulation of infected material in the dependent bronchi.

Etiopathogenesis

Most cases follow recurrent episodes of respiratory infections such as bronchitis, bronchiolitis, post measles or post pertussis pulmonary infections, cystic fibrosis and pneumonitis in infancy and early childhood. Infections damage the bronchial wall and cause segmental areas of collapse, which exert a negative pressure on the damaged bronchi, causing them to dilate. The bronchial dilation is widespread and patchy. The bronchi may show cylindrical, fusiform or saccular dilatation.

Aspiration of foreign body, food, or mucus plug in the bronchus may occlude the bronchial lumen and cause segmental areas of collapse. The bronchi are dilated due to negative pressure by the collapsed segment. If the occlusion is relieved before the stagnant secretions are infected and the bronchial wall is damaged, the bronchiectasis is reversible. The bronchial dilatations are generally segmental or lobar. Extrinsic compression by the tuberculous lymph nodes often causes collapse of right middle lobe.

Congenital disorders of bronchi such as bronchomalacia, communicating type of bronchial cyst or sequestrated lung may be the cause of bronchiectasis in some cases. Kartagener syndrome is characterized by bronchiectasis, situs inversus and sinusitis and is attributed to disorder to ciliary motility (immotile cilia syndrome). Cystic fibrosis is characterised by recurrent lower respiratory infections associated with malabsorption. Immunodeficiency syndromes may be responsible for recurrent pulmonary infections and bronchiectasis.

Clinical Manifestations

The onset is generally insidious. The respiratory infections tend to persist longer and recur frequently with waxing and waning. Often the illness can be traced back to an episode of measles or whooping cough. A history of inhalation of foreign body is usually not forthcoming as it is often forgotten.

The most prominent symptom is cough with copious mucopurulent expectoration. Cough is more marked in some postures because of irritation of the infected secretions draining into fresh areas of lung. Likewise the cough is more marked when the child wakes up in the morning due to a change of posture. Younger children may not expectorate out the sputum which they swallow.

In the course of illness, the sputum may become blood streaked or even frank hemoptysis may occur. In chronic cases clubbing of fingers is seen.

The general health is poor, with recurrent infections. The patient complains of loss of appetite, irritability and poor weight gain.

Investigations

X-ray film of the chest shows honeycombing of the involved area indicating multiple small abscess cavities. Bronchography which was considered as gold standard for diagnosis of bronchiectasis has been replaced with high resolution computerized scan (HRCT of chest). Bronchoscopy is undertaken where structural abnormalities of airway is considered. Sputum should be sent for culture and sensitivity. Tuberculin reaction is done to exclude tuberculosis. Pilocarpine iontophoresis is done for estimating sweat chloride in cases suspected to be suffering from cystic fibrosis.

Prevention

Most cases follow acute respiratory infections, which are inadequately treated. All pulmonary infections should be treated promptly and adequately till the chest is clear of all signs, long after the fever has subsided. Even in ordinary pulmonary infections, airway should be kept patent by encouraging postural drainage. Measles and whooping cough should be prevented by specific immunization. Prompt medical help should be sought if there is any suspicion of inhalation of a foreign body.

Management

During acute exacerbations, bacterial infections should be controlled and airway kept clear of secretions. This is facilitated by effective cough at regular intervals and postural drainage. Assistance by a specially trained pulmonary physiotherapist may be useful. Surgical resection of the involved area should be undertaken only in children who have marked symptoms despite adequate the medical treatment and in whom the disease is localized. Extrinsic compression of bronchi by mediastinal masses requires surgical intervention. In young children with generalized disease associated with recurrent pulmonary infections, ill advised surgery may make the patient worse. If the child cannot cooperate in post surgery postural coughing, segmental or lobar collapse may occur in the postoperative period and new bronchiectatic lesions may appear. Children with generalized disease may improve significantly clinically with medical treatment alone during adolescence.

CYSTIC FIBROSIS

Cystic fibrosis (CF) is the most common life limiting recessive genetic disorder in Caucasians with an incidence of approximately 1 in 2500 children born in the United Kingdom. It is less common in African Americans (1 in 15000) and in Asian Americans (1:31000). It also affects other ethnic groups such as black population with an incidence of 1 in 17,000 and the native American population with an approximate incidence of 1 in 80,000.

The incidence in migrant Indian populations in the UK has been estimated between 1 in 10000 to 12000. The precise incidence of CF among Indians is unknown.

Molecular Genetics

The basic defect in CF is a mutation in the gene for chloride conductance channel, i.e. cystic fibrosis transmembrane conductance regulator (CFTR). The failure of chloride conductance by epithelial cells leads to dehydration of secretions that are too viscid and difficult to clear. The defective gene is located at long arm of chromosome 7. Till now more than 1400 mutations in the gene have been recognized. Commonest mutation is Delta F 508 and constitute upto 70% in Caucasian population. The frequency of mutation in Indian children is 25–30%.

Clinical Manifestations

The clinical features depend on age of diagnosis, supportive care received and treatment. The common clinical presentation includes meconium ileus in neonatal period, recurrent bronchiolitis in infancy and early childhood, recurrent lower respiratory tract infections, chronic lung disease, bronchiectasis, steatorrhea and with increasing age pancreatitis, and azoospermia. Pancreatic insufficiency is present in > 85% of CF patients (Table 13.10).

Diagnosis

The diagnosis of CF should be suspected by the presence of a typical phenotype or family history and confirmed by the demonstration of a high sweat chloride (>60 mEq/L) on at least two occasions and/or by identifying two CF causing mutations. Nasal potential difference measurements can be used as an adjunct to sweat test but is not widely available.

Management

The treatment of cystic fibrosis in children includes respiratory management, nutritional care, anticipation and early diagnosis of liver disease, diabetes and other organ dysfunction.

Respiratory Management

The principle components of care includes airway clearance techniques, antibiotics and antiinflammatory agents

Nutritional Management

The main aim of nutritional management is to achieve normal growth and development of children. Nutritional management of CF include:

13

Table 13.10: Common clinical features of cystic fibrosis(%)

0–2 years	%
Meconium ileus	10–15
Obstructive jaundice	5–10
Bleeding diathesis	5–10
Heat prostration/hyponatremia	5–10
Failure to thrive	60–70
Steatorrhea	85
Rectal prolapse	20
Bronchitis/bronchiolitis	10
Staphylococcal pneumonia	40–50
2–12 years	
Malabsorption	85
Recurrent pneumonia	60
Nasal polyposis	6–36
Intussusception	1–5
> 13 years	
Chronic pulmonary disease	70
Clubbing	60
Abnormal glucose tolerance	20-30
Diabetes mellitus	7
Chronic intestinal obstruction	1–20
Focal biliary cirrhosis	
Portal hypertension	25
Gallstones	4–14
Azoospermia	98

i. Increasing caloric intake by encouraging parents to feed the child more frequently. If appetite is poor due to persistent infection, feeding may be given by nasogastric route or by gastrostomy.
ii. *Supplement fat soluble vitamins:* Due to pancreatic insufficiency, there will be deficiency of fat soluble vitamins. Vitamin A, D and E are supplemented in twice the recommended doses. These should be given along with food and enzymes.
iii. *Replace pancreatic enzymes:* Enteric coated tablets or spherules of pancreatic enzymes are given with each feed. Enzymes are started at doses of 1000–2000 IU of lipase/Kg in divided doses and modified bsaed on weight gain, nature of stool (frequency, amount and smell) and abdominal symptoms.

Suggested reading

1. Kabra S K, Kabra M, Lodha R, Shastri S. Cystic fibrosis in India. Pediatric Pulmonology 2007; 42: 1087–1094.
2. Kabra SK, Kabra M, Gera S, Lodha R, Sridevi KN, Chacko S, Mathew J, Shastri S, Ghosh M An indigenously developed method for sweat collection and estimation of chloride for diagnosis of cystic fibrosis. Indian Pediatrics 2002; 39:1039–1043.

ACUTE RESPIRATORY DISTRESS SYNDROME (ARDS)

It is defined as pulmonary edema not originating from the heart. The most common cause is severe pneumonia followed by sepsis. Other predisposing factors include shock, tissue injury, aspiration, toxins, microthrombi, intravascular coagulation, uremia and increased intracranial pressure.

There is increased permeability of alveolar capillary membrane leading to aggregation of leukocytes in pulmonary circulation. Mediators such as free oxygen radicals and platelet activating factors are released and injure vascular epithelium. In the acute stage there is edema and hyaline membrane formation. Subsequently fibrosis occurs. Microthrombi formation in vessels contributes to increased pulmonary vascular resistance and right to left shunting.

Clinical Features

ARDS can occur at any age. Initially symptoms are less and lungs are clear. Later on within 6–8 hours, patient becomes breathless. After 12 hours of insult, refractory hypoxia occurs followed by hypercapnia. Radiologically most lung fields are affected with reticular opacities. Mortality is very high, being 50–60% even in good centers.

Treatment

Patient is to be managed in an intensive care unit with cardiorespiratory monitoring and artificial ventilation. Ventilation is achieved by high PEEP or inverse ratio ventilation. Cause of ARDS is to be treated simultaneously.

Suggested reading

Lodha R, Kabra SK, Pandey RM. Acute respiratory distress syndrome: experience at a tertiary care hospital. Indian Pediatrics 2001; 38: 1154–59.

DIAGNOSTIC APPROACH TO CHRONIC COUGH

Chronic cough can be quite distressing.

Type of Cough

Staccato paroxysms of cough suggest whooping cough or chlamydia infection. Barking or brassy cough associated with changes in the voice indicate laryngotracheal disease. In case of postnasal drip, cough appears to be like an attempt to clear the throat and described as a hawking cough. Cough of psychogenic nature has a honking character (Table 13.11).

Sputum

Purulent sputum indicates the presence of suppurative lung disease. Although sputum is mucoid in cases of asthma, a yellowish sputum may be present in some cases due to the presence of a large number of eosinophils in it. Hemoptysis indicates the possibility of bronchiectasis, tuberculosis, mitral stenosis, cystic fibrosis or foreign body in the bronchus.

Wheezing

Wheezing is indicative of asthma.

Table 13.11: Diagnosis of chronic cough with relation to age

Age	*Cases*
Onset from birth	Laryngeal webs, vascular rings or H type tracheoesophageal fistula
Starting in first month	Congenital infections (rubella, CMV) leading to interstitial pneumonia
Early infancy	Gastroesophageal reflux leading to vomiting and aspiration
During late infancy	Bronchitis, asthma, cystic fibrosis, whooping cough
Pre-school age	Recurrent bronchitis, allergic bronchitis, asthma, foreign body, chronic suppurative lung disease, pulmonary eosinophilia
At all ages	Asthma, whooping cough, viral bronchitis, tuberculosis, foreign body aspiration.

Seasonal Cough

Chronic cough which is more common in certain seasons during the year should arouse the suspicion of asthma. Chronic cough occurring only in winter months is usually indicative of viral etiology.

Nutrition of the Child

Severe nutritional disturbance in association with chronic cough is found in cases of tuberculosis, bronchiectasis, pertussis, cystic fibrosis, severe chronic asthma or immune deficiency syndromes.

Investigations

Chest X-ray film, examination of the sputum, blood counts and tuberculin test may be necessary for arriving at a definitive diagnosis. Bronchoscopy may be necessary in some cases. CT scan of chest is a non invasive investigation.

Non-specific Therapy

Cough suppressants are preferably avoided in children. These are indicated only, if the cough is dry and exhausting or, if it disturbs sleep and prevents adequate nutrition, e.g. in whooping cough. Dextromethorphan is an effective cough suppressant and is non-habit forming.

Bronchodilators are useful in the treatment of children with cough due to occult asthma because of retained tracheobronchial secretions. Mucociliary transport of secretions is helped by the beta-adrenergic agonists and the xanthine group of drugs both in the asthmatic as well as in non-asthmatic children with chronic bronchitis.

Physiotherapy, e.g. chest clapping, vibrations and postural drainage are useful in facilitating removal of bronchial secretions.

Suggested reading

Marchant JM, Masters IB, Taylor SM, Cox NC, Seymour GJ, Chang AB. Evaluation and outcome of young children with chronic cough. Chest 2006;129:1132–41.

EMPYEMA THORACIS

Empyema thoracis is collection of pus in the pleural cavity. This is commonly caused as a complication of pneumonia or rupture of subdiaphragmatic or liver abscess in the pleura. Commonly it is sequel of staphylococcal pneumonia. It can occur secondary to pneumonia due to other organisms including *S. pneumoniae,* gram-negative bacilli and mycoplasma.

Clinical features include fever, breathing difficulty, toxic appearance of child. There is decreased movement of respiration with decreased air entry and vocal resonance. Percussion note is dull. Occasionally it may manifest as a pulsatile swelling over chest and is called empyema necessitans.

An X-ray film of chest shows shift in mediastinum with obliteration of costophrenic angle and varying degree of opacification. A pleural tap may show purulent material full of pus cells with high protein and low sugar. Gram stain and culture may show causative agent. Empyema should be differentiated from other causes of pleural effusion including tubercular and neoplastic.

Therapy of emyema consists of administration of antibiotics active against staphylococcus, i.e. cloxacillin, vancomycin. The pus is drained by putting continuous under water seal intercostal drainage tube. One time drainage of fluid under thoracoscopy is preferred if facility exists. After antibiotics and drainage if lung is not expanding or there is loculations in the pleura a CT scan of chest for evidence of thickening of pleura or loculated empyema can be obtained and patient considered for decortication by thoracotomy or thoracoscopy.

14 Disorders of Cardiovascular System

CONGESTIVE CARDIAC FAILURE

Every cardiac patient has a potential for developing congestive cardiac failure (CCF). Congestive cardiac failure by itself is not a diagnosis. It is a clinical syndrome due to an underlying anatomical or pathological cause, which is the primary diagnosis.

CCF is defined as *Inability of the heart to maintain an output, at rest or during stress, necessary for the metabolic needs of the body (systolic failure) and inability to receive blood into the ventricular cavities at low pressure during diastole (diastolic failure)*. Thus, due to systolic failure, it is unable to propel blood into the aorta and in diastolic failure, it receives inadequate amount of blood. Diastolic failure is recognized by clinical features of heart failure with evidence of increased filling pressures with preserved systolic function and, in many instances, cardiac output. An increase in left-sided filling pressures results in dyspnea from pulmonary congestion. An increase in right-sided filling pressures results in tender hepatomegaly and edema. Besides hypertrophied ventricles, diastolic failure occurs in restrictive heart disease and constrictive pericarditis. While mitral and tricuspid valve stenoses result in elevated atrial pressure, they are not, in the strictest sense, diastolic heart failure. Systolic failure, however, is a much more common clinical problem.

Etiopathogenesis

The causes of diastolic failure are indicated in Table 14.1. The management of diastolic failure has been covered with each condition. The causes of systolic failure or mixed systolic and diastolic failure can be classified according to age (Table 14.2). Rheumatic fever (RF) and rheumatic heart disease (RHD) are typically encountered beyond 5 years of age. In regions where it is common (mostly underserved and rural populations) it is a common cause of heart failure. Its prevalence is declining in urban populations.

Congenital Heart Disease

Keith pointed out over 50 years ago that if a patient of congenital heart disease does not develop CCF within the first year of life, he is not likely to do so in the next 10 years, unless complicated by anemia, infection or infective endocarditis. This statement is largely true but for a few exceptions. These include congenital heart defects associated with valve regurgitation and/or severe hypoxia.

Table 14.1: Heart failure due to diastolic dysfunction

Mitral or tricuspid valve stenosis*
Constrictive pericarditis
Restrictive cardiomyopathy
Acute ventricular volume overload (acute aortic or mitral valve regurgitation)
Myocardial ischemia#
Marked ventricular hypertrophy (hypertrophic cardiomyopathy, storage disorders of myocardium, hypertension, severe aortic or pulmonary valve stenosis)
Dilated cardiomyopathy#

*Mitral or tricuspid stenosis result in elevated atrial pressures with normal ventricular diastolic pressures

#Often associated with combined systolic and diastolic dysfunction

Table 14.2: Causes of congestive cardiac failure

Infants	*Children*
Congenital heart disease	Rheumatic fever, rheumatic heart disease
Myocarditis, primary myocardial disease	Congenital heart disease complicated by anemia, infection or endocarditis
Rhythm disorders (tachy-, bradyarrhythmias)	Systemic hypertension
Kawasaki disease with coronary occlusion	Myocarditis, primary myocardial disease
Anemia	Pulmonary hypertension (primary, secondary)
Miscellaneous	
Infections	
Hypoglycemia	
Hypocalcemia	
Neonatal asphyxia	
Persistent pulmonary hypertension of neonate (PPHN)	

Left to right shunts: Patients with left to right shunts tend to develop CCF around 6–8 weeks of life. At birth, the pulmonary vascular resistance is high, and the pulmonary artery pressure more or less equals the systemic pressure. The left to right shunt is small, whether the communication is at the atrial, ventricular or pulmonary artery level. The *maximum fall in the pulmonary vascular resistance occurs, in the first few weeks of life* and then more slowly for a few months. The size of the shunt gradually increases and reaches its maximum around the age of six weeks. If the baby is going to develop CCF due to a large shunt, he will do so at this time. The chances of a later increase in the shunt are minimal. Therefore, if CCF is not apparent by this time it is not likely to occur, unless the left to right shunt is associated with arch obstruction or regurgitation of the atrioventricular valve. Associated anemia or infection may also precipitate CCF at an earlier age. Prematurity results in a relatively early regression of the pulmonary vasculature and left to right shunts tend to manifest at even 3–4 weeks of age with CCF.

Right to left shunts: The patients with right to left shunts at the *ventricular* or *pulmonary artery level* have either pulmonic stenosis or pulmonary arterial hypertension. Since the right ventricle is decompressed by the right to left shunt, CCF does not occur. Right to left shunt at the *atrial level* can be secondary to obstruction at the right ventricular outlet or inlet. The former presents with CCF in first few days of life, if the obstruction is severe or there is atresia. With less severe obstruction, CCF develops late. The commonest obstruction at the right ventricular inlet is tricuspid atresia. If patients with tricuspid atresia manifest signs of right-sided congestion, they do so because they have a small communication at the atrial level. It is a form of mechanical obstruction like tricuspid valve stenosis or mitral stenosis.

Obstructive lesions: In congenital obstructive lesions of the heart, CCF is a relatively late phenomenon. However, atresia or critical stenosis of aortic, mitral or pulmonary valve can result in CCF within the first few days of life. If the lesion is mild, they may go on for years before the increasing severity makes the child symptomatic. Coarctation of the aorta can result in CCF within the first few weeks or months of life. However, if these patients do not manifest CCF in the first year of life, collaterals develop and prevent onset of failure by decompressing the obstruction. Therefore, obstructive lesions show CCF either soon after birth or later when the child is older.

Transpositions: Patients with transposition of great arteries (TGA) typically present early in the first 1–2 weeks of life with severe hypoxia resulting from poor mixing of systemic and pulmonary venous blood. CCF may be associated with intense hypoxia with resultant myocardial dysfunction. More commonly, CCF is the result of a large VSD or PDA occurring in association with transposition with markedly increased pulmonary blood flow. These infants may present as early as 4 weeks because of the substantial increase in pulmonary blood flow. The hypoxia is typically less than transposition with intact ventricular septum because of better mixing.

Total anomalous pulmonary venous return (TAPVR): This condition refers to anomalous drainage of the pulmonary venous blood into the right side (either to the right atrium or one of the veins draining into the right atrium). The obstructed form of TAPVR is associated with obstruction to pulmonary venous drainage (often at the level of the vein that finally communicates with the systemic veins). This presents early in the neonatal period or sometimes during the first weeks of life with severe pulmonary hypertension, heart failure and severe hypoxia. The unobstructed form may present in the first few months of life with heart failure and varying degrees of pulmonary hypertension. Occasionally, unobstructed TAPVR is undetected in infancy and manifests late in life.

Congenital atrioventricular valve regurgitation: Unlike left to right shunts, mitral or tricuspid valve regurgitation can result in CCF at an early age. Congenital TR manifests early because the elevated pulmonary artery pressure increases its severity. If the TR is not severe, it may improve with time as pulmonary vascular resistance declines.

The age of occurrence of CCF suggests the underlying cause (Table 14.3). The occurrence of CCF at an unexpectedly early age for a patient thought to have a simple shunt lesion should prompt search for an associated condition, such as coarctation.

Myocardial Disease

Dilated cardiomyopathy (DCM) refers to a group of conditions of diverse etiology in which both ventricles are enlarged with reduced contractility. It is considered the result of a variety of disease processes affecting the heart muscle. Causes of DCM include infections, metabolic derangements, hereditary disorders, nutritional

Table 14.3: Time of onset of congestive failure

Age	*Lesion*
Birth–72 hr	Pulmonary, mitral and aortic atresias
4 days–1 week	Hypoplastic left and right heart syndromes, transposition and malposition of great arteries
1–4 weeks	Transposition and malposition complexes, endocardial fibroelastosis, coarctation of aorta
1–2 months	Transposition and malposition complexes, endocardial cushion defects, ventricular septal defect, patent ductus arteriosus, total anomalous pulmonary venous return, anomalous left coronary artery from pulmonary artery
2–6 months	Transposition and malposition complexes, ventricular septal defect, patient ductus arteriosus, total anomalous pulmonary venous return, aortic stenosis, coarctation of aorta

deficiencies and exposure to drugs and toxins; a majority is classified as 'idiopathic' because the cause is not identifiable. Viral myocarditis may be the initial insult in many patients. Since it is difficult to distinguish myocarditis from cardiomyopathy, particularly in infants and young children, these terms are sometimes interchanged or termed 'DCM-myocarditis'.

The myocarditis and primary myocardial disease groups are recognized by *cardiac enlargement,* predominantly involving the left ventricle, *absence of significant murmurs, CCF, gallop rhythm* and EKG showing *conduction disturbances, arrhythmias, left ventricular hypertrophy* and nonspecific *ST* and *T wave changes.*

In most other patients with DCM-myocarditis, the EKG findings are nonspecific varying from left ventricular hypertrophy to low voltage complexes. A very short PR interval and QRS complexes of a high voltage (requiring ½ of ¼ standardization for the complexes to fit the recording paper) suggests Pompe's disease. Patients with an anomalous left coronary artery from pulmonary artery have an anterolateral myocardial infarction pattern on the EKG.

Arrhythmias

The third important cause of CCF in infancy is paroxysmal supraventricular tachycardia. Almost three-fourths of patients are below 4 months of age. Heart rates above 180/ minute tend to precipitate CCF. There is usually no failure in the first 24 hr. If the tachycardia persists for 36 hr, about 20% will develop CCF and almost 50% at 48 hr. There is a tendency for recurrences of tachycardia if the onset is after 4 months of age. Any long-standing tachyarrhythmia can be associated with ventricular dysfunction (tachycardiomyopathy) that may mimic a cardiomyopathy. Typical examples include ectopic atrial tachycardia (EAT) and permanent junctional re-entrant tachycardia (PJRT). In PJRT, P waves are inverted in leads II, III and aVF. P waves of EAT are different from those during sinus rhythm. It is, therefore, important to examine the EKG in any infant presenting with heart failure, ventricular dysfunction and heart failure. Often this difference is quite subtle. The presence of very rapid rates and, irregularities resulting from transient AV block provide help in making the diagnosis. If tachycardiomyopathy is suspected, 24-hr ambulatory EKG (Holter) may be useful in confirming the diagnosis. This is especially useful in EAT where heart rate accelerations are associated with only subtle variations in P wave morphology. Severe bradycardia, typically from complete heart block, can also result in heart failure.

Anemia

With a normal heart, hemoglobin levels of 5g/dL can result in CCF. In a heart compromised by disease, CCF may be precipitated even with higher hemoglobin levels of 7–8 g/dL. Younger infants are more susceptible to develop failure with anemia.

Infections

Severe infections, especially of the upper and lower respiratory tract may cause CCF. At times, it may be difficult to differentiate pulmonary infection from CCF in infants, as tachycardia, tachypnea and a palpable liver may be present in both. Not infrequently, CCF in an infant with heart disease may be associated with infection. Differentiation from infection is based on presence or absence of cardiac enlargement. In the absence of cardiac enlargement, the diagnosis of CCF is equivocal, except in the neonates. Even they show a rapidly enlarging heart in the course of a few days to a week. Hypoglycemia, neonatal asphyxia and hypocalcemia may result in CCF in neonates.

Three conditions, which may result in CCF without cardiac enlargement, are congenital mitral stenosis, cortriatriatum and the obstructive variety of total anomalous pulmonary venous connection, which are physiologically identical, in having pulmonary venous obstruction.

Rheumatic Fever

The most common cause of CCF in older children is *acute rheumatic fever* with *carditis* and *rheumatic heart disease.* It is necessary to emphasize that in India it cannot be considered axiomatic that a child with rheumatic heart disease who is in CCF has active carditis. The manifestations of rheumatic disease are different in India. Symptomatic mitral valve obstruction occurs at an early age, without the latent period of two decades as seen elsewhere. Patients of gross mitral and/or aortic regurgitation in CCF, without evidence of rheumatic activity are frequent.

Anemia and Infections Complicating Congenital Heart Disease

The next important cause of CCF in older children is congenital heart disease complicated by systemic or endocardial infection, anemia, unrelated myocarditis and systemic hypertension. The reasons for congenital heart disease resulting in CCF before the age of one year and its rarity up to the age of 10 years has been emphasized.

Hypertension

Systemic hypertension specially associated with acute glomerulonephritis or non-specific (idiopathic) obstructive aortitis, resulting in CCF, is not infrequently seen in the older children. In our experience, the most common cause of CCF in older children is nonspecific aortitis, if complicated congenital heart disease and systemic hypertension from renal parenchymal disease are excluded.

Clinical Features

The recognition of CCF in older children is based on the same features as in adults. Its diagnosis in infants and smaller children is based on subtle signs and symptoms.

Slow weight gain is related to two factors. The infant takes small feeds because of easy fatiguability and there is an excessive loss of calories from increased work of breathing associated with CCF. Uncommonly, there may be an unusual gain in weight due to collection of water, manifesting as facial puffiness or rarely as edema on the feet. The difficulty in feeding may manifest itself as 'poor feeder', a complaint that the baby does not take more than one to two ounces of milk at a time or that he is hungry within a few minutes after taking a small feed. Shortness of breath or fatigue from feeding results in the baby accepting only a small amount of milk at a time. A few minutes rest relieves him and since he is still hungry, he starts crying. The result is an irritable infant crying all the time. Often a mother may state that the baby breathes too fast while feeding or that the baby is more comfortable and breathes better when held against the shoulder—which is the equivalent of orthopnea in older children. Not infrequently, the baby may be brought with the complaints of persistent hoarse crying, wheezing, excessive perspiration and less commonly, puffiness of face (Table 14.4).

Table 14.4: Symptoms of congestive cardiac failure

Poor weight gain
Difficulty in feeding
Breathes too fast; breathes better when held against the shoulder
Persistent cough and wheezing
Irritability, excessive perspiration and restlessness
Pedal edema

Left-sided failure is indicated by tachypnea and tachycardia. Persistent cough, especially on lying down, hoarse cry and wheezing are other evidences of left-sided failure. The well known and familiar basal rales in the chest are hardly ever audible. Right-sided failure is indicated by hepatomegaly and facial puffiness. Examination of the neck veins in small babies is not helpful. Firstly, it is difficult to evaluate the short neck with baby fat and secondly, studies show that the right atrial pressure stays normal in more than one-half of infants with CCF. Edema on the feet occurs late. Common to both left and right-sided failure is the presence of *cardiac enlargement, third sound gallop and poor peripheral pulses with or without cyanosis* (Table 14.5).

Table 14.5: Signs of congestive cardiac failure in infants

Left-sided failure	*Failure of either side*	*Right-sided failure*
Tachypnea	Cardiac enlargement	Hepatomegaly
Tachycardia	Gallop rhythm (S3)	Facial edema
Cough	Peripheral cyanosis	Jugular venous
Wheezing	Small volume pulse	engorgement
Rales in chest	Absence of weight gain	Edema on feet

Treatment of Congestive Cardiac Failure

CCF means "inadequate cardiac output." The management of CCF consists in a determined "four-pronged attack" for the correction of the inadequate output.

i. Reducing cardiac work
ii. Augmenting myocardial contractility
iii. Improving cardiac performance
iv. Correcting the underlying cause

CCF represents an emergency in newborns; identification of the cause is necessary since initiating specific treatment can be life-saving; examples include duct dependent systemic circulation (critical coarctation, aortic stenosis, interrupted aortic arch). These newborns require prostaglandin infusion for stabilization.

Reducing Cardiac Work

The work of the heart is reduced by *restricting the patient's activities, sedatives, treatment of fever, anemia, obesity, and using vasodilators.* Neonates should be nursed in an incubator with minimal handling. The baby is kept propped up at an incline of about 30°; pooling of edema fluid in dependent areas reduces its collection in lungs, reducing the work of breathing.

At a temperature of 36 to 37°C, the overall circulatory and metabolic needs are minimal, thus reducing work of heart. Humidified oxygen to maintain a concentration of 40–50%, improves impaired oxygenation secondary to pulmonary congestion, thus reducing the work of heart by reducing requirements of cardiac output. If the patient is restless or dyspneic, sedatives are used. Morphine sulfate in doses of 0.05 mg/kg SC provides effective sedation. A benzodiazepine such as midazolam is also useful for sedation in selected circumstances. Sedatives reduce anxiety and lower catecholamine secretion, reducing physical activity, the respiratory and heart rates. The requirements of oxygen fall, and this reduces the cardiac workload. Use of sedatives may also be useful in restricting physical activity in children.

Presence of fever, anemia or infection increases the work of the heart. In infants and small children, the presence of superadded infection in congested lungs is difficult to recognize. Antibiotics are, therefore, necessary in the management of CCF in infants. **Anemia** imposes stress on the heart because of the decreased oxygen carrying capacity of blood. Anemia results in tachycardia and in a hyperkinetic circulatory state. Correction of anemia will result in decreased cardiac work. If transfusion is indicated, packed red cells (10–20 ml/kg) can be given along with a single IV dose of frusemide (1 mg/kg). Less common conditions, which worsen cardiac function, include *pulmonary emboli, thyrotoxicosis* and *obesity.*

Vasodilators: Have been used for the management of CCF to counteract compensatory mechanisms at work to improve the inadequate cardiac output. Arteriolar and venous vasoconstriction is mediated through catecholamines. Arteriolar constriction maintains blood pressure

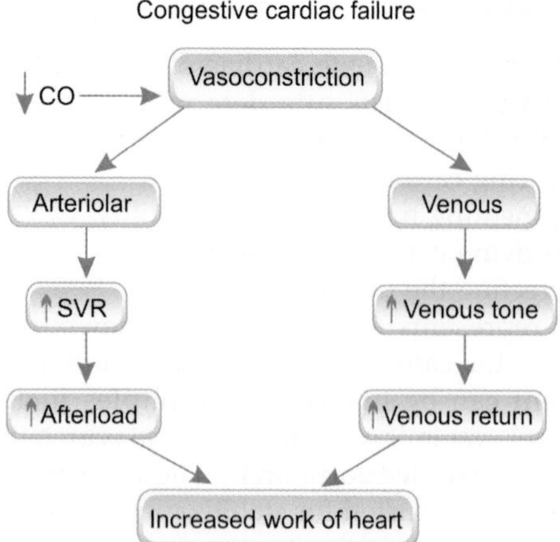

Fig.14.1: Low cardiac output (CO) results in vasoconstriction increasing systemic vascular resistance (SVR) and venous tone leading to increase in the work of heart

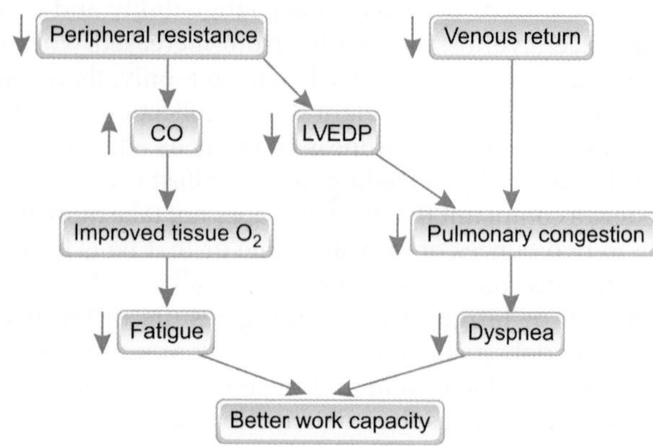

Fig. 14.2: By reducing the systemic vascular resistance and decreasing the venous tone vasodilators provide better work capacity. LVEDP—left ventricular end-diastolic pressure

14

by increasing the systemic vascular resistance, which increases cardiac work (Fig.14.1). Venoconstriction results in decreased venous capacitance and increased venous return, thereby increasing the filling pressures of the ventricles to increase the cardiac output. Since the compensatory mechanisms are inappropriately excessive, vasodilators, by reducing the arteriolar and venous vasoconstriction, reduce the work of heart (Fig. 14.2). Traditionally, nitrates were used as preferential venodilators and hydralazine as an arteriolar dilator (Table 14.6). The use of ACE inhibitors (captopril and enalapril) is now well established in infants and children. Besides being vasodilators, ACE inhibitors have other useful effects in CCF. They suppress the renin-angiotensin-aldosterone system, thus reducing vasoconstriction as well as sodium and water retention. They prevent potassium loss, reducing the risk of arrhythmias. By suppressing catecholamines, they prevent arrhythmias as well as the adverse effects of catecholamines on the myocardium. The major side effect of ACE inhibitor is cough, which can be quite troublesome. Persistent cough may necessitate the use of angiotensin receptor blockers (losartan, irbesartan, valsartan). Initially it is necessary to monitor the renal function: urinalysis, serum electrolytes, creatinine and urea once a week for 6–8 weeks after starting ACE inhibitors. Since ACE inhibitors might cause first dose hypotension, the first dose should be one quarter of the calculated dose. The patient should be recumbent for the first 6 hr to prevent unusual fall in blood pressure. Aspirin and non-steroidal antiinflammatory drugs attenuate the effects of ACE inhibitors and increase the possibility of renal toxicity. In the presence of renal dysfunction, it is preferable to use ramipril since it is excreted through kidneys as well as liver.

In the acute care setting sodium nitroprusside is often used as a vasodilator. It has effects on both the venous as well as the arterial systems. Phosphodiesterase inhibitors such as milrinone have become very popular, especially in postoperative settings. They have powerful vasodilatory and inotropic effects. The indications for use of vasodilators include, acute mitral or aortic regurgitation, ventricular dysfunction due to myocarditis, anomalous coronary artery from pulmonary artery and in postoperative setting.

Although β-adrenergic blockers are known to precipitate CCF, they have been found to improve survival especially in patients with DCM, who continue to have inappropriate tachycardia. The most useful agents include metoprolol and carvedilol. The latter is preferred because it combines the properties of β-blockers with peripheral

Table 14.6: **Dose and mode of administration of vasodilators**

Agent	*Action*	*Dose*	*Tolerance*
Nitroglycerine	Venous	0.05–20 µg/kg/min IV infusion	Common
Isosorbide dinitrate	Venous	0.01 mg/kg q 6-hr PO (maximum dose 2 mg/kg/day)	Common
Nitroprusside	Venous, arteriolar	0.5–8.0 µg/kg/min IV infusion	Rare
Hydralazine	Arterial	0.5–0.1 mg/kg/IV q 6-hr; 1–7.5 mg/kg/day PO, divided doses	Occasional
Prazosin	Venous, arterial	5–25 µg/kg/dose PO q 6-hr	Common
Nifedipine	Venous, arterial	0.3 mg/kg/dose PO q 6-hr	Rare
Captopril	Venous, arterial	0.5–6 mg/kg/day, divided doses	Uncommon
Enalapril	Venous, arterial	0.1–1 mg/kg/day, divided doses	Uncommon

vasodilation. Treatment with carvedilol (begun at 0.08–0.4 mg/kg/day and increased to maximum 1 mg/kg/day) has been shown to improve survival in patients with DCM. Calcium channel blockers have been shown to have adverse effects in CCF and should be avoided, unless indicated for control of systemic hypertension.

Augmenting Myocardial Contractility

Augmenting myocardial contractility by inotropic drugs like digitalis improves cardiac output. In infants and children, only digoxin is used. It has a rapid onset of action and is eliminated quickly. It is available for oral and parenteral administration. Oral digoxin is available in white (Lanoxin-Burroughs Welcome) 0.25 mg tablets and as Digoxin elixir (1 mL contains 0.05 mg). Guidelines for use of digoxin are given in Table 14.7. Digitalis decreases heart rate and increases myocardial contractility. The strength and velocity of myocardial contraction is increased due to action on the myocardium.

Table 14.7: Digoxin and frusemide dosage

Digoxin	*Digitalizing dose mg/kg*	*Maintenance dose (fraction digitalizing dose)*
Premature, neonates	0.04	1/4
1 month–one year	0.08	1/3 to 1/4
1–3 years	0.06	1/3 to 1/4
Above 3 years	0.04	1/3
Frusemide		
1–3 mg/kg/day PO		
1 mg/kg/dose IV		

Except for premature babies, the smaller the child, the better he can tolerate digitalis. In a hospitalized patient full digitalization should be sought to maximize benefit. If one-quarter or one-half of a full digitalizing dose is given, the increase in cardiac contractility is ¼ or ½ respectively of the full digitalizing dose. Unlike adults, children should be digitalized within a 24 hr period; ½ of the calculated digitalizing dose is given initially, another 1/4 in 6–8 hr and the remaining 1/4 in next 6–8 hr. The maintenance dose varies from 1/4 to 1/3 of the daily digitalizing dose, started 24 hr after the first dose. Before the third dose is given, an EKG should be obtained to rule out digitalis toxicity. The parenteral dose is 7/10 of the oral dose.

The patient should be observed for signs of digitalis toxicity. In most patients, the toxicity can be controlled by omitting the next one-two doses. The PR interval of the EKG is a useful indicator of toxicity in children. If the PR interval widens to one and a half times of the initial PR interval, digitalis toxicity is present. In infants, the upper limit of normal PR interval is 0.14 second.

Digitalis is used with caution in the following situations (a) premature neonates; (b) CCF due to myocarditis; (c) intensely cyanotic patients; and (d) CCF associated with a large heart. The dosage for premature infants is indicated in Table 14.7. In other situations, it is better to use half the calculated digitalizing as well as the maintenance dose initially. Myocardial damage, gross cardiomegaly, hypoxia, acidosis, hepatic, renal and pulmonary insufficiency increase the sensitivity of the myocardium to digitalis. Better control for therapy and avoidance of toxicity is possible with digoxin assays.

Patients receiving combined treatment with digoxin and frusemide should preferably receive PO potassium chloride 1–2 mEq/kg/day in divided doses (15 ml of 10% solution provides 20 mEq).

Inotropic Agents

Apart from digoxin, these agents belong to two groups: (i) catecholaminic inotropic agents, e.g. dopamine and dobutamine; and (ii) non-catechol, non-digitalis glycoside agents, e.g. amrinone and milrinone. Of these, only the former are useful; amrinone, milrinone, xamoterol and flosequinon are not safe and do not prolong life. In a patient with CCF if the blood pressure is low, dopamine should be used as an infusion. At a dose less than 5 mg/kg /min, it causes peripheral vasodilation and increases myocardial contractility. The renal blood flow improves, resulting in natriuresis. In higher doses, it results in peripheral vasoconstriction. Dobutamine has certain advantages over dopamine. It does not need to be administered via a central line. The dose of dobutamine is 2–15 mg/kg/min. It should be increased gradually until the desired response is achieved.

In patients with DCM, dobutamine has been used as a 24 hr infusion once or twice a week. Another inotropic agent, used in adults is ibopamine. This is an orally effective agent, which releases epinine, with inotropic, vasodilator and natriuretic effects.

The use of digitalis for its inotropic effect is controversial. In CCF, the serum level of catecholamines is high. CCF is associated with myocardial dysfunction. If the myocardium is failing it should be provided rest using vasodilators rather than inotropic agents. Use of inotropic agents is like flogging a tired horse. High catecholamine levels have been shown to be toxic to myocardium in animals. Lastly, digitalis has a low therapeutic to toxic ratio and can result in serious life-threatening arrhythmias. A number of studies have confirmed that the use of digoxin is beneficial for symptom relief and that digoxin should be used whether the patient has mild, moderately severe or severe CCF, with or without sinus rhythm. Digoxin is a second-line drug like ACE inhibitors. Both can be combined for a synergistic effect. By increasing cardiac output, digoxin lowers the systemic impedence indirectly, thus to some extent unloading the ventricles.

Improving Cardiac Performance by Reducing Venous Return (Preload)

Diuretics reduce the blood volume, decrease venous return and ventricular filling. This tends to reduce the heart size. The larger the heart, the more the wall tension and the poorer is its performance. With reduction in heart size and volume, the myocardial function and the cardiac output improve. Diuretics reduce the total body sodium, thus reducing the blood pressure and the peripheral vascular resistance. This helps in increasing the cardiac output and reducing the work of the heart. The increase in blood volume is a compensatory phenomenon in CCF. If reduction of blood volume is vigorous, it may cause hypotension and elevation of blood urea nitrogen.

Diuretics are the first line of management in congestive failure. The action of orally administered frusemide starts within 20 minutes. Frusemide interferes with the sodium, potassium and chloride transport in the ascending limb of Henle. Patients on frusemide should receive potassium supplements. With the use of potent diuretics like frusemide, it is necessary to have frequent checks of the serum electrolytes to prevent serious electrolyte imbalance. It is preferable to combine frusemide with a potassium sparing diuretic such as spironolactone, triamterene or amiloride instead of giving potassium supplements.

Frusemide activates renin-angiotensin-aldosterone system (RAAS), which is responsible for vasoconstriction (increases work of heart) and sodium and water retention. If indicated, ACE inhibitors should be combined with frusemide; the combination further suppresses the RAAS.

The other method of altering the body fluid volume is by restricting the sodium intake. Sodium restriction cannot be practised in infants, since low sodium milks are not easily available. In older children it is not justified to restrict the salt intake excessively since children cannot be forced to eat what they do not like. Since salt-free diets are unpalatable, child stops eating and loses weight. Low sodium diets should be used only if CCF cannot be controlled with digitalis, diuretics and ACE inhibitors.

CCF increases calorie requirements. Concentrated milk formulae supplemented by soluble protein preparations provide more calories.

Correcting the Underlying Cause

Although mentioned last this has the biggest impact on survival. As treatment is initiated it is important to obtain the basic information required to identify the cause of CCF. The approach should be systematic. Non-invasive tests (especially echocardiography) allow identification of the cause in virtually all children with suspected heart disease. Catheterization with angiocardiography is seldom necessary. The investigations also establish the severity of the lesion. Many of them are tackled by curative or palliative operations. A diagnostic label of idiopathic DCM mandates careful exclusion of all conditions that are known to cause ventricular dysfunction. In practical terms, the most important purpose of clinical evaluation and diagnostic tests in children with suspected DCM is to identify correctable conditions that present with ventricular dysfunction. The commonest conditions missed are atrial tachyarrhythmias, coarctation of the aorta and obstructive aortitis.

The presence of CCF in a child with rheumatic heart disease does not necessarily mean presence of active carditis. In any patient of rheumatic heart disease, if active carditis has been excluded and an adequate trial given to medical management, operative treatment should be considered. It is important to look for sustained tachyarrhythmia on the EKG. The heart failure is corrected once the arrhythmia is managed. Anomalous origin of the left coronary artery is treated surgically. Other primary myocardial diseases do not have specific treatment. *Prolonged bedrest combined with anticongestive measures including vasodilators may be helpful.* The prognosis depends on the underlying cause. When treating these patients caution should be exercised regarding the use of digitalis. There is evidence to suggest that steroids may be hazardous in patients with Coxsackie myocarditis. Steroids should be avoided in patients of myocarditis in the acute stage, unless they have serious conduction disturbances or peripheral vascular failure. Patients with DCM may benefit from treatment with betablockers. If endocardial biopsy suggests active inflammation, treatment with steroids and immunosuppressants may be considered in selected cases. However, there is little published evidence that supports its use to improve eventual prognosis. Patients with endocardial fibroelastosis do not respond well to digitalis. Once digitalis has been started in these patients, it should be continued for a number of years. Early discontinuation may result in reappearance of CCF resistant to therapy.

Uncommon causes of CCF in infants and children include upper respiratory infection, hypoglycemia, neonatal asphyxia and hypocalcemia. Appropriate treatment depends on a high index of suspicion. Hypertrophied tonsils and adenoids by causing upper respiratory obstruction, resulting in hypoxia and hypercapnia, can cause pulmonary hypertension and CCF. Management consists of relief of the upper airway obstruction.

Stepwise Management of Congestive Failure

The most important step consists in establishing the cause of CCF accurately. Correction of the cause should be possible in most patients since rheumatic and congenital heart diseases are the two commonest causes. It is important to recognize that treatment of cause alone can have an major impact on prognosis.

Step 1 is the use of frusemide combined with digoxin and ACE inhibitors if the patient is not doing well. **Step 2** consists of adding isosorbide nitrate if the problem is pulmonary congestion (avoid hydralazine, which may have adverse effects) or carvedilol if the heart rate is too fast (patient in sinus rhythm). **Step 3** involves addition of either nitrates or carvedilol, whichever was not used earlier. Therapy with once-daily spironolactone has been shown to improve outcome. Careful monitoring of serum potassium is required; combined therapy of potassium sparing diuretics, oral potassium supplements and ACE inhibitors should be avoided. **Step 4** is the intermittent use of dobutamine or dopamine with dobutamine (separate infusion), if the blood pressure is low. **Step 5** involves making sure that the patient is getting all advised medications. Those not adequately controlled need either medical or surgical correction of the cause of CCF. The only patients who do not respond to the above measures and do not have a correctable cause would be patients with myocarditis or DCM. For them, **Step 6** involves a myocardial biopsy and treatment with corticosteroids if evidence for active myocarditis is present. In the absence of active myocarditis, therapy with β-blockers (e.g. carvedilol) should be increased to maximum tolerable levels. **Step 7** is the use of ventricular assist devices or cardiac transplantation. It is necessary to emphasize that the last two steps are applicable only to rare patients with, e.g. DCM.

Prognosis

The mortality of CCF in infants is very high (40%), despite best medical treatment. This indicates that early recognition and referral to specialized centers for infant care providing both medical and surgical help, is essential to improve outcome.

ACUTE RHEUMATIC FEVER

Rheumatic fever is an immunological disorder initiated by group A beta-hemolytic streptococcus. Recent studies suggest that besides group A streptococci, group E and G may also cause rheumatic fever. Antibodies produced against some streptococcal cell wall proteins and sugars react with the connective tissues of the body and heart and result in rheumatic fever. There is no single test for the confirmation of diagnosis. There is a strong relationship with streptococcal infection and it is possible to prevent rheumatic fever by appropriate treatment of streptococcal infection with the use of penicillin.

Epidemiology

Rheumatic heart disease constitutes 10–50% of the cardiac patients in Indian hospitals. The prevalence rate for rheumatic heart disease in the village population near Agra was 2/1000 and in the urban population of Chandigarh it was 2.07/1000 for women and 1.23/1000 for men. Similar figures were obtained in Delhi. A survey of 11 cities in India showed a prevalence rate of 0.55 to 0.67/1000. A survey conducted by the Indian Council of Medical Research (ICMR) involving 133,000 children 6 to 16 years in age showed the incidence to be 5.3/1000. Selected parts of India are now reporting a significant decline in RF incidence and RHD prevalence. Surveys conducted at Chandigarh, Indore, Cochin and Vellore involving more than 100,000 children (2004–2007) indicate that the prevalence has dropped to below 1/1000 to as low as 0.5 to 0.6/1000.

The incidence of rheumatic fever following streptococcal sore throat in western countries is 0.3% in the general population and 1–3% in crowded communities like army barracks.

Age and sex: The most common age group is 5–15 yr. Though rheumatic fever is believed to be less common below the age of 5 yr, it is unlikely to be so in India, since established juvenile rheumatic mitral stenosis is often seen in children below the age of 12 years. The sexes are nearly equally affected, mitral valve disease and chorea being more common in females, whereas aortic valve involvement is more often seen in males.

Predisposing factors: Poor socioeconomic conditions leading to unhygienic living conditions and overcrowded households are predisposing factors since they help spread infections. Undernutrition, by altering the immune response, may increase susceptibility. However, recent epidemics in United States have occurred in upper middle class families in the absence of overcrowding and with good medical facilities.

Etiopathogenesis

The etiology of rheumatic fever is unknown. A strong association with β-hemolytic streptococci is indicated by the following:

i. A history of preceding sore throat is available in approximately 50% patients.
ii. Epidemics of streptococcal infection are followed by a high incidence of rheumatic fever.
iii. The seasonal variation of rheumatic fever and streptococcal infection are identical.
iv. In patients with established rheumatic heart disease, streptococcal infection is followed by recurrence of acute rheumatic fever.
v. Penicillin prophylaxis for streptococcal infection prevents recurrences of rheumatic fever in those patients who have had it earlier.
vi. More than 85% patients with acute rheumatic fever consistently show elevated levels of anti-streptococcal antibody titer.

Though these features indicate the association of rheumatic fever with streptococcal infection, streptococci have never been isolated from lesions in joints, heart or the blood. Considerable evidence suggests that the rheumatic fever is an antigen-antibody reaction. Following streptococcal sore throat, there is a latent period of 10 days to several weeks before the onset of rheumatic fever. This latent period is similar to the other antigen-antibody diseases like serum sickness.

It has been suggested that patients of rheumatic fever produce antibodies against streptococcal cell wall and cell membrane proteins. The streptococcal antigen and human myocardium appear to be identical antigenically. These antibodies might react with human connective tissue especially the cardiac muscle, striated muscle and vascular smooth muscle. By immunofluorescence, the antibodies have been seen attached to sarcolemma of the cardiac muscle. Streptococcal products against which antibodies have been demonstrated include streptolysin, hyaluronidase, erythrogenic toxin, streptokinase and deoxyribonuclease.

The hyaluronic acid capsule of streptococci prevents phagocytosis by leukocytes. Below the capsule, hair-like fimbriae containing lipoteichoic acid as well as the M, T and R proteins are present. Lipoteichoic acid provides the mucosal attachment (destroyed by penicillin). The M, T and R proteins are utilized for typing the streptococci. The M protein is believed to be the virulence factor of the streptococcus. Each strain has a type specific M protein. A component of the streptococcal cell wall carbohydrate, N-acetyl glucosamine is also present in human connective tissue. Compounds containing N-acetyl glucosamine cross-react with antiserum against human connective tissue.

Thus, streptococcal cell wall proteins as well as carbohydrates have the capacity to produce antibodies capable of reacting with human connective tissue, resulting in rheumatic fever. Rheumatic fever appears to be the result of the host's unusual response at both the cellular and humoral level to streptococcus. Antibodies against the heart muscle (anti-heart antibodies) and nervous tissue (anti-neuronal antibodies) are found in high titers in patients with carditis and chorea. The antibodies are specific in that they react with rheumatic tissue, but not other tissue. However, their exact significance is not clear. These features, however, do not explain why some people are susceptible while others are not so susceptible to rheumatic fever following streptococcal infection. Human leucocyte antigen (HLA) studies suggest an association with HLA-DR3. Serum 883, a B-cell alloantigen is identified in 100% patients with rheumatic fever. Another antibody labeled D 8/17 identified 100% patients in USA but only 60% in India. The findings favor genetic susceptibility to rheumatic fever, perhaps inherited in Mendelian recessive pattern.

Clinical Features

The clinical features of rheumatic fever consists of streptococcal sore throat with fever followed 10 days to a few weeks later by recurrence of fever and various manifestations of acute rheumatic fever. History of sore throat is available in less than 50% patients. Guidelines for the clinical diagnosis of acute rheumatic fever, originally suggested by Duckett Jones were revised by the American Heart Association. The guidelines consist of major, minor and essential criteria (Table 14.8). *Two major or one major and two minor criteria are required in the presence of essential criteria to diagnose acute rheumatic fever.* It is important to emphasize that these guidelines are meant to enable the diagnosis of rheumatic fever and *do not mean that a physician should not use his clinical judgment in making a diagnosis in the absence of these criteria.*

Major Criteria

Carditis: The rheumatic carditis is a pancarditis involving the pericardium, myocardium and the endocardium. Carditis occurs in 50–60% of patients with acute rheumatic fever. It is an *early* manifestation of rheumatic fever so that by the time a patient seeks help, he already has evidence of carditis. Almost 80% of those patients who develop carditis do so within the first 2 weeks of the onset of rheumatic fever.

Pericarditis: Pericarditis results in precordial pain, which may be quite severe; a friction rub is present on auscultation. Clinical pericarditis is seen in approximately 15% of those who have carditis. The EKG may show ST and T wave changes consistent with pericarditis. Rheumatic pericarditis is associated with only small effusions and does not result in tamponade or constrictive pericarditis. A patient of rheumatic pericarditis *always has additional mitral or mitral and aortic regurgitation murmurs.* If after the disappearance of the pericardial friction rub there are no murmurs, one can safely exclude rheumatic fever as the cause of pericarditis. The importance of pericarditis lies in identifying the presence of carditis as well as the presence of acute rheumatic fever.

Myocarditis: The features of myocarditis are (i) cardiac enlargement, (ii) soft first sound, (iii) protodiastolic (S3) gallop, (iv) CCF and (v) Carey Coombs' murmur.

Table 14.8: Criteria for diagnosis of rheumatic fever

Major criteria	*Minor criteria*
Carditis Arthritis Subcutaneous nodules Chorea Erythema marginatum	A. *Clinical* i. Fever ii. Arthralgia iii. Previous rheumatic fever, rheumatic heart disease B. *Laboratory* i. Acute phase reactants: leukocytosis, elevated sedimentation rate and C-reactive protein ii. Prolonged PR interval on EKG
Essential criteria	
Evidence for recent streptococcal infection, as indicated by a. Increased antistreptolysin O titer b. Positive throat culture c. Recent scarlet fever	

Myocarditis *per se* plays little, if any role, in the morbidity of rheumatic fever.

Carey Coombs' murmur is a delayed diastolic mitral murmur heard during the course of acute rheumatic fever. It tends to disappear after the myocarditis subsides. Although believed to indicate myocarditis, it is unlikely that the murmur is due to myocarditis *per se*. No other myocarditis results in a mitral diastolic murmur unless associated with significant mitral regurgitation. Most likely it is due to increased diastolic flow, secondary to mitral regurgitation, across inflamed cusps. The disappearance can be explained by the decrease in the left ventricular size following subsidence of myocarditis, and better function of the mitral valve—papillary muscle complex.

Evidence for absence of myocarditis playing any role in the morbidity and mortality of rheumatic fever is based on the following findings:

1. Troponin T, a marker of myocardial damage, has been found not to increase during acute rheumatic fever with carditis indicating absence of significant myocardial damage.
2. Radionuclide evaluation using antimyosin antibody indicates insignificant myocardial uptake (hence absence of significant damage) in the absence of pericarditis and CCF.
3. Myocardial biopsies during acute rheumatic fever with carditis have failed to provide information regarding presence of myocarditis because of paucity of myocardial damage.
4. Echocardiographic evaluation of the left ventricular function indicates that the myocardial contractility (the capacity of myocardium to contract) remains normal even in the presence of CCF.
5. Pathological evaluation of the myocardium indicates that the amount of myocardial damage is insufficient to explain the mortality.
6. Surgical replacement of mitral and/or aortic valve during acute rheumatic fever results in a rapid control of CCF and decrease in heart size, despite investigational evidence for ongoing active rheumatic fever. The surgical findings thus indicate that it is the acute hemodynamic overload secondary to valvar regurgitation, which is responsible for CCF and the morbidity and mortality of acute rheumatic fever.

Endocarditis: The endocarditis is represented by a pansystolic murmur of mitral regurgitation with or without an associated aortic regurgitation murmur. Pathologically mitral valve is involved in 100% cases of rheumatic fever who have carditis. Clinically, however, 5–8% patients may present as pure aortic regurgitation. Thus, almost 95% patients have mitral regurgitation murmur, a quarter of them also having an aortic regurgitation murmur and only 5% pure aortic regurgitation. Tricuspid valvulitis resulting in tricuspid regurgitation occurs in 10–30% cases. Isolated tricuspid valvulitis as a manifestation of acute rheumatic endocarditis does not occur. Clinical evidence of pulmonary valve involvement in acute rheumatic fever is never seen.

The acute hemodynamic overload resulting from acute mitral regurgitation and/or aortic regurgitation leads to left ventricular failure and is the main reason for the morbidity and mortality of rheumatic fever and rheumatic heart disease. The severity of the valvar endocarditis causing acute and later chronic hemodynamic overload determines the prognosis of individual patients.

Arthritis: Rheumatic arthritis is a polyarthritis involving large joints like knees, ankles and elbows. Uncommonly smaller joints may also be involved. It is a migratory polyarthritis with the affected joints showing redness, warmth, swelling, pain and limitation of movement. It is an *early* manifestation and occurs in 70–75% cases according to western literature. However, the figures from India indicate that arthritis is seen in 30–50% patients. The pain and swelling appear rather quickly, last 3–7 days and subside spontaneously to appear in some other joint. There is no *residual damage to the joint.* One clinical observation regarding arthritis is that the younger the patient with acute rheumatic fever, the less the arthritis and the older the patient, the more the arthritis.

14

Subcutaneous nodules: Subcutaneous nodules appear on bony prominences like elbows, shins, occiput and spine. They vary in size from pinhead to an almond. They are non-tender. Subcutaneous nodules are a *late* manifestation and appear around 6 weeks after the onset of rheumatic fever though they have been described as early as 3 weeks from the onset. They occur in about 3–20% cases of rheumatic fever in India. Patients who have subcutaneous nodules almost always have carditis. They last from a few days to weeks but have been known to last for almost a year.

Chorea: Sydenham's chorea is a *late* manifestation occurring about 3 months after the onset of acute rheumatic fever. Generally, when a patient manifests chorea, the signs of inflammation in the form of elevated sedimentation rate have returned to normal. Chorea consists of purposeless, jerky movements resulting in deranged speech, muscular incoordination, awkward gait and weakness. The affected child is emotionally disturbed and drops things she or he is carrying. It is 3–4 times more common in females as compared to males. *Untreated, it has a self-limiting course of 2–6 weeks.*

Erythema marginatum: Although considered more specific than other varieties of skin manifestations, it is extremely rare in Indians. The rash is faintly reddish, not raised above the skin and non-itching. It starts as a red spot with a pale center, increasing in size to coalesce with adjacent spots to form a serpiginous outline. We believe that the inability to recognize erythema marginatum is not because it does not occur but because of the dark complexion of the skin. Anyone who has seen erythema marginatum would recognize the futility of searching it in a dark complexioned person. It is an early manifestation, predominantly seen over the trunk.

Minor Criteria

Clinical

i. *Fever:* Rheumatic fever is usually associated with fever. The temperature rarely goes above 39.5°C. In the initial attack, it is present in almost 90% patients.
ii. *Arthralgia:* Arthralgia is defined as subjective pain whereas arthritis means subjective symptoms as well as objective signs of joint inflammation. Whereas arthritis is a major manifestation, arthralgia is a minor manifestation. Figures from India indicate that arthritis and arthralgia together occur in about 90% patients.
iii. *Previous rheumatic fever or rheumatic heart disease:* This minor criterion is applicable only for a second attack of rheumatic fever.

Laboratory

i. *Acute phase reactants* consist of polymorphonuclear leukocytosis, increased sedimentation rate and presence of C-reactive protein. The leukocyte count is usually 10,000–15,000 per cu mm. The sedimentation rate is usually elevated during acute rheumatic fever and remains so for 4–10 weeks in almost 80% patients. In a small proportion of patients, it may remain elevated even beyond 12 weeks. Although CCF tends to bring the sedimentation rate down toward normal, it is unlikely that a patient of acute rheumatic fever with CCF will have a normal sedimentation rate. C-reactive protein is a β-globulin, which is increased uniformly in all patients of acute rheumatic fever. It subsides rapidly if a patient is on steroids. Absence of C-reactive protein is strongly against the diagnosis of acute rheumatic fever. Presence of C-reactive protein, however, is not diagnostic since it becomes positive in many other infections.
ii. *Prolonged PR interval in the EKG:* Prolonged PR interval is a non-diagnostic criterion since it can get prolonged in many infections. It is also not diagnostic of carditis. Higher grades of block like second degree atrioventricular block, especially of the Wenckebach type, may also be seen. Complete atrioventricular block is rare. Prolongation of QTc (corrected QT interval) is also suggestive of myocarditis.

Essential Criteria

The essential criteria include evidences for recent streptococcal infection. The most useful is the presence of antibodies against the streptococci. The commonest in use is the antistreptolysin 'O' titer (ASO). Considerable confusion exists regarding its value as well as the levels, which should be considered significant. Elevated levels of ASO only indicate previous streptococcal infection and not rheumatic fever. Although generally the higher the level the more likely one can conclude a recent streptococcal infection, lower levels considered "normal" do not necessarily exclude a recent streptococcal infection. For example, if the basal ASO titer of an individual is 50 units and it goes up to 250 units, it is indicative of recent streptococcal infection. An isolated figure of 250, if the previous levels are not known, is not helpful in taking a decision. Rising titer of ASO is a strong evidence for a recent streptococcal infection.

Positive throat culture for streptococci is relatively uncommon, when a patient presents with acute rheumatic fever. Positive throat culture can also not be equated with the diagnosis of rheumatic fever. Positive throat culture means that streptococci are present in the throat. The patient may or may not have rheumatic fever. The third feature suggestive for the diagnosis of recent streptococcal infection is the presence of residua of scarlet fever. The desquamation of skin of palms and soles indicates that the patient has had scarlet fever within the previous two weeks.

Echocardiography

It is a very sensitive investigation for the diagnosis of rheumatic carditis. Features indicative of rheumatic carditis consist of annular dilatation, elongation of the chordae to the anterior leaflet of the mitral valve causing prolapse and lack of coaptation of the two leaflets resulting in mitral regurgitation. The jet of mitral regurgitation is directed toward the posterolateral wall. There is focal nodular thickening of the tips of the mitral leaflets, which do not have an independent chaotic movement seen with infective endocarditis. In addition, there is variable degree of increase in the left atrial and ventricular size. Involvement of the aortic valve is recognized as aortic regurgitation.

Though the revised Jones criteria do not include echocardiographic and Doppler findings for the diagnosis of carditis, these investigations have improved the recognition of carditis, which at times is not possible clinically. This has led to the recognition of the entity of subclinical carditis in which although there are no clinical findings, the echocardiographic findings indicate mitral regurgitation.

Treatment

There is no specific treatment. Management is symptomatic combined with suppressive therapy. The patients need secondary prophylaxis, and long-term follow-up to establish the natural course of the clinically silent disease.

Bedrest: All patients with acute rheumatic fever should be kept on bedrest and in those with carditis; the bedrest should be prolonged until evidence of activity subsides. Such end points are at times difficult to determine. Patients who do not have carditis can be ambulatory in 2–3 weeks, whereas if carditis is present, immobilization is continued for one to three months, especially in the presence of CCF.

Diet: In the absence of cardiac involvement, there should be no restriction in salt intake. Even in the presence of cardiac involvement, salt restriction is not necessary unless CCF is present and not responding well to treatment.

Penicillin: After obtaining throat cultures, the patient should be treated with penicillin. Initially the patient is given therapeutic doses of penicillin, 400,000 units of procaine penicillin, intramuscularly, twice daily for 10 days. This is followed by treatment with benzathine penicillin 1.2 million units every 21 days, or 0.6 million units every 15 days. The dose is decided by the patients' muscle mass, since the injections are painful.

Suppressive Therapy

Aspirin or *steroids* are given as suppressive therapy. Since untreated rheumatic fever subsides in 12 weeks in 80% patients, either of the two suppressive agents is given for 12 weeks. Steroids are a more potent suppressive agent as compared to aspirin. However, there is no proof that the use of steroids results in less cardiac damage as compared to aspirin. A number of observations indicate that steroids act faster and are superior in the initial phases. Pericardial friction rub tends to disappear within 3–5 days after starting the steroids and a new friction rub does not appear. Despite adequate doses of aspirin, a new friction rub may still make its appearance. Similarly subcutaneous nodules tend to disappear faster with the use of steroids as compared to aspirin. Lastly, patients who have carditis with CCF have higher mortality if aspirin is used compared to steroids. In selecting the suppressive drug for an individual patient, the following guidelines are followed:

i. If a patient has carditis with CCF, the use of corticosteroids is mandatory.
ii. Carditis without CCF: one may use either steroids or aspirin; steroids are preferred.
iii. If the patient does not have carditis, it is preferable to use aspirin.

The duration of course for the suppressive agent, aspirin or steroids, is 12 weeks. With aspirin, the full doses are given for 10 weeks and then tapered off in next two weeks. Full doses of steroids are given for three weeks and then tapered very gradually in the next nine weeks. The steroid most commonly used is prednisone. The dose is 60 mg/day for patients weighing more than 20 kg and 40 mg/day for patients weighing less than 20 kg. This is continued for 3 weeks and then reduced to 50 mg/day for 1 week and 40 mg/day for another week. Following this, the reduction in dose is by 5 mg/week. The dose of aspirin is 90 to 120 mg/kg/day in four divided doses. If facilities for estimation of blood levels of salicylate are available, these are maintained between 20–25 mg/dL.

Management of congestive cardiac failure is dealt with previously. It is emphasized that surgical replacement of the mitral and/or aortic valve is indicated if the patient is deteriorating despite aggressive anticongestive measures. Hemodynamic overload due to mitral and/or aortic regurgitation is the main cause of mortality.

Management of Chorea

Chorea is a late manifestation. By the time a patient presents as chorea the sedimentation rate as well as the ASO may be normal. The patient as well as the parents should be reassured and told about the self-limiting course of the disease. The patient should be provided complete physical and mental rest. Phenobarbitone 30 mg thrice daily is given. Other drugs, including chlorpromazine, diazepam, diphenhydramine (Benadryl) or promethazine (Phenergan) can be administered. Although aspirin and steroids are supposed not to have a place in the management of chorea, we have seen dramatic response in some patients not doing well on a combination of chlorpromazine and phenobarbitone. Long-term follow up studies in patients of chorea have shown appearance of heart disease in 20% patients in twenty years and 30% in thirty years. Penicillin prophylaxis is essential to prevent recurrence of rheumatic fever.

Prevention of Rheumatic Fever

It would be ideal to provide primary prevention of rheumatic fever.

Primary prevention: It requires identification of streptococcal sore throat and its treatment with penicillin. It depends on the awareness of parents regarding dangers of sore throat. For primary prevention, it is necessary to educate the community regarding the consequences of streptococcal sore throat. Logistically it is difficult since it requires (i) identification of sore throat, (ii) rapidly confirming that the sore throat is streptococcal, and (iii) provision of appropriate treatment.

Data from recent epidemics of rheumatic fever in United States indicates that 30–80% of sore throats resulting in rheumatic fever can be asymptomatic. *Rheumatic fever could not be prevented in patients of streptococcal pharyngitis treated by adequate doses of oral penicillin for ten days. As such intramuscular benzathine penicillin is mandatory for prevention of rheumatic fever.* Because asymptomatic streptococcal pharyngitis can result in rheumatic fever, primary prevention can only be possible by using an antistreptococcal vaccine. Such a vaccine is under development.

Secondary prevention: It consists in giving long-acting benzathine penicillin. The dose is 1.2 million units once every 3 weeks or 0.6 million units every 15 days, depending on patient age and muscle mass. The injection is painful and some patients get fever for 24–36 hr following the injection. It is preferable to give the injection on a Saturday afternoon to avoid loss of studies for the child.

Ideally, penicillin prophylaxis should continue life long. Less than the ideal would be to continue it until the age of 35 years. The least satisfactory approach is to give for 5 years from the last attack of rheumatic fever. The responsibility of continuing prophylactic penicillin lies on the parents, however, unless a physician takes time in explaining the seriousness of the problem and the necessity of continuing penicillin on a long-term basis, the physician has done his job inadequately.

RHEUMATIC HEART DISEASE

In the pediatric age group, the sequelae of rheumatic fever consist of mitral, aortic and tricuspid valve disease. The mitral valve involvement manifests predominantly as mitral regurgitation and much less commonly as mitral stenosis. The aortic valve and tricuspid valve involvement presents exclusively as aortic and tricuspid regurgitation respectively. Rheumatic aortic stenosis has never been described below the age of 15 years.

Mitral Regurgitation

Mitral regurgitation is the commonest manifestation of acute as well as previous rheumatic carditis. In our own study of 850 patients of rheumatic heart disease below the age of 12 years, 750 patients had pure or dominant mitral regurgitation.

Hemodynamics

Mitral regurgitation results in a systolic leak of blood to the left atrium. The regurgitant volume of blood reaches the left atrium during ventricular systole at almost systemic pressure, however, during diastole it can pass freely across the mitral valve. Thus, although the left atrial pressure increases during systole, it drops during diastole. The mean left atrial pressure, therefore, stays normal or is only slightly increased. There is thus no increase in pulmonary venous pressure and no pulmonary congestion. The increased volume of blood handled by the left atrium and left ventricle results in an increase in the size of both these chambers. Mitral regurgitation provides two exits for the left ventricular blood—the forward flow through the aortic valve into the systemic circulation and the backward leak into the left atrium. The forward output becomes insufficient during exertion. This decrease in the systemic output results in fatigue, the commonest symptom of significant mitral regurgitation. Absence of pulmonary congestion prevents occurrence of dyspnea unless the mitral regurgitation is severe or the left ventricular myocardium is failing. With failing left ventricle, the left ventricular diastolic pressure increases, the left atrial and pulmonary venous pressure increase and pulmonary congestion appears. There is an increase in pulmonary arterial pressure and features of pulmonary arterial hypertension appear. Thus presence of features of pulmonary arterial hypertension in a patient having pure mitral regurgitation suggests (i) severe mitral regurgitation, or (ii) failing left ventricular myocardium, or (iii) acute mitral regurgitation.

The mitral regurgitation developing during acute rheumatic fever is of sudden onset. It results in an acute hemodynamic overload over the left ventricle. The features of left ventricular failure can occur even with relatively moderate leaks during the acute illness. The size of the left atrium also plays a significant role in mitral regurgitation. With acute mitral regurgitation the left atrial size is normal and the increased volume reaching the left atrium increases the left atrial and the pulmonary venous pressure, resulting in pulmonary congestion and features of left ventricular failure. With long standing mitral regurgitation the left atrium increases in size to accommodate the regurgitant volume without increasing the left atrial pressure and features of left ventricular failure are absent. Another important adjustment consists of *decrease in the systemic vascular resistance to help increase the forward flow.* The maximum ejection of blood into the aorta takes place during early systole. The combination of these two factors results in an increased systolic and decreased diastolic pressure in the systemic circuit. The pulse pressure is, therefore, increased resulting in the *small water hammer pulse* of mitral regurgitation.

Clinical Features

On examination the pulse pressure is relatively wide. The resting pulse rate is increased to maintain an adequate cardiac output. In the absence of pulmonary congestion the respiratory rate is normal. Features of left ventricular failure are absent and appear late unless the mitral regurgitation is *acute, severe* or left ventricular *myocardium is failing.* The heart size is dependent on the severity of mitral regurgitation as well as the status of the left ventricular myocardium. The cardiac apex is displaced downward and outward with forcible apex and hyperkinetic precordium. Less than 10% patients have a systolic thrill. The reason for this is the direction of the regurgitant stream, which is backwards into the left atrium. Since the left atrium cannot be felt anteriorly over the precordium, the murmur remains impalpable as a thrill. The first sound may be soft, normal or occasionally accentuated. Generally, it is inaudible as it is masked by the systolic murmur. The second sound is normally split with mild mitral regurgitation. With moderate or severe mitral regurgitation the second sound is widely split but the width of splitting varies with respiration becoming narrower during expiration and wider with inspiration. The wide splitting is due to an early aortic component of the second sound. With failing left ventricle the wide splitting disappears. Except with very mild mitral regurgitation, *a third sound is audible at the apex and indicates increased early rapid filling* of the left ventricle. With severe mitral regurgitation a delayed diastolic mitral murmur starting with the third sound is audible. The delayed diastolic murmur is *secondary to a large flow* across the mitral valve during diastole. Not infrequently this *delayed diastolic murmur* may be palpable as a short diastolic thrill. In pure mitral regurgitation, the delayed diastolic murmur always ends somewhere in *mid-diastole* and there is *no late diastolic (presystolic) accentuation. It may appear unusual but a diastolic thrill in severe mitral regurgitation* is more common than a systolic thrill. The classical diagnostic sign is the pansystolic murmur, best heard at the apex and widely radiating to the axilla and back as well as to the left sternal border (Fig. 14.3). The pansystolic murmur of rheumatic mitral regurgitation is generally not well heard at the second left interspace by the side of the sternum.

EKG shows sinus tachycardia and a normal axis. Signs of left ventricular hypertrophy may be present with long-standing and severe mitral regurgitation. The thoracic

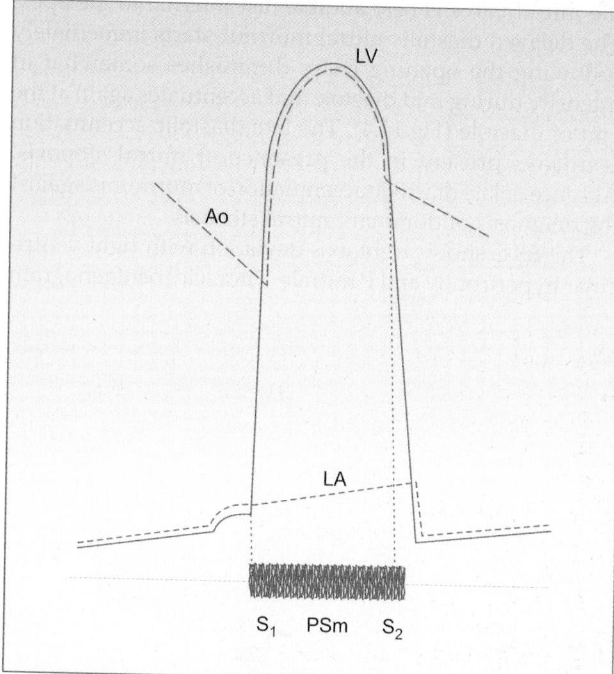

Fig. 14.3: The characteristic pansystolic murmur. As the left ventricular (LV) pressure exceeds the left atrial pressure (LA) the first sound (S_1) occurs. However, the murmur of mitral regurgitation will also start at the same time masking the S_1. Since the maximum difference in the LV and LA pressure is quickly reached and maintained throughout systole, the murmur maintains the same intensity throughout systole appearing pansystolic. Finally as the LV pressure drops below the aortic (Ao) pressure the A_2 occurs. The LV pressure is higher than LA pressure at this time and the murmur goes beyond the A_2 thus masking both the S_1 and and the A_2. (PSm Pansystolic murmur)

roentgenogram shows cardiac enlargement secondary to left ventricular enlargement, the size depending on the severity of mitral regurgitation. Left atrial enlargement may be inferred from the elevation of left bronchus but is more clearly outlined with barium swallow in right anterior oblique position. In the absence of left ventricular failure, there is absence of prominence of pulmonary veins as well as features of pulmonary congestion. Echocardiogram shows enlarged left atrium and ventricle. Doppler echo can quantitate mitral regurgitation non-invasively.

Differential Diagnosis

Besides rheumatic fever, other causes of mitral regurgitation in the pediatric age group include (i) atrial septal defect of the primum variety; (ii) coarctation of the aorta with mitral regurgitation (congenital); (iii) left ventricular fibroelastosis; (iv) congenital corrected transposition of great arteries; (v) papillary muscle dysfunction in dilatation of left ventricle from any cause including myocarditis; (vi) atrial septal defect of the secundum type with floppy mitral valve; (vii) Marfan and Hurler syndrome, and (viii) anomalous origin of left coronary artery from pulmonary artery.

14

Treatment

Mild to moderate mitral regurgitation is tolerated for long periods. The severity of mitral regurgitation increases with time. Medical management consists in the use of digitalis, diuretics and vasodilators besides prophylactic penicillin for prevention of recurrences of rheumatic fever. In the presence of severe mitral regurgitation, operation is indicated. The treatment of choice is mitral valve repair, however, the commonest surgical approach is prosthetic valve repair or replacement. It is indicated if the cardiothoracic ratio is more than 55%. It is necessary to emphasize that valve replacement is not a cure. The patients have to be on anticoagulants as long as they have a prosthetic valve. Putting a 10–12 years old child on anticoagulants and continuing it indefinitely is a major undertaking. Before consideration of valve replacement, one should assess the feasibility of long-term anticoagulation.

Mitral Stenosis

Rheumatic mitral stenosis is less common than mitral regurgitation in children. In our analysis of 850 patients of rheumatic heart disease up to the age of 12 years, the diagnosis of pure mitral stenosis was made in 96 patients. Pediatric mitral stenosis constitutes 10% of all rheumatic mitral stenosis patients.

Hemodynamics

Mitral stenosis results in obstruction to flow of blood across the mitral valve during left ventricular diastole. The left atrium compensates for this obstruction by increasing its pressure. This increase in pressure results in hypertrophy of the left atrial wall. However, the left atrium is a thin walled chamber and the capacity for its hypertrophy is limited. The increase in left atrial pressure prevents decrease in the blood flow across the mitral valve. Since there are no valves between the left atrium and the pulmonary veins, the increased left atrial pressure is transmitted to pulmonary veins as well. The increased pulmonary venous pressure results in pulmonary capillary engorgement and pulmonary congestion, which produces dyspnea, the commonest symptom of mitral stenosis. The pulmonary arterial pressure increases to maintain forward flow from the pulmonary artery to the left side of the heart. Clinically the pulmonary arterial hypertension is recognized by accentuation of the pulmonary component of the second sound. The right ventricle hypertrophies and its systolic pressure increases as pulmonary arterial hypertension increases, since it is the right ventricle that has to maintain the pulmonary pressure as well as the flow.

14

In the absence of tricuspid regurgitation the right ventricular hypertrophy is concentric without an increase in the size of right ventricular chamber. The heart size stays normal. With mild or moderate mitral obstruction, the forward flow through the mitral valve remains normal. With severe mitral obstruction, the forward flow through the mitral valve is diminished. If the flow to the left ventricle decreases, the cardiac output diminishes and peripherally one feels a small volume pulse. The diminished cardiac output in severe mitral stenosis is recognized on the bedside as cold extremities, with or without peripheral cyanosis and a small volume pulse.

The two most unfortunate aspects of mitral stenosis are (i) its occurrence distal to a thin walled left atrium with a limited capacity for hypertrophy, and (ii) absence of valves between the left atrium and the pulmonary veins. The former is the main reason because of which the cardiac output cannot be increased significantly with exercise and if for any reason the systemic pressure falls and the patient goes into shock it is extremely difficult to resuscitate the patient. The latter results in pulmonary congestion and dyspnea with exercise, limiting the capacity of the patient to work even with mild obstruction. In the presence of limited capacity to increase the forward flow, exercise can precipitate pulmonary edema more readily. The right ventricular hypertension can result in tricuspid regurgitation, which is seen in 30% patients with moderate to severe mitral stenosis.

Clinical Features

Boys are affected twice as commonly as girls. The youngest patient with pure mitral stenosis seen in our clinic was 5 years-old. In another patient seen by us at the age of 8 years, the diagnosis of mitral stenosis was made at the age of 4 years elsewhere. Of the operated patients, the youngest was 6 years with histological evidence of rheumatic mitral stenosis, based on evaluation of surgically removed left atrial appendage. The patients of mitral stenosis give history of shortness of breath on exertion or even at rest depending on the severity. Other important symptoms consist of cough, hemoptysis, paroxysmal nocturnal dyspnea, attacks of acute pulmonary edema and atypical angina.

On examination the pulse is of small volume. The respiratory rate is increased except in patients with mild mitral obstruction. Depending on the severity, there may or may not be signs of right sided congestion, in the form of engorged neck veins and enlarged tender liver. The liver may have systolic pulsations if there is associated tricuspid regurgitation, the jugular venous pulse shows prominent 'a' waves. If tricuspid regurgitation is present, the jugular veins show dominant 'V' waves. With moderate or severe mitral stenosis signs of pulmonary congestion in the form of rales are present.

Examination of the precordium reveals a normal sized heart with a tapping apex beat, parasternal impulse and an apical diastolic thrill. The second sound may be palpable at the second left interspace. On auscultation the first sound is accentuated, the second sound normally split with a loud pulmonary component. An opening snap of the mitral valve is best audible just internal to the apex. The delayed diastolic mitral murmur starts immediately following the opening snap, diminishes somewhat in intensity during mid diastole and accentuates again at the end of diastole (Fig.14.4). The late diastolic accentuation is always present in the presence of mitral stenosis. Absence of late diastolic accentuation of murmur is against the diagnosis of dominant mitral stenosis.

The EKG shows right axis deviation with right ventricular hypertrophy and P mitrale. Thoracic roentgenogram

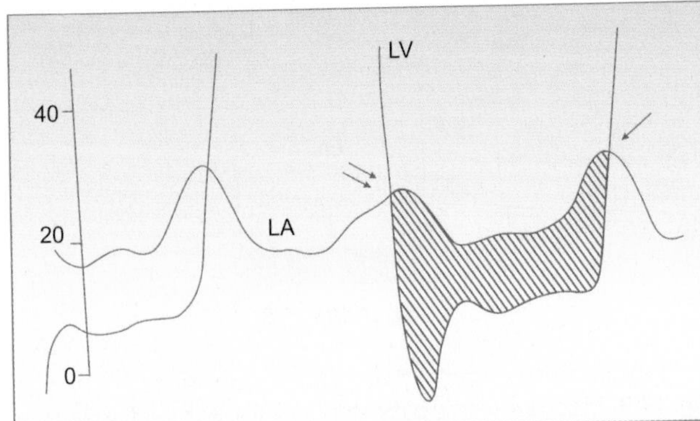

Fig. 14.4: Mitral stenosis. Simultaneous left ventricular (LV) and left atrial (LA) tracing. The shaded area represents the gradient between LV and LA. During this period the delayed diastolic murmur of mitral stenosis is heard. The shape of the murmur on auscultation corresponds to the shape of the diastolic gradient. Presence of gradient at the end diastole (arrow) indicates significant mitral stenosis. The murmur starts after opening snap which will occur when the LV pressure drops below LA pressure (double arrow)

shows a normal sized heart with features of pulmonary venous and arterial hypertension, as well as left atrial enlargement. Echocardiogram shows decreased EF slope, paradoxical posterior leaflet motion, left atrial enlargement and pulmonary arterial hypertension. 2D echo can identify the narrowed mitral opening. Doppler echo provides transmitral gradient accurately noninvasively.

Assessment of severity: The criteria for the clinical diagnosis of mitral stenosis are *accentuated first sound,* the *mitral opening snap* and the *delayed diastolic murmur* with *late diastolic accentuation.* When assessing the severity, one has to separate the severity of mitral obstruction from the degree of pulmonary arterial hypertension. The *severity of mitral stenosis is clinically judged by the distance between the opening snap and the aortic component of the second sound.* The closer the opening snap to the second sound, the more severe is the obstruction. The intensity or duration of the diastolic murmur does not correlate with the severity since mild as well as severe mitral stenosis may result in very soft murmurs. The duration of the murmur depends on the heart rate. An indirect way of assessing the severity of mitral stenosis is by assessing for pulmonary arterial hypertension. Whereas mild pulmonary arterial hypertension may be present with mild, moderate or severe mitral obstruction, severe pulmonary hypertension occurs only with severe obstruction. Echocardiogram combined with Doppler gradient gives more precise assessment of severity. Atrial fibrillation is rare in children.

Differential Diagnosis

Isolated congenital mitral stenosis is very rare. The opening snap is less commonly heard in congenital mitral stenosis. Cortriatriatum, obstruction of pulmonary veins and left atrial myxoma should be excluded.

Treatment

The management of mitral stenosis is essentially surgical. The patients should be digitalized and given diuretics. Digitalis helps by (i) reducing the heart rate and increasing the left ventricular filling; (ii) increasing the left atrial contractility; and (iii) maintaining a slow heart rate and thus a better forward flow.

Closed mitral valvotomy is still the best surgical approach in India. While closed valvotomy can relieve commissural fusion, it cannot accomplish much for subvalvar fusion and shortening of the chordae tendinae. The more the subvalvar pathology, the less satisfactory is the final result. Closed valvotomy, therefore, is not expected to give uniformly good results in all patients. Mitral valvuloplasty may also be done using a balloon, which is introduced through the femoral vein, passed through the atrial septum, positioned in the mitral valve and inflated to reopen the stenosed valve. The results of balloon mitral valvotomy are comparable to closed valvotomy, although the cost and complication rates are higher.

Aortic Regurgitation

Aortic valve involvement in rheumatic heart disease results in aortic regurgitation. Rheumatic aortic stenosis has *not been described in the children.* Clinically pure aortic regurgitation, without associated mitral valve disease, is rare and occurs in 5–8% patients. Pathologically pure rheumatic aortic valve disease is almost unknown.

Hemodynamics

Aortic regurgitation is a backward leak from the aorta into the left ventricle during diastole. This increases the volume of blood reaching the left ventricle. The left ventricle increases in size to accommodate the extra volume. The size of the left ventricle is thus directly related to the degree of aortic leak, unless there is myocardial disease. Because of the backward flow of blood the forward flow is impaired. This is compensated by peripheral vasodilatation as well as increased ejection from the left ventricle during early part of the systole. However, significant aortic regurgitation results in low forward output. The peripheral pulse pressure is wide because of increased systolic and lowered diastolic pressure. Signs of wide pulse pressure in the form of exaggerated arterial and arteriolar pulsations are present unless the aortic regurgitation is mild. Slowing of heart rate increases the diastolic period and increases the regurgitant volume of blood in aortic regurgitation. With good left ventricular myocardial function even moderate aortic regurgitation is tolerated well for long periods. If the left ventricular myocardium is failing the left ventricular diastolic pressure goes up and results in an increase in left atrial pressure and pulmonary congestion.

Significant dilatation of the left ventricle is accompanied with abnormal stress on the mitral valve—papillary muscle complex. This may result in inadequate apposition of the mitral leaflets and appearance of mitral regurgitation.

Clinical Features

Aortic valve disease is more common in boys compared to girls. The main symptom is palpitation, related to the large stroke volume. With mild to moderate aortic regurgitation the forward flow can be raised effectively on exercise. Fatigue is not an early symptom. The pulse pressure is wide. The wider the pulse pressure, the more severe the aortic leak. The diastolic blood pressure may be recorded as zero with severe aortic regurgitation. Prominent carotid pulsations (Corrigan's sign), visible arterial pulsations over the extremity vessels (dancing peripheral arteries) and visible pulsations of the abdominal aorta are evidences of wide pulse pressure from any cause. Holding the middle of the forearm or leg and elevating it discloses a sharply rising and abruptly falling pulse (Corrigan pulse or water hammer pulse). Nodding of head may be present with each systole (de Musset's sign) due to sudden filling of the carotid vessels in severe aortic regurgitation.

Arteriolar pulsations may be seen over the nail bed, uvula, lips, ear lobes and in the eye grounds. There is also exaggeration of the systolic pressure difference between the brachial and femoral arteries (Hill's sign). Normally the difference between the systolic pressure in the brachial artery and the femoral artery is less than 20 mm of mercury, the femoral systolic pressure being higher. Systolic pressure difference between 20 to 40 mm of mercury suggests mild aortic regurgitation. If the difference is between 40 to 60 mm of mercury, it suggests moderate aortic regurgitation. A difference of more than 60 mm of mercury indicates severe aortic regurgitation.

If the stethoscope is put over the brachial or the femoral artery without applying any pressure pistol shot sounds may be heard in moderate or severe aortic regurgitation. A systolic murmur may be heard if pressure is applied to partially occlude the artery proximal to the chest piece and a diastolic murmur if pressure is applied distally. This combination of systolic and diastolic murmurs is the Duroziez sign.

14

Examination of the precordium shows cardiac enlargement with the apex displaced downward and outward. The size itself depends on the degree of aortic leak. The apex is forcible or heaving. With large leaks the whole chest wall may show a *back and forth* movement. Uncommonly a diastolic thrill may be palpable at the upper left or right sternal border. The first sound is soft and the aortic component of the second sound may be audible or may be masked by the regurgitant diastolic murmur. The murmur of aortic regurgitation is a high pitched, decrescendo diastolic murmur starting with the aortic component of the second sound. The intensity and the length of the murmur do not correlate with the severity of aortic regurgitation. The murmur is best heard along the left sternal border and radiates to the apex and even beyond the apex. With large aortic leaks there is also an ejection systolic murmur at the second right interspace, conducted to the neck and not infrequently associated with a systolic thrill. The systolic murmur is the result of a large stroke volume, passing across rough valves. It does not indicate aortic stenosis if the pulse pressure is wide and the carotid upstroke is brisk.

The EKG shows increase in left ventricular voltages with deep 'S' waves in V1 and tall 'R' waves in V6. There are also deep 'Q' waves in left chest leads with tall 'T' waves. The pattern of deep 'Q' waves and tall 'T' waves has been called diastolic overloading of the left ventricle. Chest X-ray shows left ventricular cardiomegaly and dilated ascending aorta. Echocardiogram shows enlarged left ventricle, dilated aorta and flutter of anterior mitral leaflet. A Doppler study quantitates the severity of valvar lesion.

Differential Diagnosis

The differential diagnosis of rheumatic aortic regurgitation includes: (i) *conditions associated with a wide pulse pressure* like patent ductus arteriosus, arteriovenous fistulae, ventricular septal defect with aortic regurgitation, ruptured sinus of Valsalva, anemia and thyrotoxicosis, (ii) *conditions associated with a non-rheumatic regurgitant diastolic murmur* like pulmonary regurgitation, aortic regurgitation with ventricular septal defect, ruptured sinus of Valsalva and congenital aortic valve disease. Congenital aortic valve disease is either a leaking bicuspid aortic valve or aortic stenosis. Pure congenital aortic regurgitation is extremely rare. Other conditions, which may result in aortic regurgitation, include Marfan syndrome, Hurler syndrome and idiopathic aortoarteritis.

Management

Mild to moderate aortic regurgitation is well tolerated for years. Significant aortic regurgitation, if associated with either angina like chest pain or signs of left ventricular failure, can only be managed surgically. Surgical treatment consists of aortic valve replacement, by either homograft or a prosthetic valve. Operative treatment is indicated for patients who have symptoms of either left ventricular failure or angina. Better surgical results are claimed in patients whose cardiothoracic ratio is less than 60%. Cardiothoracic ratio is an unreliable index especially in children. If in a good inspiratory film the cardiothoracic ratio is more than 55%, cardiac enlargement is present.

Before recommending valve replacement surgery one should consider: (i) has rheumatic activity and thus active myocarditis subsided, since active myocarditis by itself can cause cardiac enlargement; (ii) is there any suggestion for progressive deterioration; (iii) is the patient's cardiac status bad enough to warrant prosthetic valve replacement and thus commitment to life long anticoagulation.

Digitalis can be used if the patient has CCF, however, by slowing the heart rate, digitalis increases the regurgitant volume of blood. Treatment with vasodilators, especially ACE inhibitors, is useful.

Aortic Stenosis

Since rheumatic aortic stenosis is not seen in children, this is discussed later in this chapter.

Tricuspid Regurgitation

Features indicative of tricuspid regurgitation are seen in almost 20–50% patients with rheumatic heart disease in our country. In an individual patient it is difficult to decide whether the tricuspid regurgitation is organic or functional.

Hemodynamics

Tricuspid regurgitation results in a systolic backflow of blood from the right ventricle to the right atrium. The systolic leak thus results in a systolic murmur and a volume overload of the right atrium as well as the right ventricle. The volume overload results in an increase in the size of the right atrium as well as the right ventricle, which is *displaced downward and outward.* Usually all patients with tricuspid regurgitation also have pulmonary arterial hypertension. The systolic backflow under pressure results in a prominent systolic wave, the V wave, in the jugular venous pulse as well as the liver. During inspiration the increased venous return increases the flow across the tricuspid valve. Thus both the systolic as well as the diastolic murmurs at the tricuspid valve become louder during inspiration. In patients of rheumatic heart disease the tricuspid regurgitation may be associated either with mitral stenosis or with mitral regurgitation. If the tricuspid regurgitation is associated with mitral stenosis it may be either organic or functional due to pulmonary arterial hypertension. If, on the other hand, the tricuspid regurgitation is associated with dominant or pure mitral regurgitation it is most likely organic. This is because mitral regurgitation of a severity to result in pulmonary arterial hypertension of a degree to cause functional tricuspid regurgitation is rare.

Clinical Features

There are no specific symptoms of tricuspid regurgitation. It is possible that with the onset of tricuspid regurgitation the dyspnea may be relieved to some extent in patients of mitral stenosis. The patients may give history of pain in the right hypochondrium due to a congested liver and of fatigue due to a decrease in systemic output. Specific features of tricuspid regurgitation consist of (i) prominent V waves in the jugular venous pulse, (ii) systolic pulsations of the liver, and (iii) a systolic murmur at the lower left sternal border increasing in intensity with inspiration. With milder degrees of regurgitation it is not unusual to have no systolic murmur during expiration, whereas a grade II–III ejection or pansystolic murmur appears during inspiration. With severe tricuspid regurgitation a loud grade III to IV pansystolic murmur is heard at the lower left sternal border, which varies little with inspiration and can be associated with a thrill, (iv) a right ventricular third sound or a short tricuspid delayed diastolic murmur increasing in intensity during inspiration, may be audible in marked tricuspid regurgitation.

In addition to the above features there are signs of pulmonary hypertension and mitral valve disease. In association with mitral stenosis, severe tricuspid regurgitation may result in marked dilatation of the right ventricle and the whole of the anterior surface, including the apex may be formed by the right ventricle. In such patients the apex beat is not only displaced outward but also downward. This should not be mistaken for left ventricular enlargement. In these cases the pansystolic murmur of tricuspid regurgitation may be heard from the lower left sternal border to the apex. Since the left ventricle is displaced backwards, the mitral stenosis murmur may be audible only in the axilla or may not be made out at all. It is not uncommon for these patients to be diagnosed as those of mitral regurgitation. Besides the peripheral signs of tricuspid regurgitation, the EKG is helpful in separating these cases from mitral regurgitation. Patients of tricuspid regurgitation of this severity almost always show severe right ventricular hypertrophy on EKG. Contrast echo and Doppler can document and quantitate the severity of tricuspid regurgitation as well as findings of left sided disease.

Management

All patients with findings of tricuspid regurgitation should be put on anticongestive measures whether the tricuspid regurgitation is associated with mitral stenosis or with mitral regurgitation. This will help in reducing the severity of tricuspid regurgitation. Further management depends on the associated mitral valve lesion. Patients of mitral stenosis may loose all evidences of tricuspid regurgitation following mitral valvotomy. Patients of tricuspid regurgitation in association with mitral regurgitation generally have severe mitral regurgitation. They should initially be treated conservatively. If, however, there is evidence of deterioration or lack of improvement during follow up, the patient may have to be sent up for mitral valve repair or replacement. At the time of operation the tricuspid valve can be inspected and tricuspid annuloplasty or repair performed.

Clinical Problems in Patients with Rheumatic Heart Disease

There are two major problems that one faces in patients of rheumatic heart disease: (i) Does the patient have active or inactive rheumatic fever? and (ii) in a febrile patient, is it active rheumatic fever or infective endocarditis?

Active or Inactive Rheumatic Fever?

A lot of 'judgment' or personal bias is generally involved in this decision. For the diagnosis of activity one has to use the Jones criteria. Presence of cardiac involvement cannot be used as a major criterion since the carditis may be the result of a previous attack of rheumatic fever. However, presence of a pericardial friction rub is evidence of active carditis. If the patient has well documented cardiac findings then the appearance of a new murmur or a significant increase in a pre-existing murmur is very suggestive for active rheumatic fever. History of arthralgia or arthritis within a period of less than 12 weeks is suggestive of active rheumatic fever specially if associated with elevated sedimentation rate and ASO titer. Despite CCF it is unusual for the sedimentation rate to be normal in a patient of active rheumatic fever. All patients of rheumatic heart disease must have elevated ASO titer before they can be labeled as *active*. The difficulty arises in those patients who have relatively low levels of the ASO titer. In such cases unless serial serum samples are available it is difficult to decide whether there has been a rise in the level of the ASO titer.

While foreign literature has emphasized that the presence of CCF in children suggests active carditis, this is not true in India. Patients of severe mitral stenosis with tricuspid regurgitation and CCF are not infrequent in India, though unknown in western countries. Patients with severe mitral regurgitation and CCF without rheumatic activity are also common. Presence of CCF cannot therefore be equated with rheumatic activity.

In a Febrile Patient, is it Active Rheumatic Fever or Infective Endocarditis?

At times separation of rheumatic activity from infective endocarditis can be difficult. The arguments used above for separating active from inactive rheumatic fever can be employed for the diagnosis of active rheumatic fever. The diagnosis of infective endocarditis should be suspected in any cardiac patient who has *unexplained fever* of 7–10 days in the presence of embolic phenomena. Embolic phenomena, however, are rarely diagnosed unless the central nervous system is involved. The term unexplained fever indicates that causes of fever like typhoid fever, malaria should be investigated and excluded.

14

Patients of infective endocarditis have loss of appetite, general weakness, malaise, headache and loss of weight. They may show petechiae, splinter hemorrhages, Roth's spots, clubbing and splenomegaly. Janeway lesions and Osler's nodes are rare in children, however, arthralgia is not uncommon. The temperature in the subacute variety of infective endocarditis generally does not go beyond 38.5°C. It is not uncommon, however, especially in patients who seek help late in the course of endocarditis or those who have received antibiotics in inadequate doses to have low grade fever. They may show occasional spikes when the temperature goes up to 37.5°C but mostly fluctuates around 36.8°C.

Investigations show normocytic normochromic anemia with hemoglobin level of 7–10 g/dL. The leukocyte count is less than 10,000/cu mm in 50%; thrombocytopenia may occur. Urine examination shows mild albuminuria and microscopic hematuria. Multiple fresh urine specimens should be examined. The diagnostic investigation is blood culture. Both aerobic and anaerobic cultures should be obtained. At least three cultures are taken at half-hr intervals, each sample of 10 mL. Despite best efforts only about 50% patients yield positive culture; the antibiotic sensitivity guides the choice of antibiotics. The culture should be preserved through subcultures so that the effectiveness of the treatment can be ascertained. Five days after starting treatment, patient's serum is used in dilutions to determine whether adequate bactericidal levels are achieved. Echocardiogram is a highly sensitive non-invasive technique for identifying endocarditis. Vegetations of 2 mm or more can be detected.

If the separation of rheumatic activity from infective endocarditis is in doubt because of negative cultures or low levels of ASO titer, it is best to give a therapeutic trial. Since infective endocarditis is more serious, the patient should first be treated for this condition.

Suggested reading

1. Committee of the American Heart Association. Jones criteria (revised) for guidance in the diagnosis of rheumatic fever. Circulation 1965; 32: 664.
2. Guidelines for the diagnosis of rheumatic fever. JAMA 1992; 268: 2069–2073.
3. Narula J, et al. Rheumatic fever. Am Registry Path AFIP. Washington DC, 1999.

INFECTIVE ENDOCARDITIS

Infection of the endocardial lining of the heart is called infective endocarditis. Infection may occur over the endocardium of the valves or the mural endocardium as well as the endothelium of the blood vessels. The most common site of infection is generally a diseased valve from where the infection can spread to the mural endocardium or the vascular endothelium. Initially the term used was bacterial endocarditis, acute and subacute. Following the realization that infective organisms other than bacteria, like fungi or rickettsiae, can also result in infection the term used is infective endocarditis. Infective endocarditis has significant morbidity, and mortality, at times, changing the prognosis of an otherwise benign lesion markedly. It should be considered as a medical emergency since it can damage the valves, the myocardium and other parts of the body like the brain and the kidneys.

Predisposing Factors

Infective endocarditis predominantly occurs in a diseased heart. In children the common underlying disease could be congenital heart disease including mitral valve prolapse syndrome or rheumatic heart disease. Rarely infection can occur in an otherwise normal heart as part of generalized septicemia, presenting as acute endocarditis. The commonest congenital lesions involved in infective endocarditis are those with a ventricular septal defect (VSD) or aortic valve disease. Thus isolated VSD, VSD with aortic regurgitation, Fallot's tetralogy, tricuspid atresia, valvar aortic stenosis or a bicuspid aortic valve in coarctation of the aorta are generally the commonest lesions associated with endocarditis. Endocarditis can occur following a shunt as in Blalock Taussig shunt. Other congenital lesions not uncommonly associated with endocarditis are patent ductus arteriosus, pulmonic stenosis and mitral valve prolapse syndrome. It is rare in atrial septal defect of the secundum type unless associated with mitral valve prolapse. Endocarditis affects the mitral or aortic valve in patients with rheumatic heart disease. Patients with prosthetic valves or those with recent cardiac surgery are prone to endocarditis. Infections anywhere in body, e.g. pyoderma, tooth abscess, ear infection, urinary infection or osteomyelitis may result in endocarditis. Although interventions like dental procedures, cardiac catheterization, genitourinary procedures or bronchoscopy can result in endocarditis, it is rare to identify a predisposing event. The most common predisposition for endocarditis in children is poor dental hygiene.

Drug addicts, especially those using the parenteral route, are prone to right sided endocarditis, involving the tricuspid or pulmonary valve; endocarditis can also affect mitral and/or aortic valves.

Pathogenesis

The pathogenesis of endocarditis depends on the invasiveness and virulence of the infective organisms. The earlier nomenclature of subacute or acute endocarditis was dependent on the course of the disease. In the pre-antibiotic era patients with acute endocarditis (septicemia) died within six weeks whereas the subacute type of endocarditis, almost always lethal, caused death in about six months. The infection generally starts at a jet lesion, that is, where the high pressure jet in a ventricular septal defect or aortic stenosis hits the endocardium or the endothelium. The right ventricular mural endocardium or the tricuspid valve in ventricular septal defect, aortic endothelium in aortic stenosis or coarctation of the aorta, ventricular surface of the aortic valve in aortic regurgitation are the usual sites.

Bacteremia resulting from an infection such as a boil, furuncle, otitis media or initiated by an intervention such as cardiac or urinary catheterization or dental extraction is necessary for the initiation of endocarditis. Bacteremia may also result from simple day to day events such as brushing teeth. Bacteria that are deposited on the endocardium are covered by fibrin and platelets forming vegetations. Almost any species of bacteria and some species of fungi can cause endocarditis. *S. viridians, S. aureus,* enterococci, *P. aeruginosa* and some gram negative bacilli are responsible for endocarditis. Fungal endocarditis may occur in hospitalized patients with indwelling central venous catheters.

Clinical Features

The presence of unexplained fever of 7–10 days duration in a patient with known heart disease should raise the suspicion of endocarditis. Patients may also show other features of endocarditis. *S. viridans* results in a subacute form of illness while *S. aureus* and other pyogenic organisms cause a fulminant (acute) and rapidly progressive illness. It is possible, however, for an organism like staphylococci to cause a subacute form of illness. Identification of endocarditis by the organism is preferable, as it helps in deciding the choice of antibiotics as well. Another useful way for identifying endocarditis is by the underlying setting, e.g. postoperative endocarditis, prosthetic valve endocarditis, endocarditis in drug addicts, etc.

Infective endocarditis is rare below the age of two years. The clinical features are divided into (i) indicating the presence of an infection; (ii) indicating involvement of the cardiovascular system; and (iii) indicating the presence of an immunological reaction to infection. The features indicating the presence of infection consist of fever, chills, rigors, night sweats, general malaise, weakness, loss of appetite, weight loss and amenorrhea in females. Arthralgia and diffuse myalgia can occur, however, arthritis does not occur except in acute endocarditis as part of septicemia when it is likely to be monarticular.

Features indicative of the involvement of the cardiovascular system may be absent in the initial stages. The acute occurrence of left or right heart failure, development of a new murmur or change in a pre-existing murmur, and features suggesting embolic events (e.g. hemiparesis from stroke, hematuria from renal infarct, left flank pain from splenic infarct, and gastrointestinal hemorrhage from mesenteric embolism) is suggestive. Murmurs due to aortic, mitral or tricuspid regurgitation may appear; the regurgitant lesions progress rapidly causing hemodynamic changes, resulting in CCF.

Features of immunological response presenting as vasculitis due to infection consist of arthralgia, myalgia, petechiae, Osler's nodes, Janeway lesion, clubbing, splenomegaly and microscopic hematuria. Splinter hemorrhages are hemorrhagic spots under the nails, though suggestive, are not specific for endocarditis as they can result from minor injuries. Petechiae over the skin or mucous membranes and conjunctiva are seen in about 50% patients. Petechiae in the retina are called Roth's spots. Osler's nodes are tender erythematous nodules over the pulp of finger tips, but are relatively rare. Janeway lesions are non-tender erythematous patches on the palms and soles. Clubbing and splenomegaly tend to appear 3-weeks after the onset of endocarditis.

In the acute form the symptoms progress rapidly with high fever, chills and rigors. Perforation of valve cusps results in acute aortic or mitral regurgitation with progressive downhill course and death within 6-weeks from the onset. In acute endocarditis, metastatic lesions causing abscesses in the central nervous system or elsewhere in the body (acute arthritis, splenic or mesenteric abscess, brain abscess or osteomyelitis) are common. Metastatic abscesses are rare in subacute endocarditis.

Patients with endocarditis of the right side such as the tricuspid or the pulmonary valve throw emboli to the lungs. The embolic episodes to lungs may present as repeated episodes of pneumonitis or septic infarcts resulting in lung abscesses. This is common with intravenous drug abusers and patients with VSD.

Postoperative endocarditis is classified as early (within 60 days) and late (after 60 days). Early endocarditis is due to pyogenic organisms (staphylococcus, pseudomonas, gram negative bacilli) introduced at the time of operation. The patients have high fever with chills and rigors and features of septicemia. Late endocarditis is like native valve endocarditis and the commonest organisms are *S. viridans* and gram negative bacilli. The patients tend to follow the subacute course. Cardiac surgery is an important risk factor for gram negative endocarditis. Prosthetic valve endocarditis may also be early or late; fungal infection of prosthetic valves is associated with high mortality.

The risk of ***fungal endocarditis*** has increased especially following cardiac surgery and in intensive care settings. Candida is the commonest fungus responsible; infection with histoplasma, blastomyces, aspergillus, cryptococcus and mucor may occur. Predisposing factors for fungal endocarditis include intravenous drug abuse, indwelling catheters, intensive antibiotic therapy, prolonged steroid administration, radiation, immunosuppressive therapy and prosthetic valves. The incidence of embolism is high, since fungal vegetations tend to be large.

Diagnosis

A positive blood culture, in a patient with underlying heart disease, suspected to have endocarditis is confirmatory for the diagnosis. Three blood cultures, each of 10 mL, taken with meticulous aseptic precautions every half hour are recommended. It has been shown that three blood cultures shall detect over 95% cases with a positive blood culture. Unfortunately in most reports in our country almost 50% patients with endocarditis have negative blood cultures, the commonest cause being previous antibiotic therapy. Arterial sampling does not offer any advantage over venous sampling. Other causes of culture negative endocarditis are technical errors in obtaining specimens and inappropriate culture techniques. Infection with unusual organisms, anaerobic organisms and fungi require special culture media and incubation for 2–3 weeks.

Other investigations, which provide supportive evidence for diagnosis, are:

a. *Normocytic normochromic anemia:* Hemoglobin level around 10 g/dL.
b. *White cell count:* In subacute presentation, leukocyte counts are normal in approximately 50% patients. In acute endocarditis, leukocyte counts are usually elevated.
c. *Platelet count* may be reduced.
d. *Elevated sedimentation rate* in almost all patients. In the presence of advanced CCF or renal insufficiency, sedimentation rates can be normal.
e. *Microscopic hematuria* and albuminuria are present in 90% cases.
f. *Immunological investigations:* Investigations, which suggest endocarditis, include increased gamma globulins, false positive serology for syphilis, cryoglobulinemia, low complement levels and circulating immune complexes. Specific antibodies against causative organism may be increased, e.g. high ASO titer in streptococcal endocarditis and anti-teichoic acid antibodies in staphylococcal endocarditis. Rheumatoid factor is positive in approximately 50% cases and normalizes after treatment.

Echocardiography is a sensitive diagnostic tool for detecting vegetations, including in patients with culture negative endocarditis. Echocardiography also identifies complications like ruptured chordae, perforated cusps and flail cusps resulting from endocarditis. Vegetations more than 2 mm can be identified by echocardiography. The sensitivity of echocardiographic identification of endocarditis is dependent on the site of involvement. For aortic and mitral valves the sensitivity is more than 90%, and for tricuspid and pulmonary valves it is 70%. The presence of vegetations correlates well with the diagnosis of infective endocarditis. If vegetations can be demonstrated, the probability of having endocarditis is around 94%. If vegetations are absent, the probability of not having endocarditis is 92%. However, echocardiography is an operator dependent investigation and its utility depends on how meticulously it is performed. Potential limitations of echocardiography in older children can be overcome by transesophageal echocardiography (TEE). Occasionally in smaller children too, TEE proves valuable in arriving at a diagnosis. TEE is particularly useful in prosthetic valve endocarditis and when complications such as a valve ring abscess are suspected.

Complications

Damage to valve cusps or perforation, rupture of chordae tendinae result in acute regurgitant lesions causing sudden hemodynamic deterioration. Migration of vegetations may result in embolic neurological deficit, renal infarcts with hematuria, mesenteric infarct and melena, loss of fingers or toes due to obstruction of blood supply. Damage to the vasa vasorum of blood vessels due to vasculitis may result in the formation of mycotic aneurysms, which can rupture and result in massive bleeding. Sinus of Valsalva aneurysms following endocarditis of the aortic valve are not uncommon.

The kidneys may be affected in many ways. They may have embolic infarct with hematuria, or show postinfectious GN or membranoproliferative GN resulting in albuminuria, microscopic hematuria and acute renal dysfunction. The finding of IgG, IgM and complement deposits on the glomerular basement membrane indicate that it is an immune complex nephritis. Renal insufficiency tends to appear beyond three weeks of the onset of endocarditis and is progressive until the endocarditis has been cured. Hematuria can persist for three to six months even after the endocarditis has been cured. However, even advanced renal insufficiency tends to regress and renal function tends to return toward normal after the endocarditis has been cured. Presence of mild to moderate renal insufficiency should not be viewed as a poor prognostic sign.

Treatment

The treatment of endocarditis can be considered under two headings: (a) treatment of the current episode, and (b) prevention of endocarditis. Principles of management are: (i) identification of the organism; (ii) determining its antibiotic sensitivity; (iii) starting treatment as early as possible; and (iv) using bactericidal antimicrobial agent(s) for an appropriate duration to obtain cure and prevent relapse.

If the blood culture is positive, the choice of antibiotics is dictated by the antibiotic sensitivity. If the culture is negative empirical therapy covering a wide range of organisms is necessary. Once an organism is detected, the culture plate should not be discarded. After starting treatment, the patient's serum, diluted 1:8 parts or more, may be used to determine if it shall inhibit the growth of the organism, indicating the efficacy of treatment. Organisms causing endocarditis, choice of antibiotics and duration of treatment is shown in Table 14.9.

Penicillin sensitive *S. viridans* endocarditis is treated with penicillin combined with an aminoglycoside (gentamicin or amikacin). Patients allergic to penicillin should receive cefazolin. Patients sensitive to both penicillin and cephalosporins should be treated with vancomycin. For *S. fecalis,* the regimen of choice is a combination of ampicillin combined with an aminoglycoside. Endocarditis secondary to infection with *S. aureus* is treated with the combination of cloxacillin and an aminoglycoside or combination of vancomycin with an aminoglycoside. Fungal endocarditis is treated with either amphotericin alone or its combination with flucytosine. Surgical excision of the infected valve may be necessary; relapses of endocarditis may occur.

Culture negative endocarditis: Patients with culture negative endocarditis need empiric treatment. The choice of treatment lies between a combination of ampicillin with an aminoglycoside or combination of cloxacillin and an aminoglycoside.

Prophylaxis

Prophylaxis of endocarditis in patients with known valvar or congenital heart disease is the responsibility of the treating physician. The patients should be warned regarding the possibility of endocarditis if extracardiac infections are not treated properly. The recommended antibiotic prophylaxis is as follows.

Dental treatment: Penicillin V 2 g by mouth on an empty stomach one hour before dental treatment, followed by 0.5 g every 6 hours for 3 days; *or* crystalline penicillin G one million units mixed with 600,000 U of procaine penicillin given IM 30–60 minutes before procedure, followed by oral penicillin V as above; *or* single dose of amoxicillin 50 mg/kg by mouth one hour earlier. Alternatively the patient can receive a single injection of various forms of penicillin (300,000 units of crystalline, 300,000 units of procaine and 600,000 units of benzathine penicillin) one hr before the procedure. Patients with prosthetic heart valves should receive IM penicillin with streptomycin or gentamicin one hr before the procedure.

Genitourinary and gastrointestinal operations: Amoxicillin 25 mg/kg by mouth one hr before and 2 mg/kg IM gentamicin 30 minutes before the operation. Patients who are going in for gastrointestinal operations should be given metronidazole in addition. Amoxicillin and gentamicin are repeated at least for two more doses after the procedure.

Summary

Infective endocarditis is a life threatening disease with high mortality (30%) and morbidity. Recovery of renal function following cure of endocarditis is satisfactory. It is the responsibility of the treating physicians to advise patients and parents regarding prevention of endocarditis. The patients should be treated aggressively with bactericidal antibiotics, according to sensitivity and for a long enough period to prevent relapses.

Suggested reading

1. Durack DT. Prevention of infective endocarditis. NEJM 1995; 332: 38–44.
2. Durack DT, Crawford MH. Infective endocarditis. Cardiology Clinics. Saunders, Pennsylvania, 2003.

FETAL CIRCULATION

Most of the information regarding fetal circulation has been obtained from animal studies specially the sheep.

Table 14.9: Choice of antibiotics and duration of treatment for infective endocarditis

Organism	*Antibiotic of choice*		*Duration*
	Option I	*Option II*	
Streptococcus viridians	Penicillin and aminoglycoside	Cefazolin and aminoglycoside	4 wks
Group A streptococci	Penicillin and aminoglycoside	Cefazolin and aminoglycoside	4 wks
Streptococcus fecalis	Ampicillin and aminoglycoside	Vancomycin and aminoglycoside	6 wks
Staphylococcus aureus	Cloxacillin and aminoglycoside	Vancomycin and aminoglycoside	6 wks
Escherichia coli	Ceftriaxone and aminoglycoside	Ampicillin and aminoglycoside	6 wks
Pseudomonas	Ticarcillin and aminoglycoside		6 wks
Culture negative	Ampicillin and aminoglycoside	Cloxacillin and aminoglycoside	6 wks

14

Observations obtained from human fetuses, indicate that the course of circulation is quite similar to that found in fetal lambs. The heart assumes its normal four-chambered shape by the end of six weeks of intrauterine life. From then on only minor changes occur and consist mainly in the growth of the heart as a whole with increasing age of the fetus. However, significant differences exist between the fetal circulation and postnatal circulation.

For the exchange of gases, the fetus is dependent on placental circulation, whereas the neonate is dependent on the lungs. Following birth, with the first inspiration, the lungs expand with air and the gas exchange function is transferred from the placenta to the lungs. This necessitates circulatory adjustments following birth to transform the fetal circulation to the postnatal circulation. The route of blood flow in the fetus is different from that in the postnatal state. Blood oxygenated in the placenta is returned by way of the umbilical veins, which enter the fetus at the umbilicus and course through to join the portal vein. The ductus venosus provides a low resistance bypass between the portal vein and the inferior vena cava. Most of the umbilical venous blood shunts through the ductus venosus to the interior vena cava. Only a small proportion mixes with the portal venous blood and passes through the liver. The inferior vena cava blood comprising the streams of hepatic veins, umbilical veins and that reaching the inferior vena cava directly from lower extremities and kidneys enters the right atrium. On reaching the right atrium the bloodstream is divided into two portions by the inferior margin of the septum secundum—the crista dividens. About one-third of the total inferior vena cava blood enters the left atrium, through the foramen ovale, the rest two-thirds mixes with the venous return from the superior vena cava to enter the right ventricle.

The blood reaching the left atrium from the right atrium mixes with the small amount of blood reaching the left atrium through the pulmonary veins and passes to the left ventricle. The left ventricle pumps out the blood into the ascending aorta for distribution to the coronaries, head and upper extremities. The superior vena cava stream, comprising blood returning from the head and arms, passes almost directly to the right ventricle. Only minor quantities (1–3%) of this stream reaches the left atrium. The right ventricle pumps out blood into the pulmonary trunk. A small amount of this blood enters the pulmonary circulation, the rest passes through the ductus arteriosus into the descending aorta to mix with the small amount of blood reaching the descending aorta from the aortic arch (derived from the left ventricle).

In summary the main differences between the fetal circulation and postnatal circulation consist of (i) presence of placental circulation which provides the gas exchange for the fetus; (ii) absence of gas exchange in the collapsed lungs; this results in very little flow of blood to the lungs and consequently very little pulmonary venous return to the left atrium; (iii) presence of ductus venosus, joining the portal vein with the inferior vena cava thus providing a low resistance bypass for umbilical venous blood to reach the inferior vena cava; (iv) widely open foramen ovale to provide a route to the oxygenated blood coming through the umbilical veins to reach the left atrium and ventricle for distribution to the coronaries and the brain; and lastly (v) widely open ductus arteriosus to allow the right ventricular blood to reach the descending aorta since the lungs are non-functioning.

Distribution, Oxygen Saturation and Partial Pressures of Oxygen

The umbilical venous blood has a saturation of about 80% and a pO_2 of 32–35. The mixing of umbilical venous blood with inferior vena cava stream results in a reduction of oxygen saturation to about 70%. The inferior vena caval blood represents approximately 65–70% of total venous return to the heart. One-third of the inferior vena caval stream enters the left atrium after crossing the foramen ovale. It mixes with the pulmonary venous return comprising of about 8% of the total venous return to the heart. The blood reaching the left ventricle has a saturation of about 65% and a pO_2 of 26–28. The left ventricular output is approximately a half of the right ventricular output. The right ventricle receives most of the superior vena caval blood, which constitutes about 22–25% of the total venous return to the heart. The superior vena caval blood has a saturation of about 40% and pO_2 of 12–14. It mixes with the inferior vena caval stream reaching the right ventricle as well as the coronary sinus flow. The blood reaching the pulmonary artery has a saturation of about 50–55% and a pO_2 of 16–18. The saturation of blood in the descending aorta is about 55–60% and pO_2 20–22 mm.

In postnatal life the blood leaving the right ventricle, after coursing through the lungs, reaches the left ventricle. Two ventricles are connected in series and therefore, the outputs of right and left ventricles are approximately identical. In the fetus very little of the right ventricular output reaches the left ventricle through the lungs, the rest goes through the ductus arteriosus into the descending aorta. The two ventricles are, therefore, in parallel. The left ventricle supplies the head and upper extremities, while the right ventricle supplies the trunk, viscera and the lower extremities.

Intravascular Pressures in the Fetus

The aorta and the pulmonary trunk are connected by a wide ductus arteriosus. This results in identical pressures in the two great arteries (aorta and pulmonary trunk), approximately 70/45 mm Hg. The systolic pressure in the right and left ventricles are also identical and approximate 70 mm Hg. The volume of blood reaching the right atrium is considerably larger than that reaching the left atrium. In fact the latter's main source of blood is through the right atrium. The right atrial mean pressure (4 mm Hg) is slightly higher than the mean pressure of the left atrium

(3 mm). In the fetal lamb the pulmonary trunk and right ventricular pressures are about 5–8 mm of Hg higher than the left ventricular and aortic pressures toward the end of the pregnancy.

The blood flow to various organs in the fetus is determined by local vascular resistance. In postnatal life, all pressure measurements are in relation to the atmospheric pressure. The intravascular pressures of the fetus, indicated above, are expressed in relation to the intra-amniotic pressure. The intra-amniotic pressure is 10–12 mm Hg higher than the atmospheric pressure. The intra-amniotic pressure varies directly with intra-abdominal pressure and with uterine contractions. Intravascular pressures of the fetus are, therefore, affected by changes in the intra-amniotic pressures. The fetal heart rate decreases and the blood pressure rises, with increasing maturity of the fetus.

Circulatory Adjustments at Birth

Circulatory adjustments occur immediately following birth and continue to occur for a variable period of time following birth. This change is brought about because of a shift from placental dependence for gas exchange in the fetus to pulmonary gas exchange in the neonate. Loss of placental circulation and clamping of the umbilical cord, after birth, results in a sudden increase in systemic vascular resistance due to loss of the low resistance placental circulation. This tends to increase the aortic blood pressure and the left ventricular systolic pressure. The left ventricular diastolic pressure also tends to rise and increases the left atrial pressure. The loss of placental circulation results in a sudden reduction of flow through the ductus venosus, which closes off. Flow through the ductus venosus disappears by the 7th day of postnatal life. The loss of placental flow results in a decrease in the volume of blood returning to the right atrium. The right atrial pressure decreases. The left atrial pressure becomes higher than the right atrial pressure and the septum primum, which acts as a valve of the fossa ovalis, approximates with the septum secundum to close off the foramen ovale. Functional closure of the foramen ovale occurs very quickly. Over a period of months to year, the septum primum and septum secundum become adherent resulting in anatomical closure of the foramen ovale.

Sudden expansion of lungs with the first few breaths causes a fall in pulmonary vascular resistance and an increased flow into the pulmonary arteries. The pulmonary artery pressure falls due to lowering of pulmonary vascular resistance. The pressure relations between the aorta and pulmonary trunk are reversed so that the flow through the ductus is reversed. Instead of blood flowing from the pulmonary artery to aorta, the direction of flow through the ductus, is from the aorta to pulmonary trunk. Although the exact mechanism for the closure of ductus arteriosus is not known, the musculature of the ductus arteriosus has been shown to be sensitive to change in oxygen saturation. An increase in the blood oxygen saturation causes the muscle of the ductus arteriosus to constrict and close. In full term neonates, the ductus arteriosus closes within 10–21 days.

This results in the establishment of the postnatal circulation. The blood reaching the right atrium through the superior and inferior vena cava is emptied into the right ventricle and pumped into the pulmonary trunk. After gas exchange in the lungs, it reaches the left atrium and ventricle. The latter pumps it out for oxygenation of the tissues. The venous return again comes back to the right atrium. The two ventricles are connected in series and have identical outputs. Over the next several weeks, the pulmonary vascular resistance, pulmonary artery and right ventricular pressures continue to decline. The adult relationship of pressures and resistances in the pulmonary and systemic circulations is established by the end of 2–3 weeks (Fig. 14.5).

CONGENITAL HEART DISEASE

The purpose of this chapter is not to give a detailed account of individual congenital cardiac lesions. Excellent textbooks are available for the reader who is interested in details of individual lesions. We intend to approach the problem faced by a pediatrician when evaluating a child with a heart murmur. The questions that the pediatrician has to answer are:

I. Does the child have heart disease?
II. Is it congenital heart disease?
III. If it is congenital heart disease, what is the lesion?
IV. What is the severity of the lesion?

Firstly, a decision has to be made in any patient whether the murmur represents heart disease or is it the so-called

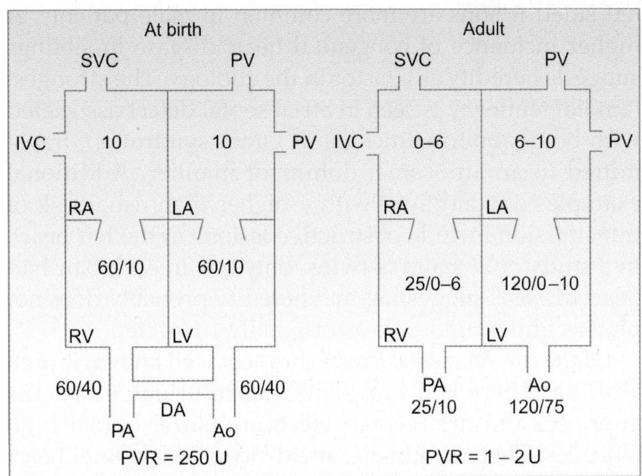

Fig. 14.5: Pressure and resistance in the right and left-sided chambers and vessels at birth compared to adults. SVC superior vena cava; IVC inferior vena cava; RA right atrium; LA left atrium; RV right ventricle; LV left ventricle; PV Pulmonary vein; PA pulmonary artery; Ao aorta; PVR peripheral vascular resistance; DA ductus arteriosus

"functional" murmur. If heart disease is present then we have to separate congenital from non-congenital lesions. Based on the classical features of the individual lesions one can then make a specific diagnosis. Once the specific diagnosis is made, the decision as to what is to be done for the patient depends on the severity of the lesion. Let us not forget that palliation or curative treatment is most often surgical treatment. Cardiac operations are major operations. The diagnosis has to be precise and accurate. The decision regarding operation is dependent on the type and severity of the lesion as well as the type of surgical help available.

Incidence

The prevalence of congenital cardiac lesions in India is not known. The incidence of congenital cardiac lesions at birth was originally estimated to be 6–8 per 1000 live births in the Western countries. Recently it has been realized that the incidence is higher, especially if all of the newborns are followed up to the age of 1-year, since some of the conditions may not be manifest in the first few weeks of life. Recent figures from the Western literature suggest the incidence to be about 1/100 live births. This figure does not include congenital bicuspid aortic valve (2/1000) or congenital mitral valve prolapse syndrome (6/1000). Congenital heart diseases comprise 17% of all cardiac cases in the outpatient cardiac clinic of the AIIMS hospital.

Etiology

The etiology of the majority of congenital heart diseases is not known and in most situations no specific directions can be given regarding prevention of congenital cardiac lesions. Both genders are equally affected, though for individual lesions there may be some differences. Right sided lesions are more common in female patients and left sided lesions are more common in male patients. A higher incidence of congenital heart disease in siblings suggests heredity as a factor in the etiology. The strongest familial tendency is seen in atrial septal defect associated with bony abnormalities (Holt Oram syndrome), transmitted in an autosomal dominant manner. Additional examples of conditions with a higher than usual risk of transmission include obstructive lesions in the left heart. In a study of 26 pairs of twins, only one in each pair had heart disease, suggesting that heredity probably does not play as important a role as originally suspected.

Of the *environmental factors* the most well known is high altitude. There is a higher incidence of patent ductus arteriosus and atrial septal defects in children born at high altitudes. There is a higher incidence of congenital heart disease in children of mothers with diabetes mellitus. The occurrence of rubella in the first trimester of pregnancy may result in patent ductus arteriosus and/or branch pulmonary artery stenosis. Maternal intake of thalidomide or alcohol and maternal phenylketonuria are known to result in specific types of congenital heart disease.

Genetic and chromosomal aberrations are also known to predispose to congenital heart disease. The list of specific chromosomal disorders linked to congenital heart defects is growing. Trisomy 21, 13 and 18 and Turner syndrome are associated with a high frequency of congenital heart disease. Marfan syndrome, Ehler-Danlos syndrome and Hurler syndromes may be associated with congenital heart disease. Partial deletion of chromosome 22 (CATCH 22 syndrome, Di-George syndrome) is being increasingly recognized in association with conotruncal malformations (e.g. tetralogy of Fallot, persistent truncus arteriosus, ventricular septal defect with interruption of the aortic arch).

Diagnostic Implications of Circulatory Changes at Birth

In the section on fetal circulation, it was pointed out that the lungs are sparingly perfused since the oxygen and nutritional requirements of the fetus are derived from the mother through the placenta. After birth, the lungs expand and provide oxygenation of blood. *The increased flow of blood* to the pulmonary artery passing through the lungs and reaching the left atrium, *increases the left atrial pressure.* The effect of this is that the septum primum approximates with the septum secundum and the foramen ovale closes functionally. Clamping of the cord increases the systemic vascular resistance (resistance to flow of blood in the systemic arteries). Thus the systemic pressure increases, while the pulmonary artery pressure falls due to lowering of the pulmonary vascular resistance. As a result, flow of blood through the ductus arteriosus reverses. Instead of blood flowing from the pulmonary artery to the aorta, as in the fetus, the blood flows from aorta to the pulmonary artery. The ductus arteriosus constricts and closes off. The pulmonary and systemic circulations thus separate from each other soon after birth.

At this time, however, the pulmonary pressure and resistance is equal or only slightly lower than the systemic pressure. Therefore, even if there is a communication between the two sides like atrial or ventricular septal defect or patent ductus arteriosus, there is very little flow from left to the right side. The pulmonary vascular resistance *falls rapidly* to reach normal adult levels by *2–3 weeks in normal babies.* In the presence of a *ventricular septal defect or patent ductus arteriosus* however, *the fall in pulmonary vascular resistance and pressure is slower and reaches adult values by 6–10 weeks.* Since there is little flow across the abnormal communications like atrial or ventricular septal defect or patent ductus arteriosus, they do not manifest in the first few days of life. The ventricular septal defect or patent ductus arteriosus murmurs tend to appear by the middle or the end of the first week of life. It gradually increases in intensity as the pressure and resistance in the pulmonary circuit fall. Only by 6–10 weeks when the resistance may have reached its lowest value, the maximum shunt would become apparent. In *atrial septal defect*, on the other hand, the *right ventricular hypertrophy, present at birth, prevents a large shunt.* A thick ventricle cannot expand well in diastole to accommodate a large volume of blood. The right ventricular hypertrophy takes *six months or more to regress.* Thus, the murmur of atrial septal defect takes even longer i.e. 6 months, before these patients are identified.

On the other hand, *obstructive lesions like aortic stenosis or pulmonic stenosis and valvular leaks like mitral or tricuspid regurgitation are operative from birth.* As such the murmur of obstructive lesions as well as valvular leaks are audible immediately after birth. The clinical manifestations of congenital lesions associated with atrial, ventricular or aortopulmonary communication, therefore, show rapid changes in the first few weeks or months of life. Even if the evaluation of an infant at the age of one week has been felt to be normal, it does not rule out the presence of congenital heart disease. It is also not possible to correctly estimate the severity of the lesion in the first few weeks of life.

Diagnostic Implications of Pressures and Resistances in the Cardiac Chambers and Great Vessels

The pressures and resistances in the pulmonary and systemic circulations are indicated in Table 14.10. The pulmonary and systemic flows are equal if there are no abnormal communications between the two sides. According to Poiseuille's equation, modified for application to blood flow through vessels:

Pressure = Flow × Resistance

The pressure is measured in mm Hg, flow in liters/min and resistance in dynes/sec/cm^5 or units (each unit being 80 dynes/ sec/cm^5). Although this equation is not accurate when applied to flow of blood in pulmonary and systemic circuits, it helps in understanding the hemodynamics. When applied to systemic and pulmonary circuits, it can be rewritten as:

Systemic pressure = Systemic flow × Peripheral vascular resistance
Pulmonary arterial pressure = Pulmonary flow × Pulmonary vascular resistance

Table 14.10: Pressure and resistance in the pulmonary and systemic circuits

Pressures	mm Hg	
Superior vena cava	0–6	Left atrium 6–10
Right atrium	0–6	Left ventricle 80–120/5–10
Right ventricle	25/0–6	Systemic artery 80–120/60–85
Pulmonary artery	25/10	
Resistance	dynes/sec/cm^5 (units)	
Pulmonary	80–240 (1–3)	Systemic 800–1600 (10–20)

It is thus obvious that the pressure in a vessel is dependent on the *flow* through the vessel and the *resistance*, offered by the vessel to the flow of blood. It is possible to increase the pressure in a vessel either by increasing the flow or by increasing the resistance. Increase in flow through the pulmonary artery means a left to right shunt, as occurs in atrial or ventricular septal defect or patent ductus arteriosus. Generally, this increase in flow is not associated with significant increase in pressure as the *resistance falls* or *remains the same.* At the same time, the distensibility characteristics of the pulmonary artery are such that it can accommodate almost three times the normal flow without an increase in pressure. Hence, *large left to right shunts can take place without an increase in pressure.*

Increase in pulmonary vascular resistance means obstructive disease in the pulmonary circuit. The pulmonary vessels develop medial hypertrophy and later intimal changes are added, to further obstruct the flow of blood through the pulmonary circulation. *After a certain stage, it is an irreversible process.* The increase in resistance to flow in the pulmonary circuit is associated with *reduction in flow.* The increase in pressure in the pulmonary artery associated with normal resistance is called *hyperkinetic pulmonary arterial hypertension* whereas when the pressure is increased due to increase in pulmonary vascular resistance, it is called *obstructive pulmonary arterial hypertension.* Clinically both situations are seen and can be separated from each other on the bed side.

Table 14.10 indicates that the pressures in the right sided chambers and the pulmonary artery are lower than the pressures on the left side. As such, if there is a communication between the two sides, the flow will be from the left to the right side. The difference in pressure between the two atria is small. As such in an *atrial septal defect* there is absence of a significant transmission of pressure from the left atrium to the right atrium. In the presence of a *ventricular septal defect,* however, the flow of blood from the left ventricle to the right ventricle is at a considerable difference in systolic pressures between the two ventricles. There will be some increase in right sided pressure and this depends on the size of the ventricular septal defect. The smaller the defect, the less the transmission of the ventricular pressure to the right ventricle. With large defects the pressures in the two ventricles may be identical. The flow of blood from left to right will depend on the pulmonary vascular resistance. When the ductus arteriosus is patent, the blood flows from the aorta to the pulmonary artery during both systole as well as diastole, because there is considerable difference in the pressures between the two great arteries in both phases of the cardiac cycle. The size of the ductus arteriosus determines how much of the aortic pressure will be directly transmitted to the pulmonary artery. With a large patent ductus arteriosus, the pressures in the aorta and pulmonary artery become identical. The flow into the pulmonary artery then depends on the pulmonary vascular resistance. If the pulmonary vascular resistance is low, there will be flow of blood from the aorta to the pulmonary artery.

Another aspect of left to right shunts, which has clinical significance, is that in *atrial septal defect* the right ventricle accommodates the extra volume of the shunted blood during diastole. An atrial septal defect, therefore, causes a *diastolic overload of the right ventricle. In ventricular septal defects the shunt from left ventricle to the right ventricle is during systole, as such, the shunted blood reaches the right ventricle while the latter is also actively contracting and becoming smaller. This results in the flow from the left ventricle going to the pulmonary artery more or less directly.* The right ventricle acts simply as a conduit and the shunt is not a volume load for the right ventricle. The shunted blood passes through the lungs and finally leads to a diastolic volume overload of the left ventricle. In patent ductus arteriosus the flow from the aorta to the pulmonary artery, is during both systole as well as diastole. Thus, it results in a systolic as well as a diastolic volume load of the pulmonary artery. For the left ventricle, patent ductus arteriosus results in a diastolic volume overload.

14

Diagnostic Implications of the Second Heart Sound

Auscultation of the heart provides important diagnostic information. Assessment of the second heart sound is important (Fig. 14.6).

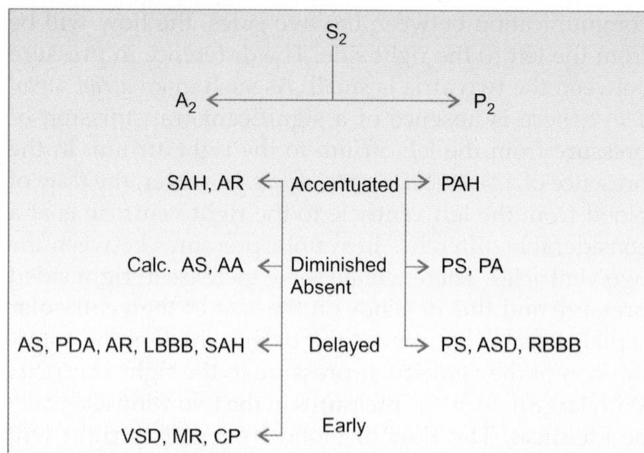

Fig.14.6: Second sound (S_2): The aortic component (A_2) is accentuated in systemic hypertension (SAH) and aortic regurgitation (AR). It is diminished or absent in aortic atresia (AA) and calcific aortic stenosis (AS). A_2 is delayed in AS, patent ductus arterious (PDA), AR, left bundle branch block (LBBB) and SAH. A_2 comes earlier in mitral regurgitation (MR), ventricular septal defect (VSD) and constrictive pericarditis (CP).
The pulmonic component (P_2) is accentuated in pulmonary arterial hypertension (PAH), diminished or absent in pulmonic stenosis (PS) and pulmonary atresia (PA). P_2 is delayed in PS, atrial septal defect (ASD) and right bundle block (RBBB).

The normal second heart sound can be described in three parts:

i. It has two components, the aortic closure sound (A_2) and the pulmonary closure sound (P_2).
ii. During quiet breathing both the components are superimposed on each other during expiration. Thus, only a single second sound is heard. During inspiration, the aortic component comes slightly early whereas the pulmonary component is delayed, resulting in a splitting of the second sound in which the A_2 precedes the P_2.
iii. *The aortic component is louder than the pulmonary component,* except in infants below the age of 3–6 months. When we say that the second sound is normal, it means that we have carefully observed the three parts of the second sound. Abnormalities of the second sound occur in each of the three parts.

Abnormalities of the Aortic Component (A_2) of the Second Sound

The A_2 may be *accentuated or diminished* in intensity. It can also occur early or late in timing. The A_2 is accentuated in systemic hypertension and in aortic regurgitation. The A_2 is diminished in intensity or may be absent when the aortic valve is immobile because of fibrosis or calcification or when the aortic valve is absent as in aortic valve atresia. The *A_2 is delayed* in timing when the left ventricular ejection is prolonged as in aortic valvar or subvalvar stenosis, patent ductus arteriosus with a large left to right shunt, aortic regurgitation, left bundle branch block and left ventricular failure. The *A_2 occurs early* in ventricular septal defect, mitral regurgitation and constrictive pericarditis.

The recognition of delayed or early A_2 on the bed side will be explained below.

Abnormalities of the Pulmonic Component (P_2) of the Second Sound

The P_2 may be *accentuated or diminished* in intensity or *delayed* in timing. Although it may be occurring early in tricuspid regurgitation, it is not recognized as such on the bedside since tricuspid regurgitation as an isolated lesion (without pulmonary arterial hypertension) is rare. *Accentuated P_2* is present in pulmonary arterial hypertension from any cause. The *P_2 is diminished* in intensity in pulmonic stenosis. It is absent when the pulmonary valve is absent as in pulmonary valvar atresia. The *P_2 is delayed* in pulmonic stenosis, atrial septal defect, right bundle branch block, total anomalous pulmonary venous connection and type A WPW syndrome.

Abnormalities in Splitting of the Second Sound (S_2)

As indicated above the normal S_2 is single (or closely split, less than 0.03 sec) in expiration and split in inspiration with the louder A_2 preceding the P_2. *Wide splitting of the second sound* is defined as splitting during expiration due to an early A_2 or late P_2 that is, the A_2–P_2 interval is 0.03

sec or more during expiration. During *inspiration* if the A_2–P_2 interval increases further, it is called wide variable splitting. If the A_2–P_2 interval is the same in expiration and inspiration, it is called widely split and fixed, second sound. *Wide and variable splitting* of the S_2 is seen in pulmonic stenosis, mitral regurgitation and ventricular septal defect. In pulmonic stenosis it is due to a delay in P_2 whereas in mitral regurgitation and ventricular septal defect it is due to an early A_2. *Wide and fixed splitting* of the S_2 occurs in atrial septal defect, right bundle branch block and total anomalous pulmonary venous connection and is due to a delay in P_2.

The delay in A_2 results in closely split, single or paradoxically split S_2. This is recognized on the bedside only if one is looking for it. The S_2 is split in expiration but during inspiration the split becomes narrower or disappears (Fig. 14.7). A single second sound means that it is either A_2 or P_2 or a combination of both A_2 and P_2. The decision whether it is A_2 or P_2 or a combination of both A_2 and P_2 depends not on the location or intensity of the single second sound but on an analysis of the total clinical profile. For example, in tetralogy of Fallot only a single S_2 is heard and it is the A_2 since P_2 is delayed and so soft that it is inaudible. In ventricular septal defect with pulmonary arterial hypertension and right to left shunt (Eisenmenger complex) again a single S_2 is heard and represents a combination of A_2 and P_2. Based on auscultation alone one may not be able to differentiate between tetralogy of Fallot and Eisenmenger complex. However, history and thoracic roentgenogram can easily separate them. Thus, the interpretation of the single second sound is not dependent on auscultation alone.

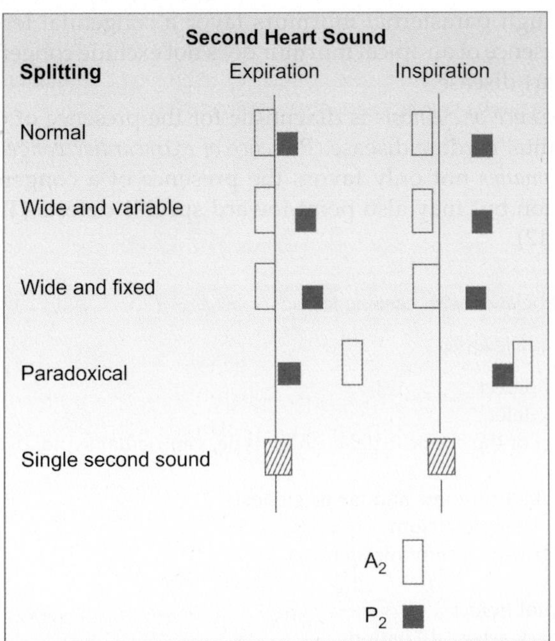

Fig. 14.7: Second sound (S_2): The relationship of aortic (A_2) and pulmonic component (P_2) in inspiration and expiration. Single S_2 means that it may be either A_2 or P_2 or a combination of both

Assessment for Presence of Heart Disease

The assessment of a child for the presence of heart disease may be done using *Nadas' criteria*. Presence of one major or two minor criteria indicate heart disease (Table 14.11).

Table 14.11: Nadas' criteria

Major	*Minor*
Systolic murmur grade III or more	Systolic murmur less than grade III
Diastolic murmur	Abnormal second sound
Cyanosis	Abnormal ECG
Congestive cardiac failure	Abnormal X-ray
	Abnormal blood pressure

Major Criteria

Systolic murmur grade III or more in intensity: Systolic murmurs are classified into ejection systolic murmurs and pansystolic murmurs. *A pansystolic murmur is always abnormal* no matter what is its intensity. There are only three lesions which produce a pansystolic murmur and these are (*a*) ventricular septal defect, (*b*) mitral regurgitation and (*c*) tricuspid regurgitation.

An ejection systolic murmur may be due to an organic cause or a "functional" murmur. An ejection systolic murmur with a thrill is an organic murmur. A functional grade III ejection systolic murmur may be heard in anemia or high fever especially in smaller children. *Almost 50% of children at the age of 5 years may have an ejection systolic murmur.* If accompanied with a normal second sound, then it is unlikely to be significant. Before discarding a murmur as of no significance, it is necessary to obtain an EKG and a thoracic roentgenogram. If they are normal, one can probably exclude heart disease, though another evaluation after 6 months is preferable.

Diastolic murmur: Presence of a diastolic murmur always indicates the presence of organic heart disease. The only two exceptions are severe systemic hypertension and severe anemia. In severe systemic hypertension, reduction of blood pressure may cause an aortic regurgitation murmur to disappear. Anemia may also result in delayed diastolic murmurs across the tricuspid and mitral valves.

Cyanosis: Central cyanosis suggest that either unoxygenated blood is entering the systemic circulation through a *right to left shunt* or *the blood passing through the lungs is not getting fully oxygenated.* The oxygen saturation of the arterial blood is less than normal, the normal being around 98%. If the blood is not fully oxygenated in the lungs, it is called *pulmonary venous unsaturation* and indicates severe lung disease. Cyanosis due to a right to left shunt indicates presence of heart disease. The central cyanosis is present in fingers and toes as well as in the mucous membranes of the mouth and tongue. It results in *polycythemia and clubbing of* fingers and toes. Presence of central cyanosis indicates presence of heart disease if lung disease is excluded.

Congestive cardiac failure: Presence of CCF indicates heart disease, except in neonates and infants who can get cardiac failure from hypoglycemia and anemia.

Minor Criteria

Systolic murmur less than grade III in intensity: The value of murmurs has already been discussed above. It is necessary to emphasize that soft, less than grade III murmurs by themselves do not exclude heart disease.

Abnormal second sound: Abnormalities of the second sound always indicate presence of heart disease. It has been included as a minor criterion only because auscultation is an individual and subjective finding. *No one is perfect in auscultation and anyone can be wrong.* If the auscultatory abnormality can be substantiated by a phonocardiogram it becomes objective evidence and indicates presence of heart disease.

14

Abnormal electrocardiogram: Its main value lies in determining the mean QRS axis, right or left atrial hypertrophy and right or left ventricular hypertrophy. Criteria for ventricular hypertrophy, based only on voltage criteria are not diagnostic for the presence of heart disease. The voltage of the QRS complexes can be affected by changes in blood viscosity, electrolyte imbalance, position of the electrode on the chest wall and thickness of the chest wall. If a patient is asymptomatic, the physical examination and chest X-ray are normal but the EKG is abnormal, the presence of heart disease is not likely. Such a patient should be carefully reevaluated before diagnosing heart disease.

Abnormal X-ray: The reasons for considering abnormal X-ray as a minor criterion are twofold. In small children, the heart size varies with expiration and inspiration. If there is cardiomegaly on a good inspiratory film, it is suggestive of heart disease. The second reason which leads to difficulty in assessing the cardiac size is the presence of thymus in children up to the age of 2-years, which may fallaciously suggest cardiomegaly. Fluoroscopy is useful in separating the thymic shadow from the heart.

Abnormal blood pressure: It is difficult to obtain accurate blood pressure in smaller children. If the cuff is small it would give a falsely high reading of blood pressure, whereas if it is too large it gives low readings. The blood pressure cuff should cover at least two-thirds of the length of the arm and most of the circumference.

Based on the presence of one major or two minor criteria a decision can be taken that the child has heart disease. These guidelines are meant to help in identifying the presence of heart disease. It does not follow that the pediatrician should not use his judgment and common sense for identifying the presence or absence of heart disease.

Features Indicative of the Presence of Congenital Cardiac Lesions

If the heart disease was diagnosed at or soon after birth, it favors the presence of congenital cardiac disease. As indicated above, *murmurs of obstructive and regurgitant lesions should be audible immediately after birth whereas murmurs of left to right shunts tend to appear somewhat later.* If the presence of a heart murmur is known within the first year of life, it is a strong pointer toward the diagnosis of a congenital lesion. The murmurs produced by congenital lesions tend to be parasternal. However, apical pansystolic murmur of mitral regurgitation may be heard in atrial septal defect of the endocardial cushion type defect. Hence, though parasternal murmurs favor a congenital lesion, presence of an apical murmur does not exclude congenital heart disease.

Presence of cyanosis is diagnostic for the presence of congenital cardiac disease. *Presence of extracardiac congenital anomalies* not only favors the presence of a congenital lesion but may also point toward specific defects (Table 14.12).

Table 14.12: Extracardiac anomalies associated with cardiac lesions

Extracardiac anomalies	*Likely congenital cardiac lesion*
Bony abnormalities; absence of radius or ulna	Ventricular septal defect
Syndactyly, polydactyly	Ventricular septal defect
Trisomy 21 (Down syndrome)	Atrial septal defect of the endocardial cushion type, ventricular septal defect
Arachnodactyly	Atrial septal defect
Turner syndrome	Coarctation of aorta, pulmonic and aortic stenosis
Ellis-van Creveld syndrome	Atrial septal defect, single atrium
Rubella syndrome	Patent ductus arteriosus, pulmonic stenosis
Moon facies and hypertelorism	Pulmonic stenosis
Holt Oram syndrome	Familial atrial septal defect
Marfan syndrome	Aortic or pulmonary artery dilatation
Hurler syndrome	Mitral or aortic regurgitation
Trisomy 13–15	Ventricular septal defect
Trisomy 17–18	Ventricular septal defect, patent ductus arteriosus

Classification of Congenital Heart Diseases

For the purpose of diagnosing individual anomalies it is helpful to classify patients of congenital heart disease into three groups:

Group I	Left to right shunts
Group II	Right to left shunts (cyanotic lesions)
Group III	Obstructive lesions

Left to right shunts: Patients of left to right shunts are characterized by *frequent chest infections.* Each attack of cold seems to turn into bronchopneumonia, which lasts longer than usual. It is not uncommon for these patients to have six to eight attacks of pneumonia in the first year of life. Patients of left to right shunts do not have cyanosis. They have a tendency for increased sweating, which is related to their tendency for developing CCF. Frequent chest infections with tachypnea result in the soft rib cage being drawn inward at the diaphragmatic attachments of the ribs. This combined with cardiac enlargement gives them a *precordial bulge.* On palpation, the precordium is *hyperkinetic.* On auscultation, they have either a *tricuspid or a mitral delayed diastolic murmur.* Evaluation of the thoracic roentgenogram shows hyperemic or plethoric lung fields, as well as cardiomegaly.

Right to left shunts: Patients of right to left shunts are characterized by the presence of cyanosis, which leads to *polycythemia* and *clubbing. Cyanotic* patients, however, belong to two subgroups. Some of these patients are associated with normal or decreased pulmonary arterial pressure, while others are associated with elevated pulmonary arterial pressure. The patients who have diminished pulmonary arterial pressure, also have diminished pulmonary blood flow, due to the presence of pulmonary stenosis. Cyanotic patients with increased pulmonary arterial pressure (pulmonary arterial hypertension), may have either *increased pulmonary blood flow* or *diminished pulmonary blood flow* due to pulmonary vascular obstructive disease. The latter are particularly unfortunate since they have most probably reached the stage of irreversible pulmonary arterial hypertension. Patients with increased pulmonary blood flow are mildly cyanotic; those with normal or diminished pulmonary blood flow are moderately to severely cyanotic.

`Thus cyanotic patients have either pulmonic stenosis or *pulmonary arterial hypertension. Cyanotic patients with pulmonic stenosis* are characterized by an *ejection systolic murmur, delayed and diminished* P_2 and *ischemic lung fields* in thoracic roentgenogram. *Cyanotic patients with pulmonary arterial hypertension* have *accentuated and palpable* P_2 *an ejection systolic murmur and large, main as well as right and left branches of the pulmonary artery* in the thoracic roentgenogram. The appearance of chest X-ray depends on the pulmonary blood flow. If the pulmonary blood flow is increased, the lung fields appear plethoric throughout and cardiomegaly is present. If the pulmonary blood flow is normal or diminished, the radiograph shows the paradoxical finding of prominent and large hilar pulmonary arteries with clear or ischemic peripheral lung fields.

Within these two subgroups of cyanotic patients some patients can be separated from others because of the presence of abnormal mixing of blood resulting in a right to left as well as a left to right shunt. Majority of these patients present in early infancy or neonatal life with a combination of *cyanosis, cardiomegaly, congestive cardiac failure, increased sweating, absence of weight gain* (failure to thrive) and mostly plethoric lung fields. These patients have *transposition of great arteries, total anomalous pulmonary venous connection, persistent truncus arteriosus* or *malposition of great arteries.*

Obstructive lesions: The diagnostic features of the patients of obstructive lesions consist of *absence of frequent chest infections and cyanosis, absence of precordial bulge, presence of a forcible or heaving cardiac* impulse due to concentric hypertrophy of the ventricles without cardiac enlargement, a systolic thrill associated with an *ejection systolic murmur, absence of tricuspid and mitral delayed diastolic murmurs,* and presence of *delayed corresponding second sound.* The only right sided obstructive lesion is *pulmonary stenosis* whereas the two left sided obstructive lesions are *aortic stenosis* and *coarctation of the aorta.* The chest X-ray shows a *normal sized heart and normal pulmonary vasculature.* The EKG not only indicates whether the obstructive lesion is right or left sided, but is also helpful in indicating the severity of the obstruction.

LEFT TO RIGHT SHUNTS

The three main left to right shunts are *atrial septal defect* of the ostium secundum and ostium primum variety (endocardial cushion defect), *ventricular septal defect* and *patent ductus arteriosus.* They can be separated by physical examination, EKG and chest X-ray.

Atrial Septal Defect

Atrial septal defect is an abnormal communication between the two atria. The ostium secundum type of atrial septal defect is generally anatomically located at the fossa ovalis. It can also be superior or posterior to the fossa ovalis. The ostium primum type of the defect (endocardial cushion defect) is situated inferior to the fossa ovalis. It is associated with a cleft in the anterior leaflet of the mitral valve, with or without a cleft in the septal tricuspid leaflet. Atrial septal defect constitutes 13% of patients with congenital heart disease. The secundum type is ten times more common than the endocardial cushion type.

Hemodynamics

Physiologically atrial septal defect results in leaking of oxygenated blood from the left to the right atrium at a minor difference in pressure between the two atria. The left to right shunt is thus *silent on auscultation.* The right atrium receives blood not only through the superior and inferior vena cava but also the blood, shunted from the left atrium. The right atrium enlarges in size to accommodate the extra volume of blood. The large volume received by the right atrium passes through a normal sized tricuspid valve producing a *delayed diastolic murmur* audible on the bedside at the lower left sternal border. The *right ventricle enlarges* in size to accommodate the large volume reaching it. Because of the large volume of blood passing across a normal pulmonary valve a *pulmonary ejection murmur is produced.* The large volume also results in *prolonged ejection phase* of the right ventricle. The pulmonary valve closes late and the P_2 is delayed. Since the right ventricle is fully loaded, further increase in the right ventricular volume during inspiration cannot occur. The second sound is, therefore, *widely split and fixed:* the P_2 is accentuated. The cardiac apex is formed by the enlarged right ventricle and the accentuated P_2 is well audible at the apex as well. Hence audible P_2 at the apex in atrial septal defect does not mean pulmonary hypertension. The pulmonary artery and its branches enlarge to accommodate the left to right shunt and the lung fields are plethoric.

14

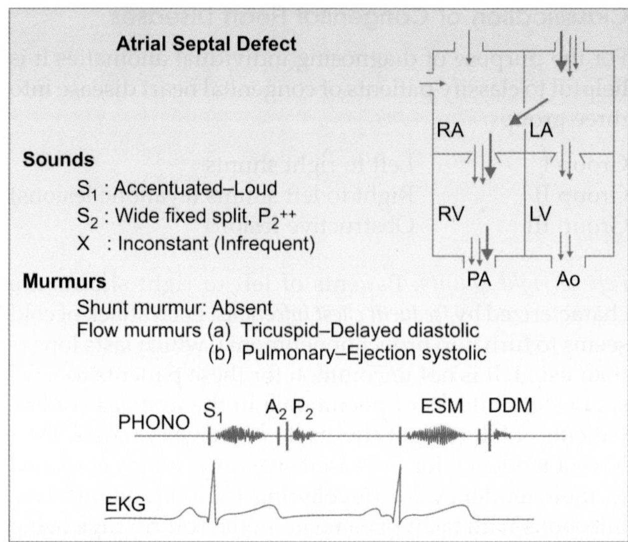

Fig. 14.8: Summary of auscultatory findings in the atrial septal defect, S_1 = first sound, S_2 = second sound, P_2 = pulmonic component of the second sound, X = click, A_2 = aortic component of the second sound, ESM = ejection systolic murmur, RA = right atrium, LA = left atrium, RV = right ventricle, LV = left ventricle, PA = pulmonary artery, Ao = aorta

Clinical Features

Patients of atrial septal defect are generally asymptomatic. Mild effort intolerance and frequent chest infections are the only symptoms. CCF is rare. On physical examination patients of atrial septal defect have a *parasternal impulse.* A systolic thrill may be palpable at the second left interspace in 10% patients. *The cardiac enlargement is only mild to moderate.* Marked cardiomegaly suggests additional lesions like mitral valve obstruction (Lutembacher syndrome) or mitral regurgitation. The first sound is normal or may be loud due to a loud tricuspid component of the first sound. The second sound is widely split and fixed with the P_2 being accentuated and widely transmitted along the left sternal border and up to apex. There is an ejection systolic murmur (grade 3 or less) at the second and third left interspaces. *It is widely transmitted all over the chest.* There is also a *delayed diastolic murmur at* the lower left sternal border. The tricuspid delayed diastolic murmur may be mistaken for an early diastolic murmur or a pericardial friction rub at the bedside. The error occurs as the tricuspid delayed diastolic murmur starts earlier in the diastolic period because the tricuspid valve opens before the mitral valve and the gap between the delayed P_2 and the start of the diastolic murmur may be missed. Systolic and diastolic murmurs produced at the tricuspid valve have, at times, a scratchy superficial character almost like a pericardial friction rub (Fig. 14.8).

Presence of a pansystolic murmur of mitral regurgitation at the apex in a patient with atrial septal defect suggests four possibilities:

i. If the EKG reveals left axis deviation of more than–30°, it suggests *ostium primum* atrial septal defect.
ii. The patient may have *a floppy mitral valve* with a midsystolic click and a late ejection systolic or even a pansystolic murmur (mitral valve prolapse syndrome).
iii. Ostium secundum defect associated with rheumatic *mitral regurgitation;* and
iv. Secundum atrial septal defect rarely associated with cleft mitral valve resulting in mitral regurgitation.

The last three conditions have right axis deviation on the EKG. The EKG of ostium secundum atrial septal defect is characterized by right axis deviation and right ventricular hypertrophy. The characteristic configuration of the precordial lead V_1 is rsR′ seen in almost 90% patients (Fig. 14.9). Presence of left axis deviation beyond –30° suggests the ostium primum type of atrial septal defect (Fig. 14.10).

The thoracic roentgenogram shows mild to moderate cardiomegaly, right atrial and right ventricular enlargement, prominent main pulmonary artery segment, a relatively small aortic shadow and plethoric lung fields.

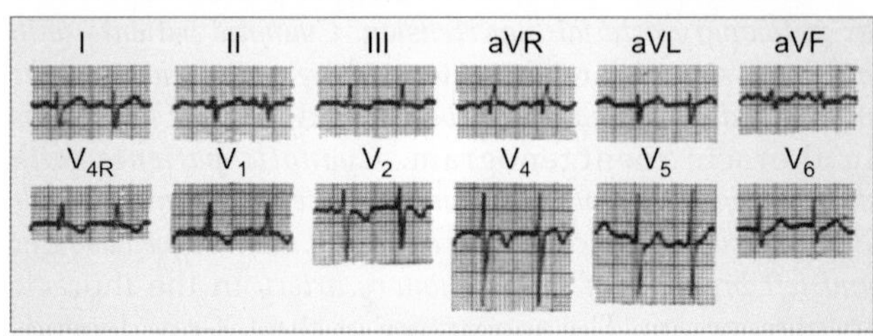

Fig. 14.9: Electrocardiogram of atrial septal defect of the secundum type. Mean QRS axis is +130°. Lead V_1 shows rsR′ characteristic of the defect

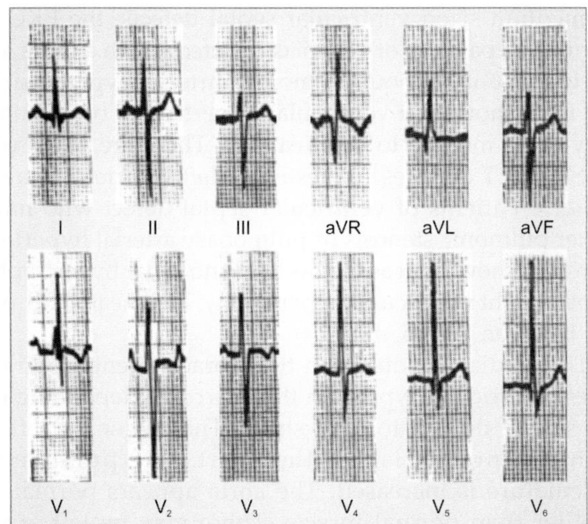

Fig. 14.10: Electrocardiogram of atrial septal defect of the primum type (endocardial cushion or atrioventricular canal defect). The mean QRS axis is –45°

The left atrium does not enlarge in size in atrial septal defect. Enlarged left atrium without associated anomalies like mitral regurgitation excludes the diagnosis of atrial septal defect. Echocardiogram shows increased size of the right ventricle with paradoxical ventricular septal motion. 2D echo in subcostal four chambered view identifies the defect.

Assessment of the Severity

The size of the left to right shunt is directly proportional to the intensity of the two murmurs and the heart size. The larger the shunt the more the cardiomegaly and the louder the pulmonary and tricuspid murmurs.

Complications

Pulmonary arterial hypertension due to pulmonary vascular obstructive disease is rare *below the age of 20-years.* It is recognized by the disappearance of the systolic and diastolic murmurs, appearance of a constant pulmonary ejection click and loud palpable P_2. *The second sound continues to be widely split and fixed.*

Treatment

The medical management consists in treating chest infections. *Infective endocarditis is very rare* in patients of ostium secundum atrial septal defect, unless floppy mitral valve is present. The risk of operation for closure of atrial septal defect is so low that asymptomatic patients are referred for surgery. Most surgeons prefer correction with the use of heart lung bypass. The ideal age for operation is between 2–5 years. With use of hypothermia, patients are being operated below the age of 2-years without extra risk. Definitive cure is possible with device closure in selected patients (see later).

Ventricular Septal Defect

It is a communication between the ventricles; 90% defects are located in the membranous part of the ventricular septum with extension into the adjoining muscular part. Others are located in the muscular septum and can be multiple. This is the commonest congenital cardiac lesion, accounting for 27% of congenital heart disease in our clinic.

Hemodynamics

A ventricular septal defect results in shunting of oxygenated blood from the left to the right ventricle. The left ventricle starts contracting before the right ventricle. The flow of blood from the left ventricle to the right ventricle starts early in systole and a pressure gradient is maintained between the two ventricles throughout systole. The murmur resulting from the left to right shunt, starts early, masking the first sound and continues throughout the systole with almost the same intensity appearing as a pansystolic murmur on auscultation and palpable as a thrill. Toward the end of systole, the declining left ventricular pressure becomes lower than the aortic pressure. This results in closure of the aortic valve and occurrence of A_2. At this time, however, the left ventricular pressure is still higher than the right ventricular pressure and the left to right shunt continues. The pansystolic murmur, therefore, ends beyond A_2 completely masking it.

The left to right ventricular shunt occurs during systole at a time when the right ventricle is also contracting and its volume is decreasing. The left to right shunt, therefore, streams to the pulmonary artery more or less directly. This flow of blood across the normal pulmonary valve results in an *ejection systolic murmur at the pulmonary valve.* On the bedside, however, the ejection systolic murmur cannot be separated from the pansystolic murmur. The effect of the ejection systolic murmur is a *transmission of the pansystolic murmur to the upper left sternal border,* where its ejection character is recognized since it does not mask the aortic component of the second sound.

The large volume of blood passing through the lungs is recognized on the X-ray as *pulmonary plethora.* The increased volume of blood finally reaches the left atrium and may result in *left atrial enlargement.* Passing through a normal mitral valve the large volume of blood results in a *delayed diastolic murmur at the apex.* The intensity and duration of the delayed diastolic murmur at the apex is directly related to the size of the shunt. The large flow across the normal mitral valve also results in *accentuated first sound,* not appreciable on the bedside as it is drowned by the pansystolic murmur. Since the left ventricle has two outlets, the aortic valve allowing forward flow and the ventricular septal defect resulting in a backward leak, it empties relatively early. This results in an early A_2. *Since the ejection into the right ventricle and pulmonary artery is increased because of the left to right shunt the P_2 is delayed.* Therefore, the second sound is *widely split but varies with respiration* in patients of ventricular septal defect with a large left to right shunt. There is also an increase in the intensity of the P_2.

Clinical Features

The patients of ventricular septal defect can become symptomatic around 6–10 weeks of age. They can develop CCF at this time. Premature babies with a ventricular septal defect can become symptomatic even earlier. Palpitation, dyspnea on exertion and frequent chest infection are the main symptoms in older children. On examination the pulse pressure is relatively wide. The precordium is *hyperkinetic with a systolic thrill* at the left sternal border. The heart size is enlarged with a left ventricular type of apex. *The first and the second sounds are masked by a pansystolic murmur* at the left sternal border. The second sound can, however, be made out at the second left interspace or higher. It is *widely split and variable* with accentuated P2. A third sound may be audible at the apex. A loud pansystolic murmur is present at the left sternal border. The maximum intensity of the murmur may be in the third, fourth or the fifth left interspace. It is well heard at the second left interspace but not conducted beyond the apex. A delayed diastolic murmur, starting with the third sound is audible at the apex (Fig. 14.11).

The EKG in ventricular septal defect is quite variable. All children are born with right ventricular hypertrophy. As such initially all patients of ventricular septal defect have right ventricular hypertrophy. Because of the delay in the fall of pulmonary vascular resistance due to the presence of ventricular septal defect, the regression of pulmonary arterial hypertension is delayed and right ventricular hypertrophy regresses more slowly. In small or medium sized ventricular septal defects, the EKG is normal. In patients of ventricular defects with a large left to right shunt, without pulmonary arterial hypertension, the EKG shows left ventricular hypertrophy by the time they are 6 months to one-year-old. There are, however, no ST and T changes suggestive of left ventricular strain pattern. Patients of ventricular septal defect who have either pulmonic stenosis or pulmonary arterial hypertension may show right as well as left ventricular hypertrophy or pure right ventricular hypertrophy. The mean QRS axis lies between +30 to +90°.

The cardiac silhouette in the thoracic roentgenogram is left ventricular type with the heart size depending on the size of the left to right shunt. The bigger the left to right shunt, the larger the heart. The pulmonary vasculature is increased. The aorta appears normal or smaller than normal in size. There may be left atrial enlargement in patients with a large left to right shunt. Patients of ventricular septal defect with a small shunt either because the ventricular defect is small or because of the associated pulmonic stenosis or pulmonary arterial hypertension have a normal sized heart. The pulmonary vasculature is normal with small defects or if there is associated pulmonic stenosis. The pulmonary vasculature is plethoric if there is associated pulmonary arterial hypertension. Echocardiogram shows increased left atrial and ventricular size as well as exaggerated mitral valve motion. 2D echo can identify the site and size of defect in 90% cases as well as pick up the presence or absence of pulmonic stenosis or pulmonary hypertension.

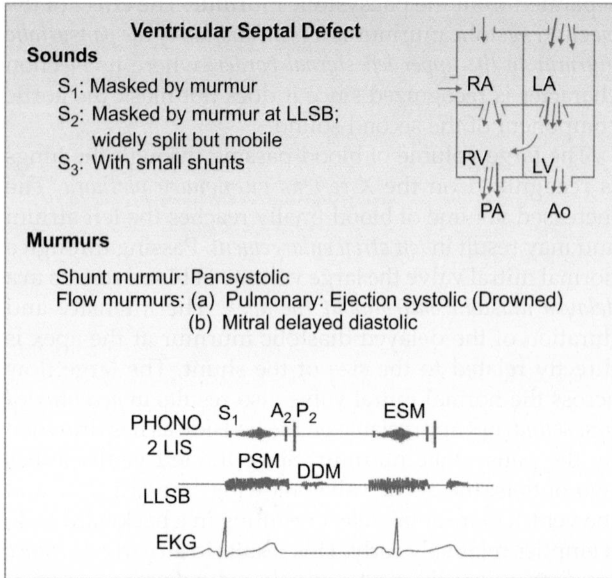

Fig. 14.11: Summary of auscultatory findings in ventricular septal defect. LLSB = lower left sternal border. 2 LIS = second left interspace. PSM = pansystolic murmur

Assessment of Severity

If the *ventricular septal defect is small, the left to right shunt murmur continues to be pansystolic* but since the shunt is small, the second sound is normally split and the intensity of P_2 is normal. There is also *absence of the delayed diastolic mitral murmur.* If the ventricular septal defect is very small it acts as a stenotic area resulting in an ejection systolic murmur. This is the commonest cause of the so-called functional systolic murmurs in children, which disappear because of spontaneous closure of small defects.

If the *ventricular septal defect is large it results in transmission of left ventricular systolic pressure to the right ventricle.* The right ventricular pressure increases and the difference in the systolic pressure between the two ventricles decreases. The *left to right shunt murmur becomes shorter and softer* and on the bedside appears as an ejection systolic murmur. If there is right ventricular outflow obstruction due to associated *infundibular pulmonic stenosis,* the right ventricular pressure increases and the ventricular septal defect murmur becomes an ejection systolic murmur. In the former situation, the pulmonary artery pressure is increased and results in an accentuated P_2; in the latter, the pulmonary artery pressure is normal or decreased and the P_2 is diminished in intensity and delayed in timing resulting in a widely split, variable S_2 with soft P_2.

Patients of ventricular septal defect may have either *hyperkinetic pulmonary arterial hypertension or obstructive pulmonary arterial hypertension.* The P_2 is accentuated in both. In the former there is a large left to right shunt whereas the latter is associated with a small left to right shunt. In *hyperkinetic pulmonary arterial hypertension the cardiac impulse is hyperkinetic with a pansystolic murmur and thrill, widely split and variable S_2 with accentuated P_2 and a mitral delayed diastolic murmur. The obstructive pulmonary arterial hypertension is associated with a forcible parasternal impulse, the thrill is absent or faint, the systolic murmur is ejection type, the S_2 is normally but closely split with accentuated P_2 and there is no mitral murmur.*

Based on physical findings, it is thus possible to distinguish very small, small, medium sized and large ventricular septal defects. It is also possible to determine if there is associated pulmonic stenosis or pulmonary arterial hypertension of the hyperkinetic or obstructive variety. Doppler echo can provide the gradient between the left and right ventricles, helping in the assessment of right ventricular and pulmonary pressures.

Course and Complications

Patients of ventricular septal defects can have a very variable course. They may develop congestive cardiac failure in infancy, which is associated with a high mortality. It is estimated that 70–80% of all ventricular defects become smaller or disappears; the latter is called spontaneous closure. Most (90%) patients who show spontaneous closure, do so by the age of 3 years, though it may occur later as well.

Patients born with an uncomplicated ventricular septal defect may develop *pulmonic stenosis* due to hypertrophy of the right ventricular infundibulum, develop *pulmonary arterial hypertension* or rarely *aortic regurgitation* due to prolapse of the right coronary or the non-coronary cusp of the aortic valve. Development of pulmonary arterial hypertension is a dreaded complication, since if it is of the obstructive type the patient becomes inoperable. Patients of ventricular defects may develop CCF in adult life around the age of 30–40 years. It is also possible for a patient with a relatively small ventricular septal defect to go through the whole life without any symptoms or difficulty. Lastly, the ventricular septal defect is the *commonest congenital lesion complicated by infective endocarditis.* The incidence of infective endocarditis has been estimated as 2/100 patients in a follow up of 10-years, that is 1 per 500 patient year. The incidence of endocarditis is small enough that it cannot be considered as an indication for operation in small defects.

Treatment

Medical management consists in control of congestive cardiac failure, treatment of repeated chest infections, and prevention and treatment of anemia and infective endocarditis. The patients should be followed carefully to assess the development of pulmonic stenosis, pulonary arterial hypertension or aortic regurgitation.

Surgical treatment is indicated if (i) congestive cardiac failure occurs in infancy and does not respond to medical management; (ii) the left to right shunt is large (pulmonary flow more than twice the systemic flow); and (iii) there is associated pulmonic stenosis, pulmonary arterial hypertension or aortic regurgitation. Surgical treatment is not indicated in patients with a small ventricular septal defect and in those patients who have developed pulmonary arterial hypertension of a severity that a right to left shunt has appeared.

The *operative treatment* consists in closure of the ventricular septal defect with the use of a patch. The operation can be performed through the right atrium, which is the preferred approach, or through a right ventriculotomy, which leaves majority of the patients with right bundle branch block. The operation can be done as early as a few months after birth if congestive failure cannot be controlled with medical management. With evidence of pulmonary hypertension, the operation should be performed as early as possible. Most modern centers are able to close the defect surgically in young infants. It is unwise to make the sick infants wait for a certain weight threshold, since most infants with large defects do not gain weight satisfactorily. Episodes of lower respiratory infections require hospitalization and are difficult to manage. For very sick infants with pneumonia who require mechanical ventilation, early surgery should be considered.

The major complications of the ventricular defect surgery are: (i) complete heart block, (ii) bifascicular block and (iii) reopened or residual ventricular septal defect. These complications are fortunately rare. The risk of surgery in uncomplicated defects is now less than 1% in most centers in our country.

Catheter closure of ventricular septal defects is possible for muscular defects in relatively older children (>8–10 kg). There is a device designed for perimembranous defects as well. However, the risk of complete heart block with the membranous defect occluder is significant. Device closure of ventricular septal defect requires considerable technical expertise and should be attempted at dedicated centers.

Patent Ductus Arteriosus

Patent ductus arteriosus (PDA) is a communication between the pulmonary artery and the aorta. The aortic attachment of the ductus arteriosus is just distal to the left subclavian artery. The ductus arteriosus is present in the fetal life but closes functionally and anatomically soon after birth. The incidence of PDA in our clinic is 11%.

Hemodynamics

PDA results in a left to right shunt from the aorta to the pulmonary artery. *The flow occurs both during systole and diastole as a pressure gradient is present throughout the cardiac*

14

cycle between the two great arteries, if the pulmonary artery pressure is normal. The flow of blood results in a murmur, which starts in systole, after the first sound and reaches a peak at the second sound. The murmur then diminishes in intensity and is audible during only a part of the diastole. Thus, it is a continuous murmur.

The PDA results in a systolic as well as diastolic overloading of the pulmonary artery. The increased flow after passing through the lungs reaches the left atrium that enlarges in size. The increased volume of blood reaching the left atrium enters the left ventricle in diastole, across a normal mitral valve. The passage of this increased flow across the mitral valve results in *an accentuated first sound as well as a mitral delayed diastolic murmur.* The intensity of the delayed diastolic murmur is directly related to the size of the left to right shunt. With small shunts, there is no mitral diastolic murmur. With moderate sized shunts, a left ventricular third sound is audible due to rapid early filling of the left ventricle. With large shunts, there is a mitral delayed diastolic murmur. The left ventricle, as in ventricular septal defects, receives the increased volume of blood during diastole. As such, both these lesions cause diastolic overloading of the left ventricle. The large volume of blood in the left ventricle causes a prolongation of the left ventricular systole and an increase in the size of the left ventricle to accommodate the extra volume. The prolonged left ventricular systole results in *delayed closure of the aortic* valve and a late A2. With large left to right shunts, the S2 *may be paradoxically split.* The large left ventricular volume ejected into the aorta results in *dilatation of the ascending aorta.* A dilated ascending aorta results in an *aortic ejection click,* which is audible all over the precordium and precedes the start of the continuous murmur. The large volume of blood from the left ventricle passing through a normal aortic valve results in an aortic ejection systolic murmur that, however, on the bedside is drowned by the continuous murmur.

Clinical Features

Patients of PDA may become symptomatic in early life and develop CCF around 6–10 weeks of age. Older children give history of effort intolerance, palpitation and frequent chest infections. The flow from the aorta to the pulmonary artery is a leak from the systemic flow. This results in a *wide pulse pressure* and many of the signs of *wide pulse pressure* seen in patients with aortic regurgitation are present in patients who have a PDA. On the bedside, presence of prominent carotid pulsations in a patient with features of a left to right shunt is suggestive of the diagnosis. The cardiac impulse is hyperkinetic with a left ventricular type of apex. A systolic or a continuous thrill may be palpable at the second left interspace. *The first sound is accentuated and the second narrowly or paradoxically split with large left to right shunts.* With small shunts, the second sound is normally split. The P_2 is louder than normal. It is difficult to evaluate the S_2 in patients of PDA, since the maximum intensity of the continuous murmur occurs at S_2 and tends to mask the S_2. Clinically there is no point in evaluating the second sound if the patient has a continuous murmur. The continuous murmur indicates presence of both a systolic as well as a diastolic difference in pressure between the aorta and pulmonary artery, thus excluding significant pulmonary arterial hypertension. *The murmur starts after the first sound and reaches the peak at the second sound. The murmur then diminishes in intensity and is audible only during a part of the diastole.* The peak at S_2 differentiates the PDA murmur from other causes of a continuous murmur. Additionally the systolic portion of the murmur is grating and rough. It appears to be broken into multiple systolic sounds, the multiple clicks. The murmur is best heard at the second left interspace and *also below the left clavicle* where it maintains its continuous character. There is a third sound at the apex, followed by a delayed diastolic murmur in large shunts (Fig. 14.12).

The EKG shows normal axis with left ventricular dominance or hypertrophy. Deep Q waves in left chest leads with tall 'T' waves are characteristic of the volume overloading of left ventricle. The EKG almost never shows ST and T changes suggestive of left ventricular "strain" in uncomplicated PDA below the age of 15-years. Presence of ST and T changes suggests presence of additional aortic stenosis or fibroelastosis. The chest X-ray exhibits cardiac enlargement with a left ventricular silhouette. The cardiac size depends on the size of the left to right shunt. The larger the shunt the bigger the cardiac size. There may be left atrial enlargement. The ascending aorta and the aortic knuckle are prominent. The pulmonary vasculature is

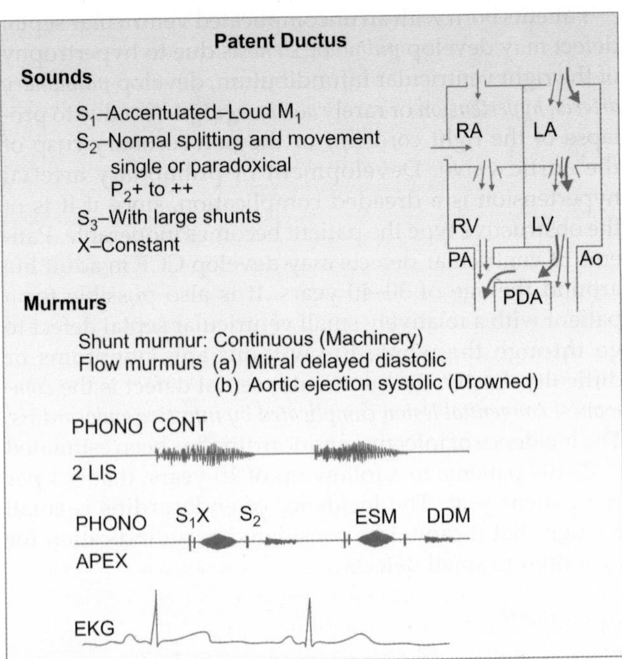

Fig. 14.12: Summary of auscultatory findings in patent ductus arteriosus (PDA) M_1=mitral component of first sound; ESM ejection systolic murmur; DDM delayed diastolic murmur; CONT continuous

plethoric. 2D echocardiogram can identify the PDA, which is confirmed by Doppler.

Assessment of Severity

The evaluation of the size of the left to right shunt depends on a number of features: (i) the larger the heart size the larger the left to right shunt; (ii) absence of third sound and delayed diastolic murmur indicates a small left to right shunt. Presence of the third sound indicates a moderate left to right shunt whereas an audible delayed diastolic murmur suggests a large left to right shunt; (iii) the wider the pulse pressure the larger the shunt.

Course and Complications

Neonates and infants have pulmonary hypertension at birth. The regression of pulmonary hypertension occurs slowly in the presence of PDA. The murmur is an ejection systolic murmur to start with and assumes the continuous character some weeks or months later. It thus remains indistinguishable from a ventricular septal defect murmur in early life. Differentiation between PDA and ventricular septal defect from the location of the maximum intensity of the murmur is also not possible since the infant chest is so small. Palpation in the suprasternal notch may help in differentiating PDA from a ventricular septal defect since the large aorta in ductus becomes palpable. CCF may occur within the first six weeks of life but can be controlled medically in most cases. Patients of PDA tend to develop pulmonary arterial hypertension earlier than patients of ventricular septal defect. Those patients who develop pulmonary arterial hypertension lose the diastolic difference in the aortic and pulmonary pressures first. Thus with increasing pulmonary arterial hypertension the diastolic component becomes shorter and may disappear altogether, leaving only an ejection systolic murmur.

PDA may be associated with hyperkinetic or obstructive pulmonary arterial hypertension as in ventricular septal defects. In both situations the murmur loses its diastolic component and the P_2 is accentuated. The hyperkinetic pulmonary hypertension is associated with a large heart and mitral delayed diastolic murmur, whereas the obstructive variety is accompanied with a normal heart size and absence of the mitral diastolic murmur. With severe pulmonary arterial hypertension and a right to left shunt through a PDA, the normal splitting of S2 is maintained but the murmur disappears and the patients develop differential cyanosis.

Differential Diagnosis

The differential diagnosis of PDA includes conditions capable of giving a continuous murmur over the precordium. In addition, combination of a pansystolic murmur with an early diastolic murmur, which are partly superimposed on each other, may simulate a continuous murmur over the precordium. Differential diagnosis of a continuous murmur includes: (i) coronary arteriovenous fistula; (ii) ruptured sinus of Valsalva fistulae into the right side, (iii) aortico-pulmonary septal defect; (iv) systemic arteriovenous fistula over the chest; (v) bronchial collateral murmurs; (vi) pulmonary arteriovenous fistula; (vii) peripheral pulmonic stenosis; (viii) venous hum including the one which is associated with total anomalous pulmonary venous connection; and (ix) small atrial septal defect associated with mitral stenosis.

The impression of continuous murmur due to a combination of a pansystolic murmur and regurgitant diastolic murmur occurs most commonly in ventricular septal defect associated with aortic regurgitation. This difficulty may also occur in combinations of mitral and/or tricuspid regurgitation with aortic regurgitation. Combination of aortic stenosis and aortic regurgitation never gives an auscultatory impression of a continuous murmur since a gap between the two murmurs can always be appreciated.

Treatment

A large PDA is better tolerated by term newborns when compared to preterm newborns. Premature newborns with a hemodynamically significant PDA that results in heart failure, respiratory distress or necrotizing enterocolitis require prompt management. Indomethacin or ibuprofen is often attempted. It is likely to be effective before the age of 2-weeks in preterm newborns and is unlikely to be useful in term babies. The dose is 0.1 mg/kg/dose, orally, 12 hourly for three doses. Hepatic or renal insufficiency or bleeding tendency are contraindications. Newborns not responding to these agents require surgical ligation. The PDA in term infants may close spontaneously as late as one month after birth and it is worth waiting to a month even if the duct is large unless CCF is refractory.

Large PDA may result in congestive cardiac failure in infancy. Echocardiography allows ready confirmation of the diagnosis and estimation of hemodynamic severity of the PDA. Catheter-based treatment (occlusive devices or coils) are now realistic in many patients. They are technically challenging in small infants especially those <5 kg and should be performed in centers that are accustomed to doing them. Today, indications for surgery for PDA include, small infants with large ducts, preterm infants, and ducts that are very large (larger than the size of available devices). In our country, surgery is more affordable in many centers and many patients can only be offered surgery. Occlusive devices are particularly expensive and often cost 3–4 times that of surgery.

Patients who have a PDA with pulmonary arterial hypertension are considered inoperable if a right to left shunt has appeared because of pulmonary arterial hypertension. Since the right to left shunt through the PDA flows down the descending aorta, cyanosis is present in toes but not in fingers. This is called *differential cyanosis* and is characteristic of PDA with pulmonary arterial hypertension and right to left shunt.

RIGHT TO LEFT SHUNTS

As indicated earlier, patients who are cyanotic have either pulmonic stenosis or pulmonary arterial hypertension.

Right to Left Shunts with Pulmonic Stenosis

Examples of this combination include tetralogy of Fallot, tricuspid atresia and Ebstein's anomaly.

Tetralogy of Fallot

Tetralogy of Fallot (TOF) is the commonest cyanotic congenital heart disease in children above the age of two years, constituting 75% of all patients. Its incidence in our clinic is 17%. Anatomically TOF consists of ventricular septal defect associated with obstruction to the right ventricular outflow in the form of infundibular or infundibular plus valvular pulmonic stenosis. The constituents of TOF are (i) ventricular septal defect, (ii) pulmonic stenosis, (iii) overriding or dextroposed aorta, and (iv) right ventricular hypertrophy.

14

Hemodynamics

Physiologically the pulmonic stenosis causes concentric right ventricular hypertrophy without cardiac enlargement and increase in right ventricular pressure (Fig. 14.13). When the right ventricular pressure is as high as the left ventricular or the aortic pressure, a right to left shunt appears to decompress the right ventricle. Once the right and left ventricular pressures have become identical, increasing severity of pulmonic stenosis reduces the flow of blood into the pulmonary artery and increases the right to left shunt. As the systolic pressures between the two ventricles are identical there is little or no left to right shunt and the ventricular septal defect is silent. The right to left shunt is also silent since it occurs at insignificant difference in pressure between the right ventricle and the aorta. The flow from the right ventricle into the pulmonary artery occurs across the pulmonic stenosis producing an ejection systolic murmur. The more severe the pulmonic stenosis, the less the flow into the pulmonary artery and the bigger the right to left shunt. Thus the more severe the pulmonic stenosis, the shorter the ejection systolic murmur and the more the cyanosis. *Thus, the severity of cyanosis is directly proportional to the severity of pulmonic stenosis, but the intensity of the systolic murmur is inversely related to the severity of pulmonic stenosis.* The ventricular septal defect of TOF is always large enough to allow free exit to the right to left shunt. Since the right ventricle is effectively decompressed by the ventricular septal defect, CCF never occurs in TOF. The exceptions to this rule are (i) anemia; (ii) infective endocarditis; (iii) systemic hypertension; (iv) unrelated myocarditis complicating TOF; and (v) aortic or pulmonary valve regurgitation.

The right ventricular outflow obstruction results in a delay in the P_2. Since the pulmonary artery pressure is

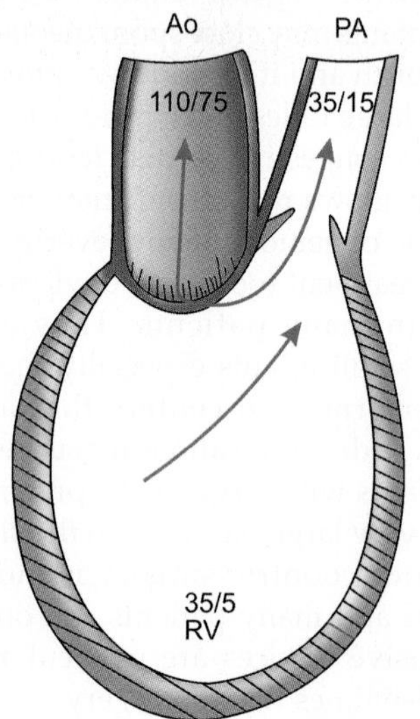

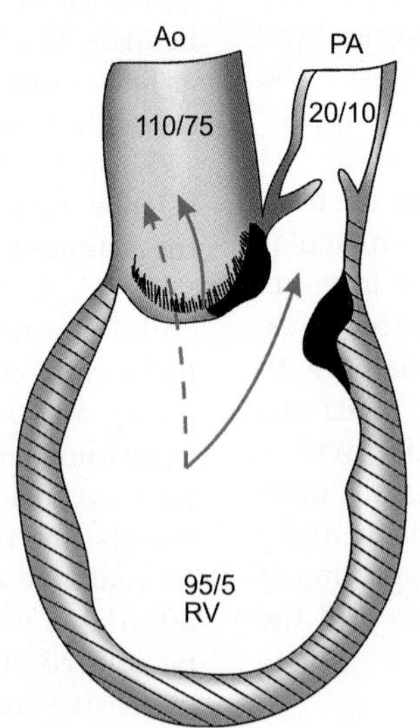

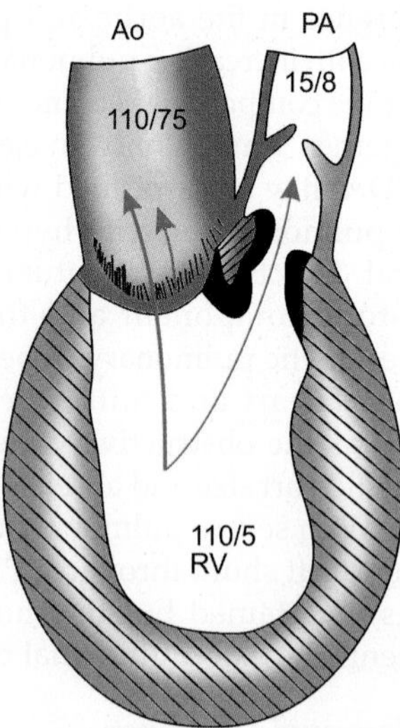

Fig. 14.13: Digrammatic portrayal: (A) ventricular septal defect, (B) ventricular septal defect with moderate pulmonic stenosis, and (C) Fallot's tetralogy. (A) In the absence of pulmonic stenosis the right ventricular (RV) and the pulmonary artery (PA) pressures are normal or slightly elevated. Since the left ventricular (LV) pressure is higher, there is a systolic flow of blood from the LV into the PA through the RV. (B) If a VSD is associated with moderate pulmonic stenosis, the RV systolic pressure increases and there is RV hypertrophy. The left to right shunt decreases and the VSD murmur becomes softer. The pulmonic stenosis murmur, however, is loud. (C). In Fallot's tetralogy the RV and LV pressures are identical. There is no left to right shunt and as such the VSD is silent. The flow from RV to PA decreases, decreasing the intensity of pulmonic stenosis murmur. A right to left shunt occurs from RV to Aorta (Ao) at identical pressures. As such the right to left shunt is silent

reduced, the P_2 is also reduced in intensity. The late and soft P_2 is generally inaudible in TOF. The S_2 is, therefore, single and the audible sound is A_2. Since the aorta is somewhat anteriorly displaced, the audible single A_2 is quite loud. The ascending aorta in TOF is large and may result in an aortic ejection click. On auscultation the diastolic interval is completely clear in TOF as there is no third or fourth sound or a diastolic murmur.

Concentric right ventricular hypertrophy reduces the distensibility of the right ventricle during diastole. The right atrial contraction at the end of diastole causes a relatively large 'a' waves. Although the 'a' waves are prominent in the jugular venous pulse, they are not too tall unless right ventricular dysfunction is present.

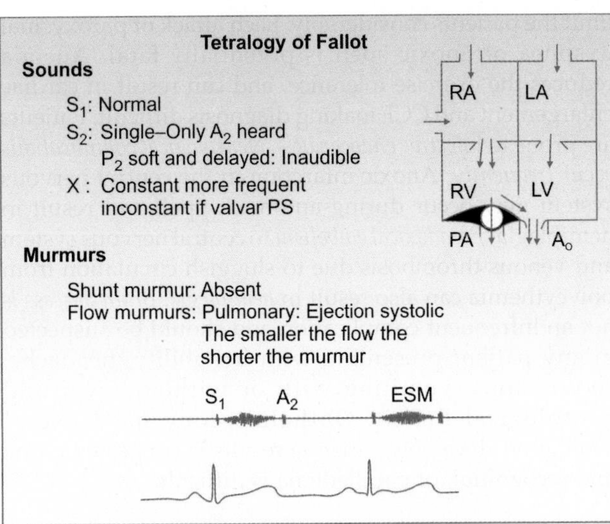

Fig. 14.14: Summary of auscultatory findings in Fallot's tetralogy. X = Systolic click

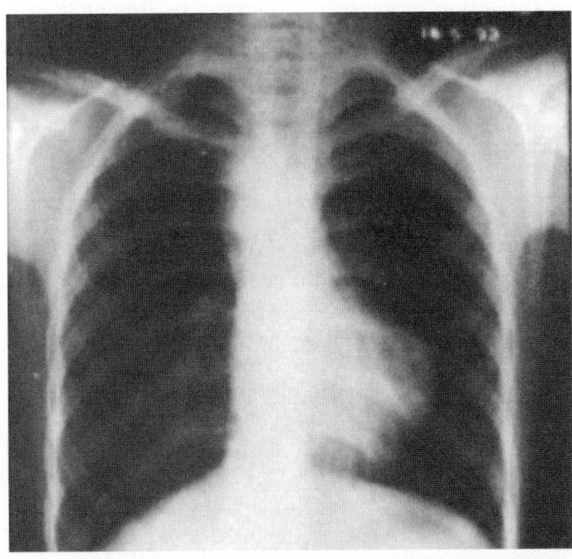

Fig. 14.15: Thoracic roentgenogram of Fallot's tetralogy. The cardiac size is normal, main pulmonary artery segment is concave, cardiac configuration is right ventricular. The lung fields are ischemic and the aorta is large in size

Clinical Features

Patients with TOF may become symptomatic any time after birth. Neonates as well as infants may develop anoxic spells (paroxysmal attacks of dyspnea). Cyanosis may be present from birth or make its appearance some years after birth. The commonest symptoms are dyspnea on exertion and exercise intolerance. The patients assume a sitting posture (squatting) as soon as they get dyspneic. Although squatting is not specific for TOF, it is the commonest cardiac lesion in which squatting is noted.

Anoxic spells occur predominantly after waking up or following exertion. The child starts crying, becomes dyspneic, bluer than before and may lose consciousness. Convulsions may occur. The frequency varies from once in a few days to numerous attacks every day.

Physical examination discloses *cyanosis, clubbing, slightly prominent 'a' waves in the jugular venous pulse, normal sized heart with a mild parasternal impulse, a systolic thrill in less than 30% patients, normal first sound, single second sound and an ejection systolic murmur which ends before the audible single second sound.* The only additional auscultation findings can be a constant ejection click due to a large aorta or an inconstant ejection click due to additional valvular pulmonic stenosis (Fig. 14.14).

EKG shows right axis deviation with right ventricular hypertrophy. The 'T' waves are inverted in right precordial leads. 'P' pulmonale may be present, but is uncommon. V_1 may show pure 'R' but transition to R/S complex occurs at V_2. The X-ray shows a normal sized heart with upturned apex, suggestive of right ventricular hypertrophy. The absence of main pulmonary artery segment gives the shape described as *cor-en sabot*. The aorta is enlarged and a right aortic arch is present in 30%; the latter is recognized by its concave impression on the right side of trachea. The pulmonary fields are oligemic (Fig. 14.15). Echocardiogram identifies the large overriding aorta, right ventricular hypertrophy and outflow obstruction; aortic-mitral valve continuity is maintained.

Assessment of Severity

As pointed out above the more the severity of cyanosis and the shorter the murmur, the more the severity of tetralogy. Paroxysmal attacks of dyspnea can be present with mild as well as severe TOF. However, effort intolerance is directly related to the severity.

Diagnosis

Echocardiography allows confirmation of diagnosis and also provides additional information required for surgery. Cardiac catheterization is seldom necessary.

Course and Complications

The pulmonic stenosis becomes progressively more severe with age. The dyspnea and increasing exercise intolerance limit the patients considerably. Each attack of paroxysmal dyspnea or anoxic spell is potentially fatal. Anemia reduces the exercise tolerance, and can result in cardiac enlargement and CCF making diagnosis difficult. Patients are prone to *infective endocarditis. Neurological complications occur frequently.* Anoxic infarction in the central nervous system may occur during an anoxic spell and result in hemiplegia. *Paradoxical embolism* to central nervous system and venous thrombosis due to sluggish circulation from polycythemia can also result in *hemiplegia. Brain abscess* is not an infrequent complication and should be suspected in any patient presenting with irritability, headache, convulsions, vomiting with or without fever and neurological deficit. Opthalmoscopy need expert evaluation since polycythemia results in congested retina and recognition of papilledema is difficult.

Treatment

The medical management of TOF is limited to management of complications including anoxic spells (Table 14.13) and correction of anemia. Operative treatment is of two types, palliative and definitive. *Palliative treatment* consists of anastomosing a systemic artery with the pulmonary artery to increase the pulmonary blood flow and thus increase the amount of oxygenated blood reaching the systemic circulation. While these procedures prolong life and increase the exercise tolerance, the basic disease remains unaltered.

Table 14.13: Management of anoxic spells
Knee chest position
Humidified oxygen
Morphine 0.1 to 0.2 mg/kg, SC
Obtain venous pH; sodium bicarbonate 1–3 ml/kg (diluted) IV
Propranolol 0.1 mg/kg/IV (during spell); 0.5–1 mg/kg/6 hourly orally (Alternatives: metoprolol, esmolol)
Vasopressors: methoxamine (Vasoxyl) IM or IV drip
Correct anemia
Consider surgery

The most common procedure is the modified *Blalock-Taussig shunt,* which consists of subclavian artery to pulmonary artery anastomosis using a Goretex graft. Shunts of historic importance include:

i. Classical Blalock-Taussig shunt: subclavian artery (side opposite the aortic arch) pulmonary artery anastomosis.
ii. Pott's shunt: descending aorta anastomosed to the pulmonary artery.
iii. Waterston's shunt: ascending aorta right pulmonary artery anastomosis.

The definitive operation consists of closing the ventricular septal defect and resecting the infundibular obstruction. The risk of operation is less than 5%; 85–90% patients return to normal life after surgery. With suitable anatomy, the operation can be performed at any age if pulmonary arteries are of adequate size and the anterior descending coronary artery is from the left coronary artery. Major complications include complete heart block, right bundle branch block, left anterior hemiblock, residual ventricular septal defect and residual pulmonic stenosis. Since the pulmonary valve is frequently excised, patients show pulmonary regurgitation and right ventricular dilatation. Long term risks following surgery include heart failure and ventricular tachyarrhythmias.

Tricuspid Atresia

Congenital absence of the tricuspid valve is called tricuspid atresia (Fig. 14.16). The right ventricle is hypoplastic and inflow portion absent. Tricuspid atresia constitutes 2% of all congenital heart disease in our clinic.

Hemodynamics

Atresia of the tricuspid valve results in the absence of a communication between the right atrium and the right ventricle. The right ventricle is underdeveloped, the inflow portion being absent. The only exit for the systemic venous blood coming to the right atrium through the inferior and superior vena cava is by way of the patent foramen ovale or an atrial septal defect. There is complete mixing of the systemic venous and pulmonary venous blood in the left atrium from where the blood passes to the left ventricle. A ventricular septal defect provides communication between the left ventricle and the outflow portion of the right ventricle. The pulmonary artery is connected to the right ventricular outflow and the aorta arises from the left ventricle in 70% cases. In 30% patients, aorta arises from the right ventricle and the pulmonary artery from the left ventricle. The latter group of patients is called tricuspid atresia with transposition of great arteries. The left ventricle, therefore, maintains both the systemic as well as the pulmonary circulation. The saturation of blood in the pulmonary artery and the aorta is identical. The saturation of blood in the aorta depends on the size of pulmonary blood flow. The larger the pulmonary blood flow, the more the oxygenated blood coming back to the left atrium to mix with the unoxygenated blood coming from the right atrium and the higher the final mixed saturation. The pulmonary blood flow is dependent on the size of the ventricular defect, which in tricuspid atresia is always a muscular defect. The smaller the ventricular septal defect, the less the pulmonary blood flow.

Clinical Features

Clinical presentation depends on the state of pulmonary flow, which may be diminished or increased. Patients with diminished pulmonary blood flow constitute 90% of all cases. Symptoms and physical signs are identical to TOF. Features suggesting tricuspid atresia are (i) left ventricular

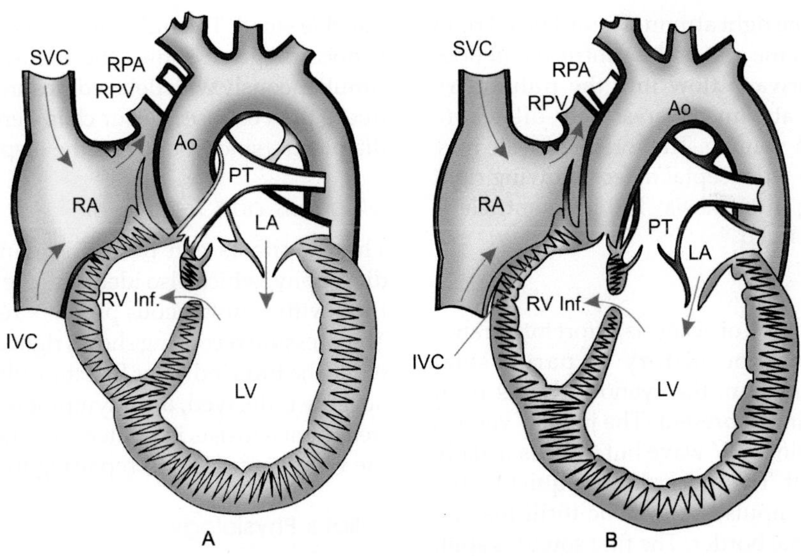

Fig. 14.16: Tricuspid atresia

(A) Normally related great arteries. Systemic venous blood reaching the RA through the superior (SVC) and inferior vena cava (IVC) reaches the LA through an atrial defect (or patent foramen ovale). There is complete mixing of the systemic and pulmonary venous blood in the LA. The LV is large. Aorta (Ao) arises from the LV. A muscular ventricular septal defects is the only route through which blood can reach the hypoplastic right ventricle (RV Inf.). The pulmonary trunk (PT) arises from the right ventricle. RPV and LPV = right and left pulmonary veins. (B) Transposed great arteries with tricuspid atresia. The PT is arising from the LV whereas the Ao is arising from RV (RA=Right artium, LA=Left artium, SVC and IVC=Superior and inferior vena cava, RV and LV=Right and left ventricle, RV Inf.=Right ventricular infundibulum, RPA and LPA = right and left pulmonary artery)

type of apical impulse; (ii) prominent large a waves in jugular venous pulse; (iii) enlarged liver with presystolic pulsations (a waves); and (iv) EKG showing left axis deviation and left ventricular hypertrophy. The mean QRS axis is around –45°. The P waves may show both right and left atrial hypertrophy. The chest X-ray shows oligemic lung fields, left ventricular configuration of the cardiac silhouette and a prominent superior vena cava. Echocardiogram identifies a large single ventricular cavity. In the four-chambered view, atretic tricuspid valve can be recognized and great vessel relationship established.

Patients of tricuspid atresia with increased pulmonary blood flow cannot generally be diagnosed accurately clinically.

Course

The patients of tricuspid atresia are relatively sicker compared to TOF. They show cyanosis from birth; anoxic spells and squatting may be present.

Treatment

The medical management is the same as for TOF. From the standpoint of surgical treatment, tricuspid atresia is classified under single ventricle physiology. This broad category includes all anatomic examples of single ventricle. In addition, this also includes situations when one atrioventricular valve is atretic or one of the ventricles is hypoplastic. Surgical management of single ventricle physiology is often in stages. The first stage involves early pulmonary arterial band (usually under the age of 3 months) for patients who have increased pulmonary blood flow and the modified Blalock-Taussig shunt for those who have reduced pulmonary blood flow with cyanosis. The second operation is the bidirectional Glenn shunt, where the superior vena cava is anastomosed to the right pulmonary artery. This surgery allows effective palliation until the age of 4–6 years. The Fontan operation is finally required for elimination of cyanosis. Here all the systemic venous return (from both vena cava) is routed to the pulmonary artery. This is at best a palliative procedure and there are important long-term issues in a substantial proportion of survivors.

Ebstein Anomaly

An unusual and rare cyanotic congenital heart disease with diminished pulmonary blood flow results from an abnormality of the tricuspid valve. The posterior as well as the septal leaflet of the tricuspid valve is displaced downwards to a variable extent. The result is an attachment to the posterior wall of the right ventricle. In addition, the leaflets are malformed and fused resulting in obstruction to flow of blood into the right ventricle. The portion of the right ventricle above the leaflet attachment thins out and is called atrialized right ventricle. The right ventricular contraction is also abnormal.

Hemodynamics

The tricuspid valve anomaly results in obstruction to forward flow of blood as well as its regurgitation from

14

the right ventricle into the right atrium. The atrialized right ventricle contracts with the rest of the ventricle and does not allow effective forward flow into the pulmonary circulation. The right atrium progressively dilates, to accommodate the extra volume. The foramen ovale may be patent or there is an atrial septal defect allowing right to left shunt, resulting in cyanosis. The left ventricle is hypertrophied and enlarged.

Clinical Features

Patients present with history of cyanosis, effort intolerance and fatigue; there may be history of paroxysmal tachycardia. On examination, the cyanosis varies from slight to severe. Clubbing is present. The jugular venous pulse may show a dominant 'V wave but there is usually no venous engorgement. The precordium is quiet with a left ventricular apical impulse. A systolic thrill may be palpable at the left sternal border. The first sound is split, however, the tricuspid component cannot be made out, resulting in a single, normally audible first sound. The abnormal tricuspid valve may produce a mid systolic click. The second sound is widely split, but variable with a soft pulmonic component. A right ventricular third sound and/or a right atrial fourth sound may be audible. The abnormal tricuspid valve may produce a mid systolic click. Thus, triple or quadruple sounds are usually heard. The murmur may be a midsystolic ejection or pansystolic murmur. There is also a short tricuspid delayed diastolic murmur. The systolic and the diastolic murmurs have a scratchy character, not unlike a pericardial friction rub.

The EKG characteristically shows P pulmonale, P mitrale and right bundle branch block. The R wave in V_1 does not exceed 7 mm; lead V_6 shows relatively tall R and broad S waves. Wolff Parkinson White type of conduction abnormality may be seen (Fig. 14.17). Chest X-ray shows right atrial and ventricular enlargement. The main pulmonary artery segment is prominent and the aortic knuckle small. The pulmonary vasculature is diminished. Echocardiogram shows the tricuspid and mitral valves simultaneously with delayed closure of the tricuspid valve (more than 65 msec). Four chambered view in 2D echo is diagnostic, since it outlines the displaced tricuspid valve.

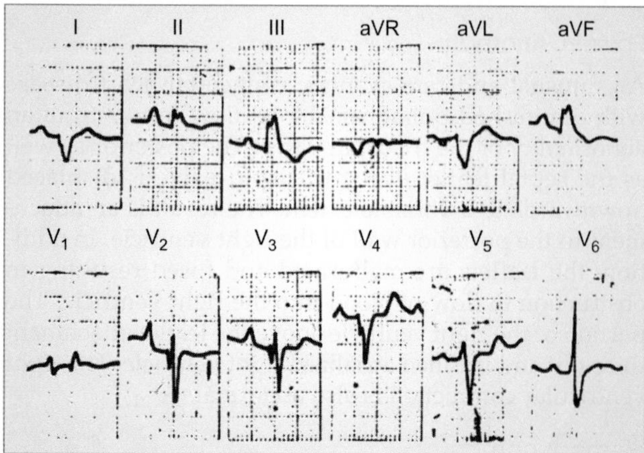

Fig. 14.17: Electrocardiogram typical of Ebstein anomaly. Right bundle branch block with 'R' of less than 7 mm is present

Diagnosis and Treatment

The diagnosis can be easily confirmed by echocardiography, which also identifies the severity. Intracardiac EKG with simultaneous pressure recording is of interest. The pressure recording shows right atrial type of pressure, while the EKG indicates that the catheter is in the ventricle. Surgery is delayed, until symptoms develop. The surgical treatment consists in obliterating the atrialized portion of the right ventricle and repairing the tricuspid valve.

Fallot's Physiology

The concept of Fallot's physiology is useful for the bedside identification of a group of conditions clinically presenting with similar symptoms and signs. *The diagnosis of TOF is made in a cyanotic child with a normal sized heart, mild parasternal impulse, normal first sound and an ejection systolic murmur ending before a single second sound.* History of paroxysmal attacks of dyspnea and squatting may be present. Identical symptoms and physical findings are present in (i) complete transposition of great arteries with ventricular septal defect and pulmonic stenosis, (ii) double outlet right ventricle with pulmonic stenosis and a large subaortic ventricular septal defect, (iii) tricuspid atresia with diminished pulmonary blood flow, (iv) single ventricle with pulmonic stenosis, and (v) corrected transposition of great arteries with ventricular septal defect and pulmonic stenosis. The above described symptoms and physical findings are related to the presence of a large ventricular septal defect associated with pulmonic stenosis. Clinically with the help of EKG and chest X-ray it is not always possible to separate TOF from the above conditions, except tricuspid atresia (which shows left axis deviation and left ventricular hypertrophy). Fallot's physiology identifies these six anomalies, which are surgically treatable and potentially correctable. 2D echocardiography can distinguish and identify these anomalies fairly accurately.

Tetralogy of Fallot (TOF): EKG shows right axis deviation (axis between 90–150°). Echo identifies aortic overriding of the septum, aortic valve mitral valve continuity and the posterior great vessel being the aorta.

Transposition of great vessels with ventricular septal defect and pulmonic stenosis: EKG is similar to that seen in TOF. Echocardiogram identifies that the aorta is to the right of and anterior to the posterior great vessel, the pulmonary artery. Aorta is connected to the right ventricle and the pulmonary artery to the left ventricle. The pulmonary valve and mitral valve are continuous.

Tricuspid atresia: EKG is diagnostic; echo identifies only one atrioventricular valve and one ventricle. The atretic tricuspid valve is better seen in the apical four-chambered view.

Single ventricle with pulmonic stenosis: EKG shows left axis deviation with right ventricular hypertrophy or right axis deviation with left ventricular hypertrophy. Monophasic or equiphasic QRS complexes in all the precordial leads are also suggestive of single ventricle. Echocardiogram can identify a single large ventricular cavity receiving both atrioventricular valves.

Corrected transposition of great vessels, ventricular septal defect, pulmonic stenosis: EKG may show right or left axis deviation; precordial leads show qR complexes in the right sided and absent Q waves in left chest leads; complete heart block is associated. Echo shows inversion of ventricles.

Double outlet right ventricle, pulmonic stenosis, large ventricular septal defect: EKG shows right axis deviation with right ventricular hypertrophy. Echocardiography shows separation between the posterior great vessel and the mitral valve and that both great vessels are connected to the right ventricle.

Transposition of Great Vessels

Transposition of great vessels (TGA) is defined as *aorta arising from the right ventricle and pulmonary artery from the left ventricle.* By definition, therefore, the great vessels (aorta, pulmonary artery) arise from inappropriate ventricles, both of which must be present and identifiable. Anatomically TGA is divided into the *complete variety* and the *physiologically corrected type.* In complete TGA, the right atrium empties into the right ventricle from which aorta arises. The left atrium drains into the left ventricle to which the pulmonary artery is connected. This results in complete separation of the systemic and pulmonary circulation. In the physiologically corrected TGA (also known as L-TGA) the right atrium is connected to an inverted morphologically left ventricle, which is connected to the pulmonary artery whereas the left atrium is connected to the inverted morphologically right ventricle connected to aorta. Thus, the route of blood flow is normal and hence the name corrected TGA (Fig. 14.18).

Hemodynamics

In complete TGA the aorta generally lies anterior and to the right of the pulmonary artery. For this reason, this is also referred to as D-TGA. Since the systemic and pulmonary circulations are separate, survival depends on the presence of atrial, ventricular or aortopulmonary communications. Complete TGA is classified into (*a*) with intact ventricular septum, and (*b*) with ventricular septal defect. The latter is subdivided into cases with and without pulmonic stenosis. Patients with complete TGA,

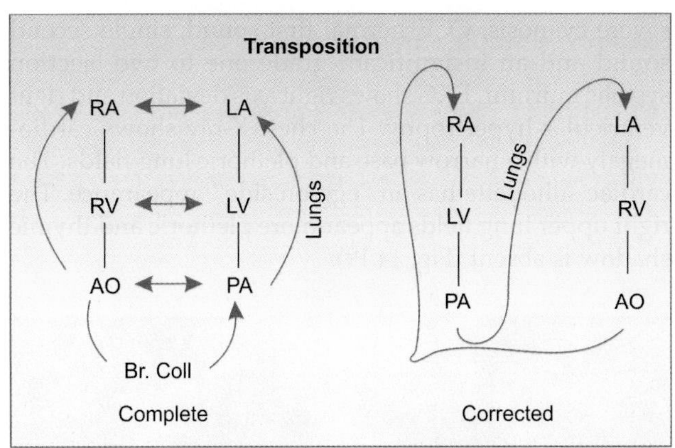

Fig. 14.18: The route of blood flow in complete TGA results in two separate circulations and survival depends on mixing. The mixing can occur at the atrial, ventricular or great vessel level. Bronchial collaterals (Br. Coll.) also increase pulmonary blood flow: In corrected TGA the route of blood flow is normal. Hemodynamics depend on associated anomalies

ventricular septal defect and pulmonic stenosis have been covered in Fallot's physiology. In patients with TGA, the oxygenated pulmonary venous blood recirculates in the lungs whereas the systemic venous blood recirculates in the systemic circulation. The pulmonary artery saturation is thus always higher than the aortic saturation. Survival depends on the mixing available between the two circulations. In patients with intact ventricular septum, the mixing site is the atrial communication. Generally, the atrial communication is the patent foramen ovale and being small the mixing is very poor. Neonates thus are symptomatic due to severe hypoxemia and systemic acidosis within the first few days after birth.

Presence of a ventricular septal defect of adequate size results in good mixing. As the fetal pulmonary vasculature regresses, the pulmonary blood flow increases and results in CCF around 4–10 weeks of age. The failing left ventricle and large pulmonary blood flow increase the left atrial pressure. The patients, therefore, have pulmonary venous hypertension as well. The mixing with a large ventricular septal defect can be so good that at times cyanosis can be missed. The presence of a large ventricular septal defect equalizes pressures in the two ventricles as well as the great arteries. The pulmonary artery also carries a large flow. Patients with TGA and large ventricular septal defect develop pulmonary vascular obstructive disease (Eisenmenger physiology) early in life.

Clinical Features

Patients of complete TGA with intact ventricular septum are cyanotic at birth. Since the interatrial communication results in poor mixing, the neonates present with rapid breathing and CCF secondary to hypoxemia within the first week of life. The heart size can be normal in the first two weeks of life but enlarges rapidly. Examination shows severe cyanosis, CCF, normal first sound, single second sound and an insignificant grade one to two ejection systolic murmur. EKG shows right axis deviation and right ventricular hypertrophy. The chest X-ray shows cardiomegaly with a narrow base and plethoric lung fields. The cardiac silhouette has an "egg on side" appearance. The right upper lung fields appear more plethoric and thymic shadow is absent (Fig. 14.19).

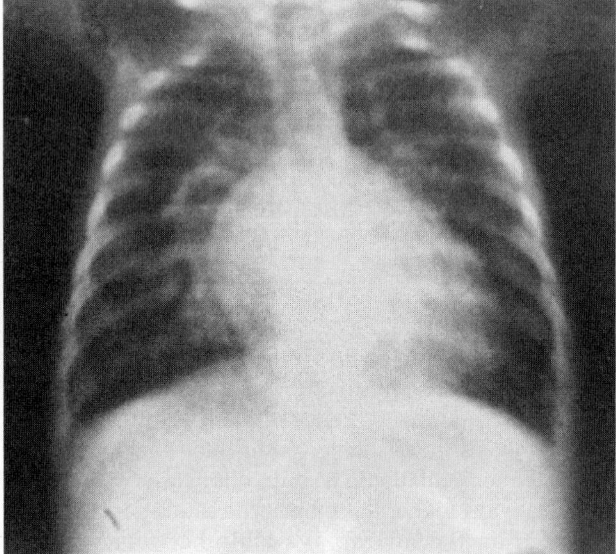

Fig. 14.19: Egg on side appearance in transposition

Patients of complete TGA with ventricular septal defect have a large pulmonary blood flow, good mixing at the ventricular level and as such the cyanosis is relatively mild. They develop CCF around 4–10 weeks of age. Physical findings consist of cyanosis, cardiomegaly, congestive failure, normal first sound, single or normally split second sound and a grade two to four ejection systolic murmur. Apical third sound gallop or a middiastolic rumble may be present. EKG shows right axis deviation with biventricular, right ventricular or left ventricular hypertrophy; chest X-ray shows cardiomegaly, plethoric lung fields and some features of pulmonary venous hypertension.

Treatment

Medical management has little to offer. Oxygenation can hardly be improved by administering oxygen. The best approach consists in doing balloon atrial septostomy following confirmation of the diagnosis. This procedure can be accomplished in the cardiac catheterization laboratory or on the patient's bedside. The septostomy is successful only up to the age of 6–12 weeks. Septostomy gives temporary relief by providing better mixing as well as reducing the left atrial pressure. If the diagnosis can be established below the age of two weeks and facilities for operation at this age are available, the patient can be subjected to definitive repair by the arterial switch operation (Jatene's repair). The pulmonary artery and aorta are transected. The distal aorta is anastomosed to the proximal pulmonary stump (neoaortic root) and the pulmonary artery to the proximal aortic stump (neopulmonary artery). The coronary arteries are moved along to the neoaortic root along with a cuff of aortic tissue to allow suturing without compromising coronary blood flow. The other operation available for complete TGA is atrial switch operation (Mustard or Senning) in which the pulmonary venous blood is redirected to the right ventricle and the systemic venous blood to the left ventricle, thus establishing normal route of blood flow. Jatene's switch operation is preferable to atrial switch since the latter results in complications like right ventricular failure and atrial arrhythmias in later life. Most cardiac centers strive to achieve excellence with the arterial switch because the long-term results are satisfying.

If a ventricular septal defect is present it can be closed at the same time. If facilities for definitive repair are not available, pulmonary artery banding can be done in patients with a ventricular septal defect to protect the pulmonary vasculature. Since PDA results in early pulmonary vascular disease, it should be divided as early as possible. Since patients with TGA tend to develop pulmonary vascular obstructive disease (Eisenmenger physiology) early in life even if they have only an atrial communication, they should be operated as early as possible, ideally below the age of three months.

Corrected TGA

In corrected TGA the aorta lies anterior and to the left of the pulmonary artery. The ascending aorta forms the left upper border of the cardiac silhouette. Since the route of blood flow is normal, it is the associated anomalies, which determine the clinical features. The associated anomalies, present in more than 98%, include (i) ventricular septal defect with or without pulmonic stenosis; (ii) left sided Ebstein's anomaly of the tricuspid valve (clinically simulates mitral regurgitation); and (iii) atrioventricular conduction defects including complete atrioventricular block. The most useful clue for the diagnosis of corrected TGA is related to inversion of the ventricles. The precordial leads V_{4R}, V_1, and V_2 may show a Q wave which is absent in the left precordial leads. The chest roentgenogram shows a smooth left upper border corresponding to the ascending aorta. The diagnosis depends on echocardiographic identification of ventricular inversion as well as additional anomalies.

Total Anomalous Pulmonary Venous Connection

Total anomalous pulmonary venous connection (TAPVC) is an uncommon condition. The pulmonary veins instead of joining the left atrium are connected anomalously to result in the total pulmonary venous blood reaching the right atrium. TAPVC is classified into supracardiac, cardiac, infracardiac and mixed varieties. In supracardiac

TAPVC, the pulmonary veins join together to form a common pulmonary vein that drains into the left innominate vein or the right superior vena cava. In the cardiac TAPVC, the veins join the coronary sinus or enter the right atrium directly. In the infracardiac variety, the common pulmonary vein drains into the portal vein.

Hemodynamics

TAPVC results in the pulmonary venous blood reaching the right atrium, which also receives the systemic venous blood. This results in almost complete mixing of the two venous returns. The blood flow to the left atrium is through a patent foramen ovale or atrial septal defect. The oxygen saturation in the pulmonary artery is higher or identical to that in the aorta because of mixing of the blood in the right atrium. Physiologically TAPVC can be divided into (a) patients with pulmonary venous obstruction, and (b) patients without pulmonary venous obstruction. Pulmonary venous obstruction results in pulmonary hypertension as well as restriction to pulmonary blood flow. In the absence of pulmonary venous obstruction, the pulmonary blood flow is large and results in CCF between 4–10 weeks of age. TAPVC of the infracardiac type is always obstructive, while cardiac and supracardiac types may or may not have pulmonary venous obstruction.

Clinical Features

TAPVC of the non-obstructive type is commoner than the obstructive type. Patients present with cyanosis and CCF as the fetal pulmonary vasculature regresses, typically around 4–10 weeks of age. With large pulmonary blood flow, the cyanosis may be minimal or clinically not recognizable. The patients are irritable and have failure to thrive. They also show hyperkinetic precordium, normal or accentuated first sound, widely split and fixed second sound with accentuated pulmonic component, grade II–IV pulmonary ejection systolic murmur and a tricuspid flow murmur. The physical findings are identical to that of an atrial septal defect. Presence of CCF at this age suggests TAPVC since CCF in atrial septal defect at this age is very rare. A continuous venous hum may be audible at the upper left or right sternal border or in the suprasternal notch.

Patients with obstructive type of TAPVC present with marked cyanosis and CCF within the first 1–2 weeks of life. Physical findings consist of a normal sized heart with parasternal heave, normal first sound, accentuated pulmonic component of S_2 and insignificant murmurs. Tricuspid regurgitation can occur and results in cardiomegaly.

Diagnosis

EKG in TAPVC with or without pulmonary venous obstruction shows right axis deviation and right ventricular hypertrophy. In obstructive TAPVC, P pulmonale is common. The chest X-ray shows cardiomegaly with plethoric lung fields in non-obstructive TAPVC. In the first two years of life, characteristic pattern of the 'snowman' or figure of '8' configuration in the supracardiac TAPVC draining to left innominate vein is not seen. Chest X-ray in obstructive TAPVC consists of a normal sized heart with severe pulmonary venous hypertension resulting in a ground glass appearance of the lungs. Echocardiography allows confirmation of the diagnosis, definition of the individual pulmonary veins and assessment of the site of obstruction if present.

The diagnosis of obstructive TAPVC is considered in a cyanotic neonate with a normal sized heart and ground glass lung fields. The diagnosis of non-obstructive TAPVC is suspected if auscultatory features of atrial septal defect are associated with either cyanosis or congestive failure in the first 2–3 months of life.

Management

Operation is indicated as early as possible since 80% of infants die within the first three months of life without surgical help. Obstructed TAPVC constitute a surgical emergency. The results of surgery for both forms of TAPVC are satisfactory but newborns and infants with obstructed TAPVC might develop pulmonary hypertensive crisis in the postoperative period and need expert management.

Cyanosis with Increased Pulmonary Blood Flow

A large number of conditions result in the combination of cyanosis with increased pulmonary blood flow. Common to these conditions is the presence of abnormal mixing of pulmonary venous blood with the systemic venous blood and absence of obstruction to pulmonary blood flow. The anomalies included in this group of conditions are transposition of great vessels, total anomalous pulmonary venous connection, single ventricle without obstruction to pulmonary blood flow, persistent truncus arteriosus, tricuspid atresia with absence of obstruction to pulmonary blood flow and double outlet right ventricle without pulmonic stenosis. Patients present with CCF in the neonatal period and are characterized by the presence of cyanosis, cardiomegaly and failure to thrive. Almost 80% die within the first 3 months of life due to CCF or pulmonary infection. Those who survive develop pulmonary hypertension due to pulmonary vascular obstructive disease and become inoperable and thus incurable. Echocardiography or cardiac catheterization with angiography are necessary for the specific diagnosis. Operative treatment is not possible without the correct diagnosis. Since mortality of unoperated patients is high and patients develop Eisenmenger syndrome early, it is necessary that patients presenting with cyanosis and increased pulmonary blood flow be referred to centers where facilities for care for such patients is available.

Cyanotic Congenital Heart Disease with Pulmonary Arterial Hypertension

This group of patients are also termed Eisenmenger syndrome, implying the presence of severe pulmonary arterial hypertension resulting in a right to left shunt at the atrial, ventricular or pulmonary arterial level. Eisenmenger complex consists of pulmonary arterial hypertension with a ventricular septal defect providing the right to left shunt.

Hemodynamics

14

The pulmonary arterial hypertension is due to pulmonary vascular obstructive disease. If a communication is present at the pulmonary arterial level or the ventricular level, the right ventricular pressure cannot go beyond the systemic pressure. The right to left shunt decompresses the right ventricle. The right ventricle has only concentric hypertrophy without significant increase in the size. In patients who have PDA or ventricular septal defect, there is only a mild parasternal impulse without a significant heave. In patients who do not have a ventricular septal defect or PDA, the right ventricle, besides hypertrophy, also dilates. The right to left shunt at the atrial level is an indication of right ventricular failure to accommodate this volume and push into the pulmonary artery. Thus, patients of Eisenmenger syndrome with communication at the atrial level only, exhibit a parasternal heave and cardiac enlargement. The right ventricular pressure may even be higher than the systemic pressure.

A right to left shunt at the atrial level or the ventricular level reaches the ascending aorta and is thus distributed to the whole systemic circulation. This results in equal cyanosis of fingers and toes. A right to left shunt through a PDA is directed into the descending aorta, since the ductus joins the arch of aorta distal to the origin of left subclavian artery. This results in the right to left shunt reaching only the distribution of descending aorta. The fingers remain pink while the toes show cyanosis and clubbing; *differential cyanosis* is characteristic of pulmonary arterial hypertension with a PDA.

The etiology of pulmonary arterial hypertension is not known. High pulmonary artery oxygen saturation, high flow through the pulmonary artery and hyperreactive pulmonary vasculature have been considered as possible explanations.

Clinical Features

Patients present with history of cyanosis, fatigue, effort intolerance and dyspnea. There may be history of repeated chest infections in childhood; examination shows cyanosis and clubbing. The features indicative of pulmonary arterial hypertension consist of parasternal impulse and palpable S_2. The pulmonary component of S_2 is accentuated and louder than the aortic component. The splitting of S_2 remains wide and fixed in atrial septal defect. Due to superimposition of A_2 and P_2 the second sound is single in patients who have a ventricular septal defect. Patients with PDA continue to have a normally split S2. A pulmonary ejection click, which unlike patients of valvar pulmonic stenosis, is well heard during inspiration and expiration. A functional pulmonary regurgitation murmur can be present along the left sternal border. Patients with atrial septal defect, in whom Eisenmenger physiology is uncommon, can develop tricuspid regurgitation (Fig. 14.20).

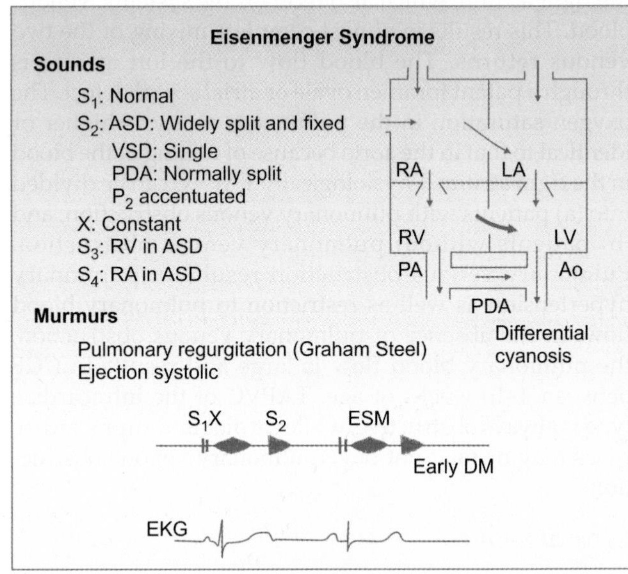

Fig. 14.20: Summary of auscultatory findings in Eisenmenger syndrome

EKG shows right axis deviation and right ventricular hypertrophy; P pulmonale may be present. The chest X-ray is characteristic with prominent pulmonary arterial segment and large right and left main pulmonary arteries, but oligemic lung fields. Thus, the hilar area shows pulmonary plethora while the peripheral fields suggest oligemia.

Treatment

There is no role for surgical treatment. Medical management consists in treating chest infections, correcting anemia and managing CCF. Intermittent use of oxygen may help relieve syncope, severe headaches and angina-like chest pain. Ideally, pulmonary vascular obstructive disease should be prevented from developing. This means careful evaluation and follow up of patients of ventricular septal defect and PDA in the first two years of life, when pulmonary arterial hypertension is generally reversible. Patients with cyanosis and increased pulmonary blood flow develop Eisenmenger physiology very early and need to be operated by two to three months of age. Patients who have features of pulmonary arterial hypertension should be operated early to prevent the development of irreversible pulmonary arterial hypertension.

Medications have recently become available for the management of pulmonary hypertension. These include agents that reduce pulmonary hypertension. The phosphodiestrase-5 inhibitors (sildenafil, tadalafil) selectively increase the local availability of cyclic GMP in the pulmonary vascular smooth muscles, promoting pulmonary vasodilation. Bosentan, sitaxsentan and ambrisentan are endothelin receptor blockers, which inhibit the pulmonary vasoconstrictor effects of endothelin, promote vasodilation and enable vascular remodeling. Prostacyclin analogs promote pulmonary vasodilation. The results of preliminary studies with these agents in Eisenmenger syndrome are promising.

OBSTRUCTIVE LESIONS

Aortic Stenosis

Congenital aortic stenosis constitutes about 8% of all congenital cardiac lesions in our clinic. Pathologically the obstruction is at the valve, above the valve (supravalvar) or below the valve (subvalvar). At the valve level, the aortic stenosis results from either unicuspid or bicuspid aortic valve. Rarely the aortic valve ring may itself be small. The unicuspid aortic valve is stenotic from its design and the patients are symptomatic early in life. The bicuspid aortic valve results in significant obstruction when the valves become thicker and relatively immobile, usually at 30–40 years of age. ***Supravalvar aortic stenosis*** results from obstruction in the root of aorta, above the aortic valve. It is typically associated with Williams' syndrome.

Subvalvar aortic stenosis is of many varieties:

i. *Discrete membranous subvalvar stenosis:* Results from a membrane, with a central or eccentric hole, at the left ventricular outflow tract. It may be very close to the aortic valve or just below the valve ring.
ii. *Fibromuscular subvalvar aortic stenosis:* Fibromuscular tissue present below the aortic valve narrows down the left ventricular outflow. The fibromuscular tissue extends from the septal wall of the left ventricle to the anterior (aortic) leaflet of the mitral valve.
iii. *Idiopathic hypertrophic subaortic stenosis:* It is also called asymmetrical septal hypertrophy or hypertrophic obstructive cardiomyopathy. The ventricular septum, hypertrophied out of proportion to the rest of the ventricular wall, results in narrowing of the left ventricular outflow tract.

Hemodynamics

Obstruction at the aortic valve level is overcome by raising the systolic pressure of the left ventricle. This is brought about by concentric hypertrophy of the left ventricle. Because of a powerful, muscular left ventricle, the emptying of the left ventricle is complete but the duration of the systole is prolonged. The prolongation of left ventricular ejection time causes delayed closure of the aortic valve resulting in delayed A2. The flow across the obstruction results in the aortic ejection systolic murmur, which is typically diamond shaped, starting after the first sound and ending before the aortic component of the second sound with a mid-systolic peak. The systolic murmur is always palpable as a thrill at the second right interspace, suprasternal notch and the carotid vessels. The powerful left ventricle can maintain a normal forward cardiac output. The prolonged ejection results in the characteristic pulse, which can be best described as slowly rising to a peak, which is sustained and then has a slow down-slope. The peak is low so that the pulse is of low amplitude and prolonged duration.

Concentric hypertrophy of the left ventricle results in decreased distensibility of the left ventricle in diastole-reduced compliance. In severe aortic stenosis, therefore, with marked left ventricular hypertrophy, the left ventricular diastolic pressure also rises. With increase in left ventricular diastolic pressure, the left atrial pressure must increase to be able to fill the left ventricle during diastole. Hence, with severe aortic stenosis accompanied with marked left ventricular hypertrophy, a forceful left atrial contraction results in a palpable as well as audible fourth sound (S_4). When the left ventricle starts failing in aortic stenosis, besides hypertrophy dilatation also appears and causes increase in heart size. With left ventricular failure a third sound (S_3) becomes audible.

In valvar aortic stenosis there is post stenotic dilatation of the ascending aorta, visible in the posteroanterior thoracic roentgenogram. In supravalvar and subvalvar aortic stenosis the post stenotic dilatation is absent. A dilated ascending aorta is associated with an ejection click. In valvar aortic stenosis, the first sound is followed by an ejection click, which precedes the starts of the murmur. The aortic ejection click is well heard at the apex, and along the left sternal border.

Clinical Features

The patients of mild to moderate aortic stenosis are asymptomatic. With severe aortic stenosis the initial symptom is generally dyspnea on exertion. The patients may also give history of angina on effort and syncope. Presence of any one of these three symptoms suggests severe aortic stenosis. The blood pressure is normal with mild aortic stenosis. *The more the severity of aortic stenosis, the narrower the pulse pressure.* This gives the characteristic low amplitude prolonged duration pulse. The cardiac size remains normal unless left ventricular failure is present. The apical impulse is forcible or heaving. In severe aortic stenosis the fourth sound may be palpable. If left ventricular failure is present the third sound may be palpable. A systolic thrill is palpable at the second right interspace, suprasternal notch and the carotid arteries. The first sound is normal and followed by an ejection click in valvar aortic stenosis. The aortic component of the *second sound (A_2) is delayed but not diminished in intensity in* aortic stenosis. The delay results in normally but closely split,

14

single or paradoxically split second sound according to the severity of obstruction. With severe aortic stenosis an S4 is audible. In aortic stenosis associated with left ventricular failure S3 is palpable and audible. The ejection systolic murmur starting after the ejection click reaches a peak in mid-systole. (Fig. 14.21). With increasing severity of aortic stenosis the peak is delayed so that the maximum intensity of the murmur is closer to the end rather than being midsystolic. With immobile valves either due to severe fibrosis or calcification the systolic click as well as the A2 diminish in intensity and may become inaudible (Fig. 14.22).

The discrete subvalvar aortic stenosis is differentiated from valvar aortic stenosis by the absence of click and the post stenotic dilatation of the ascending aorta in the thoracic roentgenogram. In most of these patients an aortic regurgitation murmur is audible if carefully looked for. The aortic regurgitation murmur results from the blood, trapped between the closed aortic valve and the discrete diaphragm, leaking during diastole into the main ventricular cavity. There are no specific features based on which fibromuscular subaortic obstruction can be separated clinically from discrete membranous subaortic stenosis. The aortic regurgitation murmur may or may not be present. The maximum intensity of the systolic

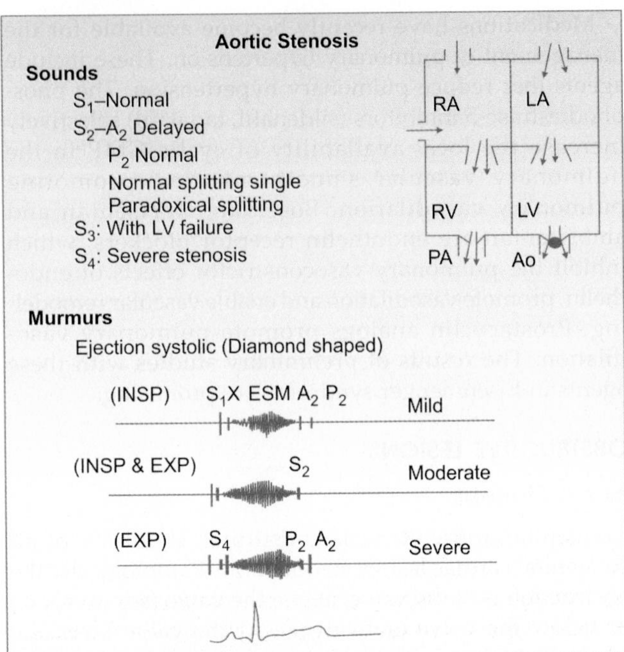

Fig. 14.22: Summary of auscultatory findings in aortic stenosis: S_4 fourth sound; X aortic click

murmur and thrill may be in the third or fourth left interspace.

Supravalvar aortic stenosis is associated with characteristic "elfin" facies, mental retardation, dental abnormalities, strabismus and peripheral arterial stenosis. It is closely related to idiopathic hypercalcemia and may be due to hypervitaminosis D. Since the obstruction is above the aortic valve, the pressure in the segment of the aorta before the obstruction is also elevated and results in a loud A2. The jet through the supravalvar narrowing may be directed toward the innominate artery resulting in a slightly higher systolic pressure in the right arm compared to the left arm.

EKG reveals left ventricular hypertrophy; presence of ST and T wave changes suggest severe aortic stenosis. *However, a normal EKG does not exclude severe aortic stenosis.* The chest X-ray exhibits a normal sized heart with dilated ascending aorta in valvar aortic stenosis. In supravalvar and subvalvar aortic stenosis, the roentgenogram may be normal. Presence of cardiac enlargement indicates severe aortic stenosis. Echocardiogram can not only identify the site of aortic stenosis, but also assess the gradient across the obstruction accurately.

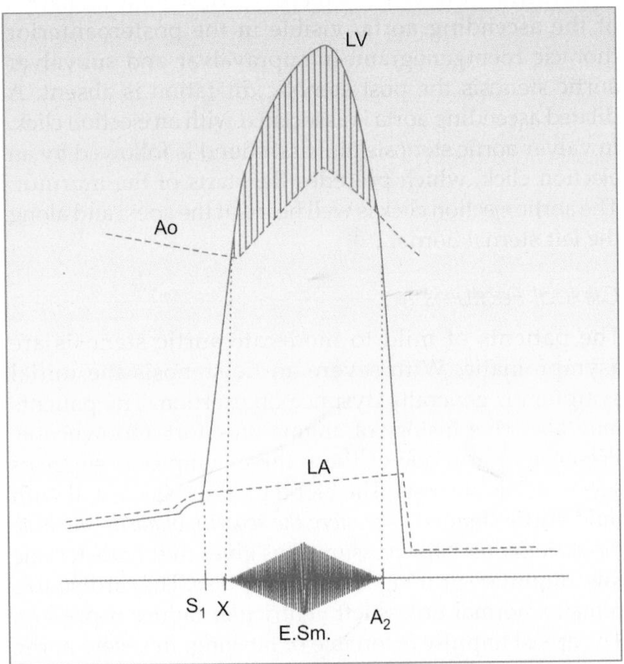

Fig. 14.21: Aortic stenosis: Diagrammatic portrayal of the hemodynamic basis for aortic stenosis murmur. The first sound (S_1) occurs as the left ventricular (LV) pressure increases above left atrial (LA) pressure. This is followed by the ejection click (X) occurring after the aortic valve opens. The shape of the gradient between LV and aorta (Ao) corresponds to the shape of the aortic ejection systolic murmur (ESm). The murmur ends before the aortic components of the second sound (A_2)

Assessment of Severity

In every patient it is necessary to assess the severity of aortic stenosis. Absence of an indication of severity means incomplete diagnosis. The clinical assessment of severity depends on the following

a. Symptomatic patients have severe aortic stenosis. If the patient is asymptomatic, it does not exclude severe aortic stenosis.

b. Narrower the pulse pressure, the more severe the aortic stenosis.
c. Presence of a systolic thrill at the second right interspace suggests at least moderately severe aortic stenosis. If the thrill is felt only in the suprasternal notch and not at the second right interspace, it favors mild or critical aortic stenosis in failure.
d. The later the peak of the ejection systolic murmur, the more severe the narrowing.
e. The delay in the A_2 is reasonably well correlated with severity. With mild aortic stenosis the S_2 is normally split, with moderate aortic stenosis it is closely split, with severe or critical aortic stenosis it is single or paradoxically split.
f. Presence of S_4 is indirect evidence for severe aortic stenosis.
g. Presence of S_3 indicates severe aortic stenosis and congestive cardiac failure.
h. ST and T changes on the EKG favor severe aortic stenosis.
i. Cardiac enlargement indicates severe aortic stenosis with left ventricular failure.
j. Doppler echo can quantitate the gradient across the aortic valve very accurately.

Left ventricular myocardial disease may alter the findings to favor a more severe lesion.

Treatment

Patients with aortic stenosis should be followed closely, noting the blood pressure, second heart sound and pulse pressure on each visit. An EKG should be obtained every 6–12 months. Symptoms should be carefully evaluated, if necessary by direct questioning. Doppler echo can be used to quantitate the gradient at each visit. Aortic stenosis is a progressive lesion becoming more severe with time. It is a bad disease since it is *one of the few lesions that can cause sudden death.* The patients should be discouraged from outdoor games, athletics, competitive sports and strenuous exercises if the stenosis is significant (gradients of 50 mm Hg or more). If the clinical assessment is in doubt, the patient must have echo and Doppler studies for proper assessment. If there is evidence for CCF, the patient should be digitalized.

Balloon aortic valvuloplasty is an established technique for non-operative relief of aortic obstruction. A balloon introduced through the femoral artery can be placed at the aortic valve and inflated to tear the valve along the commissure. It is indicated if the gradient is above 75 mm; the procedure may be repeated if restenosis occurs. Significant aortic regurgitation is a contraindication for balloon valvotomy. Supravalvar and subvalvar aortic stenosis do not respond to balloon dilation.

Surgical treatment is indicated if significant aortic regurgitation is associated.

The two main operations being done at present are aortic valvotomy and aortic valve replacement. Surgical valvotomy is done if balloon valvotomy is unsuccessful. The operative treatment for aortic valve is unsatisfactory since a patient who has had valvotomy may develop aortic regurgitation. Over the next 5–10 years, the valve may become immobile resulting in reappearance of aortic stenosis and necessitating valve replacement. Patients who get valve replacement also cannot be considered cured, since none of the prosthetic valves or homograft valves will last indefinitely. The patients have to be kept on anticoagulants if they have a prosthetic valve replacement and need very careful follow up to ensure that they do not develop infective endocarditis.

Coarctation of the Aorta

Congenital coarctation of the aorta is located at the junction of the arch with the descending aorta. It is a sharp indentation involving the anterior, lateral and the posterior wall of the aorta. The medial wall is spared in the narrowing. It may be distal or proximal to the ductus or ligamentum arteriosus and also the left subclavian artery. Forty to 80% patients have a bicuspid aortic valve.

Hemodynamics

The previous classification of preductal (infantile) and postductal (adult) coarctation is no more used. Physiologically the difference between the preductal and postductal coarctation depends on the absence or presence of collateral anastomosing vessels. In the fetal life, the right ventricular output passes down the descending aorta through a wide ductus arteriosus. The left ventricular output empties into the innominate, left carotid and left subclavian arteries. Very little of the left ventricular output reaches the descending aorta. The portion of the aorta distal to the left subclavian and before the portion where the ductus arteriosus joins is called the isthmus. At birth, normally the isthmus is the most narrow part of the aorta. If the fetus has a preductal coarctation it does not interfere with his normal hemodynamics and collaterals are not formed as they are not necessary. On the other hand if a postductal coarctation is present it is operative in the fetal life as it interferes with the right ventricular output reaching the descending aorta. This stimulates formation of collaterals even in the fetal life. After birth when the right ventricular output is directed into the pulmonary arteries and there is no flow from the pulmonary artery into the aorta, the descending aorta must receive its total supply from the left ventricle via the ascending aorta. Since in preductal coarctation there are no collaterals, the neonate becomes symptomatic immediately, hypertension resulting in left ventricular failure. Neonates who have a postductal coarctation already have some collaterals and are spared from developing severe hypertension and congestive cardiac failure.

The exact mechanism for the production of systemic hypertension in coarctation is not known. The aortic obstruction is certainly partly responsible for it. The narrowed pulse pressure in the descending aorta distal to the coarctation has been implicated in the renal mechanism for the causation of hypertension in coarctation.

The obstruction stimulates growth of collateral vessels between the proximal and distal segments. The intercostal vessels also participate in decompressing the hypertensive upper segment. They enlarge and become palpable at the lower borders of the ribs. Palpable collaterals are also felt at the medial and inferior angle of scapula. Because of the decompression of the upper segment by the collaterals, the resting blood pressure in the upper extremities may even be normal. On exercise, however, the systolic pressure always is unduly accentuated.

Clinical Features

The only symptoms in uncomplicated coarctation may be intermittent claudication, pain and weakness of legs and dyspnea on running. Examination shows delayed and weak or impalpable femorals compared to strong brachial arteries. It is possible for the femorals to be impalpable whereas the dorsalis pedis vessels may be well felt since the distal pulse pressure is wider. As a rule if the femorals are well felt in an infant the diagnosis can be excluded. Rarely it is possible for the patients to continue to have pulmonary arterial hypertension. A patent ductus arteriosus may support the distal segment of the aorta. In such a situation good femoral pulsations may be present in spite of coarctation, which would be preductal in location and associated with cyanosis in toes. It is important to remember that the site of coarctation does not determine whether the flow through the PDA is from left to right or from right to left. Whether the coarctation is preductal or postductal, the flow is from left to right since the distal segment of the aorta in coarctation almost never has a mean pressure below 50 mm of Hg. If the flow through the PDA is from right to left, it indicates that there is severe pulmonary arterial hypertension.

The heart size remains normal with a left ventricular forcible or heaving apex. A systolic thrill may be palpable in the suprasternal notch. There are prominent arterial pulsations in the suprasternal notch and the carotid vessels. The first sound is accentuated and followed by a loud constant ejection click. The second sound is normally split with a loud aortic component. A variable intensity ejection systolic murmur is heard with the point of maximum intensity over the back in the interscapular area. The murmur may be well heard over the precordium. The murmur starts late in systole after a considerable gap from the first sound and click. It may appear to go through the second sound suggesting a continuous murmur. This is because of the delay in the transmission of pulse from the heart to the site of coarctation. Continuous murmurs may be audible over the collaterals in the chest wall but are uncommon. An aortic ejection systolic murmur and/or an aortic regurgitation murmur may be present because of the bicuspid aortic valve (Fig. 14.23).

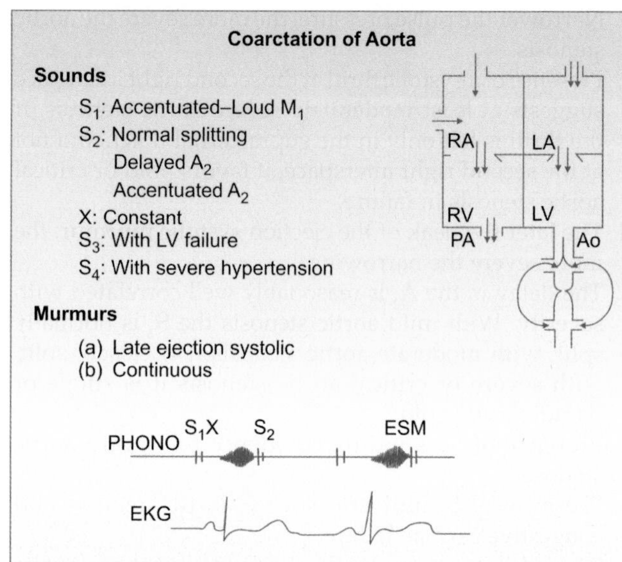

Fig. 14.23: Summary of auscultatory findings in coarctatioon of the aorta. S_3 third sound

EKG shows left ventricular hypertrophy; presence of ST and T wave changes suggests additional aortic stenosis or endocardial fibroelastosis. Chest X-ray shows a normal sized heart with prominent ascending aorta, and the aortic knuckle. In an over penetrated film, the site of coarctation can be localized as the proximal segment is dilated and there is post stenotic dilatation of the distal segment. Barium swallow shows the characteristic 'E' sign and confirms the site of coarctation (Fig. 14.24). The characteristic notching of the lower borders of ribs appears

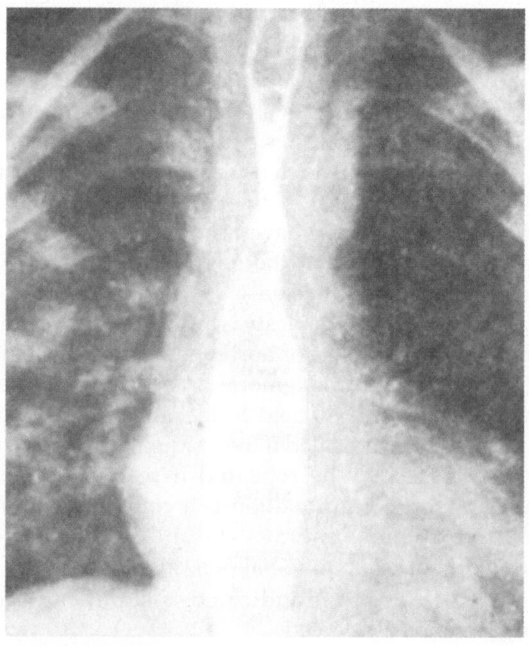

Fig. 14.24: Barium swallow showing 'E' sign secondary to coarctation

beyond the age of 10 years. Using suprasternal approach, coarctation can be visualized by echocardiogram and the gradient estimated.

Assessment of Severity

The degree of systemic hypertension determines the severity of coarctation. Cardiac enlargement indicates left ventricular failure and severe coarctation.

Course and Complications

Coarctation may result in congestive failure in infancy. If congestive failure does not occur in infancy, it is unlikely to occur throughout the pediatric age group unless complicated by infective endocarditis or anemia. The complications of coarctation include rupture of berry intracranial aneurysm, rupture of an intercostal aneurysm and dissection of aorta. These complications are rare in the pediatric age group. Infective endocarditis may occur. The site of endocarditis may be either the wall of aorta distal to coarctation or the bicuspid aortic valve.

Treatment

Medical management consists in control of congestive failure in infancy. Except in complicated coarctation of aorta, medical management should be able to control congestive failure. The patients can be operated at any age, but the risk is lowest between the ages of 1–10 years. Beyond the age of 15 years the risk is higher since the tissues become friable. Ideally, the patients should be operated as early as possible after the age of 1-year.

It is likely that coarctation of aorta is not a localized disease at the junction of arch and descending aorta. There is a generalized weakness of the arterial media. Resection of coarctation does not guarantee freedom from complications like dissection of aorta. Systemic hypertension can persist following operation and recoarctation of aorta can also occur. This has been explained as failure of expansion of surgically anastomosed site. Recoarctation is amenable to treatment by balloon angioplasty. Balloon angioplasty is being increasingly utilized for relief of recoarctation as well as the primary mode of treatment in place of operative treatment.

Newborns with coarctation require surgery because balloon angioplasty invariably results in restenosis presumably from the constricting ductal tissue at the coarctation site that remains in the aortic wall.

Pulmonic Stenosis

Anatomically pulmonic stenosis is located at the valvar or subvalvar level. The subvalvar pulmonic stenosis is called infundibular pulmonic stenosis. Uncommonly pulmonic stenosis may be in the pulmonary artery above the valve or in the main right or left branches or the peripheral branches. These are called supravalvar, right and left main branch stenosis and peripheral pulmonic stenosis respectively, however, peripheral pulmonic stenosis gives a wrong impression in the sense that like coarctation it results in the proximal area being hypertensive.

Hemodynamics

Flow across the narrow pulmonary valve results in a pulmonary ejection systolic murmur. To keep the flow normal the right ventricle increases its systolic pressure and develops concentric right ventricular hypertrophy. The pulmonary artery beyond the obstruction shows post-stenotic dilatation visible on the thoracic roentgenogram as a dilated pulmonary arterial segment. Because of the obstruction, the right ventricular systole is prolonged resulting in delayed closure of the pulmonic component (P_2) of the second sound. The delay in the P_2 results in a widely split second sound. The split is variable becoming wider in inspiration. The width of splitting in expiration is directly related to the severity of pulmonary valvar obstruction. Similarly the duration of the systolic murmur is also directly related to the severity of obstruction. Thus the more severe the pulmonic stenosis, the longer the systolic murmur and the wider the splitting of the second sound. In valvar pulmonic stenosis a pulmonary ejection click is audible during expiration but disappears or becomes softer during inspiration. It precedes the start of the murmur. The more severe the pulmonic stenosis the closer the click to the first sound. In severe pulmonic stenosis the click almost merges with the first sound, which then appears to be louder in expiration compared to inspiration. The concentric hypertrophy results in maintaining a normal heart size and at the same time reduces the right ventricular distensibility. In severe pulmonic stenosis with marked right ventricular hypertrophy, the right ventricular diastolic pressure also increases. The right atrial pressure increases to be able to fill the right ventricle and results in a right atrial fourth sound (S_4) as well as prominent 'a' waves in the jugular venous pulse.

Clinical Features

Patients of mild to moderate pulmonic stenosis are asymptomatic. With severe pulmonic stenosis dyspnea on effort appears. If the foramen ovale is patent, a right to left shunt at the atrial level may occur in severe pulmonic stenosis and result in cyanosis. Palpitation, easy fatigability and rarely angina like chest pain can also occur. On examination the patients are characteristically described as having a round face and hypertelorism. Port-wine angiomatous malformation may be present over the skin. Turner's phenotype without chromosomal abnormalities (Noonan syndrome) is associated with pulmonic stenosis. Except in severe pulmonic stenosis with right to left shunt at the atrial level there is absence of cyanosis. The cardiac size is normal and the hypertrophied right ventricle results in a left parasternal heave. A systolic thrill is palpable at the second and third left interspace. It may also be felt in the suprasternal notch. The first sound remains normal and the intensity of P_2 is also normal. Moderate pulmonic stenosis results in wide variable splitting of the second sound. Severe pulmonic stenosis results in a further widening of the split. In critical pulmonic stenosis the P_2 is also diminished in intensity and may be so widely split in expiration that further widening during inspiration may not be appreciated on auscultation suggesting a fixed split second sound. A pulmonary ejection click varying with the respiration follows the first sound. Fourth sound is audible in severe as well as critical pulmonic stenosis (Fig. 14.25). If the right ventricle fails, a right ventricular third sound may be audible. Rarely with right ventricular failure, tricuspid regurgitation may appear. Since the right atrium offers less resistance to flow of blood than the obstruction at the pulmonary valve, the flow through the pulmonary valve diminishes reducing the intensity as well as the duration of the pulmonary ejection systolic murmur. These patients present with significant cyanosis as in Fallot's tetralogy. The pulmonary systolic murmur is a diamond shaped murmur with mild pulmonic stenosis. With increasing severity of pulmonic stenosis the duration and intensity of the murmur increase and the peak is delayed. With moderately severe pulmonic stenosis, the murmur ends just short of the aortic component of the second sound. In critical pulmonic stenosis the pulmonary ejection murmur goes through the aortic component of the second sound, partially or completely masking it.

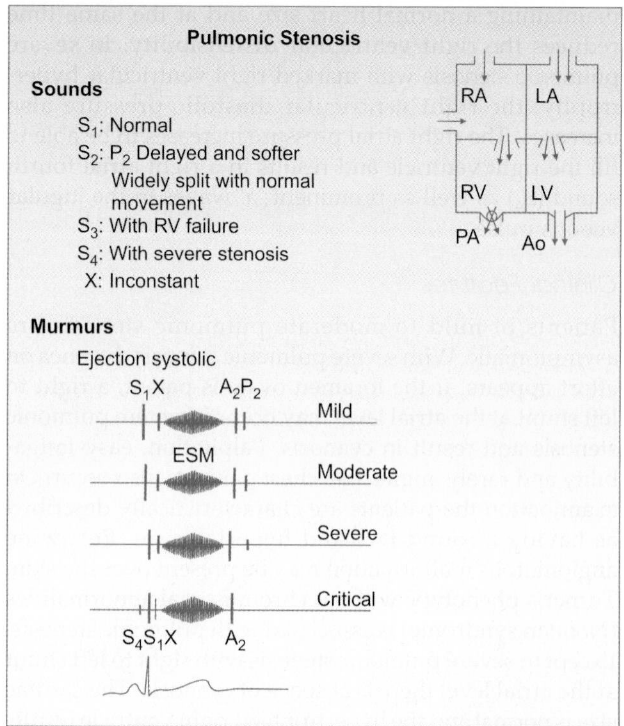

Fig. 14.25: Summary of auscultatory findings in pulmonic stenosis

The EKG shows right axis deviation and right ventricular hypertrophy. Pulmonic stenosis is a systolic overload for the right ventricle. The systolic overloading pattern in the electrocardiogram is suggested by a pure 'R' or a 'qR' type of complex in V_{4R} and V_1 leads. This is not very specific and rsR type of complex can be present. P pulmonale suggests severe pulmonic stenosis. The thoracic roentgenogram shows a normal sized heart with normal pulmonary vasculature in mild, moderate as well as severe pulmonic stenosis. Pulmonary oligemia occurs only when the patients develop a right to left shunt at the atrial level in severe or critical pulmonic stenosis. The main pulmonary artery segment exhibits post stenotic dilatation. Echocardiogram can identify the site and using Doppler assess the severity of pulmonic obstruction.

Infundibular pulmonic stenosis is separated from valvar pulmonic stenosis by (i) absence of click in infundibular type; (ii) absence of post stenotic dilatation in the thoracic roentgenogram; and (iii) a relatively lower point of maximum intensity of the systolic murmur in the third and fourth left interspace.

Assessment of Severity

The severity of pulmonic stenosis can be assessed by the following:

i. Symptomatic patients have severe pulmonic stenosis.
ii. Cyanosis and cardiac enlargement indicate severe pulmonic stenosis.
iii. The closer the pulmonary ejection click to S_1, the more severe the stenosis.
iv. The wider the splitting of S_2, the more severe the stenosis.
v. The longer the murmur the more severe the stenosis. Murmur ending before, at or beyond the aortic component of the second sound indicate moderately severe, severe and critical pulmonic stenosis respectively.
vi. A pure R in V_1 of 20 mm and appearance of S wave in left precordial leads suggests severe stenosis.
vii. Cardiomegaly and decreased pulmonary flow indicate severe pulmonic stenosis.
viii. Doppler echo can quantitate the gradient accurately.

Treatment

Unlike valvar aortic stenosis, valvar pulmonic stenosis does not increase in severity with time. Patients with mild pulmonic stenosis (Doppler gradient less than 50 mm Hg) do not require intervention. Balloon valvuloplasty is the treatment of choice for isolated valvar pulmonic stenosis. Surgical treatment is indicated if balloon valvotomy is unsuccessful, as in dysplastic valves or if the pulmonary valve annulus is small. The operation is done under cardiopulmonary bypass with a low risk. Infundibular stenosis requires surgical resection either through atrial or right ventriculotomy.

ENDOMYOCARDIAL DISEASES

Endomyocardial diseases may be defined as those diseases, which primarily affect endocardium or the myocardium of a known or unknown etiology. They are characterized by CCF, cardiomegaly and arrhythmias. Generally, there are no murmurs. However, dilatation of the ventricles may result in functional mitral or tricuspid regurgitation murmurs.

Endocardial Fibroelastosis

The etiology of endocardial fibroelastosis is not known. Hypoxia, interference with lymphatic drainage, maternal toxins, toxoplasmosis, mumps and coxsackie B infection are considered possible etiological factors. Fetal myocarditis might result in a dilated chamber, which develops fibroelastosis as a secondary phenomenon. Left atrium, mitral valve and aortic valve may show milky white thickening of the endocardium. In the common dilated type, left ventricle is enlarged. In the uncommon contracted type, the left ventricle is small but is not hypoplastic.

Endocardial fibroelastosis restricts the systolic ejection as well as the diastolic filling. As a result the ejection fraction is reduced resulting in low cardiac output. Elevation of end-diastolic pressure causes pulmonary venous and arterial hypertension. The end-diastolic volume is increased in the common dilated left ventricle type of endocardial fibroelastosis.

The symptoms of CCF start in the first week of life. Cardiomegaly and S_3 gallop are present. Murmur of mitral regurgitation may be heard. EKG shows findings suggestive of left ventricular hypertrophy, with deep S waves in right precordial leads and qR with tall R waves in the left chest leads, ischemic ST segment changes are also present. Chest X-ray shows cardiomegaly with pulmonary venous hypertension. On fluoroscopy, cardiac pulsations are poor. 'M' mode echocardiogram shows enlarged left ventricle with a thick poorly contracting septum and the posterior left ventricular wall. The left atrium is also enlarged. The mitral valve shows reduced EF slope due to low cardiac output. 2D echo shows poorly contracting dilated left ventricle/with thickened endocardium.

Treatment consists of treatment of CCF. The younger the patient at the onset of symptoms, the poorer the prognosis. If the patient responds well to digoxin, it should be continued for several years. In the presence of significant mitral regurgitation, mitral annuloplasty or replacement may be required.

Myocarditis

Infection with ECHO, coxsackie B, rubella, herpes and influenza virus are known to cause myocarditis; diphtheritic myocarditis is not uncommon in India. Myocarditis generally occurs in the newborn period and early infancy. The onset may be abrupt with cardiovascular collapse or gradual with left and right heart failure. Arrhythmias and conduction disturbances are common. There is cardiomegaly, tachycardia, muffled heart sounds and features of CCF. The electrocardiogram shows low voltage and non-specific ST-T changes. Chest X-ray reveals cardiomegaly and pulmonary venous hypertension.

Treatment consists in management of CCF and antiarrhythmic drugs. Digoxin should be used cautiously, preferably at one-half to three-quarters of the standard dose. Steroids may be of some benefit in the presence of conduction disturbances and cardiovascular collapse. They should not be used in the acute phase, when viremia may be present. Use of ACE inhibitors is recommended.

Cardiomyopathies

The term cardiomyopathy is defined as intrinsic disease of the myocardium in which there is no structural deformity of the heart. It is called *primary cardiomyopathy* or primary myocardial disease when the etiology is unknown. If the myocardial disease is secondary to a systemic disease, it is termed as *secondary cardiomyopathy* (Table 14.14). The myocardial diseases are classified clinically as (i) dilated type, (ii) restrictive type, and (iii) hypertrophic type. The hypertrophic cardiomyopathy may occur (a) without outflow obstruction, or (b) with outflow obstruction. Obstructive cardiomyopathy is also known as idiopathic hypertrophic subaortic stenosis or asymmetrical septal hypertrophy or hypertrophic obstructive cardiomyopathy (HOCM).

Dilated cardiomyopathy is the commonest form of myocardial disease seen in children. The onset of CCF may be acute or subacute; cardiomegaly and S_3 gallop are present. Murmur of mitral regurgitation and uncommonly

Table 14.14: Secondary cardiomyopathies
Infection
Viral, bacterial, fungal, rickettsial, parasitic.
Collagen disorders
Systemic lupus erythematosus, dermatomyositis.
Metabolic, endocrine disorders
Beri beri, glycogen storage disease type II (Pompe), amyloidosis.
Mucopolysaccharidoses, uremia, pheochromocytoma, porphyria.
Neurological, muscular disorders
Friedreich ataxia, muscle dystrophies.
Medications, toxins
Adriamycin, phenothiazine, lead, emetine, chloroquine.
Hematological
Sickle cell anemia, thrombotic thrombocytopenic purpura.
Neoplastic
Rhabdomyoma, myxoma, leukemia, lymphoma.
Miscellaneous
Idiopathic aortitis, cystic fibrosis, glomerulonephritis.

that of tricuspid regurgitation may be present. The patients are prone to have embolic phenomena. The EKG is variable and may show non-specific ST and T changes with or without left ventricular hypertrophy. Conduction disturbances, arrhythmias or pseudoinfarction pattern may be present. Echocardiogram shows dilated ventricular cavity without hypertrophy of the free wall of the left ventricle or the septum. The left ventricular contractility is markedly reduced.

Treatment consists in prolonged bedrest and anticongestive therapy including vasodilators, especially ACE inhibitors. Bed rest and anticongestive therapy, over a long period, result in gradual improvement in most patients. If the patient does not show improvement in 2–3 weeks, hospitalization is essential. A myocardial biopsy may be necessary in patients with refractory symptoms, to determine further management. The role of immunosuppressive agents and immunoglobulin infusions is not clear.

β-blockers were contraindicated in the past since they might precipitate CCF. However, in patients with dilated cardiomyopathies where treatment of the cause is not possible, their use has been shown to be beneficial. Since catecholamine levels are high in CCF and there is down regulation of β-receptors, β-blockers control the heart rate, reduce vasoconstriction and upgrade b-receptors. They may also prevent or retard myocardial damage related to high catecholamine levels. The most commonly used b-blockers include metoprolol and carvedilol. Treatment with intermittent infusions of dopamine or dobutamine is promising. Some patients benefit from treatment with carnitine (100 mg/kg/day in divided doses for two days, followed by 50 mg/kg/day).

Anomalous Left Coronary Artery from Pulmonary Artery (ALCAPA)

ALCAPA needs specific mention as a cause of congestive cardiomyopathy since the diagnosis is made by EKG and the treatment is specific. If a patient presenting with congestive cardiomyopathy with or without a mitral regurgitation murmur shows anterolateral myocardial infarction pattern on the EKG, the diagnosis is that of ALCAPA. Echocardiogram shows a large right coronary artery and absence of the origin of left coronary artery from the aorta. The left coronary artery is seen to arise from the pulmonary artery and usually shows flow in the reverse direction in the left anterior descending artery and the left circumflex artery. This flow reversal results from collateral flow into the left coronary system from the right coronary artery. Angiography is rarely necessary for the diagnosis of ALCAPA. The treatment is mobilization and translocating the origin from pulmonary artery to aorta.

Restrictive Cardiomyopathy (RCM)

It is relatively uncommon in children. There is restriction to ventricular filling. Endocardial fibroelastosis with a normal or smaller than normal left ventricle and endomyocardial fibrosis (EMF) are the two common types. Endomyocardial fibrosis is endemic in the state of Kerala but rare in North India. Pathologically, there is dense fibrosis in the apical and inflow regions of the left and the right ventricles, which restricts diastolic ventricular filling. The papillary muscles and chordae may be tethered by the connective tissue, resulting in severe mitral or tricuspid regurgitation. Patients with predominant left sided involvement have symptoms of dyspnea, nocturnal dyspnea, hemoptysis and embolic phenomena. On examination, there is cardiomegaly with or without findings of mitral regurgitation. Cardiac output is low and there are features of pulmonary venous and arterial hypertension. With predominant right sided involvement, the patients present with fatigue from low cardiac output, edema on feet and ascites. There is cardiomegaly with prominent cardiac pulsations in the second to fourth left interspace from a dilated right ventricular outflow. S_3 gallop and tricuspid regurgitation murmur may be present. Treatment consists of decongestive therapy. Decortication or stripping of the endocardium with mitral valve replacement has been tried with success.

Restrictive cardiomyopathy of other varieties is characterized by a combination of features of left and right sided failure with a normal sized heart. Clinically or even following cardiac catheterization, it may be difficult to distinguish it from constrictive pericarditis. Echocardiogram is useful in excluding constrictive pericarditis.

Hypertrophic Cardiomyopathy (HCM)

The hypertrophic cardiomyopathy with obstruction (HCM) is uncommon in children. It has been reported with or without familial involvement even in neonates. Pathologically there is asymmetrical hypertrophy of the ventricular septum. The free walls of the left and right ventricles are hypertrophied to a lesser extent. The ventricular septum bulges into the left ventricle, the malaligned anterior mitral valve leaflet causes obstruction in the left ventricular outflow during systole. Uncommonly, there may be right ventricular outflow obstruction as well. The abnormally oriented mitral valve becomes regurgitant.

The patients usually present with exertional dyspnea, anginal type of chest pain, palpitation and syncope or a murmur may have been detected. Sudden death can occur.

The pulse has a sharp upstroke with a bisferiens character. The apex beat is forcible or heaving. The fourth sound may be palpable at the apex. Double or triple apical impulse may be present. The second sound may be normally split, single or paradoxically split, depending on the severity of the left ventricular outflow obstruction. An ejection systolic murmur of varying intensity is heard at left sternal edge. A pansystolic murmur or mitral regurgitation and a fourth sound may be heard at the apex.

The ejection systolic murmur increases in intensity by maneuvers, which increase the myocardial contractility or decrease the volume of the left ventricle. The murmur decreases in intensity by procedures, which increase left ventricular volume or decrease the myocardial contractility. Thus, sudden squatting decreases the intensity of the murmur, while standing upright from sitting position (by decreasing venous return and left ventricular size) increases the intensity of the systolic murmur. EKG shows left ventricular hypertrophy, with or without ischemic changes; WPW type changes may be present. Echocardiogram shows disproportionate hypertrophy of the ventricular septum, systolic anterior motion of the anterior leaflet of the mitral valve and midsystolic closure of the aortic valve. Cardiac catheterization and angiography are rarely required. It may be necessary to increase the left ventricular contractility with isoprenaline to increase the magnitude of obstruction during catheterization, or during echocardiographic evaluation.

The younger the age of the onset, the poorer the prognosis. The disease may be progressive and sudden death may occur in spite of medical and/or surgical treatment. β-blocking drugs and more recently verapamil have been used to decrease the myocardial contractility and thus the obstruction. For the control of arrhythmias, disopyramide or amiodarone are the drugs of choice, the former reduces myocardial contractility as well.

Hypertrophic cardiomyopathy has an autosomal dominant pattern of inheritance with a variable but high degree of penetrance. It is believed to be linked to mutations in β–myosin, troponin T and alpha-tropomyosin genes. Some other genetic factors play a role in hypertrophy in hypertrophic cardiomyopathy. Angiotensin converting enzyme (ACE) gene have three alleles, DD, ID and II. Patients of HCM with ACE genotype DD have more left ventricular hypertrophy than if the genotype is II. ACE inhibitors are known to reduce the muscle mass, which is desirable in patients with hypertrophied left ventricle. However, ACE inhibitors reduce the systemic pressure and may adversely affect the outflow obstruction in patients with HCM. In the absence of outflow obstruction, a carefully monitored use of ACE inhibitors is justified.

It is essential that patients with HCM should have a 24-hr Holter to document for arrhythmias. In children who can do exercise, the effect of exercise on the rhythm is ascertained. Patients of HCM should be restrained from strenuous games and exercise. Digitalis and other inotropic drugs as well as diuretics and nitrates are contraindicated in patients with hypertrophic obstructive cardiomyopathy.

PERICARDIAL DISEASES

Inflammatory diseases of the pericardium may present as acute dry pericarditis, pericarditis with effusion or chronic constrictive pericarditis (Table 14.15).

Table 14.15: Etiology of pericardial diseases

Acute	*Chronic*
Bacterial (septicemia)	Constrictive pericarditis
Viral	Tuberculous
Tuberculous	Non-specific (idiopathic)
Rheumatic	Post-pyogenic
Collagen disorders	Post-traumatic
Idiopathic	Pericardial defects
Uremic	Pericardial cyst
Postoperative	

Acute Pericarditis

Acute pericardial inflammation causes precordial pain, which may be dull, sharp or stabbing in character. Occasionally, the pain may be felt over the neck and shoulder and may worsen on lying down. Child becomes dyspneic and has cough. The pattern of fever and toxemia depends on the etiology. The bedside diagnostic physical sign is the presence of pericardial friction rub, which is a rough scratchy sound, made up of three components, a systolic, a diastolic and a presystolic scratch. It can be heard anywhere over the precordium, is unrelated to the respiratory cycle and increases on pressing the chest piece of stethoscope over the precordium. The EKG shows generalized ST elevation in the initial stages. Later the ST segment becomes iso-electric and the T waves become inverted. Still later, the ST segment may be depressed.

If effusion develops, the cardiac silhouette increases in size. The heart sounds become muffled and evidence of peripheral congestion in the form of raised jugular venous pressure, hepatomegaly and edema may develop. The pericardial friction rub may persist or disappear. If the fluid accumulates rapidly, there is marked interference with cardiac filling and features of cardiac tamponade as evidenced by (i) rising jugular venous pressure; (ii) paradoxical inspiratory filling of the neck veins; (iii) increasing heart rate; (iv) falling pulse pressure with; and (v) pulsus paradoxus appear. The EKG shows non-specific generalized ST and T changes with low voltage tracings. The chest X-ray shows cardiomegaly with smooth outline and blunting of the cardio-hepatic angle. The echocardiogram shows an echo-free space behind the posterior left ventricular wall. Pericardiocentesis should be done to determine the etiology as well as to relieve cardiac tamponade if present. Treatment will depend on the etiology. Surgical drainage is rarely indicated unless the fluid is thick and fibrinous.

Chronic Constrictive Pericarditis

Constrictive pericarditis is not an uncommon disease in our country. Generally it is secondary to tuberculous infection; less commonly the etiology is obscure or it may follow pyogenic pericarditis. There is fibrous thickening of both layers of the pericardium. There is an encasement around the heart, which restricts the filling of both the ventricles equally. Calcification rarely occurs during childhood. The myocardium is not involved in the early stages but in longstanding cases the fibrous process infiltrates the myocardium as well. This results in myocardial dysfunction in addition to cardiac restriction. Fibrosis makes the surgical correction difficult. It also prevents complete normalization after the operation.

Dyspnea, fatigue and progressive enlargement of the abdomen are the commonest symptoms. Some patients complain of paroxysmal nocturnal dyspnea. Jugular venous pressure is always elevated with equally prominent 'a' and 'v' waves and a prominent 'y' descent. Inspiratory filling of the neck veins (Kussmaul sign) is seen in about a half of the cases. Liver is pulsatile, both 'a' and 'v' waves being felt. Spleen may be enlarged and ascites is common. Unilateral or bilateral pleural effusion is a common finding. Pulse is fast and of low volume. Pulsus paradoxus may be present.

Normal EKG is against the diagnosis of constrictive pericarditis; all cases show non-specific ST-T changes and 75% cases have low voltage. Occasionally, there is right axis deviation or right ventricular hypertrophy pattern. Left atrial overload pattern is uncommon in our patients. The chest X-ray reveals normal sized heart with ragged or shaggy borders, prominent superior vena cava shadow merging with the right atrial margin. The lungs may show pleural effusion and plate atelectasis. Hemodynamic studies reveal elevation of right atrial mean pressure, right ventricular end-diastolic pressure, pulmonary artery diastolic pressure and the pulmonary artery wedge pressures. The right ventricular end-diastolic pressure is more than one-third of the systolic pressure (Fig. 14.26). The cardiac index may be normal or reduced, but the stroke volume is low.

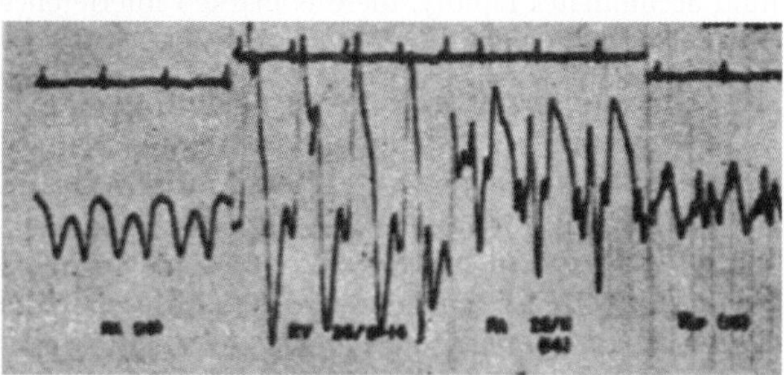

Fig. 24.26: Constrictive pericarditis. Tracing of the right atrium (RA), right ventricle (RV), pulmonary artery (PA) and the pulmonary artery wedge pressure (PcP) from a case of constrictive pericarditis

The treatment is surgical decortication of the pericardium. It results in normalization of the hemodynamic abnormalities in most cases. Some cases of long standing constrictive pericarditis who have myocardial dysfunction may improve slowly or may have residual myocardial dysfunction. Except post-pyogenic pericarditis cases, all of our patients have been treated with a 6-week course of antitubercular drugs before being operated, since majority of these are post-tuberculous pericarditis. Full course of antitubercular treatment follows pericardiectomy.

Suggested reading

Marian AJ, Roberts R. Recent advances in the molecular genetics of hypertrophic cardiomyopathy. Circulation 1995; 92: 1336–1347.

CARDIAC RHYTHM DISORDERS

Cardiac arrhythmias are not infrequent and may be potentially life threatening. The reported incidence of supraventricular tachycardia (SVT) in children ranges from 1 in 250 to 1 in 1000. Recognition of arrhythmias is not always easy and requires a high index of suspicion. It is important to arrive at a precise diagnosis and initiate specific treatment.

Recognizing Arrhythmia

The clinical features suggestive of an underlying arrhythmia are listed in Table 14.16.

Table 14.16: **Clinical features in arrhythmias**
Irregular heart beat.
Heart rate that is inappropriate for the clinical condition.
Unexplained heart failure.
Underlying cardiac anomaly known to be associated with rhythm disorders.
Syncope, palpitations, chest discomfort.
Family history of sudden cardiac events.

Irregular heart rate: The most common cause of an irregular heart rate is physiological sinus arrhythmia. This can be easily recognized by an increase in heart rate with inspiration and a decrease with expiration. Sinus arrhythmia is usual following a febrile illness and by drugs that increase vigil tone (e.g. digoxin), and abolished by exercise. Irregularities of sinus rhythm are common in premature infants especially bradycardia associated with apnea spells. Other common causes of heart rate irregularity in children include atrial and ventricular premature beats and conduction disturbances. Less common but potentially serious causes are listed in Table 14.17.

Inappropriate heart rate: A heart rate that is inappropriately fast or slow should arouse the suspicion of an underlying arrhythmia. Inappropriately slow heart rate in a child complaining of fatigue, giddiness or syncope should arouse the suspicion of complete heart block. Inappropriately fast rates suggest tachyarrhythmias, such as SVT.

Unexplained heart failure: Arrhythmias such as ectopic atrial tachycardia (EAT), permanent junctional re-entrant tachycardia (PJRT) and some forms of ventricular tachycardia can present as heart failure. At initial evaluation, the heart rates may not be inappropriate for the degree of failure. Diagnosis may be missed, particularly in EAT and PJRT.

Table 14.17: Causes of irregular heart beat

Sinus arrhythmia.
Other common and usually benign causes.
Supraventricular (atrial and junctional premature beats).
Ventricular premature beats.
Transient conduction disturbances (Wenckebach type), atrioventricular and sinoatrial blocks.
Transient bradycardia in a premature infant.
Uncommon but potentially serious causes.
Mobitz type II heart block.
Ectopic atrial tachycardia; multifocal atrial tachycardia.
Polymorphic ventricular tachycardia and Torsades.
Atrial fibrillation, with or without WPW syndrome.
Atrial flutter with variable conduction.
Tachyarrhythmias can manifest as irregular heart rate, if identified at onset or offset or if brief duration.

These conditions should be considered in the differential diagnosis of dilated cardiomyopathy, especially if the heart rate is relatively fixed.

Underlying conditions: A number of congenital and acquired heart diseases and certain systemic conditions are associated with arrhythmias (Table 14.18). Ventricular and supraventricular arrhythmias can follow cardiac surgery for correction of congenital heart disease. Operations resulting in scar formation in the right ventricle such as repair of tetralogy of Fallot are associated with ventricular tachycardia. The Fontan operation for single ventricle physiology, or the Senning or Mustard procedure for transposition are associated with high incidence of re-entrant atrial arrhythmias. Organophosphate exposure, tricyclic antidepressant overdose, digoxin toxicity, antiarrhythmic drug treatment and substance abuse can be associated with arrhythmias.

Table 14.18: Arrhythmias suggestive of specific congenital heart disease

Sick sinus syndrome
Sinus venosus, atrioventricular canal defect, Holt Oram syndrome with atrial septal defect (ASD).
Narrow QRS tachycardias
Ebstein anomaly; corrected transposition with Ebstein anomaly.
Atrioventricular canal, ASD.
Pulmonic stenosis, total anomalous pulmonary venous connection, tricuspid atresia (older patients).
Atrial fibrillation and flutter Congenital mitral stenosis, total anomalous pulmonary venous connection, coronary AV fistula, primary pulmonary hypertension (late).
WPW and pre-excitation syndromes Ebstein anomaly; corrected transposition with Ebstein anomaly
Wide QRS tachycardias Anomalous left coronary artery from pulmonary artery, coronary AV fistula, arrhythmogenic right ventricle
Atrio-ventricular conduction defects Corrected transposition of great arteries; Ebstein anomaly
Postoperative patients Supraventricular, ventricular arrhythmias

Syncope, palpitations and chest discomfort: The most common cause of syncope in children is mediated *via* the autonomic nervous system, known as vasovagal syncope. Only a fraction of syncopal episodes result from cardiac arrhythmias. Life threatening ventricular tachycardia, such as one associated with long QT syndrome, characteristically results in syncope. It is important to differentiate them from vasovagal episodes. Vasovagal syncope characteristically occurs in situations like prolonged standing in a hot environment, sight of blood, painful stimulus, emotional stress or following a recent illness. A brief period of syncope may follow a breath holding spell. Older children may complain of episodic palpitations. Occasionally, there is a sensation of chest discomfort or pain during tachyarrhythmias.

14

Diagnostic Work-up

It is necessary to address issues listed in Table 14.19 to enable diagnosis and specific treatment. A 12-lead EKG should be obtained and cardiac rhythm monitoring initiated.

Table 14.19: Initial assessment of arrhythmia

Can the clinical condition result from a cardiac arrhythmia?
Is there hemodynamic instability?
Is the arrhythmia incessant or episodic?
Is this a re-entrant arrhythmia or does it involve an automatic focus?
Where is the arrhythmic focus or circuit located?
Is there an underlying structural heart disease?

Management of hemodynamic instability: All tachyarrhythmias and bradyarrhythmias influence hemodynamics adversely. In clinical terms, this adverse influence manifests as a spectrum ranging from no detectable manifestations to circulatory collapse. Children tolerate a wide range of heart rates and an infant may appear comfortable with rates exceeding 200/min. Extreme hemodynamic instability is relatively rare in childhood arrhythmias, particularly in the absence of structural heart disease. If present, it requires emergency treatment, discussed under individual arrhythmias.

Figure 14.27 depicts a useful algorithm to treat most tachyarrhythmias. Emergency treatment options for bradyarrhythmias are shown in Table 14.20.

Re-entrant vs. automatic tachyarrhythmias: Tachyarrhythmias result from one of the three mechanisms:

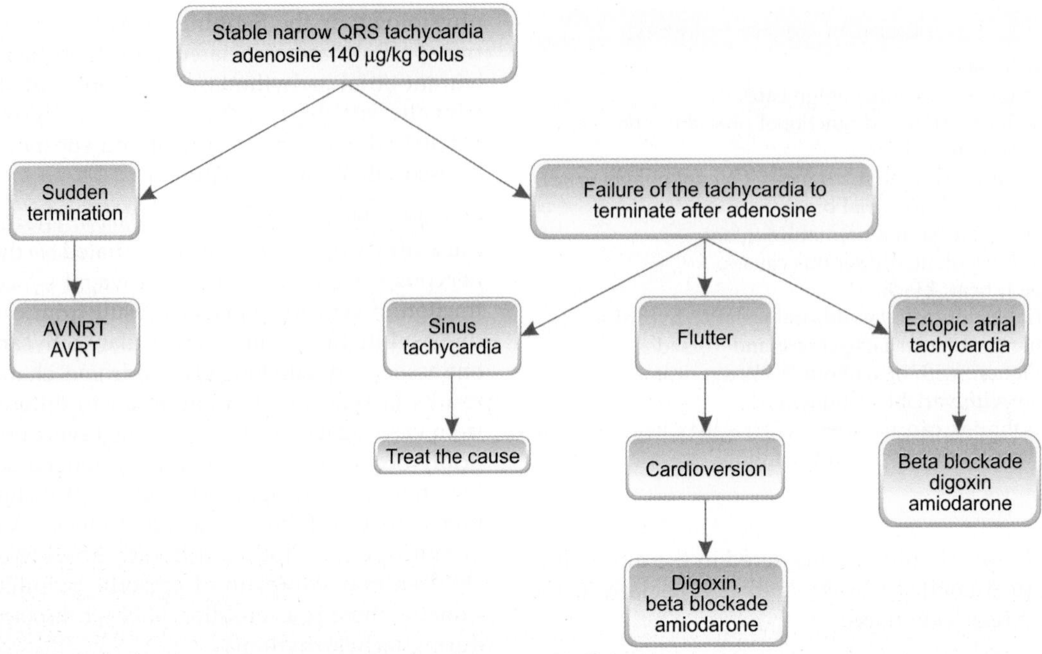

Fig. 14.27: Management algorithm for stable narrow QRS tachycardia. AVNRT : atrioventricular nodal re-entrant tachycardia; AVRT : atrioventricular re-entrant tachycardia

14

Table 14.20: Emergency treatment for bradyarrhythmias

Modality	*Indication*	*Dose*
Atropine	Severe sinus bradycardia, AV block with narrow QRS (supraventricular) escape	0.02 mg/kg IV bolus
Isoproterenol	Lack of response to atropine, AV block with wide QRS (ventricular) escape	0.1–2 μg/kg/min IV infusion
Transcutaneous pacing	Severe symptomatic bradycardia, asystole (not suitable for infants, young children)	Twice the capture threshold
Transvenous pacing	As an alternative to transcutaneous pacing for infants and young children	Twice the capture threshold

re-entry, increased automaticity and triggered activity. In children, the first two mechanisms account in most cases. Clinical and EKG features together with response to medications and maneuvers distinguish re-entrant tachyarrhythmias from those due to increased automaticity. Re-entrant arrhythmias have a relatively sudden onset and termination. Successful termination with DC cardioversion or overdrive pacing (pacing at rates faster than arrhythmia rate) suggests re-entrant mechanism. Automatic arrhythmias have a relatively slow onset, gradual acceleration (warm-up to peak rates at onset) and deceleration (cool down at termination).

Diagnosis and Management of Tachyarrhythmias

A combined strategy that simultaneously addresses both diagnosis and treatment is appropriate. This is determined by the QRS duration on the initial EKG and presence or absence of hemodynamic instability. Based on the QRS duration, arrhythmias are classified as narrow or wide. This is a useful classification and serves as an excellent guide to initial treatment. Age specific normal values for QRS duration are given in Table 14.21.

Table 14.21: Normal QRS duration at various age groups

Age group	*QRS duration in seconds*
0–6 months	0.03–0.07 (0.05)
1–5 years	0.04–0.08 (0.06)
10–15 years	0.04–0.09 (0.07)
>15 years	0.06–0.09 (0.08)

Values represent range (mean)

As a preliminary step, sinus tachycardia should be excluded. Rates as high as 240/min can occasionally be recorded during sinus tachycardia. There is always an underlying cause for sinus tachycardia, including fever, peripheral circulatory failure, extreme dehydration, accidental ingestion of drugs or toxic substances.

Narrow QRS tachycardia : Most narrow QRS tachycardias (Table 14.22) are well tolerated and allow initial diagnostic work-up. If a patient is seen during an arrhythmia, all attempts should be made to obtain data before terminating the arrhythmia. Information that should be sought during a narrow QRS tachycardia include the P wave morphology and P-QRS relationship. P waves that appear normal during the arrhythmia suggest sinus tachycardia. Ectopic atrial tachycardia is suggested by abnormal P wave morphology. Inverted P waves may be seen when atria are activated in a retrograde fashion, e.g. re-entrant tachyarrhythmias involving accessory pathways (AV re-entrant tachycardia). Often P waves are not clearly seen on the baseline EKG but are unmasked by adenosine. Evidence of 2:1 AV conduction, as suggested by a 2:1 P to QRS ratio during a narrow QRS tachycardia, indicates atrial flutter. Evidence of complete AV dissociation (no consistent P-QRS relationship) indicates junctional ectopic tachycardia.

Adenosine administration is diagnostic and therapeutic (Table 14.23). It acts by producing a marked slowing of AV node conduction; its effect lasts for a few seconds. Side effects are short-lived and include flushing, chest pain and dyspnea. It is imperative to obtain an EKG record or a rhythm strip during adenosine administration. The medication is administered rapidly at a dose of 50–300 mcg/kg, followed by a rapid push of normal saline as a bolus. Most re-entrant tachycardias, where AV node is a part of the circuit (AV node re-entrant tachycardia, AV re-entrant tachycardia) are terminated by adenosine, while atrial flutter is seldom terminated. The transient AV block that results from adenosine administration can unmask flutter waves on the surface EKG, confirming the diagnosis. Similarly, transient slowing of AV conduction can unmask ectopic atrial tachycardia. If adenosine is not available, vagal maneuvers can be attempted. For infants and young children, an ice filled plastic bag placed on the face is effective. Older children can be encouraged to perform

14

Table 14.22: Causes of narrow QRS tachycardia

Site	*Re-entrant arrhythmias*	*Automatic arrhythmias*
Sinus node	Sinus node re-entry	Sinus tachycardia
Atrium	Intra atrial re-entrant arrhythmias following cardiac surgery (Fontan, Senning operations)	Ectopic atrial tachycardia
	Atrial flutter Atrial fibrillation	Multifocal atrial tachycardia
AV node	AV node re-entry	Junctional ectopic tachycardia
Accessory pathway	Atrioventricular re-entry involving concealed or manifest (WPW) pathway Permanent junctional re-entrant tachycardia	

Table 14.23: Differential diagnosis of narrow QRS tachycardia

Arrhythmia	*P waves*	*P-QRS relationship*	*Response to adenosine*
Sinus tachycardia	Normal	1:1	Transient slowing; AV block
Sinus node-entry	Normal	Usually 1:1	No effect or transient AV block
Ectopic atrial tachycardia	Abnormal and different from baseline	Usually 1:1	No effect or transient AV block
Atrial flutter	Saw tooth appearance, rates exceed 240/min	2:1 or 1:1	Transient AV block may unmask flutter waves; rarely arrhythmia terminates
Postoperative intra atrial re-entry*	Slow atrial flutter, P waves different from baseline; rates 130–240/min	Variable, often 1:1	Transient AV block may unmask flutter waves; rarely arrhythmia terminates
Multifocal atrial tachycardia	Multiform	Usually 1:1	No effect or transient AV block
Junctional ectopic tachycardia	Normal (AV dissociation) or inverted (1:1 retrograde conduction)	Complete AV dissociation is diagnostic	No effect on rate; transient retrograde VA conduction block unmasks AV dissociation
AV nodal tachycardia	Usually not visible (masked by RS complexes)	1:1	Sudden termination is characteristic
AV re-entrant tachycardia	Inverted (retrograde VA conduction)	1:1	Sudden termination
Permanent junctional re-entrant tachycardia	Inverted (long VA conduction time)	1:1	No effect or transient termination

*Postoperative intraatrial re-entry may follow surgery that results in atrial scarring, e.g. Fontan operation, Senning operation

the Valsalva maneuver or carotid sinus massage. Eye ball pressure for vagal stimulation is contraindicated in infants.

Unstable narrow QRS tachycardia: This is uncommon, especially in the absence of structural heart disease. Low energy (0.5–2 J/kg) synchronized DC cardioversion should be performed. Cardioversion should be preceded by administration of a short acting benzodiazepine such as midazolam (0.1–0.2 mg/kg/dose).

Wide QRS tachycardia: Wide QRS complex tachycardias usually result from foci or circuits in the ventricles. Some supraventricular tachycardias can also result in a wide QRS configuration. The overall approach is quite similar to narrow QRS tachycardias. Identify P waves, define P-QRS relationship and determine QRS axis configuration in precordial leads (Figs 14.28 and 14.29). Demonstrable AV dissociation (inconsistent P-QRS relationship) clearly suggests ventricular tachycardia (VT). In most situations, however, it is not easy to distinguish VT from supraventricular tachycardia. If the patient is stable administration of adenosine will terminate or unmask the latter. If there is no response to adenosine, treatment for VT should be initiated.

In stable patients, it is better to initiate pharmacologic treatment of VT before considering cardioversion since the response to initial treatment can help decides long-term medications. Lignocaine is the initial choice and procainamide an effective alternative. Other medications include amiodarone, sotalol, mexeletine and flecanide.

Unstable wide QRS tachycardia: Wide QRS tachycardia with hemodynamic instability is an emergency. Synchronized cardioversion (0.5–2 J/kg) should be performed; CPR is initiated for pulseless patients. Subsequent treatment should follow standard guidelines for pulseless patients with VT or ventricular fibrillation (Fig. 14.30).

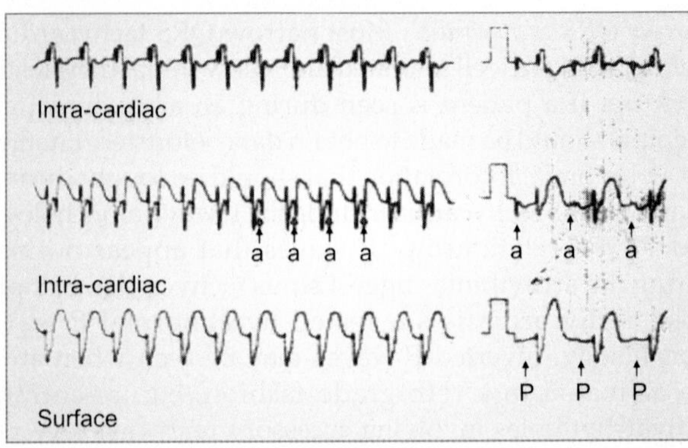

Fig. 14.28: Wide QRS tachycardia resulting from a re-entrant circuit involving an accessory pathway in a patient with right bundle branch block. Surface ECG, can be mistaken for ventricular tachycardia. ECG of the top two rows has been obtained directly from the atrium using post operative atrial wires as electrodes. The bottom strip is the surface ECG from a monitoring lead. Conversion to sinus rhythm after adenosine is seen in the last four complexes on the right. a=artial contraction, p = p wave.

Irregular wide QRS tachycardia: Sustained and irregular wide QRS tachycardia is uncommon and usually suggests a diagnosis of Wolf Parkinson White (WPW) syndrome with atrial fibrillation. In the presence of hemodynamic instability, synchronized high energy cardioversion (1–2 J/kg) is indicated. If the patient is stable, procainamide infusion may be tried.

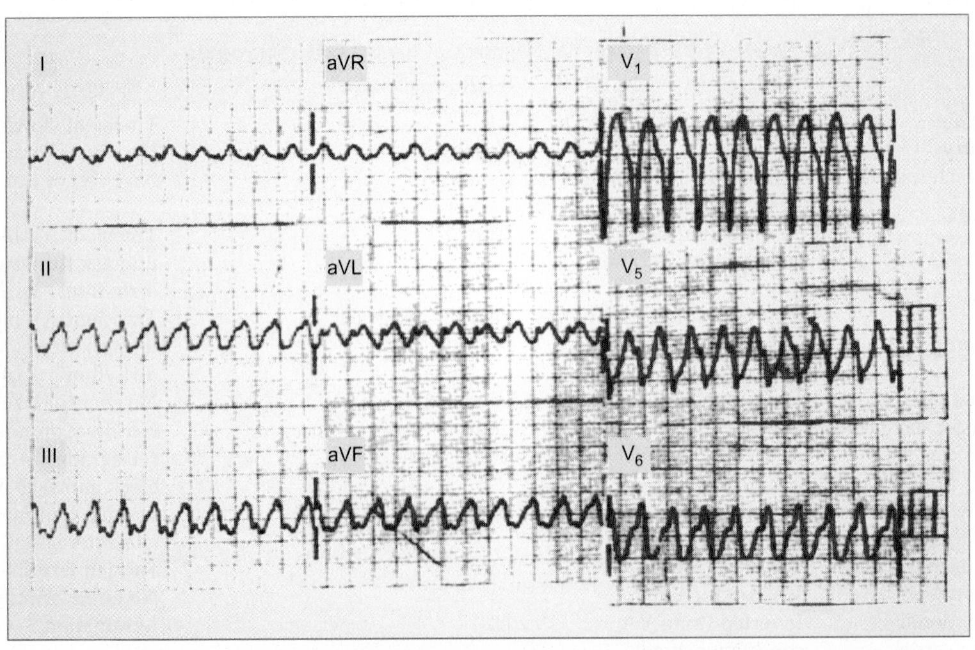

Fig. 14.29: Wide QRS tachycardia. Supraventricular tachycardia in a patient with left bundle branch block can be mistaken for ventricular tachycardia. Rate of 230/min is more in favour of SVT

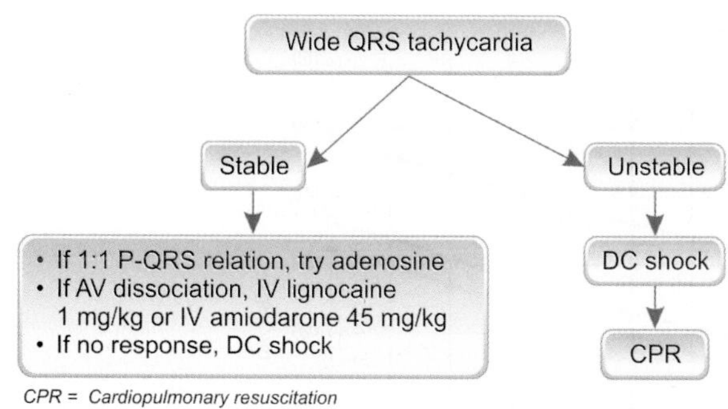

Fig. 14.30: Management of wide QRS tachycardia

Follow-up

Once the arrhythmia has been taken care of, recurrences need to be prevented. Follow up evaluation includes an echocardiogram (to rule out structural heart disease), Holter test (24-hr ambulatory EKG recording) and an esophageal electrophysiological study. Invasive intracardiac electrophysiological study is often combined with radiofrequency ablation therapy. This modality offers a prospect of cure, by permanently modifying the arrhythmic substrate. Most accessory pathways can now be treated by radiofrequency ablation. Because of long-term concerns, radiofrequency ablation is recommended for children older than 4–6 years.

Suggested reading

Walsh EP, Saul JP. Cardiac arrhythmias. In: Fyler DC, ed. Nadas' Pediatric Cardiology. Philadelphia: Hanley & Belfus, 1992, pp 377–435.

HYPERTENSION

Normative charts show that both systolic and diastolic blood pressures vary with age, gender and height percentiles. Blood pressure is also influenced by physical activity, anxiety and emotions. Blood pressure should therefore be recorded when the child is at rest for at least 10 minutes; high values should be rechecked on more than one occasions.

The Fourth US Task Force Report on Hypertension in children and adolescents and the Indian Society of Pediatric Nephrology recommend that hypertension be diagnosed and staged as follows:

Pre-hypertension:	Systolic or diastolic blood pressure 90th-95th percentile
Hypertension:	Systolic or diastolic blood pressure >95th percentile
Stage I hypertension:	Systolic or diastolic blood pressure between 95th percentile and 99th percentile + 5 mm Hg
Stage II hypertension:	Systolic or diastolic blood pressure > 99th percentile + 5 mm Hg

Table 14.24 gives rough estimates of blood pressure in children and adolescents. Normative data on blood pressure values, based on gender, age and height percentiles, derived from a large multiethnic cohort, have been used to define the 50th, 90th, 95th, and 99th percentiles of blood pressure for age, gender and height percentiles. These tables are available at http://www.nhlbi.nih.gov/health/prof/heart/hbp/hbp_ped.htm. The Indian Society of Pediatric Nephrology recommends the use of charts provided for screening and staging of hypertension in boys and girls respectively (Figs 14.31 and 14.32). If percentiles of systolic and diastolic pressures are different, the higher percentile is used for defining and staging hypertension.

Table 14.24: Blood pressure measurement (auscultatory method, mm Hg)

Age	*Systolic pressure*	*Diastolic pressure*
1–3 months	75 ± 5	50 ± 5
4–12 months	84 ± 5	65 ± 5
1–8 years	95 ± 5	65 ± 5
9–14 years	105 ± 5	65 ± 5

Since many patients with stage I hypertension are asymptomatic, it is difficult to estimate the true prevalence of hypertension in children, but is considered to range between 1–4%.

Measuring Blood Pressure

Auscultatory method: Blood pressure is measured in the same manner as in adults. Blood pressure cuff width should be between 50–75% of the circumference of the arm. A narrow cuff gives falsely high readings. Appropriate cuff sizes for different ages are: infants 2.5 cm; 1–12 months 5 cm; 1–8 years 9 cm; older children 12.5 cm. The cuff is inflated rapidly to occlude the brachial artery in the cubital fossa and deflated gradually, systolic pressure is indicated at the onset of Korotkov sounds and diastolic pressure when the heart sounds disappear.

Palpatory method: It is done in the same manner as the auscultatory method. Radial pulse is palpated instead of auscultation. Return of the pulse indicates systolic pressure, which is 5–10 mm Hg less than that recorded by auscultatory method.

Oscillometry: Concerns regarding the environmental risks of mercury have resulted in replacement of mercury sphygmomanometers by electronic devices, of which the most commonly used are the oscillometric instruments. The blood pressure cuff is inflated and deflated electronically. The instrument records the onset and peak oscillations over the brachial artery. It provides an estimate of systolic and diastolic pressures, and heart rate.

Doppler ultrasound: Instead of the oscillometer, an electronic transducer is used. When systolic pressure is reached, movements of the arterial wall cause a Doppler effect (change in frequency of reflected wave, which is transformed into sounds). Recordings are thus comparable to auscultatory method. Electronic instruments should be calibrated periodically.

14

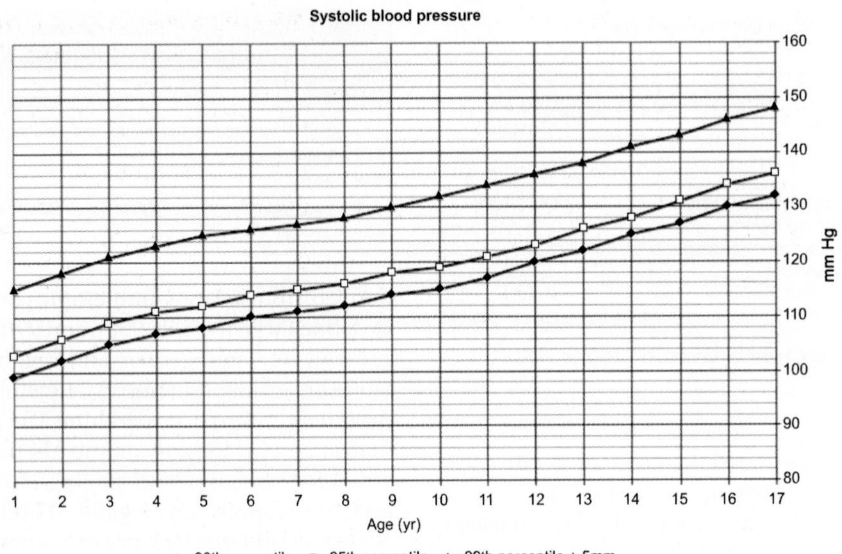

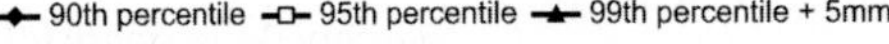

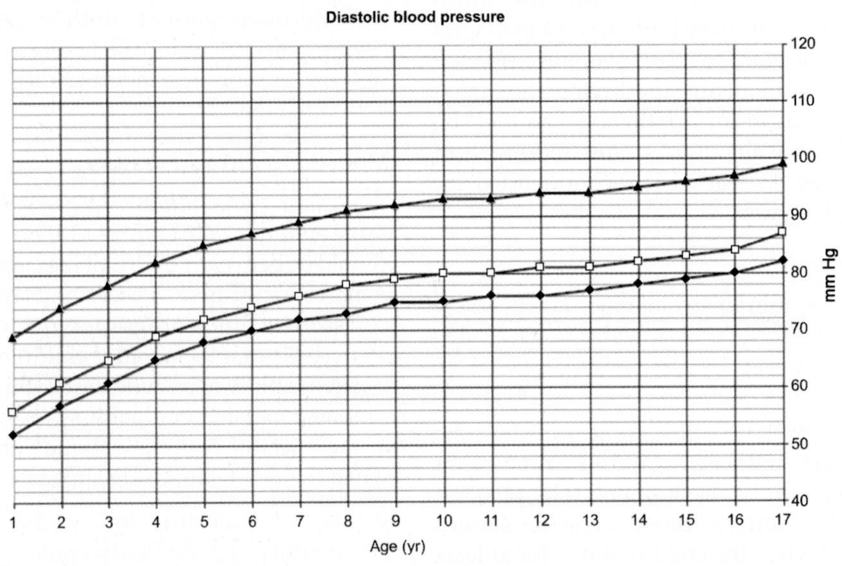

Fig. 14.31: Blood pressure levels for boys at 50th percentile for height. Chart depicting 90th (closed diamonds), 95th (open squares) and 99th + 5 mm (closed triangles) percentile values for (A) systolic and (B) diastolic blood pressures, representing cut off values for the diagnosis of pre-hypertension, stage I and stage II hypertension respectively in boys (based on the Fourth US Task Force Report on Hypertension). (Reproduced with permission)

Etiology

The relative frequency of the etiology hypertension in children is different from adults. Essential hypertension is relatively uncommon in children and accounts for about 5–10% cases. However, it is being increasingly realized that adult essential hypertension does not occur suddenly. As shown by tracking studies, children destined to develop essential hypertension in adults show blood pressure values between 90–95th percentile during childhood. Children with essential hypertension show mild (stage I) elevation in systolic or diastolic pressure; these patients are usually asymptomatic. The presence of markedly elevated (stage II) or symptomatic hypertension suggests an underlying renal or endocrine cause.

Most cases of symptomatic hypertension in children are secondary to an underlying cause. Londe reviewed literature to show that 78% were related to renal parenchymal disease, 12% to renovascular disease, 2% had coarctation and 0.5% had pheochromocytoma. Cushing syndrome, renal tumors, polyarteritis and primary aldosteronism are extremely rare causes of hypertension in children. Idiopathic (Takayasu) aortoarteritis, often involving renal arteries, is a more common cause of hypertension in Asian children than reported in the West.

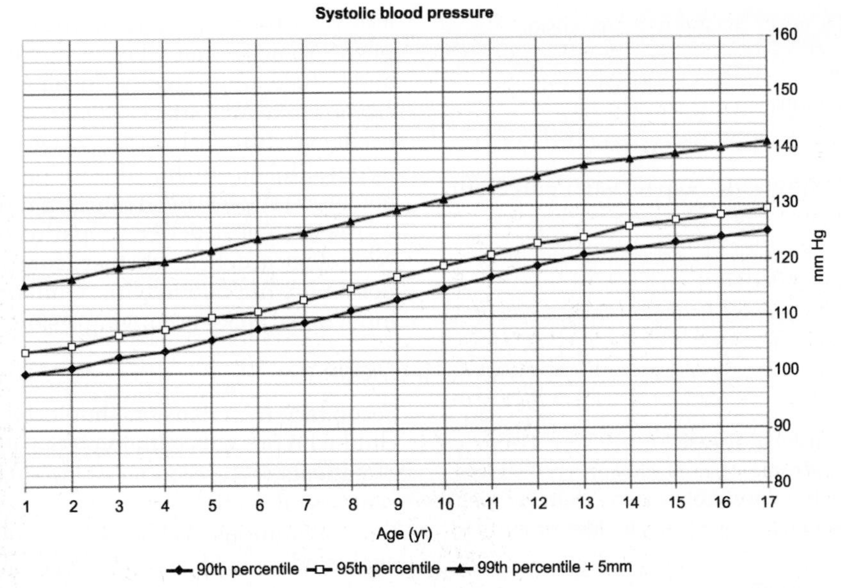

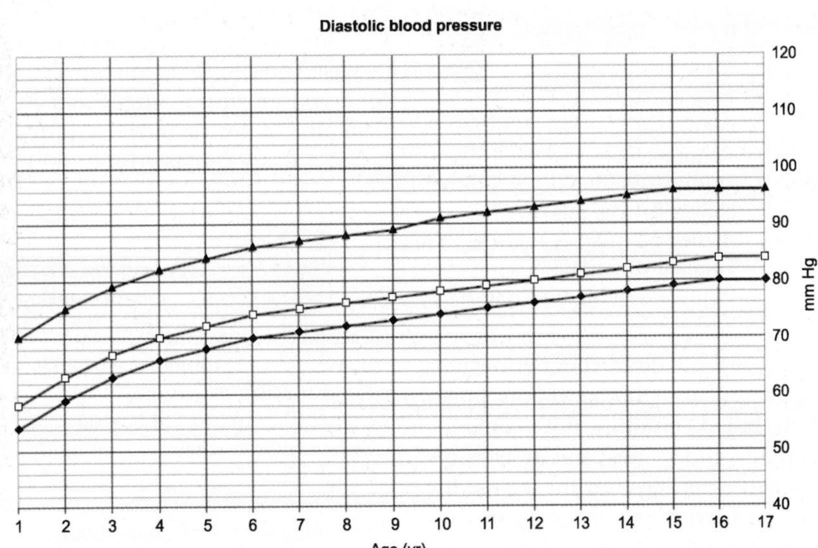

Fig. 14.32: Blood pressure levels for girls at 50th percentile for height. Chart depicting 90th (closed diamonds), 95th (open squares) and 99th + 5 mm (closed triangles) percentile values for (A) systolic and (B) diastolic blood pressures, representing cut off values for the diagnosis of pre-hypertension, stage I and stage II hypertension respectively in girls (based on the Fourth US Task Force Report on Hypertension).(Reproduced with permission)

Tables 14.25 and 14.26 show common causes of persistent and transient hypertension.

Clinical Features

Hypertension per se is asymptomatic. Presence of symptoms indicates end organ disease. Symptoms attributed to hypertension include headache, nausea, vomiting, dizziness, irritability and epistaxis. The clinical features relate to the underlying disease, renal or endocrine. Patients with chronic renal damage may show polyuria, polydipsia, weakness, fatigue, pallor, weight loss and edema. In coarctation of the aorta, femoral pulsations are weak and the blood pressure in lower limbs is less than in the upper limbs. In pheochromocytoma, there are episodes of palpitation, sweating and flushing. Weight loss is an important finding in pheochromocytoma. Patients with Cushing disease have plethoric facies with buffalo hump type obesity, hirsutism and abdominal striae.

With severe hypertension, patients may present in hypertensive crisis with loss of vision, convulsions, nerve palsies and other neurologic deficits (hypertensive encephalopathy). Prolonged hypertension results in *hypertensive retinopathy*. Congestive cardiac failure as a manifestation of systemic hypertension is extremely rare in children. If present, it should suggest acute glomerulonephritis or idiopathic aortoarteritis.

Table 14.25: Causes of persistent hypertension

Intrinsic renal diseases
Chronic glomerulonephritis
Reflux nephropathy
Obstructive uropathy
Congenital lesions (dysplastic, hypoplastic, polycystic kidneys)
Renovascular
Idiopathic (Takayasu) aortoarteritis
Renal artery stenosis
Essential hypertension
Coarctation of aorta
Endocrine
Pheochromocytoma, Cushing disease
Liddle syndrome, syndrome of mineralocorticoid excess, glucocorticoid remediable aldosteronism, congenital adrenal hyperplasia, neuroblastoma, primary hyperaldosteronism
Renal tumors
Wilm's tumor, nephroblastoma

14

Table 14.26: Causes of transient hypertension

Renal	*Miscellaneous*
Acute post-streptococcal GN	Landry Guillain Barré syndrome
Hemolytic uremic syndrome	Poliomyelitis
Renal trauma	Corticosteroids, contraceptives intake
Henöch Schönlein purpura	Hypernatremia
Postrenal transplant	Familial dysautonomia
Renal vein thrombosis	Acute intermittent porphyria

Grading of hypertensive retinopathy: In grade I hypertensive retinopathy, the arterioles appear as broad yellow lines (copper wire). In grade II, blood column is not visible in the arterioles (seen as broad yellow lines) and at arterio-venous crossings, thickened arterioles nip the veins. In grade III, hemorrhages and exudates are seen in the fundus. Arterioles are narrowed and their diameter is about ¼ of the diameter of veins. Arterioles appear as broad white silvery lines in which blood column is not visible, but there is dilatation of the vein distal to it. *In grade IV retinopathy, indicating malignant hypertension, papilledema is superadded over changes of grade III retinopathy.*

Physical Examination and Differential Diagnosis

Blood pressure should be obtained in both arms and at least one leg. Asymmetrical pressure with right arm pressure higher than left arm can occur in coarctation of the aorta, supravalvar aortic stenosis and obstructive aortoarteritis. Higher blood pressure in arms compared to legs occurs in coarctation and obstructive aortitis. Renal artery stenosis and aortoarteritis and essential hypertension may result in an abdominal bruit. Pallor combined with edema suggests chronic renal failure. Weight loss due to a hypermetabolic state, attacks of headache, palpitation, flushing, sweating and postural hypotension indicate the possibility of pheochromocytoma. Obesity, hirsutism, abdominal striae and buffalo hump signify Cushing's syndrome. Polyuria, cramps or tetanic attacks, generalized weakness, absence of edema with attacks of severe weakness suggest primary hyperaldosteronism. Abdominal mass and history of hematuria suggest renal tumor or renal mass of hydronephrosis from obstructive uropathy, or polycystic kidney. Neurological deficit, whether acute or subacute signify the possibility of poliomyelitis, Guillain-Barre syndrome or intracranial space occupying lesion.

Diagnosis

Secondary hypertension should be considered in every child who presents with hypertension. Since the majority of patients with secondary hypertension have a renal or renovascular etiology, tests are designed to screen for these conditions (Table 14.27). Patients should also be evaluated for evidence of target organ damage, by retinal fundus examination, urine biochemistry for proteinuria, EKG and an echocardiogram. The utility of peripheral PRA in screening for renovascular hypertension is limited.

Based on clinical features and initial evaluation, a cause for hypertension is suggested in most instances. Confirmation of the diagnosis requires specific investigations tailored to specific needs (Table 14.28).

Table 14.27: Screening investigations for patients with hypertension

Complete blood counts
Blood urea, creatinine, electrolytes, glucose, uric acid
Lipid profile
Urinalysis, culture (if necessary)
24-hr urinary protein or spot albumin to creatinine ratio
Chest X-ray
Ultrasonography for kidneys, adrenals
Screening for target organ damage
Retinal fundus examination
Urine spot protein to creatinine ratio
ECG, echocardiography

Table 14.28: Diagnostic tests for sustained hypertension

Condition	*Investigations*
Glomerulo-nephritis	Complement, autoantibodies, renal biopsy
Reflux nephropathy	Micturating cystourethrogram, DMSA scintigraphy
Renovascular hypertension	Doppler flow studies, captopril renography, angiography
Coarctation of aorta	Echocardiography, angiography
Endocrine causes	Plasma renin activity, aldosterone; plasma, and urinary cortisol; Plasma, urine catecholamines; MIBG scan; CT/MR imaging; thyroid functions

Management

Each patient must be appropriately evaluated. Efforts must be made to determine the etiology of hypertension.

Salt restriction: Salt restriction is useful but difficult to implement in children. During summer months with excess of sodium loss in sweat as is common in tropical countries, salt restriction is not desirable except in patients who have hypertensive cardiac failure. In essential hypertension, which is usually inherited, the whole family should be advised to restrict salt in cooking.

Long-term Medication

Sufficient experience in children on the use of many anti hypertensive medications is not available. Therefore, these should be used under supervision.

Thiazide: group of diuretics are commonly employed. Hydrochlorothiazide is more potent than chlorothiazide. Since these cause hypokalemia, potassium salts should be given as supplements. Hyperuricemia, at times observed in association with thiazide treatment, is not usual in childhood. Recently, frusemide has been used to treat mild and moderate hypertension. While this agent is less effective for treatment of hypertension than thiazides, it is better used in patients with impaired renal function. Spironolactone (antagonist of aldosterone) should be used in hypertension secondary to hyperaldosteronism. Side effects include gynecomastia in boys and menstrual irregularities in girls.

Beta-adrenergic antagonists are effective agents for initial therapy of hypertension. It is preferable to use agents that require single or twice daily dosing, e.g. metoprolol or atenolol. Labetalol, an α and β-blocker, is effective in patients refractory to other medications. The use of propranolol has declined in view of the need for multiple daily doses and frequent side effects.

Angiotensin converting enzyme (ACE) inhibitors and angiotensin receptor blockers are effective antihypertensive agents. They reduce the blood pressure effectively especially when combined with diuretics. A large number of agents are now available. Of the ACEI, captopril (chiefly used in young infants) requires dosing every 6–8 hr. Beyond infancy, enalapril (1–2 daily doses) is preferred. Newer ACEI (lisinopril, ramipril) require once daily dosing and have fewer side effects. Angiotensin receptor blockers approved for use in children include losartan and irbesartan.

Nifedipine and amlodepine are effective *calcium channel blockers* for children. The availability of long acting preparations permit once or twice daily dosing. Some patients require therapy with additional agents, including clonidine, prazosin, hydralazine and minoxidil. Table 14.29 provides a list of antihypertensive drugs used in children.

Table 14.29: Oral antihypertensive medications

Drug	Dose
Captopril	0.3–6 mg/kg/day; three divided doses
Enalapril	0.1–0.6 mg/kg/day; single daily dose
Lisinopril	0.06–0.6 mg/kg/day; single daily dose
Losartan	0.7–1.4 mg/kg/day; single daily dose
Amlodepine	0.05–0.5 mg/kg/day; once-twice daily dose
Nifedipine (extended release)	0.25–3 mg/kg/day; once-twice daily dose
Atenolol	0.5–2 mg/kg/day; once-twice daily dose
Metoprolol	1–6 mg/kg/day; two divided doses
Labetalol	1–40 mg/kg/day; two-three divided doses
Clonidine	5–25 µg/kg/day; three-four divided doses
Prazosin	0.05–0.5 mg/kg/day; two divided doses
Hydralazine	1–8 mg/kg/day; four divided doses
Frusemide	0.5–6 mg/kg/day; one-two doses
Spironolactone*	1–3 mg/kg/day; one-two doses
Hydrochlorothiazide	1–3 mg/kg/day; once daily

Management of Hypertensive Emergency

Appropriate treatment of hypertensive emergencies reduces mortality and improves renal function. Therapy for such emergencies should preferably start with parenteral agents (Table 14.30). Intravenous infusion of *sodium nitroprusside* is very effective in reducing blood pressure in the most resistant cases. However, its use should be restricted, as it requires careful monitoring in an intensive care setting. Other IV agents that may be used include labetalol and nicardipine. Sublingual nifedipine acts within minutes to control the blood pressure and may be used if therapy with IV agents is not feasible.

As soon as the condition of the child permits, oral antihypertensive regimen should be started. Patients with post-streptococcal glomerulonephritis may be initially treated with oral frusemide. In cases of crisis associated with pheochromocytoma, an adrenergic blocker, phentolamine may be used.

Table 14.30: Drugs for hypertensive emergencies

Drug	Dose
Sodium nitroprusside	50 mg is dissolved in a liter of 5% dextrose solution to give a concentration of 5 µg/ml. IV infusion: 0.3–8 µg/kg/min; most managed by 2 µg/kg/min. Protect infusate from light
Nitroglycerine	IV infusion: 1–3 µg/kg/min, increase by 0.5–1 µg/kg/min every 30 min
Labetalol	IV infusion: 0.25–3 mg/kg/hr; or bolus: 0.2-1 mg/kg/dose; may repeat every 5–10 min to maximum 40 mg
Nifedipine	PO: 0.25 mg/kg
Nicardipine	IV infusion: 0.5–5 µg/kg/min; maximum 5 mg/hr
Phentolamine	IV bolus: 0.1–0.2 mg/kg (maximum 5 mg); repeat 2–4 hr

14

Stepwise Treatment of Hypertension

Since essential hypertension is a lifelong problem, an attempt must be made to change the life style of the patient. A diet low in salt and animal proteins, reduction in weight, ensuring regular exercise as well as periods of relaxation may be effective and not require medications. Therapy with antihypertensive agents is required for patients with: (i) stage II hypertension, (ii) stage I or II hypertension with evidence of end-organ damage or (iii) sustained stage I hypertension that is not controlled despite 6-months of life style modification, including exercise and weight reduction. Principles of antihypertensive therapy include:

i. Start with ACE inhibitors (e.g. enalapril, lisinopril, ramipril).
ii. If the blood pressure is not controlled, add a thiazide diuretic.
iii. If the blood pressure is still not controlled, add a calcium channel blocker, e.g. amlodipine.
iv. Finally, consider addition of a beta blocker (atenolol, carvedilol, labetalol).
v. If ACE inhibitors are associated with cough, shift to angiotensin receptor blockers (losartan).

14

Suggested reading

1. Indian Pediatric Nephrology Group, Indian Academy of Pediatrics. Evaluation and management of hypertension. Indian Pediatr 2007; 44: 103–121
2. National High Blood Pressure Education Program Working Group. The Fourth report on the diagnosis, evaluation and treatment of high blood pressure in children and adolescents. Pediatrics 2004; 114 (suppl): 555–576.

INTERVENTIONAL CARDIOLOGY

Interventions in the cardiac catheterization laboratory and utilizing echocardiography have significantly changed the management of children with heart diseases. It is emphasized that *interventional procedures are always performed in cooperation with surgical colleagues.* Interventions in absence of surgical cover are unethical. The available procedures are outlined in Table 14.31.

Creation of Defects

Atrial septostomy: Creation of a large communication between the right and left atrium may be required to provide better mixing of blood as in complete transposition of great arteries with intact ventricular septum. Other indications include relief of left atrial hypertension (as in hypoplastic left heart syndrome or mitral atresia) and relief of right atrial hypertension or increase the right to left shunting of blood (as in total anomalous pulmonary venous connection and tricuspid atresia).

The technique consists in passing a catheter with an inflatable balloon from the femoral vein through the inferior vena cava to the right atrium and then to the left atrium through the foramen ovale or the atrial septal defect. The balloon is inflated in the left atrium and pulled into the right atrium so as to tear the atrial septum and thus allow free communication between the two atria (Figs 14.33A and B). The procedure is generally successful only up to the age of four weeks or so, since beyond that age the septum becomes too thick. In such cases, the atrial

Table 14.31: Interventional procedures

Creation of defects
Balloon and blade atrial septostomy
Opening narrow areas
Stenotic valves
Narrow arteries
Stenotic veins
Closing abnormal openings or vessels
Closure of septal defects
Closure of patent ductus and abnormal arterial channels
Closure of abnormal venous channels
Arrhythmia management

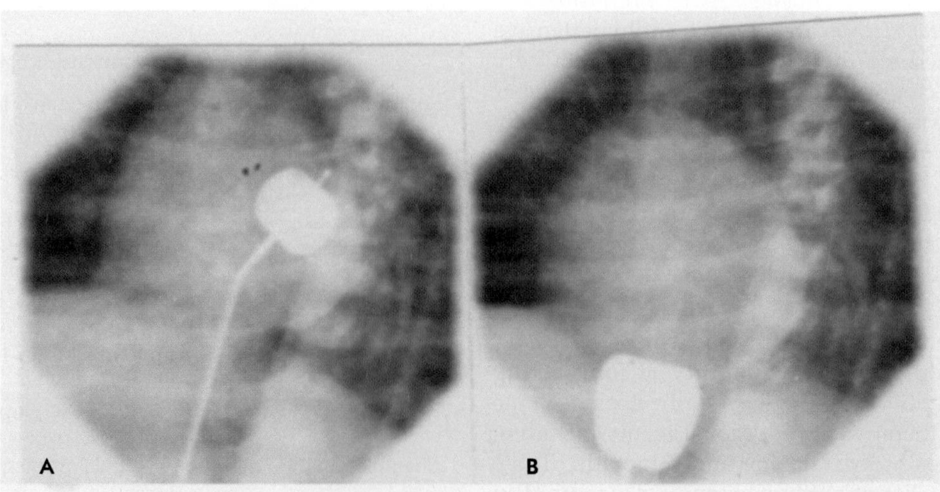

Figs 14.33A and B: Atrial septostomy. (A) Balloon catheter in left atrium (B) balloon pulled through the atrial septum in the right atrium

septal defect can be enlarged using non elastic inflatable balloon dilation. A retractable blade atrial septostomy is possible for older babies where balloon septostomy does not work. In hypoplastic left heart syndrome, it may be necessary to stent the atrial septum to provide a reliable opening.

Opening Narrow Areas

Balloon valvuloplasty: A non-elastic, inflatable balloon is positioned in a stenotic aortic, pulmonary, tricuspid or mitral valve to dilate them and relieve the obstruction. For valvar pulmonic stenosis, balloon valvotomy is the procedure of choice even in neonates. Surgical correction of valvar pulmonic stenosis is indicated only if balloon valvotomy fails to relieve the obstruction, e.g. dysplastic pulmonary valves in Noonan's syndrome (Fig. 14.34).

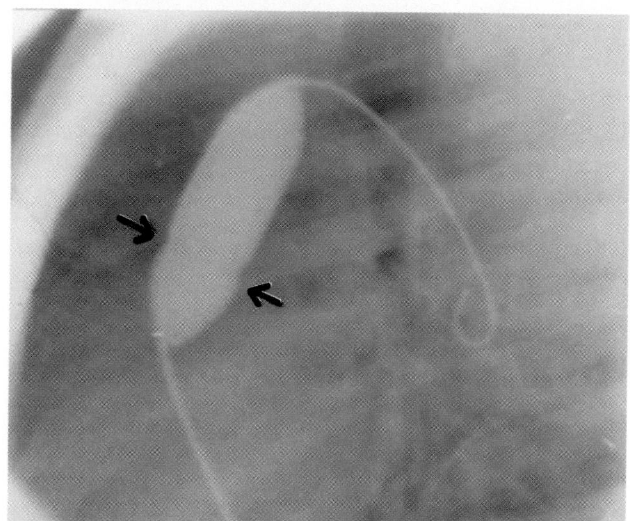

Fig. 14.34: Pulmonary valvotomy. Catheter passed from inferior vena cava to right atrium, right ventricle and pulmonary artery. The tip is in the lung. Inflated balloon at the level of pulmonary valve (indent – arrows)

Aortic stenosis responds well to balloon valvuloplasty and has been utilized even in neonates with critical stenosis. The non-elastic inflatable balloon catheter is introduced percutaneously through the femoral artery and inflated in the aortic valve to relieve the obstruction (Fig. 14.35). The indication for balloon valvotomy is the same as for surgical valvotomy. Both procedures allow the child to grow to an age when valve replacement can be performed. The complication of aortic regurgitation is probably slightly higher than that following surgical valvotomy. Balloon aortic valvuloplasty is specially useful in neonates and infants where the surgical mortality is high. One major concern in this age group, however, is a high incidence of loss of femoral artery pulses (30%) and possible impairment of limb growth. This can be avoided by dilating the

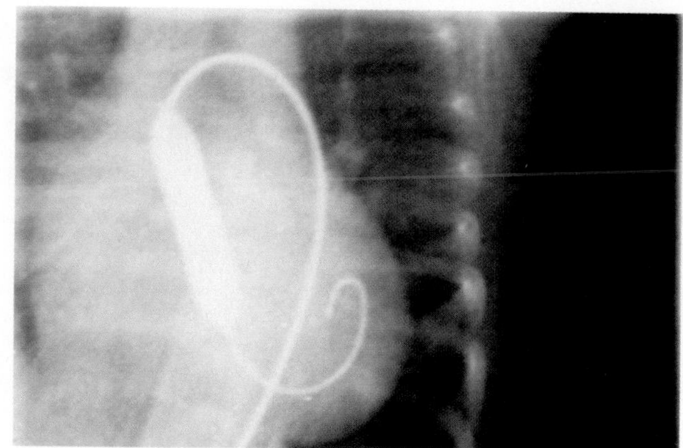

Fig. 14.35: Aortic valvotomy. Catheter passed via aorta into the left ventricle. Inflated balloon is across the aortic valve

valve via the femoral vein approach (through a patent foramen ovale). In the absence of aortic regurgitation balloon dilation can be repeated if necessary to allow growth of the child to an age when valve replacement becomes necessary as the definitive treatment. Discrete membranous sub-valvar aortic stenosis, with the membrane less than 2 mm in thickness and a gradient of 75 mm Hg or more, can be dilated with a balloon catheter. Indication for interference is the same as for valvar aortic stenosis. The membrane tends to regrow, hence, a close follow-up is essential.

Mitral valvotomy via percutaneous femoral vein approach, using a transseptal puncture to reach the left atrium has become an acceptable therapeutic modality for rheumatic mitral stenosis. The results are as good as those obtained by surgical valvotomy. The frequency of significant mitral regurgitation requiring valve replacement as an emergency procedure is no more than that of closed mitral valvotomy, however, if it does occur emergency surgical valve repair or replacement becomes essential. Congenital mitral stenosis is rarely amenable to balloon dilation. *Tricuspid valvuloplasty* can be performed using balloon catheter but is almost never needed in children.

Arterial obstruction: Coarctation of the aorta with a pressure gradient of 20 mm Hg in the presence of systemic hypertension or congestive failure requires relief of obstruction. Balloon dilatation of unoperated (referred to as native) coarctation of the aorta is now an acceptable therapeutic modality (Figs 14.36A and B). Balloon dilatation causes a circumferential tear of the intima and media. In the majority of patients, adverse clinical events are absent. Balloon dilatation of native coarctation is currently the treatment of choice for children older than three months. Below the age of three months controversy regarding preference for balloon dilatation versus surgical correction is still present. For patients who develop recoarctation of the aorta following surgical correction, balloon dilatation is the procedure of choice. Metal mesh formed into a tube,

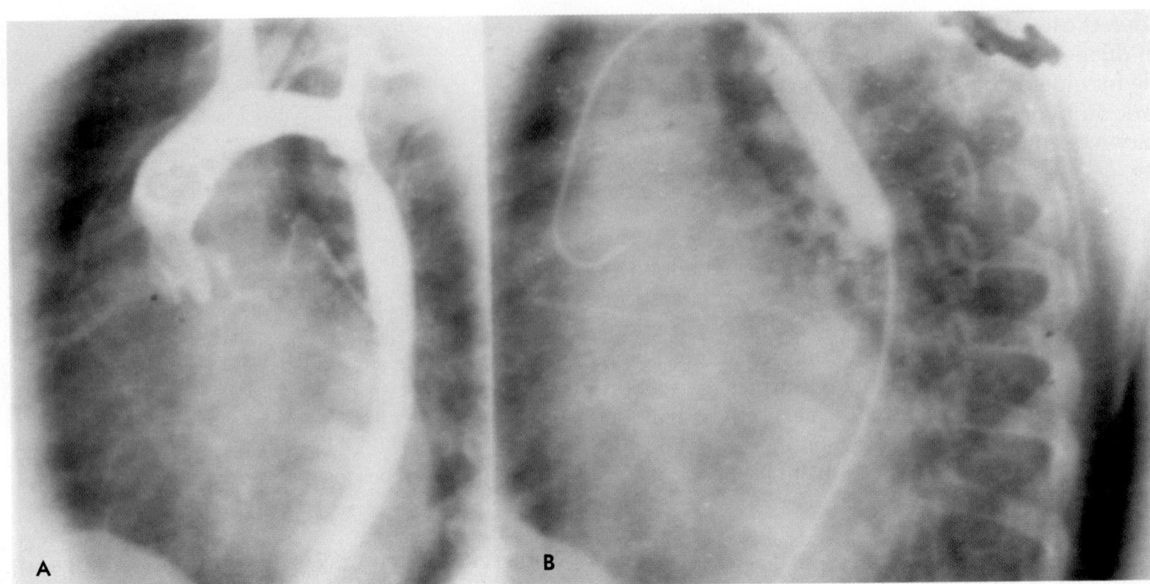

Figs 14.36A and B: (A) Coarctation of the aorta (B) balloon dilatation of the coarctation

called ***stents***, are now being utilized to prevent reappearance of the narrowing. Newer stents, which are self expandable or can be expanded or dilated to increase the size of the lumen are now available and being increasingly deployed. The disadvantage of using stents in infants and children is the need for redilation in a growing child.

Obstructive aortoarteritis is an important cause of severe hypertension and congestive failure in children in India. Balloon dilatation of the aorta, branches of the aorta as well as renal arteries has been utilized with excellent results. The need for anticongestive and antihypertensive treatment may disappear or the requirement of drug management considerably reduce following balloon dilatation with or without a stent.

Branch pulmonary artery stenosis referred to as peripheral pulmonic stenosis does not respond well to balloon dilation alone. Use of self expandable or balloon expandable stents have allowed dilation of branch (or distal) pulmonary artery stenosis not treatable surgically. Peripheral pulmonic stenosis could be an isolated lesion but is more commonly found in association with lesions constituting Fallot's physiology. It results in persistent pulmonary arterial hypertension following definitive repair of these lesions. Following balloon dilatation and placement of stent the pulmonary artery pressure decreases and the forward flow increases. Restenosis is uncommon but if the stents are placed at a young age, growth of the child may require redilatation.

Venous obstruction: Dilatation of superior or inferior vena cava and pulmonary vein stenosis have been performed successfully, however, the numbers are small and guidelines for their management not clearly established. The major problem in the management of venous obstruction is the problem of tear of the thin walled veins. However many venous channels are not surgically correctable and balloon dilatation is the only approach available even with a high risk.

Closing Abnormal Openings or Vessels

Closure of septal defects: Non-operative closure of *secundum atrial septal defect* (ASD) located at fossa ovalis area is possible. Device closure of atrial septal defects has become increasingly realistic after the introduction of the Amplatzer double disc device. The device (Fig. 14.37) is relatively easy to deploy and in many centers it is offered as the first line for treatment for ASD.

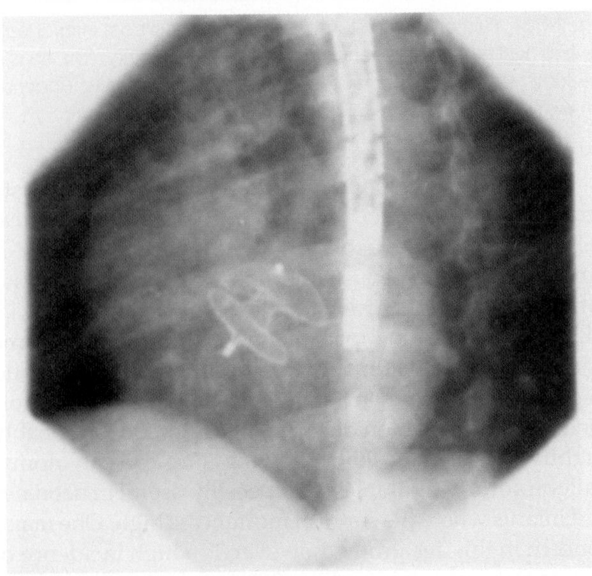

Fig. 14.37: Amplatzer device after closing a secundum atrial septal defect

Most (90%) *ventricular defects* (VSD) are sub-aortic perimembranous in location and not amenable to device closure. Muscular VSD can be closed with occluding devices. While the technique is cumbersome, it avoids a ventriculotomy scar on the myocardium. VSD closure is done under echocardiographic control in the laboratory, thus reducing radiation exposure.

Closure of arterial channels : Non-surgical closure of *patent ductus arteriosus* (PDA) is done using a number of techniques, e.g. foam plug and coil embolization. A relatively small PDA, up to 3 mm can be very effectively closed using coil embolization. The coils are made of stainless steel wire, which when pushed out of the delivery catheter form a coiled spring. They are coated with Dacron fiber to enhance clotting of blood around the coil. It is the clotting of blood and formation of thrombus that results in the closure of the PDA. Closure of larger PDA using Amplatzer device is rapidly gaining acceptance because of its ability to close larger ducts (up to 10 mm) with almost 100% success.

A number of congenital arterial anomalies can potentially be successfully closed using coils or detachable balloons. These include (a) aortopulmonary collaterals in patients of Fallot's physiology, (b) surgically created shunts in patients with Fallot's physiology, (c) coronary arteriovenous fistulae, (d) systemic arteriovenous fistulae and (e) pulmonary arteriovenous fistulae or any other unwanted abnormal channels. The biggest advantage is avoiding a surgical procedure and shortened hospital stay.

Arrhythmia Management

Identification of accessory pathways using electrophysiological studies in pre-excitation syndromes and using radiofrequency ablation results in a permanent cure of paroxysmal supraventricular tachycardias. Radiofrequency ablation is avoided in infancy because many patients show spontaneous recovery from the condition. Patients with supraventricular tachycardias starting after the age of one year, especially those occurring beyond the age of 6 years are best treated using radiofrequency ablation rather than medical therapy, which may be lifelong. Radiofrequency ablation of ectopic atrial or junctional tachycardias is rewarding since they respond poorly to drug therapy. Permanent form of junctional reciprocating tachycardia, atrial flutter in postoperative patients of Mustard or Senning surgery can also be managed by this procedure. Some forms of ventricular tachycardia can be managed by radiofrequency ablation rather than medications.

Suggested reading

Bahl VK, *et al*. Non-coronary cardiac interventions. The first report of the non-coronary cardiac intervention. Registry of India. Indian Heart J 1997; 49: 97–101.

15 Disorders of Kidney and Urinary Tract

RENAL ANATOMY AND PHYSIOLOGY

Kidneys excrete the end products of metabolism and help to keep the composition and volume of body fluids within normal range. They are also involved in the regulation of blood pressure and erythropoiesis, synthesis of ammonia, and metabolism of vitamin D, hormones and cytokines.

Each kidney is composed of approximately a million nephrons, each consisting of a glomerulus and renal tubule. The glomerulus is made of a tuft of capillaries and a central region of mesangium. The capillaries arise from the afferent arteriole and join to form the efferent arteriole, the entry and exit being at the hilum of the kidney. The capillary wall consists of a fenestrated endothelium, glomerular basement membrane and foot processes (podocytes) of visceral epithelial cells. The basement membrane is made of type IV collagen, laminin and heparan sulfate proteoglycan. The Bowman's space leads into the proximal tubule that has an initial convoluted portion and a straight segment. The latter leads to the descending and ascending limbs of the loop of Henle and the distal tubule. Six to eight distal tubules join to form the collecting ducts that finally enter the renal pelvis. The renal cortex consists of glomeruli, proximal and distal tubules. Renal medulla contains the descending and ascending limbs of the loop of Henle and the collecting ducts.

Renal Vasculature

The renal artery divides into segmental arteries that branch to form interlobar and arcuate arteries. The latter give rise to the intralobar arteries, which provide the afferent arterioles for the glomeruli. The efferent arterioles from the glomeruli form a meshwork of peritubular venous capillaries that empty into intralobar veins.

Juxtaglomerular Apparatus (JGA)

The early part of the distal tubule on its ascent from the medulla to the cortex lies near the glomerulus of the same nephron. The cells of the tubule that come in contact with the afferent arteriole of the glomerulus are denser than the rest, and are called macula densa. The smooth muscle cells of the afferent arteriole, in this region, contain prominent cytoplasmic granules that are the site of renin activity. The JGA is composed of the afferent and efferent arterioles, the macula densa and lacis cells located between these structures. The JGA is involved in systemic blood pressure regulation, electrolyte homeostasis and tubuloglomerular feedback.

Renal Physiology

Glomerular filtration depends upon the higher pressure in afferent arterioles. The filtration barrier is constituted by the endothelium with slit pores, basement membrane and podocytes of visceral epithelial cells. Filtration of solutes depends upon their molecular size, shape and electrical charge.

The filtrate from the glomerular capillaries passes from the Bowman's capsule into the proximal convoluted tubule, loop of Henle, distal tubule and collecting ducts. The filtrate contains all the diffusible and ultrafiltrable substances present in plasma. Small quantities of protein are usually present, but are reabsorbed in proximal tubule. Bulk of the glomerular filtrate is reabsorbed into the peritubular capillaries and only 0.5% is excreted as urine.

Tubular Reabsorption

The proximal tubules reabsorb about 80% of the glomerular filtrate. Normally about 65% of sodium is reabsorbed in the proximal tubule, through several active transport systems. Sodium transport is dependent on the parallel transport of bicarbonate, chloride, amino acids and glucose. Tubular reabsorption of sodium and other permeable solutes is promoted by the phenomenon of *solvent drag* during transport of water across the tubular epithelium.

The glomerular filtration rate is regulated by tubuloglomerular feedback that depends upon the functional integrity of the JGA. Increased delivery of chloride to the macula densa results in local activation of renin-angiotensin mechanism. The differential constrictive action of angiotensin on the afferent and efferent arterioles causes a reduction in glomerular filtration. The renin-angiotensin-aldosterone system, prostaglandins, catecholamines, kinins and natriuretic peptides are involved in sodium handling. Potassium is completely reabsorbed in the proximal tubule; the amount seen in urine depends upon its secretion in the distal tubule. Amino acids are also totally reabsorbed in the proximal tubules by different pathways.

Distal tubules and collecting ducts are responsible for urinary acidification, urinary concentration and regulation of sodium balance. Exchange of potassium or hydrogen ions for sodium takes place in the distal tubules under the regulation of aldosterone. Antidiuretic hormone mediates absorption of water through insertion of 'water, channels (aquaporins) on the luminal surface of cells in the collecting tubules. Low levels of the hormone, as in central diabetes insipidus, result in large amounts of dilute urine. The converse occurs during dehydration.

The kidney helps in regulation of acid-base balance by maintaining plasma bicarbonate concentration at 24–26 mEq/L. Filtered bicarbonate is almost completely reabsorbed, 85 to 90% in the proximal tubules and the rest in distal tubules and collecting ducts. Bicarbonate, consumed in the buffering of nonvolatile acids, is regenerated by the renal excretion of titratable acid and ammonia. Chronic acidosis augments the production of ammonia and thus elimination of acid.

Suggested reading

Srivastava RN, Bagga A. Renal anatomy and physiology. In: Pediatric Nephrology, 4th edn. Jaypee, New Delhi, 2005;1–19.

DEVELOPMENT OF STRUCTURE AND FUNCTION

Differentiation of the primitive kidney is stimulated by penetration of the metanephros, during the fifth week of gestation, by the ureteric bud; the latter is an outgrowth of the mesonephric duct. Division of the ureteric bud within the metanephros induces the development of nephrons. The ureteric bud gives rise to the intrarenal collecting system, renal calyces, pelvis and ureter. The most active period of nephrogenesis is from 20–36 weeks. The full number of nephrons is present around 36 weeks. Dysgenesis at various stages of development accounts for the large variety of congenital anomalies of the kidney and urinary tract. Postnatal growth of kidneys parallels somatic growth and is due to increase in the size of individual nephrons. However, the latent capacity of the kidneys to hypertrophy continues well into adulthood. Thus, unilateral nephrectomy is usually followed by hypertrophy of the other kidney.

Glomerular Filtration

Glomerular filtration begins between 9–12 weeks of gestation, initiating urine formation. Fetal urine is a major component of the amniotic fluid after 15–16 weeks. The fetal kidney receives about 2–4% of cardiac output, whereas in the neonate renal blood flow amounts to 15–18% of cardiac output. The serum creatinine level is high at birth reflecting the maternal value but falls rapidly to about 0.4 mg/dL by the end of the first week. 92% neonates pass urine within the first 48 hr. Depending on solute intake, a healthy infant excretes 15–30 mL/kg/day of urine on the first two days of life and 25–120 mL/kg/day during the next 4 weeks. The GFR is low at birth (15–20 mL/min/1.73 m^2 in the first 3 days in term, 10–15 mL/min/1.73 m^2 in preterm infants). These values increase rapidly to 35–45 mL/min/1.73 m^2 at 2 weeks and 75–80 mL/min/1.73 m^2 by 2 months of life.

Tubular Function

During the first weeks of life, tubular function follows a pattern similar to GFR but at a lower level. Compared to adults, there is reduced sodium and bicarbonate reabsorption and limited hydrogen ion excretion. The pH of urine in newborns is inappropriately high for the degree of acidemia.

Plasma Osmolality

The capacity of the kidneys to concentrate or dilute urine is limited in neonates. An infant can concentrate his urine to a maximum of 700–800 mOsm/kg whereas the older child can achieve 1200–1400 mOsm/kg. Growing babies utilize most of the protein available for growth rather than catabolize it to urea. Decreased production and excretion of urea result in a relatively hyposmolar interstitium resulting in reduced urinary concentration compared to older children. The newborn can dilute his urine to a minimum of 50 mOsm/kg, like an older child. However, the time taken to excrete a water load is much longer in the neonate. Thus, delayed feeding, and overdiluted or concentrated feeds are potentially harmful.

Maturation of Renal Function

Renal function continues to improve during the first two years of life, at the end of which, various parameters of renal function approach adult values, if corrected to standard surface area. Structural growth parallels the functional maturation.

Suggested reading

1. Srivastava RN, Bagga A. Diseases of the newborn. In: Pediatric Nephrology, 4th edn. Jaypee, New Delhi, 2005;413–42.
2. Hughson MD. Low birth weight and kidney function: is there a relationship and is it determined by the intrauterine environment? Am J Kidney Dis 2007; 50(4):531–534.

DIAGNOSTIC EVALUATION

Common manifestations of renal disorders include edema, hematuria, oligoanuria, dysuria and abnormalities of micturition, flank pain and ureteric colic. Serious renal disease may be present with subtle or no symptoms. Awareness of differences in the pattern of renal disease at various ages helps in their evaluation.

Neonatal Period

Congenital anomalies of kidney and urinary tract manifest commonly in neonatal period. These may be detected antenatally on maternal ultrasonographic examination.

Appropriate imaging procedures are needed to confirm and define their severity. Abnormal urinary stream or dribbling of urine suggests an anomaly of the distal urinary tract. The causes of acute renal failure in the newborn are different from those in older children.

Infancy to 3 Years

During infancy, unexplained fever may be the only feature of urinary tract infection (UTI). UTI may also be suggested by other nonspecific symptoms such as failure to thrive, diarrhea and vomiting. It is important to diagnose these infections since urinary tract anomalies may be present. An abdominal mass at this age is likely to be a Wilms' tumor, hydronephrosis or multicystic renal dysplasia. Hemolytic uremic syndrome (HUS) most commonly occurs during this age group. About 20% patients with minimal change nephrotic syndrome have onset of the disease between 2–3 years. Renal tubular disorders such as renal tubular acidosis and Fanconi syndrome are most often detected at this age.

3 to 6 Years

Minimal change nephrotic syndrome is a common condition at this age. Acute post-streptococcal glomerulonephritis (GN), rare below the age of 3 yr, is usual in older children. Rickets at this age is rarely due to vitamin D deficiency, unless there is malabsorption or chronic liver disease.

6 to 14 Years

Acute post-streptococcal glomerulonephritis (GN) is common; nephrotic syndrome beginning beyond 8–10 years of age may be of the non-minimal type. Acute-on-chronic renal failure, previously undetected chronic renal failure, symptomatic hypertension and collagen vascular diseases are common.

Clinical Features of Renal Disease

Abnormalities of Micturition

A poor urinary stream in boys, especially in presence of a full bladder, suggests obstruction, most commonly due to posterior urethral valves. Persistent dribbling indicates abnormal ureteric insertion distal to bladder neck. All infants with meningomyelocele should be evaluated for bladder dysfunction.

Edema

Acute GN presents with facial puffiness and gross hematuria; the edema is turgid and does not pit readily on pressure. If fluid intake is not restricted, the edema may increase and involve hands, feet and legs. In nephrotic syndrome, edema develops insidiously, starting with eyelid puffiness most noticeable in the morning. Over a period of several days, there is swelling over the feet and legs. Edema is soft and easily pits on pressure. Facial swelling is often mistaken for allergy or insect bite.

Hematuria

Gross hematuria in acute GN is typically smoky brown or cola colored. Bright red blood suggests a non-glomerular cause, as in renal or vesical calculi. Gross hematuria is rare in UTI. Other conditions, which might impart a red color to urine include hemoglobinuria, myoglobinuria, porphyria and ingestion of beetroot.

Oliguria

Oliguria defined as urine volume less than 1 mL/kg per hr, commonly results from gastroenteritis and hypovolemia. Oliguria is also an important feature of moderate or severe acute GN, acute tubular necrosis and other conditions causing severe glomerular injury (e.g. HUS, vasculitis).

Dysuria, Flank Pain, Ureteric Colic

These features suggest UTI or urinary tract calculi.

Polyuria, Polydipsia

Impairment of urinary concentration is an early feature of obstructive uropathy and tubulointerstitial disorders. Polyuria is also seen in conditions associated with deficiency or resistance to antidiuretic hormone, diabetes mellitus, persistent hypokalemia (e.g. distal renal tubular acidosis) and hypercalcemia.

Enuresis

Most children with nocturnal enuresis have no evidence of renal disease. Urinalysis and culture are recommended in children who show enuresis after having achieved continence.

Hypertension

Assessment of blood pressure is necessary in all patients with disorders of the kidneys or urinary tract. Symptomatic hypertension in children is chiefly due to a renal parenchymal or renovascular cause; endocrine conditions are uncommon.

Growth Retardation

Physical retardation is an important feature of chronic renal insufficiency and renal tubular disorders.

Anemia

Normocytic normochromic anemia is striking in patients with chronic renal failure. Patients with unexplained anemia should be evaluated for a renal disease.

Abdominal Mass

Multicystic renal dysplasia, polycystic kidneys, renal vein thrombosis, hydronephrosis (secondary to pelviureteric junction or urethral obstruction) and Wilms' tumor may cause palpable renal masses.

INVESTIGATIONS IN RENAL DISEASE

Examination of Urine

Urinalysis is an important assessment of patients with diseases of the kidneys and urinary tract. It must be done meticulously, or important abnormalities may be overlooked.

Collection of Specimen

The first morning specimen is preferred. It should be collected in a clean container and enough quantity sent so that the specific gravity can be measured. Specimens for culture should be collected carefully. After local cleaning, a 'clean catch' sample is collected in a sterile container. If facilities for immediate processing are not available, this specimen may be stored at 4°C for 12–14 hours.

It is often difficult to obtain satisfactory specimens in children below 2-year-old. In small infants, urine may be collected using a sterile bag that is applied after cleaning the perineum with soap and water. The bag is removed as soon as the baby has voided; these specimens should not be used for urine culture. Urine may be collected in infants by percutaneous suprapubic bladder puncture or transurethral catheterization. Specimens obtained through these methods are adequate for urine culture.

Protein

Boiling test is satisfactory. Ten to 15 mL of urine is taken in a test tube and the upper portion boiled. If turbidity appears, 3 drops of concentrated acetic acid are added and specimen boiled again. A zero to 4+ grading is used to record the concentration; 1+ reaction is slight turbidity through which fine print can be read and signifies 15–30 mg of protein/dL; 3+ reaction is a white, cloudiness with fine precipitate through which black lines are not visible and amounts to 150–350 mg/dL. Proteinuria can also be semi-quantitatively tested using 10% sulfosalicylic acid. Five drops are added to a test tube half-filled with urine and turbidity graded from negative to 4+. X-ray contrast media and massive doses of penicillin may cause false positive reactions. Dipstick methods (Uristix), widely used for testing proteinuria, are convenient and equally reliable. Composite strips that also examine for glucose, pH, hematuria, leukocyte esterase and nitrite are also available.

Reducing Substances

Benedict's test detects reducing substances. The glucose oxidase method, available on dipsticks, is specific for glucose.

Microscopic Examination

A fresh, well-mixed specimen should be examined; presence of cellular elements and casts is noted. More than 5 red cells/HPF in a centrifuged specimen is abnormal. Red cell casts indicate glomerular inflammation. Leukocytes may occasionally be absent despite significant bacteriuria. On the other hand, isolated presence of leukocytes does not indicate UTI. The detection of bacteriuria in fresh, uncentrifuged urine is significant.

Blood Tests

Blood levels of creatinine and urea are used to assess renal function. The normal levels of serum creatinine are 0.2–0.5 mg/dL in children below 6 years and 0.4–0.8 mg/dL in older children. Blood urea ranges between 20–35 mg/dL during childhood. However, it is important to realize the limitations of these investigations. Normal values of blood urea or creatinine do not exclude impaired renal function, since they do not increase even when glomerular filtration rate is reduced by 50%. The level of serum creatinine is dependent on muscle mass and is, therefore low in malnutrition. Bilirubin may interfere with creatinine measurements. Blood urea levels are low on a protein deficient diet and high with tissue breakdown, trauma, gastrointestinal bleeding and use of corticosteroids. Estimation of blood levels of cystatin-C, which does not depend on the nutritional status, has been proposed to be a sensitive indicator of glomerular function.

Other investigations that are useful in specific instances include serum albumin, cholesterol, anti-streptococcal antibody titers, complement, immunoglobulins and autoantibodies. Measurements of blood pH, bicarbonate, electrolytes and osmolality are important in evaluating patients with tubular disorders and/or renal failure.

Glomerular Filtration Rate (GFR)

While clearance of inulin is regarded as the reference for estimating GFR, the test involves accurate IV infusion of inulin followed by measurement of its levels in timed urine and blood samples. Measurement of the creatinine clearance is adequate for assessing GFR in most cases.

Creatinine Clearance

The child voids at 8 am and urine is discarded. Subsequently all urine specimens are saved in a clean glass bottle until 8 am the next day. This specimen is added to the 24-hr collection, and the total urine volume is measured. A blood specimen for creatinine is obtained. Creatinine clearance is estimated by the formula:

$$\text{Creatinine clearance} = UV \div P$$

Where, U = urinary creatinine (mg/dL), V = urine flow per minute (24-hr urine in mL divided by 1440), P = plasma creatinine (mg/dL). Since creatinine clearance depends upon the body size, the values are normalized to surface area. The normal creatinine clearance is 80–120 mL/minute per 1.73 m^2.

GFR can also be computed from serum creatinine and the child's height.

GFR (mL/minute per 1.73 m^2) = K × height (cm) ÷ serum creatinine (mg/dL).

The value of the constant K is 0.55, except in infants (K 0.45) and pubertal boys (K 0.7).

Radionuclide Clearance

Disappearance curves of the radionuclides, ^{125}I-iothalamate, ^{99m}Tc-DTPA or ^{51}Cr-EDTA following a single IV injection can be used to accurately compute GFR.

Urinary Concentration Test

Following a few hours of fluid deprivation, under careful observation, desamino-8-D-arginine vasopressin (DDAVP) is administered nasally (5–10 μg in neonates and infants, 20 μg in children) or by IM injection (0.4–1.0 μg in infants and young children, 2 μg in older children). Urine is collected every hr for the next 2–3 hr. Following administration of DDAVP, patients with nephrogenic diabetes insipidus fail to show a rise of urine osmolality that remains below 300 mOsm/kg water (normal >800 mOsm/kg water). Those with deficiency of the antidiuretic hormone concentrate urine appropriately.

Imaging of the Urinary Tract

Plain X-Ray

The child is given a liquid diet and laxative on the previous night. A plain film of the abdomen provides information on renal size, shape and outline and radiopaque calculi. The length of normal kidney approximates the height of first four lumbar vertebrae. A small kidney may indicate hypoplasia or chronic damage. The opposite kidney, unless diseased, shows compensatory hypertrophy. The utility of information provided by plain films has reduced following availability of ultrasonography.

Ultrasonography

Ultrasonography is the initial modality for imaging of the kidney and urinary tract in most renal diseases. This investigation is readily available, non-invasive and can be performed even in uncooperative patients, small infants and those with renal failure. The procedure is operator dependent and should be done by an experienced radiologist. Anatomic details of the kidneys, ureters and bladder are examined; Doppler sonography is useful in studying renal blood flow.

Intravenous Pyelogram (IVP)

A carefully done IVP gives valuable information about renal anatomy and function. The patient is prepared as for a plain X-ray. The contrast medium is injected IV and films are taken at 2, 5, 10 and 30 minutes. IVP provides satisfactory details on renal size, shape, cortical outlines and calyceal pattern. The use of IVP has declined following the availability of radionuclide imaging.

Micturating Cystourethrogram (MCU)

MCU is necessary for studying the lower urinary tract. A sterile catheter is introduced into the bladder, which is filled with contrast medium; films are taken during and end-micturition. MCU provides precise details of the anatomy of the bladder and urethra, presence of vesicoureteric reflux and obstruction in the lower urinary tract (e.g. posterior urethral valves, urethral stenosis).

Radionuclide Imaging

Imaging of the kidney and urinary tract has been simplified by radionuclide methods, which have replaced conventional radiocontrast studies such as the IVP, MCU and angiography. Radionuclide procedures are non-invasive, highly sensitive and expose patients to less radiation compared to radiocontrast studies.

The compounds, labeled with radioactive ^{99m}technetium, commonly used include dimercaptosuccinic acid (DMSA), diethylenetriamine pentacetic acid (DTPA) and mercaptotriacylglycine (MAG-3). Following IV injection, DMSA attains high concentration in the renal cortex and provides very high quality images of renal morphology. This is particularly useful in detection and follow-up of renal parenchymal defects associated with urinary tract infections (Fig. 15.1A). DTPA is freely filtered at the glomerulus with no tubular reabsorption or excretion. A DTPA renogram is useful for evaluating perfusion and function of each kidney. Obstruction to the urine flow can be diagnosed by studying the effect of IV frusemide on the renogram. Normally there is a prompt washout of the radionuclide, but this clearing may not occur in subjects with upper urinary tract obstruction (Fig. 15.1B). Renal arterial narrowing results in reduced renal blood flow and an abnormal pattern on the DTPA renogram. This effect is accentuated by administration of angiotensin converting enzyme inhibitors, thus increasing its sensitivity in diagnosis of renal artery stenosis. MAG-3 provides highly satisfactory information on renal structure and function.

A ^{99m}Tc-labeled radionuclide scan can be used instead of the radiocontrast MCU. Radionuclide cystography is sensitive for detecting vesicoureteric reflux with minimal radiation exposure. However, this procedure does not provide sufficient anatomic details of the bladder and urethra to recommend its use for initial evaluation of patients with suspected urinary tract obstruction, nor for grading of vesicoureteric reflux.

Suggested reading

1. Guignard JP; Santos F. Laboratory investigations: In: Pediatric Nephrology, 5th ed. Avner ED, Harmon WE, Niaudet P. Lippincott Williams and Wilkins, Philadelphia 2004;399–424.
2. Avni FE, Hall M, Diagnostic imaging. In Pediatric Nephrology, 5th ed.Avner ED, Harmon WE, Niaudet P. Lippincott Williams and Wilkins, Philadelphia 2004;449–473.
3. Gupta AK. Imaging of the urinary tract. In: Pediatric Nephrology, 4th ed. Eds. Srivastava RN, Bagga A. Jaypee, New Delhi, 2005, 30–44.
4. Zaffanello M, Franchini M, Fanos V. Is serum cystatin-C a suitable marker of renal function in children? Ann Clin Lab Sci 2007; 37(3): 233–40.

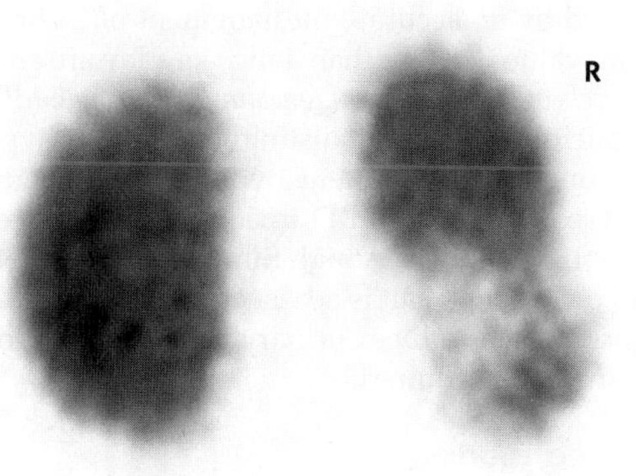

Fig. 15.1A: Dimercaptosuccinic acid (DMSA) renal scan showing loss of volume with scars in middle and lower pole of right kidney; features suggestive of reflux nephropathy

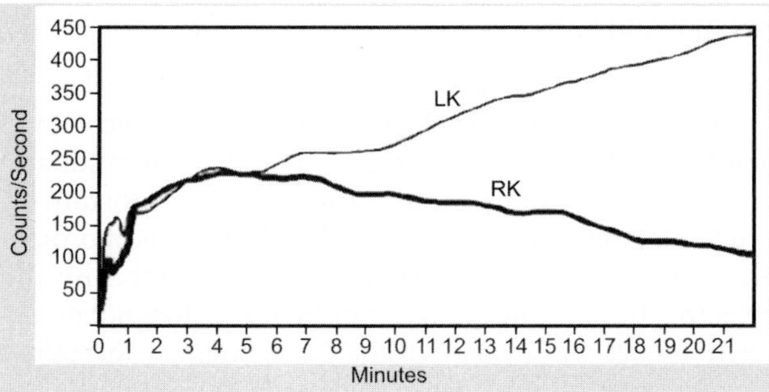

Fig. 15.1B: Diethylenetriamine pentacetic acid (DTPA) renal scan showing normal uptake and excretion of radiolabeled dye in right kidney. Left kidney shows adequate concentration but non-excretion of the dye, suggesting obstruction at the pelviureteric junction

HEMATURIA

The presence of blood in urine imparts it a color, which includes various shades of deep red, smoky brown, cola-color and faint pink. Parents may mistake very concentrated urine for that containing blood. Microscopic examination of urine will show red blood cells. Reagent coated dipsticks detect free hemoglobin and myoglobin. Alternatively benzedine or guaic test may be performed. Red urine may be present in porphyria and following sugarbeet ingestion. Urine appears orange-colored after administration of rifampicin or pyridium. Uric acid crystals may also impart a pink tinge to the nappy.

In childhood, the commonest cause of gross hematuria is post-infectious GN. Urinary tract stones are not infrequent. Gross hematuria is rare in acute pyelonephritis. Important causes of hematuria are listed in Table 15.1. Conditions that cause persistent microscopic hematuria include idiopathic hypercalciuria, benign familial hematuria, Alport syndrome, IgA nephropathy and membranoproliferative GN.

Table 15.1: Important causes of hematuria
Renal
Glomerular. Acute GN (see Table 15.2), crescentic GN, Alport syndrome, membranoproliferative GN
Renovascular. Renal vein thrombosis
Hematological
Disseminated intravascular coagulation, thrombocytopenia, hemophilia, sickle cell disease
Ureteric, vesical
Calculi, hemorrhagic cystitis (drug-induced, adenovirus), idiopathic hypercalciuria
Others
Polycystic kidneys, hydronephrosis, birth asphyxia, neoplasms (bladder papilloma, Wilms' tumor), urinary tract infections, renal trauma

GN glomerulonephritis

Diagnostic Evaluation

A history of pain in the flank or suprapubic region, dysuria and edema should be obtained. Physical examination should include assessment of growth and features of acute or chronic kidney disease such as edema, hypertension, unexplained pallor, bony abnormalities and abdominal mass. An audiogram and a detailed eye examination may be needed.

A fresh specimen of urine is examined for red cells, red cell casts and protein. Absence of large number of red cells in a grossly bloody urine suggests hemoglobinuria (seen in acute intravascular hemolysis) or myoglobinuria. In glomerular disease, urine shows dysmorphic red cells, of different shapes, whereas in bleeding from renal pelvis or the lower urinary tract, the red cells maintain normal morphology (Fig. 15.2). Presence of significant proteinuria (2+ or more) and/or red cell casts also suggests glomerular disease. Hypercalciuria should be excluded by the

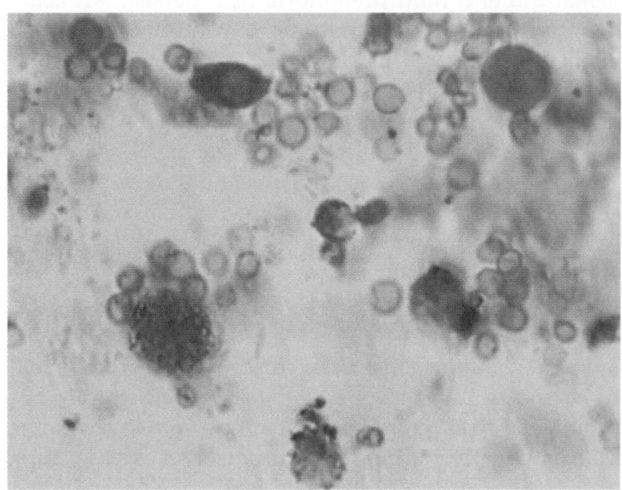

Fig.15.2: Hematuria. Note normal morphology of red cell

determination of urinary calcium to creatinine ratio on one or more random urine samples.

A plain X-ray film of the abdomen and abdominal ultrasound is done to exclude major renal and urinary tract anomalies and calculi. Blood levels of urea and creatinine are measured; other specialized blood tests depend on the clinical suspicion of the likely etiology. Surgical conditions that cause hematuria can be diagnosed by appropriate imaging methods. Invasive procedures such as cystoscopy are rarely indicated.

In a significant proportion of cases, mild microscopic hematuria spontaneously disappears over a period of several years. Other family members may have a similar urinary abnormality. If there is no family history of renal disease, a renal biopsy is not urgently indicated and the patient kept under long-term observation.

Renal Biopsy

Renal biopsy should be done if hematuria is associated with persistent or heavy (3+ or more) proteinuria, there is history of renal disease in the family or evidence of chronic kidney disease in the patient, or if renal impairment or hypertension are seen during follow up. A biopsy is also considered in children showing persistent microscopic hematuria for two or more years even in the absence of the above features. This procedure is necessary to diagnose IgA nephropathy, Alport syndrome, thin basement membrane disease (typically presents as familial, benign hematuria) and chronic GN. The biopsy is evaluated by light, immunofluorescence and electron microscopy.

IgA Nephropathy

Predominant deposition of IgA in the glomeruli, chiefly in the mesangium and occasionally in capillary walls, characterizes this disorder. The most common clinical manifestation is recurrent episodes of gross hematuria that are precipitated by upper respiratory infections, and last for 2–5 days. In between these episodes, microscopic hematuria and mild proteinuria may persist. An acute nephritic or nephrotic syndrome may rarely be the initial manifestation. Renal histology shows mesangial proliferation of varying severity. Patients with hematuria and non-nephrotic proteinuria are treated using angiotensin converting enzyme inhibitors (e.g. enalapril, ramipril). Therapy with prednisolone and other immunosuppressive agents is indicated in patients showing nephrotic range proteinuria or deranged renal function. A small proportion of patients progress to chronic renal failure.

Idiopathic Hypercalciuria

This is a common cause of microscopic and gross hematuria, and urolithiasis. A family history of hematuria or urolithiasis may be present. Urinary calcium to creatinine ratio in the early morning 'spot' urine serves as a screening test. The upper limit of normal is 0.2 (mg/mg); higher values suggest hypercalciuria. The diagnosis may be confirmed by an accurate measurement of 24-hr urinary calcium; values greater than 4 mg/kg/day are abnormal. *Blood levels of calcium and magnesium are normal.* Idiopathic hypercalciuria should be distinguished from hypercalciuria secondary to persistent hypercalcemia (e.g. hyperparathyroidism, vitamin D toxicity) or associated with renal tubular acidosis. A high fluid intake and diet low in animal protein and salt is advised. Therapy with thiazide diuretics, which reduces urinary calcium excretion, may occasionally be required.

Suggested reading

1. Pan CG. Evaluation of gross hematuria. Pediatr Clin North Am 2006; 53:401–412
2. Indian Pediatric Nephrology Group. Consensus statement on evaluation of hematuria. Indian Pediatr 2006; 43: 965–973
3. Halachmi S, Kakiashvili D, Meretyk S. A review on hematuria in children. Scientific World Journal 2006; 6: 311–317

PROTEINURIA

The glomerular capillary walls provide an effective barrier to filtration of proteins. The presence of anionic charge (contributed by glucosaminoglycans and heparan sulfate) along the basement membrane is also important in preventing filtration of proteins. Small amounts of protein are filtered but almost completely reabsorbed by the proximal tubule. The degree of proteinuria does not necessarily reflect the severity of the glomerular abnormality; massive proteinuria often occurs in minimal change nephrotic syndrome, in which glomeruli appear normal or show very mild changes.

The presence of more than trace amounts of protein in the urine is abnormal. Persistent and heavy proteinuria especially if associated with hematuria should be promptly evaluated. Absence of proteinuria does not exclude renal disease.

Quantification of Proteinuria

Protein concentration of 100–1000 mg/m^2/day indicates mild to moderate proteinuria; more than that is heavy (nephrotic range) proteinuria. Accurate quantitative measurements of 24-hr urinary protein are not needed if careful semi-quantitative tests are done on a concentrated (first morning) specimen. Normally the protein to creatinine ratio, in the first morning urine specimen, is below 0.1 (mg/mg); a ratio of 0.1–1 indicates mild to moderate, and >1 heavy proteinuria. The latter usually corresponds to 3+ or 4+ reaction on boiling or dipstick test.

Fever, dehydration and heavy exercise may cause transient and mild proteinuria. Mild proteinuria may also occur in UTI, hydronephrosis and renal tuberculosis. In proximal tubular defects (e.g. Fanconi syndrome) mild proteinuria may occur, being chiefly composed of low molecular weight globulins. Heavy proteinuria (predominantly albumin) usually indicates glomerular disease.

Important causes of asymptomatic proteinuria include orthostatic proteinuria, chronic glomerular diseases, reflux nephropathy, renal hypoplasia and rarely renal tubular disorders. In orthostatic (postural) proteinuria, protein is absent in urine specimen collected after overnight recumbence. The pathogenesis of this condition is not clear but the long-term outcome is good. Continued follow-up is necessary until proteinuria disappears. Chronic renal damage from vesicoureteric reflux and UTI may manifest with proteinuria. Several forms of glomerular diseases, especially focal segmental glomerulosclerosis, may cause persistent, asymptomatic proteinuria; microscopic hematuria is often associated. A renal biopsy is indicated in the presence of persistent or heavy proteinuria. Long-term observation is necessary to monitor clinical course and renal function. Prolonged treatment with angiotensin converting enzyme inhibitors or angiotensin receptor blockers is effective in reducing persistent proteinuria.

Suggested reading

Srivastava RN. Isolated asymptomatic proteinuria. Indian J Pediatr 2002, 69: 1055–1058.

ACUTE GLOMERULONEPHRITIS

Acute glomerulonephritis (GN) is characterized by relatively abrupt onset of hematuria, oliguria, edema and hypertension. The clinical and histological severity varies considerably and is not always correlated. A child with mild disease may go undetected, while in a severe case anuria, hypertensive encephalopathy and heart failure may be present. Acute GN following streptococcal infection is the commonest type in children. A similar presentation may, however, be present in the conditions enumerated in Table 15.2.

Appropriate laboratory investigations are carried out to reach a diagnosis. A renal biopsy may be required if GN does not appear to be resolving within two weeks.

POST-STREPTOCOCCAL GLOMERULONEPHRITIS

Acute GN following infection by group A beta-hemolytic streptococci is a common disorder in hospital practice. It mainly involves school-age children and is uncommon below the age of 3 years; boys are more frequently affected.

Table 15.2: Conditions presenting as acute glomerulonephritis
Post-infectious: Streptococci, staphylococci, hepatitis B and C, bacterial endocarditis, infected ventriculoatrial shunts and prosthesis
Systemic vasculitis: Henoch-Schönlein purpura, systemic lupus erythematosus, polyarteritis nodosa, Wegener's granulomatosis
Membranoproliferative glomerulonephritis
IgA nephropathy
Familial nephropathy: Alport syndrome

Epidemiological studies have shown that asymptomatic cases are frequent. The streptococcal infection is usually of the throat or skin, and precedes the onset of nephritis by 1 to 4 weeks. Only a few strains of streptococci are nephritogenic, e.g. types 4 and 12 causing pharyngitis and type 49 causing pyoderma. Post-streptococcal GN is a typical example of an immune complex disease. The streptococcal antigen-antibody complexes are trapped in the glomerular capillaries where they activate complement and initiate inflammatory changes.

Pathology

On light microscopy, the glomeruli are enlarged and ischemic, and the capillary loops narrowed. There is proliferation of mesangial cells and infiltration with neutrophils. Immunofluorescence shows granular deposits of IgG and complement (C3) along the capillary walls. Electron-microscopy shows deposits on the subepithelial side of the glomerular basement membrane.

Clinical Features

The onset is rapid, with puffiness around the eyes and pedal edema. Edema may be more pronounced if fluids have been given in the presence of oliguria. Urine is characteristically cola-colored. The degree of oliguria usually correlates with the severity of the disease. Hypertension is common. Atypical presentations include (i) convulsions due to hypertensive encephalopathy; (ii) left ventricular failure and pulmonary edema, due to malignant hypertension and hypervolemia; and (iii) acute renal failure.

15

Laboratory Findings

Urine shows 1+ to 2+ protein with red cells, and red cell and granular casts. White cells, indicative of glomerular inflammation, are also present and should not be regarded as evidence of UTI. Hemodilution may result in normocytic anemia; ESR is often raised. Blood levels of urea and creatinine are elevated reflecting renal impairment; hyponatremia and hyperkalemia occur with continuing oliguria. The chest X-ray may show prominent vascular markings suggesting hypervolemia. Throat swab culture may rarely show β-hemolytic streptococci. Serologic evidence for streptococcal infection is present in most patients with pharyngitis, though antibiotic therapy may blunt this response. The ASO titer is increased in more than 80% patients. Anti-DNase B is elevated in cases of streptococcal skin infection. These titers decrease to low levels within 4 to 6 weeks. The level of serum C3 is low in 90% patients but normalizes by 5–6 weeks. Persistent low C3 levels indicate other forms of GN.

Management

Patients with mild oliguria and normal blood pressure can be managed at home. Others are best treated in a hospital since close attention to blood pressure and dietary intake is essential. Strict bedrest is not necessary. Once acute GN has occurred, treatment with penicillin has no effect on the course of the disease, but may be given if active pharyngitis or pyoderma is present.

The principles of management of patients with severe oliguria and azotemia are discussed later in the chapter.

Diet: The intake of protein, sodium and potassium should be restricted until blood levels of urea reduce and urine output increases. Carbohydrates and fats are allowed. Overhydration is a dangerous complication as it may increase hypertension and precipitate left ventricular failure. Urine output should be accurately measured. Fluid intake should be restricted to an amount equal to insensible losses and 24-hr urine output.

Weight: The child should be weighed daily. In the presence of severe oliguria, he should lose about 0.5% body weight per day because of endogenous catabolism. A gain in weight necessitates reduction in fluid intake.

Diuretics: Patients showing modest edema are treated with oral frusemide at a dose of 1–3 mg/kg; the edema disappears with the return of renal function. Therapy with IV frusemide (2–4 mg/kg) is necessary in subjects with pulmonary edema.

15

Hypertension: Mild hypertension may be controlled by restriction of salt and water intake. Effective anti-hypertensive agents include amlodepine, nifedipine, atenolol or diuretics. Patients with hypertensive emergencies need prompt treatment with IV nitroprusside or labetalol.

Left ventricular failure: Hypertension should be controlled and IV frusemide given to induce diuresis, leading to improvement in heart failure. If immediate diuresis is not seen, steps are taken to initiate urgent dialysis. Venesection with removal of 100–200 mL blood or tying rotating tourniquets, to reduce venous return to the heart, is seldom used. Respiratory support with positive end-expiratory pressure may be needed.

Prolonged oliguria: Treatment, as outlined above, should be continued and levels of blood urea and electrolytes monitored. *Dialysis is required in children with severe renal failure and prolonged oligoanuria, fluid overload and life-threatening electrolyte disturbances.* Occurrence of secondary infections should be avoided.

Outcome and Prognosis

Acute post-streptococcal GN has an excellent prognosis in childhood. The symptoms begin to resolve in the first week with loss of edema and fall in blood pressure. In most cases, gross hematuria and significant proteinuria disappear within two weeks. Microscopic hematuria and slight proteinuria may persist for several months, and is of no significance. Hypertension subsides within two to three weeks, but rarely may persist for several weeks. Patients with acute GN of non-streptococcal etiology have variable and unpredictable outcome. Close follow up of these cases with periodic urinalyses and measurements of blood pressure is needed.

Renal biopsy: A biopsy is rarely indicated in those suspected to have post-streptococcal GN except when renal function is severely impaired beyond 7–10 days or serum C3 remains depressed beyond 6–8 weeks. Patients with unresolving acute GN (persistent oliguria or azotemia past 7–10 days, hypertension or gross hematuria past 2–3 weeks) or those with features of a systemic illness (e.g. systemic lupus) require a kidney biopsy.

CRESCENTIC GLOMERULONEPHRITIS

Rapidly progressive GN (RPGN) is defined as an acute nephritic illness accompanied by rapid loss of renal function over days to weeks. The histopathological correlate is the presence of crescents (crescentic GN) involving 50% or more glomeruli (Fig. 15.3). The presence of crescents is a histologic marker of severe glomerular injury, which may occur in a number of conditions including postinfectious GN, systemic vasculitides and Goodpasture syndrome. The severity of clinical and histological features often correlates. Patients with circumferential crescents involving more than 80% glomeruli show advanced renal failure; those with noncircumferential crescents in fewer glomeruli have an indolent course. Renal biopsy should, therefore, be done in patients with severe nephritic features, which do not resolve within 1–2 weeks.

The outcome is related to prompt institution of therapy and histological severity. Without appropriate treatment, patients are at risk for chronic renal failure. Satisfactory results have been obtained with administration of IV methylprednisolone, followed by oral prednisolone and cyclophosphamide. Plasmapheresis is beneficial in

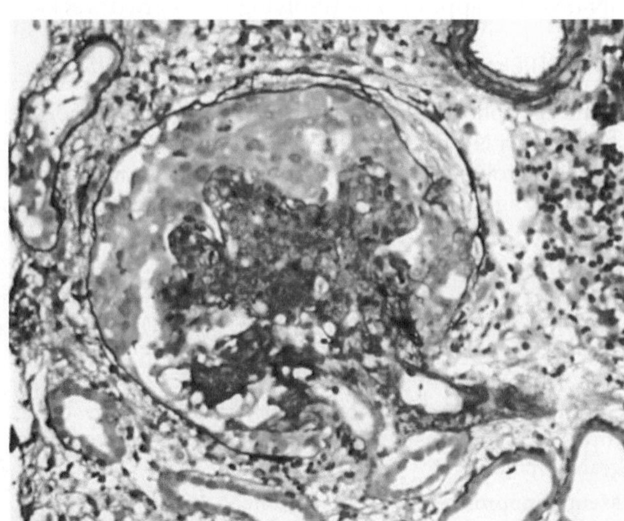

Fig. 15.3: Cellular crescent with compression of the glomerular tuft, Silver Methanamine stain × 800

patients with systemic vasculitides and Goodpasture syndrome.

NEPHRITIS IN HENOCH-SCHÖNLEIN PURPURA (HSP)

HSP is one of the most common vasculitis in children (Fig. 15.4). Mild renal involvement indicated by microscopic hematuria and mild proteinuria is common. Serum IgA levels may be elevated. Renal biopsy shows mesangial proliferation with mesangial deposition of IgA. Most patients recover without any specific treatment. However, long-term observation is necessary to detect insidious renal damage. Rarely a patient may present with nephritic or nephrotic syndrome, hypertension, azotemia and crescentic GN. Therapy with a combination of steroids, cyclophosphamide and azathioprine is recommended; the long-term outcome may not be satisfactory.

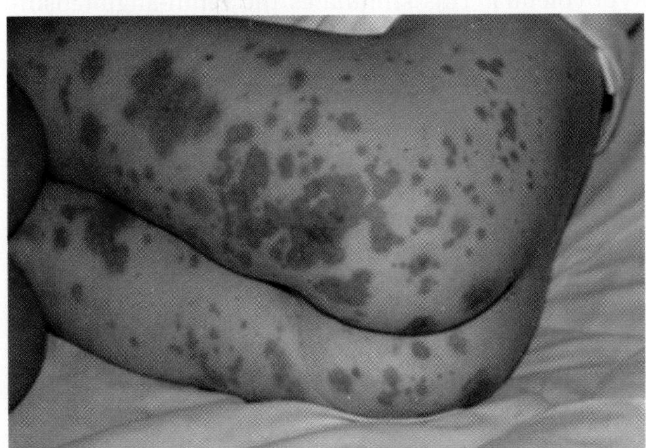

Fig. 15.4: Henoch-Schönlein purpura; extensive rash over lower extremities and gluteal region

RENAL INVOLVEMENT IN SYSTEMIC LUPUS ERYTHEMATOSUS

A variety of clinical and renal histological patterns are observed. Asymptomatic proteinuria and/or hematuria, acute nephritic syndrome and nephrotic syndrome are most common. Rarely renal involvement may be manifested as rapidly progressive GN. Renal biopsy may show almost normal glomeruli, focal or diffuse proliferative GN or membranous nephropathy. Immunofluorescence studies show mesangial and capillary wall deposits of IgG and C3, and usually C1q and IgA. Antinuclear and double-stranded DNA autoantibodies are present in the blood of most cases with lupus nephritis; C3 levels are reduced.

Remissions and relapses, and progressive renal damage characterize the course of the disease. Infections and end stage renal disease is the chief cause of mortality. Management with judicious use of corticosteroids, cytotoxic drugs (cyclophosphamide, mycophenolate mofetil and azathioprine) and cyclosporin A, and appropriate treatment of infections has significantly improved the outcome.

Suggested reading

1. Coppo R, Amore A. New perspectives in treatment of glomerulonephritis. Pediatr Nephrol 2004;19:256–265.
2. Coppo R. Pediatric IgA nephropathy: clinical and therapeutic perspectives. Semin Nephrol 2008;28(1):18–26.
3. Hogg RJ. IgA nephropathy: What's new? Pediatr Nephrol 2007; 22:1809–1814.
4. Fervenza FC. Henoch–Schönlein purpura nephritis. Int J Dermatol 2003; 42: 170–177.
5. Perfumo F, Martini A. Lupus nephritis in children. Lupus 2005; 14:83–88.
6. Hejaili FF, Moist LM, Clark WF. Treatment of lupus nephritis. Drugs 2003;63:257–274.

HEMOLYTIC UREMIC SYNDROME

The hemolytic uremic syndromes are a heterogeneous group of disorders that are a common cause of acute renal failure in children. *They are characterized by microangiopathic hemolytic anemia, thrombocytopenia and acute renal insufficiency.* Two broad subgroups are recognized: the first is common in young children and associated with a diarrheal prodrome (D+ or typical HUS), whereas the second is much rarer and not associated with antecedent diarrhea (D– or atypical HUS).

15

D+ HUS

The diarrheal illness that precedes HUS is caused by verotoxin-producing *E. coli* (usually *E. coli* O157: H7) in North America and Europe; in the Indian subcontinent *Shigella dysenteriae 1* is the chief pathogen. Cytotoxin-mediated injury to the endothelium in the renal microvasculature leads to localized coagulation and fibrin deposition. As red cells and platelets traverse these damaged vessels, they are injured and sequestered. Though the brunt of the microvascular injury is on the kidney, other organs especially the brain may be affected.

Clinical Features

Children less than 2–3 years are usually affected. Following a prodrome of acute diarrhea or dysentery, patients show sudden onset of pallor and oliguria. Blood pressure may be high. Focal or generalized seizures and alteration of consciousness are common.

Investigations

The blood film shows broken and distorted red cells, increased reticulocyte count and high blood levels of LDH; Coombs' test is negative. Thrombocytopenia and neutrophilic leukocytosis are usually present. Urine shows microscopic hematuria and mild proteinuria. Blood levels of urea and creatinine are elevated reflecting the severity of the renal failure. On renal biopsy, the endothelial cells are swollen and separated from the basement membrane with accumulation of foamy material in the subendothelial space. The capillary lumen is narrowed by swollen endothelial cells, blood cells and fibrin thrombi. Arterioles may show similar changes. Patchy or extensive renal cortical necrosis may be present. HUS is diagnosed on clinical and laboratory features, and a renal biopsy is rarely required.

D– HUS

This condition, seen at any age, lacks the prodromal history of diarrhea or dysentery. The onset may be insidious and occasionally present with a rapidly progressive illness. The microangiopathic lesions chiefly affect interlobular arteries and result in severe hypertension and progressive renal insufficiency. Predisposing factors include inherited abnormalities in the complement regulatory pathway, infection with neuraminidase-producing organisms (pneumococci) or HIV, cobalamin deficiency, systemic lupus and drugs (e.g. cyclosporin, mitomycin).

Treatment

The treatment includes management of complications of renal failure, and hypertension and correction of anemia. Proper nutrition must be ensured. Peritoneal or hemodialysis dialysis might be necessary to prevent complications of renal insufficiency. Plasmapheresis and/or infusion of fresh frozen plasma may benefit patients with D– HUS. The prognosis of the illness has improved with aggressive supportive measures.

Outcome

Mortality during the acute episode of D+ HUS is low. On follow up, 20–30% patients show varying degree of residual renal damage. Factors suggestive of poor outcome include oligoanuria for more than 2 weeks, severe neurological involvement and presence of renal cortical necrosis. The acute and long-term outcome in patients with D– HUS is often unsatisfactory; recurrent episodes of the illness may occur.

Suggested reading

1. Besbas N, Karpman D, Landau D, Loirat C. A classification of hemolytic uremic syndrome and thrombotic thrombocytopenic purpura and related disorders. Kidney Int 2006; 70: 423–431.
2. Siegler R, Oakes R. Hemolytic uremic syndrome; pathogenesis, treatment, and outcome. Curr Opin Pediatr 2005; 17(2): 200–4.
3. Ardalan MR. Review of thrombotic microangiopathy (TMA) and post-renal transplant TMA. Saudi J Kidney Dis Transpl 2006; 17: 235–244.

NEPHROTIC SYNDROME

Nephrotic syndrome is characterized by massive proteinuria, hypoalbuminemia and edema; hyperlipidemia is often associated. Some patients show hematuria and hypertension. Heavy proteinuria (more than 1 g/m^2 per day) is the basic abnormality, leading to hypoalbuminemia (serum albumin below 2.5 g/dL). The resultant fall in plasma oncotic pressure leads to interstitial edema and hypovolemia. This stimulates the renin-angiotensin-aldosterone axis and antidiuretic hormone secretion that enhances sodium and water retention. The pathogenesis of edema may however be different in patients with significant glomerular lesions, who show primary sodium retention and expanded intravascular volume. Hypoalbuminemia also induces hepatic synthesis of β-lipoproteins resulting in hypercholesterolemia.

More than 90% of childhood nephrotic syndrome is primary (or idiopathic). Other causes such as amyloidosis, vasculitis, systemic lupus erythematosus, post-infectious GN and hepatitis B nephropathy are infrequent. Nephrotic syndrome in children can be divided into two groups based on renal histological characteristics:

(i) Minimal change nephrotic syndrome (MCNS) (ii) Nephrotic syndrome with significant lesions (Table 15.3).

Steroid sensitive nephrotic syndrome (which is usually MCNS) has a satisfactory long-term outcome. In contrast, steroid resistant nephrotic syndrome (usually associated with significant glomerular lesions) has a less satisfactory course and a significant proportion progress to chronic renal failure.

Table 15.3: Features of idiopathic nephrotic syndrome

Features	*Minimal lesion (MCNS)*	*Significant lesions*
Age at onset	2–6 yr	Older children
Sex incidence	Higher in boys	Equal
Hematuria	Rare	Usual
Blood pressure	Normal	Normal or increased
GFR	Normal	Normal or decreased
Renal biopsy	Normal glomeruli; mild mesangial proliferation; often IgM deposits	Changes of varying severity; C3, immunoglobulin deposits
Serum C3	Normal	Low in MPGN
Selectivity of proteinuria	High	Low
Response to steroids	Remission in >95%	Proteinuria persists in most
Prognosis	Good; relapses stop by second decade	Variable progression of renal damage

MPGN membranoproliferative glomerulonephritis; GFR glomerular filtration rate

MINIMAL CHANGE NEPHROTIC SYNDROME

MCNS accounts for 80% cases of nephrotic syndrome in children. Renal biopsy does not show significant abnormalities on light microscopy (Fig. 15.5A). Electron microscopy shows non-specific obliteration of epithelial foot processes. Immunofluorescence studies do not demonstrate deposition of immune reactants except occasional mesangial IgM. On ther other hand, patients with focal segmental glomerulosclerosis (FSGS) show evidence of sclerosis involving a segment of the glomerular tuft (Fig. 15.5B). The pathogenesis of MCNS is obscure. There is evidence to suggest perturbation of the cell-mediated immunity, which through yet undefined mechanisms alters the permselectivity of the glomerular filter, resulting in massive proteinuria. A primary abnormality of the epithelial foot processes (podocytes) is also postulated.

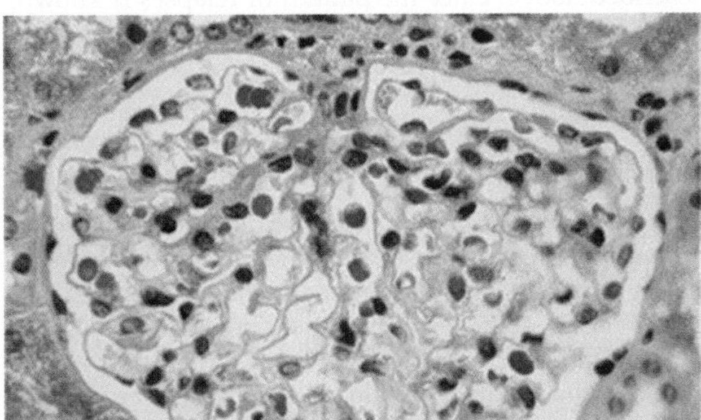

Fig. 15.5A: Renal histology in a 4-year-old boy with steroid dependent nephrotic syndrome. There is normal morphology of glomerular capillary loops, mesangial matrix and cells suggestive of minimal change disease

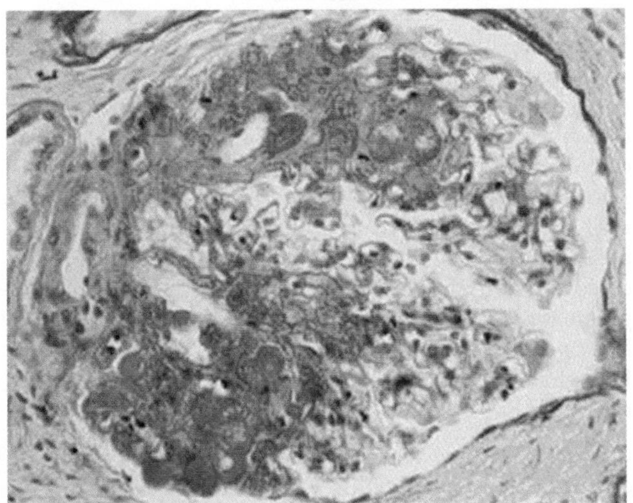

Fig. 15.5B: Histological features in a 6-year-old girl with steroid resistant nephrotic syndrome secondary to focal segmental glomerulosclerosis. Note the hilar sclerosis involving large areas of the glomerulus and adhesions to the Bowman's capsule

Clinical Features

The onset is insidious with edema first noticed around the eyes and subsequently on legs. It is soft and pits easily on pressure. Gradually edema becomes generalized, with ascites, hydrothorax and hydrocele (Fig. 15.6). With increasing edema, urine output may fall. The blood pressure is usually normal; sustained elevation suggests the possibility of significant glomerular lesions. The bloated appearance and relative well being of the child is misleading and after the loss of edema, severe muscle wasting is revealed. Infections may be present at the onset and during relapses.

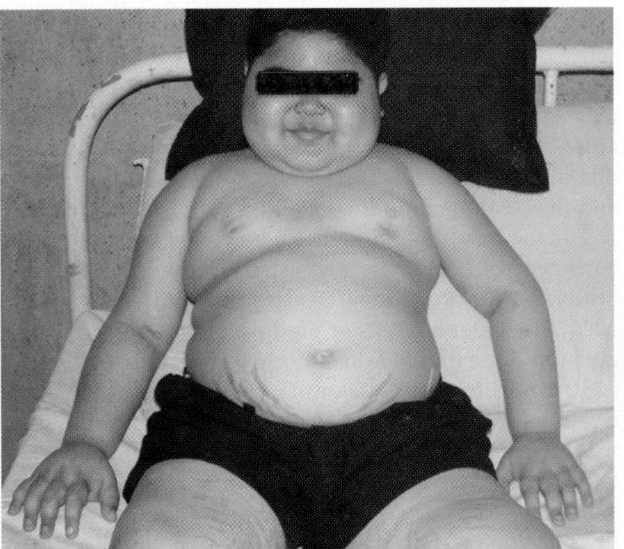

Fig. 15.6: An 8-year-old boy with steroid dependent nephrotic syndrome. Anasarca is seen affecting upper limbs (including dorsa of hands), trunk and ascites. Note the Cushingoid features, striae on lower abdominal wall and upper legs

Laboratory Findings

Urine examination shows heavy (3+ to 4+) proteinuria. Gross hematuria or persistent microscopic hematuria suggests the likelihood of significant glomerular lesions. Hyaline and granular casts may be present. Serum albumin is low and values less than 1 g/dL are often obtained. Hypercholesterolemia may impart a milky appearance to the plasma. Blood urea and creatinine values are usually within the normal range, except when there is hypovolemia and fall in renal perfusion.

Blood levels of IgG are low and those of IgM elevated; C3 level is normal. The severity of glomerular damage is reflected in the passage of proteins of large molecular weight, chiefly globulin. Protein selectivity is the ratio of the clearance of high molecular weight (e.g. IgG) to low molecular weight proteins (e.g. transferrin, albumin). A low ratio indicates highly selective proteinuria, as in MCNS. However, this information does not offer diagnostic help.

A renal biopsy is not required to confirm the diagnosis of MCNS prior to starting treatment. A biopsy is recommended in children with atypical features at the onset (age below 12 months, gross or persistent microscopic hematuria, low blood C3, hypertension or impaired renal function). Patients who continue to show nephrotic range proteinuria despite appropriate steroid therapy require a biopsy to determine the underlying disorder.

Management

Initial Episode

The child should receive a high protein diet. Salt is restricted to the amount in usual cooking with no extra salt given. Any associated infection is treated. The presence of tuberculosis should be looked for. Diuretics are administered only if edema is significant. Frusemide (1–4 mg/kg/d in 2 divided doses) alone or with an aldosterone antagonist, spironolactone (2–3 mg/kg/d in 2 divided doses) is adequate. Diuretics should be used cautiously and overzealous fluid loss avoided.

15

For the past three decades, a modified version of the corticosteroid regimen suggested by the International Study Group on Kidney Disease in Children has been used. The latter consists of prednisolone 60 mg/m^2/day given in three divided doses for 4 weeks, followed by 40 mg/m^2 on alternate days for the next 4 weeks, after which treatment is discontinued. A number of studies indicate that intensive prednisolone therapy for the initial episode has beneficial effect on the long-term course of nephrotic syndrome. The current recommendation is to administer prednisolone at a dose of 2 mg/kg/day in divided doses for 6 weeks, followed by 1.5 mg/kg on alternate days (as a single morning dose) for another 6 weeks; therapy is then stopped. Other regimens are being explored.

About 90–95% children with MCNS will respond to prednisolone with diuresis, loss of edema and abolition of proteinuria, usually by 10–14 days. Steroid therapy results in cushingoid features and hypertension that might need treatment.

Parent Education

The parents should be explained about the disease and the usual outcome, and their cooperation ensured. They are taught how to examine urine for protein, which should be done periodically to detect a relapse early. During the periods of remission, no dietary or physical restrictions are imposed.

Subsequent Course

A small proportion of patients have only a single episode of the illness, while the majority shows relapses. Some patients have three or less relapses in a year (infrequent relapsers), while others have four or more relapses (frequent relapsers). About 15% remain in remission while on prednisolone therapy and relapse whenever the dose is reduced or within 2 weeks of its discontinuation (steroid dependent). About 20–5% patients either do not respond to the initial treatment with prednisolone, or do so transiently and later cease to respond (steroid resistant).

Management of Relapse

An upper respiratory infection or a febrile episode often precipitates a relapse; occasionally there is no obvious cause. Mild proteinuria (1+ to 2+) may sometime occur during such infections and spontaneously disappear. It is prudent to wait for a few days before starting treatment. However, if urine shows 3+ or 4+ protein (for more than 3–4 days) or if edema appears, prednisolone should be promptly administered (2 mg/kg daily) for 10–14 days, which induces remission, followed by alternate day treatment (1.5 mg/kg) for the next 4 weeks.

The first 2–3 relapses are treated in the manner described above. Once the pattern of relapses is known, therapy is individualized. Figure 15.7 outlines the management of patients with steroid sensitive nephrotic syndrome.

Treatment of Patients with Frequent Relapses

Long-term alternate day prednisolone: Following completion of treatment for a relapse, alternate day prednisolone is slowly tapered to a minimum maintenance dose (usually 0.3–0.7 mg/kg) that keeps the patient in remission without causing steroid toxicity. This dose is maintained for 9–12 months. Relapses, while on this therapy, are treated with daily prednisolone until urine is protein-free for 3 days, after which alternate-day therapy is resumed. Treatment for repeated breakthrough relapses may cause steroid toxicity. Such children should not be exposed to further large doses of prednisolone and given one of the second-line drugs discussed below.

Levamisole: This immunomodulator is effective in reducing relapse rates in a proportion of patients with frequent relapsing or steroid dependent nephrotic syndrome. After inducing remission, levamisole is administered at a dose of 2–2.5 mg/kg on alternate days. Alternate day prednisolone is given in decreasing doses, until a dose of 0.3–0.5 mg/kg is reached, for 3–6 months; it is occasionally possible to further reduce the dose of prednisolone or discontinue it altogether. Treatment with levamisole is given for 1–2 years or longer. The chief side effect is leukopenia, which should be monitored every 2 months. Encephalopathy with seizures and skin rash are reported rarely.

Cyclophosphamide: Treatment with alkylating agents is effective in many patients with frequent relapsing or steroid dependent nephrotic syndrome. A 12-week course of treatment with cyclophosphamide or chlorambucil may induce long-lasting remission in 50% cases. The former is preferred in view of comparative safety and wider

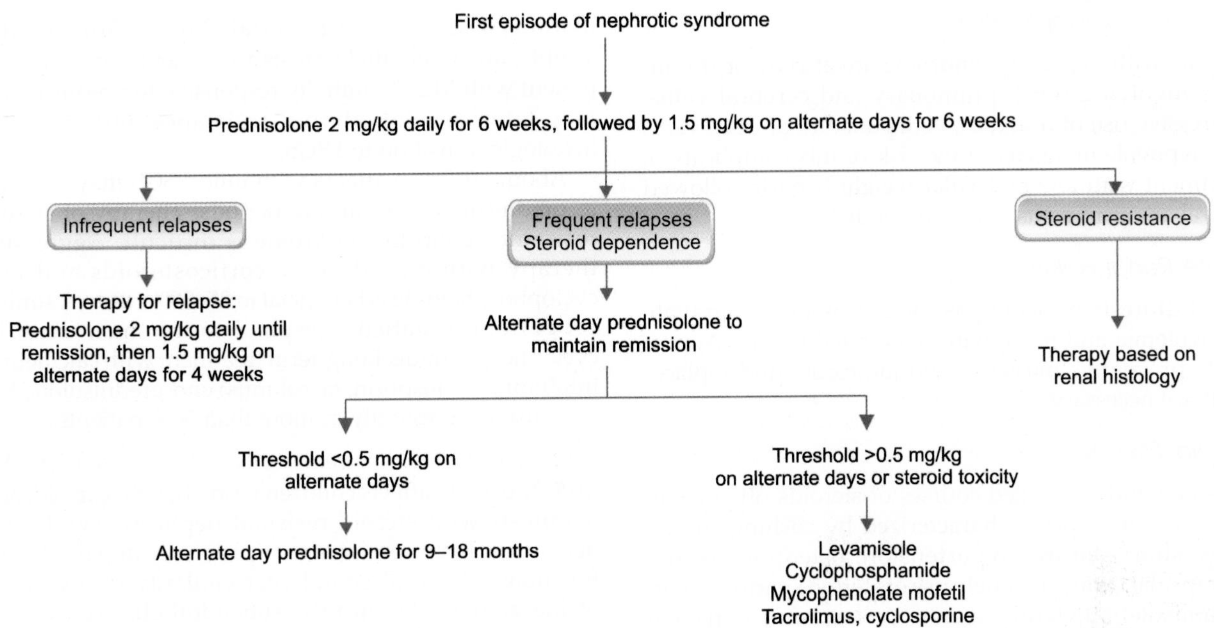

Fig. 15.7: Management of patients with steroid sensitive nephrotic syndrome

experience. Side effects include leukopenia (requiring fortnightly monitoring), nausea and vomiting; a high fluid intake is ensured to prevent hemorrhagic cystitis. Alkylating agents are associated with a risk of gonadal toxicity and malignancies, although in the doses and duration used these risks are minimal. Repeat courses of either agent are avoided.

Cyclosporin A: Cyclosporin, a calcineurin inhibitor, is used in patients who do not benefit significantly from levamisole or cyclophosphamide, continue to relapse and show significant steroid toxicity. The drug is administered daily along with small dose of alternate day prednisolone. Cyclosporin is effective in maintaining remission in most cases. Side effects include hirsutism, gum hyperplasia and hypertension; long-term treatment may result in nephrotoxicity. Another calcineurin inhibitor, tacrolimus has similar efficacy as cyclosporin but is free of cosmetic side effects. A renal biopsy is advisable before commencing treatment with these agents.

Mycophenolate mofetil: Prolonged treatment with this agent is useful in reducing relapse rates and corticosteroid requirements. The lack of renal, hemodynamic and metabolic toxicity makes it an attractive alternative to calcineurin inhibitors. Chief side effects include gastrointestinal discomfort, diarrhea and leukopenia.

Some patients who respond to therapy with levamisole, mycophenolate mofetil and calcineurin inhibitors may relapse once these medications are discontinued. Relapses during or following therapy with these agents are treated with prednisolone as described above.

Complications in Nephrotic Syndrome

The patient should be maintained in remission, as far as possible. Relapses should be promptly treated so that the child does not develop more than minimal edema. Several complications that are associated with massive edema and ascites can thus be avoided.

Edema

Edema is controlled with salt restriction and oral hydrochlorothiazide (1–2 mg/kg/day) or frusemide for a few days. Salt must not be totally stopped and the usual amounts used in cooking should be allowed. For massive edema and anasarca, higher doses of frusemide along with spironolactone may be needed. Infusion of albumin may be necessary in intractable cases where the serum albumin levels are extremely low causing poor renal perfusion and oliguria.

Infections

The nephrotic state and corticosteroid therapy render children susceptible to infections. Infection with *Streptococcus pneumoniae,* gram-negative organisms and varicella are common and serious. Children may present with serious pyogenic infections, e.g. peritonitis, cellulitis, pneumonia and meningitis. The symptoms and signs may be subtle. Peritonitis may manifest with low grade fever, diarrhea and abdominal discomfort. Infections must be detected and treated promptly. Immunization with pneumococcal and varicella vaccines is recommended once the patient is off steroids for 4–6 weeks.

Thrombotic Complications

Patients with nephrotic syndrome are at risk for thrombosis involving renal, pulmonary and cerebral veins. Aggressive use of diuretics, venepuncture of deep veins and hypovolemia increase the risk of this complication. Treatment with low molecular weight heparin followed by oral anticoagulants is recommended.

Acute Renal Failure

Rapid diuresis or acute gastroenteritis may aggravate hypovolemia and precipitate acute renal failure. Appropriate preventive measures and judicious fluid replacement are necessary.

Steroid Toxicity

Repeated and prolonged courses of steroids often result in significant toxicity, characterized by cushingoid features, short stature, hypertension, osteoporosis and subcapsular cataract. Timely use of steroid sparing agents (levamisole, alkylating agents, cyclosporin) is recommended.

Long-Term Outcome

Children with MCNS usually have an excellent prognosis. The frequency of relapses decreases with time and a majority of patients outgrow the condition by adulthood. It is unfortunately not possible to predict when a particular patient will stop getting relapses. The mortality rate of 1–4% is associated with infections and hypovolemia that should be preventable.

NEPHROTIC SYNDROME WITH SIGNIFICANT LESIONS

In about 10–15% of children with nephrotic syndrome, significant glomerular abnormalities are present. These are of several distinct types with variable course and outcome. Mesangial proliferative GN and focal segmental glomerulosclerosis are more common while membranous nephropathy is rare. Some of these conditions are caused by the deposition of immune complexes in the glomeruli, with subsequent activation of complement. Inflammatory processes and coagulation mechanisms are important in the production of glomerular injury. The antigen responsible is usually not known, though *Plasmodium malariae, Treponema pallidum*, HIV and parvovirus are incriminated. Hepatitis B and C viruses may cause membranous nephropathy or membranoproliferative GN.

Mesangial proliferative GN: This is a common histologic abnormality in nephrotic syndrome with significant glomerular lesions. There is diffuse, mild to severe proliferation in the mesangial region and prominence of mesangial matrix. A proportion of patients respond to corticosteroids and/or cyclophosphamide.

Focal segmental glomerulosclerosis (FSGS): FSGS is characterized by obliteration of segments of glomeruli by hyaline, PAS-positive material (Fig. 15.5B); tubular atrophy and interstitial fibrosis are present. An occasional patient with MCNS, initially responsive to prednisolone, may later develop steroid resistance and apparent histologic transition to FSGS.

About 20–25% patients with mild FSGS may respond to prednisolone for varying periods. Therapy of steroid resistant nephrotic syndrome is difficult. Aggressive therapy with high dose IV corticosteroids and oral cyclophosphamide is beneficial in 25–30% cases. A similar proportion of patients respond to treatment with IV cyclophosphamide. Long-term treatment with calcineurin inhibitors (cyclosporin, tacrolimus) and prednisolone has been used successfully in more than 50% patients.

Membranoproliferative (mesangiocapillary) GN (MPGN): MPGN usually affects children more than 8-year-old, and manifests with steroid-resistant nephrotic syndrome, hematuria, hypertension and occasionally impaired renal functions. Glomeruli show hypercellularity and extension of mesangial cells into the subendothelial space with significantly reduced capillary lumen. The glomerular basement membrane is intact (MPGN type I). In about 30%, the glomerular basement membrane shows dense deposits, persistent low serum C3, and abundant immunoglobulin and C3 deposits (MPGN type II). The long-term prognosis is poor although periods of spontaneous remission are observed. Long-term administration of prednisolone (1–1.5 mg/kg on alternate days) retards progressive kidney disease.

Supportive Care of Resistant Nephrotic Syndrome

Patients who fail to respond to various specific regimens are treated symptomatically. Hypertension must be controlled and infections managed appropriately. In most cases edema can be minimized with judicious use of diuretics. The use of intravenous albumin should be limited to cases with (i) symptomatic hypovolemia, (ii) symptomatic edema or (iii) marked ascites that is causing respiratory compromise. In cases with hypovolemia, 10–20 mL/kg of 4.5–5% albumin should be infused. Severe symptomatic edema or ascites may be treated with 0.75–1 g/kg of 20% albumin, infused over 2 hours, to expand the circulating volume followed by frusemide 1 mg/kg. Close monitoring is essential to avoid fluid overload and pulmonary edema. Albumin infusion has been shown to augment diuresis when co-administered with frusemide in severely hypoalbuminemic patients whose edema is refractory to diuretics.

Angiotensin converting enzyme inhibitors, such as enalapril are used to reduce the severity of proteinuria. The antiproteinuric effect of these medications is due to alteration of the capillary permeability and reduction in glomerular hydrostatic pressure. Reduction of proteinuria is associated with increased serum albumin and reduced edema. Therapy with HMG coenzyme-A reductase inhibitors is useful in lowering blood levels of cholesterol in subjects with persistent hypercholesterolemia.

Suggested reading

1. Hodson EM, Willis NS, Craig JC. Corticosteroid therapy for nephrotic syndrome in children. Cochrane Database Syst Rev 2007; (4): CD001533.
2. Indian Pediatric Nephrology Group. Indian Academy of Pediatrics. Management of steroid sensitive nephrotic syndrome. Revised guidelines. Indian Pediatr 2008; 45: 203–214.
3. Vats AN. Genetics of idiopathic nephrotic syndrome. Indian J Pediatr 2005; 72: 777–783.
4. Bagga A, Mantan M. Nephrotic syndrome in children. Indian J Med Res 2005; 122: 13–28.
5. Habashy D, Hodson E, Craig J. Interventions for idiopathic steroid-resistant nephrotic syndrome in children. Cochrane Database Syst Rev, 2004; (2): CD003594. Update in: Cochrane Database Syst Rev, 2006; (2): CD003594.
6. Moudgil A, Bagga A, Jordan SC. Mycophenolate mofetil therapy in frequently relapsing steroid-dependent and steroid-resistant nephrotic syndrome of childhood. Pediatr Nephrol 2005; 20: 1376–1381.

CHRONIC GLOMERULONEPHRITIS

Chronic GN is not a single disease entity, but comprises advanced stages of several forms of GN. In most cases, the glomerular disease is primary and not part of a systemic disorder. However, chronic GN may occur in systemic lupus erythematosus, microscopic polyarteritis, familial nephropathies and nephropathies due to drugs and toxins. Variable glomerular deposition of immunoglobulin, complement and fibrin is found on immunofluorescence studies. Renal biopsy examination in early stages shows one of several patterns.

i. Proliferative GN (mesangial proliferative GN, crescentic GN, MPGN)
ii. Focal segmental glomerulosclerosis
iii. Membranous nephropathy

In late stages, renal histologic changes are nonspecific. Most glomeruli are sclerosed with corresponding tubular, interstitial and vascular changes. It is usually very difficult to determine the type of GN that led to such changes. Post-streptococcal acute GN seldom leads to chronic GN.

Clinical Features

The patient may be asymptomatic and the disease detected on routine urine examination. Others may show failure to thrive, persistent anemia, moderate to severe hypertension, edema, nocturia, microscopic or gross hematuria, bone pains and deformities.

Differential Diagnosis

It may, at times, be difficult to distinguish chronic from acute GN. The presence of anemia, growth retardation, evidence of long-standing hypertension (hypertensive retinopathy, left ventricular hypertrophy) and radiological skeletal changes indicate impaired renal function of long duration. Examination of the renal biopsy is valuable in confirming the diagnosis.

Laboratory Findings

Urinalysis shows protein, often in large amounts, hematuria, white cells and casts. Urine specific gravity is fixed and low (around 1010). Blood urea and creatinine levels are raised and the glomerular filtration rate usually less than 30 mL/min/1.73 m^2. Ultrasonography shows small kidneys with regular outline and lack of calyceal deformities.

Management

There is no specific treatment for chronic GN. Treatment with steroids and other immunosuppressive drugs does not usually offer any benefit. The blood pressure should be controlled and infections treated. If renal function is severely compromised, the treatment is that of chronic renal failure.

INTERSTITIAL NEPHRITIS

This is a focal or diffuse inflammatory reaction of the renal interstitium with secondary involvement of the tubules, and rarely, glomeruli. Acute interstitial nephritis is usually due to infections or drugs (e.g. ampicillin, cephalosporins). The common causes of chronic interstitial nephritis include urinary tract obstruction and vesicoureteric reflux. Interstitial nephritis may also be a feature of a systemic disorder (e.g. systemic lupus, vasculitis, associated with uveitis); autoantibodies to the tubular basement membrane are found in some cases. In many instances, no cause is determined.

The clinical features are non-specific and include abdominal pain, anorexia, pallor, headache and edema. Hypertension is generally absent. The presence of progressive renal insufficiency associated with satisfactory urine output, and urinary abnormalities such as hyposthenuria and mild proteinuria suggest the diagnosis. Leukocytes are frequently seen in the urine and Wright's stain of the urine sediment may reveal eosinophils, especially in drug-associated disease. The blood eosinophil count may be increased.

A renal biopsy establishes the diagnosis and helps assess severity. Drug-related interstitial nephritis is treated with stoppage of the offending drug; treatment with corticosteroids is beneficial. Systemic illness, if any, should be appropriately managed. The treatment of chronic interstitial nephritis is symptomatic.

Suggested reading

Alon US. Tubulointerstitial nephritis. In: Pediatric Nephrology, 5th edn. Eds. Avner ED, Harmon WE, Niaudet P. Lippincott Williams and Wilkins, Anner ED. Philadelphia 2004;817–83.

URINARY TRACT INFECTIONS

Urinary tract infections (UTI) are a common medical problem affecting 6–8% girls and 1.5–2% boys. They are an important cause of morbidity and might result in renal damage, often in association with vesicoureteric reflux (VUR). During infancy, UTI are as common in boys and girls, since (i) the route of infection is often hematogenous, and (ii) boys have a higher incidence of urinary tract anomalies, particularly posterior urethral valves. Beyond infancy, the incidence of UTI and asymptomatic bacteriuria is higher in girls.

Microbiology

UTI, in most cases, are caused by *E. coli* that forms the predominant periurethral flora. *Klebsiella, Enterobacter, Proteus, Pseudomonas,* enterococcus and *Candida* are encountered in presence of obstruction, instrumentation and poor immune state.

The adhesion of bacteria to epithelial cells may have a central role in UTI. Bacterial adhesion is mediated by fimbriae, which are proteinaceous, hair-like extensions from the bacterial cell surface. The fimbriae recognize specific receptors on the epithelial cell membrane. P-blood group antigens are the receptors for *E. coli* having fimbriae on their surface. Such organisms are an important cause of acute pyelonephritis in the absence of VUR. Some *E. coli* strains possess invasive toxins and hemolysins, and are more pathogenic.

Predisposing Factors

VUR, obstructive uropathy and neurogenic bladder predispose to UTI in almost 30–40% children. Obstructive uropathy is more common in boys. Neurogenic bladder may be associated with meningomyelocele, or follow neoplasm or trauma to the lumbosacral region. Children with malnutrition, renal parenchymal disease or those receiving immunosuppressive therapy are also susceptible to UTI. There is evidence that circumcision may protect against UTI, especially in infancy.

Pathology

UTI may be confined to bladder (cystitis) or renal parenchyma (pyelonephritis). In cystitis, the bladder is inflamed and edematous; when associated with distal urinary obstruction, its wall is thickened and fibrosed, causing distortion of ureterovesical junction. The ureter and pelvis may be dilated and renal parenchyma inflamed.

Clinical Features

The clinical features depend upon the age and the severity of UTI. Neonates show features of sepsis with fever, vomiting, diarrhea, jaundice, poor weight gain and lethargy. The older infant has unexplained fever, frequent micturition and occasionally convulsions. Distal UTI in older children presents with dysuria, hypogastric pain, frequency and urgency. Patients with pyelonephritis have fever, systemic toxicity, chills and rigors with flank pain. Gross hematuria is uncommon. The presence of crying or straining during voiding, dribbling, weak or abnormal urine stream and palpable bladder suggest urinary obstruction.

Diagnosis

The diagnosis of UTI is confirmed by urine culture. Urine is obtained by suprapubic bladder aspiration or urethral catheterization in children below 2 yr, and a careful 'clean-catch' procedure in older children. The specimen is stored at 4° C until transported to the laboratory. An uncentrifuged urine specimen may be examined in a counting chamber. The presence of more than 10 white cells/cu mm is abnormal. The presence of bacteriuria on oil immersion microscopy of a fresh uncentrifuged urine specimen suggests significant bacteriuria. Dipstick examination (combining detection of leukocyte esterase and nitrite) is as sensitive as microscopic urinalysis in screening for UTI.

The definitive diagnosis of UTI depends on the urine culture showing 10^5 or more bacteria per mL. However, infants with symptomatic UTI may show colony counts of 10^4 to 10^5/mL. Any colony growth in urine obtained by suprapubic aspiration is significant. Tests to differentiate upper from lower UTI are of little practical value.

Treatment

Once UTI is suspected, a urine specimen is sent for culture and treatment started. *The choice of initial treatment depends on the age and clinical condition of the patient, and presence of complications or structural abnormalities.* Antibiotic therapy is modified, if required, once culture result is available. *Following treatment of the first episode of UTI, plans are made for evaluation of the urinary tract.* Treatment with prophylactic antibiotics is given until results of imaging are available.

General measures: The child is encouraged to take large amount of fluids and empty the bladder frequently to prevent stasis of urine.

UTI in early infancy: In the neonate and young infant (below 3 months old), UTI is often associated with sepsis. The treatment should be with a combination of ampicillin and an aminoglycoside (e.g. gentamicin, amikacin) for 10–14 days. Alternatively, a third generation cephalosporin (e.g. ceftriaxone, cefotaxime) may be used. Fluid and electrolyte balance should be maintained and other supportive care provided. An ultrasound of the abdomen is done to exclude major anomalies. Further imaging is usually done 4 weeks following recovery.

UTI in older children: The management depends upon the clinical evaluation of the severity of UTI. Prompt institution of therapy is crucial. If pyelonephritis is suspected (indicated by fever, systemic toxicity and flank pain) antibiotics are administered initially parenterally, as above. The antibiotic may be administered orally, once toxicity declines and the child is accepting by mouth.

In patients who are not toxic and accepting orally, treatment may be started with oral amoxicillin, co-amoxiclav, cephalexin or cefixime. With appropriate therapy, fever and systemic toxicity reduce and the urine culture is sterile within 24–36 hr. Failure to obtain such a result suggests either lack of bacterial sensitivity to the medication or presence of an underlying anomaly of the urinary tract. Treatment is given for 7–10 days. Commonly used drugs for treatment of UTI are listed in Table.15.4. Routine urine culture after completion of antibiotic therapy is not required.

Urine cultures are repeated if suspecting recurrence of a UTI, as in patients with unexplained fever, dysuria, flank pain or foul smelling urine. Recurrent UTI in the absence of VUR or obstruction seldom lead to renal scarring. Bacteriuria in absence of any symptoms is called *asymptomatic bacteriuria*. It has been shown to be innocuous and need not be treated.

Short term therapy: Lower UTI has been treated in adults with single dose or short-term (3-day) antibiotics. Such regimens are not advised in children.

Diagnostic Imaging Studies

The primary concerns following the diagnosis of UTI are the presence of an underlying urologic anomaly (obstruction or vesicoureteric reflux) and involvement of the kidney (pyelonephritis). Recommended radiological evaluation includes a combination of ultrasound abdomen (examining the kidney, ureter and bladder), micturating cystourethrogram (MCU) and radionuclide renal scan. Intensive imaging is preferred in children below 2-yr-old.

Ultrasonography is a useful investigation for detection of major renal anomalies. MCU detects the presence of VUR or other anomalies (especially posterior urethral valve). Renal cortical ^{99m}Tc DMSA scans are used to diagnose acute pyelonephritis especially in infants, in whom clinical clues are less reliable. They are also the most sensitive technique for detecting renal cortical scars as a sequel of UTI (Fig. 15.1A).

Suggested reading

1. Indian Pediatric Nephrology Group. Indian Academy of Pediatrics. Consensus statement on management of urinary tract infections. Indian Pediatr 2001; 38: 1106–15.
2. Hari P, Mantan M, Bagga A. Management of urinary tract infections. Indian J Pediatr 2003; 70(3): 235–9.
3. Bauer R, Kogan BA. New developments in the diagnosis and management of pediatric UTIs. Urol Clin North Am 2008; 35: 47–58.
4. Watson AR. Management of urinary tract infection in children. BMJ 2007; 335(7616): 356–357.
5. Mori R, Lakhanpaul M, Verrier-Jones K. Diagnosis and management of urinary tract infection in children: summary of NICE guidelines. BMJ 2007; 335(7616): 395–7.

VESICOURETERIC REFLUX

Vesicoureteric reflux (VUR) refers to the retrograde flow of urine from the bladder to the upper urinary tract. The rise in intravesical pressure occurring during micturition is freely transmitted to the ureter, renal pelvis, papillary collecting ducts and renal tubules. Pathogenic organisms that might be present in the bladder can gain access to the renal parenchyma, initiate inflammation and renal scarring (*reflux nephropathy*). VUR is present in 30–35% of children with febrile UTI and is a major risk factor for acute pyelonephritis and reflux nephropathy. The latter may result in hypertension, renal insufficiency and cause morbidity during pregnancy. Significant VUR may occur *in utero* and be associated with varying degrees or renal dysplasia. VUR may be familial in 30–35% patients. Young siblings (especially below 5-yr-old) of children with VUR should therefore be screened for the condition.

Two techniques are commonly used to detect VUR. The radiocontrast MCU is most commonly used since in addition to showing VUR it provides excellent anatomical details. The severity of VUR is graded from I to V (Figs 15.8A and B). Isotope radionuclide cystography is more sensitive for detecting VUR, and causes less radiation exposure than the former but provides less anatomical details. Follow-up screening of patients diagnosed to have reflux (on radiocontrast study) may be done by radionuclide cystography.

15

Table 15.4: Drugs for treatment of urinary infections

Drug	*Dose (mg/kg/day)*[1]	*Doses/ day*	*Remarks*
Cotrimoxazole/	6–8 (of trimethoprim)	2	Broad spectrum; rash, nausea, marrow depression
Amoxicillin[2]	30–50	2–3	Effective against *E. coli*, *Proteus*; rash, diarrhea,
Co-amoxiclav			resistance develops fast
Cefixime	10–20	2	Broad spectrum; rapid resistance
Ciprofloxacin[3]	10–15	2	Effective against gram negative bacteria; rapidly
Ofloxacin			develops resistance
Gentamicin[4]	5–7	1–2	Effective against gram-negative bacteria; may be used
Amikacin[4]	15		in single dose; renal and auditory toxicity
Cefotaxime[4]	100	2–3	Broad spectrum agent; may cause rash, minimal
Ceftriaxone[4]	75	1–2	nephrotoxicity

[1] Dose adjustment required in renal insufficiency
[2] Amoxicillin may be used alone or in combination with clavulanic acid (co-amoxiclav)
[3] Avoid the use of fluoroquinolones as first-line agents
[4] Parenteral use for pyelonephritis

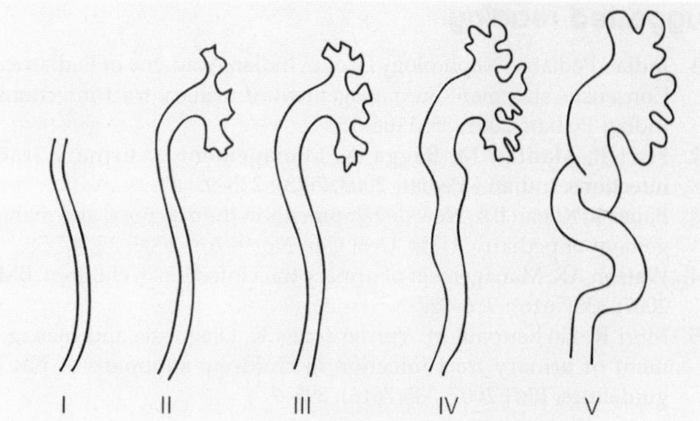

Fig. 15.8A: Grading of vesicoureteric reflux

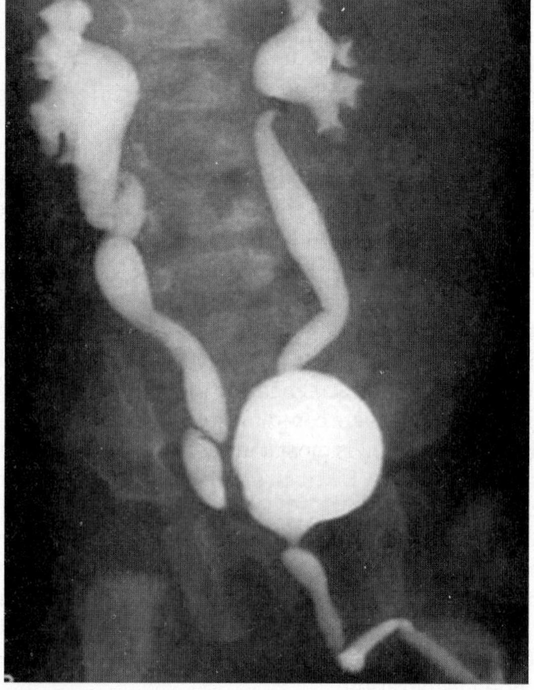

Fig. 15.8B: Micturating cystourethrogram showing bilateral grade IV primary vesicoureteric reflux

Management

The primary goal of treatment is prevention of pyelonephritis and complications of reflux nephropathy. Medical therapy is based on the principle that VUR resolves with time, and antibiotics maintain urine sterility and prevent infections while awaiting spontaneous resolution. The basis for surgical therapy is that, in select situations, ongoing VUR has the potential to cause significant renal injury and elimination of reflux will minimize this likelihood. Long-term controlled studies have shown that outcomes such as recurrence of UTI, and renal scarring, growth and functions are similar when patients are treated with antibiotic prophylaxis or surgery.

Continuous antibiotic prophylaxis is recommended as the initial treatment for almost all children with VUR. Cotrimoxazole or nitrofurantoin is given as a bedtime dose, which is one-fifth of the usual therapeutic dose (see below). In view of nausea and abdominal discomfort associated with nitrofurantoin, therapy with cotrimoxazole is preferred. Trimethoprim alone is as effective as cotrimoxazole but is not available in India. Treatment with cephalexin is preferred in infants less than 4-months-old and children with G6PD deficiency. Drugs that tend to select resistant bacteria in the bowel including amoxicillin, nalidixic acid and other quinolones are not suitable for prophylaxis. Breakthrough infections during prophylaxis are treated with appropriate antibiotics.

The indications for surgical correction of primary VUR are limited and include poor compliance or intolerance to medical treatment. Surgery might also be indicated in patients showing recurrent breakthrough UTI despite prophylaxis, appearance of new scars or persistence of grade IV-V reflux beyond 2-yr of age. Surgical procedures of ureteric reimplantation have cure rates of 95–97%. The precise indications for endoscopic submucosal injection (e.g. of Teflon or other biocompatible products) at the ureteric orifice are not defined.

Follow up evaluation should be performed annually with urinalysis and measurement of height, weight and blood pressure. Urine cultures should be obtained in presence of symptoms suggestive of a UTI. Follow up renal ultrasonography and cystography should be performed every 12–18 months.

General measures: These include a liberal fluid intake, regular and complete bladder emptying and local toilet. Constipation should be avoided.

Reflux Nephropathy

This is characterized by renal cortical scarring, predominantly at the poles. The underlying calyces lose their normal concave shape and show clubbing. Such scarring occurs early in life when the kidneys are still growing; formation of fresh scars after 5–6 yr of age is uncommon. Reflux nephropathy is an important cause of hypertension and end stage renal disease in children.

Long-Term Prophylaxis in Children with UTI

The indications for antibiotic prophylaxis are as follows:

1. Children below 3 yr of age who have received treatment for the first UTI and are being investigated for an underlying etiology.
2. Children with normal urinary tract and no VUR, but with three or more UTI in one year. Prophylaxis is continued until the child is free of UTI for 6 months.
3. UTI with VUR. Prophylaxis until the child is free from reflux.

Medications used for prophylaxis are listed in Table 15.5.

Table 15.5: Antibiotics for long-term prophylaxis

Drug	*Dosage (mg/kg/day)**	*Remarks*
Cotrimoxazole	1–2 of trimethoprim	Maintain adequate fluid intake; avoid in infants under 6 weeks; contraindicated in G6PD deficiency
Nitrofurantoin	1–2	May cause gastrointestinal upset; contraindicated in: G6PD deficiency, infants < 3 months; resistance rare
Cephalexin	10	Safe in young infants
Trimethoprim	1–2	Safe and effective; not available in India

* Usually administered as a single bedtime dose

Suggested reading

1. Greenbaum LA, Mesrobian HG. Vesicoureteral reflux. Pediatr Clin North Am 2006; 53(3): 413–427.
2. Hodson EM, Wheeler DM, Vimalchandra D, Smith GH, Craig JC. Interventions for primary vesicoureteric reflux. Cochrane Database Syst Rev 2007; (3): CD001532.
3. Williams GJ, Wei L, Lee A, Craig JC. Long-term antibiotics for preventing recurrent urinary tract infection in children. Cochrane Database Syst Rev 2006; 3: CD001534.
4. Callewaert PR. What is new in surgical treatment of vesicoureteric reflux? Eur J Pediatr 2007; 166: 763–768.

ACUTE RENAL FAILURE

Acute renal failure (ARF) denotes an acute impairment of renal function resulting in retention of nitrogenous wastes and other biochemical derangement. Oliguria or anuria is a prominent feature, though rarely urine output may be normal. ARF is a common, life-threatening situation in childhood, where proper assessment and adequate treatment are crucial.

In the absence of a standard definition of ARF and recognizing that the occurrence of azotemia represents the end-result of a variety of conditions, the term **acute kidney injury** (AKI) is proposed to reflect the entire spectrum of the disorder. Patients are considered to have AKI if there is abrupt (within 48-hr) reduction in kidney function, defined as either (i) an absolute increase in serum creatinine of more than or equal to 0.3 mg/dl or increase in serum creatinine of more than or equal to 1.5 fold from baseline, or (ii) reduction in urine output (oliguria of less than 0.5 ml/kg per hour for >6-hr).

Incidence and Etiology

ARF (not including functional oliguria that rapidly responds to fluid volume repletion) accounts for 2–5% admissions to general pediatric wards across the world. In developing countries, common causes for ARF in children include gastroenteritis with dehydration, serious infections, D+ hemolytic uremic syndrome (HUS), post-infectious and crescentic glomerulonephritis (GN) and intravascular hemolysis (in patients with G6PD deficiency). In developed countries, ARF follows major surgical procedures, D+ HUS and severe systemic infections. A list of common causes is shown in Table 15.6.

The causes of ARF are broadly divided into *pre-renal*, *intrinsic renal* and *post-renal*. Pre-renal failure is renal insufficiency due to systemic hypovolemia or renal hypoperfusion. In the early stages, this is rapidly reversible by infusion of fluids but, if prolonged or severe, may lead to acute tubular necrosis. Post-renal failure occurs consequent to mechanical obstruction in the collecting system.

Acute-on-Chronic Renal Failure

Occasionally a patient with undetected chronic renal disease may present for the first time with acute onset of

Table 15.6: Important causes of acute renal failure

PRE-RENAL	
Acute gastroenteritis, hemorrhage, shock, congestive heart failure	
INTRINSIC RENAL	
Acute tubular necrosis	***Glomerulonephritis***
Fluid loss, hemorrhage, shock	Acute glomerulonephritis
Sepsis	Crescentic glomerulonephritis
Nephrotoxic drugs, toxins	Renal vasculitis
Intravascular hemolysis	
Interstitial nephritis	***Hemolytic uremic syndrome***
Infections, drugs	
Autoimmune	***Renal vein thrombosis***
Idiopathic	
POST-RENAL	
Calculus, posterior urethral valves	

15

anuria or oliguria. On careful inquiry, a history of previous renal disease may be obtained. The presence of the following suggests the possibility of a chronic kidney disease (i) retardation of physical growth, (ii) severe anemia, (iii) hypertensive retinopathy, (iv) hypocalcemia and hyperphosphatemia, (v) radiologic features of osteodystrophy and (vi) small contracted kidneys on imaging.

Pathophysiology

Glomerular filtration rate and renal blood flow are markedly reduced, often by 50 to 75%. Leakage of glomerular filtrate back into the circulation across the damaged tubular epithelium, and tubular obstruction from impaction of casts and cellular debris is considered to lead to oliguria. The importance of tubular obstruction, back-leak of filtrate and renal vasoconstriction vary, depending on the cause and duration of renal failure. Intravascular coagulation may play an important role in sepsis and hemolytic uremic syndrome. Patients with glomerulonephritis have severe glomerular inflammation and often large crescents. Ischemic changes consist of focal or patchy necrosis in the tubules, most frequently distal tubules at the corticomedullary junction. Nephrotoxic agents cause uniform epithelial damage, especially in the proximal tubules, without disruption of tubular basement membrane.

Diagnostic Approach

In a child with oligoanuria, it is important to look for pre-renal factors that lead to renal hypoperfusion. A history of diarrhea, vomiting, fluid or blood loss is taken and an assessment of fluid intake in the previous 24 hr made. In pre-renal azotemia, the renal tubular function is intact and reabsorption of water and sodium is increased. The urine is thus highly concentrated with low sodium content. Impaired tubular function in intrinsic renal failure results in increased sodium excretion and failure to concentrate urine. Determination of urine sodium and osmolality, and fractional excretion of sodium help in differentiating functional oliguria (pre-renal) from established (intrinsic) renal failure (Table 15.7).

Fluid Repletion

Pre-renal ARF rapidly responds to fluid replacement with improved renal perfusion and increased urine output. Dehydration is corrected by infusion of 20–30 mL/kg of normal saline or Ringer's lactate over 45–60 minutes. If hemorrhage accounts for vascular collapse, blood transfusion should be given. Potassium should not be administered until urine flow is established; care is taken to avoid overhydration. Patients with renal hypoperfusion, in whom the only reason for oliguria is intravascular volume depletion, respond to fluids with increase in urine output (2–4 mL/kg over the next 2–3 hr). Appropriate fluid therapy should then be continued. However, if no diuresis occurs despite *correction of dehydration*, frusemide (2–3 mg/kg IV) may be given. Its administration results in a urine flow of 2–4 mL/kg over the next 2–3 hr if renal tubular function is intact. The use of mannitol is not recommended in children. If these measures fail to induce diuresis, a diagnosis of established ARF is made.

Biochemical Derangement

Increased blood levels of urea and creatinine are striking, and a reliable indicator of the severity of renal failure. Metabolic acidosis results from failure to excrete hydrogen ions. Serum potassium level may be elevated. Factors that aggravate hyperkalemia are acidosis, which causes potassium to shift from the intracellular compartment, infection, hemolysis and tissue damage. Fluid retention is often a complicating factor, and results from excessive oral or parenteral fluids. It may lead to edema, hypertension and heart failure. Hyponatremia usually reflects overhydration.

Clinical Features

A history of anuria or severe oliguria is present. In a small proportion, (e.g. gentamicin toxicity, intravascular hemolysis) urine output may not be diminished (non-oliguric renal failure). Depending upon the underlying cause and duration of renal failure, the child may look remarkably well or extremely sick. Features of the underlying illness are usually present.

Table 15.7: Differentiation of functional oliguria from Intrinsic renal failure (indices for neonates are in parentheses)

Index	*Functional oliguria*	*Intrinsic renal failure*
Urinary sodium (mEq/L)	<20 (<30)	>40 (>60)
Urinary osmolality (mOsm/kg)	>500 (>400)	<300 (<350)
Blood urea to creatinine ratio	>20: 1	<20: 1
Urine to plasma osmolality ratio	>1.5 (>2)	<0.8-1.2 (<1.1)
FENa* (%)	<1 (<3)	>1 (>10)

$$\text{* Fractional excretion of sodium} = \frac{\text{urine sodium} \times \text{serum creatinine}}{\text{serum sodium} \times \text{urine creatinine}} \times 100$$

Abnormalities directly related to the derangement caused by loss of renal function include acidotic breathing, alteration of sensorium and irregularities of cardiac rate and rhythm. In acute tubular necrosis, clinical examination may reveal no abnormality except for dehydration. The oliguric phase lasts about 3–10 days, during which period the biochemical and clinical abnormalities gradually worsen; more rapidly if infection, trauma and bleeding are associated. Subsequently urine output increases steadily. A diuretic phase may be observed, usually lasting for a week, during which large amounts of water and electrolytes, particularly potassium may be lost. The patient may get dehydrated if these losses are not adequately replaced.

Laboratory Evaluation

These include complete blood counts, and estimation of blood levels of urea, creatinine, electrolytes, pH and bicarbonate, and urinalysis. An EKG is done to examine for evidence of hyperkalemia and chest X-ray for pulmonary plethora and cardiac enlargement. Ultrasonography is a useful imaging tool because of its non-dependence on renal function. It allows visualization of the pelvicalyceal system, and assessment of renal size, structural anomalies and calculi. Additional tests are done, where appropriate, to determine the cause of ARF.

Management

Prompt clinical and laboratory evaluation is necessary. Complications such as dehydration or fluid overload, hypertension, heart failure, severe anemia, hyperkalemia and acidosis may already be present and require urgent treatment.

Fluid and Electrolytes

Fluid and electrolyte intake must be meticulously regulated. The daily fluid requirement amounts to insensible water losses (300–400 mL/m^2), urinary output and extrarenal fluid losses. Insensible fluid losses should be replaced with 5% glucose solution with little or no potassium. The composition of urinary and extrarenal losses should be analyzed and replaced accordingly. It is usually possible to administer the required amounts of fluid by mouth.

Fluid therapy is guided by intake and output analysis, weight, physical examination and serum sodium. If fluid in an appropriate volume and composition is given, the patient should lose 0.5–1% of his weight every day because of tissue breakdown. The serum sodium concentration should stay within the normal range. A rapid weight loss and rising serum sodium suggest inadequate fluid replacement, while an absence of weight loss and low serum sodium indicate fluid excess.

Diet

Patients with ARF have increased metabolic needs. Adequate nutritional support with maximization of caloric intake should be achieved as early as possible. A diet containing 0.8–1.0 g/kg of protein in infants and 0.6–0.8 g/kg in older children and a minimum of 50–60 Cal/kg is recommended. The latter requirement can be met by adding liberal amounts of carbohydrates and fats to the diet. Vitamin and micronutrient supplements are provided. In patients with oligoanuria and fluid overload, daily caloric requirement cannot be met due to fluid restriction. These patients require early initiation of dialysis to allow adequate caloric intake.

Treatment of Complications

In a child with ARF, immediate attention is directed towards detection and management of life-threatening complications.

Fluid overload: Children with pulmonary edema and congestive cardiac failure are treated using standard guidelines. If the condition does not improve, patients require endotracheal intubation and assisted ventilation.

Hyperkalemia: Hyperkalemia is an emergency as the resultant cardiac toxicity may cause sudden death. Urgent treatment is instituted depending on blood potassium levels and EKG changes. Concomitant metabolic acidosis should be corrected. Calcium antagonizes the cardiotoxicity of hyperkalemia; for immediate effect, the dose is 0.5–1 mL/kg of 10% calcium gluconate given IV over 5–10 minutes. Administration of sodium bicarbonate also lowers serum potassium by favoring its uptake by cells; 1–2 mL/kg of a 7.5% solution is infused over 10–20 minutes. Nebulized administration of salbutamol (5–10 mg) may be beneficial through a similar mechanism, the effect is seen within 20–30 minutes. Cellular uptake of potassium is also achieved by administration of glucose 0.5 g/kg along with soluble insulin 0.1 U/kg IV over 90 minutes. Exchange resins (calcium resonium 1 g/kg/day) may be given orally or by enema to eliminate potassium from the gut. The onset of action of resins is slow and their role in treatment of life-threatening hyperkalemia limited.

The benefit following administration of calcium gluconate, salbutamol, sodium bicarbonate and glucose-insulin is transient, and most patients with hyperkalemia secondary to ARF require dialysis.

Metabolic acidosis: Severe acidosis is treated by administration of sodium bicarbonate, 1–2 mEq/kg, aiming to raise the serum bicarbonate level to 15–17 mEq/L. Patients should be monitored for fluid retention and hypertension; correction of acidosis may precipitate hypocalcemic seizures. Persistence of acidosis requires dialysis treatment.

Hypertension: Severe hypertension may occur with acute glomerulonephritis and hemolytic uremic syndrome, leading to encephalopathy and heart failure. The symptoms of hypertensive encephalopathy are usually related to the rapidity of rise rather than the absolute value of the blood pressure.

Symptomatic hypertension needs to be lowered gradually: Too rapid reduction may result in ischemia and infarction of regions in the brain, spinal cord and retina. Blood pressure is reduced by one-third of the total desired reduction during the first 6–8 hr, a further third over the next 12–24 hr and the final third over the following 2–3 days. Infusion of nitroprusside (0.5–8 μg/kg per minute) causes a predictable reduction in blood pressure; the rate of infusion can then be titrated depending on the response. Since the half-life of this drug is in minutes, it may be stopped if there is a precipitous fall in blood pressure. Frusemide (1–2 mg/kg IV) is given if there are features of fluid excess. IV infusion of labetalol is as effective as sodium nitroprusside.

Once the patient is asymptomatic, maintenance oral therapy is instituted using a calcium channel blocker (nifedipine, amlodepine), beta-adrenergic blocker (atenolol), or vasodilator (prazosin) alone or in combination.

Hyponatremia: Hyponatremia (serum sodium <130 mEq/L) usually is the result of excessive fluid administration rather than salt loss. Plasma sodium concentration >125 mEq/L is rarely symptomatic. Sodium concentration between 120–125 mEq/L may be associated with encephalopathy, lethargy and seizures. Fluid restriction is the primary mode of therapy. Treatment with hypertonic saline is reserved for those with symptomatic hyponatremia or level <115–120 mEq/L. A dose of 6 mL/kg of 3% saline (given over 30–60 minutes) raises serum sodium by 5 mEq/L. Hypertonic saline must be used cautiously because of potential complications of fluid overload and hypertension.

15

General Supportive Care

Patients with ARF should be managed under intensive care conditions. Accurate records of intake and output and daily weight should be maintained. Urine should be collected by condom drainage; bladder should preferably not be catheterized. The risk of infection is high and appropriate preventive measures are necessary. Prophylactic antibiotics are not recommended but infections should be promptly detected and treated. The dosage of antibiotics often needs to be modified.

Dialysis

The purpose of dialysis is to remove endogenous and exogenous toxins and maintain fluid, electrolyte and acid-base balance until renal function recovers. The indications for dialysis are listed in Table 15.8. It is important to assess the clinical situation and anticipate the course of ARF in each case, depending on the type and severity of renal injury. *Dialysis should be started early to prevent occurrence of complications, especially in hypercatabolic states* (e.g. extensive trauma and infections).

Both hemodialysis and peritoneal dialysis are effective in the management of ARF. Peritoneal dialysis does not require vascular access and sophisticated equipment, and is easy to perform even in neonates. This makes it the preferred dialysis procedure in children (Table 5.8).

Table 15.8: Indications for dialysis in acute renal failure
Severe hyperkalemia (serum potassium >6.5 mEq/L)
Dysnatremia (serum sodium <130 or >150 mEq/L)
Severe acidosis (pH <7.2, TCO_2 <12 mEq/L)
Uremic encephalopathy
Pulmonary edema; congestive heart failure

Peritoneal dialysis: The abdominal skin is prepared as for a surgical procedure. After ensuring that the bladder is empty, lignocaine is infiltrated in the midline at a point midway between the umbilicus and pubic symphysis. Dialysis fluid 20 mL/kg is infused to distend the peritoneal cavity. A small incision is made in the skin and linea alba and the peritoneal catheter introduced and advanced into the paracolic gutter. It is fixed to the skin with purse-string sutures. The dialysis fluid is infused 30–50 mL/kg, left in the peritoneal cavity for 30 to 45 minutes and then allowed to flow, using a siphon effect, into the draining bottle. The entire system is kept as an air-free, closed system. Thirty-40 cycles are carried out. Potassium is not added in the first 5–10 cycles, to enable correction of hyperkalemia. Later, 3–4 mEq/L potassium chloride is added to the dialysis fluid. Overhydration and pulmonary edema can be relieved using concentrated dialysis fluid.

The results of peritoneal dialysis are gratifying. In acute tubular necrosis, often a single dialysis is adequate. The procedure can, however, be repeated if necessary. If the need for prolonged dialysis is anticipated, a silastic Tenckhoff catheter should be surgically placed. The most important complication is peritonitis. Meticulous aseptic precautions will minimize its incidence. The dialysate should be examined for white cells and bacteria and cultured.

Continuous hemofiltration: Continuous hemofiltration employs a filtration cartridge that permits efficient removal of excess fluid as protein-free plasma. An appropriate vascular access allows adequate blood inflow and outflow. The patient's cardiac output provides the driving force for the hemofilter. The procedure is particularly useful for the management of patients with severe fluid overload, and renal failure secondary to cardiovascular and abdominal surgery, burns, heart failure and septic shock. Continuous hemofiltration provides smoother control of ultrafiltered volume and gradual correction of metabolic abnormalities in unstable patients with multi-organ failure.

Outcome

ARF carries a mortality of 20–40%, chiefly related to the underlying etiology and duration of renal failure. Patients with septicemia and hemolytic uremic syndrome with prolonged anuria are associated with a poor prognosis. The outcome in crescentic glomerulonephritis and vasculitis depends on the severity of the renal injury and promptness in initiation of specific therapy. The outlook is satisfactory in acute tubular necrosis without complicating factors. Other factors associated with poor outcome include delayed referral, presence of complicating infections and cardiac, hepatic or respiratory failure. Maintenance of nutrition and prevention of infections is extremely crucial in improving outcome.

Suggested reading

1. Srivastava RN, Bagga A . Acute renal failure. In: Pediatric Nephrology, 4th edn. Jaypee, New Delhi, 2004;158–76.
2. Barletta GM, Bunchman TE. Acute renal failure in children and infants. Curr Opin Crit Care 2004;10:499–504.
3. Strazdins V, Watson AR, Harvey B; European Pediatric Peritoneal Dialysis Working Group. Renal replacement therapy for acute renal failure in children: European guidelines. Pediatr Nephrol 2004; 19(2): 199–207.
4. Srivastava RN, Bagga A. Acute renal failure in north Indian children. Indian J Med Res 1990; 92: 404–408.

ACUTE RENAL FAILURE IN THE NEWBORN

Important causes of renal failure in the neonate include perinatal asphyxia, shock, septicemia, respiratory distress syndrome and intravascular volume depletion following surgery for cardiac and other congenital defects. Bilateral renal artery thrombosis may occur after umbilical artery catheterization.

Renal vein thrombosis is suspected in asphyxiated, dehydrated or polycythemic neonates with hematuria, enlarging flank mass, thrombocytopenia and azotemia. Renal failure may occasionally be the first manifestation of a congenital anomaly of the urinary tract. Features suggestive of urinary tract obstruction include an abdominal mass, hypertension, oligoanuria or polyuria.

The levels of serum creatinine and urea should be monitored in sick neonates. Renal failure is suspected in the presence of (i) oliguria (urine output <1 mL/kg/hr); (ii) blood creatinine >1.2 mg/dL. Serum creatinine levels are high at birth (reflecting maternal levels) and decrease to below 0.5 mg/dL by 5–7 days of age. Failure of reduction or rise of serum creatinine indicates impaired renal function. Urinary indices should be interpreted with caution (Table 15.7).

The principles of management are similar to that for older children. Fluid given should be limited to insensible (30 mL/kg per day for full-term, 50–100 mL/kg per day for preterm neonates), gastrointestinal and renal losses. Extremely premature neonates nursed in radiant warmers require extra fluids. Systolic blood pressure more than 95–100 mm Hg may need treatment.

Extra care should be taken while dialyzing these children; peritoneal dialysis is technically easier and preferred. Sudden distention of peritoneal cavity may cause respiratory embarrassment or apnea. Hypothermia should be avoided by carefully warming the dialysis fluid. A number of drugs are dialyzable and appropriate amounts should be added to supplement for their losses.

Mortality rates for oliguric renal failure are approximately 40–50%; non-oliguric patients have a better prognosis. The outcome is related to the underlying condition unless the renal failure is prolonged beyond a few days. Infants with tubular necrosis usually show complete recovery; those with cortical or medullary necrosis may only partly regain renal function and show chronic kidney disease.

Suggested reading

1. Moghal NE, Embleton ND. Management of acute renal failure in the newborn. Semin Fetal Neonatal Med 2006; 11(3): 207–213.
2. Andreoli SP. Acute renal failure in the newborn. Semin Perinatol 2004; 28(2): 112–23.

CHRONIC KIDNEY DISEASE

The terms chronic renal failure (CRF) and end stage renal disease denote advanced kidney damage for which renal replacement is the only definitive option. It is important to recognize various conditions that have the potential to cause progressive loss of kidney function and eventually lead to CRF. The term chronic kidney disease (CKD) is used to describe patients with kidney damage or decreased level of renal function for three months, or more, irrespective of the underlying etiology. CKD is divided into 5 stages, based on level of GFR (estimated from level of serum creatinine and height using the Schwartz formula) (Table 15.9). This classification has resulted in standardized definitions and categorization of the disease. Important conditions resulting in CKD are listed in Table 15.10.

Chronic Renal Failure

Chronic renal failure (CRF) implies permanent, severe decrease in renal function. Regardless of the etiology, once

Table 15.9: Stages of chronic kidney disease

Stage	*Description*	*GFR ml/min/1.73 m^2*
I	Slight kidney damage with normal or increased filtration	More than 90
II	Mild decrease in kidney function	60–89
III	Moderate decrease in kidney function	30–59
IV	Severe decrease in kidney function	15–29
V	Kidney failure: requiring dialysis or transplantation	<15

GFR glomerular filtration rate

Table 15.10: Common causes of chronic kidney disease

Glomerulonephritis: Idiopathic (e.g. focal segmental glomerulosclerosis); secondary (to systemic lupus erythematosus, IgA nephropathy, microscopic polyarteritis, Henoch Schonlein purpura).
Reflux nephropathy
Obstructive uropathy: Posterior urethral valves, pelviureteric junction obstruction, renal stones.
Developmental anomalies: Bilateral renal hypoplasia, dysplasia.
Familial nephropathy: Nephronophthisis, Alport syndrome, polycystic kidneys.
Others: Hemolytic uremic syndrome, amyloidosis, renal vein thrombosis, renal cortical necrosis.

there is a critical loss of nephron mass, the renal failure is progressive, and the symptom complex similar in most cases. Most children with CKD stage I-III (GFR more than 30 ml/min/1.73 m^2) are asymptomatic; reduction of GFR below this level is associated with symptoms. End stage renal disease (ESRD) is characterized by decline of renal function to a degree when life cannot be sustained without chronic dialyses or transplantation. This usually corresponds to GFR of 5–10 mL/min/1.73 m^2.

15

Pathophysiology and Clinical Features

Loss of urinary concentrating ability results in frequent passage of urine, nocturia and increased thirst. Anemia that is usually normocytic and normochromic is chiefly due to reduced renal erythropoietin production. Mild hemolysis and blood loss from gastrointestinal tract may also contribute.

Resistance to the action of growth hormone, the levels of which are increased, is considered to be responsible for growth failure. Anorexia, malnutrition and skeletal deformities contribute to growth retardation. Abnormalities in metabolism of calcium and phosphate and bone disease results from hyperphosphatemia, lack of renal formation of 1,25 dihydroxyvitamin D3, deficiency of calcium, chronic acidosis and secondary hyperparathyroidism. Systemic acidosis is secondary to loss of nephrons with decreased ammonia formation and consequent failure to buffer hydrogen ions.

The blood pressure may be increased and optic fundi show hypertensive retinopathy. Severe proximal muscle weakness, peripheral neuropathy, itching, purpura and pericarditis are late features. Infections are common and may acutely worsen renal function. *Failure to thrive, growth retardation, anemia, hypertension and bony deformities may often be the presenting features of chronic renal failure, without a previous history of renal disease.*

Investigations

The patient should be investigated to find the cause of renal failure and detect reversible factors (e.g. urinary tract obstruction, UTI, severe hypertension, drug toxicity and dehydration). Appropriate imaging studies are done. Blood counts and levels of urea, creatinine, electrolytes, pH, bicarbonate, calcium, phosphate, alkaline phosphatase, parathormone, protein and albumin are obtained. Blood levels of ferritin and transferrin saturation are obtained in patients with anemia. GFR can be estimated based on serum creatinine and height; its accurate assessment by creatinine clearance or radionuclide methods is rarely necessary.

Management

Optimal management of chronic renal failure involves a team approach involving pediatric nephrologist, trained nurse, dietitian, social worker and orthopedic surgeon. Every attempt is made to keep the child ambulatory and active. Constant encouragement and emotional support are necessary. At the initial stages, management aims at maintaining nutrition and retarding progression of the renal failure. Later, treatment of complications and renal replacement therapy in the form of dialysis or transplantation is required.

Retarding Progression of Renal Failure

Children should consume the recommended dietary intake of protein, avoiding excessive intake. Hypertension should be adequately controlled. Long term therapy with angiotensin converting enzyme inhibitors has been shown to reduce proteinuria and may retard progression of renal failure.

Diet

Careful attention to diet is essential Recommended daily amounts of calories should be ensured. A diet high in polyunsaturated fats, such as corn oil and medium chain triglycerides and complex carbohydrates is preferred. Water restriction is usually not necessary, except in ESRD or presence of fluid overload. Excessive use of diuretics, overzealous restriction of salt and gastroenteritis may lead to dehydration that should be corrected.

i. *Proteins:* The protein intake should be 1–2 g/kg/day; proteins consumed should be of high biologic value.
ii. *Sodium:* Since renal regulation of sodium reabsorption is impaired, its dietary intake needs to be individualized. Some infants are polyuric and lose large amounts of sodium requiring salt supplementation. Children with chronic glomerulonephritis retain sodium and water, which contributes to hypertension. These patients require salt and water restriction and may benefit from diuretics.
iii. *Potassium:* Renal regulation of potassium balance is maintained until very late, but the capacity to rapidly excrete a potassium load is reduced. Dietary items with large potassium content should be avoided.
iv. *Calcium and phosphorus:* Calcium supplements are given as calcium carbonate or acetate. Excessive

consumption of dairy products should be avoided to restrict phosphate intake.

v. *Vitamins:* Vitamins B_1, B_2, folic acid, pyridoxine and B12 are supplemented.

Hypertension

Hypertension in patients with proteinuria and glomerular filtration rate >30 ml/min/1.73 m^2 should preferably be treated with angiotensin converting enzyme inhibitors (e.g. enalapril). Beta-adrenergic blockers (atenolol) and calcium channel antagonists (nifedipine, amlodipine) are also effective agents; the latter are the preferred initial choice in CKD stage IV-V. Additional treatment with loop diuretics is beneficial in those with fluid overload. Patients with severe hypertension, uncontrolled with the above medications, may require additional treatment with clonidine or prazosin.

Anemia

Subcutaneous administration of recombinant human erythropoietin allows satisfactory increase in levels of hemoglobin. Patients should receive iron and folic acid supplements. Patients on hemodialysis should receive intravenous iron supplementation. The dose of erythropoietin should be adjusted to achieve target hemoglobin of 11–12 g/dL. Inadequate response to erythropoietin may occur due to iron deficiency, chronic infection, aluminum toxicity and severe hyperparathyroidism. Patients with hemoglobin level below 6 g/dL who are unable to afford erythropoietin, should receive leukocyte-poor, packed red cell transfusions to raise levels. Blood should be transfused slowly, since it may aggravate hypertension and heart failure.

Infections

Urinary tract and other infections should be promptly treated with effective and least toxic drugs. The dosage of most drugs requires modification (reduction of dosage and/or increase in dosing interval), depending on the severity of renal failure.

Growth

Optimization of caloric and protein intake and treatment of mineral bone disease is important. Administration of recombinant human growth hormone improves growth velocity in children with chronic renal failure. The high cost of this treatment, however, limits its use.

Mineral Bone Disease

Mineral bone disease is a serious problem in children as it occurs during the period of active growth. (Fig. 15.9). Its prevention and adequate treatment is crucial. The proximal nephron is the chief site of synthesis of 1, 25 dihydroxyvitamin D3 (calcitriol), the most potent metabolite of vitamin D. Its decreased production is an important factor in the pathogenesis of secondary hyperparathyroidism in CRF. With reduction of renal function, phosphate balance is initially maintained by its increased excretion from the normal nephrons. However, when the GFR falls below 25%, blood phosphate levels rise.

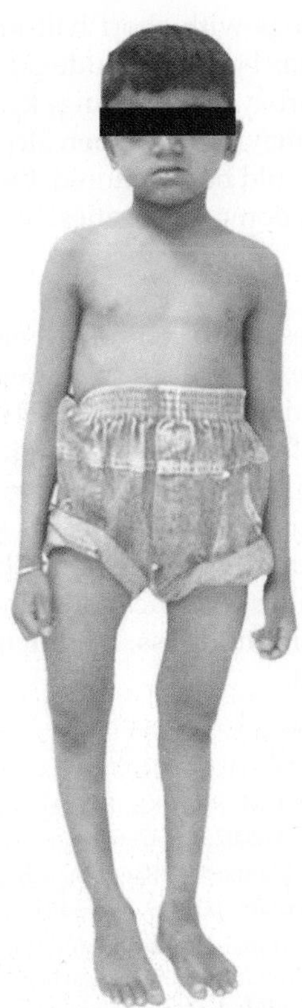

Fig. 15.9: Mineral bone disease in a 10-year-old boy with stage 5 chronic kidney disease secondary to neurogenic bladder. Note the short stature (height 108 cm), frontal bossing, chest wall and lower limb deformities

The symptoms are vague and nonspecific. Bone pain, muscle weakness, growth retardation and skeletal deformities are prominent. Blood examination shows hypocalcemia, hyperphosphatemia and raised levels of alkaline phosphatase and parathyroid hormone. X-rays reveal metaphyseal changes suggestive of rickets. Radiologic features of secondary hyperparathyroidism are initially seen in the phalanges and clavicles.

Treatment is based on dietary restriction of phosphate, and administration of phosphate binders and vitamin D. When GFR is reduced below 50%, phosphate containing dietary articles (e.g. dairy products) are restricted. Blood phosphate levels should be maintained in the normal range. Calcium carbonate or acetate, 0.5–1 g/day with meals, reduces intestinal absorption of phosphate. The renal excretion of aluminum, in children with renal failure, is poor; its accumulation may increase the risk of bone disease and aluminum-related encephalopathy. Prolonged administration of aluminum hydroxide as a phosphate binder is therefore avoided.

Vitamin D analogs with short half-life are preferred. Medications that may be used include calcitriol (20–50 ng/kg/day) or 1α-hydroxy D3 (25–50 ng/kg/day). Excessive vitamin D intake may cause hypercalcemia and hypercalciuria, which should be monitored. Osteotomy may be required to correct bony deformities.

Long-Term Care

The rate of progression of chronic renal injury is very variable. In some disorders (e.g. hemolytic uremic syndrome, crescentic GN), stage V CKD is present within few weeks or months. In others (e.g. reflux nephropathy and some forms of chronic GN), the rate of deterioration of renal function may be slow. Patients showing a rapid deterioration of renal function should be evaluated for potentially reversible complications (infection, urinary outflow obstruction, fluid loss, hypertension and use of nephrotoxic drugs).

Suggested reading

1. Chan JC, Williams DM, Roth KS. Kidney failure in infants and children. Pediatr Rev 2002; 23: 47–60.
2. Hari P, Singla IK, Mantan M, Bagga A. Chronic renal failure in children. Indian Pediatr 2003; 40: 1035–1042.
3. Hogg RJ, et al. National Kidney Foundation's Kidney Disease Outcomes Quality Initiative. Clinical practice guidelines for chronic kidney disease in children and adolescents. Pediatrics 2003; 111: 1416–1421.
4. Haycock GB. Management of acute and chronic renal failure in the newborn. Semin Neonatol 2003; 8: 325–334.

RENAL REPLACEMENT THERAPY

Preparation of a child for end stage care should be discussed in advance with the family members. The financial resources and the family support available should be addressed. The different forms of renal replacement therapy available are chronic peritoneal dialysis, hemodialysis and renal transplantation. In children with stage V CKD (ESRD), transplantation is the desired form of therapy. Social and economic reasons have precluded the availability of renal replacement therapy for children in developing countries.

Chronic Peritoneal Dialysis (PD)

Chronic PD is done through a Tenckhoff catheter tunneled through the abdominal wall into the peritoneum. Chronic PD can be done manually (ambulatory PD) or with the help of an automatic cycler (cyclic PD). The duration of dialysis is usually 10–12 hr a day during which 4–6 cycles are performed. Chronic PD is preferred to chronic hemodialysis since it is done at home, without the need for hospital visits. Patients on chronic PD have less restriction on fluid and caloric intake; control of hypertension is better and hematocrit is maintained. The success of chronic PD, however, relies upon the motivation of families to carry out the procedure.

Chronic Hemodialysis (HD)

Chronic HD is mostly carried out in the hospital setting. These children require vascular access either an arteriovenous fistula or graft, or a double lumen indwelling catheter in a central vein (e.g. internal jugular, femoral or subclavian vein). Dialysis is done for 3–4 hours/session, with a frequency of 3 sessions/week.

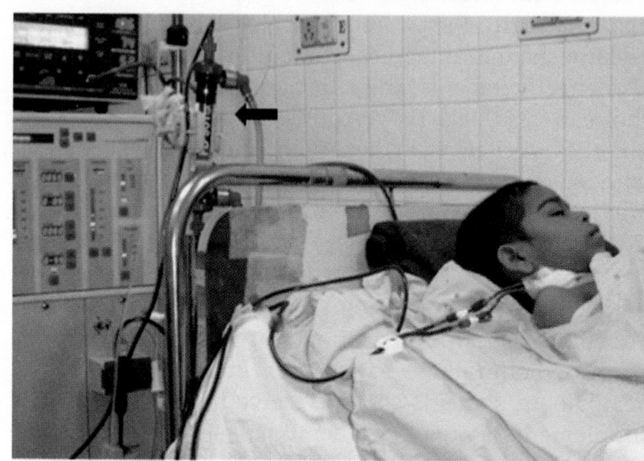

Fig. 15.10: Hemodialysis in a patient with end stage renal disease. Note the vascular access through a catheter in the internal jugular vein, hemodialysis machine and the dialyzer (solid arrow)

During a hemodialysis session, blood is circulated through an extracorporeal circuit that includes a hollow fiber dialyzer (artificial kidney) (Fig. 15.10). Anticoagulation of the circuit is achieved by systemic heparinization. The procedure requires high degree of technical expertise and need for continuous monitoring.

Renal Transplantation

The feasibility and efficacy of renal transplantation as standard therapy for ESRD in children is well established. Advances in surgical skills, availability of better immunosuppressive medications and ability to prevent and treat infections, has improved the short and long term outcome. The usual immunosuppressive therapy is a combination of a calcineurin inhibitor (cyclosporin, tacrolimus), purine synthesis inhibitor (azathioprine, mycophenolate mofetil) and prednisolone. Long-term allograft survival is better with live compared to deceased donors. Following successful renal transplantation the child can lead a normal life and resume physical activity and schooling. The allograft survival varies between 10–17 years.

Suggested reading

1. Hari P, Kanitkar M, Mantan M, Bagga A. Hemodialysis in children. Indian Pediatr 2002 39: 375–80.
2. White CT, Gowrishankar M, Feber J. Peritoneal Dialysis Working Group. Clinical practice guidelines for pediatric peritoneal dialysis. Pediatr Nephrol 2006; 21: 1059–1066.

3. Fischbach M, Edefonti A, Schröder C, Watson A; The European Pediatric Dialysis Working Group. Hemodialysis in children: general practical guidelines. Pediatr Nephrol 2005; 20: 1054–1066.
4. White CT, Trnka P, Matsell DG. Selected primary care issues and comorbidities in children who are on maintenance dialysis: a review for the pediatric nephrologist. Clin J Am Soc Nephrol 2007; 2: 847–857.

DISORDERS OF RENAL TUBULAR TRANSPORT

In comparison to glomerular diseases, tubular disorders are less common. Early and correct diagnosis is essential since specific management is possible in many cases. The diagnosis of a *primary* tubular disorder implies that there is no significant impairment of glomerular function or tubulointerstitial inflammation. A tubular disorder may be congenital or acquired and involve a single function of a tubule (renal glucosuria, nephrogenic diabetes insipidus) or multiple functions (Fanconi syndrome).

Initial Evaluation

Children with primary defects in tubular function usually present during infancy. Table 15.11 shows important clinical features of patients with such disorders. Most renal tubular disorders can be diagnosed following careful interpretation of urine and plasma biochemistry. Urine dipstick analysis may reveal glucosuria and proteinuria. Detection of low molecular weight proteinuria (e.g. retinol binding protein, β-2 microglobulin) suggests proximal tubular dysfunction. The osmolality of early morning urine sample (first urine passed on awakening) is a useful test of renal concentrating ability; a value of >700–800 mOsm/kg is normal. Levels of electrolytes, calcium, creatinine and amino acids may be measured on a random urine sample. These values are usually expressed as the solute/creatinine ratio to allow for differences in urine concentration. Blood levels of sodium, potassium, chloride, calcium, magnesium and phosphate are determined; tubular reabsorption of phosphate and other solutes can be calculated. If metabolic acidosis is detected, estimation of plasma and urine anion gap and urine pH is recommended.

Table 15.11: Features suggesting renal tubular disorder
Growth retardation, failure to thrive
Delayed motor milestones
Polyuria, polydipsia
Recurrent episodes of unexplained fever, vomiting, dehydration; episodic weakness
Rickets, bone pains
Constipation
Craving for salt and savory foods
Renal, ureteric calculi

RENAL TUBULAR ACIDOSIS (RTA)

RTA encompasses conditions characterized by a defect of renal acidification, which result in hyperchloremic metabolic acidosis and inappropriately high urine pH. The plasma anion gap [Na^+ –(Cl^- + HCO_3^-)] is in the normal range of 10–14 mEq/L. The renal function is normal or only mildly impaired. Two main forms are recognized: distal RTA (type I) and proximal RTA (type II). A third variety (type IV) distinguished by the presence of hypoaldosteronism and hyperkalemia is not common in children. Incomplete and mixed forms often occur.

Renal acidification: Depending on dietary protein intake, children produce about 1–3 mEq/kg/day of non-volatile acids. The reabsorption of filtered bicarbonate as well as excretion of acid is mediated by tubular secretion of hydrogen ions (H^+). In the proximal tubule, filtered HCO_3^- combines with H^+ to form H_2CO_3 that rapidly dissociates to H_2O and CO_2 (catalyzed by carbonic anhydrase at the brush border of the tubular basement membrane). CO_2 diffuses along its concentration gradient into the tubular cell, combining with H_2O to generate HCO_3^- that is absorbed by the peritubular capillaries. The proximal tubule reabsorbs 80–90% of the filtered HCO_3^-; the remainder is reabsorbed distally. In the distal tubule, the secreted H^+ ions combine with the major urinary buffers, sodium hydrogen phosphate (Na_2HPO_4) and ammonia (NH_3) to form NaH_2PO_4 and NH_4^+ (measured in urine as titratable acidity and ammonium ion respectively). The distal nephron generates and maintains a steep pH gradient between the blood and urine, but its capacity to secrete H^+ ions is small. Thus, even a slight increase in distal HCO_3^- delivery results in increase in urine pH. Extracellular fluid volume and potassium balance also regulate H^+ secretion and HCO_3^- reabsorption.

Distal RTA

Distal (type I) RTA is due to defective secretion of H^+ in the distal tubule. Children present with failure to thrive, polyuria and polydipsia, hypokalemic muscle weakness and rickets. Ultrasonography may show nephrocalcinosis. The condition is often sporadic, but may be inherited (dominant, recessive or X-linked). There is an association with systemic diseases (systemic lupus erythematosus, Wilson disease) and with drug toxicity (lithium, analgesics, amphotericin B).

Diagnosis: The biochemical abnormalities include hyperchloremic metabolic acidosis, hypokalemia, increased urinary excretion of calcium and decreased urinary citrate. Urinary net acid excretion (titratable acid and ammonium) is markedly reduced. Despite moderate to severe acidosis, patients cannot lower urine pH below 6. Proximal bicarbonate absorption is usually normal though younger children may occasionally show some bicarbonate wasting. Measurement of the difference between urinary and blood CO_2, during the passage of alkaline urine, is a reliable indicator of distal tubular acidification. Normally the difference is more than 20 mm Hg, provided the urine pH is >7.5. In children with distal RTA, the urine to blood CO_2 gradient is reduced below 10 mm Hg.

Treatment: Hypokalemia should be treated before correction of acidosis. Acidosis is treated by administration of sodium bicarbonate (initially 2–3 mEq/kg in divided doses); the dose of alkali can be increased until the blood bicarbonate level is normal. Treatment of acidosis reduces potassium losses and promotes growth and healing of rickets. Vitamin D supplements are not required.

Proximal (Type II) RTA and Fanconi Syndrome

Proximal RTA is due to reduced proximal tubular reabsorption of HCO_3^-, so that at normal levels of plasma HCO_3^-, marked bicarbonaturia is found. Once the plasma HCO_3^- falls below 16 mEq/L, it is mostly reabsorbed. At steady state, daily acid loads are excreted successfully. The distal acidification mechanism is intact. Thus, children with proximal RTA have less severe acidosis than distal RTA. Proximal RTA is usually a part of global proximal tubular dysfunction (Fanconi syndrome) when tubular proteinuria, aminoaciduria, glucosuria, phosphaturia and uricosuria are present in addition to bicarbonaturia.

15

Fanconi syndrome may be (i) idiopathic, or secondary to (ii) a metabolic disorder (cystinosis, galactosemia, tyrosinemia, Lowe syndrome, fructosemia, some forms of glycogen storage disease, Wilson disease and mitochondrial disorders), (iii) drugs (ifosfamide, aminoglycosides, cisplatin), (iv) toxins (cadmium, lead, mercury) and (v) tubulointerstitial nephritis.

Clinical features and diagnosis: Failure to thrive and physical retardation are the chief clinical features. Irritability, anorexia and listlessness may be present. Rickets is rare in isolated proximal RTA but common in Fanconi syndrome. Those with secondary Fanconi syndrome may also have features of the underlying disorder. The blood pH and HCO_3^- levels are low and urine pH relatively alkaline. However if the blood HCO_3^- falls below 14–16 mEq/L, urine pH falls to <5.5. Urinary calcium and citrate excretion is normal. Demonstration of a high fractional excretion of HCO_3^- (>15%), following bicarbonate infusion to raise the plasma HCO_3^- level above 22 mEq/L, is confirmatory.

Treatment: The correction of acidosis requires administration of 5–20 mEq/kg of alkali daily. Since administration of large amounts of alkali result in massive HCO_3^- wasting, it is prudent to give a modest amount of sodium bicarbonate (5–8 mEq/kg/day in divided doses) along with restriction of dietary sodium. The latter causes contraction of extracellular fluid volume and increased proximal HCO_3^- reabsorption. Administration of hydrochlorothiazide has a similar effect. Part of the alkali is replaced as potassium citrate. Children with Fanconi syndrome also need supplements of phosphate (neutral phosphate, Joulie solution). Treatment with vitamin D is necessary in children with rickets.

Cystinosis

This autosomal recessive disorder presents in infancy with features of severe Fanconi syndrome. Affected patients later show photophobia and enlarged liver and spleen; some have blond hair. Presence of cystine crystals in cornea (on slit lamp microscopy) and elevated levels of leukocyte cystine is useful in diagnosis. Most patients show progression to end stage renal failure by 10–12 yr of age. Early initiation of treatment with cysteamine may retard progression of systemic disease. Long-term complications include hypothyroidism and diabetes mellitus.

Lowe Syndrome

This X-linked condition presents within the first few months of life with Fanconi syndrome, severe rickets, ocular defects (cataract, buphthalmos, corneal degeneration, strabismus), hypotonia and developmental delay. Most children die in early childhood.

NEPHROGENIC DIABETES INSIPIDUS

Congenital nephrogenic diabetes insipidus is an X-linked (rarely autosomal recessive) disorder of water reabsorption, due to a defect in the interaction of ADH with its receptor. Absorption of water in the distal tubules and collecting ducts is significantly impaired. The usual history is of a boy who, within a few weeks of life, shows failure to thrive, excessive thirst, recurrent episodes of dehydration and unexplained fever. These infants are often suspected of having some infection and undergo extensive laboratory tests. An observant mother may notice that the infant continues to pass urine even when dehydrated. Polyuria and polydipsia are striking in older children.

Hypernatremia with low urine sodium is characteristic. The urine osmolality is inappropriately low (usually below 150–200 mOsm/kg) for the elevated plasma osmolality. Further, urine osmolality does not increase despite administration of DDAVP. This allows nephrogenic diabetes insipidus to be differentiated from deficiency of the ADH (central diabetes insipidus). The latter show normal response to DDAVP with increase in urine osmolality to more than 600–800 mOsm/kg. Treatment consists of increased fluid intake and sodium restriction. Administration of hydrochlorothiazide, alone or in combination with amiloride, reduces polyuria and leads to clinical improvement. Indomethacin may also reduce urine volume, but its use is limited beyond infancy.

RENAL GLUCOSURIA

Renal glucosuria is an autosomal recessively transmitted, isolated defect of tubular glucose transport. It is recognized by the presence of glucose in the urine, despite its normal blood levels. Glucose metabolism and other renal tubular transport mechanisms are normal. The disorder is asymptomatic and benign.

CYSTINURIA

This autosomal recessive disorder is characterized by impaired proximal tubular reabsorption of cystine and dibasic amino acids (ornithine, lysine and arginine). Supersaturation of urine with cystine crystals may lead to formation of recurrent radiopaque calculi. A high fluid intake and urinary alkalization should be ensured. Administration of penicillamine may prevent formation of calculi.

BARTTER SYNDROME

Bartter syndrome results from excessive chloride, potassium and sodium wasting in the thick ascending limb of the loop of Henle. Clinical features include failure to thrive, polyuria, polydipsia and recurrent episodes of dehydration. The neonatal form of the disease is particularly severe with maternal polyhydramnios, postnatal polyuria, dehydration, hypercalciuria and nephrocalcinosis. Patients show marked hypokalemia with high urinary potassium, hypochloremic metabolic alkalosis and increased levels of plasma renin and aldosterone. Hyperplasia of the juxtaglomerular apparatus is seen.

Bartter syndrome should be differentiated from other conditions with persistent hypokalemic metabolic alkalosis by the presence of normal blood pressure, and high urinary chloride and calcium excretion. Treatment with potassium chloride supplements is necessary. Use of prostaglandin synthase inhibitors (indomethacin 2–3 mg/kg/day or ibuprofen 20–30 mg/kg/day) is beneficial.

Suggested reading

1. Bagga A, Dillon M. Inherited disorders of sodium and water handling. In: Comprehensive Clinical Nephrology. Eds. Johnson RJ, Feehally J. Mosby, London, 2000;52.1–52.12.
2. Bagga A, Bajpai A, Menon S. Approach to renal tubular disorders. Indian J Pediatr 2005;72(9): 771–6.
3. Bagga A, Sinha A. Evaluation of renal tubular acidosis. Indian J Pediatr 2007; 74(7): 679-86.
4. Majzoub JA, Srivatsa A. Diabetes insipidus. Pediatr Endocrinol Rev 2006; 4 Suppl 1: 60–65.

UROLITHIASIS

Calculus disease of the urinary tract may affect the urinary bladder or kidneys. Symptoms include dysuria, hypogastric pain, hematuria and occasionally urinary infections. Children with a metabolic abnormality are likely to form recurrent and multiple stones. Ultrasonography detects most radiopaque and radiolucent calculi and nephrocalcinosis. High resolution computerized tomography detects even minute calculi; intravenous pyelography is useful if ureteric calculus is suspected.

Endemic Vesical Calculi

Vesical calculi are common in young boys (below 5-yr-old) in some parts of the country, e.g. Rajasthan, Andhra Pradesh and north-eastern states, having become less prevalent in most regions of the country. They are common in neighboring countries including Pakistan and Afghanistan.

These stones are usually single, and composed of ammonium acid urate and calcium oxalate. Consumption of a predominantly cereal (wheat or jowar) based, low calcium and phosphate, and high oxalate diet is related to its etiology. Recurrent diarrheal episodes may contribute by causing dehydration, and an acidic, concentrated urine. A high intake of dairy products and animal proteins has led to reduction in the prevalence of these stones. Treatment is surgical with suprapubic cystolithotomy. The risk of recurrence is very low.

Renal Calculi

These are uncommon in children. Detailed investigations should be done to determine the underlying etiology. The commonest metabolic cause is idiopathic hypercalciuria. Other causes include hyperoxaluria, distal RTA, hyperparathyroidism and cystinuria. Magnesium ammonium phosphate (struvite) calculi may occur due to recurrent UTI, often with underlying urinary obstruction. No underlying cause is found in a significant proportion of cases.

15

Stones less than 5–7 mm in size may pass spontaneously. Extracorporeal shock wave lithotripsy (ESWL) may suffice for small stones. Percutaneous nephrolithotomy may be appropriate in patients with relative contraindication for ESWL or with stones too large for lithotripsy. Ureteroscopy is useful for distal and mid ureteric calculi. Open surgery is necessary for stones more than 3 cm in size or those with associated pelviureteric junction obstruction. UTI should be treated and a large fluid intake ensured. Patients with idiopathic hypercalciuria may benefit from a low salt intake; dietary calcium restriction is not necessary. Persistent hypercalciuria is treated with oral potassium citrate, an inhibitor of crystallization. Thiazide diuretics reduce urine calcium excretion, reducing the risk of stone formation; their long-term use is, however, restricted due to side effects. Prolonged alkali supplementation is necessary in patients with distal RTA.

Suggested reading

1. Nicoletta JA, Lande MB. Medical evaluation and treatment of urolithiasis. Pediatr Clin North Am 2006; 53: 479–491.
2. Durkee CT, Balcom A. Surgical management of urolithiasis. Pediatr Clin North Am 2006; 53: 465–477.
3. Mantan M, Bagga A, Virdi VS, Menon S, Hari P. Etiology of nephrocalcinosis in northern Indian children. Pediatr Nephrol 2007; 22: 829–833.
4. Mohamed J, Riadh M, Abdellatif N. Urolithiasis in infants. Pediatr Surg Int 2007; 23: 295–299.

CONGENITAL ABNORMALITIES

Congenital abnormalities of kidney and urinary tract are common. Some are of no clinical significance; others may be symptomatic, present problems in management and account for about 25% cases of CKD in children.

Renal Agenesis, Hypoplasia

The presence of bilateral renal agenesis or hypoplasia is not compatible with life. Neonates show low set ears, flat nose, prominent epicanthic folds and small chin (Potter facies). Owing to lack of fetal urine production, there are oligohydramnios and limb anomalies. Pulmonary hypoplasia is the usual cause of mortality. Unilateral agenesis is not uncommon and usually asymptomatic; the contralateral kidney shows hypertrophy.

Renal Ectopia, Renal Fusion

An ectopic kidney may lie in the pelvis or the iliac fossa. It may be structurally normal or hypoplastic. The patient may be asymptomatic, or have abdominal discomfort or dysuria. If identical poles of both kidneys are fused, horseshoe kidney results. Patients with horseshoe kidney show vesicoureteric reflux in 30%.

Renal Dysplasia, Multicystic Kidney

Renal dysplasia implies abnormal development of renal parenchyma. Primitive ducts surrounded by connective tissue, metaplastic cartilage, poorly differentiated glomeruli and dilated tubules are present. A multicystic kidney is a large, dysplastic, non-functioning kidney containing cysts of varying sizes. No intervention is usually necessary since it shows progressive involution. The contralateral kidney and ureter may show structural anomalies or vesicoureteric reflux, which should be excluded by appropriate imaging. Bilateral total renal dysplasia is fatal in the neonatal period.

Obstructive Uropathy

Obstructive anomalies of the urinary tract are an important cause of irreversible renal damage in childhood. The common lesions include posterior urethral valves and pelviureteric junction obstruction. Chronic obstruction may result in distal renal tubular dysfunction with impaired urinary concentration and acidification, and affect vitamin D metabolism. Thus, polyuria, polydipsia, failure to thrive, refractory rickets and systemic acidosis may be present.

Pelviureteric Junction (PUJ) Obstruction

Stenosis of the PUJ may be unilateral or bilateral and leads to hydronephrosis. Obstruction is more common in patients with ectopic, malrotated or horseshoe kidney. PUJ obstruction may present as an asymptomatic flank mass or be associated with upper abdominal pain and UTI. Ultrasonography, IVP and radionuclide (DTPA) renal scan are useful in diagnosis and assessment of renal function. Once the diagnosis is confirmed, surgical treatment is necessary.

Posterior Urethral Valves

These constitute an important cause of distal urinary tract obstruction in boys. Dribbling, abnormal urinary stream, palpable bladder and recurrent UTI are the usual presenting features. The presence of severe obstruction in the urinary tract *in utero* may lead to renal dysplasia. Mild to moderate impairment of renal function may be present at birth. The diagnosis is confirmed on MCU, which shows dilated posterior urethra and valves at its junction with the anterior urethra. The bladder is enlarged and may show diverticuli and trabeculations; secondary vesicoureteric reflux is common. Endoscopic fulguration of the valves is performed as early as possible. Alternatively, temporary urinary diversion by vesicostomy or bilateral ureterostomies is necessary. Long-term follow up after surgery is necessary since a significant proportion of patients may show progressive kidney disease.

Renal Duplication

A duplex (duplicated) system is a kidney with two pyelocalyceal systems. In patients with partial or incomplete duplication, either a single or bifid ureter is present; in those with complete duplication, two ureters from the affected side empty separately into the bladder. Evaluation consists of imaging of the upper tract (ultrasonography, DTPA renal scan, intravenous pyelography) to evaluate for obstruction, and lower tract (MCU) for vesicoureteric reflux.

Meatal Stenosis

Significant narrowing of urethral meatus is rarely a cause of urinary tract obstruction. The treatment consists of meatal dilatation, failing which meatoplasty may be needed.

Phimosis

Normally up to the age of 2 years, the prepuce cannot be fully retracted because of its congenital adhesions with the glans. The diagnosis of phimosis, therefore, should be made with caution in young children. Phimosis, in infancy, may predispose to recurrent UTI.

ANTENATAL DETECTION OF URINARY TRACT ANOMALIES

Extensive use of antenatal ultrasonography has lead to increasing detection of urinary tract anomalies. On antenatal ultrasound, hydronephrosis is identified in 4–5% pregnancies. However, it is emphasized that antenatal detection of a dilated urinary tract does not always indicate anatomical obstruction. More than 80% of such neonates show normal amount of amniotic fluid and are asymptomatic at birth. These children need to be evaluated with a renal ultrasound at 4–7 days of life. Neonates showing hydronephrosis should undergo a MCU and/or DTPA renal scan to detect vesicoureteric reflux and/or urinary tract obstruction, and evaluate differential renal function. Neonates with posterior urethral valve, solitary kidney or bilateral hydronephrosis and impaired renal function require prompt management. In a majority, hydronephrosis is non-obstructive and spontaneous resolution occurs by 2–5 years of age. Most patients, therefore, require a period of waiting and close clinical and radiological follow up. Surgery is indicated in presence of symptoms (e.g. abdominal mass, recurrent UTI, hypertension) or deterioration of differential renal function.

Suggested reading

1. Indian Pediatric Nephrology Group, Indian Academy of Pediatrics. Consensus statement on management of antenatally detected hydronephrosis. Indian Pediatr 2001, 38: 1244–1251.
2. Carr MC. Prenatal management of urogenital disorders. Urol Clin North Am 2004; 31(3): 389–97.
3. Nakai H, Asanuma H, Shishido S, Kitahara S, Yasuda K. Changing concepts in urological management of the congenital anomalies of kidney and urinary tract, CAKUT. Pediatr Int 2003; 45: 634–641.
4. Becker A, Baum M. Obstructive uropathy. Early Hum Dev 2006; 82: 15–22.

HEREDITARY NEPHROPATHIES

Hereditary renal diseases are an important cause of chronic kidney disease in children and young adults. Polycystic kidney disease, Alport syndrome and nephronophthisis are relatively common (Table 15.12). In recent years, the gene loci, for many of these conditions have been identified. While improving understanding of the pathogenesis, genetic tools have enabled rapid and precise diagnosis of these conditions.

Polycystic Kidneys

The infantile form of polycystic kidney disease is inherited in an autosomal recessive manner. The kidneys are large and palpable and filled with masses of cysts. Prenatal ultrasound is a reliable screening procedure and may be performed in 'at-risk' families. The onset of hypertension and renal insufficiency is in early childhood but the prognosis is variable. Congenital hepatic fibrosis may be associated and cause portal hypertension.

The adult form of polycystic kidneys (inheritance autosomal dominant) usually manifests with episodic hematuria, hypertension and palpable kidneys during the third decade of life, but may present in childhood. Renal insufficiency develops gradually. Cysts may occur in the liver, spleen and pancreas; cardiac valvular anomalies and berry aneurysms of the cerebral arteries are associated. Cystic kidneys may occasionally be found on screening a parent or grandparent.

15

Suggested reading

1. Grünfeld JP. Congenital/inherited kidney diseases: how to identify them early and how to manage them. Clin Exp Nephrol 2005; 9: 192–194.
2. Rizk D, Chapman AB. Cystic and inherited kidney diseases. Am J Kidney Dis 2003; 42:1305–1317.
3. Niaudet P, Gubler MC. WT1 and glomerular diseases. Pediatr Nephrol 2006; 21: 1653–1660.

Table 15.12: Common inherited renal disorders

Condition	*Important features*
Alport syndrome	X-linked inheritance; mutations in gene encoding alpha subunit of collagen 4 *(COL4A1)*. Microscopic/gross hematuria, proteinuria; sensorineural deafness; ocular defects (lenticonus, cataract); progression to renal failure. *Electron microscopy:* variable thickness of glomerular basement membrane; marked attenuation to broadening and lamination.
Nephronophthisis	AR inheritance; mutations in gene encoding nephrocystin *(Neph 1, Neph 2, Neph 3)*. Polyuria, polydipsia; retinal degeneration; metabolic acidosis; anemia; progression to renal failure. Small kidneys with cysts on ultrasound, CT scans. *Histology:* tubular dilatation and atrophy, interstitial fibrosis; cysts located in collecting ducts. *Electron microscopy:* thickened, laminated tubular basement membrane.
'Finnish' congenital nephrotic syndrome	AR; mutations in gene encoding nephrin *(NPHS1)*. Congenital nephrotic syndrome (presenting first 3 months of life); failure to thrive; recurrent infections; progression to renal failure by 2–3 yr. *Histology:* microcystic dilation of proximal tubules. High levels of AFP in maternal serum and amniotic fluid enable antenatal screening.
Denys-Drash syndrome	Mutations in *WT1* gene. Congenital nephrotic syndrome; male pseudohermaphroditism; risk of bilateral Wilms' tumor. *Histology:* diffuse mesangial sclerosis.

AR autosomal recessive; AFP alpha-fetoprotein

16 Endocrine and Metabolic Disorders

GENERAL PRINCIPLES

Hormones are substances secreted by endocrine glands that act at sites away from the source of their production. Besides the classical *endocrine* action, hormones also have *paracrine* (on tissues close to the source of production) and *autocrine* (on the source of production) effects. Most endocrine disorders respond dramatically to specific treatment making their identification a desirable goal. Endocrine work-up is however resource-intensive emphasizing the need for careful patient selection and step-wise evaluation.

Source

Hormones are produced by the endocrine glands. They differ from exocrine glands, involved in secretion of mucus and enzymes, in that their secretion is released directly into the bloodstream. This allows their widespread effects. Endocrine glands are small, but play a crucial role in maintenance of body physiology and homeostasis (the adrenal gland accounts for only 0.05% of body weight, but its agenesis is incompatible with life.). The hypothalamic-pituitary axis is the master endocrine gland and regulates other endocrine glands including thyroid, adrenals, and gonads and processes like growth and water regulation.

Chemical Structure

Hormones are derivatives of amino acids (e.g. peptide hormones, glycoproteins, thyroxine and epinephrine) or cholesterol (e.g. steroid hormones, vitamin D, adrenal and gonadal steroids). Their chemical structure has significant impact on their action. The peptide hormones (pituitary hormones, parathyroid hormone – PTH, growth hormone – GH and insulin) do not bind to circulating binding proteins. This results in their rapid elimination and a short half-life. They do not cross the plasma membrane, but act on membrane receptors. The steroid hormones on the other hand bind to circulating proteins resulting in prolonged half-life. They traverse the cell membranes due to their lipophilic nature and act on intracellular receptors (Table 16.1).

Table 16.1: Comparison of peptide and steroid hormones

Features	*Peptide hormones*	*Steroid hormones*
Chemical nature	Amino acid derivative	Cholesterol derivative
Half-life	Short	Prolonged
Plasma protein binding	None	Specific protein, albumin
Receptors	Extracellular	Intracellular
Actions	Fast	Slow
Examples	GH, insulin, LH, FSH, PTH, vasopressin	Cortisol, aldosterone, estrogen, testosterone, calcitriol

Mechanism of Action

Hormone action is mediated by specific receptors. They may be extracellular (peptide hormones) or intracellular (steroid and thyroid hormones). *Extracellular receptors* have intrinsic catalytic activity (e.g. tyrosine kinase for insulin, ACTH and GH receptors) or are linked to a catalytic protein (e.g. G protein for anterior pituitary hormone receptors and PTH). Binding of hormones to these receptors activates a catalytic process (phosphorylation of tyrosine residues or activation of adenylate cyclase, phosphodiesterase or phospholipase-C) that results in production of second messengers (cyclic AMP, cyclic GMP or diacyl glycerol– DAG). These second messengers induce structural changes in other intracellular proteins culminating in the hormone effect (Fig. 16.1). Steroids and thyroxine act on *intracellular receptors*. The hormone-receptor complex then binds to the hormone response elements in the target gene resulting in regulation of transcription (Fig. 16.2). The effect of these hormones is slower than those acting through extracellular receptors (Table 16.2).

Regulation

Hormone secretion is regulated by a feedback system that includes regulatory hormones, hormone levels and hormone effects. The feedback operates at the level of the endocrine gland as well as the hypothalamic-pituitary axis.

Metabolism

Peptide hormones are rapidly inactivated by plasma enzymes resulting in a short duration of action. Steroid

Table 16.2: Comparison of intracellular and extracellular hormone receptors

Features	*Extracellular receptor*	*Intracellular receptors*
Location	Cell membrane	Cytoplasm, nucleus
Ligand	Peptide hormones	Steroids, thyroxine
Secondary effect	Tyrosine kinase, G protein	DNA binding
Mediator	cAMP, cGMP, Ca^+, DAG	Transcription regulation
Response time	Fast	Slow

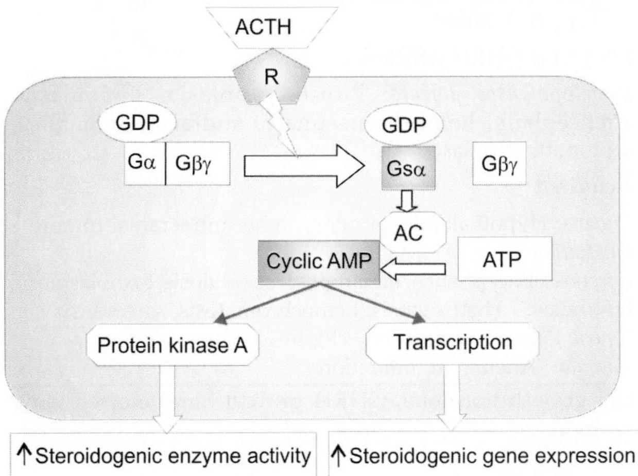

Fig.16.1: Mechanism of action of extracellular G protein coupled ACTH receptor. Note that ACTH receptor has a small extracellular and intracellular receptor. Activation of the ACTH receptor stimulates Gsα, resulting in increased intracellular cyclic AMP that stimulate steroidogenesis by activating cyclic AMP dependent kinases

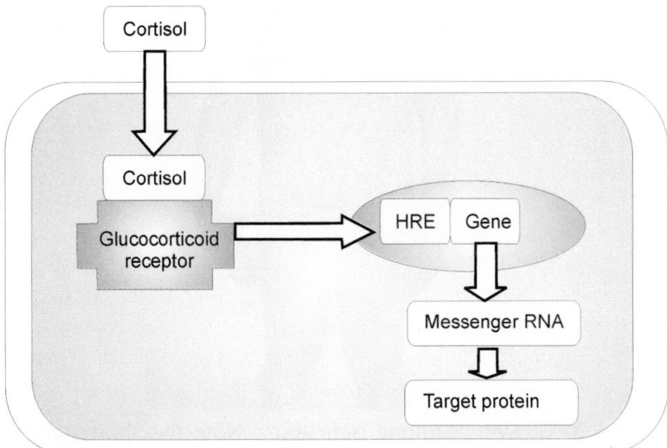

Fig. 16.2: Mechanism of action of intracellular cortisol receptor. HRE hormone response element

hormones are metabolized by the liver and excreted in the urine. Hormone metabolism is an important part of their regulation. Metabolism of hormones (e.g. androgen to estrogen, testosterone to dihydrotestosterone and calcidiol to calcitriol) is vital for their actions. Inactivation of hormones at the site of action prevents their excess effects (e.g. inactivation of cortisol by 11β-hydroxysteroid dehydrogenase prevents its action on mineralocorticoid receptor). Peripheral conversion also plays an important role in hormone functions (e.g. production of active form of thyroid hormone).

Assessment

Endocrine assessment relies on the assessment of basal hormone levels (thyroid disorders), their urinary metabolites (adrenal disorders), hormone effects (insulin-like growth factor-1 levels in GH deficiency, urinary osmolality for diabetes insipidus), stimulation tests (GH deficiency, adrenal insufficiency) and suppression tests (GH excess, Cushing syndrome). Pulsatile secretion of most hormones makes the assessment of endocrine status with a single blood test difficult in most situations. This could be overcome by pooling multiple blood samples taken over time (cortisol and gonadotropins) or by pharmacological stimulation tests (GH deficiency, delayed puberty or adrenal insufficiency). The feedback mechanism also helps in assessment of endocrine disorders. Elevated pituitary hormones in the setting of endocrine deficiency (LH and FSH with delayed puberty and ACTH with adrenal insufficiency) indicate primary organ failure, while low levels suggest a hypothalamic-pituitary dysfunction. The feedback mechanism also provides the basis for dynamic endocrine tests for diagnosis of hormone excess states (dexamethasone suppression test for Cushing syndrome, glucose suppression test for GH excess).

16

DISORDERS OF PITUITARY GLAND

The pituitary gland is believed to be the master endocrine gland that regulates other endocrine glands. Disorders of pituitary functions are implicated in a wide variety of endocrine disorders.

Physiology

The anterior and posterior parts of pituitary gland are distinct embryologically and functionally. The anterior pituitary develops from the Rathke's pouch, while posterior pituitary originates from the infundibulum, which is a downgrowth from the floor of the diencephalon. The pituitary lies in sella turcica in the sphenoid bone, and three-fourths of it is constituted by the anterior pituitary.

The principal hormones produced by the anterior pituitary are thyroid stimulating hormone (TSH), adrenocorticotropic hormone (ACTH), follicle-stimulating hormone (FSH), luteinizing hormone (LH), growth hormone (GH) and prolactin (PRL). These hormones regulate actions of adrenals (ACTH), thyroid (TSH) and gonads (LH and FSH). The secretion of anterior pituitary hormones is regulated by hypothalamic peptides (growth hormone releasing hormone—GHRH, gonadotropin releasing hormone—GnRH, corticotropin releasing hormone—CRH and thyrotropin releasing hormone—TRH) and hormones produced by the target glands. The hypothalamic tropic hormones are transported to the anterior pituitary by the hypothalamic-pituitary-hypophyseal portal system. GH has specific growth promoting action on protein synthesis, skeletal growth and intermediary metabolism. These effects are mediated through synthesis of insulin-like growth factor 1 (IGF-1). IGF-1 in turn circulates bound to binding proteins called IGFBP; the major one being IGFBP3. The levels of IGF-1 and IGFBP3 are thus surrogate markers of GH action.

Posterior pituitary hormones (arginine vasopressin—AVP and oxytocin) are secreted by neurons located in the hypothalamic nuclei. AVP (also known as the antidiuretic hormone, ADH) is the key regulator of body water and osmolality.

GROWTH HORMONE DEFICIENCY (GHD)

16

Growth hormone deficiency (GHD) may follow congenital CNS malformations (midline defects or holoprosencephaly), genetic defects (POU1FI, PROP1 and HESX1 mutations) or acquired neurological insults (neurosurgery, trauma, radiation and tumor) (Table 16.3). These children have normal growth at birth. Growth retardation is usually apparent around one year of age. Midfacial crowding, round facies, mild obesity and immature facial appearance are common (Fig. 16.3). Body proportions are normal. These children appear overweight for their height with markedly increased subcutaneous fat. The development of teeth is delayed. Other features include crowding of midfacial structures, frontal bossing, depressed nasal bridge, prominent philtrum, high pitched voice, increased skin-fold thickness, truncal obesity, single central incisor tooth and hypoplastic penis and scrotum. The facial appearance is "doll like" and these children look much younger than their actual age. Bone age is delayed. The height age is less than the bone age and chronological age. Newborns may present with severe hypoglycemic seizures and ACTH deficiency. Associated gonadotropin deficiency causes delay in sexual development. This may not be clinically evident till the age of puberty.

Resistance to growth hormone action (growth hormone insensitivity, Laron syndrome) presents with severe growth retardation and elevated baseline GH levels.

Table 16.3: Etiology of growth hormone deficiency

Congenital
Genetic defects:
Isolated GH deficiency
Type I : Autosomal recessive
Type II: Autosomal dominant
Type III: X-linked recessive
Multiple pituitary deficiencies
Type I: Autosomal recessive
Type II: X-linked
Idiopathic GHRH deficiency
Developmental defects: Pituitary aplasia, hypoplasia, anencephaly, holoprosencephaly, midfacial anomalies, septooptic dysplasia
Acquired
Tumors: Hypothalamic, pituitary, other intracranial tumors
Irradiation
Infections: Encephalitis, meningitis, tuberculosis, toxoplasmosis
Infiltration: Histiocytosis, hemochromatosis, sarcoidosis
Injury: Perinatal insult (breech), head injury, surgery
Vascular: Aneurysm, infarction

GH growth hormone, GHRH growth hormone releasing hormone

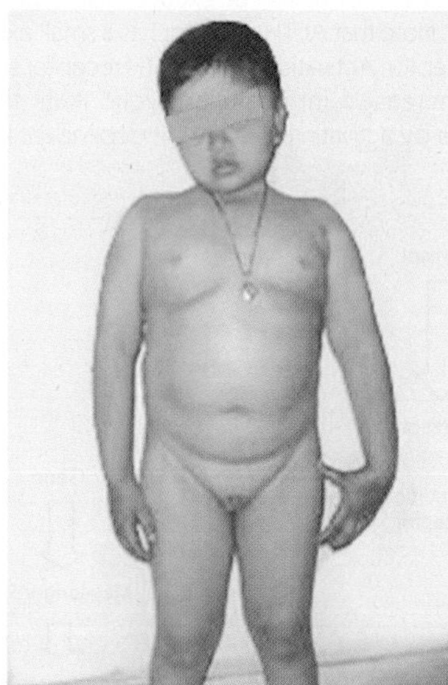

Fig. 16.3: Growth hormone deficiency. Note the short stature, immature facies, excess subcutaneous fat and micropenis

Other endocrine causes: Hypothyroidism is associated with severe growth retardation and may present with short stature alone. Children with pseudohypoparathyroidism and rickets have short stature along with the other more evident features. Prolonged insulin deficiency as in type 1 diabetes mellitus has been shown to produce severe growth retardation with hepatomegaly (Mauriac syndrome).

Evaluation

The need for evaluation of a short child is based on height and growth velocity. No work-up is required if height is more than –2 SDS (third percentile) or growth velocity is above 25th percentile. On the other hand, immediate evaluation is warranted if height SDS is less than –3 (first percentile). Children with height SDS between –2 to –3 should be followed-up. Work-up is required if growth velocity is below 25th percentile.

History: Perinatal history, birth weight and length should be recorded. History of birth asphyxia, breech presentation, neonatal hypoglycemia, and prolonged jaundice may be the early indicators of GHD. Features of chronic infections, cardiopulmonary disorders, malabsorption and raised intracranial tension should be looked for. Presence of polyuria and polydipsia suggests diabetes insipidus, diabetes mellitus and/or renal tubular acidosis. Constipation, delayed milestones, lethargy and cold intolerance are indicative of hypothyroidism. Accurate estimation of dietary recall forms an integral part of evaluation of short stature. Family history of short stature or delayed puberty may suggest the diagnosis of familial short stature (FSS) or constitutional delay of puberty and growth.

Examination: The first step in evaluation is detailed anthropometric assessment (weight, weight for height and head circumference). Weight loss is suggestive of nutritional etiology (malnutrition, systemic illness, and malabsorption) while weight is preserved in most endocrine disorders. Body proportions are helpful in identifying skeletal dysplasia. Lower segment (LS) is measured from the pubic symphysis to the feet. Upper segment (US) is obtained by subtracting it from height. The US:LS ratio is 1.7:1 at birth and decreases by 0.07–0.1 each year to reach 1:1 by 7–10 years of age. Increased US:LS ratio suggests hypothyroidism, achondroplasia (Fig. 16.4) and Turner syndrome while reduced US:LS ratio is seen in disorders like Morquio syndrome and spondyloepiphyseal dysplasia. Body proportions are normal in GHD. The clinician should look for specific features of an underlying etiology such as GHD, hypothyroidism, Turner syndrome and rickets (Table 16.4). Evaluation for dysmorphism, skeletal deformities and sexual maturity rating are essential.

Investigations: Laboratory evaluation of short stature involves step-wise application of diagnostic tests to determine the etiology (Fig. 16.5).

Step 1: The first step in investigation is to rule out common causes of short stature in the community. This involves exclusion of malnutrition, chronic systemic illnesses and recurrent infections. These could be done performing complete blood counts with erythrocyte sedimentation rate, urine and stool examinations, chest X-ray with tuberculin testing (if indicated), blood urea, creatinine, calcium, phosphorus, alkaline phosphatase, and liver and renal function tests. Investigations for malabsorption and venous blood gas for renal tubular acidosis should be performed. Estimation of skeletal maturation forms an important aspect of evaluation of short stature. This is done by comparing X-ray of left wrist with age specific norms.

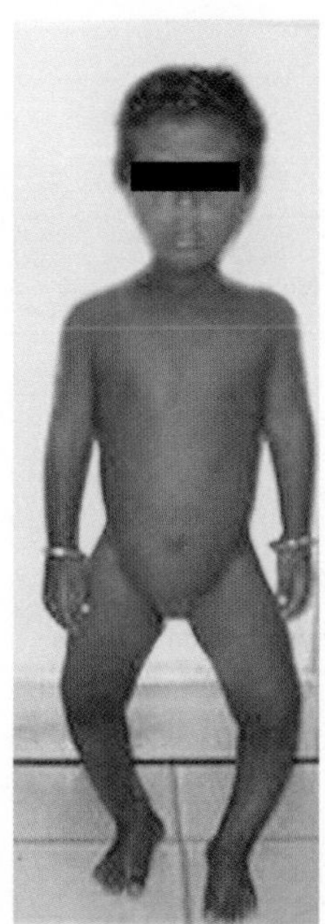

Fig. 16.4: Achondroplasia: Note the abnormal body proportions and facies

Table 16.4: Pointers to the etiology of short stature

Pointer	*Etiology*
Midline defects, micropenis	Growth hormone deficiency
Rickets	Renal failure, malabsorption, renal tubular acidosis
Pallor	Renal failure, malabsorption, nutritional anemia
Malnutrition	Protein energy malnutrition, malabsorption, celiac disease, cystic fibrosis
Obesity	Hypothyroidism, Cushing syndrome, Prader Willi syndrome
Metacarpal shortening	Turner syndrome, pseudohypoparathyroidism
Cardiac murmur	Turner syndrome, congenital heart disease
Mental retardation	Hypothyroidism, Down syndrome, Turner syndrome, pseudohypoparathyroidism

Step 2: The next step in evaluation involves evaluation for hypothyroidism, Turner syndrome and celiac disease. Turner syndrome should be excluded in all girls with short stature irrespective of clinical features. Serological tests for celiac disease are helpful. Presence of disproportion would indicate evaluation for skeletal dysplasias.

16

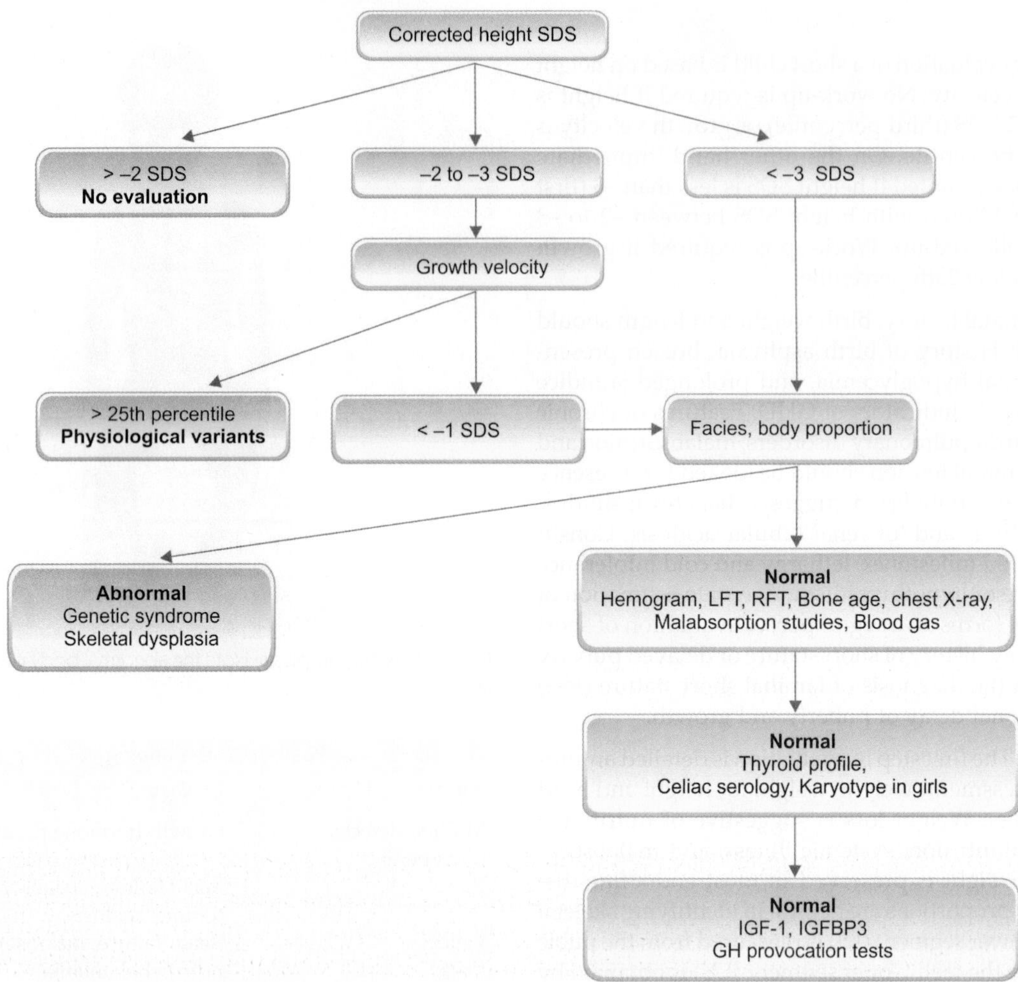

16

Fig. 16.5: Approach to a child with short stature. SDS standard deviation score; LFT liver function tests; RFT renal function tests; IGF-1 insulin-like growth factor-1, IGFBP3 IGF binding protein-3; GH growth hormone

Step 3: Evaluation for GH-IGF axis is performed only after other common causes of growth retardation have been excluded. This is important as systemic illness and hypothyroidism influence the GH-IGF axis. Random or fasting blood GH level measurements are not helpful in diagnosis of GHD due to pulsatile secretion of GH. The diagnosis of GHD requires pharmacological stimulation tests. Diagnosis of GHD is suspected when the peak level of GH is less than 10 ng/mL following stimulation. The common provocative agents used are insulin, arginine, glucagon, L dopa, and clonidine. Other tests are based on the use of physiological stimuli and include physical exercise, food intake, stress and sleep. Levels of IGF1 and IGFBP3 are helpful to diagnose GHD and Laron syndrome. GHD is associated with other pituitary hormone deficiencies and investigations should be carried out to determine deficiency of these hormones if GHD is present. CT or MRI scans of hypothalamic and pituitary regions are essential to rule out developmental or acquired CNS lesions.

Management

Management involves correction of underlying cause and provision of adequate nutrition intake.

Nonspecific: Patients should be advised high protein and calorie diet. They should be encouraged to increase physical activity. Iron and vitamin deficiencies should be corrected. Zinc supplementation (10 mg/day for 3–6 months) is effective in improving growth in idiopathic short stature.

Specific: Initiation of specific treatment is effective in restoration of growth in hypothyroidism (thyroxine), celiac disease (gluten free diet) and renal tubular acidosis (bicarbonate). Short course of testosterone should be given in boys with constitutional delay of puberty and growth. Treatment of genetic syndromes and skeletal dysplasia is extremely difficult. Bone lengthening (Ilizarov technique) has been used with variable success in these children.

Growth hormone: GH is highly effective in GHD. This can result in an increase in height by 20–30 cm. The treatment is given as daily nighttime injections (25–50 μg/kg/day)

till epiphyseal closure. The treatment is very expensive and should be started only if it could be given for at least 2 years. Growth hormone has also been recommended for Turner syndrome, chronic renal failure, small for gestational age infants, Prader Willi syndrome and idiopathic short stature.

Suggested reading

1. Lifshitz F, Botero D. Worrisome growth. In: Pediatric Endocrinology, 4th edn. Eds: Lifshitz F, Marcel Dekker, New York, 2003;1–47.
2. Rosenfeld GR, Cohen P. Disorders of growth hormone/insulin like growth factor and action. In: Pediatric Endocrinology, 2nd Edn. Eds: Sperling MA. Saunders, Philadelphia. 2002, 211–288.
3. Patel L, Clayton PE. Normal and disordered growth. In: Clinical Pediatric endocrinology, 5th edn. Eds: Brook CGD, Clayton PE, Brown RS. Blackwell Publishers, London. 2005;90–112.
4. Reiter EO, Rosenfeld RG. Normal and aberrant growth. In Williams Textbook of Endocrinology, 10th edn. Eds: PR Larsen, HM Kronenberg, S Melmed, KS Polonsky, Philadelphia: WB Saunders., 2003;1003–1114.
5. Bajpai A, Sharma J, Menon PSN (eds). Short Stature. In: Practical Pediatric Endocrinology. Jaypee Brothers Medical Publishers Pvt Ltd, New Delhi. 2003;3–8.
6. Bajpai A, Menon PSN. Insulin like growth factors axis and growth disorders. Indian J Pediatr 2006;73:67–71
7. Bajpai A, Menon PS. Growth hormone therapy. Indian J Pediatr 2005;72:139–144.

GROWTH HORMONE EXCESS

Pituitary gigantism is rare in children but may be the only clue to underlying pituitary adenoma, which may be isolated or associated with multiple endocrine involvements in the setting of multiple endocrine neoplasia or McCune Albright syndrome.

GH excess results in somatic overgrowth or gigantism. Its increased secretion after the fusion of skeletal epiphyses causes features of acromegaly. Features are coarse with prominent jaw, broad nose, enlarged tongue, bushy eyebrows, thick skin and dorsal kyphosis. Muscle weakness, bony and cartilaginous overgrowth, cardiomyopathy and pigmentation of skin may be present. Destruction of the anterior pituitary by adenoma may result in hypothyroidism and hypogonadism. Headache, visual field defects such as bitemporal hemianopsia and enlargement of the blind spot are common.

The diagnosis is based on clinical examination, serial photographs of the child, growth assessment and investigations. Skull X-ray films show enlarged sella turcica with erosion of the margins. Tufting of the phalanges and increased heel pad thickness may be present. CT or MRI scan determines the extent of the tumor. GH levels are elevated to as high as 400 ng/mL; these are not suppressed by a glucose tolerance test.

GH excess should be differentiated from *Sotos syndrome* (cerebral gigantism) characterized by large size at birth, excessive growth in early childhood, advanced height, weight and bone age. The skull is large with prominent forehead and jaw, high arched palate, hypertelorism and antimongoloid slant of the palpebral fissure. Mental retardation is present in about 85% cases, affecting expressive language, motor development and attention deficits. GH secretion and activity are normal. *Hereditary tall stature, obesity, precocious puberty, Marfan syndrome* and *lipodystrophy* should be ruled out by appropriate tests.

Medical management involves the use of long acting somatostatin analog like octreotide. GH receptor antagonist (Pegviosomant) is also proposed for treatment. Partial or complete resection of pituitary adenoma is indicated if there is evidence of raised intracranial tension.

Suggested reading

Patel L, Clayton PE. Normal and disordered growth. In: Clinical Pediatric Endocrinology, 5th edition. Eds: Brook CGD, Clayton PE, Brown RS, Blackwell Publishers, London. 2005;90–112.

DIABETES INSIPIDUS AND POLYURIA

Polyuria (urine output more than 5 ml/kg/hour or 2 L/m^2/day) is a common pediatric problem. Careful evaluation of polyuria is essential, as it may be the only manifestation of serious disease (diabetes mellitus, brain tumor, renal tubular acidosis).

Physiology

Maintenance of water balance involves regulation of urine output and thirst. Thirst is controlled by the hypothalamus under the effect of osmoreceptors. Urine output is determined by solute load, hydration status and urine concentration capacity. Increased solute load as in diabetes mellitus results in polyuria. Fluid homeostasis involves close interaction of AVP, renin-angiotensin-aldosterone system and atrial natriuretic peptide (ANP). *AVP* secreted by the hypothalamus, acts on the V2 receptors in collecting duct to increase free water resorption. This involves migration of aquaporin water channels. AVP secretion is regulated by plasma osmolality with minor effect of blood volume. The *renin-angiotensin-aldosterone system* is central to the regulation of sodium, fluid and blood pressure. The system is activated by the production of renin by the juxtaglomerular cells in response to volume depletion and low blood pressure. Renin acts on angiotensinogen to form angiotensin I. Angiotensin I is then converted by the angiotensin convertase enzyme to angiotensin II. Angiotensin II acts on adrenal cortex to increase aldosterone production and blood vessels to cause vasoconstriction. Aldosterone acts on the distal convoluted tubule and collecting duct to increase sodium and fluid resorption and potassium excretion.

Etiology

Polyuria may result from increased solute load or impaired renal concentrating capacity (Table 16.5).

Diabetes mellitus: Diabetes mellitus is an important cause of polyuria. The condition presents with polydipsia, polyphagia, recurrent infections and weight loss.

Table 16.5: Causes of polyuria
Increased fluid intake
Iatrogenic
Compulsive water drinking (psychogenic polydipsia)
Increased urinary solute excretion
Osmotic diuresis—Diabetes mellitus, mannitol treatment
Salt loss—Adrenal insufficiency, diuretics, cerebral salt wasting, aldosterone resistance
Impaired urinary concentration
Inefficient AVP action (Diabetes insipidus, DI)
Central DI (Neurogenic DI)
Genetic defects—Autosomal recessive, autosomal dominant, DIDMOAD syndrome
Malformations—Septo-optic dysplasia, holoprosencephaly, anencephaly
Neurological insults—Head trauma, neurosurgery, infection, brain death
Infiltrative disorders—Sarcoidosis, histiocytosis
CNS tumors—Craniopharyngioma, germinoma, pinealoma
Nephrogenic DI
Genetic—X linked (V2 receptor), AR, AD (aquaporin defect)
Acquired—Hypokalemia, hypercalcemia, obstructive uropathy, nephrocalcinosis
Renal disorders
Renal tubular acidosis
Bartter syndrome
Gitelman syndrome

Renal disorders: While most renal parenchymal diseases present with decreased urine output; polyuria is common in obstructive uropathy. Polyuria is often the presenting feature of tubular disorders like renal tubular acidosis (RTA), Bartter syndrome and Gitelman syndrome. These conditions are associated with severe failure to thrive and bony deformity.

Diabetes Insipidus

Inefficient AVP action (diabetes insipidus, DI) is an important cause of polyuria. The condition presents with low urine osmolality in the wake of high plasma osmolality. DI is due to decreased AVP production (central DI) or action (nephrogenic DI). Dehydration is unusual in the absence of abnormality in thirst mechanism. Infants are at a high risk of developing hypernatremic dehydration.

Central DI is commonly related to intracranial pathology (brain tumor, malformation, neurosurgery, trauma and infection). *Craniopharyngioma* presents with diabetes insipidus, growth retardation and skull calcification. A strategically located tumor in the pituitary stalk like *germinoma,* on the other hand, may be missed on neuroimaging emphasizing the need of periodic neuroimaging. *CNS malformations* such as septo-optic dysplasia and holoprosencephaly, display central DI and anterior pituitary defects. *Histiocytosis* is the commonest infiltrative disorder associated with central DI. *CNS infections* including tuberculosis have also been linked with the development of central DI.

Nephrogenic DI results from inherited or acquired resistance to AVP. Hypokalemia and hypercalcemia are important causes of nephrogenic DI. The genetic defects associated with nephrogenic DI include X-linked AVP receptor mutation and rare autosomal recessive aquaporin mutations. Acquired causes include obstructive uropathy, nephrocalcinosis and exposure to drugs (lithium and demeclocycline).

Inefficient aldosterone action: These conditions include adrenal insufficiency, isolated aldosterone deficiency or aldosterone resistance. They present with hyponatremia, hyperkalemia and dehydration. The condition may be lethal if undiagnosed. Failure to thrive is common. Pigmentation is characteristic of adrenal insufficiency. Polyuria and salt wasting in the neonatal period should prompt evaluation for congenital adrenal hyperplasia. Genital ambiguity in girls may be the only clue to diagnosis.

Excessive water drinking: The condition is extremely rare and is a diagnosis of exclusion. Low urine osmolality makes it difficult to differentiate from diabetes insipidus.

Evaluation

Subjective estimates of urine output and nocturia may suggest polyuria; they however cannot substitute measurement of 24-hour urine output (or fluid intake). Urine output in excess of 2 L/m^2/day or 5 ml/kg/hour is suggestive of polyuria. Once confirmed, the child needs work up for the etiology.

Clinical: Diabetes mellitus is suggested by features like polyphagia, recurrent infections and failure to thrive. Renal tubular acidosis is suggested by acidotic breathing, bony deformities or muscle weakness. History of head trauma, neurosurgery, exposure to radiation and features of focal deficits and raised intracranial tension should be evaluated. Neurological and fundus examination should be performed. Careful search for features of histiocytosis like ear discharge, proptosis, rash, organomegaly, lymphadenopathy, bony defects and seborrheic dermatitis is essential (Table 16.6).

Investigations: Initial investigations should include urine sugar and early morning specific gravity or osmolality. Blood gas, urea, electrolytes, calcium and creatinine should be estimated. High plasma osmolality (more than 300 mOsm/kg or serum sodium more than 145 mmol/L) and low urine osmolality (less than 300 mOsm/kg, urine specific gravity less than 1.005) is suggestive of DI, which should be classified further on the basis of response to AVP. Patients with normal plasma osmolality and low urine osmolality (less than 700 mOsm/kg) should undergo water deprivation test. Urinary osmolality more than 700 mOsm/kg (specific gravity more than 1.010) excludes DI.

Table 16.6: Pointers to diagnosis of polyuria

Feature	*Diagnosis*
Mid line defects	Central diabetes insipidus (DI)
Rickets	Renal tubular acidosis (RTA), renal failure
Failure to thrive	Nephrogenic DI, RTA, congenital adrenal hyperplasia , Bartter syndrome
Rash, seborrhea, bone defects	Histiocytosis
Hyperpigmentation	Adrenal insufficiency
Muscle weakness, neck flop	Hypokalemia (RTA, Bartter syndrome)
Genital ambiguity	Congenital adrenal hyperplasia
Mental retardation	CNS malformations, nephrogenic DI

MRI of the hypothalamic-pituitary region and anterior pituitary evaluation should be done in central DI. Evaluation of nephrogenic DI includes renal imaging and serum electrolytes.

Water deprivation test : The test is indicated in children with polyuria, low urinary osmolality and normal plasma osmolality. The aim is to increase plasma osmolality above 300 mOsm/kg (or serum sodium above 145 mmol/L) to allow opportunity for maximal renal concentration. Renal failure and renal tubular acidosis should be excluded before the test. Water deprivation test is not required in the presence of hypernatremia. The test should be done in an inpatient basis due to risk of dehydration. Water deprivation is started early in the morning. The child should be weighed and target weight loss calculated (5% of total body weight). Samples for blood sodium, potassium, sugar, osmolality and urine osmolality should be obtained. Body weight, urine output and urine and blood osmolality should be monitored hourly. The test should be stopped when urine osmolality increases above 700 mOsm/kg (or specific gravity more than 1.010; excludes DI), plasma osmolality increases above 300 mOsm/kg (or serum sodium above 145 mmol/L; target achieved) or weight loss is more than 5% (risk of dehydration). Urine osmolality below 300 mOsm/kg in the presence of plasma osmolality above 300 mOsm/kg is diagnostic of DI and should be further evaluated with response to vasopressin. Children with urine osmolality between 300–700 mOsm/kg with plasma osmolality above 300 mOsm/kg may have partial central or nephrogenic DI.

Vasopressin response test: This test is performed for differentiation of complete central DI from nephrogenic DI. Urine osmolality is measured one and four hours after vasopressin injection. An increase in urine osmolality by more than 50% of baseline levels is diagnostic of central DI while lower increase is suggestive of nephrogenic DI.

Management

Management of polyuria is guided by the underlying cause. Treatment of diabetes mellitus (insulin), adrenal insufficiency (hydrocortisone) and renal tubular acidosis (bicarbonate) is effective in reducing urine output. Behavioral therapy is recommended for psychological polydipsia.

Central DI: Central DI is managed with vasopressin analogs. Desmopressin, a vasopressin analog has increased potency and prolonged duration of action. It is given intranasal (2.5–10 mg 12 hourly) or orally (50–200 µg 12 hourly). Patients should be allowed to have at least one urine output before giving the next dose of the drug to avoid fluid overload. Patients with idiopathic DI should be followed for evolving brain tumors.

Nephrogenic DI: Hydrochlorothiazide-amiloride combination (1–2 mg/kg/day) reduces urine output by 40%. This paradoxical effect results from decreased delivery of free water to collecting ducts and distal tubule (site of AVP action) due to increased sodium absorption in the proximal tubule. Addition of indomethacin to this regimen reduces urine output to 50–70%. This should be combined with salt restriction and reduction in solute load.

Suggested reading

1. Bajpai A, Sharma J, Menon PSN (eds). Diabetes insipidus. In: Practical Pediatric Endocrinology. Jaypee Brothers Medical Publishers, New Delhi. 2003;17–23.
2. Ghirardello S, Malattia C, Scagnelli P, Maghnie M. Current Perspectives on the pathogenesis of central diabetes insipidus. J Pediatr Endocrinol Metab. 2005;18:631–45.
3. Muglia LJ. Majzoub JA. Disorders of the posterior pituitary. In: Pediatric Endocrinology, Eds: Sperling MA. WB Saunders 2002, Philadelphia, 289–322.

DISORDERS OF THYROID

Thyroid hormones play an important role in the regulation of growth, development and homeostasis. Disorders of thyroid glands are one of the most common pediatric endocrine diseases.

Physiology

The thyroid gland is formed by an invagination of endoderm of the foregut with a pouch in the floor of the pharynx migrating to the thyroid cartilage. The gland migrates from foramen cecum located at the base of tongue to its position in the neck. Thyroid hormone biosynthesis involves interaction of iodine, tyrosine, thyroglobulin and thyroid peroxidase enzyme. The first step is transport of iodine using sodium-iodine co-transporter. Iodine is then organified to monoiodotyrosine (MIT) and diiodotyrosine (DIT). This is followed by production of T4 (by coupling of 2 DIT molecules) and T3 (by coupling of one DIT and one MIT molecule). Thyroid peroxidase, the enzyme regulating this process, is the rate-limiting enzyme in thyroid hormone synthesis. This is followed by proteolysis and release of thyroid hormones in to the circulation. This process is controlled by thyroid stimulating hormone (TSH). TSH secretion is in turn under direct control of the thyrotropin-releasing hormone (TRH) released from the hypothalamus and feedback control of thyroxine. Most T3 in the circulation is produced by peripheral conversion of T4 by the enzyme, monodeiodinase. This process is stimulated in thyroid depleted states as a protective mechanism to produce more T3. T3 levels thus are the last to fall in hypothyroidism and are not a reliable indicator of the disease. TSH is the most sensitive indicator of primary hypothyroidism. Thyroid hormones bind to intracellular receptors and activate transcription factors.

Thyroid hormones are involved in the regulation of somatic and intellectual growth, intermediary metabolism and thermoregulation. There is a critical phase in the early neonatal period for the effect of thyroid hormone on mental development. This underscores the need of early diagnosis and appropriate management of congenital hypothyroidism. TSH levels increase immediately after birth resulting in increase in T3 and T4 levels, reaching their maximum by 24 hours. Their levels fall to normal in the next few weeks. TSH levels should be estimated either at birth or at day 3 for neonatal screening.

Assessment of Thyroid Function

Thyroid functions are assessed by estimation of TSH free and total T3 and T4. TSH is the most sensitive indicator of primary hypothyroidism but has no value in the diagnosis of central hypothyroidism. T4 levels are better indicator of thyroid status than T3 due to increased conversion of T4 to T3 during thyroid deplete state. Considering the wide variability in the levels of circulating thyroid binding globulin (TBG), estimation of free thyroid hormone is superior to total levels in the diagnosis of hypothyroidism. Low FT4 and TSH levels are suggestive of central hypothyroidism while high TSH levels indicate primary hypothyroidism. Repeated elevation in TSH in the presence of normal FT4 is suggestive of compensated primary hypothyroidism.

HYPOTHYROIDISM

Decreased production of thyroid hormones has significant impact on growth and development. Thus while untreated congenital hypothyroidism has devastating intellectual and developmental consequences, acquired hypothyroidism adversely affects growth and school performance.

Etiology

Hypothyroidism could be caused by defects in the hypothalamus, pituitary, thyroid gland or in the peripheral sensitivity to thyroxin (Table 16.7).

Table 16.7: Etiology of hypothyroidism

Central

- *Malformations:* Septo-optic dysplasia, holoprosencephaly
- *Genetic defects*
- *CNS insults*: Trauma, surgery, radiation, infection
- *CNS tumors:* Craniopharyngioma, germinoma

Primary

- *Dysgenesis:* Aplasia, dysplasia, ectopic
- *Enzyme defects*: Trapping, organification, thyroglobulin
- *Iodine deficiency:* Endemic goiter
- *Autoimmune thyroiditis*: Hashimoto's thyroiditis, polyglandular autoimmune syndrome types I, II and III·
- *Ablation of thyroid:* Surgery, radiation, infection
- *Goitrogens*: Thiocyanates, thionamides, lithium, amiodarone
- *Transient causes*: Transplacental passage of antibody, drugs, goitrogens
- *Systemic disease*: Cystinosis, histiocytosis

Peripheral

- Resistance to thyroxine

Primary hypothyroidism: Defects in thyroid hormone synthesis, disordered development or destruction of thyroid gland are the causes of primary hypothyroidism. Iodine deficiency is the commonest cause of hypothyroidism in certain parts of India. In certain endemic iodine deficient areas, the incidence of congenital hypothyroidism is significantly higher compared to nonendemic regions. Thyroid dysgenesis is the most common cause of congenital hypothyroidism in nonendemic areas (75% of all cases). The disorder encompasses a spectrum ranging from complete agenesis, partial agenesis and ectopic thyroid. As most of these disorders are sporadic, no genetic association has been observed. Increased incidence of thyroid dysgenesis is noted in Down syndrome. Biosynthetic defects include disorders affecting iodine transport, peroxidation, thyroglobulin synthesis and deiodination. *Pendred syndrome*, a disorder of the pendrin gene, is associated with decreased intracellular transport of iodine and deafness. Thyroid enlargement is common and takes the form of smooth rounded colloid goiter. Transient congenital hypothyroidism may occur following transplacental passage of TSH receptor blocking antibodies, iodine exposure and treatment with drugs like amiodarone.

Autoimmune thyroiditis is the most common cause of acquired hypothyroidism. The disorder is more common in girls and presents with subtle clinical features. Short stature may be the only manifestation. Goiter is often nodular and firm in contradistinction to the soft and uniform goiter in patients with dyshormonogenesis. Thyroid peroxidase and thyroglobulin antibodies are usually present. Autoimmune thyroiditis may be associated with other autoimmune endocrinopathies like adrenal insufficiency, type 1 diabetes mellitus and hypoparathyroidism.

The association with type 1 DM is in particular important to identify, as 30% of newly diagnosed children with type 1 DM having anti-thyroid antibodies and 10% having biochemical features of hypothyroidism.

Central hypothyroidism: Central hypothyroidism is caused by defects in the hypothalamic-pituitary axis. These disorders are characterized by low TSH levels and are frequently associated with other anterior pituitary hormone deficiencies. CNS malformations and genetic defects of the hypothalamic-pituitary region can cause these disorders in the neonatal period. Acquired causes include head trauma, neuro-surgery, radiation exposure, tumors and CNS infections. Isolated TSH deficiency is extremely rare.

Thyroid hormone resistance: Features of hypothyroidism in the presence of elevated thyroid hormone levels characterize this disorder of resistance to thyroid hormones. The resistance could be at the level of the pituitary, peripheral tissue or both providing a spectrum of clinical manifestations.

Congenital Hypothyroidism

Congenital hypothyroidism is an important preventable cause of mental retardation, deafness and short stature. Iodine deficiency, dysgenesis and defects in thyroid hormone biosynthesis are the common causes of congenital hypothyroidism. Congenital hypothyroidism may rarely be a result of hypothalamic-pituitary dysfunction, TSH receptor blocking antibodies and intake of maternal antithyroid drugs.

Clinical Features

Features of congenital hypothyroidism are nonspecific and difficult to identify in the neonatal period. These features become prominent with increasing age; the window period for neurological intervention has however lapsed in most of these patients by this time. This underlines the need for neonatal screening. Clinical manifestations include hoarse cry, facial puffiness, umbilical hernia, hypotonia, mottling of skin and lethargy (Fig. 16.6). Prolonged jaundice, constipation and unexplained hypothermia may also be indicators of hypothyroidism. Open posterior fontanel is an important indicator of congenital hypothyroidism (Table 16.8).

Evaluation

Maternal thyroid disease or ingestion of antithyroid medications should be enquired. Family history of hypothyroidism suggests dyshormonogenesis, while recurrent transient hypothyroidism indicates maternal TSH receptor antibody related disease. Residence in iodine deficient area may provide a clue to the diagnosis of iodine deficiency. Goiter should prompt evaluation for transplacental passage of antithyroid drugs or disorders of thyroid hormone biosynthesis. Hypoglycemia, micropenis and midline facial defects are pointers to hypothalamic causes.

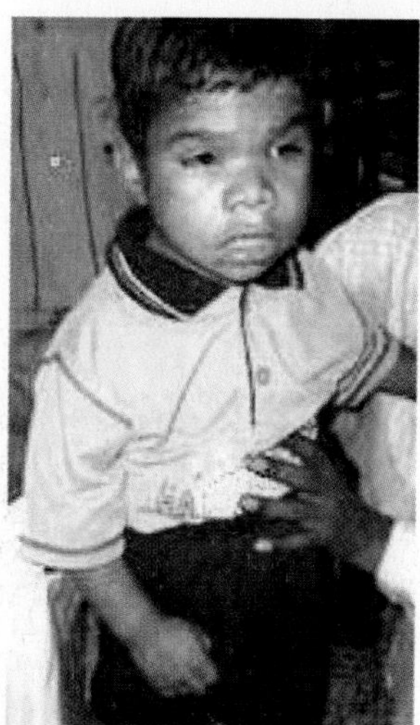

Fig. 16.6: Congenital hypothyroidism: Note the characteristic facial features

Table 16.8: Clinical features of hypothyroidism

Congenital	*Acquired*
Open posterior fontanel	Growth retardation
Umbilical hernia	Delayed skeletal maturation
Edematous, characteristic facies	Delayed dental development
Constipation	Delayed puberty
Pallor	Myopathy
Hypothermia	Enlarged sella
Large tongue	Pseudotumor cerebri
Rough dry skin	
Hypotonia	
Large abdomen	

Investigations should include radionuclide uptake, ultrasound, antithyroid antibodies and 24 hour urine iodine. Children with low TSH levels should be worked up for other pituitary defects. Radiotracer uptake study with radioactive iodine or technetium should be done as soon as the diagnosis of primary congenital hypothyroidism has been established (Fig 16.7). Children with no radioactive tracer uptake should be subjected to ultrasound examination for the site and size of thyroid gland. Thyroid dysgenesis should be diagnosed if no thyroid tissue is visualized on ultrasound. Children with absent radiotracer uptake but normal thyroid on ultrasound could be suffering from defects in iodine transport, TSH receptor defects or transplacental passage of TSH blocking antibody. Increased radioactive tracer uptake is indicative of iodine deficiency or dyshormonogenesis (Table 16.9).

Management

Thyroid replacement should be started immediately after diagnosis. In central hypothyroidism cortisol replacement

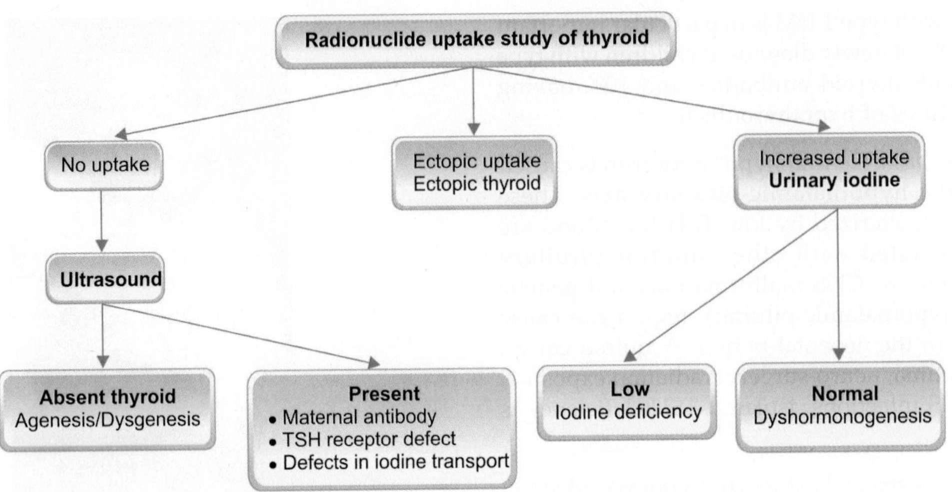

Fig. 16.7: Approach to a child with congenital hypothyroidism

Table 16.9: Comparison of different forms of primary congenital hypothyroidism

Type	*Goiter*	*Radioactive iodine uptake*	*Urine iodine*	*Ultrasound thyroid*	*Diagnostic investigation*
Dysgenesis	No	No	Normal	Absent	Scan
Ectopic	No	Ectopic	Normal	Absent	Scan
Iodine deficiency	Yes	High	Low	Eutopic	Urine iodine
TSHRAb	No	No	Normal	Eutopic	Antibody
Enzyme defects	Yes	Normal	Normal	Eutopic	Perchlorate discharge

TSHRAb antibody to TSH receptor

should precede thyroid replacement as it could precipitate adrenal insufficiency. Thyroxine (T4) should be initiated in a dose of 10–15 µg/kg/day. T4 and TSH levels are expected to normalize over one week and one month respectively with this treatment. The drug should be given as tablets as liquid preparations are unreliable. Follow-up should be done monthly during infancy, at every 3 months between 1 and 3 years, and six monthly thereafter. FT4 and TSH should be measured at each visit. Thyroxine dose should be adjusted to achieve FT4 levels in the upper normal range for the age. Lifelong thyroid replacement is required in most cases. Thyroid replacement should be stopped for one month at the age of 3 years in suspected transient congenital hypothyroidism. Treatment may be discontinued in the absence of any abnormality on investigations and normal levels of thyroid hormones.

Outcome: Outcome is universally poor in children with congenital hypothyroidism who have been diagnosed beyond the neonatal period. Mental retardation and short stature are common sequels. Early diagnosis and treatment following neonatal screening has resulted in normal intellectual outcomes.

Acquired Hypothyroidism

Acquired hypothyroidism is most commonly caused by autoimmune destruction of thyroid as a part of chronic lymphocytic thyroiditis (Hashimoto's thyroiditis). Rarely congenital abnormalities like thyroid dysgenesis or an inborn error of thyroid hormone synthesis may present in older children and at adolescence. Iodine deficiency and goitrogens are other causes of primary hypothyroidism in older children. Secondary hypothyroidism due to combined hypothalamic-pituitary defects could be a manifestation of CNS insults or tumors.

Clinical Features

Feature of acquired hypothyroidism are subtle compared to congenital hypothyroidism. Short stature may be the only manifestation. Cold intolerance, lethargy, constipation, delay in dentition and poor school performance may indicate hypothyroidism. All children with unexplained mental retardation and short stature should be evaluated for hypothyroidism. Most patients with hypothyroidism have delayed puberty; however, uncontrolled longstanding hypothyroidism may trigger precocious puberty. Goiter is common in iodine deficiency, chronic lymphocytic thyroiditis or dyshormonogenesis. Hypothyroidism has been associated with Down syndrome, Turner syndrome, celiac disease and type 1 DM. All children with these disorders should be periodically screened for hypothyroidism even in the absence of symptoms.

Evaluation

Severe short stature and mental retardation point towards missed congenital hypothyroidism. Round uniform smooth goiter is suggestive of iodine deficiency or disorder of thyroid hormone synthesis; firm nodular goiter indicates autoimmune thyroiditis. Family history of acquired hypothyroidism is suggestive of autoimmune thyroiditis. Children with central hypothyroidism should be evaluated with pituitary function tests and MRI of the hypothalamic-pituitary region. Antibodies to thyroid peroxidase enzyme (anti-TPO) and thyroglobulin (anti-TBG) should be estimated in acquired primary hypothyroidism. Patients with no evidence of thyroid autoimmunity should be worked up for other causes of hypothyroidism by radionuclide scan, ultrasound examination and urinary iodine excretion.

Management

Treatment of acquired hypothyroidism should be gradual. A dose of 100 μg/m^2/day is recommended (Table 16.10). Initial treatment should be started at 25–50% of these doses with gradual build up every 3–4 weeks as required. The drug should be given empty stomach at morning. Feeds should be withheld for 30 minutes to avoid interference with the absorption of the drug. Follow-up should be done every three months during the first two years of therapy and six monthly thereafter. The doses should be modified to maintain TSH levels in the normal range. TSH levels should be estimated during routine visit, in the presence of features of hypo or hyper-thyroidism or six weeks after modification of dose. Annual estimation of bone age should be done. Children with nongoitrous hypothyroidism need lifelong treatment. A trial of discontinuation of thyroid hormone may be considered in patients with goitrous hypothyroidism after regression of the goiter. TSH levels should be repeated six weeks later. Patients with elevated TSH levels should be restarted on thyroid hormone and would require lifelong treatment.

Table 16.10: Recommended dose schedule of thyroxine

Age	*Thyroxine dose* μg/kg/day
Neonatal period	10–15
1–6 months	6–10
1–5 years	4–6
5–12 years	3–5
12–18 years	2–3
> 18 years	1–2

Screening for Congenital Hypothyroidism

Difficulty in early identification of congenital hypothyroidism and the disastrous consequences of delayed diagnosis have led to neonatal screening for hypothyroidism. These screening programs use dried blood sample collected at the postnatal age of 2 to 4 days. Primary TSH approach is the most commonly used strategy. This has higher sensitivity compared to T4 based approach. *Primary TSH approach* does not identify central hypothyroidism. *T4 first approach* can identify these children, but has the disadvantage of missing cases with compensated hypothyroidism. Overall TSH first approach appears to be superior to T4 first approach (Table 16.11). Thyroid functions should be repeated if TSH levels are above 20 mU/L. Confirmation of hypothyroidism should be followed by etiological investigations (thyroid scan and ultrasound). Thyroid hormone replacement should be started as soon as these investigations have been performed. Neonatal screening has significantly improved intellectual outcome in congenital hypothyroidism with IQ scores similar to general population.

Table 16.11: Strategies for neonatal thyroid screening

Feature	*TSH first*	*T4 first*
Initial investigation	TSH	T4
Cut-off for evaluation	> 20 mU/L	< 84 μg/dL
Back-up investigation	TSH	T4
False positive	High	Low
False negative	Low	High
Detection of compensated hypothyroidism	Yes	No
TBG deficiency	Yes	No
Thyroid hormone resistance	Yes	No
Central hypothyroidism	No	Yes

TBG Thyroid binding globulin

Goiter

Goiter refers to the enlargement of the thyroid gland. From a clinical standpoint thyromegaly is diagnosed when the lateral lobe of the thyroid is larger than the terminal phalanx of the thumb of the child.

Etiology

Goiter may be congenital or acquired, sporadic or endemic. Goiter may be associated with diminished, normal or increased thyroid function (Table 16.12). Thyroid enlargement may represent increase in size in response to compensatory TSH secretion (hypothyroidism), infiltration (autoimmune thyroiditis, neoplastic or hemochromatosis), or presence of TSH receptor stimulatory antibody (Graves disease). Important causes of congenital goiter include maternal antithyroid medications, dyshormonogenesis and iodine deficiency. Autoimmune thyroiditis is

Table 16.12: Causes of goiter
Physiological
• Puberty goiter
Pathological
• Inflammatory—Acute suppurative thyroiditis, subacute thyroiditis
• Infiltration—Autoimmune thyroiditis, neoplastic infiltration, hemochromatosis
• Increased TSH levels—Dyshormonogenesis, iodine deficiency, unilateral agenesis
• TSH stimulating antibody—Graves disease
• Colloid goiter.

the most common cause in childhood followed by iodine deficiency, dyshormonogenesis and Graves disease. Subtle defects in thyroid hormone synthesis or mild iodine deficiency may result in mild goiter during pubertal growth spurt. Nontoxic diffuse goiter also known as simple goiter, colloid goiter or adolescent goiter is an acquired thyroid enlargement with normal thyroid function not due to an inflammatory or neoplastic process. It is found exclusively in girls (95%) usually around puberty (Fig. 16.8). Clinically it presents as a painless thyroid enlargement, firm in consistency, occasionally asymmetrical or nodular. Differential diagnosis includes chronic lymphocytic thyroiditis, diffuse nodular goiter, benign adenoma, thyroid cyst and occasionally a carcinoma. Histological examination is normal showing variable follicular size, dense colloid with flat epithelium.

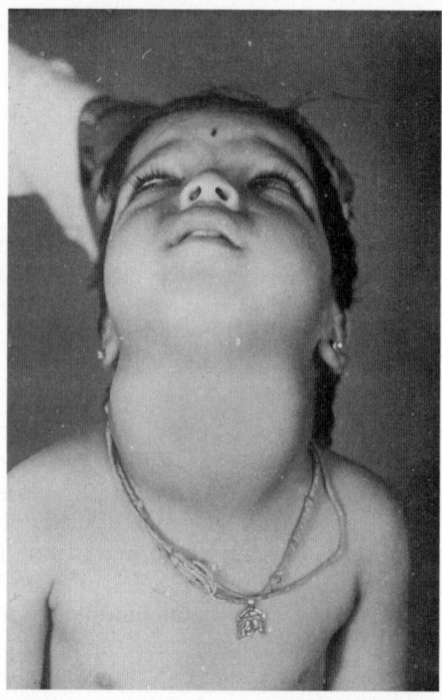

Fig. 16.8: Diffuse goiter in a child secondary to dyshormonogenesis

Evaluation

During clinical evaluation goiter is usually classified into diffuse and nodular goiter. Either form can be produced by autoimmune thyroiditis and colloid goiter. An acutely painful thyroid enlargement is usually due to hemorrhage or active inflammation, whereas a firm goiter is characteristic of chronic lymphocytic thyroiditis. Multiple nodular goiter may be seen in chronic lymphocytic thyroiditis, iodine deficiency and colloid goiter. Isolated enlargement of one lobe indicates hemiagenesis. A well-circumscribed nodule is usually due to a benign cyst. A single firm or hard painless irregular nodule is suggestive of malignancy. Diffuse goiter in the newborn may be due to Graves' disease, dyshormonogenesis or goitrogenic drugs. Investigations should include thyroid function tests. Anti-TPO and TGA antibodies should be measured to identify autoimmune thyroiditis. Positive antibodies indicate a risk of hypothyroidism even if the thyroid functions are normal. Iodine deficiency should be excluded with estimation of urinary iodine excretion. Ultrasound and fine needle aspiration should be performed if no clue to etiology is identified.

Management

Treatment should be directed by the cause (antithyroid medications in Graves disease, thyroxine in hypothyroidism). Children with autoimmune thyroiditis should be followed with annual thyroid function tests. Trial of thyroxine in a dose of 100–200 µg daily should be given in children with "physiological goiter." This produces complete regression in about 30% of cases by two years. Surgery should be avoided unless the goiter is large enough to cause respiratory embarrassment.

Iodine Deficiency Disorders

The term iodine deficiency disorders (IDD) refers to the wide spectrum of effects of iodine deficiency on growth and development. It includes endemic goiter, endemic cretinism, impaired mental function in children and adults with goiter and increased stillbirths and perinatal and infant mortality. Evidence is now available that these conditions can be prevented by correction of iodine deficiency. Endemic goiter is present when the prevalence in a defined population exceeds 10%. Endemic goiter is graded by the method of WHO (Table 16.13). Screening of neonatal hypothyroidism has also been suggested as a method for ascertaining the presence and significance of an endemic disease. Estimates of iodine intake are usually derived from 24 hour urinary iodine excretion values or urinary iodine concentration expressed in relation to creatinine concentration as given in Table 16.14.

Clinical Features

Endemic goiter does not differ from nontoxic diffuse sporadic goiter and the diagnosis is established by epidemiologic criteria. Usually TSH is elevated with low T4 and T3 levels.

Table 16.13: Estimation of thyroid size by palpation	
Stage 0	No goiter
Stage 1A	Goiter detectable only by palpation and not visible even when the neck is fully extended.
Stage 1B	Goiter palpable but visible only when the neck is fully extended (this stage also includes nodular glands even if not goitrous).
Stage 2	Goiter visible when the neck is in normal position; palpation not needed for diagnosis.
Stage 3	Very large goiter, which can be recognized at a considerable distance.

Table 16.14: Classification of severity of iodine deficiency	
Grade I	Mean daily urinary excretion of more than 50 μg but less than 100 μg iodine per 24 hr, per gm of creatinine or per liter of urine. At this level goiter will be rare.
Grade II	Mean daily excretion between 25–50 μg per 24 hrs, per gm of creatinine or per liter of urine. At this level goiter is frequent with nodular goiter and hypothyroidism of varying degrees.
Grade III	Mean daily excretion below 25 μg per 24 hrs, per gm of creatinine or per liter of urine. Goiter will be frequent and cretinism is very common at this level

Endemic cretinism is a disorder associated with endemic goiter and severe iodine deficiency with characteristic clinical features, which include deafmutism, squint, mental retardation and characteristic spastic or rigid neuromotor disorder. Two types of endemic cretinism are described. The neurological cretinism is characterized by deaf-mutism, squint, proximal spasticity and rigidity more in the lower extremities, disorders of stance and gait with preservation of vegetative functions, occasional signs of cerebellar or oculomotor disturbance and severe mental deficiency. Myxedematous cretinism is characterized by retarded psychomotor development, severe short stature, coarse facial features and myxedema without deafmutism. The pathogenesis of endemic cretinism is poorly understood. Iodine deficiency is also associated with poor school performance in children and recurrent pregnancy loss in women.

Prevention and Control

Iodine deficiency disorders are best prevented as treatment is usually ineffective. Iodinated salt or iodized oil are highly efficacious in preventing iodine deficiency. Goiters while on treatment may shrink with appearance of nodules. Treatment of endemic cretinism may eliminate signs of hypothyroidism but neuromotor and intellectual deficiency are irreversible. Surgical removal of large goiters is useful in airway obstruction and for cosmetic reasons.

The National Goiter Control Program of the Ministry of Health in India began in 1962 with the establishment of salt iodination plants. The program is directed towards control of iodine deficiency disorders and working to ensure that only iodized salt will be used in India. The recommended daily intake of iodine is 40–120 μg for children up to the age of 10; 150 μg for older children and adults and an additional 25 and 50 μg during pregnancy and lactation respectively. Based on an assumption of a mean intake of salt of 5 gm/day, the recommended level of iodination is one part of iodine in 25,000 to 50,000 parts of salt.

HYPERTHYROIDISM

Hyperthyroidism is uncommon in children. It is most commonly seen in young girls, caused by Graves disease (Table 16.15).

Table 16.15: Etiology of hyperthyroidism
Infancy
Transplacental passage of thyroid antibodies
TSH receptor activating mutation
After infancy
Graves disease (TSH receptor stimulating antibody)
Release of preformed thyroid hormone - Subacute thyroiditis
Toxic thyroid nodule, toxic multinodular goiter
Iatrogenic
Pituitary resistance to T3

The condition should be suspected in children with weight loss with increased appetite, tremors, diarrhea, warm extremities, increased sweating and anxiety. Inability to concentrate, personality changes, mood instability and poor school performance are common. The diagnosis is confirmed by the demonstration of elevated serum free T4 and T3 levels. Frequently serum T4 levels may remain normal with elevated serum T3 (T3 toxicosis). Clinical examination reveals firm homogeneous goiter. Eye signs are common and are related to sympathetic overactivity (lid lag, ophthalmoplegia, absence of wrinkling) or autoimmune infiltration (chemosis, proptosis). Tachycardia, cardiac arrhythmia and high output cardiac failure may occur.

The presence of goiter, infiltrative eye signs and hyperthyroidism is suggestive of Graves disease. Absence of goiter should raise the possibility of transient hyperthyroidism as part of autoimmune thyroiditis. TSH levels are usually undetectable in Graves disease. Ultrasonography, nuclear scan and RAIU are helpful in diagnosing toxic nodule or diffuse goiter.

Antithyroid drugs are ineffective in the acute phase due to significant lag period in their onset of action. Treatment with propylthiouracil (5 mg/kg/day) is preferred to methimazole (0.5 mg/kg/day) in the acute stage. Beta blockers (propranolol 2 mg/kg/day in two divided dose) are effective in amelioration of sympathetic symptoms. Iodinated contrast (idopate 0.001 μg/kg/day) and Lugol's iodine (5% iodine and 10% potassium iodide; 126 mg/ml iodine, 1 drop 8 hourly) are effective in reversal of features of hyperthyroidism. Prednisolone (1–2 mg/kg/day) inhibits peripheral conversion of T4 to T3 and is useful in treatment of hyperthyroid storm. Cardiac failure refractory to these measures requires treatment with digitalis.

Surgery and radioiodine ablation should be considered in patients showing failure of medical management. Patients with large or toxic nodular goiter require partial or total thyroidectomy. Radioiodine (I^{131}) is now increasingly used in the management.

Congenital hyperthyroidism: One percent of babies born to mothers with Graves disease show fetal thyrotoxicosis and cardiac failure. Management includes maternal antithyroid drugs and digitalis. Presentation usually occurs within the first week of life but may be delayed if mother is on antithyroid medications or has concomitant TSH receptor blocking antibody. Treatment should include antithyroid drugs, propranolol and corticosteroids. The condition is self-limiting and resolves over 3–6 months.

DISORDERS OF CALCIUM METABOLISM

Calcium plays an important role in the regulation of neurotransmission, muscular contractility, cardiac function and hormone signaling. Disorders of calcium homeostasis present as acute emergency as well as a chronic disorder.

16

Physiology

Calcium homeostasis involves interaction of gastrointestinal absorption, bone resorption and renal excretion. Most body calcium (99%) is stored in the bone and is in constant equilibrium with serum calcium. Regulation of bone resorption is responsible for acute calcium homeostasis while renal excretion and gastrointestinal absorption regulates chronic calcium status. Parathyroid hormone (PTH), vitamin D and calcitonin are the key regulators of calcium metabolism. *Calcium sensing receptor* present in the parathyroid gland and kidneys senses serum calcium levels. Reduced action of the receptor in the presence of low serum calcium levels results in increased PTH secretion and inhibition of renal calcium excretion. *PTH* increases serum calcium by stimulating bone resorption (osteoblast), calcitriol production (proximal tubule) and renal calcium resorption (distal tubule). PTH also increases phosphate excretion resulting in hypophosphatemia. *Calcitriol* is the only hormone that regulates calcium absorption. Calcitriol is formed by activation of vitamin D in the liver (25-hydroxylation) and kidney (1-hydroxylation). Sunlight is the major source of vitamin D with minor contribution from dietary sources. 1α-hydroxylase enzyme in the kidneys is the rate limiting step of calcitriol synthesis. The activity of the enzyme is affected by serum calcium, PTH and vitamin D levels. *Calcitonin*, secreted by the parafollicular cells of thyroid in response to elevated calcium levels, lowers serum calcium levels by decreasing bone resorption and increasing urinary calcium excretion.

HYPOCALCEMIA

Hypocalcemia (total calcium lower than 8 mg/dL) is an important metabolic condition. Estimation of ionic calcium is important for confirmation of hypocalcemia (ionic calcium less than 1.1 mmol/L). Empirical formula for calculation of ionic calcium may be used if ionic levels are not available.

$$\text{Ionized Ca} = \text{Total Ca} - 0.8 \times (\text{albumin g/dL} - 4)$$

Clinical Features

In the neonatal period, subtle clinical features like lethargy, jitteriness and poor feeding are characteristic of hypocalcemia. Seizures are common and hypocalcemia is the commonest biochemical abnormality associated with neonatal seizures. In the postneonatal period, the commonest presentation is with tetany (simultaneous contraction of groups of muscles). This is most commonly observed in hands (adduction of thumbs along with extension of the proximal interphalangeal joints and flexion of distal interphalangeal joints) and feet (flexion and internal rotation of lower limbs) resulting in carpopedal spasm. In milder cases, latent tetany can be detected by tests of neuromuscular excitability. Tapping of facial nerve at the angle of jaw results in contraction of facial muscles (Chvostek sign). Inflating blood pressure cuff above the systolic blood pressure for more than 5 minutes triggers spasm of the hand muscles (Trousseau sign). Severe hypocalcemia presents with laryngeal spasm and cardiac failure. Hypocalcemia should be considered in children with seizures, dilated cardiomyopathy and unexplained stridor. The diagnosis is confirmed by the demonstration of prolonged QT interval on ECG (Q_oT_c more than 0.2 seconds).

$$Q_oT_c = Q_oT \div \sqrt{RR}$$

(Q_oT = Interval from beginning of Q wave to beginning of T wave; RR = RR interval)

Etiology

Hypocalcemia may be caused by chelation of calcium or inefficient PTH or vitamin D (Table 16.16) action.

PTH related: Inefficient PTH action caused by decreased production (hypoparathyroidism) or action (pseudohypoparathyroidism) is an important cause of hypocalcemia. These disorders are characterized by *high phosphate levels* due to impaired phosphaturic action of PTH. Hypoparathyroidism may occur as part of congenital malformation (isolated or genetic syndromes) or acquired destruction of the parathyroid glands (autoimmune, infiltration or surgery).

Autoimmune hypoparathyroidism is the most common form in older children and frequently associated with

Table 16.16: Etiology of hypocalcemia

PTH deficiency (Hypoparathyroidism)
Aplasia: DiGeorge syndrome
Autoimmune destruction: Polyglandular autoimmune disorders I and II
Infiltration: Wilson disease, hemochromatosis, thalassemia
Transient: Hypomagnesemia, maternal hyperparathyroidism, post-surgery
PTH resistance (Pseudohypoparathyroidism)
Vitamin D deficiency
Nutritional: Poor intake, malabsorption
1α-hydroxylase deficiency: Renal failure, VDDR I
Calcitriol resistance: VDDR II
Increased inactivation: Phenytoin, phenobarbitone
Chelation
Phosphate load
Tumor lyses
Rhabdomyolyis
Top feeds

VDDR: Vitamin D dependent rickets

autoimmune polyendocrinopathy type 1. DiGeorge syndrome characterized by abnormal development of third and fourth pharyngeal pouches, is caused by deletion of part of chromosome 22q. This results in maldevelopment of thymus (resulting in T cell immunodeficiency), parathyroid (resulting in hypoparathyroidism), heart (resulting in conotruncal defects) and face (abnormal facies).

Hypomagnesemia is an important cause of transient hypoparathyroidism and should be excluded in children with refractory hypocalcemia.

PTH resistance (pseudohypoparathyroidism, PHP), is caused by inactivating mutation in the gene encoding for stimulatory subunit of G protein (Gsα). This presents with clinical features of hypoparathyroidism in the wake of elevated PTH levels. PHP may be associated with the phenotype of Albright's hereditary osteodystrophy (AHO) such as round facies, brachydactyly, short stature, obesity, short fourth and fifth metacarpals (brachymetacarpia), subcutaneous calcifications and various bony deformities.

Vitamin D related: Vitamin D deficiency (nutritional, malabsorption), decreased 1α-hydroxylase action (renal failure, vitamin D dependent rickets - VDDR I), increased inactivation of vitamin D (antiepileptic drugs) and calcitriol resistance (VDDR II) are associated with hypocalcemia. Phosphate levels are low due to secondary hyperparathyroidism. *Vitamin D deficiency* is the most common cause of hypocalcemia in children. The condition usually presents in infancy or adolescence. Rickets may be absent. Maternal vitamin D deficiency is common in India and results in reduced calcium and vitamin D stores in children. These infants develop hypocalcemia during periods of rapid bone growth (4–8 weeks of life). *VDDR* presents with early onset severe hypocalcemia and rickets.

Increased chelation: Increased calcium binding results in reduction of ionic calcium and features of hypocalcemia. This is most commonly related to *high phosphate* levels (renal failure or release of intracellular phosphate due to hemolysis, tumor lysis or rhabdomyolyis). Increased phosphate levels in cow's milk and commercial formula is an important cause of neonatal hypocalcemia. *Metabolic or respiratory alkalosis* increases albumin binding of calcium resulting in hypocalcemia.

Evaluation

Evaluation is directed towards identification of etiology and assessment of the severity of illness.

Clinical: Adequacy of airway, breathing and circulation should be assessed. Detailed history of the age of onset, presenting features, frequency of episodes of hypocalcemia and family history should be obtained. Neonates should be screened for prematurity, birth asphyxia, maternal hyperparathyroidism and initiation of top feeds. History suggestive of renal failure, liver disease, malnutrition, decreased exposure to sunlight indicates vitamin D related causes. Congestive cardiac failure, recurrent infections and abnormal facies are suggestive of DiGeorge syndrome.

Investigations: Initial evaluation should include serum phosphate levels, renal and liver function tests and serum alkaline phosphatase (Table 16.17, Fig. 16.9). Phosphate regulation is dependent on PTH and inefficient PTH action results in hyperphosphatemia. Hypocalcemia due to decreased vitamin D action is associated with secondary hyperparathyroidism and low phosphate levels. Thus hypocalcemia with hyperphosphatemia in the absence of phosphate load (exogenous or tissue lysis) and normal renal function suggests parathyroid insufficiency. Hypomagnesemia should be considered in patients with refractory hypocalcemia and normal or low phosphate levels. 25-hydroxyvitamin D levels should be measured in children with rickets to identify vitamin D deficiency. Therapeutic trial to vitamin D may be used if these levels are not available. No response to vitamin D should prompt evaluation for renal failure, renal tubular acidosis, liver disease and malabsorption. Normal work-up for these conditions is suggestive of vitamin D dependent rickets.

Management

When the clinical picture is suggestive of hypocalcemia and tests are not available, parenteral calcium should be administered (2 mL/kg intravenously over 5–10 minutes) after obtaining blood sample for calcium. Calcium gluconate (5% 9 mg calcium per mL) is the preparation of choice. Care should be taken to administer the drug slowly (to avoid cardiac effects) and avoid extravasation (to prevent skin necrosis). Parenteral calcium should be

Table 16.17: Laboratory features of common causes of hypocalcemia

Disorder	*Phosphate*	*Alkaline phosphatase*	*25-hydroxyvitamin D*	*PTH*
Vitamin D deficiency	Low, normal	High	Low	High
Renal failure	High	High	Normal	High
Phosphate load	High	Normal	Normal	High
Hypoparathyroidism	High	Normal	Normal	Low
Pseudohypoparathyroidism	High	Normal	Normal	High
Hypomagnesemia	Low, normal	Normal	Normal	Low

PTH: Parathormone

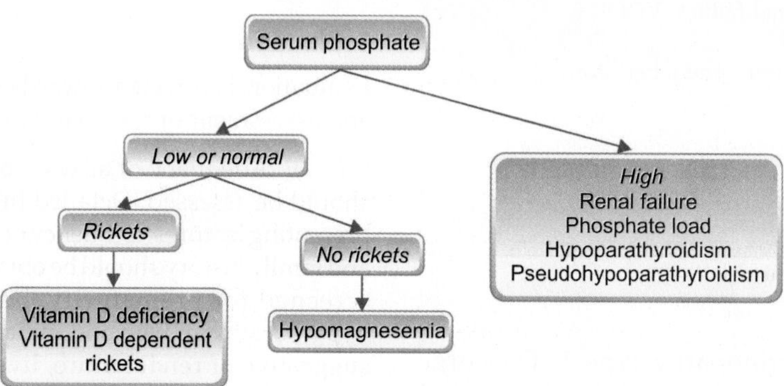

Fig. 16.9: Evaluation of a child with hypocalcemia. Investigation include estimates of blood levels of phosphate, creatinine, magnesium and parathormone. Levels of vitamin D metabolites may also require to be determined

16

started at a dose of 80 mg/kg/day and should be gradually tapered over two days. Oral calcium carbonate should be started from day 2. Short course activated vitamin D (calcitriol or 1α-vitamin D, 20–40 ng/kg/day in three divided doses for 2 days) should be given to children with vitamin D deficiency and acute hypocalcemia. This should be combined with high dose vitamin D (300,000– 600,000 IU) to replenish body stores of the vitamin. Long term management for PTH defective states includes activated vitamin D (30–60 ng/kg/day) and calcium (50 mg/kg/day) in the form of calcium carbonate. VDDR is managed with activated vitamin D and calcium phosphate. Higher doses of vitamin D may be required in patients with VDDR II.

HYPERCALCEMIA

Hypercalcemia (serum calcium more than 11 mg/dL) is rare in children. Its causes include increased bone resorption (hyperparathyroidism, malignancy and immobilization) or excessive vitamin D action (iatrogenic excess; increased 1α-hydroxylase activity).

Hyperparathyroidism is the commonest cause of chronic hypercalcemia in children. Homozygous inactivating mutations of the calcium sensing receptor present with severe neonatal hyperparathyroidism. Parathyroid adenoma is rare before the age of 10 years. Rarely, hypercalcemia may be associated with other conditions, e.g. William syndrome (supravalvular aortic stenosis, abnormal facies) or hypophosphatasia (inactivating mutation of alkaline phosphatase). Vitamin D related hypercalcemia most commonly occurs in patients with overdose of vitamin D. Increased 1α-hydroxylase activity may occur in patients with granulomatous diseases (tuberculosis, sarcoidosis) or fat necrosis.

Clinical features are often nonspecific, including muscular weakness, anorexia, nausea, vomiting, constipation, polydipsia and polyuria. Ectopic calcification in the kidney, basal ganglia and skin are common. Bony deformities and pathological fractures may be present. Infants present with failure to thrive, poor feeding, hypotonia and seizures. Serum total and ionized calcium levels are elevated with low levels of phosphate. Hyperparathyroidism is associated with elevated levels of parathormone (PTH).

Treatment of acute hypercalcemia involves high fluid intake followed by frusemide (1 mg/kg). Bisphosphonates and antiresorptive agents are indicated if there is no response to these measures. Hemodialysis may be required in refractory cases. Surgical exploration is indicated in all cases of hyperparathyroidism. The glands should be carefully inspected and adenoma, if present, should be removed. Short course of glucocorticoids (prednisolone 2 mg/kg/day for 3 weeks) is indicated in children with iatrogenic vitamin D excess or increased 1α-alpha hydroxylase action (fat necrosis or sarcoidosis).

DISORDERS OF ADRENAL GLANDS

The adrenal cortex produces important hormones involved in the regulation of fluid and electrolyte homeostasis, glucose regulation and response to stress.

Physiology

Adrenal cortex produces three important groups of hormones—the glucocorticoids, mineralocorticoids and androgens. The outermost zona glomerulosa synthesizes aldosterone, while the zona reticularis and fasciculata synthesize glucocorticoids (cortisol) and androgens (dehydroepiandrosterone—DHEA, and androstenedione). The process of steroidogenesis involves conversion of cholesterol to steroid hormones through a series of enzymatic processes. Cholesterol is transferred into the mitochondria in a process mediated by the steroidogenic acute regulatory protein (StAR), an ACTH-dependent protein. The most clinically relevant step in steroidogenesis is 21-hydroxylation of progesterone and 17-hydroxyprogesterone (17OHP) to deoxicorticosterone (DOC) and 11-deoxicorticosterone (11DOC) respectively. This is mediated by the enzyme 21-hydroxylase (P450c21) and is crucial for the production of cortisol and aldosterone.

Cortisol, the major glucocorticoid hormone has an important role in intermediary metabolism causing increased blood glucose levels and enhanced catabolism of proteins and lipids. *Aldosterone* acts on distal renal tubules and collecting ducts of kidneys to promote sodium and fluid reabsorption. Aldosterone deficiency causes urinary salt wasting resulting in salt wasting crisis. Hyponatremia, hyperkalemia and metabolic acidosis are characteristic. *Adrenal androgens* are necessary for the development of pubic and axillary hair.

Adrenocorticotropic hormone (ACTH), a polypeptide secreted by the anterior pituitary, is the principle regulator of glucocorticoid and androgen synthesis. Intravascular volume, serum potassium levels and renin-angiotensin system are the chief regulators of aldosterone synthesis. ACTH has only a minor role in aldosterone regulation. ACTH deficiency is therefore not associated with salt wasting crisis. ACTH secretion is stimulated by hypothalamic CRH and suppressed by cortisol as part of feedback loop.

ADRENOCORTICAL HYPERFUNCTION AND CUSHING SYNDROME

Hyperfunction of the adrenal cortex may be associated with excess glucocorticoid, mineralocorticoid, androgen or estrogen production. The most common disorder of adrenocortical hyperfunction is Cushing syndrome, to describe features caused by prolonged glucocorticoid excess. The term Cushing disease refers to hypercortisolism caused by an ACTH-producing pituitary tumor.

Cushing Syndrome

Classic features of Cushing syndrome such as central obesity, striae, moon facies and buffalo hump are rare in children (Fig. 16.10). Growth failure and obesity are common; other features include hypertension, hirsutism, delayed puberty, behavioral problems, bone pain and muscle weakness.

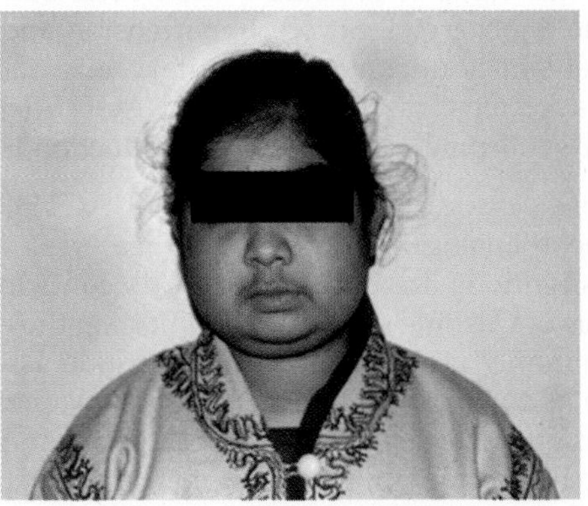

Fig. 16.10: Cushing disease secondary to pituitary adenoma: Note the moon face and hypertrichosis over forehead and upper lip

Cushing syndrome may be caused by increased endogenous production or exogenous administration (Table 16.18). Prolonged steroid treatment is the commonest cause of childhood Cushing syndrome. Increased adrenal glucocorticoid production may be related to increased ACTH levels or represent autonomous adrenal hyperfunction. Adrenal pathology is more likely in young children, while pituitary causes are common after puberty. Ectopic ACTH production is rare.

16

Table 16.18: Etiology of Cushing syndrome
ACTH dependent causes
Hypothalamic lesions: Increased CRH production Pituitary lesions: Microadenoma, macroadenoma Ectopic lesions: Neuroblastoma, carcinoid tumor, Wilms tumor
ACTH independent causes
Adrenal tumor: Carcinoma, adenoma Pigmented nodular hyperplasia McCune Albright syndrome
Exogenous administration
Glucocorticoids: Oral, parenteral, topical, inhaled ACTH

ACTH-independent causes: Autonomous adrenal production is the most common cause of Cushing syndrome in young children and may be due to adrenal adenoma, carcinoma or nodular hyperplasia. Adrenal adenomas almost always secrete cortisol with minimal secretion of mineralocorticoids or sex steroids, while carcinomas tend to secrete excess cortisol, mineralocorticoids and androgens. The likelihood of adrenal carcinoma is higher in children with early age at onset, rapid progression, concomitant hyperandrogenism and a large abdominal mass.

ACTH-dependent causes: Increased pituitary ACTH production is the chief cause of endogenous Cushing syndrome. Pigmentation due to increased melanocyte stimulating hormone is observed. Severe hypertension and hyperandrogenism is uncommon. Pituitary microadenoma accounts for most cases of childhood ACTH-dependent Cushing syndrome. Ectopic ACTH production is rare.

Exogenous causes: Prolonged intake of ACTH, hydrocortisone or analogs results in similar features.

Investigations are directed towards confirming the diagnosis of Cushing syndrome and finding the etiology. The commonly used screening tests include assessment of diurnal cortisol rhythm, overnight dexamethasone suppression test and urine free cortisol (Table 16.19). Loss of diurnal rhythm is the earliest marker of hypercortisolism. Estimation of morning and evening cortisol has been used for screening of Cushing syndrome. Individual variation in cortisol levels limits the diagnostic value of this test. The estimation of midnight cortisol, the time of physiological nadir of cortisol, is a useful screening test for Cushing syndrome. Overnight dexamethasone suppression test involves estimation of cortisol levels after a single midnight dose of dexamethasone (0.3 mg/m^2; maximum dose 1 mg). Lack of suppression of cortisol levels to less than 5 μg/dL favors the diagnosis of Cushing syndrome. 24-hr urine free cortisol is a useful screening test; levels >75 μg/m^2/day are highly suggestive. Low dose dexamethasone suppression test is commonly used for confirmation of the diagnosis. This involves measurement of serum cortisol after eight doses of oral dexamethasone (5 μg/kg per dose, every six hours for two days or 1.25 mg/m^2/day divided into four doses given over two days). Serum cortisol levels >5 μg/dL is diagnostic of Cushing syndrome.

The most important part of evaluation of a child with Cushing syndrome is to differentiate ACTH-dependent causes from autonomous adrenal steroid production (Table 16.20). ACTH levels differentiate ACTH-independent (ACTH levels <5 pg/mL) from ACTH-dependent conditions (ACTH levels >15 pg/mL). Ectopic ACTH production should be suspected in children with extremely high ACTH levels (>100 pg/mL). High dose dexamethasone suppression test is based on the principle that high doses of this agent suppress ACTH production in individuals with pituitary lesions but not in those with ectopic ACTH production. The test involves estimation of cortisol levels after eight doses of dexamethasone (20 μg/kg/dose every 6 hours for 2 days or 3.75 mg/m^2/day divided into four doses given over two days).

Adrenal tumors in children are usually large and identifiable on ultrasound. Size greater than 10 cm, vascular invasion, loss of capsule and elevated metabolites (dehydroepiandrosterone sulphate, androstenedione and 17-OHP) are suggestive of carcinoma. Magnetic resonance imaging of the hypothalamic-pituitary region should be performed in children with ACTH-dependent Cushing syndrome. Inferior petrosal sinus sampling is the test for identifying the source of ACTH production and should be performed in children with ACTH-dependent Cushing syndrome with normal neuroimaging.

Resection of adrenal lesion is recommended for adrenal adenoma and carcinoma. Prolonged cortisol excess causes suppression of the normal contralateral adrenal gland. This mandates close monitoring for adrenal insufficiency

Table 16.19: Screening tests for Cushing syndrome

Test	*Sensitivity*	*Specificity*	*Cut-off level*	*Comments*
Morning cortisol	Low	Low	>10 μg/dL	Not recommended
Overnight dexamethasone suppression test	High	Low	>5 μg/dL	Screening test
Urine free cortisol	High	High	>75 μg/m^2/day	Screening test*
Low dose dexamethasone suppression test	High	High	>5 μg/dL	Diagnostic test

* Diagnostic of Cushing syndrome if levels greater than 3 to 4 times the normal range

Table 16.20: Laboratory findings of common causes of Cushing syndrome

Disorder	*UFC*	*HDDST*	*ACTH*	*CRH test*
Adrenal lesion	High	Not suppressed	Low	Negative
Pituitary lesion				
Microadenoma	High	Suppressed	High	Positive
Macroadenoma	High	Not suppressed	High	Positive
Ectopic ACTH	High	Not suppressed	High	Negative
Exogenous	Low	Not suppressed	Low	Negative

UFC – 24-hour urine free cortisol, HDDST- High dose dexamethasone suppression test, ACTH- Adrenocorticotropic hormone, CRH- Corticotrophin releasing hormone in the perioperative period. Adrenal carcinoma is highly malignant and has a high rate of recurrence. Pigmented nodular hyperplasia should be treated with bilateral adrenalectomy. Trans-sphenoidal resection of pituitary adenoma is recommended for Cushing disease.

Medical management of Cushing syndrome with inhibitors of steroidogenesis (ketoconazole, aminogluthemide, cyproheptadine, metyrapone, mitotane) has been tried with variable results.

ALDOSTERONE EXCESS

Primary hyperaldosteronism due to increased adrenal aldosterone production is extremely rare. Secondary hyperaldosteronism results from factors that activate renin–angiotensin system.

Primary hyperaldosteronism may be caused by diffuse hyperplasia or adenoma. *Glucocorticoid-remediable aldosteronism* (GRA), a genetic disorder involving switch of Cyp11 and Cyp11AS gene, is characterized by regulation of aldosterone secretion by ACTH resulting in hyperaldosteronism. Primary hyperaldosteronism should be differentiated from secondary hyperaldosteronism (renal failure, congestive cardiac failure, liver disease and nephrotic syndrome) and apparent mineralocorticoid excess (Liddle syndrome, deficiencies of 11β-hydroxysteroid dehydrogenase, and congenital adrenal hyperplasia due to deficiency of 11β-hydroxylase and 17α-hydroxylase) (Table 16.21).

Table 16.21: Etiology of hyperaldosteronism
Primary hyperaldosteronism
Adenoma, hyperplasia Glucocorticoid remediable hyperaldosteronism
Secondary hyperaldosteronism
Renal artery stenosis, renin secreting tumor Cardiac failure, nephrotic syndrome, liver disease
Apparent mineralocorticoid excess
Liddle syndrome Congenital adrenal hyperplasia, 11β-hydroxysteroid dehydrogenase

Hyperaldosteronism is associated with fluid and sodium retention along with increased urinary loss of potassium. The most common clinical features of primary hyperaldosteronism are hypertension and hypokalemic alkalosis.

Hypokalemic alkalosis in a child with low renin hypertension should prompt evaluation for true or apparent aldosterone excess. High aldosterone level in this setting is suggestive of primary hyperaldosteronism or GRA. The conditions may be differentiated by dexamethasone suppression test. Decrease in aldosterone levels and resolution of clinical and laboratory features after dexamethasone suppression suggests GRA; no effect is seen in primary hyperaldosteronism. Diagnosis of primary hyperaldosteronism should be confirmed by adrenal imaging.

Hyperaldosteronism should be managed with salt restriction and anti-aldosterone agents, spironolactone or eplerenone. Physiological hydrocortisone replacement suppresses ACTH secretion in GRA resulting in resolution of hyperaldosteronism and hypertension. Surgery is the treatment of choice for adrenal adenoma.

PHEOCHROMOCYTOMA

Pheochromocytoma is a catecholamine-secreting tumor, arising from the chromaffin cells of adrenal medulla. It can also arise from the abdominal sympathetic chain, periadrenal area, or in the thoracic cavity. The condition is extremely rare in children and co-exits with other syndromes such as neurofibromatosis, von Hippel Lindau disease and multiple endocrine neoplasia type II.

Excessive secretion of catecholamines results in hypertension, which is usually sustained and occasionally paroxysmal. The clinical symptoms include headache, palpitation, pallor, sweating, nausea, vomiting, visual disturbances and occasionally convulsions. The diagnosis should be considered only after other common causes of childhood hypertension like renal parenchymal disorders, renal artery stenosis and coarctation of aorta have been excluded. Diagnosis is established by demonstration of increased urinary excretion of catecholamines and their derivatives. Ultrasound, CT scan, MRI scan, and ^{123}I MIBG (metaiodiobenzylguanidine) scintigraphy are used for localization. Often the tumors are multiple.

Surgery is the treatment of choice. Transabdominal exploration of all the sites with removal of tumors is advocated. Preoperative alpha blockade is needed and earlier phenoxybenzamine and prazosin were used. Recently calcium channel blocking agents have been used successfully.

ADRENAL INSUFFICIENCY

Adrenal insufficiency may be related to adrenal loss (primary adrenal insufficiency; autoimmune destruction, infection, hemorrhage), decreased ACTH production (secondary adrenal insufficiency) or ACTH resistance. Autoimmune adrenal dysfunction is the commonest cause of primary adrenal failure (Addison disease). Autoimmune adrenal failure is often associated with autoimmune polyendocrinopathies type 1 and 2. Infections like tuberculosis and HIV are associated with primary adrenal failure. Adrenal hemorrhage in the setting of meningococcal and other bacterial infections (Waterhouse-Friderichsen syndrome) is an important cause of insufficiency. Congenital adrenal hypoplasia and steroidogenic defects (StAR, 21-hydroxylase and 3β-hydroxysteroid dehydrogenase deficiencies) present with adrenal insufficiency in the neonatal period. Secondary adrenal insufficiency is caused by congenital malformations (holoprosencephaly, midline defects) genetic defects or acquired insult (neurosurgery, tumor, radiation). This is usually associated with other anterior pituitary hormone deficiency as well. Mineralocorticoid function is preserved and salt wasting is not observed. Prolonged steroid treatment is associated with suppression of the hypothalamic-pituitary axis resulting in adrenal insufficiency after discontinuation of medications.

Defects in steroid synthesis and congenital adrenal hypoplasia manifest in the early neonatal period with polyuria, failure to thrive, recurrent vomiting and shock. Acquired adrenal insufficiency presents with slowly progressive lethargy, vomiting, salt craving, fatigue, postural hypotension, fasting hypoglycemia and episodes of shock during severe illness. Adrenal insufficiency is manifest only after 90% of adrenal is damaged. The clinico-biochemical picture of shock, hyponatremia, hyperkalemia, and hemoconcentration is characteristic of acute adrenal insufficiency and warrants immediate steroid replacement. Primary adrenal insufficiency is characterized by hyperpigmentation due to elevated levels of MSH. Hyperpigmentation is present in sun-exposed areas as elbows and palmar creases and areas that are normally hyperpigmented such as areola and genitalia.

All patients suspected to have adrenal insufficiency should have urgent serum electrolytes and blood sugar test. Basal levels of cortisol are low but can be in the normal range. Elevated plasma renin activity (PRA) indicates mineralocorticoid deficiency. ACTH stimulation test (cortisol estimation 60 minutes after 0.25 mg of ACTH injection IM) is the best test for adrenocortical reserve. Serum cortisol levels lower than 18 μg/dl are suggestive of adrenal insufficiency. The next step in evaluation of adrenal insufficiency is estimation of ACTH levels. Elevated ACTH levels suggest primary adrenal pathology while low levels points towards pituitary defect. Further evaluation of primary adrenal insufficiency includes abdominal CT scan, estimation of anti-adrenal antibodies and workup for tuberculosis.

The initial management of salt wasting crisis includes correction of shock by fluid boluses. Hydrocortisone is given immediately at a dose of 50 mg/m^2 followed by 100 mg/m^2/day. Frequent monitoring of hemodynamic parameters, urine output and serum electrolytes are required. Once the child is hemodynamically stable, hydrocortisone can be tapered to the physiological dose (10 mg/m^2/day). Fludrocortisone acetate (0.1 mg/day) should be added once the hydrocortisone dose is less than 50 mg/m^2/day. Long-term management of adrenal insufficiency requires lifelong replacement of glucocorticoids and mineralocorticoids. Parents should be educated about the need of increasing dose during periods of stress. The dose of glucocorticoid should be increased 2–3 times in conditions of minor stress (fever and mild infection) and 4–5 times in severe stress (severe infection or surgery). These doses should continue throughout the period of stress. Patients with secondary adrenal insufficiency require lower dose of glucocorticoids (6–10 mg/m^2/day); mineralocorticoid replacement is not necessary.

CONGENITAL ADRENAL HYPERPLASIA

Congenital adrenal hyperplasia (CAH), a group of autosomal recessive defects in steroid synthesis, is characterized by deficiency of adrenocortical hormones on one hand and excess of steroid precursors on the other (Fig 16.11). CAH is the commonest adrenal disorder in childhood.

21-hydroxylase Deficiency

21-hydroxylase deficiency is the commonest form of CAH accounting for over 90% of all cases. This disorder is associated with diminished synthesis of the cortisol and aldosterone. Low cortisol levels stimulate ACTH synthesis. Elevated ACTH level causes accumulation of steroid precursors (DHEA, androstenedione and 17OHP). There is wide variation in presentation of 21-hydroxylase deficiency ranging from acute life threatening salt wasting crises to virilization and premature adrenarche. The disease forms a spectrum of presentation ranging from severe form presenting in the neonatal period with salt wasting crisis to milder form presenting with virilization alone to mild hyperandrogenism in late childhood.

Salt wasting (SW) form: These patients are the most severely affected and present in the neonatal period with virilization and salt wasting. Diagnosis is often missed in boys as they lack specific clinical features. They present after second week of life with failure to thrive, polyuria, hyperpigmentation, and shock. Early diagnosis is mandatory to prevent mortality. 21-hydroxylase deficiency should be suspected in neonates with ambiguous genitalia, polyuria, shock, recurrent vomiting and features of sepsis with negative septic screen. The diagnosis should be confirmed immediately by hormonal assay. If these are not available, the child should be managed empirically in the lines of adrenal insufficiency.

Simple virilizing (SV) form: A subset of patients with 21-hydroxylase deficiency (25%) synthesize enough aldosterone to prevent adrenal crises. These patients have features of androgen excess in the form of virilization in girls and peripheral precocious puberty in boys (Fig. 16.12).

Non-classic (NC) form: This disorder is associated with partial 21-hydroxylase deficiency. Cortisol and aldosterone levels are normal. Clinical manifestations are related to mild hyperandrogenism which presents with hirsutism, acne and menstrual irregularity.

Diagnosis

Diagnosis of salt washing form is established by demonstration of extreme elevation of 17OHP levels

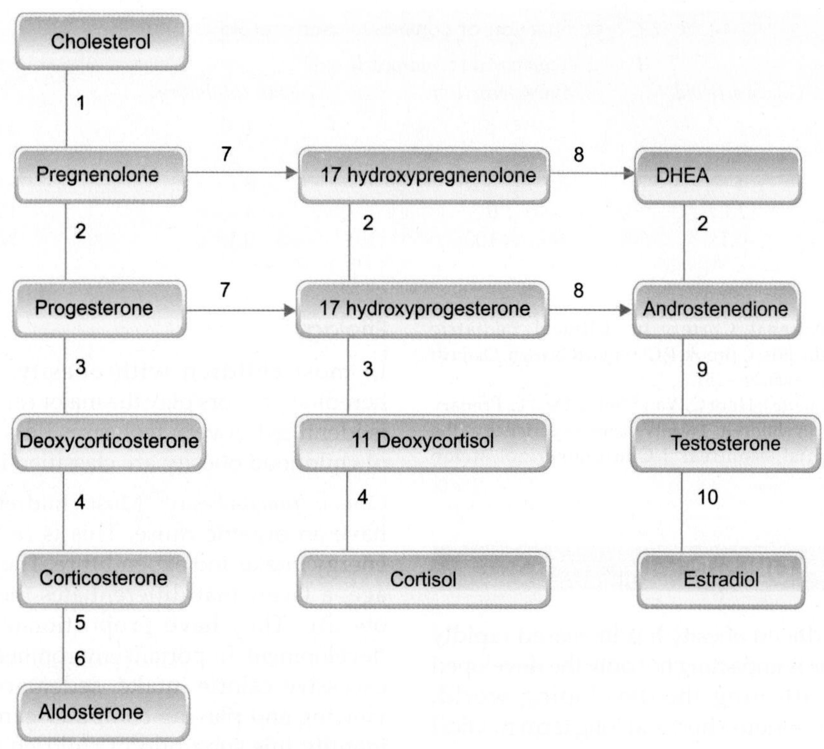

Fig. 16.11: Steroidogenic pathway

1 = Cholesterol side chain cleavage enzyme (CYP11A); 2 = 3β-hydroxysteroid dehydrogenase; 3 = 21α-hydroxylase (CYP21); 4 = 11β-hydroxylase (CYP11B1); 5 = 18-hydroxylase (CYP11B2); 6 = 18-oxidase (CYP11B2); 7 = 17α-hydroxylase (CYP17); 8 = 17, 20-lyase (CYP17); 9 = 17β-hydroxysteroid dehydrogenase; 10 = aromatase (CYParom).

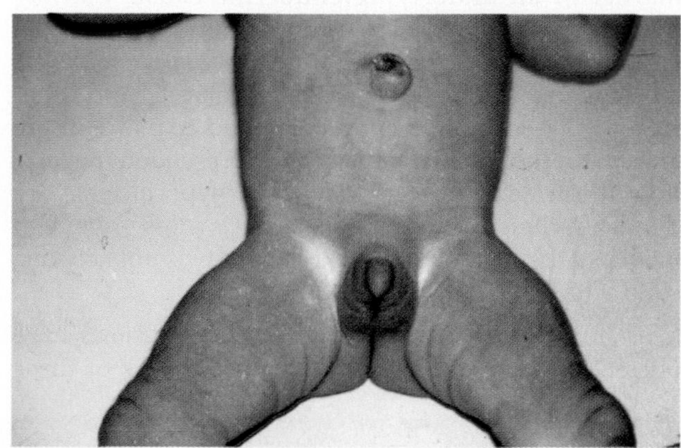

Fig. 16.12: Congenital adrenal hyperplasia secondary to 21-hydroxylase deficiency: Note the clitoral hypertrophy, hyperpigmentation and increased rugosity of the labial folds almost giving a male appearance to the female genitalia.

(10000-20000 ng/dL, normal <90 ng/dL) in the presence of clinical and laboratory features of adrenal insufficiency. 17OHP levels are elevated to a lesser extent in those with simple virilizing and non classic forms. The best method of diagnosing these patients is the estimation of 17OHP levels before and 60 minutes after an intramuscular injection of ACTH (0.25 mg).

Management

These patients require lifelong treatment. Patients with salt washing and virilizing forms should be treated with hydrocortisone (10–15 mg/m^2/day) and fludrocortisone (0.1 mg/day). Doses should be increased under stressful conditions as for adrenal insufficiency. After completion of growth, synthetic glucocorticoid preparations (dexamethasone, prednisolone) can be used (Table 16.22).

Other Variants

Enzyme deficiencies other than 21-hydroxylase deficiency account for less than 10% of cases of CAH. Patients with 11β-hydroxylase deficiency and 17α-hydroxylase deficiency present with hypertension and should be managed with hydrocortisone alone. Deficiencies of StAR and 3β-hydroxysteroid dehydrogenase manifest as salt wasting crisis and require addition of mineralocorticoid.

Suggested reading

1. Arnaldi G, Angeli A, Atkinson AB, et al. Diagnosis and classification of Cushing syndrome: a consensus statement. J Clin Endocrinol Metab 2003,88:5593–5602.
2. Findling JW, H Raff. Screening and diagnosis of Cushing's syndrome. Endocrinol Metab Clin North Am 2005;34:385–402.
3. Hopkins RL, Leinung MC. Exogenous Cushing syndrome and glucocorticoid withdrawal. Endocrinol Metab Clin North Am 2005;34:371–84.

Table 16.22: **Comparison of commonly used steroid preparations**

Preparation	*Potency (compared to hydrocortisone)*			*Biological half life*
	Glucocorticoid	*Mineralocorticoid*	*Growth inhibitory*	
Hydrocortisone	1	1	1	6 hours
Cortisone	0.8	1.25	1.25	5 hours
Prednisolone	4	0.25	8	8 hours
Dexamethasone	20	0	40	12 hours
Fludrocortisone	0.1	100	0.1	12 hours

4. Miller WL. The Adrenal Cortex. In: Clinical Pediatric Endocrinology, 5th edn. Eds: C Brook, P Clayton, R Brown, Oxford: Blackwell Publishing. 2005;293–351.
5. Perry R, Kecha O, Paquette J, Huot C, Van Vliet G, Deal C. Primary adrenal insufficiency in children: Twenty years' experience at the Sainte-Justine Hospital, Montreal. J Clin Endocrinol Metab 2005;90:3243–50.

OBESITY

The incidence of childhood obesity has increased rapidly in the last decade. This is impacting not only the developed countries but also affecting the developing world. Childhood obesity has serious short and long term medical consequences.

Criteria for Obesity

16

Obesity implies excessive fat and not merely excess weight. Body weight is thus not a reliable criterion for defining obesity. As methods of measuring body fat are cumbersome and expensive, several clinical and anthropometric parameters are used as markers of obesity.

Body mass index: Body mass index (BMI) is the most widely used parameter to define obesity. It takes into account weight as well as the height. It is calculated by the formula:

$$\text{BMI} = \text{Weight (kg)} \div \text{height (m)}^2$$

Children with BMI more than 85 percentile for age are considered at-risk for obesity while those more than 95 percentile for age are obese. BMI is a good indicator of body fat but is unreliable in short muscular individuals.

Weight for height: This compares the child's weight to the expected weight for his/her height. Weight for height more than 120% is diagnosed as obesity.

Skin fold thickness: Skin fold thickness measured over the subscapular, triceps or biceps regions is an indicator for subcutaneous fat. Age specific percentile cut-offs should be used with values more than 85 percentile being abnormal.

Waist circumference: This is a marker of abdominal adiposity, a key risk factor for metabolic and cardiovascular effects of obesity.

Etiology

In most children with obesity, environmental and hereditary factors play the major role. Underlying etiology is identified in very few cases (less than 1%). The causes of childhood obesity are classified in Table 16.23.

Constitutional obesity: Most children with obesity do not have an organic cause. This is caused by imbalance in energy intake and expenditure. These children are tall for age, a factor that differentiates them from pathological obesity. They have proportional obesity and normal development. Important environmental influences include excessive calorie intake, sedentary lifestyle, television viewing and playing computer games. It is important to identify this subgroup of children to avoid unnecessary investigations.

Endocrine causes: Though rare, identification of endocrine etiology of obesity has important management implications. Growth failure in an obese child is an important marker of an underlying endocrine cause. *Cushing syndrome* is characterized by central obesity, hypertension, striae and retarded skeletal maturation. *Hypothyroidism* is an extremely rare cause of isolated obesity and other features like developmental delay and coarse skin are always present. In GH deficiency and pseudohypoparathyroidism, growth retardation and hypocalcemia are dominant clinical features and obesity is a less prominent manifestation. Endocrine cause of obesity is unlikely in a child with normal growth.

Genetic syndromes: A variety of genetic syndromes have obesity as their major clinical feature. Many of these

Table 16.23: **Etiology of obesity**

Constitutional

Environmental factors (over 95% of all cases)

Pathological

- Endocrine: Cushing syndrome, GH deficiency, hypothyroidism, pseudohypoparathyroidism
- Hypothalamic: Head injury, infection, brain tumor, radiation, post-neurosurgery
- Drugs: Antiepileptic drugs, steroids, estrogen
- Genetic syndromes: Prader Willi, Laurence Moon Biedl Bardet, Beckwith Weidemann, Carpenter syndromes
- Monogenic disorders: Leptin deficiency, leptin resistance, abnormalities of MC4 receptor and proconvertase

syndromes are associated with hypogonadism or hypotonia (Prader Willi, Carpenter and Laurence Moon Biedl Bardet syndromes).

Hypothalamic obesity: CNS insults due to surgery, radiation, tumors and trauma results in rapid onset obesity. These disorders are associated with excessive appetite, signs and symptoms of CNS involvement and other hypothalamic-pituitary defects.

Monogenic obesity: Monogenic obesity represents a very small proportion of children with obesity. They are more likely in the presence of early onset of obesity, morbid obesity and strong family history. Leptin deficiency was the first monogenic cause of obesity identified. Inefficient leptin action (deficiency or resistance) results in uncontrolled appetite and obesity. Abnormalities in mineralocorticoid receptor and proconvertase have also been associated with obesity.

Evaluation

Initial evaluation is guided to differentiate constitutional from pathological obesity (Table 16.24). Normal growth, generalized pattern and lack of developmental delay or dysmorphism suggests constitutional obesity and against the need for extensive investigations.

Table 16.24: Comparison of constitutional and pathological obesity

Feature obesity	*Constitutional obesity*	*Pathological*
Distribution	Generalized	Usually central
Growth	Accelerated	Retarded
Bone age	Advanced	Retarded
Dysmorphism	Absent	May be present

Clinical: Family history of obesity and its complications should be recorded. Detailed history of physical activity, dietary recall and periods of inactivity should be assessed. Increased appetite in a child with recent onset obesity may indicate the possibility of a hypothalamic lesion. Delayed development points towards genetic syndromes associated with obesity. Features of raised intracranial tension along with history of CNS infection, head trauma or neurosurgery should point towards the diagnosis of CNS cause of obesity. Intake of drugs linked with development of obesity like steroids and antiepileptics should be inquired. Features of daytime somnolence or sleep apnea are suggestive of obesity severe enough to produce respiratory embarrassment. Examination for features of endocrinopathies, dysmorphic syndromes and complications such as hypertension and acanthosis nigricans should be performed. Special emphasis should be given to sexual maturity and ocular examination. Hypogonadism is an important feature of obese children with Laurence Moon Biedl syndrome and Prader Willi syndromes (Figs 16.13 and 16.14, Tables 16.25 and 16.26).

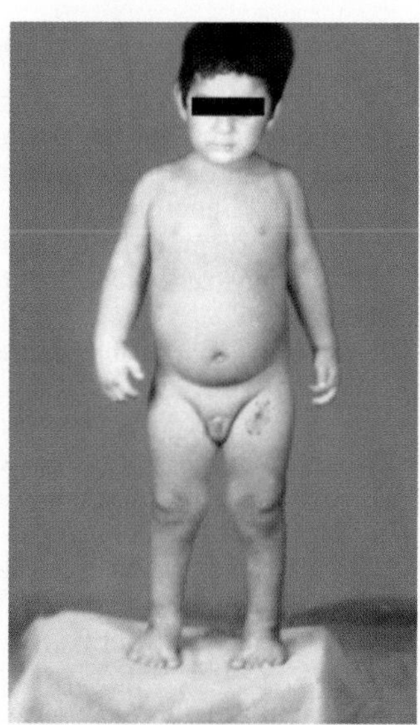

Fig. 16.13: Laurence Moon Biedl Bardet syndrome: Note the central obesity and hypoplastic genitalia

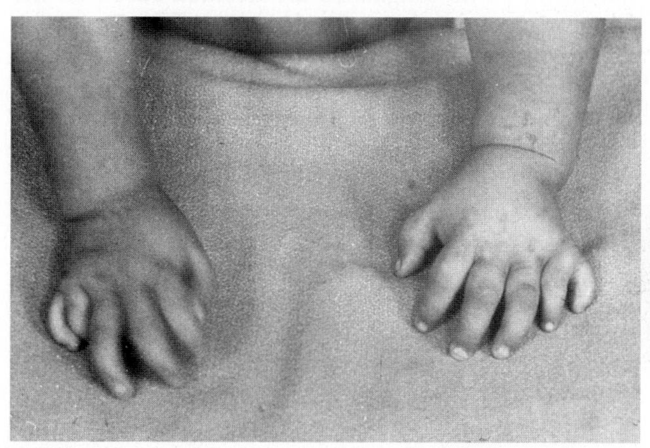

Fig. 16.14: Laurence Moon Biedl Bardet syndrome: Note the polydactyly

Table 16.25: Pointers to diagnosis to obesity

Feature	*Etiology*
Hypogonadism	Laurence Moon Biedl Bardet, Prader Willi syndrome
Retinitis pigmentosa	Alstrom syndrome, Laurence Moon Biedl Bardet syndrome
Ear lobe creases, organomegaly	Beckwith Weidemann syndrome
Short hand and feet, almond shaped eyes	Prader Willi syndrome
Polydactyly	Laurence Moon Biedl Bardet syndrome, Alstrom syndrome
Buffalo hump, striae	Cushing syndrome
Metacarpal shortening	Pseudohypoparathyroidism
Mental retardation	Prader Willi syndrome, hypothyroidism, pseudohypoparathyroidism

16

Table 16.26: Features of pathological obesity

Disorder	*Features*
Prader Willi syndrome	Infantile hypotonia, hyperphagia, almond like eyes, acromicria, hypogonadism, behavioral abnormality
Laurence Moon Biedl Bardet syndrome	Hypogonadism, retinitis pigmentosa, polydactyly, renal abnormalities, mental retardation
Beckwith Wiedemann syndrome	Organomegaly, ear lobe creases, hemihypertrophy
Cushing syndrome	Hirsutism, central obesity, growth retardation, striae, buffalo hump, hypertension, myopathy
Hypothyroidism	Growth retardation, coarse facies, developmental delay
Pseudohypo-parathyroidism	Tetany, osteodystrophy
Constitutional	Increased growth rate, normal facies, family history

Investigations: Investigations are decided based on the degree of obesity and associated complications. Endocrine investigations are done only in the presence of pointers to diagnosis such as growth failure, clinical features, developmental delay, and dysmorphism. Screening for complications is indicated in obese children (BMI more than 95th percentile). Investigations are also recommended for overweight children in the presence of family history of cardiovascular complications or type 2 DM or rapid increase in obesity. This evaluation should include oral glucose tolerance test, serum cholesterol and liver function tests.

16

Complications

Childhood obesity is associated with significant complications (Table 16.27).

Table 16.27: Complications of obesity

System	*Complication*
Central nervous system	Benign intracranial hypertension
Respiratory	Obstructive sleep apnea
Cardiovascular	Atherosclerosis, hypertension
Hepatobiliary	Nonalcoholic steatohepatitis (NASH), gall stone disease
Endocrine	Polycystic ovarian disease, type 2 diabetes mellitus, dyslipidemia
Orthopedic	Slipped capital femoral epiphyses, Blount's disease, osteoarthritis

Cardiovascular: Obesity has been linked with hyperlipidemia, hypertension and coronary artery disease. This is associated with significant risk of adverse cardiovascular effects in early adulthood. Metabolic syndrome, a combination of insulin resistance, hypertension and hyperlipidemia, is in particular an important complication of obesity.

Endocrine: Most important endocrine complication of obesity is insulin resistance. This presents as a spectrum of changes ranging from elevated insulin levels to impaired glucose tolerance to type 2 DM. A characteristic clinical feature is *acanthosis nigricans*, dark and rough areas on the exposed areas of skin including back of neck, axilla and thigh (Fig. 16.15). Ovarian hyperandrogenism leading to premature adrenarche and polycystic ovarian syndrome is an important feature of obesity.

Respiratory: Obesity is associated with restrictive (decreased respiratory movements due to obesity) as well as obstructive pulmonary disease (fat deposition in the airway). The most severe respiratory complication is the obesity-hypoventilation syndrome associated with hypoxia and features of cor pulmonale. In its milder form, it is associated with snoring, irritability, hyperactivity and daytime somnolence.

Orthopedic: Obese children are prone to slipped femoral epiphyses, flat feet, Blount's disease (tibia vara) and early onset osteoarthritis.

Hepatobiliary: Insulin resistance in obesity is associated with fatty infiltration in liver. This may vary from mild infiltration with no effect to steatohepatitis to chronic liver disease. The incidence of cholelithiasis is greater in obese children and has been shown to increase with treatment for obesity.

Management

Management of childhood obesity is challenging with major impetus on lifestyle measures (Fig 16.16). Specific management is available for only a few conditions. Diet, activity and behavioral measures are the cornerstones of therapy with intensive measures like drug therapy and surgery reserved for morbid cases.

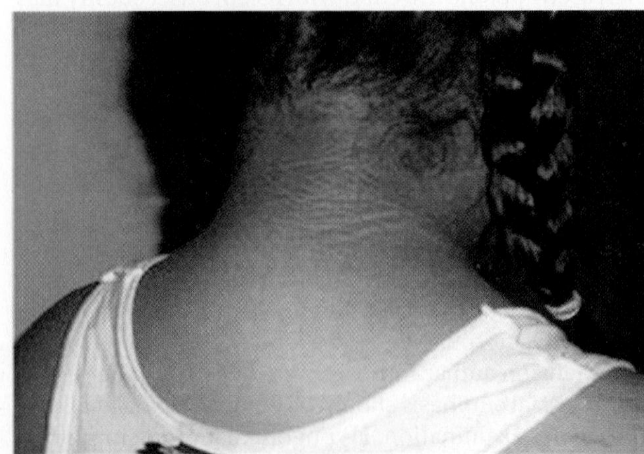

Fig. 16.15: Acanthosis nigricans on the back of neck in a girl with obesity

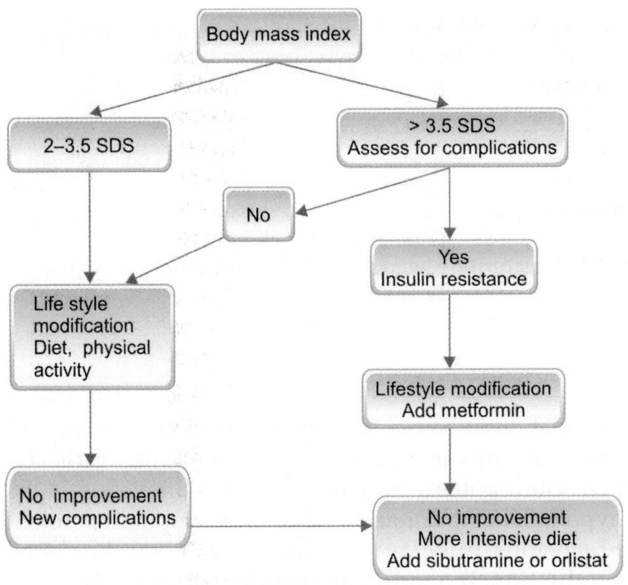

Fig. 16.16: Approach to management of obesity

Dietary measures: Initial dietary measure includes mild caloric restriction and alteration in dietary habits. Intake of 1200–1800 calories depending upon the age of the individual with 30–40% restriction is recommended. Over-aggressive dietary restriction is associated with poor compliance and growth faltering. Apart from restricting calorie intake, efforts should be directed towards improving the nutritive value of the diet. Reduction in consumption of junk foods, carbonated drinks and saturated fat along with an increase in fiber, fruits and vegetable intake are helpful in improving body composition. Regular meal consumption with fixed portion size is an effective strategy in inducing weight gain.

Lifestyle modification: Increase in physical activity along with reduction in sedentary lifestyle is an important part of obesity management. Swimming, running and playing outdoor games should be encouraged. Physical activity for at least 30–45 minutes per day should be recommended. Activities like television viewing, videogames and internet surfing should be restricted.

Drugs: Drug therapy is reserved only for severe cases of obesity. There is limited data regarding the use of anti-obesity drugs in children. The only drugs that have been tried in adolescents include *orlistat* (gastric lipase inhibitor) and *sibutramine* (neurotransmitter modulator). *Metformin* is indicated in children with insulin resistance. It has the added advantage of inducing weight loss. Leptin (for those with leptin deficiency) and octreotide (for hypothalamic obesity) are promising approaches for subgroups of children with obesity. The efficacy of pharmacological therapy for obesity has however been modest compared to surgery.

Surgery: Surgery for obesity is the last resort in treatment. It is indicated for morbid obesity (BMI more than 40 kg/m^2 with complications) when other measures have failed. Laparoscopic gastric banding is the procedure of choice and is directed at reducing gastric capacity. This results in reduced appetite and weight loss. Experience with obesity surgery in children is limited but has been shown to cause significant reduction in body weight sustained for a period of 1 year.

Initial management should be directed towards lifestyle modification with increased physical activity and nutritional advice. Metformin should be considered if clinical or laboratory features of insulin resistance are present. Children with morbid obesity with no response to lifestyle measures are candidates for surgery and medications.

Suggested reading

1. Alemzadeh R, Rising R, Cedillo M, Lifshitz F. Obesity in children. In: Pediatric Endocrinology, 4th edn. Eds: Lifshitz F, Marcel Dekker, New York. 2003;823–858.
2. Speiser PW, Rudolf MCJ, Anhalt H et al on behalf of the obesity consensus working group. Consensus statement: Childhood obesity. J Clin Endocrinol Metab 2005;90:1871–1887.

PUBERTAL DISORDERS

Puberty is the phase of life when secondary sexual characteristics appear and mature and capability of reproduction is attained. Deviations from the normal pattern of puberty have significant diagnostic and therapeutic implications.

16

Physiology

Puberty involves development of primary (testicular and penile growth in boys and breast and uterine growth in girls) and secondary sexual characteristics (pubic and axillary hair growth, acne and axillary odor). Sex hormones (estrogen in girls and testosterone in boys) play an important role in development of primary sexual characteristics, while adrenal androgens are involved in the development of secondary sexual characteristics. These processes are distinct and under separate endocrine control (gonadarche controlled by GnRH and adrenarche by ACTH). Gonadal hormone synthesis is controlled by gonadotropins, which are in turn produced after stimulation by hypothalamic gonadotropin-releasing hormone (GnRH).

Pulsatile GnRH secretion is the triggering event for puberty. Initially GnRH pulses occur only during nights followed by secretion during both day and night. This results in increase in the levels of gonadotropin and thereby sex hormones. LH levels increase around 25 times during puberty as compared to FSH levels, which increase by only 2.5 fold. This makes LH a better indicator of pubertal status compared to FSH. Pulsatile secretion of GnRH makes basal gonadotropin levels an unreliable indicator of pubertal status. Recently kisspeptin, a hypothalamic peptide, has been shown to be the key regulator of puberty. Acting as the "on-off switch" of puberty, kisspeptin initiates GnRH pulses.

The hypothalamic-pituitary-gonadal axis is under feedback control. Thus secretion of LH is inhibited by sex hormones (testosterone and estrogen) produced by the Leydig cells and theca cells. Inhibin produced by the Sertoli and granulosa cells inhibits production of FSH.

Patterns of Pubertal Development

The pattern of pubertal development is different in girls and boys. Puberty starts at around the age of 10 years in girls (range 8–12 year) and is completed in 5 years. Breast enlargement (*thelarche*) is the first event followed by the development of pubic hair (*pubarche*) and onset of menstrual cycles (*menarche*). Breast development may be asymmetrical in the initial phase. Menarche usually occurs 2.5 years after thelarche. Discordant pubertal development (menarche within one year of thelarche) suggests hyperestrogenic states with withdrawal bleeding. In boys, puberty starts with testicular enlargement at 11.5 years (range 9 years to 14 years). This is followed by penile enlargement and pubarche. *Spermarche* occurs by the age of 14 years.

The stage of pubertal assessment is assessed using Tanner staging system (Table 16.28). Breast development beyond Tanner II in girls and testicular volume greater than 4 ml indicates onset of puberty. Maximum growth spurt occurs during early puberty in girls (Tanner II–III) compared to boys where it occurs later (Tanner III–IV) (Table 16.29). Menstrual periods are irregular in the first few years before attainment of regular ovulatory cycles. It is important to differentiate adrenarche (pilosebaceous development related to increase in adrenal steroids) from gonadarche (genital development related to increase in GnRH) due to implications in clinical assessment.

Table 16.29: Comparison of pattern of pubertal development in boys and girls

Feature	*Girls*	*Boys*
Onset	10–12 years	12–14 year
First sign	Breast development	Testicular enlargement
Growth spurt	Early (Tanner I and II)	Late (Tanner III and IV)
Sexual maturity	Menarche 14 years	Spermarche 15 years

PRECOCIOUS PUBERTY

Pubertal onset before the age of 8 years in girls and 9.5 years in boys is suggestive of precocious puberty. Precocious puberty may be related to stimulation of the hypothalamic-pituitary axis (gonadotropin-dependent precocious puberty) or autonomous sex hormone production (gonadotropin-independent). Pubertal development may involve all aspects of pubertal development or restricted to one component (premature thelarche, adrenarche or menarche).

Precocious Puberty in Girls

Precocious puberty is common in girls and may represent normal variation in the age at onset of puberty. In most cases, puberty is slowly progressive with no long-term adverse effect. Endocrine workup should therefore be restricted to girls with progressive forms of puberty.

Etiology

Gonadotropin-dependent precocious puberty (GPP) or central precocious puberty is much more common than gonadotropin-independent precocious puberty (GIPP) (Table 16.30). In more than 90% of these cases, no underlying cause is

Table 16.28: Sexual maturity rating

Stage	*Breast*	*Pubic hair*
GIRLS		
I	No breast tissue	Same as abdominal hair
II	Breast bud, enlargement of areola	Minimally pigmented, mainly over labia
III	Further enlargement of breast bud and areola	Darker and coarser hair on mons pubis
IV	Secondary mound formed by papilla and areola	Adult type, less distribution
V	Adult contour with projection of papilla alone	Adult feminine distribution

Stage	*Genital changes*	*Testicular volume*	*Pubic hair*
BOYS			
I	Prepubertal	< 4 ml	Same as abdominal hair
II	Early penile growth, scrotal enlargement, pink scrotum	4–10 ml	Fine pubic hair at the base of penis
III	Increase in penile length, scrotal growth	10–15 ml	Increase in number of hair, darkening
IV	Increase in penile length and width, pigmented scrotum	15–20 ml	Spread around thigh, less than adult distribution
V	Adult size	> 20 ml	Adult male distribution

Table 16.30: Etiology of precocious puberty in girls
Gonadotropin-dependent or central precocious puberty (GPP)
Idiopathic
CNS tumors: Hamartoma, pituitary adenoma, craniopharyngioma, glioma
CNS infections: Neurotuberculosis, meningitis
CNS insults: Head trauma, neurosurgery, cranial irradiation
CNS malformations: Arachnoid cyst, hydrocephalus, Septo-optic dysplasia
Gonadotropin-independent or peripheral precocious puberty (GIPP)
Hypothyroidism
Ovarian estrogen: McCune Albright syndrome, cyst, tumor, aromatase excess
Adrenal estrogen: Estrogenic adrenal adenoma
Exogenous estrogen exposure
Incomplete variants
Isolated thelarche
Isolated pubarche (adrenarche)
Isolated menarche

identified. Onset after the age of six years, slow progression and lack of neurological features suggests idiopathic GPP. GPP may be caused by a number of CNS pathologies including infection, birth asphyxia, hydrocephalus, trauma, surgery, radiation and space occupying lesions. *Hypothalamic hamartoma*, a neuronal migration defect, is the commonest cause of organic central precocious puberty (Figs 16.17 and 16.18). The disorder presents with early onset and rapid progression of puberty, seizures and uncontrolled laughter episodes (gelastic epilepsy).

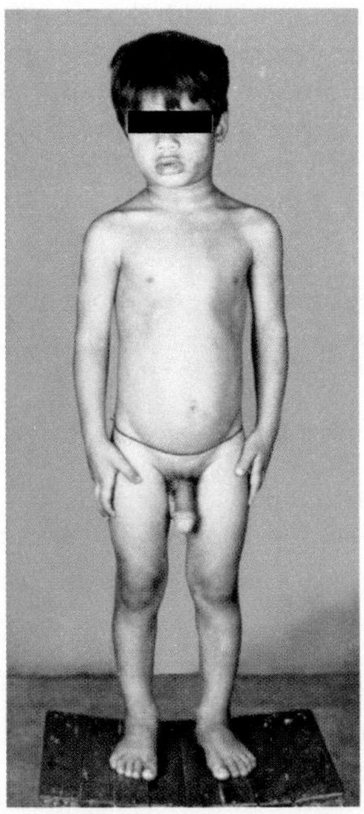

Fig. 16.17: Central precocious puberty secondary to hypothalamic hamartoma

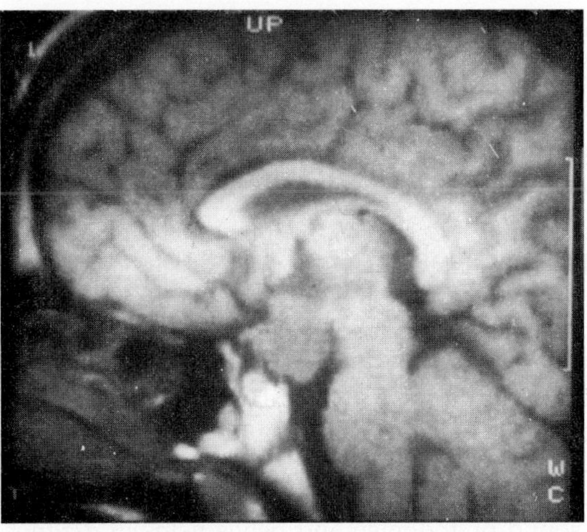

Fig. 16.18: MRI scan of brain showing an isodense mass suggestive of hypothalamic hamartoma

Gonadotropin-independent precocious puberty (GIPP) or peripheral precocious puberty is rare and usually caused by *estrogenic ovarian cysts*. Fluctuating pubertal development and early vaginal bleeding (due to hyperestrogenic state) is common. The condition is usually self-resolving and there is no need for treatment. Recurrent ovarian cysts should raise the possibility of *McCune Albright syndrome*, a somatic activating mutation of stimulatory G protein. The condition presents with constellation of cutaneous (multiple dark brown café-au-lait spots), skeletal (multiple fibrous dysplasia) and endocrine abnormalities (hyperthyroidism, rickets and GH excess). Precocious puberty occurs at an early age and is rapidly progressive. Advancement of skeletal maturation may trigger GPP. Prolonged untreated primary hypothyroidism may induce early puberty due to action of TSH on FSH receptor. Delayed bone age and growth is characteristic. Estrogenic adrenal tumor is an extremely rare cause of GIPP.

Evaluation

Aims of evaluation include confirmation of diagnosis, identification of underlying etiology and determination of prognosis and treatment.

Clinical: History should include the onset, progression and extent of puberty. Exposure to steroids, estrogens and androgens should be enquired. Family history of precocious puberty and early menarche points towards idiopathic central precocious puberty. History indicative of intracranial space occupying lesion, CNS infections, neurosurgery, radiotherapy and head trauma should be noted. Features of hypothyroidism should be assessed. Advanced growth is characteristic of precocious puberty; growth retardation is indicative of hypothyroidism or concomitant GH deficiency. Examination of vaginal mucosa for estrogen effect provides clues regarding the pubertal status of the patient. Red, glistening mucosa suggests lack of estrogens while pink mucosa with mucus is indicative of estrogen effect. Abdominal examination for adrenal or ovarian mass should be done. Features of McCune Albright syndrome in the form of café-au-lait spots, polyostotic fibrous dysplasia, bony deformities and polyendocrinopathy should be looked for.

Investigations: Assessment of pubertal status is based on basal or stimulated gonadotropin levels. Pooled gonadotropin levels are preferred due to their pulsatile secretion. LH is a better indicator compared to FSH as LH levels increase significantly during puberty. LH levels in the pubertal range with LH/FSH ratio more than 1 is suggestive of development of puberty. In unequivocal situations, LH levels should be measured 30, 60 and 90 minutes after GnRH injection (GnRH stimulation test). Ultrasound of abdomen and pelvis helps in diagnosing follicular cysts and ovarian and adrenal mass. Thyroid function should be assessed to rule out hypothyroidism. Bone age helps in assessing the height compromise and in predicting final height. MRI of brain should be done in girls with onset of puberty before 6 years of age, rapid progression and associated neurological features. Pituitary functions should be assessed in girls with organic GPP.

Advanced bone age (more than two years ahead of chronological age) is suggestive of progressive precocious puberty, while normal bone age indicates slowly progressive puberty. Retarded growth and skeletal maturation is diagnostic of hypothyroidism. Pubertal LH levels are suggestive of GPP and should be followed with an MRI of brain. Girls with GIPP should undergo ultrasound of ovary and adrenals (for ovarian cyst and adrenal tumor) and skeletal survey (for fibrous dysplasia in McCune Albright syndrome).

Management

Aims of treatment include treatment of underlying cause, management of associations, suppression of puberty and achievement of target height potential. The significant long-term consequence of precocious puberty is short stature. Growth is accelerated at presentation. This is associated with disproportionately advanced bone age resulting in premature epiphyseal fusion culminating in compromised final height. Significant psychosocial issues including pubertal development at an early age and practical issues of menstruation in a young girl need to be addressed.

Gonadotropin-dependent precocious puberty: Treatment includes management of underlying cause and suppression of puberty. Drugs used for pubertal suppression include medroxyprogesterone acetate (MPA), cyproterone and GnRH analogs. MPA does not improve height outcome and may be considered in girls with intellectual disability where final height is not important. Long acting GnRH analogs are the only agents effective in improving height outcome. They cause sustained stimulation and desensitization of pituitary leading to reversal of pubertal changes. GnRH analogs should be considered in girls with early onset (before 6 years of age) rapidly progressive puberty and height compromise (bone age to chronological age difference more than two years). Triptorelin (60 µg/kg) or leuprolide (300 µg/kg) administered as a deep intramuscular injection every 4 weeks is the most commonly used agent. The treatment is discontinued at the chronological age of 11 years and bone age of 12.5 years. This is followed by gradual reappearance of secondary sexual characters. Menarche is attained around 12–18 months following discontinuation of treatment.

Gonadotropin-independent precocious puberty: Thyroxine replacement results in reversal of pubertal changes in hypothyroidism. Treatment for McCune Albright syndrome is directed towards inhibiting estrogen production (aromatase inhibitors like anastrazole or letrozole) or estrogen action (tamoxifen). Treatment of ovarian cysts is guided by size and morphological features.

Precocious Puberty in Boys

Precocious puberty is less common in boys, but when present is usually associated with significant pathology. This mandates prompt evaluation and treatment of all boys with precocious puberty.

Etiology

Gonadotropin-dependent and independent precocious puberty accounts for similar number of cases in boys (Table 16.31).

Gonadotropin-dependent precocious puberty (GPP): The etiology is similar to girls with the exception that organic etiology is more common. Hypothalamic hamartoma, craniopharyngioma, hydrocephalus and tubercular meningitis are important causes. These disorders are associated with increase in testicular volume and elevated basal and GnRH stimulated LH.

Table 16.31: Etiology of precocious puberty in boys
Gonadotropin-dependent or central precocious puberty
Idiopathic
CNS tumors: Hamartoma, craniopharyngioma, glioma
CNS infections: Tubercular meningitis, meningitis
CNS injury: Head trauma, surgery, radiation
CNS malformation: Arachnoid cyst, hydrocephalus
Gonadotropin-independent or peripheral precocious puberty
Congenital adrenal hyperplasia: 21-hydroxylase deficiency, 11β-hydroxylase deficiency
Adrenal tumors: Adenoma, carcinoma
Testicular tumors: Seminoma, germinoma
Testotoxicosis–activation of LH receptor
hCG secreting tumor: Germinoma, hepatoblastoma
Exogenous androgen exposure: Testosterone cream

Gonadotropin-independent precocious puberty (GIPP): This is caused by increased androgen production by testis and adrenals in the setting of prepubertal LH levels. Adrenal overproduction due to *congenital adrenal hyperplasia* is the commonest cause of peripheral precocious puberty. Rarely adrenal tumors may present with precocious puberty. Penile enlargement with prepubertal testicular volume is characteristic. *Human chorionic gonadotropin (hCG) secreting germ cell tumors* of the liver, mediastinum or brain may present with precocious puberty. Testicular volume is only slightly increased as only Leydig cells are enlarged. *Testotoxicosis,* a disorder associated with constitutional activation of LH receptor, presents with early onset gonadotropin-independent precocious puberty. *Androgen secreting testicular tumors* present with precocious puberty and unilateral testicular enlargement.

Evaluation

Evaluation is directed towards confirming the diagnosis and establishing the underlying cause.

Clinical: History should include age at onset of pubertal development, progression of puberty, neurological features, family history of precocious puberty and androgen exposure. Detailed anthropometric and neurological examination should be performed. Pointers to CAH (hyperpigmentation and hypertension) should be identified. Estimation of testicular volume forms an integral part of assessment. Prepubertal testicular volume (less than 4 ml) is characteristic of CAH and adrenal tumors, while unilateral enlargement is seen in testicular tumors. Pubertal testicular enlargement indicates GPP while milder enlargement is observed in hCG secreting tumors and testotoxicosis.

Investigations: Initial investigations should include LH, FSH and testosterone levels and bone age. All patients with pubertal LH levels should undergo visual field examination and MRI of brain. If CNS pathology is identified, detailed pituitary evaluation should be performed. In the presence of prepubertal LH levels, imaging for adrenals (preferably a CT scan) and 17OHP levels should be done. hCG levels should be estimated if these investigations are noncontributory.

Management

Management includes treatment of underlying CNS pathology and GnRH analog therapy. GnRH analog should be continued till the age of 12 years and a bone age of 17.5 years is achieved. CAH is managed with hydrocortisone and fludrocortisone. Surgery is the treatment of choice for adrenal and testicular tumors, while radiotherapy is effective in hCG secreting tumors. Aromatase inhibitors and antiandrogens are indicated in testotoxicosis.

Incomplete Variants

These disorders usually represent normal variants and do not require specific treatment. Their identification helps in restricting the extent of diagnostic work-up and counselling.

Isolated thelarche: Isolated breast development may represent isolated thelarche or first manifestation of central precocious puberty or GPP. Bone age, gonadotropin levels and pelvic ultrasound helps in differentiating the two conditions. Normal growth, prepubertal LH, age appropriate bone age and small uterine size suggest isolated thelarche. Advanced bone age, elevated LH levels and increased uterine size indicate precocious puberty and need for GnRH analog therapy.

Isolated adrenarche: Premature adrenarche refers to development of pubic hair and acne in the absence of breast development or menarche. Most cases are physiological variants. Rarely androgen excess due to adrenal (CAH due to 21-hydroxylase deficiency, 11β-hydroxylase deficiency or adrenal tumor) or ovarian (tumor or polycystic ovarian disease) causes may be identified. Normal bone age and absence of virilization suggest premature adrenarche and no treatment. Girls with virilization and advanced bone age should be investigated for hyperandrogenic states.

Isolated menarche: Menarche in the absence of thelarche is against the diagnosis of GPP. Vaginal bleeding may occur early in course of estrogen excess states like ovarian cysts, hypothyroidism and McCune Albright syndrome. Vaginal bleeding without breast development should prompt evaluation of local causes like infection, foreign body, sexual abuse and tumors.

DELAYED PUBERTY

Delayed puberty is more common in boys than girls. Most children with delayed puberty have constitutional delay emphasizing the need for watchful monitoring and conservative approach.

Delayed Puberty in Girls

Delayed puberty is defined as lack of secondary sexual characteristics by the age of 17 years. Absence of menarche by the age of 16 years or 5 years after pubertal onset also indicates pubertal delay.

Etiology

Delayed puberty may be caused by defects in the hypothalamic-pituitary axis, ovaries or genital tract (Table 16.32). Patients with anatomical defects present with amenorrhea with normal breast development. Defects in the hypothalamic-pituitary axis are associated with low gonadotropin levels (*hypogonadotropic hypogonadism*). This may be related to reversible causes like systemic diseases, malnutrition, eating disorders, hyperprolactinemia and hypothyroidism. Irreversible defects include destruction of the hypothalamic-pituitary axis by infection, surgery, radiation or tumor. *Kallmann syndrome,* a neuronal

Table 16.32: Etiology of delayed puberty in girls

Hypogonadotropic hypogonadism

Transient
- Systemic disorders: Renal failure, liver disease, celiac disease, renal tubular acidosis, cystic fibrosis
- Nutritional disorders: Malnutrition, anorexia nervosa
- Endocrine disorders: Hypothyroidism, hyperprolactinemia, type 1 diabetes

Permanent
- Isolated hypogonadotropic hypogonadism
  Genetic: KAL1, GnRH receptor, LH, FSH, DAX1 mutations
  Dysmorphic syndromes: CHARGE, Prader Willi, Laurence Moon Biedl Bardet syndromes
- Multiple pituitary hormone deficiency
  - Malformations: Holoprosencephaly, septo-optic dysplasia, midline defects
  - Genetic disorders: PROP1, LH gene deletions
  - Brain tumors: Craniopharyngioma, germinoma, glioma
  - CNS insults: Surgery, infection, radiation, trauma
  - Infiltrative disorders: Histiocytosis, autoimmune disorders

Hypergonadotropic hypogonadism
- Gonadal dysgenesis: Turner syndrome, SRY deletion, trisomy 18, 13, 21
- Steroidogenic defects: CAH due to StAR, 17α- hydroxylase, 17β-hydroxysteroid dehydrogenase, aromatase deficiency
- Ovarian insults: Surgery, radiation, alkylating agents, infections
- Autoimmune ovarian failure: Autoimmune polyendocrinopathy
- Gonadotropin resistance: LH and FSH receptor mutations

Isolated amenorrhea
- Structural malformations: Müllerian agenesis, vaginal septum, imperforate hymen
- Inefficient androgen action: Complete androgen insensitivity syndrome

16

migration defect due to mutation of KAL1 gene, is characterized by defective smell sensation, low GnRH levels and hypogonadotropic hypogonadism. *Hypergonadotropic hypogonadism* is associated with defective estrogen production by ovaries and elevated gonadotropin levels. Turner syndrome, ovarian failure and enzymatic defects in estrogen synthesis production are important causes of this condition.

Evaluation

Goals of evaluation include identification of constitutional delay, organic etiology requiring neuroimaging and decision regarding treatment.

Clinical: Family history of delayed puberty provides a clue to constitutional delay in puberty. Features of chronic systemic diseases such as renal, hepatic and cardiac disease should be inquired. Features of head injury, neurosurgery and intracranial space occupying lesions suggest a defect in the hypothalamic-pituitary axes. Poor smell sensation is indicative of Kallmann syndrome. Patients with amenorrhea with normal secondary sexual characteristics are likely to have anatomical defects and should be evaluated accordingly. Neurological examination including that for olfactory sensation should be performed. Features of Turner syndrome and hypothyroidism should be looked into. Galactorrhea points towards hypothyroidism or hyperprolactinemia.

Investigations: Initial workup is directed towards excluding systemic disorders such as liver disease, renal disease and malabsorption. This should be followed by measurement of FSH levels. Karyotype should be done if FSH levels are high. Steroidogenic defects are likely, if karyotype and pelvic ultrasound are normal. In patients with low/normal FSH levels, prolactin and thyroid profile should be measured to exclude reversible causes. Neuroimaging and pituitary function tests should be done if these levels are normal.

Management

All patients with hypergonadotropic hypogonadism and irreversible hypogonadotropic hypogonadism need hormone replacement. Hormone replacement should be deferred till the age of 12 years to avoid deleterious effects on height. The goal of treatment is to initiate and maintain sexual characteristics and to prevent osteoporosis. Treatment should be started with low dose estrogens (5 µg ethinyl estradiol or 0.3 mg conjugated estrogen every day) and gradually increased every 3 months till adult doses (20 µg of ethinyl estradiol or 1.25 mg of conjugated estrogen daily by 2 years) are reached. Medroxyprogesterone acetate (MPA 5–10 mg from day 11 to 21) should be added two years after initiation of treatment or once withdrawal bleeding has started.

Delayed Puberty in Boys

Delayed puberty is more common in boys than girls and is usually due to a constitutional delay. Lack of pubertal changes by the age of 14 years is suggestive of delayed puberty.

Etiology

Constitutional delay in growth and puberty (CDPG) is the commonest cause of delayed puberty in boys (Table 16.33). These boys have growth retardation and delayed bone age. Family history of delayed puberty is present. Gonadotropin levels are prepubertal similar to hypogonadotropic hypogonadism.

Hypogonadotropic hypogonadism may be reversible due to systemic illnesses or permanent due to neurological insult (infection, surgery, radiation or tumor). *Kallmann syndrome* is an important cause of isolated gonadotropin deficiency and presents with impaired smell sensation. Delayed puberty is common in dysmorphic syndromes like Prader

DISORDERS OF SEXUAL DIFFERENTIATION

Disorders of sexual differentiation (DSD), previously termed as intersex disorders, are rare but constitute a medical, social and psychological emergency. Careful clinical and laboratory evaluation is essential for identifying the underling disorder, need of emergent therapeutic intervention and decision about sex of rearing.

Physiology

Sexual differentiation is a complex process involving a close interaction of genetic, phenotypic and psychological factors. Usually genetic sex guides gonadal sex, which is responsible for the determination of phenotypic manifestations and gender identity. Any deviation from this pattern results in DSD. Sexual differentiation involves development of gonads in accordance to the genetic signals, development of internal sexual organs and secondary sexual characters (Fig. 16.20).

Gonadal differentiation: Germ cells arise from the celomic epithelium of hindgut and migrate to the gonadal ridge at 4–6 weeks of gestation. These cells combine with somatic cells to give rise to the bipotential gonad. A transcriptional factor present on Y chromosome called the sex determining region of the Y chromosome (SRY), is one of the most important regulators of sexual differentiation. SRY acts in conjunction with other genes like Wilms tumor gene 1 (WT1), SOX 9 and DAX1 to induce testicular development. In the absence of SRY, the bipotential gonad develops into ovary.

Genital differentiation: Following development of testis, antimüllerian hormone (AMH) secreted by Sertoli cells induces regression of müllerian ducts. Testosterone produced by Leydig cells is responsible for sustenance of Wolffian ducts. Dihydrotestosterone (DHT), produced by action of 5α-reductase on testosterone, is responsible for male external genital development (scrotal fusion and development of corpus spongiosum and penile corpus cavernosa). Feminization is the default process of sexual development. In the absence of AMH and testosterone, müllerian ducts differentiate into fallopian tubes, uterus and the upper third of the vagina. Labioscrotal swellings and urethral folds do not fuse and give rise to labia majora and minora respectively. The genital tubercles form the clitoris while canalization of the vaginal plate creates the lower portion of the vagina. Prenatal exposure to androgens may lead to labioscrotal fusion, while exposure thereafter usually causes clitoromegaly alone and no labial fusion.

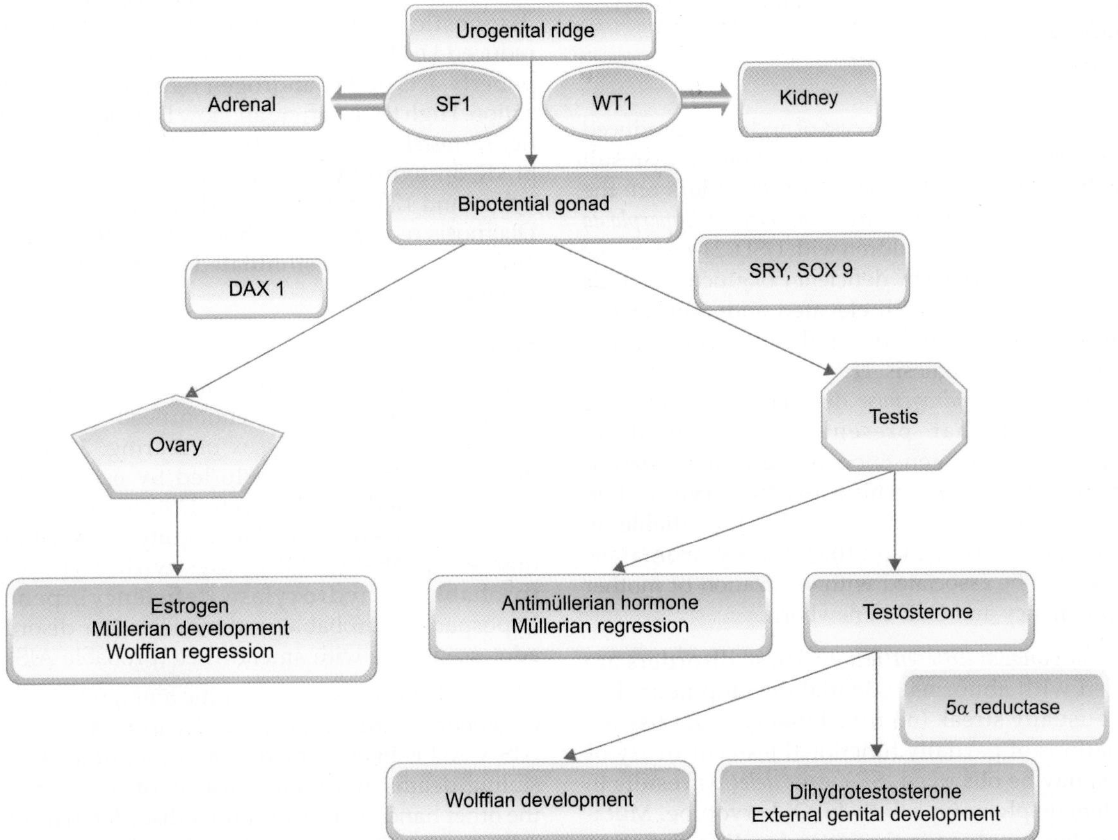

Fig. 16.20: The process of sexual development and its disorders

16

Classification

DSD may be caused by defects in gonadal differentiation (gonadal dysgenesis), androgen production (increased in females and reduced in males) or action (androgen insensitivity syndrome). Intersex disorders were conventionally classified into four major categories of male pseudohermaphroditism, female pseudohermaphroditism, mixed gonadal dysgenesis, and true hermaphroditism. This has been replaced by the new etiology based classification (Table 16.37).

Table 16.37: Karyotype based classification of disorders of sexual differentiation

Karyotype	*Normal genital appearance**	*Genital ambiguity*
46,XX	SRY insertion Severe 21OHD	Congenital adrenal hyperplasia Aromatase deficiency Maternal virilization Maternal drug intake
46,XY	SRY deletion SF1 defect	Testicular dysgenesis Steroidogenic defects
	Gonadal dysgenesis Severe StAR defect Complete AIS	Partial AIS 5ARII deficiency
46,XY/45,X		Gonadal dysgenesis Ovotesticular DSD

* Discordant to genotypic sex

Increased androgen production: Excess of androgen produced during the critical period of fetal development may result in masculinization of a female. These disorders are the commonest form of DSD. *Congenital adrenal hyperplasia* should be excluded in all children with DSD. *21-hydroxyase deficiency* is characterized by deficiency of glucocorticoids and mineralocorticoids with elevated androgen levels. Delay in diagnosis could be fatal, underscoring the importance of early diagnosis. *11-hydroxylase deficiency* and *3β-hydroxysteroid dehydrogenase* deficiency are the other forms of CAH that present with virilization. Transplacental androgen exposure due to maternal medications or hyperandrogenism may lead to virilization in newborn. These disorders are readily identifiable by history of virilization in mother. Rarely aromatase deficiency may be associated with virilization of mother during pregnancy and DSD in newborn.

Disorders of gonadal differentiation: These disorders are associated with abnormal gonadal development. The gonad is usually streak (no functional gonadal tissue). Combinations of partially functional testis or ovary or ovotestis may be observed. *SRY gene deletion* results in normal female phenotype with 46,XY karyotype. Mutations in genes involved in the testicular differentiation (WT1, SOX9, SF1 and DAX1) are other causes of 46,XY gonadal dysgenesis. These disorders are associated with renal (WT1 mutation), skeletal (SOX9) and adrenal abnormalities (DAX1). An important feature of these disorders is the presence of müllerian structures that differentiates them from disorders of inefficient androgen action. 46,XY gonadal dysgenesis is associated with risk of development of gonadoblastoma. Asymmetric gonadal location may result in asymmetric genital appearance. 46,XX gonadal dysgenesis is usually caused by SRY translocation and presents as normal appearing male. *Ovotesticular DSD*, new term for true hermaphroditism, is characterized by the presence of both ovarian and testicular tissue in the same individual.

Inefficient androgen action: These disorders result from decreased production, activation or action of androgens. *Androgen insensitivity syndrome (AIS)*, (previously referred to as testicular feminization syndrome), an X-linked disorder of androgen action, is the commonest cause and is characterized by resistance to androgens. The disease forms a spectrum ranging from a normal female to boy with hypospadias, to a male with infertility. Complete androgen insensitivity presents in the neonatal period as a girl with inguinal masses and primary amenorrhea in older girls. Absent or sparse pubic and axillary hair is common. Increasing testosterone levels during puberty result in increased estrogen level and further feminization. Müllerian structures are absent. High DHT levels are diagnostic. *5α-reductase deficiency* is associated with reduced DHT production. Increased testosterone during puberty acts on the androgen receptor leading to virilization. High testosterone and low DHT levels are diagnostic. *Testosterone biosynthetic defects* include deficiency of StAR, 3β-hydroxysteroid dehydrogenase, 17α- hydroxylase and 17β-hydroxysteroid dehydrogenase enzymes. Diagnosis requires estimation of testosterone precursors and basal and hCG stimulated testosterone and androstenedione levels.

Evaluation

Aims of evaluation include identification of the child requiring immediate intervention, need of further workup and decision about the sex of rearing. 21-hydroxylase deficiency should be excluded by estimating serum electrolytes and 17OHP levels. DSD workup is indicated in the infants with genital ambiguity, girls with inguinal masses (probable AIS), boys with cryptorchidism (probable 21-hydroxylase deficiency), penoscrotal hypospadias (probable undervirilization disorder) and adolescent girls with amenorrhea (probable AIS).

Clinical: Family history of genital ambiguity is suggestive of genetic disorders such as 21-hydroxylase deficiency or AIS. CAH is likely if there is a history of fetal losses and sibling deaths and family history of consanguinity. On the other hand, history of similar disorder in healthy male relatives (brothers and maternal uncles) is suggestive of AIS. Gonads in complete AIS might have been mistaken for inguinal hernia and operated. Intake of progestational drugs during first trimester and features of virilization in mother should be enquired. Failure to thrive, polyuria and lethargy indicate 21-hydroxylase deficiency (Table 16.38). Virilization during puberty is suggestive of 5α-reductase deficiency, while feminization indicates AIS. General examination should include assessment for facial dysmorphism and hyperpigmentation. Maternal examination for features of hyperandrogenism like hirsutism, acne and change in voice should be done.

Table 16.38: Pointers to etiology of Disorders of sexual differentiation (DSD)

Pointer	*Likely diagnosis*
Pigmentation	Congenial adrenal hyperplasia, SF1 defect
Genital asymmetry	Mixed gonadal dysgenesis, ovotesticular DSD
Hypertension	11α or 17α hydroxylase defect
Hemihypertrophy	WT1 mutation
Renal failure	Denys Drash syndrome

Genital examination: The most important step is identification of gonads. Bilaterally rounded structures below the inguinal canal are most likely to be testis. Unilateral gonads are suggestive of mixed gonadal dysgenesis. The labioscrotal region should be evaluated for the extent of fusion (Fig. 16.21). Müllerian structures can be confirmed by a good rectal examination. The length of phallus and number of openings in the urogenital region should be recorded. Asymmetrical labioscrotal region is suggestive of gonadal dysgenesis or ovotesticular DSD. The genitalia should be staged according to the classification proposed by Prader from grades I to V with grade I representing female with clitoromegaly and V male with cryptorchidism.

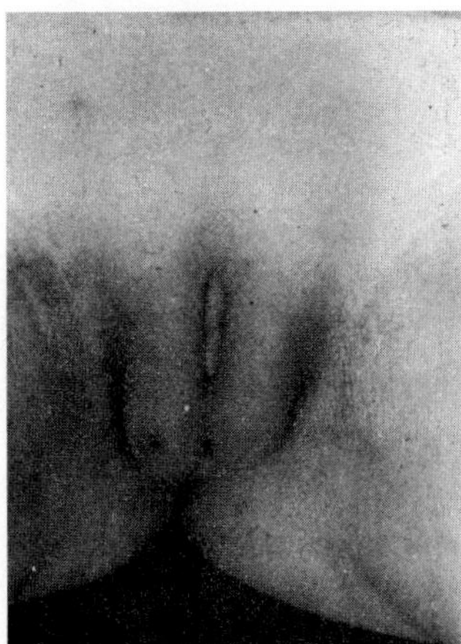

Fig. 16.21: Disorder of sexual development—partial androgen insensitivity syndrome—Note the female appearance of the genitalia with an underdeveloped buried penis and poorly developed scrotum and testes

Investigations: Initial investigations should include karyotyping, estimation of electrolytes, 17OHP and pelvic ultrasound. FISH for Y component provides rapid information about the genetic status. Identification of müllerian structures is an important part of evaluation of ambiguous genitalia. Genitogram is helpful in determination of level of fusion, which is of surgical importance. Further investigations are guided by clinical and laboratory evaluation.

Müllerian structures with no palpable gonads indicate androgen excess state and need for estimation of 17OHP levels. Absence of müllerian structures is suggestive of inefficient testosterone action and should be evaluated with estimation of testosterone and DHT levels. The presence of both müllerian structures and palpable gonads indicate gonadal dysgenesis or ovotesticular DSD. Absent gonads and müllerian structure may be caused by vanishing testis syndrome or dysfunctional intra-abdominal testis. Estimation of levels of AMH and hCG stimulation test are helpful in differentiating the two conditions. Children with vanishing testis will have low levels of AMH and inappropriate response to hCG stimulation.

Management

Management involves parental counseling, decision about sex of rearing, timing of surgical correction and gonadectomy. This requires a multidisciplinary team including pediatrician interested in endocrinology, pediatric surgeon, geneticist, psychologist and social worker. Specific management should be initiated for conditions like 21-hydroxylase deficiency.

16

Parental counseling: Birth of a child with DSD generates significant parental anxiety and stress. The most important aspect of counseling is reassurance of parents that the child is healthy and the condition is amenable to surgical treatment. Gender specific connotation (his or her, testis, ovary) should be avoided and neutral terms like gonads and phallus be used. The process of sexual differentiation should be explained. This should be followed by explanation of child's appearance and possible diagnosis. Future implications regarding sexual and fertility prospects should be discussed.

Decision about sex of rearing: Gender assignment should depend on the potential for future sexual and reproductive function, anatomical status, feasibility of reconstructive surgery and social acceptance and norms. Girls with virilization disorders usually have potential for fertility and should be reared as females. Individuals with complete AIS should also be reared as females. Decision of sex of rearing is difficult in disorders of inefficient androgen action. This should depend on genital appearance and surgical feasibility. There has been a trend of performing early surgeries before gender identity is established. Most centers perform clitoroplasty at the age of 1 year with vaginoplasty reserved during puberty for girls with vaginal stenosis. Gonadectomy should be done in gonadal dysgenesis or ovotesticular DSD, if a Y cell line is present.

Cryptorchidism (Undescended Testes)

Cryptorchidism is present in about 3% of full-term infants and 20% of premature infants. In most boys testis descend spontaneously by the age of one year with a decrease in the prevalence to around 1%. Spontaneous testicular descent is highly unlikely after the age of one year and the prevalence in adult population is around 0.8%.

Etiology

Most children with undescended testis do not have an identifiable underlying cause. Endocrine causes account for only a small proportion of boys with undescended testis. The possibility of salt wasting 21-hydroxylase deficiency presenting with sex reversal should be considered in newborns with bilateral cryptorchidism. Undescended testis may be associated with hypopituitarism, dysmorphic syndromes and disorders of androgen production and action.

Evaluation

It is important to differentiate true undescended testis from retractile or ectopic testis due to therapeutic and prognostic implications (Fig. 16.22). Poorly developed scrotum and inability to bring down the testis to the scrotal sack suggests true undescended testis. *Retractile testis* is an otherwise fully descended testis that has an active cremasteric reflex, which retracts it into the groin.

16

Penoscrotal hypospadias and genital ambiguity is suggestive of disorders of androgen production or action. Features of dysmorphic syndromes like Prader Willi, Laurence Moon Biedl Bardet, Noonan and DeLange syndromes are usually evident on examination. The hCG stimulation test should be done in boys with bilateral nonpalpable testis to differentiate abdominal testis from anorchia.

Management

Undescended testis is associated with significant complications like torsion, trauma, inguinal hernia, testicular dysfunction and development of malignancy. These children should be treated early because of the increased risk for malignancy and infertility in later life. The optimal time of therapy is before the age of one year. The most commonly used medical treatment is human chorionic gonadotropin (hCG) 250 units below 1 year, 500 units between 1 and 5 years and 1,000 units above 5 years administered twice a week for 5–6 weeks. Good response occurs within a month. Alternately GnRH in the form of an intramuscular injection or nasal spray may be tried. Retraction rate of testes after cessation of therapy is high. If the response to hCG is poor, patient should be treated early with orchiopexy.

Micropenis

A penis whose length in stretched position is less than 2 SD below the mean for the age is termed micropenis. Micropenis may be isolated or may be associated with

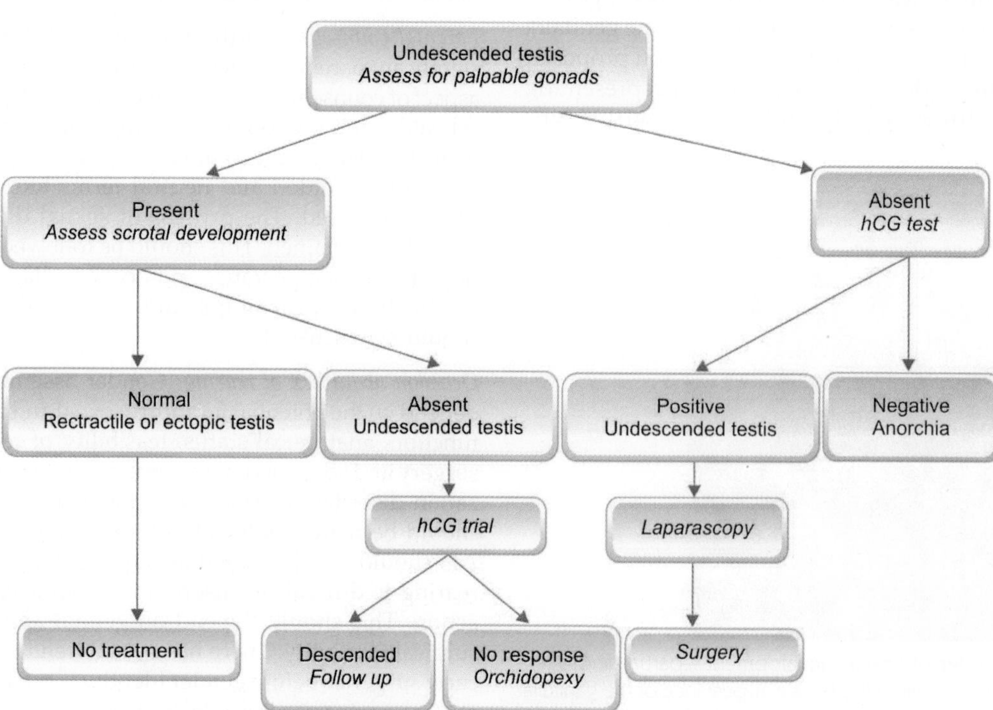

Fig. 16.22: Approach to cryptorochidism; hCG human chorionic gonadotropin

genital and structural abnormalities. Most often it is the result of primary or secondary testicular failure.

Etiology

Micropenis results from decreased androgen action during fetal life. It may be due to hypogonadotropic hypogonadism as in Kallmann syndrome, Prader Willi syndrome, septooptic dysplasia, idiopathic hypogonadotropic hypogonadism (primary) with isolated micropenis, Klinefelter syndrome or Robinow syndrome. It may be a manifestation of partial androgen insensitivity syndrome or testosterone biosynthetic defects.

Evaluation

Penile length should be measured in a fully stretched state by grasping the glans between thumb and forefinger. A firm ruler or caliper should be pressed against the pubic ramus to depress the suprapubic fat pad. The measurement should be made along the dorsum to the tip of the glans penis excluding the length of foreskin. Penile size is often underestimated in boys with obesity (due to the suprapubic fat) and hypospadias (due to chordee). Investigations should include estimation of gonadotropin and testosterone levels. Boys with low gonadotropin and testosterone levels (hypogonadotropic hypogonadism) should undergo anterior pituitary hormone tests (IGF-1, IGFBP3, serum cortisol, thyroid function tests and urine osmolality) and MRI of the brain. Elevated gonadotropin levels (hypergonadotropic hypogonadism) should prompt evaluation for testicular dysgenesis, steroidogenic defects or AIS.

Management

All boys with micropenis are treated with a course of *low dose testosterone* (25 mg testosterone enanthate or cypionate monthly for three doses). The aim of this short course of testosterone treatment is to increase penile length and not to induce puberty. Boys with micropenis should be reared as males as normal sexual function is usually attainable with early intervention.

Suggested reading

1. Bajpai A, Sharma J, Menon PSN (eds). Ambiguous genitalia. In: Practical Pediatric Endocrinology. JP Brothers 2003;97–101.
2. Hutson JM, Hasthorpe S. Testicular descent and cryptorchidism: the state of the art in 2004. J Pediatr Surg 2005;40:297–302.
3. Warne GL, Zajac JD. Evaluation of a child with ambiguous genitalia: A practical guide to diagnosis and management. In: Pediatric Endocrine Disorders. Eds: Desai MP, Bhatia V, Menon PSN. Orient Longman, Hyderabad. 2003;257–276.

DIABETES MELLITUS

Diabetes mellitus is a metabolic disorder that is characterized by hyperglycemia and glycosuria. Hyperglycemia resulting from diabetes mellitus causes damage to multiple organs. Hence diabetes mellitus is the leading cause of end stage renal disease, (ESRD), non-traumatic leg amputation, and adult blindness.

The incidence of both type 1 and type 2 diabetes is increasing worldwide. Sedentary lifestyles and changes in dietary habits are believed to be contributing to this increase.

Classification

Diabetes mellitus is classified based on pathogenic processes that result in hyperglycemia (Table 16.39). Previous terms of insulin-dependent (IDDM) and non-insulin-dependent diabetes mellitus (NIDDM) are not used, since many patients with type 2 diabetes eventually require insulin to control hyperglycemia. The classification is based on pathogenesis rather that modality of treatment. Though most patients with type I diabetes present under the age of 30 years, 5–10% individuals develop type 1 diabetes after 30 years. Likewise type 2 diabetes is being increasingly diagnosed in adolescents who are obese.

Table 16.39: Classification of diabetes mellitus
Type 1 Diabetes mellitus
Absolute insulin deficiency resulting from β-cell destruction
Type 2 Diabetes mellitus
Progressive insulin secretary defect in the background of insulin resistance
Gestational diabetes mellitus (GDM)
Diabetes mellitus manifesting in pregnancy
Other specific types of diabetes mellitus
Genetic defects in β-cell function or insulin action, diseases of exocrine pancreas and drug or chemical induced diabetes

Most patients can be clearly classified as type 1 or 2 diabetes mellitus (Table 16.39). However, occasionally an adolescent with type 2 diabetes may present with ketoacidosis and similarly patients with type 1 diabetes mellitus may present late and progress slowly appearing like type 2 diabetes. The correct diagnosis, however, becomes obvious with time.

Epidemiology

Diabetes has been more commonly diagnosed over the past two decades. The prevalence rates of impaired fasting glucose are also increasing. Type 2 diabetes is increasing in prevalence more rapidly than type 1 due to increasing obesity and less active lifestyles of children. There is a significant geographic variation in the incidence of diabetes mellitus. Scandinavia has the highest incidence of type 1 diabetes mellitus, with Finland having the incidence of 35/100,000/year. China and Japan have a much lower incidence of 1–3/100,000/year. Indian data suggest an incidence of 10.5/100,000/year. India would have 79 million diabetics by 2030, the highest for any country in the world. The variability in incidence in type

1 diabetes is believed to be due to differences in frequency of high risk HLA alleles in various ethnic groups. Type 1 diabetes is uncommon in infants. Diabetes mellitus in the newborn period is usually transient, although occasionally a more permanent diabetes is seen. The incidence of diabetes mellitus increases in children with advancing age all the way to adolescence, with peaks at 5 and 12 years of age. Seasonal variation has been noted with a higher incidence in spring and fall.

Diagnosis

The World Health Organization has outlined diagnostic criteria for diabetes mellitus (Table 16.40).

Random blood sugar of 200 mg/dl or more associated with the classic symptoms of diabetes mellitus (polydipsia, polyuria, and weight loss) is diagnostic. Oral glucose tolerance is not routinely recommended. Fasting blood sugar is also a reliable and convenient test. Elevated hemoglobin A_{1C} is diagnostic of diabetes mellitus. However, it is not completely reliable when dealing with mild elevations of blood sugars.

Table 16.40: Criteria for the diagnosis of diabetes mellitus

- Symptoms of diabetes and a random blood glucose concentration ≥11.1mmol/L (200 mg/dL) *or*
- Fasting blood sugar 7 mmol/L (126 mg/dL) *or*
- Two hour plasma glucose ≥11.1 mmol/L (200 mg/dL) during an oral glucose tolerance test

16

Screening

Epidemiologic studies indicate that the disease is often present for over a decade in patients eventually diagnosed with type 2 diabetes mellitus. 50% or more patients with Type 2 diabetes have one or more of the complications of diabetes at the time of diagnosis. High risk adolescents should therefore be screened for diabetes.

Insulin Synthesis, Secretion and Action

Insulin is produced by the β cells of the pancreatic islets. Proinsulin is an 86 amino-acid precursor of insulin, which is produced by the cleavage of preproinsulin. Proinsulin is cleaved to produce C-peptide and the A and B insulin chains (connected by disulphide bonds). C-peptide is less degradable by the liver and a useful marker of insulin secretion. Glucose is the key regulator of insulin secretion. GLUT2 (glucose transporter) transports glucose into the β cells. Glucose phosphorylation in the β cells is the rate limiting step in insulin secretion. Glucose 6 phosphate metabolism during glycolysis generates ATP; this ATP, inhibits ATP sensitive K^+ channels; simultaneously, voltage dependent Ca^{2+} channel are opened and the influx of Ca^{2+} into the cell causes insulin release. Insulin is released in small secretary bursts of 80–150 minutes and also as large bursts following meals 50% insulin is degraded in the liver. Insulin binds to receptors at target sites, where glucose transporters are translocated to the surface (GLUT4) for glucose uptake. Activation of other receptor signaling pathway induces glycogen synthesis, protein synthesis and lipogenesis.

Pathogenesis

Type 1 diabetes develops consequent to immune - mediated destruction of pancreatic β cells, resulting in severe impairment of insulin secretion in genetically susceptible children. The immunologic process has often been going on for years before endogenous insulin secretion declines to levels resulting in clinical diabetes. Genetic, environmental and autoimmune factors are believed to result in the development of type 1 diabetes.

Genetics

Genetic susceptibility to diabetes involves multiple genes. The major susceptibility genes are located in the HLA region on chromosome 6. Polymorphisms in the HLA complex account for almost 50% of the genetic risk of developing type I diabetes. This region contains genes that encode for class II MHC (major histocompatibilty complex) molecules. These genes are responsible for appropriate presentation of antigen to helper T cells involved in initiating the immune response. Studies have indicated that certain haplotypes confer significant risk of acquiring diabetes while yet others are protective.

Inheritance of diabetes is polygenic. Most individuals with predisposing haplotypes do not develop diabetes. Hence most individuals with type 1 diabetes do not have first-degree relatives with type 1 diabetes. Concordance of type I diabetes in identical twins ranges from 30–70%. 7% of children whose fathers have type 1 diabetes develop type 1 diabetes. Mothers with type 1 diabetes do not confer a similar risk. Siblings are not at higher risk of developing type 1 diabetes.

Environmental Factors

Many environmental agents have been thought to trigger the development of type 1 diabetes mellitus. However, none has been proven to be directly causative. The identification of an environmental trigger has been difficult since diabetes develops many years after the onset of pancreatic damage. Triggers of autoimmune damage include viruses, bovine milk protein (presented in infancy by the early introduction of cow milk protein) and nitrosourea compounds.

Autoimmune Factors and Autoimmunity

Individuals susceptible to development of diabetes have normal β cell mass at birth. Autoimmune destruction affects only the β cells of the islets, even though the α and δ cells are functionally and embryologically similar to the β cells. Autoimmune destruction of islets progresses over many years resulting in a decline in insulin secretion and β cell mass. The pancreatic islets are infiltrated with lymphocytes in a process called insulinitis. Once the islet cells are completely destroyed the inflammatory process abates and the islet gets atrophic. The immunologic process is thought to be trigged by infectious or environmental factors. In most patients markers of autoimmune destruction can be measured after the onset of autoimmunity and decline once clinical diabetes is established. Clinical diabetes occurs when the pancreas loses 80% or more of its insulin secretory ability. Residual pancreatic β cells remain which are functionally active and transiently secrete insulin during the immediate treatment phase resulting in the honeymoon phase of diabetes. During this transient, fleeting phase, insulin requirements decrease. This can last for a few days to several weeks. The autoimmune process eventually destroys the remaining islet cells and the individual becomes completely insulin deficient.

Islet cell antibodies (ICA) can be measured in the serum of 70–80% patients at the time of diagnosis. These include antibodies directed at pancreatic islet molecules such as insulin, IA–2/ICA–512 and GAD–65. The presence of these antibodies predates the clinical presentation of diabetes and declines after clinical disease has manifested. Autoantibody production in Indian children is less pronounced, both in frequency and duration compared to Caucasian children.

Clinical Features

Children and adolescents usually present with symptoms of diabetes that have often been ongoing for a month or two prior to seeking physician contact, with an acute increase in symptoms over the last week. Symptoms of type 1 diabetes mellitus include polyuria, nocturia, polydipsia, recent weight loss, polyphagia and fatigue. Recent acute infection is often noted at presentation. Approximately 50% children present with acute complication of diabetes or diabetic ketoacidosis.

Course of Illness

Most children respond to insulin therapy. Once insulin is initiated, blood sugars gradually decline. Often, after around a week of insulin therapy, the need for exogenous insulin declines, due to a transient recovery of insulin secretion. This phase is called the honeymoon phase of diabetes. Some children can go completely insulin free during this time. The honeymoon phase generally lasts from a few days to a month. It can rarely extend as long as one year. Insulin needs increase over time till such time as when the pancreas can no longer secrete insulin. At this point the child's daily insulin requirement plateaus at 0.8–1 unit /kg/day.

Treatment

The goals of therapy of type 1 and 2 diabetes mellitus are:

- Eliminate symptoms related to hyperglycemia
- Reduce and delay the complications
- Achieve a normal lifestyle and normal emotional and social development
- Achieve normal physical growth and development
- Detect associated diseases early.

A comprehensive approach is adopted to achieve these goals. Symptoms of diabetes abate with blood sugars <200 mg/dL, making the first goal relatively easier to achieve. However, achieving the other goals require focus on diabetes education, medical nutritional therapy (MNT) and well-planned appropriate insulin therapy that is customized to the unique needs of each patient. The availability of insulin analogs and insulins with long duration of action with minimal/absent peaks allows insulin therapy to match glucose excursions with meals and at the same time provide baseline insulin for endogenous glucose production without significant hypoglycemia. Advances in self blood glucose monitoring (SBGM), development of insulin pumps for accurate insulin delivery, continuous glucose monitoring systems (CGMS) and development of a team approach to the management of diabetes care has greatly improved diabetes care. These developments and strategies have allowed many children and adolescents to achieve glycemic goals of near normal blood sugars; goals that were previously almost impossible to achieve, with conventional insulin therapy of two injections a day.

The current therapeutic regimen, which involves frequent blood sugar monitoring and multiple insulin injections or continuous subcutaneous injection infusion (CSII), along with dietary modifications, is called intensive insulin therapy. Intensive insulin therapy involves frequent communication between the physician and the diabetes educator to accomplish insulin adjustments in a timely manner, with the goal of achieving near normal blood sugar at all times. Intensive therapy results in reduced late complications of diabetes by 39–60%.

16

Team Approach

Most diabetes centers adopt a team approach to diabetes care. In this approach, a group of professionals trained in diabetes care provide comprehensive education and care. Diabetes education is the main focus. Individualized goals are set based on the strengths of the patient and family. The team typically comprises of a pediatric endocrinologist, a diabetes educator, a dietician, a social worker and a psychologist.

Insulin Preparations

Current insulin preparations are generated using recombinant DNA technology. Animal insulins should no longer be used. Amino acid substitutions on human insulin will alter insulin pharmacokinetics and this has been used to synthesize "designer" insulin preparations with particular desired characteristics. Insulin analogue – Lispro (Lys(B28)Pro(B29) human insulin) allows better control of blood sugar as its onset of action is faster than regular insulin and duration of action is shorter. Insulin Aspart also has shorter onset of action but it's duration of action is longer than Lispro insulin. These modifications in insulin enable improved glycemic control during fasting as well as postprandial state. Table 16.41 provides the pharmacokinetics and specific characteristics of currently available insulins.

Insulin Therapy

Insulin requirements generally range from 0.5–1 unit/kg/day.

At diagnosis, insulin therapy is initiated with four doses of short acting insulin. The dose is evaluated and an appropriate home regimen of insulin is planned. The goal of therapy is to provide background insulin to maintain glycemic control during the fasting state, and to punctuate this with multiple boluses of short acting insulins to maintain euglycemia during postprandial states in a titrate-able manner. The rest is a mere detail related to the pharmacokinetic characteristics of the insulin being used.

As of now, the most accurate method of achieving glycemic control uses the *insulin pump*. It utilizes insulin delivery devices to accurately deliver a small baseline continuous infusion of insulin, coupled with parameters for bolus therapy – related to food intake and activity levels. The bolus insulin is determined by the amount of carbohydrate intake and the blood sugar level.

16

In most traditional regimens, intermediate or long-acting insulin is utilized to provide background insulin to maintain glycemic control during the fasting state. Short acting insulin is used to provide glycemic control in the postprandial state. Insulin regimens in varying combinations are utilized to achieve near normal blood sugars at all times with minimal hypoglycemia. There are two main classes of insulin regimen: (i) NPH with short acting insulin analogues and (ii) long acting insulin, typically insulin Glargine (Lantus) with short acting insulin; as depicted in Fig. 16.23.

In the NPH regimen two to three injections are given per day routinely: a combination of NPH and short acting before breakfast, short acting at dinner and NPH at dinner or bedtime. In this regimen usually two-thirds of the total daily insulin is prescribed in the morning prior to breakfast and one-third is given in the evening. Pre-breakfast: two-third of the morning insulin is given as NPH and one-third as short acting insulin. Pre-dinner or pre-bedtime: 1/2–2/3 of the evening insulin is given as NPH and 1/3–1/2 of the evening insulin is given as short acting insulin prior to dinner. When drawing up a mixed dose of insulin, short acting insulin is drawn before intermediate acting cloudy insulin. An accidental introduction of longer acting

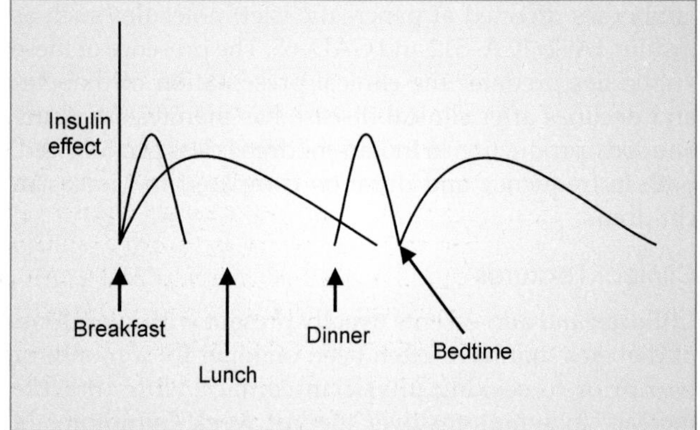

Fig. 16.23: Intermediate and short acting insulin regimen

Table 16.41: Features of different insulin preparation

Preparation	*Properties*	*Onset*	*Peak*	*Effective duration*
Short acting				
Lispro	Faster onset and shorter duration	15 minutes	0.5–1.5 hr	3–4 hr
Insulin Aspart	Faster onset	15 minutes	0.5–1.5 hr	3–6 hr
Regular		30 min	2 hr	3–6 hr
Intermediate				
NPH insulin	Slower onset and longer duration	2–4 hr	6–10 hr	10–16 hr
Lente	Slower onset and longer duration	3–4 hr	6–12 hr	12–18 hr
Long acting				
Ultra Lente	Slower onset and longer duration	6–10 hr	10–16 hr	18–20 hr
Glargine (Lantus)	Slower onset and longer duration no peak	4 hr	—	24 hr

Combinations of intermediate and short acting insulin as 70% / 30% and 50% / 50% are available.

insulin in short acting insulin can result in increasing the duration of short acting insulin. A meal plan, incorporating three meals and two or three snacks, is planned. Insulin is adjusted by reviewing blood sugars. Blood sugars are monitored at least four times a day (prior to meals and at bedtime). It is important to follow the diet outlined in the plan and to adhere to meal timings. Variation in meal amounts and timings can result in wide fluctuations in blood sugars, with high blood sugars from eating excessively and low blood sugars with insufficient food intake and delayed meals. Variations in physical activity and exercise will also affect the insulin/blood sugar dynamic. This plan is typically chosen for children who are young and have difficulty with insulin injections. A child who eats at scheduled times and is able to follow the meal plan is the best candidate. This regimen does not generate near normal blood sugars as desired for optimal control of diabetes. The insulin dose in such regimen should be adjusted based on SMBG results. The fasting blood sugar is primarily determined by the prior evening NPH insulin. The pre-lunch insulin is determined by the morning short acting insulin. The pre-dinner glucose is determined by the morning NPH. Insulin doses are adjusted by 10–20% of the day's dose.

A more physiologic insulin regimen utilizes multiple daily injections of Lispro or Aspart with baseline insulin levels achieved using Glargine insulin (Lantos). In this regimen, insulin Glargine is given once daily either in the morning or evening. Short acting insulin is given with every meal and snack. The dose of the short acting insulin is determined by the amount of carbohydrate intake and the level of blood sugar. The dose of the short acting insulin is calculated based on a carbohydrate ratio (units of insulin per gram of carbohydrate ingested). Most infants and young children are on one unit of insulin per 20–30 grams of carbohydrates, while older children on one unit per 10–15 grams of carbohydrate. Adolescents can require as much as 1 unit of insulin per 5 grams of carbohydrate. *Example: If a child's insulin dose is 1 unit per 15 grams of carbohydrate and he is consuming 60 grams of carbohydrate (1 cup of rice and 1 cup of yoghurt) at a meal, the insulin dose for this meal will calculate as 60/15=4 units.* If the blood sugar is high, additional insulin, called correction dose, is advised to correct the high blood sugar. The correction dose is dependent on the sensitivity of the patient to insulin which is suggested by the total daily insulin dose. If a child is on 100 units of daily insulin the child is less sensitive to insulin compared to another patient who is on 50 units a day. The goal of additional insulin therapy is to correct the high blood sugar to the 120 to 180mg/ dL range; depending on the age of the child and the time of dose. Higher targets are set for bedtime and night, and for younger children, particularly those under age 3 years. An algorithm/formula for assessing correction dose is taught to patients. Example Correction Insulin= Blood Sugar –140/Correction Factor. Correction factor for insulin Lispro and Aspart is 1800/TDD (total daily dose). *Example: If a child is on 60 units of daily insulin, correction factor is 30 (1800/60). A correction factor of 30 indicates that 1 unit of short acting insulin will bring a child's blood sugar down by 30 points.*

Continuous subcutaneous insulin infusion (CSII) via insulin pump is being increasingly used in the western world. The principle involved is essentially a refinement of the regimen above (insulin Glargine. Insulin pumps are being increasingly used in the western world and are continuously being improved upon. Use of pumps in India has been limited, thus far. The infusion pump has significant advantages over MDI. These include: (i) the ability to vary the basal insulin during the day and night by using multiple basal rates allowing adjustment of insulin for nocturnal and daytime requirements; (ii) usefulness in preventing early morning hyperglycemia secondary to dawn phenomenon due to morning hormonal surges; (iii) allowing alteration of basal rates during exercise and hence preventing post-activity hypoglycemia; (iv) allowing boluses to be given in different wave forms (extended, dual wave, etc.) to account for variable absorption from different foods. High fat foods takes longer to metabolize and result in delayed hyperglycemia which can be addressed using complex boluses with dual wave infusion with a greater proportion of insulin given two hours after food intake. Extended boluses are used for food consumed over two–three hours or longer in small portions.

The disadvantages of insulin pump therapy are: infection at the infusion site, obstruction of the infusion set resulting in unexplained hyperglycemia if site is completely obstructed; high cost of care; and the nuisance of the insulin pump which is always attached to the child, being a constant reminder of diabetes.

Insulin pumps have been used in conjunction with sensor devices that measure trans-dermal blood sugars. These measurements enable development of graphs with trends of high or low blood sugars that provide a more accurate and detailed and dynamic record of blood sugar profile.

Medical Nutrition Therapy (MNT)

MNT in diabetes is important in preventing and treating existing diabetes. The goal of nutritional therapy is to match nutritional intake with appropriate insulin. Insulin therapy and self blood glucose monitoring are integrated with appropriate nutrition and caloric intake. Flexibility in caloric intake, especially to allow exercise, is desired. Nutritional plan which allows deviation in food intake incorporating individuals likes and dislikes is implemented.

Nutritional plans are aimed at optimizing blood sugar, weight, and lipids. Rigid nutritional plans are no longer recommended.

An individualized nutritional plan is formulated for each patient. The plan takes into account meal and snack times as well as food consumption prior to the onset of diabetes. A flexible plan is determined to facilitate compliance with nutritional therapy. Simple sugars are discouraged. Foods with a low glycemic index are encouraged. Fiber intake is encouraged. Caloric intake is determined based on the formula: age in years × 100 +1000 (example: for a 10 years old child, ideal caloric intake is calculated as 10 × 100 + 1000 = 2000 calories/day). Nutritional therapy is based on the insulin regimen selected.

NPH /short acting insulin regimens: A typical plan includes 3 meals and 3 snacks (midmorning, afternoon and bedtime). Number of servings of carbohydrate, protein and fat are determined for each meal and snack. Food choices are discussed. In general, these plans tend to be less flexible.

Basal-bolus insulin regimens (Glargine-multiple injections and pump therapy): Carbohydrate counting is taught to patient and families along with basic principles of nutrition. Whole grains and complex carbohydrates are encouraged.

Carbohydrates
- 55–60 % of total caloric intake
- Monitoring carbohydrate by carbohydrate counting or exchanges is suggested
- Refined sugars are reduced to <30 % of total carbohydrates.
- Naturally occurring sugars in fruits are not limited; however fruit juices are not encouraged.

Fiber
- High fiber diet reduces blood sugar
- Intake of 25–35 grams /day is suggested

16

Protein
- Intake is evaluated based on kidney function, growth and glycemic function
- 15%–20% of total caloric intake is provided as protein
- Protein intake is reduced to 8–10% of caloric intake in adolescents with diabetic nephropathy or microalbuminuria

Fats
- The amount of dietary fat impacts adult coronary artery disease
- Saturated fats should be limited
- Intake of trans fats should be minimized.

Sweeteners
- 5 sweeteners are approved (acesulfame, aspartame, neotame, saccharin, sucralose)
- Sucrose does not increase glycemia any more than isocaloric starch. Sucrose and sucrose containing food need not be limited.

Exercise

Physical activity is important for children with diabetes. It increases glucose utilization and increases insulin sensitivity; consequently, it greatly assists in metabolic control. It also builds self esteem. Long tem outcome of children with diabetes is better with regular exercise. Recommended activities include walking, jogging and swimming and organized sports.

Type 2 diabetes mellitus in children and adolescents The incidence of type 2 diabetes in children and adolescents is rising and parallels the increase in childhood obesity, at least in the West and in the more affluent sections of Indian society. Change in dietary habits and lifestyle changes seem to have contributed to this increase. Increase in TV watching and an increase in time spent playing videogames rather than outdoor play have resulted in children acquiring a sedentary lifestyle. Distinguishing between type 1 and 2 diabetes in children can be difficult (Table 16.42). Often children with type 2 diabetes may have weight loss and ketoacidosis as the presenting feature. Sometimes autoantibodies are also measured in children with type 2 diabetes. These children are typically overweight, and have a significant family history of type 2 diabetes. They are noted to have acanthosis nigricans, which is a characteristic skin appearance seen typically in the neck crease, axilla, antecubital area, groin and the periumblical area. The skin appears dark, thickened and velvety. Children who present with ketosis are treated with insulin initially and transitioned to oral hypoglycemics once their endogenous glucose secretion recovers. These children and adolescents should be evaluated for hyperlipidemia, diabetic retinopathy, and nephropathy at diagnosis. It is recommended that children at risk of type 2 diabetes be screened for diabetes. The risk factors include obesity, presence of acanthosis nigricans, and first degree relatives with type 2 diabetes.

Table 16.42: Distinguishing features of type 1 and type 2 diabetes mellitus

Features	*Type 1*	*Type 2*
Onset	Rapid	Slow
Age of onset	Before age 30 years	After 30 years
Obesity	Usually thin; have weight loss	Usually overweight
HLA association	+++	Not increased
Family history	10%	+++
Concordance in twins	25–50%	50–70%
Islet cell autoimmunity	>80%	<5%
Ketoacidosis	Frequent	Absent
Microvascular complications	Rare at diagnosis	May be present at diagnosis
Insulin therapy	100%	Many years after diagnosis

Plasma Blood Sugar and Hemoglobin Goals for Children and Adolescents with Type 1 Diabetes

Goals need to be set, but nevertheless are individualized and planned. Blood sugar goals may need to be higher for children with hypoglycemic unawareness (see below) or who have frequent and serious hypoglycemia. Goals may be set lower if achievable without complication and risk. Younger children have a higher risk of hypoglycemia. Pre-pubertal children are at a lower risk for long-term complication than are post-pubertal children. Therefore, goals for an acceptable range for blood sugars and for glycosylated hemoglobin can safely be set a little higher for younger children.

The goals recommended by the ADA and published in 2007 practice guidelines are shown below (Table 16.43).

Table 16.43: Goals of blood sugar and Hb A1C

Toddlers and preschoolers (0–6 years)
Pre-meal glucose: 100–180 mg/dL
Bedtime and overnight: 110–200 mg/dL
HbA_{1C}: <8.5%
School age (6–12 years)
Pre-meal glucose: 90–180 mg/dL
Bedtime and overnight: 100–180 mg/dL
HbA_{1C}: <8.0%
Adolescents and young adult
Pre-meal glucose: 90–130 mg/dL
Bedtime and overnight: 90–150 mg/dL
HbA_{1C}: <7.5%

Sick Day Care

Children with diabetes require careful intervention at home when they are ill or ketotic. If timely intervention is not provided they can develop diabetic ketoacidosis (DKA) a serious and life-threatening complication of diabetes. Children who are noted to have high blood sugars >240 mg/dL and or are ill should be tested for ketosis. β hydroxybutyrate and aceto-acetic acid can be measured in blood or urine. Based on the level of ketosis additional insulin is provided every 2 hours. This ranges from 5–20% of the total daily dose as short acting insulin. Blood sugar is monitored and parents are advised to push fluids. If child is vomiting, 30 ml of fluid is given every 15 minutes. The choice of fluid is dependent on blood sugar level. Sugar containing fluids are given if blood sugar is normal or low. Scheduled insulin is never omitted. If child is vomiting and unable to drink or eat substantially, the day's insulin is split in small frequent doses. At these times the daily requirement of insulin increases. Parents are advised to bring the child to the emergency room if the child is noted to have altered sensorium, rapid breathing, fruity odor, signs of dehydration, persistent vomiting and persistent ketosis.

COMPLICATIONS OF DIABETES

Diabetic Ketoacidosis

Diabetic ketoacidosis (DKA) is the most common severe complication of diabetes mellitus. DKA is a state of hyperglycemic dehydration and ketotic acidemia. It is characterized by hyperglycemia, acidosis and ketosis. Blood sugar is typically over 250 mg/dL, ketonemia with ketones greater than 1:2 dilution, serum pH <7.3 and serum bicarbonate <15 mmol/L. In moderate DKA, serum pH is <7.2 and serum Bicarbonate<10 mmol/L. Severe DKA is characterized by serum pH< 7.1 and serum bicarbonate<5 mmol/L. It can occur in both type 1 and type 2 diabetes. Hyperglycemic hyperosmolar state (HHS) is hyperglycemic state seen primarily seen in adolescents with type 2 diabetes. Both disorders are associated with absolute or relative insulin deficiency, volume depletion and acidosis. DKA can occur as the initial presentation of type 1 diabetes. 15–70% of all newly diagnosed diabetic children present with DKA. The rate of DKA is inversely proportional to the rate of diabetes in the community. The overall rate of DKA in community has remained consistent at 25%. The prevalence of DKA decreases with age from 36% in children < 5 years of age to 16% in those > 14 years. Mortality rates in children with DKA vary from 0.15–0.3%. However if cerebral edema occurs, death occurs in 20–25% patients and there is significant morbidity in survivors. Cerebral edema accounts for 60–90% of all DKA related deaths in children.

DKA most commonly occurs in children and adolescents who are non compliant to insulin therapy. Recently it has also been seen in patients on insulin pump therapy due to acute interruption of insulin due to pump malfunction. In young patients with type 1 diabetes, psychological problems complicated by eating disorders may be a contributing factor in 20% of recurrent ketoacidosis. Factors that may lead to insulin omission in younger patients include fear of weight gain with improved metabolic control, fear of hypoglycemia, rebellion from authority, and stress of chronic disease. Infection is believed to be one of the main precipitating factors.

Pathophysiology

The most important factor that contributes to pathogenesis of DKA is insulin deficiency. This coupled with an increase in counter-regulatory hormones namely glucagon, growth hormone and cortisol augments glucose production from glycogenolysis and gluconeogenesis while limiting glucose utilization. These hormonal alterations result in hyperglycemia and lipolysis resulting in increased free fatty acid production. Oxidation of fatty acids in liver generate β-hydroxybutyrate and acetoacetic acid (ketones) which results in acidosis and ketosis. Hyperglycemia results in osmotic diuresis causing dehydration and hypovolemia and can progress to severe dehydration and shock. Dehydration also causes lactic acidosis which increases acidosis. Ketosis and acidosis results in electrolyte imbalances and other most diagnostic manifestations of DKA including fruity odor and rapid respirations (Kaussmaul's breathing). Acidosis causes shift of intracellular ions most importantly potassium and phosphate to the extracellular compartment. These are lost in urine in excess amounts resulting in total body potassium and phosphate depletion. However, serum levels of potassium are variable, depending on the stage of DKA. Initially serum potassium levels are high and once treatment with insulin is initiated the child becomes hypokalemic. Phosphate is a major component of 2, 3 DPG and its depletion results in decrease in 2–3 DPG and oxygen delivery to the tissues. Hypertriglyceridemia and hyperglycemia also falsely lower serum sodium resulting in pseudohyponatremia. Each 100 mg/dL elevation in blood sugar lowers serum sodium by 1.6 meq/dL. For example, a patient with plasma glucose of 600 mg/dL would be expected to have serum sodium of 8 m/Eq/L lower than normal.

Clinical Features

The symptoms and physical signs of DKA are listed in Table 16.44.

Though the metabolic derangements of DKA may take a long time to develop, the signs and symptoms develop in 24 hours. Nausea and vomiting are almost always present. Abdominal pain is usually severe and mistaken for acute appendicitis and other causes of severe abdominal pain are considered. Dehydration is usually severe. Hypotension and shock can be seen in severe DKA. Acidosis and acetone accumulation result is classic signs of DKA: rapid respiration known as Kussmaul breathing and fruity odor. Lethargy and CNS depression may evolve into coma. Cerebral edema is a serious complication of DKA and is more frequently seen in children. Children may also have signs of infection including fever which precipitate DKA.

16

Table 16.44: Manifestations of DKA

Symptoms	*Physical findings*
Abdominal pain	Tachycardia
Nausea and vomiting	Dry mucous membrane/reduced skin turgor,/hypotension
Polyuria/polydipsia	Tachypnea/Kussmaul respirations/ respiratory distress
Shortness of breath	Abdominal tenderness Lethargy/cerebral edema/coma

Laboratory Evaluation

Criteria for confirmation of diagnosis of DKA include blood glucose >250 mg/dL, blood pH <7.3 and serum bicarbonate <15 mmol/dL. Serum K^+ may be elevated or normal initially but declines with therapy. Serum Na^+ is low and elevated and creatinine are reflective of dehydration. Leukocytosis and hypertriglyceridemia are found. In DKA serum ketones are elevated and β-hydroxybutyrate is three fold higher than acetoactate. Acetoacetate is preferentially detected by ketosis detection reagent (nitroprusside). Serum ketones are present in significant levels (positive at serum dilution of >1:8). Plasma assays of β- hydroxybutyrate more accurately reflect the true ketone body level.

Management

The goal of treatment is slow correction of dehydration and acidosis preventing development of cerebral edema. The reversal of metabolic derangements occurs over 24 hours with judicious fluid, electrolyte and IV insulin therapy (See management guidelines for details).

A practical approach to the management of diabetes ketoacidosis is shown in Table 16.45.

Nonketotic Hyperosmolar State

This condition is characterized by severe hyperglycemia usually >600 mg/dL, hyperosmolality (>350 mOs/kg), plasma ketones negative or <1:2 dilution and dehydration. Although it is usually a complication of NIDDM, it can occur in IDDM at any age if insulin is present to prevent ketoacidosis, but is insufficient to control the blood sugar. The principles of treatment include judicious fluid replacement, regular insulin if fluid therapy for two hours does not decrease blood sugar and treatment for underlying problem.

Cerebral Edema

Risk factors for cerebral edema include: new onset diabetes, younger age, poor glucose control and longer duration of DKA symptoms prior to therapy. The diagnosis is suspected when there is a sudden change in mental status and child is difficult to arouse. Urgent CT scan of head is required.

Hypoglycemia

Hypoglycemia is defined as blood sugar less than 60 mg/dL. Low blood sugar usually occurs when there is mismatch of food and insulin or the child has been unusually active and insulin and/or food has not been adjusted for increase in activity. Counter-regulatory hormones namely adrenalin, glucagon and cortisol are secreted in the body's attempt to correct the hypoglycemia. Adrenergic symptoms such as tremors, pallor, tachycardia, and sweating can be seen. If left untreated, more severe symptoms from neuroglycopenia (decreased availability of glucose to the brain) may rapidly ensue; these include seizures, fainting and coma. Prevention of hypoglycemia should be discussed with the patient and family during diabetes education sessions. Treatment involves a rule of 15, i.e. 15 grams of free sugar are given in form of sugar, honey, juice or carbonated drink, followed by recheck of blood sugar in 15 minutes. If the child is unconscious glucagon is administered intramuscularly. The dose is dependent on the age and weight of the child. (Infants 0.3 mg, child <25 kg: 0.5 mg and child> 25 kg 1.0 mg). If glucagon is unavailable intravenous dextrose is given.

Intermediate Complications

Lipoatrophy is fat atrophy at the injection site. This can be prevented by rotation of injection sites.

Table 16.45: Practical guide for assessment and management of diabetic ketoacidosis

INITIAL ASSESSMENT

History

1. New onset diabetes: Evaluate onset and duration of symptoms
2. Known diabetic, evaluate :
   - Precipitating factors (insulin dose, illness, stress, dietary indiscretions)
   - History of diabetes (date of diagnosis, previous hospital admissions related to diabetes, insulin dose).
   - Duration of symptoms
   - Recent home glucose levels; duration of urine ketones if tested at home
   - Most recent insulin dose and timing

Physical examination

- Vital signs; hydration status; infections
- CNS status—Glasgow coma scale
- Signs of acidosis

Laboratory

- Bedside blood glucose; urine for glucose and ketones.
- Complete metabolic panel, Hb_{A1C}, lipid profile, insulin autoantibodies, anti GAD-65 antibodies, anti islet cell antibodies.
- Blood gas and serum electrolytes every 4 hours
- Calcium, magnesium and phosphate every 12 hours
- Appropriate cultures, X-rays

ACUTE MANAGEMENT

A. ***Fluids and electrolytes*** (Goal: correct dehydration over 24–48 hours)
   1. Initial fluid bolus should be determined based on blood pressure and capillary refill
      - Usually 10–20 mL/kg as normal saline bolus is given over the first hour
      - Hypovolemic shock—continue fluids for another hour
      - Isotonic fluids (normal saline) to be continued till blood sugar 300 mg/dL
   2. Calculate fluids based on 10% dehydration.
   3. Total fluids **must not** exceed 4000 ml/m^2/day, unless patient is in hypovolemic shock.
   4. IV fluids are without glucose until blood glucose (BG) is 250–300 mg/dL. Add 5% dextrose when BG is 250–300 mg/dL and 10% glucose when BG is <180 mg/dL.
   5. Potassium (20–40 mEq/L; ½ KCl and ½ KPO_4) is added in fluids after urine flow is established and serum K^+ is <5.5 mEq/L.

B. ***Use of bicarbonate***
   1. Bicarbonate is not used routinely in management of DKA
   2. To be considered if pH does not improve and arterial pH remains <7.0 (venous pH <6.9) and serum bicarbonate is less than 5–10 mEq/L. Do not use bicarbonate when serum bicarbonate is >10 mEq/L.
   3. Plan **half correction** of deficit in 24 hours. (Assume total bicarbonate 25 mEq/L for arterial and 27 mEq/L for venous blood.)
   4. Calculate deficit as follows: (Normal bicarbonate – actual bicarbonate) × 0.6 × patients Wt in kg = Total deficit.
   5. Start correction with adding ½ deficit in IV fluids to run over 24 hours.
   6. Discontinue bicarbonate in IV fluids when serum bicarbonate reaches ≥10 mEq/L and serum pH > 7.1.

C. ***Insulin therapy***
   1. Start insulin drip at 0.1 units/kg/hour. If patient is a known diabetic and has received insulin subcutaneously start lower insulin dose 0.05 u/kg/hr
   2. When blood glucose <300 mg/dL, change IV fluids to 5% dextrose with 0.45 saline.
   3. If blood glucose drops to <180 mg/dL, inspite of D5 in IV fluids, change IV fluid to 10% dextrose in 0.45 saline.
   4. If blood glucose drops to <150 mg/dL, reduce insulin drip in decrements of 0.02 unit/kg/hour.
   5. The rate of fall of plasma glucose should be 80–100 mg/hr or 40 mg/hr in the presence of severe infection. If there is no change in plasma glucose in 2 × 3 hours, increase the insulin infusion (0.15 U/kg/hr).
   6. When patient is acidotic and ketotic *never* decrease insulin infusion below 0.05 U/kg/hr and *never* discontinue insulin infusion until after subcutaneous insulin has been given.
   7. Monitor blood glucose every 30 minutes when changing insulin drip or if blood glucose drops <150 mg/dL.
   8. Insulin must be continued until pH >7.36 or serum bicarbonate >20 mEq/L.

D. ***Monitoring***
   - Fluid balance: intake and output hourly to adjust IV rate every four hours.
   - Vital signs: every hour; neurological signs: alertness, Glasgow coma scale, pupils every 2 hours; weight daily
   - Venous pH, serum HCO_3^- and serum ketones every two hours initially and then less frequently. If acidosis is severe and bicarbonate is being given, hourly pH is indicated.
   - Bedside blood sugar hourly; serum electrolytes every two hours; if stable, every four hours.

Limited joint mobility is typically noted in the hands. This occurs due to flexion contractures of the metacarpophalangeal and proximal interphalangeal joints.

Growth failure occurs in children whose diabetes is not well controlled. *Mauriac syndrome* occurs with poor control of diabetes. These children have hepatomegaly, pale skin and extreme short stature.

Delay in sexual maturation is associated with inadequate control of diabetes. These children have delayed bone age.

Hypoglycemic unawareness is caused by frequent hypoglycemia associated with tight metabolic control of diabetes. It is due to impaired counter regulatory response to hypoglycemia. Raising blood sugar targets and prevention of hypoglycemia usually causes reversal of hypoglycemic unawareness.

Chronic Complications

Retinopathy in diabetes is characterized by microaneurysms and proliferative disease. Previously 80–90% of individuals developed eye disease by 15 years of diabetes. With intensive management of diabetes this occurrence is being delayed. Virtually all children and adolescents with well controlled diabetes have lack of retinopathy in the pediatric years.

Nephropathy causes significant morbidity and mortality in the adult years. It is defined by leaking of albumin in the urine. It is preceded by microalbuminuria. Treatment with ACE inhibitors can delay the progression of nephropathy.

Peripheral neuropathy is unusual in children and adolescents. This results in decreased nerve conduction velocity and sensory changes are common. An abnormality in vibration perception is first noted.

16

Screening for Chronic Complications in Type 1 Diabetes Mellitus

Nephropathy

- Annual screening of microalbuminuria should be initiated once the child is 10 years of age or has had diabetes for 5 years.
- Screening is done by testing random spot urine for microalbumin to creatinine ratio.
- Abnormal screening test is confirmed with 24 hour urine microalbumin /creatinine ratio. Patients with elevated microalbumin/creatinine ratio are treated with ACE inhibitors.

Dyslipidemia

Fasting blood levels of lipids are estimated annually. The goal of therapy is to maintain LDL < 100 mg/dL.

Retinopathy

- First ophthalmologic exam is suggested once child is ≥ 10 years of age and has had diabetes for 3–5 years
- Annual follow up is suggested.

Celiac Disease

Evaluation for celiac disease involves testing for serum IgA, anti-gliadin antibodies, and transglutaminase antibodies. Further evaluation is suggested if these antibodies are elevated.

Suggested reading

Dunger DB, Sperling MA, Acerini CL, Bohn DJ et al. European Society for pediatric endocrinology/Lawson Wilkins Pediatric Endocine Society Consensus Statement on diabetic ketocidosis in children and adolescents. Pediatrics 2004;113:e133–140.

17 Central Nervous System

INTRODUCTION

Diseases of the nervous system are common in pediatric practice. Neurological symptoms are encountered in a variety of systemic illnesses. Almost 20–30% of children encounter acute, chronic or recurrent neurological illnesses. These are major contributors to childhood morbidity and disability. Accurate early diagnosis in children is likely to be more rewarding than in adults.

Asphyxia, infections, birth trauma, congenital malformations, neurometabolic disorders and developmental disabilities are common in childhood. Brain tumors are the second most frequent malignancy in childhood. Spectrum of neurological disorders of infancy and childhood is more diverse than in adults. With the advent of newer diagnostic modalities such as computerized tomography, magnetic resonance imaging, functional imaging by PET and SPECT scans newer electroencephalographic techniques and evoked potentials it is now possible to accurately diagnose and delineate many neurological ailments.

Development of the CNS occurs in three stages, i.e. cytogenesis, histogenesis and organogenesis. Final composition and shape of the nervous system is determined by organogenesis, through blending of neural and extraneural tissues. Disturbances in their blending lead to arteriovenous malformations such as Sturge-Weber's syndrome. Inappropriate blending of neural tissue with ectoderm results in formation of hamartoma, craniopharyngioma, pinealoma, etc. These lesions occur along the midline of neural axis.

Destructive, inflammatory lesions and vascular insults of the brain may destroy the brain structure to cause gross brain malformations, porencephaly or hydranencephaly.

APPROACH TO NEUROLOGICAL DIAGNOSIS

History

An accurate and sequential clinical history of evolution of the disease gives more information than a time-consuming detailed neurological examination and expensive investigations.

Onset of illness: The mode of onset gives information about the etiology. Head trauma, vascular causes and acute infections are sudden in onset. Subacute onset is characteristic of infections with organisms of low virulence and neurodegenerative processes. Degenerative and neoplastic disorders are generally insidious in onset. Course of illness gives a clue to the nature of illness. Meningococcal meningitis has a galloping course, whereas tuberculous meningitis may go on for weeks.

Developmental history: It helps in differentiating a normal neurodevelopment from developmental delay, defining the time of onset and impact of the ailment on the neurodevelopment. All the developmental milestones are delayed if the disease begins at or near the time of birth of the child. Development may retrogress with acquired insults or degenerative disease of the nervous system. Also, one should ask for consanguineous marriages and family history of neurological disorders.

Physical Examination

Useful information about the nervous system can be obtained even in an uncooperative and unconscious child by good observation and capacity to correlate and analyze the findings. Inspection is a crucial part of neurological examination. One should observe the child for posture, strength and symmetry of spontaneous movements, behavior, apathy, interest in surroundings, hyperkinesis, involuntary movements such as tremors, athetosis, chorea, myoclonus and convulsions. A mental record should be made of spontaneous movements, since it is not easy to elicit active movements on command. The child winces in response to a painful stimulus; it may be difficult to elicit response to light touch.

Cranial nerves: Light and consensual reflexes show integrity of second and third cranial nerves. Extrinsic ocular muscle ophthalmoplegia and paralytic squint indicate involvement of third cranial nerve. Ptosis with anhidrosis of the face and miosis implies Horner syndrome or involvement of C8 and T1 sympathetic ganglia. Down and out movement of the affected eye indicates fourth cranial nerve involvement. The head may be tilted to one side in patients with visual defects, cerebellar disease or squint. Fifth nerve integrity can be checked by conjunctival or corneal reflex in an unconscious child. Sixth nerve paralysis is diagnosed by a convergent paralytic squint. It may be a false localizing sign. Facial asymmetry, loss of nasolabial fold on the ipsilateral side, pulling of the angle of the mouth on contralateral side and drooling of saliva indicates paralysis of seventh nerve. Wincing or closing of eyes in response to noise indicates intact auditory functioning. Ninth and tenth nerve integrity is determined by gag reflex, nasal twang, nasal regurgitation and position of the uvula. If the child can shrug his shoulders, eleventh nerve (accessory) is intact. In twelfth nerve palsy, the tip of the tongue is turned to the side of the lesion.

Motor Examination

Best power in all limbs, during spontaneous movement and against gravity and resistance should be recorded.

Deep tendon reflexes: These are best elicited when the concerned muscle groups are relaxed. Exaggerated deep tendon reflexes imply upper motor neuron lesions and diminished reflexes are observed in lower motor neuron disease, neuropathies, advanced muscle diseases and disuse atrophy. Cerebellar lesions cause pendular jerks. Plantar response may be normally extensor until the age of one year.

Developmental Examination

This aims to confirm the milestones stated by the mother. In infancy, besides tone, posture, neonatal reflexes, head control, appearance of protective reflexes, and the ability to attain gross motor functions should be examined, using standard tests/charts of development to confirm delayed development in various domains.

INVESTIGATIONS FOR NEUROLOGICAL DISEASES

Neurological investigations may serve to (i) confirm the diagnosis and etiology; (ii) identify the site of lesion; (iii) rule out other conditions; (iv) review the progress of disease; and (v) evaluate the response to treatment.

Lumbar Puncture

Lumbar puncture is indicated in inflammatory CNS disorders, neonatal sepsis, neurologic malignancies (to determine CNS spread and for therapy), autoimmune diseases, demyelinating illnesses, slow virus infections specially subacute sclerosing panencephalitis (SSPE) (for virological studies, oligoclonal bands and immune response), and certain neurometabolic disorders (for CNS metabolites). Lumbar puncture is not indicated in every case of febrile convulsions except in infants or if meningoencephalitis needs to be excluded.

Fundus must be examined prior to procedure to exclude papilledema, as sudden release of cerebrospinal fluid pressure following lumbar puncture may result in medullary coning and cardiorespiratory arrest. Full aseptic conditions should be maintained while doing lumbar puncture to obviate iatrogenic infection. Cerebrospinal fluid (CSF) pressure appears low when there is thick pus in the subarachnoid space which cannot easily come out of the thin LP needle.

The CSF should be examined grossly for its appearance and microscopically for number and type of cells. Protein, sugar and chloride content estimation is routinely performed. Culture and serology of CSF should be carried out if infection is suspected.

Electroencephalogram (EEG)

Electroencephalogram is a common and conventionally employed electroneurophysiological test. Electrical activity from the surface of the brain is recorded by placing a set of electrodes in a specific arrangement on the scalp (montages). Recorded rhythms are evaluated by their rate, amplitude (μV), symmetry and morphology. The various rhythms include fast activity beta rhythm at 14–20 Hz (cycles/sec), alpha rhythm at 8–13 Hz, theta rhythm at 4–7 Hz and slow rhythm or delta at 1–3 Hz. Activity faster than beta is an artifact from the scalp muscles. Fig. 17.1 depicts a normal EEG record.

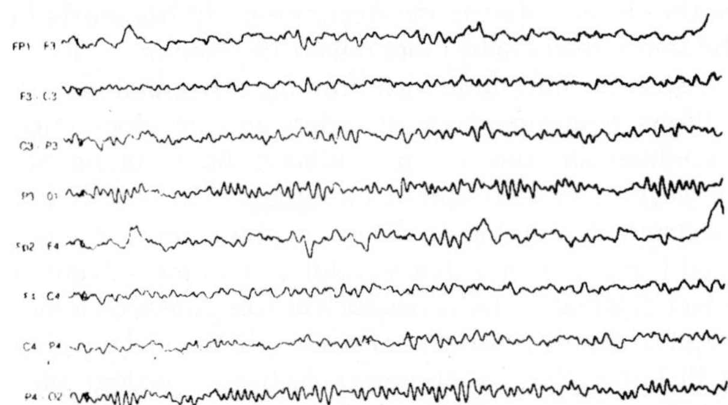

Fig. 17.1: Normal EEG, in a 5-year-old child. Note normal posterior dominant alpha background activity

Indications: EEG is useful in classifying and diagnosing electrical correlates in epilepsy. The EEG is essential to distinguish between a seizure and non-seizure state, e.g. fainting spells, hypoxic episodes and breath holding spells. EEG is especially helpful for making the diagnosis of absence attacks, herpes encephalitis and myoclonic epilepsies, nonconvulsive status and epilepsy syndromes, and to correlate background rhythm with metabolic/organ failure. EEG is not indicated in typical febrile convulsions.

There is no indication to stop anticonvulsants before an EEG, in case the child is already receiving them. A natural sleep record obtained by asking the mother to wake the child early on the day of EEG is useful. A sleep deprivation EEG record is useful where an initial EEG is normal yet seizures are suspected.

Abnormalities: The common abnormalities of background include slow/abnormal or asymmetric rhythms; these may be generalized, localized or lateralized to one side and thus help to localize anatomic lesions. In addition, spikes, sharp waves, polyspikes or hypsarrhythmia may be seen in seizure disorders (Fig. 17.2).

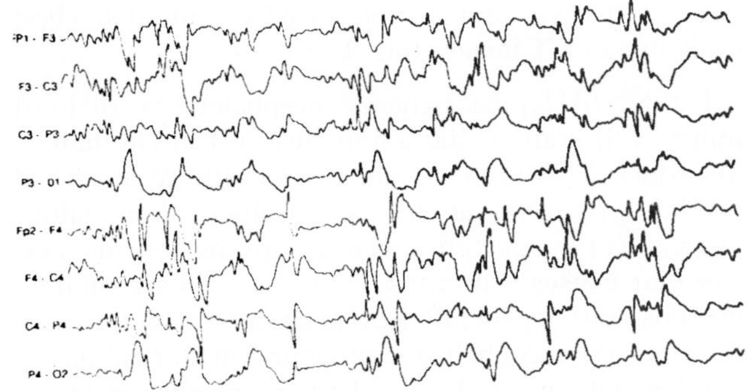

Fig. 17.2: Abnormal EEG, in a 4-month child, showing abnormal slow chaotic background with multifocal spikes suggestive of hypsarrhythmia

Spikes are transient discharges that stand out from background, last less than 70 milliseconds and may be associated with a compensatory slow rhythm. When spikes occur very closely, they are called polyspikes. Spike discharges have great significance in the diagnosis of seizure disorders. Sharp waves have duration of 70–200 milliseconds and are less pointed.

Presence of focal, lateralized, slow rhythms with waves, spike wave discharges are useful to identify a focus in partial epilepsies. A *three per second spike and wave discharge* is observed in typical absence attacks (Fig. 17.3). Brief bursts of polyspikes are common in myoclonic epilepsies. In benign focal epilepsies of childhood, clusters of high amplitude, spike wave complexes are seen in Rolandic areas. High voltage (>100 μV), generalized, chaotic slow waves (hypsarrhythmia) and spikes are common in infantile spasms.

Subacute sclerosing panencephalitis (SSPE) is characterized by periodic epileptiform discharges recurring at similar intervals throughout the record. The discharges are similar in morphology and amplitude and often superimposable (Fig 17.4).

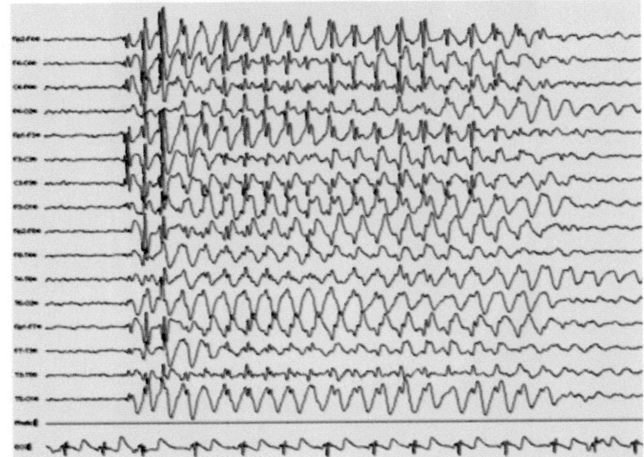

Fig. 17.3: Synchronous 3 Hz spike wave discharges in a child with absence epilepsy

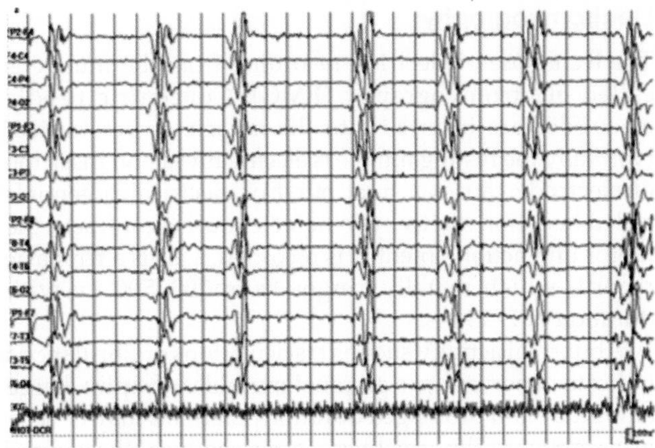

Fig. 17.4: High amplitude periodic sharp waves in a child with subactue sclerosing panencephalitis (SSPE)

Herpes encephalitis may be associated with periodic lateralized slow waves or high voltage complexes. Focal slowing may be observed in inflammatory granulomas cerebral abscesses and infarctions. A focal flattening may suggest subdural effusion. Generalized slowing of the background is seen in encephalitic syndromes. Barbiturates and benzodiazepines produce generalized fast beta activity.

Limitations of EEG: Two percent of the normal population may have abnormal EEG records with spikes that have no clinical consequence or diagnostic utility. Patients with epilepsies may have normal interictal records. Treatment should not be based on EEG alone; correlation with the clinical condition is important. EEG is also not a technique for determining when to stop antiepileptic drugs in epilepsy, though it may be useful in some states.

Video EEG and EEG-telemetry are useful in identifying surgical foci of epilepsy and in management of intractable epilepsies. Magnetoencephalography records the magnetic field generated instead of electrical potentials and can localize the focus three dimensionally.

Evoked Potential Response

Evoked potentials in response to visual, brainstem, auditory or somatosensory stimuli are useful tools to assess conduction, processing of information and integrity of specific sensory pathways. It also helps to determine the site of pathology. Brainstem auditory evoked potentials (BAEP) and otoacoustic emissions (OAE) can detect early defects of hearing and post-kernicteric damage to the newborn. Visual evoked responses (VER) are useful to determine site and severity of neurological insult and evaluate children with neurological visual loss. These tools also have diagnostic utility in assessment of deeply comatose patients and in certain neurodegenerative disorders to distinguish sensory pathway *vs.* neuronal insult.

Electromyography

The technique of electrical recording from the muscle is called electromyography (EMG). Concentric needle electrodes are inserted into the muscle to be studied. Normally the resting muscle is electrically silent. Insertion of electrode causes a brief burst of electrical potentials called insertional activity. When the muscle contracts, the motor unit action potential is recorded. This is a triphasic record, which usually ranges from 200–500 μv with duration of 2–15 ms.

Abnormal activity such as fasciculations or fibrillations indicate denervation, e.g. spinal muscular atrophy. Large amplitude and prolonged duration potentials may be seen in neurogenic abnormalities. In myopathies, these units are of low voltage and shorter duration. Myasthenic syndromes reveal a decremental response on prolonged or repeated stimulation. When requisitioning an EMG, a partly involved muscle should be sampled rather than an atrophic or a normal muscle.

EMG is especially helpful to distinguish between neurogenic and myogenic weakness in a floppy infant and characterization of muscle disorders.

Nerve Conduction Study

Nerve conduction studies are useful for diagnosing specific nerve lesions, neuropathies and for characterizing the effect of systemic disorders on both motor and sensory peripheral nerve function. Diminished nerve conduction velocities, which imply diseases of myelin, can be observed in patients with peripheral neuropathies and dysmyelinopathies. Nerve conduction studies are useful in distinguishing poliomyelitis from Guillain-Barré syndrome.

Neuroimaging

Ultrasonography: It is an investigation of choice in newborns and infants with a neurological illness and can be performed through the open anterior fontanel. It can be performed at bedside and provides quick and useful information. The ventricles, part of cortex and periventricular tissue are very well visualized with ultrasonography. Sedation is rarely necessary. A color Doppler ultrasound evaluates many vascular malformations and congenital anomalies in a 2-dimensional way. The peripheral cortex and posterior fossa is poorly visualized. It is an investigation of great practical utility in the diagnosis and follow-up of newborns with hypoxic ischemic encephalopathy.

Computerized tomography (CT scan): The cross-sectional image produced from the brain section under investigation is analyzed by computerized technology. This slices the brain into thin sections up to thickness of few mm. Newer modifications and sophisticated scanners provide 3-D images, volumetric data and quick sequential images. CT evaluates anatomy of supratentorial brain structures reasonably well. Myelination, posterior fossa and brain stem structures are not well visualized. Calcification is best evaluated by CT images (Fig. 17.5).

Indications: (i) Hypoxic ischemic encephalopathy; (ii) head injury; (iii) craniofacial anomalies, (iv) inflammatory disorders: CNS tuberculosis, neurocysticercosis, basal exudates, pyogenic abscesses and other inflammatory lesions; (v) suspected space occupying lesions; (vi) vascular causes – infarcts, sinus thrombosis, malformations; (vii) degenerative brain disorders; (viii) hydrocephalus, porencephaly and structural malformations.

CT is not very useful in a large proportion of neurometabolic, neuromigration and genetic disorders. Most patients with mental subnormality do not yield significant diagnostic information on the CT scan. In vascular, inflammatory, infectious or neoplastic lesions a plain scan followed by contrast enhanced scan improves diagnostic yield.

Magnetic resonance imaging (MRI): MRI provides anatomical delineation, gray-white matter distinction, and allows detection of myelination and congenital abnormalities, vascular anomalies and migration defects with far greater diagnostic detail than CT. The midline structures, posterior fossa and brainstem structures can be visualized well. Sagittal and coronal views are appropriate for volume evaluation of CNS structures. Abnormalities of spine can also be diagnosed by MRI technique. Some degenerative disorders can be picked up early by MRI. MRI is also of particular use in patients with intractable epilepsy as it helps in anatomic localization of lesion. MR spectroscopy is being increasingly used as an investigative tool.

Functional scans: Functional scans like *positron emission tomography* (PET) help to demonstrate perfusion, oxygen

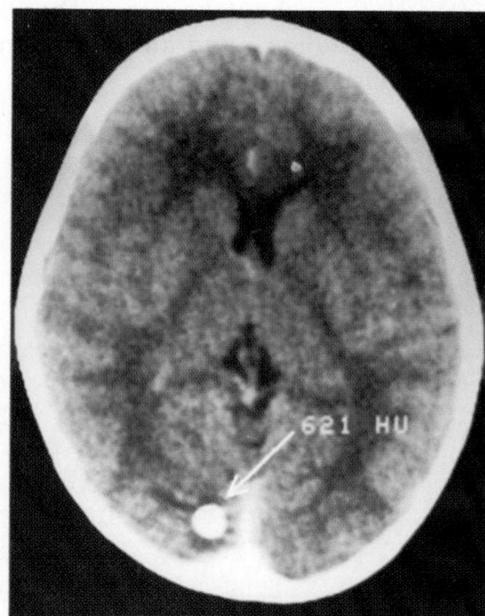

Fig. 17.5: Non contrast enhanced CT of brain showing a calcified cyst

and glucose uptake in different parts of brain like cerebrum, cerebellum, thalamus and basal ganglia. These scans are of practical utility in the evaluation of surgically resectable lesions in intractable epilepsy, cerebral tumors and head injuries. PET scans can be modified to assess cerebral blood volume, cerebral blood flow, oxygen and cerebral glucose metabolism. These have been used as research tools for assessing brain development, speech and vision dysfunction. PET is extremely useful for localization of an anatomic focus in presurgical work up of intractable epilepsy.

SPECT scans utilizing HMPAO and ECD are now widely available. They are useful to identify perfusion in ictal and interictal states. Increased perfusion in the ictal phase is suggestive of an epileptogenic focus. It has become an important presurgical investigation of intractable epilepsies.

Others

Digital subtraction cerebral angiography is done to evaluate cerebrovascular disorders. *Carotid Doppler* studies can be used to study flow patterns. *Myelography* is used for investigating compression of the spinal cord. Metrizamide myelogram can be performed to evaluate compressive myelopathies on the CT scan. In some cases *needle biopsy* of the brain may be obtained for histochemical studies. *Psychometric tests* are carried out for measuring cognitive ability and intelligence of patients with suspected mental retardation.

Suggested reading

1. Brett EM. Normal development and neurologic examination beyond the newborn period. In: Brett EM. Pediatric Neurology. 3rd edn. London: Churchill Livingstone 1997; 25–50.
2. Swaiman KF, Ashwal S, Ferriero DM. Pediatric Neurology; Principals & Practice. 4th edn. Philadelphia: Mosby 2006

CONVULSIONS

Convulsions are caused by abnormal electrical discharges from the brain resulting in abnormal involuntary, paroxysmal, motor, sensory, autonomic or sensorial activity. About 5 percent children experience convulsions during the first five years of life. Motor movements consisting of tonic and clonic components are the most commonly observed phenomenon, except in the newborn period.

Several times, a child may present with a condition that can mimic or be misinterpreted as a seizure. These conditions include convulsive syncope with or without cardiac dysarrhythmia, decerebrate posturing, psychogenic events, dystonia, migraine and many other depending upon the age of the patient. A seizure has to be differentiated from these conditions as misdiagnosis can have significant therapeutic implications.

Neonatal seizures often present with twitching of the limbs, fluttering of the eyelids, sucking movements and conjugate deviation of the eyes. These should be distinguished from jitteriness, tremors, startle response to stimuli, sudden jerks on awakening and tremulousness of the hungry child.

Common causes of convulsions are better classified according to the age at onset (Table 17.1).

Approach to a Child with Convulsions

A good description of the seizures including mode of onset, details of aura, type of seizure, automatism, associated behavioral abnormalities and the postictal phase should be obtained. An accurate seizure description is more informative than detailed neurological examination or investigations. Perinatal, developmental, and family history of seizures help in determining the cause. The child should be examined for evidence of raised intracranial tension, degenerative, metabolic or congenital disorders.

Table 17.1: Causes of convulsions
Early neonatal period
Birth asphyxia, difficult obstructed labor
Intraventricular, intracerebral hemorrhage
Pyridoxine dependency, hypoglycemia, hypocalcemia, dysnatremia
Inborn errors of metabolism
Maternal withdrawal of medications
Injection of local anesthetic into the fetal scalp during the paracervical block given to the mother
Neonatal period
Hypocalcemia, hypomagnesemia, hypoglycemia, dyselectrolytemia
Kernicterus
Developmental malformations, microcephaly, porencephaly, arteriovenous (AV) fistulae, agenesis of corpus callosum
Meningitis, septicemia, tetanus neonatorum, intrauterine infections
Metabolic errors: Phenylketonuria, maple syrup urine disease, galactosemia, urea cycle disorders, homocystinuria
One month to three years
Simple febrile convulsions
Neurological infections: Bacterial meningitis, intrauterine infections, tuberculous meningitis, aseptic meningitis, encephalitis, cerebral malaria, tetanus, Reye's syndrome
Epilepsy
Metabolic causes: Dyselectrolytemia, hypocalcemia, hypomagnesemia, inborn errors of metabolism
Space occupying lesions: Neoplasm, brain abscess, tuberculoma, cysticercosis
Vascular: AV malformations, intracranial thrombosis, hemorrhage
Miscellaneous: Hypertensive encephalopathy, sequelae of birth trauma and birth asphyxia, gray matter degeneration, storage disorders
Postinfectious or postvaccinal encephalopathy: mumps, measles or varicella infection; pertussis vaccination
Drugs, poisons: Phenothiazines, salicylates, phenytoin, strychnine, carbon monoxide, lead

Role of Investigations

Biochemical tests should be ordered if there is clinical suspicion of a metabolic cause. Estimation of glucose, calcium and screening tests for neurometabolic causes usually suffice. Metabolic/cytogenetic studies screening of amino acids, blood ammonia, and blood and CSF lactate/pyruvate levels are indicated if inborn errors of metabolism are suspected and in familial seizures.

Electroencephalography (EEG): A normal interictal EEG record does not exclude a clinical diagnosis of epilepsy. It is the best supplementary test for classification and diagnosis of epilepsy. It should be ordered, to confirm a clinically doubtful convulsion, to characterize the type of seizure, to locate an epileptic focus and to determine its anatomical basis. EEG does not always help in determining the duration of therapy. Considerable discrepancy may exist between the type of clinical seizure and electroencephalographic manifestations.

Cranial imaging: X-ray films of the skull are not helpful, except in microcephaly, scattered calcification and thickening of the calvarium. MR imaging, CT scans and functional imaging are indicated in partial seizures, seizures with focal neurological deficits, dysmorphic features, or skin lesions suggesting neuroectodermatoses, and in the presence of raised intracranial pressure. Focal EEG abnormalities justify the need for imaging. Important pathologies to be identified include atrophies, inflammatory, malformations, migration defects, neoplasia, vascular malformation, etc.

STATUS EPILEPTICUS

17

Status epilepticus (SE) implies prolonged single seizure or multiple episodes of seizures lasting more than 30 minutes without regaining consciousness in between. This precise definition of SE is now revised downwards, so that potentially life-threatening complications are avoided.

SE can be classified as *convulsive* (tonic-clonic, clonic, tonic, or myoclonic) or *non-convulsive* (absence, non convulsive speech sensorial alteration). Convulsive SE is the most important, and is associated with significant morbidity and mortality. The neurological sequelae following SE depend upon etiology, age and duration of SE. The risk of complications increases substantially with duration (>60 minutes). Neurological residua include mental retardation, focal neurological deficits, behavioral disorders and chronic epilepsy. The occurrence of further unprovoked seizures in patients with no prior seizure disorder is between 25 and 75%. The mortality rate is 10%; most deaths are attributable to the patient's underlying pathology. Only 1 to 2% of mortality is related to SE *per se*.

In over 50% of cases, SE is the patient's first seizure. It has been estimated that about 3% of epileptics will experience a SE in their lifetime. Approximately 25% of childhood SE is idiopathic, 25% is associated with fever or meningoencephalitis, while 25% of patients have congenital or neurodevelopmental abnormality or acquired CNS insult. SE may be a symptom of acute disorder, e.g. head trauma, stroke, drug intoxication, subarachnoid bleed, pyridoxine deficiency or metabolic abnormality (hypoglycemia, hyponatremia).

Pathophysiology of SE

SE results from excessive and persistent excitation, or ineffective recruitment of inhibition. Excitatory neurotransmitters that have a major role in SE include glutamate, aspartate and acetylcholine, and the dominant inhibitory neurotransmitter is gamma-aminobutyric acid. The blockage of N-methyl-d-aspartate (NMDA) channels by magnesium ions seems to be important in the pathogenesis of neuronal damage in SE. There is also evidence that heat-shock protein is induced in some neurons in SE and that it may have a neuroprotective role. Associated hypoxia, hypotension, acidosis and hyperpyrexia further exacerbate the neuronal damage.

Evaluation in the Emergency Department

One should obtain careful description of the event, preliminary symptoms, progression of the clinical pattern, duration of the event including the postictal period, presence of incontinence or biting of the tongue. History of seizures, non compliance with antiepileptic drugs (AEDs) or change of AED, and history of prior neurological development are important. One should carefully observe the seizure type, state of consciousness and vital signs, look for systemic disease and perform relevant physical examination.

Postictal confusion usually resolves over several hours; failure to improve gradually should prompt a search for other causes such as hypoglycemia, CNS infection, CNS vascular event, drug toxicity, psychiatric disorders and nonconvulsive status epilepticus (SE). In particular, nonconvulsive SE can present with subtle behavioral changes, which can be easily discounted unless the clinician maintains a high index of suspicion. Nonconvulsive SE can be diagnosed by continuous EEG monitoring.

Investigations

Whether laboratory tests are indicated in the emergency room for patients presenting after having had a seizure for the first time, and are alert and oriented and have no clinical findings, is controversial except for serum glucose estimation. All other tests have a very low yield in this group. Patients with suspected underlying medical disorder need detailed investigations. In known epileptics AED levels are essential to determine noncompliance. If there is history of fever, blood counts, smear and spot tests for malaria and blood culture should be done. Screening for organ failure (LFT/RFT) and arterial blood gas should be done. Sample should be stored for possible poisoning.

Patients who are in convulsive SE require comprehensive diagnostic testing which includes serum glucose, electrolyte, urea, creatinine, calcium, magnesium (if indicated), a complete blood cell count, arterial blood gas analysis, determination of anticonvulsant level (if on anticonvulsants) renal and liver function tests. Lumbar puncture is considered only in patients suspected to have a CNS infection. If meningitis is suspected but lumbar puncture cannot be performed, antibiotics should be administered immediately.

Neuroimaging: It is an important investigation, though the yield varies from 3–41%. The proportion may be higher in developing countries because of high incidence of neurocysticercosis. A head CT is informative for acute head trauma, malignancy, fever, meningoencephalitis, neurometabolic disorders, persistent headache or in presence of focal neurological signs. Brain imaging is eventually necessary in children with nonfebrile status epilepticus and uncontrolled epilepsy. Skull radiograph is rarely of use except in trauma.

Electroencephalography (EEG): An urgent EEG in the emergency room is recommended for those patients with SE especially if nonconvulsive SE is suspected.

Management

There are four goals of therapy: (i) ensure adequate vitals, systemic and cerebral oxygenation, (ii) terminate seizure activity, (iii) prevent seizure recurrence, (iv) establish the diagnosis and treat the underlying disorder.

Emergency Supportive Treatment

Emergency management of convulsing patient focuses on securing the airway, maintaining oxygenation, ensuring perfusion by obtaining intravenous access, and protecting the patient from injury. Head and neck should be positioned to keep the airway open. An oral or nasal airway may need to be inserted. If necessary, airway should be suctioned. Oxygen should be administered by nasal cannula or mask. If the need for respiratory assistance persists after the patient has been supported by bag-valve-mask, endotracheal intubation should be considered. Two lines of IV access should be rapidly secured. Immediate determination of blood sugar is required. Blood sample is procured for other laboratory studies as discussed. 10–25% dextrose (2mL/kg) should be given empirically. Hypotension can potentiate or exacerbate any derangement in cerebral physiology and function. Systolic BP should be maintained at normal levels. Hyperthermia occurs frequently in SE; rectal temperature should be recorded and treated promptly by passive cooling.

Anticonvulsant Treatment

The goal of anticonvulsant treatment is rapid termination of clinical and electrical seizure activity by the prompt administration of appropriate drugs in adequate doses, with attention to the possibility of complicating apnea, hypoventilation and other metabolic abnormalities. The dosage schedule, route and rate of administration of the common anticonvulsant drugs used to treat acute seizures and SE are outlined in Tables 17.2 and 17.3.

Table 17.2: Anticonvulsants in management of acute seizures

Drug	*Route*	*Intial dose (mg/kg)*	*Rate of infusion*	*Remarks*
Diazepam	IV	0.1–0.3	1 mg/min	Must be followed by phenytoin loading
	Rectal	0.2-0.5		can cause apnea,respiratory depression
Lorazepam	IV	0.05–0.1	1 mg/min	Longer duration of action, less respiratory depression than diazepam
	Rectal	0.1–0.4		Slower onset of action than rectal diazepam
Midazolam	IV	0.05–0.2	1–18 μg/kg/min	
	IM	0.1–0.2		
	Buccal	0.1–0.2		Equally effective as rectal diazepam
	Nasal	0.1–0.2		
Valproic acid	IV	20		Emerging as a good drug for status epilepticus
	Rectal	20		Dilute with equal amount of sterile water
Paraldehyde	IM	0.15 mL/kg		Use glass syringe
	Rectal	0.3 mL/kg		Dilute one part with three parts of olive/coconut oil
Phenytoin	IV	15–20	0.5–1 mg/kg/min	Mix only in normal saline, may cause dysarrhythmia and hypotension
Fosphenytoin	IV/IM	15–20 PE/kg	3 mg/kg/min	Less risk of hypotension, data not available in young children
Phenobarbitone	IV	10–20	1–2 mg/kg/min	Hypotension, respiratory depression, especially if used after benzodiazepines

IV intravenous, IM intramuscular, PE: phenytoin equivalents

Table 17.3: Drugs for management of refractory status epilepticus

Drug	*Initial IV dose (mg/kg)*	*Maintenance infusion*	*Remarks*
Pentobarbital	5–15	0.5–5 mg/kg/hr	Titrate drip to seizure control/burst suppression on EEG
Propofol	1–3	2–10 mg/kg/hr	Rapid infusion can cause apnea
Midazolam	0.05–0.2	1–18 μg/kg/min	Fewer hemodynamic adverse effects than pentobarbital
Diazepam	0.1–0.3	0.1–1 mg/kg/hr	Cardiorespiratory monitoring
Lignocaine	1–2	3–5 mg/kg/hr	Proconvulsant at higher doses

Early and effective treatment is essential to prevent a refractory status and long-term neurological sequelae. Many anticonvulsant protocols and treatment guidelines are reported from various institutions and groups. Most importantly, every institution should have a well-established treatment protocol depending upon the local availability of drugs. A proposed management protocol is shown in Fig. 17.6.

Domiciliary Treatment

Pre-hospital treatment is advocated for all children with recurrent prolonged seizures. Home use of anticonvulsants in chronic epileptics can reduces hospitalization episodes, cost and status. The drug that is most commonly used is oral midazolam or rectal diazepam. Diazepam in the injection (5 mg/mL) or syrup (2 mg/5 mL) form can be used. The usual rectal dose for diazepam is 0.2 to 0.5 mg/kg. A size 8 feeding tube after lubricating with xylocaine/paraffin is injected per rectum up to 4 cm. The required dose of the drug is injected through the feeding tube and then flushed with tap water. Only a single prehospital dose of rectal diazepam should be given by the caretakers to avoid possibility of respiratory depression.

The rectal route of administration is not always acceptable or convenient. A promising alternative is midazolam by buccal or nasal route. A few studies have found buccal and nasal midazolam to be as effective as rectal diazepam in the acute treatment of seizures.

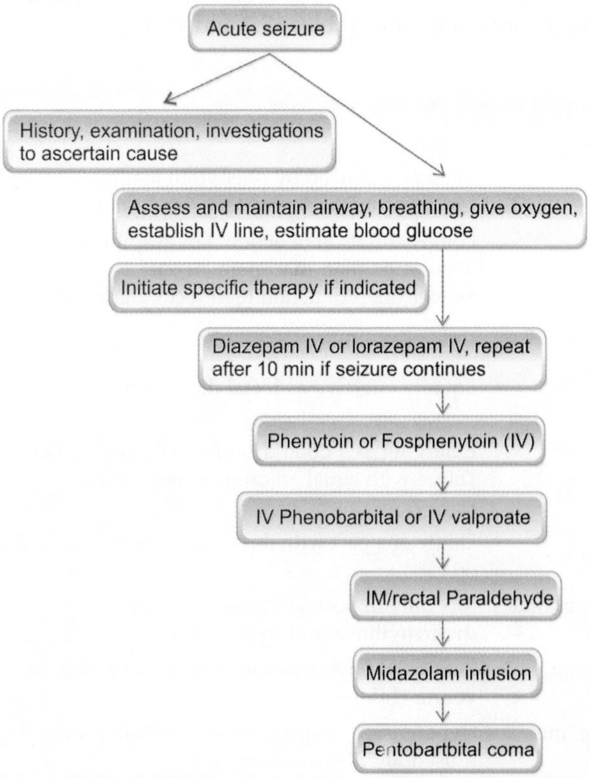

Acute seizure
History, examination, investigations to ascertain cause
Assess and maintain airway, breathing, give oxygen, establish IV line, estimate blood glucose
Initiate specific therapy if indicated
Diazepam IV or lorazepam IV, repeat after 10 min if seizure continues
Phenytoin or Fosphenytoin (IV)
IV Phenobarbital or IV valproate
IM/rectal Paraldehyde
Midazolam infusion
Pentobartbital coma

Fig. 17.6: Algorithm for management of status epilepticus

Hospital Treatment

Any child who presents actively convulsing to emergency room should be assumed to be in SE and managed aggressively. The benzodiazepines are potent first line agents. The drug routinely recommended is lorazepam or diazepam. If diazepam is used when treating SE, a long acting anticonvulsant such as phenytoin must be administered concurrently with diazepam to prevent recurrent convulsions. Diazepam should be administered by the intravenous (IV) route, if IV line has been expeditiously established. Diazepam stops convulsion within 5 minutes in 80% of patients. The usual IV dosage for diazepam is 0.1 to 0.3 mg/kg given at a rate of 1 mg/min. This dose can be repeated two or three times every 5 to 10 minutes if seizures persist up to a maximum dose of 10 mg. Many centers prefer use of lorazepam (0.05–0.1 mg/kg I/V) as a first line anticonvulsant as it has a longer duration of action (12–24 hours), less respiratory depression and repeated doses are less often required than with diazepam. A second long-acting anticonvulsant is also not required because of longer duration of action. Maintenance drugs should be added to control further seizures.

If IV access cannot be immediately obtained, then other routes of administration (rectal, oral) should be considered. The intraosseous route requires an invasive procedure. Rectal lorazepam is not preferred as it has a slower onset of action compared with rectal diazepam. The liquid formulation of valproic acid per rectally in a dose of 20 mg/kg can also be used but response to rectal valproate is slower than with rectal diazepam.

Coupled with potent anticonvulsant properties and the ease of administration by intramuscular, nasal or buccal route, *midazolam* may prove to be an important drug for the initial management of acute seizure when IV access is not available. The dose used is 0.1 to 0.2 mg/kg. The safety, optimal dosing and the clinical trials of midazolam for initial management of SE, however, needs further evaluation.

Phenytoin is useful for maintaining a prolonged antiseizure effect after rapid termination of seizures with a benzodiazepine or when they fail. The loading dose is 15 to 20 mg/kg infused at a rate of 0.5 to 1.0 mg/kg/min (maximum 50 mg/min). A therapeutic effect can be seen in 20 minutes. Saline solution should be used for infusion because phenytoin can precipitate in dextrose solution. The side-effects include hypotension, cardiac dysarrhythmia, phlebitis and tissue necrosis from extravasation, movement disorder and cerebellar ataxia.

Fosphenytoin is a water-soluble ester of phenytoin that is rapidly converted to phenytoin by systemic phosphatases. Fosphenytoin can also be thus administered intramuscularly. The dose of fosphenytoin is expressed in phenytoin equivalents (PE) and is 15–20 mg/kg, infused at a rate of no more than 3 mg/kg/min (maximum 150 mg/min). Phlebitis is less common with fosphenytoin but its primary disadvantage is high cost.

In case of no response to benzodiazepines and phenytoin, *phenobarbitone* is administered in a loading dose of 10 to 20 mg/kg at a rate of 1 to 2 mg/kg/min. Potential side effects include hypotension, respiratory depression, sedation and bradycardia. It must be used with caution in patients who have already received a benzodiazepine because respiratory depression may be exacerbated. Phenobarbitone is the drug of choice in neonatal seizure, hypersensitivity to phenytoin and cardiac conduction abnormality.

If the patient is already receiving phenytoin or phenobarbitone, 5–10 mg/kg of the drug should be given before repeating the dose of diazepam or starting another drug because drug withdrawal is the most likely cause of SE in such cases. Determine the phenytoin level in the acute phase to avoid toxicity.

Paraldehyde can be administered per rectally (0.3 mL/kg diluted 1: 3 in olive or coconut oil) or intramuscularly (0.15 mL/kg deep IM due to high incidence of sterile abscesses) in case seizures are continuing. Paraldehyde should be given in a glass syringe as it dissolves plastic. If signs and symptoms of raised intracranial pressure are present, mannitol can be administered in a dose of 5 mL/kg (20%) IV over 10 minutes to decrease cerebral edema. Maintenance therapy should be simultaneously started with appropriate AED.

Refractory Status Epilepticus

When the seizure has not responded to at least two doses of diazepam intravenously or rectally in succession followed by phenytoin or phenobarbitone or both or seizure lasting more than 60 minutes after treatment has been started, it is labeled as refractory SE. It is associated with potentially fatal complications including severe hemodynamic and respiratory compromise. Patients with refractory SE must be ideally managed in a tertiary health care center with intensive care unit where facility for artificial ventilation is available. The modalities for treatment of refractory SE include barbiturate coma, midazolam or diazepam infusion, lignocaine, intravenous valproate, propofol, and inhalation anesthesia.

In a recent meta-analysis, midazolam infusion was found to be a good choice for initial treatment of refractory SE. Compared to pentobarbital, midazolam has fewer hemodynamic consequences minimizing the need for invasive monitoring. The need for endotracheal intubation and mechanical ventilation is also less frequent with midazolam. Patient recovery is also quicker allowing earlier assessment after SE, and shortening the duration of ICU stay. A bolus dose of 0.15 mg/kg of midazolam is followed by continuous infusion at a rate of 1 μg/kg/min increasing by 1 μg/kg/min every 15 minutes until a maximum of 18 μg/kg/min or seizure control. The optimum rate of infusion at which seizure control is achieved is maintained for a period of 48 hours. Subsequently the infusion rate is gradually decreased by 1 μg/kg/min every two hours. Any seizure activity during the weaning period requires an immediate resumption of the infusion to achieve again a seizure-free period of 48 hours.

Both pentobarbital and thiopental have been used for barbiturate coma. Patients requiring barbiturate coma must be intubated and mechanically ventilated with close hemodynamic and continuous EEG monitoring. Pentobarbital is given in a loading dose of 5 mg/kg followed by an infusion of 0.5–3 mg/kg/hr. The patient is monitored for a burst suppression pattern by EEG. The patient remains in barbiturate coma for 12 to 24 hours. The patient is then weaned and observed for recurrence of seizure activity. If seizure recurs, the patient is placed back into the barbiturate coma and weaning is again tried after another 24 hours. Barbiturate coma is advantageous over the use of general anesthesia.

General anesthesia with isoflurane or halothane in conjunction with a neuromuscular blockade can also be used for refractory SE. Neuromuscular blockade results in muscle paralysis and facilitates mechanical ventilation. Continuous EEG is necessary to ensure that burst suppression has occurred when the patient is paralyzed.

First Time Seizure: When to Initiate Long-Term Anticonvulsant Drugs?

The decision for therapy is based on the underlying cause of the seizure, the results of the head CT or MRI and EEG. All of these data are rarely available before discharge from the emergency room, consequently the decision to initiate therapy must be based on the predicted risk for seizure recurrence, which depends on the underlying etiology of the seizure. When no etiology is identified and the EEG findings are normal, the recurrence risk is 24% at 2 years. Patients who have structural lesion on CT or patients with focal seizure that secondarily generalize have a risk of recurrence of up to 65% and are the group of patients that probably benefit from initiating long-term anticonvulsant therapy.

Suggested reading

1. Rosenow F, Arzimanoglou A, Baulac M. Recent developments in treatment of status epilepticus: A review. Epileptic Disord. 2002;4 Suppl 2:S41–51.
2. Bleck TP. Management approaches to prolonged seizures and status epilepticus. Epilepsia 1999;40 Suppl 1:S59–63.
3. Bleck TP.Intensive care unit management of patients with status epilepticus.Epilepsia 2007;48 Suppl 8:59–60.
4. Brevoord JC, Joosten KF, Arts WF, et al. Status epilepticus: clinical analysis of a treatment protocol based on midazolam and phenytoin. J Child Neurol 2005;20:476–481.
5. Hanhan UA, Fiallos MR, Orlowski JP. Status epilepticus. Pediatr Clin North Am 2001;48:683–694.
6. Prasad K, Al-Roomi K, Krishnan PR, Sequeira R. Anticonvulsant therapy for status epilepticus. Cochrane Database Syst Rev 2005 Oct 19; (4): CD003723.
7. Abend NS, Dlugos DJ.Treatment of refractory status epilepticus: literature review and a proposed protocol.Pediatr Neurol 2008;38:377–390.

FEBRILE CONVULSIONS

Febrile convulsions are the commonest provoked seizures and 3–5% of children experience them. They are defined as seizures during fever occurring between 6 months to 5 years age in the absence of infection of the central nervous system in a neurologically normal child. Febrile seizures are frequently genetically determined. The convulsions are not related to the degree of temperature rise but are frequent if temperature rises abruptly. The febrile convulsions may be (i) simple, benign; or (ii) atypical, complex.

17

Simple benign febrile convulsions: The fits occur within 24 hours of the onset of fever, last less than 10 minutes and are usually single per febrile episode. Convulsions are generalized; 4–18% may show focal convulsions. There is no post-ictal neurological deficit. There may be a family history of febrile convulsions in the siblings.

Atypical febrile seizures: Atypical or complex febrile convulsions should always be distinguished from simple febrile convulsions by the clinical criteria enumerated above. Presence of family history of epilepsy, neurodevelopmental retardation and atypical episodes increase recurrence risk of febrile episodes and subsequent epilepsy.

Convulsions due to neurological damage may also be precipitated by fever, as the cerebral threshold for seizures is reduced with the elevation of temperature. These are distinct from febrile convulsions, which occur in a neurodevelopmentally normal child.

Differentiation from meningitis : Infections of the central nervous system such as meningitis or encephalitis, are important causes of convulsions associated with fever and can be easily confused with simple febrile convulsions. LP should be performed in the first episode of febrile seizure, in infants below 1 year or where meningitis is suspected. In all patients with febrile convulsions, a lumbar puncture is not required routinely. EEG and neuroimaging have no role in febrile seizures.

Treatment: Febrile convulsions are managed by prompt reduction of temperature with antipyretics or hydrotherapy to comfort the patient. Supportive therapy, nursing in semi-prone position, adequate airway and oxygen should be assured. An intravenous line should be started to maintain hydration, to give anticonvulsant medication or to obtain blood specimens for investigation. Possibility of meningitis should be excluded by a lumbar puncture if indicated. Aspirin should be avoided because of apprehension of development of Reye's syndrome. Injection of diazepam (0.2–0.3 mg/kg/dose) slow push IV (maximum of 5 mg/dose) is given for control of seizures. Phenobarbitone is slower acting than diazepam but has a more sustained action. When given IV, action starts within 5–10 minutes but peak concentration in brain is reached in 30 to 60 minutes.

Febrile Seizure Prophylaxis

Prophylaxis of febrile convulsions is indicated if febrile episodes are recurrent (30–40%). Prophylaxis may be continuous or intermittent.

Intermittent prophylaxis is currently the desirable form of therapy during episodes of fever. Intermittent drug prophylaxis is indicated for the first three days of fever as majority of episodes occur within this period. A drug that attains drug levels quickly and prevents febrile convulsions should be used. Diazepam and other benzodiazepines attain desired levels quickly and may be given as a solution per rectum, suppository or via oral route. Oral diazepam, midazolam and clobazam are effective prophylactics. Other agents given orally do not attain desired concentrations quickly and are hence unreliable for intermittent therapy. Intermittent phenobarbitone is of little use as blood levels are not achieved by intermittent use. Antipyretics, hydrotherapy and meticulous temperature recording should be advocated for all patients. Domiciliary care is recommended.

Continuous prophylaxis in the form of antiepileptic drug therapy is advocated in the event of failure of intermittent therapy, especially in recurrent atypical seizures or family history of epilepsy. Only sodium valproate (10–20 mg/kg/day) or phenobarbitone (3–5 mg/kg/day) are effective for febrile seizure prophylaxis. Carbamazepine and phenytoin are ineffective. The duration of therapy should be for 1–2 years or until 5 years of age, whichever comes earlier.

Prognosis: Recurrence risk of febrile convulsions varies from 30–50% and is greater with younger age, female sex, presence of risk factors and atypical prolonged episodes. About 1–2% of children with simple febrile convulsions and up to 5% of those with recurrent complex seizures are likely to develop epilepsy. Parents of the child should be reassured that the risk of epilepsy after simple febrile seizure is not significantly greater than the general population. The risk of developing epilepsy is higher if the seizures are atypical, i.e. last more than 15 minutes, are focal, electroencephalogram is persistently abnormal, if the child has abnormal neurodevelopment or a family history of epilepsy. Complex partial seizures may manifest after several years of prolonged atypical/febrile convulsions. The role of febrile seizures as an etiological cause for temporal lobe epilepsy is uncertain.

Suggested reading

1. American Academy of Pediatrics. Practice parameters: Febrile seizures. Pediatrics 1996; 97: 769–775.
2. Dubé CM, Brewster AL, Richichi C, Zha Q, Baram TZ.Fever, febrile seizures and epilepsy.Trends Neurosci. 2007;30(10):490–6. Epub 2007 Sep 25.
3. RJ.Technical report: treatment of the child with simple febrile seizures.Pediatrics. 1999;103(6):e86.
4. Jankowiak J, Malow B.Seizures in children with fever: Generally good outcome.Neurology 2003 Jan 28;60(2):E1–2.
5. Cendes F.Febrile seizures and mesial temporal sclerosis.Curr Opin Neurol 2004 Apr;17(2):161–4.

EPILEPSY

Definition

Epilepsy is characterized by recurrent, episodic, paroxysmal, involuntary clinical events associated with abnormal electrical activity from the neurons. The patient may present with motor, sensory or psychomotor phenomena, often with alteration in sensorium.

Epidemiology

Five percent of children are estimated to experience one or more seizures in childhood, less than 1% have epilepsy. The incidence is highest in the preschool years. Intrafamilial recurrence of convulsions, especially simple febrile convulsions, is common.

Classification

Epilepsy is classified by appraisal of (*a*) seizure type, (*b*) etiology and (*c*) electroencephalographic data. If the underlying etiology is identified it is symptomatic epilepsy otherwise it is called idiopathic. In cryptogenic a cause is presumed. A simplified modified version of the classification proposed by the International League Against Epilepsy (ILAE) is given in Table 17.4.

Table 17.4: Classification of epilepsy

Generalized
Generalized epilepsy may be (i) tonic clonic (grand mal), (ii) tonic, (iii) clonic, (iv) absence (petit mal), (v) atonic, akinetic (minor, motor), (vi) bilateral epileptic myoclonus syndromes *Idiopathic.* (i) benign neonatal convulsions, (ii) childhood absence, (iii) juvenile absence, (iv) juvenile myoclonic epilepsy, (v) grand mal seizures on awakening, (vi) generalized idiopathic *Cryptogenic.* (i) West syndrome (infantile spasms), (ii) Lennox Gastaut syndrome (childhood epileptic encephalopathy), (iii) myoclonic-astatic seizures, (iv) myoclonic absences
Localized
Simple partial (elementary symptoms, no impairment of consciousness) with (i) motor, (ii) sensory, (iii) autonomic, (iv) mixed symptoms *Complex partial* (impaired consciousness) (i) simple partial but with loss of consciousness; and (ii) with automatism
Syndromes
Idiopathic. Benign childhood focal epilepsy with centrotemporal spikes or Rolandic epilepsy. Epilepsy with occipital paroxysms *Symptomatic.* (i) Chronic progressive epilepsy; (ii) epilepsia partialis continua
Undetermined syndromes
Neonatal seizures Severe myoclonic epilepsy of infancy Epilepsy with continuous spike waves during slow wave sleep Acquired epileptic aphasia

Clinical Features of Epilespy

For the purpose of clinical description epilepsy may be broadly described as generalized or partial (focal). Generalized seizures may be (i) tonic, clonic or tonic-clonic; (ii) absence fits (petit mal); (iii) atonic, akinetic or minor motor; and (iv) myoclonic.

Tonic-Clonic Seizures (Grand Mal Type)

Generalized tonic-clonic seizures are the most frequent form of childhood epilepsy. Classic form has four phases viz. (i) aura; (ii) tonic; (iii) clonic; and (iv) postictal phase.

Aura: A transitory premonitory symptom or aura heralds the onset of a seizure. The child may recognize the impending seizure by the aura and adopt measures for self-protection. Aura may be sensory, visceral, motor or autonomic. Only one-third of patients can describe the aura properly.

Tonic phase: During this phase, skeletal muscles go into a sustained spasm. Spasm of the laryngeal muscles forces the air out from the lungs through a partially closed glottis resulting in a shrill cry. The muscular rigidity is most marked in the antigravity muscles, such as flexors of arms and extensors of lower extremities. The child becomes unconscious and falls on the ground. The face appears pale, pupils are dilated and eyes are rolled either upward or to the side. There is frothing from the mouth. Urine or stools may be passed involuntarily. Later, the face appears suffused. This phase lasts for about thirty seconds.

17

Clonic phase: It is characterized by rhythmic alternating contractions of muscle groups, which persist for a few minutes. In many patients, epileptic phases overlap each other.

Postictal phase: The child may complain of headache, confusion, perform automatic actions, of which he has little recollection later. Rarely, the child develops a transient paresis, may lose bladder/bowel control or injure himself. Unlike in adults, personality changes are unusual in children. EEG shows generalized burst of spikes and irregular 4–6 Hz spike-wave complex.

Absence Attacks

Absence seizures start abruptly in childhood; the peak prevalence is between 6–8 years. Even in children, absence seizures are less common than tonic-clonic seizures. A typical attack of absence seizures is not preceded by an aura. The patients have a brief abrupt lapse of awareness or consciousness. Patient may show sudden discontinuation of the activity being performed with staring spell, eye fluttering, or rhythmic movements. The seizure lasts less than 30 seconds. There is no loss of posture, incontinence of urine/stools or breathing difficulty. Other neurological manifestations and postictal phenomena are absent and development is normal. Unaware of the nature of their illness, schoolteachers may consider them inattentive pupils.

Postictal drowsiness and confusion do not occur and the patient can resume normal work soon after the seizure. Hyperventilation for 3 minutes often precipitates the attacks. Absence seizures may occur in multiples, every day. Attacks following in close succession indicate *petit mal* status or *pyknolepsy*.

About half of patients become seizure-free and the rest develop tonic-clonic fits. This is particularly common in children with a very early or late onset of absence fits. Learning disabilities and behavior disorders when present are probably related to associated conditions. Electroencephalogram shows a characteristic 3 per second spike and slow wave pattern. Absence fits are distinguished from complex partial seizures by shorter duration (10 seconds), absence of aura and abrupt return of full consciousness.

17

Partial Seizures

Partial seizures account for 60% of seizures in childhood. Common causes include inflammatory granulomas, atrophic lesions, vascular insults, birth asphyxia, head trauma and neoplasms. In some geographic areas including India, neurocysticercosis has emerged as a common cause. Neurocutaneous syndrome, arteriovenous malformations and infarcts are less frequent. Magnetic resonance imaging may help to clarify the etiology more accurately than CT scanning.

Partial seizures are classified as

i. *Simple partial* without loss of consciousness, with motor, sensory, autonomic or mixed symptoms.
ii. *Complex partial* with impairment of consciousness and automatisms, psychomotor or limbic system symptoms.
iii. *Partial with secondary generalization.*

Simple partial seizures begin with a focal epileptiform discharge, howsoever brief. The symptoms are generally motor or sensory depending on the cerebral focus. Sensory symptoms include tingling, pain, sensation of cold, burning or special symptoms. Sometimes visual, olfactory, auditory or taste hallucinations may be complained of. Consciousness is not impaired. When the simple seizure spreads from one area of body to the other according to the representation in the precentral gyrus of the motor cortex, it is called a *Jacksonian march*. Interictal EEG shows focal spikes or sharp waves.

Complex partial seizures with motor manifestations: These events occur secondary to the involvement of parietal or temporal lobe. Partial seizures may be associated with automatisms or with loss of consciousness, even if seizures are not generalized. Underlying neurocysticercosis or tuberculoma is the most important cause.

Complex partial seizures originating from temporal lobe (psychomotor epilepsy): The clinical profile is protean and the episodes are frequently misdiagnosed for absence or other seizure types, behavior problems or malingering. Brief visceral, olfactory or visual aura are followed by peculiar posture, tonic jerks of the face and or limbs, or one-sided dystonia. Inappropriate repetitive movements such as lip smacking, chewing and fidgetiness may occur. Patients may perform complex automatisms, acts, or simply wander aimlessly. There is no memory for the events and consciousness is impaired. It manifests, as memory disturbances like forced thinking or dreamy states, transitory fear, visual or other hallucinations. Postural tone is reduced and the child tends to fall gradually. Vasomotor changes such as circumoral pallor are often present. Tonic or clonic movements characteristic of grand mal are usually absent but may follow in about 15% of cases.

The behavior might superficially appear normal, but the child has no recollection of what has happened. In complex-partial seizures associated behavioral abnormalities are more frequent.

Benign Childhood Epilepsy with Centrotemporal Spikes

The syndrome has five characteristic features viz., (i) the age of onset is between 2 and 13 years; (ii) there is no neurological or intellectual deficit; (iii) seizures generally occur in sleep, are simple partial with motor signs and involve mouth area (abnormal sensation tingling and numbness of tongue and lips). Speech involvement, dysarthria and somatosensory symptoms are common; (iv) interictal EEG shows a spike focus over the centrotemporal or Rolandic area; and (v) may be self-limiting with spontaneous remission around adolescence. These seizures account for about one-fourth of cases of epilepsy in mid childhood. It is most likely to have an autosomal dominant inheritance. Treatment with carbamazepine or valproate controls the attacks.

Neonatal Seizures

Incidence ranges from 1–2% to almost 20% in preterm infants. Seizures may be a signal for underlying neurological diseases severe asphyxia or a metabolic cause (approximately 25%).

Poor myelination and incomplete dendritic arborization result in clinical manifestations that are different from older children. Neonatal seizures present in decreasing order of frequency as (i) subtle; (iii) focal clonic; (iii) multifocal clonic; (iv) generalized tonic; and (v) myoclonic.

Subtle seizures may manifest as eyelid blinking, fluttering or buccal-lingual movement. There may be pedaling or automatic movements because of subcortical neuronal discharges. The common causes are hypoxic ischemic encephalopathy (almost half), sepsis and bacterial meningitis. Metabolic seizures due to hypoglycemia, hypocalcemia, dyselectrolytemia and hypomagnesemia account for almost one fourth. Intracranial bleeding, developmental anomalies and inborn errors of metabolism need to be excluded. Malformations and dysgenetic states are important causes of tonic or myoclonic type of jerks. About one-third are multifactorial and idiopathic.

It is important to establish the cause of neonatal seizures; investigations for hypoglycemia, hypocalcemia, hypomagnesemia, hypoxia, sepsis should be performed. Lumbar puncture for the diagnosis of meningitis is advised. Clinical trial with intravenous injection of glucose and calcium is essential, before anticonvulsants are started.

Myoclonic Epilepsies

West syndrome (infantile spasms): The onset is usually between 3–8 months of life. It is characterized by a combination of salaam spells (sudden dropping of the head and flexion of arms), mental retardation and hypsarrhythmia on EEG (diffuse high voltage slow spike and chaotic activity). Common cause of infantile spasms are: (i) hypoxic ischemic encephalopathy; (ii) neurocutaneous syndromes specially tuberous sclerosis; (iii) perinatal infections; (iv) hemorrhage; (v) injury; (vi) metabolic disorders; and (viii) localized structural malformations. No cause may be identified in a large number of cases. The spasms occur in clusters usually on waking. Prognosis for normal mental development is poor. ACTH and corticosteroids frequently help, the course varies from 2–12 weeks, depending upon response. Vigabatrin is a satisfactory choice, especially in tuberous sclerosis.

Lennox-Gastaut syndrome: Onset is usually in late infancy or childhood, is characterized by mixed seizures, including myoclonic, atypical absence, generalized tonic-clonic or partial seizures. Intellectual regression is invariable. Very slow background and slow generalized spike wave discharges (2 per second) are observed on EEG. This diffuse form of encephalopathy may result from factors such as head injury, anoxia, cardiopulmonary arrest, post-vaccinal encephalopathy and CNS infections. Drugs of choice are valproic acid, benzodiazepines and ACTH. Prognosis is often unsatisfactory. Newer anti-epileptic drugs, lamotrigine, topiramate and zonisamide are promising.

Common Errors in Diagnosing Epilepsy

A wrong label of epilepsy may be given to 20–30% children reporting to epilepsy clinics. A variety of paroxysmal disorders, which mimic seizures, should be excluded. These include syncope, breath holding spells, acute psychiatric states, migraine variants, abnormal movement disorders, paroxysmal disturbances of sleep like night terrors, narcolepsy and lastly hysteria. Careful history and EEG are useful to rule out these conditions.

If in doubt, treatment should be deferred until the diagnosis becomes obvious on follow-up of the natural course of the disease. In severe cases, the seizures repeat themselves and in mild cases there is no emergency in rushing to therapy. Certain types of epilepsies may be missed or underdiagnosed, these include brief absence spells, mild myoclonus and abdominal epilepsy. Such cases are relatively uncommon. The vast majority of errors are of overdiagnosis of epilepsy.

Management of Epilepsy

A chronic illness like epilepsy produces emotional and psychosocial disturbances. A physician must therefore give due consideration to them besides medical aspects such as drug therapy, side-effects of drugs and identifying etiology. Child should be protected from injury or accidents during seizures, yet permitted a near normal life. Vocational guidance should be given regarding choice of profession with minimal environmental risks. Epilepsy requires management under supervision of a physician for prolonged period extending over 1 to 4 years.

Drug Therapy

The first line anti-epileptic drugs (AED) include phenytoin, phenobarbitone, sodium valproate and carbamazepine. The indications, dose and side-effects of commonly used drugs is depicted in Table 17.5. Age, sex, economic factors and seizure type determine choice of AED.

Tonic-clonic seizures: Carbamazepine is an effective drug for partial and generalized tonic-clonic seizures. It has the advantage of very few side-effects. Phenobarbitone is the drug of choice in the first year of life. Almost 20% develop hyperkinesia and learning disabilities after first year of life. Phenytoin is often used as initial choice if economic constraints exist. Therapy should be initiated with lowest anticonvulsant doses. The drug dose should be increased gradually. If the seizures control is inadequate or if signs of toxicity appear, an alternate antiepileptic drug should be

Table 17.5: Medications used in epilepsy				
Medication	*Indication*	*Dose*	*Half-life*	*Side effects; remarks*
Carbamazepine	Partial, tonic clonic, atonic, akinetic	10–30 mg/kg/day; start with low doses	13–18 hr	GI symptoms, hepatitis, rash, bone marrow depression
Phenytoin	Tonic clonic, atonic akinetic	5–10 mg/kg/day; 1–2 doses	2–20 hr	Hirsutism, gingival hyperplasia; toxicity if blood level >20 mg/ml. Ataxia, nystagmus, diplopia, drowsiness, seizures (phenytoin encephalopathy), rash, lymphoma. Interferes with calcium metabolism, megaloblastic anemia
Sodium valproate	Broad spectrum	20–60 mg/kg/day; 2–3 doses	7–11 hr	Idiosyncratic fatal hepatic necrosis (especially infants); use L-carnitine if dose >30 mg/kg/d or if high blood ammonia. Nausea, sedation, weight gain, hair loss; false positive urine ketones
Ethosuximide	Absence seizures	20–25 mg/kg; 1–2 doses	4–30 hr	Photophobia, leukopenia, drowsiness, nausea. Rarely blood dyscrasia, myasthenia syndrome
ACTH	West syndrome	20–40 U/day IM for 4–6 weeks; reduce dose next 3–6 months		Hypercortisolism
Clonazepam	Atonic, akinetic Resistant absence seizures	0.02–0.2 mg/kg/day; 2–3 doses		Fatigue, somnolence, hypotonia, excessive secretions
Phenobarbitone	Tonic clonic, akinetic, febrile seizures	5–10 mg/kg; single dose	20–80 hr	Not a preferred agent; drowsiness, hyperkinesia, drug dependency
Lamotrigine	Broad spectrum; partial, absence seizures	5–10 mg/kg/day; 1–5 mg/kg/day single dose with valproate, 10–15 mg/kg/day with enzyme inducing agents	14–50 hr	Dizziness, drowsiness, blurred vision, rash, Steven-Johnson syndrome
Topiramate	Refractory partial, secondary generalized seizures	2–10 mg/kg/day; 2–3 doses	18–23 hr	Weight loss, acidosis, neuropsychiatric symptoms
Vigabatrin	Simple partial; complex partial; infantile spasms in tuberous sclerosis	50–150 mg/kg/day; 2–3 doses	5–8 hr	Drowsy, fatigue, loss of peripheral vision, retinal degeneration, aggravates absence seizures
Levetiracetam	Partial, generalized seizures; myoclonus; photosensitive epilepsy	10–60 mg/kg/day;2 doses	6–8 hr	Behavioral changes particularly in retarded children, sedation
Zonisamide	Refractory infantile spasms Progressive myoclonic epilepsy Partial seizures	2–10 mg/kg/day; 2 doses	24–60 hr	Weight loss, renal stones
Clobazam (add on)	Partial, generalized epilepsy	0.3–2 mg/kg/day; 1–2 doses		Sedation, ataxia, drooling, hyperactivity
Tiagabine (add on)	Partial seizures, with/ without generalization	Starting dose 0.2 mg/ kg/day; 4–6 mg/kg/day	4–7 hr	Exacerbate primary generalized seizures, unsteadiness; avoid in hepatic disease
Acetazolamide	Refractory seizures	10–20 mg/kg/day; 2–3 doses	4–10 hr	Metabolic acidosis, paresthesia, anorexia, weight loss

17

tried and the initial drug tapered. Sodium valproate should be used as single agent. As a rule, monotherapy should be practiced. Polypharmacy should be discouraged, because doses and side-effects of the individual drugs become difficult to monitor. If the above drugs fail to relieve seizures with monotherapy, addition of a second drug is necessary.

Duration of treatment varies from 2–3 years except in severe neurodevelopment delay or structural malformation neurological deficits where risk of breakthrough and recurrence of seizures is higher. Antiepileptic plasma drug level monitoring is not required routinely. It helps in better and safer control of therapy: (i) if high dose levels are being used; (ii) in mixed seizure disorders; (iii) in polydrug therapy; (iv) to assess drug compliance; and (v) to determine plasma level before discarding a major drug.

Complex-partial seizures: The drug of choice is carbamazepine, 10–30 mg/kg/day in 2–3 divided doses. It has a positive psychotropic effect. Slow release preparations may have advantage. In resistant seizures, alternate first line drugs or polypharmacy may be required. Re-evaluation of missed etiological diagnosis should be considered. Other antiepileptic drugs may be useful. Newer drugs and surgery should be restricted for selected patients.

Newer antiepileptic drugs: The more commonly tried newer antiepileptic drugs, lamotrigine, topiramate, vigabatrine, gabapentin, zonisamide, oxcarbazine, etc. Lamotrigine and topiramate have wide spectrum and are useful adjunct after primary failure in partial and generalized epilepsies. Familiarization of drug use and side effects is essential. Oxcarbazine may be useful for partial epilepsies; and vigabatrine for infantile spasms.

Absence seizures: Effective agents include ethosuximide (currently not available in India), sodium valproate, lamotrigine and benzodiazepines

Myoclonic and akinetic seizures: In West's syndrome, ACTH gel 20–40 units per day may be given by IM injections for two weeks. Half and then one-third of this dose is given for a further period of 8–10 weeks. Prednisolone, 2 mg/kg/day in 2 divided doses may be used. The result is almost similar to ACTH. These agents abolish fits and EEG improves; there is little effect on the mental status. Sodium valproate and benzodiazepines such as clonazepam, nitrazepam or clobazam may be used alternatively.

Surgical Treatment

Severe disabling, medically resistant cases of epilepsy may be treated surgically after a careful selection and work up. Possible surgical choices include lesional resection of epileptic areas, resection of corpus callosum and focal resection of parts of cerebral cortex such as temporal lobe and extra-temporal regions involved in epileptogenesis . Surgical treatment should be increasingly used by identification of anatomic lesions to cure epilepsy.

Duration of Therapy and Prognosis

Drug withdrawal should be attempted slowly over 3 months, usually after 1–2 years in absence attacks and 2 year seizure free period in tonic-clonic seizures. Partial complex seizures are more difficult to control. Drug compliance is essential. It is difficult to give a precise prognosis. Almost 10–15% patients relapse after an adequate course of AED's. Risk is low if the seizures were controlled easily, certain genetic types, normal neurodevelopment, etc. Relapse rate is low in generalized tonic-clonic seizures and absence fits. Treatment has to be continued lifelong in juvenile myoclonic epilepsy. Normal neurological and psychological profile indicate better prognosis. It is difficult to control seizures in children with neuro-developmental handicaps and post-traumatic epilepsy.

Social Aspects

One should encourage full participation in educational and extracurricular activities. Competitive sports, which may endanger the child's life should be avoided. Parents must be cautioned regarding the necessity of regular treatment and continuous follow up. In adolescence, epilepsy may merit dose/drug reconsideration. One should reassure that with regular treatment, generally the seizures can be brought under control and children do not suffer intellectual deterioration.

Suggested reading

1. Wheless JW, Clarke DF, Carpenter D.Treatment of pediatric epilepsy: expert opinion, 2005. J Child Neurol. 2005 Dec;20 Suppl 1:S1–56;
2. Berg AT. Risk of recurrence after a first unprovoked seizure. Epilepsia. 2008;49 Suppl 1:13–8.
3. Wheless JW, Clarke DF, Arzimanoglou A, Carpenter D. Treatment of pediatric epilepsy: European expert opinion, 2007. Epileptic Disord. 2007 Dec;9(4):353–412.
4. Nabbout R, Dulac O.Epileptic syndromes in infancy and childhood.Curr Opin Neurol. 2008 Apr;21(2):161–6.
5. Camfield P, Camfield C.Special considerations for a first seizure in childhood and adolescence.Epilepsia. 2008;49 Suppl 1:40–4.
6. Blumstein MD, Friedman MJ. Childhood seizures. Emerg Med Clin North Am. 2007 Nov;25(4):1061–86, vii.

COMA

The word coma is derived from the Greek word: *Koma*, meaning deep sleep. The unarousable sleep and disturbance of consciousness usually results from pathological status affecting reticular formation of the brainstem, the hypothalamus or the cerebral hemispheres.

A clinical definition of coma entails an altered state of consciousness combined with a reduced capacity for arousal and decreased responsiveness to visual, auditory and tactile stimulation. Intelligible speech is affected though the patient may respond to noxious stimuli by purposeful withdrawal, he or she cannot localize pain with discrete, defensive movements.

Causes of coma are given in Table 17.6.

Pathophysiology

Human conscious behavior requires interplay between the cerebral cortex and subcortical structures in the diencephalon, midbrain and upper pons. The anatomic substrate for this arousal system is the ascending reticular activating system (ARAS), a portion of the larger reticular formation that constitutes the central core of the brain stem and extends from the caudal medulla to the rostral midbrain. The ARAS is strategically located and systematically arranged to initiate long-sustained behavioral arousal, during which time higher cortical functions can be accomplished.

Table 17.6: Causes of coma

Causes without focal neurological signs
Cerebrospinal fluid is normal
i. Poisonings, narcotic agents, toxins
ii. Metabolic disorders, e.g. hypoglycemia, diabetic acidosis, uremia, hepatic encephalopathy
iii. Head injury, concussion
iv. Septicemia
v. Postictal
vi. Hyperpyrexia, febrile encephalopathy
vii. Water intoxication
Cerebrospinal fluid is abnormal
i. Meningitis
ii. Encephalitis
iii. Subarachnoid hemorrhage
iv. Cerebral vein thrombosis
v. Midline cerebral tumors
Causes associated with focal neurological signs
i. Demyelinating disorders
ii. Post-ictal coma
iii. Intracerebral bleed, vascular malformation
iv. Tumors, infarcts, strokes
v. Infections: brain abscess, subdural empyema, encephalitis
vi. Head injury, intracranial hemorrhage
Miscellaneous
Systemic illnesses, hypertension, shock

Four pathophysiologic variables indicate the functional level, severity of involvement and the rate and extent of the disease process. These functions include pattern of respiration, size and reactivity of the pupils, spontaneous and induced eye movements, verbal responses and motor responses.

Grades of Coma

17

Stage 1 or stupor: The patient can be aroused briefly and shows verbal or motor responses to stimuli.

Stage 2 or light coma: The patient cannot be aroused easily, except with painful stimuli.

Stage 3 or deep coma : There is no response to painful stimuli. The limbs may be kept in a primitive reflex posture. Cortical control over the motor functions is lost. When the brainstem is intact, the arms are flexed on the chest, the fists are closed and legs are extended (*decorticate posture*). In dysfunction of the midbrain, the comatose child adopts a *decerebrate posture*. The arms are rigidly extended and pronated and legs are extended.

Stage 4 or brain death: All cerebral functions are lost. Pupillary reflexes are absent. There is no spontaneous respiratory effort. However, local spinal reflexes may be preserved.

Glasgow Coma Scale

The score is useful for evaluating progress of cases with disturbed consciousness and is calculated from the figures given in parenthesis.

E. Eye opening: Spontaneous (4), in response to call (3), in response to painful stimuli (2), no response (1).

M. Best motor response: Obeys commands (6), localizes (5), withdraws limb on irritation (4), abnormal flexion of extremities (3), extensor response (2), no movement (1).

V. Best verbal response: Well oriented (5), confused conversation (4), inappropriate words are spoken (3), incomprehensible sounds (2), no vocal response (1).

Score of less than 7 suggest coma, while score of 9 or more excludes coma. Most cases with score of 8 are also comatose.

Approach to Diagnosis of Coma

The airways, breathing and circulatory status should be immediately attended. Intravenous access should be obtained and respiration, blood pressure, capillary refill time recorded. Look for fever, injury, raised intracranial pressure. A detailed neurologic examination should be carried out to rule out involvement of cranial nerves, motor deficits and bladder/bowel dysfunction.

If respiratory depression or circulatory collapse is present, prepare for intubation, assisted ventilation and vasopressor support.

History: A proper detailed history of events preceding coma, background illnesses, exposure to drugs and toxins provides useful information. The acuteness of onset, presence of fever, history of trauma and suggestions of possible bacterial, viral, or parasitic infestations is important. History of immunocompromised states and malignancy may suggest opportunistic infections. Family history of tuberculosis, malarial prevalence may be useful information to elicit. History of headache, vomiting and diplopia suggest raised intracranial pressure. Failure to thrive, vomiting, peculiar skin and urinary odor suggest a metabolic cause. Endocrinal dysfunction, dyselectrolytemia, hypo/ hyperglycemic states, uremia, hyperammonemia suggest metabolic basis for coma. History of preceding seizure may indicate post-ictal coma.

Onset: Determine if the loss of consciousness was sudden or preceded by other symptoms. Sudden onset may be due to trauma, poisoning, intracranial vascular episodes, post-ictal phase, acute hypoxia, hydrocephalus due to obstruction of cerebrospinal pathway in cases of brain tumor.

Systemic examination: It includes accurate recording of temperature, pulse, respiration rate, blood pressure, pupil size and reactivity, coma scale, airway patency, pattern and adequacy of respiration. Skin and mucosa should be inspected for bleeding diathesis, exanthem or systemic disease. Organ failures are suggested by associated jaundice, anemia, etc.

Respiration: Periodic or *Cheyne-Stoke type breathing* indicates bilateral damage to the cerebral cortex with an intact brain stem. It occurs in transtentorial herniation, congestive cardiac failure and some metabolic disorders. It is attributed to an abnormally increased ventilatory response to CO_2 followed by post-hyperventilation apnea. *Hyperventilation* occurs in metabolic coma with acidosis and in brainstem lesions. *Prolonged inspiratory cramp followed by expiratory pause* indicates pontine lesions. *Irregular or ataxic* breathing indicates involvement of respiratory center in the medulla.

Depth of unconsciousness: Presence of yawning, swallowing or licking movements of the lips, is an evidence of intact functioning of the brainstem. In these cases deep coma is unlikely. If a child resists when his hand is allowed to fall towards his face, he is not in coma. However flexion, extension and adduction movements may be seen in comatose patients as they are mediated at lower spinal reflex level.

Involuntary movements: Repetitive, multifocal, myoclonic jerks are seen in anoxic, metabolic or toxic encephalopathies. In infections of the central nervous system, multifocal seizures may occur.

Pupillary signs: Pupils are generally *small, equal* and *reactive* in toxic, metabolic cause of coma. Pupils are *moderately dilated* in midbrain damage; they do not react to light but fluctuate slightly. *Pinpoint pupils* indicate pontine lesion or morphine poisoning. *Bilateral fixed dilated pupils* are seen in terminal states or severe ischemic brain damage, atropine or belladonna poisoning. *Unilateral unreactive dilated pupils* indicate third nerve damage, often associated with transtentorial herniation of the temporal lobe or traction of third cranial nerve against posterior cerebral artery.

Eye movements: Stimulation of cortical center for gaze, results in conjugate eye movements to the contralateral side, whereas ablation produces conjugate deviation of the eyes to the ipsilateral side.

Doll's eye response: If the head is suddenly turned to one side, there is a conjugate deviation of eye in the opposite direction. This response occurs if the brainstem is intact. Doll's eye movement is not seen in normal conscious infants and is absent when brainstem centers for eye movements are damaged.

Oculovestibular response: If the external auditory canal is irrigated with cold water, the eyes normally deviate towards the stimulated side. This response is lost in pontine lesions, labyrinthitis and coma due to drugs such as sedatives and phenytoin.

The hallmark of metabolic encephalopathy consists of loss of oculocephalic and oculovestibular reflexes with preservation of the pupillary light reflex.

Motor responses: Structural lesions within the cerebral hemispheres involving cortical or subcortical motor centers lead to contralateral hemiparesis and hemifacial weakness. In the comatose patient, these motor abnormalities may manifest as alternation in muscular tone, deep tendon reflex or spontaneous activity when compared with the contralateral side.

Flexion of one or both upper extremities with or without extension of the legs (decorticate posture) denotes a predominantly cerebral cortical and subcortical disturbance with relative preservation of all brainstem structures. Decerebrate posturing (extension of all extremities) is observed in bilateral cerebral cortical disease with or without brainstem dysfunction as far caudal as the upper pons. Decerebrate rigidity can result from increased ICP originating in the posterior fossa, metabolic disease, cerebral hypoxia, hypoglycemia and liver dysfunction (Reye's syndrome). Both decorticate and decerebrate posturing is stimulus-sensitive and may require the induction of pain for their appearance.

Flaccidity occurs when a lesion has abolished cortical and brainstem function, at least as low as the pontomedullary junction.

Investigations

Laboratory studies should be carried out to exclude hypo or hyperglycemia, uremia, hepatic dysfunction, dyselectrolytemia and other metabolic abnormalities. Blood ammonia, lactate, acid base disturbances, toxins and poisoning should be investigated on suspicion by preserving appropriate samples. Ferric chloride test shows purple color with ketones and aspirin poisoning. It gives green color with phenothiazine and isoniazid intoxication. Inflammatory causes of the CNS should be excluded by a lumbar puncture and blood/CSF culture and a sepsis screen. In febrile coma, peripheral smear should be examined for malarial parasite. Cranial imaging (CT) helps to identify intracranial bleeds, infarct raised ICP meningeal enhancement, hydrocephalus, etc.

Treatment

Airway should be kept patent and tongue should be prevented from falling back. Blood pressure should be monitored and aspiration should be prevented. Dyselectrolytemia and fluid imbalance should be corrected. In situations where inappropriate secretion of antidiuretic hormone is likely, maintenance fluid may be reduced to two-third of the requirement. Hyper and hypothermia should be managed. Bladder/bowel care and care of the eyes and back to avoid bed sores is imperative. Raised intracranial pressure should be treated.

Fever with acute onset coma of uncertain origin with no evidence of meningitis merits treatment for as cerebral malaria in endemic areas.

Specific treatment should be given for hypoglycemia (IV glucose) diabetic coma (see chapter on diabetes mellitus), inflammatory disease of brain or meninges, metabolic causes or organ failure. Raised intracranial pressure is treated with IV infusion of mannitol, at a dose of 0.5 g/kg every 6–8 hr for 6 doses. Hypertonic saline also may be used. In some cases especially TBM, dexamethasone (0.15 mg /kg every 6-hr) may be used. In cases of hepatic coma, attempt is made to eliminate intestinal bacteria and their products, such as ammonia and false neurotransmitter such as phenylethanolamine and octopomine. Parenteral systemic antibiotics, vitamin and non-absorbable synthetic disaccharide lactulose is given (10–15 mL/day in divided doses) by nasogastric tube or per rectum. Dietary protein is reduced. Hypoprothrombinemia is treated with injectable vitamin K or blood transfusion. Exchange transfusion, plasmapheresis and peritoneal dialysis are indicated in specific situations. Corticosteroids have been used in certain metabolic encephalopathies and post-viral encephalopathies, they are contraindicated in cerebral malaria. The benefit is inconsistent in other states. Metabolic coma due to inborn metabolic errors requires specific treatment.

Suggested reading

1. Giacino JT. Disorders of consciousness: differential diagnosis and neuropathologic features. Semin Neurol 1997; 17: 105.
2. Kirkham FJ. Non-traumatic coma in children. Arch Dis Child. 2001; 85: 303–12.
3. Ranjit S. Emergency and intensive care management of a comatose patient with intracranial hypertension, current concepts. Indian Pediatr 2006 May;43(5):409–15.
4. Halley MK, Silva PD, Foley J, Rodarte A.Loss of consciousness: when to perform computed tomography? Pediatr Crit Care Med 2004 May;5(3):230–3.

ACUTE BACTERIAL MENINGITIS

Acute bacterial meningitis, a major cause of morbidity and mortality in young children, occurs both in epidemic and sporadic pattern.

Epidemiology

17

Age: Acute bacterial meningitis is commoner in neonates and infants than in older children because their immune mechanism and phagocytic functions are not fully matured. The common organisms implicated in the neonatal period are *Escherichia coli, Streptococcus pneumoniae, Salmonella* species, *Pseudomonas aeruginosa, Streptococcus fecalis* and *Staphylococcus aureus*. From the age of three months onward to 2–3 years, the infection is most often due to *Hemophilus influenzae, S. pneumoniae* and meningococci (*Neisseria meningitides*). Beyond 3 years, the two most common organisms causing meningitis are *S. pneumoniae* and *N. meningitides*.

Host: Patients with diminished host resistance (compliment/immunoglobulin/polymorph function defects) are predisposed, also malignancies, patients on immunosuppressive drugs are more susceptible to develop meningitis, specially by fungi, *Listeria* and *Mycoplasma*.

Pathogenesis

The infection spreads hematogenously to meninges from bacterial sepsis or distant foci, etc., e.g. pneumonia, empyema, pyoderma and osteomyelitis. Purulent meningitis may follow head injury. Rarely, the infection may extend from contiguous septic foci, e.g. infected para nasal sinuses, mastoiditis, osteomyelitis and fracture of the base of skull.

Recurrent meningitis may be associated with pilonidal sinus, CSF rhinorrhea, traumatic lesions of the cribriform plate and ethmoidal sinus or congenital fistulae, besides immune deficiency disorders.

Pathology

The leptomeninges are infiltrated with inflammatory cells. The cortex of the brain shows edema, exudate and proliferation of microglia. Ependymal cells are destroyed and purulent exudate collects at the base of the brain. The subarachnoid space is filled with a cloudy or opaque fluid most marked in interpeduncular and chiasmatic cisterns. Exudates may block the foramina of Luschka and Magendie resulting in internal hydrocephalus. Thrombophlebitis of the cerebral vessels may occur leading to infarction and neurological sequelae. Permanent neurological sequelae result from infarction, necrosis and hydrocephalus. In cases of meningococcal meningitis, the illness may be fulminating and death may occur within a few hours because of endotoxic shock.

Subcellular pathogenetic mechanisms: Bacterial pathogens on destruction liberate cell wall and membrane active components (teichoic acids, endotoxins and peptidoglycans). In response the host cells and capillary endothelia produce tumor necrosis factor, cytokines and platelet activating factors. Their interaction with the blood brain barrier and neurons results in extensive host damage. Cerebral edema (vasogenic) results due to endothelial cell injury or cytotoxins, leukocyte products and toxic radicals. The role of dexamethasone in reducing host damage due to blockage of the above mechanisms has been demonstrated in both experimental and clinical settings.

Clinical Features

The onset is usually acute and febrile. In the initial phase, the child becomes irritable, resents light, has bursting headache either diffuse or in the frontal region, spreading to the neck and the eyeballs. The infant may have projectile vomiting, shrill cry and a bulging fontanel.

Seizures are a common symptom and may occur at the onset or during the course of the illness. Varying grades of alterations in sensorium may occur. Photophobia is marked. There is generalized hypertonia and marked neck rigidity. Flexion of the neck is painful and limited. *Kernig sign* is present, i.e. extension of knee is limited to less than 135 degrees. Due to spasm and pain in the back of the thigh or muscles of the back. In *Brudzinski sign*, the knees are flexed as neck of the child is passively flexed. The fundus is either normal or shows congestion and papilledema. Extrinsic ocular palsies may lead to squint, diplopia and ptosis. If skin of the abdomen is lightly scratched, flushing may be seen (*tache cerebrale*). The muscle power in the limbs is preserved. Reflexes are normal, diminished or exaggerated. Neurological deficits like hemiparesis, cranial nerve palsies and hemianopsia may develop. Respiration may become periodic or Cheyne-Stokes type often with shock in the late stages of illness.

Meningitis in neonates and young infants: Bacterial meningitis in the newborn and the first 4 to 6 months of life has many atypical features. Neck rigidity and Kernig sign are seldom prominent. Anterior fontanel may or may not be bulging.

Symptoms and signs, which arouse suspicion of bacterial meningitis are: (i) presence of sepsis; (ii) vacant stare; (iii) alternating irritability and drowsiness; (iv) persistent vomiting with fever; (v) refusal to suck; (vi) poor tone; (vii) poor cry; (viii) shock, circulatory collapse; (ix) fever or hypothermia; (x) tremor or convulsions; and (xi) neurological deficits of varying types.

Newborn babies are at a higher risk for developing meningitis under the following circumstances: prematurity, low birth weight, complicated labor, prolonged rupture of membranes, maternal sepsis and babies given artificial respiration or intensive care.

Special Features

Meningococcal meningitis: Epidemics of meningococcal meningitis are generally caused by serotype A and less commonly by Type C. Type B generally cause sporadic disease. Other serotypes of *N. meningitides* include D, X, Y, Z, W–135, etc. Children living in overcrowded houses are specially predisposed. Carrier state is common in children.

Besides classical features of meningitis, these children show petechial hemorrhages on the skin or mucosa. It is a good practice to look for petechiae over the conjunctiva if there are no hemorrhagic spots or rashes on the skin. Meningococcemia may be associated with acute fulminating illness and adrenal insufficiency. The child is severely prostrated, has hypotension, shock and quickly goes into coma. This is called *Waterhouse Freiderichsen syndrome*. It occurs due to hemorrhage and necrosis in the adrenal glands during the course of meningococcal septicemia. The syndrome may also occur in other types of septicemia.

Rarely a chronic form of meningococcemia may occur. This manifests with intermittent fever, chills, joint pains and maculopapular hemorrhagic rash lasting for several days. Meningococci are very fragile organisms and are destroyed very easily if there is delay in CSF culture.

Pneumococcal meningitis: Pneumococcal meningitis occurs at all ages except for the first few months of life. It usually follows otitis media, sinusitis, pneumonia or head injury. Exudates are common on the cortex, subdural effusion is a usual complication.

Staphylococcal meningitis: Neonatal staphylococcal meningitis is often associated with umbilical sepsis, pyoderma or septicemia. In older children it follows otitis media, mastoiditis, sinus thrombosis, pneumonia, arthritis and septic lesions of the scalp or skin.

Hemophilus influenzae type B meningitis: It is frequent in children between the ages of 3 and 12 months. Subdural effusion should be suspected in infants in whom focal neurological signs and fever persist even after the CSF clears biochemically and microbiologically. Convulsions are common. Residual auditory deficit is a common complication. HiB vaccine is strongly recommended to reduce the community prevalence of this infection.

Complications

CNS complications include subdural effusion or empyema, ventriculitis, arachnoiditis, brain abscess and hydrocephalus. CNS complications should be suspected if infants and children fail to respond to treatment, or if fever, focal neurological signs and constitutional symptoms recur after a lapse of few days. Long-term neurological deficits include hemiplegia, aphasia, ocular palsies, hemianopsia, blindness, deafness, sensorineural auditory impairment (deafness) and mental retardation. *Systemic complications* include shock, myocarditis, status epilepticus and syndrome of inappropriate ADH secretion (SIADH).

Diagnosis

Acute bacterial meningitis should be suspected in children presenting with a brief history of fever, irritability, photophobia, headache, vomiting, convulsions and altered sensorium. Diagnosis should be substantiated by examination of the cerebrospinal fluid. Cells should be examined within half an hour and stained to identify their morphology, rather than mere reporting of cell type on the Neubauer chamber.

The CSF has elevated pressure, is turbid with an elevated cell count, often >1,000/mm^3 and mostly polymorphonuclear. Proteins are elevated above 100 mg/dL and sugar in the CSF is reduced significantly to below 50% of blood sugar or below 40 mg/dL. Thus, it is desirable to obtain the blood glucose level concurrently with the CSF glucose. Microscopic examination of the sediment stained with Gram's stain helps to identify organisms. Collect the CSF for culture on a transport medium.

In partially treated meningitis, CSF may be clear with predominant lymphocytes; culture is usually sterile. Biochemistry may be variably altered.

CT scan is not necessary for diagnosis, but is useful to exclude the presence of subdural effusion, brain abscess, hydrocephalus, exudates and vascular complication. It is also useful to distinguish partially treated pyogenic meningitis from tuberculous meningitis.

Rapid diagnostic tests may be used to distinguish between viral, bacterial and tuberculous meningitis based on antigen or antibody demonstration, e.g. counter current immune-electrophoresis, latex particle agglutination, coagglutination, ELISA and its modified techniques.

Besides being rapid, they are unaltered by previous antibiotic usage. Latex agglutination and ELISA are most popular with sensitivity and specificity of almost 80%. Polymerase chain reaction is used for diagnosis of infection with herpes simplex, enteroviruses, meningococci, tuberculosis, etc.

Non-specific tests including C-reactive protein, lactic dehydrogenase and CSF lactic acid level may help to broadly differentiate pyogenic from non-pyogenic meningitis. CSF CRP and tumor necrosis factor is also elevated in pyogenic meningitis.

Differential Diagnosis

Meningism: This may occur in inflammatory cervical lesions and apical pneumonia. There are no neurological signs and the cerebrospinal fluid is normal. Generalized infection associated with toxemia such as due to *H. influenzae* and typhoid fever may be confused with meningitis.

Partially treated bacterial meningitis: If the child has received prior antibiotics, the cerebrospinal fluid becomes sterile. Biochemistry may be altered and pleocytosis persists, though type of cellular response change. It poses a difficult problem in the differential diagnosis from tuberculous meningitis and aseptic meningitis. The onset, clinical course, rapid diagnostic tests and other ancillary investigations may be useful.

Aseptic meningitis: The clinical and laboratory profile is similar to pyogenic meningitis. The CSF pressure is elevated, shows mild pleocytosis and moderate increase in protein with near normal sugar. The CSF lactic acid is not elevated. No organisms are cultured.

17

Tuberculous meningitis: The onset is insidious with lethargy, low-grade fever, irritability, vomiting and weight loss. Features of meningeal irritation are less prominent and course of the illness is prolonged. Neurological features include seizures, gradually progressive unconsciousness, cranial nerve deficits, motor deficits and visual involvement. Features of hydrocephalus and decerebration are relatively common. Evidence of systemic tuberculosis and family contact should be looked for. Mantoux test may be positive and primary complex may be present on chest X-ray. Cerebrospinal fluid is clear and a cobweb coagulum is formed on standing. It appears as a basketball net suspended from the upper end of fluid in the test-tube. The cell count is in tens to hundreds with majority of lymphocytes; the sugar is less reduced than in pyogenic meningitis. Early stage may pose a diagnostic problem.

Cryptococcal meningitis: It usually occurs in an immunocompromised host. There is low-grade fever, mild cough and pulmonary infiltration. Meningeal involvement has a gradual onset with a protracted course. The clinical features are not specific. The CSF shows the fungus as thick walled budding yeast cells, surrounded by a large gelatinous capsule in India ink preparation. The organism grows well on Sabouraud medium.

Viral encephalitis: Acute onset with early disturbances of sensorium, raised intracranial pressure and variable neurological deficit. The CSF is clear and may show mild pleocytosis, mild elevation of protein and normal sugar. PCR for viral antigens and rising CSF antibody titers are useful diagnostic clues.

Poliomyelitis: It should be suspected as a cause of mild nuchal rigidity during epidemics of poliomyelitis in the community. CSF shows an increase in protein and lymphocytes with normal sugar.

Subarachnoid hemorrhage: Sudden headache and sensorial alteration occur without preceding fever. The course of illness is rapid and signs of meningeal irritation are marked. CT scan is diagnostic. CSF reveals many crenated RBCs.

Lyme disease: It is an infection of central nervous system with *Borrelia burgdorferi*, a tick-borne spirochete. Patients develop encephalopathy-polyneuropathy, leukoencephalitis and hearing loss (ceftriaxone is given IV for two weeks for treatment).

Treatment

Initial Empiric Therapy

Initial therapy recommended is a third generation cephalosporins such as ceftriaxone or cefotaxime. A combination of ampicillin (200 mg/kg) and chloramphenicol (100 mg/kg/24 hours) for 10–14 days is also effective as initial empiric choice. If fever or meningeal signs persist after 48 hours of therapy, CSF should be repeated and antibiotics reviewed.

Specific Antimicrobial Therapy

All antibiotics are to be given intravenously.

Meningococcal or pneumococcal meningitis: Penicillin 4–500,000 units/kg/day q4 hourly. Cefotaxime (150–200 mg/kg/day q8 hourly IV) or ceftriaxone (100–150 mg/kg/day q12 hourly IV) are also effective.

H. influenzae meningitis: Ceftriaxone or cefotaxime IV is used as a single agent. Alternatively, combination of ampicillin (300 mg/kg/d IV q6 h) and chloramphenicol (100 mg/kg/day) may be administered.

Staphylococcal meningitis: Vancomycin is the treatment of choice if methicillin or penicillin resistance is suspected. Addition of rifampicin to the regime increases the CSF penetrance and killing power of these drugs.

Listeria: Ampicillin (300 mg/kg/day IV q6 h) and aminoglycoside (gentamicin, amikacin or netilmicin) are preferred.

Gram negative rods: Cefotaxime/ceftazidime/ceftriaxone may be used. A cheaper alternative consists of a combination of ampicillin and aminoglycoside.

Pseudomonas: A combination of ceftazidime and an aminoglycoside is used. Ceftazidime may also be replaced with ticarcillin or mezlocillin. Meropenem or cefepime are good broad spectrum agents, useful if above drugs fail.

Duration of Therapy

Generally, patients with bacterial meningitis show distinct improvement in 10 days and treatment is rarely necessary beyond 10–14 days except for staphylococcal meningitis and some patients with Gram negative infection. Routine lumbar puncture at the end of therapy is not recommended any more. However, in cases with delayed or partial clinical response, a repeat CSF examination is indicated. Therapy is stopped if child is afebrile, cerebrospinal fluid protein and sugar become normal, and the cell count in the cerebrospinal fluid is less than $30/mm^3$.

Steroid Therapy

Dexamethasone in a dose of 0.15 mg/kg IV 6 hourly for 2–4 days is recommended. The first dose of corticosteroids should precede antibiotic use by at least 15 minutes. This helps to reduce the incidence of residual neurological complications, such as sensorineural deafness and possibly internal hydrocephalus, and behavioral disturbances. This is especially useful in *Hemophilus* meningitis. There is no role of dexamethasone in neonatal meningitis.

Symptomatic Therapy

Increased intracranial pressure: Lumbar puncture should be done very carefully in the presence of increased intracranial pressure. Osmotic diuresis with 0.5 g/kg of mannitol as a 20% solution is administered intravenously every 4–6 hours for a maximum of 6 doses.

Convulsions: Administer diazepam 0.3 mg/kg (maximum 5 mg) IV, followed by phenytoin 10 to 15 mg/kg as initial treatment. Subsequently, phenytoin is given 5 mg/kg/day PO or IV until the antibiotics are continued.

Fluid and electrolyte homeostasis: Restricted fluids (two-third of maintenance) may be required due to inappropriate ADH secretion in some patients. If unconscious, child may be fed through the nasogastric tube.

Hypotension: Fall in blood pressure should be corrected by intravenous infusion of fluids and vasopressors such as dopamine and dobutamine.

Nursing care: The oral cavity, eyes, bladder and bowel should be taken care of. Management of constipation prevents atony of the rectum. Retention of the urine is managed by gentle suprapubic pressure or a hot water bottle. Bedsores are prevented by repeated change of posture in the bed and application of methylated spirit on the skin to harden it. Soft foam rubber mattress or air cushion is used to prevent pressure on the bony points.

Treatment of complications: Post-treatment complications are attributed to exudates, vascular insults and release of endotoxin in the cerebrospinal fluid.

Subdural empyema: Drainage of the subdural space along with intensive antibiotic therapy.

Hydrocephalus: Ventriculomegaly may occur in the acute phase and generally regresses. Ventriculoatrial or ventriculoperitoneal shunt is rarely required.

Follow-Up and Rehabilitation

All cases of bacterial meningitis should be followed up for early detection of residual neurological handicaps and provided appropriate rehabilitation. Auditory evaluation should be carried out at the time of discharge and 6 weeks later.

Suggested reading

1. El Bashir H, Laundy M, Booy R. Diagnosis and treatment of bacterial meningitis. Arch Dis Child 2003; 88: 615–20.
2. Tunkel AR: Bacterial meningitis. LWW 2001, Philadelphia USA
3. van de Beek D, de Gans J,McIntyre P, Prasad K. Corticosteroids for acute bacterial meningitis. Cochrane Database of Systematic Reviews 2007, Issue 1. Art. No.: CD004405.
4. Tunkel AR, Hartman BJ,Kaplan SL. Practice Guidelines for the Management of Bacterial Meningitis. Clinical Infectious Diseases 2004; 39:1267–84
5. Maconochie I, Baumer H, Stewart MER. Fluid therapy for acute bacterial meningitis. Cochrane Database of Systematic Reviews 2008, Issue 1. Art. No.: CD004786.

TUBERCULOUS MENINGITIS

Meningitis is a serious complication of childhood tuberculosis. It may occur at any age, but is most common between 6 and 24 months of age, there is usually a focus of primary infection with tuberculosis or concomitantly with miliary tuberculosis. Mortality rate has reduced but survivors may be left with serious disabling neurological sequelae.

Pathogenesis

The tuberculous infection usually reaches the meninges by hematogenous route, and less commonly through the intracranial lymphatics or the cervical lymph nodes. Tubercle bacilli are immobilized in the end arteries and lead to formation of submeningeal tubercular foci. These may discharge the tubercle bacilli into the subarachnoid space intermittently. The bacilli proliferate and cause perivascular exudation followed by caseation, gliosis and giant cell formation. Tuberculous meningitis may occur as a part of the generalized miliary tuberculosis, with tubercles in the choroid plexus directly infecting the meninges.

Pathology

The meningeal surface and ependyma are inflamed, covered with yellow grayish exudates and tubercles. These are most severe at the base, in the region of the temporal lobes and along the course of the middle cerebral artery. The subarachnoid space and the arachnoid villi are obliterated resulting in poor reabsorption of cerebrospinal fluid and dilation of the ventricles, the exudate may block cerebrospinal fluid pathway resulting in hydrocephalus.

The choroid plexus is congested, edematous and studded with tubercles. There is cerebral edema. There may be infarcts in the brain due to vascular occlusion. Tuberculous encephalopathy results in diffuse edema of brain simulating postinfective, allergic encephalopathy. Necrotizing or hemorrhagic leukoencephalopathy may occur in some cases.

Clinical Manifestations

The clinical course of tuberculous meningitis is described in three stages. This differentiation is arbitrary as one-stage merges into the other.

Prodromal stage or stage of invasion: The onset is insidious and vague with low-grade fever, loss of appetite and disturbed sleep. The child who was active and playful earlier becomes peevish, irritable and restless. Vomiting is frequent and the older children may complain of headache. He may exhibit head banging and resents exposure to bright sunlight (photophobia). Constipation is usual.

Stage of meningitis: During this stage, neck rigidity is demonstrated and Kernig sign is positive. The temperature is elevated, usually up to 39°C and may be remittent or intermittent. The pulse is slow but usually regular in rhythm and volume. Breathing may be disturbed. The patient may be drowsy or delirious. Muscle tone may be increased. As the disease progresses, convulsions and neurological deficits like monoplegia and hemiplegia may occur; sphincter control is usually lost.

Stage of coma: This stage is characterized by loss of consciousness, rise of temperature and altered respiratory pattern. Pupils are dilated, often unequal, with nystagmus and squint. Ptosis and ophthalmoplegia are frequent. With the progression of the disease, the coma deepens; episodic decerebration is observed which progresses in severity. The respiration becomes Cheyne-Stokes or Biot type, bradycardia is common. Untreated illness is lethal in about four weeks.

According to Udani, *et al.* the frequency of various neurological manifestations is as follows: hemiplegia (20%), quadriplegia (19%), monoplegia (3%), hemiballismus (11%), tremors (6.1%), midline cerebellar syndromes (4%), cranial nerve palsies (14%), decerebrate rigidity (13%), decorticate rigidity (3%), and cerebellar hemispheric lesions (1.0%).

Diagnosis

Lumbar puncture: Lumbar puncture should always be done in children with low-grade pyrexia, unexplained recurrent vomiting, unusual irritability and lassitude. The cerebrospinal fluid pressure is elevated to 30–40 cm H_2O (normal 3–4 cm H_2O). The CSF may be clear and colorless, spinal block may cause xanthochromia. On standing, a pellicle or a cobweb coagulum is formed in the center of the tube. It is composed of cells and tubercle bacilli enmeshed in fibrin. The CSF reveals increased cells 100–400/mm^3, polymorphonuclear cells may predominate in early stages but are replaced soon by lymphocytes. The CSF protein is increased above 40 mg/dL, and sugar usually reduced to about 2/3 of the blood sugar. The chloride level is less than 600 mg/dL. Cerebrospinal fluid does not confirm the etiological diagnosis, but is adequate evidence for starting antitubercular therapy before more definite evidence of tuberculosis is available. Demonstration of acid fast bacilli by direct smear, culture and guinea pig inoculation is seldom positive. Bactec and PCR are useful tests where available.

CT scan: Computerized tomography is useful in tubercular meningitis and identifies many pathological correlates of tubercular meningitis. Basal exudates, inflammatory granulomas, hypodense lesions or infarcts and hydrocephalus both communicating and less commonly obstructive type may be seen (Fig. 17.7). X-ray of the chest may provide supportive evidence for tuberculosis. Tuberculin test should be done. A negative reaction does not always exclude the diagnosis.

Serological tests: for the diagnosis of tuberculous meningitis are not very sensitive; ELISA is also not very useful. ***Bactec*** and ***PCR*** for tuberculosis carry better sensitivity and specificity. Tests for HIV should be performed on all suspected subjects.

Differential Diagnosis

Purulent meningitis: The onset is acute with rapid progression. The cerebrospinal fluid is turbid or purulent

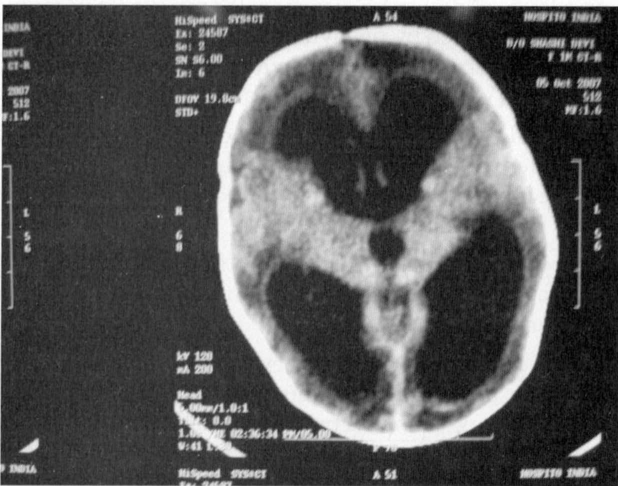

Fig. 17.7: Contrast enhanced CT of brain showing communicating hydrocephalous and periventricular ooze in a child with tubercular meningitis

with a significant increase in the number of polymorphonuclear leukocytes in the CSF. Protein content is elevated and sugar level is markedly decreased. The etiological agent is demonstrated by the examination of smear, culture or serology.

Partially treated purulent meningitis: Poses a difficult diagnostic dilemma. The clinical picture and cerebrospinal fluid changes are often indistinguishable from tuberculous meningitis. Rapid diagnostic tests to rule out specific bacterial antigens should be performed if available. PCR and Bactec provide supportive evidence for tuberculosis. Treat with a combination of antipyogenic and antitubercular regimen for 10 days and repeat the lumbar puncture to evaluate response. Bacterial meningitis cases are likely to improve substantially and the antitubercular treatment may then be discontinued.

Encephalitis: The onset is acute with fever, seizures, disturbances of sensorium, drowsiness and diffuse or focal neurological signs. The cerebrospinal fluid reveals mild pleocytosis, normal or mildly elevated proteins and normal sugar. CT scan is normal. EEG may be abnormal.

Typhoid encephalopathy: Typhoid patients with severe toxemia may appear drowsy and develop neurological deficits without meningeal signs. The clinical picture may simulate tuberculous meningitis. Cerebrospinal fluid is normal. Blood culture is positive for *Salmonella typhi* and Widal test may be positive.

Brain abscess: Patients present with irregular low-grade fever, localized neurological symptoms and features of raised intracranial pressure. A prior history of congenital cyanotic heart disease or pyogenic lesions (suppurative otitis media, mastoiditis, lung abscess, osteomyelitis, etc.) should be asked for. The cerebrospinal fluid is normal except when the abscess communicates with the subarachnoid space; CT scan is diagnostic.

Brain tumor: The onset is slow with history of headache, recurrent vomiting, disturbances of vision and localizing neurological signs. The patients are usually afebrile. CT or MRI helps in diagnosis.

Chronic subdural hematoma: There may be a history of head injury or trivial trauma, symptoms of failure to thrive, headache, vomiting, localizing neurological signs and features of increased intracranial pressure. The fundus shows papilledema or choked disks. The sutures may be separated. The cerebrospinal fluid is normal. CT scan or ultrasound is useful. The subdural tap shows fluid with high protein concentration.

Amebic meningoencephalitis: Free living amebae, i.e. *Naeglaria* and *Acanthameba* can cause meningoencephalitis. While *Naeglaria* meningoencephalitis presents acutely, *Acanthameba* meningoencephalitis presents as chronic granulomatous encephalitis. It is more common in immunocompromised hosts. Non-response to antipyogenic or antitubercular therapy should arouse suspicion. Diagnosis is made by demonstration of motile amebae in the fresh CSF preparation. Culture is confirmatory.

Prognosis

The prognosis is related to the age of the patient, stage at which diagnosis is made, adequacy of treatment and presence of complications. The prognosis is poorer in younger children. Early diagnosis, adequate and prolonged therapy improves the prognosis. Untreated cases die within 4 to 8 weeks.

Recovery is a rule in Stage 1 disease. The mortality in Stage 2 is 20–25% and of the survivors, 25% would have neurological deficits. Stage 3 disease has 50% mortality and almost all the survivors would have neurological sequelae. The long-term sequelae include mental retardation, seizures and motor/cranial nerve deficits. Hydrocephalus is practically universal. Visual complications and optic atrophy are common. Arachnoiditis, spinal block may cause motor and bladder/bowel symptoms.

Treatment

Antitubercular therapy: The treatment of tuberculous meningitis should be prompt, adequate and prolonged for at least 12 months. Short course chemotherapy is not recommended. At least 4 antitubercular drugs should be used for initial 2 months comprising (i) isoniazid (5 mg/kg/day, maximum 300 mg per day); (ii) rifampicin (10 mg/kg/orally, once empty stomach in the morning, maximum dose 600 mg/day); (iii) ethambutol (15–20 mg/kg/day); and (iv) pyrazinamide (30 mg/kg/day PO). Streptomycin (30–40 mg/kg/day IM) may be used initially for 2–3 weeks. The first two drugs are continued to complete one year of therapy.

Steroids: Parenteral dexamethasone 0.15 mg/kg every 6 hr IV; change to oral drug (prednisolone) once brain edema settles. Oral corticosteroids may be continued for 6 weeks and tapered over next two weeks. Steroids reduce the intensity of cerebral edema, risk of development of arachnoiditis, fibrosis and spinal block.

Symptomatic therapy of raised intracranial pressure, seizures, dyselectrolytemia should be done. The patient should be kept under observation for development of papilledema, optic atrophy or increasing head circumference. Decerebration is common in advanced cases in the acute phase. Ventriculocaval shunt may be required in cases with increasing hydrocephalus and persistent decerebration.

Suggested reading

1. Kent SJ, Crowe SM, Yung A, et al. Tuberculous meningitis: a 30 year review. Clin Infect Dis 1993; 17: 987.
2. Shah GV. Central nervous system tuberculosis: imaging manifestations. Neuroimaging Clin N Am 2000; 10: 355–74.
3. Tung YR, Lai MC, Lui CC, et al. Tuberculous meningitis in infancy. Pediatr Neurol 2002; 27: 262–6.

Table 17.7: Etiology of encephalitis and encephalopathies
Encephalitis
Viral
RNA viruses (mumps, measles, rubella, enteroviruses)
DNA viruses (Herpes simplex, cytomegalovirus, Epstein Barr, Pox group)
Arthropod borne (Japanese B, West Nile, Russian spring summer, equine viruses)
HIV, rabies, lymphocytic choriomeningitis, dengue
Slow virus infections, prion infections
Non-viral
Rickettsia; fungi (cryptococcus); protozoa (*T. gondii*); bacteria (tuberculous meningitis, listeria)
Encephalopathies
Acute disseminated encephalomyelopathy (ADEM). Allergic, post-exanthematous, post-vaccinial
Postinfectious. Typhoid, shigella, Reye syndrome
Hypoxic encephalopathy, heat hyperpyrexia
Metabolic. Diabetic acidosis, uremic coma, hepatic coma, neonatal hyperbilirubinemia, lactic acidosis, inborn errors of metabolism
Fluid and electrolyte disturbances. Water intoxication, hypernatremia, hyponatremia, alkalosis, acidosis
Toxic. Heavy metals (lead, mercury, arsenic), insecticides, *Cannabis indica*, carbon monoxide
Malignancies
Mitochondrial disorders

4. Garg RK Classic diseases revisited: Tuberculosis of the central nervous system. Postgrad. Med. J. 1999;75;133–140.
5. Tuberculosis: clinical diagnosis and management of tuberculosis, and measures for its prevention and control. London: Royal College of Physicians, 2006.
6. Thwaites GE, Nguyen DB, Nguyen HD et al. Dexamethasone for the treatment of tuberculous meningitis in adolescents and adults. New Eng J Med 2004;351:1741–1751.

ENCEPHALITIS AND ENCEPHALOPATHIES

Encephalitis is defined as an inflammatory process of the central nervous system with dysfunction of the brain. The term encephalopathy implies cerebral dysfunction due to circulating toxins, poisons, abnormal metabolites or intrinsic biochemical disorders affecting neurons but without inflammatory response.

Etiopathology

Encephalitis and encephalopathies may result from a variety of infective and non-infective causes. These are summarized in the Table 17.7.

The pathological changes are non-specific except in herpes simplex encephalitis and rabies, where specific inclusions are demonstrable. Gross examination of the brain usually shows diffuse edema, congestion and hemorrhages. Microscopically, there may be perivascular cuffing with lymphocytes and neutrophils. The neurons show necrosis and degeneration, associated with neuronophagocytosis. The ground substance may show glial proliferation.

Clinical Manifestations

The clinical manifestations of encephalitis depend on: (i) severity of infection; (ii) susceptibility of the host; (iii) localization of the agent; and (iv) presence of raised intracranial pressure. A wide variety of clinical manifestations may occur ranging from an inapparent, mild abortive type of illness, aseptic meningitis syndrome or severe encephalomyelitis with or without radiculitis.

Onset: The onset of illness is generally sudden but may at times be gradual.

Initial symptoms: The initial symptoms are high fever, mental confusion, headache, vomiting, irritability, apathy or loss of consciousness, often associated with seizures. Sudden severe rise of intracranial pressure may result in decerebration, cardiorespiratory insufficiency, hyperventilation and autonomic dysfunction. The child may develop disturbances of speech and other neurological deficits such as ocular palsies, hemiplegia and cerebellar syndromes. Extrapyramidal symptoms are common in Japanese B encephalitis and lateralization to one side with temporal or frontal involvement is common in herpes encephalitis.

Typical features: Include increased intracranial pressure and papilledema with evidence of brainstem dysfunction. Unchecked brain swelling may lead to herniation at tentorial hiatus, compression of the midbrain causing deterioration in consciousness, pupillary abnormalities, ptosis, sixth nerve palsy, opthalmoplegia, paralysis of upward gaze, Cheyne-Stoke breathing, hyperventilation and bradycardia. Herniation of cerebellum through the foramen magnum causes distortion and compression of medulla oblongata with severe disturbances of vital centers leading to respiratory or cardiac arrest.

Prognosis

The course of illness is variable, from a mild illness with spontaneous complete recovery to very severe forms. There may be severe neurological residua, which may totally incapacitate the child. Metabolic encephalopathies may have an intermittent or progressive course despite treatment. Inborn metabolic errors may have an intermittent course.

Diagnosis

Every effort should be made to arrive at a precise etiological diagnosis by a careful history, systemic examination, account of recent illnesses or exposure to toxins. Lumbar puncture must always be done if there is no papilledema. The cerebrospinal fluid is examined biochemically, cytologically and by viral/bacterial cultures. Serum electrolytes, blood sugar, urea, blood ammonia, metabolic screening, serum lactate, urinary ketones and urinalysis should be done. Toxicologic studies should be undertaken in suspected patients. One should exclude treatable causes such as enteric encephalopathy, malaria, shigella, toxins, poisoning, diabetes mellitus and renal disease. Virological studies should include viral culture and PCR on CSF and blood. IgM Elisa on CSF serum should be done for arbo/entero/herpes/measles virus. Rising titers of sera are obtained for antibodies to neurotropic viruses, typhoid, etc. Serum lead levels should be estimated if there is a possible exposure of the child to lead contaminated environment.

Acute disseminated encephalomyelitis (ADEM): Acute immune demyelination of the brain, spinal cord following a variety of insults to oligodendroglia. Damage is perivenular in location commonly at the gray-white zone and occurs commonly after infections or vaccination usually a monophasic illness, permanent deficits after the initial severe manifestation occasionally. Acute stage is characterized by seizures, sensorial alternation and multifocal neurological signs, raised intracranial pressure visual disturbances, etc. Cerebrospinal fluid usually normal, mild pleocytosis, mildly elevated protein and normal glucose. Imaging may be normal, generally reveals multiple hypodensities in white matter, which enhance with contrast MRI may also show spinal cord, basal ganglia lesions in addition to white matter involvement. Therapy with pulse corticosteroids is useful.

Management

Treatment aims to save life, prevent neurological residua, relieve symptoms.

Emergency treatment: Airway should be kept patent and assisted respiration given if necessary. Hyperpyrexia should be managed with vigorous hydrotherapy and antipyretics. Shock is managed by infusion of appropriate fluid, dextran or vasopressors. Dopamine or dobutamine are added to the infusion to maintain blood pressure. Seizures are controlled by intravenous diazepam and phenytoin. Raised intra-cranial pressure is managed by IV infusion of 20% mannitol solution (1 g of mannitol/kg body weight) given in 30 minutes and corticosteroids such as dexamethasone. The role of corticosteroids in most encephalitides is not proven except in acute disseminated encephalomyelitis and where an autoimmune mechanism is postulated.

Herpes simplex encephalitis: Herpes simplex type I virus is the causative organism. Type II virus causes perinatal herpes infections. Clinical picture includes fever of sudden onset, mental confusion, vomiting, meningeal irritation, headache and papilledema. In addition to seizures neurological deficits are common. Localizing signs (focal seizures, focal paralyses, focal EEG changes), presence of RBCs in the CSF and focal involvement of the temporal lobe on CT scan are important diagnostic clues. Diagnosis can be established by CSF culture or PCR. The drug of choice is acyclovir (30 mg/kg/day) administered in 3 divided doses per day for a 10 days period. Early therapy is crucial for recovery. Prognosis is variable; about half the patients recover after timely therapy.

Suggested reading

1. Shoji H, Azuma K, Nishimura Y, et al. Acute viral encephalitis: the recent progress. Intern Med 2002; 41: 420–8.
2. Bulakbasi N, Kocaoglu M.Central nervous system infections of herpes virus family. Neuroimaging Clin N Am. 2008 Feb;18(1): 53–84; viii.
3. Shankar SK, Mahadevan A, Kovoor JM.Neuropathology of viral infections of the central nervous system.Neuroimaging Clin N Am. 2008 Feb;18(1):19–39; vii.
4. Fitch MT, Abrahamian FM, Moran GJ, Talan DA.Emergency department management of meningitis and encephalitis. Infect Dis Clin North Am. 2008;22(1):33–52, v-vi.
5. Mizuguchi M, Yamanouchi H, Ichiyama T, Shiomi M.Acute encephalopathy associated with influenza and other viral infections. Acta Neurol Scand Suppl 2007;186:45–56.
6. Amin R, Ford-Jones E, Richardson SE et al.Acute childhood encephalitis and encephalopathy associated with influenza: a prospective 11-year review. Pediatr Infect Dis J 2008; 27(5):390–5.

REYE SYNDROME

The first description of this syndrome was probably made by Najib Khan in Jamshedpur, in 1956 (Jamshedpur fever). Reye and colleagues in Australia in 1964 described a diffuse fatty infiltration of the liver, to a lesser extent of the kidney, and cerebral edema with diffuse mitochondrial injury.

Pathogenesis

It is an acute self-limiting metabolic insult of diverse etiology resulting in generalized mitochondrial dysfunction due to inhibition of fatty acid β-oxidation. Salicylates or viral infections can precipitate this metabolic impairment. An inborn error of coenzyme A dehydrogenase, reduction in medium chain acyl-A and accumulation of unusual Co-A esters is suspected. Viruses like varicella and influenza B have been incriminated. Contamination of food with aflatoxin has also been implicated. There is some epidemiological evidence that use of aspirin or salicylate used for certain viral acute respiratory infections might precipitate Reye syndrome. Neuroglucopenia and hyperammonemia result from mitochondrial and sodium pump failure. Encephalopathy appears to be secondary to the liver damage.

Clinical Features

A mild prodromal illness may be followed by an acute onset of the disease. The child has vomiting for one or two days along with anorexia, listlessness, followed by rapid disturbances of sensorium, irregular breathing, decerebration, pupillary changes and rapidly developing coma. Seizures occur in more than 80% patients. There are hardly any focal neurological or meningeal signs. Hepatomegaly is present in half the cases. Jaundice is infrequent. The clinical features may be described in four stages:

Stage I: Vomiting, anorexia, mild confusion, listlessness, apathy.

Stage II: Delirium, restlessness, irritability, lack of orientation, frightened, agitated states.

Stage III: Coma, decorticate posture which later becomes decerebrate, patients may die.

Stage IV: Flaccidity, areflexia, apnea, dilated pupils not reacting to light, severe hypotension.

Laboratory Investigations

There may be some degree of hypoglycemia with low levels of glucose in the cerebrospinal fluid. Serum ammonia levels are elevated. Prothrombin time is prolonged and hepatic enzymes are increased. Liver biopsy shows fatty change and glycogen depletion but no necrosis of the liver cells, EEG shows generalized slow waves.

Prognosis

Prognosis is poor with 25–70% mortality. Survivors may have neurological sequelae.

Management

Hepatic failure needs appropriate management. The patient is given low protein diet with adequate calories. Intravenous infusion of mannitol (20% solution; 0.5 g/kg/IV q6 hourly) and dexamethasone are used to reduce the brain edema. Hypoglycemia should be corrected by IV 10–25% glucose. Acidosis, hypoxia and dyselectrolytemia should be corrected. Double volume exchange transfusion has been used in Stage III. Vitamin K and fresh frozen plasma may be required. Surgical decompression of the raised intracranial pressure may be required to save life.

Suggested reading

17

1. Casteels-Van Daele M, Van Geet C, Wouters C, et al. Reye syndrome revisited: a descriptive term covering a group of heterogeneous disorders. Eur J Pediatr 2000; 159: 641–8.
2. Glasgow JF, Middleton B. Reye syndrome—insights on causation and prognosis. Arch Dis Child 2001; 85: 351–3.
3. Schrör K.Aspirin and Reye syndrome: A review of the evidence. Paediatr Drugs 2007;9(3):195–204.

INTRACRANIAL SPACE OCCUPYING LESIONS

Intracranial space occupying lesions (ICSOL) include brain tumors, masses of congenital origin and inflammatory disorders such as brain abscess, neurocysticercosis, tuberculoma and subdural fluid collection, etc. Brain edema may also simulate space occupying lesions. ICSOL may present with features of increased intracranial tension, altered sensorium and/or localizing signs. These are detailed below:

Increased Intracranial Tension (ICT)

The intracranial space and its contents (brain, CSF & blood) are in a state of delicate equilibrium. After closure of sutures and fontanel the adaptive mechanisms to changes in contents and pressure in the brain is through the displacement of CSF from the intracranial cavity, compensatory hemodynamic changes ensue. Heart rate slows, respiratory rate is altered and blood pressure rises to maintain the cerebral circulation. Average pressure of cerebrospinal fluid is 180 mm of water is subject to many factors such as patency of the ventricular system, straining, sleep, position and size of the lumbar puncture needle and the kind of fluid.

The signs of raised ICT appear early in infratentorial tumors and are relatively late in supratentorial neoplasms. Common clinical features of raised ICT include either one or a combination of the following clinical features.

Increased head size and/or papilledema: In infants, there is separation of the cranial sutures, wide fontanels and increased head circumference. The fontanel should be examined with the baby relaxed and placed in the upright position. A delayed fontanel closure or a tense and non-pulsatile fontanel is significant. Separation of the sutures compensates for increase in the intracranial pressure.

The *MacEwen's or crackpot sign* indicates raised intracranial pressure after sutures have closed. Papilledema is unusual in infant unless the increase in intracranial pressure is very high. The changes include loss of cupping of the disk, absent venous pulsations and raised disk margins. In severe cases, hemorrhages may be observed. Tests, such as enlargement of the blind spot on visual field examination are helpful in differentiating papilledema from other conditions.

Vomiting: Unexplained projectile vomiting not associated with nausea, especially in the morning should arouse suspicion of a brain tumor. It is attributed to direct pressure on the medullary centers. Headache may or may not present.

Headache: Young children often do not complain of headache. Persistent headache in young children, prominent in early morning is highly suspicious. During the night, when the child is inactive and is lying in a horizontal position, the ventricular pressure above the mass increases and sleep is interrupted because of headache. During the day, partial obstruction is overcome, facilitated by the effect of gravity and symptoms may abate. Parents erroneously impute the early morning headache, coinciding with the time of going to school as malingering and thus delay seeking medical intervention.

Diplopia and sixth nerve palsy: Increased pressure displaces the brainstem downwards, thus stretching the sixth nerve and resulting in paralysis of the lateral gaze and diplopia.

Localizing Signs

These signs are helpful to detect the anatomical site of the lesion.

Cranial nerve palsies: Multiple cranial nerve palsies occur in brainstem lesions along with involvement of pyramidal tract and cerebellar pathways. Sixth nerve palsy usually has no localizing value. If 6th nerve palsy is associated with supranuclear seventh nerve involvement, it may be suggestive of pontine lesion. In supranuclear hypoglossal paralysis, tongue is tilted to contralateral side. In pseudobulbar palsy, uvula, gag reflex and movements remain intact, though swallowing is affected. Nasopharyngeal masses, rhabdomyosarcoma, lymphosarcoma and inflammatory masses may involve cranial nerves in their course.

Head tilt: Head tilt is seen in superior oblique paralysis, cerebellar lesions and posterior fossa tumors.

Ataxia: Ataxia occurs in cerebellar, spinocerebellar tract, frontal lobe or thalamic lesions.

Motor deficit: This may occur in cerebral, brainstem and spinal cord lesions.

Seizures: These indicate cortical or subcortical lesion. Intermittent decerebrate posturing may be due to infratentorial pathology.

Nystagmus : Both irritative and destructive lesions in any part of cerebello-vestibular system may cause nystagmus with quick and slow components in opposite direction. Unilateral cerebellar lesion may produce bilateral manifestations because of compression across the midline. Brainstem lesions cause vertical nystagmus. The site of lesion is towards the side of the coarse nystagmus. Nystagmus also occurs with increased intracranial pressure, degenerative syndromes and with toxicity of anti-epilepsy drugs such as phenytoin and phenobarbitone.

Vision: It is difficult to evaluate visual acuity and field of vision in children. Impaired vision not corrected by glasses should arouse suspicion of lesion near optic nerve, chiasma, optic radiations or cortical blindness. Bitemporal hemianopsia may indicate compression over chiasma but it may also be seen in optic atrophy.

Personality disturbances: Infants may become irritable, lethargic and show disturbances of behavior or speech. Loss of cortical sensation as described in supratentorial tumors of adults is difficult to interpret in children. There may be a decline in intellectual function.

Personality disturbances, inappropriate sphincter control and grasp response suggest localization of tumor near the frontal lobe. There may be optic atrophy in the fundus of the same side and papilledema in the opposite eye (*Foster Kennedy syndrome*).

BRAIN TUMORS

Tumors arising from the brain are the second most common group of neoplasms in children next only to hematologic malignancies. Metastatic tumors are rare during childhood. Certain genetic syndrome and familial factors increase risk of occurrence of brain tumors. Primary brain tumors may be malignant or benign. Benign tumors may, however, become life-threatening if these are located near a vital area of the brain.

Over two-thirds of brain tumors in children are infratentorial. *About one-third to half of these are medulloblastomas and one-third are astrocytomas of cerebellum.* Brain stem gliomas and ependymomas account for the rest. Most of these tumors occur near the midline. Therefore they commonly obstruct CSF circulation and cause hydrocephalus early in disease. In adults, infratentorial tumors account for less than 10% of brain neoplasms. Common supratentorial tumors are astrocytomas, ependymomas, craniopharyngioma and malignant gliomas. Papillomas of choroid plexus and pineal body tumors are less common. Meningiomas, acoustic neuromas and pituitary adenomas are rare in childhood. Ataxia telengiectasia and neurocutaneous syndromes are associated with a higher incidence of brain tumors. Imaging technology is the mainstay of diagnosis. CT gives adequate information about ventricular size, tumor and surrounding edema. It is useful for follow-up. MRI provides better information regarding mass size, infratentorial and spinal cord extension and tumor detail.

Cerebellar Tumors

Medulloblastoma: These are midline cerebellar tumors. They occur in infancy, are fast growing, malignant, craniospinal spread along neuraxis is common and death occurs early. They cause truncal ataxia, early papilledema, unsteadiness in sitting position and a tendency to walk with a broad base. Radiation, chemotherapy and a VP shunt are generally required.

Astrocytoma: These are common in the cerebellar hemisphere. There is ataxia and incoordination more on the side of the lesion. Nystagmus is observed on lateral gaze of the child to the affected side. Areflexia and hypotonia are present. The head is tilted to the side of lesion to relieve the increased intracranial pressure caused by herniation of tumor or cerebellar tonsils through the foramen magnum. Complete surgical excision of the tumor is often feasible. Chemotherapy with tomustin, vincristine and cisplatin is advised. Brachytherapy is now used in a variety of brain tumors to limit radiation necrosis and provide local irradiation to improve prognosis.

Brainstem Tumors

Signs of increased intracranial tension are minimal yet vomiting occurs due to infiltration of medullary vomiting center. Hemiparesis, cranial nerve deficits and personality changes are common; reflexes in the lower limbs are exaggerated. The pontine tumors affect the 6th and 7th cranial nerves.

Glioma of the brainstem causes bilateral involvement of the cranial nerves and long tracts. Cerebellar dysfunction is often present. The usual age of onset is in the later half of the first decade. Brainstem gliomas carry the worst prognosis. Most children die within 18 months. Surgical excision is difficult and not very promising. Hyperfractionation radiotherapy is being evaluated. Chemotherapy does not have significant role.

Ependymoma of the fourth ventricle: It occurs in the first decade of life. The flow of cerebrospinal fluid is obstructed, causing an early rise in the intracranial pressure. These patients may present with subarachnoid hemorrhage. The tumors metastasize along the neuraxis. Surgical excision is rarely possible, patients may be treated with radiotherapy. Survival of the child for a long period is unusual.

Supratentorial Tumors

Craniopharyngioma: These can present at any time during childhood. The tumor is congenital and arises from squamous epithelial cell rests of the embryonic Rathke pouch. The neoplasm is usually cystic and benign. Clinical features include (i) growth failure; (ii) bitemporal hemianopsia, asymmetric or unilateral visual field defects; (iii) signs of increased intracranial pressure; and (iv) endocrine abnormalities such as diabetes insipidus and delayed puberty (in less than 10% of cases). X-ray films may show calcification. Cranial imaging reveals the mass its extent and its nature. Bone age is retarded. Surgical excision is possible but difficult. The tumor cyst may be aspirated or malignant ones are treated with radiotherapy or implants.

Glioma of the cerebral hemispheres: These usually occur during the first and second decade of the life. The patient presents with seizures and hemiparesis. Rarely, involvement of fronto-pontine cerebellar fibers may cause ataxia. Vomiting, headache and papilledema are relatively late features of supratentorial tumors. Incidence of gliomas is higher in children with neurocutaneous syndromes. The histological types include astrocytoma, oligodendroglioma and glioblastoma.

17

Ependymoma and sarcoma of cerebral hemisphere may be clinically indistinguishable. There may be optic atrophy in the fundus of the same side and papilledema in the opposite eye in frontal lobe tumor.

Hypothalamic glioma: These rare tumors cause diencephalic syndrome in infants. The children fail to thrive, the subcutaneous fat is lost, and have sleep and respiratory disturbances. Older children may present with precocious puberty. Histological types observed are glioma, pinealoma, teratomas and hamartomas.

Glioma of optic nerve: Visual disturbances, squint, proptosis, exophthalmos and optic atrophy are the usual presenting features. The skull film shows enlarged optic foramen and CT of the orbit is diagnostic. Incidence of optic glioma is higher in cases of neurofibromatosis. Progression of tumor is relatively slow. Surgery is possible if the lesion is limited to one side.

Tumors of deep structures: in the cerebral hemispheres such as basal ganglia, thalamus and ventricular system are not associated with early seizures, disturbances of consciousness, behavior, vision, speech or cortical sensation.

Diagnosis

The diagnosis should be based on clinical history, physical examination and supported by computerized tomography (CT scan) and magnetic resonance imaging (MRI or NMR). Gadolinium-enhanced MRI increases its usefulness for evaluation of brain tumors and for follow-up. Electroencephalograms have limited role, ventriculography is obsolete and carotid angiography is required for specific information only.

INFLAMMATORY GRANULOMAS

Inflammatory granulomas are an important cause of raised intracranial pressure and partial seizures in childhood. These may be tubercular, parasitic, fungal or bacterial in origin. Neurocysticercosis and tuberculomas are the commonest granulomas.

Neurocysticercosis

It is caused by larval stage of *Taenia solium.*

Pathogenesis: Evolution occurs from a non-attenuating cyst, to a ring with perilesional edema, to a disc lesion; which may disappear, persist or even calcify. Neurocysticercosis can be classified as parenchymal, intraventricular, meningeal, spinal or ocular depending on the site of involvement.

Clinical features: Parenchymal neurocysticercosis –seizures are the commonest manifestations (80%), followed by raised intracranial pressure, focal deficits or rarely meningeal signs. Seizures may be generalized or partial (2:3) – simple or complex partial seizures, mainly with motor manifestations. Intraventricular neurocysticercosis presents with features of raised intracranial pressure, focal neurological deficits and hydrocephalus. Meningeal signs are indicative of a meningeal cyst. Visual symptoms or blindness results from cysts within the eye. *Spinal neurocysticercosis* presents with features of spinal cord compression or transverse myelitis.

Diagnosis: Neurocysticercosis is the most common cause of a ring enhancing lesion on CT scan of the brain (Fig. 17.8). The lesion is disc or ring like image with a hypodense center. Lesion may be single or multiple. A scolex is often present within the ring. There is often considerable edema surrounding the lesion. The midline shift is not significant. Lesion is usually supratentorial but may occur in infratentorial regions. MRI is more useful than a CT scan in doubtful cases.

ELISA for cysticercosis is positive in almost half the patients with single rings; the positivity is greater in periventricular and multiple lesions. Cerebrospinal fluid may be examined for cells, cysticercal antigens and PCR, though its diagnostic utility is variable. Cerebrospinal fluid and serum ELISA with newer immunoblot together have a greater yield.

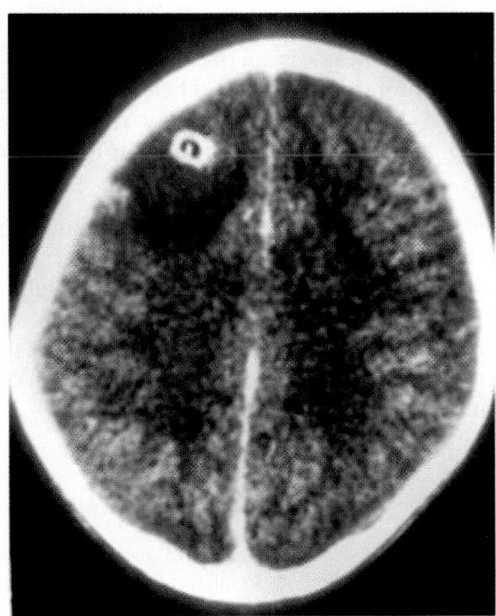

Fig. 17.8: Contrast enhanced CT of brain showing a degenerating ring enhancing cyst with eccentric scolex and perilesional edema in right frontal lobe

Therapy: Cysticidal therapy is not necessary for inactive and calcified lesions. There may be benefit to treat single active and multiple lesions. Cysticidal drugs commonly used include albendazole and praziquantel. Albendazole is the preferred drug because of efficacy, and is less expensive. The dose (15 mg/kg/day) may be given for varying periods from 5 to 28 days. Corticosteroids (prednisolone 1–2 mg/kg/d) are started 2–3 days before initiating therapy and continued during cysticidal therapy. Symptomatic treatment includes anticonvulsants for 6–9 months or until resolution of the lesions. Calcified lesions require anticonvulsant therapy for 2–3 years.

Tuberculoma

The clinical presentation is similar to neurocysticercosis. On CT scan, there is a single or multiple ring enhancing lesions. Tuberculoma rings are usually larger. The lesion often has a thick (≥20 mm) irregular wall and may be associated with a midline shift and severe perilesional edema (Fig 17.9). Focal deficits are more frequent in tuberculomas. A precise differentiation from neurocysticercosis may be difficult. Presence of basal exudates should arouse suspicion of tuberculoma. Ancillary evidence for tuberculosis in the form of a positive chest radiograph or tuberculin test should be looked for. The diagnosis is often suspected based on family history of contact, positive tuberculin reaction, other evidences of tuberculosis and subacute course of the illness.

Antituberculous therapy is recommended for 1 year (2 HRZE + 10 HR) as for tubercular meningitis along with corticosteroids for initial 6–8 weeks.

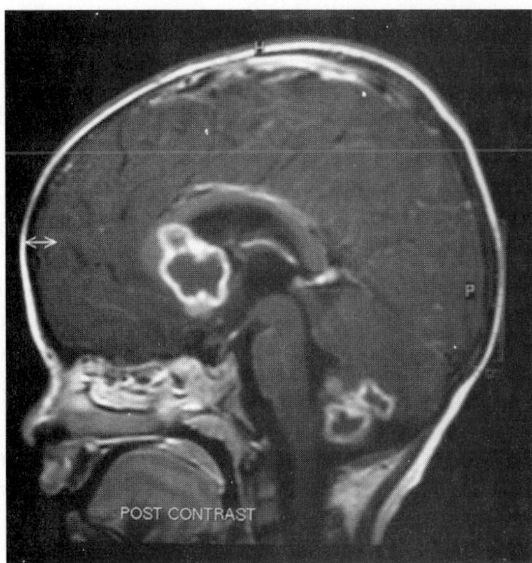

Fig. 17.9: Contrast enhanced MRI (sagittal view) of brain showing enhancing irregular ring like multiple tuberculomas

Suggested reading

1. Kraft R.Cysticercosis: an emerging parasitic disease. Am Fam Physician. 2007 Jul 1;76(1):91–6.
2. Mazumdar M, Pandharipande P, Poduri A.Does albendazole affect seizure remission and computed tomography response in children with neurocysticercosis? A Systematic review and meta-analysis. J Child Neurol. 2007 Feb;22(2):135–42.
3. Ito A, Takayanagui OM, Sako Y et al. Neurocysticercosis: clinical manifestation, neuroimaging, serology and molecular confirmation of histopathologic specimens. Southeast Asian J Trop Med Public Health. 2006;37 Suppl 3:74–81.
4. Nash TE, Singh G, White AC, et al. Treatment of neurocysticercosis: current status and future research needs. Neurology. 2006 Oct 10;67(7):1120–7.
5. Takayanagui OM, Odashima NS. Clinical aspects of neurocysticercosis.Parasitol Int. 2006;55 Suppl:S111–5. Epub 2005 Dec 5.
6. Garcia HH, Del Brutto OH; Cysticercosis Working Group in Peru.Neurocysticercosis: updated concepts about an old disease.Lancet Neurol. 2005 Oct;4(10):653–61.
7. Del Brutto OH.Neurocysticercosis. Semin Neurol. 2005 Sep;25(3):243–51.

BRAIN ABSCESS

Brain abscess is an important differential diagnosis among children with unexplained fever, altered sensorium, elevated intracranial pressure, localized neurological findings and headache.

Predisposing factors include head injury, meningitis or systemic sepsis. Congenital cyanotic heart disease patients have increased risk since the septic emboli pass to the brain, through the right to left shunt and the hypoxic brain provides a good growth medium, especially for the anaerobic bacilli. Brain abscess may occur by contiguous infection from the middle ear, mastoids, paranasal sinuses and skull bones. At times, metastasis may occur from lung abscess or osteomyelitis.

Etiology: Anerobic organisms, streptococci, *Staphylococcus aureus*, pneumococci, *Proteus* and *Hemophilus influenzae* are the common infecting organisms. The abscesses are observed more often in the cerebrum compared to infratentorial compartment.

Clinical features of brain abscess may be described under 4 broad headings: (i) features of raised intracranial pressure; (ii) manifestations of intracranial suppuration such as irritability, drowsiness, stupor, and meningeal irritation; (iii) features suggesting toxemia, e.g. fever, chills, and leukocytosis; and (iv) focal neurological signs such as focal convulsions, cranial nerve palsies, aphasia, ataxia, visual field defects and neurological deficit.

Diagnosis is established by CT scan or MRI. Lumbar puncture is not necessary to diagnose brain abscess and should be done only if necessary to exclude other diagnosis and very cautiously since the procedure may precipitate herniation of the brainstem.

Management includes investigation for source of infection, treatment of precipitating cause, management of raised intracranial pressure and symptoms. Empirical therapy should begin with a third generation cephalosporin, vancomycin and metronidazole and continued for at least 3 weeks. Surgical drainage or excision of the abscess should be done in case of abscesses of > 2.5 cm, located in posterior fossa, fungal abscess or if gas is identified inside the abscess.

Suggested reading

1. Calfee DP, Wispelwey B. Brain abscess. Semin Neurol 2000; 20: 353–60.
2. Goodkin HP, Harper MB, Pomeroy SL. Intracerebral abscess in children: historical trends at Children's Hospital Boston. Pediatrics. 2004 Jun;113(6):1765–70.
3. Leotta N, Chaseling R, Duncan G, Isaacs D. Intracranial suppuration.J Paediatr Child Health. 2005 Sep-Oct;41(9–10):508–12.
4. Lu CH, Chang WN, Lin YC et al. Bacterial brain abscess: microbiological features, epidemiological trends and therapeutic outcomes. QJM. 2002 Aug;95(8):501–9.
5. Foerster BR, Thurnher MM, Malani PN, Petrou M, Carets-Zumelzu F, Sundgren PC.Intracranial infections: clinical and imaging characteristics.Acta Radiol. 2007 Oct;48(8):875–93.

SUBDURAL EFFUSION

Subdural effusion may be acute or chronic. In infancy, subdural effusions are often associated with bacterial meningitis. These are generally acute, small and regress spontaneously. Rarely a large effusion may result in increased intracranial pressure and focal neurological signs. The arachnoid membrane may permit spread of infection from subarachnoid to the subdural space. Chronic subdural presents as raised intracranial pressure. The protein content of this fluid is high and vascular membrane forms around the subdural effusion. This may require surgical intervention.

Clinical features are non-specific. Convulsions, vomiting, irritability and drowsiness are present. There is persistent fever, anterior fontanel bulges and head size increases. In the newborn period, the skull may show increased transillumination. CT/MRI or subdural tap establishes the diagnosis.

Treatment: Small collections are absorbed spontaneously. Large effusions may need to be aspirated every 24 to 48 hours until these become small or are completely dried up. Surgical irrigations with indwelling drains may be considered if the effusion persists for more than 2 weeks. Surgical excision of the subdural membrane is difficult and results are not encouraging.

Suggested reading

1. Ersahin Y. Subdural fluid collections in infants. Pediatr Neurosurg 2001; 34: 280.
2. Tolias C, Sgouros S, Walsh AR, et al. Outcome of surgical treatment for subdural fluid collections in infants. Pediatr Neurosurg 2000; 33: 194–7.
3. Osman Farah J, Kandasamy J, May P, Buxton N, Mallucci C.Subdural empyema secondary to sinus infection in children.Childs Nerv Syst. 2008 Jun 25. PMID: 18575871.
4. Laupland KB.Vascular and parameningeal infections of the head and neck. Infect Dis Clin North Am. 2007 Jun;21(2):577–90, viii.
5. Ziai WC, Lewin JJ 3rd.Advances in the management of central nervous system infections in the ICU. Crit Care Clin. 2006 Oct;22(4):661–94.

HYDROCEPHALUS

The CSF is secreted at the choroid plexus within the ventricles by ultrafiltration and active secretion. It passes from the lateral ventricles to the third ventricle, fourth ventricle exits from Foramen of Luschka and Magendie reaches the basal cisterns, and then the cerebral and spinal subarachnoid spaces where it is absorbed via the arachnoid villi (granulations) into the venous channels and sinuses. About 20 mL of CSF is secreted in an hour and its turnover is 3 or 4 times in a day.

Etiology: Hydrocephalus results from an imbalance between production and absorption of cerebrospinal fluid. Hydrocephalus may be (i) communicating; or (ii) non-communicating (obstructive).

Communicating hydrocephalus: There is no blockage between the ventricular system, the basal cisterns and the spinal subarachnoid space.

Obstructive or non-communicating hydrocephalus: The block is at any level in the ventricular system, commonly at the level of aqueduct or foramina of Luschka and Magendie (Fig. 17.10).

Excess CSF may be produced in papilloma of choroid plexus. In hydrocephalus the ventricles are dilated above the block in obstructive type under increased CSF pressure. In cerebral atrophy, ventricles are dilated but pressure is not raised (*hydrocephalus ex vacuo*). Presence of

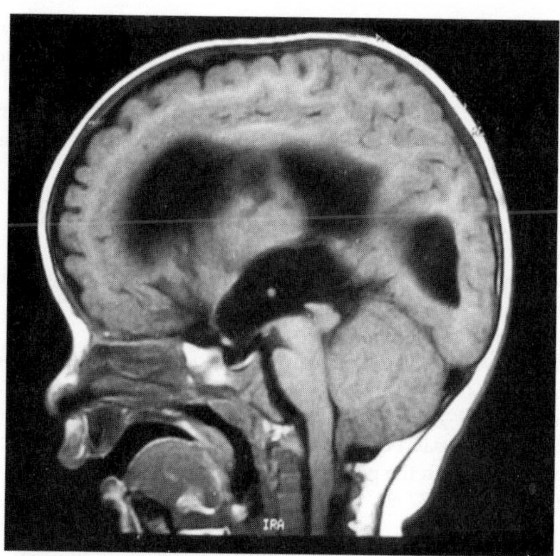

Fig. 17.10: Arnold Chiari II malformation: MRI T1W sagittal view showing obstructive hydrocephalus stretched brainstem and tonsillar herniation (patient also had a meningomyelocele)

periventricular ooze on CT/MR imaging helps to identify the former.

Hydrocephalus may be congenital or acquired (Table 17.8).

Pathology: Ventricles are dilated, at times unevenly. Ependymal lining of ventricles is disrupted resulting in periventricular ooze. Subependymal edema occurs. White matter is compressed. Cortex is generally preserved until late but cortical atrophy may occur. The process may be reversible if the treatment is started early.

Clinical features: Hydrocephalus may manifest with enlarging head size, delayed closure of fontanel and sutures. Associated symptoms include headache, nausea, vomiting, personality and behavior disturbances such as irritability, head banging, apathy and drowsiness.

Table 17.8: **Causes of hydrocephalus**
Congenital Hydrocephalus
Intrauterine infections: Rubella, cytomegalovirus, toxoplasmosis, intracranial bleeds, intraventricular hemorrhage
Congenital malformations: Aqueduct stenosis, Dandy-Walker syndrome (posterior fossa cyst continuous with fourth ventricle), Arnold-Chiari syndrome (portions of cerebellum and brainstem herniating into cervical spinal canal, blocking the flow of CSF to the posterior fossa)
Midline tumors obstructing CSF flow
Acquired Hydrocephalus
Tuberculosis, chronic and pyogenic meningitis
Post-intraventricular hemorrhage
Posterior fossa tumors: Medulloblastoma, astrocytoma, ependymoma
Arteriovenous malformation, intracranial hemorrhage, ruptured aneurysm
Hydrocephalus *ex vacuo*

Papilledema, pyramidal tract signs and cranial nerve palsies may occur. Skull contour becomes abnormal and forehead is prominent. Scalp veins become prominent and dilated. A sunset sign is seen in the eyes, i.e. sclera above the cornea becomes visible. Upward gaze is impaired. Limbs become spastic because of stretching of cortical fibers. Distortion of the brainstem may lead to bradycardia, systemic hypertension and altered respiration rate.

Congenital hydrocephalus starts in fetal life and may manifest or even develop subsequently. The large head size at birth causes difficulty in delivery of the head during labor. There may be associated congenital malformations.

Diagnosis: Accurate serial recording of the head circumference is essential for early diagnosis of hydrocephalus and should be supported by serial USG. An increase in the head circumference in the first 3 months of life >1 cm every fortnight should arouse suspicion of hydrocephalus. Brain grows very rapidly in the first few weeks of life and therefore sagittal and coronal sutures may be separated up to 0.5 cm. This physiological separation disappears after the first fortnight of life. Persistent widening of squamoparietal sutures is not physiological and should arouse suspicion of hydrocephalus. Cranial ultrasound and computed tomography help to evaluate serial ventricular size while the latter gives information about cortical mantle, periventricular ooze and etiology of hydrocephalus. MRI/CT may be necessary to determine the site of obstruction and in congenital hydrocephalus to identify associated malformation. Arnold Chiari malformation has downward displacement of cerebellum and medulla, obstruction of CSF pathway or migration defects. Dandy Walker malformation reveals a cystic malformation, atresia of outlet foramina or any brain malformations.

Differential Diagnosis of Large Head

Megalencephaly: There are no signs of increased intracranial pressure. The ventricles are not large, nor under increased pressure. Causes include Hurlers' syndrome, metachromatic leukodystrophy and Tay Sach's disease. *Chronic subdural hematoma* causes large head, mostly located in the parietal region without prominent scalp veins or sunset sign. Large head size is also observed in hydranencephaly, rickets, achondroplasia, hemolytic anemias and familial macrocephalies.

Treatment

Management includes making a precise etiological diagnosis and identification of associated malformations, clinical course and severity of hydrocephalus.

If hydrocephalus is arrested spontaneously, surgical intervention may not be necessary. Medical management should be instituted if surgery is not indicated. Acetazolamide at a dose of 25–100 mg/kg/day diminishes CSF production in mild, slowly progressive hydrocephalus.

Oral glycerol has also been used for similar purpose. A conservative approach is better in most cases.

If the head size enlarges rapidly, or is associated with progressive symptoms, where vision or life is endangered it is desirable to treat surgically before irreparable damage occurs. In congenital obstructive hydrocephalus, acquired hydrocephalus, periventricular ooze with hydrocephalus a ventriculo-atrial or preferably a ventriculo-peritoneal shunt should be done to drain the CSF directly into the circulation or into the peritoneal cavity. Third ventriculotomy by endoscopic approach is another option particularly in children with obstructive hydrocephalus. In cases of bacterial meningitis, an acute hydrocephalus may set in which is self-limited. Patients with tuberculous meningitis and progressive hydrocephalus require a shunt, specially if it is obstructive.

A variety of shunts are now available. It is usually necessary to keep the shunt for the entire life. As the child grows in size it may be necessary to revise the shunt, using a longer tube. Blockage and infection are the two most common shunt complications. Shunt revision may also be necessary if there is bacterial colonization of the shunt.

Prognosis: Even with the best of treatment, prognosis is guarded. Almost two-third of children have variable mental and developmental disabilities. Prognosis of hydrocephalus associated with spina bifida is not satisfactory.

PSEUDOTUMOR CEREBRI (BENIGN INTRACRANIAL HYPERTENSION)

It is a benign self-limiting disorder with generally a favorable outcome. The intracranial pressure is elevated, ventricular system is either normal or small. Generally there are no focal neurological signs. Onset of symptoms of raised intracranial pressure may be sudden or gradual extending over a week or so. Visual field shows enlargement of blind spot.

It may follow use of outdated tetracycline, high doses of vitamin A, quinolones, lateral sinus thrombosis (following otitis media, mastoiditis especially on the right side) and obstruction of venous outflow due to pressure on superior vena cava. Pulmonary disease with CO_2 retention may also be responsible. It may occur during withdrawal of corticosteroid therapy, Addison's disease, hypoparathyroidism besides systemic lupus erythematosus. EEG shows excessive slow wave activity. Isotope brain scan, CT or MRI are normal. The patient improves spontaneously after a few months. Acetazolamide (carbonic anhydrase inhibitors) or oral glycerol helps in symptomatic relief. Dexamethasone may be required. Cerebral decompression or optic nerve sheath fenestration is rarely necessary.

Suggested reading

1. Garg BP, Walsh L. Clinical approach to the child with a large head. Indian J Pediatr 2001; 68: 867–71.
2. Vertinsky AT, Barnes PD.Macrocephaly, increased intracranial pressure, and hydrocephalus in the infant and young child.Top Magn Reson Imaging. 2007 Feb;18(1):31–51.
3. Beni-Adani L, Biani N, Ben-Sirah L, Constantini S.The occurrence of obstructive vs absorptive hydrocephalus in newborns and infants: relevance to treatment choices.Childs Nerv Syst. 2006 Dec;22(12):1543–63.
4. Waluza JJ. Management of hydrocephalus.Trop Doct. 2006 Oct;36(4):197–8.
5. Duhaime AC.Evaluation and management of shunt infections in children with hydrocephalus. Clin Pediatr (Phila). 2006 Oct;45(8):705–13.
6. Matthews YY.Drugs used in childhood idiopathic or benign intracranial hypertension. Arch Dis Child Educ Pract Ed. 2008 Feb;93(1):19–25.
7. Kesler A, Bassan H.Pseudotumor cerebri - idiopathic intracranial hypertension in the pediatric population. Pediatr Endocrinol Rev. 2006 Jun;3(4):387–92.

NEURAL TUBE DEFECTS

Neural tube defects (NTD) are one of the most common structural congenital anomalies and imply a failure of proper closure of neural tube and covering mesoderm and ectoderm. These defects occur in about 1.5 per 1,000 live births; the risk in second sibling is 5 per 100 births. The incidence in North India is as high as 3.9–9/1,000 live births.

Etiology

Primary neural tube defects have multi-factorial inheritance. Maternal risk factors include alcohol, radiation exposure, insulin dependent diabetes mellitus (IDDM), valproate and carbamazepine, zinc and folate deficiency. Chromosomal abnormalities including trisomy 13 and 15 have been reported.

Maternal malnutrition is an important risk factor for development of NTD. Studies until date have shown decreased maternal folate levels in NTD affected pregnancies. Periconceptional folic acid supplementation has shown to decrease both the occurrence and recurrence of NTD, though the exact mechanism for this protective effect remains unknown.

Clinical Features

The defect is obvious at birth or through fetal sonography. It varies in severity from an occult anomaly to severe life threatening problem. Lumbosacral region is the commonest site, but any part of the spine may be affected. The defect may extend over a variable length of the spinal cord.

The spectrum includes spina bifida (meningocele, meningomyelocele, spina bifida occulta), anencephaly (absence of brain calvaria, total or partial), encephalocele (herniation of brain and meninges through defect in calvaria), craniorachischisis (anencephaly associated with continuous bony defect of spine and exposure of neural tissue) and iniencephaly (dysraphism of occipital region accompanied by retroflexion of neck and trunk).

Neural tube defects may be associated with other congenital anomalies and dysfunction of organ systems. Affected children may have lower body paralysis, bladder and bowel dysfunction, learning disabilities, hydrocephalus due to Arnold-Chiari Type 2 malformation and endocrinal abnormalities. Anencephaly is an important cause of fetal and infant mortality. Severe cases die *in utero*, or in the early neonatal period. Long term sequelae include neurological and motor significant physical disability, psychosocial maladjustments and increased financial burden on family.

Spina bifida occulta constitues about 5% cases and is asymptomatic. Meningocele or myelomeningocele, presents clinically as a raw red fleshy plaque, consists of meninges, CSF, nerve roots and dysplastic spinal cord. In ***meningocele***, the sac is covered only by skin and generally there is no neurologic deficit. Arnold-Chiari malformation associated meningomyelocele may have a variety of associated CNS anomalies like heterotopias, hypoplasia and ventricular abnormalities.

In ***meningomyelocele*** the neurologic deficit includes varying degrees of flaccid, areflexic paraparesis and sensory deficit in the trunk and legs correspond to the involved segments of the dysplastic cord. The cord distal to the site of the lesion is severely affected. Involvement of bowel and bladder results in fecal and urinary incontinence. Hydrocephalus is usually present in varying degrees and a shunt is required generally. Arnold-Chiari malformation may cause facial weakness and swallowing difficulty. Tongue movements may be impaired and there may be laryngeal stridor.

Management

Prenatal diagnosis of myelodysplasia is possible by estimating alpha-fetoprotein level in the maternal blood between 14 and 16 weeks of gestation, or in the amniotic fluid in early pregnancy where the test is more specific. Additional test in amniotic fluid includes acetyl cholinesterase estimation. Ultrasound pick-up rate is around 100%, maternal blood alpha fetoprotein (16–18 weeks) has accuracy of 60–70%, amniocentesis for alpha fetoprotein and acetylcholinesterase has accuracy of 97%. There is no indication for preinduction cesarian section except craniomegaly, large protruding lesions and obstetric indications.

Investigations: They include ultrasound of head and sac (if possible kidney also), CXR and X-ray spine, culture from lesion and draining CSF and complete blood counts.

Treatment: Management of NTD requires a team approach with the cooperation of pediatrician, neurologist, neurosurgeon, urologist and orthopedic surgeon with assistance from physiotherapist, social worker and psychiatrist. Parents should be counseled actively. The degree of paralysis, presence of hydrocephalus, kyphosis, congenital malformation, evidence of infection of nervous system influences decisions.

Surgery includes surgery of the defect and a VP shunt (if associated with hydrocephalus). Early closure prevents neurological deterioration. Open lesions draining CSF should be closed within 24 hours. Closed lesions should be operated within 48 hours. In case, the lesion is infected, the child should be given parenteral antibiotics. Surgery is done only when three 24 hours CSF cultures are sterile.

Lorber's criteria for selective surgery: Surgery is not recommended if there is severe paraplegia at or below L3 level, kyphosis or scoliosis, gross hydrocephalus, associated gross congenital anomalies, intracerebral birth injuries and neonatal ventriculitis before closure of back. Ninety percent would die in the neonatal period.

Prognosis

Delay in intervention causes increase in complications like worsening of neurologic deficit, infection (local or ventriculitis), progressive hydrocephalus, etc. Late complications include: hydrocephalus in 80–90% because of Chiari II malformation, urinary tract infections, enuresis, fecal incontinence or constipation, sexual dysfunction, intellectual deterioration, delayed neurological problems (tethered cord, intradural mass lesions), epilepsy in 10–30%, ocular problems (30%), shunt infection (25%), psychosocial problems and motor deficits. 2% die during initial hospitalization. 15% die by ten years of age. The mortality rate plateaus by 4 years of age.

Prevention

Primary prevention includes folate supplementation to all prospective mothers including first pregnancy. Food fortification is another possible approach. Counseling of family with a previous child with NTD is essential. The risk of recurrence is 3.5% with 1 affected child, 10% with 2 affected children and 25% with 3 affected children. MTHFR polymorphism should be studied. Advise periconceptional folate and offer prenatal diagnosis in subsequent pregnancy. Folate supplementation reduces recurrence risk by 70%. Zinc and vitamin A supplementation is also advised.

Dose for primary prevention is 0.4 mg per day. A mother who has previously delivered a child with NTD should receive 5 mg per day of folic acid in subsequent pregnancies. Secondary prevention is imperative after an index case. Duration of supplementation is 2 months before and 3 months after conception.

17

Suggested reading

1. Birnbacher R, Messerschmidt AM, Pollak AP. Diagnosis and prevention of neural tube defects. Curr Opin Urol 2002;12: 461–4.
2. Lonely J, Watson L, Watson T, Bover C. Periconceptional supplementation with folate and/or multivitamins for preventing neural tube defects. Cochrane Database Sys Rev 2000; 2: CD 00156.
3. Verity C, Firth H, French-Constant C. Congenital abnormalities of the central nervous system. J Neurol Neurosurg Psychiatry 2003; 74 : 3–8.
4. Shaer CM, Chescheir N, Schulkin J.Myelomeningocele: a review of the epidemiology, genetics, risk factors for conception, prenatal

diagnosis, and prognosis for affected individuals. Obstet Gynecol Surv. 2007 Jul;62(7):471–9.
5. Kibar Z, Capra V, Gros P.Toward understanding the genetic basis of neural tube defects. Clin Genet. 2007 Apr;71(4):295–310.
6. Pitkin RM.Folate and neural tube defects. Am J Clin Nutr. 2007 Jan; 85(1):285S–288S.

ACUTE HEMIPLEGIA OF CHILDHOOD

Acute hemiplegia of childhood is most often due to cerebrovascular disorders. The exact cause often remains obscure despite modern diagnostic aids and extensive investigations.

Causes

1. ***Occlusive diseases of the cerebrovascular system***
   a. *Venous thrombosis of dural sinus:* Congenital cyanotic heart disease, dehydration, paranasal sinuses, leukemia
   b. *Thrombosis (arterial):* Sickle cell disease, homocystinuria, iron deficiency anemia, dysproteinemias, thrombotic thrombocytopenic purpura, Takayasu disease, polyarteritis nodosa, lupus erythematosus, trauma to internal carotid artery, retropharyngeal abscess, protein C or S deficiency, Moyamoya disease, NADH coenzyme and reductase deficiency, mitochondrial encephalopathy, stroke syndromes
   c. *Cerebral embolism:* Subacute or acute bacterial endocarditis, air embolism, fracture causing fat embolism, umbilical vein catheterization in the newborn, sepsis
2. ***Intracranial hemorrhage:*** Arteriovenous malformations, coagulopathy, platelet vascular defects, hypertension, trauma, intracranial aneurysm, Sturge-Weber syndrome
3. ***Inflammatory:*** Inflammatory granulomas
4. ***Porencephaly:*** Cerebral abscess, meningitis, encephalitis, intracranial space occupying lesions
5. ***Idiopathic:*** Mitochondrial disorders also produce recurrent stroke like episodes and lactic acidosis in both arterial blood and CSF. The stroke does not clearly follow vascular distribution. MR imaging helps in suspecting the diagnosis.

17

Clinical Features

Mode of onset: The rapidity of onset varies with the cause. Emboli occur abruptly with maximum neurological signs at onset. There is improvement with passage of time. Seizures are frequently associated. Although intracranial hemorrhage also occurs acutely, it takes some time before the full clinical picture manifests with headache and nuchal rigidity. Cerebrovascular thrombosis is relatively less rapid in onset.

History and physical examination: History of ear, throat mastoid infection, intraoral or neck trauma, associated cardiac disease or hematological disorders may be helpful in determining the cause.

In mild hemiparesis, when the child is running or walking, there is circumduction and movements of the upper extremities are asymmetric. If the child is pushed from sitting position the child extends his arm to protect himself from a fall. This is called lateral propping reaction. In spastic hemiplegia, this reaction is asymmetric. Absent propping reaction in infants after the age 8 to 9 months is always abnormal.

Benign intracranial hypertension occurs in lateral sinus thrombosis. Multifocal seizures, raised intracranial pressure and vomiting are common in superior sagittal sinus thrombosis. Arterial occlusions generally occur in the first two years of life. These may be associated with hemiparesis and seizures, which are difficult to control with medication. Hemiparesis, cerebral hemiatrophy and cerebral porencephaly may result.

Localization

Cortical lesions: Cortical lesions are characterized by the specific pattern of motor deficit, depending on the vascular distribution of the artery involved. Seizures and cortical sensory loss are usual.

In the left-sided lesion, aphasia is a dominant clinical feature. The child has difficulty in reading, writing and comprehension. Organization of space and body image are affected. In right parietal lesions, the child exhibits lack of attention for objects on his left side. He may ignore the left side of a picture placed before him or may not even recognize his left hand. He has difficulty in copying simple figures (indicating constructional apraxia). He gets lost easily and confuses directions given to him because of spatial disorganization.

Corona radiata: The hemiplegia is generally complete and seizures are usually absent.

Internal capsule: Hemiplegia is complete, often with sensory loss.

Brainstem

a. *Midbrain*: Hemiplegia on the contralateral side and paralysis of 3rd and 4th cranial nerves on the same side (Weber syndrome).
b. *Pons*: Hemiplegia on the opposite side and involvement of 6th and 7th cranial nerves on the same side (Millard-Gubler syndrome).
c. *Medulla oblongata:* Contralateral hemiplegia with ipsilateral involvement of several cranial nerves.

Management

Investigate for the predisposing illness. Platelet count, hemoglobin, MCV, MCH, serum iron and iron binding capacity, nitroprusside reaction for homocystinuria, sickle cell preparation of blood, antinuclear antibody tests, protein C and S estimation, APLA, serum lactate/pyruvate, CSF lactate/pyruvate, chest X-ray and ECG. Metabolic tests if indicated.

Neurological work-up includes CT scan, electroencephalogram and MR angiography. Lumbar puncture is indicated for inflammatory CNS disease.

Treatment: Specific treatment depends on the etiology of hemiplegia. The role of T-plasminogen activator in childhood stroke is not established. In thrombotic stroke, heparin may be indicated. Seizures should be controlled and hydration should be maintained. Physiotherapy and speech therapy should be started early.

Treatment of acute cerebral thrombosis is directed towards increasing cerebral perfusion, limiting brain edema, and preventing recurrences. Salicylates are used for preventing recurrence. Calcium channel blockers have been found useful in some. Seizures often persist and anticonvulsants may be required.

Vasodilators and platelet inhibitors have been used in treatment. Free radical scavengers and coenzyme Q may have limited utility.

Prognosis

Prognosis with regard to seizures and mental retardation is worse in acute idiopathic hemiplegia below 3 years of age. Hemiplegic side may be atrophied and post-hemiplegia athetosis may be seen in these cases. Cerebral hemiatrophy with flattening of the skull and porencephaly secondary to parenchymal damage may occur.

Suggested reading

1. Bernard TJ, Goldenberg NA.Pediatric arterial ischemic stroke. Pediatr Clin North Am. 2008;55(2):323–38, viii.
2. Mackay MT, Monagle P.Perinatal and early childhood stroke and thrombophilia. Pathology. 2008;40(2):116–23.
3. Seidman C, Kirkham F, Pavlakis S.Pediatric stroke: current developments. Curr Opin Pediatr. 2007;19(6):657–62.
4. Carpenter J, Tsuchida T, Lynch JK.Treatment of arterial ischemic stroke in children. Expert Rev Neurother. 2007;7(4):383–92.
5. Carpenter J, Tsuchida T.Cerebral sinovenous thrombosis in children. Curr Neurol Neurosci Rep. 2007;7(2):139–46.
6. Jordan LC, Hillis AE.Hemorrhagic stroke in children.Pediatr Neurol. 2007 Feb;36(2):73–80.
7. Nelson KB, Lynch JK.Stroke in newborn infants.Lancet Neurol. 2004;3(3):150–8.

PARAPLEGIA AND QUADRIPLEGIA

Paraplegia refers to motor weakness of both lower limbs. Quadriplegia is the nomenclature used for neurological weakness of all four limbs; the involvement is more in the upper limbs as compared to the lower extremities. Neurological weakness may be (i) ***spastic*** — spasticity, exaggerated tendon reflexes, extensor plantar or (ii) ***flaccid*** — flaccidity, diminished tendon reflexes, flexor plantar response and muscle wasting. Incomplete paralysis is known as paraparesis or quadriparesis. It may be acute, or insidious in onset and have a variable course. The vascular, traumatic and post-infective lesions are usually acute in onset with variable gradual recovery. Compressive/ neoplastic lesions have insidious onset with gradually progressive deficit. Degenerative disorders have an insidious onset with slowly progressive course and characteristic spinal tract deficit distribution.

Flaccid weakness may result from spinal cord, nerve root, nerves and myopathic disorders. Acute onset follows demyelinating polyneuropathy, polio, vascular and traumatic spinal cord insults. Chronic causes include spinal muscular atrophy (SMA), peripheral neuropathies and myopathies. Table 17.9 enlists the common causes of paraplegia and quadriplegia.

It should be remembered that symmetrically brisk tendon reflexes with flexor plantar response may be normal in children and do not necessarily indicate any pathological process. In case of doubt between plantar reflex and withdrawal response, the dorsilateral aspect of

Table 17.9: Causes of paraplegia or quadriplegia
A. Spastic
a. ***Compressive***
Tuberculosis spine with or without paraspinal abscess.
Extradural, e.g. metastasis from neuroblastoma, leukemia, lymphoma; inflammatory process, such as epidural abscess (usually posterior to the spinal cord), bony abnormalities such as achondroplasia, Morquio disease, hemivertebrae and occipitalization of atlas vertebra, atlantoaxial dislocation
Intradural. Neurofibroma and dermoid cyst
Intramedullary. Glioma, ependymoma, hemato- or hydromyelia
b. ***Non-compressive myelopathies***
Vascular anomalies of the spinal cord (AV malformations, angiomas and telengiectasia)
Spinal cord trauma or transaction of cord
Transverse myelitis/myelopathy. Viral, neuromyelitis optica, segmental necrosis due to vascular occlusion, e.g. of anterior spinal artery
Familial spastic paraplegia, white matter degenerations
Lathyrism due to consumption of toxic pulse *Lathyrus sativum*
Degenerative spinal cord disease
c. ***Supra-cord lesions***
Cerebral palsy
Hydrocephalus
Bilateral cortical disease
Bilateral white matter disease
B. Flaccid weakness
Spinal shock in the initial stages of spinal cord damage, e.g. after trauma, vascular, inflammatory, neoplastic lesions, or transverse myelopathy
Acute inflammatory demyelinating polyneuropathy, acute motor axonal neuropathy
Acute poliomyelitis
Spinal muscular atrophies
Demyelinating neuropathies
Motor sensory neuropathy
Botulism, Riley Day syndrome, asymptomatic areflexia
C. Pseudoparalysis
Surgery, osteomyelitis, fractures, myositis, metabolic myopathy

the foot should be stroked (Chaddock maneuver) to obtain the plantar response. In lesions above the level of midbrain, jaw reflex becomes brisk. Abdominal reflexes should be elicited by stroking the skin over the abdomen close to the umbilicus. Examine patient carefully for sensory involvement and sensory level, wasting at the segments of the lesion, posterior column involvement and bladder bowel involvement.

Management

In acute myelitis, high dose of dexamethasone (5 mg/kg/ day) or IV methylprednisolone pulse therapy for 3–5 days may be useful. In tuberculosis, appropriate drugs, corticosteroids and local management suffice. In acute trauma and paraplegia due to neoplasia the treatment may be surgical.

Paraplegia is initially flaccid but later becomes spastic with development of painful flexor spasms due to the stimulation of pain fibers. Decubitus ulcers may occur. The child should be frequently turned in bed and nursed on foam mattress. Physiotherapy should be done. Bladder must be emptied regularly by compression or repeated catheterization to prevent it being distended and becoming atonic. Later bladder may become spastic with frequent but partial reflex emptying. Urinary tract infection may supervene due to inadequate drainage of the bladder. It should be appropriately treated. In severe spasticity, drugs that reduce tone provide relief.

GUILLAIN-BARRÉ SYNDROME/ACUTE INFLAMMATORY DEMYELINATING POLYNEUROPATHY

Etiology

The disorder is most likely an autoimmune process. The peripheral lymphocytes are sensitized to a protein component of the myelin (p2, neuritogenic peptide); the basic myelin protein may be altered and rendered immunogenic by the infection. These immune mechanisms cause demyelination. Molecular mimicry of bacterial/viral with neuronal gangliosides may cause AMAN and AMSAN syndromes.

In two-thirds of cases, there is a history of preceding viral infection about two or three weeks prior to the illness. Neurologic manifestations usually begin 2–4 weeks after the viral illness such as infectious mononucleosis (Epstein-Barr virus infection), mumps, measles and those caused by echo, coxsackie and influenza viruses. The conditions can follow rabies infection, or administration of neural vaccines for rabies. *Campylobacter* infections have been strongly associated with severe forms and acute motor axonal neuropathy (AMAN) syndrome.

Clinical Features

The disorder is characterized by symmetric weakness of the muscles, diminished reflexes and subjective sensory involvement. Pain in the muscles is an early symptom. This is followed by weakness developing in a few days, at first in the legs and then spreading to the upper extremities and trunk muscles. Weakness is more marked in the proximal muscle groups. Tendon reflexes are diminished, plantar reflex is normal and there is hypotonia. Cranial nerve involvement (most often the facial nerve) is seen in three-fourths of the cases. Early in disease the involvement may at times be unilateral or the degree of weakness may be different on two sides. Sensory symptoms are subjective rather than objective. Involvement of the autonomic nervous system is indicated by urinary retention, hypertension or postural hypotension. Respiratory insufficiency may occur if the intercostal muscles are paralyzed. A variant of infectious polyneuritis may also present with ataxia.

Diagnosis

The cerebrospinal fluid shows a characteristic albuminocytological dissociation. The protein is elevated $\geq$45 mg/ dL in almost 80% subjects but cell number is normal. The rise in protein begins in late first week and maximizes by 2–3 weeks. The disorder should be distinguished from poliomyelitis (asymmetric paralysis and CSF pleocytosis), polymyositis (normal CSF, elevated CPK and muscle pains, no bladder/bowel involvement), transverse myelitis (spasticity, exaggerated tendon jerks and extensor plantar response after the initial flaccidity for a few days) and cerebellar ataxia. Heavy metal intoxication, porphyria, botulism, spinal cord compression (Froin syndrome), and post-diphtheric paralysis may mimic Guillain-Barré syndrome.

Treatment

The natural course of the disease is generally self-limited with gradual recovery in majority of the patients. Few patients develop severe paralysis at onset often associated with respiratory muscle involvement. These patients definitely require treatment. Recent trials have shown a good response with intravenous immunoglobulin, administered at a dose of 400 mg/kg/day for 5 days. Response is best if treatment is offered within 3–4 days of onset. Plasmapheresis is another therapeutic modality shown to have benefit. Respiratory failure may warrant assisted ventilation.

Recovery is complete in most cases, but may take 6 months to 2 years for restoration of full function. Physiotherapy remains the mainstay to prevent handicaps.

Suggested reading

1. Hughes RAC, Cornblath DR. Guillain-Barré syndrome. Lancet 2005; 366: 1653–66.
2. Hughes RAC, Wijdicks EFM, Barohn,R et al. Practice parameter: Immunotherapy for Guillain–Barré syndrome: Report of the Quality Standards Subcommittee of the American Academy of Neurology. Neurology 2003; 61;736–740.
3. Korinthenberg R, Schessl J, Kirschner J. Clinical presentation and course of childhood Guillain-Barré syndrome: A prospective multicentre study. Neuropediatrics. 2007;38:10–7.

ACUTE FLACCID PARALYSIS

Acute flaccid paralysis (AFP) refers to acute onset (<4 weeks) flaccid, i.e. floppy or limp paralysis of the affected limb(s). Tone is diminished on examination by palpation or passive movement of joints, but sensation is not affected. A case of AFP is defined as any child aged <15 years who has acute onset of flaccid paralysis for which no obvious cause (such as severe trauma or electrolyte imbalance) is found, or paralytic illness in a person of any age in which polio is suspected.

Anatomically AFP can be classified into 4 groups based on four levels of motor unit namely muscle, neuromuscular junction, motor fibers, and anterior horn cells. Most of the lesions are acquired often after an acute illness and has rapidly progressive weakness. Localization of disorder in the motor unit can be done based on clinical features (Table 17.10).

Common causes of AFP in our country include poliomyelitis, Guillain-Barré syndrome (GBS), transverse myelitis and traumatic neuritis. Their differentiating features are detailed in the Table 17.11.

AFP Surveillance

It should be stressed that surveillance is carried out for all cases of AFP and not just for poliomyelitis. Therefore, all AFP cases should be reported, regardless of the final diagnosis. Because paralytic poliomyelitis is one cause of AFP, maintaining a high sensitivity of AFP reporting will ensure that all cases of paralytic poliomyelitis are detected, reported, and investigated, resulting in preventive control measures to interrupt transmission of disease. The aim of AFP surveillance is to detect poliovirus transmission and the earlier stool is collected the greater the chance that poliovirus may be detected.

Historically, poliomyelitis has often been referred to as infantile paralysis. Occasionally, poliomyelitis may occur in older children. Therefore, AFP surveillance must focus on children aged <15 years, it must be flexible to capture the occasional case that may occur in older children or adults. It should be noted that AFP in a person aged >15 years is unlikely to be polio. Any case of AFP, regardless of the age, should be reported and investigated if poliomyelitis is a possible cause.

Experience in other parts of the world indicates that at least 1 case of non-polio AFP occurs for every 1,00,000 children aged <15 years per year. This is referred to as the "background" rate of AFP among children. The other non-polio causes of AFP, such as Guillain-Barré syndrome (GBS), transverse myelitis, traumatic neuritis, account for this background rate, regardless of whether acute poliomyelitis exists in the community.

Special effort should be made to obtain 2 stool specimens from AFP cases within 14 days of paralysis onset. Outbreak response efforts should be started promptly without waiting for the laboratory results, which might take up to 8 weeks. All cases that are classified as "discarded," not polio, require thorough justification and should be reported with the final diagnosis. When a case of AFP is seen late in the field, stool specimens may be collected up to 60 days after onset of paralysis. The chances of finding poliovirus in the stool after that length of time are extremely remote. However, it should be noted that with a functioning and sensitive surveillance system for AFP, late detection of AFP cases indicates surveillance failure. The aim should always be to detect AFP cases early so that adequate specimens can be collected.

Adequate specimen can be defined as 2 specimens, at least 24 hours apart, collected within 14 days of paralysis onset; each of adequate volume (8–10 g) and arriving at a WHO accredited laboratory in good condition. Good condition means no desiccation, no leakage, adequate documentation and evidence that the cold chain was maintained. Surveillance is carried out for all cases of AFP, not just for poliomyelitis.

Table 17.10: Clinical features of conditions causing acute flaccid paralysis

Site	*Clinical features*	*Conditions*
Muscles	Neck, limb girdle, proximal muscles affected Possible cardiomyopathy Occasional respiratory muscle involvement	Myoglobinuric myopathy, hypokalemic paralysis, toxic paralysis, myopathy of intensive care
Neuromuscular junction	Cranial, limb girdle and proximal muscles May affect respiratory muscles Autonomic signs (presynaptic) Fatigability (post synaptic)	Myasthenia gravis Botulism, hypermagnesemia
Peripheral nerve	Weakness: distal, symmetrical, sensory May have associated autonomic signs May involve cranial nerves Deep tendon reflexes reduced/lost early	Guillain-Barré syndrome Diphtheric neuropathy Porphyria, lead neuropathy Hypophosphatemia, cobalamin deficiency
Anterior horn cells	Predominantly motor signs, hyporeflexia Sensory symptoms uncommon Often asymmetric	Poliomyelitis Other enteroviruses

Table 17.11: Differential diagnosis of acute flaccid paralysis

Feature	*Poliomyelitis*	*Guillain Barré Syndrome*	*Transverse myelitis*	*Traumatic neuritis*
Progression to full paralysis	24–48 hour	Hours to days	Hours to 4 days	Hours to 4 days
Fever onset	High, always present at onset of paralysis	No	Present before paralysis	No
Flaccidity	Acute, asymmetrical, proximal	Acute, symmetrical, distal, ascending	Acute, symmetrical, lower limbs	Acute, asymmetric
Muscle tone	Diminished	Diminished	Diminished in lower limbs	Diminished
Deep tendon reflexes	Decreased or absent	Absent	Absent early, hyper-reflexia late	Decreased or absent
Sensation	Severe myalgia and backache, no sensory changes	Cramps, tingling, hypoanesthesia of palms and soles	Anesthesia of lower limbs with sensory level	Pain in gluteal region
Cranial nerves	Only when bulbar and bulbospinal	Often present, affecting nerves VII, IX, X, XI, XII	Absent	Absent
Respiratory insufficiency	Only when bulbar and bulbospinal	In severe cases	Sometimes	Absent
CSF examination	High leukocytes; normal or slightly increased protein	Less than 10 leukocytes; high protein	Cellular or acellular; normal or slightly increased protein	Normal
Bladder dysfunction	Absent	Transient	Present	Never
EMG at 3 weeks (wk)	Abnormal	Normal	Normal	May show abnormality
Nerve conduction velocity at 3 wk	Normal	Abnormal, demyelination or axonal damage	Normal	Abnormal
Sequelae at 3 months	Severe, asymmetrical atrophy; skeletal deformities appear later	Symmetrical atrophy of distal muscles, recovery in milder cases	Diplegia, atrophy after years, recovery in milder cases	Moderate atrophy in affected limb

Suggested reading

1. Francis PT. Surveillance of acute flaccid paralysis in India. The Lancet 2007; 369: 1322–1323.
2. Field Guide - Surveillance of Acute Flaccid Paralysis. 3rd edition. New Delhi: Ministry of Health and Family Welfare, Government of India; 2005.
3. Progress towards interruption of wild poliovirus transmission in 2005. Wkly Epidemiol Rec 2006;17:165–172 18.24.

SYDENHAM CHOREA (RHEUMATIC CHOREA)

Chorea may precede or follow manifestations of rheumatic fever. There is a significant epidemiological association of chorea with rheumatic fever. Nearly one-third of these patients develop rheumatic valvular heart disease. Concurrent association of chorea with rheumatic polyarthritis is rare although authentic cases have been recorded. This is attributed to the fact that chorea generally supervenes later in the course of rheumatic activity. Chorea is a major criterion for the diagnosis of rheumatic activity.

Clinical Features

Sydenham chorea is more common in girls than in boys. The usual age of onset is 5 to 15 years. Classically, choreiform movements are described as irregular, non-repetitive, quasipurposive and involuntary. They are usually proximal but may affect fingers, hands, extremities and face. The clinical picture may be variable depending on the severity of the illness. The child may appear clumsy, have mild tick like jerks and deterioration in handwriting. Movements may be limited to one side of the body as in hemiballismus. The movements are aggravated by attention, stress or excitement, but disappear during sleep. Emotional lability, hypotonia and a jerky speech are common associations.

The following clinical maneuvers are helpful in arriving at the diagnosis:

1. When the hand is outstretched above the head, forearms tend to pronate.
2. When hands are stretched forwards, he flexes the wrist and hyperextends the fingers.
3. The child relaxes hand grip on and off as if he is milking a cow (*Milkmaid's grip*).
4. The child cannot maintain the tongue in protruded position (*darting tongue*).
5. During speech an audible click is heard.
6. The knee reflex may show a sustained contraction resulting in a hung up reflex. Otherwise there may be a pendular knee reflex.

Investigations: The neurological investigations are generally unrewarding. ASLO titer may not be elevated because the onset of chorea is late.

Prognosis: The disorder is generally self-limiting and may last from a few weeks to few months (up to 2 years). Relapses or recurrences are not uncommon.

Treatment: The child should be protected from injury; bedding should be well padded. These children may be treated with chlorpromazine, haloperidol, sodium valproate or carbamazepine. Doses may be determined by minimum doses required for symptom suppression. Aspirin or steroids help to limit the course of chorea and the important modalities of treatment in resistant cases not responding to symptomatic therapy. Antistreptococcal prophylaxis with penicillin G should be given to prevent recurrence of rheumatic activity.

Suggested reading

1. Weiner SG, Normandin PA.Sydenham chorea: a case report and review of the literature.Pediatr Emerg Care. 2007 Jan;23(1):20-4.
2. Pavone P, Parano E, Rizzo R, Trifiletti RR.Autoimmune neuropsychiatric disorders associated with streptococcal infection: Sydenham chorea, PANDAS, and PANDAS variants.J Child Neurol. 2006 Sep;21(9):727–36.
3. Mink JW.Paroxysmal dyskinesias.Curr Opin Pediatr. 2007 Dec;19(6):652–6.

ATAXIA

Ataxia is not unusual in childhood. Movements of the limbs are uncoordinated even in absence of weakness. The child is unsteady, tends to sway while standing with feet together or walking in a tandem fashion. Nystagmus, dysarthria, posterior column signs and evidence of labyrinth or cerebellar disease and raised intracranial pressure should be looked for. A history of drug, toxins and recent infections is important (Table 17.12).

Acute Cerebellar Ataxia

Acute cerebellar ataxia may result from many causes: the common being post-viral, drugs and para-neoplastic states. Epstein-Barr virus and chickenpox virus have been implicated.

The usual age of onset is between 1 and 5 years. Ataxia may develop within a few hours following a febrile illness. The patient has hypotonia, dysarthria, significant ataxia of gait and some incoordination in extremities. The tendon jerks are often pendular and nystagmus is common. The cerebrospinal fluid shows mild pleocytosis. Changes in electroencephalogram are minimal. Prognosis is good. Corticosteroids are useful and a quick response is observed. Recurrence is uncommon. In the post viral group other diagnoses should be entertained in the event of recurrence or non-response.

Table 17.12: Causes of ataxia

Acute Ataxia
1. Acute cerebrellar ataxia
2. Toxicity with phenylhydantoin or lead
3. Benign paroxysmal vertigo of children. (Basilar artery migraine) recurrent episodic
4. Guillain-Barré syndrome variant with ataxia
5. Occult malignancy such as neuroblastoma
Chronic Ataxia
1. Tumor of posterior fossa
2. Ataxia telangiectasia
3. Friedreich ataxia
4. Wilson disease
5. Refsum syndrome
6. Metachromatic leukodystrophy
7. Abetalipoproteinemia
8. Hartnup and maple syrup urine disease
9. Degenerative disorders

Ataxia Telengiectasia

This is an autosomal recessive disorder localized to long arm of chromosome 11, characterized by progressive cerebellar ataxia starting between the ages of one and three years. A few years later, telengiectasia over the conjunctivae and skin may be observed. These children often have diminished immunological competence (IgA deficiency and impaired cell mediated immunity), frequent sinopulmonary infections and increased predisposition to lymphoreticular malignancies. They have elevated alphafetoprotein levels and defects in DNA repair. Serum IgA should be estimated in cases presenting with chronic ataxia.

Friedreich Ataxia

It is a familial disorder with recessive inheritance. These cases present in later part of the first or second decades. The classical changes include degeneration of three long spinal tracts *viz.*, dorsal, pyramidal and spinocerebellar tracts.

There is loss of position and vibration sense, ataxia nystagmus, dysarthria and areflexia (due to cerebellar dysfunction). Plantar response is usually extensor because of pyramidal involvement. Intellect is not affected. In addition, these children show skeletal abnormalities such as pes cavus and kyphoscoliosis. Cardiac lesions may be present as evidenced by a large heart with ECG abnormalities. Optic atrophy is usually seen. There is a higher incidence of diabetes mellitus in these cases.

Occult Neuroblastoma

A child with acute cerebellar ataxia, who shows irregular, hyperkinetic spontaneous movement of eyes in many directions (opsoclonus) and myoclonic jerks of face and body should always be investigated for occult malignancy especially neuroblastoma.

Refsum Disease

It is due to disturbances in phytanic acid metabolism. Clinical features include ataxia, atypical retinitis pigmentosa with night blindness, deafness, ichthyosis and conduction defects in the heart. Protein level in CSF is high. These patients should be treated by withholding green vegetables (which are rich in phytanic acid chlorophyll) from the diet.

Demyelinating/Storage Diseases

Ataxia is an important component of disorders of demyelination. Visual involvement, pyramidal tract involvement and a waxing and waning course may be observed. Lipidoses can also present with cerebellar features.

Developmental Disorders

Cerebellar ataxia may also occur due to rudimentary development of cerebellar folia. It may be associated with diplegia, both spastic and flaccid, congenital chorea and mental defect. These are non-progressive and may appear to improve with physiotherapy.

Suggested reading

1. Bernard G, Shevell MI.Channelopathies: a review. Pediatr Neurol. 2008 Feb;38(2):73–85.
2. Nandhagopal R, Krishnamoorthy SG.Unsteady gait.Postgrad Med J. 2006 May;82(967):e7–8.

INFANTILE TREMOR SYNDROME

Infantile tremor syndrome as reported from Indian subcontinent is a self-limiting clinical disorder in infants and young children. It is characterized by acute or gradual onset with mental and pychomotor changes, pigmentary disturbances of hair and skin, pallor and tremors. The disease is now encountered less frequently.

Etiopathogenesis

17

The clinical features suggest a disorder of the extra-pyramidal system. The course of the illness is self-limiting, hence it is unlikely to be a progressive degenerative disorder. Etiologic possibilities are malnutrition, vitamin B12 deficiency and viral infections but none have been conclusively proven.

Malnutrition: Due to its close resemblance with Kahn's nutritional recovery syndrome, malnutrition was postulated as a possible etiology but majority of children are not malnourished, look chubby and their serum proteins are within normal range.

Vitamin B12 deficiency: A similar clinical entity with low vitamin B12 levels, megaloblastic bone marrow and a prompt response to vitamin B12 therapy was described but not substantiated.

Magnesium deficiency: Low magnesium levels in the serum and cerebrospinal fluids are reported in some cases.

Infections: Seasonal incidence and cortical biopsy suggest that it might be a form of meningoencephalitis, but failure to isolate any viral antigen, consistently normal CSF, presence of pigmentary changes and pallor do not support this hypothesis.

Toxin: Epidemiological evidence does not support the view that infantile tremor syndrome is due to a toxin.

Enzyme defect: A transient tyrosine metabolism defect might lead to interference in melanin pigment production. Depigmentation of substantia nigra may explain the tremor. This needs further confirmation.

Clinical Features

Infantile tremor syndrome occurs in apparently plump normal or underweight and exclusively breast-fed children in the age of 5 months to 3 years. Boys are twice as commonly affected as girls. Most cases occur in summer months in children belonging to the low socio-economic group.

The prodromal phase lasts for 2 weeks to 2 months. In a typical case, the onset is heralded by mental/motor regression characterized by apathy, vacant look, inability to recognize the mother, lack of interest in surroundings, lethargy and poor response to bright and colored objects. There is hyperpigmentation, especially over the dorsum of hands, feet, knees, ankles, wrists and terminal phalanges. Pigmentary changes over thighs may be reticular or honeycomb-like. Hair become light brown, sparse, thin, silky and lusterless. There is mild to moderate pallor. At times there may be fever, upper respiratory tract infections, diarrhea, edema, hepatomegaly and a tremulous cry.

The next phase is characterized by abrupt onset of tremors, which are usually generalized. Tremors are coarse, fast, 6–12 cycles per second, of low amplitude, initially intermittent but become continuous later on. Rate of tremors may vary from one limb to the other. Head is tossed from side to side and trunk may show twisting or wriggling dystonic movements. Tremors disappear during sleep and are aggravated during crying, playing or feeding. Some infants assume a typical bird with wings spread out posture. Tone is variable. Consciousness is retained. Average duration of this phase is two to five weeks. Condition remains static for some time before disappearing altogether.

During the post-tremor phase, pallor and pigmentation become less, the child becomes more alert. Improvement in psychomotor function is relatively slow. This phase usually lasts for one to six months but the course may be unduly prolonged with associated infections. Mortality is never directly related to the disease but may be attributed to concurrent infections. Subnormal intelligence is the only long-term sequel.

Investigations

Laboratory investigations are not pathognomonic. There is mild to moderate anemia with hemoglobin between 6–11 g/dL. Morphology of red cells is variable (normocytic, microcytic, macrocytic or dimorphic). Bone marrow shows normoblastic, dimorphic or megaloblastic changes. Cerebrospinal fluid is normal. Histological changes of liver, skin, muscle, rectum and nerve are non-contributory. Cortical biopsies reveal mild inflammatory changes. Phenumoencephalography reveals cortical atrophy. CT scan shows no abnormalities or mild atrophy. EEG may show epileptiform activity. Virological studies are negative.

Differential Diagnosis

Kahn's nutritional recovery syndrome, infection of the central nervous system, chronic liver diseases, hypoglycemia, hypomagnesemia, heredofamilial degenerative diseases, phenothiazine toxicity, hyperthyroidism and megaloblastic anemia may be considered in the differential diagnosis.

Treatment

Treatment is largely empirical, symptomatic and supportive. Iron, calcium, magnesium, vitamin B6 supplements and injectable vitamin therapy is reported to help some patients. Phenobarbitone, phenytoin and anti parkinsonism drugs do not shorten the duration of tremors. Tremors may considerably diminish after administration of propranolol. We have successfully used carbamazepine for this condition in a few cases.

Nutrition should be maintained with dietary supplementation. Parents should be reassured. Associated infections and secondary complications must be treated.

Suggested reading

1. Kumar A. Movement disorders in the tropics. Parkinsonism Relate Discord 2002; 9: 69–75.
2. Vora RM, Tullu MS, Bartakke SP, Kamat JR.Infantile tremor syndrome and zinc deficiency. Indian J Med Sci. 2002 Feb;56(2): 69–72.

CEREBRAL PALSY

Cerebral palsy (CP) is defined as a non-progressive neuromotor disorder of cerebral origin. It includes heterogeneous clinical states of variable etiology and severity ranging from minor incapacitation to total handicap. Most of the cases have multiple neurological deficits and variable mental handicap. The term does not include progressive, degenerative or metabolic disorders of the nervous system.

It is difficult to estimate the precise magnitude of the problem since mild cases are likely to be missed. Approximately 1–2 per 100 live births is a reasonable estimate of the incidence.

Etiopathogenesis

Factors may operate prenatally, during delivery or in the postnatal period. Maldevelopment and disorderly anatomic organization of the brain, perinatal hypoxia, birth trauma, chorioamnionitis, prothrombotic factors, acid base imbalance, indirect hyperbilirubinemia, metabolic disturbances and intrauterine or acquired infections may operate. The role of mild birth asphyxia as an etiological insult for cerebral palsy is questionable. Most infants have multiple risk factors. Prematurity is an important risk factor for cerebral diplegia while term weight babies get quadriparesis or hemiparesis and a poorer mental outcome. The mechanism of CP in a large proportion of cases remains unclear and primary neurological aberrations may be unfolded in future. The importance of role of birth asphyxia has been questioned by recent data, and asphyxia may be manifestation of the brain damage rather than the primary etiology.

A variety of pathological lesions such as cerebral atrophy, porencephaly, migration defects, microcephaly, leukomalacia, degeneration of basal ganglia and cerebellar lesions may be observed. Gliosis of the contralateral hemispheres may result from vascular occlusions.

Cerebral palsy is classified on basis of topographic distribution, neurologic findings and etiology .

Spastic Cerebral Palsy

This is the commonest form (65%). Depending on distribution of spasticity it may be a spastic quadriparesis, diplegia or hemiparesis. Early diagnostic features of neural damage include abnormally persistent neonatal reflexes, feeding difficulties, persistent cortical thumb after 3 months age and a firm grasp. On vertical suspension, the infant goes into scissoring due to adductor spasm with an extensor posture and does not flex his knees or thigh. The stretch tendon reflexes are always brisk. They have variable degrees of mental, visual handicaps and behavioral problems.

Spastic quadriparesis is more common in term babies, and exhibits severe signs including opisthotonic posture, pseudobulbar palsy, feeding difficulties, restricted voluntary movements and multiple deficits.

Spastic diplegia is commoner in preterm babies and is associated with periventricular leukomalacia. The lower limbs are more severely affected with extension and adduction posturing, brisk tendon jerks and tendency to contractures.

Spastic hemiplegia is usually recognized after 4–6 months age. Abnormal persistent fisting, abnormal posture or gait disturbance may be the presenting complaint. Vascular insults, porencephaly or cerebral anomalies may be associated.

Seizures are common in all forms and require therapy. A thorough screen for associated handicaps and developmental assessment is warranted.

Hypotonic (Atonic) Cerebral Palsy

Despite pyramidal involvement, these patients are atonic or hypotonic. Tendon reflexes are normal or brisk and Babinski response is positive. They are often severely mentally retarded. In cerebellar involvement, hypotonia is not associated with exaggerated reflexes. Muscles may show fiber disproportion and delayed CNS maturation is common.

Extrapyramidal CP

The clinical manifestations include dyskinesia such as athetosis, choreiform movements, dystonia, tremors and rigidity. Arms, leg, neck and trunk may be involved. These cases account for about 30% of the patients. Mental retardation and hearing deficits may be present. High tone audiometry should be performed. Early diagnostic indicators are inability to reach for and grasp a dangling ring by the age of 6 months. Cerebral damage following bilirubin encephalopathy is a classical example, and deafness a common association.

Cerebellar Involvement

Occurs in less than 5% of the patients. There is hypotonia and hyporeflexia. Ataxia and intention tremors appear by the age of 2 years. Nystagmus is unusual, mental status may be near normal in some of these patients.

Mixed Type

A proportion of the patients have features of diffuse neurological involvement of the mixed type.

Severity of Lesion

Mild cases of cerebral palsy are ambulatory and account for only 20% of patients. Moderately involved patients achieve ambulation by help. These may be treated at out patient level and 50% of the patients are placed in this category. Severely affected and multiple deficit children account for the rest.

Holistic Evaluation

Eyes: Nearly half the patients may have strabismus, paralysis of gaze, cataracts, coloboma, retrolental fibroplasia, perceptual and refractive errors.

Ears: Partial or complete loss of hearing is usual in kernicterus. Brain damage due to rubella may be followed by receptive auditory aphasia.

Speech: Aphasia, dysarthria and dyslalia are common among dyskinetic individuals.

Sensory defects: Astereognosis and spatial disorientation are seen in one-third of the patients.

Seizures: Spastics usually have generalized or focal tonic seizures. Seizures are more in the disorders acquired postnatally. These patients respond poorly to antiepileptic agents. Electroencephalograms show gross abnormalities.

Intelligence: About a quarter of the children may have borderline intelligence (IQ 80–100); and half of them are severely mentally retarded.

Miscellaneous: Inadequate thermoregulation and problems of social and emotional adjustment are present in many cases. These children may have associated dental defects and are more susceptible to infections.

Diagnosis

The diagnosis of cerebral palsy should be suspected if a child with a low birth weight, perinatal insult has increased tone, feeding difficulties and does not keep pace with the anticipated normal range of neurological and behavioral development. Abnormalities of tone posture, involuntary movements and neurological deficits should be recorded. Evaluation includes perinatal history, detailed neurological and developmental examination and assessment of language and learning disabilities. Inborn errors of metabolism may need to be excluded by screening of the plasma and urine. CT and MRI help delineate the extent of cerebral damage in a case of cerebral palsy.

Differential Diagnosis

Neurodegenerative disorders: Progressively increasing symptoms, familial pattern of disease, consanguinity, specific constellation of symptoms and signs are usual clues for neurometabolic disorders. Failure to thrive, vomiting, seizures are significant symptoms. Laboratory investigations are necessary.

Hydrocephalus and subdural effusion: Head size is large, fontanel may bulge and sutures may separate.

Brain tumors or space occupying lesions: Lesion is progressive and features of increased intracranial pressure are evident.

Muscle disorders: Congenital myopathies, muscular dystrophies and muscle-eye-brain diseases can mimic cerebral palsy. Distribution of muscle weakness and other features is characteristic, hypotonia is associated with diminished reflexes. The enzyme creatine phosphokinase may be elevated. EMG and muscle biopsy are diagnostic.

Ataxia telengiectasia: Ataxia may appear before the ocular telengiectasia are evident. But progressive course is usually evident.

Prevention

Prevention of maternal infection, fetal or perinatal insults, good maternal care and freedom from postnatal damage reduces prevalence. Recent evidence points that asphyxia at birth may be a manifestation of poor establishment of respiration in a brain damaged child and is not always an etiological factor. Early diagnosis, prompt adequate management plans can reduce the residual neurological and psychosocial emotional handicaps for the child and his family.

Management

The management plan should be holistic, involve the family and be directed to severity, type of neurological deficits and associated problems. Stress on improving posture, reducing tone preventing contractures and early stimulation is necessary. Identification of associated deficits is important for appropriate physiotherapy and occupational therapy. Symptomatic treatment is prescribed for seizures. Tranquilizers are administered for behavior disturbances and muscle relaxants may be used for improving the muscle function. Baclofen and tizanidine help to reduce spasticity. Diazepam may ameliorate spasticity and athetosis. Dantrolene sodium helps in relaxation of skeletal muscles. Local phenol blocks provide relief for few months. Plastic orthoses may help to prevent contractures, surgical procedures for spasticity and contractures may be required in carefully selected patients. Botulinum toxin is the new, albeit costly alternative for reducing muscle tone.

Occupational therapy: The beginning is made with simple movements of self-help in feeding and dressing with progressive development of more intricate activities like typing.

Educational: The defects of vision, perception, speech and learning are managed by adequate special education experiences.

Orthopedic support: Light weight splints may be required for tight tendo-Achilles and cortical thumb.

Social: The family should be given social and emotional support to help it to live with the child's handicap.

Rehabilitation and vocational guidance: Parents should help the child to adjust in the society and if possible to become self-reliant and independent by proper vocational guidance and rehabilitation. Several handicapped children may need to be institutionalized.

Suggested reading

1. Rosenbaum P. Cerebral palsy: what parents and doctors want to know. BMJ 2003; 326: 970–4.
2. Nelson KB, Chang T.Is cerebral palsy preventable? Curr Opin Neurol. 2008 Apr;21(2):129–35.
3. Anttila H, Autti-Rämö I, Suoranta J, Mäkelä M, Malmivaara A.Effectiveness of physical therapy interventions for children with cerebral palsy: a systematic review.BMC Pediatr. 2008 Apr 24;8:14.
4. O'Shea M.Cerebral palsy.Semin Perinatol. 2008 Feb;32(1):35–41.
5. Garne E, Dolk H, Krägeloh-Mann I, Holst Ravn S, Cans C; SCPE Collaborative Group.Cerebral palsy and congenital malformations.Eur J Paediatr Neurol. 2008 Mar;12(2):82–8.
6. Jones MW, Morgan E, Shelton JE.Primary care of the child with cerebral palsy: a review of systems (part II).J Pediatr Health Care. 2007 Jul-Aug;21(4):226–37.

DEGENERATIVE BRAIN DISORDERS

A wide variety of hereditary and acquired disorders cause progressive degeneration of the central nervous system. In these disorders, new developmental skills are not achieved. As the disease advances, skill already acquired may also be lost. The degeneration may primarily involve the gray or white matter, resulting in corresponding clinical profile.

Late cases may have common features. A fluctuant course with recurrent seizures, mental deterioration, failure to thrive, infections, bad odor, skin and hair changes may point to inborn errors of metabolism. Some common causes of neurodegeneration are described below.

Infantile Gaucher Disease (Type II)

It is a metabolic disorder with autosomal recessive inheritance. The lysosomal enzyme glucocerebroside beta-glucosidase is deficient. Glucocerebroside accumulates in various tissues. Foamy reticulum cells are present in the bone marrow. Acid phosphatase is raised in the blood and tissues. The deficient enzyme can be identified in leukocytes/fibroblasts. Most cases terminate fatally before they are 3 years old. Clinically, these children show a characteristic triad of retroflexed head, trismus and squint. They may show hypertonia, marked feeding problems vomiting and dysphagia. Splenomegaly and hepatomegaly are observed later. Enzyme replacement has been tried for juvenile and adult forms of this disease. It has a very different clinical profiles.

Tay-Sach Disease (GM2 gangliosidosis)

Inheritance is autosomal recessive. A history of consanguinity is usually obtained. It was earlier reported in Ashkenazi Jews but has been reported in other racial groups also. Several cases have been documented in India. Low serum beta-hexosaminidase level is the characteristic metabolic defect. As a result GM2 ganglioside accumulates in the neurons. Death occurs by 2 to 4 years. Initially, milestones are delayed. Later, there is retrogression of development. The baby has an abnormal startle response to noise. Convulsions, rigidity of the extensor group of muscles and blindness supervene after the first year.

A cherry red spot is seen over the macular region of the retina. The head size increases. Liver and spleen are not enlarged. Sandhoff disease is described in non-Jewish people. It resembles Tay-Sach's disease clinically except for later onset, mild visceromegaly and progressive ataxia. Both hexosominidase A and B are deficient. These cases may show congestive heart failure and enlarged liver.

Metachromatic Leukodystrophy

Inheritance is autosomal recessive and the gene is located on chromosome 22. The characteristic metabolic defect is decreased urinary or leukocyte aryl sulphatase A activity. Clinically, the illness manifests as ataxia, stiffness starting in the second year of life. A little later, signs of bulbar involvement and intellectual deterioration are observed. Initially there is hypotonia, but later spasticity supervenes. Characteristically, distal tendon reflexes are lost due to associated peripheral neuropathy. Progressive intellectual impairment, optic atrophy and loss of speech develop in the course of illness. Convulsions may occur in some cases but are not a prominent feature. These children go into decerebrate posture terminally. CT scan and MR imaging reveal abnormal white matter finger like projections, sural nerve biopsy may reveal metachromatic granules and the enzyme (ara-A) is low; parents may reveal a carrier state.

Mucopolysaccharidoses

This is a group of disorders. Inheritance is autosomal recessive. Deficiency of L-iduronidase is the characteristic metabolic defect. Heparan and dermatan sulphate excretion in the urine is increased. Metachromatic cytoplasmic inclusion bodies are seen in the lymphocytes. Clinically, delayed milestones become apparent by the age of 1 year. The facies is coarse. The child appears a dwarf with gibbus at the level of L1 vertebra. The abdomen is prominent. Liver and spleen are enlarged. Hands are short and stubby. Deafness and haziness of cornea are also seen. Valvular heart disease may be there. Most cases die by the age of 10 to 20 years. Scheie syndrome is milder.

Subacute Sclerosing Panencephalitis

This condition is believed to follow several months to years after an attack of measles. The usual age of onset is between 5 and 15 years. In the early stages, minor personality changes may be observed and school performance deteriorates. Later, slow myoclonic jerks in the limbs and trunk are observed. Progressive neurologic deterioration occurs. Electroencephalogram shows characteristic periodic slow waves with high voltage and a burst suppression pattern.

MENTAL RETARDATION

Mental retardation is defined as subaverage general intelligence, manifesting during early developmental period. The child has diminished learning capacity and does not adjust well socially.

Grades of Mental Handicap

17

Intellect comprises perception, memory, recognition, conceptualization, convergent and divergent reasoning (classification and creativity), *verbal facility* and *motor competence*. Intelligence tests devised to measure different parameters of intelligence in the different age groups include the following:

Gesell's Developmental Schedules, Bayley Infant Scales, Griffith's Mental Development Scale, Wechsler Preschool and Primary Scale of Intelligence (W.P.P.S.I.), Wechsler Intelligence Scale for Children (W.I.S.C.), Stanford-Binet Tests (Terman-Merrill revision), Raven's Matrices, Denver II Development Screening Test, Good enough Draw-a-man Test, A.A.M.D. Adaptive Behavior Scale.

Indian adaptations of some of these are: Kulshrestha or Kamath adaptations of the Stanford-Binet test, Phatak's adaptation of the Bayley Scales, Malin's adaptation of the WISC, Vineland Social Maturity Scale and Bhatia's Battery of Performance Tests.

The *intelligence quotient (IQ)* is calculated according to the formula: mental age divided by chronological age, multiplied by 100.

The degree of mental handicap is designated *mild, moderate, severe and profound,* for IQ levels of 51–70, 36–50, 21–35 and 0–20, respectively. An IQ level of 71 to 90 is designated *borderline intelligence* and is not included in mental handicap. The terms *educable* and *trainable* are used for mild and moderate mental handicap, respectively, while the severe and profoundly handicapped are designated *custodian*. However, all levels of mentally retarded children are educable and trainable to some extent.

Prevalence

In the general population, 2 to 3% of children have an IQ below 70. Nearly three-fourth of such cases are mildly handicapped. About 4 per 1,000 (or 0.4%) of the general population, are more severally handicapped with an IQ below 50.

Etiology

Mild mental retardation is due to interplay of several biomedical, sociocultural and psychological factors. It is often difficult to incriminate only a single factor in etiology. Majority of cases are idiopathic. Specific causes may be described under three headings *viz.*, prenatal, natal and postnatal. In moderate to severe mental retardation the cause is easier to identify.

Prenatal factors
Aminoacidopathies: Organic acidemia, phenylketonuria, homocystinuria, histidinemia, organic aciduria
Carbohydrate disorders: Glycogen storage defects, glucose transport defects, galactosemia
Mucopolysaccharidoses
Chromosomal disorders: Down syndrome, fragile X syndrome, Klinefelter syndrome
Iodine deficiency
Neuroectodermal dysplasia: Tuberous sclerosis
Developmental defects: Microcephaly, craniostenosis, porencephaly, cerebral migration defects

Maternal factors
Use of teratogens in first trimester of pregnancy
Intrauterine infections (rubella, toxoplasmosis, CMV, herpes, syphilis, HIV)
Placental insufficiency, toxemia of pregnancy, antepartum hemorrhage
Radiation during pregnancy

Natal factors
Birth injuries
Hypoxic, ischemic encephalopathy
Intracerebral hemorrhage

Postnatal or acquired factors
Infections of central nervous system
Head injuries
Thrombosis of cerebral vessels
Post-vaccinal encephalopathies
Kernicterus, hypoglycemia
Hypoxia, hypothyroidism
Malnutrition, child abuse
Autism

Predisposing Factors

Low socio-economic strata: These children are exposed to several environmental causes of mental handicap, such as inadequate nutrition of mother and child, poor antenatal and obstetric care, lack of immunization, delayed and inappropriate treatment of infections, and unsatisfactory environmental stimulation.

Low birth weight: The small for gestational age (SGA) infant has a poorer long-term prognosis for postnatal development than preterm infants of equal weight, who are appropriate for gestational age. However, even the preterm infant is at risk for cerebral hemorrhage, anoxia and infections. The SGA infant is subjected to adverse genetic or prenatal environmental influences, which may occasionally result in brain damage.

Advanced maternal age: Chromosomal anomalies such as Down syndrome as well as intrauterine factors, such as fetal deprivation and hypoxia are commoner in offspring of older mothers. Birth trauma is more frequent in the infant of the older primipara.

Consanguinity of parents is associated with a high incidence of genetically transmitted mental handicap.

Clinical Presentation and Diagnosis

The mental age is below the chronological age. Most of them present with the behavior syndrome of cerebral dysfunction, such as hyperactivity, short span of attention, distractibility, poor concentration, poor memory, impulsiveness, awkward clumsy movements, disturbed sleep, emotional instability, low frustration tolerance and wide scatter in intellectual function.

Associated defects of the musculoskeletal system, of vision, or speech and hearing are often found in mentally handicapped children. Congenital anomalies of other systems, apart from the neurological system, may be associated, when cause is prenatal. Convulsions are common in the mentally handicapped.

History should include developmental and family history. A complete physical examination will usually help in the diagnosis. It should include an examination of the fundus and a developmental assessment.

Various syndromes in which mental handicap is a feature should be looked for. These often indicate etiology, such as cretinism, dysmorphic states, rubella syndrome and Down syndrome. Additional investigations are necessary in only a small portion of cases, depending on the probable diagnosis. These are:

Urine tests including chromatography for conditions such as metachromatic leukodystrophy, phenylketonuria, homocystinuria, galactosemia, etc.

Investigations for hypothyroidism; bone age, thyroid hormone, TSH estimation.

Chromosomal studies for suspected chromosomal anomalies, Down syndrome, fragile X syndrome.

Biopsy (bone marrow, liver, rectum, brain, skin) to confirm storage/other disorders.

Blood examination for appropriate enzymes; excessive or deficient metabolites.

Serological tests for intrauterine infections.

X-ray skull, CSF examination, EEG

Computed tomography, MRI may define hydrocephalus, porencephaly, absence of corpus callosum, tuberous sclerosis, migration defects, white matter diseases, cortical atrophy.

Risk of Occurrence or Recurrence

The overall risk of Down syndrome is 1 in 650 births. The risk varies with maternal age, from 1 in 1850 at maternal age of 15–19 years, 1 in 1600 at 20–24 years, 1 in 1350 at 25–29 years, 1 in 800 at 30–34 years, 1 in 260 at 35–39 years, 1 in 100 at 40–44 years, to 1 in 50 at 45 years and over.

Recurrence risk in trisomy G with normal parents is under 5%. In a carrier mother with a balanced D-G translocation, the theoretical risk of producing a child with Down syndrome is 1 in 3, but the observed risk is 1 in 10, since most of such concepts are aborted. In parental GG-translocation, the risk of producing a child with Down syndrome is 100%.

Two mentally handicapped partners can produce children, with normal intelligence. When only one parent was mentally handicapped, 27% of the offspring were normal. When one sibling is mentally handicapped, the risk of mental handicapped of other siblings is 50% for autosomal dominant conditions, 25% for autosomal recessive conditions and under 5% for idiopathic mental handicap.

Prevention

Genetic counseling: The risk of disorders with autosomal recessive inheritance is high in consanguineous marriages. Parents should be informed about the chance of birth of an affected baby in a subsequent pregnancy, if a sibling is retarded due to a metabolic cause. Mothers older than 35-year should be screened for Down syndrome during pregnancy.

Vaccination of girls with rubella vaccine should be encouraged to prevent fetal rubella syndrome.

During pregnancy, good *antenatal care* and advice on avoidance of teratogens, hormones, iodides and anti-thyroid drugs is given. Mothers should be protected from contact with patients suffering from viral diseases. When indicated, amniocentesis may be done for study of amniotic fluid for tissue culture, chromosome studies, alpha-fetoprotein and enzyme for prenatal diagnosis.

During labor, *good obstetric and postnatal supervision* is essential to prevent occurrence of birth asphyxia, injuries, jaundice and sepsis.

Postnatally: Neonatal and neurological infections should be diagnosed and treated promptly. Hyperbilirubinemia should be managed with phototherapy and/or exchange transfusion. Cretinism and galactosemia, if diagnosed and treated in early infancy, have a satisfactory prognosis. Patients with progressive neurologic disease or severe reaction to whole cell pertussis vaccine should receive the acellular vaccine instead. Screening of all newborn infants for metabolic disorders such as phenylketonuria and homocystinuria permits early treatment, averting irreversible brain damage.

Management

The parents should be counseled together. The diagnosis, principles of early stimulation and management should be explained, emphasizing the prognosis. Parental guilt and the home situation should be discussed. Mentally handicapped children need essential basic care as any other child. Minimal criticism and high appreciation, short-term goals and structured learning results in less withdrawal, aggressive and hostile reactions.

Associated diseases and dysfunctions, e.g. of musculoskeletal system, vision, hearing, locomotion and feeding should be appropriately managed. Anticonvulsive treatment is prescribed for seizures, medications such as phenobarbitone should be avoided. Patients with hyperactivity often respond to amphetamines including methylphenidate. Specific management of any well-defined syndrome such as metabolic or endocrine disease should be done.

Institutionalization should be avoided. Day care centers and schools, integrated schools, vocational training centers, sheltered farms and workshops are useful. Classes should be taken to educate mothers and families in caring for the handicapped and in trying to develop their potential to the maximum, in an effort to make these children as independent as possible.

Suggested reading

1. Sherr EH, Shevell MI. Mental Retardation and Global developmental delay. In Swaiman KF, Ashwal S Ferriero DM. Pediatric Neurology Principles & Practice 4th ed. Philadelphia Mosby, 2006.
2. Moeschler JB.Genetic evaluation of intellectual disabilities. Semin Pediatr Neurol. 2008;15(1):2–9.
3. McDonald L, Rennie A, Tolmie J, Galloway P, McWilliam R.Investigation of global developmental delay.Arch Dis Child. 2006;91(8):701–5.
4. Shevell M, Ashwal S, Donley D, et al.Practice parameter: evaluation of the child with global developmental delay: report of the Quality Standards Subcommittee of the American Academy of Neurology and The Practice Committee of the Child Neurology Society. Neurology. 2003 11;60(3):367.

NEUROCUTANEOUS SYNDROMES

There are five major neurocutaneous syndromes viz. (i) neurofibromatosis; (ii) tuberous sclerosis; (iii) von Hippel Landau disease; (iv) Sturge-Weber syndrome; and (v) ataxia-telengiectasia. All of these are inherited disorders except for Sturge-Weber syndrome. Clinical profile of these syndromes is diverse, varying from the mild abortive forms to severe potentially fatal disorders.

Neurofibromatosis

Inheritance is autosomal dominant. There are two types: type NF1 (von Recklinghausen disease or peripheral NF1) and type NF2 (central neurofibromatosis). Deletion or inactivation of the NF gene in chromosome 17 is responsible for NF1. Gene for NF2 is probably located on chromosome 22.

NF1: Two or more of the following are present: (i) 6 or more cafe-au-lait spots, each over 5 mm in diameter before puberty or over 15 mm diameter in older persons; (ii) 2 or more neurofibromas or one plexiform neuroma; (iii) freckling in axillary or inguinal regions; (iv) optic glioma; (v) Two or more Lisch nodules; dysplasia of the sphenoid bone or thinning of the cortex of long bones with or without pseudoarthrosis; and (vi) a first degree relative with NF1.

NF2: Presence of bilateral auditory neuroma; unilateral auditory neuroma along with a first degree relative with meningioma, schwannoma or juvenile posterior subcapsular lenticular opacity.

Management: Management comprises of supportive care, surveillance for and treatment of new manifestations and surgical management of spinal deformities. Genetic counseling is necessary.

Tuberous Sclerosis Complex

Tuberous sclerosis is a neurocutaneous disorder inherited as an autosomal dominant trait. The presenting features vary with age.

Cardinal features are skin lesions, convulsion and mental retardation. Early skin lesions are hypopigmented, ash-leaf shaped macules (Fig 17.11), red or pink papules (angiofibromas) called adenoma sebaceum on face .These appear and also enlarge with age. Other lesions are shagreen patches, subungual fibromas and oral fibromas.

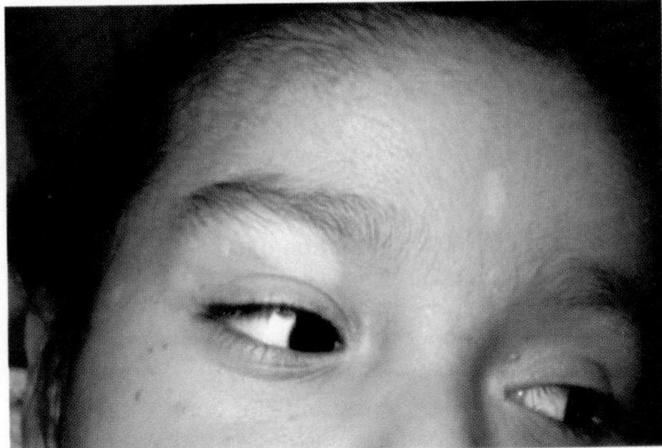

Fig. 17.11: Facial skin showing multiple ash leaf spots in a child with tuberous sclerosis

Retinal hamartoma may be present. In early life tumors in heart and kidneys may be detected on ultrasonography. In infancy, myoclonic jerks often lead to detection of this entity and are an important cause of West syndrome; vigabatrine is a useful medication in these cases. Parents and siblings should be examined for stigmata of tuberous sclerosis.

Sturge-Weber Syndrome

Sturge-Weber syndrome is characterized by facial nevus flammens (usually in the distribution of first branch of trigeminal nerve but not limited to it), contralateral focal seizures, calcification of the cortex and subcortical structures and glaucoma on the same side as the skin lesions.

von-Hippel-Landau Disease

In this disorder, there are retinal and cerebellar hemangioblastomas besides the spinal cord angiomas and cystic tumors of pancreas, kidneys and epididymis. Patients may show nystagmus, ataxia and signs of increased intracranial pressure.

Ataxia Telengiectasia

It is an autosomal recessively inherited disease that has been mapped to chromosome 11q. The syndrome manifests with progressive cerebellar ataxia, oculocutaneous telengiectasia, choreoathetosis, pulmonary and sinus infections, immune deficiency and lymphoreticular malignancies.

Ataxia begins between 12–15 months age and progresses relentlessly making children wheel chair bound by 10–12 years age. Telengiectasia appears by 2–7 years on bulbar conjunctiva and even skin. Increased incidence of abnormal movements, vitiligo, abnormal GTT are observed. Investigations reveal decreased serum IgA in three-fourths of the patients. Alfa-fetoprotein is almost universally elevated. Increased chromosomal breaks on chromosome 14 are common. Neuroimaging reveals cerebellar atrophy. Treatment is symptomatic.

Suggested reading

1. Kandt RS. Tuberous sclerosis complex and neurofibromatosis Type 1: the two most common neurocutaneous diseases. Neurol Clin 2002; 20: 941–64.
2. Leung AK, Robson WL.Tuberous sclerosis complex: a review. J Pediatr Health Care. 2007 Mar-Apr;21(2):108–14.
3. Ferner RE, Huson SM, Thomas N, Moss C, Willshaw H, Evans DG, Upadhyaya M, Towers R, Gleeson M, Steiger C, Kirby A.Guidelines for the diagnosis and management of individuals with neurofibromatosis 1.J Med Genet. 2007 Feb;44(2):81–8.
4. Quigg M, Miller JQ.Clinical findings of the phakomatoses: tuberous sclerosis. Neurology. 2005 Nov 22;65(10):E22–3.

17

18 Neuromuscular Disorders

MUSCULAR DYSTROPHIES

The muscular dystrophies are genetically determined, progressive, primary disorders of muscle. Common presenting symptoms include delayed motor milestones, abnormal mode of walking, difficulty in running, climbing stairs and getting up from floor, frequent falls, weakness of arms or face, ocular symptoms, enlargement or wasting of muscles and recurrent chest infections. The symptoms are progressive and a family history of similar illness may be obtained. A genetic classification of muscular dystrophies is depicted in Table 18.1.

Table 18.1: Classification of muscular dystrophies

X-linked dystrophies	
Duchenne, Becker	XR
Emery-Dreifuss	XR
Limb-girdle muscular dystrophies (LGMD)	
LGMD 1A-C	AD
LGMD 2A-H	AR
Congenital muscular dystrophies	
1. *With involvement of central nervous system*	
Fukuyama dystrophy	AR
Walker-Warburg dystrophy	AR
Muscle-Eye-Brain dystrophy	AR
2. *Without involvement of central nervous system*	
Merosin-deficient classic type	AR
Merosin-positive classic type	AR
Integrin-deficient dystrophy	AR
Distal dystrophies	AD/AR
Facioscapulohumeral dystrophy	AD
Oculopharyngeal dystrophy	AD
Myotonic dystrophy	AD

AD autosomal dominant; AR autosomal recessive; XR X-linked recessive.

DYSTROPHINOPATHIES: DUCHENNE AND BECKER MUSCULAR DYSTROPHIES

Duchenne muscular dystrophy (DMD) is a severe muscle wasting disorder, resulting in early confinement to wheel chair and often death by the age of 20 years. Becker muscular dystrophy (BMD) is a milder form of the same disease with later onset and a slower progression.

Genetics

Incidence: DMD and BMD display an X-linked recessive pattern of inheritance. Expression of the disease is essentially confined to males. Females are affected if the X chromosome carrying the normal allele is lost or inactivated. The incidence of DMD is approximately 1 in 3500 male births; one-third of the cases occur secondary to fresh mutations. The incidence of BMD is 5.4/100,000 with a mutation rate which is about 5% of that for DMD.

Affected gene: The gene responsible for DMD and BMD (*the DMD gene*) maps to the short arm of the X chromosome at band Xp21 and extends over 79 exons, and a 2.5 Mb genomic region. Approximately 60% of affected individuals have a deletion of one or more exons of the gene. Another 5% have duplication of exons, while the remaining 35% have a variety of subtle mutations, including point mutations. The mutation rate in BMD is much lower.

Dystrophin: The primary product of the DMD gene is a high molecular weight cytoskeletal protein. It is part of the dystrophin-glycoprotein complex, an ensemble of membrane-associated proteins that span the muscle sarcolemma, providing linkage between the intracellular cytoskeleton and the extracellular matrix (Fig. 18.1). Dystrophin is expressed in skeletal and smooth muscles, brain, peripheral nerves and other tissues. Boys with DMD have little or no functional dystrophin whereas in the milder disease BMD, dystrophin may be reduced in amount or altered in size.

Clinical Features

In the classical DMD, the perinatal history is normal. Early development of the child is normal or slightly delayed. When the child starts walking in the early part of the second year, he may appear clumsy while walking on even surface and may fall when walking or running on uneven ground. The gait is waddling with a compensatory lumbar lordosis. The toddler has difficulty in climbing up the stairs. He places his hand on the next step to lift himself up and always uses the support of the railing or the wall.

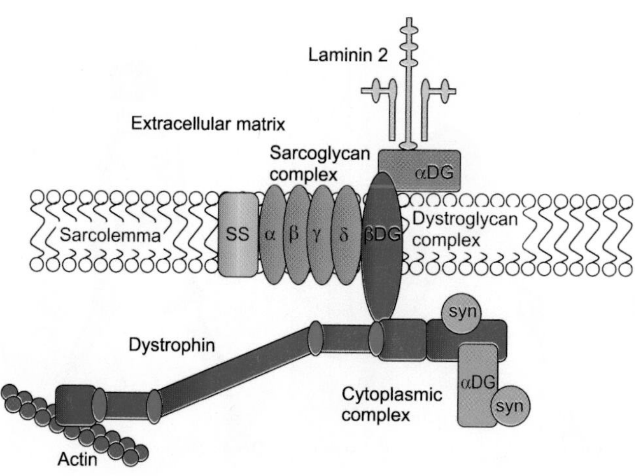

Fig. 18.1: Molecular architecture of dystrophin and dystrophin-associated proteins on the cell membrane

The diagnosis is suspected, especially if there is a positive family history of similar illness. Hypertrophy of calf muscles may be observed by the age of 4–5 years (Fig. 18.2). The weakness of shoulder girdles is demonstrated by inability to raise the hand above shoulder or comb the hair.

Distribution of the apparently hypertrophied (pseudohypertrophied) and atrophied muscles is characteristic. The calf muscles, glutei, deltoid, serrati anterior, brachioradialis and tongue muscles appear large. Sternal head of the pectoralis major and supraspinatus are atrophied. The condition shows relentless progression, with weakness and wasting affecting the proximal lower extremity muscles more profoundly. Eventually all the muscles atrophy. As the disease progresses, contractures develop at the ankles and hips. Wheel chair dependency typically occurs by about 12 years of age. Death in DMD most commonly results from pulmonary insufficiency and respiratory infections at about 20 years of age. In BMD, the pattern of muscle wasting closely resembles that seen in DMD.

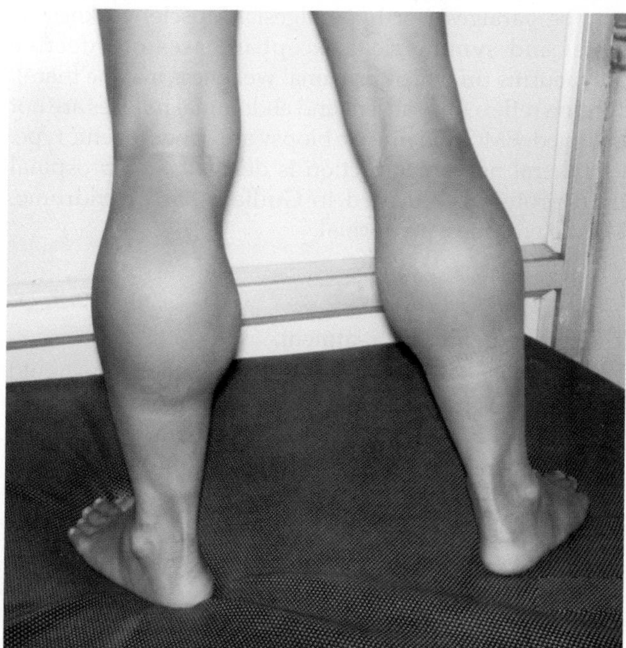

Fig. 18.2: Prominent calf hypertrophy in a child with Duchenne muscular dystrophy

Gower sign: The child has difficulty in standing up from the recumbent position. He turns to side, lifts his trunk up by supporting his weight on his arms and then stands up as if climbing upon his body by supporting it with his hand. This sign indicates weakness of the pelvic girdle muscles (Figs 18.3A to D).

Cardiac involvement in DMD is common; the onset being usually after the age of 10 years. Almost all patients beyond the age of 18 years will have some manifestations of cardiomyopathy. The heart demonstrates fibrosis in the posterobasal portion of the left ventricular wall. Congestive heart failure and cardiac arrhythmias usually occur only in the late stages and especially during times of stress from intercurrent infections. In about 10% of cases, death is due to cardiac dysfunction.

Acute gastric dilatation (intestinal pseudo-obstruction): It consists of sudden episodes of vomiting associated with abdominal pain and distension, and may lead to death if not treated appropriately.

Intelligence: The average intelligence quotient is approximately one standard deviation below the mean. One-third of DMD children have an IQ below 75. Mental retardation is a pleiotropic effect of dystrophin mutation. The site or size of deletion has no correlation with severity of retardation.

Course of the Disease

The natural history of the illness permits distinction between DMD and BMD. The majority of Becker patients initially experience difficulties between the ages of 5–15 years, although an onset in the third and fourth decade, or even later, can occur. By definition, Becker patients ambulate beyond the age of 15 years, allowing clinical distinction from DMD. Becker patients have a reduced life expectancy, but majority of patients survive at least into the fourth or fifth decade.

A great heterogeneity of clinical presentation and course of illness can be recognized, emphasizing a continuous spectrum ranging from very severe to very mild. A well-recognized subgroup of patients with an intermediate course between DMD and BMD patients are referred to as *outliers*, representing an intermediate form of dystrophinopathy. In both DMD and BMD, about 5–10% of female carriers show asymmetric muscle weakness and frequently have enlarged calf muscles.

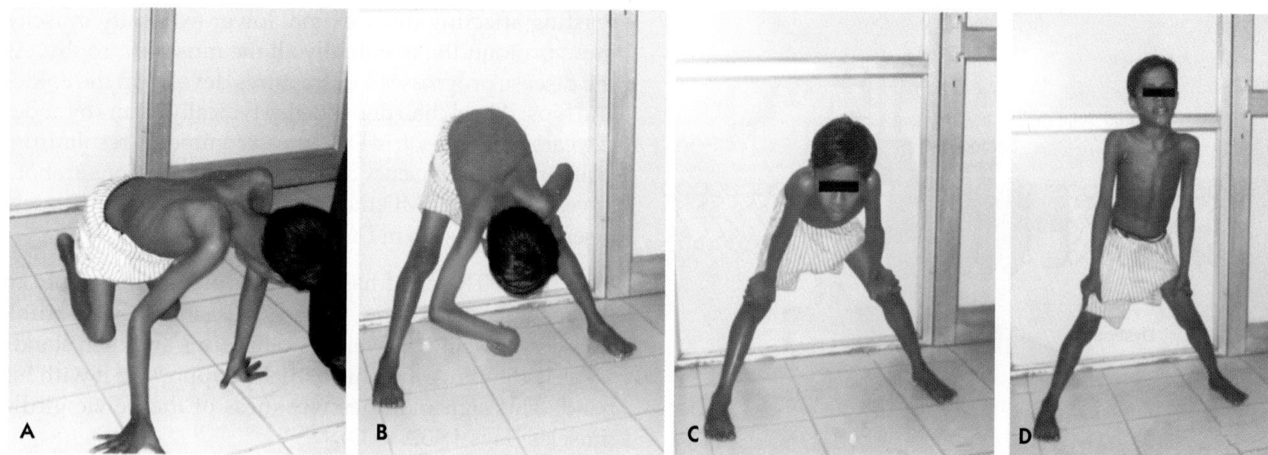

Figs 18.3A to D: Gower sign. Note how the child with hip girdle muscle weakness climbs up on himself to get to upright position

Diagnosis

The serum levels of the enzyme, creatine phosphokinase (CPK), are elevated up to 15,000–20,000 U/L range and even higher, especially in early stages, even before the clinical manifestations become obvious. Raised CPK occurs secondary to its leakage from the muscle fiber due to damage at the sarcolemma membrane. Levels may decrease in very advanced disease. Measurements of CPK can detect two-thirds of the carrier females.

Electromyography (EMG) is rarely necessary to identify a myopathic process when the CPK is high and clinical features are typical. EMG is useful, if the serum CPK is not elevated to the degree expected for dystrophin deficiency. The amplitude and duration of motor unit potential is decreased and the frequency of polyphasic potentials is increased.

Histopathology of muscle fibers shows diffuse changes of degeneration and regeneration. Ultimately, muscle is replaced by fat and degenerative changes. In contrast, muscular atrophies secondary to neurological disease show bundles of degenerated muscle fibers interspersed with those of normal muscles bundles.

Immunohistochemistry for dystrophin I, II and III reveals absent dystrophin in DMD and reduced, patchy dystrophin staining in BMD. In such cases, western blot analysis of the protein helps to identify alteration in amount or altered molecular weight of dystrophin.

Gene deletion can be identified by multiplex PCR. Common exon deletion sites should be investigated. In deletion negative patients, linkage studies using CA repeat markers are used for carrier detection and prenatal diagnosis. A small proportion has duplications and rest have point mutations. Neither the size of the deletion nor its location bears any consistent relation to the clinical severity of the condition.

Differential Diagnosis

Muscular dystrophy should be distinguished from myelopathies and polyneuritis.

Myelopathies: Sensory changes and distribution of weakness are variable. Deep tendon reflexes are brisk and abdominal reflexes are often absent. Sphincter involvement is usually present. Fasciculations may be present, especially if there is slow degeneration of anterior horn cells. EMG shows neurogenic pattern. Peripheral nerve conduction time is normal in early stage. Muscle enzymes are within the normal range.

Polyneuritis: Sensory changes are usually present. There may be paralgesia or hyperalgesia. Muscle weakness is distal and symmetrical except in cases of infective polyneuritis (in which proximal weakness may be there). Tendon reflexes are absent and abdominal reflexes are not involved. EMG and muscle biopsy are of neurogenic type. Peripheral nerve conduction is delayed. Cerebrospinal fluid protein is elevated in Guillain-Barre syndrome. Muscle enzymes are normal.

Management

There is no definitive treatment.

Encourage ambulation: Prolonged immobilization should be avoided as it hastens deterioration in muscle function. Ambulation is maintained by physiotherapy, exercises, daily walking and use of tricycle. Contractures are postponed by exercises and use of standing boards so that the Achilles tendon is placed on constant stretch for 20 minutes twice a day. Prolong the period of active walking by fitting of leg braces at the stage when the child is losing the ability to get around independently. Subcutaneous tenotomy is done for severe contractures. This is followed by early ambulation by application of walking casts and bracing.

Cardiorespiratory care: Respiratory exercises should begin as soon as the diagnosis is made. Infections are managed with appropriate antibiotic therapy and postural drainage. Cardiomyopathy and congestive cardiac failure are managed by conventional approaches.

Supportive care: Low fat diet is given to prevent obesity as these patients would ultimately become non-ambulatory and it is difficult to manage an obese child. Scoliosis is prevented by the use of tight fitting braces. Emotional support is given to the patient and the family. Prognosis should be explained.

Drug therapy: The only drug useful to some extent in DMD is prednisolone. Randomized controlled trials have demonstrated improved muscle strength within 3–6 months of therapy. Prednisolone given in a dose of 0.75 mg/kg/day reduces the rate of progression but the disease continues unabated. The drug is continued as long as the child is ambulatory. Prednisolone may prolong ambulation by a maximum of only 2 years. Prednisolone is not beneficial in patients with BMD. Deflazacort may be used as an alternative. Experimental therapies include exon skipping, gene therapy and stem cell therapy.

Follow-Up

Patients should be followed at 6-monthly intervals for observing progression of weakness in skeletal muscles, drug side-effects, cardiac status, development of deformities, muscle charting, timed functional activities and cardiac monitoring by ECG. Timed functional activities including walking a predefined distance, time to get up from floor and climb a series of steps are useful in initial evaluation, monitoring progression of disease and evaluating response to treatment.

Prevention

Carrier detection: Identification of carrier status of females by CPK estimation and genetic studies in families of DMD patients is of crucial importance in reducing community burden of DMD.

Prenatal diagnosis by chorionic villus sample at 11th week of gestation is conducted if the index patient has a disease related mutation in the family or if linkage is informative. Further tests are necessary only for a male fetus. These include a multiplex PCR to detect a deletion or linkage studies using CA repeat markers.

Suggested reading

1. Metules T. Duchenne muscular dystrophy. Rev Neurol 2002;65: 39–44
2. Wells DJ. Treatments for muscular dystrophy: Increased treatment options for Duchenne and related muscular dystropies. Gene Ther 2008;15(15):1077–8.
3. Manzur AY, Kuntzer T, Pike M, Swan A. Glucocorticoid corticosteroids for Duchenne muscular dystrophy. Cochrane Database Syst Rev 2008 23;(1):CD003725.
4. Angelini C. The role of corticosteroids in muscular dystrophy: a critical appraisal. Muscle Nerve. 2007 Oct;36(4):424–35.

Emery Dreifuss Muscular Dystrophy (EDMD)

EDMD is an X-linked disorder characterized by a specific pattern of contractures at elbow, ankle and neck, cardiomyopathy, conduction disturbances and slowly progressive weakness into adult life. The muscle weakness is predominantly proximal in upper limbs (scapulohumeral) and distal in lower limbs (peroneal). CPK levels are moderately elevated. The basic defect in EDMD are mutations in genes encoding nuclear envelope proteins (emerin, lamins A & C). The most common X-linked EDMD has been localized to the end of the long arm of the X chromosome (Xq28)and encodes for Emerin protein. Rarer autosomal dominant and recessive forms have also been described

Limb-Girdle Muscular Dystrophies (LGMD)

These are inherited as either autosomal dominant (LGMD 1A, 1B and 1C) or autosomal recessive (LGMD 2A-H) disorders. Autosomal recessive LGMDs are now known as sarcoglycanopathies.

Sarcoglycan (SG) complex consists of a distinct group of five dystrophin-associated transmembrane proteins (α, β, γ, δ, and ε-sarcoglycans), expressed on the sarcolemma (Fig. 18.1). This transmembrane complex links the cytoskeleton to the extracellular matrix and is essential for the preservation of the integrity of the muscle cell membrane. Pathogenic mutations in any of the SG genes (except ε-SG) disrupt the entire SG complex and leads to secondary deficiency of the other SG proteins.

Sarcoglycanopathies are caused by mutations in any of the four sarcoglycan genes: α (LGMD 2D), β (LGMD 2E), γ (LGMD 2C) and δ (LGMD 2F).

Most LGMD phenotypes demonstrate weakness in a limb-girdle distribution with sparing of the facial, extraocular and pharyngeal muscles. The degree of weakness is extremely variable. Calf hypertrophy is common in the recessively inherited LGMDs but is not an invariable feature. Mentation is spared. Cardiomyopathy is less predictable. CPK levels are higher in the recessive than dominant LGMD cases. Muscle biopsy is characteristic on immunohistochemistry for sarcoglycans (Fig. 18.4).

Congenital Muscular Dystrophies

Children present with hypotonia and proximal muscular weakness at birth or within the first few months of life. Most affected children might eventually be able to stand with some support, but few learn to walk. Muscle weakness is usually nonprogressive, but joint contractures may develop. CNS involvement may be present. Several different forms are recognized, with and without mental retardation. CPK levels are moderately elevated. Muscle

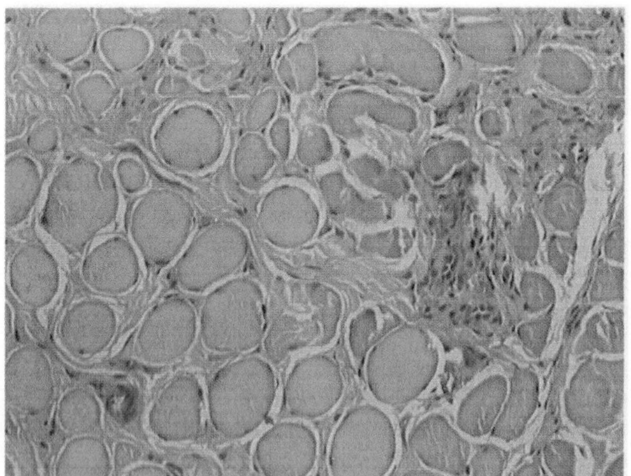

Fig. 18.4: Gamma sarcoglycanopathy. Muscle biopsy shows variation in fiber size, myophagocytosis and endomysial and perimysial fibrosis (H&E). (*Courtesy: MC Sharma and C Sarkar*)

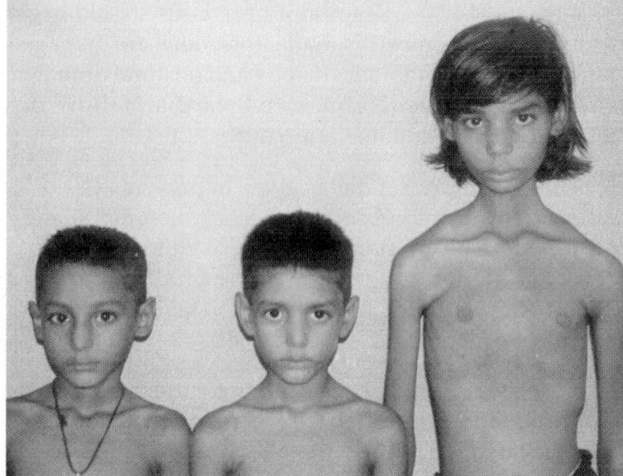

Fig. 18.5: A family with 3 siblings affected with facioscapulohumeral dystrophy with characteristic muscle involvement

biopsy shows signs of dystrophy, a marked increase in endomysial and perimysial connective tissue, and fiber size variability. Deficiency of merosin can be shown by western blot analysis or muscle immunohistochemistry and also with chorionic villus material for prenatal diagnosis. MRI of the brain shows white matter changes in some.

Fukuyama Congenital Muscular Dystrophy (FCMD)

This is muscle disease is associated with severe CNS defects, cardiomyopathy and ocular abnormalities. The condition is found predominantly in Japan. Seizures are common. Most FCMD patients never learn to walk. Patients usually become bed-ridden before 10 years of age and most die by 20 years of age. Severe mental retardation is observed in all cases.

18

Facioscapulohumeral Dystrophy

This relatively benign muscular dystrophy manifests around puberty. Facial, shoulder girdle and proximal arm muscles are involved. Patients cannot close the eyes forcefully, whistle or hold air in the oral cavity. Smiling or grimacing produces faint muscle movements (Fig. 18.5). Winging and elevation of scapulae occur due to weakness of the scapular muscles. Foot drop results from weak peroneal and anterior tibial muscle. Progression of weakness is relatively slow. Pelvic-girdle involvement is late and less marked. Hypertrophy does not occur. Neurological involvement occurs in form of sensorineural hearing loss. Cardiac muscles and mental functions are notably spared. CPK levels may be slightly elevated. Muscle biopsy and EMG frequently show changes suggestive of a neurogenic origin, along with myopathic changes.

Myotonic Dystrophy

It is a multisystem disorder, involving heart, smooth muscle, central nervous system, eye, and endocrine glands as well as skeletal muscle. The common presenting features in decreasing order of frequency include muscle weakness, myotonia (delayed muscular relaxation interpreted as stiffness), positive family history, mental retardation, cataract and neonatal problems. The neonate has a tented upper lip, difficulty in sucking and swallowing, generalized hypotonia, respiratory distress, delayed motor development, mental retardation and immunodeficiency.

Myotonia is nearly always absent in affected infants, but usually develops by the age of 10 years. Other systemic manifestations include ptosis, ophthalmoplegia, cardiac conduction disturbances, cardiomyopathy, dysphagia, aspiration, constipation, dysarthria, gall stones and abnormal renal handling of calcium.

Muscle enzymes do not reveal any abnormalities in adult form of myotonic dystrophy. In children, EMG is usually normal. EMG demonstrates myotonia along with diminished action potential amplitude and polyphasic potentials.

No cure is available. Antimyotonia medications (phenytoin, mexeletine, procainamide, quinine) have been used to reduce myotonia with marginal benefit.

To summarize, salient differentiating features of major types of childhood muscular dystrophies are depicted in Table 18.2.

Suggested reading

1. Linksnorwood F, De Visser M, Eymard B, Lochmüller H, Bushby K; EFNS Guideline Task Force.EFNS guideline on diagnosis and management of limb Girdle Muscular Dystrophies. Eur J Neurol. 2007;14:1305–12.
2. Linkstrip J, Drost G, Van Engelen BG, Faber CG. Drug Treatment for Myotonia. Cochrane Database Syst Rev. 2006;25:CD004762.

Table 18.2: Characteristic features of muscular dystrophies

Type	*Genetics; Characteristic features*	*Age at onset*	*Involvement*	*Progression*
Duchenne	Xp-linked recessive; Pseudohypertrophy of calf muscles, subnormal intelligence	2–5 years	Pelvic girdle; shoulder girdle and heart	Fast
Becker	Xp-linked recessive; Pseudohypertrophy; pes cavus	8–10 years	Pelvic girdle	Slow
Emery Dreifuss	Xq 28-linked recessive/ autosomal dominant; Cardiac arrhythmias	5–15 years	Biceps, triceps and peroneal muscles	Slow
Limb girdle	Autosomal recessive/ dominant	10–30 years	Pelvic and shoulder girdles	Slow
Distal	Autosomal recessive/ dominant	12–30 years	Gastrocnemius; mainly distal muscles	Slow
Myotonic dystrophy	Autosomal dominant (19q13.3)	Newborn to adult	Face, girdles, sterno-cleidomastoids	Slow, multisystem involvement

3. Linksmuchir A, Worman HJ. Emery-Dreifuss Muscular Dystrophy. Curr Neurol Neurosci Rep. 2007;7:78–83.
4. Linkspandya S, King WM, Tawil R. Facioscapulohumeral Dystrophy. Phys Ther. 2008;88:105–13.
5. Danièle N, Richard I, Bartoli M. Ins and outs of therapy in Limb Girdle Muscular Dystrophies. Int J Biochem Cell Biol. 2007;39:1608–24.
6. Straub V, Bushby K. The Childhood Limb-Girdle Muscular Dystrophies. Semin Pediatr Neurol. 2006;13:104–14.
7. Linkscardamone M, Darras BT, Ryan MM. Inherited myopathies and muscular dystrophies. Semin Neurol 2008;28: 50–9.
8. Thirion C, Lochmüller H. Current status of gene therapy for Muscle Diseases. Drug News Perspect. 2007;20:357–63.
9. Muntoni F, Wells D. Genetic treatments in muscular dystrophies. Curr Opin Neurol. 2007;20:590–4.

OTHER MYOPATHIES

Myopathies are congenital or secondary to inflammatory, metabolic and endocrine abnormalities.

Congenital Myopathies

The 'structural' congenital myopathies include central core disease, minicore disease, multicore disease, nemaline myopathy, myotubular myopathy, myotubular myopathy with type 1 fiber hypotrophy, severe congenital X-linked myotubular myopathy, congenital fiber type disproportion, myopathies with abnormality of other subcellular organelles and nonspecific congenital myopathies. There is also frequently a genetic element and the inheritance may be autosomal dominant or autosomal recessive, and occasionally X-linked.

Clinical Features

Not all cases are strictly 'congenital' with symptoms at birth, and many may indeed present much later. As a rule, *these myopathies tend to be relatively non-progressive.* It is clinically difficult to readily distinguish between the various congenital myopathies, since they all tend to present in a somewhat similar, non-specific way. This may take the form of a floppy infant syndrome at birth or in early infancy, or may present later with features of muscle weakness. In some children this weakness will be predominantly proximal and of girdle distribution, in others it may be more generalized and may also affect facial muscles. Ocular muscles are frequently affected in myotubular myopathy. Nemaline myopathy has a higher incidence of associated dysmorphic features and respiratory deficit.

Diagnosis

Investigations such as CPK and EMG are not of much help in diagnosis as CPK levels are frequently normal and the EMG may be normal or may show mild, non-specific changes. Muscle biopsy, supplemented by immunocytochemistry, histochemical analysis and electron microscopy, is the only certain way of making an accurate diagnosis.

Endocrine Myopathies

Thyroid Myopathies

Thyrotoxicosis causes proximal muscle weakness and wasting accompanied by myopathic electromyogram (EMG) changes. Thyroxine binds to myofibrils and in excess impairs contractile function. Hyperthyroidism may also induce myasthenia gravis and hypokalemic periodic paralysis.

Hypothyroidism: Produces hypotonia and a proximal muscle weakness. The serum CPK level is elevated and returns to normal after replacement therapy. Muscle biopsy reveals myofiber necrosis and sometimes central cores.

Hyperparathyroidism

Most patients with primary hyperparathyroidism develop weakness, fatigability, and muscle wasting that is reversible after removal of the parathyroid adenoma.

Steroid-induced Myopathy

Both natural Cushing disease and the iatrogenic Cushing syndrome due to exogenous corticosteroid administration may cause progressive proximal weakness, increased serum CPK levels and a myopathic EMG. Myosin filaments may be selectively lost. Fluorinated steroids (e.g. dexamethasone) are the most likely to produce steroid myopathy.

Hyperaldosteronism (Conn Syndrome)

It is accompanied by episodic and reversible weakness similar to that of periodic paralysis. The proximal myopathy may become irreversible in chronic cases. Elevated CPK levels and even myoglobinuria sometimes occur during acute attacks.

Metabolic Myopathies

Potassium-related Periodic Paralysis

Episodic muscular weakness is associated with transient alterations in serum potassium levels, usually hypokalemia but occasionally hyperkalemia. The disorder is inherited as an autosomal dominant trait. It is precipitated in some patients by hyperaldosteronism or hyperthyroidism, by administration of amphotericin B, or by ingestion of licorice. The defective genes are at the 17q13.1–13.3 locus in hyperkalemic periodic paralysis and at the 1q31–32 locus in hypokalemic periodic paralysis.

The paralysis is often an episodic event; patients are unable to move after awakening and gradually recover muscle strength during the next few minutes or hours. Muscles that remain active in sleep, such as the diaphragm and cardiac muscle, are not affected. Patients are normal between attacks, but in adult life the attacks become more frequent, and the disorder causes progressive myopathy with permanent weakness even between attacks.

Alterations in serum potassium level occur only during acute episodes and are accompanied by T-wave changes in the electrocardiogram (ECG). The CPK level may be mildly elevated at those times. Muscle biopsy taken during the episode may reveal a vacuolar myopathy.

18

Malignant Hyperthermia

This syndrome is usually inherited as an autosomal dominant trait. It occurs in patients with central core disease but is not limited to that particular myopathy. Acute episodes are precipitated by exposure to general anesthetics and occasionally to local anesthetic drugs. Patients suddenly develop extreme fever, rigidity of muscles, and metabolic and respiratory acidosis; the serum CPK level rises to as high as 35,000 IU/L. Myoglobinuria may result in tubular necrosis and acute renal failure. The muscle biopsy during an episode of malignant hyperthermia or shortly afterward shows widely scattered necrosis of muscle fibers (rhabdomyolysis). Between attacks, the muscle biopsy findings are normal. The attacks may be prevented by administering dantrolene sodium before an anesthetic is given.

Mitochondrial Disorders

Mitochondrial disorders are multisystem diseases with very heterogeneous clinical manifestations. They have been linked to seizures, strokes, ataxia, optic atrophy, neuropathy, myopathy, cardiomyopathy, cardiac conduction disturbances, sensorineural hearing loss, diabetes mellitus and other clinical features.

Classic syndromes linked to mitochondrial DNA mutations include Leber's hereditary optic neuropathy; mitochondrial encephalomyopathy, lactic acidosis and stroke like episodes (MELAS); myoclonic epilepsy with ragged-red fibers (MERRF), chronic progressive external ophthalmoplegia; neuropathy, ataxia and retinitis pigmentosa; Kearns-Sayre syndrome, etc.

Skeletal muscle biopsy reveals ragged-red fibers. Electron microscopy reveals abnormal proliferation of mitochondria with intramitochondrial paracrystalline inclusions. Elevation of blood and CSF lactate, myopathic potentials on electromyography, axonal and demyelinating peripheral neuropathy on nerve conduction studies, sensorineural hearing loss and basal ganglia calcification or focal signal abnormalities on MRI may be present.

Use of agents that modify mitochondrial function (coenzyme Q10 and idebenone) may have a role.

Inflammatory Myopathies

These myopathies are characterized by inflammation in skeletal muscle resulting in muscle fiber damage and subsequent clinical muscle weakness. There are two major categories: idiopathic and infectious (Table 18.3). The classic idiopathic inflammatory myopathies are usually considered autoimmune diseases with a genetic predisposition. Dermatomyositis is the most common form in childhood and discussed in detail elsewhere (Chapter 20). Polymyositis is relatively uncommon in children and is

Table 18.3: Inflammatory myopathies
Idiopathic
Juvenile dermatomyositis
Polymyositis
Inclusion body myositis
Myositis as overlap syndrome
Others: (i) eosinophilic myositis, (ii) focal nodular myositis, (iii) sarcoid myopathy
Infectious
Viral myositis: (i) influenza; (ii) human immunodeficiency virus; (iii) others
Parasitic myositis: (i) trichinosis; (ii) toxoplasmosis; (iii) cysticercosis
Bacterial myositis
Fungal myositis

usually seen as an overlap syndrome with other connective tissue disorders. Inclusion body myositis is almost exclusively a disease of adults.

Suggested reading

1. D'Amico A, Bertini E. Congenital myopathies. Curr Neurol Neurosci Rep. 2008; 8:73–9.
2. Jackson Ce. A clinical approach to muscle diseases. Semin Neurol. 2008; 28:228–40.

MYASTHENIA GRAVIS

Myasthenia gravis in children is divided into neonatal transient and juvenile types:

Neonatal transient myasthenia gravis occurs in infants of myasthenic mothers. Placental transfer of AChR-antibody or immunocytes results in transient impairment of neuromuscular transmission in the neonate. Findings such as a weak suck or cry, ptosis, dysphagia, generalized weakness, decreased spontaneous movement, or respiratory distress are usually present in the first few hours of life but may not be evident until the third day. Hypotonia may be the primary manifestation. The symptoms usually resolve in the first 4 weeks but may persist for months.

Juvenile myasthenia gravis represents the childhood onset of autoimmune myasthenia seen in adults. Isolated ocular involvement is a common presentation followed by generalization or may be generalized at onset. Onset is usually after 10 years of age. Ptosis is the most common clinical finding, frequently accompanied by ophthalmoparesis. Facial and oropharyngeal weakness results in dysarthria, dysphagia and chewing difficulty. Limb weakness is usually proximal. Weakness improves after rest/sleep and is worsened by exertion.

Myasthenia is frequently associated with other diseases of an immune etiology such as rheumatoid arthritis, thyroiditis, SLE and diabetes mellitus.

Diagnosis

Edrophonium (Tensilon) Test

Edrophonium (0.15–0.2 mg/kg; maximum 10 mg) is administered intravenously. The best indication of a positive test is a significant increase in the palpebral fissure aperture or the opening of a completely ptotic eye. False positive results may be obtained in drug-induced myasthenia, botulism, brainstem gliomas and Guillain-Barre syndrome. Intramuscular neostigmine is an alternative.

Repetitive Stimulation

EMG reveals a decremental response of the compound muscle action potential in response to repetitive stimulation of a motor nerve. *Single fiber electromyography* is a more sensitive measure of neuromuscular transmission than repetitive stimulation.

Antibody Testing

Demonstration of AChR-antibody in the serum is the most specific test for supporting the diagnosis. However, absence of AChR-antibody does not rule out presence of the disease.

Treatment

Neonates with transient myasthenia are at risk of respiratory and bulbar dysfunction. If there is no significant respiratory or swallowing impairment, medications are not necessary. In more severe cases, oral pyridostigmine is given at a recommended daily dose of 7 mg/kg in divided doses, 30 minutes before feeding. For neonates unable to swallow, intramuscular (IM) pyridostigmine should be given; 1 mg of IM pyridostigmine is equivalent to 30 mg oral dose. Intramuscular neostigmine has more muscarinic side effects. Treatment for 4 to 6 weeks is all that is required.

Patients with juvenile myasthenia who require maintenance therapy are treated with anticholinesterase agents with or without immunosuppressive medications. Therapy with pyridostigmine is recommended initially. Corticosteroids and other immunosuppressive agents, e.g. azathioprine, cyclosporine and cyclophosphamide have been useful. Prednisolone is considered an effective agent; therapy is initiated at a dose of 1.5–2 mg/kg daily. Once clinical improvement occurs, the medication is reduced to an alternate-day dose of 1.5 mg/kg, for 6–8 months.

Treatment with plasmapheresis and IV gamma globulin is reserved for patients with refractory disease or for those in myasthenic crisis. Thymectomy may be useful in treating older children. Certain drugs can exacerbate myasthenic symptoms and should be avoided. The notable ones are antibiotics (aminoglycosides, erythromycin, penicillin, sulfonamides, fluoroquinolones), cardiovascular drugs (beta-blockers, procainamide, quinidine), anesthetic agents (neuromuscular blocking agents, lidocaine, procaine), phenytoin, iodinated contrast media, corticosteroids, chloroquine and penicillamine.

Suggested reading

1. Mahadeva B, Phillips LH 2nd, Juel VC. Autoimmune disorders of neuromuscular transmission. Semin Neurol. 2008; 28:212–27.
2. Gajdos P, Chevret S, Toyka K. Intravenous immunoglobulin for myasthenia gravis. Cochrane Database Syst Rev. 2008; 1: CD002277.
3. Juel VC, Massey JM. Myasthenia gravis. Orphanet J Rare Dis. 2007; 2:44.
4. Parr JR, Jayawant S. Childhood myasthenia: clinical subtypes and practical management. Dev Med Child Neurol. 2007; 49:629–35.

FLOPPY INFANT

Floppy infant is an infant with marked hypotonia of the muscles and variable associated weakness. This may be associated with frequent respiratory infections, feeding difficulties, facial weakness, ptosis, ophthalmoplegia and dislocated hips. Contractures may develop in later stages. Common causes of a floppy infant are given in Table 18.4.

Diagnosis

A clinical diagnosis of hypotonia is usually suggested by relative immobility, bizarre and unusual postures of the infant, diminished resistance to passive movements or an excessive range of joint mobility. After the neonatal period, they usually present with delay in motor milestones.

Posture

The floppy infant assumes a frog-like posture. On ventral suspension, the baby cannot maintain limb posture against gravity and assumes the position of a rag doll.

Movements

Spontaneous movements are reduced. There is diminished resistance to passive movement of the limbs and the range of movement of the peripheral joints is increased.

Scarf Sign

Put the child in a supine position and hold one of the infant's hands. Try to put it around the neck as far as possible around the opposite shoulder. Observe how far the elbow goes across the body. In a floppy infant, the elbow easily crosses the midline.

Pull to Sit

When pulled up from the supine to the sitting position, the head of the baby lags.

Table 18.4: Causes of floppy infant syndrome

Central nervous system

Perinatal asphyxia, neonatal encephalopathy, kernicterus, cerebral palsy (atonic type), intracranial hemorrhage, chromosomal anomalies including Down syndrome, inborn errors of metabolism (aminoaciduria, mucopolysaccharidosis, cerebral lipidosis)

Spinal cord

Anterior horn cell disease: Werdnig Hoffman (spinal muscular atrophy), poliomyelitis

Peripheral nerves

Familial dysautonomia, hereditary motor sensory neuropathy

Myoneural junction

Neonatal myasthenia gravis, infantile botulism, following antibiotic therapy

Muscles

Muscular dystrophies, congenital myotonic dystrophies, congenital myopathies (central core disease, nemaline myopathy), polymyositis, glycogen storage disease, arthrogryphosis multiplex congenita

Miscellaneous

Protein energy malnutrition, hypothyroidism, rickets, Prader-Willi syndrome, Ehler-Danlos syndrome, cutis laxa

18

Ascertaining Etiology

The diagnosis of the precise etiological cause of hypotonia is difficult without detailed investigations. Apart from hypotonia, which is ubiquitously present in these children, several other features should be looked for, that may help in determining the cause. These features include the extent (in terms of involvement of various muscle groups), and distribution (proximal *vs.* distal) of neurological weakness, as well as presence or absence of deep tendon reflexes. Additional confirmatory evidence can be provided by an electromyogram (EMG) and muscle biopsy.

The first decision to make is whether one is dealing with a neuromuscular problem or whether the hypotonia is symptomatic of a disorder in the central nervous system or some other system. If the hypotonia is of neuromuscular origin the main causes are likely to be spinal muscular atrophy (Werdnig Hoffman disease), congenital myotonic dystrophy, congenital muscular dystrophy, one of the congenital myopathies or other less frequent conditions. The degree and distribution of weakness may help to distinguish between these causes.

Routine nerve conduction and electromyography (EMG) are helpful in trying to establish a neuromuscular cause, either a denervation process or a myopathy. In all cases with weakness this should be followed by a muscle biopsy, which is the only accurate way of establishing a definitive diagnosis, since the serum enzymes as well as EMG may be completely normal in some floppy infants with congenital myopathies, even in the presence of marked weakness.

Table 18.5 shows characteristic features of a floppy infant according to the site of involvement.

Spinal Muscular Atrophy

Childhood spinal muscular atrophy (SMA) is a common autosomal recessive disorder characterized by muscle weakness due to degeneration of motor neurons in the spinal cord and brainstem nuclei. It can be inherited as autosomal dominant, X recessive or sporadic. Its incidence is 1 in 6,700 to 1 in 25,000 live births and prevalence is 0.12 to 25 per 10,000. Progression of the disease is due to loss of anterior horn cells, thought to be caused by unregulated apoptosis. Positional cloning strategies have revealed several candidate genes including the 'survival motor neuron' and 'neuronal apoptosis inhibitory protein' genes on chromosome 5.

Clinical Features

Characteristic features include generalized symmetrical weakness more in proximal muscle groups, accompanied by hypotonia and fasciculations of tongue. The trunk is commonly involved. Weakness in the legs is characteristically greater than in the arms. The child is alert. Feeding behavior and cry are poor. Deep tendon reflexes are absent. History of affected siblings in the family may be available. CPK is normal or mildly elevated.

Table 18.5: **Differentiating features of a floppy infant according to site of involvement**

Site of involvement	Extent of weakness: Face	Arms	Legs	Proximal vs. distal weakness	Deep tendon reflexes	EMG	Muscle biopsy
Central	–	+	+	> or =	Normal or increased	Normal	Normal
Anterior horn cell	±	++++	++++	> or =	Absent	Denervation potentials, Fasciculations	Neurogenic atrophy
Peripheral nerve	–	++	+++	<	Decreased/ absent	Abnormal NCS, ± Denervation potentials	Denervation pattern
Neuromuscular junction	+++	++	++	=	Normal	Decremental response on repetitive stimulation	Normal
Muscle	Variable	++	+++	>	Decreased	Short duration, polyphasic potentials	Characteristic

EMG electromyography; NCS nerve conduction studies

Fibrillations, positive sharp waves and fasciculations have been reported on EMG. Muscle biopsy shows neurogenic type of atrophy or presence of atrophied muscle spindles in groups (Fig. 18.6). The gene encoding survival motor neuron is deleted in approximately 95% of SMA cases. Prenatal diagnosis is possible.

Types

SMA type I is commonly known as Werdnig-Hoffmann disease. A classical patient presents within first 6 months and is never able to sit. More than 90% die by 10 years of age; age of onset determines the age of death.

Type II manifests in the first year of life. Unaided sitting is possible but walking is not achieved. More than 90% survive beyond 10 years.

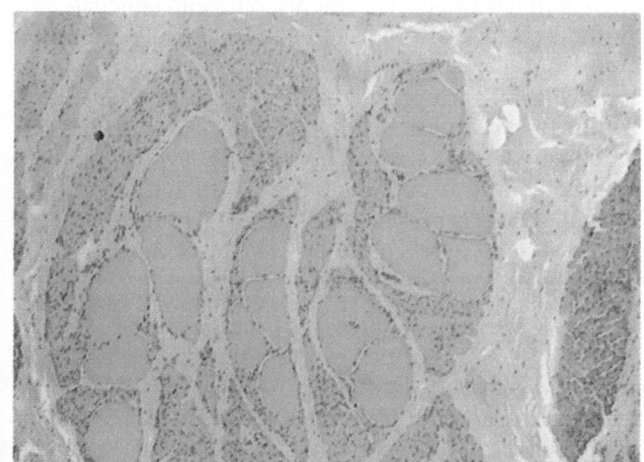

Fig. 18.6: Spinal muscular atrophy showing group atrophy (H&E). (*Courtesy: MC Sharma and C Sarkar*)

Type III can achieve walking without aids and lifespan is not markedly reduced.

Type IV presents after 30 years of age. The severity is variable and lifespan is unaffected.

Treatment

There is no effective therapy. Management consists of preventing or treating complications. Complications of severe weakness include restrictive lung disease, poor nutrition, orthopedic deformities, immobility and psychosocial problems. Possible therapeutic strategies include the use of neurotropic agents and embryonic grafts. Potential treatment modalities include gabapentin and valproate.

Hypotonic Cerebral Palsy

Many children are hypotonic due to a central cause (hypotonic cerebral palsy) and may be mentally retarded. In spite of hypotonia, reflexes are present or brisk in patients with cerebral palsy. Floppy infant due to cerebral causes is associated with lethargy, poor feeding, lack of alertness, poor Moro's reflex and seizures during the neonatal period. The diagnosis of hypothyroidism, Down syndrome, congenital myopathies, arthrogryposis and muscle dystrophies should be excluded. The diagnosis of Pompe disease is suspected if the child has hepatomegaly, cardiomegaly and generalized hypotonia.

Prader-Willi Syndrome

The syndrome presents with profound hypotonia at birth and marked feeding difficulty but there are no associated respiratory difficulties. The cry is often weak and high-pitched. Facies are characteristic with a high forehead, dolicocephaly, small almond-shaped eyes and an open triangular-shaped mouth. Such babies are mentally retarded and obese. Diabetes mellitus occurs later in life. Testes may be undescended. It has been shown to be associated with deletion in the short arm of chromosome 15, especially the paternal chromosome.

Ehlers-Danlos Syndrome

The basic manifestations are joint hypermobility, skin hyperextensibility, dystrophic scarring of the skin, easy bruising and connective tissue fragility. Wound healing is delayed and there are freely movable subcutaneous nodules. Molecular genetics has helped to characterize 11 different types of Ehlers-Danlos syndrome, based predominantly on the associated features.

Suggested reading

1. Erazo-Torricelli R. Neonatal hypotonia. Rev Neurol 2000; 31: 252–62.
2. Richer LP, Shevell MI, Miller SP. Diagnostic profile of neonatal hypotonia: An 11-year study. Pediatr Neurol 2001; 25: 32–7.
3. Bodensteiner JB. The evaluation of the hypotonic infant. Semin Pediatr Neurol. 2008; 15:10–20.

Peripheral Neuropathies

The term peripheral neuropathy indicates disease of peripheral nerves. Two-thirds of such cases are chronic. Of the latter group, roughly 70% are hereditary, 20% indeterminate and 10% acquired.

Hereditary Neuropathies

These clinically and genetically heterogeneous disorders produce progressive deterioration of the peripheral nerves with secondary muscle wasting and weakness in a distal distribution. Depending on the predominant clinical involvement, hereditary neuropathies are divided in broad categories of (i) **hereditary motor;** (ii) **hereditary sensory and autonomic**; and (iii) **hereditary motor and sensory neuropathies.**

18

Hereditary motor and sensory neuropathies (HMSN): Dyck and Lambert's classification divided the HMSN into HMSN I-VII and X. Hereditary motor sensory neuropathy types I and II are often referred to as **Charcot-Marie-Tooth disease**, which is characterized by weakness of the extremities and foot deformities including pes cavus and permanently flexed "hammer" toes. Variable loss of sensations is present. This condition is also referred to as peroneal muscular atrophy, because of the characteristic muscle involvement early in the illness. Inheritance is autosomal dominant, though autosomal recessive and X-linked forms are also known.

HMSN Type I: The peripheral nerves are often easily palpated because they are hypertrophied as a result of excessive Schwann cell and fibroblast activity. This creates redundant wrappings of Schwann cell investments around nerve fibers accompanied by excessive collagen deposition, known as onion bulbs. Sural nerve biopsies disclose a loss of myelinated fibers, especially the large myelinated fibers.

The disease is typically recognized during the first decade of life or in early adolescence, but it may be evident even at birth. Early onset, although uncommon, usually results in greater disability later in life than that seen in individuals with later onset, who are often able to ambulate and work until old age.

HMSN Type I presents with distal lower extremity muscle wasting. Progressive weakness of the anterior tibialis muscle is associated with the development of the high arch of the foot or *pes cavus*. The hammer toe deformities occur as the long toe extensors attempt to make up for the foot dorsiflexor (anterior tibialis) atrophy and weakness. Gradual loss of sensation is noted, especially loss of proprioception, which causes unsteady gait in darkness and a positive Romberg sign. Vibration and big toe joint position sense are both diminished. Tendon reflexes are usually lost early at the ankle and later at the knee. Muscle wasting and weakness slowly spread proximally. Motor and sensory conduction velocity is less than 60% of normal values in infants, and in patients older than 3 years it is less than 38 m/sec in all peripheral nerves.

Treatment is supportive. Early in the course of the disease, strengthening exercises for the feet and legs with active stretching of the feet may be beneficial. Using ankle-foot orthoses to stabilize the feet and correct the foot drop may help reduce the likelihood of falls.

HMSN Type II: Clinical manifestations tend to develop later than in Type I. Muscle atrophy and weakness are milder and more prominent than sensory deficits compared to Type I disorder. Pathology is marked by axonal degeneration. Nerve hypertrophy and palpable nerve enlargement are not present. Onion bulb formation typical of Type I disease is rarely seen.

HMSN Type III (Dejerine-Sottas disease): Schwann cells are incapable of forming normal myelin. Histologically, they are characterized by the presence of thin myelin sheaths, often with few or poorly compacted myelin lamellae, and by the presence of onion bulbs. Hypomyelination is a prominent element. In the majority of cases, hypotonia and delay in developmental milestones or both are noted within the first year of life. Walking is often delayed beyond the second year, but most HMSN Type III toddlers eventually do walk, although coordination is never fully normal. Ataxia is present in all patients, probably due to a proprioceptive deficit. Distal weakness, more marked in the lower limbs, is present.

Hereditary sensory and autonomic neuropathies (HSAN): At least five clinical entities exist under HSAN including hereditary sensory radicular neuropathy, congenital sensory neuropathy, familial dysautonomia, congenital insensitivity to pain and anhidrosis. All of them are characterized by a progressive loss of function that predominantly affects the peripheral sensory nerves.

These conditions are less common than hereditary motor and sensory neuropathies. The clinical presentation depends on the population of affected neurons or axons. When degeneration of the large diameter afferent fibers occurs, position sense is primarily involved. When the small afferent and autonomic fibers are affected, an increased threshold to nociception and thermal discrimination occurs, accompanied by autonomic and trophic changes.

Metabolic Neuropathies

Diabetes mellitus: Slowed sensory nerve conduction velocities and impaired autonomic function have been reported in 25% of diabetic children at the time of diagnosis. Despite multiple daily doses of insulin and good blood sugar levels, peripheral neuropathy is inevitable in 10% children and adolescents with insulin-dependent diabetes mellitus. Features include mild distal weakness, loss of touch and pain sensation, and decreased ankle tendon reflexes. Changes are bilaterally symmetric and more in the lower extremities.

Uremic neuropathy: It is rarely diagnosed in children. When recognized, it is characterized by burning sensations in the feet and a symmetric motor sensory neuropathy with progressive muscle weakness. Motor and sensory nerve conduction velocities are decreased early in the course of the disease, often before clinical symptoms appear. Proximal nerves are affected earlier.

Acute intermittent porphyria: This rare inborn error of metabolism, inherited on an autosomal-dominant basis, is caused by defects in the gene encoding hydroxymethylbilane synthase on the long arm of chromosome 11. Acute, severe, colicky abdominal pain is a typical manifestation of an acute episode accompanied by central nervous system and peripheral nervous system impairment. Peripherally, motor weakness is most striking, but sensory impairment may also occur. A flaccid paralysis resembling Guillain-Barre syndrome has been observed. The proximal muscles may be more involved than distal muscles. Reflexes are often diminished or absent.

Thiamine deficiency: Vitamin B1 deficiency in children causes peripheral neuropathy, encephalopathy and high-output cardiac failure.

Abetalipoproteinemia: Abetalipoproteinemia is characterized by progressive ataxic neuropathy, retinitis pigmentosa, steatorrhea, hypolipidemia, deficiency of fat-soluble vitamins and acanthocytosis.

Toxic Neuropathies

Diphtheria: The onset may occur between 1 to 16 weeks following the infection. Blurred vision and swallowing difficulties mark the onset of diphtheric neuropathy. A generalized motor sensory demyelinating polyneuropathy with distal, symmetric involvement is recognized. Lower cranial nerves are affected. Proximal and distal muscle weakness and muscle tenderness are present.

Serum sickness: It is a systemic illness resulting from hypersensitivity to an injected foreign protein, such as tetanus or diphtheria antisera, producing encephalomyelitis, neuropathy or brachial plexus neuropathies.

Botulism: Three forms of botulism exist, the most common being the infantile form that occurs between 1 and 38 weeks of age. A heat-labile neurotoxin is elaborated by *C. botulinum* under anaerobic conditions. The toxin produces a presynaptic blockade to prevent the release of acetylcholine from cholinergic nerve endings. The toxin seems to block the exocytosis of acetylcholine-containing vesicles at presynaptic release sites.

Infantile botulism: A history of constipation in a 1–6 month old infant followed by a subacute progression over 4 to 5 days of bulbar and extremity weakness with feeding difficulties, ptosis, hypotonia and respiratory embarrassment should suggest this condition.

Classic botulism: It develops 12 to 36 hours after ingestion of the toxin-containing food. Early symptoms are blurred vision, diplopia, dizziness, dysarthria and dysphagia followed by a descending paralysis and dyspnea.

Wound botulism: Wound contamination with *C. botulinum* leads to subsequent production of botulinum toxin after bacterial incubation, producing clinical botulism 4 to 14 days after the wound has been infected.

Drug-induced Neuropathy

Chloramphenicol can cause mild, primarily sensory peripheral neuropathy after long-term use at relatively high doses. Nitrofurantoin can cause a severe motor and sensory peripheral neuropathy with an acute to subacute time course. Isoniazid causes an axonal neuropathy responsive to pyridoxine therapy in 1% to 2% of patients. The primarily sensory neuropathy begins with paresthesia. Ethambutol occasionally causes a sensory neuropathy associated with optic neuritis. Metronidazole may also produce neuropathy. Pyridoxine taken in large dose can cause a sensory neuropathy with paresthesia, diffuse sensory loss, sensory ataxia and autonomic dysfunction.

Peripheral neuropathy may develop after the use of chemotherapeutic agents to treat neoplasms. Sensorimotor peripheral neuropathy may develop after high-dose cytosine arabinoside therapy. Vincristine is perhaps the best known chemotherapeutic agent, causing peripheral neuropathy and, less commonly, autonomic and cranial nerve neuropathy. Tingling sensations, absent reflexes particularly at the ankles, distal weakness and impaired vibration and superficial sensation develop secondary to vincristine use. Cisplatin may cause profound axonal loss in peripheral nerves, producing a sensory neuropathy.

Heavy metal neuropathy: Lead toxicity may cause a motor neuropathy. Lower extremities are particularly affected. Other clinical features include abdominal pain, constipation, anemia and encephalopathy. Rarely, arsenic poisoning produces an axonal, primarily sensory neuropathy. Exposure may be by overdose, producing a subacute neuropathy, or may be more chronic, causing a slowly progressing neuropathy. Organic mercury poisoning in children produces acrodynia or pink disease consisting of generalized erythema, especially of the hands, feet and face with swelling of the hands and feet. Chronic exposure results in sensory and motor neuropathy, encephalopathy, and autonomic dysfunction. Accidental ingestion of rat poison or insecticides or thallium products causes an acute or subacute syndrome of gastrointestinal disturbance and neuropathy.

Suggested reading

1. Klein CJ.The inherited neuropathies. Neurol Clin 2007; 25:173–207.
2. Reilly MM. Sorting out the inherited neuropathies. Pract Neurol. 2007;7:93–105.
3. Parman Y. Hereditary neuropathies. Curr Opin Neurol 2007; 20:542–7.
4. Ouvrier R, Geevasingha N, Ryan MM. Autosomal-recessive and X-linked forms of hereditary motor and sensory neuropathy in childhood. Muscle Nerve 2007;36:131–43.
5. Jani-Acsadi A, Krajewski K, Shy ME. Charcot-Marie-Tooth neuropathies: diagnosis and management. Semin Neurol 2008;28:185–94.
6. Young P, De Jonghe P, Stögbauer F, Butterfass-Bahloul T. Treatment for Charcot-Marie-Tooth disease. Cochrane Database Syst Rev 2008;1:CD006052.

LIMPING

A limp in the child is generally of serious concern to the parents and the physician. The differential diagnosis for a child with lower extremity limb pain or limp is quite diverse; only a few conditions require urgent treatment. Most cases of limp are transient and may improve with time without any specific treatment.

Limp may be the result of disorders in any part of the weight-bearing structures including spine, hips, knees, ankle and feet. Diseases causing tenderness, weakness or asymmetry of the weight-bearing apparatus, result in a limping gait.

History

The diagnosis is based on the *history* including age of the child, time of onset, duration, severity of pain, location of pain, aggravating factors, posture of the child, history of trauma, course of illness and accompanying clinical features (fever, weight loss, malaise). Certain diagnoses are more common at different ages.

A physician must be familiar with normal motor developmental milestones and gait pattern and be able to appreciate abnormal gait. Most children can "cruise" or walk holding onto objects before the age of 1 year and walk independently by 14 to 18 months. By 3 years of age, children usually develop a mature walking pattern. By the age of 9 years a child usually assumes a well-developed adult type of gait. Generally, limp is a reflex response to weight bearing on a painful weak or imbalanced limb. The time of stance on affected limb is reduced and the stride length of the normal limb is shortened. As a result the child quickly bears weight on the normal limb.

Examination

An attempt is made to localize the cause of the limp in the spine, hips, knees, ankle or neuromuscular apparatus. The differential diagnosis of a limping child depending on the part involved is detailed in Table 18.6.

A child with painful knee walks with extended knee to avoid motion in the joint. In spinal disease, the trunk is held rigidly. One with septic arthritis of hip refuses to walk. In Legg-Calve-Perthes disease glutei muscles on the affected side cannot keep the pelvis at level when the affected limb bears the weight, so that pelvis is tilted to the unaffected side (Trendlenburg gait). The level of pelvis is checked by placing a hand on the iliac crest. Diseases of

Table 18.6: Common conditions resulting in a limp
Neuromuscular disorders
Paralysis of muscles, e.g. (acute poliomyelitis, traumatic neuritis)
Hemiplegia, acute hemiplegia of childhood
Myopathies and muscular dystrophies
Hemi-hypertrophy of muscles
Disorders of bones and joints
Hip
Congenital dislocation of hip
Pyogenic arthritis; tuberculosis
Transient synovitis
Trauma
Rickets
Slipped epiphysis
Osteochondritis (Perthe's disease)
Knee and ankle
Tuberculosis
Rheumatoid arthritis
Transient synovitis
Trauma
Osteochondritis
Foot
Painful lesions of the nails, toes and soles, e.g. warts, corns, blisters, paronychia, ingrowing toe nail, fracture
Ill-fitting shoes
Osteochondritis
Spine
Tuberculosis
Scoliosis
Congenital defects

neuromuscular system affect walking in several ways because of flaccidity or spasticity. These should be excluded by looking for atrophy, asymmetry or torsion.

Children who present with an obvious orthopedic diagnosis such as trauma with suspected fracture may need nothing more than radiographic studies. At initial presentation, however, the history and physical examination may not be sufficient in eliciting a diagnosis and certain laboratory and radiographic studies may be beneficial.

The management depends on the specific cause. Besides medical and surgical management, acute and long-term rehabilitation are also important.

Suggested reading

1. Leung AK, Lemay JF. The limping child. J Pediatr Health Care 2004;18:219–23.
2. Abbassian A. The limping child: a clinical approach to diagnosis.Br J Hosp Med (Lond) 2007;68:246–50.
3. Wyndham M. The limping child. Community Pract 2007; 80:42.

19 Childhood Malignancies

Childhood cancers are rare, but are an important cause of morbidity and mortality in children younger than 15 years. Malignancies are difficult to detect in children because the signs and symptoms are nonspecific and mimic many common disorders. Pediatric cancers differ from that in adults since they are more aggressive and consequently more responsive to chemotherapy. Common malignancies in children include leukemia (30%), brain tumors (20%) and lymphoma (12%), followed by neuroblastoma, retinoblastoma, and tumors affecting soft tissues, kidneys, bones and gonads. The majority of pediatric cases of acute leukemia, neuroblastoma, Wilms' tumor, retinoblastoma and primary liver cancer occur below the age of 5-year. Hodgkin and, non-Hodgkin lymphoma and bone tumors occur frequently in children over 10-years-old. At all ages, boys are affected more frequently than girls. Advances in diagnosis, multi-modality therapy, rational use of chemotherapy and improved supportive care have improved the survival rates tremendously and over 70% of all childhood cancers are now curable.

LEUKEMIA

Leukemia is a malignancy that arises from clonal proliferation of abnormal hematopoietic cells leading to disruption of normal marrow function and various manifestations of leukemia. Leukemia is the most common cancer in children. There are two main subtypes, acute lymphoblastic leukemia (ALL) and acute myeloid leukemia (AML). A small proportion may have chronic myeloid leukemia (CML).

ACUTE LYMPHOBLASTIC LEUKEMIA

ALL is the most common malignancy accounting for one-fourths of all childhood cancer and three-fourths of all newly diagnosed patients with leukemia. Its incidence is approximately 3–4 cases per 100,000 children below 15-years of age. Boys have higher rates than girls, especially in adolescents with T-cell ALL. There is a peak in the incidence of childhood ALL, between the ages of 2- and 5-years, due to ALL associated with a pre-B lineage (referred to as *common ALL*).

The etiology of ALL remains unknown in a majority of cases. However, several genetic syndromes have been associated with an increased risk of leukemia. In particular, there is a 10–20 fold increased risk of leukemia (ALL and AML) in children with Down syndrome. Other genetic syndromes associated with leukemia include Bloom syndrome, Fanconi anemia, neurofibromatosis, Klinefelter syndrome, immunodeficiency and ataxia telangiectasia. Exposure to ionizing radiation, certain pesticides and parental smoking are associated with a higher incidence of ALL. Patients having received therapeutic irradiation and aggressive chemotherapy (alkylating agents, epipodophyllotoxins) are also at higher risk of developing acute leukemia.

Classification

Morphology

The classification of ALL has evolved over the years from one that was primarily morphology based to one which is currently based on immunophenotyping, karyotyping and molecular biology techniques. ALL cells can be classified using the French-American-British (FAB) criteria into morphologic subtypes (Table 19.1). L1 lymphoblasts, the most common in children (80–85%), have scant cytoplasm and inconspicuous nucleoli; these are associated with a better prognosis (Fig. 19.1). Patients in the L2 category, accounting for 15% cases, show large, pleomorphic blasts with abundant cytoplasm and prominent nucleoli. Only 1–2% patients with ALL show L3 morphology in which cells are large, have deep cytoplasmic basophilia and prominent vacuolation; these cells show surface immunoglobulin and should be treated as Burkitt lymphoma.

Immunophenotype

Monoclonal antibodies classify ALL into B-cell precursor, B-cell or T-cell leukemia in more than 99% cases. Precursor B-cell ALL is subdivided into early pre-B and pre-B. B-cell precursors include CD19, CD20, CD22 and CD79. Mature B-cells are characterized by immunoglobulins on their surface, while the T-cell ALL carry the immunophenotypes CD3, CD7, CD5 or CD2. The specific myeloid markers include CD13, CD14 and CD33. Rarely the cells

Table 19.1: **FAB classification of acute lymphoblastic leukemia**

Cytologic features	*L1 (80–85%)*	*L2 (15%)*	*L3 (1–2%)*
Cell size	Small cells predominate, homogenous	Large, heterogenous in size	Large, homogenous
Amount of cytoplasm	Scanty	Variable; often moderately abundant	Moderately abundant
Nucleoli	Small, inconspicuous	One or more, often large	One or more, prominent
Nuclear chromatin	Homogenous	Variable, heterogenous	Stippled, homogenous
Nuclear shape	Regular, occasional clefts	Irregular clefts, indentation	Regular, oval to round
Cytoplasmic basophilia	Variable	Variable	Intensely basophilic
Cytoplasmic vacuolation	Variable	Variable	Prominent

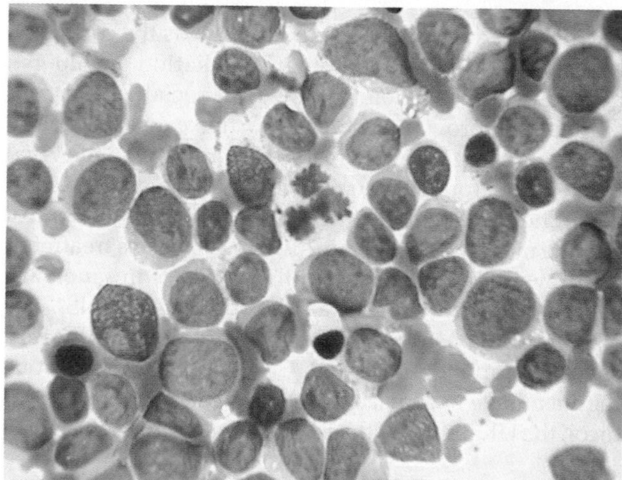

Fig. 19.1: Bone marrow aspirate from child with acute leukemia shows reduced normal marrow elements and replacement with blasts

may express both myeloid and lymphoid antigens (biphenotypic leukemia).

Cytogenetics

Technological improvements enable demonstration of abnormalities in chromosomal number and/or structure in most cases of ALL. The presence of hyperdiploidy (chromosome number >50) is associated with good prognosis in contrast to the poor prognosis in patients with hypoploidy (chromosome number <45 per cell). Specific chromosomal translocations in ALL, including t(8;14) in B-cell ALL, t(4;11) in infant leukemia and t(9;22) translocation that forms the Philadelphia chromosome, are associated with a poor prognosis.

Prognostic Factors and Risk Assessment

The two most important prognostic factors include age at diagnosis and the initial leukocyte count. Children less than 1-year-old have an unsatisfactory prognosis; infant leukemia is often associated with t(4;11) translocation and high leukocyte counts. Children between the ages of 1- and 9-years do well. The presence of leukocyte count more than 50,000/mm^3 at diagnosis is associated with a bad prognosis. Relapse rates are higher in boys. While patients with B-cell leukemia (L3 morphology) previously had unsatisfactory outcome, the prognosis has improved with specific B-cell leukemia directed protocols. The presence of T-cell leukemia is *per se* not a bad prognostic factor unless associated with other risk factors, including high leukocyte count, mediastinal mass or disease affecting the central nervous system at diagnosis. Patients showing hyperdiploidy have a good prognosis, while presence of hypodiploidy is associated with an unsatisfactory outcome. Philadelphia positive t(9;22) ALL and translocation t(4;11) which is present in infant leukemia are associated with poor prognosis. Response to treatment with prednisolone is considered an *in vivo* prognostic factor; patients showing ≥1000/mm^3 blasts in peripheral blood following 7-days treatment with prednisolone and an intrathecal dose of methotrexate are likely to have an adverse outcome.

B cell ALL, age between 1–9 years, total leukocyte count less than 50,000/mm^3 at diagnosis, female sex, absence of mediastinal widening, lymphadenopathy and organomegaly, absence of CNS disease, hyperploidy and certain chromosomal abnormalities (trisomy 4 and 10) at diagnosis constitute low risk ALL; all other patients are considered as high risk.

Clinical Presentation

The duration of symptoms in a child with ALL may vary from days to weeks and in some cases few months. However, most patients present with 3–4 weeks' history. The clinical features of ALL are those of bone marrow infiltration with leukemic cells (bone marrow failure) and the extent of extramedullary disease spread. Common features include manifestations of anemia, thrombocytopenia and neutropenia. These include pallor and fatigue, petechiae, purpura and bleeding, and infections. Lymphadenopathy, hepatomegaly and splenomegaly are present in more than 60% patients. Bone or joint pain and tenderness may occur due to leukemic involvement of the periosteum of bones or joints. Infants and young children may present with a limp or refusal to walk. Few (2–5%) show central nervous system (CNS) involvement at diagnosis; most are asymptomatic but some have features of raised intracranial pressure. The diagnosis of CNS leukemia is made on examination of the cerebrospinal fluid; even a single blast is sufficient for this diagnosis. Overt testicular leukemia may be seen in about 1% of cases. It presents with firm, painless, unilateral or bilateral swelling of the testes; the diagnosis is confirmed by testicular biopsy. Other rare sites of extramedullary involvement include heart, lungs, kidneys, ovaries, skin, eye or the gastrointestinal tract.

Differential Diagnosis

These include infectious mononucleosis, acute infectious lymphocytosis, idiopathic thrombocytopenic purpura, aplastic anemia and viral infections like cytomegalovirus and others that result in leukemoid reactions and pancytopenia. Idiopathic thrombocytopenic purpura is the most common cause of acute onset of petechiae and purpura in children. Ordinarily children with ITP have no evidence of anemia and have a normal leukocyte count and differential count. Bone marrow smear reveals normal hematopoiesis and normal or increased number of megakaryocytes. A bone marrow examination is recommended prior to initiation of steroid treatment for presumed ITP, in order to exclude leukemia. ALL must be differentiated from aplastic anemia, which may present with pancytopenia. The condition may also be mistaken for juvenile rheumatoid arthritis in patients presenting with fever, joint symptoms (limp, arthritis or arthralgia), pallor, splenomegaly and leukocytosis. ALL should be distinguished from other malignancies (neuroblastoma, non-Hodgkin lymphoma, rhabdomyosarcoma, Ewing sarcoma and retinoblastoma) that present with bone marrow involvement. Morphologic, cytochemical, immunophenotypic and cytogenetic characteristics of the malignant cells should be done. Occasionally patients with ALL may present with hypereosinophilia or as an emergency with life threatening infections, hemorrhage, organ dysfunction secondary to leukostasis or signs and symptoms of superior vena cava syndrome.

Management

The management of acute leukemia needs the combined effort of the pediatric oncologist, radiation oncoloigst, nursing team, psychologist, medical social worker and dietician. Improvements in supportive care and chemotherapeutic regimes has resulted in improved survival from <5% before 1965 to 80% for children diagnosed in 2000. The successful treatment of ALL requires the control of bone marrow or systemic disease, as well as treatment (or prevention) of extramedullary disease in sanctuary sites, particularly the central nervous system (CNS). The cornerstone of this strategy is systemic combination chemotherapy together with CNS prophylaxis. Various regimen have been used to treat ALL like MCP 841 protocol, the UK protocol, the BFM protocol, etc. (Table 19.2).

Table 19.2: MCP 841 protocol for acute lymphoblastic leukemia

Cycle	*Chemotherapy*	*Dose and schedule*
Induction 1(I1)	Prednisolone	40 mg/m^2 p.o. days 1–28
	Vincristine	1.4 mg/m^2 i.v. days 1, 8, 15, 22 and 29
	Daunorubicin	30 mg/m^2 i.v. days 8, 15, 29
	L–Asparaginase	6000 U/m^2 i.m. QOD × 10 doses days 2–20
	Methotrexate	12 mg IT days 1, 8, 15, 22*
Induction 2 (I2)	6–Mercaptopurine	75 mg/m^2 p.o. days 1–7 and days 15–21
	Cyclophosphamide	750 mg/m^2 i.v. days 1 and 15
	Methotrexate	12 mg IT days 1, 8, 15 and 22*
	Cranial irradiation	200 cGy × 9 days (total 1800 cGy)
Repeat Induction 1 (RI1)	Same as Induction 1	Doses and schedule as per I1
Consolidation (C)	Cyclophosphamide	750 mg/m^2 i.v. days 1 and 15
	Vincristine	1.4 mg/m^2 i.v. days 1 and 15
	Cytosine arabinoside	70 mg/m^2 s.c. every 12 hours x 6 doses, days 1–3 and days 15–17
	6–Mercaptopurine	75 mg/m^2 p.o. days 1–7 and days 15–21
Maintenance (M) 6 cycles	Prednisolone	40 mg/m^2 p.o. days 1–7
	Vincristine	1.4 mg/m^2 i.v. day 1
	Daunorubicin	30 mg/m^2 i.v. day 1
	L–Asparaginase	6000 U/m^2 i.m. on days 1, 3, 5 and 7
	6–Mercaptopurine	75 mg/m^2 p.o. daily, 3 weeks out of every four for a total of 12 weeks. Begin on day 15
	Methotrexate	15 mg/m^2 p.o. once a week missing every 4th week for a total of 12 weeks. Begin on day 15

* Intrathecal (IT), in 5 to 10 mL 0.9% sodium chloride injection on days 1, 8, 15 and 22. Dosages are age-adjusted: 1–2 yr (8 mg); 2–3 yr (10 mg); >3 yr (12 mg).

The treatment of ALL is divided into 4 stages: (i) **Induction therapy** (to attain remission), (ii) **CNS prophylaxis** or **CNS preventive therapy**, (iii) **Intensification** (consolidation) and (iv) **Maintenance therapy** (continuation). The intensification (consolidation) phase, following induction of remission, may not be required in *low risk* patients, though recent studies suggest benefits in long-term survival with intensification therapy in both low risk and high risk patients. The average duration of treatment in ALL ranges between 2–2½ year; there is no advantage of treatment exceeding 3-years.

Induction Therapy

The drug regimen combining vincristine and prednisolone induces remission in 80–95% patients with ALL. Since the remission rate and duration are improved by the addition of a third and fourth drug (L-asparaginase and/or anthracycline) to vincristine and prednisolone, current induction regimens include vincristine, prednisolone, L-asparaginase and an anthracycline, with remission achieved in 95–98% of cases. The induction therapy lasts for 4–6 weeks.

CNS Preventive Therapy

The concept of CNS preventive therapy is based on the fact that most children with leukemia have subclinical CNS involvement at the time of diagnosis and this acts as a sanctuary site where leukemic cells are protected from systemic chemotherapy because of the blood brain barrier. The early institution of CNS prophylaxis is essential to eradicate leukemic cells which have passed the blood brain barrier. CNS prophylaxis has enabled increased survival rates in leukemia. Most children receive a combination of intrathecal methotrexate and cranial irradiation. However, there is considerable concern regarding long term neurotoxicity and risk of development of brain tumors following this therapy. In order to achieve effective CNS prophylaxis while minimizing neurotoxicity, experts now recommend a lower dose of cranial irradiation (1800cGy) with intrathecal methotrexate. Other alternative regimens for CNS prophylaxis include the use of triple intrathecal therapy consisting of methotrexate, hydrocortisone and cytarabine without cranial irradiation. Others propose that cranial irradiation should be limited for patients with high risk features at diagnosis, including T-cell ALL with leukocyte count >100,000/mm^3, Philadelphia chromosome positive and presence of CNS leukemia.

Intensification (Consolidation) Therapy

This is a period of intensified treatment administered shortly after remission induction, with administration of new chemotherapeutic agents to tackle the problem of drug resistance. There is clear evidence that 'intensification' has improved the long term survival in patients with ALL, especially those with high risk disease. Commonly used agents for intensification therapy include high dose methotrexate, L-asparaginase, epipodophyllotoxin, cyclophosphamide and cytarabine. Use of these medications has resulted in prolonged periods of granulocytopenia and the need for improved supportive care, liberal use of broad spectrum antibiotics and blood products.

Maintenance (Continuing) Therapy

It has been estimated that approximately two to three logs of leukemic blasts are killed during the induction therapy, leaving a leukemic cell burden in the range of 10^9–10^{10}. Additional therapy is therefore necessary to prevent a relapse.

Once remission is achieved, maintenance therapy is continued for an additional 2–2.5 years. Without such therapy, patients of ALL relapse within the next 2–4 months. The exception are those with B-cell ALL, who are treated with short term (<6 months) high-dose chemotherapy. A number of drug combination and schedules are used, some based on periodic reinduction, others on continued delivery of effective drugs. The main agents used include 6-mercaptopurine daily and methotrexate once a week given orally, with or without pulses of vincristine and prednisolone or other cytostatic drugs. Monthly pulses of vincristine and prednisolone appear to be beneficial. In intermediate high risk ALL most investigators use aggressive treatment and additional drugs during maintenance therapy. It is imperative to monitor children for drug toxicity and compliance. For better outcome, methotrexate and 6-mercaptopurine should be given to the limits of tolerance as determined by absolute neutrophil counts.

Supportive Care

Because of the potential complications encountered with treatment and the need for aggressive supportive care like blood component therapy, detection and management of infections, nutritional and metabolic needs and psychosocial support, these children should be treated by a specialist in a cancer center or hospital with all support facilities. These children should be given cotrimoxazole as prophylaxis against pneumocytis carinii pneumonia They are vaccinated against hepatitis B infection and screened for HIV infection. Oral hygiene is taken care of by batadine gargles. They are vaccinated against hepatitis B infection and screened for HIV infection. Oral hygiene is taken care of by betadine gargles. The survival rates of children with malignancies are enhanced through access to state-of-the-art treatment given according to well defined protocols in specialized centers.

Treatment After Relapse

Despite the success of modern treatment, 20–30% of children with ALL relapse. The main cause of treatment failure in leukemia is relapse of the disease. The most common site of relapse is in the bone marrow (20%), followed by CNS (5%) and testis (3%). The prognosis for a child with ALL who relapses depends on the site and time of relapse. Early bone marrow relapse before completing maintenance therapy has the worst prognosis and long time survival of only 10–20%, while late relapses occurring after cessation of maintenance therapy have a better prognosis (30–40% survival). Relapse in extra-medullary sites, particularly testes, is more favorable in terms of survival. The treatment of relapse must be more aggressive than the first line therapy with use of new drugs to overcome the problem of drug resistance.

Allogeneic bone marrow transplantation offers a better chance of cure than conventional chemotherapy for children with ALL who enter a second remission after hematologic relapse. In addition to the treatment related morbidity and mortality, lack of a suitable matched donor limits widespread application of allogeneic transplantation. Facilities for bone marrow transplantation are available in all major centers in India including Bombay, Vellore, Chennai and Delhi.

Late Effects of Treatment

Long term effects of treatment, which may take years to become apparent, are of particular concern. Continued evaluation of these patients for prolonged periods is necessary. Patients who have received cranial irradiation at a younger age are at risk for cognitive and intellectual impairment and development of CNS neoplasms. There is a risk of development of secondary AML after the intensive use of epipodophyllotoxins (etoposide or tenoposide) therapy. Endocrine dysfunctions leading to short stature, obesity, precocious puberty, osteoporosis, thyroid dysfunction and growth retardation (growth hormone deficiency) are reported. Patients having received treatment with an anthracycline are at risk of cardiac toxicity.

Survival Trends in India

There has been a significant improvement in the outcome of ALL in India. Multicentric trials suggest a 5-year patient survival ranging from 50–60% in our country. Economic reasons result in poor compliance and large number of dropouts, contributing to the decreased survival. The high incidence of infections, lack of good supportive care and poor tolerance to chemotherapy in malnourished patients also contributes to the mortality. T-cell leukemia and cytogenetic abnormalities, which predict poor outcome, are more common in Indian patients.

ACUTE MYELOID LEUKEMIA

Acute myeloid leukemia (AML) also termed as acute non-lymphoblastic leukemia accounts for 15–20% of leukemia in children. AML is much more complex and resistant disease than ALL. Progress has been slower and therapy more complicated, but with intensive myelosuppressive induction and post-remission therapy, about 40–50% patients can achieve long term survival.

Epidemiology

The ratio of AML to ALL is approximately 1:4. AML can occur at any age but the incidence is more during adolescence; males are affected as frequently as females. Congenital leukemia (occurring during first 4–weeks of life) is mostly AML. While the etiology of AML is not known, there is an association following exposure to ionizing radiation. Down syndrome is the most common genetic predisposing factor associated with risk of developing AML during the first three years of life. Other predisposing factors are Fanconi anemia, Bloom syndrome, Kostmann syndrome and Diamond Blackfan anemia. Medications associated with risk of AML include alkylating agents and epipodophyllotoxins.

Classification

AML can be divided into several subgroups according to the FAB classification: M_0 undifferentiated, M_1 acute myeloblastic leukemia with minimal maturation, M_2 acute myeloblastic leukemia with maturation, M_3 acute promyelocytic leukemia, M_4 acute myelomonocytic leukemia, M_5 acute monoblastic leukemia, M_6 erythroblastic leukemia, M_7 acute megakaryoblastic leukemia. About 30–40% patients with AML are M_1 and M_2, and about same percentage is M_4 and M_5. M_3 type of AML constitutes about 5–10% and M_7 is strongly associated with Down syndrome. Specific chromosomal abnormalities are found in the various subgroups. Translocation between chromosome 8 and 21 t(8;21) translocation is found almost exclusively in M_1 and M_2. Almost all patients with M_3 carry the translocation t(15;17) and M_5 is associated with t(9;11). Abnormalities of chromosome 16 are seen in mainly M_4 subtype. FAB classification along with the most commonly employed histochemical stains is usually sufficient to distinguish with AML and its subtypes from ALL. Staining for myeloperoxidase activity and positive stain with Sudan black B is observed in AML. Auer rods, needle shaped accumulation of primary granules, are commonly found in M_2, M_3 and M_5 subtypes of AML (Fig. 19.2).

Clinical Features

Most patients with AML present with pallor, fatigue, bleeding or fever as manifestations of underlying anemia, thrombocytopenia and neutropenia. Unlike ALL, lymphadenopathy and massive hepatosplenomegaly is not very common in AML. However, infants and toddlers with AML have more organomegaly, high leukocyte counts and CNS disease at diagnosis. They are mostly M_4 and M_5 subtypes. Disseminated intravascular coagulation may occur with any subgroup, but is common in acute promyelocytic leukemia (M_3). Chloromas are localized

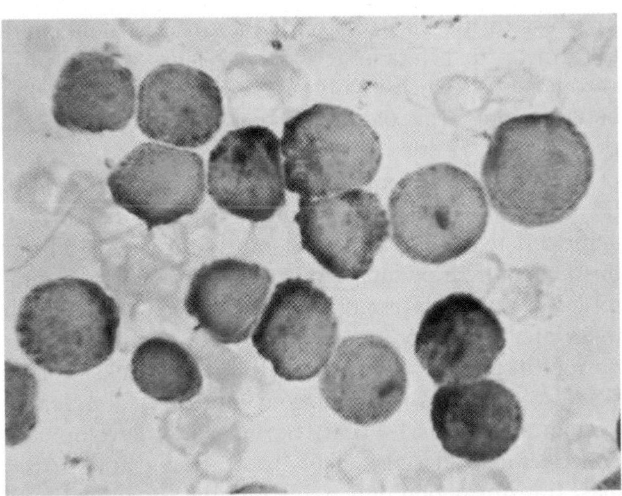

Fig. 19.2: A case of acute myeloid leukemia: the blast cells are positive for cytochemistry stain myeloperoxidase. This confirms myeloid lineage of the blast cells

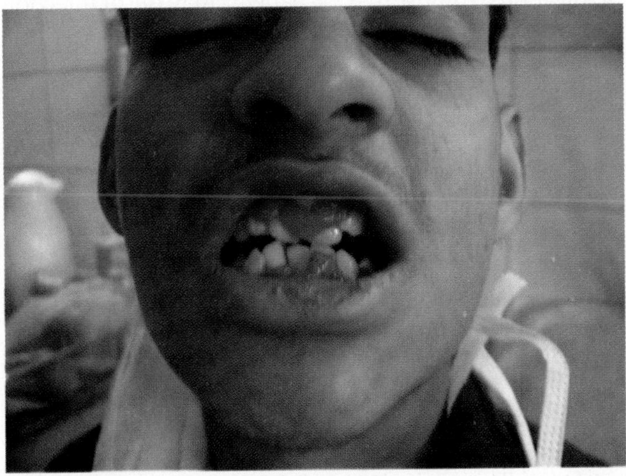

Fig. 19.4: Gum hyperplasia is seen in acute myeloid leukemia, characteristically in subtype AML-M4 and M5

collections of leukemic cells seen exclusively in patients with AML. They may occur at any site including CNS, bones (typically orbit) (Fig. 19.3) and skin. Gingival hypertrophy may be present (Fig. 19.4). Diagnosis must be confirmed by bone marrow examination; the morphologic, cytochemical, immunophenotypic and genetic characteristics of the blast cells should be determined.

Sometimes the diagnosis of AML is preceded by a prolonged preleukemic phase lasting several weeks or months. Usually this is characterized by a lack of one of the normal blood cell lineages, resulting in refractory anemia, a moderate neutropenia or thrombocytopenia. The condition is referred to as a myelodysplastic syndrome. Some patients may show hypoplastic bone marrow that may develop later into an acute leukemia.

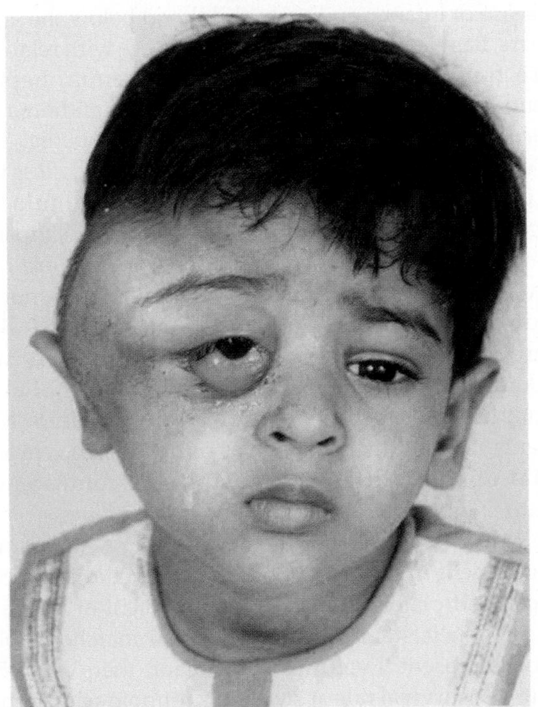

Fig. 19.3: Chloroma in a child with AML

Treatment

Compared to ALL, the cure rate is hampered by a lower remission rate, an increased relapse rate due to the development of resistance to multiple chemotherapeutic drugs and a greater risk of death in remission due to infections and hemorrhage. Nevertheless, during the past two decades, the long term survival for children with AML has increased from less than 10% to almost 50%. This is due to intensification of therapy along with improved supportive care. The main drugs used for induction therapy are combination of cytosine arabinoside and an anthracycline (doxorubicin or daunorubicin). The induction regimen most commonly used is cytosine arabinoside (100 mg/m^2/day given as continuous infusion for 7 days) plus daunorubicin (45 mg/m^2/day for 3 days) with or without additional drugs (etoposide, thioguanine). With the current regimen, remission is induced in about 70–80% patients. However, without further therapy most children relapse within one year. Post remission therapy (consolidation therapy) includes high dose chemotherapy including cytosine arabinoside and etoposide. Allogeneic bone marrow transplantation during early remission is associated with a better long term survival. Patients with acute promyelocytic leukemia (M3), which accounts for about 10–15% of patients of AML, are treated differently with all transretinoic acid or arsenic and systemic chemotherapy.

Since patients with AML are at high risk for myelosuppression following chemotherapy, they require intensive blood component support including platelet transfusions and broad spectrum antibiotics for control of infections. Almost 10–12% patients may die of infection and bleeding during induction therapy.

Suggested reading

1. Arya LS. Childhood cancer—challenges and opportunities. Indian J Pediatr 2003;70:159–162.
2. Magrath T, et al. Treatment of acute lymphoblastic leukemia in countries with limited resources: lessons from use of a single protocol in India over a twenty year period. Eur J Cancer 2005; 41:1570–1583.
3. Margolin JF, et al. Acute lymphoblastic leukemia. In: Principles and Practice of Pediatric Oncology. Eds Pizzo PA, Poplack DG. Lippincott Williams & Wilkins, Philadelphia 2006;538–590.
4. Golub TR, Arceci RJ. Acute myelogenous leukemia. In: Principles and Practice of Pediatric Oncology. Eds. Pizzo PA, Poplack DG. Lippincot Williams & Wilkins, Philadelphia, 2006; 591–644.
5. Woods WG. Curing childhood acute myeloid leukemia at the halfway point: Promises to keep and miles to go before we sleep. Pediatr Blood Cancer 2006; 46: 565–569.
6. Vardiman JW, et al. The World Health Organization (WHO) classification of the myeloid neoplasms. Blood 2002; 100: 2292–2302.
7. Creutzig U, et al. Treatment strategies and long term results in paediatric patients treated in four consecutive AML-BFM trials. Leukemia 2005; 19: 2030–2042.

CHRONIC MYELOID LEUKEMIA

Chronic myeloid or myelogenous leukemia (CML) is a myeloproliferative disorder. CML is primarily a disease of middle age; the peak incidence is in the fourth and fifth decade. However, it may occur at any age including infants and young children. Two main types of well-differentiated myelogenous leukemia have been recognized. One is clinically and hematologically comparable with the adult form of chronic myelogenous leukemia and occurs in children above the age of 4 years. The other presents earlier in infancy and early childhood usually below the age of 4 years, called juvenile chronic myelogenous leukemia (JCML) has a much more rapid course. The environmental factor implicated in the etiology of CML is ionizing radiation.

Adult Variety of CML (ACML)

Though ACML is one of the commonest leukemias in adults, it is rare in children accounting for 3–5% cases. The natural history is divided into chronic, accelerated and blast phases. In the chronic phase, patient has nonspecific symptoms such as fever, malaise and weight loss. Occasionally, patients present with acute symptoms such as bone or joint pain or priapism. Splenomegaly is the most common physical finding and is usually massive. Mild hepatomegaly and lymphadenopathy may be present. Leukocytosis is present in all cases and 80% patients have leukocyte counts above 100,000/mm^3. The differental count shows all forms of myeloid cells from promyelocytes to polymorphonuclear leukocytes; basophilia is common. Mild anemia and thrombocytosis are common, but thrombocytopenia is rare. Bone marrow aspirate demonstrates a shift in the myeloid series to immature forms that increase in number as patients progress to the blast phase of the disease. Leukocyte alkaline phosphatase activity is low. Philadelphia chromosome, which involves a reciprocal translocation between long arms of chromosomes 22 and 9; t(9;22) is present in 90% cases.

The aim of treatment during chronic phase is to control the increasing white cell counts. This can usually be achieved by single agent chemotherapy with either busulfan or hydroxyurea. However, these agents are being replaced with α-interferon and more recently imatinib mesylate. The blood counts returns to normal or near normal in almost all patients within 6–8 weeks. Spleen size also decreases. With the conventional treatment, the average survival is 3–4 years. Survival after development of accelerated phase is usually less than a year and after blast transformation only a few months. Treatment with α-interferon may produce partial or complete remission in the chronic phase. Recently the invention of imatinib, which is a tyrosine kinase inhibitor has shown promising results in CML. Imatinib achieves high rates of complete hematological and cytogenetic remission; the rate of progression to accelerated or blast crisis is decreased. Allogeneic stem cell transplantation is the only documented curative therapy for patients with CML.

Juvenile Chronic Myeloid Leukemia

JCML, also termed as juvenile myelomonocytic leukemia, is an uncommon hematological malignancy accounting for less than 2% leukemias in children. Patients with neurofibromatosis are at high risk for development of JCML (Figs 19.3 and 19.4). Compared to ACML, JCML is a disease of infancy and early childhood below the age of 5-years, has a more acute and severe course with relatively more frequent lymphadenopathy, anemia, hepatosplenomegaly, skin involvement (eczema, xanthoma and *café-au-lait* spots), infection and thrombocytopenia.

Peripheral smear shows leukocytosis (usually less than 100,000/mm^3) with the full spectrum of granulocytic precursors and increased normoblasts; monocytosis is often striking. Thrombocytopenia and anemia are common. The leukocyte alkaline phosphatase score is normal or low and fetal hemoglobin levels are elevated. Bone marrow aspirates show an increased cellularity with predominance of granulocytic cells in all stages of maturation; megakaryocytes are normal or decreased. Most patients have normal karyotypes or nonspecific chromosomal abnormalities. Philadelphia chromosome is negative; monosomy 7 is found in 30% patients.

JCML has a fulminant and rapidly fatal course. Management involves supportive care including packed red cell and platelet transfusions, treatment of infections and allogeneic stem cell transplant if a matched sibling donor is present. Even with transplant, there is 30–50% event-free survival rate at 3 year. Cis retinoic acid has been tried with some benefit in JMML.

Suggested reading

1. Altman AJ. Chronic leukemias of childhood. In: Principles and Practice of Pediatric Oncology Eds. Pizzo PA, Poplack DG. Lippincot Williams & Wilkins, Philadelphia 2006;645–672.
2. Goldman JM. How I treat chronic myeloid leukemia in the imatinib era? Blood 2007;110:2828–2837.

LYMPHOMA

Lymphomas are the third most common malignancy in children and adolescents, after leukemia and brain tumors. About 60% are non-Hodgkin's lymphoma and 40% are Hodgkin's disease. Lymphomas are uncommon below the age of 5 years and the incidence increases with age.

NON-HODGKIN LYMPHOMA

Pediatric non-Hodgkin lymphomas (NHL) are different from lymphomas in adults. Low grade lymphomas, which are common in adults are rare in children. Pediatric NHL are high grade, diffuse and aggressive with propensity for wide spread dissemination.

Epidemiology

The relative frequency and incidence of NHL show significant geographic variations. There is male preponderance, with male to female ratio of 3:1. In equatorial Africa, 50% of all cancers are lymphomas (Burkitt lymphoma being predominant). In United States and Europe, one-third of childhood NHL are lymphoblastic, one-half small, noncleaved cell lymphomas (Burkitt and non Burkitt or Burkitt like) and the rest are large cell lymphomas. In India, lymphoblastic lymphoma is more common. NHL is also characterized on basis of their T- or B-cell nature. Lymphoblastic lymphomas are T-cell derived, while undifferentiated lymphomas (Burkitt and non-Burkitt) are B-cell derived. NHL may follow previous chemotherapy for Hodgkin's disease, or be associated with immunodeficiency and DNA repair deficiency syndromes (Wiskott Aldrich syndrome, X-linked lymphoproliferative disorders, ataxia telangiectasia), acquired immunodeficiency syndrome and organ transplantation (post-transplant lymphoproliferative disease). Infection with malaria and EB virus are considered risk factors for Burkitt lymphoma.

Clinical Presentation

Patients with NHL present with clinical features that correlate with histologic subtype and stage or extent of the disease. Children with NHL typically present with extranodal disease involving the mediastinum, abdomen or head and neck region. Intrathoracic NHL, most often T-cell lymphoma, might present with cough, dyspnea, dysphagia, chest pain or the superior vena cava syndrome. There may be associated pleural and/or pericardial effusion. Cervical lymphadenopathy, abdominal pain, ascites, palpable abdominal mass, intestinal obstruction or intussusception (typical B-cell disease), cranial nerve palsy, bone involvement, jaw swelling (Burkitt lymphoma) and pancytopenia due to bone marrow involvement may occur. Jaw is most frequentl involved site in African Burkitt lymphoma, but rare elsewhere.

Diagnosis

NHL are rapidly growing tumors; prompt diagnosis is therefore essential. Almost two-thirds of patients have widespread disease at the time of diagnosis, involving bone marrow, central nervous system or both. Selection of the appropriate lymph node or mass for histological diagnosis is necessary. Histology is the primary means for diagnosis and is supplemented, if possible, with immunophenotypic and cytogenetic studies. If the clinical condition is not suitable for biopsy, due to a large mediastinal mass causing superior vena cava syndrome, the diagnosis may be made with less invasive procedures, e.g. percutaneous needle aspiration of accessible lymph node, examination of body fluids or bone marrow.

Table 19.3 shows the St. Judes'staging system, which is applicable to all types of childhood NHL. In newly diagnosed patients, a detailed workup and relevant investigations should be done (Table 19.4).

Table 19.3: Staging system for non Hodgkin lymphoma

Stage I: A single tumor or nodal area is involved, excluding the abdomen and mediastinum.
Stage II: Disease extent limited to a single tumor with regional node involvement, 2 or more tumors or nodal areas involved on one side of the diaphragm, or a primary gastrointestinal tract tumor (completely resected) with or without regional node involvement.
Stage III : Tumors or involved lymph node areas, occur on both sides of the diaphragm. Also includes any primary intrathoracic (mediastinal, pleural, or thymic) disease, extensive primary intra-abdominal disease, or any paraspinal or epidural tumors.
Stage IV: Bone marrow and/or central nervous system disease, regardless of other sites of involvement.

Table 19.4: Evaluation of patient with non Hodgkin lymphoma

- Complete blood count.
- Surgical biopsy for histology; cytochemical, immunologic, cytogenetics and molecular studies.
- Bone marrow aspiration and biopsy.
- Cytology: cerebrospinal fluid; if available, pleural, pericardial or peritoneal fluid.
- Liver function tests, renal function tests, electrolytes, LDH, uric acid.
- Chest radiograph; ultrasonography.
- CT scan, MRI of chest and abdomen.
- Optional: gallium scan, positron emission tomography.

Management

The dramatic improvement in the survival of patients with NHL is because of development of highly effective chemotherapy and supportive care. Surgery has limited role in treatment other than for diagnostic purposes. Radiotherapy is also restricted to emergency situations, e.g. superior vena cava syndrome or spinal cord compression due to paraspinal disease. Different chemotherapeutic regimens are used for treatment of B- and T-cell lymphomas. The regimens for lymphoblastic lymphoma are usually based on protocols for ALL. Most successful protocols are the German BFM (Burlin, Frankfurt, Munster) protocols and a modified version of LSA_2L_2 protocol. These are intensive protocols that use combinations of 8 to 10 drugs. Cranial irradiation or prophylactic intrathecal chemotherapy is given in stage III and IV diseases. Chemotherapy is given for a period of 1 to 2 years depending on the stage and extent of the disease. The long term survival in patients with lymphoblastic lymphoma with limited disease is 80–90% and for advanced disease 70–80%.

The chemotherapeutic regimens for B-cell lymphoma (Burkitt and non Burkitt) is different. Most protocols consist of short duration (6-months), intensive alkylating agent therapy (cyclophosphamide or ifosphamide) with high dose methotrexate, vincristine, anthracyclines, etoposide and cytarabine; CNS prophylaxis is provided with intrathecal chemotherapy. Long term survival is highly satisfactory with survival in more than 90% patients with limited disease and 75–85% in patients with extensive disease. Survival rates in patients with bone marrow disease have also improved dramatically. The use of anti-CD20 monoclonal antibodies (rituximab) directed against B-cell antigens has been safely combined with standard chemotherapy to improve survival.

Suggested reading

1. Link MP, Weinstein HJ. Malignant non-Hodgkin's lymphomas in children. In: Principles and Practice of Pediatric Oncology. Eds. Pizzo PA, Poplack DG, Lippincott Williams and Wilkins, Philadelphia, 2006; 722–747.
2. Cairo MS, Spostos R, Perkins SL et al. Burkitt's and non Burkitt like lymphoma in children and adolescents. Br J Hematol 2003;120:660–670.
3. Srinivas V, Soman CS, Naresh KN. Study of the distribution of 289 non-Hodgkin's lymphomas using the WHO classification among children and adolescents in India. Med Pediatr Oncol 2002 ;39: 40–43.

HODGKIN LYMPHOMA

Hodgkin lymphoma is characterized by progressive enlargement of lymph nodes. The disease is considered unicentric in origin and has a predictable pattern of spread by extension to contiguous nodes. While its etiology is unknown, the biology of the disease confirms malignant behavior.

Epidemiology

The annual incidence of Hodgkin lymphoma is approximately 5–7 cases per million children and it accounts for 5–6% malignancies. The age specific incidence of Hodgkin lymphoma exhibits a characteristic bimodal distribution. In developed countries, the early peak occurs in the age group of 20 to 30 years and the second peak after the age of 50 years. In developing countries, however, the early peak occurs before adolescence; it is more common in males. Hodgkin lymphoma is rare before the age of four years. The condition is more common in individuals with an underlying immunodeficiency disease such as ataxia telangiectasia and AIDS.

Pathology

Lymph nodes are the most common tissue on which the diagnosis of Hodgkin lymphoma is made. However, liver, spleen, bone marrow or lung may provide the material for histologic examination. It is necessary to obtain the entire node by excision biopsy for proper histologic examination. Fine needle aspiration biopsy and frozen section material are not optimal for histology. The diagnosis of Hodgkin lymphoma is made with the identification of the Reed Sternberg cells (large multinucleated giant cells with abundant cytoplasm and either multiple or multilobed nuclei). Presence of these cells is, however, not pathognomonic, since they can be seen in reactive lymphoid hyperplasia, NHL and non-lymphoid malignancies.

Hodgkin's disease is divided into four histopathologic subtypes: lymphocytic predominance, nodular sclerosis, mixed cellularity and lymphocyte depletion. Nodular sclerosing is the most common type in developed countries, whereas in developing countries including India, the mixed cellularity type is common, accounting for nearly 60% cases. The WHO classification of Hodgkin lymphoma recognizes two major subtypes: (i) nodular lymphocyte predominant Hodgkin lymphoma and (ii) classical Hodgkin lymphoma, which includes four subtypes (nodular sclerosing, mixed cellularity, lymphocyte rich and lymphocyte depleted).

Clinical Features

Children with Hodgkin lymphoma usually present with painless cervical or supraclavicular lymphadenopathy; the nodes are firm and rubbery in consistency. Cervical lymph nodes are the most frequent (80%) site of primary involvement; 50% patients may also have mediastinal adenopathy (Fig. 19.5). Less commonly, axillary or inguinal lymphadenopathy is the presenting feature. About 20–30% of children present with systemic (B) symptoms, as defined by the Ann Arbor staging criteria, with fever over 38°C, night sweats and unexplained weight loss of >10% body weight at presentation. The frequency of these symptoms increases with advanced

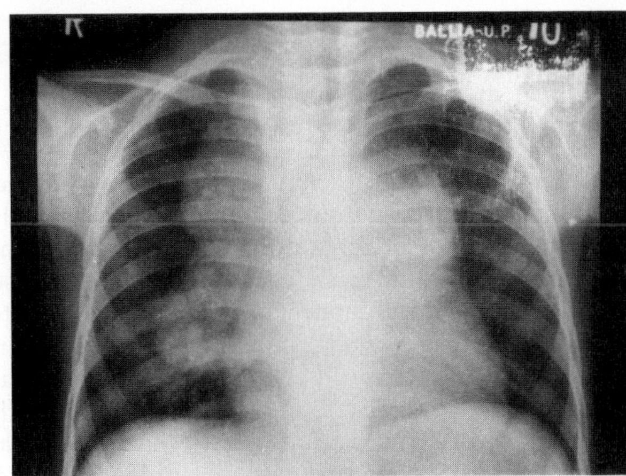

Fig. 19.5: Superior mediastinal widening with lobulated lymph node masses (Courtesy: Dr. O.P. Mishra, Varanasi)

disease and indicate an unfavorable prognosis. Besides presence of 'B' symptoms, other prognostic factors include stage of disease, histopathological subtype (risk increases from lymphocyte predominant to nodular sclerosis to mixed cellularity to lymphocyte depletion), bulky mediastinal disease, extensive splenic involvement and more than 5 nodal sites in stage III.

Diagnostic Work Up and Staging

Evaluation of a patient includes careful physical examination with assessment of all lymph node bearing areas. Chest radiograph provides information about enlargement of the mediastinum. CT scan of the chest provides information about pulmonary parenchyma, chest wall, pleura and pericardium that may not be apparent on chest X-ray. CT scan of the abdomen and pelvis is done to examine for involvement of the viscera and lymph nodes. Although lymphangiography is a reliable method for retroperitoneal lymph nodes, it is rarely performed in children. Bone marrow biopsy should be performed in all children with systemic symptoms and in advanced stage (III and IV) disease. A staging laparotomy is not performed because of concerns related to operative morbidity and splenectomy. The diagnostic workup and staging are outlined in Tables 19.5 and 19.6.

Treatment

The purpose of therapy is to cure children with least possible immediate and long-term complications and provide optimal quality of life. Most pediatric protocols prescribe multi-agent combination chemotherapy, either alone or with low dose radiation therapy to the involved field. The addition of radiation to combination chemotherapy improves disease-free survival in patients with bulky disease and presence of 'B' symptoms. High dose (35–44 Gy) radiation therapy alone is reserved for grown up children and adolescents with localized disease (Stage I or stage II A).

Table 19.5: Diagnostic evaluation for children with Hodgkin lymphoma

- Physical examination with measurement of lymph nodes
- Hemogram differential counts, ESR, CRP, liver and renal function tests, serum alkaline phosphatase, LDH
- Lymph node biopsy
- Chest X-ray P/A and lateral views; measurement of mediastinal mass thoracic cavity ratio
- CT scan of neck and chest
- CT or MRI of abdomen and pelvis
- Bone marrow biopsy (all children except stages IA/IIA)
- Bone scan (recommended in children with bone pains or raised SAP)
- CSF examination (if indicated)
- CT scan brain (if indicated)
- Gallium or PET scan (may identify more sites than conventional imaging, more accurate for residual mass)
- Surgical staging with lymph node sampling and lymphangiography (selected cases)

ESR erythrocyte sedimentation rate, CRP C reactive protein, LDH lactate dehydrogenase, P/A postero-anterior, CT computed tomography, MRI magnetic resonance imaging, SAP serum alkaline phosphatase, CSF cerebrospinal fluid, PET position emission tomography.

Table 19.6: Ann Arbor staging classification for Hodgkin lymphoma

Stage	*Definition*
I	Involvement of single lymph node region (I) or of a single extralymphatic organ or site (IE) by direct extension
II	Involvement of two or more lymph node regions on the same side of the diaphragm (II) or localized involvement of an extralymphatic organ or site and one or more lymph node regions on the same side of the diaphragm (IIE)
III	Involvement of lymph node regions on both sides of the diaphragm (III), which may be accompanied by involvement of the spleen (IIIS) or by localized involvement of an extralymphatic organ or site (IIIE) or both III (E + S)
IV	Diffuse or disseminated (multifocal) involvement of one or more extralymphatic organs or tissues with or without associated lymph node involvement

Systemic symptoms

Each stage is subdivided into A and B subcategories, B for those with defined systemic symptoms and A for those without any. The B designation is given to patients with: (i) unexplained loss of > 10% of body weight in 6 months before diagnosis (ii) unexplained fever with temperature above 38°C for 3 consecutive days (iii) drenching night sweats. Pruritus alone does not qualify for B classification, nor does a short febrile illness associated with an infection.

After work up and staging, all patients with early stage (I, II) Hodgkin lymphoma are given combination chemotherapy (e.g. 2–4 cycles of ABVD comprising adriamycin, bleomycin, vinblastine, dacarbazine) with or without radiotherapy. Those with advanced stage of Hodgkin lymphoma are given 4–6 cycles of chemotherapy (e.g. ABVD) with or without radiotherapy. Other combinations of chemotherapy include 6–8 cycles of MOPP (nitrogen mustard, vincristine, procarbazine and prednisolone); and COPP regime in which nitrogen mustard is replaced by cyclophosphamide). Some also use alternating regimes of ABVD and COPP (4 cycles of each (Table 19.7). Depending on the stage of the disease 70–90% patients with Hodgkin lymphoma are cured.

Increasing attention is now focused on minimizing late complications of therapy. In growing children low dose, involved field radiation therapy is preferred along with combination chemotherapy in advanced Hodgkin lymphoma. High dose radiation therapy might result in diminished growth of soft tissue and bone, hypothroidism, gonadal dysfunction and secondary malignancies. High cumulative doses of anthracyclines, bleomycin and alkylating agents are avoided to reduce cardiopulmonary and gonadal toxicity.

Suggested reading

1. Hudson MM, Onciu M, Donaldson SS. Hodgkin's lymphoma. In: Principles and Practice of Oncology. Eds. Pizzo PA, Poplack DG. Lippincott Williams and Wilkins, Philadelphia, 2006 pp 695–721.
2. Dinand V, Arya LS. Epidemiology of childhood Hodgkin's disease; is it different in developing countries? Indian Peditr 2006; 43(2): 141–147.
3. Arya LS, et al. Hodgkin's disease in Indian children: outcome with chemotherapy alone. Pediatr Blood Cancer 2006; 46: 26–34.
4. Diehl V, Franklin J, Pfreundschuh M, et al. Standard and increased—dose BEACOPP chemotherapy compared with COPP—ABVD for advanced Hodgkin's disease. N Engl J Med 2003;348:2386–2395.
5. Engert A, Franklin J, Eich HT, et al: Two cycles of doxorubicin, bleomycin, vinblastine and dacarbazine plus extended—field radiotherapy is superior to radiotherapy alone in early favorable Hodgkin's lymphoma: final results of the GHSG HD7 Trial J Clin Oncol 2007;25:3495–3502.

OTHER MALIGNANCIES

NEUROBLASTOMA

Neuroblastoma is the most common intra-abdominal solid tumor in children, accounting for 7–8% of all cancers. It is a malignant tumor of the autonomic nervous system derived from the neural crest. Neuroblastoma is a disease of early childhood with approximately 90% of patients presenting before 5-years of age and almost 50% within the first 2-years of life. The etiology is not known but familial cases occur, and there is an association with neurofibromatosis, Hirschsprung disease, heterochromia, fetal hydantoin and fetal alcohol syndromes, and Friedreich ataxia. Rearrangement or deletion of the short arm of chromosome 1 has been found in 80% cases.

Clinical Features

The clinical features are related to the localization of the sympathetic nervous system and site of metastasis. The most common sites of primary tumors are the adrenal gland (30%), paravertebral retroperitoneum (28%), posterior mediastinum (15%), pelvis (5%) and cervical area. The patient may be asymptomatic with a paraspinal, localized intrathoracic or retroperitoneal mass found incidentally. This presentation has an excellent prognosis. At the other extreme is an anxious, febrile patient with periorbital ecchymoses, scalp nodules and bone pain from widespread metastasis (Fig. 19.6). Unusual presentations include an infant with increasing hepatomegaly from neuroblastoma in the liver, with or without skin or bone marrow involvement (stage IV-S disease, associated with good prognosis). Another is the patient with spinal cord signs secondary to 'dumb-bell' tumor growth. The primary paraspinal tumor grows through the intervertebral foramen and forms an intraspinal mass with neurologic signs, including paraplegia. Metastasis, present in 60–70% children, are usually to the skeleton (facial bones, skull), bone marrow and lymph nodes. Less

Table 19.7: ABVD and COPP chemotherapy protocols for Hodgkin lymphoma

Drug	*Route*	*Dose (mg/m²)*	*Schedule*
COPP cycle*			
Cyclophosphamide	IV	600	days 1, 8
Oncovin (vincristine sulfate)	IV	1.5 (maximum 2.0 mg)	days 1, 8
Procarbazine	p.o	100	days 1–14
Prednisone	p.o	40 (maximum 60 mg)	days 1–14
ABVD cycle*			
Adriamycin (doxorubicin)	IV	25	days 1, 15
Bleomycin	IV	10	days 1, 15
Vinblastine	IV	6	days 1, 15
Dacarbazine	IV	375	days 1, 15

*Each cycle to be started on day 29 of the previous cycle, alternating 4 COPP cycles with 4 ABVD cycles. IV intravenous.

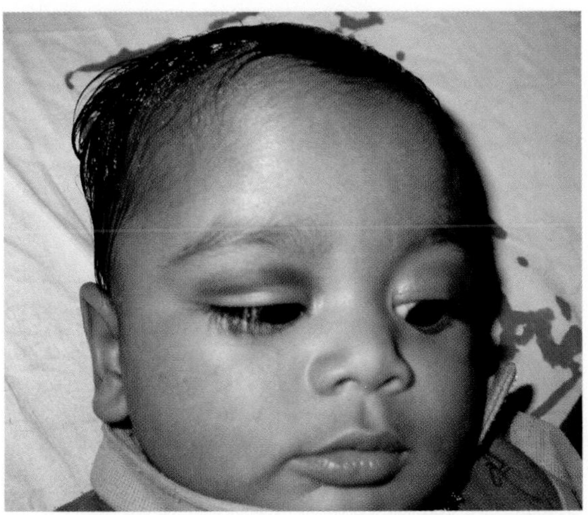

Fig. 19.6: Raccoon eyes-blackish discoloration around eyes seen frequently in neuroblastoma (Courtesy: Dr. Sandeep Agarwala, Pediatric Surgery, AIIMS)

frequent features are sweating, diarrhea, hypertension, cerebellar signs, and opsoclonus (dancing eyes) attributed to metabolic and immunologic disturbances.

Investigations

The gold standard for the diagnosis of neuroblastoma is examination of tumor tissue by histopathology and immunohistochemistry. Other investigations include blood counts, urinary catecholamine excretion, bone marrow aspiration and biopsy, liver function tests, abdominal ultrasound, and X-rays and bone scan for metastasis. Nuclear scanning with I^{123} or I^{131} MIBG detects tumors and metastasis accurately. Quantitation of serum neuron-specific enolase and ferritin, amplification of the *N-myc* oncogene, tumor cell ploidy and age-based histologic classification of the tumor are of prognostic value. Children with neuroblastoma can be divided into two groups: those with favorable and those with unfavorable features. The favorable group has a survival expectancy of 90% or more. It is characterized by young age (<1.5 year), favorable stage (I, II and IV-S), normal levels of serum ferritin and favorable histology. Older patients with stage III or IV disease, serum ferritin levels greater than 150 mg/ml and tumors of unfavorable histology have survival rates of 20% or less. The International Neuroblastoma Staging System is shown in Table 19.8.

Table 19.8: International neuroblastoma staging system

Stage I: Localized tumor confined to the area of origin; complete excision, with or without microscopic residual disease; identifiable ipsilateral and contralateral lymph nodes negative microscopically.

Stage IIA: Localized tumor with incomplete gross excision; identifiable ipsilateral and contralateral lymph nodes negative microscopically.

Stage IIB: Localized tumor with complete or incomplete gross excision; with positive ipsilateral regional lymph nodes; identifiable contralateral lymph nodes negative microscopically.

Stage III: Tumor infiltrating across the midline with or without regional lymph node involvement; or unilateral tumor with contralateral regional lymph node involvement; or midline tumor with bilateral regional lymph node involvement.

Stage IV: Tumor disseminated to distant lymph nodes, bone, bone marrow, liver or other organs (except Stage IV-S).

Stage IV-S: Localized primary tumor as defined for Stage 1 or 2 with dissemination limited to liver, skin, and/or bone marrow (limited to infants less than one year of age).

Treatment

Age and clinical stage are the two most important independent prognostic factors. Even with advanced disease, children less than 1-year-old at diagnosis have a better outcome than those diagnosed later. Localized neuroblastoma has better prognosis; it can be treated with surgery alone and does not require chemotherapy. Treatment modalities for neuroblastoma include chemotherapy, surgery and radiation therapy. Chemotherapy is the mainstay of treatment for most patients with neuroblastoma in advanced stage. Chemotherapy includes vincristine and alkylating agents in combination with anthracycline and epipodophyllotoxins. Chemotherapy regimens widely used are OPEC (vincristine, cyclophosphamide, cisplatinum, teniposide (VM-26), CADO (vincristine, cyclophosphamide, doxorubicin), and PE-CADO (vincristine, cyclophosphamide, doxorubicin, cisplatinum, tenoposide), etc. In all treatments good remissions are reached, but the recurrence rate is high. Treating advanced neuroblastoma is not very rewarding.

Suggested reading

Brodeur GM, Maris JM. Neuroblastoma. In: Principles and Practice of Pediatric Oncology. Eds. Pizzo PA, Poplack DG. Lippincott Williams & Wilkins, Philadelphia, 2006; 933–970.

WILMS' TUMOR

Wilms' tumor (nephroblastoma) is the most common malignant tumor of the kidney, accounting for 6–7% of all malignancies. Eighty percent of patients with Wilms' tumor present under 5-years of age; the frequency is similar in boys and girls. The peak age at diagnosis is 2–3 years; 6% patients have bilateral disease and 1% cases are familial. Bilateral disease is more common in patients with familial Wilms' tumor. Genitourinary anomalies like horseshoe or fused kidney, hypospadias, cryptorchidism, Denys Drash syndrome (male pseudohermaphroditism, diffuse mesangial sclerosis with congenital nephrotic syndrome) and renal dysplasia are found in 4–6%. Genetic syndromes, particularly aniridia, hemihypertrophy, Beckwith Wiedemann syndrome (macroglossia, gigantism, umbilical hernia, hemihypertrophy), WAGR

(Wilms' tumor, aniridia, genitourinary malformations and mental retardation) and trisomy 18 may be associated. Cytogenetic abnormalities include deletion in 11p13 and tumor specific loss of heterozygosity on the short arm of chromosome 1.

Clinical Features

Most patients present with an asymptomatic abdominal mass detected by their parents or physician during routine examination. Common features at diagnosis include hematuria (10–25%), hypertension (25%), abdominal pain (30%), fever (20%), anorexia and vomiting. Wilms' tumor should be considered in any child with abdominal mass (Fig. 19.7). Important differential diagnosis includes neuroblastoma, other flank masses including hydronephrosis, multicystic kidney, and rarely abdominal lymphoma and retroperitoneal rhabdomyosarcoma.

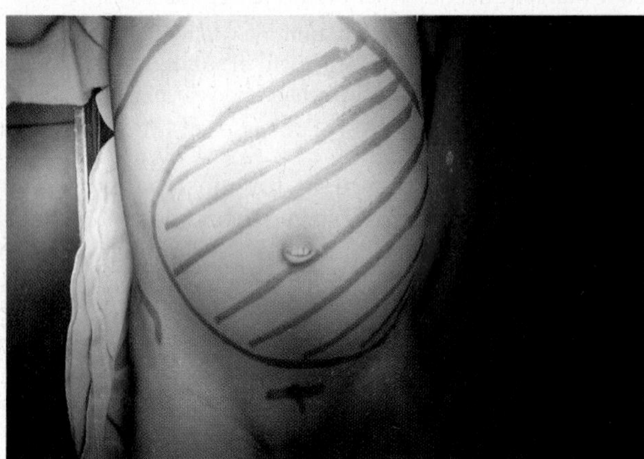

Fig. 19.7: Child with Wilms' tumor showing marking of mass. The children are usually asymptomatic so a high index of suspicion is required to identify these cases. (Courtesy: Dr Sandeep Agarwala, Pediatric Surgery, AIIMS)

Investigations

Ultrasonography is the most important investigation since it can differentiate solid from cystic renal mass. CT scan and MRI provide detailed view of the extent of the tumor (Fig. 19.8). Intravenous pyelography is seldom necessary. An X-ray chest is done to examine for pulmonary metastasis. Metastasis in the liver can be detected on ultrasonography and CT scan. Complete blood counts, urinalysis and assessment of renal and liver function is done in all cases.

Prognostic Factors

The prognostic factors are determined by staging:
Stage I: Tumor confined to kidney and completely excised.
Stage II: Tumor extends beyond kidney but completely excised.
Stage III: Tumor infiltrates renal fat; residual tumor after surgery. Lymph node involvement of hilum, paraaortic region or beyond.

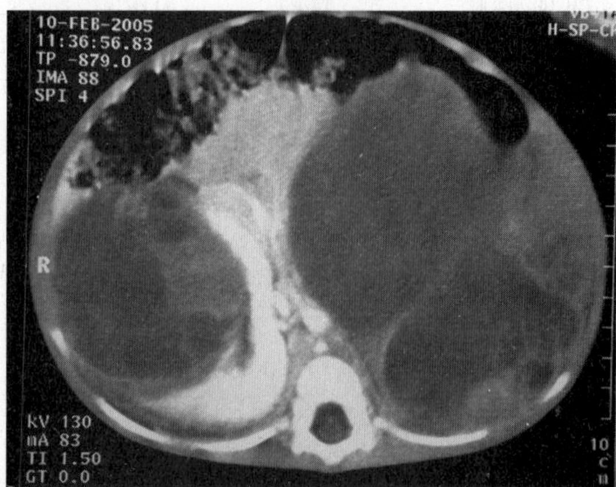

Fig. 19.8: CT scan showing bilateral Wilms' tumor. This poses many challenges to the treating team

Stage IV: Metastasis in lung or liver, rarely bone and brain.
Stage V: Bilateral renal involvement.

Another prognostic factor is pathology. 3% tumors show *favorable pathology* for which only surgical excision is necessary. Another 6% have *unfavorable histology*; these tumors are pleomorphic and ruptured, and show early metastasis to bones. The majority of patients have *standard histology*, where precise treatment is determined by staging. Ploidy is another prognostic sign, diploid tumors have a better prognosis than hyperdiploid tumors.

Treatment

Therapy for Wilms' tumor is based on stage of the disease and histology. Usually, all modalities of treatment: surgery, chemotherapy and radiotherapy are required. The immediate treatment for unilateral disease is removal of the affected kidney. Many experts prefer preoperative chemotherapy because it diminishes the size of the tumor and allows better staging. By preoperative chemotherapy, using actinomycin D and vincristine for a period of 4 weeks, 85% of the patients may not require any local radiotherapy. Stage I and II tumors with favorable histology are usually treated postoperatively with vincristine and actinomycin D. The commonly used drugs for advanced Wilms' tumor are a combination of vincristine, actinomycin D and adriamycin along with abdominal radiation. With the modern therapy, 80–90% of patients with Wilms' tumor are cured.

Suggested reading

1. Green DM. The treatment of stages I-IV favorable histology Wilms' tumor. J Clin Oncol 2004; 22:1366–1372.
2. Dome JS, et al. Renal tumors. In: Principles and Practice of Pediatric Oncology. Eds. Pizzo PA, Poplack DG. Lippincott Williams & Wilkins, Philadelphia, 2006; 905–932.

RHABDOMYOSARCOMA

Rhabdomyosarcoma is the most common soft-tissue sarcoma in children under 15-years of age. Nearly half of these cases are diagnosed below the age of 5-years and two-thirds by 10-years of age. These tumors are associated with several conditions including Li-Fraumeni syndrome, neurofibromatosis and the fetal alcohol syndrome. The histologic classification includes embryonal (60%), alveolar (20%) variants; the remainder are pleomorphic and undifferentiated. Embryonal histology is present most often in tumors of head and neck and genitourinary areas and have good prognosis. Alveolar rhabdomyosarcoma, which occurs mostly in the extremities and perineal region in older children is associated with an unsatisfactory outcome.

Rhabdomyosarcoma may occur at any anatomic site where striated muscle is present. In general, they present as a mass without antecedent trauma. The most common primary site is the head and neck region (35%) (Fig. 19.9) followed by the genitourinary tract, extremities, trunk and retroperitoneum. Rhabdomyosarcoma is the most common non-ocular orbital tumor in young children, usually presenting with proptosis or swelling of the eyelid. Parameningeal tumors (nose, nasopharynx, middle ear, mastoid and paranasal sinuses) have a tendency for intracranial extension. Genitourinary tumors may present as a pelvic mass, bladder and prostate enlargement or a polypoid mass in the vagina. Extremity and truncal primaries are generally of alveolar histology with poor prognosis. About 25% of patients present with metastasis at the time of diagnosis, commonly in the lung, bone marrow and bone.

Assessing the extent of the tumor is important, because therapy and prognosis depend on the degree to which the mass has spread beyond the primary site. The optimal therapy involves multimodality approach, including chemotherapy, surgery and radiotherapy. The commonly used chemotherapeutic drugs are vincristine, actinomycin D, cyclophosphamide and doxorubicin. Patients with metastasis show less than 25% long term survival.

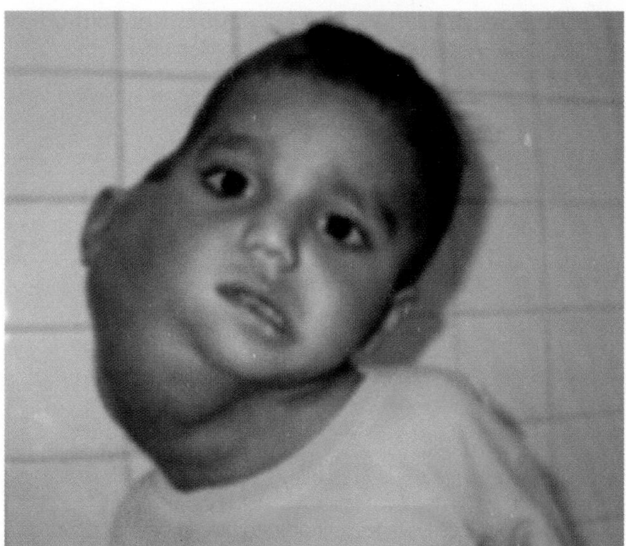

Fig. 19.9: Rhabdomyosarcomas are common in the head and neck region. They usually present as painless soft tissue masses. (Courtesy: Dr. Sandeep Agarwala, Pediatric Surgery, AIIMS)

Suggested reading

1. Wexler LH, et al. Rhabdomyosarcoma and the other undifferentiated sarcomas. In: Principles and Practice of Pediatric Oncology. Eds. Pizzo PA, Poplack DG. Lippincott Williams & Wilkins, Philadelphia, 2006; 971–1001.
2. Stevens MC. Treatment for childhood rhabdomyosarcoma. The cost of cure. Lancet Oncol 2005; 6:77–84.

BONE TUMORS

Osteogenic sarcoma and Ewing's sarcoma are the two major types of bone tumors in children and adolescents. Both the tumors occur more commonly during second decade of life and show male predominance.

Osteogenic Sarcoma

The peak incidence of osteogenic sarcoma is during adolescence, correlating with the rapid bone growth; it is rare below the age of 5-years. The distal femur and proximal tibia are the most frequent sites followed by proximal humerus and middle and proximal femur. Flat bones, e.g. vertebrae, pelvic bones and mandible may rarely be involved. Radiation exposure is a documented causal factor for osteogenic sarcoma. Localized painful swelling in the bone is the usual presentation which may be mistakenly attributed to traumatic or infective conditions, delaying the diagnosis by months. Metastasis occurs early to the lungs and other bones.

Radiographic examination shows sclerotic or lytic bone lesions and periosteal new bone formation over the metaphyseal region. The differential diagnosis includes osteomyelitis and other bone tumors. Biopsy must be done to confirm the diagnosis. This is a pleomorphic, spindle cell tumor that forms extracellular matrix or osteoid. Imaging studies include CT chest and radionuclide bone scan to rule out metastasis. MRI provides accurate assessment of tumor extent.

Successful treatment requires multiagent chemotherapy with complete surgical resection. Limb sparing surgery by wide resection of the primary tumor is followed by replacement of missing bone by a prosthesis. Amputation is rarely needed with present day management comprising chemotherapy and surgery. Chemotherapeutic agents include doxorubicin, cisplatin, ifosfamide, cyclophosphamide and high dose methotrexate. The tumor is unresponsive to radiotherapy. With current treatments, more than two-thirds of patients presenting without metastasis have long term survival and are cured.

Ewing's Sarcoma

Ewing's sarcoma is the second most common malignant bone tumor in children and adolescents. Ewing's sarcoma occurs most often in the second decade, but can occur below the age of 10-years. They most often arise from flat bones such as pelvis, chest wall and vertebrae and the diaphyseal region of long bones. Common sites of metastasis are lungs and other bones; bone marrow metastasis is not uncommon.

The typical presentation is with pain, swelling, a lump and/or a limp. Systemic symptoms such as fever and weight loss may be present. The duration of symptoms varies from few weeks to sometimes more than a year. Osteomyelitis and Langerhan cell histiocytosis particularly eosinophilic granuloma are the differential diagnosis. Other small round cell tumors, which metastasize into the bone marrow are neuroblastoma, rhabdomyosarcoma and NHL. Plain radiographs may show destructive lesions of the diaphysis of bone in the form of lytic or mixed lytic and sclerotic lesions with a classical appearance called 'onion skinning'. Biopsy must be done to confirm the diagnosis. Chest CT, bone scan and bone marrow biopsy are performed to evaluate for metastasis.

These tumors are very well responsive to both chemotherapy and radiotherapy. Local surgery is also an effective way to treat Ewing's sarcoma, however surgical amputation is rarely indicated. Tumor control with radiotherapy requires moderately high doses ranging from 5500 to 6000 cGy. Multiagent combination chemotherapy includes vincristine, dactinomycin, cyclophosphamide and doxorubicin. Some investigators add ifosfamide and/or etoposide to the above medications. In localized disease, without metastasis the cure rate is nearly 60%, while in metastatic disease it is less than 30%.

Suggested reading

1. Bernstein M, et al. Ewing sarcoma family of tumors. In: Principles and Practice of Pediatric Oncology. Eds Pizzo PA, Poplack DG. Lippincott Williams & Wilkins, Philadelphia, 2006; 1002–1032.
2. Link MP, et al. Osteosarcoma. In: Principles and Practice of Pediatric Oncology. Eds Pizzo PA, Poplack DG. Lippincott Williams & Wilkins, Philadelphia, 2006; 1074–1115.
3. Carvajal R, Meyers P. Ewing's sarcoma and primitive neuroectodermal family of tumors. Hematol Oncol Clin North Am 2005; 19: 501–525
4. Miser JS, et al. Treatment of metastatic Ewing's sarcoma: evaluation of combination ifosfamide and etoposide - a Children's Cancer Group and Pediatric Oncology Group study. J Clin Oncol 2004; 22:2873–2876

RETINOBLASTOMA

Retinoblastoma is the most common primary ocular tumor of childhood, a tumor of the embryonic neural retina. It has an incidence of 11 new cases per million population (age less than 5-years). About 90% cases are diagnosed by age 3–4 years and 98% by 5 years. Bilateral disease is diagnosed earlier then unilateral disease. There is increased frequency of retinoblastoma in some developing countries especially Latin America, Africa and Asia including India. Approximately 20–30% of cases are bilateral and 10% of patients have family history of retinoblastoma; all these patients have a germ line mutation of the retinoblastoma gene (*Rb*) encoded on chromosome 13q14. Approximately 10–12% of unilateral cases have a germline mutation of the *Rb* gene as well. Of all cases, about 40% are hereditary. The tumor predisposition is inherited in an autosomal dominant pattern with high penetrance. Germ line mutations of the *Rb* gene are associated with increased risk of developing secondary malignancies (e.g. osteosarcoma, soft tissue sarcoma), affecting up to 35% of patients 30-years after diagnosis.

Most patients with retinoblastoma in the developed countries are diagnosed early when the tumor remains intraocular. By contrast, in developing countries including India, late diagnosis is the rule. The most common sign is white reflex, termed leukocoria (Fig. 19.10) of one or both eyes. The next common presenting sign is strabismus followed by painful gluacoma, redness of the eye and diminished vision. In developing countries, retinoblastoma presents very late in its extraocular stage, either with an orbital mass (proptosis) or with distant metastasis in the bone, bone marrow, lymph nodes and central nervous system.

Where possible, both eyes should be examined under general anesthesia. Proper staging requires ultrasonography and CT scan of the orbit and brain, for assessment of orbital and intracranial extension. Bone marrow biopsy and CSF examination for cytology is done in advanced cases.

Retinoblastoma is curable when the disease is intraocular. For intraocular tumors, the standard treatment approach has been enucleation in unilateral cases. In bilateral cases, enucleation is reserved for eyes with local loss of vision and/or those with high risk for extraocular spread. In the remaining bilateral cases, the practice is to rely on local therapy for individual lesions either with cryotherapy, photo (laser) coagulation, brachytherapy

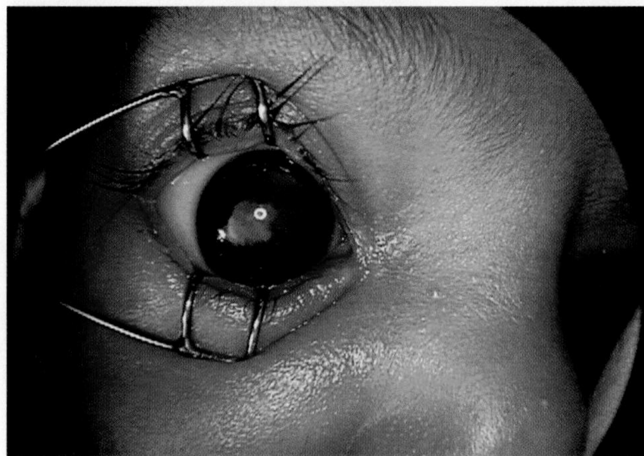

Fig. 19.10: In the early stages retinoblastoma can be picked up by a change in the normal red reflex of the eye to a yellow reflex. This can easily be tested using an ophalmoscope/other light source and can be part of the well baby examination. (Courtesy: Prof. R.V. Azad, Ophthalmology, AIIMS)

(plaque radiation) and/or external beam radiotherapy. The use of chemotherapy has previously been reserved for patients with extraocular disease including regional or distant metastasis. Several reports have documented long-term survival of patients with metastatic disease treated with high dose chemotherapy with autologous bone marrow transplantation.

Suggested reading

1. Hurwitz RL, et al. Retinoblastoma. In: Principles and Practice of Pediatric Oncology. Eds. Pizzo PA, Poplack DG. Lippincot Williams & Wilkins, Philadelphia, 2006; 865–886.
2. Friedman DL, et al. Chemoreduction and local ophthalmic therapy for intraocular retinoblastoma. J Clin Oncol 2000; 18: 12–17.
3. Chintagumpala M, et al. Retinoblastoma: review of current management. Oncologist 2007; 12: 1237–1246.

THE HISTIOCYTOSES

The childhood histiocytoses are a rare and diverse group of disorders that presented difficulties for diagnosis and treatment. The International Histiocyte Society has proposed a classification based on the relation of these lesions to normal histiocytic and reticulum cell subsets, as follows:

Class I	Langerhans cell histiocytosis (LCH) (previously called histiocytosis X)
Class II	Hemophagocytic lymphohistiocytosis
Class III	Malignant histiocytosis; acute monocytic leukemia; true histiocytic lymphoma

Class I Histiocytosis

LCH is a reactive proliferative disease characterized by abnormal histiocytes, along with lymphocytes, eosinophils, and normal histiocytes to form infiltrates typical for the disease. The hallmark of LCH is the presence of Birbeck granules on electron microscopy and positivity for S-100 protein and CD1a positivity. These infiltrates cause osteolytic lesions and/or involvement of various other organs. The etiology of LCH is unknown and its pathogenesis not understood. Currently, the disease is widely accepted to be a reactive process rather than a malignancy.

The spectrum of LCH (eosinophilic granuloma, Hand-Schuller-Christian disease, Letterer-Siwe disease) reflects varying extents of the disease. The course of disease is unpredictable, varying from rapid progression and death, to repeated recurrence and recrudescence with chronic sequelae, to spontaneous regression and resolution. Patients with disease that is localized (skin or bone) have a good prognosis and are felt to need minimum or even no treatment. In contrast, multiple organ involvement, particularly in young children (under 2-year-old), carries relatively poor prognosis.

The most common involvement is of the skeleton (80%). Bone lesions can be single or multiple affecting skull bones, long bones, vertebrae, mastoid and mandible. The lesions may be painless or present with pain and local swelling; X-rays show sharp lytic lesions with nonhealing borders (Fig. 19.11). Clinical manifestations include vertebral collapse and spinal compression, pathological fractures in long bones, chronic draining ears and early eruption of teeth. Other manifestations include seborrheic skin rash (Fig. 19.12) in scalp area and back (60%), lymphadenopathy (33%), hepatosplenomegaly (20%) and parenchymal lung infiltrates (15%). Bilateral infiltration of retroorbital area may cause exophthalmos. Gingival mucous membrane may be involved with lesions, which look like candidiasis. Pituitary dysfunction may result in growth retardation and/or diabetes insipidus. Severe disease is characterized by fever, weight loss, malaise, failure to thrive and liver dysfunction. Liver involvement may result in sclerosing cholangitis and cirrhosis. Bone marrow involvement may lead to anemia and thrombocytopenia.

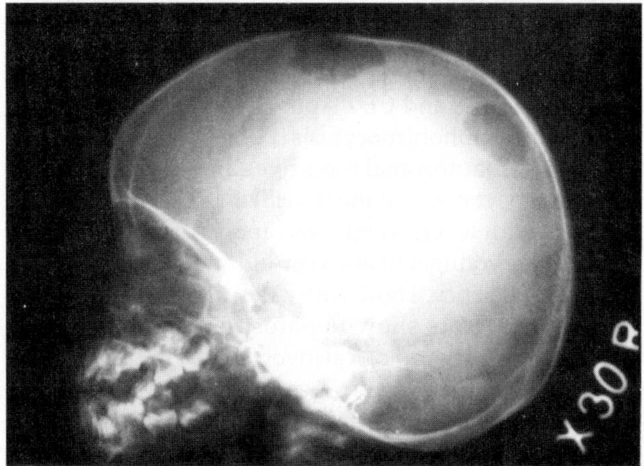

Fig. 19.11: X-ray skull showing two large osteolytic lesions in histiocytosis (LCH). (Courtesy: Dr. O.P. Mishra; Varanasi)

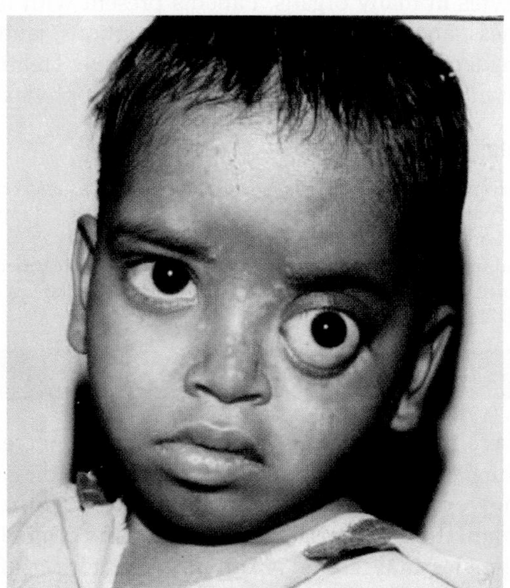

Fig. 19.12: Skin rash and proptosis in LCH

19

Diagnostic work up should include complete blood count, liver function tests, coagulation studies, skeletal survey, chest X-ray and urine specific gravity. In addition, evaluation of involved organ system should be undertaken. Bone marrow biopsies are required to exclude infiltration.

Treatment for localized disease or single bony lesion include curettage and low dose radiation (600 rads). Multisystem disease is treated with chemotherapy, combining vinblastine (weekly IV) and prednisone given daily for 36 months. Other agents include etoposide, methotrexate and 6-mercaptopurine, chlorodeoxyadenosine, cyclosporine and interferon. Multiorgan dysfunction is associated with poor prognosis. About 10–15% patients develop diabetes insipidus and require appropriate screening and follow up.

Class II Hemophagocytic Lymphohistiocytoses

The class II histiocytoses are characterized by accumulation of antigen processing cells (macrophages), which lack Birbeck granules and CD1 a positivity. Familial erythrophagocytic lymphohistiocytosis (FEL) is the only inherited histiocytosis (autosomal recessive). Infection associated hemophagocytic syndrome (IAHS) and FEL both present similarly with fever, weight loss and irritability. Patients with FEL are younger than 4-year-old and may have severe immune deficiency. Those with IAHS may present in older children; patients show hepatosplenomegaly, organ dysfunction and neurological involvement. FEL is a rapidly progressive fatal disorder. Treatment of any underlying infection should be undertaken.

Class III Histiocytosis

These conditions represent malignancies of the monocyte macrophage system with proliferation of malignant histiocytes in many organs. Patients present with fever, weakness, anemia, weight loss, skin eruptions, jaundice lymphadenopathy and hepatosplenomegaly. Treatment is with intensive chemotherapy and CNS prophylaxis.

Suggested reading

1. Ladisch S, Jaffe ES. The Histiocytoses. In: Principles and Practice of Pediatric Oncology. Eds. Pizzo PA, Poplack DG. Lippincot Williams & Wilkins, Philadelphia, 2006;768–785.
2. Gadner H, et al. LCH-I: A randomized trial of treatment for multisystem Langerhans cell histiocytosis. J Pediatrics 2001; 138:728.

ONCOLOGIC EMERGENCIES

The overall survival of children with cancer has increased over the past 25 years as a result of advances in diagnosis and newer therapies including hematopoietic cell transplantation and use of growth factors. Oncologic emergencies may come as initial presentation of the malignancy, during course of the disease or as a consequence of therapy. A solid tumor may invade or compress vital organs like trachea, esophagus or superior vena cava. Effusions into the pleural space or pericardium may compromise functions of heart and lung. Metastasis into the brain may lead to cerebral edema and features of raised intracranial tension. Spinal cord tumor involvement by malignancy may lead to cord compression. Bone marrow involvement results in anemia, bleeding due to thrombocytopenia or coagulation abnormalities (disease/chemotherapy), leukostasis, thrombosis, cerebrovascular episodes and infections. Hormonal problems can occur because of paraneoplastic secretions. Metabolic complications may occur prior to/at onset of chemotherapy following lysis of tumor cell. Finally, therapy related complications, include myocardial dysfunction (anthracyclines), extravasation of drugs (anthracyclines, vinca alkaloids), hemorrhagic cystitis (cyclophosphamide), cerebrovascular accidents (methotrexate, l-asparaginase), and pancreatitis (l-asparginase, corticosteroids) may be encountered. Early diagnosis and urgent management of these conditions will save the life of the child and allow for treatment of the underlying malignancy.

Cardiovascular and Pulmonary Emergencies

Superior vena cava syndrome, cardiac tamponade, pericardial and pleural effusions are some serious complications, which need early diagnosis and management.

Superior Vena Cava Syndrome

Superior vena cava syndrome (SVC) is the compression of the superior vena cava. Tracheal compression may coexist (superior mediastinal syndrome). Patients may present with symptoms of hoarseness, cough, dyspnea, orthopnea, headache, lethargy or irritability. Chief signs include swelling of face, neck and upper extremities, facial plethora and cyanosis, chemosis of conjunctivae, prominent neck veins, stridor and pulsus paradoxus. Malignancies implicated include non-Hodgkin lymphoma, Hodgkin lymphoma, acute lymphoblastic leukemia, neuroblastoma and germ cell tumors.

Minimally invasive techniques should be utilized to establish a diagnosis. Steroids or chemotherapy should be started immediately; occasionally radiotherapy may be required.

Cardiac Tamponade

This occurs due to massive pericardial effusion, constrictive pericarditis from radiation, intracardiac thrombus or tumors. Symptoms of tamponade include chest pain, cough, and dyspnea while signs include tachycardia, cyanosis, hypotension and pulsus paradoxus. Treatment includes provision of oxygen, hydration and percutaneous pericardial drainage. The fluid must be sent for relevant diagnostic investigations.

Spinal Cord Compression

Spinal cord compression is a relatively common complication in the pediatric setting. The tumor encroaches on the epidural space or subarachnoid space. Magnetic resonance imaging with gadolinium is the investigation study of choice. Steroids should be started immediately; occasionally surgical intervention may be required.

Infectious Emergencies

Infectious complications are the most common emergencies seen in children with cancer. Neutropenia occurs due to disease and as a consequence of treatment with chemotherapy and/or radiation. Disruption of the skin and mucosal barriers increases the risk of infection. The severity of neutropenia is categorized as mild when the absolute neutrophil count (ANC) is 1000–1500 cells per mm^3, moderate when the ANC is 500–1000 cells per mm^3, and severe when the ANC is less than 500 cells per mm^3. The risk of bacterial infection is related to both the severity and duration of neutropenia. The child should be evaluated for a focus of infection such as pneumonia, typhlitis, perianal abscess, bacteremia, central line infections, and urine or skin infections. Blood cultures and cultures from specific sites of infection must be sent. A chest X-ray should be obtained. Specific treatment includes intravenous broad-spectrum antibiotics targeted against gram positive and negative organisms. Combinations usually used include an aminoglycoside (amikacin, tobramycin or gentamycin) with a broad-spectrum agent (e.g. ceftazidime, cefoperazone, piperacillin with tazobactum or meropenem). The choice of antibiotics should depend on culture sensitivity patterns and incidence of organisms with extended spectrum β-lactamase production.

Metabolic Emergencies

Common metabolic emergencies include those associated with different tumors (e.g. diabetes insipidus, hypercalcemia, tumor lysis syndrome) or as complications of treatment (e.g. diabetes mellitus, syndrome of inappropriate antidiuretic hormone production).

Tumor lysis syndrome is caused by cell lysis resulting in hyperuricemia, hyperkalemia, hypocalcemia and hyperphosphatemia. This may occur prior to or after initiation of therapy. Burkitt's lymphoma and T-cell lymphoblastic lymphomas are the most common causes. Prevention of tumor lysis syndrome is by ensuring adequate hydration (2–4 times maintenance fluid; given intravenously without additional potassium) to enable appropriate urine output, alkalinization (with sodium bicarbonate to maintain urine pH about 7.5), allopurinol (300 mg/m^2 per day, orally) and measures to combat hyperkalemia and hyperphosphatemia. Hypocalcemia may lead to prolonged QTc interval, however calcium supplementation needs to be done carefully in presence of high phosphate levels (to avoid calcium-phosphate product >60). Patients with tumor lysis syndrome may require careful management of electrolyte balance and occasionally hemodialysis.

Syndrome of inappropriate antidiuretic hormone (SIADH) secretion may occur due to various chemotherapeutic agents (cyclophosphamide, vinca alkaloids, cisplatin) or with certain malignancies (craniopharyngioma, nasopharyngeal carcinoma). The management consists of fluid restriction and treatment of cause if possible.

Gastrointestinal Emergencies

The main acute gastrointestinal complications include acute abdomen, ileus, massive hepatomegaly and typhlitis. These conditions need early diagnosis; usually conservative management is preferred over surgical intervention. Infants with stage IV neuroblastoma may present with massive hepatomegaly sufficient to cause respiratory compromise. This needs urgent diagnosis and initiation of chemotherapy or irradiation. Typhlitis presents usually with fever, neutropenia and acute abdominal pain. It is a necrotizing colitis caused by bacterial invasion of the cecum that may progress to bowel infarction and perforation. Typhilitis requires IV antibiotics and aggressive supportive care. Hemorrhagic pancreatitis, due to L-asparaginase or other causes, is treated with IV imipenem, providing parenteral fluids and nutrition, and management of pain.

Hyperleukocytosis

Hyperviscosity associated symptoms are frequent in acute myeloid leukemia. Presenting symptoms include dyspnea, hypoxemia and right ventricular failure; neurological features comprise of blurred vision and altered sensorium; priapism may occasionally occur. These patients are at risk for bleeds in the brain or pulmonary parenchyma. Thrombocytopenia is managed by platelet transfusions; anemia is difficult to manage since transfusions may exacerbate symptoms of hyperviscosity. Therapy includes ensuring adequate fluid intake, and treatment with hydroxyurea (10–20 mg/kg) and allopurinol.

Urologic Emergencies

Priapism occurs mostly in chronic myeloid leukemia, and is treated with ensuring adequate hydration, and treatment with allopurinol and hydroxyurea. If leukocytosis and electrolyte problems persist, leukopheresis is recommended. If priapism does not respond to treatment within 48–72 hours, the child may be left with persistent deformity.

Obstructive uropathy is seen in patients with bladder rhabdomyosarcomas, large retroperitoneal sarcomas or bulky retroperitoneal lymphomas. A CT scan helps to confirm the diagnosis. Placement of urinary catheter or stents may be helpful, until definitive therapy of the malignancy results in resolution of the obstruction.

Suggested reading

Cohen KJ, Helman LJ. Pediatric emergencies. In: Oncology Emergencies, Oxford University Press, 2002; 239–252.

20 Rheumatological Disorders

APPROACH TO DIAGNOSIS OF ARTHRITIS

Arthritis is a common complaint in children. It is said to be present if there is swelling or effusion in a joint or if there are any 2 of the following 4 features: limitation of range of motion, pain, tenderness and increased heat. It can be the manifestation of an underlying illness (infectious or noninfectious) or may be a primary disease condition in itself. It may not always be easy to differentiate these two categories but there are almost always important leads which can be picked up from a good clinical evaluation. A convenient way to classify arthritis is based on the usual duration of illness at the time of presentation (Table 20.1).

Transient Synovitis

Transient synovitis is a common condition seen in young children and is characterized by sudden onset of pain in the hips, thighs or knees following an upper respiratory catarrh. It is a self-limiting disorder, lasts only 2–4 days and must not be confused with a septic arthritis or acute osteomyelitis. Aspiration of the affected joint results in dramatic improvement. Skin traction and judicious use of non-steroidal anti-inflammatory drugs (NSAIDs) is usually all that is required.

Table 20.1: Classification of arthritis

Acute arthritis (usually <2 weeks)
1. Arthritis associated with acute rheumatic fever
2. Transient (toxic) synovitis
3. Arthritis associated with Kawasaki disease, Henoch-Schönlein purpura
4. Septic arthritis (*Staphylococcus aureus, Hemophilus influenzae, Neisseria meningitidis*)
Subacute arthritis (2–6 weeks)
1. Reactive arthritis
2. Arthritis associated with systemic lupus erythematosus, dermatomyositis, polyarteritis nodosa
3. Associated with leukemia, neuroblastoma
4. Arthritis associated with Lyme disease, brucellosis
5. Sickle cell disease
6. Arthritis associated with hypogammaglobulinemia
Chronic arthritis (>6 weeks)
1. Juvenile rheumatoid arthritis
2. Ankylosing spondylitis
3. Tubercular arthritis
4. Legg-Calve-Perthes disease
5. Psoriasis

Reactive Arthritis

Reactive arthritis is not as common in children as in adults. It is diagnosed on the basis of Berlin criteria: (i) Typical peripheral arthritis—usually a lower limb asymmetric oligoarthritis; (ii) Evidence of preceding infection (commonly gastrointestinal or genitourinary), usually by shigella, chlamydia or yersinia; (iii) Exclusion of other causes of arthritides.

Arthritic presentation of Acute Leukemia

A small proportion of children with acute lymphocytic leukemia may appear to have an 'arthritic' presentation. Bone pain (more marked at night) rather than joint swelling is the predominant complaint. A bone marrow examination is mandatory in such cases.

Arthritis associated with Hypogammaglobulinemia

X-linked agammaglobulinemia (Bruton disease) may sometimes be associated with an unusual 'aseptic' arthritis but accompanying respiratory and other infections are also present. This arthritis is caused by infection due to mycoplasma.

Legg-Calve-Perthes Disease

Legg-Calve-Perthes disease is characterized by an avascular necrosis of the femoral head occurring usually in boys 5–10 years of age. It is now believed to be a manifestation of an underlying hypercoagulable state and the possible etiologies include the presence of the factor V Leiden mutation or a deficiency of protein C/protein S. Affected children present with a limp. Initial X-rays may be normal and it is necessary to perform isotope bone scans and magnetic resonance imaging if the index of suspicion is high. Subsequent X-rays show a characteristic sequential progression: (i) widening of joint space, (ii) fragmentation of epiphysis with patchy areas of increased lucency/density, (iii) abnormalities of shape of femoral head and neck, (iv) deformed head. Treatment options include femoral varus osteotomies or containment splints.

Tubercular Arthritis

Tubercular arthritis is not very common in our experience. It can result from an actual infection with the organism *Mycobacterium tuberculosis* or else may result from an allergic phenomenon (Poncet's disease). The former type usually presents as a monoarthritis (e.g. hip or ankle joint) while the latter type presents as a polyarthritis with a strongly positive Mantoux reaction.

Suggested reading

1. Cassidy JT, Petty RE. Textbook of Pediatric Rheumatology, 5th edn. Elsevier Saunders, Philadelphia, 2005.
2. Singh S, Khubchandani R. Pediatric rheumatology in India —in need of a joint effort. Indian Journal of Pediatrics 2002; 69:19–20.
3. Salaria M, Singh S, Dutta U, Sehgal S, Kumar L. Arthritis as the presenting feature of hypogammaglobulinemia. Indian Pediatrics 1998; 35:367–370.
4. Salaria M, Singh S, Kumar L. Reiter's Syndrome: A case report. Indian Pediatrics 1997; 34: 943–944.
5. Chaudhuri MK, Singh S, Kumar L. Poncet's Disease- Tuberculous rheumatism. Indian Journal of Pediatrics 1995; 62: 363–365.

JUVENILE RHEUMATOID ARTHRITIS (JRA)

The term JRA comprises a group of conditions characterized by chronic inflammatory changes of one or more joints. It cannot be overemphasized that JRA is a clinical diagnosis. The American College of Rheumatology (ACR) has defined it as arthritis of one or more joints with onset below the age of 16 years and persisting for at least 6 weeks, with explicit exclusion of other specific diseases such as juvenile ankylosing spondylitis (JAS), juvenile psoriatic arthritis (JPsA), arthritides associated with inflammatory bowed disease (AAIBD), infectious and postinfectious arthritis and other rheumatic diseases. The terminology used for childhood arthritides is somewhat confusing. For instance, the European League Against Rheumatism (EULAR) has suggested the use of the term 'Juvenile Chronic Arthritis' (JCA) in place of JRA, and the suggested cut-off for duration of arthritis is 3 months rather than 6 weeks as in JRA. Moreover, the EULAR definition does not exclude conditions like JAS, JPsA and AAIBD. The International League of Associations for Rheumatology (ILAR) has recently proposed the use of the term 'Juvenile Idiopathic Arthritis' and subdivided the group into seven different categories, but this classification is rather complex and more suited for research purposes rather than day to day clinical work. The ACR criteria, on the other hand, are 'user friendly' and easy to apply.

It must be clearly understood that JRA is, by no means, the pediatric counterpart of adult type of rheumatoid arthritis—the two conditions are quite distinct clinically and biologically.

JRA is not a rare disease—the estimated prevalence rates being in the range of 0.4–1.3 per 1000 children. It is the commonest rheumatological disorder of childhood and one of the most common causes of disability, chronic morbidity and school absenteeism in children. While the western studies suggest that JRA is more common in girls, in India the ratio appears to be almost equal.

Etiology

JRA is an autoimmune disease and the immune system is intimately involved in the evolution of the disease. There also appears to be a major histocompatibility complex (MHC) associated genetic predisposition. For instance, HLA DR5, DR6, DR8 and A2 are linked to early onset oligoarthritis (seen more in girls), B27 to late onset oligoarthritis (seen more in boys) and DR4, Dw4 and DR1 to rheumatoid factor positive polyarthritis. JRA does not appear to be a single disease entity and the different subtypes may, in fact, be representing separate clinical conditions.

The etiopathogenesis of JRA remains an enigma. Several environmental triggers (e.g. infection with rubella virus, parvovirus B19, *Mycobacterium tuberculosis*, *Mycoplasma pneumoniae* and enteric organisms; physical trauma; psychological stress) have been linked to the onset of JRA but the exact role that each has to play is not clear.

Complement activation and consumption probably play an important role in the initiation and perpetuation of the inflammatory response. Levels of circulating immune complexes (CICs) parallel the activity of the disease and systemic features. Such CICs have been found in the synovium and synovial fluid. T lymphocytes in the synovium have increased expression of activation markers (i.e. CD3+ IL-2R+). These are believed to secrete inflammatory cytokines like tumor necrosis factor-α (TNF-α) and interferon-γ (IFN-γ). The cytokine profile of the 3 types of JRA appears to be quite distinct – increased levels of IL-1α are associated with polyarthritis, TNFα and IL-1β with oligoarthritis and IL-6 with systemic onset disease.

A number of autoantibodies (for instance antinuclear, anti-smooth muscle) may be seen in the sera of children with JRA. The classical IgM rheumatoid factor (RF) is usually negative but it is believed that some children may have hidden RF (especially IgA) in the circulating immune complexes.

Clinical Features

Three major types of onset are described according to the presentation during the first 6 months of disease, viz. pauciarticular (4 or fewer joints involved), polyarticular (5 or more joints involved) and systemic (with fever and rash).

Pauciarticular Onset JRA

Pauciarticular onset is the most frequent type of JRA accounting for about 60% of patients. Four or fewer joints (usually large) are affected and the involvement is often asymmetrical. Joint swelling rather than joint pain is the usual complaint. Two subtypes are described:

Type I: More common in young girls, typically 3–5 years of age. The knees, ankles, and elbows are commonly affected. Small joints of the hands and feet are not involved. Asymptomatic, and potentially blinding, iridocylitis can be seen in 25% of patients by slit lamp examination. Secondary glaucoma and cataract may also occur.

Type II: More common in boys, typically older than 8 years. Large joints of lower extremities are commonly affected. Many children are HLA B27 positive and a proportion of these may go on to develop ankylosing spondylitis later as adults. However, sacroiliitis and spondylitis is usually not a significant complaint in the pediatric age. Self-limiting acute iritis may occur in some patients but it does not progress on to the chronic iridocyclitis seen in type I. A family history of ankylosing spondylitis, psoriasis, Reiter's disease and low back pain may be obtained in these children.

Polyarticular Onset JRA

It occurs in 30% of patients and is more common in girls. Five or more joints (both large and small) are affected within the first 6 months of onset of disease. Joint pain out of proportion to the degree of joint swelling is the usual complaint. Fever and malaise can be significant. Two subtypes are known:

Rheumatoid factor positive: Age at onset is late childhood or early adolescence. The arthritis is symmetrical, additive, severe and deforming and typically involves the small joints of the hand, especially the metacarpophalangeal and the first interphalangeal. Cervical spine and temporomandibular joints can also be affected. This subtype is the only category of JRA which is somewhat similar to the adult onset rheumatoid arthritis. Rheumatoid nodules are present in some patients and they represent the most severe forms of the disease.

Rheumatoid factor negative: This subtype may occur at any age in childhood. The knees, wrists and hips are the joints usually affected. Small joints of hands and feet are less commonly involved and rheumatoid nodules are not seen. Joint disease in this subtype of JRA is far less severe than that seen in rheumatoid factor positive polyarthritis category.

Systemic Onset JRA

About 10% of patients with JRA may have an acute onset of the disease with prominent systemic features. It may be noted that these systemic features may precede the joint manifestations by weeks or months and consequently this condition should be considered in the differential diagnosis of any child with prolonged fever. In infants and young children it may be a very difficult clinical diagnosis to arrive at, especially at the stage when joint symptoms are not clearly manifest. Systemic onset JRA can occur at any age and is slightly more common in boys. The illness usually begins as an intermittent fever rising up to 39–40°C with a characteristic twice daily peak. Fever is usually more prominent in the evening hours. Affected children have marked irritability which typically decreases with the subsidence of fever. Fever is accompanied by a characteristic evanescent maculopapular rash with central clearing. This rash may be seen anywhere on the body but is usually more prominent on the trunk. It can be very difficult to recognize in individuals with dark skin. Systemic involvement in the form of pericarditis and interstitial lung disease may be present. Hepatosplenomegaly and lymphadenopathy are common at presentation and can lead to diagnostic confusion. There is a moderate neutrophilic leukocytosis and elevated erythrocyte sedimentation rate. The rheumatoid factor is almost always negative.

Laboratory Investigations

From the pediatrician's point of view it is important that one learns to recognize the differing patterns of joint involvement in various types of JRA. This 'pattern recognition' is often the most important diagnostic clue. Laboratory investigations seldom help in arriving at a diagnosis. Synovial fluid aspiration for microscopy and culture is indicated in children with monoarthritis because septic arthritis may need to be excluded. It must, however, be noted that the joint aspirate in children with JRA would also show a predominantly polymorphonuclear response with low sugar and decreased complement—a picture not unlike that of septic arthritis.

Full blood counts should be ordered along with an erythrocyte sedimentation rate. Acute lymphocytic leukemia can sometimes have an arthritic presentation and such children may be mistakenly diagnosed as having JRA. Bone marrow aspiration must, therefore, be carried out (to exclude leukemia) if use of corticosteroids is being contemplated for treatment of JRA or else such patients may go into partial remission and further complicate therapeutic decision making.

C-reactive protein measurements are a surrogate marker of disease activity and are helpful on follow-up. Plain radiographs of affected joints are obtained at the time of initial diagnosis and may be repeated for assessment of erosive disease. It should be noted that screening for RF is not a useful test for diagnosis of childhood arthritis, but it is an important prognostic factor.

Treatment

Management of JRA involves many specialities. A good physiotherapy and occupational therapy team is required so that the therapy can be tailored to cater to the specific needs of an individual child. This would not only prevent development of deformities but would also facilitate 'mainstreaming' and rehabilitation. Physical therapy helps in relieving pain, enables maintenance of posture and joint mobility, improves muscle strength and prevents fixed flexion deformities.

All children with JRA must be assessed initially by an ophthalmologist so that uveitis can be detected early and treated appropriately. Children with pauciarticular onset JRA type I need regular follow-up with an ophthalmologist as uveitis can develop at any time. Some families find it very difficult to accept the long term implications of a diagnosis of JRA and need psychosocial support.

Medical Therapy

NSAIDs are the mainstay of symptomatic management. The conventional NSAIDs inhibit both isoforms of the enzyme cyclo-oxygenase, i.e. COX1 (which is constitutive and mediates physiologic prostaglandin production necessary for gastrointestinal mucosal integrity and adequacy of renal blood flow) and COX2 (which is inducible and mediates pathologic prostaglandin production especially at sites of inflammation). The NSAIDs commonly used in children are naproxen and ibuprofen. Indomethacin is believed to be of particular use in HLA B27 associated spondyloarthropathies. Doses of commonly used NSAIDs are given in Table 20.2.

Table 20.2: Doses of commonly used NSAIDs

	Dose (mg/kg/day)	*Maximum dose (mg/day)*	*Frequency of administration (hr)*
Naproxen	15–20	750	q12
Ibuprofen	35–45	2400	q6
Indomethacin	1–2	150	q8
Diclofenac	2–3	150	q6
Piroxicam	0.3–0.6	20	q24

The analgesic dose is usually half the anti-inflammatory dose

Development of Reye's syndrome is a distinct possibility while a child is receiving NSAIDs, especially if there is an intercurrent viral illness. All children with NSAIDs must be closely monitored for gastrointestinal side effects. The recently introduced selective COX2 inhibitor NSAIDs (e.g. rofecoxib, valdecoxib) may have lower gastrointestinal side-effects but these drugs are not recommended for use in children. Pseudoporphyria is a peculiar side effect of naproxen. Although the mechanism of action of all NSAIDs is the same, idiosyncratic responses are well known and a given child may respond to one NSAID and not to the other. Response to therapy is usually slow and this fact must be explained to the parents. Treatment must continue for at least 4–6 weeks before a decision to switch over to another NSAID is made.

Disease modifying anti-rheumatic drugs (DMARDs) need to be started in almost all children with polyarticular onset JRA. In the past a number of drugs (e.g. hydroxychloroquin, d-penicillamine and gold salts) were believed to have significant DMARD activity. However, controlled studies have failed to show a significant benefit as compared to placebo. Oral weekly methotrexate (15–25 mg/m^2/week) has revolutionized the management of severe forms of JRA. It is perhaps the only 'true' DMARD. It should be given empty stomach. The drug can be continued for years together if considered necessary. Children seem to tolerate methotrexate better than adults and also have fewer side effects. Once the child is in stable remission, the drug can be tapered off to the minimum effective dose and then gradually stopped. Methotrexate should, however, only be given under close medical supervision. Periodic testing of liver functions is mandatory while the child is on this drug. Development of hepatic fibrosis is a dreaded side-effect.

Intraarticular injections of corticosteroids (usually triamcinolone) are the preferred therapy for children with pauciarticular onset JRA. In addition, local ocular steroid instillation is done for associated iridocyclitis. Systemic corticosteroids (usually prednisolone 1–2 mg/kg/day) are necessary for severe unremitting arthritis, systemic manifestations (e.g. pericarditis, myocarditis, vasculitis) and rapidly progressive disease. Prednisolone, when used in this manner, is usually given as bridge therapy for a few weeks while awaiting the clinical response of DMARDs. A small minority of children, however, may require long-term steroids.

Newer modalities of treatment include therapies targeted against tumor necrosis factor (TNFα). These include use of a recombinant soluble TNF receptor p-75 fusion protein (etanercept) and a monoclonal antibody directed to TNF α (infliximab). Both of these are powerful biological agents and can be very effective in patients with arthritis which is non-responsive to more conventional therapy. Leflunomide, an inhibitor of pyrimidine synthesis, is a useful 'add-on' drug in adults with rheumatoid arthritis but experience in children is limited. Cyclosporin A is also a useful modality of therapy in difficult cases.

Course of Illness

Pauciarticular onset JRA type I usually has a good prognosis but asymmetric growth of limbs with localized deformities can be seen. Blindness due to progressive uveitis is a known but preventable complication. Children with pauciarticular JRA type II can develop spondylitis and sacroiliitis later in life, especially if they are HLA B27 positive.

Patients with seropositive polyarticular JRA have a disease pattern similar to adults with rheumatoid arthritis. The arthritis can be erosive and deforming, if not treated aggressively. Response to therapy, however, is not predictable. The prognosis is relatively better for seronegative polyarticular JRA as remissions are obtained more often and residual joint lesions may be minimal.

The course of systemic disease can be extremely variable and the response to therapy is not always satisfactory. Approximately 50% of patients with systemic disease undergo remission with minor residual joint involvement while others may develop progressive arthritis or have recurrent episodes of systemic disease. The presence of HLA-DR4 is usually associated with severe, persistent arthritis.

Inappropriately treated or untreated patients with JRA may develop flexion contractures of hips, knees and elbows resulting in permanent disability. Neck stiffness is an especially debilitating problem and can result in torticollis. Temporomandibular joint involvement results in restricted opening of the mouth and may require surgical intervention.

Complications

Anemia is almost always present in children with persistent active arthritis and serial hemoglobin levels mirror disease activity rather closely. For instance, a child with JRA having a hemoglobin level of 6–8 gm/dL can be assumed to be having long-standing active disease, while a child whose hemoglobin is above 10 gm/dL would usually be well controlled. Anemia is believed to be mainly due to chronic ongoing inflammation, but blood loss induced by NSAIDs can also be a contributory factor.

Chronic anterior uveitis may be clinically silent and potentially blinding. Girls below 6 years of age with pauciarticular onset JRA and who have antinuclear antibodies are at highest risk of developing this complication. Majority of children are completely asymptomatic and the condition can only be diagnosed by regular screening on slit lamp examination. Screening is warranted every 6 months for all patients with pauciarticular onset JRA type I. Children with other forms of JRA should be screened once at the time of initial diagnosis and annually thereafter. Treatment includes local instillation of steroids and mydriatrics.

Joint contractures result from pain associated with synovial inflammation, raised intraarticular pressure and muscle spasm. Joint replacement is required in children with deforming arthritis but this option can only be exercised after active growth has ceased.

Growth disturbances and limb length discrepancies are not unusual. There may be localized overgrowth (such as leg lengthening due to knee synovitis) or undergrowth (such as premature fusion of finger epiphyses). Generalized growth failure may occur secondary to severe inflammation or treatment with corticosteroids. Treatment with recombinant human growth hormone may be an option in children with severe growth disturbances.

20

Secondary amyloidosis is a rare but dreaded complication of JRA. It presents with asymptomatic proteinuria and hypoalbuminemia and is often irreversible. It is our policy to carry out screening for amyloidosis in all children with long-standing active JRA. This can be easily done on fine needle aspiration cytology from the abdominal fat pad. Methotrexate and chlorambucil have been used for treatment of secondary amyloidosis.

Suggested reading

1. Cassidy JT, Petty RE. Textbook of Pediatric Rheumatology, 5th edn. Elsevier Saunders, Philadelphia, 2005.
2. Singh S, Salaria M,Kumar L, Datta V, Sehgal S. Clinico-immunological profile of juvenile rheumatoid arthritis at Chandigarh. Indian Pediatrics 1999;36:449–454.
3. Jain V, Singh S, Sharma A. Keratoconjunctivitis sicca is not uncommon in children with juvenile rheumatoid arthritis. Rheumatology International 2001;20:159–62.
4. Goraya JS, Singh G, Singh S, Gill SS, Goyal A, Mitra SK, Kumar L. Arteriovenous malformation of knee masquerading as juvenile arthritis. Scandinavian Journal of Rheumatology 1998;27:313.
5. Beri A, Singh S, Gupta A, Khullar M. Comparison of serum nitric oxide levels in active juvenile rheumatoid arthritis with those of patients in remission. Rheumatology International 2004;24:264–266.

PSORIATIC ARTHRITIS

Arthritis may precede, accompany or follow the occurrence of psoriasis in children. Presence of a typical psoriatic rash comprises the major criterion for the diagnosis of juvenile psoriatic arthritis (JPsA), while nail pitting (onycholysis), family history of psoriasis (in first or second degree relatives), a psoriasis-like rash and dactylitis comprise the 4 minor criteria. Definite JPsA is diagnosed in the presence of arthritis and a typical psoriatic rash or arthritis with 3 of the 4 aforementioned minor criteria. Probable JPsA is diagnosed when there is arthritis with only 2 minor criteria.

LYME DISEASE

Lyme disease is characterized by recurrent episodes of fever, a characteristic macular annular rash (erythema migrans), joint symptoms (usually an asymmetric migratory arthritis of large joints typically with accompanying myositis) and involvement of the central nervous system (headache, aseptic meningitis, cranial nerve palsies). Ocular involvement in the form of uveitis and optic neuritis can also occur. Unlike adults, carditis is rare in children. In view of the multisystem involvement the clinical presentation can be very variable and one has to have a high index of suspicion. It has not been reported very frequently from our country but there is no reason to believe that it would be rare in India. It is caused by a tick (*Ixodes sp.*) borne spirochete (*Borrelia burgdorferi*). The diagnosis can be confirmed by direct tests such as culture (technically difficult, results may take many weeks), polymerase chain reaction (specificity low) and histochemistry on synovial tissue (interpretation requires experience) or by indirect serological tests such as ELISA (low specificity) or Western blotting (high specificity). According to the criteria given by the Centers for Disease Control and Prevention, a definitive diagnosis of Lyme disease can be made when there is erythema migrans (> 5 cm diameter) or any one of the typical clinical features (arthritis, meningitis, radiculoneuritis, mononeuritis, carditis) in the presence of specific antibodies. These criteria have, however, not been validated in children. It may be noted that all serological tests may be negative in the first few weeks of the illness and the treating physician may get virtually no help from the laboratory. Early disease can be treated with oral amoxycillin (50 mg/kg/day) while for disseminated disease or late cases parenteral ceftriaxone (100 mg/kg/day) is the drug of choice. Duration of therapy is 4 weeks. Children treated late or incompletely can have a smouldering chronic course often resistant to any form of therapy and resulting in considerable morbidity.

SYSTEMIC LUPUS ERYTHEMATOSUS (SLE)

SLE is an autoimmune disorder characterized by inflammation of blood vessels and connective tissues resulting in multisystemic involvement. The clinical manifestations can be extremely variable and the course unpredictable. Childhood SLE is usually more severe and has a poorer prognosis than adult SLE. The hallmark of SLE is the presence of antinuclear antibodies (ANA). The marked female predominance characteristic of adult SLE is usually not that apparent in young children.

Diagnosis

The diagnosis of SLE can be facilitated by the criteria given by American College of Rheumatology (ACR) in 1982. Presence of four of these criteria, either at presentation or sequentially, gives a sensitivity and specificity of 96% in adults. It must, however, be understood that SLE remains essentially a clinical diagnosis—the criteria only provide helpful guidelines for arriving at a diagnosis. In many patients (especially children), treatment may have to be started even when they do not fulfil the requisite number of criteria. The ACR criteria have never been prospectively validated in children. The revised 1997 version of the ACR criteria is given in Table 20.3.

Table 20.3: ACR 1997 criteria for classification of systemic lupus erythematosus

1. Malar rash
2. Discoid rash
3. Photosensitivity
4. Oral/nasal mucocutaneous ulcerations
5. Nonerosive arthritis
6. Nephritis (proteinuria > 0.5 g/day or cellular casts)
7. Encephalopathy (seizures or psychosis)
8. Pleuritis or pericarditis
9. Cytopenia
10. Positive immunoserology (antibodies to dsDNA/Sm nuclear antigen) or positive finding of antiphospholipid antibodies (IgG/IgM anticardiolipin antibodies or lupus anticoagulant or VDRL)
11. Positive antinuclear antibody test

The malar rash, which is virtually pathognomonic of SLE, may not be very apparent initially. It involves the cheek, bridge of nose and lower eyelids but spares the nasolabial folds. Discoid lesions are rare in childhood onset SLE. Oral ulcerations may involve the buccal mucosa or palate and are characteristically painless. Arthritis is usually mild and always non-erosive.

Renal involvement is a dreaded complication of SLE and one of the commonest causes of mortality in children. Lupus nephritis can be classified as follows:

Class I: Normal; *Class II:* Mesangial proliferation; *Class III:* Focal proliferative glomerulonephritis; *Class IV:* Diffuse proliferative glomerulonephritis; *Class V:* Membranous glomerulonephritis; *Class VI*: Glomerulosclerosis. Class III and Class IV lesions are associated with the poorest prognosis and require the most aggressive forms of therapy.

Neurological features may include psychosis, seizures and chorea. There may be no correlation between the severity of clinical involvement and findings on neuroimaging. Hematologic abnormalities may include a Coombs' positive hemolytic anemia, leukopenia, lymphopenia and thrombocytopenia. In addition, there may be coagulation abnormalities due to secondary antiphospholipid antibody syndrome. Cardiac manifestations may include a pericarditis, myocarditis, or a verrucous (Libman-Sacks) endocarditis.

Serology

Almost all patients with SLE have demonstrable ANA. Presence of anti-double-stranded DNA antibodies is highly specific of SLE. The titers of these antibodies usually correlate with disease activity. Anti-histone antibodies are characteristic of drug-induced lupus (e.g. following dilantin, isoniazid, hydralazine) but in such cases anti-ds DNA antibodies are usually absent and serum complement (C3) level is not decreased. Anti-Ro antibodies are believed to play a role in the development of congenital heart blocks characteristic of neonatal lupus syndromes. These heart blocks are permanent. Anti-Sm antibodies are believed to be a marker for CNS lupus.

Treatment

Glucocorticoids form the mainstay of therapy. Prednisolone is usually started in doses of 1–2 mg/kg/day and then gradually tapered according to disease activity. Arthritis usually responds to NSAIDs. Sunscreen lotions (with a sun protection factor of 15–20) must be prescribed for all such children and should be applied 3–4 times/day. These should be used even on cloudy days.

Life-threatening complications (e.g. Class IV lupus nephritis, mycocarditis, encephalopathy) may warrant use of intravenous pulses of methyl prednisolone or dexamethasone for 3–5 days, followed by oral prednisolone. Use of monthly pulses of intravenous cyclophosphamide (600–750 mg/m^2) has considerably improved the long-term outcome in children with severe forms of lupus nephritis. Once remission is achieved, the patient can be put on long-term maintenance azathioprine. Mycophenolate mofetil is being increasingly used for the therapy of severe forms of lupus nephritis in children.

For almost all patients with SLE, low dose prednisolone (e.g. 2.5–5 mg/day) has to be continued for many years. Once a child has been in stable remission for a 'reasonable' period of time, hydroxychloroquin (5–6 mg/kg/day) can be started and further tapering of steroids can be carried out under very careful supervision. Maintenance steroids should only be stopped after careful deliberation.

Infections must be treated aggressively with appropriate antimicrobials and the steroid dose hiked up during such episodes. With appropriate therapy, the long-term outlook of SLE in children now is quite encouraging.

Suggested reading

1. Cassidy JT, Petty RE. Textbook of Pediatric Rheumatology, 5th edn. Elsevier Saunders, Philadelphia, 2005.
2. Singh S, Devidayal, Minz R, Nada R, Joshi K. Childhood lupus nephritis: 12 years experience from North India. Rheumatol Int 2006; 26: 604–607.
3. Singh S, Devi Dayal, Kumar L, Joshi K. Mortality patterns in childhood lupus—10 years experience in a developing country. Clin Rheumatol 2002; 21: 462–65.
4. Singh S, Dayal D, Kumar L. Childhood SLE: A single center experience from a developing country. Lupus 2001, 10 (Suppl.): S82.

THE ANTIPHOSPHOLIPID ANTIBODY (APLA) SYNDROME

The APLA syndrome is a common accompaniment of systemic lupus erythematosus but can be seen in association with other rheumatological disorders as well. It was first described by Hughes and co-workers from London in the early eighties. The syndrome can, at times, arise *de novo* when it is known as primary APLA syndrome. It is a common cause of hypercoagulable states in children and can manifest with arterial and venous thrombosis, livedo reticularis and thrombocytopenia. The presentation can sometimes be catastrophic and may result in fatality. Laboratory diagnosis is based on the detection of anticardiolipin antibodies (IgM and IgG) and the lupus anticoagulant test. Treatment is with long term oral anticoagulation.

Suggested reading

1. Ahluwalia J, Singh S, Garewal G. Antiphospholipid antibodies in children with systemic lupus erythematosus: a prospective study from Northern India. Rheumatol Int 2005;25:530–535.
2. Khetarpal R, Goraya JS, Singh M, Singh S, Kumar L. Pulmonary hypertension as presenting feature of childhood SLE: Association with lupus anticoagulant. Scand J Rheumatol 1998, 26:325–326.

20

JUVENILE DERMATOMYOSITIS

Juvenile dermatomyositis (JDM) is a multisystem disease characterized by non-suppurative inflammation of striated muscle and skin and a systemic vasculopathy. Unlike adults, pure polymyositis (i.e. in absence of dermatological changes) is uncommon in children. The diagnosis can be made on the basis of criteria provided by Bohan and Peter:

1. Characteristic heliotrope discoloration over the upper eyelids
2. Symmetrical proximal muscle weakness
3. Elevated levels of muscle enzymes (AST, ALT, CK, aldolase)
4. Electromyographic evidence of myopathy
5. Muscle biopsy showing myonecrosis, myophagocytosis, and perifascicular atrophy.

A 'definite' diagnosis of JDM can be made if a child fulfils the first criterion along with any three of the remaining four; it is considered 'probable' if two of the four criteria are met and 'possible' if only one of the four criteria is met in addition to the first criterion. Other typical dermatological changes include Gottron's papules (collodion patches) over the dorsal aspects of metacarpophalangeal and interphalangeal joints of fingers (toes usually not involved), edema over eyelids, photosensitivity, a truncal rash and calcinosis. From the clinical point of view a child with characteristic dermatological findings along with proximal muscle weakness can be confidently diagnosed as having JDM and started on treatment irrespective of the biopsy findings. Magnetic resonance imaging (MRI) shows characteristic hyperintense signals on T2-weighted images suggestive of muscle edema and inflammation while the T1-weighted images may show fibrosis, atrophy and fatty infiltration. Typical findings on MRI may preclude the need for a muscle biopsy.

Treatment involves use of intravenous boluses of parenteral steroids (methylprednisolone 30 mg/kg/day or dexamethasone 5 mg/kg/day) for 3–5 days followed by oral prednisolone (1.5–2 mg/kg/day). Steroids are then gradually tapered depending on the clinical response. Oral weekly methotrexate (15–25 mg/m^2/week) is now increasingly being used as first-line therapy in combination with prednisolone. The usual duration of therapy is 18–24 months. Rapid tapering of steroids may result in disease relapse. The long-term prognosis is excellent.

Suggested reading

1. Cassidy JT, Petty RE. Textbook of Pediatric Rheumatology, 5th edn. Elsevier Saunders, Philadelphia, 2005.
2. Singh S, Bansal A. Twelve years experience of juvenile dermatomyositis in North India. Rheumatol Int 2006;26:510–515.
3. Verma S, Singh S, Bhalla AK, Khullar M. Study of subcutaneous fat in children with juvenile dermatomyositis. Arthritis Rheumatism 2006; 55: 564–568.

SCLERODERMA

The term scleroderma refers to 'hardening of the skin'. It can be classified as follows:

1. Systemic scleroderma (e.g. diffuse cutaneous, limited cutaneous)

2. Overlap syndromes
3. Localized scleroderma (e.g. morphea, linear scleroderma, eosinophilic fasciitis)
4. Chemically induced scleroderma (e.g. associated with polyvinyl chloride, pentazocine, bleomycin).
5. Pseudosclerodermas (e.g. phenylketonuria, scleredema, progeria and porphyria cutanea tarda).

Diffuse cutaneous systemic scleroderma is usually associated with widespread visceral involvement including the gastrointestinal tract, heart, lungs and kidneys. It is believed that fetomaternal graft-versus-host reactions are involved in the pathogenesis of this condition. Onset of disease is insidious and may be difficult to recognize in the initial stages. The child presents with skin tightening (edema, atrophy and acrosclerosis), Raynaud phenomenon (i.e. blanching, cyanosis and erythema), soft tissue contractures, arthralgias and myalgias, dysphagia (regurgitation, reflux, and aspiration), dyspnea (interstitial fibrosis, low diffusing capacity) and characteristic subcutaneous calcifications. In addition many children have abnormalities of nail fold capillaries which can be seen as capillary dropouts and dilated loops with a magnifying glass or the +40 lens of the ophthalmoscope. Onset of hypertension and proteinuria usually indicate renal involvement and should be a cause for serious concern.

Systemic scleroderma is rare in children but can result in severe disability. Investigations show presence of antinuclear antibodies (with the characteristic nucleolar pattern on immunofluorescence) and antibodies to Scl-70 (DNA-topoisomerase 1) or centromere. No form of drug therapy has been found to be curative. Penicillamine and colchicine can produce beneficial results in some patients, especially if used early in the course of disease. Pulse dexamethasone therapy has also been shown to be effective. Monthly pulses of intravenous cyclophosphamide (followed by maintenance daily azathioprine or weekly methotrexate) can be life-saving in patients with interstitial lung disease. Nifedipine is useful for management of Raynaud phenomenon while enalapril can result in control of blood pressure and stablization of renal function. The latter is also the drug of choice for scleroderma renal crises. With appropriate management, 10-year survival rates of up to 90% have been reported in children.

Scleredema is a benign, self-limiting condition characterized by non-pitting indurated edema over face, neck, shoulders and chest but always excluding the hands and feet.

Suggested reading

1. Cassidy JT, Petty RE. Textbook of Pediatric Rheumatology, 5th edn. Elsevier Saunders, Philadelphia, 2005.
2. Dayal D, Singh S, Kumar L, Radotra BD. Disabling pansclerotic morphea of childhood and hypogammaglobulinemia: A curious association. Rheumatol Int 2002, 21 :158–60.
3. Dayal D, Singh S, Radotra BD, Kumar L. Scleredema of Buschke : a clinical series of 5 patients. APLAR J Rheumatol 2001, 4:175–77.

MIXED CONNECTIVE TISSUE DISEASE (MCTD)

MCTD is a multisystemic overlap syndrome characterized by features of rheumatoid arthritis, systemic scleroderma, SLE and dermatomyositis occurring in conjunction with high titers of anti-ribonucleoprotein (RNP) antibodies (specific for U1 RNP). Nephritis is usually less common and less severe than in SLE. Many children show good response to low-dose glucocorticoids and NSAIDs. Oral weekly methotrexate is also a useful therapeutic option. Treatment must be individualized and should focus on the particular disease component which is predominating in a given child.

VASCULITIDES

The vasculitides can be best classified according to the size of the vessel involved as follows:

1. Large vessel (i.e. aorta and major branches) vasculitis, e.g. Takayasu arteritis, giant cell arteritis.
2. Medium vessel (i.e. coronary, renal, hepatic, mesenteric) vasculitis, e.g. Kawasaki disease, polyarteritis nodosa
3. Small vessel (i.e. arterioles, capillaries, venules) vasculitis, e.g. Henoch-Schönlein purpura, Wegener's granulomatosis, microscopic polyangiitis, Churg-Strauss syndrome, cutaneous leukocytoclastic angiitis.

Suggested reading

1. Ozen S, Ruperto N, Dillon MJ, Bagga A, Kamorz K, Davin JC et al. EULAR/PreS endorsed consensus criteria for the classification of childhood vasculitis. Annals Rheum Dis 2006, 65: 936–941.
2. Singh S, Das R. Clinical approach to vasculitis in children. Indian J of Pediatr 2002;69: 27–34.

Takayasu Arteritis

This is characterized by a segmental inflammatory panarteritis resulting in stenosis and aneurysms of aorta and its major branches causing weak arterial pulses. It is believed to be the commonest cause of renovascular hypertension in India. It is classified according to the site of involvement: *Type I*-aortic arch; *Type II*-descending aorta; *Type III*-aortic arch and descending aorta; *Type IV*-aorta and pulmonary artery involvement. Many children with Takayasu arteritis show a strongly positive Mantoux reaction. The classification criteria for childhood Takayasu arteritis are given in Table 20.4.

Table 20.4: Classification criteria for Takayasu arteritis

Table 20.4: Classification criteria for Takayasu arteritis
Angiographic abnormalities (conventional, CT or MR) of the aorta or its main branches
plus
at least one of the following four features:
1. Decreased peripheral artery pulse(s) and/or claudication of extremities.
2. Blood pressure difference >10 mmHg
3. Bruits over aorta and/or its major branches
4. Hypertension (based on childhood normative data)

20

Diagnosis is confirmed by angiography. Treatment involves long-term immunosuppression with prednisolone and methotrexate (used in weekly doses). Angioplasty procedures are now being increasingly performed even in small children and have shown promising results. Cyclophosphamide or azathioprine may be required in children who fail to show an adequate response to steroids. Hypertension must be managed appropriately. The 5 year survival rates are more than 90%.

Suggested reading

1. Singh S, Bali HK, Salaria M, Lal S, Pandav SS, Kumar L. Takayasu's arteritis in young children—a potentially treatable condition. Indian Pediatr 1999, 36:291–296.
2. Jain S, Sharma N, Singh S, Bali HK, Kumar L, Sharma BK. Takayasu arteritis in children and young Indians. Int J Cardiol 2000, 75 (S) : 153–57
3. Kakkar N, Vasishta RK, Banerjee AK, Singh S, Kumar L. Pulmonary capillary hemangiomatosis as a cause of pulmonary hypertension in Takayasu's aortoarteritis. Respiration 1997, 64:381–383.

Kawasaki Disease (KD)

KD is an acute febrile mucocutaneous lymph node syndrome mainly affecting infants and young children. More than 80% of cases are seen in children below 5 years of age. It is perhaps the commonest vasculitic disorder of childhood and has replaced acute rheumatic fever as the leading cause of acquired heart disease in children in many countries. KD has been reported from all parts of the world. In Japan alone, more than 5000 new cases are reported and treated every year. In India, this condition is now being increasingly recognized but the vast majority of patients still continue to remain undiagnosed probably because of lack of awareness amongst pediatricians and physicians treating children.

It is important to remember that the diagnosis of KD is based entirely on the recognition of a temporal sequence of characteristic clinical findings and that there is no specific laboratory test. The diagnostic criteria for KD are as follows:

A. Fever lasting for at least 5 days

B. Presence of 4 of the following 5 conditions:
   1. Bilateral non-purulent conjunctival injection
   2. Changes of mucosae of oropharynx (e.g. injected pharynx, injected lips, strawberry tongue)
   3. Changes of peripheral extremities (e.g. edema/erythema of hands/feet in acute stage; desquamation, which usually begins periungually, in convalescent stage)
   4. Polymorphous rash
   5. Cervical lymphadenopathy (at least 1 node > 1.5 cm)

C. Illness not explained by any other known disease process.

20

It should be noted that the above clinical features evolve sequentially over a period of few days and all need not be present at one particular point of time. This partly explains the difficulty that the clinician experiences in arriving at a correct diagnosis of KD. Most children have high grade fever and are extremely irritable. In fact, it is this irritability which often provides the first clinical clue to the diagnosis. KD must be considered in the differential diagnosis of all children below 5 years of age who have fever without apparent focus lasting more than 5 days.

The basic lesion is a necrotizing vasculitis of medium-sized muscular arteries (especially coronaries), which may result in aneurysms, dilatations, and stenoses in untreated patients.

Treatment involves use of a single dose of intravenous immunoglobulin (2 g/kg) and aspirin in anti-inflammatory doses (75–80 mg/kg) till the child becomes afebrile. Low dose aspirin (3–5 mg/kg/day) is then continued for a few weeks for its antiplatelet activity. In appropriately treated children, the long-term prognosis is excellent with less than 1% patients developing coronary artery abnormalities as compared to 20–30% in the untreated category.

Suggested reading

1. Singh S. Kawasaki disease: A clinical dilemma. Indian Pediatr 1999, 36:871–875.
2. Singh S, Bansal A, Gupta A, Kumar RM, Mittal BR. Kawasaki disease—a decade of experience from North India. Int Heart J 2005, 46:679–689.
3. Singh S, Gupta MK, Bansal A, Kumar RM, Mittal BR. A comparison of the clinical profile of Kawasaki disease in children from Northern India above and below 5 years of age. Clin Exper Rheumatol 2007;25:654–657.
4. Mitra A, Singh S, Devidayal, Khullar M. Serum lipids in North Indian children treated for Kawasaki disease. Int Heart J 2005;46:811–817.
5. Kushner HI, Macnee R, Burns JC. Impressions of Kawasaki syndrome in India. Indian Pediatr 2006;43:939–942.

Polyarteritis Nodosa (PAN)

PAN is rare in childhood. The clinical manifestations can be variable because of multisystemic involvement and include fever, hypertension, abdominal pain, arthritis, myalgia, skin involvement (especially livedo reticularis), CNS involvement (seizures, encephalopathy) and peripheral neuropathy. Pathological diagnosis consists of demonstration of fibrinoid necrosis in medium-sized arteries with segmental involvement and a predilection for bifurcation of vessels. On angiography, aneurysms may be demonstrable in the renal arteries or celiac axis. The diagnostic criteria for childhood PAN have been recently revised (Table 20.5). Treatment consists of long-term immunosuppression with prednisolone and cyclophosphamide.

Suggested reading

1. Kumar L, Sarkar B, Singh S, Bajwa RPS, Joshi K, Malik N. Polyarteritis nodosa—a few unusual findings. Indian Pediatr 1996;33:459–464.
2. Sood M, Singh S, Khandelwal N, Kumar L. Bilateral sudden loss of vision: An unusual presentation of childhood polyarteritis nodosa. APLAR J Rheumatol 2001; 4:187–89.

Table 20.5: Classification criteria for childhood polyarteritis nodosa

Illness characterized by the presence of either a biopsy showing small and mid-size artery necrotizing vasculitis or angiographic abnormalities[#] (aneurysms or occlusions)

plus

at least 2 of the following:

1. Skin involvement
2. Myalgia or muscle tenderness
3. Systemic hypertension (based on childhood normative data)
4. Abnormal urine analysis and/or impaired renal function
5. Mononeuropathy or polyneuropathy
6. Testicular pain or tenderness
7. Signs or symptoms suggesting vasculitis of any other major organ systems (gastrointestinal, cardiac, pulmonary or central nervous system)

Should include conventional angiography if magnetic resonance angiography is negative

Henoch-Schönlein Purpura

Henoch-Schönlein purpura (HSP) is one of the most common vasculitides of childhood and is characterized by the presence of a non-thrombocytopenic (and usually palpable) purpura, a transient arthralgia (occasionally arthritis) and abdominal symptoms. The criteria for diagnosis of childhood HSP are given in Table 20.6.

The illness begins with a purpuric rash more prominent over the extensor aspects of lower extremities and buttocks. It may be macular, maculopapular or even urticarial to begin with and can be difficult to diagnose in the first few days of the illness. Glomerulonephritis is seen in approximately half of the patients but only 10–20% of these have azotemia or nephrotic range proteinuria. Clinically, it may manifest as isolated hematuria, hypertension or a nephritic/nephrotic syndrome. This is the only long-term complication of HSP. Significant renal involvement is uncommon in children below 6 years of age. Gastrointestinal manifestations usually occur in the first 7–10 days of the illness. Affected children may be erroneously diagnosed as having a 'surgical abdomen' and even subjected to unnecessary surgery. Abdominal pain is usually intermittent, colicky and periumbilical.

Table 20.6: Classification criteria for Henoch-Schönlein purpura

Palpable purpura in the presence of at least one of the following 4 features:

1. Diffuse abdominal pain
2. Any biopsy showing predominant IgA deposition
3. Arthritis or arthralgia
4. Renal involvement (any hematuria and/or proteinuria)

Vomiting occurs in about 60% of patients but hematemesis and melena are relatively less common.

Most clinical features are self-limiting and resolve in a few days. Rare manifestations of HSP include CNS vasculitis, coma, Guillain-Barre syndrome, pulmonary hemorrhage, carditis and orchitis.

Laboratory Investigations

HSP is a clinical diagnosis and none of the laboratory features are pathognomonic. There may be a non-specific increase in total serum IgA levels. Many children may have microscopic hematuria and proteinuria. Skin biopsy from the involved sites may show the characteristic leukocytoclastic vasculitis but this is not pathognomonic of HSP. On indirect immunofluorescence there are deposits of IgA and C3 in skin as well as renal biopsies. Ultrasound examination may need to be repeated at frequent intervals for evolving abdominal findings.

Treatment

Management is generally supportive with maintenance of hydration and pain relief. Prednisolone (1–1.5 mg/kg/day) is often given in children with gastrointestinal involvement and is usually continued for 2–3 weeks depending on the clinical response. There is, however, no clear evidence that steroids alter the natural course of the disease.

HSP nephritis is a sinister complication and can result in chronic renal failure if not managed appropriately. There is evidence to suggest that long-term treatment with prednisolone and azathioprine can result in prolonged remissions.

Prognosis

The disease usually runs its entire course in 4 weeks and majority of the children have no permanent sequelae even when the short-term morbidity is quite significant. Children older than 6 years with significant renal involvement (especially children with rapidly progressive glomerulonephritis and fibrous crescents) need to be followed up and the long-term prognosis is guarded. Overall 1–5% of children with HSP nephritis progress to end-stage renal disease.

Suggested reading

1. Kumar L, Singh S, Goraya JS, Uppal B, Kakkar S, Walker R, Sehgal S. Henoch-Schönlein purpura—the Chandigarh experience. Indian Pediatr 1997;35:19–25.
3. Singh S, Dayal D, Minz RW, Joshi K, Datta U, Kumar L. Severe Henoch-Schönlein nephritis: Treatment with azathioprine and steroids. Rheumatol Int 2002, 22:133–137.
4. Goraya JS, Singh S, Kumar L. Acute abdomen in Henoch-Schonlein purpura: A surgical dilemma. APLAR J Rheumatol 2000;4:79–80.

Wegener's Granulomatosis (WG)

WG is rare in children. It is characterized by a necrotizing granulomatous angiitis affecting the respiratory tract and kidneys. Constitutional symptoms are quite common. Presence of anti-neutrophil cytoplasmic antibodies (ANCAs), especially c-ANCA, are virtually pathognomonic of WG. The diagnostic criteria for childhood Wegener's granulomatosis are given in Table 20.7. With steroids and cyclophosphamide, the long-term outlook is excellent.

Table 20.7: Classification criteria for childhood Wegener's granulomatosis
Three of the following six features should be present:
1. Abnormal urinalysis
2. Granulomatous inflammation on biopsy
3. Nasal sinus inflammation
4. Subglottic, tracheal or endobronchial stenosis
5. Abnormal chest X-ray or CT scan
6. Positive c-ANCA staining

Behcet's Disease

This is an extremely uncommon vasculitic disorder. The clinical manifestations can be quite variable. These may be classified as:

1. **Major:** Aphthous stomatitis, genital ulceration, cutaneous manifestations and ocular disease.
2. **Minor:** Gastrointestinal disease, thrombophlebitis, arthritis, family history and neurological involvement.

Behcet's disease is characterized by multiple relapses with the ocular and neurological manifestations resulting in significant disability. Many patients show a positive pathergy test (cutaneous pustular reaction following needle pricks). HLA B5 and B51 haplotypes have been associated with this syndrome. Drug therapy involves use of colchicine and thalidomide. Methotrexate and chlorambucil have also been used.

21 Genetic Disorders

PHYSIOLOGICAL CONSIDERATIONS

The pattern of inheritance is determined by the genetic material in the nuclei of cells, which is distributed into 23 pairs of chromosomes. The two members of 22 pairs of chromosomes are apparently alike (or homologous) in both sexes. These are called autosomes. The 23rd pair of chromosomes is homologous only in females with two X chromosomes. In the male the 23rd pair of chromosomes has one X chromosome, and a much smaller Y chromosome. These are called sex chromosomes.

Chromosomes are the agents for inheritance of characteristics and these are derived from both parents in equal number. In the germ cells of both sexes, the cell division is not of the usual mitotic variety, but is a reduction division or meiosis. The cells which are obtained after meiosis have only one representative of each pair of chromosomes, so that in human beings they have only 23 chromosomes. In the course of meiosis, not only is the number of chromosomes halved, there is also some exchange of genetic material between the two members of a pair. This phenomenon is called crossover. Some of these cells (having half the usual quota of chromosomes) form gametes.

The female gamete (ovum) has 22 autosomes and one X chromosome, while the male gamete (sperm) can have two types of chromosomal pattern, 22 + X or 22 + Y. The fertilization of an ovum by an X-bearing sperm will result in a female offspring and by a Y-bearing sperm will result in a male offspring. Since the progeny inherits half their chromosomes from the father and half from the mother, they have some characteristics of both. Since the parents had also inherited their chromosomes in the same way, and so did their parents, and so on, the chromosomes of an individual have the entire ancestral history inscribed on them. The segregation of chromosome pairs at meiosis is a random process and occurs independently for each pair.

The portion of a chromosome which codes for a 'character' is called a gene. The position of a gene on a chromosome is called its locus. Corresponding loci on the two members of a pair carry genes for the same character. The character coded by the two chromosomes may have different forms. For instance, one of them may code for black iris, and another for blue iris. Such alternative forms of a gene are known as alleles. If the alleles code for the same forms, these are said to be present in the homozygous state; if they code for different traits, they are in heterozygous state. If an allele clinically manifests itself even in the heterozygous state, it is called a dominant gene or character. Its alternate form or allele which does not express itself clinically when the other allele from the other parent is normal is called a recessive gene. Recessive genes will manifest features of the disease only when present on both chromosomes in the pair (homozygous state) or when the specific abnormal gene is inherited from both parents. Therefore, clinically manifest characters of an individual may not always indicate his or her genetic constitution since recessive alleles are masked in the heterozygous state. The genetic make up of a person is called the genotype, and the clinically manifest characters are known as the phenotype.

Sometimes a gene may express itself in several slightly modified forms without adverse effect on the health of the individual. This is referred to as genetic polymorphism.

From Chromosomes to Characters

Chemically, the chromosomes are made up of deoxyribonucleic acid (DNA) and histones. Only about 3% of DNA in the human genome symbolizes genes. About 93% has apparently no clear cut function and is flippantly termed as "junk DNA". Many copies of the latter type of DNA are scattered at random over the chromosomes intermingled with genes. These are called repetitive sequences. These are useful for fingerprinting of the human genome. There are about 30,000 genes in the human beings. Roughly 20% of these are specific genes which regulate the production of structural or functional proteins. About 80% genes are housekeeping genes responsible for basic cell functioning. Highly related genes are clustered in a particular region of chromosomes. DNA determines the type of messenger ribonucleic acid (mRNA) that is synthesized by a cell; mRNA is responsible for the type of protein manufactured by the cell. The proteins that are manufactured may be structural proteins or enzymes. Together these determine how the cell looks and what it does. The characteristics of individual cells collectively make up the characteristics of the whole organism.

MOLECULAR GENETICS

Our understanding of molecular genetics has tremendously advanced because of development of new techniques. It is now possible to cleave DNA at specific points by restriction endonucleases derived from bacteria. DNA probes can be made to detect specific base sequences in the DNA. Southern blotting technique helps in identification of small fragments of DNA obtained after the action of application of restriction endonucleases followed by initial separation on agarose gel electrophoresis and subsequent transfer to a nitrocellulose paper filter (NCP). The most fascinating advance in molecular genetics is the ability to form large number of copies of DNA sequences in a short time. This amplification of genetic material is now possible with polymerase chain reaction (PCR). In PCR, the double stranded DNA fragment is first denatured by heating resulting in two single strands of DNA. These are annealed by a synthetic primer. Then the enzyme, a DNA polymerase, supplied along with nucleotides, starts to extend the primer. The primer is extended along the length of the DNA fragment of interest, thereby duplicating it. This process (denaturation/annealing/extension) is repeated several times resulting in a million copies of DNA sequence. There are many more molecular genetic techniques available, like high throughput PCR and microarray techniques through which thousands of samples can be analyzed in a very short time.

The Human Genome Project

The Human Genome Project (HGP) began formally in 1990 and is a 13 year effort coordinated by the US Department of Energy and the National Institute of Health (NIH). It finalized almost two years earlier than expected. It was an enormous task as the aim was to sequence 3 billion base pairs and identify approximately 30,000 genes.

The genome is defined as the total genetic material contained within the chromosomes of an organism. It can be said to be the total genetic information which is carried by the DNA. **Transcriptome** is the transcribed messenger RNA (mRNA) complement and the **Proteome** is the translated protein constitution.

Impact on Human Disease and Clinical Practice

Isolation of disease genes: Many genes are known to cause human diseases when mutated, but there are others which may have an indirect influence. The major effort of modern molecular medicine is to identify association of genes with human diseases.

Isolation of diseased genes can be done by two major strategies : functional cloning and positional cloning. In functional cloning there is knowledge about the function of the gene product (protein) and the identification of gene follows. In positional cloning identification of the gene follows the establishment of its position on the genome. The various markers identified all over the genome on different chromosomes help in gene identification. Positional cloning is used in majority of disorders as the function of gene products is seldom known. The isolation of the gene is followed by identification of disease causing mutations.

Comparative biology of humans and other organisms: Study of comparative biology was a major component of HGP. It helps in developing strategies, techniques and infrastructure for studying human DNA. This is based on the fundamental knowledge that all organisms are related and share same general type of DNA blueprint and there is significant conservation. This approach helps in understanding gene structure and function.

Advances in molecular diagnostics: Molecular diagnostics have tremendous scope and usefulness in clinical practice. The disorders which can be tested are of wide range which include hereditary, neoplastic and infectious diseases. The HGP has and will help in development of molecular diagnostics in two major ways. Firstly by identification of disease genes and disease causing mutations and secondly use of wider range of more refined technologies in clinical practice. PCR is being extensively used in clinical practice already. With the availability of high-throughput PCR testing hundreds/thousands of PCRs can be performed in a day. An important discovery is this area is DNA chips or micro arrays.

Therapeutic benefits: The therapeutic benefits encompass pre-symptomatic diagnosis and use of preventive measures (like lifestyle alterations and surveillances), prenatal diagnosis in lethal or chronic disabling disorders and actual therapeutics. The therapeutic advances would include gene therapy, development of better pharmacological agents. An interesting area in pharmacogenomics is studying the genetic basis of drug responsiveness and resistance.

Ethical, legal and social implications: There are various issues which need serious thought and discussion. Some of the important ones are as follows:

i. Who should have access to this data
ii. Use of genetic information to discriminate people, like carriers being stigmatized or health insurance being denied asymptomatic persons.
iii. Pre-symptomatic diagnosis and susceptibility to disease (e.g. late onset neurological disorders and malignancy predisposition).
iv. Misuse in prenatal testing.
v. Interpretation of tests and pre and post test counseling issues.

GENETICS AND DISEASE

Most disease have a probable genetic and an environmental basis. The genetic component may be the major or the only factor leading to manifestation of the disease, or it may merely predispose the individual to get a disease in response to environmental stresses. Different diseases can be considered to be at different regions of the spectrum between the genetic and environmental reasons in causation of the disease. Thus, based on genetic mechanism, the disease may be one of five types: (i) chromosomal disorders, (ii) single gene disorders, (iii) polygenic disorders, (iv) mitochondrial disorders and (v) somatic cell (genetic) disorders.

CHROMOSOMAL DISORDERS

Mechanisms of Chromosomal Anomalies

Chromosomes contain a large number of genes. Loss or gain of a whole chromosome due to abnormalities in cell division may cause such profound disturbances in the genetic constitution of the fetus that it may affect its survival and the fetus may be aborted. If the fetus is born alive it may die soon after birth. Even if the disturbances are not lethal, the sufferer may be malformed, mentally retarded or infertile. At times, only a part of the chromosome may be deleted or lost, causing less severe genetic disturbances. Generally speaking, loss of a whole chromosome except that of one X chromosome (as in Turner syndrome) is lethal. Surveys in still-born or abortuses (aborted fetuses) have shown large proportion of chromosomal anomalies. Of all live newborns, 0.5% may have a chromosomal anomaly.

Each chromosome has a short arm (p) and a long arm (q) joined by a centromere. Chromosomes are numbered based on their size and position of the centromere (Fig. 21.1).

Chromosomal abnormalities are generally sporadic and therefore, the risk of their recurrence in the offsprings is low (except in situation when either parent is a balanced translocation carrier). There are two types of chromosomal abnormalities—numerical (aneuploidies) and structural. There are several mechanisms which lead to chromosomal abnormalities.

Inversion

One or two breaks may occur along the length of the chromosome arm. The broken pieces may rearrange themselves in a new way. If there is no loss or gain of

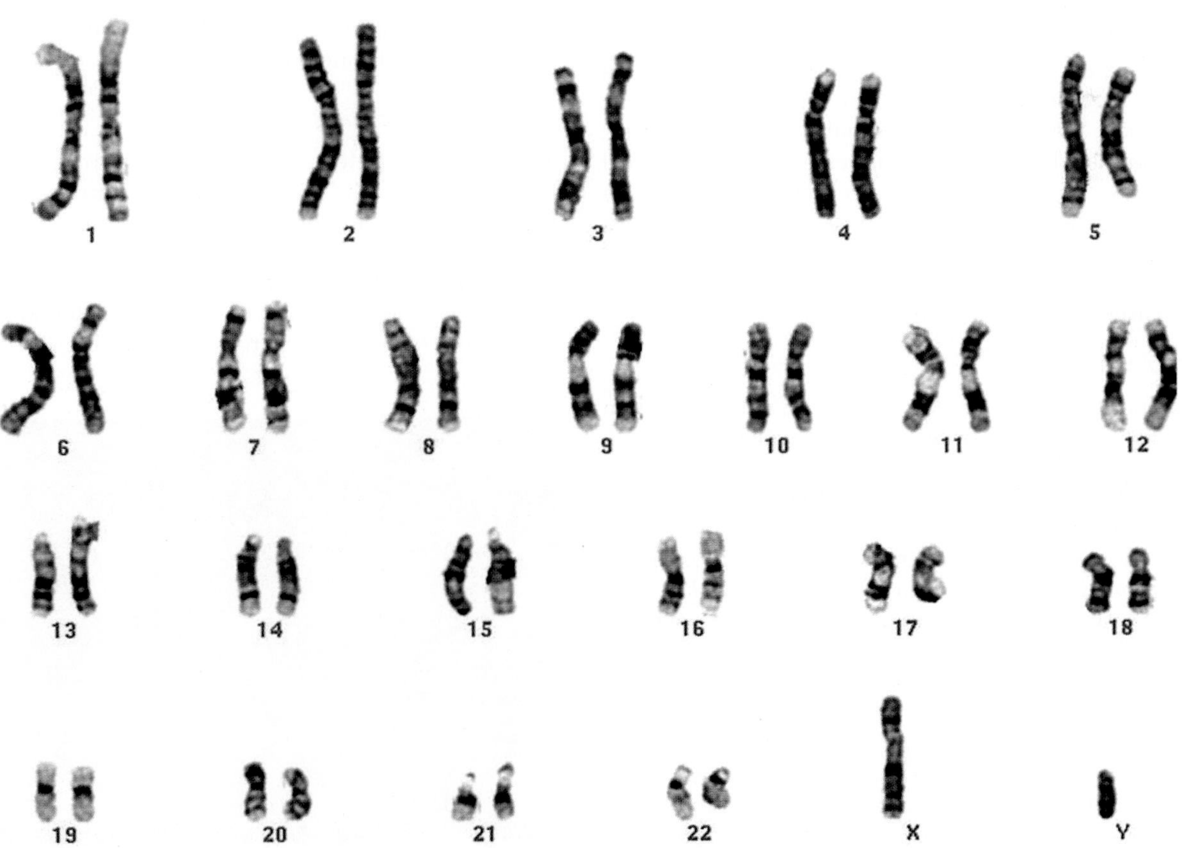

Fig. 21.1: Conventional G banded karyotype

genetic material, there may be no significant clinical manifestations. Break point is important if it disrupts a vital gene.

Isochromosome

During mitotic cell division, the chromosome divides longitudinally. Rarely it may divide transversely across the centromere. Half of the chromosome replicates to form its complement. Thus instead of normal chromosomes, two new types of chromosomes are formed—one having both the long arms and the other with both the short arms. These are known as isochromosomes. Each isochromosome thus has excess of some genetic material and deficiency of some other genetic material, e.g. in some cases of Turner syndrome.

Anaphase Lag

In the first meiotic division, the chromosomes are arranged in pairs in the equatorial plane during the metaphase. During anaphase if one of the chromosomes is slow in its migration, it might be excluded and thus be lost.

Nondisjunction

During the first meiotic division, both members of a pair of chromosomes may move jointly during anaphase to either of the daughter cells. Thus, whereas one daughter cell may have both members of a pair of chromosomes; i.e. 22 + 2 or 24 chromosomes, the other cell may have only 22 chromosomes without any representation of the erring pair. When such gametes mate with other gametes with normal chromosomal complement, the zygote will either have 47 or 45 chromosomes. Nondisjunction leads to aneuploidies. Common aneuploidies seen in live born babies include Down syndrome (Trisomy 21), Edward Syndrome (Trisomy 18), Patau syndrome (Trisomy 13) and Turner syndrome (monosomy X).

Mosaicism

If the nondisjunction occurs in the first mitotic division instead of meiosis, of the two new cells which are formed, one has 47 chromosomes and the other cell has 45 chromosomes. The error is perpetuated by repeated mitotic divisions. Thus, two cell lines with 47 and 45 chromosomes are observed in the same individual. If the nondisjunction occurs after a few mitotic division have already occurred, more than two cell lines may be observed, some with normal and the others with abnormal complement of chromosomes.

Translocation

A chromosome or a segment of a chromosome may break off from the parent chromosome and be joined to another chromosome. This phenomenon is called translocation. Thus one chromosome may appear shortened in this process, no loss or gain of the genetic material occurs, the translocation is balanced and the person is phenotypically normal. Translocated chromosome may be transmitted to either gamete during meiosis and when it mates with normal gamete, the resulting zygote may either have excess or deficiency of the genetic material. Such an offspring is abnormal. Viability of such zygotes would depend on the essentiality of the genes carried on translocated portion of the chromosome.

Deletion

A segment of chromosome may break off and be lost. Loss of a portion of chromosomal material large enough to be seen by light microscope is often lethal or poorly tolerated. Submicroscopic deletions are detected on special chromosomal staining or fluorescent in situ hybridization (FISH) (Fig. 21.2). DNA probes have been developed that make it possible for FISH to be used for diagnosis. Gene deletion syndromes are characterized by loss of a cluster of genes, giving rise to a consistent pattern of congenital anomalies and developmental problems. Examples of these are William syndrome (7 q 11.23); retinoblastoma with mental retardation and dysmorphic facies (13 q 14.1); Prader Willi syndrome (hypotonia, mental retardation and obesity, 15q 11); Rubinstein - Taybi syndrome (microcephaly, broad thumbs and big toes, dysmorphism and mental retardation, 16 q 13); and DiGeorge syndrome (congenital heart defect, hypoplasia of parathyroid and thymus, facial anomalies, palate anomalies, 22 q 11).

Genomic Imprinting

Maternal and paternal sets of genes are not always functionally equal. Some genes are preferentially expressed from maternal or paternal side. Example: Prader-Willi syndrome (microdeletion on paternal side or inheritance of both copies from maternal side) and Angelman syndrome (microdeletion on maternal side or inheritance of both copies from paternal side).

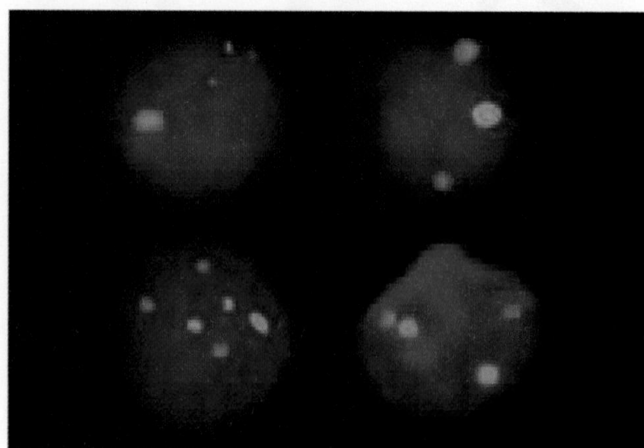

Fig. 21.2: Fluorescent signals on FISH testing. Reduction or increased number of signals indicates aneuploidy

Down Syndrome

This is the most common chromosomal disorder occurring with a frequency of 1:800 to 1:1000 newborns. Chromosome number 21 is present in triplicate, the origin of the extra chromosome 21 being either maternal or paternal. In most cases the extra chromosome is from the mother. Down syndrome occurs more often in offspring of mothers conceiving at older age; the risk in the newborn is 1:1550 if maternal age is between 15 and 29 years, 1:800 at 30–34 years, 1:270 at 35 to 39 years, 1:100 at 40 to 44 years and 1:50 after 45 years. This is attributed to the exposure of the maternal oocyte to harmful environmental influences for a longer period since graffian follicles are present in the fetal life and exist through female reproductive life. The sperm has a short life span and has therefore less chances of an injurious exposure.

Cytogenetics

Regular trisomy is found in about 94% cases of Down syndrome. Approximately 1% of cases are mosaic and the rest (5%) are due to translocations, most commonly involving chromosomes 21 and 14. Karyotype of the parents is only required if the affected child has translocation Down syndrome.

Clinical Features and Diagnostic Considerations

Patients with Down syndrome have mental and physical retardation, flat facies, an upward slant of eyes and epicanthal folds. Oblique palpebral fissure is obvious only when the eyes are open. The nose is small with flat nasal bridge. Mouth shows a narrow short palate with small teeth and furrowed protruding tongue. There is significant hypotonia. The skull appears small, brachycephalic with flat occiput. Ears are small and dysplastic. There is a characteristic facial grimace on crying. Hands are short and broad. Clinodactyly (hypoplasia of middle phalanx with a single flexion crease of 5th finger) and simian crease are usual. There is a wide gap between the first and the second toe (sandle gap). Figures 21.3A and B show characteristic facial features.

Other Abnormalities

Congenital heart disease (CHD): About 40% children with Down syndrome have CHD. Endocardial cushion defects account for about 40–60% cases. Presence of CHD is the most significant factor in determining survival. All children with Down syndrome should have a cardiac evaluation before 9 months of age and it should ideally include an ECHO.

Gastrointestinal malformations: Atresias are present in around 12% of cases, especially duodenal atresia. There is an increased risk of Hirschsprung disease.

Eye problems: There is an increased risk of cataract, nystagmus, squint, and abnormalities of visual acuity. Routine evaluation in first year (or earlier if indicated) and then every year is recommended.

Hearing defects: 40–60% patients have conductive hearing loss and are prone to serous otitis media (50–70% during first year). Routine evaluation in first year and then every year is advisable. Audiological evaluation at least once between 5–13 years and then every year is recommended.

Thyroid dysfunction: About 13–54% of children with Down syndrome have hypothyroidism. Thyroid function tests (T3, T4 and TSH) are recommended once in the neonatal period/at first contact and then every year. This should ideally include anti-thyroid antibodies specially in older children as etiology is more likely to be autoimmune.

Atlanto-occipital subluxation: The incidence is variable, reported in 10–30% of cases. Lateral neck radiograph is recommended once between 3–5 years, before surgery, for participation in special games, or earlier, if signs and symptoms suggest cord compression.

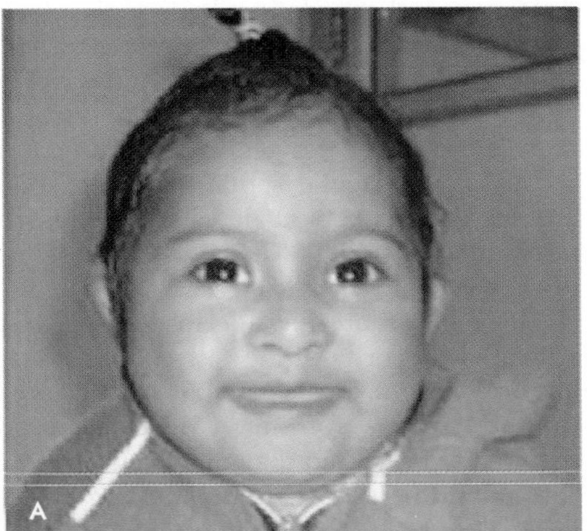

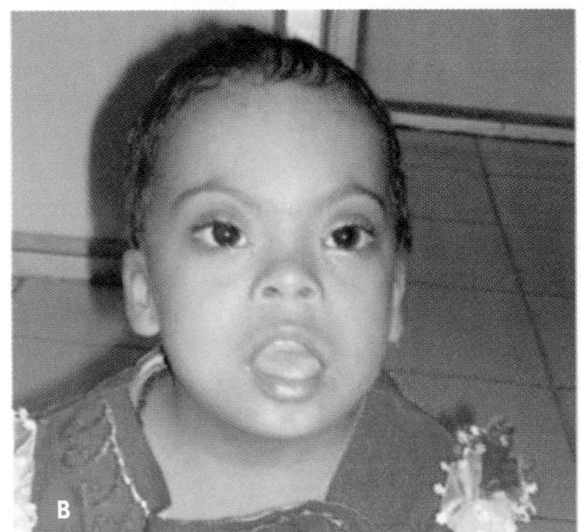

Figs 21.3A and B: Two babies with characterstic features of Down syndrome. showing characteristic flat facies, upward eye slant and open mouth appearance

21

Physical growth: Regular follow-up for height and weight is a must. Linear growth is retarded as compared to normal, children tend to become obese with age. Special growth charts for Down syndrome children should ideally be used.

Muscle tone tends to improve with age, whereas the rate of developmental progress slows with age. The mainstay of management is early stimulation, physiotherapy and speech therapy. Fortunately, social performance is usually achieved beyond that expected for mental age. Generally they behave as good babies and happy children, like mimicry, are friendly, have a good sense of rhythm and enjoy music. The major cause for early mortality is congenital heart disease, and almost 50% of those with cardiac anomalies die in infancy. Chronic rhinitis, conjunctivitis and periodontal disease are common. Lower respiratory tract infections pose a threat to life. They are more prone to develop hematological malignancies.

Counseling

The parents of a child with Down syndrome (DS) should be counseled with tact, compassion and truthfulness. Briefly one should:

1. Inform about the disorder as early as possible after diagnosis is confirmed
2. Counsel in presence of both the parents in privacy, with the mother holding the baby comfortably
3. Talk in simple and positive language giving hope, and allow sufficient time to the parents to ask questions
4. Discuss known problems and associated disorders
5. Highlight importance of early stimulation
6. Not talk about institutionalisation and adoption, unless asked. Both these options should be discouraged
7. Ask the parents to contact the local Down syndrome association, if one exists
8. Talk about genetics only after chromosomal analysis.
9. Inform about recurrence risks and possibilities of prenatal diagnosis
10. Schedule future appointments.

Risk of Recurrence

Women 35 years of age or less who have a child with trisomy have a 1% risk of having another, which is significantly greater than the general population. The risk is little increased, if any, over the usual maternal age dependent frequency if the mother at risk is 35 years or older. For translocations inherited from the mother, the risk is about 10%, whereas it is about 4–5% when father is the carrier.

Prenatal Diagnosis

Parents who wish to get a prenatal diagnosis have a number of options. They can directly get a fetal karyotype by chorionic villus sampling or amniocentesis. Alternatively (if the parents do not want invasive testing) an initial screening may be performed with maternal serum markers—PAPP-A and free βhCG in first trimester and serum α feto protein, human chorionic gonadotrophin, unconjugated estriol and inhibin A in second trimester. If the risk of bearing a Down syndrome child is more than 1 : 250, prenatal fetal karyotyping can be offered.

Fetal ultrasonography helps to detect fetuses who are at high risk for chromosomal abnormalities. Important findings in the second trimester which are markers of Down syndrome include increased nuchal fold thickness (measured over the occiput and not over the spine), short femur and humerus length and duodenal atresia. In the first trimester nuchal translucency and nasal bone are very robust markers. Ultrasound findings help in counselling specially if the parents have opted for initial screening with maternal serum markers. Both maternal serum screening and fetal USG are screening techniques and cannot rule out Down syndrome.

Prenatal karyotyping can be done by various invasive procedures. Chorionic villus sampling (CVS) can be carried out between 10–12 weeks of pregnancy (transcervical or transabdominal). This allows diagnosis in the first trimester. The options for the couples who come late or opt for the initial screening with serum markers and ultrasonography are karyotyping by amniocentesis (16–18 weeks) or transabdominal CVS, or cordocentesis (after 18 weeks). The karyotype results are available within a week with cord blood samples and direct CVS preparations. The results of amniotic fluid cultures take about 2–3 weeks. The risk of fetal loss after CVS is about 3–4% and with cordocentesis it is about 3%. Amniocentesis poses the lowest risk of about 0.5–1%.

Trisomy 18 (Edward Syndrome)

Next to Down syndrome, this is the second most common autosomal trisomy among live births. Frequency is about 1:3000 births.

This disorder is characterized by failure to thrive, developmental retardation, hypertonia, elongated skull, low set and malformed ears, micrognathia, shield-shaped chest, short sternum, joint abnormalities including flexion deformity of fingers, limited hip abduction and short dorsiflexed hallux. Congenital heart disease is common - mostly as ventricular septal defect and patent ductus arteriosus. Most subjects have simple dermal arches on nearly all of the digits. They often have very short fourth digits with only a single crease.

The mean maternal age in cases of trisomy 18 is advanced. Majority of the cases are post-mature with a low birth weight. Most infants are usually feeble, and have limited capacity for survival. Resuscitation is often required at birth, and they may have apneic episodes in the neonatal period. Poor sucking capability may necessitate nasogastric feeding, but even with optimal management they fail to thrive. The median survival is about 3 months.

Trisomy 13 (Patau Syndrome)

The incidence of this syndrome is about one per 5000 births. It is characterized by severe developmental and physical retardation, microcephaly with sloping forehead and holoprosencephaly type of defect with varying degrees of incomplete development of forebrain, olfactory and optic nerves. There is microphthalmia, coloboma of iris, retinal dysplasia and cataract. Malformations of ears, and cleft lip with or without cleft palate are common (Fig. 21.4A); many children are deaf. Capillary hemangiomata are characteristic. There are frequent abnormalities of fingers and toes such as polydactyly, flexion deformities and long and hyperconvex nails (Fig. 21.4B). Congenital heart disease is present in almost 80% of patients. Common defects are ventricular septal defect, patent ductus arteriosus and atrial septal defect.

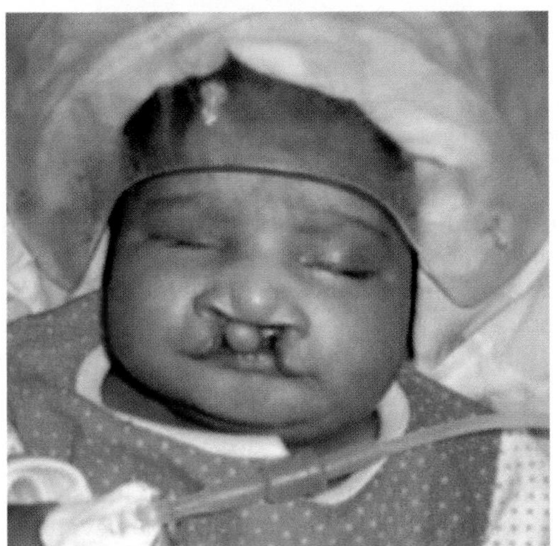

Fig. 21.4A: Clinical photograph of a baby with trisomy 13 showing cleft lip and palate

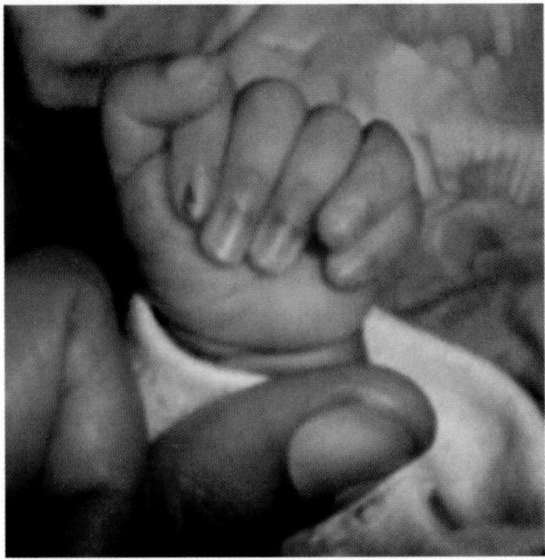

Fig. 21.4B: Clinical photograph of a baby with trisomy 13 showing polydactyly

There is an overlap between the clinical features of trisomies 13 and 18. The highest discriminating values are for ectodermal scalp defects and harelip and cleft palate in trisomy 13, and an elongated skull and simple arches on all digits for trisomy 18. However, it is easy to recognize typical cases.

Majority of cases die in the first six months of life. Survivors have severe mental defects and seizures and they fail to thrive.

Klinefelter Syndrome

Klinefelter syndrome refers to a form of hypogonadism comprising small testes with hyalinized seminiferous tubules, failure of development of secondary sex characters and increased gonadotrophins. The frequency of this syndrome is about 1.32 per 1000 among newborns, about 79/1000 among mentally subnormal population, while 10–20% of males attending infertility clinics have this syndrome. Cases of Klinefelter syndrome usually seek medical consultation near puberty due to the failure of appearance of secondary sexual characters. There are reports that even in the prepubertal age the testes and penis are smaller in size for the age. The patients tend to be tall and underweight. They have relatively elongated legs and more eunuchoid proportions. Occasionally hypospadias or cryptorchidism is present. The diagnosis should also be considered in all boys with mental retardation, as well as in children with psychosocial, learning or school adjustment problems. Pubertal development is delayed. The growth of pubic and facial hair is often late; and the pubic hair is generally feminine in distribution. About 40% of adults have gynecomastia, appearing usually soon after puberty between the ages of 14 and 16 years. Characteristically the testes are small.

The testicular histology shows small, shrunken and hyalinized seminiferous tubules, while some are lined exclusively by sertoli cells. Leydig cells show hypertrophy and clumping.

Chromosomal analysis reveals 47 XXY karyotype. Individuals with XXY/XY mosaicism have a better potential prognosis.

Klinefelter Variants

As the number of X chromosomes increases beyond two, the clinical manifestations (mental retardation, impairment of virilization, somatic defects such as bony abnormalities at the elbow leading to restricted supination and flexion) increase correspondingly.

This syndrome should be suspected in a male with learning disabilities, language difficulties, attention deficit, psychosocial problems with hypogonadism, small tests, infertility and gynecomastia.

Management includes behavioral and psychosocial rehabilitation. Testosterone therapy should be started in middle to late adolescence with monitoring of levels.

Testosterone enanthate is used in the dose of 200 mg every 10–14 days IM (adults), 100 mg every 10–14 days (adolescents), and is increased to 150 mg and then 200 mg.

XYY Males

The incidence of XYY males is approximately 1 in 840 newborns. They are seldom detected in childhood or adolescence. These individuals have tendency towards tall stature with dull mentality but IQ is usually within normal limits. Behavioural abnormalities can be problematic during childhood and adolescence. The initial belief of these individuals being more juvenile delinquents does not seem to be significant. The onset of puberty may be delayed but most individuals are fertile. Occasionally cryptorchidism, small penis, hypospadias, radio ulnar synostosis, and EEG and EKG abnormalities (prolonged PR interval) have been reported.

Turner Syndrome

Turner syndrome having 45 X chromosomal constitution, has an incidence of about 1:3000 newborns. However, chromosomal studies of spontaneous abortions have clearly shown that majority of 45 X fetuses are likely to be aborted. The precise reason for this is not known. In this syndrome there is a considerable degree of chromosomal mosaicism, e.g. 45 X/46 XX. Formation of isochromosome of long arms of X chromosome may also lead to Turner phenotype with 46 chromosomes because of absence of short arms. The advanced maternal age effect is not apparent. For this reason, it has been suggested that this syndrome does not arise from gametic nondisjunction.

Clinical Features

The disorder may be recognizable at birth. Patients have lymphedema of the dorsum of hands and feet, and there are loose skin folds at the nape of neck. Manifestations include short stature, short neck with webbing and low posterior hairline. There are anomalous ears, prominent narrow and high arched palate, small mandible and epicanthal folds. Chest is broad shield-like with widely spaced hypoplastic nipples. There is increased carrying angle at elbow. Knee anomalies include medial tibial exostosis. Short fourth metacarpals and metatarsals are seen. Later, pigmented nevi may appear. At puberty, sexual maturation fails to occur. Adult stature is less than 145 cm. The phenotype is highly variable. It has been recommended that in all short girls diagnosis of Turner syndrome should be kept in mind.

Associated congenital defects are common in the kidney (horse-shoe kidney, double or cleft renal pelvis), heart (coarctation of aorta) and ears (perceptive hearing defect). Congenital lymphedema usually recedes in early infancy, leaving only puffiness over the dorsum of fingers and toes. Linear growth proceeds at about half to three-fourths the usual rate. Figure 21.5 shows typical features.

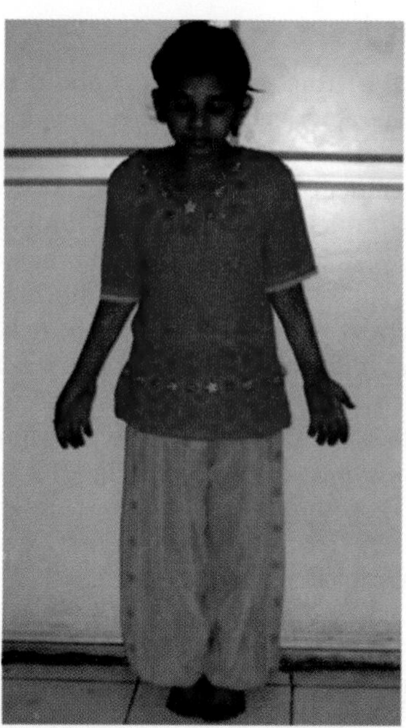

Fig. 21.5: Turner syndrome in a 10-year-old girl. Note the short neck and wide carrying angle

The clinical manifestations are milder in Turner syndrome mosaicism. It has been suggested that whereas the loss of a whole chromosome or of the short arm of the X chromosome leads to both ovarian dysgenesis and somatic abnormalities, the loss of only the long arm of the X chromosome results only in ovarian dysgenesis.

Management

Height monitoring using normal growth charts for Turner syndrome girls should be done. Cardiac evaluation at baseline and every year is recommended. Regular measurement of blood pressure and ECHO at baseline and every year is advisable. Growth hormone therapy is useful and may increase the final height by 8–10 cm, but decision to treat should be left to the parents as the cost of treatment is prohibitive. Counseling regarding behavioral problems due to short stature, amenorrhoea and sterility is an integral part of management. Evaluation for thyroid dysfunction in infancy and early childhood is recommended only if growth is abnormal as compared to normal girls with Turner syndrome. TSH measurement every year should be done starting at about 10 years.

Ovarian hormone replacement should be started around 14 years. To start with, conjugated estrogen at 0.3 mg/day or ethinyl estradiol 5–10 mg/day used for 3–6 months; then increased to 0.625 mg or 1.25 mg (conjugated estrogen) or 20–50 μg/day (ethinyl estradiol). After 6 months–1 year, cyclical therapy with estrogen and progesterone is started.

Regular audiometry should done in adults or earlier if indicated. Evaluation for renal malformation by USG at first contact should be done. Prophylactic gonadectomy in Turner syndrome patients with Y chromosome is recommended due to chances of developing gonadoblastoma.

SINGLE GENE DISORDERS

Drawing and interpreting a pedigree is an integral part of genetic diagnosis. Table 21.1 gives symbols used for pedigree drawing.

Autosomal Dominant Disorders

Generally, the autosomal dominant mutations cause faults in the synthesis of structural or non-enzyme proteins, e.g. Huntington's chorea and connective tissue disorders. These disorders manifest even if only one of the alleles of the abnormal gene is affected. The autosomal dominant disorders are generally milder than the recessive disorders. However, physical examination of other siblings and the parents should be done to uncover milder forms of the disorder. Homozygotes for the dominant mutant genes usually die prenatally, as in the case of the gene for achondroplasia. If the child is the only affected member, it is very likely that the observed mutation has occurred de novo and is not inherited. In such cases other siblings are not likely to be affected. However, one-half of the offsprings of the affected individual are likely to inherit the disorder. New dominant gene mutations are more likely to occur if the paternal age is high. Examples: Neurofibromatosis, achondroplasia, Marfan syndrome, Crouzon disease, etc. A typical pedigree is shown in Fig. 21.6.

Table 21.1: Common pedigree symbols, definitions and abbreviations

Instructions

- **Key should contain all information relevant to interpretation of pedigree (e.g. define shading)·**
- **For clinical (non-published) pedigrees, include:**
  a. family names/initials, when appropriate
  b. name and title of person recording pedigree
  c. historian (person relaying family history information)
  d. date of intake/update.
- **Recommended order of information placed below symbol (below to lower right, if necessary):**
  a. age/date of birth or age at death
  b. evaluation
  c. pedigree number (e.g. I-1, I-2, I-3)

	Male	*Female*	*Sex unknown*	*Comments*
Individual	b. 1925	30 y	4 month	Assign gender by phenotype. Square represents male; circle represents a female; a diamond represents whose sex is not known. Age/date of birth can be given at the bottom or right hand corner.
Affected individual				Fillings can be shading, hatches, dots, lines, etc.
				For ≥ 2 conditions the symbols are partitioned correspondingly, each quadrant with different fillings/patterns representing different features.
Multiple individuals; number known	6	6	6	Number of the siblings is written inside the symbols; affected individuals should not be grouped.
Multiple individuals; number unknown				"?" is used in the place of "n"
Deceased individual	d. 35 y	d. 4 mo		If known, write "d" with age at death below symbol.

Contd.

Contd.

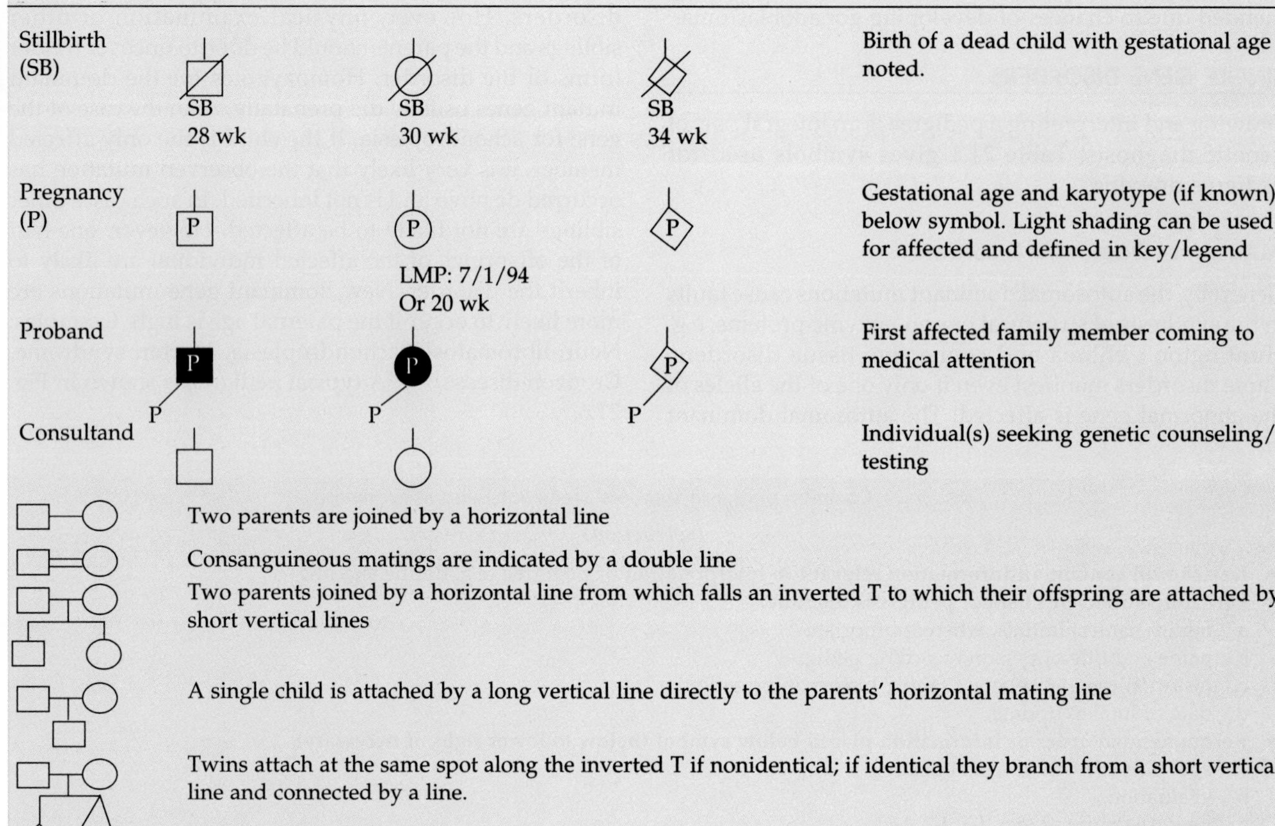

Stillbirth (SB)	SB 28 wk	SB 30 wk	SB 34 wk	Birth of a dead child with gestational age noted.
Pregnancy (P)	P	P LMP: 7/1/94 Or 20 wk	P	Gestational age and karyotype (if known) below symbol. Light shading can be used for affected and defined in key/legend
Proband	P P	P P	P P	First affected family member coming to medical attention
Consultand				Individual(s) seeking genetic counseling/testing

Two parents are joined by a horizontal line

Consanguineous matings are indicated by a double line

Two parents joined by a horizontal line from which falls an inverted T to which their offspring are attached by short vertical lines

A single child is attached by a long vertical line directly to the parents' horizontal mating line

Twins attach at the same spot along the inverted T if nonidentical; if identical they branch from a short vertical line and connected by a line.

Pedigree symbols and abbreviations for pregnancies not carried to term

Instructions

- Symbols are smaller than standard ones and individual's line is shorter. (Even if sex is known, triangles are preferred to a small square/circle; symbol may be mistaken for symbols given in the previous table, especially in hand drawn pedigrees)·
- If gender and gestational age known, write below symbol in that order.

	Male	*Female*	*Sex unknown*	*Comments*
Spontaneous abortion (SAB)	Male	Female	ECT	If ectopic pregnancy, write ECT below symbol
Affected SAB	Male	Female	16 week	If gestational age known, write below symbol. Key/legend used to define shading
Termination of pregnancy (TOP)	Male	Female		Other abbreviations (e.g. TAB, VTOP, Ab) not used for sake of consistency
Affected TOP	Male	Female		Key/legend used to define shading

- Parents who are unaffected and unrelated may be omitted from the pedigree.
- To save space, huge pedigrees are sometimes drawn in circular or spiral form rather than in a rectangular form.

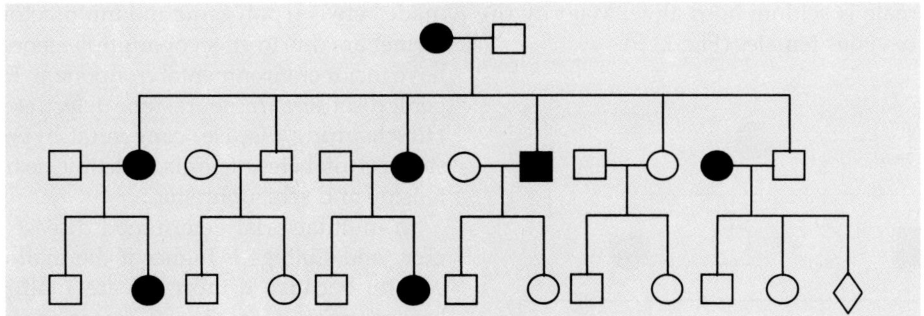

Fig. 21.6: Autosomal dominant inheritance

Autosomal Recessive Disorders

Autosomal recessive disorders manifest only in homozygous states, i.e. both the alleles are mutant genes. Generally autosomal recessive mutations affect synthesis of enzyme proteins, leading to inborn errors of metabolism. The parents of the affected individuals are apparently normal but carry the mutant genes. As they are heterozygous, the mutant recessive gene does not express itself in the phenotype. In such matings, one-fourth of the offsprings are affected (homozygous for the mutant genes), one-fourth are normal (both normal alleles) and half are carriers (heterozygote with one mutant allele and one normal allele).

For obvious reasons, recessive disorders are more common in consanguineous marriage or in closed communities like Jews and Parsis. It is now possible to detect carrier status by biochemical and molecular techniques in a number of autosomal recessive disorders. Examples are beta-thalassemia, phenylketonuria and galactosemia. A classical pedigree is shown in Fig. 21.7.

X-Linked Recessive Disorders

Males have an X and a shorter Y chromosome. There may be no corresponding locus for a mutant allele of the X-chromosome on the shorter Y chromosome. The mutant recessive gene on X chromosome, therefore, expresses as a clinical disorder in the male child because it is not being suppressed by a normal allele. In the female, the disorder does not manifest clinically, if the mutant gene is kept in check by the normal allele in the other X chromosome. The females thus act as carriers of the mutant allele. Half of their male children inherit the mutant allele and are affected. It is now possible to detect carrier state in the female child in case of some disorders, e.g. hemophilia, Duchenne muscular dystrophy and mucopolysaccharidosis type II (Hunter syndrome). Color blindness also has an X-linked recessive inheritance. Figure 21.8 shows a family with X-linked recessive inheritance.

X-Linked Dominant Inheritance Disease

Dominant X-linked conditions are rare. Both the heterozygous female and hemizygous males are affected. All the sons of the affected males are normal and all the daughters are affected. The affected females transmit the disease to half of the sons and half of the daughters. Examples : Hypophosphatemic type of vitamin D-resistant rickets, oro-facio-digital syndrome and incontinentia pigmenti. The effect of the mutant gene on development is so severe

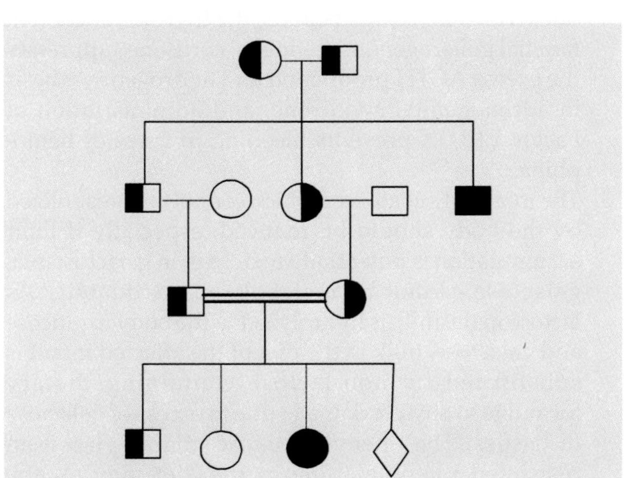

Fig. 21.7: Autosomal recessive inheritance

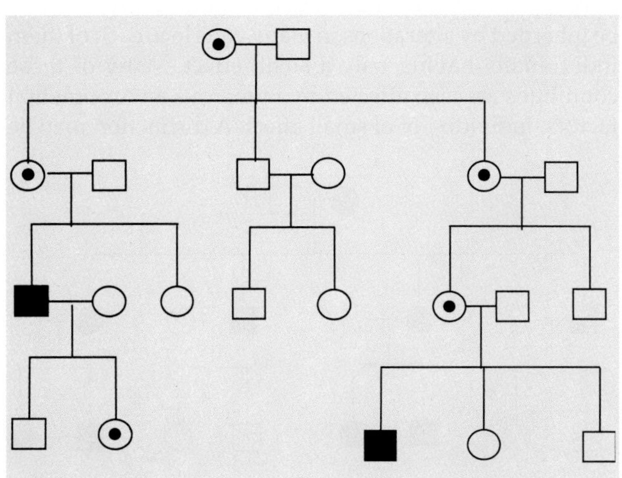

Fig. 21.8: X-linked recessive inheritance

that the affected male is seldom born alive. Majority of patients are heterozygous females (Fig. 21.9).

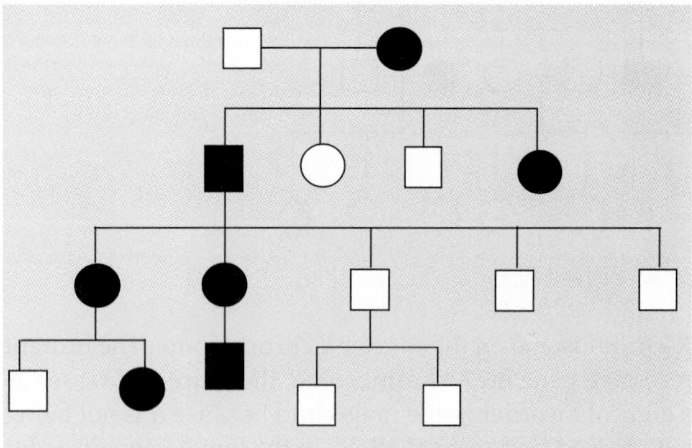

Fig. 21.9: X-linked dominant inheritance

MITOCHONDRIAL INHERITANCE

Mutations within a mitochondrial gene can lead to phenotypic defects and show a pattern of maternal genetic transmission. In this type, the inheritance is maternal. All offsprings born to an affected female will be affected. The reason is that the mitochondria are only present in ovum and not in sperms. All affected daughters will transmit the disease. Sons will be affected but will not transmit the disease (Fig. 21.10). Examples : Leigh disease (movement disorder, regression, respiratory dyskinesia), and mitochondrial encephalopathy, lactic acidosis and stroke like syndrome (MELAS).

POLYGENIC INHERITANCE

In a number of conditions, the affected individuals do not have a sharp division between the normal and the abnormal, but merely represent a spectrum of a continuously variable attribute. Such conditions are likely to be inherited by alterations in many gene loci, each of them individually having only a small effect. Many of these conditions are also affected by numerous environmental factors, individually of small effect. A distinction may be made between polygenic and multifactorial diseases. The former are due to effect of multiple genes, while the latter have major environmental component. Examples of polygenic disorders are: neural tube defect, cleft lip, cleft palate, Hirschsprung disease, congenital hypertrophic pyloric stenosis, diabetes mellitus, ischemic heart disease, hypertension and schizophrenia.

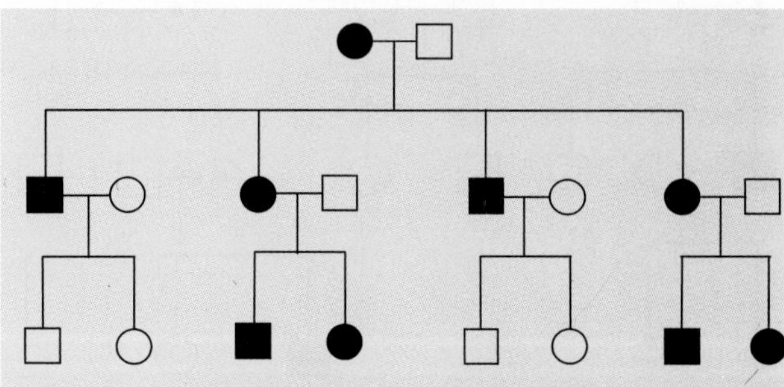

Fig. 21.10: Mitochondrial inheritance

In multifactorial determined disease, the risk to progeny and siblings is higher if the malformation is more severe, because a more severe malformation can be looked upon as a bigger deviation from the normal threshold, e.g. the risk of recurrence of Hirschsprung disease in a family is higher if the aganglionic segment of the colon is longer. When these diseases have a marked sex predilection, the risk of recurrence in the family is higher if the index patient belongs to the less often affected sex. This is so, because the mutant genes are likely to be more severe so as to produce the disease in the sex with an inherent resistance to the disease. For example, pyloric stenosis has a male to female ratio of 5 to 1. Among the children of female patients, 19% of their sons and 7% of daughters are likely to be affected, whereas in case of male patients, 5% of their sons and 2.5% of daughters are prone to suffer from the disease.

SOMATIC CELL (GENETIC) DISORDERS

These include cancers which can arise due to genetic changes in somatic cells.

THERAPY FOR GENETIC DISORDERS

Genetic disorders cannot generally be cured completely. However, symptoms of many disorders can be ameliorated and the irreversible damage or handicap can be prevented or reduced through several therapeutic approaches.

1. The deficiency of the metabolic end product may be made up by replacement or administration of the product. Thus, thyroxine restores the thyroid function in familial goiterogenous cretinism; cortisone suppresses the excess ACTH production and androgen synthesis in adrenogenital syndrome, and administration of Factor VIII/IX prevents bleeding in cases of hemophilia.
2. The intake of substances which cannot be metabolized by the body should be reduced, especially if their accumulation is potentially toxic; e.g. in galactosemia, galactose cannot be metabolized adequately. As lactose in the milk is hydrolyzed in the body to glucose and galactose, milk in the diet of the affected infant is substituted by non-lactose containing dietary formulae to obviate damage due to excess of galactose in tissues. The phenylketonuric infants placed on restricted phenylalanine in the diet may escape irreversible neurological damage.

3. Certain drugs which precipitate adverse symptoms in metabolic disorders such as barbiturates in porphyria hepatica and oxidating agents in glucose-6 phosphate dehydrogenase deficiency, should never be administered in these patients.
4. Patients with hemophilia and osteogenesis imperfecta should be protected from trauma and other environmental hazards to prevent excessive bleeding and fractures respectively.
5. Surgery helps to reduce the functional or cosmetic disability in many structural defects.
6. The excretion of certain toxic metabolites can be promoted by chelating agents; e.g. penicillamine promotes excretion of copper in patients with Wilson disease, or desferrioxamine can be used to chelate iron in cases of thalassemia and hemochromatosis.
7. Certain drugs may inhibit production of substances which are accumulated, e.g. allopurinol inhibits xanthine oxidase and thus reduces the synthesis of uric acid, and hence is useful in cases of gout.
8. Certain enzyme systems which may be immature or reduced at certain phases of life may be induced or stabilized by the use of chemical agents such as phenobarbitone for inducing hepatic microsomal enzymes like glucuronyl transferase, in cases of neonatal hyperbilirubinemia or Crigler-Najjar syndrome.
9. In a number of metabolic disorders, enzymatic block can be bypassed by administration of large quantities of the coenzyme; for example, pyridoxine in homocystinuria.
10. Enzyme replacement therapy has become a reality with the use of deficient enzyme in Gaucher disease, Hurler syndrome, Morquio syndrome, Fabry disease and Pompe's disease. The cost of the treatment is prohibitive.
11. Gene therapy is the ultimate goal for genetic disorders. Though significant research has gone in this field, gene therapy has been effectively tried only for adenosine deaminase deficiency, familial hypercholesterolemia and some cancers. The aim is to introduce the normal gene in the affected individual. This is done by using viral or non viral vectors for introducing normal functioning genes. The therapy can be invivo (i.e. direct introduction in the body/tissues), or exvivo (when cells with the normal functioning gene are grown outside and then introduced), which is the preferred mode. As the exact regulation of gene function of single gene disorders is very complex, the implementation of gene therapy is complicated.

POSSIBILITIES OF PREVENTION OF GENETIC DISORDERS

Carrier Screening

It is now possible to detect the carrier state in case of a large number of autosomal recessive or X-linked recessive disorders. Female carriers of Duchenne muscular dystrophy may show high serum levels of the enzyme creatinine phosphokinase. Female carriers of glucose-6-phosphate dehydrogenase deficiency can be detected by demonstrating relatively low level of enzymes in their erythrocytes. HbA2 levels for β thalassemia carrier status in high risk communities is useful. Molecular techniques are now being increasingly used for carrier detection. Individuals who are more likely to give birth to offspring with hereditary disorders can be recognized by precise diagnostic procedures. Genetic counseling for restriction on selection of the mate or procreation, will limit the spread of the genetic disorder.

Genetic Metabolic Screening

Newborn infants are screened routinely for some inborn errors of metabolism in developed countries. This is of special value for detecting the affected cases during the newborn period, so that the handicap can be prevented or minimized by early treatment, e.g. in cases of phenylketonuria, galactosemia, familial hypercholesterolemia, congenital hypothyroidism, tyrosinosis, etc.

Prevention of neural tube defects (NTD) with the use of folic acid periconceptionally has been proved beyond doubt. Four mg of folic acid taken every day one month before to three months after conception is recommended for prevention of recurrence. It has also been recommended that all expectant mothers should consume about 0.4 mg of folic acid daily to prevent first occurrence of NTD. Food fortification with folic acid is being considered in western countries.

Prenatal diagnosis and selective termination of affected fetuses is a successfully used modality for preventing birth of affected babies and reducing the load of lethal/chronically disabling/untreatable/difficult to treat genetic disorders in the community.

The prenatal screening/diagnostic modalities can be noninvasive or invasive. Noninvasive techniques include fetal inspection using ultrasonography (rarely, other techniques like fetoscopy, radiology or MRI are also used). Fetal ultrasonography has became a very important tool for diagnosing fetal malformation with leaping improvements in this technology like level II/III scans and 3D ultrasonography.

Maternal serum biochemical screening using triple markers test (alpha-fetoprotein, hCG and estriol) in the second trimester (16–20 weeks) has a detection rate of about 70% for Down syndrome. First trimester screening using PAPP-A and free beta hCG is also widely studied and is equally useful. Alpha-fetoprotein and estriol are low whereas hCG is high in pregnancies with Down syndrome fetuses. Alpha-fetoprotein level in maternal blood is also a very sensitive marker for open neural tube defects, the levels being high if fetus is affected. Invasive prenatal testing includes chorionic villus biopsy, amniocentesis and cord blood sampling. The timings,

21

indications and risks of these techniques are summarized in Table 21.2.

These samples can be used for chromosomal studies, DNA based tests or enzyme assays. Amniotic fluid is the preferred sample for chromosomal studies and chorionic villus tissue for DNA based tests. Many single gene disorders can be diagnosed prenatally. Same examples are α-thalassemia, sickle cell anemia, hemophilia, duchenne muscular dystrophy, cystic fibrosis, lysosomal storage disorders, etc.

GENETIC COUNSELING

Genetic counseling is a communication process, which deals with problems associated with the occurrence and recurrence of a genetic disorder in a family. Counseling should be undertaken by a physician with proper understanding of the genetic mechanisms. Some important indications for genetic counseling are as follows:

- Known or suspected hereditary disease in a patient or family
- Birth defects in previous children
- Unexplained mental retardation/dysmorphism/ multiple malformations in a child
- Consanguinity
- Exposure to a teratogen during pregnancy
- Identification of malformation(s) by ultrasonography during pregnancy.

Objectives are:

- To make precise diagnosis (if possible), explaining the cause and course of the disease and treatment options, if available.
- To reduce anxiety/guilt.
- Providing risk figures for future offspring/relatives based on genetic facts.
- To provide information about prenatal diagnostic possibilities and the risks involved.
- To help the couples make decision by nondirective counseling.

The essentials of counseling are:

1. Precise diagnosis based on a detailed family history, constructing a pedigree, clinical examination and investigations. History of consanguinity is important to elicit.
2. Calculation of the risk of recurrence based on inheritance pattern, empiric risk figures or laboratory tests.
3. Nondirective counseling with good communication maintaining truth and confidentiality.

Points to remember:

1. Hereditary diseases may manifest at the time of birth or several years later in life.
2. All congenital defects observed at the time of birth are not necessarily inherited. Some of these may be due to teratogenic effect of drugs, infections or irradiation during the first trimester of pregnancy.
3. All familial diseases are not necessarily inherited disorders. Children share not only genes, but also the environment.
4. Different genetic disorders may result in similar clinical picture. Thus several clinical syndromes, which were once considered as a single entity are now known to be caused by several different genes. This is called genetic heterogeneity. It is therefore, necessary to make a precise diagnosis of the genetic disorder, to provide accurate genetic counseling.
5. A degree of clinical variability exists in the presentation of certain genetic disorders. This variable expression of the mutant gene is attributed to the degree of penetration of the gene. Thus one member of the family may show all the features of a genetic disease, while his or her siblings may show only mild forms of the disorders with one or the other sign.

Table 21.2: Prenatal diagnostic procedures

Procedure		*Timing*	*Indications*	*Risks*
Chorionic villus sample (CVS)*	Transcervical Transabdominal	≥ 11 weeks ≥ 11 weeks	Molecular testing, cytogenetic testing, biochemical assay, intrauterine infection	2–5% fetal loss, limb defects, fetomaternal hemorrhage
Amniocentesis	Early	≤15 weeks	As above	1% fetal loss
	Classical	16–18 weeks	As above + alfa-fetoprotein	fetomaternal hemorrhage
Cord blood sample		≥ 18 weeks	Cytogenetic, molecular and biochemical testing intrauterine infection	1–3% fetal loss, fetomaternal hemorrhage

* CVS should not be done preferably before 10 weeks of pregnancy. Choice of route is an individual decision. Transabdominal route can be used before 12 weeks also.

6. Difficulty in genetic counseling may arise if the socially accepted father is not the real biologic father.
7. Genetic counselor should interpret the anticipated risk of recurrence of the inherited disorder in the future siblings in a meaningful manner, so that the family can arrive at a rational decision. The counselor has a particularly important responsibility in reassuring the parents that the risk of recurrence is low in case of disorders with multifactorial inheritance. In sporadic mutations and most of chromosomal disorders, there is only a small or no risk of recurrence.
8. While conveying information to the parents the physician should be extremely cautions. He should take special care not to infuse a sense of guilt in the parents. In case of X-linked disorders, it will be desirable to temper the blame on the mother, lest she is castigated by her husband or in-laws (Indian scenario).

Suggested readings

1. Rimori DL, Cooner JM, Pyeritz RE, Korf BR. Principles and Practice of Medical Genetics, 4th edn., Churchill Livingstone, Philadelphia, 2006.
2. Harper PS. Practical Genetic counseling, 5th edn. Wright Publishers, Bristol 2004.
3. Health supervision for children with Down syndrome, American Academy of Pediatrics Committee on Genetics of Pediatrics. 1994;93:855–859.

22 Inborn Errors of Metabolism

INTRODUCTION

Inborn errors of metabolism (IEM) are conditions caused by genetic defects related to synthesis, metabolism, transport or storage of biochemical compounds. The metabolic error usually results in deficiency of one or more enzymes required for the formation or transport of proteins.

Worldwide incidence of IEM has been estimated to be about 3–4/1000 live births. More than 300 such defects are known. Most IEMs are inherited in an autosomal recessive manner, some are X-linked.

Depending on the biochemical defect, these disorders can be grouped into defects of (a) **amino acid**: aminoacidurias (*phenylketonuria, cystinuria, alkaptonuria*), urea cycle defects (*CPS deficiency, citrullinemia, argininemia*), (b) **organic acidemias** (*isovaleric acidemia, propionic acidemia, methylmalonic acidemia (MMA)*), branched chain disorders (*maple syrup urine disease*); (c) **lipid**: mitochondrial fatty acid oxidation defects (*acyl CoA dehydrogenase deficiency*), peroxisomal disorders (*Zellweger syndrome, adrenoleukodystrophy*), lysosomal disorders [lipidoses (*GM1 gangliosidosis, Tay Sachs disease, Gaucher disease, Niemann Pick disease, metachromatic leukodystrophy*), mucopolysaccharidoses and mucolipidoses (*sialidosis, Canavan disease*)], lipoprotein defects (*familial hypercholesterolemia*); (d) **carbohydrates:** glycogen storage disease (GSD), disorders of galactose (*UDPG epimerase deficiency*), fructose (*intolerance, fructosuria*), pyruvate (*pyruvate dehydrogenase deficiency, Leigh disease*), and gluconeogenesis; (e) **purines and pyrimidines**: *Lesch-Nyhan syndrome, AMP deaminase deficiency, orotic aciduria, DHP dehydrogenase deficiency;* and (f) **miscellaneous** diseases: *porphyria, Wilson disease, alpha 1 antitrypsin deficiency.*

In this chapter, we shall confine our discussion to common and potentially debilitating or life threatening disorders.

CLINICAL CLASSIFICATION

The clinical classification (Table 22.1) gives an insight into the manifestations and pathogenesis of neuromuscular disorders (NMDs). As evident from this classification, the neurological deterioration can be of intoxication or energy deficiency type. Manifestations may differ in these two types of diseases. Common presentation are as follows:

Table 22.1: Classification of inherited neurometabolic disorders

Clinical features	*Acute encephalopathy*	*Chronic (progressive) encephalopathy*
Age at presentation	Neonatal or early infancy	Late infancy, childhood, or adolescence
Initial central nervous system symptoms	Gray matter Cognitive impairment Seizures Vision impairment	White matter Spasticity Ataxia Hyperreflexia
Metabolite	Small-molecule	Large-molecule
Clinical course	Intoxication Vomiting Lethargy or coma Abnormal respiration	Energy deficiency or intoxication Liver dysfunction Cardiomyopathy Weakness

Intoxication

- Initial symptom free interval
- Poor feeding usually first reported
- Unexplained coma, respiratory abnormalities, hiccups, apnea, bradycardia and hypothermia
- Changes in muscle tone and involuntary movements. Hypertonia, opisthotonus, axial hypotonia and limb hypertonia, myoclonic jerks.

Energy Deficiency Type

- More variable, less dramatic features
- May not have initial symptom free interval
- Hypotonia
- Cardiac signs, malformations, dysmorphism, organomegaly.

APPROACH TO METABOLIC DISORDERS

When to Suspect IEM

Detection of IEM is usually delayed because the manifestations mimic many of the common pediatric illnesses like neonatal sepsis and hypoxic ischemic encephalopathy.

A physician has to pick up the important clues in history, physical examination and routine laboratory investigations to suspect IEM.

Neonatal Period

IEMs should be suspected in a previously well newborn presenting with lethargy, poor feeding, persistent vomiting, intractable seizures, tachypnea, floppiness, unusual body/urine odor, failure to thrive, etc. where other common problems like sepsis, hypoxic ischemic encephalopathy and hypoglycemia have been ruled out. If undiagnosed, these disorders are frequently fatal. History of previous unexplained neonatal deaths or parental consanguinity are important clues.

Physical examination may reveal skin and hair changes, cataract, hepatomegaly, jaundice, hypotonia, unexplained neurologic signs and coma. Presence of ambiguous genitalia suggests congenital adrenal hyperplasia (CAH). **Acute metabolic encephalopathy** is the term given to a syndrome of lethargy, poor feeding, seizures, altered sensorium and abnormalities of tone in a child suspected to be having IEM. Symptoms are absent at birth because toxic fetal metabolites are cleared by the placenta.

Laboratory investigations like persistent/recurrent hypoglycemia, intractable metabolic acidosis, unexplained leukopenia, thrombocytopenia (possibility of organic acidurias) and hyperammonemia are indications for evaluation.

Older Children

The onset of illness may be delayed in intermittent or milder forms of IEM. Recurrent episodes of sensorial derangement, vomiting, hypotonia, hypoglycemia and acidosis warrant investigations. Unexplained developmental delay with or without seizures, mental retardation, organomegaly, coarse facies, cataract, dislocated lenses, chronic skin lesions, abnormal hair, abnormal urine color on standing and failure to thrive, etc. are also important clues. Table 22.2 provides a list of some important signs and symptoms seen in IEMs.

Table 22.2: Clinical pointers to neurometabolic disorders

Cutaneous abnormality: Perioral eruption (multiple carboxylase deficiency), increased pigmentation (adrenoleukodystrophy, decreased pigmentation (phenylketonuria).

Abnormal urinary or body odor: Musty (phenylketonuria), maple syrup (maple syrup urine disease), sweaty feet (isovaleric acidemia, glutaric acidemia type II), cat urine (multiple carboxylase deficiency), sulphurous (homocystinuria).

Hair abnormalities: Alopecia (multiple carboxylase deficiency), kinky hair (Menke's disease), arginosuccinemic aciduria, multiple carboxylase deficiency.

Dysmorphic features: Zellweger syndrome, glutaric acidemia type II.

Ocular abnormalities: Cataract (galactosemia, Zellweger syndrome, homocystinuria), iris heterochromia/retinitis pigmentosa (Zellweger syndrome), KF ring (Wilson disease)

Hepatomegaly: Galactosemia, glycogen storage disease (GSD) tyrosinemia

Hepatosplenomegaly: Storage disorders – Niemann-Pick, Gaucher disease, mucopolysaccharidosis

Renal enlargement: Zellweger syndrome, GSD I, tyrosinemia

Clinical Syndromes

Basically IEMs can present as four types of clinical syndromes—neurologic, hepatic, cardiac and storage and dysmorphism.

Neurologic Syndromes

Neurologic syndromes can present as acute encephalopathy, chronic encephalopathy, movement disorders, myopathy and psychiatric problems.

1. *Acute encephalopathy:* This presents as an acute emergency and needs to be differentiated from many acquired conditions. Encephalopathy in acutely presenting IEM has certain characteristics.
   - It usually occurs with little warning in a previously health individual.
   - Early signs may be taken as behavioral problem
   - Often progresses rapidly
   - Consciousness may fluctuate
   - Usually not associated with focal neurological deficits.
   - History of recurrent similar episodes may be present

   The initial investigations in acute encephalopathy are shown in Fig. 22.1. Examples of acutely presenting IEMs are organic acidurias, urea cycle disorders, fatty acid oxidation defects and mitochondrial disorders.

2. *Chronic encephalopathy:* Psychomotor retardation/developmental delay is the commonest manifestation of IEM. The retardation tends to be global and progressive. History of regression of milestones may be present. Irritability, aggressiveness, hyperactivity and lack of night sleep are commonly associated. In addition retardation is often associated with objective neurological signs like tone changes, pyramidal or extra-pyramidal deficits. Initial approach to a chronic encephalopathy is shown in Fig. 22.2.

   Seizures, visual failure and extrapyramidal disturbances are signs of gray matter disease. Seizures occur early in disease course, are associated with other neurologic signs, are usually complex partial or myoclonic and are resistant to conventional therapy.

   Involvement of non-neural tissue like hepatosplenomegaly gives important clue to diagnosis. Hepatosplenomegaly is commonly seen in lysosomal storage disorders. IEMs commonly presenting as chronic, encephalopathy include neuronal ceroid lipofuscinosis, storage disorders and homocystinuria.

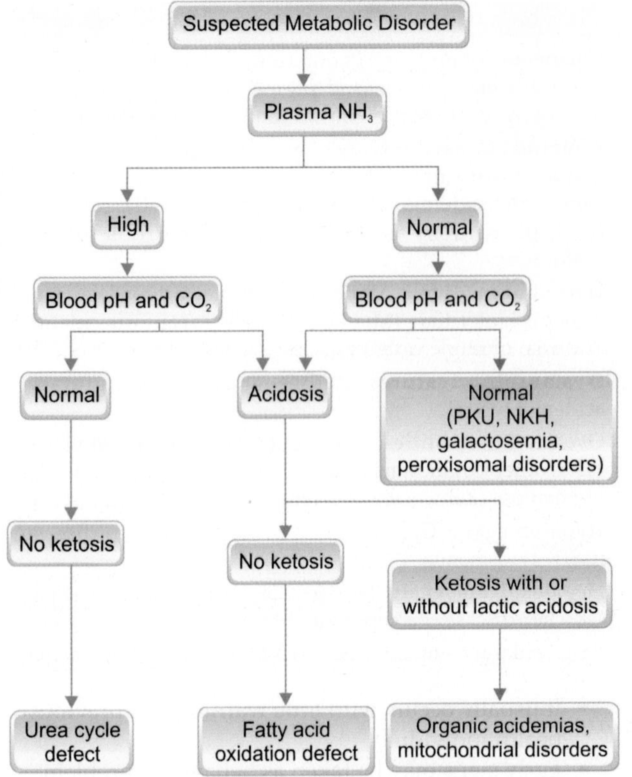

Fig. 22.1: Approach to a newborn infant with suspected metabolic defect. NH_3 ammonia, PKU phenylketonuria, NKH nonketotic hyperglycinemia

3. *Movement disorders* in patients with IEM can be seen in a vast variety of disorders and are usually associated with other neurologic signs. Movement abnormalities can be intermittent or progressive. They may be in the form of ataxias, dystonia, choreoathetosis and parkinsonism. Common examples of IEMs presenting as movement disorder are organic acidurias, neuronal ceroid lipofuscinosis (late onset forms), lysosomal storage disorders and urea cycle disorders, etc.

4. *Myopathy:* IEMs presenting with myopathy are usually due to defects in energy metabolism. The myopathy can be progressive muscle weakness (GSD II & III), exercise intolerance with cramps and myoglobinuria (GSD V, VI) or myopathy as a part of multi-system disease (mitochondrial myopathies).

Hepatic Syndrome

Liver involvement is seen in a number of IEMs. There are four possible presentations:

- Jaundice may be unconjugated (G6PD deficiency, Gilbert and Crigler-Najjar syndromes) or conjugated (galactosemia, tyrosinemia, fructose intolerance).
- Hepatomegaly–asymptomatic hepatomegaly is common, e.g. GSD, tyrosinemia.
- Hypoglycemia–Galactosemia, GSD.
- Hepatocellular dysfunction–Galactosemia, GSD (IV and III), Niemann Pick type B, α_1 antitrypsin deficiency.

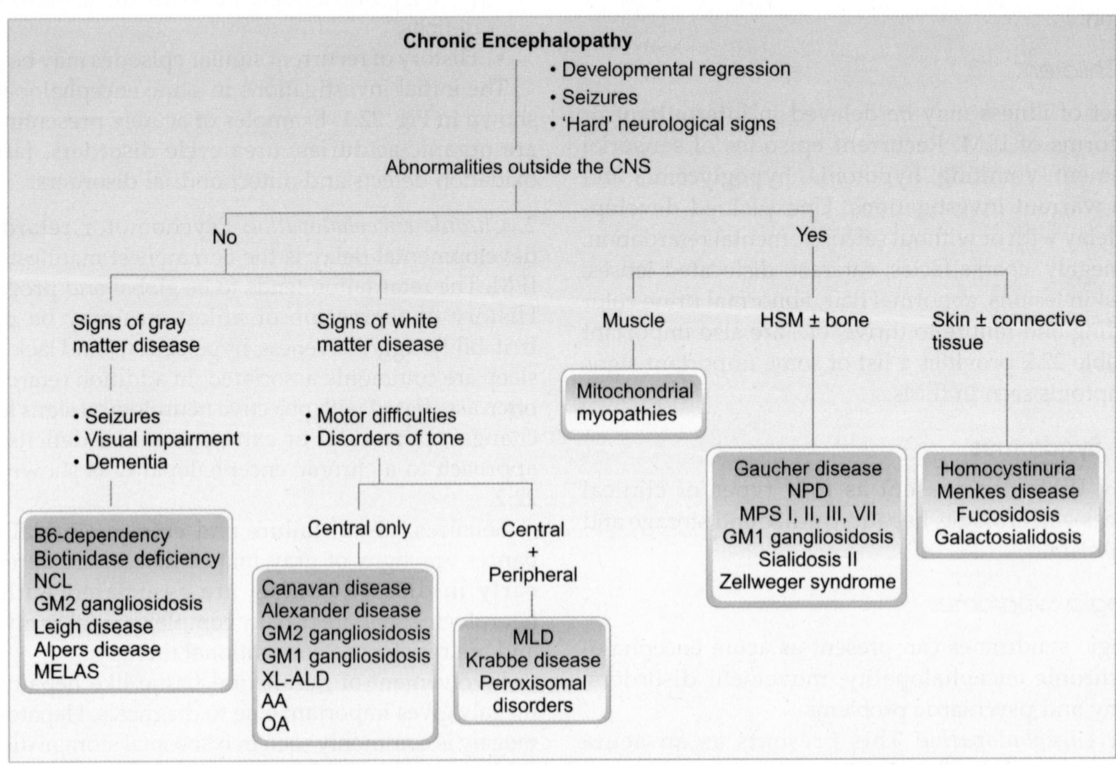

Fig. 22.2: Approach to IEM presenting as chronic encephalopathy. HSM hepatosplenomegaly; NCL neuronal ceroid lipofuscinosis; MELAS mitochondrial encephalopathy, lactic acidosis, stroke; XL-ALD X linked-adrenoleukodystrophy; AA aminoaciduria; OA organic aciduria; MLD metachromatic leukodystrophy; NPD Niemann Pick disease; MPS mucopolysaccharidosis

Cardiac Syndromes

Serious cardiac disease has been found to be associated particularly with fatty acid oxidation defects, mitochondrial disorders and GSD II. Syndromes may present as cardiomyopathy (GSD, fatty acid oxidation defects, mitochondrial disorders, methylmalonic acidemia, Fabry disease, mucopolysaccharidosis, GM1 gangliosidosis) arrhythmias (Kearns Sayre syndrome, Fabry disease) and coronary artery disease (familial hypercholesterolemia).

Storage Syndromes and Dysmorphism

Dysmorphic features in IEM, though not common, may be characteristic in certain situation. It usually becomes more prominent with age and is associated with ultrastructural pathological abnormalities. Mucopolysaccharidosis and peroxisomal disorders are important examples. Storage syndromes may have dysmorphic facies along with organomegaly and skeletal abnormalities.

Laboratory Work-up

The investigations should be done during the episode. Biochemical tests may be totally normal in between episodes when the child is asymptomatic. Initial routine investigations should include:

1. *Blood investigations:* Total and differential counts; blood sugar, electrolytes, ammonia, lactate and pyruvate, liver enzymes and arterial blood gases.
2. *Urine metabolic screen:* pH, ketones, odor, reducing substances, special urine tests such as ferric chloride, dinitrophenylhydrazine, nitroprusside and toluidine blue spot test.
3. *Specialized tests* are required for reaching a conclusive diagnosis.

Table 22.3 describes tests required for diagnosis of acutely presenting IEMs. Based on the results of four screening tests, IEM can be classified in major categories (Table 22.4).

Biochemical Autopsy

In a severely ill or dying child, where a metabolic disease is suspected but not diagnosed, parents should be convinced about the need for a biochemical autopsy for confirmation of diagnosis. After taking informed written consent, the following material should be obtained postmortem to facilitate diagnosis.

- **Blood:** 5–10 mL each in heparin (for plasma) and EDTA (leukocytes). Keep frozen at –20°C;
- **Urine:** Obtain as much as possible (may be taken by suprapubic aspiration). Keep at –20°C

Table 22.3: Investigations for inborn errors of metabolism presenting acutely

	Investigations
Urine	Smell (special odor) Look (special color) Acetone Reducing substances Ketoacids
Blood	Blood cell count Electrolytes (anion gap) Glucose, calcium Blood gases (pH, pCO_2, HCO_3^-, pO_2) Prothrombin time Transaminases (and other liver tests) Ammonia Lactic and pyruvic acids (arterial blood sample)
Miscellaneous	Lumbar puncture Chest X-ray Echocardiography, electromyography Cerebral ultrasound CT, MRI, EEG
Specialized Investigations	High performance liquid chromatography (HPLC) for aminoacidopathies Gas chromatography mass spectroscopy (GCMS) for organic acidurias Tandem mass spectroscopy (TMS) screening for aminoacidopathies and organic aciduria; diagnostic for fatty acid oxidation defects Blood on filter paper (as "Guthrie test") Enzymes and molecular studies

CT computed tomography, MRI magnetic resonance imaging, EEG electroencephalography

22

Table 22.4: Four basic tests for inherited metabolic disorders

Group	*Acidosis*	*Ketosis*	*Lactate*	*Ammonia*	*Diagnosis*
I	–	+	–	–	MSUD
II	+	+	–	–	Organic aciduria
III	+	+	+	–	Lactic acidosis
IV	–	–	–	+	Urea cycle disorder
V	–	–	–	–	NKH, sulfite oxidase deficiency, peroxisomal disorders, PKU, galactosemia

MSUD maple syrup urine disease, NKH nonketotic hyperglycinemia, PKU phenylketonuria

- Cerebrospinal fluid
- **Skin biopsy** including dermis in culture medium or saline with glucose at 37°C
- **Liver, muscle, kidney or heart biopsy** should be done and tissue must be frozen
- **Clinical photograph** for dysmorphism
- **Infantogram** for skeletal malformations.

MANAGEMENT

Principles

- Treatment may have to be instituted empirically without a specific diagnosis.
- To reduce the formation of toxic metabolites by decreasing substrate availability (by stopping feeds and preventing endogenous catabolism).
- To provide adequate calories.
- To enhance excretion of toxic metabolites.
- To institute co-factor therapy for specific disease and also empirically if diagnosis not established.

Immediate Steps (for Acutely Ill Child)

- Stop oral feeds, process/store blood and urine samples before stopping feeds.
- Start parenteral fluids (appropriate for age).
- Correct dehydration, acidosis and dyselectrolytemias.
- Start specific therapy if any (e.g. sodium benzoate for hyperammonemic states).
- Monitor and maintain vitals, blood sugar, pH, electrolytes.
- Transfer to a tertiary center.

Further Management

- Cardiorespiratory support (mechanical ventilation if needed).
- In case of non response/worsening with previous therapy/peritoneal dialysis, hemodialysis, exchange transfusion may be done to get rid of toxic metabolites.
- Specific therapy–special diets, vitamins.

Genetic Counseling and Prenatal Diagnosis

Most IEMs are inherited in autosomal recessive manner and risk of recurrence in subsequent pregnancy is 25%. Few disorders are X-linked, autosomal dominant and mitochondrial in inheritance. Prenatal diagnosis is possible by enzyme assays in chorionic villus biopsy/ amniotic fluid, metabolites in amniotic fluid and using fetal DNA for molecular tests.The details are discussed in Chapter 21.

Suggested reading

1. Clarke TR Joe. A Clinical Guide to Inherited Metabolic Diseases. Cambridge University Press
2. Scriver CR, Beaudet AL, Sly WS Valle D. The Metabolic and Molecular Bases of Inherited Disease. 8th Edition, McGraw Hill; Vol. 1 : 2001.
3. Carballo EC. Detection of inherited neurometabolic disorders—A practical clinical approach. Pediatr Clin North Am 1992;39: 801–820.
4. Leonard JV, Morris AA. Inborn errors of metabolism around time of birth. Lancet 2000;356:583–7.
5. Ogier de Baulny H. Management and emergency treatments of neonates with a suspicion of inborn errors of metabolism. Semin Neonatol 2002;7:17–26.

DISORDERS OF METABOLISM OF AMINO ACIDS

Phenylketonuria

Phenylketonuria (PKU) is a well known metabolic disorder with autosomal recessive inheritance. The level of hepatic enzyme *phenylalanine hydroxylase* is low, therefore, phenylalanine cannot be converted to tyrosine. Phenylalanine accumulates in the blood, cerebrospinal fluid and tissues. Accessory metabolic pathways start operating, which convert phenylalanine into phenylpyruvic acid, phenyl-lactic acid and o-hydroxyphenyl-acetic acid. These metabolites are excreted in the urine (Fig. 22.3).

The cells are not able to effectively utilize other amino acids because of high concentration of phenylalanine. However, the absorption of phenylalanine by the cells is also not significantly increased. The brain cells are deprived of amino acids, which are essential nutrients for their maturation and myelination during the period of rapid neurological development. Phenylalanine metabolites are not directly toxic to the brain.

Clinical Features

The child is usually normal in the first month of life. Neurological signs such as irritability, tremors, convulsions, hyperkinesis and muscular hypertonia manifest after some weeks. Development is markedly retarded resulting in gross intellectual impairment. High phenylalanine levels result in competitive inhibition of tyrosinase

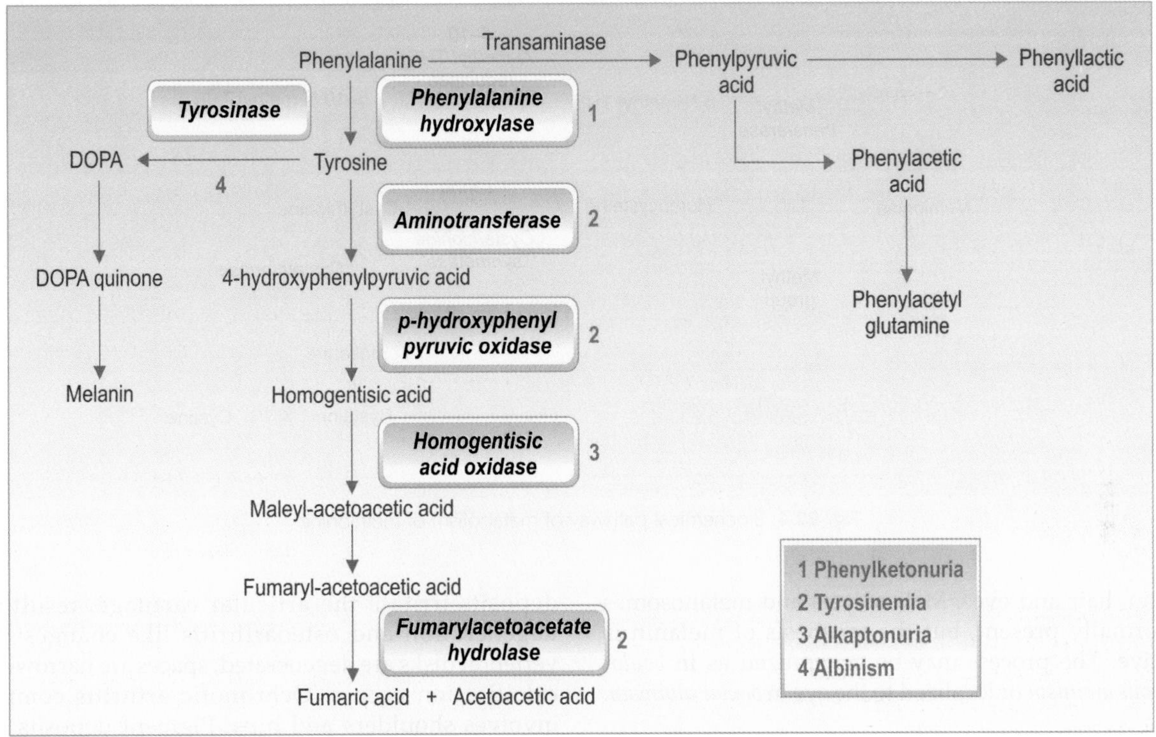

Fig. 22.3: Biochemical pathway of metabolism of phenylalanine and tyrosine

which converts tyrosine to melanin. This accounts for blond hair, blue iris and fair skin of the patients. Skin is more vulnerable to minor inflammatory lesions, rashes and eczema. Accumulation of phenylacetic acid and other metabolites causes characteristic musty body odor.

Diagnosis

Diagnostic criteria for PKU are: (i) on a normal diet, phenylalanine level in excess of 20 mg/dL/24 hr on two occasions, (ii) blood tyrosine level >5 mg/dL, and (iii) presence of abnormal urinary metabolites of phenylalanine detected by Guthrie or ferric chloride test. In the newborn period, the diagnosis can be made by routine screening of all neonates.

Treatment

Phenylalanine should be restricted in the diet of infants. However, it should not be completely eliminated as it is necessary for normal growth. If the dietary treatment is initiated within a few weeks of birth and blood phenylalanine levels are carefully monitored, mental retardation may be preventable. Biochemical abnormalities, other neurological signs and pigmentary changes of skin and hair improve within a few weeks of starting the therapy. Dietary restriction must continue for about 8–10 years.

Suggested reading

1. Cederbaum S. Phenylketonuria: an update. Curr Opin Pediatr 2002;14:702–6.
2. NIH Consensus Statement. Phenylketonuria (PKU): Screening and management. 2000;17:1–33.

Tyrosinemia

Most commonly, there is decreased activity of the enzyme *fumaryl acetoacetate hydrolase*. Tyrosine and methionine levels in the blood are high (Fig. 22.4). The clinical features include chronic liver disease and disturbances in renal tubular reabsorption. The latter leads to excretion of excess phosphates in urine, along with glycosuria, proteinuria and aminoaciduria (Fanconi syndrome). Phosphaturia results in hypophosphatemia, secondary hyperparathyroidism and rickets.

These patients develop hepatosplenomegaly, hyperbilirubinemia and hemorrhages. Acidosis may be present. Growth is retarded.

Treatment

Restriction of phenylalanine, tyrosine and methionine in the diet may result in some improvement, but the effect on liver function is not consistent and the progression persists. Inhibition of enzyme hydroxyl phenylpyruvate deoxygenase by NTBC has been shown to be of help but follow-up studies are required for long-term effects. Liver transplant is the most effective therapy.

Albinism

Albinism is an inherited disorder due to deficiency of the enzyme *tyrosinase* with diminished or absent melanin in

22

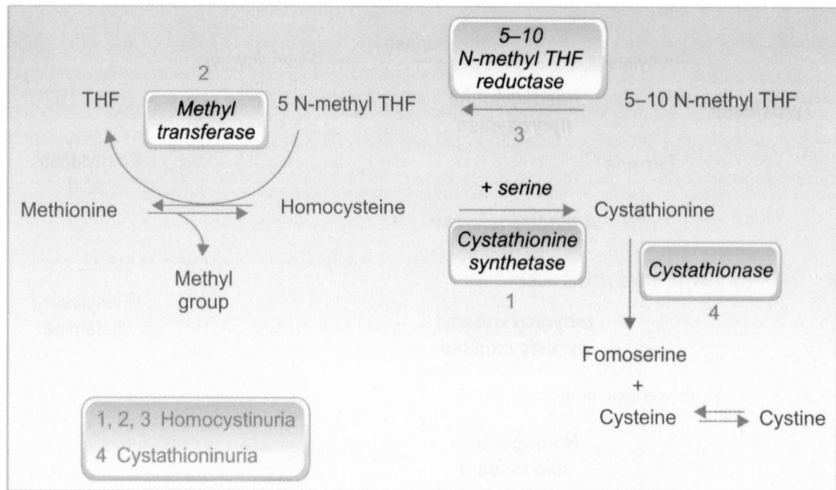

Fig. 22.4: Biochemical pathway of metabolism of methionine

the skin, hair and eyes. Melanocytes and melanosomes are normally present, but the synthesis of melanin is defective. The process may be generalized as in *oculocutaneous albinism* or localized to the eye in *ocular albinism*.

Clinical Features

The skin is depigmented. It does not tan but burns on exposure to sunlight. The hair is white and silky in texture and the iris is pinkish or bluish. The light passes through the iris causing photophobia. Visual acuity is diminished and nystagmus is often present. Intelligence remains normal.

Chediak Higashi syndrome comprises oculocutaneous albinism, neutropenia and susceptibility to pyogenic infections.

Suggested reading

1. Moss C. Genetic skin disorders. Semin Neonatol 2000;5:311–20.
2. Oetting WS. Albinism. Curr Opin Pediatr 1999;11:565–71.
3. Russell-Eggitt I. Albinism. Ophthalmol Clin North Am 2001;14: 533–46.

Alkaptonuria

Alkaptonuria is a rare metabolic disorder due to deficiency of the enzyme *homogentisic acid oxidase* in the liver and kidney. This inhibits the breakdown of homogentisic acid, which is excreted unchanged in urine. Accumulation of homogentisic acid (HGA) leads to destruction of connective tissue.

Clinical Features

The urine becomes dark on standing, especially if the pH of urine is alkaline. A black pigment is deposited in the sclera (between the cornea and the canthi) and the ear and nose cartilage (*ochronosis*). It is rarely noticed before the age of 20 to 30 years. The pigment in ochronosis is probably a polymer of homogentisic acid. Pigment deposits irritate the articular cartilage, resulting in degeneration and osteoarthritis like changes. Intervertebral disks are degenerated, spaces are narrowed and calcification occurs. Ochronotic arthritis commonly involves shoulders and hips. Pigment deposits in the kidney manifest as renal stones and nephrosis. The urine shows a black reaction with Fehling or Benedict reagents but no reaction with glucose oxidase.

Treatment

No specific therapy is known. Administration of ascorbic acid may prevent deposition of the ochronotic material in the cartilage but has no effect on the basic metabolic defect. Nitisinone inhibits the enzyme that produces HGA and may prove useful.

Suggested reading

Phornphutkul C, Introne WJ, Perry MB, et al. Natural history of alkaptonuria. N Engl J Med 2002;347:2111–21.

Homocystinuria

Homocystinuria is a relatively common metabolic error with autosomal recessive inheritance. In the most common situation, type 1, cystathionine is not synthesized from homocysteine and serine because the enzyme cystathionine synthetase in the liver is deficient (Fig. 22.4). Although the precursor, homocysteine accumulates in the tissues, it is rapidly oxidized to homocystine. The plasma level of homocystine is elevated and it is excreted in the urine. Methionine donates its methyl (CH_3) group to form homocysteine. The reaction is catalyzed by an enzyme methyl transferase. The methyl group for this is derived either from N^5 methyltertrahydrofolate or betaine which is a derivative of choline. Thus methionine level in the blood is elevated.

Clinical Features

The usual age of presentation is 3–4 years. The patients develop subluxation of the lens, recurrent thromboembolic episodes and have marfanoid features. The deficiency of cystine (which is formed from cystathionine) causes lesions of the lens. Thrombi in vessels are attributed to increased stickiness of the platelets and activation of Hageman factor, caused by accumulation of homocysteine. High methionine level in the brain is responsible for mental retardation, which is observed in only half of the reported cases. As cystine is necessary for collagen formation, its deficiency expresses itself as generalized osteoporosis. Convulsions and cerebrospinal lesions are due to thromboembolic phenomena in blood vessels of the nervous system. N^5 methyl-tetrahydrofolate, which donates a methyl group for methylation of homocysteine is excessively utilized and therefore, the plasma level of folate (derived from N^5 methyl-tetrahydrofolate) is low. These patients should be treated by restriction of methionine in the diet starting very early in life. Small proportion of cases are pyridoxine responsive and large doses of pyridoxine should be tried. Some patients do not improve till folic acid (1–5 mg/day) is also given.

Variants

Type II is due to a deficiency of enzyme N^5-methyl-tetrahydrofolate methyl transferase. This requires methyl B12 for its activity. In these patients methionine level is low. Clinical features include dementia, seizures and megaloblastic anemia. Methionine should not be restricted and large doses of vitamin B12 should be given.

Type III is due to deficiency of the enzyme $N^{5,10}$ methylene tetrahydrofolate reductase. This enzyme is responsible for the synthesis for N^5-methyl-tetrahydrofolate. These patients suffer from mental retardation. The symptoms improve on administration of folate. Methionine should not be restricted in diet as its level is low in these cases.

Patients with type II or type III disease do not show skeletal changes, ectopia lentis or thromboembolic phenomena. Presence of homocysteine in the urine is detected by the cyanide nitroprusside test. Elevated levels of methionine and homocystine are diagnostic.

Suggested reading

Rosenblatt DS, Whitehead VM. Cobalamin and folate deficiency: acquired and hereditary disorders in children. Semin Hematol 1999;36:19–34.

Cystinuria

Cystinuria is a metabolic disorder with autosomal recessive inheritance. The transport of cystine across both renal tubular cells and intestines is defective. There is a selective increase in the renal clearance and urinary excretion of basic amino acids, i.e. cystine, lysine, arginine and ornithine. Other amino acids are not excreted in excessive quantities. As the concentration of cystine in the urine is high, it tends to precipitate, leading to the formation of radio-opaque cystine renal calculi. Cystine appears as transparent, hexagonal crystals which are soluble in alkaline urine. Cyanide nitroprusside reaction in the urine is positive.

Treatment

The formation of cystine stones can be reduced by maintaining a good flow of urine (>1.5 L/m^2/d) and urinary alkalinization up to pH 7.5 by giving sodium bicarbonate and/or potassium citrate. In resistant cases (cystine excretion >750 mg/d), sulfhydryl agents such as D-penicillamine or tiopronin,which form highly soluble mixed disulfides with cystine moieties, are added. Excessive dietary intake of methionine should be avoided as methionine is the substrate necessary for endogenous production of cystine. Captopril produces marked reduction in cystine excretion.

Suggested reading

1. Joly D, Rieu P, Mejean A, et al. Treatment of cystinuria. Pediatr Nephrol 1999;13:945–50.
2. Pietrow PK, Auge BK, Weizer AZ, et al. Durability of the medical management of cystinuria. J Urol 2003;169:68–70.

Hartnup Disease

Hartnup disease is a rare inherited disorder. The transport of *monoamino-monocarboxylic acids* sharing a common pathway across the renal tubular cells is defective. Massive aminoaciduria is observed without a corresponding increase in plasma amino acid level. The absorption of these amino acids from jejunum is also delayed and incomplete. The amino acids remain in the intestines for longer periods and are decomposed there by bacteria into indole and indoxyl derivatives, which are then absorbed and excreted in the urine. Tryptophan level in the plasma is low. As tryptophan is metabolized into indole and indoxyl compounds, less of it is available for kynurenine nicotinamide metabolic pathway. As the end product of the kynurenine pathway is nicotinamide, nicotinamide production is diminished.

Clinical Features

The clinical features simulate pellagra. The skin shows photosensitivity and becomes rough and reddish on exposure to the sunlight. Neurologic lesions of cerebellar ataxia and psychologic disturbances are attributed to the lack of nicotinamide and toxic effects of retained indolic acids.

Treatment

High protein diet should be given to balance losses of amino acids in the urine. Intestinal antiseptic agents prevent the degradation of tryptophan. Oral administration of nicotinamide alleviates pellagra like symptoms.

DISORDERS OF METABOLISM OF BRANCHED CHAIN AMINO ACIDS AND ORGANIC ACIDS

Branched chain organic acidurias are a group of disorders that result from an abnormality of specific enzymes involving the catabolism of branched chain amino acids (leucine, isoleucine, valine). Maple syrup urine disease (MSUD), isovaleric acidemia (IVA), propionic aciduria (PA) and methylmalonic aciduria (MMA) represent the most commonly encountered abnormal organic acidurias. All these four disorders present in neonates as a neurologic distress of the intoxication type with either ketosis or ketoacidosis and hyperammonemia. The symptoms are nonspecific but some important clues may help in diagnosis; e.g. maple syrup odor in MSUD, sweaty feet odor in isovaleric aciduria, etc. There is a free interval between birth and clinical symptoms. MMA, PA and IVA present with severe dehydration, leuconeutropenia and thrombopenia which can mimic sepsis. All these disorders can be diagnosed by identifying acylcarnitine and other organic acid compounds in plasma and urine by gas chromatography mass spectrometry or tandem MS-MS.

Treatment

Treatment of acute episode includes correction of dehydration and acidosis. Adequate calorie intake is ensured, either orally or intravenously with proteins. Measures are taken to reduce ammonia levels if hyperammonemia is present. Severe cases many require exchange transfusion or peritoneal dialysis.

Specific treatment for multiple carboxylase deficiency is biotin supplementation, which results in dramatic response. Large doses of Vitamin B12 are useful in methylmalonic aciduria. Oral administration of carnitine is also useful in some forms of organic acidurias.

Suggested reading

Ogier de Baulny H, Saudubray JM. Branched-chain organic acidurias. Semin Neonatol 2002;7:65–74.

Maple Syrup Urine Disease

Maple syrup urine disease (MSUD) is an autosomal recessive disorder. Impaired activity of the branched-chain 2-oxoacid dehydrogenase complex (BCOA-DH) causes accumulation of branched-chain L-amino (BCAA) and 2-oxoacids (BCOA) in the serum, cerebrospinal fluid and urine which may exert neurotoxic effects. Levels of branched chain amino acids (leucine, isoleucine and valine), which are remote precursors of the keto acids, are also elevated. High levels of branched chain amino acids in the body fluids disturb the transport of other amino acids across the cell membrane. The synthesis of protein, lipoproteins and myelin is diminished. Branched chain keto acids inhibit glutamic acid decarboxylation in the brain.

Clinical Features

Patients are born normal. Symptoms of poor feeding, lethargy and vomiting appear within the first week of life. Ataxia, convulsions and spasticity are noted. There is rapid and progressive degeneration of the nervous system. Patient becomes comatosed and death occurs within a few weeks or months. These features are due to toxicity of accumulated metabolites, especially leucine. The smell of maple syrup is due to ketoacids. Hypoglycemic attacks occur due to high level of leucine in the blood.

Diagnosis

Ferric chloride gives navy blue color with the patient's urine, whereas 2–4 dinitrophenylhydrazine (DNPH) produces a yellow precipitate with the patient's urine. Guthrie's test is also useful in picking up these cases. Increased levels of leucine, isoleucine and valine are diagnostic.

Treatment

Treatment comprises dietary management with strictly reduced quantities of protein and BCAA as well as aggressive intervention during acute neonatal and subsequent metabolic complications. MSUD is regarded as a metabolic disorder with potentially favorable outcome when the patients are kept on a carefully supervised long-term therapy. Few patients with classical form of the disease have received orthotopic whole liver transplantation.

Suggested reading

1. Puliyanda DP, Harmon WE, Peterschmitt MJ, et al. Utility of hemodialysis in maple syrup urine disease. Pediatr Nephrol 2002:17:239–42.
2. Wendel U, Saudubray JM, Bodner A, et al. Liver transplantation in maple syrup urine disease. Eur J Pediatr 1999;158:S60–4.

Organic Acidurias

These small molecule disorders may have two types of clinical presentations: an insidious onset with few to no acute crises; and an acute metabolic encephalopathy, often brought on by illness and increased catabolism.

Most organic acidemias become clinically apparent during the newborn period or early infancy. After an initial period of well-being, affected children develop a life-threatening episode of metabolic acidosis characterized by an increased anion gap. The usual clinical presentation is that of a toxic encephalopathy and includes vomiting, poor feeding, neurologic symptoms such as seizures and abnormal tone, and lethargy progressing to coma. In the older child or adolescent, variant forms of the organic acidurias can present as loss of intellectual function, ataxia or other focal neurologic signs, Reye syndrome, recurrent keto-acidosis, or psychiatric symptoms.

Clinical pointers to specific organic acidurias

- **Cutaneous abnormalities:** Perioral eruption (multiple carboxylase deficiency)
- **Abnormal urinary or body odor:** Maple syrup/burnt sugar [maple syrup urine disease (MSUD)], sweaty feet [isovaleric acidemia (IVA)], cat urine (multiple carboxylase deficiency)
- **Hair abnormalities:** Alopecia (multiple carboxylase deficiency), kinky hair (multiple carboxylase deficiency)
- **Dysmorphic features:** Mevalonic aciduria and 3-OH-isobutyric aciduria
- **Hypoglycemia and neurological symptoms:** Organic acidurias including late onset MSUD
- **Acute ataxia:** Late onset MSUD, methylmalonic acidemia (MMA), IVA, multiple carboxylase deficiency
- **Acute metabolic encephalopathies:** Glutaryl-CoA dehydrogenase deficiency, IVA, MSUD, MMA, multiple carboxylase deficiency, propionic aciduria
- **Acute hemiplegia and metabolic disease (metabolic stroke):** MMA and propionic acidemia (PA), glutaric aciduria type 1, methylcrotonyl-CoA carboxylase deficiency

Management

Immediate management includes stopping oral feeds, (process/store blood and urine samples before stopping feeds), intravenous fluids, correction of dehydration, acidosis and dyselectrolytemias. Specific therapy may be started (e.g. sodium benzoate for hyperammonemic states). In cases of refractory acidosis dialysis may be required.

Adjunctive compounds to dispose of toxic metabolites: Examples include use of thiamine to treat thiamine-responsive MSUD and hydroxocobalamin, but usually not cyanocobalamin to treat methylmalonic acidemia. For the disorders of propionate metabolism, intermittent administration of non-absorbed antibiotics can reduce the production of propionate by gut bacteria. The various cofactors and adjunctive therapy is detailed in Table 22.5.

DISORDERS OF UREA CYCLE

Catabolism of amino acids leads to production of free ammonia. Ammonia is converted into urea through the five steps of urea cycle (Fig. 22.5). Two moles of ammonia are excreted as 1 mole of urea per cycle, at a net cost of 3 moles ATP. Urea cycle may be blocked at any stage. Deficiency of any of the five enzymes in the urea cycle results in the accumulation of ammonia (> 200 μmol/L) and leads to encephalopathy. A defect in the stage III results in citrullinemia; stage IV defect causes argininosuccinic acidemia. Hyperargininemia results from the metabolic block in the last stage of the urea cycle.

Clinical Features

All metabolic defects of urea cycle, whether due to accumulation of ammonia (I and II stage), citrulline (III

Table 22.5: Cofactor/adjunctive therapy

Disorders	*Vitamin/cofactor/adjunctive therapy (dose)*
Maple syrup urine disease	Thiamine (5 mg/kg/day)
Methylmalonic acidemia	B12 (1–2 mg/day); L-Carnitine (100 mg/kg/d); Metronidazole (10–20 mg/kg/day)
Propionic acidemia	L-Carnitine (100 mg/kg/d); Metronidazole (10–20 mg/kg/day)
Isovaleric acidemia	L-carnitine (50–100 mg/kg/day); L-glycine (150–300 mg/kg/day)
Glutaric aciduria	Carnitine
Multiple carboxylase	Biotin (10–40 mg/day)

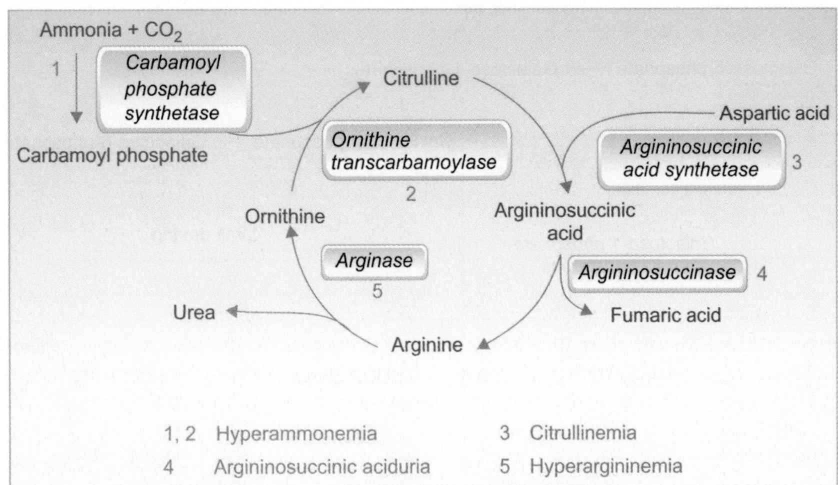

Fig. 22.5: Disorders of metabolism of amino acids of urea cycle

stage), argininosuccinic acid or arginine (IV and V stage) are toxic for the brain. These patients are intolerant to protein food and show a dislike for these. Recurrent vomiting and irritability are observed early in life. The disease progresses rapidly to lethargy, coma, ataxia and convulsions. Clinical features include mental retardation, muscular rigidity, opisthotonos and delayed development.

22

Patients of argininosuccinic acidemia have dry, breakable and short hair. Blood urea levels are nearly normal, thus indicating that the metabolic blocks are not complete.

Treatment

Hyperammonemic states (organic acidemias, urea cycle defects)—appropriate dietary restriction of proteins (in acute stage 0.25 g/kg/d as a mixture of essential amino acids and later 1–1.5 g/kg/day). Low protein diets are also available commercially. Sodium benzoate (250–500 mg/kg/day in 4-6 divided doses orally) can be administered as it conjugates with NH_3 and forms a nontoxic metabolite that is easily excreted. Sodium phenylacetate (250–500 mg/kg/day) and arginine (200–800 mg/kg/day) are also effective. Carnitine supplementation has also been recommended with phenylacetate and benzoate. Catabolic states triggering hyperammonemia should be avoided. Gene therapy is under investigation.

Hemodialysis, peritoneal dialysis or hemofiltration should be instituted if serum ammonia exceeds 500 mmol/L. Sustained ammonia levels greater than 800 mmol/L for >24 h are associated with irreversible neurological damage.

Suggested reading

1. Burton BK. Urea cycle disorders. Clin Liver Dis 2000; 4: 815–830.
2. Lee B, Goss J. Long-term correction of urea cycle disorders. J Pediatr 2001;138:S62–71.
3. Leonard JV, Morris AA. Urea cycle disorders. Semin Neonatol 2002; 7: 27–35.
4. Summar M, Tuchman M. Proceedings of a consensus conference for the management of patients with urea cycle disorders. J Pediatr 2001;138:S6–10.
5. Urea Cycle Disorders Conference group. Consensus statement from a conference for the management of patients with urea cycle disorders. J Pediatr 2001;138:S1–5.

DEFECTS OF CARBOHYDRATE METABOLISM

Galactosemia

Galactose absorbed from the gut is phosphorylated to galactose-1-phosphate, the reaction being catalyzed by the enzyme *galactokinase*. Galactose-1-phosphate combines with UDP glucose (uridyl diphosphoglucose) to form UDP galactose and glucose-1-phosphate (Fig. 22.6). This reaction is catalyzed by the enzyme galactose-1-phosphate uridyl transferase. Deficiency of either galactokinase or galactose-1-phosphate uridyl transferase results in accumulation of galactose and of galactose-1-phosphate which act as cellular toxins. Galactose is excreted in urine. Alternative metabolic pathways of galactose are utilized excessively. Galactose is reduced to galactilol by the enzyme aldose reductase. Galactitol is not metabolized further and is excreted in urine. A small amount of galactose may be oxidized to galactonic acid by the enzyme galactose dehydrogenase.

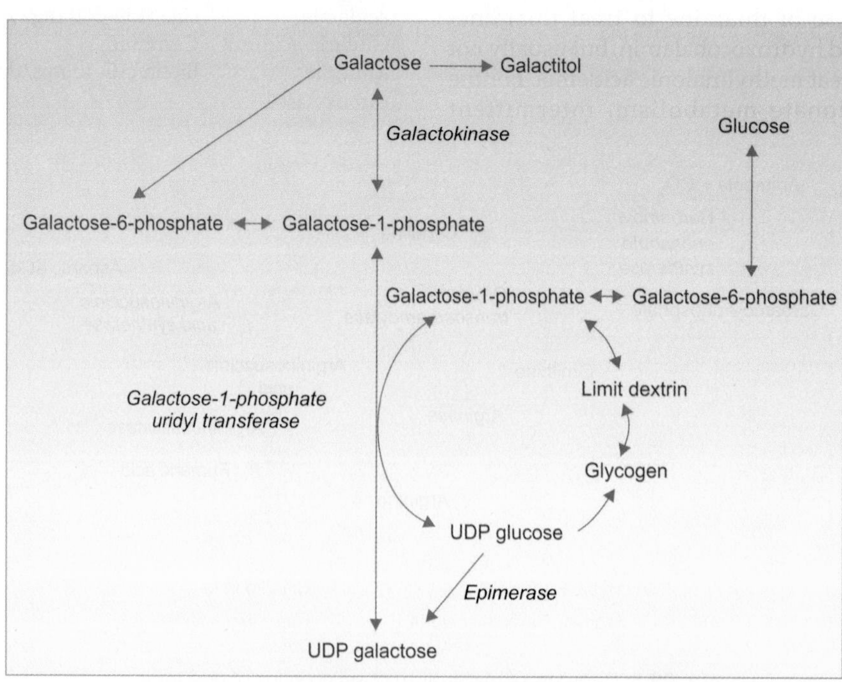

Fig. 22.6: Schematic metabolism of galactose and glucose

Galactose-1-Phosphate Uridyl Transferase Deficiency

It is an autosomal recessive disorder manifesting within a few days or weeks after birth (after ingestion of milk). The physiological jaundice of the newborn period persists longer than usual. The liver is enlarged and cataract appears within a few weeks. There is evidence of liver dysfunction. The children become mentally retarded. Vomiting, diarrhea and failure to thrive are early and common manifestations. The mechanism of toxicity is obscure, but cataract is believed to be due to accumulation of galactitol. Mental retardation and hepatic cirrhosis are attributed to galactose-1-phosphate.

Galactokinase Deficiency

Manifestations are milder. Mental retardation, liver damage and cachexia do not occur. The only significant abnormality is cataract due to accumulation of galactilol.

Treatment

Galactose free diet, if started early, leads to rapid clinical improvement and prevents further damage. Mental retardation (classical galactosemia), if already present does not improve with therapy.

Glycogen Storage Disorders

A major part of ingested carbohydrate is absorbed as glucose via the portal system. The glucose is phosphorylated to several intermediate compounds (glucose-6-phosphate and glucose-1-phosphate) and is ultimately stored as glycogen. Glycogen is an extensively branched polysaccharide formed by glucose units linked together by alpha 1–4 and alpha 1–6 bonds. When the peripheral glucose is utilized and blood glucose level falls, the glycogen in the liver is depolymerized, the bonds at branch points are split and free glucose is released into the blood by hydrolytic dephosphorylation. The final reaction is mediated by the enzyme glucose-6-phosphatase. The series of reactions causing release of glucose are called glycogenolysis (Fig. 22.7).

Theoretically, there may be a deficient synthesis of glycogen or glycogen may be stored excessively in the liver and other tissues due to inadequate depolymerization. In some types, glycogen may have an abnormal chemical structure.

Several well-defined disorders of glycogen metabolism have been described (Table 22.6). These are numbered

Table 22.6: Enzymatic deficiencies in glycogenesis

Type	Enzyme
Type I	Glucose-6-phosphatase
Type II	Lysosomal alpha-1, 4-glucosidase (acid and neutral maltase)
Type III	Amylo-1, 6-glucosidase or oligo-1, 4-1, 4-glucano-transferase (debrancher enzyme)
Type IV	Alpha-1, 4 glucan:alpha-1, 4 glucan-6-alpha glucosyl tranferase (brancher enzyme)
Type V	Muscle phosphorylase
Type VI	Liver phosphorylase
Type VII	Phosphofructokinase
Type VIII	Phosphoglucose isomerase
Type IX	Phosphorylase kinase
Type X	Phosphorylase kinase
Type XI	3, 5-cyclic AMP dependent kinase
Type XII	Phosphoglucose isomerase
Type XIII	Triose phosphate isomerase
Type XIV	Phosphoglycerate mutase, M isoenzyme

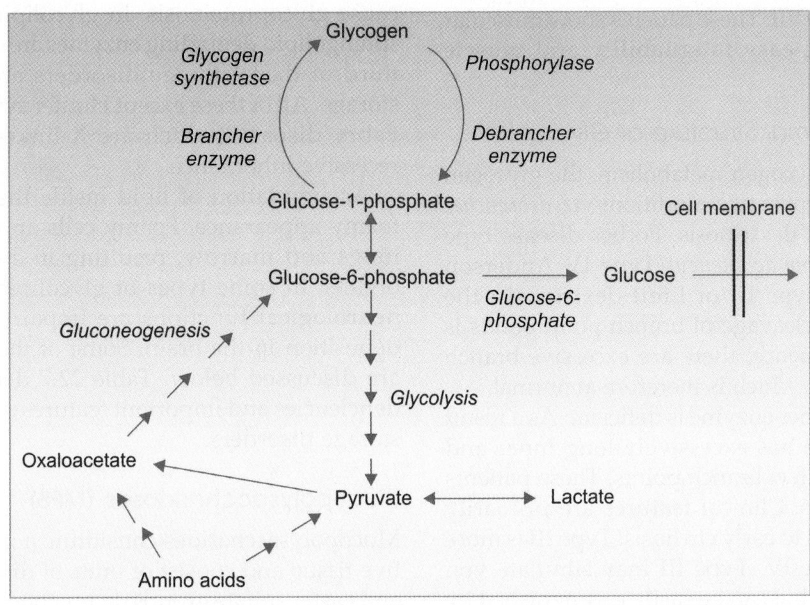

Fig. 22.7: Schematic glucose and glycogen metabolism in the liver

according to the sequence of their discovery. However, it may be more convenient for the physician to consider these according to the principal organ involved.

Disorders in which Liver is the Main Affected Organ

22 These include type I (von Gierke disease), type III (Forbes or limit dextrinosis), type IV (amylopectinosis) types VI, VII, IX and X.

In type I GSD the usual clinical features include hepatomegaly, failure to thrive, hypoglycemia, ketosis and acidosis. Hypoglycemia becomes worse after overnight fasting and is attributed to the inability of the liver to release glucose in the blood. Consequently free fatty acids are mobilized excessively to provide for the energy needs of the body. This results in hyperlipemia in type I. Administration of glucose ameliorates ketosis. In type I, the blood glucose level does not rise on administration of glucagon.

Disorders in which Cardiac Muscle is Affected

Type IIa (Pompe disease): Signs and symptoms of this disease result from lysosomal storage of glycogen in skeletal muscles, cardiac muscles and central nervous system. The heart is enlarged and appears globular. Electrocardiogram shows left axis deviation, short PR interval and large QRS. Heart failure with dyspnea and cyanosis may occur. Skeletal muscles show hypotonia and marked weakness. The tongue is large and protruding. Death usually occurs before the age of 1 year. The diagnosis is suggested by low levels of the enzyme *acid maltase* in leukocytes, liver, muscles and fibroblasts. Enzyme replacement therapy is available and very effective but the cost is prohibitive.

Disorders with Skeletal Muscle Involvement

Type IIb, type III (Forbes or limit dextrinosis), type V (McArdle disease), type VII. These patients show muscular hypotonia, weakness, easy fatiguability and muscle cramps.

Disorders with Abnormal Structure of Glycogen

In most disorders of glycogen metabolism, the glycogen structure is normal except in two conditions viz. *debrancher enzyme deficiency* (limit dextrinosis, Forbes disease type III) and *brancher enzyme deficiency* (Type IV Anderson amylopectinosis). In type III or limit dextrinosis, the enzyme necessary for cleavage of branch point bonds is deficient. As a consequence, there are excessive branch points on the glycogen, which is therefore abnormal.

In type IV, the brancher enzyme is deficient. As a result the glycogen molecule has excessively long inner and outer chains with very few branch points. These patients do not develop ketosis. Clinical features are primarily related to liver and lead to early cirrhosis. Type III is more common than the type IV. Type III may simulate von Gierke disease (type I), but can be easily distinguished by galactose infusions, which promptly causes hyperglycemia, because there is no defect of dephosphorylation. Prognosis is relatively better. Usually, these patients present with isolated massive hepatomegaly and deranged liver function. Patients should be treated with high protein and low fat diet. Small frequent feeds are preferable. Intercurrent infections should be treated promptly.

Treatment

Carbohydrate metabolism in liver is responsible for glucose homeostasis. Treatment is designed mainly to maintain normoglycemia and is achieved by continuous nasogastric infusion of glucose or oral uncooked starch. Depending on the response frequent day time feeds and continuous nasogastric feeding at night may be given. Uncooked starch acts as a slow release form of glucose. This is specially useful in type I, III and IV but most demanding in type I. Enzyme replacement therapy is available for type II GSD.

Suggested reading

1. Clayton PT. Inborn errors presenting with liver dysfunction. Semin Neonatol 2002;7:49–63.
2. Wright EM, Turk E, Martin MG. Molecular basis for glucose-galactose malabsorption. Cell Biochem Biophys 2002;36:1 15–21.

LYSOSOMAL STORAGE DISORDERS

This comprises of a group of about 40 disorders. Deficiency of a lysosomal enzyme may result in impaired intralysosomal degradation of exogenous and endogenous macromolecules and deposition of these metabolites in several body tissues. Enzyme deficiencies in the degradation pathway of glycosaminoglycans cause mucopolysacchariosis, and deficiencies affecting glycopeptides cause glycoproteinosis. In glycolipid storage disorders, sphingolipid degrading enzymes are deficient. About two-third of these storage disorders are due to glycolipid storage. All of these except Hunter syndrome (MPS II) and Fabry disease (which are X-linked) have autosomal recessive inheritance.

Accumulation of lipid inside the cells gives them a foamy appearance. Foamy cells appear in liver, spleen, lungs and marrow, resulting in enlargement of these organs. In some types of glycolipid storage disorders, neurological functions are impaired due to abnormal deposition in the brain. Some of the common disorders are discussed below. Table 22.7 depicts the enzymatic deficiencies and important features of common lysosomal storage disorders.

Mucopolysaccharidoses (MPS)

Mucopolysaccharides consititute a major part of connective tissue and consist of units of disaccharides, nitrogen and easter sulfate groups. In mucopolysaccharidoses, acid mucopolysaccharides are abnormally deposited in the

Table 22.7: Clinical features of common lysosomal storage disorders

Disorder	*Cherry-red spot*	*Visceromegaly*	*Skeletal lesions*	*Mental retardation*	*Bulbar signs*
Gangliosidosis GM1	+	+	+	+	–
Gaucher disease	–	+	+	+	+
Krabbe disease	–	–	–	+	–
Metachromatic leukodystrophy	+	–	–	+	–
Multiple sulfatase deficiency	+	+	+	+	–
Niemann-Pick disease	+	+	–	+	–
Sandhoff disease	+	+	+	–	–
Tay-Sachs disease	+	–	–	+	–

tissues and excreted in the urine. Acid mucopolysaccharides yield N'acetyl-hexosamine (a substituted sugar) and uronic acid. Neutral mucopolysaccharides comprise N'acetyl hexosamine and a hexose. Major acid mucopolysaccharides are hyaluronic acid, chondroitin 4-sulfate, chondroitin 6-sulfate, dermatan sulfate, heparin sulfate and heparin. Keratan sulfate (of cornea or bones) is a neutral mucopolysaccharide. The sulfated mucopolysaccharides are linked with protein to form macromolecules. Due to lack of degradation, mucopolysaccharides accumulate in the lysosomes causing disorganization of the cell structure and function. Partially degraded mucopolysaccharides are excreted in the urine. At least 8 genetic variants of mucopolysaccharidosis are recognized. Their clinical features are summarized in Table 22.8.

Metabolic Defect

1. Accumulation of dermatan sulfate and heparan sulfate in the tissues and their excretion in the urine occurs in Hurler syndrome (type IH), Scheie syndrome (type IS), Hunter syndrome (type II) and type VII.
2. Heparan sulfate accumulates in tissues, and is excreted in the urine in Sanfilippo disease (type IIIA and B).
3. Keratan sulfate and chondroitin sulfate are excreted in the urine in cases of Morquio syndrome (type IV).
4. Dermatan sulfate is excreted in the urine in Maroteaux-Lamy syndrome (type VI).
5. Excretion of keratin sulfate like material in the urine and accumulation in the tissue occurs in type VIII.

Inheritance is autosomal recessive in all the types of mucopolysaccharidosis except type II which is X-linked recessive.

Clinical Features

Mental retardation is severe in type III and VII, moderate in type I, mild in type II, rare in type IV (Morquio) and IS (previously called type V). It is absent in type VI (Maroteaux Lamy).

Cloudy cornea is observed in types I, IS and VI but it may occur in some cases of type IV, cloudiness of cornea is minimal in type III, but is not seen in type II.

Bone changes are most marked in type IV, marked in type I, II, VI and VII but are mild in types III and IS. The type of skeletal changes observed include the following: Thickening of the skull, marked deformity of the sella turcica, broad spatula like ribs, beak shaped vertebrae especially around the L1 vertebra and heavy bones of the hands.

In Morquio disease (type IV) the trunk is short with flattened narrow vertebrae, barrel shaped chest with sternum protruding forwards. Other features include short neck, broad mouth, widely spaced teeth, prominent maxilla and hands reaching up to knees.

Facies are coarse in type IH, the lips are thick, tongue is enlarged, teeth are peg-like and widely separated. Bridge of the nose is depressed. The features are very coarse and may be mistaken with cretinism.

Table 22.8: Clinical features of mucopolysaccharidoses (MPS)

Eponym/MPS	*Clinical Features*				
Number	*Mental retardation*	*Coarse facies*	*Hepatosplenomegaly*	*Dysostosis multiplex*	*Corneal clouding*
Hurler/IH	+	+	+	+	+
Scheie/IS	–	–	–	–	+
Hunter/II	+	+	+	+	–
Sanifilipo/III	+	–	–	–	–
Morquio/IV	–	–	–	+	+
Maroteaux-Lamy/VI	–	–	–	+	+
Sly/VII	–	–	+	+	–

Hepatosplenomegaly is present in types I, II, VI and VII and multiple sulphatase deficiency.

Figure 22.8 shows a classical facies of MPS I and Fig. 22.9 shows important skeletal changes.

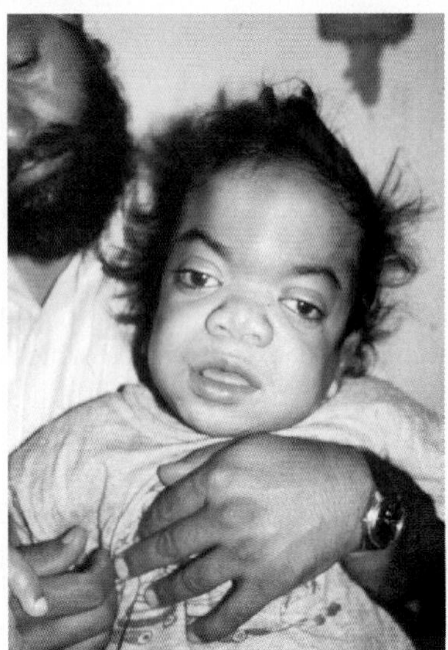

Fig. 22.8: Hurler syndrome

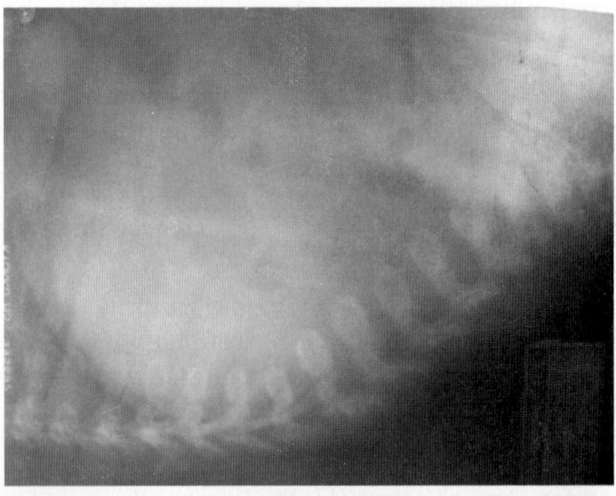

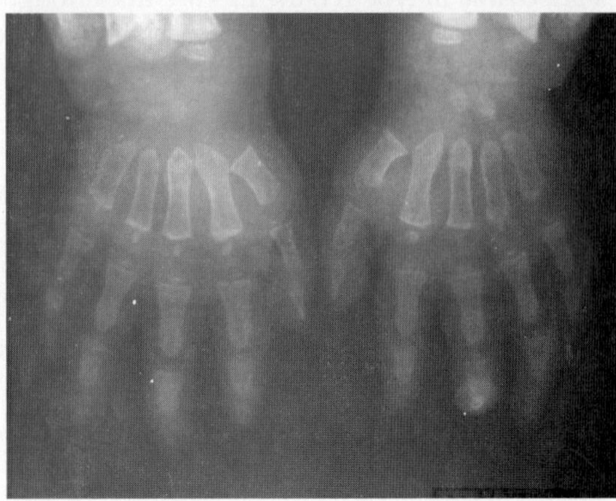

Fig. 22.9: Typical radiological findings of MPS. Note beaking of vertebrae and proximal tapering of metacarpals

Diagnosis is made by testing urinary excretion of glycosaminoglycans (GAG) and specific enzyme assays.

Treatment

Enzyme replacement therapy is available for type I and type VI but the cost is prohibitive. Trials are on for other types of disease. Bone marrow transplantation has been found to be effective in MPS I and VI.

Suggested reading

1. Froissart R, Moreira da Silva I, Guffon N, et al. Mucopolysaccharidosis -genotype/phenotype aspects. Acta Paediatr 2002;91:S82–7.
2. Rigante D, Segni G. Cardiac structural involvement in mucopolysaccharidoses. Cardiology 2002;98:18–20.
3. Saxonhouse MA, Behnke M, Williams JL, et al. Mucopolysaccharidosis Type VII presenting with isolated neonatal ascites. J Perinatol 2003;23:73–5.

Gaucher Disease

Gaucher disease is a relatively common metabolic disorder with autosomal recessive inheritance. There is deficiency of the tissue enzyme *glucocerebrosidase* which splits glucose from glucosyl ceramide. As a result, *glucosyl ceramide*, a cerebroside, accumulates in the cell of reticuloendothelial system. The cerebroside laden cells are large and have eccentric nuclei; the cytoplasm appears like crumpled silk (*Gaucher cells*).

Clinical Features

The spleen is always markedly enlarged and there are signs of hypersplenism, e.g. leucopenia and thrombocytopenia. The liver is enlarged and the marrow cavity is widened, due to deposits of Gaucher cells. Expansion of the bone is prominent, especially at the lower end of the femur and humerus. Diagnosis is made by doing *glucocerebrosidase* enzyme levels in leucocytes or skin fibroblasts.

Three clinical variants are described: In type I (chronic non-neuronopathic), the course of illness is chronic, and the visceral involvement is prominent, but there are no neurological signs. The disease may be detected in older persons.

In type II (acute neuronopathic), the disease starts early and death occurs before the age of 2 years. Neurological symptoms are prominent.

In type III (chronic neuronopathic), the onset is in the second year; the course is subacute and both visceral and neurological manifestations occur.

Treatment

This was the first storage disorder for which the treatment became available. Enzyme replacement is done with natural or recombinant glucocerebrosidase. It is effective but expensive. Bone marrow transplantation is another treatment option. OGT-918 slows the rate of accumulating glycolipids and is under trial.

Suggested reading

Elstein D, Abrahamov A, Dweck A, et al. Gaucher disease: pediatric concerns. Paediatr Drugs 2002;4:417–26.

Metachromatic Leukodystrophy

Sulfated glycososphingolipids accumulate in the white matter of the central nervous system, peripheral nerves, liver and kidney. The myelin degenerates but neuronal cells are affected to a lesser degree. Granular masses accumulate in the white matter of the brain. Acidified cresyl violet stains them purple with a brown background. This metachromatic staining gives the name to the disease.

Clinical Features

The disorder has infantile and juvenile forms. Early clinical manifestations including disturbances of gait, incoordination and progressive mental deterioration appear in the second year of life. Knee jerk is brisk but ankle reflex and plantar response may be absent because of involvement of peripheral nerves. Death occurs before the age of 10 years. Diagnosis is confirmed by level of the enzyme arylsulphatase A in the white cells.

Treatment

There is no effective treatment. Bone marrow transplantation has been tried in few cases.

Suggested reading

Kaye EM. Update on genetic disorders affecting white matter. Pediatr Neurol 2001;24:11–24.

GM1 Gangliosidoses

In type I, the onset is at birth. There is severe cerebral degeneration. Facial features resemble mucopolysaccharidosis type I H. Hepatosplenomegaly and cherry red spot on the macular region are present. X-ray of the bones show dysostosis. These children die of respiratory infections before the age of 2 years.

In type II, the onset of illness is between 1 and 2 years and death occurs before the age of 10 years. Liver and spleen are not enlarged. Radiological abnormalities are minimal but psychic and motor disturbances are severe.

GM2 Gangliosidosis

The inborn errors of GM2 ganglioside metabolism cause GM2 ganglioside to accumulate within the lysosomes of the nerve cells. The majority of the patients are infants with the ***Tay-Sachs*** form (Type I) of the disease associated with a severe deficiency of beta-N-acetylhexosaminidase A (hexosaminidase A). Both hexosaminidase A and B are deficient in ***Sandhoff disease*** (type II).

Tay-Sachs Disease

Tay-Sachs disease is an autosomal recessively inherited metabolic defect, common in Ashkenazi Jews. It is now reported from all over the world including India. A history of consanguinity is usually obtained. There is deficiency of ganglioside GM2 hexosaminidase, leading to accumulation of ganglioside GM2 within the ganglion cells of the nervous system. Myelin is degenerated.

The disorder manifests clinically by the age of 6 months. Apathy, hypotonia, visual defects and developmental retardation occur early. The child progressively becomes spastic, blind and demented. The fundus examination shows cherry red spot over the macular region in the retina. Death occurs within 3–4 years.

Sandhoff Disease

In Sandhoff disease, visceral involvement is present in addition to features of Tay-Sachs disease.

Niemann Pick Disease

Niemann Pick disease is an autosomal recessive storage disorder of sphingomyelin and cholesterol in the lysosomes. In the classical form (type A), clinical manifestations begin in early life with feeding difficulties, failure to thrive and developmental delay and later neuroregression. There is protuberant abdomen with hepatosplenomegaly. Cherry red spot on fundus examination is seen in about half the cases. Late onset variants are associated with extrapyramidal manifestations. Diagnosis is confirmed by measurement of sphingomyelinase levels. There is no specific treatment available presently. Type B disease is a milder form with hepatosplenomegaly but no neurological involvement.

Suggested reading

1. Christopher R, Rangaswamy GR, Shetty KT. GM2 gangliosidoses: a review of cases confirmed by beta-N-acetylhexosaminidase assay. Indian J Pediatr 1995;62:479–83.
2. Gelbart M. Tay-Sachs disease. Nurs Times 1998;94:39.

DEFECTS OF LIPID METABOLISM

The main function of lipoproteins is to transport water insoluble compounds in the serum. The lipoproteins are classified according to the relative proportion of their constituents, viz. protein, cholesterol, phospholipids and triglycerides. Disorders include familial hypercholeslerolemias, hypertriglyceridemias and abetalipoproteinemia.

Abetalipoproteinemia

Abetalipoproteinemia is an inherited disease characterized by the virtual absence of apolipoprotein B (apoB)-containing lipoproteins from plasma. Possible genetic defects may be (i) deficient synthesis of apoprotein of low density beta-lipoproteins, (ii) increased utilization of apoproteins, or (iii) difficulty in incorporation of apoprotein into the lipoprotein. Beta-lipoproteins are necessary for formation of chylomicrons which are absent in the plasma. The plasma cholesterol and triglyceride levels are low. Clinically the patients have abnormally crenated thorny erythrocytes (acanthocytes), malabsorption of fats, retinitis pigmentosa and neurological signs of ataxia, tremors, athetosis, and loss of vibration and position sense. Though fats are normally digested and assimilated through the intestinal mucosa, these cannot be transported to plasma from there because of the inability to form chylomicrons. Lipoproteins may be necessary for the transport of some essential nutrients to erythrocytes. Therefore their absence may interfere with the synthesis of red cell membrane, thus causing acanthocytosis. Pathogenesis of the eye and brain changes is obscure.

Suggested reading

1. Finch LA, Nowicki MJ, Mitchell TE, et al. Abetalipoproteinemia. J Pediatr Gastroenterol Nutr 2001;32:310,315.
2. Ohashi K, Ishibashi S, Osuga J, et al. Novel mutations in the microsomal triglyceride transfer protein gene causing abetalipoproteinemia. J Lipid Res 2000;41:1199–204.
3. Padma MV, Jain S, Maheshwari MC. Abetalipoproteinemia in an Indian family. Indian J Pediatr 1996;63:263–9.

PEROXISOMAL DISORDERS

Peroxisomes are subcellular organelles. A number of enzymatic reactions such as oxidation of long chain fatty acids, catalases and phytanic acid occur in these. *Zellweger syndrome* (ZS), neonatal *adrenoleukodystrophy* (NALD), and infantile *Refsum disease* (IRD) are clinically overlapping syndromes, collectively called **peroxisome biogenesis disorders**, with clinical features being most severe in ZS and least pronounced in IRD. Inheritance of these disorders is autosomal recessive. The peroxisome biogenesis disorders are genetically heterogeneous, having at least 12 different complementation groups (CG). The gene affected in CG1 is *PEX1*. Approximately 65% of the patients harbor mutations in PEX1.

These multisystemic disorders are characterized by invariable neurological involvement. Symptoms include seizures, nystagmus, hearing defects, progressive upper motor neuron deficits and neurologic deterioration, optic atrophy and adrenal atrophy. MRI demonstrates white matter changes in brain. Urinary organic acid analysis is indeed useful for screening subjects with peroxisomal disorders.

Suggested reading

1. Barth PG, Gootjes J, Bode H, et al. Late onset white matter disease in peroxisome biogenesis disorder. Neurology 2001;57:1949–55.
2. Raymond GV. Peroxisomal disorders. Curr Opin Neurol 2001;14:783–7.

MISCELLANEOUS DISORDERS

Alpha-1-Antitrypsin Deficiency

α-1-antitrypsin, a protease inhibitor (Pi), is synthesized in the liver and protects lung alveolar tissues from destruction by neutrophil elastase. Over 70% of people in normal population are PiM type. Their alpha-1-antitrypsin level ranges between 0.8 to 1.8 g/L.

Deficiency

Deficiency leads to retention of abnormal polymerized α-1-antitrypsin in hepatocytes; emphysema results from alveolar damage. At least 24 alleles of the gene have been recognized. PiZ mutant is responsible for majority of cases. The alpha-1-antitrypsin concentration is usually below 0.6 g/L in PiZ and nil in those with Pi null. Other homozygous and heterozygous states have intermediate levels.

Clinical Manifestations

Clinical manifestations in childhood include late hemorrhagic disease of infancy, cholestasis or chronic liver disease. Lungs are affected in adulthood. Glomerulonephritis, vasculitis and panniculitis are the other rare manifestations. Diagnosis can be made by estimating serum levels, genotyping and *Pi* phenotyping.

Treatment

Replacement therapy with intravenous α-1-antitrypsin improves the serum levels but is of little benefit in infants with liver disease; though it can prevent or treat lung disease in adults. There are promising early results with gene therapy. Efforts are on to move polymerized α-1-antitrypsin from liver to lung where it might be beneficial. Liver replacement therapy has been used successfully for severe liver injury. An increasing number of patients with severe emphysema have undergone lung transplantation.

Suggested reading

1. Pashankar D, Schreiber RA. Neonatal cholestasis: a red alert for the jaundiced newborn. Can J Gastroenterol 2000;14:67D–72D.
2. Perlmutter DH. Alpha-1-antitrypsin deficiency. Semin Liver Dis 1998;18:217–25.
3. Primhak RA, Tanner MS. Alpha-1 antitrypsin deficiency. Arch Dis Child 2001;85:2–5.

Wilson Disease

Wilson disease is a inborn error of copper metabolism autosomal recessive inheritance; the defective gene is mapped to chromosome 13. Either the lysosomal copper is excreted in insufficient quantities in the bile or the binding of copper by metallothionine is increased four fold due to aberrant chemical structure of this intracellular storage protein copper.

Copper accumulates in the cytoplasm of liver cells, reaching a level of 500 to 2000 μg/g of dry weight. Liver cells are damaged, copper is released in the serum and then deposited in other tissues and cells. Red blood cells are damaged, resulting in hemolysis. Proximal renal tubules are affected. The toxic effects of copper on the brain cells cause neurologic disturbances. Deposition in the cornea results in Kayser-Fleischer rings.

Low serum levels of ceruloplasmin are characteristic. This is probably secondary to hepatic damage and not the primary metabolic defect as was believed earlier. As most of the copper in serum is bound to ceruloplasmin, total serum copper level is reduced.

Clinical Features

The clinical presentation can be extremely varied, viz. acute or chronic liver disease with or without neurological disease, psychiatric problems, bony deformities, hemolytic anemia and endocrine manifestations.

Hepatic dysfunction: The patients are younger, generally between 6 and 15 years of age. The illness starts acutely with jaundice and hepatomegaly, progressing rapidly to hepatic coma and death. The course of the illness may simulate chronic active hepatitis.

Neurological presentation: These patients are generally older and present with symptoms of basal ganglia involvement, e.g. rigidity, tremors, difficulty in speech, poor handwriting and abnormal posture. There may also be psychiatric disturbances. Performance at the school may deteriorate. The illness appears as a combination of cerebellar ataxia and Parkinsonism. Although the liver may be enlarged, jaundice is usually absent. Kayser Fleischer ring appears rusty brown in color usually along with upper and lower borders of cornea. It should be looked for by slit lamp examination. Absence of the ring does not exclude the diagnosis of Wilson disease, especially in the first decade of life.

Diagnosis

Low ceruloplasmin, high 24 h urinary copper and presence of KF rings help in diagnosis. The serum ceruloplasmin level is less than 20 mg/dL and serum copper concentration is below 20 μg/dL. More than 100 μg of copper is excreted in the urine in 24 hours. Urinary copper estimation is usually done with a penicillamine challenge. Liver copper concentration exceeds 250 μg/g of dry weight. Liver function tests are abnormal.

Low serum copper and ceruloplasmin levels are not characteristic of Wilson disease in infants up to the age of 6 months and in patients with nephrosis, kwashiorkor or severe malabsorption syndrome. Serum copper levels are increased in biliary cirrhosis and toxic cirrhosis.

22

Treatment

Dietary intake of copper rich foods, e.g. liver, shellfish, nuts and chocolate is to be reduced. Copper already deposited in tissues is chelated by administration of d-penicillamine a dose of 10–30 mg/kg/day in 3–4 divided doses, at 30 minutes before meals. This increases the urinary excretion of copper. The treatment has to be continued for life. Some patients may develop fever, skin rash, adenopathy, arthralgia, leucopenia and thrombocytopenia. These symptoms may be temporary. Treatment may have to be discontinued if the patient develops nephrotic syndrome, lupus-like syndrome or immune complex glumerulitis. In such patients, triethylene tetraamine dihydrochloride may be tried. All siblings must be screened for the disease.

Suggested reading

1. Pandit A, Bavdekar A, Bhave S. Wilsons' disease. Indian J Pediatr 2002;69:785–9.
2. Perez-Aguilar F. Wilson's disease: physiopathological, clinical and therapeutic considerations. Gastroenterol Hepatol 2003;26:42–51.
3. Tao TY, Gitlin JD. Hepatic copper metabolism: insights from genetic diseases. Hepatology 2003;37:1241–7.

23 Eye Disorders

Children may present to pediatricians with common eye problems which can often be taken care of by the primary care pediatric physician then and there. This helps the child to get promptly treated and saves the parents from having to search for another medical professional to solve the case. In addition, several systemic diseases have ocular manifestations, some of which may actually be the presenting features, which are important to be recognized for making the correct diagnosis and instituting appropriate management. Finally, some diseases require treatments which are known to have ocular side effects which need to be recognized, noted and monitored or taken care of accordingly.

THE NORMAL EYE AND VISUAL SYSTEM

The visual system involves optical elements constituting a focusing apparatus, an imaging system and a relaying network of connections running from the retina to the brain. The 'eye' essentially acts as an image-capturing instrument like a video camera and transmits the information as impulse to the visual cortex which gives us 'vision' or the 'ability to see'. The entire process is complex and involves a marvelous combination of elements in each eye and an intricate coordination mechanism to combine the image created by the two eyes into a single visual experience. An interplay of anatomy, physiology, biochemistry and neurobiology is involved in providing the same. Hence, a complex arrangement involving the motor apparatus, i.e. the extraocular (the four rectus muscles, two oblique muscles, levator palpebrae superioris and the orbicularis oculi) and intraocular muscles (sphincter and dilator pupillae for controlling pupil size and ciliary muscles for accommodation), optical elements within each eye (cornea and lens for focusing the image, clear aqueous and vitreous humor for transmitting light undiverted), sensory apparatus for forming the image (neurosensory retina) and complex neural connections transmitting the information to the brain exists for what we take for granted as 'normal vision'.

IMPORTANT EYE DISORDERS IN CHILDHOOD

At Birth or During Infancy (0-12 Months)

- Congenital cataract
- Retinopathy of prematurity
- Congenital glaucoma
- Congenital corneal opacity
- Developmental abnormalities of the globe or adnexa
- Craniofacial anomalies and syndromes
- Nutritional deficiency
- Infections and inflammatory diseases.

Early Childhood (1–6 Years)

- Retinoblastoma
- Strabismus
- Amblyopia
- Refractive errors (myopia, hypermetropia, astigmatism)
- Nystagmus
- Developmental cataract
- Developmental glaucoma
- Trauma-induced injuries and their sequelae
- Nutritional deficiency
- Infections and inflammatory diseases
- Dystrophies and degenerative diseases of the cornea, retina and optic nerve
- Metabolic disorders and storage diseases
- Vascular abnormalities
- Phacomatoses
- Orbital tumors

Later Childhood (7–12 Years) and Teenage Period (13–18 Years)

- Strabismus
- Refractive errors (myopia, hypermetropia, astigmatism)
- Developmental cataract
- Developmental glaucoma
- Trauma induced injuries and their sequelae
- Infections and inflammatory diseases
- Dystrophies and degenerative diseases of the cornea, retina, and optic nerve
- Metabolic disorders and storage diseases
- Vascular abnormalities and phacomatoses
- Orbital tumors.

PEDIATRIC EYE SCREENING

The concept of screening children for eye diseases arose because physicians are aware that infants and very young children are not able to communicate their symptoms or difficulties. In addition, there are several potentially blinding and some life-threatening diseases which affect this age group which, if detected and treated in time, can be cured or controlled appropriately to limit ocular morbidity and prevent irreversible blindness. Depending on the disease, the age group and resources available, pediatric eye screening can be undertaken by the obstetrician, pediatrician, ophthalmologist, general physician, trained nurse or birth attendant, school teacher or community health care worker.

The basic goal of pediatric eye screening is to detect eye and vision problems in children or identify risk factors known to lead to ocular and vision problems so that the child can then be referred for detailed ophthalmic evaluation, confirmation of diagnosis and appropriate medical management.

History

Screening examination

- Assessment of visual acuity
- External inspection including examination of pupils
- Corneal light reflection (Hirschberg) test
- Cover testing for ocular alignment and motility
- Examination of the red reflex

Referral for comprehensive eye evaluation, if necessary.

COMPREHENSIVE PEDIATRIC MEDICAL EYE EVALUATION

Examination

- Assessment of visual acuity and fixation pattern
- Observation of ocular alignment and motility
- Testing binocularity and stereoacuity
- Sensorimotor evaluation
- External examination of the eye and adnexa
- Anterior segment examination
- Examination of pupils and their reaction to light, darkness and accommodation
- Noting of red reflex or binocular red reflex (Brückner) test
- Cycloplegic retinoscopy (refraction)
- Examination of the fundus with an ophthalmoscope

Additional tests

- Testing of color vision
- Measurement of intraocular pressure
- Assessment of central corneal thickness
- Testing of visual fields
- Baseline documentation with clinical photography

Diagnosis and management

- Prescription of spectacles
- Medication or surgical intervention, counseling of parents and follow-up
- Referral to a geneticist, if indicated.

Practical Guidelines

Ocular history should include enquiries regarding any eye problems, known disease, previous diagnoses if any, and prior and current treatments.

Systemic history should also be taken and this will include relevant prenatal and perinatal history that may be relevant or useful such as history of any maternal illness; alcohol, drug and tobacco use during pregnancy; mode of delivery; birth weight; any history of past hospitalizations or surgery; general health, growth and development including major milestones, current medications and any known allergies.

Family history of eye conditions and relevant systemic diseases should be documented.

Social history, including racial or ethnic heritage, is required for certain diagnostic considerations such as in cases suspected or known to have sickle cell anemia or Tay-Sachs disease. In cases of suspected child abuse or substance abuse by the child, social history including family background and enquiring about friends and social circle may be helpful. History of smoking by family members may be useful in establishing contributory factors in respiratory diseases which may also have an indirect bearing on ocular allergies.

Presence of any of the following risk factors would be indications for referral for a comprehensive ophthalmic evaluation:

- *General health problems, systemic disease, or prior use of medications that are known to be associated with eye disease and visual abnormalities*
  - Prematurity (birth weight less than 1500 g or gestational age ≤30 weeks)
  - Suspected retinopathy of prematurity
  - Intrauterine growth retardation
  - Perinatal complications
  - Neurological disorders
  - Juvenile rheumatoid arthritis
  - Thyroid disease
  - Craniofacial abnormalities
  - Diabetes mellitus
  - Syndromes with known ocular manifestations
  - Chronic steroid therapy or other medications known to affect the eyes
  - Suspected child abuse
- *A family history of conditions known to be associated with eye or vision problems*
  - Retinoblastoma
  - Childhood cataract
  - Childhood glaucoma
  - Retinal dystrophy or degeneration
  - Strabismus and/or amblyopia
  - Refractive errors in early childhood

- Sickle cell disease
- Syndromes with ocular manifestations
- Family history of non-traumatic childhood blindness

- *Signs or symptoms of eye problems reported by the family, health care provider or school teacher*
  - Defective ocular fixation or visual interactions
  - Abnormal appearance of the eyes
  - Squinting or tendency to close one eye in certain situations
  - Any obvious ocular alignment, movement abnormality, head tilt or nystagmus
  - Large and/or cloudy eyes
  - Drooping of the eyelids
  - Lumps or swelling around the eyes
  - Persistent or recurrent tearing, sticky discharge, redness, itching or photophobia
  - Learning disabilities or dyslexia

Guidelines for Examination

Children are best examined in a comfortable and friendly environment. Very young children can remain in the lap of their mother while older children can be distracted with toys and colorful objects. When the child first enters the room, simple observation of behavior, fixation, movement and general awareness of the surroundings are good indicators of the child's general visual status, and any gross abnormalities can be detected.

Steady fixation and uniform steady alignment of the eyes develops in the first 4–6 weeks. Visual acuity assessment in children less than 6 months of age is limited to seeing if the child attempts to fix and follow light. A child 6–12 months of age can follow and even reach out towards colorful objects and this permits a very crude assessment of gross visual ability. A more objective assessment can be made with electrophysiological tests using a pattern-induced visual evoked response using chequered patterns of varying degrees of resolution (pattern VER) or by observing the optokinetic response or nystagmus induced by the child's attempt to view a striped pattern on a moving drum (OKN nystagmus). Both these tests are an assessment of the resolution acuity or power of the eye to distinguish patterns of varying degrees of separation or width. However, both tests are expensive and not readily available in routine clinics so are practically only used at tertiary levels of care. For most preverbal children up to the age of 3 years, a simple observation of fixation pattern and behavior, ability to see, follow or pick up small objects like toys or candy beads, preferential looking tests using Teller acuity cards or preferential looking cards are used to estimate the visual status. Unilateral loss is also tested for by observing if the child resists closure or occlusion of one eye over the other.

Vision of children 3–5 years of age can be assessed using picture tests and symbols with matching cards such as the Kays symbols, tumbling E or HOTV card tests where one relies on the child's ability to recognize the shape and match the shape with a similar one on a card. Children 5 years or older can be tested with more conventional vision testing methods using a Snellens visual acuity chart with either alphabets or tumbling E or Landoldts C symbols.

Ocular movements and external examination of the eye can be performed by using adequate illumination with a torch and aided by toys or colorful pictures to capture the child's attention and interest to cooperate with the examiner. Pupillary reactions must be tested and fundus examination should be attempted with a direct ophthalmoscope through the undilated pupil to view the disc and macula. In case required, for more detailed eye examination of the fundus and retinal periphery, the pupils can be dilated with mydriatic eye drops such as 2.5% phenylephrine or short acting cyloplegic-mydriatic drops such as tropicamide 0.5% or cyclopentolate 1% eye drops. The retina is best viewed with an indirect ophthalmoscope as this gives the maximum field of view and the examination can be completed efficiently. In general, as far as possible, most of the examination should be completed without touching or going too close to the child so that the child is comfortable and does not feel intimidated. Once, one has gained the trust and confidence of the child, one can attempt further examination such as digital assessment of the intraocular pressure, eversion of the lids, slit lamp examination, etc. In certain situations, an examination under anesthesia is required and should be done only after obtaining the parents' informed consent after explaining why the procedure is to be done and what exactly is planned.

CONGENITAL AND DEVELOPMENTAL ABNORMALITIES

This group of diseases may or may not manifest at birth. If the disease is detected at birth it is 'congenital' such as lid coloboma, severe corneal opacity, total cataract with a white opaque lens, etc. Sometimes the disease is present at birth, but detected later on, for example a partial cataract or mild congenital glaucoma. Sometimes the disease is a defect of development but manifests later, such as developmental cataract or juvenile glaucoma.

Disorders in Development of the Whole Eyeball (Globe Abnormalities)

A child may be born with a small eye (microphthalmos or nanophthalmos), absent eyeball (anophthalmos) with or without an orbital cyst, or more complex abnormalities associated with craniofacial dysgenesis.

Abnormalities of Development of the Orbit, Eyelids and Adnexa (Lacrimal Drainage System and Glands)

Children are sometimes born with the eyes completely covered by the eyelids so that the globe is not apparent or visible (cryptophthalmos). A blocked nasolacrimal duct may manifest at birth as a dacryocystocoele or later on as dacryocystitis. Lacrimal diverticulae or a fistula are other abnormalities which may or may not be immediately apparent at birth. Telangiectasias and vascular abnormalities such as capillary or cavernous hemangioma, lymphangioma, arteriovenous malformations and orbital varices may be present as isolated abnormalities or part of other syndromes such as the phakomatoses.

Other abnormalities of the lids include abnormal shape and position such as blepharophimosis, ptosis, prominent epicanthic folds, lid coloboma, congenital ichthyosis, entropion, ectropion, etc. Early oculoplastic reconstruction needs to be undertaken if the visual axis is covered or the cornea is at risk of exposure keratopathy due to lagophthalmos or inadequate lid closure.

Diseases affecting the Conjunctiva and Anterior Segment

Some of the important conditions that may be seen include conjunctival telangiectasia, hazy or opaque cornea (causes can be memorized using the mnemonic STUMPED, i.e. **s**clerocornea, birth **t**rauma , **u**lcer, **m**ucopolysaccharidosis, **P**eter's anomaly, **e**ndothelial dystrophy or **e**ndothelial dysfunction secondary to congenital glaucoma, **d**ermoid); flat cornea (cornea plana); anterior segment dysgenesis, aniridia, iris coloboma; primary congenital or juvenile developmental glaucoma; lens opacity or cataract, lens coloboma, displaced or subluxated lens or ectopia lentis, abnormal shape of lens such as microspherophakia, lens coloboma, lenticonus and persistent hyperplastic primary vitreous (Fig. 23.1).

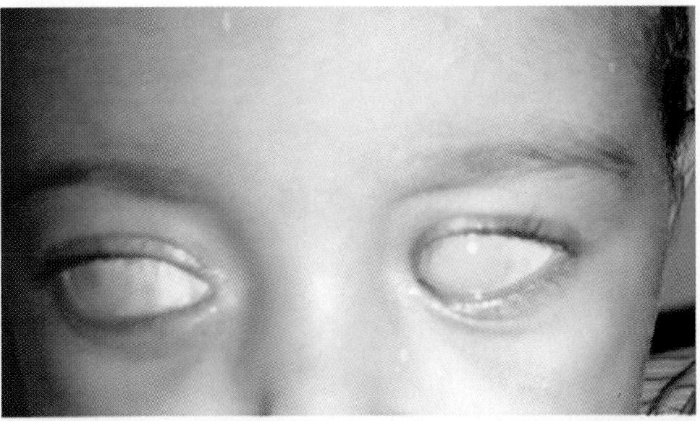

Fig. 23.1: Child with bilateral congenital corneal opacity. Differential diagnosis includes all causes of congenital corneal opacity (STUMPED) and also congenital glaucoma with buphthalmos and corneal edema due to raised intraocular pressure. Absence of watering, photophobia, blepharospasm and normal intraocular pressure ruled out glaucoma. Systemic examination ruled out mucopolysaccharidoses and there was no history of birth trauma or infection to suggest an ulcer. The uniform, bilaterally symmetrical opacification of the whole cornea favors a diagnosis of congenital hereditary endothelial dystrophy over Peter's anomaly and the child requires corneal transplantation to restore vision and prevent irreversible sensory deprivation amblyopia. Long-term visual prognosis is poor as anticipated problems include graft survival, secondary infection, graft rejection, secondary glaucoma, refractive error related to astigmatism and amblyopia.

Retinopathy of Prematurity

This is a condition seen in preterm babies due to early exposure to oxygen and other environmental factors by a premature, underdeveloped retinal vascular system. Main risk factors are prematurity especially birth before 32 weeks of gestation, birth weight less than 1500 g and presence of other contributory risk factors such as supplemental oxygen therapy, hypoxemia, hypercarbia and concurrent illness like septicemia. The clinical features are graded in stages of severity depending on the retinal signs and the zone of retina involved. Children at risk should be screened periodically to look for evidence of developing what is considered as 'threshold' disease, i.e. requiring ablative laser treatment of the avascular zone of the retina to check further progression and prevent blinding stages of the disease which would then require surgical intervention to treat the ensuing retinal detachment and other complications.

ACQUIRED EYE DISEASES

Nutritional Disorders

The most important condition in this category is vitamin A deficiency which can be catastrophic in very young children if severe enough to produce keratomalacia (melting of the cornea which is usually bilateral, but can be asymmetric). Up to the age of six months, children should have adequate reserves of vitamin A stored in their liver deposited during pregnancy and augmented by breast milk during the lactating period. However, if the mother's nutrition is poor or the infant is not properly fed after birth, severe vitamin A deficiency may be precipitated by an attack of acute respiratory infection such as measles or pneumonia or acute gastroenteritis which could lead to bilateral blindness due to severe melting of the cornea. Milder forms of vitamin A deficiency in older children may manifest with xerosis of the conjunctiva, Bitot's spot and nyctalopia or night blindness. Adequate nutritional advice to the pregnant and lactating mother and proper weaning with vitamin A rich fruits and vegetables should be routine in antenatal and postnatal care to prevent the problem. Keratomalacia is treated with oral vitamin A 200,000 IU stat followed by a second dose after 24 hours and a third dose after 2 weeks. In case the child is vomiting and cannot retain oral supplement an intramuscular injection of vitamin A may be given instead. For children less than 1 year of age and those weighing less than 10 kg, half the dose is given to avoid vitamin A toxicity and vitamin A induced intracranial hypertension.

Other forms of nutrition related problems could be vitamin B12 deficiency associated with loss of vision due to optic neuropathy or similar disorders secondary to heavy metal poisoning, drug toxicity and 'toxic amblyopia' (Fig. 23.2).

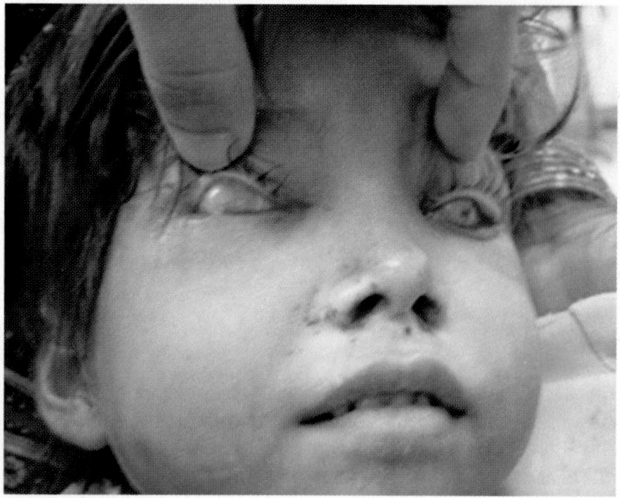

Fig. 23.2: Bilateral keratomalacia in a child with protein energy malnutrition (PEM) and acute exacerbation of severe vitamin A deficiency precipitated by an episode of pneumonia. Note the bilateral stromal melting and keratolytic effect with bilateral corneal opacification, complete loss of vision in both eyes and corneal perforation in the left eye. The child requires an emergency tectonic corneal allograft transplant from a suitable cadaveric donor (keratoplasty) in the left eye, treatment with vitamin A supplementation and measures to reverse the PEM. Later further visual rehabilitation with an optical keratoplasty in the right eye can be undertaken. Prognosis for long term vision is poor due to problems of amblyopia, graft survival, secondary infection and secondary glaucoma. The parents need to be counseled on family planning and nutritional advice should be given

Infections

Preseptal cellulitis and orbital cellulitis manifest as swelling and inflammation of the eyelids, are differentiated clinically and often occur due to spread of infection from the lids or adnexa or the paranasal sinuses or following trauma. They are potentially dangerous infections as they involve the anatomical 'dangerous area of the face', and if not treated promptly and adequately, can spread intracranially resulting in meningitis or cavernous sinus thrombosis. Ultrasonography is required to detect an orbital abscess which has to be drained, and CT scan or MRI is required if involvement of adjacent paranasal sinuses or intracranial involvement is suspected. Treatment requires systemic antibiotics and antiinflammatory agents, supplemented with topical antibiotics and supportive measures, like lubricating eyedrops to prevent corneal damage if proptosis is present.

Other infections involving the eyelids include blepharitis, hordeolum externum (stye), hordeolum internum (infected chalazion), molluscum contagiosum and phthyriasis of the eyelashes. Lid hygiene, hot fomentation and local antibiotic ointments are useful along with instructions for personal hygiene. Phthyriasis will require mechanical removal of nits adhering to the eyelashes and local application of 20% fluorescein sodium to the lid margins, along with systemic ivermectin therapy for recalcitrant cases, supplemented with advice on hygiene and treatment of any other affected family members.

Common infections of the ocular surface include conjunctivitis which could be bacterial, viral or chlamydial. Conjunctivitis occurring within the first month after birth is called ophthalmia neonatorum. Every effort should be made to identify the etiologic agent, especially in cases of ophthalmia neonatorum as gonococcal conjunctivitis can be vision threatening in the newborn. Conjunctival smears and swabs can be sent for microbiological evaluation. Mucopurulent conjunctivitis is treated with topical antibiotic eyedrops and supportive measures such as cleansing the eye with clean water, lubricating eyedrops and cold compresses.

More severe infection of the ocular surface includes keratitis and corneal ulcers. Trauma is the most common underlying predisposing factor, but poor hygiene and lowering of local immunity secondary to chronic inflammation, viral infections and use of topical steroids are other risk factors for bacterial and fungal infections of the cornea. Trauma with vegetative matter such as a thorn, tree branches or wooden broom stick (often used for making 'bows and arrows' for playing), predisposes to fungal infections. Corneal ulcers require an examination under anesthesia for detailed examination and corneal scraping to send specimens for microbiological analysis. Empirical therapy for bacterial corneal ulcers is first started with a combination of freshly prepared fortified topical antibiotics such as 5% cephazolin and 1.3% tobramycin eyedrops hourly, half hourly alternately round the clock for the first 48 hours. After 48 hours, the culture report should be checked and clinical response reviewed. If there is no substantial clinical improvement, the antibiotic can be changed by consulting the microbiology results and antibiogram. If the culture report has failed to isolate any organisms, a repeat specimen can be sent. If clinically responding to therapy, the frequency of antibiotics can be reduced to use during waking hours only, followed two days later by two hourly application and then reduced to 4 hourly, 6 hourly and discontinued a week after the ulcer has healed. Supportive measures include topical cycloplegics, hot fomentation, analgesics, antiglaucoma medication if secondary glaucoma is present, antibiotic ointment at night, and later, addition of lubricating eyedrops in the healing stage. Fungal keratitis is treated with topical Natamycin 5% 1 hourly with supportive measures. Herpes simplex viral keratitis is treated with topical acyclovir 3% eye ointment for epithelial involvement and systemic acyclovir for herpetic keratouveitis or recurrent disease (Fig. 23.3).

Other infections include endophthalmitis (traumatic, metastatic or iatrogenic following intraocular surgery), parasitic infestations such as toxoplasmosis, toxocariasis, and cysticercosis of the eye, extraocular muscles or orbit.

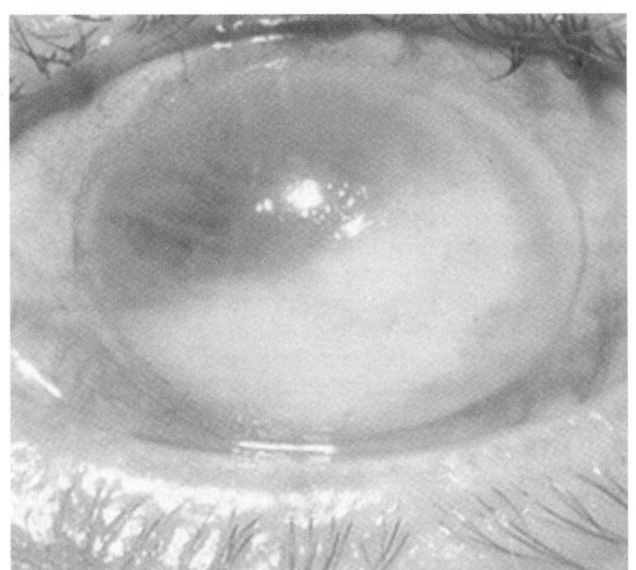

Fig. 23.3: A partially treated hypopyon corneal ulcer. The overlying epithelial defect has healed, but there is a deep corneal abscess, corneal edema and pus, i.e. a hypopyon in the anterior chamber

Allergic and Inflammatory Diseases

Children may develop allergic diseases of the skin around the eye and the ocular surface and conjunctiva. Dermatitis may be an allergic reaction to local ophthalmic medication or sometimes secondary to a local insect bite, application of traditional eye medicines or herbal remedies, use of local creams or lotions, etc. In addition a variety of environmental and hereditary factors may interplay to produce a variety of allergic conjunctival manifestations such as seasonal allergic conjunctivitis, hay fever conjunctivitis, perennial or chronic allergic conjunctivitis, atopic allergic conjunctivitis and vernal keratoconjunctivitis. Itching, redness, discomfort, gritty or foreign body sensation, watering, mucoid or thick ropy discharge, photophobia and blepharospasm are all seen in different combinations and varying degrees of severity. Treatment includes cold compresses, topical antihistaminic eyedrops for mild cases and counseling to avoid rubbing the eyes. Topical corticosteroid eyedrops give quick relief but are best avoided in mild cases because of the danger of self-medication and unsupervised chronic topical use complicated by steroid induced glaucoma and secondary corneal infection and ulceration. More severe allergies may have secondary consequences in the form of dry eye, keratopathy and corneal ulceration. These are best referred to ophthalmologists for expert management and careful follow up.

Other inflammations include phlyctenular conjunctivitis or keratoconjunctivitis (believed to be an 'allergic' immunological reaction to tubercular antigen), interstitial keratitis secondary to infections like rubella, syphilis, leprosy, tuberculosis, etc.; uveitis, either idiopathic or associated with juvenile chronic arthritis, psoriasis, tuberculosis, sarcoidosis, toxoplasma induced chorioretinitis, etc. Acute anterior uveitis (iritis, cyclitis and iridocyclitis) usually presents with a red inflamed eye with photophobia and diminution of vision. Chronic uveitis may be less symptomatic with decreased vision due to complicated cataract. Intermediate and posterior uveitis (pars planitis, vitritis, retinitis, choroiditis and retinochoroiditis) are usually painless with symptoms of decreased vision (due to hazy media and retinal or optic nerve swelling and inflammation) and floaters (due to inflammatory cells in the vitreous). Treatment is with topical cycloplegic agents and steroids, supplemented with, systemic steroids, and specific therapy for any underlying disease, such as tuberculosis, if identified. Sometimes stronger immunosuppressive medications such as cyclosphosphamide or methotrexate are required. As such, a patient with uveitis needs detailed thorough examination with a slit lamp biomicroscope to identify the inflammatory response, ophthalmoscopy to view the fundus, and specialist ophthalmic care and follow up to control the inflammation and minimize the morbidity related with the disease and its treatment.

Sometimes intraocular (retinoblastoma or juvenile xanthogranuloma) or systemic malignant disorders may masquerade as uveitis syndrome due to outpouring of malignant cells into the eye and vascular uveal tracts.

Optic neuritis is another important inflammatory disease which could be idiopathic, secondary to infections or associated with demyelinating disorders. Classical features include a rapid drop in vision usually in one eye which is accompanied by a relative afferent pupillary defect and normal fundus (retrobulbar neuritis) or inflammatory swelling of the optic disc (papillitis) and retinal edema and/or exudates (neuroretinitis) on ophthalmoscopic examination. The condition needs to be treated in consultation with a neurophthalmologist after appropriate investigations to identify the underlying cause.

Metabolic Diseases and Endocrine Disorders

Homocystinuria is associated with subluxation of the lens, and secondary glaucoma can be seen as a secondary complication. The lens is usually subluxated downwards and this causes poor vision due to displacement and astigmatism. Surgical lens removal has to be done under general anesthesia taking suitable precautions, as the patients are prone to thromboembolism. Optical rehabilitation is usually done with spectacles or contact lenses, though in some cases intraocular lenses can be fitted using scleral or bag fixation augmented with bag fixation devices.

Various storage disorders such as cerebral storage disease, lipidosis and gangliosidosis may be associated with a 'cherry red spot' due to abnormal deposition in the retina, corneal clouding as in some of the mucopolysaccharidoses and Kayser Fleisher ring in the peripheral cornea in Wilson disease. Juvenile diabetes mellitus may be associated with cataract and diabetic retinopathy and thyroid dysfunction with dysthyroid eye disease. Tyrosinase deficiency could be associated with ocular albinism with foveal hypoplasia and poor vision.

Musculoskeletal, Neurodegenerative Diseases and Phakomatoses

Marfan and Ehlers-Danlos syndromes may be associated with subluxated lenses and possible consequent secondary glaucoma. Marfan syndrome is usually associated with upward and outward displacement of the lenses and myopia with consequent blurred vision. Retinal detachments are also common. Surgical lens removal becomes necessary if the vision is non-correctible with spectacles or contact lenses. Leukodystrophies and demyelinating diseases may be associated with extra-ocular muscle weakness, ptosis and optic neuropathy. Phakomatoses like neurofibromatosis, Sturge-Weber syndrome and nevus of Ota may be associated with *café au lait* spots and plexiform neurofibromas of the lids and orbit, Lisch nodules on the iris and glaucoma.

Local muscular dystrophies or degenerations such as chronic progressive external ophthalmoplegia result in ptosis and restriction of eye movements. Duchenne muscular dystrophy may be associated with cataracts.

Tumors and Neoplastic Diseases

Benign tumors include dermoids of orbit, lids or on cornea; hamartomas, osteoma, vascular malformations or hemangiomas of various types and neurofibromas. Malignant intraocular tumors are confined to retinoblastoma, juvenile xanthogranuloma, medulloepithelioma and metastatic lesions from neuroblastomas, Ewings sarcoma, leukemias and lymphomas. Orbital tumors include rhabdomyosarcoma, Langerhans cell histiocytosis, extraocular spread of retinoblastoma, metastatic spread of Ewings sarcoma, neuroblastoma, leukemias and lymphomas (Fig. 23.4).

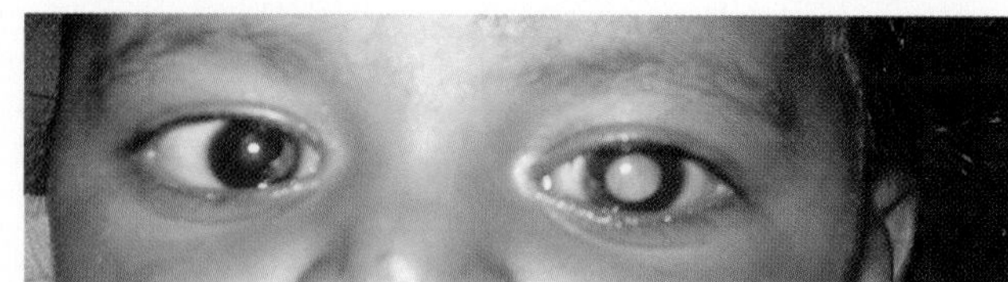

Fig. 23.4: 'Leokocoria' or white pupil in an infant. Note the white appearance is seen to be from a structure more posteriorly, has a slight yellowish pinkish tinge due to vascularization and the appearance is unlike that seen due to a cataract. An ultrasonography can confirm the diagnosis straight away as to the site of origin and the nature of the lesion. The diagnosis is retinoblastoma and this appearance should not be mistaken for a cataract. An immediate referral to a tertiary care centre with an explanation to the parents about the possible etiology is mandatory to ensure prompt diagnosis and treatment of this potentially life-threatening disease. A CT scan to demonstrate calcification and map the extent of the tumor, screening of the other eye and siblings will form part of the management protocol. Depending on the size , extent and spread of the tumor, treatment options include enucleation, local treatment with laser or radiotherapy, and systemic chemotherapy

REFRACTIVE ERRORS

An abnormality in the refractive and focusing apparatus of the eye thereby making it difficult for parallel rays of light from the distance to be accurately focused on the retina is a deviation from the normal emmetropic state and is termed as 'ametropia' or refractive error. This manifests usually as poor or blurred vision which may be noticed by parents, relatives, friends, school teachers or reported by the child as a difficulty in viewing clearly. Sometimes, indirect evidence is reported as 'eye rubbing', 'squinting', 'going too close to the television, holding objects too close to the eyes, etc. An assessment of visual acuity followed by cycloplegic refraction and fundus evaluation is required in addition to routine ophthalmic evaluation. Refractive errors may be myopia, hypermetropia and astigmatism and spectacles must be prescribed accordingly. Associated amblyopia or strabismus must be taken care of and any additional features like nystagmus or extraocular muscle imbalance ruled out. Patients need to be carefully monitored with respect to improvement of vision with spectacles and compliance with follow up. Failure to show an improvement of vision with spectacles warrant further investigations to rule out any associated subtle pathology such as microstrabismus, retinal macular degeneration, retinitis pigmentosa, congenital hereditary cone dystrophy, delayed visual maturation, dyslexia, Leber's amaurosis, etc.

STRABISMUS AND AMBLYOPIA

Strabismus is defined as the condition when the visual axes of the two eyes do not meet at the point of regard. In other words, the motor and sensory alignment of the two eyes and their images in the brain are not synchronized. The cause may be a basic abnormality of development as in essential esotropia or exotropia (concomitant or comitant squint when the angle of deviation or separation of the two eyes is uniform, irrespective of the direction or position of gaze) or secondary to extraoocular muscle paralysis, i.e. paralytic squint, local orbital space occupying lesion, myositis or orbital inflammation as in orbital pseudotumor syndrome, orbital musculofascial abnormality like Duane's retraction syndrome or Brown's superior oblique tendon sheath syndrome (incomitant or non-concomitant squint where the deviation is more in certain positions and less or even absent in some positions of gaze).

An inward deviation of the eye is termed esotropia and outward deviation is termed exotropia. The child initially suffers diplopia due to the different images being presented to the visual cortex by the two eyes, but learns to suppress one image eventually developing amblyopia or a 'lazy eye' with a loss of binocularity and stereopsis. Very young children will not report their symptoms and presence of an intermittent or constant squint or misalignment of the eyes should be indications for referral to an ophthalmologist.

Amblyopia or 'lazy eye' is a condition of subnormal vision defined as two lines less than normal or less than the fellow eye on the visual acuity chart with no anatomical cause detectable on examination, i.e. no media opacity and a normal fundus. Amblyopiogenic factors have their maximum impact on the immature developing visual system, i.e. during the first 6 years of life and include sensory deprivation or abnormal binocular interaction. The former would refer to a corneal opacity or cataract which, even if taken care of surgically, do not indicate good chances of restoration of normal vision. Similarly abnormal binocular interaction occurs in the presence of strabismus or anisometropia (difference in the refractive power of the two eyes), in which case, one eye takes over and the visual cortical neurons meant to receive stimuli from the other eye are unable to develop normally leading to a 'lazy eye'. These changes are potentially reversible with appropriate therapy in the first decade, but become irreversible and permanent if left uncorrected. Treatment involves first restoration of clear vision with correction of any refractive error with spectacles, removal of any media opacity if present such as corneal opacity (by corneal transplantation) or cataract (cataract removal with intraocular lens implantation or other appropriate optical correction), patching therapy by part time patching of the 'good' eye to enable the 'lazy' eye to catch up and strabismus surgery to restore ocular alignment if required.

CATARACT

A visible lenticular opacity in the eye is termed as a cataract. It is congenital if present since birth, developmental if appears later on and traumatic if occurs after an episode of eye trauma. A central opacity is onsidered visually significant if it impairs visual acuity and on clinical assessment is obstructing a clear view of the fundus. A cataract may be unilateral or bilateral and then symmetric or symmetric. In view of the risk of sensory deprivation amblyopia, visually significant cataract should be treated surgically as soon as possible after birth. Functional success is highest if operated within the first few weeks after birth, provided the child is medically fit to undergo general anesthesia. Unilateral cataracts must be supplemented with postoperative patching therapy to take care of any amblyopic effect. Optical and visual rehabilitation for the aphakic state resulting from lens removal includes the implantation of an intraocular lens (IOL) for children above two years of age. Generally intraocular lenses are avoided for children less than two years old as there are significant problems of change in lens power requirements as the maximum growth of the eyeball takes place during the first two years of life as also higher risk of complications of glaucoma and intraocular inflammation and fibrosis. In very young children, therefore, a capsule rim is left for subsequent secondary IOL implantation and temporary optical rehabilitation is provided with spectacles or contact lenses supplemented with patching for amblyopia in unilateral cases (Fig. 23.5).

GLAUCOMA

Primary congenital and developmental juvenile glaucoma are now recognized to be inherited diseases. Primary congenital glaucoma is associated with CYP1B1 gene (2p21) which had a predominantly autosomal recessive mode of inheritance, and mutations in the myocillin (MYOC) gene. Photophobia, blepharospasm, watering and an enlarged eyeball are classic symptoms. Suspicion of glaucoma or buphthalmos warrants urgent referral to

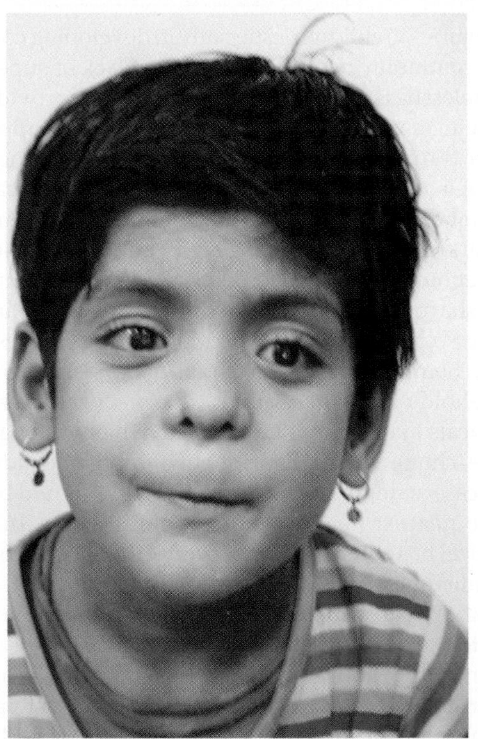

Fig. 23.5: A child with bilateral developmental cataract. Note that the cataract is partial so as the child had some vision, the parents did not notice the problem till it was pointed out by the school teacher to have the eyes tested. The child has a cataract in both eyes visible as a whitish opacity behind the pupil. Also note that the child has a convergent squint. The child also has impaired hearing and congenital heart disease, suspected to be due to congenital rubella syndrome. Proper immunization of the mother for rubella would have prevented this disabling ocular and systemic disease and further emphasizes the importance of proper community coverage by immunization programs.

an ophthalmologist. An examination under anesthesia is required to measure the corneal diameter, the intraocular pressure and visualize the optic disc. Once glaucoma is confirmed, medical therapy to lower the pressure is started and patient prepared for surgery. If the cornea is clear enough to allow visualization of the angle structures, a goniotomy is attempted. If the glaucoma is more severe or the cornea very edematous, a glaucoma drainage procedure for opening of alternative aqueous drainage channels such as a trabeculectomy and trabeculotomy is undertaken. If the cornea fails to clear after adequate control of the intraocular pressure, a corneal transplantation is required to restore vision and prevent irreversible sensory deprivation amblyopia.

Children can also develop secondary glaucoma due to chronic use of topical corticosteroid eyedrops, following eye trauma particularly if associated with traumatic hyphema (blood in the anterior chamber) or angle recession, after surgery for developmental cataract and after chronic uveitis.

EYE TRAUMA AND TRAUMA RELATED PROBLEMS

Eye injuries in children, especially in developing countries, most commonly occur as the result of lack of supervision or carelessness on the part of the adult care provider. The eye being a very small and delicate structure, apparently minor trauma can also have serious consequences. Eye injuries are considered to be an important cause of preventable blindness and every effort must be made to educate the community in general and mothers in particular about the importance of not allowing children to play with sharp pointed toys like bows and arrows and firecrackers, chemicals including colors during Holi festival or other chemicals like edible 'chuna'. Sharp and dangerous household objects like knives, scissors, needles, etc. and chemicals like cleaning liquid, acid, whitewash paint and edible 'chuna' should be kept out of reach of children.

In case an injury is sustained, the child should be taken to the nearest health centre without delay. In case a chemical has entered the eye, every effort should be made to immediately wash the eyes thoroughly with locally available clean water such as drinkable water, and then rush to the nearest hospital without delay.

Perforating injuries of the globe require surgical repair under general anesthesia under cover of systemic and topical antibiotics and tetanus prohylaxis. The child should be told not to rub the eyes and given only fluids while rushing the child to hospital so that there is no unnecessary delay in preparing the patient for general anesthesia and planning surgery on reaching the hospital. Meticulous repair of the wounds should be undertaken as soon as possible to minimize the risk of secondary complications such as endophthalmitis, expulsion of intraocular contents and later risk of sympathetic ophthalmitis or an inflammatory panuveitis in the normal other eye due to sensitization of the immune system to the sequestered antigens in the exposed uveal tissue hitherto protected from direct access to lymphatic drainage (Figs 23.6A and B).

RETINAL DISEASES

Children can be affected by a wide variety of retinal diseases. Retinal detachment can occur secondary to trauma or spontaneously in cases with high or pathological myopia. Classical symptoms such as sudden loss of vision with floaters and photopsia may not be reported by children and the detachment may not be detected till much later. Retinal detachment requires surgical treatment and the sooner the surgery is performed, the greater are the chances of functional recovery of vision. Other diseases that can affect the retina in childhood include degenerative and hereditary conditions like retinitis pigmentosa and a variety of different forms of macular degeneration such as Stargardt's disease. These diseases lead to gradual, painless, bilateral diminution of vision in the first or second decade of life which may be accompanied by defective dark adaptation or abnormal color vision. No specific treatment modalities are available, but refractive correction, low vision aids, visual rehabilitation and genetic counseling are ancillary measures which must be undertaken.

Vascular abnormalities of the retina such as hemangiomas, arteriovenous malformations and exudative vitreoretinopathies like Coat's disease may be seen. Retinal

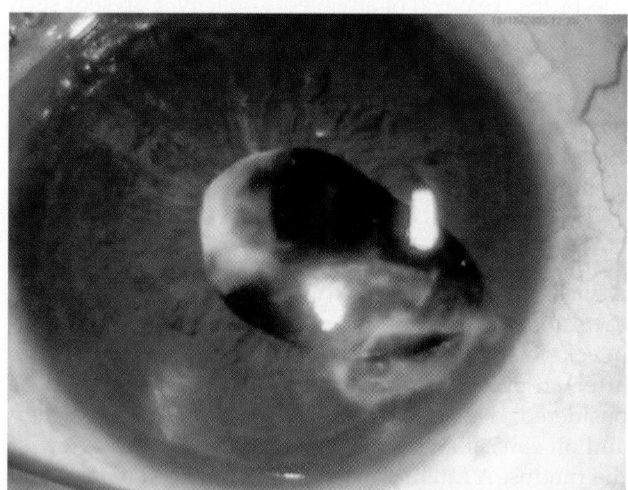

Fig. 23.6A: The sequelae of ocular trauma. The child sustained an injury to the eye with a wooden stick from an ordinary broom which was being used to play a game of bows and arrows with friends. The child had a corneal perforation which was repaired as an emergency and associated traumatic cataract was surgically removed and an intraocular lens implanted during a second surgery performed 6 weeks later. Note the irreversible anatomical damage with corneal scar, distorted iris and pupil and lens capsular opacification. Permanent functional handicap includes astigmatism, loss of accommodation requiring the use of spectacles with near correction for reading, glare and photophobia from the pupil damage, and a long-term risk of secondary glaucoma

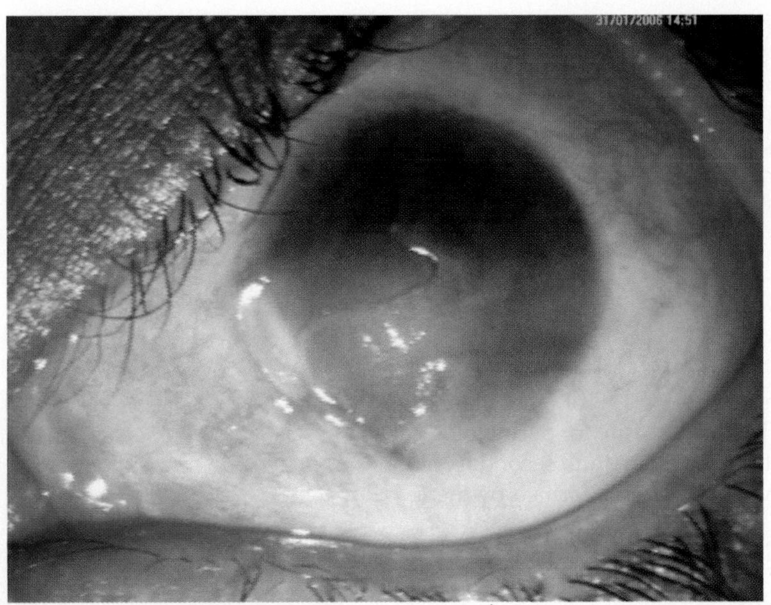

Fig. 23.6B: The long term consequences of chemical injury. The child was playing with a packet of edible 'chuna' dispensed in a thin plastic pouch at the local 'paan' shop. While squeezing the packet the thin cellophane plastic covering burst and the 'chuna' squirted into the child's eye. Though the parents tried to wash the eye with water, the child would not let them wash the eye thoroughly due to severe pain and burning. The parents delayed seeking medical attention until the next morning. A thorough irrigation of the eye with normal saline was performed in the emergency department and an examination under anesthesia was required with double eversion of the upper lid to remove residual chunks of solid 'chuna' from underneath the upper lid hidden in the superior fornix. The child was treated with topical antibiotics to prevent secondary infection of the raw inflamed ocular surface, topical steroids to control inflammation, topical cycloplegic, topical ascorbate and citrate drops to replenish ascorbate levels, promote collagen synthesis and promote corneal healing. Supplementary therapy with amniotic membrane transplantation to restore the ocular surface and prevent excessive scarring and vascularization was also undertaken with subsequent use of preservative-free topical lubricants. Note that despite the best efforts and successful clinical result considering the severity of injury, the long-term sequelae include residual conjunctival inflammation with limbal stem cell deficiency and a scarred, irregular and opacified corneal surface. Further therapeutic options include limbal stem cell transplantation by an autograft from the fellow eye or an allograft from an HLA-matched relative

vasculitis may be seen in Eales' disease and other inflammatory disorders. Diabetic retinopathy and hypertensive retinopathy can occur if these systemic disorders are present in sufficient grade of severity predisposing to these manifestations for an adequate duration of time.

Suggested reading

For a review of relevant anatomy, physiology, optics and description of important diseases, differential diagnosis and management in keeping with the undergraduate syllabus: Parsons diseases of the eye. 20th edn. Eds Ramanjit Sihota R, Tandon R. Elsevier India, Delhi.

23

24 Skin Disorders

Skin disorders account for nearly 1/3 of ailments in the pediatric population. The prerequisite for dermatological diagnosis is identification of primary and secondary skin lesions as well as the various patterns formed by them.

BASICS OF CLINICAL DERMATOLOGY

Morphology of Lesions

Primary Lesions

The basic or characteristic lesions of a disease are the primary lesions.

Macules: Macule is a circumscribed area of change in skin color without any change in consistency (Fig. 24.1). A macule may be hyperpigmented (e.g. café au lait macule), hypopigmented (e.g. leprosy), depigmented (e.g. vitiligo) or erythematous (e.g. drug rash).

Papules and nodules: Papule is a solid lesion <0.5 cm in diameter with a major part of it projecting above the skin (Fig. 24.2A). Papules may be dome shaped, flat topped, conical, filiform (finger-like), umbilicated (with crater on surface) or verrucous (having multiple closely packed firm elevations). A papule which is >0.5 cm in size is called a **nodule** (Fig. 24.2B).

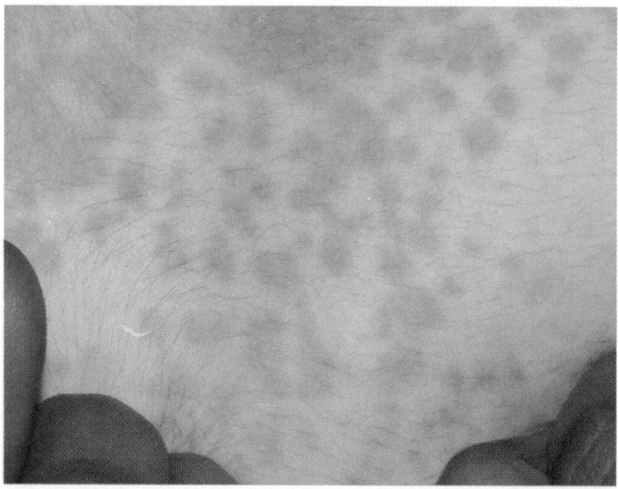

Fig. 24.1: Macule: circumscribed area of change in skin color without any change in consistency

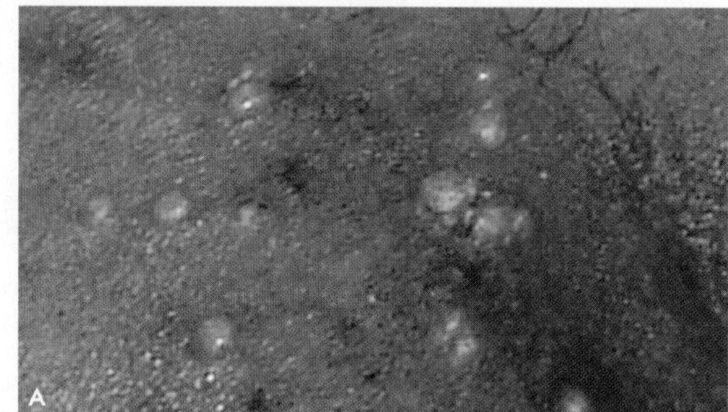

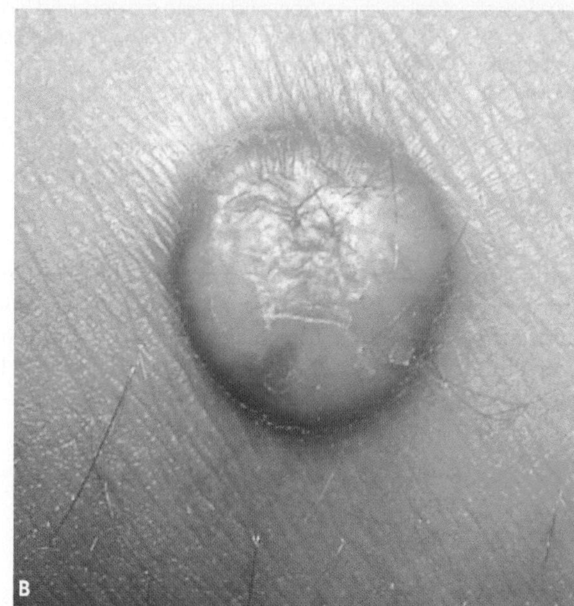

Figs 24.2A and B: (A) Papule: solid lesion, <0.5 cm. (B) Nodule: solid lesion, > 0.5 cm

Plaque: Plaque is an area of altered skin consistency, the surface area of which is greater than its depth (Fig. 24.3). A plaque can be elevated, depressed or flat.

Wheal: Wheal, which is the characteristic lesion in urticaria, is an evanescent, pale/erythematous raised lesion which disappears within 24–48 hours (Fig. 24.4). Wheals are due to dermal edema and when the edema extends into

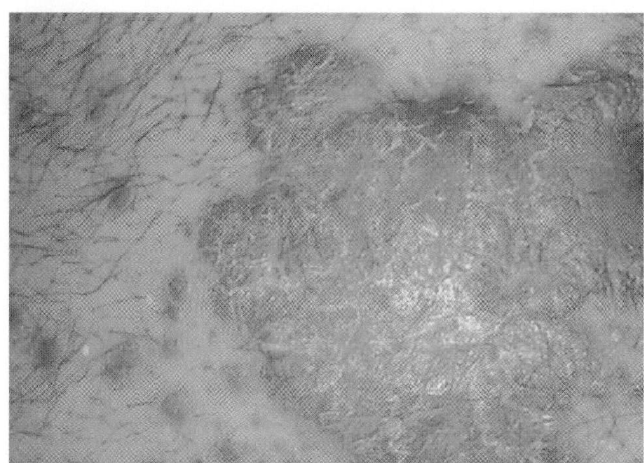

Fig. 24.3: Plaque: area of altered skin consistency, the surface area of which is greater than its depth

Fig. 24.4: Wheal: evanescent, pale erythematous raised lesion which disappears within 24–48 hours

subcutis, they are called angioedema. When the wheals are linear, the phenomenon is called dermographism.

Blisters: Blister is a circumscribed elevated, superficial fluid filled cavity (Fig. 24.5). If <0.5 cm, it is called a vesicle and if >0.5 cm in size it is called a bulla.

Secondary Lesions

Secondary lesions are the basic lesions, modified by secondary events.

Scales: Scales are flakes of stratum corneum (Fig. 24.6) and are diagnostic in certain dermatoses, e.g. silvery easily

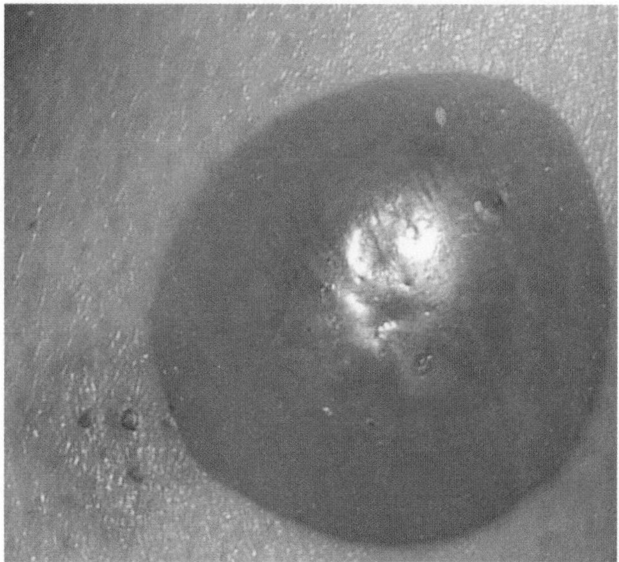

Fig. 24.5: Blister: circumscribed, elevated, superficial fluid filled cavity

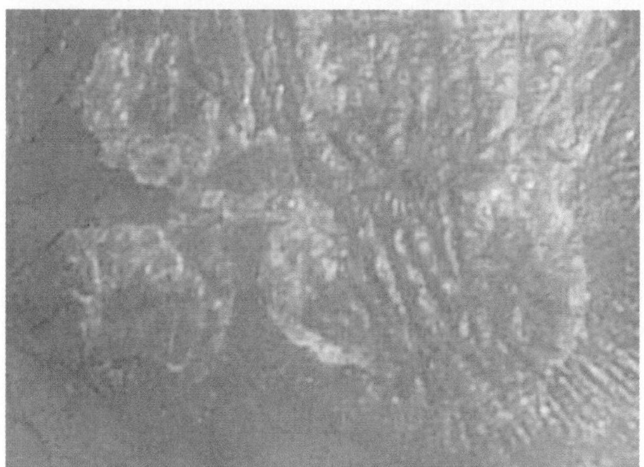

Fig. 24.6: Scale: flakes of stratum corneum

detachable (psoriasis), branny (pityriasis versicolor) and fish-like (ichthyosis).

Crusts: Crusts are formed when serum, blood or pus dries on the skin surface (Fig. 24.7).

Erosions and ulcers: A defect, which involves only the epidermis and heals without a scar (Fig. 24.8A) is called an erosion while an ulcer is a defect in the skin which extends into the dermis or deeper and heals with scarring (Fig. 24.8B).

Atrophy: Atrophy is the reduction of some or all layers of skin. In epidermal atrophy, thinning of the epidermis leads to loss of skin texture and cigarette-paper like wrinkling without depression and in dermal atrophy, loss of connective tissue of the dermis leads to depression of the lesion.

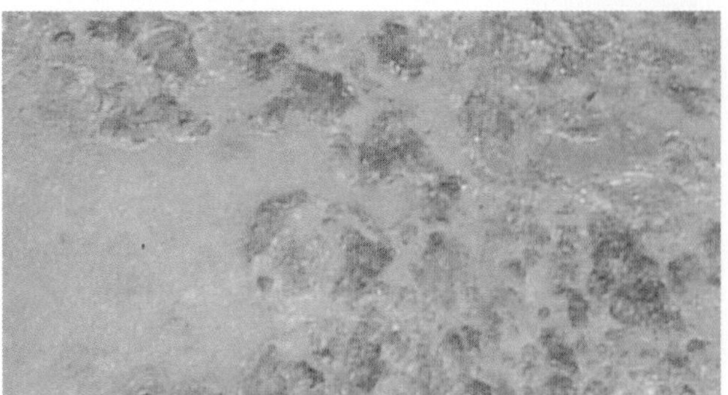

Fig. 24.7: Crust: yellow brown collection of keratin and serum

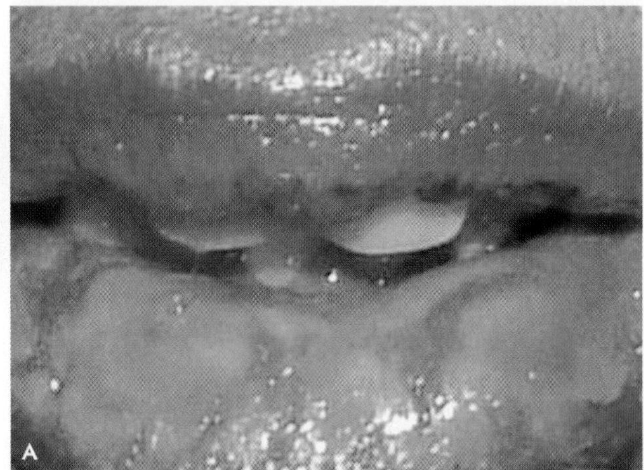

Figs 24.8A and B: Erosions and ulcers: (A) Erosions are due to complete or partial loss of epidermis without loss of dermis. (B) Ulcer is a defect in the skin which extends into the dermis or deeper and heals with scarring

Lichenification: Lichenification consists of triad of thickening of skin, hyperpigmentation and increased skin markings (Fig. 24.9). It is caused by repeated scratching.

Specific Lesions

These lesions are diagnostic of the disease.

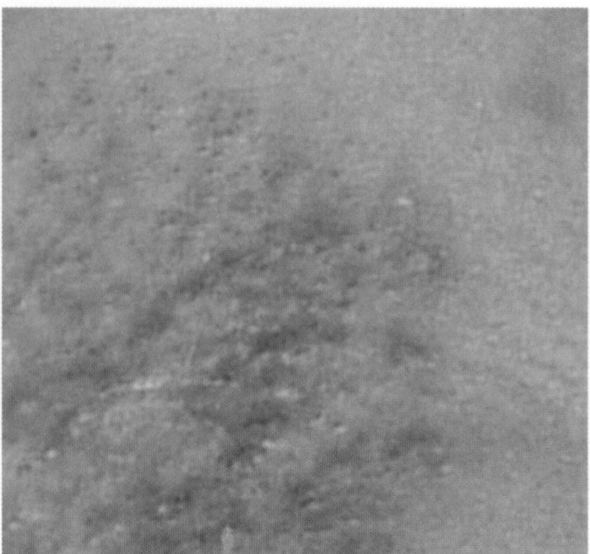

Fig. 24.9: Lichenification: thickening and hyperpigmentation of skin with increased skin markings

Burrow: Burrow is a dark serpentine, curvilinear lesion with a minute papule at one end and it is diagnostic of scabies (Fig. 24.10).

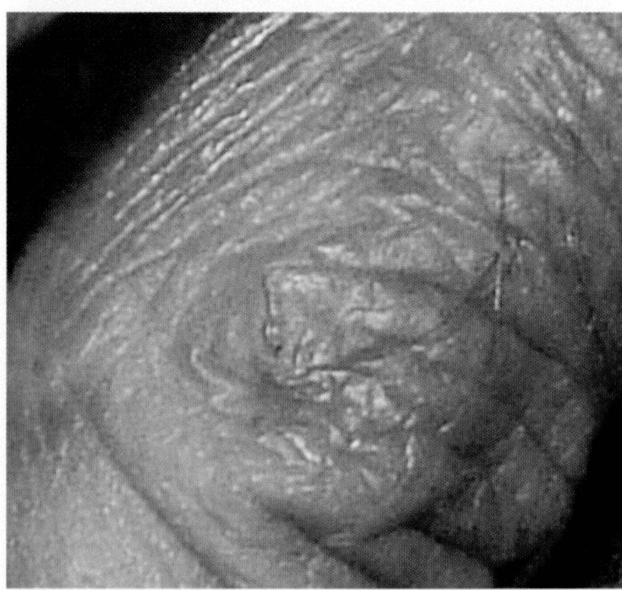

Fig. 24.10: Burrow: serpentine, thread-like, grayish curvilinear lesion, diagnostic of scabies

Comedones: Keratin plugs that form within follicular ostia and they can be open or closed (Fig. 24.11). They are diagnostic of acne.

Arrangement of Lesions

Arrangement of skin lesions can help in diagnosis (Table 24.1).

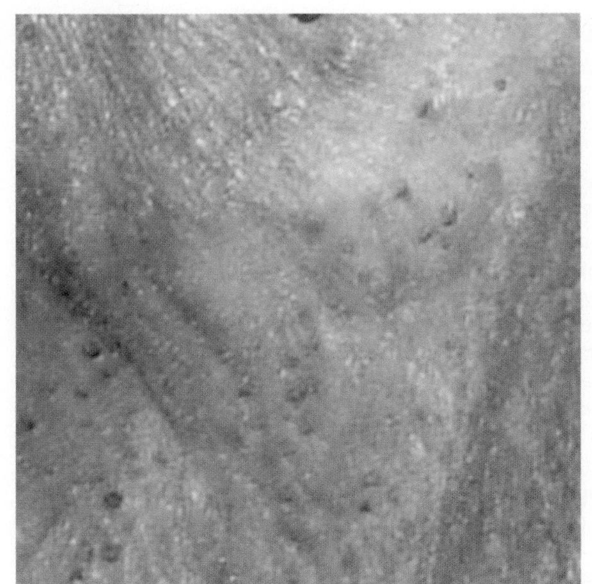

Fig. 24.11: Comedones: keratin plugs that form within follicular ostia

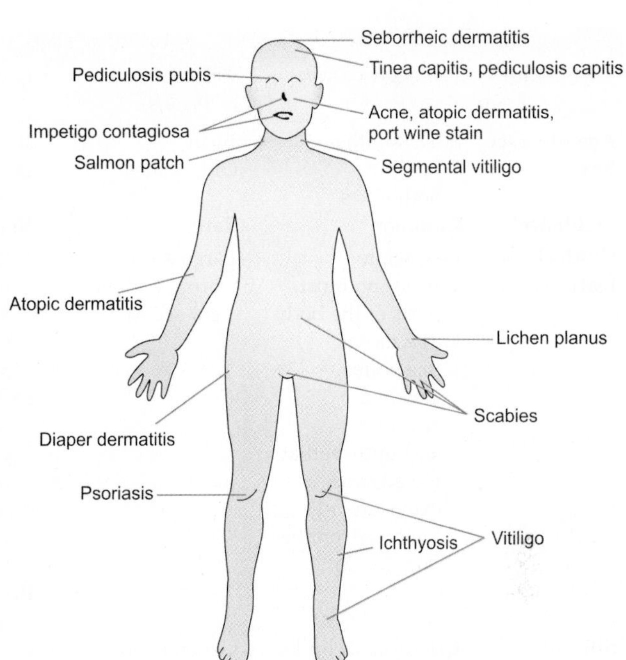

Fig. 24.12: Sites of predilection of common skin diseases

Table 24.1: Arrangement of skin lesions

Arrangement	*Example*
Linear	Verrucous epidermal nevus
Grouped	Herpes simplex
Dermatomal	Herpes zoster
Arcuate	Granuloma annulare

Sites of Predilection

Sites of predilection are important for dermatological diagnosis (Fig. 24.12).

GENODERMATOSES

Genodermatoses are the group of inherited single gene cutaneous disorders that manifest themselves wholly or in part in the skin, mucous membranes, hair and nails.

Ichthyosis

Ichthyosis are a heterogeneous group disorders characterized by the presence of fish-like scales.

Classification

- Ichthyosis vulgaris (IV)
- X-linked ichthyosis (XLI)
- Lamellar ichthyosis (LI)
- Non-bullous ichthyosiform erythroderma (NBIE)
- Epidermolytic hyperkeratosis (EHK)

Etiology

Ichthyosis vulgaris: Autosomal dominant. Due to reduced or absent filagrin (responsible for formation of keratin filaments).

X-linked ichthyosis: Deficiency of steroid sulfatase enzyme.

Lamellar ichthyosis: Autosomal recessive; abnormality of gene encoding for transglutaminase.

Non-bullous ichthyosiform erythroderma: Autosomal recessive. Several defects identified.

Epidermolytic hyperkeratosis: Autosomal dominant. Defect in keratin synthesis or degradation.

Clinical Features

The clinical features of various forms of ichthyosis are shown in Table 24.2.

Treatment

Symptomatic treatment

- Hydration (by immersing in water), and immediate lubrication with petroleum jelly or urea containing creams and lotions, form mainstay of treatment.
- Keratolytic agents (hydroxyacids, propylene glycol and salicylic acid) when moderately severe.
- Oral retinoids (acetretin) given in collodoin baby and severe cases of lamellar ichthyosis and epidermolytic hyperkeratosis.

Treatment of complications: Short course of topical steroid-antibiotic combination in eczematized skin.

Epidermolysis Bullosa (EB)

It is a heterogeneous group of disorders characterized by a tendency to develop blisters even after trivial trauma.

24

Table 24.2: Clinical features of ichthyosis

Main features	*Ichthyosis vulgaris*	*X-Linked ichthyosis*	*Lamellar ichthyosis*	*NBIE*	*EHK*
Age of onset	3–12 months	Birth	Birth	Birth	Birth
Sex	Equal in both sexes	Only males	Equal in both sexes	Equal in both sexes	Equal in both sexes
Incidence	Common	Rare	Very rare	Rare	Rare
Clinical features	Fine white scales on most parts of the body Large mosaic-like scales, attached at centre and upturned at the edge on extensors of lower extremities (Fig. 24.13)	Large dark brown adherent scales	Collodion baby, ensheathed in a shiny lacquer-like membrane at birth (Fig. 24.14) Diffuse large thick brown pasted (plate-like) scales (Fig. 24.15) develop later which persist for life. Erythema is minimal	Collodion baby at birth Fine branny scales and marked erythema develop later	Generalized erythema with blistering at birth. Followed by development of brownish, warty, broad, linear plaques Scales may fall off in small areas leaving bald patches (skip areas)
Sites of predilection	Extensors of limbs; major flexures always spared and face is usually spared	Generalized involvement with no sparing of flexures. Palms and soles spared.	Generalized with accentuation on lower limbs and flexures	Generalized erythema and scaling	Generalized with accentuation in flexures
Associated features	Hyperlinear palms soles Keratosis pilaris Atopic diathesis	Corneal opacities Cryptorchidism	Ectropion, and eclabium Crumpled ears Palmar and plantar keratoderma	Palmar and plantar keratoderma less frequent	Palmar and plantar keratoderma in >60%.

NBIE non-bullous ichthyosiform erythroderma; EHK epidermolytic hyperkeratosis

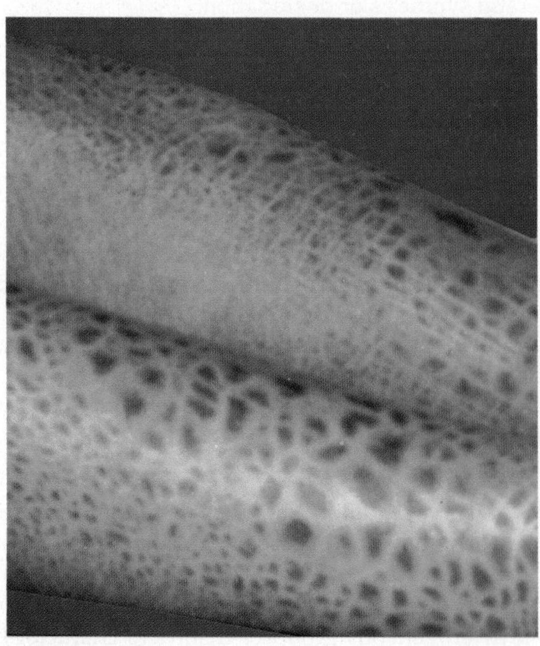

Fig. 24.13: Ichthyosis vulgaris: large scales on extremities which are attached at the center and turned up at the edge

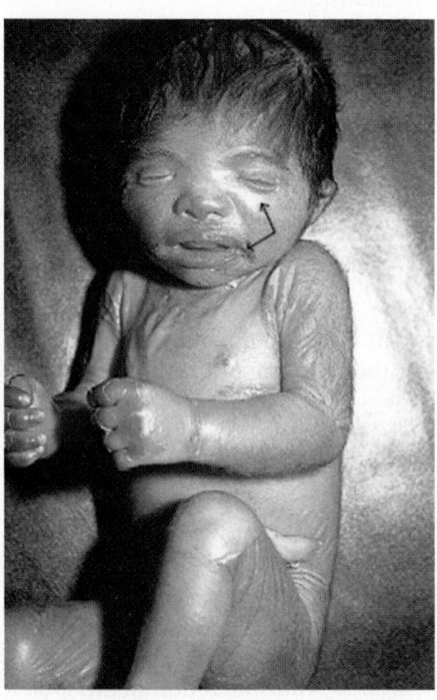

Fig. 24.14: Collodion baby: baby is ensheathed in a shiny lacquer-like membrane

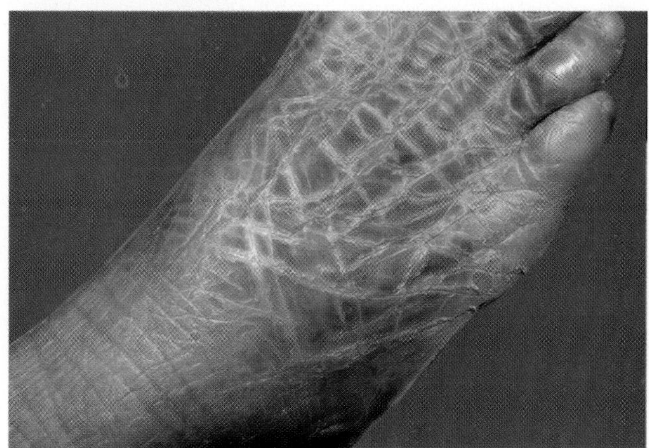

Fig. 24.15: Lamellar ichthyosis: large pasted scales with continuous rippling around ankle

Classification

Inherited EB

- EB simplex: autosomal dominant; defective keratin gene.
- Junctional EB: autosomal recessive
- Dominant dystrophic EB: autosomal dominant; defective collagen 7 gene
- Recessive dystrophic EB: autosomal recessive

Acquired EB

- EB acquisita immune mediated.

Clinical Features (Table 24.3)

Treatment

General measures

- Avoiding friction and trauma, wearing soft well ventilated shoes, gentle handling of child.
- Wound management.
- Nutritional support.
- Infection control.

Specific measures

- Gene therapy, especially for junctional variant.
- Phenytoin is of doubtful value in autosomal recessive EB.
- Empirical use of vitamin E.

Surgical measures

Surgery is required for release of fused digits, correction of limb contractures and esophageal strictures.

INFECTIONS

Bacteria, viruses and fungi can cause infections of the skin.

Pyodermas

Classification: Based on predisposing factors, pyodermas are classified as:

Primary: When there is no underlying skin disease.

Secondary: When there is an underlying skin disease, e.g. scabies, pediculosis, dermatophytic infection, atopic dermatitis or miliaria.

Based on morphology, pyodermas are classified as shown in Table 24.4.

Localized pyoderma

- Bullous impetigo — *Staphylococcus aureus*
- Impetigo contagiosa — *S. aureus*, *S. pyogenes*, both
- Ecthyma — *S. aureus*, *S. pyogenes*, both

- ***Spreading pyodermas***
  - Erysipelas — *S. pyogenes*
  - Cellulitis — *S. pyogenes*
- ***Follicular pyodermas*** — *S. aureus*

Predisposing factors

- Underlying skin disease (scabies, pediculosis, fungal infection)
- Poor hygiene
- Carrier states
- Systemic diseases: diabetes.

Table 24.3: **Clinical features of epidermolysis bullosa (EB)**

	EB simplex	*Junctional EB*	*Autosomal dominant dystrophic EB*	*Autosomal recessive dystrophic EB*
Age of onset	Early childhood	At birth	At birth/early infancy	At birth
Skin lesions	Non-hemorrhagic bullae develop on normal skin	Large flaccid bullae which heal slowly	Hemorrhagic blisters which heal with scarring and milia	Hemorrhagic blisters which heal with severe scarring (Fig 24.16)
Sites	Sites of repeated trauma (hands and feet)	Perioral and perianal areas and sites of trauma	Sites of friction (knees, elbows, fingers)	Generalized
Mucosal lesions	Mucosae spared	Involved	Mucosal involvement minimal	Mucosal involvement severe
Nail involvement	–	+	+	++
Complications	Heal without scarring	One variant is lethal	Scarring and milia formation	Severe scarring: • Webbing of digits (mitten hand) • Esophageal strictures

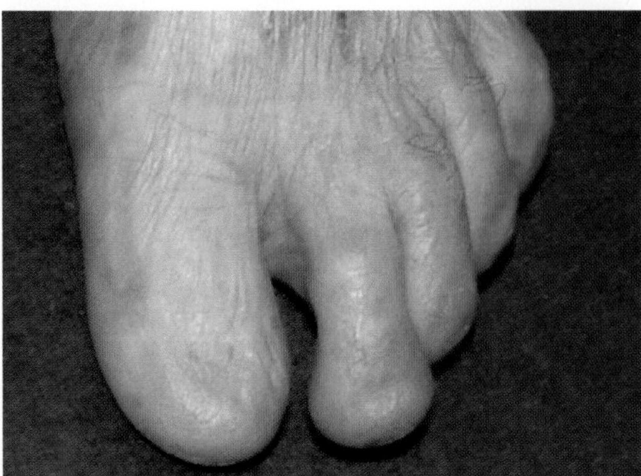

Fig. 24.16: EB dystrophica: Bullae heal with scarring. Note loss of nails

24

Table 24.4: Classification of pyodermas

		Superficial	*Deep*
Non-follicular	Localized	Impetigo contagiosa, Bullous impetigo	Ecthyma
	Spreading	Erysipelas	Cellulitis
Follicular	Folliculitis	Superficial folliculitis	Deep folliculitis
	Perifolliculitis	Furuncle	Carbuncle

Clinical features

Clinical features of different types of pyodermas are discussed in Tables 24.5 to 24.7.

Treatment

General measures

- Local hygiene.
- Rest and limb elevation in case of spreading pyodermas
- NSAIDs, if pain and constitutional symptoms are present.

Specific measures

- Topical antibiotics like mupirocin, sodium fusidate and nadifloxacin, for localized lesions.
- Systemic antibiotics for wide spread lesions, presence of constitutional symptoms and lymphadenopathy and spreading infection.
  - Antistreptococcal antibiotics (e.g. injectable procaine penicillin) for erysipelas and cellulitis.
  - Erythromycin group for impetigo contagiosa and ecthyma.
  - Antistaphylococcal antibiotics (e.g. cloxacillin) for bullous impetigo and follicular infections.
- For recurrent infections, rule out underlying skin disease, evaluate for carrier state and treat accordingly.

Staphylococcal Scalded Skin Syndrome (SSSS)

Etiology

SSSS is mediated by hematogenously spread exotoxin produced by *S. aureus* present in infection at a site distant

Table 24.5: Clinical features of non-follicular pyodermas

	Impetigo contagiosa	*Bullous impetigo*	*Ecthyma*
Age	Children	Infants	Any age
Clinical features	Thin-walled blisters on erythematous base. Rupture rapidly to leave honey-colored crusts (Fig. 24.17) Lesions spread without central clearing. Lymphadenopathy frequent	Thick-walled, persistent blisters on bland skin. Rupture only after a few days to leave thin varnish-like crusts (Fig. 24.18) Lesions heal in center to form annular plaques. Lymphadenopathy rare	Crusted, tender erythematous indurated plaque Heals with scarring
Sites of predilection	Face, especially around the mouth and nose	Face and other parts of body	Buttocks, thighs, legs
Complications	Post streptococcal glomerulonephritis (PSGN) Eczematization	Staphylococcal scalded skin syndrome	PSGN Eczematization Scarring

Table 24.6: Clinical features of spreading pyodermas

	Erysipelas	*Cellulitis*
Clinical features	Red, hot edematous well defined rapidy spreading plaques with superficial vesiculation Constitutional symptoms	Red, hot edematous rapidly spreading, ill defined, deep plaques. Constitutional symptoms
Sites of predilection	Face	Lower extremities

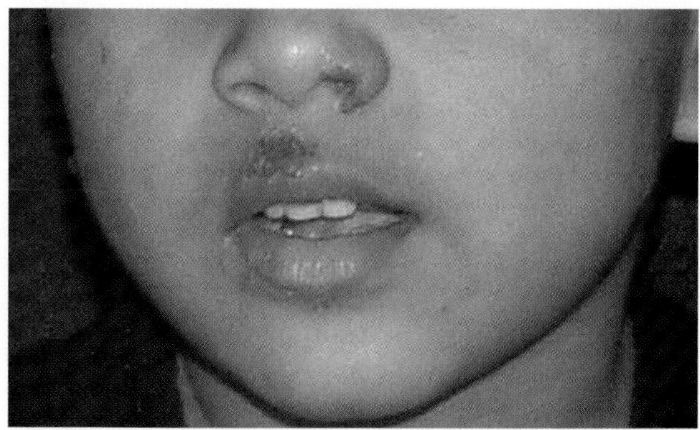

Fig. 24.17: Impetigo contagiosa: honey-colored crusts around mouth

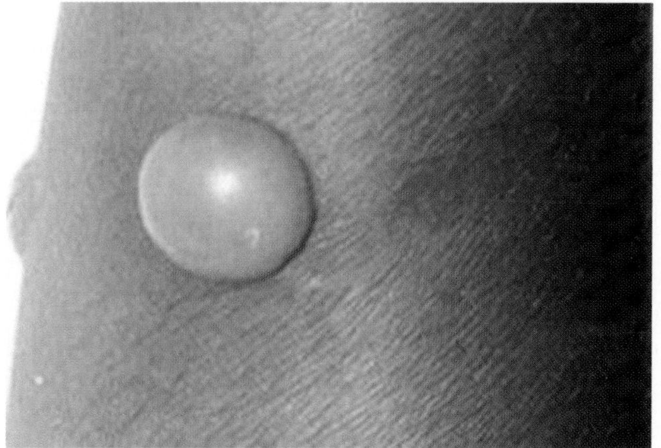

Fig. 24.18: Bullous impetigo: thick-walled, persistant blisters on bland skin

Table 24.7: Clinical features of follicular pyodermas		
	Folliculitis	*Furuncle*
Clinical features	Erythematous follicular papules, often surmounted by pustules (Fig. 24.19).	Firm red follicular nodules which discharge pus and heal with minimal scarring.
Sites of predilection	Face, lower extremities	Buttocks, lower extremities

from the involved, skin, (e.g. otitis media, pneumonitis) and rarely in skin.

Clinical features
- Usually seen in newborns and infants <2 years of age.
- Erythema and tenderness is followed by superficial peeling of skin in thin sheets, giving the appearance of scalding (Fig. 24.20). Constitutional symptoms are minimal.

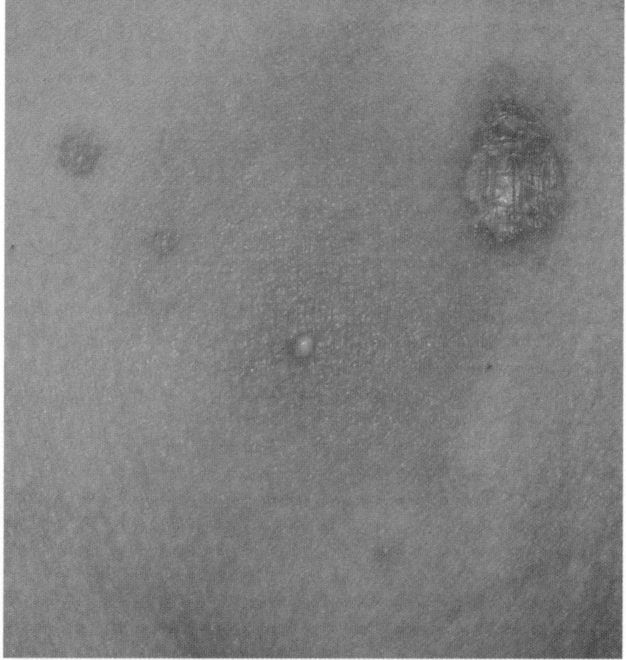

Fig. 24.19: Folliculitis: erythematous follicular papule often surmounted by pustules

Treatment
- Supportive measures.
- Antistaphylococcal antibiotics, administered initially parenterally then orally.

Cutaneous Tuberculosis

Clinical features

Clinical presentation is highly variable and depends on immunity of the individual as well as route of inoculation of organism.

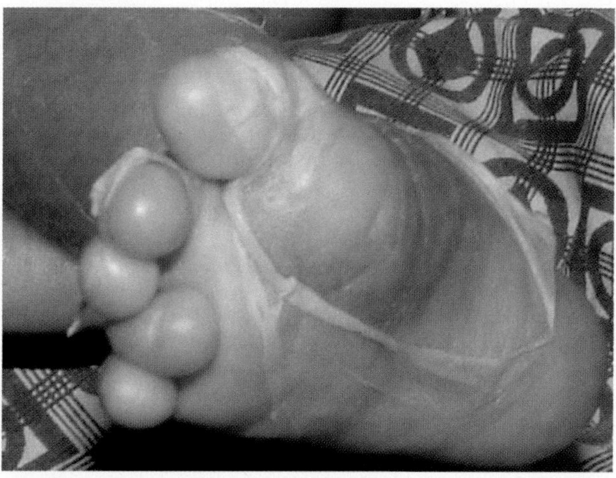

Fig. 24.20: Staphylococcal scalded skin syndrome (SSSS): erythema and superficial peeling of skin in thin sheets

Lupus vulgaris

- Characterized by solitary, well defined, reddish-brown plaque which slowly spreads centrifugally (Fig. 24.21). On diascopy, i.e. pressing the lesion with a clean glass slide, apple jelly nodules are identified. Center becomes atrophic and scarred with time but often develops nodules.
- Seen on head, neck and buttocks, upper limbs.

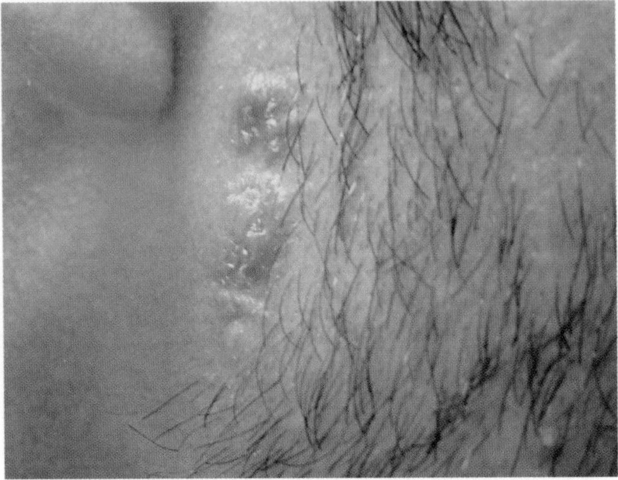

24

Fig. 24.21: Lupus vulgaris: solitary, well defined annular plaque with central scarring

Scrofuloderma

- Occurs by contiguous spread from tubercular lymph nodes, bones or joints.
- Manifests initially as firm subcutaneous nodules which break open to form sinuses. The mouth of the sinus is serpiginous with undermined edges.

Tuberculosis verrucosa cutis

- Presents at trauma-prone sites.
- Single papule with a violaceous halo which evolves to warty, firm plaque having clefts and fissures that discharge pus. There may be scarring at center.

Diagnosis

Diagnosis is confirmed by histopathology.

Treatment

Intensive phase: of 8 weeks with

- Isoniazid 5 mg/kg
- Rifampicin 10 mg/kg
- Ethambutol 15 mg/kg
- Pyrazinamide 30 mg/kg

Maintenance phase: of 16 weeks with

- Isoniazid 5 mg/kg
- Rifampicin 10 mg/kg

Leprosy

The mode of transmission is uncertain but possibly nasal droplet infection is important. The type of disease which develops depends on the hosts immunological response. If the host mounts good cell-mediated immunity (CMI), the infection is localized, while if the CMI is poor, the infection is extensive with visceral involvement.

Classification

The Ridley Jopling classification, which is based on clinicopathological, immunological and bacteriological parameters, classifies leprosy into:

- ***Indeterminate***
- ***Determinate***
  - Polar (stable) leprosy:
    - Tuberculoid leprosy (TT)
    - Lepromatous leprosy (LL)
  - Borderline (unstable) leprosy
    - Borderline tuberculoid leprosy (BT)
    - Borderline leprosy (BB)
    - Borderline lepromatous leprosy (BL)

Clinical features

Skin lesions: Macules, plaques and nodules which can be hypopigmented, anesthetic/hypoesthetic. Skin appendages (hair, sweating) on the lesions are reduced and there is epidermal atrophy.

Nerve involvement: Nerves can be thickened and tender and there may be associated sensory and motor impairment.

Acid-fast bacilli (AFB): AFB can be demonstrated in some forms (usually LL, BL and less frequently BB).

The profile of different clinical types of leprosy is discussed in Table 24.8.

Lepra reactions

Two types of acute episodes are seen in course of leprosy.

- ***Type 1 lepra reaction:***
  - Is due to alteration in host's CMI
  - Occurs in borderline spectrum (BT, BB, BL).
  - It can be an upgrading (reversal reaction) with improvement of CMI or a downgrading reaction (as seen in natural course of disease) when CMI decreases.
  - Characterized by edema and erythema of preexisting lesions and neuritis which may result in sensory and motor impairment.
- ***Type 2 lepra reaction (erythema nodosum leprosum)***
  - Is an immune complex reaction.
  - Occurs in BL and LL.
  - Characterized by several tender erythematous, transient nodules on face, flexures and legs. It is also associated with neuritis, orchitis, iridocyclitis, arthralgia and fever.

Table 24.8: Clinical profile of spectrum of leprosy

	Indeterminate	*TT*	*BT*	*BB*	*BL*	*LL*
Skin lesions						
– Number	Single	Single/few	Few	Several	Numerous	Innumerable
– Size	Variable	Variable	May be large	Variable	Small	Small
– Sensations	Variable	Anesthetic	Hypoesthetic	Hypoesthetic	Hypoesthetic	Normoesthetic
– Symmetry	Asymmetrical	Asymmetrical	Asymmetrical	Bilateral but asymmetrical	Tendency to symmetry	Symmetrical
– Morphology	Always macule on face of child (Fig. 24.22)	Macule/ plaque; well defined	Plaques; well defined with satellite lesions (Fig. 24.23).	Macules/plaque; with sloping edge (inverted saucer appearance)	Macules/papules, nodules, plaques; ill-defined.	Macules/papules, nodules, plaques; ill-defined Diffuse infiltration of face (leonine facies)
Nerves	+/–	Single trunk/ feeder nerve related to lesion thickened/ nodular	Asymmetrical. Few nerves thickened. Anesthesia in distribution of nerve	Asymmetrical. Several nerves thickened	Almost symmetrical. Several nerves thickened. Glove and stocking anesthesia	Symmetrical. Several nerves thickened. Glove and stocking anesthesia
Systemic involvement					Lymphadenopathy, hepatosplenomegaly, ocular and testicular involvement.	
Reactions	–	Stable	Type I	Type I	Type I/ Type II	Type II
Lepromin	+/–	+	+/–	–	–	–
AFB	+/–	–	–	+/–	+/++	+++

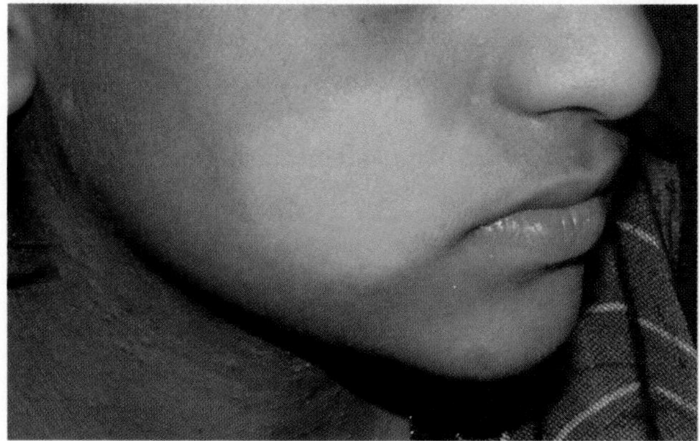

Fig. 24.22: Indeterminate leprosy: ill-defined hypopigmented, hypoesthetic macule on the face

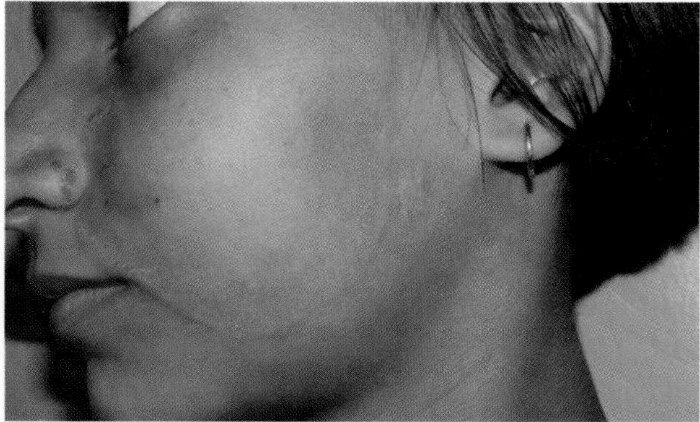

Fig. 24.23: Borderline tuberculoid: well defined erythematous plaque with satellite lesions

Complications of leprosy

The following complications may develop:

- Trophic ulcers.
- Deformities: like claw hand, clawing of toes, foot drop and saddle nose deformity.
- Ophthalmologic complications: diminished corneal sensation, lagophthalmos and recurrent iridocyclitis.
- Renal involvement.

Investigations

The following investigations need to be done to establish the diagnosis and for classification.

Slit skin smears: Slit skin smears are taken from the lesions, and ear lobules. These are stained with modified Ziehl-Neelsen method.

Lepromin test: Lepromin test is of prognostic value.

24

Histopathology: Granulomas and neural involvement are seen.

Treatment

- The patient (and parents) needs reassurance, counseling regarding treatment and care of hands, feet and eyes.
- For the purpose of treatment, leprosy is classified into paucibacillary and multibacillary leprosy. Multi drug therapy (MDT) is instituted based on number of lesions (Table 24.9).
- ***Newer drugs:*** Newer drugs are required in case of resistance or intolerance to conventional therapy. These include ofloxacin, sparfloxacin, minocycline and clarithromycin.
- ***Treatment of reactions***

  Acute lepra reactions may be of variable severity and are managed as depicted in Table 24.10.

24

Viral Infections

Several viruses infect the skin, either primarily or as part of the viremia.

Verruca (Warts)

Etiology

Caused by human papilloma virus, of which there are more than 100 types. They are transmitted by close contact and auto-inoculation.

Clinical features

In children, nongenital warts are common, with an incidence of upto 10%. The main features of various types of warts are given in Table 24.11.

Treatment

Several modalities of treatment used, depending on the type of wart:

- ***Verruca vulgaris:*** Cryotherapy, electric cautery and radiofrequency ablation.
- ***Verruca plana:*** Trichloroacetic acid touches, retinoic acid (0.025–0.05%) locally at night.
- ***Palmoplantar warts:*** Wart paint after soaking in water to soften skin and protecting surrounding skin, cryotherapy and formalin soaks.
- ***Filiform warts:*** Electric cautery and radiofrequency ablation.

Molluscum Contagiosum

Clinical features

- ***Morphology:*** Multiple pearly white, dome-shaped papules with central umbilication (Fig. 24.26). Cheesy material can be expressed from the lesion.
- ***Site:*** Seen on any part of the body. Widespread lesions are seen in atopics and immunocompromised patients.
- ***Course:*** Usually self limiting, clears within a year's time.
- ***Complications:*** Secondary infection.

Treatment

Application of wart paint and mechanical removal under cover of topical anesthetic EMLA.

Table 24.10: Treatment of reactions

	Type 1 reaction	*Type 2 reaction*
Mild	NSAIDS	NSAIDS
Moderate	NSAIDS Oral corticosteroids	NSAIDS Thalidomide* Chloroquine Clofazamine
Severe	NSAIDS Oral corticosteroids	Thalidomide* Corticosteroids Antimony (parenteral)

*Not to be used in girls in the reproductive age group.
NSAIDs non-steroidal anti-inflammatory drugs

Table 24.9: WHO recommendation for treatment of leprosy in children aged 10–15 years

	*Paucibacillary**	*Multibacillary**
Definition	5 or < lesions	>5 lesions
Duration of therapy	6 months of treatment to be completed in 9 months	12 months to be completed in 18 months
Drugs		
Supervised (monthly)	Rifampicin 450 mg	Rifampicin 450 mg + Clofazimine 150 mg
Unsupervised (daily)	Dapsone 50 mg	Dapsone 50 mg + Clofazimine 25 mg

*In children < 10 years of age, dose is given according to weight. Rifampicin: 10 mg/ kg body weight; clofazimine: 1 mg/ kg body weight daily, 6 mg/ kg monthly; dapsone: 2 mg/ kg body weight.

Table 24.11: Main features of different types of warts

	Verruca vulgaris (common warts)	*Verruca plana (plane warts)*	*Palmoplantar warts*	*Filiform warts*
Clinical features	Single or multiple firm papules with hyperkeratotic, clefted surface (Fig. 24.24).	Skin-colored Flat smooth papules with slight elevation (Fig. 24.25). Koebner's phenomenon may be seen due to auto-inoculation.	Superficial (mosaic): Usually painless, hyperkeratotic papules and plaques Deep (myrmecia): Painful, deep seated papules with a horny collar	Thin elongated, firm projections on a horny confluent base.
Site	Any part of body, most commonly on back of hands, on fingers and knees	Face and back of hands.	Soles and less often palms	Face

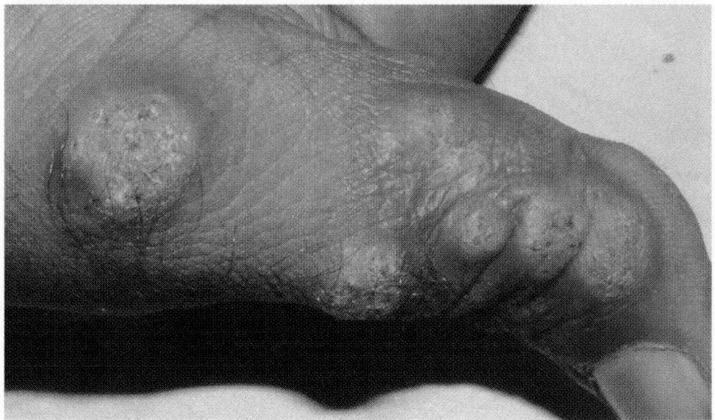

Fig. 24.24: Verruca vulgaris: firm papules with hyperkeratotic, clefted surface

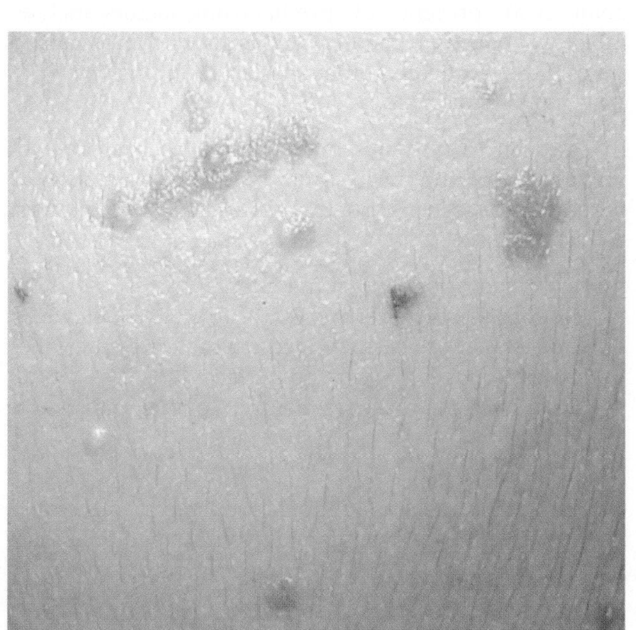

Fig. 24.25: Verruca plana: multiple skin-colored papules

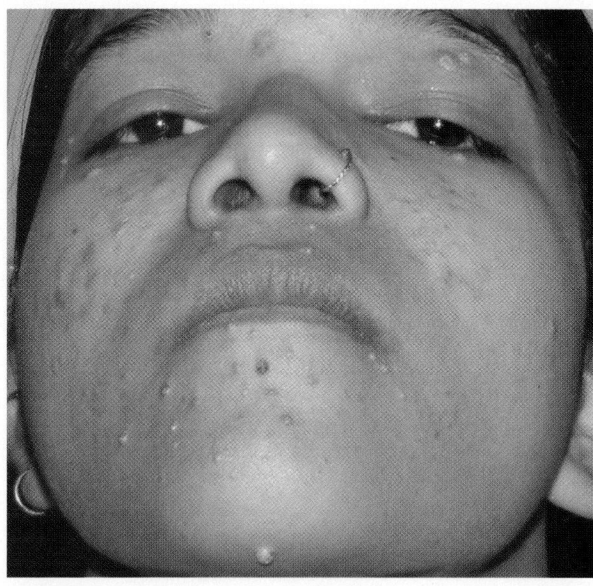

Fig. 24.26: Molluscum contagiosum: pearly white dome-shaped papules with central umbilication

Fungal Infections

Superficial fungal infections are common in childhood.

Dermatophytoses (Ringworm)

Etiology

Three genera of fungus cause dermatophytoses *Trichophyton, Epidermophyton and Microsporum*. The infection is given different names depending on the site affected. Dermatophyte infection of glabrous skin is known as tinea corporis, of groin as tinea cruris, of hands as tinea manuum, of feet as tinea pedis, of nails as tinea unguium, and of scalp as tinea capitis.

Clinical features

Classical lesion of tinea is an annular or arcuate plaque with the active edge showing papulovesiculation and scaling and a clear centre. These features are modified by site.

24

Tinea capitis
Is common in preadolescent children and three patterns are seen:

Non-inflammatory or epidemic type: Caused by anthropophilic organisms and so is responsible for epidemics. It presents as a patch of alopecia with marked scaling at periphery (Fig. 24.27). Hair break off easily and inflammation is minimal.

Inflammatory type or kerion: Caused by zoophilic organisms and so does not cause epidemics. It presents as a boggy swelling which drains pus from multiple openings (Fig. 24.28). Hair is easily pluckable without pain. Usually associated with occipital lymphadenopathy.

Favus: Caused by *T. schonleinii*, presents as yellowish, foul smelling cup-shaped crusts with matting of hair.

Tinea corporis
- Shows classical features of tinea and is usually inflammatory in children.

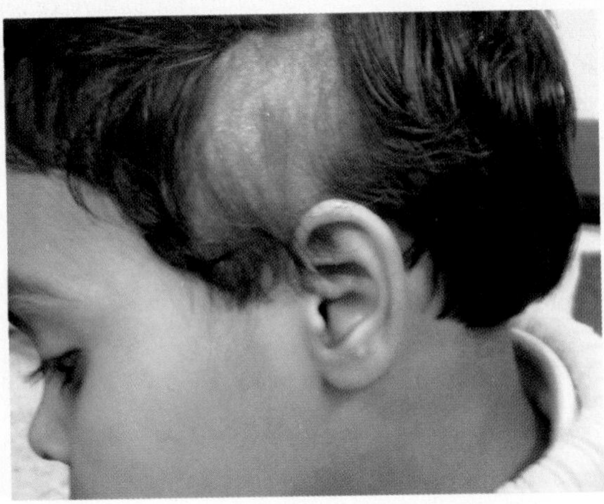

Fig. 24.27: Tinea capitis: area of non-scarring alopecia with minimal inflammation

- Most frequently seen on exposed parts.
- Tinea faciale (tinea of face) common in children.

Diagnosis
KOH test is simple, quick, inexpensive and sensitive test. Culture is confirmatory and required for identification of species.

Treatment
Tinea capitis
- Griseofulvin (15 mg/kg/day of ultramicrosized formulation for 8 weeks) is drug of choice.
- Terbinafine (5 mg/kg/day for 4 weeks) is effective in non-inflammatory tinea capitis. Longer treatment (8 weeks) needed for kerion.
- Washing with ketoconazole shampoo helps to reduce transmission. Also avoid sharing combs and other head wear.

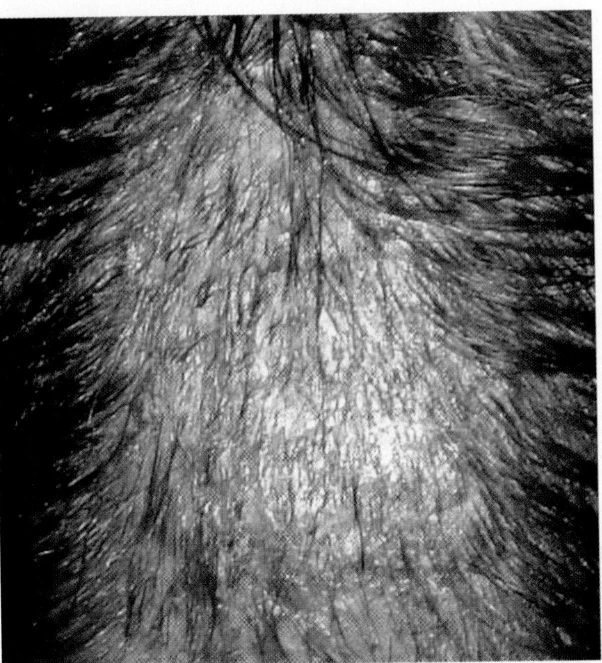

Fig. 24.28: Kerion: boggy swelling of scalp

Tinea corporis
- Localized lesions treated with topical therapy (azoles available as clotrimazole, miconazole or ketoconazole in lotion, gel and cream formulations)
- Widespread lesions require systemic antifungal therapy with griseofulvin (for 4 weeks) or terbinafine (2 weeks).

Candidiasis

Candida albicans, a normal commensal, becomes pathogenic in the presence of predisposing factors such as moisture, obesity, diabetes and immunocompromised states. Less frequently, other species like *C. glabrata*.

Clinical features
In children candidiasis may present as oral thrush, vulvovaginitis, intertrigo, candidal diaper dermatitis or paronychia as seen in chronic mucocutaneous candidiasis.

Oral thrush
- Seen in new born breast fed infants.
- Presents as soft, creamy white to yellow, elevated plaques, that are easily wiped off to leave an erythematous, eroded or ulcerated surface.
- Buccal mucosa (most frequently), tongue, palate and gingiva.

Candidal intertrigo
Occurs in skin folds as erythematous, moist, macerated lesion with a frayed irregular edge with satellite lesions.

Candidal diaper dermatitis
- Begins in perianal region, spreading to perineum, upper thighs, lower abdomen and lower back.

- Presents as well defined weeping eroded lesions with scalloped border with a collar of overhanging scales and satellite pustules.

Candidal paronychia

- In children, candidal paronychia is rare except in those with chronic mucocutaneous candidiasis in which condition it may be associated with candidal onychomycosis.
- Nail plate is thickened and dystrophic. There is loss of cuticle with redness and swelling of nail fold. Small beads of pus can be expressed from under the proximal nail fold.

Diagnosis

KOH test shows budding yeasts and pseudohyphae and culture confirms the diagnosis.

Treatment

- Predisposing factors should be addressed and the area should be kept dry.
- Topical therapy with imidazoles (clotrimazole, miconazole and ketoconazole), amphotericin, and nystatin is effective for thrush.
- Systemic therapy with weekly fluconazole or pulse itraconazole is given for onychomycosis.

Pityriasis Versicolor

Caused by commensal yeast *Malasezzia* species of which *M. furfur* is most incriminated.

Clinical features

- Seen in adolescents.
- Characterized by scaly, perifollicular macules with variable pigmentation (from hypopigmented to erythematous to hyperpigmented). The fine branny scales can be accentuated by gentle abrasion with a glass slide.
- Most frequently seen on upper torso (both anterior and posterior), neck and sometimes also on proximal part of upper extremities.

Diagnosis

KOH mount shows a mixture of short branched hyphae and spores (spaghetti and meatball appearance).

Treatment

Topical therapy with imidazoles (ketaconazole 2%) for 3 consecutive days or selenium sulphide 2.5% lotion applied once a week for 4 weeks.

INFESTATIONS

Scabies

Caused by *Sarcoptes scabei var hominis* and transmitted by close contact with infested humans. Animal scabies acquired from infested animals, but does not spread from one human to another.

Clinical Features

Symptoms: Severe itching, more intense at night.

Primary lesion: Burrow, a grey thread-like serpentine line with a minute papule at the end. Also seen are papules and papulovesicles.

Secondary lesions: Pustules, eczematized lesions and nodules.

Sites of predilection: Lesions characteristically seen in webs of hands, on wrists, ulnar aspects of forearms, elbows, axillae, umbilical area, genitalia, feet and buttocks. Face is usually spared except in infants in whom scalp, palms and soles (Fig. 24.29 A) are also involved. Nodular lesions are seen on genitalia (Fig. 24.29 B).

Complications: Secondary infections, acute glomerulonephritis (following secondary streptococcal infection) and eczematization.

Treatment

24

- All close contacts of the patient, even if asymptomatic, should be treated. However, overzealous laundering of bed linen and clothes is not necessary.
- Topical scabicide should be applied all over body below the neck including on the free edge of nails, genitals, soles of feet after hydration of body with a bath. Scabicides available include:
  - *Permethrin 5%:* Overnight single application is treatment of choice beyond 2 months of age.
  - *Crotamiton 10%:* Two applications daily for 14 days.
  - *Benzyl benzoate, 25%:* Three applications at 12 hourly intervals.
  - *Gamma benzene hexacloride, 1%:* Single application. To be avoided in infants.
- *Ivermectin,* single oral dose of 200 μg /kg body weight, in children older than 5 years.
- Antibiotics need to be given, if secondary infection is present.
- Antihistamines need to be given for 1–2 weeks.

Pediculosis

Head louse infestation is common in children while pubic louse infestation is infrequent but when it occurs it involves eyelashes and eyebrows. Louse is an obligate ectoparasite and 2 species infest humans:

- *Pediculosis humanus* (*P. humanus capitis*, head louse and *P. humanus corporis*, body louse).
- *Phthirus pubis* (pubic louse).

Head louse infestation is transmitted by close contact and pubic louse infestation is acquired by children from infested parents.

Clinical Features

Symptoms: Severe pruritis.

Findings: Though adults are difficult to find, nits (egg-capsules) are easily seen firmly cemented to hair on which they can be slided but not flicked off.

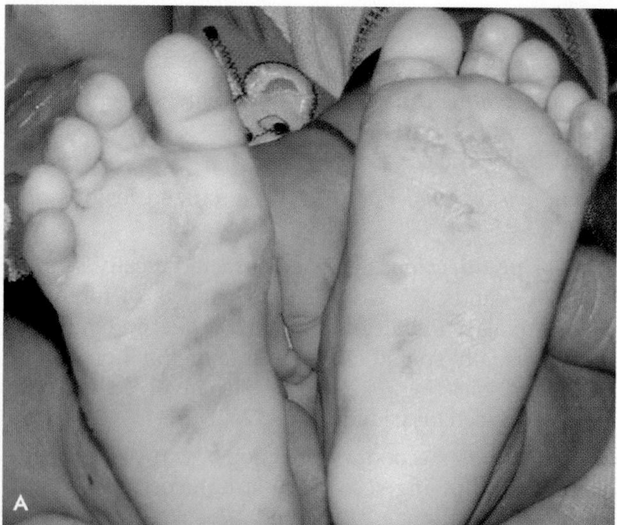

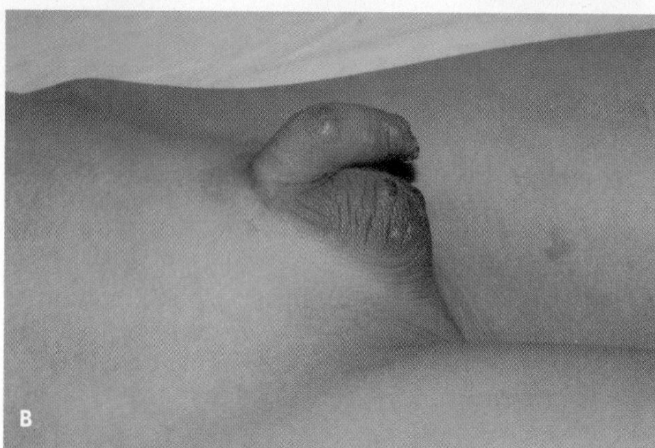

Figs 24.29A and B: Infantile scabies: (A) multiple papulo-vesicular lesions on soles. (B) nodular lesions on genitalia

Complications: Secondary infection, eczematization and occipital lymphadenopathy.

Treatment

Pediculosis capitis

- All family members should be treated.
- ***Pediculocides***
  - Permethrin, 1% lotion, single 10 minute application to wet hair followed by rinsing. Second application after 7 days.
  - Gamma benzene hexachloride, 1% single overnight application to dry hair followed by rinsing. Second application used after 7 days.
  - Malathion, 0.5% water based lotion, applied on dry hair for 6 hours. Has residual effect, so 2nd application not needed.

Pediculosis pubis infestation of lashes

Petrolatum (twice daily for 7–10 days) is used, with good results, for eyelash infestation. The petrolatum covers the lice and their nits, preventing respiration. The dead lice are removed mechanically with tweezers.

DRUG ERUPTIONS

Drug eruptions are adverse events that occur after systemic or topical administration of a drug. (Table 24.12)

Diagnosis

- Diagnosis is based on clinical features and temporal relation to drug use. Though any drug can cause a reaction after any length of treatment, some drugs are more suspect and the most recent introduction most likely cause.
- Prick tests and *in vitro* tests are of little value. The role of drug provocation test is controversial but may be needed to find the culprit drug in patients on multiple drugs as well as to find safe alternative drugs.

Treatment

Withdrawal of drug: Is most effective approach but is not always easy as the child may be taking several drugs or the suspected drug may be difficult to withdraw as it is essential. Sometimes chemically unrelated drug substitute may not be available.

Symptomatic therapy

- Urticaria: Antihistaminics.
- Anaphylactic reactions: Airway maintenance, adrenaline, chlorpheniramine maleate, hydrocortisone.
- Exanthematous reactions: Topical, and if severe, systemic steroids.
- SJS-TEN complex: Supportive treatment including fluid-electrolyte balance. Role of systemic corticosteroids controversial.

NEVI

Nevus is a developmental disorder characterized by hyperplasia of epidermal/dermal structures in a circumscribed area of skin.

Melanocytic Nevi

Melanocytic nevi are circumscribed pigmented lesions composed of groups of melanocytic nevus cells.

Classification

- Congenital melanocytic nevi
- Acquired:
  - Junctional melanocytic nevi
  - Compound melanocytic nevi
  - Intradermal melanocytic nevi (seen in adults).

Clinical Features

Table 24.13 delineates the clinical features that distinguish the different types of melanocytic nevi.

Treatment

Congenital nevi: Especially those larger than 20 cm, need to be watched for malignant transformation.
Acquired nevi: Can be left alone.

Table 24.12: Common drug eruptions

Pattern	Morphology	Drugs implicated
Exanthematous eruptions	Commonest drug eruption. Symmetric erythematous macules and papules surmounted by scales.	Penicillins, sulphonamides, anticonvulsants, antitubercular drugs,
Erythroderma (exfoliative dermatitis)	Entire skin surface becomes erythematous, scaly and edematous.	Penicillins, sulphonamides, barbiturates, isoniazid and gold.
Stevens Johnson syndrome-toxic epidermal necrolysis (SJS-TEN) complex	Initial lesions targetoid, followed by diffuse, intense erythema. Flaccid blisters, followed by large areas of skin denudation. Mucosae always involved.	Sulphonamides, pencillin, quinolones, barbiturates phenytoin, frusemide, hydralazine, NSAIDS.
Fixed drug eruption	Well demarcated, erythematous plaques, recurring at same site each time implicated drug is taken. Subside with hyperpigmentation.	Phenolphthalein, barbiturates, sulphonamides, tetracyclines, salicylates.
Photosensitive eruption	Pruritic papules and plaques on sun-exposed areas.	Thiazides, sulphonamides, tetracyclines, quinolones, phenothiazines, psoralens.
Vasculitis	Can manifest as palpable purpura, urticarial vasculitis, necrotic ulcers nodular vasculitis.	NSAIDS, phenytoin, sulphonamides, tetracyclines, ampicillin.
Urticaria and angioedema	Can occur independently or as a part of a severe generalized reaction with bronchospasm and circulatory collapse (anaphylaxis).	Aspirin, indomethacin, opiates, sulphonamides, pencillin.

24

Dermal Melanocytosis

Mongolian Spot

- Consists of grey blue macules presenting at birth in Asian infants.
- Seen commonly in lumbosacral region.
- Is due to ectopic melanocytes in dermis.
- Disappear spontaneously by early childhood.

Nevus of Ota

- Consists of mottled slate grey and brown hyperpigmented macules presenting at birth or infancy. Pigmentation of sclera (slate grey) and conjunctiva (brown) is common.
- Seen in the distribution of maxillary division of trigeminal nerve.
- Persists for life but can be treated with lasers.

Epidermal Nevi

Heterogeneous group of disorders characterized by hyperplasia of epidermal structures in a circumscribed area of skin.

Clinical Features

- Usually present at birth.
- Presents as multiple brown papular lesions arranged linearly (Fig. 24.30)
- Several variants described:
  - Verrucous epidermal nevus
  - Inflammatory linear verrucous epidermal nevus
  - Nevus comedonicus
  - Nevus sebaceous.

Treatment

Topical retinoic acid and dermabrasion are helpful.

Vascular Nevi

Clinical features of vascular nevi are detailed in Table 24.14 and 24.15.

Treatment

Salmon patch: None required.

Strawberry hemangioma: Small lesions resolve spontaneously. Large symptomatic lesions need treatment with systemic steroids in the proliferative phase. Pulsed tunable dye laser is useful for cosmetic results.

Portwine stain: Cosmetic camouflage. Laser ablation with pulsed tunable dye laser.

Table 24.13: Clinical features of melanocytic nevi

	Congenital nevus	Junctional nevus	Compound nevus
Age of onset	Birth	Early childhood	Childhood
Morphology	Single/multiple dark brown-black lesions Become cerebriform over time. Usually have coarse hair.	Brown-dark brown macules with color variation within lesion. Smooth margin	Brown-black dome shaped smooth lesion. Color variation present but less than junctional nevus. May have hair.
Site	Giant lesions on trunk.	Palms, soles, genitals	Face

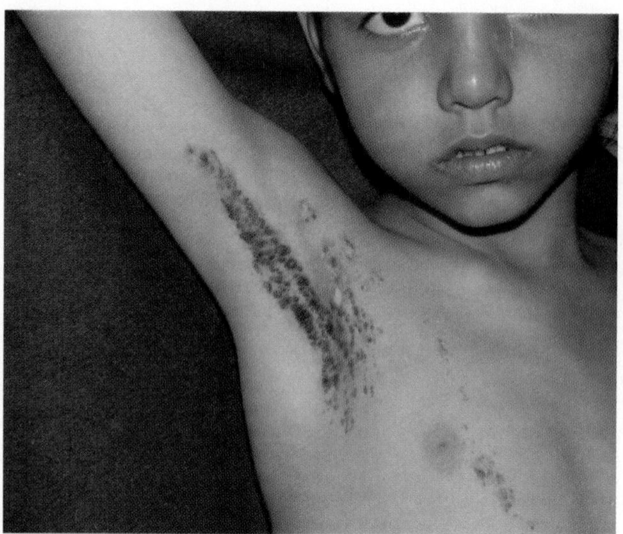

Fig. 24.30: Verrucous epidermal nevus: multiple brown papular lesions arranged linearly

24

Lymphangioma: Surgery, CO_2 laser, radiofrequency ablation.

ECZEMATOUS DERMATITIS

Eczematous dermatitis manifest clinically in acute phase as papulovesiculation and in chronic phase as thickened dry and sometimes lichenified skin.

Atopic Dermatitis

Atopic dermatitis (AD) is an acute, subacute or chronic relapsing, endogenous eczema, characterized by dry skin and pruritic, recurrent, symmetric dermatitic lesions.

Etiology

- Genetic predisposition is an important factor but the inheritance pattern has not been ascertained.
- Immunological changes include elevated IgE levels, increased levels of specific IgE to allergens and abnormalities of lymphocytes.

Table 24.14: Classification of vascular nevi

	Malformations	*Hemangiomas*
	Capillary • Salmon patch • Portwine stain Arterial Venous Combined	• Capillary • Cavernous • Mixed
Onset	Always present at birth	Usually begin after birth
Evolution	Growth proportionate to growth of child and then persists	Initial growth followed by involution
Underlying skeletal defects	Frequent	Infrequent

Table 24.15: Clinical features of vascular nevi

	Salmon patch	*Strawberry hemangioma*	*Portwine stain (PWS)*	*Lymphangioma*
Onset	At birth	After birth	At birth	At birth
Morphology	Telangiectatic macules	Soft, bright nodule with pale stippling (Fig. 24.31)	Light pink to deep red macules (Fig. 24.32). Become bosselated with age	Cluster of thin-walled vesicles (frog spawn)
Site	Nape of neck, forehead and eyelids	Face and neck	Face	Trunk
Complications	None	Interfere with function. Bleeding or ulceration	Trigeminal PWS (Sturge Weber syndrome) associated with hamartomas of CNS resulting in seizures and ophthalmological deficits	Prone to repeated trauma
Course	Involutes by age of one.	Grows for few months and then spontaneous regresses.	Persists throughout life	Persists

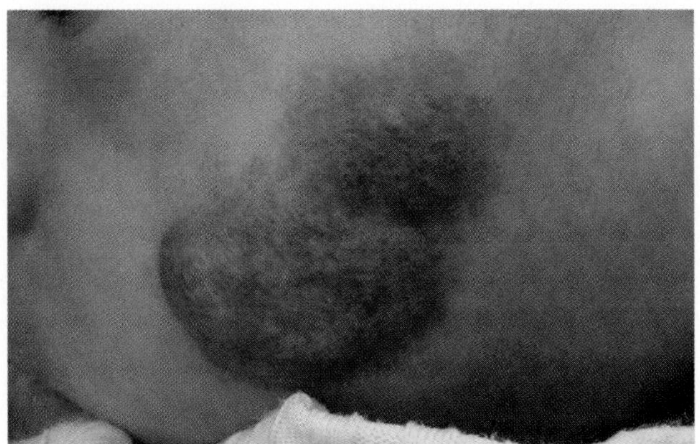

Fig. 24.31: Strawberry hemangioma: soft bright red nodule with pale stippling

Fig. 24.32: Portwine stain: light pink to deep red macule

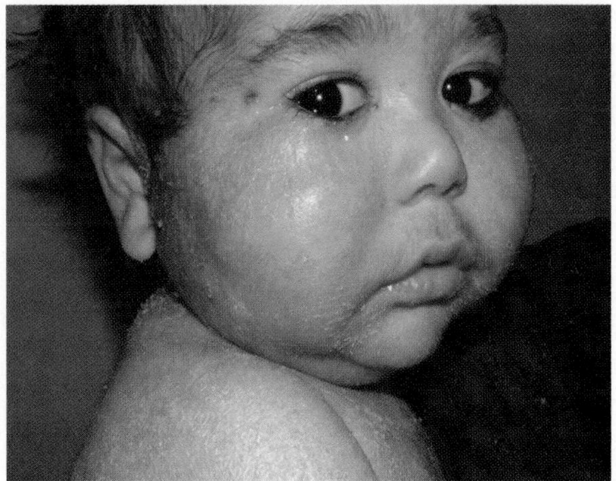

Fig. 24.33: Infantile eczema: papulo-vesicular lesions on the face

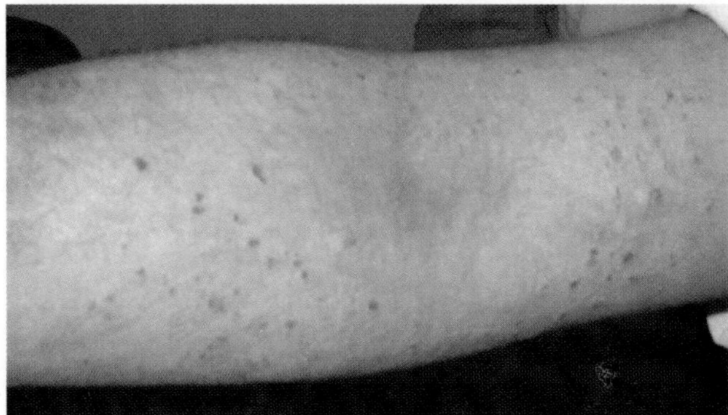

Fig. 24.34: Atopic dermatitis in childhood: dry plaques in the flexures

Clinical Features

Patterns

Two distinct patterns of AD are seen in children.

- ***Infantile pattern***
  - Begins after 3 months of age as extremely itchy erythematous papulovesicles.
  - Begins usually on face (Fig. 24.33) with in involvement of rest of the body over period of time.
  - Clears by 18 months of age in 40% and in 60% changes into childhood pattern.
- ***Childhood pattern***
  - Dry lichenified and crusted plaques.
  - Seen mainly on cubital (Fig. 24.34) and popliteal fossa, the neck and face.
  - 70% clear by 10 years of age.

Complications

- Infections: bacterial (impetigo), viral (herpes, molluscum) and fungal infections.
- Disturbed sleep and poor growth.

Diagnosis (Table 24.16)

Diagnosis of AD is clinical and several criteria have been devised to make the diagnosis. Of these Hanifin and Rajka's criteria for diagnosis of AD have been extensively validated.

Treatment

General measures

Parents and the child should be educated about the disease and its chronic course.

Avoid scratching

- Avoiding contact with irritants, like woolens, chemicals
- Using mild soaps and cleansing lotions
- Avoiding house dust mite: Often (not necessarily always) measures like using barriers on pillows and mattresses, regular vacuuming of rooms, etc. help.

Dietary restrictions

- Role of dietary restrictions is controversial.
- Breast feeding of infant at risk may decrease the chance of child developing AD.

Vaccinations

No contraindication to vaccination except in children specifically allergic to eggs, in whom measles, influenza and yellow fever vaccines are best avoided.

Symptomatic treatment

Acute eczema

Best treated with:

- Wet dressings, topical steroids and topical antibiotics, when indicated.
- Though role of oral antihistaminics is controversial, the sedating antihistamines are routinely used.
- Oral antibiotics are used in case of infected lesions and also empirically in extensive dermatitis.

Chronic eczema

- Hydration followed by application of emollients like petrolatum.
- Topical antiinflammatory agents like glucocorticoids. Corticosteroids are combined with keratolytic agents like salicylic acid in lichenified lesions. Potent steroids should be avoided on face and genitalia.
- Topical immunomodulators like tacrolimus and pimecrolimus are useful because of their steroid sparing action and rapid reduction in itching.

24

Table 24.16: Hanifin and Rajka's criteria for diagnosis of atopic dermatitis

Major features (Must have 3 or more):
Pruritis
Typical morphology and distribution:
• Facial and extensor involvement in infants and children.
• Flexural lichenification in adults
Dermatitis, chronic or chronically relapsing
Personal or family history of atopy (asthma, allergic rhinitis or atopic dermatitis)
Minor features (Must have 3 or more):
Cataracts (anterior subcapsular)
Cheilitis
Conjunctivitis, recurrent
Facial pallor/erythema
Food intolerance
Hand dermatitis: nonallergic, irritant
Ichthyosis
Elevated levels of IgE
Immediate (type I) skin test reactivity
Infections
Itching, when sweating
Keratoconus
Keratosis pilaris
Nipple dermatitis
Orbital darkening
Palmar hyperlinearity
Perifollicular accentuation
Pityriasis alba
White dermographism
Wool intolerance
Xerosis

- Oral antihistaminics are used to break the itch-scratch cycle.
- Narrow band UVB, psoralens with UVA (PUVA) and cyclosporine useful in resistant cases.

Infantile Seborrheic Dermatitis

Malassezia furfur, a commensal yeast is incriminated in the pathogenesis.

Clinical Features

- There is erythema with yellow-orange scales and crusts on the scalp (cradle cap) (Fig. 24.35). Eczematous lesions may be present in the major flexures and trunk.
- Self-limiting disease, course.

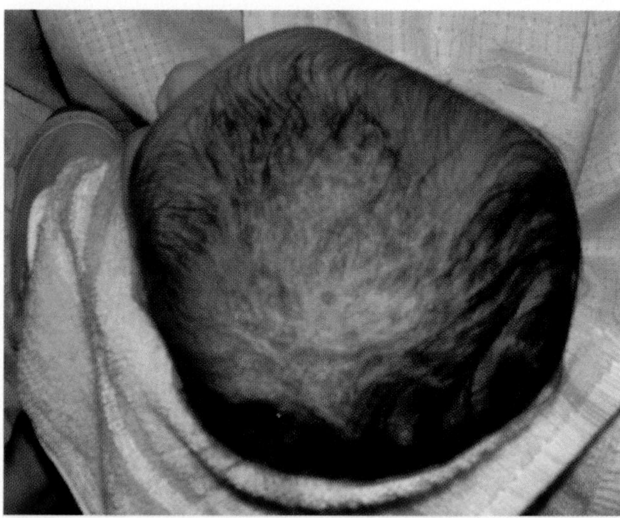

Fig. 24.35: Infantile seborrheic dermatitis: erythema with yellow orange scales and crust on the scalp

Treatment

- The crusts of cradle cap should be removed by warm olive oil.
- Application of 2% ketaconazole shampoo, mild topical steroid or 1% pimecrolimus cream hastens subsidence.

Diaper Dermatitis

Etiology

An irritant dermatitis in infants caused by prolonged contact with feces and ammonia (produced by the action of urea splitting organism on urine).

Clinical Features

The area in contact with diapers (the convexity of buttocks) shows moist, glazed erythematous lesions with sparing of depth of flexures (Fig. 24.36).

Prevention

- Keeping area clean, dry and avoiding use of disposable diapers.

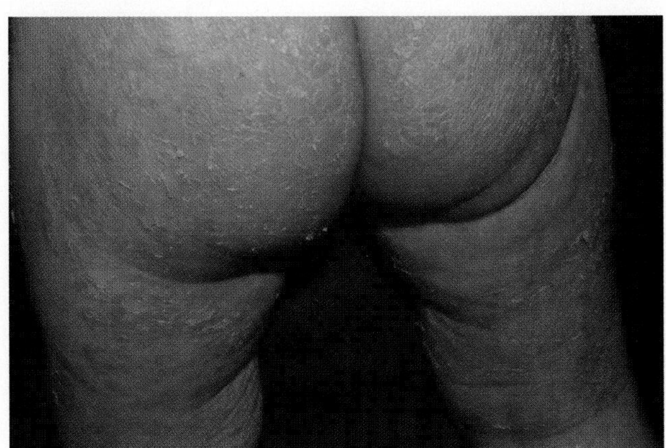

Fig. 24.36: Diaper dermatitis: moist, glazed erythematous lesions with sparing of flexures

- Rinsing washed cotton diapers well (preferably in diluted lemon juice).

Treatment

Emollients and mild topical steroids with antifungal agents useful in acute phase.

DISORDERS OF SKIN APPENDAGES

Acne Vulgaris

Acne vulgaris is a polymorphic eruption due to inflammation of pilosebaceous units.

Etiology

Etiology of acne vulgaris is multifactorial.

- ***Increased sebum secretion:*** Sebaceous glands are more sensitive to androgens due to enhanced end organ sensitivity leading to increased sebum secretion.
- ***Microbial colonization:*** *Propionibacterium acnes* (a normal commensal) is most commonly implicated.
- ***Occlusion of pilosebaceous orifice:*** Pilosebaceous orifice is occluded by keratin plugs leading to retention of sebum and consequent growth of microorganism, setting up a vicious cycle.

Clinical Features

- Affects 85% of adolescents.
- Consists of a polymorphic eruption of comedones (open and closed), papules, pustules, nodules and cysts on a background of oily skin (Fig. 24.37). Lesions heal usually with pitted scars. Comedones are pathognomonic lesions.

Variants

Infantile acne: Caused by maternal hormones. Presents at birth lasting upto 3 years. It is more common in males and lesions are similar to adolescent acne.

Acne conglobata: Is a severe form of acne characterized by abscesses, cysts and intercommunicating sinuses.

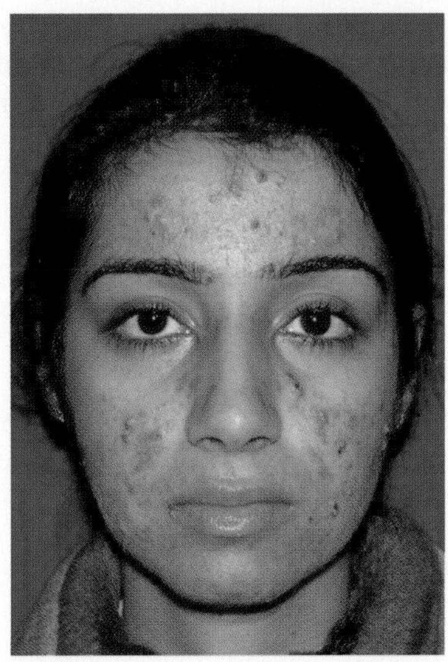

Fig. 24.37: Acne vulgaris: polymorphic eruptions with comedones

24

Drug-induced acne: Can be caused by steroids, androgens, anticonvulsants and consists of monomorphic lesions of papules or pustules.

Treatment

General measures

- Oil and oil-based skin care products need to be avoided. There is no restriction with regard to use of soaps and cleansers.
- No dietary restrictions are usually needed.

Specific measures

Mild acne

- Benzoyl peroxide (2.5–5%), in gel formulation.
- Topical retinoids in the form of tretinoin (0.025–0.05%) and adapalene (0.1%). Need to be applied at night to reduce the photosensitivity.
- Topical antibiotics (clindamycin and erythromycin).
- Azaleic acid (10–20%).

Moderate acne

Oral antibiotics (doxycycline, minocycline and azithromycin) are added to topical agents.

Severe acne

Oral isotretinoin

- Indicated in cystic, conglobate acne or acne refractory to conventional treatment. But since, the drug is potentially teratogenic it needs to be given with caution in girls (only after a negative pregnancy test and ensuring double contraception for 1 month prior to and 3 months following cessation of therapy).
- Given in a dosage of 0.5–1 mg/ kg body weight for a period of 12–16 weeks leads to complete long-lasting remission in majority of patients.

- Side effects like dry skin, cheilitis, and dry eyes (seen in all patients) are treated symptomatically. Careful monitoring of liver function tests and lipid profile is essential at baseline and every 6 weeks.

Cyproterone acetate
- Should not be used in boys.
- Used cyclically in combination with ethinyl estradiol in girls who have a polycystic ovary disease.

Physical modalities

Intralesional corticosteroids for stubborn cysts and laser therapy, cryotherapy, dermabrasion and collagen injections are used for treatment of scars.

Alopecia Areata

Etiology

Autoimmunity is the most likely cause of alopecia areata.

24

Clinical Features

- Affects children and young adults.
- Typically discoid areas of noncicatricial alopecia with exclamation mark hair at periphery (Fig. 24.38).
- Most commonly occurs on the scalp, eyelashes and brows. Alopecia totalis is total absence of terminal scalp hair while alopecia universalis is total loss of terminal hair from body and scalp. Ophiasis is a band-like pattern of hair loss from the periphery of scalp.
- *Course:* Spontaneous remission is common. Initially, the regrowing hairs are grey, but regain color over period of time. Poor prognostic features include onset in childhood, ophiasis, association of atopy and widespread alopecia.

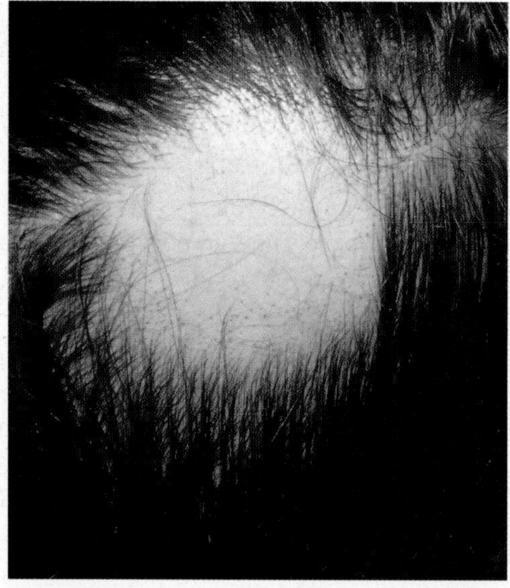

Fig. 24.38: Alopecia areata: non-cicatricial, non-inflammatory discoid lesions with exclamation mark hair at periphery

Treatment

Single or few lesions of <6 months duration: Observed, as spontaneous recovery common.
Single or few lesions of >6 months duration: Treated with following:
- Topical corticosteroids.
- Intralesional triamcinolone acetonide.
- Topical minoxidil.
- Topical psoralens in combination with UVA/sunlight.

Extensive lesions
- Oral corticosteroids.
- Oral psoralens with UVA/sunlight.
- Induction of allergic contact dermatitis with agents such as diphencyprone.

Miliaria

Etiology

Miliaria is due to obstruction and rupture of eccrine sweat ducts resulting in spillage of sweat into adjacent tissue.

Clinical Features

Milaria occurs at any age and depending on level of rupture 3 different morphologically variants seen:
Miliaria crystallina: Usually seen during high fever. Characterized by tiny, non-inflamed vesicles.
Miliaria rubra: Characterized by small erythematous papules commonly surmounted by vesicles.
Miliaria profunda: Characterized by large erythematous papules.

Treatment

- General measures are avoiding humidity, wearing cotton clothes.
- Calamine lotion and mild topical steroids are useful.

DISORDERS OF PIGMENTATION

Vitiligo

Vitiligo is chracterized by depigmented macules. It affects both sexes equally and peak incidence is seen between 10–30 years.

Etiology

Genetic factors: 20–30% of patients have a positive family history.

Autoimmune hypothesis: Association with autoimmune disorders, e.g. thyroid disorders and alopecia areata, presence of antibodies to melanocytes and lymphocytes in early lesions points to autoimmune etiology.

Neurogenic hypothesis: In some patterns of vitiligo.

Clinical Features

Morphology: Characterized by depigmented (chalky white or pale white) macules which are sharply marginated. The outline of macules is scalloped and these coalesce to form geographical patterns. Hairs in the lesions may be normal or depigmented (leucotrichia).

Sites of predilection: It can affect any part of the body, but areas prone to trauma are frequently affected.

Patterns

- *Focal type:* Characterized by 1 or more macules at a single site.
- *Segmental type:* Unilateral, dermatomal lesion(s), seen in children usually along the distribution of mandibular division of facial nerve. Stable type, which responds poorly to medical treatment.
- *Acrofacial vitiligo*: Involves skin around eyes, mouth and acral parts (Fig. 24.39). Lip-tip pattern is characterized by depigmentation of skin around mouth, finger tips and toes, lips, nipples, genitalia (tip of penis and vulva) and perianal area.
- *Vitiligo universalis:* extensive generalized vitiligo due to confluence of patches.

Course: Slowly progressive, though can sometimes progress rapidly. Spontaneous pigmentation is seen in 10% of patients. Segmental vitiligo has a stable course and like acrofacial vitiligo is more resistant to treatment. Predictors of poor prognosis include long standing disease, leucotrichia and lesions on resistant areas (bony prominences, non-hairy, non-fleshy areas and mucosae).

Associations: Look for cutaneous associations (alopecia areata, atopic dermatitis), endocrine disorders (diabetes mellitus, Addisons disease, hypoparathyroidsim and thyroid disorders) and pernicious anemia.

Treatment

Reassurance (more of parents, due to associated social stigma) , sunscreens and cosmetic coverup may be needed.

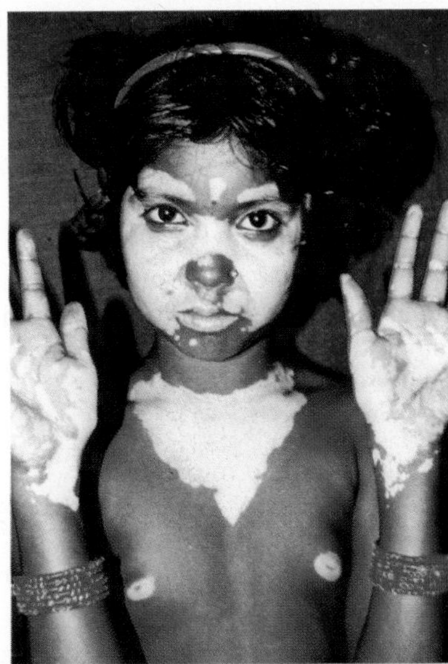

Fig. 24.39: Acrofacial vitiligo: involvement of face and acral parts

Medical treatment

Topical photochemotherapy: Is used for localized lesions and employs topical psoralen and UVA/sunlight.

Systemic photochemotherapy: Is used for extensive lesions in children older than 6 years and employs systemic psoralen and UVA/sunlight.

Narrow-band UVB (311): Is the treatment of choice in children older than 6 years of age and does not require psoralens.

Corticosteroids and immunomodulators

Topical steroids: Are used for single or few macules of recent origin.

Systemic glucocorticoids: Are used in case of intolerance to psoralens, rapidly progressive vitiligo and non-responsiveness to psoralens.

Topical calcineurin inhibitors: Tacrolimus and pimecrolimus used for facial lesions.

Surgical treatment

In refractory and stable segmental vitiligo surgical techniques like punch grafting, split skin grafting, blister grafting and melanocytes transfer can be tried.

24

Freckles and Lentigines

- Both are characterized by presence of discrete hyperpigmented macules.
- Lesions of freckles seen in red-haired, very fair children. Lentigines show no such predilection. Lesions of freckles seen in photoexposed parts of body (face, V of neck and dorsolateral aspect of forearms) with conspicuous absence on covered skin. Lentigines show no such predilection and may also be seen on mucosae (Peutz Jegher syndrome). Freckles are lighter, with less delineated edges and show variegation in color including darkening on sun exposure. Lentigines are darker, sharply defined and do not darken on sun exposure.
- Important to differentiate the two as lentigines may be cutaneous marker of multisystem syndromes.

PAPULOSQUAMOUS DISORDERS

Lichen Planus (LP)

It is an acute or chronic dermatosis involving skin and/ or mucous membranes.

Etiology

Unknown. An eruption resembling lichen planus and termed lichenoid eruption is seen after intake of drugs like chloroquin and as a manifestation of graft-vs-host disease.

Clinical Features

Morphology: Characterized by pruritic, polygonal, violaceous and flat-topped papules (Fig. 24.40) with white

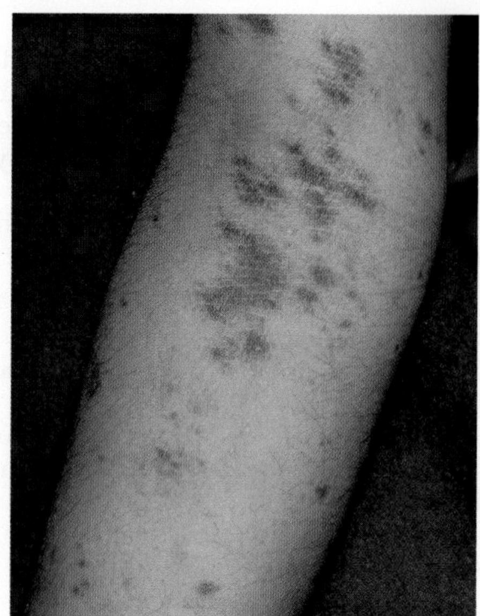

Fig. 24.40: Lichen planus: plane polygonal, violaceous papules

24

streaks (Wickhams striae) on the surface (visualized best with hand lens after application of mineral oil).

Sites of predilection: Lesions seen on wrists, around ankles and may appear at sites of trauma (Koebners phenomenon).

Variants: Several variants like linear, actinic, hypertrophic, follicular.

Mucosal membranes: Mucosal involvement seen 25% patients in form of reticulate lacey pattern on buccal mucosa, tongue and gingiva or superficial erosions on tongue and buccal mucosa, annular lesions are seen on genitalia.

Scalp lesions: Scarring alopecia.

Nail changes: Longitudinal grooves, tenting of nail plates and pterygium formation.

Diagnosis

Diagnosis is based on clinical features and can be confirmed by histopathology.

Treatment

Localized lichen planus:	Topical steroids and oral antihistamines.
Extensive lichen planus:	PUVA, oral steroids and acitretin
Lichen planus of nails:	Oral steroids
Lichen planus of scalp:	Oral steroids
Mucosal lichen planus:	Dapsone + steroids in orabase, oral steroids, acitretin

Psoriasis

Psoriasis is a chronic, recurring dermatosis which may have onset in childhood/adolescence (type I psoriasis) and in adults (type II psoriasis). Type I psoriasis is characterized by:

- Onset in second decade.
- Positive family history.
- Severe disease.
- Prominent Koebners phenomenon.
- Frequent association with HLA Cw6.
- Prolonged course, requiring relatively more aggressive therapy.

Etiology

Etiology is unknown but several factors are incriminated:

Heredity: Psoriasis is polygenic trait.

Triggers: Physical trauma, infections (β hemolytic streptococci, HIV infection) and drugs (lithium, NSAIDS, antimalarials).

Immunological factors: T cells play a pivotal role in pathogenesis of psoriasis.

Classification

- ***Chronic***
  - Psoriasis vulgaris
  - Erythroderma
- ***Acute onset***
  - Acute guttate
  - Pustular psoriasis

Clinical Features

Psoriasis vulgaris

Morphology: Characterized by well demarcated, indurated, erythematous scaly (silvery, loose) lesions. Lesions become polycyclic due to confluence and annular because of central clearing.

Sites of predilection: Symmetrical involvement of knees, elbows and extensors, lower back, scalp and sites of trauma (Koebners/isomorphic phenomenon). Face and photo-exposed areas generally spared.

Bedside tests

- *Grattage test:* Accentuation of scales on grating lesion with a glass slide.
- *Auspitz sign:* Removal of scales by scraping with a glass slide reveals a glistening white membrane (Burkleys membrane) and on removing the membrane, punctate bleeding points become visible.

Guttate psoriasis

- Occurs in children and adolescents.
- May be precipitated by streptococcal tonsillitis.
- Crops as small erythematous scaly papules.
- Predominantly on trunk.

Pustular psoriasis

Two rare variants described in children:

Annular pustular psoriasis. Characterized by sudden onset of fiery red erythema rapidly covered by cluster of very superficial creamy white pustules which in children form circinate/annular lesions (Fig. 24.41).

Infantile and juvenile pustular psoriasis. Rare; seen in infants as annular/circinate lesions (Fig. 24.42). Runs a

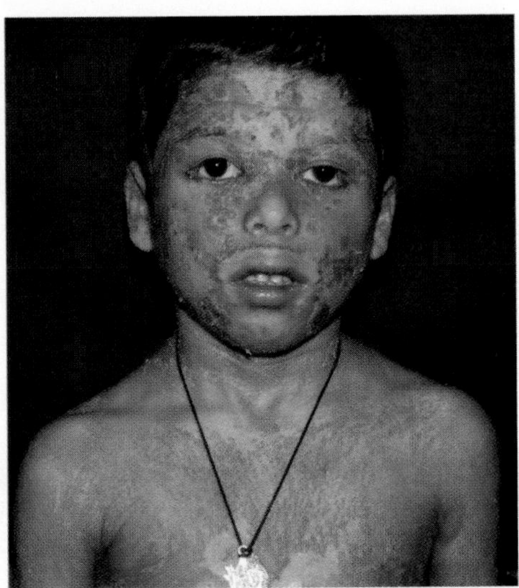

Fig. 24.41: Pustular psoriasis: superficial pustules which coalesce to form circinate lesions

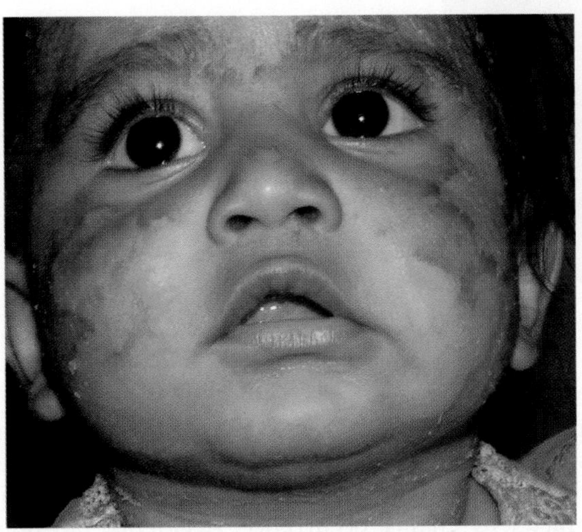

Fig. 24.42: Juvenile psoriasis: annular/circinate lesions seen in infants

benign course and often confused with seborrheic and napkin dermatitis.

Associations

Nail changes: Seen in 10–50% of children and include pitting, thickening, subungual hyperkeratosis, onycholysis, discoloration and oil spots or staining of nail bed.
Joint: 10% patients have joint involvement.

Diagnosis

Diagnosis is based on history and clinical features. A biopsy (which is confirmatory) is however, not necessary.

Treatment

- It is important to counsel the parents (and the child) about the chronic nature of the disease and the likelihood of relapses.
- Several options are available, depending on the type and extent of disease (Table 24.17).

Suggested reading

1. Chemotherapy of leprosy: report of a WHO study group [1993]. WHO Study Group on Chemotherapy of Leprosy, 1993; Geneva, Switzerland.
2. Khanna, N. Illustrated Synopsis of Dermatology and Sexually Transmitted Diseases 3e, Elsevier, New Delhi 2008.
3. Bhutani, L.K. and Khanna, N. Bhutanis Color Atlas of Dermatology, Mehta Publishers, New Delhi, 2006

Table 24.17: **Treatment options in psoriasis**

	Treatment of choice	*Alternative modalities*
Psoriasis vulgaris		
• Localised (<30% BSA)	Coal tar, short-contact dithranol	Topical steroids + salicylic acid
• Extensive (>30% BSA)	Narrow band UVB PUVA*/ PUVA sol	Methotrexate, acitretin cyclosporin A
• Facial lesions	Topical steroids	
Guttate psoriasis	Antibiotics + emollients PUVA*/ PUVAsol**	Coal tar, tacrolimus, mild topical steroids
Pustular psoriasis	Methotrexate, acitretin	

*PUVA: Psoralen + UVA. Patient ingests 8 methoxypsoralen, 0.6 mg/ kg and exposes after 2 hours to gradually increasing doses of UVA (provided either from artificial sources or from sunlight PUVAsol**) after applying an emollient on the lesions. Should not be used in children <6 years of age.

Figures 24.10, 24.14, 24.16, 24.28 and 24.34 in this chapter are reproduced from Khanna, N: *Illustrated Synopsis of Dermatology and Sexually Transmitted Diseases*, 2/e, with permission of the publishers, Elsevier, New Delhi.

25 Poisonings, Injuries and Accidents

A poison is any agent of self-injury absorbed into the system through epithelial surfaces. An accident is a sudden unexpected event of an afflictive or unfortunate character by chance occurrence. Accidents, poisoning, vehicular trauma and falls are an important cause of childhood mortality and morbidity. Toddlers are especially predisposed as they are mobile, inquisitive, and cannot differentiate between harmful and harmless things. It is important to implement strategies involving careful supervision and interventions to reduce incidence of accidents and poisoning, especially in children less than five-yr-old.

POISONING

In developing countries, pesticides and plants are the commonly encountered poisoning in children while pharmaceuticals and chemicals form the major cause of poisoning in the developed world. Common causes of poisoning in north India include kerosene oil (25%), barbiturates (12%), organophosphate compounds (10%) and corrosives (5%). Majority (>90%) of toxic exposures in children occur at home, involving a single substance. These products are familiar, visually appealing in glossy containers and tasty to young children. Dermal, inhalation and ophthalmic routes of exposure are rare.

Two distinct patterns of poisoning are observed: accidental poisoning in children younger than 11-yr and self poisoning in older children. Toxic exposures in adolescents are primarily intentional (suicide, abuse) or occupational.

Databases on toxicology, hazardous chemicals, environmental health, and toxic releases on the worldwide web is available at (TOXNET) **toxnet.nlm.nih.gov**

DIAGNOSIS OF POISONING

Identification of poisoning in children requires a high index of suspicion. A history of ingestion of a chemical/poison, though seldom available, should be sought whenever any hyperacute onset of symptoms occur in an apparently healthy child or in the presence of unexplained multisystem involvement (Table 25.1).

Table 25.1: Clinical features suggesting poisoning

- Hyperacute onset of symptoms (e.g. encephalopathy in an apparently healthy child with inconclusive, bizarre clinical features)
- Unexplained multisystem involvement, metabolic acidosis
- Acute renal failure, acute liver failure
- Arrhythmias, in a child with no known cardiac illness

High index of suspicion in children between 1–3 yr-old

Table 25.2: Presenting features of common poisoning

Toxin	*Symptoms and signs*	*Differential diagnosis*
Paracetamol	Acute liver failure	Fulminant hepatic failure
Theophylline	Hyperglycemia, ketosis	Diabetic ketoacidosis
Salicylates	Fever, tachypnea	Pneumonia
Strychnine	Spasms	Tetanus
Arsenic	Diarrhea	Cholera
Ethanol	Non-ketotic hypoglycemia	Glycogen storage disease
Ecstasy	CNS depression, fits, pyrexia	Febrile convulsion

Strychnine often used in homeopathic treatments
Ecstasy: MDMA (methylenedioxy amphetamine)

Sometimes, common poisonings may mimic other common conditions in children in clinical features (Table 25.2). A drug or treatment history of family members, immediate care givers, recent visitors in a household with toddlers may hold important clues to the nature of drug/chemical or ingredient involved. A history of comorbid neurological (e.g. complex partial seizures) or neuropsychiatric illness may explain the circumstances of the poisoning. On examination, specific signs like tachycardia, bradycardia, miosis, mydriasis may point towards the incriminating agent of injury (Table 25.3). The time of onset and progression of cluster of symptoms helps in identifying the specific toxidrome. Signs that are useful in distinguishing different toxidromes are discussed in Table 25.4.

Table 25.3: Clinical clues to nature of poisoning

Features	*Toxin*
Bradycardia	Digoxin, organophosphorus compounds, β-blockers
Tachycardia	Atropine, salicylates
Acidotic breathing	Salicylates
Hypertension	Phenylpropanolamine
Hypothermia	Barbiturates
Fever	Atropine, salicylates, theophylline, quinine
Ataxia	Phenytoin
Paralysis	Botulism, heavy metals
Miosis	Organophosphates, opioids, barbiturates
Mydriasis	Atropine, amphetamines
Jaundice	Acetaminophen, carbon tetrachloride
Cyanosis	Methemoglobinemia, carbon monoxide
Flushed appearance (red)	Carbon monoxide, cyanide
Characteristic smell	Acetone, cyanide, alcohol, kerosene

Bedside Tests for Toxin Identification

These tests provide an idea about the possible toxin before the reports of other tests are available.

Urine Tests

Urine should be examined for abnormal color. In phenol poisoning, smoky dark green color occurs on standing. Oxalate crystals indicate the possibility of ethylene glycol poisoning. *Ferric chloride test* may help in identifying the incriminated toxin. Add 5–10 drops of freshly prepared 10% ferric chloride solution to 10 ml of boiled and acidified urine. Change of color to red suggests exposure to salicylates; purple green and violet indicate phenothiazine and phenol exposure respectively. Ketones in urine suggest exposure to acetone, salicylate and isopropyl alcohol.

Blood Tests

Blood appears chocolate color in patients with methemoglobinemia. This turns pink on addition of potassium cyanide. Measurement of anion gap and osmolal gap detects accumulation of unmeasured ions and osmotically active agents in blood.

Gastric Aspirate

Addition of two drops of 30% hydrogen peroxide and deferoxamine (0.5 ml, 125 mg/ml) to 1 ml of gastric fluid leads to color change in iron poisoning.

Efforts to identify the poison should not jeopardize general measures, which are effective in most cases.

Laboratory Evaluation

Poisoning is associated with accumulation of toxins in the body. The aim of laboratory evaluation is to identify the toxin, assess the amount of exposure and detect organ dysfunction and metabolic derangements produced by the toxin. Initial samples in any child with suspected poisoning should include vomitus or gastric aspirate for identification of the incriminating agent and urine and blood for qualitative and quantitative assessment respectively.

Hemogram with complete blood count, ECG, chest X-ray, liver and renal function tests and blood gas analysis should be performed in all children with significant intoxication. The effect of toxins on metabolism may produce characteristic abnormalities that may help in identification of the toxin (Table 25.5).

25

MANAGEMENT

Early suspicion and appropriate management forms the mainstay of therapy. General measures should be instituted immediately, since early treatment is associated with improved outcome.

If the child is brought in the ***pre-toxic phase***, decontamination is the highest priority and treatment is based on history. The maximum potential toxicity based on greatest possible exposure should be assumed. During ***toxic phase,*** the time between the onset of poisoning and the peak effects, management is based primarily on clinical and laboratory findings. Resuscitation and stabilization are the first priority. During ***resolution phase***, supportive care and

Table 25.4: Common toxidromes

Findings	*Adrenergic*	*Anticholinergic*	*Anticholinesterase (cholinergic)*	*Opioid*	*Sedative, hypnotic*
Heart rate	Increased	Increased	Decreased	Decreased	Arrhythmia, QT prolongation
Temperature	Increased	Increased	No change	No change	No change
Pupil	Dilated	Dilated	Constricted	Constricted	Dilated
Mucosa	Wet	Dry	Wet	No change	No change
Skin	Diaphoresis	Dry	Diaphoresis	Normal	No change
Respiratory	Tachypnea	Tachypnea, secretions ++	Wheeze, tachypnea	Hypoventilation	Hypoventilation
Neurologic	Agitated, tremors, seizures, hallucinations	Agitated/ hallucinations	Coma, fasciculations	Sedation	Convulsions, coma, myoclonus, hyperreflexia

Table 25.5: Laboratory pointers to identification of toxins

Observation	*Possible toxin*
Hypocalcemia	Ethylene glycol, oxalate
Hypokalemia	Beta agonists, diuretics, theophylline
Hyperkalemia	Beta blockers, digoxin, alpha agonist
Hyperglycemia	Acetone, theophylline, calcium channel blockers
Hypoglycemia	Oral hypoglycemic agents, ethanol, quinine, salicylates
Increased anion gap	Methanol, ethanol, ethylene glycol, salicylate, isoniazid
Decreased anion gap	Lithium, bromide
Increased osmolal gap	Mannitol, ethylene glycol, isopropyl alcohol, glycerol, acetone, sorbitol
Pulmonary edema	Carbon monoxide, cyanide, irritant gas
Radiopaque density	Calcium, heavy metal
Bradycardia, AV block	Beta blockers, digoxin, calcium channel blockers
Prolonged QRS complex	Hyperkalemia, membrane active agents

monitoring should continue until clinical and laboratory abnormalities have resolved.

25

Airway Maintenance

Establishing airway may be difficult in children with poisoning due to caustic and thermal upper airway injuries, neck and facial injuries, or angioedema. *In any child with altered mental status, respiratory depression and pupillary constriction, a trial of naloxone should be given before intubation.* Bag and mask ventilation is associated with a higher risk of aspiration. This can be minimized by synchronized and gentle ventilation, Sellick's maneuver and aspiration of gastric contents prior to ventilation.

Breathing

Adequacy of breathing should be assessed by respiratory effort, chest movement, air entry and oxygen saturation.

Circulation

Fluid boluses, repeated if needed, under monitoring for fluid overload, constitute the initial management of shock particularly in poisoning due to cardiotoxic agents and children with cardiopulmonary diseases. In an unresponsive shock, dopamine is the agent of choice except in poisoning due to tricyclic antidepressant or MAO inhibitors. Exposure to myocardial depressant or vasodilator toxin or concomitant conditions like visceral injuries, pulmonary embolism, ruptured aortic aneurysm, sepsis or severe acidosis makes the hypotension refractory to these measures.

Supportive Therapy

The goals of supportive therapy include maintenance of homeostasis and prevention and treatment of complications. Indications for intensive care include: (i) evidence of severe poisoning, coma, respiratory depression, hypotension, cardiac conduction abnormalities, arrhythmias, hypothermia or hyperthermia; (ii) need for antidote or enhanced elimination therapy; and (iii) progressive clinical deterioration.

Prevention of Further Absorption of Poison

These measures target preventing absorption of the toxin and depend upon the site and route of poisoning and patient's age and general condition.

Dilution: This involves application of water in an effort to reduce the duration of exposure to the toxin. The mechanism depends upon the site of exposure.

In patients with corrosive burns and organophosphorous poisoning (readily absorbed from skin), all clothes should be removed and the contaminated area washed with liberal amount of water and soap. *Neutralization of an agent (using alkali for acid exposure or vice versa) is harmful and contraindicated.* Skin cleaning should be done irrespective of duration of exposure to the toxin. Lubricating solutions like grease or cream may cause poison to stick on to skin.

Oral and ocular mucosa is washed with plenty of water. Eyes should be irrigated with lids fully retracted for at least 20 minutes. This may be achieved by keeping normal saline bottle and infusion set near the eye. In patients with corrosive ingestion, liberal amounts of water or clear fluid (5 ml/kg) should be given orally as soon as possible. It is contraindicated in poisoning due to tablets as it may cause increased absorption.

Gastrointestinal decontamination: Gastric emptying is a cardinal principle of management of ingested toxins. The desired outcome is prevention of continued absorption of poison from the gut into the bloodstream in asymptomatic children.

The procedure of choice for decontamination, if needed, is activated charcoal, with whole bowel irrigation being used for a few indications. Ipecac induced emesis and cathartics are not recommended as gastric emptying procedures. Orogastric lavage may be considered for uncommon situations.

Routine administration of *syrup of ipecac* in the emergency department in children with poisoning may remove 30 to 40% of ingested toxin when administered soon after the ingestion. It has been abandoned except as a home remedy before child is transported to emergency room. Other emetics like apomorphine, detergent, raw egg and dry mustard powder are also not used.

The role of *gastric lavage* in children is not clear. It is contraindicated in corrosive poisoning. The procedure should be reserved for conditions where a potentially lethal toxin has been recently (within 60 minutes) ingested. Gastric lavage should be performed with a large tube with multiple lateral holes at the distal end and funnel at the proximal end. Size of tube is selected according to age (neonates 28 Fr, older children 36 Fr). Narrow tubes are ineffective in removing solid substances.

Gastric lavage should be performed only after the gag reflex has been assessed. In patients with impaired consciousness and absent gag response, intubation should be performed before gastric lavage. The length of lavage tube should be measured before insertion. *The child should be kept in lateral decubitus position with lowering of head end.* Lavage should be done with 15 ml/kg of normal saline until clear fluid is drained. Activated charcoal should be instilled after the lavage is completed.

Binding agents: Activated charcoal, clay and cholestyramine may be helpful in reducing absorption of ingested toxins. *Activated charcoal* is produced by destructive distillation of organic materials like wood, coconut and petroleum. The distillate is treated at high temperature using steam. These procedures increase the adsorptive capacity of the compound by increasing surface area, removing adsorbed material and reduction in particle size. Activated charcoal acts by binding and elimination of the toxin. The total surface (adsorptive) of activated charcoal is 1600 to 1800 m^2/g making it ideal as binding agent.

Activated charcoal is used at a dose of 1–2 g/kg. The drug is available as a 400 mg tablet and should be crushed before administration, made into slurry and administered. Under most circumstances, a single dose is effective. Multiple doses of activated charcoal (every 4-hr) have been shown to decrease elimination half lives of drugs through gut dialysis. The greatest benefit is within one-hr of ingestion. Multiple doses may be indicated in patients with massive ingestion of toxin and desorption of toxin from activated charcoal.

Activated charcoal is an effective nonspecific adsorbent and should be considered in all cases of poisoning, irrespective of interval since ingestion. It should be avoided in patients with corrosive ingestion, ileus, intestinal hemorrhage and patient with unprotected airway at risk of aspiration. Other binding agents including various attapulgite, bentonite, fuller's earth, kaolin-pectin are less effective. The burnt toast in universal antidote possesses little, if any adsorption capacity, and has been abandoned. Cholestyramine has been found effective in paracetamol and digitalis toxicity but it is less well tolerated.

Cathartics: Routine use of cathartics either alone or with activated charcoal is not recommended.

Whole bowel irrigation with polyethylene glycol has been used in patients with poisoning and drug overdosage. It is the only procedure, which decontaminates beyond the pylorus without inducing emesis or causing fluid overload and dyselectrolytemia. It is, however, not a substitute for activated charcoal. It is particularly useful following ingestion of sustained release drugs, slowly dissolving agents, ingested crack vials and drug packs. The procedure is not helpful in the management of ingestion of rapidly absorbed drugs, liquids, parenteral drugs and caustics. Whole bowel irrigation can be achieved with administration of 500 ml/hour of polyethylene glycol over 4–6 hr. The procedure is safe, with rare side effects of rectal itching and vomiting.

Enhancing Elimination

Procedure directed towards enhancing elimination is indicated in patients with significant delay following poisoning or when methods for prevention of absorption are ineffective or not applicable. Diuresis, alteration of urine pH and dialysis are commonly used for enhancing drug elimination.

Manipulation of pH and diuresis: The rate of elimination of ingested substances can be increased by increasing GFR or altering urine pH for the toxins that are excreted by kidneys. Acidification of urine to enhance elimination of weak bases should be avoided. Alkalization of urine may be used in patients with poisoning due to weak acids like salicylate, phenobarbital and herbicides. This is achieved by administration of sodium bicarbonate at a dose of 1–2 mEq/kg given every 3–4 hr, in order to maintain urine pH between 7 and 8. Sodium bicarbonate is also effective in reducing the toxicity of tricylic antidepressants, quinine and some antiarrythmic drugs.

25

Dialysis: The indications of dialysis are given in Table 25.6. The mode of dialysis depends upon clinical condition, available resources and type of ingestion.

Peritoneal dialysis is more effective in children due to larger peritoneal surface in relation to body surface area. It enhances elimination of compounds like alcohol, lithium and salicylates. It has the disadvantages of gradual removal of toxins and decreased efficacy in hypotensive subjects. The procedure may however be a temporizing measure before hemodialysis or hemoperfusion.

Hemodialysis is the preferred method for removal of compounds like bromide, chloral hydrate, ethanol, methanol, ethylene glycol, lithium and salicylates. In addition to removing toxins, it also rapidly corrects metabolic abnormalities and fluid overload. The procedure has risks of bleeding or thrombosis, hypotension, nosocomial infection and possible elimination of agents like folinic acid and ethanol, administered therapeutically during acute poisoning.

Hemoperfusion is the procedure (of pumping blood through a cartridge containing activated charcoal or carbon with large surface area) and is effective in removal of substances adsorbed by activated charcoal. The procedure has the advantage of being not limited by protein binding and is the preferred method for elimination of carbamazepine, phenobarbital, phenytion and theophylline. Substances, which are not adsorbed by activated charcoal, like alcohol, lithium, many heavy metal poisons are not removed. The procedure may be associated with complications like thrombocytopenia, leukopenia and hypocalcemia.

Exchange transfusion may be performed in neonates and infants. It removes poisons affecting the red blood cells (as in methemoglobinemia or arsine-induced hemolysis). The elimination of heavy metals is enhanced by chelation and removal of carbon monoxide can be increased by hyperbaric oxygen.

Table 25.6: Indications of dialysis in a patient with suspected poisoning

Patient related	*Toxin related*
Anticipated prolonged coma	Satisfactory membrane permeability
Hepatic and renal failure	Correlation between plasma concentration and toxicity
Serious underlying illness	Plasma levels in fatal range
	Significant quantity of agent metabolized to toxic substances, e.g. barbiturates, chloral hydrate, ethylene glycol, theophylline, salicylates, heavy metals

25

Administration of Antidotes

Antidotes counteract the effects of poisons by neutralizing them or by antagonizing their physiologic effects (activation of opposing nervous system activity, provision of metabolic or receptor substrate). Antidotes significantly reduce the morbidity and mortality, but are potentially toxic. Their safe use requires correct identification of specific poisoning or syndrome. Table 25.7 lists the common antidotes used for management of poisonings.

Prevention of re-exposure

Poisoning is a preventable illness: The elegance and delicacy of the development of a human from conception through adolescence affords particular windows of vulnerability to hazards. The best approach to prevent poisoning in children is to limit the access to poison. In households where children live or visit, alcoholic beverages, medications, household products (automotive, cleaning, fuel, pet-care, toiletry products), non-edible plants and vitamins, should be kept out of reach or in locked or child proof cabinets. Poison prevention education should be an integral part of all well child visits, even before a child is mobile. Counseling parents and other caregivers about potential poisoning risks, how to "poison-proof" a child's environment, and what to do if a poisoning occurs diminishes the likelihood of serious morbidity or mortality from an exposure.

Adolescents with suicidal poisoning or drug addiction need proper counseling before discharge. Unless pediatricians are aware, the likelihood of early diagnosis and appropriate management of suspected cases of poisoning or drug abuse are dramatically decreased. A potentially healthy adulthood is irreparably harmed.

COMMON POISONINGS

Acetaminophen (Paracetamol)

It is the most common analgesic, antipyretic used in children. The toxic dose is usually >200 mg/kg in children <12-yr-old. Overdosage is treated with N-acetylcysteine used orally within 16-hr after ingestion at a loading dose of 140 mg/kg diluted to 5% solution orally, followed by 70 mg/kg q 4-hr for another 2 days.

Organophosphorous Compounds (Insecticides and Pesticides)

Pesticides are the most important poison throughout the tropics, being both common and associated with a high mortality rate. Pesticides include insecticides, herbicides, fungicides, nematocides, rodenticides, fumigants, *Bacillus thuringiensis* and unconventional pest control agents (e.g. sulphur). Exposure in children may be acute or chronic. Chronic exposure may be dietary or nondietary. Aggregate exposure refers to total exposure to a single pesticide through food, water and non-dietary exposure. Cumulative exposure is the summated exposure to multiple pesticides with a common mode of action.

Table 25.7: Antidotes for common poisonings

Poison	*Antidote*	*Dose*
Acetaminophen	N-acetyl cysteine	Loading dose 140 mg; maintenance 70 mg/kg q 4 hr × 17 doses
Anticholinergics	Physostigmine	0.02 mg/kg slow IV
Benzodiazepines	Flumazenil	0.01 mg/kg bolus, or total dose of 1–3 mg
Digoxin	Digoxin immune antibody fragment	10–20 vials IV bolus in emergency
Methemoglobinemia	Methylene blue	1–2 mg/kg slow IV
Opioids	Naloxone	0.4–2 mg IV
Organophosphates	Atropine	0.1 mg/kg IV; repeat dose titrated to effect
Salicylates	Sodium bicarbonate	150 mEq + 40 mEq KCl in 1 L of 5% dextrose
Ethylene glycol Methanol	Fomepizole	15 mg/kg IV stat; 10 mg/kg/dose q12 hr × 4 doses

Children are at higher risk in view of higher body surface area and high body mass ratio; significantly greater minute ventilation rates in young children result in increased pulmonary exposure. These agents are absorbed through the skin and mucosa. Symptoms of excessive parasympathetic activity including blurring of vision, headache, giddiness, nausea, pain in the chest, profuse salivation and sweating occur within a few hours. Pupils are constricted and papilledema may occur. Carbamates are less toxic than organophosphorus pesticides. Death is usually due to respiratory failure.

Treatment includes reduction of dermal contact and gastric emptying. Atropine sulphate is the primary antidote (0.03–0.04 mg/kg IV; ampoule 1 mg/ml); the dose is repeated after 15 minutes and then every hour until atropinization (maximum 1 mg/kg in 24-hr). Atropine, a competitive antagonist of muscarinic receptors, reverses the peripheral symptoms (secretions and airway resistance) and arrests the early phase of convulsions when given within 5 minutes of exposure. It is a satisfactory antidote for mildly affected victims as an anti-sialogogue or as a peripheral parasympatholytic. This agent does not cross the blood-brain barrier and is ineffective for those with symptoms involving central nervous system. It is an effective antidote, but causes profound neurological effects, including sedation.

Pralidoxime aldoxime methiodide (2-PAM) hydrolytically cleaves the organophosphate from the enzyme, acetylcholinesterase restoring enzymatic function. It is given at a dose of 25–50 mg/kg IM to a maximum of 2000 mg/hr every 12-hr (maximum for infants 0.25 g). It is highly effective in reversing nicotinic effects (e.g. muscle fasciculations, weakness, respiratory depression). It is not given in carbamate poisoning alone. Common untoward effects include dizziness, transient diplopia, and blurred vision. Dose adjustment in individuals with renal insufficiency is required, because 2-PAM is excreted almost entirely unchanged by the kidneys. Rapid IV administration can cause laryngospasm and rigidity. Hypertension is the most serious untoward effect at higher doses. Intravenous fluids are given if needed.

Toxicity with DEET (diethyl toluamide, the component of most insect repellant creams) may occur through covered skin surfaces or ingestion. Seizures are the most severe manifestation but are most often self limited.

For DDT poisoning, phenobarbitone is given for convulsions. Cholestyramine, an anion exchange resin should be administered to all symptomatic patients of DDT poisoning.

Hydrocarbon Poisoning

Aliphatic hydrocarbons, including kerosene, turpentine, lubricating oils and tar, have the greatest risk of aspiration and pulmonary symptoms. Aromatic compounds include benzene compounds and have mainly neurological and hepatic toxicity. The type of toxicity with a hydrocarbon depends on its volatility, viscosity or surface tension. The lower the viscosity, higher is the risk of pulmonary aspiration. Thus substances with low viscosity and volatility (mineral oil, kerosene, furniture polish) have a higher risk of aspiration. Substances with high volatility and low viscosity (benzene derivatives like toluene, xylene used in solvents and degreasers, gasoline, naphtha in lacquer diluent) may also act as toxins through inhalation, manifesting with neurological depression.

Kerosene and paraffin oils are common household energy sources in the developing world. Often kept in unsafe containers (soft drink and beer bottles), these oils are a major cause of accidental poisoning among young children. The incidence of kerosene ingestion has decreased to less than half. Respiratory symptoms, as a result of chemical pneumonitis, restlessness, fever and abdominal distension are common. Convulsions and coma may occur. Radiological changes, which might occur within one-hr include basilar infiltrates, emphysema, pleural effusion and pneumatoceles. *Management is symptomatic with preservation of the airway in unconscious patients.* Gastric emptying is contraindicated and is done only when large quantities of turpentine have been ingested or the hydrocarbon product contains benzene, toluene, halogenated hydrocarbons, heavy metals, pesticides or aniline dyes. Mortality ranges from 2–10% and is higher in malnourished children. Steroids have no role in treatment.

Iron Intoxication

Ingestion of tablets of ferrous sulfate may cause acute poisoning, characterized by GI toxicity, followed by a period of relative stability and then circulatory shock with metabolic acidosis and myocardial dysfunction. Hepatic necrosis and gastric scarring are long-term effects. The lethal dose is 300 mg/kg of iron. The child may develop complications within a few hr or after a latent period of 1–2 days.

Treatment includes gastric emptying, followed by stomach wash with sodium bicarbonate. IV sodium bicarbonate (3 ml/kg diluted twice with 5% dextrose) is given for treatment of acidosis. Fluid resuscitation may be necessary. Iron is chelated with IV infusion of deferioxamine (dose 15 mg/kg/hr) until the serum iron is <300 mg/dl or until 24-hr after the child has stopped passing 'vine rose' colored urine. In case of renal failure, dialysis to remove deferioxamine-Fe complex may be required.

Dhatura (Belladona) Poisoning

Accidental ingestion of dhatura seeds cause delirium, confusion, visual disturbances, photophobia, dilated sluggishly reacting pupils, dryness of skin and mouth, fever, tachycardia and urinary retention. Treatment is by gastric lavage and physostigmine at a dose 0.1 mg/kg (max 2 mg) IV slowly.

Resource guide listing multiple information sources on poisoning is available at: www.cehn.org, www.ace.orst.edu/info/nptm

HELP CENTRE

National Poison Information Centre

All India Institute of Medical Sciences, New Delhi

Telephone 91-11-26593677, 26589391, 26593282

Fax 91-11-26588663, 26589691

Information available at http://www.aiims.edu/aiims/departments/NPIC/NPICintro.htm
email npicaiims@hotmail.com

INJURIES AND ACCIDENTS

An injury is defined as a bodily lesion at the organic level, resulting from acute exposure to energy (mechanical, thermal, electrical, chemical or radiant) in amounts that exceed the threshold of physiological tolerance; in some cases (e.g. drowning, strangulation, freezing), the injury results from an insufficiency of a vital element.

25

Injury vs. Accident

Perhaps the single most important barrier to progress in injury control is the perception that injuries are random chance occurrences that cannot be predicted or prevented. The use of the term 'accident' implies this unpredictability. However, most injuries occur under fairly predictable circumstances in high-risk children and hence the term 'accident prevention' has been replaced by 'injury control'. Injuries (or accidents) in children, among the leading causes of death in children who survive beyond their first birthday, represent a major epidemic of non-communicable disease throughout the world. As per WHO estimate >10% of those killed due to accident (any type) were children.

In today's high-tech world, there are dangers for children everywhere, on roads, at home, at school and on playgrounds. Most accidents occur in the age group of 2–5 yr, mostly in boys. India has one of the highest road traffic accidents in the world. Burn injuries are second only to motor vehicle accidents as the cause of accidental death in children 1–4 yr of age. During the well baby visit, developmentally oriented safety surveys should be done. Target messages should be discussed with parents as per a schedule (Table 25.8).

Injuries are of two types –*unintentional* and *intentional.* The former can be broadly divided into three categories – injuries at home, sports injuries and road injuries. Intentional injuries such as homicide and suicide are rare in children but not uncommon in adolescents. This section deals only with management of unintentional injuries.

Injury Control

Injury control operates in three phases: prevention, minimization of damage and post injury care. In planning injury prevention, the following principles deserve emphasis.

- Passive injury prevention strategies are preferred over active strategies; e.g. automatic locks for cabinets with medicines.
- Specific instructions (e.g. keep water heater temperature lower than 120° F) are more likely to be followed than general advice (e.g. reduce the temperature of hot water tap in your home).
- Individual education reinforced by community-wide education programs are more effective than isolated education sessions.

FIRE AND BURNS

Injury following burns is an important cause of death in India. Scald burns secondary to household accidents predominate in most series, constituting 70% of all thermal injuries in infants, toddlers and pre-school children. Most of these injuries are potentially preventable. Burns may also occur with chemicals (particularly corrosives), cigarettes (child abuse) and electric current. Burns in children have higher mortality than adults since they have (i) thinner and more sensitive skin, (ii) markedly increased ratio of body surface area to body mass, with limited physiological reserve, (iii) significant metabolic and systemic disturbances and (iv) immature immune system and (v) increased fluid requirements.

First Aid for Burns and Scalds

While approaching a child with fire, keep a blanket or coat between the rescuer and the burning child. The victim may be rolled on the ground to extinguish the flames, or covered with a blanket or coat.

In case of minor burns or scalds- pour cold water/apply cold water soaks/submerge the burned portion immediately in water and continue it until pain disappears. Do not apply any ointment, grease, soda, oil, powder, butter or herbs. If the skin is blistered, do not rupture it; instead, cover it with a cloth as clean as possible. Remove the charred cloth only if it comes out easily. Cover with clean sheets of sterile dressing and patient should be wrapped in blanket or foil. Wrapping with wet sheets or the application of ice should be avoided since the resultant hypothermia leads to serious arrhythmia and compromises the outcome. Inhalation injury, frequently associated with large burns, is an important early predictor of mortality and is the commonest cause of death during the first hour postburn. The singeing of the nasal vibrissae is common in facial burns, but is not a reliable indicator of inhalation injury.

Electrical Burns

The power supply should be switched off using nonconductor material like dry wooden stick.

Table 25.8: Advice to parents for prevention of injuries

Type of injury	DO	DON'T
At play	• Choose toys, games appropriate to child's age • Regular inspection of condition of toys in use • Set mattresses at lower levels as activity increases • Healthy, safe playgrounds and playing conditions	• Don't allow children to fly kites in rain, terrace • Don't allow playing with plastic bags, electric cords, dupatta, sharps, beads, coins, small toys with detachable or moving parts
Falls	• Use beds with rails for children aged < 6 years • Set a good example: avoid standing on a rocking chair • Remove/replace torn or frayed carpet/linen; fix a *non-skid* device under the rugs laid on polished floors	• Don't allow children to play on the stairs/balconies without railings/terrace without parapet wall • Don't leave oil/grease/liquid soap on the floor • Don't keep chair or furniture near open windows or galleries • Don't keep large toys in the crib (stepping–stone for the infant)
Cuts	• Remove rusty nails and broken bottles immediately • Teach the child how to handle tools and mechanical instruments safely	• Don't leave any sharp objects near the vicinity of the child • Don't allow to run or play with sticks (even lollipop stick) or any sharp objects
Burns	• Keep children far away from the stove while cooking; Be careful while using portable stoves • Always have an adequate fireguard hooked in place • Allow the child to play with firecrackers under supervision by an adult	• Don't let him enter the kitchen to recover a toy· • Don't leave hot utensils/pans in the kitchen within the child's reach • Don't leave an electric iron switched on close to a child
Scalds	• Keep children away from pots cooking on the stove • Turn pan handles away from the front of the stove • Always check the temperature of the milk before feeding the child	• Don't drink/pass hot tea/coffee while holding the infant
Electro-cution	• Use electric points of the safe variety so that the child cannot insert a lead pencil or other object through the hole • Keep all switch boards in good condition	• Don't keep electric equipments plugged on when not in use • Don't keep electric cables within the reach of children
Poisoning	• Keep all medicines/cleaning agents/drugs/kerosene/pesticides out of reach of children in their original containers and not in fruit juice/colored bottles • Instruct elder siblings not to give any medications to their brother/sisters	• Don't leave any medicines in the child's bedroom; • Don't store inedible products in food shelves. • Don't take medicines in front of your child
Drowning	• If the child is close to water, remove him before answering any call	• Don't leave young children and those with seizure disorders unattended in bath tubs or near swimming pools/ponds/beaches/full buckets in bathroom
Suffo-cation	• Remove broken rattle and other play items immediately • Keep plastic bags, scarves, ropes, cords out of reach of children • Leave cupboards/wardrobes/refrigerators unlocked	• Don't give (pea) nuts to children <2 year of age • Don't give bolus of food to infants or toddlers • Don't allow children to run about with food in the mouth or to play while eating
Fire injuries	• Always turn off the gas after use • Store inflammables in child-proof containers	• Don't light firecrackers in hand; bend over while lighting crackers; touch half-lit firecrackers
Road traffic injuries	• Teach older children how to cross the road safely and other safety rules • Ensure adequate lightning, construction of side walks, and roadway barriers in areas of high pedestrian traffic • Ensure that your child's bicycle is maintained in good condition; make him wear properly fitting approved cycle helmets and shoes while riding • Be sure that the child is not riding when he is receiving tranquillizing drugs • Ensure use of reflectors, mirrors and bright reflecting clothes	• Don't keep the door open when the child is at home • Don't allow younger children to cross the streets alone • Don't allow doubling on the bicycle, especially with infants • Don't carry more than one child on a 2-wheeler; allow child to stand in front of a rider • Don't ride at night; play near/on roads • Don't allow children to occupy front seat of car, lean out of vehicle windows or take any body part out of the window

Chemical Burns

The burnt area is flushed with plenty of running cold water. If an eye is burnt by chemical especially an acid or an alkali, it is flushed gently but thoroughly with tap water for long time. The burn wound should be kept as clean as possible, protected from dirt, dust and flies.

Management

Estimate Burn Size

The primary determinant of survival in patients with burn injury is patient age below 4-yr and the size and depth of the burn wound. Young children do not tolerate thermal injury as well as adults. The Berkow body surface area chart and the rule of nines, used to estimate surface area of burn injuries in adults, are not applicable to children. The Lund and Browder modification, which divides the body into small portions and takes into account childhood differences in body proportions, is preferred.

Hospitalization

Minor burns can be treated at home with topical ointments. Indications for hospitalization are patients having: (i) 5% total body surface area (TBSA) third-degree burns, (ii) 10% TBSA second- and third-degree burns, or (iii) burn injuries involving the face, hands or genitalia. Principles of therapy include: (i) adequate fluid replacement, (ii) correction of hypoxia and ventilatory disturbances, (iii) prevention of hypothermia and (iv) management of pain and anxiety. Patients with inhalation injury are managed by endotracheal intubation and supportive ventilation; hyperventilation with 100% oxygen shortens the half-life of carbon monoxide elimination from 4 hr to 40 minutes.

25

Adequate Fluid Replacement

The goal of fluid resuscitation is to restore and maintain perfusion and tissue oxygen delivery at optimal levels in order to protect the zone of ischemia in burned tissues without overloading the circulation. Oliguria occurs as a result of several factors, including excessive secretion of antidiuretic hormone. Urine output should be maintained between 0.7–1 ml/kg/hr. Isotonic solutions (normal saline or Ringer lactate) should be administered initially at a rate of 20 ml/kg/hr until calculation of appropriate replacement can be made. Potassium is not administered during the first 12–24 hr, or until normal kidney function is demonstrated.

Topical Therapy

Sixty-five per cent of pediatric burns heal spontaneously, without the need for skin grafting, with topical therapy alone. The most commonly used topical agents are 0.5% silver sulphadiazine, 0.5% silver nitrate and mafenide acetate. These agents limit bacterial proliferation but do not sterilize the wound. Silver sulphadiazine offers advantages in small children; its application is painless, it has a soothing effect and restricts fluid and heat loss from the burn surface. It can cause skin rash, leukopenia and thrombocytopenia. Silver nitrate is not an effective antibacterial agent because of poor penetration of the burn eschar; it can cause hyponatraemia, hypokalaemia, hypochloremia and hypocalcemia. Mafenide acetate penetrates the burn eschar effectively; its application can be painful and may be associated with skin reaction and metabolic acidosis (being a carbonic anhydrase inhibitor). Daily dressing changes are required after thorough cleansing. Maintaining such dressings intact in a young child is difficult over the face and hands. MEBO (moist exposed burn ointment) is promising in this regard. A judicious combination of topical therapy, eschar excision and skin grafting helps in quick healing. Decompressive escharotomy of circumferential burns of the chest, abdomen and extremities must be performed without delay at the bedside

Analgesia

Adequate control of pain and anxiety is essential to minimize the stress response in burn injury. Narcotics are the commonest form of analgesia in major burns. Requirement for analgesia is generally higher in adults with burn injuries.

Nutrition

Attention to the nutritional needs of a burned child is an essential component of management. High caloric and nitrogen intake is crucial for survival. Adult nutritional calculation formulas are not well suited to children. Calorie requirements are best estimated by the following formula

- *Infants:* 2100 Cal/m^2 + 1000 Cal/m^2 burn surface area
- *Children:* 1800 Cal/m^2 + 1300 Cal/m^2 burn surface area
- *Adolescents:* 1500 Cal/m^2 surface area and burn surface area.

Adequate protein (2–3 g /kg body weight), supplementation of trace elements, vitamins and minerals is necessary. Whenever feasible, particularly in patients with less than 15–20% burns, nutrients should be administered by the enteral route. Tube feeding is started on the first day of admission with rapid advancement towards intake goals. In children with more extensive burns, inhalation injury or prolonged paralytic ileus, parenteral nutrition is considered.

Others

Assessment of physical abilities and enabling full range of joint movements by physical and occupational therapy and play therapy is encouraged. Family support and evaluation of the child's social environment should not be overlooked.

DROWNING

Drowning is a form of asphyxial death in which the access of air to the lungs is prevented by the submersion of the body in water or other fluid medium. In India, drowning is an important cause of child mortality. Though drowning occurs most frequently in natural bodies of water like ponds, lakes, river, deaths due to drowning in swimming pool and bath tubs are increasing. The risk of drowning is directly related to physical development of a child and his aquatic skills.

Aspiration, Suffocation

Many young children die every year due to suffocation caused by ingestion of foreign objects. Safety pins lead the list of ingested object in infants. More than 50% accidental deaths among infants were caused by aspiration of food during or after feeding. Peanuts are mostly responsible for aspiration related suffocation fatalities in 2–4 yr-olds. Eating rapidly, improper chewing, running with food in mouth or holding a potential foreign body in the mouth (such as a pin, nail or small toy) is responsible for such mishaps. Less common reasons include accidental suffocation due to pacifier cords, cords of cradles, small chains, necklace and rarely by being crushed by adults sleeping in the same bed as a young infant.

Most of the injuries can be prevented by ensuring discipline, an attribute that has not received sufficient emphasis in injury prevention. Discipline may not prevent a toddler from getting into trouble, but it can prevent an older child from becoming involved in accidents. It includes immediate stopping of all dangerous practices such as door banging, throwing objects around the room, playing on the stairs, *etc.* Even a young child of 1 to 1½ years can be trained to keep away from the kitchen stove or electrical connections. Parents should not tolerate any dangerous habits such as turning on the gas taps that are done for attention seeking. However, they should be aware that excessive discipline and over-strictness may force their children to rebel against restrictions making them vulnerable to injuries.

Suggested reading

1 Riordan M, et al. Poisoning in children. General management. Arch Dis Child 2002;87:392–396.
2. Riordan M, et al: Poisoning in children 3: Common medicines. Arch Dis Child 2002;87:400–402.

26 Pediatric Critical Care

INTRODUCTION

While neonatal and adult intensive care is well advanced, pediatric intensive care is still a developing area. In tertiary care hospitals, 5–10% of total pediatric beds should be for ICU and this should be greater if the hospital has surgical units.

Instability of homeostatic mechanisms, functional immaturity of vital organs and occurrence of multiple problems simultaneously in critically ill children lead to a complex picture. In addition, children have special needs. In order to optimize resource utilization, it is essential to understand indications of admission into the PICU (Table 26.1).

Table 26.1: Indications for admission into PICU

- Hemodynamic instability, shock, cardiac arrhythmias or cardiorespiratory arrest
- Severe anemia or hemorrhage
- Acute poisoning
- Respiratory failure: Impending or established
- Altered sensorium, encephalopathies, status epilepticus or raised intracranial pressure
- Hepatic failure and complications
- Renal failure and complications
- Severe metabolic abnormalities such as severe hyper- or hypokalemia, severe hyper- or hyponatremia, hypoglycemia or diabetic ketoacidosis
- Severe infections like severe malaria
- For procedures such as peritoneal dialysis, exchange transfusion, central venous cannulation
- For postoperative monitoring and care.

The optimal number of beds in an ICU is 6–10. Proper attention has to be paid to the ICU layout; 200–250 square feet area should be provided per bed. This area will provide space for the bed and various equipments. The unit should have an uninterrupted power supply. The unit preferably should be air-conditioned. The type and arrangement of beds should be such to allow rapid access to the head end for airway management. A crash cart containing all the drugs and necessary equipment for resuscitation should be ready at all times. In addition, the unit should have a central station where the nursing and physician staff can observe all the patients. There should be adequate space for various utilities and storage.

The ICU should also have various equipments for cardio-respiratory monitoring, ECG monitoring, pulse oximeters, devices for oxygen therapy, mechanical ventilators, nebulizers, devices for IV therapy including infusion pumps, weighing scales and plenty of disposables.

More important than anything else, it is the ICU team that has a key role in care of critically ill children. The team consists of physicians trained in intensive care and well versed with resuscitation and intravascular access, and well trained and dedicated nursing staff. It is desirable to have a multidisciplinary team.

The ICU should have access to laboratory facilities, preferably relying on micro-methods. Rapid diagnostic tests for glucose estimation and for determination of various compounds in the urine should be available in the ICU. There should be facility for complete blood counts and blood gas and electrolyte estimations. Portable X-ray units and ultrasonography are desirable.

Care of a child in ICU requires regular assessment and monitoring (particularly the trends). This relies heavily on physical examination and use of various monitoring equipments. However, the equipments are not a substitute to clinical methods. In fact, intensive care is labor intensive. The decision making in the ICU goes in the continuous cycle of evaluation, intervention and re-evaluation. The success of intensive care is greatly dependent on early identification of a sick child.

In addition to caring for the primary disorder, particular attention should also be paid to nutrition, sedation and analgesia and infection control.

Suggested reading

Consensus guidelines for pediatric intensive care units in India: Indian Pediatr 2002; 39: 43–50.

ASSESSMENT/IDENTIFICATION OF A SERIOUSL ILL CHILD

In order to improve the survival of seriously ill children, it is mandatory to recognize a sick child at the earliest. This early identification is required on arrival to the emergency services and also in children already admitted in the hospital. Such an assessment will ensure provision of more intensive care to these children, which should improve the survival.

Identification of a critically sick child relies on observation of the child, history and physical examination. At first contact, the ABCs are quickly assessed-patency of **A**irway, adequacy of **B**reathing and **C**irculation (this aspect is discussed in the section on pediatric life support). If there is an abnormality in any of these, life support/ resuscitation must be initiated.

The important symptoms in seriously ill children include:

- Drowsiness
- Seizure activity
- Excessive irritability
- Decreased activity
- Difficulty in breathing
- Cold extremities (particularly in the absence of cold environment)
- Decreased feeding/decreased intake of fluids
- Decrease in the urine output (e.g. less than 4 wet nappies in the previous 24 hours)
- Apneic episodes/cyanosis
- Bilious vomiting.

These features are predictive of a serious illness, particularly in young infants. In addition, the history should identify any underlying chronic illness.

An assessment of whether a child appears to be well or ill can also be made on grading the degree of compromise in a variety of age-specific behavioral and activity parameters. Various clinical scoring systems are available for describing the severity of illness. The parameters objectively evaluated in some of these scores include: the respiratory effort, level of activity, color, temperature, playfulness, quality of cry, reaction to parental stimulation, and hydration status. Some of the scores are Yale Observation Score, Young Infant Observation Scale, and Severity Index Score. These scores help in objectivising the assessment; however, none of these are 100% sensitive and specific.

Examination is targeted at picking up abnormalities in various organ systems. As mentioned earlier, it begins with assessment of ABCs. Pulse rate, character of the pulse, respiratory rate and effort, temperature, capillary refill time, and oxygen saturation (if available) should be accurately measured. In addition, one should look for pallor, icterus, edema, wasting and signs of dehydration; examine the central nervous system for alteration of sensorium, any neurological deficits, and signs of meningeal irritation; and assess the renal function by recording the urine output.

If facility is available for pulse oximetry, the same should always be included in the assessment of a child. In a sick child, commonly performed investigations include: complete blood counts, blood glucose and electrolytes, and if feasible, arterial blood gas estimation. The rest of the work up should be tailored according to the clinical profile.

Once a sick child is identified and assessed completely, appropriate interventions are performed and the child periodically reexamined to assess improvement or worsening even with intervention and also to identify any fresh problems.

For management of a critically sick child it is mandatory to have good clinical skills; there is no substitute for these. Once the child is examined, it is important to identify the problems; for this, a sound knowledge of normal and abnormal is required. Appropriate intervention is then performed and the child reassessed in the same cycle.

MONITORING

Monitoring of critically ill children is an essential component of management. The purposes of monitoring are:

i. To measure intermittently or continuously key physiologic indices that help in diagnosis and management,
ii. To provide alarms that notify the health care team that important changes have occurred in the child's condition, and
iii. To create and evaluate trends that would help in the assessment of treatment and prognosis.

Respiratory Monitoring

Physical examination: The child should be observed for respiratory rate and pattern, chest retractions, nasal flaring, use of accessory muscles and color. On auscultation, check for asymmetry of air entry, type of breath sounds and presence of stridor, rhonchi or crepitations.

Use of monitors: Respiratory rate can be monitored continuously by impedence pneumography, which requires the presence of three electrodes over the chest. One must be aware about the normal rates at different ages to be able to detect abnormality (Table 26.2).

Table 26.2: Respiratory rates (RR) and heart rates (HR) at different ages

Age (years)	*RR (breaths/min)**	*HR (beats/min)**
1	30 (22–38)	120 (80–160)
2	25 (17–33)	110 (80–130)
4	23 (17–27)	100 (80–120)
6	21 (15–26)	100 (75–115)
8	20 (15–26)	90 (70–110)
10	18 (15–25)	90 (70–110)
12	18 (14–26)	85 (65–105)
14	17 (15–23)	80 (60–100)
16	17 (12–22)	75 (55–95)

* Figures in parentheses give the range

Pulse oximetry has made it possible to non-invasively measure percent oxygen saturation of hemoglobin. The technique is based on Beer-Lambert law and the ratio of oxyhemoglobin to the sum of total hemoglobin (reduced hemoglobin and oxyhemoglobin) estimated by measuring absorption at wavelengths of 660 nm (red) and 940 nm (infrared). Pulse oximetry is fairly reliable in most settings. However, some conditions lead to inaccuracies: dyshemoglobinemias (methemoglobin), dyes and pigments (methylene blue), poor peripheral perfusion, increased venous pulsations, and optical interference with external light sources like phototherapy unit or fluorescent light.

Transcutaneous blood gas monitoring is now feasible and it makes continuous monitoring of pCO_2 and pO_2 possible. However, it has the limitations of need for frequent calibration, high cost, and occasional burns.

Capnography is the graphic waveform produced by variations in CO_2 concentration throughout the respiratory cycle as a function of time. A sidestream or mainstream sampler samples the gases inspired and expired by the patient. CO_2 is estimated in these samples by infrared spectroscopy. End-tidal CO_2 can be used as a substitute for $PaCO_2$. Also, it has a role in determining endotracheal tube placement, dead space, and mechanical ventilation failures.

In mechanically ventilated children, respiratory mechanics help in better understanding of respiratory pathophysiology.

Apart from these continuous monitoring modalities, chest radiography and arterial blood gas analyses are performed periodically.

Hemodynamic Monitoring

Hemodynamic monitoring provides information about perfusion of a child's vital organs.

Physical examination: Repeated examination of a critically ill child is the cornerstone of hemodynamic monitoring. The rate and character of pulse should be examined. The heart rates are dependent on the age and one must be aware of these to pick up abnormalities.

Blood pressure can be monitored by noninvasive or invasive methods. The pressures may be determined manually using sphygmomanometers or by use of automated systems. Invasive methods rely on placement of a catheter in an artery and pressure measurement by manometer. In children with hemodynamic compromise, blood pressures may not drop significantly until the compromise is severe.

The state of microcirculation can be assessed by **capillary filling time**. Firm pressure is applied over sternum or forehead by ball of the thumb for 5 seconds- this leads to blanching. On removal of pressure, the color returns and the time taken for complete return of color is noted. The normal capillary filling time is 3 seconds or lesser. Any prolongation signifies impairment of microcirculation. This helps in diagnosing hemodynamic compromise earlier than drop in arterial blood pressures.

Another way of determining adequacy of the peripheral perfusion is noting the core-peripheral temperature gradient. A gradient of more than 5°C indicates hypoperfusion.

Abnormality in the intensity of the heart sounds and the presence of murmurs may indicate underlying heart disease.

Continuous ECG monitoring is mandatory in critically ill children admitted in ICU.

Central venous pressures (CVP) are monitored by placing a catheter through a large vein into the right atrium. This pressure gives information about the venous return and the preload. Normal right atrial pressure is less than 6 mm Hg. If the pressures are low in a child with hypotension, it signifies a low intravascular fluid volume. On the other hand, CVP may be increased due to myocardial dysfunction, fluid overload or increased pulmonary artery pressures.

In some children, particularly after cardiac surgery, monitoring of cardiac output and pulmonary artery pressures may be useful. Echocardiography is a non-invasive modality to assess cardiac structure and function.

In addition, vital organ perfusion can be assessed by monitoring urine output, which is a surrogate marker of renal perfusion and function. Urine output less than 0.5 ml/kg/hr in a child with normal kidneys signifies poor renal perfusion or excessive ADH. Poor perfusion may be due to depletion of intravascular volume or conditions like congestive cardiac failure or shock. Monitoring of the sensorium and neurologic status also gives information about vital organ perfusion.

Monitoring of Other Organ Systems

Other monitoring depends on the child's diagnosis and the affected organ systems. This would include monitoring of the hepatic, renal and hematologic parameters.

Level of consciousness can be assessed by Glasgow Coma Scale (GCS). Modified GCS can be used in small kids upto 5 years of age (Table 26.3).

Suggested reading

1. Robertson MA, Molyneux EM. Triage in the developing world—can it be done? Arch Dis Child 2001;85:208–13.
2. Nolan T, Angos P, Cunha AJ, Muhe L, Qazi S, Simoes EA et al. Quality of hospital care for seriously ill children in less-developed countries. Lancet 2001; 357: 106–10.
3. Cheifetz IM Venkataram ST, Hamel DS. Respiratory monitoring. In Nichols DG. Roger's Textbook of Pediatric Intensive Care. Baltimore, Lipincott Williams and Wilkins 2008;662–85.
4. Halley GC, Tibby S. Hemodynamic monitoring. In: Nichols DG Rogerts Textbook of Pediatric Intensive Care. Baltimore. Lippincott Williams and Wilkins 2008;1039–63.
5. Talman A, Warren A, Development of modified pediatric coma scale in intensive care practice. Arch Dis Child 1997;77:519–21.

Table 26.3: The Glasgow Coma Scale		
≤ 5 years	*>5 years*	*Score*
Eye opening response		
Spontaneous	Spontaneous	4
To speech	To speech	3
To pain	To pain	2
None	None	1
Verbal response		
Alert, coos, words-normal	Oriented	5
Irritable cry	Confused	4
Cries to pain	Inappropriate words	3
Moans to pain	Incomprehensive sounds	2
No response to pain	None	1
Motor response		
Normal spontaneous movements	Obeys commands	6
Localizes (> 9 months)	Localizes to supra-orbital stimulus	5
Withdraws	Withdraws	4
Abnormal flexion (decorticate posturing)	Abnormal flexion (decorticate posturing)	3
Abnormal extension (decerebrate response)	Abnormal extension (decerebrate response)	2
None	None	1

PEDIATRIC BASIC AND ADVANCED LIFE SUPPORT

Cardiopulmonary arrest in children is much less common than adults. The major causes of death in infants and children are respiratory failure, sudden infant death syndrome (SIDS), sepsis, neurologic diseases, submersion or drowning and injuries. In contrast to adults, sudden cardiac arrest in children is uncommon, and cardiac arrest does not usually result from a primary cardiac cause. More often it is the terminal event of progressive respiratory failure or shock, also called an asphyxial arrest.

Basic life support (BLS) refers to a protocol mandatory in cases of cardiopulmonary arrest providing cardio-pulmonary resuscitation (CPR) with or without devices and bag-mask ventilation till advanced life support can be provided. Two major objectives of cardiopulmonary resuscitation are to preserve organ viability during cardiac arrest and to help return of spontaneous circulation (ROSC).

SEQUENCE OF CPR/BLS

To maximize survival and intact neurological status in post-resuscitation stage strict adherence to the BLS sequence is needed. Basic life support (BLS) guidelines give a series of skills performed sequentially to assess and restore effective ventilation and circulation to the child with respiratory or cardio-respiratory arrest. Evaluation and interventions in pediatric BLS should be simultaneous processes. The sequence for BLS is described as

1. Assess responsiveness
2. Airway
3. Breathing
4. Circulation.

Assess Responsiveness

The pediatrician should quickly assess the presence and extent of injury, if present and determine the level of consciousness (whether the child is responsive or not). The child who has sustained head or neck trauma should not be shaken. A child, who is responsive but having respiratory distress, will require opening of airway to optimize the ventilation and circulatory support. **If the child is unresponsive, seek help and be prepared for BLS.** If second rescuer is present during assessment, he can initiate the BLS activation of emergency system to get proper medical help.

Airway

Infants and children are at a higher risk of having respiratory obstruction and failure due to following reasons: smaller size of upper airway in comparison to adults; large size of tongue in relation to the size of oropharynx; smaller and compliant subglottic area more prone for collapse and/or obstruction; relatively compliant chest wall and rib cage; and limited oxygen reserve.

Position of the Victim

If the child is unresponsive, the child should be placed on a hard surface in face up or supine position. If head or neck trauma is suspected, head and torso should be moved as a unit and the neck immobilized.

Open the Airway

Tongue is the most common cause of respiratory obstruction in unresponsive children and all the measures are targeted to lift the tongue away from the posterior pharynx to keep the airway patent.

Head tilt chin lift maneuver: If the victim is unresponsive and trauma is not suspected, the airway is opened by tilting the head back and lifting the chin (Fig. 26.1). One

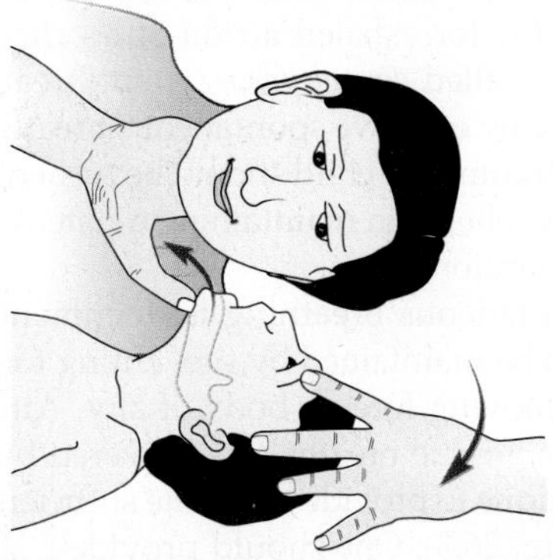

Fig. 26.1: Head tilt-chin lift maneuver

26

hand is placed over the child's forehead and the head is gently tilted back. At the same time the fingers of the other hand are placed on the lower jaw to lift the chin to open the airway. This maneuver should not to be used in suspected cases of trauma.

Jaw thrust: Two or three fingers are placed under each side of lower jaw at its angle to lift the jaw upwards and outwards (Fig. 26.2). If this method is unsuccessful, the head may slightly be extended and another attempt is made. This method should be used in all victims with blunt trauma, craniofacial injury and those having Glasgow Coma Scale score of less than 8. This method is no longer recommended for lay rescuer because it is difficult to learn and perform, is often not an effective way to open the airway, and may cause spinal movement.

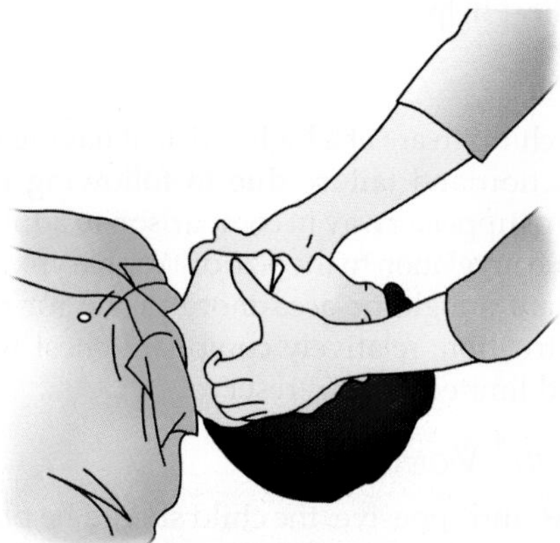

Fig. 26.2: Opening the airway with jaw thrust

Foreign body airway obstruction: If this is suspected, one should open the mouth and look for a foreign body. If seen, it should be carefully removed under vision. Trained healthcare provider should perform a tongue-jaw lift to look for obstructing objects.

Breathing

Check for Breathing

After opening of child's airway, one should *look* for signs of breathing, i.e. rhythmic chest and abdominal movements; *listen* for exhaled breath sounds at the nose and mouth, and *feel* for exhaled air on one's cheek. Periodic gasping, also called *agonal gasps,* is not breathing. If the patient is having effective spontaneous breathing with no evidence of trauma the child should be turned to recovery position which helps in maintaining a patent airway and prevents aspiration.

If no spontaneous breathing is documented, airway patency is to be maintained by preventing tongue falling back and removing foreign body, if any. After taking in deep breaths, rescue breaths are delivered by mouth-to-mouth technique to provide a volume sufficient for child's chest rise (Fig. 26.3). One should provide 2 slow breaths to the victim (1–1.5 sec per breath) with pausing in

Fig. 26.3: Rescue breathing in a child

between to increase the oxygen content in the delivery breath. Current recommendations suggest that between 2 to 5 rescue breaths should be provided initially to ensure at least 2 effective ventilations provided. If victim is < 1 year of age, rescuer should place the mouth over the infant's mouth and nose to create a seal and blow/exhale to result in chest rise. A good head position should be maintained to keep the airway patent in between. Mouth-to-nose breathing is a reasonably good alternative method of providing rescue breaths to an infant. In case of a larger child (1–8 years of age) mouth-to-mouth breathing should be provided. Mouth-to-mouth rescue breaths may not be acceptable in some cases due to high chances of transmission of infectious diseases. Barrier devices may improve the aesthetics for the rescuers but have not been documented to reduce the risk of disease transmission. Two broad categories of barrier devices are available; these are masks and face, shields. Most masks have one way valve preventing victim's exhaled air from entering the rescuer's mouth.

Firm but gentle pressure on the cricoid cartilage during ventilation can reduce gastric distention and regurgitation during rescue breaths. This maneuver helps in compressing esophagus and reducing air entry to stomach and subsequent regurgitation.

Bag and Mask Ventilation

Self-inflating bags should be used in CPR/BLS, which are available in pediatric and adult sizes. Flow inflating bags need an oxygen flow for inflation and can be used in hospital setup. For full term neonates, infants and children <8 years of age, ventilation bags of minimum volume 450–500 ml should be used to deliver adequate amount of tidal volume. Neonatal size bags (250 ml) may be useful for preterm neonates. Regardless the size of ventilation bag, adequate amount of tidal volume should be used to cause visible chest rise. Excessive expansion may compromise cardiac output, increasing the chances of regurgitation by distending stomach and increases chances of air leak. In patients with small airway obstruction like asthma, bronchiolitis, excessive ventilation volume may lead to air leak and compromised cardiac output. In patients with head injury or cardiac arrest, excessive ventilation may adversely affect neurological outcome.

The self-inflating bag delivers only room air unless it is connected to an oxygen source. Pediatric bag-valve device without any reservoir if connected to an oxygen inflow of 10 L/min delivers 30% to 80% of oxygen to the patient. If used with a reservoir it may deliver 60% to 95% of oxygen and oxygen inflow of 15 L/min is necessary to provide an adequate oxygen volume in the reservoir.

Techniques of bag-mask ventilation: Bag-mask ventilation can be as effective as endotracheal intubation and safer when providing ventilation for short periods. But bag-mask ventilation requires training and periodic retraining. One should select a bag with reservoir and mask of proper size for the patient. The mask must cover the patient's nose and mouth completely without covering the eyes or overlapping chin. The bag-mask system is connected to oxygen supply, the airway is opened and a proper face-mask seal is ensured. When no signs of neck trauma are present, victim's head is to be tilted back to a semi extended position to keep airway open. If trauma is suspected, no head and neck movement is to be done. One should place the thumb and index finger in a 'C' shape over the mask and exert downward pressure on the mask to achieve air seal. The jaw lifting and mask-face seal are done by one hand, which is called as 'E-C clamp' technique. After applying the mask to face properly, the ventilation bag is compressed with the other hand to achieve visible chest rise. Two rescuers can achieve better bag-mask ventilation; one maintains the proper airway patency and mask-face seal while the other rescuer delivers ventilation. Gastric distention can be reduced by the placement of an orogastric or nasogastric tube.

Circulation

After opening the airway and providing 2 effective rescue breaths, heart rate is checked to determine whether the patient is in cardiac arrest and requires chest compression. Pulse check can be taken as a sign of circulation. Carotid artery is palpated in children and brachial artery is palpated in infants. This should not take more than 10 seconds.

Indications for *chest compression* are absence of signs of circulation after delivering rescue breaths (no spontaneous breathing, coughing, movement or pulse) or the child is pale or cyanosed or heart rate/pulse rate <60 beats per minute with signs of poor perfusion after rescue breaths.

Chest compressions are serial rhythmic compressions of the chest that cause blood flow to the vital organs (heart, lungs and brain) in an attempt to keep them viable until Advanced Life Support (ALS) is available. Chest compressions provide circulation as a result of increase in intrathoracic pressure and/or direct compression of the heart and should be provided with ventilation in infants and children. One should compress the lower half of sternum to a relative depth of approximately one third to half of the antero-posterior diameter of chest at a rate at least 100 compressions per minute in infants and 80 per minute in children. The xiphoid process should be avoided while providing chest compression and compression should be adequate to produce a palpable pulse during resuscitation. To provide optimum chest compression, victim should be lying supine on a hard and flat surface. In an infant with no signs of head or neck trauma, CPR may be successfully done supporting the infant's back with palm of one hand while the other hand gives the chest compression.

Chest Compression in Infants (<1 Year)

Two-finger technique: If you are alone or you cannot physically encircle the victim's chest, compress the chest with 2 fingers. Place two fingers of one hand vertically over the sternum just below the inter-mammary line (between the two nipples) ensuring that the fingers are not over xiphoid process. One can keep one hand under the infant supporting the body and head and the other hand can perform the compression.

Two-thumb technique: Encircle the infant's chest with both hands; spread your fingers around the thorax, and place your thumbs together over the lower half of the sternum avoiding xiphisternum. Forcefully compress the sternum with your thumbs as you squeeze the thorax with your fingers for counter pressure. The 2 thumb–encircling hands technique is preferred because it produces higher coronary artery perfusion pressure, more consistently results in appropriate depth or force of compression, and may generate higher systolic and diastolic pressures. Provider should perform chest compressions while the other maintains the airway and performs ventilations at a ratio of 15:2 with as short a pause in compressions as possible. Do not ventilate and compress the chest simultaneously with either mouth-to-mouth or bag-mask ventilation.

Chest Compression Technique in the Child (1–8 Years Age)

Heel of one hand should be placed over lower half of sternum avoiding pressure over xiphoid with fingers lifted above the chest wall to prevent compression of rib cage (Fig. 26.4). Rescuer should place/position him/herself vertically above the victim's chest.

Chest Compression for Large Children and Above 8 Years of Age

Two-hand method for chest compression should be used to achieve an adequate depth of compression in these

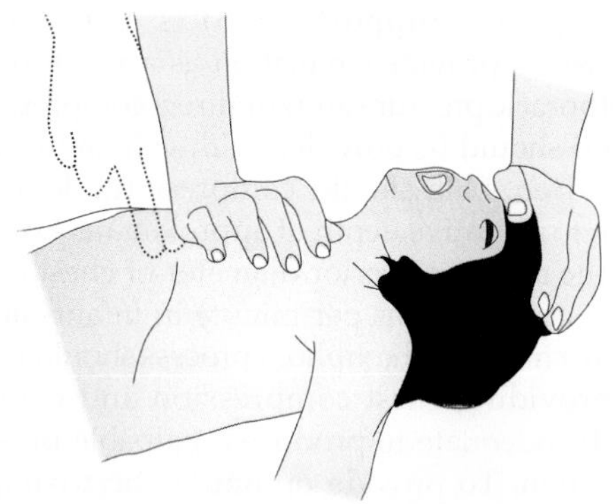

Fig. 26.4: Chest compression in a child

children. This is achieved by placing heel of one hand over the lower half of sternum and heel of the other hand over the first hand, interlocking the fingers of both hands with fingers lifted above the chest wall. Compress the sternum to depress approximately one third to half of the anteroposterior diameter of chest. After compression, release the pressure without taking off the fingers or thumb from the surface of chest wall. Chest compression should be delivered in a smooth fashion with equal time in compression and relaxation phases.

Ventilations are relatively less important during the first minute of CPR for victims of sudden arrhythmia induced cardiac arrest than they are after asphyxia-induced arrest, but even in asphyxial arrest, a minute ventilation that is lower than normal is likely to maintain an adequate ventilation-perfusion ratio because cardiac output and, therefore, pulmonary blood flow produced by chest compressions is quite low.

The lay rescuers should use a 30:2 compression-ventilation ratio for all (infant, child, and adult) victims. For one healthcare provider, the compression-ventilation ratio should be 30:2 for all age groups and for two rescuers, the compression-ventilation ratio should be 30:2 for all adult CPR and 15:2 compression ventilation ratio for infant and child up to the start of puberty.

Two or more rescuers should rotate the compressor role approximately every 2 minutes to prevent fatigue and deterioration in quality and rate of chest compressions. The switch should be accomplished as quickly as possible (ideally in less than 5 seconds) to minimize interruptions in chest compressions.

External chest compression in children and infants should always be accompanied by rescue breathing. Reassess the victim after 2 minutes or after 5 cycles.

If signs of spontaneous circulation have reappeared, chest compression should be stopped and only ventilation to continue till return of adequate spontaneous breathing.

PEDIATRIC ADVANCED LIFE SUPPORT (PALS)

Pediatric advanced life support (PALS) refers to the assessment and support of pulmonary and circulatory function in the periods before an arrest, during and after an arrest. PALS target the prevention of causes of arrest and early detection and treatment of cardiopulmonary compromise and arrest in critically ill or injured child.

Components of PALS

- Basic life support (BLS)
- Use of equipments and techniques to establish and maintain effective oxygenation, ventilation and perfusion
- Clinical and ECG monitoring with arrhythmia detection and management
- Establishing and maintaining vascular access
- Identification and treatment of reversible causes of cardiopulmonary arrest
- Emergency treatment of patients with cardiac and respiratory arrest
- Treating patients with trauma, shock, respiratory failure or other pre-arrest conditions.

Adjuncts for Airway and Ventilation

All fluids from patients should be treated as potentially infectious and standard universal precautions be followed. Oxygen should be given to all seriously ill or injured children with respiratory insufficiency, shock and trauma. During mouth-to-mouth rescue breathing, 16–17% oxygen is delivered with alveolar oxygen pressure of 80 mm Hg, and optimal external chest compressions provide only a fraction of cardiac output resulting in reduced tissue perfusion and oxygen delivery. Ventilation-perfusion mismatch during CPR and underlying respiratory conditions causes right to left shunting resulting in reduced oxygenation. Oxygen can be administered by facemask, nasal cannula, pharyngeal mask, laryngeal mask and tracheal tubes with ventilation.

Endotracheal Intubation

If used properly, this is the most effective and reliable method of ventilation. The advantages of endotracheal intubation are: (a) ensures adequate ventilation, (b) reduced risk of aspiration of gastric contents, (c) inspiratory time and peak inspiratory pressure can be controlled, (d) suction can be done to keep airway patent, and (e) positive end-expiratory pressure can be provided.

Indications for endotracheal intubations are excessive work of breathing leading to fatigue, inadequate CNS control of ventilation leading to apnea or poor respiratory effort, functional or anatomical airway obstruction, need for higher peak inspiratory pressure or positive end-expiratory pressure to maintain effective alveolar gas exchange, lack of airway protective reflexes, and for prolonged duration CPR. Airway in the child is more compliant with relatively large tongue, anteriorly placed glottis and proportionately smaller airway, making it different from adults. As the subglottic area is the narrowest part of the pediatric airway, uncuffed endotracheal tubes are used in children <8 years of age. In certain circumstances (e.g. poor lung compliance, high airway resistance, or a large glottic air leak) a cuffed tube may be preferable provided that attention is paid to endotracheal tube size, position, and cuff inflation pressure. The cuff inflation pressure should be kept <20 cm H_2O.

Size of the tracheal tube and suction catheter for the tube can be determined according to the age of the child/ infant as per the following chart (Table 26.4):

Beyond 1 year of age, the size of tracheal tube can be estimated according to the formula:

Tracheal tube size (in mm)

= (Age in years/4) + 4 in case of uncuffed tube

= (Age in years/4) + 3 in case of cuffed tube

In general, tubes of size 0.5 mm smaller and 0.5 mm larger than the estimated should be available for use. The size of suction catheter (in Fr) is usually twice the internal diameter of the tracheal tube in mm, i.e. 8 Fr suction catheter for tracheal tube of size 4 mm.

Table 26.4: Selecting the sizes of ET tube and suction catheters in newborn and infants

Age	*Tracheal tube size (in mm)*	*Suction catheter size (in Fr)*
Premature newborn <1 Kg	2.5	5
Premature newborn 1–2 Kg	3.0	5–6
Newborn 2–3 kg	3.0–3.5	6–8
Newborn > 3 kg	3.5–4.0	8
Infant (0 month–1 year)	3.5–4.0	8

Intubation Procedure

Intubation should always be preceded by supplemental oxygen and attempt should not exceed approximately 30 seconds as hypoxia created during prolonged intubation attempts increases the morbidity. Intubation should be interrupted with development of bradycardia (HR <60 bpm), if color or perfusion deteriorates, oxygen saturation by pulse oximetry falls to an unacceptable level. In these conditions assisted ventilation should be continued by bag-mask ventilation with supplemental oxygen until child's condition improves. In conditions like ARDS, requiring high peak inspiratory pressure that cannot be maintained by bag-mask ventilation, intubation should be considered despite presence of bradycardia or cyanosis.

Straight blade laryngoscope is usually used for infants and curved ones for children beyond 1–2 years of age. Blade tip is passed over epiglottis followed by blade traction to lift the base of tongue and epiglottis anteriorly, exposing the glottis. Endotracheal intubation should be attempted after visualizing the glottic opening. Appropriate depth of insertion of the tracheal tube from the angle of mouth can be estimated according to the formula:

Depth of insertion (cm) = Internal diameter of the tracheal tube (in mm) × 3.

In newborn the depth of insertion of endotracheal tube depends on the birth weight:

Depth of insertion (cm) = birth weight (kg) + 6

In children >2 years of age:

Depth of insertion (in cm) = (age in years/2) + 12.

While intubating, the black mark on the tracheal tube should be kept at the level of vocal cords to place the tube in proper position.

After intubation, the position of the tracheal tube should be assessed to ensure adequate ventilation and avoiding complications like segmental collapses. Chest rise should be bilaterally symmetrical with equal air entry in both axillae. Breath sounds should be checked over upper abdomen to rule out esophageal intubation and due to close proximity breath sounds may be heard over chest in infants and young children. Check for exhaled CO_2 if there is a perfusing rhythm. If the child has a perfusing rhythm and is <20 kg, one may use an esophageal detector device to check for evidence of esophageal placement. Check oxygen saturation with a pulse oximeter. Following hyper oxygenation, the oxyhemoglobin saturation detected by pulse oximetry may not demonstrate a fall indicative of incorrect endotracheal tube position (i.e. tube displacements) for as long as 3 minutes. If there is uncertainty about the tube position, direct laryngoscopy can be performed to visualize the tube passing between the vocal cords. Tracheal tube position should be confirmed by chest radiograph.

Establishing and Maintaining Vascular Access

26

Intravenous Access

During CPR the preferred venous access is the largest, most easily accessible one which does not require interruption of the resuscitation. Central venous lines provide more secure access to the circulation with more rapid action and higher peak drug level than peripheral venous administration. Femoral vein is the safest and easiest to access. Subclavian veins may be considered. Central venous lines provide more secure access to circulation and permit administration of drugs that might injure the peripheral sites if extravasated, such as vasopressors, hypertonic sodium bicarbonate and calcium. The agents with short half-life such as vasopressors, adrenaline and adenosine act better if given through central venous access. Catheter lengths of 5 cm in infant, 8 cm in young child and 12 cm in older child are usually suitable.

Intraosseous access should be tried to administer fluids, drugs, blood products during resuscitation, in cases where vascular access cannot be achieved. The usual site for the intraosseous access is anterior tibial bone marrow and other sites include distal femur, medial malleous and anterior superior iliac spine. Drugs like adrenaline, adenosine, vasopressors, can be administered via this route. It can be used to take samples for chemical analysis, blood grouping and cross matching.

Tracheal route may be used for administration of lipid-soluble drugs like lidocaine, epinephrine, atropine and naloxone (LEAN) until vascular access is established. According to the data from animal models and adult human studies, the suggested dosage for tracheal use is approximately 10 times of IV dose.

Administration of resuscitation drugs into the trachea can result in lower blood concentrations than the same dose given intravascularly. Furthermore, recent animal studies suggest that the lower epinephrine concentrations achieved when the drug is delivered by the endotracheal route may produce transient β-adrenergic effects. These effects can be detrimental, causing hypotension, lower coronary artery perfusion pressure and flow, and reduced potential for return of spontaneous circulation. Thus, although endotracheal administration of some resuscitation drugs is possible, IV or IO drug administration is preferred because it will provide a more predictable drug delivery and pharmacologic effect.

Non–lipid-soluble drugs (e.g. sodium bicarbonate and calcium) may injure the airway and should not be administered via the endotracheal route.

Fluid Therapy

Early restoration of the circulating blood volume is important to prevent progression to refractory shock or cardiac arrest. Volume expansion is best achieved with isotonic crystalloid fluids, such as Ringer lactate or normal saline. Blood replacement is indicated in patients with severe hemorrhagic shock who remain in shock even after infusion of 40–60 ml/kg of crystalloid. Dextrose solutions should not be used for initial resuscitation as they don't expand the intravascular volume effectively and may cause hyperglycemia leading to osmotic diuresis setting a vicious cycle of polyuria and hypovolemia. Recommendation cannot be made about use of colloid solutions in fluid resuscitation of infants and children due to lack of studies.

Hypoglycemia, if suspected or documented, should be managed readily with intravenous glucose with measures to prevent recurrence.

Drugs used for Cardiac Arrest and Resuscitation

Table 26.5 shows the commonly used drugs during resuscitation.

Arrhythmias

Most pediatric arrhythmias are the consequences of hypoxemia, acidosis, hypotension but children with myocarditis, cardiomyopathy and after cardiac surgery are at increased risk of primary arrhythmia. Drugs in therapeutic or toxic doses can lead to arrhythmia. About 10% of pediatric cardiac arrest patients have VF or pulseless VT.

Bradyarrhythmias

Hypoxemia, hypothermia, acidosis, hypotension, and hypoglycemia depress the sinus node function and slow conduction through the myocardium. In addition to these,

26

Table 26.5: Drugs used during cardiopulmonary resuscitation

Drug	*Indications*	*Dosage*	*Remarks*
Epinephrine	Symptomatic bradycardia, pulse less arrest	IV/IO: 0.01 mg/kg (1:10,000, 0.1 ml/kg) ET: 0.1 mg/kg (of 1: 1000 flush with 1–2 ml of saline) Repeat every 3–5 minutes, if required.	Tachyarrhythmia and hypertension may occur
Atropine	Bradyarrhythmias	0.02 mg/kg (minimum dose: 0.1 mg)	Tachycardia and pupil dilatation may occur but not fixed dilated pupils
Calcium gluconate (10% = 9 mg/ ml elemental calcium)	Hypocalcaemia, hypermagnesemia, hyperkalemia	1 ml/kg IV/IO (slow push)	Monitor HR, bradycardia may occur
Glucose	Suspected or documented hypoglycemia	0.5–1 g/kg	Avoid hyperglycemia
Sodium bicarbonate	Severe metabolic acidosis, hyperkalemia	1 mEq/kg IV/IO slowly	Use only if ventilation is adequate
Adenosine	SVT	0.1 mg/kg; repeat dose 0.2 mg/kg. Rapid bolus IV/IO	Monitor ECG during dose
Amiodarone	Pulseless VF/VT	5 mg/kg IV/IO	Monitor ECG during dose
Lidocaine	VF/VT	1 mg/kg IV/IO followed by infusion: 20–50 µg/kg/min	Monitor ECG during dose
Naloxone	Opioid intoxication	0.1 mg/kg IV/IO/ET	Repeated doses may be required.
Magnesium sulfate	Torsades, suspected hypomagnesemia, acute severe asthma	25–50 mg/kg rapid push for first 2 indications and an infusion over 30 min for asthma	Watch for respiratory depression and hypotension.

IV intravenous, IO: intraosseous; VF ventricular fibrillation; VT ventricular tachycardia excessive vagal stimulation, raised intracranial pressure or brain stem compression may cause bradycardia. Sinus bradycardia, sinus node arrest with junctional or idioventricular rhythm, AV blocks are usual pre-terminal rhythms observed in infants and children. All slow rhythms resulting in hemodynamic instability require immediate treatment. Adrenaline or epinephrine is the most useful drug in treating symptomatic bradycardia unless due to heart block or vagal overtone. For suspected bradycardia due to vagal overtone, atropine is the drug of choice. If no positive or transient effect is observed after ventilation and oxygenation, continuous infusion of epinephrine or dopamine should be considered.

Pulseless Electrical Activity (PEA)

It is a state of electrical activity observed on a monitor or ECG in absence of detectable cardiac activity. This is often the pre terminal state preceding asystole representing the electrical activity of a hypoxic and acidotic myocardium. Occasionally the PEA may be due to sudden impairment of cardiac output with normal ECG rhythm and heart rate increased or rapidly decreasing. Pulses or other evidence of cardiac output are absent and child appears lifeless. This category of PEA is called electromechanical dissociation (EMD). The reversible causes of EMD are 4H's and 4T's. The 4 H's are severe hypovolemia, hypoxia, hypothermia, hyperkalemia and other metabolic imbalances whereas the 4 T's are tension pneumothorax, toxins and drugs, pericardial tamponade, pulmonary thromboembolism. Treatment of PEA and EMD are same as treatment of asystole with identification of reversible causes and treating accordingly.

Please refer to section on tachyarrhythmia for treatment of supraventricular tachycardis, ventricular tachycardia and fibrillation.

Defibrillation

Defibrillation is the asynchronous depolarization of a critical mass of myocardium that successfully terminates VF or pulse less VT. It is successful in cases of sudden onset VF having oxygenated normothermic myocardium without significant acidosis. Larger size defibrillator paddles, i.e. 8–10 cm in diameter are recommended in children weighing more than 10 kg weight to maximize the current flow. Smaller paddles are used in infants and children weighing less than 10 kg. One paddle is placed over the right side of the upper chest and the other one over the apex of the heart (to the left of the nipple over the left lower ribs). Alternatively electrodes may be placed in anterior-posterior position with one placed to left of sternum and the other one over back.

Optimal electrical energy dose to defibrillate is not conclusively established in children but the available data suggests an initial dose of 2J/kg. If this is unsuccessful, energy dose should be doubled and repeated if needed. First 3 episodes should be given in rapid successions with pauses to check the presence of VF. Simultaneous correction of hypoxia, acidosis, and hypothermia should be done if present to improve the outcome of defibrillation. After failure of 3 attempts, trial of defibrillation should be given after epinephrine and CPR for 30 to 60 seconds. After the 4th failed defibrillation, use amiodarone (5 mg/kg bolus), lidocaine (1 mg/kg) or high dose epinephrine followed by defibrillation with 4 J/kg within 30 to 60 seconds after each drug if VF/VT persists.

In cases of children > 8 years of age those who weigh >50 kg, adult dose defibrillation should be used. Increase in the dose is not indicated when defibrillation is initially successful but rhythm reverts back to VF. Adjunctive medications (amiodarone, lidocaine, sotalol) with defibrillation may improve the outcome. The reversible causes of VF/VT (hypoxia, hypothermia, hyper/hypokalemia, hypovolemia and metabolic disorders) should be looked for and treated accordingly.

Suggested reading

1. Guidelines 2005 for cardiopulmonary resuscitation and emergency cardiovascular care: Pediatric basic life support. Circulation 2005; 112 (suppl part 11): 156–66.
2. Guidelines 2005 for cardiopulmonary resuscitation and emergency cardiovascular care: Pediatric advanced life support. Circulation 2005; 112 (suppl part 12):167–87.

RESUSCITATION IN TRAUMA: BASIC PRINCIPLES

26

A large number of children are injured in accidents both in and outside the home. While minor injuries can be managed easily, serious injuries need expert care to improve the outcomes. As with other emergencies, it is mandatory to start with the assessment of ABC. A few specific considerations are given here.

Airway

Often, children injured in road traffic accidents or due to fall from height have cervical injury and improper handling may lead to irreparable damage. In such cases, the cervical spine should be immobilized with a semi-rigid cervical collar. Ensure that head is in neutral position. Cervical collar should not be removed till radiographs and physical examination have ruled out the spine injury. Always inspect for foreign body, blood or broken teeth in the upper airway. For airway stabilization, head-tilt/chin-lift procedure is contraindicated because of converting an incomplete spinal cord injury into a complete one. Cricothyrotomy may be required in the presence of severe orofacial trauma.

Breathing

The considerations for endotracheal intubation and ventilation are the same as discussed earlier. Inspect for pneumothorax or hemothorax.

Circulation

External bleeding may be control by direct pressure to the sites with sterile gauze dressings. Watch for features of circulatory compromise. Hypotension may occur only after the child loses 25–30% of blood volume acutely. Intravascular access with two large bore cannulae should be established within 90 seconds or three attempts; in case of failure to do so, intra-osseous access should be sought. The fluid management in case of shock is discussed in the section on shock. Arrange for blood and blood products at the earliest.

Once the ABCs have been taken care of, remove the patient's entire clothing and perform thorough head-to-toe examination. Make sure that the child is hemodynamically stable during this evaluation. Evaluate the head and neck for external injuries. Examine the nervous system for evidence of focal deficits and features of raised intracranial tension. Look for any chest wall abnormality, paradoxical movements and rib fractures. Serial abdominal examinations should be performed for tenderness, distension, and flank ecchymoses. Pelvis should be assessed for symmetry, tenderness and stability. Blood at urinary meatus suggests urethral injury; do not catheterize in this situation. Watch for any external injury, deformity or fractures in the extremities.

Basic radiologic evaluation includes radiographs of cervical spine, chest, head, pelvis and extremities (if fracture is suspected). Special studies include a CT of the head (indicated in a child with unconsciousness, change in mental status, seizures, focal neurologic deficit, severe headache or other features of raised intracranial tension). If abdominal trauma is suspected, CT of the abdomen should be performed.

Close monitoring is essential. Heart rate, respiratory rate, blood pressure, capillary filling time, oxygen saturation should be monitored. In addition, serial assessment of Glasgow coma scale scores and neurological status, and urine output should be performed.

SHOCK

Definition

An acute syndrome that occurs because of cardiovascular dysfunction and inability of circulatory system to provide adequate oxygen and nutrients to meet the metabolic demands of vital organs. Despite this academic definition, shock remains a clinical diagnosis and can exist without hypotension.

Causes of Shock

Table 26.6 shows various types of shock and common causes:

Table 26.6: Types of shock

Hypovolemic	*Distributive*	*Cardiogenic*	*Septic**
Dehydration	Anaphylaxis	Heart disease	Bacterial
Gastroenteritis	Neurogenic	Anoxia	Viral
Deprivation	Drug toxicity	Cardiomyopathy	Fungal
Hemorrhage	Burns	Tamponade	

* Septic shock actually has components of several groups including distributive, cardiogenic and hypovolemia

Pathophysiology of Blood Pressure Regulation

Body has a host of regulatory systems designed to maintain adequate perfusion to vital vascular beds. These are broadly divided into neural reflexes and humoral reflexes.

Neural sympathetic reflexes via vasomotor center:
a. Baroreceptors-carotid body, aortic arch
b. Volume receptors-right atrium, pulmonary bed
c. Chemoreceptors-aortic and carotid body, medullary receptors
d. Cerebral ischemic response.

Humoral response:
a. Adrenal medulla-catecholamines
b. Hypothalamic-pituitary response-ACTH and vasopressin
c. Renin-angiotensin-aldosterone system.

Baroreceptors

Reduction in MAP or pulse pressure results in decreased stimulation of carotid sinus and aortic arch baroreceptors which leads to vasoconstriction by inhibition of vasomotor center. Vasoconstriction is severe in skeletal muscles, splanchnic, cutaneous vascular bed whereas flow is preserved in cerebral, coronary, retinal circulation (auto regulation).

Chemoreceptors

Hypotension causes local tissue hypoxia and acidosis due to reduced perfusion leading to firing of signals from chemoreceptors. Increased signals from these receptors cause respiratory stimulation, increased vasoconstriction and cardiac function.

Humoral Receptors

Release of epinephrine and nor-epinephrine from adrenal medulla and systemic adrenergic nerve endings (nor-epinephrine) as a result of hypotension causing vasoconstriction, ionotropic and chronotropic effect. Release of vasopressin from neurohypophysis leads to vasoconstriction and free water reabsorption from renal tubules and collecting tubules.

Renin-Angiotensin-Aldosterone System

Reduced renal perfusion stimulates release of renin from JG cells of kidney. Renin enhances conversion of angiotensinogen to angiotensin-I, which is subsequently converted to angiotensin-II by angiotensin converting enzyme (ACE). Angiotensin-II is a potent vasoconstrictor and also stimulates release of aldosterone enhancing renal sodium reabsorption.

Mediators of Tissue Damage in Shock

Altered oxygen metabolism: Hypoxia and ischemic (oxygen and substrate deficiency) injury occurs at some time during all types of shock. Cellular hypoxia results from either atmospheric low oxygen input abnormal lungs with V/Q mismatch, stagnant anoxia, anemic hypoxia. Reduced ATP production, depressed mitochondrial function, intracytoplasmic calcium, dysfunction of Na^+ K^+ ATPase pump lead to cellular edema which subsequently causes release of lysosomal enzymes resulting in tissue damage.

Microcirculatory abnormality: Spasm of precapillary sphincters and arterioles cause anoxia and damage to capillary endothelium. This leads to blockage of capillary bed with platelet aggregation and fibrin deposit further compromising the tissue circulation.

Diagnosis

A child, who is lethargic, ashen gray, tachypneic, cold with diminished peripheral pulses and hypotension is easily diagnosed as having shock. But the successful outcome of interventions at this state is limited. Diagnosis of shock/impending shock at an early stage and intervening may improve the outcome.

Early diagnosis of shock requires a high degree of suspicion and knowledge of conditions predisposes children to shock. The children who are febrile, have an identifiable source of infection or are hypovolemic due to any cause are at great risk of developing shock.

Signs of early shock include tachycardia, mild tachypnea, prolonged capillary refill (>3 sec), orthostatic change in BP or pulse and mild irritability. Unexplained tachycardia may be an earliest indicator of shock. Decreased tissue perfusion can be identified by changes in body temperature (cold extremities), decreased capillary refill (rate of refill after firm pressure over soft tissues or nail bed for 3 seconds) are sensitive indicators of shock. Vital organ hypoperfusion can be assumed to occur if oliguria or altered mentation occurs. Most significant physical finding in shock results from autonomic response to stress like tachycardia. Physical finding of acidosis is mostly respiratory resulting from CNS medullary stimulation by chemoreceptors leading to tachypnea, hyperpnea and hyperventilation.

Alteration in pulse pressure (narrowing) is the early finding of shock due to reduction in systolic blood pressure (SBP) and mild increase in diastolic blood pressure (DBP). SBP decreases with the fall in the stroke volume but the vascular tone maintains DBP and mean arterial pressure (MAP) that drop late in the course of shock.

Physical findings may vary according to the type and stage of shock. Shock may be early compensated and late or uncompensated according to the duration. Features of shock are present in cases of absolute hypovolemia, which may be due to any cause. The signs of early shock include tachycardia, mild tachypnea, slightly delayed capillary refill (>2–3 sec), orthostatic changes in blood pressure or pulse and mild irritability. But early septic shock reveals increased peripheral pulses, warm and over perfused extremities, widened pulse pressure and hyper dynamic precardium.

If the shock state continues, the compensatory mechanisms are not enough to maintain the metabolic needs of the tissues. The cellular ischemia and inflammatory mediators released affect the microcirculation to reveal the signs of brain, kidney and cardiac compromise. Increase in tachypnea due to metabolic acidosis leads to reduction in $PaCO_2$ and respiratory alkalosis. Skin shows features of reduced capillary refill and mottling. Hypotension and oliguria sets in with hypothermia. Mental changes in the form of agitation, confusion, stupor and finally coma may occur.

Classification/Etiology of the Shock

Recognition and treatment of shock depends upon the classification/etiology of the shock. The commonly used analogy of the circulatory system includes three components, a pump (the Heart), plumbing (the vascular system) and fluid (circulating blood volume). In order to assure adequate perfusion each of these systems needs to be functioning, otherwise shock will ensue. Consequently the three main types of shock, plus septic shock are listed below.

Hypovolemic shock (problems with the fluid) arises essentially because of loss of preload. Clues in the history that suggest hypovolemic shock include (i) Fluid losses due to diarrhea, vomiting, blood loss, profuse and prolonged sweating, or polyuria or a combination of these, and (ii) Decreased intake due to vomiting, poor appetite, or fluid deprivation. Clues in the physical examination that would make one think about hypovolemic shock are dry mucous membranes, absence of tears, and decreased urine output. Others features that go along with shock are poor perfusion, delayed capillary refill, diminished peripheral pulses and poor color. The central venous pressure is usually low. Laboratory investigations may reveal elevated blood urea and to a lesser extent creatinine, elevated uric acid levels and small cardiac silhouette on chest X-ray.

Cardiogenic shock (problems with the pump) results from loss of contractility. Clues in the history are diagnosis of congenital heart disease, recent cardiac surgery, other diseases associated with heart problems (e.g. Duchenne muscular dystrophy), or recent viral infection. Clues in the physical examination are presence of a murmur, particularly if new, extra heart sounds (S3, gallop), elevated JVP, hepatomegaly, or friction rub. Central venous pressure is usually elevated. Chest X-ray film may show a large silhouette and pulmonary edema. Troponin may be elevated in infectious etiology.

Distributive shock (problems with the plumbing) results from loss of after load or systemic vascular resistance. Clues in the history include recent allergic exposure (insect bite, other agent with history of severe reaction) or spinal cord injury (traumatic, surgical). Clues in the physical examination are bounding pulses, well perfused skin, and a very low blood pressure requiring large volumes of fluid.

Septic shock has components of all the three above-mentioned types: loss of preload, loss of after load/SVR, and loss of *contractility*. There may be a varying contribution by these components. Clues in the history that should make one suspect septic shock are fever, a focus of infection, immunosuppression, or exposure to particular infectious agents (e.g. meningococcus). On physical examination the triad of fever, tachycardia and tachypnea is common in infections in children. Septic shock is suspected in a child if in addition to these, there are features of decreased perfusion in form of altered mentation, prolonged capillary refill of >3 sec (cold shock) or flash capillary refill (warm shock), diminished or bounding peripheral pulses, or decreased urine output of < 1 mL/kg/hr. Hypotension being a late feature of shock may or may not be present on clinical examination, however its presence is confirmatory. A focus of infection should always be looked for. A rash should raise the suspicion of meningococcemia.

Clues in laboratory study include a high or very low white blood cell count and presence of coagulopathy.

Monitoring

Proper monitoring of the patients who are in shock or impending shock is done to detect the alteration in physiologic status and intervene at the earliest. It can also give clue to the effectiveness of the intervention done. These patients should be admitted to the pediatric intensive care unit. Clinical parameters to be monitored are pulse rate and pulse volume, respiratory rate and pattern, temperature, skin colour, BP, sensorium, urine out put along with ECG and pulse oximetry. Metabolic parameters to be monitored are blood glucose, electrolytes, blood gases (preferably arterial) to prevent and correct the abnormality at the earliest. Invasive pressure monitoring should be done wherever possible including central venous pressure (CVP) and pulmonary arterial catheterization by Swan-Ganz catheter.

Treatment

Always start with ABCs. The therapy essentially depends on the type of shock. In hypovolemic shock, replacement of intravascular volume by isotonic intravenous fluid is the mainstay of therapy. In cardiogenic shock, inotropic support is required. In some cases of cardiogenic shock, reduction of afterload by use of vasodilators may prove beneficial.

Fluid Therapy

Vascular Access

Large bore intravenous cannula/catheter should be placed in large peripheral veins like femoral vein. In older children and adolescents, cannulation of internal jugular, external jugular, subclavian veins can also be considered.

Choice of Fluids and Blood Products

First choice of fluid should be 0.9% normal saline or Ringer's lactate for acute stage of resuscitation. Large volumes of fluid for acute stabilization in children have not been shown to increase the rate of acute respiratory distress syndrome or cerebral edema. Crystalloids are the fluid of choice in acute phase but when the fluid requirement is high colloids (Dextran, gelatin, 5% albumin) may be of use. Experiences with starch, hypertonic saline or hyperoncotic albumin is limited in pediatric practice. Packed RBC should be given at 10mL/kg to maintain hematocrit of 30% or hemoglobin 10 g/dL.

Volume of Fluids

Fluid infusion is best started with boluses of 20 ml/kg titrated with clinical parameters of cardiac output like heart rate, capillary refill, sensorium. The ideal first fluid should be 0.9% normal saline or Ringer lactate and infused rapidly over 5–10 minutes. If no significant improvement is noticed, repeat boluses of 20 ml/kg should be given. Large volume fluid deficits may require 40 to 60 ml/kg and maximum up to 200 ml/kg over first hour for replenishing the deficit. The patients who do not respond to rapid boluses of 40–60 ml/kg in first hour of therapy are labeled as fluid refractory shock and should be given inotropic support. Such patients require invasive monitoring and also one should consider intubation and mechanical ventilation.

Use of Vasoactive Drug

Vasopressor Therapy

Dopamine is accepted as the first line inotrope of choice for shock in both children and newborn (Table 26.7). Dopamine increases cardiac output with dosages of 5–10 μg/kg/min. Vasoconstrictor effect of dopamine is evident at doses >15 μg/kg/min due to release of nor-epinephrine from sympathetic vesicles which may not be well developed in young infants (<6 months). Earlier belief of low dose dopamine (2–5 μg/kg/min) increasing the renal blood flow is no longer accepted. Dopamine refractory shock responds to norepinephrine or high does of epinephrine. Some may prefer to use low dose nor-epinephrine as the first line agent for warm hyperdynamic shock. Use of vasopressors can be titrated with perfusion pressure (MAP-CVP) or the systemic vascular resistance that ensures optimum urine output and creatinine clearance.

Table 26.7: Vasopressor drugs

Drug	*Dose Range (μg/kg/min)*	*Receptor Activity*	*Use*	*Risk*
Dopamine	5–20	$D_1/D_2 > \beta > \alpha$	Early inotropy needs, septic shock	Peripheral vasoconstriction
Epinephrine	0.01–2*	$\beta_1 = \beta_2 > \alpha$	Anaphylaxis, cardiogenic shock	Ischemia, hypertension
Norepine-phrine	0.05–1	$\alpha > \beta_1$	Severe vasodilatation, hypotension	Acidosis from poor perfusion, ischemic injury

* Vasocontrictive dose is > 0.2 μg/kg/min

Inotropic Therapy

After initial fluid resuscitation, myocardial contractility should be augmented to improve the cardiac output to meet the metabolic demand and catecholamines are the most useful drugs for this effect (Table 26.8). Dobutamine and mid dose dopamine are used as first line ionotropic agents in adults but children may be less responsive. Epinephrine infusion usually acts in cases of dopamine or dobutamine refractory shock. Low dose epinephrine may be used as first line choice for cold hypo dynamic shock, i.e. low cardiac output states.

In children remaining normotensive with low output state and high vascular resistance despite epinephrine and vasodilator, use of type III Phosphodiesterase inhibitors should be considered. These agents increase cyclic AMP and potentate the β receptor stimulating effect on cardiac vascular tissue. These drugs should be discontinued at the first sign of tachyarrhythmia, hypotension or diminished systemic vascular resistance due to long half life of the drugs. Hypotension can be overcome by stopping epinephrine and starting norepinephrine by stimulating α receptor activity.

Vasodilator Therapy

Vasodilators are of use in pediatric patients remaining in hypodynamic with high systemic vascular resistance shock despite fluid and ionotropic support (Table 26.9).

Figure 26.5 outlines the plan of management of a child with septic shock.

Acid Base Normalization

Sodium bicarbonate infusion/therapy rarely maintains the arterial pH without optimizing perfusion and ventilation. So, it should be considered as a temporary and immediate therapy to improve the myocardial function, only when the pH is less than 7. Improved circulation and oxygenation improves the acid-base homeostasis.

Other Metabolic Corrections

Hypoglycemia and hypocalcemia should be rapidly diagnosed and corrected along with attempt to prevent recurrence.

Other Medications

Antibiotic Administration

For a successful outcome, it is important that appropriate antibiotics are administered at the earliest in adequate doses to a child in septic shock. The choice of antibiotics depends on the focus of infection and the most likely pathogen that may be responsible. If there is no focus of infection on clinical evaluation, the child must be administered broad spectrum antibiotics to cover both gram negative and gram positive bacterial infections (e.g. 3rd generation cephalosporin with vancomycin).

Table 26.8: Inotropic drugs

Drug	*Dosing Range (μg/kg/min)*	*Receptors*	*Use*	*Risk*
Dopamine	5–20	$D_1/D_2 > \beta > \alpha$	Early inotropy needs, septic shock	Peripheral vasoconstriction
Dobutamine	3–20	$\beta_1 > \beta_2 > \alpha$	Contractility	Tachycardia, vasodilation
Epinephrine	0.01–2	$\beta_1 = \beta_2 > \alpha$	Contractility, vasoconstriction (higher doses)	Tachycardia, vasoconstriction
Milrinone	0.3–0.7	Phosphodiesterase inhibitor	Inotropy, vasodilation	Tachycardia, vasodilation
Amrinone	5–10	Phosphodiesterase inhibitor	Inotropy, vasodilation	Tachycardia, vasodilation

Table 26.9: Vasodilator agents

Drug	*Dosing range (μg/kg/min)*	*Site of action*	*Use*	*Risk*
Nitroprusside	0.3–7	Arteries > veins	Afterload reduction	Cyanide toxicity, hypotension
Nitroglycerin	0.5–5	Veins > arteries	Preload and afterload reduction	Hypotension

26

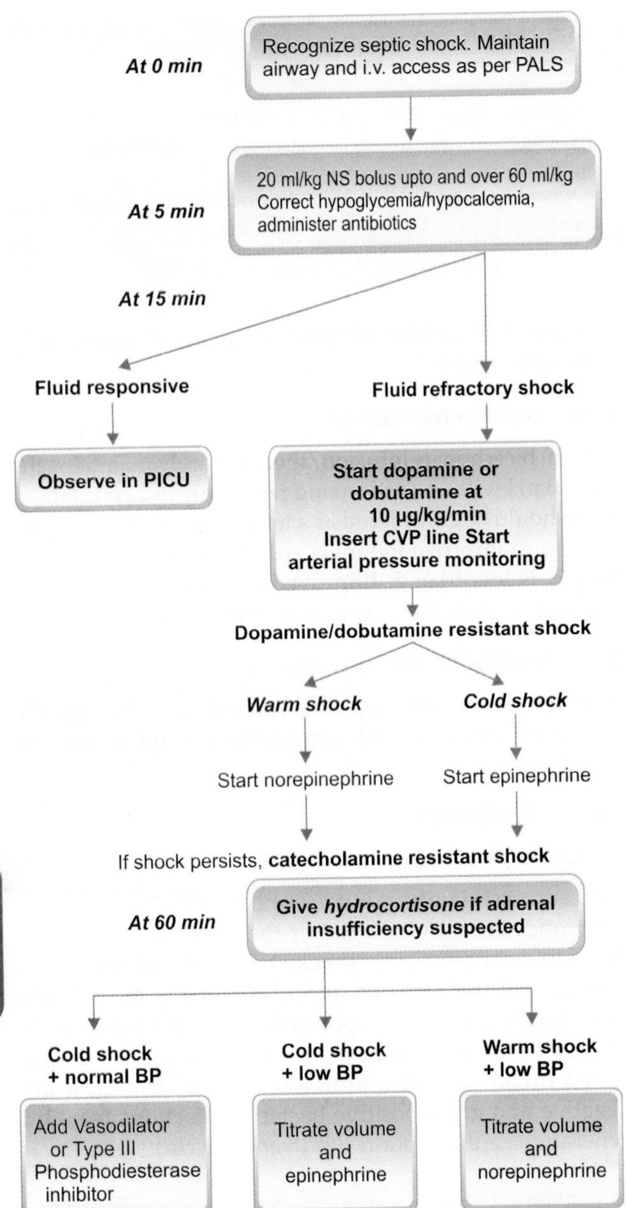

Fig. 26.5: Guidelines to manage septic shock

26

Clinical evaluation, the child must be administered broad.

Source Control

If the child has pus collections, e.g. abscesses, empyema thoracis, collection in soft tissues and intra-abdominal collections, the appropriate surgical drainage should be ensured.

Steroids

Steroids should be reserved for catecholamine refractory shock and suspected or proven adrenal insufficiency. Adrenal insufficiency and a low aldosterone may be more common in children with septic shock than previously thought. But there is lack of randomized controlled study to establish the benefits of steroid administration in septic shock children.

Immunotherapy

Trials are ongoing to target the inflammatory mediators responsible for the manifestation or pathogenesis of shock. These agents can be categorized into three major categories as agent aimed at blocking the effect of microbial products, agent blocking cytokine effects, agent reducing or preventing nitric oxide production. Although there was much optimism that these agents would reduce the morbidity and detrimental effects of inflammatory mediators, subsequent animal and human studies have revealed mixed results. In fact some of these studies have been associated with an increased mortality. Naloxone hydrochloride, an opioid antagonist, may block the endorphin effect that occurs in sepsis and may improve the hemodynamics in patients with septic shock. However, its routine usage is not recommended. Inhibition of nitric oxide release by methylene blue has been shown to improve the mean arterial pressure in adult patients with septic shock.

Activated Protein C (Drotrecogin Alfa)

Studies in adults have shown the beneficial effects in patients with severe sepsis when used as a 96 hours continuous infusion, but pediatric studies have shown the detrimental effects. At present, the use of activated protein C is not recommended in children.

ECMO Therapy

ECMO is a viable therapy for refractory shock in neonates. It is less successful in refractory pediatric shock with 30 to 50% survival.

Suggested reading

1. Dellinger RP, Lovy MM, Carlet JM, et al. Surviving Sepsis campaign: International guidelines for management of severe sepsis and septic shock 2008. Crit Care Med 2008;36:296–327.
2. Tabbutt S. Heart failure in pediatric septic shock: utilizing inotropic support. Crit Care Med. 2001; 29 (10 Suppl): S231–6.
3. Krismer AC, Wenzel V, Mayr VD, Voelckel WG, Strohmenger HU, Luries K, Lindner KH. Arginine vasopressin during cardiopulmonary resuscitation and vasodilatory shock: current experience and future perspectives. Curr Opin Crit Care. 2001;7:157–69.

MECHANICAL VENTILATION

Respiratory System Mechanics

The respiratory system includes the lungs, extra pulmonary airways, and the chest wall. The respiratory structures can be classified as either tube-like (e.g. upper airway, trachea, and bronchi) or bag like (e.g. alveoli, diaphragm, and abdominal wall). Tube-like structures are conduits for gases; their mechanics can be characterized by the relationship of the gas flow through the tube (F) and the pressure difference (P_2–P_1) that produces the flow. Bag-like inflatable structures contain gas; their mechanics are characterized by the relationship between the contained gas volume (V) and the pressure difference displacing the wall.

Lungs are a combination of both types of structures. To simplify the matters, lung can be viewed as a single compartment, consisting of a single, cylindrical flow-conducting tube (i.e. the conducting airways) connected to a single, spherical, elastic compartment (i.e. alveoli). The transrespiratory pressure (Ptr) necessary to achieve inflation has two components:

i. the transairway pressure (Pta) necessary to overcome the resistance to flow, and
ii. the transthoracic pressure (Ptt) which is the pressure required to deliver the tidal volume against the elastic recoil.

When a patient is ventilated, the Ptr is equal to the airway pressure (Paw)

$$Paw = Ptt + Pta$$

The change in Pta is proportional to the change in flow rate (F) and the constant of proportionality $\Delta P/\Delta F$ is resistance (R). The change in the lung volume is directly proportional to the corresponding change in the Ptt. The constant $\Delta V/\Delta P$ is called compliance (C), and its reciprocal elastance. If a system is highly compliant, it means that only a small change in pressure is required to achieve inflation; on the other hand if compliance is reduced, a larger change in pressure is required to produce the same change in volume. Therefore, the equation of motion of the respiratory system for inspiration is: $Paw = V/C + F R$. The equation of motion for expiration is: $V/C = -F R$, as during passive exhalation, the elastic component of the lungs (i.e. the elastic recoil) provide the necessary pressure to drive the flow.

Principles of Mechanical Ventilation

The maintenance of normal gas exchange depends on adequate oxygenation and ventilation. For easy understanding, the two can be separated and will be dealt with separately.

Oxygenation

This essentially depends on the fraction of O_2 (FiO_2) and the extent of ventilation-perfusion mismatch. Increasing the FiO_2 increases the alveolar PO_2 (P_AO_2) and thereby increases the P_aO_2.

$$P_AO_2 = PiO_2 - P_ACO_2$$
$$= FiO_2 (P_{atm} - P_{H_2O}) - P_aCO_2 / \text{Respiratory quotient.}$$

This equation shows that P_AO_2 can be increased by increasing the FiO_2. The other way, not commonly used, is to administer oxygen at higher pressures i.e. hyperbaric oxygen therapy.

Ventilation perfusion mismatch is usually due to atelectasis or poorly ventilated alveolar units (these act as R→ L shunt). These units can be recruited by increasing the mean airway pressure (MAP). This recruitment reduces the mismatch and also increases the end expiratory volume, thereby improving the compliance of the lung. The MAP is dependent on the peak inspiratory pressure (PIP), positive end expiratory pressure (PEEP), inspiratory time (Ti), expiratory time (Te), and the characteristics of the waveform (k).

$$MAP = k [(Ti \times PIP) + (Te \times PEEP)]/(Ti + Te)$$

From this equation, one can predict the effects of change in PIP, PEEP, Ti, etc. on the MAP.

Alveolar Ventilation

The P_aCO_2 depends on the CO_2 production and the alveolar ventilation. While the CO_2 production can be manipulated by dietary modifications and modification of the metabolic rates, the same cannot be done for effecting acute changes in P_aCO_2. So, for practical purposes the changes in the P_aCO_2 depend on alveolar ventilation.

Alveolar ventilation = [Tidal volume (V_T)–dead space volume (V_D)] × Respiratory frequency (f).

Therefore, the P_aCO_2 can be altered by regulating V_T and frequency. In a mechanically ventilated child, efforts should be made to minimize the dead space , e.g. ET tube should be cut short, ventilator circuit dead space should be minimized. Usually an increase in V_T would decrease P_aCO_2. However, this will depend on the dead space and changes in the metabolic rate.

At end of this discussion it is clear that to improve oxygenation, the following can be done: increase FiO_2, or PIP, or PEEP, or Ti. To reduce P_aCO_2, increase the V_T or the frequency (f). V_T in turn is dependent on the driving pressure i.e. PIP-PEEP, the resistance, compliance, and the Ti.

Indications for Mechanical Ventilation

1. Established or imminent respiratory failure resulting from:
   i. Pulmonary disease
   ii. Hypoventilation/apnea caused by central nervous system pathology
2. Defective ventilatory pump: neuromuscular diseases, chest wall trauma
3. Post resuscitation for circulatory arrest
4. To reduce the of work of breathing: in children with shock
5. Hyperventilation for reducing raised intracranial pressure
6. Prophylactic indications: during and after surgery.

Mechanical Ventilators

Mechanical ventilators are designed to assist or replace the work of the respiratory muscles and the thorax to maintain the gas exchange function of the lungs. There are many types of ventilators available. Chatburn developed a useful classification, which is easy to understand. This is based on the equation of motion:

Pressure= (Volume/compliance) + Flow × Resistance.

The main headings to describe a ventilator are:

a. Power input,
b. Power transmission,
c. Control scheme,
d. Output waveform, and
e. Alarms.

Modes of Mechanical Ventilation

A mechanical ventilator can allow/ deliver 4 different types of breaths: mandatory, assisted, supported, or spontaneous; or a combination of these.

Mandatory Ventilation/Controlled Ventilation

In controlled ventilation, all breaths are triggered, limited, and cycled by the ventilator. This mode is used when the patient's ventilatory drive is limited or absent or has been suppressed using drugs or when the patients has been therapeutically paralyzed.

Pressure control ventilation: In this mode, ventilators deliver a positive pressure up to a predetermined pressure limit above PEEP during the selected Ti and at a set frequency. The tidal volume delivered will depend on the mechanics of the respiratory system. This mode is preferred in newborns and young infants, where volume controlled ventilation has some problems.

26

Volume control ventilation: In this mode, a preset tidal volume is delivered during the set inspiratory time with a set frequency and constant inspiratory flow. This has certain advantages over the pressure control ventilation as fixed tidal volume and minute ventilation are maintained. However, in newborns and young infants, the tidal volume required is small. In this scenario, the losses in the ventilator circuit may significantly reduce the effective volume delivered to the lungs leading to ineffective ventilation.

Pressure regulated volume control ventilation: This mode combines the features of both volume and pressure control modes. This mode uses a decelerating inspiratory flow waveform to deliver a set tidal volume during the selected Ti and at set frequency. The advantage of this mode over volume control is that it ventilates at lower pressures, thereby reducing the barotrauma.

Assisted Ventilation

Assisted ventilation is identical to the controlled modes except that the patient's inspiratory effort triggers the ventilator to deliver the breath using preselected limit and cycle variables, i.e. the patient performs the triggering work, the ventilator completes the rest. Assisted ventilation aims at reducing patient effort and optimizing comfort. Modes of assisted ventilation can be used in large number of situations to work in synchrony with patient effort. This is because most ventilated patients continue to breathe on their own except if their CNS is highly damaged, if their $PaCO_2$ is maintained lower than the apnea threshold, or if they are deeply sedated or paralyzed. These modes are also used during weaning.

Assist control ventilation (ACV): ACV is a mode of mechanical ventilation where the ventilator provides a preset V_T or pressure in response to every patient-initiated breath. If the patient fails to initiate a breath within a preselected time period, the ventilator delivers the V_T or pressure at the predetermined frequency. Since every patient inspiratory effort that is detected by the machine results in a mechanical breath there is a risk of hyperventilation and respiratory alkalosis.

Synchronized intermittent mandatory ventilation (SIMV): In this mode, the mechanical breaths are delivered at a preset frequency; the machine tries to deliver these breaths in response to the patient's spontaneous inspiratory efforts. For example, we chose SIMV frequency of 20/min. this means that a breath is due every 3 seconds. If the machine detects patient's inspiratory effort during a small time window when the breath is due, it synchronizes the breath. If no such effort is detected during the time window, the machine delivers the breath on its own (this is similar to a controlled breath). In between the mandatory breaths, the patient can breathe spontaneously. Unlike ACV, there is no risk of hyperventilation even if patient is breathing rapidly because only the set SIMV frequency will be delivered. While this mode has conventionally been used as a weaning mode, this mode can be used as a starting mode.

Supported Ventilation

Supported ventilation is defined as breaths that are triggered by the patient, limited by the ventilator, and cycled by the patient.

Pressure support ventilation (PSV): In this mode, the patient triggers the ventilator to deliver a flow of gas sufficient to meet the patient's demands while the pressure in the circuit increases because of the closure of the expiratory valve. Inspiration is terminated when the inspiratory flow decreases to a percentage of its initial peak value. PSV decreases inspiratory work and abolishes diaphragmatic muscle fatigue. PSV can also compensate the inspiratory work because of the endotracheal tube impedence. PSV is of help in difficult to wean patients.

Assessment of the Child after Initiation of Mechanical Ventilation

Soon after the initiation of mechanical ventilation, clinical assessment should be performed by evaluation of chest movements/expansion, air entry, breath sounds, and the color of the skin. Pulse oximetry is useful adjunct. The patient ventilator interaction should be evaluated carefully and efforts should be made to improve synchronization. After a short time of stabilization, ABGs should be measured and necessary adjustments should be made.

Continuing Ventilatory Support and Weaning from Mechanical Ventilation

Most children need ventilatory support for a few days only; however, a small number require mechanical ventilation for prolonged periods. After starting mechanical ventilation, subsequent adjustments are made after evaluating the child's disease status, spontaneous effort, and ABGs. In case of worsening, the settings have to be increased (as discussed earlier). Usually one variable is modified at a time and then its effect seen on ABGs. However, if worsening is severe or or acute, multiple variables, e.g. FiO_2, rate, PEEP, etc. may have to be adjusted to achieve improvement in oxygenation and/or ventilation.

Weaning is basically the process of liberation from ventilator. As the child improves the need for ventilatory support decreases. A child's condition has to be carefully followed so that our support keeps pace with the child; decreasing support earlier than indicated imposes greater work of breathing while delaying this would delay extubation.

Suggested reading

1. Lodha R, Kapoor V, Kabra SK, Mechanical ventilation. In: Kabra SK, Lodha R, eds. Essentials of Pediatric Pulmonology. Nobel Vision 2006;233–257.
2. Heulitt MT, Wolf GK, Arnold JH. Mechanical ventilation. In Nichols DG (ed). Roger's Textbook of Pediatric Intensive Care. Baltimore. Lipincott Williams and Wilkins. 2008;508–31.

NUTRITION IN CRITICALLY ILL CHILDREN

A critically ill child is particularly prone to develop malnutrition. Decreased intake, accelerated demands brought by severe illness, and increased needs associated with growth contribute to malnutrition. In sick children, reduced nutrition intake can have deleterious effects. As children have less energy and substrate reserves, they are more dependent on substrate supply than adults. Malnutrition in hospitalized patient is increasingly being recognized as an important factor determining outcome of the disease. Children with any grade of malnutrition are at increased risk of mortality with acute severe illness. There is growing evidence that early and appropriate goal oriented nutritional support in the ill child aids recovery.

Stress results in increase in resting energy expenditure, proteolysis, gluconeogenesis, urinary nitrogen loss, glucose intolerance and resistance to insulin. Provision of glucose alone does not suppress 'auto-cannibalism'. It is essential to provide adequate nutrition early in course of severe illness in order to improve the outcomes.

Two routes are available for administration of nutrients: enteral and parenteral. Enteral route is the preferred one, provided the intestines are functioning. It is safer and more cost effective than total parenteral nutrition (TPN). Enteral nutrition helps in maintaining the gut barrier and prevents the ulcerative complications. It also preserves the indigenous flora and prevents the overgrowth of the pathogens there by reducing the risk of bactermia and pneumonia. The enteral feeding prevents the gut mucosal atrophy so that the early resumption of full oral feeds is easier during recovery period.

Elemental and non-elemental diets are available. Simplest kind of feed is a milk based feed. Various commercial formulas are available. The elemental formulae contain carbohydrates as oligosaccharides, maltodextrins or hydrolyzed cornstarch; nitrogen as peptides or free amino acid and lipids as various oils or medium-chain triglycerides. In addition, special formulae are also available, e.g., low lactose or lactose free diets. Start with 10–15 ml/kg/d of feeds and increase by 10–15 ml/kg/d till target categories are achieved. Enteral feeds may be delivered directly into the stomach by nasal/oral routes. Small-bowel feedings are useful in cases of gastroparesis. Supplementation of vitamins and minerals is best done with enteral route.

The disadvantage of enteral route is, most patients with sepsis may have the septic ileus, which would take 3–7 days to resolve precluding the early administration of enteral route. The other common clinical conditions where the enteral feeding is contraindicated are severe GI hemorrhage, recent GI surgery, intestinal obstruction. The complications of enteral feeding are intolerance, misplacement of the feeding tube, esophagitis and esophageal ulceration. There can be reflux which may lead to pulmonary aspiration. Diarrhea may occur because of hyperosmolar formulae, infection, or malabsorption. Rarely there can be nutritional recovery syndrome in a child who is severely malnourished and is given high caloric and protein diet.

Parenteral nutrition refers to the delivery of all the nutrients directly into the blood stream: amino acid mixtures, lipids, glucose, and trace mineral and vitamins. These may be infused into a peripheral or central vein. The use of peripheral veins is limited by the osmolality of infusate (should be < 700 mOsm/l). Thus, for delivery of adequate calories, central venous access is essential.

The goal for calories is age dependent. For infants, the need is about 100 cal/kg. Glucose infusions are started at about 5–6 mg/kg/minute and increased gradually; insulin may be used if there is hyperglycemia. Amino acids are begun at 1g/kg/d; then increased over 2–3 days to 2.5 g/kg/d. Lipids are infused at 0.5 g/kg on day 1 and increased to 2–2.5 g/kg/d over 4–5 days. Appropriate combination can be achieved by considering fluid requirements. Trace elements and vitamin preparations are added.

Use of TPN requires regular monitoring blood glucose thrice a day; serum electrolytes and urea twice a week; and serum chemistry, triglycerides, and complete blood counts once a week. Weight is recorded daily, other anthropometric measurements recorded once a week.

The complications include catheter related infections, liver dysfunction, hyperglycemia, hyperlipidemia, acidosis, and electrolyte imbalances.

Once parenteral nutrition is started, enteral feeds are added as soon as gut function improves.

Immunonutrition

The use of enteral formulae supplemented with immunonutrients has been demonstrated to modulate gut function, inflammatory and immune responses. In critical illness, it is desirable to have reinforcement of mucosal barrier and cellular defense and some down-regulation of local or systemic inflammatory response. This may be achieved by use of immunonutrients: glutamine, arginine, w-3 fatty acids, nucleotides, taurine, cysteine, certain complex carbohydrates and probiotic bacteria. Use of immunonutrition has been shown to reduce morbidity and the risk of infectious complications in critically ill patients.

Suggested reading

1. Biolo G, Grimble G, Preiser JC, et al. Metabolic basis of nutrition in intensive care unit patients. Intensive Care Med 2002; 28: 1512– 20.
2. de Carvalho WB Leite HP. Nutritional Support in the critically ill child. In Nichols DG (ed). Roger's Textbook Pediatric Intensive Care. Baltimore. Lippincott Williams and Wilkins. 2008;1500–15.
3. Briassoulis G, Zavras N, Hatzis T. Malnutrition, nutritional indices, and early enteral feeding in critically ill children. Nutrition. 2001; 17: 548–57.

SEDATION, ANALGESIA, PARALYSIS

The management of acute pain and anxiety in children undergoing therapeutic and diagnostic procedures outside the operating theater has improved substantially. The goal of sedation is safe and effective control of pain, anxiety, and motion so as to allow a necessary procedure to be performed and to provide appropriate amnesia or decreased awareness. The need for sedation and analgesia is significantly higher in intensive care units.

The state of sedation varies from conscious sedation to deep sedation to general anesthesia. In *conscious sedation,* the consciousness is depressed but the protective airway reflexes are maintained and the child can respond appropriately to verbal command or physical stimulation. *Deep sedation* refers to a medically controlled state of depressed consciousness from which the child is not easily aroused. This is accompanied by partial or complete loss of protective reflexes and the child cannot respond purposefully to physical stimulation or verbal commands. For safe sedation, it is essential to have skilled personnel capable of rapidly identifying and treating cardiorespiratory complications. The child should be carefully assessed before sedation. This includes evaluation of underlying medical problems, medication use, allergies and time and nature of last oral intake.

Monitoring is very important during sedation. The child's face, mouth and movement of chest wall must be continuously observed. The vital regions should be measured before, after the administration of the drugs, on completion of the procedure, during recovery and at completion of recovery. ECG monitoring and pulse oximetry are useful adjuncts. The sedation and procedure room should have all the equipment for airway management and the essential drugs for resuscitation.

Table 26.10 summarizes the details of commonly used drugs for sedation and analgesia. Table 26.11 lists various clinical scenarios requiring sedation/analgesia. For children undergoing mechanical ventilation, continuous infusion of midazolam/diazepam may be used for better control of ventilation. In addition, intermittent doses or continuous infusion of fentanyl or morphine may be used for pain control.

Neuromuscular Blocking Drugs

The use of neuromuscular blocking drugs (NMBD) drugs is common in intensive care units. Various drugs are now available to allow the clinician to tailor a regimen to child's specific needs. Succinyl choline is the only depolarizing muscle relaxant available. The non-depolarizing drugs include pancuronium, atracurium, vecuronium, rocuronium.

The possible indications for use of neuromuscular blocking drugs in intensive care units are as follows:

Short Term

i. Facilitation of airway instrumentation
ii. Facilitation of invasive procedures

Long Term

i. Facilitation of mechanical ventilation, to overcome patient-ventilation dyssynchrony, and to facilitate ventilation at high settings.
ii. Reduction of work of breathing/metabolic demand.
iii. Treatment of agitation unresponsive to maximum sedation and analgesia
iv. Treatment of tetanus
v. Facilitation of treatment of status epilepticus under continuous EEG monitoring.

Limiting asynchronous patient-ventilator interactions has been one of the major indications of use of NMBDs in intensive care units. However, improved ventilator techniques and development of ventilators that can synchronize with child's own inspiratory efforts have reduced the use of NMBDs.

Table 26.12 shows the characteristics and doses of various neuromuscular blocking drugs.

Children receiving neuromuscular blocking drugs should be monitored very carefully. Particular attention should be paid towards position of artificial airway and

Table 26.10: Commonly used drugs for sedation and analgesia

Drug	*Clinical effects*	*Dose*	*Onset of action*	*Duration of action*
1. Chloral hydrate	Sedation, motion control, anxiolysis, No analgesia	25–100 mg/kg body weight P.O.	15–30 min	60–120 min
2. Triclofos	Sedation, motion control, no analgesia	20–100 mg/kg P.O.	30–45 min	4–6 hours
3. Midazolam	Sedation, motion control, anxiolysis. No analgesia	I.V. 0.05–0.1 mg/kg – adjusted to 0.4–0.6 mg/kg Infusion: 0.5–3.0 μg/kg/min	2–3 min	45–60 min
4. Diazepam	Sedation, motion control, anxiolysis. No analgesia	I.V. 0.2–0.3 mg/kg Infusion: 0.1–0.5 mg/kg/hr	2–5 min	60–120 min
5. Propofol	Sedation, motion control. No analgesia.	I.V. 0.5–1 mg/kg; then 0.1–0.5 mg/kg every 3–10 min. Infusion: 5–10 μg/kg/min	1 min	10 min
Analgesic agents				
1. Morphine	Analgesia, sedation	0.1 mg/kg i.v.	2–3 min	30–60 min
2. Fentanyl	Analgesia	1 μg/kg/dose, may be repeated every 3 min Infusion: 1–5 μg/kg/hr		
3. Ketamine	Analgesia, dissociation, amnesia, motion control	I.V. 1–1.5 mg/kg over 1–2 min	1 min	15–60 min
		I.M. 3–5 mg/kg	3–5 min	15–150 min

Table 26.11: Various clinical scenarios for sedation and analgesia

Clinical Scenarios	*Examples*	*Sedation strategy*
Non-invasive procedure	CT Echocardiography EEG MRI Ultrasonography	Comforting alone in older children Chloral hydrate P.O. Triclofos P.O. Midazolam I.V.
Procedures associated with low level of pain and high anxiety	Intravenous cannulations Phlebotomy Lumbar puncture Flexible bronchoscopy	Comforting and local anesthesia
Procedures associated with high level of pair and high anxiety	Central catheter placement Bone marrow aspiration Endoscopy, Abscess-incision and drainage Interventional radiology Procedures Intercostal drainage Paracentesis.	Midazolam and fentanyl/morphine I.V. Ketamine I.V. or I.M.

Table 26.12: Neuromuscular blocking drugs

Drug	*Initial Drug Dose (mg/kg)*	*Onset of action (min)*	*Duration (min)*	*Infusion rate (μg/kg/min)*
Parcuronium	IN 0.1 CH 0.15	2–5	20–25	IN 0.4–0.6 CH 0.5–1.0
Atracurium	IN 0.3 CH 0.5	1–3	20–25	IN 10–20 CH 10–20
Vecuronium	IN 0.1 CH 0.15	1–3	20–25	IN 1–15 CH 15–25
Recuronium	IN 0.5 CH 0.8	1–3	20–25	—
Succinylcholine	IN 3 CH 2	0.5–1	4–5	—

IN infant, CH child

adequate ventilation. Sedation should always be given to any child who is requiring paralysis.

The use of these drugs is associated with some complications. Prolonged usage of NMBDs can cause muscle atrophy and joint contractures. This can be reduced by passive movements and splinting of joints in functional position. Pressure sores and skin ulcers are likely to develop because of immobilization and impaired skin perfusion. Absence of eye blink may lead to corneal drying and abrasions. This can be avoided by use of lubricating ointment and artificial tears and gentle closing of the eyelid. If a child is receiving NMBDs, he/she should simultaneously receive a sedative and analgesic for overcoming anxiety no pain. Some children experience prolonged muscle weakness after discontinuation of NMBD. Use of succinyl chloride may lead to vagal-mediated bradycardia, sinus arrest or functional rhythms; larger doses may lead to tachycardia, ventricular arrhythmias and hypertension.

Suggested reading

1. Krauss B, Steven SM. Sedation and analgesia for procedures in children N Engl J Med 2000; 342: 938–45.
2. Young C, Knudsen N, Hilton A, Reves JG. Sedation in intensive care unit. Crit Care Med 2000; 28: 854–66.
3. Martin LD, Bratton SL, O'Rourke PP. Clinical uses and controversies of neuromuscular blocking agents in infants and children. Crit Care Med 1999; 27: 1358–68.
4. Nair MNG, Jatane SK. Sedation Analgesia in Pediatric Intensive Care. Indian J Pediatr 2004;71;145–49.

NOSOCOMIAL INFECTIONS IN PICU

Nosocomial or hospital acquired infections are all infections that occur during a patient's hospitalization and not present or incubating at admission. Also any infection that appears to have been acquired in hospital but does not manifest until after discharge is judged to be a nosocomial infection. Therefore, all infections diagnosed 48 hours after admission till 72 hours after discharge should be considered as nosocomial.

Nosocomial infections are a significant problem in pediatric intensive care units. The infections in pediatric intensive care units (PICU) are more widespread than in general pediatric wards. The increased risk of infection probably results both from the greater severity of the underlying disease and from the frequent interventions and use of devices that bypass natural barriers to infection.

The estimated rate of infection is 10–20 nosocomial infections per 1000 patient days for pediatric ICUs. The overall nosocomial infection rates in the PICUs are reported to be 6–10%. These rates are lower than those seen in adult intensive care units. The primary bloodstream infections are the commonest nosocomial infections (25–30%) in PICUs followed by the lower respiratory tract infections (20–25%) and urinary tract infection (UTI) (15–20%). In adults, UTI is the commonest nosocomial infection followed by surgical infection and lower respiratory tract infections. Staphylococcous aureus, coagulase negative staphaylococci, *E.coli*, *Pseudomonas aeruginosa*, *Klebseilla*, *enterococci* and Candida are the significant pathogens in pediatric services in the various sites examined.

The risk of nosocomial infections in a PICU is the direct consequence of the severity of illness, the level of invasive monitoring, the indiscriminate use of anti-microbial and the nature of diagnostic procedures. The duration of stay in an ICU is an important determinant of nosocomial infection. The use of invasive devices (endotracheal tubes, intravascular catheters, urinary catheters) has an important role in development of nosocomial infections. It is observed that about 90% of all bloodstream infections occurred in children with central venous lines, 95% of nosocomial pneumonias occurred in those on mechanical ventilation and 75% of UTIs in children with urinary catheters. These figures highlight the important role of various devices in nosocomial infections.

Nosocomial infections may be caused by organisms that originate from exogenous sources in hospital or from endogenous sources such as child's own flora. Because of alteration of child's flora associated with the illness and hospitalization, such distinction may not be easy. The altered flora mainly included gram-negative bacilli and Staphylococcus aureus, which were often antibiotic resistant.

The hospital environment may contribute to acquisition and spread of most endemic nosocomial infections. Even if environmental surfaces are contaminated with microbes, they can be spread to patients by hand contact only. Occasionally, environment may be responsible for life threatening nosocomial infections such as aspergillus in immunocompromised individuals.

It is estimated that the overall mortality attributed to nosocomial infections is about 10%. The mortality is associated with nosocomial infections is multifactorial; some of these factors are the type of patient, the number of altered organs, and the microbes responsible for the infection. Blood stream infections caused by Klebsiella pneumoniae or the fungi have mortality range of 18–20%. The nosocomial infections increase the duration of stay in hospital and also the cost of therapy.

Strategies to Reduce the Incidence of Nosocomial Infections

For reducing the incidence of nosocomial infection, each PICU should have an infection control program. There should be a written description of the goals, objectives, and structure of program. A team of health professionals should ensure implementation of the policies and compliance on the part of the PICU team. Well-directed infection control activities can reduce the nosocomial infection rates by up to 50%.

The importance of **hand washing** and hand disinfection is well understood. The appropriate hand washing technique includes wetting the hands, taking soap, rubbing hands to produce a lather, and performing wash movements that include rubbing palm to palm, right palm over left dorsum and vice versa, palm to palm with fingers interlaced, backs of fingers to opposing palm with fingers interlocked, rotational rubbing of right thumb clasped in left palm and vice versa, rotational rubbing with clasped fingers of right hand in palm of left hand and with changed roles (Fig. 26.6). The whole procedure should not take less

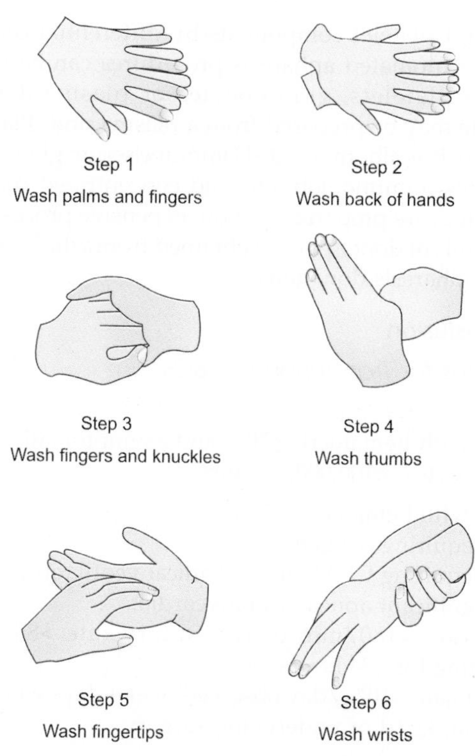
Step 1
Wash palms and fingers
Step 2
Wash back of hands
Step 3
Wash fingers and knuckles
Step 4
Wash thumbs
Step 5
Wash fingertips
Step 6
Wash wrists

Fig. 26.6: Six steps of hand washing

than 30 seconds. After washing, hands should be dried with disposable paper or cloth towel. It has been noticed that health personnel practice hand washing in only 25–50% of the opportunities. In order to improve compliance, various hygienic hand rubs can be used. Rubbing of 3–5 ml of a fast acting antiseptic preparation on to both hands can be an effective substitute to hand washing. The various preparations available include n-propanol, isopropanol, ethanol, and chlorhexidine diacetate.

In addition to the specific measures mentioned earlier for prevention of specific nosocomial infections, proper **sterilization/disinfection** of various medical items is mandatory. Aseptic precautions should be followed strictly whenever any invasive procedure is being carried out.

A well-nourished child is less likely to acquire nosocomial infection than a malnourished one. Enteral nutrition appears to be better than parenteral nutrition. Enteral nutrition may have a favorable impact on gastrointestinal immunologic function and infectious morbidity. There has been considerable interest in the role of immune-enhancing enteral diets (containing glutamine, arginine, mRNA, omega-3 fatty acids from fish oil) in reduction of nosocomial infections and mortality in ICUs.

Appropriate and rational prescription of antibiotics is essential to prevent emergence of resistant strains. There should be constant surveillance and periodic review of the antibiotic policies and prescriptions. With careful microbiologi monitoring, cycling of antibiotics for empiric therapy can help in reducing the emergence of drug resistance.

Adequate and well-trained staff—both nursing staff and physicians—are essential for infection control. Education of the staff about various infection control practices and procedure-specific guidelines has an important role in the reduction of incidence of nosocomial infections. The education program should be on a continuing basis with periodic evaluation of the knowledge and practices.

Surveillance of nosocomial infections is an essential element of any infection control program. The most important goal of surveillance is to reduce the risk of acquiring nosocomial infections. This provides data useful for identifying infected patients, determining the site of infections and identifying the factors that contribute to nosocomial infections. Control measures can be evaluated objectively if the surveillance is good.

Specific Preventive Measures

Prevention of Nosocomial Pneumonias

The colonization of upper airways by pathogenic microbes and thereby, the risk of nosocomial pneumonia can be reduced by several measures. Effective hand washing by the health care personnel can reduce the risk of nosocomial pneumonias. Various chemicals such as chlorhexidine or rubs containing alcohol may be used. The reduction in the number of microorganisms on hands is related to the volume and number of times they are used. In addition, the hospital workers should comply with hospital infection control policies.

The gastrointestinal tract is an important source for endogenous upper airway colonization. Use of antacids and H_2 blockers raise gastric pH and facilitate gastric microbial colonization. When indicated, instead of H_2 blockers and antacids, sucralfate may be used for prophylaxis against gastric bleeding as the gastric pH remains low with its use. The use of selective decontamination of the gut using antimicrobial such as tobramycin, gentamycin, polymyxin and nystatin is controversial and is not recommended.

Contaminated respiratory therapy equipments have been implicated in nosocomial pneumonias. Resuscitation bags, ventilator tubings, nebulizers should be disinfected. Only sterile fluids should be nebulized or used in humidifiers. Personnel taking care of intubated children should wash their hands before and after delivering care. The ventilator circuit tubings should be changed no more often than every 48 hours. Care should be taken to prevent contamination during suctioning; endotracheal suctioning should be performed as needed to remove secretions. Positioning of patients with head end elevation does reduce the risk of aspiration and nosocomial pneumonia.

Prevention of Bloodstream Infections

The major factors associated with development of catheter-related nosocomial infections are: (i) the sterility of the

26

technique of insertion and maintenance of the catheter throughout its life, (ii) type of solution being administered through the intravenous line, (iii) number of "break ins" into the catheters system and intravenous tubing, (iv) the presence of infection elsewhere in the body. The following measures may help in reducing catheter-related infections:

- Selection of subclavian, basilic or cephalic vein site rather then femoral or internal jugular vein.
- Using maximal aseptic technique for catheter "insertion"
- Mupirocin ointment may reduce the risk of bacterial colonization of catheters but may increase colonization rate of fungi.
- Using cotton gauze rather than transparent dressing.
- Having an experienced physician insert the catheter.
- Avoid use of TPN catheters for other than infusion of TPN.
- Have adequate staff for management of patients with central venous catheters.

Prevention of Nosocomial Urinary Tract Infections

The catheterizations should be kept to a minimum. The need for catheterization must be strictly evaluated and catheterization must be replaced by closed condom drainage whenever possible. When thought to have fulfilled their need the catheters must be immediately removed. Strict asepsis should be maintained during insertion of the catheter using sterile gloves, drapes, and local antiseptics.

Closed drainage must be strictly maintained and this has been shown to bring down the rates of infection. The closed drainage must be maintained with the collection tubing and bag below the level of the patient's bladder and the tubing must always be above the level of the bag. When in place the closed drainage system must be handled and manipulated as infrequently as possible. Antibiotic prophylaxis does reduce the frequency of infections but is not universally recommended as it selects multidrug resistant strains when the infection occurs.

Suggested reading

1. Lodha R, Natchu UCM, Nanda M, Kabra SK. Nosocomial infections in pediatric intensive care units. Indian J Pediatr 2001;68:1063–1070.
2. Banerjee SN, Grohskopf LA, Sinlowitz-Cochran RL, Jarvis WR, National Nosocomial infections Surveillance Systems; Pediatric Prevention Network. Incidence of Pediatric and neonatal intensive care unit-acquired infections. Infect Control Hosp Epidemiol 2006;27;561–70.

BLOOD TRANSFUSIONS

Blood component transfusion is an integral part of the treatment plan of many children and adolescents cared for in an ICU. Blood products are prepared from collected whole blood or apharesis donation. Donated whole blood units are separated as required into red blood cells (RBC), plasma and platelet components by differential centrifugation. Automated apharesis procedures can be used to collect platelets, granulocytes or plasma. Cryoprecipitate may be prepared from a plasma unit. Plasma proteins such as albumin, anti-D immune serum globulins, intravenous immunoglobulins and concentrated coagulation factors are prepared by more expensive processing of large polls of donor plasma obtained from whole blood or plasmapharesis donations.

RBC Transfusion

Indications for Transfusion of RBCs

Small volume transfusion

1. Infant with hematocrit ≤20% and asymptomatic with reticulocytes <100,000/cu mm.
2. Infant with hematocrit ≤30%
   requiring oxygen <35%;
   requiring CPAP or mechanical ventilation;
   and significant apnea or bradycardia;
   heart rate >180/min or respiratory rate >80/min persisting for >24 hours; or
   weight gain <102g/day observed over 4 days while on ≥100 cal/kg/d or undergoing surgery.
3. Infant with hematocrit ≤35%
   if receiving oxygen >35% or
   getting mechanical ventilation.

Transfusion in children

1. Hb 4 g/dL or less (Hematocrit 12%) irrespective of the clinical condition group
2. Hb 4–6 g/dL (Hematocrit 13–18%) with
   Features of hypoxia, acidosis causing dyspnea or impaired consciousness
3. Hyperparasitemia in malaria (>20%)
4. Features of cardiac decompensation.

Transfusion for acute blood loss

If patient is not stabilized after 2 boluses of 20 mL/kg of isotonic crystalloid and the suspected blood loss is >30%.

Transfusion for chronic anemia

Children with chronic anemia usually tolerate Hb levels as low as 4 g/dl and the underlying cause of anemia should be detected for better therapy as only transfusion is not the definitive therapy. So the patient should be investigated and monitored for any evidence of abnormal physical signs of cardiovascular decompensation, which indicates transfusion. Along with transfusion the definitive therapy should also be given to improve the outcome and reduce the need of further transfusion.

Choice of Blood Group

For RBC transfusion, the choices are based on the principle that the recipient plasma must not contain antibodies corresponding to donor A and /or B antigens. For plasma and platelet transfusion, donor plasma must not contain

A /B antibodies corresponding to recipient A/B antigens. Patients who are RhD antigen positive may receive RhD positive or negative RBCs but patients who are RhD negative should receive only RhD negative RBCs. Ideally the same blood group RBC which is compatible with the recipient plasma should be transfused. The acceptable choices of ABO blood groups for RBC, plasma and platelet transfusions are shown in the following Table 26.13.

Table 26.13: Possible choices of ABO blood groups for RBCs, plasma and platelet transfusions

Recipient blood group	*Acceptable ABO group of blood component to be transfused*		
	RBCs	*Plasma*	*Platelets*
O	O	O A,B,AB	O A,B,AB
A	A, O	A, AB	A, AB
B	B, O	B, AB	B, AB
AB	AB, A, B, O	AB	AB

Quantity of Transfusion

The quantity of blood administered depends on the hematocrit of RBC unit, pretransfusion Hb level and patient's weight. If the Hb level is ≥5 g/dl and CPDA-1 RBC is used (Hematocrit 0.7–0.75), a transfusion of 10 ml/kg usually raises Hb level by 2.5 g/dl. If anemia has developed slowly and Hb level is <5 g/dl, RBC transfusion should be given slowly or in small quantities to avoid precipitating cardiac failure from circulatory overload.

Platelets

Platelet concentrates are usually prepared from whole blood donation but it may be collected by apharesis technique. The usual platelet bags contains 5.5×10^{10} platelets/unit, about 50 ml plasma, trace to 0.5 ml of RBCs and varying number of leukocytes upto 10^8/unit. Apharesis platelet units contain 3×10^{11} platelets, approximately 250–300 ml plasma, trace to 5 ml of RBCs and 10^6–10^9 leukocytes. It can be stored upto 5 days at 20–24°C.

Indications for platelet transfusion are:

i. Platelet count <10 × 10^9/L
ii. Platelet count <20 × 10^9/L and bone marrow infiltration, severe mucositis, DIC, anticoagulation therapy
iii. Platelet count <30–40 x 10^9/L and DIC
iv. Platelet count <50–60 x 10^9/L and major surgical intervention.

Plasma

Plasma is prepared from a whole blood donation by centrifugation and it can be collected using automated apharesis techniques. A unit of plasma contains 150–250 mL when prepared from whole blood donations. Immediately following collection from a normal donor, plasma contains approximately 1 unit/ml of each of coagulation factors. Coagulation factors V and VIII are labile and are not stable in plasma stored at 1–6°C. Plasma frozen within 8 hours of donation contains at least 0.7 u/ml of factor VIII and is called fresh frozen plasma (FFP). Plasma after 24 hours of donation contains <15% of factor V and VIII. FFP may be stored for 12 months at temperature –18°C or colder.

Use of FFP is limited exclusively to the treatment or prevention of clinically significant bleeding due to deficiency of one or more plasma coagulation factors and such situations can be:

- Use of vitamin K antagonist
- Severe liver disease
- Disseminated intravascular coagulation (DIC)
- Massive/large volume transfusion
- Isolated congenital coagulation factor deficiency.

Dosage and Administration

Compatibility tests before plasma transfusion are not necessary and plasma should be ABO compatible with recipients RBCs. Usually RhD group need not be considered unless in cases where large volume of FFP is needed. FFP may be thawn in a water bath at 30–70° C or in a microwave designed for this purpose. Dose of FFP depends on the clinical situation and the underlying disease. If used at a dose 10–20 ml/kg, it increases the level at coagulation factors by 20% immediately after infusion.

Cryoprecipitate

Cryoprecipitate is the precipitate formed when FFP is thawed at 4°C. It is then refrozen within 1 hour in 10–15 ml of the donor plasma and stored at –18°C or less for a period up to one year. This unit contains 80–100 units of factor VIII, 100–250 mg of fibrinogen, 40–60 mg of fibronectins, 40–70% of vWF and 30% of factor XIII.

Indication

Hemophilia and Von willebrand disease, congenital deficiencies of fibrinogen or factor XIII.

Dosage

Compatibility testing of cryoprecipitate units is not necessary but ABO compatible units should be used. Rh group need not be considered. 1 unit/5–10 kg of recipient weight as rapidly as the patients clinical condition permits and the duration should not exceed 4 hours.

Risks of Transfusion

Before prescribing blood/blood products for a patient, it is always essential to weigh up the risks of transfusion against the risks of not transfusion.

Red Cell and Plasma Transfusion

1. Risk of serious hemolytic transfusion reaction
2. Transmission of infections agents including HIV, HBV, HCV, Syphilis, Malaria, CMV.
3. Any blood product can be contaminated with bacteria due to inappropriate method of collection/storage.

Transfusion reactions: Table 26.14 summarises various adverse effects of transfusion of blood or blood products.

Time Limit for Infusion

There is a risk of bacterial proliferation or loss of function in blood products once they have been removed from the correct storage conditions.

Whole Blood/RBCs

Transfusion should be started within 30 min of removing the pack from storage temperature (+2°C to +6°C). It should complete within 4 hours of starting infusion if the

Table 26.14: Adverse effects of use of blood and blood products

Category	*Signs*	*Symptoms*	*Cause*	*Treatment*
• Mild	Urticaria, rash	Pruritus	Hypersensitivity reaction	Slow the infusion-Antihistaminic (Chlorpheniramine maleate 0.1 mg/kg) If no improvement in 30 minutes treat as category 2
• Moderately severe	Flushing Urticaria Rigors Fever Restlessness Tachycardia	Anxiety Itching Palpitation Mild dyspnea Headache	Hypersensitivity reaction	Stop infusion and replace IV set Notify blood bank Sample from the bag and patient for repeat cross matching Antihistaminic Antipyretic Steroid(IV) and bronchodilator if needed Urine sample for hemolysis If improve restart infusion slowly If no improvement in 15 minutes treat as category 3
• Life threatening	Rigor Fever Restlessness Hypotension Tachycardia Hemoglobinuria (red urine) DIC(bleeding)	Anxiety Chest pain Pain at IV site Respiratory distress Backache Headache Dyspnea	Hemolysis Bacterial contamination Fluid overload Anaphylaxis Transfusion associated lung injury Septic shock	Stop infusion Change IV set Normal saline 20 ml/kg and repeat if needed Ionotropes if needed Elevate the legs O_2 and airway opening Adrenaline (1:1000) 0.01 mg/kg IV/SC Steroid(IV) and bronchodilator (if needed) Notify blood bank Sample from the bag and patient for repeat cross matching Urine sample for hemolysis If bleeding (DIC) give platelets, cryoprecipitates, FFP or factor concentrates If acute renal failure: Check fluid balance `Frusemide (1 mg/kg); Dialysis if needed If bacteremia –send blood c/s and antibiotics
Other delayed complications				
• Delayed hemolytic reaction (after 5–10 days)	Fever Anemia Jaundice			No treatment if hypotension—treat as acute intravascular hemolysis
• Post transfusion purpura (after 5–10 days)	Increase bleeding tendency Thrombocytopenia			High dose steroid, IVIG (intravenous immunoglobulins), plasma exchange
• Graft *vs* host disease (after 10–12 days)	Fever Rash and desquamation diarrhea, hepatitis pancytopenia			Supportive care
• Iron overload	Cardiac and liver failure in transfusion dependent patients			Iron chelating agents, desferioxamine (subcutaneous infusion), deferiprone (oral)

hospital temperature is between 22°C to 25°C. In case of high ambient temperature shorter out of refrigeration times should be used.

Platelets

As soon as they have been received and should be completed in about 20 min.

FFP

In adult FFP one unit 200–300 ml in 20 min (start within 30 min) and in children depending on the clinical condition.

These products should be infused through a new, sterile blood administration set containing an integral 170–200 μm filter and should be changed 12 hourly if multiple transfusions are needed.

For platelet transfusion a fresh set primed with saline should be used.

The child should be monitored frequently during infusion of blood or blood products.

Massive Transfusion

The replacement of blood loss equivalent to or greater than the patients total blood volume with stored blood in less than 24 hours (70 ml/kg) in adults and 80–90 ml/km children/infants).

The complications of massive transfusion are acidosis, hyperkalemia, citrate toxicity and hypocalcemia, depletion of fibrinogen and coagulation factors, depletion of platelets. DIC, hypothermia, reduced 2,3 DPG and microaggregates.

Suggested reading

1. Lacroix J, Luban NLC, Wong ECC. Blood Products in PICU. In. Nichols DG (Ed). Roger's Textbook of Pediatric Intensive care. Baltimore Lippincott William and Wilkins 2008;584–99.
2. Easley RB, Brady KM, Tobias JD. Hemotologic to Emergencies. In. Nichols DG (Ed). Roger's Textbook of Pediatric Intensive Care, Baltimore Lippincott William and Wilkins 2008;1725–58.

PREDICTORS OF MORTALITY AND SCORING SYSTEMS

Severity of illness assessment has been crucial from time long-for a wide range of pediatric, neonatal and intensive care users, including quality assessment, controlling for severity of illness in clinical studies and study of intensive care unit resource utilization and management.

The basic aim of intensive care is highest possible quality. Quality of care cannot be improved in the absence of objective predictors of outcome; the reason being that clinical effectiveness of critical care cannot be evaluated. Outcome of a patient in intensive care unit which can be assessed in terms of mortality, morbidity, functional health status and quality of life is possible only if baseline and data thereafter is comparable, which in the absence of appropriate case mix and objective assessment of severity of illness would seem irrelevant. In resource poor settings, based on initial progression and severity of illness, effort can be made to rationalize the admissions to intensive care unit. This helps channelising the resources for both patient care and resource management. Moreover once the clinical and laboratory parameters have been assigned specific values, it becomes easy to analyze the data for the purpose of cohort comparison and medical audit. To sum up, role of predictors of outcome in intensive care in today's scenario is to draw an association between a dependent and independent variable in the form of a mathematical equation for the purpose of comparative audit, evaluative research and clinical management.

Determining the Predictors of Outcome

Once admitted in to intensive care unit, the parameters which would decide the final outcome of the patient are: the illness, its severity, the care received in the intensive care unit and the complications of care thereafter. When it comes to determine as to which factors would seem applicable, the two parameters which come into the picture are physiological criteria and laboratory parameters at the time the patient is admitted to the intensive care unit.

Illness can be assessed in terms of parameters that are markers of severity of illness and organ dysfunction.

Scoring Systems

For ease of application to routine clinical care simple method to objectivise the severity of illness has been devised. Scoring systems enable matching of patients for evaluation of treatment protocols and new drugs, defining criteria for admission to special care facilities by identifying life threatening clinical situation and prognostication of outcome. The rising cost of medical services in recent years has created the need to evaluate cost effectiveness of different medical facilities and treatment modalities again stressing the need for an objective measure of disease severity.

The commonly used scoring systems are PRISM, PRISM III, TISS, and PIM. The PRISM (Pediatric Risk of Mortality) score was developed and validated in intensive care unit setting by Pollack et al. This scoring system assesses the severity of illness according to 14 physiological and laboratory parameters. The parameters are: heart rate, systolic and diastolic blood pressure, respiratory rate, PaO_2/FiO_2 ratio, $PaCO_2$, Glasgow coma score, pupillary reactions, prothrombin time, total bilirubin, potassium, calcium, glucose, and bicarbonate. Each variable is then assigned a particular score and further age dependent variables are individually categorized. Thereafter, the sum total of all scores is fed into a predecided equation and the final PRISM score is used for mortality and dynamic objective risk assessment. There are some problems with PRISM. Because it is calculated from the most abnormal values of 14 variables over a 24 hour period, it is very difficult to collect the large amount of information needed to calculate PRISM, so that many pediatric intensive care units do not calculate it routinely. Later this score was refined and PRISM III score was developed and validated.

Shann et al developed and validated PIM (Pediatric index of mortality) and PIM2. PIM2 is a simple model based on eight explanatory variables collected at the time of admission to the intensive care unit starting from whether admission to intensive care unit was elective or not, presence of underlying high risk diagnosis, acid base parameters-PaO_2, FiO_2, base excess, systolic blood pressure, need for mechanical ventilation, and pupillary reaction.

Some parameters which have not been included in the scoring systems mentioned above namely infection status (focus of infection, counts, c-reactive protein); malnutrition (nutritional parameter assessment –weight, height, weight for height, etc.); underlying illness also need to be evaluated.

Suggested reading

1. Pollack MM, Patel KM, Ruttimann UE. PRISM III: an updated pediatric risk of mortality score. Crit Care Med 1996; 24:743–752
2. Pollack M. Severity-of-illness scoring system. In. Nichols DG (ed). Roger's Textbook of Pediatric Intensive Care. Baltimore. Lippincott Williams and Wilkins. 2008;106–13.

27 Common Medical Procedures

REMOVAL OF ASPIRATED FOREIGN BODY

The management of foreign body aspiration in children varies according to the presentation and age of the patient. If the child presents with acute signs and symptoms of upper airway obstruction and can cough, breathe, or speak, the child should be encouraged to utilize his or her cough to dislodge the foreign body. However, if the child is observed to have either complete obstruction or partial obstruction with either cyanosis or poor air exchange, or if the child's cough is ineffective in expelling the foreign body, then the rescuer should intervene. Blind finger-sweeps should be avoided in infants and children because the foreign body could be pushed back into the airway, causing further obstruction.

A choking infant younger than 1-year-old should be placed face down over the rescuer's arm, with the head positioned below the trunk. Five measured back blows are delivered rapidly between the infant's scapulas with the heel of the rescuer's hand (Fig. 27.1). If obstruction persists, the infant should be rolled over and five rapid chest compressions performed (similar to cardiopulmonary resuscitation). This sequence is repeated until the obstruction is relieved. In a choking child older than 1-yr of age, abdominal thrusts (Heimlich maneuver) may be performed, with special care in younger children because of concern about possible intra-abdominal organ injury (Fig. 27.2).

When initial interventions fail, a jaw thrust should be performed, with the hope of partially relieving the obstruction. If the foreign body can be visualized, it should be manually removed, using Magill or other large forceps. In the unconscious, nonbreathing child, a tongue-jaw lift can be performed by grasping both the tongue and lower jaw between the thumb and finger and lifting. For children who present with signs and symptoms suggestive of bronchial foreign body aspiration beyond the oropharynx, endoscopy should be performed by those experienced with the procedure.

INSERTION OF NASOGASTRIC TUBE

Indications

1. Decompression of the stomach and proximal bowel for obstruction or trauma.
2. Gastric lavage in the child with upper gastrointestinal bleeding or accidental ingestion.
3. Administration of medications or for nutrition.

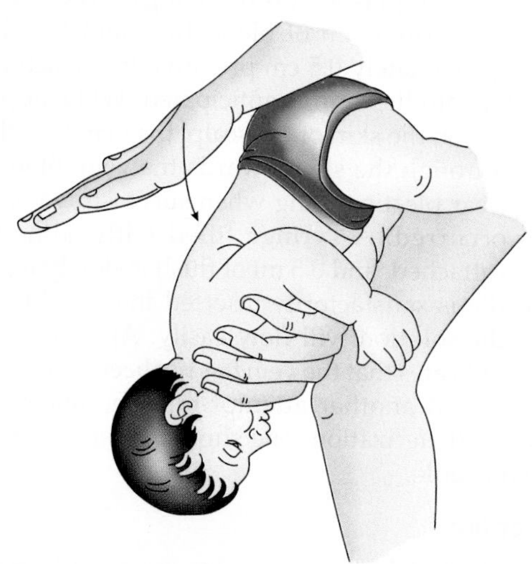

Fig. 27.1: Back blows in a choking infant

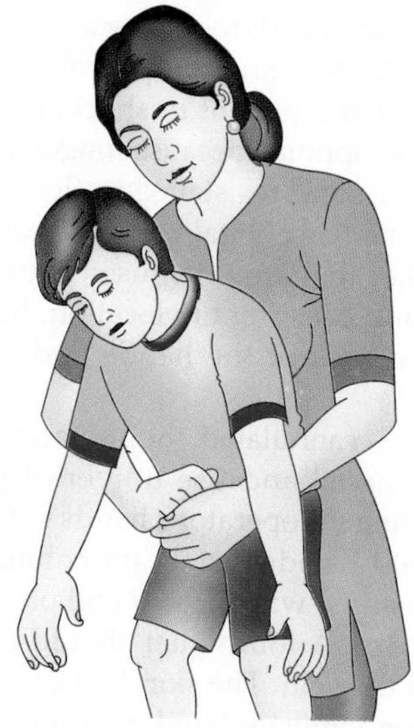

Fig. 27.2: Heimlich maneuver in a child

Procedure

One should choose the largest size tube feasible, without causing undue discomfort to the child; an 8-Fr tube in newborns, 10-Fr for l-yr-old and 14–16 Fr for teenagers are appropriate. The length of tubing to be passed is estimated by adding 8–10 cm to the distance from the nares to the xiphoid process. One should prepare the child by explaining the procedure as fully as possible; sedation is rarely required. Infants and obtunded children require the supine position with their head turned to the side.

The curved tube is straightened out and its patency is checked with a syringe. Lubricant is applied to facilitate atraumatic nasal passage. The tube is grapsed 5 to 6 cm from the distal end and advanced posteriorly along the floor of the nose. It is inserted with the natural curve of the tube pointing downward in order to pass the bend the posterior pharynx makes. If the child coughs or gags persistently or the tube emerges from the mouth, one should temporarily discontinue the procedure.

When the tube is successfully passed to the measured length, its position is checked by attaching a 5 ml syringe filled with air to the proximal end and, while depressing the plunger rapidly, listening with a stethoscope for gurgling over the stomach. The tube is taped securely to the nose.

Complications

The nasogastric tube insertion may be associated with complications such as (i) tracheal intubation, (ii) nasal or pharyngeal trauma and (iii) vomiting.

VENOUS CATHETERIZATION

PERIPHERAL PERCUTANEOUS VENOUS CATHETERIZATION

27

Small-caliber plastic catheters and small over-the-needle catheters (22–24 gauge) are available to cannulate even the small veins of the hand, foot, or scalp of neonates. Selection of catheter size and peripheral venous site are important issues. For a patient in shock, the widest and shortest catheter is optimal, because longer and narrower catheters result in more resistance to flow. The greater saphenous vein, median cubital vein and external jugular vein are three sites that are often used because they are relatively large and consistent in location. In older children, veins in the back of the hands and forearms are commonly used.

Before the vein is cannulated, the operator should wash his or her hands well and use universal precautions, including protecting the operator's hands with gloves. The extremities should be adequately immobilized, and the site should be cleansed with alcohol and povidone iodine and allowed to dry. A tourniquet should be applied in order to distend the vein. The skin is stretched taut with the operator's nondominant hand in order to immobilize the vein. The operator should puncture the skin at a 15 to 30° angle, 5 to 10 mm distal to the expected entrance site into the vein. The vein is subsequently punctured by the needle, with blood return into the catheter hub. When this blood return is noted, the catheter is advanced a few millimeters to ensure that the catheter tip, as well as the needle, is in the lumen of the vein. The catheter is then advanced over the needle into the vein, and the needle is removed. The tourniquet is released, and saline is flushed intravenously to ensure patency of the catheter and vein.

Adequate immobilization of the extremity is an important aspect of successful peripheral vein cannulation. Moreover, it is important to adequately secure and protect the catheter after successful cannulation. The most common complication of peripheral venous cannulation is catheter displacement and infiltration of the tissues with the infusing fluid.

SCALP VEIN CATHETERIZATION

Indication

To achieve intravenous access for delivering fluid and/or medication in an infant usually younger than one year of age, when peripheral extremity veins are unavailable.

Technique

The infant younger than one year of age has several easily accessible scalp veins. These include the frontal, supraorbital, posterior facial, superficial temporal and posterior auricular veins and their tributaries. The patient is restrained in a supine position with an assistant stabilizing the infant's head. An area large enough to expose not only the desired veins, but an area of surrounding scalp for adequate taping of the infusion needle is shaved . In this area, a vein is selected such that it has a straight segment that is as long as the part of the needle that is to be inserted.

The skin is prepared by cleansing with povidone–iodine solution followed by alcohol. A Butterfly scalp vein needle is grasped by the plastic tabs or "wings." The needle is inserted in the direction of blood flow and the skin is pierced approximately 0.5 cm proximal to the actual site where entry into the vein is anticipated. While applying mild traction on the skin of the scalp, the needle is slowly advanced through the skin towards the vein. Blood will enter the clear plastic tubing when successful venipuncture has occurred. A syringe filled with saline flush solution is attached, and 0.5 ml of flush is slowly injected. If the needle is satisfactorily inserted into the lumen of the vein, the solution will flow easily. Appearance of a skin weal indicates that the vein has not been satisfactorily cannulated and another attempt must be made. After successful catheterization, one should carefully tape the scalp vein needle.

Complications

Inadvertent arterial puncture, ecchymoses and hematoma are rare complications.

CENTRAL VENOUS CANNULATION

Indications

1. Unattainable access to the peripheral circulation.
2. Access for drugs and fluids that require central administration (e.g. vasopressors, hyper-alimentation fluids, contrast medications).
3. To monitor central venous pressure.
4. Access for hemodialysis, plasmapheresis and continuous renal replacement therapy.

The venous sites preferred for various indications are showed in Table 27.1.

Table 27.1: Preferred venous access sites for various pediatric conditions

Indication	*First choice*	*Second choice*
Emergency airway management, CPR	Femoral vein	Subclavian vein
Long-term parenteral nutrition	Subclavian vein	Internal jugular vein
Acute hemodialysis or plasmapheresis	Internal jugular vein	Femoral vein
Coagulopathy	Femoral vein	External jugular vein
General access (i.e. for surgery, medicine)	Internal jugular vein	Femoral vein or subclavian vein

CPR: Cardiopulmonary resuscitation

Procedure

There are some common principles applicable to all central venous catheter procedures. These include: (i) need for strict asepsis during and at the time of catheter insertion; (ii) use of the Seldinger technique; (iii) need for adequate sedation to minimize movement; (iv) exclusion of bleeding diathesis before insertion; (v) ensuring proper catheter tip location, avoiding areas of high risk like ventricles and left atrium. It is important to verify catheter position with regular chest X-rays; and (vi) constant monitoring of the patient's vital signs and oxygen saturation.

Sites for Central Venous Cannulation

External Jugular Vein

The external jugular vein can be identified easily. There is a less risk of pneumothorax. Complications are minimal because of the superficial position of the cannulation vein (Fig. 27.3) and the ability to compress the vein to prevent hemorrhage.

Internal Jugular Vein

Internal jugular vein cannulation provides an excellent approach to the central circulation with a high success rate and minimal complications. Carotid artery puncture and pneumothorax are the most common complications.

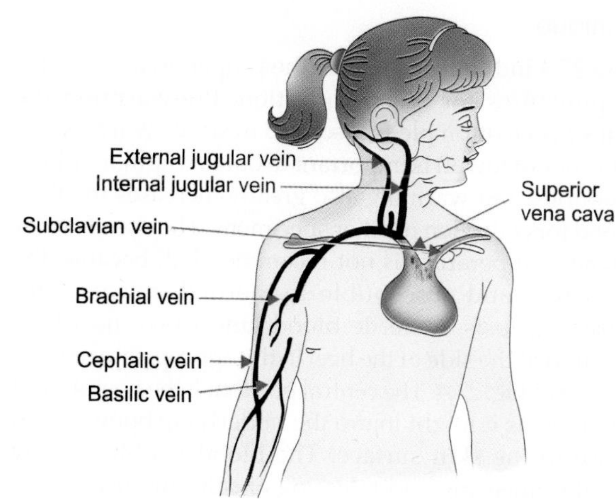

Fig. 27.3: Venous anatomy of the neck and the upper extremity

With left-sided cannulation there is potential for injury to the thoracic duct, and there is a higher risk for pneumothorax because the apex of the left lung is higher than on the right.

Subclavian Vein

The subclavian vein is the preferred site in patients with long-term catheter requirements because of its relatively high level of patient comfort and ease of catheter maintenance. In patients with hypovolemia, the subclavian vein does not collapse as readily as some of the other major vessels because of its fibrous attachments directly below the clavicle. The major complications include pneumothorax, subclavian artery puncture, hemothorax and risk of subclavian vein stenosis.

Femoral Vein

Femoral vein cannulation is the most common site for central vein cannulation as it is easily accessible and avoids possible pleura and lung complications. The Trendelenburg position is not needed and serious complications are rare. All of these reasons make it popular in the pediatric patient, especially in the patient needing airway management or cardiopulmonary resuscitation. At the inguinal ligament, the vein lies in the femoral sheath just below the skin line. It lies just medial to the femoral artery, which is just medial to the femoral branch of the genitofemoral nerve. The main complications are the risk of arterial puncture, infections and rarely deep vein thrombosis (more common with long-dwelling catheters in adolescents).

CAPILLARY BLOOD (HEEL PRICK)

Indications

To obtain arterialized capillary blood for blood gas analysis, bilirubin, glucose, hematocrit and other biochemical parameters.

Technique

Figure 27.4 indicates in shades the proper area to use for heel punctures for blood collection. Pre-warming the infant's heel (cotton pledget soaked in sterile warm water at 40°C or hot towel) is important to obtain capillary blood gas samples and warming also greatly increases the flow of blood for collection of other specimens. The use of water at higher temperature is not recommended, because the skin is thin and susceptible to thermal injury. After ensuring asepsis, a sterile blood lancet or a needle is punctured at the side of the heel in the appropriate regions as shown in Fig. 27.4. The central portion of the heel should be avoided as it might injure the underlying bone, which is close to the skin surface. The blood is obtained by alternate squeezing and releasing of calf muscles.

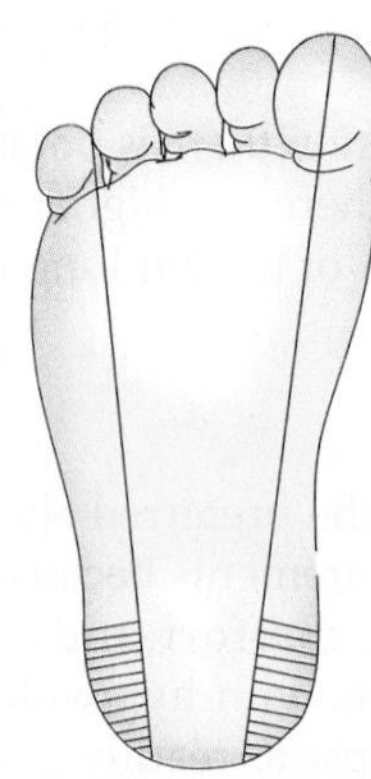

Fig. 27.4: Recommended sites for neonatal capillary blood sampling. Hatched areas indicate safe areas for puncture sites

27

ARTERIAL CATHETERIZATION

Indications for arterial lines include the need to monitor (i) blood pressure continuously especially for hemodynamically unstable patients and (ii) blood samples frequently, especially arterial blood gases. Radial artery cannulation is a primary site of arterial cannulation in infants and children. Right radial artery cannulation is selected when pre-ductal arterial oxygen tensions are important in evaluating and treating infants with congenital heart disease.

Complications

i. Disconnection of the catheter from the infusion system.
ii. Ischemia; remove radial artery cannula if ischemic changes develop.
iii. Emboli; result in arteriolar spasm or ischemic necrosis.
iv. Infection at the site of the insertion, with risk of septicemia.

INTRAOSSEOUS INFUSION

Intraosseous infusions can be performed rapidly and reliably, even in patients with shock. Medical personnel can usually attain intraosseous access in less than 1 minute during emergencies. The bone marrow cavity is effectively a noncollapsible vascular space, even in the setting of shock or cardiac arrest. Therefore, intraosseous access is the initial vascular access site of choice in patients with life-threatening problems such as cardiopulmonary arrest or decompensated shock.

Almost any medication that can be administered into a central or peripheral vein can be safely infused into the bone marrow. Crystalloid solutions, colloid solutions and blood products can be safely infused through the bone marrow, as can hypertonic solutions.

Procedure

The technique of intraosseous infusion is rapid and simple. The most commonly used sites are the proximal tibia, distal tibia and distal femur (Fig. 27.5). Due to differences in cortical thickness, the proximal tibia along the flat anteromedial surface of the shaft, 1 to 2 cm below the tibial tuberosity, is the preferred site in infants and young children. The distal tibia at the junction of the medial malleolus and the shaft of the tibia is the preferred site in older children. The distal one third of the femur along the midline and approximately 3 cm above the sternal condyle can also be used.

Technique

i. Using aseptic technique, the site is prepared with iodine solution.
ii. The skin is injected with 1% lidocaine for anesthesia in the awake patient.

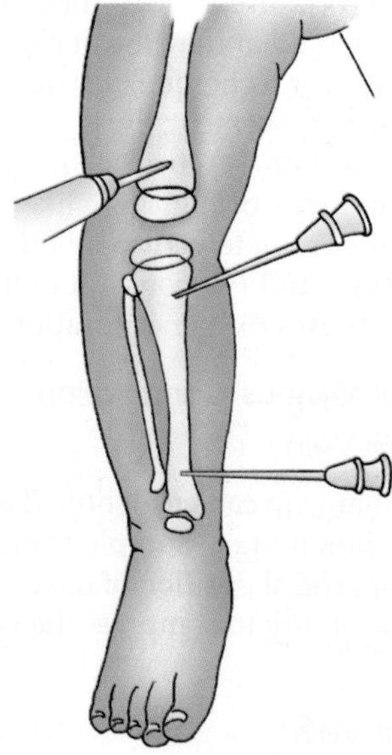

Fig. 27.5: Insertion sites for intraosseous infusion in the proximal tibia, 1 cm to 2 cm anteromedial from the tibial tuberosity, the distal tibia at the junction of medial malleoulus and the shaft of the tibia, and the distal one-third of the femur

iii. The needle is inserted at an angle of 10–15° from the vertical, away from the joint space (caudad for the proximal tibia, cephalad for the distal tibia and femur). Apply pressure and a to-and-fro rotary motion. As the needle passes into the marrow, a "give away" will be felt. The needle should stand without support.

iv. Evidence for successful entrance into the marrow includes (a) the lack of resistance (or a "give way") after the needle passes through the cortex, (b) the ability of the needle to remain upright without support, (c) aspiration of the bone marrow into a syringe, and (d) free flow of the infusion without significant subcutaneous infiltration. Aspiration of bone marrow into the intraosseous needle is not always possible, especially in a very dehydrated patient.

v. One should then remove the stylet. Proper placement is confirmed by aspiration of bone marrow into a 5-ml syringe or freely flowing heparinized saline flush.

vi. The needle is connected to the desired intravenous tubing and solution.

vii. One should observe for extravasation of fluids into the surrounding soft tissue. This indicates superficial needle placement or that the bone has been pierced posteriorly.

Complications

Potential complications include osteomyelitis, subcutaneous abscess, extravasation of fluid into subcutaneous tissue, epiphyseal trauma and fat embolism.

LUMBAR PUNCTURE

Indications

To obtain cerebrospinal fluid (CSF) for the diagnosis of meningitis, meningoencephalitis, subarachnoid hemorrhage and other neurologic syndromes.

Procedure

Lateral Decubitus Position

The patient is restrained in the lateral decubitus position as shown in Fig. 27.6A. The spine is maximally flexed without compromising the upper airway. Frequently, in young infants, the patient's hands can be held down between the flexed knees with one of the assistant's hands. The other hand can flex the infant's neck at the appropriate time. The spinal cord ends at approximately the level of the L1 and L2 vertebral bodies. Caudal to L2, only the filum terminale is present. The desired sites for lumbar puncture are the interspaces between the posterior elements of L3 and L4 or L4 and L5. One should locate these spaces by palpating the iliac crest. An imaginary "plumb line" is followed from the iliac crest to the spine. The interspace encountered is L4 to L5.

The skin is cleansed with povidone iodine solution and alcohol. One should begin at the intended puncture site and sponge in widening circles until an area of 10 cm in diameter has been cleaned and allow it to dry. The child is draped beneath his or her flank and over the back with the spine accessible to view. Local anesthesia should be used in children older than 1-yr of age. The site is anesthetized by injecting 1% lidocaine intradermally to raise a weal, then the needle is advanced into desired interspace injecting anesthetic, being careful not to inject it into a blood vessel or spinal canal.

The spinal needle is checked to ensure that the stylet is secure. One should grasp the spinal needle firmly with the bevel facing "up" toward the ceiling, making the bevel parallel to the direction of the fibers of the ligamentum flavum. The patient's position should be checked again to ensure that the needle's trajectory is midsagittal to his or her back. The needle is inserted into the skin over the selected interspace in the midline sagittal plane. The needle should be inserted slowly, aiming slightly cephalad toward the umbilicus. When the ligamentum flavum and then the dura are punctured, a "pop" and decreased resistance are felt. One should then remove the stylet and check for flow of spinal fluid. If no fluid is obtained, one should reinsert the stylet, advance the needle slowly and check frequently for the appearance of CSF.

About 1 ml of CSF is collected in each of the three sterile tubes. The CSF is sent for routine culture, glucose and protein determination and cell count. Additional tubes are collected as indicated. One should then reinsert the stylet and remove the spinal needle with one quick motion. The back is cleansed and the puncture site is covered.

Sitting Position

The infant is restrained in the seated position with maximal spinal flexion (Fig. 27.6B). The assistant should hold the infant's hands between his or her flexed legs with one hand and flex the infant's head with the other hand. Drapes are placed underneath the child's buttocks and on the shoulders with an opening near the intended spinal puncture site. One should choose the interspace as noted earlier and follow the procedure as outlined for the lateral position. The needle is inserted such that it runs parallel to the spinal cord.

Complications

Lumbar puncture may be associated with headache, local back pain and infection. Brainstem herniation may occur in the presence of symptomatic intracranial hypertension.

THORACOCENTESIS

Indications

Thoracocentesis is performed to evacuate fluid from the patient's pleural space.

Diagnostic

Pleural effusion or empyema.

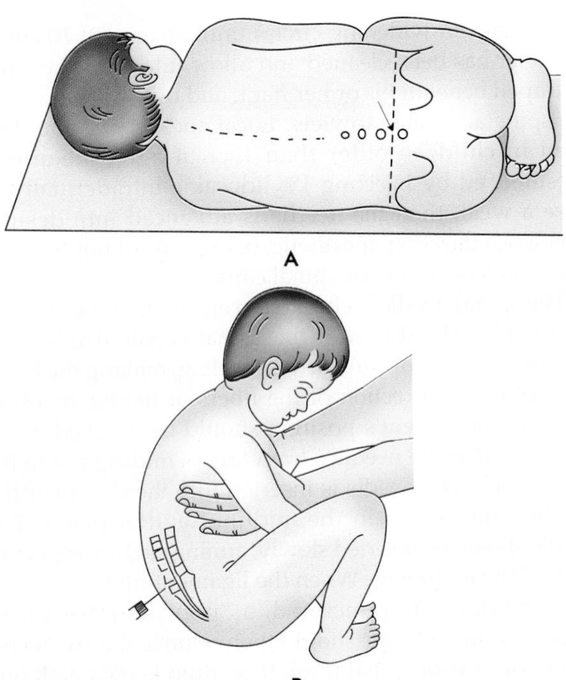

Figs 27.6A and B: Lumbar puncture with the child in (A) decubitus position (B) sitting position. Arrow indicates site for needle insertion

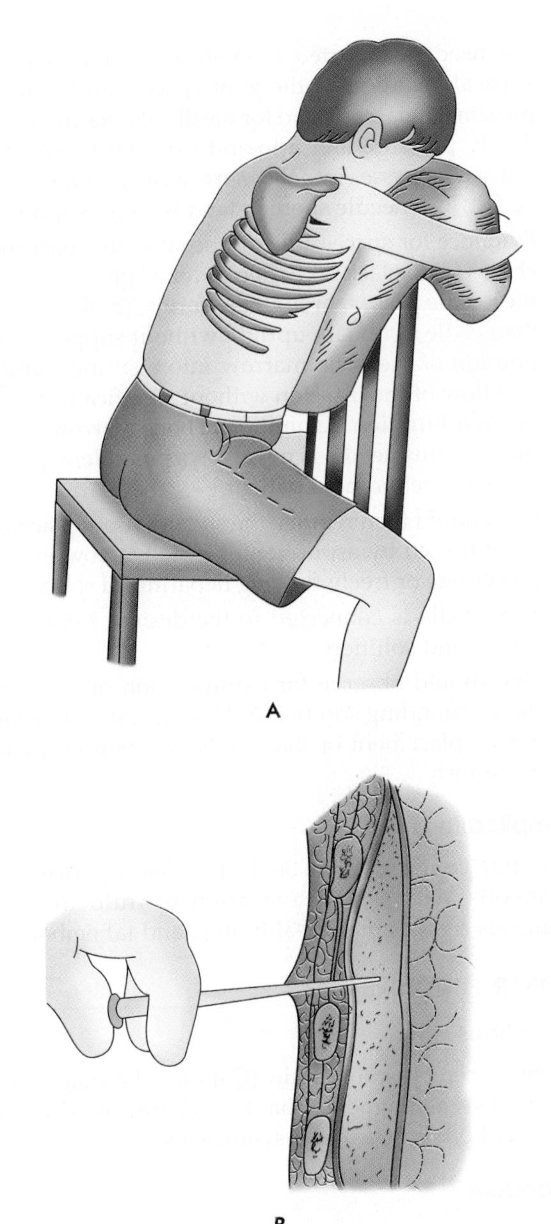

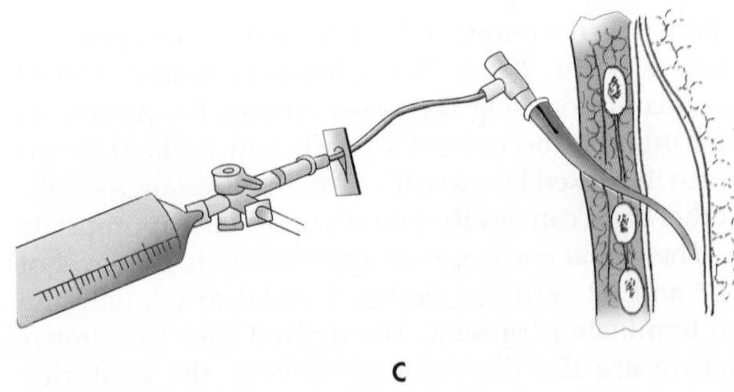

Figs 27.7A to C: Thoracocentesis: (A) The landmark for thoracocentesis is the angle of the scapula that corresponds approximately to the eighth rib interspace. (B) The needle is introduced immediately above the superior edge of the rib to avoid puncturing the intercostals vessels. (C) After inserting the catheter in the pleural space, the catheter is connected to a three-way stopcock and a syringe

Therapeutic

When large collections of pleural fluid compromise ventilatory function, the procedure should be done carefully in subjects with uncorrected coagulopathy. Persistent inability to draw fluid suggests a loculated effusion, and the operator should withhold further attempts until the procedure can be performed under radiographic guidance (i.e. CT scan, ultrasound).

Technique

The first step in thoracocentesis is to ensure that fluid is present in the area of thoracocentesis by clinical and radiological methods. Decubitus films are helpful in demonstrating free fluid that shifts with movement. The procedure (Figs 27.7A to C) is carried out with the patient appropriately sedated and properly positioned. Standard positioning for the patient is with the patient positioned upright and leaning forward. The procedure is carried out under aseptic precautions. The site of entry is anesthetized with local anesthetic. The landmark for evacuation of the fluid is the angle of the scapula that corresponds approximately to the eighth rib interspace. An appropriate catheter is used over the needle. The needle is introduced immediately above the superior edge of the rib to avoid puncturing the intercostal artery and vein. Once the pleural space is entered and fluid is aspirated, the catheter is advanced as the needle is withdrawn. The catheter is connected to a three-way stopcock and syringe (10–20 ml). It is important to control the aspiration of fluid such that air is not allowed to enter the pleural space from the outside.

Complications

i. Intercostal artery puncture with severe hemorrhage.
ii. Development of pneumothorax or hemothorax.
iii. Malpositioned needle, leading to abdominal viscera or lung parenchymal injury.

ABDOMINAL PARACENTESIS

Indications

Diagnostic

Determine etiology of ascites; diagnose peritonitis.

Therapeutic

Remove large volumes of ascitic fluid (if causing respiratory compromise).

Technique

The patient is placed in a supine position, and the bladder is emptied. The common sites for paracentesis are shown in Fig. 27.8. These sites are chosen to avoid puncture of underlying vessels or viscera. Usually the left lower quadrant is preferred to the right in critically ill children because they may have cecal distention. Following local infiltration of xylocaine, the skin is then tiled anteriorly so that further infiltration into the subcutaneous tissue is in a different plane (Z tracking). A needle or over-the-needle catheter is then advanced using the Z tracking technique and at an angle perpendicular to the skin. Continued aspiration of the needle is used until peritoneal fluid is aspirated. Approximately 10–15 ml of fluid is aspirated for studies, which include culture, Gram stain and cytology; levels of amylase, lactate dehydrogenase (LDH), bilirubin, albumin and protein are estimated. If the paracentesis is performed for therapeutic purposes, a catheter should be placed.

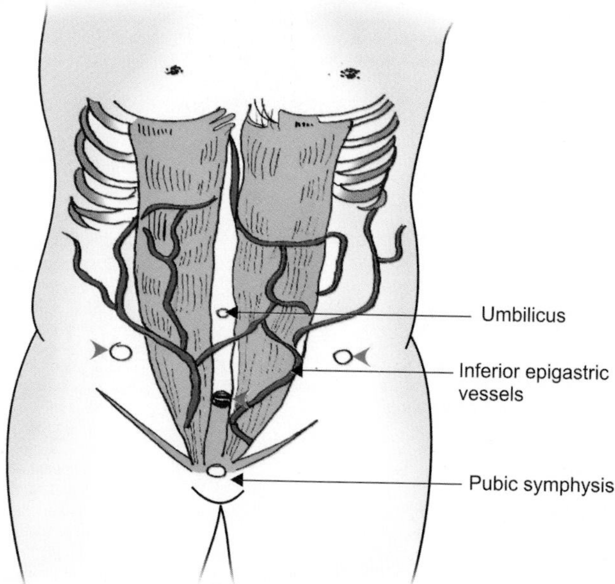

Fig. 27.8: Sites for abdominal paracentesis. The preferred sites are the linea alba (midway between the umbilicus and the pubic symphysis) and lateral to the rectus abdominis muscle. Arrowheads (◀) indicate common sites for paracentesis

Complications

The complications of abdominal paracentesis are hemorrhage, fluid leak, intestinal or bladder perforation and hypotension, if large volumes are removed.

CATHETERIZATION OF BLADDER

Indications

Bladder catheterization is done in bedridden patients who need short-term assistance. It is also required in patients with (i) polytrauma, especially for evaluation of the urinary tract in an unconscious child; (ii) shock; (iii) acute urinary retention; and (iv) to obtain a urine specimen for urinalysis.

Complications

Injury to urethra or urinary bladder, and inadvertent catheterization of the vagina may occur. Absence of aseptic precautions might result in urinary tract infection.

Procedure

Restrain the patient as necessary. Prepare the urethral meatus and penis or the perineal area by cleansing with povidone iodine solution; select a Foley catheter of the appropriate size (8 Fr in the newborn, 10 Fr in most children and 12 Fr in older children). The catheter tip should be well lubricated to minimize local trauma.

Male

Gently grasp and extend the penile shaft to straighten out the urethral pathway. Hold the catheter near the distal tip and advance it up the urethra unless resistance or an obstruction is encountered. If resistance is encountered, select a smaller catheter. The catheter should be passed into the bladder all the way to the Y-connection; this is important because urine may begin to flow while the catheter is in the proximal urethra, and inflation of the balloon in the urethra may lead to complications. Inflate the balloon after advancing the catheter all the way to the Y-connection. Tape the catheter to the child's leg.

Female

In the female, the principles of catheterization are similar to those in the male. Have an female assistant carefully spread the labia. Introduce a well-lubricated, pretested Foley catheter into the bladder. Again, advance the catheter its entire length before inflating the balloon. A catheter that is passed in its entirety has not been inadvertently located in the small vagina of the young girl. After withdrawing the catheter until a dunking sensation is appreciated, secure it with tape.

LIVER BIOPSY

Liver biopsy is used to determine the cause of "acute or chronic liver disease," assess prognosis, determine response to therapy and monitor effects of hepatotoxic drugs. Analysis of the biopsy specimen can include histology, metal content, biochemical or enzyme assay, culture for viral, bacterial or fungal pathogens, and electron microscopy.

Liver biopsy can be performed percutaneously at the bedside or with ultrasound guidance. The latter is preferred because of lower complication rate and the opportunity to visualize the liver and target focal lesions. The biopsy can be performed by either an anterior, subdiaphragmatic or right lateral approach, the last being the most commonly used. The biopsy site is typically just anterior to the right midaxillary line, at about the tenth intercostal space. Absolute contraindications include inability to remain still and maintain expiration for the procedure, or a bleeding tendency. Relative contraindications include severe anemia, peritonitis, marked ascites, high-grade biliary obstruction and a subphrenic or right pleural effusion. Major complications (e.g. intra-abdominal hemorrhage, bile peritonitis, lacerated liver) are rare.

Transjugular venous biopsy of the liver is used in patients with risk of bleeding. Surgical liver biopsy obtains liver tissue *via* laparotomy or laparoscopy and is utilized in instances when the percutaneous technique is contraindicated. The surgical methods allow for better hemostasis when the patient has a coagulopathy.

RENAL BIOPSY

The usual indications are children with steroid resistant nephrotic syndrome, rapidly progressive glomerulonephritis, recurrent gross hematuria with significant proteinuria, and unexplained acute renal failure. In most instances, a percutaneous biopsy is done using a spring-loaded biopsy needle that is guided with ultrasonography. In children, the procedure can be done with sedation. The procedure is relatively safe in experienced hands. The tissue obtained is processed with standard histochemical stains, and examined by light, immunofluoroscence and electron microscopy.

Suggested reading

1. Dieckmann RA, Fiser DH, Selbst SM editors: Illustrated textbook of pediatric emergency and critical care procedures 1st edn, Philadelphia, Mosby, 1997.
2. Carlson DW, Digiulic GA, Gennitz MH, Givens TG, Handler SD, Hodge D, et al: Illustrated techniques of pediatric emergency procedures. In Fleisher GR, Ludwigs editors: Synopsis of pediatric emergency medicine; 4th edition, Philadelpha; Williams and Wilkins, 2000.
3. Fuhrman BP, Zimmerman JJ editors: Pediatric critical care, 3rd edn, Philadelphia, Mosby, 2006

28 Rational Drug Therapy

INTRODUCTION

Drugs play a vital role in protecting, maintaining and restoring the health of people, if used rationally. Most drugs are chemicals and their indiscriminate consumption may lead to toxicity and adverse reactions. Expected benefits and possible side effects of the drug should always be kept in mind. It is better to use those drugs with which the physician is familiar. Indiscriminate and injudicious use of drug may be potentially harmful. Some general guidelines for rational drug therapy are given below.

i. There should be a genuine indication for the use of a drug in the patient.
ii. A minimum number of appropriate, familiar and inexpensive drugs of good quality should be used.
iii. Drugs should preferably be prescribed by generic name.
iv. The dosage of the drug should be optimum to achieve the desired clinical benefits.
v. It is desirable to administer drugs as far as possible through oral route in children.
vi. Adverse drug reactions should be anticipated, monitored and appropriately managed.

Examples of true *synergism* are rare; the most notable exception being cotrimoxazole incorporating trimethoprim and sulphamethoxazole. Combination of antibiotic agents may be necessary when the causative agent is not known. *Multidrug therapy* is indicated to prevent bacterial resistance to individual drugs during long-term management of tuberculosis and leprosy and also to reduce toxicity of individual drugs. Bactericidal drugs ordinarily act best when the organism is actively multiplying. Therefore, bacteriostatic drugs are not the best agents to combine with bactericidal drugs.

The response to different drugs may vary at different ages due to developmental factors and may depend on the genetic factors controlling their metabolism. Doses of drugs need to be modulated according to the individual responses. The dosages of the drugs may vary in specific disease, e.g. meningitis, subacute bacterial endocarditis, pyogenic arthritis, etc. All doses given below are approximate doses used in common practice. The reader is advised to consult the prescribing information on the drug package.

Key words: M^2 = square meter of body surface; PO= per oral; SC = subcutaneous; PR = rectal; T = topical; IM = intramuscular; IV= intravenous; ITH= intrathecal; Wt.= weight; D = day; h = hour; Y = age in years; g = gram; kg = kilogram; mg = milligram. Names of some popular proprietary preparations are given in parenthesis.

ANALGESICS, ANTIPYRETICS AND NON-STEROIDAL ANTI-INFLAMMATORY DRUGS (NSAIDS)

Non-Narcotic Analgesics

Aspirin: Anti-inflammatory dose in rheumatic disease: 90–130 mg/kg/day PO q 4 h. Antipyretic dose: 30–60 mg/kg/day PO q 4–6 h. Salicylates should be avoided on empty stomach. *Side effects:* Hypersensitivity, hypoprothrombinemia. There is an epidemiologic association between salicylate use and Reye's encephalopathy. Therefore its use for upper respiratory tract infection and fevers of undetermined origin in children is not advisable.

Paracetamol: 40–60 mg/kg/PO q 4–6 h. Injection 5 mg/kg IM. *Side effects:* Skin rashes, hepatotoxicity. Occasionally renal damage.

Ibuprofen: 20–30 mg/kg/day q 6–8 h oral Avoid in infants < 6 months age. *Side effects:* Nausea, vomiting, rashes.

Nimesulide: 5 mg/kg/day q 8–12 h. *Side effects:* Hepatic enzyme elevation. Use with caution in hepatocellular disease or when combining with another hepatotoxic drug. Safety not established in children under 6 month of age.

Narcotic Analgesics (Opioids)

Fentanyl: 0.5–5 μg/kg/dose q 1–4 h IV, may be administered as a continuous infusion 1–5 μg/kg/h. Potent narcotic analgesic, 0.1 mg dose possesses an equivalent analgesic activity to 10 mg of morphine.

Pentazocine: 0.5 to 1 mg/kg per dose 4 times a day. (30–60 mg IM equivalent to 10 mg of morphine. Orally 50 mg equals 60 mg of codeine). Contraindications. Head injury, raised intracranial tension, porphyria.

Codeine: For pain: 3 mg /kg/D PO q 4 h. For cough: 0.2 mg/kg/dose 4 hourly.

Pethidine: 1–2 mg/kg/dose IM or IV.

Morphine: 0.1–0.2 mg/kg/dose q 4 h (max. 15 mg) IV, IM or SC. *Caution:* Keep naloxone (0.01 mg/kg IV) ready as antidote in case of respiratory depression.

Non-Steroidal Anti-Inflammatory Drugs (NSAIDs)

Quick acting

a. *Salicylates*
b. *Propionic acid derivatives;* Ibuprofen, 20–30 mg/kg/D q 6 h for fever; 30 mg/kg/D for Juvenile rheumatoid arthritis (JRA); ketoprofen and naproxen 5 mg/kg per dose two times a day
c. *Anthranilic acid derivatives* (mefenamic acid 8 mg/kg/dose three times a day).
d. *Aryl acetic acid derivatives* (diclofenac sodium 2–5 mg/kg/day q 8h PO).
e. *Indole derivatives* (indomethacin 3 mg/kg/D PO q 8h, for ductus closure use 0.2 mg/kg/dose for 3 doses IV or PO).

Slow acting

a. *Hydroxychloroquine* 5–10 mg/kg/D.
b. *Penicillamine* 15 mg/kg/D q 8 h; (c) *gold* 3–6 mg single dose daily of auronofin. Refer to Chapter 19, on juvenile rheumatoid arthritis, for details of dosages.

ANTIARRHYTHMICS

Adenosine: 0.05–0.2 mg/kg/dose rapid IV (over 1–3 secs), if no response in 1–2 min, double the dose and continue to double the dose 1–2 min until response occurs. Max single dose 0.25 mg/kg. Indicated for supraventricular tachycardia. *Side effects:* Transient chest pain, dyspnea, flushing, bronchospasm.

Atropine sulfate: 0.01 mg/kg/dose SC or IV. The dose can be repeated after 2 h (max 4–6 times a day). Antidote to organo-phosphorus poisoning: 0.02–0.05 mg/kg every 10–20 min until atropine effect, then every 1–4 hourly for at least 24 hours. *Side effects:* Dry mouth, blurred vision, tachycardia, urinary retention, constipation, dizziness, hallucinations, restlessness.

Bretylium: 5–20 mg/kg/D q 8 h PO or 5–10 mg/kg IM or IV for ventricular arrhythmias. Repeated 1 to 2 hr if arrhythmia persists and subsequently given 6–8 hrs for 3 to 5 days.

Lidocaine hydrochloride (Xylocard, Gesicard): 1 mg/kg/dose IV. May repeat after 5–10 min. Continuous IV infusion 0.02–0.05 mg/kg/min. Max dose 5 mg/kg/D. *Side effects:* Hypotension, seizures, asystole, respiratory arrest.

Phenytoin sodium (Eptoin): *For arrhythmia:* Loading 1.25 mg/kg IV over 3 min and repeat every 5–10 min to a maximum total dose of 15 mg/kg or until arrhythmia reverts or hypotension develops; maintenance 5–10 mg/kg/D q 12 h PO. *For status epilepticus:* loading 15–20 mg/kg IV, do not exceed 1–3 mg/kg/min. Maintain with 5–8 mg/kg/D PO or IV q 12–24 h. *Side effects:* Gum hypertrophy, hirsutism, hypersensitivity, megaloblastic anemia, osteomalacia, vestibulocerebellar syndrome.

Procainamide (Pronestyl): 2 mg/kg/dose IV followed by 0.5 mg/kg/h by constant IV infusion. PO dose 50 mg/kg/D q 3–4 h. *Side effects:* Thrombocytopenia, coomb's positive hemolytic anemia, lupus like syndrome. *Contraindication:* Heart blocks, myasthenia gravis.

Propranolol: 0.01–0.25 mg/kg/dose IV. May repeat in 15 minutes. Then 4–8 hrly. Orally 0.5–1 mg/kg/D q 6 h. *Side effects:* Life threatening increase in pulmonary resistance, fatigue, bradycardia.

Quinidine: Test dose 2 mg/kg PO followed by 30 mg/kg/D PO q 6 h. *Side effects:* Thrombocytopenia, tinnitus, hypotension, blood dyscrasias. Contraindicated in heart blocks, congestive heart failure.

Verapamil: 2–4 mg/kg/D q 8 hr PO, 0.1–0.2 mg/kg IV over 2 min in infants and 0.1–0.3 mg/kg IV over 2 min in children. *Contraindication:* Cardiogenic shock, AV block, children below 2 years of age.

ANTIMYASTHENIC AGENTS

Edrophonium chloride (Tensilon): *Initial dose:* 0.04 mg/kg dose (maximum 1 mg for <30 kg). If no response after 1 min, may give 0.16 mg/kg/dose for a total of 0.2 mg/kg (total maximum dose is 5 mg for <30 kg).

Neostigmine bromide (Prostigmin): Neonate 1 mg q 4 h, 30 min before feed. Children 1–3 mg/kg/D PO q 4–6 h. Begin with lower dose and increase gradually till symptoms disappear. Use with atropine for non-depolarizing neuromuscular blocking agents. *Side effects:* Cholinergic.

Pyridostigmine (Mestinon): 7 mg/kg/D PO q 4–6 h. Start with lower dose and increase gradually.

DRUGS USEFUL AGAINST INFECTIONS

ANTIBIOTICS

Antibiotics in common use are classified below:

A. *Inhibitors of synthesis of or activate enzymes that destroy bacterial cell wall:* Penicillins, cephalosporins, bacitracins.
B. *Inhibitors of protein' synthesis:* Aminoglycosides, tetracyclines, chloramphenicol, macrolides (erythromycin), lincosamides (lincomycin and clindamycin).
C. *Inhibitors of bacterial cell membrane function (increasing permeability and leakage of intracellular compounds):* Polymyxins, amphotericin B, nystatin.
D. *Inhibitors of nucleic acid metabolism:* Griseofulvin and actinomycin, rifampin (inhibit DNA-dependent RNA polymerase).

E. *Alter protein synthesis and result in cell death:* Aminoglycosides.
F. *Antimetabolities:* Sulphonamides and trimethoprim.
G. *Nucleic acid analogs:* Acyclovir.
H. *Inhibitors of DNA gyrase:* Quinolones.

Penicillin

Common nucleus of natural or semi-synthetic penicillin is, 6-aminopenicillanic acid (6-APA). Benzyl penicillin is still the drug of choice for Gram positive and Gram negative cocci. Gram negative bacilli such as *Listeria, Clostridia* and *spirochetes* also respond to penicillin G. Bacterial resistance to penicillins is due to production of beta-lactamase by the bacteria. Beta-lactamase (penicillinase) splits the beta-lactam ring and inactivates the penicillin. Addition of a side chain to the basic structure of penicillin reduces the effect of beta-lactamase on the antibiotic. By altering the chemical structure of penicillin, a range of broad spectrum antibiotics have been developed.

Penicillin may cause hypersensitivity reactions in about 1% of individuals. Hypersensitivity reaction may be immediate (lgE mediated type IV- T cell mediated). Symptoms include urticaria, angioneurotic edema, anaphylactic shock, asthma, laryngeal edema, hypotension. Delayed reactions are fixed drug eruption, serum sickness, hemolytic anemia, and recurrent arthralgia.

Penicillins (Penicillinase-sensitive)
Benzyl penicillin G (sodium or potassium)
4,00,000 units PO q 6 h
50,000–60,000 units/kg/D IM q 6 h
2,00,000–4,00,000 units/kg/D (meningitis) IV q 4–6 h
Benzathine penicillin G 1.2 mega units IM once in 3–4 weeks
Procaine penicillin G 4,00,000 units IM q 12–24 h

Acid-resistant penicillins	
Phenoxy-methyl-penicillin V (Pencillin V)	10 mg/kg/D PO q 6 h
Pencillinase resistant penicillins	
Methicillin sodium	100 mg/kg/D IM or IV q 6h
Oxacillin	50 mg/kg/D PO or IV q 6h
Cloxacillin	50–100 mg/kg/D PO cr IV q 6 h
Broad spectrum penicillins (aminopenicillins)	
Ampicillin	50–100 mg/kg/D PO or IV q 6 h
For meningitis	200–400 mg/kg/D IV q 4–6h
Amoxycillin	25–50 mg/kg/D PO q 8 h

Amoxycillin and potassium clavulanate
Can be used with lactamase producing bacteria. Doses same as with amoxycillin.

Ampicillin and sulbactam sodium
150 mg/kg/D q 8 h IM or IV. Contains 100 mg ampicillin and 50 mg sulbactam.

Anti-pseudomonas penicillins	
Carbenicillin	50–500 mg/kg/D IM or IV q 6 h
Ticarcillin	50–300 mg/kg/D IV infusion q4–6h
Piperacillin	100–300 mg/kg/D IV infusion q 4–8 h.

Cephalosporins

These groups of antibiotics have a common peptide nucleus, 7-aminocephalosporanic acid. These antibiotics resist hydrolysis by beta-lactamase (penicillinase).

First generation cephalosporins have similar spectrum as penicillin. More recently introduced cephalosporins have greater activity against Gram negative bacilli. Approximately 10% of penicillin-hypersensitive patients show allergy to cephalosporin and even a fatal anaphylaxis may occur. Oral cephalosporins cause gastrointestinal symptoms such as loss of appetite, nausea, vomiting and diarrhea. Some parenteral cephaloridines may cause serious renal toxicity. First and second generation cephalosporins have anti- staphyloccal activity. However, third generation are not effective against staphylococci.

Drug	*Dosage (mg/kg/day)*	
First generation cephalosporins		
Cephalexin	25–50	PO q 6 h
Cefazolin	50–100	IM or IV q 6–8 h
Cefadroxil	30	PO q 12 h
Second generation cephalosporins		
Cefaclor	20–40	PO q 6–8 h
Cephamandole	50–150	IM or IV q 8–12 h
Cefuroxime	50–100	IM or IV q 6–8 h
Third generation cephalosporins		
Cefotaxime	100–150	IM or IV q 8–12 h
Cefoperazone	50–200	IM q 8–12 h
Ceftriaxone	80–150	IV q 12–24 h
Ceftazidime	100–150	IV q 8–12 h
Ceftizoxime	100–150	IV q 8–12 h, IM
Cefixime	8–10	PO q 12 h
Third generation drugs attain high CSF concentrations and are widely used in meningitis.		
Fourth generation cephalosporins		
Cefpirome	30–60	IM or IV 12 h
Cefpodoxime	8–10	PO q 12 h

Aminoglycosides

These are composed of amino sugars linked by glycoside linkage and are prepared by fermentation of various species of streptomyces. Gentamicin is fermented from *Micromonospora purpura*. Amikacin and netilmicin are semisynthetic aminoglycosides prepared from kanamycin and sisomicin. These antibiotics are bactericidal and mainly useful against Gram negative bacilli. Organisms may become resistant to aminoglycosides by mutation.

Streptomycin has auditory and vestibular toxicity. Hypersensitivity can also occur. Rashes and drug fevers occur in about 5% of patients. Kanamycin may show ototoxicity (cochlear damage). Gentamicin and other aminoglycosides cause vestibular damage and reversible kidney dysfunction (proteinuria and azotemia).

Drug	*Dosage (mg/kg/day)*	
Streptomycin	30–40	IM q 12 h
Gentamicin	5–7.5	IM or IV q 8–12 h
Amikacin	15-20	IM or IV q 8–12 h
Tobramycin	6–7.5	IM or IV q 6–8 h
Netilmicin	6–7.5	IM or IV q 8 h
Sisomicin	5–7.5	IM or IV q 8 h

Dosage should be reduced and interval between dosage should be increased in case of renal damage and raised urea and creatinine levels.

Tetracyclines

Tetracyclines are deposited in growing teeth and bones. If the drug is used in children between the ages of 2 months and 8 years, both deciduous and permanent teeth may show irreversible staining, hypoplasia of enamel and proneness to caries. Deposition in bones may lead to stunting. Doxycycline does not bind to calcium as intimately. Tetracyclines are not recommended in children below 8 years of age.

Drug	*Dosage (mg/kg/day)*	
Tetracyclines	25–50	PO q 6 h
	15–25	IM q 8–12 h
Doxycycline	2–5	PO q 12–24 h

28

Chloramphenicol

It is a bacteriostatic drug. Indicated in *H. influenzae* meningitis and enteric fever. Most important toxicity is bone marrow depression after prolonged administration of the drug and is dose related. It may reverse on stoppage of drug. A more serious type of aplasia may occur due to idiosyncracy to the drug and may follow a single dose or prolonged therapy. Incidence varies between 1 in 10,000 to 1 in 50,000. This toxic reaction is unpredictable and may terminate fatally. Drug fever, skin rashes and angioneurotic edema may occur as hypersensitivity reaction. GI disturbances are also seen. Newborn infants especially prematures on full dose of chloramphenicol develop grey-baby syndrome, resulting in abdominal distension, vomiting, refusal to suck and dyspnea. The baby develops gray color due to cyanosis and peripheral circulatory collapse with death occurring in half of cases.

Chloramphenicol	50–100 mg/kg/D PO, IM or IV q 6 h
Ophthalmic ointment	0.5 and 1%

Macrolides

Macrolides are bacteriosatic. These can be used for infections with *Staphylococcus aureus*, streptococci, *Mycoplasma pneumoniae, Chlamydia, Corynebacterium diphtherae,* tetanus bacilli, *B. pertussis* and *Campylobacter jejuni*. Erythromycin is generally safe with occasional gastrointestinal *side effects*. Azithromycin has increased activity against Gram negative organism and is better tolerated as compared to erythromycin.

Drug	*Dosage (mg/kg/day)*	
Erythromycin	30–50	PO q 6–8 h
Roxithromycin	5–8	PO 12 h
Azithromycin	10	PO 24 h
Clarithromycin	15	PO q 12 h

Quinolones

These act by inhibiting the enzyme DNA gyrase and are useful in a wide variety of enteric, urinary, respiratory, skin, bone, joint and systemic infections. Except nalidixic acid (used widely for dysentery), none of the quinolones are officially recommended for use in children.

Drug	*Dosage (mg/kg/day)*	
Nalidixic acid	50–60	PO q 8 h
Ciprofloxacin	20–30	PO q 12h
	10–20	IV q 12 h
Gatifloxacin	10	PO 24 h
Norfloxacin	10–15	PO q 12 h
Levofloxacin	10–15	PO or IV 24 hr
Ofloxacin	15	PO q 12 h
	5–10	IV q 12 h
Pefloxacin	12	PO q 12 h
Sparfloxacin	4	PO q 24 h

Sulphonamides

Cotrimoxazole

It is a mixture of trimethoprim and sulphamethoxazole. Its antibacterial action results from the action of two-sequential steps in the synthesis of tetrahydrofolic acid. Toxic Side effects are blood dyscrasias, exfoliative dermatitis, serum sickness, drug fever, etc. Each tablet contains of 80 mg of trimethoprim and 400 mg of sulphamethoxazole. Dosage is 5–8 mg of trimethoprim equivalent/kg/D PO q 12 h.

Anti-Leprosy Drugs

Refer to Chapter 24.

Antitubercular Drugs

Refer to Chapter 9.

Miscellaneous

Drug	*Dosage (mg/kg/day)*	
Aztreonam	90–300 mg	IV or IM Q 6–8 h
Clindamycin	15–20 mg	PO IV q 6 h
Colistin	5–15 mg	PO q 6–8 h
Furazolidine	6 mg	PO q 8 h
Imipenem	60–100 mg	IM or IVq 6 h
Lincomycin	30 mg	PO q 6 h
Polymyxin B	20,000 IU	PO q 8 h
Vancomycin	30–60 mg	IV q 6–8 h
Teicoplanin	10 mg/kg 12 h for 3 doses and then 6–10 mg/kg/D every 24 h IM or IV	

ANTIFUNGAL AGENTS

Amphotericin B (Fungizone): Start at 0.25 mg/kg/D and increase every day by 0.25 mg till a maximum dose of 1mg/kg/D. Total dose not to exceed 30–35 mg/kg over 4 to 6 weeks. Dilute in D5W, compatible with saline. Protect from light. Test dose 0.1 mg/kg IV. *Side effects:* Febrile reactions, nephrotoxic and blood dyscrasias.

Fluconazole: 3–6 mg/kg/D q 24 hrs. *Side effects:* Dizziness, skin rash, hepatic dysfunction.

Flucytosine (Ancobon): 50–150 mg/kg/day PO q 6h. *Side effects:* Neutropenia, thrombocytopenia, colitis, hepatotoxic.

Griseofulvin (Grisovin): 10 mg/kg/day PO q 6–12 h. Double dose in extensive lesions. *Side effects:* Urticaria, paresthesia, proteinuria, leucopenia.

Hamycin: Local application for oral thrush q 6 h.

Ketoconazole (Nizoral, Fungicide): 3–6 mg/kg/day PO single dose. *Side effects:* Abdominal pain, headache, dizziness, somnolence, photophobia, thrombocytopenia. It inhibits androgen and therefore may precipitate gynecomastia in adolescents.

Miconazole: 40 mg/kg/D PO or IV. Local application 2% dermatologic cream. *Side effects:* Pruritis, rash thrombocytopenia.

Nystatin: 1 to 2 million units/D q 8 h PO for diarrhea due to *Candida albicans*. For topical application to mucosa dissolve 1,00,000 units nystatin per mL of glycerine.

Terbinafine: Not recommended below 2 years. 62.5 mg q 24 h for ≤ 20 kg, 125 mg q 24 h for 20–40 kg, 250 mg q 24 h for > 40 kg for 2–6 weeks. *Indications:* Fungal infection of skin, nail, hair.

ANTHELMINTHICS

Albendazole (Alminth, Nubend, Zentel): Used for single or mixed intestinal infestations with roundworms, whip worms, threadworms, hookworms, tapeworms, *Strongyloides stercoralis,* hydatid cyst, cysticercosis in large doses for prolonged period.

200 mg single dose for children between 1–2 years. 400 mg single dose for children of >2 years and adults. For *Strongyloides,* teniasis and H. *nana,* 400 mg daily for 3 days. For hydatid cyst 400 mg twice daily for 28 days (3 cycles at 14 days interval). For neurocysticercosis 15–20 mg/kg/day for 2–3 weeks. *Side effect:* Anorexia, nausea, vomiting.

Diethylcarbamazine citrate (Banocide, Hetrazan): 6 mg/kg/day PO q 8h for 2 weeks, for filariasis; 10 mg/kg/day PO q 8 h for 1 month, for tropical eosinophilia; 15 mg/kg single dose for 4 days for Loeffler syndrome. *Side effects:* Gastrointestinal upset, drowsiness.

Ivermectin: Drug of choice for scabies and onchocerciasis, strongyloides; alternative drug for single dose treatment of filariasis, ascaris, enterobius and trichuris. Dose 200 µg/kg PO single dose. Contraindicated in children <5 y old.

Levamisole (Decaris, Vermisol): 2 mg/kg/day PO single dose for ascariasis. For hookworm infestation 50 mg PO q 6 h for 4 doses. As an immunopotentiating agent 2 mg/day 3 days in a week for 4–6 weeks. *Side effects:* Gastrointestinal upset, drowsiness.

Mebendazole (Mebex, Wormin): 100 mg PO twice daily for 3 days. Repeat after two weeks.

Niclosamide (Niclosan): 1 g. PO empty stomach followed by another dose after one hour. Brisk purgative two hours after the last dose. Half dose to children below 6 years old. *Side effects:* Gastrointestinal disturbances.

Parmomycin: For tapeworm 11 mg/kg/dose q 15 min 4 doses and *H.nana* 45 mg/kg/dose once a day PO for 7 days.

Piperazine salts (Antepar): Enterobiasis: 50 mg/kg/day for 7 days. Ascariasis: 150 mg/kg/PO single dose for 2 days. *Side effects:* Vomiting, blurred vision, uriticaria. Contraindicated in patients with epilepsy.

Praziquantel: 50 mg/kg/D q 8 h PO for 10–14 days for neurocysticercosis. Single dose 10–20 mg/kg for tapeworms. For liver fluke infestation 75 mg/kg/D q 8 h for 2 days.

Pyrantel pamoate (Combantrin, Nemocid): 10 mg/kg PO single dose with a maximum of 1 g. Repeat after one week. *Indications:* Roundworms, pinworms, *Strongyloides, stercoralis* mixed infestations.

Quinacrine: Effective for tapeworms. Children 5–10 yrs, 100 mg q 10 min PO four doses and 11–14 yrs; 200 mg q 10 min PO three doses.

Thiabendazole: 50 mg/kg/day q 12 hr upto a maximum dose of 3 g/day. Duration of therapy for strongyloides 2 days, intestinal nematodes 2 days, cutaneous larva migrans 2–5 days, visceral larva migrans 5–7 days, trichinosis 204 days.

ANTIMALARIALS

Tissue schizonticides: (For causal prophylaxis) Pyrimethamine. (To prevent relapses in vivax malaria) Primaquine.
Blood schizonticides: (i) Classical: Chloroquine, quinine. (ii) Drugs which inhibit dihydrofolate reductase: Chloroguanide, pyrimethamine.
Gametocides: Primaquine for *P. falciparum*. Quinine and chloroquine for *P. vivax* and *P. malariae.*

Sporontocides: Primaquine, pyrimethamine and chloroguanide.

Artemether: 3.2 mg/kg IM on first day followed by 1.6 mg/kg daily subsequently for a total of 5 days. Indicated in severe variety (including cerebral) of multidrug resistant malaria.

Artesunate: 4 mg/kg IM on first day followed by 1 mg/kg daily for a total of 7 days. Therapy can be given orally when patient is able to take. 4 mg/kg/D single dose oral for 7 days or for 3 days followed by a single dose of mefloquine 25 mg/kg. *Indication:* Multidrug resistant malaria.

Chloroquine phosphate (Lariago, Resochin, Nivaquin): 10 mg of base/kg stat, followed by 5 mg/kg after 6 h and then once a day for 2 days. Parenteral dose: 0.8 mg of base/kg per hour in continuous infusion for 30 hours or 3.5–5 mg of base/kg IM or slow IV every 12 hours to obtain a total dose of 25 mg/kg.

For malarial prophylaxis 5 mg/kg/D PO per week from 2 weeks before till 8 weeks after the last exposure in the endemic area. *Side effects:* Nausea, vomiting, encephalopathy.

Mefloquine: Treatment of drug resistant uncomplicated *P. falciparum* malaria: 15 mg/kg single dose oral for partially immune. For non-immune patients, a second dose of 10 mg/kg is given 8–24 hrs later. Prophylaxis of chloroquine resistant malaria: 3.5 mg/kg of base weekly.

28

Primaquine: 0.3 mg/kg/day (base) oral for 5 days for radical cure and prevention of relapse in *Plasmodium vivax* and ovale infections. In case of *P. falciparum* infection it may be given to interrupt transmission (by destroying gametocytes) 0.7 mg/kg single dose. *Side effects:* Intravascular hemolysis in patients with G-6-PD deficiency.

Pyrimethamine (Daraprim): 0.5 mg/kg/week PO for chemoprophylaxis (starting 2 week before entering and continuing 8 week after leaving malarial endemic zone). *Side effects:* Anemia, leucopenia, thrombocytopenia.

Pyrimethamine and sulphadoxine (Reziz, Crydoxin FM, Malocide): For treatment of chloroquine resistant uncomplicated *P. falciparum* infections known to be sensitive to pyrimethamine; Equivalent to 1 mg/kg of pyrimethamine or 20 mg/kg of sulphadoxine PO single dose.

Quinine dihydrochloride: For severe falciparum malaria. 20 mg/kg of salt given in a concentration of 1 mg/ml of normal saline or 5% dextrose infused over a period of 4 hours as a loading dose followed by 10 mg/kg 8 hourly as a 4 hour infusion. Quinine dihydrochloride 12 mg of salt is equivalent to 10 mg base. Shift to oral therapy as soon as possible. If the patient is critically ill for more than 48 hr or develops acute renal failure and requires continuation of IV quinine, the dose should be reduced to ½ to avoid quinine toxicity. Total duration of therapy is 7–10 days. Intramuscular route is as efficacious as IV and can be given in a loading dose of 20 mg/kg (diluted to 60 mg/ml divided and injected into both anterior and lateral aspects of thighs and buttocks) followed by 10 mg/kg 8 hr.

Quinine sulphate: For uncomplicated chloroquine resistant *P. falciparum* infections 25–30 mg/kg/day of salt q 8 hr oral for 7 days. It is preferably used in combination with either tetracycline (40 mg/kg/day q 6 hr for 10 days) or clindamycin (20–40 mg/kg/day q 8 hr for 3 days) or pyrimethamine (0.75 mg/kg/day q 12 hr for 3 days) or sulfadiazine (150 mg/kg/day q 8 hr for 6 days) to prevent emergence of drug resistance.

ANTIPROTOZOAL

Chloroquine (Lariago): 10 mg/kg/day PO q 8 h for 14–21 days for extraintestinal amebiasis.

Dehydroemetine dihydrochloride: 1–3 mg/kg/day PO q 8 h for 10–15 days or 1 mg/kg/day IM for 7–10 days. *Side effects:* Renal and cardiac toxicity.

Diloxanide furoate (Furamide): (For luminal amebic infection, cysts) 20 mg/kg/day PO q 8 h for 10 days.

Furazolidone (Furoxone): (For giardiasis) 5–8 mg/kg/day PO q 6–8 h. *Side effects:* Hemolytic anemia in G-6-PD deficiency, hypotension, hypoglycemia.

Metronidazole (Flagyl, Metrogyl): Giardiasis 10 mg/kg/day PO q 8 h for 10 days. Amebiasis (systemic infection) 20 mg/kg/day PO q 8 h for 21 days or 50 mg/kg/day PO q 8 h for 7 days. *Side effects:* Diarrhea: leucopenia, metallic taste.

Pentamidine: For leishmaniasis 4 mg/kg/day IM or slow IV infusion single daily dose. Course of treatment 12 to 15 doses. A second course may be given after 2 weeks. *Side effects:* Breathlessness, tachycardia, dizziness, fainting fits, headache and vomiting.

Secnidazole (Secnyl): 30 mg/kg PO single dose. In case of hepatic amebiasis give for 5 days.

Sodium stibogluconate: 20 mg/kg/day IM or IV for 20 days for cutaneous leishmaniasis; for 30 days for mucocutaneous leishmaniasis and systemic *Leishmania* infection.

Tinidazole (Tiniba): 50 mg/kg PO single dose in a day for 2–3 days. *Side effects:* Same as for metronidazole.

ANTIVIRAL AGENTS

A. **Antiretroviral—HIV drugs**

Abacavir: 8 mg/kg 12 hr for children >3 months of age with max dose of 300 mg. Use as second line drug.

Didanosine: Neonatal dose upto 90 days: 50 mg/m^2 q 12 hr. Pediatric dose: 120 mg/m^2 q 12 hr (range: 90–150 mg/m^2); max dose 200 mg/dose. Adolescent dose: <60 kg 125 mg BD and, >60 kg 200 mg BD give 30 minutes before or 2 hours after meals. *Side effects:* Headache, pancreatitis, peripheral neuropathy, optic neuritis, liver dysfunction.

Efavirenz (EFV): Pediatric dose for 10 to <15 kg 200 mg OD, 15 to <20 kg 250 mg OD, 20 to <25 kg 300 mg OD, 25 to <32.5 kg 350 mg OD, 32.5 to <40 kg 400 mg OD, >40 kg 600 mg OD.; If using a oral suspension, use a 30% higher dose. *Caution:* Severe CNS and psychiatric symptoms can be precipitated

Lamivudine (3TC): Neonates 4 mg/kg/day PO q 12 hrly, children 4 mg/kg/dose PO q 12 hr. Maximum dose is 150 mg. Reverse transciptase inhibitor used in combination with zidovudine and/or other anti-HIV drugs.

Nelfinavir: Child over 2 years 50–55 mg/kg twice per day with max dose 2 gm. Use as second line drug.

Nevirapine (NVP): Neonates 2 mg/kg single dose for use for prevention of mother to child transmission. Children: 160– 200 mg/m^2/dose oral q 12 hr. Induction dose: once daily for first 14 days; it is generally half the daily maintenance dose given. It is a non nucleosides reverse transcriptase inhibitor specific for HIV–1 transcriptase (not HIV-2) or human polymerase. *Side effects:* Rash, Stevens Johnson syndrome, liver dysfunction

Lopinavir/Ritonavir: 6 month to 12 year: 7- <15 kg: 12 mg/kg lopinavir/3 mg/kg ritonavir q 12 hr with food; 15–40 kg: 10 mg/kg lopinavir/2.5 mg/kg ritonavir q 12 hr with food. > 12 yr: 400 mg lopinavir/100 mg ritonavir q 12 hr with food. Administer with food to enhance bioavailibility.

Stavudine (d4T): 1 mg/kg/dose q 12 hr PO. Adolescents >60 kgs 40 mg BD, < 60 kg 30 mg BD. *Side effects:* Peripheral neuropathy, pancreatitis, nausea, headache.

Zalicitabine (ddc): Pediatric usual dose 0.01 mg/kg q 8 hourly. Adolescents 0.75 mg q. 8 hourly. One hour before or two hours after meals.

Zidovudine (ZDV, AZT): Premature infants: 1.5 mg/kg IV or 2 mg/kg 8–12 hourly. Neonates/infants <3 months: oral 2 mg/kg q 6 hours, IV 1.5 mg/kg q 6 hours. Pediatric oral dose is 90–180 mg/m^2 q 6–8 hrs.

> *Nevirapine based regimen uses combination of stavudine, lamivudine and nevirapine while efavirenz based regimen uses stavudine, lamivudine and efavirenz*

B. **Acyclovir (acivir, ocuvir)**

For neonatal herpes simplex; use 30 mg/kg/D q 8 h IV. Older children with herpes simplex require 250 mg/M^2/D IV q 8 h. PO dosing is not well established and generally not recommended. Orally, this drug is used for treatment or chronic prophylaxis of genital HSV (200 mg PO 5 times a day; for 5 days and 6–12 months in acute cases and for prophylaxis respectively). Herpes zoster or chickenpox in adolescents 400–800 mg 24 hrs for 7 days.

C. **Other antiviral agents**

Ribavirin: Dilute 6 gm of ribavirin in 300 ml of sterile water and nebulize for 12–18 hr/d for 3–7 days. 10 mg/kg/day oral q 6–8 hrs with maximum dose of 150 mg/day upto 10 yrs and 200 mg/day after 10 yrs after 10 yrs for respiratory syncytial virus and measles virus. *Side effects:* Seizures, congestive heart failure, urinary retention, leucopenia.

Adenine arabinoside (Vidarabine): In neonate 15 mg/kg/D IV constant infusion for 10 days. In older children one-half the dose is given. *Side effects:* Hepatic and hematologic dysfunction.

Amantadine: 4–8 mg/kg/D q 8 h oral. Maximum dose of 150 mg/D upto 10 years and 200 mg/D after 10 years.

Ganciclovir: 15 mg/kg/D IV q12 h for 14–21 days. For long-term suppression 10 mg/kg 3 days in a week for 3 months. *Indications:* Acquired CMV retinitis, congenital CMV pneumonia.

Isoprinosine: 50–100 mg/kg/D q 12h oral in subacute sclerosing panencephelitis.

Idoxuridine (Kerecide): Topical application in the eyes for herpetic keratitis.

Idoxuridine (Inosiplex): 50–100 mg/kg/D PO q 12 h. Trifluorothymidine (Viroptic). Topical application in the eyes for herpetic keratitis.

D. **Interferons (IFNs)**

The interferons are a family of proteins, produced and secreted by peripheral blood leucocytes, fibroblasts and epithelial cells. The major subtypes of IFNs on the basis of antigenicity, biologic and chemical properties are: alpha, beta and gamma. Human interferon alfa is commercially available as alfa-n3 alfa-2a, and alfa-2b which are of recombinant DNA origin and exist as single interferon subtype preparations.

The action of IFNs appears to result from a complex cascade of biologic modulation and pharmacologic effects. They influence many cell functions. These include restoration, augmentation and/or modulation of the host's immune system; direct antiproliferative and antineoplastic activities; and modulation of cell differentiation, transcription and translation, including a reduction in oncogene expression.

Clinical Applications

Viral infections: IFN alfa is indicated in chronic hepatitis B and chronic non-A non-B (including hepatitis C). IFN alfa causes a decrease in hepatitis B virus DNA polymerase activity. Seroconversion to anti HBe occurs in approximately one-third of patients with chronic hepatitis B infections treated with this drug. The goals of IFN alfa-therapy is to inhibit hepatitis B viral replication, long-term control of hepatic necrosis resulting inflammation, prevention of cirrhosis, and malignant transformation of hepatocytes.

Therapy with 2.5–10 million units generally given daily for about one week, then 3 times weekly for a total 1–6 months in patients with chronic infection has been associated with a response rate of improvement 25–40% of cases. Other data also suggest that IFN alfa can produce clinical, biochemical, and serologic remissions with hepatitis B virus-related renal injury. IFN alfa has also been used along with acyclovir and vidarabine, steroids and other lymphokines in an attempt to improve response rates.

It is also tried in management of some malignancies (chronic myeloid leukemia).

ANTICANCER DRUGS

Doses of anti-cancer drugs are modified by different workers for specific uses. Consult current protocols.

Actinomycin D: 10 to 15 mg/kg/day for 5 days. *Side effects:* Thrombocytopenia, agranulocytosis, myalgia, erythema, nausea, vomiting.

L-asparaginase: 1000 units/kg/D IM or IV for 10 to 20 days. *Side effects:* Uremia, CNS disturbances, hyperglycemia, pancreatitis.

Azathioprine: 1–5 mg/kg/D q 24h PO. *Side effects:* Leucopenia, fever, liver damage, pancreatitis.

Bleomycin: 12–20 mg/M^2 once or twice weekly 300 mg/kg, SC, IV or IM. *Side effects:* Rash, pruritus, vesiculation, pulmonary fibrosis.

Busulphan: 60 µg/kg/D PO. *Side effects:* Thrombocytopenia, cataract, pulmonary fibrosis, hyperpigmentation.

Chlorambucil: 200 mg/kg/D. *Side effects:* Bone marrow depression.

28

Cisplatin: 15–20 mg/M^2/D for 5 days. *Side effects:* Bone marrow depression, nephrotoxic, ototoxic.

Cyclophosphamide: 2–3 mg/kg/U PO or IV is a conservative dose for susceptible neoplasms. Higher dose of 4–8 mg/kg IV for 6 days followed by oral dose of 1–5 mg/kg may be used. *Side effects:* Leucopenia, alopecia, hemorrhagic cystitis.

Cyclosporin A: 10–25 mg/kg/D PO. IV dose 5–6 mg/kg/D in slow infusion. *Side effects:* Nephrotoxic, gastrointestinal disturbances, hirustism, gum hypertrophy, angioedema.

Cytarabine (cytosine arabinosides): 2 mg/kg/D IV. *Side effects:* Granulocytopenia, megaloblastic anemia, neurotoxic, nephrotoxic, flu-like syndrome.

Dacarbazine DTIC: 2–4.5 mg/kg/IV. *Side effects:* Pancytopenia, paresthesia, flushing.

Daunorubicin: 25–50 mg/M^2 IV max dose 550 mg/M^2. *Side effects:* Pancytopenia, cardiotoxic, rashes, red colored urine.

Doxorubicin: 60–75 mg/M^2 IV max dose 550 mg/M^2. *Side effects:* Same as daunorubicin.

Hydroxyurea: 20–30 mg/kg/D PO. *Side effects:* Bone marrow suppression, megaloblastic changes, impairment of renal function.

6-mercaptopurine: 2.5 mg/kg/D PO. *Side effects:* Bone marrow depression, jaundice, hepatotoxic, hematuria.

Methotrexate: Standard dose 2.5–5 mg for children PO 2.5–10 mg for adults PO. Higher doses of 30 mg/M^2 have been used three times a week. *Side effects:* Bone marrow depression, ulceration of mouth, megaloblastic anemia, diarrhea, hepatoxic.

Mustine hydrochloride: Total dose 0.4 mg/kg or 6–10 mg/M^2 given in 2 or 4 daily consecutive IV injection. *Side effects:* 13 one marrow depression, tinnitus, vertigo, deafness.

Procarbazine: 50 mg/M^2/D PO during first week followed by 100 mg/M^2/D. *Side effects:* Bone marrow depression, somnolence, depression, agitation, peripheral neuropathy.

Vinblastine: 2.5 mg/M^2 IV increased by 1.25 mg/M^2 weekly to a maximum of 7.5 mg/M^2. *Side effects:* Bone marrow depression, headache, depression, psychosis, neuromyopathy, peripheral neuritis, convulsions.

Vincristine: 1.5–2 mg/M^2 IV weekly. *Side effects:* Same as vinblastine, bone marrow depression less common.

ANTICOAGULANTS

Acenocumarol (Sintrom): Dose is 1–8 mg/day PO single dose. Maintain prothrombin time 1.5 times of normal.

Heparin: IV: 50 u/kg IV bolus followed by 10–25 u/kg/hr as IV infusion or 50–100 u/kg/dose q 4 hr IV. SC: 25–50 u/kg q 12 hr*. DVT prophylaxis: 5000 u/dose SC q 8–12 hr until ambulatory.

Antidote: Protamine sulfate (1 mg neutralizes 1 mg : heparin). *Side effects:* Skin rash, alopecia. Contraindicated in ulcerative colitis, shock, hidden hemorrhage.

Phenindione: 0.5 to 4 mg/kg/day q 12 hr oral.

Warfarin: 0.05 to 0.34 mg/kg/day oral or parenteral. Adjust the dose to maintain desired prolongation of prothrombin time.

*The dose is adjusted by maintaining clotting time at twice the normal.

ANTICONVULSANTS

Refer to Chapter 17.

ANTIDOTES

Ipecac syrup: < 1 yr 5–10 mL/dose, others 15–20 mL/dose. Do not use in semi-comatose child or after charcoal administration.

Deferoxamine (Desferal): 20 mg/kg IM or IV. Slow subcutaneous infusion every 6 h; dose to be adjusted depending upon the response. *Side effects:* Hypotension, shock, cramps, diarrhea. Contraindicated in renal insufficiency.

Dimercaprol (BAL): 2.5 mg /kg PO every 4 hours on the first day, every 6 hours on the next 2 days, every 12 hours for the next 10 days and thereafter 24 hourly for the next 10 days. *Side effects:* Burning sensation, muscle aches, fever, hemolysis in G-6-PD deficiency.

Edetate calcium disodium: 12.5–30 mg/kg/dose IV 12 hourly for 5 days. *Side effects:* Proteinuria, hematuria.

Methylene blue: 1–2 mg/kg/dose IV (in 5 minutes).

Nalorphine (Lethidrone): 0.1 mg/kg/dose IM or IV.

Naloxone (Narcan): 0.01 mg/kg/dose IM or IV. Repeat if needed.

Penicillamine (Cuprimid): Infants 5 mg/kg/dose 3–4 c times daily. *Side effects:* Nephrotoxic, hepatotoxic, leucopenia, thrombocytopenia, cataract, bleeding diathesis.

Digoxin specific Fab antibody (Digibind) is a recently introduced preparation for digoxin poisoning. Given by IV infusion. Approximately 60 mg binds 1 mg of digoxin.

ANTIEMETICS

Dimenhydrinate: 5 mg/kg/day q 6 hr oral, 1M or IV. Avoid in children below 2 years. Maximum dose 2–6 yrs: 75 mg/day, 6–12 yrs: 150 mg/day.

Domeperidone (Domstal): 0.3 mg/kg/dose PO, IM may be repeated after 4 to 8 hours. *Side effects:* Mild extra-pyramidal symptoms.

Metoclopramide (Perinorm, Reglan): 0.5 to 2 mg/kg/D PO, IM q 6–8 h. *Side effects:* Extrapyramidal symptoms.

Ondansetron hydochloride: Oral dose <4 yr: 2 mg q 4 hr, 4–11 yrs: 4 mg q 4 hr, >12 yr: 8 mg q 4 hr. IV dose for >3 yrs old 0.15–0.45 mg/kg/dose at 30 min before and 4 and 8 hr after emetogenic drugs. Indicated in chemotherapy and radiotherapy induced emesis (not indicated below 4 years of age).

Cisapride: 0.5 mg/kg/D PO q 6–8 h. Indicated for gastroesophageal reflux, chronic constipation.

Prochlorperazine (Stemetil): 0.5 mg/kg/D PO q 8 h. IM dose is half of oral dose. *Side effects:* Bone marrow depression, CNS depression, extrpyramidal symptoms.

Promethazine theoclate: 0.5 mg/kg/dose q 8–12 hr oral. Administer first dose 1–2 hr before travel. *Indications:* Motion sickness. C/I: children <2 yrs; asthma, sleep apnea.

Triflupromazine (Siquil): 0.5 mg/kg/day q 8 h PO. IM dose is half. *Side effects:* Drowsiness, hypotension.

ANTIHISTAMINICS

Most antihistaminics are histamine H1 blocking agents and exert their action by competing with H1 receptors. These do not prevent release of histamine but have varying degrees of anticholinergic and antiserotonergic activity.

Astemizole (Stemiz, Astelong): 2 mg/10 kg body weight. Below 6 yr not recommended. Single daily dose. Should be taken half an hour before meals. *Side effects:* Weight gain with prolonged use.

Cetrizine (Alerid): Non sedating long acting. Dose 0.2 mg/kg once day PO.

Clemastine (Tavegyl): 1 to 3 yrs: 0.25 mg – 0.5 mg BD, 3–6 yrs: 0.5 mg BD, 6–12 yrs: 0.5–1 mg BD; > 12 year: 1 mg BD. Avoid below 1 year of age. Useful for urticaria, contact dermatitis.

Chlorpeniramine maleate: Children 0.35 mg/kg/day q 4–6 hr. According to age: 2–6 yrs: 1 mg, 6–12 yrs: 2 mg, >12 yrs: 4 mg q 4 to 6 hrly. *Side effects:* Hypotension, sedation, urinary retention, oculogyric spasms may occur with higher doses and after a few days of therapy.

Cyproheptadine hyprochloride: 0.25 mg/kg/D q 8 h PO. *Side effects:* Same as chlorpheniramine.

Dimethindene maleate: Children >12 yrs; 1–2 mg q 8 hrly or 2.5 mg SR twice a day.

Diphenhydramine hydrochloride: 5 mg/kg/day q 6 hr oral, maximum dose 300 mg/24 hr. For anaphylaxis or phenothiazine overdose 1–2 mg /kg IV slowly.

Fexofenadine: 30 mg BD for children < 12 years and 60 mg BD or 120 mg OD for children >12 yrs.

Hydroxyzine hydrochloride: 2 mg/kg/day q 6 hrly oral; 0.5–1 mg/kg/dose q 4–6 hr IM.

Ketotifen: 1 mg twice daily for children. Indicated in prophylaxis of allergic bronchial asthma, symptomatic treatment of allergic rhinitis and conjunctivitis. *Side effects:* None.

Loratadine: It is a long acting selective periheral H1 antagonist with minimal sedation. Above 3 yrs upto 30 kg weight 5 mg oral per day; 12 yrs 10 mg once a day oral.

Methdilazine hydrochloride: >3 yrs 4 mg q 6–12 hrly.

Pheniramine maleate (avil): 0.5 mg/kg/D PO, I.M or IV q 8h. *Side effects:* Same as chlorpheniramine.

Promethazine hydrochloride (Phengran): 0.1 mg/kg/day q 6 to 8 hr and 0.5 mg/kg/dose at HS oral PRN.

Nausea and vomiting or sedation : 0.25–1 mg/kg/dose q 4 to 6 hr oral, IM, IV or PR.

Motion sickness: 0.5 mg/kg/dose q 12 hr oral (1st dose 30 minutes before journey).
Side effects: Same as chlorpheniramine.

Pseudoephedrine: Children <12 yrs 4 mg/kg/day q 6 to 8 hr oral, >12 yrs: 30–60 mg/dose q 6–8 hr PO. Maximum dose 240 mg per day.

ANTIHYPERTENSIVES

Refer to Chapter 13.

ANTISPASMODICS

Dicyclomine hydrochloride (Cyclominol, Colimex): Infants below 6 months: 5–10 drops (colimex) 15 min before feeds, 6 month to 2 yrs: 10–20 drops 15 min before feeds, above 2 yrs 1 ml every 6 hr. *Side effects:* Dry mouth, urinary retention.

Hyoscine butylbromide (Buscopan): 6–12 years 10 mg q 8 h PO, 10–20 mg IV or IM bolus.

Oxyphenonium bromide (Antrenyl): 0.8 mg/kg/day q 6 hr oral. Give 5–10 drops in preschool children and 10–20 drops in older children q 6 hr. *Side effects:* Dry mouth, blurred vision, retention of urine, dizziness, fatigue, tremors.

Pipenzolate methyl bromide: 2.5–5 mg every 8 hr oral. Below 6 months 4 drops, 6 month to 1 year 8–10 drops, 1–3 yrs 16 drops before feed.

ANTITOXINS AND IMMUNOGLOBULINS

Anti-Rh D immunoglobulin: For prevention of rhesus sensitization of Rh negative mother. The baby or abortus should be Rh-positive and indirect Coomb's test during pregnancy should be negative. For antenatal prophylaxis give 300 mcg IM at 28 weeks and 34 weeks of gestation or a single dose within 72 hours of delivery. In twin pregnancy, give double the dose. In case of abortion, evacuation, procedures (CVS, amniocentesis, external cephalic version) and trauma give 250 mcg IM.

Antisnake venom: It contains a mixture of four enzyme-refined lyophilized polyvalent antisnake venom serum (common Krait, Cobra, Russell's viper and saw-scaled viper). The total dose of antivenin serum is around 5 vials (50 ml) for mild, 5–15 vials for moderate manifestations and 15–20 vials (150–200 ml) for severe cases. Smaller children may require one and half times of this dose because they receive larger dose of venom per unit body weight. The antivenin is given IV diluted in 250 ml of one-fifth saline. It is safe to maintain an infusion rate of 20 ml/kg/hr. Use steroids and antihistamines in addition. Exclude horse serum allergy by injecting intradermal 0.02 ml of 1:10 diluted antivenin. In subjects with hypersensitivity careful desensitization is undertaken. *Side effects:* Serum sickness, anaphylaxis.

Diphtheria antitoxin: *For Schick test positive contacts.* One dose of diphtheria toxoid should be given in one arm and 500–2000 units of diphtheria antitoxin IM in other arm. Six weeks later, give prophylactic toxoid in order to complete the course of active immunization in form of 3 doses of toxoid at monthly intervals. *For treatment,* the dose is not related to age and weight of the patient: Pharyngeal or laryngeal diphtheria of 48 hours duration 20,000–40,000 units IV. Nasopharyngeal diphtheria, 40,000–60,000 units IV. Extensive disease of more than 3 days duration with neck swelling, 80,000–1,20,000 units IV.

Human normal immunoglobulin: For prophylaxis and treatment of viral diseases, bums, bacterial infections, and primary immunodeficiency disorders:

Primary immunodeficiency disorders 0.2 mL/kg IM every 4 weeks.

Attenuation of disease among close contacts of *Measles.* 0.25 mL/kg IM within 6 days of exposure; *Hepatitis A.* 0.02–0.04 mL/kg/IM of a 10% solutions.; *Hepatitis B (Hepatitis B immune globulin).* 0.06 mL/kg IM to maximum of 3–5 mL given within 7 days of exposure. Repeat 30 days after exposure. *Side effects:* Coagulopathy, thrombocytopenia. Contraindicated in IgA deficiency and allergy to human immunoglobulin.

Human tetanus specific immunoglobulin: Prophylactic: 250 IU IM; Therapeutic: 30–300 IU/kg IV; Intrathecal: 250–500 IU single dose.

Intravenous immune gamma-globulin (IVIG): Dose 0.4 to 1g/kg/D IV infusion over 2 hours daily for 5 days or 2 g/kg IV infusion over 10–12 hrs as a single dose. *Possible uses.* (i) Idiopathic thrombocytopenic purpura, (ii) Kawasaki disease, (iii) myasthenia gravis, (iv) autoimmune neutropenia, (v) systemic lupus erythematosus, (vi) juvenile rheumatoid arthritis, (vii) Guillaine-Barré syndrome, (viii) dermatomyositis, (ix) psoriasis, and (x) atopic allergy.

Human rabies specific immunoglobulin: 20 units/kg. Half for infiltration at the site of bite and half IM over gluteal region if patient presents within 24 hours. The total dose is given IM, if patient presents between 1–7 days. The rabies vaccine should be administered simultaneously.

Tetanus antitoxin: Prophylactic: 3,000–5,000 units SC, IM; Therapeutic: 10,000 units IM or IV; Intrathecal: 250–500 units q 24 h for 3 days. *Side effects:* Serum sickness, anaphylaxis.

Varicella zoster immunoglobulin (VZIG): 125 units/kg IM within 48 hours or at least within 96 hours of exposure to varicella.

BRONCHODILATORS AND ANTI-ASTHMA AGENTS

Adrenaline: 0.01 mL/kg/dose (maximum 0.5 mL/dose) of 1 : 1000 solution SC. Repeat the dose after 15–20 min. *Side effects:* Palpitations, anxiety.

Aminophylline: 5–7 mg/kg/dose PO every 8 h. For status asthmaticus 5–7 mg/kg loading dose IV followed by 0.9 mg/kg/h. If patient is already receiving oral aminophylline do not use loading dose. For apneic attacks in preterm infants 5 mg/kg loading dose slow IV followed by 2 mg/kg PO or IV q 8 h. *Side effects:* Irritability, convulsions.

Bambuterol: An oral long acting prodrug of terbutaline with 24 hr duration of action. 2–5 yr: 5 mg, 6–12 yr: 10 mg single dose. May be useful in nocturnal asthma. Presently recommended for use in children above 2 yrs of age.

Beclomethasone dipropionate (Beclate inhaler): Inhalation of 50–100 µg of beclomethasone 3–4 times per day (maximum 10 inhalations in 24 hours) in children with chronic asthma requiring corticosteroid therapy for 10–12 weeks.

Budesonide (Pulmicort inhaler): Inhalation of 100 µg of budesonide 2–3 times a day (maximum 8 inhalations in 24 hours). Meter dose inhalers are used with a spacer, while rotacaps with a rotahaler. Baby mask can be used in infants.

Ciclosonide: Long acting steroid one (80 mcg) or two (160 mcg) puff/day. Not to be used below 12 years of age.

Formoterol fumarate: 12 mcg inhalation twice daily. It is a long acting selective beta-2 adrenergic stimulant. Not for treatment of acute asthma.

Fluticasone propionate: 50–500 mcg/day in two divided doses. (Mild persistent asthma 50–100 mcg/day; moderate persistent 100–200 mcg/day; severe persistent 200–500 mcg/d). Adults 100–1000 mcg/day.

Orciprenaline (Alupent): 0.3–0.5 mg/kg/dose PO with maximum of 1 mg/kg/D.

Ipratropium bromide (Ipravent): As neubliser 250 mcg to be diluted in 2–4 ml of saline and given over 10 minutes, every 20 minutes for 3 doses followed by 250 mcg nebulization every 2–4 hours. Ipratropium MDI 1–2 puffs thrice daily.

Ketotifen: Children >2 yrs 1 mg twice daily for children. Start at lower dosage at night for 2 to 3 days.

Montelukast sodium: 2–6 years: 4 mg once a day, 6–14 years: 5 mg once daily, >14 yr: 10 mg oral once daily in the evening. *Indications:* exercise induced asthma, alternate to long acting B 2 agonist.

Salbutamol (Albuterol, Ventorlin): 0.1–0.4 mg/kg/dose PO every 8 hours. Inhaler 1–2 puffs of 100 µg every 6–8 hours. Injection 4–6 ug/kg/dose SC, IM or IV q 6–8 h. It is given effectively through nebulizer with an airflow of 6 L/min delivering 2–5 micron size particles. *Side effects:* Headache, tremor, irritability.

Salmeterol: 1–2 puffs twice a day. Maximum 4 puffs twice a day or rotacap once or twice a day. It is long acting and provides prolonged bronchodilation. (Not recommended for children below 4 years of age).

Sodium cromoglycate: Initiating dose is 1–2 puffs (5 mg per MDI dose) 3–4 times/d or 1 rotacap (20 mg/cap) 3–4 times/d. Maintenance dose: 1 puff 3–4 times/day or 2–3 rotacaps per day. Adults 2 puffs 4 times daily. Continuous prophylaxis is required, may take 4–6 week for evident beneficial effect.

Terbutaline (Bricanyl): 0.1–0.15 mg/kg/D q 8 h orally. 0.005 to 0.01 mg/kg/D SC, IM or slow IV divided doses 8 hourly. Inhaler 1–2 puffs of 250 µg every 6–8 h. *Side effects:* Same as salbutamol.

Zafirlukast: 40 mg/d in 2 divided dose for prophylaxis and treatment of asthma in children older than 12 years.

Note: Metered dose inhalers should be used with spacers. For infants MDI with spacer can be used with a baby face mask. Rotacap dose is double of the inhaler dose. Rotacaps are administered using Rotahaler.

CARDIOTONICS

Inotropic Agents

Dobutamine (Dobutrex): 2.5–25 µg/kg/min IV continuous infusion. *Side effects:* Tachycardia, hypertension, arrhythmias.

Dopamine: 2–5 µg/kg/min IV continuous infusion increased slowly to 20 µg/kg/min. Adjust the dose for the desired effects. Maximum recommended dose is up to 30 µg/kg/min. *Side effects:* Tachyarrhythmias, hypertension, vasoconstriction, vomiting. Extravasation may cause tissue necrosis.

Digoxin: Digitalizing dose: for *premature infants* 0.04 mg/kg/D, *mature neonates* 0.06 mg/kg/D, infants (1–12 month) 0.06–0.08 mg/kg/D, older children 0.04 mg/kg/D PO (parenteral dose is 2/3rd of this amount). One half of digitalizing dose is given stat followed by 1/4th dose after 8 hours and 1/4th of digitalizing dose after 16 hours. The maintenance dose is 1/4th of digitalizing dose and given once a day. *Side effects:* Nausea, vomiting, pulsus bigeminy, extra systoles, partial or complete heart blocks, sinus arrhythmia, atrial or ventricular tachycardia.

Milirinone: 50–75µg/kg loading dose, followed by 0.25–1.0 µg/kg/min continuous infusion. Inotropic and vasodilatory action.

Mephentermine (Mephentine): 0.4 mg/kg/dose IV blous or slow infusion.

Norepinephrine: 0.05–0.1 µg/kg/min. Titrate dose to desired effect (maximum dose 2 µg/kg/min). Used in vasodilatory and septic shock.

Isoproterenol hydrochloride: 0.05–0.5 µg/kg/min IV.

DIURETICS

Acetazolamide (Diamox): As diuretic 5 mg/kg/D PO in divided—doses 8 hourly. For treatment of hydrocephalus 50–70 mg/kg/D PO in divided doses 8 hourly. Also useful in epilepsy and glaucoma. *Side effects:* Drowsiness, crystalluria, renal calculi, convulsion, acidosis.

Bumetanide (Burnet): 0.01–0.02 mg/kg/dose oral, if needed may be repeated at intervals of 6–12 hrs. Patients refractory to furosemide may respond to bumetanide. It is approximately 40 times more potent on a milligram per milligram basis than furosemide. *Side effects:* Muscle cramps, nausea, vomiting, gynecomastia, leucopenia, thrombocytopenia.

Chlorthalidone (Hythalton): 1–2 mg/kg/D PO single dose.

Chlorthiazide (Chlortride): 20 mg/kg/D PO in 2 doses q 12h. *Side effects:* Hyperglycemia, glycosuria, blood dyscrasias, neonatal thrombocytopenia, hypokalemia, hypotension.

Ethacrynic acid (Ethacrine): 0.5–1.0 mg/kg/dose IV every 12–24 hours or 3 mg/kg/D PO. *Side effects:* Hyponatremia, hypokalemia, hypotension, nerve deafness.

Frusemide (Lasix): 2–4 mg/kg/D PO or 1–2 mg/kg/D IV. *Side effects:* Electrolyte disturbances, dermatitis, blurring of vision, hypokalemia, hypotension, thrombocytopenia.

Hydrochlorthiazide (Hygrotone): 1–2 mg/kg/D PO q 12 h. *Side effects:* Same as chlorthiazide.

Metalazone: 0.2–0.4 mg/kg /day q 24 hrs.

Spironolactone (Aldactone): 2–3 mg Ikg/D PO q 8 h. *Side effects:* Drowsiness, confusion, gynecomastia.

Triamterene (Dytide): 2–4 mg/kg/D PO q 12 h. *Side effects:* Hyperkalemia (it is a potassium sparing diuretic), hyponatremia, dry mouth, headache.

HORMONES AND DRUGS FOR ENDOCRINAL DISORDERS

Adrenal

Beclomethasone diproprionate (Beclate): Aerosol 50 to 100 µg per puff every 6–8 hours (max 10 puffs per day). Nasal spray 50–100 µg/d q 12–24 h.

Betamethasone (Betnesol): 0.1–0.2 mg/kg daily in divided doses oral. 750 mcg is equivalent to 5 mg prednisolone. Upto 1 year: 1 mg, 1–5 years: 2 mg, 6–12 years: 4 mg daily. Adult dose 0.5 – 6 mg /day. *Indications:* Congenital adrenal hyperplasia, brain edema, severe attack of bronchial asthma and autoimmune disorders. For enhancing fetal lung maturity, when labor starts before 34 weeks, administer to the mother 12 mg IM in 2 doses 24 hr apart.

Cortisone acetate (Cortin): 0.7 mg/kg/D PO for physiological requirement. Therapeutic dose is 2.5–10 mg/kg/D PO every 8 hours. *Side effects:* Immediate-moon facies, acne, increased appetite, reduced resistance to infections, headache, papilledema, gastritis, peptic ulcer, hypertension, electrolyte disturbances, activation of tuberculosis, glaucoma, pseudotumor cerebri. *Prolonged therapy.* Myopathy, osteoporosis, growth retardation, cataract, adrenal cortical atrophy.

Dexamethasome (Decadron): 0.05–0.5 mg/kg/day oral. For CAH 0.5 to 1.5 mg per day oral. Adult 10–50 mg stat then 4–8 mg 4 hrly, reduce 2mg 8 hrly. For cerebral edema 0.5 mg/kg/dose q 6 hr IM or IV. For high dose pulse dexamethasone therapy for autoimmune disorders affecting skin, joints and kidneys give 5 mg/kg as a slow infusion (not to exceed 100 mg).

Hydrocortisone (Efcorlin): For status asthmaticus 25–50 mg/kg/dose q 4–6 h IV. For endotoxic shock 50 mg/kg initial dose followed by 50–150 mg/kg/D q 6 h IV for 48–72 h. For acute adrenal insufficiency 1–2 mg/kg/dose IV bolus, then 25–150 µg/kg/D q 6 h. CAH initial dose 0.5–0.7mg/kg/D divided 1/4 in morning 1/4 at noon and 1/2 at night; maintenance dose 0.3–0.4 mg/kg/D divided as above.

Prednisolone (Wysolone, deltacortril): Dose 1/5 of cortisone. 2 mg/kg/D PO divided doses 6–8 hourly or single dose in the morning.

Methylprednisolone (Solumedrol): 0.4–1.7 mg/kg/D IM or IV. For emergency higher doses of 30 mg/kg IV bolus over 10 to 20 minutes and repeated after 4 hours if necessary. For pulse therapy 30 mg/kg daily for 3–5 days. Shock 30 mg/kg/dose q 6 h for 2–3 days.

Triamcinolone (Kenacort): Oral upto 24 mg daily in divided doses. Deep IM 40 mg or intra-articular 2.5–15 mg. No sodium retention effect. Avoid in children below 6 years.

Pituitary

ACTH (Acthargel): 1.6 units/kg/IM or IV single dose. For infantile spasms give 20–40 units/kg/D in 2 divided doses.

Vasopressin (Pitressin): 5–20 units every 4 hours for diabetes insipidus. For bleeding esophageal varices, 20 units IV over 15 minutes followed by 0.2 U/min or 0.33 U/kg/hr. For central diabetes insipidus, 1.5–10 mU/kg/min. For catecholamine refractory vasodilatory septic shock, 0.3–2.0 mU/kg/min. *Side effects:* Hypertension, water intoxication.

Desmopressin (DDAVP): Analogue of vasopressin for nasal instillation. Devoid of pressor activity. 5–30 µg once or twice daily for diabetes insipidus. For primary nocturnal enuresis 20 µg at bed time increased to 40 µg (never use for >28 days period). IM or IV injection 4 µg.

Growth hormone: 0.09–0.2 unit/kg/day SC or IM daily three times per week till accepted height is achieved or bone fusion occurs. For Turner Syndrome 0.09–0.1 unit/kg SC daily can be increased to 0.11–0.14 unit /kg daily.

Thyroid

Carbimazole (Neomercazole): 1–2 mg/kg/D PO divided doses 8 hourly. *Side effects:* Urticaria, loss of taste, alopecia, pigmentation, bone marrow depression.

Liothyronine sodium: 0.5–1.5 µg/kg/day single dose oral. For hypothyroid coma 5–20 µg IV every 12 hours.

Potassium iodide: 1 ml saturated Lugol's iodine solution per day q 8 hr oral or potassium iodide 50–150 mg/day q 8 hr oral. Max 0.4 mol/kg/hr; min oral dose 1 mmol/kg <5 yrs and age >5 yrs 0.5 mmol/kg

Propylthiouracil: 1–4 mg/kg/day. Under 10 years 50–150 mg/day q 8 hr and >10 years 150–300 mg/day q 8 hr. Maintenance dose 50 mg twice daily.

Thyroxine sodium: 10–15 µg/kg/day in newborn babies and 5 µg/kg/day in children, single dose oral empty stomach in the morning. (By 5 years of age 100 µg per day is reached and by 12 years 200–250 µg per day).

Pancreas

Insulin (Plain): Insulin for diabetic ketoacidosis.

High dose schedule: Soluble insulin 2 units/kg, half IV and half SC stat. If initial blood glucose is more than 500 mg/dl, administer additional 1 unit/kg IV after one hour, followed by 1 unit/kg SC every 2 hours till blood sugar falls below 250mg/dl.

Low dose schedule: 0.1 unit/kg IV bolus followed by 0.1 unit/kg/hour continuous infusion in normal saline with the help of an infusion pump till blood sugar comes down to 300 mg/dl. Switch over to N/2 saline in 5% dextrose and give 0.25 units/kg q 6 hr SC.

TRACE METALS

Magnesium sulphate: 2–3 mEq/kg/D as maintenance needs in cases of protein energy malnutrition. Magnesium sulphate 50% solution provides 4 mEq/mL. 20–100 mg/kg/dose as 1% solution by slow IV infusion not more than 100 mg per minute. 100 mg/kg/dose as 50% solution if given IM.

Zinc sulphate: For deficiency 0.5 mg/kg/day for infants; 10 mg/kg/day for older children and 6 mg/kg/d for acrodermatitis enteropathica.

SEDATIVES, HYPNOTICS AND ANTIDEPRESSANTS

Diazepam: Sedative and anxiolytic in doses of 2–5 mg PO. As an anticonvulsant 0.2 mg/kg/dose IV (max 10 mg). May repeat in 15 minutes.

Lorazepam: Dose 0.1 mg/kg IV. Duration of action is longer than diazepam. Can repeat after 5 minutes. Oral dose 0.03–0.05 mg/kg/dose q 8–12 h.

Clonazepam: 0.03 mg/kg/D PO q 8 h. Gradually increase till maximum dose of 0.1–0.3 mg/kg/D is achieved.

Butyrophenones (Haloperidol): 0.25 mg PO q 12 h (for anxiety). 5–10 mg/D PO q 12 h (for chorea). *Side effects:* Extrapyramidal reactions, dyskinesia.

Tricyclic antidepressants. (Imipramine): 1.5 mg/kg/D PO single or divided doses. For nocturnal enuresis 25 mg at bed time. For children over 10 years old, 50 mg may be given. Duration of treatment 6–8 weeks. *Side effects:* Anticholinergic effects, dry mouth constipation, urinary retention, blurred vision, tremors, hypotension.

Chloral hydrate: 5–10 mg/kg/dose for sedation and 20–75 mg/kg/dose for heavy sedation.

Chlorpromazine: 2.5–6 mg/kg/day q 6 hr oral. In chorea start with 50 mg/day oral and increase by 25 mg/day till chorea is controlled or maximum dose of 300 mg/day is achieved. For neonatal tetanus, 1 to 2 mg/kg per dose 2 to 4 hourly.

Fluoxetine hydrochloride: Children >5 yr give 5–10 mg oral once a day, maximum dose 20 mg per day.

Haloperidol: Infantile autism: 0.025–0.05 mg/kg/d, psychotic disorder: 0.05–0.15 mg/kg/d q 8–12 hr, non-psychotic behaviour disorder: 0.05–0.075 mg/kg/d, agitation 0.01–0.03 mg/kg/d q 8–12 hr.

Ketamine: For IV induction 0.5–2 mg/kg at a rate not to exceed 0.5 mg/kg/min; IM, oral, rectal 3–10 mg/kg/dose; nasal and sublingual 3–5 mg/kg/dose. Minor procedures 0.5–1.0 mg/kg. Sedative dose 2 mg/kg. The concomitant use of midazolam is beneficial.

Midazolam: 0.07–0.2 mg/kg/dose IM or IV for preoperative sedation or conscious sedation during mechanical ventilation. IV 0.2 mg/kg bolus followed by 0.4–0.6 µg/kg/min as continuous infusion. Oral or rectal 0.5–0 0.75 mg/kg/dose. Nasal or sublingual 0.2–0.5 mg/kg/dose.

Triclofos (Tricloryl): 20 mg/kg/dose for sedation.

VASODILATORS

Captopril: (Venous and arteriolar) Infants: 0.5 –6.0 mg/kg/day q8 hr oral, children: 12.5 mg q12 hr oral. Monitor total leukocyte count and renal functions

Hydralazine: (Arterial) 0.1–0. 5 mg/kg /dose IV 6 hr, 1–7.5 mg/kg /day q 6–8 hr.

Isosorbide dinitrate (Venous): 0.1 mg/kg/D PO q 6–8 h. *Side effects:* Flushing, headache.

Isoxuprine hydrochloride (Duvadilan): 0.5–1 mg/kg/D PO IM or IV q 8 h. *Side effects:* Hypotension.

Nifedipine: (Venous and arteriolar) 0.3 mg/kg/dose oral q 6hr

Prazosin: (Venous and arteriolar) 5–25 μg /kg/dose oral q 6hr. *Side effects:* Postural hypotension, dizziness, faintness, nasal stuffiness, priapism.

Sodium nitroprusside: (Venous and arteriolar) 0.5–8.0 μg /kg/min IV infusion. 50 mg is dissolved in one liter of 5% dextrose to provide concentration of 50 μg/ml.

Tolazoline: Used for pulmonary hypertension in newborns with RDS 1–2 mg/kg IV over 10 min followed by 1–2 mg/kg/hour in continuous infusion.

Xanthinol nicotinate (Complamina): 5–10 mg/kg/D IM or IV PO q 8 h. *Side effects:* Hypotension, flushing.

CEREBRAL ACTIVATORS

Pyritinol (Enecephabol): Improves cerebral metabolism and enhances neurotransmission, used in delayed development and sequelae of neurological illnesses.

Piracetam: Cerebral activator, used in mental subnormality. Dose: 150 mg/kg/D PO q 8 h.

Doxapram: Used for neonatal apnea 0.5–2.5 mg/kg/h continuous infusion.

Pemoline: Used for minimal brain dysfunction in older children in a dose of 1 mg/kg/D PO every day single dose. Increase weekly by 0.5 mg/kg till a maximum dose of 3 mg/kg/D. Not recommended for children less than 3 years of age.

MISCELLANEOUS

Acetazolamide (Diamox): 30–50 mg/kg/D PO q 6–8h.

Allopurinol: 10 mg/kg/D PO q 12 h.

Aminocaproic acid: 100 mg/kg/dose 4–6 hourly IV, PO, may cause hypercoagulation, nausea, vomiting.

Bisacodyl (Dulcolax): 5–10 mg to be given 6 hr before the desired effect.

Calcitriol (1, 25-dihydroxycholecalciferol): In renal failure, use 0.01–0.05 μg/kg/24 hour.

Calcium gluconate (Elemental calcium 9%): 1–2 ml/kg of 10% solution. IV infusion is given very slowly under cardiac monitoring.

Cimetidine: 20–40 mg/kg/D PO, IV q 6 h.

Dantrolene: 0.5 mg/kg/twice daily. Increase dose till desired effect is reached in cases of chronic spasticity, for example, cerebral palsy. Intravenously, the drug is used for malignant hyperthermia.

Ergocalciferol: Used for renal osteodystrophy in a dose of 25,000–2,50,000 i.u./D PO, decrease the dose once healing occurs.

Famotidine: 1–1.2 mg/kg/D, PO q 12 h. Maximum dose is 40 mg per day.

Glycerol: 05–1 g/kg/dose PO 6 hr.

Human albumin: 1 g/kg/dose IV over 30–120 minutes for hypoprotinemia.

Ketamine: 0.5–2.0 mg/kg stat IV 3–7 mg/kg stat supplemental dose 1/3rd of initial dose. Increases respiratory secretions. Atropine is helpful.

Lactulose: For cases of hepatic coma, <2 yrs 2.5 mL/D PO, PR q 12 h (5 mL contains 3.35 g). >2 yrs 5–10 mL PO, PR q12h. *Side effects:* Diarrhea.

Magnesium sulfate: As cathartic 250 mg/kg/dose PO. For hypomagnesemia 100 mg/kg/dose IM 4–6 h (1% solution contains 10 mg magnesium/mL (0.08 mEq/mL). For asthma 50–100 mg/kg/dose IV.

Mannitol: 0.5–3 g/kg/dose IV single dose. It should be given over 30–60 min.

Pancuronium: Neonates 0.05–1.0 mg/kg/dose 1V undiluted over 5 minutes. More than one month 0.04–0.1 mg/kg/dose q 1–4 h. 0.05–0.2 mg/kg/h as continuous infusion.

Physostigmine: 0.001–0.03 mg/kg/dose IM, SC, IV. Repeat q 15–20 min to desired effect or maximum dose of 20 mg.

Potassium chloride: 1–2 mEq/kg/D q8 h PO. Maximum IV dose is 20 mEq/h of infusate.

Pralidoxime (PAM): 25–50 mg/kg stat repeat for organophosphorus poisoning.

Probenecid: 20–40 mg/kg/D q 8 h with initial loading dose of 25 mg/kg PO.

Prostaglandin E1: Useful to maintain the patency of ductus arteriosus prior to surgery in neonates; dose 0.05–0.4 μg/kg/min. Usual maintenance dose is 0.01–0.4 μg/kg/min.

Pulmonary surfactant: *Survanta* 4 mL/kg/dose intratracheally. *Exosurf* 5 mL/kg/dose. *Neosurf* 5.0 mL/kg/dose.

Ranitidine: 2 mg/kg/D PO, IM or IV q 12 h. *Side effects:* Renal impairment.

Sodium bicarbonate: 1–2 mEq/kg/dose or calculated on basis of base deficit as follows:
Base deficit × weight in kgs × 0.6 = mEq, or mL of 7.5% solution of sodium bicarbonate required for correction.

29 Integrated Management of Neonatal and Childhood Illnesses

Child health has remained an essential component of most of the national health programs in India from Expanded Program of Immunization (EPI) in 1974 to the most recent National Rural Health Mission. Introduction of several new technologies in early 1980's have made it possible to prevent major infectious diseases of childhood through mass immunization campaigns and treatment of diarrheal dehydration and malaria at low cost. However, the current child health scenario indicates that common childhood illnesses like acute respiratory infections, diarrhea, measles, malaria, and malnutrition continue to result in high mortality among children less than 5 years of age. The available trends of under five mortality rate (U5MR) suggest that the national goal to reduce U5MR to 42 per 1000 live births by 2015 is not a realistic projection, even with the currently available interventions. Even though effective interventions to manage these conditions are available, the current child health scenario is not likely to change significantly unless new strategies are introduced to reduce child mortality and improve child health and development. Integrated Management of Childhood Illness (IMCI) strategy optimizes public health approach for improving children's health through the delivery of essential child health interventions.

Why Integrated Management?

Many well known interventions like universal immunization, essential newborn care, exclusive breastfeeding during first 6 months of life, appropriate complementary feeding, oral rehydration therapy, and timely and appropriate use of antibiotics in pneumonia have proven to be effective. While each of these interventions is successful, there is evidence to suggest that an integrated approach is needed to manage sick children. Besides, sick children often present with overlapping signs and symptoms common to different illnesses and often suffer from more than one illness which may necessitate different treatments. Another reason for integrated approach is the need for incorporating preventive strategies such as immunization and nutrition along with curative care.

INTEGRATED MANAGEMENT OF NEONATAL AND CHILDHOOD ILLNESS (IMNCI) STRATEGY

Integrated Management of Childhood Illness (IMCI) strategy, developed by World Health Organization in collaboration with UNICEF and many other agencies in mid-1990s, combines improved management of common childhood illnesses as well as prevention of diseases and promotion of health by dealing with counselling on feeding and immunization. This strategy has been adapted and expanded in India to include neonatal care at home as well as in the health facilities and renamed as ***Integrated Management of Neonatal and Childhood Illness (IMNCI).***

Essential Components of IMNCI Strategy

The IMNCI strategy includes both preventive and curative interventions that aim to improve practices in health facilities, the health system and at home. At the core of the strategy is integrated case management of the most common neonatal and childhood problems with a focus on the most common causes of death in children < 5 years of age.

The strategy includes three main components:

- Improvements in the case-management skills of health staff through use of locally adapted guidelines
- Improvements in the overall health system; and
- Improvements in family and community health care practices.

This chapter elaborates the clinical guidelines for the treatment of sick children in an outpatient or primary care setting.

IMNCI Clinical Guidelines

The IMNCI clinical guidelines target children less than 5 years old, the age group that bears the highest burden of morbidity and mortality. The guidelines represent an evidence-based, syndromic approach to case management that includes rational, effective and affordable use of drugs. Careful and systematic assessment of common symptoms, using well-selected reliable clinical signs, helps to guide rational and effective actions.

An evidence-based syndromic approach can be used to determine: (a) health problem(s) the child may have, (b) severity of the child's condition and (c) actions that can be taken to care for the child (e.g. refer the child immediately, manage with available resources, or manage at home). In addition the guidelines suggest the adjustments required to manage with the capacity of health system and active involvement of family members in health care practices.

The Principles of Integrated Care

Depending on a child's age, various clinical signs and symptoms differ in their degrees of reliability and diagnostic value and importance. IMNCI clinical guidelines focus on children up to 5 years of age. The treatment guidelines have been broadly described under two age categories:

- Young infants age up to 2 months.
- Children age 2 months up to 5 years.

The IMNCI guidelines are based on the following principles:

- All children under 5 years of age must be examined for conditions which indicate ***immediate referral.***
- Children must be ***routinely assessed*** for major symptoms, nutritional and immunization status, feeding problems and other problems.
- Only a limited number of carefully ***selected clinical signs*** are used for assessment.
- ***Classification*** - a combination of individual signs is used to classify the severity of illness which calls for specific action rather than a 'diagnosis'. Classifications are colour coded and suggest referral **(pink)**, initiation of treatment in health facility **(yellow)** or management at home **(green).**
- IMNCI guidelines address ***most common***, but not all pediatric problems.
- IMNCI management protocols use a limited number of ***essential drugs.***
- Caretakers are ***actively involved*** in the treatment of children.
- IMNCI includes counselling of caretakers about ***home care*** including feeding, fluids and when to return to health facility.

IMNCI Case Management Process (Fig. 29.1)

Steps of case management process are:
Step 1: Assess the young infant/child
Step 2: Classify the illness
Step 3: Identify treatment
Step 4: Treat the young infant/child
Step 5: Counsel the mother
Step 6: Follow up care

29

Classification Tables

IMNCI classification table describes the steps of case management process: Assess, Classify and Identify Treatment (See chart). There are separate classification boxes for main symptoms, nutritional status and anemia. Classification tables are used starting with the **pink** rows. If the young infant/ child does not have the severe classifications, look at the **yellow** rows. For the classification tables that have a **green** row, if the young infant/ child does not have any of the signs in the pink or yellow rows, select the classification in the green row. If the young infant/child has signs from more than one row, the more severe classifications is selected. However, if the classification table has ***more than one arm*** (e.g. possible bacterial infection/jaundice, diarrhea in a sick child), one may have more than one classification from that box.

IMNCI classifications are not necessarily specific diagnoses, but they indicate what *action* needs to be taken. All classifications are colour coded: **pink** calls for hospital referral or admission, **yellow** for initiation of treatment, and **green** means that the child can be sent home with careful advice on when to return.

Effective Communication with the Mother/Care Provider

It is critical to communicate effectively with the infant's mother or caretaker. Proper communication helps to reassure the mother or caretaker that the infant will receive appropriate care. In addition, the success of home treatment depends on how well the mother or caretaker knows about giving the treatment and understands its importance.

OUTPATIENT MANAGEMENT OF YOUNG INFANTS AGE UP TO 2 MONTHS

Assess and Classify Sick Young Infants

Young infants (infants age <2 months) have special characteristics that must be considered when classifying their illness. They can become sick and die very quickly from serious bacterial infections. They frequently have only general signs such as few movements, fever or low body temperature. Mild chest indrawing is normal in young infants because their chest wall is soft. For these reasons, assessment, classification and treatment of young infant is somewhat different from an older infant or young child. The assessment procedure for this age group includes a number of important steps that must be followed by the health care provider, including: (1) history taking and communicating with the caretaker about the young infant's problem; (2) checking for possible bacterial infection/jaundice; (3) assessing for diarrhea if present ; (4) checking for feeding problem or malnutrition; (5) checking immunization status; and (6) assessing other problems.

Checking for Possible Bacterial Infection/Jaundice

In the first step all sick young infants are first examined to assess for signs of possible bacterial infection and jaundice. The bacterial infection can be serious bacterial infection or a localized infection such as skin infection or ear infection.

The clinical signs which point to possible serious bacterial infection are : *Convulsions* (as part of the current illness), *fast breathing* (the cut-off rate to identify fast

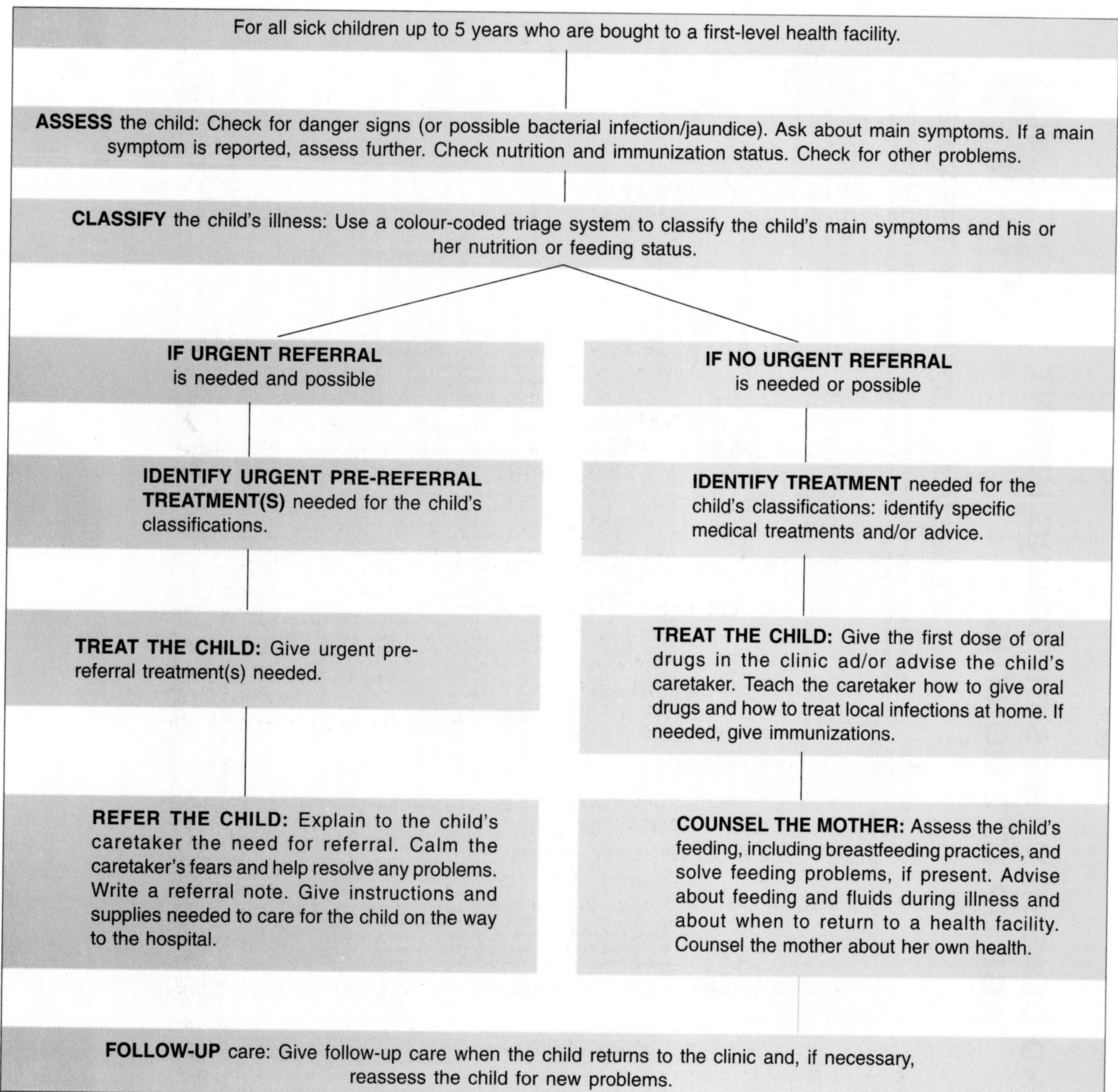

For all sick children up to 5 years who are bought to a first-level health facility.
ASSESS the child: Check for danger signs (or possible bacterial infection/jaundice). Ask about main symptoms. If a main symptom is reported, assess further. Check nutrition and immunization status. Check for other problems.
CLASSIFY the child's illness: Use a colour-coded triage system to classify the child's main symptoms and his or her nutrition or feeding status.
IF URGENT REFERRAL is needed and possible
IF NO URGENT REFERRAL is needed or possible
IDENTIFY URGENT PRE-REFERRAL TREATMENT(S) needed for the child's classifications.
IDENTIFY TREATMENT needed for the child's classifications: identify specific medical treatments and/or advice.
TREAT THE CHILD: Give urgent pre-referral treatment(s) needed.
TREAT THE CHILD: Give the first dose of oral drugs in the clinic ad/or advise the child's caretaker. Teach the caretaker how to give oral drugs and how to treat local infections at home. If needed, give immunizations.
REFER THE CHILD: Explain to the child's caretaker the need for referral. Calm the caretaker's fears and help resolve any problems. Write a referral note. Give instructions and supplies needed to care for the child on the way to the hospital.
COUNSEL THE MOTHER: Assess the child's feeding, including breastfeeding practices, and solve feeding problems, if present. Advise about feeding and fluids during illness and about when to return to a health facility. Counsel the mother about her own health.
FOLLOW-UP care: Give follow-up care when the child returns to the clinic and, if necessary, reassess the child for new problems.

Fig. 29.1: IMNCI Case Management Process

breathing in young infants is 60 breaths per minute or more; if the count is 60 breaths or more, the count should be repeated, because the breathing rate of a young infant is often irregular. If the second count is also 60 breaths or more, the young infant has fast breathing); *severe chest indrawing; nasal flaring; grunting; bulging fontanelle; >10 skin pustules; axillary temperature >37.5°C or <35.5°C; lethargy or unconsciousness;* and *less than normal movements.* Presence of any of these signs indicates possible serious bacterial infection which may be a part of sepsis or pneumonia. A young infant with possible serious bacterial infection is referred urgently to hospital after giving first dose of antibiotics. The mother is advised to continue breast feeding and to keep the baby warm on the way to hospital.

Pus or redness around the umbilicus or presence of <10 skin pustules or pus draining from ear is classified as local bacterial infection and treated with oral antibiotics.

Jaundice is the visible manifestation of hyperbilirubinemia. Occurrence of jaundice within first 24 hours of birth or after 14 days of age or deep jaundice visible as yellow palms and soles suggests pathological jaundice and is classified as a severe illness necessitating urgent referral to a hospital for evaluation. (Chart 29.1). An infant age 1–13 days who has jaundice but palms and soles are not yellow

29

Chart 29.1

ASSESS AND CLASSIFY THE SICK YOUNG INFANT AGE UP TO 2 MONTHS

ASSESS — CLASSIFY — IDENTIFY TREATMENT

ASK THE MOTHER WHAT THE YOUNG INFANT'S PROBLEMS ARE
- Determine if this is an initial or follow-up visit for this problem.
  - If follow-up visit, use the follow-up instructions on the bottom of this chart.

USE ALL BOXES THAT MATCH INFANT'S SYMPTOMS

A child with a pink classification needs URGENT attention, complete the assessment and pre-referral treatment immediately so referral is not delayed

CHECK FOR POSSIBLE BACTERIAL INFECTION / JAUNDICE

ASK:
- Has the infant had convulsions?

LOOK, LISTEN, FEEL:
- Count the breaths in one minute. Repeat the count if elevated.
- Look for severe chest indrawing.
- Look for nasal flaring.
- Look and listen for grunting.
- Look and feel for bulging fontanelle.

(YOUNG INFANT MUST BE CALM)

- Look for pus draining from the ear.
- Look at the umbilicus. Is it red or draining pus?
- Look for skin pustules. Are there 10 or more skin pustules or a big boil?
- Measure axillary temperature (if not possible, feel for fever or low body temperature).
- See if the young infant is lethargic or unconscious.
- Look at the young infant's movements. Are they less than normal?
- Look for jaundice? Are the palms and soles yellow?

	SIGNS	CLASSIFY AS	IDENTIFY TREATMENT (Urgent pre-referral treatments are in bold print.)
Classify ALL YOUNG INFANTS	• Convulsions or • Fast breathing (60 breaths per minute or more) or • Severe chest indrawing or • Nasal flaring or • Grunting or • Bulging fontanelle or • 10 or more skin pustules or a big boil or • If axillary temperature 37.5°C or above (or feels hot to touch) or temperature less than 35.5°C (or feels cold to touch) or • Lethargic or unconscious or • Less than normal movements.	**POSSIBLE SERIOUS BACTERIAL INFECTION**	➢ ***Give first dose of intramuscular ampicillin and gentamicin.*** ➢ ***Treat to prevent low blood sugar.*** ➢ ***Warm the young infant by skin to skin contact if temperature less than 36.5°C (or feels cold to touch) while arranging referral.*** ➢ ***Advise mother how to keep the young infant warm on the way to the hospital.*** ➢ ***Refer URGENTLY to hospital#***
	• Umbilicus red or draining pus or • Pus discharge from ear or • <10 skin pustules.	**LOCAL BACTERIAL INFECTION**	➢ ***Give oral co-trimoxazole or amoxycillin for 5 days.*** ➢ Teach mother to treat local infections at home. ➢ Follow up in 2 days.
And if the infant has jaundice	• Palms and soles yellow or • Age < 24 hours or • Age 14 days or more	**SEVERE JAUNDICE**	➢ ***Treat to prevent low blood sugar.*** ➢ ***Warm the young infant by skin to skin contact if temperature less than 36.5°C (or feels cold to touch) while arranging referral.*** ➢ ***Advise mother how to keep the young infant warm on the way to the hospital.*** ➢ ***Refer URGENTLY to hospital.***
	• Palms and soles not yellow	**JAUNDICE**	➢ Advise mother to give home care for the young infant. ➢ Advise mother when to return immediately. ➢ Follow up in 2 days.
And if the temp. is between 35.5 – 36.4°C	• Temperature between 35.5 – 36.4°C	**LOW BODY TEMPERATURE**	➢ Warm the young infant using skin to skin contact for one hour and REASSESS. ➢ Treat to prevent low blood sugar.

*# If referral is not possible, see the section **Where Referral Is Not Possible** in the module **Treat the Young Infant and Counsel the Mother**.*

THEN ASK:

Does the young infant have diarrhoea?*

IF YES, ASK:

- For how long?
- Is there blood in the stool?

LOOK AND FEEL:

- Look at the young infant's general condition. Is the infant:
  - Lethargic or unconscious?
  - Restless and irritable?
- Look for sunken eyes.
- Pinch the skin of the abdomen. Does it go back:
  - Very slowly (longer than 2 seconds)?
  - Slowly?

Classify DIARRHOEA

for DEHYDRATION

Signs	Classification	Treatment
Two of the following signs: • Lethargic or unconscious. • Sunken eyes. • Skin pinch goes back very slowly.	**SEVERE DEHYDRATION**	➢ ***Give first dose of intramuscular ampicillin and gentamicin.*** ➢ ***If infant also has low weight or another severe classification:*** – ***Refer URGENTLY to hospital with mother giving frequent sips of ORS on the way.*** – ***Advise mother to continue breastfeeding.*** – ***Advise mother how to keep the young infant warm on the way to the hospital.*** ***OR*** ➢ If infant does not have low weight or any other severe classification: – Give fluid for severe dehydration (Plan C) and then refer to hospital after rehydration.
Two of the following signs: • Restless, irritable. • Sunken eyes. • Skin pinch goes back slowly.	**SOME DEHYDRATION**	➢ ***If infant also has low weight or another severe classification*** – ***Give first dose of intramuscular ampicillin and gentamicin*** – ***Refer URGENTLY to hospital with mother giving frequent sips of ORS on the way.*** – ***Advise mother to continue breastfeeding.*** – ***Advise mother how to keep the young infant warm on the way to the hospital.*** ➢ *If infant does not have low weight or another severe classification:* - Give fluids for some dehydration (Plan B). - Advise mother when to return immediately. - Follow up in 2 days.
• Not enough signs to classify as some or severe dehydration.	**NO DEHYDRATION**	➢ Give fluids to treat diarrhoea at home (Plan A). ➢ Advise mother when to return immediately. ➢ Follow up in 5 days if not improving.

and if diarrhoea 14 days or

Signs	Classification	Treatment
• Diarrhoea lasting 14 days or more.	**SEVERE PERSISTENT DIARRHOEA**	➢ Give first dose of intramuscular ampicillin and gentamicin if the young infant has low weight, dehydration or another severe classification. ➢ Treat to prevent low blood sugar. ➢ Advise how to keep infant warm on the way to the hospital. ➢ Refer to hospital.#

and if blood in stool

Signs	Classification	Treatment
• Blood in the stool.	**SEVERE DYSENTERY**	➢ Give first dose of intramuscular ampicillin and gentamicin if the young infant has low weight, dehydration or another severe classification. ➢ Treat to prevent low blood sugar. ➢ Advise how to keep infant warm on the way to the hospital. ➢ Refer to hospital.#

* ***What is diarrhoea in a young infant?***
If the stools have changed from usual pattern and are many and watery (more water than fecal matter). The normally frequent or loose stools of a breastfed baby are not diarrhoea.

If referral is not possible, see the section ***Where Referral Is Not Possible*** *in the module* ***Treat the Young Infant and Counsel the Mother****.*

THEN CHECK FOR FEEDING PROBLEM & MALNUTRITION:

ASK:

- Is there any difficulty feeding?
- Is the infant breastfed? If yes, how many times in 24 hours?
- Does the infant usually receive any other foods or drinks? If yes, how often?
- What do you use to feed the infant?

LOOK, FEEL:

- Determine weight for age.

IF AN INFANT: **Has any difficulty feeding, or**
Is breastfeeding less than 8 times in 24 hours, or
Is taking any other foods or drinks, or
Is low weight for age,

AND

Has no indications to refer urgently to hospital:

ASSESS BREASTFEEDING:

- Has the infant breastfed in the previous hour?

If the infant has not fed in the previous hour, ask the mother to put her infant to the breast. Observe the breastfeed for 4 minutes.
(If the infant was fed during the last hour, ask the mother if she can wait and tell you when the infant is willing to feed again.)

- Is the infant able to attach?
  no attachment at all　*not well attached*　*good attachment*

> *TO CHECK ATTACHMENT, LOOK FOR:*
> - *Chin touching breast*
> - *Mouth wide open*
> - *Lower lip turned outward*
> - *More areola visible above than below the mouth*
>
> (All of these signs should be present if the attachment is good)

- Is the infant suckling effectively (that is, slow deep sucks, sometimes pausing)?
  not suckling at all　*not suckling effectively*　*suckling effectively*
  Clear a blocked nose if it interferes with breastfeeding.
- Look for ulcers or white patches in the mouth (thrush).

- Does the mother have pain while breastfeeding?

If yes, look and feel for:
- Flat or inverted nipples, or sore nipples
- Engorged breasts or breast abscess

Classify FEEDING

Signs	Classify as	Treatment
• Not able to feed or • No attachment at all or • Not suckling at all or • Very low weight for age.	**NOT ABLE TO FEED - POSSIBLE SERIOUS BACTERIAL INFECTION OR SEVERE MALNUTRITION**	➢ ***Give first dose of intramuscular ampicillin and gentamicin.*** ➢ ***Treat to prevent low blood sugar.*** ➢ ***Warm the young infant by skin to skin contact if temperature less than 36.5°C (or feels cold to touch) while arranging referral.*** ➢ ***Advise mother how to keep the young infant warm on the way to the hospital.*** ➢ ***Refer URGENTLY to hospital#***
• Not well attached to breast or • Not suckling effectively or • Less than 8 breastfeeds in 24 hours or • Receives other foods or drinks or • Thrush (ulcers or white patches in mouth) or • Low weight for age or • Breast or nipple problems	**FEEDING PROBLEM OR LOW WEIGHT**	➢ If not well attached or not suckling effectively, teach correct positioning and attachment. ➢ If breastfeeding less than 8 times in 24 hours, advise to increase frequency of feeding. ➢ If receiving other foods or drinks, counsel mother about breastfeeding more, reducing other foods or drinks, and using a cup and spoon. ➢ If not breastfeeding at all, advise mother about giving locally appropriate animal milk and teach the mother to feed with a cup and spoon. ➢ If thrush, teach the mother to treat thrush at home. ➢ If low weight for age, teach the mother how to keep the young infant with low weight warm at home. ➢ If breast or nipple problem, teach the mother to treat breast or nipple problems. ➢ Advise mother to give home care for the young infant. ➢ Advise mother when to return immediately. ➢ Follow-up any feeding problem or thrush in 2 days. ➢ Follow-up low weight for age in 14 days.
• Not low weight for age and no other signs of inadequate feeding.	**NO FEEDING PROBLEM**	➢ Advise mother to give home care for the young infant. ➢ Advise mother when to return immediately. ➢ Praise the mother for feeding the infant well.

\# *If referral is not possible, see the section* ***Where Referral Is Not Possible*** *in the module* ***Treat the Young Infant and Counsel the Mother.***

is advised home care but should be advised to come for follow up after 2 days and advised when to return immediately.

In addition to possible bacterial infection and jaundice, sick young infants with temperature between 35.5°–36.5°C are classified as low body temperature. This may be due to environmental factors or can be due to infection. Such infants are warmed using skin to skin contact and reassessed after 1 hour. If the temperature becomes normal and the infant has no other pink classification he can be sent home after advising the mother on how to keep the baby warm. If the temperature is still below 36.5°C the infant should be referred to the hospital.

Assessing for Diarrhea

Diarrhea is a main symptom, which is assessed if the mother says it is present. Exclusively breastfed infants normally pass frequent soft stools. This should not be confused with diarrhea. A young infant is said to have diarrhea if the stools have changed from usual pattern and the child is passing many and watery stools (more water than fecal matter).

Clinical Assessment and Classification

All infants with diarrhea should be assessed for presence of dehydration. A number of clinical signs are used to determine the level of dehydration: *infant's general condition* (lethargic or unconscious or restless /irritable); *sunken eyes* and elasticity *of skin* (skin pinch goes back very slowly, slowly or immediately). In addition the infant is assessed for persistent diarrhea and dysentery.

Persistent diarrhea is an episode of diarrhea, with or without blood, which begins acutely and lasts at least 14 days. Persistent diarrhea is usually associated with weight loss and often with serious non-intestinal infections. Persistent diarrhea in a young infant is considered as severe illness and requires urgent referral. Similarly visible blood in stool in a young infant is classified as severe dysentery and the infant should be referred to hospital.

All young infants with diarrhea are classified for degree of dehydration and in addition may be classified if they have persistent diarrhea and /or dysentery. Young infants with severe dehydration will need IV fluids while those with some dehydration are treated as plan B with oral rehydration. Young infants with no dehydration will require more fluid to prevent dehydration (see chapter on diarrhea).

Checking for Feeding Problems or Malnutrition

All sick young infants seen in outpatient health facilities should be routinely evaluated for adequate feeding and have their weight checked. Weight for age compares the young infant's weight with the infants of the same age in the reference population (WHO-NCHS reference). The *very low weight for age* identifies children whose weight is –3 standard deviations below the mean weight of infants in the reference population (Z score <–3). The *low weight for age* identifies children whose weight is –2 standard deviations below the mean weight of infants in the reference population (Z score <-2). Infants who are very low weight for age are given pink classification and should be referred to a hospital. Infants who are low weight for age need special attention to how they are fed and on keeping them warm.

To assess the young infant for feeding problems the mother is asked specific questions about infant feeding to determine if the feeding practices are optimal. The weight of the child and feeding history is taken in to consideration to determine if breast feeding technique needs to be checked. Thus an exclusively breast fed infant who is not low weight for age does not require any intervention and is therefore not observed for breast feeding. If the mother gives history of feeding problem or the infant is low weight for age and has no indication for referral the mother is observed for breast feeding. Breast feeding is observed to see the signs of attachment and whether the infant is suckling effectively. Mothers of infants with problem in feeding are counselled appropriately. Infants who are not low weight for age and have no feeding problem are classified as "no feeding problem" and counselled about home care of young infant.

Checking Immunization Status

Immunization status should be checked in all sick young infants. A young infant who is not sick enough to be referred to a hospital should be given the necessary immunizations before s/he is sent home.

Assessing Other Problems

All sick young infants need to be assessed for other potential problems mentioned by the mother or observed during the examination. If a potentially serious problem is found or there are no means in the clinic to help the infant, s/he should be referred to hospital.

Identify Treatment and Treat

The next step is to **identify treatment** required for the young infant according to the classification. All the treatments required are listed in the "Identify Treatment" column of the *ASSESS and CLASSIFY THE SICK YOUNG INFANT,* Chart 29.1. If a sick young infant has more than one classification, treatment required for all the classifications must be identified. The first step is to determine if there is need to refer the child to hospital.

All infants and children with a severe classification (pink) are referred to a hospital as soon as assessment is completed and necessary pre-referral treatment is administered. Successful referral of severely ill infants to the hospital depends on effective counselling of the caretaker. The first step is to give urgent pre-referral treatment (written in bold font in identify treatment section of chart). This may be:

- Administering first dose of antibiotic.

- Treatment of severe dehydration.
- Warming the young infant using skin to skin contact (kangaroo mother care) and keeping the infant warm on the way to the hospital.
- Prevention of hypoglycemia with breastmilk; if young infant is not able to swallow give expressed breast milk/ appropriate animal milk with added sugar by nasogastric tube.
- In young infants with diarrhea, giving frequent sips of ORS solution on the way to the hospital.

Treatment in Outpatient Clinic and at Home

Young infants who have local infection, feeding problem or low weight, or diarrhea with some dehydration should have treatment initiated in clinic which is to be continued at home (Table 29.1). Counselling a mother/caretaker is critical for home care. The health professional should use good communication skills while counselling the mother/ caretaker for treatment (Box 29.1).

OUTPATIENT MANAGEMENT OF SICK CHILD AGE 2 MONTHS UP TO 5 YEARS

Assess and Classify Sick Child

The assessment procedure is similar to that of young infant including: (1) history taking and communicating with the caretaker about the child's problem; (2) checking for general danger signs; (3) checking main symptoms; (4) checking for malnutrition; (5) checking for anemia; (6) assessing the child's feeding; (7) checking immunization status; and (8) assessing other problems (Chart 29.2).

Table 29.1: Treatment guidelines for managing sick young infant in outpatients and at home

- **Treatment of local infections.**
  - Local bacterial infection: Give oral cotrimoxazole or amoxicillin × 5 days (avoid cotrimoxazole in infants < 1 month of age who are premature or jaundiced).
  - Skin pustules or umbilical infection: Teach to apply gentian violet paint twice daily at home.
  - Discharge from ear: Teach to dry the ear by wicking.
- **Some and no dehydration.**
  - Treat dehydration as per WHO guidelines for treatment of dehydration.
- **Feeding problem or low weight.**
  - Teach correct positioning and attachment for breast-feeding.
  - Teach the mother to manage breast and nipple problems.
  - Treat thrush: Tell the mother to paint the mouth of the young infant with gentian violet 0.25% twice daily.
  - Feeding with a cup and spoon: Wherever indicated teach the mother correct technique of feeding.
  - Counsel the mother/caretaker about other feeding problems.
- **Keep the young infant warm.**
  - Teach the mother how to keep the young infant with low weight or low body temperature warm (do not bathe the young infant but sponge with lukewarm water to clean, provide skin to skin contact; keep the room warm : clothe the baby in 3-4 layers properly covering the head with a cap and hands and feet with gloves and socks respectively, cover the baby and the mother with additional quilt or shawl, especially in cold weather).

Box 29.1: Effective Communication and Counselling–APAC

Ask and listen: Ask the mother/caretaker and listen carefully to find out the young infant/ child's problems and what the mother/caretaker is already doing for the young infant/child
Praise: Praise the mother/ caretaker for what she has done well.
Advise and teach: Advise the mother/ caretaker how to take care of young infant/ child at home (for tasks which require mother/caretaker to carry out treatment at home: give information, show an example, and let her practice).
Check: Before the mother/ caretaker leaves, always check her understanding by asking questions to find out what she understands and what needs further explanation.

Checking for General Danger Signs

A sick child brought to an outpatient facility may have signs that clearly indicate a specific problem. For example, a child may present with cough and chest indrawing which indicate severe pneumonia. However, some children may present with serious, non-specific signs called "***General Danger Signs***" that do not point to a particular diagnosis. For example, a child who is lethargic or unconscious may have meningitis, severe pneumonia, cerebral malaria or any other severe disease. Great care should be taken to ensure that these general danger signs are not overlooked because they suggest that a child is severely ill and needs urgent attention. The following **general danger signs** should be routinely checked in all children: (i) History of convulsions during the present illness, (ii) unconsciousness or lethargy, (iii) inability to drink or breastfeed when mother tries to breastfeed or to give the child something to drink, and (iv) child vomits everything.

If a child has ***one or more*** of these signs, he must be considered ***seriously ill*** and will almost always need referral. In order to start treatment for severe illnesses without delay, the child should be quickly assessed for the main symptoms and malnutrition and referred urgently to a hospital.

Assessing For Main Symptoms

After checking for general danger signs, the health care provider must enquire about the following main symptoms: (a) cough or difficult breathing; (b) diarrhea; (c) fever; and (d) ear problems. If the symptom is present the child is evaluated for that symptom (Chart 29.2).

a. **Cough or difficult breathing:** A child with cough or difficult breathing may have pneumonia or severe respiratory infection. In developing countries, pneumonia is often due to bacteria. The most common are *Streptococcus pneumoniae* and *Hemophilus influenzae.*

Chart 29.2

ASSESS AND CLASSIFY THE SICK CHILD AGE 2 MONTHS UP TO 5 YEARS

ASSESS | CLASSIFY | IDENTIFY TREATMENT

ASK THE MOTHER WHAT THE CHILD'S PROBLEM ARE

- Determine if this is an initial or follow-up visit for this problem.
  - if follow-up visit, use the follow-up instructions on *TREAT THE CHILD* chart.
  - if initial visit, assess the child as follows:

CHECK FOR GENERAL DANGER SIGNS

ASK:	*LOOK:*
• Is the child able to drink or breastfeed? • Does the child vomit everything? • Has the child had convulsions?	• See if the child is lethargic or unconscious.

A child with any general danger sign needs URGENT attention; complete the assessment and any pre-referral treatment immediately so referral is not delayed.

USE ALL BOXES THAT MATCH THE CHILD'S SYMPTOMS AND PROBLEMS TO CLASSIFY THE ILLNESS.

THEN ASK ABOUT MAIN SYMPTOMS:

Does the child have cough or difficult breathing?

IF YES, ASK:	*LOOK, LISTEN:*		
• For how long?	• Count the breaths in one minute. • Look for chest indrawing. • Look and listen for stridor.	CHILD MUST BE CALM	***Classify COUGH or DIFFICULT BREATHING***

If the child is:	Fast breathing is:
2 months up to 12 months	**50** breaths per minute or more
12 months up to 5 years	**40** breaths per minute or more

SIGNS	CLASSIFY AS	IDENTIFY TREATMENT (Urgent pre-referral treatments are in bold print.)
• Any general danger sign or • Chest indrawing or • Stridor in calm child.	**SEVERE PNEUMONIA OR VERY SEVERE DISEASE**	➢ ***Give first dose of injectable chloramphenicol (If not possible give oral amoxycillin).*** ➢ ***Refer URGENTLY to hospital.#***
• Fast breathing.	**PNEUMONIA**	➢ ***Give Cotrimoxazole for 5 days.*** ➢ Soothe the throat and relieve the cough with a safe remedy if child is 6 months or older. ➢ Advise mother when to return immediately. ➢ Follow-up in 2 days.
• No signs of pneumonia or very severe disease.	**NO PNEUMONIA: COUGH OR COLD**	➢ If coughing more than 30 days, refer to assessment. ➢ Soothe the throat and relieve the cough with a safe home remedy if child is 6 months or older. ➢ Advise mother when to return immediately. ➢ Follow-up in 5 days if not improving.

*# If referral is not possible, see the section **Where Referral Is Not Possible** in the module **Treat the Child**.*

Does the child have diarrhoea?

IF YES, ASK:

- For how long?
- Is there blood in the stool?

LOOK AND FEEL:

- Look at the child's general condition.
  Is the child:
  - Lethargic or unconscious?
  - Restless and irritable?
- Look for sunken eyes.

  Offer the child fluid.
  Is the child:
  - Not able to drink or drinking poorly?
  - Drinking eagerly, thirsty?
- Pinch the skin of the abdomen.
  Does it go back:
  - Very slowly (longer than 2 seconds)?
  - Slowly?

Classify DIARRHOEA

for DEHYDRATION

Signs	Classify as	Treatment
Two of the following signs: • Lethargic or unconscious • Sunken eyes • Not able to drink or drinking poorly • Skin pinch goes back very slowly.	**SEVERE DEHYDRATION**	➢ If child has no other severe classification: – Give fluid for severe dehydration (Plan C). ➢ ***If child also has another severe classification :*** ***Refer URGENTLY to hospital***[#] **with mother giving frequent sips of ORS on the way. Advise the mother to continue breastfeeding.** ➢ ***If child is 2 years or older and there is cholera in your area, give doxycycline for cholera.***
Two of the following signs: • Restless, irritable • Sunken eyes • Drinks eagerly, thirsty • Skin pinch goes back slowly.	**SOME DEHYDRATION**	➢ Give fluid and food for some dehydration (Plan B). ➢ ***If child also has a severe classification:*** ***Refer URGENTLY to hospital***[#] ***with mother giving frequent sips of ORS on the way. Advise the mother to continue breastfeeding.*** ➢ Advise mother when to return immediately. ➢ Follow-up in 5 days if not improving.
Not enough signs to classify as some or severe dehydration.	**NO DEHYDRATION**	➢ Give fluid and food to treat diarrhoea at home (Plan A). ➢ Advise mother when to return immediately. ➢ Follow-up in 5 days if not improving.

and if diarrhoea 14 days or more

Signs	Classify as	Treatment
• Dehydration present.	**SEVERE PERSISTENT DIARRHOEA**	➢ **Treat dehydration before referral unless the child has another severe classification.** ➢ **Refer to hospital.**[#]
• No dehydration.	**PERSISTENT DIARRHOEA**	➢ Advise the mother on feeding a child who has PERSISTENT DIARRHOEA. ➢ Give single dose of vitamin A. ➢ Give zinc sulphate 20 mg daily for 14 days. ➢ Follow-up in 5 days.

and if blood in stool

Signs	Classify as	Treatment
• Blood in the stool.	**DYSENTERY**	➢ ***Treat for 5 days with cotrimoxazole.*** ➢ Follow-up in 2 days.

If referral is not possible, see the section ***Where Referral Is Not Possible*** *in the module* ***Treat the Child.***

Does the child have fever?

(by history or feels hot or temperature 37.5°C* or above)

IF YES:
Decide Malaria Risk: High or Low

THEN ASK:

- Fever for how long?
- If more than 7 days, has fever been present every day?
- Has the child had measles within the last 3 months?

LOOK AND FEEL:

- Look or feel for stiff neck.
- Look and feel for bulging fontanelle.
- Look for runny nose.

Look for signs of MEASLES

- Generalized rash and
- One of these: cough, runny nose, or red eyes.

If the child has measles now or within the last 3 months:

- Look for mouth ulcers. Are they deep and extensive?
- Look for pus draining from the eye.
- Look for clouding of the cornea.

Classify FEVER

High Malaria Risk

HIGH MALARIA RISK

Signs	Classify as	Treatment
• Any general danger sign or • Stiff neck or • Bulging fontanelle.	**VERY SEVERE FEBRILE DISEASE**	➢ ***Give first dose of IM quinine after making a blood smear.*** ➢ ***Give first dose of IV or IM chloramphenicol (If not possible, give oral amoxycillin).*** ➢ ***Treat the child to prevent low blood sugar.*** ➢ ***Give one dose of paracetamol in clinic for high fever (temp. 38.5°C or above).*** ➢ ***Refer URGENTLY to hospital#.***
• Fever (by history or feels hot or temperature 37.5°C or above).	**MALARIA**	➢ ***Give oral antimalarials for HIGH malaria risk area after making a blood smear.*** ➢ ***Give one dose of paracetamol in clinic for high fever (temp. 38.5°C or above)*** ➢ Advise mother when to return immediately. ➢ Follow-up in 2 days if fever persists. ➢ If fever is present every day for more than 7 days, refer for assessment.

Low Malaria Risk

LOW MALARIA RISK

Signs	Classify as	Treatment
• Any general danger sign or • Stiff neck or • Bulging fontanelle.	**VERY SEVERE FEBRILE DISEASE**	➢ ***Give first dose of IM quinine after making a blood smear.*** ➢ ***Give first dose of IV or IM chloramphenicol (If not possible, give oral amoxycillin).*** ➢ ***Treat the child to prevent low blood sugar.*** ➢ ***Give one dose of paracetamol in clinic for high fever (temp. 38.5°C or above).*** ➢ ***Refer URGENTLY to hospital#.***
• NO runny nose and NO measles and NO other cause of fever.	**MALARIA**	➢ ***Give oral antimalarials for LOW malaria risk area after making a blood smear.*** ➢ ***Give one dose of paracetamol in clinic for high fever (temp. 38.5°C or above).*** ➢ Advise mother when to return immediately. ➢ Follow-up in 2 days if fever persists. ➢ If fever is present every day for more than 7 days, refer for assessment.
• Runny nose PRESENT or • Measles PRESENT or • Other cause of fever PRESENT**	**FEVER - MALARIA UNLIKELY**	➢ ***Give one dose of paracetamol in clinic for high fever (temp.38.5°C or above).*** ➢ Advise mother when to return immediately. ➢ Follow-up in 2 days if fever persists. ➢ If fever is present every day for more than 7 days, refer for assessment.

If MEASLES Now or within last 3 months, Classify

Signs	Classify as	Treatment
• Any general danger sign or • Clouding of cornea or • Deep or extensive mouth ulcers.	**SEVERE COMPLICATED MEASLES***	➢ ***Give first dose of Vitamin A.*** ➢ ***Give first dose of injectable chloramphenicol (If not possible give oral amoxycillin).*** ➢ ***If clouding of the cornea or pus draining from the eye, apply tetracycline eye ointment.*** ➢ ***Refer URGENTLY to hospital.***
• Pus draining from the eye or • Mouth ulcers.	**MEASLES WITH EYE OR MOUTH COMPLICATIONS***	➢ ***Give first dose of Vitamin A.*** ➢ ***If pus draining from the eye, treat eye infection with tetracycline eye ointment.*** ➢ If mouth ulcers, treat with gentian violet. ➢ Follow-up in 2 days.
• Measles now or within the last 3 months.	**MEASLES**	➢ ***Give first dose of Vitamin A.***

** This cutoff is for axillary temperatures; rectal temperature cutoff is approximately 0.5°C higher.*
*** Other causes of fever include cough or cold, pneumonia, diarrhoea, dysentery and skin infections.*

** Other important complications of measles - pneumonia, stridor, diarrhoea, ear infection, and malnutrition - are classified in other tables.*

If referral is not possible, see the section* ***Where Referral Is Not Possible*** *in the module* ***Treat the Child.***

29

Does the child have an ear problem?

IF YES, ASK:

- Is there ear pain?
- Is there ear discharge? If yes, for how long?

LOOK AND FEEL:

- Look for pus draining from the ear.
- Feel for tender swelling behind the ear.

Classify EAR PROBLEM

Signs	Classification	Treatment
• Tender swelling behind the ear.	**MASTOIDITIS**	➤ ***Give first dose of injectable chloramphenicol (If not possible give oral amoxycillin).*** ➤ ***Give first dose of paracetamol for pain.*** ➤ ***Refer URGENTLY to hospital***[#].
• Pus is seen draining from the ear and discharge is reported for less than 14 days, or • Ear pain.	**ACUTE EAR INFECTION**	➤ ***Give cotrimoxazole for 5 days.*** ➤ Give paracetamol for pain. ➤ Dry the ear by wicking. ➤ Follow-up in 5 days.
• Pus is seen draining from the ear and discharge is reported for 14 days or more.	**CHRONIC EAR INFECTION**	➤ Dry the ear by wicking. ➤ Follow-up in 5 days.
• No ear pain, and • No pus seen draining from the ear.	**NO EAR INFECTION**	No additional treatment.

*If referral is not possible, see the section **Where Referral Is Not Possible** in the module **Treat the Child.***

THEN CHECK FOR MALNUTRITION

LOOK AND FEEL:
- Look for visible severe wasting.
- Look for oedema of both feet.
- Determine weight for age.

Classify NUTRITIONAL STATUS

Signs	Classification	Treatment
• Visible severe wasting or • Oedema of both feet.	**SEVERE MALNUTRITION**	➢ ***Give single dose of Vitamin A.*** ➢ ***Prevent low blood sugar.*** ➢ ***Refer URGENTLY to hospital#.*** ➢ ***While referral is being organized, warm the child.*** ➢ ***Keep the child warm on the way to hospital.***
• Very low weight for age.	**VERY LOW WEIGHT**	➢ Assess and counsel for feeding. ➢ Advise mother when to return immediately. ➢ Follow-up in 30 days.
• Not very low weight for age and no other signs of malnutrition.	**NOT VERY LOW WEIGHT**	➢ If child is less than 2 years old, assess the child's feeding and counsel the mother on feeding according to the FOOD box on the *COUNSEL THE MOTHER* chart. - If feeding problem, follow-up in 5 days. ➢ Advise mother when to return immediately.

THEN CHECK FOR ANAEMIA

LOOK:
- Look for palmar pallor. Is it:
  - Severe palmar pallor?
  - Some palmar pallor?

Classify ANAEMIA

Signs	Classification	Treatment
• Severe palmar pallor	**SEVERE ANAEMIA**	➢ ***Refer URGENTLY to hospital#.***
• Some palmar pallor	**ANAEMIA**	➢ ***Give iron folic acid therapy for 14 days.*** ➢ Assess the child's feeding and counsel the mother on feeding according to the FOOD box on the *COUNSEL THE MOTHER* chart. – If feeding problem, follow-up in 5 days. ➢ Advise mother when to return immediately. ➢ Follow-up in 14 days.
• No palmar pallor	**NO ANAEMIA**	➢ ***Give prophylactic iron folic acid if child 6 months or older.***

THEN CHECK THE CHILD'S IMMUNIZATION *, PROPHYLACTIC VITAMIN A & IRON-FOLIC ACID SUPPLEMENTATION STATUS

IMMUNIZATION SCHEDULE:

AGE	VACCINE
Birth	BCG + OPV-0
6 weeks	DPT-1 + OPV-1 (+ HepB-1**)
10 weeks	DPT-2 + OPV-2 (+ HepB-2**)
14 weeks	DPT-3 + OPV-3 (+ HepB-3**)
9 months	Measles + Vitamin A
16–18 months	DPT Booster + OPV + Vitamin A
60 months	DT

PROPHYLACTIC VITAMIN A

Give a single dose of vitamin A:

100,000 IU at 9 months with measles immunization
200,000 IU at 16–18 months with DPT Booster
200,000 IU at 24 months
200,000 IU at 30 months
200,000 IU at 36 months

PROPHYLACTIC IFA

Give 20 mg elemental iron +100 mcg folic acid (one tablet of Pediatric IFA or 5 ml of IFA syrup or 1 ml of IFA drops) for a total of 100 days in a year after the child has recovered from acute illness **if:**
- ➢ The child 6 months of age or older, and
- ➢ Has not received Pediatric IFA tablet/syrup/drops for 100 days in last one year.

*** A child who needs to be immunized should be advised to go for immunization the day vaccines are available at AW/SC/PHC**
**** Hepatitis B to be given wherever included in the immunization schedule**

ASSESS OTHER PROBLEMS

MAKE SURE CHILD WITH ANY GENERAL DANGER SIGN IS REFERRED after first dose of an appropriate antibiotic and other urgent treatments.
Exception: Rehydration of the child according to Plan C may resolve danger signs so that referral is no longer needed.

*# If referral is not possible, see the section **Where Referral Is Not Possible** in the module **Treat the Child.***

Many children are brought to the clinic with less serious respiratory infections. Most children with cough or difficult breathing have only a mild infection. They do not need treatment with antibiotics. Their families can manage them at home. Very sick children with cough or difficult breathing need to be identified as they require antibiotic therapy. Fortunately, one can identify almost all cases of pneumonia by checking for these two clinical signs: fast breathing and chest indrawing. Chest indrawing is a sign of severe pneumonia.

Clinical assessment and classification: A child presenting with cough or difficult breathing should first be assessed for general danger signs. This child may have pneumonia or another severe respiratory infection. Three key clinical signs are used to assess a sick child with cough or difficult breathing: *fast breathing* (cut-off respiratory rate for fast breathing is 50 breaths per minute or more for a child 2 months up to 12 months, and 40 breaths per minute or more for 12 months up to 5 years); *lower chest wall indrawing and stridor in a calm child.* Based on a combination of the above clinical signs, children presenting with cough or difficult breathing can be classified into one of the three categories. A child with general danger sign or chest indrawing or stridor is classified as severe pneumonia or very severe disease and merits urgent referral to the hospital. A sick child with cough who has fast breathing is classified as pneumonia and his treatment initiated in clinic with oral antimicrobials. A child with cough with none of these signs is classified as cough and cold and given home remedies to soothe throat and counselled for home care.

A child with cough or cold normally improves in one or two weeks. However, a child with chronic cough (more than 30 days) needs to be further assessed (and, if needed, referred) to exclude tuberculosis, asthma, whooping cough or any other problem).

b. **Diarrhea:** A child with diarrhea passes stools with more water than normal. A child with diarrhea may have (1) acute watery diarrhea (including cholera); (2) dysentery (bloody diarrhea); or (3) persistent diarrhea (diarrhea that lasts 14 days or more).

Most diarrheal episodes are caused by agents for which antimicrobials are not effective and therefore antibiotics should not be used routinely for treatment of diarrhea. Anti-diarrheal drugs do ***not*** provide practical benefits for children with acute diarrhea, and some may have dangerous side effects. Therefore these drugs should never be given to children.

29

Clinical assessment and classification: **All** children with diarrhea should be assessed for dehydration based on the following clinical signs: *child's general condition* (lethargic or unconscious or restless/irritable); *sunken eyes; child's reaction when offered to drink* (not able to drink or drinking poorly or drinking eagerly/ thirsty or drinking normally) and *elasticity of skin* (skin pinch goes back very slowly, slowly or immediately). In addition a child with diarrhea should be asked how long the child has had diarrhea and if there is blood in the stool. This will allow identification of children with persistent diarrhea and dysentery.

Children with severe dehydration require immediate IV infusion according to WHO treatment guidelines described in plan C. Children with some dehydration require active oral treatment with ORS as per plan B. Patients with diarrhea and no dehydration are advised to give more fluid than usual to prevent dehydration according to WHO treatment plan A.

All children with persistent diarrhea are classified based on presence or absence of dehydration. Children with persistent diarrhea and dehydration are classified as severe persistent diarrhea and need to be referred to hospital after treatment of dehydration. Children with persistent diarrhea and no dehydration can be safely managed on outpatient basis with appropriate feeding. Children with dysentery are given effective antibiotics for shigellosis.

c. **Fever:** Fever is a very common condition and is often the main reason for bringing children to the health center. It may be caused by minor infections, but may also be the most obvious sign of a life-threatening illness, e.g. *P. falciparum* malaria or meningitis. When diagnostic capacity is limited, it is important first to identify those children who need urgent referral with appropriate pre-referral treatment (antimalarial or antibacterial). **All** sick children should be assessed for fever if it is reported by mother or fever is present on examination.

Clinical assessment and classification: In endemic areas the risk of malaria transmission is defined by areas of high and low malaria risk in the country. National Anti-Malaria Program (NAMP) has defined areas depending on malaria risk. A child presenting with fever is assessed and classified depending on risk of malaria. History of duration of fever is important in evaluating fever. If fever has persisted daily for more than seven days the child needs to be referred to hospital for assessment and diagnostic tests. The other signs looked for in a child with fever include general danger signs (assessed earlier) and signs of meningitis, e.g. *bulging fontanelle and stiff neck.* Besides these, signs of measles and runny nose are also looked for.

If the child has measles currently or within the last three months, he should be assessed for possible complications. Some complications of measles are assessed as main symptoms, e.g. cough/difficult breathing, diarrhea and ear infections. Clouding of cornea and mouth ulcers are assessed along with measles. Clouding of cornea is a dangerous eye complication. If not treated, cornea can ulcerate and cause blindness. An infant with corneal clouding needs urgent treatment with vitamin A.

Before classifying fever, one should check for other obvious causes of fever.

Children with fever are classified based on the presence of any of the general danger signs, stiff neck, level of malaria risk in the area and presence/absence of symptoms like runny nose, measles or clinical signs of other possible infection. In high malaria risk area all children with fever need to get antimalarial treatment as per NAMP guidelines. In areas with low malaria risk children with fever with no other obvious cause are classified as malaria and should be evaluated with blood smear and treated with oral antimalarial drugs (chloroquine). In low malaria risk area children with fever with another cause of fever (e.g. cough and cold or ear infection or diarrhea) are classified as fever, malaria unlikely and given symptomatic treatment for fever. Since the malaria risk may change with time malaria is treated as per national guidelines.

d. **Ear problems:** A child with an ear problem may have otitis. It may be acute or chronic infection. If the infection is not treated, the ear drum may perforate. Ear infections are the main cause of deafness in low-income areas, which in turn leads to learning problems. The middle ear infection can also spread from the ear and cause mastoiditis and/or meningitis. The sick child is assessed for ear infection if any ear problem is reported.

   Clinical assessment and classification: The mother is asked about history of ear *pain* and ear *discharge or pus.* The child is examined for tender *swelling behind the ear.* Based on these clinical findings a child can be classified as mastoiditis, acute ear infection, chronic ear infection or no ear infection. Children with mastoiditis are classified as severe illness and referred urgently to hospital. Children with acute ear infection are given oral antibiotics and those with chronic ear infection are advised to keep the ear dry by wicking.

Checking for Malnutrition

After assessing for general danger signs and the four main symptoms, ***all* children should be assessed for malnutrition.** There are two main reasons for routine assessment of nutritional status in sick children: (1) to identify children with severe malnutrition who are at increased risk of mortality and need urgent referral to provide active treatment; and (2) to identify children with sub-optimal nutritional status resulting from ongoing deficits in dietary intake plus repeated episodes of infection and who may benefit from nutritional counseling.

Clinical Assessment and Classification

Visible severe wasting : This is defined as severe wasting of the shoulders, arms, buttocks, and legs, with ribs easily seen, and indicates presence of marasmus. When wasting is extreme, there are many folds of skin on the buttocks and thigh. It looks as if the child is wearing baggy pants. The face of a child with visible severe wasting may still look normal. The child's abdomen may be large or distended.

Edema of both feet: The presence of oedema in both feet may signal kwashiorkor.

Weight for age: Plotting weight for age in the growth chart, based on reference population, helps to identify children with ***low*** (Z score less than –2) or ***very low*** (Z score less than –3) weight for age, those who are at increased risk of infection and poor growth and development.

Classification of nutritional status: Using a combination of the simple clinical signs above, children can be classified as **severe malnutrition** (visible wasting with or without edema), **very low weight** or **not very low weight.**

Checking for Anemia

All children should also be assessed for anemia. The most common cause of anemia in young children in developing countries is nutritional or because of parasitic or helminthic infections.

Clinical assessment and classification: Palmar pallor can help to identify sick children with severe anemia. Wherever feasible, diagnosis of anemia can be supported by using a simple laboratory test for hemoglobin estimation. For clinical assessment of anemia the color of the child's palm is compared with examiner's own palm. If the skin of the child's palm is pale, the child has ***some palmar pallor.*** If the skin of the palm is very pale or so pale that it looks white, the child has ***severe palmar pallor.*** Based on palmar pallor it is classified as severe anemia, anemia or no anemia.

Assessing the Child's Feeding

All children ***less than 2 years old*** and ***all children classified as*** **anemia or very low weight** need to be assessed for feeding even if they have a normal Z-score. Feeding assessment includes questioning the mother or caretaker about feeding history. The mother or caretaker should be given appropriate advice to help overcome any feeding problems found.

To assess feeding, ask the mother: does she breastfeed her child (how many times during the day and night), does the child take any other food or fluids (what food or fluids, how many times a day, how the child is fed, how large are the servings, does the child receive his own serving, who feeds the child) and during the illness, has the child's feeding changed, (if yes, how?).

Identify feeding problems: When counselling a mother about feeding, one should use good communication skills. It is important to complete the assessment of feeding by referring to age appropriate feeding recommendations and identify all the feeding problems before giving advice. In addition to differences from the feeding recommendations, some other problems may become apparent from the mother's answers. Other common feeding problems are: *Difficulty breastfeeding, use of feeding bottle, lack of active feeding and not feeding well during illness.* IMNCI guidelines recommend locally acceptable, available and affordable foods for feeding a child during sickness and health. A sample of such recommendations is given in the IMNCI chart which needs to be adapted to local conditions.

Checking Immunization, Vitamin A and Folic Acid Supplementation Status

The immunization status of ***every sick child*** brought to a health facility should be checked. Children who are well enough to be sent home can be immunized.

After checking immunization status, determine if the child needs vitamin A supplementation and/or prophylactic iron folic acid supplementation.

Assessing Other Problems

The IMNCI clinical guidelines focus on five main symptoms. In addition, the assessment steps within each main symptom take into account several other common problems. For example, conditions such as meningitis, sepsis, tuberculosis, conjunctivitis, and different causes of fever such as ear infection and sore throat are routinely assessed within the IMNCI case management process. If the guidelines are correctly applied, children with these conditions will receive presumptive treatment or urgent referral. Nevertheless, health care providers still need to consider other causes of severe or acute illness.

Identify Treatment and Treat

All the treatments required are listed in the "Identify Treatment" column of the *ASSESS and CLASSIFY THE SICK CHILD AGE 2 MONTHS UP TO 5 YEARS* (Chart 29.2). ***All sick children*** with a severe classification (pink) are referred to a hospital as soon as assessment is completed and necessary pre-referral treatment is administered. If a child only has severe dehydration and no other severe classification, and IV infusion is available in the outpatient clinic, an attempt should be made to rehydrate the sick child. The principles of referral of a sick child are similar to those described for a sick young infant.

Referral of Children Age 2 Months up to 5 Years

29

Possible pre-referral treatment (s) includes:

- For **convulsions** diazepam IV or rectally. If convulsions continue after 10 minutes give a second dose.
- First dose of appropriate intramuscular antibiotic—Chloramphenicol or ampicillin + gentamicin or ceftriaxone (for **severe pneumonia or severe disease; very severe febrile disease; severe complicated measles; mastoiditis**). Give oral antibiotic if injectable antibiotics are not available.
- First dose of quinine (for **severe malaria**) as per national guidelines.
- Vitamin A (**persistent diarrhea, measles, severe malnutrition**).
- Prevention of hypoglycemia with breast milk or sugar water.
- Oral antimalarials as per guidelines.
- Paracetamol for high fever (38.5°C or above) or pain.
- Tetracycline eye ointment (if clouding of the cornea or pus draining from eye).
- Frequent sips of ORS solution on the way to the hospital in sick children with diarrhea.

If a child does not need ***urgent*** referral, check to see if the child needs ***non-urgent referral*** for further assessment; for example, for a cough that has lasted more than 30 days, or for fever that has lasted seven days or more. These referrals are not as urgent, and other necessary treatments may be done before transporting for referral.

Treatment in Outpatient Clinics and at Home

Identify the treatment associated with each non-referral classification (***yellow and green***) in the IMNCI chart. Treatment uses a minimum of affordable essential drugs. Following guidelines for treatment need to be followed:

- Counselling a mother/caretaker for looking after the child at home is very important. Good communication skills based on principles of *APAC* are helpful for effective counselling.
- Give appropriate treatment and advice for 'yellow' and 'green' classifications as detailed in Table 29.2.

Counseling A Mother or Caretaker

A child who is seen at the clinic needs to continue treatment, feeding and fluids at home. The child's mother or caretaker also needs to recognize when the child is not improving, or is becoming sicker. The success of home treatment depends on how well the mother or caretaker knows how to give treatment, understands its importance and knows when to return to a health care provider. Some advice is simple; other advice requires teaching the mother or caretaker **how to do a task**. When you teach a mother how to treat a child, use three basic teaching steps: *give information; show an example; let her practice.*

- Advise to continue feeding and increase fluids during illness;
- Teach how to give oral drugs or to treat local infection;
- Counsel to solve feeding problems (if any);
- Advise when to return (Table 29.3). Every mother or caretaker who is taking a sick child home needs to be advised about when to return to a health facility. The health care provider should (a) teach signs that mean to return immediately for further care, (b) advise when to return for a follow-up visit and (c) schedule the next well-child or immunization visit.

REVISION IN IMNCI CLINICAL AND MANAGEMENT GUIDELINES

IMNCI strategy recommends adaptation of clinical and management guidelines based on the local epidemiologic

Table 29.2: Treatment guidelines for managing sick child in outpatients and at home

- **Pneumonia, acute ear infection:** Give the first dose of the antibiotics in the clinic and teach the mother how to give oral drugs, cotrimoxazole (first line) or amoxicillin (second line)*.
- **Dysentery:** Give the first dose of the antibiotics in the clinic and teach the mother how to give oral drugs, cotrimoxazole (first line) or nalidixic acid (second line)*.
- **Cholera:** In areas where cholera can not be excluded, children more than 2 years old with severe dehydration should be given a single dose of doxycycline.
- **Dehydration and persistent diarrhea:** Treat 'some' and 'no' dehydration and persistent diarrhoea as per standard WHO Guidelines.
- **Persistent diarrhea:** Give zinc (20 mg elemental zinc) daily for 14 days and a single dose of vitamin A.
- **Malaria:** Treat as per recommendations
- **Anemia:** Give iron folic acid for 14 days.
- **Cough and cold:** If the child is 6 months or older use safe home remedies (continue breastfeeding, use honey, tulsi, ginger and other safe local home remedies).
- **Local infection:** Teach the mother or caretaker how to treat the infection at home. Instructions may be given about how to: Treat eye infection with tetracycline eye ointment; dry the ear by wicking to treat ear infection; treat mouth ulcers with gentian violet.

* Give a second-line drug only if first-line drug is not available or if the child has not responded to first-line drug

Table 29.3: Counsel mother when to return

Mother should report immediately if she notices following symptoms :

Young infant (age 0–2 months)	*Sick child (2 months–5 yrs)*
• Breastfeeding or drinking poorly • Becomes sicker • Develops fever or cold to touch • Fast/difficult breathing • Blood in stools (if infant has diarrhea) • Yellow palms and soles (if jaundiced)	**Any child** – Not able to drink or breastfeed – becomes sicker – develops fever **Child with cough and cold** – develop fast/difficult breathing **Child with diarrhoea** – has blood in stool – drinking poorly

- *Mother should bring infant for follow up visit* *
- *Mother should come for scheduled immunization visit*

* *See section on identify treatment*

scenario and management guidelines, which are evidence-based, pertain to majority of common childhood illnesses, are locally relevant and feasible. Evaluation and providing justification for revision of these guidelines is a continuous process. With the availability of more epidemiological data on common childhood illnesses in India, there is a possibility of future inclusion of conditions like HIV/AIDS, dengue fever and asthma at national or state level revision of IMNCI guidelines.

During the last decade, there has been a significant breakthrough in introducing newer concepts and recommendations pertaining to management of childhood illnesses. With the availability of more evidence based information, some of these guidelines have already been revised by World Health Organization and incorporated in national health programs. Future adaptation of IMNCI guidelines is likely to have following revisions:

- **Management of diarrhea:** WHO recommends use of reduced osmolarity ORS with 75 mEq/l of sodium and 75 mmol/l of glucose (osmolarity 245 mOsm/l) as the universal solution for all causes of diarrhea and at all ages and supplementation of elemental zinc (20 mg in children older than 6 months and 10 mg per day in infants less than 6 months) to be started as soon as diarrhea starts and continued for a total period of 14 days. Reduced osmolarity ORS has been introduced in the National Health Programme in 2002 and a policy decision has been taken for including zinc in the RCH/National Rural Health Mission by the Government of India.
- **Management of dysentery:** In view of wide spread resistance to cotrimoxazole, the Indian Academy of Pediatrics Task Force recommends ciprofloxacin as first line drug in areas where resistance rates to cotrimoxazole exceeds 30%.

Suggested reading

1. Murray CJL, Lopez AD. The global burden of disease: A comprehensive assessment of mortality and disability from diseases, injuries and risk factors in 1990 and projected to 2020. In: Global Burden of Disease and Injury Series (vol. I), Cambridge, MA, Harvard School of Public Health, 1996.
2. Gove S. For the WHO Working Group on Guidelines for Integrated Management of the Sick Child. Bull WHO 1997, 75: 7–24.
3. World Health Organization. Integrated Management of the Sick Child. Bull WHO 1995; 73:735–740.
4. World Health Organization. Management of the Child with a Serious Infection or Severe Malnutrition: Guidelines for care at the first-referral level in developing countries. WHO, Geneva, 2000.
5. World Health Organization. Integrated Management of Childhood Illness. WHO/CHD/97.3.A –3.G, WHO, Geneva, 1997.
6. Integrated Management of Neonatal and Childhood Illness. Training Modules for Physicians. Ministry of Health and Family Welfare, Govt. of India, 2003.

30 Rights of Children

The Constitution of India guarantees equality before the law to all citizens, and pledges special protections for children. In 1974, India adopted a National Policy for Children and declared it a *supreme national asset*. In 1992, India accepted the obligations of the UN Convention on the Rights of the Child. The National Commission for Protection of Child Rights has been set up as a statutary body under the Commission for Protection of Child Rights Act, 2005 to protect, promote and defend child rights in the country.

Physicians should have a knowledge of child rights and advocate them in their daily practice. This chapter discusses major concerns and strategies of rights of every child in the area of child survival, identity, development, protection and participation.

Child Survival: Major Concerns

High infant and newborn mortality: The infant mortality rate has declined to 57 (National Family Health Survey 2005), mainly due to survival of post-neonatal infants (between 29 days and 1 year). The current neonatal mortality rate (39 per 1000 live births) accounts for two-thirds of all infant deaths and half of under-5 child mortality. One-fourth of all neonates are low birth weight (birth weight <2.5 kg); they have a 15-fold higher risk of dying during the newborn period.

Nutrition security is a basic right: Millions of children lack protection against hunger. Based on data from the Third National Family Health Survey, 46% of children less than 3-year are stunted and 75% young children are anemic.

Infectious diseases: Diarrhea and respiratory tract infections, rising rates of tuberculosis, infection with HIV and persistence of malaria pose serious threats to child survival.

Gender inequality: Girls are denied equal right to life. The birth of girls is being prevented and girl infants are dying. Female feticide is increasing despite being banned. Prebirth sex selection is on the rise. The 2001 Census reveals that the 0–6 sex ratio is now 927 girls to 1,000 boys. This is a serious threat to India's population balance.

Strategies for Child Survival

Invest in child survival: Children should have access to preventive, protective and curative services, ensuring (i) tracking in relation to health, nutrition and education; (ii) universal immunization against vaccine-preventable diseases; (iii) early identification for special health needs and appropriate referrals; (iv) promotion of breastfeeding; (v) control of common infectious diseases; and (vi) that services are of good quality, affordable and accessible for all.

Provide better public health services: (i) Ensure safe drinking water, sanitation, and environmental protection, giving the most disadvantaged communities access to common resources; (ii) Combat hunger and malnutrition by ensuring food security to families and nutrition security to children; supplementary nutrition and provision of midday meals; (iii) Universalize ICDS services to all 0–3-year-old; ensure survival support and childhood care.

Child Identity

Birth registration and identity is a child's first civil right. International standards recognize all people up to 18-year-old as children. India has acknowledged this basic principle in 1992, but this is not reflected in the laws. India must recognize all persons up to the age of 18-years as children, and reflect this uniformly in all its laws and practices.

Child Development

Education: About half of India's children of school-going age are not in school. At present, the 86th Constitutional Amendment pledging free and compulsory education as a fundamental right serves only the 6–14 yr age group, denying learning rights to children below 6-yr and leaving out children above 14-yr.

Health care, nutrition, shelter and security should be provided for the underserved children. Children with disabilities or special needs are seriously underserved. Only 5% of children with disability are reached by any kind of services; only 2% can access schooling. Children on the street or those not accessible through family channels cannot avail of development opportunities. The budget allocation for children is 2.3% of total budget.

Strategies Enabling Child Development

Every child should receive services that support early childhood care and development. Pediatricians can advocate, supervise or assist the government agencies to develop and operate a network of child care and development services including ICDS, crèches and preschools for young children. Pediatricians can advocate, supervise or assist the government agencies to increase investment in primary education. Quality standards for education, teaching content and methods, and curriculum reforms should be ensured. Other strategies include ensuring food and nutrition security, especially for the poor and most disadvantaged, providing basic health care and immunization.

Child Protection

Children have the right to be protected against all forms of abuse (physical, sexual or emotional), neglect, exploitation and corporal punishment. All forms of child labor are an abuse of basic child rights. Lack of family or adult support results in denial of basic services; such children deserve special protection and assistance. Children are targeted in communal violence as never before. They also suffer discrimination and denial in post-riot situations. Children of indigenous and tribal communities suffer neglect, discrimination and alienation and are affected by armed conflict and other civil violence.

Children have the right to special protection against trafficking, communal and political violence, armed conflict, terrorist activities and migrant situations. Every child has the right to adequate housing and shelter, including in urban and tribal settings. The State needs effective legislation to punish and deter abuse, sexual abuse and trafficking in children as well as prenatal sex determination, feticide and infanticide. Street children should be provided with safe shelter services and opportunities for relevant education and vocational training. Children should have access to contact services to help them in case of emergency or distress. The emergency toll-free phone service for children in distress (Child Line 1098) should be expanded and awareness generated about such help lines. Orphanages and shelter homes are required to assist children without families. Adoption should give first priority to the best interests of the child concerned.

CHILD ABUSE AND NEGLECT

Definition

The WHO defines child abuse as forms of physical and/or emotional ill-treatment, sexual abuse, neglect or negligent treatment, commercial or other exploitation, resulting in actual or potential harm to the child's health, survival, development or dignity in the context of a relationship of responsibility, trust or power. Major types of child abuse by caregiver or other adults include: (i) *physical abuse* - acts of commission that cause actual physical harm or have the potential for harm; (ii) *sexual abuse* - caregiver uses a child for sexual gratification; (iii) *emotional abuse*-failure of a caregiver to provide an appropriate and supportive environment, including acts that have an adverse effect on the emotional health and development, (iv) *neglect* - failure of a parent/guardian to provide for the development of the child, where the parent is in a position to do so, in one or more of the following areas: health, education, emotional development, nutrition, shelter and safe living conditions. Neglect is thus distinguished from circumstances of poverty in that neglect can occur only in cases where reasonable resources are available to the family or caregiver.

Extent of the Problem in India

The recent study on child abuse in India (2007) by Ministry of Women and Child Development highlights the high prevalence of all forms of child abuse in our country. The term *child abuse* has different connotations in different cultural milieu and socioeconomic situations. In the Indian context, it is important to include children being deprived of education, early development, basic health care and nutrition. Child labor is the worst kind of child abuse and neglect.

Manifestations of Child Abuse and Neglect

Injuries inflicted by a caregiver on a child can take many forms. Death in abused children is most often the consequence of a head injury or injury to the internal organs. Abuse is suggested by patterns of injury to the skin and skeletal manifestations including multiple fractures at different stages of healing. There is evidence that about one-third of severely shaken infants die and that the majority of the survivors suffer long-term consequences such as mental retardation, cerebral palsy or blindness. Children who have been sexually abused exhibit symptoms of infection, genital injury, abdominal pain, constipation, chronic or recurrent urinary tract infections or behavioral problems. To be able to detect child sexual abuse requires a high index of suspicion and familiarity with the verbal, behavioral and physical indicators of abuse. Many children will disclose abuse to caregivers or others spontaneously, though there may also be indirect physical or behavioral signs. Emotional and psychological abuse has received less attention globally due to cultural variations in different countries. However, corporal punishment of children, e.g. slapping, punching, kicking or beating, is a significant phenomenon in schools and other institutions. Child neglect can manifest as failure to thrive, failure to seek basic health care and immunization, deprivation of education and basic nutrition needs. A neglected child may be exposed to environmental hazards, substance abuse, inadequate supervision, poor hygiene and abandonment.

Strategies to Reduce Child Abuse and Neglect

In India, the problems of socially marginalized and economically backward groups are immense, particularly amongst children in urban slums, street and working children, children of construction workers, etc. Although child labor cannot be abolished in presence of poverty, it is necessary to ensure that working children are not exploited. They must get time for education and must receive health care. Laws for protection of children against all forms of abuse and exploitation should be enforced.

Child protection services should reach the rural areas, where a large proportion of the population resides. A comprehensive approach to child protection in these areas must involve the Panchayati Raj institution. The panchayat officials should be given the responsibility to ensure that basic education, nutrition, health care and sanitation available for proper development of every child in their village. The panchayat should be duty bound to ensure that every child is in school and thus protected from agrarian and allied rural occupations as a part of family or individual child labor.

Pediatricians are the best advocates for children and for protection of their rights. They can contribute by recognizing, responding to and reporting child abuse. Physicians in developed countries are required by law to report cases of child abuse and neglect. They are protected in cases of erroneous reporting, as long as it is done in good faith to protect a child. A similar legislation that makes child abuse reporting mandatory for pediatricians and certain professional groups is welcome. In addition, pediatricians can work with the community, NGOs and administrators in government and reach out to the neglected, deprived and abused children for their comprehensive needs that include education, health aspects, protection and rehabilitation.

The Constitution of India guarantees many fundamental rights to children, however, the approach to fulfil these rights has been needs based rather than rights based. Child abuse is a basic violation of the child's rights. The adoption of rights based approach is needed to provide care and protection to the large numbers of children in our country. There is an urgent need for the State to create an enabling environment through legislation, schemes and enhanced budget to address the problem of child abuse and neglect in our country.

Suggested reading

1. National Family Health Survey, India, 2006. http://www.nfhsindia.org/nfhs3.html
2. UNICEF. Convention on the Rights of the Child, 2004. http://www.kidzee.com/images/unicef.pdf
3. Study on Child Abuse. Ministry of Women and Child Development, Government of India, 2007
4. International Society for Prevention of Child Abuse and Neglect. World perspective on child abuse, 6th edn, 2006. http://www.ispcan.org

ADOPTION

Adoption is an important alternative for the rehabilitation of children who are destitute and abandoned or for social reasons cannot be brought up by their parents. Medical practitioners and pediatricians play a vital role in influencing health and social decisions of their adoptive patients and need to work closely with counselors and allied health professionals.

'Right to a family' is proposed as a fundamental right by the United Nations. Adoption agencies need to ensure that these rights are protected.

Legal Aspects

In India, only agencies recognized by the Government can deal with adoption placement. Direct adoption placement by hospitals, maternity and nursing homes is not permitted. Prior to 2000, adoption was allowed to Hindus under the Hindu Adoption and Maintenance Act; other religious groups were governed by the Guardianship and Wards Act. The Juvenile Justice (Care and Protection of Children) Act, passed by the Parliament in 2000, enables citizens of all religions the freedom to adopt a minor child, irrespective whether he/she is a single parent and/or such adoptive parent/s adopt a child of the same sex, irrespective of the number of living biological sons or daughters.

Adoption Procedures

A child, who has been relinquished by his/her biological parents or found abandoned, must first be presented to the Child Welfare Committee. This committee has the sole authority to declare the child free for adoption under the current law. In case of an abandoned child, the committee, after due investigations, declares the child as destitute and free for adoption. In case the biological parents want to relinquish a child, they have to execute a document in favor of the adoption agency, duly witnessed by any authority of the hospital and a relative. A waiting period of 2 months is given to the biological parents to reconsider the decision, following which the child is free for adoption.

Prospective Adoptive Parents

A child can be adopted by a married couple having infertility or voluntarily opting for adoption. Even single persons are eligible to adopt. Couples who have taken a decision to adopt should go to a registered agency, which is licensed to process adoption by both state government and the Central Adoption Resource Authority (an autonomous body under the Ministry of Women and Child Development, Government of India). Recognized placement agencies alone can process the application of abandoned children for in country and inter-country adoptions of Indian children. Applications for inter-country adoption, of a child born in India, should be forwarded by an accredited agency of the country of the adoptive parents, to a recognized placement agency in India along with all documents to Central Adoption Resource Authority.

A social worker from the adoption agency provides guidelines and support to preadoptive parents, and helps them make informed decisions (pre-adoption counseling). A home study is conducted by the professional social worker. Additionally, parents are required to submit documents regarding their health, financial status, etc. Once their application is approved, a suitable child is shown to them. After they accept the child, placement is legalized. The placement is followed up to a period of 3 years or such time until legal adoption is complete. The adoptive parents are assured confidentiality and provided support as needed.

Role of a Pediatrician

Pediatricians are in the position where families take them into confidence and seek their advice in many situations.

- All essential tests (HIV, hepatitis B) which have a window period may be repeated at 3 and 6 months, before placement.
- They can counsel and teach the public about the process of adoption.
- Parents who wish to relinquish their children due to any reason must be told about correct procedure; leaving young children in public places or in unhealthy surroundings is unsafe and traumatizing.
- Doctors should discourage private adoptions, since these are illegal.
- Babies in placement agencies are usually taken for a second opinion to a pediatrician, where the child should be examined carefully and a realistic diagnosis and prognosis should be explained to the adoptive parents.
- A supporting and understanding attitude encourages adoptive parents to overcome their fears.

Suggested reading

Central Adoption Resource Agency; www.adoptionindia.nic.in

them make informed decisions (pre-adoption counselling). A home study is conducted by the professional social worker. Additionally, parents are required to submit documents regarding their health, financial status, etc. Once their application is approved, a suitable child is shown to them. After they accept the child, placement is facilitated. The placement is followed up for a period of a year or such time until legal adoption is complete. The adoptive parents are assured confidentiality and provided support as needed.

Role of a Pediatrician

Pediatricians are in the position where families take them into confidence and seek their advice in many situations.

- All essential tests (HIV, hepatitis B) which have a window period may be repeated at 3 and 6 months before placement.
- They can counsel and teach the public about the process of adoption.
- Parents who wish to relinquish their children due to any reason must be told about correct procedure; leaving young children in public places or in unhealthy surroundings is unsafe and traumatizing.
- Doctors should discourage private adoptions, since these are illegal.
- Babies in placement agencies are usually taken for a second opinion to a pediatrician; the child should be examined carefully and a realistic diagnosis and prognosis should be explained to the adoptive parents.
- A supporting and understanding attitude encourages adoptive parents to overcome their fears.

Suggested reading

Central Adoption Resource Agency. www.adoptionindia.nic.in

Index